AMERICAN ISSUES

THE SOCIAL RECORD

Fourth Edition

EDITED BY MERLE CURTI, PROFESSOR OF
HISTORY, UNIVERSITY OF WISCONSIN; WILLARD
THORP, PROFESSOR OF ENGLISH, PRINCETON
UNIVERSITY; AND CARLOS BAKER, PROFESSOR
OF ENGLISH, PRINCETON UNIVERSITY

J. B. LIPPINCOTT COMPANY
CHICAGO   PHILADELPHIA   NEW YORK

THIS IS AN ENLARGED EDITION OF THE AUTHORS'
WORK OF THE SAME TITLE, COPYRIGHT 1941,
1944 AND 1955 BY J. B. LIPPINCOTT COMPANY

PRINTED IN THE UNITED STATES OF AMERICA

FOREWORD

WHEN, IN 1941, we wrote the preface to the first edition of *American Issues*, we saw no need to apologize for adding another anthology to those collections of historical and literary documents already available. No anthology hitherto published had made an adequate critical distinction between selections whose bearing and interest are primarily social and selections which stand on their own merits as literature. On the other hand, none of the previous anthologies had been so designed as to enable the student, with a minimum of inconvenience, to study the literature of America against the magnificent panorama of its history. *American Issues*, which appeared in two volumes, *The Social Record* and *The Literary Record*, answered the needs and problems we had ourselves experienced in our teaching of American social and intellectual history at Columbia and American literature at Princeton.

The rapid development of American Studies as a field after World War II still further justified the pioneering that the first edition of *American Issues* represented. Other anthologies inevitably appeared, some of which reflected an approach similar to ours. But none of these, we believe, lent themselves as well as *American Issues* did to a wide variety of needs of both teachers and students. In some cases, *The Literary Record*, which included such writing as can honestly be said to show the artist's hand at work, consciously shaping his material, was used without its companion volume. In other instances, courses were so organized that instructors preferred to make use of *The Social Record* alone. In still others, the two volumes have been used together with satisfying results.

The Social Record presents those records—speeches, reports, pamphlets, letters, autobiographies—which best elucidate the dominant issues at work in American society, on many fronts, in many regions, at many levels, and through all the periods of our history since English ships brought the first colonists to our shores. Visible in this volume, as in the log of one of those early vessels, is the record of storm and stress, of action and reaction, of progress and recession, which has resulted from our constant struggle to advance American democracy and to realize the American dream. Some of these documents have inspired men to fight for the ideas they contain. On some the very destiny of the nation has depended. Some pose problems still unsolved, while others demonstrate that there is nothing new under the sun. Indeed, many of the questions here discussed are no more indigenous to our soil than were the original colonists. But whenever an issue of foreign origin has taken root here, we have sought to show how it was transplanted, how adapted, how transformed by native circumstances into an important American issue. For any student of American civilization, in this country or abroad, these documents, or comparable ones, ought to be required reading. In 1941, we considered it an important purpose of this anthology to make widely available certain important historical items which were otherwise accessible only in rare editions; this purpose continues to be served by the present volume despite the appearance in recent years of paperback editions of several records first to appear in accessible form in the original edition of *The Social Record*.

In retrospect, we are confirmed in our original judgment that it was wise to include substantial selections of the records chosen rather than mere illustrative samplings. We are also of the opinion that the essential organization, which gives emphasis both to conflict and to consensus, was sound and foresighted. The essays prefacing each major theme or issue and the biographical and bibliographical material have proved useful to teacher and student alike.

v

FOREWORD

In the revised edition of 1955, new materials, largely retained in the present edition, were included to depict varying points of view on domestic problems and foreign relations during and after World War II. The additional selections in the present edition (fourth edition, 1960, 1962) illustrate the principal issues of the American people and their leaders in the years just behind us. Special attention has been given in the field of domestic issues to civil rights, race relations, mass communications, and the impact of the newer behavioral sciences on such traditional American values as freedom, individualism, and social well-being. In the field of foreign relations, the problems associated with the "cold war" and the uses and control of atomic energy are also illuminated by fresh and readable selections. As in the preceding topics and periods in earlier editions, the selections depict varying points of view. It seemed likely, in 1960, as it does in 1962, that the problems considered in the new materials would continue to be major American issues in the years ahead.

In the preparation of the original edition of *The Social Record*, Miss Regina Wilbur and Miss Royce Moch gave much appreciated help, and Judith Greene surveyed large bodies of material which proved useful in making the selections for the fourth edition.

THE EDITORS

ACKNOWLEDGMENTS

THE EDITOR gratefully acknowledges the permission of the following publishers and individuals to reprint material in this book:

Louis Adamic: for a selection from *My America*.

George Ade: for two fables from *More Fables*.

Mary Antin: for a selection from *They Who Knock at Our Gates*.

D. Appleton-Century Company: for selections from *Prose Writings* by William Cullen Bryant, edited by Parke Godwin; from *Speeches of John C. Calhoun;* and from *Complete Works of Abraham Lincoln,* edited by John G. Nicholay and John Hay.

The Association for the Study of Negro Life and History: for a selection from the *Journal of Negro History*.

Atlantic Monthly, for the use of the essay by Herbert Ravenel Sass, "Mixed Schools and Mixed Blood," in the issue for November, 1956.

Ray Stannard Baker: for selections from *The Reign of Lawlessness*.

Charles A. Beard: for *The Myth of Rugged Individualism*.

Mrs. Albert J. Beveridge: for a selection from *The Meaning of the Times,* by Albert J. Beveridge.

The Bobbs-Merrill Company: for the selection from *The Meaning of the Times,* by Albert J. Beveridge, copyright, 1908, 1936, used by special permission of the publishers, The Bobbs-Merrill Company.

Albert & Charles Boni: for a selection from *The Journal of William Maclay*.

Brown, Son & Ferguson, Ltd.: for the song "Across the Western Ocean," from *Sea Songs and Shanties,* by Captain W. B. Whall.

Mrs. Andrew Carnegie: for a selection from *The Empire of Business,* by Andrew Carnegie.

The University of Chicago Press: for excerpts from "Country Versus City," by Warren H. Wilson, in *Papers and Proceedings, Tenth Annual Meeting of the American Sociological Society, 1915,* volume XI, "The Sociology of Rural Life," and for a selection from W. Lloyd Warner, *American Life: Dream and Reality,* 1953.

Miss Joanna Colcord: for the song, "The Black Ball Line," from *Songs of American Sailormen*.

Mrs. Bernice Congdon Colwell: for "We Stand at Armageddon," by C. H. Congdon.

Cousins, Norman, for the inclusion of "Wanted—Two Billion Angry Men," *Sat. Review,* Feb. 1, 1955.

Coward-McCann, Inc.: for a selection from Henry Ford's *My Philosophy of Industry,* an interview by Fay Leone Faurote, copyright, 1928, by Coward-McCann, Inc.

Criterion Books, Inc., for the selection from Edward Teller and Albert E. Latter, *Our Nuclear Future,* 1958.

F. S. Crofts & Company: for a selection from *American Problems of Today,* by Louis M. Hacker.

Curtis Publishing Company, for the editorial "Quiz Scandals are Only a Symptom," *Saturday Evening Post,* December 12, 1959.

The John Day Company, Inc.: for *The Myth of Rugged Individualism,* by Charles A. Beard.

Department of Archives and History, Jackson, Mississippi: for a selection from *Jefferson Davis, Constitutionalist, His Letters, Papers, and Speeches*.

John Dewey: for a selection from *The Influence of Darwin on Philosophy*.

J. Frank Dobie: for the poem "Mustang Gray," from *Publications of the Texas Folk-Lore Society*.

Doubleday, Doran and Company: for selections from *American Individualism,* by Herbert Hoover, copyright, 1922; from *Up from Slavery,* by Booker T. Washington, copyright, 1901, 1909; from *The New Freedom,* by Woodrow Wilson, copyright, 1913; from *The Constitution of the United States,* by James M. Beck, copyright, 1924; and from *Leaves of Grass,* by Walt Whitman, copyright, 1924.

William O. Douglas: for a selection from "The Black Silence of Fear," in *New York Times Magazine* for January 13, 1952.

ACKNOWLEDGMENTS

W. E. B. Du Bois: for a selection from "Social Planning for the Negro," in the *Journal of Negro Education*.

Mrs. F. P. Dunne: for two selections from *Observations by Mr. Dooley*, by Finley Peter Dunne.

E. P. Dutton and Company: for a selection from *Letters from an American Farmer*, by Michel-Guillaume Jean de Crèvecœur.

Elaine Goodale Eastman: for a selection from *The Indian Today*, by Charles Alexander Eastman.

Henry Pratt Fairchild: for a selection from *The Melting-Pot Mistake*.

Leo Feist, Inc.: for verses of the song, "Over There," copyright, 1917.

Mrs. Harry Fine: for selections from *Shelburne Essays*, by Paul Elmer More.

Henry Ford: for a selection from *My Philosophy of Industry*.

Fortune: for a selection from *U.S.A. Permanent Revolution*, 1951.

The Forum: for a selection from *The Drift of Population to the Cities: Remedies*, by Henry J. Fletcher.

Funk and Wagnalls Company: for a selection from *Speeches of William Jennings Bryan*.

Henry George School of Social Science: for a selection from *Significant Paragraphs*, by Henry George.

Harcourt, Brace and Company: for three songs from *The American Songbag*, by Carl Sandburg; and for selections from *The Autobiography of Lincoln Steffens*, copyright, 1931, and from *Middletown in Transition*, by Robert S. and Helen Merrell Lynd, copyright, 1937.

Harper and Brothers: for selections from *Charles W. Eliot, The Man and His Beliefs*, edited by Allan Neilson; *My America*, by Louis Adamic; *I'll Take My Stand*, by Twelve Southerners, and the selection from James Luther King, Jr., *Stride Toward Freedom*, 1958.

Henry Holt and Company: for selections from *The Federalist*, by Paul Leicester Ford; *The Influence of Darwin on Philosophy and Other Essays*, by John Dewey; and *The Frontier in American History*, by Frederick Jackson Turner.

Herbert Clark Hoover: for a selection from *American Individualism*.

Houghton Mifflin Company: for selections from *Mosses from an Old Manse*, by Nathaniel Hawthorne; from *Outlooks on Society, Literature and Politics*, by Edwin Percy Whipple; from *The Writings of Henry David Thoreau* (Riverside Edition); from *Looking Backward*, by Edward Bellamy; from *They Who Knock at Our Gates*, by Mary Antin; from *Contemporaries*, by Thomas Wentworth Higginson; from *Over the Teacups*, by Oliver Wendell Holmes; from *The Education of Henry Adams*, by Henry Adams; from *Prose Works of John Greenleaf Whittier;* from *Works*, by Ralph Waldo Emerson; and from *Unguarded Gates*, by Thomas Bailey Aldrich.

Elbert Hubbard II: for a selection from *A Message to Garcia*, by Elbert Hubbard.

Charles H. Kerr and Company: for a selection from *The Autobiography of Mother Jones*.

Martin Luther King, Jr.: for a selection from *Stride Toward Freedom, The Montgomery Story*.

Alfred A. Knopf: for selections from *Notes on Democracy*, by H. L. Mencken; from *The American Democrat*, by James Fenimore Cooper; from *The Partisan Leader*, by Nathaniel Beverley Tucker; and from *Recollections of the Last Ten Years*, by Timothy Flint.

Little, Brown and Company: for selections from *Orations and Speeches*, by Edward Everett; from *Nationality in Literature*, by James Russell Lowell; from *The Oregon Trail*, by Francis Parkman; from *The Writings and Speeches of Daniel Webster;* and from *U. S. Foreign Policy: Shield of the Republic*, by Walter Lippmann.

Walter Lippmann: for a selection from "Philosophy and United States Foreign Policy," 1947.

Mrs. Charmian K. London: for a selection from *The War of the Classes*, by Jack London.

Longmans, Green and Company: for selections from *The Will to Believe* and *The Moral Equivalent of War*, by William James.

The Macmillan Company: for selections from John Woolman's *Journal and Essays*, edited by Gummere; from *Peace and Bread in Time of War* and *The Spirit of Youth and the City Streets*, by Jane Addams; and from *A Ten Years' War*, by Jacob Riis.

Lyle Evans Mahan: for a selection from *The Interest of America in Sea Power*, by Alfred Thayer Mahan.

The Manning Association: for a selection from *The Key of Libberty*.

H. L. Mencken: for a chapter of *Notes on Democracy*.

Music Publishers Holding Corporation: for verses of the song, "Brother, Can You Spare a Dime," from *Americana;* words by E. Y. Harburg and music by Jay Gorney.

National Resources Planning Board: for a selection from *The National Planning Board Final Report 1933–34.*

Nebraska Writers' Project: for the ballad, "But the Mortgage Worked the Hardest."

Reinhold Niebuhr: for a selection from "An Adequate Faith for the World Crisis," 1947.

W. W. Norton and Company: for the song, "The Black Ball Line," from *Songs of American Sailormen,* by Joanna Colcord.

Paull-Pioneer Music Corporation: for the chorus of the song, "The Sidewalks of New York," copyright, 1894, reproduced by permission of the Corporation, owners of the copyright.

G. P. Putnam's Sons: for selections from *A Rebel's Recollections,* by George C. Eggleston; from *Recollections of a Private Soldier in the Army of the Potomac,* by Frank Wilkeson; from *The Writings of Thomas Jefferson,* edited by Paul Leicester Ford; from *The Works of Henry Clay;* from *Eldorado,* by Bayard Taylor; from *The Age of Reason,* by Thomas Paine; from *The Works of Alexander Hamilton;* and from *Speeches, Correspondence, and Political Papers of Carl Schurz,* by Carl Schurz.

Random House: for a selection from *The Public Papers and Addresses of Franklin D. Roosevelt.*

Ratner, Victor M., "Television: Standards of Taste v. Freedom of Taste," *New York Times,* December 23, 1959.

Rogers, Professor Carl R., "Certain Issues Concerning the Control of Human Behavior," in *Science,* in the issue of November, 1956.

Sass, Marion Hutson, for permission to use his father's essay, "Mixed Schools and Mixed Blood," in the *Atlantic Monthly* for November, 1956.

Laurence Sears and *The American Scholar:* for a selection from "Security and Liberty," 1951.

Charles Scribner's Sons: for selections from *Christian Nurture,* by Horace Bushnell; from *The Silent South,* by George W. Cable; from *Autobiography,* by David Crockett; and from *Readings in Recent American Constitutional History, 1876–1926,* by Allen Johnson and William E. Robinson.

Upton Sinclair: for a selection from *The Jungle.*

Skinner, Professor B. F., "Some Issues Concerning the Control of Behavior," in *Science,* November 30, 1956.

Socialist Labor Party: for a selection from *Reform or Revolution,* by Daniel De Leon.

Elsie Strong: for a selection from *The Twentieth Century City* and from *Our Country,* by Josiah Strong.

Trustees Under the Will of Mary Baker Eddy: for "One Cause and Effect," in *Miscellaneous Writings,* by Mary Baker Eddy, copyrighted 1896 and renewed in 1924; and for the poem, "Satisfied," by Mary Baker Eddy.

Vanguard Press: for a selection from *The Dissenting Opinions of Mr. Justice Holmes.*

Viking Press: for selections from *The Higher Learning in America,* by Thorstein Veblen, copyright 1918; and *The Letters of Sacco and Vanzetti,* edited by Marion D. Frankfurter and Gardner Jackson, copyright 1928.

Vital Speeches: for selections from Dwight D. Eisenhower's "An Atomic Stockpile for Peace" (1953), Herbert C. Brownell's "The Fight Against Communism" (1954), Harry S. Truman's "The Faith by Which We Live" (1949), Walter Lippmann's "Philosophy and United States Foreign Policy" (1947) and George C. Marshall, "European Unity" (1947).

Mrs. Woodrow Wilson: for a selection from *The Public Papers of Woodrow Wilson, 1925–1929,* edited by W. E. Dodd and R. S. Baker.

Ella Winter: for a selection from *Autobiography* and from *The Shame of the Cities,* by Lincoln Steffens.

Yale University Press: for "Reply to a Socialist," by William Graham Sumner, in *Challenge of Facts,* edited by Albert Galloway Keller, 1924.

CONTENTS

The Other World or This, 1630-1790

The Struggle for Freedom, 1630-1776

The Rise of Americanism, 1783-1825

Democracy and Aristocracy, 1783-1840

Agrarianism and Commercial Capitalism, 1800-1850

The East and the Frontier, 1800-1860

Nationalism and Cosmopolitanism, 1825-1860

Life Everlasting, 1790-1860

The Second American Revolution, 1860-1865

North and South: The New Nationalism, 1865-1900

The Passing of the Frontier, 1850-1890

Class Conflicts and Class Protests, 1870-1896

Country and City, 1890-1920

Immigration and Its Restriction, 1865-1930

Naturalism and Supernaturalism, 1860-1910

Reform and the Conservative Defense, 1900-1917

Imperialism, War, and Pacifism, 1880-1920

The Big Money, 1920-1929

Depression and Reconstruction, 1929-1940

The Second World War, 1941–1945

Internal Adjustments and External Anxieties, 1945–

» » *The Other World or This* « «

1630-1790

» »   « «

PSALM 23

By Eliot, Weld, and Mather

1. The Lord to mee a shepheard is,
     want therefore shall not I
2. Hee in the folds of tender grasse,
     doth cause me downe to lie:

   To waters calme me gently leads
3.   Restore my soule doth hee:
   he doth in paths of righteousnes:
     for his names sake leade mee.

4. Yea, though in valley of deaths shade
     I walk, none ill I'll feare:
   Because thou are with mee, thy rod,
     and staffe my comfort are.

5. For mee a table thou hast spread,
     in presence of my foes:
   thou dost anoynt my head with oyle,
     my cup it over-flowes.

6. Goodnes & mercy surely shall
     all my dayes follow mee:
   and in the Lords house I shall dwell
     so long as dayes shall bee.

This song appeared in the *Bay Psalm Book*. Psalm singing was the only music which was permitted in the Puritan church. The Plymouth colonists first used the Ainsworth *Psalter*, which they had brought with them from England; the Massachusetts church preferred the versions of Sternhold and Hopkins. In 1640 Massachusetts provided itself with a Psalter of its own making, the famous *Bay Psalm Book*, the first book printed in the colonies. It was enormously popular, not only in America (seventy editions through 1773), but in England and Scotland as well. The versifiers of the psalms in it were three ministers, Richard Mather, Thomas Weld, and John Eliot, the "Apostle to the Indians."

» »   « «

The Other World or This

ONE OF the most pervasive conflicts in colonial life was that between supernatural and naturalistic outlooks and values. Some of the seventeenth century founders succeeded fairly well in setting up colonies in which the Word of God exerted far-reaching power over daily activities. But the claims of this world were like the pull of the ocean tide. Even in New England's Bible Commonwealths the advance of commercial interests made it increasingly hard for the theocracy to enforce its regulations over economic and social life. And although Anglican piety was more pronounced in the planting colonies than many have supposed, by the early eighteenth century a worldly plantation class had emerged which, like the merchants in the northern colonies, subordinated spiritual to temporal interests. This tendency was, perhaps, somewhat less marked among the more humble farmers. But the sturdy yeomen in Virginia, ardent though they were in demanding freedom to worship God as they saw fit, were, like farmers elsewhere, enterprising folk with loyalties that sometimes competed with religion. This was true even among groups which, like the pious Germans of Pennsylvania, often succeeded in maintaining a quite remarkable balance between the spiritual and the worldly. Even the Quakers, who began as humble and unworldly people, were taken to task by one of their own members, John Woolman, for truckling to the temptations and values of the world. Yet it would be easy to overemphasize the advance of secularism. Many remained traditionally pious and devout. In the mid-eighteenth century a wave of evangelical revivals, known as the Great Awakening, reinforced old-fashioned piety and moral codes.

The intellectually minded among both the established clergy and the merchant and the planting classes, however, stood in large measure apart from the emotional fervor of the Great Awakening. These groups had been, consciously or unconsciously, touched by the claims of natural science and rationalism. They tended increasingly to doubt many of the superstitions which sought to provide supernatural explanations for baffling phenomena. They looked with distrust on the belief in witchcraft and in a Deity given to constant interferences of a miraculous sort in man's daily life. It was not only that many of them had read the writings of Newton and the great scientists and rationalistic philosophers of Europe. Nor was it that the more privileged classes had heard some of these concepts applied by their own parsons who sought in rationalism and in science additional support for revelation. In the struggles with a hostile sea and an unfriendly forest, science frequently proved to be more serviceable than faith in supernaturalism. Merchants had to cultivate the science of navigation with its auxiliaries, mathematics, astronomy, and geography. Entrepreneurs engaged in exploiting naval stores and in opening up iron mines had to know something of natural history (the term given to geology and biology). Aware of the rapidity with which soil was impoverished, planters concerned themselves, in growing numbers, with scientific agriculture. In search of "cures" for a bewildering variety of ills of the flesh, men turned to the strange New World flora and fauna for "specifics." Thus moved by natural curiosity, as well as by utilitarian needs, American colonials made contributions to science and were duly honored by the Royal Society in London.

The delimitation of the area of supernaturalism was also furthered by the reception in certain circles of deism. By a curious circumstance parsons themselves were sometimes responsible for the ingress of deism. Influenced by Newtonianism and the growing authority

3

of science generally, they sought to "reconcile" science and religion, to show that religion was itself in harmony with naturalistic outlooks. By the middle of the eighteenth century colonial intellectuals were greatly influenced by the deistic conception of a law-governed, rational universe, in which the Supreme Architect was little more than an objectification of natural laws. Even the plain people got at least a hint of these newer ideas in the almanacs of Benjamin Franklin and Nathaniel Ames. The Great Awakening checked the spread of deistic beliefs among the rank and file but had less effect on the outlooks of intellectuals and men of substance.

Moreover, the traditional concern of religion with the lot of the unfortunate received new emphasis in the eighteenth century. If the efforts of Cotton Mather to advance piety through neighborly good works were inspired by his religion, such activities nevertheless emphasized the importance of earthly well-being. Even Jonathan Edwards, who formulated anew the deterministic Calvinism, ministered to the Indians. John Woolman denounced slavery, against which the Puritan judge, Samuel Sewall, had earlier protested. The Anglican Society for the Propagation of the Gospel and allied groups devoted much energy to the welfare of depressed groups.

Humanitarianism, which owed much to religion, was also enriched by the doctrines of the Enlightenment. The conviction that social environment was responsible for social ills, and that these would disappear in a more rational society, made advances. Man was not innately depraved, people began to think, and destined for a grim future, but potentially divine and capable of happiness on this earth. These ideas, together with utilitarian studies, sought entrance in the curriculum of educational institutions which, on the secondary and college level, had largely, though never entirely, been dominated by religious ideals. The Enlightenment, with interest in the lot of mankind on this earth, with a faith in a rational universe, in the possibility if not the inevitability of progress, knocked at the door and found it partly open.

» »   « «

INCREASE MATHER

1639–1723

BY FAMILY POSITION, training, and temperament Increase Mather belonged to and did much to support the theocratic oligarchy of Massachusetts Bay. A rigid Calvinist in theology and in polity, he opposed the relatively democratic conception of church government which the Independents had favored and did what he could to augment the power of the clergy. He also did much to prevent the transformation of the virtually autonomous Massachusetts Bay Colony into a royal province: for a time, at least, he saved some part of the old order by his skillful diplomacy in England during the early years of the reign of William and Mary. In 1701 he was forced from the presidency of Harvard College by the more liberal party; and though as a leader of vast erudition and personal force he continued, from the pastorate of North Church, Boston, to exert much influence, his dominance waned long before his death in 1723.

From Increase Mather's fertile pen more than one hundred and fifty writings on theology, church government, science, and history issued. *A Relation of the Troubles which have happened in New-England, By Reason of the Indians there* (1667) is an important account of King Philip's War. But he is best remembered for *An Essay for the Recording of Illustrious Providences, Wherein an Account is given of many Remarkable and very Memorable Events, which have happened in this last age; Especially in New England* (1684). That so erudite a scholar could subscribe to such old-wives' tales and superstition is evidence of the sway of supernaturalism at that time. Increase Mather did take a less vigorous role in supporting the "witchcraft delusion" than his son Cotton Mather. Indeed, he published in 1693 *Cases in Conscience Concerning Evil Spirits*, a pioneer protest against admitting as evidence the recitations of what "bewitched" persons claimed to have seen during their paroxysms.

T. J. Holmes, *Increase Mather, a Bibliography of His Works*, 2 vols., Cleveland, 1931.
Remarkable Providences Illustrative of the Earlier Days of American Colonization, G. Offor, ed., London, 1856, 1890.
K. B. Murdock, *Increase Mather, the Foremost American Puritan*, Cambridge, 1925.

» » *From:* REMARKABLE PROVIDENCES « «

ILLUSTRATIVE OF THE EARLIER DAYS OF AMERICAN COLONISATION

CHAPTER V

CONCERNING THINGS PRETER-NATURAL WHICH HAVE HAPNED IN NEW ENGLAND

Inasmuch as things which are preternatural, and not accomplished without diabolical operation, do more rarely happen, it is pitty but that they should be observed. Several Accidents of that kind have hapned in New-England; which I shall here faithfully Relate so far as I have been able to come unto the knowledge of them.

Very Remarkable was that Providence wherein Ann Cole of Hartford in New-England was concerned. She was and is accounted a person of real Piety and Integrity. Nevertheless, in the Year 1662, then living in her Fathers House (who has likewise been esteemed a godly Man) She was taken with very strange Fits, wherein her Tongue was improved by a Dæmon to express things which she herself knew nothing of. Sometimes the Discourse would hold for a considerable time. The general purpose of which was, that such and such persons (who were named in the Discourse which passed from her) were consulting how they might carry on mischievous designs against her and several others, mentioning sundry wayes they should take for that end, particularly that

they would afflict her Body, spoil her Name, etc. The general answer made amongst the Dæmons, was, She runs to the Rock. This having been continued some hours, the Dæmons said, Let us confound her Language, that she may tell no more tales. She uttered matters unintelligible. And then the Discourse passed into a Dutch-tone (a Dutch Family then lived in the Town), and therein an account was given of some afflictions that had befallen [10] divers; amongst others, what had befallen a Woman that lived next Neighbour to the Dutch Family, whose Arms had been strangely pinched in the night, declaring by whom and for what cause that course had been taken with her. The Reverend Mr. Stone (then Teacher of the Church in Hartford) being by, when the Discourse hapned, declared, that he thought it impossible for one not familiarly acquainted with the Dutch (which Ann Cole [20] had not in the least been) should so exactly imitate the Dutch-tone in the pronunciation of English. Several Worthy Persons (*viz.*, Mr. John Whiting, Mr. Samuel Hooker, and Mr. Joseph Hains) wrote the intelligible sayings expressed by Ann Cole, whilest she was thus amazingly handled. The event was, that one of the persons (whose Name was Greensmith, being a lewd and ignorant Woman, and then in Prison on suspicion for Witch-craft), men- [30] tioned in the Discourse as active in the mischief done and designed, was by the Magistrate sent for; Mr. Whiting and Mr. Haines read what they had written; and the Woman being astonished thereat, confessed those things to be true, and that she and other persons named in this preternatural Discourse, had had familiarity with the Devil: Being asked whether she had made an express Covenant with him, she answered, she had not, only as she promised to go with him when he called, which accordingly she had sundry times done; and that the Devil told her that at Christmass they would have a merry Meeting, and then the Covenant between them should be subscribed. The next day she was more particularly enquired of concerning her Guilt respecting the Crime she was accused with. She then acknowledged, that though when Mr. Hains began to read what he had taken down in Writing, her rage was such that she could have torn him in pieces, and was as resolved as might be to deny her guilt (as she had done before), yet after he had read awhile, she was (to use her own expression) as if her flesh had been pulled from her bones, and so could not deny any longer: she likewise declared, that the Devil first appeared to her in the form of a Deer or Fawn, skipping about her, wherewith she was not much affrighted, and that by degrees he became very familiar, and at last would talk with her; moreover, she said that the Devil had frequently the carnal knowledge of her Body. And that the Witches had Meetings at a place not far from her House; and that some appeared in one shape, and others in another; and one came flying amongst them in the shape of a Crow. Upon this Confession, with other concurrent Evidence, the Woman was Executed; so likewise was her husband, though he did not acknowledge himself guilty. Other persons accused in the Discourse made their escape. Thus doth the Devil use to serve his Clients. After the suspected Witches were either executed or fled, Ann Cole was restored to health, and has continued well for many years, approving herself a serious Christian.

There were some that had a mind to try whither the Stories of Witches not being able to sink under water were true; and accordingly a Man and Woman, mentioned in Ann Cole's Dutch-toned discourse, had their hands and feet tyed, and so were cast into the water, and they both apparently swam after the manner of a Buoy, part under, part above the Water. A by-stander, imagining that any person in that posture would be so born up, offered himself for trial, but being in the like matter gently laid on the Water, he immediately sunk right down. This was no legal Evidence against the suspected persons, nor were they proceeded against on any such account; However doubting that an Halter would choak them, though the Water would not, they very fairly took their flight, not having been seen in that part of the World since. Whether this experiment were lawful, or rather Superstitious and Magical, we shall (συν θεω) enquire afterwards.

Another thing which caused a noise in the Countrey, and wherein Satan had undoubtedly a great influence, was that which hapned at Groton. There was a Maid in that Town (one Elizabeth Knap) who in the Moneth of October, Anno 1671, was taken after a very strange manner, sometimes weeping, sometimes laughing, sometimes roaring hideously, with violent motions and agitations of her body, crying out Money, Money, etc. In November following, her Tongue for many hours together was drawn like a semicircle up to the roof of her Mouth, not to be removed, though some tried with their fingers to do it. Six Men were scarce able to hold her in some of her fits, but she would skip about the House yelling and looking with a most frightful Aspect. *December* 17, Her Tongue was drawn out of her mouth to an extraordinary length; and now a Dæmon began manifestly to speak in her. Many words were uttered wherein are the Labial Letters, without any motion of her Lips, which was a clear demonstration that the voice was not her own. Sometimes Words were spoken seeming to proceed out of her throat, when her Mouth was shut. Sometimes with her Mouth wide open, without the use of any of the Organs of speech. The things then uttered by the Devil were chiefly Railings and Revilings of Mr. Willard (who was at that time a Worthy and Faithful Pastor to the Church in Groton). Also the Dæmon belched forth most horrid and nefandous Blasphemies, exalting himself above the most High. After this she was taken speechless for some time. One thing more is worthy of Remark concerning this miserable creature. She cried out in some of her Fits, that a Woman (one of her Neighbours) appeared to her, and was the cause of her Affliction. The Person thus accused was a very sincere, holy Woman, who did hereupon with the Advice of Friends, visit the poor Wretch; and though she was in one of her Fits, having her Eyes shut, when the innocent person impeached by her came in; yet could she (so powerful were Satans Operations upon her) declare who was there, and could tell the touch of that Woman from any ones else. But the gracious Party thus accused and abused by a malicious Devil, Prayed earnestly with and for the Possessed creature; after which she confessed that Satan had deluded her, making her believe evil of her good Neighbour without any cause. Nor did she after that complain of any Apparition or Disturbance from such an one. Yea, she said, that the Devil had himself in the likeness and shape of divers tormented her, and then told her it was not he but they that did it.

As there have been several Persons vexed with evil Spirits, so divers Houses have been wofully Haunted by them. In the Year 1679, the house of William Morse, in Newberry in New-England, was strangely disquieted by a Dæmon. After those troubles began, he did by the Advice of Friends, write down the particulars of those unusual Accidents. And the account which he giveth thereof is as followeth:—

On *December* 3, in the night time, he and his Wife heard a noise upon the roof of their House, as if Sticks and Stones had been thrown against it with great violence; whereupon he rose out of his Bed, but could see nothing. Locking the Doors fast, he returned to Bed again. About midnight they heard an Hog making a great noise in the House, so that the Man rose again, and found a great Hog in the house, the door being shut, but upon the opening of the door it ran out.

On *December* 8. in the Morning, there were five great Stones and Bricks by an *invisible hand* thrown in at the west end of the house while the Mans Wife was making the Bed, the Bedstead was lifted up from the floor, and the Bedstaff flung out of the Window, and a Cat was hurled at her; a long Staff danced up and down in the Chimney; a burnt Brick, and a piece of a weatherboard were thrown in at the Window: The Man at his going to Bed put out his Lamp, but in the Morning found that the Saveall of it was taken away, and yet it was unaccountably brought into its former place. On the same day, the long Staff but now spoken of, was hang'd up by a line, and swung to and fro, the Man's Wife laid it in the fire, but she could not hold it there, inasmuch as it would forcibly fly out; yet after

much ado with joynt strength they made it to burn. A shingle flew from the Window, though no body near it, many sticks came in at the same place, only one of these was so scragged that it could enter the hole but a little way, whereupon the Man pusht it out, a great Rail likewise was thrust in at the Window, so as to break the Glass.

At another time an Iron Crook that was hanged on a Nail, violently flew up and down, also a Chair flew about, and at last lighted on the Table where Victuals stood ready for them to eat, and was likely to spoil all, only by a nimble catching they saved some of their Meal with the loss of the rest, and the overturning of their Table.

People were sometimes Barricado'd out of doors, when as yet there was no body to do it: and a Chest was removed from place to place, no hand touching it. Their Keys being tied together, one was taken from the rest, & the remaining two would fly about making a loud noise by knocking against each other. But the greatest part of this *Devils* feats were his mischievous ones, wherein indeed he was sometimes Antick enough too, and therein the chief sufferers were, the Man and his Wife, and his Grand-Son. The Man especially had his share in these *Diabolical* Molestations. For one while they could not eat their Suppers quietly, but had the Ashes on the Hearth before their eyes thrown into their Victuals; yea, and upon their heads and Clothes, insomuch that they were forced up into their Chamber, and yet they had no rest there; for one of the Man's Shoes being left below, 'twas filled with Ashes and Coals, and thrown up after them. Their Light was beaten out, and they being laid in their Bed with their little Boy between them, a great stone (from the Floor of the Loft) weighing above three pounds was thrown upon the mans stomach, and he turning it down upon the floor, it was once more thrown upon him. A Box, and a Board were likewise thrown upon them all. And a Bag of Hops was taken out of their Chest, wherewith they were beaten, till some of the Hops were scattered on the floor, where the Bag was then laid, and left.

In another Evening, when they sat by the fire, the Ashes were so whirled at them, that they could neither eat their Meat, nor endure the House. A Peel struck the Man in the face. An Apron hanging by the fire, was flung upon it, and singed before they could snatch it off. The Man being at Prayer with his Family, a

Beesom gave him a blow on his head behind, and fell down before his face.

On another day, when they were Winnowing of Barley, some hard dirt was thrown in, hitting the Man on the Head and both the Man and his Wife on the back; and when they had made themselves clean, they essayed to fill their half Bushel but the foul Corn was in spite of them often cast in amongst the clean, and the Man being divers times thus abused was forced to give over what he was about.

On *January* 23 (in particular) the Man had an iron Pin twice thrown at him, and his Inkhorn was taken away from him while he was writing, and when by all his seeking it he could not find it, at last he saw it drop out of the Air, down by the fire: a piece of Leather was twice thrown at him; and a shoe was laid upon his shoulder, which he catching at, was suddenly rapt from him. An handful of Ashes was thrown at his face, and upon his clothes: and the shoe was then clapt upon his head, and upon it he clapt his hand, holding it so fast, that somewhat unseen pulled him with it backward on the floor.

On the next day at night, as they were going to Bed, a lost Ladder was thrown against the Door, and their Light put out; and when the Man was a bed, he was beaten with an heavy pair of Leather Breeches, and pull'd by the Hair of his Head and Beard, Pinched and Scratched, and his Bed-board was taken away from him; yet more in the next night, when the Man was likewise a Bed; his Bed-board did rise out of its place, notwithstanding his putting forth all his strength to keep it in; one of his Awls wa[s] brought out of the next room into his Bed, and did prick him; the clothes wherewith he hoped to save his head from blows were violently pluckt from thence. Within a night or two after, the Man and his Wife received both of them a blow upon their heads, but it was so dark that they could not see the stone which gave it; the Man had his Cap pulled off from his head while he sat by the fire.

The night following, they went to bed undressed, because of their late disturbances, and the Man, Wife, Boy, presently felt themselves pricked, and upon search found in the Bed a Bodkin, a knitting Needle, and two sticks picked at both ends. He received also a great blow, as on his Thigh, so on his Face, which fetched blood: and while he was writing a Candlestick was twice thrown at him, and a

great piece of Bark fiercely smote him, and a pail of Water turned up without hands. On the 28 of the mentioned Moneth, frozen clods of Cow-dung were divers times thrown at the man out of the house in which they were; his Wife went to milk the Cow, and received a blow on her head, and sitting down at her Milking-work had Cow-dung divers times thrown into her Pail, the Man tried to save the Milk, by holding a Piggin side-wayes under the Cowes belly, but the Dung would in for all, and the Milk was only made fit for Hogs. On that night ashes were thrown into the porridge which they had made ready for their Supper, so as that they could not eat it; Ashes were likewise often thrown into the Man's Eyes, as he sat by the fire. And an iron Hammer flying at him, gave him a great blow on his back; the Man's Wife going into the Cellar for Beer, a great iron Peel flew and fell after her through the trapdoor of the Cellar; and going afterwards on the same Errand to the same place, the door shut down upon her, and the Table came and lay upon the door, and the man was forced to remove it e're his Wife could be released from where she was; on the following day while he was Writing, a dish went out of its place, leapt into the pale, and cast Water upon the Man, his Paper, his Table, and disappointed his procedure in what he was about; his Cap jumpt off from his head, and on again, and the Pot-lid leapt off from the Pot into the Kettle on the fire.

February 2. While he and his Boy were eating of Cheese, the pieces which he cut were wrested from them, but they were afterwards found upon the Table under an Apron, and a pair of Breeches: And also from the fire arose little sticks and Ashes, which flying upon the Man and his Boy, brought them into an uncomfortable pickle; But as for the Boy, which the last passage spoke of, there remains much to be said concerning him, and a principal suf- ferer in these afflictions: For on the 18. of *De- cember*, he sitting by his Grandfather, was hurried into great motions and the Man thereupon took him, and made him stand between his Legs, but the Chair danced up and down, and had like to have cast both Man and Boy into the fire: and the Child was afterwards flung about in such a manner, as that they feared that his Brains would have been beaten out; and in the evening he was tossed as afore, and the Man tried the project of holding him, but ineffectually. The Lad was soon put to Bed, and they presently heard an huge noise, and demanded what was the matter? and he answered that his Bed-stead leaped up and down: and they (*i.e.* the Man and his Wife) went up, and at first found all quiet, but before they had been there long, they saw the Board by his Bed trembling by him, and the Bed-clothes flying off him, the latter they laid on immediately, but they were no sooner on than off; so they took him out of his Bed for quietness.

December 29. The Boy was violently thrown to and fro, only they carried him to the house of a Doctor in the Town, and there he was free from disturbances, but returning home at night, his former trouble began, and the Man taking him by the hand, they were both of them almost tript into the fire. They put him to bed, and he was attended with the same iterated loss of his clothes, shaking off his Bed-board, and Noises, that he had in his last conflict; they took him up, designing to sit by the fire, but the doors clattered, and the Chair was thrown at him, wherefore they carried him to the Doctors house, and so for that night all was well. The next morning he came home quiet, but as they were doing somewhat, he cried out that he was prickt on the back, they looked, and found a three-tin'd Fork sticking strangely there; which being carried to the Doctors house, not only the Doctor himself said that it was his, but also the Doctors Servant affirmed it was seen at home after the Boy was gone. The Boys vexations continuing they left him at the Doctors, where he remained well till awhile after, and then he complained he was pricked, they looked and found an iron Spindle sticking below his back; he complained he was pricked still, they looked, and found Pins in a Paper sticking to his skin; he once more complained of his Back, they looked, and found there a long Iron, a bowl of a Spoon, and a piece of a Pansheard. They lay down by him on the Bed, with the Light burning, but he was twice thrown from them, and the second time thrown quite under the Bed; in the Morning the Bed was tossed about with such a creaking noise, as was heard to the Neighbours; in the afternoon their knives were one after another brought, and put into his back, but pulled out by the Spectators; only one knife which was missing seemed to the standers by to come out of his Mouth: he was bidden to read his Book, was taken and thrown about several times, at last hitting the Boys Grandmother on the head. Another time he was thrust

out of his Chair and rolled up and down without cries, that all things were on fire; yea, he was three times very dangerously thrown into the fire, and preserved by his Friends with much ado. The Boy also made for a long time together a noise like a Dog, and like an Hen with her Chickens, and could not speak rationally.

Particularly, on *December* 26. He barked like a Dog, and clock't like an Hen, and after long distraining to speak, said, there's *Powel*, I am pinched; his Tongue likewise hung out of his mouth, so as that it could by no means be forced in till his Fit was over, and then he said 'twas forced out by *Powel*. He & the house also after this had rest till the ninth of *January:* at which time the Child, because of his intolerable ravings, lying between the Man and his Wife, was pulled out of Bed, and knockt vehemently against the Bed-stead Boards, in a manner very perillous and amazing. In the Day time he was carried away beyond all possibility of their finding him. His Grandmother at last saw him creeping on one side, and drag'd him in, where he lay miserable lame, but recovering his speech, he said, that he was carried above the Doctors house, and that *Powel* carried him, and that the said *Powel* had him into the Barn, throwing him against the Cart-wheel there, and then thrusting him out at an hole; and accordingly they found some of the Remainders of the Threshed Barley which was on the Barn-floor hanging to his Clothes.

At another time he fell into a Swoon, they forced somewhat Refreshing into his mouth, and it was turned out as fast as they put it in; e're long he came to himself, and expressed some willingness to eat, but the Meat would forcibly fly out of his mouth; and when he was able to speak, he said *Powel* would not let him eat: Having found the *Boy* to be best at a Neighbours house, the Man carried him to his Daughters, three miles from his own. The Boy was growing antick as he was on the Journey, but before the end of it he made a grievous hollowing, and when he lighted, he threw a great stone at a Maid in the house, and fell on eating of Ashes. Being at home afterwards, they had rest awhile, but on the 19 of *January* in the Morning he swooned, and coming to himself, he roared terribly, and did eat Ashes, Sticks, Rug-yarn. The Morning following, there was such a racket with the Boy, that the Man and his Wife took him to Bed to them. A Bedstaff was thereupon thrown at them, and a

Chamber pot with its Contents was thrown upon them, and they were severely pinched. The Man being about to rise, his Clothes were divers times pulled from them, himself thrust out of his Bed, and his Pillow thrown after him. The Lad also would have his clothes plucked off from him in these Winter Nights, and was wofully dogg'd with such fruits of Devilish spite, till it pleased God to shorten
10   the Chain of the wicked *Dæmon.*

All this while the Devil did not use to appear in any visible shape, only they would think they had hold of the Hand that sometimes scratched them; but it would give them the slip. And once the Man was discernably beaten by a Fist, and an Hand got hold of his Wrist which he saw, but could not catch; and the likeness of a *Blackmore* Child did appear from under the Rugg and Blanket, where the Man
20   lay, and it would rise up, fall down, nod & slip under the clothes when they endeavoured to clasp it, never speaking any thing.

Neither were there many Words spoken by Satan all this time, only once having put out their Light, they heard a scraping on the Boards, and then a Piping and Drumming on them, which was followed with a Voice, singing *Revenge! Revenge! Sweet is Revenge!* And they being well terrified with it, called upon
30   God; the issue of which was, that suddenly with a mournful Note, there were six times over uttered such expressions as *Alas! Alas! me knock no more! me knock no more!* and now all ceased.

The Man does moreover affirm, that a Seaman (being a Mate of a Ship) coming often to visit him, told him that they wronged his Wife who suspected her to be guilty of Witchcraft; and that the Boy (his Grandchild) was the
40   cause of this trouble; and that if he would let

him have the Boy one day, he would warrant him his house should be no more troubled as it had been; to which motion he consented. The Mate came the next day betimes, and the Boy was with him until night; after which his house he saith was not for some time molested with evil Spirits.

Thus far is the Relation concerning the *Dæmon* at *William Morse* his House in *Newbery.* The true Reason of these strange disturbances is as yet not certainly known: some (as has been hinted) did suspect *Morse's* Wife to be guilty of Witchcraft.

One of the Neighbours took Apples which were brought out of that house and put them into the fire; upon which they say, their houses were much disturbed. Another of the Neighbours, caused an Horse-shoe to be nailed before the doors, & as long as it remained so, they could not perswade the suspected person to go into the house; but when the Horse-shoe was gone, she presently visited them. I shall not here inlarge upon the vanity and superstition of those Experiments, reserving that for another place: All that I shall say at present is, that the *Dæmons* whom the blind Gentiles of old worshipped, told their Servants, that such things as these would very much affect them; yea, and that certain Characters, Signs and Charms would render their power ineffectual; and accordingly they would become subject, when their own directions were obeyed. It is sport to the Devils when they see silly Men thus deluded and made fools of by them. Others were apt to think that a Seaman or some suspected to be a Conjurer, set the Devil on work thus to disquiet *Morse's* family. Or it may be some other thing as yet kept hid in the secrets of providence might be the true original of all this Trouble.* * *   1684

COTTON MATHER

1663–1728

THE SON of Increase Mather and the active head of his father's church in Boston after 1688, Cotton Mather was a curiously complex figure. On the one hand, as his *Diary* reveals, he was pedantic, morbidly introspective, and eccentric; on the other, as his philanthropic activities and his *Essays to do Good* (1710) prove, he was a faithful and helpful pastor, a friend of missions, temperance, and popular education. The fact is, Cotton Mather looked both backward and forward. His *Magnalia Christi Americana* (1702), notable for the rich dignity of its Elizabethan prose, glorified the ideals and the characters of the Puritan fathers and argued for the preservation of their values in a society which was rapidly departing from the old order. Cotton Mather's *Memorable Providences Relating to Witchcraft and Possessions* (1689) and *The Wonders of the Invisible World* (1693) not only record the "witchcraft delusion" which he supported with considerable fanaticism, but justify what was done. At the same time he agreed with his father in holding that "spectral evidence," or the testimony of "bewitched" persons regarding their visions during paroxysm, should not be admitted; and he favored leniency in punishments.

Cotton Mather also interested himself in science and was nominated for membership in the Royal Society in 1713. His championship of inoculation against smallpox was not only notably courageous: it also marked him as a "progressive." *The Christian Philosopher* (1721), written in part to reconcile science and religion, reveals traces, at least, of deistic thought. His humanitarianism and his interest in practical methods for higher living influenced Franklin. In all these respects Cotton Mather was responding to the newer influences which were undermining the old Puritanism, to which he clung with stubborn melancholy. His vast writings, which number five hundred titles, make him New England's leading scholar and most industrious man of letters.

Thomas O. Holmes, *Cotton Mather, A Bibliography of his Works*, 3 vols., Cambridge, 1940.
The Diary of Cotton Mather, 2 vols., New York, 1957.
Magnalia Christi Americana, T. Robbins and others, ed., Hartford, 1853–1855.
K. B. Murdock, *Selection from the Works of Cotton Mather*, New York, 1925.
Barrett Wendell, *Cotton Mather, The Puritan Priest*, New York, 1891, 1926.
N. R. and L. Boas, *Cotton Mather, Keeper of the Puritan Conscience*, New York, 1928.

» » *From:* THE WONDERS OF THE INVISIBLE WORLD « «

ENCHANTMENTS ENCOUNTRED

§II. The *New-Englanders* are a People of God settled in those, which were once the *Devils* Territories; and it may easily be supposed that the *Devil* was Exceedingly disturbed, when he perceived such a People here accomplishing the Promise of old made unto our Blessed Jesus, *That He should have the Utmost parts of the Earth for his Possession.* There was not a greater Uproar among the *Ephesians,* when the Gospel was first brought among them, than there was among, *The Powers of the Air* (after whom those *Ephesians* walked) when first the *Silver Trumpets* of the Gospel here made the *Joyful Sound.* The Devil thus Irritated, immediately try'd all sorts of Methods to overturn this poor Plantation: and so much of the Church, as was *Fled into this Wilderness,* immediately found, *The Serpent cast out of his Mouth a Flood for the carrying of it away.* I believe, that never were more *Satanical Devices*

used for the Unsetling of any People under the Sun, than what have been Employ'd for the Extirpation of the *Vine* which God has here *Planted, Casting out the Heathen, and preparing a Room before it, and causing it to take deep Root, and fill the Land; so that it sent its Boughs unto the* Attlantic *Sea* Eastward, *and its Branches unto the* Connecticut *River* Westward, *and the Hills were covered with the Shadow thereof.* But, All those Attempts of Hell, have hitherto been Abortive, many an *Ebenezer* has been Erected unto the Praise of God, by his Poor People here; and, *Having obtained Help from God, we continue to this Day.* Wherefore the Devil is now making one Attempt more upon us; an Attempt more Difficult, more Surprizing, more snarl'd with unintelligible Circumstances than any that we have hitherto Encountred; an Attempt so *Critical,* that if we get well through, we shall soon Enjoy *Halcyon* Days with all the *Vultures* of Hell, *Trodden under our Feet.* He has

10

20

wanted his *Incarnate Legions* to Persecute us, as the People of God have in the other Hemisphere been Persecuted: he has therefore drawn forth his more *Spiritual* ones to make an Attacque upon us. We have been advised by some Credible Christians yet alive, that a Malefactor, accused of *Witchcraft* as well as *Murder,* and Executed in this place more than Forty Years ago, did then give Notice, of, *An Horrible*
10 *PLOT against the Country by* WITCHCRAFT, *and a Foundation of* WITCHCRAFT *then Laid, which if it were not seasonably Discovered, would probably Blow up, and pull down all the Churches in the Country.* And we have now with Horror seen the *Discovery* of such a *Witchcraft!* An Army of *Devils* is horribly broke in upon the place which is the *Center,* and after a sort, the *First-born* of our *English* Settlements: and the Houses of the Good
20 People there, are fill'd with the doleful Shrieks of their Children and Servants, Tormented by Invisible Hands, with Tortures altogether preternatural. After the Mischiefs there Endeavoured, and since in part Conquered, the terrible Plague, of *Evil Angels,* hath made its Progress into some other places, where other Persons have been in like manner Diabolically handled. These our poor Afflicted Neighbours, quickly after they become *Infected* and *In-*
30 *fested* with these *Dæmons,* arrive to a Capacity of Discerning those which they conceive the *Shapes* of their Troublers; and notwithstanding the Great and Just Suspicion, that the *Dæmons* might Impose the *Shapes* of Innocent Persons in their *Spectral Exhibitions* upon the Sufferers, (which may perhaps prove no small part of the *Witch-Plot* in the issue) yet many of the Persons thus Represented, being Examined, several of them have been Con-
40 victed of a very Damnable *Witchcraft:* yea, more than One *Twenty* have *Confessed,* that they have Signed unto a *Book,* which the Devil show'd them, and Engaged in his Hellish

Design of *Bewitching,* and *Ruining* our Land. *We* know not, at least *I* know not, how far the *Delusions* of Satan may be Interwoven into some Circumstances of the *Confessions;* but one would think, all the Rules of Understanding Humane Affayrs are at an end, if after so many most Voluntary Harmonious *Confessions,* made by Intelligent Persons of all Ages, in sundry Towns, at several Times, we must not Believe the *main strokes* wherein those *Confessions* all agree: especially when we have a thousand preternatural Things every day before our eyes, wherein the *Confessors* do acknowledge their Concernment, and give Demonstration of their being so Concerned. If the Devils now can strike the minds of men, with any *Poisons* of so fine a Composition and Operation, that Scores of Innocent People shall Unite, in *Confessions* of a Crime, which we see actually committed, it is a thing prodigious, beyond the Wonders of the former Ages, and it threatens no less than a sort of a Dissolution upon the World. Now, by these *Confessions* 'tis Agreed, *That the Devil* has made a dreadful Knot of *Witches* in the Country, and by the help of *Witches* has dreadfully increased that Knot: *That* these *Witches* have driven a Trade of Commissioning their *Confederate Spirits,* to do all sorts of Mischiefs to the Neighbours, whereupon there have ensued such Mischievous consequences upon the Bodies and Estates of the Neighbourhood, as could not otherwise be accounted for: yea, *That* at prodigious *Witch-Meetings,* the Wretches have proceeded so far, as to Concert and Consult the Methods of Rooting out the Christian Religion from this Country, and setting up instead of it, perhaps a more gross *Diabolism,* than ever the World saw before. And yet it will be a thing little short of *Miracle,* if in so *spread* a Business, as this, the Devil should not get in some of his Juggles, to confound the Discovery of all the rest.   1693

» » *From:* THE CHRISTIAN PHILOSOPHER « «

ESSAY XXXII

OF MAN

Hear now the Conclusion of the Matter. To enkindle the *Dispositions* and the *Resolutions* of PIETY in my Brethren, is the *Inten-*

tion of all my ESSAYS, and must be the *Conclusion* of them.

Atheism is now for ever chased and hissed out of the World, every thing in the World concurs to a Sentence of *Banishment* upon it. *Fly, thou Monster, and hide, and let not the darkest Recesses of Africa itself be able to cherish thee; never dare to shew thyself in a World where every thing stands ready to overwhelm thee!* A BEING that must be *superior to Matter,* even the *Creator* and *Governor* of all *Matter,* is every where so conspicuous, that here can be nothing more *monstrous* than *to deny the God that is above.* No *System* of *Atheism* has ever yet been offered among the Children of Men, but what may presently be convinced of such *Inconsistences,* that a Man must ridiculously believe *nothing certain* before he can imagine them; it must be a *System* of *Things which cannot stand together!* A Bundle of *Contradictions* to themselves, and to all *common Sense.* I doubt it has been an *inconsiderate* thing to pay so much of a Compliment to *Atheism,* as to bestow solemn *Treatises* full of learned *Arguments* for the Refutation of a *delirious Phrenzy,* which ought rather to be put out of countenance with the most *contemptuous Indignation.* And I fear such Writers as have been at the pains to put the *Objections* of Atheism into the most plausible Terms, that they may have the honour of *laying a Devil when they have raised him,* have therein done too *unadvisedly.* However, to so much notice of the raving *Atheist* we may condescend while we go along, as to tell him, that for a Man to question the *Being* of a GOD, who requires from us an *Homage* of *Affection,* and *Wonderment,* and Obedience to Himself, and a perpetual Concern for the Welfare of the *Human Society,* for which He has in our *Formation* evidently *suited* us, would be an *exalted Folly,* which undergoes especially two Condemnations; it is first condemned by this, that every Part of the *Universe* is continually *pouring in* something for the *confuting* of it; there is not a Corner of the whole World but what supplies a *Stone* towards the Infliction of such a *Death* upon the *Blasphemy* as justly belongs to it: and it has also this condemning of it, that Men would soon become *Canibals* to one another by embracing it; Men being utterly destitute of any Principle to keep them *honest in the Dark,* there would be no *Integrity* left in the World, but they would be as the *Fishes of the Sea to one another,* and worse than *the creeping Things, that have no Ruler over them.* Indeed from every thing in the World there is this Voice more audible than the loudest Thunder to us; *God hath spoken, and these two things have I heard!* First, *Believe and adore a glorious GOD, who has made all these Things*

and know thou that He will bring thee into Judgment! And then *be careful to do nothing but what shall be for the Good of the Community which the glorious GOD has made thee a Member of.* Were what God *hath spoken* duly regarded, and were these *two things* duly complied with, the World would be soon revived into a desirable *Garden of God,* and Mankind would be fetch'd up into very comfortable Circumstances; till *then* the World continues in a wretched Condition, *full of doleful Creatures,* with *wild Beasts crying* in its *desolate Houses, Dragons* in its most *pleasant Palaces.* And now declare, O *every thing that is reasonable,* declare and pronounce upon it whether it be possible that *Maxims* absolutely *necessary* to the *Subsistence* and *Happiness* of Mankind, can be *Falsities?* There is no possibility for this, that *Cheats* and *Lyes* must be so *necessary,* that the *Ends* which alone are worthy of a glorious GOD, cannot be attain'd without having *them* imposed upon us!

Having dispatch'd the *Atheist,* with bestowing on him *not many* Thoughts, yet *more* than could be deserved by such an *Idiot;* I will proceed now to propose two general Strokes of *Piety,* which will appear to a *Christian Philosopher* as unexceptionable as any Proposals that ever were made to him.

First, the Works of the glorious God exhibited to our View, 'tis most certain they do *bespeak,* and they should *excite our Acknowledgments of His Glories* appearing in them: the Great GOD is infinitely *gratified* in beholding the Displays of His own infinite *Power,* and *Wisdom,* and *Goodness,* in the Works which He has made; but it is also a most acceptable Gratification to Him, when such of His Works as are the *rational Beholders* of themselves, and of the rest shall with devout Minds *acknowledge* His Perfections, which they see shining there. Never does one endued with *Reason* do any thing more evidently *reasonable,* than when he makes every thing that occurs to him in the vast Fabrick of the World, an *Incentive* to some agreeable Efforts and Salleys of *Religion.* What can any Man living object against the *Piety* of a Mind awaken'd by the sight of God in His Works, to such Thoughts as these: *Verily, there is a glorious* GOD! *Verily, the GOD who does these things is worthy to be feared, worthy to be loved, worthy to be relied on! Verily, all possible Obedience is due to such a* GOD;

and most abominable, most inexcusable is the Wickedness of all Rebellion against Him! A Mind kept under the Impression of such Thoughts as these, is an *holy* and a *noble* Mind, a *Temple* of God, *a Temple filled with the Glory of God.* There is nothing but what will afford an *Occasion* for the *Thoughts;* the oftner a Man improves the *Occasion,* the more does he *glorify* GOD, and answer the *chief End of Man;* and why should he not *seek occasion* for it, by visiting for this purpose the several *Classes* of the Creatures (for *Discipulus in hác Scholâ erit Peripateticus*) [1] as he may have opportunity for so generous an Exercise! But since the horrid Evil of all *Sin* is to be inferred from this; *it is a Rebellion against the Laws of the glorious* GOD, *who is the Maker and the Ruler of all Worlds;* and *it is a disturbance of the good Order wherein the glorious Maker and Ruler of all Things has placed them all;* how much ought a quickned *Horror of Sin* to accompany this Contemplation, and produce this most agreeable Resolution, *My God, I will for ever fear to offend thy glorious Majesty!* Nor is this all the *Improvement* which we are to make of what we see in the *Works of God;* in our *improving* of them, we are to accept of the *Rebuke* which they give to our *Presumption,* in pretending to criticize upon the *dark things* which occur in the Dispensations of His *Providence;* there is not any one of all the *Creatures* but what has those *fine things* in the *Texture* of it, which have never yet been reached by our *Searches,* and we are as much at a loss about the *Intent* as about the *Texture* of them; *as yet* we know not what the glorious God *intends* in His forming of those *Creatures,* nor what *He has to do* in them, and with them; He therein proclaims this Expectation, *Surely they will fear me, and receive Instruction.* And the Point wherein we are now instructed is this: 'What! Shall I be so vain as to be *dissatisfied* 'because I do not *understand* what is done by 'the glorious GOD in the Works of His *Provi-* 'dence!' *O my Soul, hast thou not known, hast thou not heard concerning the everlasting God, the Lord, the Creator of the Ends of the Earth, that there is no searching of His Understanding?*

And then, secondly, the CHRIST of God must not be forgotten, who is *the Lord of all. I am not ashamed of the Gospel of* CHRIST, of which I will *affirm constantly,* that if the *Philosopher* do not call it in, he *paganizes,* and leaves the finest and brightest Part of his Work unfinished. Let *Colerus* persuade us if he can, that in the Time of *John Frederick* the Elector of *Saxony* there was dug up a *Stone,* on which there was a Representation of our *crucified Saviour;* but I cannot forbear saying, there is not a *Stone* any where which would not look *black* upon me, and *speak* my Condemnation, if my *Philosophy* should be so *vain* as to make me lay aside my Thoughts of my *enthroned Saviour.* Let *Lambecius,* if he pleases, employ his Learning upon the Name of our Saviour CHRIST, found in Letters naturally engraven at the bottom of a large *Agate-Cup,* which is to be seen among the Emperor's Curiosities; I have never drank in that *Cup,* however I can more easily believe it than I can the *Crucifixus ex Radice Crambres enatus,* or the *Imago Virginis cum Filiolo, in Minervâ Ferri expressa,*[2] and several more such things, which the Publishers of the *German Ephemerides* have mingled with their better Entertainments: but I will assert, that a glorious CHRIST is more to be considered in the *Works of Nature* than the *Philosopher* is generally aware of; and my CHRISTIAN *Philosopher* has not fully done his Part, till He who is *the First-born of every Creature* be come into Consideration with him. *Alsted* mentions a *Siclus Judaeo-Christianus,* which had on one side the Name JESUS, with the Face of our *Saviour,* and on the other the Words that signify *the King Messiah comes with Peace, and God becomes a Man;* and *Leusden* says he had a couple of these *Coins* in his possession. I have nothing to say on the behalf of the *Zeal* in those *Christianized Jews,* who probably were the Authors of these *Coins,* a *Zeal* that *boil'd* into so needless an Expression of an Homage, that indeed cannot be too much expressed in the *instituted ways* of it to a Redeemer, whose *Kingdom is not of this World:* but this I will say, *all the Creatures in this World are part of His Kingdom;* there are no *Creatures* but what are His *Medals,* on every one of them the Name of JESUS is to be found inscribed. Celebrate, O *Danhaver,* thy *Granatilla,* the *Peruvian Plant,* on which a strong Imagination finds a Representation of the *Instruments* employed in the *Sufferings* of our Saviour, and especially the *bloody Sweat* of His Agonies; were the Representation as really and lively made as has been

---

[1] *A disciple in that school will be a Peripatetic philosopher.*

[2] *The Crucifix sprang forth from the root of a cabbage. The image of the Madonna and Child is visible in a vein of iron ore.* Mather holds these examples up as the height of the ridiculous.

ımagined, I would subscribe to the Epigram upon it, which concludes:

Flos hic ita formâ vincit omnes Flosculos,
Ut totus optet esse Spectator Oculus.[3]

But I will, with the Exercise of the most *solid Reason*, by every part of the World, as well as the *Vegetables*, be led to my *Saviour*.

A *View of the Creation* is to be taken, with suitable Acknowledgments of the glorious CHRIST, in whom the *eternal Son of God* has personally united Himself to ONE of His *Creatures*, and becomes on *his* account propitious to *all the rest;* our *Piety* indeed will not be *Christianity* if HE be left unthought upon.

This is HE, of whom we are instructed, Col. 1. 16, 17. *All things were created by Him, and for Him; and He is before all things, and by Him all things consist.* It is no contemptible Thought wherewith *De Sabunde* has entertained us: *Productio Mundi à Deo facta de Nihilo, arguit aliam productionem, summam, occultam, & æternam in Deo, quæ est de sua propria Natura, in qua producitur Deus de Deo, & per quam ostenditur summa Trinitas in Deo.*[4] And certainly he that as a *Father* does produce a *Son,* but as an *Artist* only produce an *House,* has a Value for the *Son* which he has not for the *House;* yea, we may say, if GOD had not first, and from Eternity, been a *Father* to our *Saviour,* He would never have exerted Himself as an *Artist* in that *Fabrick,* which He has built *by the Might of His Power, and for the Honour of His Majesty!*

The Great Sir *Francis Bacon* has a notable Passage in his *Confession of Faith: I believe that God is so holy, as that it is impossible for Him to be pleased in any Creature, tho the Work of his own Hands, without beholding of the same in the Face of a Mediator;—without which it was impossible for Him to have descended to any Work of Creation, but He should have enjoyed the blessed and individual Society of three Persons in the Godhead for ever; but out of His eternal and infinite Goodness and Love purposing to become a Creature, and communicate with His Creatures, He ordained in His eternal Counsel that one Person of the Godhead should be united to one Nature, and to one particular of His Creatures;* that so in the Person of the Mediator the true Ladder might be fixed, whereby God might descend to His Creatures, and His Creatures ascend to Him.*

It was an high Flight of *Origen,* who urges, that our *High-Priest's* having *tasted of Death,* ὑπὲρ παυτος, FOR ALL, is to be extended even to the very *Stars,* which would otherwise have been *impure* in the sight of God; and thus are ALL THINGS restored to the *Kingdom* of the Father. Our Apostle *Paul* in a famous Passage to the *Colossians* (i. 19, 20.) may seem highly to favour this Flight. One says upon it, 'If this be so, we need not break the 'Glasses of *Galilaeo,* the *Spots* may be washed 'out of the *Sun,* and *total Nature* sanctified to 'God that made it.'

Yea, the sacred Scriptures plainly and often invite us to a Conception, which Dr. *Goodwin* has chosen to deliver in such Terms as these: 'The *Son of God personally and actually exist-* 'ing as the *Son* of God with God, afore the 'World or any Creature was made, *He* under- 'taking and covenanting with God to become 'a *Man, yea, that Man* which He hath now 'taken up into one Person with Himself, as 'well for *this End,* as for *other Ends* more 'glorious; God did in the Fore-knowledge of 'that, and in the Assurance of that *Covenant* 'of His, proceed to the *creating* of all things 'which He hath made; and without the Intui- 'tion of *this,* or having *this* in His Eye, He 'would not have made any thing which He 'hath made.'

O CHRISTIAN, *lift up now thine Eyes, and look from the place where thou art to all* Points of the Compass, and concerning *whatever thou seest,* allow that all these things were formed *for the Sake* of that Glorious-One, who is now *God manifest in the Flesh* of our JESUS; 'tis on His Account that the eternal Godhead has the *Delight* in all these things, which preserves them in their Being, and grants them the *Help,* in the *obtaining* whereof they *continue to this day.*

But were they not all made *by the hand,* as well as *for the Sake* of that Glorious-ONE? They were verily so. *O my JESUS, it was that Son of God who now dwells in thee, in and by whom the Godhead exerted the Power, which could be exerted by none but an all-powerful GOD, in the creating of the World!* He is that Word of GOD *by whom all things were made, and without whom was not any thing made that was made.*

---

[3] *By its form this flower surpasses all little flowers to such a degree that the spectator wishes to be all eye.*

[4] *God's creation of the world out of nothing argues another creation, highest, hidden, and everlasting in God, which is of his own nature, in which God is produced from God, and by which is shown the sublime trinity in God.* The reference here is apparently to the Saviour.

10

20

30

40

50

This is not all that we have to think upon; we see an incomparable *Wisdom* of GOD in His *Creatures;* one cannot but presently infer, *What an incomprehensible Wisdom then in the Methods and Affairs of that Redemption, whereof the glorious GOD has laid the Plan in our JESUS!* Things which the *Angels desire to look into.* But, O *evangelized Mind,* go on, mount up, soar higher, think at this rate; *the infinite Wisdom which formed all these things is peculiarly seated in the Son of God;* He is that *reflexive Wisdom* of the eternal Father, and that *Image of the invisible God, by whom all things were created;* in *Him* there is after a peculiar manner the original *Idea and Archetype* of every thing that offers the infinite *Wisdom* of GOD to our Admiration. Wherever we see the *Wisdom* of God admirably shining before us, we are invited to such a Thought as this; *this Glory is originally to be found in thee, O our Immanuel!* 'Tis in Him *transcendently.* But then 'tis impossible to stop without adding, *How glorious, how wondrous, how lovely art thou, O our Saviour!*

Nor may we lay aside a grateful Sense of this, that as the *Son* of God is *the Upholder of all Things in all Worlds,* thus, that it is owing to his potent *Intercession* that the *Sin of Man* has made no more havock on this *our World.* This *our World* has been by the *Sin of Man* so perverted from the *true Ends* of it, and rendred full of such loathsome and hateful Regions, and such *Scelerata Castra,* that the Revenges of God would have long since rendred it as a *fiery Oven,* if our blessed JESUS had not *interceded* for it: *O my Saviour, what would have become of me, and of all that comforts me, if thy Interposition had not preserved us!*

We will add one thing more: Tho the one GOD in His *three Subsistences* be the *Governor* as well as the *Creator* of the World, and so the *Son* of God ever had what we call the *natural Government* of the World, yet upon the *Fall* of Mankind there is a *mediatory Kingdom* that becomes expedient, that so *guilty Man,* and that which was *lost,* may be brought to God; and the singular Honour of this *mediatory Kingdom* is more *immediately* and most *agreeably* assign'd to the *Son of God,* who assumes the Man JESUS into His own Person, and has *all Power in Heaven and Earth given to Him;* all things are now commanded and ordered by the *Son of God* in the *Man upon the Throne,* and this *to the Glory*

of the Father, by whom the *mediatory Kingdom* is erected, and so conferred. This *peculiar Kingdom* thus managed by the *Son of God* in our JESUS, will cease when the illustrious Ends of it are all accomplished, and *then* the *Son of God* no longer having such a *distinct Kingdom* of His own, shall return to those eternal Circumstances, wherein He shall reign with the *Father* and the *Holy Spirit,* one God, blessed for ever. In the mean time, what Creatures can we behold without being obliged to some such Doxology as this; *O Son of God, incarnate and enthroned in my JESUS, this is part of thy Dominion! What a great King art thou, and what a Name hast thou above every Name, and how vastly extended is thy Dominion! Dominion and Fear is with thee, and there is no Number of thine Armies! All the Inhabitants of the Earth, and their most puissant Emperors, are to be reputed as nothing before thee!*

But then at last I am losing myself in such Thoughts as these: *Who can tell* what *Uses* our Saviour will put all these *Creatures* to at the *Restitution of all things,* when He comes to rescue them from the *Vanity* which as yet captivates them and incumbers them; and His raised People in the *new Heavens* will make their Visits to a *new Earth,* which they shall find flourishing in *Paradisaick* Regularities? *Lord, what thou meanest in them, I know not now, but I shall know hereafter!* I go on, *Who can tell* how sweetly our Saviour may *feast* His *chosen People* in the *Future State,* with Exhibitions of all these *Creatures,* in their various *Natures,* and their curious *Beauties* to them? *Lord, I hope for an eternally progressive Knowledge, from the Lamb of God successively leading me to the Fountains of it!*

I recover out of my more *conjectural Prognostications,* with resolving what may *at present* yield to a serious Mind a *Satisfaction,* to which this World knows none superior: When in a way of *occasional Reflection* I employ the *Creatures* as my *Teachers,* I will by the *Truths* wherein those ready *Monitors* instruct me, be led to my glorious JESUS; I will consider the *Truths as they are in* JESUS, and count my Asceticks deficient, till I have some Thoughts of HIM and of His Glories awakened in me. To conclude, It is a good Passage which a little Treatise entitled, *Theologia Ruris,* or, *The Book of Nature,* breaks off withal, and I might make it my Conclusion: 'If we mind 'Heaven whilst we live here upon *Earth,* this

'*Earth* will serve to conduct us to *Heaven,* 'thro the Merits and Mediation of the *Son of* '*God,* who was made the *Son of Man,* and 'came thence on purpose into this lower World 'to convey us up thither.'

I will finish with a Speculation, which my most valuable Dr. *Cheyne* has a little more largely prosecuted and cultivated.

All *intelligent compound Beings* have their whole Entertainment in these three Principles, the DESIRE, the OBJECT, and the SENSATION arising from the *Congruity* between them; this *Analogy* is preserved full and clear thro the *Spiritual World, yea,* and thro the *material* also; so *universal* and *perpetual* an *Analogy* can arise from nothing but its *Pattern* and *Archetype* in the infinite God or Maker; and could we carry it up to the Source of it, we should find the TRINITY of Persons in the eternal GODHEAD admirably exhibited to us. In the GODHEAD we may first apprehend a *Desire,* an infinitely active, ardent, powerful *Thought,* proposing of *Satisfaction;* let this represent GOD the FATHER: but it is not possible for any Object but God Himself to *satisfy Himself,* and fill His *Desire* of Happiness; therefore HE Himself *reflected* in upon Himself, and contemplating His own infinite Perfections, even the *Brightness of His Glory,* and the *express Image of His Person,* must answer this glorious Intention; and this may represent to us GOD the SON. Upon this Contemplation, wherein GOD Himself does behold, and possess, and enjoy Himself, there cannot but arise a *Love,* a *Joy,* an *Acquiescence* of God Himself within Himself, and worthy of a God; this may shadow out to us the third and the last of the Principles in this *mysterious Ternary,* that is to say, the Holy SPIRIT. Tho these *three Relations* of the Godhead in itself, when derived analogically down to Creatures, may appear but *Modifications* of a *real Subsistence,* yet in the supreme Infinitude of the Divine Nature, they must be infinitely *real* and *living* Principles. Those which are but *Relations* when transferred to *created Beings,* are glorious realities in the infinite God. And in this View of the Holy Trinity, low as it is, it is impossible the SON should be without the FATHER, or the FATHER without the SON, or both without the Holy SPIRIT; it is impossible the SON should not be necessarily and eternally begotten of the Father, or that the Holy SPIRIT should not necessarily and eternally proceed both from Him and from the SON. Thus from what occurs throughout the whole Creation, *Reason* forms an imperfect Idea of this incomprehensible Mystery.

But it is time to stop here, and indeed how can we go any further!

FINIS

1721

JONATHAN EDWARDS

1703–1758

JONATHAN EDWARDS was descended from intellectual and vigorous men and women. During his studies at Yale, he became familiar with the liberal thought of Locke, Newton, and Berkeley. Indulging his precocious mind in remarkable exercises in natural science and his poetic fancy in philosophical speculations, he might well have become one of the heralds of the Enlightenment or even of the still more remote intuitionism of Emerson. Instead, he turned his remarkable intellectual gifts to pastoral work, to logic, theology, and missionary enterprises. During his ministry at Northampton, Massachusetts (1727–1750), he opposed the growing liberalism in religion and took a firm stand for the strict morals and the harsh Calvinistic doctrine of the old order. Yet his poetic and mystical impulses shone through the grim and deterministic Calvinistic dogma which he preached with zeal in the evangelical movement known as "The Great Awakening."

Some of these revival sermons well illustrate the quality of his supernatural faith. At Stockbridge, Massachusetts, to which he retired as a missionary to the Indians after his dismissal from his pastorate at Northampton, he wrote some of his impressive theological works, including *A Careful and strict Enquiry into the modern prevailing Notions of that Freedom of the Will, Which is Supposed to be essential to Moral Agency, Virtue and Vice, Reward and Punishment, Praise and Blame* (1754).

Edwards died as a result of the effects of inoculation against smallpox before he had an opportunity to exert much influence on the College of New Jersey, to the presidency of which he had been chosen.

The selections given here illustrate some of the remarkable qualities of Edwards's mind.

Works, Perry Miller, ed., New Haven, 1957–

C. H. Faust and T. H. Johnson, *Jonathan Edwards, Representative Selections* (American Writers Series), New York, 1935.

H. B. Parkes, Jr., *Jonathan Edwards, the Fiery Puritan*, New York, 1930.

A. C. McGiffert, Jr., *Jonathan Edwards*, New York, 1932.

Ola E. Winslow, *Jonathan Edwards, 1703–1758*, New York, 1940.

Perry Miller, *Jonathan Edwards*, New York, 1949.

» » *From:* SOME THOUGHTS CONCERNING THE PRESENT « «
REVIVAL OF RELIGION IN NEW-ENGLAND

Northampton, March 19, 1737.

We in this town were, the last Lord's day, (March 13th) the spectators, and many of us the subjects, of one of the most amazing instances of Divine preservation, that perhaps was ever known in the world. Our meeting-house is old and decayed, so that we have been for some time building a new one, which is yet unfinished. It has been observed of late,
10 that the house we have hitherto met in, has gradually spread at the bottom; the sills and walls giving way, especially in the foreside, by reason of the weight of timber at top pressing on the braces, that are inserted into the posts and beams of the house. It has done so more than ordinarily this spring: which seems to have been occasioned by the heaving of the ground, through the extreme frosts of the winter past, and its now settling again on that
20 side which is next the sun, by the spring thaws. By this means, the underpinning has been considerably disordered, which people were not sensible of, till the ends of the joists, which bore up the front gallery, were drawn off from the girts on which they rested, by the walls giving way. So that in the midst of the public exercise in the forenoon, soon after the beginning of the sermon, the whole gallery—full of people, with all the seats and timbers, suddenly and without any warning—sunk, and
30 fell down, with the most amazing noise, upon

the heads of those that sat under, to the astonishment of the congregation. The house was filled with dolorous shrieking and crying; and nothing else was expected than to find many people dead, or dashed to pieces.

The gallery, in falling, seemed to break and sink first in the middle; so that those who were upon it were thrown together in heaps before the front door. But the whole was so sudden, that many of those who fell, knew nothing what it was, at the time, that had befallen them. Others in the congregation, thought it had been an amazing clap of thunder. The falling gallery seemed to be broken all to pieces, before it got down; so that some who fell with it, as well as those who were under, were buried in the ruins; and were found pressed under heavy loads of timber, and could do nothing to help themselves.

But so mysteriously and wonderfully did it come to pass, that every life was preserved; and though many were greatly bruised, and their flesh torn, yet there is not, as I can understand, one bone broken, or so much as put out of joint, among them all. Some, who were thought to be almost dead at first, are greatly recovered; and but one young woman, seems yet to remain in dangerous circumstances, by an inward hurt in her breast: but of late there appears more hope of her recovery.

None can give an account, or conceive, by

what means people's lives and limbs should be thus preserved, when so great a multitude were thus imminently exposed. It looked as though it was impossible, but that great numbers must instantly be crushed to death, or dashed in pieces. It seems unreasonable to ascribe it to any thing else but the care of Providence, in disposing the motions of every piece of timber, and the precise place of safety where every one should sit and fall, when none were in any capacity to care for their own preservation. The preservation seems to be most wonderful, with respect to the women and children in the middle alley, under the gallery where it came down first, and with greatest force, and where there was nothing to break the force of the falling weight.

Such an event, may be a sufficient argument of a Divine providence over the lives of men. We thought ourselves called on to set apart a day to be spent in the solemn worship of God, to humble ourselves under such a rebuke of God upon us, in time of public service in his house, by so dangerous and surprising an accident; and to praise his name for so wonderful, and as it were miraculous, a preservation. The last Wednesday was kept by us to that end; and a mercy, in which the hand of God is so remarkably evident, may be well worthy to affect the hearts of all who hear it.

1737

Northampton, Dec. 12, 1743.
Rev and dear Sir,[1]

Ever since the great work of God, that was wrought here about nine years ago, there has been a great and abiding alteration in this town, in many respects. There has been vastly more religion kept up in the town, among all sorts of persons, in religious exercises, and in common conversation; there has been a great alteration among the youth of the town, with respect to revelry, frolicking, profane and licentious conversation, and lewd songs; and there has also been a great alteration, amongst both old and young, with regard to tavern-haunting. I suppose the town has been in no measure, so free of vice in these respects, for any long time together for sixty years, as it has been these nine years past. There has also been an evident alteration, with respect to a charitable spirit to the poor: though I think with regard to this, we in this town, as well as the land in general,

come far short of gospel rules. And though after that great work nine years ago, there has been a very lamentable decay of religious affections, and the engagedness of people's spirit in religion; yet many societies for prayer and social worship, were all along kept up, and there were some few instances of awakening, and deep concern about the things of another world, even in the most dead time.

In the year 1740, in the spring, before Mr. Whitefield came to this town, there was a visible alteration: there was more seriousness and religious conversation; especially among young people: those things that were of ill tendency among them, were forborne; and it was a very frequent thing for persons to consult their minister upon the salvation of their souls; and in some particular persons, there appeared a great attention, about that time. And thus it continued, until Mr. Whitefield came to town, which was about the middle of October following: he preached here four sermons in the meeting-house, (besides a private lecture at my house,) one on Friday, another on Saturday, and two upon the Sabbath. The congregation was extraordinarily melted by every sermon; almost the whole assembly being in tears for a great part of sermon time. Mr. Whitefield's sermons were suitable to the circumstances of the town; containing a just reproof of our backslidings, and in a most moving and affecting manner, making use of our great professions, and great mercies, as arguments with us to return to God, from whom we had departed. Immediately after this, the minds of the people in general appeared more engaged in religion, shewing a greater forwardness to make religion the subject of their conversation, and to meet frequently for religious purposes, and to embrace all opportunities to hear the word preached. The revival at first, appeared chiefly among professors, and those that had entertained hope that they were in a state of salvation, to whom Mr. Whitefield chiefly addressed himself; but in a very short time, there appeared an awakening and deep concern among some young persons, that looked upon themselves in a christless state; and there were some hopeful appearances of conversion, and some professors were greatly revived. In about a month or six weeks, there was a great attention in the town, both as to the revival of professors and the awakening of others. By the middle of December, a considerable work of God appeared among those that were very

[1] This letter, addressed to the Rev. Mr. Prince, in Boston, originally appeared in *Christian History* (Boston), June 11 and 18, 1743.

young; and the revival of religion continued to increase, so that in the spring an engagedness of spirit, about the things of religion, was become very general amongst young people and children, and religious subjects almost wholly took up their conversation, when they were together.

In the month of May, 1741, a sermon was preached to a company, at a private house:
10 Near the conclusion of the discourse, one or two persons, that were professors, were so greatly affected with a sense of the greatness and glory of divine things, and the infinite importance of the things of eternity, that they were not able to conceal it—the affection of their minds overcoming their strength, and having a very visible effect upon their bodies. When the exercises were over, the young people that were present, removed into the
20 other room for religious conference; and particularly that they might have opportunity to enquire of those, that were thus affected, what apprehensions they had: and what things they were, that thus deeply impressed their minds; and there soon appeared a very great effect of their conversation; the affection was quickly propagated throughout the room; many of the young people and children, that were professors, appeared to be overcome with a sense
30 of the greatness and glory of divine things, and with admiration, love, joy, and praise, and compassion to others, that looked upon themselves as in a state of nature; and many others at the same time were overcome with distress, about their sinful and miserable estate and condition; so that the whole room was full of nothing but outcries, faintings, and the like. Others soon heard of it in several parts of the town, and came to them; and what they saw
40 and heard there, was greatly affecting to them, so that many of them were overpowered in like manner, and it continued thus for some hours; the time being spent in prayer, singing, counselling and conferring. There seemed to be a consequent happy effect of that meeting, to several particular persons, and on the state of religion in the town in general. After this, were meetings from time to time, attended with like appearances. But a little after it, at the con-
50 clusion of the public exercises on the Sabbath, I appointed the children that were under seventeen years of age, to go from the meeting-house to a neighbouring house, that I might there further enforce what they had heard in public, and might give in some counsels proper for

their age. The children were there very generally and greatly affected with the warnings and counsels that were given them, and many exceedingly overcome; and the room was filled with cries; and when they were dismissed, they almost all of them went home crying aloud through the streets, to all parts of the town. The like appearances attended several such meetings of children, that were appointed. But their affections appeared by what followed, to be of a very different nature: in many, they appeared indeed but childish affections, and in a day or two would leave them as they were before: others were deeply impressed; their convictions took fast hold of them, and abode by them: and there were some that, from one meeting to another, seemed extraordinarily affected for some time, to but little purpose, their affections presently vanishing from time to time; but yet afterwards, were seized with abiding convictions, and their affections became durable.

About the middle of the summer, I called together the young people that were communicants, from sixteen to twenty-six years of age, to my house; which proved to be a most happy meeting: many seemed to be very greatly and most agreeably affected with those views, which excited humility, self-condemnation, self-abhorrence, love and joy: many fainted under these affections. We had several meetings that summer, of young people, attended with like appearances. It was about that time, that there first began to be cryings out in the meeting house; which several times occasioned many of the congregation to stay in the house after the public exercises were over, to confer with those who seemed to be overcome with religious convictions and affections, which was found to tend much to the propagation of their impressions, with lasting effect upon many; conference being, at these times, commonly joined with prayer and singing. In the summer and autumn, the children in various parts of the town, had religious meetings by themselves, for prayer, sometimes joined with fasting; wherein many of them seemed to be greatly and properly affected, and I hope some of them savingly wrought upon.

The months of August and September, were the most remarkable of any this year, for appearances of the conviction and conversion of sinners, and great revivings, quickenings, and comforts of professors, and for extraordinary external effects of these things. It was a very frequent thing, to see an house full of out-cries, fainting, convulsions, and such like, both with distress, and also with admiration and joy. It was not the manner here, to hold meetings all night, as in some places, nor was it common to continue them till very late in the night: but it was pretty often so, that there were some that were so affected, and their bodies so overcome, that they could not go home, but were obliged to stay all night where they were. There was no difference, that I know of here, with regard to these extraordinary effects, in meetings in the night and in the day time: the meetings in which these effects appeared in the evening, being commonly begun, and their extraordinary effects, in the day, and continued in the evening; and some meetings have been very remarkable for such extraordinary effects, that were both begun and finished in the day time. There was an appearance of a glorious progress of the work of God upon the hearts of sinners, in conviction and conversion, this summer and autumn, and great numbers, I think we have reason to hope, were brought savingly home to Christ. But this was remarkable: the work of God in his influences of this nature, seemed to be almost wholly upon a new generation—those that were not come to years of discretion in that wonderful season, nine years ago, children, or those that were then children: Others, who had enjoyed that former glorious opportunity, without any appearance of saving benefit, seemed now to be almost wholly passed over and let alone. But now we had the most wonderful work among children, that ever was in Northampton. The former outpouring of the Spirit, was remarkable for influences upon the minds of children, beyond all that ever been before; but this far exceeded that. Indeed, as to influences on the minds of professors, this work was by no means confined to a new generation. Many, of all ages, partook of it: but yet in this respect, it was more general on those that were of the young sort. Many, who had been formerly wrought upon, and in the time of our declension had fallen into decays, and had in a great measure left God, and gone after the world, now passed under a very remarkable new work of the Spirit of God, as if they had been the subjects of a second conversion. They were first led into the wilderness, and had a work of conviction; having much deeper convictions of the sins of both nature and practice, than ever before; though with some new circumstances, and something

new in the kind of conviction in some, with great distress, beyond what they had felt before their first conversion. Under these convictions, they were excited to strive for salvation, and the kingdom of heaven suffered violence from some of them, in a far more remarkable manner than before; and after great convictions and humblings, and agonizing with God, they had Christ discovered to them anew, as an all sufficient Saviour, and in the glories of 10 his grace, and in a far more clear manner than before; and with greater humility, self-emptiness and brokenness of heart, and a purer, a higher joy, and greater desires after holiness of life; but with greater self-diffidence and distrust of their treacherous hearts. One circumstance, wherein this work differed from that, which had been in the towns five or six years before, was, that conversions were frequently wrought more sensibly and visibly; the 20 impressions stronger, and more manifest by their external effects; the progress of the Spirit of God in conviction, from step to step, more apparent; and the transition from one state to another, more sensible and plain; so that it might, in many instances, be as it were seen by bystanders. The preceding season had been very remarkable on this account, beyond what had been before; but this more remarkable than that. And in this season, these apparent or 30 visible conversions, (if I may so call them,) were more frequently in the presence of others, at religious meetings, where the appearances of what was wrought on the heart, fell under public observation. * * *

With respect to the late season of revival of religion amongst us, for three or four years past, it has been observable, that in the former part of it, in the years 1740 and 1741, the work seemed to be much more pure, having less of 40 a corrupt mixture, than in the former great outpouring of the Spirit, in 1735 and 1736. Persons seemed to be sensible of their former errors, and had learned more of their own hearts, and experience had taught them more of the tendency and consequences of things. They were now better guarded, and their affections were not only stronger, but attended with greater solemnity, and greater humility and self distrust, and greater engagedness after holy 50 living and perseverance; and there were fewer errors in conduct. But in the latter part of it, in the year 1742, it was otherwise: the work continued more pure till we were infected from abroad: Our people hearing of, and some of them seeing, the work in other places, where there was a greater visible commotion than here, and the outward appearances were more extraordinary, were ready to think that the work in those places far excelled what was amongst us, and their eyes were dazzled with the high profession and great show that some made, who came hither from other places.

10 That those people went so far beyond them in raptures and violent emotions of the affections, and a vehement zeal, and what they called *boldness for Christ,* our people were ready to think was owing to far greater attainments in grace, and intimacy with heaven: they looked little in their own eyes, in comparison with them, and were ready to submit themselves to them, and yield themselves up to their conduct, taking it for granted, that

20 every thing was right that they said and did. These things had a strange influence on the people, and gave many of them a deep and unhappy tincture from which it was a hard and long labour to deliver them, and from which some of them are not fully delivered, to this day.

The *effects* and *consequences* of things among us plainly show the following things, viz. That the degree of *grace* is by no means

30 to be judged of by the degree of *joy,* or the degree of *zeal;* and that indeed we cannot at all determine by these things, who are gracious and who are not; and that it is not the *degree* of religious affections, but the *nature* of them, that is chiefly to be looked at. *Some* that have had very great raptures of joy, and have been extraordinarily *filled,* (as the vulgar phrase is,) and have had their bodies overcome, and that very often, have manifested far less of

40 the temper of christians in their conduct since, than some others that have been still, and have made no great outward show. But then again, there are *many others,* that have had extraordinary joys and emotions of mind, with frequent great effects upon their bodies, that behave themselves stedfastly, as humble, amiable, eminent christians.

'Tis evident that there may be great religious affections in individuals, which may, in show

50 and appearance, resemble gracious affections, and have the same effects upon their bodies, but are far from having the same effect on the temper of their minds and the course of their lives. And likewise, there is nothing more manifest, by what appears amongst us, than that

the good estate of individuals is not chiefly to be judged of by any exactness of steps, and method of experiences, in what is supposed to be the first conversion; but that we must judge by the spirit that breathes, the effect wrought upon the temper of the soul in the time of the work and remaining afterwards. Though there have been very few instances among professors, amongst us, of what is ordinarily called scandalous sins, known to me; yet the temper that some of them show, and the behaviour they have been of, together with some things in the nature and circumstances of their experiences, make me much afraid least there be a considerable number, that have wofully deceived themselves. Though, on the other hand, there is a great number, whose temper and conversation is such, as justly confirms the charity of others towards them; and not a few, in whose disposition and walk, there are amiable appearances of eminent grace. And notwithstanding all the corrupt mixtures that have been in the late work here, there are not only many blessed fruits of it, in particular persons that yet remain, but some good effects of it upon the town in general. A spirit of party has more extensively subsided. I suppose there has been less appearance, these three or four years past, of that division of the town into two parties, which has long been our bane, than has been, at any time during the preceding thirty years; and the people have apparently had much more caution, and a greater guard on their spirit and their tongues, to avoid contention and unchristian heats, in town-meetings, and on other occasions. And 'tis a thing greatly to be rejoiced in, that the people very lately came to an agreement and final issue, with respect to their grand controversy relating to their common lands; which has been, above any other particular thing, a source of mutual prejudices, jealousies and debates, for fifteen or sixteen years past. The people also seem to be much more sensible of the danger of resting in old experiences, or what they were subjects of at their supposed first conversion; and to be more fully convinced of the necessity of forgetting the things that are behind, and pressing forward and maintaining earnest labour, watchfulness and prayerfulness, as long as they live.

I am, Rev. Sir,

Your friend and brother,

JONATHAN EDWARDS.

1743

CHARLES CHAUNCY

1705-1787

NO RELIGIOUS LEADER in New England in the eighteenth century, save Jonathan Edwards, was more significant than Charles Chauncy, for fifty years pastor of the First Church in Boston. A stout opponent of Episcopacy, Chauncy wrote frequently and ably against the establishment of a bishopric and a theological school for the training of Anglican clergymen as well as against the theory of episcopacy itself. Chauncy also, with other liberal ministers such as Jonathan Mayhew, opposed the harsher tenets of Calvinism. In *All Men Illustrated and Vindicated as a Scriptural Doctrine* (1782) and, especially, in *The Benevolence of the Deity* (1784) Chauncy defended a position similar to that of the later Unitarians and Universalists. He also vigorously opposed the *Great Awakening* on the ground that evangelical revivals overemphasized the emotional at the expense of the rational elements in religion. *Seasonable Thoughts on the State of Religion in New England* (1743), *Letters to Whitefield* (1744, 1745), and *A Sermon on Enthusiasm* (1742) are all notable criticisms of evangelical revivalism.

P. L. Ford, *Bibliographia Chaunciana: A List of the Writings of Charles Chauncy*, No. 6, Elzevir Club Series, Brooklyn, N. Y., 1884.
W. B. Sprague, *Annals of the American Pulpit*, 9 vols., New York, 1857–1869, II, 8–13.
Williston Walker, *Ten New England Leaders*, New York, 1901.

From: ENTHUSIASM DESCRIBED

» » AND CAUTIONED AGAINST « «

I am in the first place, to give you some account of *Enthusiasm*. And as this is a thing much talk'd of at present, more perhaps than at any other time that has pass'd over us, it will not be tho't unseasonable, if I take some pains to let you into a true understanding of it.

The word, from its Etymology, carries in it a good meaning, as signifying *inspiration from God:* in which sense, the prophets under the old testament, and the apostles under the new, might properly be called *Enthusiasts*. For they were under a divine influence, spoke as moved by the *Holy Ghost*, and did such things as can be accounted for in no way, but by recurring to an immediate extraordinary power, present with them.

But the word is more commonly used in a bad sense, as intending an *imaginary*, not a *real* inspiration: according to which sense, the Enthusiast is one who has a conceit of himself as a person favored with the extraordinary presence of the Deity. He mistakes the workings of his own passions for divine communica-tions, and fancies himself immediately inspired by the Spirit of God, when all the while, he is under no other influence than that of an over-heated imagination.

The cause of this enthusiasm is a bad temperament of the blood and spirits; 'tis properly a disease, a sort of madness, and there are few, perhaps none at all, but are subject to it; though none are so much in danger of it as those in whom melancholy is the prevailing ingredient in their constitution. In these it often reigns, and sometimes to so great a degree that they are really beside themselves, acting as truly by the blind impetus of a wild fancy, as though they had neither reason nor understanding.

And various are the ways in which the enthusiasm discovers itself.

Sometimes, it may be seen in their countenance. A certain wildness is discernible in their general look and air, especially when their imaginations are moved and fired.

Sometimes, it strangely loosens their tongues

and gives them such an energy, as well as fluency and volubility in speaking, as they themselves, by their utmost efforts, can't so much as imitate, when they are not under the enthusiastic influence.

Sometimes, it affects their bodies, throws them into convulsions and distortions, into quakings and tremblings. This was formerly common among the people called Quakers. I was myself, when a lad, an eye-witness to such violent agitations and foamings in a boisterous female speaker as I could not behold but with surprise and wonder.

Sometimes, it will unaccountably mix itself with their conduct and give it such a tincture of that which is freakish or furious as none can have an idea of, but those who have seen the behavior of a person in a frenzy.

Sometimes, it appears in their imaginary peculiar intimacy with heaven. They are, in their own opinion, the special favorites of God, have more familiar converse with Him than other good men, and receive immediate, extraordinary communications from Him. The thoughts which suddenly rise up in their minds, they take for suggestions of the Spirit; their very fancies are divine illuminations; nor are they strongly inclined to anything, but 'tis an impulse from God, a plain revelation of His will.

And what extravagances, in this temper of mind, are they not capable of, and under the specious pretext, too, of paying obedience to the authority of God? Many have fancied themselves acting by immediate warrant from heaven, while they have been committing the most undoubted wickedness. There is indeed scarce anything so wild, either in speculation or practice, but they have given in to it. They have, in many instances, been blasphemers of God and open disturbers of the peace of the world.

But in nothing does the enthusiasm of these persons discover itself more than in the disregard they express to the dictates of reason. They are above the force of argument, beyond conviction from a calm and sober address to their understandings. As for them, they are distinguished persons; God himself speaks inwardly and immediately to their souls. "They see the light infused into their understandings, and cannot be mistaken; 'tis clear and visible there, like the light of bright sunshine; shows itself and needs no other proof but its own

evidence. They feel the hand of God moving them within and the impulses of His Spirit, and cannot be mistaken in what they feel. Thus they support themselves, and are sure reason hath nothing to do with what they see and feel. What they have a sensible experience of, admits no doubt, needs no probation." And in vain will you endeavor to convince such persons of any mistakes they are fallen into. They are certainly in the right, and know themselves to be so. They have the Spirit opening their understandings and revealing the truth to them. They believe only as he has taught them: and to suspect they are in the wrong is to do dishonor to the Spirit; 'tis to oppose his dictates, to set up their own wisdom in opposition to his, and shut their eyes against that light with which he has shined into their souls. They are not, therefore, capable of being argued with; you had as good reason with the wind.

And as the natural consequence of their being thus sure of everything, they are not only infinitely stiff and tenacious, but impatient of contradiction, censorious, and uncharitable; they encourage a good opinion of none but such as are in their way of thinking and speaking. Those, to be sure, who venture to debate with them about their errors and mistakes, their weaknesses and indiscretions, run the hazard of being stigmatized by them as poor unconverted wretches, without the Spirit, under the government of carnal reason, enemies to God and religion, and in the broad way to hell.

They are likewise positive and dogmatical, vainly fond of their own imaginations, and invincibly set upon propagating them; and in the doing of this, their powers being awakened and put as it were, upon the stretch, from the strong impressions they are under that they are authorized by the immediate command of God himself, they sometimes exert themselves with a sort of ecstatic violence; and 'tis this that gives them the advantage, among the less knowing and judicious, of those who are modest, suspicious of themselves, and not too assuming in matters of conscience and salvation. The extraordinary fervor of their minds, accompanied with uncommon bodily motions and an excessive confidence and assurance, gains them great reputation among the populace, who speak of them as men of God in distinction from all others, and too commonly hearken to and revere their dictates, as though they really were, as they pretend, immediately communicated to them from the Divine Spirit.

This is the nature of Enthusiasm, and this its operation, in a less or greater degree, in all who are under the influence of it. 'Tis a kind of religious frenzy, and evidently discovers itself to be so whenever it rises to any great height.

And much to be pitied are the persons who are seized with it. Our compassion commonly works towards those who, while under distraction, fondly imagine themselves to be kings and emperors; and the like pity is really due to those who, under the power of enthusiasm, fancy themselves to be prophets, inspired of God and immediately called and commissioned by him to deliver his messages to the world. And though they should run into disorders and act in a manner that cannot but be condemned, they should notwithstanding be treated with tenderness and lenity; and the rather, because they do not commonly act so much under the influence of a bad mind as a deluded imagination. And who more worthy of Christian pity than those who, under the notion of serving God and the interest of religion, are filled with zeal and exert themselves to the utmost while all the time they are hurting and wounding the very cause they take so much pains to advance. 'Tis really a pitiable case; and though the honesty of their intentions won't legitimate their bad actions, yet it very much alleviates their guilt. We should think as favorably of them as may be and be dispos'd to judge with mercy, as we would hope to obtain mercy.

. . . Let us beware of charging God *foolishly*, from what we have heard of the *nature*, and *influence* of *enthusiasm*. This may appear a dark article in God's government of the world; but it stands upon the same foot with his permission of other evils, whether *natural* or *moral*. And, if we shou'd not to be able to see perfectly into the reason of this dispensation, we shou'd rather attribute it to our own ignorance, than reply against God. We may assure ourselves, a wise, and good, and holy God, would not have suffered it thus to be, if there were not some great and valuable ends to be hereby answered.

Greater advantages may, in the end, accrue to true religion, by the sufferance of an *en-* *thusiastic* spirit, and the prevalence of it, at certain times, than we may be capable of discerning at present.

It may furnish both opportunity and occasion for the trial of those, who call themselves Christians; whether they have just notions of religion, and courage and faithfulness to stand up for *real* truths, against meer *imaginary* ones.—It may serve as a foil to set off the beauty and glory of true, genuine Christianity. —It may tend to the encouragement of reasonable and solid religion; and, in the run of things, recommend it, in the most effectual manner, to men's choice and practice.—In a word, it may put men upon a more thorough examination into the grounds of the Christian religion, and be the means of their being, more generally, established in its truth, upon the best and most reasonable evidence.

These are some of the ends capable of being answered by the permission of a *spirit of enthusiasm*, and the prevalence of it, for a while. And as to the persons themselves led aside by it, it is, in the same way to be reconciled with the general goodness of GOD towards men, as in the case of *distraction*, and the evil effects consequent thereupon. The persons, heated with *enthusiastic* imaginations, are either, in a faulty sense, accessory to this unhappy turn of mind, or they are not: if the *latter*, they may depend upon the pity and mercy of *God*, notwithstanding the extravagancies they may run into; yea, if they are good men, as is doubtless, sometimes the case, it may be hoped, that this evil which has happened to them, will, after the manner of other sufferings, work together for good to them. But if thro' the pride of their hearts, a vain-glorious temper, accompanied with rashness and arrogance, or the like, they are really accessory to their own delusion, and mad conduct following therefrom, let them not think to cast the blame on GOD: They do but reap the fruit of what they themselves have sown. And if they shou'd be totally delivered up, as has sometimes been the case, to the devices of their own hearts, and the *lying inspirations* of *wicked spirits*, they can fault nobody but themselves. God is just while he makes them an example for the warning of others, lest they also be given up to believe lies. And he is *good* as well as just; good to others, in putting them hereby upon their guard, and severe towards *them*.   1742

WILLIAM PENN

1644–1718

IN 1682 WILLIAM PENN inaugurated the "Holy Experiment" by landing a company of settlers on the site of Philadelphia. His subsequent relations with his colony reveal the conflict in his own social philosophy. As the son of Admiral Sir William Penn, a courtier and a man of wealth, Penn inclined toward the view that his colony was to be administered efficiently and with some regard for the material fortunes of his family. But as a loyal convert to Quakerism Penn tempered his aristocratic and worldly views by a deep concern with piety and spiritual values, by democratic concessions to the colonists, by zeal for religious tolerance, and by fair treatment of the Indians. He stayed in America only four years; but his influence on Pennsylvania was considerable.

Penn's writings include accounts of the province which were designed to serve as promotion literature to attract immigration. The liberal *Frame of Government* (1682) and the *Essay towards the Present and Future Peace of Europe* (1693) are political writings which admirably combine practicality with social vision. *No Cross, No Crown* (1669), the *Brief Account of the Rise and Progress of the People Called Quakers* (1694), and *Fruits of a Father's Love* (1726) testified to the intensity of his religious faith. *Fruits of Solitude* (1693) provides a good illustration of the fusion in this Quaker's thought of the worldly and the unworldly.

M. K. Spence, *William Penn, A Bibliography*, Harrisburg, 1932.

A Collection of the Works of William Penn, 2 vols., London, 1726, is more nearly complete than the editions of 1771, 1782, and 1825. A definitive edition was begun in 1910 by A. C. Myers.

The Peace of Europe: The Fruits of Solitude, and other Writings, Everyman's Lib. Ser., New York, 1916.

Catherine Owens Peare, *John Woolman: Child of Light*, New York, 1954.

E. C. O. Beatty, *William Penn as a Social Philosopher*, New York, 1939.

» » From: SOME FRUITS OF SOLITUDE « «

EDUCATION

4. We are in Pain to make them Scholars, but not *Men!* To talk, rather than to know, which is true *Canting*.

5. The first thing obvious to Children is what is sensible; and that we make no Part of their Rudiments.

6. We press their Memory too soon, and puzzle, strain and load them with Words and Rules; to know *Grammer* and *Rhetorick*, and a strange Tongue or two, that it is ten to one may never be useful to them; leaving their natural *Genius* to *Mechanical* and *Physical* or natural Knowledge uncultivated and neglected; which would be of exceeding Use and Pleasure to them through the whole Course of their Life.

7. To be sure, Languages are not to be despised or neglected. But Things are still to be preferred.

8. Children had rather be making of *Tools* and *Instruments* of Play; *Shaping, Drawing, Framing,* and *Building,* &c. than getting some Rules of Propriety of Speech by heart: And those also would follow with more Judgment, and less Trouble and Time.

9. It were happy if we studied Nature more in natural things; and acted according to Nature; whose Rules are *few, plain* and *most reasonable.*

10. Let us begin where she begins, go her Pace, and close always where she ends, and we cannot miss of being good *Naturalists*.

11. The Creation would not be longer a

Riddle to us: The *Heavens, Earth,* and *Waters,* with their respective, various and numerous Inhabitants: Their Productions, Natures, Seasons, Sympathies and Antipathies; their Use, Benefit and Pleasure, would be better understood by us: And an *eternal Wisdom, Power, Majesty* and *Goodness,* very *conspicuous* to us; through those sensible and passing Forms: The World wearing the *Mark* of it's Maker, whose Stamp is every where *visible,* and the *Characters* very *legible* to the Children of Wisdom.

12. And it would go a great Way to caution and direct People in their Use of the World, that they were better studied and knowing in the Creation of it.

13. For how could Men find the Confidence to abuse it, while they should see the Great Creator stare them in the Face, in all and every Part thereof?

14. Their Ignorance makes them insensible, and that Insensibility hardy in misusing this noble Creation, that has the Stamp and Voice of a *Deity* every where, and in every Thing to the Observing.

15. It is Pity therefore that Books have not been composed for *Youth,* by some curious and careful *Naturalists,* and also *Mechanicks,* in the *Latin* Tongue, to be used in Schools, that they might learn Things with Words: Things *obvious* and *familiar* to them, and which would make the Tongue easier to be attained by them.

16. Many able *Gardiners* and *Husbandmen* are yet ignorant of the *Reason* of their Calling; as most *Artificers* are of the Reason of their own Rules that govern their excellent Workmanship. But a Naturalist and Mechanick of this Sort, is Master of the Reason of both, and might be of the Practice too, if his Industry kept Pace with his Speculation; which were very commendable; and without which he cannot be said to be a *compleat* Naturalist or Mechanick.

17. Finally, if Man be the *Index* or *Epitomy* of the World, as *Philosophers* tell us, we have only to read our *selves* well to be *learn'd* in it. But because there is nothing we less regard than the *Characters* of the Power that made us, which are so clearly written upon us and the World he has given us, and can best tell us what we are and should be, we are even Strangers to our own *Genius:* The *Glass* in which we should see that true instructing and agreeable Variety, which is to be observed in Nature, to the Admiration of that Wisdom and Adoration of that Power which made us all.

CENSORIOUSNESS

41. We are apt to be very pert at *censuring others,* where we will not endure Advice our selves. And nothing, shews our *Weakness* more than to be so sharp-sighted at spying other Men's Faults, and so *purblind* about our own. 1c

42. When the Actions of a Neighbour are upon the Stage, we can have all our Wits about us, are so quick and critical we can split an Hair, and find out every Failure and Infirmity: *But are without feeling, or have but very little Sense of our own.*

43. Much of this comes from *ill Nature,* as well as from an inordinate Value of our selves: For we love rambling better than Home, and blaming the unhappy, rather than covering 2c and relieving them.

44. In such Occasions some shew their Malice and are witty upon *Misfortunes;* others their Justice, they can reflect a pace: but few or none their *Charity;* especially if it be about Money Matters.

45. You shall see an *old Miser* come forth with a set Gravity, and so much Severity against the *Distressed,* to *excuse his Purse,* that he will, 'ere he has done, put it out of all 3c Question, That RICHES is *Righteousness* with him. *This,* says he, *is the Fruit of your Prodigality* (as if, poor Man, *Covetousness* were no Fault) Or, *of your Projects, or grasping after a great Trade:* While he himself would have done the same thing, but that he had not the *Courage* to venture so much ready Money *out of his own trusty Hands,* though it had been to have brought him back the *Indies* in Return. But the Proverb is just, *Vice should* 4c *not correct Sin.*

46. They have a Right to censure, that have an *Heart* to help: The rest is Cruelty, not Justice.

TEMPERANCE

59. To this a *spare* Dyet contributes much. Eat therefore to *live,* and do not live to eat. That's like a Man, but this below a *Beast.*

60. Have wholesome. but not *costly* Food, 5c and be rather cleanly than *dainty* in ordering it.

61. The *Receipts* of Cookery are *swell'd* to a Volume, but a *good Stomack* excels them all; to which nothing contributes more than *Industry* and *Temperance.*

62. It is a cruel Folly to offer up to *Ostentation* so many Lives of Creatures, as make up the State of our Treats; as it is a prodigal one to spend more in Sauce than in Meat.

63. The Proverb says, *That enough is as good as a Feast:* But it is certainly better, if Superfluity be a Fault, which never fails to be at Festivals.

64. If thou rise with an Appetite thou art sure never to sit down without one.

65. Rarely drink but when thou art dry; nor then, between Meals, if it can be avoided.

66. The *smaller* the Drink, the *clearer* the Head, and the *cooler* the *Blood;* which are great Benefits in Temper and Business.

67. Strong Liquors are good at some times, and in small Proportions; being better for *Physick* than Food, for *Cordials* than common Use.

68. The most *Common* things are the most *useful;* which shews both the *Wisdom* and *Goodness* of the great Lord of the Family of the World.

69. What therefore he has made *rare,* don't thou use *too commonly:* Lest thou shouldest invert the Use and Order of Things; become Wanton and Voluptuous; and thy *Blessings* prove a *Curse.*

70. *Let nothing be lost,* said our Saviour: But that is *lost* that is *misused.*

71. Neither urge another to that thou wouldst be unwilling to do thy self; nor do thy self what looks to thee *unseemly,* and intemperate in another.

72. All Excess is ill: but *Drunkenness* is of the worst Sort: It *spoils* Health, *dismounts* the Mind, and unmans Men: It *reveals Secrets,* is *Quarrelsome, Lascivious, Impudent, Dangerous* and *mad:* In fine, he that is Drunk is not a Man; because he is so long void of *Reason,* that distinguishes a Man from a Beast.

APPAREL

73. Excess in *Apparel* is another *costly* Folly: The very Trimming of the vain World would *cloath* all the *naked* one.

74. Chuse thy Cloaths by thine owne Eyes, not anothers. The more plain and simple they are, the better. Neither unshapely nor Fantistical; and for Use and Decency, and not for Pride.

75. If thou art clean and warm, it is sufficient; for more doth but rob the *Poor,* and please the *Wanton.*

76. It is said of the true Church, *The King's Daughter is all glorious* 𝔴𝔦𝔱𝔥𝔦𝔫. Let our Care therefore be of our *Minds* more than of our *Bodies,* if we would be of her Communion.

77. We are told with Truth, that *Meekness* and *Modesty* are the Rich and Charming Attire of the Soul: And the plainer the Dress, the more distinctly, and with greater Lustre, their Beauty shines.

78. It is a great Pity such Beauties are so *rare,* and those of *Jezebel's* Forehead are so *common:* Whose Dresses are Incentives to Lust; but *Bars* instead of Motives, to *Love* or *Vertue.*

RIGHT MARRIAGE

79. Never Marry but *for Love;* but see that thou lov'st what is *lovely.*

80. If Love be not thy *chiefest* Motive, thou wilt soon grow *weary* of a Married State, and *stray* from thy Promise, to search out thy Pleasures in *forbidden* Places.

81. Let not Enjoyment *lessen,* but augment Affection; it being the basest of Passions *to like when we have not, what we slight when we possess.*

82. It is the Difference betwixt *Lust* and *Love,* that this is fix't, that Volatile. Love grows, Lust wasts by Enjoyment: And the Reason is, that one springs from an *Union of Souls, and the other from an Union of Sense.*

83. They have divers Originals, and so are of different Families: That *inward* and *deep,* this superficial; this transient, and that permanent.

84. They that Marry for *Money,* cannot have the true Satisfaction of Marriage; the requisite Means being wanting.

85. Men are generally more careful of the *Breed* of their *Horses* and *Dogs* than of their Children.

86. Those must be of the best Sort, for *Shape, Strength, Courage* and *good Conditions*: But as for these, their own Posterity, *Money shall answer all Things.* With such, it makes the *Crooked Streight,* sets *Squint-Eyes right, cures Madness, covers Folly, changes ill Conditions, mends the Skin, gives a sweet Breath, repairs Honours, makes Young, works Wonders.*

87. O how *sordid* is *Man* grown! Man, the Noblest Creature of the World, as a *God* on *Earth,* and the *Image* of him that made it; thus to *mistake* Earth for Heaven, and *Worship Gold* for God!

FRIENDSHIP

106. *Friendship* is the next Pleasure we may hope for: And where we find it not at Home, or have no home to find it in, we may seek it abroad. It is an Union of *Spirits*, a Marriage of *Hearts*, and the Bond thereof *Virtue*.

107. There can be no Friendship where there is no *Freedom*. Friendship loves a *free* Air, and will not be penned up in streight and narrow Enclosures. It will speak *freely*, and *act* so too; and take nothing ill, where no Ill is meant; nay where it is, 'twill *easily* forgive, and forget too, upon small Acknowledgments.

108. Friends are true *Twins* in Soul; they Sympathize in every thing, and have the same Love and Aversion.

109. One is not happy without the other, nor can either of them be miserable *alone*. As if they could change *Bodies*, they take their *Turns* in Pain as well as in Pleasure; *relieving* one another in their most adverse Conditions.

110. What one enjoys, the other cannot Want. Like the Primitive Christians, they have all things in common, and no *Property but in one another*.

QUALITIES OF A FRIEND

111. A true Friend unbosomes *freely*, advises *justly*, assists *readily*, adventures *boldly*, takes all *patiently*, defends *couragiously*, and continues a Friend *unchangeably*.

112. These being the Qualities of a Friend, we are to find them before we chuse one.

113. The *Covetous*, the *Angry*, the *Proud*, the *Jealous*, the *Talkative*, cannot but make ill Friends, as well as the *False*.

114. In short, chuse a Friend as thou dost a Wife, *till Death separate you*.

115. Yet be not a Friend beyond the *Alter:* But let *Virtue* bound thy *Friendship:* Else it is not Friendship, but an evil Confederacy.

116. If my *Brother* or *Kinsman* will be my Friend, I ought to prefer him before a Stranger, or I shew little Duty or *Nature* to my *Parents*.

117. And as we ought to prefer our *Kindred* in Point of Affection, so too in Point of *Charity*, if *equally* needing and deserving.

KNOWLEDGE

162. *Knowledge* is the *Treasure*, but *Judgment* the Treasurer of a *wise* Man.

163. He that has more Knowledge than Judgment, is made for *another Man's* Use more than his own.

164. It cannot be a good Constitution, where the Appetite is great and the Digestion weak.

165. There are some Men like *Dictionaries;* to be lookt into upon Occasion, but have no Connection, and are little entertaining.

166. Less Knowledge than Judgment will always have the Advantage upon the *Injudicious* knowing Man.

167. A wise Man makes what he learns his *own*, 'tother shews he's but a *Copy*, or a Collection at most.

WIT

168. *Wit* is an happy and striking Way of expressing a Thought.

169. 'Tis not often tho' it be lively and mantling, that it carries a great Body with it.

170. Wit therefore is fitter for Diversion than Business, being more grateful to Fancy than Judgment.

171. Less Judgment than Wit, is *more Sail than Ballast*.

172. Yet it must be confest, that Wit gives an *Edge* to Sense, and recommends it extreamly.

173. Where Judgment has Wit to express it, there's the *best* Orator.

ART AND PROJECT

227. *Art*, is Good, where it is beneficial. *Socrates* wisely bounded his Knowledge and Instruction by *Practice*.

228. Have a Care therefore of *Projects:* And yet despise nothing rashly, or in the *Lump*.

229. *Ingenuity*, as well as Religion, sometimes suffers between two *Thieves; Pretenders* and *Despisers*.

230. Though injudicious and dishonest Projectors often discredit Art, yet the most *useful* and *extraordinary* Inventions have not, at first, escap'd the Scorn of *Ignorance;* as their Authors, rarely, have cracking of their Heads, or breaking of their Backs.

231. Undertake no Experiment, in Speculation, that appears not *true in Art;* nor then, at thine *own* Cost, if costly or hazardous in making.

232. As many Hands make light Work, so *several Purses* make *cheap* Experiments.

INDUSTRY

233. *Industry* is certainly very commendable, and *supplies* the Want of Parts.

234. *Patience* and *Diligence,* like Faith, *remove Mountains.*

235. Never give out while there is *Hope;* but hope not beyond Reason, for that shews more Desire than Judgment.

236. It is a profitable Wisdom to know when we have done enough: Much Time and Pains are spared, in not flattering ourselves against Probabilities.

BALLANCE

309. We must not be concern'd above the Value of the Thing that engages us; nor raised *above* Reason, in maintaining what we think reasonable.

310. It is too common an Error, to invert the Order of Things; by making an *End* of that which is a *Means,* and a *Means* of that which is an *End.*

311. *Religion* and *Government* escape not this *Mischief:* The first is too often made a *Means* instead of an End; the other an End instead of a Means.

312. Thus Men seek Wealth rather than Subsistence; and the End of Cloaths is the least Reason of their Use. Nor is the satisfying of our Appetite our End in Eating, so much as the pleasing of our Pallate. The like may also be said of Building, Furniture, &c. where the Man rules not the Beast, and Appetite submits not to Reason.

313. It is great Wisdom to proportion our Esteem to the Nature of the Thing: For as that way things will not be undervalued, so neither will they engage us *above* their intrinsick *Worth.*

314. If we suffer little Things to have great Hold upon us, we shall be as *much* transported for them, as if they deserved it.

315. It is an old Proverb, *Maxima Bella ex levissimis Causis:* The greatest Feuds have had the smallest Beginnings.

316. No matter what the Subject of the Dispute be, but what Place we give it in our Minds: For that governs our Concern and Resentment.

317. It is one of the fatalest Errors of our Lives, when we spoil a good Cause by an ill Management: And it is not impossible but we may *mean well* in an *ill* Business; but that will not defend it.

318. If we are but sure the End is Right, we are too apt to gallop over all Bounds to compass it; not considering that lawful Ends may be very *unlawfully* attained.

319. Let us be careful to take *just ways* to compass just Things; that they may *last* in their Benefits to us.

320. There is a troublesome Humor some Men have, that if they may not lead, *they will not follow;* but had rather a thing were never done, than not done their own way, tho' other ways very desirable.

321. This comes of an *over-fulness* of our selves, and shews we are more concern'd for *Praise,* than the *Success* of what we think a good Thing.

RELIGION

. . . 550. I find all sorts of People *agree,* whatsoever were their Animosities, when *humbled* by the Approaches of Death: *Then they forgive, then they pray for, and love one another:* Which shews us, that it is not our Reason, but our *Passion,* that makes and holds up the *Feuds* that reign among Men in their Health and Fulness. They, therefore, that live *nearest* to that which they should die, must certainly live *best.*

551. Did we *believe* a Final Reckoning and Judgment, or did we think *enough* of what we do *believe,* we would allow *more* Love in Religion than we do; since *Religion* it self is nothing else but *Love to God and Man.*

552. *He that lives in Love lives in God,* says the Beloved Disciple: And to be sure a Man can live *no where better.*

553. It is more reasonable Men should value that Benefit, which is most *durable.* Now Tongues shall cease, and Prophecy fail, and Faith shall be *consummated* in Sight, and Hope in Enjoyment; but *Love remains.*

554. Love is indeed Heaven upon Earth; since Heaven above would not be Heaven without it: For where there is not Love; there is Fear: But *perfect Love casts out Fear.* And yet we naturally *fear most* to offend what we *most Love.*

555. What we Love, we'll Hear; and what we love, we'll trust; and what we love we'll serve, ay, and suffer for too. *If you love me* (says our Blessed Redeemer) *keep my Commandments.* Why? Why then he'll *Love us;* then we shall be his *Friends;* then he'll send us the *Comforter;* then whatever we ask, we

shall receive; and then where he is *we shall be also and that for ever.* Behold the Fruits of *Love;* the *Power, Vertue, Benefit,* and *Beauty* of *Love!*

556. *Love* is above all; and when it prevails in us all, we shall all be *Lovely,* and in *Love* with *God* and *one* with *another*. Amen.

1693

JOHN WOOLMAN

1720–1772

FROM Mount Holly, New Jersey, John Woolman, schoolmaster, clerk, and tailor, journeyed as a Quaker preacher to the settlements of Friends in various parts of the colonies. He raised his voice again and again in behalf of justice to the Indian; he decried "reaping the unrighteous profits of that iniquitous practice of dealing in Negroes." He was, in addition, an able spokesman against war. His social philosophy, which also deprecated riches and unfairness toward labor and advocated equitable distribution of this world's goods, was rooted in his simple piety and in his intuitive faith in divine and human goodness. Religiously inspired though his humanitarianism was, and notable though his *Journal* is for its spiritual poise and for its reflection of the doctrine of supernatural communion of the individual soul with the Holy Spirit, Woolman nevertheless showed by his example as well as by his pen his deep concern for man's worldly lot.

Catherine Owens Peare, *William Penn*, Phila., 1957.
The Journal and Essays of John Woolman, A. M. Gummere, ed., New York, 1922. This includes an excellent biography and bibliography.

» » *From:* A PLEA FOR THE POOR « «

CHAPTER I

Wealth desired for its own sake Obstructs the increase of Virtue, and large possessions in the hands of selfish men have a bad tendency, for by their means too small a number of people are employed in things usefull, and therefore some of them are necessitated to labour too hard, while others would want business to earn their Bread, were not employments invented, which having no real use, serve only to please the vain mind.

Rents set on lands are often so high, that persons who have but small substance are straitened in hiring a plantation and while Tenants are healthy, and prosperous in business, they often find Occasion to labour harder than was intended by our Gracious Creator.

Oxen & Horses are often seen at work, when through Heat & too much labour, their eyes, and the emotion of their Bodies manifest that they are oppressed. Their loads in Wagons are frequently so heavy, that when weary with halling it far, their drivers find occasion in going up Hills, or through mire, to raise their spirits by whiping to get forward. Many poor people are so thronged in their business, that it is difficult for them to provide Shelter sutable for their animals, in great storms. These things are common when in health; but through Sickness and inability to labour through loss of Creatures, and miscarriage in business, many are straitened; & much of their increase goes to pay rent or Interest, that they have not wherewith to hire so much as their case requires. Hence one poor woman in attending on her Children, providing for her family, & helping the sick, does as much business as would for the time be Sutable Employment for two or three, and honest persons are often straitened to give their children sutable learning.

The mony which the wealthy receive from

the poor, who do more than a proper share of business in raising it, is frequently paid to other poor people for doing business which is foreign to the true use of things.

Men who have large possessions, & live in the spirit of Charity, who carefully inspect the circumstance of those who occupy their Estates, and, regardless of the Customs of the times, regulate their demands agreeably to Universal Love: these by being Righteous on a principle, do good to the poor without placing it as an act of bounty. Their Example in avoiding superfluities tends to incite others to moderation; their goodness, in not exacting what the Laws or Customs would support them in, tends to open the Channel to moderate Labour in useful Affairs, and to discourage those branches of business which have not their foundation in true wisdom.

To be busied in that which is but vanity, & serves only to please the unstable mind, tends to an alliance with those who promote that vanity, and is a snare in which many poor tradesmen are entangled.

To be employed in things connected with Virtue, is most agreeable with the Character and Inclination of an honest man.

While industrious frugal people are borne down with poverty, and opressed with too much labour in useful things, the way to apply mony, without promoting pride and Vanity, remains open to such who truly Sympathize with them in their various Difficulties.

CHAPTER II

The Creator of the earth is the owner of it. He gave us being thereon, and our nature requires nourishment, which is the produce of it. As he is kind and merciful we, as his creatures, while we live answerable to the design of our creation, are so far Entitled to a convenient Subsistence, that no man may justly deprive us of it.

By the agreements and Contracts of Our Fathers and predecessors, and by doings and proceedings of our own, some claim a much greater share of this world than others: and while those possessions are Faithfully Improved to the good of the whole, it consists with Equity. But he who with a view to self-exaltation, causeth some with their domestick Animals to labour immoderately, and, with the monys arising to him therefrom, employs others in the Luxuries of Life, Acts contrary to the Gracious designs of Him who is the true owner of the Earth, nor can any possessions, either acquired or derived from Ancestors, justify such conduct.

Goodness Remains to be goodness, and the direction of pure wisdom is obligatory on all Reasonable Creatures: that Laws and Customs are no further a Standard for our proceedings than as their Foundation is on Universal Righteousness.

Though the poor Occupy our Estates by a bargain, to which they in their poor Circumstance agreed, and we ask even less than a punctual fulfilling of their agreement; yet if our views are to lay up riches, or to live in conformity to customs which have not their Foundation in the Truth, and our demands are such as requires greater Toyl, or application to business in them, than is Consistent with pure Love, we invade their rights as Inhabitants of that World, of which a good and gracious God is proprietor, under whom we are Temants.

Where all superfluities, and the desire of outward greatness laid aside, and the right use of things universally attended to, Such a number of people might be employed in things usefull, as that moderate labour, with the Blessing of Heaven, would answer all good purposes relating to people and their Animals, and a Sufficient number have time to attend to proper Affairs of Civil Society.

CHAPTER III

While our Strength and Spirits are lively, we go cheerfully through business. Either too much or too little Action is tiresome, but a right portion is healthfull to our bodies, and agreeable to an honest mind.

Where men have great Estates, they stand in a place of Trust. To have it in their power, without difficulty, to live in that fashion which occasions much labour, and at the same time confine themselves to that use of things Prescribed by our Redeemer, and Confirmed by his Example, and the Examples of many who lived in the Early ages of the Christian Church, that they may more Extensively relieve objects of Charity;—for men possessed of great Estates to live thus, requires close attention to *Divine love.*

Our Gracious Creator cares & provides for all his Creatures. His tender mercies are over all his works & so far as his Love influences Our minds, so far we become interested in his workmanship, and feel a desire to take hold of every opportunity to lessen the distresses of the Afflicted, & increase the Happiness of the Creation. Here we have a prospect of one common interest from which our own is inseparable, that to turn all the treasures we possess in to the Channel of Universal Love, becomes the business of our lives.

Men of large estates, whose hearts are thus enlarged, are like Fathers to the poor, and in looking over their Brethren in distressed circumstances, and considering their own more easie condition, they find a Field for humble meditation, & feel the strength of those obligations they are under to be kind and tenderhearted toward them. Poor men eased of their burthens, and released from too close an application to business, are at Liberty to hire others to their assistance, to provide well for their Animals, and find time to perform those duties amongst their Acquaintance, which belong to a well guided Social life.

When these reflect on the opportunity those had to oppress them, & consider the goodness of their conduct, they behold it Lovely, & consistent with brotherhood. And as the man whose mind is conformed to Universal Love, hath in Trust Setled in God, and finds a firm Foundation to Stand on in any Changes or Revolutions that happen amongst men; so allso, the goodness of his conduct tends to spread a kind, benevolent disposition in the world.

. . .

CHAPTER X

"Are not two Sparrows sold for a Farthing, and one of them shall not fall to the Ground without your Father."

The way of Carrying on Wars, common in the world, is so far distinguishable from the purity of Christ's Religion, that many scruple to joyn in them. Those who are so redeemed from the Love of the World, as to possess nothing in a Selfish Spirit, their "Life is hid with Christ in God," and these he preserves in resignedness, even in times of Commotion.

As they possess nothing but what pertains to His family, anxious thoughts about wealth or dominion hath little or nothing in them to work upon, and they learn contentment in being disposed of according to His Will, who being Omnipotent, and always mindful of his Children, causeth all things to work for their good. But where that spirit works which loves Riches; works, & in its working gathers wealth, and cleaves to customs which have their Root in self pleasing. This Spirit thus separating from

Universal Love, seeks help from that power which stands in the Separation, and whatever name it hath, it still desireth to defend the Treasures thus gotten. This is like a Chain, where the end of one link encloses the end of another. The rising up of a desire to obtain wealth is the beginning. This desire being cherished moves to action, and riches thus gotten pleace self and while self hath a life in them it desires to have them defended.   10

Wealth is attended with Power, by which Bargains and proceedings contrary to Universal Righteousness are Supported, and here Oppression, carried on with worldly policy & order, cloathes itself with the name of Justice, and becomes like a seed of Discord in the soyl: and as this spirit which wanders from the pure Habitation prevails, so the seed of War Swells & Sprouts and grows & becomes Strong, till much fruit are ripened. Thus cometh the Harvest spoken of by the prophet, which "is a Heap, in the Day of Grief & of desperate Sorrow."   20

Oh! that we who declare against wars, and Acknowledge our trust to be in God only, may walk in the Light, and therein examine our Foundation & motives in holding great Estates: May we look upon our Treasures, and the furniture of our Houses, and the Garments in which we array ourselves, and try whether the seeds   30 of war have any nourishment in these our possessions, or not. Holding Treasures in the Self pleasing Spirit is a Strong plant, the fruit whereof ripens fast.

A day of outward Distress is coming, and Divine Love calls to prepare for it. Hearken then, O ye Children who have known the Light, and come forth! Leave every thing which our Lord Jesus Christ does not own. Think not his pattern too plain or too coarse for you. Think   40 not a Small portion in this life too little: but let us live in His Spirit, & walk as he walked, and he will preserve us in the greatest Troubles.

. . .

CHAPTER XVI

To keep Negroes as Servants till they are Thirty years of age, and hold the profits of the last nine years of their labour as our own, on a   50 Supposition that they may some time be an expense to our states, is a way of proceeding which appears to admit of improvement.

Reasons offered. *1st.* Men of mature age, who have walked orderly, and made no contract to serve, that they are entitled to freedom I expect is generally agreed to; and to make them serve as Slaves Nine years longer, may be to keep them slaves for term of Life. They may die before that age, and be no expense to us; and may leave Children to whom, with reason, they might in their last Sickness, desire to give the monies they had earned after they had paid for their own Education.

2d. The Labour of a healthy, Industrious Negro Man for nine years, I suppose at a moderate computation, may not be less than Fifty pounds proclamation money besides his Diet and Clothing. Now if this money be earned, either in the service of the Man who Educated him, or laid by in yearly proportion under the care of the said Man, and put out at a moderate interest for the Negroes Use; and to be applied to his future necessities, or to such honest purposes as he by his last will might direct, this would appear to us a more brotherly way of proceeding, were we in the Negroes Condition.

3d. Pure goodness tendeth to beget its own likeness, and where men are convinced that the conduct of those who have power over them is Equitable, it naturally Yields encouragement for them to provide against old age. The pure witness being reached, a care is thereby incited that they may not become a burden on the states of those whom they have found to be honest Men, and true Friends to them, but where men have laboured without wages nine years longer than is common with other Men amongst whom they dwell, and then set free; and at going off, are Assured that those who so detained them are largely in their debt, but expect not to recover the debt except they become needy when unable to help themselves —Such would naturally be induced to think this treatment unbrotherly; To think of the Reasonableness of their wages being some time paid; To think that the state in which they laboured might reasonably assist them in old age, and thus be tempted to decline from a wise application to business.

4th. If I see a Man want relief, and know he hath money in my Hands which must some time be paid, with reasonable use, either to him, or to others by his direction, there appears in this case no Temptation to withhold it at the time I saw that he wanted it, but if selfishness so far prevail in me, that I looked upon the money which I had in trust, with a desire to keep it from the true owner, and through the strength of desire, joined with expectation,

at length so far consider it a part of my estate, as to apply it in promoting myself or my Family in the World, and therewith entered into expenses which a humble follower of Christ might have shuned: here, by joyning with one temptation there is great danger of falling into more, and of not attending to the wants of the Man who had monies in my Hands, with that care and diligence which I might have done, had the Tempter found no entrance into my Mind.

5th. If we righteously account for the monies which we have in Security, with a reasonable use thereon, and frugally expend the whole in relieving the Man who earned it; and more being wanted, the public refuseth to bear any part of the expense; if our states have not been benefited aforetime by the labours of his Fathers nor Ancestors, this appears to be a case wherein the Righteous suffer for the Testimony of a good Conscience; and from which it faithfully attended to they might in time, I trust, hope for relief.

6th. The negroes have been a suffering people, and we as a civil society are they by whom they have suffered. Now where persons have been injured as to their outward substance and died without having recompense, their children appear to have a right to that which was Equitably due to, and detained from their Fathers. (My heart is Affected with Sorrow while I write on this Subject, on account of the great injuries committed against these Gentiles, and against their children who have been born in that Captivity which is an unrighteous Captivity. When the Ancestors of these people were imported from Africa, some, I believe, bought them with intent to treat them kindly as slaves. They bought them as though those violent men had a Right to sell them, but I believe without weightily considering the nature and tendency of such a bargain, and thus building on an Unrighteous Foundation, a vail was gradually drawn over a practice very grievous, and Afflicting to great numbers of the Gentiles. A care is now reviveing in many Places that this Vail may be yet further removed, and that this Disorder may be searched to the bottom, and my concern is that we may not only bear in Mind that the Negroes have been a Suffering people under us as a Civil Society, but that we may in true Humiliation, feel for that pure Influence which alone is able to guide us in the way where healing and restoration is experienced.)

Having thus far spoken of the negroes as

equally entitled to the benefit of their Labour with us, I feel it on my mind to mention that debt which is due to many negroes of the present age. Where men within certain limmits are so formed into a Society as to become like a large body consisting of many members, here whatever injuries are done to others not of this Society, by members of this Society, if the Society in whose power it is, doth not use all reasonable endeavours to execute justice and Judgment, nor publicly disown those unrighteous proceedings, the iniquities of Individuals become chargeable on such Civil Society to which they remain united. And where persons have been injured as to their outward Substance, and died without having recompense, so that their children are kept out of that which was equitably due to their parents; here such children appear to be justly entitled to receive recompense from that Civil Society under which their parents suffered.

My heart is affected with sorrow while I write on this Subject, on account of the great injuries committed against these Gentiles, and against their children born in Captivity. Had the active members of Civil Society when those injuries were first attempted, united in a firm opposition to those violent proceedings; had others in a selfish spirit attempted the like afterward, and met with a firm opposition, and been made to do justice to the injured persons, till the prospect of gain by such unrighteous proceedings appeared so doubtful that no further Attempts had been made,—how much better had it been for these American Colonies and Islands!

When the ancestors of these people were brought from Africa, some I believe bought those poor sufferers with intent to treat them kindly as slaves. They bought them as though those violent men had a right to sell them, but I believe without entering deep enough into the consideration of the consequence of such proceedings. Others I believe bought them with views of outward ease and profit, and thus those violent men found people of reputation who purchased their booty, and built on that purchase as a foundation to exercise the Authority of Masters, and thus encouraged them in this horrible Trade, till their proceedings were so far approved by Civil Society as to consider those men as members, without proceeding to punish them for their crimes, and hence a veil was gradually drawn over a practice, the most foreign to Righteousness, and the

face of things so disguised that under the most lamentable injustice but few appeared to be alarmed at it, or zealously labour to have justice done to the sufferers & their posterity.

The poor Africans were people of a strange language, & not easie to converse with; & their Scituation as Slaves, too generally destroyed that brotherly freedom which frequently subsists between us and inoffensive Strangers.

In this adverse condition, how reasonable is it to suppose, that they would revolve in their distressed minds, the iniquities committed against them, and mourn! Mourn without any to comfort them!

Though through gradual proceedings in unrighteousness, dimness hath come over many minds, yet the nature of things is not altered. Long oppression hath not made Oppression consistent with Brotherly Love, nor length of time through several ages made recompense to the posterity of those injured Strangers. Many of them lived, and died without having their suffering cases heard and determined according to Equity, and under a degree of Sorrow on account of the wantonness, the Vanity and Superfluity too common amongst us as a Civil Society, even while a heavy load of unrighteous proceedings lies upon us, do I now under a feeling of universal Love & in a fervent concern for the real interest of my fellow members in Society, as well as the Interest of my fellow creatures in general, express these things.

Suppose an inoffensive youth, forty years ago, was violently taken from Guinea, Sold here as a Slave, and laboured hard till old age, and hath children who are now living. Though no sin may properly be mentioned as an equal reward for the total deprivation of Liberty; yet if the sufferings of this man be computed at no more than fifty pounds, I expect candid men will suppose it within bounds, and that his Children have an Equitable right to it.

Fifty pounds at three per cent, adding the Interest to the Principal once in ten years appears in forty years to make upward of one hundred & forty pounds.

Principal 50^{l}......................	50
Interest 10 year at 3p^{r}cent...............	15
	65
Interest 10 year........................	19
	84
Interest 10 year........................	25
	109
Interest 10 year........................	32
	141

10

20

30

40

Now when our minds are thoroughly divested of all prejudice in relation to the difference of colour, and the Love of Christ, in which there is no partiality, prevails upon us, I believe it will appear that a heavy account lies against us as a Civil Society for oppressions commited against people who did not injure us; and that if the particular case of many individuals were fairly stated, it would appear that there was considerable due to them.

I conclude with the words of that Righteous Judge in Israel, Behold here I am: witness against me before the Lord, and before his anointed; whose ox have I taken? or whose ass have I taken? or whom have I defrauded? whom have I oppressed? or of whose hand have I received any bribe, to blind mine eyes therewith; and I will restore it to you. I Samuel xii. 3.

1763

BENJAMIN FRANKLIN

1706–1790

THE OUTLINE of Franklin's life is well known: it is one of the first of American "success" stories and it is the most impressive. Son of a humble Boston candle-maker, at the age of twelve he began an apprenticeship in his brother's printing shop. By diligently improving his mind and by shrewd common sense he did well as the proprietor of his own printing establishment in Philadelphia. *Poor Richard's Almanack*, with its sprightly wit and homely utilitarianism, was a profitable venture; and Franklin also enjoyed success as a newspaper publisher. But money was not an end in itself. It gave him greater leisure to indulge his interest in natural science, invention, and writing. Above all, it made it possible for him to give much time to the civic improvement of his adopted city. The intellectual life of the time was broadened through the discussion clubs he founded, through the library he promoted, and through the educational institutions he supported. Intellectual life was deepened through his own scientific work and that of his associates in the American Philosophical Society, which owed much to him. In the struggle for freedom Franklin, as we shall see, played a leading part.

It has become customary to contrast Franklin with Edwards. Franklin had little of the aestheticism, mysticism, and supernaturalism of Jonathan Edwards. Although, as a deist, he accepted the doctrine that a Supreme Being had planned the universe, and although he saw much pragmatic value in many of the moral and ethical values of Christianity, Franklin was far more interested in this world than in the next. The way to truth for him was the way of the inductive scientist. Experiment and observation promised man more understanding of the universe than revelation. He studied the little-known and terrifying phenomenon known as electricity, and proved that it was mobile, not static; that it was subject to at least some degree of control. He observed nature in many other aspects and made contributions to geology, meteorology, and mathematics. In the spirit of Bacon, Franklin put his knowledge of science to social uses: the Franklin stove, bifocal glasses, the lightning rod, all contributed to the amelioration of day-by-day living conditions.

Franklin advocated religious tolerance and utilitarian morals. His *Almanacks* did much to familiarize the plain people with the Newtonian theory of the universe, and to weaken the hold which the biblical account of Creation held on the popular mind. For his scientific achievements he was recognized and honored abroad as one of the leading "philosophers" of the Enlightenment.

Franklin was a son of the Enlightenment also in his zeal for humanitarianism. He befriended the cause of the poor debtor and the slave. He pointed to the evils of war and did something to turn men's minds toward the possibility of achieving peace. He took an advanced view in regarding women as human beings equal, in all potentialities of mental achievement, to men. Although he did not subscribe without qualification to the doctrine of inevitable progress, he did believe that the rational elements in man's mind and in his society might be increased through the extension and diffusion of knowledge.

Papers, Leonard W. Larabee and others, eds., New Haven, 1959–
I. Bernard Cohen, *Benjamin Franklin: His Contribution to the American Tradition*, Indianapolis, 1953.
Carl Van Doren, *Benjamin Franklin*, New York, 1938.
Verner W. Crane, *Benjamin Franklin and a Rising People*, Boston, 1954.

» » *From:* THE AUTOBIOGRAPHY « «

[SCIENTIFIC EXPERIMENTS]

In 1746, being at Boston, I met there with a Dr. Spence, who was lately arrived from Scotland, and show'd me some electric experiments. They were imperfectly perform'd, as he was not very expert; but, being on a subject quite new to me, they equally surpris'd and pleased me. Soon after my return to Philadelphia, our library company receiv'd from Mr. P. Collinson, Fellow of the Royal Society of London, a present of a glass tube, with some account of the use of it in making such experiments. I eagerly seized the opportunity of repeating what I had seen at Boston; and, by much practice, acquir'd great readiness in performing those, also, which we had an account of from England, adding a number of new ones. I say much practice, for my house was continually full, for some time, with people who came to see these new wonders.

To divide a little this incumbrance among my friends, I caused a number of similar tubes to be blown at our glass-house, with which they furnish'd themselves, so that we had at length several performers. Among these, the principal was Mr. Kinnersley, an ingenious neighbor, who, being out of business, I encouraged to undertake showing the experiments for money, and drew up for him two lectures, in which the experiments were rang'd in such order, and accompanied with such explanations in such method, as that the foregoing should assist in comprehending the following. He procur'd an elegant apparatus for the purpose, in which all the little machines that I had roughly made for myself were nicely form'd by instrument-makers. His lectures were well attended, and gave

great satisfaction; and after some time he went thro' the colonies, exhibiting them in every capital town, and pick'd up some money. In the West India Islands, indeed, it was with difficulty the experiments could be made, from the general moisture of the air.

Oblig'd as we were to Mr. Collinson for his present of the tube, etc., I thought it right he should be inform'd of our success in using it, and wrote him several letters containing accounts of our experiments. He got them read in the Royal Society, where they were not at first thought worth so much notice as to be printed in their Transactions. One paper, which I wrote for Mr. Kinnersley, on the sameness of lightning with electricity, I sent to Dr. Mitchel, an acquaintance of mine, and one of the members also of that society, who wrote me word that it had been read, but was laughed at by the connoisseurs. The papers, however, being shown to Dr. Fothergill, he thought them of too much value to be stifled, and advis'd the printing of them. Mr. Collinson then gave them to *Cave* for publication in his Gentleman's Magazine; but he chose to print them separately in a pamphlet, and Dr. Fothergill wrote the preface. Cave, it seems, judged rightly for his profit, for by the additions that arrived afterward they swell'd, to a quarto volume, which has had five editions, and cost him nothing for copy-money.

It was, however, some time before those papers were much taken notice of in England. A copy of them happening to fall into the hands of the Count de Buffon, a philosopher deservedly of great reputation in France, and, indeed, all over Europe, he prevailed with M. Dalibard to translate them into French, and

they were printed at Paris. The publication offended the Abbé Nollet, preceptor in Natural
Philosophy to the royal family, and an able
experimenter, who had form'd and publish'd a
theory of electricity, which then had the general vogue. He could not at first believe that
such a work came from America, and said it
must have been fabricated by his enemies at
Paris, to decry his system. Afterwards, having
been assur'd that there really existed such a
person as Franklin at Philadelphia, which he
had doubted, he wrote and published a volume
of Letters, chiefly address'd to me, defending
his theory, and denying the verity of my experiments, and of the positions deduc'd from
them.

I once purpos'd answering the abbé, and actually began the answer; but, on consideration
that my writings contain'd a description of experiments which any one might repeat and
verify, and if not to be verifi'd, could not be defended; or of observations offer'd as conjectures, and not delivered dogmatically, therefore
not laying me under any obligation to defend
them; and reflecting that a dispute between
two persons, writing in different languages,
might be lengthened greatly by mistranslations,
and thence misconceptions of one another's
meaning, much of one of the abbé's letters being founded on an error in the translation, I
concluded to let my papers shift for themselves,
believing it was better to spend what time I
could spare from public business in making
new experiments, than in disputing about those
already made. I therefore never answered M.
Nollet, and the event gave me no cause to repent my silence; for my friend M. le Roy, of
the Royal Academy of Sciences, took up my
cause and refuted him; my book was translated
into the Italian, German, and Latin languages;
and the doctrine it contain'd was by degrees
universally adopted by the philosophers of
Europe, in preference to that of the Abbé; so
that he lived to see himself the last of his sect,
except Monsieur B——, of Paris, his *élève* and
immediate disciple.

What gave my book the more sudden and
general celebrity, was the success of one of its
proposed experiments, made by Messrs. Dalibard and De Lor at Marly, for drawing lightning from the clouds. This engag'd the public
attention every where. M. de Lor, who had an
apparatus for experimental philosophy, and
lectur'd in that branch of science, undertook
to repeat what he called the *Philadelphia Ex-*

periments; and, after they were performed before the king and court, all the curious of Paris
flocked to see them. I will not swell this narrative with an account of that capital experiment, nor of the infinite pleasure I receiv'd in
the success of a similar one I made soon after
with a kite at Philadelphia, as both are to be
found in the histories of electricity.

Dr. Wright, an English physician, when at
Paris, wrote to a friend, who was of the Royal
Society, an account of the high esteem my experiments were in among the learned abroad,
and of their wonder that my writings had been
so little noticed in England. The Society, on
this, resum'd the consideration of the letters
that had been read to them; and the celebrated
Dr. Watson drew up a summary account of
them, and of all I had afterwards sent to England on the subject, which he accompanied
with some praise of the writer. This summary
was then printed in their Transactions; and
some members of the Society in London, particularly the very ingenious Mr. Canton, having verified the experiment of procuring lightning from the clouds by a pointed rod, and
acquainting them with the success, they soon
made me more than amends for the slight with
which they had before treated me. Without my
having made any application for that honour,
they chose me a member, and voted that I
should be excus'd the customary payments,
which would have amounted to twenty-five
guineas; and ever since have given me their
Transactions gratis. They also presented me
with the gold medal of Sir Godfrey Copley for
the year 1753, the delivery of which was accompanied by a very handsome speech of the
president, Lord Macclesfield, wherein I was
highly honoured.　　　　　1771, 1784–1789

[DEISM]

Before I enter upon my public Appearance
in Business it may be well to let you know the
then State of my Mind, with regard to my
Principles and Morals, that you may see how
far those influenc'd the future Events of my
Life. My Parent's had early given me religious
Impressions, and brought me through my
Childhood piously in the Dissenting Way. But
I was scarce 15 when, after doubting by turns
of several Points as I found them disputed in
the different Books I read, I began to doubt of
Revelation it self. Some Books against Deism
fell into my Hands; they were said to be the

Substance of Sermons preached at Boyle's Lectures. It happened that they wrought an Effect on me quite contrary to what was intended by them: For the Arguments of the Deists which were quoted to be refuted, appeared to me much Stronger than the Refutations. In short I soon became a thorough Deist. My arguments perverted some others, particularly Collins and Ralph: but each of them having afterwards wrong'd me greatly without the least Compunction and recollecting Keith's Conduct towards me, (who was another Freethinker) and my own towards Vernon and Miss Read, which at Times gave me great Trouble, I began to suspect that this Doctrine tho' it might be true, was not very useful.—My London Pamphlet, which had for its Motto these Lines of Dryden

> *Whatever is, is right. Tho' purblind Man*
> *Sees but a Part of the Chain, the nearest Link,*
> *His Eyes not carrying to the equal Beam,*
> *That poises all, above;*

and from the Attributes of God, his infinite Wisdom, Goodness and Power concluded that nothing could possibly be wrong in the World, and that Vice and Virtue were empty Distinctions, no such Things existing: appear'd now not so clever a Performance as I once thought it; and I doubted whether some Error had not insinuated itself unperceiv'd, into my Argument, so as to infect all that follow'd, as is common in metaphysical Reasonings.—I grew convinc'd that *Truth, Sincerity* and *Integrity* in Dealings between Man and Man, were of the utmost Importance to the Felicity of Life, and I form'd written Resolutions, (wch still remain in my Journal Book) to practice them everwhile I lived. Revelation had indeed no weight with me as such; but I entertain'd an Opinion, that tho' certain Actions might not be bad *because* they were forbidden by it, or good *because* it commanded them; yet probably those Actions might be forbidden *because* they were bad for us, or commanded *because* they were beneficial to us, in their own Natures, all the Circumstances of things considered. And this Persuasion, with the kind hand of Providence, or some guardian Angel, or accidental favourable Circumstances and Situations, or all together, preserved me (thro' this dangerous Time of Youth and the hazardous Situations I was sometimes in among Strangers, remote from the Eye and Advice of my Father) without any *wilful* gross Immorality or Injustice that might have been expected from my Want of Religion. I say *wilful*, because the Instances I have mentioned, had something of *Necessity* in them, from my Youth, Inexperience, and the Knavery of others. I had therefore a tolerable Character to begin the World with, I valued it properly, and determin'd to preserve it.— . . .

I had been religiously educated as a Presbyterian; and tho' some of the dogmas of that persuasion, such as *the eternal decrees of God, election, reprobation, etc.*, appeared to me unintelligible, others doubtful, and I early absented myself from the public assemblies of the sect, Sunday being my studying day. I never was without some religious principles. I never doubted, for instance, the existence of the Deity; that he made the world, and govern'd it by his Providence; that the most acceptable service of God was the doing good to man; that our souls are immortal; and that all crime will be punished, and virtue rewarded, either here or hereafter. These I esteem'd the essentials of every religion; and, being to be found in all the religions we had in our country, I respected them all, tho' with different degrees of respect, as I found them more or less mix'd with other articles, which, without any tendency to inspire, promote, or confirm morality, serv'd principally to divide us, and make us unfriendly to one another. This respect to all, with an opinion that the worst had some good effects, induc'd me to avoid all discourse that might tend to lessen the good opinion another might have of his own religion; and as our province increas'd in people, and new places of worship were continually wanted, and generally erected by voluntary contribution, my mite for such purpose, whatever might be the sect, was never refused.

Tho' I seldom attended any public worship, I had still an opinion of its propriety, and of its utility when rightly conducted, and I regularly paid my annual subscription for the support of the only Presbyterian minister or meeting we had in Philadelphia. He us'd to visit me sometimes as a friend, and admonish me to attend his administrations, and I was now and then prevail'd on to do so, once for five Sundays successively. Had he been in my opinion a good preacher, perhaps I might have continued, notwithstanding the occasion I had for the Sunday's leisure in my course of study; but his discourses were chiefly either polemic arguments, or explications of the peculiar doctrines of our sect, and were all to me very dry, uninteresting, and unedifying, since not a single moral principle was inculcated or enforc'd, their aim seeming to be rather to make us Presbyterians than good citizens.

At length he took for his text that verse of the fourth chapter of Philippians, *"Finally, brethren, whatsoever things are true, honest, just, pure, lovely, or of good report, if there be any virtue, or any praise, think on these things."* And I imagin'd, in a sermon on such a text, we could not miss of having some morality.
10 But he confin'd himself to five points only, as meant by the apostle, viz.: 1. Keeping holy the Sabbath day. 2. Being diligent in reading the holy Scriptures. 3. Attending duly the publick worship. 4. Partaking of the Sacrament. 5. Paying a due respect to God's ministers.

These might be all good things; but, as they were not the kind of good things that I expected from that text, I despaired of ever meeting with them from any other, was disgusted, and attended his preaching no more. I had some years before compos'd a little Liturgy, or form of prayer, for my own private use (viz., in 1728), entitled *Articles of Belief and Acts of Religion.* I return'd to the use of this, and went no more to the public assemblies. My conduct might be blameable, but I leave it, without attempting further to excuse it; my present purpose being to relate facts, and not to make apologies for them.

1771, 1784–1789

From: ARTICLES OF BELIEF
» » AND ACTS OF RELIGION « «

FIRST PRINCIPLES

I believe there is one supreme, most perfect Being, Author and Father of the Gods themselves. For I believe that Man is not the most perfect Being but one, rather that as there are many Degrees of Beings his Inferiors, so there are many Degrees of Beings superior to him.

Also, when I stretch my Imagination thro'
30 and beyond our System of Planets, beyond the visible fix'd Stars themselves, into that Space that is every Way infinite, and conceive it fill'd with Suns like ours, each with a Chorus of Worlds forever moving round him, then this little Ball on which we move, seems, even in my narrow Imagination, to be almost Nothing, and myself less than nothing, and of no sort of Consequence.

When I think thus, I imagine it great Vanity
40 in me to suppose, that the *Supremely Perfect* does in the least regard such an inconsiderable Nothing as Man. More especially, since it is impossible for me to have any positive clear idea of that which is infinite and incomprehensible, I cannot conceive otherwise than that he *the Infinite Father* expects or requires no Worship or Praise from us, but that he is even infinitely above it.

But, since there is in all Men something like
50 a natural principle, which inclines them to DEVOTION, or the Worship of some unseen Power;

And since Men are endued with Reason superior to all other Animals, that we are in our World acquainted with;

Therefore I think it seems required of me, and my Duty as a Man, to pay Divine Regards to SOMETHING.

I conceive then, that the INFINITE has created many beings or Gods, vastly superior to Man, who can better conceive his Perfections than we, and return him a more rational and glorious Praise.

As, among Men, the Praise of the Ignorant or of Children is not regarded by the ingenious Painter or Architect, who is rather honour'd and pleas'd with the approbation of Wise Men & Artists.

It may be that these created Gods are immortal; or it may be that after many Ages, they are changed, and others Supply their Places.

Howbeit, I conceive that each of these is exceeding wise and good, and very powerful; and that Each has made for himself one glorious Sun, attended with a beautiful and admirable System of Planets.

It is that particular Wise and good God, who is the author and owner of our System, that I propose for the object of my praise and adoration.

For I conceive that he has in himself some of those Passions he has planted in us, and that, since he has given us Reason whereby we are capable of observing his Wisdom in the Creation, he is not above caring for us, being pleas'd with our Praise, and offended when we slight Him, or neglect his Glory.

I conceive for many Reasons, that he is a *good Being;* and as I should be happy to have so wise, good, and powerful a Being my Friend, let me consider in what manner I shall make myself most acceptable to him.

Next to the Praise resulting from and due to his Wisdom, I believe he is pleas'd and delights in the Happiness of those he has created; and since without Virtue Man can have no Happiness in this World, I firmly believe he delights to see me Virtuous, because he is pleased when he sees Me Happy.

And since he has created many Things, which seem purely design'd for the Delight of Man, I believe he is not offended, when he sees his Children solace themselves in any manner of pleasant exercises and Innocent Delights; and I think no Pleasure innocent, that is to Man hurtful.

I *love* him therefore for his Goodness, and I *adore* him for his Wisdom.

Let me then not fail to praise my God continually, for it is his Due, and it is all I can return for his many Favours and great Goodness to me; and let me resolve to be virtuous, that I may be happy, that I may please Him, who is delighted to see me happy. Amen!

1728

» » PROPOSED NEW VERSION OF THE BIBLE « «

[To the Printer of * * *]

Sɪʀ,

It is now more than one hundred and seventy years since the translation of our common English Bible. The language in that time is much changed, and the style, being obsolete, and thence less agreeable, is perhaps one reason why the reading of that excellent book is of late so much neglected. I have therefore thought it would be well to procure a new version, in which, preserving the sense, the turn of phrase and manner of expression should be modern. I do not pretend to have the necessary abilities for such a work myself; I throw out the hint for the consideration of the learned; and only venture to send you a few verses of the first chapter of Job, which may serve as a sample of the kind of version I would recommend.   A. B.

PART OF THE FIRST CHAPTER OF JOB MODERNIZED

Oʟᴅ Tᴇxᴛ	Nᴇᴡ Vᴇʀsɪᴏɴ
Verse 6. Now there was a day when the sons of God came to present themselves before the Lord, and Satan came also amongst them.	Verse 6. And it being *levée* day in heaven, all God's nobility came to court, to present themselves before him; and Satan also appeared in the circle, as one of the ministry.
7. And the Lord said unto Satan, Whence comest thou?	7. And God said to Satan, You have been some time absent;

Then Satan answered the Lord, and said, From going to and fro in the earth, and from walking up and down in it.

8. And the Lord said unto Satan, Hast thou considered my servant Job, that there is none like him in the earth, a perfect and an upright man, one that feareth God, and escheweth evil?

9. Then Satan answered the Lord, and said, Doth Job fear God for naught?

10. Hast thou not made an hedge about his house, and about all that he hath on every side? Thou hast blessed the work of his hands, and his substance is increased in the land.

11. But put forth thine hand now, and touch all that he hath, and he will curse thee to thy face.

where were you? And Satan answered [,] I have been at my country-seat, and in different places visiting my friends.

8. And God said, Well, what think you of Lord Job? You see he is my best friend, a perfectly honest man, full of respect for me, and avoiding every thing that might offend me.

9. And Satan answered, Does your Majesty imagine that his good conduct is the effect of mere personal attachment and affection?

10. Have you not protected him, and heaped your benefits upon him, till he is grown enormously rich?

11. Try him;—only withdraw your favor, turn him out of his places, and withhold his pensions, and you will soon find him in the opposition. 1779

» » PARABLES « «

A PARABLE AGAINST PERSECUTION [1]

1. And it came to pass after these things, that Abraham sat in the door of his tent, about the going down of the sun.

2. And behold a man, bent with age, coming from the way of the wilderness, leaning on a staff.

3. And Abraham arose and met him, and said unto him, Turn in, I pray thee, and wash thy feet, and tarry all night, and thou shalt arise early in the morning, and go on thy way.

4. But the man said, Nay, for I will abide under this tree.

5. And Abraham pressed him greatly; so he turned, and they went into the tent; and Abraham baked unleavened bread, and they did eat.

6. And when Abraham saw that the man blessed not God, he said unto him, Wherefore dost thou not worship the most high God, Creator of heaven and earth?

7. And the man answered and said, I do not worship thy God, neither do I call upon his name; for I have made to myself a god, which abideth always in mine house, and provideth me with all things.

8. And Abraham's zeal was kindled against the man, and he arose and fell upon him, and drove him forth with blows into the wilderness.

9. And God called unto Abraham, saying, Abraham, where is the stranger?

10. And Abraham answered and said, Lord, he would not worship thee, neither would he call upon thy name; therefore have I driven him out from before my face into the wilderness.

11. And God said, Have I borne with him these hundred and ninety and eight years, and nourished him, and cloathed him, notwithstanding his rebellion against me; and couldst not thou, who art thyself a sinner, bear with him one night?

12. And Abraham said, Let not the anger of the Lord wax hot against his servant; lo, I have sinned; lo, I have sinned; forgive me, I pray thee.

13. And Abraham arose, and went forth

[1] For an account of this hoax see L. S. Livingston's *Benjamin Franklin's Parable against Persecution. With an Account of the Early Editions*, Cambridge, Mass., 1916.

into the wilderness, and sought diligently for the man, and found him, and returned with him to the tent; and when he had entreated him kindly, he sent him away on the morrow with gifts.

14. And God spake again unto Abraham, saying, For this thy sin shall thy seed be afflicted four hundred years in a strange land;

15. But for thy repentance will I deliver them; and they shall come forth with power, and with gladness of heart, and with much substance. 1774

A PARABLE ON BROTHERLY LOVE

1. In those days there was no worker of iron in all the land. And the merchants of Midian passed by with their camels, bearing spices, and myrrh, and balm, and wares of iron.

2. And Reuben bought an axe of the Ishmaelite merchants, which he prized highly, for there was none in his father's house.

3. And Simeon said unto Reuben his brother, "Lend me, I pray thee, thine axe." But he refused, and would not.

4. And Levi also said unto him, "My brother, lend me, I pray thee, thine axe"; and he refused him also.

5. Then came Judah unto Reuben, and entreated him, saying, "Lo, thou lovest me, and I have always loved thee; do not refuse me the use of thine axe."

6. But Reuben turned from him, and refused him likewise.

7. Now it came to pass, that Reuben hewed timber on the bank of the river, and his axe fell therein, and he could by no means find it.

8. But Simeon, Levi, and Judah had sent a messenger after the Ishmaelites with money, and had bought for themselves each an axe.

9. Then came Reuben unto Simeon, and said, "Lo, I have lost mine axe, and my work is unfinished; lend me thine, I pray thee."

10. And Simeon answered him, saying, "Thou wouldest not lend me thine axe, therefore will I not lend thee mine."

11. Then went he unto Levi, and said unto him, "My brother, thou knowest my loss and my necessity; lend me, I pray thee, thine axe."

12. And Levi reproached him, saying, "Thou wouldest not lend me thine axe when I desired it, but I will be better than thou, and will lend thee mine."

13. And Reuben was grieved at the rebuke of Levi and being ashamed, turned from him, and took not the axe, but sought his brother Judah.

14. And as he drew near, Judah beheld his countenance as it were covered with grief and shame; and he prevented him, saying, "My brother, I know thy loss; but why should it trouble thee? Lo, have I not an axe that will serve both thee and me? Take it, I pray thee, and use it as thine own."

15. And Reuben fell on his neck, and kissed him, with tears, saying, "Thy kindness is great, but thy goodness in forgiving me is greater. Thou are indeed my brother, and whilst I live, will I surely love thee."

16. And Judah said, "Let us also love our other brethren; behold, are we not all of one blood?"

17. And Joseph saw these things, and reported them to his father Jacob.

18. And Jacob said, "Reuben did wrong, but he repented. Simeon also did wrong; and Levi was not altogether blameless.

19. "But the heart of Judah is princely. Judah hath the soul of a king. His father's children shall bow down before him, and he shall rule over his brethren."   1774

» » LETTERS « «

[To Ezra Stiles]

Philadelphia, March 9, 1790.

REVEREND AND DEAR SIR:

I received your kind letter of January 28, and am glad you have at length received the portrait of Governor Yale from his family, and deposited it in the College Library. He was a great and good man, and had the merit of doing infinite service to your county by his munificence to that institution. The honour you propose doing me by placing mine in the same room with his, is much too great for my deserts; but you always had a partiality for me, and to that it must be ascribed. I am, however, too much obliged to Yale College, the first learned society that took notice of me and adorned me with its honours, to refuse a request that comes from it thro' so esteemed a friend. But I do not think any one of the portraits you mention, as in my possession, worthy of the place and company you propose to place it in. You have an excellent artist lately arrived. If he will undertake to make one for you, I shall cheerfully pay the expence, but he must not delay setting about, or I may slip thro' his fingers, for I am now in my eighty-fifth year, and very infirm. . . .

You desire to know something of my religion. It is the first time I have been questioned upon it. But I cannot take your curiosity amiss, and shall endeavor in a few words to gratify it. Here is my creed.

I believe in one God, creator of the universe. That he governs it by his Providence. That he ought to be worshipped. That the most acceptable service we render to him is doing good to his other children. That the soul of man is immortal, and will be treated with justice in another life respecting its conduct in this. These I take to be the fundamental principles of all sound religion, and I regard them as you do in whatever sect I meet with them.

As to Jesus of Nazareth, my opinion of whom you particularly desire, I think the system of morals, and his religion, as he left them to us, the best the world ever saw or is likely to see; but I apprehend it has received various corrupting changes, and I have, with most of the present dissenters in England, some doubts as to his divinity; tho' it is a question I do not dogmatize upon, having never studied it, and think it needless to busy myself with it now, when I expect soon an opportunity of knowing the truth with less trouble. I see no harm, however, in its being believed, if that belief has the good consequence, as it probably has, of making his doctrines more respected and better observed; especially as I do not perceive that the Supreme takes it amiss, by distinguishing the unbelievers in his government of the world with any peculiar marks of his displeasure.

I shall only add, respecting myself, that,

having experienced the goodness of that being in conducting me prosperously thro' a long life, I have no doubt of its continuance in the next, though without the smallest conceit of meriting such goodness. My sentiments on this head you will see in the copy of an old letter enclosed, which I wrote in answer to one from a zealous religionist, whom I had relieved in a paralytic case by electricity, and who, being afraid I should grow proud upon it, sent me his serious though rather impertinent caution. I send you also the copy of another letter, which will shew something of my disposition relating to religion. With great and sincere esteem and affection, I am,

　　Your obliged old friend and most obedient humble servant,　　　　　B. FRANKLIN.

P. S. Had not your college some present of books from the King of France? Please to let me know, if you had an expectation given you of more, and the nature of that expectation. I have a reason for the inquiry.

　　I confide that you will not expose me to criticism and censure by publishing any part of this communication to you. I have ever let others enjoy their religious sentiments, without reflecting on them for those that appeared to me unsupportable and even absurd. All sects here, and we have a great variety, have experienced my good will in assisting them with subscriptions for building their new places of worship; and as I have never opposed any of their doctrines, I hope to go out of the world in peace with them all.　　　　　　1790

»　» THE SPEECH OF POLLY BAKER[1]　«　«

The Speech of Miss Polly Baker before a Court of Judicature, at Connecticut near Boston in New England; where she was prosecuted the fifth time, for having a Bastard Child: Which influenced the Court to dispense with her Punishment, and which induced one of her Judges to marry her the next Day—by whom she had fifteen Children.

　　"May it please the honourable bench to indulge me in a few words: I am a poor, unhappy woman, who have no money to fee lawyers to plead for me, being hard put to it to get a living. I shall not trouble your honours with long speeches; for I have not the presumption to expect that you may, by any means, be prevailed on to deviate in your Sentence from the law, in my favour. All I humbly hope is, that your honours would charitably move the governor's goodness on my behalf, that my fine may be remitted. This is the fifth time, gentlemen, that I have been dragg'd before your court on the same account; twice I have paid heavy fines, and twice have been brought to publick punishment, for want of money to pay those fines. This may have been agreeable to the laws, and I don't dispute it; but since laws are sometimes unreasonable in themselves, and therefore repealed; and others bear too hard on the subject in particular circumstances, and therefore there is left a power somewhere to dispense with the execution of them; I take

the liberty to say, that I think this law, by which I am punished, both unreasonable in itself, and particularly severe with regard to me, who have always lived an inoffensive life in the neighbourhood where I was born, and defy my enemies (if I have any) to say I ever wrong'd any man, woman, or child. Abstracted from the law, I cannot conceive (may it please your honours) what the nature of my offense is. I have brought five fine children into the world, at the risque of my life; I have maintain'd them well by my own industry, without burthening the township, and would have done it better, if it had not been for the heavy charges and fines I have paid. Can it be a crime (in the nature of things, I mean) to add to the king's subjects, in a new country, that really wants people? I own it, I should think it rather a praiseworthy than a punishable action. I have debauched no other woman's husband, nor enticed any other youth; these things I never was charg'd with; nor has any one the least cause of complaint against me, unless, perhaps, the ministers of justice, because I have had children without being married, by which they have missed a wedding fee. But can this be a fault of mine? I appeal to your honours. You are pleased to allow I don't want sense; but I must be stupified to the last degree, not to prefer the honourable state of wedlock to the condition I have lived in. I always was, and still am willing to enter into it; and doubt not my behaving well in it, hav-

---

[1] For an interesting note on this "Speech," which appeared in the *Gentleman's Magazine*, April, 1747, see A. H. Smythe, *The Writings of Benjamin Franklin* (10 vols., New York, 1905–1907), II, 463–464.

ing all the industry, frugality, fertility, and skill in economy appertaining to a good wife's character. I defy any one to say I ever refused an offer of that sort: on the contrary, I readily consented to the only proposal of marriage that ever was made me, which was when I was a virgin, but too easily confiding in the person's sincerity that made it, I unhappily lost my honour by trusting to his; for he got me with child, and then forsook me.

"That very person, you all know, he is now become a magistrate of this country; and I had hopes he would have appeared this day on the bench, and have endeavoured to moderate the Court in my favour; then I should have scorn'd to have mentioned it; but I must now complain of it, as unjust and unequal, that my betrayer and undoer, the first cause of all my faults and miscarriages (if they must be deemed such), should be advanced to honour and power in this government that punishes my misfortunes with stripes and infamy. I should be told, 'tis like, that were there no act of Assembly in the case, the precepts of religion are violated by my transgressions. If mine is a religious offense, leave it to religious punishments. You have already excluded me from the comforts of your church communion. Is not that sufficient? You believe I have offended heaven, and must suffer eternal fire: Will not that be sufficient? What need is there then of your additional fines and whipping? I own I do not think as you do, for, if I thought what you call a sin was really such, I could not presumptuously commit it. But, how can it be believed that heaven is angry at my having children, when to the little done by me towards it, God has been pleased to add his divine skill and admirable workmanship in the formation of their bodies, and crowned the whole by furnishing them with rational and immortal souls?

"Forgive me, gentlemen, if I talk a little extravagantly on these matters; I am no divine, but if you, gentlemen, must be making laws, do not turn natural and useful actions into crimes by your prohibitions. But take into your wise consideration the great and growing num- ber of batchelors in the country, many of whom, from the mean fear of the expences of a family, have never sincerely and honourably courted a woman in their lives; and by their manner of living leave unproduced (which is little better than murder) hundreds of their posterity to the thousandth generation. Is not this a greater offense against the publick good than mine? Compel them, then, by law, either to marriage, or to pay double the fine of forni- cation every year. What must poor young women do, whom customs and nature forbid to solicit the men, and who cannot force them- selves upon husbands, when the laws take no care to provide them any, and yet severely punish them if they do their duty without them; the duty of the first and great command of nature and nature's God, *encrease and multiply*; a duty, from the steady performance of which nothing has been able to deter me, but for its sake I have hazarded the loss of the publick esteem, and have frequently endured publick disgrace and punishment; and therefore ought, in my humble opinion, instead of a whipping, to have a statue erected to my memory." 1747

» » ADVICE TO A YOUNG TRADESMAN « «

To my Friend, A. B.:

As you have desired it of me, I write the following hints, which have been of service to me, and may, if observed, be so to you.

Remember, that *time* is money. He that can earn ten shillings a day by his labour, and goes abroad, or sits idle, one half of that day, though he spends but sixpence during his diversion or idleness, ought not to reckon *that* the only expense; he has really spent, or rather thrown away, five shillings besides.

Remember, that *credit* is money. If a man lets his money lie in my hands after it is due, he gives me the interest, or so much as I can make of it during that time. This amounts to a considerable sum where a man has good and large credit, and makes good use of it.

Remember, that money is of the prolific, generating nature. Money can beget money, and its offspring can beget more, and so on. Five shillings turned is six, turned again it is seven and three-pence, and so on till it be- comes an hundred pounds. The more there is of it, the more it produces every turning, so that the profits rise quicker and quicker. He that kills a breeding sow, destroys all her offspring to the thousandth generation. He that murders a crown, destroys all that it might have produced, even scores of pounds.

Remember, that six pounds a year is but a groat a day. For this little sum (which may be daily wasted either in time or expense unperceived) a man of credit may, on his own security, have the constant possession and use of an hundred pounds. So much in stock, briskly turned by an industrious man, produces great advantage.

Remember this saying, *The good paymaster is lord of another man's purse.* He that is known to pay punctually and exactly to the time he promises, may at any time, and on any occasion, raise all the money his friends can spare. This is sometimes of great use. After industry and frugality, nothing contributes more to the raising of a young man in the world than punctuality and justice in all his dealings; therefore never keep borrowed money an hour beyond the time you promised, lest a disappointment shut up your friend's purse for ever.

The most trifling actions that affect a man's credit are to be regarded. The sound of your hammer at five in the morning, or nine at night, heard by a creditor, makes him easy six months longer; but, if he sees you at a billiardtable, or hears your voice at a tavern, when you should be at work, he sends for his money the next day; demands it, before he can receive it, in a lump.

It shows, besides, that you are mindful of what you owe; it makes you appear a careful as well as an honest man, and that still increases your credit.

Beware of thinking all your own that you possess, and of living accordingly. It is a mistake that many people who have credit fall into. To prevent this, keep an exact account for some time, both of your expenses and your income. If you take the pains at first to mention particulars, it will have this good effect: you will discover how wonderfully small, trifling expenses mount up to large sums, and will discern what might have been, and may for the future be saved, without occasioning any great inconvenience.

In short, the way to wealth, if you desire it, is as plain as the way to market. It depends chiefly on two words, *industry* and *frugality;* that is, waste neither *time* nor *money,* but make the best use of both. Without industry and frugality nothing will do, and with them every thing. He that gets all he can honestly, and saves all he gets (necessary expenses excepted), will certainly become *rich,* if that Being who governs the world, to whom all should look for a blessing on their honest endeavours, doth not, in his wise providence, otherwise determine.

An Old Tradesman.

1748

The Struggle for Freedom

1630-1776

THE LIBERTY SONG

Come join hand in hand, brave Americans all,
And rouse your bold hearts at fair Liberty's call;
No tyrannous acts shall suppress your just claim,
Nor stain with dishonor America's name.
   In freedom we're born, and in freedom we'll live;
     Our purses are ready,
     Steady, friends, steady,
   Not as slaves, but as freemen our money we'll give.

Our worthy forefathers—let's give them a cheer—
To climates unknown did courageously steer;
Thro' oceans to deserts, for freedom they came,
And, dying, bequeath'd us their freedom and fame.

Their generous bosoms all dangers despis'd,
So highly, so wisely, their birthrights they priz'd;
We'll keep what they gave, we will piously keep,
Nor frustrate their toils on the land or the deep.

The Tree their own hands had to Liberty rear'd,
They lived to behold growing strong and rever'd;
With transport then cried, "Now our wishes we gain,
For our children shall gather the fruits of our pain."

How sweet are the labors that freemen endure,
That they shall enjoy all the profit, secure—
No more such sweet labors Americans know,
If Britons shall reap what Americans sow.

Swarms of placemen and pensioners soon will appear,
Like locusts deforming the charms of the year:
Suns vainly will rise, showers vainly descend,
If we are to drudge for what others shall spend.

Then join hand in hand, brave Americans all,
By uniting we stand, by dividing we fall;
In so righteous a cause let us hope to succeed,
For Heaven approves of each generous deed.

All ages shall speak with amaze and applause,
Of the courage we'll show in support of our laws;

To die we can bear—but to serve we disdain,
For shame is to freemen more dreadful than pain.

This bumper I crown for our sovereign's health,
And this for Britannia's glory and wealth;
That wealth, and that glory immortal may be,
If she is but just, and we are but free.
    In freedom we're born, etc.

Shortly after the refusal of the Massachusetts Legislature to rescind the Circular Letter of February 11, 1768, John Dickinson, author of the famous *Letters from a Farmer in Pennsylvania to the Inhabitants of the British Colonies,* sent this song to James Otis for use in the colonists' cause. Published in the *Boston Gazette* and soon sung to an English tune, "Hearts of Oak," it was instantly popular. According to Mr. S. Foster Damon, the Sons of Liberty adopted it for their official song.

» » « «

THE YANKEE'S RETURN FROM CAMP

Father and I went down to camp,
    Along with Captain Gooding,
And there we see the men and boys,
    As thick as hasty pudding.
        Chorus—Yankee Doodle, keep it up,
            Yankee Doodle, dandy,
              Mind the music and the step,
                And with the girls be handy.

And there we see a thousand men,
    As rich as 'Squire David;
And what they wasted every day,
    I wish it could be savèd.

The 'lasses they eat every day,
    Would keep a house a winter;
They have so much that, I'll be bound,
    They eat it when they're a mind to.

And there we see a swamping[1] gun,
    Large as a log of maple,
Upon a deuced little cart,
    A load for father's cattle.

And every time they shoot it off,
    It takes a horn of powder,

[1] big.

And makes a noise like father's gun,
    Only a nation louder.

I went as nigh to one myself,
    As Siah's underpinning;
And father went as nigh again,
    I thought the deuce was in him.

Cousin Simon grew so bold,
    I thought he would have cock'd it;
It scar'd me so, I shrink'd it off,
    And hung by father's pocket.

And Captain Davis had a gun,
    He kind of clapped his hand on't,
And stuck a crooked stabbing iron
    Upon the little end on't.

And there I see a pumpkin shell
    As big as mother's basin;
And every time they touch'd it off,
    They scamper'd like the nation.

I see a little barrel too,
    The heads were made of leather,
They knock'd upon't with little clubs,
    And call'd the folks together.

And there was Captain Washington,
    And gentlefolks about him,
They say he's grown so tarnal proud,
    He will not ride without 'em.

He got him on his meeting clothes,
    Upon a slapping stallion,
He set the world along in rows,
    In hundreds and in millions.

The flaming ribbons in his hat,
    They look'd so tearing fine ah,
I wanted pockily to get,
    To give to my Jemimah.

I see another snarl of men
    A digging graves, they told me,
So tarnal long, so tarnal deep,
    They 'tended they should hold me.

It scar'd me so, I hook'd it off,
Nor stopp'd, as I remember,
Nor turned about, till I got home,
Lock'd up in mother's chamber.

The early history of "Yankee Doodle" (actually the name of the tune) is obscure. The best guess is that it originated as a burlesque of Yankee manners and was soon taken over by the Yankees themselves. A New York State legend maintains that the words were written at Fort Crailo, across the river from Albany, by a young surgeon on General Abercrombie's staff who was amused by the raw recruits enlisting under this inept general, soon to lose the battle of Ticonderoga (1758). The tune was known in the colonies as early as 1767.

The Struggle for Freedom

THE FOUNDERS of the English-speaking colonies initiated in the New World a planned order which greatly curtailed the freedom of the individual. If the individual did not conform to the religious doctrines of the controlling group and if he belonged to the indentured servant class, or even to the plain people, his freedom was still further restricted. And although the colonists enjoyed varying degrees of freedom from British control, they were seldom free from some consciousness that their liberty was also being restricted in the interest of the home land. This became especially true during the Restoration period and throughout the eighteenth century.

The colonial period merged into the Revolution with many of the traditional restrictions on freedom still in full force. Yet one of the great issues in colonial history has been the struggle between authority and freedom. And on every front, religious, political, economic, and social, impressive gains for freedom had been won.

In the religious sphere the conception of uniformity was challenged almost from the start. Anne Hutchinson, Roger Williams, and the Quakers introduced disturbing elements into Massachusetts Bay; and although religious uniformity was upheld by arguments and by authority, it was whittled away. Rhode Island from the start divorced church from state and granted a large measure of religious freedom. So did Pennsylvania, and, at times, Maryland. The increasingly large number of non-Anglicans in Virginia and the Carolinas greatly weakened the established Church of England. Before the outbreak of the Revolution dissenters were struggling for the religious freedom which liberal-minded men like Jefferson did so much to effect during the Revolutionary period.

In the economic sphere the early efforts to enforce a planned economy broke down with an enlarged degree of liberty for the individual. The collectivistic elements in the Bible Commonwealths, which included price-fixing and the regulation of wages, went by the board when the ever more powerful merchants made their will the order of the day. Efforts to control economy in the planting colonies met with some measure of success but at the same time encountered great obstacles. In Virginia the Culpepper Rebellion indicated that the planters had no stomach for governmental efforts to control the production of the staple, tobacco. But the growth of individual economic freedom for the middle class was most marked in relationships with the mother country. It proved virtually impossible for the British government to reserve forests for future naval supplies: interlopers bent on profits felled the great trees in the King's forests which they regarded as gifts of Nature for the entrepreneur. Land speculators and promoters fumed against British efforts to restrict advance on the frontier, efforts designed partly to protect British fur trade interests and partly to prevent Indian troubles. The Navigation Acts, designed to balance the economy of the entire empire as well as to enhance the profits of the merchant capitalists of Great Britain, were violated right and left by colonial merchants. In zeal for profits colonists even trafficked with pirates on whose heads London had set a price. The increasing effort of the British government to enforce the acts of trade and to compel the colonies to share the growing burden of imperial defense was the precipitating cause of the struggle for independence.

Although the middle class made constant gains in economic freedom, even the lower economic strata could, in a much greater degree than in the Old World, improve their lot.

After terms of indentureship had been served, many of the redemptioners and servants made their way as artisans or as freehold farmers in the newer regions along the frontier. Humble folk, indeed, were subject to many restrictions: in general they had no political power at all. But under the leadership of such men as Nathaniel Bacon, Jacob Leisler, and John Coode they showed, in the later years of the seventeenth century, a spirit of genuine revolt. In the 1740's the "country party" in Massachusetts challenged the control of the clerical-merchant combination, the Paxson boys in the 1760's threatened Philadelphia with violence in their effort to win political privileges, and about the same time the Regulators of frontier North Carolina and the tidewater ruling class made civil war. Furthermore, the common man resisted the efforts of quasi-feudal land-proprietors to collect quitrents, and looked with disfavor on the primogeniture and entails which facilitated the upbuilding of large family estates.

In the struggle for political freedom, both on the domestic stage and in relation with the mother country, colonial Americans tended to make a stand on their constitutional rights as Englishmen. This was true in the tussles of the lower houses of the provincial assemblies with the royal governors, and it was true in the early stages of the agitation which led to the Declaration of Independence—John Dickinson is a representative of this position. But in the natural-rights philosophy, with its doctrine of popular sovereignty and the right of revolution, colonists had an even more powerful weapon. New England clergymen, such as John Wise, had elaborated the natural-rights doctrines in local issues over the form of church government, and had shown the political implications of these doctrines. As constitutional arguments seemed to avail little in the heated controversies with England in the 1760's, New Englanders like James Otis and Samuel Adams, artisans like "the Liberty Boys," and lawyers like Patrick Henry resorted increasingly to the natural rights philosophy. The Declaration of Independence is the great monument to this school of thought. But the idea of resistance to constituted authority met with sturdy opposition.

» » « «

JOHN WINTHROP

1588–1649

A GRADUATE of Trinity College, Cambridge, and a lawyer who enjoyed membership in the Inner Temple, John Winthrop, lord of Groton Manor, Suffolk, commanded considerable influence among the local gentry. In 1629 he was made governor of the newly established Massachusetts Bay Company, and he supervised the departure of the colonists who sailed in 1636. His letters to his wife reveal an affectionate tenderness, but outwardly Governor Winthrop was an intense Puritan and a zealous autocrat. His unwillingness to permit religious dissent and to admit any democratic influence into the oligarchic theocracy merely reflected, it is true, the ideals of the founders of the colony, who had set their hearts on establishing a "Bible Commonwealth." The following passages illustrate the subordination of the individual in his economic activities to a collectivistic concern for the well-being of the social structure and the dominant conception of the proper restraints on political and other freedom. The

"Little Speech on Liberty" was occasioned when Winthrop was acquitted from the charge brought against him by certain elements who opposed the unlimited control of the oligarchy in elections.

Winthrop Papers, 5 vols., Mass. Hist. Soc., 1929–1947.
Edmund S. Morgan, *The Puritan Dilemma: The Story of John Winthrop*, Boston, 1958.
Winthrop's Journal, J. K. Hosmer, ed., 2 vols., New York, 1908.

» » From: THE JOURNAL OF JOHN WINTHROP « «

[REGULATION OF ECONOMIC LIFE]

The scarcity of workmen had caused them to raise their wages to an excessive rate, so as a carpenter would have three shillings the day, a laborer two shillings and sixpence, etc.; and accordingly those who had commodities to sell advanced their prices sometime double to that they cost in England, so as it grew to a general complaint, which the court, taking knowledge of, as also of some further evils, which were springing out of the excessive rates of wages, they made an order, that carpenters, masons, etc., should take but two shillings the day, and laborers but eighteen pence, and that no commodity should be sold at above four pence in the shilling more than it cost for ready money in England; oil, wine, etc., and cheese, in regard of the hazard of bringing, etc., [excepted]. The evils which were springing, etc., were: 1. Many spent much time idly, etc., because they could get as much in four days as would keep them a week. 2. They spent much in tobacco and strong waters, etc., which was a great waste to the commonwealth, which, by reason of so many foreign commodities expended, could not have subsisted to this time, but that it was supplied by the cattle and corn, which were sold to new comers at very dear rates, viz., corn at six shillings the bushel, a cow at £20,—yea, some at £24, some £26,—a mare at £35, an ewe goat at 3 or £4; and yet many cattle were every year brought out of England, and some from Virginia. Soon after order was taken for prices of commodities, viz., not to exceed the rate of four pence in the shilling above the price in England, except cheese and liquors, etc.   1633

[REPRESENTATIVE GOVERNMENT]

Order was taken for ministering an oath to all house keepers and sojourners, being twenty years of age and not freemen, and for making a survey of the houses and lands of all freemen.

Notice being sent out of the general court to be held the 14th day of the third month, called May, the freemen deputed two of each town to meet and consider of such matters as they were to take order in at the same general court; who, having met, desired a sight of the patent, and, conceiving thereby that all their laws should be made at the general court, repaired to the governor to advise with him about it, and about the abrogating of some orders formerly made, as for killing of swine in corn, etc. He told them, that, when the patent was granted, the number of freemen was supposed to be (as in like corporations) so few, as they might well join in making laws; but now they were grown to so great a body, as it was not possible for them to make or execute laws, but they must choose others for that purpose: and that howsoever it would be necessary hereafter to have a select company to intend that work, yet for the present they were not furnished with a sufficient number of men qualified for such a business, neither could the commonwealth bear the loss of time of so many as must intend it. Yet this they might do at present, viz., they might, at the general court, make an order, that, once in the year, a certain number should be appointed (upon summons from the governor) to revise all laws, etc., and to reform what they found amiss therein; but not to make any new laws, but prefer their grievances to the court of assistants; and that no assessment should be laid upon the country without the consent of such a committee, nor any lands disposed of.   1634

Mr. Vane and Mr. Peter, finding some distraction in the commonwealth, arising from some difference in judgment, and withal some alienation of affection among the magistrates and some other persons of quality, and that hereby factions began to grow among the people, some adhering more to the old governor, Mr. Winthrop, and others to the late governor, Mr. Dudley,—the former carrying matters with more lenity, and the latter with more severity,— they procured a meeting, at Boston, of the governor, deputy, Mr. Cotton, Mr. Hooker, Mr. Wilson, and there was present Mr. Winthrop, Mr. Dudley, and themselves; where, after the Lord had been sought, Mr. Vane declared the occasion of this meeting, (as is before noted,) and the fruit aimed at, viz., a more firm and friendly uniting of minds, etc., especially of the said Mr. Dudley and Mr. Winthrop, as those upon whom the weight of affairs did lie, etc., and therefore desired all present to take up a resolution to deal freely and openly with the parties, and they each with other, that nothing might be left in their breasts, which might break out to any jar or difference hereafter, (which they promised to do). Then Mr. Winthrop spake to this effect: that when it pleased Mr. Vane to acquaint him with what he had observed, of the dispositions of men's minds inclining to the said faction, etc., it was very strange to him, professing solemnly that he knew not of any breach between his brother Dudley and himself, since they were reconciled long since, neither did he suspect any alienation of affection in him or others from himself, save that, of late, he had observed, that some new comers had estranged themselves from him, since they went to dwell at Newtown; and so desired all the company, that, if they had seen any thing amiss in his government or otherwise, they would deal freely and faithfully with him, and for his part he promised to take it in good part, and would endeavor, by God's grace, to amend it. Then Mr. Dudley spake to this effect: that for his part he came thither a mere patient, not with any intent to charge his brother Winthrop with any thing; for though there had been formerly some differences and breaches between them, yet they had been healed, and, for his part, he was not willing to renew them again; and so left it to others to utter their own complaints. Whereupon the governor, Mr. Haynes, spake to this effect: that Mr. Winthrop and himself had been always in good terms, etc.; therefore he was loath to give any offence to him, and he hoped that, considering what the end of this meeting was, he would take it in good part, if he did deal

openly and freely, as his manner ever was. Then he spake of one or two passages, wherein he conceived, that [he] dealt too remissly in point of justice; to which Mr. Winthrop answered, that his speeches and carriage had been in part mistaken; but withal professed, that it was his judgment, that in the infancy of plantation, justice should be administered with more lenity than in a settled state, because people were then more apt to transgress, partly of ignorance of new laws and orders, partly through oppression of business and other straits; but, if it might be made clear to him, that it was an error, he would be ready to take up a stricter course. Then the ministers were desired to consider of the question by the next morning, and to set down a rule in the case. The next morning, they delivered their several reasons, which all sorted to this conclusion, that strict discipline, both in criminal offences and in martial affairs, was more needful in plantations than in a settled state, as tending to the honor and safety of the gospel. Whereupon Mr. Winthrop acknowledged that he was convinced, that he had failed in over much lenity and remissness, and would endeavor (by God's assistance) to take a more strict course hereafter. Whereupon there was a renewal of love amongst them, and articles drawn to this effect:—

1. That there should be more strictness used in civil government and military discipline.

2. That the magistrates should (as far as might be) ripen their consultations beforehand, that their vote in public might bear (as the voice of God).

3. That, in meetings out of court, the magistrates should not discuss the business of parties in their presence, nor deliver their opinions, etc.

4. That trivial things, etc., should be ended in towns, etc. . . .

6. That the magistrates shall be more familiar and open each to other, and more frequent in visitations, and shall, in tenderness and love, admonish one another, (without reserving any secret grudge,) and shall avoid all jealousies and suspicions, each seeking the honor of another, and all, of the court, not opening the nakedness of one another to private persons; in all things seeking the safety and credit of the gospel.

7. To honor the governor in submitting to him the main direction and ordering the business of the court. . . . **1636**

[ON LIBERTY]

I suppose something may be expected from me, upon this charge [of exceeding the powers of deputy governor] which has befallen me, which moves me to speak now to you; yet I intend not to intermeddle in the proceedings of the court, or with any of the persons concerned therein. Only I bless God, that I see an issue of this troublesome business. I also acknowledge the justice of the court, and, for mine own part, I am well satisfied, I was publicly charged, and I am publicly and legally acquitted, which is all I did expect or desire. And though this be sufficient for my justification before men, yet not so before the God, who hath seen so much amiss in my dispensations (and even in this affair) as calls me to be humble. For to be publicly and criminally charged in this court, is matter of humiliation, (and I desire to make a right use of it,) notwithstanding I be thus acquitted. If her father had spit in her face, (saith the Lord concerning Miriam,) should she not have been ashamed seven days? Shame had lien upon her, whatever the occasion had been. I am unwilling to stay you from your urgent affairs, yet give me leave (upon this special occasion) to speak a little more to this assembly. It may be of some good use, to inform and rectify the judgments of some of the people, and may prevent such distempers as have arisen amongst us.

The great questions that have troubled the country, are about the authority of the magistrates and the liberty of the people. It is yourselves who have called us to this office, and being called by you, we have our authority from God, in way of an ordinance, such as hath the image of God eminently stamped upon it, the contempt and violation whereof hath been vindicated with examples of divine vengeance. I entreat you to consider, that when you choose magistrates, you take them from among yourselves, men subject to like passions as you are. Therefore when you see infirmities in us, you should reflect upon your own, and that make you bear the more with us, and not be severe censurers of the failings of your magistrates, when you have continual experience of the like infirmities in yourselves and others. We account him a good servant, who breaks not his covenant. The covenant between you and us is the oath you have taken of us, which is to this purpose, that we shall govern you and judge your causes by the rules of God's laws and our own, according to our best skill. When you agree with a workman to build you a ship or house, etc., he undertakes as well for his skill as for his faithfulness, for it is his profession, and you pay him for both. But when you call one to be a magistrate, he doth not profess nor undertake to have sufficient skill for that office, nor can you furnish him with gifts, etc., therefore you must run the hazard of his skill and ability. But if he fail in faithfulness, which by his oath he is bound unto, that he must answer for. If it fall out that the case be clear to common apprehension, and the rule clear, also, if he transgress here, the error is not in the skill, but in the evil of the will: it must be required of him. But if the case be doubtful, or the rule doubtful, to men of such understanding and parts as your magistrates are, if your magistrates should err here, yourselves must bear it.

For the other point concerning liberty, I observe a great mistake in the country about that. There is a twofold liberty, natural (I mean as our nature is now corrupt) and civil or federal. The first is common to man with beasts and other creatures. By this, man, as he stands in relation to man simply, hath liberty to do what he lists; it is a liberty to evil as well as to good. This liberty is incompatible and inconsistent with authority, and cannot endure the least restraint of the most just authority. The exercise and maintaining of this liberty makes men grow more evil, and in time to be worse than brute beasts: *omnes sumus licentia deteriores*.[1] This is that great enemy of truth and peace, that wild beast, which all the ordinances of God are bent against, to restrain and subdue it. The other kind of liberty I call civil or federal, it may also be termed moral, in reference to the covenant between God and man, in the moral law, and the politic covenants and constitutions, amongst men themselves. This is the proper end and object of authority, and cannot subsist without it; and it is a liberty to that only which is good, just, and honest. This liberty you are to stand for, with the hazard (not only of your goods, but) of your lives, if need be. Whatsoever crosseth this, is not authority, but a distemper thereof. This liberty is maintained and exercised in a way of subjection to authority; it is of the same kind of liberty wherewith Christ hath made us free. The woman's own choice makes such

---

[1] *We are all the worse for freedom.*

a man her husband; yet being so chosen, he is her lord, and she is to be subject to him, yet in a way of liberty, not of bondage; and a true wife accounts her subjection her honor and freedom, and would not think her condition safe and free, but in her subjection to her husband's authority. Such is the liberty of the church under the authority of Christ, her king and husband; his yoke is so easy and sweet to her as a bride's ornaments; and if through frowardness or wantonness, etc., she shake it off, at any time, she is at no rest in her spirit, until she take it up again; and whether her lord smiles upon her, and embraceth her in his arms, or whether he frowns, or rebukes, or smites her, she apprehends the sweetness of his love in all, and is refreshed, supported, and instructed by every such dispensation of his authority over her. On the other side, ye know who they are that complain of this yoke and say, let us break their bands, etc., we will not have this man to rule over us. Even so, brethren, it will be between you and your magistrates. If you stand for your natural corrupt liberties, and will do what is good in your own eyes, you will not endure the least weight of authority, but will murmur, and oppose, and be always striving to shake off that yoke; but if you will be satisfied to enjoy such civil and lawful liberties, such as Christ allows you, then will you quietly and cheerfully submit unto that authority which is set over you, in all the administrations of it, for your good. Wherein, if we fail at any time, we hope we shall be willing (by God's assistance) to hearken to good advice from any of you, or in any other way of God; so shall your liberties be preserved, in upholding the honor and power of authority amongst you. 1645

ROGER WILLIAMS

c. 1604–1683

THE STORMY CAREER of Roger Williams from the time that he landed at Boston in 1630 centered in his theological and political radicalism. Six years later he was forced to leave Massachusetts Bay, largely because, as pastor of the church in Salem, he had crossed swords with the dominant theocrats. He insisted that every individual not only had the right to worship as he pleased but that he also might associate mutually with others to form a government more satisfactory than the one under which he lived. In espousing the idea of separation of church and state Williams further alienated the ruling group. A true Independent, he opposed the program of the union of churches into a presbytery. To make matters still worse, he insisted that the colonists had no right to their land unless they had bought it from the Indians.

Although Williams devoted much of his time and energy to work among the Indians and to the problems of the colony which he founded at Providence, his place in the history of American social thought largely rests on his writings in defense of freedom of conscience. When the Reverend John Cotton of Boston maintained that a certain prisoner in Newgate was being justly punished for his nonconformity, Williams, in *The Bloudy Tenent, of Persecution, for the cause of Conscience, discussed in a Conference between Truth and Peace* (1644), took the contrary view. Williams's plea for toleration, which was published in London in the same year as Milton's *Areopagitica*, was answered by Cotton. By insisting on freedom of conscience and on the compact theory of the state, Roger Williams contributed to the formulation of the American doctrines of separation of church and state, of individualism, and of democracy.

The Works of Roger Williams, 6 vols., Narragansett Club, Providence, 1866–1874.
Perry Miller, *Roger Williams: His Contributions to the American Tradition*, Indianapolis, 1953.
Ola E. Winslow, *Master Roger Williams*, New York, 1957.
S. H. Brockunier, *The Irrepressible Democrat: Roger Williams*, New York, 1940.

» » *From:* THE BLOUDY TENENT [&c] « «

CHAPTER II

[AGAINST PERSECUTION]

[PEACE]: Deare *Truth,* I have two sad *Complaints:*

First, the most sober of thy *Witnesses,* that dare to *plead* thy *Cause,* how are they charged to be *mine Enemies, contentious, turbulent,* 10 *seditious?*

Secondly, Thine *Enemies,* though they speake and raile against thee, though they outragiously *pursue, imprison, banish, kill* thy faithfull *Witnesses,* yet how is all vermillion'd o're for *Justice* 'gainst the *Hereticks?* Yea, if they kindle coales, and blow the flames of *devouring Warres,* that leave neither *Spirituall* nor *Civill State,* but burns up *Branch* and *Root,* yet how doe all pretend an *holy War?* 20 He that *kills,* and hee that's *killed,* they both cry out, It is for *God,* and for their *conscience.*

Tis true, nor one nor other seldome dare to plead the mighty Prince *Christ Jesus* for their *Authour,* yet both (both *Protestant* and *Papist*) pretend they have spoke with *Moses* and the *Prophets,* who all, say they (before *Christ* came) allowed such *holy persecutions, holy Warres* against the enemies of holy *Church.*

30 TRUTH. *Deare Peace* (to ease thy first *complaint*) tis true, thy dearest *Sons,* most like their mother, *Peace-keeping, Peace-making* Sons of *God,* have borne and still must beare the *blurs* of *troublers* of *Israel,* and turners of the *World* upside downe. And tis true againe, what *Salomon* once spake: The *beginning* of *strife* is as when one letteth out *Water,* therefore (saith he) leave off *contention* before it be medled with. This *Caveat* 40 should keepe the *bankes* and *sluces* firme and strong, that *strife,* like a *breach of waters,* breake not in upon the sons of men.

Yet *strife* must be distinguished: It is *necessary* or *unnecessary, godly* or *ungodly, Christian* or *unchristian,* &c.

It is *unnecessary, unlawfull, dishonourable, ungodly, unchristian,* in most cases in the world, for there is a *possibility* of keeping *sweet Peace* in most cases, and if it be *possible,* 5c it is the expresse command of *God* that *Peace* be kept, *Rom.* 13.

Againe, it is *necessary, honourable, godly,* &c. with *civill* and earthly *weapons* to *defend* the *innocent,* and to *rescue* the oppressed from the violent *pawes* and *jaws* of oppressing persecuting *Nimrods, Psal.* 73. *Job* 29.

It is as *necessary,* yea more *honourable, godly,* and *Christian,* to *fight* the *fight* of *faith,* with *religious* and *spirituall Artillery,* and to *contend earnestly* for the *faith* of *Jesus,* once delivered to the *Saints* against all *opposers,* and the *gates* of *earth* and *hell, men* or *devils,* yea against *Paul* himselfe, or an *Angell* from *heaven,* if he bring any other *faith* or *doctrine, Jude vers.* 4. *Gal.* 1. 8.

PEACE. With the *clashing* of such *Armes* am I never *wakened.* Speake once againe (deare Truth) to my second *complaint* of bloody *persecution,* and devouring *wars,* marching under the colours of upright *Justice,* and holy *Zeale,* &c.

TRUTH. Mine eares have long beene filled with a threefold dolefull *Outcry.*

First, of one hundred forty foure thousand *Virgins* (*Rev.* 14.) forc'd and ravisht by *Emperours, Kings,* and *Governours* to their beds of *worship* and *Religion,* set up (like *Absaloms*) on high in their severall *States* and *Countries.*

Secondly, the cry of those precious *soules* under the *Altar* (*Rev.* 6) the *soules* of such as have been persecuted and slaine for the testimony and *witnesse* of *Jesus,* whose *bloud* hath been spilt like *water* upon the *earth,* and that because they have held fast the *truth* and *witnesse* of *Jesus,* against the *worship* of the *States* and *Times,* compelling to an *uniformity* of *State Religion.*

These *cries* of *murthered Virgins* who can sit still and heare? Who can but run with zeale inflamed to prevent the *deflowring* of *chaste soules,* and spilling of the *bloud* of the *innocent? Humanity* stirs up and prompts the *Sonnes* of men to draw *materiall swords* for a *Virgins chastity* and *life,* against a *ravishing murtherer?* And *Piety* and *Christianity* must needs awaken the *Sons of God* to draw the *spiritual sword* (the Word of *God*) to preserve the *chastity* and *life* of *spirituall Virgins,* who abhorre the spirituall *defilements* of *false worship, Rev.* 14.

Thirdly, the *cry* of the *whole earth,* made *drunke* with the *bloud* of its *inhabitants,* slaughtering each other in their *blinded zeale,* for *Conscience,* for *Religion,* against the *Catholickes,* against the *Lutherans,* &c.

What fearful *cries* within these twenty years of hundred *thousands* men, women, children, fathers, mothers, husbands, wives, brethren, sisters, old and young, high and low, *plundred, ravished, slaughtered, murthered, famished?* And hence these cries, that men fling away the *spiritual sword and spiritual artillery* (in *spiritual* and *religious* causes) and rather trust for the suppressing of each others *God, Conscience,* and *Religion* (as they suppose) to an *arme* of *flesh,* and *sword* of *steele?*

TRUTH. *Sweet Peace,* what hast thou there?

PEACE. *Arguments* against *persecution* for cause of *Conscience.*

TRUTH. And what there?

PEACE. An *Answer* to such *Arguments,* contrarily maintaining such *persecution* for cause of *Conscience.*

TRUTH. These *Arguments* against such *persecution,* and the *Answer* pleading for it, written (as *Love* hopes) from godly *intentions, hearts,* and *hands,* yet in a marvellous different *stile* and *manner.* The *Arguments* against *persecution* in *milke,* the *Answer* for it (as I may say) in *bloud.*

The *Authour* of these *Arguments* (against *persecution*) (as I have beene informed) being committed by *some* then in power, *close prisoner* to *Newgate,* for the witnesse of some *truths* of *Jesus,* and having not the use of *Pen* and *Inke,* wrote these *Arguments* in *Milke,* in sheets of Paper, brought to him by the *Woman* his *Keeper,* from a friend in *London,* as the *stopples* of his *Milk bottle.*

In such Paper written with *Milk* nothing will appeare, but the way of reading it by *fire* being knowne to this *friend* who received the Papers, he transcribed and kept together the Papers, although the *Author* himselfe could not correct, nor view what himselfe had written.

It was in *milke,* tending to soule *nourishment,* even for *Babes* and Sucklings in *Christ.*

It was in *milke,* spiritually *white,* pure and innocent, like those *white horses* of the *Word of truth* and *meeknesse,* and the *white Linnen* or *Armour* of *righteousness,* in the *Army* of *Jesus. Rev.* 6. & 19.

It was in *milke,* soft, meeke, peaceable and gentle, tending both to the *peace* of *soules,* and the *peace* of *States* and *Kingdomes.*

PEACE. The *Answer* (though I hope out of milkie pure intentions) is returned in *bloud: bloudy* & slaughterous *conclusions; bloudy* to the *souls* of all men, forc'd to the *Religion* and *Worship* which every civil State or Commonweale agrees on, and compells all subjects to in a dissembled *uniformitie.*

Bloudy to the *bodies,* first of the holy *witnesses* of *Christ Jesus,* who testifie against such invented worships.

Secondly, of the *Nations* and Peoples slaughtering each other for their severall respective Religions and Consciences.

CHAPTER VI

[CHURCH AND STATE]

PEACE. The next *distinction* concerning the manner of persons holding forth the aforesaid *practices* (not onely the *waightier duties* of the *Law,* but points of *doctrine* and *worship* lesse principall.)

"Some (saith he [John Cotton]) hold them forth in a *meeke* and *peaceable* way: some with such *arrogance* and *impetuousnesse,* as of it selfe tendeth to the disturbance of *civill peace.*"

TRUTH. In the examination of this *distinction* we shall discusse,

First, what is *civill Peace,* (wherein we shall vindicate thy name the better.)

Secondly, what it is to hold forth a Doctrine or Practice in this *impetuousnesse* or *arrogancy.*

First, for *civill peace,* what is it but *pax civitatis,* the peace of the Citie, whether an *English* City, *Scotch,* or *Irish* Citie, or further abroad, *French, Spanish, Turkish* City, &c.

Thus it pleased the Father of *Lights* to define it, *Ierem.* 29. 7. Pray for the *peace* of the *City;* which *peace* of the *City,* or *Citizens,* so compacted in a *civill* way of *union,* may be intire, unbroken, safe, &c. notwithstanding so many thousands of *Gods people* the *Jewes,* were there in *bondage,* and would neither be *constrained* to the *worship* of the Citie *Babell,* nor restrained from so much of the *worship* of the true *God,* as they then could practice, as is plaine in the practice of the 3 Worthies, *Shadrach, Misach,* and *Abednego,* as also of *Daniel, Dan.* 3. & *Dan.* 6. (the peace of the *city* or *Kingdome,* being a far different Peace from the Peace of the *Religion* or Spirituall *Worship,* maintained & professed of the Citizens. This *Peace* of their *Worship* (which *worship* also in some Cities being various) being a false Peace, *Gods people* were and ought to be *Nonconformitants*, not daring either to be *restrained* from the *true*, or constrained to *false Worship*, and yet without *breach* of the Civill or *Citie-peace*, properly so called.

PEACE.   Hence it is that so many glorious and flourishing *Cities* of the World maintaine their *Civill* peace, yea the very *Americans* & wildest *Pagans* keep the peace of their *Towns* or *Cities*; though neither inn one nor the other can any man prove a true *Church* of God in those places, and consequently no spirituall and heavenly peace: The Peace *spirituall* (whether true or false) being of a higher and farre different nature from the Peace of the place or people, being meerly and essentially *civill* and *humane*.

TRUTH.   O how lost are the sonnes of men in this point? To illustrate this: The *Church* or *company* of *worshippers* (whether true or false) is like unto a Body or Colledge of *Physitians* in a *Citie*; like unto a *Corporation*, *Society*, or *Company* of *East-Indie* or *Turkie-Merchants*, or any other *Societie* or *Company* in *London*: which Companies may hold their *Courts*, keep their *Records*, hold *disputations*; and in matters concerning their *Societie*, may dissent, divide, breake into *Schismes* and *Factions*, sue and implead each other at the *Law*, yea wholly breake up and dissolve into pieces and nothing, and yet the *peace* of the *Citie* not be in the least measure impaired or disturbed; because the *essence* or being of the *Citie*, and so the *well-being* and *peace* thereof is essentially distinct from those particular *Societies; the Citie-Courts, Citie-Lawes, Citie-punishments* distinct from theirs. The *Citie* was before them, and stands absolute and intire, when such a *Corporation* or *Societie* is taken down. For instance further, The *City* or *Civill* state of *Ephesus* was essentially distinct from the *worship* of *Diana* in the Citie, or of the *whole city*. Againe, the *Church* of *Christ* in *Ephesus* (which were Gods people, converted and call'd out from the *worship* of that *City* unto *Christianitie* or *worship* of God in *Christ*) was distinct from both.

Now suppose that *God* remove the *Candle-stick* from *Ephesus*, yea though the *whole Worship* of the *Citie of Ephesus* should be altered: yet (if men be true and honestly ingenuous to *Citie-covenants, Combinations* and *Principles*) all this might be without the least impeachment or infringement of the Peace of the *City* of *Ephesus*.

Thus in the Citie of *Smirna* was the Citie it selfe or Civill estate one thing, The Spirituall or Religious state of *Smirna*, another; The Church of *Christ* in *Smirna*, distinct from them both; and the *Synagogue* of the *Jewes*, whether literally *Jewes* (as some thinke) or mystically, false *Christians*, (as others) called the *Synagogue* of *Sathan*, Revel. 2. distinct from all these. And notwithstanding these spirituall oppositions in point of *Worship* and *Religion*, yet heare we not the least noyse (nor need we, if Men keep but the Bond of *Civility*) of any *Civil breach*, or *breach* of *Civill* peace amongst them: and to persecute Gods people there for Religion, that only was a breach of Civilitie it selfe.   1644

NATHANIEL WARD

1578–1652

A GRADUATE OF Emmanuel College, Cambridge, Nathaniel Ward was excommunicated from the Church of England for his dissent from certain of its teachings. For two years after his arrival in America in 1634 he served as minister of the Church in Ipswich, Massachusetts. The *Body of Liberties*, adopted in 1641 as the code of laws for the Colony, was the result of a compromise between Ward's draft and that of the Reverend John Cotton.

When Ward returned to England in 1646 he took with him the manuscript of *The Simple Cobbler of Aggawam*. It purported to be written by a "cobbler" of Aggawam, which was in reality Ipswich. Written in simple, vigorous, but picturesque Elizabethan prose, this tract was designed in part to counteract the impression that Roger Williams's doctrine of tolerance ruled New England thought, and in part to persuade Parliament to legislate against toleration. For Ward believed that if through toleration "God hide his path, Satan is at hand to turn Convoy." The only freedom of religion tolerable to Ward was that in which "all Familists, Antinomians, Anabaptists, and other Enthusiasts shall have free liberty to keep away from us." Yet Ward's defense of intolerance included the plea for Presbyterians and Independents, King and People, to compromise their differences in the interest of stability. *The Simple Cobbler's* dislike of democracy and of innovation generally was as pronounced as his distaste for religious freedom:

> The upper world shall Rule,
> While Stars will run their race
> The nether world obey,
> While People keep their place.

The Simple Cobbler of Aggawam in America, L. C. Wroth, ed., Scholar's Facsimiles and Reprints, New York, 1937. J. W. Dean, *A Memoir of the Rev. Nathaniel Ward, A.M.*, Albany, 1868.

» » From: THE SIMPLE COBBLER OF AGGAWAM « «

[INTOLERANCE]

Either I am in an Appoplexie, or that man is in a Lethargie, who doth not now sensibly feele God shaking the heavens over his head, and the earth under his feet: The Heavens so, as the Sun begins to turne into darknesse, the Moon into blood, the Starres to fall down to the ground; So that little Light of Comfort or Counsell is left to the sonnes of men: The Earth so, as the foundations are failing, the righteous scarce know where to finde rest, the inhabitants stagger like drunken men: it is in a manner dissolved both in Religions and Relations: And no marvell; for, they have defiled it by transgressing the Lawes, changing the Ordinances, and breaking the Everlasting Covenant. The Truths of God are the Pillars of the world, whereon States and Churches may stand quiet if they will; if they will not, Hee can easily shake them off into delusions, and distractions enough.

Sathan is now in his passions, he feeles his passion approaching; hee loves to fish in royled waters. Though that Dragon cannot sting the vitals of the Elect mortally, yet that Beelzebub can fly-blow their Intellectuals miserably: The finer Religion grows, the finer hee spins his Cobwebs, hee will hold pace with Christ so long as his wits will serve him. Hee sees him-selfe beaten out of grosse Idolatries, Heresies, Ceremonies, where the Light breakes forth with power; he will therefore bestirre him to prevaricate Evangelicall Truths, and Ordinances, that if they will needs be walking, yet they shall *laborare varicibus*,[1] and not keep their path, he will put them out of time and place; Assassinating for his Engineers, men of Paracelsian parts; well complexioned for honesty; for, such are fittest to Mountebanke his Chimistry into sicke Churches and weake Judgements.

Nor shall hee need to stretch his strength over-much in this worke: Too many men having not laid their foundations sure, nor ballasted their Spirits deepe with humility and feare, are prest enough of themselves to evaporate their owne apprehensions. Those that are acquainted with Story know, it hath ever beene so in new Editions of Churches: Such as are least able, are most busie to pudder in the rubbish, and to raise dust in the eye of more steady Repayrers. Civill Commotions make roome for uncivill practises: Religious mutations, for irreligious opinions: Change of Aire, discovers corrupt bodies; Reformation of Religion, unsound mindes. Hee that hath any well-faced phansy in his Crowne, and doth not vent it now, fears the pride of his owne heart will dub him dunce for ever. Such a one

[1] *Stagger awkwardly.* Literally, *struggle because of unsound legs.*

will trouble the whole *Israel* of God with his most untimely births, though he makes the bones of his vanity stick up, to the view and griefe of all that are godly wise. The devill desires no better sport than to see light heads handle their heels, and fetch their carreers in a time, when the Roofe of Liberty stands open.

The next perplexed Question, with pious and ponderous men, will be: What should bee done for the healing of these comfortlesse exulcerations. I am the unablest adviser of a thousand, the unworthiest of ten thousand; yet I hope I may presume to assert what follows without just offense.

First, such as have given or taken any unfriendly reports of us *New-English,* should doe well to recollect themselves. Wee have beene reputed a Colluvies of wild Opinionists, swarmed into a remote wildernes to find elbow-roome for our phanatick Doctrines and practices: I trust our diligence past, and constant sedulity against such persons and courses, will plead better things for us. I dare take upon me, to bee the Herauld of *New-England* so farre, as to proclaime to the world, in the name of our Colony, that all Familists, Antinomians, Anabaptists, and other Enthusiasts shall have free Liberty to keepe away from us, and such as will come to be gone as fast as they can, the sooner the better.

Secondly, I dare averre, that God doth no where in his word tolerate Christian States, to give Toleration to such adversaries of his Truth, if they have power in their hands to suppresse them.

Here is lately brought us an extract of a *Magna Charta,* so called, compiled between the Sub-planters of a *West-Indian* Island; whereof the first Article of constipation, firmly provides free stable-room and litter for all kinde of consciences, be they never so dirty or jadish; making it actionable, yea, treasonable, to disturbe any man in his Religion, or to discommend it, whatever it be. Wee are very sorry to see such professed prophanenesse in *English* Professors, as industriously to lay their Religious foundations on the ruine of true Religion; which strictly binds every conscience *to contend earnestly for the Truth: to preserve unity of spirit, Faith and Ordinances, to be all like minded, of one accord; every man to take his brother into his Christian care: to stand fast with one spirit, with one mind, striving together for the faith of the Gospel;* and by no

meanes to permit Heresies or errronious opinions: But God abhorring such loathsome beverages, hath in his righteous judgment blasted that enterprize, which might otherwise have prospered well, for ought I know; I presume their case is generally knowne ere this.

If the devill might have his free option, I beleeve he would ask nothing else, but liberty to enfranchize all false Religions, and to embondage the true; nor should hee need: It is much to be feared, that laxe Tolerations upon State-pretences and planting necessities, will be the next subtle Stratagem he will spread to distate the Truth of God and supplant the peace of the Churches. Tolerations in things tolerable, exquisitely drawn out by the lines of the Scripture, and pensill of the Spirit, are the sacred favours of Truth, the due latitudes of Love, the faire Compartiments of Christian fraternity: but irregular dispensations, dealt forth by the facilities of men, are the frontiers of error, the redoubts of Schisme, the perillous irritaments of carnall and spirituall enmity.

My heart hath naturally detested foure things: The standing of the Apocrypha in the Bible; Forrainers dwelling in my Countrey, to crowd out native Subjects into the corners of the Earth; Alchymized coines; Tolerations of divers Religions, or of one Religion in segregant shapes: He that willingly assents to the last, if he examines his heart by daylight, his conscience will tell him, he is either an Atheist, or an Heretique, or an Hypocrite, or at best a captive to some Lust: Poly-piety is the greatest impiety in the world. True Religion is *Ignis probationis,* which doth *congregare homogenea & segregare heterogenea.*[2]

Not to tolerate things meerly indifferent to weak consciences, argues a conscience too strong: pressed uniformity in these, causes much disunity: To tolerate more than indifferents, is not to deale indifferently with God: He that doth it, takes his Scepter out of his hand, and bids him stand by. Who hath to doe to institute Religion but God? The power of all Religion and Ordinances, lies in their purity: their purity in their simplicity: then are mixtures pernicious. I lived in a City, where a Papist preached in one Church, a Lutheran in another, a Calvinist in a third; a Lutheran one part of the day, a Calvinist the other, in the same Pulpit: the Religion of that place was but

---

[2] True Religion is *an ordeal by fire,* which doth *draw together the like and separate the unlike.*

motly and meagre, their affections Leopard-like.

If the whole Creature should conspire to doe the Creator a mischiefe, or offer him an insolency, it would be in nothing more, than in erecting untruths against his Truth, or by sophisticating his Truths with humane medleyes: the removing of some one iota in Scripture, may draw out all the life, and traverse all the Truth of the whole Bible: but to authorise an untruth, by a Toleration of State, is to build a Sconce against the walls of heaven, to batter God out of his Chaire: To tell a practicall lye, is a great sin, but yet transient; but to set up a Theoricall untruth, is to warrant every lye that lyes from its root to the top of every branch it hath, which are not a few.

I would willingly hope that no Member of the Parliament hath skilfully ingratiated himselfe into the hearts of the House, that he might watch a time to midwife out some ungracious Toleration for his owne turne, and for the sake of that, some other, I would also hope that a word of generall caution should not be particularly misapplied. I am the freer to suggest it, because I know not one man of that mind, my aime is generall, and I desire may be so accepted. Yet good Gentlemen, look well about you, and remember how Tiberius play'd the Fox with the Senate of *Rome,* and how *Fabius Maximus* cropt his ears for his cunning.

That State is wise, that will improve all paines and patience rather to compose, then tolerate differences in Religion. There is no divine Truth, but hath much Celestial fire in it from the Spirit of Truth: nor no irreligious untruth, without its proportion of Antifire from the Spirit of Error to contradict it: the zeale of the one, the virulency of the other, must necessarily kindle Combustions. Fiery diseases seated in the spirit, embroile the whole frame of the body; others more externall and coole, are less dangerous. They which divide in Religion, divide in God; they who divide in him, divide beyond *Genus Generalissimum,* where there is no reconciliation, without atonement; that is, without uniting in him, who is One, and in his Truth, which is also one.

Wise are those men who will be persuaded rather to live within the pale of Truth where they may bee quiet, than in the purliev's, where they are sure to bee hunted ever and anon, doe Authority what it can. Every singular Opinion, hath a singular opinion of itself;

and he that holds it, a singular opinion of himself, and a simple opinion of all contra-sentients: he that confutes him, must confute all three at once, or else he does nothing; which will not be done without more stirre then the peace of the State or Church can indure.

. . .

That if the State of *England* shall either willingly Tolerate, or weakly connive at such Courses, the Church of that Kingdome will sooner become the Devills Dancing-Schoole, then Gods-Temple: The Civill State a Bearegarden, then an Exchange: The whole Realme a Pais base, then an *England.* And what pity it is, that that Country which hath been the Staple of Truth to all Christendome, should now become the Aviary of Errors to the whole World, let every fearing heart judge.

I take Liberty of Conscience to be nothing but a freedome from sinne, and error. *Conscientia in tantum libera, in quantum ab errore liberata.*[3] And liberty of Error nothing but a Prison for Conscience. Then small will bee the kindnesse of a State to build such Prisons for their Subjects.

The Scripture faith, there is nothing makes free but Truth, and Truth saith, there is no Truth but One: If the States of the World would make it their sumoperous Care to preserve this One Truth in its purity and Authority it would ease them of all other Politicall cares. I am sure Satan makes it his grand, if not onely task, to adulterate Truth; Falsehood is his sole Scepter, whereby he first ruffled, and ever since ruined the World.

If Truth be but One, me thinks all the Opinionists in *England* should not be all in that One Truth, some of them I doubt are out. He that can extract an unity out of such a disparity, or contract such a disparity into an unity; had need be a better Artist, then ever was *Drebell.*

If two Centers (as we may suppose) be in on Circle, and lines drawn from both to all the points of the Compasse, they will certainly crosse one another, and probably cut through the Centers themselves.

There is talke of an universall Toleration, I would talk what I could against it, did I know what more apt and reasonable Sacrifice *England* could offer to God for his late performing all his heavenly Truths, then an universall

---

[3] *Conscience is free to the extent that it is freed from error.*

Toleration of all hellish Errors, or how they shall make an universal Reformation, but by making Christs Academy the Devils University, where any man may commence Heretique *per* *saltum;* where he that is *filius Diabolicus,* or *simpliciter pessimus,* may have his grace to goe to hell *cum Publico Privilegio;* and carry as many after him, as he can.   1647

SAMUEL SEWALL

1652–1730

SAMUEL SEWALL is best known through the vivid *Diary* which for fifty-seven years chronicled many of the trivial as well as the more important happenings of Boston and its vicinity and which at the same time revealed Sewall himself as a suitor and husband, a shrewd businessman, a judge, and a prominent citizen. After graduating from Harvard and winning many successes in practical matters, he served the Colony in various political offices. Although identified with the more conservative elements in the community, Sewall was anxious to have justice done to the Indians and to unfortunates generally. He displayed considerable courage in 1696 when he did public penance for his earlier concurrence in the sentencing of nineteen persons to be hanged as witches. *The Selling of Joseph* (1700), one of the earliest American protests against slavery, was answered by John Saffin in *A Brief and Candid Answer to a late Printed Sheet, entitled, The Selling of Joseph* (1701).

Diary of Samuel Sewall, Mass. Hist. Soc. *Collections*, ser. 5, vols. V–VII, Boston, 1878–1882.
Letter Book of Samuel Sewall, Mass. Hist. Soc. *Collections*, ser. 6, vols. I–II, Boston, 1886–1888.
Samuel Sewall's Diary, Mark Van Doren, ed., New York, 1927.
N. H. Chamberlain, *Samuel Sewall and the World He Lived In*, Boston, 1897.
The Selling of Joseph, Mass. Hist. Soc. *Collections*, ser. 5, vol. VI, 1879.

» » THE SELLING OF JOSEPH « «

"Forasmuch as Liberty *is in real value next unto* Life: *None ought to part with it themselves, or deprive others of it, but upon most mature Consideration.*

"The Numerousness of Slaves at this day in the Province, and the Uneasiness of them under their Slavery, hath put many upon thinking whether the Foundation of it be firmly and well laid; so as to sustain the Vast Weight that is built upon it. It is most certain that all Men, as they are the Sons of *Adam,* are Co-heirs; and have equal Right unto Liberty, and all other outward Comforts of Life. *GOD hath given the Earth* (with all its Commodities) *unto the Sons of* Adam, *Psal.* 115. 16. *And hath made of One Blood, all Nations of Men, for to dwell on all the face of the Earth, and hath determined the Times before appointed, and* the bounds of their habitation: That they should seek the Lord. Forasmuch then as we are the Offspring of GOD &c. Act 17. 26, 27, 29. Now although the Title given by the last *ADAM,* doth infinitely better Mens Estates, respecting GOD and themselves; and grants them a most beneficial and inviolable Lease under the Broad Seal of Heaven, who were before only Tenants at Will: Yet through the Indulgence of GOD to our First Parents after the Fall, the outward Estate of all and every of their Children, remains the same, as to one another. So that Originally, and Naturally, there is no such thing as Slavery. *Joseph* was rightfully no more a Slave to his Brethren, than they were to him: and they had no more Authority to *Sell* him, than they had to *Slay* him. And if *they* had nothing to do to Sell him;

the Ishmaelites bargaining with them, and paying down Twenty pieces of Silver, could not make a Title. Neither could *Potiphar* have any better interest in him than the *Ishmaelites* had. *Gen.* 37. 20, 27, 28. For he that shall in this case plead *Alteration of Property,* seems to have forfeited a great part of his own claim to Humanity. There is no proportion between Twenty Pieces of Silver, and LIBERTY. The Commodity itself is the Claimer. If *Arabian* Gold be imported in any quantities, most are afraid to meddle with it, though they might have it at easy rates; lest if it should have been wrongfully taken from the Owners, it should kindle a fire to the Consumption of their whole Estate. 'Tis pity there should be more Caution used in buying a Horse, or a little lifeless dust; than there is in purchasing Men and Women: Whenas they are the Offspring of GOD, and their Liberty is,

"'. . . *Auro pretiosior Omni.*'[1]

"And seeing GOD hath said, *He that Stealeth a Man and Selleth him, or if he be found in his hand, he shall surely be put to Death. Exod.* 21. 16. This Law being of Everlasting Equity, wherein Man Stealing is ranked amongst the most atrocious of Capital Crimes: What louder Cry can there be made of that Celebrated Warning,

"'*Caveat Emptor!*'[2]

"And all things considered, it would conduce more to the Welfare of the Province, to have White Servants for a Term of Years, than to have Slaves for Life. Few can endure to hear of a Negro's being made free; and indeed they can seldom use their freedom well; yet their continual aspiring after their forbidden Liberty, renders them Unwilling Servants. And there is such a disparity in their Conditions, Colour & Hair, that they can never embody with us, and grow up into orderly Families, to the Peopling of the Land: but still remain in our Body Politick as a kind of extravasat Blood. As many Negro men as there are among us, so many empty places there are in our Train Bands, and the places taken up of Men that might make Husbands for our Daughters. And the Sons and Daughters of *New England* would become more like *Jacob,* and *Rachel,* if this Slavery were thrust quite out of doors. Moreover it is too well known what Tempta-

tions Masters are under, to connive at the Fornication of their Slaves; lest they should be obliged to find them Wives, or pay their Fines. It seems to be practically pleaded that they might be Lawless; 'tis thought much of, that the Law should have Satisfaction for their Thefts, and other Immoralities; by which means, *Holiness to the Lord,* is more rarely engraven upon this sort of Servitude. It is likewise most lamentable to think, how in taking Negros out of *Africa,* and Selling of them here, That which GOD has joyned together men do boldly rend asunder; Men from their Country, Husbands from their Wives, Parents from their Children. How horrible is the Uncleanness, Mortality, if not Murder, that the Ships are guilty of that bring great Crouds of these miserable Men, and Women. Methinks, when we are bemoaning the barbarous Usage of our Friends and Kinsfolk in *Africa:* it might not be unseasonable to enquire whether we are not culpable in forcing the Africans to become Slaves amongst our selves. And it may be a question whether all the Benefit received by *Negro* Slaves, will balance the Accompt of Cash laid out upon them; and for the Redemption of our own enslaved Friends out of *Africa.* Besides all the Persons and Estates that have perished there.

"Obj. 1. *These Blackamores are of the Posterity* of Cham, and *therefore are under the Curse of Slavery. Gen.* 9. 25, 26, 27.

"*Answ.* Of all Offices, one would not begg this; *viz.* Uncall'd for, to be an Executioner of the Vindictive Wrath of God; the extent and duration of which is to us uncertain. If this ever was a Commission; How do we know but that it is long since out of Date? Many have found it to their Cost, that a Prophetical Denunciation of Judgment against a Person or People, would not warrant them to inflict that evil. If it would, *Hazael* might justify himself in all he did against his Master, and the *Israelites,* from 2 *Kings* 8. 10, 12.

"But it is possible that by cursory reading, this Text may have been mistaken. For *Canaan* is the Person Cursed three times over, without the mentioning of *Cham.* Good Expositors suppose the Curse entail'd on him, and that this Prophesie was accomplished in the Extirpation of the *Canaanites,* and in the Servitude of the *Gibeonites. Vide Pareum.* Whereas the Blackmores are not descended of *Canaan,* but of *Cush.* Psal. 68. 31. *Princes shall come out of Egypt* [Misraim], *Ethiopia* [Cush] *shall soon*

[1] *More precious than all gold.*
[2] *Let the buyer beware!*

stretch out her hands unto God. Under which Names, all *Africa* may be comprehended; and their Promised Conversion ought to be prayed for. Jer. 13. 23. *Can the Ethiopian change his skin?* This shows that Black Men are the Posterity of *Cush:* Who time out of mind have been distinguished by their Colour. And for want of the true, Ovid assigns a fabulous cause of it.

"'*Sanguine tum credunt in corpora summa vocato Æthiopum populus nigrum traxisse colorem.*'[3]
Metamorph. lib. 2.

"*Obj. 2. The Nigers are brought out of a Pagan Country, into places where the Gospel is Preached.*

"*Answ.* Evil must not be done, that good may come of it. The extraordinary and comprehensive Benefit accruing to the Church of God, and to *Joseph* personally, did not rectify his brethrens Sale of him.

"*Obj. 3. The Africans have Wars one with another: Our Ships bring lawful Captives taken in those Wars.*

"*Answ.* For ought is known, their Wars are much such as were between *Jacob's* Sons and their Brother *Joseph.* If they be between Town and Town; Provincial, or National: Every War is upon one side Unjust. An Unlawful War can't make lawful Captives. And by Receiving, we are in danger to promote, and partake in their Barbarous Cruelties. I am sure, if some Gentlemen should go down to the Brewsters to take the Air, and Fish: and a stronger party from *Hull* should Surprise them, and Sell them for Slaves to a Ship outward bound: they would think themselves unjustly dealt with;

[3] *It was then* [during Phaëthon's ride], *as men think, that the peoples of Ethiopia became black-skinned, since the blood was drawn to the surface of their bodies by the heat.* [*Metamorphoses*, II, 235–236.]

both by Sellers and Buyers. And yet 'tis to be feared, we have no other kind of Title to our *Nigers. Therefore all things whatsoever ye would that men should do to you, do ye even so to them: for this is the Law and the Prophets.* Matt. 7. 12.

"*Obj. 4. Abraham had servants bought with his Money, and born in his House.*

"*Answ.* Until the Circumstances of *Abraham's* purchase be recorded, no Argument can be drawn from it. In the mean time, Charity obliges us to conclude, that He knew it was lawful and good.

"It is Observable that the *Israelites* were strictly forbidden the buying or selling one another for Slaves. *Levit.* 25. 39. 46. *Jer.* 34 8. . . .22. And GOD gaged His Blessing in lieu of any loss they might conceipt they suffered thereby. *Deut.* 15. 18. And since the partition Wall is broken down, inordinate Self love should likewise be demolished. GOD expects that Christians should be of a more Ingenuous and benign frame of spirit. Christians should carry it to all the World, as the Israelites were to carry it one towards another. And for men obstinately to persist in holding their Neighbours and Brethren under the Rigor of perpetual Bondage, seems to be no proper way of gaining Assurance that God has given them Spiritual Freedom. Our Blessed Saviour has altered the Measures of the ancient Love-Song, and set it to a most Excellent New Tune, which all ought to be ambitious of Learning. *Matt.* 5. 43, 44. *John* 13. 34. These Ethiopians, as black as they are; seeing they are the Sons and Daughters of the First *Adam,* the Brethren and Sisters of the Last ADAM, and the Offspring of GOD; They ought to be treated with a Respect agreeable.   1700

JOHN WISE

1652–1725

FOR REFUSING to pay taxes to what he regarded as the unjustifiable autocracy of the Andros regime, John Wise, son of an indentured servant and minister of the church in Ipswich, Massachusetts, was deprived of his ministerial functions and put under bond to keep the peace. But his greatest contributions to the cause of freedom were the stand which he later made against the efforts of the Mathers to transform the relatively democratic form of local self-government by the New England churches into a more centralized control. On the basis of the natural rights philosophy, which he absorbed from his reading of Locke, Puffendorf, and other political philosophers, Wise insisted that the essentially democratic contract theory was the basis of ecclesiastical as well as civil government. In 1772 his brilliant and vigorous essays, *The Churches Quarrel Espoused* (1710) and *A Vindication of the Government of New England Churches* (1717), were reprinted and did good service as arguments for the right of the colonies to determine their own political fate. Wise's *A Word of Comfort to a Melancholy County* (1721), in espousing the cause of paper money, further revealed his sympathy with the plain people.

George Allen Cook, *John Wise, Early American Democrat*, New York, 1952.

From: A VINDICATION OF THE GOVERNMENT OF NEW ENGLAND CHURCHES

» » « «

CHAPTER II

[MAN'S FREEDOM]

1. I Shall disclose several Principles of Natural Knowledge; plainly discovering the Law of Nature; or the true sentiments of Natural Reason, with Respect to Mans Being and Government. And in this Essay I shall peculiarly confine the discourse to two heads, *viz.*

1. Of the Natural [in distinction to the Civil] and then,

2. Of the Civil Being of Man. And I shall Principally take Baron *Puffendorff* for my Chief Guide and Spokesman. * * *

But to proceed under the head of a State of Natural Being, I shall more distinctly Explain the State of Humane Nature in its Original Capacity, as Man is placed on Earth by his Maker, and Cloathed with many Investitures, and Immunities which properly belong to Man separately considered. As,

1. The Prime Immunity in Mans State, is that he is most properly the Subject of the Law of Nature. He is the Favourite Animal on Earth; in that this Part of Gods Image, *viz.* Reason is Congenate with his Nature, wherein by a Law Immutable, Instampt upon his Frame, God has provided a Rule for Men in all their Actions, obliging each one to the performance of that which is Right, not only as to Justice, but likewise as to all other Moral Vertues, the which is nothing but the Dictate of Right Reason founded in the Soul of Man. *Motloy, De Mao, Præf.* That which is to be drawn from Mans Reason, flowing from the true Current of that Faculty, when unperverted, may be said to be the Law of Nature; on which account, the Holy Scriptures declare it written on Mens hearts. For being indowed with a Soul, you may know from your self, how, and what you ought to act, Rom. 2. 14. *These having not a Law, are a Law to themselves.* So that the meaning is, when we acknowledge the Law of Nature to be the dictate of Right Reason, we must mean that the Understanding of Man in Endowed with such a power, as to be able, from the Contemplation of humane Condition to discover a necessity of Living agreeably with this Law: And likewise to find out some Principle, by which the Precepts of it, may be clearly and solidly Demonstrated. The way to discover the Law of Nature in our own state, is by a narrow Watch, and accurate Contemplation of our Natural Condition, and propensions. Others say this is the way to find out the Law of Nature. *scil.* If a Man any ways doubts, whether what he is going to do to another Man be agreeable to the Law of Nature, then let him suppose himself to be in that other Mans Room; And by this Rule effectually Executed. A Man must be a very dull Scholar to Nature not to make Proficiency in the Knowledge of her Laws. But more Particularly in pursuing our Condition for the discovery of the Law of Nature, this is very obvious to view, *viz.*

1. A Principle of Self-Love, & Self-Preservation, is very predominant in every Mans Being.

2. A Sociable Disposition.

3. An Affection or Love to Mankind in General. And to give such Sentiments the force of a Law, we must suppose a God who takes care of all Mankind, and has thus obliged each one, as a Subject of higher Principles of Being, then meer Instincts. For that all Law properly considered, supposes a capable Subject, and a Superiour Power; And the Law of God which

is Binding, is published by the Dictates of Right Reason as other ways: Therefore says *Plutarch, To follow God and obey Reason is the same thing.* But moreover that God has Established the Law of Nature, as the General Rule of Government, is further Illustrable from the many Sanctions in Providence, and from the Peace and Guilt of Conscience in them that either obey, or violate the Law of Nature. But moreover, the foundation of the Law of Nature with relation to Government, may be thus Discovered. *scil.* Man is a Creature extreamly desirous of his own Preservation; of himself he is plainly Exposed to many Wants, unable to secure his own safety, and Maintenance without the Assistance of his fellows; and he is also able of returning Kindness by the furtherance of mutual Good; But yet Man is often found to be Malicious, Insolent, and easily Provoked, and as powerful in effecting mischief, as he is ready in designing it. Now that such a Creature may be Preserved, it is necessary that he be Sociable; that is, that he be capable and disposed to unite himself to those of his own species, and to Regulate himself towards them, that they may have no fair Reason to do him harm; but rather incline to promote his Interests, and secure his Rights and Concerns. This then is a Fundamental Law of Nature, that every Man as far as in him lies, do maintain a Sociableness with others, agreeable with the main end and disposition of humane Nature in general. For this is very apparent, that Reason and Society render Man the most potent of all Creatures. And finally, from the Principles of Sociableness it follows as a fundamental Law of Nature, that Man is not so Wedded to his own Interest, but that he can make the Common good the mark of his Aim: And hence he becomes Capacitated to enter into a Civil State by the Law of Nature; for without this property in Nature, *viz.* Sociableness, which is for Cementing of parts, every Government would soon moulder and dissolve.

2. The Second Great Immunity of Man is an Original Liberty Instampt upon his Rational Nature. He that intrudes upon this Liberty, Violates the Law of Nature. In this Discourse I shall wave the Consideration of Mans Moral Turpitude, but shall view him Physically as a Creature which God has made and furnished essentially with many Enobling Immunities, which render him the most August Animal in the World, and still, whatever has happened since his Creation, he remains at the upper-

end of Nature, and as such is a Creature of a very Noble Character. For as to his Dominion, the whole frame of the Lower Part of the Universe is devoted to his use, and at his Command; and his Liberty under the Conduct of Right Reason, is equal with his trust. Which Liberty may be briefly Considered, Internally as to his Mind, and externally as to his Person.

1. The Internal Native Liberty of Mans Nature in general implies, a faculty of Doing or Omitting things according to the Direction of his Judgment. But in a more special meaning, this Liberty does not consist in a loose and ungovernable Freedom, or in an unbounded Licence of Acting. Such Licence is disagreeing with the condition and dignity of Man, and would make Man of a lower and meaner Constitution then Bruit Creatures; who in all their Liberties are kept under a better and more Rational Government, by their Instincts. Therefore as *Plutarch* says, *Those Persons only who live in Obedience to Reason, are worthy to be accounted free: They alone live as they Will, who have Learnt what they ought to Will.* So that the true Natural Liberty of Man, such as really and truely agrees to him, must be understood, as he is Guided and Restrained by the Tyes of Reason, and Laws of Nature; all the rest is Brutal, if not worse.

2. Mans External Personal, Natural Liberty, Antecedent to all Humane parts, or Alliances must also be considered. And so every Man must be conceived to be perfectly in his own Power and disposal, and not to be controuled by the Authority of any other. And thus every Man, must be acknowledged equal to every Man, since all Subjection and all Command are equally banished on both sides; and considering all Men thus at Liberty, every Man has a Prerogative to judge for himself, *viz.* What shall be most for his Behoof, Happiness and Well-being.

3. The Third Capital Immunity belonging to Mans Nature, is an equality amongst Men; Which is not to be denied by the Law of Nature, till Man has Resigned himself with all his Rights for the sake of a Civil State; and then his Personal Liberty and Equality is to be cherished, and preserved to the highest degree, as will consist with all just distinctions amongst Men of Honour, and shall be agreeable with the publick Good. For Man has a high valuation of himself, and the passion seems to lay its first foundation [not in Pride, but] really in the high and admirable Frame and Constitution of

Humane Nature. The Word Man, says my Author, is thought to carry somewhat of Dignity in its sound; and we commonly make use of this as the most proper and prevailing Argument against a rude Insulter, *viz. I am not a Beast or a Dog, but am a Man as well as your self.* Since then Humane Nature agrees equally with all persons; and since no one can live a Sociable Life with another that does not own or Respect him as a Man; It follows as a Command of the Law of Nature, that every Man Esteem and treat another as one who is naturally his Equal, or who is a Man as well as he. There be many popular, or plausible Reasons that greatly Illustrate this Equality, *viz.* that we all Derive our Being from one stock, the same Common Father of humane Race. On this consideration *Bœthius* checks the pride of the Insulting Nobility.

> *Quid Genus et Proavos Strepitis?*
> *Si Primordia Vestra,*
> *Auteremque Deum Spectas,*
> *Nullus Degener Extat*
> *Nisi vitiis Perjura fovens,*
> *Proprium Deserat Orturn.*

> *Fondly our first Descent we Boast;*
> *If whence at first our Breath we Drew*
> *The common springs of Life we view,*
> *The Airy Notion soon is Lost.*

> *The Almighty made us equal all;*
> *But he that slavishly complyes*
> *To do the Drudgery of Vice,*
> *Denyes his high Original.*

And also that our Bodies are Composed of matter, frail, brittle, and lyable to be destroyed by thousand Accidents; we all owe our Existence to the same Method of propagation. The Noblest Mortal in his Entrance on to the Stage of Life, is not distinguished by any pomp or of passage from the lowest of Mankind; and our Life hastens to the same General Mark: Death observes no Ceremony, but Knocks as loud at the Barriers of the Court, as at the Door of the Cottage. This Equality being admitted, bears a very great force in maintaining Peace and Friendship amongst Men. For that he who would use the Assistance of others, in promoting his own Advantage, ought as freely to be at their service, when they want his help on the like Occasions. *One Good turn Requires another*, is the Common Proverb; for otherwise he must need esteem others unequal to himself, who constantly demands their Aid, and as constantly denies his own. And whoever is of

this Insolent Temper, cannot but highly displease those about him, and soon give Occasion of the Breach of the Common Peace. It was a Manly Reproof which *Charactacus* gave the *Romans. Num. Si vos Omnibus* &c. What! because you desire to be Masters of all Men, does it follow therefore that all Men should desire to be your Slaves, for that it is a Command of Natures Law, that no Man that has not obtained a particular and special Right, shall arrogate to himself a Larger share then his fellows, but shall admit others to equal priviledges with himself. So that the Principle of Equality in a Natural State, is peculiarly transgressed by Pride, which is when a Man without sufficient reason prefers himself to others. And though as *Hensius*, Paraphrases upon *Aristotle's* Politicks to this Purpose. *viz. Nothing is more suitable to Nature, then that those who Excel in Understanding and Prudence, should Rule and Controul those who are less happy in those Advantages,* &c. Yet we must note, that there is room for an Answer, *scil.* That it would be the Greatest absurdity to believe, that Nature actually Invests the Wise with a Sovereignty over the weak; or with a Right of forcing them against their Wills; for that no Sovereignty can be established, unless some Humane Deed, or Covenant Precede: Nor does Natural fitness for Government make a Man presently Governour over another; for that as *Ulpian* says, *by a Natural Right all Men are born free;* and Nature having set all Men upon a Level and made them Equals, no Servitude or Subjection can be conceived without Inequality; and this cannot be made without Usurpation or Force in others, or Voluntary Compliance in those who Resign their freedom, and give away their degree of Natural Being. And thus we come,

2. To consider Man in a Civil State of Being; wherein we shall observe the great difference betwen a Natural, and Political State; for in the Latter State many Great disproportions appear, or at least many obvious distinctions are soon made amongst Men; which Doctrine is to be laid open under a few heads.

1. Every Man considered in a Natural State, must be allowed to be Free, and at his own dispose; yet to suit Mans Inclinations to Society; And in a peculiar manner to gratify the necessity he is in of publick Rule and Order, he is Impelled to enter into a Civil Community; and Divests himself of his Natural Freedom, and puts himself under Government; which amongst other things Comprehends the Power

of Life and Death over Him; together with Authority to Injoyn him some things to which he has an utter Aversation, and to prohibit him other things, for which he may have as strong an Inclination; so that he may be often under this Authority, obliged to Sacrifice his Private, for the Publick Good. So that though Man is inclined to Society, yet he is driven to a combination by great necessity. For that the true

10 and leading Cause of forming Governments, and yielding up Natural Liberty, and throwing Mans Equality into a Common Pile to be new Cast by the Rules of fellowship; was really and truly to guard themselves against the Injuries Men were lyable to Interchangeably; for none so Good to Man, as Man, and yet none a greater Enemy. So that,

2. The first Humane Subject and Original of Civil Power is the People. For as they have

20 a Power every Man over himself in a Natural State, so upon a Combination they can and do bequeath this Power unto others; and settle it according as their united discretion shall Determine. For that this is very plain, that when the Subject of Sovereign Power is quite Extinct, that Power returns to the People again. And when they are free, they may set up what species of Government they please; or if they rather incline to it, they may subside into a

30 State of Natural Being, if it be plainly for the best. In the *Eastern* Country of the *Mogul*, we have some resemblance of the Case; for upon the Death of an absolute Monarch, they live so many days without a Civil Head; but in that *Interregnum*, those who survive the Vacancy, are glad to get into a Civil State again; and usually they are in a very Bloody Condition when they return under the Covert of a new Monarch; this project is to indear the People to a

40 Tyranny, from the Experience they have so lately had of an Anarchy.

3. The formal Reason of Government is the Will of a Community, yielded up and surrendered to some other Subject, either of one particular Person, or more, Conveyed in the following manner.

Let us conceive in our Mind a multitude of Men, all Naturally Free & Equal; going about voluntarily, to Erect themselves into a new

50 Common-Wealth. Now their Condition being such, to bring themselves into a Politick Body, they must needs Enter into divers Covenants.

1. They must Interchangeably each Man Covenant to joyn in one lasting Society, that

they may be capable to concert the measures of their safety, by a Publick Vote.

2. A Vote or Decree must then nextly pass to set up some Particular species of Government over them. And if they are joyned in their first Compact upon absolute Terms to stand to the Decision of the first Vote concerning the Species of Government: Then all are bound by the Majority to acquiesce in that particular Form thereby settled, though their own private Opinion, incline them to some other Model.

3. After a Decree has specified the Particular form of Government, then there will be need of a New Covenant, whereby those on whom Sovereignty is conferred, engage to take care of the Common Peace, and Welfare. And the Subjects on the other hand, to yield them Faithful Obedience. In which Covenant is Included that Submission and Union of Wills, by which a State may be conceived to be but one Person. So that the most proper Definition of a Civil State, is this, *viz.* A Civil State is a Compound Moral Person, whose Will [United by those Covenants before passed] is the Will of all; to the end it may Use, and Apply the strength and riches of Private Persons towards maintaining the Common Peace, Security, and Well-being of all. Which may be conceived as tho' the whole State was now become but one Man; in which the aforesaid Covenants may be supposed under Gods Providence, to be the Divine *Fiat*, Pronounced by God, let us make Man. And by way of resemblance the aforesaid Being may be thus Anatomized.

1. The Sovereign Power is the Soul infused, giving Life and Motion to the whole Body.

2. Subordinate Officers are the Joynts by which the Body moves.

3. Wealth and Riches are the Strength.

4. Equity and Laws are the Reason.

5. Councellors the Memory.

6. *Salus Populi*, or the Happiness of the People, is the End of its Being; or main Business to be attended and done.

7. Concord amongst the Members, and all Estates, is the Health.

8. Sedition is Sickness, and Civil War Death.

4. The Parts of Sovereignty may be considered: So,

1. As it Prescribes the Rule of Action: It is rightly termed *Legislative Power*.

2. As it determines the Controversies of Subjects by the Standard of those Rules. So is it justly Termed Judiciary Power.

3. As it Arms the Subjects against Foreign-

ers, or forbids Hostility, so its called the Power of Peace and War.

4. As it takes in Ministers for the discharge of Business, so it is called the Right of Appointing Magistrates. So that all great officers and Publick Servants, must needs owe their Original to the Creating Power of Sovereignty. So that those whose Right it is to Create, may Dissolve the being of those who are Created, unless they cast them into an Immortal Frame. And yet must needs be dissoluble if they justly forfeit their being to their Creators.

5. The Chief End of Civil Communities, is, that Men thus conjoyned, may be secured against the Injuries, they are lyable to from their own Kind. For if every Man could secure himself singly; It would be great folly for him, to Renounce his Natural Liberty, in which every Man is his own King and Protector.

6. The Sovereign Authority besides that it inheres in every State as in a Common and General Subject. So farther according as it resides in some One Person, or in a Council [consisting of some Select Persons, or of all the Members of a Community] as in a proper and particular Subject, so it produceth different Forms of Common-wealths, *viz.* Such as are either simple and regular, or mixt.

1. The Forms of a Regular State are three only, which Forms arise from the proper and particular Subject, in which the Supream Power Resides. As,

1. A Democracy, which is when the Sovereign Power is Lodged in a Council consisting of all the Members, and where every Member has the Priviledge of a Vote. This Form of Government, appears in the greatest part of the World to have been the most Ancient. For that Reason seems to shew it to be most probable, that when Men [being Originally in a condition of Natural Freedom and Equality] had thoughts of joyning in a Civil Body, would without question be inclined to Administer their common Affairs, by their common Judgment, and so must necessarily to gratifie that Inclination establish a Democracy; neither can it be rationally imagined, that Fathers of Families being yet Free and Independent, should in a moment, or little time take off their long delight in governing their own Affairs, & Devolve all upon some single Sovereign Commander; for that it seems to have been thought more Equitable, that what belonged to all, should be managed by all, when all had entered by Compact into one Community. The Original of our Gov-

ernment, says *Plato*, [speaking of the *Athenian* Common-wealth] *was taken from the Equality of our Race. Other States there are composed of different Blood, and of unequal Lines, the Consequence of which are disproportionable Soveraignty, Tyrannical or Oligarchycal Sway; under which men live in such a manner, as to Esteem themselves partly Lords, and partly Slaves to each other. But we and our Country men, being all Born Brethren of the same* [10] *Mother, do not look upon our selves, to stand under so hard a Relation, as that of Lords, and Slaves; but the Parity of our Descent incline us to keep up the like Parity by our Laws, and so yield the precedency to nothing but to Superiour Vertue and Wisdom.* And moreover it seems very manifest that most Civil Communities arose at first from the Union of Families, that were nearly allyed in Race and Blood. And though Ancient Story make frequent mention [20] of Kings, yet it appears that most of them were such that had an Influence rather in perswading, then in any Power of Commanding. So *Justin* describes that Kind of Government, as the most Primitive, which *Aristotle* stiles an Heroical Kingdom. *viz.* Such as is no ways inconsistent with a Democratical State. *De Princip. Reru.* 1. *L.* 1. *C.*

A democracy is then Erected, when a Number of Free Persons, do Assemble together, in [30] Order to enter into a Covenant for Uniting themselves in a Body: And such a Preparative Assembly hath some appearance already of a Democracy; it is a Democracy in *Embrio* properly in this Respect, that every Man hath the Priviledge freely to deliver his Opinion concerning the Common Affairs. Yet he who dissents from the Vote of the Majority, is not in the least obliged by what they determine, till by a second Covenant, a Popular Form be actu- [40] ally Established; for not before then can we call it a Democratical Government, *viz.* Till the Right of Determining all matters relating to the publick Safety, is actually placed in a General Assembly of the whole People; or by their own Compact and Mutual Agreement, Determine themselves the proper Subject for the Exercise of Sovereign Power. And to compleat this State, and render it capable to Exert its Power to answer the End of a Civil State: These Condi- [50] tions are necessary.

1. That a certain Time and Place be Assigned for Assembling.

2. That when the Assembly be Orderly met, as to Time and Place, that then the Vote of the

Majority must pass for the Vote of the whole Body.

3. That Magistrates be appointed to Exercise the Authority of the whole for the better dispatch of Business, of every days Occurrence; who also may with more Mature diligence, search into more Important Affairs; and if in case any thing happens of greater Consequence, may report it to the Assembly; and be peculiarly Serviceable in putting all Publick Decrees into Execution. Because a large Body of People is almost useless in Respect of the last Service, and of many others, as to the more Particular Application and Exercise of Power. Therefore it is most agreeable with the Law of Nature, that they Institute their Officers to act in their Name, and Stead.

2. The Second Species of Regular Government, is an Aristocracy; and this is said then to be Constituted when the People, or Assembly United by a first Covenant, and having thereby cast themselves into the first Rudiments of a State; do then by Common Decree, Devolve the Sovereign Power, on a Council consisting of some Select Members; and these having accepted of the Designation, are then properly invested with Sovereign Command; and then an Aristocracy is formed.

3. The Third Species of a Regular Government, is a Monarchy which is settled when the Sovereign Power is confered on some one worthy Person. It differs from the former, because a Monarch who is but one Person in Natural, as well as in Moral account, & so is furnished with an Immediate Power of Exercising Sovereign Command in all Instances of Government; but the fore named must needs have Particular Time and Place assigned; but the Power and Authority is Equal in each.

2. Mixt Governments, which are various and of divers kinds [not now to be Enumerated] yet possibly the fairest in the World is that which has a Regular Monarchy; [in Distinction to what is Dispotick] settled upon a Noble Democracy as its Basis. And each part of the Government is so adjusted by Pacts and Laws that renders the whole Constitution an *Elisium*. It is said of the *British* Empire, *That it is such a Monarchy, as that by the necessary subordinate Concurrence of the Lords and Commons, in the Making and Repealing all Statutes or Acts of Parliament; it hath the main advantages of an Aristocracy, and of a Democracy, and yet free from the Disadvantages and Evils of either. It is such a Monarchy, as by most Admirable Temperament affords very much to the Industry, Liberty, and Happiness of the Subject, and reserves enough for the Majesty and Prerogative of any King, who will own his People as Subjects, not as Slaves. It is a Kingdom, that of all the Kingdoms of the World, is most like to the Kingdom of Jesus Christ, whose Yoke is easie, and Burden light.* Present State of *England* 1st Part 64 *p* * * *   1717

JOHN DICKINSON

1732–1808

JOHN DICKINSON, after a youth spent on a plantation on the East Shore of Maryland, studied law in the Middle Temple in London. Returning to Philadelphia, he sided with the Penn family in its tussles with the popular party in Pennsylvania. In view of his essential conservatism his participation in the Stamp Act Congress was somewhat surprising. Nevertheless Dickinson counselled moderation in the heated discussions which preceded the outbreak of the struggle for independence. But his *Letters from a Farmer in Pennsylvania*, which appeared in three newspapers in 1767–1768, contributed to the growing conviction that America was suffering from wrongs for which the Mother country was responsible. Distinguishing between the right of Parliament to levy internal and external taxation, Dickinson drew a line which limited the powers claimed by Parliament. Within two years at least ten editions of the *Letters* appeared in pamphlet form.

Dickinson refused to sign the Declaration of Independence, which he believed to be premature. But during the War itself he supported the cause of the patriots by arms. Later, as a member of the Constitutional Convention and as Governor of Pennsylvania and Delaware, Dickinson contributed substantially to the consolidation of the new order.

The Political Writings of John Dickinson, Esq., 2 vols., Wilmington, 1801.
The Writings of John Dickinson, P. L. Ford, ed., vol. I, Philadelphia, 1895.
C. J. Stillé, *The Life and Times of John Dickinson, 1732–1808*, Philadelphia, 1891.

From: LETTERS FROM A FARMER IN PENNSYLVANIA

LETTER I

My Beloved Countrymen,

I am a *Farmer*, settled after a variety of fortunes, near the banks of the river *Delaware*, in the province of *Pennsylvania*. I received a liberal education, and have been engaged in the busy scenes of life: But am now convinced, that a man may be as happy without bustle, as with it. My farm is small; my servants are few, and good; I have a little money at interest; I wish for no more; my employment in my own affairs is easy; and with a contented grateful mind, I am compleating the number of days allotted to me by divine goodness.

Being master of my time, I spend a good deal of it in a library, which I think the most valuable part of my small estate; and being acquainted with two or three gentlemen of abilities and learning, who honour me with their friendship, I believe, I have acquired a greater share of knowledge in history, and the laws and constitution of my country, than is generally attained by men of my class, many of them not being so fortunate as I have been in the opportunities of getting information.

From infancy I was taught to love humanity and liberty. Inquiry and experience have since confirmed my reverence for the lessons then given me, by convincing me more fully of their truth and excellence. Benevolence towards mankind excites wishes for their welfare, and such wishes endear the means of fulfilling them. Those can be found in liberty alone, and therefore her sacred cause ought to be espoused by every man, on every occasion, to the utmost of his power. As a charitable but poor person does not withhold his mite, because he cannot relieve *all* the distresses of the miserable, so let not any honest man suppress his sentiments concerning freedom, however small their influence is likely to be. Perhaps he may "touch some wheel" that will have an effect greater than he expects.

These being my sentiments, I am encouraged to offer to you, my countrymen, my thoughts on some late transactions, that in my opinion are of the utmost importance to you. Conscious of my defects, I have waited some time in expectation of seeing the subject treated by persons much better qualified for the task; but being therein disappointed, and apprehensive that longer delays will be injurious, I venture at length to request the attention of the public, praying only for one thing,—that is, that these lines may be *read* with the same zeal for the happiness of *British America*, with which they were *wrote*.

With a good deal of surprize I have observed that little notice has been taken of an act of parliament, as injurious in its principle to the liberties of these colonies, as the *Stamp-Act* was: I mean the act for suspending the legislation of *New-York*.

The assembly of that government complied with a former act of parliament, requiring certain provisions to be made for the troops in *America*, in every particular, I think, except the articles of salt, pepper and vinegar. In my opinion they acted imprudently, considering all circumstances, in not complying so far, as would have given satisfaction, as several colonies did: But my dislike of their conduct in that instance, has not blinded me so much, that I cannot plainly perceive, that they have been punished in a manner pernicious to *American* freedom, and justly alarming to all the colonies.

If the *British* parliament has a legal authority to order, that we shall furnish a single article for the troops here, and to compel obedience to that order; they have the same right to order us to supply those troops with arms, cloaths, and every necessary, and to compel obedience to *that* order also; in short, to lay *any burdens* they please upon us. What is this but *taxing* us at a *certain sum,* and leaving to us only the *manner* of raising it? How is this mode more tolerable than the *Stamp-Act?* Would that act have appeared more pleasing to *Americans,* if being ordered thereby to raise the sum total of the taxes, the mighty privilege had been left to them, of saying how much should be paid for an instrument of writing on paper, and how much for another on parchment?

An act of parliament commanding us to do a certain thing, if it has any validity, is a tax upon us for the expence that accrues in complying with it, and for this reason, I believe, every colony on the continent, that chose to give a mark of their respect for *Great-Britain,* in complying with the act relating to the troops, cautiously avoided the mention of that act, lest their conduct should be attributed to its supposed obligation.

The matter being thus stated, the assembly of *New-York,* either had, or had not a right, to refuse submission to that act. If they had, and I imagine no *American* will say, they had not, then the parliament had no *right* to compel them to execute it. If they had not *that right,* they had *no right* to punish them for not executing it; and therefore had *no right* to suspend their legislation, which is a punishment. In fact, if the people of *New-York* cannot be legally taxed but by their own representatives, they cannot be legally deprived of the privileges of making laws, only for insisting on that exclusive privilege of taxation. If they may be legally deprived in such a case of the privilege of making laws, why may they not, with equal reason, be deprived of every other privilege? Or why may not every colony be treated in the same manner, when any of them shall dare to deny their assent to any impositions that shall be directed? Or what signifies the repeal of the *Stamp-Act,* if these colonies are to lose their *other* privileges, by not tamely surrendering that of *taxation?*

There is one consideration arising from the suspicion, which is not generally attended to, but shews its importance very clearly. It was not *necessary,* that this suspension should be caused by an act of parliament. The crown might have restrained the governor of *New-*

York, even from calling the assembly together, by its prerogative in the royal governments. This step, I suppose, would have been taken, if the conduct of the assembly of *New-York* had been regarded as an act of disobedience *to the crown alone:* But it is regarded as an act of "disobedience to the authority of the BRITISH LEGISLATURE." This gives the suspension a consequence vastly more affecting. It is a parliamentary assertion of the *supreme authority* of the *British* legislature over these colonies in *the point of taxation;* and it is intended to COMPEL *New-York* unto a submission to that authority. It seems therefore to me as much a violation of the liberty of the people of that province, and consequently of all these colonies, as if the parliament had sent a number of regiments to be quartered upon them, till they should comply. For it is evident, that the suspension is meant as a compulsion; and the *method* of compelling is totally indifferent. It is indeed probable, that the sight of red-coats, and the beating of drums would have been most alarming, because people are generally more influenced by their eyes and ears than by their reason: But whoever seriously considers the matter, must perceive, that a dreadful stroke is aimed at the liberty of these colonies. I say of these colonies: For the cause of *one* is the cause of *all.* If the parliament may lawfully deprive *New-York* of any of its rights, it may deprive any, or all the other colonies of their rights; and nothing can possibly so much encourage such attempts, as a mutual inattention to the interest of each other. *To divide and thus to destroy,* is the first political maxim in attacking those who are powerful by their union. He certainly is not a wise man, who folds his arms and reposeth himself at home, seeing with unconcern the flames that have invaded his neighbour's house, without any endeavours to extinguish them. When Mr. *Hampden's* ship-money cause for three shillings and four-pence was tried, all the people of *England,* with anxious expectation, interested themselves in the important decision; and when the slightest point touching the freedom of a single colony is agitated, I earnestly wish, that all the rest may with equal ardour support their sister. Very much may be said on this subject, but I hope, more at present is unnecessary.

With concern I have observed that two assemblies of this province have sat and adjourned, without taking any notice of this act.

It may perhaps be asked, what would have been proper for them to do? I am by no means fond of inflammatory measures. I detest them. I should be sorry that any thing should be done which might justly displease our sovereign or our mother-country. But a firm, modest exertion of a free spirit should never be wanting on public occasions. It appears to me, that it would have been sufficient for the assembly, to have ordered our agents to represent to the Kings' ministers, their sense of the suspending act, and to pray for its repeal. Thus we should have borne our testimony against it; and might therefore reasonably expect that on a like occasion, we might receive the same assistance from the other colonies.

"*Concordia res parvæ crescunt.*"[1]

Nov. 4. [1767]   A Farmer

LETTER III

Beloved Countrymen,

I rejoice to find that my two former letters to you have been generally received with so much favour, by such of you whose sentiments I have had an opportunity of knowing. Could you look into my heart, you would instantly perceive an ardent affection for your persons, a zealous attachment to your interests, a lively resentment of every insult and injury offered to your honour or happiness; and an inflexible resolution to assert your rights, to the utmost of my weak power, to be the only motives that have engaged me to address you.

I am no farther concerned in any thing affecting *America,* than any one of you, and when liberty leaves it, I can quit it much more conveniently than most of you. But while Divine Providence that gave me existence in a land of freedom, permits my head to think, my lips to speak, and my hand to move, I shall so highly and gratefully value the blessing received, as to take care, that my silence and inactivity shall not give my implied assent to any act, degrading my brethren and myself from the birthright, wherewith Heaven itself "hath made us free."

Sorry I am to learn, that there are some few persons, who shake their heads with solemn motion, and pretend to wonder, what can be the meaning of these letters. "*Great-Britain,*" they say, "is too powerful to contend with; she is determined to oppress us; it is in vain to speak of right on one side, when there is power

[1] *In peace, small things grow great.*

on the other; when we are strong enough to resist, we shall attempt it; but now we are not strong enough, and therefore we had better be quiet; it signifies nothing to convince us that our rights are invaded, when we cannot defend them; and if we should get into riots and tumults about the late act, it will only draw down heavier displeasure upon us."

What can such men design? What do their grave observations amount to, but this—"That these colonies totally regardless of their liberties, should commit them with humble resignation to *chance, time,* and the tender mercies of *ministers.*"

Are these men ignorant that usurpations which might have been successfully opposed at first, acquire strength by continuance, and thus become irresistable? Do they condemn the conduct of the colonies concerning the *Stamp-Act?* Or have they forgot its successful issue? Ought the colonies at that time, instead of acting as they did, to have trusted for relief to the fortuitous events of futurity? If it is needless "to speak of *rights*" now, it was as needless then. If the behaviour of the colonies was prudent and glorious then, and successful too; it will be equally prudent and glorious to act in the same manner now, if our rights are equally invaded, and may be as successful.— Therefore it becomes necessary to enquire, whether "our rights *are* invaded." To talk of "defending" them, as if they could be no otherwise "defended" than by arms, is as much out of the way, as if a man having a choice of several roads, to reach his journey, and should prefer the worst, for no other reason but because it *is* the worst.

As to "riots and tumults," the gentlemen who are so apprehensive of them, are much mistaken if they think, that grievances cannot be redressed without such assistance.

I will now tell the gentlemen what is "the meaning of these letters." The meaning of them is, to convince the people of these colonies that they are, at this moment, exposed to the most imminent dangers; and to persuade them immediately, vigorously, unanimously to exert themselves, in the most firm, and most peaceable manner, for obtaining relief.

The cause of liberty is a "cause of too much dignity, to be sullied by turbulence and tumults." It ought to be maintained in a manner suitable to her nature. Those who engage in it, should breathe a sedate yet fervent spirit, animating them to actions of prudence, justice, modesty, bravery, humanity and magnanimity.

To such a wonderful degree were the antient *Spartans,* as brave and free a people as ever existed, inspired by this happy temperature of soul, that rejecting even in their battles the use of trumpets, and other instruments, for exciting heat and rage, they marched up to scenes of havock and horror, with the sound of flutes, to the tunes of which their steps kept pace— "exhibiting," as *Plutarch* says, "at once a terrible and delightful sight, and proceeding, with a deliberate valour, full of hope and good assurance, as if some divinity had sensibly assisted them."

I hope, my dear countrymen, that you will in every colony be upon your guard against those who may at any time endeavour to stir you up, under pretences of patriotism, to any measures disrespectful to our sovereign and our mother-country. Hot, rash, disorderly proceedings injure the reputation of a people as to wisdom, valour, and virtue, without procuring them the least benefit. I pray GOD that he may be pleased to inspire you and your posterity to the latest ages with that spirit, of which I have an idea, but find a difficulty to express: To express in the best manner I can, I mean a spirit that shall so guide you, that it will be impossible to determine whether an *American's* character is most distinguishable for his loyalty to his sovereign, his duty to his mother-country, his love of freedom, or his affection for his native soil.

Every government, at some time or other, falls into wrong measures; these may proceed from mistake or passion. But every such measure does not dissolve the obligation between the governors and the governed; the mistake may be corrected; the passion may pass over. It is the duty of the governed, to endeavour to rectify the mistake, and to appease the passion. They have not at first any other right, than to represent their grievances, and to pray for redress, unless an emergence is so pressing as not to allow time for receiving an answer to their applications, which rarely happens. If their applications are disregarded, *then* that kind of opposition becomes justifiable, which can be made without breaking the laws, or disturbing the public peace. This consists in the prevention of the oppressors reaping advantage from their oppressions, and not in their punishment. For experience may teach them what reason did not; and harsh methods cannot be proper till milder ones have failed.

If at length it becomes UNDOUBTED, that an inveterate resolution is formed to annihilate the liberties of the governed, the *English* history affords frequent examples of resistance by force. What particular circumstances will in any future case justify such resistance, can never be ascertained till they happen. Perhaps it may be allowable to say, generally, that it never can be justifiable, until the people are FULLY CONVINCED, that any further submission will be destructive to their happiness.

When the appeal is made to the sword, highly probable is it, that the punishment will exceed the offence; and the calamities attending on war outweigh those preceding it. These considerations of justice and prudence will always have great influence with good and wise men.

To these reflections on this subject, it remains to be added, and ought forever to be remembered; that resistance in the case of colonies against their mother-country, is extremely different from the resistance of a people against their prince. A nation may change their kings, or race of kings, and retaining their antient form of government, be gainers by changing. Thus *Great-Britain,* under the illustrious house of *Brunswick,* a house that seems to flourish for the happiness of mankind, has found a felicity, unknown in the reigns of the *Stuarts.* But if once *we* are separated from our mother-country, what new form of government shall we accept, or where shall we find another *Britain* to supply our loss? Torn from the body to which we are united by religion, liberty, laws, affections, relations, language and commerce, we must bleed at every vein.

In truth, the prosperity of these provinces is founded in their dependance on *Great-Britain;* and when she returns to "her old good humour, and old good nature," as Lord *Clarendon* expresses it, I hope they will always esteem it their duty and interest, as it most certainly will be, to promote her welfare by all the means in their power.

We cannot act with too much caution in our disputes. Anger produces anger; and differences that might be accommodated by kind and respectful behaviour, may by imprudence be enlarged to an incurable rage.

In quarrels between countries, as well as in those between individuals, when they have risen to a certain height, the first cause of dissention is no longer remembered, the minds of the parties being wholly engaged in recollecting and resenting the mutual expressions of their dislike. When feuds have reached that fatal point, all considerations of reason and equity vanish; and a blind fury governs, or rather confounds all things. A people no longer regards their interest, but the gratification of their wrath. The sway of the *Cleons,* and *Clodius's,*[2] the designing and detestable flatterers of the prevailing passion, becomes confirmed. Wise and good men in vain oppose the storm, and may think themselves fortunate, if endeavouring to preserve their ungrateful fellow-citizens, they do not ruin themselves. Their *prudence* will be called *baseness;* their *moderation, guilt;* and if their virtue does not lead them to destruction, as that of many other great and excellent persons has done, they may survive to receive from their expiring country, the mournful glory of her acknowledgement, that their councils, if regarded, would have saved her.

The *constitutional* modes of obtaining relief, are those which I would wish to see pursued on the present occasion; that is, by petitions of our Assemblies, or, where they are not permitted to meet, of the people, to the powers that can afford us relief.

We have an excellent prince, in whose good dispositions toward us we may confide. We have a generous, sensible and humane nation, to whom we may apply. They *may* be deceived: They may, by artful men, be provoked to anger against us; but I cannot yet believe they will be cruel or unjust, or that their anger will be implacable. Let us behave like dutiful children, who have received unmerited blows from a beloved parent. Let us complain to our parents; but let our complaints speak, at the same time, the language of affliction and veneration. 10

If, however, it shall happen by an unfortunate course of affairs, that our applications to his Majesty and the Parliament for redress prove ineffectual, let us *then* take another step, by witholding from *Great-Britain,* all the advantages she has been used to receive from us. *Then* let us try, if our ingenuity, industry and frugality, will not give weight to our remonstrances. Let us all be united with one spirit in one cause. Let us invent; let us work; let us save; let us, at the same time, keep up our claims, and unceasingly repeat our complaints; but above all, let us implore the protection of that infinitely good and gracious Being, "by whom kings reign and princes decree justice." 20

"Nil desperandum."[3]

A FARMER.
1767

[2] The Greek Cleon and the Roman Clodius brought catastrophe to their respective countries.

[3] *Nothing is to be despaired of.*

BENJAMIN FRANKLIN

1706–1790

FROM THE early phases of his public career in Pennsylvania Franklin showed his sympathies with the popular cause. In espousing the proposal for paper money he was serving the indebted classes. In regarding labor as the source of wealth, and property as subject to social control, he was likewise befriending the underdog. Similarly during the struggles between the popular and proprietary parties in Pennsylvania, Franklin took his stand with the people. This does not mean that he was a hot-headed radical. On the contrary, he helped organize Philadelphia's middle classes against the threatened "revolution" of the frontiersmen who demanded policies for which the urban groups in political control had no liking. And Franklin's moderation during his agency in England on the eve of the Revolution kept the way open to compromise until events moved too fast.

Franklin signed the Declaration of Independence, and greatly contributed to the success of the American cause during his ministry to France. His part in the negotiation of the Treaty of Alliance with France, and in the settlement by which England recognized American independence, was a notable one. And Franklin also used his influence for the successful outcome of the proposals for a new Constitution.

Franklin's writings in behalf of American freedom from England are admirable examples both of his urbane style and of the political quality of his mind.

Papers, Leonard Larabee and others, eds., New Haven, 1959–

V. W. Crane, *Certain Writings of Benjamin Franklin on the British Empire and the American Colonies*, Papers of the Bibliog. Soc. of Amer., vol. XXVIII, 1934.

Carl Van Doren, *Benjamin Franklin*, New York, 1938.

RULES BY WHICH A GREAT EMPIRE MAY BE REDUCED TO A SMALL ONE

An ancient Sage boasted, that, tho' he could not fiddle, he knew how to make a *great city* of a *little one*. The science that I, a modern simpleton, am about to communicate, is the very reverse.

I address myself to all ministers who have the management of extensive dominions, which from their very greatness are become troublesome to govern, because the multiplicity of their affairs leaves no time for *fiddling*.

I. In the first place, gentlemen, you are to consider, that a great empire, like a great cake, is most easily diminished at the edges. Turn your attention, therefore, first to your *remotest* provinces; that, as you get rid of them, the next may follow in order.

II. That the possibility of this separation may always exist, take special care the provinces are never incorporated with the mother country; that they do not enjoy the same common rights, the same privileges in commerce; and that they are governed by *severer* laws, all of *your enacting*, without allowing them any share in the choice of the legislators. By carefully making and preserving such distinctions, you will (to keep to my simile of the cake) act like a wise ginger-bread-baker, who, to facilitate a division, cuts his dough half through in those places where, when baked, he would have it *broken to pieces*.

III. Those remote provinces have perhaps been acquired, purchased, or conquered, at the *sole expence* of the settlers, or their ancestors, without the aid of the mother country. If this should happen to increase her *strength*, by their growing numbers, ready to join in her wars; her *commerce*, by their growing demand for her manufactures; or her *naval power*, by greater employment for her ships and seamen, they may probably suppose some merit in this, and that it entitles them to some favour; you are therefore to *forget it all, or resent it,* as if they had done you injury. If they happen to be zealous whigs, friends of liberty, nurtured in revolution principles, *remember all that* to their prejudice, and resolve to punish it; for such principles, after a revolution is thoroughly established, are of *no more use;* they are even *odious* and *abominable*.

IV. However peaceably your colonies have submitted to your government, shewn their affection to your interests, and patiently borne their grievances; you are to *suppose* them always inclined to revolt, and treat them accordingly. Quarter troops among them, who by their insolence may *provoke* the rising of mobs, and by their bullets and bayonets *suppress* them. By this means, like the husband who uses his wife ill *from suspicion*, you may in time convert your *suspicions* into *realities*.

V. Remote provinces must have *Governors* and *Judges*, to represent the Royal Person, and execute everywhere the delegated parts of his office and authority. You ministers know, that much of the strength of government depends on the *opinion* of the people; and much of that opinion on the *choice of rulers* placed immediately over them. If you send them wise and good men for governors, who study the interest of the colonists, and advance their prosperity, they will think their King wise and good, and that he wishes the welfare of his subjects. If you send them learned and upright men for Judges, they will think him a lover of justice. This may attach your provinces more to his government. You are therefore to be careful whom you recommend for those offices. If you can find prodigals, who have ruined their fortunes, broken gamesters or stockjobbers, these may do well as *governors;* for they will probably be rapacious, and provoke the people by their extortions. Wrangling proctors and pettifogging lawyers, too, are not amiss; for they will be for ever disputing and quarrelling with their little parliaments. If withal they should be ignorant, wrong-headed, and insolent, so much the better. Attornies' clerks and Newgate solicitors will do for *Chief Justices,* especially if they hold their places *during your pleasure;* and all will contribute to impress those ideas of your government, that are proper for a people *you would wish to renounce it.*

VI. To confirm these impressions, and strike them deeper, whenever the injured come to the capital with complaints of mal-administration, oppression, or injustice, punish such suitors with long delay, enormous expence, and a final judgment in favour of the oppressor. This will have an admirable effect every way. The trouble of future complaints will be prevented, and Governors and Judges will be encouraged to farther acts of oppression and injustice; and thence the people may become more disaffected, and at length desperate.

VII. When such Governors have crammed their coffers, and made themselves so odious to the people that they can no longer remain among them, with safety to their person, *recall and reward* them with pensions. You may make them *baronets* too, if that respectable order should not think fit to resent it. All will contribute to encourage new governors in the same practice, and make the supreme government, *detestable.*

VIII. If, when you are engaged in war, your colonies should vie in liberal aids of men and money against the common enemy, upon your simple requisition, and give far beyond their abilities, reflect that a penny taken from them by your power is more honourable to you, than a pound presented by their benevolence; despise therefore their voluntary grants, and resolve to harass them with novel taxes. They will probably complain to your parliaments, that they are taxed by a body in which they have no representative, and that this is contrary to common right. They will petition for redress. Let the Parliaments flout their claims, reject their petitions, refuse even to suffer the reading of them, and treat the petitioners with

the utmost contempt. Nothing can have a better effect in producing the alienation proposed; for though many can forgive injuries, *none ever forgave contempt.*

IX. In laying these taxes, never regard the heavy burthens those remote people already undergo, in defending their own frontiers, supporting their own provincial governments, making new roads, building bridges, churches, and other public edifices, which in old countries have been done to your hands by your ancestors, but which occasion constant calls and demands on the purses of a new people. Forget the *restraints* you lay on their trade for *your own* benefit, and the advantage a *monopoly* of this trade gives your exacting merchants. Think nothing of the wealth those merchants and your manufacturers acquire by the colony commerce; their encreased ability thereby to pay taxes at home; their accumulating, in the price of their commodities, most of those taxes, and so levying them from their consuming customers; all this, and the employment and support of thousands of your poor by the colonists, you are *intirely to forget.* But remember to make your arbitrary tax more grievous to your provinces, by public declarations importing that your power of taxing them has *no limits;* so that when you take from them without their consent one shilling in the pound, you have a clear right to the other nineteen. This will probably weaken every idea of *security in their property,* and convince them, that under such a government they *have nothing they can call their own;* which can scarce fail of producing the *happiest consequences!*

X. Possibly, indeed, some of them might still comfort themselves, and say, "Though we have no property, we have yet *something* left that is valuable; we have constitutional *liberty,* both of person and of conscience. This King, these Lords, and these Commons, who it seems are too remote from us to know us, and feel for us, cannot take from us our *Habeas Corpus* right, or our right of trial *by a jury of our neighbours;* they cannot deprive us of the exercise of our religion, alter our ecclesiastical constitution, and compel us to be Papists, if they please, or Mahometans." To annihilate this comfort, begin by laws to perplex their commerce with infinite regulations, impossible to be remembered and observed; ordain seizures of their property for every failure; take away the trial of such property by Jury, and give it to arbitrary Judges of your own ap-

pointing, and of the lowest characters in the country, whose salaries and emoluments are to arise out of the duties or condemnations, and whose appointments are *during pleasure*. Then let there be a formal declaration of both Houses, that opposition to your edicts is *treason*, and that any person suspected of treason in the provinces may, according to some obsolete law, be seized and sent to the metrop-
10 olis of the empire for trial; and pass an act, that those there charged with certain other offences, shall be sent away in chains from their friends and country to be tried in the same manner for felony. Then erect a new Court of Inquisition among them, accompanied by an armed force, with instructions to transport all such suspected persons; to be ruined by the expence, if they bring over evidences to prove their innocence, or be found guilty and
20 hanged, if they cannot afford it. And, lest the people should think you cannot possibly go any farther, pass another solemn declaratory act, "that King, Lords, Commons had, hath, and of right ought to have, full power and authority to make statutes of sufficient force and validity to bind the unrepresented provinces IN ALL CASES WHATSOEVER." This will include *spiritual* with temporal, and, taken together, must operate wonderfully to your purpose; by
30 convincing them, that they are at present under a power something like that spoken of in the scriptures, which can not only *kill their bodies,* but *damn their souls* to all eternity, by compelling them, if it pleases, *to worship the Devil.*

XI. To make your taxes more odious, and more likely to procure resistance, send from the capital a board of officers to superintend the collection, composed of the most *indiscreet,*
40 *ill-bred,* and *insolent* you can find. Let these have large salaries out of the extorted revenue, and live in open, grating luxury upon the sweat and blood of the industrious; whom they are to worry continually with groundless and expensive prosecutions before the abovementioned arbitrary revenue Judges; *all at the cost of the party prosecuted,* tho' acquitted, because *the King is to pay no costs.* Let these men, *by your order,* be exempted from all the
50 common taxes and burthens of the province, though they and their property are protected by its laws. If any revenue officers are *suspected* of the least tenderness for the people, discard them. If others are justly complained of, protect and reward them. If any of the

under officers behave so as to provoke the people to drub them, promote those to better offices: this will encourage others to procure for themselves such profitable drubbings, by multiplying and enlarging such provocations, and *all will work towards the end you aim at.*

XII. Another way to make your tax odious, is to misapply the produce of it. If it was originally appropriated for the *defence* of the provinces, the better support of government, and the administration of justice, where it may be *necessary,* then apply none of it to that *defence,* but bestow it where it is *not necessary,* in augmented salaries or pensions to every governor, who had distinguished himself by his enmity to the people, and by calumniating them to their sovereign. This will make them pay it more unwillingly, and be more apt to quarrel with those that collect it and those that imposed it, who will quarrel again with them, and all shall contribute to your *main purpose,* of making them *weary of your government.*

XIII. If the people of any province have been accustomed to support their own Governors and Judges to satisfaction, you are to apprehend that such Governors and Judges may be thereby influenced to treat the people kindly, and to do them justice. This is another reason for applying part of that revenue in larger salaries to such Governors and Judges, given, as their commissions are, *during your pleasure* only; forbidding them to take any salaries from their provinces; that thus the people may no longer hope any kindness from their Governors, or (in Crown cases) any justice from their Judges. And, as the money thus misapplied in one province is extorted from all, probably *all will resent the misapplication.*

XIV. If the parliaments of your provinces should dare to claim rights, or complain of your administration, order them to be harassed with *repeated dissolutions.* If the same men are continually returned by new elections, adjourn their meetings to some country village, where they cannot be accommodated, and there keep them *during pleasure;* for this, you know, is your PREROGATIVE; and an excellent one it is, as you may manage it to promote discontents among the people, diminish their respect, and *increase their disaffection.*

XV. Convert the brave, honest officers of your *navy* into pimping tide-waiters and colony officers of the *customs*. Let those, who in time of war fought gallantly in defence of the commerce of their countrymen, in peace be taught to prey upon it. Let them learn to be corrupted by great and real smugglers; but (to show their diligence) scour with armed boats every bay, harbour, river, creek, cove, or nook throughout the coast of your colonies; stop and detain every coaster, every wood-boat, every fisherman, tumble their cargoes and even their ballast inside out and upside down; and, if a penn'orth of pins is found un-entered, let the whole be seized and confiscated. Thus shall the trade of your colonists suffer more from their friends in time of peace, than it did from their enemies in war. Then let these boats crews land upon every farm in their way, rob the orchards, steal the pigs and the poultry, and insult the inhabitants. If the injured and exasperated farmers, unable to procure other justice, should attack the aggressors, drub them, and burn their boats; you are to call this *high treason and rebellion*, order fleets and armies into their country, and threaten to carry all the offenders three thousand miles to be hanged, drawn, and quartered. *O! this will work admirably!*

XVI. If you are told of discontents in your colonies, never believe that they are general, or that you have given occasion for them; therefore do not think of applying any remedy, or of changing any offensive measure. Redress no grievance, lest they should be encouraged to demand the redress of some other grievance. Grant no request that is just and reasonable, lest they should make another that is unreasonable. Take all your informations of the state of the colonies from your Governors and officers in enmity with them. Encourage and reward these *leasing-makers;* secrete their lying accusations, lest they should be confuted; but act upon them as the clearest evidence; and believe nothing you hear from the friends of the people: suppose all *their* complaints to be invented and promoted by a few factious demagogues, whom if you could catch and hang, all would be quiet. Catch and hang a few of them accordingly; and the *blood of the Martyrs* shall *work miracles* in favour of your purpose.

XVII. If you see *rival nations* rejoicing at the prospect of your disunion with your provinces, and endeavouring to promote it; if they translate, publish, and applaud all the complaints of your discontented colonists, at the same time privately stimulating you to severer measures, let not that *alarm* or offend you. Why should it, since you all mean *the same thing?*

XVIII. If any colony should at their own charge erect a fortress to secure their port against the fleets of a foreign enemy, get your Governor to betray that fortress into your hands. Never think of paying what it cost the country, for that would look, at least, like some regard for justice; but turn it into a citadel to awe the inhabitants and curb their commerce. If they should have lodged in such fortress the very arms they bought and used to aid you in your conquests, seize them all; it will provoke like *ingratitude* added to *robbery*. One admirable effect of these operations will be, to discourage every other colony from erecting such defences, and so your enemies may more easily invade them; to the great disgrace of your government, and of course *the furtherance of your project.*

XIX. Send armies into their country under pretence of protecting the inhabitants; but, instead of garrisoning the forts on their frontiers with those troops, to prevent incursions, demolish those forts, and order the troops into the heart of the country, that the savages may be encouraged to attack the frontiers, and that the troops may be protected by the inhabitants. This will seem to proceed from your ill will or your ignorance, and contribute farther to produce and strengthen an opinion among them, *that you are no longer fit to govern them.*

XX. Lastly, invest the General of your army in the provinces, with great and unconstitutional powers, and free him from the controul of even your own Civil Governors. Let him have troops enow under his command, with all the fortresses in his possession; and who knows but (like some provincial Generals in the Roman empire, and encouraged by the universal discontent you have produced) he may take it into his head to set up for himself? If he should, and you have carefully practised these few *excellent rules* of mine, take my word for it, all the provinces will immediately join him; and you will that day (if you have not done it sooner) get rid of the trouble of governing them, and all the *plagues* attending their *commerce* and connection from henceforth and for ever.

Q. E. D.
1773

THOMAS PAINE

1737–1809

THOMAS PAINE came to Philadelphia in 1774, and, thanks to an introduction from Benjamin Franklin, became editor of the *Pennsylvania Magazine or American Museum*, which had been recently launched. On January 10, 1776, *Common Sense*, one of the most notable pamphlets evoked by the Revolution, appeared. Within three months over a hundred thousand copies had been circulated; and there is little doubt that it played an important part in enlisting for the patriot cause the support of many wavering souls, and of convincing as many more that conciliation was no longer possible, that monarchism was outmoded, and that independence was the only possible and desirable outcome. Paine enlisted in the ranks of the revolutionists and, to check discouragement and to aid in attracting volunteers to the American army, issued pamphlets periodically between 1776 and 1783, sixteen under the title *The Crisis*. After independence had been won Paine played a part in the French Revolution and in the literary warfare between advocates and foes of the natural rights philosophy and of deism.

The Writings of Thomas Paine, M. D. Conway, ed., 4 vols., New York, 1894–1906.
The Life and Works of Thomas Paine, Patriots Edition, 10 vols., New Rochelle, 1925.
The Complete Writings of Thomas Paine, 2 vols., Philip S. Foner, ed., New York, 1945.
M. D. Conway, *The Life of Thomas Paine*, 2 vols., New York, 1893.
Alfred O. Aldridge, *Man of Reason, the Life of Thomas Paine*, Phila., 1959.
H. H. Clark, "Toward a Reinterpretation of Thomas Paine," *American Literature*, V (May, 1933).

» » *From:* COMMON SENSE « «

* * * In the following pages I offer nothing more than simple facts, plain arguments, and common sense: and have no other preliminaries to settle with the reader, than that he will divest himself of prejudice and prepossession, and suffer his reason and his feelings to determine for themselves: that he will put on or rather that he will not put off the true character of a man, and generously enlarge his views beyond the present day.

Volumes have been written on the subject of the struggle between England and America. Men of all ranks have embarked in the controversy, from different motives, and with various designs; but all have been ineffectual, and the period of debate is closed. Arms as the last resource decide the contest; the appeal was the choice of the King, and the Continent has accepted the challenge.

It hath been reported of the late Mr. Pelham (who tho' an able minister was not without his faults) that on his being attacked in the House of Commons on the score that his measures were only of a temporary kind, replied, "*they will last my time.*" Should a thought so fatal and unmanly possess the Colonies in the present contest, the name of ancestors will be remembered by future generations with detestation.

The Sun never shined on a cause of greater worth. 'Tis not the affair of a City, a County, a Province, or a Kingdom; but of a Continent—of at least one eighth part of the habitable Globe. 'Tis not the concern of a day, a year, or an age; posterity are virtually involved in the contest, and will be more or less affected even to the end of time by the proceedings now. Now is the seed time of Continental union, faith, and honour. The least fracture now, will be like a name engraved with the point of a pin on the tender rind of a young oak; the wound will enlarge with the tree, and posterity read it in full grown characters.

By referring the matter from argument to arms, a new æra for politics is struck—a new method of thinking hath arisen. All plans, proposals, &c. prior to the 19th of April, *i.e.* to the commencement of hostilities, are like the almanacks of the last year; which tho' proper then, are superceded and useless now. Whatever was advanced by the advocates on either side of the question then, terminated in one and the same point, viz. a union with Great Britain; the only difference between the parties was the method of effecting it; the one proposing force the other friendship; but it hath so far happened that the first hath failed, and the second hath withdrawn her influence.

As much hath been said of the advantages of reconciliation, which like an agreeable dream, hath passed away and left us as we were, it is but right, that we should examine the contrary side of the argument, and enquire into some of the many material injuries which these Colonies sustain, and always will sustain, by being connected with and dependant on Great Britain. To examine that connection and dependance, on the principles of nature and common sense, to see what we have to trust to if separated, and what we are to expect if dependant.

I have heard it asserted by some, that as America hath flourished under her former connection with Great Britain, the same connection is necessary towards her future happiness, and will always have the same effect—Nothing can be more fallacious than this kind of argument:—we may as well assert that because a child has thrived upon milk, that it is never to have meat, or that the first twenty years of our lives is to become a precedent for the next twenty. But even this is admitting more than is true, for I answer, roundly, that America would have flourished as much, and probably much more had no European power taken any notice of her. The commerce by which she hath enriched herself are the necessaries of life, and will always have a market while eating is the custom of Europe.

But she has protected us say some. That she hath engrossed us is true, and defended the Continent at our expense as well as her own is admitted; and she would have defended Turkey from the same motive, viz. for the sake of trade and dominion.

Alas! we have been long led away by ancient prejudices and made large sacrifices to superstition. We have boasted the protection of Great Britain, without considering, that her motive was *interest* not *attachment;* and that she did not protect us from *our enemies on our account,* but from *her enemies* on *her own account,* from those who had no quarrel with us on any *other account,* and who will always be our enemies on the *same account.* Let Britain waive her pretensions to the continent, or the continent throw off the dependance, and we should be at peace with France and Spain were they at war with Britain. The miseries of Hanover ['s] last war ought to warn us against connections.

It hath lately been asserted in parliament, that the colonies have no relation to each other but through the Parent Country, *i.e.* that Pennsylvania and the Jerseys, and so on for the rest, are sister Colonies by the way of England; this is certainly a very round-about way of proving relationship, but it is the nearest and only true way of proving enemyship, if I may so call it. France and Spain never were, nor perhaps ever will be our enemies as *Americans,* but as our being the *subjects of Great Britain.*

But Britain is the parent country say some. Then the more shame upon her conduct. Even brutes do not devour their young, nor savages make war upon their families; wherefore, the assertion if true, turns to her reproach; but it happens not to be true, or only partly so, and the phrase, *parent* or *mother country,* hath been jesuitically adopted by the King and his parasites, with a low papistical design of gaining an unfair bias on the credulous weakness of our minds. Europe and not England is the parent country of America. This new World hath been the asylum for the persecuted lovers of civil and religious liberty from *every part* of Europe. Hither have they fled, not from the tender embraces of the mother, but from the cruelty of the monster; and it is so far true of England, that the same tyranny which drove the first emigrants from home, pursues their descendants still.

In this extensive quarter of the Globe, we forget the narrow limits of three hundred and sixty miles (the extent of England) and carry our friendship on a larger scale; we claim brotherhood with every European Christian, and triumph in the generosity of the sentiment.

It is pleasant to observe by what regular gradations we surmount the force of local prejudice as we enlarge our acquaintance with

the World. A man born in any town in England
divided into parishes, will naturally associate
most with his fellow parishioners (because
their interests in many cases will be common)
and distinguish him by the name of *neighbour:*
if he meet him but a few miles from home,
he drops the narrow idea of a street, and
salutes him by the name of *townsman:* if he
travel out of the country and meet him in any
10   other, he forgets the minor divisions of street
and town, and calls him *countryman,* i.e.
county-man: but if in their foreign excursions
they should associate in France, or any other
part of *Europe,* their local remembrance would
be enlarged into that of *Englishmen.* And by
a just parity of reasoning, all Europeans meeting in America, or any other quarter of the
Globe, are *countrymen;* for England, Holland,
Germany, or Sweden, when compared with
20   the whole, stand in the same places on the
larger scale, which the divisions of street, town,
and county do on the smaller ones; Distinctions
too limited for Continental minds. Not one
third of the inhabitants, even of this province,
[Pennsylvania], are of English descent. Wherefore, I reprobate the phrase of parent or mother
country applied to England only, as being
false, selfish, narrow and ungenerous.
But admitting, that we were all of English
30   descent, what does it amount to? Nothing.
Britain, being now an open enemy, extinguishes
every other name and title: and to say that
reconciliation is our duty, is truly farcical. The
first king of England, of the present line
(William the Conqueror) was a Frenchman,
and half the Peers of England are descendants
from the same country; wherefore, by the same
method of reasoning, England ought to be
governed by France.
40   Much hath been said of the united strength
of Britain and the Colonies, that in conjunction,
they might bid defiance to the world: But this
is mere presumption; the fate of war is uncertain, neither do the expressions mean any
thing; for this Continent would never suffer
itself to be drained of inhabitants, to support
the British Arms in either Asia, Africa, or Europe.
Besides, what have we to do with setting
50   the world at defiance? Our plan is commerce,
and that well attended to, will secure us the
peace and friendship of Europe because it is
the interest of all Europe to have America a
free port. Her trade will always be a protection,

and her barrenness of gold and silver secure
her from invaders.
I challenge the warmest advocate for reconciliation, to shew, a single advantage that this
Continent can reap by being connected with
Great Britain. I repeat the challenge, not a
single advantage is derived. Our corn will
fetch its price in any market in Europe, and
our imported goods must be paid for, buy them
where we will.
But the injuries and disadvantages which
we sustain by that connection, are without
number, and our duty to mankind at large, as
well as to ourselves, instruct us to renounce
the alliance: Because, any submission to, or
dependance on Great Britain, tends directly
to involve this Continent in European wars
and quarrels. [And sets us at variance with
nations, who would otherwise seek our friendship, and against whom, we have neither
anger nor complaint.] As Europe is our market
for trade, we ought to form no partial connection with any part of it. 'Tis the true interest
of America, to steer clear of European contentions, which she never can do, while by
her dependance on Britain, she is made the
make-weight in the scale of British politics.
Europe is too thickly planted with Kingdoms, to be long at peace, and whenever a
war breaks out between England and any
foreign power, the trade of America goes to
ruin, *because, of her connection with Britain.*
The next war may not turn out like the last,
and should it not, the advocates for reconciliation now, will be wishing for separation then,
because neutrality in that case, would be a
safer convoy than a man of war. Every thing
that is right or reasonable pleads for separation.
The blood of the slain, the weeping voice of
nature cries, 'TIS TIME TO PART. Even the
distance at which the Almighty hath placed
England and America, is a strong and natural
proof, that the authority of the one over the
other, was never the design of Heaven. The
time likewise at which the Continent was discovered, adds weight to the argument, and the
manner in which it was peopled encreases the
force of it.—The Reformation was preceded
by the discovery of America; as if the Almighty
graciously meant to open a sanctuary to the
persecuted in future years, when home should
afford neither friendship nor safety.
The authority of Great Britain over this
Continent, is a form of government which

sooner or later must have an end: and a serious mind can draw no true pleasure by looking forward, under the painful and positive conviction that what he calls "the present constitution," is merely temporary. As parents, we can have no joy, knowing that *this government* is not sufficiently lasting to ensure any thing which we may bequeath to posterity: And by a plain method of argument, as we are running the next generation into debt, we ought to do the work of it, otherwise we use them meanly and pitifully. In order to discover the line of our duty rightly, we should take our children in our hand, and fix our station a few years farther into life; that eminence will present a prospect, which a few present fears and prejudices conceal from our sight.

Though I would carefully avoid giving unnecessary offence, yet I am inclined to believe, that all those who espouse the doctrine of reconciliation, may be included within the following descriptions. Interested men, who are not to be trusted, weak men who *cannot see*, prejudiced men who *will not* see, and a certain set of moderate men who think better of the European world than it deserves; and this last class, by an ill-judged deliberation, will be the cause of more calamities to this continent, than all the other three.

It is the good fortune of many to live distant from the scene of present sorrow; the evil is not sufficiently brought to *their* doors to make *them* feel the precariousness with which all American property is possessed. But let our imaginations transport us a few moments to Boston; that seat of wretchedness will teach us wisdom, and instruct us for ever to renounce a power in whom we can have no trust. The inhabitants of that unfortunate city who but a few months ago were in ease and affluence, have now no other alternative than to stay and starve, or turn out to beg. Endangered by the fire of their friends if they continue within the city, and plundered by government if they leave it. In their present condition they are prisoners without the hope of redemption, and in a general attack for their relief, they would be exposed to the fury of both armies.

Men of passive tempers look somewhat lightly over the offences of Britain, and still hoping for the best, are apt to call out, *Come, come, we shall be friends again for all this.* But examine the passions and feelings of mankind: Bring the doctrine of reconciliation to the touchstone of nature, and then tell me, whether you can hereafter love, honour, and faithfully serve the power that hath carried fire and sword into your land? If you cannot do all these, then are you only deceiving yourselves, and by your delay bringing ruin upon posterity. Your future connection with Britain whom you can neither love nor honor, will be forced and unnatural, and being formed only on the plan of present convenience, will in a little time, fall into a relapse more wretched than the first. But if you say, you can still pass the violations over, then I ask, Hath your house been burnt? Hath your property been destroyed before your face? Are your wife and children destitute of a bed to lie on, or bread to live on? Have you lost a parent or a child by their hands, and yourself the ruined and wretched survivor? If you have not, then are you not a judge of those who have. But if you have, and still can shake hands with the murderers, then are you unworthy the name of husband, father, friend, or lover, and whatever may be your rank or title in life, you have the heart of a coward, and the spirit of a sycophant.

This is not inflaming or exaggerating matters, but trying them by those feelings and affections which nature justifies, and without which, we should be incapable of discharging the social duties of life, or enjoying the felicities of it. I mean not to exhibit horror for the purpose of provoking revenge, but to awaken us from fatal and unmanly slumbers, that we may pursue determinately some fixed object. 'Tis not in the power of England or of Europe to conquer America, if she doth not conquer herself by *delay* and *timidity*. The present winter is worth an age if rightly employed, but if lost or neglected, the whole continent will partake of the misfortune; and there is no punishment which that man doth not deserve, be he, who, or what, or where he will, that may be the means of sacrificing a season so precious and useful.

'Tis repugnant to reason, to the universal order of things, to all examples from former ages, to suppose, that this continent can long remain subject to any external power. The most sanguine in Britain doth not think so. The utmost stretch of human wisdom cannot at this time, compass a plan, short of separation, which can promise the continent even a year's security. Reconciliation is *now* a fallacious dream. Nature hath deserted the connection, and art cannot supply her place. For, as Milton wisely expresses "never can true reconcilement grow where wounds of deadly hate have pierced so deep."

Every quiet method for peace hath been ineffectual. Our prayers have been rejected with disdain; and hath tended to convince us that nothing flatters vanity or confirms obstinacy in Kings more than repeated petitioning —and nothing hath contributed more, than that very measure, to make the Kings of Europe absolute. Witness Denmark and Sweden. Wherefore, since nothing but blows will do, for God's sake let us come to a final separation, and not leave the next generation to be cutting throats under the violated unmeaning names of parent and child.

To say, they will never attempt it again is idle and visionary, we thought so at the repeal of the stamp-act, yet a year or two undeceived us; as well may we suppose that nations which have been once defeated will never renew the quarrel.

As to government matters 'tis not in the power of Britain to do this continent justice: The business of it will soon be too weighty and intricate to be managed with any tolerable degree of convenience, by a power so distant from us; and so very ignorant of us; for if they cannot conquer us, they cannot govern us. To be always running three or four thousand miles with a tale or a petition, waiting four or five months for an answer, which when obtained requires five or six more to explain it in, will in a few years be looked upon as folly and childishness—There was a time when it was proper, and there is a proper time for it to cease.

Small islands not capable of protecting themselves; are the proper objects for government to take under their care: but there is something very absurd, in supposing a Continent to be perpetually governed by an island. In no instance hath nature made the satellite larger than its primary planet, and as England and America with respect to each other reverse the common order of nature, it is evident that they belong to different systems. England to Europe: America to itself.

I am not induced by motives of pride, party or resentment to espouse the doctrine of separation and independence; I am clearly, positively, and conscientiously persuaded that 'tis the true interest of this continent to be so; that every thing short of that is mere patchwork, that it can afford no lasting felicity,—that it is leaving the sword to our children, and shrinking back at a time, when a little more, a little further, would have rendered this continent the glory of the earth.

As Britain hath not manifested the least inclination towards a compromise, we may be assured that no terms can be obtained worthy the acceptance of the continent, or any ways equal to the expence of blood and treasure we have been already put to.

The object contended for, ought always to bear some just proportion to the expence. The removal of North, or the whole detestable junto, is a matter unworthy the millions we have expended. A temporary stoppage of trade was an inconvenience, which would have sufficiently balanced the repeal of all the acts complained of, had such repeals been obtained; but if the whole Continent must take up arms, if every man must be a soldier, 'tis scarcely worth our while to fight against a contemptible ministry only. Dearly, dearly, do we pay for the repeal of the acts, if that is all we fight for; for in a just estimation 'tis as great a folly to pay a Bunker-hill price for law as for land. As I have always considered the independancy of this Continent, as an event which sooner or later must arrive, so from the late rapid progress of the Continent to maturity, the event could not be far off. Wherefore on the breaking out of hostilities, it was not worth the while to have disputed a matter, which time would have finally redressed, unless we meant to be in earnest: otherwise it is like wasting an estate on a suit at law, to regulate the trespasses of a tenant, whose lease is just expiring. No man was a warmer wisher for a reconciliation than myself, before the fatal 19th of April 1775, but the moment the event of that day was made known, I rejected the hardened, sullen-tempered Pharaoh of England for ever; and disdain the wretch, that with the pretended title of FATHER OF HIS PEOPLE can unfeelingly hear of their slaughter, and composedly sleep with their blood upon his soul.

But admitting that matters were now made up, what would be the event? I answer, the ruin of the Continent. And that for several reasons.

First.—The powers of governing still remaining in the hands of the king, he will have a negative over the whole legislation of this Continent: And as he hath shewn himself such an inveterate enemy to liberty, and discovered such a thirst for arbitrary power; is he, or is he not, a proper man to say to these Colonies, *You shall make no laws but what I please!*? And is there any inhabitant in America so ignorant, as not to know, that according to what is called the *present constitution,* that this Continent can make no laws but what the king gives leave to; and is there any man so unwise, as not to see, that (considering what has happened) he will suffer no laws to be made here, but such as suits his purpose? We may be as effectually enslaved by the want of laws in America, as by submitting to laws made for us in England. After matters are made up (as it is called) can there be any doubt, but the whole power of the crown will be exerted to keep this Continent as low and humble as possible? Instead of going forward, we shall go backward, or be perpetually quarrelling or ridiculously petitioning.—We are already greater than the King wishes us to be, and will he not hereafter endeavour to make us less? To bring the matter to one point, is the power who is jealous of our prosperity, a proper power to govern us? Whoever says *No* to this question is an *Independant* for independency means no more than whether we shall make our own laws, or, whether the King the greatest enemy this Continent hath, or can have, shall tell us, *there shall be no laws but such as I like.*

But the King you'll say, hath a negative in England; the people there can make no laws without his consent. In point of right and good order, there is something very ridiculous that a youth of twenty-one (which hath often happened) shall say to several millions of people older and wiser than himself, "I forbid this or that act of yours to be law." But in this place I decline this sort of reply, though I will never cease to expose the absurdity of it, and only answer that England being the King's residence, and America not so, makes quite another case. The King's negative here is ten times more dangerous and fatal than it can be in England, for there he will scarcely refuse his consent to a bill for putting England into as strong a state of defence as possible, and here he would never suffer such a bill to be passed.

America is only a secondary object in the system of British politics. England consults the good of this country no farther than it answers her own purpose. Wherefore her own interest leads her to suppress the growth of ours in every case which doth not promote her advantage, or in the least interferes with it. A pretty state we should soon be in, under such a second hand government, considering what has happened! Men do not change from enemies to friends by the alteration of a name: And in order to shew that reconciliation now is a dangerous doctrine, I affirm, *that it would be policy in the King at this time, to repeal the acts for the sake of reinstating himself in the government of the provinces;* In order that HE MAY ACCOMPLISH BY CRAFT AND SUBTLETY, IN THE LONG RUN, WHAT HE CANNOT DO BY FORCE AND VIOLENCE IN THE SHORT ONE. Reconciliation and ruin are nearly related.

Secondly.—That as even the best terms which we can expect to obtain, can amount to no more than a temporary expedient, or a kind of government by guardianship, which can last no longer than till the Colonies come of age, so the general face and state of things in the interim will be unsettled and unpromising: Emigrants of property will not choose to come to a country whose form of government hangs but by a thread, and who is every day tottering on the brink of commotion and disturbance; And numbers of the present inhabitants would lay hold of the interval to dispose of their effects, and quit the Continent.

But the most powerful of all arguments is, that nothing but independance, i.e. a continental form of government, can keep the peace of the Continent, and preserve it inviolate from civil wars. I dread the event of a reconciliation with Britain now, as it is more than probable, that it will be followed by a revolt some where or other, the consequences of which may be far more fatal than all the malice of Britain.

Thousands are already ruined by British barbarity; (thousands more will probably suffer the same fate;) Those men have other feelings than us who have nothing suffered. All they now possess is liberty, what they before enjoyed is sacrificed to its service, and having nothing more to lose, they disdain submission. Besides, the general temper of the Colonies towards a British government will be like that of a youth, who is nearly out of his time; they will care very little about her: And a government which cannot preserve the peace, is no government at all, and in that case we pay our money for nothing; and pray what is it that Britain can do, whose power will be wholly on paper, should a civil tumult break out the very day after reconciliation? I have heard some men say, many of whom I believe spoke without thinking, that they dreaded an independance, fearing that it would produce civil wars: It is but seldom that our first thoughts are truly correct, and that is the case here; for there are ten times more to dread from a patched up connection, than from independance. I make the sufferers case my own, and I protest, that were I driven from house and home, my property destroyed, and my circumstances ruined, that as a man sensible of injuries, I could never relish the doctrine of reconciliation, or consider myself bound thereby.

The Colonies hath manifested such a spirit of good order and obedience to continental government, as is sufficient to make every reasonable person easy and happy on that head. No man can assign the least pretence for his fears, on any other grounds, than such as are truly childish and ridiculous, viz., that one colony will be striving for superiority over another.

Where there are no distinctions, there can be no superiority; perfect equality affords no temptation. The Republics of Europe are all, (and we may say always) in peace. Holland and Switzerland, are without wars, foreign or domestic: Monarchical governments, it is true, are never long at rest; the crown itself is a temptation to enterprising ruffians at home; and that degree of pride and insolence ever attendant on regal authority, swells into a rupture with foreign powers in instances, where a republican government by being formed on more natural principles, would negociate the mistake.

If there is any true cause for fear respecting independance, it is because no plan is yet laid down. Men do not see their way out—Wherefore, as an opening into that business I offer the following hints; at the same time modestly affirming, that I have no other opinion of them myself, than that they may be the means of giving rise to something better. Could the straggling thoughts of individuals be collected, they would frequently form materials for wise and able men to improve into useful matter.

Let the assemblies be annual with a president only. The representation more equal. Their business wholly domestic, and subject to the authority of a Continental Congress.

Let each Colony be divided into six, eight or ten convenient districts, each district to send a proper number of Delegates to Congress, so that each Colony send at least thirty. The whole number in Congress will be at least 390. Each congress to sit and to choose a president by the following method. When the Delegates are met, let a Colony be taken from the whole thirteen Colonies by lot, after which let the Congress choose (by ballot) a president from out of the Delegates of that province. In the next Congress let a Colony be taken by lot from twelve only, omitting that Colony from which the president was taken in the former Congress, and so proceeding on till the whole thirteen shall have had their proper rotation. And in order that nothing may pass into a law but what is satisfactorily just, not less than three fifths of the Congress to be called a majority— He that will promote discord under a government so equally formed as this, would have joined Lucifer in his revolt.

But as there is a peculiar delicacy from whom, or in what manner this business must first arise, and as it seems most agreeable and consistent, that it should come from some intermediate body between the governed and the governors, that is, between the Congress and the People Let a CONTINENTAL CONFERENCE be held in the following manner, and for the following purpose,

A Committee of twenty six members of congress, viz. Two for each Colony. Two Members from each House of Assembly, or Provincial convention; and five Representatives of the people at large, to be chosen in the capital city or town of each Province, for, and in behalf of the whole Province, by as many qualified voters as shall think proper to attend from all parts of the Province for that purpose: or if more convenient, the Representatives may be chosen in two or three of the most populous parts thereof. In this CONFERENCE thus assembled, will be united the two grand principles of business, *knowledge* and *power*. The members of Congress, Assemblies, or Conventions, by having had experience in national concerns, will be able and useful counsellors, and the whole, being impowered by the people, will have a truly legal authority.

The conferring members being met, let their business be to frame a CONTINENTAL CHARTER, or Charter of the United Colonies; (answering, to what is called the Magna Charta of England) fixing the number and manner of choosing Members of Congress, Members of Assembly, with their date of sitting; and drawing the line of business and jurisdiction between them: Always remembering, that our strength and happiness is Continental, not Provincial. Securing freedom and property to all men, and above all things, the free exercise of religion, according to the dictates of conscience; with such other matter as is necessary for a charter to contain. Immediately after which, the said conference to dissolve, and the bodies which shall be chosen conformable to the said charter, to be the Legislators and Governors of this Continent, for the time being: Whose peace and happiness, may GOD preserve. AMEN.

Should any body of men be hereafter delegated for this or some similar purpose, I offer them the following extracts from that wise observer on Governments, Dragonetti. "The science" says he "of the Politician consists in fixing the true point of happiness and freedom. Those men would deserve the gratitude of ages, who should discover a mode of government that contained the greatest sum of individual happiness, with the least national expense."

But where, say some, is the King of America? I'll tell you, Friend, he reigns above, and doth not make havoc of mankind like the Royal Brute of Great Britain. Yet that we may not appear to be defective even in earthly honours, let a day be solemnly set apart for proclaiming the Charter; let it be brought forth placed on the Divine Law, the word of God; let a crown be placed thereon, by which the world may know, that so far as we approve of monarchy, that in America THE LAW IS KING. For as in absolute governments the King is law, so in free countries the law *ought* to be King; and there ought to be no other. But lest any ill use should afterwards arise, let the Crown at the conclusion of the ceremony be demolished, and scattered among the People whose right it is.

A government of our own is our natural right: and when a man seriously reflects on the precariousness of human affairs, he will become convinced, that it is infinitely wiser and safer, to form a constitution of our own, in a cool deliberate manner, while we have it in our power, than to trust such an interesting event to time and chance. If we omit it now, some Massanello may hereafter arise, who laying hold of popular disquietudes, may collect together the desperate and the discontented, and by assuming to themselves the powers of government, may sweep away the liberties of the Continent like a deluge. Should the government of America return again into the hands

of Britain, the tottering situation of things will be a temptation for some deseperate adventurer to try his fortune; and in such a case, what relief can Britain give? Ere she could hear the news, the fatal business might be done; and ourselves suffering like the wretched Britons under the oppression of the Conqueror. Ye that oppose independance now, ye know not what ye do: ye are opening a door to eternal tryanny, by keeping vacant the seat of 10 government. There are thousands, and tens of thousands, who would think it glorious to expel from the Continent, that barbarous and hellish power, which hath stirred up the Indians and the Negroes to destroy us; the cruelty hath a double guilt, it is dealing brutally by us, and treacherously by them.

To talk of friendship with those in whom our reason forbids us to have faith, and our affections wounded thro' a thousand pores instruct 20 us to detest, is madness and folly. Every day wears out the little remains of kindred between us and them, and can there be any reason to hope, that as the relationship expires, the affection will encrease, or that we shall agree better, when we have ten times more and greater concerns to quarrel over than ever?

Ye that tell us of harmony and reconciliation, can ye restore to us the time that is past? Can ye give to prostitution its former innocence? 30 Neither can ye reconcile Britain and America. The last cord now is broken, the people of England are presenting addresses against us. There are injuries which nature cannot forgive; she would cease to be nature if she did. As well can the lover forgive the ravisher of his mistress, as the Continent forgive the murders of Britain. The Almighty hath implanted in us these unextinguishable feelings for good and wise purposes. They are the guardians of his 40 image in our hearts. They distinguish us from the herd of common animals. The social compact would dissolve, and justice be extirpated from the earth, or have only a casual existence were we callous to the touches of affection. The robber and the murderer would often escape unpunished, did not the injuries which our tempers sustain, provoke us into justice.

O ye that love mankind! Ye that dare oppose not only the tyranny, but the tyrant, stand 50 forth! Every spot of the old world is over-run with oppression. Freedom hath been hunted round the globe. Asia and Africa have long expelled her.—Europe regards her like a stranger, and England hath given her warning to depart. O! receive the fugitive, and prepare in time an asylum for mankind. * * *

On these grounds I rest the matter. And as no offer hath yet been made to refute the doctrine contained in the former editions of this pamphlet, it is a negative proof that either the doctrine cannot be refuted, or that the party in favour of it are too numerous to be opposed. *Wherefore,* instead of gazing at each other, with suspicious or doubtful curiosity, let each of us hold out to his neighbour the hearty hand of friendship, and united in drawing a line, which, like an act of oblivion, shall bury in forgetfulness every former dissension. Let the names of whig and tory be extinct; and let none other be heard among us, than those of a *good citizen, an open and resolute friend,* and *a virtuous supporter of the* RIGHTS OF MANKIND, and of the FREE AND INDEPENDENT STATES OF AMERICA. 1776

PATRICK HENRY

1736–1799

AN UPCOUNTRY Virginia lawyer, Patrick Henry espoused the American patriotic cause during the Stamp Act discussion by offering, in the House of Burgesses, resolutions condemning the act and by declaring, in a speech destined to become famous: "Caesar had his Brutus; Charles the First, his Cromwell; and George the Third—may profit by their example." On March 23, 1775, before the Virginia Convention of Delegates, Henry made another patriotic address which William Wirt later reconstructed in his *Sketches of the Life and Character of Patrick Henry* (1817). Popularized in schoolreaders, Henry's reputed oration so enshrined him in the hearts of the people that he became a folk-hero. His contribution to the struggle for freedom, if exaggerated in the popular mind of the nineteenth century, was nevertheless real.

W. W. Henry, *Patrick Henry: Life, Correspondence and Speeches,* 3 vols., New York, 1891.
Jacob Axelrad, *Patrick Henry, the Voice of Freedom,* New York, 1947.
Robert D. Meade, *Patrick Henry: Patriot in the Making,* Phila., 1957.

» » SPEECH IN THE VIRGINIA CONVENTION OF DELEGATES « «

MARCH 23, 1775

No man thinks more highly than I do of the patriotism, as well as abilities, of the very worthy gentlemen who have just addressed the house. But different men often see the same subjects in different lights; and, therefore, I hope it will not be thought disrespectful to those gentlemen, if, entertaining as I do, opinions of a character very opposite to theirs, I shall speak forth my sentiments freely, and without reserve. This is no time for ceremony. The question before the house is one of awful moment to this country. For my own part, I consider it as nothing less than a question of freedom or slavery. And in proportion to the magnitude of the subject, ought to be the freedom of the debate. It is only in this way that we can hope to arrive at truth, and fulfil the great responsibility which we hold to God and our country. Should I keep back my opinions at such a time, through fear of giving offence, I should consider myself as guilty of treason towards my country, and of an act of disloyalty toward the majesty of Heaven, which I revere above all earthly kings.

Mr. President, it is natural to man to indulge in the illusions of hope. We are apt to shut our eyes against a painful truth and listen to the song of that syren, till she transforms us into beasts. Is this the part of wise men, engaged in a great and arduous struggle for liberty? Are we disposed to be of the number of those, who having eyes, see not, and having ears, hear not, the things which so nearly concern their temporal salvation? For my part, whatever anguish of spirit it may cost, I am willing to know the whole truth; to know the worst, and to provide for it.

I have but one lamp by which my feet are guided; and that is the lamp of experience. I know of no way of judging of the future but by the past. And judging by the past, I wish to know what there has been in the conduct of the British ministry for the last ten years, to justify those hopes with which gentlemen have been pleased to solace themselves and the house? Is it that insidious smile with which our petition has been lately received? Trust it not, sir; it will prove a snare to your feet. Suffer not yourselves to be betrayed with a kiss. Ask yourselves how this gracious reception of our petition comports with those warlike preparations which cover our waters and darken our land. Are fleets and armies necessary to a work of love and reconciliation? Have we shown ourselves so unwilling to be reconciled, that force must be called in to win back our love? Let us not deceive ourselves, sir. These are the implements of war and subjugation, the last arguments to which kings resort.

I ask gentlemen, sir, what means this martial array, if its purpose be not to force us to submission? Can gentlemen assign any other possible motive for it? Has Great Britain any enemy in this quarter of the world, to call for all this accumulation of navies and armies? No, sir, she has none. They are meant for us; they can be meant for no other. They are sent over to bind and rivet upon us those chains, which the British ministry have been so long forging. And what have we to oppose to them? Shall we try argument? Sir, we have been trying that for the last ten years. Have we any thing new to offer upon the subject? Nothing. We have held the subject up in every light of which it is capable; but it has been all in vain. Shall we resort to entreaty and humble supplication? What terms shall we find, which have not been already exhausted? Let us not, I beseech you, sir, deceive ourselves longer. Sir, we have done

every thing that could be done, to avert the storm which is now coming on. We have petitioned, we have remonstrated, we have supplicated, we have prostrated ourselves before the throne, and have implored its interposition to arrest the tyrannical hands of the ministry and parliament. Our petitions have been slighted; our remonstrances have produced additional violence and insult; our supplications have been disregarded; and we have been spurned, with contempt, from the foot of the throne. In vain, after these things, may we indulge the fond hope of peace and reconciliation. There is no longer any room for hope. If we wish to be free, if we mean to preserve inviolate those inestimable privileges for which we have been so long contending, if we mean not basely to abandon the noble struggle in which we have been so long engaged, and which we have pledged ourselves never to abandon, until the glorious object of our contest shall be obtained, we must fight!—I repeat it, sir, we must fight!! An appeal to arms and to the God of Hosts is all that is left us!

They tell us, sir, that we are weak, unable to cope with so formidable an adversary. But when shall we be stronger? Will it be the next week or the next year? Will it be when we are totally disarmed, and when a British guard shall be stationed in every house? Shall we gather strength by irresolution and inaction? Shall we acquire the means of effectual resistance by lying supinely on our backs, and hugging the delusive phantom of hope, until our enemies shall have bound us hand and foot? Sir, we are not weak, if we make a proper use of those means which the God of nature hath placed in our power. Three millions of people, armed in the holy cause of liberty, and in such a country as that which we possess, are invincible by any force which our enemy can send against us. Besides, sir, we shall not fight our battles alone. There is a just God who presides over the destinies of nations, and who will raise up friends to fight our battles for us. The battle, sir, is not to the strong alone; it is to the vigilant, the active, the brave. Besides, sir, we have no election. If we were base enough to desire it, it is now too late to retire from the contest. There is no retreat, but in submission and slavery! Our chains are forged. Their clanking may be heard on the plains of Boston! The war is inevitable—and let it come!! I repeat it, sir, let it come!!!

It is in vain, sir, to extenuate the matter.

Gentlemen may cry, peace, peace—but there is no peace. The war is actually begun! The next gale that sweeps from the north will bring to our ears the clash of resounding arms! Our brethren are already in the field! Why stand we here idle? What is it that gentlemen wish? What would they have? Is life so dear, or peace so sweet, as to be purchased at the price of chains and slavery? Forbid it, Almighty God! I know not what course others may take; but as for me, give me liberty, or give me death!

1775

JONATHAN BOUCHER

1738–1804

JONATHAN BOUCHER, an Anglican parson and schoolmaster in Virginia and Maryland, represents the position of the Tory who could see only evil in the agitation of the rebels. "I endeavored in my sermons," wrote Boucher, "and in various pieces published in the Gazettes of the country, to check the immense mischief that was impending, but I endeavored in vain." So great was the popular opposition to Boucher that he preached some of his sermons, on the eve of the Revolution, with his manuscript in one hand and a loaded pistol in the other. The following sermon, an answer to that of a Philadelphia minister, the Reverend Mr. Duche, was preached in Queen Anne's parish, Maryland, in 1775. Forced to leave Maryland in 1775, he returned to his native land. In 1797 Boucher published a series of his anti-revolutionary sermons in a volume entitled *A View of the Causes and Consequences of the American-Revolution in Thirteen Discourses*. In opposing the arguments of the natural rights philosophy Boucher relied on the doctrine of passive obedience to divinely constituted authority.

Reminiscences of an American Loyalist, 1738–1789, Jonathan Bouchier, ed., Boston and New York, 1925.
"Letters of Rev. Jonathan Boucher," *Md. Hist. Mag.*, VI–IX (1912–1914).
Letters of Jonathan Boucher to George Washington, W. C. Ford, ed., Brooklyn, New York, 1899.

From: A VIEW OF THE CAUSES AND
» » CONSEQUENCES OF THE AMERICAN « «
REVOLUTION

DISCOURSE XII

ON CIVIL LIBERTY, PASSIVE OBE-DIENCE, AND NON-RESISTANCE

Stand fast, therefore, in the liberty wherewith Christ hath made us free.
Galatians, ch. v. ver. 1

. . . Hence it follows, that we are free, or otherwise, as we are governed by law, or by the mere arbitrary will, or wills, of any individual, or any number of individuals. And liberty is not the setting at nought and despising established laws—much less the making our own wills the rule of our own actions, or the actions of others—and not bearing (whilst yet we dictate to others) the being dictated to, even by the laws of the land; but it is the being governed by law, and by law only. The Greeks described Eleutheria, or Liberty, as the daughter of Jupiter, the supreme fountain of power and law. And the Romans, in like manner, always drew her with the pretor's wand, (the emblem of legal power and authority,) as well as with the cap. Their idea, no doubt, was, that liberty was the fair fruit of just authority, and that it consisted in men's being subjected to law. The more carefully well-devised restraints of law are enacted, and the more rigorously they are executed in any country, the greater degree of civil liberty does that country enjoy.

To pursue liberty, then, in a manner not warranted by law, whatever the pretence may be, is clearly to be hostile to liberty: and those persons who thus *promise you liberty,* are themselves *the servants of corruption.*

"Civil liberty (says an excellent writer) [1] is a severe and a restrained thing; implies, in the notion of it, authority, settled subordinations, subjection, and obedience; and is altogether as much hurt by too little of this kind, as by too much of it. And the love of liberty, when it is indeed the love of liberty, which carries us to withstand tyranny, will as much carry us to reverence authority, and to support it; for this most obvious reason, that one is as necessary to the being of liberty, as the other is destructive of it. And, therefore, the love of liberty which does not produce this effect, the love of liberty which is not a real principle of dutiful behaviour towards authority, is as hypocritical as the religion which is not productive of a good life. Licentiousness is, in truth, such an excess of liberty as is of the same nature with tyranny. For, what is the difference betwixt them, but that one is lawless power exercised under pretence of authority, or by persons vested with it; the other, lawless power exercised under pretence of liberty, or without any pretence at all? A people, then, must always be less free in proportion as they are more licentious; licentiousness being not only different from liberty, but directly contrary to it—a direct breach upon it."

True liberty, then, is a liberty to do every thing that is right, and the being restrained from doing any thing that is wrong. So far from our having a right to do every thing that we please, under a notion of liberty, liberty itself is limited and confined—but limited and confined only by laws which are at the same time both it's foundation and it's support. It can, however, hardly be necessary to inform you, that ideas and notions respecting liberty, very different from these, are daily suggested in the speeches and the writings of the times; and also that some opinions on the subject of government at large, which appear to me to be particularly loose and dangerous, are advanced in the sermon now under consideration; and that, therefore, you will acknowledge the propriety of my bestowing some farther notice on them both.

It is laid down in this sermon, as a settled

[1] Bishop Butler, in his sermon before the House of Lords, January 30, 1740. [Boucher's note.]

maxim, that the end of government is "the common good of mankind." I am not sure that the position itself is indisputable; but, if it were, it would by no means follow that, "this common good being matter of common feeling, government must therefore have been instituted by common consent." There is an appearance of logical accuracy and precision in this statement; but it is only an appearance. The position is vague and loose; and the assertion is made without an attempt to prove it. If by men's "common feelings" we are to understand that principle in the human mind called common sense, the assertion is either unmeaning and insignificant, or it is false. In no instance have mankind ever yet agreed as to what is, or is not, "the common good." A form or mode of government cannot be named, which these "common feelings" and "common consent," the sole arbiters, as it seems, of "common good," have not, at one time or another, set up and established, and again pulled down and reprobated. What one people in one age have concurred in establishing as the "common good," another in another age have voted to be mischievous and big with ruin. The premises, therefore, that "the common good is matter of common feeling," being false, the consequence drawn from it, viz. that government was instituted by "common consent," is of course equally false.

This popular notion, that government was originally formed by the consent or by a compact of the people, rests on, and is supported by, another similar notion, not less popular, nor better founded. This other notion is, that the whole human race is born equal; and that no man is naturally inferior, or, in any respect, subjected to another; and that he can be made subject to another only by his own consent. The position is equally ill-founded and false both in it's premises and conclusions. In hardly any sense that can be imagined is the position strictly true; but, as applied to the case under consideration, it is demonstrably not true. Man differs from man in every thing that can be supposed to lead to supremacy and subjection, *as one star differs from another star in glory.* It was the purpose of the Creator, that man should be social: but, without government, there can be no society; nor, without some relative inferiority and superiority, can there be any government. A musical instrument composed of chords, keys, or pipes, all perfectly equal in size and power, might as well be expected to produce harmony, as a society composed of members all perfectly equal to be productive of order and peace. If (according to the idea of the advocates of this chimerical scheme of equality) no man could rightfully *be compelled to come in* and be a member even of a government to be formed by a regular compact, but by his own individual consent; it clearly follows, from the same principles, that neither could he rightfully be made or compelled to submit to the ordinances of any government already formed, to which he has not individually or actually consented. On the principle of equality, neither his parents, nor even the vote of a majority of the society, (however virtuously and honourably that vote might be obtained,) can have any such authority over any man. Neither can it be maintained that acquiescence implies consent; because acquiescence may have been extorted from impotence or incapacity. Even an explicit consent can bind a man no longer than he chooses to be bound. The same principle of equality that exempts him from being governed without his own consent, clearly entitles him to recall and resume that consent whenever he sees fit; and he alone has a right to judge when and for what reasons it may be resumed.

Any attempt, therefore, to introduce this fantastic system into practice, would reduce the whole business of social life to the wearisome, confused, and useless talk of mankind's first expressing, and then withdrawing, their consent to an endless succession of schemes of government. Governments, though always forming, would never be completely formed: for, the majority to-day, might be the minority to-morrow; and, of course, that which is now fixed might and would be soon unfixed. Mr. Locke indeed says, that, "by consenting with others to make one body-politic under government, a man puts himself under an obligation to every one of that society to submit to the determination of the majority, and to be concluded by it." For the sake of the peace of society, it is undoubtedly reasonable and necessary that this should be the case: but, on the principles of the system now under consideration, before Mr. Locke or any of his followers can have authority to say that it actually is the case, it must be stated and proved that every individual man, on entering into the social compact, did first consent, and declare his consent, to be concluded and bound in all cases by the vote of the majority. In making such a

declaration, he would certainly consult both his interest and his duty; but at the same time he would also completely relinquish the principle of equality, and eventually subject himself to the possibility of being governed by ignorant and corrupt tyrants. Mr. Locke himself afterwards disproves his own position respecting this supposed obligation to submit to the "determination of the majority," when he argues that a right of resistance still exists in the governed: for, what is resistance but a recalling and resuming the consent heretofore supposed to have been given, and in fact refusing to submit to the "determination of the majority?" It does not clearly appear what Mr. Locke exactly meant by what he calls "the determination of the majority": but the only rational and practical public manner of declaring "the determination of the majority," is by law: the laws, therefore, in all countries, even in those that are despotically governed, are to be regarded as the declared "determination of a majority" of the members of that community; because, in such cases, even acquiescence only must be looked upon as equivalent to a declaration. A right of resistance, therefore, for which Mr. Locke contends, is incompatible with the duty of submitting to the determination of "the majority," for which he also contends.

It is indeed impossible to carry into effect any government which, even by compact, might be framed with this reserved right of resistance. Accordingly there is no record that any such government ever was so formed. If there had, it must have carried the seeds of it's decay in it's very constitution. For, as those men who make a government (certain that they have the power) can have no hesitation to vote that they also have the right to unmake it; and as the people, in all circumstances, but more especially when trained to make and unmake governments, are at least as well disposed to do the latter as the former, it is morally impossible that there should be any thing like permanency or stability in a government so formed. Such a system, therefore, can produce only perpetual dissensions and contests, and bring back mankind to a supposed state of nature; arming every man's hand, like Ishmael's, against every man, and rendering the world an *aceldama*, or field of blood.—Such theories of government seem to give something like plausibility to the notions of those other modern theorists, who regard all governments as invasions of the natural rights of men, usurpations, and tyranny. On this principle it would follow, and could not be denied, that government was indeed fundamentally, as our people are sedulously taught it still is, an evil. Yet it is to government that mankind owe their having, after their fall and corruption, been again reclaimed, from a state of barbarity and war, to the conveniency and the safety of the social state: and it is by means of government that society is still preserved, the weak protected from the strong, and the artless and innocent from the wrongs of proud oppressors. It was not without reason, then, that Mr. Locke asserted, that a greater wrong cannot be done to prince and people, than is done by "propagating wrong notions concerning government."

Ashamed of this shallow device, that government originated in superior strength and violence, another party, hardly less numerous, and certainly not less confident than the former, fondly deduce it from some imaginary compact. They suppose that, in the decline perhaps of some fabulous age of gold, a multitude of human beings, who, like their brother beasts, had hitherto ranged the forests, *without guide, overseer, or ruler*—at length convinced, by experience, of the impossibility of living either alone with any degree of comfort or security, or together in society, with peace, without government, had (in some lucid interval of reason and reflection) met together in a spacious plain, for the express purpose of framing a government. Their first step must have been the transferring to some individual, or individuals, some of those rights which are supposed to have been inherent in each of them: of these it is essential to government that they should be divested; yet can they not, rightfully, be deprived of them, otherwise than by their own consent. Now, admitting this whole supposed assembly to be perfectly equal as to rights, yet all agreed as to the propriety of ceding some of them, on what principles of equality is it possible to determine, either who shall relinquish such a portion of his rights, or who shall be invested with such new accessory rights? By asking another to exercise jurisdiction over me, I clearly confess that I do not think myself his equal; and by his consenting to exercise such authority, he also virtually declares that he thinks himself superior. And, to establish this hypothesis of a compact, it is farther necessary that the whole assembly should concur in this opinion—a concurrence so extremely improbable, that it seems to be

barely possible. The supposition that a large concourse of people, in a rude and imperfect state of society, or even a majority of them, should thus rationally and unanimously concur to subject themselves to various restrictions, many of them irksome and unpleasant, and all of them contrary to all their former habits, is to suppose them possessed of more wisdom and virtue than multitudes in any instance in real life have ever shewn. Another difficulty respecting this notion may yet be mentioned. Without a power of life and death, it will, I presume, be readily admitted that there could be no government. Now, admitting it to be possible that men, from motives of public and private utility, may be induced to submit to many heavy penalties, and even to corporal punishment, inflicted by the sentence of the law, there is an insuperable objection to any man's giving to another a power over his life: this objection is, that no man has such a power over his own life; and cannot therefore transfer to another, or to others, be they few or many, on any conditions, a right which he does not himself possess. He only who gave life, can give the authority to take it away: and as such authority is essential to government, this argument seems very decidedly to prove, not only that government did not originate in any compact, but also that it was originally from God.

This visionary idea of a government by compact was, as Filmer says, "first hatched in the schools; and hath, ever since, been fostered by Papists, for good divinity." For some time, the world seemed to regard it merely as another Utopian fiction; and it was long confined to the disciples of Rome and Geneva, who, agreeing in nothing else, yet agreed in this. In an evil hour it gained admittance into the Church of England; being first patronized by her during the civil wars, by "a few miscreants, who were as far from being true Protestants, as true Subjects." Mankind have listened, and continue to listen to it with a predilection and partiality, just as they do to various other exceptionable notions, which are unfavourable to true religion and sound morals; merely from imagining, that if such doctrines be true, they shall no longer be subjected to sundry restraints, which, however wholsome and proper, are too often unpalatable to our corrupt natures. What we wish to be true, we easily persuade ourselves is true. On this principle it is not difficult to account for our thus eagerly following these *ignes fatui* of our own fancies or "feelings," rather than the sober steady light of the word of God; which (in this instance as well as in others) lies under this single disadvantage, that it proposes no doctrines which may conciliate our regards by flattering our pride.

If, however, we can even resolve no longer to be bewildered by these vain imaginations, still the interesting question presses on us, "Where," in the words of Plato, "where shall we look for the origin of government?" Let Plato himself instruct us. Taught then by this oracle of Heathen wisdom, "we will take our stations there, where the prospect of it is most easy and most beautiful." Of all the theories respecting the origin of government with which the world has ever been either puzzled, amused, or instructed, that of the Scriptures alone is accompanied by no insuperable difficulties.

It was not to be expected from an all-wise and all-merciful Creator, that, having formed creatures capable of order and rule, he should turn them loose into the world under the guidance only of their own unruly wills; that, like so many wild beasts, they might tear and worry one another in their mad contests for preeminence. His purpose from the first, no doubt, was, that men should *live godly and sober lives.* But, such is the sad estate of our corrupted nature, that, ever since the Fall, we have been averse from good, and prone to evil. We are, indeed, so disorderly and unmanageable, that, were it not for the restraints and the terrors of human laws, it would not be possible for us to dwell together. But as men were clearly formed for society, and to dwell together, which yet they cannot do without the restraints of law, or, in other words, without government, it is fair to infer that government was also the original intention of God, who never decrees the end, without also decreeing the means. Accordingly, when man was made, his Maker did not turn him adrift into a shoreless ocean, without star or compass to steer by. As soon as there were some to be governed, there were also some to govern: and the first man, by virtue of that paternal claim, on which all subsequent governments have been founded, was first invested with the power of government. For, we are not to judge of the Scriptures of God, as we do of some other writings; and so, where no express precept appears, hastily to conclude that none was given. On the contrary, in commenting on the Scriptures, we are frequently called upon to find out the precept from the practice. Taking this rule, then, for our direction in the present instance, we find, that, copying after the fair model of heaven itself, wherein there was government even among the angels, the families of the earth were subjected to rulers, at first set over them by God: *for, there is no power, but of God; the powers that be are ordained of God.* The first father was the first king: and if (according to the rule just laid down) the law may be inferred from the practice, it was thus that all government originated; and monarchy is it's most ancient form.

Little risque is run in affirming, that this idea of the patriarchal origin of government has not only the most and best authority of history, as far as history goes, to support it; but that it is also by far the most natural, most consistent, and most rational idea. Had it pleased God not to have interfered at all in the case, neither directly nor indirectly, and to have left mankind to be guided only by their own uninfluenced judgments, they would naturally have been led to the government of a community, or a nation, from the natural and obvious precedent of the government of a family. In confirmation of this opinion, it may be observed, that the patriarchal scheme is that which always has prevailed, and still does prevail, among the most enlightened people: and (what is no slight attestation of it's truth) it has also prevailed, and still does prevail, among the most unenlightened. According to Vitruvius, the rudiments of architecture are to be found in the cottage: and, according to Aristotle, the first principles of government are to be traced to private families. Kingdoms and empires are but so many larger families: and hence it is that our Church, in perfect conformity with the doctrine here inculcated, in her explication of the fifth commandment, from the obedience due to parents, wisely derives the congenial duty of *honouring the king and all that are put in authority under him.*

. . .

Even where the Scriptures are silent, they instruct: for, in general, whatever is not therein commanded, is actually forbidden. Now, it is certain that mankind are no where in the Scriptures commanded to resist authority; and no less certain that, either by direct injunction, or clear implication, they are commanded to *be subject to the higher powers:* and this subjection is said to be enjoined, not for our sakes only, but also *for the Lord's sake.* The glory of God is much concerned, that there should be good government in the world: it is, therefore, the uniform doctrine of the Scriptures, that it is under the deputation and authority of God alone that *kings reign and princes decree justice.* Kings and princes (which are only other words for supreme magistrates) were doubtless created and appointed, not so much for their own sakes, as for the sake of the people committed to their charge: yet are they not, therefore, the creatures of the people. So far from deriving their authority from any supposed consent or suffrage of men, they receive it from God, the source and original of all power. However obsolete, therefore, either the sentiment or the language may now be deemed, it is with the most perfect propriety that the supreme magistrate, whether consisting of one or of many, and whether denominated an emperor, a king, an archon, a dictator, a consul, or a senate, is to be regarded and venerated as the viceregent of God.

. . .

Having, then, my brethren, thus long been *tossed to and fro* in a wearisome circle of *uncertain traditions,* or in speculations and projects still more uncertain, concerning government, what better can you do than, following the Apostle's advice, *to submit yourselves to* *every ordinance of man, for the Lord's sake;* *whether it be to the King as supreme, or unto* *GOVERNORS, as unto them that are SENT* *by him for the punishment of evil-doers, and for* *the praise of them that do well? For, so is the* *will of God, that with well-doing ye may put* *to silence the ignorance of foolish men; as free,* *and not using your liberty for a cloke of maliciousness, but as the servants of God. Honour* *all men: love the brotherhood: fear God: honour the king.*   (1775)   1797

» » *The Rise of Americanism* « «

1783-1825

» » « «

THE AMERICAN STAR

Come, strike the bold anthems, the war-dogs are howling,
Already they eagerly snuff up their prey;
The red cloud of war o'er our forests is scowling,
Soft peace spreads her wings, and flies weeping away;
The infants, affrighted, cling close to their mothers;
The youths grasp their swords—for the combat prepare;
While beauty weeps fathers and lovers and brothers,
Who rush to display the American Star.

Come, blow the shrill bugle, the loud drum awaken,
The dread rifle seize, let the cannon deep roar;
No heart with pale fear or faint doubtings be shaken,
No slave's hostile foot leave a print on our shore.
Shall mothers, wives, daughters and sisters left weeping,
Insulted by ruffians be dragg'd to despair?
Oh, no!—from the hills the proud eagle comes sweeping,
And waves to the brave the American Star.

The spirits of Washington, Warren, Montgomery,
Look down from the clouds with bright aspect serene;
Come, Soldiers, a tear, and a toast to their memory;
Rejoicing, they'll see us as they once have been.
To us the high boon by the gods have [sic] been granted,
To spread the glad tidings of liberty far;
Let millions invade us, we'll meet them undaunted,
And conquer or die by the American Star.

Your hands then, dear comrades, round liberty's altar,
United; we swear by the souls of the brave,
Not one from the strong resolution shall falter,
To live independent, or sink in the grave.
Then freemen, file up! lo, the blood banners flying,
The high bird of liberty screams in the air,
Beneath her, oppression and tyranny dying—
Success to the beaming American Star.

Apparently this was the most popular war song during the War of 1812, though it has been found in the *Comic Songster* of 1809 and probably first appeared earlier than that. The words were written by the "Hibernian Bard," John M'Creery of Petersburg, Virginia. The tune is that of "The Wounded Hussar."

» »   « «

THE STAR-SPANGLED BANNER

O say, can you see, by the dawn's early light,
    What so proudly we hailed at the twilight's last gleaming—
Whose broad stripes and bright stars, through the clouds of the
    fight,
    O'er the ramparts we watched were so gallantly streaming!
And the rocket's red glare, the bombs bursting in air,
Gave proof through the night that our flag was still there;
O! say, does the star-spangled banner yet wave
O'er the land of the free, and the home of the brave?

On that shore dimly seen through the mists of the deep,
    Where the foe's haughty host in dread silence reposes,
What is that which the breeze, o'er the towering steep,
    As it fitfully blows, now conceals, now discloses?
Now it catches the gleam of the morning's first beam,
In full glory reflected now shines on the stream;
'Tis the star-spangled banner; O long may it wave
O'er the land of the free, and the home of the brave!

And where is that band who so vauntingly swore
    That the havoc of war and the battle's confusion
A home and a country should leave us no more?
    Their blood has washed out their foul footsteps' pollution.
No refuge could save the hireling and slave
From the terror of flight, or the gloom of the grave;
And the star-spangled banner in triumph doth wave.
O'er the land of the free, and the home of the brave.

O! thus be it ever, when freemen shall stand
    Between their loved homes and the war's desolation!
Blest with victory and peace, may the heav'n-rescued land
    Praise the power that hath made and preserved us a nation.
Then conquer we must, when our cause it is just,
And this be our motto,—"In God is our trust":
And the star-spangled banner in triumph shall wave
O'er the land of the free, and the home of the brave.

    During the bombardment of Fort McHenry by the British on the
night of September 13, 1814, Francis Scott Key (1779–1843), a Washington lawyer, was detained on a vessel in Baltimore harbor. When he
saw the American flag still flying over the fort at dawn, he was moved
to write this song. It was sung to the tune "To Anacreon in Heaven,"
an English drinking song of the day.

» » « «

The Rise of Americanism

THE LATE TORIES who elected to stay in the recently established republic found it to their advantage to adjust themselves as best they might to the new order which England recognized in 1783. But some among them, and not a few conservatives who achieved maturity in the years after independence, continued, sometimes for material and sometimes for sentimental reasons (often, of course, for both) to give heart and mind to the mother country which they so deeply admired. Yet the most lively issue in the newly established republic was not Anglophilism versus Americanism. Nor was it, in spite of the enthusiasm many liberals felt for the principles of the French Revolution, Jacobinism versus Americanism. The leading issue, rather, concerned the true nature of the Americanism to which the great bulk of citizenry subscribed. For notwithstanding the cleavages in American society and thought which resulted from class, state, and regional conflicts of interest, the struggle for independence, the campaign for a stronger central government, and the second war with England all greatly enhanced a pattern of ideas and feeling that may rightly be called Americanism.

On the cultural level, although there were, to be sure, marked differences, it was relatively easier for patriots of whatever economic and political convictions to join hands in demanding the encouragement of a distinctively American culture. Some contended for a language well differentiated from the mother tongue. Others clamored for an indigenous literature, art, science, and education. These were at the same time to express and to promote American values and ideas rather than those of Europe. And American values and ideas included republicanism as against monarchism, the freedom and development of the human spirit, rather than its repression, and peace rather than war. Cultural nationalism further tended to put a premium on the practical and the useful. Above all, it demanded that American writers and artists deal with American subjects. It is true that many patricians, in whose hands cultural leadership naturally lay, disparaged this crusade for Americanism in culture and insisted on the preservation of what they esteemed as the tried and the universal in the whole heritage of the past.

On the political and economic level the conflicting interpretations given to Americanism were more sharply defined. The commercial and financial class demanded a vigorous federal government which alone could promise relief from awkward state restrictions on trade and business, which alone could assist the land-promoter by repulsing the Indian who blocked the flow of settlement. Although the commercial class complained bitterly when British and French interfered with their shipping, it insisted that America should keep out of the Napoleonic war, that American interests required a policy of isolation and peace. When at length the country was involved in the maelstrom, the New England commercial class boycotted the war and in the name of Americanism strenuously opposed the movement for military conscription. But by an odd dialectic the class and sectional opposition to the War of 1812 carried with it the seeds of a new nationalism: the migration of commercial capital into manufacturing, which the closure of ports and seas necessitated, paved the way for internal improvements, for tariffs, for the expanding and tightly knit home market which was to be the most important economic factor in the development of American nationalism. To achieve that end the substantial capitalist class reverted to the early Federalist championship of a strong central government and to the doctrine of the powers implied in the Constitution for extensive federal operations.

On the other hand, the more democratic elements in the towns and the bulk of the farming and agrarian class interpreted Americanism, in the sphere of politics and economics, in very different terms. This group identified Americanism with individual freedom, the civil liberties, and a broad suffrage. These ends, in the minds of Jefferson and his followers, seemed best advanced, not by a strong centralized federal government, but by one of limited powers, one in which the states retained the larger share of sovereignty. Being largely agrarian, these Americans favored the extension of the national frontiers in the interest of agrarian dominance; and in the name of American geographical predestination the national domain was extended, not, as many hoped, through victory in the War of 1812, but by the purchase of the Floridas and Louisiana. Although the Jeffersonians identified war with the Europeanism which they despised, and although they genuinely experimented with peace experiments, they guided the country into and through the second war with England. If this war did not succeed in achieving the victories for the American principles of neutrality or for the conquest of the Canadas, it did greatly advance national self-consciousness by lessening the ties that bound us to England and by the dramatic exploits of American naval heroes.

Thus Americanism meant different things to different sections and classes, and conflicting interests were to continue to claim that their program was "American" and that of their rivals "un-American." But at the same time there was general agreement on the desirability of isolation from Europe's quarrels and on the separateness of the Western Hemisphere from the rest of the world. This doctrine, together with the ardent defenses of the American character against the charge that it was materialistic and lacking in originality, and the demand for an indigenous culture, was evidence that an Americanism transcending actual cleavages was emerging.

» »   « «

MICHEL-GUILLAUME JEAN DE CRÈVECŒUR
1735–1813

CRÈVECŒUR WAS a native of Caen, France. He explored, perhaps as a mapmaker, the borderlands of the Great Lakes and the Ohio, and served under Montcalm in the French and Indian Wars. His rovings led him in 1759 to New York, and in subsequent years he traveled in that and in neighboring colonies. He became a naturalized citizen, married an American, and settled down as a farmer in Orange County, New York, where, in spite of his Tory sympathies, he stayed until 1780. After the War he returned to New York, as French consul, and in 1790 returned again to his native land.

Crèvecœur's *Letters from an American Farmer* (1782) is marked by an astute understanding of the economy and character of late eighteenth-century America. A keen observer, his descriptions, written in a simple, charming prose, and his homespun and sagacious reflections, make his book a classic. His analysis of the effects of the mingling of the peoples on the making of the American character is, perhaps, unexcelled.

Letters from an American Farmer, London, 1782, W. P. Trent and Ludwig Lewisohn, eds., New York, 1904.
Sketches of Eighteenth Century America, H. L. Bourdin, R. H. Gabriel, and S. T. Williams, eds., New Haven, 1925.
J. P. Mitchell, *St. Jean de Crèvecœur*, New York, 1916.
H. C. Rice, *Le Cultivateur Americain; Etude sur l'œuvre de Saint John de Crèvecœur*, Paris, 1933.

» » *From:* LETTERS FROM AN AMERICAN FARMER « «

WHAT IS AN AMERICAN?

I wish I could be acquainted with the feelings and thoughts which must agitate the heart and present themselves to the mind of an enlightened Englishman, when he first lands on this continent. He must greatly rejoice, that he
10 lived at a time to see this fair country discovered and settled; he must necessarily feel a share of national pride, when he views the chain of settlements which embellishes these extended shores. When he says to himself, this is the work of my countrymen, who, when convulsed by factions, afflicted by a variety of miseries and wants, restless and impatient, took refuge here. They brought along with them their national genius, to which they principally
20 owe what liberty they enjoy, and what substance they possess. Here he sees the industry of his native country, displayed in a new manner, and traces in their works the embrios of all the arts, sciences, and ingenuity which flourish in Europe. Here he beholds fair cities, substantial villages, extensive fields, an immense country filled with decent houses, good roads, orchards, meadows, and bridges, where an hundred years ago all was wild, woody, and un-
20 cultivated!

What a train of pleasing ideas this fair spectacle must suggest! it is a prospect which must inspire a good citizen with the most heartfelt pleasure. The difficulty consists in the manner of viewing so extensive a scene. He is arrived on a new continent; a modern society offers itself to his contemplation, different from what he had hitherto seen. It is not composed, as in Europe, of great lords who possess every thing,
40 and of a herd of people who have nothing. Here are no aristocratical families, no courts, no kings, no bishops, no ecclesiastical dominion, no invisible power giving to a few a very visible one; no great manufacturers employing thousands, no great refinements of luxury. The rich and the poor are not so far removed from each other as they are in Europe.

Some few towns excepted, we are all tillers of the earth, from Nova Scotia to West Florida.
50 We are a people of cultivators, scattered over an immense territory, communicating with each other by means of good roads and navigable rivers, united by the silken bands of mild government, all respecting the laws without dreading their power, because they are equitable. We are all animated with the spirit of industry, which is unfettered, and unrestrained, because each person works for himself. If he travels through our rural districts, he views not the hostile castle, and the haughty mansion, contrasted with the clay-built hut and miserable cabbin, where cattle and men help to keep each other warm, and dwell in meanness, smoke, and indigence. A pleasing uniformity of decent competence appears throughout our habitations. The meanest of our log-houses is a dry and comfortable habitation. Lawyer or merchant are the fairest titles our towns afford; that of a farmer is the only appellation of the rural inhabitants of our country. It must take some time ere he can reconcile himself to our dictionary, which is but short in words of dignity, and names of honour. There, on a Sunday, he sees a congregation of respectable farmers and their wives, all clad in neat homespun, well mounted, or riding in their own humble waggons. There is not among them an esquire, saving the unlettered magistrate. There he sees a parson as simple as his flock, a farmer who does not riot on the labour of others. We have no princes, for whom we toil, starve, and bleed: we are the most perfect society now existing in the world. Here man is free as he ought to be; nor is this pleasing equality so transitory as many others are. Many ages will not see the shores of our great lakes replenished with inland nations, nor the unknown bounds of North America entirely peopled. Who can tell how far it extends? Who can tell the millions of men whom it will feed and contain? for no European foot has as yet travelled half the extent of this mighty continent!

The next wish of this traveller will be to know whence came all these people? they are a mixture of English, Scotch, Irish, French, Dutch, Germans, and Swedes. From this promiscuous breed, that race now called Americans have arisen. The eastern provinces must indeed be excepted, as being the unmixed descendants of Englishmen. I have heard many wish they had been more intermixed also: for my part, I am no wisher; and think it much better as it has happened. They exhibit a most conspicuous figure in this great and variegated picture; they too enter for a great share in the pleasing perspective displayed in these thirteen provinces. I know it is fashionable to reflect on them; but I respect them for what they have done; for the accuracy and wisdom with which they have settled their territory; for the decency of their manners; for their early love of letters; their ancient college, the first in this hemisphere; for their industry, which to me, who am but a farmer, is the criterion of every thing. There never was a people, situated as they are, who, with so ungrateful a soil, have done more in so short a time. Do you think that the monarchial ingredients which are more prevalent in other governments, have purged them from all foul stains? Their histories assert the contrary.

In this great American asylum, the poor of Europe have by some means met together, and in consequence of various causes; to what purpose should they ask one another, what countrymen they are? Alas, two thirds of them had no country. Can a wretch who wanders about, who works and starves, whose life is a continual scene of sore affliction or pinching penury; can that man call England or any other kingdom his country? A country that had no bread for him, whose fields procured him no harvest, who met with nothing but the frowns of the rich, the severity of the laws, with jails and punishments; who owned not a single foot of the extensive surface of this planet? No! urged by a variety of motives, here they came. Every thing has tended to regenerate them; new laws, a new mode of living, a new social system; here they are become men: in Europe they were as so many useless plants, wanting vegetative mould, and refreshing showers; they withered, and were mowed down by want, hunger, and war: but now, by the power of transplantation, like all other plants, they have taken root and flourished! Formerly they were not numbered in any civil list of their country, except in those of the poor; here they rank as citizens. By what invisible power has this surprizing metamorphosis been performed? By that of the laws and that of their industry. The laws, the indulgent laws, protect them as they arrive, stamping on them the symbol of adoption; they receive ample rewards for their labours; these accumulated rewards procure them lands; those lands confer on them the title of freemen; and to that title every benefit is affixed which

men can possibly require. This is the great operation daily performed by our laws. From whence proceed these laws? From our government. Whence that government? It is derived from the original genius and strong desire of the people, ratified and confirmed by government. This is the great chain which links us all, this is the picture which every province exhibits, Nova Scotia excepted. There the crown has done all; either there were no people who had genius, or it was not much attended to: the consequence is, that the province is very thinly inhabited indeed; the power of the crown, in conjunction with the musketos, has prevented men from settling there. Yet some part of it flourished once, and it contained a mild harmless set of people. But for the fault of a few leaders the whole were banished. The greatest political error the crown ever committed in America, was to cut off men from a country which wanted nothing but men.

What attachment can a poor European emigrant have for a country where he had nothing? The knowledge of the language, the love of a few kindred as poor as himself, were the only cords that tied him: his country is now that which gives him land, bread, protection, and consequence: *Ubi panis ibi patria*,[1] is the motto of all emigrants. What then is the American, this new man? He is either an European, or the descendant of an European; hence that strange mixture of blood, which you will find in no other country. I could point out to you a man, whose grandfather was an Englishman, whose wife was Dutch, whose son married a French woman, and whose present four sons have now four wives of different nations. *He* is an American, who, leaving behind him all his ancient prejudices and manners, receives new ones from the new mode of life he has embraced, the new government he obeys, and the new rank he holds. He becomes an American by being received in the broad lap of our great *Alma Mater.*

Here individuals of all nations are melted into a new race of men, whose labours and posterity will one day cause great change in the world. Americans are the western pilgrims, who are carrying along with them that great mass of arts, sciences, vigour, and industry, which began long since in the east; they will finish the great circle. The Americans were once scattered all over Europe; here they are incorporated into one of the finest systems of

---

[1] *Where my bread is earned, there is my country.*

population which has ever appeared, and which will hereafter become distinct by the power of the different climates they inhabit. The American ought, therefore, to love this country much better than that wherein either he or his forefathers were born. Here the rewards of his industry follow with equal steps the progress of his labour; his labour is founded on the basis of nature, *self-interest;* can it want a stronger
10 allurement? Wives and children, who before in vain demanded of him a morsel of bread, now, fat and frolicsome, gladly help their father to clear those fields whence exuberant crops are to arise to feed and to clothe them all; without any part being claimed, either by a despotic prince, a rich abbot, or a mighty lord. Here religion demands but little of him; a small voluntary salary to the minister, and gratitude to God; can he refuse these? The American is a
20 new man, who acts upon new principles; he must therefore entertain new ideas, and form new opinions. From involuntary idleness, servile dependance, penury, and useless labour, he has passed to toils of a very different nature, rewarded by ample subsistence.—This is an American.

North America is divided into many provinces, forming a large association, scattered along a coast 1,500 miles extent and about 200
30 wide. This society I would fain examine, at least such as it appears in the middle provinces; if it does not afford that variety of tinges and gradations which may be observed in Europe, we have colours peculiar to ourselves. For instance, it is natural to conceive that those who live near the sea, must be very different from those who live in the woods; the intermediate space will afford a separate and distinct class.

Men are like plants; the goodness and flavour
40 of the fruit proceed from the peculiar soil and exposition in which they grow. We are nothing but what we derive from the air we breathe, the climate we inhabit, the government we obey, the system of religion we profess, and the nature of our employment. Here you will find but few crimes; these have acquired as yet no root among us. I wish I were able to trace all my ideas; if my ignorance prevents me from describing them properly, I hope I shall be able
50 to delineate a few of the outlines, which are all I propose.

Those who live near the sea, feed more on fish than on flesh, and often encounter that boisterous element. This renders them more bold and enterprising; this leads them to neg-

lect the confined occupations of the land. They see and converse with a variety of people; their intercourse with mankind becomes extensive. The sea inspires them with a love of traffic, a desire of transporting produce from one place to another; leads them to a variety of resources, which supply the place of labour. Those who inhabit the middle settlements, by far the most numerous, must be very different; the simple cultivation of the earth purifies them; but the indulgences of the government, the soft remonstrances of religion, the rank of independent free-holders, must necessarily inspire them with sentiments, very little known in Europe among people of the same class. What do I say? Europe has no such class of man; the early knowledge they acquire, the early bargains they make, give them a great degree of sagacity. As freemen, they will be litigious; pride and obstinacy are often the cause of law suits; the nature of our laws and governments may be another. As citizens, it is easy to imagine, that they will carefully read the newspapers, enter into every political disquisition, freely blame or censure governors and others. As farmers, they will be careful and anxious to get as much as they can, because what they get is their own. As northern men, they will love the chearful cup. As christians, religion curbs them not in their opinions; the general indulgence leaves every one to think for himself in spiritual matters; the laws inspect our actions; our thoughts are left to God. Industry, good living, selfishness, litigiousness, country politics, the pride of freemen, religious indifference, are their characteristics. If you recede still farther from the sea, you will come into more modern settlements; they exhibit the same strong lineaments, in a ruder appearance. Religion seems to have still less influence, and their manners are less improved.

Now we arrive near the great woods, near the last inhabited districts; there men seem to be placed still farther beyond the reach of government, which in some measure leaves them to themselves. How can it pervade every corner? as they were driven there by misfortunes, necessity of beginnings, desire of acquiring large tracts of land, idleness, frequent want of economy, ancient debts; the reunion of such people does not afford a very pleasing spectacle. When discord, want of unity and friendship—when either drunkenness or idleness prevail in such remote districts—contention, inactivity, and wretchedness must ensue. There are not the same remedies to these evils as in a long established community. The few magistrates they have, are in general little better than the rest; they are often in a perfect state of war; that of man against man, sometimes decided by blows, sometimes by means of the law; that of man against every wild inhabitant of these venerable woods, of which they are come to dispossess them. There men appear to be no better than carnivorous animals of a superior rank, living on the flesh of wild animals when they can catch them; and when they are not able, they subsist on the grain.

He who would wish to see America in its proper light, and have a true idea of its feeble beginnings and barbarous rudiments, must visit our extended line of frontiers where the last settlers dwell, and where he may see the first labours of settlement, the mode of clearing the earth, in all their different appearances; where men are wholly left dependent on their native tempers, and on the spur of uncertain industry, which often fails, when not sanctified by the efficacy of a few moral rules. There, remote from the power of example, and check of shame, many families exhibit the most hideous parts of our society. They are a kind of forlorn hope, preceding by ten or twelve years the most respectable army of veterans which come after them. In that space, prosperity will polish some, vice and the law will drive off the rest, who uniting again with others like themselves will recede still farther; making room for more industrious people, who will finish their improvements, convert the log-house into a convenient habitation, and rejoicing that the first heavy labours are finished, will change in a few years that hitherto barbarous country into a fine, fertile, well regulated district.

Such is our progress, such is the march of the Europeans toward the interior parts of this continent. In all societies there are off-casts; this impure part serves as our precursors or pioneers; my father himself was one of that class; but he came upon honest principles, and was therefore one of the few who held fast; by good conduct and temperance, he transmitted to me his fair inheritance, when not above one in fourteen of his contemporaries had the same good fortune.

Forty years ago, this smiling country was thus inhabited; it is now purged, a general decency of manners prevails throughout; and such has been the fate of our best countries.

Exclusive of those general characteristics, each province has its own, founded on the government, climate, mode of husbandry, customs, and peculiarity of circumstances. Europeans submit insensibly to these great powers, and become in the course of a few generations, not only Americans in general, but either Pennsylvanians, Virginians, or provincials under some other name. Whoever traverses the continent, must easily observe those strong differences, which will grow more evident in time. The inhabitants of Canada, Massachusetts, the middle provinces, the southern ones will be as different as their climates; their only points of unity will be those of religion and language.

. . . Europe contains hardly any other distinctions but lords and tenants; this fair country alone is settled by freeholders, the possessors of the soil they cultivate, members of the government they obey, and the framers of their own laws, by means of their representatives. This is a thought which you have taught me to cherish; our distance from Europe, far from diminishing, rather adds to our usefulness and consequence as men and subjects. Had our forefathers remained there, they would only have crouded it, and perhaps prolonged those convulsions which had shook it so long. Every industrious European who transports himself here, may be compared to a sprout growing at the foot of a great tree; it enjoys and draws but a little portion of sap; wrench it from the parent roots, transplant it, and it will become a tree bearing fruit also. Colonists are therefore intitled to the consideration due to the most useful subjects; a hundred families barely existing in some parts of Scotland, will here in six years, cause an annual exportation of 10,000 bushels of wheat: 100 bushels being but a common quantity for an industrious family to sell, if they cultivate good land. It is here, then, that the idle may be employed, the useless become useful, and the poor become rich: but by riches I do not mean gold and silver; we have but little of those metals; I mean a better sort of wealth, cleared lands, cattle, good houses, good clothes, and an increase of people to enjoy them.

There is no wonder that this country has so many charms, and presents to Europeans so many temptations to remain in it. A traveller in Europe becomes a stranger as soon as he quits his own kingdom; but it is otherwise here. We know, properly speaking, no strangers; this is every person's country; the variety of our soils, situations, climates, governments, and

produce, hath something which must please every body. No sooner does an European arrive, no matter of what condition, than his eyes are opened upon the fair prospects; he hears his language spoke, he retraces many of his own country manners, he perpetually hears the names of families and towns with which he is acquainted; he sees happiness and prosperity in all places disseminated; he meets with hos-
10 pitality, kindness, and plenty every where: he beholds hardly any poor, he seldom hears of punishments and executions; and he wonders at the elegance of our towns, those miracles of industry and freedom. He cannot admire enough our rural districts, our convenient roads, good taverns, and our many accommodations; he involuntarily loves a country where every thing is so lovely. When in England, he was a mere Englishman; here he stands on a
20 larger portion of the globe, not less than its fourth part, and may see the productions of the north, in iron and naval stores; the provisions of Ireland, the grain of Egypt, the indigo, the rice of China. He does not find, as in Europe, a crouded society, where every place is over-stocked; he does not feel that perpetual collision of parties, that difficulty of beginning, that contention which oversets so many.
30 There is room for every body in America: has he any particular talent, or industry? he exerts it in order to procure a livelihood, and it succeeds. Is he a merchant? the avenues of trade are infinite; is he eminent in any respect? he will be employed and respected. Does he love a country life? pleasant farms present themselves; he may purchase what he wants, and thereby become an American farmer. Is he a labourer, sober and industrious; he need not
40 go many miles, nor receive many informations before he will be hired, well fed at the table of his employer, and paid four or five times more than he can get in Europe. Does he want uncultivated lands? thousands of acres present themselves, which he may purchase cheap. Whatever be his talents or inclinations, if they are moderate, he may satisfy them. I do not mean, that every one who comes will grow rich in a little time; no, but he may procure an
50 easy, decent maintenance, by his industry. Instead of starving, he will be fed; instead of being idle, he will have employment; and these are riches enough for such men as come over here. The rich stay in Europe; it is only

the middling and poor that emigrate. Would you wish to travel in independent idleness, from north to south, you will find easy access, and the most chearful reception at every house; society without ostentation, good cheer without pride, and every decent diversion which the country affords, with little expense. It is no wonder that the European who has lived here a few years, is desirous to remain; Europe with all its pomp, is not to be compared to this continent, for men of middle stations or labourers.

An European, when he first arrives, seems limited in his intentions, as well as in his views; but he very suddenly alters his scale; two hundred miles formerly appeared a very great distance; it is now but a trifle; he no sooner breathes our air than he forms schemes, and embarks in designs he never would have thought of in his own country. There the plenitude of society confines many useful ideas, and often extinguishes the most laudable schemes which here ripen into maturity. Thus Europeans become Americans.

But how is this accomplished in that croud of low, indigent people, who flock here every year from all parts of Europe? I will tell you; they no sooner arrive than they immediately feel the good effects of that plenty of provisions we possess: they fare on our best food, and are kindly entertained; their talents, character, and peculiar industry are immediately enquired into; they find countrymen every where disseminated, let them come from whatever part of Europe.

Let me select one as an epitome of the rest; he is hired, he goes to work, and works moderately; instead of being employed by a haughty person, he finds himself with his equal, placed at the substantial table of the farmer, or else at an inferior one as good; his wages are high, his bed is not like that bed of sorrow on which he used to lie: if he behaves with propriety, and is faithful, he is caressed, and becomes, as it were, a member of the family. He begins to feel the effects of a sort of resurrection; hitherto he had not lived, but simply vegetated; he now feels himself a man, because he is treated as such; the laws of his own country had overlooked him in his insignificancy; the laws of this cover him with their mantle. Judge what an alteration there must arise in the mind and thoughts of this man; he begins to forget his former servitude and dependence; his heart involuntarily swells and glows; this first swell inspires him with those new thoughts which constitute an American. What love can he entertain for a country where his existence was a burden to him! if he is a generous good man, the love of his new adoptive parent, will sink deep into his heart. He looks around, and sees many a prosperous person, who but a few years before was as poor as himself. This encourages him much; he begins to form some little scheme, the first, alas, he ever formed in his life. If he is wise, he thus spends two or three years, in which time he acquires knowledge, the use of tools, the modes of working the lands, felling trees, &c. This prepares the foundation of a good name, the most useful acquisition he can make. He is encouraged; he has gained friends; he is advised and directed; he feels bold; he purchases some land; he gives all the money he has brought over, as well as what he has earned, and trusts to the God of harvests for the discharge of the rest. His good name procures him credit; he is now possessed of the deed, conveying to him and his posterity the fee simple, and absolute property of two hundred acres of land, situated on such a river. What an epocha in this man's life! He is become a freeholder, from perhaps a German boor—he is now an American, a Pennsylvanian. He is naturalized; his name is enrolled with those of the other citizens of the province. Instead of being a vagrant, he has a place of residence; he is called the inhabitant of such a county, or of such a district, and for the first time in his life counts for something; for hitherto he had been a cypher. I only repeat what I have heard many say, and no wonder their hearts should glow, and be agitated with a multitude of feelings, not easy to describe. From nothing to start into being; from a servant to the rank of master; from being the slave of some despotic prince, to become a free man, invested with lands, to which every municipal blessing is annexed! What a change indeed! It is in consequence of that change, that he becomes an American.

This great metamorphosis has a double effect; it extinguishes all his European prejudices; he forgets that mechanism of subordination, that servility of disposition which poverty had taught him; and sometimes he is apt to forget it too much, often passing from one extreme to the other. If he is a good man, he forms

schemes of future prosperity; he proposes to educate his children better than he has been educated himself; he thinks of future modes of conduct, feels an ardour to labour he never felt before. Pride steps in, and leads him to every thing that the laws do not forbid: he respects them; with a heart-felt gratitude he looks toward that government from whose wisdom all his new felicity is derived, and under whose wings and protection he now lives. These reflexions constitute him the good man and the good subject.

Ye poor Europeans, ye, who sweat and work for the great—ye, who are obliged to give so many sheaves to the church, so many to your lords, so many to your government, and have hardly any left for yourselves—ye, who are held in less estimation than favourite hunters or useless lap-dogs—ye, who only breathe the air of nature, because it cannot be withheld from you; it is here that ye can conceive the possibility of those feelings I have been describing; it is here the laws of naturalization invite every one to partake of our great labours and felicity, to till unrented, untaxed lands!

Many, corrupted beyond the power of amendment, have brought with them all their vices, and, disregarding the advantages held out to them, have gone on in their former career of iniquity, until they have been overtaken and punished by our laws. It is not every emigrant who succeeds; no, it is only the sober, the honest, and industrious: happy those, to whom this transition has served as a powerful spur to labour, to prosperity, and to the good establishment of children, born in the days of their poverty: and who had no other portion to expect, but the rags of their parents, had it not been for their happy emigration. Others again, have been led astray by this enchanting scene; their new pride, instead of leading them to the fields, has kept them in idleness; the idea of possessing lands is all that satisfies them— though surrounded with fertility, they have mouldered away their time in inactivity, misinformed husbandry, and ineffectual endeavours. How much wiser, in general, the honest Germans than almost all other Europeans; they hire themselves to some of their wealthy landsmen, and in that apprenticeship learn every thing that is necessary. They attentively consider the prosperous industry of others, which imprints on their minds a strong desire of possessing the same advantages. This forcible idea never quits them; they launch forth, and by dint of sobriety, rigid parsimony, and the most persevering industry, they commonly succeed. Their astonishment at their first arrival from Germany is very great; it is to them a dream; the contrast must be very powerful indeed; they observe their countrymen flourishing in every place; they travel through whole counties where not a word of English is spoken; 10 and in the names and the language of the people they retrace Germany. They have been an useful acquisition to this continent, and to Pennsylvania in particular; to them it owes some share of its prosperity; to their mechanical knowledge and patience, it owes the finest mills in all America, the best teams of horses, and many other advantages. The recollection of their former poverty and slavery never quits them as long as they live.

20 The Scotch and the Irish might have lived in their own country perhaps as poor; but enjoying more civil advantages, the effects of their new situation do not strike them so forcibly, nor has it so lasting an effect. From whence the difference arises, I know not; but out of twelve families of emigrants of each country, generally seven Scotch will succeed, nine German, and four Irish. The Scotch are frugal and laborious; but their wives cannot 30 work so hard as the German women, who, on the contrary, vie with their husbands, and often share with them the most severe toils of the field, which they understand better. They have therefore nothing to struggle against, but the common casualties of nature. The Irish do not prosper so well; they love to drink and to quarrel; they are litigious, and soon take to the gun, which is the ruin of every thing; they seem, beside, to labour under a greater degree 40 of ignorance in husbandry than the others; perhaps it is that their industry had less scope, and was less exercised at home. I have heard many relate, how the land was parcelled out in that kingdom; their ancient conquest has been a great detriment to them, by over-setting their landed property. The lands, possessed by a few, are leased down *ad infinitum;* and the occupiers often pay five guineas an acre. The poor are worse lodged there than any where 50 else in Europe; their potatoes, which are easily

raised, are perhaps an inducement to laziness: their wages are too low, and their whiskey too cheap.

There is no tracing observations of this kind, without making at the same time very great allowances; as there are everywhere to be found a great many exceptions. The Irish themselves, from different parts of that kingdom, are very different. It is difficult to account for this surprising locality; one would think on so small an island all Irishmen must be alike; yet it is not so; they are different in their aptitude to, and in their love of labour.

The Scotch, on the contrary, are all industrious and saving; they want nothing more than a field to exert themselves in; and they are commonly sure of succeeding. The only difficulty they labour under is, that technical American knowledge, which requires some time to obtain; it is not easy for those who seldom saw a tree, to conceive how it is to be felled, cut up, and split into rails and posts.

. . . After a foreigner from any part of Europe is arrived, and become a citizen; let him devoutly listen to the voice of our great parent, which says to him, "Welcome to my shores, distressed European; bless the hour in which thou didst see my verdant fields, my fair navigable rivers, and my green mountains!—If thou wilt work, I have bread for thee; if thou wilt be honest, sober and industrious, I have greater rewards to confer on thee—ease and independence. I will give thee fields to feed and clothe thee; a comfortable fire-side to sit by, and tell thy children by what means thou hast prospered; and a decent bed to repose on. I shall endow thee, beside, with the immunities of a freeman. If thou wilt carefully educate thy children, teach them gratitude to God, and reverence to that government, that philanthropic government, which has collected here so many men and made them happy, I will also provide for thy progeny: and to every good man this ought to be the most holy, the most powerful, the most earnest wish he can possibly form, as well as the most consolatory prospect when he dies. Go thou, and work and till; thou shalt prosper, provided thou be just, grateful and industrious."   1793

DAVID RAMSAY

1749–1815

AFTER GRADUATING from the College of New Jersey and studying medicine at Philadelphia, Ramsay became a leading physician in Charleston and an ardent defender of the American cause during the Revolutionary struggle. He held several offices in South Carolina and represented his adopted state in the Continental Congress.

Ramsay's *History of the American Revolution* (1789) and *History of the Revolution of South Carolina* (1785) are marked by judicious patriotism and some firsthand knowledge of the events described. No one has more effectively evaluated the influence of the Revolution on the American mind than Ramsay in the following selection from the *History of the American Revolution*.

R. Y. Hayne, sketch of Dr. Ramsay in Ramsay's *History of the United States*, 3 vols., Philadelphia, 1816–1817, and in the *Universal History Americanized*, 9 vols., Philadelphia, 1819.

» » From: THE HISTORY OF THE AMERICAN « « REVOLUTION

APPENDIX NO. IV

[THE INFLUENCE OF THE REVOLUTION ON THE MINDS AND MORALS OF THE CITIZENS]

The American Revolution, on the one hand, brought forth great vices; but on the other hand, it called forth many virtues, and gave occasion for the display of abilities which, but for that event, would have been lost to the world. When the war began, the Americans were a mass of husbandmen, merchants, mechanics and fishermen; but the necessities of the country gave a spring to the active powers of the inhabitants, and set them on thinking, speaking and acting, in a line far beyond that to which they had been accustomed. The difference between nations is not so much owing to nature, as to education and circumstances. While the Americans were guided by the leading strings of the mother country, they had no scope nor encouragement for exertion. All the departments of government were established and executed for them, but not by them. In the years 1775 and 1776 the country, being suddenly thrown into a situation that needed the abilities of all its sons, these generally took their places, each according to the bent of his inclination. As they severally pursued their objects with ardor, a vast expansion of the human mind speedily followed. This displayed itself in a variety of ways. It was found that the talents for great stations did not differ in kind, but only in degree, from those which were necessary for the proper discharge of the ordinary business of civil society. In the bustle that was occasioned by the war, few instances could be produced of any persons who made a figure, or who rendered essential services, but from among those who had given specimens of similar talents in their respective professions. Those who from indolence or dissipation, had been of little service to the community in time of peace, were found equally unserviceable in war. A few young men were exceptions to this general rule. Some of these, who had indulged in youthful follies, broke off from their vicious courses, and on the pressing call of their country became useful servants of the public: but the great bulk of those, who were the active instruments of carrying on the revolution, were self-made, industrious men. These who by their own exertions, had established or laid a foundation for establishing personal independence, were most generally trusted, and most successfully employed in establishing that of their country. In these times of action, classical education was found of less service than good natural parts, guided by common sense and sound judgment.

. . .

The Americans knew but little of one another, previous to the revolution. Trade and business had brought the inhabitants of their
10 seaports acquainted with each other, but the bulk of the people in the interior country were unacquainted with their fellow citizens. A continental army, and Congress composed of men from all the States, by freely mixing together, were assimilated into one mass. Individuals of both, mingling with the citizens, disseminated principles of union among them. Local prejudices abated. By frequent collision asperities were worn off, and a foundation was laid for
20 the establishment of a nation, out of discordant materials. Intermarriages between men and women of different States were much more common than before the war, and became an additional cement to the union. Unreasonable jealouses had existed between the inhabitants of the eastern and of the southern States; but on becoming better acquainted with each other, these in a great measure subsided. A wiser policy prevailed. Men of liberal minds
30 led the way in discouraging local distinctions, and the great body of the people, as soon as reason got the better of prejudice, found that their best interests would be most effectually promoted by such practices and sentiments as were favourable to union. Religious bigotry had broken in upon the peace of various sects, before the American war. This was kept up by partial establishments, and by a dread that the church of England through the power of the
40 mother country, would be made to triumph over all other denominations. These apprehensions were done away by the revolution. The different sects, having nothing to fear from each other, dismissed all religious controversy. A proposal for introducing bishops into America before the war, had kindled a flame among the dissenters; but the revolution was no sooner accomplished, than a scheme for that purpose was perfected, with the consent and
50 approbation of all those sects who had previously opposed it. Pulpits which had formerly been shut to worthy men, because their heads had not been consecrated by the imposition of the hands of a Bishop or of a Presbytery, have since the establishment of independence, been reciprocally opened to each other, whensoever the public convenience required it. The world will soon see the result of an experiment in politics, and be able to determine whether the happiness of society is increased by religious establishments, or diminished by the want of them.

Though schools and colleges were generally shut up during the war, yet many of the arts and sciences were promoted by it. The Geography of the United States before the revolution was but little known; but the marches of armies, and the operations of war, gave birth to many geographical enquiries and discoveries, which otherwise would not have been made. A passionate fondness for studies of this kind, and the growing importance of the country, excited one of its sons, the Rev. Mr. Morse, to travel through every State of the Union, and amass a fund of topographical knowledge, far exceeding any thing heretofore communicated to the public. The necessities of the States led to the study of Tactics, Fortification, Gunnery, and a variety of other arts connected with war, and diffused a knowledge of them among a peaceable people, who would otherwise have had no inducement to study them.

The abilities of ingenious men were directed to make farther improvements in the art of destroying an enemy. Among these, David Bushnell of Connecticut invented a machine for submarine navigation, which was found to answer the purpose of rowing horizontally, at any given depth under water, and of rising or sinking at pleasure. To this was attached a magazine of powder, and the whole was contrived in such a manner, as to make it practicable to blow up vessels by machinery under them. Mr. Bushnell also contrived sundry other curious machines for the annoyance of British shipping; but from accident they only succeeded in part. He destroyed one vessel in charge of Commodore Symonds, and a second one near the shore of Long-Island.

Surgery was one of the arts which was promoted by the war. From the want of hospitals and other aids, the medical men of America, had few opportunities of perfecting themselves in this art, the thorough knowledge of which can only be acquired by practice and observation. The melancholy events of battles, gave the American students an opportunity of seeing, and learning more in one day, than they could have acquired in years of peace. It was in the hospitals of the United States, that Dr. Rush first discovered the method of curing the lock jaw by bark and wine, added to other invigorating remedies, which has since been adopted with success in Europe, as well as in the United States.

The science of government, has been more generally diffused among the Americans by means of the revolution. The policy of Great Britain, in throwing them out of her protection, induced a necessity of establishing independent constitutions. This led to reading and reasoning on the subject. The many errors that were at first committed by unexperienced statesmen, have been a practical comment on the folly of unbalanced constitutions, and injudicious laws. The discussions concerning the new constitution, gave birth to much reasoning on the subject of government, and particularly to a series of letters signed Publius, but really the work of Alexander Hamilton, in which much political knowledge and wisdom were displayed, and which will long remain a monument of the strength and acuteness of the human understanding in investigating truth.

When Great Britain first began her encroachments on the colonies, there were few natives of America who had distinguished themselves as speakers or writers, but the controversy between the two countries multiplied their number.

The stamp act, which was to have taken place in 1765, employed the pens and tongues of many of the colonists, and by repeated exercise improved their ability to serve their country. The duties imposed in 1767, called forth the pen of John Dickinson, who in a series of letters signed a Pennsylvania Farmer, may be said to have sown the seeds of the revolution. For being universally read by the colonists, they universally enlightened them on the dangerous consequences, likely to result from their being taxed by the parliament of Great Britain.

In establishing American independence, the pen and the press had merit equal to that of the sword. As the war was the people's war, and was carried on without funds, the exertions of the army would have been insufficient to effect the revolution, unless the great body of the people had been prepared for it, and also kept in a constant disposition to oppose Great Britain. To rouse and unite the inhabitants, and to persuade them to patience for several years, under present sufferings,

with the hope of obtaining remote advantages for their posterity, was a work of difficulty. This was effected in a great measure by the tongues and pens of the well informed citizens, and on it depended the success of military operations. . . .

The early attention which had been paid to literature in New-England, was also eminently conducive to the success of the Americans in resisting Great Britain. The university of Cambridge was founded as early as 1636, and Yale college in 1700. It has been computed, that in the year the Boston port act was passed, there were in the four eastern colonies, upwards of two thousand graduates of their colleges dispersed through their several towns, who by their knowledge and abilities, were able to influence and direct the great body of the people to a proper line of conduct, for opposing the encroachments of Great Britain on their liberties. The colleges to the southward of New-England, except that of William and Mary in Virginia, were but of modern date; but they had been of a standing sufficiently long, to have trained for public service, a considerable number of the youth of the country. The college of New-Jersey, which was incorporated about 28 years before the revolution, had in that time educated upwards of 300 persons, who, with a few exceptions, were active and useful friends of independence. From the influence which knowledge had in securing and preserving the liberties of America, the present generation may trace the wise policy of their fathers, in erecting schools and colleges. They may also learn that it is their duty to found more, and support all such institutions. Without the advantages derived from these lights of this new world, the United States would probably have fallen in their unequal contest with Great Britain. Union which was essential to the success of their resistance, could scarcely have taken place, in the measures adopted by an ignorant multitude. Much less could wisdom in council, unity in system, or perseverance in the prosecution of a long and self denying war, be expected from an uninformed people. It is a well known fact, that persons unfriendly to the revolution, were always most numerous in those parts of the United States, which had either never been illuminated, or but faintly warmed by the rays of science. The uninformed and the misinformed constituted a great proportion of those Americans, who preferred the leading strings of the Parent State, though encroaching on their liberties, to a government of their own countrymen and fellow citizens.

As literature had in the first instance favoured the revolution, so in its turn, the revolution promoted literature. The study of eloquence and of the Belles lettres, was more successfully prosecuted in America, after the disputes between Great Britain and her colonies began to be serious, than it ever had been before. The various orations, addresses, letters, dissertations and other literary performances which the war made necessary, called forth abilities where they were, and excited the rising generation to study arts, which brought with them their own reward. Many incidents afforded materials for the favourites of the muses, to display their talents. Even burlesquing royal proclamations by parodies and doggerel poetry, had great effects on the minds of the people. A celebrated historian has remarked, that the song of Lillibullero forwarded the revolution of 1688 in England. It may be truly affirmed, that similar productions produced similar effects in America. Francis Hopkinson rendered essential service to his country by turning the artillery of wit and ridicule on the enemy. Philip Freneau laboured successfully in the same way. Royal proclamations and other productions which issued from royal printing presses were by the help of a warm imagination, arrayed in such dresses as rendered them truly ridiculous. Trumbull with a vein of original Hudibrastic humour, diverted his countrymen so much with the follies of their enemies, that for a time they forgot the calamities of war. Humphries twined the literary with the military laurel, by superading the fame of an elegant poet, to that of an accomplished officer. Barlow increased the fame of his country and of the distinguished actors in the revolution, by the bold design of an epic poem ably executed, on the idea that Columbus foresaw in vision, the scenes that were to be transacted on the theatre of that new world, which he had discovered. Dwight struck out in the same line, and at an early period of life finished, an elegant work entitled the conquest of Canaan, on a plan which has rarely been attempted. The principles of their mother tongue, were first unfolded to the Americans since the revolution, by their countryman Webster. Pursuing an unbeaten track, he has made discoveries in the genius and construction of the English language,

which had escaped the researches of preceding philologists. These and a group of other literary characters have been brought into view by the revolution. It is remarkable, that of these, Connecticut has produced an unusual proportion. In that truly republican state, every thing conspires to adorn human nature with its highest honours.

From the later periods of the revolution till the present time, schools, colleges, societies and institutions for promoting literature, arts, manufactures, agriculture, and for extending human happiness, have been increased far beyond anything that ever took place before the declaration of independence. Every state in the union, has done more or less in this way, but Pennsylvania has done the most. The following institutions have been very lately founded in that state, and most of them in the time of the war or since the peace. An university in the city of Philadelphia; a college of physicians in the same place; Dickinson college at Carlisle; Franklin college at Lancaster; the Protestant Episcopal academy in Philadelphia; academies at York-town, at Germantown, at Pittsburgh and Washington; and an academy in Philadelphia for young ladies; societies for promoting political enquiries; for the medical relief of the poor, under the title of the Philadelphia Dispensary; for the promoting the abolition of slavery; and the relief of free negroes unlawfully held in bondage; for propagating the gospel among the Indians, under the direction of the United Brethren; for the encouragement of manufactures and the useful arts; for alleviating the miseries of prisons. Such have been some of the beneficial effects, which have resulted from that expansion of the human mind, which has been produced by the revolution, but these have not been without alloy.

To overset an established government unhinges many of those principles, which bind individuals to each other. A long time, and much prudence, will be necessary to reproduce a spirit of union and that reverence for government, without which society is a rope of sand. The right of the people to resist their rulers, when invading their liberties, forms the corner stone of the American republics. This principle, though just in itself, is not favourable to the tranquility of present establishments. The maxims and measures, which in the years 1774 and 1775 were successfully inculcated and adopted by American patriots, for oversetting the established government, will answer a similar purpose when recurrence is had to them by factious demagogues, for disturbing the freest governments that were ever devised.

War never fails to injure the morals of the people engaged in it. The American war, in particular, had an unhappy influence of this kind. Being begun without funds or regular establishments, it could not be carried on without violating private rights; and in its progress, it involved a necessity for breaking solemn promises, and plighted public faith. The failure of national justice, which was in some degree unavoidable, increased the difficulties of performing private engagements, and weakened that sensibility to the obligations of public and private honour, which is a security for the punctual performance of contracts.

In consequence of the war, the institutions of religion have been deranged, the public worship of the Deity suspended, and a great number of the inhabitants deprived of the ordinary means of obtaining that religious knowledge, which tames the fierceness, and softens the rudeness of human passions and manners. Many of the temples dedicated to the service of the most High were destroyed, and these from a deficiency of ability and inclination, are not yet rebuilt. The clergy were left to suffer, without proper support. The depreciation of the paper currency was particularly injurious to them. It reduced their salaries to a pittance, so insufficient for their maintenance, that several of them were obliged to lay down their profession, and engage in other pursuits. Public preaching, of which many of the inhabitants were thus deprived, seldom fails of rendering essential service to society, by civilizing the 10 multitude and forming them to union. No class of citizens have contributed more to the revolution than the clergy, and none have hitherto suffered more in consequence of it. From the diminution of their number, and the penury to which they have been subjected, civil government has lost many of the advantages it formerly derived from the public instructions of that useful order of men.

On the whole, the literary, political, and 20 military talents of the citizens of the United States have been improved by the revolution, but their moral character is inferior to what it formerly was. So great is the change for the worse, that the friends of public order are loudly called upon to exert their utmost abilities, in extirpating the vicious principles and habits, which have taken deep root during the late convulsions.   1789

THE FEDERALIST

WHEN THE Constitution was presented to the American electorate for ratification, its fate seemed dubious. In the bitter controversial battle fought over it, pamphlets appeared on both sides. *The Federalist*, printed originally as contributions to New York newspapers from the anonymous hands of John Jay, Alexander Hamilton, and James Madison, was probably not the decisive factor in determining the ratification of the Constitution that some have claimed. And had the Constitution been rejected, or had the Confederacy won in the Civil War, it is quite likely that Richard Henry Lee's *Letters of the Federal Farmer*, the most brilliant contemporary criticism of the Constitution, would enjoy the place which *The Federalist* does in fact. In any case, *The Federalist*, alone of the controversial pamphlets which the fight for the ratification of the Constitution brought forth, has survived to become a political classic.

In spite of serious shortcomings in *The Federalist*, its essential greatness is abundantly clear. In the words of Edward Mead Earle, it was "the first and continues to be the most important discussion of federal government, for which the Constitution of the United States set a significant precedent. It was and still is a masterly analysis and interpretation of the Constitution and of the fundamental principles upon which the government of the United States was established." It has been cited by justices of the Supreme Court as high authority; and it has been discussed by almost all serious students of political philosophy.

Any selections are inevitably an inadequate illustration of the comprehensive defense of the Constitution which *The Federalist* as a whole presents. But Madison's tenth paper calls for especial mention, for it postulates not only the theory of the economic basis of politics and of political history, but the more characteristically American doctrine that a republican and representative government can fairly and satisfactorily solve the conflicts of economic interest.

The Federalist, Sesquicentennial Edition. Introduction by Edward Mead Earle, Washington, 1938.

» » *From:* THE FEDERALIST « «

(Independent Journal, October 27, 1787)

NO. 1

INTRODUCTION

Utility of the Union—Inefficiency of confederation —Capacity of people for self-government—Opposition of state officials to new constitution—Honest differences of opinion—Political intolerance—Charges and counter charges—Publius a supporter of the proposed constitution—Outline of The Federalist—National sentiment for Union.

To the People of the State of New York:

After an unequivocal experience of the inefficiency of the subsisting federal government, you are called upon to deliberate on a new Constitution for the United States of America. The subject speaks its own importance; comprehending in its consequences nothing less than the existence of the UNION, the safety and welfare of the parts of which it is composed, the fate of an empire in many respects the most interesting in the world. It has been frequently remarked that it seems to have been reserved to the people of this country, by their conduct and example, to decide the important question, whether societies of men are really capable or not of establishing good government from reflection and choice, or whether they are forever destined to depend for their political constitutions on accident and force. If there be any truth in the remark, the crisis at which we are arrived may with propriety be regarded as the era in which that decision is to be made; and a wrong election of the part we shall act may, in this view, deserve to be considered as the general misfortune of mankind.

This idea will add the inducements of philanthropy to those of patriotism, to heighten the solicitude which all considerate and good men must feel for the event. Happy will it be if our choice should be directed by a judicious estimate of our true interests, unperplexed and unbiased by considerations not connected with the public good. But this is a thing more ardently to be wished than seriously to be expected. The plan offered to our deliberations affects too many particular interests, innovates upon too many local institutions, not to involve in its discussion a variety of objects foreign to its merits, and of views, passions, and prejudices little favorable to the discovery of truth.

Among the most formidable of the obstacles which the new Constitution will have to encounter may readily be distinguished the obvious interest of a certain class of men in every State to resist all changes which may hazard a diminution of the power, emolument, and consequence of the offices they hold under the State establishment; and the perverted ambition of another class of men, who will either hope to aggrandize themselves by the confusions of their country, or will flatter themselves with fairer prospects of elevation from the subdivision of the empire into several partial confederacies than from its union under one government.

It is not, however, my design to dwell upon observations of this nature. I am well aware that it would be disingenuous to resolve indiscriminately the opposition of any set of men (merely because their situations might subject them to suspicion) into interested or ambitious views. Candor will oblige us to admit that even such men may be actuated by upright intentions; and it cannot be doubted that much of the opposition which has made its appearance, or may hereafter make its appearance, will spring from sources, blameless, at least, if not respectable—the honest errors of minds led astray by preconceived jealousies and fears. So numerous indeed and so powerful are the causes which serve to give a false bias to the judgment, that we, upon many occasions, see wise and good men on the wrong as well as on the right side of questions of the first magnitude to society. This circumstance, if duly attended to, would furnish a lesson of moderation to those who are ever so much persuaded of their being in the right in any controversy. And a further reason for caution, in this respect, might be drawn from the reflection that we are not always sure that those who advocate the truth are influenced by purer principles than their antagonists. Ambition, avarice, personal animosity, party opposition, and many other motives not more laudable than these, are apt to operate as well upon those who support as those who oppose the right side of a question. Were there not even these inducements to moderation, nothing could be more ill-judged than that intolerant spirit which has, at all times, characterized political parties. For in politics, as in religion, it is equally absurd to aim at making proselytes by fire and sword. Heresies in either can rarely be cured by persecution.

And yet, however just these sentiments will be allowed to be, we have already sufficient indications that it will happen in this as in all former cases of great national discussion. A torrent of angry and malignant passions will be let loose. To judge from the conduct of the opposite parties, we shall be led to conclude that they will mutually hope to evince the justness of their opinions, and to increase the number of their converts by the loudness of their declamations and the bitterness of their invectives. An enlightened zeal for the energy and efficiency of government will be stigmatized as the offspring of a temper fond of despotic power and hostile to the principles of liberty. And overscrupulous jealousy of danger to the rights of the people, which is more commonly the fault of the head than of the heart, will be represented as mere pretense and artifice, the stale bait for popularity at the expense of the public good. It will be forgotten, on the one hand, that jealousy is the usual concomitant of love, and that the noble enthusiasm of liberty is apt to be infected with a spirit of narrow and illiberal distrust. On the other hand, it will be equally forgotten that the vigor of government is essential to the security of liberty; that, in the contemplation of a sound and well-informed judgment, their interest can never be separated; and that a

dangerous ambition more often lurks behind the specious mask of zeal for the rights of the people than under the forbidding appearance of zeal for the firmness and efficiency of government. History will teach us that the former has been found a much more certain road to the introduction of despotism than the latter, and that of those men who have overturned the liberties of republics, the greatest number have begun their career by paying an obsequious court to the people; commencing demagogues, and ending tyrants.

In the course of the preceding observations, I have had an eye, my fellow-citizens, to putting you upon your guard against all attempts, from whatever quarter, to influence your decision in a matter of the utmost moment to your welfare, by any impressions other than those which may result from the evidence of truth. You will, no doubt, at the same time have collected from the general scope of them, that they proceed from a source not unfriendly to the new Constitution. Yes, my countrymen, I own to you that, after having given it an attentive consideration, I am clearly of opinion it is your interest to adopt it. I am convinced that this is the safest course for your liberty, your dignity, and your happiness. I affect not reserves which I do not feel. I will not amuse you with an appearance of deliberation when I have decided. I frankly acknowledge to you my convictions, and I will freely lay before you the reasons on which they are founded. The consciousness of good intentions disdains ambiguity. I shall not, however, multiply professions on this head. My motives must remain in the depository of my own breast. My arguments will be open to all, and may be judged of by all. They shall at least be offered in a spirit which will not disgrace the cause of truth.

I propose, in a series of papers, to discuss the following interesting particulars:—*The utility of the UNION to your political prosperity—The insufficiency of the present Confederation to preserve that Union—The necessity of a government at least equally energetic with the one proposed, to the attainment of this object—The conformity of the proposed Constitution to the true principles of republican government—Its analogy to your own State constitution*—and lastly, *The additional security which its adoption will afford to the preservation of that species of government, to liberty, and to property.*

In the progress of this discussion I shall endeavor to give a satisfactory answer to all the objections which shall have made their appearance, that may seem to have any claim to your attention.

It may perhaps be thought superfluous to offer arguments to prove the utility of the UNION, a point, no doubt, deeply engraved on the hearts of the great body of the people in every State, and one which, it may be imagined, has no adversaries. But the fact is that we already hear it whispered in the private circles of those who oppose the new Constitution, that the thirteen States are of too great extent for any general system, and that we must of necessity resort to separate confederacies of distinct portions of the whole.[1] This doctrine will, in all probability, be gradually propagated, till it has votaries enough to countenance an open avowal of it. For nothing can be more evident to those who are able to take an enlarged view of the subject than the alternative of an adoption of the new Constitution or a dismemberment of the Union. It will therefore be of use to begin by examining the advantages of that Union, the certain evils, and the probable dangers, to which every State will be exposed from its dissolution. This shall accordingly constitute the subject of my next address.   PUBLIUS [HAMILTON]

(*Independent Journal,* October 31, 1787)

NO. 2

THE VALUE OF UNION

Necessity of government—Theory of separate confederacies—Geographical and racial homogeneity of the United States—Inefficiency of the articles of confederation—The Federal Convention—Consideration of the constitution—The congress of 1774—Universal belief in the necessity of Union—Project of separate confederacies.

To the People of the State of New York:

When the people of America reflect that they are now called upon to decide a question, which, in its consequences, must prove one of the most important that ever engaged their attention, the propriety of their taking a very

[1] The same idea, tracing the arguments to their consequences, is held out in several of the late publications against the new Constitution.—PUBLIUS. [This and the following footnotes are by the author of this selection.]

comprehensive, as well as a very serious, view of it, will be evident.

Nothing is more certain than the indispensable necessity of government, and it is equally undeniable that, whenever and however it is instituted, the people must cede to it some of their natural rights, in order to vest it with requisite powers. It is well worthy of consideration therefore, whether it would conduce more to the interest of the people of America that they should, to all general purposes, be one nation, under one federal government, or that they should divide themselves into separate confederacies, and give to the head of each the same kind of powers which they are advised to place in one national government.

It has until lately been a received and uncontradicted opinion that the prosperity of the people of America depended on their continuing firmly united, and the wishes, prayers, and efforts of our best and wisest citizens have been constantly directed to that object. But politicians now appear, who insist that this opinion is erroneous, and that instead of looking for safety and happiness in union, we ought to seek it in a division of the States into distinct confederacies or sovereignties. However extraordinary this new doctrine may appear, it nevertheless has its advocates; and certain characters who were much opposed to it formerly are at present of the number. Whatever may be the arguments or inducements which have wrought this change in the sentiments and declarations of these gentlemen, it certainly would not be wise in the people at large to adopt these new political tenets without being fully convinced that they are founded in truth and sound policy.

It has often given me pleasure to observe that independent America was not composed of detached and distant territories, but that one connected, fertile, wide-spreading country was the portion of our western sons of liberty. Providence has in a particular manner blessed it with a variety of soils and productions, and watered it with innumerable streams, for the delight and accommodation of its inhabitants. A succession of navigable waters forms a kind of chain round its borders, as if to bind it together; while the most noble rivers in th' world, running at convenient distances, present them with highways for the easy communication of friendly aids, and the mutual transportation and exchange of their various commodities.

With equal pleasure I have so often taken notice that Providence has been pleased to give this one connected country to one united people—a people descended from the same ancestors, speaking the same language, professing the same religion, attached to the same principles of government, very similar in their manners and customs, and who, by their joint counsels, arms, and efforts, fighting side by side throughout a long and bloody war, have nobly established general liberty and independence.

This country and this people seem to have been made for each other, and it appears as if it was the design of Providence that an inheritance so proper and convenient for a band of brethren united to each other by the strongest ties, should never be split into a number of unsocial, jealous, and alien sovereignties.

Similar sentiments have hitherto prevailed among all orders and denominations of men among us. To all general purposes we have uniformly been one people; each individual citizen everywhere enjoying the same national rights, privileges, and protection. As a nation we have made peace and war; as a nation we have formed alliances, and made treaties, and entered into various compacts and conventions with foreign states.

A strong sense of the value and blessings of union induced the people, at a very early period, to institute a federal government to preserve and perpetuate it. They formed it almost as soon as they had a political existence; nay, at a time when their habitations were in flames, when many of their citizens were bleeding, and when the progress of hostility and desolation left little room for those calm and mature inquiries and reflections which must ever precede the formation of a wise and well-balanced government for a free people. It is not to be wondered at that a government, instituted in times so inauspicious, should on experiment be found greatly deficient and inadequate to the purpose it was intended to answer.

This intelligent people perceived and regretted these defects. Still continuing no less attached to union than enamored of liberty, they observed the danger which immediately threatened the former and more remotely the latter; and being persuaded that ample security for both could only be found in a national government more wisely framed, they,

as with one voice, convened the late convention at Philadelphia, to take that important subject under consideration.

This convention, composed of men who possessed the confidence of the people, and many of whom had become highly distinguished by their patriotism, virtue, and wisdom, in times which tried the minds and hearts of men, undertook the arduous task. In the mild season of peace, with minds unoccupied by other subjects, they passed many months in cool, uninterrupted, and daily consultation; and finally, without having been awed by power, or influenced by any passions except love for their country, they presented and recommended to the people the plan produced by their joint and very unanimous councils.

Admit, for so is the fact, that this plan is only *recommended,* not imposed, yet let it be remembered that it is neither recommended to *blind* approbation, nor to *blind* reprobation; but to that sedate and candid consideration which the magnitude and importance of the subject demand, and which it certainly ought to receive. But this (as was remarked in the foregoing number of this paper) is more to be wished than expected, that it may be so considered and examined. Experience on a former occasion teaches us not to be too sanguine in such hopes. It is not yet forgotten that well-grounded apprehensions of imminent danger induced the people of America to form the memorable Congress of 1774. That body recommended certain measures to their constituents, and the event proved their wisdom; yet it is fresh in our memories how soon the press began to teem with pamphlets and weekly papers against those very measures. Not only many of the officers of government, who obeyed the dictates of personal interest, but others, from a mistaken estimate of consequences, or the undue influence of former attachments, or whose ambition aimed at objects which did not correspond with the public good, were indefatigable in their efforts to persuade the people to reject the advice of that patriotic Congress. Many, indeed, were deceived and deluded, but the great majority of the people reasoned and decided judiciously; and happy they are in reflecting that they did so.

They considered that the Congress was composed of many wise and experienced men. That, being convened from different parts of the country, they brought with them and com-

municated to each other a variety of useful information. That, in the course of the time they passed together in inquiring into and discussing the true interests of their country, they must have acquired very accurate knowledge on that head. That they were individually interested in the public liberty and prosperity, and therefore that it was not less their inclination than their duty to recommend only
10 such measures as, after the most mature deliberation, they really thought prudent and advisable.

These and similar considerations then induced the people to rely greatly on the judgment and integrity of the Congress; and they took their advice, notwithstanding the various arts and endeavors used to deter them from it. But if the people at large had reason to confide in the men of that Congress, few of
20 whom had been fully tried or generally known, still greater reason have they now to respect the judgment and advice of the convention, for it is well known that some of the most distinguished members of that Congress, who have been since tried and justly approved for patriotism and abilities, and who have grown old in acquiring political information, were also members of this convention, and carried into it their accumulated knowledge and experience.
30 It is worthy of remark that not only the first, but every succeeding Congress, as well as the late convention, have invariably joined with the people in thinking that the prosperity of America depended on its Union. To preserve and perpetuate it was the great object of the people in forming that convention, and it is also the great object of the plan which the convention has advised them to adopt. With what propriety, therefore, or for what good
40 purposes, are attempts at this particular period made by some men to depreciate the importance of the Union? Or why is it suggested that three or four confederacies would be better than one? I am persuaded in my own mind that the people have always thought right on this subject, and that their universal and uniform attachment to the cause of the Union rests on great and weighty reasons, which I shall endeavor to develop and explain
50 in some ensuing papers. They who promote the idea of substituting a number of distinct confederacies in the room of the plan of the convention, seem clearly to foresee that the rejection of it would put the continuance of the Union in the utmost jeopardy. That certainly would be the case, and I sincerely wish that it may be as clearly foreseen by every good citizen, that whenever the dissolution of the Union arrives, America will have reason to exclaim, in the words of the poet: "FAREWELL! A LONG FAREWELL TO ALL MY GREATNESS."   PUBLIUS [JAY]

(*Independent Journal,* November 21, 1787)

NO. 9

THE UNION A SAFEGUARD AGAINST DOMESTIC DISTURBANCES

Example of Greek and Italian republics—Arguments against republican government and civil liberty—Improvements in the art of government —Advantages of extended territory—Opinion of Montesquieu—Necessity for subdivision implied in Montesquieu's view—Federalization an expedient for the extension of government—Quotation from Montesquieu—Inaccurate distinction between confederation and consolidation—Definition of a confederate republic—Federal character of proposed constitution—Lycian confederacy.

To the People of the State of New York:

A firm Union will be of the utmost moment to the peace and liberty of the States, as a barrier against domestic faction and insurrection. It is impossible to read the history of the petty republics of Greece and Italy without feeling sensations of horror and disgust at the distractions with which they were continually agitated, and at the rapid succession of revolutions by which they were kept in a state of perpetual vibration between the extremes of tyranny and anarchy. If they exhibit occasional calms, these only serve as short-lived contrasts to the furious storms that are to succeed. If now and then intervals of felicity open to view, we behold them with a mixture of regret arising from the reflection that the pleasing scenes before us are soon to be overwhelmed by the tempestuous waves of sedition and party rage. If momentary rays of glory break forth from the gloom, while they dazzle us with a transient and fleeting brilliancy, they at the same time admonish us to lament that the vices of government should pervert the direction and tarnish the luster of those bright talents and exalted endowments for which the favored soils that produced them have been so justly celebrated.

From the disorders that disfigure the annals of those republics the advocates of despotism have drawn arguments, not only against the forms of republican government, but against the very principles of civil liberty. They have decried all free government as inconsistent with the order of society, and have indulged themselves in malicious exultation over its friends and partisans. Happily for mankind, stupendous fabrics reared on the basis of liberty, which have flourished for ages, have, in a few glorious instances, refuted their gloomy sophisms. And, I trust, America will be the broad and solid foundation of other edifices, not less magnificent, which will be equally permanent monuments of their errors.

But it is not to be denied that the portraits they have sketched of republican government were too just copies of the originals from which they were taken. If it had been found impracticable to have devised models of a more perfect structure, the enlightened friends to liberty would have been obliged to abandon the cause of that species of government as indefensible. The science of politics, however, like most other sciences, has received great improvement. The efficacy of various principles is now well understood, which were either not known at all, or imperfectly known to the ancients. The regular distribution of power into distinct departments; the introduction of legislative balances and checks; the institution of courts composed of judges holding their offices during good behavior; the representation of the people in the legislature by deputies of their own election: these are wholly new discoveries, or have made their principal progress towards perfection in modern times. They are means, and powerful means by which the excellences of republican government may be retained and its imperfections lessened or avoided. To this catalogue of circumstances that tend to the amelioration of popular systems of civil government, I shall venture, however novel it may appear to some, to add one more, on a principle which has been made the foundation of an objection to the new Constitution; I mean the ENLARGEMENT of the ORBIT within which such systems are to revolve, either in respect to the dimensions of a single State, or to the consolidation of several smaller States into one great Confederacy. The latter is that which immediately concerns the object under consideration. It will, however, be of use to examine the principle in its application to a single State, which shall be attended to in another place.

The utility of a Confederacy, as well to suppress faction and to guard the internal tranquillity of States, as to increase their external force and security, is in reality not a new idea. It has been practiced upon in different countries and ages, and has received the sanction of the most approved writers on the subjects of politics. The opponents of the plan proposed have, with great assiduity, cited and circulated the observations of Montesquieu on the necessity of a contracted territory for a republican government. But they seem not to have been apprised of the sentiments of that great man expressed in another part of his work, nor to have adverted to the consequences of the principle to which they subscribe with such ready acquiescence.

When Montesquieu recommends a small extent for republics, the standards he had in view were of dimensions far short of the limits of almost every one of these States. Neither Virginia, Massachusetts, Pennsylvania, New York, North Carolina, nor Georgia can by any means be compared with the models from which he reasoned and to which the terms of his description apply. If we therefore take his ideas on this point as the criterion of truth, we shall be driven to the alternative either of taking refuge at once in the arms of monarchy, or of splitting ourselves into an infinity of little jealous, clashing, tumultuous commonwealths, the wretched nurseries of unceasing discord, and the miserable objects of universal pity or contempt. Some of the writers who have come forward on the other side of the question seem to have been aware of the dilemma; and have even been bold enough to hint at the division of the larger States as a desirable thing. Such an infatuated policy, such a desperate expedient, might, by the multiplication of petty offices, answer the views of men who possess not qualifications to extend their influence beyond the narrow circles of personal intrigue, but it could never promote the greatness or happiness of the people of America.

Referring the examination of the principle itself to another place, as has been already mentioned, it will be sufficient to remark here that, in the sense of the author who has been most emphatically quoted upon the occasion, it would only dictate a reduction of the SIZE of the more considerable MEMBERS of the Union, but would not militate against their being all comprehended in one confederate government. And this is the true question, in the discussion of which we are at present interested.

So far are the suggestions of Montesquieu from standing in opposition to a general Union of the States, that he explicitly treats of a CONFEDERATE REPUBLIC as the expedient for extending the sphere of popular government, and reconciling the advantages of monarchy with those of republicanism.

"It is very probable" (says he[2]), "that mankind would have been obliged at length to live constantly under the government of a single person, had they not contrived a kind of constitution that has all the internal advantages of a republican, together with the external force of a monarchial government. I mean a CONFEDERATE REPUBLIC.

"This form of government is a convention by which several smaller *states* agree to become members of a larger *one*, which they intend to form. It is a kind of assemblage of societies that constitute a new one, capable of increasing, by means of new associations, till they arrive to such a degree of power as to be able to provide for the security of the united body.

"A republic of this kind, able to withstand an external force, may support itself without any internal corruptions. The form of this society prevents all manner of inconveniences.

"If a single member should attempt to usurp the supreme authority, he could not be supposed to have an equal authority and credit in all the confederate states. Were he to have too great influence over one, this would alarm the rest. Were he to subdue a part, that which would still remain free might oppose him with forces independent of those which he had usurped, and overpower him before he could be settled in his usurpation.

"Should a popular insurrection happen in one of the confederate states, the others are able to quell it. Should abuses creep into one part, they are reformed by those that remain sound. The state may be destroyed on one side, and not on the other; the confederacy may be dissolved, and the confederates preserve their sovereignty.

"As this government is composed of small republics, it enjoys the internal happiness of each; and with respect to its external situation,

[2] *Spirit of Laws*, Vol. i. book ix. chap. i.—PUBLIUS.

it is possessed, by means of the association, of all the advantages of large monarchies."

I have thought it proper to quote at length these interesting passages, because they contain a luminous abridgment of the principal arguments in favor of the Union, and must effectually remove the false impressions which a misapplication of other parts of the work was calculated to make. They have, at the same time, an intimate connection with the more immediate design of this paper; which is, to illustrate the tendency of the Union to repress domestic faction and insurrection.

A distinction, more subtle than accurate, has been raised between a *Confederacy* and a *consolidation* of the States. The essential characteristic of the first is said to be the restriction of its authority to the members in their collective capacities, without reaching to the individuals of whom they are composed. It is contended that the national council ought to have no concern with any object of internal administration. An exact equality of suffrage between the members has also been insisted upon as a leading feature of a confederate government. These positions are, in the main, arbitrary; they are supported neither by principle nor precedent. It has indeed happened that governments of this kind have generally operated in the manner which the distinction, taken notice of, supposes to be inherent in their nature; but there have been in most of them extensive exceptions to the practice, which serve to prove, as far as example will go, that there is no absolute rule on the subject. And it will be clearly shown, in the course of this investigation, that, as far as the principle contended for has prevailed, it has been the cause of incurable disorder and imbecility in the government.

The definition of a *Confederate Republic* seems simply to be "an assemblage of societies," or an association of two or more states into one state. The extent, modifications, and objects of the federal authority are mere matters of discretion. So long as the separate organization of the members be not abolished; so long as it exists, by a constitutional necessity, for local purposes; though it should be in perfect subordination to the general authority of the union, it would still be, in fact and in theory, an association of states, or a confederacy. The proposed Constitution, so far from implying an abolition of the State governments, makes them constituent parts of the national sovereignty, by allowing them a direct representation in the Senate, and leaves in their possession certain exclusive and very important portions of sovereign power. This fully corresponds, in every rational import of the terms, with the idea of a federal government.

In the Lycian confederacy, which consisted of twenty-three CITIES or republics, the largest were entitled to *three* votes in the COMMON COUNCIL, those of the middle class to *two*, and the smallest to *one*. The COMMON COUNCIL had the appointment of all the judges and magistrates of the respective CITIES. This was certainly the most delicate species of interference in their internal administration; for if there be anything that seems exclusively appropriated to the local jurisdictions, it is the appointment of their own officers. Yet Montesquieu, speaking of this association says: "Were I to give a model of an excellent Confederate Republic, it would be that of Lycia." Thus we perceive that the distinctions insisted upon were not within the contemplation of this enlightened civilian; and we shall be lead to conclude, that they are the novel refinements of an erroneous theory.

PUBLIUS [HAMILTON]
1787

(*New York Daily Advertiser,*
November 22, 1787)

NO. 10

THE UNION A CHECK ON FACTION

Among the numerous advantages promised by a well-constructed union, none deserves to be more accurately developed than its tendency to break and control the violence of faction. The friend of popular governments never finds himself so much alarmed for their character and fate as when he contemplates their propensity to this dangerous vice. He will not fail, therefore, to set a due value on any plan which, without violating the principles to which he is attached, provides a proper cure for it. The instability, injustice, and confusion introduced into the public councils have, in truth, been the mortal diseases under which popular governments have everywhere perished; as they continue to be the favorite and fruitful topics from which the adversaries to liberty derive their most specious declamations.

The valuable improvements made by the American constitutions on the popular models, both ancient and modern, cannot certainly be too much admired; but it would be an unwarrantable partiality, to contend that they have as effectually obviated the danger on this side as was wished and expected. Complaints are everywhere heard from our most considerate and virtuous citizens, equally the friends of public and private faith and of public and personal liberty, that our governments are too unstable; that the public good is disregarded in the conflicts of rival parties; and that measures are too often decided, not according to the rules of justice, and the rights of the minor party, but by the superior force of an interested and overbearing majority. However anxiously we may wish that these complaints had no foundation, the evidence of known facts will not permit us to deny that they are in some degree true. It will be found, indeed, on a candid review of our situation, that some of the distresses under which we labor have been erroneously charged on the operation of our governments; but it will be found, at the same time, that other causes will not alone account for many of our heaviest misfortunes; and, particularly, for that prevailing and increasing distrust of public engagements, and alarm for private rights, which are echoed from one end of the continent to the other. These must be chiefly, if not wholly, effects of the unsteadiness and injustice with which a factious spirit has tainted our public administrations.

By a faction, I understand a number of citizens, whether amounting to a majority or minority of the whole, who are united and actuated by some common impulse of passion, or of interest, adverse to the rights of other citizens or to the permanent and aggregate interests of the community.

There are two methods of curing the mischiefs of faction: the one, by removing its causes; the other, by controlling its effects.

There are again two methods of removing the causes of faction: the one, by destroying the liberty which is essential to its existence; the other, by giving to every citizen the same opinions, the same passions, and the same interests.

It could never be more truly said than of the first remedy, that it was worse than the disease. Liberty is to faction what air is to fire, an ailment without which it instantly expires. But it could not be less folly to abolish liberty, which is essential to political life, because it nourishes faction, than it would be to wish the annihilation of air, which is essential to animal life, because it imparts to fire its destructive agency.

The second expedient is as impracticable as the first would be unwise. As long as the reason of man continues fallible, and he is at liberty to exercise it, different opinions will be formed. As long as the connection subsists between his reason and his self-love, his opinions and his passions will have a reciprocal influence on each other; and the former will be objects to which the latter will attach themselves. The diversity in the faculties of men, from which the rights of property originate, is not less an insuperable obstacle to a uniformity of interests. The protection of these faculties is the first object of government. From the protection of different and unequal faculties of acquiring property, the possession of different degrees and kinds of property immediately results; and from the influence of these on the sentiments and views of the respective proprietors ensues a division of the society into different interests and parties.

The latent causes of faction are thus sown in the nature of man; and we see them everywhere brought into different degrees of activity, according to the different circumstances of civil society. A zeal for different opinions concerning religion, concerning government and many other points, as well of speculation as of practice; an attachment to different leaders ambitiously contending for pre-eminence and power, or to persons of other descriptions whose fortunes have been interesting to the human passions, have, in turn, divided mankind into parties, inflamed them with mutual animosity, and rendered them much more disposed to vex and oppress each other, than to co-operate for their common good. So strong is this propensity of mankind to fall into mutual animosities, that where no substantial occasion presents itself, the most frivolous and fanciful distinctions have been sufficient to kindle their unfriendly passions and excite their most violent conflicts. But the most common and durable source of factions has been the various and unequal distribution of property. Those who hold and those who are without property have ever formed distinct interests in society. Those who are creditors and those who are debtors fall under a like discrimination. A landed interest, a manufacturing interest, a mercantile interest, a moneyed interest, with many lesser interests, grow up of necessity in civilized nations, and divide them into different classes, actuated by different sentiments and views. The regulation of these various and interfering interests forms the principal task of modern legislation, and involves the spirit of party and faction in the necessary and ordinary operations of the government.

No man is allowed to be a judge in his own cause; because his interest would certainly bias his judgment and, not improbably, corrupt his integrity. With equal, nay, with greater reason, a body of men are unfit to be both judges and parties at the same time; yet what are many of the most important acts of legislation, but so many judicial determinations, not indeed concerning the rights of single persons, but concerning the rights of large bodies of citizens? and what are the different classes of legislators, but advocates and parties to the causes which they determine? Is a law proposed concerning private debts?—it is a question to which the creditors are parties on one side, and the debtors on the other. Justice ought to hold the balance between them. Yet the parties are, and must be, themselves the judges; and the most numerous party, or, in other words, the most powerful faction, must be expected to prevail. Shall domestic manufactures be encouraged, and in what degree by restrictions on foreign manufactures? are questions which would be differently decided by the landed and the manufacturing classes, and probably by neither with a sole regard to justice and the public good. The apportionment of taxes on the various descriptions of property is an act which seems to require the most exact impartiality; yet there is, perhaps, no legislative act in which greater opportunity and temptation are given to a predominant party, to trample on the rules of justice. Every shilling with which they overburden the inferior number is a shilling saved to their own pockets.

It is in vain to say that enlightened statesmen will be able to adjust these clashing interests and render them all subservient to the public good. Enlightened statesmen will not always be at the helm; nor, in many cases, can such an adjustment be made at all, without taking into view indirect and remote considerations, which will rarely prevail over the immediate interest which one party may find in disregarding the rights of another or the good of the whole.

The inference to which we are brought is that the causes of faction cannot be removed, and that relief is only to be sought in the means of controlling its effects.

If a faction consists of less than a majority, relief is supplied by the republican principle, which enables the majority to defeat its sinister views by regular vote. It may clog the administration, it may convulse the society; but it will be unable to execute and mask its violence under the forms of the Constitution. When a majority is included in a faction, the form of popular government, on the other hand, enables it to sacrifice to its ruling passion or interest both the public good and the rights of other citizens. To secure the public good, and private rights, against the danger of such a faction, and at the same time to preserve the spirit and the form of popular government, is then the great object to which our inquiries are directed. Let me add that it is the great *desideratum*, by which alone this form of government can be rescued from the opprobrium under which it has so long labored, and be recommended to the esteem and adoption of mankind.

By what means is this object attainable? Evidently by one of two only. Either the existence of the same passion or interest in a majority, at the same time, must be prevented; or the majority, having such coexistent passion or interest, must be rendered, by their number and local situation, unable to concert and carry into effect schemes of oppression. If the impulse and the opportunity be suffered to coincide, we well know that neither moral nor religious motives can be relied on as an adequate control. They are not found to be such on the injustice and violence of individuals, and lose their efficacy in proportion to the number combined together; that is, in proportion as their efficacy becomes needful.

From this view of the subject it may be concluded that a pure democracy, by which I mean a society consisting of a small number of citizens, who assemble and administer the government in person, can admit of no cure for the mischiefs of faction. A common passion or interest will, in almost every case, be felt by a majority of the whole; a communication and concert results from the form of government itself; and there is nothing to check the inducements to sacrifice the weaker party or an obnoxious individual. Hence it is that such democracies have ever been spectacles of turbulence and contention; have ever been found incompatible with personal security, or the rights of property, and have in general been as short in their lives as they have been violent in their deaths. Theoretic politicians, who have patronized this species of government, have erroneously supposed that by reducing mankind to a perfect equality in their political rights, they would at the same time be perfectly equalized and assimilated in their possessions, their opinions, and their passions.

A republic, by which I mean a government in which the scheme of representation takes place, opens a different prospect, and promises the cure for which we are seeking. Let us examine the points in which it varies from pure democracy, and we shall comprehend both the nature of the cure and the efficacy which it must derive from the union.

The two great points of difference between a democracy and a republic are: First, the delegation of the government, in the latter, to a small number of citizens elected by the rest; secondly, the greater number of citizens, and greater sphere of country, over which the latter may be extended.

The effect of the first difference is, on the one hand, to refine and enlarge the public views, by passing them through the medium of a chosen body of citizens, whose wisdom may best discern the true interest of their country, and whose patriotism and love of justice will be least likely to sacrifice it to temporary or partial considerations. Under such a regulation, it may well happen that the public voice, pronounced by the representatives of the people, will be more consonant to the public good than if pronounced by the people themselves, convened for the purpose. On the other hand, the effect may be inverted. Men of factious tempers, of local prejudices, or of sinister designs, may by intrigue, by corruption, or by other means, first obtain the suffrages, and then betray the interests of the people. The question resulting is, whether small or extensive republics are most favorable to the election of proper guardians of the public weal; and it is clearly decided in favor of the latter by two obvious considerations.

In the first place, it is to be remarked that, however small the republic may be, the representatives must be raised to a certain number, in order to guard against the cabals of a few; and that, however large it may be, they must be limited to a certain number, in order to guard against the confusion of a multitude. Hence, the number of representatives in the two cases not being in proportion to that of the constituents, and being proportionally greatest in the small republic, it follows that if the proportion of fit characters be not less in the large than in the small republic, the former will present a greater option, and consequently a greater probability of a fit choice.

10 In the next place, as each representative will be chosen by a greater number of citizens in the large than in the small republic, it will be more difficult for unworthy candidates to practise with success the vicious arts, by which elections are too often carried; and the suffrages of the people, being more free, will be more likely to centre in men who possess the most attractive merit and the most diffusive and established characters.

20 It must be confessed that in this as in most other cases, there is a mean, on both sides of which inconveniences will be found to lie. By enlarging too much the number of electors, you render the representative too little acquainted with all their local circumstances and lesser interests; as by reducing it too much, you render him unduly attached to these, and too little fit to comprehend and pursue great and national objects. The federal Constitution 30 forms a happy combination in this respect; the great and aggregate interests being referred to the national, the local and particular to the State, legislatures.

The other point of difference is, the greater number of citizens and extent of territory which may be brought within the compass of republican than of democratic government; and it is this circumstance principally which renders factious combinations less to be dreaded in the 40 former, than in the latter. The smaller the society, the fewer probably will be the distinct parties and interests composing it; the fewer the distinct parties and interests, the more frequently will a majority be found of the same party; and the smaller the number of individuals composing a majority, and the smaller the compass within which they are placed, the more easily will they concert and execute their plans of oppression. Extend the sphere, and 50 you take in a greater variety of parties and interests; you make it less probable that a majority of the whole will have a common motive to invade the rights of other citizens; or if such a common motive exists, it will be more difficult for all who feel it to discover their own

strength, and to act in unison with each other. Besides other impediments, it may be remarked that where there is a consciousness of unjust or dishonorable purposes, communication is always checked by distrust, in proportion to the number whose concurrence is necessary.

Hence it clearly appears that the same advantage which a republic has over a democracy, in controlling the effects of faction, is enjoyed by a large over a small republic—is enjoyed by the Union over the States composing it. Does the advantage consist in the substitution of representatives, whose enlightened views and virtuous sentiments render them superior to local prejudices, and to schemes of injustice? It will not be denied that the representation of the Union will be most likely to possess these requisite endowments. Does it consist in the greater security afforded by a greater variety of parties, against the event of any one party being able to outnumber and oppress the rest? In an equal degree does the increased variety of parties, comprised within the Union, increase this security. Does it, in fine, consist in the greater obstacles opposed to the concert and accomplishment of the secret wishes of an unjust and interested majority? Here, again, the extent of the Union gives it the most palpable advantage.

The influence of factious leaders may kindle a flame within their particular States, but will be unable to spread a general conflagration through the other States. A religious sect may degenerate into a political faction in a part of the confederacy; but the variety of sects dispersed over the entire face of it must secure the national councils against any danger from that source. A rage for paper money, for an abolition of debts, for an equal division of property, or for any other improper and wicked project will be less apt to pervade the whole body of the Union than a particular member of it; in the same proportion as such a malady is more likely to taint a particular county or district than an entire State.

In the extent and proper structure of the Union, therefore, we behold a republican remedy for the diseases most incident to republican government. And according to the degree of pleasure and pride we feel in being republicans, ought to be our zeal in cherishing the spirit and supporting the character of federalists.　　　　PUBLIUS [MADISON]
1787

THOMAS JEFFERSON

1743–1826

JEFFERSON'S CONCEPTION of "Americanism" is, in the first place, a peculiar generalization of the virtues and values of the small planter type of Virginian of the late eighteenth century. Economic independence, general intelligence, and devotion to the soil and to political freedom seemed to Jefferson traits notably present in the farming class which he tended to idealize and which, in any case, he hoped might continue to form the bulwark of the American experiment. While he came, during the Embargo period, to admit that a degree of industry might be desirable in the interest of a greater measure of economic self-sufficiency, he always abhorred the idea of an urbanized America with a demagogue-worshiping proletariat.

Jefferson's conception of American nationalism was enriched by his identification of it with many of the principles of the Enlightenment. Religious freedom, the civil liberties, world peace, the diffusion of knowledge, the limitation of authority and scientific rather than supernatural values,—all these he fondly hoped would flourish with vigor on American soil: American civilization might well be enriched by the thought and learning of Europe, and yet at the same time resist the corrupting influence of too great an infiltration of the aristocracy and the authoritarianism of the Old World. Jefferson hoped that Americans might make genuinely important contributions to the arts and sciences, and took pains to refute the imputations of such European naturalists as Buffon that the American environment had dwarfed many species common to both hemispheres.

The Papers of Thomas Jefferson, Julian P. Boyd and others, eds., 15 vols., Princeton, 1950–
Gilbert Chinard, *Thomas Jefferson, the Apostle of Americanism*, rev. ed., Ann Arbor, 1957.

» » From: NOTES ON VIRGINIA « «

The opinion advanced by the Count de Buffon,[1] is 1. That the animals common both to the old and new world are smaller in the latter. 2. That those peculiar to the new are on a smaller scale. 3. That those which have been domesticated in both have degenerated in America. and 4. That on the whole it exhibits fewer species. And the reason he thinks is, that the heats of America are less; that more waters are spread over its surface by nature, and fewer of these drained off by the hand of man. In other words, that *heat* is friendly, and *moisture* adverse to the production and development of large quadrupeds. I will not meet this hypothesis on its first doubtful ground,

whether the climate of America be comparatively more humid? Because we are not furnished with observations sufficient to decide this question. And though, till it be decided, we are as free to deny as others are to affirm the fact, yet for a moment let it be supposed. The hypothesis, after this supposition, proceeds to another: that *moisture* is unfriendly to animal growth. The truth of this is inscrutable to us by reasonings à priori. Nature has hidden from us her modus agendi. Our only appeal on such questions is to experience; and I think that experience is against the supposition. It is by the assistance of *heat* and *moisture* that vegetables are elaborated from the elements of earth, air, water, and fire. We accordingly see the more humid climates produce the greater quantity of vegetables. Vegetables are medi-

[1] Georges Louis Leclerc Buffon (1707–1788), author of the *Histoire naturelle* (44 vols., Paris, 1749–1804), was the outstanding naturalist of the later part of the eighteenth century. [This and the following notes in this selection are Jefferson's own.]

ately or immediately the food of every animal; and in proportion to the quantity of food, we see animals not only multiplied in their numbers, but improved in their bulk, as far as the laws of their nature will admit. Of this opinion is the Count de Buffon himself in another part of his work: "en general il paroit que les pays un peu *froids* conviennent mieux à nos bœufs que les pays chauds, et qu'ils sont d'autant plus gros et plus grands que le climat est plus *humide* et plus abondans en pâturages. Les bœufs de Danemarck, de la Podolie, de l'Ukraine et de la Tartarie qu'habitent les Calmouques sont les plus grands de tous." Here then a race of animals, and one of the largest too, has been increased in its dimensions by *cold* and *moisture,* in direct opposition to the hypothesis, which supposes that these two circumstances diminish animal bulk, and that it is their contraries *heat* and *dryness* which enlarge it. But when we appeal to experience, we are not to rest satisfied with a single fact. Let us, therefore, try our question on more general ground. Let us take two portions of the earth, Europe and America for instance, sufficiently extensive to give operation to general causes; let us consider the circumstances peculiar to each, and observe their effect on animal nature. America, running through the torrid as well as temperate zone, has more *heat* collectively taken, than Europe. But Europe, according to our hypothesis, is the *dryest.* They are equally adapted then to animal productions; each being endowed with one of those causes which befriend animal growth, and with one which opposes it. If it be thought unequal to compare Europe with America, which is so much larger, I answer, not more so than to compare America with the whole world. Besides, the purpose of the comparison is to try an hypothesis, which makes the size of animals depend on the heat and *moisture* of climate. If, therefore, we take a region, so extensive as to comprehend a sensible distinction of climate, and so extensive too as that local accidents, or the intercourse of animals on its borders, may not materially affect the size of those in its interior parts, we shall comply with those conditions which the hypothesis may reasonably demand. The objection would be the weaker in the present case, because any intercourse of animals which may take place on the confines of Europe and Asia, is to the advantage of the former, Asia producing certainly larger animals than Europe. Let us then take a

comparative view of the Quadrupeds of Europe and America, presenting them to the eye in three different tables, in one of which shall be enumerated those found in both countries; in a second, those found in one only; in a third, those which have been domesticated in both. To facilitate the comparison, let those of each table be arranged in gradation according to their sizes, from the greatest to the smallest, so far as their sizes can be conjectured. The weights of the large animals shall be expressed in the English avoirdupoise pound and its decimals; those of the smaller, in the same ounce and its decimals. Those which are marked thus *, are actual weights of particular subjects, deemed among the largest of their species. Those marked thus †, are furnished by judicious persons, well acquainted with the species, and saying, from conjecture only, what the largest individual they had seen would probably have weighed. The other weights are taken from Messrs. Buffon and D'Aubenton, and are of such subjects as came casually to their hands for dissection. This circumstance must be remembered where their weights and mine stand opposed; the latter being stated not to produce a conclusion in favor of the American species, but to justify a suspension of opinion until we are better informed, and a suspicion, in the meantime, that there is no uniform difference in favor of either; which is all I pretend.

A Comparative View of the Quadrupeds of Europe and of America

I. ABORIGINALS OF BOTH

	Europe llb.	America llb.
Mammoth...............		
Buffalo. Bison...........		*1800
White Bear. Outs blanc......		
Carribou. Renne...........		
Bear. Ours................	153.7	*410
Elk. Elan. Original palmated..		
Red deer. Cerf.............	288.8	*273
Fallow deer. Daim.........	167.8	
Wolf. Loup................	69.8	
Roe. Chevreuil.............	56.7	
Glutton. Glouton. Carcajou...		
Wild Cat. Chat sauvage......		†30
Lynx. Loup cervier.........	25.	
Beaver. Castor.............	18.5	*45

. . . That the last part of it is erroneous, which affirms that the species of American quadrupeds are comparatively few, is evident from the tables taken together. By these it appears that there are an hundred species aboriginal in America. Mons. de Buffon supposes about double that number existing on the whole earth. Of these Europe, Asia, and Africa, furnish suppose 126; that is, the 26 common to Europe and America, and about 100 which are not in America at all. The American species, then, are to those of the rest of the earth, as 100 to 126, or 4 to 5. But the residue of the earth being double the extent of America, the exact proportion would have been but 4 to 8.

Hitherto I have considered this hypothesis as applied to brute animals only, and not in its extension to the man of America, whether aboriginal or transplanted. It is the opinion of Mons. de Buffon that the former furnishes no exception to it.

An afflicting picture, indeed, which for the honor of human nature, I am glad to believe has no original. Of the Indian of South America I know nothing; for I would not honor with the appellation of knowledge, what I derive from the fables published of them. These I believe to be just as true as the fables of Æsop. This belief is founded on what I have seen of man, white, red, and black, and what has been written of him by authors, enlightened themselves, and writing among an enlightened people. The Indian of North America being more within our reach, I can speak of him somewhat from my own knowledge, but more from the information of others better acquainted with him, and on whose truth and judgment I can rely. From these sources I am able to say, in contradiction to this representation, that he is neither more defective in ardor, nor more impotent with his female, than the white reduced to the same diet and exercise; that he is brave, when an enterprise depends on bravery; education with him making the point of honor consist in the destruction of an enemy by stratagem, and in the preservation of his own person free from injury; or, perhaps, this is nature, while it is education which teaches us to honor force more than finesse; that he will defend himself against a host of enemies, always choosing to be killed, rather than to surrender, though it be to the whites, who he knows will treat him well; that in other situations, also, he meets death with more deliberation, and endures tortures with a firmness unknown almost

to religious enthusiasm with us; that he is affectionate to his children, careful of them, and indulgent in the extreme; that his affections comprehend his other connections, weakening, as with us, from circle to circle, as they recede from the centre; that his friendships are strong and faithful to the uttermost extremity; that his sensibility is keen, even the warriors weeping most bitterly on the loss of their children, though in general they endeavor to appear superior to human events; that his vivacity and activity of mind is equal to ours in the same situation; hence his eagerness for hunting, and for games of chance. The women are submitted to unjust drudgery. This I believe is the case with every barbarous people. With such, force is law. The stronger sex therefore imposes on the weaker. It is civilization alone which replaces women in the enjoyment of their natural equality. That first teaches us to subdue the selfish passions, and to respect those rights in others which we value in ourselves. Were we in equal barbarism, our females would be equal drudges. The man with them is less strong than with us, but their woman stronger than ours; and both for the same obvious reason; because our man and their woman is habituated to labor, and formed by it. With both races the sex which is indulged with ease is the least athletic. An Indian man is small in the hand and wrist, for the same reason for which a sailor is large and strong in the arms and shoulders, and a porter in the legs and thighs. They raise fewer children than we do. The causes of this are to be found, not in a difference of nature, but of circumstance. The women very frequently attending the men in their parties of war and of hunting, child-bearing becomes extremely inconvenient to them. It is said, therefore, that they have learned the practice of procuring abortion by the use of some vegetable; and that it even extends to prevent conception for a considerable time after. During these parties they are exposed to numerous hazards, to excessive exertions, to the greatest extremities of hunger. Even at their homes the nation depends for food, through a certain part of every year, on the gleanings of the forest; that is, they experience a famine once in every year. With all animals, if the female be illy fed, or not fed at all, her young perish; and if both male and female be reduced to like want, generation becomes less active, less productive. To the obstacles, then, of want and hazard, which nature has opposed to the multiplication of wild animals, for the purpose of restraining their numbers within certain bounds, those of labour and of voluntary abortion are added with the Indian. No wonder, then, if they multiply less than we do. Where food is regularly supplied, a single farm will show more of cattle, than a whole country of forests can of buffalos. The same Indian women, when married to white traders, who feed them and their children plentifully and regularly, who exempt them from excessive drudgery, who keep them stationary and unexposed to accident, produce and raise as many children as the white women. Instances are known, under these circumstances, of their rearing a dozen children. An inhuman practice once prevailed in this country, of making slaves of Indians. It is a fact well known with us, that the Indian women so enslaved produced and raised as numerous families as either the whites or blacks among whom they lived. It has been said that Indians have less hair than the whites, except on the head. But this is a fact of which fair proof can scarcely be had. With them it is disgraceful to be hairy on the body. They say it likens them to hogs. They therefore pluck the hair as fast as it appears. But the traders who marry their women, and prevail on them to discontinue this practice, say, that nature is the same with them as with the whites. Nor, if the fact be true, is the consequence necessary which has been drawn from it. Negroes have notoriously less hair than the whites; yet they are more ardent. But if cold and moisture be the agents of nature for diminishing the races of animals, how comes she all at once to suspend their operation as to the physical man of the new world, whom the Count acknowledges to be 'à peu près de même stature que l'homme de notre monde,' and to let loose their influence on his moral faculties? How has this 'combination of the elements and other physical causes, so contrary to the enlargement of animal nature in this new world, these obstacles to the development and formation of great germs,' been arrested and suspended, so as to permit the human body to acquire its just dimensions, and by what inconceivable process has their action been directed on his mind alone? To judge of the truth of this, to form a just estimate of their genius and mental powers, more facts are wanting, and great allowance to be made for those circumstances of their situation which call for a display of particular talents only. This done, we shall probably find that they are formed in

mind as well as body, on the same module with the 'Homo sapiens Europæus.' The principles of their society forbidding all compulsion, they are to be led to duty and to enterprise by personal influence and persuasion. Hence eloquence in council, bravery and address in war, become the foundations of all consequence with them. To these acquirements all their faculties are directed. Of their bravery and address in war we have multiplied proofs, because we have been the subjects on which they were exercised. Of their eminence in oratory we have fewer examples, because it is displayed chiefly in their own councils. Some, however, we have, of very superior lustre. I may challenge the whole orations of Demosthenes and Cicero, and of any more eminent orator, if Europe has furnished any more eminent, to produce a single passage, superior to the speech of Logan, a Mingo chief, to Lord Dunmore, when governor of this state. And as a testimony of their talents in this line, I beg leave to introduce it, first stating the incidents necessary for understanding it. In the spring of the year 1774, a robbery and murder were committed on an inhabitant of the frontier of Virginia, by two Indians of the Shawanee tribe. The neighbouring whites, according to their custom, undertook to punish this outrage in a summary way. Col. Cresap, a man infamous for the many murders he had committed on those much injured people, collected a party and proceeded down the Kanhaway in quest of vengeance. Unfortunately a canoe of women and children, with one man only, was seen coming from the opposite shore, unarmed, and unsuspecting an hostile attack from the whites. Cresap and his party concealed themselves on the bank of the river, and the moment the canoe reached the shore, singled out their objects, and at one fire, killed every person in it. This happened to be the family of Logan, who had long been distinguished as a friend of the whites. This unworthy return provoked his vengeance. He accordingly signalized himself in the war which ensued. In the autumn of the same year a decisive battle was fought at the mouth of the Great Kanhaway, between the collected forces of the Shawanese, Mingoes and Delawares, and a detachment of the Virginia militia. The Indians were defeated and sued for peace. Logan, however, disdained to be seen among the suppliants. But lest the sincerity of a treaty should be distrusted, from which so distinguished a chief absented himself, he sent, by a messenger, the following speech, to be delivered to Lord Dunmore.

"I appeal to any white man to say, if ever he entered Logan's cabin hungry, and he gave him not meat; if ever he came cold and naked, and he cloathed him not. During the course of the last long and bloody war Logan remained idle in his cabin an advocate for peace. Such was my love for the whites, that my countrymen pointed as they passed, and said, 'Logan is the friend of white men.' I had even thought to have lived with you, but for the injuries of one man. Colonel Cresap, the last spring in cold blood, and unprovoked, murdered all the relations of Logan, not sparing even my women and children. There runs not a drop of my blood in the veins of any living creature. This called on me for revenge. I have sought it: I have killed many: I have fully glutted my vengeance: for my country I rejoice at the beams of peace. But do not harbour a thought that mine is the joy of fear. Logan never felt fear. He will not turn on his heel to save his life. Who is there to mourn for Logan?—Not one."

Before we condemn the Indians of this continent as wanting genius, we must consider that letters have not yet been introduced among them. Were we to compare them in their present state with the Europeans North of the Alps, when the Roman arms and arts first crossed those mountains, the comparison would be unequal, because, at that time, those parts of Europe were swarming with numbers: because numbers produce emulation and multiply the chances of improvement, and one improvement begets another. Yet I may safely ask, how many good poets, how many able mathematicians, how many great inventors, in arts or sciences, had Europe, North of the Alps, then produced? And it was sixteen centuries after this before a Newton could be formed. I do not mean to deny that there are varieties in the race of man, distinguished by their powers both of body and mind. I believe there are, as I see to be the case in the races of other animals. I only mean to suggest a doubt, whether the bulk and faculties of animals depend on the side of the Atlantic on which their food happens to grow, or which furnishes the elements of which they are compounded? Whether nature has enlisted herself as a Cis- or Trans-Atlantic partisan? I am induced to suspect there has been more eloquence than sound reasoning displayed in support of this theory; that it is one of those cases

where the judgment has been seduced by a glowing pen; and whilst I render every tribute of honor and esteem to the celebrated Zoologist, who has added, and is still adding, so many precious things to the treasures of science, I must doubt whether in this instance he has not cherished error also by lending her for a moment his vivid imagination and bewitching language.

So far the Count de Buffon has carried this new theory of the tendency of nature to belittle her productions on this side the Atlantic. Its application to the race of whites transplanted from Europe, remained for the Abbè Raynal.[2] 'On doit etre etonnè (he says) que l'Amerique n'ait pas encore produit un bon poëte, un habile mathematicien, un homme de genie dans un seul art, ou seule science.' 7. Hist. Philos. pa. 92, edn. Maestricht, 1774. 'America has not yet produced one good poet.' When we shall have existed as a people as long as the Greeks did before they produced a Homer, the Romans a Virgil, the French a Racine and Voltaire, the English a Shakespeare and Milton, should this reproach be still true, we will inquire from what unfriendly causes it has proceeded, that the other countries of Europe and quarters of the earth shall not have inscribed any name in the roll of poets. But neither has America produced 'one able mathematician, one man of genius in a single art or a single science.' In war we have produced a Washington, whose memory will be adored while liberty shall have votaries, whose name will triumph over time, and will in future ages assume its just station among the most celebrated worthies of the world, when that wretched philosophy shall be forgotten which would have arranged him among the degeneracies of nature. In Physics we have produced a Franklin, than whom no one of the present age has made more important discoveries, nor has enriched philosophy with more, or more ingenious solutions of the phænomena of nature. We have supposed Mr. Rittenhouse[3] second to no astronomer living; that in genius he must be the first, because he is self taught. As an artist he has exhibited as great a proof of mechanical genius as the world has ever produced. He has not indeed made a world; but he has by imitation approached nearer its Maker than any man who

[2] Guillaume Thomas François Raynal (1713–1796), author of the *Histoire des Indes*, a colonial encyclopedia which enjoyed great authority.
[3] David Rittenhouse (1732–1796), a Pennsylvanian instrument-maker who was also noted as an authority on mathematics and astronomy.

has lived from the creation to this day. As in philosophy and war, so in government, in oratory, in painting, in the plastic art, we might show that America, though but a child of yesterday, has already given hopeful proofs of genius, as well as of the nobler kinds, which arouse the best feelings of man, which call him into action, which substantiate his freedom, and conduct him to happiness, as of the subor10 dinate, which serve to amuse him only. We therefore suppose, that this reproach is as unjust as it is unkind: and that, of the geniuses which adorn the present age, America contributes its full share. For comparing it with those countries where genius is most cultivated, where are the most excellent models for art, and scaffoldings for the attainment of science, as France and England for instance, we calculate thus. The United States contains three 20 millions of inhabitants; France twenty millions; and the British islands ten. We produce a Washington, a Franklin, a Rittenhouse. France then should have half a dozen in each of these lines, and Great Britain half that number, equally eminent. It may be true that France has: we are but just becoming acquainted with her, and our acquaintance so far gives us high ideas of the genius of her inhabitants. It would be injuring too many of them to name particularly a Voltaire, a Buffon, the constellation of Encyclopedists, the Abbè Raynal himself, etc. etc. We therefore have reason to believe she can produce her full quota of genius. The present war having so long cut off all communication with Great Britain, we are not able to make a fair estimate of the state of science in that country. The spirit in which she wages war, is the only sample before our eyes, and that does not seem the legitimate offspring either of science or of civilization. The sun of her glory is fast descending to the horizon. Her Philosophy has crossed the channel, her freedom the Atlantic, and herself seems passing to that awful dissolution whose issue is not given human foresight to scan.

1782

» » *From:* LETTERS « «

TO *J. BANNISTER, JUNIOR*

Paris, October 15, 1785

32 DEAR SIR:—I should sooner have answered the paragraph in your letter, of September the 19th, respecting the best seminary for the education of youth in Europe, but that it was necessary for me to make inquiries on the subject. The result of these has been, to consider the competition as resting between Geneva and Rome. They are equally cheap, and probably 40 are equal in the course of education pursued. The advantage of Geneva is, that students acquire there the habit of speaking French. The advantages of Rome are, the acquiring a local knowledge of a spot so classical and so celebrated; the acquiring the true pronounciation of the Latin language; a just taste in the fine arts, more particularly those of painting, sculpture, architecture, and music; a familiarity with those objects and processes of agriculture which 50 experience has shown best adapted to a climate like ours; and lastly, the advantage of a fine climate for health. It is probable, too, that by being boarded in a French family, the habit of speaking that language may be obtained. I do not count on any advantage to be derived, in Geneva, from a familiar acquaintance with the principles of that government. The late revolution has rendered it a tyrannical aristocracy, more likely to give ill than good ideas to an American. I think the balance in favor of Rome. Pisa is sometimes spoken of as a place of education. But it does not offer the first and third of the advantages of Rome. But why send an American youth to Europe for education? What are the objects of an useful American education? Classical knowledge, modern languages, chiefly French, Spanish, and Italian; Mathematics, Natural philosophy, Natural history, Civil history, and Ethics. In Natural philosophy, I mean to include Chemistry and Agriculture, and in natural history, to include Botany, as well as the other branches of those departments. It is true that the habit of speaking the modern languages cannot be so well acquired in America; but every other article can be as well acquired at William and Mary college, as at any place in Europe. When college education is done with, and a young man is to prepare himself for public life, he must cast his eyes (for America) either on Law or Physics. For

the former, where can he apply so advantageously as to Mr. Wythe? [4] For the latter, he must come to Europe: the medical class of students, therefore, is the only one which need come to Europe. Let us view the disadvantages of sending a youth to Europe. To enumerate them all, would require a volume. I will select a few. If he goes to England, he learns drinking, horse racing, and boxing. These are the peculiarities of English education. The following circumstances are common to education in that, and the other countries of Europe. He acquires a fondness for European luxury and dissipation, and a contempt for the simplicity of his own country; he is fascinated with the privileges of the European aristocrats, and sees, with abhorrence, the lovely equality which the poor enjoy with the rich, in his own country; he contracts a partiality for aristocracy or monarchy; he forms foreign friendships which will never be useful to him, and loses the seasons of life for forming, in his own country, those friendships which, of all others, are the most faithful and permanent; he is led, by the strongest of all the human passions, into a spirit for female intrigue, destructive of his own and others' happiness, or a passion for whores, destructive of his health, and, in both cases, learns to consider fidelity to the marriage bed as an ungentlemanly practice, and inconsistent with happiness; he recollects the voluptuary dress and arts of the European women, and pities and despises the chaste affections and simplicity of those of his own country; he retains, through life, a fond recollection, and a hankering after those places, which were the scenes of his first pleasures and of his first connections; he returns to his own country, a foreigner, unacquainted with the practices of domestic economy, necessary to preserve him from ruin, speaking and writing his native tongue as a foreigner, and therefore unqualified to obtain those distinctions, which eloquence of the pen and tongue ensures in a free country; for I would observe to you, that what is called style in writing or speaking is formed very early in life, while the imagination is warm, and impressions are permanent. I am of opinion, that there never was an instance of a man's writing or speaking his native tongue with elegance, who passed from fifteen to twenty years of age out of the country where it was spoken. Thus,

no instance exists of a person's writing two languages perfectly. That will always appear to be his native language, which was most familiar to him in his youth. It appears to me, then, that an American, coming to Europe for education, loses in his knowledge, in his morals, in his health, in his habits, and in his happiness. I had entertained only doubts on this head before I came to Europe: what I see and hear, since I came here, proves more than I had even suspected. Cast your eye over America: who are the men of most learning, of most eloquence, most beloved by their countrymen and most trusted and promoted by them? They are those who have been educated among them, and whose manners, morals, and habits, are perfectly homogeneous with those of the country.

Did you expect by so short a question, to draw such a sermon on yourself? I dare say you did not. But the consequences of foreign education are alarming to me, as an American. I sin, therefore, through zeal, whenever I enter on the subject. You are sufficiently American to pardon me for it. Let me hear of your health, and be assured of the esteem with which I am, dear Sir, your friend and servant.   1785

[TO JAMES MONROE]

Paris, June 17, 1785

. . . I sincerely wish you may find it convenient to come here. The pleasure of the trip will be less than you expect but the utility greater. It will make you adore your own country, it's soil, it's climate, it's equality, liberty, laws, people & manners. My God! how little do my country men know what precious blessings they are in possession of, and which no other people on earth enjoy. I confess I had no idea of it myself. While we shall see multiplied instances of Europeans going to live in America, I will venture to say no man now living will ever see an instance of an American removing to settle in Europe & continuing there. Come then & see the proofs of this, and on your return add your testimony to that of every thinking American, in order to satisfy our countrymen how much it is their interest to preserve uninfected by contagion those peculiarities in their government & manners to which they are indebted for these blessings.

1785

---

[4] George Wythe (1726–1806), signer of the Declaration of Independence, professor of law at William and Mary College, and Chancellor of Virginia. [Jefferson's note.]

NOAH WEBSTER

1758–1843

NOAH WEBSTER'S student days at Yale during the Revolution were followed by a period of school teaching, in which he prepared a series of pioneer textbooks on grammar and spelling. Devoted to the idea of cultural independence from Europe, Webster championed a distinctively American language and system of education. His services to cultural nationalism include, in addition to his famous "Speller" and the *Grammatical Institute of the English Language*, labors which led to the enactment of an American copyright law, the compilation of the monumental *American Dictionary of the English Language* (1828), the first American revised version of the Bible, and a notable series of literary essays. Of these, his *Sketches of American Policy* (1785) rank high in the literature which called attention to the need for a stronger and more centralized federal government. Webster's *American Magazine* (1787–1788) and *The American Minerva*, a daily newspaper edited at Hartford (1793), gave him an important place in early American journalism.

Emily Ellsworth Skeel, *A Bibliography of the Writings of Noah Webster*, Edwin H. Carpenter, ed., New York, 1958.
H. R. Warfel, *Noah Webster: Schoolmaster to America*, New York, 1936.
E. E. F. Ford, *Notes on the Life of Noah Webster*, 2 vols., New York, 1912.
Letters, Harry R. Warfel, ed., New York, 1953.
G. P. Krapp, *The English Language in America*, 2 vols., New York, 1925.
H. L. Mencken, *The American Language*, New York, 1919; 4th ed. revised, 1936.

From: AN ESSAY ON THE NECESSITY, ADVANTAGES
»   »   AND PRACTICABILITY OF REFORMING THE   «   «
MODE OF SPELLING

It has been observed by all writers on the English language, that the orthography or spelling of words is very irregular; the same letters often representing different sounds, and the same sounds often expressed by different letters. For this irregularity, two principal causes may be assigned.

1. The changes to which the pronunciation of a language is liable, from the progress of science and civilization.

2. The mixture of different languages, occasioned by revolutions in England, or by a predilection of the learned, for words of foreign growth and ancient origin. . . .

But such is the state of our language. The pronunciation of the words which are strictly *English,* has been gradually changing for ages, and since the revival of science in Europe, the language has received a vast accession of words from other languages, many of which retain an orthography very ill suited to exhibit the true pronunciation.

The question now occurs: ought the Americans to retain these faults which produce innumerable inconveniences in the acquisition and use of the language, or ought they at once to reform these abuses, and introduce order and regularity into the orthography of the AMERICAN TONGUE?

Let us consider this subject with some attention.

Several attempts were formerly made in England to rectify the orthography of the language.[1] But I apprehend their schemes failed of success, rather on account of their intrinsic

[1] The first by Sir Thomas Smith, secretary of state to Queen Elizabeth; another by Dr. Gill, a celebrated master of St. Paul's school in London; another by Mr. Charles Butler, who went so far as to print his book in his proposed orthography; several in the time of Charles the First; and in the present age, Mr. Elphinstone, published a treatise in a very ridiculous orthography. [This and the other footnotes in this selection are Webster's own.]

difficulties than on account of any necessary impracticability of a reform. It was proposed, in most of these schemes, not merely to throw out superfluous and silent letters, but to introduce a number of new characters. Any attempt on such a plan must undoubtedly prove unsuccessful. It is not to be expected that an orthography, perfectly regular and simple, such as would be formed by a "Synod of Grammarians on principles of science," will ever be substituted for that confused mode of spelling which is now established. But it is apprehended that great improvements may be made, and an orthography almost regular, or such as shall obviate most of the present difficulties which occur in learning our language, may be introduced and established with little trouble and opposition.

The principal alterations necessary to render our orthography sufficiently regular and easy, are these:

1. The omission of all superfluous or silent letters; as *a* in *bread.* Thus *bread, head, give, breast, built, meant, realm, friend,* would be spelt *bred, hed, giv, brest, bilt, ment, relm, frend.* Would this alteration produce any inconvenience, any embarrassment or expense? By no means. On the other hand, it would lessen the trouble of writing, and much more, of learning the language; it would reduce the true pronunciation to a certainty; and while it would assist foreigners and our own children in acquiring the language, it would render the pronunciation uniform, in different parts of the country, and almost prevent the possibility of changes.

2. A substitution of a character that has a certain definite sound for one that is more vague and indeterminate. Thus by putting *ee* instead of *ea* or *ie,* the words *mean, near, speak, grieve, zeal,* would become *meen, neer, speek, greev, zeel.* This alteration would not occasion a moment's trouble; at the same time it would prevent a doubt respecting the pronunciation; whereas the *ea* and *ie* having different sounds, may give a learner much difficulty. Thus *greef* should be substituted for *grief; kee* for *key; beleev* for *believe; laf* for *laugh; dawter* for *daughter; plow* for *plough; tuf* for *tough; proov* for *prove; blud* for *blood;* and *draft* for *draught.* In this manner *ch* in Greek derivatives should be changed into *k;* for the English *ch* has a soft sound, as in *cherish;* but *k* always a hard sound. Therefore *character, chorus, cholic, architecture,* should be written *karacter, korus, kolic, arkitecture;* and were they thus written,

no person could mistake their true pronunciation.

Thus *ch* in French derivatives should be changed into *sh; machine, chaise, chevalier,* should be written *masheen, shaze, shevaleer;* and *pique, tour, oblique,* should be written *peek, toor, obleek.*

3. A trifling alteration in a character or the addition of a point would distinguish different sounds, without the substitution of a new character. Thus a very small stroke across *th* would distinguish its two sounds. A point over a vowel, in this manner, *ȧ,* or *ȯ,* or *ī,* might answer all the purposes of different letters. And for the diphthong *ow,* let the two letters be united by a small stroke, or both engraven on the same piece of metal, with the left hand line of the *w* united to the *o.*

These, with a few other inconsiderable alterations, would answer every purpose, and render the orthography sufficiently correct and regular.

The advantages to be derived from these alterations are numerous, great and permanent.

1. The simplicity of the orthography would facilitate the learning of the language. It is now the work of years for children to learn to spell; and after all, the business is rarely accomplished. A few men, who are bred to some business that requires constant exercise in writing, finally learn to spell most words without hesitation; but most people remain, all their lives, imperfect masters of spelling, and liable to make mistakes, whenever they take up a pen to write a short note. Nay, many people, even of education and fashion, never attempt to write a letter, without frequently consulting a dictionary.

But with the proposed orthography, a child would learn to spell, without trouble, in a very short time, and the orthography being very regular, he would ever afterwards find it difficult to make a mistake. It would, in that case, be as difficult to spell *wrong* as it is now to spell *right.*

Besides this advantage, foreigners would be able to acquire the pronunciation of English, which is now so difficult and embarrassing that they are either wholly discouraged on the first attempt, or obliged, after many years' labor, to rest contented with an imperfect knowledge of the subject.

2. A correct orthography would render the pronunciation of the language as uniform as the spelling in books. A general uniformity thro the United States would be the event of such a

reformation as I am here recommending. All persons, of every rank, would speak with some degree of precision and uniformity.[2] Such a uniformity in these states is very desirable; it would remove prejudice, and conciliate mutual affection and respect.

3. Such a reform would diminish the number of letters about one sixteenth or eighteenth. This would save a page in eighteen; and a saving of an eighteenth in the expense of books, is an advantage that should not be overlooked.

4. But a capital advantage of this reform in these states would be, that it would make a difference between the English orthography and the American. This will startle those who have not attended to the subject; but I am confident that such an event is an object of vast political consequence. For

The alteration, however small, would encourage the publication of books in our own country. It would render it, in some measure, necessary that all books should be printed in America. The English would never copy our orthography for their own use; and consequently the same impressions of books would not answer for both countries. The inhabitants of the present generation would read the English impressions; but posterity, being taught a different spelling, would prefer the American orthography.

Besides this, a *national language* is a band of *national union*. Every engine should be employed to render the people of this country *national;* to call their attachments home to their own country; and to inspire them with the pride of national character. However they may boast of independence, and the freedom of their government, yet their *opinions* are not sufficiently independent; an astonishing respect for the arts and literature of their parent country, and a blind imitation of its manners, are still prevalent among the Americans. Thus an habitual respect for another country, deserved indeed and once laudable, turns their attention from their own interests, and prevents their respecting themselves.

. . .

Sensible I am how much easier it is to propose improvements than to *introduce* them. Everything *new* starts the idea of difficulty; and yet it is often mere novelty that excites the appearance; for on a slight examination of the proposal, the difficulty vanishes. When we firmly *believe* a scheme to be practicable, the work is *half* accomplished. We are more frequently deterred by fear from making an attack than repulsed in the encounter.

Habit also is opposed to changes; for it renders even our errors dear to us. Having surmounted all difficulties in childhood, we forget the labor, the fatigue, and the perplexity we suffered in the attempt, and imagine the progress of our studies to have been smooth and easy.[3] What seems intrinsically right is so merely thro habit.

Indolence is another obstacle to improvements. The most arduous task a reformer has to execute, is to make people *think;* to rouse them from that lethargy which, like the mantle of sleep, covers them in repose and contentment.

But America is in a situation the most favorable for great reformations; and the present time is, in a singular degree, auspicious. The minds of men in this country have been awakened. New scenes have been, for many years, presenting new occasions for exertion; unexpected distresses have called forth the powers of invention; and the application of new expedients has demanded every possible exercise of wisdom and talents. Attention is roused; the mind expanded; and the intellectual faculties invigorated. Here men are prepared to receive improvements, which would be rejected by nations whose habits have not been shaken by similar events.

Now is the time, and *this* the country, in which we may expect success, in attempting changes favorable to language, science and government. Delay, in the plan here proposed, may be fatal; under a tranquil general government, the minds of men may again sink into indolence; a national acquiescence in error will follow; and posterity will be doomed to struggle with difficulties, which time and accident will perpetually multiply.

Let us then seize the present moment, and establish a *national language,* as well as a national government. Let us remember that there is a certain respect due to the opinions of other

---

[2] I once heard Dr. Franklin remark, "that those people spell best, who do not know how to spell"; that is, they spell as their ears dictate, without being guided by rules, and thus fall into a regular orthography.

[3] Thus most people suppose the present mode of spelling to be really the *easiest* and *best.* This opinion is derived from habit; the new mode of spelling proposed would save three fourths of the labor now bestowed in learning to write our language. A child would learn to spell as well in one year as he can now in four. This is not a supposition: it is an assertion capable of proof; and yet people, never knowing, or having forgot the labor of learning, suppose the present mode to be the easiest. No person, but one who has taught children, has any idea of the difficulty of learning to spell and pronounce our language in its present form.

nations. As an independent people, our reputation abroad demands that in all things we should be federal; be *national;* for if we do not respect *ourselves,* we may be assured that *other nations* will not respect us. In short, let it be impressed upon the mind of every American that to neglect the means of commanding respect abroad is treason against the character and dignity of a brave independent people.

1789

GEORGE WASHINGTON

1732–1799

ALTHOUGH HIMSELF a revolutionist, Washington had no heart or mind for any subversive or revolutionary movement which threatened the dearly-bought national freedom and the precarious national unity inaugurated by the Constitution. Convinced that the opposition in western Pennsylvania to the federal imposition and collection of a tax on whiskey was not merely a defiance of federal authority in the crucial matter of the raising of a revenue, but a plot for the overthrow of the central government, he called upon the militias to suppress the "western insurrection." In so doing Washington also revealed his sympathy with the conservative class, for the Westerners had genuine grievances. But Washington's humanity and practicality tempered his class loyalty: he granted full pardon to all insurgents who swore allegiance to the United States.

Washington's devotion to the ideal of a strong union and central government was reflected in his "Farewell Address" as well as in his proclamation on the Whiskey Insurrection. As if in vindication of his course as President, he warned his countrymen against factional opposition to existing authority, opposition which in his eyes was incompatible with good government and the preservation of liberty. The diffusion of knowledge, the inculcation of morality, and the preservation of national independence against foreign wiles and intrigues, with good faith toward all nations and favoritism toward none, also stand high in the values of "the Father of His Country."

L. D. Baldwin, *Whiskey Rebels: The Story of a Frontier Uprising,* Pittsburgh, 1939.
J. C. Fitzpatrick, *The Writings of George Washington from the Original Manuscript Sources, 1745–1799,* 26 vols., Washington, 1931–1938.
Douglas S. Freeman, *George Washington,* A Biography, 7 vols., New York, 1948–1957.
Marcus Cunliffe, *George Washington, Man and Monument,* Boston, 1958.

» » *From:* THE FAREWELL ADDRESS « «

Friends and Fellow-Citizens:

The period for a new election of a citizen to administer the Executive Government of the United States being not far distant, and the time actually arrived when your thoughts must be employed in designating the person who is to be clothed with that important trust, it appears to me proper, especially as it may conduce to a more distinct expression of the public voice, that I should now apprise you of the resolution I have formed to decline being considered among the number of those out of whom a choice is to be made.

I beg you at the same time to do me the justice to be assured that this resolution has not been taken without a strict regard to all the considerations appertaining to the relation which binds a dutiful citizen to his country; and that in withdrawing the tender of service, which silence in my situation might imply, I am influenced by no diminution of zeal for your future interest, no deficiency of grateful respect for your past kindness, but am supported by a full conviction that the step is compatible with both.

The acceptance of and continuance hitherto in the office to which your suffrages have twice called me have been a uniform sacrifice of inclination to the opinion of duty and to a deference for what appeared to be your desire. I constantly hoped that it would have been much earlier in my power, consistently with motives which I was not at liberty to disregard, to return to that retirement from which I had been reluctantly drawn. The strength of my inclination to do this previous to the last election had even led to the preparation of an address to declare it to you; but mature reflection on the then perplexed and critical posture of our affairs with foreign nations and the unanimous advice of persons entitled to my confidence impelled me to abandon the idea. I rejoice that the state of your concerns, external as well as internal, no longer renders the pursuit of inclination incompatible with the sentiment of duty or propriety, and am persuaded, whatever partiality may be retained for my services, that in the present circumstances of our country you will not disapprove my determination to retire.

The impressions with which I first undertook the arduous trust were explained on the proper occasion. In the discharge of this trust I will only say that I have, with good intentions, contributed toward the organization and administration of the Government the best exertions of which a very fallible judgment was capable. Not unconscious in the outset of the inferiority of my qualifications, experience in my own eyes, perhaps still more in the eyes of others, has strengthened the motives to diffidence of myself; and every day the increasing weight of years admonishes me more and more that the shade of retirement is as necessary to me as it will be welcome. Satisfied that if any circumstances have given peculiar value to my services they were temporary, I have the consolation to believe that, while choice and prudence invite me to quit the political scene, patriotism does not forbid it.

In looking forward to the moment which is intended to terminate the career of my political life my feelings do not permit me to suspend the deep acknowledgment of that debt of gratitude which I owe to my beloved country for the many honors it has conferred upon me; still more for the steadfast confidence with which it has supported me, and for the opportunities I have thence enjoyed of manifesting my inviolable attachment by services faithful and persevering, though in usefulness unequal to my zeal. If benefits have resulted to our country from these services, let it always be remembered to your praise and as an instructive example in our annals that under circumstances in which the passions, agitated in every direction, were liable to mislead; amidst appearances sometimes dubious; vicissitudes of fortune often discouraging; in situations in which not unfrequently want of success has countenanced the spirit of criticism, the constancy of your support was the essential prop of the efforts and a guaranty of the plans by which they were effected. Profoundly penetrated with this idea, I shall carry it with me to my grave as a strong incitement to unceasing vows that Heaven may continue to you the choicest tokens of its beneficence; that your union and brotherly affection may be perpetual; that the free Constitution which is the work of your hands may be sacredly maintained; that its administration in every department may be stamped with wisdom and virtue; that, in fine, the happiness of the people of these States, under the auspices of liberty, may be made complete by so careful a preservation and so prudent a use of this blessing as will acquire to them the glory of recommending it to the applause, the affection, and adoption of every nation which is yet a stranger to it.

Here, perhaps, I ought to stop. But a solicitude for your welfare which can not end but with my life, and the apprehension of danger natural to that solicitude, urge me on an occasion like the present to offer to your solemn contemplation and to recommend to your frequent review some sentiments which are the result of much reflection, of no inconsiderable observation, and which appear to me all important to the permanency of your felicity as a people. These will be offered to you with the more freedom as you can only see in them the disinterested warnings of a parting friend, who can possibly have no personal motive to bias his counsel. Nor can I forget as an encourage-

ment to it your indulgent reception of my sentiments on a former and not dissimilar occasion.

Interwoven as is the love of liberty with
every ligament of your hearts, no recommendation of mine is necessary to fortify or confirm
the attachment.

The unity of government which constitutes
you one people is also now dear to you. It is
justly so, for it is a main pillar in the edifice of
your real independence, the support of your
tranquility at home, your peace abroad, of your
safety, of your prosperity, of that very liberty
which you so highly prize. But as it is easy to
foresee that from different causes and from
different quarters much pains will be taken,
many artifices employed, to weaken in your
minds the conviction of this truth, as this is
the point in your political fortress against
which the batteries of internal and external
enemies will be most constantly and actively
(though often covertly and insidiously) directed, it is of infinite moment that you should
properly estimate the immense value of your
national union to your collective and individual
happiness; that you should cherish a cordial,
habitual, and immovable attachment to it; ac-
customing yourselves to think and speak of it
as of the palladium of your political safety and
prosperity; watching for its preservation with
jealous anxiety; discountenancing whatever
may suggest even a suspicion that it can in
any event be abandoned, and indignantly
frowning upon the first dawning of every attempt to alienate any portion of our country
from the rest or to enfeeble the sacred ties
which now link together the various parts.

For this you have every inducement of
sympathy and interest. Citizens by birth or
choice of a common country, that country has
a right to concentrate your affections. The
name of American, which belongs to you in
your national capacity, must always exalt the
just pride of patriotism more than any appellation derived from local discriminations. With
slight shades of difference, you have the same
religion, manners, habits, and political principles. You have in a common cause fought and
triumphed together. The independence and
liberty you possess are the work of joint councils and joint efforts, of common dangers, sufferings, and successes.

But these considerations, however powerfully they address themselves to your sensibility, are greatly outweighed by those which
apply more immediately to your interest. Here

every portion of our country finds the most
commanding motives for carefully guarding
and preserving the union of the whole.

The *North,* in an unrestrained intercourse
with the *South,* protected by the equal laws of
a common government, finds in the productions
of the latter great additional resources of maritime and commercial enterprise and precious
materials of manufacturing industry. The
South, in the same intercourse, benefiting by
the same agency of the *North,* sees its agriculture grow and its commerce expand. Turning partly into its own channels the seamen of
the *North,* it finds its particular navigation
invigorated; and while it contributes in different ways to nourish and increase the general
mass of the national investigation, it looks forward to the protection of a maritime strength
to which itself is unequally adapted. The *East,*
in a like intercourse with the *West,* already
finds, and in the progressive improvement of
interior communications by land and water will
more and more find, a valuable vent for the
commodities which it brings from abroad or
manufactures at home. The *West* derives from
the *East* supplies requisite to its growth and
comfort, and what is perhaps of still greater
consequence, it must of necessity owe the
secure enjoyment of indispensable *outlets* for
its own productions to the weight, influence,
and the future maritime strength of the Atlantic side of the Union, directed by an indissoluble community of interest as *one nation.*
Any other tenure by which the *West* can hold
this essential advantage, whether derived from
its own separate strength or from an apostate
and unnatural connection with any foreign
power, must be intrinsically precarious.

While, then, every part of our country thus
feels an immediate and particular interest in
union, all the parts combined can not fail to
find in the united mass of means and efforts
greater strength, greater resource, proportion-
ably greater security from external danger, a
less frequent interruption of their peace by
foreign nations, and what is of inestimable
value, they must derive from union and exemption from those broils and wars between themselves which so frequently afflict neighboring
countries not tied together by the same governments, which their own rivalships alone
would be sufficient to produce, but which opposite foreign alliances, attachments, and intrigues would stimulate and imbitter. Hence,
likewise, they will avoid the necessity of those

overgrown military establishments which, under any form of government, are inauspicious to liberty, and which are to be regarded as particularly hostile to republican liberty. In this sense it is that your union ought to be considered as a main prop of your liberty, and that the love of the one ought to endear to you the preservation of the other.

These considerations speak a persuasive language to every reflecting and virtuous mind, and exhibit the continuance of the union as a primary object of patriotic desire. Is there a doubt whether a common government can embrace so large a sphere? Let experience solve it. To listen to mere speculation in such a case were criminal. We are authorized to hope that a proper organization of the whole, with the auxiliary agency of governments for the respective subdivisions, will afford a happy issue to the experiment. It is well worth a fair and full experiment. With such powerful and obvious motives to union affecting all parts of our country, while experience shall not have demonstrated its impracticability, there will always be reason to distrust the patriotism of those who in any quarter may endeavor to weaken its bands.

In contemplating the causes which may disturb our union it occurs as matter of serious concern that any ground should have been furnished for characterizing parties by *geographical* discriminations—*Northern* and *Southern, Atlantic* and *Western*—whence designing men may endeavor to excite a belief that there is a real difference of local interests and views. One of the expedients of party to acquire influence within particular districts is to misrepresent the opinions and aims of other districts. You can not shield yourselves too much against the jealousies and heartburnings which spring from these misrepresentations; they tend to render alien to each other those who ought to be bound together by fraternal affection. . . .

To the efficacy and permanency of your union a government for the whole is indispensable. No alliances, however strict, between the parts can be an adequate substitute. They must inevitably experience the infractions and interruptions which all alliances in all times have experienced. Sensible of this momentous truth, you have improved upon your first essay by the adoption of a Constitution of Government better calculated than your former for an intimate union and for the ef-

ficacious management of your common concerns. This Government, the offspring of our own choice, uninfluenced and unawed, adopted upon full investigation and mature deliberation, completely free in its principles, in the distribution of its powers, uniting security with energy, and containing within itself a provision for its own amendment, has a just claim to your confidence and your support. Respect for its authority, compliance with its laws, acquiescence in its measures, are duties enjoined by the fundamental maxims of true liberty. The basis of our political systems is the right of the people to make and to alter their constitutions of government. But the constitution which at any time exists till changed by an explicit and authentic act of the whole people is sacredly obligatory upon all. The very idea of the power and the right of the people to establish government presupposes the duty of every individual to obey the established government. . . .

Toward the preservation of your Government and the permanency of your present happy state, it is requisite not only that you steadily discountenance irregular oppositions to its acknowledged authority, but also that you resist with care the spirit of innovation upon its principles, however specious the pretexts. One method of assault may be to effect in the forms of the Constitution alterations which will impair the energy of the system, and thus to undermine what can not be directly overthrown. In all the changes to which you may be invited remember that time and habit are at least as necessary to fix the true character of governments as of other human institutions; that experience is the surest standard by which to test the real tendency of the existing constitution of a country; that facility in changes upon the credit of mere hypothesis and opinion exposes to perpetual change, from the endless variety of hypothesis and opinion; and remember especially that for the efficient management of your common interests in a country so extensive as ours a government of as much vigor as is consistent with the perfect security of liberty is indispensable. Liberty itself will find in such a government, with powers properly distributed and adjusted, its surest guardian. It is, indeed, little else than a name where the government is too feeble to withstand the enterprises of faction, to confine each member of the society within the limits prescribed by the laws, and to maintain all in the secure and tranquil enjoyment of the rights of person and property.

I have already intimated to you the danger of parties in the State, with particular reference to the founding of them on geographical discriminations. Let me now take a more comprehensive view, and warn you in the most solemn manner against the baneful effects of the spirit of party generally.

This spirit, unfortunately, is inseparable from our nature, having its root in the strongest passions of the human mind. It exists under different shapes in all governments, more or less stifled, controlled, or repressed; but in those of the popular form it is seen in its greatest rankness and is truly their worst enemy. . . .

It serves always to distract the public councils and enfeeble the public administration. It agitates the community with ill-founded jealousies and false alarms; kindles the animosity of one part against another; foments occasionally riot and insurrection. It opens the door to foreign influence and corruption, which find a facilitated access to the government itself through the channels of party passion. Thus the policy and the will of one country are subjected to the policy and will of another.

There is an opinion that parties in free countries are useful checks upon the administration of the government, and serve to keep alive the spirit of liberty. This within certain limits is probably true; and in governments of a monarchical cast patriotism may look with indulgence, if not with favor, upon the spirit of party. But in those of the popular character, in governments purely elective, it is a spirit not to be encouraged. From their natural tendency it is certain there will always be enough of that spirit for every salutary purpose; and there being constant danger of excess, the effort ought to be by force of public opinion to mitigate and assuage it. A fire not to be quenched, it demands a uniform vigilance to prevent its bursting into a flame, lest, instead of warming, it should consume.

It is important, likewise, that the habits of thinking in a free country should inspire caution in those intrusted with its administration to confine themselves within their respective constitutional spheres, avoiding in the exercise of the powers of one department to encroach upon another. The spirit of encroachment tends to consolidate the powers of all the departments in one, and thus to create, what-

ever the form of government, a real despotism. A just estimate of that love of power and proneness to abuse it which predominates in the human heart is sufficient to satisfy us of the truth of this position. The necessity of reciprocal checks in the exercise of political power, by dividing and distributing it into different depositories, and constituting each the guardian of the public weal against invasions by the others, has been evinced by experiments ancient and modern, some of them in our country and under our own eyes. To preserve them must be as necessary as to institute them. If in the opinion of the people the distribution or modification of the constitutional powers be in any particular wrong, let it be corrected by an amendment in the way which the Constitution designates. But let there be no change by usurpation; for though this in one instance may be the instrument of good, it is the customary weapon by which free governments are destroyed. The precedent must always greatly overbalance in permanent evil any partial or transient benefit which the use can at any time yield.

Of all the dispositions and habits which lead to political prosperity, religion and morality are indispensable supports. In vain would that man claim the tribute of patriotism who should labor to subvert these great pillars of human happiness—these firmest props of the duties of men and citizens. The mere politician, equally with the pious man, ought to respect and to cherish them. A volume could not trace all their connections with private and public felicity. Let it simply be asked, Where is the security for property, for reputation, for life, if the sense of religious obligation *desert* the oaths which are the instruments of investigation in courts of justice? And let us with caution indulge the supposition that morality can be maintained without religion. Whatever may be conceded to the influence of refined education on minds of peculiar structure, reason and experience both forbid us to expect that national morality can prevail in exclusion of religious principle.

It is substantially true that virtue or morality is a necessary spring of popular government. The rule indeed extends with more or less force to every species of free government. Who that is a sincere friend to it can look with indifference upon attempts to shake the foundation of the fabric? Promote, then, as an object of primary importance, institutions for the general diffusion of knowledge. In proportion as the structure of a government gives force to public opinion, it is essential that public opinion should be enlightened.

As a very important source of strength and security, cherish public credit. One method of preserving it is to use it as sparingly as possible, avoiding occasions of expense by cultivating peace, but remembering also that timely dis-
10 bursements to prepare for danger frequently prevent much greater disbursements to repel it; avoiding likewise the accumulation of debt, not only by shunning occasions of expense, but by vigorous exertions in time of peace to discharge the debts which unavoidable wars have occasioned, not ungenerously throwing upon posterity the burthen which we ourselves ought to bear. The execution of these maxims belongs to your representatives; but it is necessary that
20 public opinion should cooperate. To facilitate to them the performance of their duty it is essential that you should practically bear in mind that toward the payment of debts there must be revenue; that to have revenue there must be taxes; that no taxes can be devised which are not more or less inconvenient and unpleasant; that the intrinsic embarrassment inseparable from the selection of the proper objects (which is always a choice of difficulties), ought to be a
30 decisive motive for a candid construction of the conduct of the Government in making it, and for a spirit of acquiescence in the measures for obtaining revenue which the public exigencies may at any time dictate.

Observe good faith and justice toward all nations. Cultivate peace and harmony with all. Religion and morality enjoin this conduct. And can it be that good policy does not equally enjoin it? It will be worthy of a free, enlightened,
40 and at no distant period a great nation to give to mankind the magnanimous and too novel example of a people always guided by an exalted justice and benevolence. Who can doubt that in the course of time and things the fruits of such a plan would richly repay any temporary advantages which might be lost by a steady adherence to it? Can it be that Providence has not connected the permanent felicity of a nation with its virtue? The experiment, at
50 least, is recommended by every sentiment which ennobles human nature. Alas! is it rendered impossible by its vices?

In the execution of such a plan nothing is more essential than that permanent, inveterate antipathies against particular nations and pas-

sionate attachments for others should be excluded, and that in place of them just and amicable feelings toward all should be cultivated. The nation which indulges toward another an habitual hatred or an habitual fondness is in some degree a slave. It is a slave to its animosity or to its affection, either of which is sufficient to lead it astray from its duty and its interest. Antipathy in one nation against another disposes each more readily to offer insult and injury, to lay hold of slight causes of umbrage, and to be haughty and intractable when accidental or trifling occasions of dispute occur.

Hence frequent collisions, obstinate, envenomed, and bloody contests. The nation prompted by ill will and resentment sometimes impels to war the government contrary to the best calculations of policy. The government sometimes participates in the national propensity, and adopts through passion what reason would reject. At other times it makes the animosity of the nation subservient to projects of hostility, instigated by pride, ambition, and other sinister and pernicious motives. The peace often, sometimes perhaps the liberty, of nations has been the victim.

So, likewise, a passionate attachment of one nation for another produces a variety of evils. Sympathy for the favorite nation, facilitating the illusion of an imaginary common interest in cases where no real common interest exists, and infusing into one the enmities of the other, betrays the former into a participation in the quarrels and wars of the latter without adequate inducement or justification. It leads also to concessions to the favorite nation of privileges denied to others, which is apt doubly to injure the nation making the concessions by unnecessarily parting with what ought to have been retained, and by exciting jealousy, ill will, and a disposition to retaliate in the parties from whom equal privileges are withheld; and it gives to ambitious, corrupted, or deluded citizens (who devote themselves to the favorite nation) facility to betray or sacrifice the interests of their own country without odium, sometimes even with popularity, gilding with the appearances of a virtuous sense of obligation, a commendable deference for public opinion, or a laudable zeal for public good the base or foolish compliances of ambition, corruption, or infatuation.

As avenues to foreign influence in innumerable ways, such attachments are particularly alarming to the truly enlightened and independent patriot. How many opportunities do they afford to tamper with domestic factions, to practice the arts of seduction, to mislead public opinion, to influence or awe the public councils! Such an attachment of a small or weak toward a great and powerful nation dooms the former to be the satellite of the latter. Against the insidious wiles of foreign influence (I conjure you to believe me, fellow-citizens) the jealousy of a free people ought to be *constantly* awake, since history and experience prove that foreign influence is one of the most baneful foes of republican government. But that jealousy, to be useful, must be impartial, else it becomes the instrument of the very influence to be avoided, instead of a defense against it. Excessive partiality for one foreign nation and excessive dislike for another cause those whom they actuate to see danger only on one side, and serve to veil and even second the arts of influence on the other. Real patriots who may resist the intrigues of the favorite are liable to become suspected and odious, while its tools and dupes usurp the applause and confidence of the people to surrender their interests.

The great rule of conduct for us in regard to foreign nations is, in extending our commercial relations to have with them as little *political* connection as possible. So far as we have already formed engagements let them be fulfilled with perfect good faith. Here let us stop.

Europe has a set of primary interests which to us have none or a very remote relation. Hence she must be engaged in frequent controversies, the causes of which are essentially foreign to our concerns. Hence, therefore, it must be unwise in us to implicate ourselves by artificial ties in the ordinary vicissitudes of her politics or the ordinary combinations and collisions of her friendships or enmities.

Our detached and distant situation invites and enables us to pursue a different course. If we remain one people, under an efficient government, the period is not far off when we may defy material injury from external annoyance; when we may take such an attitude as will cause the neutrality we may at any time resolve upon to be scrupulously respected; when belligerent nations, under the impossibility of making acquisitions upon us, will not lightly hazard the giving us provocation; when we may choose peace or war, as our

interest, guided by justice, shall counsel.

Why forego the advantages of so peculiar a situation? Why quit our own to stand upon foreign ground? Why, by interweaving our destiny with that of any part of Europe, entangle our peace and prosperity in the toils of European ambition, rivalship, interest, humor, or caprice?

It is our true policy to steer clear of permanent alliances with any portion of the foreign world, so far, I mean, as we are now at liberty to do it; for let me not be understood as capable of patronizing infidelity to existing engagements. I hold the maxim no less applicable to public than to private affairs that honesty is always the best policy. I repeat, therefore, let those engagements be observed in their genuine sense. But in my opinion it is unnecessary and would be unwise to extend them.

Taking care always to keep ourselves by suitable establishments on a respectable defensive posture, we may safely trust to temporary alliances for extraordinary emergencies.

Harmony, liberal intercourse with all nations are recommended by policy, humanity, and interest. But even our commercial policy should hold an equal and impartial hand, neither seeking nor granting exclusive favors or preferences; consulting the natural course of things; diffusing and diversifying by gentle means the streams of commerce, but forcing nothing; establishing with powers so disposed, in order to give trade a stable course, to define the rights of our merchants, and to enable the Government to support them, conventional rules of intercourse, the best that present circumstances and mutual opinion will permit, but temporary and liable to be from time to time abandoned or varied as experience and circumstances shall dictate; constantly keeping in view that it is folly in one nation to look for disinterested favors from another; that it must pay with a portion of its independence for whatever it may accept under that character; that by such acceptance it may place itself in the condition of having given equivalents for nominal favors, and yet of being reproached with ingratitude for not giving more. There can be no greater error than to expect or calculate upon real favors from nation to nation. It is an illusion which experience must cure, which a just pride ought to discard. . . .

Though in reviewing the incidents of my Administration I am unconscious of intentional error, I am nevertheless too sensible of my defects not to think it probable that I may have committed many errors. Whatever they may be, I fervently beseech the Almighty to avert or mitigate the evils to which they may tend. I shall also carry with me the hope that my country will never cease to view them with indulgence, and that, after forty-five years of my life dedicated to its service with an upright zeal, the faults of incompetent abilities will be consigned to oblivion, as myself must soon be to the mansions of rest.

Relying on its kindness in this as in other things, and actuated by that fervent love toward it which is so natural to a man who views in it the native soil of himself and his progenitors for several generations, I anticipate with pleasing expectation that retreat in which I promise myself to realize without alloy the sweet enjoyment of partaking in the midst of my fellow-citizens the benign influence of good laws under a free government—the ever-favorite object of my heart, and the happy reward, as I trust, of our mutual cares, labors, and dangers.   Go. WASHINGTON

1796

» » PROCLAMATION ON THE WHISKEY REBELLION « «

Whereas combinations to defeat the execution of the laws laying duties upon spirits distilled within the United States and upon stills have from the time of the commencement of those laws existed in some of the western parts of Pennsylvania; and

Whereas the said combinations, proceeding in a manner subversive equally of the just authority of government and of the rights of individuals, have hitherto effected their dangerous and criminal purpose by the influence of certain irregular meetings whose proceedings have tended to encourage and uphold the spirit of opposition by misrepresentations of the laws calculated to render them odious; by endeavors to deter those who might be so disposed from accepting offices under them through fear of public resentment and of injury to person and property, and to compel those who had accepted such offices by actual violence to surrender or forbear the execution of them; by circulating vindictive menaces against all those who should otherwise, directly or indirectly, aid in the execution of the said laws, or who, yielding to the dictates of conscience and to a sense of obligation, should themselves comply therewith; by actually injuring and destroying the property of persons who were understood to have so complied; by inflicting cruel and humiliating punishments upon private citizens for no other cause than that of appearing to be the friends of the laws; by intercepting the public officers on the highways, abusing, assaulting, and otherwise ill treating them; by going to their houses in the night, gaining admittance by force, taking away their papers, and committing other outrages, employing for these unwarrantable purposes the agency of armed banditti disguised in such manner as for the most part to escape discovery; and

Whereas the endeavors of the Legislature to obviate objections to the said laws by lowering the duties and by other alterations conducive to the convenience of those whom they immediately affect (though they have given satisfaction in other quarters), and the endeavors of the executive officers to conciliate a compliance with the laws by explanations, by forbearance, and even by particular accommodations founded on the suggestion of local considerations, have been disappointed of their effect by the machinations of persons whose industry to excite resistance has increased with every appearance of a disposition among the people to relax in their opposition and to acquiesce in the laws, insomuch that many persons in the said western parts of Pennsylvania have at length been hardy enough to perpetrate acts which I am advised amount to treason, being overt acts of levying war against the United States, the said persons having on the 16th and 17th July last past proceeded in arms (on the second day amounting to several hundreds) to the house of John Neville, inspector of the revenue for the fourth survey of the district of Pennsylvania; having repeatedly attacked the said house with the persons therein, wounding some of them; having seized David Lenox, marshal of the district of Pennsylvania, who previous thereto had been fired upon while in the execution of his duty by a party of armed men, detaining him for some time prisoner, till for the preservation of his life and the obtaining of his liberty, he found it necessary to enter into stipulations to forbear the execution of certain official duties touching processes issuing out of a court of the United States; and having finally obliged the said inspector of the said revenue and the said marshal from considerations of personal safety to fly from that part of the country, in order, by a circuitous route, to proceed to the seat of Government, avowing as the motives of these outrageous proceedings an intention to prevent by force of arms the execution of the said laws, to oblige the said inspector of the revenue to renounce his said office, to withstand by open violence the lawful authority of the Government of the United States, and to compel thereby an alteration in the measures of the Legislature and a repeal of the laws aforesaid; and

Whereas by a law of the United States entitled "An act to provide for calling forth the militia to execute the laws of Union, suppress insurrections, and repel invasions," it is enacted "that whenever the laws of the United States shall be opposed or the execution thereof obstructed in any State by combinations too powerful to be suppressed by the ordinary course of judicial proceedings or by the powers vested in the marshals by that act, the same being notified by an associate justice or the district judge, it shall be lawful for the President of the United States to call forth the militia of such State to suppress such combinations and to cause the laws to be duly executed. And if the militia of a State where such combinations may happen shall refuse or be insufficient to suppress the same, it shall be lawful for the President, if the Legislature of the United States shall not be in session, to call forth and employ such numbers of the militia of any other State or States most convenient thereto as may be necessary; and the use of the militia so to be called forth may be continued, if necessary, until the expiration of thirty days after the commencement of the ensuing session: *Provided always,* That whenever it may be necessary in the judgment of the President to use the military force hereby directed to be called forth, the President shall forthwith, and previous thereto, by proclamation, command such insurgents to disperse and retire peaceably to their respective abodes within a limited time"; and

Whereas James Wilson, an associate justice, on the 4th instant, by writing under his hand, did from evidence which had been laid before him notify to me that "in the counties of Washington and Allegany, in Pennsylvania, laws of the United States are opposed and the execution thereof obstructed by combinations too powerful to be suppressed by the ordinary course of judicial proceedings or by the powers vested in the marshal of that district"; 10 and

Whereas it is in my judgment necessary under the circumstances of the case to take measures for calling forth the militia in order to suppress the combinations aforesaid, and to cause the laws to be duly executed; and I have accordingly determined so to do, feeling the deepest regret for the occasion, but withal the most solemn conviction that the essential interests of the Union demand it, that the very 20 existence of Government and the fundamental principles of social order are materially involved in the issue, and that the patriotism and firmness of all good citizens are seriously called upon, as occasions may require, to aid in the effectual suppression of so fatal a spirit:

Wherefore, and in pursuance of the proviso above recited, I, George Washington, President of the United States, do hereby command all 30 persons being insurgents as aforesaid, and all others whom it may concern, on or before the 1st day of September next to disperse and retire peaceably to their respective abodes. And I do moreover warn all persons whomsoever against aiding, abetting, or comforting the perpetrators of the aforesaid treasonable acts, and do require all officers and other citizens, according to their respective duties and the laws of the land, to exert their utmost en- 40 deavors to prevent and suppress such dangerous proceedings.

In testimony whereof I have caused the seal of the United States of America to be affixed to these presents, and signed the same with my hand.

(Seal.) *Done at the City of Philadelphia, the*
7th day of August, 1795, and of the
Independence of the United States 50
of America the nineteenth.

Go. WASHINGTON

By the President:
EDM: RANDOLPH

1794

HENRY CLAY

1777–1852

A SELF-MADE MAN, Henry Clay had come, by 1810, to represent the aspirations of the Ohio Valley pioneers with whom he had identified himself after a brief study of law in Virginia, his native state. Federal protection against the Northwest Indians and their British mentors, together with the acquisition of Canadian lands to satisfy the never-quenched thirst for lands which pioneers always experienced, were the "national" interests on which was based Clay's ardently patriotic plea for the aggressive conduct of the second war with Great Britain. This he, as one of the Western "war hawks," helped to bring on. In his later career Clay's championship of internal improvements at federal expense and a protective tariff for the development of home markets, similarly concealed sectional and class interests under a "nationalistic" banner. Clay's love of the Union was, however, sincere, and his efforts to preserve it, notably in his labors for compromise of sectional antagonisms in 1833 and again in 1850, identify him with a cause which had the future on its side.

Clay's speech in the House of Representatives in 1813, contrasting as it does with Webster's criticism of the War and of the proposal for conscription, represents his nationalism and illustrates his oratorical skill.

The Papers of Henry Clay, James F. Hopkins, ed., Lexington, 1959–
Clement Eaton, *Henry Clay and the Art of American Politics*, Boston, 1957.
Richard Current, *Daniel Webster and the Rise of National Conservatism*, Boston, 1955.
G. G. Van Deusen, *The Life of Henry Clay*, Boston, 1937.

» » From: THE NEW ARMY BILL « «

. . . Considering the situation in which this country is now placed—a state of actual war with one of the most powerful nations on the earth—it may not be useless to take a view of the past, and of the various parties which have at different times appeared in this country, and to attend to the manner by which we have been driven from a peaceful posture to our present warlike attitude. Such an inquiry may assist in guiding us to that result, an honorable peace, which must be the sincere desire of every friend to America. The course of that opposition, by which the administration of the government had been unremittingly impeded for the last twelve years, was singular, and, I believe, unexampled in the history of any country. It has been alike the duty and the interest of the administration to preserve peace. It was their duty, because it is necessary to the growth of an infant people, to their genius, and to their habits. It was their interest,

because a change of the condition of the nation brings along with it a danger of the loss of the affections of the people. The administration has not been forgetful of these solemn obligations. No art has been left unessayed, no experiment, promising a favorable result, left untried to maintain the peaceful relations of the country. When, some six or seven years ago, the affairs of the nation assumed a threatening aspect, a partial nonimportation was adopted. As they grew more alarming, an embargo was imposed. It would have accomplished its purpose, but it was sacrificed upon the altar of conciliation. Vain and fruitless attempt to propitiate! Then came along nonintercourse; and a general non-importation followed in the train. In the mean time, any indications of a return to the public law and the path of justice, on the part of either belligerent, are seized upon with avidity by the administration. . . . No matter with what unfeigned sincerity, with what real effort, the administration cultivates peace, the opposition insists that it alone is culpable for every breach that is made between the two countries. . . . Restriction after restriction has been tried; negotiation has been resorted to, until further negotiation would have been disgraceful. While these peaceful experiments are undergoing a trial, what is the conduct of the opposition? They are the champions of war—the proud—the spirited—the sole repository of the nation's honor—the men of exclusive vigor and energy. The administration, on the contrary, is weak, feeble, and pusillanimous—"incapable of being kicked into a war." The maxim, "not a cent for tribute, millions for defense," is loudly proclaimed. Is the administration for negotiation? The opposition is tired, sick, disgusted with negotiation. They want to draw the sword, and avenge the nation's wrongs. When, however, foreign nations, perhaps emboldened by the very opposition here made, refuse to listen to the amicable appeals, which have been repeated and reiterated by the administration, to their justice and to their interest—when, in fact, war with one of them has become identified with our independence and our sovereignty, and to abstain from it was no longer possible, behold the opposition veering round and becoming the friends of peace and commerce. They tell you of the calamities of war, its tragical events, the squandering away of your resources, the waste of the public treasure, and the spilling of innocent blood. "Gorgons, hydras, and chimeras dire." They tell you that honor is an illusion! Now, we see them exhibiting the terrific forms of the roaring king of the forest. Now the meekness and humility of the lamb! They are for war and no restrictions, when the administration is for peace. They are for peace and restrictions, when the administration is for war. You find them, sir, tacking with every gale, displaying the colors of every party, and of all nations, steady only in one unalterable purpose—to steer, if possible, into the haven of power.

. . . True to our principles, we are now struggling for the liberty of our seamen against foreign oppression. True to theirs, they oppose a war undertaken for this object. They have, indeed, lately affected a tender solicitude for the liberties of the people, and talk of the danger of standing armies, and the burden of the taxes. But it must be evident to you, Mr. Chairman, that they speak in a foreign idiom.

Their brogue evinces that it is not their vernacular tongue. What! the opposition who, in 1798 and 1799, could raise a useless army to fight an enemy three thousand miles distant from us [France], alarmed at the existence of one raised for a known and specified object—the attack of the adjoining provinces of the enemy! What! the gentleman from Massachusetts [Josiah Quincy], who assisted by his vote to raise the army of twenty-five thousand, alarmed at the danger of our liberties from this very army!

But, sir, I must speak of another subject which I never think of but with feelings of the deepest awe. The gentleman from Massachusetts, in imitation of some of his predecessors of 1799, has entertained us with a picture of cabinet plots, presidential plots, and all sorts of plots, which have been engendered by the diseased state of the gentleman's imagination. I wish, sir, that another plot of a much more serious and alarming character—a plot that aims at the dismemberment of our Union—had only the same imaginary existence. But no man who has paid any attention to the tone of certain prints, and to transactions in a particular quarter of the Union, for several years past, can doubt the existence of such a plot. It was far, very far from my intention to charge the opposition with such a design. No, I believe them generally incapable of it. But I can not say as much for some, who have been unworthily associated with them in the quarter of the Union to which I have referred. The gentleman can not have forgotten his own sentiments, uttered even on the floor of this House, "peaceably if we can, FORCIBLY if we must," nearly at the very time Henry's mission to Boston was undertaken.[1] The flagitiousness of that embassy had been attempted to be concealed by directing the public attention to the price which, the gentleman says, was given for the disclosure. As if any price could change the atrociousness of the attempt on the part of Great Britain, or could extenuate, in the slightest degree, the offense of those citizens who entertained and deliberated upon a proposition so infamous and unnatural! There was a most remarkable coincidence between some of the things which that man states, and certain

[1] John Henry, a British subject, visited Boston in 1809 and wrote to the Governor-General of Canada detailed reports of his conversations with leading Federalists. After British authorities refused to buy these letters, the federal government purchased them for fifty thousand dollars. The letters, apart from revealing the well-known Federalist discontent with the Republican administration, were quite commonplace.

events in the quarter alluded to. In the contingency of war with Great Britain, it will be recollected that the neutrality and eventual separation of that section of the Union was to be brought about. . . .

. . . The war was declared, because Great Britain arrogated to herself the pretension of regulating our foreign trade, under the delusive name of retaliatory orders in council—a pretension by which she undertook to proclaim to American enterprise, "thus far shalt thou go, and no further"—orders which she refused to revoke, after the alleged cause of their enactment had ceased; because she persisted in the practice of impressing American seamen; because she had instigated the Indians to commit hostilities against us; and because she refused indemnity for her past injuries upon our commerce. I throw out of the question other wrongs. The war in fact was announced, on our part, to meet the war which she was waging on her part. So undeniable were the causes of the war, so powerfully did they address themselves to the feeling of the whole American people, that when the bill was pending before this House, gentlemen in the opposition, although provoked to debate, would not, or could not, utter one syllable against it. It is true, they wrapped themselves up in sullen silence, pretending they did not choose to debate such a question in secret session. . . .

. . . I am far from acknowledging that, had the orders in council been repealed, as they have been, before the war was declared, the declaration of hostilities would of course have been prevented. In a body so numerous as this is, from which the declaration emanated, it is impossible to say, with any degree of certainty, what would have been the effect of such a repeal. Each member must answer for himself. As to myself, I have no hesitation in saying, that I have always considered the impressment of American seamen as much the most serious aggression. But, sir, how have those orders at last been repealed? Great Britain, it is true, has intimated a willingness to suspend their practical operation, but she still arrogates to herself the right to revive them upon certain contingencies, of which she constitutes herself the sole judge. She waives the temporary use of the rod, but she suspends it *in terrorem* over our heads. Supposing it to be conceded to, gentlemen, that such a repeal of the orders in council as took place on the 23d of June last, exceptional as it is, being known before the

war was proclaimed, would have prevented it; does it follow that it ought to induce us to lay down our arms, without the redress of any other injury of which we complain?

Does it follow, in all cases, that what **would** in the first instance have prevented would **also** terminate the war? By no means. It requires a strong and powerful effort in a nation, prone to peace as this is, to burst through its habits, and encounter the difficulties and privations of war. Such a nation ought but seldom to embark in a belligerent contest; but when it does, it should be for obvious and essential rights alone, and should firmly resolve to extort, at all hazards their recognition. The war of the Revolution is an example of a war begun for one object and prosecuted for another. It was waged, in its commencement, against the right asserted by the parent country to tax the colonies. Then no one thought of absolute independence. The idea of independence was repelled. But the British government would have relinquished the principle of taxation. The founders of our liberties saw, however, that there was no security short of independence, and they achieved that independence. When nations are engaged in war, those rights in controversy, which are not acknowledged by the treaty of peace, are abandoned. And who is prepared to say, that American seamen shall be surrendered as victims to the English principle of impressment? And, sir, what is this principle? She contends, that she has a right to the services of her own subjects; and that, in the exercise of this right, she may lawfully impress them, even although she finds them in American vessels, upon the high seas, without her jurisdiction. Now I deny that she has any right, beyond her jurisdiction, to come on board our vessels, upon the high seas, for any other purpose than in the pursuit of enemies, or their goods, or contraband of war. But she further contends, that her subjects can not renounce their allegiance to her, and contract a new obligation to other sovereigns. I do not mean to go into the general question of the right of expatriation. If, as is contended, all nations deny it, all nations at the same time admit and practice the right of naturalization. Great Britain herself does this. Great Britain, in the very case of foreign seamen, imposes, perhaps, fewer restraints upon naturalization than any other nation. Then, if subjects can not break their original allegiance, they may, according to universal usage, contract a new allegiance. . . .

The honorable gentleman from New York [Mr. Bleeker], in the very sensible speech with which he favored the committee, made one observation which did not comport with his usual liberal and enlarged views. It was, that those who are most interested against the practice of impressment, did not desire a continuance of the war on account of it; while those (the southern and western members) who had no interest in it, were the zealous advocates of American seamen. It was a provincial sentiment unworthy of that gentleman. It was one which, in a change of condition, he would not express, because I know he could not feel it. Does not that gentleman feel for the unhappy victims of the tomahawk in the western wilds, although his quarter of the Union may be exempted from similar barbarities? I am sure he does. If there be a description of rights which, more than any other, should unite all parties in all quarters of the Union, it is unquestionably the rights of the person. No matter what his vocation; whether he seeks subsistence amid the dangers of the deep, or draws them from the bowels of the earth, or from the humblest occupations of mechanic life; wherever the sacred rights of an American freeman are assailed, all hearts ought to unite, and every arm should be braced to vindicate his cause.

The gentleman from Delaware sees in Canada no object worthy of conquest. According to him it is a cold, sterile, and inhospitable region. And yet such are the allurements which it offers, that the same gentleman apprehends that if it be annexed to the United States, already too much weakened by the extension of territory, the people of New England will rush over the line and depopulate that section of the Union! That gentleman considers it honest to hold Canada as a kind of hostage, to regard it as a sort of bond for the good behavior of the enemy. But he will not enforce that bond. The actual conquest of that country would, according to him, make no impression upon the enemy; and yet the very apprehension only of such a conquest would, at all times, have a powerful operation upon him! Other gentlemen consider the invasion of that country as wicked and unjustifiable. Its inhabitants are represented as harmless and unoffending; as connected with those of the bordering States by a thousand tender ties, interchanging acts of kindness, and all the offices of good neighborhood. Canada . . . innocent! Canada un-offending! Is it not in Canada that the tomahawk of the savage has been molded into its death-like form? Has it not been from Canadian magazines, Malden and others, that those supplies have been issued which nourish and continue the Indian hostilities—supplies which have enabled the savage hordes to butcher the garrison of Chicago, and to commit other horrible excesses and murders? Was it not by the joint co-operation of Canadians and Indians that a remote American fort, Michilimackinac, was assailed and reduced while in ignorance of a state of war? But, sir, how soon have the opposition changed their tone! When the administration was striving, by the operation of peaceful measures, to bring Great Britain back to a sense of justice, they were for old-fashioned war. And now they have got old-fashioned war their sensibilities are cruelly shocked, and all their sympathies lavished upon the harmless inhabitants of the adjoining provinces. What does a state of war present? The united energies of one people arrayed against the combined energies of another; a conflict in which each party aims to inflict all the injury it can, by sea and land, upon the territories, property, and citizens of another; subject only to the rules of mitigated war practiced by civilized nations. The gentlemen would not touch the continental provinces of the enemy, nor, I presume, for the same reason, her possessions in the West Indies. The same humane spirit would spare the seamen and soldiers of the enemy. The sacred person of his majesty must not be attacked; for the learned gentlemen on the other side are quite familiar with the maxim, that the king can do no wrong. Indeed, I know of no person on whom we may make war upon the principles of the honorable gentlemen but Mr. Stephen, the celebrated author of the orders in council, or the Board of Admiralty who authorize and regulate the practice of impressment!

The disasters of the war admonish us, we are told, of the necessity of terminating the contest. If our achievements by land have been less splendid than those of our intrepid seamen by water, it is not because the American soldier is less brave. On the one element, organization, discipline, and a thorough knowledge of their duties, exist, on the part of the officers and their men. On the other, almost every thing is yet to be acquired. We have, however, the consolation that our country abounds with the richest materials, and that in no instance, when engaged in action, have our arms been tarnished. . . .

It is alleged that the elections in England are in favor of the ministry, and that those in this country are against the war. If, in such a cause (saying nothing of the impurity of their elections) the people of that country have rallied round their government, it affords a salutary lesson to the people here; who, at all hazards, ought to support theirs, struggling as it is to maintain our just rights. But the people here have not been false to themselves; a great majority approve the war, as is evinced by the recent re-election of the chief magistrate. Suppose it were even true, that an entire section of the Union were opposed to the war; that section being a minority, is the will of the majority to be relinquished? In that section the real strength of the opposition had been greatly exaggerated. Vermont has, by two successive expressions of her opinion, approved the declaration of war. In New Hampshire, parties are so nearly equipoised, that out of thirty or thirty-five thousand votes, those who approved and are supporting it, lost the election by only one thousand or one thousand five hundred. In Massachusetts alone have they obtained any considerable accession. If we come to New York, we shall find that other and local causes have influenced her elections.

. . . An honorable peace is attainable only by an efficient war. My plan would be, to call out the ample resources of the country, give them a judicious direction, prosecute the war with the utmost vigor, strike wherever we can reach the enemy, at sea or on land, and negotiate the terms of a peace at Quebec or at Halifax. We are told that England is a proud and lofty nation, which, disdaining to wait for danger, meets it half way. Haughty as she is, we once triumphed over her, and, if we do not listen to the counsels of timidity and despair, we shall again prevail. In such a cause, with the aid of Providence, we must come out crowned with success; but if we fail, let us fail like men, lash ourselves against our gallant tars, and expire together in one common struggle, fighting for FREE TRADE AND SEAMEN'S RIGHTS.

1813

DANIEL WEBSTER

1782–1852

FOUR YEARS after his graduation from Dartmouth College in 1801, Daniel Webster began his distinguished career in law. Early identifying himself with the commercial interest of New England, he was in 1813 elected to the House of Representatives as a Federalist representative from Massachusetts. New England had no heart for the War with England which the Madison administration was pursuing; in fact, the conservative commercial interests of that section virtually boycotted the War. When a proposal was made to introduce military conscription, Webster, as the representative of the war opposition, boldly and brilliantly spoke against it. His speech, delivered before the House on December 9, 1814, is, then, not only an example of his oratory, but of a position which fused pacifism and humanitarianism with devotion to the class and sectional interests which he represented. Only after commercial capital in New England had flowed into manufacturing enterprises did Webster shift his allegiance from mercantile wealth and free trade to industrial wealth and a protective tariff. This shift also marked an important step in his development as a nationalist.

The Writings and Speeches of Daniel Webster, National Edition, 18 vols., Boston, 1903.

Richard N. Current, *Daniel Webster and the Rise of National Conservatism*, Boston, 1955.

» » *From:* SPEECH ON THE CONSCRIPTION BILL « «

(HOUSE OF REPRESENTATIVES, DECEMBER 9, 1814)

MR. CHAIRMAN: After the best reflection which I have been able to bestow on the subject of the bill before you, I am of the opinion that its principles are not warranted by any provision of the Constitution. It appears to me to partake of the nature of those other propositions for military measures which this session, so fertile in inventions, has produced. It is of the same class with the plan of the Secretary of War; [1] with the bill reported to this House by its own Committee for filling the ranks of the regular army, by classifying the free male population of the United States; and with the resolution recently introduced by an honorable gentleman from Pennsylvania (Mr. Ingersoll), and which now lies on your table, carrying the principle of compulsory service in the regular army to its utmost extent.

This bill indeed is less undisguised in its object, and less direct in its means, than some of the measures proposed. It is an attempt to exercise the power of forcing the free men of this country into the ranks of an army, for the general purposes of war, under color of a military service. To this end it commences with a classification which is in no way connected with the general organization of the militia, nor, to my apprehension, included within any of the powers which Congress possesses over them. All the authority which this Government has over the militia, until actually called into its service, is to enact laws for their organization and discipline. This power it has exercised. It now possesses the further power of calling into its service any portion of the militia of the States, in the particular exigencies for which the Constitution provides, and of governing them during the continuance of such service. Here its authority ceases. The classification of the whole body of the militia, according to the provisions of this bill, is not a measure which respects either their general organization or their discipline. It is a distinct system, introduced for new purposes, and not connected with any power which the Constitution has conferred on Congress.

But, sir, there is another consideration. The

[1] James Monroe.

services of the men to be raised under this act are not limited to those cases in which alone this Government is entitled to the aid of the militia of the States. These cases are particularly stated in the Constitution, "to repel invasion, suppress insurrection, or execute the laws." But this bill has no limitation in this respect. The usual mode of legislating on the subject is abandoned. The only section which would have confined the service of the militia, proposed to be raised, within the United States has been stricken out; and if the President should not march them into the Provinces of England at the north, or of Spain at the south, it will not be because he is prohibited by any provision in this act.

This, sir, is a bill for calling out the militia, not according to its existing organization, but by draft from new created classes;—not merely for the purpose of "repelling invasion, suppressing insurrection, or executing the laws," but for the general objects of war—for defending ourselves, or invading others, as may be thought expedient;—not for a sudden emergency, or for a short time, but for long stated periods; for two years, if the proposition of the Senate should finally prevail; for one year, if the amendment of the House should be adopted. What is this, sir, but raising a standing army out of the militia by draft, and to be recruited by draft, in like manner, as often as occasion may require?

This bill, then, is not different in principle from the other bills, plans, and resolutions which I have mentioned. The present discussion is properly and necessarily common to them all. It is a discussion, sir, of the last importance. That measures of this nature should be debated at all, in the councils of a free government, is cause of dismay. The question is nothing less than whether the most essential rights of personal liberty shall be surrendered, and despotism embraced in its worst form.

I have risen, on this occasion, with anxious and painful emotions, to add my admonition to what has been said by others. Admonition and remonstrance, I am aware, are not acceptable strains. They are duties of unpleasant performance. But they are, in my judgment, the duties which the condition of a falling State imposes. They are duties which sink deep in his conscience, who believes it probable that they may be the last services which he may be able to render to the Government of his country. On the issue of this discussion, I believe the fate of this Government may rest. Its duration is incompatible, in my opinion, with the existence of the measures in contemplation. A crisis has at last arrived, to which the course of things has long tended, and which may be decisive upon the happiness of present and of future generations. If there be anything important in the concerns of men, the considerations which fill the present hour are important. I am anxious, above all things, to stand acquitted before God and my own conscience, and in the public judgment, of all participations in the counsels which have brought us to our present condition and which now threaten the dissolution of the Government. When the present generation of men shall be swept away, and that this Government ever existed shall be matter of history only, I desire that it may be known that you have not proceeded in your course unadmonished and unforewarned. Let it then be known, that there were those who would have stopped you, in the career of your measures, and held you back, as by the skirts of your garments, from the precipice over which you are plunging and drawing after you the Government of your country.

. . .

It is time for Congress to examine and decide for itself. It has taken things on trust long enough. It has followed executive recommendation, till there remains no hope of finding safety in that path. What is there, sir, that makes it the duty of this people now to grant new confidence to the administration, and to surrender their most important rights to its discretion? On what merits of its own does it rest this extraordinary claim? When it calls thus loudly for the treasure and the lives of the people, what pledge does it offer that it will not waste all in the same preposterous pursuits which have hitherto engaged it? In the failure of all past promises, do we see any assurance of future performance? Are we to measure out our confidence in proportion to our disgrace and now at last to grant away everything, because all that we have heretofore granted has been wasted or misapplied? What is there in our condition that bespeaks a wise or an able government? What is the evidence that the protection of the country is the object principally regarded? In every quarter that protection has been more or less abandoned to the States. That every town on the coast is not now in possession of the enemy, or in ashes, is owing to the vigilance and exertion of the States themselves, and to no protection granted to them by those on whom the whole duty of their protection rested.

Or shall we look to the acquisition of the professed objects of the war, and there find grounds for approbation and confidence? The professed objects of the war are abandoned in all due form. The contest for sailors' rights is turned into a negotiation about boundaries and military roads, and the highest hope entertained by any man of the issue, is that we may be able to get out of the war without a cession of territory.

. . .

. . . Let us examine the nature and extent of the power which is assumed by the various military measures before us. In the present want of men and money, the Secretary of War has proposed to Congress a military conscription. For the conquest of Canada, the people will not enlist; and if they would, the treasury is exhausted, and they could not be paid. Conscription is chosen as the most promising instrument, both of overcoming reluctance to the service, and of subduing the difficulties which arise from the deficiencies of the exchequer. The administration asserts the right to fill the ranks of the regular army by compulsion. It contends that it may now take one out of every twenty-five men, and any part, or the whole of the rest, whenever its occasions require. Persons thus taken by force, and put into an army, may be compelled to serve there during the war, or for life. They may be put on any service, at home or abroad, for defence or for invasion, according to the will and pleasure of the Government. This power does not grow out of any invasion of the country, or even out of a state of war. It belongs to government at all times, in peace as well as in war, and it is to be exercised under all circumstances, according to its mere discretion. This, sir, is the amount of the principle contended for by the Secretary of War.

Is this, sir, consistent with the character of a free government? Is this civil liberty? Is this the real character of our Constitution? No, sir, indeed it is not. The Constitution is libelled, foully libelled. The people of this country have not established for themselves such a fabric of despotism. They have not purchased at a vast expense of their own treasure and their own blood a Magna Charta to be slaves. Where is it written in the Constitution, in what article or section is it contained, that you may take children from their parents, and parents from their children, and compel them to fight the battles of any war in which the folly or the wickedness of government may engage it? Under what concealment has this power lain hidden which now for the first time comes forth, with a tremendous and baleful aspect, to trample down and destroy the dearest rights of personal liberty? Who will show me any constitutional injunction which makes it the duty of the American people to surrender everything valuable in life, and even life itself, not when the safety of their country and its liberties may demand the sacrifice, but whenever the purposes of an ambitious and mischievous government may require it? Sir, I almost disdain to go to quotations and references to prove that such an abominable doctrine has no foundation in the Constitution of the country. It is enough to know that that instrument was intended as the basis of a free government, and that the power contended for is incompatible with any notion of personal liberty. An attempt to maintain this doctrine upon the provisions of the Constitution is an exercise of perverse ingenuity to extract slavery from the substance of a free government. It is an attempt to show, by proof and argument, that we ourselves are subjects of despotism, and that we have a right to chains and bondage, firmly secured to us and our children by the provisions of our government. It has been the labor of other men, at other times, to mitigate and reform the powers of government by construction; to support the rights of personal security by every species of favorable and benign interpretation, and thus to infuse a free spirit into governments not friendly in their general structure and formation to public liberty.

The supporters of the measures before us act on the opposite principle. It is their task to raise arbitrary powers, by construction, out of a plain written charter of National Liberty. It is their pleasing duty to free us of the delusion, which we have fondly cherished, that we are the subjects of a mild, free, and limited government, and to demonstrate by a regular chain of premises and conclusions, that government possesses over us a power more tyrannical, more arbitrary, more dangerous, more allied to blood and murder, more full of every form of mischief, more productive of every sort and degree of misery than has been exercised by any civilized government, with a single exception, in modern times.

The Secretary of War has favored us with an argument on the constitutionality of this power. . . .

Congress having, by the Constitution, a power to raise armies, the secretary contends that no restraint is to be imposed on the exercise of this power, except such as is expressly stated in the written letter of the instrument. In other words, that Congress may execute its powers, by any means it chooses, unless such means are particularly prohibited. But the general nature and object of the Constitution impose as rigid a restriction on the means of exercising power as could be done by the most explicit injunctions. It is the first principle applicable to such a case, that no construction shall be admitted which impairs the general nature and character of the instrument. A free constitution of government is to be construed upon free principles, and every branch of its provisions is to receive such an interpretation as is full of its general spirit. No means are to be taken by implication which would strike us absurdly if expressed. And what would have been more absurd than for this Constitution to have said that to secure the great blessings of liberty it gave to government an uncontrolled power of military conscription? Yet such is the absurdity which it is made to exhibit, under the commentary of the Secretary of War.

But it is said that it might happen that an army could not be raised by voluntary enlistment, in which case the power to raise armies would be granted in vain, unless they might be raised by compulsion. If this reasoning could prove anything, it would equally show, that whenever the legitimate power of the Constitution should be so badly administered as to cease to answer the great ends intended by them, such new powers may be assumed or usurped, as any existing administration may deem expedient. This is the result of his own reasoning, to which the secretary does not profess to go. But it is a true result. For if it is to be assumed, that all powers were granted, which might by possibility become necessary, and that government itself is the judge of this possible necessity, then the powers of government are precisely what it chooses they should be. Apply the same reasoning to any other power granted to Congress, and test its accuracy by the result. Congress has power to borrow money. How is it to exercise this power? Is it confined to voluntary loans? There is no express limitation to that effect, and, in the language of the secretary, it might happen, indeed it has happened, that persons could not be found willing to lend. Money might be borrowed then in any other mode. In other words, Congress might resort to a *forced* loan. It might take the money of any man by force, and give him in exchange exchequer notes or certificates of stock. Would this be quite constitutional, sir? It is entirely within the reasoning of the secretary, and it is a result of his argument, outraging the rights of individuals in a far less degree than the practical consequences which he himself draws from it. A compulsory loan is not to be compared, in point of enormity, with a compulsory military service.

If the Secretary of War has proved the right of Congress to enact a law enforcing a draft of men out of the militia into the regular army, he will at any time be able to prove, quite as clearly, that Congress has power to create a Dictator. The arguments which have helped him in one case, will equally aid him in the other, the same reason of a supposed or possible state necessity, which is urged now, may be repeated then, with equal pertinency and effect.

Sir, in granting Congress the power to raise armies, the people have granted all the means which are ordinary and usual, and which are consistent with the liberties and security of the people themselves, and they have granted no others. To talk about the unlimited power of the Government over the means to execute its authority, is to hold a language which is true only in regard to despotism. The tyranny of arbitrary governments consists as much in its means as in its ends; and it would be a ridiculous and absurd constitution which should be less cautious to guard against abuses in the one case than in the other. All the means and instruments which a free government exercises, as well as the ends and objects which it pursues, are to partake of its own essential character, and to be conformed to its genuine spirit. A free government with arbitrary means to administer it is a contradiction; a free government without adequate provision for personal security is an absurdity; a free government, with an uncontrolled power of military conscription, is a solecism, at once the most ridiculous and abominable that ever entered into the head of man.

Sir, I invite the supporters of the measures before you to look to their actual operation. Let the men who have so often pledged their own fortunes and their own lives to the support of this war, look to the wanton sacrifice which they are about to make of their lives and fortunes. They may talk as they will about substitutes, and compensations, and exemptions. It must come to the draft at last. If the Government cannot hire men voluntarily to fight its battles, neither can individuals. If the war should continue, there will be no escape, and every man's fate and every man's life will come to depend on the issue of the military draft. Who shall describe to you the horror which your orders of conscription shall create in the once happy villages of this country? Who shall describe the distress and anguish which they will spread over those hills and valleys, where men have heretofore been accustomed to labor, and to rest in security and happiness? Anticipate the scene, sir, when the class shall assemble to stand its draft, and to throw the dice for blood. What a group of wives and mothers and sisters, of helpless age and helpless infancy, shall gather round the theatre of this horrible lottery, as if the stroke of death were to fall from heaven before their eyes on a father, a brother, a son, or a husband. And in a majority of cases, sir, it will be the stroke of death. Under present prospects of the continuance of the war, not one half of them on whom your conscription shall fall will ever return to tell the tale of their sufferings. They will perish of disease and pestilence, or they will leave their bones to whiten in fields beyond the frontier. Does the lot fall on the father of a family? His children, already orphans, shall see his face no more. When they behold him for the last time, they shall see him lashed and fettered, and dragged away from his own threshold, like a felon and an outlaw. Does it fall on a son, the hope and the staff of aged parents? That hope shall fail them. On that staff they shall lean no longer. They shall not enjoy the happiness of dying before their children. They shall totter to their grave, bereft of their offspring and unwept by any who inherit their blood. Does it fall on a husband? The eyes which watch his parting steps may swim in tears forever. She is a wife no longer. There is no relation so tender or so sacred that by these accursed measures you do not propose to violate it. There is no happiness so perfect that you do not propose to destroy it. Into the paradise of domestic life you enter, not indeed by temptations and sorceries, but by open force and violence.

But this father, or this son, or this husband goes to the camp. With whom do you associate him? With those only who are sober and virtuous and respectable like himself? No, sir. But you propose to find him companions in the worst men of the worst sort. Another bill lies on your table offering a bounty to deserters from your enemy. Whatever is most infamous in his ranks you propose to make your own. You address yourselves to those who will hear you advise them to perjury and treason. All who are ready to set heaven and earth at defiance at the same time, to violate their oaths and run the hazard of capital punishment, and none others, will yield to your solicitations. And these are they whom you are allowing to join your ranks, by holding out to them inducements and bounties with one hand, while with the other you are driving thither the honest and worthy members of your own community, under the lash and scourge of conscription. In the line of your army, with the true levelling of despotism, you propose a promiscuous mixture of the worthy and the worthless, the virtuous and the profligate; the husbandman, the merchant, the mechanic of your own country, with the beings whom war selects from the excess of European population, who possess neither interest, feeling, nor character in common with your own people, and who have no other recommendation to your notice than their propensity to crimes.

Nor is it, sir, for the defence of his own house and home, that he who is the subject of military draft is to perform the task allotted to him. You will put him upon a service equally foreign to his interests and abhorrent to his feelings. With his aid you are to push your purposes of conquest. The battles which he is to fight are the battles of invasion,—battles which he detests perhaps and abhors, less from the danger and the death that gather over them, and the blood with which they drench the plain, than from the principles in which they have their origin. Fresh from the peaceful pursuits of life, and yet a soldier but in name, he is to be opposed to the veteran troops, hardened under every scene, inured to every privation, and disciplined in every service. If, sir, in this strife he fall—if, while ready to obey every rightful command of government, he is forced from his home against right, not to contend for the defence of his country, but to prosecute a miserable and detestable project of invasion, and in that strife he fall, 'tis murder. It may stalk above the cognizance of human law, but in the sight of Heaven it is murder; and though millions of years may roll away, while his ashes and yours lie mingled together in the earth, the day will yet come when his spirit and the spirits of his children must be met at the bar of omnipotent justice. May God in his compassion, shield me from any participation in the enormity of this guilt.

I would ask, sir, whether the supporters of these measures have well weighed the difficulties of their undertaking. Have they considered whether it will be found easy to execute laws which bear such marks of despotism on their front, and which will be so productive of every sort and degree of misery in their execution? For one, sir, I hesitate not to say that they cannot be executed. No law professedly passed for the purpose of compelling a service in the regular army, nor any law which, under color of military draft, shall compel men to serve in the army, not for the emergencies mentioned in the Constitution, but for long periods, and for the general objects of war, can be carried into effect. In my opinion it ought not to be carried into effect. The operation of measures thus unconstitutional and illegal ought to be prevented by a resort to other measures which are both constitutional and legal. It will be the solemn duty of the State Governments to protect their own authority over their own militia, and to interpose between their citizens and arbitrary power. These are among the objects for which the State Governments exist; and their highest obligations bind them to the preservation of their own rights and the liberties of their people. I express these sentiments here, sir, because I shall express them to my constituents. Both they and myself live under a constitution which teaches us that "the doctrine of nonresistance against arbitrary power and oppression is absurd, slavish, and destructive of the good and happiness of mankind." [2] With the same earnestness with which I now exhort you to forebear from these measures, I shall exhort them to exercise their unquestionable right of providing for the security of their own liberties.

[2] N. H. Bill of Rights. [Editor of Webster's *Writings*.]

In my opinion, sir, the sentiments of the free population of this country are greatly mistaken here. The nation is not yet in a temper to submit to conscription. The people have too fresh and strong a feeling of the blessings of civil liberty to be willing thus to surrender it. You may talk to them as much as you please, of the victory and glory to be obtained in the enemy's provinces; they will hold those objects in light estimation if the means be a forced military service. You may sing to them the song of Canada Conquest in all its variety, but they will not be charmed out of the remembrance of their substantial interests and true happiness. Similar pretences, they know, are the graves in which the liberties of other nations have been buried, and they will take warning.

. . .

Allusions have been made, sir, to the state of things in New England, and, as usual, she has been charged with an intention to dissolve the Union. The charge is unfounded. She is much too wise to entertain such purposes. She has had too much experience, and has too strong a recollection of the blessings which the Union is capable of producing under a just administration of government. It is her greatest fear, that the course at present pursued will destroy it, by destroying every principle, every interest, every sentiment, and every feeling which have hitherto contributed to uphold it. Those who cry out that the Union is in danger are themselves the authors of that danger. They put its existence to hazard by measures of violence, which it is not capable of enduring They talk of dangerous designs against government, when they are overthrowing the fabric from its foundations. They alone, sir, are friends to the union of the States, who endeavor to maintain the principles of civil liberty in the country, and to preserve the spirit in which the Union was framed.   1814

JOHN QUINCY ADAMS

1767–1848

THE ELDEST SON of John and Abigail Adams, John Quincy Adams has been less remembered for the breadth and depth of his culture and his services to intellectual life than for his career in diplomacy and politics. In crystallizing the national foreign policy which President Monroe incorporated in his famous message, Secretary of State Adams was merely expressing one phase of his nationalism. He was devoted to the larger interests of the nation, which he identified with the preservation and extension of the rights of man and the promotion of general well-being. It was this devotion, no less than his stubborn independence and his Puritanical aloofness, which made his political career a stormy one.

His first inaugural address as President advanced the doctrine, cherished by the fathers of the republic, that the federal government should promote the general welfare not only through internal improvements but through subsidies to scientific enterprises. This alarmed the strict constructionists who feared that an extension of federal power might jeopardize local and class interests. Unable to carry his point in regard to a cultural program under federal auspices, Adams did promote learning through his celebrated report on weights and measures and his services in connection with the organization of the Smithsonian Institution. The breadth of Adams's learning as well as his zeal for the civic liberties and for human rights are revealed not only in his many uncollected addresses but also in *The Diary of John Quincy Adams, 1794–1845*, one of the great diaries of nineteenth-century America.

J. W. Cronin and W. H. Wise, *Bibliography of John Adams and John Quincy Adams*, Washington, D. C., 1935.
The Writings of John Quincy Adams, W. C. Ford, ed., 7 vols., New York, 1913–1917.
Samuel Flagg Bemis, *John Quincy Adams and the Union*, New York, 1956.

From: JOHN QUINCY ADAMS' FIRST MESSAGE
TO CONGRESS

. . . Upon this first occasion of addressing the Legislature of the Union, with which I have been honored, in presenting to their view the execution so far as it has been effected of the measures sanctioned by them for promoting the internal improvement of our country, I can not close the communication without recommending to their calm and persevering consideration the general principle in a more enlarged extent. The great object of the institution of civil government is the improvement of the condition of those who are parties to the social compact, and no government, in whatever form constituted, can accomplish the lawful ends of its institution but in proportion as it improves the condition of those over whom it is established. Roads and canals, by multiplying and facilitating the communications and intercourse between distant regions and multitudes of men, are among the most important means of improvement. But moral, political, intellectual improvement are duties assigned by the Author of Our Existence to social no less than to individual man. For the fulfillment of those duties governments are invested with power, and to the attainment of the end—the progressive improvement of the condition of the governed—the exercise of delegated powers is a duty as sacred and indispensable as the usurpation of powers not granted is criminal and odious. Among the first, perhaps the very first, instrument for the improvement of the condition of men is knowledge, and to the acquisition of much of the knowledge adapted to the wants, the comforts, and enjoyments of human life public institutions and seminaries of learning are essential. So convinced of this was the first of my predecessors in this office, now first in the memory, as, living, he was first in the hearts, of our countrymen, that once and again in his addresses to the Congresses with whom he cooperated in the public service he earnestly recommended the establishment of seminaries of learning, to prepare for all the emergencies of peace and war—a national university and a military academy. With respect to the latter, had he lived to the present day, in turning his eyes to the institution at West Point he would have enjoyed the gratification of his most earnest wishes; but in surveying

the city which has been honored with his name he would have seen the spot of earth which he had destined and bequeathed to the use and benefit of his country as the site for an university still bare and barren.

In assuming her station among the civilized nations of the earth it would seem that our country had contracted the engagement to contribute her share of mind, of labor, and of expense to the improvement of those parts of knowledge which lie beyond the reach of individual acquisition, and particularly to geographical and astronomical science. Looking back to the history only of the half century since the declaration of our independence, and observing the generous emulation with which the Governments of France, Great Britain, and Russia have devoted the genius, the intelligence, the treasures of their respective nations to the common improvement of the species in these branches of science, is it not incumbent upon us to inquire whether we are not bound by obligations of a high and honorable character to contribute our portion of energy and exertion to the common stock? The voyages of discovery prosecuted in the course of that time at the expense of those nations have not only redounded to their glory, but to the improvement of human knowledge. We have been partakers of that improvement and owe for it a sacred debt, not only of gratitude, but of equal or proportional exertion in the same common cause. Of the cost of these undertakings, if the mere expenditures of outfit, equipment, and completion of the expeditions were to be considered the only charges, it would be unworthy of a great and generous nation to take a second thought. One hundred expeditions of circumnavigation like those of Cook and La Pérouse would not burden the exchequer of the nation fitting them out so much as the ways and means of defraying a single campaign in war. But if we take into the account the lives of those benefactors of mankind of which their services in the cause of their species were the purchase, how shall the cost of those heroic enterprises be estimated, and what compensation can be made to them or to their countries for them? Is it not by bearing them in affectionate remembrance? Is it not still more by imitating their example—by enabling countrymen of our own to pursue the same career and to hazard their lives in the same cause?

In inviting the attention of Congress to the subject of internal improvements upon a view thus enlarged it is not my design to recommend the equipment of an expedition for circumnavigating the globe for purposes of scientific research and inquiry. We have objects of useful investigation nearer home, and to which our cares may be more beneficially applied. The interior of our own territories has yet been very imperfectly explored. Our coasts along many degrees of latitude upon the shores of the Pacific Ocean, though much frequented by our spirited commercial navigators, have been barely visited by our public ships. The River of the West, first fully discovered and navigated by a countryman of our own, still bears the name of the ship in which he ascended its waters, and claims the protection of our armed national flag at its mouth. With the establishment of a military post there or at some other point of that coast, recommended by my predecessor and already matured in the deliberations of the last Congress, I would suggest the expediency of connecting the equipment of a public ship for the exploration of the whole northwest coast of this continent.

The establishment of an uniform standard of weights and measures was one of the specific objects contemplated in the formation of our Constitution, and to fix that standard was one of the powers delegated by express terms in that instrument to Congress. The Governments of Great Britain and France have scarcely ceased to be occupied with inquiries and speculations on the same subject since the existence of our Constitution, and with them it has expanded into profound, laborious, and expensive researches into the figure of the earth and the comparative length of the pendulum vibrating seconds in various latitudes from the equator to the pole. These researches have resulted in the composition and publication of several works highly interesting to the cause of science. The experiments are yet in the process of performance. Some of them have recently been made on our own shores, within the walls of one of our own colleges, and partly by one of our own fellow-citizens. It would be honorable to our country if the sequel of the same experiments should be countenanced by the patronage of our Government, as they have hitherto been by those of France and Britain.

Connected with the establishment of an university, or separate from it, might be undertaken the erection of an astronomical observatory, with provision for the support of an astronomer, to be in constant attendance of observation upon the phenomena of the heavens, and for the periodical publication of his observations. It is with no feeling of pride as an American that the remark may be made that on the comparatively small territorial surface of Europe there are existing upward of 130 of these light-houses of the skies, while throughout the whole American hemisphere there is not one. If we reflect a moment upon the discoveries which in the last four centuries have been made in the physical contribution of the universe by the means of these buildings and of observers stationed in them, shall we doubt of their usefulness to every nation? And while scarcely a year passes over our heads without bringing some new astronomical discovery to light, which we must fain receive at second hand from Europe, are we not cutting ourselves off from the means of returning light for light while we have neither observatory nor observer upon our half of the globe and the earth revolves in perpetual darkness to our unsearching eyes?

When, on the 25th of October, 1791, the first President of the United States announced to Congress the result of the first enumeration of the inhabitants of this Union, he informed them that the returns gave the pleasing assurance that the population of the United States bordered on 4,000,000 persons. At the distance of thirty years from that time the last enumeration, five years since completed, presented a population bordering upon 10,000,000. Perhaps of all the evidences of a prosperous and happy condition of human society the rapidity of the increase of population is the most unequivocal. But the demonstration of our prosperity rests not alone upon this indication. Our commerce, our wealth, and the extent of our territories have increased in corresponding proportions, and the number of independent communities associated in our Federal Union has since that time nearly doubled. The legislative representation of the States and people in the two Houses of Congress has grown with the growth of their constituent bodies. The House, which then consisted of 65 members, now numbers upward of 200. The Senate, which consisted of 26 members, has now 48. But the executive and, still more, the judiciary departments are yet in a great measure confined to their primitive organization, and are now not adequate to the urgent wants of a still growing community.

The naval armaments, which at an early period forced themselves upon the necessities of the Union, soon led to the establishment of a Department of the Navy. But the Departments of Foreign Affairs and of the Interior, which early after the formation of the Government had been united in one, continue so united to this time, to the unquestionable detriment of the public service. The multiplication of our relations with the nations and Governments of the Old World has kept pace with that of our population and commerce, while within the last ten years a new family of nations in our own hemisphere has arisen among the inhabitants of the earth, with whom our intercourse, commercial and political, would of itself furnish occupation to an active and industrious department. The constitution of the judiciary, experimental and imperfect as it was even in the infancy of our existing Government, is yet more inadequate to the administration of national justice at our present maturity. . . .

The laws relating to the administration of the Patent Office are deserving of much consideration and perhaps susceptible of some improvement. The grant of power to regulate the action of Congress upon this subject has specified both the end to be obtained and the means by which it is to be effected, "to promote the progress of science and useful arts by securing for limited times to authors and inventors the exclusive right to their respective writings and discoveries." If an honest pride might be indulged in the reflection that on the records of that office are already found inventions the usefulness of which has scarcely been transcended in the annals of human ingenuity, would not its exultation be allayed by the inquiry whether the laws have effectively insured to the inventors the reward destined to them by the Constitution—even a limited term of exclusive right to their discoveries?

On the 24th of December, 1799, it was resolved by Congress that a marble monument should be erected by the United States in the Capitol at the City of Washington; that the family of General Washington should be requested to permit his body to be deposited under it, and that the monument be so designed as to commemorate the great events of his military and political life. In reminding Congress of this resolution and that the monument contemplated by it remains yet with execution, I shall indulge only the remarks that the works at the Capitol are approaching completion; that the consent of the family, desired by the resolution, was requested and obtained; that a monument has been recently erected in this city over the remains of another distinguished patriot of the Revolution, and that a spot has been reserved within the walls where you are deliberating for the benefit of this and future ages, in which the mortal remains may be deposited of him whose spirit hovers over you and listens with delight to every act of the representatives of his nation which can tend to exalt and adorn his and their country.

The Constitution under which you are assembled is a charter of limited powers. After full and solemn deliberation upon all or any of the objects which, urged by an irresistible sense of my own duty, I have recommended to your attention should you come to the conclusion that, however desirable in themselves, the enactment of laws for effecting them would transcend the powers committed to you by that venerable instrument which we are all bound to support, let no consideration induce you to assume the exercise of powers not granted to you by the people. But if the power to exercise exclusive legislation in all cases whatsoever over the district of Columbia; if the power to lay and collect taxes, duties, imposts, and excises, to pay the debts and provide for the common defense and general welfare of the United States; if the power to regulate commerce with foreign nations and among the several States and with the Indian tribes, to fix the standard of weights and measures, to establish post-offices and post-roads, to declare war, to raise and support armies, to provide and maintain a navy, to dispose of and make all needful rules and regulations respecting the territory of other property belonging to the United States, and to make all laws which shall be necessary and proper for carrying these powers into execution—if these powers and others enumerated in the Constitution may be effectually brought into action by laws promoting the improvement of agriculture, commerce, and manufactures, the cultivation and encouragement of the mechanic and of the elegant arts, the advancement of literature, and the progress of the sciences, ornamental and profound, to refrain from exercising them for the benefit of the people themselves would be to hide in the earth the talent committed to our charge—would be treachery to the most sacred of trusts.

The spirit of improvement is abroad upon the earth. It stimulates the hearts and sharpens the faculties not of our fellow-citizens alone, but of the nations of Europe and of their rulers. While dwelling with pleasing satisfaction upon the superior excellence of our political institutions, let us not be unmindful that liberty is power; that the nation blessed with the largest portion of liberty must in proportion to its numbers be the most powerful nation upon earth, and that the tenure of power by man is, in the moral purposes of his Creator, upon condition that it shall be exercised to ends of beneficence, to improve the condition of himself and his fellowmen. While foreign nations less blessed with that freedom which is power than ourselves are advancing with gigantic strides in the career of public improvement, were we to slumber in indolence or fold up our arms and proclaim to the world that we are palsied by the will of our constituents, would it not be to cast away the bounties of Providence and doom ourselves to perpetual inferiority? In the course of the year now drawing to its close we have beheld, under the auspices and at the expense of one State of this Union, a new university unfolding its portals to the sons of science and holding up the torch of human improvement to eyes that seek the light. We have seen under the persevering and enlightened enterprise of another State the waters of our Western lakes mingle with those of the ocean. If undertakings like these have been accomplished in the compass of a few years by the authority of single members of our Confederation, can we, the representative authorities of the whole Union, fall behind our fellow-servants in the exercise of the trust committed to us for the benefit of our common sovereign by the accomplishment of works important to the whole and to which neither the authority nor the resources of any one State can be adequate?

Finally, fellow-citizens, I shall wait with cheering hope and faithful cooperation the result of your deliberations, assured that, without encroaching upon the powers reserved to the authorities of the respective States or to the people, you will, with a due sense of your obligations to your country and of the high responsibilities weighing upon yourselves, give efficacy to the means committed to you for the common good. And may He who searches the hearts of the children of men prosper your exertions to secure the blessings of peace and promote the highest welfare of our country.

1825

» » Democracy and Aristocracy « «

1783-1840

TIPPECANOE

Tippecanoe has no chariot to ride in,
No palace of marble has he to reside in,
No bags of gold eagles, no lots of fine clothes—
But he has a wealth far better than those;
The love of a nation, free, happy and true,
Are the riches and portion of Tippecanoe.

Proud Martin rides forth in his splendor and pride,
And broad are his lands upon Kinderhook side,
The roof of a palace is over his head,
And his table with plate and with dainties is spread;
But a log cabin shelters a patriot true—
'Tis the home of our Hero, bold Tippecanoe!

Our hero has never grown rich on the State;
No sneaking sub-treasurers bow at his gate;
No fat office-holders he keeps in his thrall;
But millions of freemen will rise at his call—
Then shout every lover of liberty true:
Huzza for the Hero of Tippecanoe!

In the hilarious presidential campaign of 1840 the Whigs did their best to picture Van Buren, the candidate of the Democrats, as a champagne-drinking dandy with perfumed whiskers. Their own candidate, General Harrison, the hero of the battle of Tippecanoe (1811), was be-rhymed as a real son of the people, content with hard cider and a humble log cabin. This campaign song is from *The Log Cabin Song-Book*, published in New York in 1840. It was sung to the tune of "Alan-a-dale."

» » « «

Democracy and Aristocracy

THE CONTROVERSY between Federalists and Republicans as to what really constituted Americanism was in large measure a conflict between aristocratic and democratic interests and principles. It is, indeed, hardly too much to say that the most important issue in the first half century of national existence was that of aristocracy *versus* democracy. The aristocrats often seemed to be on the top; yet the period as a whole is one in which their influence waned until finally in 1828 the democracy of Jackson triumphed. It would, of course, be historically incorrect to picture the more democratic forces of this period, represented by Jefferson and the leaders of his party, as democratic in the sense in which Jackson's movement was democratic. For the leaders of Jeffersonian democracy were patricians; and most of them believed in a natural aristocracy, that is to say, in one based on the gifts of nature and destined to guide and to direct the less talented. Yet the Jeffersonian democrats, particularly in the period of the French Revolution, contained a left-wing which, in accepting the principles of liberty, equality, and fraternity, was both militant and equalitarian. The discontented farmers who followed Daniel Shays likewise endeavored to keep alive the more democratic concepts of the American Revolution, especially the appeal to direct action in behalf of what were regarded as natural rights.

In the political and economic sphere the conflict between aristocracy and democracy expressed itself in the efforts of the agrarians to broaden the franchise and to curb the hold of the substantial and directing classes on the machinery of government. They tried to organize themselves into "democratic societies"; and one spokesman, at least, favored a national union of farmers and workers in behalf of their common interests, which the commercial and plantation aristocrats, with their professional allies, opposed. Thanks to the effective political leadership of Jefferson and his lieutenants, the Federalists lost control of the national government in 1800. But once in power, the Jeffersonians adopted some measures which resembled those of the Federalists; power and responsibility tended to bring to the fore the conservatism implicit in their conception of a patrician-led democracy. Yet the Jeffersonian party in office was sufficiently democratic to be regarded by the great commercial interests as dangerously subversive.

Culturally the forces of democracy demanded a modification of the monopoly the privileged classes had enjoyed. Freedom of the press, a broader basis of education, and the diffusion of knowledge generally bulked large in the democratic program. While many leaders and some of the rank and file subscribed to deism and to the general principles of the Enlightenment, the conservative aristocrats won back to orthodox religion many of Jefferson's humble supporters. For while many conservatives in politics and in economics showed favor to deism, they tended to take a less advanced position when deism showed signs of spreading among the masses. Unitarianism promised a midway refuge which combined a certain liberalism in matters of faith with an institutional check on too subversive doctrines. And many conservatives in politics and economics, alarmed at the spread of Jacobin principles, insisted on a stronger alliance between orthodox Christians and defenders of the existing political and economic order.

Socially the controversy between the aristocrats and democrats centered in the question of titles and the nature of classes. Some, like John Adams, stood firmly for the adoption of titles of dignity for the highest personages in the governing class. Others tried to establish a "republican court" as near to that of a monarchy as New World conditions permitted. Still others clung to the idea that nature had distributed talent and merit to different classes as such, rather than to individuals as such.

On the other hand, democrats scorned the idea that a republic needed either titles or a "court." To them such trappings suggested the deplorable tendency to imitate Europe rather than to throw off once and for all the shackles of the Old World. With equal vigor democrats protested against the idea that talents, by an inevitable decree of fate, followed class lines. They insisted, rather, that inequalities in wealth and cultural opportunities were reflected in differences in talent. They looked with favor on the environmentalist theory of human nature. They put great faith in the power of the diffusion of knowledge to elevate the masses. There might indeed be natural aristocrats, as Jefferson held; but no natural aristocracy, the champions of democracy contended, was synonomous with inherited rank or wealth.

» »   « «

» » SHAYS'S REBELLION « «

WHEN THE Massachusetts legislature, which was responsive to the dominant commercial and politically privileged class, refused to hearken to the appeals of the distressed farmers for relief from the burdensome poll tax and from foreclosures on lands, and was deaf to their cry for political reforms, Captain Daniel Shays, a former Revolutionary officer, led a rebellion against the constituted authorities. Farm prices had fallen disastrously, and the rural areas were badly affected not only by special grievances but also by the prevailing depression. Mobs broke up the meetings of courts and threatened to seize the armory at Springfield. The well-to-do were alarmed, and took measures to suppress the rebellion, which was finally put down by the militia.

The following address presents the conservative view of the rebellion, a view somewhat weakened by the previous indifference of the legislature to genuine grievances and to proper appeals for relief, but also by the fact that the government itself, in granting many of the demands once the rebellion was crushed, recognized their validity.

J. T. Adams, *New England in the Republic*, Boston, 1926.
Robert J. Taylor, *Western Massachusetts in the Revolution*, Providence, 1954.
Marion L. Starkey, *A Little Rebellion*, New York, 1955.

From: AN ADDRESS FROM THE GENERAL COURT TO
« «   THE PEOPLE OF THE COMMONWEALTH OF   « «
MASSACHUSETTS

At a period, when grievances are complained of, in divers counties of the State; when the symptoms of discontent are manifest and alarming, and individuals resort to arms, to support their disaffection, and oppose the Courts of Justise; it becomes the duty of the Legislature, to investigate, and, as far as may be, to remove the grounds of complaint; to undeceive those.

who are misguided by false representation; and if lenient means are ineffectual, to vindicate by vigorous and decisive measures, the honor of government, and provide for the security of the State.

The General Court have therefore employed the greater part of the present session, hitherto, in examining the causes of uneasiness, and the objections made to the measures of government; and in providing (as far as honor and justice would allow) relief from the burthens, under which the citizens of the Commonwealth have laboured: and we now request the attention of our constituents, to the state of public affairs; and the reasons, why a compliance with the wishes of some of them, would be dishonorable to us, and injurious to themselves.

We have no doubt, that endeavours are used by evil and designing men, to alienate the affections of the people in general, from those who are concerned in the administration of government; but conscious of the rectitude of our intentions, we are convinced, that if the public measures are examined with candour, the confidence you lately reposed in us, will not be lessened; and that however great the public burthens are, attempts have not been wanting on our part, to alleviate them: no man in the community is exempt from those burthens; the members of the Legislature have their full share; and can it be thought they would designedly impose unnecessary burthens on themselves; or omit any thing that might tend to their relief from such burthens? Their duty and their interest, would equally forbid it, for the relief of their constituents would be their own.

. . .

The sitting of the General Court in Boston, has occasioned uneasiness; doubtless it would be more convenient for a part of the State, if it was holden at some other place; but the interest and wishes of a part, are not to be considered alone: Boston has long been thought the most convenient place: some of the General Court have supposed otherwise; but the major part were against a removal, and must the minor part therefore rise against the government? Because they could not have every thing as they wished, could they be justified in resorting to force? Such a principle would destroy all society. Attention, however, has been paid to the instruction of many towns respecting the removal of the General Court out of the town of Boston, and a Committee consisting of a member from each county, has been appointed to consider the subject and report.

It never can be the case, that the whole community shall be of the same opinion; in a republican government the major part must govern: if the minor part governs, it becomes an aristocracy: if every one opposes at his pleasure, it is no government, it is anarchy and confusion.

In some parts of the Commonwealth, it is frequently said, if our Representative goes to Court, he will do us no service; for the measures he is in favour of, will not be adopted: but *why* will they not be adopted? Every measure that is proposed, is attended to, and considered; and if finally rejected, it is because the majority think it inexpedient; and how absurd and contradictory would the proceedings of the Court be, if every proposition should be acceded to.

The complaints in different parts of the State are repugnant, and petitions from different places, request measures directly opposite; it is impossible therefore, that all should be gratified: what then shall be done? Unless we submit to be controuled by the greater number, the Commonwealth must break in pieces; but neither will the inhabitants of any county or town be all of the same sentiments, each man therefore must be a part, and the whole reduced to a state of nature.

If then it is plain, that the vote of the major part must govern, the question is, where shall that vote be taken? Not in a country convention; because nine-tenths of the State are not represented, and their interest is not attended to. The constitution has pointed out the mode of representation; and will any one suppose, that because the persons chosen, are called a General Court, they have less integrity or patriotism, than if they were called a convention?

It is said by some, that a new constitution is necessary; and although the sentiments of the persons, who complain, are opposite on this point, the subject may demand some attention. The objection made to the present constitution, is the expence of the government. From the foregoing statement of that expence for the last five years, we find, that if the expence of the House of Representatives is included, it will not exceed eighteen thousand, one hundred and nine pounds by the year; as there are in the State, more than ninety-four thousand polls, if the whole sum was paid by the polls, each poll must pay three shillings and ten pence and no more; but as about two-thirds of the taxes are paid by the estates, the tax upon a poll, according to the present mode of assessment, would be less than sixteen-pence.

It has been alleged, that the salaries given to the officers of government, are a great burthen.

The Governour has per annum	£ 1100 0 0
The Secretary	250 0 0
The Treasurer	350 0 0
The Judges of the Supreme Court	1775 0 0
The Commissary-General	150 0 0
Total.	3625 0 0

If this sum was wholly paid by the polls, the tax would be no more than nine-pence half-penny upon a poll; it must therefore be apparent to every reasonable man, that the large taxes we have paid have not been applied to the support of civil government.

We have but lately heard that the Senate has been thought by any one to be a grievance; if it has been so considered, we think it must have been owing to inattention; for we are convinced that every judicious man who attends to the nature of our government, will consider that as an important and necessary branch of the Legislature.

Before the constitution was formed every town in the State had a right to send one or more Representatives; the people at that time were very tenacious of this right; it is highly probable they would be so at the present time; perhaps the very persons who complain would not be willing to part with it, for if they preferred a Legislature elected by counties, to one chosen by the several towns, such an assembly would be constituted like the present Senate, and differ only in name; however, the cost of an experiment would far exceed the sum proposed to be saved, as a revision of the constitution may take place in 1795, when it is to be hoped the minds of men will be in a more tranquil state.

An attempt to form the present constitution was begun in the year 1777; and was not compleated until the year 1780; the cost and trouble attending it, we all remember were exceeding great, and perhaps nothing would finally have been agreed to, if an unusual spirit of mutual condescendsion had not prevailed; a sense of common danger from abroad produced internal harmony and union: But what hope could we now have of that mutual compliance, which would be necessary to agree upon a form of government; when the tempers of so many are in a state of irritation? Should the present government be overthrown, a state of general confusion would ensue; and after we had experienced all the horrors of anarchy, and the effects of unrestrained violence and revenge, our dear earned freedom, would probably be swallowed up, by domestic despotism or foreign dominion.

The constitution is as free and popular as the preservation of society will admit; and indeed some have feared, it is more so; it has been highly applauded by foreigners and approved by the people: all persons employed in the legislative or executive parts of government, depend annually upon the people for their choice; if the people are dissatisfied with their conduct, they have an opportunity yearly to appoint others, in whom they can more fully confide. Can there be any necessity then, of resorting to irregular, or violent measures, to obtain redress of grievances?

That the people are overburthened with taxes is said to be a grievance: the taxes have indeed been very great; perhaps the General Court have misjudged of the abilities of their constituents, but it may be that those who complain, if they knew the state of the public debt, and the motives of the Legislature, would be satisfied. We shall therefore state them.

The sums applied to the use of the United States, were esteemed by Congress to be indispensably necessary; and the General Court in former years supposed they could not with any regard to their duty as a part of the union, refuse the payment; nor could we think ourselves under less obligations to provide for the payment of that part of the tax granted in March last, which is appropriated to the use of the Continent.

The necessity of a speedy payment of the before mentioned part of that tax, is complained of as a grievance. By the resolve of Congress of Sept. 27th, 1785, it was provided, that the Commissioners of the Continental Loan-Office should not on any pretence whatever, issue any certificates for the interest of the Continental debt, until the State for which he was Loan-Officer, should have passed a Legislative act, complying with the requisition in the said resolve; and by the same resolve it was required, that the Legislature of each State should provide in the act complying with that requisition, that if on the first day of January, 1787, the said certificates should not be in the hands of some proper officer, the deficiency should be paid in specie: it was therefore absolutely necessary, that the act should be constructed as it was, otherwise no certificates could have been issued; notwithstanding which, application is now made to Congress, that the term for receiving those certificates may be prolonged.

The army notes were made payable, one third part in 1784, one third in 1785, and the remainder in 1786. The service of the officers and soldiers of the late army, was acknowledged by all to be exceedingly meritorious, and perhaps no part of the community had greater reason to complain of grievances than they. It was represented that many of them were urgent to have the notes redeemed: they were issued upon this express condition, that they should be receivable in the first taxes after they should become payable, and the General Court well knew, that if the abilities of the people were sufficient, it would be greatly for their advantage to redeem them.

We think the observations that have been made will explain the necessity of that part of the taxes, which has been applied to the support of civil government. With regard to the residue of the taxes, it is apparent, from the manner in which the expenditures have been made, that they were occasioned by the war. When the war first commenced, the people solemnly engaged to each other to carry it on until they obtained security of their rights, altho' their *lives* and *fortunes* should be the *price* of *the purchase*: if there was the least truth or sincerity in these declarations, could it be supposed, they would individually grudge the contribution of their part of the expence, when the event exceeded their most sanguine expectations?

Public credit is one of the most important trusts committed to the Legislature; in proportion as that declines, the State is weakened and in danger. It is of the same importance to a community, as a character for truth is to individuals. The want of a paper currency has been complained of as a grievance; but we find that in divers places where complaints have arisen, the idea of a paper currency is rejected with marks of great disapprobation. Indeed a little attention to the subject, we conceive, must satisfy every intelligent and unprejudiced mind, that the emission of

such a currency would be exceedingly prejudicial. If it could be carried into circulation, the solid coin would be exported, the morals of the people would become more depraved, designing men would practice innumerable frauds; and if it should ever afterwards be redeemed, it would plunge the State in deeper distress: If it should not be redeemed, it would cause the ruin of many individuals, and brand the State with infamy. And upon whom would that ruin fall? Not upon the artful and unprincipled, they would gain by the fraud; not upon the prudent and discerning, they would be guarded against it; but the loss would chiefly happen to the *widow* and the *orphan*, the simple and unwary; the most innocent and defenceless part of the community; that part, whose interests the Legislature ought to defend with peculiar attention. The widow and orphan are the special charge of the Supreme Being, and all are enjoined to exercise vigilance and tenderness for their welfare. This injunction every man, possessed of natural affections, must feel the force of; for who can tell how soon his wife and his children may fall a prey to sharpers and speculators, if a paper money system shall be adopted.

A full experiment of this State's ability to uphold the credit of a paper medium, was made in the case of the new emission: the faith of the United States, and of this State, were both pledged for its support; a fund was provided, sufficient to pay the interest; and although, when it first came into circulation, it passed at the rate of one and seven-eighths for one, interest to a large amount in silver was paid upon the nominal sum; notwithstanding which, at the very time the interest was paying, the currency rapidly depreciated.

We presume there is not a man in the State who supposes, that if we emitted a paper currency, it would not depreciate; and if it depreciates, it will pass at different rates, in different places, and to different persons, at the same time; it will therefore produce the same effect as divers weights and divers measures, which we are assured are an abomination.

We feel in common with our neighbours the scarcity of money; but is not this scarcity owing to our own folly? At the close of the war, there was no complaint of it; since that time, our fields have yielded their increase, and heaven has showered its blessings on us, in uncommon abundance; but are we not constrained to allow, that immense sums have been expended, for what is of no value, for the gewgaws imported from Europe, and the more pernicious produce of the West-Indies; and the dread of a paper currency impedes the circulation of what remains: It is said however, that such a currency would give us present relief; but like the pleasure of sin, it would be but for a reason; and like that too, it would be a reproach to the community, and would produce calamities without end.

Until the people can forget the injuries and frauds occasioned by paper currencies, in their own time; we think they must be satisfied, of the inexpediency and injustice, of making new emissions.

Within a few years the habits of luxury have exceedingly increased, the usual manufactures of the country have been little attended to. That we can buy goods cheaper than we can make them, is often repeated, and is even become a maxim in economy, altho' a most absurd and destructive one. While these habits continue, the wisest Legislature will not be able to remove our complaints. The emission of a paper currency, and such like expedients, may seem to refresh us for a moment; but they will serve to fan the flame, that must eventually consume us.

Without a reformation of manners, we can have little hope to prosper in our public or private concerns. At the close of the war we greedily adopted the luxurious modes of foreign nations. Although our country abounds with all the necessaries of life, the importations from abroad, for our own consumption, have been almost beyond calculation; we have indulged ourselves in fantastical and expensive fashions and intemperate living; by these means our property has been lessened and immense sums in specie have been exported. Government is complained of, as if *they* had devoured them; and the cry of many persons now is, make us paper money. This request is next in point of imprudence, to that of the Israelites to Aaron, to make them a calf; and a compliance would be but a little more honorable or advantageous, in the one case, than it was in the other.

As the difficulty in paying debts increased, a disregard to honesty, justice and good faith, in public and private transactions has become more manifest. That virtue, which is necessary to support a Republic, has declined; and as a people, we are now in the precise channel, in which the liberty of States has generally been swallowed up. But still our case is not desperate; by recurring to the principles of integrity and public spirit, and the practice of industry, sobriety, economy, and fidelity in contracts, and by acquiescing in laws necessary for the public good, the impending ruin may be averted, and we become respectable and happy.—By such means, we may falsify the invidious predictions of our enemies, that we should crumble to pieces, and should be too corrupt to maintain republican freedom. In such a cause we may hope, that the God of our fathers, who has defended us hitherto, will prosper the work of his own hands, and save the fair structure of American liberty from falling into ruin.

We make no boast of uncommon skill in legislation; but sacredly regarding the oaths we have taken, we claim the merit of upright designs, and of pursuing as far as we can judge, a system formed on the principles of justice, and calculated to promote the honor, the safety and happiness of the State.

In a Commonwealth, where a spirit of unreasonable jealousy and a complaining temper, are indulged and countenanced, it will be impossible to give satisfaction to the people: if Angels in such case were to govern us, opposition would be made to their administration; indeed we have a striking instance that when such humours prevail, even the authority of the Supreme Being will be thought a grievance. The people of Israel were under his particular care and government; He was their Lawgiver and Judge; He delivered them from their oppressors; He led them through the sea; He rained them down the corn of Heaven, and sent them meat to the full; but notwithstanding, they complained of His government and wantonly provoked His anger; like that people, we have experienced astonishing testimonies of the divine favour. God forbid! that like them, we should requite him with murmuring and ingratitude, and provoke him to destroy us.

When the people are distressed with the conduct of any government, it may at least deserve a reflection, whether the difficulty is not with themselves. At the last election in this State, perhaps a greater number of new Members were returned, than at any former period; they came together with a fixed design, to gratify their constituents, in every thing which the interest of the community would permit; and they never lost sight of that object; notwithstanding which, greater dissatisfaction with public measures is expressed at this time, than ever before since the revolution. The Legislature have attended to all the petitions that have been presented, and all the complaints that have been made; so far as justice will allow, they will comply with the requests in those petitions and remove the grounds of those complaints. If they possess abilities and integrity equal to the other members of the community, the advantages they derive from the information collected from all parts of the State, and a public discussion of subjects, render them more capable to judge, of the fitness of public measures; but if they are to have the favour of the people, and a voice in the public Counsels, only on condition of their establishing iniquity by law, they are willing to lose the shameful pre-eminence.

The General Court have heard with inexpressible concern, of the insurrections in several counties of the State. The pretence that the Court of Common Pleas, is a grievance, affords but a wretched excuse for such outrageous proceedings; that Court, except a small alteration in the name, has existed time immemorial; no complaints were heard against it in former times; no application has been made to the Legislature before this session to abolish it. The fees, except those of Jurors and witnesses, are in many instances less, and we think in none greater than they were before the war. Provision has been made to enable the citizens to settle their demands without resorting to that Court, if they are disposed to do it; several years since, the Justices of the Peace were authorized to take acknowledgements of debts, even to the largest amount; and more lately an act was passed to enable any persons in difference, who could agree to refer their disputes, to resort to a Justice, and enter into a rule for that purpose, without being subject to the expence of an action. But if the Court of Common Pleas has been by any supposed unnecessary, how surprising then, the idea, that any persons could think themselves justified, in opposing by force, an ancient institution, without taking a single step to obtain redress in a regular method. But not content with obstructing the Courts of Common Pleas, the disaffected have taken arms to prevent the sitting of the Supreme Judicial Court, against which, not a single complaint has been uttered. These proceedings are the more alarming, as they can be accounted for, only on the supposition, that the instigators wish to subvert all order and government, and reduce the Commonwealth, to the most deplorable state of wretchedness and contempt.

In this view, our situation appears exceedingly alarming; sufficiently so, to arrest the most serious attention, and summon the united efforts, of all orders in the State. Some persons have artfully affected to make a distinction between the government and people, as though their interests were different and even opposite; but we presume, the good sense of our constituents will discern the deceit and falsity of those insinuations. Within a few months the authority delegated to us will cease, and all the citizens will be equally candidates in a future election; we are therefore no more interested to preserve the constitution and support the government, than others: but while the authority given us continues, we are bound to exercise it for the benefit of our constituents. And we now call upon persons of all ranks and characters to exert themselves for the public safety. Upon the Ministers of religion, that they inculcate upon the minds of their people, the principles of justice and public virtue; that they earnestly endeavour to impress them with sentiments of reverence to the Deity and benevolence to men, and convince them of the ruinous effects of luxury and licentiousness. Upon the officers of every denomination, that they endeavour to inform the ignorant; and by their examples of economy, to induce others to the practice of the same virtue; and that they use their utmost efforts to suppress the insurrections of such lawless and violent men, as may wish to pull down the fabric of law and government, and level it with the dust. And upon the whole body of the people, that they provide for the instruction of the rising generation; that they practice all those virtues which are the ornament and strength of society, and abstain from those vices and follies, that weaken the State, and have a tendency to its ruin; and especially that they oppose with fortitude and perseverance, all attempts to impede the course of justice and render their own lives and property insecure.

Many who disapprove insurrections against the government, neglect to afford their aid, in suppressing them; but to stand still, inactive spectators in such case, is like a man who when his house is in flames, should stand with folded arms, and console himself with this, that he did not set it on fire.

We persuade ourselves, that the far greater

part of those who have been concerned in the late dangerous tumults, have been deluded by the false representations of men who go about to deceive; and we with them to reflect how fatal such proceedings may prove in the issue, to themselves and their children; that they must increase the public burthens, and embarrass the measures calculated for relief; that it is their own constitution and laws they are endeavouring to overthrow; that this constitution and these laws were formed for the safety of every member of the State; and that the man who attempts to subvert those laws, and that constitution, does in effect make an attempt upon the life, liberty and property of every member of the community; and we conjure them, by all that they hold dear and sacred, forthwith to desist from such ruinous pursuits.

Perhaps there are some, who deaf to the voice of reason, and lost to all sense of justice and virtue, may resolve to continue in their dangerous course; but let them be assured, although they flatter themselves that the considerations of friendship and affinity, may delay the time of recompence; yet the vengeance of an injured community, must one day, pursue and overtake them.   1786

NOAH WEBSTER

1758–1843

NOAH WEBSTER'S nationalism, important as it was in his thought, was by no means his exclusive interest. In his social philosophy he shifted from a democratic and deistic position to an aristocratic and orthodox religious faith. The following selections from his *Essays* illustrate his conservatism.

Noah Webster, *Collection of Essays and Fugitive Writings on Moral, Historical, Political, and Literary Subjects*, Boston, 1790.

H. R. Warfel, *Noah Webster: Schoolmaster to America*, New York, 1936.

» » THE DEVIL IS IN YOU « «

That the political body, like the animal, is liable to violent diseases, which, for a time, baffle the healing art, is a truth which we acknowledge, and which most of us lament. But as most of the disorders, incident to the human frame, are the consequence of an intemperate indulgence of its appetites, or of neglecting the most obvious means of safety; so most of the popular tumults, which disturb government, arise from an abuse of its blessings, or an inattention to its principles. A man of a robust constitution, relying on its strength, riots in gratifications which weaken the *stamina vitæ;* the surfeiting pleasures of a few years destroy the power of enjoyment; and the full fed voluptuary feels a rapid transition to the meagre valetudinarian. Thus people who enjoy an uncommon share of political privileges, often carry their freedom to licentiousness, and put it out of their power to enjoy society by destroying its support.

Too much health is a *disease,* which often requires a very strict regimen; *too much liberty* is the worst of *tyranny;* and *wealth* may be accumulated to such a degree as to *impoverish* a State. If *all* men attempt to become *masters,* the *most* of them would necessarily become *slaves* in the attempt; and could *every man* on earth possess millions of joes,[1] *every man* would be *poorer* than *any man* is now, and infinitely more wretched, because they could not procure the necessaries of life.

[1] A Portuguese and Brazilian gold coin worth from 8 to 9 dollars. [*Century Dict. and Ency.*]

My countrymen, it is a common saying now, that *the devil is in you.* I question the influence of the devil, however, in these affairs. Divines and politicians agree in this, to father all evil upon the devil; but the effects ascribed to this prince of evil spirits, both in the moral and political world, I ascribe to the wickedness and ignorance of the human heart. Taking the word *Devil* in this sense, he is *in* you, and *among* you, in a variety of shapes.

In the first place, the *weakness of our federal government is the devil.* It prevents the adoption of any measures that are requisit for us, as a nation; it keeps us from paying our honest debts; it also throws out of our power all the profits of commerce, and this drains us of cash. Is not this the devil? Yes, my countrymen, an empty purse is the *devil.*

You say you are jealous of your rights, and dare not trust Congress. Well, that jealousy is an evil spirit, and all evil spirits are *devils.* So far the devil is in you. You act, in this particular, just like the crew of a ship, who would not trust the helm with *one* of their number, because he might *possibly* run her ashore, when by leaving her without a pilot, they were *certain* of shipwreck. You act just like men, who in raising a building, would not have a master workman, because he *might* give out wrong orders. You will be masters yourselves; and as you are not all ready to lift at the same time, one labors at a stick of timber, then another, then a third; you are then vexed that it is not raised; why let a master order thirteen of you to take hold together, and you will lift it at once. Every family has a *master* (or a *mistress* —I beg the ladies' pardon). When a ship or a house is to be built, there is a master; when highways are repairing, there is a master; every little school has a master; the continent is a great school; the boys are numerous, and full of roguish tricks, and there is no *master.* The boys in this great school play truant, and there is no person to chastise them. Do you think, my countrymen, that America is more easily governed than a school? You do very well in small matters; extend your reason to great ones. Would you not laugh at a farmer who would fasten a cable to a plough, and yet attempt to draw a house with a cobweb? "And Nathan said unto David, *thou art the man."* You think a master necessary to govern *a few* harmless children in a school or family; yet leave thousands of great rogues to be governed by *good advice.* Believe me, my friends, for

I am *serious; you lose rights,* because you will not giv your magistrates authority to *protect them.* Your liberty is despotism, because it has no control; your power is nothing, because it is not united.

But further, luxury rages among you, and luxury is *the devil.* The war has sent this evil demon to impoverish people, and embarrass the public. The articles of rum and tea alone, which are drank in this country, would pay all its taxes. But when we add, sugar, coffee, feathers, and the whole list of baubles and trinkets, what an enormous expense? No wonder you want paper currency. My countrymen are all grown very tasty! Feathers and jordans must all be imported! Certainly gentlemen, the devil is among you. A Hampshire man, who drinks forty shillings worth of rum in a year, and never thinks of the expense, will raise a mob to reduce the governor's salary, which does not amount to three pence a man per annum. Is not this the devil?

My countrymen—A writer appeared, not long ago, informing you how to redress grievances. He givs excellent advice. Let every man make a little box, and put into it *four pence* every day. This in a year will amount to six pounds one shilling and eight pence, a sum more than sufficient to pay any poor man's tax. Any man can pay three or four pence a day, though no poor man can, at the end of a year, pay six pounds. Take my advice, every man of you, and you will hardly feel your taxes.

But further, a *tender law is* the *devil.* When I trust a man, a sum of money, I expect he will return the full value. That Legislature which says my debtor may pay me with *one third* of the value he received, commits a deliberate act of villany; an act for which an *individual,* in any government, would be honored with a whipping post, and in most governments, with a gallows. When a man makes dollars, one third of which only is silver, and passes them for good coin, he must lose his ears, &c.

But Legislatures can, with the solemn face of rulers, and guardians of justice, boldly give currency to an *adulterated coin,* enjoin it upon debtors to cheat their creditors, and enforce their systematic knavery with legal penalties. The differences between the man who makes and passes counterfeit money, and the man who tenders his creditor one third of the value of the debt, and demands a discharge, is the same as between a thief and a robber. The first cheats his neighbor in the dark, and takes his property without his knowledge: the last boldly meets him at noon day, tells him he is a rascal, and demands his purse.

My countrymen, the devil is among you. Make *paper* as much as you please; make it a tender in all *future contracts,* or let it rest on its own bottom: But remember that past contracts are *sacred things;* that Legislatures have
10 no right to interfere with them; they have no right to say, a debt shall be paid at a discount, or in any manner which the parties never intended. It is the business of justice to fulfil the intention of parties in contracts, not to defeat them. To pay *bona fide* contracts for cash, in paper of little value, or in old horses, would be a dishonest attempt in an individual; but for Legislatures to frame laws to support and encourage such detestable villany, is like a judge
20 who should inscribe the arms of a rogue over the seat of justice, or clergymen who should convert into bawdy-houses the temples of Jehovah. My countrymen, the world says, the devil is in you: Mankind detest you as they would a nest of robbers.

But lastly, mobs and conventions are devils. Good men love law and legal measures. Knaves only fear law, and try to destroy it. My countrymen, if a constitutional Legislature cannot
30 redress a grievance, a mob never can. Laws are the security of life and property; nay, what is more, of liberty. The man who encourages a mob to prevent the operation of law, ceases to be *free or safe;* for the same principle which leads a man to put a bayonet to the breast of

a judge will lead him to take property where he can find it; and when the judge dare not act, where is the loser's remedy? Alas, my friends, too much liberty is no liberty at all. Giv me any thing but mobs; for mobs are the devil in his worst shape. I would shoot the leader of a mob, sooner than a midnight ruffian. People may have grievances, perhaps, and no man would more readily hold up his hand to redress them than myself; but mobs rebel against laws of their own, and rebellion is a crime which admits of no palliation.

My countrymen, I am a private, peaceable man. I have nothing to win or to lose by the game of paper currency; but *I revere justice.* I would sooner pick oakum all my life, than stain my reputation, or pay my creditor one farthing less than his honest demands.

While you attempt to trade to advantage, without a *head* to combine all the States into systematic, uniform measures, the world will laugh at you for fools. While merchants take and giv credit, the world will call them idiots, and laugh at their ruin. While farmers get credit, borrow money, and mortgage their farms, the world will call them fools, and laugh at their embarrassments. While all men liv beyond their income, and are harrassed with duns and sheriffs, no man will pity them, or giv them relief. But when mobs and conventions oppose the courts of justice, and Legislatures make paper or old horses a legal tender in all cases, the world will exclaim with one voice—*Ye are rogues, and the devil is in you!*
                                                    1786

»   »   ADVICE TO CONNECTICUT FOLKS   «   «

41   . . . Now, good people, I have a word of advice for you. I will tell you how to pay your taxes and debts, without feeling them.

1st. Fee no lawyers.

You say lawyers have too high fees. I say they have not. They cost me not one farthing. Do as I have always done, and lawyers' fees will be no trouble at all. If I want a new coat, or my wife wants a new gown, we have agreed
50 to wear the old ones until we have got cash or produce to pay for them. When we buy, we pay in hand; we get things cheaper than our neighbors; merchants never dun us, and we have no lawyers' fees to pay. When we see sheriffs and duns knocking at the doors of our

neighbors, we laugh at their folly. Besides, I keep a little drawer in my desk, with money enough in it to pay the next tax; and I never touch a farthing until the collector calls. Now, good folks, if you will take the same method, you will save out of lawyers' fees and court charges, on the most moderate calculations, 20,000l. a year.

2dly. I allow my family but two gallons of rum a year. This is enough for any family, and too much for most of them. I drink cyder and beer of my own manufacture; and my wife makes excellent beer, I assure you. I advise you all to do the same. I am astonished at you, good folks. Not a mechanic or a laborer goes to work for a merchant, but he carries home a bottle of rum. Not a load of wood comes to town, but a gallon bottle is tied to the cart stake to be filled with rum. Scarcely a woman comes to town with tow cloth, but she has a wooden gallon bottle in one side of her saddle bags, to fill with rum. A stranger would think you to be a nation of Indians by your thirst for this paltry liquor. Take a bit of advice from a good friend of yours. Get two gallons of rum in a year; have two or three frolics of innocent mirth; keep a little spirit for a medicine, and let your common drink be the produce or manufacture of this country. This will make a saving of almost 400,000 gallons of rum, or 80,000l. a year.

3dly. Never buy any useless clothing.

Keep a good suit for Sundays and other public days; but let your common wearing apparel be good substantial cloths, and linens of your own manufacture. Let your wives and daughters lay aside their plumes. Feathers and fripperies suit the Cherokees or the wench in your kitchen; but they little become the fair daughters of America.[1] Out of the dry goods imported, you may save 50,000l. a year.

These savings amount to 150,000l. a year.

[1] I would just mention to my fair readers, whom I love and esteem, that feathers and other frippery of the head, are disreputable in Europe. [Webster's note.]

This is more than enough to pay the interest of all our public debts.

My countrymen, I am not trifling with you: I am serious. You feel the facts I state; you know you are poor, and ought to know, the fault is all your own. Are you not satisfied with the food and drink which this country affords? The beef, the pork, the wheat, the corn, the butter, the cheese, the cyder, the beer, those luxuries which are heaped in profusion upon 10 your tables? If not, you must expect to be poor. In vain do you wish for mines of gold and silver. A mine would be the greatest curse that could befal this country. There is gold and silver enough in the world, and if you have not enough of it, it is because you consume all you earn in useless food and drink. In vain do you wish to increase the quantity of cash by a mint, or by paper emissions. Should it rain millions of joes into your chimnies, on your present 20 system of expenses, you would still have no money. It would leave the country in streams. Trifle not with serious subjects, nor spend your breath in empty wishes. Reform; economize. This is the whole of your political duty. You may reason, speculate, complain, raise mobs, spend life in railing at Congress and your rulers; but unless you import less than you export, unless you spend less than you earn, you will eternally be poor.   1786

THOMAS JEFFERSON

1743–1826

J EFFERSON'S RESPONSE to Shays's Rebellion was in striking contrast with that of Noah Webster. In the following letters the Virginia statesman's general philosophy of the relations of the governed to the governors is given some interesting specific applications.

The Papers of Thomas Jefferson, Julian P. Boyd and *others,* eds., Princeton, 1950–

» » LETTERS « «

TO COLONEL EDWARD CARRINGTON

Paris, january 16, 1787

. . .

The tumults in America I expected would have produced in Europe an unfavorable

opinion of our political state. But it has not. On the contrary, the small effect of these tumults seems to have given more confidence in the firmness of our governments. The interposition of the people themselves on the side of government has had a great effect on the opinion here. I am persuaded myself that the good sense of the people will always be found to be the best army. They may be led astray for a moment, but will soon correct themselves. The people are the only censors of their governors; and even their errors will tend to keep these to the true principles of their institution. To punish these errors too severely would be to suppress the only safeguard of the public liberty. The way to prevent these irregular interpositions of the people, is to give them

10 full information of their affairs through the channel of the public papers, and to contrive that those papers should penetrate the whole mass of the people. The basis of our governments being the opinion of the people, the very first object should be to keep that right; and were it left to me to decide whether we should have a government without newspapers, or newspapers without a government, I should not hesitate a moment to prefer the latter. But

20 I should mean that every man should receive those papers, and be capable of reading them. I am convinced that those societies (as the Indians) which live without government, enjoy in their general mass an infinitely greater degree of happiness than those who live under the European governments. Among the former, public opinion is in the place of law, and restrains morals as powerfully as laws ever did anywhere. Among the latter, under pretence

30 of governing, they have divided their nations into two classes, wolves and sheep. I do not exaggerate. This is a true picture of Europe. Cherish, therefore, the spirit of our people, and keep alive their attention. Do not be too severe upon their errors, but reclaim them by enlightening them. If once they become inattentive to the public affairs, you and I, and Congress and Assemblies, Judges and Governors, shall all become wolves. It seems to be the law

40 of our general nature, in spite of individual exceptions; and experience declares that man is the only animal which devours his own kind; for I can apply no milder term to the governments of Europe, and to the general prey of the rich on the poor. The want of news has led me into disquisition instead of narration, forgetting you have every day enough of that. I shall be happy to hear from you sometimes, only observing that whatever passes through

50 the post is read, and that when you write what should be read by myself only, you must be so good as to confide your letter to some passenger, or officer of the packet. I will ask your permission to write to you sometimes, and to assure you of the esteem and respect with

which I have honor to be, dear Sir, your most obedient, and most humble servant.　　1787

TO JAMES MADISON

Paris, January 30, 1787

DEAR SIR,—My last to you was of the 16th of December; since which, I have received yours of November the 25th, and December the 4th, which afforded me, as your letters always do, a treat on matters public, individual and economical. I am impatient to learn your sentiments on the late troubles in the eastern States. So far as I have yet seen, they do not appear to threaten serious consequences. Those States have suffered by the stoppage of the channels of their commerce, which have not yet found other issues. This must render money scarce, and make the people uneasy. This uneasiness has produced acts absolutely unjustifiable; but I hope they will provoke no severities from their governments. A consciousness of those in power that their administration of the public affairs has been honest, may, perhaps, produce too great a degree of indignation; and those characters, wherein fear predominates over hope, may apprehend too much from these instances of irregularity. They may conclude too hastily, that nature has formed man insusceptible of any other government than that of force, a conclusion not founded in truth nor experience. Societies exist under three forms, sufficiently distinguishable. 1. Without government, as among our Indians. 2. Under governments, wherein the will of every one has a just influence; as is the case in England, in a slight degree, and in our States, in a great one. 3. Under governments of force; as is the case in all other monarchies, and in most of the other republics. To have an idea of the curse of existence under these last, they must be seen. It is a government of wolves over sheep. It is a problem, not clear in my mind, that the first condition is not the best. But I believe it to be inconsistent with any great degree of population. The second state has a great deal of good in it. The mass of mankind under that, enjoys a precious degree of liberty and happiness. It has its evils, too; the principal of which is the turbulence to which it is subject. But weigh this against the oppressions of monarchy, and it becomes nothing. *Malo periculosam libertatem quam quietam servitutem.*[1] Even this evil is productive of good.

---

[1] *Rather a dangerous liberty than a peaceful servitude.*

It prevents the degeneracy of government, and nourishes a general attention to the public affairs. I hold it, that a little rebellion, now and then, is a good thing, and as necessary in the political world as storms in the physical. Unsuccessful rebellions, indeed, generally establish the encroachments on the rights of people, which have produced them. An observation of this truth should render honest republican governors so mild in their punishment of rebellions, as not to discourage them too much. It is a medicine necessary for the sound health of government. . . .   1787

WILLIAM MACLAY

1734–1804

NO CONTEMPORARY RECORD of the early days of the Republic is more justly celebrated than the piquant and racy *Journal of Senator William Maclay of Pennsylvania*. Not edited and published until 1880 and 1890, this *Journal* is the only complete record of the debates in the first session of the Senate. Maclay was a Scotch-Irish Pennsylvanian who had organized defense against the Indians during the war of the Revolution and taken part, in various capacities, in the politics of the state prior to his election to the United States Senate in 1789. Maclay, as the representative of rural Pennsylvania, opposed the Federalist policies of Hamilton, denounced the rage for speculation, and held up to scorn the efforts of conservatives to fasten aristocratic forms on the new nation. Aware of the economic bases of politics and given to caustic and witty remarks on all the leading personalities of the day, Maclay's *Journal* is of unparalleled value in its frank revelation of the contest between the more democratic and aristocratic forces of the time.

L. R. Harley, *William Maclay, United States Senator from Pennsylvania 1789–1791*, Philadelphia, 1909.
Journal of William Maclay, C. A. Beard, ed., New York, 1927.

» » *From:* THE JOURNAL OF WILLIAM MACLAY « «

CHAPTER I

ON TITLES AND CEREMONIALS

30th April, Thursday.—This is a great, important day. Goddess of etiquette, assist me while I describe it. The Senate stood adjourned to half after eleven o'clock. About ten dressed in my best clothes; went for Mr. Morris' lodgings, but met his son, who told me that his father would not be in town until Saturday. Turned into the Hall. The crowd already great. The Senate met. The Vice-President rose in the most solemn manner. This son of *Adam* seemed impressed with deeper gravity, yet what shall I think of him? He often, in the midst of his most important airs—I believe when he is at loss for expressions (and this he often is, wrapped up, I suppose, in the contemplation of his own importance)—suffers an unmeaning kind of vacant laugh to escape him. This was the case to-day, and really to me bore the air of ridiculing the farce he was acting. "Gentlemen, I wish for the direction of the Senate. The President will, I suppose, address the Congress. How shall I behave? How shall we receive it? Shall it be standing or sitting?"

Here followed a considerable deal of talk from him which I could make nothing of. Mr. Lee began with the House of Commons (as is usual with him), then the House of Lords, then the King, and then back again. The result of his information was, that the Lords sat and the Commons stood on the delivery of the King's speech. Mr. Izard got up and told how often he had been in the Houses of Parliament. He said a great deal of what he had seen there. [He] made, however, this sagacious discovery, that the Commons stood because they had no seats to sit on, being arrived at the bar of the House of Lords. It was discovered after some time that the King sat, too, and had his robes and crown on.

Mr. Adams got up again and said he had been very often indeed at the Parliament on those occasions, but there always was such a crowd, and *ladies along,* that for his part he could not say how it was. Mr. Carrol got up to declare that he thought it of no consequence how it was in Great Britain; they were no rule to us, etc. But all at once the Secretary, who had been out, whispered to the Chair that the Clerk from the Representatives was at the door with a communication. Gentlemen of the Senate, how shall he be received? A silly kind of resolution of the committee on that business had been laid on the table some days ago. The amount of it was that each House should communicate to the other what and how they chose; it concluded, however, something in this way: That everything should be done with all the *propriety* that was *proper.* The question was, Shall this be adopted, that we may know how to receive the Clerk? It was objected [that] this will throw no light on the subject; it will leave you where you are. Mr. Lee brought the House of Commons before us again. He reprobated the rule; declared that the Clerk should not come within the bar of the House; that the proper mode was for the Sergeant-at-Arms, with the mace on his shoulder, to meet the Clerk at the door and receive his communication; we are not, however, provided for this ceremonious way of doing business, having neither mace nor sergeant nor Masters in Chancery, who carry down bills from the English Lords.

Mr. Izard got up and labored unintelligibly to show the great distinction between a communication and a delivery of a thing, but he was not minded. Mr. Elsworth showed plainly enough that if the Clerk was not permitted to deliver the communication, the Speaker might as well send it inclosed. Repeated accounts came [that] the Speaker and Representatives were at the door. Confusion ensued; the members left their seats. Mr. Read rose and called the attention of the Senate to the neglect that

had been shown Mr. Thompson, late Secretary. Mr. Lee rose to answer him, but I could not hear one word he said. The Speaker was introduced, followed by the Representatives. Here we sat an hour and ten minutes before the President arrived—this delay was owing to Lee, Izard, and Dalton, who had stayed with us while the Speaker came in, instead of going to attend the President. The President advanced between the Senate and Representatives, bowing to each. He was placed in the chair by the Vice-President; the Senate with their president on the right, the Speaker and the Representatives on his left. The Vice-President rose and addressed a short sentence to him. The import of it was that he should now take the oath of office as President. He seemed to have forgot half what he was to say, for he made a dead pause and stood for some time, to appearance, in a vacant mood. He finished with a formal bow, and the President was conducted out of the middle window into the gallery, and the oath was administered by the Chancellor. Notice that the business done was communicated to the crowd by proclamation, etc., who gave three cheers, and repeated it on the President's bowing to them.

As the company returned into the Senate chamber, the President took the chair and the Senators and Representatives their seats. He rose, and all arose also, and addressed them (see the address). This great man was agitated and embarrassed more than ever he was by the leveled cannon or pointed musket. He trembled, and several times could scarce make out to read, though it must be supposed he had often read it before. He put part of the fingers of his left hand into the side of what I think the tailors call the fall of the breeches [corresponding to the modern side-pocket], changing the paper into his left [right] hand. After some time he then did the same with some of the fingers of his right hand. When he came to the words *all the world,* he made a flourish with his right hand, which left rather an ungainly impression. I sincerely, for my part, wished all set ceremony in the hands of the dancing-masters, and that this first of men had read off his address in the plainest manner, without ever taking his eyes from the paper, for I felt hurt that he was not first in everything. He was dressed in deep brown, with metal buttons, with an eagle on them, white stockings, a bag, and sword.

From the hall there was a grand procession

to Saint Paul's Church, where prayers were said by the Bishop. The procession was well conducted and without accident, as far as I have heard. The militia were all under arms, lined the street near the church, made a good figure, and behaved well.

The Senate returned to their chamber after service, formed, and took up the address. Our Vice-President called it *his most gracious speech*. I can not approve of this. A committee was appointed on it—Johnson, Carrol, Patterson. Adjourned. In the evening there were grand fireworks. The Spanish Ambassador's house was adorned with transparent paintings; the French Minister's house was illuminated, and had some transparent pieces; the Hall was grandly illuminated, and after all this the people went to bed.

May 1st.—Attended at the Hall at eleven. The prayers were over and the minutes reading. When we came to the minute of the speech it stood, *His most gracious speech*. I looked all around the Senate. Every countenance seemed to wear a blank. The Secretary was going on: I must speak or nobody would. "Mr. President, we have lately had a hard struggle for our liberty against kingly authority. The minds of men are still heated: everything related to that species of government is odious to the people. The words prefixed to the President's speech are the same that are usually placed before the speech of his Britannic Majesty. I know they will give offense. I consider them as improper. I therefore move that they be struck out, and that it stand simply address or speech, as may be judged most suitable."

Mr. Adams rose in his chair and expressed the greatest surprise that anything should be objected to on account of its being taken from the practice of that Government under which we had lived so long and happily formerly; that he was for a dignified and respectable government, and as far as he knew the sentiments of people they thought as he did; that for his part he was one of the first in the late contest [the Revolution], and, if *he could have thought of this, he never would have drawn his sword.*

Painful as it was, I had to contend with the Chair. I admitted that the people of the colonies (now States) had enjoyed formerly great happiness under that species of government, but the abuses of that Government under which they had smarted had taught them what they had to fear from that kind of government;

that there had been a revolution in the sentiments of people respecting government equally great as that which had happened in the Government itself; that even the modes of it were now abhorred; that the enemies of the Constitution had objected to it the facility there would be of transition from it to kingly government and all the trappings and splendor of royalty; that if such a thing as this appeared on our minutes, they would not fail to represent 10 it as the first step of the ladder in the ascent to royalty. The Vice-President rose a second time, and declared that he had mentioned it to the Secretary; that he could not possibly conceive that any person could take offense at it. I had to get up again and declare that, although I knew of it being mentioned from the Chair, yet my opposition did not proceed from any motive of contempt; that, although it was a painful task, it was solely a sense of duty 20 that raised me.

The Vice-President stood during this time; said he had been long abroad, and did not know how the temper of people might be now. Up now rose Mr. Read, and declared for the paragraph. He saw no reason to object to it because the British speeches were styled *most gracious*. If we chose to object to words because they had been used in the same sense in Britain, we should soon be at a loss to do 30 business. I had to reply. "It is time enough to submit to necessity when it exists. At present we are at no loss for words. The words speech or address without any addition will suit us well enough." The first time I was up Mr. Lee followed me with a word or two by way of seconding me; but when the Vice-President, on being last up, declared that he was the person from whom the words were taken, Mr. Lee got up and informed the Chair that 40 he did not know that circumstance, as he had been absent when it happened. The question was put and carried for erasing the words without a division.

After the House adjourned the Vice-President took me to one side, declared how much he was for an efficient Government, how much he respected General Washington, and much of that kind. I told him I would yield to no person in respect to General Washington; that 50 our common friends would perhaps one day inform him that I was not wanting in respect to himself [Adams]; that my wishes for an efficient Government were as high as any man's, and begged him to believe that I did myself great violence when I opposed him in the chair, and nothing but a sense of duty could force me to it. He got on the subject of checks to government and the balances of power. His tale was long. He seemed to expect some answer. I caught at the last word, and said undoubtedly without a balance there could be no equilibrium, and so left him hanging in geometry.

10 The unequivocal declaration that he would never have drawn his sword, etc., has drawn my mind to the following remarks: that the motives of the actors in the late Revolution were various can not be doubted. The abolishing of royalty, the extinguishing of patronage and dependencies attached to that form of government, were the exalted motives of many revolutionists, and these were the improvements meant by them to be made of the war 20 which was forced on us by British aggression —in fine, the amelioration of government and bettering the condition of mankind. These ends and none other were publicly avowed, and all our constitutions and public acts were formed in this spirit. Yet there were not wanting a party whose motives were different. They wished for the loaves and fishes of government, and cared for nothing else but a translation of the diadem and scepter from London to 30 Boston, New York, or Philadelphia; or, in other words, the creation of a new monarchy in America, and to form niches for themselves in the temple of royalty.

This spirit manifested itself strongly among the officers at the close of the war, and I have been afraid the army would not have been disbanded if the common soldiers could have been kept together. This spirit they developed in the Order of Cincinnati, where I trust it 40 will spend itself in a harmless flame and soon become extinguished. That Mr. Adams should, however, so unequivocally avow this motive, at a time when a republican form of government is secured to every State in the Union, appears to me a mark of extreme folly.[1]

Mem.,[2] 1790.—It is worthy of remark that about this time a spirit of reformation broke out in France which finally abolished all titles and every trace of the feudal system. Strange, 50 indeed, that in that very country [America], where the flame of freedom had been kindled, an attempt should be made to introduce these

[1] "John Adams was included by Jefferson among the believers in monarchy."—Randall's Life of Jefferson, vol. i, p. 586. [Maclay's note.]
[2] Memorandum.

absurdities and humiliating distinctions which the hand of reason, aided by our example, was prostrating in the heart of Europe. I, however, will endeavor (as I have hitherto done) to use the resentment of the Representatives to defeat Mr. Adams and others on the subject of titles. The pompous and lordly distinctions which the Senate have manifested a disposition to establish between the two Houses have nettled the Representatives, and this business of titles may be considered as part of the same tune. While we are debating on titles I will, through the Speaker, Mr. Muhlenberg, and other friends, get the idea suggested of answering the President's address without any title, in contempt of our deliberations, which still continue on that subject. This once effected, will confound them [the Senators] completely, and establish a precedent they will not dare to violate.

. . .

May 8th.—Attended a joint committee on the papers of the old Congress. Made progress in the business. Agreed to meet at half-past ten on Monday and report. Senate formed. The Secretary, as usual, had made some mistakes, which were rectified, and now Mr. Elsworth moved for the report of the Joint Committee to be taken up on the subject of titles. It was accordingly done. Mr. Lee led the business. He took his old ground—all the world, civilized and savage, called for titles; that there must be something in human nature that occasioned this general consent; that, therefore, he conceived it was right. Here he began to enumerate many nations who gave titles—such as Venice, Genoa, and others. The Greeks and Romans, it was said, had no titles, "but" (making a profound bow to the Chair) "you were pleased to set us right in this with respect to the Conscript Fathers the other day." Here he repeated the Vice-President's speech of the 23d ultimo [April], almost verbatim all over.

Mr. Elsworth rose. He had a paper in his hat, which he looked constantly at. He repeated almost all that Mr. Lee had said, but got on the subject of kings—declared that the sentence in the primer of fear God and honor the king was of great importance; that kings were of divine appointment; that Saul, the head and shoulders taller than the rest of the people, was elected by God and anointed by his appointment.

I sat, after he had done, for a considerable

time, to see if anybody would rise. At last I got up and first answered Lee as well as I could with nearly the same arguments, drawn from the Constitution, as I had used on the 23d ult. I mentioned that within the space of twenty years back more light had been thrown on the subject of governments and on human affairs in general than for several generations before; that this light of knowledge had diminished the veneration for titles, and that mankind now considered themselves as little bound to imitate the follies of civilized nations as the brutalities of savages; that the abuse of power and the fear of bloody masters had extorted titles as well as adoration, in some instances from the trembling crowd; that the impression now on the minds of the citizens of these States was that of horror for kingly authority.

Izard got up. He dwelt almost entirely on the antiquity of kingly government. He could not, however, well get further back than Philip of Macedon. He seemed to have forgot both Homer and the Bible. He urged for something equivalent to nobility having been common among the Romans, for they had three names that seemed to answer to honorable, or something like it, before and something behind. He did not say Esquire. Mr. Carrol rose and took my side of the question. He followed nearly the track I had been in, and dwelt much on the information that was now abroad in the world. He spoke against kings. Mr. Lee and Mr. Izard were both up again. Elsworth was up again. Langdon was up several times, but spoke short each time. Patterson was up, but there was no knowing which side he was of. Mr. Lee considered him as against him and answered him, but Patterson finally voted with Lee. The Vice-President repeatedly helped the speakers for titles. Elsworth was enumerating how common the appellation of President was. The Vice-President put him in mind that there were presidents of fire companies and of a cricket club. Mr. Lee at another time was saying he believed some of the States authorized titles by their Constitutions. The Vice-President, from the chair, told him that Connecticut did it. At sundry other times he interfered in a like manner. I had been frequently up to answer new points during the debate.

I collected myself for a last effort. I read the clause in the Constitution against titles of nobility; showed that the spirit of it was against not only granting titles by Congress, but against the permission of foreign potentates granting *any titles whatever;* that as to kingly government, it was equally out of the question, as a republican government was guaranteed to every State in the Union; that they were both equally forbidden fruit of the Constitution. I called the attention of the House to the consequences that were like to follow; that gentlemen semed to court a rupture with the other House. The Representatives had adopted the report, and were this day acting on it, or according to the spirit of the report. We were proposing a title. Our conduct would mark us to the world as actuated by the spirit of dissension, and the characters of the Houses would be as aristocratic and democratical.

The report [of the Committee on Titles] was, however, rejected. "Excellency" was moved for as a title by Mr. Izard. It was withdrawn by Mr. Izard, and "highness" with some prefatory word, proposed by Mr. Lee. Now long harangues were made in favor of this title. "Elective" was placed before. It was insisted that such a dignified title would add greatly to the weight and authority of the Government both at home and abroad. I declared myself totally of a different opinion; that at present it was impossible to add to the respect entertained for General Washington; that if you gave him the title of any foreign prince or potentate, a belief would follow that the manners of that prince and his modes of government would be adopted by the President. (Mr. Lee had, just before I got up, read over a list of the titles of all the princes and potentates of the earth, marking where the word "highness" occurred. The Grand Turk had it, all the princes of Germany had [it], sons and daughters of crown heads, etc.) That particularly "elective highness," which sounded nearly like "electoral highness," would have a most ungrateful sound to many thousands of industrious citizens who had fled from German oppression; that "highness" was part of the title of a prince or princes of the blood, and was often given to dukes; that it was degrading our President to place him on a par with any prince of any blood in Europe, nor was there one of them that could enter the list of true glory with him.

But I will minute no more. The debate lasted till half after three o'clock, and it ended in appointing a committee to consider of a title to be given to the President. This whole silly

business is the work of Mr. Adams and Mr. Lee; Izard follows Lee, and the New England men, who always herd together, follow Mr. Adams. Mr. Thompson says this used to be the case in the old Congress. I had, to be sure, the greatest share in this debate, and must now have completely sold (no, sold is a bad word, for I have got nothing for it) every particle of court favor, for a court our House seems de-
10 termined on, and to run into all the fooleries, fopperies, fineries, and pomp of royal etiquette; and all this for Mr. Adams.

May 9th.—Attended the Hall at ten o'clock to go on the Judicial Committee. Met many of the members. I know not the motive, but I never was received with more familiarity, nor quite so much, before by the members. Elsworth in particular seemed to show a kind of fondness. The Judicial Committee did no busi-
20 ness. Senate formed. It took a long time to correct the minutes. Otis keeps them miserably. At length the committee came in and reported a title—*His Highness the President of the United States of America and Protector of the Rights of the Same.* Mr. Few had spoken a word or two with me, and signified his unwillingness to do anything hastily. He got up and spoke a great deal against hasty measures. He did not pointedly move for postponement,
30 but it amounted nearly to it. The Clerk of the other House in the mean time appeared at the bar and announced the adoption of the report of the Joint Committee (rejecting titles).

I got up and expressed my opinion that what had fallen from the honorable gentleman from Georgia amounted to a motion for postponement, and asked leave to second him. I then pointed out the rupture that was likely to ensue with the other House; that this was a
40 matter of very serious import, and I thought it our indispensable duty to avoid any inconvenience of that kind; that by the arrangement between the Houses in case of disagreement a conference might be requested; that my intention was, if the postponement was carried, to move immediately for a committee of conference to be appointed on the difference between the Houses, and I had hopes that by these means all subject of debate would be
50 done away. Mr. Read got up and moved that the report might be adopted. He was not seconded, but the motion was in itself idle. Mr. Strong spoke in favor of the postponement, and was interrupted from the Chair. Mr. Dalton after some time spoke in favor of it.

I could now see a visible anxiety in the Chair.

I had a fine, slack, and easy time of it to-day. Friends seemed to rise in succession. Lee went over his old ground twice, but owned at last there was great difficulty every way, but said plainly the best mode was for the House to adopt the report, and then the other House would follow. He found, however, the current began to turn against him, and he laid his head on his hand as if he would have slept. Mr. Strong was up again. He said among many things that he thought the other House would follow, but there was a risk in it.

Mr. Izard got up at last. He, too, was for a postponement. I could see the Vice-President kindled at him. Mr. Izard said we knew the other House had adopted the report [rejecting titles]. The Vice-President interrupted him and said no; we had no right to know it nor could we know it until after the Clerk had this morning given official information. The members fixed themselves, and the question was called for.

Up now got the Vice-President, and for forty minutes did he harangue us from the chair. He began first on the subject of order, and found fault with everything almost, but down he came to particulars, and pointedly blamed a member for disorderly behavior. The member had mentioned the appearance of a captious disposition in the other House. This was disorderly and spoke with asperity. The member meant was Mr. Izard. All this was only prefatory. On he got to his favorite topic of titles, and over the old ground of the immense advantage of, the absolute necessity of them. When he had exhausted this subject he turned a new leaf, I believe, on the conviction that the postponement would be carried and perhaps the business lost by an attention to the other House.

"Gentlemen, I must tell you that it is you and the President that have the making of titles. Suppose the President to have the appointment of Mr. Jefferson at the court of France. Mr. Jefferson is, in virtue of that appointment, the most illustrious, the most powerful, and what not. But the President must be himself something that includes all the dignities of the diplomatic corps and something greater still. What will the common people of foreign countries, what will the sailors and the soldiers say, 'George Washington, President of the United States'? They will despise him *to all eternity*. This is all nonsense to the philosopher, but so is all government whatever."

The above I recollect with great precision, but he said fifty more things, equally injudicious, which I do not think worth minuting. It is evident that he begins to despair of getting the article of titles through the House of Representatives, and has turned his eye to get it done solely by the Senate.

Having experienced relief by the interference of sundry members, I had determined not to say another word, but his new leaf appeared so absurd I could not help some animadversions on it. I rose. Mr. President, the Constitution of the United States has designated our Chief Magistrate by the appellation of the *President of the United States of America*. This is his title of office, nor can we alter, add to, or diminish it without infringing the Constitution. In like manner persons authorized to transact business with foreign powers are styled *Ambassadors, Public Ministers*, etc. To give them any other appellation would be an equal infringement. As to grades of orders or titles of nobility, nothing of the kind can be established by Congress.

Can, then, the President and Senate do that which is prohibited to the United States at large? Certainly not. Let us read the Constitution: *No title of nobility shall be granted by the United States*. The Constitution goes further. 10 The servants of the public are prohibited from accepting them from any foreign state, king, or prince. So that the appellations and terms given to nobility in the Old World are contraband language in the United States, nor can we apply them to our citizens consistent with the Constitution. As to what the common people, soldiers, and sailors of foreign countries may think of us, I do not think it imports us much. Perhaps the less they think, or have 20 occasion to think of us, the better.

JOEL BARLOW

1754–1812

BARLOW, who was the son of a Connecticut farmer, outgrew his early parochial and conservative surroundings and became one of the most nationalistic and at the same time one of the most cosmopolitan of Americans. Teaching, preaching, writing, business, and the law absorbed his energies after graduation from Yale in 1778. His first notable poem, *The Vision of Columbus* (1787), celebrated in grandiose couplets the glories of his country, past and present; and he contributed to some of the joint-products of the conservative "Hartford Wits."

If Barlow's agency in France for the Scioto land company was a failure, his residence abroad greatly widened his outlook. Becoming a true son of the Enlightenment, he helped Thomas Paine publish *The Age of Reason* and was made a citizen of France for his literary defense of the Revolution. In 1792 his *Advice to the Privileged Orders* still further augmented his fame as a champion of the principles of popular government. The following year his *Letter Addressed to the People of Piedmont* summarized his glorification of the French Revolution.

After his return to America in 1805 he completed the revision of his pretentious epic which was published as *The Columbiad* two years later. Barlow also tried to promote the establishment of a national institution for research and instruction in the arts and sciences. He died in Poland while on a mission designed to persuade Napoleon to deal more gently with American merchant vessels.

The Political Writings of Joel Barlow, New York, 1796.
James L. Woodress, *A Yankee's Odyssey*, Phila., 1958.
Theodore Zunder, *The Early Days of Joel Barlow, a Connecticut Wit*, New Haven, 1934.
V. C. Miller, *Joel Barlow: Revolutionist, 1791–1792*, Hamburg, 1932.
P. H. Boynton, "Joel Barlow Advises the Privileged Orders," *New Eng. Quart.* XII (September, 1939), 477–499.

A LETTER ADDRESSED TO THE PEOPLE
OF PIEDMONT

» 　 »　　　　　　　　　　　　　　　　　　«　 «

Chambery, December 27, 1792

CITIZENS OF PIEDMONT,

You occupy one of the strongest frontiers of
a country which nature seems to have destined
to be the happiest in Europe. But a number of
imperious circumstances, of which you have
been rather the victims than the authors, have
for many centuries inverted the order of things,
and deprived you of those advantages which
ought to attend your situation. I am a stranger
in this part of the world; Italy is known to me
only from its history, and your present condition only from distant observation and report.
It is not probable that I shall ever have the
pleasure of seeing you or any part of your
country. You must, therefore, acquit me of
entertaining any desire to mislead you, as I can
have no possible interest in addressing you
this letter, but the interest the human heart
naturally takes in uttering the truth on a very
important subject. You are my fellow-creatures;
as such I love you, and cherish the ties which
ought to be mutual between us. You are in a
condition which appears to me to call upon you
to burst the bands of slavery; in this view, I am
ready to hail you as brothers, and wish to aid
you in your work.

I presume in the first place, and I think I am
not deceived, that you are discontented with
your present situation. I believe you are convinced that you cannot be happy, as a people,
while the powers of your government remain
as they now are, as relative to the church, the
state, and the army. If this be true, you must
wish for a change; provided such change can
be within your power, and provided you are
convinced that it would be for your advantage.
Let us examine these two points: whether you
are able to effect a revolution in your government; and if you are, whether you would be
benefited by it.—For it is not my wish to hurry
you into measures, of which you cannot see the
issue, and for which you are not prepared.

I. *Are you able to effect a revolution in your
government?*

The question need never be asked of any
people, when considered with reference to
themselves only, without regard to their neighbours. A whole people is essentially sovereign.

They can at all times do as they please with
their own affairs, unless they are overpowered
by surrounding nations. It is the people who
support the government as it now is; and the
same sovereign people can at any time change
its form, and support it in whatever manner it
shall please them best. The question has no
difficulty in it, but when viewed with reference
to the interest which other governments may
have in preventing a revolution in their neighbourhood.

The enquiry, pursued in this connection, becomes more extensive; especially when applied
to a country of small dimensions, and to a
nation less powerful than some of its neighbours. Such is Piedmont. Had you been called
upon seven years ago to look into your affairs,
and take the government into your own hands,
you must have considered it as a dangerous experiment. Even supposing the weight of your
sufferings to have been as great then as they are
now, and supposing you had been possessed of
the same information which you have since
drawn from the progress of liberty in Europe,
it would scarcely have been prudent for you to
have engaged in so daring an enterprise. All the
tyrants in your neighbourhood would have
brought forward their armies of slaves to crush
the rebellion. The French court would have
been, at that time, as much your enemy as the
French nation is now your friend. And the
house of Austria, with all the subdivisions of
its power in Italy, posted at your gates, would
have united with that of Bourbon, to have
guaranteed your king in every possible extent
of his oppression.

Under these disadvantages your struggles
for liberty might have been vain; they might
even have produced a new injury, instead of
relieving you from the old. But the ground is
now changed; the duty you owe to yourselves
is clearly pointed out by the natural current of
events; and the work you have to do, in establishing a perfect and undisturbed liberty, is in
my opinion much easier than you imagine.
France is at this time, not only the most powerful nation in Europe, but when engaged, as she
now is, in defence of liberty, she is a match for
all the other powers of Europe, when united in
defence of tyranny. France is now your natural

friend, the friend of all people and the enemy of all tyrants. She is indeed the only friend you have as a nation in this part of the world. France has brought liberty to your doors; and she invites you, in the name of all that is dear to you as men, in the name of all that can bind you to the interests of human nature in general, to accept the blessing at her hands. She has done more; she has taught you and all other people how public happiness is to be acquired and preserved. She has addressed herself to the great principles of reason which are common to all men; she has cleared away the mass of prejudice, of false doctrine, of superstition in the science of morals; a mass which the complicated abuses of tyranny, continued for many centuries, had accumulated on the human mind. She has laid down and clearly defined the rights and duties of man and of citizens, explained the great doctrine of equality, the true design of government, the nature of the trust to be reposed in public officers, as servants of the people, by whom they are created and by whom they are paid. She has taught you a great practical truth, which is too consoling to be rejected, and too clear to be called in question, *that you are the sovereigns in your own country*; that you have not, that you cannot have a master, unless you choose to give up your reason, and renounce the character of men; that for any man to call himself your sovereign is a blasphemy against God the sovereign of nature, and against men the proprietors of the earth.

Obligations of gratitude are due to the French nation from you, and from every people in Europe. She has conquered liberty for all men, and laid the foundation for universal public felicity. Other nations have only to build the superstructure, of which the model is given them in the constitution of this great republic.

But let us not amuse ourselves with words, nor rest the argument on theoretical principles, however incontestible they may be. Let us speak of facts that are passing before our eyes, and call to mind the events of the great year that is now drawing to a close. You have seen the principal tyrants and the most formidable armies of Europe, combined and marching in full career of promised victory against the liberties of France.—These armies after sweeping over half of Europe and famishing whole countries in their way to the French frontiers, have there been cut to pieces by a handful of freemen, and driven out of their country. Lib-

erty has marched on the heels of the fugitives; the arch tyrant of Austria, at the head of this fatal conspiracy of kings, has lost the finest part of his dominions; many of the subaltern princes of the empire have lost the whole of theirs, and are now beggars abroad among their brother brigands, who are in expectation of the same inevitable fate. The standard of liberty has reached the borders of the Rhine by the miscarriage of the same combination which 10 has brought it to the summit of the Alps.

All the crowned heads in Europe are now covered with thorns. The man of Turin, who calls himself your king, has been forced to relinquish one half of the usurpations of his ancestors, and is now menacing you with destruction for fear you should reclaim the rest. The Dutchy of Savoy and the country of Nice, more fortunate than you, have been the first to cast off his yoke, and are now ready to assist 20 you with their arms to follow their example. The pope and the other Italian despots, are occupied in restraining the spirit of liberty at home; so that no one of the neighbouring powers is in a condition to take any considerable part in your affairs, except the French; and the French are wishing to give you every aid that you may ask.

Under these circumstances, we need no longer enquire whether you are able to effect a 30 revolution; the more natural question is, are you able to resist it? It is true, the French have renounced all ideas of conquest, and have declared that they will never make war against the liberty of any people. But you will observe that this principle contains in itself a declaration of war against all tyrants who are hostile to the liberty of France; especially against those whose vicinity renders them dangerous to the internal peace of the new republic, by 40 fostering its fugitive traitors, and being the centre of new conspiracies against the rights of man. The court of Turin comes under this description. It is hostile to the liberties of France; it has been so from the beginning; the nature of its external connections and of its internal constitution requires that it should be so to the end. The court of Turin must, therefore, be overturned; the government of your country must be changed, and its powers re- 50 stored to you, to whom they naturally belong.

This is a simple view of facts, which may serve to indicate the present crisis of your affairs, of which it is proper that you should be apprised; that by a due consideration of the causes you may not be astonished at the effects. I make known to you my opinion, with all the frankness that the solemnity of the subject demands; and it seems almost impossible that you should fail to turn the consequences to your advantage.

II. *The more important question to be discussed is, Whether you will be benefited by a revolution in your government?*

10   Many of you will doubtless consider this enquiry as superfluous, because your condition can scarcely be rendered worse, and the means of rendering it better are so obvious that they cannot escape the slightest observation. But those of you who are accustomed to reflect on the principles of liberty will pardon the simplicity of the enquiry, in favour of the great mass of the people whom it is our duty to instruct. There has been so much falsehood and 20 folly imposed on that class of mankind, in order to debase and brutalize their minds to the level of their condition, that their ignorance has become preter natural; it is almost necessary to begin their instruction by informing them that they are human creatures. But, citizen of Italy, defendants of Brutus and Cato, this state of degradation is not the condition designed for man. The God of equal liberty has allotted you a different birthright; you are now 30 invited to reclaim your inheritance, to take possession of your portion among your brethren, to enjoy it in peace, and restore harmony to the great family of men.

You have been fatally misinformed with respect to the nature of the French revolution, and the events that have attended it. Your religious teachers and your political masters have an interest in deceiving you. They unite their efforts for this purpose; they blind your eyes, 40 as you blind the eyes of a mill-horse, that he may not see his harness, nor consider the weight he draws. If the mill-horse could know that he has only a feeble child for a conductor, and that he is made to go constantly round in the same small circle, so that he cannot hope to come nearer his journey's end; especially if he could look into the neighbouring fields and see the other horses enjoying their liberty, he would soon revolt against his little despot, he 50 would grow discouraged with the same unpromising round of fatigue, and refuse to do his work. It is for this reason that you blind his eyes. My friends, the same arts are used with you. The clergy and the nobles of your country, with a man at their head whom they call a king,

do nothing but live upon your labours. They cannot support their luxury by any other means than by keeping you constantly at work. They know that if you were to be informed of their weakness and of your own strength, you would refuse to be their drudges. They are sensible that the moment you open your eyes, you will see that they are but men, that all men are equal in their rights, that they have no more right or power to be kings and lords over you, than you have to be kings and lords over them; and that in consequence of this, you would immediately overturn that abominable system of public robbery which they call a government, and establish a new and equal government, which should secure to every man the fruits of his own labours, protect the innocent, punish the guilty, and instruct every member of society in his duties and rights.

This is precisely what the people of France have done; and the performance of this great work, so necessary to the happiness of mankind, is called the French revolution. It is the knowledge of this revolution which your court and clergy wish to conceal from you lest you should follow the example. They prevent the French newspapers from coming into your country; they forbid the reading of all books that treat of this revolution, and all conversation on that or any other political subject; they have shut up the popular theatres at Turin, and left open none but that of the nobility, from which the citizens are excluded; they have suppressed the great university of that capital, called *the University of the Provinces,* which used to bring students from all parts of Italy, and a considerable emolument to the town; they have doubled the number of their spies, and increased the powers of the police.

All this is to keep you ignorant of the French revolution, that you may not be disposed to follow the example. Observe the insult offered to your understanding. If the example were bad, your good sense would teach you to shun it; it would need only to be known, to be despised; and it ought to be explained to all people, that they might learn to avoid such a dangerous innovation. If it be good, it ought to be taught by your teachers, and imitated by all the world. But be assured that the very caution they use to prevent your coming to the knowledge of the fact, is a proof that such a revolution would be an advantage to you and a disadvantage to them.

But this is not all; they have invented a

thousand falsehoods to supply the place of truth. They have told you lies, in order to excite your enmity against your best friends, and to rouse you to war against those principles which ought to be as dear to you as to the French; because they are the principles of equal liberty and national happiness, applicable to all people. They have told you that the French nation is a race of robbers, assassins, and atheists; they have overturned the religion of their country, waged war against all property and against the lives of its owners. These are impudent falsehoods which never could have been imposed upon you for a moment, had you been permitted to judge for yourselves.

With regard to religion, I only request you to look into the first principles of liberty, as declared by the national assembly. You will find them conformable to the system of catholic faith, as taught by the apostles and recognized in your country, before the church was connected with the civil government, and before the ministers of the altar became tyrants of the state. The French constitution has declared, that all men shall be free to worship God in their own way, and to follow the dictates of their conscience. If any man shall tell you that this is destroying your religion, he is a liar, and not worthy to be your teacher. The gospel of Jesus Christ preaches to you in the strongest language the great doctrine of equality; that all men are equal in the sight of God, and that you shall call no man your master upon earth. —This is the very language of the French revolution. But its authors have gone farther; and, to silence all cavillers who could persuade you or others that they have destroyed the catholic religion, they have done more to maintain it than any legislative body ever did before; they have ordained that the priests and bishops, chosen by the people, shall be salaried and paid out of the national purse.

It is true, they have suppressed those haunts of idleness, hypocrisy, and vice, known by the name of monasteries and convents. This is an advantage to religion, instead of being against it; for religion teaches men to do good, and to labour for their living; but these institutions teach them to do nothing, and live upon the labours of others. Be assured therefore, that the French have done nothing to the disadvantage of religion; but, on the contrary, they have done much to maintain it in its native purity and independence. But I intreat you in the sincerity of my heart not to receive this fact on the strength of my assertion, or that of any other man; but to look into their conduct and judge for yourselves.

You have been likewise taught to believe that the French have violated private property. This is a malicious calumny, which every step of their revolution will contradict, the moment you become acquainted with it. In all the decrees of the national assembly, in all the irregular movements and insurrections of the people, whatever was the object, you will find they have paid a most sacred regard to individual property. Their conduct in this respect has been more laudable within the last three years than that of any other government in Europe. The same thing may be observed with regard to the private morals of the people; they are essentially better than they formerly were. There have been less instances of theft and robbery in France since the revolution, than at any former period; and probably less, in proportion to its population, than in any of the neighbouring countries during the same period.

. . .

The act of the assembly declaring the church lands to be the property of the nation, the suppression of tithes and other feudal claims, have been often mentioned as violations of property. Those who really consider them in this light are weak men, or they have not examined the subject; those who persuade you to think so, without believing it themselves, are wicked men, and not to be trusted. As to the church lands, this act of the assembly did not change the property of them at all. They belonged to the nation before.—What the assembly did, was to change the mode of paying the clergy, equalize their salaries and reduce the number of ecclesiastics. That laborious and more useful class of the clergy, who before were starving upon a beggarly pittance, have had their salaries raised; that idle and overgrown class, who, without doing any duty, were living in the style of princes and tyrants, have been reduced to a moderate income. All are now chosen by the people, and all paid by the nation. With regard to the feudal claims, they were founded in usurpation. The landlords and nobles, to whom they were attributed, had no right to them or property in them, any more than the king of Sardinia has property in you, or in the people of Jerusalem, of which he likewise styles himself king. These feudal claims were mere badges of servitude, which the establishment of equal liberty and the abolition of hereditary titles rendered it necessary to destroy. The nation has in all instances showed itself able to distinguish between the empty superstition of pomp, which serves only to debase mankind, and the solid principles of society on which the revolution is founded.

You have heard it likewise asserted that the French revolution has been marked with cruelty and murder. This is unfortunately true. But it has likewise been marked with treachery, with bribery, with perjury, with all the complicated wiles of expiring despotism. All the cruelty, all the crimes of every name or denomination, that have attended this revolution, have proceeded from royalty, the adherents of royalty, and the refractory priests. The court of Versailles had been for ages a school of falsehood and deceit; and the execution of the penal laws served as a public exhibition of torture, to familiarize the people with the most sanguinary punishments. If the court of Turin and the laws of Piedmont are any better, it is happier for you; you will have the less wickedness to combat in the course of your revolution. But I fear in some respects they are worse. These circumstances in France had trained up in all parts of the kingdom a numerous class of men versed in every art of treachery and perfidy. In this situation of things the great mass of the people, who are naturally honest and good, set

themselves seriously to work in the business of the revolution; which might have been carried on with the greatest harmony; as it had nothing in view but the welfare of the whole. But these deceitful men, being enemies of the revolution, and finding that they could not oppose it by open force, assumed the mask of patriotism, and brought themselves into places of trust in every department of the legislative and executive power. The effect of this was that these good people found themselves deceived and betrayed in every stage of their affairs, from the beginning of the revolution in 1789, till the tenth of August, 1792. Being surrounded by traitors, and not knowing whom to trust even with the execution of their own vengeance, it was natural and sometimes necessary that they should assume this terrible task upon themselves. In some instances indeed this popular vengeance has been ill directed, and has fallen on innocent heads. But these instances are rare.

The limits, I prescribe to my letter, will not allow of my entering into details on a subject so intricate and extensive. This, however, may be relied on as an undeniable truth, that nothing is more human, generous and just, than the general spirit of the revolution; and whatever particular acts, may seem to contravene these principles, those acts are chargeable upon its enemies, and not upon its friends.   1796

WILLIAM MANNING

1747–1814

WILLIAM MANNING, of Billerica, Massachusetts, like the yeoman class to which he belonged, distrusted governors and government, aristocrats and men of affairs, scholars, and lawyers. In contrast with well-to-do merchants, he felt a sickening horror for the financial policies of Hamilton; and with Jefferson, whose disciple he was, he disliked equally much the pro-British attitude of the Federalists. In the French Revolution he saw, not the bondage that it appeared to be in the eyes of orthodox clergymen and people of substance, but rather a welcome emancipation of the downtrodden masses, the greatest blessing in all history. Manning believed that the only hope for the survival of the democratic forces in America was in their enlightenment by true information, that they might know what their true interest was, and by the organization of common folk in a great national union. These measures alone, he insisted, could hold the privileged and selfish few in check.

Unlettered though he was (six months' schooling was all he ever had) Manning felt impelled, in the days of reaction of 1798, to write a series of essays for the *Independent Chronicle*, Boston's

Jeffersonian journal. As Samuel Eliot Morison observes, it is not hard to understand why the editor of this sheet turned Manning's contribution down. No newspaper editor could look with favor on his proposal for a national union of laborers and farmers with an independent press. Manning's *Key of Libberty* is an amazingly salty account. It is, moreover, an invaluable record of the way in which the issue between democracy and aristocracy appeared to a simple, unschooled farmer.

William Manning, *The Key of Libberty, Showing the Causes why a Free Government has always Failed, and a Remedy Against It*, with notes and a foreword by Samuel Eliot Morison, Billerica, Mass., 1922.

» » *From:* THE KEY OF LIBBERTY « «

3dly. Shews how the Few & Many Differ in their Interests in its operation

In the swet of thy face shall thou git thy bread untill thou return to the ground, is the erivarsable sentance of Heaven on Man for his rebellion. To be sentanced to hard Labour dureing life is very unplesent to humane Nature. Their is a grate avartion to it purceivable in all men—yet it is absolutely nesecary that a large majority of the world should labour, or we could not subsist. For Labour is the soul parrant of all property—the land yealdeth nothing without it, & their is no food, clothing, shelter, vessel, or any nesecary of life but what costs Labour & is generally esteemed valuable according to the Labour it costs. Therefore no person can posess property without labouring, unless he git it by force or craft, fraud or fortun out of the earnings of others.

But from the grate veriety of capacietyes strength & abilityes of men, their always was, & always will be, a very unequel distribution of property in the world. Many are so rich that they can live without Labour. Also the marchent, phisition, lawyer & divine, the philosipher and school master, the Juditial & Executive Officers, & many others who could honestly git a living without bodily labours. As all these professions require a considerable expence of time & property to qualify themselves therefor, & as no person after this qualifying himselfe & making a pick on a profession by which he meens to live, can desire to have it dishonourable or unproductive, so all these professions naturally unite in their skems to make their callings as honourable & lucrative as possable. Also as ease & rest from Labour are reaconed amongue the gratest pleasurs of Life, pursued by all with the gratest avidity & when attained at once creates a sense of superiority & as pride & ostentation are natural to the humain harte, these ordirs of men generally asotiate together and look down with two much contempt on those that labour.

On the other hand the Labourer being contious that it is Labour that seports the hole, & that the more there is that live without Labour & the higher they live or the grater their saleryes & fees are, so much the harder he must work, or the shorter he must live, this makes the Labourer watch the other with a jelous eye & often has reason to complain of real impositions. But before I proseed to shew how the few & many differ in money matters I will give a short description of what Money is.

Money is not property of itself but ondly the Representitive of property. Silver & Gold is not so valuable as Iron & Steel for real use, but receives all its value from the use that is made of it as a medium of trade. Money is simply this—a thing of lighter carrage than property that has an established value set upon it eyther by law or general Consent, For Instance, if a doller or a peace of paper, or a chip, would pass throughout a nation or the world for a burshel of corne or any other property to the value of said corne, then it would be the representitive of so much property.

Also Money is a thing that will go where it will fetch the most as naturally as water runs down hill, for the posessor will give it whare it will fetch the most. Also when their is an addition to the quantity or an extrodinary use of barter & credit in commerce the prices of property will rise. On the other hand if Credit is ruened & the medium made scarser the price of all kinds of property will fall in proportion. Here lays the grate shuffel betwen the few & many. As the interests & incomes of the few lays chiefly in money at interest, rents, salaryes, & fees that are fixed on the nominal value of money, they are interested in haveing mony scarse & the price of labour & produce as low as possable. For instance if the prices of labour & produce should fall one halfe if [it] would be just the same to the few as if their rents fees & salleryes ware doubled, all which they would git out of the many. Besides the fall of Labour and produce & scarsety of money always brings the many Into destress & compels them into a state of dependance on the few for favours & assistance in a thousand ways.

On the other hand, if the many could rais the price of Labour, &c one halfe & have the mony circulate freely they could pay their debts, eat & drink & injoy the good of their labour with out being dependant on the few for assistance. Also high prices opperates as a bounty on industry & economy—an industrious & prudent man may presently lay up something against time of need when prices are high but if a person leaves off worke & lives high when prices are up his mony or property will last him but little while.

But the gratest dainger the Many are under in these money matters are from the Juditial & Executive Officers, espatssilly so as their incomes for a living are almost holly gotten from the follys and destresse of the Many, & they being governed by the same selfish prinsaples as other men are. They are the Most interested in the destreses of the many of any in the Nation. the scarser money is & the grater the destreses of the many are, the better for them. It not ondly doubles the nominal sume of their pay, but it doubles & thribbles their bisness, & the many are obliged to come to them cap in hand & beg for mercy patience & forbearance. This gratifyes both their pride & covetousness, when on the other hand when money is plenty & prices high they have little or nothing to do. This is the Reason why they aught to be kept intirely from the Legislative Body & unless their can be wisdom anough in the Peopel to keep the three Departments of Government intirely seperate a free Government cant be seported. For in all these conceived differenc of interests, It is the bisness and duty of the Lejeslative Body to determine what is Justis or what is Right & Rong, & the duty of every individual in the nation to regulate his conduct according to their detisions. And if the Many ware always fully & fairly represented in the Lejeslative Body they neaver would be oppresed or find fault so as to trouble the Govern-

ment, but would always be zelous to seport it.

The Reasons why a free government has always failed is from the unreasonable demands & desires of the few. They cant bare to be on a leavel with their fellow cretures, or submit to the determinations of a Lejeslature whare (as they call it) the Swinish Multitude [1] are fairly represented, but sicken at the eydea, & are ever hankering & striving after Monerca or Aristocracy whare the people have nothing to do in maters of government but to seport the few in luxery & idleness.

For these & many other reasons a large majority of those that live without Labour are ever opposed to the prinsaples & operation of a free Government, & though the hole of them do not amount to one eighth part of the people, yet by their combinations, arts & skeems have always made out to destroy it soner or later, which I shall indeavour to prove by considering—

4thly. The Meens by which the few Destroy it

This I will indever to do by making a few remarks on the doings of the few on the eight following things, Viz. 1t on the Ignorance of the Many—2d on the Combinations of the few. 3 on Larning—4 on knowledge—5t on Constitutions 6tly on Money or the Medium—7th on Elections 8thly on wars.

1. On the Ignorance of the Many

Solomon said, Train up a Child in the way he should go, & when he is old he will not depart from it. And it is as true that if a child is trained up in the way he should not go, when he is old he will keep to it. It is the universal custom & practis of monorcal & dispotick government to train up their subjects as much in ignorance as they can in matters of government, & to teach them to reverance & worship grate men in office, & to take for truth what ever they say without examining for themselves.

Consiquently when ever Revolutions are brought about & free governments established it is by the influence of a few leeding men, who after they have obtained their object (like other men) can neaver receiv compensation & honours anough from the people for their serv-

---

[1] "Learning will be cast into the mire and trodden down under the hoofs of a swinish multitude." Burke's *Reflections on the Revolution in France* (1791). [Samuel Eliot Morison, editor of Manning's *Key*.]

ices, & the people being brought up from their uths to reverance & respect such men they go on old ways & neglect to search & see for themselves & take care of their own interists. Also being naturally very fond of being flattered, they redily hear to measures proposed by grate men who they are convinced have done them good services. This is the prinsaple ground on which the few work to Destroy a free government.

2. On the Combinations of the Few

In a free government the few, finding their scheems & vues of interest borne down by the many, to gain the power they cant constitutionally obtain, Always indevour to git it by cunaing & corruption, contious at the same time that userpation when once began the safty of the userper consists ondly in grasping the hole. To efect this no cost nor pains is spared, but they first unite their plans & scheems by asotiations, conventions, & coraspondances with each other. The Marchents asotiate by themselves, the Phitisians by themselves, The Ministers by themselves, the Juditial & Executive Officers are by their professions often called together & know each others minds, & all letirary men & the over grown rich, that can live without labouring, can spare time for consultation. All being bound together by common interest, which is the stronges bond of union, join in their secret corraspondance to counter act the interests of the many & pick their pockets, which is efected ondly for want of the meens of knowledg amongue them.

3. On Larning

Larning is of the gratest importance to the seport of a free government, & to prevent this the few are always crying up the advantages of costly collages, national acadimyes & grammer schooles, in ordir to make places for men to live without work, & so strengthen their party. But are always opposed to cheep schools & woman schools, the ondly or prinsaple means by which larning is spred amongue the Many.

4. On Knowledge

The gratest & best meens of obtaining the knowledge nesecary for a free man to have, is by the Liberty of the Press, or publick Newspapers. To counter act and destroy this privi-

ledge the few spare no pains to make them as costly as posable & to contradict everything in them that favours the interests of the Many, puting Darkness for Light, & Light for Darkness, falsehood for truth, & truth for falsehood, &cc.

5. On Constitutions & Laws

The few have a grate advantage over the Many in forming & constructing Constitutions & Laws, & are highly interested in haveing them numerous, intricate & as inexplicit as posable. By this they take to themselves the right of giving them such explanations as suits their interests, & make places for numerous lawyers & Juditial & Executive officers, which ads grately to their strength by numbers. 10

6. On the Medium of Trade

Money or a Medium of trade is of such a nature that their are innumerable ways by which the few can manage it to the injury of the Many, such as erecting banks & useing parshality in remitances, ruining publick & private credit, & stoping the circulation of money &cc; by which they can bring the Many into destress & set them to quariling & sewing one another, & so make a plenty of bisness for their party. 22

30

7. On Elections

This is a grate object with the few, to carry their points in elections, this being the ondly meens by which the Many can seporte their Rights. Consiquently the few all unite in extoling the goodness & abilityes of their candidates, & of runing down & blackgarding the candidates on the other side. Also they will appeal to the electors in a veriaty of ways. Some they will flatter by promises of favours, such as being customers to them, or helping them out of debt, or other difficultyes; or help them to a good bargain, or treet them, or trust them, or lend them money, or even give them a little money, if they will vote for such & such a man. Others they will thretten, 'if you dont vote for such & such a man,' or 'if you do' &cc, 'you shall pay me what you owe me,' or 'I will sew you'—'I will turne you out of my house' or 'off of my farm'—'I wont be your customer any longer'—'I will wager a ginna that you dare not vote for such a man—if you do you shall have a bloody nose for it,' Or they will hire 40

50

some body to communicate these things to the electors. Also they will hinder votes from being counted or returned right, & often will themselves (or hire others to) put in two or three votes apeace. All these things have bin practised & may be again.

8. *On Wars*

10 So apt are Mankind to be rought up into a pashon by false reports & slight ofences that it is an easy matter for cunning men to set peasable familyes & frinds at variance, whare their is no grounds for it on either side. In the same manner Towns States & Nations may be set at war against each other, & I have no dout but that it has bin the case many a time, that thousands & Millions have bin slain on both sides equilly thinking that they have bin fighting in
20 a good cause, when the hole matters in dispute would have mad little or no dispute between honest neighbours. Nor do I despute but that it has bin agreed upon by Rulers of Nations to make war on each other, ondly that they might have a pretense to raise & keep up standing armies to deprive their own subjects of their Rights & Libbertyes. This is a grate object with the few, & when they attain it, It ads so much to their number, strength & importance that
30 they have but little more to fear, and the Many have but little reason to expect that they can maintain their Libertyes Long.

In the foregoing remarks I have but just touched on the prinsaple meens by which the few destroy free governments.

I Shall now proseed

5thly. To Elustrate them by Sundry Remarks on the Operation of these Causes in our own Governments

43 I Shall not here atempt to say any thing on the want of knowledge amongue the peopel, seposeing that it will fully oppear by the remarks I shall make on the combinations & doings of the few.

Remarks on the Society of Cincinaty

51 Toards the close of the late War the Officers of the Continental army ware considerably borne upon, by not being paid according to contract, & many of them thought they ware not notifed anough in the fraiming of the State Constitutions. At the close of the War they formed themselves into a Sociaty by the name of Cincinaty. This Institution caused grate alarm & many pointed publications in newspapers, considering it as a daingerous Body.

This uneasiness caused them at their first General Meeting to make very assential alterations in their Constitution, which they published together with a very plausible Circular Letter, indevouring in it to make the world believ that they neaver would nor could prove any harme. But from that time their was a continual noys & wrighting from one end of the Continent to the other against the badness of publick credit, & the weekness & insefitiancy of the Federal Government.

When the shais affair happened in Masachusets it was heded by one of this ordir & many of the rest of them put under pay to surpress it.

Immediately after a Convention was caled to amend the federal Government, when a hard tusel was made chiefly by this ordir to establish a monorcal government in ordir to have their president made King. But though they failed in that yet by some meens or other they have rigeled themselves into almost all the posts of profit & honour in the federal Government. And from this ordir also origenated the funding sistim, by which those that labour for a living will have millions and millions of dollors to pay, for which the publick neaver riceived nor the posessor naver gave one single farthing for. Also from this ordir originated the Indian war which has cost us thousands of lives & six millions of dollors without the least advantage to us. From this ordir also originated the breach of the federal Constitution & a breach of the French Aliance by makeing the Brittish Treety, which has brought us almost to the brink of ruen.

When I charge these things to Cincinaty I do not meen that they did them alone but as planners & leaders in them, for to them also may be charged the organisation of allmost all the ordirs of the few who follow after & seport them in their diabolical masures—which I will remark upon seperately as followeth.

On Speculators, Stock & Land Jobers

These ordirs of men ar made up prinsaply of Cincinaty, & by the funding sistem have risen like a black cloud over the Continant, & have gained welth like the Nabobs of the East.

They have got the prinsaple command of our funds, & not ondly swindle honest individuals out of their property, but by their bribery & corruption have grate influence in our elections, & agitate our publick Counsels. By their land speculations & bribery they shook the government of Jorgia almost to its foundation & agitated the federal Government so that one of the Senetors chellenged one of the Representitives for a Duel, right in the midst of one of the most important debates they Ever was or ever will be ingaged in.

On Doctors

The Doctors have established their Meditial Societyes & have both their State & County Meetings, by which they have so nearly enielated Quacary of all kinds, that a poor man cant git so grate cures of them now for a ginna, as he could 50 years ago of an old Squaw for halfe a pint of Rhum. The bisness of a Midwife could be purformed 50 years ago for halfe a doller & now it costs a poor man 5 hole ones.

On Marchents

The Marchents have organised themselves & have their Chambers of Commerce & corraspondance from one end of the Continent to the other. Although they are in many respects a grate advantage to the Many, by makeing vent for our produce & furnishing us with nesecaryes & conveniences from other cuntryes, yet if we should be drawn into a war by their adventures we should pay very dear for all the advantages we receive from them. Besides, forron trade not well regulated is the most dangerous to the interest of the Many of any thing we have to fear. Our money may be all carryed off from amongue us for that which will do us no good.

Foron manufactoryes may be cheepest at first cost but not in the long run. Marchents may grow rich on the ruens of our mecanicks & manufactoryes, & bring us into as bad a condition as we ware in 1786, for they look ondly to their own interests. It is evident that a large parte of the marchents were in favour of the Brittish treaty & fond of carrying on a trade with that sinking Nation, which trade leaves a ballence against Amarica of more than 4 million of dollers annually, which will ruen ous in a few years unless it is Stopt.

On Literary Men & Coledges

The true prinsaples of Republicanisam & a free government may be taught to the Uths in some of our Coleges & Acadimies for aught I know, but it is evident that other political prinsaples are admited in many of them, or we should not be stunded with Exhibitions in favour of Monocyes & runing down Republican prinsaples as we often be. One thing is prity cartain, that the Schollers are taught to keep up the dignity of their professions, for if we apply for a preacher or a School Master, we are told the price is So Much, & they cant go under, for it is agreed upon & they shall be disgrased if they take less, let their abilityes for the servis be what they will.

On Ministers of the Gospel

The Ministers of the Congeragational ordir & others for aught I know have formed them selves in to Societyes & many of them are incorporated & have their State & County Meetings which may be of grate service or absolutly nesecary in their Sacred functions. But it is no brech of Charity to sepose that they have some political purposes in them, nor do I deny their right to meddle in politicks. But as they receive their seport for teaching piety, religion, morality & things relitive to another world, & their hearers being not at all of them capable of desarning betwen divinity & politicks, they aught when ever they teach obediance to the sivil Laws or reprove for disobediance &cc., to teach & explain to them the true prinsaples of our free government as Established in our Constitutions. Insted of preaching about & praying for Officers of government as infalible beings, or so perfect that we aught to submit to & prais them for all they do, (when in fact they are all our servents & at all times accountable to the peopel) they aught to teach their hearers to be watchfull of men in power, & to gard their own Rights & priviledges, with a jelous eye, & teach them how to do it in a Constitutional way.

If their prinsaples forbid this they had better let politicks intirely alone, for if they use their grate influence to mislead & prejudice their hearers against the true prinsaples of a free government (as Many of them have done of late) by praising our Executive for making the British treety, & in short by praising Monorcal & Dispotick government, & running down & blackgarding Republican prinsaples & the French Nation, they are in fact acting a treesonable & rebellious part & doing all in their power to destroy the Government, & their hearers aught not to attend on such teachings. It is this conduct in Ministers that is the prinsaple reason for the neglect of publick worship & Religious Institutions that is so much complained of by the Ministers now.

Ministers have it more in their power to turn the minds of their hearers Right or Rong than any other ordir of men, & it has bin the general practis of all arbitrary governments to prostitute Religion to political purposes, & make a handle of this ordir of men to misleed, flatter, & drive the people, by the terrors of the other world into submission to their political scheems & interests. Consiquently they aught to be watched & garded against above all other ordirs, espatially when they preach politicks.

. . .

On Larning

No person who is a frind to Libberty will be against a large expence in Larning, but it aught to be promoted in the cheepest & best manner possable, which in my oppinnion would be:—For every State to maintain as many Coledges in conveniant parts thereof as would be attended upon to give the highest Degrees of Larning, & for every County to keep as many Grammer Schools or Acadimies in conveniant parts thereof as would be attended too by both sects summer & winter, & no student or scholer to pay anything for tuition, and for the County Schooles to pay a purticuler attention to teaching the Inglish langueg & qualifying its scholars to teach & govern Common Schools for little children.

And for Every Town to be obliged to keep as Much as six weeks of wrighting school in the winter & twelve weeks of a woman school in the summer in every parte of the town. So that none should be thronged with two many schollers, nor none have too far to travel, & every person be obliged to send his children to school, for the publick are as much interested in the Larning of one child as an other.

If this method of Larning was established we should soone have a plenty of school masters & mistrises as cheep as we could hire other labour, & Labour & Larning would be conected together & lesen the number of those that live without work. Also we should have a plenty of

men to fill the highest offices of State for less than halfe we now give. But insted of this mode of Larning the few are always striving to oblige us to maintain grait men with grate salleryes & to maintain Grammer Schools in every town to teach our Children a b c all which is ondly to give imploy to gentlemens sons & make places for men to live without worke. For their is no more need of a mans haveing a knowledge of all the languages to teach a Child to read write & cifer than their is for a farmer to have the marinors art to hold plow.

On Knowlidge

The prinsaple knowledge nesecary for a free man to have is obtained by the Libberty of the press or publick newspapers. But this kind of knowledge is almost ruened of late by the doings of the few. But a few years ago we could have the hole news by one paper in a week, & could put some dependance on what was printed. But the few, being closely combined & detarmined to destroy our Government, find it nesecary to destroy the Liberty of the press first. To efect this they imploy no printers, but those that will adhear strictly to their vuies & interests, & use all the arts & retrick hell can invent to blackgard the Republican printers & all they print, & strive to make the peopel believe falsehood for truts & truts for falsehood, & as they have money & lasure they have their papers every day in the week. Consiquently the Republican printers double their papers, so that a labouring man must now be at the expence of three or four dollers anually & read & studdy halfe his time, & then be at a loss to know what is true & what not—thus the few have almost ruened the Libberty of the press.

On Elections

The hole interest of the Many lays in giting and keeping fully & fairly represented in the several branches of government, & this depends intirely in the Electors haveing a knoledge of the carictor, abilityes & politicle sentiments of those they vote for, & it is imposible for all to have a personal knoledge of them. In large towns their are some instances wheir the electors do not all know those they vote for in them. The State Senetors are more unknown, the govenour & federal Representitives are furder off still, & the Electors of president, being chosen ondly for a single Act & not accountable for his Conduct in that all Important Act. I have often wondered that under the present meens of knowledge, and in opposition to the numerous arts of flatery, deception thretnings & falsehoods practised by the few in elections, that the Many git so fully represented as they do, & that their are so many Representitives that expose themselves to the abuse of the few by Seporting our caws, when we seport them so poorly, & all the hopes I have of seporting our Libbertyes is by a reformation or improvement in this thing.

. . .

On the Shais Affair in Masachusets [2]

As I lived near wheir this afair hapned, & received some frouns from the acttors on both sides of the actt because I was apposed to their measures, I will indaver to give a more full but impartial account of it.

At the close of the late war with Brittan, although our paper money had dyed away, & left the peopel grately in debt by it, & a large publick det on us by the war, Yet their was a large quantity of hard mony amongue us sefitient for a Medium. But for want of a proper regulation of trade, & the prices of Labour & produce being higher here than in other cuntryes, our marchents shiped it off lode after load by the hundred thousand dollers together untill their was but little left, & taxes ware extreemly high. Some countyes ware two or three years behind, & the price of Labour & produce falling very fast, creditors calling for old debts that they would not take in paper Money, & those that had money demanding 30, 40, & some 50 pursent interest, fee officers demanding double, thribble & some 4 times so much as the law alowed them, and all of them so crouded with bisness that it was hard to git any done, & property selling every day by execution for less than halfe its value, & jales crouded with debttors; & the peopel being ignorant that all their help lay in being fully and fairly represented in the Legeslature, many towns neglected to send Representitives in ordir to save the cost, so that the few ondly ware Represented at cort, with an Aristrocratical Bodoin [3] as Govenour at their head.

Under all these circumstances the peopel

ware drove to the gratest extremity. Many countyes took to Conventions, Remonstrances & petition to a Corte where they ware not halfe represented. But not being heard to or in some instances charged with saditious metings & intentions some countyes ware so follish as to stop the Corts of Justis by force of armes. This shook the government to its foundation, for insted of fatherly councals & admonitions, the dog of war was let loose upon them & they ware declared in a state of Insurrection & Rebellion. In these circomstances, the few ware all alive for the seporte of Government, & all those who would not be continually crying Government—Government—or dared to say a word against any of their measures ware called Shasites & Rebels & thretned with prosicutions &cc. But a large majority of the peopel, thinking that their was blame on both sides, or vueing one side as knaves & the other as fooles, it was with grate difficulty & delay before a sefitient number could be raised & sent to surpress them. But it was done with the loss of but few lives.

This put the peopel in the most zelous sarches after a remidy for their greviences. Thousands & thousands of miles ware rode to consult each other on the afair, & they hapily efected it in a few months. Ondly by useing their priviledges as electors, Bodoin was turned out from being govenour (& in a few years sickened & dyed) & Hancok was almost unanimously Chosen in his rome. Many of the old Representitives shaired the same fate, & a full Representation sent to Cort from every parte of the State, which soone found out meens to redress the grevances of the peopel, though they ware attended with the most dificult circumstances. So that everything appeared like the clear & plesent sunshine after a most tremendious storme. This is a streiking demonstration of the advantages of a free elective government, & shews how a peopel may run themselves into the gratest difficultyes by inatention in elections & retreve their circumstances again by attending theirtoo.

This Shais afair neaver would have hapned if the peopel had bin posesed of a true knowledge of their Rights, Dutyes, & Interests, or if the government had done their duty according to the oaths they ware under, & if they had have had such a govenour as Hancok at that time. Even after the Corts ware stoped he would have Settled the hole afare for less than a thousand dollers. But as it was maniged it

---

[2] Shays's Rebellion of 1786. [Samuel Eliot Morison, editor.]
[3] James Bowdoin.

cost the State seaveral hundred thousands dollers, & this is always the way in wars. The few that are imployed to manage them make them as costly as posable & if the mater was sarched to the bottom it would be found that some of the ordir of Cincinaty have bin at the botom of all these wars, & got into bisness & grone rich by them & the farmers & Labourers have yet the cost to pay & So it will be again if we have a war with France.   1798

JOHN ADAMS (1735–1826) and THOMAS JEFFERSON (1743–1826)

AFTER THE ELECTION of 1800, in which John Adams and Thomas Jefferson were rivals for the presidency, their friendship lapsed. Twelve years of estrangement and silent misunderstanding followed, after which a reconciliation was effected. From that time until July 4, 1826, when the two patriots died within a span of a few hours, their correspondence was unbroken. It is marked by wit, gossip, and profound speculation. They exchanged views on the classics, on history, on religion and philosophy, and on politics. In their discussion of democracy the conflicting views of the two men represented, in reality, deep cleavages in American life and thought.

The Adams-Jefferson Letters, 2 vols., Lester J. Cappon, ed., Chapel Hill, 1959.
Catherine Drinker Bowen, *John Adams and the American Revolution*, Boston, 1950.

» » LETTERS « «

JOHN ADAMS TO THOMAS JEFFERSON

Quincy, July 9, 1813

. . . I recollect, near some thirty years ago, to have said carelessly to you that I wished I could find time and means to write something upon aristocracy. You seized upon the idea, and encouraged me to do it with all that friendly warmth that is natural and habitual to you. I soon began, and have been writing on that subject ever since. I have been so fortunate as never to be able to make myself understood.

Your "ἄριϛτοι" are the most difficult animals to manage of anything in the whole theory and practice of government. They will not suffer themselves to be governed. They not only exert all their own subtlety, industry and courage, but they employ the commonalty to knock to pieces every plan and model that the most honest architects in legislation can invent to keep them within bounds. Both patricians and plebeians are as furious as the workmen in England, to demolish labor-saving machinery.

But who are these "ἄριϛτοι"? Who shall judge? Who shall select these choice spirits from the rest of the congregation? Themselves? We must first find out and determine who themselves are. Shall the congregation choose? Ask Zenophon; perhaps hereafter I may quote you Greek. Too much in a hurry at present, English must suffice. Zenophon says that the ecclesia always chooses the worst men they can find, because none others will do their dirty work. This wicked motive is worse than birth or wealth. Here I want to quote Greek again. But the day before I received your letter of June 27th, I gave the book to George Washington Adams, going to the academy at Hingham. The title is Ἐθικὴ Ποίησις,[1] a collection of moral sentences from all the most ancient Greek poets. In one of the oldest of them, I read in Greek, that I cannot repeat, a couplet, the sense of which was: "Nobility in men is worth as much as it is in horses, asses, or rams; but the meanest blooded puppy in the world, if he gets a little money, is as good a man as the best of them." Yet birth and wealth together have prevailed over virtue and talents in all

[1] *Formation of character.*

ages. The many will acknowledge no other "ἄριϛτοι."

Your experience of this truth will not much differ from that of your best friend.   1813

JEFFERSON TO JOHN ADAMS

Monticello, October 28, 1813

DEAR SIR,—According to the reservation between us, of taking up one of the subjects of our correspondence at a time, I turn to your letters of August the 16th and September the 2nd. The passage you quote from Theognis, I think has an ethical rather than a political object. The whole piece is a moral *exhortation* . . . and this passage particularly seems to be a reproof to man, who, while with his domestic animals he is curious to improve the race, by employing always the finest male, pays no attention to the improvement of his own race, but intermarries with the vicious, the ugly, or the old, for considerations of wealth or ambition. It is in conformity with the principle adopted afterwards by the Pythagoreans, and expressed by Ocellus in another form . . . which, as literally as intelligibility will admit, may be thus translated: "concerning the inter-procreation of men, how, and of whom it shall be, in a perfect manner, and according to the laws of modesty and sanctity, conjointly, this is what I think right. First to lay it down that we do not commix for the sake of pleasure, but of the procreation of children. For the powers, the organs and desires for coition have not been given by God to man for the sake of pleasure, but for the procreation of the race. For as it were incongruous, for a mortal born to partake of divine life, the immortality of the race being taken away, God fulfilled the purpose by making the generations uninterrupted and continuous. This, therefore, we are especially to lay down as a principle, that coition is not for the sake of pleasure." But nature, not trusting to this moral and abstract motive, seems to have provided more securely for the perpetuation of the species, by making it the effect of the *œstrum* implanted in the constitution of both sexes. And not only has the commerce of love been indulged on this unhallowed impulse, but made subservient also to wealth and ambition by marriage, without regard to the beauty, the healthiness, the understanding, or virtue of the subject from which we are to breed. The selecting the best male for a Harem of well chosen females also,

which Theognis seems to recommend from the example of our sheep and asses, would doubtless improve the human, as it does the brute animal, and produce a race of veritable ἄριϛτοι. For experience proves, that the moral and physical qualities of man, whether good or evil, are transmissible in a certain degree from father to son. But I suspect that the equal rights of men will rise up against this privileged Solomon and his Harem, and oblige us to continue acquiescence under the 'Αμαύρωσις γένεος ἀϛῶν" [2] which Theognis complains of, and to content ourselves with the accidental aristoi produced by the fortuitous concourse of breeders. For I agree with you that there is a natural aristocracy among men. The grounds of this are virtue and talents. Formerly, bodily powers gave place among the aristoi. But since the invention of gunpowder has armed the weak as well as the strong with missile death, bodily strength, like beauty, good humor, politeness and other accomplishments, has become but an auxiliary ground of distinction. There is also an artificial aristocracy, founded on wealth and birth, without either virtue or talents; for with these it would belong to the first class. The natural aristocracy I consider as the most precious gift of nature, for the instruction, the trusts, and government of society. And indeed, it would have been inconsistent in creation to have formed man for the social state, and not to have provided virtue and wisdom enough to manage the concerns of the society. May we not even say, that that form of government is the best, which provides the most effectually for a pure selection of these natural aristoi into the offices of government? The artificial aristocracy is a mischievous ingredient in government, and provision should be made to prevent its ascendency. On the question, what is the best provision, you and I differ; but we differ as rational friends, using the free exercise of our own reason, and mutually indulging its errors. You think it best to put the pseudo-aristoi into a separate chamber of legislation, where they may be hindered from doing mischief by their co-ordinate branches, and where, also, they may be a protection to wealth against the Agrarian and plundering enterprises of the majority of the people. I think that to give them power in order to prevent them from doing mischief, is arming them for it, and increasing instead of remedying the evil. For if the co-ordinate

---

[2] *Weakening of the breed of citizens.*

branches can arrest their action, so may they that of the co-ordinates. Mischief may be done negatively as well as positively. Of this, a cabal in the Senate of the United States has furnished many proofs. Nor do I believe them necessary to protect the wealthy; because enough of these will find their way into every branch of the legislation, to protect themselves. From fifteen to twenty legislatures of our own, in action for thirty years past, have proved that no fears of an equalization of property are to be apprehended from them. I think the best remedy is exactly that provided by all our constitutions, to leave to the citizens the free election and separation of the aristoi from the pseudo-aristoi, of the wheat from the chaff. In general they will elect the really good and wise. In some instances, wealth may corrupt, and birth blind them; but not in sufficient degree to endanger the society.

It is probable that our difference of opinion may, in some measure, be produced by a difference of character in those among whom we live. From what I have seen of Massachusetts and Connecticut myself, and still more from what I have heard, and the character given of the former by yourself, who know them so much better, there seems to be in those two States a traditionary reverence for certain families, which has rendered the offices of the government nearly hereditary in those families. I presume that from an early period of your history, members of those families happening to possess virtue and talents, have honestly exercised them for the good of the people, and by their services have endeared their names to them. In coupling Connecticut with you, I mean it politically only, not morally. For having made the Bible the common law of their land, they seem to have modeled their morality on the story of Jacob and Laban. But although this hereditary succession to office with you, may, in some degree, be founded in real family merit, yet in a much higher degree, it has proceeded from your strict alliance of Church and State. These families are canonised in the eyes of the people on common principles, "you tickle me, and I will tickle you." In Virginia we have nothing of this. Our clergy, before the revolution, having been secured against rivalship by fixed salaries, did not give themselves the trouble of acquiring influence over the people. Of wealth, there were great accumulations in particular families, handed down from generation to generation, under the English law of entails. But the only object of ambition for the wealthy was a seat in the King's Council. All their court then was paid to the crown and its creatures; and they Philipised in all collisions between the King and the people. Hence they were unpopular; and that unpopularity continues attached to their names. A Randolph, a Carter, or a Burwell must have great personal superiority over a common competitor to be elected by the people even at this day. At the first session of our legislature after the Declaration of Independence, we passed a law abolishing entails. And this was followed by one abolishing the privilege of primogeniture, and dividing the lands of intestates equally among all their children, or other representatives. These laws, drawn by myself, laid the axe to the foot of pseudo-aristocracy. And had another which I prepared been adopted by the legislature, our work would have been complete. It was a bill for the more general diffusion of learning. This proposed to divide every county into wards of five or six miles square, like your townships; to establish in each ward a free school for reading, writing and common arithmetic; to provide for the annual selection of the best subjects from these schools, who might receive, at the public expense, a higher degree of education at a district school; and from these district schools to select a certain number of the most promising subjects, to be completed at an University, where all the useful sciences should be taught. Worth and genius would thus have been sought out from every condition of life, and completely prepared by education for defeating the competition of wealth and birth for public trusts. My proposition had, for a further object, to impart to these wards those portions of self-government for which they are best qualified, by confiding to them the care of their poor, their roads, police, elections, the nomination of jurors, administration of justice in small cases, elementary exercises of militia; in short, to have made them little republics, with a warden at the head of each, for all those concerns which, being under their eye, they would better manage than the larger republics of the county or State. A general call of ward meetings by their wardens on the same day through the State, would at any time produce the genuine sense of the people on any required point, and would enable the State to act in mass, as your people have so often done, and with so much effect by their town meetings. The law for religious freedom, which made a part of this system, having put down the aristocracy of the clergy, and restored to the citizen the freedom of the mind, and those of entails and descents nurturing an equality of condition among them, this on education would have raised the mass of the people to the high ground of moral respectability necessary to their own safety, and to orderly government; and would have completed the great object of qualifying them to select the veritable aristoi, for the trusts of government, to the exclusion of the pseudalists. . . . Although this law has not yet been acted on but in a small and inefficient degree, it is still considered as before the legislature, with other bills of the revised code, not yet taken up, and I have great hope that some patriotic spirit will, at a favorable moment, call it up, and make it the keystone of the arch of our government.

With respect to aristocracy, we should further consider, that before the establishment of the American States, nothing was known to history but the man of the old world, crowded within limits either small or overcharged, and steeped in the vices which that situation generates. A government adapted to such men would be one thing; but a very different one, that for the man of these States. Here every one may have land to labor for himself, if he chooses; or, preferring the exercise of any other industry, may exact for it such compensation as not only to afford a comfortable subsistence, but wherewith to provide for a cessation from labor in old age. Every one, by his property, or by his satisfactory situation, is interested in the support of law and order. And such men may safely and advantageously reserve to themselves a wholesome control over their public affairs, and a degree of freedom, which, in the hands of the *canaille* of the cities of Europe, would be instantly perverted to the demolition and destruction of everything public and private. The history of the last twenty-five years of France, and of the last forty years in America, nay of its last two hundred years, proves the truth of both parts of this observation.

But even in Europe a change has sensibly taken place in the mind of man. Science had liberated the ideas of those who read and reflect, and the American example had kindled feelings of right in the people. An insurrection has consequently begun, of science, talents, and courage, against rank and birth, which have fallen into contempt. It has failed in its first effort, because the mobs of the cities, the instrument used for its accomplishment, debased by ignorance, poverty, and vice, could not be restrained to rational action. But the world will recover from the panic of this first catastrophe. Science is progressive, and talents and enterprise on the alert. Resort may be had to the people of the country, a more governable power from their principles and subordination; and rank, and birth, and tinsel-aristocracy will finally shrink into insignificance, even there. This, however, we have no right to meddle with. It suffices for us, if the moral and physical condition of our own citizens qualifies them to select the able and good for the direction of their government, with a recurrance of elections at such short periods as will enable them to displace an unfaithful servant, before the mischief he meditates may be irremediable.

I have thus stated my opinion on a point on which we differ, not with a view to controversy, for we are both too old to change opinions which are the result of a long life of inquiry and reflection; but on the suggestions of a former letter of yours, that we ought not to die before we have explained ourselves to each other. We acted in perfect harmony, through a long and perilous contest for our liberty and independence. A constitution has been acquired, which, though neither of us thinks perfect, yet both consider as competent to render our fellow citizens the happiest and the securest on whom the sun has ever shone. If we do not think exactly alike as to its imperfections, it matters little to our country, which, after devoting to it long lives of disinterested labor, we have delivered over to our successors in life, who will be able to take care of it and of themselves. . . .   1813

JAMES KENT

1763–1847

JAMES KENT, who early in his life came under the influence of Hamilton's conservative Federalism, did much in his law reports and in his *Commentaries on American Law* (1826–1830) to mold the character of American jurisprudence. As chief judge in the New York supreme court and as Chancellor of the New York court of chancery, Kent incorporated into his legal scholarship the tested principles of English jurisprudence. His respect for property and individual rights profoundly influenced his work.

As a member of the New York Constitutional Convention of 1821 Kent set himself against the rising tide of political democracy by opposing the abolition of property requirements for the suffrage. His arguments well illustrate an integral segment of his social philosophy.

James Kent, *Memoirs and Letters of James Kent, LL.D., Late Chancellor of the State of New York*, Boston, 1898.
J. T. Horton, *James Kent, a Study in Conservatism, 1763–1847*, New York, 1939.
N. H. Carter, W. L. Stone, and M. T. C. Gould, *Reports of the Proceedings and Debates of the Convention of 1821*, Albany, 1821.

From: REPORTS OF THE PROCEEDINGS AND DEBATES
OF THE CONVENTION OF 1821

[CHANCELLOR KENT ON SUFFRAGE]

I am in favor of the amendment which has been submitted by my honourable colleague from Albany; and I must beg leave to trespass for a few moments upon the patience of the committee, while I state the reasons which have induced me to wish, that the senate should continue, as heretofore, the representative of the landed interest, and exempted from the control of universal suffrage. I hope what I may have to say will be kindly received, for it will be well intended. But, if I thought otherwise, I should still prefer to hazard the loss of the little popularity which I might have in this house, or out of it, than to hazard the loss of the approbation of my own conscience.

I have reflected upon the report of the select committee with attention and with anxiety. We appear to be disregarding the principles of the constitution, under which we have so long and so happily lived, and to be changing some of its essential institutions. I cannot but think that the considerate men who have studied the history of republics, or are read in lessons of ex-

perience, must look with concern upon our apparent disposition to vibrate from a well balanced government, to the extremes of the democratic doctrines. Such a broad proposition as that contained in the report, at the distance of ten years past, would have struck the public mind with astonishment and terror. So rapid has been the career of our vibration.

Let us recall our attention, for a moment, to our past history.

This state has existed for forty-four years under our present constitution, which was formed by those illustrious sages and patriots who adorned the revolution. It has wonderfully fulfilled all the great ends of civil government. During that long period, we have enjoyed in an eminent degree, the blessings of civil and religious liberty. We have had our lives, our privileges, and our property, protected. We have had a succession of wise and temperate legislatures. The code of our statute law has been again and again revised and corrected, and it may proudly bear a comparison with that of any other people. We have had, during that period, (though I am, perhaps, not the fittest person to say it) a regular, stable, honest, and enlightened administration of justice. All the peaceable pursuits of industry, and all the important interests of education and science, have been fostered and encouraged. We have trebled our numbers within the last twenty-five years, have displayed mighty resources, and have made unexampled progress in the career of prosperity and greatness. Our financial credit stands at an enviable height; and we are now successfully engaged in connecting the great lakes with the ocean by stupendous canals, which excite the admiration of our neighbours, and will make a conspicuous figure even upon the map of the United States.

These are some of the fruits of our present government; and yet we seem to be dissatisfied with our condition, and we are engaged in the bold and hazardous experiment of remodelling the constitution. Is it not fit and discreet: I speak as to wise men; is it not fit and proper that we should pause in our career, and reflect well on the immensity of the innovation in contemplation? Discontent in the midst of so much prosperity, and with such abundant means of happiness, looks like ingratitude, and as if we were disposed to arraign the goodness of Providence. Do we not expose ourselves to the danger of being deprived of the blessings we have enjoyed?—When the husbandman has gathered in his harvest, and has filled his barns and his graneries with the fruits of his industry, if he should then become discontented and unthankful, would he not have reason to apprehend, that the Lord of the harvest might come in his wrath, and with his lightening destroy them?

The senate has hitherto been elected by the farmers of the state—by the free and independent lords of the soil, worth at least $250 in freehold estate, over and above all debts charged thereon. The governor has been chosen by the same electors, and we have hitherto elected citizens of elevated rank and character. Our assembly has been chosen by freeholders, possessing a freehold of the value of $50, or by persons renting a tenement of the yearly value of $5, and who have been rated and actually paid taxes to the state. By the report before us, we propose to annihilate, at one stroke, all those property distinctions and to bow before the idol of universal suffrage. That extreme democratic principle, when applied to the legislative and executive departments of government, has been regarded with terror, by the wise men of every age, because in every

European republic, ancient and modern, in which it has been tried, it has terminated disastrously, and been productive of corruption, injustice, violence, and tyranny. And dare we flatter ourselves that we are a peculiar people, who can run the career of history, exempted from the passions which have disturbed and corrupted the rest of mankind? If we are like other races of men, with similar follies and vices, then I greatly fear that our posterity will have reason to deplore in sackcloth and ashes, the delusion of the day.

It is not my purpose at present to interfere with the report of the committee, so far as respects the qualifications of electors for governor and members of assembly. I shall feel grateful if we may be permitted to retain the stability and security of a senate, bottomed upon the freehold property of the state. Such a body, so constituted, may prove a sheet anchor amidst the future factions and storms of the republic. The great leading and governing interest of this state, is, at present, the agricultural; and what madness would it be to commit that interest to the winds. The great body of the people, are now the owners and actual cultivators of the soil. With that wholesome population we always expect to find moderation, frugality, order, honesty, and a due sense of independence, liberty, and justice. It is impossible that any people can lose their liberties by internal fraud or violence, so long as the country is parcelled out among freeholders of moderate possessions, and those freeholders have a sure and efficient control in the affairs of the government. Their habits, sympathies, and employments, necessarily inspire them with a correct spirit of freedom and justice; they are the safest guardians of property and the laws: We certainly cannot too highly appreciate the value of the agricultural interest: It is the foundation of national wealth and power. According to the opinion of her ablest political economists, it is the surplus produce of the agriculture of England, that enables her to support her vast body of manufacturers, her formidable fleets and armies, and the crowds of persons engaged in the liberal professions, and the cultivation of the various arts.

Now, sir, I wish to preserve our senate as the representative of the landed interest. I wish those who have an interest in the soil, to retain the exclusive possession of a branch in the legislature, as a strong hold in which they may find safety through all the vicissitudes which

the state may be destined, in the course of
Providence, to experience. I wish them to be
always enabled to say that their freeholds
cannot be taxed without their consent. The
men of no property, together with the crowds
of dependants connected with great manufacturing and commercial establishments, and
the motley and undefinable population of
crowded ports, may, perhaps, at some future
day, under skilful management, predominate
in the assembly, and yet we should be perfectly safe if no laws could pass without the
free consent of the owners of the soil. That security we at present enjoy; and it is that
security which I wish to retain.

The apprehended danger from the experiment of universal suffrage applied to the whole
legislative department, is no dream of the imagination. It is too mighty an excitement for the
moral constitution of men to endure. The tendency of universal suffrage, is to jeopardize the
rights of property, and the principles of liberty.
There is a constant tendency in human society,
and the history of every age proves it; there is
a tendency in the poor to covet and to share
the plunder of the rich; in the debtor to relax
or avoid the obligation of contracts; in the
majority to tyranize over the minority, and
trample down their rights; in the indolent and
the profligate, to cast the whole burthens of
society upon the industrious and the virtuous;
and *there is a tendency in wicked and ambitious men, to inflame these combustible materials.* It requires a vigilant government, and a
firm administration of justice, to counteract
that tendency. Thou shalt not covet; thou shalt
not steal; are divine injunctions induced by this
miserable depravity of our nature. Who can
undertake to calculate with any precision, how
many millions of people, this great state will
contain in the course of this and the next century, and who can estimate the future extent
and magnitude of our commercial ports? The
disproportion between the men of property,
and the men of no property, will be in every
society in a ratio to its commerce, wealth, and
population. We are no longer to remain plain
and simple republics of farmers, like the New-
England colonists, or the Dutch settlements on
the Hudson. We are fast becoming a great nation, with great commerce, manufactures, population, wealth, luxuries, and with the vices
and miseries that they engender. One seventh
of the population of the city of Paris at this day
subsists on charity, and one third of the in-

habitants of that city die in the hospitals; what
would become of such a city with universal suffrage? France has upwards of four, and England upwards of five millions of manufacturing
and commercial labourers without property.
Could these kingdoms sustain the weight of
universal suffrage? The radicals in England,
with the force of that mighty engine, would
at once sweep away the property, the laws,
and the liberties of that island like a deluge.

The growth of the city of New-York is
enough to startle and awaken those who are
pursuing the *ignis fatuus* of universal suffrage.

In 1773 it had 21,000 souls.
   1801 " "   60,000 do.
   1806 " "   76,000 do.
   1820 " "   123,000 do.

It is rapidly swelling into the unwieldly population, and with the burdensome pauperism,
of an European metropolis. New-York is destined to become the future London of America; and in less than a century, that city, with
the operation of universal suffrage, and under
skilful direction, will govern this state.

The notion that every man that works a
day on the road, or serves an idle hour in the
militia, is entitled as of right to an equal participation in the whole power of the government, is most unreasonable, and has no foundation in justice. We had better at once discard
from the report such a nominal test of merit.
If such persons have an equal share in one
branch of the legislature, it is surely as much
as they can in justice or policy demand. Society
is an association for the protection of property
as well as of life, and the individual who contributes only one cent to the common stock,
ought not to have the same power and influence
in directing the property concerns of the partnership, as he who contributes his thousands.
He will not have the same inducements to care,
and diligence, and fidelity. His inducements
and his temptation would be to divide the
whole capital upon the principles of an agrarian
law.

Liberty, rightly understood, is an inestimable
blessing, but liberty without wisdom, and without justice, is no better than wild and savage
licentiousness. The danger which we have
hereafter to apprehend, is not the want, but
the abuse, of liberty. We have to apprehend
the oppression of minorities, and a disposition
to encroach on private right—to disturb chartered privileges—and to weaken, degrade, and
overawe the administration of justice; we have

to apprehend the establishment of unequal, and consequently, unjust systems of taxation, and all the mischiefs of a crude and mutable legislation. A stable senate, exempted from the influence of universal suffrage, will powerfully check these dangerous propensities, and such a check becomes the more necessary, since this Convention has already determined to withdraw the watchful eye of the judicial department from the passage of laws.

We are destined to become a great manufacturing as well as commercial state. We have already numerous and prosperous factories of one kind or another, and one master capitalist with his one hundred apprentices, and journeymen, and agents, and dependents, will bear down at the polls, an equal number of farmers of small estates in his vicinity, who cannot safely unite for their common defence. Large manufacturing and mechanical establishments can act in an instant with the unity and efficacy of disciplined troops. It is against such combinations, among others, that I think we ought to give to the freeholders, or those who have interest in land, one branch of the legislature for their asylum and their comfort. Universal suffrage once granted, is granted forever, and never can be recalled. There is no retrograde step in the rear of democracy. However mischievous the precedent may be in its consequences, or however fatal in its effects, universal suffrage never can be recalled or checked, but by the strength of the bayonet. We stand, therefore, this moment, on the brink of fate, on the very edge of the precipice. If we let go our present hold on the senate, we commit our proudest hopes and our most precious interests to the waves.

It ought further to be observed, that the senate is a court of justice in the last resort. It is the last depository of public and private rights; of civil and criminal justice. This gives the subject an awful consideration, and wonderfully increases the importance of securing that house from the inroads of universal suffrage. Our country freeholders are exclusively our jurors in the administration of justice, and there is equal reason that none but those who have an interest in the soil, should have any concern in the composition of that court. As long as the senate is safe, justice is safe, property is safe, and our liberties are safe. But when the wisdom, the integrity, and the independence of that court is lost, we may be certain that the freedom and happiness of this state, are fled forever.

I hope, sir, we shall not carry desolation through all the departments of the fabric erected by our fathers. I hope we shall not put forward to the world a new constitution, as will meet with the scorn of the wise, and the tears of the patriot.   1821

JAMES FENIMORE COOPER

1789–1851

CONCEIVING the purpose of American literature to be the expression and promotion of "American principles," Cooper is in a way almost as important in his role of social critic as he is in that of novelist. American principles, to his way of thinking, included political liberty, respect for property rights, and the leadership of the patrician class. In other words, Cooper's "Americanism" resembled in more than one respect the Federalism of the early Republic. His dissatisfaction with the social equalitarianism and the "loco-focoism" of Jacksonian America was an emotionally tense reflex of his inability to broaden his "Americanism," or, as he would have put it, to sink it to lower political levels.

R. E. Spiller and P. C. Blackburn, *A Descriptive Bibliography of the Writings of James Fenimore Cooper*, New York, 1934.
J. F. Ross, *The Social Criticism of Fenimore Cooper*, Berkeley, Calif., 1933.
Dorothy Waples, *The Whig Myth of James Fenimore Cooper*, New Haven, 1938.
R. E. Spiller, *Fenimore Cooper, Critic of His Times*, New York, 1931.

» » From: THE AMERICAN DEMOCRAT « «

ON DISTINCTIVE AMERICAN PRINCIPLES

Distinctive American principles as properly refer to the institutions of the states as to those of the Union. A correct notion of the first cannot be formed without keeping the latter constantly in view.

The leading distinctive principle of this
10 country, is connected with the fact that all political power is strictly a trust, granted by the constituent to the representative. These representatives possess different duties, and as the greatest check that is imposed on them, while in the exercise of their offices, exists in the manner in which the functions are balanced by each other, it is of the last importance that neither class trespass on the trusts that are not especially committed to its keeping.

20 The machinery of the state being the same in appearance, in this country and in that from which we are derived, inconsiderate commentators are apt to confound their principles. In England, the institutions have been the result of those circumstances to which time has accidentally given birth. The power of the king was derived from violence, the monarch, before the act of succession, in the reign of Queen Anne, claiming the throne in virtue of
30 the conquest by William, in 1060. In America, the institutions are the result of deliberate consultation, mutual concessions, and design. In England, the people may have gained by diminishing the power of the king, who first obtained it by force; but, in America, to assail the rightful authority of the executive, is attacking a system framed by the constituencies of the states, who are virtually the people, for their own benefit. No assault can be made on
40 any branch of this government, while in the exercise of its constitutional duties, without assaulting the right of the body of the nation, which is the foundation of the whole polity.

In countries, in which executive power is hereditary, and clothed with high prerogatives, it may be struggling for liberty to strive to diminish its influence; but, in this republick, in which the executive is elective, has no absolute authority in framing the laws, serves
50 for a short period, is responsible, and has been

created by the people, through the states, for their own purposes, it is assailing the rights of that people, to attempt in any manner to impede its legal and just action.

It is a general law in politics, that the power most to be distrusted, is that which, possessing the greatest force, is the least responsible. Under the constitutional monarchies of Europe, (as they exist in theory, at least,) the king, besides uniting in his single person all the authority of the executive, which includes a power to make war, create peers, and unconditionally to name to all employments, has an equal influence in enacting laws, his veto being absolute; but, in America, the executive, besides being elective, is stripped of most of these high sources of influence, and is obliged to keep constantly in view the justice and legality of his acts, both on account of his direct responsibilities, and on account of the force of public opinion.

In this country, there is far more to apprehend from congress, than from the executive, as is seen in the following reasons:—Congress is composed of many, while the executive is one, bodies of men notoriously acting with less personal responsibilities than individuals; congress has power to enact laws, which it becomes the duty of the executive to see enforced, and the really legislative authority of a country is always its greatest authority; from the decisions and constructions of the executive, the citizen can always appeal to the courts for protection, but no appeal can lie from the acts of congress, except on the ground of unconstitutionality; the executive has direct personal responsibilities under the laws of the land, for any abuses of his authority, but the member of congress, unless guilty of open corruption, is almost beyond personal liabilities.

It follows that the legislature of this country, by the intention of the constitution, wields the highest authority under the least responsibility, and that it is the power most to be distrusted. Still, all who possess trusts, are to be diligently watched, for there is no protection against abuses without responsibility, nor any real responsibility, without vigilance.

Political partisans, who are too apt to mistake the impulses of their own hostilities and friendships for truths, have laid down many false principles on the subject of the duties of the executive. When a law is passed, it goes to the executive for execution, through the executive agents, and, at need, to the courts for interpretation. It would seem that there is no discretion vested in the executive concerning the constitutionality of a law. If he distrusts the constitutionality of any law, he can set forth his objections by resorting to the veto; but it is clearly the intention of the system that the whole legislative power, in the last resort, shall abide in congress, while it is necessary to the regular action of the government, that none of its agents, but those who are especially appointed for that purpose, shall pretend to interpret the constitution, in practice. The citizen is differently situated. If he conceive himself oppressed by an unconstitutional law, it is his inalienable privilege to raise the question before the courts, where a final interpretation can be had. By this interpretation the executive and all his agents are equally bound to abide. This obligation arises from the necessity of things, as well as from the nature of the institutions. There must be somewhere a power to decide on the constitutionality of laws, and this power is vested in the supreme court of the United States, on final appeal.

When called on to approve a law, even though its principle should have been already pronounced on by the courts, the executive is independent. He is now a legislator, and can disregard all other constructions of the constitution, but those dictated by his own sense of right. In this character, to the extent of his veto-power, he is superior to the courts, which have cognizance of no more than each case as it is presented for their consideration. The president may approve of a law that the court has decided to be unconstitutional in principle, or he may veto a law that the court has decided to be constitutional in principle. The legislator himself, is compelled to submit to the interpretation of the court, however different his own views of the law may have been in passing it, but as soon as he comes to act again as a legislator, he becomes invested with all his own high duties and rights. The court cannot make the constitution, in any case; it only interprets the law. One court may decide differently from another, and instances often occur in which the same judges see reason to

change their own decisions, and it would be, to the last degree, inexpedient, to give the court an authority beyond the necessity of the circumstances.

Although the court can render a law null, its power does not extend beyond the law already passed. Congress may re-enact it, as often as it please, and the court will still exercise its reason in rejecting it. This is the balance of the constitution, which invites inquiry, the constituencies of the states holding a legal authority to render that constitutional which the courts have declared to be unconstitutional, or vice versa, by amendments to the instrument itself; the supremacy of the court being merely temporary, conditional, and growing out of expediency and necessity.

It has been said that it is a vital principle of this government, that each of its branches should confine itself to the particular duties assigned it by the constitution, and in no manner exceed them. Many grave abuses have already arisen from loosing sight of this truth, and there is danger that the whole system will be perverted from its intention, if not destroyed, unless they are seasonably corrected. Of these, the most prevalent, the one most injurious to the public service, that which has been introduced the most on foreign and the least on American principles, is the practice of using the time and influence of the legislatures, for the purpose of acting on the public mind, with a view to affect the elections. The usage has already gained so much footing, as seriously to impede the course of legislation.

This is one of the cases, in which it is necessary to discriminate between the distinctive principles of our own government, and those of the government of the country from which we are derived. In England, by the mode in which the power of the executive has been curtailed, it is necessary that the ministerial contests should be conducted in the legislative bodies, but, in this country, such a course cannot be imitated, without the legislators' assuming an authority that does not belong to them, and without dispossessing the people, in some measure, of their rights. He who will examine the constitution for the powers of congress, will find no authority to pass resolutions on, or to waste the time, which is the property of the public, in discussing the matters, on which, after all, congress has no power to decide. This is the test of legislative authority. Congress cannot properly even discuss a subject, that congress cannot legally control, unless it be to ascertain its own powers. In cases that do not admit of question, this is one of the grossest abuses of the institutions, and ought to be classed with the usurpations of other systems.

There is a feeling connected with this subject, that it behoves every upright citizen cautiously to watch. He may be opposed to the executive, for instance, as a party-man, and yet have an immediate representative in congress, of his own particular way of thinking; and it is a weakness of humanity, under such circumstances, for one to connect himself most directly with his own immediate candidate, and to look on his political opponent with distrust. The jealousy created by this feeling, induces unreflecting men to imagine that curbing their particular representatives, in matters of this nature, is curtailing their own rights, and disposes them to defend what is inherently wrong, on personal motives.

Political systems ought to be, and usually are, framed on certain great and governing principles. These principles cannot be perverted, or lost sight of, without perverting, or rendering nugatory the system itself; and, under a popular government, in an age like this, far more is to be apprehended from indirect attacks on the institutions, than from those which are direct. It is usual to excuse these departures from the right on the plea of human propensities, but human institutions are framed expressly to curb such propensities, and no truth is more salutary than that which is contained in the homely saying, that "law makers should not be law breakers."

It is the duty of the citizen to judge of all political acts on the great principles of the government, and not according to his own political partialities, or prejudices. His own particular representative is no more a representative of the people, than the representative of any other man, and one branch of the government is no more representative than another. All are to keep within their respective spheres, and it may be laid down as a governing maxim of the institutions, *that the representative who exceeds his trusts, trespasses on the rights of the people.*

All comparisons between the powers of the British parliament and those of congress are more than useless, since they are bodies differently constituted, while one is absolute, and the other is merely a special trustee for limited and defined objects.

In estimating the powers of congress, there is a rule that may be safely confided in, and which has been already hinted at. The powers of congress are express and limited. That body, therefore, can have no right *to pass resolutions* other than those which affect their own police, or, in a moral sense, even to make speeches, except on subjects on which *they have a right to pass laws.* The instant they exceed these limits, they exceed the bounds of their delegated authority. By applying this simple test to their proceedings, any citizen may, in ordinary cases, ascertain how far the representatives of the nation abuse their trusts.

Liberty is not a matter of words, but a positive and important condition of society. Its greatest safeguards, after placing its foundations on a popular base, is in the checks and balances imposed on the public servants, and all its real friends ought to know that the most insidious attacks, are made on it by those who are the largest trustees of authority, in their efforts to increase their power.

The government of the United States has three branches. The executive, the legislative and the judicial. These several branches are independent of each other, though the first is intended to act as a check on the second, no law or resolution being legal that is not first submitted to the president for his approval. This check, however, does not render the first an integral part of the legislature, as laws and resolutions may be passed without his approval, by votes of two thirds.

In most constitutional monarchies, the legislatures, being originally secondary powers, were intended as checks on the action of the crown, which was possessed of the greatest, and, by consequence, of the most dangerous authority; whereas, the case is reversed in America, the executive using his veto as a check on congress. Such is the intention of the constitution, though the tactics of party, and the bitterness of opposition, have endeavored to interpret the instrument differently, by appealing to the ancient prejudices derived from England.

ON STATION

Station may be divided into that which is political, or publick, and that which is social, or private. In monarchies and aristocracies the two are found united, since the higher classes, as a matter of course, monopolize all the offices of consideration; but, in democracies, there is not, nor is it proper that there should be, any intimate connexion between them.

Political, or publick station, is that which is derived from office, and, in a democracy, must embrace men of very different degrees of leisure, refinement, habits and knowledge. This is characteristick of the institutions, which, under a popular government, confer on political station more power than rank, since the latter is expressly avoided in this system.

Social station is that which one possesses in the ordinary associations, and is dependent on birth, education, personal qualities, property, tastes, habits, and, in some instances, on caprice, or fashion. Although the latter undeniably is sometimes admitted to control social station, it generally depends, however, on the other considerations named.

Social station, in the main, is a consequence of property. So long as there is civilization there must be the rights of property, and so long as there are the rights of property, their obvious consequences must follow. All that democracies legitimately attempt is to prevent the advantages which accompany social station from accumulating rights that do not properly belong to the condition, which is effected by pronouncing that it shall have no factitious political aids.

They who have reasoned ignorantly, or who have aimed at effecting their personal ends by flattering the popular feeling, have boldly affirmed that "one man is as good as another"; a maxim that is true in neither nature, revealed morals, nor political theory.

That one man is not as good as another in natural qualities, is proved on the testimony of our sense. One man is stronger than another; he is handsomer, taller, swifter, wiser, or braver, than all his fellows. In short, the physical and moral qualities are unequally distributed, and, as a necessary consequence, in none of them, can one man be justly said to be as good as another. Perhaps no two human beings can be found so precisely equal in every thing, that one shall not be pronounced the superior of the other; which, of course, establishes the fact that there is no natural equality.

The advocates of exclusive political privileges reason on this circumstance by assuming, that as nature has made differences between men, those institutions which create political

orders, are no more than carrying out the great designs of providence. The error of their argument is in supposing it a confirmation of the designs of nature to attempt to supplant her, for, while the latter has rendered men unequal, it is not from male to male, according to the order of primogeniture, as is usually established by human ordinances. In order not to interfere with the inequality of nature, her laws must be left to their own operations, which is just what is done in democracies, after a proper attention has been paid to the peace of society, by protecting the weak against the strong.

That one man is not deemed as good as another in the grand moral system of providence, is revealed to us in Holy Writ, by the scheme of future rewards and punishments, as well as by the whole history of those whom God has favored in this world, for their piety, or punished for their rebellion. As compared with perfect holiness, all men are frail; but, as compared with each other, we are throughout the whole of sacred history made to see, that, in a moral sense, one man is not as good as another. The evil doer is punished, while they who are distinguished for their qualities and acts, are intended to be preferred.

The absolute moral and physical equality that are inferred by the maxim, that "one man is as good as another," would at once do away with the elections, since a lottery would be both simpler, easier and cheaper than the present mode of selecting representatives. Men, in such a case, would draw lots for office, as they are now drawn for juries. Choice supposes a preference, and preference inequality of merit, or of fitness.

We are then to discard all visionary theories on this head, and look at things as they are. All that the most popular institutions attempt, is to prohibit that one *race* of men shall be made better than another by law, from father to son, which would be defeating the intentions of providence, creating a superiority that exists in neither physical nor moral nature, and substituting a political scheme for the will of God and the force of things.

As a principle, one man is as good as another in rights. Such is the extent of the most liberal institutions of this country, and this provision is not general. The slave is not as good as his owner, even in rights. But in those states where slavery does not exist, all men have essentially the same rights, an equality, which, so far from establishing that "one man is as good as another," in a social sense, is the very means of producing the inequality of condition that actually exists. By possessing the same rights to exercise their respective faculties, the active and frugal become more wealthy than the idle and dissolute; the wise and gifted more trusted than the silly and ignorant; the polished and refined more respected and sought, than the rude and vulgar.

In most countries, birth is a principal source of social distinction, society being divided into castes, the noble having an hereditary claim to be the superior of the plebian. This is an unwise and an arbitrary distinction that has led to most of the social diseases of the old world, and from which America is happily exempt. But great care must be had in construing the principles which have led to this great change, for America is the first important country of modern times, in which such positive distinctions have been destroyed.

Still some legal differences, and more social advantages, are produced by birth, even in America. The child inherits the property, and a portion of the consideration of the parent. Without the first of these privileges, men would not exert themselves to acquire more property than would suffice for their own personal necessities, parental affection being one of the most powerful incentives to industry. Without such an inducement, then, it would follow that civilization would become stationary, or, it would recede; the incentives of individuality and of the affections, being absolutely necessary to impel men to endure the labor and privations that alone can advance it.

The hereditary consideration of the child, so long as it is kept within due bounds, by being confined to a natural sentiment, is also productive of good, since no more active inducement to great and glorious deeds can offer, than the deeply seated interest that man takes in his posterity. All that reason and justice require is effected, by setting bounds to such advantages, in denying hereditary claims to trusts and power; but evil would be the day, and ominous the symptom, when a people shall deny that any portion of the consideration of the ancestor is due to the descendant.

It is as vain to think of altogether setting aside sentiment and the affections, in regulating human affairs, as to imagine it possible to raise a nature, known to be erring and weak, to the level of perfection.

The Deity, in that terrible warning delivered from the mount, where he declares that he "will visit the sins of the fathers upon the children, unto the third and fourth generation," does no more than utter one of those sublime moral truths, which, in conformity with his divine providence, pervade nature. It is merely an announcement of a principle that cannot safely be separated from justice, and one that is closely connected with all the purest motives and highest aspirations of man.

There would be a manifest injustice in visiting the offence of the criminal on his nearest of kin, by making the innocent man participate in the disgrace of a guilty relative, as is notoriously done most, by those most disposed to rail at reflected renown, and not to allow of the same participation in the glory. Both depend upon a sentiment deeper than human laws, and have been established for purposes so evidently useful as to require no explanation. All that is demanded of us, is to have a care that this sentiment do not degenerate to a prejudice, and that, in the one case, we do not visit the innocent too severely, or, in the other, exalt the unworthy beyond the bounds of prudence.

It is a natural consequence of the rights of property and of the sentiment named, that birth should produce some advantages, in a social sense, even in the most democratical of the American communities. The son imbibes a portion of the intelligence, refinement and habits of the father, and he shares in his associations. These must be enumerated as the legitimate advantages of birth, and without invading the private arrangements of families and individuals, and establishing a perfect community of education, they are unavoidable. Men of the same habits, the same degree of cultivation and refinement, the same opinions, naturally associate together, in every class of life. The day laborer will not mingle with the slave; the skilful mechanic feels his superiority over the mere laborer, claims higher wages and has a pride in his craft; the man in trade justly fancies that his habits elevate him above the mechanic, so far as social position is concerned, and the man of refinement, with his education, tastes and sentiments, is superior to all. Idle declamation on these points, does not impair the force of things, and life is a series of facts. These inequalities of condition, of manners, of mental cultivation must exist, unless it be intended to reduce all to a common level of ignorance and vulgarity, which would be virtually to return to a condition of barbarism.

The result of these undeniable facts, is the inequalities of social station, in America, as elsewhere, though it is an inequality that exists without any more arbitrary distinctions than are indispensably connected with the maintenance of civilization. In a social sense, there are orders here, as in all other countries, but the classes run into each other more easily, the lines of separation are less strongly drawn, and their shadows are more intimately blended.

This social inequality of America is an unavoidable result of the institutions, though nowhere proclaimed in them, the different constitutions maintaining a profound silence on the subject, they who framed them probably knowing that it is as much a consequence of civilized society, as breathing is a vital function of animal life.

AN ARISTOCRAT AND A DEMOCRAT

We live in an age, when the words aristocrat and democrat are much used, without regard to the real significations. An aristocrat is one of a few, who possess the political power of a country; a democrat, one of the many. The words are also properly applied to those who entertain notions favorable to aristocratical, or democratical forms of government. Such persons are not, necessarily, either aristocrats, or democrats in fact, but merely so in opinion. Thus a member of a democratical government may have an aristocratical bias, and *vice versa*.

To call a man who has the habits and opinions of a gentleman, an aristocrat, from that fact alone, is an abuse of terms, and betrays ignorance of the true principles of government, as well as of the world. It must be an equivocal freedom, under which every one is not the master of his own innocent acts and associations, and he is a sneaking democrat, indeed, who will submit to be dictated to, in those habits over which neither law nor morality assumes a right of control.

Some men fancy that a democrat can only be one who seeks the level, social, mental and moral, of the majority, a rule that would at once exclude all men of refinement, education and taste from the class. These persons are enemies of democracy, as they at once render it impracticable. They are usually great sticklers for their own associations and habits, too, though unable to comprehend any of a nature that are superior. They are, in truth, aristocrats in principle, though assuming a contrary pretension; the ground work of all their feelings and arguments being self. Such is not the intention liberty, whose aim is to leave every man to be the master of his own acts; denying hereditary honors, it is true, as unjust and unnecessary, but not denying the inevitable consequences of civilization.

The law of God is the only rule of conduct, in this, as in other matters. Each man should do as he would be done by. Were the question put to the greatest advocate of indiscriminate association, whether he would submit to have his company and habits dictated to him, he would be one of the first to resist the tyranny; for they, who are the most rigid in maintaining their own claims, in such matters, are usually the loudest in decrying those whom they fancy to be better off than themselves. Indeed, it may be taken as a rule in social intercourse, that he who is the most apt to question the pretensions of others, is the most conscious of the doubtful position he himself occupies; thus establishing the very claims he affects to deny, by letting his jealousy of it be seen. Manners, education and refinement, are positive things, and they bring with them innocent tastes which are productive of high enjoyments; and it is as unjust to deny their possessors their indulgence, as it would be to insist on the less fortunate's passing the time they would rather devote to athletic amusements, in listening to operas for which they have no relish, sung in a language they do not understand.

All that democracy means, is as equal a participation in rights as is practicable; and to pretend that social equality is a condition of popular institutions, is to assume that the latter are destructive of civilization, for, as nothing is more self-evident than the impossibility of raising all men to the highest standard of tastes and refinement, the alternative would be to reduce the entire community to the lowest. The whole embarrassment on this point exists in the difficulty of making men comprehend qualities they do not themselves possess. We can all perceive the difference between ourselves and our inferiors, but when it comes to a question of the difference between us and our superiors, we fail to appreciate merits of which we have no proper conceptions. In face of this obvious difficulty, there is the safe and just governing rule, already mentioned, or that of permitting every one to be the undisturbed judge of his own habits and associations, so long as they are innocent, and do not impair the rights of others to be equally judges for themselves. It follows, that social intercourse must regulate itself, independently of institutions, with the exception that the latter, while they withhold no natural, bestow no factitious advantages beyond those which are inseparable from the rights of property, and general civilization.

In a democracy, men are just as free to aim at the highest attainable places in society, as to obtain the largest fortunes; and it would be clearly unworthy of all noble sentiment to say, that the grovelling competition for money shall alone be free, while that which enlists all the liberal acquirements and elevated sentiments of the race, is denied the democrat. Such an avowal would be at once, a declaration of the inferiority of the system, since nothing but ignorance and vulgarity could be its fruits.

The democratic gentleman must differ in many essential particulars, from the aristocratical gentleman, though in their ordinary habits and tastes they are virtually identical. Their principles vary; and, to a slight degree, their deportment accordingly. The democrat, recognizing the right of all to participate in power, will be more liberal in his general sentiments, a quality of superiority in itself; but, in conceding this much to his fellow man, he will proudly maintain his own independence of vulgar domination, as indispensable to his personal habits. The same principles and manliness that would induce him to depose a royal despot, would induce him to resist a vulgar tyrant.

There is no more capital, though more common error, than to suppose him an aristocrat who maintains his independence of habits; for democracy asserts the control of the majority, only in matters of law, and not in matters of custom. The very object of the institution is the utmost practicable personal liberty, and to affirm the contrary, would be sacrificing the end to the means.

An aristocrat, therefore, is merely one who fortifies his exclusive privileges by positive institutions, and a democrat, one who is willing to admit of a free competition, in all things. To say, however, that the last supposes this competition will lead to nothing, is an assumption that means are employed without any reference to an end. He is the purest democrat who best maintains his rights, and no rights can be dearer to a man of cultivation, than exemptions from unseasonable invasions on his time, by the coarse-minded and ignorant.

1838

ALEXIS CHARLES HENRI MAURICE CLÉREL DE TOCQUEVILLE

1805–1859

IN COMPANY WITH Gustave de Beaumont, Tocqueville, a gifted young French aristocrat, visited the United States in 1831, partly to observe at first hand the American penitentiary system, and partly to study democracy at work. *De la Démocratie en Amérique* (1835–1840) was the most important study of American institutions made by a foreigner up to that time, and it was destined to become a classic. Tocqueville regarded American democracy as the inevitable result of the diffusion of the principle of equality on favorable soil. Although he looked with favor on many aspects of American democracy, particularly the quickened interest of the masses in public matters, his diagnosis also emphasized certain dangers, notably the anonymous, collective despotism implicit in it. The conflict between liberty and equality, in short, bulked large in Tocqueville's analysis. His study was as significant for its demonstration of the interrelations among political, social, and economic factors, as it was for any single conclusion.

Democracy in America, by Alexis De Tocqueville, the Henry Reeve text . . . now further corrected and edited . . .
by Phillips Bradley, 2 vols., New York, 1945.
J. P. Mayer, *Alexis De Tocqueville. A Biographical Study in Political Science*, New York, 1960.
G. W. Pierson, *Tocqueville and Beaumont in America*, New York, 1938.

» » *From:* DEMOCRACY IN AMERICA « «

I have hitherto examined the institutions of the United States; I have passed their legislation in review, and I have depicted the present characteristics of political society in that country. But a sovereign power exists above these institutions and beyond these characteristic features which may destroy or modify them at its pleasure—I mean that of the people. It remains to be shown in what manner this power, which regulates the laws, acts: its propensities and its passions remain to be pointed out, as well as the secret springs which retard, accelerate, or direct its irresistible course; and the effects of its unbounded authority, with the destiny which is probably reserved for it.

[WHY THE PEOPLE MAY STRICTLY BE SAID TO GOVERN IN THE UNITED STATES]

In America the people appoints the legislative and the executive power, and furnishes the jurors who punish all offences against the laws. The American institutions are democratic, not only in their principle but in all their consequences; and the people elects its representatives directly, and for the most part annually, in order to ensure their dependence. The people is therefore the real directing power; and although the form of government is representative, it is evident that the opinions, the prejudices, the interests, and even the passions of the community are hindered by no durable obstacles from exercising a perpetual influence on society. In the United States the majority governs in the name of the people, as is the case in all the countries in which the people is supreme. The majority is principally composed of peaceful citizens who, either by inclination or by interest, are sincerely desirous of the welfare of their country. But they are surrounded by the incessant agitation of parties, which

attempt to gain their co-operation and to avail themselves of their support.

[WHAT THE REAL ADVANTAGES ARE WHICH AMERICAN SOCIETY DERIVES FROM THE GOVERNMENT OF THE DEMOCRACY]

Before I enter upon the subject of the present chapter I am induced to remind the reader of what I have more than once adverted to in the course of this book. The political institutions of the United States appear to me to be one of the forms of government which a democracy may adopt; but I do not regard the American Constitution as the best, or as the only one, which a democratic people may establish. In showing the advantages which the Americans derive from the government of democracy, I am therefore very far from meaning, or from believing, that similar advantages can only be obtained from the same laws.

[GENERAL TENDENCY OF THE LAWS UNDER THE RULE OF THE AMERICAN DEMOCRACY, AND HABITS OF THOSE WHO APPLY THEM]

Defects of a democratic government easy to be discovered—Its advantages only to be discerned by long observation—Democracy in America often inexpert, but the general tendency of the laws advantageous—In the American democracy public officers have no permanent interests distinct from those of the majority—Result of this state of things.

The defects and the weaknesses of a democratic government may very readily be discovered; they are demonstrated by the most flagrant instances, whilst its beneficial influence is less perceptibly exercised. A single glance suffices to detect its evil consequences, but its good qualities can only be discerned by long observation. The laws of the American democracy are frequently defective or incomplete; they sometimes attack vested rights, or give a sanction to others which are dangerous to the community; but even if they were good, the frequent changes which they undergo would be an evil. How comes it, then, that the American republics prosper and maintain their position?

In the consideration of laws a distinction must be carefully observed between the end at which they aim and the means by which they are directed to that end, between their absolute and their relative excellence. If it be the intention of the legislator to favor the interests of the minority at the expense of the majority, and if the measures he takes are so combined as to accomplish the object he has in view with the least possible expense of time and exertion, the law may well be drawn up, although its purpose be bad; and the more efficacious it is, the greater is the mischief which it causes.

Democratic laws generally tend to promote the welfare of the greatest possible number; for they emanate from the majority of the citizens, who are subject to error, but who cannot have an interest opposed to their own advantage. The laws of an aristocracy tend, on the contrary, to concentrate wealth and power in the hands of the minority, because an aristocracy, by its very nature, constitutes a minority. It may therefore be asserted, as a general proposition, that the purpose of a democracy in the conduct of its legislation is useful to a greater number of citizens than that of an aristocracy. This is, however, the sum total of its advantages.

Aristocracies are infinitely more expert in the science of legislation than democracies ever can be. They are possessed of a self-control which protects them from the errors of temporary excitement, and they form lasting designs which they mature with the assistance of favorable opportunities. Aristocratic government proceeds with the dexterity of art; it understands how to make the collective force of all its laws converge at the same time to a given point. Such is not the case with democracies, whose laws are almost always ineffective or inopportune. The means of democracy are therefore more imperfect than those of aristocracy, and the measures which it unwittingly adopts are frequently opposed to its own cause; but the object it has in view is more useful.

Let us now imagine a community so organized by nature, or by its constitution, that it can support the transitory action of bad laws, and that it can await, without destruction, the general tendency of the legislation: we shall then be able to conceive that a democratic government, notwithstanding its defects, will be most fitted to conduce to the prosperity of this community. This is precisely what has occurred in the United States; and I repeat, what I have before remarked, that the great advantage of the Americans consists in their being able to commit faults which they may afterward repair.

An analogous observation may be made respecting public officers. It is easy to perceive that the American democracy frequently errs in the choice of the individuals to whom it entrusts the power of the administration; but it is more difficult to say why the State prospers under their rule. In the first place it is to be remarked, that if in a democratic State the governors have less honesty and less capacity than elsewhere, the governed, on the other hand, are more enlightened and more attentive to their interests. As the people in democracies is more incessantly vigilant in its affairs and more jealous of its rights, it prevents its representatives from abandoning that general line of conduct which its own interest prescribes. In the second place, it must be remembered that if the democratic magistrate is more apt to misuse his power, he possesses it for a shorter period of time. But there is yet another reason which is still more general and conclusive. It is no doubt of importance to the welfare of nations that they should be governed by men of talents and virtue; but it is perhaps still more important that the interests of those men should not differ from the interests of the community at large; for, if such were the case, virtues of a high order might become useless, and talents might be turned to a bad account. I say that it is important that the interests of the persons in authority should not conflict with or oppose the interests of the community at large; but I do not insist upon their having the same interests as the whole population, because I am not aware that such a state of things ever existed in any country.

No political form has hitherto been discovered which is equally favorable to the prosperity and the development of all the classes into which society is divided. These classes continue to form, as it were, a certain number of distinct nations in the same nation; and experience has shown that it is no less dangerous to place the fate of these classes exclusively in the hands of any one of them than it is to make one people the arbiter of the destiny of another. When the rich alone govern, the interest of the poor is always endangered; and when the poor make the laws, that of the rich incurs very serious risks. The advantage of democracy does not consist, therefore, as has sometimes been asserted, in favoring the prosperity of all, but simply in contributing to the well-being of the greatest possible number.

• • •

[THE PRINCIPLE OF EQUALITY SUGGESTS TO THE AMERICANS THE IDEA OF INDEFINITE PERFECTIBILITY OF MAN]

Equality suggests to the human mind several ideas which would not have originated from any other source, and it modifies almost all those previously entertained. I take as an example the idea of human perfectibility, because it is one of the principal notions that the intellect can conceive, and because it constitutes of itself a great philosophical theory, which is every instant to be traced by its consequences in the practice of human affairs. Although man has many points of resemblance with the brute creation, one characteristic is peculiar to himself—he improves: they are incapable of improvement. Mankind could not fail to discover this difference from its earliest period. The idea of perfectibility is therefore as old as the world; equality did not give birth to it, although it has imparted to it, a novel character.

When the citizens of a community are classed according to their rank, their profession, or their birth, and when all men are constrained to follow the career which happens to open before them, everyone thinks that the utmost limits of human power are to be discerned in proximity to himself, and none seeks any longer to resist the inevitable law of his destiny. Not indeed that an aristocratic people absolutely contests man's faculty of self-improvement, but they do not hold it to be indefinite; amelioration they conceive, but not change: they imagine that the future condition of society may be better, but not essentially different; and whilst they admit that mankind has made vast strides in improvement, and may still have some to make, they assign to it beforehand certain impassable limits. Thus they do not presume that they have arrived at the supreme good or at absolute truth (what people or what man was ever wild enough to imagine it?) but they cherish a persuasion that they have pretty nearly reached that degree of greatness and knowledge which our imperfect nature admits of; and as nothing moves about them they are willing to fancy that everything is in its fit place. Then it is that the legislator affects to lay down eternal laws; that kings and nations will raise none but imperishable monuments; and that the present generation undertakes to spare generations to come the care of regulating their destinies.

In proportion as castes disappear and the classes of society approximate—as manners, customs, and laws vary, from the tumultuous intercourse of men—as new facts arise—as new truths are brought to light—as ancient opinions are dissipated, and others take their place—the image of an ideal perfection, forever on the wing, presents itself to the human mind. Continual changes are then every instant occurring under the observation of every man: the position of some is rendered worse; and he learns but too well, that no people and no individual, how enlightened soever they may be, can lay claim to infallibility;—the condition of others is improved; whence he infers that man is endowed with an indefinite faculty of improvement. His reverses teach him that none may hope to have discovered absolute good—his success stimulates him to the never-ending pursuit of it. Thus, forever seeking—forever falling, to rise again—often disappointed, but not discouraged—he tends unceasingly towards that unmeasured greatness so indistinctly visible at the end of the long track which humanity has yet to tread. It can hardly be believed how many facts naturally flow from the philosophical theory of the indefinite perfectibility of man, or how strong an influence it exercises even on men who, living entirely for the purposes of action and not of thought, seem to conform their actions to it, without knowing anything about it. I accost an American sailor, and I inquire why the ships of his country are built so as to last but for a short time; he answers without hesitation that the art of navigation is every day making such rapid progress that the finest vessel would become almost useless if it lasted beyond a certain number of years. In these words, which fell accidentally and on a particular subject from a man of rude attainments, I recognize the general and systematic idea upon which a great people directs all its concerns.

Aristocratic nations are naturally too apt to narrow the scope of human perfectibility; democratic nations to expand it beyond compass.

[OF INDIVIDUALISM IN DEMOCRATIC COUNTRIES]

10   I have shown how it is that in ages of equality every man seeks for his opinions within himself: I am now about to show how it is that, in the same ages, all his feelings are turned towards himself alone. Individualism [1] is a novel expression, to which a novel idea has given birth. Our fathers were only acquainted with egotism. Egotism is a passionate and exaggerated love of self, which leads a man to connect everything with his own person, and
20   to prefer himself to everything in the world. Individualism is a mature and calm feeling, which disposes each member of the community to sever himself from the mass of his fellow-creatures; and to draw apart with his family and his friends; so that, after he has thus formed a little circle of his own, he willingly leaves society at large to itself. Egotism originates in blind instinct: individualism proceeds from erroneous judgment more than
30   from depraved feelings; it originates as much in the deficiencies of the mind as in the perversity of the heart. Egotism blights the germ of all virtue; individualism, at first, only saps the virtues of public life; but, in the long run, it attacks and destroys all others, and is at length absorbed in downright egotism. Egotism is a vice as old as the world, which does not belong to one form of society more than to another: individualism is of democratic origin,
40   and it threatens to spread in the same ratio as the equality of conditions.

Amongst aristocratic nations, as families remain for centuries in the same condition, often on the same spot, all generations become as it were contemporaneous. A man almost always knows his forefathers, and respects them: he thinks he already sees his remote descendants, and he loves them. He willingly imposes duties on himself towards the former and the latter;
50   and he will frequently sacrifice his personal

[1] I adopt the expression of the original, however strange it may seem to the English ear, partly because it illustrates the remark on the introduction of general terms into democratic language which was made in a preceding chapter, and partly because I know of no English word exactly equivalent to the expression. The chapter itself defines the meaning attached to it by the author. [Translator's note.]

gratifications to those who went before and to those who will come after him. Aristocratic institutions have, moreover, the effect of closely binding every man to several of his fellow-citizens. As the classes of an aristocratic people are strongly marked and permanent, each of them is regarded by its own members as a sort of lesser country, more tangible and more cherished than the country at large. As in aristocratic communities all the citizens occupy fixed positions, one above the other, the result is that each of them always sees a man above himself whose patronage is necessary to him, and below himself another man whose co-operation he may claim. Men living in aristocratic ages are therefore almost always closely attached to something placed out of their own sphere, and they are often disposed to forget themselves. It is true that in those ages the notion of human fellowship is faint, and that men seldom think of sacrificing themselves for mankind; but they often sacrifice themselves for other men. In democratic ages, on the contrary, when the duties of each individual to the race are much more clear, devoted service to any one man becomes more rare; the bond of human affection is extended, but it is relaxed.

Amongst democratic nations new families are constantly springing up, others are constantly falling away, and all that remain change their condition; the woof of time is every instant broken, and the track of generations effaced. Those who went before are soon forgotten; of those who will come after no one has any idea: the interest of man is confined to those in close propinquity to himself. As each class approximates to other classes, and intermingles with them, its members become indifferent and as strangers to one another. Aristocracy had made a chain of all the members of the community, from the peasant to the king: democracy breaks that chain, and severs every link of it. As social conditions become more equal, the number of persons increases who, although they are neither rich enough nor powerful enough to exercise any great influence over their fellow-creatures, have nevertheless acquired or retained sufficient education and fortune to satisfy their own wants. They owe nothing to any man, they expect nothing from any man; they acquire the habit of always considering themselves as standing alone, and they are apt to imagine that their whole destiny is in their own hands. Thus not only does democracy make every man forget his ancestors, but it hides his descendants, and separates his contemporaries from him; it throws him back forever upon himself alone, and threatens in the end to confine him entirely within the solitude of his own heart.

[INDIVIDUALISM STRONGER AT THE CLOSE OF A DEMOCRATIC REVOLUTION THAN AT OTHER PERIODS]

The period when the construction of democratic society upon the ruins of an aristocracy has just been completed, is especially that at which this separation of men from one another, and the egotism resulting from it, most forcibly strike the observation. Democratic communities not only contain a large number of independent citizens, but they are constantly filled with men who, having entered but yesterday upon their independent condition, are intoxicated with their new power. They entertain a presumptuous confidence in their strength, and as they do not suppose that they can henceforward ever have occasion to claim the assistance of their fellow-creatures, they do not scruple to show that they care for nobody but themselves.

An aristocracy seldom yields without a protracted struggle, in the course of which implacable animosities are kindled between the different classes of society. These passions survive the victory, and traces of them may be observed in the midst of the democratic con-fusion which ensues. Those members of the community who were at the top of the late gradations of rank cannot immediately forget their former greatness; they will long regard themselves as aliens in the midst of the newly composed society. They look upon all those whom this state of society has made their equals as oppressors, whose destiny can excite no sympathy; they have lost sight of their former equals, and feel no longer bound by a common interest to their fate: each of them, standing aloof, thinks that he is reduced to care for himself alone. Those, on the contrary, who were formerly at the foot of the social scale, and who have been brought up to the common level by a sudden revolution, cannot enjoy their newly acquired independence without secret uneasiness; and if they meet with some of their former superiors on the same footing as themselves, they stand aloof from them with an expression of triumph and of fear. It is, then, commonly at the outset of democratic society that citizens are most disposed to live apart. Democracy leads men not to draw near to their fellow-creatures; but democratic revolutions lead them to shun each other, and perpetuate in a state of equality the animosities which the state of inequality engendered. The great advantage of the Americans is that they have arrived at a state of democracy without having to endure a democratic revolution; and that they are born equal, instead of becoming so.

1840

»» *Agrarianism and Commercial Capitalism* ««

1800-1850

»» »» «« ««

THE BLACK BALL LINE

I served my time in the Black Ball Line,
To me way-aye-aye, hurrah!
In the Black Ball Line I served my time,
Hurrah for the Black Ball Line!

The Black Ball ships they are good and true,
And they are the ships for me and you.

For once there was a Black Ball ship
That fourteen knots an hour could clip.

You will surely find a rich gold mine;
Just take a trip in the Black Ball Line.

Just take a trip to Liverpool,
To Liverpool, that Yankee school.

The Yankee sailors you'll see there,
With red-top boots and short-cut hair.

The Black Ball Line, formed in 1816, was the first company to send
packet ships between New York and Liverpool. To keep to the stiff
schedule of sailing, the ships were driven hard and, according to Miss
Joanna Colcord, "acquired a bad name among sailors for the iron discipline maintained aboard." This version of the song is given in Miss
Colcord's *Songs of American Sailormen* (1938). It is printed here
through the kind permission of Miss Colcord and the publishers,
W. W. Norton and Company.

》　》　《　《

THE RAGING CANAL

Come list to me ye heroes, ye nobles and ye braves,
For I've been at the mercy of the winds and the waves;
I'll tell you of the hardships to me that did befall
While going on a voyage up the Erie can-all;

.　.　.　.　.

We left old Albany harbor just at the close of day;
If I rightly remember 'twas the second day of May;
We trusted to our driver, altho' he was but small,
Yet he knew all the windings of that raging can-all.

It seemed as if the devil had work in hand that night,
For our oil was all out, and our lamps they gave no light;
The clouds began to gather, and the rain began to fall,
And I wished myself off and safe from the raging can-all.

. . . . .

The winds came roaring on, just like a wild cat scream;
Our little vessel pitched and tost, straining every beam,
The cook she dropt the bucket and let the ladle fall,
And the waves ran mountains high on the raging can-all.

. . . . .

The Captain bid the driver to hurry with all speed,
His orders were obeyed, for he soon cracked up his lead;
With that 'ere kind of towing, he allowed, by twelve o'clock,
We should have the old critter, right bang agin the dock.

But sad was the fate of our poor devoted bark,
For the rain kept pouring faster, and the night it grew dark;
The horse gave a stumble, and the driver gave a squall,
And they tumbled head and heels into the raging can-all.

. . . . .

The sky was rent assunder, the lightning it did flash,
The thunder rattled above, just like eternal smash;
The clouds were all upsot, and the rigging it did fall,
And we scudded under bare poles on that raging can-all.

. . . . .

We took the old cook's petticoat, for want of a better dress,
And rigg'd it out upon a pole, a signal of distress;
We pledged ourselves hand to hand, aboard the boat to bide,
And not to quit the deck while a plank hung to her side.

At length that horrid night cut dirt from the sky,
The storm it did abate, and a boat came passing by,
She soon espied our signal, while each on his knees did fall,
Thankful we escaped a grave on the raging can-all.

We each of us took a nip, and signed the pledge anew,
And wonderful as danger ceased, how up our courage grew,
The craft in sight bore down on us, and quickly was 'long side,
And we all jump'd aboard and for Buffalo did ride.

And now, my boys I'll tell you how to manage wind and weather,
In a storm hug the tow path, and lay feather to feather,
And when the weather gets bad, and rain begins to fall,
Jump right ashore, and streak it from the raging can-all.

. . . . .

The building of the Erie Canal, which was completed in 1825,
made New York our greatest commercial city and opened up the
northern regions of the country. Life along the canal was exciting in
the extreme, if we can believe the canal ballads which describe it.
This version of one of these ballads is taken from *The New Popular
Forget-Me-Not Songster*, published in Cincinnati. Only eleven of its
twenty-four stanzas are printed here.

Walter Edmonds' novel *Rome Haul* is an admirable re-creation of
the great days of the Erie.

« «   » »

BANKS OF OHIO

Come, all you young men, who have a mind to range,
Into the Western country, your station for to change;
For seeking some new pleasure we'll altogether go,
And we'll settle on the banks of the pleasant Ohio.

The land it is good boys, and you need not to fear
'Tis a garden of Eden in North America.
Come along, my lively lads, and we'll altogether go
And we'll settle on the banks of the pleasant Ohio.

There's all kinds of fish in that river for our use,
Besides, the lofty sugar tree[s] which yields us their juice;
There's all kinds of game there, besides the buck and doe,
And we'll range through the wild woods and hunt the buffalo.

This river as it murmurs, it runs for the main,
It brings us good tidings quite down from New Spain;
There's all kinds of grain there, and plenty it doth grow,
And we'll draw the Spanish gold right from Mexico.

Those blood thirsty Indians you need not to fear,
We will all united be, and we will all be free from care;
We'll march into the towns, and we'll give them their deadly blow,
And we'll fold you in our arms on the pleasant Ohio.

Come, all you fair maidens wherever you be,
Come, join in with us, and rewarded you shall be;
Girls, if you'll card, knit, and spin, we'll plough, reap, and sow,
And we'll settle on the banks of the pleasant Ohio.

Girls, if you'll card, knit, and spin, we'll plough, reap, and sow,
And we'll fold you in our arms while the stormy wind doth blow.

Published in *The Forget-Me-Not Songster, Containing a Choice
Collection of old Ballads, as Sung by our Grandmothers,* Philadelphia, c. 1842.

Agrarianism and Commercial Capitalism

URING THE WAR OF 1812 a considerable amount of capital which would normally have gone into commerce was diverted into industrial enterprises. Although sharp conflicts between commercial and industrial capitalism often became apparent, as, for example, in the issue of free trade versus tariffs for the encouragement of infant industries, the relations between commercial and industrial capitalism were sufficiently close to check any basic struggle. The conflict between commercial capitalism and agrarianism was, on the other hand, one of the sharpest and most dramatic in the first half of the nineteenth century.

With the expansion of the plantation system into the Southwest, which the cotton gin made practicable, the South, divided though it was in many respects, became increasingly identified with the agrarian interest. Its spokesmen hoped to cement an alliance between the South and the other great agrarian section, the West. At the same time they realized increasingly that commercial capitalism, with its conception of a tightly controlled and centralized monetary and banking system, ran counter to the interests of farmers and planters in almost constant need of easy capital for agricultural expansion, moving of crops, and consumers goods. Jackson is generally regarded as the most vivid exponent of agrarianism and the most bitter foe of commercial capitalism; but he found in John Taylor of Caroline a more philosophical and far-seeing critic of commercial capitalism.

Commercial capitalism also encountered sharp thrusts from another type of "agrarian." Spokesmen for the rising mechanic and artisan class cried out vigorously against "monopolies" of capital. The Loco-focos, with New York as their center, represented this position. The more radical of the laboring group went so far as to insist on the application of the "natural right of man" to an equal share in property.

The men of commercial capital were not slow in defending their interest. Sometimes they did this by trying to show Southerners that they too should develop commerce and industry. Sometimes they did it by glorifying the businessman. On other occasions they tried to prove that commerce was to the true advantage of all sections and classes. Now and again a literary man dipped his pen into bottles of satire and bespattered the apostles of agrarianism. But commercial capital depended chiefly on controlling legislatures sufficiently to prevent laws hostile to its interest and to secure such franchises and favors as best suited its needs.

» »　　« «

JOHN TAYLOR OF CAROLINE

1753–1824

OHN TAYLOR was educated at William and Mary College, and in the law. During the Revolution he served with the American forces. As a member of the Virginia legislature and as a United States senator, he was perhaps the most astute political and social theorist in the Jeffersonian camp. A consistent foe of the centralization of power or "consolidation," he severely criticized the financial and economic policies of the Federalists as unconstitutional and subversive of democracy, and as instruments for the setting up of a new type of capitalistic aristocracy. Local democracy and states rights found in him as able an exponent as government-favored banks did a trenchant and farseeing critic. His social philosophy was that of a liberal agrarian, and he popularized his own and others' ideas regarding the improvement of agricultural methods. His writings include *Arator* (1813), *Construction Construed, and Constitutions Vindicated* (1820), *Tyranny Unmasked* (1822), and *New Views of the Constitution of the United States* (1823). The following selection is from *An Inquiry into the Principles and Policy of the Government of the United States* (1814), one of his most representative and able books.

An Inquiry into the Principles and Policy of the Government of the United States, New Haven, 1950.
E. T. Mudge, *The Social Philosophy of John Taylor of Caroline,* New York, 1939.

From: AN INQUIRY INTO THE PRINCIPLES AND
» » POLICY OF THE GOVERNMENT OF THE « «
UNITED STATES

CHAPTER I

ARISTOCRACY

. . . It will be an effort of this essay to prove, that the United States have refuted the ancient axiom, "that monarchy, aristocracy and democracy, are the only elements of government," by planting theirs in moral principles, without any reference to those elements; and that by demolishing the barrier hitherto obstructing the progress of political science, they have cleared the way for improvement.

Mr. Adams's system promises nothing.[1] It tells us that human nature is always the same: that the art of government can never change; that it is contracted into three simple principles; as at Athens, Venice, or Constantinople; or those of the same principles compounded, as at London, Rome, or Lacedemon. And it gravely counts up several victims of democratic rage, as proofs, that democracy is more pernicious than monarchy or aristocracy. Such a computation is a spectre, calculated to arrest our efforts, and appal our hopes, in pursuit of political good. If it be correct, what motives of preference between forms of government remain? On one hand, Mr. Adams calls our attention to hundreds of wise and virtuous patricians, mangled and bleeding victims of popular fury; on the other, he might have

[1] In *A Defense of the Constitutions of Government of the United States of America* (1787–1788) and in *Discourses on Davila* (1805), John Adams expounded the aristocratic social philosophy which characterized the outlook of his middle and later years.

exhibited millions of plebeians, sacrificed to the pride, folly and ambition of monarchy and aristocracy; and, to complete the picture, he ought to have placed right before us, the effects of these three principles commixed, in the wars, rebellions, persecutions and oppressions of the English form, celebrated by Mr. Adams as the most perfect of the mixed class of governments. Is it possible to convince us, that we are compelled to elect one of these evils? After having discovered principles of government, distinct from monarchy, aristocracy or democracy, in the experience of their efficacy, and the enjoyment of their benefits; can we be persuaded to renounce the discovery, to restore the old principles of political navigation, and to steer the commonwealth into the disasters, against which all past ages have pathetically warned us? It is admitted, that man, physically, is "always the same"; but denied that he is so, morally. Upon the truth or error of this distinction, the truth or error of Mr. Adams's mode of reasoning and of this essay, will somewhat depend. . . .

Having apprized the reader, by these general remarks, of the political principles to be vindicated or assailed in this essay; and that an effort will be made to prove, that the policy of the United States is rooted in moral or intellectual principles, and not in orders, class or caste, natural or factitious; this effort must be postponed, until the way is opened to it, by a more particular review of Mr. Adams's system. To this, therefore, I return.

He supposes "that every society must *naturally* produce an aristocratical order of men, which it will be impossible to confine to an equality of rights with other men." To determine the truth of this position, an inquiry must be made into the mode by which these orders have been produced in those countries, placed before us by Mr. Adams, as objects of terror or imitation.

10 . . . Superior abilities constitutes one among the enumerated causes of a natural aristocracy. This cause is evidently as fluctuating as knowledge and ignorance; and its capacity to produce aristocracy, must depend upon this fluctuation. The aristocracy of superior abilities will be regulated by the extent of the space, between knowledge and ignorance. As the space contracts or widens, it will be diminished or increased; and if aristocracy

20 may be thus diminished, it follows that it may be thus destroyed.

No certain state of knowledge, is a natural or unavoidable quality of man. As an intellectual or moral quality, it may be created, destroyed and modified by human power. Can that which may be created, destroyed and modified by human power, be a natural and inevitable cause of aristocracy?

It has been modified in an extent, which

30 Mr. Adams does not even compute, by the art of printing, discovered subsequently to almost the whole of the authorities which have convinced Mr. Adams, that knowledge, or as he might have more correctly asserted, ignorance, was a cause of aristocracy.

The peerage of knowledge or abilities, in consequence of its enlargement by the effects of printing, can no longer be collected and controlled in the shape of a noble order or a

40 legislative department. The great body of this peerage must remain scattered throughout every nation, by the enjoyment of the benefit of the press. By endowing a small portion of it with exclusive rights and privileges, the indignation of this main body is excited. If this endowment should enable a nation to watch and control an inconsiderable number of that species of peerage produced by knowledge, it would also purchase the dissatisfaction of its

50 numberless members unjustly excluded; and would be a system for defending a nation against imbecility, and inviting aggression from strength, equivalent to a project for defeating an army, by feasting its vanguard.

If this reasoning is correct, the collection of that species of natural aristocracy (as Mr. Adams calls it) produced by superior abilities, into a legislative department, for the purpose of watching and controlling it, is now rendered impracticable, however useful it might have been, at an era when the proportion between ignorance was essentially different; and this impracticability is a strong indication of the radical inaccuracy of considering aristocracy as an inevitable natural law. The wisdom of uniting exclusive knowledge by exclusive privileges, that it may be controlled by disunited ignorance, is not considered as being an hypothetical question, since this aristocratical knowledge cannot now exist.

Similar reasoning applies still more forcibly to the idea of nature's constituting aristocracy, by means of exclusive virtue. Knowledge and virtue both fluctuate. A steady effect, from fluctuating causes, is morally and physically impossible. And yet Mr. Adams infers a natural aristocracy, from the error, that virtue and knowledge are in an uniform relation to vice and ignorance; sweeps away by it every human faculty, for the attainment of temporal or eternal happiness; and overturns the efficacy of law, to produce private or public moral rectitude.

Had it been true, that knowledge and virtue were natural causes of aristocracy, no fact could more clearly have exploded Mr. Adams's system, or more unequivocally have dissented from the eulogy he bestows on the English form of government. Until knowledge and virtue shall become genealogical they cannot be the causes of an inheritable aristocracy; and its existence, without the aid of superior knowledge and virtue, is a positive refutation of the idea, that nature creates aristocracy with these tools.

Mr. Adams has omitted a cause of aristocracy in the quotation, which he forgets not to urge in other places; namely, exclusive wealth. This, by much the most formidable with which mankind have to contend, is necessarily omitted, whilst he is ascribing aristocracy to nature; and being both artificial and efficacious, it contributes to sustain the opinion, "that as aristocracy is thus artificially created, it may also be artificially destroyed."

Alienation is the remedy for an aristocracy founded on landed wealth; inhibitions upon monopoly and incorporation, for one founded on paper wealth. Knowledge, enlisted by Mr. Adams under the banner of aristocracy, de-

serted her associate by the invention of alienation, and became its natural enemy. Discovering its hostility to human happiness, like Brutus,
she has applied the axe to the neck of what Mr.
Adams calls her progeny; and instead of maintaining the exclusiveness of wealth, contributes
to its division by inciting competition, and assailing perpetuities. How successfully, let England illustrate. She, no longer relying upon
nature for an aristocracy, is perpetually obliged
to repair the devastations it sustains from alienation; the weapon invented by knowledge; by
resorting to the funds of paper systems, pillage,
patronage and hierarchy, for fresh supplies.

. . . In order to illustrate the opinion, that
the aristocracy exhibited to us by Mr. Adams, as
creating a necessity for his system, is only a
ghost, let us turn our eyes for a moment towards its successor.

As the aristocracies of priestcraft and conquest decayed, that of patronage and paper
stock grew; not the rival, but the instrument of
a king; without rank or title; regardless of
honor; of insatiable avarice; and neither conspicuous for virtue and knowledge, or capable
of being collected into a legislative chamber.
Differing in all its qualities from Mr. Adams's
natural aristocracy, and defying his remedy, it
is condensed and combined by an interest, exclusive, and inimical to public good.

Why has Mr. Adams written volumes to instruct us how to manage an order of nobles,
sons of the Gods, of exclusive virtue, talents,
and wealth, and attended by the pomp and
fraud of superstition; or one of feudal barons,
holding great districts of unalienable country,
warlike, high spirited, turbulent and dangerous;
now that these orders are no more? Whilst he
passes over in silence the aristocracy of paper
and patronage, more numerous, more burdensome, unexposed to public jealousy by the
badge of title, and not too honorable or high
spirited to use and serve executive power, for
the sake of pillaging the people. Are these
odious vices, to be concealed under apprehensions of ancient aristocracies, which, however
natural, are supplanted by this modern one?

. . . For the sake of perspicuity, I shall call
the ancient aristocracy, chiefly created and supported by superstition, "the aristocracy of
the first age"; that produced by conquest,
known by the title of the feudal system, "the
aristocracy of the second age"; and that erected
on paper and patronage, "the aristocracy of the
third or present age." If aristocracy is the work

of nature, by deserting her accustomed constancy, and slily changing the shape of her
work, she has cunningly perplexed our defensive operations: to create the aristocracy of the
first age, she used Jupiter; of the second, Mars;
and of the third, Mercury. Jupiter is dethroned
by knowledge; the usurpations of Mars are
scattered by commerce and alienation; and it
only remains to detect the impostures of Mercury.

. . . Having thus conceded to Mr. Adams,
that wherever a few possess the mass of the
renown, virtue, talents and wealth of a nation,
that they will become an aristocracy, and probably ought to do so; it would be a concession,
strictly reciprocal, to admit, that wherever no
such body is to be found, an aristocracy ought
not to be created by legal assignments of wealth
and poverty. As the first species of minority
will govern, because of the power arising from
such monopolies only, so no other species can,
without these sources of power. Where its
sources are, power will be found; and hence
the great mass of wealth, created by the system of paper and patronage, has annihilated
the power of the didactick and titled peerage
of England; because it has not a sufficient mass
of virtue, renown, talents or wealth, to oppose
against stock and patronage.

The aristocracies of the first and second ages
were indebted for their power to ignorance,
fraud and superstition; now reason, sincerity
and truth, are demanded by the human mind.
It disdains to worship a pageant or fear a phantom, and is only to be guided by views of interest or happiness. This change in the human
character indicates an impossibility of reviving
the principles which sustained the aristocracies
of the first and second age, when mankind believed in the Gods of a pantheon, and in the
prophetic powers of convulsed women.

Talents and virtue are now so widely distributed, as to have rendered a monopoly of
either, equivalent to that of antiquity, impracticable; and if an aristocracy ought to have
existed, whilst it possessed such a monopoly,
it ought not also to exist, because this monopoly
is irretrievably lost. The distribution of wealth
produced by commerce and alienation, is equal
to that of knowledge and virtue, produced by
printing; but as the first distribution might be
artificially counteracted, with a better prospect
of success than the latter, aristocracy has abandoned a reliance on a monopoly of virtue, renown and abilities, and resorted wholly to a

monopoly of wealth, by the system of paper and patronage. Modern taxes and frauds to collect money, and not ancient authors, will therefore afford the best evidence of its present character.

A distribution of knowledge, virtue and wealth, produced public opinion, which ought now to govern for the reason urged by Mr. Adams in favour of aristocracy. It is the declaration of the mass of national wealth, virtue and talents. Power, in Mr. Adams's opinion, ought to follow this mass in the hands of a few, because it is the ornament of society. It is unimportant whether an aristocracy is a natural, physical or moral effect, if its cause, by means, natural, physical or moral, may be lost or transferred. Whenever the mass of wealth, virtue and talents, is lost by a few and transferred to a great portion of a nation, an aristocracy no longer retains the only sanctions of its claim; and wherever these sanctions deposit themselves, they carry the interwoven power. By spreading themselves so generally throughout a nation, as to be no longer compressible into a legislative chamber, or inheritable by the aid of perpetuity and superstition, these antient sanctions of aristocracy, become the modern sanctions of public opinion. And as its will (now the rightful sovereign upon the self-same principle, urged in favor of the best founded aristocracy) can no longer be obtained through the medium of an hereditary order, the American invention of applying the doctrine of responsibility to magistrates, is the only one yet discovered for effecting the same object, which was effected by an aristocracy, holding the mass of national virtue, talents and wealth. This mass governed through such an aristocracy. This mass has searched for a new organ, as a medium for exercising the sovereignty, to which it is on all sides allowed to be entitled; and this medium is representation.

When the principles and practice of the American policy come to be considered, one subject of inquiry will be, whether public opinion, or the declaration of the mass of national virtue, talents and wealth, will be able to exercise this its just sovereignty, in union with the system of paper and patronage. If not, it is very remarkable, that this system, denominated the aristocracy of the third age, is equally inimical to Mr. Adams's principles and to mine. We both assign political power to the mass of virtue, talents and wealth in a nation. He only contends for an aristocracy from a supposition that it must possess this mass, and be the only organ of its will; I acknowledge the sovereignty of these qualities, deny their residence in a minority compressible into an aristocracy, and contend for a different organ. In order to discover whether the aristocracy of paper and patronage, is a good organ for expressing the will of the sovereign we have agreed upon, let us return to England, and consider, whether the revolution, which finally destroyed the aristocracy of the second age, and established that of the third, has placed the government in the hands of the wealth, virtue and talents of the nation, or subjected it to the influence of public opinion.

If you had seen the vulture preying upon the entrails of the agonized Prometheus, would you have believed, though Pluto himself had sworn it, that the vulture was under the control of Prometheus? If you could not have believed this, neither can you believe, that the concubinage between a government, and the system of paper and patronage, is an organ of national opinion, or of the wealth, virtue and talents of the nation, and not a conspiracy between avarice and ambition; because, it is as impossible that a nation should derive pleasure from a government founded in the principle of voraciousness, as the man from the laceration of his bowels.

It has been said, that paper and office are property; and as by their means, a minority may bring into its coffers, the whole profit of national labour, so it ought to be considered as the nation. Had Prometheus fattened by being fed upon by the vulture, it would have given some colour to this ingenious deception.

Again it has been said, that the system of paper and patronage encourages commerce, agriculture, manufactures and conquest; it aggravated the misery of Prometheus, that his liver was made to grow for the gratification of a harpy, without appeasing its voracity.

The difficulty of producing a correct opinion of the cause and consequences of the new-born aristocracy of paper and patronage, surpasses the same difficulty in relation to the aristocracies of the first and second ages, as far as its superior importance. The two last being substantially dead, their bodies may be cut up, the articulation of their bones exposed, and the convolution of their fibres unravelled; but whenever the intricate structure of the system of paper and patronage is attempted to be dissected, we moderns surrender our intellects to yells uttered by the living monster, similar to those with which its predecessors astonished, deluded, and oppressed the world for three thousand years. The aristocracy of superstition defended itself by exclaiming, the Gods! the temples! the sacred oracles! divine vengeance! and Elysian fields!—and that of paper and patronage exclaims, national faith! sacred charters! disorganization! and security of property!

Let us moderns cease to boast of our victory over superstition and the feudal system, and our advancement in knowledge. Let us neither pity, ridicule or despise the ancients, as dupes of frauds and tricks, which we can so easily discern; lest some ancient sage should rise from his grave, and answer, "You moderns are duped by arts more obviously fraudulent, than those which deceived us. The agency of the Gods was less discernable, than the effects of paper and patronage. We could not see, that the temporal and eternal pains and pleasures, threatened and promised by our aristocracy, could not be inflicted or bestowed by it; you see throughout Europe the effects of your aristocracy. Without your light, oracles were necessary to deceive us; with the help of printing, and two detections, you are deceived by aristocracy in a third form, although it pretends neither to the divinity nor heroism claimed by its two first forms. And under these disadvantages, the impositions of our aristocracy were restrained within narrower bounds than those of yours. Did any aristocracy of the first age, extend its annual spoliation from one to thirty-five millions of pounds sterling, in less than a century?"

. . . The effect of opposite interests, one enriched by and governing the other, correctly follows its cause. One interest is a tyrant, the other its slave. In Britain, one of these interests owes to the other above ten hundred millions of pounds sterling, which would require twelve millions of slaves to discharge, at eighty pounds sterling each. If the debtor interest amounts to ten millions of souls, and would be worth forty pounds sterling round, sold for slaves, it pays twelve and an half per centum on its capitation value, to the creditor interest, for the exclusive items of debt and bank stock. This profit for their masters, made by those who are called freemen, greatly exceeds what is generally made by those who are called slaves. But as

nothing is calculated except two items, by including the payments for useless offices, excessive salaries, and fat sinecures, it is evident that one interest makes out of the other, a far greater profit than if it had sold this other, and placed the money in the most productive state of usance.

Such is the freeman of paper and patronage. Had Diogenes lived until this day, he would have unfledged a cock once more, and exhibited him as an emblem, not of Plato's man, but of a freeborn Englishman. Had Sancho known of a paper stock system, he would not have wished for the government of an island inhabited by negroes. Has Providence used this system to avenge the Africans, upon the Europeans and Americans?

Whatever destroys an unity of interest between a government and a nation, infallibly produces oppression and hatred. Human conception is unable to invent a scheme, more capable of afflicting mankind with these evils, than that of paper and patronage. It divides a nation into two groups, creditors and debtors; the first supplying its want of physical strength, by alliances with fleets and armies, and practising the most unblushing corruption. A consciousness of inflicting or suffering injuries, fills each with malignity towards the other. This malignity first begets a multitude of penalties, punishments and executions, and then vengeance.

A legislature, in a nation where the system of paper and patronage prevails, will be governed by that interest, and legislate in its favour. It is impossible to do this, without legislating to the injury of the other interest, that is, the great mass of the nation. Such a legislature will create unnecessary offices, that themselves or their relations may be endowed with them. They will lavish the revenue, to enrich themselves. They will borrow for the nation, that they may lend. They will offer lenders great profits, that they may share in them. As grievances gradually excite national discontent, they will fix the yoke more securely, by making it gradually heavier. And they will finally avow and maintain their corruption, by establishing an irresistible standing army, not to defend the nation, but to defend a system for plundering the nation.

An uniform deception resorted to by a funding system, through legislative bodies, unites with experience in testifying to its uniform corruption of legislatures. It professes that its object is to pay debts. A government must either be the fraudulent instrument of the system, or the system a fraudulent instrument of a government; or it would not utter this falsehood to deceive the people.

This promise is similar to that of protecting property. It promises to diminish, and accumulates; it promises to protect, and invades. All political oppressors deceive, in order to succeed. When did an aristocracy avow its purpose? Sincerity demanded of that of the third age, the following confession: "Our purpose is to settle wealth and power upon a minority. It will be accomplished by national debt, paper corporations, and offices, civil and military. These will condense king, lords and commons, a monied faction, and an armed faction, in one interest. This interest must subsist upon another, or perish. The other interest is national, to govern and pilfer which, is our object; and its accomplishment consists in getting the utmost a nation can pay. Such a state of success can only be maintained by armies, to be paid by the nation, and commanded by this minority; by corrupting talents and courage; by terrifying timidity; by inflicting penalties on the weak and friendless, and by distracting the majority with deceitful prefessions. That with which our project commences, is invariably a promise to get a nation out of debt; but the invariable effect of it is, to plunge it irretrievably into debt."

The English system of paper and patronage, has made these confessions by the whole current of its actions for a century, and laboured to hide them by its words. That guilt should eternally endeavour to beguile, is natural. Is it also natural, that innocence should eternally be its dupe? Is it the character of virtue, in spite of common sense, to shut her eyes upon truth, and open her ears to falsehood?

. . . The only two modes extant of enslaving nations, are those of armies and the system of paper and patronage. The European nations are subjected by both, so that their chains are doubly riveted. The Americans devoted their effectual precautions to the obsolete modes of title and hierarchy, erected several barriers against the army mode, and utterly disregarded the mode of paper and patronage. The army mode was thought so formidable, that military men are excluded from legislatures, and limited to charters or commissions at will; and the paper mode so harmless, that it is allowed to break the principle of keeping legislative, ex-

ecutive and judicative powers separate and distinct, to infuse itself into all these departments, to unite them in one conspiracy, and to obtain charters or commissions for unrestricted terms, entrenched behind publick faith, and out of the reach, it is said, of national will; which it may assail, wound and destroy with impunity. This jealousy of armies, and confidence in paper systems, can only be justified, if the following argument in its defence is correct.

"An army of soldiers have a separate interest from the nation, because they draw their subsistence from it, and therefore they will combine for their own interest against the national interest; but an army of stockjobbers have no such separate interest, and will not combine. Soldiers admitted into the legislature, would legislate in favour of soldiers; but stockjobbers will not legislate in favour of stockjobbers. Soldiers may use our arms to take our money; but stockjobbers cannot use our money to take our arms. Soldiers may adhere to a chief in preference to the nation, as an instrument for gratifying their avarice and ambition upon the nation; but stockjobbers have no avarice nor ambition to be gratified, and will not therefore adhere to a chief for that purpose. Soldiers are dangerous, because they assail the liberty of a nation by open force; stockjobbers harmless, because they do it by secret fraud. All are jealous of soldiers, and therefore they will not be watched; few are jealous of stockjobbers, and therefore they will be watched. Many instances have occurred of the oppressions by the army system; one instance only of a perfect capacity in the paper system for oppression can be adduced; and as that has lasted only a single century, it would be precipitate to detect and destroy the aristocracy of paper and patronage, in less time than was requisite to detect and destroy those of superstition and the feudal system."

Alas! is it true, that ages are necessary to understand, whilst a moment will suffice to invent, an imposture? Is it true, that the example of their venerable ancestor, groaning for a century under the oppressions of this modern system of aristocracy, is incapable of awakening the Americans; and that they themselves must also become a beacon for the benefit of a more enlightened era? Caesar profited by the failure of Marius, in the art of enslaving his country; will no nation ever profit by the failure of another in the art of preserving its liberty? . . . Thus whilst a paper system pretends to make a nation rich and potent, it only makes a minority of that nation rich and potent, at the expense of the majority, which it makes poor and impotent. Wealth makes a nation, a faction or an individual, powerful; and therefore if paper systems extracted the wealth they accumulate from the winds, and not from property and labour, they would still be inimical to the principles of every constitution, founded in the idea of national will; because the subjection of a nation to the will of individuals or factions, is an invariable effect of great accumulation of wealth; but when the accumulation of a minority, impoverishes a majority, a double operation rivets this subjection.

The delusion of all paper projects is at once detected by turning upon them their own doctrine. All boast of doing good to a nation. Suppose a nation was to decline this beneficence, and propose to reward it, by doing good to paper projects, exactly in the same way they propose to benefit the nation; that is, by taking from the owners of stock, their income, and consigning over to them the taxes and the credit attached to the debtor, with the blessing of a paper circulation; the credulity which believes, that these institutions do really impose upon nations debt and taxes, direct and indirect, from motives of public good, would be presently cured by the faltering tongues, the wan faces, and the distressing lamentations, which a proposition for this exchange would produce. These paper projects which pretend to be blessings to nations, would be deprecated as curses by themselves, if the case was thus altered.

It is said that paper systems being open to all, are not monopolies. He who has money, may buy stock. All then is fair, as every man (meaning however only every monied man) may share in the plunder.

Every man may enlist in an army, yet an army may enslave a nation. A monopoly may be open to a great number, yet those who do engage in it, may imbibe the spirit of faction; but it cannot be open to all, because no interest, which must subsist upon a nation, can consist of that nation; as I cannot fatten myself by eating myself. If every citizen should go into an army, it would transform that army into the nation itself, and its pay and subsistence would cease; in like manner the profits of paper, were they generally or universally distributed, would cease; because each citizen would be his own paymaster. Had the objection been as true in practice as it is plausible in theory, these answers suffice to prove, that it would have converted paper aristocracies into paper domocracies.

The reason, however, for this apparent common power of becoming a stockjobber, consists in the constant necessity felt for recruits by every species of aristocracy. The Mamalukes of Egypt have sufficient penetration to discover this. No individual, nor an inconsiderable number of individuals, can enslave a nation. A despot raises soldiers by bounties. This system is also recruited by bounties. The soldier sometimes deserts, or takes part with the nation, after his bounty is spent; but the bounty of paper systems is so contrived, that it is perpetually going on, and anually repeated; so that the aristocracy of an oppressive system, never deserts or takes part with the nation, as the army of an oppressive prince has sometimes done.

Where avarice and ambition beat up for recruits, too many are prone to enlist. Kings, ministers, lords and commons will be obliged to command the army, and share in the plunder, or submit to be cashiered. The makers and managers of aristocracy, gamble with a certainty of winning, for a stake extorted and increased by themselves. If they deposit their penny, they draw a pound, and augment their power. The system of paper and patronage, freights annual gallions for a government and a faction, at a national mine called industry; and bestows on the people such blessings, as those enjoy who dig up the ores of Peru and Mexico. The receivers of the profit drawn from this mine, reap wealth and power; the earners reap armies, wars, taxes, monopolies, faction, poverty and ten hundred millions of debt. This is an English picture. America hopes that her governors and citizens are neither ambitious nor avaricious, and upon this solid hope, is committing the custody of her liberty to the same system. Oh! America, America, thou art the truly begotten of John Bull! It is not proposed to follow this system throughout its deleterious effects upon the morals of private citizens. But if it is capable of corrupting publick officers, or government itself, a remark to exhibit its superior malignity over the aristocracies of the first and second ages, cannot be suppressed. The manners and principles of government, are objects of imitation, and influence national character. The aristocracy of the first age, exhibited sanctity, veneration for the Gods, and moral virtues, to the publick view; not unuseful in

their operation, and particularly so in times of
ignorance; that of the second, the virtues of
generosity, honour and bravery, not unuseful
in softening barbarism into civilization, by the
magnanimity and even the folly of chivalry;
but what virtues for imitation appear in the
aristocracy of the present age? Avarice and ambition being its whole soul, what private morals
will it infuse, and what national character will
it create? A consciousness of fraud, impels it
towards perpetration. By ever affecting, and
never practising sincerity, it teaches a perpetual
fear of treachery, and a perpetual effort to in-
snare. Its end is distrust and fraud, which convert the earth into a scene of ambuscade, man
against man. Its acquisitions inflict misery,
without bestowing happiness; because they can
only feed a rapacity which can never be satisfied, and a luxury which cannot suppress remorse. In relation to private people, this system may only encourage idleness, teach swindling, ruin individuals, and destroy morals; but
allied to a government, it presents a policy of
such unrivalled malignity, as only to be expressed by saying, "the government is a speculator upon the liberty and property of the nation."

. . . Hereafter, when our constitution is considered, the competency of its security against
the aristocracy of paper and patronage, or that
of the present age, will be computed; and then
it is not meant to shrink from the consideration
of this species of aristocracy, in reference to the
United States; on the contrary, an effort will be
made to place it in several points of view, inadmissible, whilst considering it in relation to
England.

At present, supposing that the paper and
patronage system of England, is a modern political power of vast force; that it has corrupted
or supplanted the old English form of government; that its oppressions overspread the land;
that its principles are vicious, and its designs
fraudulent; we will proceed to inquire what
ought to be done.

Superstition and noble orders were defended by the strongest sanctions within the
scope of human inventions. Penalties, temporal
and eternal; splendour, pomp and honour;
united to terrify, to dazzle, to awe and to flatter the human mind; and the real or external
virtues of charity and meekness, hospitality
and nobleness of mind, induced some to love
that, which most hated, and all feared. Yet the
intellect of the last age pierced through the delusions, behind which the oppressions of hierarchy and nobility had taken shelter.

We pity the ancients for their dullness in discovering oppressions, so clearly seen by ourselves now that they are exploded. We moderns; we enlightened Americans; we who have
abolished hierarchy and title; and we who are
submitting to be taxed and enslaved by patronage and paper, without being deluded or terrified by the promise of heaven, the denunciation of hell, the penalties of law, the brilliancy
and generosity of nobility, or the pageantry and
charity of superstition.

A spell is put upon our understandings by
the words "publick faith and national credit,"
which fascinates us into an opinion, that fraud,
corruption and oppression, constitute national
credit; and debt and slavery, publick faith.
This delusion of the aristocracy of the present
age, is not less apparent, than the ancient divinity of kings, and yet it required the labours
of Locke and Sidney to detect that ridiculous
imposture.

Publick faith is made with great solemnity
to mount the rostrum, and to pronounce the
following lecture:

"Law enacted for the benefit of a nation, is
repealable; but law enacted for the benefit of
individuals, though oppressive to a nation, is a
charter, and irrepealable. The existing generation is under the tutelage of all past generations,
and must rely upon the responsibility of the
grave for the preservation of its liberty. Posterity, being bound by the contracts of its ancestry, in every case which diminishes its
rights, man is daily growing less free by a doctrine which never increases them. A government intrusted with the administration of publick affairs for the good of a nation, has a right
to deed away that nation for the good of itself
or its partisans, by law charters for monopolies
or sinecures; and posterity is bound by these
deeds. But although an existing generation can
never reassume the liberty or property held
by its ancestor, it may recompense itself by
abridging or abolishing the rights of its descendant."

Such is the doctrine which has prevented
the eye of investigation from penetrating the
recesses of the aristocracy of the present age.
It simply offers the consolation of softening
injuries to ourselves by adding to the wretchedness of our descendants. By this artifice,
(the offspring of interest and cunning,) whenever men cut off their shackles with the sword,

they are riveted on again by the pen. A successful war, to avenge a small and temporary injury, is made to gain a great and lasting calamity. Victory over enemies is followed by defeat from friends. And an enemy destroyed abroad, is only the head of an hydra, which produces two at home. This is not exaggeration, if the idea of the aristocracy of paper and patronage is not chimerical. And thence occur these curious questions: Can the United States kill one Englishman or Frenchman, without converting two at least of their own citizens, into members of this aristocracy? Which would be most dangerous and burdensome to the union, one of these foreigners abroad, or two of these aristocrats at home?

The best argument in favour of the mortgage of a nation to a faction, is, that it is a purchase; an argument however, which does not extend to the family of law charters in general. A few of a nation, have bought the nation. Caesar by plunder and rapine, amassed the means of buying or corrupting the Roman government; was his title to despotism over the Roman people therefore sound? If Jugurtha had been rich enough to buy Rome, ought the nation to have submitted to the sale, because the bargain was made with the government? If a freeman has no right to enslave his child by selling him, can one generation sell another? And if one generation has no right to sell another, can a government which exercises the double character of seller and buyer, in erecting the aristocracy of the present age, transform the most atrocious iniquity into political or moral rectitude, by writing in its forehead "publick faith?" Then let us acquit every thief, who assumes for his motto the words "honest man."

This kind of faith and honesty, have invented the opinion "that policy and justice require a law, beneficial to individuals at the expense of a nation, to exist for the period prescribed;" to sustain which, it is necessary to reverse the elemental political maxim "that the good of the whole, ought to be preferred to the good of a few." Government is erected for the purpose of carrying this maxim into execution, by passing laws for the benefit of a nation; and shall a violation of the purpose of its institution, by passing laws injurious to a nation, in creating or fostering the aristocracy of paper and patronage, be cleansed of its guiltiness, because individuals have become the accomplices of the government?

A law or a contract, prescribing an immoral action, is void. No sanction can justify murder, perjury or theft. Yet the murder of national liberty, the perjury of a traitorous government, and the theft of national wealth, by the gradual introduction of the aristocracy of the third age, are varnished into a gloss by a cunning dogma, capable even of dazzling men, so excessively honest as to put other men to death for petty thefts, committed to appease hunger or cover nakedness.

The same mouth will solemnly assert, that the principles of equity annul every contract, which defrauds an individual; and that justice or policy requires a catalogue of law charters which defraud a nation, to exist and have their effect.

This is owing to the artful conversion of good words, into knavish dogmas. It is not new, to see errour take refuge under the garb of truth. Superstition has in all ages called itself religion. Thus law charters, with the faithless design of enslaving a nation by the introduction of the aristocracy of the present age, crouch behind the good and honest words "publick faith and national credit," to prevent a nation from destroying that, which is destroying it. And they succeed; because we are as unsuspicious that a false and fraudulent dogma, is hidden under fair language, as that a well dressed gentleman indicates a thief.

To come at truth, we ought not to stop at a verbal investigation. We must consider whether the effects of every law and every measure, by whatever names the law or measure are called, are on the side of virtue or vice.

An irrepealable law charter is a standing temptation to governments to do evil, and an invitation to individuals to become their accessaries; by its help, a predominant party may use temporary power, to enact corporate or individual emoluments for itself, at the national expense. Successive parties will repeat the same iniquity; and even the outs or opposition will be corrupted, to do obeisance at the shrine of the dogma, that they also may reap of the fruit it bestows, when a nation shall fall into their hands; which upon every change of administration, will have its hopes of reform gratified, by new pillages under the sanction of publick faith and national credit.

This modern system of law charters, is founded in the same design, with the ancient system of a social compact. Under the sanction of social compact, governments have for-

merly tyrannised over nations. Under the sanction of law charters, governments now buy a
faction, rob nations of enormous wealth, and
soar beyond responsibility. The inviolability of
a social compact was the old dogma; the inviolability of law charters is the new; for effecting the same end. The last is however an
engine in the hands of avarice and ambition,
of power far superior to the first. It is able to
10 corrupt and pillage a nation without limit.
The first was an opinion unable to purchase
partisans; the last offers every thing to its
disciples, which can gratify pernicious passions, and meets arguments with bribes. Thus
a nation, which won self-government by exploding the doctrine of the antiquated compact dogma, may lose it again in the modern
law charter dogma, and thus a nation, which
thought it morally wrong to suffer slavery
20 from troops hired by clothes, pay and rations,
may be persuaded that it is morally right to
suffer slavery from troops hired by dividends,
interest upon stock, and protecting duty
bounties.

As the English began to emerge from Gothic
ignorance, the idea of liberty by compact, and
not of natural right, led them to extort charters
from their princes; but wofully is the doctrine
of deriving a right to liberty from charters,
30 turned upon this gallant nation. By allowing
them to bestow, it was discovered that they
could destroy. Such as diminish, and not those
which enlarge national freedom, have become
the sacred charters. The errour of parchment
liberty, has made liberty the creature of parchment. A government, good or bad, can easily
take away that liberty by charters, which was
created by charters. Before the idea of deriving
liberty from charter or compact became fash-
40 ionable, the evils produced by bad governments were temporary; now, slavery, as liberty
condescended to be, is created by charters, so
as to perpetuate these evils, and to hem in the
efforts of patriotism so narrowly, as to destroy
the effect of virtue in office.

By admitting that donations of publick property by a government to individuals, should irrevocably transform it into private property,
it is obvious that the stock of publick rights
50 will be continually whittled away. Tyranny is
only a partial disposition of publick rights, in
favour of one or a few. The system of paper
and patronage, bottomed upon charters and
commissions, enables avarice and ambition to
draw more extensively upon the national stock,

than any system hitherto invented. It can convert publick property into private, with unexampled rapidity, or transfer wealth and power
from the mass of a nation to a few. Its guilt is
made its sanction. Neither "private nor publick property" is allowed to be a sanction
against the frauds and invasions of paper and
patronage, until the fraud or invasion is committed; and then "private property" (good
words, as are "publick faith and national
credit") is converted into a dogma for the protection of this fraud and invasion. Titles, tythes,
feudal services, monasteries, South Sea and
Mississippi projects, funding and banking systems, sinecure offices, and every species of
fraud, monopoly and usurpation, call the pillages of private property, private property, and
generally contrive to make it so by laws or
armies.

But in the eye of justice, property, publick
or private, cannot be transferred by fraud. A
nation erects a government for the publick
benefit, and does not empower it to bring
about the aggrandisement of itself, and its
faction, to the publick detriment. If this is effected by a transfer of property, publick or
private, the transfer is fraudulent, and void; because the nation never empowered the government, by that or any other mode, to injure
its liberty or happiness. The principles of
moral rectitude, do not forbid a nation to resume power, usurped by a government; nor
property, chartered away to individuals, by
fraudulent laws; because otherwise they could
not resume just rights, since power and law
are the vehicles in which these rights are constantly taken away.

. . . Publick faith is the moral principle,
called upon to defend monopoly and law
charter, under the name of private property.
Let us consider what this sanction is in a free
government. If the government should solemnly, by law, enter into a contract with a
number of individuals, the object of which
was to diminish the liberty and wealth of the
people, by increasing the power and wealth of
the government and these individuals, does
publick faith require from the nation a fulfilment of this contract? If the question is answered in the negative, a correct definition of
publick faith, must comprise both a faithfulness to the publick good, and also a faithfulness in contracts with individuals; nor can these
two duties be made inconsistent with each
other by publick faith, without admitting it to

be a principle of a double character, sometimes good and sometimes bad. Because, if it compels the performance of one duty, by the breach of another; and if the duty required to be fulfilled, is trivial, compared with that required to be infringed; it would bestow on publick faith a mixed character, and even a prevalence of evil. Publick faith then, considered as a good moral principle, must either include and reconcile, a loyalty both to the publick good and to contracts with individuals; or if the former is not a duty imposed by publick faith, it must be a duty of superior and superseding obligation.

The construction of publick faith by monopoly, avarice and ambition, is precisely the reverse of this. They confine it to a fulfilment of every species of contract made by a government with individuals, especially if entered into for the purpose of gratifying themselves at the expense of a nation; and thus limited, consider it as the most sacred of all duties. And so far are these glossographers from considering publick faith as a good moral principle, that they make it enforce contracts, entered into for every conceivable vicious purpose; from those of betraying nations, armies, cities and forts, down to those of perjury, theft and assassination. Under this construction, whenever the publick good and a contract with an individual come in conflict, publick faith is made to decide, that the contract shall prevail; and thus its definition will come out, "national duty to suffer oppression, and lose its liberty, by laws, charters or contracts, made by a government for that purpose, provided they convey an interest to individuals." So soon as it is thus changed from a good to a vicious principle, its effects change also. From being a pledge of publick good, it becomes the protector of political fraud; it compels a nation to be an accomplice in its own ruin; it takes from it the right of self-preservation; and it becomes the modern subterfuge of the modern aristocracy.

Hitherto, in comparing the duty of a government to a nation, and to a law charter, the comparison has been exhibited in the most favourable light for the latter, by forbearing to insist upon any degree of criminality in a faction, which accepts of a charter from a government, injurious to a nation. It is, however, questionable, whether the priesthood were innocent, which executed the evil of hierarchy; or the barons, who sustained that of the feudal aristocracy; or the solicitors and holders of sinecure offices; or those who pilfer a nation by means of a law charter. If their accomplices are not guilty, tyrants themselves must be innocent.

Individuals may be aiders and abettors in projects replete with publick evil, without discerning their tendency; but the rarity of this case is evinced, by the tacit compact and union produced by such projects. This compact and union, disclose a thorough knowledge of the interest on one side, and the injury on the other, because it is the plain effect of profit; and a fear of losing profit can only be inspired by a conviction of committing an injury in its acquisition. This fear makes every individual who is conscious of drawing wealth from a nation unjustly, the friend and encomiast of the strongest power he can find; because power is the only protector of injustice. And if he cannot find a power strong enough to protect injustice, he will exert himself to erect one. When such a power exists, the more unfaithful it is to the publick good, the more its publick faith will be celebrated by those who receive the benefit of its unfaithfulness. Lewis the fourteenth, an ignorant, fanatical and tyrannical prince, was celebrated even by philosophers, because he robbed the French nation, to give them pensions.

Individuals, who do not derive their acquisitions from projects replete with publick evil, are never formed into a tacit compact or union, because, being unconscious of drawing gain from a nation unjustly, they have nothing to fear. Being unconscious of injustice, they are not naturally the friends and encomiasts of a power, strong enough to protect injustice. And deriving no benefit from the unfaithfulness of a government to the publick good, they will not celebrate a government for it. In order to see the force of this comparison, it is only necessary to conceive a society consisting of two classes, one made up of agriculturists, professions, trades and commerce, all unconnected with banking, funding and patronage; the other, of a funding system, bank charters, pensions and patronage. Which class would be the disciple and parasite of despotism? If this is discernible, the consequence of erecting this modern species of aristocracy is also discernible.

The exact similarity in nature and principle, between laws or charters establishing funding systems, banks, or sinecure profit of any kind;

and laws or charters establishing privileged orders or endowed hierarchies; appears in their common union with, and devotion to, a power capable of protecting injustice.

It is still objected "that unless laws, beneficial to individuals, though injurious to a nation, are supported, confidence in government will be destroyed, and national credit, lost." The doctrine amounts to this: "that it is good policy in a nation, to make a few individuals its masters or owners, to excite an inclination in these few individuals to lend it money, for a handsome premium and high interest." And this policy is literally pursued, by establishing a certain number of paper systems and charters, for drawing money from the nation directly or indirectly, in order to enable a few to lend a part of this money to the nation.

To this item of the value of a confidence "that laws and charters, injurious to a nation, but beneficial to individuals, will be maintained," must be added a corruption of manners, arising from the traffick between a government and a faction, for the objects of gratifying the ambition of one dealer, and the avarice of the other; and the customary violent and wretched parties, between the commencement of this confidence and its catastrophe.

On the other hand, a confidence that laws and charters injurious to a nation, will be repealed, whenever their pernicious tendency is discovered, will prevent the destructive evils generated by a contrary opinion; will enable honest governments to correct the frauds of knavish; and will check or even cure the malevolence of factions. And one effect of inestimable value flowing from this latter confidence, would be the detection and overthrow of an insidious sanction, under cover of which the modern aristocracy of paper and patronage, is fast fettering modern nations.

The analysis of aristocracy, by the first, the second, and the third ages, has been used for the purpose of a distinct arrangement of the arguments adduced to explain the superstitious, feudal, and fiscal modes of enslaving nations, by placing the powers in the hands of a minority; an effect, however produced, denominated aristocracy, throughout this essay. But it is not intended to insinuate, that the causes of aristocracy have generally acted singly; on the contrary, they more frequently unite.

It was necessary thoroughly to understand the most prominent causes of aristocracy, before we proceeded to a closer examination of our civil policy, and Mr. Adams's principles; in order to keep in mind that we have never seen a venerated and wealthy hierarchy, an army stronger than the nation, an endowed, titled and privileged order of men, or an incorporated, enriched or united faction, without having at the same time seen the aristocracy of the first, the second, or the third age. By recollecting this testimony, derived from universal experience, an inference, equivalent to mathematical certainty, "that such ends will eternally flow from such means," will unavoidably present itself.

Few would deny these premises or the inference, if it was proposed to revive oracles or feudal services. These causes of aristocracy are distinctly seen, because they do not exist. They have no counsel in court. They are, therefore, better understood than when they flourished. But both the premises and the inference are denied, when they implicate the aristocracy of paper and patronage. This cause of aristocracy is not seen, because it does not exist; and the more oppressive it shall become, the greater will be the difficulty of discovering its existence. The two first are exposed naked to our view; and the third, disguised in the garb of republicanism, and uttering patriotick words, joins the mob in kicking them about, by way of diverting the publick attention from itself. An opinion that aristocracy can only exist in the form of a hereditary order, or a hierarchy, is equivalent to an opinion, that the science of geometry can only be illustrated by a square or a triangle.   1814

THOMAS SKIDMORE

?–1832

THOMAS SKIDMORE was a mechanic who led the wage-earners' faction in the New York Workingman's Party which emerged in the late 1820's. An advocate of the ten-hour day and of the redistribution of wealth, Skidmore barely failed of election to the Assembly at Albany. He lost a large part of his following, however, to the advocates of universal guardian-schools. His bitterness is reflected, no doubt, in his doctrine that education must follow, rather than pave the way for, social reform. Apart from his daily paper, the *Friend of Equal Rights*, Skidmore's literary contribution was limited to *The Rights of Man to Property! Being a Proposition to Make it Equal among the Adults of the Present Generation* (1829), a rough-hewn book which shows that while Skidmore's social philosophy owed something to Thomas Paine, Robert Owen, and others, it was not without originality. Skidmore analyzed the exploitation of the workers by the rich and advocated a periodical redistribution of property and the prohibition of monopoly and the inheritance of wealth.

J. R. Commons and others, *History of Labor in the United States*, 2 vols., New York, 1918, vol. I, part II, chap. 3.
F. T. Carlton, "The Workingmen's Party of New York City; 1829–1831," in *Political Science Quarterly*, XXII (1907), 401–415.

» » *From:* THE RIGHTS OF MAN TO PROPERTY! « «

CHAPTER VIII

If a man were to ask me, to what I would compare the unequal distribution of property which prevails in the world, and has ever prevailed, I would say, that it reminds me of a large party of gentlemen, who should have a common right to dine at one and the same public table; a part of whom should arrive first, sit down and eat what they chose; and then, because the remaining part came later to dinner, should undertake to monopolize the whole; and deprive them of the opportunity of satisfying their hunger, but upon terms such as those who had feasted, should be pleased to prescribe.

Such, now, is the actual condition of the whole human race. Those who have gone before us, have been the first to sit down to the table, and to enjoy themselves, without interruption, from those who came afterwards; and not content with this enjoyment, they have disposed of the whole dinner, in such a manner, that nine-tenths of the beings that now people this globe, have not wherewith to dine, but

upon terms such as these first monopolisers, or those to whom they pretend they have conferred their own power as successors, shall choose to dictate. It is, as if, after dining till they were satisfied, a general scramble ensued, for what remained on the table; and those who succeeded in filling their pockets and other receptacles, with provisions, should have something to give to their children; but those who should have the misfortune to get none, or having got it, should lose it again, through fraud, calamity, or force, should have none for theirs, to the latest generation.

Such is the exact resemblance of the present order of things. Ye proud and rich possessors of the earth, look at this, and see if it be not so; and being so, and seeing that it is in your power to consent to a more *honorable* method of obtaining title to possession; say, if ye will not do so? I do not ask you, because it is in your power to confer any favor by giving such consent; for, this community, and every other, whenever they shall understand their rights, will have power enough in their own hands to do what they shall think fit, without seeking

for any acquisition from you; but because it will be more agreeable to your own true happiness, to give such consent freely; than, with the ill, but unavailing grace of reluctance. Three hundred thousand freemen, in this State, hold votes in their hands, which no power that you can command can take out; and of these freemen, more than two hundred and fifty thousand are men whom a preceding genera-
10 tion, together with yourselves and their own ignorance of their rights have conspired to place in situations such that they have no property in the State of which they are citizens; although their title to such property is as good as that of any man that breathes.

The first possession of this State, by the ancestors of its present inhabitants, was acquired by means, partaking of the nature of fraud, cunning, purchase and conquest, the
20 latter predominating; acting upon ignorance, and want of the power of resistance. So far is this emphatically true that in 1609, on Hudson's return from the place where Albany now is, whither he went, in the very first voyage which led to the discovery of the river which bears his name, "a considerable number of Indians had assembled at the head of the island, [Manhattan, on which this city now stands,] and as he approached, assailed him
30 with a volley of arrows from their canoes. By a few discharges of cannon, and muskets, which killed several of the savages, the attack was repulsed, and the assailants put to flight." So that from this historical circumstance, in the absence of other history which I need not refer to, it is evident that some previous aggression had provoked this attack.

But it is not necessary now to say more, in objection to titles obtained, by possession, by
40 conquest, or by any other imaginary species of acquisition. It has been shown already, throughout these pages, I trust to the satisfaction of the reader, that *title* to property exists for all; and for all alike; not because others have been; nor because they have *not* been; not because they had a certain being for a parent, rather than another being; not because they appear later, or earlier, on the stage of life, than others; not because of purchase, of
50 conquest, of preoccupancy, or what not; but BECAUSE THEY ARE: BECAUSE THEY EXIST. I AM; THEREFORE IS PROPERTY MINE; as much so as any man's, and that without asking any man's permission; without paying any man price;

without knowing or caring farther than as my equal right extends, whether any other human being exists, or not. Such is the language of nature; such is the language of right; and such are the principles which will justify any people in pulling down any government; which denies, even to a *single* individual of the human race, his possession, his real tangible possession, of this unalienable right of nature; or its unquestionable equivalent. How much more so, then, is it the duty of any such people, to destroy their own government, when *more than nine-tenths*, it may be, are deprived of rights which the Creator gave them, when he gave them existence?

Before I approach the termination of this work, it may not be amiss, that we ask ourselves, how has it happened, that wealth, or in other words, possession, has succeeded in making itself so unequal in the world as it appears; and appears, almost without exception, ever to have been? Immediately there are hundreds, who are ready to cry out, "It is conquest that has done it." And having so said, they seem to say, by the acquiescent manner in which it is spoken, that having been brought about by conquest, it is, therefore, impossible to undo what conquest has done.

Conquerors, undoubtedly, have their rights, as well as other men. But, these rights they have, *as men,* and not as conquerors. Often, no doubt, with the sword, they have won what truly belonged to them of right; but, then, it was not the sword that conferred the right; it only gave possession of it. The right existed before the sword was made to belong to him who wielded it. It came into existence with his own being, and departed only with it. But its *possession,* its *enjoyment,* often may depart without it, as *has* happened, I might say, almost for ever.

But how came conquest? How came men to be willing to hire themselves out to those whom we call chieftains? To be pierced with spears and arrows? To be penetrated with sword and ball for price? How came man to set himself up, as a mark to be shot at, for sixpence a-day? We need not go to remote ages to find an answer to this question. Ask only at our Forts; enquire only of our Navy, and they will tell you. They will say, that if society had given them all *a competence,* (or rather the means of acquiring it,) such as all men might have, under proper circumstances, they would not have consented to be where they are. And this would be true of all nations. Let the men of all nations be made equal among themselves, in point of property, and then will wars be immediately self-extinguished for ever. Keep up this unnatural inequality in wealth, which now exists, and they will exist as long as two nations shall be found in existence. Nay, more, they will exist even yet longer; for when only a single nation shall be found, civil wars will not fail to appear, as they do now, and from the same causes.

It appears, then, that conquerors, grow out of a state of unequal possession of property; and without such an unequal possession, they would never have existed. It appears, also, that by destroying this inequality every where, conquerors and warriors would be destroyed also. The question, then, again comes up; how came this inequality to exist? How had it beginning? For we can all easily understand how it would continue unequal, and the inequality increase in magnitude after it has once had a beginning. For it is even proverbial that "money makes money"; whereas, the true proverb should be, that *man* makes money. It is quite as ridiculous to say, that "money makes money," as it would be to say that one plantation makes another. Between the owners of these two plantations, there may be certain relations, by which the one owner comes to be possessed of both; but still it is an absurdity of the grossest kind, to say that one plantation ought to have, that is, makes, or earns another. However, as the world now is, "money makes money." And so true is it, that if a little globe of gold, as large as that of the head of a large brass pin, say the one-sixteenth of an inch in diameter, were let out on compound interest, at 5 percent a year, in a little more than 1300 years it would amount to another solid globe of gold, greater than this whole earth! Interest, therefore, is like a magnet, which daily gains more and more power, as you append more weight to it; and that without doing anything to acquire or increase this power. But, to recur again to our question: How did inequality begin?

To ascertain, we must go to those countries, in whose first settlement conquest had no agency; and when we have arrived there, we must ascend to the earliest age of the people who inhabit it. What shall we find there? No history can tell us anything; for at such periods of time, men were not able, and if they were

able, had no motive to write one. We are, therefore, left to follow nature by analogy; and from the little we do know, to infer what we do not know.

At that early age, we may understand a great extent of country before us. We may understand, also, that there were very few people. We may consider them ignorant and helpless. Their resources of subsistence would be the fruits and roots of trees; animals and fish; and their clothing, as far as they might have any, would be, perhaps, the skins of the beasts they had killed for food. Habitation they would have none; or if any, it would be for rest, a cave, or a hollow tree, or the recess of some superimpending rock. If, in process of time, they should learn, as they would, that the animals on which they subsist, might be rendered docile and tractable, it would lead them to discover that those which they now take in the chase, with great labor and difficulty, and frequently at great intervals of time, producing great distress from hunger; might be bred up in a domestic way; and they would adopt the practice. This change would lead them from the state of hunters, to that of shepherds. At first, these would locate themselves no where. They would ramble about for food: and as there is supposed to be a great superabundance of territory, and but few people, there would be no objection, because there would be no collision of interest; and, therefore, there would arise no investigation of rights. For rights are never investigated, whenever all have more than they know what to do with. It is only when privation begins to bear hard, and oppression to manifest itself, that inquiry into rights begins to take place.

But if they did not, at this stage of their existence, inquire into the rights of this shepherd, to this *temporary* location; and of that, to another; because there was no need of it; so also did they not *inquire,* (as men, now, do not inquire into their rights,) why one should have a larger flock than another; or why one shepherd dying, a certain person, or persons, rather than any other person, or persons, should become the owner of it. All had enough for their own simple wants, and this was sufficient to render inquiry unnecessary. If, indeed, any inquiry could have arisen, at that early period, it is not to be doubted, that the principle of equal rights would have prevailed; and this, if necessary, would have proceeded to the greatest extent possible. Thus, not only would it have been forbidden to any one to monopolize one location rather than another; a larger flock rather than a smaller; but the right, in preference to another, to sleep even in a hollow tree, would have been contested, and contested with the same zeal and animosity, as that with which armies now contend for the acquisition or preservation of empire.

10   In progress of time it was discovered, that these flocks could be raised with less labor and risk, if *cultivation* were added to their store of resources. But this required a *permanent* location. It called upon the shepherd to fix upon some place. In this there would be no difficulty. For inasmuch as territory is very abundant, and population thin, there is room enough, and more than enough, for all. Why should they differ? Differ they did not; and not differing,
20   no inquiry was made, why *this* location should belong to *one* rather than to another. Had any such investigation arisen, as a matter of course, the affair must have been settled by convention. Agreement must have assigned this to this; and that to the other; and no one could have said, such and such are mine, to your exclusion. Battle would have been the consequence of such a declaration, and the right of the strongest would have prevailed; but it is
30   not to be known here, whether it would have been the right of justice. Yet, during this natural progress of things, experience has not taught them; they do not perceive, the future tenacity with which possession, *now simply not objected to,* will be retained, on the principle, as it will be called, of right in the holder, by virtue of this same possession.

During all this time, population increases; but increases slowly. Deaths happen. Parents
40   more or less keep their children around them. When the former die, as there is little wealth anywhere, little or no inquiry is started, as to whose are the flocks that the father possessed? Probably none at all. Land is abundant every where; and all have opportunity to have flocks of their own, and to cultivate, little as they may do, fields of their own. The children are, therefore, left in possession.

Nor, if two shepherds immediately adjacent
50   to each other, should die, at the same time, one having, it may be, five children, and the other only one; would inquiry arise why the one child should have the flocks of the one father, and the five children have only the flocks of the other father? In general among all such nations, and I believe, always, hospitality prevails, to a great extent, and if need should arise, for the numerous family to receive of the flocks of the richer son, hospitality would afford it. Besides, land still greatly abounding, new locations would be taken, new flocks reared, and new fields cultivated; without any investigation of their actual original rights.

I said, fields would be cultivated; but the tillage they would undergo, would hardly deserve the name of cultivation. Every thing would be extremely rude. Nor, in most cases, would those fields have any fences. The locations would be *without lines* or *limits*. There would be no boundaries, for the simple reason that there is yet more of soil than any of them want. If fence be made at all, at this period, it is such, perhaps, as that which may be sufficient to inclose their flocks, and keep them from straying, while their owner sleeps.

The handicraft arts would begin to make some progress. Accidental circumstances would give some much more taste and skill, in their prosecution, than others could acquire. This superior taste and skill would be turned to account, to supply the wants of their possessor. He would look less to land, and the ordinary resources, than others are obliged to do. He would soon become indifferent, more or less, to the possession of the soil. By imitation, too, his children and associates would, more or less, adopt his mode of life, and acquire similar facility in the same pursuits. If they did not, they still could get land as much as they might want.

In this way, society advances in numbers. The arts also advance in number, perfection, and the population engaged in them; and still there is land enough for all, and more. But they find it in their common interest to divide, almost without knowing that they have done so, their occupations. Still the principle prevails, and gains strength, that whoever is near the dying man, at and about the latter part of his life, succeeds to his possessions. Nor is there yet any great harm in it: for there would be very little alteration produced for the common benefit, if the attendants upon the dying man, (being generally his children,) should abandon his location, and take another. For as yet there is more land than any and all want.

The children of those, too, who pursue handicraft trades, succeed to the possession of their father's effects; because the principle is seen to be similar; and because it is perceived, that they will better understand the use of them; and can better employ them in the satisfaction of the wants of others.

In the course of time, however, land is taken up so much, that there begins to arise some inquiry as to the *extent* of rights; none, however, as it regards the rights themselves. Long established custom having sanctioned the latest, as well as the earliest locations, it does not occur to them, to go back to periods of times anterior to their first fixation. All they conceive they have to do, is to assign *limits* or *boundaries* to such locations, as they now find them; and this, of course, is done, by what may be called the public authority. They lose sight of that original question, which they would have had to discuss, if, instead of coming through this long and tedious process, it may be, of some thousand years, to their present condition, in point of numbers, and knowledge; they had just arrived, for the first time, to the possession of the territory they now occupy. In the latter event, they would have to enquire, why this location, rather than another, should belong to this man; or why another should belong to a second instead of a third; and why also a son or brother, rather than any other person, should have it, or either, after the assigned owner has left it. All these are questions, now, *which they do not discuss;* and for the simple reason, there is no subject requiring their interposition, but that of *boundaries* or *limits,* to each man's possessions. As yet there is land, there is property enough for all; and therefore, again, they do not enquire about their rights.

At the same time, too, that limits are assigned to these locations, they are made transmissible, like ordinary personal property; and probably now, or before this time, money is invented.

Here a great change takes place. Population continues to increase; and now they can find no more unsettled land. Of if they can, they must go farther for it, than they are disposed, or are able to afford the means necessary. Sooner than do this, they prefer to enter into a treaty with him or those who have, and may spare. For the first time, the land-holder begins to feel that he has power. He tastes the advantage of it; and his thirst increases for more. Here, then, has avarice begun. Nor could it begin, until some human being was found, out of whose distress, arising in consequence of *his wanting possessions, such as his fellows*

enjoy, the sweets of another's labor, were to be extracted.

Necessity arising from a deprivation of their natural and original right to property, compels many to make a treaty, whereby they surrender a portion; a small portion, at first, it is true, of their labor. Numbers continue to increase, but the land itself does not increase. Greater and greater exactions are made, till, at last, they become so great that more cannot be given; for more is not in being to be given. Still population increases yet more; and men, needy and wretched; finding that they cannot obtain the means of supporting life, but by engaging in the interest of some large possessor, who has cause of quarrel with another, *he consents;* and thus do we see the origin of the soldier. And so does this state of things continue to increase, in inflicting misery and wretchedness upon the race, till it arrives at the condition in which we now see mankind suffering.

In all the principles of the rights of property which are thus seen to have been almost insensibly adopted, *there is not one which has been adopted on any consideration, correct or otherwise, of its own merits.* Usage has done every thing. Custom, practice, habit, has made all the law; and made it at times, and under circumstances, in which it was of *no consequence to the generation then being,* whether the *principles involved* in the custom, were good in themselves, or not; whether they would be productive of immense injury or not, when they should come to have a dense population to act upon; whether they were consistent with the rigid rights of their own generation, or not; whether they preserved the rights of posterity, or sacrificed them with a most unsparing hand. To them, it was all the same, whether they had good principles, or bad, *or none at all.* And the latter was the fact. For it is not to be said that any *principle* prevails, where no investigation is had, of the effects which the practice, whatever it may be, will produce, when carried out to the fullest extent.

Thus, in detail, do we see, how the present state of things has had its origin. In the origin of the soldier, the material of conquest, do we see also, the origin of every other miserable and dependent human being. And when conquest has once created for itself an existence; how frightfully rapid does it transfer into its own keeping, as it were, the whole property of the globe. Look at the early history of this country, and see how vast are the possessions that owe their origin more or less, to this source. Look, also, at South America. Is there any legitimacy of title in all this? And now, that suffrage, and the printing press, have come to the redemption of man's rights; shall not man undo the wrongs of the sword? Shall he not correct those errors that gave the sword its existence and its power? Shall not man, now, even at this late date, when myriads of millions have gone to their graves, without ever having once enjoyed their rights; shall not man, now, rise in the majesty of his strength, and claim that which as much belongs to him, as does his life and liberty?

Let it not be said, that man is yet unfit to enjoy these rights. Who, or what is it, that has made him so? Is it not the very evil of which I am speaking, *if it be anything?* And is it to be said that man is to be made fit, by keeping him under the operation of the same cause that has made him otherwise? Besides, why should it be said, that man's right to property, in the light in which I present it, his real and true right, is more to be kept from his possession and enjoyment, than a right in the same person even, to property coming to him in the ordinary way? No man, now, undertakes to say, that an heir at law, as now the law is among us, shall not come into possession of a legacy, because people, whoever they may be, choose to say he is unfit to receive it. Even if he be truly unfit, he nevertheless receives it, by way of guardian or trustee. Why then is it to be said, that men generally shall not have their rights, in the acceptation in which I understand them, if they shall be of opinion, that this acceptation is correct, on similar terms? Ask *them*, when they shall have made up their minds, what their rights *are*, if they are to be kept out of their possession, by any such frivolous pretexts?

But not to treat these frivolous pretexts either with a levity or a severity unbecoming our subject, it would be easy, I think, to show, in any age, and particularly the present, that the poor and the middling classes, those whose condition would be benefited by the adoption of the system recommended in this work, are *now* possessed of higher intellectual, and better moral acquirements and habits, then belong to those whom we call rich. And the proof is, as it regards the comparison of *knowledge,* both theoretical and practical, between the two parties, that if, this day, their opportunities of displaying it, were made equal, by making property equal, those who now fill the lower ranks in life, would live better and happier, on the same amount of exertion, than those who fill the higher. This, then, I take it, is evidence of the fact. For if knowledge be not that which enables us thus to live better and happier, I have yet to learn in what it consists. Any knowledge of a character different from this, I apprehend, is not worth having, and deserves to be considered as either worthless or hostile to human happiness. He, therefore, is surely no friend to the race, who, on any such unfounded pretence, as that of unfitness, want of knowledge, etc. etc. objects to the *immediate* enjoyment, by the numerous class of whom I am speaking, of their right of property, as well as of every other right. And as to the question of comparative *morality* of the two classes, every one knows that the poorer is the most virtuous.

Besides, how ridiculously absurd must those political physicians appear, who shall oppose, or attempt to *postpone* such enjoyment of their rights by the great mass of the people, until they shall receive as the phrase is, the benefit of education. If they be sincere in their belief that such education is so very indispensable as a previous step to this enjoyment; and that the people are not now sufficiently instructed, let me ask them how, under present circumstances, is it ever *possible* to give it? Is a family, where both parents and children are suffering daily, in their animal wants; where excessive toil is required to obtain the little they enjoy; where the unkind and the unfriendly passions, generated by such a wretched condition of things, reign with full sway; is such a family in a situation to receive instruction? Even if the children *attend* public institutions of education, as punctually as may be wished, where is that equality of rank and condition, as well between their parents as between themselves, which is so necessary to banish even from among children, those envious remarks on dress, etc. etc. which now render our public schools in a measure abortive? Political dreamers! Reformers, if ye prefer that I should call you so! Feed first the hungry; clothe first the naked, or ill-clad; provide comfortable homes for all; by hewing down colossal estates among us, and equalizing all property; take care that the animal wants be supplied first; that even the *apprehension* of want be banished; and then will you have a good field and good subjects for education. Then will instruction be conveyed without obstacle; for the wants, the unsatisfied wants of the body will not interfere with it. In the mean time, let all remember, that those who undertake to *hold back* the people from their rights of property, as shown in this Work, until *education,* as they call it, can first be communicated, (though as already shown, they now know more of all that is valuable among men, than those who attempt to teach them,) either do not understand themselves, or pursue the course they *are* pursuing, for the purpose of diverting the people from the possession of these rights; that they may be held in bondage, even yet longer. It becomes the people to consider, and reflect, how far it is proper for them, *to suffer* themselves to be thus *decoyed* out of the enjoyment of their rights, even for a single hour, by any such fallacious pretexts. And fallacious they must undoubtedly appear, since the entire accomplishment of all that I have marked out in this work, as well the form of government it exhibits, as the method of bringing it into existence, is a matter as plain as that of the equal division of an estate, which the father of twelve children may have left, without a will, and therefore left to them all equally. These, although not one of them could read or write a letter or understand any thing of what is called science in all its thousand branches, could nevertheless divide it among them with the most equal and impartial justice. It would be the veriest nonsense to talk first of lecturing these heirs into knowledge; if you please, into the knowledge of Astronomy, Chemistry, Botany, Anatomy, Medicine, Painting, Sculpture, Mathematics, etc. etc. etc. knowledge which has no kind of necessary connection with any correct understanding of our rights, before giving them their property; but not more so, than it is now to say, that the people are not fit to have *their* property given to *them*, until they have first gone through a course of education.

The truth is, all men are fitted for the enjoyment of their rights, when they know what they are. And *until* that time, they do not desire them. They languish in misery and wretchedness; every new day being a new day of sorrow to them, when they do not perceive them; and seem rather disposed to charge their evil condition to some "bad luck," as they call it; to some imaginary decree of destiny; to some superstitious interference with

their happiness; than to any possession by others of property which belongs to *them*. Thus is it the case with the poor and the rich, passing now in review before us. The former does not imagine that it is the latter which renders his life miserable and wretched. He does not conceive that it is he who fills his cup with bitterness, and visits himself and his family with the afflictions of slavery. "Still, slavery, still thou art a bitter draught; and though thousands have been made to drink of thee," without knowing that thou comest in the shape of the rich man, holding in his hands that property which belongs to his fellow-men; "still thou art not the less bitter on that account." So would Sterne have said, and so say I. . . .

I approach, then, the close of this Work. I hasten to commit it to the hands, the heads and the hearts of those for whose benefit it is written. It is to them that I look, for the *power* necessary, to bring the system it recommends into existence. If they shall think I have so far understood myself, and the subject I have undertaken to discuss, as to have perceived, and marked out the path that leads them to the enjoyment of their rights, their interests and their happiness, IT WILL BE FOR THOSE WHO ARE SUFFERING THE EVILS, of which I have endeavored to point out the causes and the remedies, TO LEAD THE WAY. Those who are enjoying the sweets of the labor of others, will have no hearts to feel for the misery which the present system occasions. And the first throe of pain, which they *will* feel, will be that of *alarm*, that they are soon to be ordered to riot on the toils of others no more for ever! But those who *suffer*, will feel no cause of alarm. The very intensity of their sufferings, since now they understand their origin and cure, will add double vigor to their exertions to recover their rights. But let them understand, that much is to be done, to accomplish this recovery. IT IS TO BE THE RESULT OF THE COMBINED EXERTIONS, OF GREAT NUMBERS OF MEN. These, by no means, *now* understand their true situation; but when they do, they will be ready and willing to do what belongs to their happiness. If, then, there be truth; if there be reason; if there be force of argument, in the work which I thus commit to the hands of those for whose benefit it is written; let them read; let it be read; let it be conversed about, in the hearing of those whose *interest* it is, to hear whatever of truth, of reason, and argument it may contain; and *as often,* too, as there may be opportunity. Let them awake to a *knowledge* of their rights, and how they may be obtained, and they will not be slow (since it will *then* be so easy) to re-claim them.

Let the poor and middling classes under-stand that their oppressions come from the overgrown wealth that exists among them, on the one hand, and from entire destitution on the other; and that as this overgrown wealth is continually augmenting its possessions, in a rapid ratio, the public sufferings are continually augmenting also; and must continue to aug-ment, until the equal and unalienable rights of the people shall order otherwise. Let the parent reflect, if he be now a man of toil, that his children must be, ninety-nine cases in a hun-dred, slaves, *and worse,* to some rich proprie-tor; and that there is no alternative, but the change proposed. Let him not cheat himself with empty pretensions; for, *he who commands the property of a State, or even an inordinate portion of it,* HAS THE LIBERTY AND THE HAP-PINESS OF ITS CITIZENS IN HIS OWN KEEPING. And if there be some dozen, or fifty, or five hundred of these large proprietors, they are neither more nor less than so many additional keepers. He who can feed me, or starve me; give me employment, or bid me wander about in idleness; is my master; and it is the utmost folly for me to boast of being any thing but a slave.

In fine, let the people awake to their rights; let them understand in what they consist; let them see the course they must pursue to ob-tain them; let them follow up that course, by informing each as many as he can, his fellow citizens, of the truth which this Work contains; let all co-operate in the early and effectual accomplishment of the objects it recommends, and these objects will easily and speedily be achieved, and none will have labored in vain.

At the moment of taking leave of the reader, it occurs to me, that it would be well to add a single remark. If ever the principles of this Work are to prevail; if ever they are to find their way among men, and to restore to them their rights, it is only to be done, by each doing all he can, single and separately, to open the eyes of his fellows, to the perception of the evil that oppresses him, its origin and cure. While this is doing, and doing too in many parts of the State, of the Union, and the World,

at one and the same time; for such is the co-extensive and contemporary energy; with which the productions of the press operate; the rich, now and then, will cast their eyes on this Work; and they, too, will see that the system which it proposes, must, sooner, or later, take place. Ultimately, the whole of them will come to the same conclusion. So many of them as shall dread its approach, and shall not have the moral honesty to surrender up to the disposition of their fellow citizens, all that they have, will, of course, conceal as much as they can. And that which is the most desirable to conceal, and the easiest concealed, is money. Now, when-ever it shall appear, correctly or otherwise, it is no matter, to the rich generally, that the great mass of the people have very nearly awakened to the determination to resume their rights, and pursuant thereto, to order a General Division of property; these concealments will take place very suddenly; and, perhaps, to such an extent as to withdraw the precious metals entirely from circulation, out of the banks, as well as elsewhere. In such an event, the banks would be broken; and as there would be no circulating medium, all business would be in-stantly suspended. Those who now carry on extensive business, would have nothing with which to pay off their hands; and if they had, *they* might be as willing as others, to bury it in the earth, for the purpose of defrauding the community out of it.

In such an event, which is far from being impossible, the wished for change would arrive earlier, than is already anticipated in this work; and in manner somewhat different. For the reader understands, that I have intended, that a State Convention, to be chosen by the people, for the purpose, shall order the suspension of all business, which, by this operation of with-drawing all the gold and silver from circulation, and burying it in the earth by the rich, would be anticipated. If it should so happen, it will not be the fault of this Work, or of the great mass of the people, and may not be that even, of the majority of the rich; for even a very few of them, would be able to put away all the precious metals, that are to be found in the State; and as to other States, they could no more spare *their* precious metals than our-selves, without coming in contact with a simi-lar catastrophe; and of which, they too, will be in similar danger. Besides, as to personal prop-erty in the city of New-York, alone, there is probably more in value than all the specie money in the United States, twice, or even thrice told. So that it will be no difficult thing, if dishonesty prevail, even to a small extent among the rich, to bring about the withdrawal of which I am speaking.

Under such circumstances, it may be said, that the government has suddenly ceased to exist; that it has expired, as it were, in a fit of apoplexy; and it will then be incumbent on the people to organize a temporary committee of safety; and take care, immediately, that no property leaves the State, or is wasted, or destroyed, further than is necessary for subsistence; until a State Convention can be assembled, to form a new government, on principles corresponding with *all* the rights of man; and which, as it ensures his happiness, by preserving his equality, and that of all succeeding generations, we may confidently hope will be eternal.   1829

ANDREW JACKSON

1767–1845

JACKSON, if not as democratic as historians once regarded him, nevertheless represented many values which the masses cherished, and fought vehemently many issues dear to the "moneyed" interests. Convinced that the Second National Bank was an instrument of the financial aristocrats and that it menaced the people's control of their government, Jackson vetoed the bill which Congress had passed in the early summer of 1832 for the rechartering of the Bank. The veto message, which is given in part, is characteristic of Jackson's direct onslaughts, his rejection of the binding character of opinions of the Supreme Court, and his opposition to centralized financial institutions which controlled credit, and in which foreign capital was represented. Jackson's veto message was one of the dominant issues in the presidential campaign of 1832, and his re-election was interpreted as a popular mandate to make no concession to the Whig demand for the perpetuation of the National Bank.

J. D. Richardson, *A Compilation of the Messages and Papers of the Presidents 1789–1908*, 11 vols., New York, 1909.
Arthur M. Schlesinger, Jr., *The Age of Jackson*, Boston, 1945.
Bray Hammond, *Banks and Politics in the United States, from the Revolution to the Civil War*, Princeton, 1957.
Marquis James, *Andrew Jackson, The Border Captain*, Indianapolis, 1933.

» » *From:* JACKSON'S BANK VETO MESSAGE « «

Washington, July 10, 1832

To the Senate:

The bill "to modify and continue" the act entitled "An act to incorporate the subscribers to the Bank of the United States" was presented to me on the 4th July instant. Having considered it with that solemn regard to the principles of the Constitution which the day was calculated to inspire, and come to the conclusion that it ought not to become a law, I herewith return it to the Senate, in which it originated, with my objections.

A bank of the United States is in many respects convenient for the Government and useful to the people. Entertaining this opinion, and deeply impressed with the belief that some of the powers and privileges possessed by the existing bank are unauthorized by the Constitution, subversive of the rights of the States, and dangerous to the liberties of the people, I felt it my duty at an early period of my Administration to call the attention of Congress to the practicability of organizing an institution combining all its advantages and obviating these objections. I sincerely regret that in the act before me I can perceive none of those modifications of the bank charter which are necessary, in my opinion, to make it compatible with justice, with sound policy, or with the Constitution of our country.

The present corporate body, denominated the president, directors, and company of the Bank of the United States, will have existed at the time this act is intended to take effect twenty years. It enjoys an exclusive privilege of banking under the authority of the General Government, a monopoly of its favor and support, and, as a necessary consequence, almost a monopoly of the foreign and domestic exchange. The powers, privileges, and favors bestowed upon it in the original charter, by increasing the value of the stock far above its par value, operated as a gratuity of many millions to the stockholders.

An apology may be found for the failure to guard against this result in the consideration that the effect of the original act of incorporation could not be certainly foreseen at the time of its passage. The act before me proposes another gratuity to the holders of the same stock, and in many cases to the same men, of at least seven millions more. This donation finds no apology in any uncertainty as to the effect of the act. On all hands it is conceded that its passage will increase at least 20 or 30 per cent more the market price of the stock, subject to the payment of the annuity of $200,000 per year secured by the act, thus adding in a moment one-fourth to its par value. It is not our own citizens only who are to receive the bounty of our Government. More than eight millions of the stock of this bank are held by foreigners. By this act the American Republic proposes virtually to make them a present of some millions of dollars. For these gratuities to foreigners, and to some of our own opulent citizens the act secures no equivalent whatever. They are the certain gains of the present stockholders under the operation of this act, after making full allowance for the payment of the bonus.

Every monopoly and all exclusive privileges are granted at the expense of the public, which ought to receive a fair equivalent. The many millions which this act proposes to bestow on the stockholders of the existing bank must come directly or indirectly out of the earnings of the American people. It is due to them, therefore, if their Government sell monopolies and exclusive privileges, that they should at least exact for them as much as they are worth in open market. The value of the monopoly in this case may be correctly ascertained. The twenty-eight millions of stock would probably be at an advance of 50 per cent, and command in market at least $42,000,000, subject to the payment of the present bonus. The present value of the monopoly, therefore, is $17,000,000, and this the act proposes to sell for three millions, payable in fifteen annual installments of $200,000 each.

It is not conceivable how the present stockholders can have any claim to the special favor of the Government. The present corporation has enjoyed its monopoly during the period stipulated in the original contract. If we must have such a corporation, why should not the Government sell out the whole stock and thus secure to the people the full market value of the privileges granted? Why should not Congress create and sell twenty-eight millions of stock, incorporating the purchases with all the powers and privileges secured in this act and putting the premium upon the sales into the Treasury?

But this act does not permit competition in the purchase of this monopoly. It seems to be predicated on the erroneous idea that the present stockholders have a prescriptive right not only to the favor but to the bounty of Government. It appears that more than a fourth part of the stock is held by foreigners and the residue is held by a few hundred of our own citizens, chiefly of the richest class. For their benefit does this act exclude the whole American people from competition in the purchase of this monopoly and dispose of it for many millions less than it is worth. This seems the less excusable because some of our citizens not now stockholders petitioned that the door of competition might be opened, and offered to take a charter on terms much more favorable to the Government and country.

But this proposition, although made by men whose aggregate wealth is believed to be equal to all the private stock in the existing bank, has been set aside, and the bounty of our Government is proposed to be again bestowed on the few who have been fortunate enough to secure the stock and at this moment wield the power of the existing institution. I can not perceive the justice or policy of this course. If our Government must sell monopolies, it would seem to be its duty to take nothing less than their full value, and if gratuities must be made once in fifteen or twenty years let them not be bestowed on the subjects of a foreign government nor upon a designated and favored class of men in our own country. It is but justice and good policy as far as the nature of the case will admit, to confine our favors to our own fellow-citizens, and let each in his turn enjoy an opportunity to profit by our bounty. In the bearings of the act before me upon these points I find ample reasons why it should not become a law.

It has been urged as an argument in favor of rechartering the present bank that the calling in its loans will produce great embarrassment and distress. The time allowed to close its concerns is ample, and if it has been well managed its pressure will be light, and heavy only in case its management has been bad. If, therefore, it shall produce distress, the fault will be its own, and it would furnish a reason against renewing a power which has been so obviously abused. But will there ever be a time when this reason will be less powerful? To acknowledge its force is to admit that the bank ought to be perpetual, and as a consequence the present stockholders and those inheriting their rights as successors be established a privileged order, clothed both with great political power and enjoying immense pecuniary advantages from their connection with the Government.

The modifications of the existing charter proposed by this act are not such, in my view, as make it consistent with the rights of the States or the liberties of the people. The qualification of the right of the bank to hold real estate, the limitation of its power to establish branches, and the power reserved to Congress to forbid the circulation of small notes are restrictions comparatively of little value or importance. All the objectionable principles of the existing corporation, and most of its odious features, are retained without alleviation. . . .

In another of its bearings this provision is fraught with danger. Of the twenty-five directors of this bank five are chosen by the Government and twenty by the citizen stockholders. From all voice in these elections the foreign stockholders are excluded by the charter. In proportion, therefore, as the stock is transferred to foreign holders the extent of suffrage in the choice of directors is curtailed. Already is almost a third of the stock in foreign hands and not represented in elections. It is constantly passing out of the country, and this act will accelerate its departure. The entire

control of the institution would necessarily fall into the hands of a few citizen stockholders, and the ease with which the object would be accomplished would be a temptation to designing men to secure that control in their own hands by monopolizing the remaining stock. There is danger that a president and directors would then be able to elect themselves from year to year, and without responsibility or control manage the whole concerns of the bank during the existence of its charter. It is easy to conceive that great evils to our country and its institutions might flow from such a concentration of power in the hands of a few men irresponsible to the people.

Is there no danger to our liberty and independence in a bank that in its nature has so little to bind it to our country? The president of the bank has told us that most of the State banks exist by its forbearance. Should its influence become concentered, as it may under the operation of such an act as this, in the hands of a self-elected directory whose interests are identified with those of the foreign stockholders, will there not be cause to tremble for the purity of our elections in peace and for the independence of our country in war? Their power would be great whenever they might choose to exert it; but if this monopoly were regularly renewed every fifteen or twenty years on terms proposed by themselves, they might seldom in peace put forth their strength to influence elections or control the affairs of the nation. But if any private citizen or public functionary should interpose to curtail its powers or prevent a renewal of its privileges, it can not be doubted that he would be made to feel its influence.

Should the stock of the bank principally pass into the hands of the subjects of a foreign country, and we should unfortunately become involved in a war with that country, what would be our condition? Of the course which would be pursued by a bank almost wholly owned by the subjects of a foreign power, and managed by those whose interests, if not affections, would run in the same direction there can be no doubt. All its operations within would be in aid of the hostile fleets and armies without. Controlling our currency, receiving our public moneys, and holding thousands of our citizens in dependence, it would be more formidable and dangerous than the naval and military power of the enemy.

If we must have a bank with private stock-

holders, every consideration of sound policy
and every impulse of American feeling admonishes that it should be *purely American.*
Its stockholders should be composed exclusively of our own citizens, who at least ought to
be friendly to our Government and willing to
support it in times of difficulty and danger. So
abundant is domestic capital that competition
in subscribing for the stock of local banks has
recently led almost to riots. To a bank exclusively of American stockholders, possessing
the powers and privileges granted by this act,
subscriptions for $200,000,000 could readily be
obtained. Instead of sending abroad the stock
of the bank in which the Government must
deposit its funds and on which it must rely to
sustain its credit in times of emergency, it
would rather seem to be expedient to prohibit
its sale to aliens under penalty of absolute
forfeiture.

It is maintained by the advocates of the bank
that its constitutionality in all its features ought
to be considered as settled by precedent and
by the decision of the Supreme Court. To this
conclusion I can not assent. Mere precedent is
a dangerous source of authority, and should
not be regarded as deciding questions of constitutional power except where the acquiescence of the people and the States can be considered as well settled. So far from this being
the case on this subject, an argument against
the bank might be based on precedent. One
Congress, in 1791, decided in favor of a bank;
another, in 1811, decided against it. One Congress in 1815, decided against a bank; another
in 1816, decided in its favor. Prior to the present Congress, therefore, the precedents drawn
from that source were equal. If we resort to the
States, the expressions of legislative, judicial,
and executive opinions against the bank have
been probably to those in its favor as 4 to 1.
There is nothing in precedent, therefore, which,
if its authority were admitted, ought to weigh
in favor of the act before me.

If the opinion of the Supreme Court covered
the whole ground of this act, it ought not to
control the coordinate authorities of this Government. The Congress, the Executive, and the
Court must each for itself be guided by its own
opinion of the Constitution. Each public officer
who takes an oath to support the Constitution
swears that he will support it as he understands
it, and not as it is understood by others. It is as
much the duty of the House of Representatives,
of the Senate, and of the President to decide
upon the constitutionality of any bill or resolution which may be presented to them for
passage or approval as it is of the supreme
judges when it may be brought before them
for judicial decision. The opinion of the judges
has no more authority over Congress than the
opinion of Congress has over the judges, and
on that point the President is independent of
both. The authority of the Supreme Court
must not, therefore, be permitted to control the
Congress or the Executive when acting in their
legislative capacities, but to have only such
influence as the force of their reasoning may
deserve. . . .

On two subjects only does the Constitution
recognize in Congress the power to grant exclusive privileges or monopolies. It declares
that "Congress shall have power to promote the
progress of science and useful arts by securing
for limited times to authors and inventors the
exclusive right to their respective writings and
discoveries." Out of this express delegation of
power have grown our laws of patents and
copyrights. As the Constitution expressly delegates to Congress the power to grant exclusive
privileges in these cases as the means of executing the substantive power "to promote the
progress of science and useful arts," it is consistent with the fair rules of construction to
conclude that such a power was not intended
to be granted as a means of accomplishing any
other end. On every other subject which comes
within the scope of Congressional power there
is an ever-living discretion in the use of proper
means, which can not be restricted or abolished
without an amendment of the Constitution.
Every act of Congress, therefore, which attempts by grants of monopolies or sale of exclusive privileges for a limited time, or a time
without limit, to restrict or extinguish its own
discretion in the choice of means to execute its
delegated powers is equivalent to a legislative
amendment of the Constitution, and palpably
unconstitutional. . . .

Suspicions are entertained and charges are
made of gross abuse and violation of its charter.
An investigation unwillingly conceded and so
restricted in time as necessarily to make it incomplete and unsatisfactory discloses enough
to excite suspicion and alarm. In the practices
of the principal bank partially unveiled, in the
absence of important witnesses, and in numerous charges confidently made and as yet wholly
uninvestigated there was enough to induce a
majority of the committee of investigation—a

committee which was selected from the most able and honorable members of the House of Representatives—to recommend a suspension of further action upon the bill and a prosecution of the inquiry. As the charter had yet four years to run, and as a renewal now was not necessary to the successful prosecution of its business, it was to have been expected that the bank itself, conscious of its purity and proud of its character, would have withdrawn its application for the present, and demanded the severest scrutiny into all its transactions. In their declining to do so there seems to be an additional reason why the functionaries of the Government should proceed with less haste and more caution in the renewal of their monopoly.

The bank is professedly established as an agent of the executive branch of the Government, and its constitutionality is maintained on that ground. Neither upon the propriety of present action nor upon the provisions of this act was the Executive consulted. It has had no opportunity to say that it neither needs nor wants an agent clothed with such powers and favored by such exemptions. There is nothing in its legitimate functions which makes it necessary or proper. Whatever interest or influence, whether public or private, has given birth to this act, it can not be found either in the wishes or necessities of the executive department, by which present action is deemed premature, and the powers conferred upon its agent not only unnecessary, but dangerous to the Government and country.

It is to be regretted that the rich and powerful too often bend the acts of government to their selfish purposes. Distinctions in society will always exist under every just government. Equality of talents, of education, or of wealth can not be produced by human institutions. In the full enjoyment of the gifts of Heaven and the fruits of superior industry, economy, and virtue, every man is equally entitled to protection by law; but when the laws undertake to add to these natural and just advantages artificial distinctions, to grant titles, gratuities, and exclusive privileges, to make the rich richer and the potent more powerful, the humble members of society—the farmers, mechanics, and laborers—who have neither the time nor the means of securing like favors to themselves, have a right to complain of the injustice of their Government. There are no necessary evils in government. Its evils exist only in its abuses. If it would confine itself to equal protection, and, as Heaven does its rains, shower its favors alike on the high and the low, the rich and the poor, it would be an unqualified blessing. In the act before me there seems to be a wide and unnecessary departure from these just principles.

Nor is our Government to be maintained or our Union preserved by invasions of the rights and powers of the several States. In thus attempting to make our General Government strong we make it weak. Its true strength consists in leaving individuals and States as much as possible to themselves—in making itself felt, not in its power, but in its beneficence; not in its control, but in its protection; not in binding the States more closely to the center, but leaving each to more unobstructed in its proper orbit.

Experience should teach us wisdom. Most of the difficulties our Government now encounters and most of the dangers which impend over our Union have sprung from an abandonment of the legitimate objects of Government by our national legislation, and the adoption of such principles as are embodied in this act. Many of our rich men have not been content with equal protection and equal benefits, but have besought us to make them richer by act of Congress. By attempting to gratify their desires we have in the results of our legislation arrayed section against section, interest against interest, and man against man, in a fearful commotion which threatens to shake the foundations of our Union. It is time to pause in our career to review our principles, and if possible revive that devoted patriotism and spirit of compromise which distinguished the sages of the Revolution and the fathers of our Union. If we can not at once, in justice to interests vested under improvident legislation, make our Government what it ought to be, we can at least take a stand against all new grants of monopolies and exclusive privileges, against any prostitution of our Government to the advancement of the few at the expense of the many, and in favor of compromise and gradual reform in our code of laws and system of political economy.

I have now done my duty to my country. If sustained by my fellow-citizens, I shall be grateful and happy; if not, I shall find in the motives which impel me ample grounds for contentment and peace. In the difficulties which surround us and the dangers which

threaten our institutions there is cause for neither dismay nor alarm. For relief and deliverance let us firmly rely on that kind Providence which I am sure watches with peculiar care over the destinies of our Republic, and on the intelligence and wisdom of our countrymen. Through *His* abundant goodness and *their* patriotic devotion our liberty and Union will be preserved.   ANDREW JACKSON
1832

ABBOTT LAWRENCE

1792–1855

NO FIGURE was more thoroughly representative of New England's commerce and industry than Abbott Lawrence. Associated with his brother, Amos, in the importation of British manufactured goods during the War of 1812, Lawrence subsequently became the agent for the rising manufactures of New England and himself an entrepreneur in textiles. Founder of the city that bears the family name, and promoter of railroads, and of waterworks and other local improvements, Lawrence became one of the chief spokesmen and champions in the national arena of New England's business enterprise. His abandonment of free-trade principles accompanied his turn from an importing merchant to an entrepreneur.

Lawrence served as Whig representative of Boston in the national Congress and as ambassador at the Court of St. James. A Unitarian in religion and an active exponent of education, Lawrence was above all interested in science. Agassiz's work found in him generous support, and the Lawrence Scientific School at Harvard also sprang from his generosity.

The following passages from Lawrence's *Letters to W. C. Rives, a Virginia Senator* (1846), appeared in the *Richmond Whig* and provide a good introduction to the social philosophy of New England's industrialists.

W. H. Prescott, *Memoir of the Hon. Abbott Lawrence*, n. p. 1856.
H. A. Hill, *Memoir of Abbott Lawrence*, Boston, 1883.

» »   *From:* LETTERS FROM THE HON. ABBOTT LAWRENCE   « «
TO THE HON. WILLIAM C. RIVES

MR. LAWRENCE TO MR. RIVES

NUMBER II

Another Letter from the Hon. Abbott Lawrence.—We cheerfully give up our own space to-day, to a second Letter from the Hon. Abbott Lawrence, and feel sure that our readers will thank us for the substitution. We have taken but a mere glance at this document, but think we may safely say, it is a powerful and impressive paper—throwing much light upon subjects of particular interest to Virginia, and, indeed, to the whole country.   *Richmond Whig.*

Boston, January 16th, 1846.
MY DEAR SIR:

I stated in my letter of the 7th, that I should write to you again, upon the subject of the entire change proposed by the President of the United States, and the Secretary of the Treasury, in our Revenue Laws. It is no other, than the adoption of ad valorem for specific duties, and a reduction of the whole to 20 per cent; this being the maximum at which the Secretary supposes the largest revenue can be obtained. I shall not now discuss the rates of duty that will produce the greatest amount of revenue. I will leave the Secretary to settle that question; but shall endeavor to show what the effect will be upon the country, if his recommendation should be adopted by Congress. I deem the scheme proposed to Congress, in the main, a *currency* question, and one which, if carried out, will reach, in its operation, the occupation and business of every man in the United States. I believe the most economical member of Congress will agree that thirty millions of dollars will be required, annually, to carry on this Government, for the next five years, and that this estimate does not include large sums that may be wanted to settle our affairs with Mexico, Texas, &c.; and that this sum is to be raised from Foreign Importations and the Public Lands. The goods, subject to duty, imported the last year, amounted, in round numbers, to 90 millions of dollars, and the goods free of duty to about 25 millions. I have not the returns at hand, and may not be exactly correct as to amounts, but they are near enough to illustrate my arguments: the former paid an average duty of about 32 per cent, creating a revenue, say of 28 millions. If the revenue derived from an importation of 90 millions, gave 28 millions of dollars, what amount must be imported, to produce the same sum at 20 per cent ad valorem?

The answer is, 140 millions; add to this, the free goods, about 25 millions, and we have an importation of 165 millions of dollars. Our exports have not exceeded, nor are they likely at present to exceed 120 millions: we then have a deficit of 45 millions to provide for; and how is this balance to be paid? State Stocks are no longer current in Europe. Even the Stocks of the United States cannot be negotiated on favorable terms.

We who are merchants can answer this question, having often been obliged to make our remittances in coin, when our imports have exceeded our exports.

If we are obliged to import 140 millions of goods subject [to] duty, to meet the wants of the Government, it is quite certain that the coin must be exported, to meet the deficiency. If the importations fall short of 140 millions, we then have an empty Treasury. In one case, the country will be made bankrupt to fill the Treasury; and in the other, the Treasury will be bankrupt, and resort to Congress for Treasury Notes and Loans. It may be said that our exports will increase with our imports; this supposition I think fallacious. The policy of Great Britain, and that of all Europe, has been, and is likely to continue, to protect every thing produced either at home or in their colonies. In Great Britain, the article of Cotton is now admitted free, the duty having been repealed the very last year. This was owing to repeated representations of the Manchester spinners to Parliament as to the necessity of such a measure, in consequence of the competition from foreign countries in the coarse fabrics manufactured from cotton produced in, and shipped from, the United States. The argument presented in the House of Commons was, that the Americans had taken possession of every market, where they were admitted on the same terms with their coarse goods. This is a true representation, and I apprehend the repeal of the duty on Cotton will not enable the British manufacturer to again obtain possession of those markets, for the heavy descriptions of Cotton fabrics.

What other article of importance does the Government of Great Britain admit free of duty? I know of none. Cotton is admitted free of duty from necessity. How is it with Tobacco? A duty is paid of 1200 per cent. Wheat is prohibited by the "Sliding Scale," and in case of a total repeal of the Corn Laws, very little Wheat would be shipped from this country, inasmuch as it can be laid down, in ordinary years of harvest, much cheaper from the Baltic. Beef and Pork are burdened with a heavy duty. The duty and charges on a barrel of American Pork laid down in Liverpool, with the commissions for sales, amount to $5.75; so that the quantity of this article shipped to England must be inconsiderable, unless the prices here should be so low as to be ruinous to the farmer. I cannot find in the catalogue of our strictly agricultural products, a single article that is not burdened with a high duty, in England, or other parts of Europe, if it comes in competition with their own products; nor can I discover that there is a disposition on the part of a single European Nation to relax the stringent system of duties on imports from this country. It is possible that Great Britain may abate her Corn Laws, so far as to admit Indian Corn at a nominal duty. If it should be done, I have little faith in our being able to ship it to advantage. I state the fact, then, that exports will not increase in consequence of a reduction, or even a total repeal, of the present Tariff. The duty in Great Britain, on all the products of the United States, received in that kingdom, including cotton, is not less than 48 per cent, and exclusive of cotton, 300 per cent; and this, too, on raw produce generally, where the charge of freight constitutes from one-tenth to one-quarter of the cost here—and this is *Free Trade!*

I hope you, of Virginia, will examine this matter, and ask yourselves where the best customers are to be found for your agricultural products. I will just state to you here, that Massachusetts takes annually more Flour, Indian Corn, Pork, and many other articles, the productions of the West, as well as of Virginia, than all Europe.

The question then arises, what will be our condition after the proposed plan of low duties goes into operation? In twenty days after the bill becomes a law, it will have reached every country in Europe with which we have trade: the manufactories are all set in motion for the supply of the American market; the merchandize is shipped on account of foreigners, in many cases with double invoices, one set for the Custom House, and another for the *sales*, so that instead of the duty amounting to 20 per cent, it will not, probably, exceed 15 per cent. This has been the experience of the American Importers in New York, who, previously to the passage of the Tariff of 1842, had (most of them) abandoned the business, not being able to compete successfully with fraudulent foreigners. I will not say that all foreigners commit frauds on the revenue—far from it;—but I do say, that enormous frauds have been perpetrated by foreigners, on the revenue, under ad valorem duties, and will be again—prostrating the business of honest foreign and American importers. In less than twelve months, after the new plan shall have been in operation, this whole country will be literally surfeited with foreign merchandize; (if it be not so, the revenue will fall short of the wants of the Government;) we shall then owe a debt abroad of millions of dollars, which must be paid in coin. The exchanges go up to a point that makes it profitable to ship specie; money becomes scarce in the Atlantic cities; yet bills on England and France do not fall; the loans made to the South and West are called in; demands for debts due from those sections of country, are made; exchange cannot be obtained,—produce is purchased and shipped; and when it arrives at the North, it will not command the cost in the West: a paralysis will have struck the business of the country; produce will no longer answer to pay debts due at the North, and the next resort is to coin, which is to be collected and sent down the Mississippi, or over the mountains, to Baltimore, Philadelphia, New York and Boston. Western and Southern credits are cut off, as the people of those sections can no longer promptly meet their engagements. The new States, and the outer circle of the Republic,

are the weak points; and the first giving way of the Banks is heard from those places, where there is the least amount of capital. We see the storm approaching like a thunder shower in a summer's day; we watch its progress, but cannot escape its fall. It at last reaches the great marts of trade and the exchanges, having swept every thing in its course; and the Banks of the Atlantic cities, after a violent effort to maintain their credit and honor, are forced to yield to this Utopian experiment on the currency. I have no hesitation in stating that all this will take place within the space of eighteen months from the time this experimental bill goes into operation; and not a specie-paying Bank, doing business, will be found in the United States. Where will be the revenue which was to produce such a mighty sum under low duties? Where is the Treasury, and the Secretary? and the President and his Cabinet? The Treasury is empty; the Secretary is making his estimates of income for 1849, and preparing to ask Congress for a large *batch* of Treasury Notes; or perhaps the deficit is so large that a loan may be required. We have now come to a point of depression in the great business of the country, which has attracted the attention and anxiety of all classes of people, *all* having felt its blight, excepting the great capitalists and money holders, who are reaping golden harvests by the purchase of property, which the wants of the unfortunate throw into the market at ruinous rates. It is now seen and felt from the low wages of labor, and the great number of persons unemployed, with the cries of distress from all quarters, that it is the labor and not the capital of the country that suffers by violent revulsions caused by unwise legislation. Have the people of the South and West forgotten their troubles of 1837 to 1842—to the hour of the passage of that Law, which has redeemed the credit of the Government, and restored prosperity to the country? I have intimated that there is less capital in the new States than in many of the old ones; it will not be denied that the monied capital of this country is held in the Northern and Eastern States, and that the South and West are usually largely indebted to them. Now, I should be glad to be informed what benefit is to be derived by a Planter in Alabama or Mississippi, or a farmer in Ohio or Illinois, by a change, like that I have described, particularly, if by chance he should be in debt? Do the people of the South believe they can raise the price of Cotton, or be able to negotiate loans, to prosecute the construction of their contemplated Rail-road? Do Ohio, Louisiana, Illinois, Michigan, believe they are to create a better market for their produce, or sooner complete the Harbors, so much desired on the shores of those "Inland Seas," and be able to negotiate Loans, and obtain subscribers to the Stock of their intended Rail-roads, by the adoption of this new system of political economy? And now what say the *great States* of New York and Pennsylvania to this proposed experiment? Can they afford to try it, and are they ready? If they are, it will be adopted; if they are not, the present Law will stand, and the Country will repose for awhile in happiness and prosperity. Any one would suppose, that those States, that are now just emerging from embarrassment, which at one time seemed almost sufficient to overwhelm them in ruin, would be unwilling to try an experiment which is certain, in my judgment, to place them in a position that will be the means of destroying the fair prospects of thousands who are resting in quiet security upon the faith of what they deem a paternal and wise Government. The question of an important alteration in our Revenue Laws, should not be kept in suspense. The Treasury will feel its effects before the end of the present year. The expectation of a great reduction of duties prevents the merchants from going on with their usual business. Voyages are delayed, and orders for goods are held back, until this important question shall be settled. I say, therefore, if we are to go through this fiery ordeal, let it come at once,—we cannot probably place ourselves in a better condition than we are now, to meet the troubles that await us.

Mr. Walker [1] proposes to substitute ad valorem for specific duties, in opposition to our own experience, and that of almost every other country. I have never yet found an American merchant who has not been in favor of specific duties, wherever it can be done with convenience to the Importer and the Government. I confess it is a bold measure to propose a total and entire change of a Revenue system, which was established with the Government, and has stood the test of experience, through all the trials of political parties and Administrations, from General Washington to Mr. Polk. It appears more extraordinary at this time, as the country is in a high state of prosperity. The revenue is enough for all the reasonable wants

[1] Robert J. Walker (1801–1869), Secretary of the Treasury under Polk, and author of a report (1845) which became a classic in free trade literature.

of the Government, and the people appear to be satisfied with their condition. The resources of the country were never developing more rapidly; the increase of our population, the present year, will probably equal that of the last, which I estimate at 600,000 souls; our wealth too has been wonderfully augmented by the construction of Rail-roads; there has been a great increase of our shipping, engaged in the domestic commerce of the country; not only by sea, but upon our rivers and great lakes: the manufacturing interest has been largely extended; and the soil, too, has been made to produce vastly more than at any former period. The whole productive power of the country has been greater in three years (that is, since the passage of the Tariff of 1842,) than during any equal space of time in our national history. There have been three periods of universal distress throughout our land, since the peace of 1783, and in each case under low duties. I appeal to those who remember those periods; and to others, I refer to the annals of our country. Those periods were from 1783 (the conclusion of the Revolutionary War) to 1789, 1815 to 1824, 1837 to 1842.

I would respectfully recommend to the Secretary of the Treasury, who appears to have received new light upon the subject of our national economy, to examine the history of the legislation of Congress at the above periods. He will find in his own department of the Government, abundant evidence of the distress that existed under low duties and a deranged currency.

There is a prevalent idea abroad, that the capital of the country will suffer exceedingly by a revulsion in its business, and that the tariff of 1842, has operated in favor of the capital, and not the labor of the country. There can be no doubt that capital is generally profitably and safely employed, and well paid. The profits of capital are low, when wages are low; but capital has usually had the power to take care of itself, and does not require the aid of Congress to place it in any other position, than to put the labor in motion. Congress should legislate for the labor, and the capital will take care of itself. I will give you an example of the rate of wages under low duties, and under the tariff of 1842. In 1841 and 1842, the depression in all kinds of business became so oppressive, that many of the manufacturing establishments in New England were closed, the operatives dismissed, the mechanical trades were still, and every resource for the laboring man seemed dried up.

In the city of Lowell, where there are more than thirty large cotton mills, with from six to sixteen thousand spindles each, it was gravely considered by the proprietors whether the mills should be stopped. It was concluded to reduce the wages; this was done several times, until the reduction brought down the wages from about $2.00 to $1.50 per week, exclusive of board; this operation took place upon between 7 and 8000 females; the mills run on; no sales were made of the goods; the South and West had neither money nor credit, and finally, it was determined to hold out till Congress should act upon the tariff. The bill passed, and of course the mills were kept running, which would not have been the case, if the act had been rejected; and now the average wages paid at Lowell— taking the same number of females for the same service—is $2.00 per week, exclusive of board. Yet Mr. Walker says labor has fallen. Where are the wages for labor, I ask, lower than they were in 1842? Who is to be benefited by the adoption of a system that gives up every thing, and gives no reasonable promise of any thing?

I have succeeded, I trust, in showing that there is no probability of our exports increasing, in consequence of a reduction of the tariff, and that the products of the Western States find the best market among the manufacturers at home. In regard to the Southern and cotton growing States, they are to be greatly benefited by the increase of consumption of their staples at home. No appreciable quantity can be shipped to England, if the tariff should be repealed, it being already free of duty. The establishment and successful prosecution of the spinning of cotton in this country, has enabled the planters to obtain for several years past at least, an additional cent per pound on the whole crop, and perhaps even more. The Americans are the greatest spinners of cotton in the world, the British excepted. The competition has kept the price from falling to a ruinous point on several occasions, and it has been acknowledged by many of the most intelligent planters in the South. Our consumption reached, the last year, one hundred and seventy-six millions of pounds, which is equal to the whole crop of the Union in 1825, and equal to the whole consumption of Great Britain in 1826. This is a striking fact, and one that should be remembered by the planters. The history of the production and

manufacture of cotton is so extraordinary, that I propose to send to you some statistics on the subject, furnished me by a friend. I hope you will not deem me over sanguine, when I tell you that it is my belief that the consumption of cotton in this country will double in 8 or 9 years, and that it will reach 400 millions of pounds in 1856; and further, that we are not only destined to be the greatest cotton growers, but the most extensive cotton spinners, in the world. We have all the elements among ourselves to make us so. The manufacture of cotton is probably in its infancy; but a moderate portion of mankind have yet been clothed with this healthful and cheap article. Nothing can stop the progress of this manufacture, but some suicidal legislation, that will prostrate the currency of the country, and deprive the people of the means of consuming. There can be no legislation that will break down the manufacture of cotton and wool, excepting through the operations of the currency. We may be disturbed by low duties; the finer descriptions of cotton and woolens, printed goods, and worsted fabrics, would be seriously affected by low ad valorem duties, but the coarser fabrics, such as are generally consumed by the great body of the people, will be made here under any and all circumstances. If we have competition from abroad, the labor must, and will come down; this has been often tested, and our experience establishes the fact.

In Virginia and other Southern States, and even at the West, many persons have believed that the protective system was made by, and for New England, and that New England, and particularly Massachusetts, could not thrive without it. Now, this is an error; the South and West began the system of high protective duties, for the purpose of creating a market for their produce, (although the principle of discrimination was recognized and established when the first tariff was enacted.) It is not true, that we are more dependent on a protective tariff, than the Middle Western, or Southern States. Those States that possess the smallest amount of capital, are the most benefited by a protective tariff. We have in New England, a great productive power; in Massachusetts far greater than any other State, in proportion to population. We have a hardy, industrious, and highly intelligent population, with a perseverance that seldom tires, and we have also acquired a considerable amount of skill, which is increasing every day; besides this, we have already accomplished a magnificent system of intercommunication between all parts of this section of the country by railroads; this is the best kind of protective power, having reduced the rate of carriage to a wonderful extent; this being done, we have money enough remaining, to keep all our labor employed, and prosecute our foreign and domestic commerce, without being in debt beyond the limits of our own State. Now I ask, how *we* shall stand, compared with Pennsylvania, Ohio, Alabama, Georgia, or Louisiana, when the day of financial trial shall come. I do not deny we shall suffer, but as it has been in times past, we shall go into and come out of the troubles far stronger than any other State out of New England. It is not my purpose to present to you the balance sheet of Massachusetts, but it is due to her character, and her dignity, that she should stand before you in her true position. I have never advocated a protective tariff for my own or the New England States exclusively, nor have those gentlemen with whom I have been associated in this cause, at any time, entertained a narrow or sectional view of the question. We have believed it to be for the interest of the whole country, that its labor should be protected, and so far as I have had to do with the adjustment of those difficult combinations embraced in a tariff bill, I have endeavored to take care that the interests of all the States were protected, whether they were large or small. I say now to you, and it should be said in Congress, and to the country, that Massachusetts asks no exclusive legislation. If Pennsylvania, New York and Ohio, the three great States, with Kentucky, Georgia, Missouri, Alabama and Louisiana, wish to try an experiment on iron, coal, hemp bagging, sugar, &c., &c., I am ready, as one citizen of Massachusetts, to meet it, and await in patient submission the result, which I doubt not will be found, within eighteen months, in the realization of all I have predicted. I say again, I would not, if I could, have a tariff made for Massachusetts alone. If, however, there should be a new one, let *our* interests, with those of every other in the Union, share that protection to which we are all entitled, and of which *we* claim our *full* share. I can with confidence, assure you, that we shall go upward and onward. *We will work.* If 12 hours' labor in the 24 will not sustain us, we can, and will work 14; and at the same

time feel that Congress cannot take the sinews from our arms, or rob us of the intelligence acquired from our public schools, established by the foresight and wisdom of our fathers.

At the risk of writing a long letter, I cannot forbear alluding to the fact, that the habitual agitation of this question of the tariff, has worked, in the main, to the advantage of New England.

We were, previous to the war of 1812, an agricultural and navigating people. The American system was forced upon us, and was adopted for the purpose of creating a home market for the products of the soil of the South and West; we resisted the adoption of a system, which, we honestly believed, would greatly injure our navigation, and drive us from our accustomed employments, into a business we did not understand. We came into it, however, reluctantly, and soon learned that, with the transfer of our capital, we acquired skill and knowledge in the use of it—and that, so far from our foreign commerce being diminished, it was increased, and that our domestic tonnage and commerce were very soon more than quadrupled. The illustrations were so striking in every department of labor, that those who, fifteen years ago, were the strongest opponents of the protective tariff among us, have given up their theories, and acknowledged that the revelations are such as to satisfy the most skeptical. We have gone forward steadily, till many descriptions of manufactures are as well settled in New England as the raising of potatoes. Our experience has given us skill—and, of course, we have confidence in our own resources, that does not exist elsewhere.

When I converse with gentlemen from the South and West, respecting the establishment of manufactures—they reply that they should long ago have engaged in them, but the repeal of the tariff, the action of the government, prevented them. Now you cannot blame us, if this constant agitation of the tariff question has tended to give New England not a monopoly, but advantages which she has not been instrumental in bringing about. I have no doubt we have been gainers, on the whole, by these agitations, yet we have at times been great sufferers. I wish those States that have withheld their energies from entering upon these industrial pursuits, to examine this matter—and, if I am right, to *take an observation and a new departure.* We have no jealousy, whatever, concerning the establishment of manufactories in all parts of the country; on the contrary, I believe those gentlemen from the South and West, who have been here, will bear witness to the desire on the part of the people who are engaged in manufactures, to impart all the information in their power; there is room for us all. When the southern and western States shall manufacture their own clothing, we shall have become extensive exporters of the variety of manufactures produced here. We have the ships, and the men to navigate them. We shall pursue an extensive foreign commerce with manufactures, and bring home the produce of other countries, such as coffee, tea, &c., &c., and pay for the produce of the South and West, with foreign luxuries, and necessaries of life. It has often been said here by us, who advocate protection to American labor, that in wearing British cottons, woolens, &c., &c., we were consuming British wheat, beef, pork, &c. I am happy to find authority of the highest respectability for this opinion, in the person of one of the most eminent merchants, as well as one of the best and most honorable men in England, Mr. William Brown, of Liverpool—lately the free trade candidate for Parliament, from the county of Lancaster. In a letter to John Rolfe, Esq., a landholder, upon the advantages of free trade, he says: "You next allude to the League wishing to injure you. I presume it will not be denied, that all interests in the Kingdom are so linked together, that none of them can suffer without the others being injured. We must sink or swim together! Paradoxical as it may appear, I think Great Britain is the largest *grain exporting* country in the world, although it is impos-

sible to estimate accurately what quantity of grain &c., is consumed in preparing £ 50,000,-000 value of exports, by which you are so greatly benefited. It is placed in the laboratory of that wonderful intellectual machine, man, which gives him the physical power, aided by steam, of converting it into broadcloth, calico, hardware, &c., &c., and in these shapes, your wheats find their way to every country in the world."

. . .

. . . I am aware that I have written a long letter, but I could not well abridge it, consistently, with glancing at many topics in which I could take a deep interest. The subject is boundless, and I would cheerfully carry out by illustrations, and examples, many of the points, upon which I have touched, but I forbear for the present. When I have the pleasure to meet you, we can discuss all these questions, embracing not only the present condition, but the future prospects and destiny of our beloved country, for which I entertain the strongest attachment. Our strength and glory is in upholding and maintaining the Union.

I shall send, in a few days, statistics furnished me by a friend, who is intelligent, careful and accurate in these matters, and who holds himself responsible for all that will be stated.

I pray you, my dear sir, to accept the assurances with which I remain, most faithfully, your friend, and obediant servant,

ABBOTT LAWRENCE.

To the Hon. William C. Rives,
Castle Hill, Albemarle County, Virginia.

1846

CHARLES AUGUSTUS DAVIS

1795-1867

A PIG-IRON MERCHANT, Charles A. Davis was a member of a New York literary circle that included Fitzgreene-Halleck and Philip Hone. Davis was best known for the *Letters of J. Downing, Major, Downingville Militia, Second Brigade, to His Old Friend, Mr. Dwight of the N. Y. Daily Advertiser* (1834). These letters, which went through ten editions within two years, are not to be confused with Seba Smith's *The Select Letters of Major Jack Downing* (1834), originally published in the Portland Courier (1830–1833) and to which, in the Philadelphia edition of 1834, a few of the Downing letters of Davis were added. Davis was a

Whig, and his satire on Jackson and the Jacksonians is a keen and witty thrust which illustrates the lighter aspects of the bitter controversy between the friends and foes of the Second National Bank.

M. A. Wyman, *Two American Pioneers, Seba Smith and Elizabeth Oakes Smith*, New York, 1927.
Jennette Tandy, *Crackerbox Philosophers in American Humor and Satire*, New York, 1925.

» » From: LETTERS OF J. DOWNING, MAJOR « «

LETTER XIX

The President's Plan for managing the Bank and the Country—Hunt for lost Spectacles—How and where they were found.

To my old friend Mr. Dwight, of the N. Y. Daily Advertiser.

Washington, 12th November, 1833.

I have always been tellin the Gineral, as you know, that of all troubles there was none so tuff to git round as money troubles, and when such matters git in a snarl it was worse than tryin to straiten a melitia line arter dinner. I was always afraid that we was gittin too many folks to handle the money, and to be figerin at the 'counts. Ever since I was a boy I always had a notion that the fewer hands in countin the better, and the less you handle money the better, for the more you handle it, somehow, the less it grows. And then agin I tell'd the Gineral, over and over agin, 'Don't meddle with the Bank,' says I; 'the money is safe enuff there, and one pocket,' says I, 'Gineral, is better than twenty.' But you know when I was in New-York with Zekel Bigelow tryin to find out the cause of money bein scarce, and when Zekel broke his watch showin me how the United States Bank worked among other banks, the folks somehow got round the Gineral, and the deposits was removed.

I have been lookin out for trouble ever since, though I was bound to stick to the Gineral, right or wrong, as I told him I would.

Tother day, when we came to that part of the message where we have to speak of mony matters, we sent for Mr. Taney, our new Secretary of the Treasury, to bring in his accounts. He warn't quite ready, for he ain't as quick at siferin yet as he will be to rights; so we waited for him a spell, and left a place here and there in the message, jest big enuff to put in figers: and so last night the Gineral sent agin, and said he must have the 'counts, 'ready or not ready,' and up they came, sure enuff, and not more than half-cooked; but the Gineral won't wait for nothin when he's in a hurry. 'Now,' says he, 'Major, turn to and see how they stand with last year.' And so at it I went, comparin all the amounts of out lays, the Gineral all the while smokin and thinkin pretty hard, with his feet up on the mantle. I figered up the sums pretty quick, considerin there was a good many on 'em called *estimates;* and when I got to the eend on't, 'Now,' says I, 'Gineral, you know I tell'd you that we could git up and put down nullification in no time—we could turn out a cabinet and appint other folks—we could send ministers abroad, and let 'em come home as soon as they pleased, and send other folks in their places, and give all full pay too—we could nock the United States Bank and Squire Biddle all into splinters—we could let our folks go on the Ingin lands in one place and drive them off in other places, and git up an Ingin War—and appint new officers here and there —and have new auditers to settle 'counts—and let things go on in the Post Office and Land Office pretty much to suit the folks there—and instead of havin one Bank for our mony, scatter it about among the banks of our friends. All this we could do, and have done, and have taken the responsibility too, and the folks like us the better for it; but,' says I, 'when they come to see what it all costs there'll be trouble, now I tell you,' says I.

'Why, Major,' says the Gineral, 'what's the matter? ain't 'the Goverment' economical?' says he: 'do you expect to make reforms without costin somethin? Can you clear up swamps, and cut ditches, and remove old stumps without expense?' 'Yes,' says I, 'Gineral, that's all true. But, plague on't,' says I, 'it's ben goin on so now nigh upon 5 years; and,' says I, 'it keeps costin more and more, and we are nearer bein swamp'd and stump'd than ever—here,' says I, 'now jest look and see what 'the Government' costs now, and what it cost when Mr. Adams was President; and that ain't the worst on't,' says I, 'our money is here, there, and everywhere; and I don't see how we shall find it when we want it.'

As soon as I mention'd the amount of the sums I had figered up, the Gineral jumps up, and he did stomp about a spell, I tell you—he smash'd down his pipe, and it flew into more than forty pieces—says he, 'Major, ain't you mistaken?' 'No,' says I, 'thare's no mistake about me, Gineral.' 'Let me see them accounts,' says he; and he begun to feel for his spectacles, first in one pocket, and then in another—for he had no less than 7 pockets besides his watch fob—and he couldn't find his spectacles—says he, 'Major, have you seen my spectacles?' 'No,' says I, 'Gineral, I hain't—where do you keep 'em?' says I—'Why,' says he, 'I used always to keep 'em in this side breast-pocket, but I have been so pester'd lately, I must have chang'd pockets' —'That's bad,' says I, 'Gineral, especially,' says I, 'when one wants any thing in a hurry. Now,' says I, 'I only keep one pocket; and I got that notion,' says I, 'from Squire Biddle, for he keeps eny most every thing in one pocket, and he can tell in a minit pretty much all about eny thing.'

The Gineral kept all the while feelin and turnin his pockets inside out, but no spectacles. Says he, 'Major, I reckon them 'ere spectacles are somewhere in one of these pockets, and I'll find 'em,' says he, 'if I have to take my shirt off'; and at it he went, and he off coat and jacket, and I don't know what all, and I all the while shakin 'em to find the spectacles—by-and-by I see a hole in his pantaloons-pocket; 'I'm on track now,' says I, 'Gineral; here's a hole': and, sure enuff, when he came to take off his boots, there was his best gold-rim specs, and all broke to flinders—and if we hadn't been lookin for 'em, and if I hadn't seen that 'ere hole, you never would say they ever had been specs, for they were all jam'd to nothin.

There was a curious notion then jest come into my head, and I stood stock still, holdin the Gineral's pantaloons in one hand and his right boot upside down in tother, and there lay the specs on the floor (or what there was left on 'em); and the Gineral stood lookin at me with eny most nothin on him, and the Message and the Treasury 'counts and my slate lay on the table—there warn't a word said for more than 10 minits—an awful time to stand so.

So to rights the Gineral he spoke, and says he, 'Major, what are you thinkin on?' 'Why,' says I,

'Gineral, I was thinkin,' says I, 'if you had kept your spectacles in your side breast-pocket, they would be on your nose now; but,' says I, 'that ain't the worst on't, I'm afeard,' says I, 'Gineral, we've got too many pockets for our money, and when we want it we shall all have to come to our shirts and boots before we find it.'

The Gineral got as hornety as all nature at this; and says he, 'Major, I wish now you was only Calhoun, or Biddle, or Clay, or M'Duffy, or Don Pedro, or Black Hawk, or any one but Major Downing—for I feel as if I should like to give some one a thrashing.' 'Why,' says I, 'Gineral, you ain't mad nor nothin, be you? for I am too,' says I; 'and ev'ry time I look at the 'counts,' says I, 'I feel as if I would like to git hold of some one, and thrash 'em too,'—and so we stomped about a spell, cussin and discussin most things, till we got cool agin—but it was a considerable of a storm, I tell you.

Your friend,
J. DOWNING, Major,
Downingville Militia, 2d Brigade.

LETTER XXII

Character of Mr. Clay—Art of War—A pitched and drawn Battle on the U. S. Bank—Amnesty and Overtures—Truce—*Statu quo ante bellum* —A Walk—A Button off—Tailor's Shop—The Button Scene—The Major's Success at a New Trade—The Bank worth a Button.

To my old friend Mr. Dwight, of the N. Y. Daily Advertiser.

Washington, Dec. 14th, 1833.

We have got business enuf now on our hands, I tell you; and nigh upon every day we have a squall that brings all hands to the helm. We have had fair wind so long, that few on us know exactly how to steer now-a-days, when every wind comes right in our teeth. I hain't had my coat off since Congress met; and the Gineral says we must watch them fellows closely. 'Keep a sharp look out, Major,' says he, 'on Clay—he is a *bold, independent* fellow, and will speak out his notions if the devil stands at the door; and if he had the people with him,' says the Gineral, 'as I have, there is no tellin what trouble he would give us. He would make as good a Gineral as ever was. But it will never do *to trust that man with power.*' 'Very well,' says I, 'General—but, plague on't,' says I, 'the crittur somehow keeps law on his side all the while.' 'That's true enuf,' says the Gineral, 'and therefore we must keep a sharper eye on him, and the time is come now, Major, when we must all on us try our popularity—for when the law is agin us, we shan't have nothin else to stand on.—There is nothin,' says the Gineral, 'like war-times, Major—for then, when these troublesome fellows talk about law I'd give 'em martial law, and that makes short work.'

Jest after breakfast yesterday, I and the Gineral had a high time together. I had ben expecting every day to see the Bank come out with a *reply;* and I tell'd the Gineral, says I, 'Gineral, I'm afraid we'll git a stumper from Philadelphy one of these days, that will nock us all into kindlin-wood.' But he kept sayin there was no fear of that. 'Why,' says he, 'Major, you forgit that we first give the Bank a most mortal weltin 3 years ago and left 'em no other defence than to print reports and speeches; and that show'd they hadn't much spunk; and we have been criplin on 'em ever since. And when I see they began to stagger, I give 'em our hull battery, and opened upon 'em in flank, front, and rear, our sharp shooters, headed by that amazin cute little District Attorney, open'd first on 'em. Then come my Proclamation—and then my Message—and then Mr. Tany's report—and the Globe all the while throwin shells and rockets. Why,' says the Gineral, gittin up and takin his Hickory, and givin it a whack on the floor—'if the Bank stands all that racket, Major, it's tuffer than a pepperage log. No, no, Major,' says the Gineral, 'don't you fear that the Bank will ever say a word in reply—it's as dead now,' says the Gineral, 'as a skin'd racoon.' And the words warn't out of his mouth afore in came a hull bundle of letters and newspapers, and the first thing I see among 'em was the 'Bank reply.' 'Now,' says I, 'Gineral, here's trouble!—here's the very thing,' says I, 'I've been afraid on all the while.' The Gineral laft a spell; and says he, 'Major, suppose you and I now jest take a bout, and you'll see how easy I can nock that reply into nothin.' 'Well,' says I, 'Gineral, its a bargain.—Now,' says I, 'let us sit down, and you may take,' says I, 'the Globe, or our District Attorney's report, or your Proclamation, or your Message, or Mr. Tany's report—ary one on 'em,—or,' says I, 'come to think on't, you may take 'em all together,—for they are pretty much *all one*—and I'll take this 'Bank reply,' and then let's see what kind of a

fight it will turn out.' 'Well,' says the Gineral, 'you are a man of spunk, Major, and I like you for it: and if I make a prisoner on you, I'll treat you like a brave soldier.' 'And so will I you, Gineral,' says I, 'and if you fall in the fight,' says I, 'Gineral, I'll bury you,' says I, 'with the honors of war'; and then we shook hands. 'Now, Major,' says the Gineral, 'as I am to begin the fight, don't you fire till I fire, and then we'll go threw, shot by shot.' 'Well,' says I, 'I want to know first, if I have a right to fire back *your shot,* if they miss me, and I can pick 'em up?' 'O yes,' says the Gineral, 'that's fair in war.' 'Use the enemies shot and shells, and guns too, if you can, Major,—*that's the true art of war.*' The Gineral all the while kept fixing his papers all in a string on one side the table. He put his own Messages and Proclamation in the middle, and flank'd off with our District Attorney and Mr. Tany's reports; and then he sifted the Globe about, and call'd them *scouts* and *foragers*—'There,' says he, 'Major, I am now nearly ready'; and he took off his specs, and gin 'em a good rubbin and put 'em on agin. 'Now, Major,' says he, 'take your station.' And I went round tother side, and sat down. 'Are you ready?' says the Gineral.—'All ready,' says I—and at it we went. The Gineral, he open'd his fire first, as agreed; and he fir'd away from his first Message—And then his second —then he took the Globe, and then the reports,—and he blaz'd away like all wrath, for an hour; and as soon as he stop'd to take breath—'Now,' says I, 'its my time,'—and I read the reply a spell, and answered all he said in three minits. And I gin him a look! The Gineral twisted his face most shockin, and scratched his head too. But he went at it agin as spunky as ever; for he is an amazin tuff crittur in a fight, and hangs on like a snappin turtle when he gits hold. He banged away a spell agin like all natur; and jest as he took his specs off to give 'em a rub, I gin him the reply agin. The Gineral gin his face another plagy hard rumple; and I sot waitin for him to fire agin. Says he, 'Major, that's a sharp piece you are firin with there.' 'It's a peeler,' says I, 'Gineral, I tell you—but you hain't got the best on't yet—it's jest gettin warm,' says I.

'Major,' says the Gineral, 'suppose we change batteries—let me take that reply, and you take all these documents. I like to fight,' says the Gineral, 'when there is ten to one agin me.' 'So do I,' says I, 'Gineral, and so we'd better fight it out as we sit.'

The Gineral looked a spell at his paper agin; and, says he, 'Major, I reckon we had better have a truce.' 'Not now,' says I, 'I've got my hand in now, and want to see the fight out.' 'Well,' says the Gineral, 'you see, Major, what comes when any one attempts to drive the executive'; and with that he got up, and took off his specs, and put 'em in his pocket, and put on his hat and took his Hickory, and fetched a whack on the table,—'VETO,' says he—'That's enuff,' says I, 'Gineral.'

'And now,' says the Gineral, 'let's go and take a walk'—and so we went. The Gineral didn't say nothin for more than a mile, and I nother. So, to rights, says he, 'Major, everybody says money is very scarce.' 'That's true enuf,' says I, 'and it's not got as scarce as it will be afore winter is over'; and then I tell'd the Gineral the cause on't. 'Well,' says the Gineral, 'I believe you are right; and if the worst comes to the worst,' says he, 'we'll have a new Bank, and that will make money plenty agin, wont it?' 'Yes,' says I, 'I suppose so; but we can't git a new Bank, Gineral, afore this one's time is out, and that's nigh three years yet; and long afore that time,' says I, 'there will be trouble enuf, as this one must all the while be collectin in its own money; and folks will fail, and be bankrupt; and then twenty new Banks will do them no good.' 'I don't see that,' says the Gineral. 'If we could make a new Bank now,' says I, 'right off, and let it take up the business of the old one, it wouldn't make much odds. But the law won't allow that, you know, Gineral.' And jest then the Gineral got in a way he has of twitchin with his suspender buttons behind; and to rights he broke one off. 'There,' says he, 'Major, here is this confounded button off agin.' 'Well,' says I, 'that's a small matter—here is a tailor's shop,—let's go in and make him put it on'—and so in we went. The tailor happened to be one of our party, and was tickled to death to see the President, and thought he was goin to git an office right off, and was plagily cut down when he come to find it was ony a button off; and so he jumped back on his board, and sat down on his heels agin, and said if the Gineral would take off his pantaloons, he'd put it on in a few minutes.— I looked at the Gineral and he looked at me—and we both looked at the tailor. 'Why,' says the Gineral, 'this is the worst thing, Major, I ever met—I'm stump'd completely! It will never do to risk walking home with this button off; for if 'tother one comes off, it's all

over with me; and if I sit here without my pantaloons till that fellow puts on a button, I'll kitch my death of cold! Look here, Major,' says the Gineral, 'that other button is taken all the strain, and it will come off in less than five minutes—what is to be done? It seems to me, Major,' said the Gineral, 'that no man is placed so often in such real trouble as I am.'—'Yes,' says I, 'Gineral, but it's fortunate for you, you always have me with you.' 'I know it, Major,' says he, 'and I hope you will be as true a friend now as ever you have been.'—And with that, says I to the tailor, 'Can't you fix things now, so as to git over all this trouble?' 'There is only one way,' says the tailor, 'and that I've stated, and another thing,' says he, 'the Gineral wants a new pair.' 'You rascal,' says the Gineral, 'you can't make a better pair, and one that fits me better, if you try a month—these pantaloons,' said the Gineral, 'are better than a new pair; and if they only had new buttons here they would last me to my dying day.— It takes me weeks and months to git a pair to sit easy. I won't have a new pair,' says the Gineral, 'that I'm determined on. I see,' says the Gineral, 'what you are after—you want a new job.'

'Well,' says I, 'Gineral, let me try'—and with that I wax'd a thread, and got a new button; and whilst the Gineral stood up, I sot down behind him, and stitched on the button in three minits—the Gineral all the while shakin his hickory at the tailor, and tellin him that he had no more brains in his head than he had in his thimble.—'You are a pritty fellow to belong to my party,' says he; 'I should have been soon in a pritty condition, if I had taken your advice,' says the Gineral. 'Let me ever ketch you at the White House agin.' So to rights, the tailor got mad too, and said he didn't belong to the Gineral's party—he was a Tany-Kindle-Van-Buren-Jackson-man; he knew which side his bread was butter'd; and he looked plagey knowin too—it was jest as much as I could do to keep the Gineral from smashin him—so says I, 'Come, Gineral, let's be movin'; and we went home—the Gineral all the while talkin about his escape from an awful state that tailor was about getting him in.—'Well,' says I, 'Gineral, little things sometimes give us a kink and a notion of bigger ones; and now,' says I, 'do you know, Gineral, we are in a scrape now, pretty much like that one we jest got out on.' 'How so?' says the Gineral. 'Why,' says I, 'the Bank, there it is,' says I, 'jest like your pantaloons, *better than new;* and only wants a new button; and some of these ere political tailors about us here want us to sit shiverin and shakin, and runnin the risk of gettin a rheumatiz that will last us our lives, jest for them to get the job of makin a new one.'

'And now,' says I, 'I guess you and I had better disappoint 'em, as we did the tailor jest now—stitch on a new button, and things will go smooth agin.' The Gineral didn't say a word; but he got thinkin plagey hard, till we got home agin, and he got his pipe, and I got mine, and jest as were lighten 'em, says he, 'Major, there are some fellows about us here that pester me most desperately—we must all go as a 'Unit,' or I must blow 'em all up, and git a new set. We'll think of it,' said the Gineral, and with that we cock'd our feet on the mantle-tree, and in less than five minutes you couldn't see no more on us than our toes.

Your Friend,
J. DOWNING, Major,
Downingville Militia, 2d Brigade.
1834

FREEMAN HUNT

1804-1858

LIKE MANY OTHER well-known Americans, Freeman Hunt rose to prominence through the printing trade. His rapid advancement began as the result of an editor's appreciation of his contribution to a Boston newspaper. In 1828 Hunt entered the publishing field, bringing out, with his partner, newspapers, magazines, and books. For nineteen years his energies were, however, exclusively absorbed in *Hunt's Merchants Magazine,* the first American magazine devoted exclusively to commerce. He also publicized the careers of merchants in his widely appreciated *Lives of American Merchants* (1858). The following selections from his *Worth and Wealth* illustrate his sympathy for those struggling against obstacles and, especially, his conviction that commerce is as dignified a calling as any of the professions and therefore deserving of a rationale, a guide to successful achievement.

Freeman Hunt, Jr., *Memorial Biographies of the New England Historic Genealogical Society,* Boston, 1883.

» » *From:* WORTH AND WEALTH « «

Self-reliance, to the merchant, and indeed to all who would succeed in the accomplishment of a laudable purpose or pursuit, is indispensable. It was this trait, perhaps, more than any other, that enabled an Astor, a Girard, a Gray, in our own country, to work out for themselves vast fortunes—to accumulate millions. An eminent writer has somewhere said, if our young men miscarry in their first enterprise, they lose all heart. If the young merchant fails, men say he is ruined. If the finest genius studies in one of our colleges, and is not installed in an office in one year afterwards, it seems to his friends and to himself that he is right in being disheartened, and in complaining the rest of his life. A sturdy Yankee who in turn tries all the professions, who teams it, farms it, peddles, keeps a school, preaches, edits a newspaper, goes to Congress, buys a township, and so forth, in successive years, and always, like a cat, falls on his feet, is worth a hundred of these city dolls. He walks abreast with his days, and feels no shame in not studying a profession, for he does not postpone his life, but lives already. He has not one chance! Let a stoic arise who shall reveal the resources of man, and tell men they are not leaning willows, but can and must detach themselves; that, with the exercise of self-trust, new powers shall appear; that a man is the word made flesh,

born to shed healing to the nations; that he should be ashamed of our compassion; and that the moment he acts from himself, tossing the laws, the books' idolatries and customs, out of the window, we pity him no more, but thank him and revere him—and that teacher shall restore the life of man to splendor, and make his name dear to all history. It is easy to see that a greater self-reliance—a new respect
10 for the divinity in man—must work a revolution in all the offices and relations of men: in their religion; in their education; in their pursuits; their modes of living; their association; in their property; in their speculative views.

A man of business should be able to fix his attention on details, and be ready to give every kind of argument a hearing. This will not
20 encumber him, for he must have been practised before-hand in the exercise of his intellect, and be strong in principles. One man collects materials together, and there they remain, a shapeless heap; another, possessed of method, can arrange what he has collected; but such a man as I would describe, by the aid of principles, goes farther, and builds with his materials.

He should be courageous. The courage,
30 however, required in civil affairs, is that which belongs rather to the able commander than the mere soldier. But any kind of courage is serviceable.

Besides a stout heart, he should have a patient temperament, and a vigorous but disciplined imagination; and then he will plan boldly, and with large extent of view, execute calmly, and not be stretching out his hand for things not yet within his grasp. He will let op-
40 portunities grow before his eyes until they are ripe to be seized. He will think steadily over possible failure, in order to provide a remedy or a retreat. There will be the strength of repose about him.

He must have a deep sense of responsibility. He must believe in the power and vitality of truth, and in all he does or says, should be anxious to express as much truth as possible.

His feeling of responsibility and love of truth
50 will almost inevitably endow him with diligence, accuracy and discreetness—those commonplace requisites for a good man of business, without which all the rest may never come to be "translated into action."

Almost every merchant has been rich, or at least prosperous, at some point of his life; and if he is poor now, he can see very well how he might have avoided the disaster which overthrew his hopes. He will probably see that his misfortunes arose from neglecting some of the following rules:—

Be industrious. Everybody knows that industry is the fundamental virtue in the man of business. But it is not every sort of industry which tends to wealth. Many men work hard to do a great deal of business, and, after all, make less money than they would if they did less. Industry should be expended in seeing to all the details of business—in the careful finishing up of each separate undertaking, and in the maintenance of such a system will keep everything under control.

Be economical. This rule, also, is familiar to everybody. Economy is a virtue to be practised every hour in a great city. It is to be practised in pence as much as in pounds. A shilling a day saved, amounts to an estate in the course of a life. Economy is especially important in the outset of life, until the foundations of an estate are laid. Many men are poor all their days, because, when their necessary expenses were small, they did not seize the opportunity to save a small capital, which would have changed their fortunes for the whole of their lives.

Stick to the business in which you are regularly employed. Let speculators make their thousands in a year or day; mind your own regular trade, never turning from it to the right hand or the left. If you are a merchant, a professional man, or a mechanic, never buy lots or stocks unless you have surplus money which you wish to invest. Your own business you understand as well as other men; but other people's business you do not understand. Let your business be some one which is useful to the community. All such occupations possess the elements of profits in themselves, while mere speculation has no such element.

Never take great hazards. Such hazards are seldom well balanced by the prospects of profit; and if they were, the habit of mind which is induced is unfavorable, and generally the result is bad. To keep what you have, should be the first rule; to get what you can fairly, the second.

Do not be in a hurry to get rich. Gradual gains are the only natural gains, and they who are in haste to be rich, break over sound rules, fall into temptations and distress of various sorts, and generally fail of their object. There is no use in getting rich suddenly. The man who keeps his business under his control, and saves something from year to year, is always rich. At any rate, he possesses the highest enjoyment which riches are able to afford.

Never do business for the sake of doing it, and being counted a great merchant. There is often more money to be made by a small business than a large one; and that business will in the end be most respectable which is most successful. Do not get deeply in debt; but so manage as always, if possible, to have your financial position easy, so that you can turn any way you please.

Do not love money extravagantly. We speak here merely with reference to getting rich. In morals, the inordinate love of money is one of the most degrading vices. But the extravagant desire of accumulation induces an eagerness, many times, which is imprudent, and so misses its object from too much haste to grasp it.

Success in life mainly depends upon perseverance. When a man has determined to follow a certain line of business, he must at the same time resolve to persevere until success crowns his efforts. He must never be cast down by the difficulties which may beset his path—for whoever conquers difficulty, conquers a weakness of his own frail nature likewise. How many men have commenced business under the most favorable auspices, and yet when a cloud has momentarily overshadowed their path, have lost all command over themselves and fled before the temporary gloom, instead of persevering on until the cloud has been dispersed, and sunshine once more smiled upon their efforts. Others, more fickle, have thought their business, in some minor departments, unworthy of their perseverance and energy, and forgetting the golden maxim that, "whatever is worth doing is worth doing well," have ceased to persevere in small matters, until sloth has entered deeply into their minds, and their whole business greatly neglected.

We are too apt to attribute success in business to good fortune, instead of great perseverance. This is a great evil, and should be eschewed, as it leads many to suppose that Dame Fortune will do that for them which they are unwilling to do for themselves.

The history of every great success in business is the history of great perseverance. By perseverance the mind is strengthened and invigorated, and the difficulty that once seemed so formidable is a second time surmounted with ease and confidence.

Energy and great perseverance are never thrown away on a good cause, or left unrewarded; and to every man of business, perseverance should be his motto, and then he may look with confidence to fortune as his reward. 10

There is a class of men whose patronage of art has been princely in its munificence, as their wealth has equalled that of princes, whose interests have become a chief concern of statesmen, and have involved the issues of peace and war; whose affairs afford a leading subject of the legislation of States, and fill the largest space in the volumes of modern jurists. 20 This class has produced men who have combined a vast comprehensiveness with a most minute grasp of details, and whose force of mind and will in other situations would have commanded armies and ruled States; they are men whose plans and combinations take in every continent, and the islands and the waters of every sea; whose pursuits, though peaceful, occupy people enough to fill armies and man navies; who have placed science and invention 30 under contribution, and made use of their most ingenious instruments and marvellous discoveries in aid of their enterprises; who are covering continents with railroads and oceans with steamships; who can boast the magnificence of the Medici, and the philanthropy of Gresham and of Amos Lawrence; and whose zeal for science and zeal for philanthropy have penetrated to the highest latitude of the Arctic seas, ever reached by civilized man, in the 40 ships of Grinnell.

Modern scholars have seen the important bearing of the history of commerce upon the history of the world; have seen, rather,—as who, in this most commercial of all eras, can fail to see?—how large a chapter it forms in the history of the world, although crowded out of the space it ought to fill by the wars and crimes which destroy what it creates. Hume was among the first to call attention to this 50 branch of historical inquiry, and Heeren has investigated with much learning the commerce of the ancients. If we were in possession of lives of the great merchants of antiquity, what light would they not throw upon the origin of

States, the foundation of cities, and inventions and discoveries, of which we now do not even know the dates?

Trade planted Tyre, Carthage, Marseilles, London, and all the Ionic colonies of Greece. Plato was for a while a merchant; Herodotus, they say, was a merchant. Trade was honorable at Athens, as among all nations of original and vigorous thought; when we find discredit attached to it, it is among nations of a secondary and less original civilization, like the Romans.

But if commerce forms so large a chapter in the history of the world, what would the history of America be if commerce and men of commerce were left out? Trade discovered America in the vessels of adventures, seeking new channels to the old marts of India; trade planted the American colonies, and made them flourish, even in New England, say what we please about Plymouth Rock; our colonial growth was the growth of trade—revolution and independence were the results of measures of trade and commercial legislation, although they undoubtedly involved the first principles of free government: the history of the country, its politics and policy, has ever since turned chiefly upon questions of trade and of finance, sailor's rights, protection, banks, and cotton.

1856

» » *The East and the Frontier* « «

1800-1860

» » « «

OH! SUSANNA

I came from Alabama wid
  My banjo on my knee,
I'm gwine to Louisiana,
  My true love for to see.
It rain'd all night de day I left,
  De weather it was dry,
De sun so hot I froze to death;
  Susanna, don't you cry.

Chorus
Oh! Susanna, Oh don't you cry for me,
I've come from Alabama, wid my banjo on my knee.

I jumped aboard de telegraph,
  And trabeled down de riber,
De 'lectric fluid magnified,
  And killed five hundred nigger.
De bullgine bust, de horse run off,
  I really thought I'd die;
I shut my eyes to hold my breath,
  Susanna, don't you cry.

I had a dream de odder night,
  When ebery ting was still;
I thought I saw Susanna,
  A coming down de hill.
De buckwheat cake war in her mouth,
  De tear war in her eye,
Says I, I'm coming from de South,
  Susanna, don't you cry.

I soon will be in New Orleans,
  And den I'll look all round,
And when I find Susanna,
  I'll fall upon de ground.
But if I do not find her,
  Dis darkie'll surely die,
And when I'm dead and buried,
  Susanna, don't you cry.

Stephen Foster's "Oh! Susanna" was sung "possibly for the first
time, at Andrews' Eagle Ice Cream Saloon in Pittsburgh, September

11, 1847." After its publication early in 1848 the song appeared in a great variety of arrangements and was soon heard around the world. Bayard Taylor reports having heard a minstrel sing it in Delhi, India, in 1853. But it was the gold rush of 1849 that made "Oh! Susanna" the favorite it has since been. With new verses added to Foster's original whenever the occasion required them, it echoed along the trail from Independence to the Sacramento.

» »　« «

SWEET BETSEY FROM PIKE

Oh, don't you remember sweet Betsey from Pike
Who crossed the big mountains with her lover, Ike,
With two yokes of cattle, a large yellow dog—
A tall Shanghai rooster and one spotted hog?

Chorus
Tooral lal looral lal looral la la
Tooral lal looral lal looral la la.

One evening quite early they camped on the Platte
'Twas near by the road on a green shady flat,
Where Betsey, sore-footed, lay down to repose,
With wonder Ike gazed on that Pike County rose.

Their wagon broke down with a terrible crash,
And out on the prairie rolled all kinds of trash,
A few little baby clothes done up with care,
'Twas rather suspicious, but all on the square.

The Shanghai ran off and their cattle all died,
That morning the last piece of bacon was fried,
Poor Ike was discouraged and Betsey got mad,
The dog dropped his tail and looked wondrously sad.

They stopped at Salt Lake to inquire the way,
When Brigham declared that sweet Betsey should stay;
But Betsey got frightened and ran like a deer,
While Brigham stood pawing the ground like a steer.

They soon reached the desert, where Betsey gave out,
And down in the sand she lay rolling about,
While Ike, half-distracted, looked on with surprise,
Saying, "Betsey, get up, you'll get sand in your eyes."

Sweet Betsey got up in a great deal of pain
Declared she'd go back to Pike County again,
But Ike gave a sigh, and they fondly embraced,
And they traveled along with his arm 'round her waist.

They suddenly stopped on a very high hill,
With wonder looked down upon old Placerville,
Ike sighed when he said as he cast his eyes down,
"Sweet Betsey, my darling, we've got to Hangtown."

Long Ike and Sweet Betsey attended a dance;
Ike wore a pair of his Pike County pants;
Sweet Betsey was covered with ribbons and rings,
Says Ike, "You're an angel, but where are your wings?"

Through the writings of western humorists like "John Phoenix"
(George Horatio Derby) and story-tellers like Bret Harte, the typical
California immigrant came to be known as a "Pike," though com-
paratively few of the new arrivals could actually have come from
Pike County, Missouri. This lusty song, celebrating the adventures of
a "Pike" and his "Betsey," was printed, perhaps for the first time, in
Put's Golden Songster, San Francisco, 1858. The tune is that of
"Villikins and his Dinah."

» »   « «

The East and the Frontier

SECTIONAL CONFLICT in the pre-Civil War period was by no means limited to controversies between the North and South over the tariff, states rights, and slavery. Rivalry between the East and the West created controversies. These arose from the almost magically quick development of the Ohio Valley in the early decades of the nineteenth century and the extension of the frontier in subsequent years into Michigan, Wisconsin, and Iowa. This growth of the West was the result of more than the appeal of adventure. In hard times Eastern farmers and their sons became discouraged and sought better opportunities beyond the Alleghenies. As the soil of the older states became impoverished, the Eastern farmer found it even harder to compete with the farmer on the rich lands of the West. And with the growth of cities and of industrialization the Eastern farmer found his whole way of life altered. Many preferred to go West rather than to try to make the difficult adjustments which vast economic changes demanded. At the same time land promoters spread stories of fabulous wealth to be won in the new country; and after '49 the gold in California was a magnet.

Many Easterners felt alarmed both because of the depletion of population of their own states and because of fear that the political power which the West would presently have in its hands might be used to fasten on the nation "financial vagaries" such as wildcat banks, inflation, and state repudiation of the obligations owed to creditors. Conservatives in the East also shuddered at the idea that crude frontiersmen, if left in ignorance, might ultimately destroy all the cultural and religious values dear to them.

These fears found concrete expression not only in writing but in action. Men of wealth in the East were called upon to contribute to the struggling educational and religious institutions in the West on the ground that these and these alone could civilize near-barbarians, could dampen the ardor for social measures inimical to the interests of the status quo. Messengers of Eastern culture—schoolteachers, missionaries, ministers—were sent to the West by organizations formed for that purpose. The fear that the West might also become the scene of the triumph of Catholicism, which immigrants to that section carried with them, stimulated Eastern Protestants to still greater activity.

But Eastern conservatism did not stop with an effort to extend its cultural and social values into the new country beyond the Appalachians. Not only Southern planters but their allies in control of Northern factories opposed the movement for free homesteads lest the too rapid settlement of the West reduce the value of lands in the older areas and drain away the labor supply so necessary to mill-owners. Eastern capitalists did, however, favor the program for internal improvements—roads, canals, railways—by which East and West were tied together to make feasible the selling of goods in the ever expanding Western market. Such ties also weakened the alliance of South and West, agrarian sections both, and strengthened sentiment for the Union.

The West itself believed thoroughly in itself, in its grand future. It not only visioned a great material civilization, but also looked forward to the development of a cultural life superior to that of the East in vigor, originality, and inclusiveness. Some Easterners who visited the West reported favorably on its natural beauty and way of life. One or two became professional champions of the new country. Even those who disapproved of much in the West, agreed at least that experiences in the wilderness had made a new type of people. The most American characteristics tended to be exaggerated on the frontier. Social democracy, individualism, versatility, independence, and optimism marked the Westerner. However hard times might be—and they were hard—he was confident that the future was with him.

» » « «

TIMOTHY DWIGHT

1752–1817

TIMOTHY DWIGHT was President of Yale, poet, theologian, and controversialist. He wrote his *Travels in New-England and New-York* (1821–1822), a four-volume work, to show how "New England appeared, or to my own eye would have appeared, eighty or a hundred years before," and to refute foreign criticisms of the United States. The *Travels* abound with descriptions of the landscape, with historical and statistical information, and with comments on political, economic, social, and educational conditions. A staunch and even dyed-in-the-wool New Englander, Dwight had little sympathy with those elements in the population who became pioneers. His antagonism toward the West was characteristic of his class and his region.

J. P. Thompson, *A Memoir of the Late Timothy Dwight, With the Sermon Delivered on the Occasion of His Death,* New Haven, 1844.
Charles E. Cunningham, *Timothy Dwight, A Bibliography,* New York, 1942.
M. A. de W. Howe, *Classic Shades; Five Leaders of Learning and their Colleges,* Boston, 1928.

» »   *From:* TRAVELS IN NEW-ENGLAND AND   « «
                    NEW-YORK

Vermont has been settled entirely from the other States of New-England. The inhabitants have, of course, the New-England character, with no other difference besides what is accidental. In the formation of Colonies, those who are first inclined to emigrate are usually such as have met with difficulties at home. These are commonly joined by persons, who, having large families and small farms, are induced for the sake of settling their children comfortably to seek for new and cheaper lands. To both are always added the discontented, the enterprizing, the ambitious, and the covetous. Many of the first and some of all these classes are found in every new American country, within ten years after its settlement has commenced. From this period kindred, friendship, and former neighborhood prompt others

to follow them. Others still are allured by the prospect of gain, presented in every new country to the sagacious from the purchase and sale of lands: while not a small number are influenced by the brilliant stories, which everywhere are told concerning most tracts during the early progress of their settlement.

A considerable part of all those who *begin* the cultivation of the wilderness may be denominated *foresters*, or *Pioneers*. The business of these persons is no other than to cut down trees, build log-houses, lay open forested grounds to cultivation, and prepare the way for those who come after them. These men cannot live in regular society. They are too idle, too talkative, too passionate, too prodigal, and too shiftless to acquire either property or character. They are impatient of the restraints of law, religion, and morality; grumble about the taxes by which Rulers, Ministers, and Schoolmasters are supported; and complain incessantly, as well as bitterly, of the extortions of mechanics, farmers, merchants, and physicians to whom they are always indebted. At the same time they are usually possessed, in their own view, of uncommon wisdom; understand medical science, politics, and religion better than those who have studied them through life; and, although they manage their own concerns worse than any other men, feel perfectly satisfied that they could manage those of the nation far better than the agents to whom they are committed by the public. After displaying their own talents and worth, after censuring the weakness and wickedness of their superiours, after exposing the injustice of the community in neglecting to invest persons of such merit with public offices in many an eloquent harangue, uttered by many a kitchen fire, in every blacksmith's shop, and in every corner of the streets, and finding all their efforts vain, they become at length discouraged and under pressure of poverty, the fear of a gaol, and the consciousness of public contempt, leave their native places and betake themselves to the wilderness.

Here they are obliged either to work or to starve. They accordingly cut down some trees and girdle others; they furnish themselves with an ill-built log-house and a worse barn; and reduce a part of the forest into fields, half-enclosed and half-cultivated. The forests furnish browse; and their fields yield a stinted herbage. On this scanty provision they feed a few cattle: and with these and the penurious products of their labour, eked out by hunting and fishing, they keep their families alive.

A farm, thus far cleared, promises immediate subsistence to a better husbandman. A log-house, thus built, presents, when repaired with moderate exertions, a shelter for his family. Such a husbandman is therefore induced by these little advantages, where the soil and situation please him, to purchase such a farm, when he would not plant himself in an absolute wilderness. The proprietor is always ready to sell: for he loves this irregular, adventurous, half-working, and half-lounging life; and hates the sober industry and prudent economy by which his bush pasture might be changed into a farm, and himself raised to thrift and independence. The bargain is soon made. The forester, receiving more money for his improvements than he ever before possessed and a price for the soil somewhat enhanced by surrounding settlements, willingly quits his house to build another like it, and his farm to girdle trees, hunt, and saunter in another place. His wife accompanies him only from a sense of duty or necessity, and secretly pines for the quiet, orderly, friendly society to which she originally bade a reluctant farewell. Her husband, in the meantime, becomes less and less a civilized man: and almost every thing in the family which is amiable and meritorious is usually the result of her principles, care, and influence.

The second proprietor is commonly a *farmer*, and with an industry and spirit, deserving no small commendation, changes the desert into a fruitful field.

This change is accomplished much more rapidly in some places than in others, as various causes, often accidental, operate. In some instances a settlement is begun by farmers and assumes the aspect of regular society from its commencement. This, to some extent, is always the fact: and the greater number of the first planters are, probably, of this description: but some of them also are foresters, and sometimes a majority.

You must have remarked a very sensible difference in the character of different towns through which I have passed. This diversity is in no small degree derived from the original character of the planters in the different cases.

The class of men who have been the principal subject of these remarks have already straggled onward from New-England, as well as from other parts of the Union, to Louisiana. In a political view their emigration is of very serious utility to the ancient settlements. All countries contain restless inhabitants, men impatient of labour; men who will contract debts without intending to pay them, who had rather talk than work, whose vanity persuades them that they are wise and prevents them from knowing that they are fools, who are delighted with innovation, who think places of power and profit due to their peculiar merits, who feel that every change from good order and established society will be beneficial to themselves, who have nothing to lose and therefore expect to be gainers by every scramble, and who, of course, spend life in disturbing others with the hope of gaining something for themselves. Under despotic governments they are awed into quiet; but in every free community they create, to a greater or less extent, continual turmoil, and have often overturned the peace, liberty, and happiness of their fellow-citizens. In the Roman Commonwealth, as before in the Republics of Greece, they were emptied out as soldiers upon the surrounding countries, and left the sober inhabitants in comparative quiet at home. It is true, they often threw these States into confusion and sometimes overturned the government. But if they had not been thus thrown off from the body politic, its life would have been of a momentary duration. As things actually were, they finally ruined all these States. For some of them had, as some of them always will have, sufficient talents to do mischief, at times, very extensive. The Gracchi, Clodius, Marius, and Mark Antony were men of this character. Of this character is every demagogue, whatever may be his circumstances. Power and profit are the only ultimate objects which every such man, with a direction as steady as that of the needle to the pole, pursues with a greediness unlimited and inextinguishable.

Formerly the energetic government established in New-England, together with the prevailing high sense of religion and morals and the continually pressing danger from the French and the savages, compelled the inhabitants into habits of regularity and good order, not surpassed perhaps in the world. But since the American Revolution, our situation has become less favourable to the existence, as well as to the efficacy, of these great means of internal peace. The former exact and decisive energy of the government has been obviously weakened. From our ancient dangers we have been delivered, and the deliverance was a distinguished blessing: but the sense of danger regularly brings with it a strong conviction that safety cannot be preserved without exact order and a ready submission to lawful authority.

The institutions and the habits of New-England, more I suspect than those of any other country, have prevented or kept down this noxious disposition, but they cannot entirely prevent either its existence or its effects.

In mercy, therefore, to the sober, industrious, and well-disposed inhabitants, Providence has opened in the vast Western wilderness a retreat sufficiently alluring to draw them away from the land of their nativity. We have many troubles even now: but we should have many more if this body of foresters had remained at home.

It is however to be observed that a considerable number even of these people become sober, industrious citizens merely by the acquisition of property. The love of property to a certain degree seems indispensable to the existence of sound morals. I have never had a servant in whom I could confide except such as were desirous to earn and preserve money. The conveniences and the character, attendant on the preservation of property, fix even these restless men at times, when they find themselves really able to accumulate it, and persuade them to a course of regular industry. I have mentioned that they sell the soil of their first farms at an enhanced price, and that they gain for their improvements on them what, to themselves at least, is a considerable sum. The possession of this money removes, perhaps for the first time, the despair of acquiring property, and awakens the hope and the wish to acquire more. The secure possession of property demands, every moment, the hedge of law, and reconciles a man, originally lawless, to the restraints of government. Thus situated, he sees that reputation also is within his reach. Ambition forces him to aim at it, and compels him to a life of sobriety and decency. That his children may obtain this benefit, he is obliged to send them to school, and to unite with those around him in supporting a school-master. His neighbours are disposed to build a church and settle a Minister. A regard to his own character, to the character and feelings of his family, and very often to the solicitations of his wife, prompts him to contribute to both these objects; to attend, when they are compassed, upon the public worship of God; and perhaps to become in the end a religious man.   (1810) 1821

TIMOTHY FLINT

1780–1840

TIMOTHY FLINT, whom the Missionary Society of Connecticut sent into the wilderness to establish Presbyterianism and culture, resided in the Ohio Valley from 1815 to 1825. Notwithstanding his spread-eagle patriotism and his religious and political partisanship, few men portrayed the civilization of the frontier more realistically. In the following passage from his *Recollections of the Last Ten Years* he defends the West against the criticisms emanating from conservative Easterners. His position on the Indian question is also characteristic of the frontiersman. Flint, in spite of his failure to persuade the West to accept culture as rapidly as he wished, was an excellent spokesman for a developing region.

J. E. Kirkpatrick, *Timothy Flint, Pioneer, Missionary, Author, Editor, 1780–1840*, Cleveland, 1911.

» » *From:* RECOLLECTIONS OF THE LAST TEN YEARS « «

LETTER XVII

ST. CHARLES

The people in the Atlantic states have not yet recovered from the horror, inspired by the term "backwoodsman." This prejudice is particularly strong in New England, and is more or less felt from Maine to Georgia. When I first visited this country, I had my full share, and my family by far too much for their comfort. In approaching the country, I heard a thousand stories of gougings, and robberies, and shooting down with the rifle. I have travelled in these regions thousands of miles under all circumstances of exposure and danger. I have travelled alone, or in company only with such as needed protection, instead of being able to impart it; and this too, in many instances, where I was not known as a minister, or where such knowledge would have had no influence in protecting me. I never have carried the slightest weapon of defence. I scarcely remember to have experienced any thing that resembled insult, or to have felt myself in danger from the people. I have often seen men that had lost an eye. Instances of murder, numerous and horrible in their circumstances, have occurred in my vicinity. But they were such lawless rencounters, as terminate in murder every where, and in which the drunkenness, brutality, and violence were mutual. They were catastrophes, in which quiet and sober men would be in no danger of being involved. When we look round these immense regions, and consider that I have been in settlements three hundred miles from any court of justice, when we look at the position of the men, and the state of things, the wonder is, that so few outrages and murders occur. The gentlemen of the towns, even here, speak often with a certain contempt and horror of the backwoodsmen. I have read, and not without feelings of pain, the bitter representations of the learned and virtuous Dr. Dwight, in speaking of them. He represents these vast regions, as a grand reservoir for the scum of the Atlantic states. He characterizes in the mass the emigrants from New England, as discontented coblers, too proud, too much in debt, too unprincipled, too much puffed up with self-conceit, too strongly impressed that their fancied talents could not find scope in their own country, to stay there. It is true there are worthless people here, and the most so, it must be confessed, are from New England. It is true there are gamblers, and gougers, and outlaws; but there are fewer of them, than from the nature of things, and the character of the age and the world, we ought to expect. But it is unworthy of the excellent man in question so to designate this people in the mass. The backwoodsman of the west, as I have seen him, is generally an amiable and

virtuous man. His general motive for coming here is to be a freeholder, to have plenty of rich land, and to be able to settle his children about him. It is a most virtuous motive. And notwithstanding all that Dr. Dwight and Talleyrand have said to the contrary, I fully believe, that nine in ten of the emigrants have come here with no other motive. You find, in truth, that he has vices and barbarisms, pe-
10 culiar to his situation. His manners are rough. He wears, it may be, a long beard. He has a great quantity of bear or deer skins wrought into his household establishment, his furniture, and dress. He carries a knife, or a dirk in his bosom, and when in the woods has a rifle on his back, and a pack of dogs at his heels. An Atlantic stranger, transferred directly from one of our cities to his door, would recoil from a rencounter with him. But remember,
20 that his rifle and his dogs are among his chief means of support and profit. Remember, that all his first days here were passed in dread of the savages. Remember, that he still encounters them, still meets bears and panthers. Enter his door, and tell him you are benighted, and wish the shelter of his cabin for the night. The welcome is indeed seemingly ungracious: "I reckon you can stay," or "I suppose we must let you stay." But this apparent ungraciousness
30 is the harbinger of every kindness that he can bestow, and every comfort that his cabin can afford. Good coffee, corn bread and butter, venison, pork, wild and tame fowls are set before you. His wife, timid, silent, reserved, but constantly attentive to your comfort, does not sit at the table with you, but like the wives of the patriarchs, stands and attends on you. You are shown to the best bed which the house can offer. When this kind hospitality has been
40 afforded you as long as you choose to stay, and when you depart, and speak about your bill, you are most commonly told with some slight mark of resentment, that they do not keep tavern. Even the flaxen-headed urchins will turn away from your money.

In all my extensive intercourse with these people, I do not recollect but one instance of positive rudeness and inhospitality. . . .

With this single exception, I have found the
50 backwoodsmen to be such as I have described; a hardy, adventurous, hospitable, rough, but sincere and upright race of people. I have received so many kindnesses from them, that it becomes me always to preserve a grateful and affectionate remembrance of them. If we were to try them by the standard of New England customs and opinions, that is to say, the customs of a people under entirely different circumstances, there would be many things in the picture, that would strike us offensively. They care little about ministers, and think less about paying them. They are averse to all, even the most necessary restraints. They are destitute of the forms and observances of society and religion; but they are sincere and kind without professions, and have a coarse, but substantial morality, which is often rendered more striking by the immediate contrast of the graceful bows, civility, and professions of their French Catholic neighbours, who have the observances of society and the forms of worship, with often but a scanty modicum of the blunt truth and uprightness of their unpolished neighbours.

In the towns of the upper country on the Mississippi, and especially in St. Louis, there is one species of barbarism, that is but too common; I mean the horrid practice of duelling. But be it remembered, this is the barbarism only of that small class that denominate themselves "the gentlemen." It cannot be matter of astonishment that these are common here, when we recollect, that the fierce and adventurous spirits are naturally attracted to these regions, and that it is a common proverb of the people, that when we cross the Mississippi, "we travel beyond the Sabbath."

. . .

. . . Missouri and Illinois have imported from abroad many men respectable for their talents and acquirements. Many more have come here from abroad, expecting to eclipse every thing of brightness that was already in the country, and who have very unexpectedly found themselves eclipsed. Of the itinerant preachers, I did not hear one who approached to mediocrity. They may have been pious men, but, for the most part, they defy all criticism. I heard one gentleman, who was for a while esteemed a great orator at St. Louis, twice use a figure, which I think Swift would have selected, as a fine example of bathos. Speaking of the love of God, as naturally raising the soul to the object of that love, he illustrated the idea, by saying that the stream would always rise as high as the fountain. He added, that every lady had an explanation of this fact before her, when she saw the water rising as high in the nose, as in the body of the teapot!

I heard him quote Greek to the Missourians, and his knowledge of Greek was of a piece with the figure of the teapot.

I heard the Rev. Dr. B. the favourite orator of Tennessee, preach. I would not wish to laud him in the same affected strain, with the encomiums of the blind minister of Virginia. But he is certainly an extraordinary man in his way. His first appearance is against him, indicating a rough and uncouth man. He uses many low words, and images and illustrations in bad taste. But perhaps, when you are getting tired, almost disgusted, every thing is reversed in a moment. He flashes upon you. You catch his eye and you follow him; he bursts upon you in a glow of feeling and pathos, leaving you not sufficiently cool to criticise. We may affect to decry the talent of moving the inmost affections. After all, I am inclined to think it the most important qualification, which a minister can possess. He possesses this in an eminent degree. He has the electric eye, the thrilling tones, the unction, the feeling, the universal language of passion and nature, which is equally understood and felt by all people. He has evidently been richly endowed by nature; but his endowments owe little to discipline or education.

. . .

The people here are not yet a reading people. Few good books are brought into the country. The few literary men that are here, seeing nothing to excite or reward their pursuits, seeing other objects exclusively occupy all minds, soon catch the prevailing feeling. The people are too busy, too much occupied in making farms and speculations, to think of literature.

America inherits, I believe, from England a taste for puffing. She has improved upon her model. In your quarter, as well as here, the people are idolaters to the "golden calves." Some favourite man, fashion, or opinion, sweep every thing before them. This region is the paradise of puffers. One puffs up, and another down. As you draw near the influence of the "lord of the ascendant," you will find opinions graduated to his *dicta*. The last stranger that arrives from Kentucky, or the Atlantic country, is but poorly introduced to his new residence, if he have not one of these great men to puff a breeze in the sail of his skiff, as he puts himself afloat.

I have been amused in reading puffing advertisements in the newspapers. A little subscription school, in which half the pupils are abecedarians, is a college. One is a Lancastrian school, or a school of "instruction mutuelle." There is the Pestalozzi establishment, with its appropriate emblazoning. There is the agricultural school, the missionary school, the grammar box, the new way to make a wit of a dunce in six lessons, and all the mechanical ways of inoculating children with learning, that they may not endure the pain of getting it in the old and natural way. I would not have you smile exclusively at the people of the West. This ridiculous species of swindling is making as much progress in your country as here. The misfortune is, that these vile pretensions finally induce the people to believe, that there is a "royal road" to learning. The old and beaten track, marked out by the only sure guide, experience, is forsaken. The parents are flattered, deceived, and swindled. Puffing pretenders take the place of the modest man of science, who scorns to compete with him in these vile arts. The children have their brains distended with the "east wind," and grow up at once empty and conceited.

These founders of new schools, for the most part, advertise themselves from London, Paris, Philadelphia, New York, Boston, and have all performed exploits in the regions whence they came, and bring the latest improvements with them. As to what they can do, and what they will do, the object is to lay on the colouring thick and threefold. A respectable man wishes to establish himself in a school in those regions. He consults a friend, who knows the meridian of the country. The advice is, Call your school by some new and imposing name. Let it be understood, that you have a new way of instructing children, by which they can learn twice as much, in half the time, as by the old ways. Throw off all modesty. Move the water, and get in while it is moving. In short, depend upon the *gullibility* of the people. A school, modelled on this advice, was instituted at St. Louis, while I was there, with a very imposing name. The masters,—professors, I should say,—proposed to teach most of the languages, and all the sciences. Hebrew they would communicate in twelve lessons; Latin and Greek, with a proportionate promptness. These men, who were to teach all this themselves, had read Erasmus with a translation, and knew the Greek alphabet, and in their public discourses,—for they were ministers,—sometimes dealt very abusively with the "king's English."

Town-making introduces another species of puffing. Art and ingenuity have been exhausted in devising new ways of alluring purchasers, to take lots and build in the new town. There are the fine rivers, the healthy hills, the mineral springs, the clear running water, the eligible mill-seats, the valuable forests, the quarries of building-stone, the fine steam-boat navigation, the vast country adjacent, the central position, the connecting point between the great towns, the admirable soil, and last of all the cheerful and undoubting predictions of what the town must one day be. I have read more than an hundred advertisements of this sort. Then the legislature must be tampered with, in order to make the town either the metropolis, or at least the seat of justice. In effect, we were told that in Illinois, two influential men, who both had Tadmors [1] to be upreared, took a hand of cards, to ascertain which should resign his pretensions to legislative aid in building his town, in favour of the other.

A coarse caricature of this abomination of town-making, appeared in the St. Louis papers. The name was "Ne plus ultra." The streets were laid out a mile in width; the squares were to be sections, each containing six hundred and forty acres. The mall was a vast standing forest. In the centre of this modern Babylon, roads were to cross each other in a meridional line at right angles, one from the south pole to Symmes's hole in the north, and another from Pekin to Jerusalem.

In truth, while travelling on the prairies of the Illinois and Missouri, and observing such immense tracts of rich soil, of the blackness of ink, and of exhaustless fertility,—remarking the beautiful simplicity of the limits of farms, introduced by our government, in causing the land to be all surveyed in exact squares, and thus destroying here the barbarous prescription, which has in the settled countries laid out the lands in ugly farms; and bounded them by zigzag lines,—contemplating the hedge of verdure that will bound the squares on these smooth and fertile plains,—remarking the beauty of the orchards and improvements, that must ensue,—being convinced that the climate will grow salubrious with its population and improvement,—seeing the guardian genius,

1 An allusion to a city built by King Solomon in the wilderness. See 2 Chronicles 8:4.

Liberty, hovering over the country,—measuring the progress of the future, only by the analogy of the past,—it will be difficult for the imagination to assign limits to the future growth and prosperity of the country. Perhaps on one of these boundless plains, and contiguous to some one of these noble rivers, in view of these hoary bluffs, and where all these means of the subsistence and multiplication of the species are concentered in such ample abundance, will arise the actual "Ne plus ultra." On looking at the astonishing change, which the last ten years have introduced over the whole face of the United States, and anticipating the change of a century, I have sometimes found the famous wish of Franklin stealing into my mind, with respect to the interesting country which I am describing.

LETTER XVI

ST. CHARLES

Our government can be contemplated in no point of view, more calculated to inspire affection and respect to it, than in the steady dignity, moderation, benevolence, and untiring forbearance, which it has constantly exercised towards the Indians. I have had great opportunities to see the strictness of its provisions to prevent the sale of whiskey among them, and to see the generous exertions which it has made to preserve them from destroying themselves, and from killing each other. It appears to have been the guiding maxim of the government, to ward off all evil, and to do all practicable good to this unhappy and declining race of beings. It seems to have been, too, an effort of disinterested benevolence. Had it been the policy of the government, as has been charged against it, to exterminate the race, it would only be necessary to use but a small part of the ample means in its power, to let them loose, the one tribe upon the other, and they would mutually accomplish the work of self-destruction. Nothing farther would be needed, than to unkennel them, excite their jealousies, and stir up their revenge. We have heard and read the benevolent harangues upon the guilt of having destroyed the past races of this people, and of having possessed ourselves of their lands. Continual war is the natural instinct of this race. It was equally so when white men first trod the American forest. It is not less so now, that the government exercises a benevolent restraint, and keeps them from killing each other. We firmly believe, that all ideas of property in the lands over which they roamed after game, or skulked in ambush to kill one another, all notions of a local habitation, have been furnished them by the Americans. When they were in one place to day, defending themselves against a tribe at the east, and ready to march tomorrow to dispossess another tribe at the west, and they in their turn to dispossess another tribe still beyond them, it never occurred to them to consider the land over which they marched for war or for game, as their own in permanent property, until they were taught its value by the idea which the whites attached to it. No fact is more questionable, than that ages before the whites visited these shores, they were divided into a thousand petty tribes, engaged,—as but for our government they would be now,—in endless and exterminating wars, in which they dashed the babe into the flames, and drank the warm blood of their victim, or danced and yelled around the stake where he was consuming in the fire. The process of their depopulation had been, in all probability, going on as rapidly before the discovery of the country by the whites, as since. I shall elsewhere speak of the manifest proofs of an immensely greater population in these regions than now exists. Did this race exterminate that, of which the only remaining trace is the numberless mounds, filled with human bones, which rise in the lonely prairies of the west? Certain it is, that war is the instinctive appetite of the present race, and that a state of peace is a forced and unnatural state.

I am perfectly aware, that these are not the views, which have been fashionable of late, in discussing this subject. You will do me the justice to believe, that I have aimed at but one thing,—to describe things just as they are; or at least, as they appeared to me. Truth, simple, undisguised truth is my object; and upon this, as upon all other subjects, it will ultimately prevail. Perhaps it may be said, that it is not in the vicinity of Fort Mims, or among the frontier people, that the most flattering views of the savages are to be obtained. I grant it; but I think that in the history of the ancient Canadian wars, and in the regions where I have so long sojourned, are to be found the most just, if not the most flattering views of this people. They are not the less to

be pitied, because they are a cruel people by nature. They are not less to be the objects of our best wishes and our prayers, because they have no sympathy with suffering. From my inmost soul I wish them to become the followers of Jesus Christ. I venerate the men who will venture on the hard and unpromising task of attempting their conversion. But with all these wishes, I could not disguise from myself, that such as I have represented, is the natural character of this people.

Something may be said, no doubt, in opposition to these views of the subject; as, that the frontier people have been often the aggressors in Indian quarrels. The character of the frontier people, has been much misrepresented. They are generally a harmless and inoffensive race. I have not a doubt that most of these quarrels originate in the natural jealousies of the Indians. I have been present in two instances, where they had committed murders, attended the inquest, and heard the evidence. In both cases the murders were entirely unprovoked, even the parties themselves being witnesses. They are a people extremely jealous, addicted to what the French call "tracasserie," to suspicions, and whisperings. A tribe never hunts long on our immediate frontier, without stealing horses, getting into broils, and committing murder, either among our people, or among themselves. But, it is objected, they are intoxicated, and we furnish them the means. It is true, they will be drunk, whenever they can, and this is not a very favourable trait. It is also true, that the government has established the most rigid regulations to prevent their getting whiskey, and has enforced these regulations with heavy penalties for their violation, and I have frequently seen these penalties imposed.

I remember to have seen a young Chactaw warrior, very finely dressed and painted, drunk at the piazza of the house where I lived. He made every effort to quarrel with the white people, who were about the house, and was extremely abusive and insulting. When he found that no one would quarrel with him, in revenge he plunged his knife into the neck of a beautiful horse which he was holding by the halter.

A respectable trader at the post of Arkansas had informed against another trader in the village, who had sold whiskey to the Indians. This thing always incurs their extreme resentment. I heard this gentleman in conversation

with two drunken Indians, who had slept the preceding night under his piazza. They were insolent and quarrelsome in the morning. He observed to me that could he find who had enabled them to get drunk, he would inform against him. He asked them, where they had purchased their whiskey? They gave him a bitter smile, and intimated, that they well understood his object, in asking the question.
10 He somewhat sternly repeated the question, "Where did you purchase your whiskey?" They held their bottles up in the air, and informed him, that the "great Kentucky captain," pointing to the clouds, had rained the whiskey into their bottles.

In the immense extent of frontier, which I have visited, I have heard many an affecting tale of the horrible barbarities and murders of the Indians, precisely of a character with
20 those, which used to be recorded in the early periods of New England history. I saw two children, the only members of a family—consisting of a father, mother, and a number of children—that were spared by the Indians. It was on the river Femme-Osage. A party of Sacs and Foxes, that had been burning and murdering in the vicinity, came upon the house, as the father was coming in from abroad. They shot him, and he fled, wounded,
30 a little distance and fell. They then tomahawked the wife, and mangled her body. She had been boiling the sap of the sugar-maple. The Indians threw two of the children into the boiling kettles. The younger of the two orphans that I saw, was but three years old. His sister two years older, drew him under the bed before they were seen by the Indians. It had, in the fashion of the country, a cotton counterpane that descended to the floor. The
40 howling of these demons, the firing, the barking of the dogs, the shrieking of the children that became their victims, never drew from these poor things, that were trembling under the bed, a cry, or the smallest noise. The Indians thrust their knives through the bed, that nothing concealed there, might escape them, and went off, through fear of pursuit, leaving these desolate beings unharmed.

You will see the countenances of the frontier
50 people, as they relate numberless tragic occurrences of this sort, gradually kindling. There seems, between them and the savages, a deeprooted enmity, like that between the seed of the woman and the serpent. They would be

more than human, if retaliation were not sometimes the consequence. They tell you, with a certain expression of countenance, that in former days when they met an Indian in the woods, they were very apt to see him suffer under the falling-sickness. This dreadful state of things has now passed away, and I have seldom heard of late of a murder committed by the whites upon the Indians. Twenty years ago, the Indians and whites both considered, when casual rencounters took place in the woods, that it was a fair shot upon both sides. A volume would not contain the cases of these unrecorded murders.

The narrations of a frontier circle, as they draw round their evening fire, often turn upon the exploits of the old race of men, the heroes of the past days, who wore hunting shirts, and settled the country. Instances of undaunted heroism, of desperate daring, and seemingly of more than mortal endurance, are recorded of these people. In a boundless forest full of panthers and bears, and more dreadful Indians, with not a white within a hundred miles, a solitary adventurer penetrates the deepest wilderness, and begins to make the strokes of his axe resound among the trees. The Indians find him out, ambush, and imprison him. A more acute and desperate warrior than themselves, they wish to adopt him, and add his strength to their tribe. He feigns contentment, uses the savage's insinuations, outruns him in the use of his own ways of management, but watches his opportunity, and when their suspicion is lulled, and they fall asleep, he springs upon them, kills his keepers, and bounds away into unknown forests, pursued by them and their dogs. He leaves them all at fault, subsists many days upon berries and roots, and finally arrives at his little clearing, and resumes his axe. In a little palisade, three or four resolute men stand a siege of hundreds of assailants, kill many of them, and mount calmly on the roof of their shelter, to pour water upon the fire, which burning arrows have kindled there, and achieve the work amidst a shower of balls. A thousand instances of that stern and unshrinking courage which had shaken hands with death, of that endurance which defied all the inventions of Indian torture, are recorded of these wonderful men. The dread of being roasted alive by the Indians, called into action all their hidden energies and resources.

1826

DANIEL WEBSTER

1782–1852

IN HIS FIRST BUNKER HILL oration and in his address at Plymouth, Webster, who had by 1828 become the representative of New England's rising industrialism, showed a remarkable ability to persuade his listeners to identify the values of New England with those of the country as a whole. But Webster realized that the interests of industrial New England, which no doubt he sincerely did believe to be identical with those of the nation, could not be realized in national policy unless the Northeast enjoyed the alliance of the West in the federal Congress. The election of Jackson in 1828 had, however, effected an entente between the agricultural South and West. When Senator Foot of Connecticut introduced in 1830 a resolution asking for an inquiry into the expediency of limiting the sale of western lands, Senator Hayne of South Carolina, anxious to cement this alliance, endeavored to persuade the West that the East had always selfishly tried to restrict the growth of the West.

Webster took up the challenge and in his great debate with Hayne endeavored to disprove this contention. He further told the West, in effect, that its own interests could be best served by an alliance with the East for the promotion of internal improvements and the protection of industry against foreign competition. But what made Webster's replies to Hayne live in oratorical literature and in the hearts of a rising generation of Northern and Western youth was the skill which he displayed in endearing to them the symbol of the Union. Until 1850 Webster remained a great hero in the North. When, in that year, he gave his support to the compromise measures which he felt alone could preserve the union, the antislavery forces of the North regarded him as a traitor to their standard.

The Writings and Speeches of Daniel Webster, National Edition, 18 vols., Boston, 1903.
F. J. Turner, *The United States, 1830–1850*, New York, 1935.
Richard N. Current, *Daniel Webster and the Rise of National Conservatism*, Boston, 1955.

» » From: FIRST SPEECH ON FOOT'S RESOLUTION[1] « «

. . . I now proceed, Sir, to some of the opinions expressed by the gentleman from South Carolina. Two or three topics were touched by him, in regard to which he expressed sentiments in which I do not at all concur.

In the first place, Sir, the honorable gentleman spoke of the whole course and policy of the government towards those who have purchased and settled the public lands, and seemed to think this policy wrong. He held it to have been, from the first, hard and rigorous; he was of opinion, that the United States had acted towards those who had subdued the Western wilderness in the spirit of a stepmother; that the public domain had been improperly regarded as a source of revenue; and that we had rigidly compelled payment for that which ought to have been given away. He said we ought to have imitated the example of other governments, which had acted on a much more liberal system than ours, in planting colonies. He dwelt, particularly, upon the settlement of America by colonies from Europe; and reminded us, that their governments had not exacted from those colonies payment for the soil. In reference to them, he said, it had been thought that the conquest of the wilderness was itself an equivalent for the soil, and he lamented that we had not fol-

[1] Delivered in the Senate of the United States, on the 20th of January, 1830. [The editor of Webster's *Writings*.]

lowed that example, and pursued the same liberal course towards our own emigrants to the West.

Now, Sir, I deny, altogether, that there has been any thing harsh or severe in the policy of the government towards the new States of the West. On the contrary, I maintain that it has uniformly pursued towards those States a liberal and enlightened system, such as its own duty allowed and required, and such as their interest and welfare demanded. The government has been no step-mother to the new States. She has not been careless of their interests, nor deaf to their requests; but from the first moment when the territories which now form those States were ceded to the Union, down to the time in which I am now speaking, it has been the invariable object of the government, to dispose of the soil according to the true spirit of the obligation under which it received it; to hasten its settlement and cultivation, as far and as fast as practicable; and to rear the new communities into new and independent States, at the earliest moment of their being able, by their numbers, to form a regular government.

. . . I come now, Mr. President, to that part of the gentleman's speech which has been the main occasion of my addressing the Senate. The East! the obnoxious, the rebuked, the always reproached East!—we have come in, Sir, on this debate, for even more than a common share of accusation and attack. If the honorable member from South Carolina was not our original accuser, he has yet recited the indictment against us with the air and tone of a public prosecutor. He has summoned us to plead on our arraignment; and he tells us we are charged with the crime of a narrow and selfish policy; of endeavoring to restrain emigration to the West, and, having that object in view, of maintaining a steady opposition to Western measures and Western interests. And the cause of all this narrow and selfish policy, the gentleman finds in the tariff; I think he called it the accursed policy of the tariff. This policy, the gentleman tells us, requires multitudes of dependent laborers, a population of paupers, and that it is to secure these at home that the East opposes whatever may induce to Western emigration. Sir, I rise to defend the East. I rise to repel, both the charge itself, and the cause assigned for it. I deny that the East has, at any time, shown an illiberal policy towards the West. I pronounce the whole accusation to be

without the least foundation in any facts, existing either now or at any previous time. I deny it in the general, and I deny each and all its particulars. I deny the sum total, and I deny the detail. I deny that the East has ever manifested hostility to the West, and I deny that she has adopted any policy that would naturally have led her in such a course.

But the tariff! The tariff!! Sir, I beg to say in regard to the East, that the original policy of the tariff is not hers, whether it be wise or unwise. New England is not its author. If gentlemen will refer to the tariff of 1816, they will find that this was not carried by New England votes. It was truly more a Southern than an Eastern measure. And what votes carried the tariff of 1824? Certainly not those of New England. It is known to have been made matter of reproach, especially against Massachusetts, that she would not aid the tariff of 1824; and a selfish motive was imputed to her for that, also. In point of fact, it is true that she did, indeed, oppose the tariff of 1824. There were more votes in favor of that law in the House of Representatives, not only in each of a majority of the Western States, but even in Virginia herself, than in Massachusetts. It was literally forced upon New England; and this shows how groundless, how void of all probability, must be any charge of hostility to the growth of the Western States, as naturally flowing from a cherished policy of her own.

But leaving all conjectures about causes and motives, I go at once to the fact, and I meet it with one broad, comprehensive, and emphatic negative. I deny that, in any part of her history, at any period of the government, or in relation to any leading subject, New England has manifested such hostility as is charged upon her. On the contrary, I maintain that, from the day of the cession of the territories by the States to Congress, no portion of the country has acted either with more liberality or more intelligence, on the subject of the public lands in the new States, than New England.

This statement, though strong, is no stronger than the strictest truths will warrant. Let us look at the historical facts. So soon as the cessions were obtained, it became necessary to make provision for the government and disposition of the territory. The country was to be governed. This, for the present, it was obvious, must be by some territorial system of administration. But the soil, also, was to be granted and settled. Those immense regions, large enough almost for an empire, were to be appropriated to private ownership. How was this best to be done? What system for sale and disposition should be adopted? Two modes for conducting the sales presented themselves; the one a Southern, and the other a Northern mode. It would be tedious, Sir, here, to run out these different systems into all their distinctions, and to contrast the opposite results. That which was adopted was the Northern system, and is that which we now see in successful operation in all the new States. That which was rejected was the system of warrants, surveys, entry, and location; such as prevails south of the Ohio. It is not necessary to extend these remarks into invidious comparisons. This last system is that which, as has been expressively said, has *shingled* over the country to which it was applied with so many conflicting titles and claims. Every body acquainted with the subject knows how easily it leads to speculation and litigation,—two great calamities in a new country. From the system actually established, these evils are banished. Now, Sir, in effecting this great measure, the first important measure on the whole subject, New England acted with vigor and effect, and the latest posterity of those who settled the region northwest of the Ohio will have reason to remember, with gratitude, her patriotism and her wisdom. The system adopted was her own system. She knew, for she had tried and proved its value. It was the old-fashioned way of surveying lands before the issuing of any title papers, and then of inserting accurate and precise descriptions in the patents or grants, and proceeding with regular reference to metes and bounds. This gives to original titles, derived from government, a certain and fixed character; it cuts up litigation by the roots, and the settler commences his labor with the assurance that he has a clear title. It is easy to perceive, but not easy to measure, the importance of this in a new country. New England gave this system to the West; and while it remains, there will be spread over all the West one monument of her intelligence in matters of government, and her practical good sense.

At the foundation of the constitution of these new Northwestern States lies the celebrated Ordinance of 1787. We are accustomed, Sir, to praise the lawgivers of antiquity; we help to perpetuate the fame of Solon and Lycurgus; but I doubt whether one single law of any lawgiver, ancient or modern, has produced effects of more distinct, marked, and lasting character than the Ordinance of 1787. That instrument was drawn by Nathan Dane, then and now a citizen of Massachusetts. It was adopted, as I think I have understood, without the slightest alteration; and certainly it has happened to few men to be the authors of a political measure of more large and enduring consequence. It fixed for ever the character of the population in the vast regions northwest of the Ohio, by excluding from them involuntary servitude. It impressed on the soil itself, while it was yet a wilderness, an incapacity to sustain any other than freemen. It laid the interdict against personal servitude, in original compact, not only deeper than all local law, but deeper, also, than all local constitutions. Under the circumstances then existing, I look upon this original and seasonable provision as a real good attained. We see its consequences at this moment, and we shall never cease to see them, perhaps, while the Ohio shall flow. It was a great and salutary measure of prevention. Sir, I should fear the rebuke of no intelligent gentleman of Kentucky, were I to ask whether, if such an ordinance could have been applied to his own State, while it yet was a wilderness, and before Boone had passed the gap of the Alleghanies, he does not suppose it would have contributed to the ultimate greatness of that commonwealth? It is, at any rate, not to be doubted, that, where it did apply, it has produced an effect not easily to be described or measured, in the growth of the States, and the extent and increase of their population. Now, Sir, as I have stated, this great measure was brought forward in 1787, by the North. It was sustained, indeed, by the votes of the South, but it must have failed without the cordial support of the New England States. If New England had been governed by the narrow and selfish views now ascribed to her, this very measure was, of all others, the best calculated to thwart her purposes. It was, of all things, the very means of rendering certain a vast emigration from her own population to the West. She looked to that consequence only to disregard it. She deemed the regulation a most useful one to the States that would spring up on the territory, and advantageous to the country at large. She adhered to the principle of it perseveringly, year after year, until it was finally accomplished.

Leaving, then, Mr. President, these two great and leading measures, and coming down to our own times, what is there in the history of recent measures of government that exposes New England to this accusation of hostility to Western interests? I assert, boldly, that, in all measures conducive to the welfare of the West, since my acquaintance here, no part of the country has manifested a more liberal policy. I beg to say, Sir, that I do not state this with a view of claiming for her any special regard on that account. Not at all. She does not place her support of measures on the ground of favor conferred. Far otherwise. What she has done has been consonant to her view of the general good, and therefore she has done it. She has sought to make no gain of it; on the contrary, individuals may have felt, undoubtedly, some natural regret at finding the relative importance of their own States diminished by the growth of the West. But New England has regarded that as the natural course of things, and has never complained of it. Let me see, Sir, any one measure favorable to the West, which has been opposed by New England, since the government bestowed its attention on these Western improvements. Select what you will, if it be a measure of acknowledged utility, I answer for it, it will be found that not only were New England votes for it, but that New England votes carried it. Will you take the Cumberland Road? who has made that? Will you take the Portland Canal? whose support carried that bill? Sir, at what period beyond the Greek kalends could these measures, or measures like these, have been accomplished, had they depended on the votes of Southern gentlemen? Why, Sir, we know that we must have waited till the constitutional notions of those gentlemen had undergone an entire change. Generally speaking, they have done nothing, and can do nothing. All that has been effected has been done by the votes of reproached New England. I undertake to say, Sir, that if you look to the votes on any one of these measures, and strike out from the list of ayes the names of New England members, it will be found that, in every case, the South would then have voted down the West, and the measure would have failed. I do not believe any one instance can be found where this is not strictly true. I do not believe that one dollar has been expended for these purposes beyond the mountains, which could have been obtained without cordial coöperation and support from New England.

Sir, I put the question to the West itself. Let gentlemen who have sat here ten years come forth and declare, by what aids, and by whose votes, they have succeeded, in measures deemed of essential importance to their part of the country. To all men of sense and candor, in or out of Congress, who have any knowledge upon the subject, New England may appeal for refutation of the reproach it is now attempted to cast upon her in this respect.

I take the liberty to repeat, that I make no claim on behalf of New England, or on account of that which I have now stated. She does not profess to have acted out of favor; for it would not become her so to have acted. She asks for no especial thanks; but, in the consciousness of having done her duty in these things uprightly and honestly, and with a fair and liberal spirit, be assured she will repel, whenever she thinks the occasion calls for it, an unjust and groundless imputation of partiality and selfishness.

The gentleman alluded to a report of the late Secretary of the Treasury, which, according to his reading or construction of it, recommended what he calls the tariff policy, or a branch of that policy; that is, the restraining of emigration to the West, for the purpose of keeping hands at home to carry on manufactures. I think, Sir, that the gentleman misapprehended the meaning of the Secretary, in the interpretation given to his remarks. I understand him only as saying, that, since the low price of lands at the West acts as a constant and standing bounty to agriculture, it is, on that account, the more reasonable to provide encouragement for manufactures. But, Sir, even if the Secretary's observation were to be understood as the gentleman understands it, it would not be a sentiment borrowed from any New England source. Whether it be right or wrong, it does not originate in that quarter.

1830

EDWARD EVERETT

1794–1865

IN EDWARD EVERETT New England's conservative interests found a talented representative. Unitarian clergyman, scholar, President of Harvard, orator, and political leader,
Everett showed no hesitation in taking sides in controversial issues. As representative in Congress (1825–1835) he deferred to the Southern position on slavery, a position congenial to
the interests of Massachusetts industrialists whose economic ties with the planters of the South
were close and profitable. Everett also upheld the United States Bank, and, as governor of
Massachusetts, lent support to railroad projects and to the newly established state board of
education. On the other hand, the "Levellers" or Jacksonian radicals found in Everett an
able foe. His devotion to the cause of the Union and to "Americanism," evident both in his
florid orations and in his diplomatic career as ambassador to Great Britain and as secretary
of state, in no way ran counter to his essential conservatism in political and economic matters.

Like other New England conservatives, Everett saw with alarm the growth of the West,
as it appeared to be given to such economic vagaries as cheap money, decentralized banking,
and other policies inimical to the creditor and property-conscious class. His appeal to philanthropists to support Western academic institutions as "civilizing agents" shows again the
fusion of his loyalty to his class, his section, and the nation as a whole.

Orations and Speeches on Various Occasions, 4 vols., Boston, 1853–1892.
P. R. Frothingham, *Edward Everett, Orator and Statesman,* Boston and New York, 1925.

» » *From:* EDUCATION IN THE WESTERN STATES « «

The lucid exposition which has been made of
the object of the meeting by the right reverend
bishop (McIlvaine) lightens the task of recommending it to an audience like this. I do not
know but I should act more advisedly to leave
his cogent and persuasive statement to produce
its natural effect, without any attempt on my
part to enforce it. But as we have assembled to
communicate our mutual impressions on the
subject,—to consult with each other whether
we *can* do any thing, and whether we *will* do
any thing, to promote the object in view,
(which, I own, seems to me one of high moment,) I will, with the indulgence of the meeting, and at the request of those by whom it is
called, briefly state the aspect in which the
matter presents itself to my mind.

I understand the object of the meeting to be,
to aid the funds of a rising seminary of learning in the interior of the state of Ohio, particularly with a view to the training up of a well-

educated ministry of the gospel in that part of
the United States; and to consider the claims of
such an object on this community.

As to the general question of the establishment and support of places of education, there
are principally *two courses* which have been
pursued in the practice of nations. One is, to
leave them, so to say, as an after-thought,—the
last thing provided for;—to let the community
grow up, become populous, rich, powerful; an
immense body of unenlightened peasants,
artisans, traders, soldiers, subjected to a small
privileged class;—and then let learning creep
in with luxury; be itself esteemed a luxury, endowed out of the surplus of vast private fortunes, or endowed by the state; and instead of
diffusing a wholesome general influence, of
which all partake, and by which the entire
character of the people is softened and elevated, forming itself but another of those circumstances of disparity and jealous contrast of

condition, of which too many were in existence before; adding the aristocracy of learning, acquired at expensive seats of science, to that of rank and wealth. This is, in general, the course which has been pursued with respect to the establishment of places of education in some countries of Europe. The other method is that introduced by our forefathers, namely, to lay the foundations of the commonwealth on the corner-stone of religion and education; to make the means of enlightening the community go hand in hand with the means for protecting it against its enemies, extending its commerce, and increasing its numbers; to make the care of the mind, from the outset, a part of its public economy; the growth of knowledge, a portion of its public wealth.

This, sir, is the New England system. It is the system on which the colony of Massachusetts was led, in 1647, to order that a school should be supported in every town; and in every town containing a hundred families, the school was required to be one where youth could "be fitted for the university." On the same system, eleven years earlier, the foundations of Harvard College were laid, by an appropriation out of the scanty means of the country, and at a period of great public distress, of a sum equal to the whole amount raised during the year for all other public charges. I do not know in what words I can so well describe this system, as in those used by our fathers themselves. Quoted as they have been, times innumerable, they will bear quoting again, and seem to me peculiarly apposite to this occasion: "After God had carried us safe to New England, and we had builded our houses, provided necessaries for our livelihood, reared convenient places for God's worship, and settled the civil government, one of the next things we longed for and looked after was to advance learning, and perpetuate it to posterity; dreading to leave an illiterate ministry to the churches, when the present ministers shall be in the dust."

Now, sir, it is proposed to assist our brethren in Ohio to lay the foundations of their commonwealth on this good old New England basis; and if ever there was a region where it was peculiarly expedient that this should be done, most assuredly the western part of America—and the state of Ohio as much as any other portion of it—is that region. It is two centuries since New England was founded, and its population by the last census fell short of two

millions. Forty years ago, Ohio was a wilderness, and, by the same enumeration, its population was little less than a million. At this moment, the population of Ohio (the settlement of which was commenced in 1788, by a small party from our counties of Essex and Middlesex) is almost twice as large as that of our ancient and venerable Massachusetts. I have seen this wonderful state, and the terraqueous globe does not contain a spot more favorably situated. Linked to New Orleans on one side by its own beautiful river and the father of waters, and united to New York on the other side by the lake and the Erie Canal, she has, by a stupendous exertion of her own youthful resources, completed the vast circuit of communication between them. The face of the country is unusually favorable to settlement. There is little waste or broken land. The soil is fertile, the climate salubrious; it is settled by as truehearted and substantial a race as ever founded a republic; and there they now stand, a million of souls, gathered into a political community in a single generation!

Now, it is plain that this extraordinary rapidity of increase requires extraordinary means to keep the moral and intellectual growth of the people on an equality with their advancement in numbers and prosperity. These last take care of themselves. They require nothing but protection from foreign countries, and security of property, under the ordinary administration of justice. But a system of institutions for education—schools and colleges—requires extra effort and means. The individual settler can fell the forest, build his log-house, reap his crops, and raise up his family, in the round of occupations pursued by himself; but he cannot, of himself, found or support a school, far less a college; nor can he do as much towards it as a single individual in older states, where ampler resources and a denser population afford means, coöperation, and encouragement at every turn. The very fact, therefore, that the growth of the country in numbers has been unexampled, instead of suggesting reasons why efforts in the cause of education are superfluous, furnishes an increased and increasing claim on the sympathy and good offices of all the friends of learning and education.

What, then, are the reasonable grounds of the claim, as made on us? I think I perceive several.

We live in a community comparatively ancient, possessed of an abundance of accumulated capital, the result of the smiles of Providence on the industry of the people. We profess to place a high value on intellectual improvement, on education, on religion, and on the institutions for its support. We habitually take credit that we do so. To whom should the infant community, destitute of these institutions, desirous of enjoying their benefits, and as yet not abounding in disposable means,—to whom should they look? Whither shall they go, but to their brethren, who are able to appreciate the want, and competent to relieve it? Some one must do it. These institutions, struggling into existence, must be nurtured, or they sink. To what quarter can they address themselves, with any prospect of success, if they fail here? Where will they find a community more likely to take an interest in the object, to feel a livelier sympathy in the want, more liberal, more able to give, more accustomed to give?

It is not merely in the necessity of things, that young and rising communities, if assisted at all, should derive that assistance from the older and richer; but the period is so short, since we ourselves stood in that relation to the mother country, and derived, from her bounty, benefactions to our institutions, that the obligation to requite these favors, in the only practicable way, is fresh and strong, and like that which requires a man to pay his debts. Dr. Franklin was accustomed, sometimes, to bestow a pecuniary favor on a young man, and, instead of requiring payment, to enjoin the object of his bounty, when advanced in life, and in prosperous circumstances, to give the same sum of money, with a like injunction, to some other meritorious and needy young person. The early annals of our country contain many instances of liberality from beyond the ocean. Our own University and that of New Haven were largely indebted—particularly ours—to pious and benevolent individuals in England. I know no mode of requiting these favors (which we cannot repay to the country from which we received them; she wants nothing we can give) more natural and more simple, than by imitating the liberality of which we have profited, and supplying the wants of others, at that stage of their social progress, at which our own were supplied.

The inducements to such an exercise of liberality, on our part, towards our brethren in the west, are certainly stronger than those which could have influenced England to assist the rising institutions of America. The settlers of the western country are not the aggrieved and persecuted children of the older states. We have not driven them out from among us, by cruel Star Chamber edicts; nor have they, in leaving us, shaken off from their feet the dust of an unfriendly soil. They have moved away from the paternal roof, to seek a new but not a foreign home. They have parted from their native land, neither in anger nor despair; but full of buoyant hope and tender regret. They have gone to add to the American family, not to dismember it. They are our brethren, not only after the flesh, but after the spirit also, in character and in feeling. We, in our place, regard them neither with indifference, jealousy, nor enmity, but with fraternal affection and true good will. Whom, in the name of Heaven, should we assist, if we refuse to assist them? What, sir, can we minister to the intellectual and spiritual wants of Syria, and of Greece, of Burmah, of Ceylon, and of the remotest isles of the Pacific? Have we enough, and to spare, for those remote nations and tribes, with whom we have no nearer kindred, than that Adam is our common parent, and Christ our common Savior; and shall we shut our hands on the call for the soul's food, which is addressed to us, by these our brethren, our schoolmates; whose fathers stood side by side with ours, in the great crisis of the country's fortune; whose forefathers rest side by side with ours, in the sacred soil of New England? I say nothing, sir, in disparagement of the efforts made to carry the gospel to the farthest corners of the earth. I wish, with all my heart, entire success to those efforts. But, surely, the law of Christian love will not permit us, in our care for the distant heathen, to overlook the claims of our fellow-citizens at home.

On a theme like this, I am unwilling to appeal to any thing like interest; nor will I appeal to an interest of a low and narrow character; but I cannot shut my eyes on those great considerations of an enlarged policy, which demand of us a reasonable liberality towards the improvements of these western communities. In the year 1800, the state of Ohio sent one member to Congress; and Massachusetts—not then separated from Maine—sent twenty-one. Now, Ohio sends nineteen; and Massachusetts—recently, and I am constrained to add, in my judgment, unfairly,[1] deprived of one of her

[1] By adopting a ratio of representation which left Massachusetts with an unrepresented fraction, sufficient, within a few hundreds, for another member. [Everett's note.]

members—sends but twelve. Nor will it stop here. "They must increase," and we, in comparison, "must decrease." At the next periodical enumeration Ohio will probably be entitled to nearly thirty representatives, and Massachusetts to little more than a third of this number. Now, sir, I will not, on this occasion, and in this house of prayer, unnecessarily introduce topics and illustrations, better befitting other resorts.
10 I will not descant on interests and questions, which, in the divided state of the public councils, will be decided, one way or the other, by a small majority of voices. I really wish to elevate my own mind, and, as far as lies in me, the minds of those I have the honor to address, to higher views. I would ask you, not in reference to this or that question, but in reference to the whole complexion of the destinies of the country, as depending on the action of the gen-
20 eral government,—I would ask you as to that momentous future which lies before us and our children,—By whom, by what influence, from what quarter is our common country, with all the rich treasure of its character, its hopes, its fortunes, to be controlled, to be sustained, and guided in the paths of wisdom, honor, and prosperity, or sunk into the depth of degeneracy and humiliation? Sir, the response is in every man's mind, on every man's lips. The balance
30 of the country's fortunes is in the west. There lie, wrapped up in the folds of an eventful futurity, the influences which will most powerfully affect our national weal and woe. We have, in the order of Providence, allied ourselves to a family of sister communities, springing into existence and increasing with unexampled rapidity. We have called them into a full partnership in the government; the course of events has put crowns on their heads and scep-
40 tres in their hands; and we must abide the result.
But has the power indeed departed from us —the efficient, ultimate power? That, sir, is in a great measure as we will. The real government, in this country, is that of opinion. Towards the formation of the public opinion of the country, New England, while she continues true to herself, will, as in times past, contribute vastly beyond the proportion of her numerical strength.
50 But besides the general ascendency which she will maintain through the influence of public opinion, we can do two things to secure a strong and abiding interest in the west, operating, I do not say in our favor, but in favor of principles and measures which we think sound and

salutary. The first is, promptly to extend towards the west, on every fitting occasion which presents itself, consistently with public and private duty, either in the course of legislation or the current of affairs, those good offices which of right pertain to the relative condition of the two parts of the country; to let the west know, by experience, both in the halls of Congress and the channels of commercial and social intercourse, that the east is truly, cordially, and effectively her friend, not her rival nor enemy.
The kindly influence thus produced will prove of great power and value, and will go far to secure a return of fraternal feeling and political sympathy; but it will not, of itself, on great and trying occasions of a supposed diversity of sectional interest, always prove strong enough to maintain a harmony of councils. But we can do another thing, of vastly greater moment. We can put in motion a principle of influence, of a much higher and more generous character. We can furnish the means of building up institutions of education. We can, from our surplus, contribute towards the establishment and endowment of those seminaries, where the mind of the west shall be trained and enlightened. Yes, sir, we can do this; and it is so far optional with us, whether the power to which we have subjected ourselves shall be a power of intelligence or of ignorance; a reign of reflection and reason, or of reckless strength; a reign of darkness, or of light. This, sir, is true statesmanship; this is policy, of which Washington would not be ashamed. While the partisan of the day plumes himself upon a little worthless popularity, gained by bribing the interest of one quarter, and falling in with the prejudices of another; it is truly worthy of a patriot, by contributing towards the means of steadily, diffusively, and permanently enlightening the public mind, as far as opportunity exists, in every part of the country, to secure it in a wise and liberal course of public policy.
Let no Bostonian capitalist, then,—let no man who has a large stake in New England, and who is called upon to aid this college in the centre of Ohio,—think that he is called upon to exercise his liberality at a distance, towards those in whom he has no concern. Sir, it is his own interest he is called upon to promote. It is not their work he is called upon to do; it is his own work. It is my opinion—which, though it may sound extravagant, will, I believe, bear examination—that, if the question were propounded to us, this moment, whether

it were most for the benefit of Massachusetts to give fifty thousand dollars towards founding another college in Middlesex, Hampshire, or Berkshire, or for the support of this college in Ohio, we should, if well advised, decide for the latter. We have Harvard, Amherst, Williams;—we do not want another college. In the west is a vast and growing population, possessing a great and increasing influence in the political system of which we are members. Is it for our interest, strongly, vitally for our interest, that this population should be intelligent and well educated; or ignorant, and enslaved to all the prejudices which beset an ignorant people?

When, then, the right reverend bishop and the friends of the west ask you, on this occasion, to help them, they ask you, in effect, to spare a part of your surplus means for an object, in which, to say the least, you have a common interest with them. They ask you to contribute to give security to your own property, by diffusing the means of light and truth throughout the region where so much of the power to preserve or shake it resides. They ask you to contribute to perpetuate the Union, by training up a well-educated population in the quarter which may hereafter be exposed to strong centrifugal influences. They ask you to recruit your waning strength in the national councils, by enlisting on your side their swelling numbers, reared in the discipline of sound learning and sober wisdom; so that, when your voice in the government shall become comparatively weak, instead of being drowned by a strange and unfriendly clamor, from this mighty region it may be reëchoed, with increased strength and a sympathetic response, from the rising millions of the North-western States. Yes, sir, they do more. They ask you to make yourselves rich, in their respect, good will, and gratitude;—to make your name dear and venerable, in their distant shades. They ask you to give their young men cause to love you, now, in the spring-time of life, before the heart is chilled and hardened; to make their old men, who, in the morning of their days, went out from your borders, lift up their hands for a blessing on you, and say, "Ah, this is the good old-fashioned liberality of the land where we were born!" Yes, sir, we shall raise an altar in the remote wilderness. Our eyes will not behold the smoke of its incense, as it curls up to heaven. But there the altar will stand; there the pure sacrifice of the spirit will be offered up; and the worshipper who comes, in all future time, to pay his devotions before it, will turn his face to the eastward, and think of the land of his benefactors.   1833

FRANCIS PARKMAN

1823–1893

NURTURED IN a family of wealth, culture, and social position, Francis Parkman, after graduating from Harvard and traveling in Europe, turned his attention to historical investigation. Taking as his theme the struggle of France and England for North America, Parkman equipped himself for his task by familiarizing himself with the details for the topography of the relevant locale and by making a critical investigation of the documentary sources, a task the more laborious by virtue of defective eyesight and almost chronic ill-health. His books, notable for their picturesque literary charm as well as for their vivid portraits of personalities and dramatic episodes, established him both as America's leading historian and as an eminent literary figure. Parkman's historical work was, however, far from being objective. In the words of William Dean Howells, "One moral is traced from beginning to end,—that spiritual and political despotism is bad for men and that no zeal, or self-devotion, or heroism, can overcome its evil effects."

The Oregon Trail (1847) recaptures much of the flavor of the westward migration which followed that trail in the pursuit of new homes beyond the Missouri. It was dictated to the companion of his explorations of the trail and was first published serially in the *Knickerbocker Magazine*.

Works of Francis Parkman, Frontenac Edition, Boston, 1902.
The Journals of Francis Parkman, Mason Wade, ed., New York, 1947.
W. L. Schramm, *Francis Parkman*, New York, 1938.
W. L. Schramm, "A New Englander on the Road to Oregon," *New England Quarterly*, vol. XIII (March, 1940).

» » From: THE OREGON TRAIL « «

CHAPTER VI

THE PLATTE AND THE DESERT

We were now at the end of our solitary journeyings along the St. Joseph trail. On the evening of the twenty-third of May we encamped near its junction with the old legitimate trail of the Oregon emigrants. We had ridden long that afternoon, trying in vain to find wood and water, until at length we saw the sunset sky reflected from a pool encircled by bushes and rocks. The water lay in the bottom of a hollow, the smooth prairie gracefully rising in ocean-like swells on every side. We pitched our tents by it; not, however, before the keen eye of Henry Chatillon had discerned some unusual object upon the faintly-defined outline of the distant swell. But in the moist, hazy atmosphere of the evening, nothing could be clearly distinguished. As we lay around the fire after supper, a low and distant sound, strange enough amid the loneliness of the prairie, reached our ears,—peals of laughter, and the faint voices of men and women. For eight days we had not encountered a human being, and this singular warning of their vicinity had an effect extremely impressive.

About dark a sallow-faced fellow descended the hill on horseback, and splashing through the pool, rode up to the tents. He was enveloped in a huge cloak, and his broad felt hat was weeping about his ears with the drizzling moisture of the evening. Another followed, a stout, square-built, intelligent-looking man, who announced himself as leader of an emigrant party, encamped a mile in advance of us. About twenty wagons, he said, were with him; the rest of his party were on the other side of the Big Blue, waiting for a woman who was in the pains of childbirth, and quarrelling meanwhile among themselves.

These were the first emigrants that we had overtaken, although we had found abundant and melancholy traces of their progress throughout the course of the journey. Sometimes we passed the grave of one who had sickened and died on the way. The earth was usually torn up, and covered thickly with wolf-tracks. Some had escaped this violation. One morning, a piece of plank, standing upright on the summit of a grassy hill, attracted our notice, and riding up to it, we found the following words very roughly traced upon it, apparently with a red-hot piece of iron:—

MARY ELLIS.

Died May 7th, 1845.

Aged two months.

Such tokens were of common occurrence.

We were late in breaking up our camp on the following morning, and scarcely had we ridden a mile when we saw, far in advance of us, drawn against the horizon, a line of objects stretching at regular intervals along the level edge of the prairie. An intervening swell soon hid them from sight, until, ascending it a quarter of an hour after, we saw close before us the emigrant caravan, with its heavy white wagons creeping on in slow procession, and a large drove of cattle following behind. Half a dozen yellow-visaged Missourians, mounted on horseback, were cursing and shouting among them, their lank angular proportions enveloped in brown homespun, evidently cut and adjusted by the hands of a domestic female tailor. As we approached, they called out to us: "How are ye, boys? Are ye for Oregon or California?"

As we pushed rapidly by the wagons, children's faces were thrust out from the white coverings to look at us; while the care-worn, thin-featured matron, or the buxom girl, seated in front, suspended the knitting on which most of them were engaged to stare at us with wondering curiosity. By the side of each wagon stalked the proprietor, urging on his patient oxen, who shouldered heavily along, inch by inch, on their interminable journey. It was easy to see that fear and dissension prevailed among them; some of the men—but these, with one exception, were bachelors—looked wistfully upon us as we rode lightly and swiftly by, and then impatiently at their own lumbering wagons and heavy-gaited oxen. Others were unwilling to advance at all, until the party they had left behind should have rejoined them. Many were murmuring against the leader they had chosen, and wished to depose him; and this discontent was fomented by some ambitious spirits, who had hopes of succeeding in his place. The women were divided between regrets for the homes they had left and fear of the deserts and savages before them.

We soon left them far behind, and hoped that we had taken a final leave; but our companions' wagon stuck so long in a deep muddy ditch that before it was extricated the van of the emigrant caravan appeared again, descending a ridge close at hand. Wagon after wagon plunged through the mud; and as it was nearly noon, and the place promised shade and water, we saw with satisfaction that they were resolved to encamp. Soon the wagons were wheeled into a circle: the cattle were grazing over the meadow, and the men, with sour, sullen faces, were looking about for wood and water. They seemed to meet but indifferent success. As we left the ground, I saw a tall, slouching fellow, with the nasal accent of "down east," contemplating the contents of his tin cup, which he had just filled with water.

"Look here, you," said he; "it's chock-full of animals!"

The cup, as he held it out, exhibited in fact an extraordinary variety and profusion of animal and vegetable life.

Riding up the little hill, and looking back on the meadow, we could easily see that all was not right in the camp of the emigrants. The men were crowded together, and an angry discussion seemed to be going forward. R____ was missing from his wonted place in the line, and the captain told us that he had remained behind to get his horse shod by a blacksmith attached to the emigrant party. Something whispered in our ears that mischief was on foot; we kept on, however, and coming soon to a stream of tolerable water, we stopped to rest

and dine. Still the absentee lingered behind. At last, at the distance of a mile, he and his horse suddenly appeared, sharply defined against the sky on the summit of a hill; and close behind, a huge white object rose slowly into view.

"What is that blockhead bringing with him now?"

A moment dispelled the mystery. Slowly and solemnly, one behind the other, four long trains of oxen and four emigrant wagons rolled over the crest of the hill and gravely descended, while R____ rode in state in the van. It seems that, during the process of shoeing the horse, the smothered dissensions among the emigrants suddenly broke into open rupture. Some insisted on pushing forward, some on remaining where they were, and some on going back. Kearsley, their captain, threw up his command in disgust. "And now, boys," said he, "if any of you are for going ahead, just you come along with me."

Four wagons, with ten men, one woman, and one small child, made up the force of the "go-ahead" faction, and R____, with his usual proclivity toward mischief, invited them to join our party. Fear of the Indians—for I can conceive no other motive—must have induced him to court so burdensome an alliance. At all events, the proceeding was a cool one. The men who joined us, it is true, were all that could be desired; rude indeed in manners, but frank, manly, and intelligent. To tell them we could not travel with them was out of the question. I merely reminded Kearsley that if his oxen could not keep up with our mules he must expect to be left behind, as we could not consent to be farther delayed on the journey; but he immediately replied, that his oxen *should* keep up; and if they couldn't, why, he allowed, he'd find out how to make 'em."

On the next day, as it chanced, our English companions broke the axle-tree of their wagon, and down came the whole cumberous machine lumbering into the bed of a brook. Here was a day's work cut out for us. Meanwhile our emigrant associates kept on their way, and so vigorously did they urge forward their powerful oxen, that, what with the broken axle-tree and other mishaps, it was full a week before we overtook them; when at length we discovered them, one afternoon, crawling quietly along the sandy brink of the Platte. But meanwhile various incidents occurred to ourselves.

It was probable that at this stage of our

journey the Pawnees would attempt to rob us. We began therefore to stand guard in turn, dividing the night into three watches, and appointing two men for each. Deslauriers and I held guard together. We did not march with military precision to and fro before the tents: our discipline was by no means so strict. We wrapped ourselves in our blankets, and sat down by the fire; and Deslauriers, combining his culinary functions with his duties as sentinel, employed himself in boiling the head of an antelope for our breakfast. Yet we were models of vigilance in comparison with some of the party; for the ordinary practice of the guard was to lay his rifle on the ground, and, enveloping his nose in his blanket, meditate on his mistress, or whatever subject best pleased him. This is all well enough when among Indians who do not habitually proceed further in their hostility than robbing travellers of their horses and mules, though, indeed, a Pawnee's forbearance is not always to be trusted; but in certain regions farther to the west, the guard must beware how he exposes his person to the light of the fire, lest some keen-eyed skulking marksman should let fly a bullet or an arrow from the darkness.

Among various tales that circulated around our camp-fire was one told by Boisverd, and not inappropriate here. He was trapping with several companions on the skirts of the Blackfoot country. The man on guard, knowing that it behooved him to put forth his utmost precaution, kept aloof from the fire-light, and sat watching intently on all sides. At length he was aware of a dark, crouching figure, stealing noiselessly into the circle of the light. He hastily cocked his rifle, but the sharp click of the lock caught the ear of the Blackfoot, whose senses were all on the alert. Raising his arrow, already fitted to the string, he shot it in the direction of the sound. So sure was his aim, that he drove it through the throat of the unfortunate guard, and then, with a loud yell, bounded from the camp.

As I looked at the partner of my watch, puffing and blowing over his fire, it occurred to me that he might not prove the most efficient auxiliary in time of trouble.

"Deslauriers," said I, "would you run away if the Pawnees should fire at us?"

"Ah! oui, oui, Monsieur!" he replied very decisively.

At this instant a whimsical variety of voices, —barks, howls, yelps, and whines,—all mingled together, sounded from the prairie, not far off, as if a conclave of wolves of every age and sex were assembled there. Deslauriers looked up from his work with a laugh, and began to imitate this medley of sounds with a ludicrous accuracy. At this they were repeated with redoubled emphasis, the musician being apparently indignant at the successful efforts of a rival. They all proceeded from the throat of one little wolf, not larger than a spaniel, seated by himself at some distance. He was of the species called the prairie-wolf: a grim-visaged, but harmless little brute, whose worst propensity is creeping among horses and gnawing the ropes of raw hide by which they are picketed around the camp. Other beasts roam the prairies, far more formidable in aspect and in character. These are the large white and gray wolves, whose deep howl we heard at intervals from far and near.

At last I fell into a doze, and awaking from it, found Deslauriers fast asleep. Scandalized by this breach of discipline, I was about to stimulate his vigilance by stirring him with the stock of my rifle; but, compassion prevailing, I determined to let him sleep awhile, and then arouse him to administer a suitable reproof for such forgetfulness of duty. Now and then I walked the rounds among the silent horses, to see that all was right. The night was chili, damp, and dark, the dank grass bending under the icy dewdrops. At the distance of a rod or two the tents were invisible, and nothing could be seen but the obscure figures of the horses, deeply breathing, and restlessly starting as they slept, or still slowly champing the grass. Far off, beyond the black outline of the prairie, there was a ruddy light, gradually increasing, like the glow of a conflagration; until at length the broad disk of the moon, blood-red, and vastly magnified by the vapors, rose slowly upon the darkness, flecked by one or two little clouds, and as the light poured over the gloomy plain, a fierce and stern howl, close at hand, seemed to greet it as an unwelcome intruder. There was something impressive and awful in the place and the hour; for I and the beasts were all that had consciousness for many a league around.

Some days elapsed, and brought us near the Platte. Two men on horseback approached us one morning, and we watched them with the curiosity and interest that, upon the solitude of the plains, such an encounter always excites. They were evidently whites, from their mode of riding, though, contrary to the usage of that region, neither of them carried a rifle.

"Fools!" remarked Henry Chatillon, "to ride that way on the prairie; Pawnee find them—then they catch it."

Pawnee *had* found them, and they had come very near "catching it"; indeed, nothing saved them but the approach of our party. Shaw and I knew one of them,—a man named Turner, whom we had seen at Westport. He and his companion belonged to an emigrant party encamped a few miles in advance, and had returned to look for some stray oxen, leaving their rifles, with characteristic rashness or ignorance, behind them. Their neglect had nearly cost them dear; for, just before we came up, half-a-dozen Indians approached, and, seeing them apparently defenceless, one of the rascals seized the bridle of Turner's horse and ordered him to dismount. Turner was wholly unarmed; but the other jerked a pistol out of his pocket, at which the Pawnee recoiled; and just then some of our men appearing in the distance, the whole party whipped their rugged little horses and made off. In no way daunted, Turner foolishly persisted in going forward.

Long after leaving him, and late that afternoon, in the midst of a gloomy and barren prairie, we came suddenly upon the great trail of the Pawnees, leading from their villages on the Platte to their war and hunting grounds to the southward. Here every summer passes the motley concourse: thousands of savages, men, women, and children, horses and mules, laden with their weapons and implements, and an innumerable multitude of unruly wolfish dogs, who have not acquired the civilized accomplishment of barking, but howl like their wild cousins of the prairie.

The permanent winter villages of the Pawnees stand on the lower Platte, but throughout the summer the greater part of the inhabitants are wandering over the plains,—a treacherous, cowardly banditti, who, by a thousand acts of pillage and murder, have deserved chastisement at the hands of government. Last year a Dahcotah warrior performed a notable exploit at one of these villages. He approached it alone, in the middle of a dark night, and clambering up the outside of one of the lodges, which are in the form of a half-sphere, looked in at the round hole made at the top for the escape of smoke. The dusky light from the embers showed him the forms of the sleeping inmates; and dropping lightly through the opening, he

unsheathed his knife, and, stirring the fire, coolly selected his victims. One by one, he stabbed and scalped them; when a child suddenly awoke and screamed. He rushed from the lodge, yelled a Sioux war-cry, shouted his name in triumph and defiance, and darted out upon the dark prairie, leaving the whole village behind him in a tumult, with the howling and baying of dogs, screams of women, and the yells of the enraged warriors.

Our friend Kearsley, as we learned on rejoining him, signalized himself by a less bloody achievement. He and his men were good woodsmen, well skilled in the use of the rifle, but found themselves wholly out of their element on the prairie. None of them had ever seen a buffalo; and they had very vague conceptions of his nature and appearance. On the day after they reached the Platte, looking towards a distant swell, they beheld a multitude of little black specks in motion upon its surface.

"Take your rifles, boys," said Kearsley, "and we'll have fresh meat for supper." This inducement was quite sufficient. The ten men left their wagons, and set out in hot haste, some on horseback and some on foot, in pursuit of the supposed buffalo. Meanwhile a high, grassy ridge shut the game from view; but mounting it after half an hour's running and riding, they found themselves suddenly confronted by about thirty mounted Pawnees. Amazement and consternation were mutual. Having nothing but their bows and arrows, the Indians thought their hour was come, and the fate that they were conscious of richly deserving about to overtake them. So they began, one and all, to shout forth the most cordial salutations, running up with extreme earnestness to shake hands with the Missourians, who were as much rejoiced as they were to escape the expected conflict.

A low, undulating line of sand-hills bounded the horizon before us. That day we rode ten hours, and it was dusk before we entered the hollows and gorges of these gloomy little hills. At length we gained the summit, and the long-expected valley of the Platte lay before us. We all drew rein, and sat joyfully looking down upon the prospect. It was right welcome; strange, too, and striking to the imagination, and yet it had not one picturesque or beautiful feature; nor had it any of the features of grandeur, other than its vast extent, its solitude, and its wildness. For league after league, a plain as level as a lake was outspread beneath us; here and there the Platte, divided into a dozen thread-like sluices, was traversing it, and an occasional clump of wood, rising in the midst like a shadowy island, relieved the monotony of the waste. No living thing was moving throughout the vast landscape, except the lizards that darted over the sand and through the rank grass and prickly pears at our feet.

We had passed the more tedious part of the journey; but four hundred miles still intervened between us and Fort Laramie; and to reach that point cost us the travel of three more weeks. During the whole of this time we were passing up the middle of a long, narrow, sandy plain, reaching like an outstretched belt nearly to the Rocky Mountains. Two lines of sandhills, broken often into the wildest and most fantastic forms, flanked the valley at the distance of a mile or two on the right and left; while beyond them lay a barren, trackless waste, extending for hundreds of miles to the Arkansas on the one side, and the Missouri on the other. Before and behind us, the level monotony of the plain was unbroken as far as the eye could reach. Sometimes it glared in the sun, an expanse of hot, bare sand; sometimes it was veiled by long coarse grass. Skulls and whitening bones of buffalo were scattered everywhere; the ground was tracked by myriads of them, and often covered with the circular indentations where the bulls had wallowed in the hot weather. From every gorge and ravine, opening from the hills, descended deep, well-worn paths, where the buffalo issue twice a day in regular procession to drink in the Platte. The river itself runs through the midst, a thin sheet of rapid, turbid water, half a mile wide, and scarcely two feet deep. Its low banks, for the most part without a bush or a tree, are of loose sand, with which the stream is so charged that it grates on the teeth in drinking. The naked landscape is, of itself, dreary and monotonous enough; and yet the wild beasts and wild men that frequent the valley of the Platte make it a scene of interest and excitement to the traveller. Of those who have journeyed there, scarcely one, perhaps, fails to look back with fond regret to his horse and his rifle.

Early in the morning after we reached the Platte, a long procession of squalid savages approached our camp. Each was on foot, leading his horse by a rope of bull-hide. His attire consisted merely of a scanty cincture, and an old buffalo robe, tattered and begrimed by use, which hung over his shoulders. His head was close shaven, except a ridge of hair reaching over the crown from the middle of the forehead, very much like the long bristles on the back of a hyena, and he carried his bow and arrows in his hand, while his meagre little horse was laden with dried buffalo meat, the produce of his hunting. Such were the first specimens that we met—and very indifferent ones they were—of the genuine savages of the prairie.

They were the Pawnees whom Kearsley had encountered the day before, and belonged to a large hunting-party, known to be ranging the prairie in the vicinity. They strode rapidly by, within a furlong of our tents, not pausing or looking towards us, after the manner of Indians when meditating mischief, or conscious of ill desert. I went out to meet them, and had an amicable conference with the chief, presenting him with half a pound of tobacco, at which unmerited bounty he expressed much gratification. These fellows, or some of their companions, had committed a dastardly outrage upon an emigrant party in advance of us. Two men, at a distance from the rest, were seized by them, but, lashing their horses, they broke away and fled. At this the Pawnees raised the yell and shot at them, transfixing the hindmost through the back with several arrows, while his companion galloped away and brought in the news to his party. The panic-stricken emigrants remained for several days in camp, not daring even to send out in quest of the dead body.

Our New-England climate is mild and equable compared with that of the Platte. This very morning, for instance, was close and sultry, the sun rising with a faint oppressive heat; when suddenly darkness gathered in the west, and a furious blast of sleet and hail drove full in our faces, icy cold, and urged with such demoniac vehemence that it felt like a storm of needles. It was curious to see the horses; they faced about in extreme displeasure, holding their tails like whipped dogs, and shivering as the angry gusts, howling louder than a concert of wolves, swept over us. Wright's long train of mules came sweeping round before the storm, like a flight of snow-birds driven by a winter tempest. Thus we all remained stationary for some minutes, crouching close to our horses' necks, much too surly to speak, though once the captain looked up from between the collars of his coat, his face blood-red, and the muscles of his mouth contracted by the cold into a most ludicrous grin of agony.

He grumbled something that sounded like a curse, directed, as we believed, against the unhappy hour when he had first thought of leaving home. The thing was too good to last long; and the instant the puffs of wind subsided we pitched our tents, and remained in camp for the rest of a gloomy and lowering day. The emigrants also encamped near at hand. We being first on the ground, had appropriated all the wood within reach; so that our fire alone blazed cheerily. Around it soon gathered a group of uncouth figures, shivering in the drizzling rain. Conspicuous among them were two or three of the half-savage men who spend their reckless lives in trapping among the Rocky Mountains, or in trading for the Fur Company in the Indian villages. They were all of Canadian extraction; their hard, weather-beaten faces and bushy moustaches looked out from beneath the hoods of their white capotes with a bad and brutish expression, as if their owners might be the willing agents of any villany. And such in fact is the character of many of these men.

On the day following we overtook Kearsley's wagons, and thenceforward, for a week or two, we were fellow-travellers. One good effect, at least, resulted from alliance; it materially diminished the fatigues of standing guard; for the party being now more numerous, there were longer intervals between each man's turns of duty.   1849

» » *Nationalism and Cosmopolitanism* « «

1825-1860

» » « «

THE HOD-CARRIER'S SONG

I am a bold Hodman, I live by my trade,
  I mix up my mortar, with my hoe and my spade;
And mount up the ladder, though ever so tall,
  When the man of the trowel for mortar doth call.

Chorus

  Sing tural, li tural, li tu ral lol la,
  Why don't you sing tu ral, li tu ral lol la.

With my badge on my shoulder, fill'd with mortar or brick,
  In my march up the ladder I'm nimble and quick,
With a heart light and cheerful, I whistle and sing,
  Like a lark in the morning as she mounts on the wing.

As I stand on the scaffold, with hod by my side,
  I cast my eyes homeward, o'er the deep rolling tide;
O'er the wide spread Atlantic, to the land of my birth,
  More dear to my heart, than any spot on this earth.

For there dwell the Father and Mother I love,
  And the maid I adore, my sweet turtle dove;
Whilst I, a poor Hodman, am exile from home,
  On freedom's fair shore a wanderer roam.

But a voice sweet I hear from the Emerald Isle,
  The voice of the maiden I left on the style [sic]
Be constant, dear Patrick, we'll soon meet again,
  And that joy will reward us for all of our pain.

Yes, I hope soon to meet thee, fond maid of my heart,
  And trust that again we never shall part;
At the thought of that meeting, my heart bounds with joy,
  Where no vile intruder can our pleasures annoy.

The great migration of the Irish to these shores made popular the
sentimental songs they brought with them and others which were
written to describe their life as the hod-carriers, ditch-diggers and
rail-layers in the era of industrial expansion. This song, sung to the
tune of "Villikins and his Dinah," was published as a broadside ballad
about 1860.

« « » »

Nationalism and Cosmopolitanism

ON POLITICAL, economic, and cultural levels alike sectional and class tensions checked the development of nationalism. The essential fact that Americans were not certain about their nationality was a further hindrance to the growth of nationalism: some maintained that the English strain was and rightly was the dominant one, while others contended that the polyglot population for which immigration was responsible was the true proof of a new and unique nationality. This was the background for controversies which cut deeply into cultural life.

The conviction of many men in the early days of the Republic that a truly national culture must be created continued to be cherished. This conviction, indeed, took on much of the zeal and militancy that characterized the spread-eagleism of the Jacksonian period. But even among the champions of Americanism in culture there was no agreement. Some insisted that Americanism merely meant the repudiation of the monarchism, clericalism, and aristocracy of Europe. Others held that it involved a positive insistence on the superiority of American republicanism, but that it did not require the wholehearted acceptance of political and social democracy. Still others contended that Americanism demanded the incorporation of the democratic spirit in literature and the arts; and some interpreted the democratic spirit in terms of humanitarianism and cosmopolitanism.

In the camp of the cosmopolitans the argument most frequently heard was that a unique landscape was insufficient as the basis for a literature, and that this also held for the so-called American character and institutions. Literature must concern itself, the cosmopolitans urged, with eternal and universal human values. The distant past and the rich treasure-houses of Europe were indispensable to American culture and letters. Besides, we could not, even if we would, turn our backs to these, for we had sprung from the Old World and were still tied closely to it in innumerable ways.

The champions of American nationalism often, but not always, looked with concern on the open-door policy which admitted millions of immigrants to our cities and countryside. Those who did so derived support from American labor, which had no desire to compete with that of European peasant and proletariat. But more articulate and influential were the ardent Protestants, who were horrified at the growth of Catholicism which every boatload of immigrants augmented. They proposed a limitation of immigration, or, at least, a careful supervision of the immigrant once he landed.

On the other hand many ardent nationalists believed that the true national policy was to welcome the immigrant with open arms. America, they argued, was an asylum for the oppressed of all the world; and this fact was her unique distinction. Idealists and humanitarians who took this position were also supported by industrialists who found the Irish immigrants willing to work for less than American workingmen, and to work harder. Land speculators and railroad promoters saw in the immigrant a fruitful source of revenue. And in the name of Americanism these interests acclaimed immigration as a blessed boon. Occasionally an immigrant himself pointed to the contributions his kind had made to his new home. In defining Americanism in the framework of cosmopolitan humanitarianism and democracy, the articulate immigrant helped to crystallize and to deepen this conception of Americanism in the minds of many among the older inhabitants.

» » « «

WILLIAM CULLEN BRYANT

1794–1878

IN 1826 William Cullen Bryant, already known as the author of *Thanatopsis* and *To a Water-fowl*, began his association with the *New York Evening Post*. By 1829, when he assumed the editorship which he held until his death, he had broken with the sectional and conservative sympathies of his New England youth. He gave generous and valuable support to the labor unions in their struggles with obstinate employers and harsh courts; he opposed infringements of free speech; he denounced corporate monopolies. In short, he was a good Jacksonian Democrat. His sympathies with abolition, however, led him to drift away from the Democratic party, and to help launch the Free Soil party. Subsequently Bryant played an important part in the establishment of the new and, in many respects, radical Republican party.

Bryant staunchly defended the widely cherished conviction that Americans had at hand the materials for the creation of a literature characteristic of American life and of the genius of America's free institutions. This sentiment is well expressed in the following selection, which first appeared in the *North American Review* as a review of Catherine Sedgwick's *Redwood*.

Prose Writings, Parke Godwin, ed., 2 vols., New York, 1884.
Harry H. Peckham, *Gotham Yankee; A Bibliography of William Cullen Bryant*, New York, 1950.
John Bigelow, *William Cullen Bryant*, Boston and New York, 1890.
Allan Nevins, *The Evening Post: A Century of Journalism*, New York, 1922.

» » AMERICAN SOCIETY AS A FIELD FOR FICTION « «

On more than one occasion we have already given our opinion somewhat at large of the fertility of our country, and its history, in the materials of romance. If our reasonings needed any support from successful examples of that kind of writing, as a single fact is worth a volume of ingenious theorizing, we have had the triumph of seeing them confirmed, beyond all controversy, by the works of a popular American author, who has shown the literary world into what beautiful creations those materials may be wrought. In like manner, we look upon the specimen before us as a conclusive argument that the writers of works of fiction of which the scene is laid in familiar and domestic life, have a rich and varied field before them in the United States. Indeed, the conviction on this subject, which till lately prevailed among us, that works of this kind, descriptive of the manners of our countrymen, could not succeed, never seemed to us to rest on a very solid foundation. It was rather a sweeping inference, drawn from the fact that

no highly meritorious work of the kind had appeared, and the most satisfactory and comfortable way of accounting for this was to assert that no such could be written. But it is not always safe to predict what a writer of genius will make of a given subject. Twenty years ago, what possible conception could an English critic have had of the admirable productions of the author of "Waverley," and of the wonderful improvement his example has effected in that kind of composition? Had the idea of one of those captivating works, destined to take such strong hold on all minds, been laid before him by the future author, he would probably only have wondered at his vanity.

There is nothing paradoxical in the opinion which maintains that all civilized countries— we had almost said all countries whatever— furnish matter for copies of real life, embodied in works of fiction, which shall be of lasting and general interest. Wherever there are human nature and society there are subjects for the novelist. The passions and affections, virtue and vice, are of no country. Everywhere love comes to touch the hearts of the young, and everywhere scorn and jealousy, the obstacles of fortune and the prudence of the aged, are at hand to disturb the course of love. Everywhere there exists the greed of wealth, the lust of power, and the wish to be admired; courage braving real dangers, and cowardice shrinking from imaginary ones; friendship and hatred, and all the train of motives and impulses which affect the minds and influence the conduct of men. They not only exist everywhere, but they exist, infinitely diversified and compounded, in various degrees of suppression and restraint, or fostered into unnatural growth and activity, modified by political institutions and laws, by national religions and subdivisions of those religions, by different degrees of refinement and civilization, of poverty or of abundance, by arbitrary usages handed down from indefinite antiquity, and even by local situation and climate. Nor is there a single one of all these innumerable modifications of human character and human emotion which is not, in some degree, an object of curiosity and interest. Over all the world is human sagacity laying its plans, and chance and the malice of others are thwarting them, and fortune is raising up one man and throwing down another. In none of the places of human habitation are the accesses barred against joy or grief; the kindness of the good carries gladness into families, and the treachery of the false friend brings sorrow and ruin; in all countries are tears shed over the graves of the excellent, the brave, and the beautiful, and the oppressed breathe freer when the oppressor has gone to his account. Everywhere has Nature her features of grandeur and beauty, and these features receive a moral expression from the remembrances of the past and the interests of the present. On her face, as on an immense theatre, the passions and pursuits of men are performing the great drama of human existence. At every moment, and in every corner of the world, these mighty and restless agents are perpetually busy, under an infinity of forms and disguises, and the great representation goes on with that majestic continuity and uninterrupted regularity which mark all the courses of nature. Who, then, will undertake to say that the hand of genius may not pencil off a few scenes acted in our vast country, and amid our large population, that shall interest and delight the world?

It is a native writer only that must and can do this. It is he that must show how the infinite diversities of human character are yet further varied by causes that exist in our own country, exhibit our peculiar modes of thinking and action and mark the effect of these upon individual fortunes and happiness. A foreigner is manifestly incompetent to the task; his observation would rest only upon the more general and obvious traits of our national character, a thousand delicate shades of manner would escape his notice, many interesting peculiarities would never come to his knowledge, and many more he would misapprehend. It is only on his native soil that the author of such works can feel himself on safe and firm ground, that he can move confidently and fearlessly, and put forth the whole strength of his powers without risk of failure. His delineations of character and action, if executed with ability, will have a raciness and freshness about them which will attest their fidelity, the secret charm which belongs to truth and nature, and without which even the finest genius cannot invest a system of adscititious and imaginary manners. It is this quality which recommends them powerfully to the sympathy and interest even of those who are unacquainted with the original from which they are drawn, and makes such pictures from such hands so delightful and captivating to the foreigner. By superadding to the novelty of the manners described the interest of a narrative, they create a sort of illusion which places him in the midst of the country where the action of the piece is going on. He beholds the scenery of a distant land, hears its inhabitants conversing about their own concerns in their own dialect, finds himself in the bosom of its families, is made the depositary of their secrets and the observer of their fortunes, and becomes an inmate of their firesides without stirring from his own. Thus it is that American novels are eagerly read in Great Britain, and novels descriptive of English and Scottish manners as eagerly read in America.

It has been objected that the habits of our countrymen are too active and practical; that they are too universally and continually engrossed by the cares and occupations of business to have leisure for that intrigue, those plottings and counter-plottings, which are necessary to give a sufficient degree of action and eventfulness to the novel of real life. It is said that we need for this purpose a class of men whose condition in life places them above the necessity of active exertion, and who are driven to the practice of intrigue because they have nothing else to do. It remains, however, to be proved that any considerable portion of this ingredient is necessary in the composition of a successful novel. To require that it should be made up of nothing better than the manœuvres of those whose only employment is to glitter at places of public resort, to follow a perpetual round of amusements, and to form plans to outshine, thwart, and vex each other, is confining the writer to a narrow and most barren circle. It is requiring an undue proportion of heartlessness, selfishness, and vice in his pictures of society. It is compelling him to go out of the wholesome atmosphere of those classes, where the passions and affections have their most salutary and natural play, and employ his observations on that where they are the most perverted, sophisticated, and corrupt.

But will it be seriously contended that he can have no other resource than the rivalries and machinations of the idle, the frivolous, and the dissolute, to keep the reader from yawning over his pictures? Will it be urged that no striking and interesting incidents can come to pass without their miserable aid? If our country be not the country of intrigue, it is at least the country of enterprise; and nowhere are the great objects that worthily interest the passions and call forth the exertions of men pursued with more devotion and perseverance. The agency of chance, too, is not confined to the shores of Europe; our countrymen have not attained a sufficient degree of certainty in their calculations to exclude it from ours. It would really seem to us that these two sources, along with that blessed quality of intrigue which even the least favorable view of our society will allow us, are abundantly fertile in interesting occurrences for all the purposes of the novelist. Besides, it should be recollected that it is not in any case the dull diary of ordinary occupations or amusements that forms the groundwork of his plot. On the contrary, it is some event, or at least a series of events, of unusual importance, standing out in strong relief from the rest of the biography of his principal characters, and to which the daily habits of their lives, whatever may be their rank or condition, are only a kind of accompaniment.

But the truth is that the distinctions of rank and the amusements of elegant idleness are but the surface of society, and only so many splendid disguises put upon the reality of things. They are trappings which the writer of real genius, the anatomist of the human heart, strips away when he would exhibit his characters as they are, and engage our interest for them as beings of our own species. He reduces them to the same great level where distinctions of rank are nothing and difference of character everything. It is here that James I and Charles II and Louis IX and Bob Roy and Jeanie Deans and Meg Merrilies are, by the author of the "Waverley Novels," made to meet. The monarch must come down from the dim elevation of his throne; he must lay aside the assumed and conventional manners of his station, and unbend and unbosom himself with his confidants before that illustrious master will condescend to describe him. In the artificial sphere in which the great move, they are only puppets and pageants, but here they are men. A narrative the scene of which is laid at the magnificent levees of princes, in the drawing-rooms of nobles, and the bright assemblies of fashion, may be a very pretty, showy sort of thing, and so may a story of the glittering dances and pranks of fairies. But we soon grow weary of all this and ask for objects of sympathy and regard; for something the recollection of which shall dwell on the heart, and to which it will love to recur; for something, in short, which is natural, the unaffected traits of strength and weakness, of the tender and the comic, all which the pride of rank either removes from observation or obliterates.

If these things have any value, we hesitate not to say that they are to be found abundantly in the characters of our countrymen, formed as they are under the influences of our free institutions, and shooting into a large and vigorous, though sometimes irregular, luxuriance. They exist most abundantly in our more ancient settlements, and amid the more homogeneous races of our large populations, where the causes that produce them have operated longest and with most activity. It is there that the human mind has learned best to enjoy our fortunate and equal institutions, and to profit by them. In the countries of Europe the laws chain men down to the condition in which they were born. This observation, of course, is not equally true of all those countries, but, when they are brought into comparison with ours, it is in some degree applicable to them all. Men spring up and vegetate and die without thinking of passing from the sphere in which they find themselves any more than the plants they cultivate think of removing from the places where they are rooted. It is the tendency of this rigid and melancholy destiny to contract and stint the intellectual faculties, to prevent the development of character and to make the subjects of it timid, irresolute, and imbecile. With us, on the contrary, where the proudest honors in the State and the highest deference in society are set equally before all our citizens, a wholesome and quickening impulse is communicated to all parts of the social system. All are possessed with a spirit of ambition and a love of adventure, an intense competition calls forth and exalts the passions and faculties of men, their characters become strongly defined, their minds acquire a hardihood and an activity which can be gained by no other discipline, and the community, throughout all its conditions, is full of bustle and change and action.

Whoever will take the pains to pursue this subject a little into its particulars will be surprised at the infinite variety of forms of character which spring up under the institutions of our country. Religion is admitted on all hands to be a mighty agent in moulding the human character; and, accordingly, with the perfect allowance and toleration of all religions, we see among us their innumerable and diverse influences upon the manners and temper of our people. Whatever may be his religious opinions, no one is restrained by fear of consequences from avowing them, but is left to nurse his peculiarities of doctrine into what importance he pleases. The Quaker is absolved from submission to the laws in those particulars which offend his conscience, the Moravian finds no barriers in the way of his work of proselytism and charity, the Roman Catholic is subjected to no penalty for pleasing himself with the magnificent ceremonial of his religion, and the Jew worships unmolested in his synagogue. In many parts of our country we see communities of that strange denomination, the Shakers, distinguished from their neighbors by a garb, a dialect, an architecture, a way of worship, of thinking, and of living, as different as if they were in fact of a different origin, instead of being collected from the families around them. In other parts we see small neighborhoods of the Seventh Day Baptists, retaining their simplicity of manners and quaintness of language delivered down from their fathers. Here we find the austerities of puritanism preserved to this day, there the rights and doctrines of the Church of England are shown in their effect on the manners of the people, and yet in another part of the country springs up a new and numerous sect, who wash one another's feet and profess to revive the primitive habits of the apostolic times.

It is in our country also that these differences of character, which grow naturally out of geographical situation, are least tampered with and repressed by political regulations. The adventurous and roving natives of our sea-coasts and islands are a different race of men from those who till the interior, and the hardy dwellers of our mountainous districts are not like the inhabitants of the rich plains that skirt our mighty lakes and rivers. The manners of the Northern States are said to be characterized by the keenness and importunity of their climate, and those of the Southern to partake of the softness of theirs. In our cities you will see the polished manners of the European capitals, but pass into the more quiet and unvisited parts of the country, and you will find men whom you might take for the first planters of our colonies. The descendants of the Hollanders have not forgotten the traditions of their fathers, and the legends of Germany are still recited, and the ballads of Scotland still sung, in settlements whose inhabitants derive their origin from those countries. It is hardly possible that the rapid and continual growth and improvement of our country, a circumstance wonderfully exciting to the imagination and altogether unlike anything witnessed in other countries, should not have some influence in forming our national character. At all events, it is a most fertile source of incident. It does for us in a few short years what in Europe is a work of centuries. The hardy and sagacious native of the Eastern States settles himself in the wilderness by the side of the emigrant from the British Isles; the pestilence of the marshes is braved and overcome; the bear and wolf and catamount are chased from their haunts; and then you see cornfields and roads and towns springing up as if by enchantment. In the mean time pleasant Indian villages, situated on the skirts of their hunting-grounds, with their beautiful green plats for dancing and martial exercises, are taken into the bosom of our extending population, while new States are settled and cities founded far beyond them. Thus a great deal of history is crowded into a brief space. Each little hamlet in a few seasons has more events and changes to tell of than a European village can furnish in a course of ages.

But, if the writer of fictitious history does not find all the variety he wishes in the various kinds of our population, descended, in different parts of our country, from ancestors of different nations, and yet preserving innumerable and indubitable tokens of their origin, if 10 the freedom with which every man is suffered to take his own way in all things not affecting the peace and good order of society does not furnish him with a sufficient diversity of characters, employments, and modes of life, he has got other resources. He may bring into his plots men whose characters and manners were formed by the institutions and modes of society in the nations beyond the Atlantic, and he may describe them faithfully as things which he 20 has observed and studied. If he is not satisfied with indigenous virtue, he may take for the model of his characters men of whom the Old World is not worthy, and whom it has cast out from its bosom. If domestic villany be not dark enough for his pictures, here are fugitives from the justice of Europe come to prowl in America. If the coxcombs of our own country are not sufficiently exquisite, affected, and absurd, here are plenty of silken fops from the capitals of foreign kingdoms. If he finds himself in need of a class of men more stupid and degraded than are to be found among the natives of the United States, here are crowds of the wretched peasantry of Great Britain and Germany, flying for refuge from intolerable suffering, in every vessel that comes to our shores. Hither, also, resort numbers of that order of men who, in foreign countries, are called the middling class, the most valuable part of the communities they leave, to enjoy a moderate affluence, where the abuses and exactions of a distempered system of government cannot reach them to degrade them to the condition of the peasantry. Our country is the asylum of the persecuted preachers of new religions and the teachers of political doctrines which Europe will not endure; a sanctuary for dethroned princes and the consorts of slain emperors. When we consider all these innumerable differences of character, native and foreign, this infinite variety of pursuits and objects, this endless diversity and change of fortunes, and behold them gathered and grouped into one vast assemblage in our own country, we shall feel little pride in the sagacity or the skill of that native author who asks for a richer or a wider field of observation.

1825

WILLIAM ELLERY CHANNING

1780–1842

DURING A RESIDENCE as tutor on a Virginia plantation, William Ellery Channing, a young Harvard graduate, broadened his somewhat parochial background not only by reading the writings of the great European disciples of the Enlightenment but by observing the admirable features as well as the shortcomings of a section of his country other than his own. Although Channing was by no means the first outspoken champion of nationalism in literature, his *Remarks on National Literature* (1830) was an important step in our intellectual history. The point of departure for Channing in this essay, which first appeared in the *Christian Examiner*, was Charles J. Ingersoll's *A Discourse concerning the Influence of America on the Mind*, an address delivered before the American Philosophical Society in 1823. Ingersoll had emphasized, as the peculiar American genius, practicality in affairs. Channing insisted that a national literature must reflect superior minds, be the subjects what they may. Yet Channing also criticized very forcefully the tendency of American writers to lean on English models and to draw inspiration from English themes rather than from those of their own country. Among the characteristics which he felt American literature should assume none was more important than an intellectual freedom for bold experiments, with the enlightened and humane values of a new and better age.

The Works of William Ellery Channing, Boston, 1886.
David P. Edgell, *William Ellery Channing; An Intellectual Portrait*, Boston, 1955.

» » REMARKS ON NATIONAL LITERATURE « «

By national literature we mean the expression of a nation's mind in writing. We mean the production among a people of important works in philosophy, and in the departments of imagination and taste. We mean the contributions of new truths to the stock of human knowledge. We mean the thoughts of profound and original minds, elaborated by the toil of composition, and fixed and made immortal in books. We mean the manifestation of a nation's intellect in the only forms by which it can multiply itself at home, and send itself abroad. We mean that a nation shall take a place, by its authors, among the lights of the world. It will be seen that we include under literature all the writings of superior minds, be the subjects what they may. We are aware that the term is often confined to compositions which relate to human nature and human life; that it is not generally extended to physical science; that mind, not matter, is regarded as its main subject and sphere. But the worlds of matter and mind are too intimately connected to admit of exact partition. All the objects of human thought flow into one another. Moral and physical truths have many bonds and analogies, and, whilst the former are the chosen and noblest themes of literature, we are not anxious to divorce them from the latter, or to shut them up in a separate department. The expression of superior mind in writing we regard, then, as a nation's literature. We regard its gifted men, whether devoted to the exact sciences, to mental and ethical philosophy, to history and legislation, or to fiction and poetry, as forming a noble intellectual brotherhood; and it is for the purpose of quickening all to join their labors for the public good that we offer the present plea in behalf of a national literature.

To show the importance which we attach to the subject, we begin with some remarks on what we deem the distinction which a nation should most earnestly covet. We believe that more distinct apprehensions on this point are needed, and that, for want of them, the work of improvement is carried on with less energy, consistency, and wisdom, than may and should be brought to bear upon it. The great distinction of a country, then, is, that it produces superior men. Its natural advantages are not to be disdained. But they are of secondary importance. No matter what races of animals a country breeds, the great question is, Does it breed a noble race of men? No matter what its soil may be, the great question is, How far is it 10 prolific of moral and intellectual power? No matter how stern its climate is, if it nourish force of thought and virtuous purpose. These are the products by which a country is to be tried, and institutions have value only by the impulse which they give to the mind. It has sometimes been said that the noblest men grow where nothing else will grow. This we do not believe, for mind is not the creature of climate or soil. But were it true, we should say 20 that it were better to live among rocks and sands than in the most genial and productive region on the face of the earth.

As yet the great distinction of a nation on which we have insisted has been scarcely recognized. The idea of forming a superior race of men has entered little into schemes of policy. Invention and effort have been expended on matter much more than on mind. Lofty piles have been reared; the earth has groaned under 30 pyramids and palaces. The thought of building up a nobler order of intellect and character has hardly crossed the most adventurous statesman. We beg that we may not be misapprehended. We offer these remarks to correct what we deem a disproportioned attention to physical good, and not at all to condemn the expenditure of ingenuity and strength on the outward world. There is a harmony between all our great interests, between inward and outward 40 improvements; and by establishing among them a wise order all will be secured. We have no desire to shut up man in his own spiritual nature. The mind was made to act on matter, and it grows by expressing itself in material forms. We believe, too, that in proportion as it shall gain intellectual and moral power it will exert itself with increased energy and delight on the outward creation; will pour itself forth more freely in useful and ornamental arts; will rear more magnificent structures, and will call forth new beauties in nature. An intelligent and resolute spirit in a community perpetually extends its triumphs over matter. It can even subject to itself the most unpromising region. Holland, diked from the ocean,—Venice, rising amidst the waves,—and New England, bleak and rock-bound New England, converted by a few generations from a wilderness into smiling fields and opulent cities,—point us to the mind as the great source of physical good, and teach us that, in making the culture of man our highest end, we shall not retard, but advance the cultivation of nature.

The question which we most solicitously ask about this country is, what race of men it is likely to produce. We consider its liberty of value only as far as it favors the growth of men. What is liberty? The removal of restraint from human powers. Its benefit is that it opens new fields for action and a wider range for the mind. The only freedom worth possessing is that which gives enlargement to a people's energy, intellect, and virtues. The savage makes his boast of freedom. But what is its worth? Free as he is, he continues for ages in the same ignorance, leads the same comfortless life, sees the same untamed wilderness spread around him. He is indeed free from what he calls the yoke of civil institutions. But other and worse chains bind him. The very privation of civil government is in effect a chain; for, by withholding protection from property, it virtually shackles the arm of industry, and forbids exertion for the melioration of his lot. Progress, the growth of power, is the end and boon of liberty; and, without this, a people may have the name, but want the substance and spirit of freedom.

We are the more earnest in enlarging on these views because we feel that our attachment to our country must be very much proportioned to what we deem its tendency to form a generous race of men. We pretend not to have thrown off national feeling; but we have some stronger feelings. We love our country much, but mankind more. As men and Christians, our first desire is to see the improvement of human nature. We desire to see the soul of man wiser, firmer, nobler, more conscious of its imperishable treasures, more beneficent and powerful, more alive to its connection with God, more able to use pleasure and prosterity aright, and more victorious over poverty, adversity, and pain. In our survey of our own and other countries, the great question which comes to us is this, Where and under what institutions are men most likely to advance? Where are the soundest minds and the purest hearts formed? What nation possesses, in its history, its traditions, its government, its religion, its manners, its pursuits, its relations to other communities, and especially in its private and public means of education, the instruments and pledges of a more resolute virtue and devotion to truth than we now witness? Such a nation, be it where it may, will engage our warmest interest. We love our country, but not blindly. In all nations we recognize one great family, and our chief wish for our native land is that it may take the first rank among the lights and benefactors of the human race.

These views will explain the vast importance which we attach to a national literature. By this, as we have said, we understand the expression of a nation's mind in writing. It is the action of the most gifted understandings on the community. It throws into circulation through a wide sphere the most quickening and beautiful thoughts which have grown up in men of laborious study or creative genius. It is a much higher work than the communication of a gifted intellect in discourse. It is the mind giving to multitudes, whom no voice can reach, its compressed and selected thoughts in the most lucid order and attractive forms which it is capable of inventing. In other words, literature is the concentration of intellect for the purpose of spreading itself abroad and multiplying its energy.

Such being the nature of literature, it is plainly among the most powerful methods of exalting the character of a nation, of forming a better race of men; in truth, we apprehend that it may claim the first rank among the means of improvement. We know nothing so fitted to the advancement of society as to bring its higher minds to bear upon the multitude; as to establish close connections between the more or less gifted; as to spread far and wide the light which springs up in meditative, profound, and sublime understandings. It is the ordinance of God, and one of his most benevolent laws, that the human race should be carried forward by impulses which originate in a few minds, perhaps in an individual; and in this way the most interesting relations and dependencies of life are framed. When a great truth is to be revealed, it does not flash at once on the race, but dawns and brightens on a superior understanding, from which it is to emanate and to illuminate future ages. On the faithfulness of great minds to this awful function, the progress and happiness of men chiefly depend. The most illustrious benefactors of the race have been men who, having risen to great truths, have held them as a sacred trust for their kind and have borne witness to them amid general darkness, under scorn and persecution, perhaps in the face of death. Such men, indeed, have not always made contributions to literature, for their condition has not allowed them to be authors; but we owe the transmission, perpetuity, and immortal power of their new and high thoughts to kindred spirits, which have concentrated and fixed them in books.

The quickening influences of literature need not be urged on those who are familiar with the history of modern Europe, and who of course know the spring given to the human mind by the revival of ancient learning. Through their writings the great men of antiquity have exercised a sovereignty over these later ages not enjoyed in their own. It is more important to observe that the influence of literature is perpetually increasing; for, through the press and the spread of education, its sphere is indefinitely enlarged. Reading, once the privilege of a few, is now the occupation of multitudes, and is to become one of the chief gratifications of all. Books penetrate everywhere, and some of the works of genius find their way to obscure dwellings which, a little while ago, seemed barred against all intellectual light. Writing is now the mightiest instrument on earth. Through this the mind has acquired a kind of omnipresence. To literature we then look as the chief means of forming a better race of human beings. To superior minds, which may act through this, we look for the impulses by which their country is to be carried forward. We would teach them that they are the depositaries of the highest power on earth, and that on them the best hopes of society rest.

We are aware that some may think that we are exalting intellectual above moral and religious influence. They may tell us that the teaching of moral and religious truth, not by philosophers and boasters of wisdom, but by the comparatively weak and foolish, is the great means of renovating the world. This truth we indeed regard as "the power of God unto salvation." But let none imagine that its chosen temple is an uncultivated mind, and that it selects, as its chief organs, the lips of the unlearned. Religious and moral truth is indeed appointed to carry forward mankind, but not as conceived and expounded by narrow minds, not as darkened by the ignorant, not as debased by the superstitious, not as subtilized by the visionary, not as thundered out by the intolerant fanatic, not as turned into a drivelling cant by the hypocrite. Like all other truths, it requires for its full reception and powerful communication a free and vigorous intellect. Indeed, its grandeur and infinite connections demand a more earnest and various use of our faculties than any other subject. As a single illustration of this remark, we may observe that all moral and religious truth may be reduced to one great and central thought, perfection of mind, a thought which comprehends all that is glorious in the divine nature, and which reveals to us the end and happiness of our own existence. This perfection has as yet only dawned on the most gifted human beings, and the great purpose of our present and future existence is to enlarge our conceptions of it without end, and to embody and make them manifest in character and life. And is this sublime thought to grow within us, to refine itself from error and impure mixture, to receive perpetual accessions of brightness from the study of God, man, and nature, and especially to be communicated powerfully to others, without the vigorous exertion of our intellectual nature? Religion has been wronged by nothing more than by being separated from intellect, than by being removed from the province of reason and free research into that of mystery and authority, of impulse and feeling. Hence it is that the prevalent forms or exhibitions of Christianity are comparatively inert, and that most which is written on the subject is of little or no worth. Christianity was given not to contradict and degrade the rational nature, but to call it forth, to enlarge its range and its powers. It admits of endless development. It is the last truth which should remain stationary. It ought to be so explored and so expressed as to take the highest place in a nation's literature, as to exalt and purify all other literature. From these remarks it will be seen that the efficacy which we have ascribed to literary or intellectual in-

fluence in the work of human improvement is
consistent with the supreme importance of
moral and religious truth.

If we have succeeded in conveying the impressions which we have aimed to make, our
readers are now prepared to inquire with interest into the condition and prospects of literature among ourselves. Do we possess, indeed,
what may be called a national literature? Have
we produced eminent writers in the various
departments of intellectual effort? Are our
chief resources of instruction and literary enjoyment furnished from ourselves? We regret
that the reply to these questions is so obvious.
The few standard works which we have produced, and which promise to live, can hardly,
by any courtesy, be denominated a national
literature. On this point, if marks and proofs
of our real condition were needed, we should
find them in the current apologies for our
deficiencies. Our writers are accustomed to
plead in our excuse our youth, the necessities of
a newly settled country, and the direction of
our best talents to practical life. Be the pleas
sufficient or not, one thing they prove, and that
is, our consciousness of having failed to make
important contributions to the interests of the
intellect. We have few names to place by the
side of the great names in science and literature
on the other side of the ocean. We want those
lights which make a country conspicuous at a
distance. Let it not be said that European envy
denies our just claims. In an age like this, when
the literary world forms a great family, and the
products of mind are circulated more rapidly
than those of machinery, it is a nation's own
fault if its name be not pronounced with honor
beyond itself. We have ourselves heard, and
delighted to hear, beyond the Alps, our country
designated as the land of Franklin. This name
had scaled that mighty barrier, and made us
known where our institutions and modes of
life were hardly better understood than those
of the natives of our forests.

We are accustomed to console ourselves for
the absence of a commanding literature by urging our superiority to other nations in our institutions for the diffusion of elementary knowledge through all classes of the community. We
have here just cause for boasting, though perhaps less than we imagine. That there are gross
deficiencies in our common schools, and that
the amount of knowledge which they communicate, when compared with the time spent
in its acquisition, is lamentably small, the com-

munity begin to feel. There is a crying need
for a higher and more quickening kind of instruction than the laboring part of society have
yet received, and we rejoice that the cry begins
to be heard. But, allowing our elementary institutions to be ever so perfect, we confess that
they do not satisfy us. We want something
more. A dead level of intellect, even if it should
rise above what is common in other nations,
would not answer our wishes and hopes for
our country. We want great minds to be
formed among us,—minds which shall be felt
afar, and through which we may act on the
world. We want the human intellect to do its
utmost here. We want this people to obtain a
claim on the gratitude of the human race by
adding strength to the foundation, and fulness
and splendor to the development of moral and
religious truth; by originality of thought, by
discoveries of science, and by contributions to
the refining pleasures of taste and imagination.

With these views, we do and must lament
that, however we surpass other nations in providing for and spreading elementary instruction, we fall behind many in provision for the
liberal training of the intellect, for forming
great scholars, for communicating that profound knowledge, and that thirst for higher
truths, which can alone originate a commanding literature. The truth ought to be known.
There is among us much superficial knowledge, but little severe, persevering research;
little of that consuming passion for new truth
which makes outward things worthless; little
resolute devotion to a high intellectual culture.
There is nowhere a literary atmosphere, or
such an accumulation of literary influence, as
determines the whole strength of the mind to
its own enlargement, and to the manifestation
of itself in enduring forms. Few among us can
be said to have followed out any great subject
of thought patiently, laboriously, so as to know
thoroughly what others have discovered and
taught concerning it, and thus to occupy a
ground from which new views may be gained.
Of course, exceptions are to be found. This
country has produced original and profound
thinkers. We have named Franklin, and we
may name Edwards, one of the greatest men of
his age, though unhappily his mind was lost,
in a great degree, to literature, and we fear
to religion, by vassalage to a false theology. His
work on the Will throws, indeed, no light on
human nature, and, notwithstanding the nobleness of the subject, gives no great or elevated

thoughts; but, as a specimen of logical acuteness and controversial power, it certainly ranks in the very highest class of metaphysical writings. We might also name living authors who do honor to their country. Still, we may say we chiefly prize what has been done among us as a promise of higher and more extensive effort. Patriotism, as well as virtue, forbids us to burn incense to national vanity. The truth should be seen and felt. In an age of great intellectual activity, we rely chiefly for intellectual excitement and enjoyment on foreign minds; nor is our own mind felt abroad. Whilst clamoring against dependence on European manufactures, we contentedly rely on Europe for the nobler and more important fabrics of the intellect. We boast of our political institutions, and receive our chief teachings, books, impressions, from the school of monarchy. True, we labor under disadvantages. But, if our liberty deserves the praise which it receives, it is more than a balance for these. We believe that it is. We believe that it does open to us an indefinite intellectual progress. Did we not so regard it, we should value it little. If hereditary governments minister most to the growth of the mind, it were better to restore them than to cling to a barren freedom. Let us not expose liberty to this reproach. Let us prove, by more generous provisions for the diffusion of elementary knowledge, for the training of great minds, and for the joint culture of the moral and intellectual powers, that we are more and more instructed by freedom in the worth and greatness of human nature, and in the obligation of contributing to its strength and glory.

We have spoken of the condition of our literature. We now proceed to the consideration of the causes which obstruct its advancement; and we are immediately struck by one so prevalent as to deserve distinct notice. We refer to the common doctrine that we need, in this country, useful knowledge rather than profound, extensive, and elegant literature, and that this last, if we covet it, may be imported from abroad in such variety and abundance as to save us the necessity of producing it among ourselves. How far are these opinions just? This question we purpose to answer.

That useful knowledge should receive our first and chief care we mean not to dispute. But in our views of utility we may differ from some who take this position. There are those who confine this term to the necessaries and comforts of life, and to the means of producing them. And is it true that we need no knowledge but that which clothes and feeds us? Is it true that all studies may be dispensed with but such as teach us to act on matter, and to turn it to our use? Happily, human nature is too stubborn to yield to this narrow utility. It is interesting to observe how the very mechanical arts, which are especially designed to minister to the necessities and comforts of life, are perpetually passing these limits,—how they disdain to stop at mere convenience. A large and increasing proportion of mechanical labor is given to the gratification of an elegant taste. How simple would be the art of building, if it limited itself to the construction of a comfortable shelter! How many ships should we dismantle, and how many busy trades put to rest, were dress and furniture reduced to the standard of convenience! This "utility" would work a great change in town and country, would level to the dust the wonders of architecture, would annihilate the fine arts and blot out innumerable beauties which the hand of taste has spread over the face of the earth. Happily human nature is too strong for the utilitarian. It cannot satisfy itself with the convenient. No passion unfolds itself sooner than the love of the ornamental. The savage decorates his person, and the child is more struck with the beauty than the uses of its raiment. So far from limiting ourselves to convenient food and raiment, we enjoy but little a repast which is not arranged with some degree of order and taste; and a man who should consult comfort alone in his wardrobe would find himself an unwelcome guest in circles which he would very reluctantly forego. We are aware that the propensity to which we have referred often breaks out in extravagance and ruinous luxury. We know that the love of ornament is often vitiated by vanity, and that, when so perverted, it impairs, sometimes destroys, the soundness and simplicity of the mind and the relish for true glory. Still it teaches, even in its excesses, that the idea of beauty is an indestructible principle of our nature, and this single truth is enough to put us on our guard against vulgar notions of utility.

We have said that we prize, as highly as any, useful knowledge. But by this we mean knowledge which answers and ministers to our complex and various nature; we mean that which is useful, not only to the animal man, but to the intellectual, moral, and religious man,—useful to a being of spiritual faculties, whose happiness is to be found in their free and harmonious exercise. We grant that there is primary necessity for that information and skill by which subsistence is earned and life is preserved; for it is plain that we must live in order to act and improve. But life is the means; action and improvement the end; and who will deny that the noblest utility belongs to that knowledge by which the chief purpose of our creation is accomplished? According to these views, a people should honor and cultivate, as unspeakably useful, that literature which corresponds to and calls forth the highest faculties; which expresses and communicates energy of thought, fruitfulness of invention, force of moral purpose, a thirst for the true, and a delight in the beautiful. According to these views we attach special importance to those branches of literature which relate to human nature, and which give it a consciousness of its own powers. History has a noble use, for it shows us human beings in various and opposite conditions, in their strength and weakness, in their progress and relapses, and thus reveals the causes and means by which the happiness and virtue of the race may be enlarged. Poetry is useful, by touching deep springs in the human soul; by giving voice to its more delicate feelings; by breathing out and making more intelligible the sympathy which subsists between the mind and the outward universe; by creating beautiful forms of manifestations for great moral truths. Above all, that higher philosophy, which treats of the intellectual and moral constitution of man, of the foundation of knowledge, of duty, of perfection, of our relations to the spiritual world, and especially to God,—this has a usefulness so peculiar as to throw other departments of knowledge into obscurity; and a people among whom this does not find honor has little ground to boast of its superiority to uncivilized tribes. It will be seen from these remarks that utility with us has a broad meaning. In truth, we are slow to condemn as useless any researches or discoveries of original and strong minds, even when we discern in them no bearing on any interests of mankind; for all truth is of a prolific nature, and has connections not immediately perceived; and it may be that what we call vain speculations may, at no distant period, link themselves with some new facts or theories, and guide a profound thinker to the most important results. The ancient mathematician, when absorbed in solitary thought, little imagined that his theorems, after the lapse of ages, were to be applied by the mind of Newton to the solution of the mysteries of the universe, and not only to guide the astronomer through the heavens, but the navigator through the pathless ocean. For ourselves, we incline to hope much from truths which are particularly decried as useless; for the noblest and most useful truth is of an abstract or universal nature: and yet the abstract, though susceptible of infinite application, is generally, as we know, opposed to the practical.

We maintain that a people which has any serious purpose of taking a place among improved communities should studiously promote within itself every variety of intellectual exertion. It should resolve strenuously to be surpassed by none. It should feel that mind is the creative power through which all the resources of nature are to be turned to account, and by which a people is to spread its influence, and establish the noblest form of empire. It should train within itself men able to understand and to use whatever is thought and discovered over the whole earth. The whole mass of human knowledge should exist among a people not in neglected libraries, but in its higher minds. Among its most cherished institutions should be those which will ensure to it ripe scholars, explorers of ancient learning, profound historians and mathematicians, intellectual laborers devoted to physical and moral science, and to the creation of a refined and beautiful literature.

Let us not be misunderstood. We have no desire to rear in our country a race of pedants, of solemn triflers, of laborious commentators on the mysteries of a Greek accent or a rusty coin. We would have men explore antiquity, not to bury themselves in its dust, but to learn its spirit and so to commune with its superior minds as to accumulate on the present age the influences of whatever was great and wise in former times. What we want is, that those among us whom God has gifted to comprehend whatever is now known, and to rise to new truths, may find aids and institutions to fit them for their high calling, and may become at once springs of a higher intellectual life to their own country, and joint workers with the great of all nations and times in carrying forward their race.

We know that it will be said that foreign scholars, bred under institutions which this country cannot support, may do our intellectual work, and send us books and learning to meet our wants. To this we have much to answer. In the first place we reply that, to avail ourselves of the higher literature of other nations, we must place ourselves on a level with them. The products of foreign machinery we can use without any portion of the skill that produced them. But works of taste and genius, and profound investigations of philosophy, can only be estimated and enjoyed through a culture and power corresponding to that from which they sprung.

In the next place we maintain that it is an immense gain to a people to have in its own bosom, among its own sons, men of distinguished intellect. Such men give a spring and life to a community by their presence, their society, their fame; and what deserves remark, such men are nowhere so felt as in a republic like our own; for here the different classes of society flow together and act powerfully on each other, and a free communication, elsewhere unknown, is established between the gifted few and the many. It is one of the many good fruits of liberty that it increases the diffusiveness of intellect; and accordingly a free country is, above all others, false to itself in withholding from its superior minds the means of enlargement.

We next observe—and we think the observation important—that the facility with which we receive the literature of foreign countries, instead of being a reason for neglecting our own, is a strong motive for its cultivation. We mean not to be paradoxical, but we believe that it would be better to admit no books from abroad than to make them substitutes for our own intellectual activity. The more we receive from other countries, the greater the need of an original literature. A people into whose minds the thoughts of foreigners are poured perpetually, needs an energy within itself to resist, to modify this mighty influence, and without it will inevitably sink under the worst bondage, will become intellectually tame and enslaved. We have certainly no desire to complete our restrictive system by adding to it a literary non-intercourse law. We rejoice in the increasing intellectual connection between this country and the Old World; but sooner would we rupture it than see our country sitting passively at the feet of foreign teachers. It were better to have no literature than form ourselves unresistingly on a foreign one. The true sovereigns of a country are those who determine its mind, its modes of thinking, its tastes, its principles; and we cannot consent to lodge this sovereignty in the hands of strangers. A country, like an individual, has dignity and power only in proportion as it is self-formed. There is a great stir to secure to ourselves the manufacturing of our own clothing. We say, Let others spin and weave for us, but let them not think for us. A people whose government and laws are nothing but the embodying of public opinion should jealously guard this opinion against foreign dictation. We need a literature to counteract and to use wisely the literature which we import. We need an inward power proportionate to that which is exerted on us as the means of self-subsistence. It is particularly true of a people whose institutions demand for their support a free and bold spirit that they should be able to subject to a manly and independent criticism whatever comes from abroad. These views seem to us to deserve serious attention. We are more and more a reading people. Books are already among the most powerful influences here. The question is, Shall Europe, through these, fashion us after its pleasure? Shall America be only an echo of what is thought and written under the aristocracies beyond the ocean?

Another view of the subject is this. A foreign literature will always in a measure be foreign. It has sprung from the soul of another people, which, however like, is still not our own soul. Every people has much in its own character and feelings which can only be embodied by its own writers, and which, when transfused through literature, makes it touching and true, like the voice of our earliest friend.

We now proceed to an argument in favor of native literature which, if less obvious, is, we believe, not less sound than those now already adduced. We have hitherto spoken of literature as the expression, the communication of the higher minds in a community. We now add that it does much more than is commonly supposed to *form* such minds, so that without it a people wants one of the chief means of educating or perfecting talent and genius. One of the great laws of our nature, and a law singularly important to social beings, is that the intellect enlarges and strengthens itself by expressing worthily its best views. In this as in other respects it is more blessed to give than to receive. Superior minds are formed, not merely by solitary thought, but almost as much by communication. Great thoughts are never fully possessed till he who has conceived them has given them fit utterance. One of the noblest and most invigorating labors of genius is to clothe its conceptions in clear and glorious forms, to give them existence in other souls. Thus literature creates, as well as manifests, intellectual power, and without it the highest minds will never be summoned to the most invigorating action.

We doubt whether a man ever brings his faculties to bear with their whole force on a subject until he writes upon it for the instruction or gratification of others. To place it clearly before others, he feels the necessity of viewing it more vividly himself. By attempting to seize his thoughts and fix them in an enduring form, he finds them vague and unsatisfactory to a degree which he did not suspect, and toils for a precision and harmony of views of which he had never before felt the need. He places his subject in new lights,—submits it to a searching analysis, compares and connects with it his various knowledge, seeks for it new illustrations and analogies, weighs objections, and through these processes often arrives at higher truths than he at first aimed to illustrate. Dim conceptions grow bright. Glorious thoughts which had darted as meteors through the mind are arrested, and gradually shine with a sun-like splendor, with prolific energy on the intellect and heart. It is one of the chief distinctions of a great mind that it is prone to rush into twilight regions, and to catch faint glimmerings of distant and unbounded prospects; and nothing perhaps aids it more to pierce the shadows which surround it than the labor to unfold to other minds the indistinct conceptions which have dawned on its own. Even where composition yields no such fruits, it is still a great intellectual help. It always favors comprehensive and systematical views. The laborious distribution of a great subject, so as to assign to each part or topic its just position and due proportion, is singularly fitted to give compass and persevering force of thought.

If we confine ourselves simply to the consideration of style, we shall have reason to think that a people among whom this is neglected wants one important intellectual aid. In this great power is exerted, and by exertion increased. To the multitude, indeed, language seems so natural an instrument that to use it with clearness and energy seems no great effort. It is framed, they think, to the writer's hand, and so continually employed as to need little thought or skill. But in nothing is the creative power of a gifted writer seen more than in his style. True, his words may be found in the dictionary. But there they lie disjointed and dead. What a wonderful life does he breathe into them by compacting them into his sentences! Perhaps he uses no term which has not yet been hackneyed by ordinary writers; and yet with these vulgar materials what miracles does he achieve! What a world of thought does he condense into a phrase! By new combinations of common words what delicate hues or what a blaze of light does he pour over his subject! Power of style depends very little on the structure or copiousness of the language which the writer of genius employs, but chiefly, if not wholly, on his own mind. The words arranged in his dictionary are no more fitted to depict his thoughts than the block of marble in the sculptor's shop to show forth the conceptions which are dawning in his mind. Both are inert materials. The power which pervades them comes from the soul; and the same creative energy is manifested in the production of a noble style as in extracting beautiful forms from lifeless stone. How unfaithful, then, is a nation to its own intellect in which grace and force of style receive no culture!

The remarks now made on the importance of literature as a means of educating talent and genius, we are aware, do not apply equally to all subjects or kinds of knowledge. In the exact or physical sciences a man may acquire much without composition, and may make discoveries without registering them. Even here, however, we believe that by a systematic development of his views in a luminous style, he will bring great aid to his own faculties as well as to others. It is on the vast subjects of morals and human nature that the mind especially strengthens itself by elaborate composition; and these, let it be remembered, form the staple of the highest literature. Moral truth, under which we include everything relating to mind and character, is of a refined and subtile as well as elevated nature, and requires the joint and full exercise of discrimination, invention, imagination, and sensibility, to give it effectual utterance. A writer who would make it visible and powerful must strive to join an austere logic to a fervent eloquence; must place it in various lights; must create for it interesting forms; must wed it to beauty; must illuminate it by similitudes and contrasts; must show its correspondence with the outward world, perhaps must frame for it a vast machinery of fiction. How invigorating are these efforts! Yet it is only in writing, in elaborate composition, that they are deliberately called forth and sustained, and without literature they would almost cease. It may be said of many truths, that greater intellectual energy is required to express them with effect than to conceive them, so that a nation which does not encourage this expression impoverishes so far its own mind. Take, for example, Shakespeare's Hamlet. This is a development of a singularly interesting view of human nature. It shows us a mind to which life is a burden; in which the powers of meditation and feeling are disproportioned to the active powers; which sinks under its own weight, under the consciousness of wanting energies commensurate with its visions of good, with its sore trials, and with the solemn task which is laid upon it. To conceive clearly this form of human nature shows indeed the genius of the writer. But what a new power is required to bring it out in such a drama as Shakespeare's; to give it life and action; to invent for it circumstances and subordinate characters fitted to call it forth; to give it tones of truth and nature; to show the hues which it casts over all the objects of thought! This intellectual energy we all perceive; and this was not merely *manifested* in Shakespeare's work, but without such a work it would not have been awakened. His invention would have slumbered, had he not desired to give forth his mind in a visible and enduring form. Thus literature is the nurse of genius. Through this, genius learns its own strength, and continually accumulates it; and of course, in a country without literature, genius, however liberally bestowed by the Creator, will languish, and will fail to fulfil its great duty of quickening the mass amidst which it lives.

We come now to our last—and what we deem a weighty—argument in favor of a native literature. We desire and would cherish it, because we hope from it important aids to the cause of truth and human nature. We believe that a literature springing up in this new soil would bear new fruits, and, in some respects, more precious fruits than are elsewhere produced. We know that our hopes may be set down to the account of that national vanity which, with too much reason, is placed by foreigners among our besetting sins. But we speak from calm and deliberate conviction. We are inclined to believe that, as a people, we occupy a position from which the great subjects of literature may be viewed more justly than from those which most other nations hold. Undoubtedly we labor under disadvantages. We want the literary apparatus of Europe,— her libraries, her universities, her learned institutions, her race of professed scholars, her spots consecrated by the memory of sages, and a thousand stirring associations which hover over ancient nurseries of learning. But the mind is not a local power. Its spring is within itself, and under the inspiration of liberal and high feeling it may attain and worthily express nobler truth than outward helps could reveal.

The great distinction of our country is, that we enjoy some peculiar advantages for understanding our own nature. Man is the great subject of literature, and juster and profounder views of man may be expected here than elsewhere. In Europe political and artificial distinctions have, more or less, triumphed over and obscured our common nature. In Europe we meet kings, nobles, priests, peasants. How much rarer is it to meet *men;* by which we mean human beings conscious of their own nature, and conscious of the utter worthlessness of all outward distinctions compared with what is treasured up in their own souls. Man does not value himself as man. It is for his blood, his rank, or some artificial distinction, and not for the attributes of humanity, that he holds himself in respect. The institutions of the Old World all tend to throw obscurity over what we most need to know, and that is, the worth and claims of a human being. We know that great improvements in this respect are going on abroad. Still, the many are too often postponed to the few. The mass of men are regarded as instruments to work with, as materials to be shaped for the use of their superiors. That consciousness of our own nature which contains, as a germ, all nobler thoughts, which teaches us at once self-respect and respect for others, and which binds us to God by filial sentiment and hope,—this has been repressed, kept down by establishments founded in force; and literature, in all its departments, bears, we think, the traces of this inward degradation. We conceive that our position favors a juster and profounder estimate of human nature. We mean not to boast, but there are fewer obstructions to that moral consciousness, that consciousness of humanity, of which we have spoken. Man is not hidden from us by so many disguises as in the Old World. The essential equality of all human beings, founded on the possession of a spiritual, progressive, immortal nature, is, we hope, better understood; and nothing more than this single conviction is needed to work the mightiest changes in every province of human life and of human thought.

We have stated what seems to us our most important distinction. But our position has other advantages. The mere circumstance of its being a new one gives reason to hope for some new intellectual activity, some fresher views of nature and life. We are not borne down by the weight of antiquated institutions, time-hallowed abuses, and the remnants of feudal barbarism. The absence of a religious establishment is an immense gain, as far as originality of mind is in question; for an establishment, however advantageous in other respects, is, by its nature, hostile to discovery and progress. To keep the mind where it is, to fasten the notions of one age on all future time, is its aim and proper business; and if it happened, as has generally been the case, to grow up in an age of strife and passion, when, as history demonstrates, the church was overrun with error, it cannot but perpetuate darkness and mental bondage. Among us, intellect, though far from being free, has broken some of the chains of other countries, and is more likely, we conceive, to propose to itself its legitimate object, truth,—everlasting and universal truth.

We have no thought of speaking contemptuously of the literature of the Old World. It is our daily nutriment. We feel our debt to be immense to the glorious company of pure and wise minds which in foreign lands have bequeathed us in writing their choicest thoughts and holiest feelings. Still, we feel that all existing literature has been produced under influences which have necessarily mixed with it much error and corruption; and that the whole of it ought to pass, and must pass, under rigorous review. For example, we think that the history of the human race is to be rewritten. Men imbued with the prejudices which thrive under aristocracies and state religions cannot understand it. Past ages, with their great events and great men, are to undergo, we think, a new trial, and yield new results. It is plain that history is already viewed under new aspects, and we believe that the true principles for studying and writing it are to be unfolded here, at least as rapidly as in other countries. It seems to us that in literature an immense work is yet to be done. The most interesting

questions to mankind are yet in debate. Great principles are yet to be settled in criticism, in morals, in politics; and, above all, the true character of religion is to be rescued from the disguises and corruptions of ages. We want a reformation. We want a literature in which genius will pay supreme, if not undivided, homage to truth and virtue; in which the childish admiration of what has been called greatness will give place to a wise moral judgment, which will breathe reverence for the mind and elevating thoughts of God. The part which this country is to bear in this great intellectual reform we presume not to predict. We feel, however, that, if true to itself, it will have the glory and happiness of giving new impulses to the human mind. This is our cherished hope. We should have no heart to encourage native literature, did we not hope that it would become instinct with a new spirit. We cannot admit the thought that this country is to be only a repetition of the Old World. We delight to believe that God, in the fulness of time, has brought a new continent to light, in order that the human mind should move here with a new freedom, should frame new social institutions, should explore new paths and reap new harvests. We are accustomed to estimate nations by their creative energies; and we shall blush for our country if, in circumstances so peculiar, original, and creative, it shall satisfy itself with a passive reception and mechanical reiteration of the thoughts of strangers.

We have now completed our remarks on the importance of a native literature. The next great topic is the means of producing it. And here our limits forbid us to enlarge; yet we cannot pass it over in silence. A primary and essential means of the improvement of our literature is, that, as a people, we should feel its value, should desire it, should demand it, should encourage it, and should give it a hearty welcome. It will come if called for; and, under this conviction, we have now labored to create a want for it in the community. We say that we must call for it, by which we mean not merely that we must invite it by good wishes and kind words, but must make liberal provision for intellectual education. We must enlarge our literary institutions, secure more extensive and profound teaching, and furnish helps and resources to men of their superior talent for continued laborious research. As yet intellectual labor, devoted to a thorough investigation and a full development of great subjects, is almost unknown among us; and without it we shall certainly rear few lasting monuments of thought. We boast of our primary schools. We want universities worthy of the name, where a man of genius and literary zeal may possess himself of all that is yet known, and may strengthen himself by intercourse with kindred minds. We know it will be said that we cannot afford these. But it is not so. We are rich enough for ostentation, for intemperance, for luxury. We can lavish millions on fashion, on furniture, on dress, on our palaces, on our pleasures; but we have nothing to spend for the mind. Where lies our poverty? In the purse or in the soul?

We have spoken of improved institutions as essential to an improved literature. We beg, however, not to be misunderstood, as if these were invested with a creating power, or would necessarily yield the results which we desire. They are the means, not causes, of advancement. Literature depends on individual genius, and this, though fostered, cannot be created by outward helps. No human mechanism can produce original thought. After all the attempts to explain by education the varieties of intellect, we are compelled to believe that minds, like all the other products of nature, have original and indestructible differences, that they are not exempted from that great and beautiful law which joins with strong resemblances as strong diversities; and, of consequence, we believe that the men who are to be the lights of the world bring with them their commission and power from God. Still, whilst institutions cannot create, they may and do unfold genius; and, for want of them, great minds often slumber or run to waste, whilst a still larger class, who want genius, but possess admirable powers, fail of that culture through which they might enjoy and approach their more gifted brethren.

A people, as we have said, are to give aid to literature by founding wise and enlarged institutions. They may do much more. They may exert a nobler patronage. By cherishing in their own breasts the love of truth, virtue, and freedom, they may do much to nurse and kindle genius in its favored possessors. There is a constant reaction between a community and the great minds which spring up within it, and they form one another. In truth, great minds are developed more by the spirit and character of the people to which they belong than by all other causes. Thus a free spirit, a thirst for new and higher knowledge in a community, does infinitely more for literature than the most splendid benefactions under despotism. A nation under any powerful excitement becomes fruitful of talent. Among a people called to discuss great questions, to contend for great interests, to make great sacrifices for the public weal, we always find new and unsuspected energies of thought brought out. A mercenary, selfish, luxurious, sensual people, toiling only to secure the pleasures of sloth, will often communicate their own softness and baseness to the superior minds which dwell among them. In this impure atmosphere the celestial spark burns dim; and well will it be if God's great gift of genius be not impiously prostituted to lust and crime.

In conformity with the views now stated, we believe that literature is to be carried forward, here and elsewhere, chiefly by some new and powerful impulses communicated to society; and it is a question naturally suggested by this discussion from what impulse, principle, excitement, the highest action of the mind may now be expected. When we look back, we see that literature has been originated and modified by a variety of principles,—by patriotism and national feeling, by reverence for antiquity, by the spirit of innovation, by enthusiasm, by scepticism, by the passion for fame, by romantic love, and by political and religious convulsions. Now we do not expect from these causes any higher action of the mind than they have yet produced. Perhaps most of them have spent their force. The very improvements of society seem to forbid the manifestation of their former energy. For example, the patriotism of antiquity and the sexual love of chivalrous ages, which inspired so much of the old literature, are now seen to be feverish and vicious excesses of natural principles, and have gone, we trust, never to return.

Are we asked, then, to what impulse or power we look for a higher literature than has yet existed? We answer, To a new action or development of the religious principle. This remark will probably surprise not a few of our readers. It seems to us that the energy with which this principle is to act on the intellect is hardly suspected. Men identify religion with superstition, with fanaticism, with the common forms of Christianity; and seeing it arrayed against intellect, leagued with oppression, fettering inquiry, and incapable of being blended with the sacred dictates of reason and conscience, they see in its progress only new encroachments on free and enlightened thinking. Still, man's relation to God is the great quickening truth, throwing all other truths into insignificance, and a truth which, however obscured and paralyzed by the many errors which ignorance and fraud have hitherto linked with it, has ever been a chief spring of human improvement. We look to it as the true life of the intellect. No man can be just to himself —can comprehend his own existence, can put forth all his powers with an heroic confidence, can deserve to be the guide and inspirer of other minds—till he has risen to communion with the Supreme Mind; till he feels his filial connection with the Universal Parent; till he regards himself as the recipient and minister of the Infinite Spirit; till he feels his consecration to the ends which religion unfolds; till he rises above human opinion, and is moved by a higher impulse than fame.

From these remarks it will be seen that our chief hopes of an improved literature rest on our hopes of an improved religion. From the prevalent theology which has come down to us from the dark ages, we hope nothing. It has done its best. All that can grow up under its sad shade has already been brought forth. It wraps the divine nature and human nature in impenetrable gloom. It overlays Christianity with technical, arbitrary dogmas. True faith is of another lineage. It comes from the same source with reason, conscience, and our best affections, and is in harmony with them all. True faith is essentially a moral conviction; a confidence in the reality and immutableness of moral distinctions; a confidence in disinterested virtue or in spiritual excellence as the supreme good; a confidence in God as its fountain and Almighty Friend, and in Jesus as having lived and died to breathe it into the soul; a confidence in its power, triumphs, and immortality; a confidence through which outward changes, obstructions, disasters, sufferings, are overcome, or rather made instruments of perfection. Such a faith, unfolded freely and powerfully, must "work mightily" on the intellect as well as on practice. By revealing to us the supreme purpose of the Creator, it places us, as it were, in the centre of the universe, from which the harmonies, true relations, and brightest aspect of things are discerned. It unites calmness and enthusiasm, and the concord of these seemingly hostile elements is essential to the full and healthy action of the creative powers of the soul. It opens the eye to beauty and the heart to love. Literature, under this influence, will become more ingenuous and single-hearted; will penetrate farther into the soul; will find new interpretations of nature and life; will breathe a martyr's love of truth, tempered with a never-failing charity; and, whilst sympathizing with all human suffering, will still be pervaded by a helpful cheerfulness, and will often break forth in tones of irrepressible joy, responsive to that happiness which fills God's universe.

We cannot close our remarks on the means of an improved literature without offering one suggestion. We earnestly recommend to our educated men a more extensive acquaintance with the intellectual labors of continental Europe. Our reading is confined too much to English books, and especially to the more recent publications of Great Britain. In this we err. We ought to know the different modes of viewing and discussing great subjects in different nations. We should be able to compare the writings of the highest minds in a great variety of circumstances. Nothing can favor more our own intellectual independence and activity. Let English literature be ever so fruitful and profound, we should still impoverish ourselves by making it our sole nutriment. We fear, however, that at the present moment English books want much which we need. The intellect of that nation is turned now to what are called practical and useful subjects. Physical science goes forward; and, what is very encouraging, it is spread with unexampled zeal through all classes of the community. Abuses of government, of the police, of the penal code, of charity, of poor-laws, and corn-laws, are laboriously explored. General education is improved. Science is applied to the arts with brilliant success. We see much good in progress. But we find little profound or fervid thinking expressed in the higher forms of literature. The noblest subjects of the intellect receive little attention. We see an almost total indifference to intellectual and moral science. In England there is a great want of philosophy, in the true sense of that word. If we examine her reviews, in which much of the intellectual power of the nation is expended, we meet perpetually a jargon of criticism, which shows a singular want of great and general principles in estimating works of art. We have no ethical work of any living English writer to be compared with that of

Degerando, entitled "Du Perfectionnement Moral"; and, although we have little respect for the rash generalizations of the bold and eloquent Cousin, yet the interest which his metaphysics awaken in Paris is, in our estimation, a better presage than the lethargy which prevails on such topics in England. In these remarks we have no desire to depreciate the literature of England, which, taken as a whole, we regard as the noblest monument of the human mind. We rejoice in our descent from England, and esteem our free access to her works of science and genius as among our high privileges. Nor do we feel as if her strength were spent. We see no wrinkles on her brow, no decrepitude in her step. At this moment she has authors, especially in poetry and fiction, whose names are "familiar in our mouths as household words," and who can never perish but with her language. Still, we think that at present her intellect is laboring more for herself than for mankind, and that our scholars, if they would improve our literature, should cultivate an intimacy not only with that of England, but of continental Europe.

We have now finished our remarks on the importance and means of an improved literature among ourselves. Are we asked what we hope in this particular? We answer, Much. We see reasons for anticipating an increased and more efficient direction of talent to this object. But on these we cannot enlarge. There is, however, one ground of expectation to which we will call a moment's attention. We apprehend that literature is to make progress through an important change in society, which civilization and good institutions are making more and more apparent. It seems to us that, through these causes, political life is less and less regarded as the only or chief sphere for superior minds, and that influence and honor are more and more accumulated in the hands of literary and thinking men. Of consequence, more and more of the intellect of communities is to be drawn to literature. The distinction between antiquity and the present times, in respect to the importance attached to political life, seems to us striking; and it is not an accidental difference, but founded on permanent causes which are to operate with increased power. In ancient times everything, abroad and at home threw men upon the public, and generated an intense thirst for political power. On the contrary, the improvement of later periods inclines men to give importance to literature. For example, the instability of the ancient republics, the unsettled relations of different classes of society, the power of demagogues and orators, the intensity of factions, the want of moral and religious restraints, the want of some regular organ for expressing the public mind, the want of precedents and precise laws for the courts of justice, —these and other circumstances gave to the ancient citizen a feeling as if revolutions and convulsions were inseparable from society, turned his mind with unremitting anxiety to public affairs, and made a participation of political power an important, if not an essential, means of personal safety. Again, the ancient citizen had no home, in our sense of the word. He lived in the market, the forum, the place of general resort, and of course his attention was very much engrossed by affairs of state. Again, religion, which now more than all things throws a man upon himself, was in ancient times a public concern, and turned men to political life. The religion of the heart and closet was unknown. The relation of the gods to particular states was their most prominent attribute; and, to conciliate their favor to the community, the chief end of worship. Accordingly, religion consisted chiefly in public and national rites. In Rome the highest men in the state presided at the altar, and, adding to their other titles that of Supreme Pontiff, performed the most solemn functions of the priesthood. Thus the whole strength of the religious principle was turned into political channels. The gods were thought to sustain no higher office than a political one, and of consequence this was esteemed the most glorious for men. Once more, in ancient times political rank was vastly more efficient, whether for good or for evil, than at present, and of consequence was the object of a more insatiable ambition. It was almost the only way of access to the multitude. The public man held a sway over opinion, over his country, perhaps over foreign states, now unknown. It is the influence of the press and of good institutions to reduce the importance of the man of office. In proportion as private individuals can act on the public mind; in proportion as a people read, think, and have the means of expressing and enforcing their opinions; in proportion as laws become fixed, known, and sanctioned by the moral sense of the community; in proportion as the interest of the state, the principles of administration, and all public measures are subjected to free and familiar discussion,—government becomes a secondary influence. The power passes into the hands of those who think, write, and spread their minds far and wide. Accordingly, literature is to become more and more the instrument of swaying men, of doing good, of achieving fame. The contrast between ancient and modern times in the particulars now stated is too obvious to need illustration, and our great inference is equally clear. The vast improvements which in the course of ages have taken place in social order, in domestic life, in religion, in knowledge, all conspire to one result, all tend to introduce other and higher influences than political power, and to give to that form of intellectual effort which we call literature dominion over human affairs. Thus truth, we apprehend, is more and more felt; and from its influence, joined with our peculiar condition and free institutions, we hope for our country the happiness and glory of a pure, deep, rich, beautiful, and ennobling literature.   1830

JAMES RUSSELL LOWELL

1819–1891

LOWELL'S VENERATION for the past dominated his social thought in spite of his sympathy, during his young manhood, for radical abolitionism and, in his later life, for the reforms designed to shake the hold of corrupt vested interests in public places. This reverence for the past, together with the scholarship which was closely related to it, kept Lowell from espousing without qualification the enthusiastic clamor for an "American" literature free from all traces of the culture of the European past. His sympathy for England, which served the advocates of an Anglo-American entente well, not only during his residence as ambassador at the Court of St. James but throughout much of his life, did not, on the other hand, stand in the way of Lowell's "Americanism." But his "Americanism" was that of the cultured class of the Atlantic seaboard, not that of the West, not that, certainly, of the mass of plain Americans with a penchant for "spread-eagleism" as well as for equalitarianism. The following review of Longfellow's "Kavanaugh," which first appeared in the *North American Review* in 1849, represents the cosmopolitan's protest against the extreme type of cultural nationalism.

G. W. Cooke, *A Bibliography of James Russell Lowell*, Boston and New York, 1906.
The Complete Writings of James Russell Lowell, 16 vols., Cambridge, 1904.
The Letters of James Russell Lowell, C. E. Norton, ed., 2 vols., New York, 1894.
Leon Howard, *Victorian Knight-Errant: A Study of the Early Literary Career of James Russell Lowell*, Berkeley, 1952.
Benjamin T. Spencer, *The Quest for Nationality*, Syracuse, 1957.

» » NATIONALITY IN LITERATURE « «

Time is figured with scythe, hour-glass, wallet, and slippery forelock. He is allegorized as the devourer of his own offspring. But there is yet one of his functions, and that not the least important, which wants its representative among his emblems. To complete his symbolic outfit, a sieve should be hung at his back. Busy as he must be at his mowing, he has leisure on his hands, scents out the treacherous saltpetre in the columns of Thebes, and throws a handful of dust over Nineveh, that the mighty hunter Nimrod may not, wanting due rites of sepulture, wander, a terrible shadow, on this side of the irrepassable river. A figurative personage, one would say, with quite enough to do already, without imposing any other duty upon him. Yet it is clear that he finds opportunity also thoroughly to sift men and their deeds, winnowing away with the untired motion of his wings, monuments, cities, empires, families, generations, races, as chaff.

We must go to the middle of a child's bunch of cherries to be sure of finding perfect fruit. The outer circles will show unripened halves, stabs of the robin's bill, and rain-cracks, so soon does the ambition of quantity deaden the nice conscience of quality. Indeed, with all of us, men as well as children, amount passes for something of intrinsic value. But Time is more choice, and makes his sieve only the coarser from age to age. One book, one man, one action, shall often be all of a generation busy with sword, pen, and trowel, that has not slipped irrevocably through the ever-widening meshes.

We are apt to forget this. In looking at the literature of a nation, we take note only of such names as Dante, Shakespeare, Goethe, not remembering what new acres have been added to the wide chaff-desert of Oblivion, that we may have these great kernels free from hull and husk. We overlook the fact that contemporary literature has not yet been put into the sieve, and quite gratuitously blush for the literary shortcomings of a whole continent. For ourselves, we have long ago got rid of this national (we might call it hemispherical) sensitiveness, as if there were any thing in our western half-world which stimulated it to produce great rivers, lakes, and mountains, mammoth pumpkins, Kentucky giants, two-headed calves, and what not, yet at the same time rendered it irremediably barren of great poets, painters, sculptors, musicians, and men generally. If there be any such system of natural compensations, whereby geological is balanced against human development, we may, at least, console ourselves with the anticipation, that America can never (from scientifically demonstrable inability) incur the odium of mothering the greatest fool.

There is, nevertheless, something agreeable in being able to shift the responsibility from our own shoulders to the broader ones of a continent. When anxious European friends inquire after our Art and our Literature, we have nothing to do but to refer them to Mount Washington or Lake Superior. It is their concern, not ours. We yield them without scruple to the mercies of foreign reviewers. Let those generously solicitous persons lay on and spare

not. There are no such traitors as the natural features of a country which betray their sacred trusts. They should be held strictly to their responsibilities, as, in truth, what spectacle more shameful than that of a huge, lubberly mountain, hiding its talent under a napkin, or a repudiating river? Our geographers should look to it, and instil proper notions on this head. In stating the heights of our mountains and the lengths of our rivers they should take care to graduate the scale of reproach with a scrupulous regard to every additional foot and mile. They should say, for example, that such a peak is six thousand three hundred feet high, and has never yet produced a poet; that the river so-and-so is a thousand miles long, and has wasted its energies in the manufacture of alligators and flatboatmen. On the other hand, they should remember to the credit of the Mississippi, that, being the longest river in the world, it has very properly produced the longest painter, whose single work would overlap by a mile or two the pictures of all the old masters stitched together. We can only hope that it will never give birth to a poet long in proportion.

Since it seems to be so generally conceded, that the form of an author's work is entirely determined by the shape of his skull, and that in turn by the peculiar configuration of his native territory, perhaps a new system of criticism should be framed in accordance with these new developments of science. Want of sublimity would be inexcusable in a native of the mountains, and sameness in one from a diversified region, while flatness could not fairly be objected to a dweller on the prairies, nor could eminent originality be demanded of a writer bred where the surface of the country was only hilly or moderately uneven. Authors, instead of putting upon their titlepages the names of previous works, or of learned societies to which they chance to belong, should supply us with an exact topographical survey of their native districts. The Himalaya mountains are, we believe, the highest yet discovered, and possibly society would find its account in sending the greater part of our poets thither, as to a university, either by subscription or by a tax laid for the purpose. How our literature is likely to be affected by the acquisition of the mountain ranges of California, remains to be seen. Legislators should certainly take such matters into consideration in settling boundary lines, and the General Court of Massachusetts should weigh well the responsibility it may incur to posterity, before transfering to New York the lofty nook of Boston Corner with its potential Homers and Miltons.

But perhaps we have too hastily taken the delinquency of our physical developments for granted. Nothing has hitherto been demanded of rivers and lakes in other parts of the world, except fish and mill privileges, or, at most, a fine waterfall or a pretty island. The received treatises on mountainous obstetrics give no hint of any parturition to be expected, except of mice. So monstrous a conception as that of a poet is nowhere on record; and what chloroform can we suggest to the practitioner who should be taken unawares by such a phenomenon?

At least, before definitive sentence be passed against us, the period of gestation which a country must go through, ere it bring forth a great poet, should be ascertained with scientific exactness. Let us not be in any hurry to resort to a Caesarian operation. Poets, however, valuable in their own esteem, are not, after all, the most important productions of a nation. If we can frame a commonwealth in which it shall not be a misfortune to be born, in which there shall never be a pair of hands nor a mouth too much, we shall be as usefully employed as if we should flower with a Dante or so, and remain a bony stalk forever after. We can, in the meantime, borrow a great poet when we want one, unless the pleasure and profit which we derive from the works of a great master, depend upon the proprietary right in him secured to us by compatriotism. For ourselves, we should be strongly inclined to question any exclusive claim to Shakespeare on the part of our respected relative, John Bull, who could do nothing better than look foolish when the great dramatist was called *bizarre,* and who has never had either the taste or the courage to see a single one of his most characteristic plays acted as he wrote it.

The feeling that it was absolutely necessary to our respectability that we should have a literature, has been a material injury to such as we have had. Our criticism has oscillated between the two extremes of depreciation and overpraise. On the one hand, it has not allowed for the variations of the magnetic needle of taste, and on the other, it has estimated merit by the number of degrees west from Greenwich. It seems never to have occurred to either sect of critics, that there were such things as

principles of judgment immutable as those of mathematics. One party has been afraid to commend lest an English Reviewer might afterward laugh; the other has eulogized because it considered so terrible a catastrophe probable. The Stamp Act and the Boston Port Bill scarcely produced a greater excitement in America than the appalling question, *Who reads an American book?* It is perfectly true, that the amount of enlightenment which a reader will receive from a book depends upon the breadth of surface which he brings within its influence, for we never get *something* for *nothing;* but we would deferentially suggest for the relief of many a still trembling soul, repeating to itself the *quid sum miser tunc dicturus*[1] to that awful question from the Edinburgh judgment-seat, that it is barely possible that the *power* of a book resides in the book itself, and that real books somehow compel an audience without extraneous intervention. From the first, it was impossible that Art should show here the successive stages of growth which have characterized it in the Old World. It is only geographically that we can call ourselves a new nation. However else our literature may avoid the payment of its liabilities, it can surely never be by a plea of infancy. Intellectually, we were full-grown at the start. Shakespeare had been dead five years, and Milton was eleven years old, when Mary Chilton leaped ashore on Plymouth Rock.

In looking backward or forward mentally, we seem to be infected with a Chinese incapacity of perspective. We forget the natural foreshortening, taking objects as they are reflected upon our retina, and neglecting to supply the proper interstices of time. This is equally true whether we are haruspicating the growth of desired opinions and arts, or are contemplating those which are already historical. Thus, we know statistically the amount which any race or nation has stored in its intellectual granaries, but made no account of the years of scarcity, of downright famine even, which have intervened between every full harvest. There is an analogy between the successive stages of a literature and those of a plant. There is, first of all, the seed, then the stalk, and then the seed again. What a length of stalk between Chaucer and Spenser, and again between Milton and Wordsworth! Except in India, perhaps, it would be impossible to affirm confidently an indigenous literature. The seed has been im-

[1] *What, then, am I, poor fellow, going to say?*

ported, accidentally or otherwise, as the white-weed and Hessian fly into America. Difference of soil, climate, and exposure will have their legitimate influence, but characteristics enough ordinarily remain for the tracing of the pedigree. The locality of its original production is as disputable as that of the garden of Eden. Only this is certain, that our search carries us farther and farther eastward.

No literature, of which we have authentic record or remains, can be called national in this limited and strict sense. Nor, if one could be found, would the calling it so be commendation. The best parts of the best authors in all languages can be translated; but, had they this element of exclusive nationality, the idea would demand a lexicon as well as the language which enveloped it. This shell within a shell would give more trouble in the cracking than any author can safely demand of his readers. Only a Dante can compel us to take an interest in the petty local politics of his day. No grubs were ever preserved in such amber. No Smiths and Browns were ever elevated upon so sublime and time-defying pinnacles of love, horror, and pity. The key by which we unlock the great galleries of Art is their common human interest. Nature supplies us with lexicon, commentary, and glossary to the great poems of all ages.

It would be hard to estimate the immediate indebtedness of Grecian literature; easier to reckon how much must have been due to the indirect influence of a religion and philosophy, whose esoteric ideas were of Egyptian derivation. Aristophanes is perhaps the only Grecian poet who is characterized by that quality of nationality of which we are speaking. Nay, it is something intenser than mere nationality in which his comedy is steeped. It is not the spirit of Greece, not even of Attica, but of Athens. It is cockneyism, not nationality. But his humor is more than Athenian. Were it not so, it would be dreary work enough deciphering jokes, as it were, in a mummypit, by the dim light of the scholiast's taper, too choked with dust and smoke to do any thing but cough when we are solemnly assured that we have come to the point.

There is a confusion in men's minds upon this subject. Nationality and locality are not distinguished from one another; and, were this jumble fairly cleared up, it would appear that there was a still farther confounding of truth to nature with fidelity of local coloring. Mere nationality is no more nor less than so much pro-vincialism, and will be found but a treacherous antiseptic for any poem. It is because they are men and women, that we are interested in the characters of Homer. The squabbles of a score of petty barbarian chiefs, and the siege of a city which never existed, would have been as barren and fruitless to us as a Welsh genealogy, had the foundations of the Iliad been laid no wider and deeper than the Troad. In truth, the only literature which can be called purely national is the Egyptian. What poetry, what philosophy, the torch of the Arab has fruitlessly lighted up for European eyes, we as yet know not; but that any ideas valuable to mankind are buried there, we do not believe. These are not at the mercy of sand, or earthquake, or overflow. No race perishes without intellectual heirs, but whatever was locally peculiar in their literature, their art, or their religious symbols, becomes in time hieroglyphical to the rest of the world, to be, perhaps, painfully deciphered for the verification of useless history, but incapable of giving an impulse to productive thought. Literature survives, not because of its nationality, but in spite of it.

After the United States had achieved their independence, it was forthwith decided that they could not properly be a nation without a literature of their own. As if we had been without one! As if Shakespeare, sprung from the race and the class which colonized New England, had not been also ours! As if we had no share in the puritan and republican Milton, we who had cherished in secret for more than a century the idea of the great puritan effort, and at last embodied it in a living commonwealth! But this ownership in common was not enough for us, and, as partition was out of the question, we must have a drama and an epos of our own. It must be national, too; we must have it all to ourselves. Other nations kept their poets, and so must we. We were to set up a literature as people set up a carriage, in order to be as good as our neighbors. It was even seriously proposed to have a new language. Why not, since we could afford it? Beside, the existing ones were all too small to contain our literature whenever we should get it. One enthusiast suggested the ancient Hebrew, another a fire-new tongue of his own invention. Meanwhile, we were busy growing a literature. We watered so freely, and sheltered so carefully, as to make a soil too damp and shaded for any thing but mushrooms; wondered a little why no oaks came up; and ended by voting the mushroom an oak, an American variety. Joel Barlow made the lowest bid for the construction of our epos, got the contract, and delivered in due season the Columbiad, concerning which we can only regret that it had not been entitled to a still higher praise of nationality by being written in one of the proposed new languages.

One would think that the Barlow experiment should have been enough. But we are still requested by critics, both native and foreign, to produce a national literature, as if it were some school exercise in composition to be handed in by a certain day. The sharp struggle of a day or a year may settle the question of a nation's political independence, but even for that, there must be a long moral preparation. The first furrow drawn by an English plough in the thin soil of Plymouth was truly the first line in our Declaration of Independence. Jefferson was not the prophet looking forth into the future, but the scribe sitting at the feet of the past. But nationality is not a thing to be won by the sword. We may safely trust to the influence of our institutions to produce all of it that is valuable. Let us be content that, if we have been to blame for a Columbiad, we have also given form, life, and the opportunity of entire development to social ideas ever reacting with more and more force upon the thought and the literature of the Old World.

The poetry and romance of other nations are assumed to be national, inasmuch as they occupy themselves about local traditions or objects. But we, who never had any proper youth as a nation, never had our mythic period either. We had no cradle and no nursery to be haunted with such bugaboos. One great element of external and immediate influence is therefore wanting to our poets. They cannot, as did Goethe in his Faust, imbue an old legend, which already has a hold upon the fancy and early associations of their countrymen, with a modern and philosophical meaning which shall make it interesting to their mature understandings and cultivated imaginations.

. . . This demand for a nationality bounded historically and geographically by the independent existence and territory of a particular race or fraction of a race, would debar us of our rightful share in the past and the ideal. It was happily illustrated by that parochially national Gascon, who would have been edified by the sermon had it been his good fortune to belong to the parish. Let us be thankful that there is no court by which we can be excluded from

our share in the inheritance of the great poets of all ages and countries, to which our simple humanity entitles us. No great poet has ever sung but the whole human race has been, sooner or later, the wiser and better for it. Above all, let us not tolerate in our criticism a principle which would operate as a prohibitory tariff of ideas. The intellect is a diœcious plant, and books are the bees which carry the quickening pollen from one to another mind. It detracts nothing from Chaucer that we can trace in him the influences of Dante and Boccaccio; nothing from Spenser that he calls Chaucer master; nothing from Shakespeare that he acknowledges how dear Spenser was to him; nothing from Milton that he brought fire from Hebrew and Greek altars. There is no degradation in such indebtedness. Venerable rather is this apostolic succession, and inspiring to see the *vitai lampada* [2] passed thus from consecrated hand to hand.

Nationality, then, is only a less narrow form of provincialism, a sublimer sort of clownishness and ill-manners. It deals in jokes, anecdotes, and allusions of such purely local character that a majority of the company are shut out from all approach to an understanding of them. Yet so universal a demand must have for its basis a more or less solid substratum of truth. There are undoubtedly national, as truly as family, idiosyncrasies, though we think that these will get displayed without any special schooling for that end. The substances with which a nation is compelled to work will modify its results, as well intellectual as material. The still renewing struggle with the unstable desert sands gave to the idea of durability in the Egyptian imagination a preponderance still further increased by the necessity of using granite, whose toughness of fibre and vagueness of coloring yielded unwillingly to fineness of outline, but seemed the natural helpmates of massiveness and repose. The out-of-door life of the Greeks, conducing at once to health and an unconscious education of the eye, and the perfection of physical development resulting from their palaestral exercises and constantly displayed in them, made the Greeks the first to perceive the noble symmetry of the human figure, for embodying the highest types of which Pentelicus supplied the fittest material. Corporeal beauty and strength, therefore, entered largely into their idea of the heroic, and perhaps it was rather policy than dandyism which

[2] *torch of life.*

hindered Alcibiades from learning to play the flute. With us, on the other hand, clothed to the chin in the least graceful costume ever invented by man, and baked half the year with stoves and furnaces, beauty of person has gradually receded from view, and wealth or brain is the essential of the modern novelist's hero. It may not be fanciful to seek in climate, and its resultant effects upon art, the remote cause of that fate-element which entered so largely into the Greek drama. In proportion as sculpture became more perfect, the images of the gods became less and less merely symbolical, and at last presented to the popular mind nothing more than actual representations of an idealized humanity. Before this degradation had taken place, and the divinities had been vulgarized in marble to the common eye, the ideas of the unseen and supernatural came to the assistance of the poet in giving interest to the struggles or connivances between heroes and gods. But presently a new and deeper chord of the imagination must be touched, and the unembodiable shadow of Destiny was summoned up, to move awe and pity as long as the human mind is incapable of familiarizing by precise definition the fearful and the vague. In that more purely objective age, the conflict must be with something external, and the struggles of the mind with itself afforded no sufficient theme for the poet. With us introspection has become a disease, and a poem is a self-dissection.

That Art in America will be modified by circumstances, we have no doubt, though it is impossible to predict the precise form of the moulds into which it will run. New conditions of life will stimulate thought and give new forms to its expression. It may not be our destiny to produce a great literature, as, indeed, our genius seems to find its kindliest development in practicalizing simpler and more perfect forms of social organization. We have yet many problems of this kind to work out, and a continent to subdue with the plough and the railroad, before we are at leisure for aesthetics. Our spirit of adventure will take first a material and practical direction, but will gradually be forced to seek outlet and scope in unoccupied territories of the intellect. In the meantime we may fairly demand of our literature that it should be national to the extent of being as free from outworn conventionalities, and as thoroughly impregnated with humane and manly sentiment, as is the idea on which our political fabric rests. Let it give a true reflection of our social, political, and household life. The "Poems on Man in the Republic," by Cornelius Mathews, disfigured as they were by gross faults of dialect and metre, had the great merit of presenting the prominent features of our civilization in an American light. The story of "Margaret"[3] is the most emphatically *American* book ever written. The want of plan and slovenliness of construction are characteristic of a new country. The scenery, character, dialect, and incidents mirror New England life as truly as Fresh Pond reflects the sky. The moral, also, pointing forward to a new social order, is the intellectual antitype of that restlessness of disposition, and facility of migration which are among our chief idiosyncrasies. The mistake of our imaginative writers generally is that, though they may take an American subject, they *costume* it in a foreign or antique fashion. The consequence is a painful vagueness and unreality. It is like putting Roman drapery upon a statue of Washington, the absurdity of which does not strike us so forcibly because we are accustomed to it, but which we should recognize at once were the same treatment applied to Franklin. The old masters did exactly the reverse of this. They took ancient or foreign subjects, but selected their models from their own immediate neighborhood.

. . . For ourselves, we confess, we have hopes. The breed of poets is not extinct, nor has Apollo shot away all the golden, singing arrows in his quiver. We have a very strong persuasion, amounting even to faith, that eyes and ears will yet open on this Western Continent, and find adequate utterance. If some of our birds have a right to feel neglected, yet other parts of our natural history have met with due civility; and if the pine tree complain of the tribute which Emerson has paid it, we surrender it to the lumberer and the saw-mill without remorse. It must be an unreasonable tree, wooden at head and heart.

Nay, how are we to know what is preparing for us at this very moment? What herald had Chaucer, singing the matins of that grand cathedral-service whose vespers we have not yet heard, in England? What external circumstance controlled the sweet influence of Spenser? Was Gorboduc a prologue that should have led us to expect Hamlet? Did the Restoration furnish the score for those organ-strains of Milton, breaking in with a somewhat unexpected

[3] Sylvester Judd's *Margaret* (1845), a novel of rural Massachusetts during the period after the Revolutionary War.

voluntary to drown the thin song of pander and parasite with its sublime thunders of fervor and ascription? What collyrium of nationality was it that enabled those pleasant Irish eyes of Goldsmith to pierce through the artificial tinsel and frippery of his day to that little clump of primroses at Wakefield? England had long been little better than a province of France in song, when Wordsworth struck the note of independ-
10　ence, and led the people back to the old worship. While we are waiting for our literature, let us console ourselves with the following observation with which Dr. Newman commences his History of the Hebrew Monarchy. "Few nations," he says, "which have put forth a wide and enduring influence upon others, proclaim themselves to have been indigenous on the land of their celebrity." Or, if the worst come, we can steal a literature like the Romans, and thus
20　acquire another point of similarity to that remarkable people, whom we resemble so much, according to the Quarterly Review, in our origin.

Mr. Longfellow has very good-naturedly and pointedly satirized the rigid sticklers for nationality in one of the chapters of his "Kavanagh," which we have taken for the text of some remarks we have long intended to make on this subject. It is time that we should say something
30　about the book itself . . .

. . . "Kavanagh" is, as far as it goes, an exact daguerreotype of New England life. We say *daguerreotype*, because we are conscious of a certain absence of motion and color, which detracts somewhat from the vivacity, though not from the truth, of the representation. From Mr. Pendexter with his horse and chaise, to Miss Manchester painting the front of her house, the figures are faithfully after nature. The story, too, is remarkably sweet and touching. The two friends, with their carrier-dove correspondence, give us a pretty glimpse into the trans-boarding-school disposition of the maiden mind, which will contrive to carry everyday life to romance, since romance will not come to it. The accident by which Alice discovers Kavanagh's love for Cecilia is a singularly beautiful invention; but we should wish to see with our own eyes before we believed that a king*fisher* ever pursued a dove, or, indeed, any thing but a fish. Even the king-*bird*, which does carry on a guerilla warfare with crows and hawks (slow-flighted birds,) would hardly pursue a pigeon, the swiftest of all flyers.

It is not unusual to make a single work the opportunity for passing definitive judgment upon an author. This is not our view of the duty of a critic. He is limited to the book before him, and all departures from it are impertinences. We hope that Mr. Longfellow may live a great many years yet, and give us a great many more books. We shall not undertake to pass a sentence which he may compel us to revise. We shall only say that he is the most popular of American poets, and that this popularity may safely be assumed to contain in itself the elements of permanence, since it has been fairly earned, without any of that subservience to the baser tastes of the public which characterizes the quack of letters. His are laurels honorably gained and gently worn. Without comparing him with others, it is enough if we declare our conviction, that he has composed poems which will live as long as the language in which they are written.　　　1849

WALT WHITMAN

1819–1892

IN VIEW OF THE FACT that Walt Whitman, a Brooklyn newspaper man and literary free-lance, knew the South and West at first hand only superficially, and New England scarcely at all, the nationalism that marks the preface of the first edition of *Leaves of Grass* (1855) is all the more remarkable. The preface is not without the suggestion, at least, of the later somewhat mystical internationalism which Whitman expressed in some of his greatest poems; but it is on the whole the culmination, the synthesis, of all the "calls" for an American literature and faith which men of letters had repeated again and again. Of Old World traditions, superstitions, tags of feudalism and monarchy and priesthood, Whitman will have none. His Americanism is of the spread-eagle variety so prevalent in the decade which was punctuated by the Mexican War. But it is Whitman's faith that America, more than any other spot on earth, is the home of the ordinary man, that makes his nationalism so central to the democratic individualism of his time. Whitman saw America absorbing all the peoples that sought her shores for asylum, all the immigrants and minority groups. He believed that a new race was emerging, a new order. The new race was to be made up of athletic comrades, of intensely individualistic men and women living together in fraternal bonds. And the poet's love for all the peculiarities of the different states was transcended by his mystical love for the whole, a love which the Civil War was to deepen and to lift to new levels of emotional expression.

The Uncollected Poetry and Prose of Walt Whitman, Emory Holloway, ed., New York, 2 vols., 1921.
Newton Arvin, *Whitman*, New York, 1938.
Gay Wilson Allen, *The Solitary Singer*, New York, 1955.

» » PREFACE TO "LEAVES OF GRASS" « «

America does not repel the past or what it has produced under its forms or amid other politics or the idea of castes or the old religions . . . accepts the lesson with calmness . . . is not so impatient as has been supposed that the slough still sticks to opinions and manners and literature while the life which served its requirements has passed into the new life of the new forms . . . perceives that the corpse is slowly borne from the eating and sleeping rooms of the house . . . perceives that it waits a little while in the door . . . that it was fittest for its days . . . that its action has descended to the stalwart and wellshaped heir who approaches . . . and that he shall be fittest for his days.

The Americans of all nations at any time upon the earth have probably the fullest poetical nature. The United States themselves are essentially the greatest poem. In the history of the earth hitherto the largest and most stirring appear tame and orderly to their ampler largeness and stir. Here at last is something in the doings of man that corresponds with the broadcast doings of the day and night. Here is not merely a nation but a teeming nation of nations. Here is action untied from strings necessarily blind to particulars and details magnificently moving in vast masses. Here is the hospitality which forever indicates heroes. . . . Here are the roughs and beards and space and ruggedness and nonchalance that the soul loves. Here the performance disdaining the trivial unapproached in the tremendous audacity of its crowds and groupings and the push of its perspective spreads with crampless and flowing breadth and showers its prolific and splendid extravagance. One sees it must indeed own the riches of the summer and winter, and need never be bankrupt while corn grows from the ground or the orchards drop apples or the bays contain fish or men beget children upon women.

Other states indicate themselves in their deputies . . . but the genius of the United States is not best or most in its executives or legislatures, nor in its ambassadors or authors or colleges or churches or parlors, nor even in its newspapers or inventors . . . but always most in the common people. Their manners, speech, dress, friendships—the freshness and candor of their physiognomy—the picturesque looseness of their carriage . . . their deathless attachment to freedom—their aversion to anything indecorous or soft or mean—the practical acknowledgment of the citizens of one state by the citizens of all other states—the fierceness of their roused resentment—their curiosity and susceptibility to a slight—the air they have of persons who never knew how it felt to stand in the presence of superiors—the fluency of their speech—their delight in music, the sure symptom of manly tenderness and native elegance of soul . . . their good temper and openhandedness—the terrible significance of their elections—the President's taking off his hat to them not they to him —these too are unrhymed poetry. It awaits the gigantic and generous treatment worthy of it.

The largeness of nature or the nation were monstrous without a corresponding largeness and generosity of the spirit of the citizen. Not nature nor swarming states nor streets and steamships nor prosperous business nor farms nor capital nor learning may suffice for the ideal of man . . . nor suffice the poet. No reminiscences may suffice either. A live nation can always cut a deep mark and can have the best authority the cheapest . . . namely from its own souls. This is the sum of the profitable uses of individuals or states and of present action and grandeur and of the subjects of poets.—As if it were necessary to trot back generation after generation to the eastern records! As if the beauty and sacredness of the demonstrable must fall behind that of the mythical! As if men do not make their mark out of any times! As if the opening of the western continent by discovery and what has transpired since in North and South America were less than the small theatre of the antique or the aimless sleepwalking of the middle ages! The pride of the United States leaves the wealth and finesse of the cities and all returns of commerce and agriculture and all the magnitude of geography or shows of exterior victory to enjoy the breed of full sized men or one full sized man unconquerable and simple.

The American poets are to enclose old and new for America is the race of races. Of them a bard is to be commensurate with a people. To him the other continents arrive as contributions . . . he gives them reception for their sake and his own sake. His spirit responds to his country's spirit . . . he incarnates its geography and natural life and rivers and lakes. Mississippi with annual freshets and changing chutes, Missouri and Columbia and Ohio and Saint Lawrence with the falls and beautiful masculine Hudson, do not embouchure where they spend themselves more than they embouchure into him. The blue breadth over the inland sea of Virginia and Maryland and the sea off Massachusetts and Maine and over Manhattan bay and over Champlain and Erie and over Ontario and Huron and Michigan and Superior, and over the Texan and Mexican and Floridian and Cuban seas and over the seas off California and Oregon, is not tallied by the blue breadth of the waters below more than the breadth of above and below is tallied by him. When the long Atlantic coast stretches longer and the Pacific coast stretches longer he easily stretches with them north or south. He

spans between them also from east to west and reflects what is between them. On him rise solid growths that offset the growths of pine and cedar and hemlock and liveoak and locust and chestnut and cypress and hickory and limetree and cottonwood and tuliptree and cactus and wildvine and tamarind and persimmon . . . and tangles as tangled as any canebrake or swamp . . . and forests coated with transparent ice and icicles hanging from the boughs and crackling in the wind . . . and sides and peaks of mountains . . . and pasturage sweet and free as savannah or upland or prairie . . . with flights and songs and screams that answer those of the wildpigeon and highhold and orchard-oriole and coot and surf-duck and red-shouldered-hawk and fish-hawk and white-ibis and indian-hen and cat-owl and water-pheasant and qua-bird and pied sheldrake and blackbird and mockingbird and buzzard and condor and night-heron and eagle. To him the hereditary countenance descends both mother's and father's. To him enter the essences of the real things and past and present events—of the enormous diversity of temperature and agriculture and mines—the tribes of red aborigines —the weatherbeaten vessels entering new ports or making landings on rocky coasts—the first settlements north or south—the rapid stature and muscle—the haughty defiance of '76, and the war and peace and formation of the constitution . . . the union always surrounded by blatherers and always calm and impregnable —the perpetual coming of immigrants—the wharf-hem'd cities and superior marine—the unsurveyed interior—the loghouses and clearings and wild animals and hunters and trappers . . . the free commerce—the fisheries and whaling and gold-digging—the endless gestation of new states—the convening of Congress every December, the members duly coming up from all climates and the uttermost parts . . . the noble character of the young mechanics and of all free American workmen and workwomen . . . the general ardor and friendliness and enterprise—the perfect equality of the female with the male . . . the large amativeness— the fluid movement of the population—the factories and mercantile life and laborsaving machinery—the Yankee swap—the New-York firemen and the target excursion—the southern plantation life—the character of the northeast and of the northwest and southwest—slavery and the tremulous spreading of hands to protect it, and the stern opposition to it which shall never cease till it ceases or the speaking of tongues and the moving of lips cease. For such the expression of the American poet is to be transcendant and new. It is to be indirect and not direct or descriptive or epic. Its quality goes through these to much more. Let the age and wars of other nations be chanted and their eras and characters be illustrated and that finish the verse. Not so the great psalm of the republic. Here the theme is creative and has vista. Here comes one among the wellbeloved stonecutters and plans with decision and science and sees the solid and beautiful forms of the future where there are now no solid forms.

Of all nations the United States with veins full of poetical stuff most need poets and will doubtless have the greatest and use them the greatest. Their Presidents shall not be their common referee so much as their poets shall. Of all mankind the great poet is the equable man. Not in him but off from him things are grotesque or eccentric or fail of their sanity. Nothing out of its place is good and nothing in its place is bad. He bestows on every object or quality its fit proportions neither more nor less. He is the arbiter of the diverse and he is the key. He is the equalizer of his age and land . . . he supplies what wants supplying and checks what wants checking. If peace is the routine out of him speaks the spirit of peace, large, rich, thrifty, building vast and populous cities, encouraging agriculture and the arts and commerce—lighting the study of man, the soul, immortality—federal, state or municipal government, marriage, health, free trade, intertravel by land and sea . . . nothing too close, nothing too far off . . . the stars not too far off. In war he is the most deadly force of the war. Who recruits him recruits horse and foot . . . he fetches parks of artillery the best that engineer ever knew. If the time becomes slothful and heavy he knows how to arouse it . . . he can make every word he speaks draw blood. Whatever stagnates in the flat of custom or obedience or legislation he never stagnates. Obedience does not master him, he masters it. High up out of reach he stands turning a concentrated light . . . he turns the pivot with his finger . . . he baffles the swiftest runners as he stands and easily overtakes and envelops them. The time straying toward infidelity and confections and persiflage he withholds by his steady faith . . . he spreads out his dishes . . . he offers the sweet firmfibred meat that grows men and women. His brain is the ultimate brain. He is no arguer . . . he is judgment. He judges not as the judge judges but as the sun falling around a helpless thing. As he sees the farthest he has the most faith. His thoughts are the hymns of the praise of things. In the talk on the soul and eternity and God off of his equal plane he is silent. He sees eternity less like a play with a prologue and denouement . . . he sees eternity in men and women . . . he does not see men and women as dreams or dots. Faith is the antiseptic of the soul . . . it pervades the common people and preserves them . . . they never give up believing and expecting and trusting. There is that indescribable freshness and unconsciousness about an illiterate person that humbles and mocks the power of the noblest expressive genius. The poet sees for a certainty how one not a great artist may be just as sacred as the greatest artist. . . . The power to destroy or remould is freely used by him but never the power of attack. What is past is past. If he does not expose superior models and prove himself by every step he takes he is not what is wanted. The presence of the greatest poet conquers . . . not parleying or struggling or any prepared attempts. Now he has passed that way see after him! there is not left any vestige of despair or misanthropy or cunning or exclusiveness or the ignominy of a nativity or color or delusion of hell or the necessity of hell . . . and no man thenceforward shall be degraded for ignorance or weakness or sin.

The greatest poet hardly knows pettiness or triviality. If he breathes into any thing that was before thought small it dilates with the grandeur and life of the universe. He is a seer . . . he is individual . . . he is complete in himself . . . the others are as good as he, only he sees it and they do not. He is not one of the chorus . . . he does not stop for any regulations . . . he is the president of regulation. What the eyesight does to the rest he does to the rest. Who knows the curious mystery of the eyesight? The other senses corroborate themselves, but this is removed from any proof but its own and foreruns the identities of the spiritual world. A single glance of it mocks all the investigations of man and all the instruments and books of the earth and all reasoning. What is marvelous? what is unlikely? what is impossible or baseless or vague? after you have once just opened the space of a peachpit and given audience to far and near and to the sunset and had all things enter with electric swiftness softly and duly without confusion or jostling or jam.

The land and sea, the animals fishes and birds, the sky of heaven and the orbs, the forests, mountains and rivers, are not small themes . . . but folks expect of the poet to indicate more than the beauty and dignity which always attach to dumb real objects . . . they expect him to indicate the path between reality and their souls. Men and women perceive the beauty well enough . . . probably as well as he. The passionate tenacity of hunters, woodmen, early risers, cultivators of gardens and orchards and fields, the love of healthy women for the manly form, seafaring persons, drivers of horses, the passion for light and the open air, all is an old varied sign of the unfailing perception of beauty and of a residence of the poetic in outdoor people. They can never be assisted by poets to perceive . . . some may but they never can. The poetic quality is not marshalled in rhyme or uniformity or abstract addresses to things nor in melancholy complaints or good precepts, but is the life of these and much else and is in the soul. The profit of rhyme is that it drops seeds of a sweeter and a more luxuriant rhyme, and of uniformity that it conveys itself into its own roots in the ground out of sight. The rhyme and uniformity of perfect poems show the free growth of metrical laws and bud from them as unerringly and loosely as lilacs or roses on a bush, and take shapes as compact as the shapes of chestnuts and oranges and melons and pears, and shed the perfume impalpable to form. The fluency and ornaments of the finest poems or music or orations or recitations are not independent but dependent. All beauty comes from beautiful blood and a beautiful brain. If the greatnesses are in conjunction in a man or woman it is enough . . . the fact will prevail through the universe . . . but the gaggery and gilt of a million years will not prevail. Who troubles himself about his ornaments or fluency is lost. This is what you shall do: Love the earth and sun and the animals, despise riches, give alms to every one that asks, stand up for the stupid and crazy, devote your income and labor to others, hate tyrants, argue not concerning God, have patience and indulgence toward the people, take off your hat to nothing known or unknown or to any man or number of men, go freely with powerful uneducated persons and with the young and with the mothers of families, read these leaves in the open air every season of every year of your life, re-examine all you have been told at school or church or in any book, dismiss whatever insults your own soul, and your very flesh shall be a great poem and have the richest fluency not only in its words but in the silent lines of its lips and face and between the lashes of your eyes and in every motion and joint of your body. . . . The poet shall not spend his time in unneeded work. He shall know that the ground is always ready plowed and manured . . . others may not know it but he shall. He shall go directly to the creation. His trust shall master the trust of everything he touches . . . and shall master all attachment.

The known universe has one complete lover and that is the greatest poet. He consumes an eternal passion and is indifferent which chance happens and which possible contingency of fortune or misfortune and persuades daily and hourly his delicious pay. What balks or breaks others is fuel for his burning progress to contact and amorous joy. Other proportions of the reception of pleasure dwindle to nothing to his proportions. All expected from heaven or from the highest he is rapport with in the sight of the daybreak or a scene of the winterwoods or the presence of children playing or with his arm round the neck of a man or woman. His love above all love has leisure and expanse . . . he leaves room ahead of himself. He is no irresolute or suspicious lover . . . he is sure . . . he scorns intervals. His experience and the showers and thrills are not for nothing. Nothing can jar him . . . suffering and darkness cannot—death and fear cannot. To him complaint and jealousy and envy are corpses buried and rotten in the earth . . . he saw them buried. The sea is not surer of the shore or the shore of the sea than he is of the fruition of his love and of all perfection and beauty.

The fruition of beauty is no chance of hit or miss . . . it is inevitable as life . . . it is exact and plumb as gravitation. From the eyesight proceeds another eyesight and from the hearing proceeds another hearing and from the voice proceeds another voice eternally curious of the harmony of things with man. To these respond perfections not only in the committees that were supposed to stand for the rest but in the rest themselves just the same. These understand the law of perfection in masses and floods . . . that its finish is to each for itself and onward from itself . . . that it is profuse and impartial . . . that there is not a minute of the light or dark nor an acre of the earth or sea without it—nor any direction of the sky nor any trade or employment nor any turn of events. This is the reason that about the proper expression of beauty there is precision and balance . . . one part does not need to be thrust above another. The best singer is not the one who has the most lithe and powerful organ . . . the pleasure of poems is not in them that take the handsomest measure and similes and sound.

Without effort and without exposing in the least how it is done the greatest poet brings the spirit of any or all events and passions and scenes and persons some more and some less to bear on your individual character as you hear or read. To do this well is to compete with the laws that pursue and follow time. What is the purpose must surely be there and the clue of it must be there . . . and the faintest indication is the indication of the best and then becomes the clearest indication. Past and present and future are not disjoined but joined. The greatest poet forms the consistence of what is to be from what has been and is. He drags the dead out of their coffins and stands them again on their feet . . . he says to the past, Rise and walk before me that I may realize you. He learns the lesson . . . he places himself where the future becomes present. The greatest poet does not only dazzle his rays over character and scenes and passions . . . he finally ascends and finishes all . . . he exhibits the pinnacles that no man can tell what they are for or what is beyond . . . he glows a moment on the extremest verge. He is most wonderful in his last half-hidden smile or frown . . . by that flash of the moment of parting the one that sees it shall be encouraged or terrified afterwards for many years. The greatest poet does not moralize or make applications of morals . . . he knows the soul. The soul has that measureless pride which consists in never acknowledging any lessons but its own. But it has sympathy as measureless as its pride and the one balances the other and neither can stretch too far while it stretches in company with the other. The inmost secrets of art sleep with the twain. The greatest poet has lain close betwixt both and they are vital in his style and thought.

The art of art, the glory of expression and the sunshine of the light of letters is simplicity. Nothing is better than simplicity . . . nothing can make up for excess or for the lack of definiteness. To carry on the heave of impulse and pierce intellectual depths and give all subjects their articulations are powers neither common nor very uncommon. But to speak in literature with the perfect rectitude and insouciance of the movements of animals and the unimpeachableness of the sentiment of trees in the woods and grass by the roadside is the flawless triumph of art. If you have looked on him who has achieved it you have looked on one of the masters of the artists of all nations and times. You shall not contemplate the flight of the graygull over the bay or the mettlesome action of the blood horse or the tall leaning of sunflowers on their stalk or the appearance of the sun journeying through heaven or the appearance of the moon afterward with any more satisfaction than you shall contemplate him. The greatest poet has less a marked style and is more the channel of thoughts and things without increase or diminution, and is the free channel of himself. He swears to his art, I will not be meddlesome, I will not have in my writing any elegance or effect or originality to hang in the way between me and the rest like curtains. I will have nothing hang in the way, not the richest curtains. What I tell I tell for precisely what it is. Let who may exalt or startle or fascinate or sooth I will have purposes as health or heat or snow has and be as regardless of observation. What I experience or portray shall go from my composition without a shred of my composition. You shall stand by my side and look in the mirror with me.

The old red blood and stainless gentility of great poets will be proved by their unconstraint. A heroic person walks at his ease through and out of that custom or precedent or authority that suits him not. Of the traits of the brotherhood of writers savans musicians inventors and artists nothing is finer than silent defiance advancing from new free forms. In the need of poems philosophy politics mechanism science behaviour, the craft of art, an appropriate native grand-opera, shipcraft, or any craft, he is greatest forever and forever who contributes the greatest original practical example. The cleanest expression is that which finds no sphere worthy of itself and makes one.

The messages of great poets to each man and woman are, Come to us on equal terms, Only then can you understand us, We are no better than you, What we enclose you enclose, What we enjoy you may enjoy. Did you suppose there could be only one Supreme? We affirm there can be unnumbered Supremes, and that one does not countervail another any more than one eyesight countervails another . . . and that men can be good or grand only of the consciousness of their supremacy within them. What do you think is the grandeur of storms and dismemberments and the deadliest battles and wrecks and the wildest fury of the elements and the power of the sea and the motion of nature and of the throes of human desires and dignity and hate and love? It is that something in the soul which says, Rage on, Whirl on, I tread master here and everywhere, Master of the spasms of the sky and of the shatter of the sea, Master of nature and passion and death, And of all terror and all pain.

The American bards shall be marked for generosity and affection and for encouraging competitors. . . . They shall be kosmos . . . without monopoly or secrecy . . . glad to pass any thing to any one . . . hungry for equals night and day. They shall not be careful of riches and privilege, they shall be riches and privilege . . . they shall perceive who the most affluent man is. The most affluent man is he that confronts all the shows he sees by equivalents out of the stronger wealth of himself. The American bard shall delineate no class of persons nor one or two out of the strata of interests nor love most nor truth nor the soul most nor the body most . . . and not be for the eastern states more than the western or the northern states more than the southern.

Exact science and its practical movements are no checks on the greatest poet but always his encouragement and support. The outset and remembrance are there . . . there are the arms that lifted him first and brace him best . . . there he returns after all his goings and comings. The sailor and traveler . . . the atomist chemist astronomer geologist phrenologist spiritualist mathematician historian and lexicographer are not poets, but they are the lawgivers of poets and their construction underlies the structure of every perfect poem. No matter what rises or is uttered they sent the seed of the conception of it . . . of them and by them stand the visible proofs of souls . . . always of their fatherstuff must be begotten the sinewy races of bards. If there shall be love and content between the father and the son and if the greatness of the son is the exuding of the greatness of the father there shall be love between the poet and the man of demonstrable science. In the beauty of poems are the tuft and final applause of science.

Great is the faith of the flush of knowledge and of the investigation of the depths of qualities and things. Cleaving and circling here swells the soul of the poet yet is president of itself always. The depths are fathomless and therefore calm. The innocence and nakedness are resumed . . . they are neither modest nor immodest. The whole theory of the special and supernatural and all that was twined with it or educed out of it departs as a dream. What has ever happened . . . what happens and whatever may or shall happen, the vital laws enclose all . . . they are sufficient for any case and for all cases . . . none to be hurried or retarded . . . any miracle of affairs or persons inadmissible in the vast clear scheme where every motion and every spear of grass and the frames and spirits of men and women and all that concerns them are unspeakably perfect miracles all referring to all and each distinct and in its place. It is also not consistent with the reality of the soul to admit that there is anything in the known universe more divine than men and women.

Men and women and the earth and all upon it are simply to be taken as they are, and the investigation of their past and present and future shall be unintermitted and shall be done with perfect candor. Upon this basis philosophy speculates ever looking toward the poet. ever regarding the eternal tendencies of all toward happiness never inconsistent with what is clear to the senses and to the soul. For the eternal tendencies of all toward happiness make the only point of sane philosophy. Whatever comprehends less than that . . . whatever is less than the laws of light and of astronomical motion . . . or less than the laws that follow the thief the liar the glutton and the drunkard through this life and doubtless afterward . . . or less than vast stretches of time or the slow formation of density or the patient upheaving of strata—is of no account. Whatever would put God in a poem or system of philosophy as contending against some being or influence, is also of no account. Sanity and ensemble characterise the great master . . . spoilt in one principle all is spoilt. The great master has nothing to do with miracles. He sees health for himself in being one of the mass . . . he sees the hiatus in singular eminence. To the perfect shape comes common ground. To be under the general law is great for that is to correspond with it. The master knows that he is unspeakably great and that all are unspeakably great

. . . that nothing for instance is greater than to conceive children and bring them up well . . . that to be is just as great as to perceive or tell.

In the make of the great masters the idea of political liberty is indispensable. Liberty takes the adherence of heroes wherever men and women exist . . . but never takes any adherence or welcome from the rest more than from poets. They are the voice and exposition of liberty. They out of ages are worthy the grand idea . . . to them it is confided and they must sustain it. Nothing has precedence of it and nothing can warp or degrade it. The attitude of great poets is to cheer up slaves and horrify despots. The turn of their necks, the sound of their feet, the motions of their wrists, are full of hazard to the one and hope to the other. Come nigh them awhile and though they neither speak nor advise you shall learn the faithful American lesson. Liberty is poorly served by men whose good intent is quelled from one failure or two failures or any number of failures, or from the casual indifference or ingratitude of the people, or from the sharp show of the tushes of power, or the bringing to bear soldiers and cannon or any penal statutes. Liberty relies upon itself, invites no one, promises nothing, sits in calmness and light, is positive and composed, and knows no discouragement. The battle rages with many a loud alarm and frequent advance and retreat . . . the enemy triumphs . . . the prison, the handcuffs, the iron necklace and anklet, the scaffold, garrote and leadballs do their work . . . the cause is asleep . . . the strong throats are choked with their own blood . . . the young men drop their eyelashes toward the ground when they pass each other . . . and is liberty gone out of that place? No never. When liberty goes it is not the first to go nor the second nor third to go . . . it waits for all the rest to go . . . it is the last. . . . When the memories of the old martyrs are faded utterly away . . . when the large names of patriots are laughed at in the public halls from the lips of the orators . . . when the boys are no more christened after the same but christened after tyrants and traitors instead . . . when the laws of the free are grudgingly permitted and laws for informers and blood-money are sweet to the taste of the people . . . when I and you walk abroad upon the earth stung with compassion at the sight of numberless brothers answering our equal friendship and calling no man master— and when we are elated with noble joy at the

sight of slaves . . . when the soul retires in the cool communion of the night and surveys its experience and has much extasy over the word and deed that put back a helpless innocent person into the gripe of the gripers or into any cruel inferiority . . . when those in all parts of these states who could easier realize the true American character but do not yet—when the swarms of cringers, suckers, doughfaces, lice of politics, planners of sly involutions for their own preferment to city offices or state legislatures or the judiciary or congress or the presidency, obtain a response of love and natural deference from the people whether they get the offices or no . . . when it is better to be a bound booby and rogue in office at a high salary than the poorest free mechanic or farmer with his hat unmoved from his head and firm eyes and a candid and generous heart . . . and when servility by town or state or the federal government or any oppression on a large scale or small scale can be tried on without its own punishment following duly after in exact proportion against the smallest chance of escape . . . or rather when all life and all the souls of men and women are discharged from any part of the earth—then only shall the instinct of liberty be discharged from that part of the earth.

As the attributes of the poets of the kosmos concentre in the real body and soul and in the pleasure of things they possess the superiority of genuineness over all fiction and romance. As they emit themselves facts are showered over with light . . . the daylight is lit with more volatile light . . . also the deep between the setting and rising sun goes deeper many fold. Each precise object or condition or combination or process exhibits a beauty . . . the multiplication table its—old age its—the carpenter's trade its—the grand-opera its . . . the hugehulled cleanshaped New-York clipper at sea under steam or full sail gleams with unmatched beauty . . . the American circles and large harmonies of government gleam with theirs . . . and the commonest definite intentions and actions with theirs. The poets of the kosmos advance through all interpositions and coverings and turmoils and stratagems to first principles. They are of use . . . they dissolve poverty from its need and riches from its conceit. You large proprietor they say shall not realize or perceive more than any one else. The owner of the library is not he who holds a legal title to it having bought and paid for it. Any one and every one is owner of the library who can read the same through all the varieties of tongues and subjects and styles, and in whom they enter with ease and take residence and force toward paternity and maternity, and make supple and powerful and rich and large. . . . These American states strong and healthy and accomplished shall receive no pleasure from violations of natural models and must not permit them. In paintings or mouldings or carvings in mineral or wood, or in the illustrations of books or newspapers, or in any comic or tragic prints, or in the patterns of woven stuffs or anything to beautify rooms or furniture or costumes, or to put upon cornices or monuments or on the prows or sterns of ships, or to put anywhere before the human eye indoors or out, that which distorts honest shapes or which creates unearthly beings or places or contingencies is a nuisance and revolt. Of the human form especially it is so great it must never be made ridiculous. Of ornaments to a work nothing outre can be allowed . . . but those ornaments can be allowed that conform to the perfect facts of the open air and that flow out of the nature of the work and come irrepressibly from it and are necessary to the completion of the work. Most works are most beautiful without ornament. . . . Exaggerations will be revenged in human physiology. Clean and vigorous children are jetted and conceived only in those communities where the models of natural forms are public every day. . . . Great genius and the people of these states must never be demeaned to romances. As soon as histories are properly told there is no more need of romances.

The great poets are also to be known by the absence in them of tricks and by the justification of perfect personal candor. Then folks echo a new cheap joy and a divine voice leaping from their brains: How beautiful is candor! All faults may be forgiven of him who has perfect candor. Henceforth let no man of us lie, for we have seen that openness wins the inner and outer world and that there is no single exception, and that never since our earth gathered itself in a mass have deceit or subterfuge or prevarication attracted its smallest particle or the faintest tinge of a shade—and that through the enveloping wealth and rank of a state or the whole republic of states a sneak or sly person shall be discovered and despised . . . and that the soul has never been once fooled and never can be fooled . . . and thrift

without the loving nod of the soul is only a fœtid puff . . . and there never grew up in any of the continents of the globe nor upon any planet or satellite or star, nor upon the asteroids, nor in any part of ethereal space, nor in the midst of density, nor under the fluid wet of the sea, nor in the condition which precedes the birth of babes, nor at any time during the changes of life, nor in that condition that follows what we term death, nor in any stretch of abeyance or action afterward of vitality, nor in any process of formation or reformation anywhere, a being whose instinct hated the truth.

Extreme caution or prudence, the soundest organic health, large hope and comparison and fondness for women and children, large alimentiveness and destructiveness and causality, with a perfect sense of the oneness of nature and the propriety of the same spirit applied to human affairs . . . these are called up of the float of the brain of the world to be parts of the greatest poet from his birth out of his mother's womb and from her birth out of her mother's. Caution seldom goes far enough. It has been thought that the prudent citizen was the citizen who applied himself to solid gains and did well for himself and his family and completed a lawful life without debt or crime. The greatest poet sees and admits these economies as he sees the economies of food and sleep, but has higher notions of prudence than to think he gives much when he gives a few slight attentions at the latch of the gate. The premises of the prudence of life are not the hospitality of it or the ripeness and harvest of it. Beyond the independence of a little sum laid aside for burial-money, and of a few clapboards around and shingles overhead on a lot of American soil owned, and the easy dollars that supply the year's plain clothing and meals, the melancholy prudence of the abandonment of such a great being as a man is to the toss and pallor of years of moneymaking with all their scorching days and icy nights and all their stifling deceits and underhanded dodgings, or infinitesimals of parlors, or shameless stuffing while others starve . . . and all the loss of the bloom and odor of the earth and of the flowers and atmosphere and of the sea and of the true taste of the women and men you pass or have to do with in youth or middle age, and the issuing sickness and desperate revolt at the close of a life without elevation or naïveté, and the ghastly chatter of a death without serenity or majesty, is the great fraud upon modern civilization and forethought, blotching the surface and system which civilization undeniably drafts, and moistening with tears the immense features it spreads and spreads with such velocity before the reached kisses of the soul. . . . Still the right explanation remains to be made about prudence. The prudence of the mere wealth and respectability of the most esteemed life appears too faint for the eye to observe at all when little and large alike drop quietly aside at the thought of the prudence suitable for immortality. What is wisdom that fills the thinness of a year or seventy or eighty years to wisdom spaced out by ages and coming back at a certain time with strong reinforcements and rich presents and the clear faces of wedding-guests as far as you can look in every direction running gaily toward you? Only the soul is of itself . . . all else has reference to what ensues. All that a person does or thinks is of consequence. Not a move can a man or woman make that affects him or her in a day or a month or any part of the direct lifetime or the hour of death but the same affects him or her onward afterward through the indirect lifetime. The indirect is always as great and real as the direct. The spirit receives from the body just as much as it gives to the body. Not one name of word or deed . . . not of venereal sores or discolorations . . . not the privacy of the onanist . . . not of the putrid veins of gluttons or rumdrinkers . . . not peculation or cunning or betrayal or murder . . . no serpentine poison of those that seduce women . . . not the foolish yielding of women . . . not prostitution . . . not of any depravity of young men . . . not of the attainment of gain by discreditable means . . . not any nastiness of appetite . . . not any harshness of officers to men or judges to prisoners or fathers to sons or sons to fathers or husbands to wives or bosses to their boys . . . not of greedy looks or malignant wishes . . . nor any of the wiles practised by people upon themselves . . . ever is or ever can be stamped on the programme but it is duly realized and returned, and that returned in further performances . . . and they returned again. Nor can the push of charity or personal force ever be any thing else than the profoundest reason, whether it brings arguments to hand or no. No specification is necessary . . . to add or subtract or divide is in vain. Little or big, learned or unlearned, white or black, legal or illegal, sick or well, from the first inspiration down the windpipe to the last expiration out of it, all that

a male or female does that is vigorous and benevolent and clean is so much sure profit to him or her in the unshakable order of the universe and through the whole scope of it forever. If the savage or felon is wise it is well . . . if the greatest poet or savan is wise it is simply the same . . . if the President or chief justice is wise it is the same . . . if the young mechanic or farmer is wise it is no more or less . . . if the prostitute is wise it is no more nor less. The interest will come round . . . all will come round. All the best actions of war and peace . . . all help given to relatives and strangers and the poor and old and sorrowful and young children and widows and the sick, and to all shunned persons . . . all furtherance of fugitives and of the escape of slaves . . . all the self-denial that stood steady and aloof on wrecks and saw others take the seats of the boats . . . all offering of substance or life for the good old cause, or for a friend's sake or opinion's sake . . . all pains of enthusiasts scoffed at by their neighbors . . . all the vast sweet love and precious suffering of mothers . . . all honest men baffled in strifes recorded or unrecorded . . . all the grandeur and good of the few ancient nations whose fragments of annals we inherit . . . and all the good of the hundreds of far mightier and more ancient nations unknown to us by name or date or location . . . all that was ever manfully begun, whether it succeeded or not . . . all that has at any time been well suggested out of the divine heart of man or by the divinity of his mouth or by the shaping of his great hands . . . and all that is well thought or done this day on any part of the surface of the globe . . . or on any of the wandering stars or fixed stars by those there as we are here . . . or that is henceforth to be well thought or done by you whoever you are, or by any one—these singly and wholly inure at their time and inure now and will inure always to the identities from which they sprung or shall spring. . . . Did you guess any of them lived only its moment? The world does not so exist . . . no parts palpable or impalpable so exist . . . no result exists now without being from its long antecedent result, and that from its antecedent, and so backward without the farthest mentionable spot coming a bit nearer to the beginning than any other spot. . . . Whatever satisfies the soul is truth. The prudence of the greatest poet answers at last the craving and glut of the soul, is not contemptuous of less ways of

prudence if they conform to its ways, puts off
nothing, permits no let-up for its own case or
any case, has no particular sabbath or judg-
ment-day, divides not the living from the dead
or the righteous from the unrighteous, is satisfied with the present, matches every thought
or act by its correlative, knows no possible forgiveness or deputed atonement . . . knows
that the young man who composedly periled
his life and lost it has done exceeding well for
himself, while the man who has not periled his
life and retains it to old age in riches and ease
has perhaps achieved nothing for himself worth
mentioning . . . and that only that person has
no great prudence to learn who has learnt to
prefer real longlived things, and favors body
and soul the same, and perceives the indirect
assuredly following the direct, and what evil or
good he does leaping onward and waiting to
meet him again—and who in his spirit in any
emergency whatever neither hurries or avoids
death.

The direct trial of him who would be the
greatest poet is today. If he does not flood
himself with the immediate age as with vast
oceanic tides . . . and if he does not attract
his own land body and soul to himself and
hang on its neck with incomparable love and
plunge his semitic muscle into its merits and
demerits . . . and if he be not himself the age
transfigured . . . and if to him is not opened
the eternity which gives similitude to all periods
and locations and processes and animate and
inanimate forms, and which is the bond of
time, and rises up from its inconceivable vagueness and infiniteness in the swimming shape of
today, and is held by the ductile anchors of life,
and makes the present spot the passage from
what was to what shall be, and commits itself
to the representation of this wave of an hour
and this one of the sixty beautiful children of
the wave—let him merge in the general run
and wait his development. . . . Still the final
test of poems or any character or work remains.
The prescient poet projects himself centuries
ahead and judges performer or performance
after the changes of time. Does it live through
them? Does it still hold on untired? Will the
same style and the direction of genius to
similar points be satisfactory now? Has no new
discovery in science or arrival at superior planes
of thought and judgment and behaviour fixed
him or his so that either can be looked down
upon? Have the marches of tens and hundreds
and thousands of years made willing detours

to the right hand and the left hand for his
sake? Is he beloved long and long after he is
buried? Does the young man think often of
him? and the young woman think often of him?
and do the middle-aged and the old think of
him?

A great poem is for ages and ages in common
and for all degrees and complexions and all departments and sects and for a woman as much
as a man and a man as much as a woman. A
great poem is no finish to a man or woman but
rather a beginning. Has any one fancied he
could sit at last under some due authority and
rest satisfied with explanations and realize and
be content and full? To no such terminus does
the greatest poet bring . . . he brings neither
cessation or sheltered fatness and ease. The
touch of him tells in action. Whom he takes
with firm sure grasp into live regions previously
unattained . . . thenceforward is no rest . . .
they see the space and ineffable sheen that turn
the old spots and lights into dead vacuums.
The companion of him beholds the birth and
progress of stars and learns one of the meanings. Now there shall be a man cohered out of
tumult and chaos . . . the elder encourages
the younger and shows him how . . . they two
shall launch off fearlessly together till the new
world fits an orbit for itself and looks unabashed
on the lesser orbits of the stars and sweeps
through the ceaseless rings and shall never be
quiet again.

There will soon be no more priests. Their
work is done. They may wait awhile . . . perhaps a generation or two . . . dropping off by
degrees. A superior breed shall take their place
. . . the gangs of kosmos and prophets en
masse shall take their place. A new order shall
arise and they shall be the priests of man, and
every man shall be his own priest. The churches
built under their umbrage shall be the churches
of men and women. Through the divinity of
themselves shall the kosmos and the new breed
of poets be interpreters of men and women and
of all events and things. They shall find their
inspiration in real objects today, symptoms of
the past and future. . . . They shall not deign
to defend immortality or God or the perfection
of things or liberty or the exquisite beauty and
reality of the soul. They shall arise in America
and be responded to from the remainder of the
earth.

The English language befriends the grand
American expression . . . it is brawny enough
and limber and full enough. On the tough stock

of a race who through all change of circumstances was never without the idea of political liberty, which is the animus of all liberty, it has attracted the terms of daintier and gayer and subtler and more elegant tongues. It is the powerful language of resistance . . . it is the dialect of common sense. It is the speech of the proud and melancholy races and of all who aspire. It is the chosen tongue to express growth faith self-esteem freedom justice equality friendliness amplitude prudence decision and courage. It is the medium that shall well nigh express the inexpressible.

No great literature nor any like style of behavior or oratory or social intercourse or household arrangements or public institutions or the treatment by bosses or employed people, nor executive detail or detail of the army or navy, nor spirit of legislation or courts or police or tuition or architecture or songs or amusements or the costumes of young men, can long elude the jealous and passionate instinct of American standards. Whether or no the sign appears from the mouths of the people, it throbs a live interrogation in every freeman's and freewoman's heart after that which passes by or this built to remain. Is it uniform with my country? Are its disposals without ignominious distinctions? Is it for the evergrowing communes of brothers and lovers, large, well-united, proud beyond the old models, generous beyond all models? Is it something grown fresh out of the fields or drawn from the sea for use to me today here? I know that what answers for me an American must answer for any individual or nation that serves for a part of my materials. Does this answer? or is it without reference to universal needs? or sprung of the needs of the less developed society of special ranks? or old needs of pleasure overlaid by modern science and forms? Does this acknowledge liberty with

audible and absolute acknowledgement, and set slavery at naught for life and death? Will it help breed one goodshaped and wellhung man, and a woman to be his perfect and independent mate? Does it improve manners? Is it for the nursing of the young of the republic? Does it solve readily with the sweet milk of the nipples of the breasts of the mother of many children? Has it too the old ever-fresh forbearance and impartiality? Does it look with the same love on the last born and those hardening toward stature, and on the errant, and on those who disdain all strength of assault outside of their own?

The poems distilled from other poems will probably pass away. The coward will surely pass away. The expectation of the vital and great can only be satisfied by the demeanor of the vital and great. The swarms of the polished deprecating and reflectors and the polite float off and leave no remembrance. America prepares with composure and goodwill for the visitors that have sent word. It is not intellect that is to be their warrant and welcome. The talented, the artist, the ingenious, the editor, the statesman, the erudite . . . they are not unappreciated . . . they fall in their place and do their work. The soul of the nation also does its work. No disguise can pass on it . . . no disguise can conceal from it. It rejects none, it permits all. Only toward as good as itself and toward the like of itself will it advance halfway. An individual is as superb as a nation when he has the qualities which make a superb nation. The soul of the largest and wealthiest and proudest nation may well go half-way to meet that of its poets. The signs are effectual. There is no fear of mistake. If the one is true the other is true. The proof of a poet is that his country absorbs him as affectionately as he has absorbed it.   1855

SAMUEL F. B. MORSE

1791–1872

THE ELDEST SON of the orthodox Congregationalist minister and famous geographer, Jedidiah Morse, Samuel F. B. Morse graduated from Yale in 1810 and studied painting in London under Washington Allston. Although some of his paintings are meritorious, he found the financial problem of the artist in America so keen that he turned to invention. While his invention of the telegraph was anticipated by others, Morse's contribution was both brilliant and, of course, of incalculable practical significance.

Morse stoutly upheld a democratic conception of the place of art in the national culture, and was a lively controversialist in other fields. The following selection illustrates the ideology of the Nativist, anti-Catholic movement which endeavored in the 1830's to restrict the influence of Catholic immigrants.

R. A. Billington, *The Protestant Crusade, 1800–1860*, New York, 1938.
Carleton Mabee, *The American Leonardo, a Life of Samuel F. B. Morse*, New York, 1944.

From: IMMINENT DANGERS TO THE FREE
»   » INSTITUTIONS OF THE UNITED STATES THROUGH «   «
FOREIGN IMMIGRATION

NO. VI

Recapitulation of Facts.—The necessity and propriety of discussing the political nature of the Roman Catholic System.

I have set forth in a very brief and imperfect manner the evil, the great and increasing evil, that threatens our free institutions from *foreign interference.* Have I not shown that there is real cause for alarm? Let me recapitulate the facts in the case, and see if any one of them can be denied; and if not, I submit it to the calm decision of every American, whether he can still sleep in fancied security, while incendiaries are at work; and whether he is ready quietly to surrender his liberty, civil and religious, into the hands of foreign powers.

1. It is a fact, that in this age the subject of civil and religious liberty agitates in the most intense manner the various European governments.

2. It is a fact, that the influence of American free institutions in subverting European despotic institutions is greater now than it has ever been, from the fact of the greater maturity, and long-tried character, of the American form of government.

3. It is a fact, that Popery is opposed in the very nature to Democratic Republicanism; and it is, therefore, as a political system, as well as religious, opposed to civil and religious liberty, and consequently to our form of government.

4. It is a fact, that this truth, respecting the intrinsic character of Popery, has lately been clearly and demonstratively proved in public lectures, by one of the Austrian Cabinet, a devoted Roman Catholic, and with the evident design (as subsequent events show) of exciting the Austrian government to a great enterprise in support of absolute power.

5. It is a fact, that this Member of the Austrian Cabinet [Frederick Schlegel], in his lectures, designated and proscribed this country by name, as the *"great nursery of destructive principles; as the Revolutionary school for France and the rest of Europe,"* whose contagious example of Democratic liberty had given, and would still give, trouble to the rest of the world, unless the evil were abated.

6. It is a fact, that very shortly after the delivery of these lectures, a Society was organized in the Austrian capital, called the St. Leopold Foundation, for the purpose "of promoting the greater activity of Catholic Missions in America."

7. It is a fact, that this Society is under the patronage of the Emperor of Austria,—has its central direction at Vienna,—is under the supervision of Prince Metternich,—that it is an extensive combination, embodying the civil, as well as the ecclesiastical *officers,* not only of the *whole Austrian Empire,* but of the neighbouring Despotic States,—that it is actively at work, collecting moneys, and sending agents to this country, to carry out into effect its designs.

8. It is a fact, that the agents of these foreign despots, are, for the most part, Jesuits.

9. It is a fact, that the effects of this society are already apparent in the otherwise unaccountable increase of Roman Catholic cathedrals, churches, colleges, convents, nunneries, &c., in every part of the country; in the sudden increase of Catholic emigration; in the increased clanishness of the Roman Catholics, and the boldness with which their leaders are

experimenting on the character of the American people.

10. It is a fact, that an unaccountable disposition to riotous conduct has manifested itself within a few years, when exciting topics are publicly discussed, wholly at variance with the former peaceful, deliberative character of our people.

11. It is a fact, that a species of police, unknown to our laws, has repeatedly been put in requisition to keep the peace among a certain class of foreigners, who are Roman Catholics, viz., Priest-police.

12. It is a fact, that Roman Catholic Priests have interfered to influence our elections.

13. It is a fact, that politicians on both sides have propitiated these priests, to obtain the votes of their people.

14. It is a fact, that numerous Societies of Roman Catholics, particularly among the Irish foreigners, are organized in various parts of the country, under various names, and ostensibly for certain benevolent objects; that these societies are united together by correspondence, all which may be innocent and praiseworthy, but viewed in connexion with the recent aspect of affairs, are at least suspicious.

15. It is a fact, that an attempt has been made to organize a military corps of Irishmen in New York, to be called the O'Connel Guards; thus commencing a military organization of foreigners.

16. It is a fact, that the greater part of the foreigners in our population is composed of Roman Catholics.

Facts like these I have enumerated might be multiplied, but these are the most important, and quite sufficient to make every American settle the question with himself, whether there is, or is not, danger to the country from the present state of our Naturalization Laws. I have stated what I believe to be facts. If they are *not* facts they will easily be disproved, and I most sincerely hope they will be disproved. If they are facts, and my inferences from them are wrong, I can be shown where I have erred, and an inference more rational, and more probable, involving less, or perhaps no, danger to the country, can be deduced from them, which deduction, when I see it, I will most cheerfully accept, as a full explanation of these most suspicious doings of Foreign Powers.

I have spoken in these numbers freely of a particular religious sect, the Roman Catholics, because from the nature of the case it was unavoidable; because the foreign political conspiracy is identified with that creed. With the *religious tenets* properly socalled, of the Roman Catholic, I have not meddled. If foreign powers hostile to the principles of this government, have combined to spread any religious creed, no matter of what denomination, that creed does by that very act become a subject of political interest to all citizens, and must and will be thoroughly scrutinized. We are compelled to examine it. We have no choice about it. If instead of combining to spread with the greatest activity the Catholic Religion throughout our country, the Monarchs of Europe had united to spread Presbyterianism, or Methodism, I presume, there are few who would not see at once the propriety and the necessity of looking most narrowly at the political bearings of the peculiar principles of these Sects, or of any other Protestant Sects; and members of any Protestant Sects too, would be the last to complain of the examination. I know not why the Roman Catholics in this land of scrutiny are to plead exclusive exemption from the same trial.

NO. XI

The imperious necessity of a change in the Naturalization Laws.—The dangers from the alarming increase and present character of foreign immigration.—The political changes in Europe double the dangers to the country from foreign immigration.—The test of the existence and strength of the conspiracy in the country, and the first step in the defence against it.

The propriety, nay, the imperious necessity of a change in the Naturalization Laws, is the point to which it is indispensable to the safety of the country, that the attention of Americans, as a whole people, should at this moment be concentrated. It is a national question, not only separate from, but *superior* to all others. All other questions which divide the nation, are peculiarly of a domestic character; they relate to matters between American and American. Whether the *bank system* is, or is not, adverse to our democratic institutions; whether *internal improvement* is constitutionally intrusted to the management of the general government, or reserved to the states respectively; whether *monopolies* of any kind are just or unjust; whether the *right of instructing* representatives is to be allowed or resisted; whether the *high offices* of the nation are safest administered by these or by those citizens; all these, and many kindred questions, are entirely of a domestic character, to be settled between ourselves, in the just democratic mode, by majority, by the prevailing voice of the American people declared through the *ballot box*. But the question of *naturalization*, the question whether *foreigners, not yet arrived,* shall or shall not be admitted to the American right of balloting is a matter in which the American people are in a certain sense, on one side as the original and exclusive possessors of the privilege, and foreigners on the other, as petitioners for a participation in that privilege; for the privilege of expressing their opinion upon, and assisting to decide all the other questions I have enumerated. It is, therefore, a question separate and *superior* to all these. It is a fundamental question; it affects the very foundation of our institutions, it bears directly and vitally on the *principle of the ballot* itself, that principle which decides the gravest questions of policy among Americans, nay, which can decide the very existence of the government, or can change its form at any moment. And surely this vital principle is amply protected from injury? To secure this point, every means which a people jealous of their liberties could devise was doubtless gathered about it for its preservation? It is not guarded. Be astonished, Americans, at the oversight. The mere statement of the provisions of the Naturalization Law, is sufficient, one would think, to startle any American who reflects at all. FIVE YEARS' RESIDENCE GIVES THE FOREIGNER, WHATEVER BE HIS CONDITION OR CHARACTER, THIS MOST SACRED PRIVILEGE OF ASSISTING TO CONTROL, AND ACTUALLY OF CONTROLLING (*there is not a guard to prevent,*) ALL THE DOMESTIC INTERESTS OF AMERICA. A simple *five years' residence,* allows any foreigner, (no matter what his character, whether friend or enemy of freedom, whether an exile from proscription, or a pensioned Jesuit, commissioned to serve the interests of Imperial Despots,) to handle this *"lock of our strength."* How came it to pass? How is it possible that so vital a point as the ballot box was not constitutionally surrounded with double, ay, with treble guards? How is it that this *heart* of Democracy was left so exposed; yes; this very *heart* of the body politic, in which, in periodical pulsations, the opinions of the people meet, to go forth again as law to the extremities of the nation; this *heart* left so

absolutely without protection, that the murderous eye of Imperial Despots across the deep, can, not only watch it in all its movements, but they are invited from its very nakedness, to reach out their hands to stab it. The figure is not too strong; their blow is aimed, now, whilst I write, at this very heart of our institutions. How is it that none of our sagacious statesmen foresaw this danger to the republic through the unprotected ballot box? It was foreseen. It did not escape the prophetic eye of Jefferson. He foresaw, and from the beginning foretold the evil, and uttered his warning voice. *Mr. Jefferson denounced the encouragement of emigration.* And, oh! consistency, where is thy blush? he who is now urging Jefferson's own recommendation on this vital point, is condemned by some who call themselves Jeffersonian democrats; by some journalists who in one column profess Jeffersonian principles, while in the next they denounce both the principles and the policy of Jefferson, and (with what semblance of consistency let them show if they can,) defend a great political evil, against which Jefferson left his written protest. It may be convenient, for purposes best known to themselves, for such journalists to desert their democratic principles, while loudly professing still to hold them; but the people, who are neither blind nor deaf, will soon perceive whose course is most consistent with that great apostle of democratic liberty. Do they ask, would you defend Mr. Jefferson's opinions when they are wrong?—I answer, prove them to be wrong, and I will desert them. Truth and justice are superior to all men. I advocate Jefferson's opinions, not because they are Jefferson's, but because his opinions are in accordance with truth and sound policy.—Let me show that Mr. Jefferson's opinions in relation to emigration are proved by experience to be sound.

What were the circumstances of the country when laws so favourable to the foreigner were passed to induce him to emigrate and settle in this country? The answer is obvious. Our early history explains it. In our national infancy we needed the strength of *numbers.* Powerful nations, to whom we were accessible by fleets, and consequently also by armies, threatened us. Our land had been the theatre of contests between French, and English, and Spanish armies, for more than a century. Our numbers were so few and so scattered, that as a people we could not unite to repel aggression. The war of Independence, too, had wasted us. We wanted *numerical strength;* we felt our weakness in numbers. *Safety,* then, national *safety,* was the motive which urged us to use every effort to increase our population, and to induce a foreign emigration. Then foreigners seemed all-important, and the policy of alluring them hither, too palpable to be opposed successfully even by the remonstrances of Jefferson. We could be benefited by the emigrants, and we in return could bestow on them a gift beyond price, by simply making them citizens. Manifest as this advantage seemed in the increase of our numerical strength, Mr. Jefferson looked beyond the advantage of the moment, and saw the distant evil. His reasoning, already quoted in a former number, will bear to be repeated. "I beg leave," says Mr. Jefferson, "to propose a doubt. The present desire of America is to produce rapid population by as great importations of foreigners as possible. But is this founded in good policy? *The advantage proposed, is the multiplication of numbers.* But are there no inconveniences to be thrown into the scale against the advantage expected from a multiplication of numbers by the importation of foreigners? It is for the happiness of those united in society to harmonize as much as possible in matters which they must of necessity transact together."

"Civil government being the sole object of forming societies, its administration must be conducted by common consent. Every species of government has its specific principles. Ours, perhaps, are more peculiar than those of any other in the universe. It is a composition of the freest principles of the English constitution, with others derived from the natural right and natural reason. To these nothing can be more opposed than the maxims of absolute monarchies. Yet, from such, we are to expect the greatest number of emigrants. *They will bring with them the principles of the governments they leave, imbibed in their early youth; or, if able to throw them off, it will be in exchange for an unbounded licentiousness,* passing, as is usual, from one extreme to another. It would be a miracle were they to stop precisely at the point of temperate liberty. These principles, with their language, they will transmit to their children. *In proportion to their numbers, they will share with us the legislation. They will infuse into it their spirit, warp and bias its directions, and render it a heterogeneous, incoherent, distracted mass.*"

"I may appeal to experience, for a verification of these conjectures. But if they be not *certain in event,* are they not *possible, are they not probable?* Is it not safer to wait with patience—for the attainment of any degree of population desired or expected? May not our government be more homogeneous, more peaceable, more durable?" He asks, what would be the condition of France if twenty millions of Americans were suddenly imported into that kingdom? and adds—"If it would be *more turbulent,* less happy, less strong, we may believe that the addition of *half a million of foreigners* would produce a *similar effect here.* If they come of themselves, they are entitled to all the rights of citizenship; *but I doubt the expediency of inviting them by extraordinary encouragements.*" Now, if under the most favourable circumstances for the country, when it could most be benefited, when numbers were most urgently needed, Mr. Jefferson, could discover the evil afar off, and protest against encouraging foreign immigration, how much more is the measure now to be deprecated, when circumstances have so entirely changed, that instead of *adding strength* to the country, immigration *adds weakness,* weakness physical and moral! And what overwhelming force does Mr. Jefferson's reasoning acquire, by the vast change of circumstances which has taken place both in Europe and in this country, in our earlier and in our later condition.—*Then* we were few, feeble, and scattered. *Now* we are numerous, strong, and concentrated. *Then* our accessions by immigration were real accessions of strength from the ranks of the learned and the good, from the enlightened mechanic and artisan, and intelligent husbandman. *Now* immigration is the accession of weakness, from the ignorant and the vicious, or the priest-ridden slaves of Ireland and Germany, or the outcast tenants of the poorhouses and prisons of Europe. And again. *Then* our beautiful system of government had not been unfolded to the world to the terror of tyrants; the rising brightness of American Democracy was not yet so far above the horizon as to wake their slumbering anxieties, or more than to gleam faintly, in hope, upon their enslaved subjects. *Then* emigration was natural, it was an attraction of affinities, it was an attraction of liberty to liberty. Emigrants were the proscribed for conscience' sake, and for opinion's sake, the real lovers of liberty, Europe's loss, and our gain.

Now American Democracy is denounced by name by foreign despots, waked with its increasing brilliancy. Its splendour dazzles them. It alarms them, for it shows their slaves their chains. And it must be extinguished. *Now* emigration is changed; naturalization has become the door of entrance not alone to the ever welcome lovers of liberty, but also for the priest-ridden troops of the Holy Alliance, with their Jesuit officers well skilled in all the arts of darkness. Now emigrants are selected for a service to their tyrants, and by their tyrants; not for their affinity to liberty, but for their mental servitude, and their docility in obeying the orders of their priests. They are transported in thousands, nay, in *hundreds of thousands,* to our shores, to our loss and Europe's gain.

It may be, Americans, that you still doubt the *existence* of a conspiracy, and the reality of danger from Foreign Combination; or, if the attempt is made, you yet doubt the *power* of any such secret intrigue in your society. Do you wish to test its existence and its power? It is easy to apply the test. *Test it by attempting a change in the Naturalization Law.* Take the ground that such a change must be made, that no *foreigner who comes into the country after the law is passed shall ever be allowed the right of suffrage.* Stand firmly to this single point, and you will soon discover where the enemy is, and the tactics he employs. This is the spear of Ithuriel. Apply its point. You will find your enemy, though now squat like a toad fast by the ear of our confidence, suddenly roused to show his infernal origin.

Look a moment at the proposition. You will perceive that in its very nature there is nothing to excite the opposition of a single citizen, native or naturalized, in the whole country, provided, be it distinctly borne in mind, *that he is not implicated in the conspiracy.* This prohibition, in the proposed change of the law, it is evident, touches not in any way the *native American,* neither does it touch in the slightest degree the already granted priviliges of the *naturalized citizen,* nor the *foreigner now in the country,* who is waiting to be naturalized, nor even *the foreigner on his way hither;* no, *not an individual* in the whole country is unfavourably affected by the provisions of such a law, not an individual *except alone the foreign Jesuit, the Austrian stipendiary with his intriguing myrmidons.* And how is he affected by it? He is deprived of his *passive obedience* forces; he can no longer use his power over his slaves, *to interfere in our political concerns;* he can no longer use them in his Austrian master's service; and he therefore, be assured, will resist with all the desperation of a detected brigand. He will raise an outcry. He will fill the public ear with cries of *intolerance.* He will call the measure religious bigotry, and illiberality, and religious persecution, and other popular catchwords, to deceive the unreflecting ear. But, be not deceived; when you hear him, set your mark upon him. That is the man. Try then this test. Again, I say, let the proposition be that the law of the land be so changed, that NO FOREIGNER WHO COMES INTO THE COUNTRY AFTER THE LAW IS PASSED SHALL EVER BE ENTITLED TO THE RIGHT OF SUFFRAGE. This is just ground; it is practicable ground; it is defensible ground, and it is safe and prudent ground; and I cannot better close than in the words of Mr. Jefferson: "The time to guard against corruption and tyranny is *before* they shall have gotten hold on us; IT IS BETTER TO KEEP THE WOLF OUT OF THE FOLD, THAN TO TRUST TO DRAWING HIS TEETH AND TALONS AFTER HE HAS ENTERED."　　1835

CARL SCHURZ

1829–1906

CARL SCHURZ, who fled to America after his active participation in the liberal revolutionary movement of Germany in 1848, became the most distinguished immigrant of the nineteenth century. His brilliant journalistic work on the *St. Louis Westliche Post,* the *New York Evening Post, The Nation,* and *Harper's Weekly* has been overshadowed by his career as a successful major-general in the Civil War, as Minister to Spain, and as Secretary of the Interior during the administration of President Hayes. His contributions to the Republican party were influential in swinging the support of German-Americans to Lincoln in 1860. In courageously criticizing the corruption of public life after the Civil War and in trying to check the rising tide of imperialism, Schurz showed himself to be a true reformer. The improvements which he inaugurated in the Indian administration during his secretaryship of the interior and the work which he did for the preservation of the public domain and for national parks, also entitle him to rank among Americans distinguished for their social vision.

In 1859 Schurz, a great orator and a master of the English language, delivered one of his most famous addresses, "True Americanism." In this speech he ably upheld the view of liberals in the controversy regarding the place of immigrants in the national life. This broadly conceived interpretation of "Americanism" was partly responsible for the defeat of a proposal in Massachusetts to deprive the newly naturalized from voting for a two-year period after completing his naturalization. Among Schurz's many writings his *Life of Henry Clay* (1887) and the *Reminiscences* (1907–1908) are notable.

Speeches, Correspondence and Political Papers of Carl Schurz, Frederic Bancroft, ed., 6 vols., New York, 1913.
Joseph Schafer, *Carl Schurz, Militant Liberal,* Evansville, Wis., 1930.
C. M. Fuess, *Carl Schurz, Reformer,* New York, 1932.
C. V. Easum, *The Americanization of Carl Schurz,* Chicago, 1929.

» » TRUE AMERICANISM [1] « «

MR. PRESIDENT AND GENTLEMEN:—A few days ago I stood on the cupola of your state-house, and overlooked for the first time this venerable city and the country surrounding it. Then the streets, and hills, and waters around me began to teem with the life of historical recollections, recollections dear to all mankind, and a feeling of pride arose in my heart, and I said to myself, I, too, am an American citizen. There was Bunker Hill; there Charlestown, Lexington and Dorchester Heights not far off, there the harbor into which the British tea was sunk; there the place where the old liberty-tree stood; there John Hancock's house; there Benjamin Franklin's birthplace;—and now I stand in this grand old hall, which so often resounded with the noblest appeals that ever thrilled American hearts, and where I am almost afraid to hear the echo of my own feeble voice;—oh, sir, no man that loves liberty, wherever he may have first seen

the light of day, can fail on this sacred spot to pay his tribute to Americanism. And here, with all these glorious memories crowding upon my heart, I will offer mine. I, born in a foreign land, pay my tribute to Americanism? Yes, for to me the word Americanism, *true* Americanism, comprehends the noblest ideas which ever swelled a human heart with noble pride.

It is one of the earliest recollections of my boyhood, that one summer night our whole village was stirred up by an uncommon occurrence. I say our village, for I was born not far from that beautiful spot where the Rhine rolls his green waters out of the wonderful gate of the Seven Mountains, and then meanders with majestic tranquillity through one of the most glorious valleys of the world. That night our neighbors were pressing around a few wagons covered with linen sheets and loaded with household utensils and boxes and trunks to their utmost capacity. One of our neighboring families was moving far away across a great water, and it was said that they would never again return. And I saw silent tears trickling down weather-beaten cheeks, and the hands of rough peasants firmly pressing each other, and some of the men and women hardly able to speak when they nodded to one another a last farewell. At last the train started into

[1] Speech delivered in Faneuil Hall, Boston, April 18, 1859. The legislature of Massachusetts had adopted an amendment to the constitution of the State, by which foreigners should not be permitted to vote until two years after they had become citizens of the U. S. This amendment, generally known as the "two years' amendment," was soon to be voted upon by the people. It was one of the measures brought forth by the so-called "Know-Nothing" or "American" movement, which had met with surprising successes in many parts of the U. S. It was against this spirit of proscription on account of birth, creed, or opinion, styling itself "Americanism" that the speaker directed his arguments. [Frederic Bancroft, editor of Schurz's *Works.*]

motion, they gave three cheers for *America,* and then in the first gray dawn of the morning I saw them wending their way over the hill until they disappeared in the shadow of the forest. And I heard many a man say, how happy he would be if he could go with them to that great and free country, where a man could be himself.

That was the first time that I heard of America, and my childish imagination took possession of a land covered partly with majestic trees, partly with flowery prairies, immeasurable to the eye, and intersected with large rivers and broad lakes—a land where everybody could do what he thought best, and where nobody need be poor, because everybody was free.

And later, when I was old enough to read, and descriptions of this country and books on American history fell into my hands, the offspring of my imagination acquired the colors of reality, and I began to exercise my brain with the thought of what man might be and become when left perfectly free to himself. And still later, when ripening into manhood, I looked up from my school-books into the stir and bustle of the world, and the trumpet-tones of struggling humanity struck my ear and thrilled my heart, and I saw my nation shake her chains in order to burst them, and I heard a gigantic, universal shout for Liberty rising up to the skies; and at last, after having struggled manfully and drenched the earth of Fatherland with the blood of thousands of noble beings, I saw that nation crushed down again, not only by overwhelming armies, but by the dead weight of customs and institutions and notions and prejudices which past centuries had heaped upon them, and which a moment of enthusiasm, however sublime, could not destroy; then I consoled an almost despondent heart with the idea of a youthful people and of original institutions clearing the way for an untrammeled development of the ideal nature of man. Then I turned my eyes instinctively across the Atlantic Ocean, and America and Americanism, as I fancied them, appeared to me as the last depositories of the hopes of all true friends of humanity.

I say all this, not as though I indulged in the presumptuous delusion that my personal feelings and experience would be of any interest to you, but in order to show you what America is to the thousands of thinking men in the old world, who, disappointed in their fondest hopes and depressed by the saddest experience, cling with their last remnant of confidence in human nature, to the last spot on earth where man is free to follow the road to attainable perfection, and where, unbiased by the disastrous influence of traditional notions, customs and institutions, he acts on his own responsibility. They ask themselves: Was it but a wild delusion when we thought that man has the faculty to be free and to govern himself? Have we been fighting, were we ready to die, for a mere phantom, for a mere product of a morbid imagination? This question downtrodden humanity cries out into the world, and from this country it expects an answer.

As its advocate I speak to you. I will speak of Americanism as the great representative of the reformatory age, as the great champion of the dignity of human nature, as the great repository of the last hopes of suffering mankind. I will speak of the ideal mission of this country and of this people.

You may tell me that these views are visionary, that the destiny of this country is less exalted, that the American people are less great than I think they are or ought to be. I answer, ideals are like stars; you will not succeed in touching them with your hands. But like the sea-faring man on the desert of waters, you choose them as your guides, and following them you will reach your destiny. I invite you to ascend with me the watchtower of history, overlooking the grand panorama of the development of human affairs, in which the American Republic stands in so bold and prominent relief.

He who reviews the past of this country in connection with the history of the world besides, cannot fail to discover a wonderful coincidence of great events and fortunate circumstances, which were destined to produce everlasting results, unless recklessly thrown away by imbecile generations.

Look back with me four or five centuries. The dark period of the middle ages is drawing near its close. The accidental explosion of that mysterious black powder, discovered by an obscure German monk, is the first flash of lightning preluding that gigantic thunderstorm which is to shatter the edifice of feudal society to pieces. The invention of gunpowder strips the feudal lord of his prestige as a *warrior;* another discovery is to strip him of his prestige as a *man!* Gutenberg, another obscure German, invents the printing-press, and as gunpowder blows the castles of the small feudal tyrants into the air, so the formidable artillery of printed letters batters down the citadels of ignorance and superstition. Soul and body take up arms and prepare themselves for the great battle of the Reformation. Now the mighty volcano of the German mind bursts the crust of indolence which has covered it. Luther's triumphant thunder rattles against the holy see of Rome. The world is ablaze, all the elements of society are rising up in boiling commotion—two ages are battling against each other.

This is the time when the regeneration of the old world is to take place. But the old order of things, fortified in customs and prejudices and deeply-rooted institutions, does not surrender at the first blast of trumpets. The grand but fearful struggle of the reformatory movement plunges all Europe into endless confusion. The very wheel of progress seems to grind and crush one generation after another. The ideas which concerned the highest and most sacred relations of humanity seem at the same time to call into their service the basest and most violent passions of the human heart, and in all Europe the wars of great principles degenerate into wars of general devastation.

But, meanwhile, a new country has opened its boundless fields to those great ideas, for the realization of which the old world seems no longer to be wide enough. It is as though the earth herself had taken part in the general revolution, and had thrown up from her sea-covered womb a new battle-ground for the spirit of the new era. That is America. Not only the invention of gunpowder and of the printing-press, but also the discovery of America, inaugurates the modern age.

There is the new and immense continent. The most restless and enterprising elements of European society direct their looks towards it. First, the greediness of the gold-hunting adventurer pounces upon the new conquest; but, his inordinate appetites being disappointed, he gradually abandons the field to men in whose hearts the future of the new world is sleeping, unborn.

While the coast of Virginia is settled by a motley immigration, led and ruled by men of ideas and enterprise, the sturdiest champions of principle descend upon the stony shores of New England. While the Southern colonies are settled under the auspices of lordly merchants and proprietaries, original democracy plants its stern banner upon Plymouth Rock. Mercantile speculation, aristocratic ambition and stern virtue that seeks freedom and nothing but freedom, lead the most different classes of people, different in origin, habits and persuasion, upon the virgin soil, and entrust to them the task of realizing the great principles of the age. Nor is this privilege confined to one nationality alone. While the Anglo-Saxon takes possession of New England, Virginia and Pennsylvania, the Frenchman plants his colonies on the soil of French Florida and the interior of the continent; the Hollander locates New Netherlands on the banks of the Hudson; the Swede, led there by the great mind of Oxenstiern, occupies the banks of the Delaware; the Spaniard maintains himself in peninsular Florida, and a numerous immigration of Germans, who follow the call of religious freedom, and of Irishmen, gradually flowing in, scatters itself all over this vast extent of country. Soon all the social and national elements of the civilized world are represented in the new land. Every people, every creed, every class of society has contributed its share to that wonderful mixture out of which is to grow the great nation of the new world. It is true, the Anglo-Saxon establishes and maintains his ascendancy, but without absolutely absorbing the other national elements. They modify each other, and their peculiar characteristics are to be blended together by the all-assimilating power of freedom. This is the origin of the American nationality, which did not spring from one family, one tribe, one country, but incorporates the vigorous elements of all civilized nations on earth.

This fact is not without great importance. It is an essential link in the chain of historical development. The student of history cannot fail to notice that when new periods of civilization break upon humanity, the people of the earth cannot maintain their national relations. New ideas are to be carried out by young nations. From time to time, violent, irresistible hurricanes sweep over the world, blowing the most different elements of the human family together, which by mingling reinvigorate each other, and the general confusion then becomes the starting-point of a new period of progress. Nations which have long subsisted exclusively on their own resources will gradually lose their original vigor, and die the death of decrepitude. But mankind becomes young again by its different elements being shaken together, by race crossing race and mind penetrating mind.

The oldest traditions of history speak of such great revulsions and general migrations, and if we could but lift the veil, which covers the remotest history of Asiatic tribes, we should discover the first scenes and acts of the drama, of which the downfall of the Roman Empire is a portion. When that empire had exhausted
10 its natural vitality, the dark forests of the North poured forth a barbarous but vigorous multitude, who trampled into ruins the decrepit civilization of the Roman world, but infused new blood into the veins of the old Europe, grasping the great ideas of Christianity with a bloody but firm hand—and a new period of original progress sprang out of the seeming devastation. The German element took the helm of history. But, in the course of time, the
20 development of things arrived at a new turning point. The spirit of individualism took possession of the heart of civilized humanity, and the reformatory movement of the sixteenth century was its expression. But continental Europe appeared unable to incorporate the new and progressive ideas growing out of that spirit, in organic political institutions. While the heart of Europe was ravaged by a series of religious wars, the Anglo-Saxons of England attempted
30 what other nations seemed unable to accomplish. But they also clung too fast to the traditions of past centuries; they failed in separating the Church from the State, and did not realize the cosmopolitan tendency of the new principle. Then the time of a new migration was at hand, and that migration rolled its waves towards America. The old process repeated itself under new forms, milder and more congenial to the humane ideas it represented.
40 It is now not a barbarous multitude pouncing upon old and decrepit empires; not a violent concussion of tribes accompanied by all the horrors of general destruction; but we see the vigorous elements of all nations, we see the Anglo-Saxon, the leader in the practical movement, with his spirit of independence, of daring enterprise and of indomitable perseverance; the German, the original leader in the movement of ideas, with his spirit of inquiry and
50 his quiet and thoughtful application; the Celt, with the impulsive vivacity of his race; the Frenchman, the Scandinavian, the Scot, the Hollander, the Spaniard and the Italian—all these peaceably congregating and mingling together on virgin soil, where the backwoods-

man's hatchet is the only battle-axe of civilization; led together by the irresistible attraction of free and broad principles; undertaking to commence a new era in the history of the world, without first destroying the results of the progress of past periods; undertaking to found a new cosmopolitan nation without marching over the dead bodies of slain millions. Thus was founded the *great colony of free humanity,* which has not old England along, but the *world,* for its mother-country.

This idea is, perhaps, not palatable to those who pride themselves on their unadulterated Anglo-Saxondom. To them I have to say that the destinies of men are often greater than men themselves, and that a good many are swerving from the path of glory by not obeying the true instincts of their nature, and by sacrificing their mission to one-sided pride.

The Anglo-Saxon may justly be proud of the growth and development of this country, and if he ascribes most of it to the undaunted spirit of his race, we may not accuse him of overweening self-glorification. He possesses, in an eminent degree, the enviable talent of acting when others only think; of promptly executing his own ideas, and of appropriating the ideas of other people to his own use. There is, perhaps, no other race that, at so early a day, would have founded the stern democracy of the Plymouth settlement; no other race that would have defied the trials and hardships of the original settler's life so victoriously. No other race, perhaps, possesses in so high a degree not only the daring spirit of independent enterprise, but at the same time the stubborn steadfastness necessary to the final execution of great designs. The Anglo-Saxon spirit has been the locomotive of progress; but do not forget, that this locomotive would be of little use to the world if it refused to draw its train over the iron highway and carry its valuable freight towards its destination; that train consists of the vigorous elements of all nations; that freight is the vital ideas of our age; that destination is universal freedom and the ideal development of man. That is the true greatness of the Anglo-Saxon race; that ought to be the source of Anglo-Saxon pride. I esteem the son who is proud of his father, if, at the same time, he is worthy of him.

Thus, I say, was founded the colony of free humanity on virgin soil. The youthful elements which constitute people of the new world cannot submit to rules which are not of their own making; they must throw off the fetters which bind them to an old decrepit order of things. They resolve to enter the great family of nations as an independent member. And in the colony of free humanity, whose mother country is the world, they establish *the Republic of equal rights, where the title of manhood is the title to citizenship.* My friends, if I had a thousand tongues, and a voice strong as the thunder of heaven, they would not be sufficient to impress upon your minds forcibly enough the greatness of this idea, the overshadowing glory of this result. This was the dream of the truest friends of man from the beginning; for this the noblest blood of martyrs has been shed; for this has mankind waded through seas of blood and tears. There it is now; there it stands, the noble fabric in all the splendor of reality.

They speak of the greatness of the Roman Republic! Oh, sir, if I could call the proudest of Romans from his grave, I would take him by the hand and say to him, Look at this picture, and at this! The greatness of thy Roman Republic consisted in its despotic rule over the world; the greatness of the American Republic consists in the secured right of man to govern himself. The dignity of the Roman citizen consisted in his exclusive privileges; the dignity of the American citizen consists in his holding the natural rights of his neighbor just as sacred as his own. The Roman Republic recognized and protected the *rights of the citizen,* at the same time disregarding and leaving unprotected the *rights of man;* Roman citizenship was founded upon monopoly, not upon the claims of human nature. What the citizen of Rome claimed for himself, he did not respect in others; his own greatness was his only object; his own liberty, as he regarded it, gave him the privilege to oppress his fellow-beings. His democracy, instead of elevating mankind to his own level, trampled the rights of man into the dust. The security of the Roman Republic, therefore, consisted in the power of the sword; the security of the American Republic rests in the equality of human rights! The Roman Republic perished by the sword; the American Republic will stand as long as the equality of human rights remains inviolate. Which of the two Republics is the greater—the Republic of the Roman, or the Republic of *man?*

Sir, I wish the words of the Declaration of Independence "that all men are created free and equal, and are endowed with certain inalienable rights," were inscribed upon every gate-post within the limits of this Republic. From this principle the Revolutionary Fathers derived their claim to independence; upon this they founded the institutions of this country, and the whole structure was to be the living incarnation of this idea. This principle contains the programme of our political existence. It is the most progressive, and at the same time the most conservative one; the most progressive, for it takes even the lowliest members of the human family out of their degradation, and inspires them with the elevating consciousness of equal human dignity; the most conservative, for it makes a common cause of individual rights. From the equality of rights springs identity of our highest interests; you cannot subvert your neighbor's rights without striking a dangerous blow at your own. And when the rights of one cannot be infringed without finding a ready defense in all others who defend their own rights in defending his, then, and only then, are the rights of all safe against the usurpations of governmental authority.

This general identity of interests is the only thing that can guarantee the stability of democratic institutions. Equality of rights, embodied in general self-government, is the great moral element of true democracy; it is the only reliable safety-valve in the machinery of modern society. There is the solid foundation of our system of government; there is our mission; there is our greatness; there is our safety; there, and nowhere else! This is true Americanism, and to this I pay the tribute of my devotion.

Shall I point out to you the consequences of a deviation from this principle? Look at the slave States. There is a class of men who are deprived of their natural rights. But this is not the only deplorable feature of that peculiar organization of society. Equally deplorable is it, that there is another class of men who keep the former in subjection. That there are slaves is bad; but almost worse is it, that there are masters. Are not the masters freemen? No, sir! Where is their liberty of the press? Where is their liberty of speech? Where is the man among them who dares to advocate openly principles not in strict accordance with the ruling system? They speak of a republican form of government—they speak of democracy, but the despotic spirit of slavery and mastership combined pervades their whole political life like a liquid poison. They do not dare to be

free, lest the spirit of liberty become contagious. The system of slavery has enslaved them
all, master as well as slave. What is the cause
of all this? It is that you cannot deny one class
of society the full measure of their natural
rights without imposing restraints upon your
own liberty. If you want to be free, there is
but one way: it is to guarantee an equally full
measure of liberty to all your neighbors. There
is no other.

True, there are difficulties connected with
an organization of society founded upon the
basis of equal rights. Nobody denies it. A large
number of those who come to you from foreign
lands are not as capable of taking part in the
administration of government as the man who
was fortunate enough to drink the milk of
liberty in his cradle. And certain religious denominations do, perhaps, nourish principles
which are hardly in accordance with the doctrines of true democracy. There is a conglom-
eration on this continent of heterogeneous elements; there is a warfare of clashing interest
and unruly aspirations; and, with all this, our
democratic system gives rights to the ignorant
and power to the inexperienced. And the bil-
lows of passion will lash the sides of the ship,
and the storm of party warfare will bend its
masts, and the pusillanimous will cry out—
"Master, master, we perish!" But the genius of
true democracy will arise from his slumber,
and rebuke the winds and the raging of the
water, and say unto them—"Where is your
faith?" Aye, where is the faith that led the
Fathers of this Republic to invite the weary
and burdened of all nations to the enjoyment
of equal rights? Where is that broad and
generous confidence in the efficiency of true
democratic institutions? Has the present generation forgotten that true democracy bears
in itself the remedy for all the difficulties that
may grow out of it?

It is an old dodge of the advocates of
despotism throughout the world, that the
people who are not experienced in self-government are not fit for the exercise of self-
government, and must first be educated under
the rule of a superior authority. But at the same
time the advocates of despotism will never
offer them an opportunity to acquire experience in self-government, lest they suddenly become fit for its independent exercise. To this
treacherous sophistry the fathers of this republic opposed the noble doctrine, that liberty
is the best school for liberty, and that self-

government cannot be learned but by practicing it. This, sir, is a truly American idea; this
is true Americanism, and to this I pay the
tribute of my devotion.

You object that some people do not understand their own interests? There is nothing that,
in the course of time, will make a man better
understand his interests than the independent
management of his own affairs on his own
responsibility. You object that people are ignorant? There is no better schoolmaster in the
world than self-government, independently exercised. You object that people have no just
idea of their duties as citizens? There is no
other source from which they can derive a
just notion of their duties, than the enjoyment
of the rights from which they arise. You object
that people are misled by their religious prejudices, and by the intrigues of the Roman hierarchy? Since when have the enlightened citizens of this Republic lost their faith in the
final invincibility of truth? Since when have
they forgotten that if the Roman or any other
church plants the seed of superstition, liberty
sows broadcast the seed of enlightenment? Do
they no longer believe in the invincible spirit
of inquiry, which characterizes the reformatory
age? If the struggle be fair, can the victory be
doubtful? As to religious fanaticism, it will prosper under oppression; it will feed on persecution; it will grow strong by proscription; but
it is powerless against genuine democracy. It
may indulge in short-lived freaks of passion, or
in wily intrigues, but it will die of itself, for
its lungs are not adapted to breathe the atmosphere of liberty. It is like the shark of the sea:
drag him into the air, and the monster will
perhaps struggle fearfully and frighten timid
people with the powerful blows of his tail, and
the terrible array of his teeth, but leave him
quietly to die and he will die. But engage
with him in a hand-to-hand struggle even then,
and the last of his convulsions may fatally punish your rash attempt. Against fanaticism genuine democracy wields an irresistible weapon
—it is Toleration. Toleration will not strike
down the fanatic, but it will quietly and
gently disarm him. But fight fanaticism *with*
fanaticism, and you will restore it to its own
congenial element. It is like Antæus, who
gained strength when touching his native earth.

Whoever reads the history of this country
calmly and thoroughly, cannot but discover
that religious liberty is slowly but steadily rooting out the elements of superstition, and even of

prejudice. It has dissolved the war of sects, of which persecution was characteristic, into a contest of abstract opinions, which creates convictions without oppressing men. By recognizing perfect freedom of inquiry, it will engender among men of different belief that mutual respect of true convictions which makes inquiry earnest and discussion fair. It will recognize as supremely inviolable, what Roger Williams, one of the most luminous stars of the American sky, called the sanctity of conscience. Read your history, and add the thousands and thousands of Romanists and their offspring together, who, from the first establishment of the colonies, gradually came to this country, and the sum will amount to many millions; compare that number with the number of Romanists who are now here, and you will find that millions are missing. Where are they? You did not kill them; you did not drive them away; they did not perish as the victims of persecution. But where are they? The peaceable working of the great principles which called this Republic into existence, has gradually and silently absorbed them. True Americanism, toleration, the equality of rights, has absorbed their prejudices, and will peaceably absorb everything that is not consistent with the victorious spirit of our institutions.

Oh, sir, there is a wonderful vitality in true democracy founded upon the equality of rights. There is an inexhaustible power of resistance in that system of government, which makes the protection of individual rights a matter of common interest. If preserved in its purity, there is no warfare of opinions which can endanger it —there is no conspiracy of despotic aspirations that can destroy it. But if not preserved in its purity! There are dangers which only blindness cannot see, and which only stubborn party prejudice will not see.

I have already called your attention to the despotic tendency of the slaveholding system. I need not enlarge upon it; I need not describe how the existence of slavery in the South affected and demoralized even the political life of the free States; how they attempted to press us, you and me, into the posse of the slave-catcher by that abominable act which, worse than the "alien and sedition laws," still disgraces our statute-book; how the ruling party, which has devoted itself to the service of that despotic interest, shrinks from no violation of good faith, from no adulteration of the constitutional compact, from no encroachment upon

natural right, from no treacherous abandonment of fundamental principles. And I do not hesitate to prophesy that, if the theories engendered by the institution of slavery be suffered to outgrow the equalizing tendency of true democracy, the American Republic will, at no distant day, crumble down under the burden of the laws and measures which the ruling interest will demand for its protection, and its name will be added to the sad catalogue of the broken hopes of humanity.

But the mischief does not come from that side alone; it is in things of small beginnings, but fearful in their growth. One of these is the propensity of men *to lose sight of fundamental principles, when passing abuses are to be corrected.*

Is it not wonderful how nations who have won their liberty by the severest struggles become so easily impatient of the small inconveniences and passing difficulties which are almost inseparably connected with the practical working of general self-government? How they so easily forget that rights may be abused, and yet remain inalienable rights? Europe has witnessed many an attempt for the establishment of democratic institutions; some of them were at first successful, and the people were free, but the abuses and inconveniences connected with liberty became at once apparent. Then the ruling classes of society, in order to get rid of the abuses, restricted liberty; they did, indeed, get rid of the abuses, but they got rid of liberty at the same time. You heard liberal governments there speak of protecting and regulating the liberty of the press; and, in order to prevent that liberty from being abused, they adopted measures, apparently harmless at first, which ultimately resulted in an absolute censorship. Would it be much better if we, recognizing the right of man to the exercise of self-government, should, in order to protect the purity of the ballot-box, restrict the right of suffrage?

Liberty, sir, is like a spirited housewife; she will have her whims, she will be somewhat unruly sometimes, and, like so many husbands, you cannot always have it all your own way. She may spoil your favorite dish sometimes; but will you, therefore, at once smash her china, break her kettles and shut her out from the kitchen? Let her practice, let her try again and again, and even when she makes a mistake, encourage her with a benignant smile, and your broth will be right after a while. But meddle with her concerns, tease her, bore her, and your

little squabbles, spirited as she is, will ultimately result in a divorce. What then? It is one
of Jefferson's wisest words that "he would much
rather be exposed to the inconveniences arising
from too much liberty, than to those arising
from too small a degree of it." It is a matter of
historical experience, that nothing that is wrong
in principle can be right in practice. People are
apt to delude themselves on that point; but the
ultimate result will always prove the truth of
the maxim. A violation of equal rights can
never serve to maintain institutions which are
founded upon equal rights. A contrary policy is
not only pusillanimous and small, but it is
senseless. It reminds me of the soldier who, for
fear of being shot in battle, committed suicide
on the march; or of the man who would cut
off his foot, because he had a corn on his toe.
It is that ridiculous policy of premature despair,
which commences to throw the freight overboard when there is a suspicious cloud in the
sky.

Another danger for the safety of our institutions, and perhaps the most formidable one,
arises from the general propensity of political
parties and public men to act on a policy of
mere expediency, and to sacrifice principle to
local and temporary success. And here, sir, let
me address a solemn appeal to the consciences
of those with whom I am proud to struggle
side by side against human thraldom.

You hate kingcraft, and you would sacrifice
your fortunes and your lives in order to prevent
its establishment on the soil of this Republic.
But let me tell you that the rule of political
parties which sacrifice principle to expediency,
is no less dangerous, no less disastrous, no less
aggressive, of no less despotic a nature, than
the rule of monarchs. Do not indulge in the delusion, that in order to make a government fair
and liberal, the only thing necessary is to make
it elective. When a political party in power,
however liberal their principles may be, have
once adopted the policy of knocking down their
opponents instead of voting them down, there
is an end of justice and equal rights. The history
of the world shows no example of a more arbitrary despotism, than that exercised by the
party which ruled the National Assembly of
France in the bloodiest days of the great French
Revolution. I will not discuss here what might
have been done, and what not, in those times
of a fearful crisis; but I will say that they tried
to establish liberty by means of despotism, and
that in her gigantic struggle against the united

monarchs of Europe, revolutionary France won
the victory, but lost her liberty.

Remember the shout of indignation that went
all over the Northern States when we heard
that the border ruffians of Kansas had crowded
the free-State men away from the polls and had
not allowed them to vote. That indignation was
just, not only because the men thus terrorized
were free-State men and friends of liberty, but
because they were deprived of their right of
suffrage, and because the government of that
territory was placed on the basis of force, instead of equal rights. Sir, if ever the party of
liberty should use their local predominance for
the purpose of disarming their opponents instead of convincing them, they will but follow
the example set by the ruffians of Kansas, although legislative enactments may be a gen-
teeler weapon than the revolver and bowie
knife. They may perhaps achieve some petty
local success, they may gain some small temporary advantage, but they will help to introduce
a system of action into our politics which will
gradually undermine the very foundations upon
which our republican edifice rests. Of all the
dangers and difficulties that beset us, there is
none more horrible than the hideous monster,
whose name is "Proscription for opinion's sake."
I am an anti-slavery man, and I have a right to
my opinion in South Carolina just as well as in
Massachusetts. My neighbor is a pro-slavery
man; I may be sorry for it, but I solemnly acknowledge his right to his opinion in Massachusetts as well as in South Carolina. You tell
me, that for my opinion they would mob me
in South Carolina? Sir, there is the difference
between South Carolina and Massachusetts.
There is the difference between an anti-slavery
man, who is a freeman, and a slaveholder, who
is himself a slave.

Our present issues will pass away. The slavery question will be settled, liberty will be triumphant and other matters of difference will
divide the political parties of this country. What
if we, in our struggle against slavery, had removed the solid basis of equal rights, on which
such new matters of difference may be peaceably settled? What if we had based the institutions of this country upon a difference of rights
between different classes of people? What if, in
destroying the generality of natural rights, we
had resolved them into privileges? There is a
thing which stands above the command of the
most ingenious of politicians: *it is the logic of
things and events*. It cannot be turned and

twisted by artificial arrangements and delusive settlements; it will go its own way with the steady step of fate. It will force you, with uncompromising severity, to choose between two social organizations, one of which is founded upon privilege, and the other upon the doctrine of equal rights.

Force instead of right, privilege instead of equality, expediency instead of principle, being once the leading motives of your policy, you will have no power to stem the current. There will be new abuses to be corrected, new inconveniences to be remedied, new supposed dangers to be obviated, new equally exacting ends to be subserved, and your encroachments upon the natural rights of your opponents now, will be used as welcome precedents for the mutual oppression of parties then. Having once knowingly disregarded the doctrine of equal rights, the ruling parties will soon accustom themselves to consult only their interests where fundamental principles are at stake. Those who lead us into this channel will be like the sorcerer who knew the art of making a giant snake. And when he had made it, he forgot the charmword that would destroy it again. And the giant snake threw its horrid coils around him, and the unfortunate man was choked by the monster of his own creation.

On the evening of the 2d day of November, 1855, there stood on this very platform a man, known and loved by every true son of Massachusetts, who, unmoved by the whirlwind of proscriptive movement howling around him, spoke the following words:

It is proposed to attaint men for their religion, and also for their birth. If this object can prevail, vain are the triumphs of civil freedom in its many hard-fought fields; vain is that religious toleration which we all profess. The fires of Smithfield, the tortures of the inquisition, the proscription of the Non-conformists, may all be revived. Slowly among the struggling sects was evolved the great idea of the equality of all men before the law, without regard to religious belief; nor can any party now organize a proscription merely for religious (and I may add political) belief, without calling in question this unquestionable principle.

The man who said so was Charles Sumner. Then the day was not far off when suddenly the whole country was startled by the incredible news, that his noble head had drooped under the murderous blows of a Southern fanatic, and that his warm blood had covered the floor of the Senate Chamber, the noblest sprinkling that ever fertilized a barren soil. And now I tell you, when he lay on the lounge of the antechamber, his anxious friends busy around him, and his cowardly murderers slinking away like Cain—if at that solemn moment the first question addressed to his slowly returning senses had been: Shall those who support your dastardly assailants with their votes be deprived of their suffrage? he would have raised his bleeding head, and with the fire of indignation kindling in his dim eye, he would have answered: "No! In the name of my country, no! For the honor of Massachusetts, no! For the sake of the principles for which my blood is flowing, no! Let them kill me, but let the rights of man be safe!"

Sir, if you want to bestow a high praise upon a man, you are apt to say he is an old Roman. But I know a higher epithet of praise—He is a true American! Aye, Charles Sumner is a true American; he is a representative of the truest Americanism, and to him I pay the tribute of my enthusiastic admiration.

Sir, I am coming to the close of my remarks. But I cannot refrain from alluding to a circumstance which concerns myself. I understand it has been said, that in speaking a few words on the principles of Jeffersonian democracy a few evenings since, I had attempted to interfere with the home affairs of this State, and to dictate to the Republicans their policy. Ah, sir, is there a man in Massachusetts, except he be a servant of the slave-power, who cannot hear me advocate the equal rights of man, without feeling serious pangs of conscience? Is there a son of this glorious old Commonwealth who cannot hear me draw logical conclusions from the Declaration of Independence—who cannot hear me speak of the natural right of man to the exercise of self-government, without feeling a blush fluttering upon his cheeks? If so, sir, I am sorry for him; it is his fault, not mine.

Interfere with your local matters! How could I? What influence could I, an humble stranger among you, exercise on the action of Massachusetts? But one thing I must tell you. It ought never to be forgotten that this old Commonwealth occupies a representative position. Her history is familiar to the nation; even South Carolina knows it. The nation is so accustomed to admire her glorious deed for freedom, that with this expectation their eyes are turned upon her. Massachusetts can do nothing in secret; Massachusetts can do nothing for herself alone;

every one of her acts involves a hundredfold responsibility. What Massachusetts does is felt from the Atlantic to the Pacific. But Massachusetts need only be herself, in order to be great. This is her position among the free States, recognized by all. Can there be a more honorable one? Sons of Massachusetts, you may be proud of it. Do not forget that from her greatness you cannot separate your responsibility.

10　　No, I will not meddle with your home concerns. I will however, say a word for the West. Strenuous advocate of individual rights and of local self-government as I am, if you ever hear of any movement in the West against the integrity of the fundamental principles underlying our system of government, I invite you, I entreat you, I conjure you, come one and all, and make our prairies resound and our forests shake, and our ears ring and tingle, with your
20　appeals for the equal rights of man.

Sir, I was to speak on Republicanism at the West, and so I did. This *is* Western Republicanism. These are its principles, and I am proud to say its principles are its policy. These are the ideas which have rallied around the banner of liberty not only the natives of the soil, but an innumerable host of Germans, Scandinavians, Scotchmen, Frenchmen and a goodly number of Irishmen, also. And here I tell you, those are
30　mistaken who believe that the Irish heart is devoid of those noble impulses which will lead him to the side of justice, where he sees his own rights respected and unendangered. Under this banner, all the languages of civilized mankind are spoken, every creed is protected, every right is sacred. There stands every element of Western society, with enthusiasm for a great

cause, with confidence in each other, with honor to themselves. This is the banner floating over the glorious valley which stretches from the western slope of the Alleghanies to the Rocky Mountains—that Valley of Jehoshaphat where the nations of the world assemble to celebrate the resurrection of human freedom. The inscription on that banner is not "Opposition to the Democratic party for the sake of placing a new set of men into office"; for this battle-cry of speculators our hearts have no response. Nor is it "Restriction of slavery and restriction of the right of suffrage," for this—believe my words, I entreat you—this would be the signal of deserved, inevitable and disgraceful defeat. But the inscription is "Liberty and equal rights, common to all as the air of Heaven—Liberty and equal rights, one and inseparable!"

With this banner we stand before the world. In this sign—in this sign alone, and no other—there is victory. And thus, sir, we mean to realize the great cosmopolitan idea, upon which the existence of the American nation rests. Thus we mean to fulfill the great mission of true Americanism—thus we mean to answer the anxious question of down-trodden humanity—"Has *man* the faculty to be free and to govern himself?" The answer is a triumphant "Aye," thundering into the ears of the despots of the old world that "a man is a man for all that"; proclaiming to the oppressed that they are held in subjection on false pretences; cheering the hearts of the despondent friends of man with consolation and renewed confidence.

This is true Americanism, clasping mankind to its great heart. Under its banner we march; let the world follow.　　　　　　1859

» » *Life Everlasting* « «

1790-1860

» » « «

HEBREW CHILDREN

Where are the Hebrew children?
Where are the Hebrew children?
Where are the Hebrew children?
Safe in the promised land.

Though the furnace flamed around them,
God while in their troubles found them,
He with love and mercy bound them,
Safe in the promised land.

Where are the twelve apostles? etc.
They went up through pain and sighing,
Scoffing, scourging, crucifying,
Nobly for their Master dying,
Safe in the promised land.

Where are the holy Christians etc.
Those who've washed their robes and made them
White and spotless, pure, and laid them
Where no earthly stain can fade them,
Safe in the promised land.

It is believed that the author of both the tune and the words of this camp-meeting revival song was Peter Cartwright (1785–1872), the itinerant Methodist preacher of frontier days. The tune is known to all college students, for "Where, oh where, are the verdant freshmen" (with appropriate local variations) has long been sung to it.

» » « «

O, SOMETIMES GLEAMS

O, sometimes gleams upon our sight,
Through present wrong, th' eternal right,
And step by step since time began
We see the steady gain of man.

That all of good the past hath had
Remains to make our own time glad,
Our common daily life divine,
And every land a Palestine.

Through the harsh voices of our day,
A low, sweet prelude find its way;
Through clouds of doubt and creeds of fear
A light is breaking calm and clear.

Henceforth my heart shall sigh no more
For olden time and holier shore:
God's love and blessing, then and there,
Are now and here and everywhere.

This well-loved hymn, which so well expresses the optimistic Christianity of the mid-century, is a cento made up from stanzas of Whittier's poem "The Chapel of the Hermits" (1851). It was first published as a hymn in the Boston *Hymns of the Spirit* (1864). The tune is by the best-known musician of the time, Lowell Mason.

Life Everlasting

THE ENLIGHTENMENT, it will be remembered, was only gradually received in the later colonial period, but it blossomed in the Revolution and in the years that followed. Deism spread to the middle and even lower classes; faith in the idea of progress ran into the main stream of thought; church and state were separated, and religious freedom prevailed. Plans for the diffusion of knowledge still further exemplified faith in the power of reason; and humanitarianism found devoted disciples who set about the task of emancipating the slave, improving the wretched conditions in prisons, ameliorating the criminal code, and elevating the status of women. Enthusiasm for natural science and for the teachings of the French philosophers was kindled by the alliance with France and by the migration to America of such liberal scientists as Joseph Priestley and Thomas Cooper.

But the spread of these values did not go unchallenged. Zeal for the French Revolution, which was particularly marked among the followers of Jefferson, frightened the orthodox clergy, the owners of property, the defenders of the status quo generally. As a reaction to the spread of deistic ideas, thought to mean rank materialism, evangelicism spread its wings over the land. Bible societies took root; a crusade for temperance in drinking was launched; and home missionaries, as well as foreign missions, won support. Appealing to men's emotions and especially their fear, supernatural values again won adherents all over the country.

Temporarily pushed into the background, or even driven underground, free thought and all that was associated with it again found disciples in the Jacksonian period. Frances Wright, Robert Owen, George Houston, and other Englishmen revived the memory of Thomas Paine's *Age of Reason*, and the *Free Enquirer* and other deistical and free-thought periodicals made their appearance. But since most of the reforms of the day drew much support from religion, and since supernaturalism itself was being modified by a variety of forces, radical free thought did not cut very deep. The masses, even when most militant in their opposition to the aristocracy and to the moneyed interests, stood staunchly by conventional religious faiths.

Nevertheless the lesson of Unitarianism and Universalism did much to make men think of religion in naturalistic rather than supernatural terms. Both emphasized personal character, morality, and the good life here. Even Congregationalism was forced to accept a larger measure of emphasis on these values. And the growing interest in natural science, together with the increasing secularization of life, as exemplified, for instance, in the decline of the old-fashioned strict Sabbath, extended the boundary of naturalism and delimited that of supernaturalism.

Such a growth did not, however, resolve the conflict between naturalism and supernaturalism. Throughout the period this conflict was a living issue.

» »　 « «

THOMAS PAINE

1737–1809

PAINE'S PART in crystallizing antimonarchical opinion during the early stages of the American Revolution is familiar to Americans who have appreciated the fiery qualities of his great pamphlets, *The Crisis* and *Common Sense*. His valiant defense of the French Revolution, to which as an almost professional agitator—or, at the least, a temperamental rebel—he loyally gave allegiance, met with less approval in conservative quarters. Yet *The Rights of Man* (1791, 1792) quickly became and has remained a classic in popular political thought. In *Agrarian Justice* (1797) Paine carried still further some of the implications of his conception of the pursuit of happiness as a natural right: he advocated old-age pensions and other advanced measures for social security. In his basic economic theory, however, Paine did not part company with the economic individualism so congenial to a rising commercial and industrial capitalism.

Though reared in England as a Quaker, Paine was profoundly impressed by the implications of seventeenth and eighteenth century scientific thought, especially with the Newtonian conception of the universe. It was Paine's devotion to natural science, together with his conviction that reason is the best guide in religion as in ethics and politics, that explains his hostility toward revelation, miracles, and other aspects of supernatural Christian theology. He expounded the deistic doctrine of an orderly universe governed by a Supreme Architect. Paine's *Age of Reason* was welcomed in America by apostles of the Enlightenment and bitterly assailed and misrepresented by the religiously orthodox.

The Writings of Thomas Paine, M. D. Conway, ed., 4 vols., New York, 1894–1906.
M. D. Conway, *Life of Thomas Paine*, 2 vols., New York, 1893.
M. A. Best, *Thomas Paine, Prophet and Martyr of Democracy*, New York, 1927.
H. H. Clark, "Toward a Re-interpretation of Thomas Paine," *Amer. Lit.*, vol. V (May, 1933), 133–145.

» » *From:* THE AGE OF REASON « «

THE AUTHOR'S PROFESSION OF FAITH

It has been my intention, for several years past, to publish my thoughts upon religion; I am well aware of the difficulties that attend the subject, and from that consideration, had reserved it to a more advanced period of life. I intended it to be the last offering I should make to my fellow-citizens of all nations, and that at a time when the purity of the motive that induced me to it could not admit of a question, even by those who might disapprove the work.

The circumstance that has now taken place in France, of the total abolition of the whole national order of priesthood, and of everything appertaining to compulsive systems of religion, and compulsive articles of faith, has not only precipitated my intention, but rendered a work of this kind exceedingly necessary, lest, in the general wreck of superstition, of false systems of government, and false theology, we lose sight of morality, of humanity, and of the theology that is true.

As several of my colleagues, and others of my fellow-citizens of France, have given me the example of making their voluntary and individual profession of faith, I also will make mine; and I do this with all that sincerity and frankness with which the mind of man communicates with itself.

I believe in one God, and no more; and I hope for happiness beyond this life.

I believe the equality of man, and I believe that religious duties consist in doing justice, loving mercy, and endeavouring to make our fellow-creatures happy.

But, lest it should be supposed that I believe many other things in addition to these, I shall, in the progress of this work, declare the things I do not believe, and my reasons for not believing them.

I do not believe in the creed professed by the Jewish church, by the Roman church, by the Greek church, by the Turkish church, by the Protestant church, nor by any church that I know of. My own mind is my own church.

All national institutions of churches, whether Jewish, Christian, or Turkish, appear to me no other than human inventions set up to terrify and enslave mankind, and monopolize power and profit.

I do not mean by this declaration to condemn those who believe otherwise; they have the same right to their belief as I have to mine. But it is necessary to the happiness of man, that he be mentally faithful to himself. Infidelity does not consist in believing, or in disbelieving; it consists in professing to believe what he does not believe.

It is impossible to calculate the moral mischief, if I may so express it, that mental lying has produced in society. When a man has so far corrupted and prostituted the chastity of his mind, as to subscribe his professional belief to things he does not believe, he has prepared himself for the commission of every other crime. He takes up the trade of a priest for the sake of gain, and, in order to qualify himself for that trade, he begins with a perjury. Can we conceive anything more destructive to morality than this?

Soon after I had published the pamphlet COMMON SENSE, in America, I saw the exceeding probability that an evolution in the system of government would be followed by a revolution in the system of religion. The adulterous connection of church and state, wherever it had taken place, whether Jewish, Christian, or Turkish, had so effectually prohibited, by pains and penalties, every discussion upon established creeds, and upon first principles of religion, that until the system of government should be changed, those subjects could not be brought fairly and openly before the world; but that whenever this should be done, a revolution in the system of religion would follow. Human inventions and priest-craft would be detected; and man would return to the pure,

unmixed, and unadulterated belief of one God, and no more.

[OF THE THEOLOGY OF THE CHRISTIANS; AND THE TRUE THEOLOGY]

As to the Christian system of faith, it appears to me as a species of atheism; a sort of religious denial of God. It professes to believe in a man rather than in God. It is a compound made up chiefly of manism with but little deism, and is as near to atheism as twilight is to darkness. It introduces between man and his Maker an opaque body, which it calls a redeemer, as the moon introduces her opaque self between the earth and the sun, and it produces by this means a religious or an irreligious eclipse of light. It has put the whole orbit of reason into shade.

The effect of this obscurity has been that of turning everything upside down, and representing it in reverse; and among the revolutions it has thus magically produced, it has made a revolution in Theology.

That which is now called natural philosophy, embracing the whole circle of science, of which astronomy occupies the chief place, is the study of the works of God, and of the power and wisdom of God in his works, and is the true theology.

As to the theology that is now studied in its place, it is the study of human opinions and of human fancies *concerning* God. It is not the study of God himself in the works that he has made, but in the works or writings that man has made; and it is not among the least of the mischiefs that the Christian system has done to the world, that it has abandoned the original and beautiful system of theology, like a beautiful innocent, to distress and reproach, to make room for the hag of superstition.

The Book of Job and the 19th Psalm, which even the church admits to be more ancient than the chronological order in which they stand in the book called the Bible, are theological orations conformable to the original system of theology. The internal evidence of those orations proves to a demonstration that the study and contemplation of the works of creation, and of the power and wisdom of God revealed and manifested in those works, made a great part of the religious devotion of the times in which they were written; and it was this devotional study and contemplation that led to the discovery of the principles upon which what are now called Sciences are established; and it is to the discovery of these principles that almost all the Arts that contribute to the convenience of human life owe their existence. Every principal art has some science for its parent, though the person who mechanically performs the work does not always, and but very seldom, perceive the connection.

It is a fraud of the Christian system to call the sciences *human inventions;* it is only the application of them that is human. Every science has for its basis a system of principles as fixed and unalterable as those by which the universe is regulated and governed. Man cannot make principles, he can only discover them.

For example: Every person who looks at an almanack sees an account when an eclipse will take place, and he sees also that it never fails to take place according to the account there given. This shows that man is acquainted with the laws by which the heavenly bodies move. But it would be something worse than ignorance, were any church on earth to say that those laws are an human invention.

It would also be ignorance, or something worse, to say that the scientific principles, by the aid of which man is enabled to calculate and foreknow when an eclipse will take place, are an human invention. Man cannot invent any thing that is eternal and immutable; and the scientific principles he employs for this purpose must, and are, of necessity, as eternal and immutable as the laws by which the heavenly bodies move, or they could not be used as they are to ascertain the time when, and the manner how, an eclipse will take place.

The scientific principles that man employs to obtain the foreknowledge of an eclipse, or of anything else relating to the motion of the heavenly bodies, are contained chiefly in that part of science that is called trigonometry, or the properties of a triangle, which, when applied to the study of the heavenly bodies, is called astronomy; when applied to direct the course of a ship on the ocean, it is called navigation; when applied to the construction of figures drawn by a rule and compass, it is called geometry; when applied to the construction of plans of edifices, it is called architecture; when applied to the measurement of any portion of the surface of the earth, it is called land-surveying. In fine, it is the soul of science. It is an eternal truth: it contains the *mathematical demonstration* of which man speaks, and the extent of its uses are unknown.

It may be said, that man can make or draw a triangle, and therefore a triangle is an human invention.

But the triangle, when drawn, is no other than the image of the principle: it is a delineation to the eye, and from thence to the mind, of a principle that would otherwise be imperceptible. The triangle does not make the principle, any more than a candle taken into a room that was dark, makes the chairs and tables that before were invisible. All the properties of a triangle exist independently of the figure, and existed before any triangle was drawn or thought of by man. Man had no more to do in the formation of those properties or principles, than he had to do in making the laws by which the heavenly bodies move; and therefore the one must have the same divine origin as the other.

In the same manner as, it may be said, that man can make a triangle, so also, may it be said, he can make the mechanical instrument called a lever. But the principle by which the lever acts, is a thing distinct from the instrument, and would exist if the instrument did not; it attaches itself to the instrument after it is made; the instrument, therefore, can act no otherwise than it does act; neither can all the efforts of human invention make it act otherwise. That which, in all such cases, man calls the *effect,* is no other than the principle itself rendered perceptible to the senses.

Since, then, man cannot make principles, from whence did he gain a knowledge of them, so as to be able to apply them, not only to things on earth, but to ascertain the motion of bodies so immensely distant from him as all the heavenly bodies are? From whence, I ask, *could* he gain that knowledge, but from the study of the true theology?

It is the structure of the universe that has taught this knowledge to man. That structure is an ever-existing exhibition of every principle upon which every part of mathematical science is founded. The offspring of this science is mechanics; for mechanics is no other than the principles of science applied practically. The man who proportions the several parts of a mill uses the same scientific principles as if he had the power of constructing an universe, but as he cannot give to matter that invisible agency by which all the component parts of the immense machine of the universe have influence upon each other, and act in motional unison together, without any apparent contact, and to which man has given the name of attraction, gravitation, and repulsion, he supplies the place of that agency by the humble imitation of teeth and cogs. All the parts of man's microcosm must visibly touch. But could he gain a knowledge of that agency, so as to be able to apply it in practice, we might then say that another *canonical book* of the word of God had been discovered.

If man could alter the properties of the lever, so also could he alter the properties of the triangle: for a lever (taking that sort of lever which is called a steel-yard, for the sake of explanation) forms, when in motion, a triangle. The line it descends from, (one point of that line being in the fulcrum,) the line it descends to, and the chord of the arc, which the end of the lever describes in the air, are the three sides of a triangle. The other arm of the lever describes also a triangle; and the corresponding sides of those two triangles, calculated scientifically, or measured geometrically,—and also the sines, tangents, and secants generated from the angles, and geometrically measured,—have the same proportions to each other as the different weights have that will balance each other on the lever, leaving the weight of the lever out of the case.

It may also be said, that man can make a wheel and axis; that he can put wheels of different magnitudes together, and produce a mill. Still the case comes back to the same point, which is, that he did not make the principle that gives the wheels those powers. This principle is as unalterable as in the former cases, or rather it is the same principle under a different appearance to the eye.

The power that two wheels of different magnitudes have upon each other is in the same proportion as if the semi-diameter of the two wheels were joined together and made into that kind of lever I have described, suspended at the part where the semi-diameters join; for the two wheels, scientifically considered, are no other than the two circles generated by the motion of the compound lever.

It is from the study of the true theology that all our knowledge of science is derived; and it is from that knowledge that all the arts have originated.

The Almighty lecturer, by displaying the principles of science in the structure of the universe, has invited man to study and to imitation. It is as if he had said to the inhabitants of this globe that we call ours, "I have made an earth for man to dwell upon, and I have rendered the starry heavens visible, to teach him science and the arts. He can now provide for his own comfort, AND LEARN FROM MY MUNIFICENCE TO ALL, TO BE KIND TO EACH OTHER."

Of what use is it, unless it be to teach man something, that his eye is endowed with the power of beholding, to an incomprehensible distance, an immensity of worlds revolving in the ocean of space? Or of what use is it that this immensity of worlds is visible to man? What has man to do with the Pleiades, with Orion, with Sirius, with the star he calls the north star, with the moving orbs he has named Saturn, Jupiter, Mars, Venus, and Mercury, if no uses are to follow from their being visible? A less power of vision would have been sufficient for man, if the immensity he now possesses were given only to waste itself, as it were, on an immense desert of space glittering with shows.

It is only by contemplating what he calls the starry heavens, as the book and school of science, that he discovers any use in their being visible to him, or any advantage resulting from his immensity of vision. But when he contemplates the subject in this light, he sees an additional motive for saying, *that nothing was made in vain;* for in vain would be this power of vision if it taught man nothing.

CONCLUSION

In the former part of *The Age of Reason* I have spoken of the three frauds, *mystery, miracle,* and *prophecy;* and as I have seen nothing in any of the answers to that work that in the least affects what I have there said upon those subjects, I shall not encumber this Second Part with additions that are not necessary.

I have spoken also in the same work upon what is called *revelation,* and have shewn the absurd misapplication of that term to the books of the Old Testament and the New; for certainly revelation is out of the question in reciting anything of which man has been the actor or the witness. That which man has done or seen, needs no revelation to tell him he has done it, or seen it—for he knows it already—

nor to enable him to tell it or to write it. It is ignorance, or imposition, to apply the term revelation in such cases; yet the Bible and Testament are classed under this fraudulent description of being all *revelation.*

Revelation then, so far as the term has relation between God and man, can only be applied to something which God reveals of his will to man; but though the power of the Almighty to make such a communication is necessarily admitted, because to that power all things are possible, yet, the thing so revealed (if any thing ever was revealed, and which, by the bye, it is impossible to prove) is revelation to the person *only to whom it is made.* His account of it to another is not revelation; and whoever puts faith in that account, puts it in the man from whom the account comes; and that man may have been deceived, or may have dreamed it; or he may be an impostor and may lie. There is no possible criterion whereby to judge of the truth of what he tells; for even the morality of it would be no proof of revelation. In all such cases, the proper answer should be, "When it is revealed to me, I will believe it to be revelation; but it is not and cannot be incumbent upon me to believe it to be revelation before; neither is it proper that I should take the word of man as the word of God, and put man in the place of God." This is the manner in which I have spoken of revelation in the former part of *The Age of Reason;* and which, whilst it reverentially admits revelation as a possible thing, because, as before said, to the Almighty all things are possible, it prevents the imposition of one man upon another, and precludes the wicked use of pretended revelation.

But though, speaking for myself, I thus admit the possibility of revelation, I totally disbelieve that the Almighty ever did communicate any thing to man, by any mode of speech, in any language, or by any kind of vision, or appearance, or by any means which our senses are capable of receiving, otherwise than by the universal display of himself in the works of the creation, and by that repugnance we feel in ourselves to bad actions, and disposition to good ones.

The most detestable wickedness, the most horrid cruelties, and the greatest miseries, that have afflicted the human race, have had their origin in this thing called revelation, or revealed religion. It has been the most dishonourable belief against the character of the divinity, the most destructive to morality, and the peace and happiness of man, that ever was propagated since man began to exist. It is better, far better, that we admitted, if it were possible, a thousand devils to roam at large, and to preach publicly the doctrine of devils, if there were any such, than that we permitted one such impostor and monster as Moses, Joshua, Samuel, and the Bible prophets, to come with the pretended word of God in his mouth, and have credit among us.   10

Whence arose all the horrid assassinations of whole nations of men, women, and infants, with which the Bible is filled; and the bloody persecutions, and tortures unto death and religious wars, that since that time have laid Europe in blood and ashes; whence arose they, but from this impious thing called revealed religion, and this monstrous belief that God has spoken to man? The lies of the Bible have been the cause of the one, and the lies of the Testament [of]   20 the other.

Some Christians pretend that Christianity was not established by the sword; but of what period of time do they speak? It was impossible that twelve men could begin with the sword: they had not the power; but no sooner were the professors of Christianity sufficiently powerful to employ the sword than they did so, and the stake and faggot too; and Mahomet could not do it sooner. By the same spirit that Peter cut   30 off the ear of the high priest's servant (if the story be true) he would cut off his head, and the head of his master, had he been able. Besides this, Christianity grounds itself originally upon the [Hebrew] Bible, and the Bible was established altogether by the sword, and that in the worst use of it—not to terrify, but to extirpate. The Jews made no converts: they butchered all. The Bible is the sire of the [New] Testament, and both are called the *word of*   40 *God.* The Christians read both books; the ministers preach from both books; and this thing called Christianity is made up of both. It is then false to say that Christianity was not established by the sword.

The only sect that has not persecuted are the Quakers; and the only reason that can be given for it is, that they are rather Deists than Christians. They do not believe much about Jesus Christ, and they call the scriptures a dead let-   50 ter. Had they called them by a worse name, they had been nearer the truth.

It is incumbent on every man who reverences the character of the Creator, and who wishes to lessen the catalogue of artificial miseries, and remove the cause that has sown persecutions thick among mankind, to expel all ideas of a revealed religion as a dangerous heresy, and an impious fraud. What is it that we have learned from this pretended thing called revealed religion? Nothing that is useful to man, and every thing that is dishonourable to his Maker. What is it the Bible teaches us?— rapine, cruelty, and murder. What is it the Testament teaches us?—to believe that the Almighty committed debauchery with a woman engaged to be married; and the belief of this debauchery is called faith.

As to the fragments of morality that are irregularly and thinly scattered in those books, they make no part of this pretended thing, revealed religion. They are the natural dictates of conscience, and the bonds by which society is held together, and without which it cannot exist; and are nearly the same in all religions, and in all societies. The Testament teaches nothing new upon this subject, and where it attempts to exceed, it becomes mean and ridiculous. The doctrine of not retaliating injuries is much better expressed in Proverbs, which is a collection as well from the Gentiles as the Jews, than it is in the Testament. It is there said, (xxv. 21) *"If thine enemy be hungry, give him bread to eat; and if he be thirsty, give him water to drink"*: but when it is said, as in the Testament, *"If a man smite thee on the right cheek, turn to him the other also,"* it is assassinating the dignity of forbearance, and sinking man into a spaniel.

Loving of enemies is another dogma of feigned morality, and has besides no meaning. It is incumbent on man, as a moralist, that he does not revenge an injury; and it is equally as good in a political sense, for there is no end to retaliation; each retaliates on the other, and calls it justice: but to love in proportion to the injury, if it could be done, would be to offer a premium for a crime. Besides, the word *enemies* is too vague and general to be used in a moral maxim, which ought always to be clear and defined, like a proverb. If a man be the enemy of another from mistake and prejudice, as in the case of religious opinions, and sometimes in politics, that man is different to an enemy at heart with a criminal intention; and it is incumbent upon us, and it contributes also to our own tranquillity, that we put the best construction upon a thing that it will bear. But even this erroneous motive in him makes no motive for love on the other part; and to say that we can

love voluntarily, and without a motive, is morally and physically impossible.

Morality is injured by prescribing to it duties that, in the first place, are impossible to be performed, and if they could be would be productive of evil; or, as before said, be premiums for crime. The maxim *of doing as we would be done unto* does not include this strange doctrine of loving enemies; for no man expects to be loved himself for his crime or for his enmity.

Those who preach this doctrine of loving their enemies, are in general the greatest persecutors, and they act consistently by so doing; for the doctrine is hypocritical, and it is natural that hypocrisy should act the reverse of what it preaches. For my own part, I disown the doctrine, and consider it as a feigned or fabulous morality; yet the man does not exist that can say I have persecuted him, or any man, or any set of men, either in the American Revolution, or the French Revolution; or that I have, in any case, returned evil for evil. But it is not incumbent on man to reward a bad action with a good one, or to return good for evil; and wherever it is done, it is a voluntary act, and not a duty. It is also absurd to suppose that such doctrine can make any part of a revealed religion. We imitate the moral character of the Creator by forbearing with each other, for he forbears with all; but this doctrine would imply that he loved man, not in proportion as he was good, but as he was bad.

If we consider the nature of our condition here, we must see there is no occasion for such a thing as *revealed religion*. What is it we want to know? Does not the creation, the universe we behold, preach to us the existence of an Almighty power, that governs and regulates the whole? And is not the evidence that this creation holds out to our senses infinitely stronger than any thing we can read in a book, that any imposter might make and call the word of God? As for morality, the knowledge of it exists in every man's conscience.

Here we are. The existence of an Almighty power is sufficiently demonstrated to us, though we cannot conceive, as it is impossible we should, the nature and manner of its existence. We cannot conceive how we came here ourselves, and yet we know for a fact that we are here. We must know also, that the power that called us into being, can if he please, and when he pleases, call us to account for the manner in which we have lived here; and therefore, without seeking any other motive for the belief, it is rational to believe that he will, for we know beforehand that he can. The probability or even possibility of the thing is all that we ought to know; for if we knew it as a fact, we should be the mere slaves of terror; our belief would have no merit, and our best actions no virtue.

Deism then teaches us, without the possibility of being deceived, all that is necessary or proper to be known. The creation is the Bible of the deist. He there reads, in the handwriting of the Creator himself, the certainty of his existence, and the immutability of his power; and all other Bibles and Testaments are to him forgeries. The probability that we may be called to account hereafter, will, to reflecting minds, have the influence of belief; for it is not our belief or disbelief that can make or unmake the fact. As this is the state we are in, and which it is proper we should be in, as free agents, it is the fool only, and not the philosopher, nor even the prudent man, that will live as if there were no God.

But the belief of a God is so weakened by being mixed with the strange fable of the Christian creed, and with the wild adventures related in the Bible, and the obscurity and obscene nonsense of the Testament, that the mind of man is bewildered as in a fog. Viewing all these things in a confused mass, he confounds fact with fable; and as he cannot believe all, he feels a disposition to reject all. But the belief of a God is a belief distinct from all other things, and ought not to be confounded with any. The notion of a Trinity of Gods has enfeebled the belief of *one* God. A multiplication of beliefs acts as a division of belief; and in proportion as anything is divided, it is weakened.

Religion, by such means, becomes a thing of form instead of fact; of notion instead of principle: morality is banished to make room for an imaginary thing called faith, and this faith has its origin in a supposed debauchery; a man is preached instead of a God; an execution is an object for gratitude; the preachers daub themselves with the blood, like a troop of assassins, and pretend to admire the brilliancy it gives them; they preach a humdrum sermon on the merits of the execution; then praise Jesus Christ for being executed, and condemn the Jews for doing it.

A man, by hearing all this nonsense lumped and preached together, confounds the God of the Creation with the imagined God of the Christians, and lives as if there were none.

Of all the systems of religion that ever were invented, there is none more derogatory to the Almighty, more unedifying to man, more repugnant to reason, and more contradictory in itself, than this thing called Christianity. Too absurd for belief, too impossible to convince, and too inconsistent for practice, it renders the heart torpid, or produces only atheists and fanatics. As an engine of power, it serves the purpose of despotism; and as a means of wealth, the avarice of priests; but so far as respects the good of man in general, it leads to nothing here or hereafter.

The only religion that has not been invented, and that has in it every evidence of divine originality, is pure and simple deism. It must have been the first and will probably be the last that man believes. But pure and simple deism does not answer the purpose of despotic governments. They cannot lay hold of religion as an engine but by mixing it with human inventions, and making their own authority a part; neither does it answer the avarice of priests, but by incorporating themselves and their functions with it, and becoming, like the government, a party in the system. It is this that forms the otherwise mysterious connection of church and state; the church human, and the state tyrannic.

Were a man impressed as fully and strongly as he ought to be with the belief of a God, his moral life would be regulated by the force of belief; he would stand in awe of God, and of himself, and would not do the thing that could not be concealed from either. To give this belief the full opportunity of force, it is necessary that it acts alone. This is deism.

But when, according to the Christian Trinitarian scheme, one part of God is represented by a dying man, and another part, called the Holy Ghost, by a flying pigeon, it is impossible that belief can attach itself to such wild conceits.

It has been the scheme of the Christian church, and of all the other invented systems of religion, to hold man in ignorance of the Creator, as it is of government to hold him in ignorance of his rights. The systems of the one are as false as those of the other, and are calculated for mutual support. The study of theology as it stands in Christian churches, is the study of nothing; it is founded on nothing; it rests on no principles; it proceeds by no authorities; it has no data; it can demonstrate nothing; and admits of no conclusion. Not any thing can be studied as a science without our being in possession of the principles upon which it is founded; and as this is not the case with Christian theology, it is therefore the study of nothing.

Instead then of studying theology, as is now done, out of the Bible and Testament, the meanings of which books are always controverted, and the authenticity of which is disproved, it is necessary that we refer to the Bible of the creation. The principles we discover there are eternal, and of divine origin: they are the foundation of all the science that exists in the world, and must be the foundation of theology.

We can know God only through his works. We cannot have a conception of any one attribute, but by following some principle that leads to it. We have only a confused idea of his power, if we have not the means of comprehending something of its immensity. We can have no idea of his wisdom, but by knowing the order and manner in which it acts. The principles of science lead to this knowledge; for the Creator of man is the Creator of science, and it is through that medium that man can see God, as it were, face to face.

Could a man be placed in a situation, and endowed with power of vision to behold at one view, and to contemplate deliberately, the structure of the universe, to mark the movements of the several planets, the cause of their varying appearances, the unerring order in which they revolve, even to the remotest comet, their connection and dependence on each other, and to know the system of laws established by the Creator, that governs and regulates the whole; he would then conceive, far beyond what any church theology can teach him, the power, the wisdom, the vastness, the munificence of the Creator. He would then see that all the knowledge man has of science, and that all the mechanical arts by which he renders his situation comfortable here, are derived from that source: his mind, exalted by the scene, and convinced by the fact, would increase in gratitude as it increased in knowledge: his religion or his worship would become united with his improvement as a man: any employment he followed that had connection with the principles of the creation,—as everything of agriculture, of science, and of the mechanical arts, has,—would teach him more of God, and of the gratitude he owes to him, than any theological Christian sermon he now hears. Great

objects inspire great thoughts; great munificence excites great gratitude; but the grovelling tales and doctrines of the Bible and the Testament are fit only to excite contempt.

Though man cannot arrive, at least in this life, at the actual scene I have described, he can demonstrate it, because he has knowledge of the principles upon which the creation is constructed. We know that the greatest works can be represented in model, and that the universe can be represented by the same means. The same principles by which we measure an inch or an acre of ground will measure to millions in extent. A circle of an inch diameter has the same geometrical properties as a circle that would circumscribe the universe. The same properties of a triangle that will demonstrate upon paper the course of a ship, will do it on the ocean; and, when applied to what are called the heavenly bodies, will ascertain to a minute the time of an eclipse, though those bodies are millions of miles distant from us. This knowledge is of divine origin; and it is from the Bible of the creation that man has learned it, and not from the stupid Bible of the church, that teaches man nothing.

All the knowledge man has of science and of machinery, by the aid of which his existence is rendered comfortable upon earth, and without which he would be scarcely distinguishable in appearance and condition from a common animal, comes from the great machine and structure of the universe. The constant and unwearied observations of our ancestors upon the movements and revolutions of the heavenly bodies, in what are supposed to have been the early ages of the world, have brought this knowledge upon earth. It is not Moses and the prophets, nor Jesus Christ, nor his apostles, that have done it. The Almighty is the great mechanic of the creation, the first philosopher, and original teacher of all science. Let us then learn to reverence our master, and not forget the labours of our ancestors.

Had we, at this day, no knowledge of machinery, and were it possible that man could have a view, as I have before described, of the structure and machinery of the universe, he would soon conceive the idea of constructing some at least of the mechanical works we now have; and the idea so conceived would progressively advance in practice. Or could a model of the universe, such as is called an orrery, be presented before him and put in motion, his mind would arrive at the same idea. Such an object and such a subject would, whilst it improved him in knowledge useful to himself as a man and a member of society, as well as entertaining, afford far better matter for impressing him with a knowledge of, and a belief in the Creator, and of the reverence and gratitude that man owes to him, than the stupid texts of the Bible and the Testament, from which, be the talents of the preacher what they may, only stupid sermons can be preached. If man must preach, let him preach something that is edifying, and from the texts that are known to be true.

The Bible of the creation is inexhaustible in texts. Every part of science, whether connected with the geometry of the universe, with the systems of animal and vegetable life, or with the properties of inanimate matter, is a text as well for devotion as for philosophy—for gratitude, as for human improvement. It will perhaps be said, that if such a revolution in the system of religion takes place, every preacher ought to be a philosopher. *Most certainly*, and every house of devotion a school of science.

It has been by wandering from the immutable laws of science, and the light of reason, and setting up an invented thing called "revealed religion," that so many wild and blasphemous conceits have been formed of the Almighty. The Jews have made him the assassin of the human species, to make room for the religion of the Jews. The Christians have made him the murderer of himself, and the founder of a new religion to supersede and expel the Jewish religion. And to find pretence and admission for these things, they must have supposed his power or his wisdom imperfect, or his will changeable; and the changeableness of the will is the imperfection of the judgement. The philosopher knows that the laws of the Creator have never changed, with respect either to the principles of science, or the properties of matter. Why then is it to be supposed they have changed with respect to man?

I here close the subject. I have shewn in all the foregoing parts of this work that the Bible and Testament are impositions and forgeries; and I leave the evidence I have produced in proof of it to be refuted, if any one can do it; and I leave the ideas that are suggested in the conclusion of the work to rest on the mind of the reader; certain as I am that when opinions are free, either in matters of government of religion, truth will finally and powerfully prevail.

1794–1796

TIMOTHY DWIGHT

1752–1817

IN THE DEFENSE of orthodox Calvinism against the inroads of deism and skepticism Timothy Dwight holds an important place. The grandson of Jonathan Edwards and the son of a successful merchant and landed proprietor, Dwight was identified with the economic as well as the religious status quo. Association with the Hartford Wits, and the presidency of Yale College, still further identified him with "the standing order." *The Conquest of Caanan* (1785), an epic in rhymed pentameters which mixed biblical and contemporary themes, *Greenfield Hill* (1794), a descriptive, didactic and patriotic piece, and the satirical *Triumph of Infidelity* (1788) established Dwight's reputation as a leading American poet. Among his defenses in prose of orthodoxy in religion and of Federalism in politics are *The Nature, and Danger, of Infidel Philosophy* (1798), *The Duty of Americans, at the Present Crisis* (1798), and *Theology, Explained and Defended* (1818–1819). Dwight's most enduring work was the improvement and broadening of instruction at Yale, his contribution to the development of the American missionary field, and his informative, though biased, *Travels in New-England and New-York* (1821–1822).

Charles E. Cunningham, *Timothy Dwight, a Biography*, New York, 1942.
M. C. Tyler, *Three Men of Letters*, New York, 1895.
M. A. de W. Howe, *Classic Shades; Five Leaders of Learning and Their Colleges*, Boston, 1928.

From: THE DUTY OF AMERICANS,
» » AT THE PRESENT CRISIS « «

About the year 1728, Voltaire, so celebrated for his wit and brilliancy, and not less distinguished for his hatred of Christianity and his abandonment of principle, formed a systematical design to destroy Christianity, and to introduce in its stead a general diffusion of irreligion and atheism. For this purpose he associated with himself Frederic the II, king of Prussia, and Mess. D'Alembert and Diderot, the prin-
10 cipal compilers of the Encyclopédie, all men of talents, atheists, and in the like manner abandoned. The principal parts of this system were, 1st. The compilation of the Encyclopédie; in which with great art and insidiousness the doctrines of Natural as well as Christian Theology were rendered absurd and ridiculous; and the mind of the reader was insensibly steeled against conviction and duty. 2. The overthrow of the religious orders in Catholic countries, a
20 step essentially necessary to the destruction of the religion professed in those countries. 3. The establishment of a sect of philosophists to serve, it is presumed, as a conclave, a rallying point, for all their followers. 4. The appropriation to themselves, and their disciples, of the places and honours of members of the French Academy, the most respectable literary society in France, and always considered as containing none but men of prime learning and talents. In
30 this way they designed to hold out themselves, and their friends, as the only persons of great literary and intellectual distinction in that country, and to dictate all literary opinions to the nation. 5. The fabrication of books of all kinds against Christianity, especially such as excite doubt, and generate contempt and derision. Of these they issued, by themselves and their friends, who early became numerous, an immense number; so printed, as to be purchased
40 for little or nothing, and so written, as to catch the feelings, and steal upon the approbation, of every class of men. 6. The formation of a secret Academy, of which Voltaire was the standing president, and in which books were formed, altered, forged, imputed as posthumous to deceased writers of reputation, and sent abroad with the weight of their names. These were printed and circulated, at the lowest price, through all classes of men, in an un-
50 interrupted succession, and through every part of the kingdom.

Nor were the labours of this Academy confined to religion. They attacked also morality and government, unhinged gradually the minds of men, and destroyed their reverence for every thing heretofore esteemed sacred. . . .

While these measures were advancing the great design with a regular and rapid progress, Doctor Adam Weishaupt, professor of the Canon law in the University of Ingolstadt, a city of Bavaria (in Germany) formed, about the year 1777, the order of Illuminati. This order is professedly a higher order of Masons, originated by himself, and grafted on ancient Masonic Institutions. The secrecy, solemnity, mysticism, and correspondence of Masonry, were in this new order preserved and enhanced; while the ardour of innovation, the impatience of civil and moral restraints, and the aims against government, morals, and religion, were elevated, expanded, and rendered more systematical, malignant, and daring.

In the societies of Illuminati doctrines were taught, which strike at the root of all human happiness and virtue; and every such doctrine was either expressly or implicitly involved in their system.

The being of God was denied and ridiculed.

Government was asserted to be a curse, and authority a mere usurpation.

Civil society was declared to be the only apostasy of man.

The possession of property was pronounced to be robbery.

Chastity and natural affection were declared to be nothing more than groundless prejudices.

Adultery, assassination, poisoning, and other crimes of the like infernal nature, were taught as lawful, and even as virtuous actions.

To crown such a system of falsehood and horror, all means were declared to be lawful, provided the end was good.

In this last doctrine men are not only loosed from every bond, and from every duty; but from every inducement to perform any thing which is good, and abstain from any thing which is evil; and are set upon each other, like a company of hell-hounds to worry, rend, and destroy. Of the goodness of the end every man is to judge for himself; and most men, and all men who resemble the Illuminati, will pronounce every end to be good, which will gratify their inclinations. The great and good ends proposed by the Illuminati, as the ultimate objects of their union, are the overthrow of religion, government, and human society, civil and domestic. These they pronounce to be so good, that murder, butchery, and war, however extended and dreadful, are declared by them to be completely justifiable, if necessary for these great purposes. With such an example in view, it will be in vain to hunt for ends, which can be evil.

Correspondent with this summary was the whole system. No villainy, no impiety, no cruelty, can be named, which was not vindicated; and no virtue, which was not covered with contempt.

The means by which this society was enlarged, and its doctrines spread, were of every promising kind. With unremitted ardour and diligence the members insinuated themselves into every place of power and trust, and into every literary, political and friendly society; engrossed as much as possible the education of youth, especially of distinction; became licensers of the press, and directors of every literary journal; waylaid every foolish prince, every unprincipled civil officer, and every abandoned clergyman; entered boldly into the desk, and with unhallowed hands, and satanic lips, polluted the pages of God; enlisted in their service almost all the booksellers, and of course the printers, of Germany; inundated the country with books, replete with infidelity, irreligion, immorality, and obscenity; prohibited the printing, and prevented the sale, of books of the contrary character; decried and ridiculed them when published in spite of their efforts; panegyrized and trumpeted those of themselves and their coadjutors; and in a word made more numerous, more diversified, and more strenuous exertions, than an active imagination would have preconceived.

To these exertions their success has been proportioned. Multitudes of the Germans, notwithstanding the gravity, steadiness, and sobriety of their national character, have become either partial or entire converts to these wretched doctrines; numerous societies have been established among them; the public faith and morals have been unhinged; and the political and religious affairs of that empire have assumed an aspect, which forebodes its total ruin. In France, also, Illuminatism has been eagerly and extensively adopted; and those men, who have had, successively, the chief direction of the public affairs of that country,

have been members of this society. Societies have also been erected in Switzerland and Italy, and have contributed probably to the success of the French, and to the overthrow of religion and government, in those countries. Mentz was delivered up to Custine by the Illuminati; and that General appears to have been guillotined, because he declined to encourage the same treachery with respect to Manheim. 10

Nor have England and Scotland escaped the contagion. Several societies have been erected in both of those countries. Nay in the private papers, seized in the custody of the leading members in Germany, several such societies are recorded as having been erected in America, before the year 1786.

It is a remarkable fact, that a large proportion of the sentiments, here stated, have been publicly avowed and applauded in the French 20 legislature. The being and providence of God have been repeatedly denied and ridiculed. Christ has been mocked with the grossest insult. Death, by a solemn legislative decree has been declared to be an eternal sleep. Marriage has been degraded to a farce, and the community, by the law of divorce, invited to universal prostitution. In the school of public instruction atheism is professedly taught; and at an audience before the legislature, Nov. 30, 30 1793, the head scholar declared, that he and his schoolfellows detested God; a declaration received by the members with unbounded applause, and rewarded with the fraternal kiss of the president, and with the honors of the sitting. . . .

The cautionary precept given to us by our Lord is, therefore,

That we should be eminently watchful to perform our duty faithfully, in the trying pe- 40 riod, in which our lot is cast.

To those, who obey, a certain blessing is secured by the promise of the Redeemer.

The great and general object, aimed at by this command, and by every other, is private, personal obedience and reformation of life; personal piety, righteousness, and temperance.

To every man is by his Creator especially committed the care of himself; of his time, his talents, and his soul. He knows, or may know, 50 better than any other man, his wants, his sins, and his dangers, and of course the means of relief, reformation, and escape. No one, so well as he, can watch the approach of temptation, so feelingly pray for divine assistance, or so profitably resolve on future obedience. In truth no resolutions, no prayers, no watchfulness of others, will profit him at all, unless seconded by his own. No other person can make any useful impressions on our hearts, or our lives, unless by rousing in us the necessary exertions. All extraneous labours terminate in this single point: it is the end of every doctrine, exhortation, and reproof, of every moral and religious institution . . .

10 Individuals are often apt to consider their own private conduct as of small importance to the public welfare. This opinion is wholly erroneous and highly mischievous. No man can adopt it, who believes, and remembers, the declarations of God. If "one sinner destroyeth much good," if "the effectual fervent prayer of a righteous man availeth much," if ten righteous persons, found in the polluted cities of the vale of Siddim, would have saved them 20 from destruction, the personal conduct of no individual can be insignificant to the safety and happiness of a nation. On the contrary, the advantages to the public of private virtue, faithful prayer and edifying example, cannot be calculated. No one can conjecture how many will be made better, safer, and happier, by the virtue of one.

Wherever wealth, politeness, talents, and office, lend their aid to the inherent efficacy of 30 virtue, its influence is proportionally greater. In this case the example is seen by greater numbers, is regarded with more respectful attention, and felt with greater force. The piety of Hezekiah reformed and saved a nation. Men far inferior in station to kings, and possessed of far humbler means of doing good, may still easily circulate through multitudes both virtue and happiness. The beggar on the dunghill may become a public blessing. Every parent, if a 40 faithful one, is a public blessing of course. How delightful a path of patriotism is this?

It is also to be remembered, that this is the way, in which the chief good, ever placed in the power of most persons, is to be done. If this opportunity of serving God, and befriending mankind, be lost, no other will by the great body of men ever be found. Few persons can be concerned in settling systems of faith, moulding forms of government, regulating na- 50 tions, or establishing empires. But almost all can train up a family for God, instil piety, justice, kindness, and truth, distribute peace and comfort around a neighbourhood, receive the poor and the outcast into their houses, tend the bed of sickness, pour balm into the wounds of pain and awaken a smile in the aspect of sorrow. In the secret and lowly vale of life, virtue in its most lovely attire delights to dwell. There God, with peculiar complacency, most frequently finds the inestimable ornament of a meek and quiet spirit; and there the morning and the evening incense ascends with peculiar fragrance to heaven. . . .

I have been credibly informed, that, some years before the Revolution, an eminent philosopher of this country, now deceased, declared to David Hume, that Christianity would be exterminated from the American colonies within a century from that time. The opinion has doubtless been often declared and extensively imbibed; and has probably furnished our enemies their chief hopes of success. Where religion prevails, their system cannot succeed. Where religion prevails, Illuminatism cannot make disciples, a French directory cannot govern, a nation cannot be made slaves, nor villains, nor atheists, nor beasts. To destroy us, therefore, in this dreadful sense, our enemies must first destroy our Sabbath, and seduce us from the house of God.

Religion and Liberty are the two great objects of defensive war. Conjoined, they unite all the feelings, and call forth all the energies, of man. In defense of them, nations contend with the spirit of the Maccabees; "one will chase a thousand, and two put ten thousand to flight." . . .

Without religion we may possibly retain the freedom of savages, bears, and wolves; but not the freedom of New-England. If our religion were gone, our state of society would perish with it; and nothing would be left, which would be worth defending. Our children of course, if not ourselves, would be prepared, as the ox for the slaughter, to become the victims of conquest, tyranny, and atheism. . . .

The sins of these enemies of Christ, and Christians, are of numbers and degrees, which mock account and descriptions. All that the malice and atheism of the Dragon, the cruelty and rapacity of the Beast, and the fraud and deceit of the false Prophet, can generate, or accomplish, swell the list. No personal, or national, interest of man has been uninvaded; no impious sentiment, or action, against God has been spared; no malignant hostility against Christ, and his religion, has been unattempted. Justice, truth, kindness, piety, and moral obligation universally, have been, not merely trodden under foot; this might have resulted from vehemence and passion; but ridiculed, spurned, and insulted, as the childish bugbears of drivelling idiocy. Chastity and decency have been alike turned out of doors; and shame and pollution called out of their dens to the hall of distinction, and the chair of state. Nor has any art, violence, or means, been unemployed to accomplish these evils.

For what end shall we be connected with men, of whom this is the character and conduct? Is it that we may assume the same character, and pursue the same conduct? Is it, that our churches may become temples of reason, our Sabbath a decade, and our psalms of praise Marseillais hymns? Is it, that we may change our holy worship into a dance of Jacobin phrenzy, and that we may behold a strumpet personating a Goddess on the altars of Jehovah? Is it that we may see the Bible cast into a bonfire, the vessels of the sacramental supper borne by an ass in public procession, and our children, either wheedled or terrified, uniting in the mob, chanting mockeries against God, and hailing in the sounds of Ça ira the ruin of their religion, and the loss of their souls? Is it, that we may see our wives and daughters the victims of legal prostitution; soberly dishonoured; speciously polluted; the outcasts of delicacy and virtue, and the loathing of God and man? Is it, that we may see, in our public papers, a solemn comparison drawn by an American Mother club between the Lord Jesus Christ and a new Marat; and the fiend of malice and fraud exalted above the glorious Redeemer?

Shall we, my brethren, become partakers of these sins? Shall we introduce them into our government, our schools, our families? Shall our sons become the disciples of Voltaire, and the dragoons of Marat; or our daughters the concubines of the Illuminati? . . .

But France itself has been the chief seat of the evils, wrought by these men. The unhappy and ever to be pitied inhabitants of that country, a great part of whom are doubtless of a character similar to that of the peaceable citizens of other countries, and have probably no voluntary concern in accomplishing these evils, have themselves suffered far more from the hands of philosophists, and their followers, than the inhabitants of any other country. General Danican, a French officer, asserts in his memoirs, lately published, that three millions of Frenchmen have perished in the Revolution. Of this amazing destruction the causes by which it was produced, the principles on which it was founded, and the modes in which it was conducted, are an aggravation that admits no bound. The butchery of the stall, and the slaughter of the stye, are scenes of deeper remorse, and softened with more sensibility. The siege of Lyons, and the judicial massacres at Nantes, stand, since the crucifixion, alone in the volume of human crimes. The misery of man never before reached the extreme of agony, nor the infamy of man its consummation. Collot D. Herbois and his satellites, Carrier and his associates, would claim eminence in a world of fiends, and will be marked with distinction in the future hissings of the universe. No guilt so deeply dyed in blood, since the phrenzied malice of Calvary, will probably so amaze the assembly of the final day; and Nantes and Lyons may, without a hyperbole, obtain a literal immortality in a remembrance revived beyond the grave.

In which of these plagues, my brethren, are you willing to share? Which of them will you transmit as a legacy to your children?

Would you escape, you must separate yourselves. Would you wholly escape, you must be wholly separated. I do not intend, that you must not buy and sell, or exhibit the common offices of justice and good will; but you are bound by the voice of reason, of duty, of safety, and of God, to shun all such connection with them, as will interweave your sentiments or your friendship, your religion or your policy, with theirs. You cannot otherwise fail of partaking in their guilt, and receiving of their plagues.

Another duty, to which we are no less forcibly called, is union among ourselves.

The same divine Person, who spoke in the Text, hath also said, "A house, a kingdom, divided against itself cannot stand." A divided family will destroy itself. A divided nation will anticipate ruin, prepared by its enemies. Switzerland, Geneva, Genoa, Venice, the Sardinian territories, Belgium, and Batavia, are melancholy examples of the truth of this declaration of our Saviour; beacons, which warn, with a gloomy and dreadful light, the nations who survive their ruin.

The great bond of union to every people is its government. This destroyed or distrusted, there is no center left of intelligence, counsel, or action; no system of purposes, or measures; no point of rallying, or confidence. When a nation is ready to say, "What part have we in David, or what inheritance in the son of Jesse?"

it will naturally subjoin, "Every man to his tent, O Israel!"

The candour and uprightness, with which our own government has acted in the progress of the present controversy, have forced encomiums even from its most bitter opposers, and excited the warmest approbation and applause of all its friends. Few objects could be more important, auspicious, or gratifying to Christians, than to see the conduct of their rulers such, as they can, with boldness of access, bring before their God, and fearlessly commend to his favour and protection.

In men, possessed of similar candour, adherence to our government, in the present crisis, may be regarded as a thing of course. They need not be informed, that the existing rulers must be the directors of our public affairs and the only directors; that their views and measures will not and cannot always accord with the judgment of individuals, as the opinions of individuals accord no better with each other; that the officers of government are possessed of better information than private persons can be; that, if *they* had the same information, they would probably coincide with the opinions of their rulers; that confidence must be placed in men, imperfect as they are, in all human affairs, or no important business can be done; and that men of known and tried probity are fully deserving of that confidence.

At the present time this adherence ought to be unequivocally manifested. In a land of universal suffrage, where every individual is possessed of much personal consequence as in ours, the government ought, especially in great measures, to be as secure, as may be, of the harmonious and cheerful co-operation of the citizens. All success, here, depends on the hearty concurrence of the community; and no occasion ever called for it more.

But there are, even in this State, persons who are opposed to the government. To them I observe, That the government of France has destroyed the independence of every nation which has confided in it;

That every such nation has been ruined by its internal divisions, especially by the separation of the people from their government;

That they have attempted to accomplish our ruin by the same means, and will certainly accomplish it, if they can;

That the miseries suffered by the subjugated nations have been numberless and extreme, involving the loss of national honour, the immense plunder of public and private property, the conflagration of churches and dwellings, the total ruin of families, the butchery of great multitudes of fathers and sons, and the most deplorable dishonour of wives and daughters;

That the same miseries will be repeated here, if in their power;

That there is, under God, no means of escaping this ruin, but union among ourselves, and unshaken adherence to the existing government;

That themselves have an infinitely higher interest in preserving the independence of their country, than in any thing, which *can* exist, should it be conquered;

That they must stand, or fall, with their country; since the French, like all other conquerors, though they may for a little time regard them as aids and friends with a seeming partiality, will soon lose that partiality in a general contempt and hatred for them, as Americans. That should they, contrary to all experience, escape these evils, their children will suffer them as extensively as those of their neighbours; and

That to oppose or neglect the defence of their country is to stab the breast from which they have drawn their life.

I know not that even these considerations will prevail: if they do not, nothing can be suggested by me which will have efficacy. I must leave them, therefore, to their consciences and their God.

In the mean time, since the great facts, of which this controversy has consisted, have not, during the preceding periods, been thoroughly known, or believed, by all; and since all questions of expediency will be viewed differently by different eyes; I cannot but urge a general spirit of conciliation. To men labouring under mere mistakes, and prejudices void of malignity, hard names are in most cases unhappily applied, and unkindness is unwisely exhibited. Multitudes, heretofore attached to France with great ardour, have, from full conviction of the necessity of changing their sentiments and their conduct, come forth in the most decisive language, and determined conduct, of defenders of their country. More are daily exhibiting the same spirit and measures. Almost all native Americans will, I doubt not, speedily appear in the same ranks; and none should, in my opinion, be discouraged by useless obloquy.

Another duty, injoined in the text, and highly incumbent on us at this time, is unshaken firmness in our opposition.

A steady and invincible firmness is the chief instrument of great achievements. It is the prime mean of great wealth, learning, wisdom, power and virtue; and without it nothing noble or useful is usually accomplished. Without it our separation from our enemies, and our union among ourselves, will avail to no end. The cause is too complex, the object too important, to be determined by a single effort. It is infinitely too important to be given up, let the consequence be what it may. No evils which can flow from resistance can be so great as those which must flow from submission. Great sacrifices of property, of peace, and of life, we may be called to make, but they will fall short of complete ruin. If they should not, it will be more desirable, beyond computation, to fall in the honourable and faithful defence of our families, our country, and our religion, than to survive, the melancholy, debased, and guilty spectators of the ruin of all. We contend for all that is, or ought to be, dear to man. Our cause is eminently that in which "he who seeketh to save his life shall lose it, and he who loseth it," in obedience to the command of his Master, "shall find it" beyond the grave. To our enemies we have done no wrong. Unspotted justice looks down on all our public measures with a smile. We fight for that for which we can pray. We fight for the lives, the honour, the safety of our wives and children, for the religion of our fathers, and for the liberty "with which Christ hath made us free." "We jeopard our lives" that our children may inherit these glorious blessings, be rescued from the grinding insolence of foreign despotism, and saved from the corruption and perdition of foreign atheism. I am a father. I feel the usual parental tenderness for my children. I have long soothed the approach of declining years with the fond hope of seeing my sons serving God and their generation around me. But from cool conviction I declare in this solemn place, I would far rather follow them one by one to an untimely grave, than to behold them, however prosperous, the victims of philosophism. What could I then believe, but that they were "nigh unto cursing, and that their end was to be burned.". . .

But perhaps you may be alarmed by the power and the successes of your enemies. I am warranted to declare that the ablest judge of this subject in America has said, that, if we are united, firm, and faithful to ourselves, neither France nor all Europe can subdue these States. Against other nations they contended with great and decisive advantages. Those nations were near to them, were divided, feeble, corrupted, seduced by philosophists, slaves of despotism, and separated from their government. None of these characters can be applied to us, unless we voluntarily retain those which depend on ourselves. Three thousand miles of ocean spread between us and our enemies, to enfeeble and disappoint their efforts. They will not here contend with silken Italians, with divided Swissers, nor with self-surrendered Belgians and Batavians. They will find a hardy race of freemen, uncorrupted by luxury, unbroken by despotism; enlightened to understand their privileges, glowing with independence, and determined to be free, or to die: men who love, and who will defend, their families, their country, and their religion: men fresh from triumph, and strong in a recent and victorious Revolution. Doubled, since that Revolution began, in their numbers, and quadrupled in their resources and advantages, at home, in a country formed to disappoint invasion, and to prosper defence, under leaders skilled in all the arts and duties of war, and trained in the path of success, they have, if united, firm, and faithful, every thing to hope, and, beside the common evils of war, nothing to fear.   1798

» »   « «

RALPH WALDO EMERSON

1803–1882

SINCE LEAVING the Unitarian ministry, Emerson had achieved some reputation as an essayist and lecturer. On Sunday evening, the fifteenth of July, 1838, he returned to Cambridge to give the address which startled the American clergy. In this justly famous "Divinity School Address" Emerson applied in an explicit and militant fashion the essential ideas he had advanced in *Nature* and in *The American Scholar* (1837). Yet the doctrine of self-reliance in religious matters, or, to put it another way, the idea of the sufficiency of the self in religious intuition and inspiration, was for that generation what Modernism has been for our own.

Andrews Norton of the Harvard Divinity School, in replying to Emerson the following year, took his stand on the authoritarianism of sacred literature rationally interpreted, and made it clear that Emerson's intuitionism was incompatible with any kind of authoritarianism and institutionalism. In George Ripley, on the other hand, Emerson found a champion. The controversy which Emerson aroused stirred all ecclesiastical New England. By sharpening the breach between Unitarians and those who were unable to satisfy themselves with the rationalistic formalism of that faith, the Address helped prepare the way for Transcendentalism. Harvard, the seat of Unitarianism, did not ask Emerson to reappear in her halls until after the Civil War.

G. W. Cooke, *A Bibliography of Ralph Waldo Emerson,* Boston and New York, 1908.
The Complete Work of Ralph Waldo Emerson, Centenary Edition, 12 vols., Boston and New York, 1903–1904.
J. E. Cabot, *A Memoir of Ralph Waldo Emerson,* 2 vols., Boston and New York, 1887.
Young Emerson Speaks, A. C. McGiffert, ed., Boston, 1938.
Sherman Paul, *Emerson's Angle of Vision,* Cambridge, Mass., 1952.
Ralph L. Rusk, *The Life of Ralph Waldo Emerson,* New York, 1949.

» » DIVINITY SCHOOL ADDRESS « «

In this refulgent summer, it has been a luxury to draw the breath of life. The grass grows, the buds burst, the meadow is spotted with fire and gold in the tint of flowers. The air is full of birds, and sweet with the breath of the pine, the balm-of-Gilead, and the new hay. Night brings no gloom to the heart with its welcome shade. Through the transparent darkness the stars pour their almost spiritual rays. Man under them seems a young child, and his huge globe a toy. The cool night bathes the world as with a river, and prepares his eyes again for the crimson dawn. The mystery of nature was never displayed more happily. The corn and the wine have been freely dealt to all creatures, and the never-broken silence with which the old bounty goes forward has not yielded yet one word of explanation. One is constrained to respect the perfection of this world in which our senses converse. How wide; how rich; what invitation from every property it gives to every faculty of man! In its fruitful soils; in its navigable sea; in its mountains of metal and stone; in its forests of all woods; in its animals; in its chemical ingredients; in the powers and path of light, heat, attraction and life, it is well worth the pith and heart of great men to subdue and enjoy it. The planters, the mechanics, the inventors, the astronomers, the builders of cities, and the captains, history delights to honor.

But when the mind opens and reveals the

laws which traverse the universe and make things what they are, then shrinks the great world at once into a mere illustration and fable of this mind. What am I? and What is? asks the human spirit with a curiosity new-kindled, but never to be quenched. Behold these outrunning laws, which our imperfect apprehension can see tend this way and that, but not come full circle. Behold these infinite relations, so like, so unlike; many, yet one. I would study, I would know, I would admire forever. These works of thought have been the entertainments of the human spirit in all ages.

A more secret, sweet, and overpowering beauty appears to man when his heart and mind open to the sentiment of virtue. Then he is instructed in what is above him. He learns that his being is without bound; that to the good, to the perfect, he is born, low as he now lies in evil and weakness. That which he venerates is still his own, though he has not realized it yet. *He ought.* He knows the sense of that grand word, though his analysis fails to render account of it. When in innocency or when by intellectual perception he attains to say,—"I love the Right; Truth is beautiful within and without for evermore. Virtue, I am thine; save me; use me; thee will I serve, day and night, in great, in small, that I may be not virtuous, but virtue";—then is the end of the creation answered, and God is well pleased.

The sentiment of virtue is a reverence and delight in the presence of certain divine laws. It perceives that this homely game of life we play, covers, under what seem foolish details, principles that astonish. The child amidst his baubles is learning the action of light, motion, gravity, muscular force; and in the game of human life, love, fear, justice, appetite, man, and God, interact. These laws refuse to be adequately stated. They will not be written out on paper, or spoken by the tongue. They elude our persevering thought; yet we read them hourly in each other's faces, in each other's actions, in our own remorse. The moral traits which are all globed into every virtuous act and thought,—in speech we must sever, and describe or suggest by painful enumeration of many particulars. Yet, as this sentiment is the essence of all religion, let me guide your eye to the precise objects of the sentiment, by an enumeration of some of those classes of facts in which this element is conspicuous.

The intuition of the moral sentiment is an insight of the perfection of the laws of the soul. These laws execute themselves. They are out of time, out of space, and not subject to circumstance. Thus in the soul of man there is a justice whose retributions are instant and entire. He who does a noble deed is instantly ennobled. He who does a mean deed is by the action itself contracted. He who puts off impurity, thereby puts on purity. If a man is at heart just, then in so far is he God; the safety of God, the immortality of God, the majesty of God do enter into that man with justice. If a man dissemble, deceive, he deceives himself, and goes out of acquaintance with his own being. A man in the view of absolute goodness, adores, with total humility. Every step so downward, is a step upward. The man who renounces himself, comes to himself.

See how this rapid intrinsic energy worketh everywhere, righting wrongs, correcting appearances, and bringing up facts to a harmony with thoughts. Its operation in life, though slow to the senses, is at last as sure as in the soul. By it a man is made the Providence to himself, dispensing good to his goodness, and evil to his sin. Character is always known. Thefts never enrich; alms never impoverish; murder will speak out of stone walls. The least admixture of a lie,—for example, the taint of vanity, any attempt to make a good impression, a favorable appearance,—will instantly vitiate the effect. But speak the truth, and all nature and all spirits help you with unexpected furtherance. Speak the truth, and all things alive or brute are vouchers, and the very roots of the grass underground there do seem to stir and move to bear you witness. See again the perfection of the Law as it applies itself to the affections, and becomes the law of society. As we are, so we associate. The good, by affinity, seek the good; the vile, by affinity, the vile. Thus of their own volition, souls proceed into heaven, into hell.

These facts have always suggested to man the sublime creed that the world is not the product of manifold power, but of one will, of one mind; and that one mind is everywhere active, in each ray of the star, in each wavelet of the pool; and whatever opposes that will is everywhere balked and baffled, because things are made so, and not otherwise. Good is positive. Evil is merely privative, not absolute: it is like cold, which is the privation of heat. All evil is so much death or nonentity. Benevolence is absolute and real. So much benevolence as a man hath, so much life hath he. For all things proceed out of this same spirit, which is differently named love, justice, temperance, in its different applications, just as the ocean receives different names on the several shores which it washes. All things proceed out of the same spirit, and all things conspire with it. Whilst a man seeks good ends, he is strong by the whole strength of nature. In so far as he roves from these ends, he bereaves himself of power, or auxiliaries; his being shrinks out of all remote channels, he becomes less and less, a mote, a point, until absolute badness is absolute death.

The perception of this law of laws awakens in the mind a sentiment which we call the religious sentiment, and which makes our highest happiness. Wonderful is its power to charm and to command. It is a mountain air. It is the embalmer of the world. It is myrrh and storax, and chlorine and rosemary. It makes the sky and the hills sublime, and the silent song of the stars is it. By it is the universe made safe and habitable, not by science or power. Thought may work cold and intransitive in things, and find no end or unity; but the dawn of the sentiment of virtue on the heart, gives and is the assurance that Law is sovereign over all natures; and the worlds, time, space, eternity, do seem to break out into joy.

This sentiment is divine and deifying. It is the beatitude of man. It makes him illimitable. Through it, the soul first knows itself. It corrects the capital mistake of the infant man, who seeks to be great by following the great, and hopes to derive advantages *from another*,—by showing the fountain of all good to be in himself, and that he, equally with every man, is an inlet into the deeps of Reason. When he says, "I ought"; when love warms him; when he chooses, warned from on high, the good and great deed; then, deep melodies wander through his soul from Supreme Wisdom.— Then he can worship, and be enlarged by his worship; for he can never go behind this sentiment. In the sublimest flights of the soul, rectitude is never surmounted, love is never outgrown.

This sentiment lies at the foundation of society, and successively creates all forms of worship. The principle of veneration never dies out. Man fallen into superstition, into sensuality, is never quite without the visions of the moral sentiment. In like manner, all the expressions of this sentiment are sacred and permanent in proportion to their purity. The expressions of this sentiment affect us more than all other compositions. The sentences of the oldest time, which ejaculate this piety, are still fresh and fragrant. This thought dwelled always deepest in the minds of men in the devout and contemplative East; not alone in Palestine, where it reached its purest expression, but in Egypt, in Persia, in India, in China. Europe has always owed to oriental genius its divine impulses. What these holy bards said, all sane men found agreeable and true. And the unique impression of Jesus upon mankind, whose name is not so much written as ploughed into the history of this world, is proof of the subtle virtue of this infusion.

Meantime, whilst the doors of the temple stand open, day and night, before every man, and the oracles of this truth cease never, it is guarded by one stern condition; this, namely: it is an intuition. It cannot be received at second hand. Truly speaking, it is not instruction, but provocation, that I can receive from another soul. What he announces, I must find true in me, or reject; and on his word, or as his second, be he who he may, I can accept nothing. On the contrary, the absence of this primary faith is the presence of degradation. As is the flood, so is the ebb. Let this faith depart, and the very words it spake and the things it made become false and hurtful. Then falls the church, the state, art, letters, life. The doctrine of the divine nature being forgotten, a sickness infects and dwarfs the constitution. Once man was all; now he is an appendage, a nuisance. And because the indwelling Supreme Spirit cannot wholly be got rid of, the doctrine of it suffers this perversion, that the divine nature is attributed to one or two persons, and denied to all the rest, and denied with fury. The doctrine of inspiration is lost; the base doctrine of the majority of voices usurps the place of the doctrine of the soul. Miracles, prophecy, poetry, the ideal life, the holy life, exist as ancient history merely; they are not in the belief, nor in the aspiration of society; but, when suggested, seem ridiculous. Life is comic or pitiful as soon as the high ends of being fade out of sight, and man becomes nearsighted, and can only attend to what addresses the senses.

These general views, which, whilst they are general, none will contest, find abundant illustration in the history of religion, and especially in the history of the Christian church. In that, all of us have had our birth and nurture. The truth contained in that, you, my young friends, are now setting forth to teach. As the Cultus, or established worship of the civilized world, it has great historical interest for us. Of its blessed words, which have been the consolation of humanity, you need not that I should speak. I shall endeavor to discharge my duty to you on this occasion, by pointing out two errors in its administration, which daily appear more gross from the point of view we have just now taken.

Jesus Christ belonged to the true race of prophets. He saw with open eye the mystery of the soul. Drawn by its severe harmony, ravished with its beauty, he lived in it, and had his being there. Alone in all history he estimated the greatness of man. One man was true to what is in you and me. He saw that God incarnates himself in man, and evermore goes forth anew to take possession of his World. He said, in this jubilee of sublime emotion, "I am divine. Through me, God acts; through me, speaks. Would you see God, see me; or see thee, when thou also thinkest as I now think." But what a distortion did his doctrine and memory suffer in the same, in the next, and the following ages! There is no doctrine of the Reason which will bear to be taught by the Understanding. The understanding caught this high chant from the poet's lips, and said, in the next age, "This was Jehovah come down out of heaven. I will kill you, if you say he was a man." The idioms of his language and the figures of his rhetoric have usurped the place of his truth; and churches are not built on his principles, but on his tropes. Christianity became a Mythus, as the poetic teaching of Greece and of Egypt, before. He spoke of miracles; for he felt that man's life was a miracle, and all that man doth, and he knew that this daily miracle shines as the character ascends. But the word Miracle, as pronounced by Christian churches, gives a false impression; it is Monster. It is not one with the blowing clover and the falling rain.

He felt respect for Moses and the prophets, but no unfit tenderness at postponing their initial revelations to the hour and the man that now is; to the eternal revelation in the heart. Thus was he a true man. Having seen that the law in us is commanding, he would not suffer it to be commanded. Boldly, with hand, and heart, and life, he declared it was God. Thus is he, as I think, the only soul in history who has appreciated the worth of man.

1. In this point of view we become sensible of the first defect of historical Christianity. Historical Christianity has fallen into the error that corrupts all attempts to communicate religion. As it appears to us, and as it has appeared for ages, it is not the doctrine of the soul, but an exaggeration of the personal, the positive, the ritual. It has dwelt, it dwells, with noxious exaggeration about the *person* of Jesus. The soul knows no persons. It invites every man to expand to the full circle of the universe, and will have no preferences but those of spontaneous love. But by this eastern monarchy of a Christianity, which indolence and fear have built, the friend of man is made the injurer of man. The manner in which his name is surrounded with expressions which were once sallies of admiration and love, but are now petrified into official titles, kills all generous sympathy and liking. All who hear me, feel that the language that describes Christ to Europe and America is not the style of friendship and enthusiasm to a good and noble heart, but is appropriated and formal,—paints a demigod, as the Orientals or the Greeks would describe Osiris or Apollo. Accept the injurious impositions of our early catechetical instruction, and even honesty and self-denial were but splendid sins, if they did not wear the Christian name. One would rather be

"A pagan, suckled in a creed outworn,"

than to be defrauded of his manly right in coming into nature and finding not names and places, not land and professions, but even virtue and truth foreclosed and monopolized. You shall not be a man even. You shall not own the world; you shall not dare and live after the infinite Law that is in you, and in company with the infinite Beauty which heaven and earth reflect to you in all lovely forms; but you must subordinate your nature to Christ's nature; you must accept our interpretations, and take his portrait as the vulgar draw it.

That is always best which gives me to myself. The sublime is excited in me by the great stoical doctrine, Obey thyself. That which shows God in me, fortifies me. That which shows God out of me, makes me a wart and a wen. There is no longer a necessary reason for my being. Already the long shadows of untimely oblivion creep over me, and I shall decease forever.

The divine bards are the friends of my virtue, of my intellect, of my strength. They admonish me that the gleams which flash across my mind are not mine, but God's; that they had the like, and were not disobedient to the heavenly vision. So I love them. Noble provocations go out from them, inviting me to resist evil; to subdue the world; and to Be. And thus, by his holy thoughts, Jesus serves us, and thus only. To aim to convert a man by miracles is a profanation of the soul. A true conversion, a true Christ, is now, as always, to be made by the reception of beautiful sentiments. It is true that a great and rich soul, like his, falling among the simple, does so preponderate, that, as his did, it names the world. The world seems to exist for him, and they have not yet drunk so deeply of his sense as to see that only by coming again to themselves, or to God in themselves, can they grow forevermore. It is a low benefit to give me something; it is a high benefit to enable me to do somewhat of myself. The time is coming when all men will see that the gift of God to the soul is not a vaunting, overpowering, excluding sanctity, but a sweet, natural goodness, a goodness like thine and mine, and that so invites thine and mine to be and to grow.

The injustice of the vulgar tone of preaching is not less flagrant to Jesus than to the souls which it profanes. The preachers do not see that they make his gospel not glad, and shear him of the locks of beauty and the attributes of heaven. When I see a majestic Epaminondas, or Washington; when I see among my contemporaries a true orator, an upright judge, a dear friend; when I vibrate to the melody and fancy of a poem; I see beauty that is to be desired. And so lovely, and yet with more entire consent of my human being, sounds in my ear the severe music of the bards that have sung of the true God in all ages. Now do not degrade the life and dialogues of Christ out of the circle of this charm, by insulation and peculiarity. Let them lie as they befell, alive and warm, part of human life and of the landscape and of the cheerful day.

2. The second defect of the traditionary and limited way of using the mind of Christ is a consequence of the first; this namely: that the Moral Nature, that Law of laws whose revelations introduce greatness—yea, God himself—

into the open soul, is not explored as the fountain of the established teaching in society. Men have come to speak of the revelation as somewhat long ago given and done, as if God were dead. The injury to faith throttles the preacher; and the goodliest of institutions becomes an uncertain and inarticulate voice.

It is very certain that it is the effect of conversation with the beauty of the soul, to beget a desire and need to impart to others the same knowledge and love. If utterance is denied, the thought lies like a burden on the man. Always the seer is a sayer. Somehow his dream is told; somehow he publishes it with solemn joy: sometimes with pencil on canvas; sometimes with chisel on stone; sometimes in towers and aisles of granite, his soul's worship is builded; sometimes in anthems of indefinite music; but clearest and most permanent, in words.

The man enamored of this excellency becomes its priest or poet. The office is coeval with the world. But observe the condition, the spiritual limitation of the office. The spirit only can teach. Not any profane man, not any sensual, not any liar, not any slave can teach, but only he can give, who has; he only can create, who is. The man on whom the soul descends, through whom the soul speaks, alone can teach. Courage, piety, love, wisdom, can teach; and every man can open his door to these angels, and they shall bring him the gift of tongues. But the man who aims to speak as books enable, as synods use, as the fashion guides, and as interest commands, babbles. Let him hush.

To this holy office you propose to devote yourselves. I wish you may feel your call in throbs of desire and hope. The office is the first in the world. It is of that reality that it cannot suffer the deduction of any falsehood. And it is my duty to say to you that the need was never greater of new revelation than now. From the views I have already expressed, you will infer the sad conviction, which I share, I believe, with numbers, of the universal decay and now almost death of faith in society. The soul is not preached. The Church seems to totter to its fall, almost all life extinct. On this occasion, any complaisance would be criminal which told you, whose hope and commission it is to preach the faith of Christ, that the faith of Christ is preached.

It is time that this ill-suppressed murmur of all thoughtful men against the famine of our churches;—this moaning of the heart because it is bereaved of the consolation, the hope, the grandeur that come alone out of the culture of the moral nature,—should be heard through the sleep of indolence, and over the din of routine. This great and perpetual office of the preacher is not discharged. Preaching is the expression of the moral sentiment in application to the duties of life. In how many churches, by how many prophets, tell me, is man made sensible that he is an infinite Soul; that the earth and heavens are passing into his mind; that he is drinking forever the soul of God? Where now sounds the persuasion, that by its very melody imparadises my heart, and so affirms its own origin in heaven? Where shall I hear words such as in elder ages drew men to leave all and follow,—father and mother, house and land, wife and child? Where shall I hear these august laws of moral being so pronounced as to fill my ear, and I feel ennobled by the offer of my uttermost action and passion? The test of the true faith, certainly, should be its power to charm and command the soul, as the laws of nature control the activity of the hands,—so commanding that we find pleasure and honor in obeying. The faith should blend with the light of rising and of setting suns, with the flying cloud, the singing bird, and the breath of flowers. But now the priest's Sabbath has lost the splendor of nature; it is unlovely; we are glad when it is done; we can make, we do make, even sitting in our pews, a far better, holier, sweeter, for ourselves.

Whenever the pulpit is usurped by a formalist, then is the worshipper defrauded and disconsolate. We shrink as soon as the prayers begin, which do not uplift, but smite and offend us. We are fain to wrap our cloaks about us, and secure, as best we can, a solitude that hears not. I once heard a preacher who sorely tempted me to say I would go to church no more. Men go, thought I, where they are wont to go, else had no soul entered the temple in the afternoon. A snow-storm was falling around us. The snow-storm was real, the preacher merely spectral, and the eye felt the sad contrast in looking at him, and then out of the window behind him into the beautiful meteor of the snow. He had lived in vain. He had no one word intimating that he had laughed or wept, was married or in love, had been commended, or cheated, or chagrined. If he had ever lived and acted, we were none the wiser for it. The capital secret of his profession, namely, to convert life into truth, he had not learned. Not one fact in all his experience had he yet imported into his doctrine. This man had ploughed and planted and talked and bought and sold; he had read books; he had eaten and drunken; his head aches, his heart throbs; he smiles and suffers; yet was there not a surmise, a hint, in all the discourse, that he had ever lived at all. Not a line did he draw out of real history. The true preacher can be known by this, that he deals out to his people his life,—life passed through the fire of thought. But of the bad preacher, it could not be told from his sermon what age of the world he fell in; whether he had a father or a child; whether he was a freeholder or a pauper; whether he was a citizen or a countryman; or any other fact of his biography. It seemed strange that the people should come to church. It seemed as if their houses were very unentertaining, that they should prefer this thoughtless clamor. It shows that there is a commanding attraction in the moral sentiment, that can lend a faint tint of light to dulness and ignorance coming in its name and place. The good hearer is sure he has been touched sometimes; is sure there is somewhat to be reached, and some word that can reach it. When he listens to these vain words, he comforts himself by their relation to his remembrance of better hours, and so they clatter and echo unchallenged.

I am not ignorant that when we preach unworthily, it is not always quite in vain. There is a good ear, in some men, that draws supplies to virtue out of very indifferent nutriment. There is poetic truth concealed in all the commonplaces of prayer and of sermons, and though foolishly spoken, they may be wisely heard; for each is some select expression that broke out in a moment of piety from some stricken or jubilant soul, and its excellency made it remembered. The prayers and even the dogmas of our church are like the zodiac of Denderah and the astronomical monuments of the Hindoos, wholly insulated from anything now extant in the life and business of the people. They mark the height to which the waters once rose. But this docility is a check upon the mischief from the good and devout. In a large portion of the community, the religious service gives rise to quite other thoughts and emotions. We need not chide the negligent servant. We are struck with pity, rather, at the swift retribution of his sloth. Alas for the unhappy man that is called to stand in the pulpit, and *not* give bread of life. Everything that befalls, accuses him. Would he ask contributions for the missions, foreign or domestic? Instantly his face is suffused with shame, to propose to his parish that they should send money a hundred or a thousand miles, to furnish such poor fare as they have at home and would do well to go the hundred or the thousand miles to escape. Would he urge people to a godly way of living;—and can he ask a fellow-creature to come to Sabbath meetings, when he and they all know what is the poor uttermost they can hope for therein? Will he invite them privately to the Lord's Supper? He dares not. If no heart warm this rite, the hollow, dry, creaking formality is too plain, than that he can face a man of wit and energy and put the invitation without terror. In the street, what has he to say to the bold village blasphemer? The village blasphemer sees fear in the face, form, and gait of the minister.

Let me not taint the sincerity of this plea by any oversight of the claims of good men. I know and honor the purity and strict conscience of numbers of the clergy. What life the public worship retains, it owes to the scattered company of pious men, who minister here and there in the churches, and who, sometimes accepting with too great tenderness the tenet of the elders, have not accepted from others, but from their own heart, the genuine impulses of virtue, and so still command our love and awe, to the sanctity of character. Moreover, the exceptions are not so much to be found in a few eminent preachers, as in the better hours, the truer inspirations of all, —nay, in the sincere moments of every man. But, with whatever exception, it is still true that tradition characterizes the preaching of this country; that it comes out of the memory, and not out of the soul; that it aims at what is usual, and not at what is necessary and eternal; that thus historical Christianity destroys the power of preaching, by withdrawing it from the exploration of the moral nature of man; where the sublime is, where are the resources of astonishment and power. What a cruel injustice it is to that Law, the joy of the whole earth, which alone can make the thought dear and rich; that Law whose fatal sureness the astronomical orbits poorly emulate;—that it is travestied and depreciated, that it is behooted and behowled, and not a trait, not a word of it articulated. The pulpit in losing sight of this Law, loses its reason, and gropes after it knows not what. And for want of this culture the soul of the community is sick and faithless. It wants nothing so much as a stern, high, stoical, Christian discipline, to make it know itself and the divinity that speaks through it. Now man is ashamed of himself; he skulks and sneaks through the world, to be tolerated, to be pitied, and scarcely in a thousand years does any man dare to be wise and good, and so draw after him the tears and blessings of his kind.

Certainly there have been periods when, from the inactivity of the intellect on certain truths, a greater faith was possible in names and persons. The Puritans in England and America found in the Christ of the Catholic Church and in the dogmas inherited from Rome, scope for their austere piety and their longings for civil freedom. But their creed is passing away, and none arises in its room. I think no man can go with his thoughts about him into one of our churches, without feeling that what hold the public worship had on men is gone, or going. It has lost its grasp on the affection of the good and the fear of the bad. In the country, neighborhoods, half parishes are *signing off*, to use the local term. It is already beginning to indicate character and religion to withdraw from the religious meetings. I have heard a devout person, who prized the Sabbath, say in bitterness of heart, "On Sundays, it seems wicked to go to church." And the motive that holds the best there is now only a hope and a waiting. What was once a mere circumstance, that the best and the worst men in the parish, the poor and the rich, the learned and the ignorant, young and old, should meet one day as fellows in one house, in sign of an equal right in the soul, has come to be a paramount motive for going thither.

My friends, in these two errors, I think, I find the causes of a decaying church and a wasting unbelief. And what greater calamity can fall upon a nation than the loss of worship? Then all things go to decay. Genius leaves the temple to haunt the senate or the market. Literature becomes frivolous. Science is cold. The eye of youth is not lighted by the hope of other worlds, and age is without honor. Society lives to trifles, and when men die we do not mention them.

And now, my brothers, you will ask, What in these desponding days can be done by us? The remedy is already declared in the ground of our complaint of the Church. We have contrasted the Church with the Soul. In the soul then let the redemption be sought. Wherever a man comes, there comes revolution. The old is for slaves. When a man comes, all books are legible, all things transparent, all religions are forms. He is religious. Man is the wonder-worker. He is seen amid miracles. All men bless and curse. He saith yea and nay, only. The stationariness of religion; the assumption that the age of inspiration is past, that the Bible is closed; the fear of degrading the character of Jesus by representing him as a man;—indicate with sufficient clearness the falsehood of our theology. It is the office of a true teacher to show us that God is, not was; that He speaketh, not spake. The true Christianity,— a faith like Christ's in the infinitude of man, —is lost. None believeth in the soul of man, but only in some man or person old and departed. Ah me! no man goeth alone. All men go in flocks to this saint or that poet, avoiding the God who seeth in secret. They cannot see in secret; they love to be blind in public. They think society wiser than their soul, and know not that one soul, and their soul, is wiser than the whole world. See how nations and races flit by on the sea of time and leave no ripple to tell where they floated or sunk, and one good soul shall make the name of Moses, or of Zeno, or of Zoroaster, reverend forever. None assayeth the stern ambition to be the Self of the nation and of nature, but each would be an easy secondary to some Christian scheme, or sectarian connection, or some eminent man. Once leave your own knowledge of God, your own sentiment, and take secondary knowledge, as St. Paul's, or George Fox's, or Swedenborg's, and you get wide from God with every year this secondary form lasts, and if, as now, for centuries,—the chasm yawns to that breadth, that men can scarcely be convinced there is in them anything divine.

Let me admonish you, first of all, to go alone; to refuse the good models, even those which are sacred to the imagination of men, and dare to love God without mediator or veil. Friends enough you shall find who will hold up to your emulation Wesleys and Oberlins, Saints and Prophets. Thank God for these good men, but say, "I also am a man." Imitation cannot go above its model. The imitator dooms himself to hopeless mediocrity. The inventor did it because it was natural to him, and so in him it has a charm. In the imitator something else is natural, and he bereaves himself of his own beauty, to come short of another man's.

Yourself a newborn bard of the Holy Ghost, cast behind you all conformity, and acquaint men at first hand with Deity. Look to it first and only, that fashion, custom, authority, pleasure, and money, are nothing to you,—are not bandages over your eyes, that you cannot see, —but live with the privilege of the immeasurable mind. Not too anxious to visit periodically all families and each family in your parish connection,—when you meet one of these men or women, be to them a divine man; be to them thought and virtue; let their timid aspirations find in you a friend; let their trampled instincts be genially tempted out in your atmosphere; let their doubts know that you have doubted, and their wonder feel that you have wondered. By trusting your own heart, you shall gain more confidence in other men. For all our penny-wisdom, for all our soul-destroying slavery to habit, it is not to be doubted that all men have sublime thoughts; that all men value the few real hours of life; they love to be heard; they love to be caught up into the vision of principles. We mark with light in the memory the few interviews we have had, in the dreary years of routine and of sin, with souls that made our souls wiser; that spoke what we thought; that told us what we knew; that gave us leave to be what we inly were. Discharge to men the priestly office, and, present or absent, you shall be followed with their love as by an angel.

And, to this end, let us not aim at common degrees of merit. Can we not leave, to such as love it, the virtue that glitters for the commendation of society, and ourselves pierce the deep solitudes of absolute ability and worth? We easily come up to the standard of goodness in society. Society's praise can be cheaply secured, and almost all men are content with those easy merits; but the instant effect of conversing with God will be to put them away. There are persons who are not actors, not speakers, but influences; persons too great for fame, for display; who disdain eloquence; to whom all we call art and artist, seems too nearly allied to show and by-ends, to the exaggeration of the finite and selfish, and loss of the universal. The orators, the poets, the commanders encroach on us only as fair women do, by our allowance and homage. Slight them by preoccupation of mind, slight them, as you can well afford to do, by high and universal aims, and they instantly feel that you have right, and that it is in lower places that they must shine. They also feel your right; for they with you are open to the influx of the all-knowing Spirit, which annihilates before its broad noon the little shades and gradations of intelligence in the compositions we call wiser and wisest.

In such high communion let us study the grand strokes of rectitude: a bold benevolence, an independence of friends, so that not the unjust wishes of those who love us shall impair our freedom, but we shall resist for truth's sake the freest flow of kindness, and appeal to sympathies far in advance; and—what is the highest form in which we know this beautiful element,—a certain solidity of merit, that has nothing to do with opinion, and which is so essentially and manifestly virtue, that it is taken for granted that the right, the brave, the generous step will be taken by it, and nobody thinks of commending it. You would compliment a coxcomb doing a good act, but you would not praise an angel. The silence that accepts merit as the most natural thing in the world, is the highest applause. Such souls, when they appear, are the Imperial Guard of Virtue, the perpetual reserve, the dictators of fortune. One needs not praise their courage, —they are the heart and soul of nature. O my friends, there are resources in us on which we have not drawn. There are men who rise refreshed on hearing a threat; men to whom a crisis which intimidates and paralyzes the majority,—demanding not the faculties of prudence and thrift, but comprehension, immovableness, the readiness of sacrifice,—comes graceful and beloved as a bride. Napoleon said of Massena, that he was not himself until the battle began to go against him; then, when the dead began to fall in ranks around him, awoke his powers of combination, and he put on terror and victory as a robe. So it is in rugged crises, in unweariable endurance, and in aims which put sympathy out of the question, that the angel is shown. But these are heights that we can scarce remember and look up to without contrition and shame. Let us thank God that such things exist.

And now let us do what we can to rekindle the smouldering, nigh quenched fire on the altar. The evils of the church that now is are manifest. The question returns, What shall we do? I confess, all attempts to project and establish a Cultus with new rites and forms, seem to me vain. Faith makes us, and not we it, and faith makes its own forms. All attempts to contrive a system are as cold as the new worship introduced by the French to the goddess of Reason,—today, pasteboard and filigree, and ending tomorrow in madness and murder. Rather let the breath of new life be breathed by you through the forms already existing. For if once you are alive, you shall find they shall become plastic and new. The remedy to their deformity is first, soul, and second, soul, and evermore, soul. A whole popedom of forms one pulsation of virtue can uplift and vivify. Two inestimable advantages Christianity has given us; first the Sabbath, the jubilee of the whole world, whose light dawns welcome alike into the closet of the philosopher, into the garret of toil, and into prison-cells, and everywhere suggests, even to the vile, the dignity of spiritual being. Let it stand forevermore, a temple, which new love, new faith, new sight shall restore to more than its first splendor to mankind. And secondly, the institution of preaching,—the speech of man to men,—essentially the most flexible of all organs, of all forms. What hinders that now, everywhere, in pulpits, in lecture-rooms, in houses, in fields, wherever the invitation of men or your own occasions lead you, you speak the very truth, as your life and conscience teach it, and cheer the waiting, fainting hearts of men with new hope and new revelation?

I look for the hour when that supreme Beauty which ravished the souls of those Eastern men, and chiefly of those Hebrews, and through their lips spoke oracles to all time, shall speak in the West also. The Hebrew and Greek Scriptures contain immortal sentences, that have been bread of life to millions. But they have no epical integrity; are fragmentary; are not shown in their order to the intellect. I look for the new Teacher that shall follow so far those shining laws that he shall see them come full circle; shall see their rounding complete grace; shall see the world to be the mirror of the soul; shall see the identity of the law of gravitation with purity of heart; and shall show that the Ought, that Duty, is one thing with Science, with Beauty, and with Joy.   1838

HORACE BUSHNELL

1802–1876

NO AMERICAN religious leader of the mid-nineteenth century was more significant than Horace Bushnell. Graduating from Yale College, he tried his hand at journalism, legal studies, and teaching. In 1831 a profound religious experience led him to the Yale Divinity School. As a Congregationalist minister at Hartford, Bushnell continued his speculation on religious and ethical subjects and published a series of theological writings. Bushnell's theological contributions involved new methods of thinking and expression. Revolting much as Coleridge and Schleiermacher did against rigid rationalism and precise theological dialectic, Bushnell, with the intuitions of a mystic and a poet, reinterpreted orthodox dogmas in terms of life and experience. He re-expressed the doctrines of the Trinity, of the Cross, and of miracles in such a way as to permit adjustments between faith and the advance of naturalistic thought to be effectively made.

Bushnell also reshaped the philosophy and the program of the religious education of the young. The following selection from *Christian Nurture* (1847) illustrates his thesis that "the child is to grow up a Christian, and never know himself as being otherwise." The significance of this conception of a gradual development of Christian principles can be appreciated only by contrasting it with the Calvinistic tendency to emphasize revivalistic techniques as means of conversion.

Barbara M. Cross, *Horace Bushnell: Minister to a Changing America*, Chicago, 1958.
T. T. Munger, *Horace Bushnell, Preacher and Theologian*, Boston and New York, 1899.
H. R. Heininger, *The Theological Technique of a Mediating Theologian—Horace Bushnell*, Chicago, 1935.

» » *From:* CHRISTIAN NURTURE « «

CHAPTER I

WHAT CHRISTIAN NURTURE IS

"Bring them up in the nurture and admonition of the Lord."
—*Ephesians*, vi. 4

There is then some kind of nurture which is of the Lord, deriving a quality and a power from Him, and communicating the same. Being instituted by Him, it will of necessity have a method and a character peculiar to itself, or rather to Him. It will be the Lord's way of education, having aims appropriate to Him, and, if realized in its full intent, terminating in results impossible to be reached by any merely human method.

What then is the true idea of Christian or divine nurture, as distinguished from that which is not Christian? What is its aim? What its method of working? What its powers and instruments? What its contemplated results?

Few questions have greater moment; and it is one of the pleasantest signs of the times, that the subject involved is beginning to attract new interest, and excite a spirit of inquiry which heretofore has not prevailed in our churches.

In ordinary cases, the better and more instructive way of handling this subject, would be to go directly into the practical methods of parental discipline, and show by what modes of government and instruction we may hope to realize the best results. But unhappily the public mind is preoccupied extensively by a view of the whole subject, which I must regard as a theoretical mistake, and one which will involve, as long as it continues, practical results systematically injurious. This mistaken view it is necessary, if possible, to remove. And accordingly what I have to say will take the form of an argument on the question thus put in issue; though I design to gather round the subject, as I proceed, as much of practical instruction as the mode of the argument will suffer. Assuming then the question above stated, What is the true idea of Christian education?—I answer in the following proposition, which it will be the aim of my argument to establish, viz:

That the child is to grow up a Christian, and never know himself as being otherwise.

In other words, the aim, effort, and expectation should be, not, as is commonly assumed, that the child is to grow up in sin, to be converted after he comes to a mature age; but that he is to open on the world as one that is spiritually renewed, not remembering the time when he went through a technical experience, but seeming rather to have loved what is good from his earliest years. I do not affirm that every child may, in fact and without exception, be so trained that he certainly will grow up a Christian. The qualifications it may be necessary to add will be given in another place, where they can be stated more intelligibly.

This doctrine is not a novelty, now rashly and for the first time propounded, as some of you may be tempted to suppose. I shall show you, before I have done with the argument, that it is as old as the Christian church, and prevails extensively at the present day in other parts of the world. Neither let your own experience raise a prejudice against it. If you have endeavored to realize the very truth I here affirm, but find that your children do not exhibit the character you have looked for; if they seem to be intractable to religious influences, and sometimes to display an apparent aversion to the very subject of religion itself, you are not of course to conclude that the doctrine I here maintain is untrue or impracticable. You may be unreasonable in your expectations of your children.

Possibly, there may be seeds of holy principle in them, which you do not discover. A child acts out his present feelings, the feelings of the moment, without qualification or disguise. And how, many times, would all you appear, if you were to do the same? Will you expect them to be better, and more constant and consistent, than yourselves; or will you rather expect them to be children, human children still, living a mixed life, trying out the good and the evil of the world, and preparing, as older Christians do, when they have taken a lesson of sorrow and emptiness, to turn again to the true good?

Perhaps they will go through a rough mental struggle, at some future day, and seem, to others and to themselves, there to have entered on a Christian life. And yet it may be true that there was still some root of right principle established in their childhood, which is here only quickened and developed, as when Christians of a mature age are revived in their piety, after a period of spiritual lethargy; for it is conceivable that regenerate character may exist, long before it is fully and formally developed.

But suppose there is really no trace or seed of holy principle in your children, has there been no fault of piety and constancy in your church? no want of Christian sensibility and love to God? no carnal spirit visible to them and to all, and imparting its noxious and poisonous quality to the Christian atmosphere in which they have had their nurture? For it is not for you alone to realize all that is included in the idea of Christian education. It belongs to the church of God, according to the degree of its social power over you and in you and around your children, to bear a part of the responsibility with you.

Then, again, have you nothing to blame in yourselves? no lack of faithfulness? no indiscretion of manner or of temper? no mistake of duty, which, with a better and more cultivated piety, you would have been able to avoid? Have you been so nearly even with your privilege and duty, that you can find no relief but to lay some charge upon God, or comfort yourselves in the conviction that he has appointed the failure you deplore? When God marks out a plan of education, or sets up an aim to direct its efforts, you will see, at once, that he could not base it on a want of piety in you, or on any imperfections that flow from a want of piety. It must be a plan measured by Himself and the fullness of his own gracious intentions.

Besides, you must not assume that we, in this age are the best Christians that have ever lived, or most likely to produce all the fruits of piety. An assumption so pleasing to our vanity is more easily made than verified, but vanity is the weakest as it is the cheapest of all arguments. We have some good points, in which we compare favorably with other Christians, and Christians of other times, but our style of piety is sadly deficient, in many respects, and that to such a degree that we have little cause for self-congratulation. With all our activity and boldness of movement, there is a certain hardness and rudeness, a want of sensibility to things that do not lie in action, which can not be too much deplored, or too soon rectified. We hold a piety of conquest rather than of love,—a kind of public piety, that is strenuous and fiery on great occasions, but wants the beauty of holiness, wants constancy, singleness of aim, lovliness, purity, richness, blamelessness, and,—if I may add another term not so immediately religious, but one that carries, by association, a thousand religious qualities—wants domesticity of character; wants them, I mean, not as compared with the perfect standard of Christ, but as compared with other examples of piety that have been given in former times, and others that are given now.

For some reason, we do not make a Christian atmosphere about us—do not produce the conviction that we are living unto God. There is a marvellous want of savor in our piety. It is a flower of autumn, colored as highly as it need be to the eye, but destitute of fragrance. It is too much to hope that, with such an instrument, we can fulfil the true idea of Christian education. Any such hope were even presumptuous. At the same time, there is no so ready way of removing the deficiencies just described, as to recall our churches to their duties in domestic life; those humble, daily, hourly duties, where the spirit we breathe shall be a perpetual element of power and love, bathing the life of childhood.

Thus much it was necessary to say, for the removal of prejudices that are likely to rise up in your minds, and make you inaccessible to the arguments I may offer. Let all such prejudices be removed, or, if this be too much, let them, at least, be suspended till you have heard what I have to advance; for it can not be desired of you to believe any thing more than what is shown you by adequate proofs. Which also it is right to ask that you will receive, in a spirit of conviction, such as becomes our wretched and low attainments, and with a willingness to let God be exalted, though at the expense of some abasement in ourselves. In pursuing the argument, I shall—

I. Collect some considerations which occur to us, viewing the subject on the human side, and then—

II. Show how far and by what methods God has justified, on his part, the doctrine we maintain.

There is then, as the subject appears to us—

1. No absurdity in supposing that children are to grow up in Christ. On the other hand, if there is no absurdity, there is a very clear moral incongruity in setting up a contrary supposition, to be the aim of a system of Christian education. There could not be a worse or more baleful implication given to a child, than that he is to reject God and all holy principle, till he has come to a mature age. What authority have you from the Scriptures to tell your child, or, by any sign, to show him, that you do not expect him truly to love and obey God, till after he has spent whole years in hatred and wrong? What authority to make him feel that he is the most unprivileged of all human beings, capable of sin, but incapable of repentance; old enough to resist all good, but too young to receive any good whatever? It is reasonable to suppose that you have some express authority for a lesson so manifestly cruel and hurtful, else you would shudder to give it. I ask you for the chapter and verse, out of which it is derived. Meantime, wherein would it be less incongruous for you to teach your child that he is to lie and steal, and go the whole round of the vices, and then, after he comes to mature age, reform his conduct by the rules of virtue? Perhaps you do not give your child to expect that he is to grow up in sin; you only expect that he will yourself. That is scarcely better: for that which is your expectation, will assuredly be his; and what is more, any attempt to maintain a discipline at war with your own secret expectations, will only make a hollow and worthless figment of that which should be an open, earnest reality. You will never practically aim at what you practically despair of, and if you do not practically aim to unite your child to God, you will aim at something less; that is, something unchristian, wrong, sinful.

But my child is a sinner, you will say; and how can I expect him to begin a right life, until God gives him a new heart? This is the common way of speaking, and I state the objection in its own phraseology, that it may recognize itself. Who then has told you that a child can not have the new heart of which you speak? Whence do you learn that if you live the life of Christ, before him and with him, the law of the Spirit of Life may not be such as to include and quicken him also? And why should it be thought incredible that there should be some really good principle awakened in the mind of a child? For this is all that is implied in a Christian state. The Christian is one who has simply *begun* to love what is good for its own sake, and why should it be thought impossible for a child to have this love begotten in him? Take any scheme of depravity you please, there is yet nothing in it to forbid the possibility that a child should be led, in his first moral act, to cleave unto what is good and right, any more than in the first of his twentieth year. He is, in that case, only a child converted to good, leading a mixed life as all Christians do. The good in him goes into combat with the evil, and holds a qualified sovereignty. And why may not this internal conflict of goodness cover the whole life from its dawn, as well as any part of it? And what more appropriate to the doctrine of spiritual influence itself, than to believe that as the Spirit of Jehovah fills all the worlds of matter, and holds a presence of power and government in all objects, so all human souls, the infantile as well as the adult, have a nurture of the Spirit appropriate to their age and their wants? What opinion is more essentially monstrous, in fact, than that which regards the Holy Spirit as having no agency in the immature souls of children who are growing up, helpless and unconscious, into the perils of time?

2. It is to be expected that Christian education will radically differ from that which is not Christian. Now, it is the very character and mark of all unchristian education, that it brings up the child for future conversion. No effort is made, save to form a habit of outward virtue, and, if God please to convert the family to something higher and better, after they come to the age of maturity, it is well. Is then Christian education, or the nurture of the Lord, no way different from this? Or is it rather to be supposed that it will have a higher aim and a more sacred character?

And, since it is the distinction of Christian parents, that they are themselves in the nurture of the Lord, since Christ and the Divine Love, communicated through him, are become the food of their life, what will they so naturally seek as to have their children partakers with them, heirs together with them, in the grace of life? I am well aware of the common impression that Christian education is sufficiently distinguished by the endeavor of Christian parents to teach their children the lessons of Scripture history, and the doctrines or dogmas of Scripture theology. But if they are given to understand, at the same time, that these lessons can be expected to produce no fruit till they are come to a mature age—that they are to

grow up still in the same character as other children do, who have no such instruction—what is this but to enforce the practical rejection of all the lessons taught them? And which, in truth, is better for them, to grow up in sin under Scripture light, with a heart hardened by so many religious lessons; or to grow up in sin, unvexed and unannoyed by the wearisome drill of lectures that only discourage all practical benefit? Which is better, to be piously brought up in sin, or to be allowed quietly to vegetate in it?

These are questions that I know not how to decide; but the doubt in which they leave us will at least suffice to show that Christian education has, in this view, no such eminent advantages over that which is unchristian, as to raise any broad and dignified distinction between them. We certainly know that much of what is called Christian nurture, only serves to make the subject of religion odious, and that, as nearly as we can discover, in exact proportion to the amount of religious teaching received. And no small share of the difficulty to be overcome afterwards, in the struggle of conversion, is created in just this way.

On the other hand, you will hear, for example, of cases like the following: A young man, correctly but not religiously brought up, light and gay in his manners, and thoughtless hitherto in regard to any thing of a serious nature, happens accidently one Sunday while his friends are gone to ride, to take down a book on the evidences of Christianity. His eye, floating over one of the pages, becomes fixed, and he is surprised to find his feelings flowing out strangely into its holy truths. He is conscious of no struggle of hostility, but a new joy dawns in his being. Henceforth, to the end of a long and useful life, he is a Christian man. The love into which he was surprised continues to flow, and he is remarkable, in the churches, all his life long, as one of the most beautiful, healthful, and dignified examples of Christian piety. Now, a very little miseducation, called Christian, discouraging the piety it teaches, and making enmity itself a necessary ingredient in the struggle of conversion, conversion no reality without a struggle, might have sufficed to close the mind of this man against every thought of religion to the end of life.

Such facts (for the case above given is a fact and not a fancy) compel us to suspect the value of much that is called Christian education. They suggest the possibility also that Christian piety should begin in other and milder forms of exercise, than those which commonly distinguish the conversion of adults; that Christ himself, by that renewing Spirit who can sanctify from the womb, should be practically infused into the childish mind; in other words, that the house, having a domestic Spirit of grace dwelling in it, should become the church of childhood, the table and hearth a holy rite, and life an element of saving power. Something is wanted that is better than teaching, something that transcends mere effort and will-work—the loveliness of a good life, the repose of faith, the confidence of righteous expectation, the sacred and cheerful liberty of the Spirit—all glowing about the young soul, as a warm and genial nurture, and forming in it, by methods that are silent and imperceptible, a spirit of duty and religious obedience to God. This only is Christian nurture, the nurture of the Lord.

3. It is a fact that all Christian parents would like to see their children grow up in piety; and the better Christians they are, the more earnestly they desire it and, the more lovely and constant the Christian spirit they manifest, the more likely it is, in general, that their children will early display the Christian character. This is current opinion. But why should a Christian parent, the deeper his piety and the more closely he is drawn to God, be led to desire, the more earnestly, what, in God's view, is even absurd or impossible? And, if it be generally seen that the children of such are more likely to become Christians early, what forbids the hope that, if they were riper still in their piety, living a more single and Christ-like life, and more cultivated in their views of family nurture, they might see their children grow up always in piety towards God? Or, if they may not always see it as clearly as they desire, might they not still be able to implant some holy principle, which shall be the seed of a Christian character in their children, though not developed fully and visibly till a later period in life?

4. Assuming the corruption of human nature, when should we think it wisest to undertake or expect a remedy? When evil is young and pliant to good, or when it is confirmed by years of sinful habit? And when, in fact, is the human heart found to be so ductile to the motives of religion, as in the simple, ingenuous age of childhood? How easy is it then, as compared with the stubbornness of adult years, to make all wrong seem odious, all good lovely and desirable. If not discouraged by some ill-temper

which bruises all the gentle sensibilities, or repelled by some technical view of religious character which puts it beyond his age, how ready is the child to be taken by good, as it were beforehand, and yield his ductile nature to the truth and Spirit of God, and to a fixed prejudice against all that God forbids.

He can not understand, of course, in the earliest stage of childhood, the philosophy of religion as a renovated experience, and that is not the form of the first lessons he is to receive. He is not to be told that he must have a new heart and exercise faith in Christ's atonement. We are to understand, that a right spirit may be virtually exercised in children, when, as yet, it is not intellectually received, or as a form of doctrine. Thus, if they are put upon an effort to be good, connecting the fact that God desires it and will help them in the endeavor, that is all which, in a very early age, they can receive, and that includes every thing—repentance, love, duty, dependence, faith. Nay, the operative truth necessary to a new life, may possibly be communicated through and from the parent, being revealed in his looks, manners, and ways of life, before they are of an age to understand the teaching of words; for the Christian scheme, the gospel, is really wrapped up in the life of every Christian parent, and beams out from him as a living epistle, before it escapes from the lips, or is taught in words. And the Spirit of truth may as well make this living truth effectual, as the preaching of the gospel itself.

Never is it too early for good to be communicated. Infancy and childhood are the ages most pliant to good. And who can think it necessary that the plastic nature of childhood must first be hardened into stone, and stiffened into enmity towards God and all duty, before it can become a candidate for Christian character! There could not be a more unnecessary mistake, and it is as unnatural and pernicious, I fear, as it is unnecessary.

There are many who assume the radical goodness of human nature, and the work of Christian education is, in their view, only to educate or educe the good that is in us. Let no one be disturbed by the suspicion of a coincidence between what I have here said and such a theory. The natural pravity of man is plainly asserted in the Scriptures, and, if it were not, the familiar laws of physiology would require us to believe, what amounts to the same thing. And if neither Scripture nor physiology taught us the doctrine, if the child was born as clear of natural prejudice or damage, as Adam before his sin, spiritual education, or, what is the same, probation, that which trains a being for a stable, intelligent virtue hereafter, would still involve an experiment of evil, therefore a fall and bondage under the laws of evil; so that, view the matter as we will, there is no so unreasonable assumption, none so wide of all just philosophy, as that which proposes to form a child to virtue, by simply educing or drawing out what is in him.

The growth of Christian virtue is no vegetable process, no mere onward development. It involves a struggle with evil, a fall and a rescue. The soul becomes established in holy virtue, as a free exercise, only as it is passed round the corner of fall and redemption, ascending thus unto God through a double experience, in which it learns the bitterness of evil and the worth of good, fighting its way out of one, and achieving the other as a victory. The child, therefore, may as well begin life under a law of hereditary damage, as to plunge himself into evil by his own experiment, which he will as naturally do from the simple impulse of curiosity, or the instinct of knowledge, as from any noxious quality in his mold derived by descent. For it is not sin which he derives from his parents; at least, not sin in any sense which imports blame, but only some prejudice to the perfect harmony of this mold, some kind of pravity or obliquity which inclines him to evil. These suggestions are offered, not as necessary to be received in every particular, but simply to show that the scheme of education proposed, is not to be identified with another, which assumes the radical goodness of human nature, and according to which, if it be true, Christian education is insignificant.

5. It is implied in all our religious philosophy, that if a child ever does any thing in a right spirit, ever loves any thing because it is good and right, it involves the dawn of a new life. This we can not deny or doubt without bringing in question our whole scheme of doctrine. Is it then incredible that some really good feeling should be called into exercise in a child? In all the discipline of the house, quickened as it should be by the Spirit of God, is it true that he can never once be brought to submit to parental authority lovingly and because it is right? Must we even hold the absurdity of the scripture counsel—"Children obey your parents in the Lord, for this is right?" When we speak thus of a love for what is right and good, we must of course discriminate between the mere excitement of a natural sensibility to pleasure in the contemplation of what is good (of which the worst minds are more or less capable,) and a practicable subordination of the soul to its power, a practicable embrace of its law. The child must not only be touched with some gentle emotions toward what is right, but he must love it with a fixed love, love it for the sake of its principle, receive it as a vital and formative power.

Nor is there any age, which offers itself to God's truth and love, and to that Quickening Spirit whence all good proceeds, with so much of ductile feeling and susceptibilities so tender. The child is under parental authority too for the very purpose, it would seem, of having the otherwise abstract principle of all duty impersonated in his parents, and thus brought home to his practical embrace; so that, learning to obey his parents in the Lord, because it is right, he may thus receive, before he can receive it intellectually, the principle of all piety and holy obedience. And when he is brought to exercise a spirit of true and loving submission to the good law of his parents, what will you see, many times, but a look of childish joy, and a happy sweetness of manner, and a ready delight in authority, as like to all the demonstrations of Christian experience, as any thing childish can be to what is mature?

6. Children have been so trained as never to remember the time when they began to be religious. Baxter was, at one time, greatly troubled concerning himself, because he could recollect no time when there was a gracious change in his character. But he discovered, at length, that "education is as properly a means of grace as preaching," and thus found the sweeter comfort in his love to God, that he learned to love him so early. The European churches, generally, regard Christian piety more as a habit of life, formed under the training of childhood, and less as a marked spiritual change in experience. In Germany, for example, the church includes all the people, and it is remarkable that, under a scheme so loose, and with so much of pernicious error taught in the pulpit, there is yet so much of deep religious feeling, so much of lovely and simple character, and a savor of Christian piety so generally prevalent in the community. So true is this, that the German people are every day spoken of as a people religious by nature; no other way be-

ing observed of accounting for the strong religious bent they manifest. Whereas it is due,
beyond any reasonable question, to the fact
that children are placed under a form of treatment which expects them to be religious, and
are not discouraged by the demand of an experience above their years.

Again, the Moravian Brethren, it is agreed
by all, give as ripe and graceful an exhibition
of piety, as any body of Christians living on
the earth, and it is the radical distinction of
their system that it rests its power on Christian
education. They make their churches schools of
holy nurture to childhood, and expect their
children to grow up there, as plants in the
house of the Lord. Accordingly it is affirmed
that not one in ten of the members of that
church, recollects any time when he began to
be religious. Is it then incredible that what has
been can be? Would it not be wiser and more
modest, when facts are against us, to admit
that there is certainly some bad error, either in
our life, or in our doctrine, or in both, which it
becomes us to amend?

Once more, if we narrowly examine the relation of parent and child, we shall not fail to
discover something like a law of organic connection, as regards character, subsisting between them. Such a connection as makes it
easy to believe, and natural to expect, that the
faith of the one will be propagated in the
other. Perhaps I should rather say, such a connection as induces the conviction that the character of one is actually included in that of the
other, as a seed is formed in the capsule; and
being there matured, by a nutriment derived
from the stem, is gradually separated from it.
It is a singular fact, that many believe substantially the same thing in regard to evil character,
but have no thought of any such possibility in
regard to good. There has been much speculation, of late, as to whether a child is born in
depravity, or whether the depraved character
is superinduced afterwards. But, like many
other great questions, it determines much less
than is commonly supposed; for, according to
the most proper view of the subject, a child is
really not born till he emerges from the infantile
state, and never before that time can he be said
to receive a separate and properly individual
nature.

The declarations of Scripture, and the laws
of physiology, I have already intimated, compel the belief that a child's nature is somehow
depravated by descent from parents, who are

under the corrupting effects of sin. But this,
taken as a question relating to the mere *punc-
tum temporis,* or precise point of birth, is not a
question of any so grave import as is generally
supposed; for the child, after birth, is still
within the matrix of the parental life, and will
be, more or less, for many years. And the parental life will be flowing into him all that time,
just as naturally, and by a law as truly organic,
as when the sap of the trunk flows into a limb. 10
We must not govern our thoughts, in such a
matter, by our eyes; and because the physical
separation has taken place, conclude that no
organic relation remains. Even the physical being of the child is dependent still for many
months, in the matter of nutrition, on organic
processes not in itself. Meantime, the mental
being and character have scarcely begun to
have a proper individual life. Will, in connection with conscience, is the basis of personality, 20
or individuality, and these exist as yet only in
their rudimental type, as when the form of a
seed is beginning to be unfolded at the root of
a flower.

At first, the child is held as a mere passive
lump in the arms, and he opens into conscious
life, under the soul of the parent streaming into
his eyes and ears, through the manners and
tones of the nursery. The kind and degree of
passivity are gradually changed as life ad- 30
vances. A little farther on it is observed that a
smile wakens a smile; any kind of sentiment or
passion, playing in the face of the parent, wakens a responsive sentiment or passion. Irritation
irritates, a frown withers, love expands a look
congenial to itself, and why not holy love?
Next the ear is open to the understanding of
words, but what words the child shall hear, he
can not choose, and has as little capacity to
select the sentiments that are poured into his 40
soul. Farther on, the parents begin to govern
him by appeals to will, expressed in commands,
and whatever their requirement may be, he can
as little withstand it, as the violet can cool the
scorching sun, or the tattered leaf can tame the
hurricane. Next they appoint his school, choose
his books, regulate his company, decide what
form of religion, and what religious opinions he
shall be taught, by taking him to a church of
their own selection. In all this, they infringe 50
upon no right of the child, they only fulfill an
office which belongs to them. Their will and
character are designed to be the matrix of the
child's will and character. Meantime, he approaches more and more closely, and by a grad-

ual process, to the proper rank and responsibility of an individual creature, during all which process of separation, he is having their exercises and ways translated into him. Then, at last, he comes forth to act his part in such color of evil, and why not of good, as he has derived from them.

The tendency of all our modern speculations is to an extreme individualism, and we carry our doctrines of free will so far as to make little or nothing of organic laws; not observing that character may be, to a great extent, only the free development of exercises previously wrought in us, or extended to us, when other wills had us within their sphere. All the Baptist theories of religion are based in this error. They assume, as a first truth, that no such thing is possible as an organic connection of character, an assumption which is plainly refuted by what we see with our eyes, and, as I shall by and by show, by the declarations of Scripture. We have much to say also, in common with the Baptists, about the beginning of moral agency, and we seem to fancy that there is some definite moment when a child becomes a moral agent, passing out of a condition where he is a moral nullity, and where no moral agency touches his being. Whereas he is rather to be regarded, at the first, as lying within the moral agency of the parent, and passing out, by degrees, through a course of mixed agency, to a proper independency and self possession. The supposition that he becomes, at some certain moment, a complete moral agent, which a moment before he was not, is clumsy, and has no agreement with observation. The separation is gradual. He is never, at any moment after birth, to be regarded as perfectly beyond the sphere of good and bad exercises; for the parent exercises himself in the child, playing his emotions and sentiments, and working a character in him, by virtue of an organic power.

And this is the very idea of Christian education, that it begins with nurture or cultivation. And the intention is that the Christian life and spirit of the parents, which are in and by the Spirit of God, shall flow into the mind of the child, to blend with his incipient and half-formed exercises; that they shall thus beget their own good within him—their thoughts, opinions, faith and love, which are to become a little more, and yet a little more, his own separate exercise, but still the same in character. The contrary assumption, that virtue must be the product of separate and absolutely independent choice, is pure assumption. As regards the measure of personal merit and demerit, it is doubtless true that every subject of God is to be responsible only for what is his own. But virtue still is rather a *state* of being than an act or series of acts; and, if we look at the causes which induce or prepare such a state, the will of the person himself may have a part among these causes more or less important, and it works no absurdity to suppose that one may be even prepared to such a state, by causes prior to his own will; so that, when he sets off to act for himself, his struggle and duty may be rather to sustain and perfect the state begun, than to produce a new one. Certain it is that we are never, at any age, so independent as to be wholly out of the reach of organic laws which affect our character.

All society is organic—the church, the state, the school, the family; and there is a spirit in each of these organisms, peculiar to itself, and more or less hostile, more or less favorable to religious character, and to some extent, at least, sovereign over the individual man. A very great share of the power in what is called a revival of religion, is organic power; nor is it any the less divine on that account. The child is only more within the power of organic laws than we all are. We possess only a mixed individuality all our life long. A pure, separate, individual man, living *wholly* within, and from himself, is a mere fiction. No such person ever existed, or ever can. I need not say that this view of an organic connection of character subsisting between parent and child, lays a basis for notions of Christian education, far different from those which now prevail, under the cover of a merely fictitious and mischievous individualism.

Perhaps it may be necessary to add, that, in the strong language I have used concerning the organic connection of character between the parent and the child, it is not designed to assert a power in the parent to renew the child, or that the child can be renewed by any agency of the Spirit less immediate, than that which renews the parent himself. When a germ is formed on the stem of any plant, the formative instinct of the plant may be said in one view to produce it; but the same solar heat which quickens the plant, must quicken also the germ and sustain the internal action of growth, by a common presence in both. So, if there be an organic power of character in the parent, such as that of which I have spoken, it is not a complete power in itself, but only such a power as demands the realizing presence of the Spirit of God, both in the parent and the child, to give it effect. As Paul said, "I have begotten you through the gospel," so may we say of the parent, who, having a living gospel enveloped in his life, brings it into organic connection with the soul of childhood. But the declaration excludes the necessity of a divine influence, not more in one case than in the other.

Such are some of the considerations that offer themselves, viewing our subject on the human side, or as it appears in the light of human evidence—all concurring to produce the conviction, that it is the only true idea of Christian education, that the child is to grow up in the life of the parent, and be a Christian in principle, from his earliest years.   1847

ORESTES A. BROWNSON

1803–1876

THE EARLY LIFE of Brownson, a Vermont farmboy, was characterized by a series of religious crises which resulted in his transfer of allegiance from the Presbyterian to the Universalist faiths, and from virtual agnosticism to Unitarianism. Sympathetic with the common man, Brownson helped organize the Workingman's Party and associated himself with the utopian socialist schemes of Frances Wright and Robert Dale Owen. To the *Boston Quarterly Review*, which he himself edited, he contributed many essays on social and political problems. The two papers on *The Labouring Class* postulated the doctrine of class struggle.

Although closely identified with New England's liberals and radicals, Brownson's hostility to the doctrine of unqualified popular sovereignty and his acceptance of the mediational power of Jesus led to a break with liberalism and to conversion, in 1844, to Roman Catholicism. His polemical writings in defense of his new position were no less trenchant and partisan than his earlier writings. His writings include *The American Republic; Constitution, Tendencies and Destiny* (1865), *The Convert; or, Leaves from My Experience* (1857), and a vast number of political and religious essays.

The Works of Orestes A. Brownson, H. F. Brownson, ed., 20 vols., Detroit, 1882–1887.
A. M. Schlesinger, Jr., *Orestes A. Brownson; A Pilgrim's Progress*, Boston, 1939.
Theodore Maynard, *Orestes Brownson, Yankee, Radical, Catholic*, New York, 1943.

» » From: THE CONVERT « «
Or, Leaves from My Experience

I have now completed the sketch I proposed to give of my intellectual struggles, failures, and successes, from my earliest childhood till my reception by the Bishop of Boston into the communion of the Catholic Church. I have not written to vindicate my ante-Catholic life, or to apologize for my conversion. I have aimed to record facts, principles and reasonings, trials and struggles, which have a value independent of the fact that they relate to my personal history. Yet even as the personal history of an earnest soul, working its way, under the grace of God, from darkness to light, from the lowest abyss of unbelief to a firm, unwavering, and not a blind faith in the old religion, so generally rejected and decried by my countrymen, I think my story not wholly worthless, or altogether uninstructive,—especially when taken in connection with the glimpses it incidentally affords of American thought and life during the greater portion of the earlier half of the present century. Whether what I have written proves me to have been intellectually weak, vacillating, constantly changing, all things by turns, and nothing long, or tolerably firm, consistent, and persevering in my search after truth; whether it shows that my seeking admission into the church for the reasons, and in the way and manner I did, was a sudden caprice, an act of folly, perhaps of despair, or that it was an act of deliberation, wise, judicious, and for a sufficient reason, my readers are free to judge for themselves.

This much only will I add, that, whether I am believed or not, I can say truly that, during the nearly thirteen years of Catholic experience, I have found not the slightest reason to regret the step I took. I have had much to try me, and enough to shake me, if shaken I could be, but I have not had even the slightest temptation to doubt, or the slightest inclination to undo what I had done; and have every day found new and stronger reasons to thank Almighty God for his great mercy in bringing me to the knowledge of his church, and permitting me to enter and live in her communion. I know all that can be said in disparagement of Catholics. I am well versed, perhaps no man more so, in Catholic scandals, but I have not been deceived; I have found all that was promised me, all I looked for. I have found the church all that her ministers represented her, all my imagination painted her, and infinitely more than I had conceived it possible for her to be. My experience as a Catholic, so far as the church, her doctrines, her morals, her discipline, her influences are concerned, has been a continued succession of agreeable surprises.

I do not pretend that I have found the Catholic population perfect, or that I have found in them or in myself no shortcomings, nothing to be censured or regretted; yet I have found that population superior to what I expected, more intellectual, more cultivated, more moral, more active, living, and energetic. Undoubtedly, our Catholic population, made up in great part of the humbler classes of the Catholic populations of the Old World, for three hundred years subjected to the bigotry, intolerance, persecutions, and oppressions of Protestant or *quasi*-Protestant governments, have traits of character, habits, and manners, which the outside non-Catholic American finds unattractive, and even repulsive. Certainly in our cities and large towns may be found, I am sorry to say, a comparatively numerous population, nominally Catholic, who are no credit to their religion, to the land of their birth, or to that of their adoption. No Catholic will deny that the children of these are to a great extent shamefully neglected, and suffered to grow up without the simplest elementary moral and religious instruction, and to become recruits to our vicious population, our rowdies, and our criminals. This is certainly to be deplored, but can easily be explained without prejudice to the church, by adverting to the condition to which these individuals were reduced before coming here; to their disappointments and discouragements in a strange land; to their exposure to new and unlooked-for temptations; to the fact that they were by no means the best of Catholics even in their native countries; to their poverty, destitution, ignorance, insufficient culture, and a certain natural shiftlessness and recklessness, and to our great lack of schools, churches, and priests. The proportion, too, that these bear to our whole Catholic population is far less than is commonly supposed; and they are not so habitually depraved as they appear, for they seldom or never consult appearances, and have little skill in concealing their vices. As low and degraded as they are, they never are so low or so vicious as the corresponding class of Protestants in Protestant nations. A Protestant vicious class is always worse than it appears, a Catholic vicious population is less bad. In the worst there is always some germ that with proper care may be nursed into life, that may blossom and bear fruit. In our narrow lanes, blind courts, damp cellars, and unventilated garrets, where our people swarm as bees; in the midst of filth and the most squalid wretchedness, the fumes of intemperance and the shouts and imprecations of blasphemy; in what by the outside world would be regarded as the very dens of vice, and crime, and infamy, we often find individuals who, it may well be presumed, have retained their baptismal innocence, real *Fleurs de Marie*, who remain pure and unsullied, and who, in their humble sphere, exhibit brilliant examples of the most heroic Christian virtues.

The majority of our Catholic population is made up of the unlettered peasantry, small mechanics, servant-girls, and common laborers, from various European countries; and however worthy in themselves, or useful to the country to which they have migrated, cannot, in a worldly and social point of view at least, be taken as a fair average of the Catholic population in their native lands. The Catholic nobility, gentry, easy classes, and the better specimens of the professional men, have not migrated with them. Two or three millions of the lower, less prosperous, and less cultivated, and sometimes less virtuous class of the European Catholic populations, have in a comparatively brief period been cast upon our shores, with little or no provision made for their intellectual, moral, or religious wants. Yet, if we look at this population as it is, and is every year becoming, we cannot but be struck with its marvellous energy and progress. The mental activity of Catholics, all things considered, is far more remarkable than that of our non-Catholic countrymen, and, in proportion to their numbers and means, they contribute far more than any other class of American citizens to the purposes of education, both common and liberal; for they receive little or nothing from the public treasury, and, in addition to supporting numerous schools of their own, they contribute their quota to the support of those of the state.

I do not pretend that the Catholic population of this country are a highly literary people, or that they are in any adequate sense an intellectually cultivated people. How could they be, when the great mass of them have had to earn their very means of subsistence, and have had as much as they could do to provide for the first wants of religion, and of themselves and families? Yet there is a respectable Catholic-American literature springing up among us, and Catholics have their representatives among the first scholars and scientific men in the land. In metaphysics, in moral and intellectual philosophy, they take already the lead; in natural history and the physical sciences, they are not far behind; and let once the barrier between them and the non-Catholic public be broken down, and they will soon take the first position in general and polite literature. As yet our own literary public, owing to the causes I have mentioned, I admit is not large enough to give adequate encouragement to authors, and the general public makes it a point not to recognize our literary labors. But this will not last, for it is against the interest and the genius of liberal scholarship, and Catholic authors will soon find a public adequate to their wants. Non-Catholics do themselves great wrong in acting on the principle, No good can come out of Nazareth; for we have already in what we ourselves write, in what we reprint from our brethren in the British Empire, and in what we translate from French, German, Spanish and Italian Catholics, a literature far richer and more important, even under a literary and scientific point of view, than they suspect.

I have known long and well the Protestant clergy of the United States, and I am by no means disposed to underrate their native abilities or their learning and science, and, although I think the present generation of ministers falls far below its predecessor, I esteem highly the contributions they have made and are making to the literature and science of our common country; but our Catholic clergy, below in many respects what for various reasons they should be, can compare more than favorably with them, except those among them whose mother tongue was foreign from ours, in the correct and classical use of the English language. They surpass them as a body in logical training, in theological science, and in the accuracy, and not unfrequently in the variety and extent of their erudition. Indeed, I have found among Catholics a higher tone of thought, morals, manners, and society, than I have ever found, with fair opportunities, among my non-Catholic countrymen; and taking the Catholic population of the country, even as it actually is, under all its disadvantages, there is nothing in it that need make the most cultivated and refined man of letters or of society blush to avow himself a Catholic.

Certainly, I have found cause to complain of Catholics at home and abroad, not indeed as falling below non-Catholic populations, but as falling below their own Catholic standard. I find among them, not indeed as universal, far from it, but as too prevalent, habits of thoughts and modes of action, a lack of manly courage, energy, and directness, which seem to me as unwise as they are offensive to the better class of English and American minds. In matters not of faith, there is less unanimity and less liberality, less courtesy and less forbearance, in regard to allowable differences of opinion, than might be expected. But I have recollected that I am not myself infallible, and may complain where I should not. Many things may seem to me wrong, only because I am not accustomed to them. Something must be set down to peculiarity of national temperament and development; and even what cannot be justified or excused on either ground, can in all cases be traced to causes unconnected with religion. The habits and peculiarities which I find it most difficult to like, are evidently due to the fact that the Catholics of this country have migrated for the most part from foreign Catholic populations, that have either been oppressed by non-Catholic governments directing their policy to crush and extinguish Catholicity, or by political despotisms which sprang up in Europe after the disastrous Protestant revolt in the sixteenth century, and which recognized in the common people no rights, and allowed them no equality with the ruling class. Under the despotic governments of some Catholic countries, and the bigotry and intolerance of Protestant states, they could hardly fail to acquire habits not in accordance with the habits of those who have never been persecuted, and have never been forced, in order to live, to study to evade tyrannical laws or the caprices of despotism. Men who are subjected to tyranny, who have to deal with tyrants, and who feel that power is against them, and that they can never carry their points by main force, naturally study diplomacy, and supply by art what they lack in strength. This art may degenerate into craft. That it occasionally does so with individuals here and elsewhere, it were useless to deny; but the cause is not in the church or any thing she teaches or approves. In fact, many things which Englishmen and Americans complain of in Catholics and the populations of southern Europe, have been inherited from the craft and refinement of the old Graeco-Roman civilization, and transmitted from generation to generation in spite of the church.

As yet our Catholic population, whether foreign-born or native-born, hardly dare feel themselves freemen in this land of freedom. They have so long been an oppressed people, that their freedom here seems hardly real. They have never become reconciled to the old Puritan Commonwealth of England, and they retain with their Catholicity too many reminiscences of the passions and politics of the Bourbons and the Stuarts. They are very generally attached to the republican institutions of the country, no class of our citizens more so, and would defend them at the sacrifice of their lives, but their interior life has not as yet been moulded into entire harmony with them; and they have a tendency, in seeking to follow out American democracy, to run into extreme radicalism, or, when seeking to preserve law and order, to run into extreme conservatism. They do not always hit the exact medium. But this need not surprise us, for no one can hit that medium unless his interior life and habits have been formed to it. Non-Catholic foreigners are less able than Catholic foreigners to do it, if we except the English, who have been trained under a system in many respects analogous to our own; and no small portion of our own countrymen, "to the manner born," make even more fatal mistakes than are made by any portion of our Catholic population,—chiefly, however, because they adopt a European instead of an American interpretation of our political and social order. Other things being equal, Catholic foreigners far more readily adjust themselves to our institutions than any other class of foreigners; and among Catholics, it must be observed that they succeed best who best understand and best practice their religion. They who are least truly American, and yield most to the demagogues, are those who have very little of Catholicity except the accident of being born of Catholic parents, who had them baptized in infancy. These are they who bring reproach on the whole body.

That the struggles in Europe have an influence on Catholic thought in this country is very true, and sometimes an unfavorable influence, cannot be denied. A portion of our foreign-born Catholics, subjected at home to the restraints imposed by despotism, feel on coming here that they are loosed from all restraints, and forgetting the obedience they owe to their pastors, to the prelates whom the Holy Ghost has placed over them, become insubordinate, and live more as Protestants than as Catholics; another portion, deeply alarmed at the revolutionary spirit and the evils that it has produced in the Old World, distrust the independence and personal dignity the American always preserves in the presence of authority, and are half disposed to look upon every American as a rebel at heart, if not an unbeliever. They do not precisely understand the American disposition that bows to the law, but never to persons, and is always careful to distinguish between the man and the office; and they are disposed to look upon it as incompatible with the true principle of obedience demanded by the Gospel. But I think these and their conservative brethren in Europe mistake the real American character. There is not in Christendom a more loyal or a more law-abiding people than the genuine people of the United States.

I think European Catholics of the conservative party have unfounded suspicion of our loyalty, for I think it a higher and truer loyalty than that which they seem to inculcate. I have wholly mistaken the spirit of the church, if an enlightened obedience, an obedience that knows wherefore it obeys, and is yielded from principle, from conviction, from free will, and from a sense of obligation, is not more grateful to her maternal heart than the blind, unreasoning, and cringing submission of those who are strangers to freedom. Servile fear does not rank very high with Catholic theologians; and the church seeks to govern men as freemen, as Almighty God governs them, that is, in accordance with the nature with which he has created them, as beings endowed with reason and free-will. God adapts his government to our rational and voluntary faculties, and governs us without violence to either, and by really satisfying both. The church does the same, and resorts to coercive measures only to repress disorders in the public body. Hence our ecclesiastical rulers are called shepherds, not lords, and shepherds of their Master's flock, not of their own, and are to feed, tend, protect the flock, and take care of its increase for him, with sole reference to his will, and his honor and glory. We must love and reverence them for his sake, for the great trust he has confided to them, not for their own sakes, as if they owned the flock, and governed it in their own name and right, for their own pleasure and profit. This idea of power whether in church or state, as a delegated power or trust, is inseparable from the American mind; and hence the American feels always in its presence his native equality as a man, and asserts, even in the most perfect and entire submission, his own personal independence and dignity, knowing that he bows only to the law or to the will of a common Master. His submission he yields, because he knows that it is due, but without servility or pusillanimity.

But though I entertain these views of what have been for a long time the policy of so-called Catholic governments, and, so to speak, the politics of European Catholics, I find in them nothing that reflects on the truth or efficiency of the church; for she has no responsibility in the matter, since, as I have said, she governs men, discharges her mission with a scrupulous regard to the free-will of individuals and the autonomy of states. She proffers to all every assistance necessary for the attainment of the most heroic sanctity, but she forces no man to accept that assistance. In her view, men owe all they have and are to God, but they are neither slaves nor machines.

In speaking of Catholic nations and comparing them with the Catholic standard, I find, I confess, much to regret, to deplore, and even to blame; but in comparing them with non-Catholic nations, the case is quite different, and I cannot concede that the Catholic population of any country is inferior to any Protestant population, even in those very qualities in respect to which Catholics are usually supposed to be the most deficient. In no Catholic population will you find the flunkyism which Carlyle so unmercifully ridicules in the middling classes of Great Britain; or that respect to mere wealth, that worship of the money-bag, or that base servility to the mob or to public opinion, so common and so ruinous to public and private virtue in the United States. I do not claim any very high merit for our Catholic press; it lacks, with some exceptions, dignity, grasp of thought, and breadth of view, and seems intended for an unlettered community; but it has an earnestness, a sincerity, a freedom, an independence, which will be looked for in vain in our non-Catholic press, whether religious or secular. The Catholic population of this country, too, taken as a body, have a personal freedom, an independence, a self-respect, a conscientiousness, a love of truth, and a devotion to principle, not to be found in any other class of American citizens. Their moral tone, as well as their moral standard, is higher, and they act more uniformly under a sense of deep responsibility to God and to their country. Owing to various circumstances as well as national peculiarities, a certain number of them fall easily under the influence of demagogues; but as a body, they are far less demagogical, and far less under the influence of demagogues than are non-Catholic Americans. He who knows both classes equally well, will not pretend to the contrary. The Catholics of this country, by no means a fair average of the Catholic populations of old Catholic countries, do, as to the great majority, act from honest principle, from sincere and earnest conviction, and are prepared to die sooner than in any grave matters swerve from what they regard as truth and justice. They have the principle and the firmness to stand by what they believe true and just, in good report and evil report, whether the world be with them or against them. They can, also, be convinced by arguments addressed to their reason, and moved by appeals to conscience, to the fear of God, and the love of justice. The non-Catholic has no conception of the treasure the Union possesses in these two or three millions of Catholics, humble in their outward circumstances as the majority of them are. I have never shown any disposition to palliate or disguise their faults; but, knowing them and my non-Catholic countrymen as I do, I am willing to risk the assertion that, with all their faults and shortcomings, they are the salt of the American community, and the really conservative element in the American population.

I have found valid after thirteen years of experience none of those objections to entering the Catholic communion which I enumerated in a previous chapter, and which made me for a time hesitate to follow the convictions of my own understanding. To err is human, and I do not pretend that I have found Catholics in matters of human prudence, in what belongs to them and not to the church, all that I could wish. I have found much I do not like, much I do not believe reasonable or prudent; but it is all easily explained without any reflection on the truth or efficiency of the church, or the general wisdom and prudence of her prelates and clergy. Undoubtedly our Catholic population, made up in great part of emigrants from every nation of Europe with every variety of national temper, character, taste, habit, and usage, not yet moulded, save in religion, into one homogeneous body, may present features more or less repulsive to the American wedded to his own peculiar nationality and but recently converted to the Catholic faith; but the very readiness with which these heterogeneous elements amalgamate, and the rapidity with which the Catholic body assumes a common character, falls into the current of American life, and takes, in all not adverse to religion, the tone and features of the country, proves the force of Catholicity, and its vast importance in forming a true and noble national character, and in generating and sustaining a true, generous, and lofty patriotism. In a few years they will be the Americans of the Americans, and on them will rest the performance of the glorious work of sustaining American civilization, and realizing the hopes of the founders of our great and growing republic.

Such are the views, feelings, convictions, and hopes of the Convert. But he would be unjust to himself and to his religion, if he did not say that, not for these reasons, or any like them, is he a Catholic. He loves this country, loves her institutions, he loves her freedom, but he is a Catholic because he believes the Catholic Church the church of God, because he believes her the medium through which God dispenses his grace to man, and through which alone we can hope for heaven. He is a Catholic, because he would believe, love, possess, and obey the truth; because he would know and do God's will; because he would escape hell and gain heaven. Considerations drawn from this world are of minor importance, for man's home is not here, his bliss is not here, his reward is not here, he is made for God, for endless beatitude with him, hereafter; and, let him turn as he will, his supreme good, as well as duty, lies in seeking "the kingdom of God and his justice." That the church serves the cause of patriotism; that, if embraced, it is sure to give us a high-toned and chivalric national character; that it enlists conscience in the support of our free institutions and the preservation of our republican freedom as the established order of the country, is a good reason why the American people should not oppose her, and why they should wish her growth and prosperity in our country; but the real reason why we should become Catholics and remain such, is, because she is the new creation, regenerated humanity, and without communion with her, we can never see God as he is, or become united to him as our supreme good in the supernatural order.   1857

PETER CARTWRIGHT

1785–1872

AMONG frontier evangelists Peter Cartwright was probably no more important than many others. The son of a Kentucky pioneer, he was converted to Methodism in his sixteenth year. After an initiation as an exhorter he became, in 1803, a circuit rider, operating in Kentucky and Tennessee until 1824 when he removed to Illinois, a state more congenial to his antislavery sentiments. For fifty years Cartwright, or "Uncle Peter," as he was known, made his Methodism "a joyous battlefield against the devil and rival sects." Bigoted, intense, eloquent, and militant, Cartwright enjoyed remarkable success (in spite of his failure, in 1846, to defeat his rival, Abraham Lincoln, for Congress). Anti-intellectual and thoroughly self-confident, Cartwright told his life-story in his *Autobiography* (1857) and in *Fifty Years as a Presiding Elder* (1871). He helped impress on frontier people a faith in an athletic and highly individualistic type of evangelicism.

Autobiography, Introduction by Charles L. Wallis, Nashville, Tenn., 1956.
Sidney Greenbie and Marjorie Barstow, *Hoofbeats to Heaven*, Penobscot, 1955.
W. W. Sweet, *Circuit-Rider Days Along the Ohio*, New York and Cincinnati, 1923.

» » *From:* AUTOBIOGRAPHY OF PETER CARTWRIGHT « «

CHAPTER IV

CONVERSION

In 1801, when I was in my sixteenth year, my father, my eldest half brother, and myself, attended a wedding about five miles from home, where there was a great deal of drinking and dancing, which was very common at marriages in those days. I drank little or nothing; my delight was in dancing. After a late hour in the night, we mounted our horses and started for home. I was riding my race-horse.

A few minutes after we had put up the horses, and were sitting by the fire, I began to reflect on the manner in which I had spent the day and evening. I felt guilty and condemned. I rose and walked the floor. My mother was in bed. It seemed to me, all of a sudden, my blood rushed to my head, my heart palpitated, in a few minutes I turned blind; an awful impression rested on my mind that death had come and I was unprepared to die. I fell on my knees and began to ask God to have mercy on me.

My mother sprang from her bed, and was soon on her knees by my side, praying for me, and exhorting me to look to Christ for mercy, and then and there I promised the Lord that if he would spare me, I would seek and serve him; and I never fully broke that promise. My mother prayed for me a long time. At length we lay down, but there was little sleep for me. Next morning I rose, feeling wretched beyond expression. I tried to read in the Testament, and retired many times to secret prayer through the day, but found no relief. I gave up my race-horse to my father, and requested him to sell him. I went and brought my pack of cards, and gave them to mother, who threw them into the fire, and they were consumed. I fasted, watched, and prayed, and engaged in regular reading of the Testament. I was so distressed and miserable, that I was incapable of any regular business.

My father was greatly distressed on my account, thinking I must die, and he would lose his only son. He bade me retire altogether from business, and take care of myself.

Soon it was noised abroad that I was distracted, and many of my associates in wickedness came to see me, to try and divert my mind

from those gloomy thoughts of my wretchedness; but all in vain. I exhorted them to desist
from the course of wickedness which we had
been guilty of together. The class-leader and
local preacher were sent for. They tried to point
me to the bleeding Lamb, they prayed for me
most fervently. Still I found no comfort, and
although I had never believed in the doctrine
of unconditional election and reprobation, I
was sorely tempted to believe I was a reprobate, and doomed, and lost eternally, without
any chance of salvation.

At length one day I retired to the horse-lot,
and was walking and wringing my hands in
great anguish, trying to pray, on the borders of
utter dispair. It appeared to me that I heard
a voice from heaven, saying, "Peter, look at
me." A feeling of relief flashed over me as quick
as an electric shock. It gave me hopeful feelings, and some encouragement to seek mercy,
but still my load of guilt remained. I repaired
to the house, and told my mother what had
happened to me in the horse-lot. Instantly she
seemed to understand it, and told me the Lord
had done this to encourage me to hope for
mercy, and exhorted me to take encouragement, and seek on, and God would bless me
with the pardon of my sins at another time.

Some days after this, I retired to a cave on
my father's farm to pray in secret. My soul was
in an agony; I wept, I prayed, and said, "Now,
Lord, if there is mercy for me, let me find it,"
and it really seemed to me that I could almost
lay hold of the Saviour, and realize a reconciled
God. All of a sudden, such a fear of the devil
fell upon me that it really appeared to me that
he was surely personally there, to seize and
drag me down to hell, soul and body, and such
a horror fell on me that I sprang to my feet and
ran to my mother at the house. My mother told
me that this was a device of Satan to prevent
me from finding the blessing then. Three
months rolled away, and still I did not find the
blessing of the pardon of my sins.

This year, 1801, the Western conference
existed, and I think there was but one presiding
elder's district in it, called the Kentucky District. William M'Kendree (afterward bishop)
was appointed to the Kentucky District. Cumberland Circuit, which, perhaps, was six hundred miles round, and lying partly in Kentucky
and partly in Tennessee, was one of the circuits
of this district. John Page and Thomas Wilker-
son were appointed to this circuit.

In the spring of this year, Mr. M'Grady, a

minister of the Presbyterian Church, who had
a congregation and meeting-house, as we then
called them, about three miles north of my
father's house, appointed a sacramental meeting in this congregation, and invited the Methodist preachers to attend with them, and especially John Page, who was a powerful Gospel
minister, and was very popular among the Presbyterians. Accordingly he came, and preached
with great power and success.

There were no camp-meetings in regular
form at this time, but as there was a great waking up among the Churches, from the revival
that had broken out at Cane Ridge, before
mentioned, many flocked to those sacramental
meetings. The church would not hold the tenth
part of the congregation. Accordingly, the officers of the Church erected a stand in a contiguous shady grove, and prepared seats for
a large congregation.

The people crowded to this meeting from
far and near. They came in their large wagons,
with victuals mostly prepared. The women
slept in the wagons, and the men under them.
Many stayed on the ground night and day for
a number of nights and days together. Others
were provided for among the neighbors around.
The power of God was wonderfully displayed;
scores of sinners fell under the preaching, like
men slain in mighty battle; Christians shouted
aloud for joy.

To this meeting I repaired, a guilty, wretched
sinner. On the Saturday evening of said meeting, I went, with weeping multitudes, and
bowed before the stand, and earnestly prayed
for mercy. In the midst of a solemn struggle of
soul, an impression was made on my mind, as
though a voice said to me, "Thy sins are all
forgiven thee." Divine light flashed all round
me, unspeakable joy sprung up in my soul. I
rose to my feet, opened my eyes, and it really
seemed as if I was in heaven; the trees, the
leaves on them, and everything seemed, and I
really thought were, praising God. My mother
raised the shout, my Christian friends crowded
around me and joined me in praising God; and
though I have been since then, in many instances, unfaithful, yet I have never, for one
moment, doubted that the Lord did, then and
there, forgive my sins and give me religion.

Our meeting lasted without intermission all
night, and it was believed by those who had a
very good right to know, that over eighty souls
were converted to God during its continuance.
I went on my way rejoicing for many days.

This meeting was in the month of May. In June our preacher, John Page, attended at our little church, *Ebenezer,* and there in June, 1801, I joined the Methodist Episcopal Church, which I have never for one moment regretted. I have never for a moment been tempted to leave the Methodist Episcopal Church, and if they were to turn me out, I would knock at the door till taken in again. I suppose, from the year 1786 Methodist preachers had been sent to the West, and we find among these very early pioneers, F. Poythress, presiding elder, T. Williamson, I. Brooks, Wilson Lee, James Haw, P. Massie, B. M'Henry, B. Snelling, J. Hartly, J. Talman, J. Lillard, Kobler, and others.

Perhaps the first conference holden in the West was held in Kentucky, in April, 1789, and then at different points till 1800, when the Western Conference was regularly organized, and reached from Redstone and Greenbrier to Natchez, covering almost the entire Mississippi valley. I can find at this time a record of but ninety members in 1787, and five travelling preachers. From 1787 up to 1800, Bishop Asbury visited the Western world, called together the preachers in conferences, changed them from time to time, and regulated the affairs of the infant Church in the wilderness as best he could.

Several times the Western preachers had to arm themselves in crossing the mountains to the East, and guard Bishop Asbury through the wilderness, which was infested with bloody, hostile savages, at the imminent risk of all their lives. Notwithstanding the great hazard of life, that eminent apostle of American Methodism, Bishop Asbury, showed that he did not count his life dear, so that he could provide for the sheep in the wilderness of the West.

At the time I joined the Church in 1801, according to the best accounts that I can gather, there were in the entire bounds of the Western Conference, of members, probationers, colored and all, two thousand, four hundred and eighty-four, and about fifteen travelling preachers. In the United States and territories, East and West, North and South, and Canada, seventy-two thousand, eight hundred and seventy-four. Total, in Europe and America, one hundred and ninety-six thousand, five hundred and two. The number of travelling preachers this year, for all America and Canada, was three hundred and seven; and during the same year there were eight thousand members added to the Methodist Episcopal Church.

I believe, to say nothing of some local preachers who emigrated to the West at a very early day, that James Haw and Benjamin Ogden were the first two regular itinerant preachers sent out in 1786. After travelling and preaching for several years, they both became disaffected to the Methodist Episcopal Church and withdrew, with the secession of James O'Kelly, elsewhere named in my sketches. O'Kelly left the Church in 1792. He was a popular and powerful preacher, and drew off many preachers and thousands of members with him. He formed what he called the Republican Methodist Church, flourished for a few years, and then divisions and subdivisions entered among his followers. Some of his preachers turned Arians, some Universalists, and some joined the so-called New Lights, and some returned to the Methodist Episcopal Church, and the last authentic account I had of O'Kelly he was left alone in his old age, and desired to return to the Methodist Episcopal Church again; but whether he was ever received I am not informed. And here was an end of the first grand secession from our beloved Church.

James Haw and Benjamin Ogden, we have said, became disaffected and left the church with O'Kelly's party. They soon found that they could not succeed to any considerable extent in these Western wilds. Haw veered about and joined the Presbyterians, became a pastor in one of their congregations with a fixed salary, but lived and died in comparative obscurity.

Ogden backslid, quit preaching, kept a groggery, and became wicked, and raised his family to hate the Methodists. In the year 1813, when I was on the Wabash District, Tennessee Conference, Breckenridge Circuit, at a camp-meeting in said circuit, B. Ogden attended. There was a glorious revival of religion, and Ogden got under strong conviction, and professed to be reclaimed, joined the Church again, was licensed to preach, was soon recommended and received into the travelling connection again, and lived and died a good Methodist preacher. He was saved by mercy, as all seceders from the Methodist Episcopal Church will be, if saved at all.

To show the ignorance the early Methodist preachers had to contend with in the Western wilds, I will relate an incident or two that occurred to Wilson Lee in Kentucky. He was one of the early pioneer Methodist preachers sent to the West. He was a very solemn and grave minister. At one of his appointments, at a private house on a certain day, they had a motherless pet lamb. The boys of the family had mischievously learned this lamb to butt. They would go near it, and make motions with their heads, and the lamb would back and then dart forward at them, and they would jump out of the way, so that the sheep would miss them.

A man came into the congregation who had been drinking and frolicking all the night before. He came in late, and took his seat on the end of a bench nearly in the door, and, having slept none the night before, presently he began to nod; and as he nodded and bent forward, the pet lamb came along by the door, and seeing this man nodding and bending forward, he took it as a banter, and straightway backed and then sprang forward, and gave the sleeper a severe jolt right on the head, and over he tilted him, to the no small amusement of the congregation, who all burst out into laughter; and grave as the preacher, Mr. Lee, was, it so excited his risibilities that he almost lost his balance. But recovering himself a little, he went on in a most solemn and impressive strain. His subject was the words of our Lord: "Except a man deny himself, and take up his cross, he cannot be my disciple." He urged on his congregation, with melting voice and tearful eyes, to take up the cross, no matter what it was, take it up.

There were in the congregation a very wicked Dutchman and his wife, both of whom were profoundly ignorant of the Scriptures and the plan of salvation. His wife was a notorious scold, and so much was she given to this practice, that she made her husband unhappy, and kept him almost always in a perfect fret, so that he led a most miserable and uncomfortable life. It pleased God that day to cause the preaching of Mr. Lee to reach their guilty souls and break up the great deep of their hearts. They wept aloud, seeing their lost condition, and they, then and there, resolved to do better, and from that time forward to take up the cross and bear it, be it what it might.

The congregation were generally deeply affected. Mr. Lee exhorted them and prayed for them as long as he consistently could, and, having another appointment some distance off that evening, he dismissed the congregation, got a little refreshment, saddled his horse, mounted, and started for his evening appointment. After riding some distance, he saw, a little ahead of him, a man trudging along, carrying a woman on his back. This greatly surprised Mr. Lee. He very naturally supposed that the woman was a cripple, or had hurt herself in some way, so that she could not walk. The traveller was a small man, and the woman large and heavy.

Before he overtook them Mr. Lee began to cast about in his mind how he could render them assistance. When he came up to them, lo and behold, who should it be but the Dutchman and his wife that had been so affected under his sermon at meeting. Mr. Lee rode up and spoke to them, and inquired of the man what had happened, or what was the matter, that he was carrying his wife.

The Dutchman turned to Mr. Lee and said, "Be sure you did tell us in your sarmon dat we must take up de cross and follow de Saviour, or dat we could not be saved or go to heaven, and I does desire to go to heaven so much as any pody; and dish vife is so pad, she scold and scold all de time, and dish woman is de createst cross I have in de whole world, and I does take her up and pare her, for I must save my soul."

You may be sure Mr. Lee was posed for once, but after a few moments' reflection he told the Dutchman to put his wife down, and he dismounted from his horse. He directed them to sit down on a log by the road side. He held the reins of his horse's bridle and sat down by them, took out his Bible, read to them several passages of Scripture, and explained and expounded to them the way of the Lord more perfectly. He opened to them the nature of the cross of Christ, what it is, how it is to be taken up, and how they were to bear that cross; and after teaching and advising them some time, he prayed for them by the road side, left them deeply affected, mounted his horse, and rode on to his evening appointment.

Long before Mr. Lee came around his circuit to his next appointment the Dutchman and his scolding wife were both powerfully converted to God, and when he came round he took them into the Church. The Dutchman's wife was cured of her scolding. Of course he got clear of this cross. They lived together long and happily, adorning their profession, and giving ample evidence that religion could cure a scolding wife, and that God could and did convert poor ignorant Dutch people.

This Dutchman often told his experience in

love-feasts, with thrilling effect, and hardly ever failed to melt the whole congregation into a flood of tears; and on one particular occasion which is vividly printed on my recollection, I believe the whole congregation in the love-feast, which lasted beyond the time allotted for such meetings, broke out into a loud shout.

Thus Brother Lee was the honored instrument in the hand of God of planting Methodism, amid clouds of ignorance and opposition, among the early settlers of the far West. Brother Lee witnessed a good confession to the end. At an early period of his ministry he fell from the walls of Zion with the trump of God in his hand, and has gone to his reward in heaven. Peace to his memory.

CHAPTER V

THE GREAT REVIVAL

From 1801 for years a blessed revival of religion spread through almost the entire inhabited parts of the West, Kentucky, Tennessee, the Carolinas, and many other parts, especially through the Cumberland country, which was so called from the Cumberland River, which headed and mouthed in Kentucky, but in its great bend circled south through Tennessee, near Nashville. The Presbyterians and Methodists in a great measure united in this work, met together, prayed together, and preached together.

In this revival originated our camp-meetings, and in both these denominations they were held every year, and, indeed, have been ever since, more or less. They would erect their camps with logs or frame them, and cover them with clapboards or shingles. They would also erect a shed, sufficiently large to protect five thousand people from wind and rain, and cover it with boards or shingles; build a large stand, seat the shed, and here they would collect together from forty to fifty miles around, sometimes further than that. Ten, twenty, and sometimes thirty ministers, of different denominations, would come together and preach night and day, four or five days together; and, indeed, I have known these camp-meetings to last three or four weeks, and great good resulted from them. I have seen more than a hundred sinners fall like dead men under one powerful sermon, and I have seen and heard more than five hundred Christians all shouting aloud the high praises of God at once; and I will venture to assert that many happy thousands were awakened and converted to God at these camp-meetings. Some sinners mocked, some of the old dry professors opposed, some of the old starched Presbyterian preachers preached against these exercises, but still the work went on and spread almost in every direction, gathering additional force, until our country seemed all coming home to God.

In this great revival the Methodists kept moderately balanced; for we had excellent preachers to steer the ship or guide the flock. But some of our members ran wild, and indulged in some extravagancies that were hard to control.

The Presbyterian preachers and members, not being accustomed to much noise or shouting, when they yielded to it went into great extremes and downright wildness, to the great injury of the cause of God. Their old preachers licensed a great many young men to preach, contrary to their Confession of Faith. That Confession of Faith required their ministers to believe in unconditional election and reprobation, and the unconditional and final perseverance of the saints. But in this revival they, almost to a man, gave up these points of high Calvinism, and preached a free salvation to all mankind. The Westminster Confession required every man, before he could be licensed to preach, to have a liberal education; but this qualification was dispensed with, and a great many fine men were licensed to preach without this literary qualification or subscribing to those high-toned doctrines of Calvinism.

This state of things produced great dissatisfaction in the Synod of Kentucky, and messenger after messenger was sent to wait on the Presbytery to get them to desist from their erratic course, but without success. Finally they were cited to trial before the constituted authorities of the Church. Some were censured, some were suspended, some retraced their steps, while others surrendered their credentials of ordination, and the rest were cut off from the Church.

While in this amputated condition, they called a general meeting of all their licentiates. They met our presiding elder, J. Page, and a number of Methodist ministers at a quarterly meeting in Logan County, and proposed to join the Methodist Episcopal Church as a body; but our aged ministers declined this offer, and persuaded them to rise up and embody themselves

together, and constitute a Church. They reluctantly yielded to this advice, and, in due time and form, constituted what they denominated the "Cumberland Presbyterian Church"; and in their confession of faith split, as they supposed, the difference between the Predestinarians and the Methodists, rejecting a partial atonement or special election and reprobation, but retaining the doctrine of the final uncondi-
10　tional perseverance of the saints.

What an absurdity! While a man remains a sinner he may come, as a free agent, to Christ, if he will, and if he does not come his damnation will be just, because he refused offered mercy; but as soon as he gets converted his free agency is destroyed, the best boon of Heaven is then lost, and although he may backslide, wander away from Christ, yet he *shall* be brought in. He cannot finally be lost
20　if he has ever been really converted to God.

They make a very sorry show in their attempt to support this left foot of Calvinism. But be it spoken to their credit, they do not often preach this doctrine. They generally preach Methodist doctrine, and have been the means of doing a great deal of good, and would have done much more if they had left this relic of John Calvin behind.

In this revival, usually termed in the West
30　the Cumberland revival, many joined the different Churches, especially the Methodist and Cumberland Presbyterians. The Baptists also came in for a share of the converts, but not to any great extent. Infidelity quailed before the mighty power of God, which was displayed among the people. Universalism was almost driven from the land. The Predestinarians of almost all sorts put forth a mighty effort to stop the work of God.

40　Just in the midst of our controversies on the subject of the powerful exercises among the people under preaching, a new exercise broke out among us, called the *jerks,* which was overwhelming in its effects upon the bodies and minds of the people. No matter whether they were saints or sinners, they would be taken under a warm song or sermon, and seized with a convulsive jerking all over, which they could not by any possibility avoid, and the more they
50　resisted the more they jerked. If they would not strive against it and pray in good earnest, the jerking would usually abate. I have seen more than five hundred persons jerking at one time in my large congregations. Most usually persons taken with the jerks, to obtain relief, as

they said, would rise up and dance. Some would run, but could not get away. Some would resist; on such the jerks were generally very severe.

To see those proud young gentlemen and young ladies, dressed in their silks, jewelry, and prunella, from top to toe, take the *jerks* would often excite my risibilities. The first jerk or so, you would see their fine bonnets, caps, and combs fly; and so sudden would be the jerking of the head that their long loose hair would crack almost as loud as a wagoners whip.

At one of my appointments in 1804 there was a very large congregation turned out to hear the Kentucky boy, as they called me. Among the rest there were two very finely-dressed, fashionable young ladies, attended by two brothers with loaded horsewhips. Although the house was large, it was crowded. The two young ladies, coming in late, took their seats near where I stood, and their two brothers stood in the door. I was a little unwell, and I had a phial of peppermint in my pocket. Before I commenced preaching I took out my phial and swallowed a little of the peppermint. While I was preaching, the congregation was melted into tears. The two young gentlemen moved off to the yard fence, and both the young ladies took the jerks, and they were greatly mortified about it. There was a great stir in the congregation. Some wept, some shouted, and before our meeting closed several were converted.

As I dismissed the assembly a man stepped up to me, and warned me to be on my guard, for he had heard the two brothers swear they would horsewhip me when meeting was out, for giving their sisters the jerks. "Well," said I, "I'll see to that."

I went out and said to the young men that I understood they intended to horsewhip me for giving their sisters the jerks. One replied that he did. I undertook to expostulate with him on the absurdity of the charge against me, but he swore I need not deny it; for he had seen me take out a phial, in which I carried some truck that gave his sisters the jerks. As quick as thought it came into my mind how I would get clear of my whipping, and, jerking out the peppermint phial, said I, "Yes; if I gave your sisters the jerks I'll give them to you." In a moment I saw he was scared. I moved toward him, he backed, I advanced, and he wheeled and ran, warning me not to come near him, or he would kill me. It raised the laugh on him, and I escaped my whipping. I had the pleasure, before the year was out, of seeing all four soundly converted to God, and I took them into the Church.

While I am on this subject I will relate a very serious circumstance which I knew to take place with a man who had the jerks at a camp-meeting, on what was called the Ridge, in William Magee's congregation. There was a great work of religion in the encampment. The jerks were very prevalent. There was a company of drunken rowdies who came to interrupt the meeting. These rowdies were headed by a very large drinking man. They came with their bottles of whisky in their pockets. This large man cursed the jerks, and all religion. Shortly afterward he took the jerks, and he started to run, but he jerked so powerfully he could not get away. He halted among some saplings, and, although he was violently agitated, he took out his bottle of whisky, and swore he would drink the damned jerks to death; but he jerked at such a rate he could not get the bottle to his mouth, though he tried hard. At length he fetched a sudden jerk, and the bottle struck a sapling and was broken to pieces, and spilled his whisky on the ground. There was a great crowd gathered round him, and when he lost his whisky he became very much enraged, and cursed and swore very profanely, his jerks still increasing. At length he fetched a very violent jerk, snapped his neck, fell, and soon expired, with his mouth full of cursing and bitterness.

I always looked upon the jerks as a judgment sent from God, first, to bring sinners to repentance; and, secondly to show professors that God could work with or without means, and that he could work over and above means, and do whatsoever seemeth him good, to the glory of his grace and the salvation of the world.

There is no doubt in my mind that, with weak-minded, ignorant, and superstitious persons, there was a great deal of sympathetic feeling with many that claimed to be under the influence of this jerking exercise; and yet, with many, it was perfectly involuntary. It was, on all occasions, my practice to recommend fervent prayer as a remedy, and it almost universally proved an effectual antidote.

There were many other strange and wild exercises into which the subjects of this revival fell; such, for instance, as what was called the running, jumping, barking exercise. The Methodist preachers generally preached against this extravagant wildness. I did it uniformly in my little ministrations, and sometimes gave great offense; but I feared no consequences when I felt my awful responsibilities to God. From these wild exercises, another great evil arose from the heated and wild imaginations of some. They professed to fall into trances and see visions; they would fall at meetings and sometimes at home, and lay apparently powerless and motionless for days, sometimes for a week at a time, without food or drink; and when they came to, they professed to have seen heaven and hell, to have seen God, angels, the devil and the damned; they would prophesy, and, under the pretense of Divine inspiration, predict the time of the end of the world, and the ushering in of the great millennium.

This was the most troublesome delusion of all; it made such an appeal to the ignorance, superstition, and credulity of the people, even saint as well as sinner. I watched this matter with a vigilant eye. If I opposed it, I would have to meet the clamor of the multitude; and if any one opposed it, these very visionists would single him out, and denounce the dreadful judgments of God against him. They would even set the very day that God was to burn the world, like the self-deceived modern Millerites. They would prophesy, that if any one did oppose them, God would send fire down from heaven and consume him, like the blasphemous Shakers. They would proclaim that they could heal all manner of diseases, and raise the dead, just like the diabolical Mormons. They professed to have converse with spirits of the dead in heaven and hell, like the modern spirit rappers. Such a state of things I never saw before, and I hope in God I shall never see again.

I pondered well the whole matter in view of my responsibilities, searched the Bible for the true fulfillment of promise and prophecy, prayed to God for light and Divine aid, and proclaimed open war against these delusions. In the midst of them along came the Shakers, and Mr. Rankin, one of the Presbyterian revival preachers, joined them; Mr. G. Wall, a visionary local preacher among the Methodists, joined them; all the country was in commotion.

I made public appointments and drew multitudes together, and openly showed from the Scriptures that these delusions were false. Some of these visionary men and women prophesied that God would kill me. The Shakers soon pre-

tended to seal my damnation. But nothing daunted, for I knew Him in whom I had believed, I threw my appointments in the midst of them, and proclaimed to listening thousands the more sure word of prophecy. This mode of attack threw a damper on these visionary, self-deluded, false prophets, sobered some, reclaimed others, and stayed the fearful tide of delusion that was sweeping over the coun-
10 try.

I will here state a case which occurred at an early day in the State of Indiana, in a settlement called Busroe. Many of the early emigrants to that settlement were Methodists, Baptists, and Cumberland Presbyterians. The Shaker priests, all apostates from the Baptist and the Cumberland Presbyterians, went over among them. Many of them I was personally acquainted with, and had given them letters
20 when they moved from Kentucky to that new country. There were then no Methodist circuit preachers in that region.

There was an old Brother Collins, a local preacher, who withstood these Shakers, and in private combat he was a full match for any of them, but he was not eloquent in public debate, and hence the Shaker priests overcame my old brother, and by scores swept members of different Churches away from their steadfast-
30 ness into the muddy pool of Shakerism.

The few who remained steadfast sent to Kentucky for me, praying me to come and help them. I sent an appointment, with an invitation to meet any or all of the Shaker priests in public debate; but instead of meeting me, they appointed a meeting in opposition, and warned the believers, as they called them, to keep away from my meeting; but from our former acquaintance and intimate friendship, many of
40 them came to hear me. I preached to a vast crowd for about three hours, and I verily believe God helped me. The very foundations of every Shaker present were shaken from under him. They then besought me to go to the Shaker meeting that night. I went, and when I got there we had a great crowd. I proposed to them to have a debate, and they dared not refuse. The terms were these: A local preacher I had with me was to open the debate; then
50 one or all of their preachers, if they chose, were to follow, and I was to bring up the rear. My

preacher opened up the debate by merely stating the points of difference. Mr. Brayelton followed, and, instead of argument, he turned everything into abuse and insulting slander. Then he closed, and Mr. Gill rose, but, instead of argument, he uttered a few words of personal abuse, and then called on all the Shakers to meet him a few minutes in the yard, talk a little, and then disperse.

Our debate was out in the open air, at the end of a cabin. I rose, called them to order, and stated that it was fairly agreed by these Shaker priests that I should bring up the rear, or close the argument. I stated that it was cowardly to run; that if I was the devil himself, and they were right, I could not hurt them. I got most of them to take their seats and hear me. Mr. Gill gathered a little band, and he and they left. They had told the people in the day that if I continued to oppose them, God would make an example of me, and send fire from heaven and consume me. When I rose to reply I felt a Divine sense of the approbation of God, and that he would give me success.

I addressed the multitude about three hours, and when I closed my argument I opened the door of the Church, and invited all that would renounce Shakerism to come and give me their hand. Forty-seven came forward, and then and there openly renounced the dreadful delusion. The next day I followed those that fled; and the next day I went from cabin to cabin, taking the names of those that returned to the solid foundation of truth, and my number rose to eighty-seven. I then organized them into a regular society, and the next fall had a preacher sent to them. And perhaps this victory may be considered among the first-fruits of Methodism in that part of this new country. This was in 1808.

At this meeting I collected, as well as I could, the names and places where it was supposed they wanted Methodist preaching. I made out and returned a kind of plan for a circuit, carried it to Conference, and they were temporarily supplied by the presiding elder in 1809 and 1810. In 1811 the circuit was called St. Vincennes, and was attached to the Cumberland District, and Thomas Stilwell appointed the preacher in charge.　　　　　1857

» » *The Industrial Revolution* « «

1791-1801

» » » « « «

RHYMES AND CHIMES

Oh, the world ain't now as it used to was,
  The past is like a dream, sirs,
Every thing's on the railroad plan,
  Though they don't all go by steam, sirs.

Expresses now are all the rage,
  By steamboat and balloon, sirs,
In a year or two we'll get the news
  Directly from the moon, sirs.

The electric telegraphs are now
  Both time and distance mocking,
But then, the news which they convey
  Is really very shocking.

Now when you wish to read a book,
  On the [mnemotechnic] plan, sirs,
You're only to look at the title page
  And the whole you understand, sirs.

A pint of water, an ounce of chalk,
  Together mixed make cream, sirs,
The hens have only to lay their eggs,
  And the "chickens are hatched by steam," sirs.

Should you but wish to kiss a girl,
  And not at all surprise her,
The method's as simple as A B C,
  You first must magnetise her.

But there's a doctor in Sweden I've heard,
  Whom you must acknowledge clever,
He reduces the gals to a torpid state,
  And 'tis said they live forever.

Short hand is now quite out of use,
  For when the ministers preach, sirs,
Or politicians rise to spout,
  They "Daguerreotype" the speech, sirs.

These verses, written in amazement at the wonders of the Machine Age, appear in *Elton's Songs and Melodies for the Multitude*, New York, n.d. (late 1840's), pages 291–292. Encore verses marvel at socialism, now "all the go," and laughing gas.

» » « «

The Industrial Revolution

OF ALL THE ISSUES that divided Americans, none were to be so persistent as those born of the industrial revolution. From the time when, in 1791, Samuel Slater set up the first textile mill in Rhode Island, until our own time, industrialism, in its broader sense, has profoundly affected the lives and thoughts of Americans.

In the pre-Civil War period industrialism brought in its wake some of the conditions which Jefferson had so much feared: crowded cities, in which political corruption could so easily arise; an insecure working class, exploited and restless; and a new aristocracy of wealth and power which demanded and secured special favors from the government in the form of tariffs and franchises. Few critics of industrialism, outside the South, won any wide following. But certain labor spokesmen insisted that industrialism was tantamount to slavery, that it must be democratized if democracy itself was to survive. Romantic primitivists revolted against the regimentation and standardization which they detected in industrialism, and set themselves squarely against it. Humanitarians exposed the ill-effects it had on farm-girls who tended spindles and lived in company-owned or company-managed boarding houses, and demanded a ten-hour day and legislation restricting the employment of young children in factories.

To such criticisms industrialists and their champions were not slow to reply. They insisted that industrial capitalism was essentially democratic, in that it provided a ladder by which any able man could climb to the top. They urged that the corporation itself, in making it possible for the humble rank and file to pool their savings and enjoy profits therefrom, was democratic. They insisted that such evils as had appeared were due either to low tariffs insufficient to protect American industry in its competition with factory-owners in the Old World who could employ hands at cheaper wages; or they contended that the laboring class itself was inefficient, intemperate, and improvident, and that, consequently, the ills it suffered were to be laid at its own door.

The potentialities of technology excited in the minds of some Americans a social utopianism which resembled that earlier portrayed by Bacon in the *New Atlantis*, or by Godwin in *Political Justice*. The application of science to industry and to life generally would, it was held, release man from drudgery and supply him with comforts and luxuries which even the greatest potentates of old had never enjoyed. This position marked the beginning of the effort to assimilate the machine in the framework of democracy and humanitarianism. But it was only a beginning.

» »   « «

ALEXANDER HAMILTON

1757–1804

IN HAMILTON'S mind the cause of a vigorous and powerful central government was also the cause of the propertied class which he served so well. His contribution to the establishment of a stronger union was an important one; and no one, in the early days of the Republic, did so much to make the new federal government stronger, or to inspire men of wealth with loyalty to it. Although others, notably Tenche Cox, influenced Hamilton in the formulation of his planned economic nationalism, his great work in behalf of a national bank, of the resumption of state debts by the central government, and of an excise tax to bring home to every individual the power of the federal authority, was unrivalled. The report on manufactures, here given in part, advocated economic independence from Europe through a well-balanced national economy. This was to be achieved through diversified industry, the Federal fostering of manufacturing, and, if necessary, of agriculture as well. Frederick List, H. C. Carey, and Daniel Webster subsequently pushed the implications of Hamilton's economic nationalism even further; but no one ever gave it a more effective expression than he did in writing and in action.

The Works of Alexander Hamilton, H. C. Lodge, ed., 12 vols., New York, 1904.
Louis M. Hacker, *Alexander Hamilton in the American Tradition*, New York, 1957.
John C. Miller, *Alexander Hamilton: Portrait in Paradox*, New York, 1959.
Broadus Mitchell, *Alexander Hamilton*, New York, 1957.

» » *From:* REPORT ON MANUFACTURES « «

The expediency of encouraging manufactures in the United States, which was not long since deemed very questionable, appears at this time to be pretty generally admitted. The embarrassments which have obstructed the progress of our external trade, have led to serious reflections on the necessity of enlarging the sphere of our domestice commerce. The restrictive regulations, which, in foreign markets, abridge the vent of the increasing surplus of our agricultural produce, serve to beget an earnest desire, that a more extensive demand for that surplus may be created at home; and the complete success which has rewarded manufacturing enterprise, in some valuable branches, conspiring with the promising symptoms which attend some less mature essays in others, justify a hope, that the obstacles to the growth of this species of industry are less formidable than they were apprehended to be; and that it is not difficult to find, in its further extension, a full indemnification for any external disadvantages, which are or may be experienced, as well as an accession of resources, favorable to national independence and safety.

There still are, nevertheless, respectable patrons of opinions unfriendly to the encouragement of manufactures. . . .

It ought readily to be conceded that the cultivation of the earth, as the primary and most certain source of national supply, as the immediate and chief source of subsistence to man, as the principal source of those materials which constitute the nutriment of other kinds of labor, as including a state most favorable to the freedom and independence of the human mind—one, perhaps, most conducive to the multiplication of the human species, has intrinsically a strong claim to pre-eminence over every other kind of industry.

But that it has a title to anything like an exclusive predilection in any country, ought to be admitted with great caution; that it is even more productive than every other branch of industry, requires more evidence than has yet been given in support of the position. That its real interests, precious and important, as without the help of exaggeration they truly are, will be advanced rather than injured by the due encouragement of manufactures, may, it is believed, be satisfactorily demonstrated. And it is also believed that the expediency of such encouragement, in a general view, may be shown to be recommended by the most cogent and persuasive motives of national policy. . . .

But, without contending for the superior productiveness of manufacturing industry, it may conduce to a better judgment of the policy which ought to be pursued respecting its encouragement, to contemplate the subject under some additional aspects, tending not only to confirm the idea that this kind of industry has been improperly represented as unproductive in itself, but to evince, in addition, that the establishment and diffusion of manufactures have the effect of rendering the total mass of useful and productive labor, in a community, greater than it would otherwise be. . . .

It is now proper to proceed a step further, and to enumerate the principal circumstances from which it may be inferred that manufacturing establishments not only occasion a positive augmentation of the produce and revenue of the society, but that they contribute essentially to rendering them greater than they could possibly be without such establishments. . . .

1. As to the division of labor.

It has justly been observed that there is scarcely anything of greater moment in the economy of a nation than the proper division of labor. The separation of occupations causes each to be carried to a much greater perfection than it could possibly acquire if they were blended. This arises principally from three circumstances:

1st. The greater skill and dexterity naturally resulting from a constant and undivided application to a single object. It is evident that these properties must increase in proportion to the separation and simplification of objects, and the steadiness of the attention devoted to each; and must be less in proportion to the complication of objects, and the number among which the attention is distracted.

2nd. The economy of time, by avoiding the loss of it, incident to a frequent transition from one operation to another of a different nature. This depends on various circumstances; the transition itself, the orderly disposition of the implements, machines, and materials employed in the operation to be relinquished, the preparatory steps to the commencement of a new one, the interruption of the impulse which the mind of a workman acquires from being engaged in a particular operation, the distractions, hesitations and reluctances which attend the passage from one kind of business to another.

3rd. An extension of the use of machinery. A man occupied on a single object will have it more in his power, and will be more naturally led to exert his imagination, in devising methods to facilitate and abridge labor, than if he were perplexed by a variety of independent and dissimilar operations. Besides this, the fabrication of machines, in numerous instances, becoming itself a distinct trade, the artist who follows it has all the advantages which have been enumerated for improvement in his particular art; and, in both ways, the invention and application of machinery are extended.

And from these causes united, the mere separation of the occupation of the cultivator from that of the artificer, has the effect of augmenting the productive powers of labor, and with them, the total mass of the produce or revenue of a country. In this single view of the subject, therefore, the utility of artificers or manufacturers, towards promoting an increase of productive industry, is apparent.

2. As to an extension of the use of machinery, a point which, though partly anticipated, requires to be placed in one or two additional lights.

The employment of machinery forms an item of great importance in the general mass of national industry. It is an artificial force brought in aid of the natural force of man; and, to all the purposes of labor, is an increase of hands, an accession of strength, unencumbered too by the expense of maintaining the laborer. May it not, therefore, be fairly inferred that those occupations which give the greatest scope to the use of this auxiliary contribute most to the general stock of industrious effort, and, in consequence, to the general product of industry?

It shall be taken for granted, and the truth of the position referred to observation, that manufacturing pursuits are susceptible, in a greater degree, of the application of machinery, than those of agriculture. If so, all the difference is lost to a community which, instead of manufacturing for itself, procures the fabrics requisite to its supply from other countries. The substitution of foreign for domestic manufactures is a transfer to foreign nations of the advantages accruing from the employment of machinery, in the modes in which it is capable of being employed with most utility and to the greatest extent.

The cotton-mill, invented in England, within the last twenty years, is a signal illustration of the general proposition which has been just advanced. In consequence of it, all the different processes for spinning cotton are performed by means of machines, which are put in motion by water, and attended chiefly by women and children—and by a smaller number of persons, in the whole, than are requisite in the ordinary mode of spinning. And it is an advantage of great moment, that the operations of this mill continue with convenience during the night as well as through the day. The prodigious effect of such a machine is easily conceived. To this invention is to be attributed, essentially, the immense progress which has been so suddenly made in Great Britain in the various fabrics of cotton.

3. As to the additional employment of classes of the community not originally engaged in the particular business.

This is not among the least valuable of the names by which manufacturing institutions contribute to augment the general stock of industry and production. In places where these institutions prevail, besides the persons regularly engaged in them, they afford occasional and extra employment to industrious individuals and families, who are willing to devote the leisure resulting from the intermissions of their ordinary pursuits to collateral labors, as a resource for multiplying their acquisitions or their enjoyments. The husbandman himself experiences a new source of profit and support from the increased industry of his wife and daughters, invited and stimulated by the demands of the neighboring manufactories.

Besides this advantage of occasional employment to classes having different occupations, there is another, of a nature allied to it and of a similar tendency. This is the employment of persons who would otherwise be idle, and in many cases a burthen on the community, either from the bias of temper, habit, infirmity of body, or some other cause, indisposing or disqualifying them for the toils of the country. It is worthy of particular remark that, in general, women and children are rendered more useful, and the latter more early useful, by manufacturing establishments, than they would otherwise be. Of the number of persons employed in the cotton manufactories of Great Britain, it is computed that four-sevenths, nearly, are women and children, of whom the greater proportion are children, and many of them of a tender age.

And thus it appears to be one of the attributes of manufactures, and one of no small consequence, to give occasion to the exertion of a greater quantity of industry, even by the same number of persons, where they happen to prevail, than would exist if there were no such establishments.

4. As to the promoting of immigration from foreign countries.

Men reluctantly quit one course of occupation and livelihood for another, unless invited to it by very apparent and proximate advantages. Many who would go from one country to another, if they had a prospect of continuing with more benefit the callings to which they have been educated, will often not be tempted to change their situation by the hope of doing better in some other way. Manufacturers who, listening to the powerful invitations of a better price for their fabrics or their labor, of greater cheapness of provisions, and raw materials, or an exemption from the chief part of the taxes, burthens and restraints which they endure in the Old World, of greater personal independence and consequence, under the operation of a more equal government, and of what is far more precious than mere religious toleration, a perfect equality of religious privileges, would probably flock from Europe to the United States, to pursue their own trades or professions, if they were once made sensible of the advantages they would enjoy, and were inspired with an assurance of encouragement and employment, will, with difficulty, be induced to transplant themselves, with a view to becoming cultivators of land.

If it be true, then, that it is the interest of the United States to open every possible avenue to emigration from abroad, it affords a weighty argument for the encouragement of manufactures; which, for the reasons just assigned, will have the strongest tendency to multiply the inducements to it.

Here is perceived an important resource, not only for extending the population, and with it the useful and productive labor of the country, but likewise for the prosecution of manufactures, without deducting from the number of hands which might otherwise be drawn to tillage, and even for the indemnification of agriculture for such as might happen to be diverted from it. Many, whom manufacturing views would induce to emigrate, would afterwards, yield to the temptation which the particular situation of this country holds out to agricultural pursuits. And while agriculture would, in other respects, derive many signal and unmingled advantages from the growth of manufacturers, it is a problem whether it would gain or lose, as to the article or the number of persons employed in carrying it on.

5. As to the furnishing greater scope for the diversity of talents and dispositions, which discriminate men from each other.

This is a much more powerful means of augmenting the fund of national industry than may at first sight appear. It is a just observation, that minds of the strongest and most active powers for their proper objects fall below mediocrity, and labor without effect if confined to uncongenial pursuits. And it is thence to be inferred, that the results of human exertion may be immensely increased by diversifying its objects. When all the different kinds of industry obtain in a community, each individual can find his proper element, and can call into activity the whole vigor of his nature. And the community is benefited by the services of its respective members, in the manner in which each can serve it with most effect.

If there be anything in a remark often to be met with, namely, that there is, in the genius of the people of this country, a peculiar aptitude for mechanic improvements, it would operate as a forcible reason for giving opportunities to the exercise of that species of talent, by the propagation of manufactures.

6. *As to the affording a more ample and various field for enterprise.*

This is also of greater consequence in the general scale of national exertion than might, perhaps, on a superficial view, be supposed, and has effects not altogether dissimilar from those of the circumstances last noticed. To cherish and stimulate the activity of the human mind, by multiplying the objects of enterprise, is not among the least considerable of the expedients by which the wealth of a nation may be promoted. Even things in themselves not positively advantageous sometimes become so, by their tendency to provoke exertion. Every new scene which is opened to the busy nature of man to rouse and exert itself, is the addition of a new energy to the general stock of effort.

The spirit of enterprise, useful and prolific as it is, must necessarily be contracted or expanded in proportion to the simplicity or variety of the occupations and productions which are to be found in a society. It must be less in a nation of mere cultivators than in a nation of cultivators and merchants; less in a nation of cultivators and merchants than in a nation of cultivators, artificers, and merchants.

7. *As to the creating, in some instances, a new, and securing, in all, a more certain and steady demand for the surplus produce of the soil.*

This is among the most important of the circumstances which have been indicated. It is a principal means by which the establishment of manufactures contributes to an augmentation of the produce or revenue of a country, and has an immediate and direct relation to the prosperity of agriculture.

It is evident that the exertions of the husbandman will be steady or fluctuating, vigorous or feeble, in proportion to the steadiness or fluctuation, adequateness or inadequateness of the markets on which he must depend for the vent of the surplus which may be produced by his labor; and that such surplus, in the ordinary course of things, will be greater or less in the same proportion. . . .

It may be observed, and the idea is of no inconsiderable weight, that however true it might be that a State, which, possessing large tracts of vacant and fertile territory, was at the same time secluded from foreign commerce, would find its interest and the interest of agriculture in diverting a part of its population from tillage to manufactures, yet it will not follow that the same is true of a State which, having such vacant and fertile territory, has at the same time ample opportunity of procuring from abroad, on good terms, all the fabrics of which it stands in need for the supply of its inhabitants. The power of doing this at least secures the great advantage of a division of labor, leaving the farmer free to pursue, exclusively, the culture of his land, and enabling him to procure with its products the manufactured supplies requisite either to his wants or to his enjoyments. And though it should be true that, in settled countries, the diversification of industry is conducive to an increase in the productive powers of labor, and to an augmentation of revenue and capital, yet it is scarcely conceivable that there can be anything of so solid and permanent advantage to an uncultivated and unpeopled country as to convert its wastes into cultivated and inhabited districts. If the revenue, in the meantime, should be less, the capital, in the event, must be greater.

To these observations the following appears to be a satisfactory answer:

1st. If the system of perfect liberty to industry and commerce were the prevailing system of nations, the arguments which dissuade a country, in the predicament of the United States, from the zealous pursuit of manufactures would doubtless have great force. It will not be affirmed that they might not be permitted, with few exceptions, to serve as a rule of national conduct. In such a state of things, each country would have the full benefit of its peculiar advantages to compensate for its deficiencies or disadvantages. If one nation were in a condition to supply manufactured articles on better terms than another,

that other might find an abundant indemnification in a superior capacity to furnish the produce of the soil. And a free exchange, mutually beneficial, of the commodities which each was able to supply on the best terms, might be carried on between them, supporting in full vigor the industry of each. And though the circumstances which have been mentioned, and others which will be unfolded hereafter,
10 render it probable that nations, merely agricultural, would not enjoy the same degree of opulence in proportion to their numbers as those which united manufactures with agriculture, yet the progressive improvement of the lands of the former might in the end atone for an inferior degree of opulence in the meantime; and in a case in which opposite considerations are pretty equally balanced, the option ought, perhaps, always to be in favor of leaving in-
20 dustry to its own direction.

But the system which has been mentioned is far from characterizing the general policy of nations. The prevalent one has been regulated by an opposite spirit. The consequence of it is that the United States are, to a certain extent, in the situation of a country precluded from foreign commerce. They can, indeed, without difficulty, obtain from abroad the manufactured supplies of which they are in want; but they
30 experience numerous and very injurious impediments to the emission and vent of their own commodities. Nor is this the case in reference to a single foreign nation only. The regulations of several countries, with which we have the most extensive intercourse, throw serious obstructions in the way of the principal staples of the United States.

In such a position of things, the United States cannot exchange with Europe on equal
40 terms; and the want of reciprocity would render them the victim of a system which would induce them to confine their views to agriculture and refrain from manufactures. A constant and increasing necessity, on their part, for the commodities of Europe, and only a partial and occasional demand for their own, in return, could not but expose them to a state of impoverishment, compared with the opulence to which their political and natural advantages
50 authorize them to aspire.

Remarks of this kind are not made in the spirit of complaint. It is for the nations, whose regulations are alluded to, to judge for themselves whether by aiming at too much they do not lose more than they gain. It is for the

United States to consider by what means they can render themselves least dependent on the combinations, right or wrong, of foreign policy.

It is no small consolation that already the measures which have embarrassed our trade have accelerated internal improvements, which, upon the whole, have bettered our affairs. To diversify and extend these improvements is the surest and safest method of indemnifying ourselves for any inconveniencies which those or similar measures have a tendency to beget. If Europe will not take from us the products of our soil, upon terms consistent with our interest, the natural remedy is to contract, as fast as possible, our wants of her.

2nd. The conversion of their waste into cultivated lands is certainly a point of great moment in the political calculations of the United States. But the degree in which this may possibly be retarded by the encouragement of manufactories does not appear to countervail the powerful inducements to afford that encouragement.

An observation made in another place is of a nature to have great influence upon this question. If it cannot be denied that the interests, even of agriculture, may be advanced more by having such lands of a State as are occupied under a good cultivation, than by having a greater quantity occupied under a much inferior cultivation; and if manufactories, for the reasons assigned, must be admitted to have a tendency to promote a more steady and vigorous cultivation of the lands occupied than would happen without them, it will follow that they are capable of indemnifying a country for a diminution of the progress of new settlements, and may serve to increase both the capital value and the income of its lands, even though they should abridge the number of acres under tillage.

But it does by no means follow that the progress of new settlements would be retarded by the extension of manufactures. The desire of being an independent proprietor of land is founded on such strong principles in the human breast, that, where the opportunity of becoming so is as great as it is in the United States, the proportion will be small of those whose situations would otherwise lead to it, who would be diverted from it toward manufactures. And it is highly probable, as already intimated, that the accessions of foreigners, who, originally drawn over by manufacturing views, would afterward abandon them for agricultural, would be more than an equivalent for those of our own citizens who might happen to be detached from them.

The remaining objections to a particular encouragement of manufactures in the United States now require to be examined.

One of these turns on the proposition that industry, if left to itself, will naturally find its way to the most useful and profitable employment. Whence it is inferred that manufactures, without the aid of government, will grow up as soon and as fast as the natural state of things and the interest of the community may require.

Against the solidity of this hypothesis, in the full latitude of the terms, very cogent reasons may be offered. These have relation to the strong influence of habit and the spirit of imitation; the fear of want of success in untried enterprises; the intrinsic difficulties incident to first essays toward a competition with those who have previously attained to perfection in the business to be attempted; the bounties, premiums, and other artificial encouragements with which foreign nations second the exertions of their own citizens in the branches in which they are to be rivalled.

Experience teaches that men are often so much governed by what they are accustomed to see and practise, that the simplest and most obvious improvements, in the most ordinary occupations, are adopted with hesitation, reluctance, and by slow gradations. The spontaneous transition to new pursuits, in a community long habituated to different ones, may be expected to be attended with proportionately greater difficulty.

When former occupations ceased to yield a profit adequate to the subsistence of their followers, or when there was an absolute deficiency of employment in them owing to the superabundance of hands, changes would ensue; but these changes would be likely to be more tardy than might consist with the interest either of individuals or of the society. In many cases they would not happen, while a bare support could be insured by an adherence to ancient courses, though a resort to a more profitable employment might be practicable. To produce the desirable changes as early as may be expedient may therefore require the incitement and patronage of government.

The apprehension of failing in new attempts is, perhaps, a more serious impediment. There are dispositions apt to be attracted by the mere novelty of an undertaking; but these are not always those best calculated to give it success. To this it is of importance that the confidence of cautious, sagacious capitalists, both citizens and foreigners, should be excited. And to inspire this description of persons with confidence, it is essential that they should be made to see in any project which is new—and for that reason alone, if for no other, precarious— the prospect of such a degree of countenance and support from government, as may be capable of overcoming the obstacles inseparable from first experiments.

The superiority antecedently enjoyed by nations who have preoccupied and perfected a branch of industry, constitutes a more formidable obstacle than either of those which have been mentioned, to the introduction of the same branch into a country in which it did not before exist. To maintain, between the recent establishments of one country and the long-matured establishments of another country, a competition upon equal terms, both as to quality and price, is, in most cases, impracticable. The disparity in the one, or in the other, or in both must necessarily be so considerable as to forbid a successful rivalship, without the extraordinary aid and protection of government.

But the greatest obstacle of all to the successful prosecution of a new branch of industry in a country in which it was before unknown consists, as far as the instances apply, in the bounties, premiums, and other aids which are granted, in a variety of cases, by the nations in which the establishments to be imitated are previously introduced. It is well known (and particular examples, in the course of this report, will be cited) that certain nations grant bounties on the exportation of particular commodities, to enable their own workmen to undersell and supplant all competitors in the countries to which those commodities are sent. Hence the undertakers of a new manufacture have to contend, not only with the natural disadvantages of a new undertaking, but with the gratuities and remunerations which other governments bestow. To be enabled to contend with success it is evident that the interference and aid of their own government are indispensable. . . . .

IRON

The manufactures of this article are entitled to pre-eminent rank. None are more essential in their kinds, nor so extensive in their use. They constitute, in whole or in part, the implements or the materials, or both, of almost every useful occupation. Their instrumentality is everywhere conspicuous.

It is fortunate for the United States that they have peculiar advantages for deriving the full benefit of this most valuable material, and they have every motive to improve it with systematic care. It is to be found in various parts of the United States, in great abundance, and of almost every quality; and fuel, the chief instrument in manufacturing it, is both cheap and plenty. This particularly applies to charcoal; but there are productive coal mines already in operation, and strong indications that the material is to be found in abundance in a variety of other places.

The inquiries to which the subject of this report has led have been answered with proofs that manufactories of iron, though generally understood to be extensive, are far more so than is commonly supposed. The kinds in which the greatest progress has been made have been mentioned in another place, and need not be repeated; but there is little doubt that every other kind, with due cultivation, will rapidly succeed. It is worthy of remark that several of the particular trades of which it is the basis are capable of being carried on without the aid of large capitals.

Iron works have greatly increased in the United States, and are prosecuted with much more advantage than formerly. The average price, before the Revolution, was about sixty-four dollars per ton; at present, it is about eighty—a rise which is chiefly to be attributed to the increase of manufactures of the material.

The still further extension and multiplication of such manufactures will have the double effect of promoting the extraction of the metal itself, and of converting it to a greater number of profitable purposes.

Those manufactures, too, unite, in a greater degree than almost any others, the several requisites which have been mentioned as proper to be consulted in the selection of objects.

The only further encouragement of manufactories of this article, the propriety of which may be considered as unquestionable, seems to be an increase of the duties on foreign rival commodities.

Steel is a branch which has already made considerable progress, and it is ascertained that some new enterprises, on a more extensive scale, have been lately set on foot. The facility of carrying it to an extent which will supply all internal demands, and furnish a considerable surplus for exportation, cannot be doubted. The duty upon the importation of this article, which is, at present, seventy-five cents per cwt., may, it is conceived, be safely and advantageously extended to one hundred cents. It is desirable, by decisive arrangements, to second the efforts which are making in so very valuable a branch.

The United States, already, in a great measure, supply themselves with nails and spikes. They are able, and ought certainly, to do it entirely. The first and most laborious operation, in this manufacture, is performed by water mills; and of the persons afterwards employed, a great proportion are boys, whose early habits of industry are of importance to the community, to the present support of their families, and to their own future comfort. It is not less curious than true, that, in certain parts of the country, the making of nails is an occasional family manufacture.

The expediency of an additional duty on these articles is indicated by an important fact. About one million eight hundred thousand pounds of them were imported into the United States in the course of a year, ending the 30th of September, 1790. A duty of two cents a pound would, it is presumable, speedily put an end to so considerable an importation. And it is, in every view, proper that an end should be put to it.

The manufacture of these articles, like that of some others, suffers from the carelessness and dishonesty of a part of those who carry it on. An inspection in certain cases might tend to correct the evil. It will deserve consideration whether a regulation of this sort cannot be applied, without inconvenience, to the exportation of the articles, either to foreign countries, or from one State to another.

The implements of husbandry are made in several States in great abundance. In many places it is done by the common blacksmiths. And there is no doubt that an ample supply for the whole country can, with great ease, be procured among ourselves.

Various kinds of edged tools for the use of mechanics are also made; and a considerable quantity of hollow wares, though the business of castings has not yet attained the perfection which might be wished. It is, however, improving, and as there are respectable capitals, in good hands, embarked in the prosecution of those branches of iron manufacture which are yet in their infancy, they may all be contemplated as objects not difficult to be acquired.

To insure the end it seems equally safe and prudent to extend the duty, ad valorem, upon all manufactures of iron, or of which iron is the article of chief value, to ten per cent.

Fire-arms and other military weapons may, it is conceived, be placed, without inconvenience, in the class of articles rated at fifteen per cent. There are already manufactories of these articles, which only require the stimulus of a certain demand to render them adequate to the supply of the United States.

It would also be a material aid to manufactures of this nature, as well as a means of public security, if provisions should be made for an annual purchase of military weapons, of home manufacture, to a certain determinate extent, in order to the formation of arsenals; and to replace, from time to time, such as should be drawn for use, so as to always have in store the quantity of each kind which should be deemed a competent supply.

But it may, hereafter, deserve legislative consideration, whether manufactories of all the necessary weapons of war ought not to be established on account of the government itself. Such establishments are agreeable to the usual practice of nations, and that practice seems founded on sufficient reason.

There appears to be an improvidence in leaving these essential implements of national defence to the casual speculations of individual adventure—a resource which can less be relied upon, in this case, than in most others; the articles in question not being objects of ordinary and indispensable private consumption or use. As a general rule, manufactories on the immediate account of government are to be avoided; but this seems to be one of the few exceptions which that rule admits, depending on very special reasons.

Manufactures of steel, generally, or of which steel is the article of chief value, may, with advantage, be placed in the class of goods rated at seven and a half per cent. As manufactures of this kind have not yet made any considerable progress, it is a reason for not rating them as high as those of iron; but as this material is the basis of them, and as their extension is not less practicable than important, it is desirable to promote it by a somewhat higher duty than the present.

A question arises how far it might be expedient to permit the importation of iron, in pigs and bars, free from duty. It would certainly be favorable to manufactures of the article; but the doubt is, whether it might not interfere with its production.

Two circumstances, however, abate, if they do not remove, apprehension on this score; one is the considerable increase of price which has been already remarked, and which renders it probable that the free admission of foreign iron would not be inconsistent with an adequate profit to the proprietors of iron works; the other is the augmentation of demand which would be likely to attend the increase of manufactures of the article, in consequence of the additional encouragements proposed to be given. But caution, nevertheless, in a matter of this kind is most advisable. The measure suggested ought, perhaps, rather to be contemplated subject to the lights of further experience, than immediately adopted.

FOSSIL COAL

This, as an important instrument of manufactures, may, without impropriety, be mentioned among the subjects of this report.

A copious supply of it would be of great consequence to the iron branch. As an article of household fuel, also, it is an interesting production, the utility of which must increase in proportion to the decrease of wood, by the progress of settlement and cultivation. And its importance to navigation, as an immense article of transportation coastwise, is signally exemplified in Great Britain.

It is known that there are several coal mines in Virginia now worked; and appearances of their existence are familiar in a number of places.

The expediency of a bounty on all this species of coal, of home production, and of premiums on the opening of new mines, under certain qualifications, appears to be worthy of particular examination. The great importance of the article will amply justify a reasonable expense in this way, if it shall appear to be necessary to, and shall be thought likely to answer, the end.

PRINTED BOOKS

The great number of presses disseminated throughout the Union seem to afford an assurance that here is no need of being indebted to foreign countries for the printing of the books which are used in the United States. A duty of ten per cent instead of five, which is now charged upon the article, would have a tendency to aid the business internally. . . . And with regard to books which may be specially imported for the use of particular seminaries of learning and of public libraries, a total exemption from duty would be advisable. . . .

1791

ALEXIS DE TOCQUEVILLE

1805–1859

ALTHOUGH TOCQUEVILLE thought that the greatest menace to freedom in the American system was the likelihood of tyranny by a majority, he did, in one passage in *Democracy in America*, foresee the possibility of tyranny by a manufacturing plutocracy. He did not, it is true, develop this idea adequately, or give it sufficient weight in his analysis: subsequent events proved that American democracy was less endangered by the tyranny of the majority than by that of privileged minorities, among which that of industrial capitalism was one of the most, if not the most, important.

Alexis de Tocqueville, *Democracy in America*, Henry S. Commager, ed., New York, 1947.
G. W. Pierson, *Tocqueville and Beaumont in America*, New York, 1938.

» » From: DEMOCRACY IN AMERICA « «

SECOND BOOK, CHAPTER XX

THAT ARISTOCRACY MAY BE ENGENDERED BY MANUFACTURES

I have shown that democracy is favorable to the growth of manufactures, and that it increases without limit the numbers of the manufacturing classes: we shall now see by what side road manufactures may possibly in their turn bring men back to aristocracy. It is acknowledged that when a workman is engaged every day upon the same detail, the whole commodity is produced with greater ease, promptitude, and economy. It is likewise acknowledged that the cost of the production of manufactured goods is diminished by the extent of the establishment in which they are made, and by the amount of capital employed or of credit. These truths had long been imperfectly discerned, but in our time they have been demonstrated. They have been already applied to many very important kinds of manufactures, and the humblest will gradually be governed by them. I know of nothing in politics which deserves to fix the attention of the legislator more closely than these two new axioms of the science of manufactures.

When a workman is unceasingly and exclusively engaged in the fabrication of one thing, he ultimately does his work with singular dexterity; but at the same time he loses the general faculty of applying his mind to the direction of the work. He every day becomes more adroit and less industrious; so that it may be said of him, that in proportion as the workman improves the man is degraded. What can be expected of a man who has spent twenty years of his life in making heads for pins? and to what can that mighty human intelligence, which has so often stirred the world, be applied in him, except it be to investigate the best method of making pins' heads? When a workman has spent a considerable portion of his existence in this manner, his thoughts are forever set upon the object of his daily toil; his body has contracted certain fixed habits, which it can never shake off: in a word, he no longer belongs to himself, but to the calling which he has chosen. It is in vain that laws and manners have been at the pains to level all barriers round such a man, and to open to him on every side a thousand different paths to fortune; a theory of manufactures more powerful than manners and laws binds him to a craft, and frequently to a spot, which he cannot leave: it assigns to him a certain place in society, beyond which he cannot go: in the midst of universal movement it has rendered him stationary.

In proportion as the principle of the division of labor is more extensively applied, the workman becomes more weak, more narrow-minded, and more dependent. The art advances, the artisan recedes. On the other hand, in proportion as it becomes more manifest that the productions of manufactures are by so much the cheaper and better as the manufacture is larger and the amount of capital employed more considerable, wealthy and educated men come forward to embark in manufactures which were heretofore abandoned to poor or ignorant handicraftsmen. The magnitude of the efforts required, and the importance of the results to be obtained, attract them. Thus at the very time at which the science of manufactures lowers the class of workmen, it raises the class of masters.

Whereas the workman concentrates his faculties more and more upon the study of a single detail, the master surveys a more extensive whole, and the mind of the latter is enlarged in proportion as that of the former is narrowed. In a short time the one will require nothing but physical strength without intelligence; the other stands in need of science, and almost of genius, to insure success. This man resembles more and more the administrator of a vast empire—that man, a brute. The master and the workman have then here no similarity, and their differences increase every day. They are only connected as the two rings at the extremities of a long chain. Each of them fills the station which is made for him, and out of which he does not get: the one is continually, closely, and necessarily dependent upon the other, and seems as much born to obey as that other is to command. What is this but aristocracy?

As the condition of men constituting the nation become more and more equal, the demand for manufactured commodities becomes more general and more extensive; and the cheapness which places these objects within the reach of slender fortunes becomes a great element of success. Hence there are every day more men of great opulence and education who devote their wealth and knowledge to manufactures; and who seek, by opening large establishments, and by a strict division of labor, to meet the fresh demands which are made on all sides. Thus, in proportion as the mass of the nation turns to democracy, that particular class which is engaged in manufactures becomes more aristocratic. Men grow more alike in the one—more different in the other; and inequality increases in the less numerous class in the same ratio in which it decreases in the community. Hence it would appear, on searching to the bottom, that aristocracy should naturally spring out of the bosom of democracy.

But this kind of aristocracy by no means resembles those kinds which preceded it. It will be observed at once, that as it applies exclusively to manufactures and to some manufacturing callings, it is a monstrous exception in the general aspect of society. The small aristocratic societies which are formed by some manufacturers in the midst of the immense democracy of our age, contain, like the great aristocratic societies of former ages, some men who are very opulent, and a multitude who are wretchedly poor. The poor have few means of escaping from their condition and becoming rich; but the rich are constantly becoming poor, or they give up business when they have realized a fortune. Thus the elements of which the class of the poor is composed are fixed; but the elements of which the class of the rich is composed are not so. To say the truth, though there are rich men, the class of rich men does not exist; for these rich individuals have no feelings or purposes in common, no mutual traditions or mutual hopes; there are therefore members, but no body.

Not only are the rich not compactly united amongst themselves, but there is no real bond between them and the poor. Their relative position is not a permanent one; they are constantly drawn together or separated by their interests. The workman is generally dependent on the master, but not on any particular master; these two men meet in the factory, but know not each other elsewhere; and whilst they come into contact on one point, they stand very wide apart on all others. The manufacturer asks nothing of the workman but his labor; the workman expects nothing from him but his wages. The one contracts no obligation to protect, nor the other to defend; and they are not permanently connected either by habit or by duty. The aristocracy created by business rarely settles in the midst of the manufacturing population which it directs; the object is not to govern that population, but to use it. An aristocracy thus constituted can have no great hold upon those whom it employs; and even if it succeed in retaining them at one moment, they escape the next; it knows not how to will, and it cannot act. The territorial aristocracy of former ages was either bound by law, or thought itself bound by usage, to come to the relief of its serving-men, and to succor their distresses. But the manufacturing aristocracy of our age first impoverishes and debases the men who serve it, and then abandons them to be supported by the charity of the public. This is a natural consequence of what has been said before. Between the workmen and the master there are frequent relations, but no real partnership.

I am of opinion, upon the whole, that the manufacturing aristocracy which is growing up under our eyes is one of the harshest which ever existed in the world; but at the same time it is one of the most confined and least dangerous. Nevertheless the friends of democracy should keep their eyes anxiously fixed in this direction; for if ever a permanent inequality of conditions and aristocracy again penetrate into the world, it may be predicted that this is the channel by which they will enter. 1840

DAVID CROCKETT

1786–1836

WITH SIX MONTHS' schooling and the record of a scout in the War of 1812, Crockett, a Tennessee frontiersman, was elected in 1820 to the legislature. Restless and almost constantly on the jump, he was nevertheless chosen to serve in Congress, where he represented Tennessee constituencies from 1827 to 1831, and again from 1833 to 1835. His celebrated "tour of the North" took place in 1834. On this tour he visited the Lowell mills. A vigorous anti-Jackson man, Crockett was exploited by the Whigs in their desire to compete for Jackson's frontier following. Crockett met his death at the Alamo in 1836.

It has been questioned whether David Crockett actually wrote his own autobiographical sketches. Whether or not they issued from his own pen, they are a fair expression of a racy, untutored frontiersman, self-reliant and proud of his ignorance of "book larnin'."

Davy Crockett's Own Story, as Written by Himself; the Autobiography, New York, 1955.
Marion M. Null, *The Forgotten Pioneer; the Life of Davy Crockett,* New York, 1954.
James A. Shackford, *Davy Crockett, the Man and the Legend,* Chapel Hill, 1956.
Constance Rourke, *Davy Crockett,* New York, 1937.

» » *From:* COLONEL CROCKETT'S TOUR « «

CHAPTER IV

Next morning I rose early, and started for Lowell in a fine carriage, with three gentlemen who had agreed to accompany me. I had heard so much of this place that I longed to see it; not because I had heard of the "mile of gals"; no, I left that for the gallantry of the president, who is admitted, on that score, to be abler than myself: but I wanted to see the power of machinery, wielded by the keenest calculations of human skill; I wanted to see how it was that these northerners could buy our cotton, and carry it home, manufacture it, bring it back, and sell it for half nothing; and, in the mean

time, be well to live, and make money besides.

We stopped at the large stone house at the head of the falls of the Merrimac river, and having taken a little refreshment, went down among the factories. The dinner bells were ringing, and the folks pouring out of the houses like bees out of a gum. I looked at them as they passed, all well dressed, lively, and genteel in their appearance; indeed, the girls looked as if they were coming from a quilting frolic. We took a turn round, and after dining on a fine salmon, again returned, and entered the factories.

The out-door appearance was fully sustained by the whole of the persons employed in the different rooms. I went in among the young girls, and talked with many of them. Not one expressed herself as tired of her employment, or oppressed with work: all talked well, and looked healthy. Some of them were very handsome; and I could not help observing that they kept the prettiest inside, and put the homely ones on the outside rows.

I could not help reflecting on the difference of conditions between these females, thus employed, and those of other populous countries, where the female character is degraded to abject slavery. Here were thousands, useful to others, and enjoying all the blessings of freedom, with the prospect before them of future comfort and respectability: and however we, who only hear of them, may call their houses workshops and prisons, I assure my neighbours there is every enjoyment of life realized by these persons, and there can be but few who are not happy. It cannot be otherwise: respectability depends upon being neighbour-like: here everybody works, and therefore no one is degraded by it; on the contrary, those who don't work are not estimated.

There are more than five thousand females employed in Lowell; and when you come to see the amount of labour performed by them, in superintending the different machinery, you will be astonished.

Twelve years ago, the place where Lowell now rises in all its pride was a sheep-pasture. It took its name from Francis C. Lowell, the projector of its manufactories, and was incorporated in 1826—then a mere village. The fall, obtained by a canal from the Merrimac river, is thirty-two feet, affording two levels for mills, of thirteen and seventeen feet; and the whole water of the river can be used.

There are about fourteen thousand inhabitants. It contains nine meeting-houses; appropriates seven thousand five hundred dollars for free schools; provides instruction for twelve hundred scholars, daily; and about three thousand annually partake of its benefits. It communicates with Boston by the Middlesex canal (the first ever made in the United States); and in a short time the railroad to Boston will be completed, affording every facility of intercourse to the seaboard.

This place has grown by, and must depend on, its manufactures. Its location renders it important, not only to the owners, but to the nation. Its consumption not only employs the thousands of its own population, but many thousands far away from them. It is calculated not only to give individual happiness and prosperity, but to add to our national wealth and independence; and instead of depending on foreign countries, to have our own materials worked up in our own country.

Some of the girls attended three looms; and they make from one dollar seventy-five cents to three dollars per week, after paying their board. These looms weave fifty-five yards per day; so that one person makes one hundred and sixty-five yards per day. Every thing moves on like clock work, in all the variety of employments; and the whole manufacture appears to be of the very best.

The owner of one of these mills, Mr. Lawrence, presented me with a suit of broadcloth, made out of wool bought from Mark Cockral, of Mississippi, who sold them about four thousand pounds, and it was as good cloth as the best I ever bought for best imported.

The calico made here is beautiful, and of every variety of figure and colour. To attempt to give a description of the manner in which it is stamped and coloured is far beyond my abilities. One thing I must state, that after the web is wove, and before they go further, it is actually passed over *a red-hot cylinder,* to scorch off the furze. The number of different operations is truly astonishing; and if one of my country women had the whole of the persons in her train that helped to make her gown, she would be like a captain on a field-muster: and yet, when you come to look at the cost, it would take a trunk full of them to find these same people in living for one day.

I never witnessed such a combination of industry, and perhaps never will again. I saw the whole process, from the time they put in the raw material, until it came out completely finished. In fact, it almost came up to the old story of a fellow walking into a patent machine with a bundle of wool under his arm, and coming out at the other end with a new coat on.

Nothing can be more agreeable than the attention that is paid by every one connected with these establishments. Nothing appears to be kept secret; every process is shown, and with great cheerfulness. I regret that more of our southern and western men do not go there, as it would help much to do away with their prejudices against these manufactories. At my particular request, the annexed statement was made out, which, I have no doubt, will astonish many who read this book.

I met the young gentlemen of Lowell, by their particular request, at supper. About one hundred sat down. Every thing was in grand order, and went off well. They toasted *me*, and I enlightened *them* by a speech as good as I could make: and, indeed, I considered them a good sett of fellows, and as well worth speaking to as any ones I had met with. The old saying, "them that don't work should not eat," don't apply to them, for they are the rale workies, and know how to act genteel, too; for, I assure you, I was not more kindly, and hospitably, and liberally treated any where than just by these same people.

After supper I went to my lodgings for the night. Next morning I took another range round the town, and returned to Boston.

1835

THE LOWELL OFFERING

MARVELLOUSLY here have art and labor wrought their modern miracles," wrote Whittier of the industrial center which he saw spring up at Lowell, Massachusetts. Country lasses poured into what foreign visitors and most Americans regarded as "a commercial utopia," for the dominant conception of mill life in the textile city was paternalistic. Many of the mill girls did indeed burn with a strong desire for self-culture; and the factory managers took full advantage of this, both for the sake of the operatives and for the favorable publicity which it meant for their undertakings. The *Lowell Offering* was the first American magazine produced entirely by women. From 1842 until 1847 this periodical, in which some seventy girls had some part, attracted much attention. Those who wrote for the *Lowell Offering* displayed little class-consciousness. The editors declared they would "do nothing to add to the opprobrium of which the manufacturing capitalists have already received an undue share." In view of this, and of the tendency of the periodical to inculcate habits of self-denial and contentment, it was natural for the mill-owners to take especial pride in this literary venture.

Allan Macdonald, "Lowell: A Commercial Utopia," *The New England Quarterly*, X (March, 1937), 37–62.

» » From: THE LOWELL OFFERING « «

FACTORY LABOR

Miss S: I am very happy to see you, this evening, Miss Bartlett, for I have something particular to say to you. Now do tell me if you still persist in your resolution to return to your factory employment?

Miss B: I do: I have no objection, neither have I heard any sufficiently strong to deter me.

Miss S: The idea that it is degrading in the opinion of many, would be objection enough for me without taking into the account its real tendency to promote ignorance and vice.

Miss B: By whom is factory labor considered degrading? It is by those who believe all labor degrading—by those who contemptuously speak of the farmer, the mechanic, the printer, the seamstress, and all who are obliged to toil as belonging to the lower orders—by those who seem to think the condition of labor excludes all the capacities of the mind, and the virtues of humanity. They forget that circumstances, over which they have little or no control, place them above the necessity of labor; and that circumstances may yet compel them to engage in that at which they now scoff and spurn.

Miss S: There are objections to factory labor, which serve to render it degrading—objections which cannot be urged against any other kind of female employment. For instance, to be called and to be dismissed by the ringing of a bell, savors of compulsion and slavery, and cannot cease to produce mortification, without having been destructive to self-respect.

Miss B: In almost all kinds of employment

it is necessary to keep regular established hours: more particularly so where there are as many connected as in the factories. Because we are reminded of those hours by the ringing of a bell, it is no argument against our employment, any more than it would be against going to church or to school. Our engagements are *voluntarily* entered into with our employers, with the understanding that they may be dissolved at our pleasure. However derogatory to our dignity and liberty you may consider factory labor, there is not a tinge of slavery existing in it, unless there be in every kind of labor that is urged upon us by the force of circumstances.

Miss S: Objections have been brought up against the boarding-houses, and, I think, with much plausibility. The large number of females who are there thrown together are, unavoidably, intimately connected with each other. It cannot be denied that some, guilty of immoralities, find their way into the factories and boarding-houses; the example and influence of such must be pernicious, and terminate in the increase of vice.

Miss B: It is true that the example and influence of immorality, wherever it exists, cannot be otherwise than evil. We know, also, that some exceptionable characters occasionally find a place among those employed in factories; we know it from the fact that dismissals do, now and then, occur as the consequence. But, my dear Miss S., did you ever know or hear of a class of people who could boast of perfection? among whom wrong of any description was never known?

Miss S: O, no! And, as I am no perfectionist, I never expect to know of one.

Miss B: Then, if in one case the guilt of a few has not corrupted the whole, why should it in the other? Living in a factory boarding-house, and working in a factory changes not "human nature": it is susceptible of good, and, also, of evil, there as it is elsewhere.

Miss S: I agree with you in thinking that among all classes, and in every condition in life, evil influences are at work; but in some situations in life is not the exposure to these influences much more extensive, and, therefore, more dangerous, especially to the young?

Miss B: I believe there are many kinds of female employment offered in our large towns and cities far more dangerous in this respect than factory employment, although they may be considered more desirable and respectable.

Now, the very fact that "factory girls" are so "intimately connected with each other," soon lays open the real character of all, and I can assure you, whenever the example of one is known to be otherwise than good, she is immediately removed, how expert soever she may be in her business, or profitable to her employers. I may add, that if such ones were allowed to stay, they could not, unless they had the faculty of constantly "living in hot water." Besides, if "just as the twig is bent, the tree is inclined," the characters of most are formed before ever entering a factory. And yet, after all this strictness with regard to the morals and habits of female operatives, there are those who think one cannot be honest or virtuous who has ever toiled in a factory; they are sometimes spoken of, and to, as though they were destitute of sensibility and understanding, and unworthy of sympathy, kindness, or civility. Whether this is the result of erroneous opinions of factory labor, or of the idea that all kinds of labor is dishonorable, it is not very gratifying to our love of approbation, though it will not deprive us of that dignity and self-respect which honesty of purpose and an industry that places us above dependence always beget.

Miss S: You will not acknowledge that factory labor is degrading, or that it is productive of vice, but you must own that it fosters ignorance. When there are so many hours out of each day devoted to labor, there can be no time for study and improvement.

Miss B: It is true that too large a portion of our time is confined to labor. But, first, let me remark that this is an objection which cannot be said to exist only in factory labor. It is seldom that the interest or improvement of any class of laborers is regarded by their employers in the number of hours which is called a day's work. The compensation for labor is not in proportion to the value of service rendered, but is governed by the scarcity or plenty of laborers. This is an evil which has always existed, for aught I know, and I suppose is considered remediless. We have abundant proof that unremitted toil is not always derogatory to improvement. A factory girl's work is neither hard or complicated; she can go on with perfect regularity in her duties, while her mind may be actively employed on any other subject. There can be no better place for reflection, when there must be toil, than the factory. The patronage which newspapers and periodicals find in our city, our well-worn libraries, evening schools, crowded churches and sabbath schools, prove that factory operatives find leisure to use the means for improvement both in mind and heart. But I fear I shall exhaust your patience, and will bid you good evening, with an invitation to visit me after I have returned to my mill labor; and, as far as I am able, I will show you all the wonders of our "city of spindles."   W. J. S.

1844

PARKE GODWIN

1816–1904

GODWIN'S CAREER, like that of many American liberals, began with genuine enthusiasm for social reform and tapered off into a respectable indifference to it. After graduation from Princeton in 1834 and a legal apprenticeship, he was admitted to the Kentucky bar, but returned, without establishing a practice, to New York. His friendship with William Cullen Bryant, whose daughter he married, led to a forty-five year association with the New York *Evening Post.* Imbued with Transcendental idealism, he espoused Fourieristic socialism, edited *The Harbinger,* and published *A Popular View of the Doctrines of Charles Fourier* (1844). *Democracy, Constructive and Pacific* (1844), from which the following selection is taken, is a notable analysis of the America of the early '40's in terms of its actual shortcomings when viewed in relation to the natural rights philosophy and the claims of utopian socialism. The social vision and conscience which made this book outstanding became dim as Godwin devoted his years to translating, compiling, editing, to oratory, literary criticism, and the day-by-day activities of a civic-minded New Yorker.

Parke Godwin, *Political Essays,* New York, 1856.
Parke Godwin, *Out of the Past,* New York, 1870.
Allan Nevins, *The Evening Post: A Century of Journalism,* New York, 1922.

» » *From:* DEMOCRACY, CONSTRUCTIVE AND PACIFIC « «

II. THE NEW OR CHRISTIAN AND DEMOCRATIC SOCIETY

On the ruins of the old and feudal society, there has gradually grown up the elements and forms of a new order. A change has been wrought which is manifesting itself in the development of industry, science and art, in the silent and irresistible conquests of mind over force, in the genius of creation triumphing over the genius of destruction—in the substitution of noble, sacred Work, for base, unholy War. The right of modern societies has come to be the general right; their principle is the Christian principle of the specific unity of the whole human race in humanity, whence the political dogma of the equality of all citizens before the state; and their spirit is the spirit of democracy.

True, in the older nations, the division lines of former days are still drawn; the badges of caste are still worn; the privileges and honors of nobility are perpetuated. But they are perpetuated mostly in form. They cannot be said to be the controlling spirit of the present times. The French Revolution in the old world, the American Revolution in the new, struck a battle-axe into the rotten timbers of past institutions which has shattered them into slivers. The better classes, the nobility, the monarchs may govern—but they do so virtually in the name, with the consent, and for the welfare of the people. THE MASS is a new word that has crept into all modern languages, and which indicates the existence of a new fact. The mass, through so many weary years, the despised and spoliated hewers of wood and drawers of water.

have proclaimed their equal manhood. They assert that they are an essential element in the community. They stand before us with the honest faces, the broad shoulders, the hard muscles, the swelling hearts of men; they demand of us that they be admitted into fellowship: they claim their younger brothers-share of the patrimony of the common Father. With haggard and malignant looks, their eyes darting fiery impatience and their hands grasping the red torches of fury; through streets flowing with blood and plains strewed with the dying; in the midst of agonizing cries and wild maniac rejoicings, they have fought their way to where they now stand, and there dwells not on this, nor any side, of Heaven, the power for whom it would be safe to resist their just appeals. The existence of the mass, we say, is a new fact, demonstrated in an irregular wild way—but with somewhat of significance and emphasis.

III. SEPARATION OF THE DEMOCRATIC PRINCIPLE FROM THE REVOLUTIONARY

In several of the more liberal and recent European constitutions of government; in all the constitutions, we believe, of the United States, the universal and equal Right of man is broadly asserted.

This new Right, this democratic Right, having entered into the world by revolution, having been proclaimed, established, and defended by revolution, advancing from triumph to triumph by revolution, is it at all surprising that the principle of democracy and the principle of revolution should have been confounded?

The new Right might have been incarnated in society by the consentaneous and progressive action of reform and organization, which would have completed, by peaceable means, the natural transformation of the past society in all its departments.

But this natural movement, this absorption of the old (and secretion of the new, which constitutes the healthy growth of all the organized creation, and which might have wrought the quiet and unobstructed renewal of society,) not having been seconded and directed with intelligence by those in authority; the new spirit not having been wisely and liberally guided in its mighty expansion, the work of change was left to the arbitrament of explosive violence.

It has almost invariably occurred in the contests of adverse interests, that the usurper grows selfish and the wronged furious. A wild

assault and reckless repulse is followed by long years of relentless battle,—by the impetuous shock of armies under whose tread the earth shakes to its centre,—until slow Time decides an issue which had long before been decided in the eternal laws of Providence.

When the hour has come for the Past to yield its abuses and be changed, its resistance only provokes warfare and makes its defeat the more signal. The new principle, by being resisted, 10 instead of proceeding to the task of infusing itself into existing arrangements, is exclusively absorbed in the fight with the Past; it wastes its energies in unnecessary expenditures of strength, and it confounds itself with, and takes the character of, a manifestation of mere Violent Protest—Revolution—War. This is a most grave error. It leaves the whole task of organizing the New Order, a thing to be done.

Now, this is the task which is committed to 20 our epoch—this the problem which the genius of Destiny has summoned us to solve. With the vigorous arm of a lusty youth, we have shattered what was bad in the Past. We have gone through with the terrible work of destruction. We have broken into the ancient domain of Authority and Oppression. We must now add the infinitely higher work of true democratic construction and adjustment. 29

IV. THE REVOLUTIONARY WORK FINISHED, THE DEMOCRATIC WORK HARDLY BEGUN

Our modern democratic revolutions, though they have accomplished some good, have chiefly exhibited the new principle of the Rights of man, in its abstract and negative aspects. They have swept away the last remains of the Feudal system, founded upon war and the aristocratic distinctions of birth; they have established a representative system in politics, 40 which, inasmuch as it reposes on a principle of election independent of the accident of birth, is a decided advance upon pre-existing systems; they have rendered elementary instruction more accessible to all classes of the people; and they have called into life, under the inspiration of Christianity, a deeper sense of the worth and dignity of the individual soul. This is their good. But oh! how much they have left undone! —how much is there which they could not do! 50 They have left without organization, without direction, without rule, the whole immense sphere of Industry! They have abolished the wardenships, the guilds, the corporations of the ancient time,—all of which answered the pur-

pose in a feeble way, of a partial organization
of Labor—but they have not supplied their
place by a better organization. They have
opened to a *laissez-faire* the most absolute, to
a competition the most anarchical, to a war the
most blind, and consequently to the Monopoly
of great capitalists, the whole social and economical Workshop of the World,—the vast
field on which is effected the Production and
Distribution of Universal Wealth! Here is their
grand defect; here is their radical weakness;
here is the practical vice which condemns the
entire machinery of revolution as inefficient and
unsound.

The imperfect state in which revolutionary
and destructive, or rather negative Democracy,
has left its work, keeps open a sluice by which
a deluge of wrongs is let in upon mankind. In
spite of the supposed liberality of our new
principles, in spite of the destruction of old
abuses, in spite of the constitutional equality
of citizens, in spite of the abolition of exclusive
privileges in the sphere of commerce and trade,
the actual social order, in this most democratic
of countries, is a hateful and pernicious aristocratic order,—pregnant with injustice and suffering—*not in principle nor law,* BUT IN FACT.
We are apt to imagine in our overweening
vanity that we have left behind us the odious
distinctions that prevailed among our ancestors.
We sometimes pride ourselves upon the equality of condition and happiness that marks the
society of the United States; and to a certain
extent this pride is just. Yet it is only to a
certain extent. Theoretically, constitutionally,
legally, there are no privileged classes in this
nation; the odious laws of caste are annulled.
But, practically, positively, really, we still live
under a regime of caste, we are still governed
by classes, all our social helps and appliances
are still distinguishing, partial and confined to
the few. It is not so much our legislation,
though that is somewhat to blame; it is not the
law, it is not political principle, that erects
barriers between the different categories of the
American people,—it is our economical arrangements, or to speak more accurately, our
complete want of social and industrial organization. Let this be noted!

V. THE RAPID FORMATION OF A NEW FEUDAL-ISM,—THE COLLECTIVE SERVITUDE OF LABOR

A striking phenomenon is beginning to show
itself in these days, even to the eyes of those
least observant of such things. We refer to the
rapid and powerful constitution of a new Aristocracy, of a commercial and financial Feudality, which is taking the place of the ancient
aristocracy of nobles and warriors, by the annihilation and impoverishment of the lower and
middling classes.

After the grand explosions of the American
and French Revolutions, after the overturn of
the ancient political system, after the abolition
of feudal property, of laws of primogeniture, of
trading guilds and commercial corporations,
and the bold proclamation of the great doctrine
of free-trade, society has believed itself forever
emancipated from the domination of aristocratic and exclusive powers. It has supposed
that it had achieved the enfranchisement of
every individual, that it had bequeathed to the
universal race of man the opportunity for a full
development of all its faculties.

There never was a greater mistake, as the
result most abundantly proves.

An essential element in the calculation has
been overlooked. Now that the agitation
caused by the first onset of destruction has
somewhat subsided, when matters begin to
assume their regular places, it is found that
individuals indeed enter upon the new race
of life, with perfect *freedom* to use themselves
and their natural powers as they please; but
upon what very different conditions have they
entered? They are free to run the same race,
but on most unequal and disadvantageous
terms. The same course is open to all, but
each one, to continue our sporting metaphor,
carries different weights. Nay, they cannot be
said to have been started at the same starting-
place. Some were already provided with facilities to carry them swiftly and surely along
their way,—they had fortune, talents, education, high and influential positions,—and the
accumulated experience of ages; others, and
these are the most numerous, had none of
these things; they had, nor fortune, nor rank,
nor talents developed by anterior education,
none of the aids and spurs by which the more
favored rise; they are banished to the outer
borders of civilized existence, they welter in
the lowest pools of corrupt and stagnant com-
panionships.

What must result in such a state of things,
from that industrial liberty on which we reckoned so much—from that famous doctrine of
free-trade, which was the peculiar glory of the
new science of political economy, and which

we fondly thought the last best expression of the democratic theory? What result? Let facts answer the question! They will point us to the general subjection of the masses—of the class without wealth, talent or education—to the class which is well-provisioned and equipped!

"The lists are open," say you, "all men are called to the combat, the terms are equal for all capacities." Hold! you have forgotten one thing! It is, that on this great field of battle, some are trained, disciplined, caparisoned, armed to the teeth an impenetrable hauberk and shield is round their bodies, swords and spears are in their hands—and they hold the advantageous places for assault or for flight; while others, despoiled, naked, ignorant, famished, are compelled to live from day to day, and support their wives and children, on the meagre pittance extorted from their adversaries or picked by piecemeals from the streets. Oh! most benevolent free-trader, what sort of equality is this? What fight, what resistance even, are we of the many-headed multitude to make? Your absolute liberty is only an absolute abandonment of the unarmed and destitute masses to the charity of the well-fed and well-armed few. Your democratic civilization, which began in aristocratic feudalism—the progress of which has emancipated the working-classes from direct and personal servitude only—will end in a moneyed aristocracy, will lead to a collective and indirect servitude just as oppressive as that from which we have been so lately relieved. "Gurth," says Mr. Carlyle, "born-thrall of Cedric, the Saxon, has been greatly pitied by Dryasdust and others. Gurth with a brass collar round his neck tending Cedric's pigs, in the glades of the wood, is not what I call an exemplar of human felicity; but Gurth, with the sky above him, with the free air and tinted boscage and umbrage around him, and in him the certainty of lodging and supper when he came home,—Gurth to me seems happy in comparison with many a Lancashire and Buckinghamshire man of these days, not born-thrall of anybody! Gurth's brass collar did not gall him; Cedric deserved to be his Master. The pigs were Cedric's, but Gurth too would get his parings of them. Gurth had the inexpressible satisfaction of feeling himself related indubitably, though in a rude brass-collar way, to his fellow-mortals on this earth. He had superiors, inferiors, or equals. Gurth is now "emancipated" long since; has what we call "liberty." Liberty, I am told, is a divine thing.

Liberty when it becomes the liberty to die by starvation is not so divine." There is much in that fact, Mr. Carlyle!

[*The omitted chapters, VI–IX, consider the progressive impoverishment of both the proletariat and the lower middle class, and the increasing concentration of power in the hands of a small minority.*]

X. DANGER OF SOCIAL REVOLUTIONS

A condition of things such as we have been describing, cannot long continue. Universal monopoly cannot, in the age in which we live, be endured by the oppressed and suffering working classes. The notion of individual and equal rights which has fastened itself so deeply in the minds of men within the last few centuries, will prompt the people to rise against the institutions to which they ascribe the existence of this frightful evil. The growing hatred of the poor for the rich—a hatred which it is useless to deny—will every day grow more intense. Already among the chartists of England, a "black mutinous discontent," a hot feverish hatred of the wealthy is springing up. They are getting restless under their long discipline of a thin diet and hard labor. A notion is fermenting in their brains that society is bound to do more for them than to provide dusky poorhouses and bastiles. It will be a terrific explosion this fermenting notion will make, unless the weight of their superincumbent misery be removed. Let it be looked to in time.

Human beings are not mere commodities, whose price augments and diminishes with the supply in the market. Society owes them a guaranty of life and work. They possess a right to labor, which is the most sacred of all rights. Labor is their property; the highest form and source of all property. They have intellectual and moral faculties which must be developed. God has placed them on the earth, to advance. What shall they do, then, with that society, which not only prevents them from advancing, but which degrades and brutifies them into natures worse than those of beasts? We say worse than beasts, because to the stupidity and unreasoning violence of animals, they often add the malignity of demons.

XI. THE SOCIAL HELL

Thus we have stated that blind competition tends to the formation of gigantic monopolies in every branch of labor; that it depreciates the wages of the working classes; that it excites an endless warfare between human arms, and machinery and capital,—a war in which the weak succumb; that it renders the recurrence of failures, bankruptcies, and commercial crises a sort of endemic disease; and that it reduces the middling and lower classes to a precarious and miserable existence. We have stated, on the authority of authentic documents, that while the few rich are becoming more and more rich, the unnumbered many are becoming poorer. Is anything further necessary to prove that our modern world of industry is a veritable HELL, where disorder, discord, and wretchedness reign, and in which the most cruel fables of the old mythology are more than realized? The masses—naked and destitute, yet surrounded by a prodigality of wealth; seeing on all sides heaps of gold, which by a fatal decree they cannot reach; stunned by the noise of gilded equipages, or dazzled by the brilliance of splendid draperies and dresses; their appetites excited by the magnificence of heaped-up luxuries of every climate and all arts; provoked by all that can gratify desire, yet unable to touch one jot or tittle of it—offer a terrible exemplification of Tantalus, tormented by an eternal hunger and thirst after fruits and waters, always within his reach, yet perpetually eluding his grasp. Was the penalty of Sisyphus condemned to roll his stone to a summit, from which it was forever falling, more poignant than that of many fathers of families, among the poorer classes, who, after laboring to exhaustion during their whole lives, to amass somewhat for their old age or for their children, see it swallowed up in one of those periodical crises of failure and ruin which are the inevitable attendants of our methods of loose competition? Or the story of the Danaides, compelled incessantly to draw water in vessels from which it incessantly escaped, does it not with a fearful fidelity symbolize the implacable fate of nearly two-thirds of our modern societies, who draw from the bosom of the earth and the workshops of production, by unrelaxing toil, floods of wealth, that always slip through their hands, to be collected in the vast reservoirs of a moneyed aristocracy? Walk through the streets of any of our crowded cities; see how within stone's throw of each other stand the most marked and frightful contrasts! Here, look at this marble palace reared in a pure atmosphere and in the neighborhood of pleasing prospects. Its interior is adorned with every refinement that the accumulated skill of sixty centuries has been able to invent; velvet carpets, downy cushions, gorgeous tapestries, stoves, musical instruments, pictures, statues and books. For the gratification and development of its owner and his family, industry, science, and art have been tasked to their utmost capacity of production. They bathe in all the delights, sensuous and intellectual, that human existence at this period of its career can furnish. They feel no cares; they know no interruption to the unceasing round of their enjoyments. Look you, again, to that not far distant alley, where some ten diseased, destitute and depraved families are nestled under the same rickety and tumbling roof; no fire is there to warm them; no clothes to cover their bodies; a pool of filth sends up its nauseousness perhaps in the very midst of their dwelling; the rain and keen hail fall on their almost defenceless heads; the pestilence is forever hovering over their door-posts; their minds are blacker than night with the black mists of ignorance; and their hearts are torn with fierce lusts and passions; the very sun-light blotted from the firmament and life itself turned into a protracted and bitter curse! Look you, at this, we say, and think that unless something better than what we now see is done, it will all grow worse! . . .

XII. SOMETHING TO BE DONE—AND WHAT?

What, then, in a world like this, is to be done? The question of questions is this! Either we are to close the shells of our selfishness around us, sinking down into the mire, with stupid indifference, or we are to address ourselves, at once, like noble and true-hearted men, to the solution of the difficulty. The fact of human misery is a broad and glaring one, written in characters of fire and blood across the whole earth. What is to be done with it? We iterate the question.

1. We remark that little or nothing is to be done by any form of political action, that we know of, using the word political only in its common application to the movements of government. And there are two reasons for this; first, that politics have accomplished all that it is required of them to accomplish; and second, that their sphere is so limited, that they cannot be made to touch the source of the evil. We wish to say nothing here against any of our great political parties; but we do assert that the doctrines of either of them, carried out to

the hearts' content of the most sanguine advocates of them, would achieve nothing in the way of social reform. The Whigs, by the system they propose, would only consecrate by law those abuses and distinctions which are the evidence and result of our rapid tendency to a commercial feudality. On the other hand, the Democrats, by the repeal of all restraining laws, would only give a broader field for the freer development of the elements of disorder—they would only deepen and widen the breaches in society opened by the operation of the principle of unlimited competition. The truth is, that there is everywhere spreading a secret dissatisfaction with the results of our political contests. Among our best minds, there has long been a conviction that the strife of politics was an utterly inane and useless one, fit only, like the bull-baitings and carnivals of older nations, to amuse the coarser tastes of the populace; while the people themselves are conscious of a growing indifference to the magniloquent appeals of statesmen and editors. It is now more than half a century since the controversies of our politics begun, and it would require the sharpest optics to discover in what particular they had advanced. There has been infinite labor with no progress. The same questions have been argued and reargued, without coming to a decision. We have heard speech after speech; we have seen election after election; the bar-rooms have resounded with appeals; the streets have reëchoed with clamorings; now this faction has triumphed, and now that; victory and defeat have alternated more swiftly than the changes of the moon; legislatures and senates have met, and Presidents have fulminated; yet does it not appear, after all this noise and commotion—after all this everlasting talk and expense, that we are at all nearer to a conclusion, in these days of John Tyler, than we were in the days of Thomas Jefferson. If any one would be impressed with this view, let him compare the daily newspapers of the two epochs; he will find that with the change of a few names and dates, the articles of one might well answer for the pages of the other. Our long discussion seems to have been afflicted with the curse of perpetual barrenness. This protracted struggle, this ever renewed debate, has resulted, when all is told, to the net quotient—zero.

But let us not be understood as saying that there has been no progress in American society. God forbid! How could we say it, when we know that the mighty muscles of the human hand, the mighty powers of the human mind and heart, have been at work? How could we say it, when giant miraculous Labor has been felling the forests, and turning the glebe, and whirling the spinning jennies, and putting down its thoughts in words and deeds; when the spires of an hundred thousand schoolhouses point to the skies; when the fires of truth and self-sacrifice have glowed in many more thousand breasts; when the noblest aspirations were ascending from millions of noble souls? Yes, we thank God, there has been progress: but it has not been by means of, so much as in spite of, our politics. We mean that our politics has never been thorough enough to touch the root of our social distress. It has now no vitality. All the sap has dried out and withered from our discussions. The old straw has been thrashed and rethrashed until it is reduced to the merest impalpable powder—out of which nothing can be made, not even snuff strong enough to tickle a grown man's nostrils. Something deeper—more searching, more comprehensive, more true—is wanting, to raise us from the slough into which we have lamentably fallen.

2. Our help, if any is to come to us, is to be found in the better adjustment of our social relations. The vice for which we seek a remedy is in the heart of society, not its extremities; and it is to the heart that we must apply the cure. What that cure may be, is partly indicated by the whole tenor of this essay. We have shown that capital and labor are at open war. The field of industry, in all its branches, is an eternal field of battle. Either capital tyrannizes over labor, or labor, driven to extremes, rises in insurrection against its oppressor. One or the other of these effects inevitably follow the working of the system of unrestrained competition. How obvious the suggestion, then, that this competition must be brought to an end? If we can introduce peace, where there was before war—if we can make a common feeling where there was before antagonism and hatred—if we can discover a mode of causing men to work for each other instead of against each other—then, we say, we have advanced a most important step toward the solution of the problem.

Now, the power which is able to effect this change, which can turn opposition into accord, divergence into convergence, contest into cooperation, is the principle of the ORGANIZATION

OF INDUSTRY ON THE BASIS OF A UNION OF IN-
TERESTS.

XIII. UNITY OF INTERESTS

The three productive elements of society,
the three sources of its wealth, the three wheels
of industrial mechanism, are Capital, Labor,
and Talent. Is it not conceivable that these
three powers could be wisely combined so as
to be made to work together, that these three
wheels could be made to roll into each other
with a beautiful harmony? Can we not suppose
that for the anarchical strife of blind competition; that for the war of capital against capital,
labor against labor, workman against workman and against machinery; that, for general
disorder, the universal shock of productive
forces, and the destruction of values in so many
contrary movements, might be substituted the
productive combination and useful employment of all these forces? Most assuredly such
an arrangement can be supposed; and why not
accomplished? At any rate, does it not become
our first and most imperative duty to seek out
the conditions of industrial reconciliation and
peace?

There is no radical antagonism in the nature
of these things; there is no eternal and necessary repulsion between the various elements of
production. The frightful combats of capital
against capital, of capital against labor and
talent, of laborer against laborer, of masters
against workmen and workmen against masters,
of each against all and all against each, is not
a remorseless and inexorable condition of the
life of humanity. They pertain only to the
actual mechanism of industry, to the system of
chaotic and unregulated competition, to that
false liberty of whose triumphs we have
boasted with such hollow and ill-timed joy. A
better and truer mechanism, a nobler organic
liberty, to which these awful evils do not adhere, can be found. The wisdom of man is able
to discover, if it has not already under God
discovered, an outlet to this labyrinth of suffering—a pathway upward from this dark, disordered, howling abyss.

This is what we mean by true democracy—
a state in which the highest rights and interests
of man shall be the means and appliances of a
full development; and this Democracy, constructive and pacific in its character, becomes
the object for which every benevolent and
conscientious man should labor. How far we
have already advanced toward the realization

of it, and what yet remains to be done, shall be
our topic in some future inquiry. Meanwhile,
look to it, O ye people!

. . .

Now, it is a series of co-operations that we
propose, as the means of our social reform. It
is not a mere league on the part of the followers
of a particular calling—it is not a treaty of
amity between the members of distinct classes
—not the promiscuous commingling of all
branches of trade, that we vindicate; but it is
the voluntary union of the whole of Humanity,
on definite and scientific grounds. We contend
for the solidarity of the race in organic forms;
we desire the universal association of man,
according to an universal principle: we aim
at the thorough reorganization, not of a segment, but of the whole of society, on a basis of
individual independence and freedom, and
collective harmony and progress.

Organization of the Township

This object can be attained, we think, by
the organization of the township. Let up suppose, that in a district composed of some three
hundred families, (about eighteen hundred
souls) the inhabitants should call a public
meeting, to consider their social condition, and
after the maturest deliberation, should adopt
the following resolutions:

1st. An association is formed between all
the inhabitants of this township, rich and
poor; the capital to be composed of the fixed
property of all, and of the furniture and goods
which each one may see fit to contribute, at an
appraised valuation.

2nd. Every associate shall receive in exchange for what he brings, a certificate representing the exact value of the capital relinquished to the society.

3d. Each share shall be a mortgage upon
the fixed property which it represents, and
upon the general property of the Association.

4th. Every associate, whether he have contributed fixed property or not, shall be allowed
to take part in the productive use of the common funds, for the employment of his labor
and talent.

5th. Women and children enter the society
on the same terms as the men.

6th. The annual income, the common expenses being first liquidated, shall be divided

among the members on the following terms:

(a) A first portion shall go to pay the interest on stocks.

(b) A second portion shall be divided among the laborers, according to the difficulties of their work, and the time devoted to it by each.

(c) The third and last part shall be distributed among those who have distinguished themselves, in various labors, either by intelligence, activity, or vigor.

Thus, each man, woman, and child, will be entitled to a share in each division, proportioned to their respective concurrences in the production, by their three productive faculties of Capital, Labor, and Talent.

Let us suppose, further, that the inhabitants of this township, instead of remaining in their isolated houses, should agree to dwell in a large building, or rather, in a row of buildings, separated from each other so as to secure the privacy and independence of each family, but at the same time, so connected as to render available the obvious economies of fire, light, cooking, cellars, &c. &c.: that all the different branches of labor were distributed among groups of workmen best adapted for the execution of each, including in the term of labor, domestic avocations, agriculture, mechanical art and instruction; and that each group should have the entire control of its special department, subject only to the advisory direction of a more general and superior group; we say, let this be supposed, and we shall have the outline of the simple, but most important re-organization of society which we propose.[1] We do not here assert that an organization of this kind, is the true organization for society, although we hold that the position can be proved beyond a cavil: we merely wish to show, that Society, if it would escape from the terrible evils under which it now groans, must resort to some similar organization as the next step in its progressive career. We assert that Association by townships, as here delineated, if not *the* right way, at least leads toward the right way, and is the best approximation to a Perfect Constitution of Society, that has been presented to mankind. We assert that it is the most easy, the most feasible, the most safe, the most rational, and the most desirable phasis in which we can look at the great question of Social

Reform. We assert this upon the subjoined brief views of

Its Character and Advantages

. . . It is well, therefore, that our Constitutional Reformers, would restore the usurped power of the state, to its legitimate sphere, the township. Let one township be successfully organized—and the reform would soon expand, like the concentric circles of the water, till its circumference embraced the world. Give us one example of a political community founded upon correct and progressive principles, and we will answer for the universal adoption of it —and that right soon.

In no other mode, can a system of universal reform be begun. Nature, in the formation of the manifold and wondrous series of series that go to make up her Whole, begins with a small centre of vitality, around which the parts in their beautiful and divine order, are arranged according to the glorious law of Variety in One—which is the Eternal Fact of Creation. Well, would it be for man, did he not presume to be more wise than his Maker.

2d. *It is peaceful.* As it only contemplates voluntary action, the only force which it could use, is the force of truth and moral suasion. No man's rights would be infringed by it, but on the contrary, every legitimate right would receive an additional security. It makes no violent war upon the just privileges of any class, proposes no wholesale destruction of the property of the rich, no forced distribution of goods already acquired, deals in no bitter and malignant denunciations of any party or sect. It welcomes all ranks of people, it accepts all creeds and doctrines, and shows the basis upon which all can be harmonized in variety. Goodwill, the sentiment of human brotherhood, the love of the neighbor are the only feelings to which it appeals.

. . . 4th. *It fulfills all the duties and answers all the ends of Society.* Man has a right to a living off of the Earth, or he would not have been sent here; and, for the same reason, he has a right to use all those elements which are necessary to his full growth and development. The possession of these rights, imposes corresponding *duties* on Society. It is the primary, fundamental, most important and imperative duty of Society to guaranty his rights to every human being. But, no society that ever existed, no society that now exists, has discharged this

---

[1] Our object has been to give only the most elementary view—to suggest, rather than describe. We can prove scientifically that the organization here sketched, is the one designed by God. [Godwin's note.]

duty. A majority of men have had hard work to get even bread and water enough to keep them alive, under the old arrangements, to say nothing of the higher wants of the mind and soul. Indeed, a theory has gone forth, and is earnestly vindicated in high places, that all society has to do, is to protect the person and property of the individual. A despicable theory, if it were even carried into practice! But unfortunately, this duty, small as it is, has not been met. Society has not protected property. It is true, the property of the rich has been hedged around with the thick-set fences of all law, learning and public opinion. Accumulated Labor in the shape of Capital, is the golden fruit, watched by many-headed dragons; but living, breathing Labor, which is the poor man's only property, is flung loose to the winds, left to shift for itself, without guaranty, without protection. Yet, society pays a fearful penalty for this neglect of its duty. Its armies of paupers, its alms-houses, its prisons, its soup and clothing charities, its taxes, demonstrate with vivid clearness, how much better it would be for it to stop evils at their source. This can only be done by the thorough reorganization which we propose—an organization which would secure to every man, woman, and child, (1.) the means of comfortable subsistence, such as a clean house, wholesome food, decent clothes, and the privacy of their families; (2.) the opportunities of education, in elementary branches of knowledge, in the business of life, in the positive sciences, and in the general principles of fine arts; (3.) and facilities of intercourse with their fellows, with a position to be affected by all the gentler and more refined influences of learned and polite conversation and deportment.

It is because we believe that an organization, according to our principles, would secure these ends, that we have ventured to speak of Democracy. Never was there a word more abused —never was there a word more profoundly significant. It does not mean that ferocious spirit of levelling, which, in the French Revolution, crumbled the entire Past, and even plucked God from his throne; nor yet the wild, dirty, and turbulent mobism, which, in this country, covers with the slime of its filthiness, every character that is purer and nobler than itself: but it does not mean a condition of society in which the least individual shall have his rights acknowledged, and the means and opportunities for the fullest expansion of his faculties guaranteed. It means a social state, where the whole of life, for nine-tenths of the people, shall not be a suicidal struggle for life—where the finer essences of the soul shall not be ground out to furnish bare nutriment for the body— where none of its families shall esteem it a curse to have children born to them—where honesty and diligence, not impudence and falsehood, shall be the measures of success, and where noble thoughts and generous emotions shall not be trampled out, because forsooth, they are not what the worldly-wise deem practicable or prudent. But the great fact of the Brotherhood of Man shall be recognized— that Humanity is a living organism, of which every individual is a member—each in his sphere, bound to his fellows and the whole, as the arm or the foot is bound to the body—a partaker in their wrongs—a sufferer of their diseases—a sharer in their felicity, and a co-worker with them for good and evil. Then, in the arrangements of the State, the reconciling maxims of distributive equity shall take the place of the insane and destructive doctrines of positive equality—the slavery of pauperism and vice shall be succeeded by rational freedom— and the palsying stagnation of hopeless and remediless conservatism give way to the healthful agitation of conservative progress.

5th. *It is a direct manifestation of the Spirit of Christianity.* No fact in the life of Christ, (and he was the highest form of his religion,) strikes us more forcibly than the comprehensiveness of his benevolence. Reinhard, in his admirable work, "The Plan of Jesus," attempts to prove his divinity by the very fact that he was thus universal. His utterances, his prayers, his miracles, all evince the depth and tenderness of his sympathy with Man. He took the little children into his arms; he multiplied the wine at the festivities of Galilee; he fed the poor believing crowd, not so wise as the prudent Pharisees; and he washed the feet of his sorrowing disciples, that he might show how much he loved all his fellow-men. He wished to testify that it was our chief duty to minister to each other, to call no man master, to lord it over no man, to make life a perpetual scene of mutual helpfulness and service. Such was his spirit—and this spirit he intended should be manifested in the organization of society. The outward must ever be an expression of the inward, if we would be true to our principles.

The form must correspond with the in-dwelling law—the external tenement with the idea of its inhabitant.

What then is the law which Christian Society ought to embody or incarnate: "Thou shalt love the Lord, thy God, with all thy heart, and with all thy mind, and with all thy soul. This is the first and great commandment: and the second is like unto it—Thou shalt love thy neighbor as thyself. On these two commandments hang all the law and the prophets."—(Matt. xxvii. 57.)   1844

HENRY DAVID THOREAU

1817–1862

THE UTOPIA on earth which Francis Bacon, William Godwin, and Robert Owen thought might be realized through the application of science and technology, was again brought into the foreground of discussion in England and the United States by J. A. Etzler's *The Paradise within the Reach of All Men, without Labor, by Powers of Nature and Machinery*. Etzler, a native of Germany, had published the first English edition of his book in Philadelphia in 1841. Thoreau, while appreciating the adventure which was implied in any conquest of natural obstacles, was skeptical in regard to all the overtones of Etzler's symphony. His criticism, which appeared in the *Democratic Review* in 1843, illustrates the opposition of the primitivist, the idealistic mystic and individualistic poet-naturalist, to what appeared to be the excessive materialism and regimentation of a technological earthly paradise.

F. H. Allen, *A Bibliography of Henry David Thoreau*, Boston and New York, 1908.
The Writings of Henry David Thoreau, Manuscript Edition, 20 vols., Boston and New York, 1906.
H. S. Canby, *Thoreau*, Boston, 1939, 1958.

» » *From:* PARADISE (TO BE) REGAINED « «

We learn that Mr. Etzler is a native of Germany, and originally published his book in Pennsylvania, ten or twelve years ago; and now a second English edition, from the original American one, is demanded by his readers across the water, owing, we suppose, to the recent spread of Fourier's doctrines. It is one of the signs of the times. We confess that we have risen from reading this book with enlarged ideas, and grander conceptions of our duties in this world. It did expand us a little. It is worth attending to, if only that it entertains large questions. Consider what Mr. Etzler proposes:

"Fellow Men! I promise to show the means of creating a paradise within ten years, where everything desirable for human life may be had by every man in superabundance, without labor, and without pay; where the whole face of nature shall be changed into the most beautiful forms, and man may live in the most magnificent palaces, in all imaginable refinements of luxury, and in the most delightful gardens; where he may accomplish, without labor, in one year, more than hitherto could be done in thousands of years; may level mountains, sink valleys, create lakes, drain lakes and swamps, and intersect the land everywhere with beautiful canals, and roads for transporting heavy loads of many thousand tons, and for travelling one thousand miles in twenty-four hours; may cover the ocean with floating islands movable in any desired direction with immense power and celerity, in perfect security, and with all comforts and luxuries, bearing gardens and palaces, with thousands of families, and provided with rivulets of sweet water; may explore the interior of the globe, and travel from pole to pole in a fortnight; provide himself with means, unheard of yet, for increasing his knowledge of the world, and so his intelligence; lead a life of continual happiness, of enjoyments yet unknown; free himself from almost all the evils that afflict mankind, except death, and even put death far beyond the common period of human life, and finally render it less afflicting. Mankind may thus live in and enjoy a new world, far superior to the present, and raise themselves far higher in the scale of being."

It would seem from this and various indications beside, that there is a transcendentalism in mechanics as well as in ethics. While the whole field of the one reformer lies beyond the boundaries of space, the other is pushing his schemes for the elevation of the race to its utmost limits. While one scours the heavens, the other sweeps the earth. One says he will reform himself, and then nature and circumstances will be right. Let us not obstruct ourselves, for that is the greatest friction. It is of little importance though a cloud obstruct the view of the astronomer compared with his own blindness. The other will reform nature and circumstances, and then man will be right. Talk no more vaguely, says he, of reforming the world—I will reform the globe itself. What matters it whether I remove this humor out of my flesh, or the pestilent humor from the fleshy part of the globe? Nay, is not the latter the more generous course? At present the globe goes with a shattered constitution in its orbit. Has it not asthma, ague, and fever, and dropsy, and flatulence, and pleurisy, and is it not afflicted with vermin? Has it not its healthful laws counteracted, and its vital energy which will yet redeem it? No doubt the simple powers of nature properly directed by man would make it healthy and paradise; as the laws of man's own constitution but wait to be obeyed, to restore him to health and happiness. Our panaceas cure but few ails, our general hospitals are private and exclusive. We must set up another Hygeian than is now worshipped. Do not the quacks even direct small doses for children, larger for adults, and larger still for oxen and horses? Let us remember that we are to prescribe for the globe itself.

This fair homestead has fallen to us, and how little have we done to improve it, how little have we cleared and hedged and ditched! We are too inclined to go hence to a "better land," without lifting a finger, as our farmers are moving to the Ohio soil; but would it not be more heroic and faithful to till and redeem this New-England soil of the world? The still youthful energies of the globe have only to be directed in their proper channel. Every gazette brings accounts of the untutored freaks of the wind—shipwrecks and hurricanes which the mariner and planter accept as special or general providences; but they touch our consciences, they remind us of our sins. Another deluge would disgrace mankind. We confess we never had much respect for that antediluvian race. A thoroughbred business man cannot enter heartily upon the business of life without first looking into his accounts. How many things are now at loose ends. Who knows which way the wind will blow tomorrow? Let us not succumb to nature. We will marshal the clouds and restrain the tempests; we will bottle up pestilent exhalations, we will probe for earthquakes, grub them up; and give vent to the dangerous gases; we will disembowel the volcano, and extract its poison, take its seed out. We will wash water, and warm fire, and cool ice, and underprop the earth. We will teach birds to fly, and fishes to swim, and ruminants to chew the cud. It is time we had looked into these things.

And it becomes the moralist, too, to inquire what man might do to improve and beautify the system; what to make the stars shine more brightly, the sun more cheery and joyous, the moon more placid and content. Could he not heighten the tints of flowers and the melody of birds? Does he perform his duty to the inferior races? Should he not be a god to them? What is the part of magnanimity to the whale and the beaver? Should we not fear to exchange places with them for a day, lest by their behavior they should shame us? Might we not treat with magnanimity the shark and the tiger, not descend to meet them on their own level, with spears of sharks' teeth and bucklers of tiger's skin? We slander the hyæna; man is the fiercest and cruelest animal. Ah! he is of little faith; even the erring comets and meteors would thank him, and return his kindness in their kind.

How meanly and grossly do we deal with nature! Could we not have a less gross labor? What else do these fine inventions suggest,— magnetism, the daguerreotype, electricity? Can we not do more than cut and trim the forest, —can we not assist in its interior economy, in the circulation of the sap? Now we work superficially and violently. We do not suspect how much might be done to improve our relation with animated nature; what kindness and refined courtesy there might be.

There are certain pursuits which, if not wholly poetic and true, do at least suggest a nobler and finer relation to nature than we know. The keeping of bees, for instance, is a very slight interference. It is like directing the sunbeams. All nations, from the remotest antiquity, have thus fingered nature. There are Hymettus and Hybla, and how many bee-renowned spots beside? There is nothing gross in the idea of these little herds,—their hum like the faintest low of kine in the meads. A pleasant reviewer has lately reminded us that in some places they are led out to pasture where the flowers are most abundant. "Columella tells us," says he, "that the inhabitants of Arabia sent their hives into Attica to benefit by the later-blowing flowers." Annually are the hives, in immense pyramids, carried up the Nile in boats, and suffered to float slowly down the stream by night, resting by day, as the flowers put forth along the banks; and they determine the richness of any locality, and so the profitableness of delay, by the sinking of the boat in the water. We are told, by the same reviewer, of a man in Germany, whose bees yielded more honey than those of his neighbors, with no apparent advantage; but at length he informed them that he had turned his hives one degree more to the east, and so his bees, having two hours the start in the morning, got the first sip of honey. Here, there is treachery and selfishness behind all this; but these things suggest to the poetic mind what might be done.

.   .   .

It will be seen that we contemplate a time when man's will shall be law to the physical world, and he shall no longer be deterred by such abstractions as time and space, height and depth, weight and hardness, but shall indeed be the lord of creation. "Well," says the faithless reader, "life is short, but art is long; where is the power that will effect all these changes?" This it is the very object of Mr. Etzler's volume to show. At present, he would merely remind us that there are innumerable and immeasurable powers already existing in nature, unimproved on a large scale, or for generous and universal ends, amply sufficient for these purposes. He would only indicate their existence, as a surveyor makes known the existence of a waterpower on any stream; but for their application he refers us to a sequel to this book, called the "Mechanical System." A few of the most obvious and familiar of these powers are, the Wind, the Tide, the Waves, the Sunshine. Let us consider their value.

.   .   .

[A lengthy section of the essay, here omitted, quotes extensively from Etzler's plans for the rehabilitation of the earth through the use of "innumerable and immeasurable powers already existing in nature," but as yet unharnessed—Wind, Tide, Waves, Sunshine. Etzler concludes with a picture of the world as it would be under his mechanical system were it not for man's "ignorance, prejudice, and stupid adherence to custom."]

Thus is Paradise to be Regained, and that old and stern decree at length reversed. Man shall no more earn his living by the sweat of his brow. All labor shall be reduced to "a short turn of some crank," and "taking the finished article away." But there is a crank,—oh, how hard to be turned! Could there not be a crank upon a crank,—an infinitely small crank?—we would fain inquire. No,—alas! not. But there is a certain divine energy in every man, but sparingly employed as yet, which may be called the crank within,—the crank after all,—the prime mover in all machinery,—quite indispensable to all work. Would that we might get our hands on its handle! In fact no work can be shirked. It may be postponed indefinitely, but not infinitely. Nor can any really important work be made easier by co-operation or machinery. Not one particle of labor now threatening any man can be routed without being performed. It cannot be hunted out of the vicinity like jackals and hyænas. It will not run. You may begin by sawing the little sticks, or you may saw the great sticks first, but sooner or later you must saw them both.

We will not be imposed upon by this vast application of forces. We believe that most things will have to be accomplished still by the application still by the application called Industry. We are rather pleased after all to consider the small private, but both constant and accumulated force, which stands behind every spade in the field. This it is that makes the valleys shine, and the deserts really bloom. Sometimes, we confess, we are so degenerate as to reflect with pleasure on the days when men were yoked like cattle, and drew a crooked stick for a plough. After all, the great interests and methods were the same.

It is a rather serious objection to Mr. Etzler's schemes, that they require time, men and money, three very superfluous and inconvenient things for an honest and well-disposed man to deal with. "The whole world," he tells us, "might therefore be really changed into a paradise, within less than ten years, commencing from the first year of an association for the purpose of constructing and applying the machinery." We are sensible of a startling incongruity when time and money are mentioned in this connection. The ten years which are proposed would be a tedious while to wait, if every man were at his post and did his duty, but quite too short a period, if we are to take time for it. But this fault is by no means peculiar to Mr. Etzler's schemes. There is far too much hurry and bustle, and too little patience and privacy, in all our methods, as if something were to be accomplished in centuries. The true reformer does not want time, nor money, nor co-operation, nor advice. What is time but the stuff delay is made of? And depend upon it, our virtue will not live on the interest of our money. He expects no income but our outgoes; so soon as we begin to count the cost the cost begins. And as for advice, the information floating in the atmosphere of society is as evanescent and unserviceable to him as gossamer for clubs of Hercules. There is absolutely no common sense; it is common nonsense. If we are to risk a cent or a drop of our blood, who then shall advise us? For ourselves, we are too young for experience. Who is old enough? We are older by faith than by experience. In the unbending of the arm to do the deed there is experience worth all the maxims in the world.

"It will now be plainly seen that the execution of the proposals is not proper for individuals. Whether it be proper for government at this time, before the subject has become popular, is a question to be decided; all that is to be done, is to step forth, after mature reflection, to confess loudly one's conviction, and to constitute societies. Man is powerful but in union with many. Nothing great, for the improvement of his own condition, or that of his fellow men, can ever be effected by individual enterprise."

Alas! this is the crying sin of the age, this want of faith in the prevalence of a man. Nothing can be effected but by one man. He who wants help wants everything. True, this is the condition of our weakness, but it can never be the means of our recovery. We must first succeed alone, that we may enjoy our success together. We trust that the social movements which we witness indicate an aspiration not to be thus cheaply satisfied. In this matter of reforming the world, we have little faith in corporations; not thus was it first formed.

But our author is wise enough to say, that the raw materials for the accomplishment of his purposes, are "iron, copper, wood, earth chiefly, and a union of men whose eyes and understanding are not shut up by preconceptions." Aye, this last may be what we want mainly,—a company of "odd fellows" indeed.

"Small shares of twenty dollars will be sufficient,"—in all, from "200,000 to 300,000,"—"to create the first establishment for a whole community of from 3000 to 4000 individuals"—at the end of five years we shall have a principal of 200 millions of dollars, and so paradise will be wholly regained at the end of the tenth year. But, alas, the ten years have already elapsed, and there are no signs of Eden yet, for want of the requisite funds to begin the enterprise in a hopeful manner. Yet it seems a safe investment. Perchance they could be hired at a low rate, the property being mortgaged for security, and, if necessary, it could be given up in any stage of the enterprise, without loss, with the fixtures.

Mr. Etzler considers this "Address as a touchstone, to try whether our nation is in any way accessible to these great truths, for raising the human creature to a superior state of existence, in accordance with the knowledge and the spirit of the most cultivated minds of the present time." He has prepared a constitution, short and concise, consisting of twenty-one articles, so that wherever an association may spring up, it may go into operation without delay; and the editor informs us that "Communications on the subject of this book may be addressed to C. F. Stollmeyer, No. 6, Upper Charles Street, Northampton Square, London."

But we see two main difficulties in the way. First, the successful application of the powers by machinery, (we have not yet seen the "Mechanical System,") and, secondly, which is infinitely harder, the application of man to the work by faith. This it is, we fear, which will prolong the ten years to ten thousand at least. It will take a power more than "80,000 times greater than all the men on earth could effect with their nerves," to persuade men to use that which is already offered them. Even a greater than this physical power must be brought to bear upon that moral power. Faith, indeed, is all the reform that is needed; it is itself a reform. Doubtless, we are as slow to conceive of Paradise as of Heaven, of a perfect natural as of a perfect spiritual world. We see how past ages have loitered and erred; "Is perhaps our generation free from irrationality and error? Have we perhaps reached now the summit of human wisdom, and need no more to look out for mental or physical improvement?" Undoubtedly, we are never so visionary as to be prepared for what the next hour may bring forth.

The Divine is about to be, and such is its nature. In our wisest moments we are secreting a matter, which, like the lime of the shell fish, incrusts us quite over, and well for us, if, like it, we cast our shells from time to time, though they be pearl and of fairest tint. Let us consider under what disadvantages science has hitherto labored before we pronounce thus confidently on her progress.

"There was never any system in the productions of human labor; but they came into existence and fashion as chance directed men." "Only a few professional men of learning occupy themselves with teaching natural philosophy, chemistry, and the other branches of the sciences of nature, to a very limited extent, for very limited purposes, with very limited means." "The science of mechanics is but in a state of infancy. It is true, improvements are made upon improvements, instigated by patents of government; but they are made accidentally or at hap-hazard. There is no general system of this science, mathematical as it is, which developes its principles, in their full extent, and the outlines of the application to which they lead. There is no idea of comparison between what is explored and what is yet to be explored in this science. The ancient Greeks placed mathematics at the head of their education. But we are glad to have filled our memory with notions, without troubling ourselves much with reasoning about them."

Mr. Etzler is not one of the enlightened practical men, the pioneers of the actual, who move with the slow deliberate tread of science, conserving the world; who execute the dreams of the last century, though they have no dreams of their own; yet he deals in the very raw but still solid material of all inventions. He has more of the practical than usually belongs to so bold a schemer, so resolute a dreamer. Yet his success is in theory, and not in practice, and he feeds our faith rather than contents our understand-ing. His book wants order, serenity, dignity, everything,—but it does not fail to impart what only man can impart to man of much importance, his own faith. It is true his dreams are not thrilling nor bright enough, and he leaves off to dream where he who dreams just before the dawn begins. His castles in the air fall to the ground, because they are not built lofty enough; they should be secured to heaven's roof. After all, the theories and speculations of men concern us more than their puny execution. It is with a certain coldness and langour that we loiter about the actual and so called practical. How little do the most wonderful inventions of modern times detain us. They insult nature. Every machine, or particular application, seems a slight outrage against universal laws. How many fine inventions are there which do not clutter the ground? We think that those only succeed which minister to our sensible and animal wants, which bake or brew, wash or warm, or the like. But are those of no account which are patented by fancy and imagination, and succeed so admirably in our dreams that they give the tone still to our waking thoughts? Already nature is serving all those uses which science slowly derives on a much higher and grander scale to him that will be served by her. When the sunshine falls on the path of the poet, he enjoys all those pure benefits and pleasures which the arts slowly and partially realize from age to age. The winds which fan his cheek waft him the sum of that profit and happiness which their lagging inventions supply.

The chief fault of this book is, that it aims to secure the greatest degree of gross comfort and pleasure merely. It paints a Mahometan's heaven, and stops short with singular abruptness when we think it is drawing near to the precincts of the Christian's—and we trust we have not made here a distinction without a difference. Undoubtedly if we were to reform this outward life truly and thoroughly, we should find no duty of the inner omitted. It would be employment for our whole nature; and what we should do thereafter would be as vain a question as to ask the bird what it will do when its nest is built and its brood reared. But a moral reform must take place first, and then the necessity of the other will be superseded, and we shall sail and plough by its force alone. There is a speedier way than the Mechanical System can show to fill up marshes, to drown the roar of the waves, to tame hyænas, secure agreeable environs, diversify the land, and refresh it with "rivulets of sweet water," and that is by the power of rectitude and true behavior. It is only for a little while, only occasionally, methinks, that we want a garden. Surely a good man need not be at the labor to level a hill for the sake of a prospect, or raise fruits and flowers, and construct floating islands, for the sake of a paradise. He enjoys better prospects than lie behind any hill. Where an angel travels it will be paradise all the way, but where Satan travels it will be burning marl and cinders. What says Veeshnoo Sarma? "He whose mind is at ease is possessed of all riches. Is it not the same to one whose foot is enclosed in a shoe, as if the whole surface of the earth were covered with leather?"

He who is conversant with the supernal powers will not worship these inferior deities of the wind, the waves, tide, and sunshine. But we would not disparage the importance of such calculations as we have described. They are truths in physics, because they are true in ethics. The moral powers no one would presume to calculate. Suppose we could compare the moral with the physical, and say how many horsepower the force of love, for instance, blowing on every square foot of a man's soul would equal. No doubt we are well aware of this force: figures would not increase our respect for it; the sunshine is equal to but one ray of its heat. The light of the sun is but the shadow of love. "The souls of men loving and fearing God," says Raleigh, "receive influence from that divine light itself, whereof the sun's clarity,

and that of the stars, is by Plato called but a shadow. *Lumen est umbra Dei, Deus est Lumen Luminis.* Light is the shadow of God's brightness, who is the light of light," and, we may add, the heat of heat. Love is the wind, the tide, the waves, the sunshine. Its power is incalculable; it is many horsepower. It never ceases, it never slacks; it can move the globe without a resting-place; it can warm without fire; it can feed without meat; it can clothe without garments; it can shelter without roof; it can make a paradise within which will dispense with a paradise without. But though the wisest men in all ages have labored to publish this force, and every human heart is, sooner or later, more or less, made to feel it, yet how little is actually applied to social ends. True, it is the motive power of all successful social machinery; but, as in physics, we have made the elements do only a little drudgery for us, steam to take the place of a few horses, wind of a few oars, water of a few cranks and handmills; as the mechanical forces have not yet been generously and largely applied to make the physical world answer to the ideal, so the power of love has been but meanly and sparingly applied, as yet. It has patented only such machines as the almshouses, the hospital, and the Bible Society, while its infinite wind is still blowing, and blowing down these very structures, too, from time to time. Still less are we accumulating its power, and preparing to act with greater energy at a future time. Shall we not contribute our shares to this enterprise, then?   1843

HERMAN MELVILLE

1819–1891

THIS ATTACK on the devastating effect of the machine on the lives of mill operatives is the second half of an essay by Melville entitled "The Paradise of Bachelors and the Tartarus of Maids." It appeared in *Harper's New Monthly Magazine* for April, 1855. The first part describes the "good living, good drinking, good feeling, and good talk" enjoyed by the lawyers in the Inns of Court in London. Melville had known some of the comforts of this Paradise, which he here so pointedly contrasts with the Tartarus of Maids, when he visited England in 1849.

"The Tartarus of Maids" is not the only expression of Melville's doubts about the industrial system. Scattered through his long poem *Clarel* (1876) are many bitter judgments on the new form of slavery. He saw clearly that only so long as America continued to be a land of opportunity could we expect to be free from the horrors of industrial war.

> The vast reserves—the untried fields;
> These long shall keep off and delay
> The class-war, rich-and-poor-man fray
> Of history.

Willard Thorp, *Herman Melville, Representative Selections, with Introduction, Bibliography and Notes*, New York, 1839
The Works of Herman Melville, Standard Edition, 16 vols., London, 1922–1924.
Newton Arvin, *Herman Melville*, New York, 1950.
Leon Howard, *Herman Melville, a Biography*, Berkeley, 1951.
James Baird, *Ishmael*, Baltimore, 1956.

» » THE TARTARUS OF MAIDS « «

It lies not far from Woedolor Mountain in New England. Turning to the east, right out from among bright farms and sunny meadows, nodding in early June with odorous grasses, you enter ascendingly among bleak hills. These gradually close in upon a dusky pass, which, from the violent Gulf Stream of air unceasingly driving between its cloven walls of haggard rock, as well as from the tradition of a crazy spinster's hut having long ago stood somewhere hereabouts, is called the Mad Maid's Bellows'-pipe.

Winding along at the bottom of the gorge is a dangerously narrow wheel-road, occupying the bed of a former torrent. Following this road to its highest point, you stand as within a Dantean gateway. From the steepness of the walls here, their strangely ebon hue, and the sudden contraction of the gorge, this particular point is called the Black Notch. The ravine now expandingly descends into a great, purple, hopper-shaped hollow, far sunk among many Plutonian, shaggy-wooded mountains. By the country people this hollow is called the Devil's Dungeon. Sounds of torrents fall on all sides upon the ear. These rapid waters unite at last in one turbid brick-coloured stream, boiling through a flume among enormous boulders. They call this strange-coloured torrent Blood River. Gaining a dark precipice it wheels suddenly to the west, and makes one maniac spring of sixty feet into the arms of a stunted wood of gray-haired pines, between which it thence eddies on its further way down to the invisible lowlands.

Conspicuously crowning a rocky bluff high to one side, at the cataract's verge, is the ruin of an old saw-mill, built in those primitive times when vast pines and hemlocks superabounded throughout the neighbouring region. The black-mossed bulk of those immense, rough-hewn, and spike-knotted logs, here and there tumbled all together, in long abandonment and decay, or left in solitary, perilous projection over the cataract's gloomy brink, impart to this rude wooden ruin not only much of the aspect of one of rough-quarried stone, but also a sort of feudal, Rhineland and Thurmberg look, derived from the pinnacled wildness of the neighbouring scenery.

Not far from the bottom of the Dungeon stands a large whitewashed building, relieved, like some great white sepulchre, against the sullen background of mountainside firs, and other hardy evergreens, inaccessibly rising in grim terraces for some two thousand feet.

The building is a paper-mill.

Having embarked on a large scale in the seedman's business (so extensively and broadcast, indeed, that at length my seeds were distributed through all the Eastern and Northern States, and even fell into the far soil of Missouri and the Carolinas), the demand for paper at my place became so great, that the expenditure soon amounted to a most important item in the general account. It need hardly be hinted how paper comes into use with seedsmen, as envelopes. These are mostly made of yellowish paper, folded square; and when filled, are all but flat, and being stamped, and superscribed with the nature of the seeds contained, assume not a little the appearance of business letters ready for the mail. Of these small envelopes I used an incredible quantity—several hundreds of thousands in a year. For a time I had purchased my paper from the wholesale dealers in a neighbouring town. For economy's sake, and partly for the adventure of the trip, I now resolved to cross the mountains, some sixty miles, and order my future paper at the Devil's Dungeon paper-mill.

The sleighing being uncommonly fine toward the end of January, and promising to hold so for no small period, in spite of the bitter cold I started one gray Friday noon in my pung, well fitted with buffalo and wolf robes; and, spending one night on the road, next noon came in sight of Woedolor Mountain.

The far summit fairly smoked with frost; white vapours curled up from its white-wooded top, as from a chimney. The intense congelation made the whole country look like one petrifaction. The steel shoes of my pung craunched and gritted over the vitreous, chippy snow, as if it had been broken glass. The forests here and there skirting the route, feeling the same all-stiffening influence, their inmost fibres penetrated with the cold, strangely groaned—not in the swaying branches merely, but likewise in the vertical trunk—as the fitful gusts remorselessly swept through them. Brittle with excessive frost, many colossal tough-grained maples, snapped in twain like pipe-stems, cumbered the unfeeling earth.

Flaked all over with frozen sweat, white as a milky ram, his nostrils at each breath sending forth two horn-shaped shoots of heated respiration, Black, my good horse, but six years old, started at a sudden turn, where, right across the track—not ten minutes fallen—an old distorted hemlock lay, darkly undulatory as an anaconda.

Gaining the Bellows'-pipe, the violent blast, dead from behind, all but shoved my high-backed pung uphill. The gust shrieked through the shivered pass, as if laden with lost spirits bound to the unhappy world. Ere gaining the summit, Black, my horse, as if exasperated by the cutting wind, slung out with his strong hind-legs, tore the light pung straight uphill, and sweeping grazingly through the narrow notch, sped downward madly past the ruined sawmill. Into the Devil's Dungeon horse and cataract rushed together.

With might and main, quitting my seat and robes, and standing backward, with one foot braced against the dashboard, I rasped and churned the bit, and stopped him just in time to avoid collision, at a turn, with the bleak nozzle of a rock, couchant like a lion in the way—a roadside rock.

At first I could not discover the paper-mill.

The whole hollow gleamed with the white, except, here and there, where a pinnacle of granite showed one windswept angle bare. The mountains stood pinned in shrouds—a pass of Alpine corpses. Where stands the mill? Suddenly a whirling, humming sound broke upon my ear. I looked, and there, like an arrested avalanche, lay the large whitewashed factory. It was subordinately surrounded by a cluster of other and smaller buildings, some of which, from their cheap, blank air, great length, gregarious windows, and comfortless expression, no doubt were boarding-houses of the operatives. A snow-white hamlet amidst the snows. Various rude, irregular squares and courts resulted from the somewhat picturesque clusterings of these buildings, owing to the broken, rocky nature of the ground, which forbade all method in their relative arrangement. Several narrow lanes and alleys, too, partly blocked with snow fallen from the roof, cut up the hamlet in all directions.

When, turning from the travelled highway, jingling with bells of numerous farmers—who, availing themselves of the fine sleighing, were dragging their wood to market—and frequently diversified with swift cutters dashing from inn to inn of the scattered villages—when, I say, turning from that bustling main-road, I by degrees wound into the Mad Maid's Bellows'-pipe, and saw the grim Black Notch beyond, then something latent, as well as something obvious in the time and scene, strangely brought back to my mind my first sight of dark and grimy Temple Bar. And when Black, my horse, went darting through the Notch, perilously grazing its rocky wall, I remembered being in a runaway London omnibus, which in much the same sort of style, though by no means at an equal rate, dashed through the ancient arch of Wren. Though the two objects did by no means completely correspond, yet this partial inadequacy but served to tinge the similitude not less with the vividness than the disorder of a dream. So that, when upon reining up at the protruding rock I at last caught sight of the quaint groupings of the factory-buildings, and with the travelled highway and the Notch behind, found myself all alone, silently and privily stealing through deep-cloven passages into this sequestered spot, and saw the long, high-gabled main factory edifice, with a rude tower—for hoisting heavy boxes—at one end, standing among its crowded outbuildings and boarding-houses, as the Temple Church amidst the surrounding offices and dormitories, and when the marvellous retirement of this mysterious mountain nook fastened its whole spell upon me, then, what memory lacked, all tributary imagination furnished, and I said to myself, 'This is the very counterpart of the Paradise of Bachelors, but snowed upon, and frost-painted to a sepulchre.'

Dismounting, and warily picking my way down the dangerous declivity—horse and man both sliding now and then upon the icy ledges —at length I drove, or the blast drove me, into the largest square, before one side of the main edifice. Piercingly and shrilly the shotted blast blew by the corner; and redly and demoniacally boiled Blood River at one side. A long wood-pile, of many scores of cords, all glittering in mail of crusted ice, stood crosswise in the square. A row of horse-posts, their north sides plastered with adhesive snow, flanked the factory wall. The bleak frost packed and paved the square as with some ringing metal.

The inverted similitude recurred—'The sweet, tranquil Temple garden, with the Thames bordering its green beds,' strangely meditated I.

But where are the gay bachelors?

Then, as I and my horse stood shivering in the wind-spray, a girl ran from a neighbouring dormitory door, and throwing her thin apron over her bare head, made for the opposite building.

'One moment, my girl; is there no shed hereabouts which I may drive into?'

Pausing, she turned upon me a face pale with work, and blue with cold; an eye supernatural with unrelated misery.

'Nay,' faltered I, 'I mistook you. Go on; I want nothing.'

Leading my horse close to the door from which she had come, I knocked. Another pale, blue girl appeared, shivering in the doorway as, to prevent the blast, she jealously held the door ajar.

'Nay, I mistake again. In God's name shut the door. But hold, is there no man about?'

That moment a dark-complexioned, well-wrapped personage passed, making for the factory door, and spying him coming, the girl rapidly closed the other one.

'Is there no horse-shed here, sir?'

'Yonder, the wood-shed,' he replied, and disappeared inside the factory.

With much ado I managed to wedge in horse and pung between the scattered piles of wood all sawn and split. Then, blanketing my horse, and piling my buffalo on the blanket's top, and tucking in its edges well around the breastband and breeching, so that the wind might not strip him bare, I tied him fast, and ran lamely for the factory door, stiff with frost, and cumbered with my driver's dreadnaught.

Immediately I found myself standing in a spacious place, intolerably lighted by long rows of windows, focusing inward the snowy scene without.

At rows of blank-looking counters sat rows of blank-looking girls, with blank, white folders in their blank hands, all blankly folding blank paper.

In one corner stood some huge frame of ponderous iron, with a vertical thing like a piston periodically rising and falling upon a heavy wooden block. Before it—its tame minister— stood a tall girl, feeding the iron animal with half-quires of rose-hued note-paper, which, at every downward dab of the piston-like machine, received in the corner the impress of a wreath of roses. I looked from the rosy paper to the pallid cheek, but said nothing.

Seated before a long apparatus, strung with long, slender strings like any harp, another girl was feeding it with foolscap sheets, which, so soon as they curiously travelled from her on the cords, were withdrawn at the opposite end of the machine by a second girl. They came to the first girl blank; they went to the second girl ruled.

I looked upon the first girl's brow, and saw it was young and fair; I looked upon the second girl's brow, and saw it was ruled and wrinkled. Then, as I still looked, the two—for some small variety to the monotony—changed places; and where had stood the young, fair brow, now stood the ruled and wrinkled one.

Perched high upon a narrow platform, and still higher upon a high stool crowning it, sat another figure serving some other iron animal; while below the platform sat her mate in some sort of reciprocal attendance.

Not a syllable was breathed. Nothing was heard but the low, steady, overruling hum of the iron animals. The human voice was banished from the spot. Machinery—that vaunted slave of humanity—here stood menially served by human beings, who served mutely and cringingly as the slave serves the Sultan. The girls did not so much seem accessory wheels to the general machinery as mere cogs to the wheels.

All this scene around me was instantaneously taken in at one sweeping glance—even before I had proceeded to unwind the heavy fur tippet from around my neck. But as soon as this fell from me the dark-complexioned man, standing close by, raised a sudden cry, and seizing my arm, dragged me out into the open air, and without pausing for a word instantly caught up some congealed snow and began rubbing both my cheeks.

'Two white spots like the whites of your eyes,' he said; 'man, your cheeks are frozen.'

'That may well be,' muttered I; ''tis some wonder the frost of the Devil's Dungeon strikes in no deeper. Rub away.'

Soon a horrible, tearing pain caught at my reviving cheeks. Two gaunt blood-hounds, one on each side, seemed mumbling them. I seemed Actaeon.

Presently, when all was over, I re-entered the factory, made known my business, concluded it satisfactorily, and then begged to be conducted throughout the place to view it.

'Cupid is the boy for that,' said the dark-complexioned man. 'Cupid!' and by this odd fancy-name calling a dimpled, red-cheeked, spirited-looking, forward little fellow, who was rather impudently, I thought, gliding about among the passive-looking girls—like a gold-fish through hueless waves—yet doing nothing in particular that I could see, the man bade him lead the stranger through the edifice.

'Come first and see the water-wheel,' said this lively lad, with the air of boyishly-brisk importance.

Quitting the folding-room, we crossed some damp, cold boards, and stood beneath a great wet shed, incessantly showering with foam, like the green barnacled bow of some East India-man in a gale. Round and round here went the enormous revolutions of the dark colossal water-wheel, grim with its one immutable purpose.

'This sets our whole machinery a-going, sir; in every part of all these buildings; where the girls work and all.'

I looked, and saw that the turbid waters of Blood River had not changed their hue by coming under the use of man.

'You make only blank paper; no printing of any sort, I suppose? All blank paper, don't you?'

'Certainly; what else should a paper-factory make?'

The lad here looked at me as if suspicious of my common-sense.

'Oh, to be sure!' said I, confused and stammering; 'it only struck me as so strange that red waters should turn out pale chee—paper, I mean.'

He took me up a wet and rickety stair to a great light room, furnished with no visible thing but rude, manger-like receptacles running all round its sides; and up to these mangers, like so many mares haltered to the rack, stood rows of girls. Before each was vertically thrust up a long, glittering scythe, immovably fixed at bottom to the manger-edge. The curve of the scythe, and its having no snath to it, made it look exactly like a sword. To and fro, across the sharp edge, the girls forever dragged long strips of rags, washed white, picked from baskets at one side; thus ripping asunder every seam, and converting the tatters almost into lint. The air swam with the fine, poisonous particles, which from all sides darted, subtilely, as motes in sunbeams, into the lungs.

'This is the rag-room,' coughed the boy.

'You find it rather stifling here,' coughed I, in answer; 'but the girls don't cough.'

'Oh, they are used to it.'

'Where do you get such hosts of rags?' picking up a handful from a basket.

'Some from the country round about; some from far over sea—Leghorn and London.'

''Tis not unlikely, then,' murmured I, 'that among these heaps of rags there may be some old shirts, gathered from the dormitories of the Paradise of Bachelors. But the buttons are all dropped off. Pray, my lad, do you ever find any bachelor's buttons hereabouts?'

'None grow in this part of the country. The Devil's Dungeon is no place for flowers.'

'Oh! you mean the *flowers* so called—the Bachelor's Buttons?'

'And was not that what you asked about? Or did you mean the gold bosom-buttons of our boss, Old Bach, as our whispering girls all call him?'

'The man, then, I saw below is a bachelor, is he?'

'Oh yes, he's a Bach.'

'The edges of those swords, they are turned outward from the girls, if I see right; but their rags and fingers fly so, I cannot distinctly see.'

'Turned outward.'

Yes, murmured I to myself; I see it now; turned outward; and each erected sword is so borne, edge outward, before each girl. If my reading fails me not, just so, of old, condemned state-prisoners went from the hall of judgment to their doom: an officer before, bearing a sword, its edge turned outward, in significance of their fatal sentence. So, through consumptive pallors of this blank, raggy life, go these white girls to death.

'Those scythes look very sharp,' again turning toward the boy.

'Yes; they have to keep them so. Look!'

That moment two of the girls, dropping their rags, plied each a whetstone up and down the sword-blade. My unaccustomed blood curdled at the sharp shriek of the tormented steel.

Their own executioners; themselves whetting the very swords that slay them, meditated I.

'What makes those girls so sheet-white, my lad?'

'Why'—with a roguish twinkle, pure ignorant drollery, not-knowing heartlessness—'I suppose the handling of such white bits of sheets all the time makes them so sheety.'

'Let us leave the rag-room now, my lad.'

More tragical and more inscrutably mysterious than any mystic sight, human or machine, throughout the factory, was the strange innocence of cruel-heartedness in this usage-hardened boy.

'And now,' said he, cheerily, 'I suppose you want to see our great machine, which cost us twelve thousand dollars only last autumn. That's the machine that makes the paper, too. This way, sir.'

Following him, I crossed a large, bespattered place, with two great round vats in it, full of a white, wet, woolly-looking stuff, not unlike the albuminous part of an egg, soft-boiled.

'There,' said Cupid, tapping the vats carelessly, 'these are the first beginnings of the paper; this white pulp you see. Look how it swims bubbling round and round, moved by the paddle here. From hence it pours from both vats into that one common channel yonder; and so goes, mixed up and leisurely, to the great machine. And now for that.'

He led me into a room, stifling with a strange, blood-like, abdominal heat, as if here, true enough, were being finally developed the germinous particles lately seen.

Before me, rolled out like some long Eastern manuscript, lay stretched one continuous length of iron framework—multitudinous and mysti-cal, with all sorts of rollers, wheels, and cylinders, in slowly-measured and unceasing motion.

'Here first comes the pulp now,' said Cupid, pointing to the nighest end of the machine. 'See; first it pours out and spreads itself upon this wide, sloping board; and then—look—slides, thin and quivering, beneath the first roller there. Follow on now, and see it as it slides from under that to the next cylinder. There; see how it has become just a very little 10 less pulpy now. One step more, and it grows still more to some slight consistence. Still another cylinder, and it is so knitted—though as yet mere dragon-fly wing—that it forms an air-bridge here, like a suspended cobweb, between two more separated rollers; and flowing over the last one, and under again, and doubling about there out of sight for a minute among all those mixed cylinders you indistinctly see, it re-appears here, looking now at last a little less 20 like pulp and more like paper, but still quite delicate and defective yet awhile. But—a little further onward, sir, if you please—here now, at this further point, it puts on something of a real look, as if it might turn out to be something you might possibly handle in the end. But it's not yet done, sir. Good way to travel yet, and plenty more of cylinders must roll it.'

'Bless my soul!' said I, amazed at the elongation, interminable convolutions, and deliberate 30 slowness of the machine; 'it must take a long time for the pulp to pass from end to end, and come out paper.'

'Oh, not so long,' smiled the precocious lad, with a superior and patronising air; 'only nine minutes. But look; you may try it for yourself. Have you a bit of paper? Ah! here's a bit on the floor. Now mark that with any word you please, and let me dab it on here, and we'll see how long before it comes out at the other end.' 40

'Well, let me see,' said I, taking out my pencil; 'come, I'll mark it with your name.'

Bidding me take out my watch, Cupid adroitly dropped the inscribed slip on an exposed part of the incipient mass.

Instantly my eye marked the second-hand on my dial-plate.

Slowly I followed the slip, inch by inch; sometimes pausing for full half a minute as it disappeared beneath inscrutable groups of the 50 lower cylinders, but only gradually to emerge again; and so, on, and on, and on—inch by inch; now in open sight, sliding along like a freckle on the quivering sheet; and then again wholly vanished; and so, on, and on, and on—

inch by inch; all the time the main sheet growing more and more to final firmness—when,
suddenly, I saw a sort of paper-fall, not wholly
unlike a water-fall; a scissory sound smote my
ear, as of some cord being snapped; and down
dropped an unfolded sheet of perfect foolscap,
with my 'Cupid' half faded out of it, and still
moist and warm.

My travels were at an end, for here was the
10 end of the machine.

'Well, how long was it?' said Cupid.

'Nine minutes to a second,' replied I, watch
in hand.

'I told you so.'

For a moment a curious emotion filled me,
not wholly unlike that which one might experience at the fulfilment of some mysterious
prophecy. But how absurd, thought I again;
the thing is a mere machine, the essence of
20 which is unvarying punctuality and precision.

Previously absorbed by the wheels and cylinders, my attention was now directed to a sad-
looking woman standing by.

'That is rather an elderly person so silently
tending the machine-end here. She would not
seem wholly used to it either.'

'Oh,' knowingly whispered Cupid, through
the din, 'she only came last week. She was a
nurse formerly. But the business is poor in these
30 parts, and she's left it. But look at the paper she
is piling there.'

'Ay, foolscap,' handling the piles of moist,
warm sheets, which continually were being delivered into the woman's waiting hands. 'Don't
you turn out anything but foolscap at this machine?'

'Oh, sometimes, but not often, we turn out
finer work—cream-laid and royal sheets, we
call them. But foolscap being in chief demand,
40 we turn out foolscap most.'

It was very curious. Looking at that blank
paper continually dropping, dropping, dropping, my mind ran on in wonderings of those
strange uses to which those thousand sheets
eventually would be put. All sorts of writings
would be writ on those now vacant things—
sermons, lawyers' briefs, physicians' prescrip-
tions, love-letters, marriage certificates, bills of
divorce, registers of births, death-warrants, and
50 so on, without end. Then, recurring back to
them as they here lay all blank, I could not but
bethink me of that celebrated comparison of
John Locke, who, in demonstration of his theory
that man had no innate ideas, compared the
human mind at birth to a sheet of blank paper;

something destined to be scribbled on, but
what sort of characters no soul might tell.

Pacing slowly to and fro along the involved
machine, still humming with its play, I was
struck as well by the inevitability as the evolve-
ment-power in all its motions.

'Does that thin cobweb there,' said I, pointing to the sheet in its more imperfect stage,
'does that never tear or break? It is marvellous
fragile, and yet this machine it passes through
is so mighty.'

'It never is known to tear a hair's point.'

'Does it never stop—get clogged?'

'No. It *must* go. The machinery makes it go
just *so;* just that very way, and at that very
pace you there plainly *see* it go. The pulp can't
help going.'

Something of awe now stole over me, as I
gazed upon this inflexible iron animal. Always,
more or less, machinery of this ponderous, elaborate sort strikes, in some moods, strange dread
into the human heart, as some living, panting
Behemoth might. But what made the thing I
saw so specially terrible to me was the metallic
necessity, the unbudging fatality which governed it. Though, here and there, I could not
follow the thin, gauzy veil of pulp in the course
of its more mysterious or entirely invisible advance, yet it was indubitable that, at those
points where it eluded me, it still marched on
in unvarying docility to the autocratic cunning
of the machine. A fascination fastened on me.
I stood spellbound and wandering in my soul.
Before my eyes—there, passing in slow procession along the wheeling cylinders, I seemed to
see, glued to the pallid incipience of the pulp,
the yet more pallid faces of all the pallid girls I
had eyed that heavy day. Slowly, mournfully,
beseechingly, yet unresistingly, they gleamed
along, their agony dimly outlined on the imperfect paper, like the print of the tormented face
on the handkerchief of Saint Veronica.

'Halloa! the heat of the room is too much for
you,' cried Cupid, staring at me.

'No—I am rather chill, if anything.'

'Come out, sir—out—out,' and, with the
protecting air of a careful father, the precocious
lad hurried me outside.

In a few moments, feeling revived a little, I
went into the folding-room—the first room I
had entered, and where the desk for transacting
business stood, surrounded by the blank counters and blank girls engaged at them.

'Cupid here has led me a strange tour,' said I
to the dark-complexioned man before men-

tioned, whom I had ere this discovered not only to be an old bachelor, but also the principal proprietor. 'Yours is a most wonderful factory. Your great machine is a miracle of inscrutable intricacy.'

'Yes, all our visitors think it so. But we don't have many. We are in a very out-of-the-way corner here. Few inhabitants, too. Most of our girls come from far-off villages.'

'The girls,' echoed I, glancing round at their silent forms. 'Why is it, sir, that in most factories, female operatives, of whatever age, are indiscriminately called girls, never women?'

'Oh! as to that—why, I suppose, the fact of their being generally unmarried—that's the reason, I should think. But it never struck me before. For our factory here, we will not have married women; they are apt to be off-and-on too much. We want none but steady workers: twelve hours to the day, day after day, through the three hundred and sixty-five days, excepting Sundays, Thanksgiving, and Fast-days. That's our rule. And so, having no married women, what females we have are rightly enough called girls.'

'Then these are all maids,' said I, while some pained homage to their pale virginity made me involuntarily bow.

'All maids.'

Again the strange emotion filled me.

'Your cheeks look whitish yet, sir,' said the man, gazing at me narrowly. 'You must be careful going home. Do they pain you at all now? It's a bad sign, if they do.'

'No doubt, sir,' answered I, 'when once I have got out of the Devil's Dungeon, I shall feel them mending.'

'Ah, yes; the winter air in valleys, or gorges, or any sunken place, is far colder and more bitter than elsewhere. You would hardly believe it now, but it is colder here than at the top of Woedolor Mountain.'

'I dare say it is, sir. But time presses me; I must depart.'

With that, remuffling myself in dreadnaught and tippet, thrusting my hands into my huge sealskin mittens, I sallied out into the nipping air, and found poor Black, my horse, all cringing and doubled up with the cold.

Soon, wrapped in furs and meditations, I ascended from the Devil's Dungeon.

At the Black Notch I paused, and once more bethought me of Temple Bar. Then, shooting through the pass, all alone with inscrutable nature, I exclaimed—Oh! Paradise of Bachelors! and oh! Tartarus of Maids!   1855

» » *Social Reform and Its Critics* « «

1825-1860

» » « «

COME HOME, FATHER

Father, dear father, come home with me now!
  The clock in the steeple strikes one,—
You said you were coming right home from the shop,
  As soon as your day's work was done.—
Our fire has gone out, our house is all dark,
  And mother's been watching since tea,—
With poor brother Benny so sick in her arms,
  And no one to help her but me.—
Come home, come home, come home!—
  Please,—father, dear father, come home!—
Hear the sweet voice of the child,—
  Which the night-winds repeat as they roam!
Oh, who could resist this most plaintive of pray'rs?
  Please, father, dear father, come home!

Father, dear father, come home with me now!
  The clock in the steeple strikes two;
The night has grown colder, and Benny is worse—
  But he has been calling for you.
Indeed he is worse—Ma says he will die—
  Perhaps before morning shall dawn;
And this is the message she sent me to bring—
  "Come quickly, or he will be gone."
Come home! come home! come home!
  Please, father, dear father, come home.

Father, dear father, come home with me now!
  The clock in the steeple strikes three;
The house is so lonely!—the hours are so long
  For poor weeping mother and me.
Yes, we are alone—poor Benny is dead,
  And gone with the angels of light;
And these were the very last words that he said—
  "I want to kiss Papa good night."
Come home! come home! come home!
  Please, father, dear father, come home.

Since the methods of the temperance reformers were revivalistic, a constant supply of new songs was needed for the meetings of the Washingtonian Societies and the parades of the Cold Water Army. This song, the most famous of hundreds of its kind, was composed fairly late in the history of the movement (1864) by Henry Clay Work. Like many reformers of the day, he did not limit his zeal to one evil in need of correction. He was an abolitionist as well as a temperance reformer. His name is still hated in the South, for he was also the composer of "Marching through Georgia."

» » « «

Social Reform and Its Critics

THE SOCIAL ills that sprang from the industrial revolution, together with many olde. ailments, enlisted the humanitarian zeal of devoted and heroic, as well as crotchety, souls. Many reformers fought on several fronts, lending their support to the crusades against slavery, war, and intemperance, or fighting for the emancipation of women, the cause of public education, the abolition of imprisonment for debt, or the more humane treatment of the insane, the criminal, and unfortunate classes generally. But some apostles of social justice limited their activities to a single reform cause to which they gave themselves with unstinted devotion.

The pattern of thought and activity which inspired and governed most reformers owed much to the doctrines of the Enlightenment. Faith in the perfectibility of human nature and of human society through the rational revamping of social institutions formed the cornerstone of the reform movements. But the Christian religion, both in its traditional and Unitarian forms, likewise strengthened the structure which reformers built or tried to build. And Romanticism, with its emphasis on the importance and dignity of the individual, on feeling, on brotherhood, and on utopianism, provided underpinnings for every reform cause. No doubt individual reformers were led to enlist in crusades for social betterment as a result of personal experience, sometimes of failure to make satisfactory adjustments to one or another aspect of life. But such personal motives should not be overemphasized in view of the likelihood that every region of the country had its quota of maladjusted persons, and the northeastern states and their colonies in the West were, for particular social and cultural reasons, the seat of reform activity.

In its endeavor to influence public opinion and to incorporate its position in legislation or in institutions, each reform crusade made use of more or less the same techniques. Local, state, and national organizations were formed; periodicals were edited; agents and lecturers went about the country; the support of ministers, educators, and prominent public men was enlisted. Some of the reform movements set up lobbies in the state capitals and at Washington. Many of the reformers joined hands with kindred spirits in England and on the Continent, for reform activity was not limited to the United States.

The reformers did not lack critics. In general the South was hostile, inasmuch as its ruling class devoted its energy to the defense of slavery, an institution which virtually all reformers regarded as indefensible. Moreover, many vested interests in the North itself opposed the reformers. Some fought reform openly, others assumed that indifference was the best weapon. Still others resorted to ridicule. Besides the outspoken champions of vested interests, others of a conservative turn of mind disliked the objectives and methods of the reformers. Insisting that all change must be gradual, that improvement is to be effected through the regeneration of the heart of the individual, urging that there was indeed much good in some of the institutions and practices which the reformers were trying to uproot, these conservatives stood their ground.

Many of the objectives of the reformers were gradually realized. While their contributions were often influential, in many cases the undertow of powerful social and economic forces was far more effective. Yet in focusing and in educating opinion, the reformers accelerated changes which were on the way more often than they impeded them, or failed to influence them at all. Indeed, liberal and humanitarian reform became during the Jacksonian period one of the greatest American issues; and it has, with varying fortunes, remained so ever since.

THOMAS WENTWORTH HIGGINSON

1823–1911

THE CAREER of Thomas Wentworth Higginson did much to enrich American intellectual and spiritual history. After graduating from Harvard in 1841, Higginson taught, studied divinity, and became an outspoken advocate of women's rights and of the cause of the slave. In 1852 he was called to the "Free Church" of Worcester, Massachusetts, where, in addition to preaching, he served the causes of temperance, feminism, and abolition. His antislavery views were not merely theoretical, for he participated in direct action by aiding in the liberation of fugitive slaves and by facilitating the victory of free-soil principles in Kansas. During the Civil War Higginson helped to raise and drill the first Negro regiment, which he commanded with courage and with an inspired faith in the capacity of the Negro race, a faith to which many of his men responded.

After the war Higginson, first in Newport and then in Cambridge, continued to champion various reforms, especially women's rights, and to contribute pleasant essays to such periodicals as the *Atlantic Monthly*. Higginson is also remembered as the virtual "discoverer" of Emily Dickinson. Among Higginson's memorable writings are *A Ride Through Kansas* (1856) and *Cheerful Yesterdays* (1898).

"Eccentricities of Reformers" disproves the frequently heard remark that reformers are devoid of a sense of humor!

The Writings of Thomas Wentworth Higginson, 7 vols., Boston, 1890–1900.
M. T. Higginson, *Thomas Wentworth Higginson, The Story of His Life*, Boston and New York, 1914.

» » *From:* CONTEMPORARIES « «

THE ECCENTRICITIES OF REFORMERS

"Oh, why," said an exhausted American wife to her husband, a moderate reformer, "why do the insane so cling to you?" This tendency of every reform to surround itself with a fringe of the unreasonable and half-cracked is really to its credit, and furnishes one of its best disciplines. Those who are obliged by conscience to disregard the peace and proprieties of the social world, in the paths of reform, learn by experience what a trial they are to their friends by observing what tortures they themselves suffer from those who go a few steps farther. They learn self-control by exercising moderation toward those who have lost that quality. Thomas Hughes, in his letters from America, describing some one whom he likes, adds, "He is doubtless, however, a cracked fellow, in the best sense,"—showing that, without a little crack somewhere, a man could hardly do his duty to the times. Thus it is that the insane cling to those who, though really sane, are content to be called crazy,—"fanatic named and fool," as Lowell wrote of Phillips in a sonnet. There is nothing more curious in the rich and copious memoirs of Garrison than his early cordiality of relations with John Humphrey Noyes, the man who finally became the potent head of the curious free-love community at Oneida; and Garrison was, as a result, publicly charged with holding doctrines which were to him peculiarly offensive. Dryden wrote:—

"Great wits are sure to madness near allied,
  And thin partitions do their bounds divide."

What he wrote is not more true of the coffee-house wits whom he had in mind than of the incomparably greater wits who originate and carry on reforms.

The early anti-slavery meetings in particular were severely tested in respect to patience by those who might almost be called professional lunatics, as for instance Father Lamson, Abby Folsom (Emerson's "flea of conventions"), and G. W. F. Mellen. Lamson's white habiliments and white beard seemed almost like a stage make-up for the situation; and Abby Folsom's "Interminable scroll" (Emerson again), with her shrill climax of all remarks, "It's the capitalists!" seemed like the rehearsal of a play. Yet it is not quite fair to assume that the patience of the abolitionists was invariable. There were times when it gave way: and I have seen Abby Folsom led from the hall, courteously but decisively, by Wendell Phillips on the one side and a man yet living on the other,—she still denouncing the capitalists as she reluctantly came towards the door. To the occasional policeman present, for whom the abolitionists themselves seemed as much lunatics as their allies, the petty discrimination of putting out only the craziest must have appeared an absurdity; Wendell Phillips at that very meeting had to explain the real distinction,—namely, that he and his friends were not the object of persecution because they were crazy, but because they were known not to be.

Another striking figure on the platform, who always attracted the disapproval of the profane, was Charles Burleigh, who wore not merely long curls on his shoulders, but also a long and rather ill-trimmed beard,—in a beardless period,—and had distinctly that Christ-like look which is often to be found in large gatherings of reformers. Lowell, who was one of the early beard-converts, used to be amused in going about the streets with Burleigh, a much taller man, to find himself pointed out with a sort of subsidiary emphasis, as if he were a young neophyte accompanying his father confessor. Burleigh was undoubtedly one of the ablest men in the anti-slavery conventions. Lowell, in one of his letters, describes him as "looking like one of the old apostles who had slept in the same room with a Quaker who had gone off in the morning with his companion's appropriate costume, leaving him to accommodate himself as best he might to the straight collar and the single breast of the fugitive."[1] He belonged to a gifted family, two of his brothers being poets, and he himself was a man of singular power in

[1] *Letters of James Russel Lowell*, i. 110. [Higginson's note.]

speech, with a rich and mellow voice, a benignant manner and an extremely clear and logical mind; had he also possessed humor, he would have been one of the most effective of orators. His eloquence had every essential except this, as his personal appearance had every quality of distinction but neatness.

Another man of peculiar bearing was Henry C. Wright, whose whim was never to address the presiding officer as "Mr. Chairman," but only as "Chairman," and whose erect figure and commanding voice, with the frequent recurrence of an occasional and imperious "Now, Chairman!" gave him a weight of manner which his matter did not always confirm. He had been in early life a Congregational minister, and had lost his parish, it was said, for the unclerical act (in those days) of swimming across the Connecticut River. His papers and his journals, which were profuse, are now in the Harvard College Library, and will one day, no doubt, furnish ample and quaint materials for the historian of the "Come-outers" of that day. Another noticeable person on the platform was Nathanial Peabody Rogers, the New Hampshire editor, a man of noble and beautiful character, whose journalism had a spice and zest which would not command a market on merely professional grounds; but who was a Non-resistant of non-resistants, and would, if he could have had his way, have conducted the meetings without president, secretary, or any restrictions on debate. He out-Garrisoned Garrison on this and other points, and they at last parted company, to their mutual regret. He had one of those faces of utter benignity which always surprised Southern visitors to the anti-slavery conventions, they usually expecting to find upon the platform a set of scowling stage villains.

Another picturesque and even eccentric feature upon the anti-slavery platform was the group of the Hutchinson family, raven-haired and keen-eyed as a group of Bohemians, tall and stalwart youths surrounding their rosebud of a sister, Abby. They, too, had a melodramatic look, with their wide collars and long locks; they put immense fire and fury into "The Car Emancipation" and their other anti-slavery songs. As years went on, they broke up into detached groups, extending into the second generation. The story of these experiences has been told entertainingly in a book by one of the family. Four of the brothers used to give village concerts, in which they adapted themselves to each place they visited, using local "gags" to an extent which brought out screams of laughter. I was present on one occasion, in a country town, when they had refused an encore, but when it finally had to be conceded on the special appeal of a venerable citizen; and they selected for performance one of their most absurd songs:—

"O potatoes they grow small
Over there!
O potatoes they grow small,
'Cos they plants 'em in the fall,
And they eats 'em, tops and all,
Over there."

A muffled chuckle began in all parts of the audience, and swelled to a tumult of applause incomprehensible to me till I afterwards learned that the venerable gentleman in question was known as "Small Potatoes," from an unlucky gift of a basket of such inadequate vegetables to some donation fund.

Whether the hit was wholly accidental on the part of the Hutchinsons I never knew, and the impression on the audience was soon changed when one of the brothers, who had before given evidences of insanity, came forward to make a speech to the audience, lecturing them especially on the undue love of money. He spoke to them courageously and tenderly, like a troubled father, though he still looked young; and at last said, with infinite pity, "If you wish for money, you can have it from me," and began taking silver coins from his pockets and tossing them among the audience, where they were at first eagerly picked up by boys, and then left untouched, while the spectators seemed awed and spell-bound. I never shall forget the anxious and patient look with which the brothers watched him with their large dark eyes, not, however, interfering; and even when he had emptied his pockets and turned to a box containing the receipts taken at the door, and began to throw half-dollars and quarter-dollars from that, saying to them, "May I?" they only nodded gravely, leaving him to himself. It all recalled descriptions of the reverence given by untaught persons to the acts of the insane. He soon stopped and the music was resumed, the money being honestly collected afterwards and brought back to his brothers. This member of the household finally committed suicide, after a long period during which his disordered mind evidently played with the thought of it, getting all ready for it just at the

hour when he knew he should be interrupted, as, for instance, by men coming to the barn to feed the cattle; but finally he went too far. The career of the whole family was a curious instance of the sporadic appearance of a quality akin to genius in certain households, a trait which is familiar to every student of life in New England farming towns.

Parker Pillsbury's "Acts of the Anti-Slavery Apostles" is a storehouse of facts as to the decidedly extreme attitude taken for a time by himself, Stephen Foster, Henry C. Wright, and others, of whom it could be said, as Garrison wrote to his wife about one of these, "He is remarkably successful in raising the spirit of mobocracy wherever he goes. I could wish," he adds, "that brother _____ would exercise more judgment and discretion in the presentation of his views; but it is useless to reason with him, with any hope of altering his course, as he is firmly persuaded that he is pursuing the very best course." It was during one of these mobs that Lucy Stone, urging the men who had spoken to retire from the hall through a back door, was met by them with the question, "Who will protect you?" "This gentleman will protect me," said the sweet-voiced woman, taking the arm of the ringleader of the mob as he sprang on the platform. "Yes, I will," he said, after one look at her serene face; and he piloted her safely out. So clear, however, was the conviction of these especial leaders as to the necessity of very strong statements that one excellent Quaker woman offered this resolution at the tenth anniversary meeting of the Massachusetts Anti-Slavery Society, January 28, 1842: "Resolved, That the sectarian organizations called churches are combinations of thieves, robbers, adulterers, pirates, and murderers, and as such form the bulwarks of American slavery." What she meant was simply what James G. Birney had meant in his tract, "The American Churches the Bulwarks of American Slavery"; but these specifications which she made, though logically consistent, raised natural antagonism in thousands of honest minds.

It must be remembered, on the other hand, that this was a period, even in New England, of negro pews, negro cars, and even negro stages. I can myself recall an instance, about 1840, when a colored woman was ejected from a stage on what is now Massachusetts Avenue, near the Cambridge Common; and negro cars were often provided, even on Massachusetts railways, from which the white companions of such negroes were forcibly put out, as were the colored people from white men's cars, even if they had first-class tickets. With the curious inconsistency of those times, an exception was made if the colored people were servants of whites. These outrages were particularly noticeable on the Eastern Railroad, of which a Quaker was the superintendent. In one number of "The Liberator" (xii. 56) there is a travelers' directory of the various railroads, indicating whether they do or do not have negro cars.[2] Police justices refused to punish assaults by railroad employees even on white passengers who had resisted or condemned these outrages. Under these circumstances, much was to be pardoned to the spirit of liberty.

The woman suffrage movement, involving as it did a more immediate and personal test of daily habits than the anti-slavery reform, carried with it, naturally, its own fringe of oddities. The mere fact that it coincided with the period of the Bloomer costume would have secured this; for, while it required some mental ability to lengthen one's range of thoughts, it needed none at all to shorten one's skirts. The dress, so far from being indelicate, was scrupulously and almost prudishly modest, and those who wore it would have been dismayed and horrified by the modern bathing-dress; but it brought, as I can personally testify, more discomfort to the speakers of the other sex than any trials of a platform, since the ladies who wore it had often to be escorted home through the irreverent population of a city. But, apart from this, the mere radicalism of the agitation naturally appealed to a certain number of the unbalanced, and the movement had to bear the burden.

This came over me vividly for the first time when attending a Woman's Rights meeting —this being the early designation of the enterprise—in Philadelphia. The gathering was large, and the gallery audience was made up, in a considerable degree, of young medical students, may of these being Southerners and ripe for fun. Just after the meeting had been called to order, a man of quiet appearance came to me and said, "Is Miss Ora Noon present?" Struck by the oddity of the name,— which I have slightly modified in telling this story,—I asked him why he wished to know, and he said that she was a medical student,

and some friends from out of town had arrived and wished to see her. "Will you not call for her?" he said; and I, becoming still more suspicious, referred the matter to James Mott, who was just passing. He recognized the name at once, to my great relief, called for her aloud with his usual grave dignity, and a young girl of rather odd appearance got up, made her way to the door, and went out with her friends. After a little tittering, the audience composed itself and we heard no more of the incident. But that night after returning to the hospitable home of the Motts, I was told the whole story of Ora Noon.

She was, it appeared, the daughter of a Southern slaveholder, and was to inherit negroes on coming of age. She had formed a great desire to study medicine, to which her father was vehemently opposed. After several unsuccessful efforts, she attacked him again on her twentieth birthday and requested, as a birthday gift, his assent to her wish. He still refusing, she coolly said: "Very well; in another year I shall be of age, and shall come into possession of my own property. I shall then sell my slaves, and this will give the means for my course of medical study." The father laughed at so absurd a proposal; the subject rested for a year, and on the eve of her twenty-first birthday she announced the purpose again. The father at last surrendered, made her promise not to sell her slaves, and counted out to her the money for her first year at Philadelphia. This being in her hands she quietly said: "Tomorrow I shall emancipate my slaves, instead of selling them"; and she did it. She went to Philadelphia, knowing nobody, secured a boarding-place, bought a pair of pistols, a season ticket to the pistol-gallery, and a similar ticket to a leading theatre; and thus began her professional preparations. She proved a most successful student, and led, in spite of the above little eccentricities, an irreproachable life; her success at the pistol-gallery perhaps helping to protect from any disrespect inspired by her habitual presence at the theatre. It is all a curious illustration of the erratic tendency sometimes visible, just at first, on each step in the emancipation of any class. Very probably the later demeanor of Miss Ora Noon was one of scrupulous decorum; and she may never have needed to employ her pistols against anything more formidable than clay pigeons. . . .

[2] See *Life of Garrison*, iii. 28; *Liberator*, vols. xi, xii, *passim*. [Higginson's note.]

1899

FRANCES WRIGHT

1795-1852

AMONG THE HUMANITARIAN issues that aroused sharp feelings feminism took an important place. The republication of Mary Wollstonecraft's *A Vindication of the Rights of Women* in Philadelphia in 1794 was symptomatic of the interest of such disciples of the Enlightenment as Charles Brockden Brown in women's rights; and the Quakers had traditionally granted women privileges in religious worship usually denied by other sects. But it was not until Frances Wright, a Scotswoman who came to regard America as her home, began to lecture in behalf of women's rights, labor, and education, that feminism became a genuine issue. Frances Wright did not go as far as subsequent crusaders for the overthrow of masculine supremacy, but her influence on the women's rights movement was of incalculable importance.

Frances Wright, together with Robert Dale Owen, edited the *New Harmony Gazette* and the *Free Enquirer*. In these journals, and in her *Course of Popular Lectures* (1829), she championed the cause of labor, which was beginning to organize and to enter into political struggles in New York. She also advocated the assumption by the state of the responsibility for the upbringing and education, under public auspices, of all children, as the most effective means of providing equality of opportunity and of undermining the false superstitions of religious dogma and of aristocracy. A true daughter of the Enlightenment, Frances Wright pinned her faith on the power of reason to effect reforms. Her most dramatic effort to carry out this faith was the establishment of Nashoba, a community in Tennessee, to demonstrate to planters the feasibility of the gradual emancipation of slaves through vocational education.

Frances Wright's books include *A Few Days in Athens* (1822), *Altdorf, a Tragedy* (1819), and *Views of Society and Manners in America* (1821).

W. R. Waterman, *Frances Wright*, New York, 1924.
A. J. G. Perkins and T. Wolfson, *Frances Wright, Free Enquirer*, New York, 1939.

» » From: COURSE OF POPULAR LECTURES « «

LECTURE VII

OF EXISTING EVILS, AND THEIR REMEDY

[As delivered in Philadelphia, June 2, 1829]

Having now traced with you what knowledge is in matter and in mind; what virtue is in human conduct, where its rules are to be sought, and how they may be found; tested, by the standard thus supplied, the ruling topic of discussion and instruction throughout this country; shown that, while this topic subtracts from the wealth of the nation twenty millions per annum, and from the hearts and minds of the people social fellowship and common sense, it has in nature no real existence—is not knowledge, but only imagination—is not fact, but only theory; and, having shown, moreover, that theory can supply no subject matter of instruction; that the teaching of opinions is as erroneous in principle as it is dangerous in practice; that the duty of the instructor is simply to enrich the mind with knowledge, to awaken the eye, and the ear, and the touch, to the perception of things, the judgment of their comparison and arrangement, and to leave the free unbiassed mind to draw its own conclusions from the evidence thus collected,—I shall

now present a few observations on the necessity of commencing, and gradually perfecting,
a radical reform in your existing outlays of
time and money—on and in churches, theological colleges, privileged and exclusive seminaries
of all descriptions, religious Sabbath schools,
and all their aids and adjuncts of Bibles, tracts,
missionaries, priests, and preachers, multiplied
and multiplying throughout the land, until they
10 promise to absorb more capital than did the
temple of Solomon, and to devour more of the
first fruits of industry than did the tribe of
Levi in the plenitude of its power;—on the
necessity, I say, of substituting for your present
cumbrous, expensive, useless, or rather pernicious, system of partial, opinionative, and
dogmatical instruction, one at once national,
rational, and republican; one which shall take
for its study, our own world and our own
20 nature; for its object, the improvement of man;
and for its means, the practical development of
truth, the removal of temptations to evil, and
the gradual equalization of human condition,
human duties, and human enjoyments, by the
equal diffusion of knowledge without distinction of class or sect—both of which distinctions
are inconsistent with republican institutions as
they are with reason and with common sense,
with virtue and with happiness.
30   Time is it in this land to commence this reform. Time is it to check the ambition of an
organized clergy, the demoralizing effects of
a false system of law; to heal the strife fomented by sectarian religion and legal disputes; to bring down the pride of ideal wealth,
and to raise honest industry to honour. Time
is it to search out the misery in the land, and
to heal it at the source. Time is it to remember the poor and the afflicted, ay! and the
40 vicious and the depraved. Time is it to perceive that every sorrow which corrodes the
human heart, every vice which diseases the
body and the mind, every crime which startles
the ear and sends back the blood affrighted to
the heart—is the product of one evil, the foul
growth from one root, the distorted progeny
of one corrupt parent—IGNORANCE.
      Time is it to perceive this truth; to proclaim
it on the housetop, in the market place, in city
50 and forest, throughout the land; to acknowledge it in the depths of our hearts, and to apply all our energies to the adoption of those
salutary measures which this salutary truth
spontaneously suggests. Time is it, I say, to
turn our churches into halls of science, our

schools of faith into schools of knowledge, our
privileged colleges into state institutions for
all the youth of the land. Time is it to arrest
our speculations respecting unseen worlds and
inconceivable mysteries, and to address our
inquiries to the improvement of our human
condition, and our efforts to the practical illustration of those beautiful principles of liberty and equality enshrined in the political
institutions, and, first and chief, in the national declaration of independence.
      And by whom and how, are these changes
to be effected? By whom! And do a free people ask the question! By themselves. By themselves—*the people.*
      I am addressing the people of Philadelphia
—the people of a city where Jefferson penned
the glorious declaration which awoke this nation and the world—the city, where the larum
so astounding to tyranny, so fraught with hope,
and joy, and exulting triumph to humankind,
was first sounded in the ears of Americans. I
speak to the descendants of those men who
heard from the steps of their old state house
the principles of liberty and equality first proclaimed to man. I speak to the inhabitants of
a city founded by the most peaceful, the most
humane, and the most practical of all Christian
sects. I speak to mechanics who are uniting for
the discovery of their interests and the protection of their rights. I speak to a public whose
benevolence has been long harrowed by increasing pauperism, and whose social order
and social happiness are threatened by increasing vice. I speak to sectarians who are weary
of sectarianism. I speak to honest men who
tremble for their honesty. I speak to the *dishonest* whose integrity has fallen before the
discouragements waiting upon industry; and
who, by slow degrees, or in moments of desperation, have forsaken honest labour, because
without a reward, for fraudulent speculation,
because it promised one chance of success to a
thousand chances of ruin. I speak to parents
anxious for their offspring—to husbands who,
while shortening their existence by excess of
labour, foresee, at their death, not sorrow
alone, but unrequited industry and hopeless
penury, involving shame, and perhaps infamy,
for their oppressed widows and unprotected
children. I speak to human beings surrounded
by human suffering—to fellow citizens pledged
to fellow feeling—to republicans pledged to
equal rights and, as a consequence, to equal
condition and equal enjoyments; and I call

them—oh, would that my voice were loud to reach every ear, and persuasive to reach every heart!—I call them to UNITE; and to unite for the consideration of the evils around us—for the discovery and application of their remedy.

Dreadful has been the distress exhibited during the past year, not in this city only, but in every city throughout the whole extent of this vast republic. Long had the mass of evil been accumulated, ere it attracted attention; and, would we understand how far the plague is to spread, or what is to be its termination, we must look to Europe.

We are fast traveling in the footsteps of Europe, my friends; for her principles of action are ours. We have in all our habits and usages, the same vices, and, with these same vices, we must have, as we see we have, the same evils.

The great principles stamped in America's declaration of independence, are true, are great, are sublime, and are *all her own*. But her usages, her law, her religion, her education, are false, narrow, prejudiced, ignorant, and are the relic of dark ages—the gift and bequeathment of king-governed, priest-ridden nations, whose supremacy, indeed, the people of America have challenged and overthrown, but whose example they are still following.

A foreigner, I have looked round on this land unblinded by local prejudices or national predilections; a friend to human-kind, zealous for human improvement, enamoured to enthusiasm, if you will, of human liberty, I first sought this country to see in operation those principles consecrated in her national institutions, and whose simple grandeur had fired the enthusiasm and cheered the heart of my childhood, disgusted as it was with the idle parade and pride of unjust power inherent in European aristocracy. Delighted with the sound of political liberty, the absence of bayonets and constrained taxation, I spake and published, as I felt, in praise of American institutions; and called, and, I believe, first generally awakened, the attention of the European public to their study and appreciation.

Disappointed, in common with all the friends of liberty in Europe, by the issue of the well-imagined, but ill-sustained, revolutions of the old continent, which closed, as you will remember, by the triumph of France and the holy alliance over the bands of Riego and Mina in Spain. I returned to this republic as to the last hope of the human family, anxious to inspect it through its wide extent, and to study it in all its details.

The result of my observation has been the conviction, that the reform commenced at the revolution of '76 has been but little improved through the term of years which have succeeded; that the national policy of the country was then indeed changed, but that its social economy has remained such as it was in the days of its European vassalage.

In confirmation of this, I will request you to observe, that your religion is the same as that of monarchial England—taught from the same books, and promulgated and sustained by similar means, viz. a salaried priesthood, set apart from the people; sectarian churches, in whose property the people have no share, and over whose use and occupancy the people have no control; expensive missions, treasury funds, associations, and above all, a compulsory power, compounded at once of accumulated wealth, established custom, extensive correspondence, and a system of education imbued with its spirit and all pervaded by its influence.

Again, in proof of the similarity between your internal policy and that of monarchial England, I will request you to observe that *her law is your law*. Every part and parcel of that absurd, cruel, ignorant, inconsistent, incomprehensible jumble, styled the common law of England—every part and parcel of it, I say, not abrogated or altered expressly by legislative statutes, which has been very rarely done, is at this hour the law of revolutionized America.

Farther, in proof of the identity of your fabric of civil polity with that of aristocratical England, I will request you to observe that the system of education pursued in both countries is, with little variation, one and the same. There you have endowed universities, privileged by custom, enriched by ancient royal favour, protected by parliamentary statutes, and devoted to the upholding, perpetuating, and strengthening the power and privilege to which they owe their origin. There, too, you have parish schools under the control of the parish priest, and a press every where coerced by law, swayed, bribed, or silenced by ascendant parties or tyrannous authority. And *here* have we not colleges with endowments still held by the royal charters which first bestowed them, and colleges with lands and money granted by American legislatures—not for the advantage of the American people, but for that of their rulers; for the children of privileged professions upon whom is thus entailed the privilege of their fathers, and that as certainly as the son of a duke is born to a dukedom in England. *Here* have we not also schools controlled by the clergy; nay, have we not all our public institutions, scientific, literary, judicial, or humane, ridden by the spirit of orthodoxy, and invaded, perverted, vitiated, and tormented by opinionative distinctions? And *here* have we not a press paralyzed by fear, disgraced by party, and ruled by loud-tongued fanaticism, or aspiring and threatening sectarian ambition? And more, my friends, see we not, in this nation of confederated freemen, as many distinctions of class as afflict the aristocracies of Britain, or the despotism of the Russias; and more distinctions of sect than ever cursed all the nations of Europe together, from the preaching of Peter the hermit, to the trances of Madame Krudner, or the miracles of Prince Hohenlohe?

Surely all these are singular anomalies in a republic. Sparta, when she conceived her democracy, commenced with educational equality; when she aimed at national union, she cemented that union in childhood—at the public board, in the gymnasium, in the temple, in the common habits, common feelings, common duties, and common condition. And so, notwithstanding all the errors with which her institutions were fraught, and all the vices which arose out of those errors did she [not] present for ages a wondrous sample of democratic union, and consequently of national prosperity?

What then, is wanted here? What Sparta had—a *national education*. And what Sparta, in many respects, had not—a *rational education*. Hitherto, my friends, in government as in every branch of morals, we have but too much mistaken words for truths, and forms for principles. To render men free, it sufficeth not to proclaim their liberty; to make them equal, it sufficeth not to call them so. True, the 4th of July, '76, commenced a new era for our race. True, the sun of promise then rose upon the world. But let us not mistake for the fulness of light what was but its harbinger. Let us not conceive that man in signing the declaration of his rights secured their possession; that having framed the theory, he had not, and hath not still, the practice to seek.

Your fathers, indeed, on the day from which dates your existence as a nation, opened the gates of the temple of human liberty. But think not they entered, nor that you have entered the sanctuary. They passed not, nor have you passed, even the threshold.

Who speaks of liberty while the human mind is in chains? Who of equality while the thousands are in squalid wretchedness, the millions harassed with health-destroying labour, the few afflicted with health-destroying idleness, and all tormented by health-destroying solicitude? Look abroad on the misery which is gaining on the land! Mark the strife, and the discord, and the jealousies, the shock of interests and opinions, the hatreds of sect, the estrangements of class, the pride of wealth, the debasement of poverty, the helplessness of youth unprotected, of age uncomforted, of industry unrewarded, of ignorance unenlightened, of vice unreclaimed, of misery unpitied, of sickness, hunger, and nakedness unsatisfied, unalleviated, and unheeded. Go! mark all the wrongs and the wretchedness with which the eye and the ear and the heart are familiar, and then echo in triumph and celebrate in jubilee the insulting declaration—*all men are free and equal!*

That evils exist, none that have eyes, ears, and hearts can dispute. That these evils are on the increase, none who have watched the fluctuations of trade, the sinking price of labour, the growth of pauperism, and the increase of crime, will dispute. Little need be said here to the people of Philadelphia. The researches made by the public spirited among their own citizens, have but too well substantiated the suffering condition of a large mass of their population. In Boston, in New-York, in Baltimore, the voice of distress hath, in like manner, burst the barriers raised, and so long sustained, by the pride of honest industry, unused to ask from charity what it hath been wont to earn by the sweat of the brow. In each and every city necessity has constrained inquiry; and in each and every city inquiry has elicited the same appalling facts: that the hardest labour is often without a reward adequate to the sustenance of the labourer; that when, by over exertion and all the diseases, and often vices, which excess of exertion induces, the labourer, whose patient sedulous industry supplies the community with all its comforts, and the rich with all their luxuries —when he, I say, is brought to an untimely grave by those exertions which, while sustaining the life of others, cut short his own—when he is mowed down by that labour whose products form the boasted wealth of the state, he leaves a family, to whom the strength of his manhood had barely furnished bread, to lean upon the weakness of a soul-stricken mother, and hurry her to the grave of her father.

Such is the information gleaned from the report of the committee lately appointed by the town meeting of the city and county of Philadelphia, and as verbatim reiterated in every populous city throughout the land. And what are the remedies suggested by our corporation, our newspaper editors, our religious societies, our tracts, and our sermons? Some have ordained fasts, multiplied prayers, and recommended pious submission to a Providence who should have instituted all this calamity for the purpose of fulfilling the words of a Jewish prophet, "the poor shall never cease from the land." Some, less spiritual-minded, have called for larger jails and more poor houses; some, for increased poor rates and additional benevolent societies; others, for compulsory laws protective of labour, and fixing a minimum, below which it shall be penal to reduce it; while others, and those not the least able to appreciate all the difficulties of the question, have sought the last resource of suffering poverty and oppressed industry in the humanity and sense of justice of the wealthier classes of society.

This last is the forlorn hope presented in the touching document signed by Matthew Carey and his fellow labourers.

It were easy to observe, in reply to each and all of the palliatives variously suggested for evils, which none profess to remedy, that to punish crime when committed is not to prevent its commission; to force the work of the poor in poor houses is only farther to glut an already unproductive market; to multiply charities is only to increase pauperism; that to fix by statute the monied price of labour would be impossible in itself, and, if possible, mischievous no less to the labourer than to the employer; and that, under the existing state of things, for human beings to lean upon the compassion and justice of their fellow creatures, is to lean upon a rotten reed.

I believe no individual, possessed of common sense and common feeling, can have studied the report of the committee to which I have referred, or the multitude of similar documents furnished elsewhere, without acknowledging that reform, and that not slight nor partial, but radical and universal, is called for. All must admit that no such reform—that is, that no remedy commensurate with the evil, has been suggested, and would we but reflect, we should perceive that no efficient remedy *can* be suggested, or if suggested, applied, until the people are generally engaged in its discovery and its application for themselves.

In this nation, any more than in any other nation, the mass has never reflected for the mass; the people, as a body, have never addressed themselves to the study of their own condition, and to the just and fair interpretation of their common interests. And, as it was with their national independence, so shall it be with their national happiness—it shall be found only when the mass shall seek it. No people have ever received liberty *in gift.* Given, it were not appreciated; it were not understood. Won without exertion, it were lost as readily. Let the people of America recall the ten years of war and tribulation by which they purchased their national independence. Let efforts as strenuous be now made, not with the sword of steel, indeed, but with the sword of the spirit, and their farther enfranchisement from poverty, starvation, and dependence, must be equally successful.

Great reforms are not wrought in a day. Evils which are the accumulated results of accumulated errors, are not to be struck down at a blow by the rod of a magician. A free people may boast that all power is in their hands; but no effectual power can be in their hands until knowledge be in their minds.

But how may knowledge be imparted to their minds? Such effective knowledge as shall render apparent to all the interests of all, and demonstrate the simple truths—that a nation to be strong, must be united; to be united, must be equal in condition; to be equal in condition, must be similar in habits and in feeling; to be similar in habits and in feeling, *must be raised in national institutions, as the children of a common family, and citizens of a common country.*

Before entering on the development of the means I have here suggested for paving our way to the reform of those evils which now press upon humanity, and which, carried, perhaps, to their acme in some of the nations of Europe, are gaining ground in these United States with a rapidity alarming to all who know how to read the present, or to calculate the future—I must observe, that I am fully aware of the difficulty of convincing all minds of the urgency of these evils, and of the impossibility of engaging all classes in the application of their remedy.

In the first place, the popular suffering, great as it is, weighs not with a sufficiently equal pressure on all parts of the country; and, in the second, affects not equally all classes of the population, so as to excite to that union of exertion, which once made, the reform is effected and the nation redeemed.

While the evil day is only in prospect, or while it visits our neighbour but spares ourselves, such is the selfishness generated by existing habits, and such the supineness generated by that selfishness, that we are but too prone to shrink from every effort not absolutely and immediately necessary for the supply of our own wants or the increase of our own luxuries. Yet, would the most spoiled child of worldly fortune but look around him on the changes and chances which ofttimes sweep away the best secured treasurer, and bring in a moment the capitalist to bankruptcy, and his family to want, he could not feel himself entirely removed in sympathy from the suffering portion of his fellow creatures. But let us take the case of the thriving artisan, or successful merchant—on what security does he hold that pecuniary independence which puts the bread into the mouths of his children, and protects from destitution the companion of his bosom? On sustained industry and unremitting exertions, which sickness may interrupt, a fall in the market reduce to half its value, or a few casualties or one miscalculation in a moment annihilate. Or what if death finally interrupt the father's care or the husband's tenderness— where is the stay for his orphan children? where succour for their widowed mother, now charged alone with all the weight of their provision? I have taken no extreme cases; I have taken such as may, in the course of events, be the case of every man who hears me.

Were it my disposition, which, I think, it is not, to exaggerate evils, or were I even disposed to give a fair picture of those really existing among a large mass of the American population, more especially as crowded into the cities and manufacturing districts, easy it were to harrow the feelings of the least sensitive, and, in the relation, to harrow my own.

But as the measure it is my object this evening to suggest to the people of Philadelphia, and my intention hereafter to submit to the whole American nation, must, at the first sight, win to its support the more oppressed and afflicted, I am rather desirous of addressing my prefatory arguments to that class from whence opposition is most to be apprehended.

I know how difficult it is—reared as we all are in the distinctions of class, to say nothing of sect, to conceive of our interests as associated with those of the whole community. The man possessed of a dollar, feels himself to be, not merely one hundred cents richer, but also one hundred cents *better*, then the man who is pennyless; so on through all the gradations of earthly possessions—the estimate of our own moral and political importance swelling always in a ratio exactly proportionate to the growth of our purse. The rich man who can leave a clear independence to his children, is given to estimate them as he estimates himself, and to imagine something in their nature distinct from that of the less privileged heirs of hard labour and harder fare.

This might indeed appear too gross for any of us to advance in theory, but in feeling how many must plead guilty to the prejudice! Yet is there a moment when, were their thoughts known to each other, all men must feel themselves on a level. It is when as fathers they look on their children, and picture the possibility which may render them orphans, and then calculate all the casualties which may deprive them, if rich, of their inheritance, or, if poor, grind them down to deeper poverty.

But it is first to the rich, I would speak. Can the man of opulence feel tranquil under the prospect of leaving to such guardianship as existing law or individual integrity may supply, the minds, bodies, morals, or even the fortune of their children? I myself was an orphan: and I know that the very law which was my protector, sucked away a portion of my little inheritance, while that law, insufficient and avaricious as it was, alone shielded me from spoliation by my guardian. I know, too, that my youth was one of tribulation, albeit passed in the envied luxuries of aristocracy. I know that the orphan's bread may be watered with tears, even when the worst evil be not there—*dependence*.

Can, then, the rich be without solicitude, when they leave to the mercy of a heartless world the beings of their creation? Who shall cherish their young sensibilities? Who shall stand between them and oppression? Who shall whisper peace in the hour of affliction? Who shall supply principle in the hour of temptation? Who shall lead the tender mind to distinguish between the good and the evil? Who shall fortify it against the corruption of wealth, or prepare it for the day of adversity? Such, looking upon life as it is must be the anxious thoughts even of the wealthy. What must be the thoughts of the poor man, it needs not that we should picture.

But, my friends, however differing in degree may be the anxiety of the rich and the poor, still, in its nature, is it the same. Doubt, uncertainty, apprehension, are before all. We hear of deathbed affliction. My friends, I have been often and long on the bed of mortal sickness: no fear had the threatened last sleep for me, for *I was not a parent.*

We have here, then, found an evil common to all classes, and one that is entailed from generation to generation. The measure I am about to suggest, whenever adopted, will blot this now universal affliction from existence; it will also, in the outset, alleviate those popular distresses whose poignancy and happy increase weigh on the heart of philanthropy, and crush the best hopes of enlightened patriotism. It must further, when carried into full effect, work the radical cure of every disease which now afflicts the body politic, and built up for this nation a sound constitution, embracing at once, public prosperity, individual integrity, and universal happiness.

This measure, my friends, has been long present to my mind, as befitting the adoption of the American people; as alone calculated to form an enlightened, a virtuous, and a happy community; as alone capable of supplying a remedy to the evils under which we groan; as alone commensurate with the interests of the human family, and consistent with the political institutions of this great confederated republic.

I had occasion formerly to observe, in allusion to the efforts already made, and yet making, in the cause of popular instruction, more or less throughout the Union, that, as yet, the true principle has not been hit, and that until it be hit, all reform must be slow and inefficient.

The noble example of New-England has been imitated by other states, until all not possessed of common schools blush for the popular remissness. But, after all, how can *common schools,* under their best form, and in fullest supply, effect even the purpose which they have in view?

The object proposed by common schools (if I rightly understand it) is to impart to the whole population those means for the acquirement of knowledge which are in common use: reading and writing. To these are added arithmetic, and occasionally, perhaps, some imperfect lessons in the simpler sciences. But I would ask, supposing these institutions should even be made to embrace all the branches of intellectual knowledge, and, thus, science offered gratis to all the children of the land, how are the children of the very class, for whom we suppose the schools instituted to be supplied with food and raiment, or instructed in the trade necessary to their future subsistence, while they are following these studies? How are they, I ask, to be fed and clothed, when, as all facts show, the labour of the parents is often insufficient for their own sustenance, and, almost universally, inadequate to the provision of the family without the united efforts of all its members? In your manufacturing districts you have children worked for twelve hours a day; and in the rapid and certain progress of the existing system, you will soon have them, as in England, *worked to death,* and yet unable, through the period of their miserable existence, to earn a pittance sufficient to satisfy the cravings of hunger. At this present time, what leisure or what spirit, think you, have the children of the miserable widows of Philadelphia, realizing, according to the most favourable estimate of your city and county committee, sixteen dollars per annum, for food and clothing? what leisure or what spirit may their children find for visiting a school, although the same should be open to them from sunrise to sunset? Or what leisure have usually the children of your most thriving mechanics, after their strength is sufficiently developed to spin, sew, weave, or wield a tool? It seems to me, my friends, that to build school houses now-a-days is something like building churches. When you have them, you need some measure to ensure their being occupied.

But, as our time is short, and myself somewhat fatigued by continued exertions, I must hasten to the rapid development of the system of instruction and protection which has occurred to me as capable, and alone capable, of opening the door to universal reform.

In lieu of all common schools, high schools, colleges, seminaries, houses of refuge, or any

other juvenile institution, instructional or protective, I would suggest that the state legislatures be directed (after laying off the whole in townships or hundreds) to organize, at suitable distances, and in convenient and healthy situations, establishments for the general reception of all the children resident within the said school district. These establishments to be devoted, severally, to children between a certain
10 age. Say, the first, infants between two and four, or two and six, according to the density of the population, and such other local circumstances as might render a greater or less number of establishments necessary or practicable. The next to receive children from four to eight, or six to twelve years. The next from twelve to sixteen, or to an older age if found desirable. Each establishment to be furnished with in-
20 structors in every branch of knowledge, intellectual and operative, with all the apparatus, land, and conveniences necessary for the best development of all knowledge; the same, whether operative or intellectual, being always calculated to the age and strength of the pupils.

To obviate, in the commencement, every evil result possible from the first mixture of a young population, so variously raised in error or neglect, a due separation should be made in each establishment; by which means those entering
30 with bad habits would be kept apart from the others until corrected. How rapidly reform may be effected on the plastic disposition of childhood, has been sufficiently proved in your houses of refuge, more especially when such establishments have been under *liberal* superintendence, as was formerly the case in New-York. Under their orthodox directors, those asylums of youth have been converted into jails.

It will be understood that, in the proposed
40 establishments, the children would pass from one to the other in regular succession, and that the parents who would necessarily be resident in their close neighbourhood, could visit the children at suitable hours, but, in no case, interfere with or interrupt the rules of the institution.

In the older establishments, the well directed and well protected labour of the pupil would, in time, suffice for, and then exceed their own
50 support; when the surplus might be devoted to the maintenance of the infant establishments.

In the beginning, and until all debt was cleared off, and so long as the same should be found favourable to the promotion of these best

palladiums of a nation's happiness, a double tax might be at once expedient and politic.

First, a moderate tax per head for every child, to be laid upon its parents conjointly, or divided between them, due attention being always paid to the varying strength of the two sexes, and to the undue depreciation which now rests on female labour. The more effectually to correct the latter injustice, as well as to consult the convenience of the industrious classes generally, this parental tax might be rendered payable either in money, or in labour, produce, or domestic manufactures, and should be continued for each child until the age when juvenile labour should be found, on the average, equivalent to the educational expenses, which, I have reason to believe, would be at twelve years.

This first tax on parents to embrace equally the whole population; as, however moderate it would inculcate a certain forethought in all the human family; more especially where it is most wanted—in young persons, who before they assumed the responsibility of parents, would estimate their fitness to meet it.

The second tax to be on property, increasing in per centage with the wealth of the individual. In this manner I conceive the rich would contribute, according to their riches, to the relief of the poor, and to the support of the state, by raising up its best bulwark—an enlightened and united generation.

Preparatory to, or connected with, such measures, a registry should be opened by the state, with offices through all the townships, where on the birth of every child, or within a certain time appointed, the same should be entered, together with the names of its parents. When two years old, the parental tax should be payable, and the juvenile institution open for the child's reception; from which time forward it would be under the protective care and guardianship of the state, while it need never be removed from the daily, weekly, or frequent inspection of the parents.

Orphans, of course, would find here an open asylum. If possessed of property, a contribution would be paid for its revenue to the common educational fund; if unprovided, they would be sustained out of the same.

In these nurseries of a free nation, no inequality must be allowed to enter. Fed at a common board; clothed in a common garb, uniting neatness with simplicity and convenience; raised in the exercise of common duties, in the acquirement of the same knowledge and practice of the same industry, varied only according to individual taste and capabilities; in the exercise of the same virtues, in the enjoyment of the same pleasures; in the study of the same nature; in pursuit of the same object—their own and each other's happiness—say! would not such a race, when arrived at manhood and womanhood, work out the reform of society—perfect the free institutions of America.

I have drawn but a sketch, nor could I presume to draw the picture of that which the mind's eye hath seen alone, and which it is for the people of this land to realize.

In this sketch, my friends, there is nothing but what is practical and practicable: nothing but what you yourselves may contribute to effect. Let the popular suffrage be exercised with a view to the popular good. Let the industrious classes, and all honest men of all classes, unite for the sending to the legislatures those who will represent the real interests of the many, not the imagined interests of the few—of the people at large, not of any profession or class.

To develope farther my views on this all important subject at the present time, would be to fatigue your attention, and exhaust my own strength. I shall prosecute this subject in the periodical of which I am editor,[1] which, in common with my public discourses, have been, and will ever be, devoted to the common cause of human improvement, and addressed to humankind without distinction of nation, class, or sect. May you, my fellow beings, unite in the same cause, in the same spirit! May you learn to seek truth without fear! May you farther learn to advocate truth as you distinguish it; to be valiant in its defence, and peaceful while valiant; to meet all things, and bear all things, and dare all things for the correction of abuses, and the effecting, in private and in public, in your own minds, through the minds of your children, friends, and companions, and, above all, *through your legislatures*, a radical reform in all your measures, whether as citizens, or as men! 1829

[1] The Free Enquirer, Published in New-York. [Frances Wright's note.]

JOHN GREENLEAF WHITTIER

1807–1892

THE QUAKER POET of New England's rustic beauty devoted thirty years of effort to the cause of abolition. In 1833 he printed five hundred copies of his first antislavery piece, at the cost of a large part of his year's earnings. Arthur Tappan, a well-to-do merchant, paid for the publication of five thousand copies of this tract, *Justice and Expedience: or Slavery Considered with a View to its Rightful and Effectual Abolition*. Whittier clung to, and did much to popularize the position which he took in this vigorous indictment of slavery. It came at a time when idealistic reformers were becoming more militant in their attitude toward slavery and when it was increasingly difficult for men of letters to maintain their neutrality.

T. F. Currier, *A Bibliography of John Greenleaf Whittier*, Cambridge, Mass., 1937.
The Writings of John Greenleaf Whittier, Riverside Edition, 7 vols., Boston, 1888–1892.
S. T. Pickard, *Life and Letters of John Greenleaf Whittier*, 2 vols., Boston, 1894.
Whitman Bennett, *Whittier, Bard of Freedom*, Chapel Hill, 1941.
John A. Pollard, *John Greenleaf Whittier, Friend of Man*, Boston, 1949.

» » From: JUSTICE AND EXPEDIENCE « «

Or, Slavery Considered with a View to Its Rightful and Effectual Remedy, Abolition

It may be inquired of me why I seek to agitate the subject of Slavery in New England, where we all acknowledge it to be an evil.

Because such an acknowledgement is not enough on our part: it is doing no more than the Slave-Master and Slave-trader. "We have found," says James Monroe, in his speech on the subject before the Virginia Convention, "that this evil has preyed upon the very vitals
10 of the Union; and has been prejudicial to all the States in which it has existed." All the States in their several Constitutions and declarations of right have made a similar statement. And what has been the consequence of this general belief in the evil of human servitude? Has it sapped the foundations of the infamous system? No. Has it decreased the number of victims? Quite the contrary. Unaccompanied by philanthropic action, it has been in a moral
20 point of view worthless—a thing without vitality—sightless—soulless—dead.

But, it may be said that the miserable victims of the System have our sympathies. Sympathy!—the sympathy of the Priest and Levite, looking on and acknowledging, but holding itself aloof from mortal suffering. Can such hollow sympathy reach the broken heart, and does the blessing of those who are ready to perish answer it? Does it hold back the lash from the
30 slave, or sweeten his bitter bread?

Oh, my heart is sick—my soul is weary of this sympathy—this heartless mockery of feeling;—sick of the common cant of hypocrisy, wreathing the artificial flowers of sentiment over unutterable pollution and unimaginable wrong. It is white-washing the sepulchre to make us forget its horrible deposite. It is scattering flowers around the charnel-house and over the yet festering grave to turn away our thoughts
40 "from the dead men's bones and all uncleanness"—the pollution and loathesomeness below.

No—let the TRUTH on this subject—undisguised, naked, terrible as it is, stand out before us. Let us no longer strive to forget it—let us no more dare to palliate it. It is better to meet it here with repentance than at the bar of God. The cry of the oppressed—of the millions who have perished among us as the brute perisheth,

shut out from the glad tidings of salvation, has gone there before us, to Him who as a father pitieth all his children. Their blood is upon us as a nation; woe unto us, if we repent not, as a nation, in dust and ashes. Woe unto us if we say in our hearts, "The Lord shall not see, neither shall the God Jacob regard it. He that planted the ear, shall he not hear? He who formed the eye, shall He not see?"

But it may be urged that New-England has no participation in Slavery, and is not responsible for its wretchedness.

Why are we thus willing to believe a lie? New-England not responsible? Bound by the United States Constitution to protect the slaveholder in his sins, and yet not responsible? Joining hand with crime—covenanting with oppression—leaguing with pollution, and yet not responsible! Palliating the Evil—hiding the Evil—voting for the Evil, do we not participate in it? Members of one Confederacy—children of one family—the curse and the shame—the sin against our brother, and the sin against our God—all the iniquity of Slavery which is revealed to man, and all which crieth in the ear, or is manifested to the eye of Jehovah, will assuredly be visited upon all our people. Why then should we stretch forth our hands towards our Southern brethren, and like the Pharisee thank God we are not like them? For as long as we recognize the INFERNAL PRINCIPLE that *"man can hold property in man,"* God will not hold us guiltless. So long as we take counsel of the world's policy instead of the Justice of Heaven: so long as we pursue a mistaken political expediency in opposition to the express commands of God, so long will the wrongs of the Slaves rise like a cloud of witnesses against us at the inevitable bar.

Slavery is *protected* by the constitutional compact—by the standing army—by the militia of the free states. Let us not forget that should the slaves, goaded by wrongs unendurable, rise in desperation, and pour the torrent of their brutal revenge over the beautiful Carolinas, or the consecrated soil of Virginia, New-England would be called upon to arrest the progress of rebellion,—to tread out with the armed heel of her soldiery, that spirit of freedom, which knows no distinction of cast or color; which has been kindled in the heart of the black man as well as the white.

And what is this System which we are thus protecting and upholding?

A system which holds two millions of God's creatures in bondage—which leaves one million females without any protection save their own feeble strength, and which makes even the exercise of that strength in resistance to outrage, punishable with death—which considers rational, immortal beings as articles of traffic—vendible commodities—merchantable property, —which recognises no social obligations—no natural relations—which tears without scruple the infant from the mother—the wife from the husband—the parent from the child. In the strong but just language of another—"It is the full measure of pure, unmixed, unsophisticated wickedness; and scorning all competition or comparison, it stands without a rival in the secure, indisputed possession of its detestable pre-eminence."

So fearful an evil should have its remedies.

The following are among the many which have been from time to time proposed:—

1. Placing the slaves in the condition of the serfs of Poland and Russia, fixed to the soil, and without the right on the part of the master to sell or remove them. This was intended as a preliminary to complete emancipation at some remote period; but it is impossible to perceive either its justice or expediency.

2. Gradual Abolition, an indefinite term, but which is understood to imply the draining away drop by drop of the great ocean of wrong,—plucking off at long intervals some straggling branches of the moral Uphas—holding out to unborn generations the shadow of a hope which the present may never feel,—gradually ceasing to do evil; gradually refraining from robbery, lust and murder: in brief, obeying a shortsighted and criminal policy rather than the commands of God.

3. Abstinence on the part of the people of the free states from the use of the known products of slave labor, in order to render that labor profitless. Beyond a doubt the example of conscientious individuals may have a salutary effect upon the minds of the slaveholders;—but so long as our confederacy exists, a commercial intercourse with slave-states, and a consumption of their products cannot be avoided.

4. Colonization.

The *exclusive* object of the American Colonization Society, according to the second article of its constitution, is to colonize the *free* people of color residing among us, in Africa or such other place as Congress may direct. Steadily adhering to this object it has nothing to do with Slavery; and I allude to it, as a *remedy* only because some of its friends have in view an eventual abolition or an amelioration of the evil.

Let facts speak. 10

The Colonization Society was organized in 1817. It has 218 auxiliary societies. The Legislatures of 14 States have recommended it. Contributions have poured into its treasury from every quarter of the United States. Addresses in its favor have been heard from all our pulpits.

It has been in operation 16 years. During this period nearly one million human beings have died in Slavery and the number of Slaves have 20 increased, more than half a million, or in round numbers, 550,000.

The Colonization Society has been busily engaged all this while in conveying the slaves to Africa—in other words abolishing Slavery. In this very charitable occupation it has carried away of manumitted slaves, 613.

Balance against the Society, 549,387!

But enough of its abolition tendency. What has it done for amelioration? 30

Witness the newly enacted laws of some of the slave states—laws bloody as the code of Draco, violating the laws of God and the unalienable rights of His children.

But why talk of amelioration? Amelioration of what?—of sin—of crime unutterable, of a System of wrong and outrage horrible in the eyes of God! Why seek to mark the line of a selfish policy, a carnal expediency between the criminality of Hell, and that repentance and its 40 fruits enjoined of Heaven?

For the principles and views of the Society we must look to its own statements and admissions; to its Annual Reports, to those of its Auxiliaries; to the speeches and writings of its advocates;—and to its organ, the *African Repository*.

1. *It excuses Slavery and apologizes for slave-holders. . . .*

2. *It pledges itself not to oppose the System* 50 *of Slavery. . . .*

3. *It regards God's rational creatures as property. . . .*

4. *It boasts that its measures are calculated to perpetuate the detested System of Slavery—*

*to remove the fears of the Slave-holder, and
increase the value of his stock of human beings. . . .*

    5. *It denies the power of Christian Love to
overcome an unholy prejudice against a portion
of our fellow-creatures. . . .*

    6. *It opposes strenuously the education of
the blacks in this Country, as useless, as well as
dangerous. . . .*

My limits will not admit of a more extended
examination. To the documents from whence
the above extracts have been made I would call
the attention of every real friend of humanity.
I seek to do the Colonization Society no injustice; but I wish the public generally to understand its character.

. . .

I come now to the only practicable—the
only just scheme of Emancipation:—IMMEDIATE
EMANCIPATION OF SLAVERY: an immediate acknowledgment of the great truth, that man cannot hold property in man; an immediate surrender of baneful prejudice to Christian love;
an immediate practical obedience to the command of Jesus Christ:—*"Whatsoever ye would
that men should do unto you, do ye even so to
them."*

    A correct understanding of what is meant by
Immediate Abolition must convince every candid mind, that it is neither visionary nor dangerous; that it involves no disastrous consequences of bloodshed and desolation; but, on
the contrary, that it is a safe, practicable, efficient remedy for the evils of the Slave-system.

    The term *Immediate* is used in contrast with
that of *Gradual*. Earnestly as I wish it—I do
not expect—no one expects—that the tremendous system of oppression can be instantaneously overthrown. The terrible and unrebukable
indignation of a free people has not yet been
sufficiently concentrated against it. The friends
of abolition have not forgotten the peculiar
organization of our Confederacy—the delicate
division of power between the states and the
general government. They see the many obstacles in their path-way; but they know that
public opinion can overcome them all. They
ask no aid of physical coercion. They seek to
obtain their object not with the weapons of
violence and blood, but with those of reason
and truth, prayer to God, and entreaty to man.

    They seek to impress indelibly upon every
human heart the true doctrines of the rights of
man; to establish now and forever this great

and fundamental truth of human liberty—*that
man cannot hold property in his brother;* for
they believe that the general admission of this
truth will utterly destroy the system of slavery
—based as that system is upon a denial or disregard of it. To make use of the clear exposition of an eminent advocate of Immediate
Abolition,[1] our plan of emancipation is simply
this: "To promulgate the doctrine of human
rights in high places and low places, and all
places where there are human beings. To whisper it in chimney corners, and to proclaim it
from the house-tops—yea, from the mountain-
tops. To pour it out like water from the pulpit
and the press. To raise it up with all the food
of the inner man, from infancy to gray hairs—
to give 'line upon line, and precept upon precept,' till it forms one of the foundation principles, and parts indistructible of the public
soul. Let those who contemn this plan, renounce
if they have not done it already, the gospel plan
of converting the world; let them renounce
every plan of moral reformation, and every plan
whatsoever, which does not terminate in the
gratification of their own *animal* natures."

    The friends of emancipation would urge in
the first instance an Immediate Abolition of
Slavery in the District of Columbia, and in the
Territories of Florida and Arkansas. . . .

    Here then are *twenty-six thousand* human
beings, fashioned in the image of God, the fitted
temples of His Holy Spirit, held by the Gov
ernment in the abhorrent chains of Slavery.
The power to emancipate them is clear. It is indisputable. It does not depend upon the twenty-
five slave votes in Congress. It lies with the free
states. Their duty is before them: the fear of
God, and not of man, let them perform it.

    Let them at once strike off the grievous fet-
ters. Let them declare that man shall no longer
hold his fellow-man in bondage—a beast of
burden—an article of traffic, within the Government domain. God and truth and eternal
justice demands this. The very reputation of our
fathers—the honor of our land—every principle of liberty, humanity, expediency demand it.
A sacred regard to free principles originated our
independence, not the paltry amount of practical evil complained of. And although our
fathers left their great work unfinished, it is our
duty to follow out their principles. Short of
Liberty and Equality we cannot stop without
doing injustice to their memories. If our fathers
intended that Slavery should be perpetual—

[1] Elizur Wright (1804–1885), reformer and actuary.

that our practice should for ever give the lie to our professions—why is the great constitutional compact so guardedly silent on the subject of human servitude? If State necessity demanded this perpetual violation of the laws of God and the rights of man—this continual solecism in a Government of Freedom—why is it not met as a necessity, incurable and inevitable, and formally and distinctly recognized as a settled part of our social system? State Necessity, that imperial tyrant, seeks no disguise. In the language of Sheridan, "what he does, he dares avow, and avowing, scorns any other justification than the great motives which placed the iron sceptre in his grasp."

Can it be possible that our fathers felt this State necessity strong upon them? No—for they left open the door for emancipation—they left us the light of their pure principles of liberty—they framed the great charter of American rights without employing a term in its structure to which in after times of universal freedom the enemies of our country could point with accusation or reproach.

What is *our* duty?

To give effect to the *spirit* of our Constitution; to plant ourselves upon the great Declaration and declare in the face of all the world, that political, religious and legal hypocrisy shall no longer cover as with loathsome leprosy the features of American freedom; to loose at once the bands of wickedness—to undo the heavy burdens, and let the oppressed go free.

We have indeed been authoritatively told in Congress and elsewhere that our brethren of the South and West will brook no farther agitation of the subject of Slavery. What then!—shall we heed the unrighteous prohibition? No—by our duty as Christians—as politicians—by our duty to ourselves—to our neighbor and to God *we are called upon to agitate this subject;* to give Slavery no resting place under the hallowed Ægis of a government of freedom; to tear it root and branch, with all its fruits of abomination, at least from the soil of the national domain. The slave-holder may mock us—the representatives of property—merchandise—vendible commodities, may threaten us; still our duty is imperative; the spirit of the constitution should be maintained within the exclusive jurisdiction of the Government. If we cannot "provide for the general welfare"; if we cannot "guarantee to each of the States a republican form of government," let us at least, no longer legislate for a free nation within view of the falling whip, and within hearing of the execrations of the taskmaster, and the prayer of his slave!

I deny the right of the slave-holder to impose silence on his brother of the North in reference to Slavery. What! compelled to maintain the System—to keep up the standing army which protects it, and yet be denied the poor privilege of remonstrance! Ready, at the summons of the master to put down the insurrections of his slaves—the out-breaking of that revenge which is now, and has been, in all nations, and all times, the inevitable consequence of oppression and wrong—and yet like automata, to *act* but not *speak!* Are we to be denied even the right of a slave—the right to *murmur?*

I am not unaware that my remarks may be regarded by many as dangerous and exceptionable; that I may be regarded as a fanatic for quoting the language of eternal truth, and denounced as an incendiary for maintaining, in the spirit as well as the letter, the doctrines of American Independence. But if such are the consequences of a simple performance of duty, I shall not regard them. If my feeble appeal but reaches the hearts of any who are now slumbering in iniquity—if it shall have power given it to shake down one stone from that foul temple where the blood of human victims is offered to the Moloch of Slavery—if under Providence, it can break one fetter from off the image of God, and enable one suffering African

> ———————"To feel
> The weight of human misery less, and glide
> Ungroaning to the tomb,"

I shall not have written in vain; my conscience will be satisfied.

Far be it from me to cast new bitterness into the gall and wormwood waters of sectional prejudice. No—I desire peace—the peace of universal love—of catholic sympathy—the peace of a common interest—a common feeling—a common humanity. But so long as Slavery is tolerated, no such peace can exist. Liberty and Slavery cannot dwell in harmony together. There will be a perpetual 'war in the members' of the political Mezentius—between the living and the dead. God and man have placed between them an everlasting barrier—an eternal separation. No matter under what name or law or compact their union is attempted, the ordination of Providence has forbidden it, and it cannot stand. *Peace!*—there *can* be no peace between justice and oppression—between robbery and righteousness—truth and falsehood—freedom and slavery.

The slave-holding states are not free. The name of Liberty is there, but the *spirit* is wanting. They do not partake of its invaluable blessings. Wherever Slavery exists to any considerable extent, with the exception of some recently settled portions of the country, and which have not yet felt in a great degree the baneful and deteriorating influences of slave-labor—we hear at this moment the cry of suffering. We are told of grass-grown streets—of crumbling mansions—of beggared planters and barren plantations—of fear from without—of terror within. The once fertile fields are wasted and tenantless, for the curse of Slavery—the improvidence of that labor whose hire has been kept back by fraud—has been there, poisoning the very earth beyond the reviving influence of the early and the later rain. A moral mildew mingles with and blasts the economy of nature. It is as if the finger of the everlasting God had written upon the soil of the slave-holder the language of His displeasure.

Let then the slave-holding states consult their present interest by beginning without delay the work of emancipation. If they fear not, and mock at the fiery indignation of Him, to whom vengeance belongeth, let temporal interest persuade them. They know, they must know, that the present state of things cannot long continue. Mind is the same every where, no matter what may be the complexion of the frame which it animates: there is a love of liberty which the scourge cannot eradicate—a hatred of oppression which centuries of degradation cannot extinguish. The slave will become conscious sooner or later of his strength—his physical superiority, and will exert it. His torch will be at the threshold and his knife at the throat of the planter. Horrible and indiscriminate will be this vengeance. Where then will be the pride—the beauty and the chivalry of the South? The smoke of her torment will rise upward like a thick cloud visible over the whole earth.

"Belie the negro's powers:—in headlong will,
Christian, thy brother thou shalt find him still.
Belie his virtues:—since his wrongs began,
His follies and his crimes have stamped him man."

Let the *cause* of insurrection be removed then as speedily as possible. Cease to oppress. "Let him that stole steal no more." Let the laborer have his hire. Bind him no longer by the cords of Slavery, but with those of kindness and brotherly love. Watch over him for his good. Pray for him; instruct him; pour light into the darkness of his mind.

Let this be done; and the horrible fears which now haunt the slumbers of the slave-holder will depart. Conscience will take down its racks and gibbets, and his soul will be at peace. His lands will no longer disappoint his hopes. Free labor will renovate them.

Historical facts—the nature of the human-mind—the demonstrated truths of political economy—the analysis of cause and effect, all concur in establishing,

1. That Immediate Abolition is a safe, and just and peaceful remedy for the evils of the slave-system.
2. That Free labor, its necessary consequence, is more productive, and more advantageous to the planter than slave-labor.

In proof of the proposition, it is only necessary to state the undeniable fact that immediate emancipation, whether by an individual or a community, has, in no instance been attended with violence and disorder on the part of the emancipated; but that on the contrary it has promoted cheerfulness, industry, and laudable ambition, in the place of sullen discontent, indolence and despair.

The case of St. Domingo is in point. Blood was indeed shed on that island like water, but it was not in consequence of emancipation. It was shed in the civil war which preceded it, and in the iniquitous attempt to restore the Slave-system in 1801. It flowed on the sanguine altar of slavery, not on the pure and peaceful one of emancipation. No—there, as in all the world and in all times, the violence of oppression engendered violence on the part of the oppressed, and vengeance followed only upon the iron footsteps of wrong. When, where, did justice to the injured waken their hate and vengeance? When, where did love and kindness and sympathy irritate and madden the persecuted—the broken-hearted—the foully wronged?

. . .

The present condition of Hayti may be judged of, from the following well authenticated facts. Its population is more than 700,000—its resources ample—its prosperity and happiness general—its crimes few—its labor crowned with abundance—with no paupers save the decrepit and aged—its people hospitable, respectful, orderly and contented.

The manumitted slaves, who to the number of 2000, were settled in Nova Scotia by the British Government at the close of the Revolutionary War "led a harmless life, and gained the character of an honest people from their white neighbors." Of the free laborers of Trinidad we have the same report. At the Cape of Good Hope 3000 negroes received their freedom, and with scarce a single exception betook themselves to laborious employments.

But we have yet stronger evidence. The total abolishment of Slavery in the Southern Republic has proved beyond dispute the safety and utility of Immediate Abolition. The departed Bolivar indeed deserves his glorious title of Liberator, for he began his career of freedom by striking off the fetters of his own slaves seven hundred in number.

In an official letter from the Mexican Envoy of the British Government, dated March 1826, and addressed to the Right Hon. George Canning, the superiority of free over slave labor is clearly demonstrated by the following facts:

1. The sugar and coffee cultivation of Mexico is almost exclusively confined to the great valley of Ceurnavaca and Cauntala Amilpas.

2. It is now carried on exclusively by the labor of free blacks.

3. It was formerly wholly sustained by the forced labor of slaves, purchased at Vera Cruz at $300 to $400 each.

4. Abolition in this section was effected not by the Governmental interference—not even from motives of humanity—but from an irresistible conviction on the part of the planters that their pecuniary interest demanded it.

5. The result has proved the entire correctness of this conviction; and the planters would now be as unwilling as the blacks themselves to return to the old system.

Let our Southern brethren imitate this example. It is in vain in the fact of facts like these to talk of the necessity of maintaining the abominable system—operating as it does like a double curse upon planters and slaves. Heaven and Earth deny its necessity. It is as necessary as other robberies, and no more.

Yes—putting aside altogether the righteous law of the living God—the same, yesterday, today and for ever; and shutting out the clearest political truths ever taught by man—still, in human policy—selfish expediency, would demand of the planter the immediate emancipation of his slaves.

Because slave-labor is the labor of mere *machines;* a mechanical impulse of body and limb, with which the mind of the laborer has no sympathy and from which it constantly and loathingly revolts.

Because slave-labor deprives the master altogether of the incalculable benefit of the negro's will. *That* does not co-operate with the forced toil of the body. This is but the necessary consequence of all labor which does not benefit the laborer. It is a just remark of that profound political economist Adam Smith, that "a slave can have no other interest than to eat and waste as much, and work as little as he can."

To my mind in the wasteful and blighting influences of slave-labor, there is a solemn and warning moral.

They seem the evidence of the displeasure of Him who created man after his own image, at the unnatural attempt to govern the bones and sinews, the bodies and souls of one portion of His children by the caprice, the avarice, and the lusts of another:—at that utter violation of the design of His merciful Providence, whereby the entire dependence of millions of his rational creatures, is made to centre upon the will—the existence—the ability of their fellow-mortals instead of resting under the shadow of His own Infinite Power and exceeding love.

.   .   .

Let us look at this subject in another point of view. The large sums of money necessary for stocking a plantation with slaves has an inevitable tendency to place the agricultural and slave-holding community exclusively in the hands of the wealthy,—a tendency at war with practical republicanism and conflicting with the best maxims of political economy.

Two hundred slaves at $200 per head would cost in the outset $40,000. Compare this enormous outlay for the labor of a single plantation, with the beautiful system of free labor as exhibited in New-England, where every young laborer, with health and ordinary prudence may acquire by his labor on the farms of others in a few years, a farm of his own, and the stock necessary for its proper cultivation;—where on a hard and unthankful soil, independence and competence may be attained by all.

Free labor is perfectly in accordance with the spirit of our institutions; slave labor is a relic of a barbarous, despotic age. The one like the firmament of Heaven, is the equal diffusion of similar lights, manifest, harmonious, regular; the other is the fiery predominance of some disastrous star, hiding all lesser luminaries around it in one consuming glare.

Emancipation would reform this evil. The planter would no longer be under the necessity of a heavy expenditure for slaves. He would only pay a very moderate price for his labor; a price indeed far less than the cost of the maintenance of a promiscuous gang of slaves, which the present system requires.

In an old plantation of 300 slaves, not more than 100 effective laborers will be found. Children—the old and superannuated—the sick and decrepit—the idle and incorrigibly vicious—will be found to constitute two thirds of the whole number. The remaining third perform only about one third as much work, as the same number of free laborers.

Now disburden the master of this heavy load of maintenance; let him employ *free*, able, industrious laborers only, those who feel conscious of a personal interest in the fruits of their labor, and who does not see that such a system would be vastly more safe and economical than the present?

The slave states are learning this truth by fatal experience. Most of them are silently writhing under the great curse. Virginia has uttered her complaints aloud. As yet, however, nothing has been done even there, save a small annual appropriation for the purpose of colonizing *the free colored inhabitants of the State.* Is this a remedy?

But it may be said that Virginia will ultimately liberate her *slaves* on condition of their colonization in Africa, peacefully if possible, forcibly if necessary.

Well—admitting that Virginia may be able and willing at some remote period to rid herself of the evil by commuting the punishment of her unoffending colored people, from Slavery to Exile, will her fearful remedy apply to some of the other slaveholding states?

It is a fact, strongly insisted upon by our Southern brethren as a reason for the perpetuation of Slavery, that their climate and peculiar agriculture will not admit of hard labor on the part of the whites. That amidst the fatal *malaria* of the rice plantations the white man is almost annually visited by the country fever; that few of the white overseers of these plantations reach the middle period of ordinary life:

that the owners are compelled to fly from their estates as the hot season approaches, without being able to return until the first frosts have fallen. But we are told that the *slaves* remain there, at their work—mid-leg in putrid water; breathing the noisome atmosphere, loaded with contagion, and underneath the scorching fervor of a terrible sun; that they indeed suffer; but that their habits, constitutions and their long practice enable them to labor, surrounded by such destructive influences, with comparative safety.

The conclusive answer, therefore, to those who in reality cherish the visionary hope of colonizing all the colored people of the United States in Africa or elsewhere, is this single, all-important fact:—*The labor of the blacks will not and cannot be dispensed with by the planter of the South.*

To what remedy then can the friends of humanity betake themselves but to that of Emancipation?

And nothing but a strong, unequivocal expression of public sentiment is needed to carry into effect this remedy, so far as the General Government is concerned.

And when the voice of all the non-slaveholding states shall be heard on this question; a voice of expostulation, rebuke, entreaty:—when the full light of truth shall break through the night of prejudice, and reveal all the foul abominations of slavery, will Delaware still cling to the curse which is wasting her moral strength —and still rivet the fetters upon her three or four thousand slaves?

Let Delaware begin the work; and Maryland, New Jersey, and Virginia must follow; the example will be contagious; and the great object of Universal Emancaiption will be attained.

Freemen, Christians, lovers of truth and justice! Why stand ye idle? Ours is a government of opinion, and slavery is interwoven with it. Change the current of opinion, and slavery will be swept away. Let the awful sovereignty of the people—a power which is limited only by the sovereignty of Heaven, arise and pronounce judgment against the crying iniquity. Let each individual remember that upon himself rests a portion of that sovereignty; a part of the tremendous responsibility of its exercise. The burning, withering concentration of public opinion upon the Slave system is alone needed for its total annihilation. God has given us the power to overthrow it;—a power, peaceful, yet mighty —benevolent, yet effectual—"awful without severity"—a moral strength equal to the emergency.

"How does it happen," inquires an able writer,[2] "that whenever duty is named we begin to hear of the weakness of human nature?—That same nature which outruns the whirlwind in the chase of gain—which rages like a maniac at the trumpet call of glory—which laughs danger and death to scorn when its least passion is awakened—becomes weak as childhood when reminded of its duty." But let no one hope to find an excuse in hypocrisy. The humblest individual of the community in one way or another possesses influence; and upon him as well as upon the proudest rests the responsibility of its rightful exercise and proper direction. The overthrow of a great national evil like that of Slavery, can only be effected by the united energies of the great body of the people.—Shoulder must be put to shoulder, and hand linked with hand—the whole mass must be put in motion and its entire strength applied, until the fabric of oppression is shaken to its dark foundations and not one stone is left upon another.

Let the Christian remember that the God of his worship hateth oppression; that the mystery of Faith can only be held by a pure conscience; and, that in vain is the tithe of mint, and annise, and cummin, if the weightier matters of the law, judgment, mercy and truth, are forgotten. Let him remember that all along the clouded region of slavery the truths of the Everlasting Gospel are not spoken,—that the ear of iniquity is lulled,—that those who minister between the "porch and the altar" dare not speak out the language of Eternal Justice: "Is not this the fast which I have chosen?—to loose the bands of wickedness—to undo the heavy burdens, and to let the oppressed go free?" Isa. LVIII. 6. "He that stealeth a man and selleth him; or if he be found in his hands, he shall surely be put to death." Exod. XXI. 16. Yet a little while and the voice of prayer will be heard no more in the abiding place of slavery. The truths of the Gospel—its voice of warning and exhortation will be denounced as incendiary. The night of infidelity,—the blackness of darkness—the silence—the frozen apathy of unrebuked iniquity will settle over the land, to be broken only by the upheaving Earthquake of Eternal retribution.

To the members of the religious Society of Friends, I would earnestly appeal. They have already done much to put away the evil of slavery in this country and Great Britain. The blessings of many who were ready to perish have rested upon them. But their faithful testimony must be still steadily upborne, for the great work is but begun. Let them not relax their exertions, nor be contented with a lifeless testimony—a formal protestation against the evil. Active, prayerful, unwearied exertion is needed for its overthrow. But above all, let them not aid in excusing and palliating it. Slavery has no redeeming qualities—no feature of benevolence—nothing pure—nothing peaceful; nothing just. Let them carefully keep themselves aloof from all societies and all schemes which have a tendency to excuse or overlook its crying iniquity. True to a doctrine founded on love and mercy—"peace on earth and good will to men," they should regard the suffering slave as their brother, and endeavor to "put their souls in his soul's stead." They may earnestly desire the civilization of Africa, but they cannot aid in building up the colony of Liberia so long as that colony leans for support upon the arm of *military power:* so long as it proselytes to christianity under the muzzles of its cannon; and preaches the doctrines of Christ while practicing those of Mahomet. When the Sierra Leone Company was formed, in England, not a member of the Society of Friends could be prevailed upon to engage in it, because the colony was to be supplied with cannon and other military stores. Yet the Foreign Agent of the Liberia Colony Society, to which the same insurmountable objection exists is a member of the Society of Friends, and I understand has been recently employed in providing *gun-powder,* etc. for the use of the Colony. There must be an awakening on this subject: other Woolmans and other Benezets [3] must arise and speak the truth with the meek love of James and the fervent sincerity of Paul.

To the WOMEN OF AMERICA, whose sympathies know no distinction of clime, or sect, or color, the suffering slave is making a strong appeal. Oh, let it not be unheeded! for of those to whom much is given much will be required at the last dread tribunal; and never in the strongest terms of human eulogy was woman's influence overrated. Sisters, daughters, wives, and mothers, your influence is felt every where, at the fireside, and in the halls of legislation,

[2] W. B. O. Peabody (1799–1847), Unitarian clergyman, scholar, and author.

[3] John Woolman (1720–1772) and Anthony Benezet (1713–1784) were outstanding Quaker advocates of peace and emancipation of slaves.

surrounding like the all-encircling atmosphere,
brother and father, husband and son! And by
your love of them: by every holy sympathy of
your bosoms; by every mournful appeal which
comes up to you from hearts whose sanctuary
of affections has been made waste and desolate,
you are called upon to exert it in the cause of
redemption from wrong and outrage.

Let the Patriot,—the friend of liberty and
the Union of the States, no longer shut his eyes
to the great danger—the master-evil before
which all others dwindle into insignificance.
Our Union is tottering to its foundation, and
slavery is the cause. Remove the evil. Dry up
at their source the bitter waters. In vain you
enact and abrogate your tariffs: in vain is individual sacrifice, or sectional concession. The
accursed thing is with us—the stone of stumbling and the rock of offence remains. Drag
then the Achan into light; and let National Repentance atone for National Sin.

The conflicting interests of free and slave-
labor, furnish the only ground for fear in relation to the permanency of the Union. The line
of separation between them is day by day
growing broader and deeper; geographically
and politically united, we are already, in a
moral point of view, a divided people. But a
few months ago we were on the verge of civil
war, a war of brothers—a war between the
North and the South,—between the slave-
holder and the free-laborer.[4] The danger has
been delayed for a time;—this bolt has fallen
without mortal injury to the Union—but the
cloud from whence it came still hangs above
us, reddening with the elements of destruction.

Recent events have furnished ample proof
that the slaveholding interest is prepared to
resist any legislation on the part of the General
Government which is supposed to have a tendency directly or indirectly, to encourage and
invigorate free-labor:—and that is determined
to charge upon its opposite interest the infliction of all those evils which necessarily attend
its own operation—"the primeval curse of Om-
nipotence upon slavery."

We have already felt in too many instances
the extreme difficulty of cherishing in one
common course of National Legislation the opposite interests of republican equality, and
feudal aristocracy and servitude. The truth is,
we have undertaken a moral impossibility.
These interests are from their nature irrecon-

[4] The crisis occasioned by South Carolina's stand on nullification.

cilable.—The one is based upon the purer
principles of rational liberty: the other under
the name of freedom, revives the ancient European system of barons and villains—nobles
and serfs. Indeed the state of Society which
existed among our Anglo-Saxon ancestors was
far more tolerable than that of many portions
of our *republican* confederacy. For the Anglo-
Saxon slaves had it in their power to purchase
their freedom;—and the laws of the realm
recognized their liberation and placed them
under legal protection.

To counteract the dangers resulting from a
state of society so utterly at variance, with
the Great Declaration of American Freedom,
should be the earnest endeavor of every patriotic statesman. Nothing unconstitutional, nothing violent should be attempted; but the true
doctrine of the rights of man should be steadily
kept in view; and the opposition to slavery
should be inflexible and constantly maintained.
The almost daily violation of the constitution
in consequence of the laws of some of the slave
states, subjecting free colored citizens to New
England and elsewhere, who may happen to
be on board our coasting vessels, to imprisonment immediately on their arrival in a Southern port, should be provided against. Nor
should the imprisonment of the free-colored
citizens of the Northern and Middle states, on
suspicion of being runaways, subjecting them
even after being pronounced free, to the costs
of their confinement and trial, be longer tolerated; for if we continue to yield to innovations
like these upon the constitution of our fathers,
we shall ere long have the name of a free government left us.

Dissemble as we may, it is impossible for us
to believe, after fully considering the nature of
slavery, that it can much longer maintain a
peaceable existence among us. A day of revolution must come; and it is our duty to prepare
for it. Its threatened evil may be changed into
a national blessing. The establishment of
schools for the instruction of the slave children;
a general diffusion of the lights of christianity;
and the introduction of a sacred respect for the
social obligations of marriage, and for the relations between parents and children, among our
black population, would render emancipation
not only perfectly safe, but also of the highest
advantage to the country. Two millions of freemen would be added to our population, upon
whom in the hour of danger we could safely
depend; "the domestic foe" would be changed

into a firm friend, faithful, generous, and ready to encounter all dangers in our defence. It is well known that during the last war with Great Britain, whenever the enemy touched upon our southern coast, the *slaves* in multitudes hastened to join them. On the other hand the *free blacks* were highly serviceable in repelling them. So warm was the zeal of the latter; so manifest their courage in defence of Louisiana, that the present Chief Magistrate of the United States [5] publicly bestowed upon them one of the highest eulogiums ever offered by a commander to his soldiers.

Let no one seek an apology for silence on the subject of Slavery because the laws of the land tolerate and sanction it. But a short time ago the Slave-Trade was protected by laws and treaties, and sanctioned by the example of men eminent for the reputation of piety and integrity. Yet public opinion broke over these barriers; it lifted the curtain and revealed the horrors of that most abominable traffic; and unrighteous law, and ancient custom, and avarice, and luxury, gave way before its irresistible authority. It should never be forgotten that human law cannot change the nature of human action in the pure eye of Infinite Justice; and that the ordinances of man cannot annul those of God. The Slave-System as existing in this country, can be considered in no other light than as the cause, of which the foul traffic in human flesh is the legitimate consequence. It is the parent—the fosterer—the sole supporter of the Slave-Trade. It creates the demand for slaves, and the foreign supply will always be equal to the demand of consumption. It keeps the market open. It offers inducements to the slave-trader which no severity of law against his traffic can overcome. By our laws his trade is *piracy;* while slavery, to which alone, it owes its existence, is protected and cherished, and those engaged in it are rewarded by an increase of political power proportioned to the increase of their stock of human beings! To steal the natives of Africa is a crime worthy of an ignominious death; but to steal and enslave, annually one hundred thousand of the descendants of these stolen natives, born in this country, is considered altogether excusable and proper! For my own part, I know no difference between robbery in Africa,

[5] Andrew Jackson, who, during the War of 1812, had won the battle of New Orleans.

and robbery at home. I could, with as quiet a conscience, engage in the one as the other.

"There is not one general principle," justly remarks Lord Nugent, "on which the slave-trade is to be stigmatized which does not impeach slavery itself. Kindred in iniquity, both must fall speedily—fall together; and be consigned to the same dishonorable grave.—The spirit which is thrilling through every nerve of England, is awakening America from her sleep of death. Who, among our statesmen, would not shrink from the baneful reputation of having supported by his legislative influence, the slave-trade; the traffic in human flesh? Let them then beware; for the time is near at hand when the present defenders of slavery will sink under the same fatal reputation, and leave to posterity a memory which will blacken through all future time: a legacy of infamy.

"Let us not betake us to the common arts and stratagems of nations; but fear God, and put away the evil which provokes Him: and trust not in man, but in the living God; and it shall go well for England!" This counsel, given by the pure hearted William Penn, in a former age, is about to be followed in the present. An intense and powerful feeling is working in the mighty heart of England: it is speaking through the lips of Brougam and Buxton and O'Connel, and demanding Justice in the name of humanity and according to the righteous law of God. The immediate Emancipation of 800,000 slaves is demanded with an authority which cannot much longer be disputed or trifled with. That demand will be obeyed; justice will be done; the heavy burdens will be unloosed; the oppressed set free. *It shall go well for England.*

And, when the stain on our own escutcheon shall be seen no more; when the Declaration of our Independence and the practice of our people shall agree; when Truth shall be exalted among us; when Love shall take the place of Wrong; when all the baneful pride and prejudice of caste and color shall fall forever; when under one common sun of political Liberty the slave-holding portions of our Republic shall no longer sit, like the Egyptians of old, themselves mantled in thick darkness, while all around them is glowing with the blessed light of freedom and equality,—then, and not till then, shall it go *WELL FOR AMERICA.*

1833

SARAH MARGARET FULLER

1810–1850

SARAH MARGARET FULLER, daughter of a scholarly lawyer and public man, was born in Cambridgeport, Massachusetts, in 1810. From her father she acquired a remarkable acquaintance with the classics. Brilliant and eccentric, she played an important role in New England's literary awakening. The close associate of leading Transcendentalists, Margaret Fuller edited *The Dial*, conducted "conversations" on literary and philosophical subjects, wrote for the *New York Tribune*, and traveled in Europe, where she married an Italian aristocrat, Marquis Ossoli. Outstanding among her books are *Summer on the Lakes* (1844), *Papers on Literature and Art* (1846), *Life Without and Life Within* (1859), and *Woman in the Nineteenth Century* (1855), from which the following selection is taken. Among the leaders of the woman's cause, Margaret Fuller emphasized, in more philosophical terms than her associates, the need for the intellectual emancipation of her sex as indispensable to democracy and to the decent and mutually advantageous relations of man and woman.

The Writings of Margaret Fuller, Mason Wade, ed., New York, 1941.
The Memoirs of Margaret Fuller Ossoli, 2 vols., Boston, 1852.
Madeleine B. Stern, *The Life of Margaret Fuller*, New York, 1942.
Mason Wade, *Margaret Fuller, Whetstone of Genius*, New York, 1940.

» » *From:* WOMAN IN THE NINETEENTH CENTURY « «

Man is a being of two-fold relations, to nature beneath and intelligences above him. The earth is his school, if not his birthplace; God his object; life and thought his means of interpreting nature and aspiring to God.

Only a fraction of this purpose is accomplished in the life of any one man. Its entire accomplishment is to be hoped for only from the sum of the lives of men, or Man considered as a whole.

As this whole has one soul and one body, any injury or obstruction to a part or to the meanest member affects the whole. Man can never be perfectly happy or virtuous until all men are so.

To address Man wisely, you must not forget that his life is partly animal, subject to the same laws with Nature.

But you canot address him wisely unless you consider him still more as soul, and appreciate the conditions and destiny of soul.

The growth of Man is two-fold, masculine and feminine.

So far as these two methods can be distinguished, they are so as
      Energy and Harmony;
      Power and Beauty;
      Intellect and Love;
or by some such rude classification; for we have not language primitive and pure enough to express such ideas with precision.

These two sides are supposed to be expressed in Man and Woman, that is, as the more and the less, for the faculties have not been given pure to either, but only in preponderance. There are also exceptions in great number, such as men of far more beauty than power, and the reverse. But as a general rule, it seems to have been the intention to have a preponderance on the one side that is called masculine, and on the other one that is called feminine.

There can be no doubt that if these two developments were in perfect harmony, they would correspond to and fulfill one another like hemispheres, or the tenor and bass in music.

But there is no perfect harmony in human nature; and the two parts answer one another only now and then; or if there be a persistent consonance, it can only be traced at long intervals, instead of discoursing on an obvious melody.

What is the cause of this?

Man, in the order of time, was developed first; as energy comes before harmony; power before beauty.

Woman was therefore under his care as an elder. He might have been her guardian and teacher.

But as human nature goes not straight forward but by excessive action and reaction in an undulated course, he misunderstood and abused his advantages, and became her temporal master instead of her spiritual sire.

On himself came the punishment. He educated Woman more as a servant than as a daughter, and found himself a king without a queen.

The children of this unequal union showed unequal natures and more and more men seemed sons of the handmaid rather than the princess.

At last there were so many Ishmaelites that the rest grew frightened and indignant. They laid the blame on Hagar and drove her forth into the wilderness.

But there were none the fewer Ishmaelites for that.

At last men became a little wiser and saw that the infant Moses was in every case saved by the pure instinct of Woman's breast. For as too much adversity is better for the moral nature than too much prosperity, Woman in this respect dwindled less than Man, though in other respects still a child in leading-strings.

So Man did her more and more justice and grew more and more kind.

But yet—his habits and will corrupted by the past—he did not clearly see that Woman was half himself; that her interests were identical with his; and that by the law of their common being he could never reach his true proportions while she remained in any wise shorn of hers.

And so it has gone on to our day; both ideas developing, but more slowly than they would under a clearer recognition of truth and justice, which would have permitted the sexes their due influence on one another and mutual improvement from more dignified relations.

Wherever there was pure love, the natural influences were for the time restored.

Wherever the poet or the artist gave free course to his genius, he saw the truth and expressed it in worthy forms, for these men especially share and need the feminine principle. The divine birds need to be brooded into life and song by mothers.

Whatever religion (I mean the thirst for truth and good, not the love of sect and dogma) had its course, the original design was apprehended in its simplicity, and the dove presaged sweetly from Dodona's oak.

I have aimed to show that no age was left entirely without a witness of the equality of the sexes in function, duty, and hope.

Also that when there was unwillingness or ignorance which prevented this being acted upon, women had not the less power for their want of light and noble freedom. But it was a power which hurt alike them and those against whom they made use of the arms of the servile-cunning, blandishment, and unreasonable emotion.

That now the time has come when a clearer vision and a better action are possible—when Man and Woman may regard one another as brother and sister, the pillars of one porch, the priests of one worship.

I have believed and intimated that this hope would receive an ampler fruition than ever before in our own land.

And it will do so if this land carry out the principles from which sprang our national life.

I believe that at present women are the best helpers of one another.

Let them think; let them act; till they know what they need.

We only ask of men to remove arbitrary barriers. Some would like to do more. But I believe it needs that some Woman show herself in her native dignity to teach them how to aid her, their minds are so encumbered by tradition. . . .

You ask, what use will she make of liberty when she has so long been sustained and restrained?

I answer in the first place this will not be suddenly given. . . . But were this freedom to come suddenly, I have no fear of the consequences. Individuals might commit excesses, but there is not only in the sex a reverence for decorums and limits inherited and enhanced from generation to generation, which many years of other life could not efface, but a native love, in Woman as Woman, of proportion, of "the simple art of not too much"—a Greek moderation which would create immediately a restraining party, the natural legislators and instructors of the rest, and would gradually establish such rules as are needed to guard without impeding life. But if you ask me what offices they may fill, I reply—any. I do not care what case you put; let them be sea captains if they will. I do not doubt there are women well fitted for such an office, and if so, I should be as glad to see them in it as to welcome the maid of Saragossa, or the maid of Missolonghi, or the Suliote heroine, or Emily Plater. I think women need, especially at this juncture, a much greater range of occupation than they have, to use their latent powers.

Fourier has observed these wants of women, as no one can fail to do who watches the desires of little girls or knows the ennui that haunts grown women except where they make to themselves a serene little world by art of some kind. He, therefore, in proposing a great variety of employments, in manufactures or the care of plants or animals, allows for one third of women as likely to have a taste for masculine pursuits, one third of men for feminine.

Who does not observe the immediate glow and serenity that is diffused over the life of women, before restless or fretful, by engaging in gardening, building, or the lowest department of art? Here is something that is not routine, something that draws forth life toward the infinite.

I have no doubt, however, that a large proportion of women would give themselves to the same employments as now, because there are circumstances that must lead to them. Mothers will delight to make the nest soft and warm. Nature would take care of that; no need to clip the wings of any bird that wants to soar or sing, or finds in itself the strength of pinion for a migratory flight unusual to its kind. The difference would be that *all* need not be constrained to employments for which *some* are unfit. I have urged upon the sex self-subsist-

ence, in its two forms of self-reliance and self-impulse, because I believe them to be the needed means of the present juncture.

I have urged on Woman independence of Man, not because I do not think the sexes mutually needed by one another, but because in Woman this fact has led to an excessive devotion, which has cooled love, degraded marriage, and prevented either sex from being what it should be to itself or the other.

I wish Woman to live *first* for God's sake. Then she will not make an imperfect man her god and thus sink to idolatry. Then she will not take what is not fit for her from a sense of weakness and poverty. Then if she finds what she needs in Man embodied, she will know how to love and be worthy of being loved.

By being more a soul, she will not be less Woman, for nature is perfected through spirit.

Now there is no woman, only an overgrown child. . . .

A profound thinker has said, "No married woman can represent the female world, for she belongs to her husband. The idea of Woman must be represented by a virgin."

But that is the very fault of marriage and of the present relation between the sexes, that the woman *does* belong to the man, instead of forming a whole with him.

An idea not unknown to ancient times has of late been revived, that in the metamorphoses of life the soul assumes the form first of Man and then of Woman, and takes the chances and reaps the benefits of either lot. Why then, say some, lay such emphasis on the rights or needs of Woman? What she wins not as Woman will come to her as Man.

That makes no difference. It is not Woman but the law of right, the law of growth, that speaks in us and demands the perfection of each being in its kind—apple as apple, Woman as Woman. Without adopting your theory, I know that I, a daughter, live through the life of Man; but what concerns me now is that my life be beautiful, powerful, in a word, a complete life in its kind. Had I but one more moment to live, I must wish the same.   1855

» »   « «

DOROTHEA LYNDE DIX

1802–1887

IN 1841 Dorothea Dix, a delicate and overwrought teacher of youth and author of children's books, began her investigation of the pitiful conditions of the insane in the jails, prisons, almshouses, and hovels of Massachusetts. Her *Memorial to the Legislature of Massachusetts* (1843) was based on well-tested facts, and it aroused the public conscience. The insane were generally regarded as depraved brutes, and Dorothea Dix, following the most enlightened thought of medical leaders abroad, insisted on publicly supported and controlled institutions for the therapeutic treatment of these unfortunates.

Her work as investigator of existing conditions and as champion of public responsibility and humane treatment became national in scope. She was aided by many persons of influence, but her work was creative and practical in effect. During the Civil War this timid and delicate philanthropist became "Superintendent of Women Nurses" in the War Department. After the War she resumed her work of investigating conditions of treatment of the insane, of promoting new hospitals, and of campaigning for the more generous support of those already established.

H. E. Marshall, *Dorothea Dix, Forgotten Samaritan*, Chapel Hill, 1937.
Gladys Brooks, *Three Wise Virgins*, New York, 1957.

» »   *From:* MEMORIAL TO THE LEGISLATURE OF
                    MASSACHUSETTS   « «

. . . About two years since leisure afforded opportunity and duty prompted me to visit several prisons and almshouses in the vicinity of this metropolis. I found, near Boston, in the jails and asylums for the poor, a numerous class brought into unsuitable connection with criminals and the general mass of paupers. I refer to idiots and insane persons, dwelling in circumstances not only adverse to their own physical and moral improvement, but productive of extreme disadvantages to all other persons brought into association with them. I applied myself diligently to trace the causes of these evils, and sought to supply remedies. As one obstacle was surmounted, fresh difficulties appeared. Every new investigation has given depth to the conviction that it is only by decided, prompt, and vigorous legislation the evils to which I refer, and which I shall proceed more fully to illustrate, can be remedied. I shall be obliged to speak with great plainness, and to reveal many things revolting to the taste, and from which my woman's nature shrinks with peculiar sensitiveness. But truth is the highest consideration. *I tell what I have seen*—painful and shocking as the details often are—that from them you may feel more deeply the imperative obligation which lies upon you to prevent the possibility of a repetition or continuance of such outrages upon humanity. If I inflict pain upon you, and move you to horror, it is to acquaint you with sufferings which you 10 have the power to alleviate, and make you hasten to the relief of the victims of legalized barbarity.

I come to present the strong claims of suffering humanity. I come to place before the Legislature of Massachusetts the condition of the miserable, the desolate, the outcast. I come as the advocate of helpless, forgotten, insane, and idiotic men and women; of beings sunk to a condition from which the most unconcerned 20 would start with real horror; of beings wretched in our prisons, and more wretched in our almshouses. And I cannot suppose it needful to employ earnest persuasion, or stubborn argument, in order to arrest and fix attention upon a subject only the more strongly pressing in its claims because it is revolting and disgusting in its details.

I must confine myself to few examples, but am ready to furnish other and more complete details, if required. If my pictures are displeasing, coarse, and severe, my subjects, it must be recollected, offer no tranquil, refined, or composing features. The condition of human beings, reduced to the extremest states of degradation and misery, cannot be exhibited in softened language, or adorn a polished page.

I proceed, gentlemen, briefly to call your attention to the *present* state of insane persons confined within this Commonwealth, in *cages, closets, cellars, stalls, pens! Chained, naked, beaten with rods,* and *lashed* into obedience.

As I state cold, severe *facts,* I feel obliged to refer to persons, and definitely to indicate localities. But it is upon my subject, not upon localities or individuals, I desire to fix attention; and I would speak as kindly as possible of all wardens, keepers, and other responsible officers, believing that *most* of these have erred not through hardness of heart and wilful cruelty so much as want of skill and knowledge, and want of consideration. Familiarity with suffering, it is said, blunts the sensibilities, and where neglect once finds a footing other injuries are multiplied. This is not all, for it may justly and strongly be added that, from the deficiency of adequate means to meet the wants of these cases, it has been an absolute impossibility to do justice in this matter. Prisons are not constructed in view of being converted into county hospitals, and almshouses are not founded as receptacles for the insane. And yet, in the face of justice and common sense, wardens are by law compelled to receive, and the masters of almshouses not to refuse, insane and idiotic subjects in all stages of mental disease and privation.

It is the Commonwealth, not its integral parts, that is accountable for most of the abuses which have lately and do still exist. I repeat it, it is defective legislation which perpetuates and multiplies these abuses. In illustration of my subject, I offer the following extracts from my Note-book and Journal:—

Springfield. In the jail, one lunatic woman, furiously mad, a State pauper, improperly situated, both in regard to the prisoners, the keepers, and herself. It is a case of extreme self-forgetfulness and oblivion to all the decencies of life, to describe which would be to repeat only the grossest scenes. She is much worse since leaving Worcester. In the almshouse of the same town is a woman apparently only needing judicious care, and some well-chosen employment, to make it unnecessary to confine her in solitude, in a dreary unfurnished room. Her appeals for employment and companionship are most touching, but the mistress replied "she had no time to attend to her."

. . .

Lincoln. A woman in a cage. *Medford.* One idiotic subject chained, and one in a close stall for seventeen years. *Pepperell.* One often doubly chained, hand and foot; another violent; several peaceable now. *Brookfield.* One man caged, comfortable. *Granville.* One often closely confined; now losing the use of his limbs from want of exercise. *Charlemont.* One man caged. *Savoy.* One man caged. *Lenox.* Two in the jail, against whose unfit condition there the jailer protests.

Dedham. The insane disadvantageously placed in the jail. In the almshouse, two females in stalls, situated in the main building; lie in wooden bunks filled with straw; always shut up. One of these subjects is supposed curable. The overseers of the poor have declined giving her a trial at the hospital, as I was informed, on account of expense.

. . .

Besides the above, I have seen many who, part of the year, are chained or caged. The use of cages all but universal. Hardly a town but can refer to some not distant period of using them; chains are less common; negligences frequest; wilful abuse less frequent than sufferings proceeding from ignorance, or want of consideration. I encountered during the last three months many poor creatures wandering reckless and unprotected through the country. Innumerable accounts have been sent me of persons who had roved away unwatched and unsearched after; and I have heard that responsible persons, controlling the almshouses, have not thought themselves culpable in sending away from their shelter, to cast upon the chances of remote relief, insane men and women. These, left on the highways, unfriended and incompetent to control or direct their own movements, sometimes have found refuge in the hospital, and others have not been traced. But I cannot particularize. In traversing the State, I have found hundreds of insane persons in every variety of circumstance and condition, many whose situation could not and need not be improved; a less number, but that very large, whose lives are the saddest pictures of human suffering and degradation. I give a few illustrations; but description fades before reality.

Danvers. November. Visited the almshouse. A large building, much out of repair. Understand a new one is in contemplation. Here are from fifty-six to sixty inmates, one idiotic, three insane; one of the latter in close confinement at all times.

Long before reaching the house, wild shouts, snatches of rude songs, imprecations and obscene language, fell upon the ear, proceeding from the occupant of a low building, rather remote from the principal building to which my course was directed. Found the mistress, and was conducted to the place which was called *"the home"* of the *forlorn* maniac, a young woman, exhibiting a condition of neglect and misery blotting out the faintest idea of comfort, and outraging every sentiment of decency. She had been, I learnt, "a respectable person, industrious and worthy. Disappointments and trials shook her mind, and, finally, laid prostrate reason and self-control. She became a maniac for life. She had been at Worcester Hospital for a considerable time, and had been returned as incurable." The mistress told me she understood that, "while there, she was comfortable and decent." Alas, what a change was here exhibited! She had passed from one degree of violence to another, in swift progress. There she stood, clinging to or beating upon the bars of her caged apartment, the contracted size of which afforded space only for increasing accumulations of filth, a *foul* spectacle. There she stood with naked arms and dishevelled hair, the unwashed frame invested with fragments of unclean garments, the air so extremely offensive, though ventilation was afforded on all sides save one, that it was not possible to remain beyond a few moments without retreating for recovery to the outward air. Irritation of body, produced by utter filth and exposure, incited her to the horrid process of tearing off her skin by inches. Her face, neck, and person were thus disfigured to hideousness. She held up a fragment just

rent off. To my exclamation of horror, the mistress replied: "Oh, we can't help it. Half the skin is off sometimes. We can do nothing with her; and it makes no difference what she eats, for she consumes her own filth as readily as the food which is brought her."

. . . .

Some may say these things cannot be remedied, these furious maniacs are not to be raised from these base conditions. I *know* they are. Could give *many* examples. Let *one* suffice. A young woman, a pauper, in a distant town, Sandisfield, was for years a raging maniac. A cage, chains, and *the whip* were the agents for controlling her, united with harsh tones and profane language. Annually, with others (the town's poor), she was put up at auction, and bid off at the lowest price which was declared for her. One year, not long past, an old man came forward in the number of applicants for the poor wretch. He was taunted and ridiculed. "What would he and his old wife do with such a mere beast?" "My wife says yes," replied he, "and I shall take her." She was given to his charge. He conveyed her home. She was washed, neatly dressed, and placed in a decent bedroom, furnished for comfort and opening into the kitchen. How altered her condition! As yet *the chains* were not off. The first week she was somewhat restless, at times violent, but the quiet, kind ways of the old people wrought a change. She received her food decently, forsook acts of violence, and no longer uttered blasphemies or indecent language. After a week the chain was lengthened, and she was received as a companion into the kitchen. Soon she engaged in trivial employments. "After a fortnight," said the old man, "I knocked off the chains and made her a free woman." She is at times excited, but not violently. They are careful of her diet. They keep her very clean. She calls them "father" and "mother." Go there now, and you will find her "clothed," and, though not perfectly in her "right mind," so far restored as to be a safe and comfortable inmate.

Newburyport. Visited the almshouse in June last. Eighty inmates. Seven insane, one idiotic. Commodious and neat house. Several of the partially insane apparently very comfortable. Two very improperly situated; namely, an insane man, not considered incurable, in an out-building, whose room opened upon what was called "the dead room," affording, in lieu of companionship with the living, a contempla-

tion of corpses. The other subject was a woman in a *cellar.* I desired to see her. Much reluctance was shown. I pressed the request. The master of the house stated that she was *in the cellar;* that she was *dangerous to be approached;* that she had lately attacked his wife, and *was often naked.* I persisted, "If you will not go with me, give me the keys and I will go alone." Thus importuned, the outer doors were opened. I
10 descended the stairs from within. A strange, unnatural noise seemed to proceed from beneath our feet. At the moment I did not much regard it. My conductor proceeded to remove a padlock, while my eye explored the wide space in quest of the poor woman. All for a moment was still. But judge my horror and amazement, when a door to a closet *beneath* the *staircase* was opened, revealing in the imperfect light a female apparently wasted to a
20 skeleton, partially wrapped in blankets, furnished for the narrow bed on which she was sitting. Her countenance furrowed, not by age, but suffering, was the image of distress. In that contracted space, unlighted, unventilated, she poured forth the wailings of despair. Mournfully she extended her arms and appealed to me: "Why am I consigned to hell? dark—dark —I used to pray, I used to read the Bible—I have done no crime in my heart. I had friends.
30 Why have all forsaken me!—my God, my God, why hast *thou* forsaken me!" Those groans, those wailings, come up daily, mingling with how many others, a perpetual and sad memorial. When the good Lord shall require an account of our stewardship, what shall all and each answer?

Perhaps it will be inquired how long, how many days or hours, was she imprisoned in these confined limits? *For years!* In another
40 part of the cellar were other small closets, only better, because higher through the entire length, into one of which she by turns was transferred, so as to afford opportunity for fresh whitewashing, etc.

Saugus. December 24. Thermometer below zero; drove to the poorhouse; was conducted to the master's family-room by himself; walls garnished with handcuffs and chains, not less than five pairs of the former; did not inquire how or
50 on whom applied; thirteen pauper inmates; one insane man; one woman insane; one idiotic man; asked to see them; the two men were shortly led in; appeared pretty decent and comfortable. Requested to see the other insane subject; was denied decidedly; urged the request,

and finally secured a reluctant assent. Was led through an outer passage into a lower room, occupied by the paupers; crowded; not neat; ascended a rather low flight of stairs upon an open entry, through the floor of which was introduced a stove-pipe, carried along a *few feet,* about six inches above the floor, through which it was reconveyed below. From this entry opens a room of moderate size, having a sashed window; floor, I think, painted; apartment *entirely* unfurnished; no chair, table, nor bed; neither, what is seldom missing, a bundle of straw or lock of hay; cold, very cold; the first movement of my conductor was to throw open a window, a measure imperatively necessary for those who entered. *On the floor* sat a woman, her limbs immovably contracted, so that the knees were brought upward to the chin; the face was concealed; the head rested on the folded arms. For clothing she appeared to have been furnished with *fragments* of many discharged garments. These were folded about her, yet they little benefited her, if one might judge by the constant shuddering which almost convulsed her poor crippled frame. Woful was this scene. Language is feeble to record the misery she was suffering and had suffered. In reply to my inquiry if she could not change her position, I was answered by the master in the negative, and told that the contraction of limbs was occasioned by "neglect and exposure in former years," but *since she had been crazy,* and before she fell under the charge, as I inferred, of her present *guardians.* Poor wretch! she, like many others, was an example of what humanity becomes when the temple of reason falls in ruins, leaving the mortal part to injury and neglect, and showing how much can be endured of privation, exposure, and disease without extinguishing the lamp of life.

Passing out, the man pointed to a something, revealed to more than one sense, which he called "her bed; and we throw some blankets over her at night." Possibly this is done; others, like myself, might be pardoned a doubt if they could have seen all I saw and heard abroad all I heard. The *bed,* so called, was about *three* feet long, and from a half to three-quarters of a yard wide; of old ticking or tow cloth was the case; the contents might have been a *full handful* of hay or straw. My attendant's exclamations on my leaving the house were emphatic, and can hardly be repeated.

. . . .

It may not appear much more credible than the fact above stated, that a few months since a young woman in a state of complete insanity was confined entirely naked in a pen or stall in a barn. There, unfurnished with clothes, without bed and without fire, she was left—but not alone. Profligate men and idle boys had access to the den, whenever curiosity or vulgarity prompted. She is now removed into the house with other paupers; and for this humanizing benefit she was indebted to the remonstrances, in the first instance, *of an insane man.*

Another town now owns a poorhouse, which I visited, and am glad to testify to the present comfortable state of the inmates; but there the only provision the house affords for an insane person, should one, as is not improbable, be conveyed there, is a closet in the cellar, formed by the arch upon which the chimney rests. This has a close door, not only securing the prisoners, but excluding what of light and pure air might else find admission.

Abuses assuredly cannot always or altogether be guarded against; but, if in the civil and social relations all shall have "done what they could," no ampler justification will be demanded at the great tribunal.

Of the dangers and mischiefs sometimes following the location of insane persons in our almshouses, I will record but one more example. In Worcester has for several years resided a young woman, a lunatic pauper of decent life and respectable family. I have seen her as she usually appeared, listless and silent, almost or quite sunk into a state of dementia, sitting one amidst the family, "but not of them." A few weeks since, revisiting that almshouse, judge my horror and amazement to see her negligently bearing in her arms a young infant, of which I was told she was the unconscious parent. Who was the father, none could or would declare. Disqualified for the performance of maternal cares and duties, regarding the helpless little creature with a perplexed or indifferent gaze, she sat a silent, but, oh, how eloquent, a pleader for the protection of others of her neglected and outraged sex! Details of that black story would not strengthen the cause. Needs it a mightier plea than the sight of that forlorn creature and her wailing infant? Poor little child, more than orphan from birth, in this unfriendly world! A demented mother, a father on whom the sun might blush or refuse to shine!

. . .

The greatest evils in regard to the insane and idiots in the prisons of this Commonwealth are found at Ipswich and Cambridge, and distinguish these places only, as I believe, because the numbers are larger, being more than twenty in each. Ipswich has the advantage over Cambridge in having fewer furious subjects, and in the construction of the buildings, though these are so bad as to have afforded cause for presentment by the grand jury some time since. It is said that the new County House, in progress of building, will meet the exigencies of the case. If it is meant that the wing in the new prison, to be appropriated to the insane, will provide accommodation for all the insane and idiotic paupers in the county, I can only say that it could receive no more than can be gathered in the three towns of Salem, Newburyport, and Ipswich, supposing these are to be removed, there being in Ipswich twenty-two in the prison and eight in the almshouse; in Salem almshouse, seventeen uniformly crazy, and two part of the time deranged; and in that of Newburyport eleven, including idiots. Here at once are sixty. The returns of 1842 exhibit an aggregate of one hundred and thirty-five. Provision is made in the new prison for fifty-seven of this class, leaving seventy-eight unprovided for, except in the almshouses. From such a fate, so far as Danvers, Saugus, East Bradford, and some other towns in the county reveal conditions of insane subjects, we pray they may be exempt.

I have the verbal and written testimony of many officers of this Commonwealth, who are respectable alike for their integrity and the fidelity with which they discharge their official duties, and whose opinions, based on experience, are entitled to consideration, that the occupation of prisons for the detention of lunatics and of idiots is, under all circumstances, an evil, subversive alike of good order, strict discipline, and good morals. I transcribe a few passages which will place this mischief in its true light. The sheriff of Plymouth County writes as follows: "I am decidedly of the opinion that the county jail is a very improper place for lunatics and idiots. The last summer its bad effects were fully realized here, not only by the prisoners in jail, but the disturbance extended to the inhabitants dwelling in the neighborhood. A foreigner was sentenced by a justice of the peace to thirty days' confinement in the house of correction. He was to all appearance a lunatic or madman. He destroyed every article in his room, even to his wearing apparel, his noise and disturbance was incessant for hours, day and night. I consider prisons places for the safe keeping of prisoners, and all these are equally entitled to humane treatment from their keepers, without regard to the cause of commitment. We have in jails no conveniences to make the situation of lunatics and idiots much more decent than would be necessary for the brute creation, and impossible to prevent the disturbance of the inmates under the same roof."

It is not few, but many, it is not a part, but the whole, who bear unqualified testimony to

this evil. A voice strong and deep comes up from every almshouse and prison in Massachusetts where the insane are or have been protesting against such evils as have been illustrated in the preceding pages.

Gentlemen, I commit to you this sacred cause. Your action upon this subject will affect the present and future condition of hundreds and of thousands.

In this legislation, as in all things, may you exercise that "wisdom which is the breath of the power of God."

Respectfully submitted,

D. L. Dix.
1843

HORACE MANN

1796–1859

B E ASHAMED to die until you have won some victory for humanity," counseled Horace Mann in his baccalaureate address at Antioch College in 1859. His life had well exemplified his humanitarian doctrine. Although as an antislavery Whig member of Congress from Massachusetts Mann contributed fearlessly to the growing conviction that slavery was wrong, his crusade for better free public schools was his chief contribution to social reform. Abandoning a successful law practice in Dedham and a political career in the Massachusetts state legislature, Mann accepted, in 1837, the secretaryship of the newly created state board of education. The common schools of Massachusetts had fallen to a low level, and although Mann was not the first, or the only pioneer of the educational awakening, he was perhaps the greatest. His *Common School Journal*, his reports, his lectures, his organization of teachers' conventions did much not only to improve the common schools but to popularize the theme that a generously supported public education is indispensable in a democracy, and that education is an important remedy for social ailments. With his fellow crusaders in the public school awakening, Mann made the cause one of the leading reforms of the day, and one of the most successful ones. His influence on the American public school system and on the social philosophy of American educators was both broad and deep.

Federal Writers Project, *Selective and Critical Bibliography of Horace Mann*, Roxbury, Mass., 1937.
Life and Works of Horace Mann, M. T. P. Mann, ed., Boston, 3 vols., 1865–1868.
Louise Hall Tharp, *Until Victory. Horace Mann and Mary Peabody*, Boston, 1953.
E. I. F. Williams, *Horace Mann, Educational Statesman*, New York, 1937.
Merle Curti, *The Social Ideas of American Educators*, New York, 1935, 1959.

» » From: COMMON SCHOOL JOURNAL « «

. . .

Animated by these feelings, we again enroll ourselves as a soldier in this cause,—not in the presumptious expectation that we can achieve aught that is worthy of its name; but, at the same time, not without hope that, while we uphold its banner, others may rally around it, and bear it on to victory.

Education derives arguments for its support from a more comprehensive range of considerations than ever united their advocacy for any other human interest. Health, freedom, wisdom, virtue, time, eternity, plead in its behalf. Some causes have reference to temporal interests; some to eternal;—education embraces both.

The view which invests education with the awful prerogative of projecting its consequences forward through the whole length of the illimitable future, will not be objected to by the champions of any religious creed. Those who believe that the destiny of the human soul is irrevocably fixed for weal or woe by its state or condition when its exit from life is made,—who believe that, as it is then sanctified, or unregenerate, it must go out from this world, through an opposite avenue, and into an opposite eternity,—will equally believe and maintain the tendency of intellectual and moral guidance, or neglect, especially during the impressible period of youth, to turn its course into the broad, or into the narrow way. Those, also, who believe that, although the soul should enter the spiritual world "unhouselled, unanointed, unanealed," yet that it will not be cut off from hope, but will be allowed to pass through other cycles of probation,

"Till the foul crimes done in its days of nature
Are burnt and purged away,"

will of course believe and maintain that, the lighter the burden of sin which weighs it down, at its entrance into another life, the sooner will its recuperative energies enable it to rise from its guilty fall, and to ascend to the empyrean of perfect happiness. There is still another class, who interpret the Scriptures to promise universal beatitude to the whole human race, at the instant of death. They maintain that the soul leaves every earthly impurity

in the foul tabernacle of flesh, where each had polluted the other during life, and at once springs aloft to be robed in garments of purity. But even they do not suppose that the spirit, though ransomed and cleansed by omnipotent grace, can overleap the immense moral spaces it has lost, and at once engage in the services of the upper temple, with that seraphic ardor which burns in bosoms, where its flame had been kindled while yet on earth. In other words, if the dogma of the theologians were true, that there are in heaven seven orders of celestial spirits, they will allow, that a wretch who died perpetrating sacrilege with his hands, and blaspheming God with his tongue, cannot, at once, and without a single rehearsal, strike the harp and sing hosannas in unison with the highest perfected spirits, but must forever be somewhat procrastinated in his ascent from order to order, in the celestial hierarchy.

In regard to Intellectual Education, no man can offer a single reason for arresting its progress, and confining it where it now is, which would not be equally available for reducing its present amount. He who would degrade the intellectual standing of Massachusetts to the level of Ireland, would degrade Ireland to the level of the interior of Africa, or of the Batta Islands. Nor could even the rank of savage life claim any immunity from still lower debasement. In the "lowest deep," there would be some whose selfishness would demand the opening of a still "lower deep." There would be no halting post until the race had reached the limits of degradation in troglodytes and monkeys, and the godlike faculty of reason had been lost in the mechanism of animal instinct. The useful and elegant arts that minister to the comfort of man, and gladden his eye with beauty; poetry and eloquence that ravish the soul; philosophy that comprehends the workmanship of the heavens, and reads, in the present condition of the earth, as in the leaves of a book, the records of myriads of ages gone by; language by which we are taught by all the generations that are past, and by which we may teach all the generations that are to come; —all these would be sunk in oblivion, and all the knowledge possessed by the descendants of Bacon, and Newton, and Franklin, would be to chatter and mow, to burrow in a hole, and crack nuts with the teeth. Such is the catastrophe to which we should come, could those prevail, who would make the present horizon of human knowledge stationary.

Physical Education is not only of great importance on its own account, but, in a certain sense, it seems to be invested with the additional importance of both intellectual and moral; because, although we have frequent proofs, that there may be a human body without a soul, yet, under our present earthly conditions of existence, there cannot be a human soul without a body. The statue must lie prostrate, without a pedestal; and, in this sense, the pedestal is as important as the statue.

The present generation is suffering incalculably under an ignorance of physical education. It is striving to increase the number of pleasurable sensations, without any knowledge of the great laws of health and life, and thus defeats its own object. The sexes respectively, are deteriorating from their fathers, and especially from their mothers, in constitutional stamina. The fifteen millions of the United States, at the present day, are by no means five times the three millions of the revolutionary era. Were this degeneracy attributable to mother Nature, we should compare her to a fraudulent manufacturer, who, having established his name in the market for the excellence of his fabrics, should avail himself of his reputation to palm off subsequent bales or packages, with the same stamp or earmark, but of meaner quality. Thus it is with the present race, as compared with their ancestors,—short in length, deficient in size and weight, and sleazy in texture. The activity and boldness of the sanguine temperament, and the enduring nature of the fibrous, which belonged to the olden time, are succeeded by the weak refinements of the nervous, and the lolling, lackadaisical, fashionable sentimentality of the lymphatic. The old hearts of oak are gone. Society is suffering under a curvature of the spine. If deterioration holds on, at its present rate, especially in our cities, we shall soon be a bed-rid people. There will be a land of ghosts and shadows this side of Acheron and the Elysian fields. Where are the young men, and, emphatically, where are the young women, who promise a green and vigorous age at seventy? The sweat and toil of the field and of the household are despised, and no substitute is provided for these invigorating exercises. Even professed connoisseurs, who lounge and dawdle in the galleries of art, and labor to express their weak rapture of the Jove-like stature and sublime strength of Hercules, or at the majestic figure of Venus, beneath whose ample zone there resides the energy which prevents grace from degenerating into weakness,—even they will belie, in dress and contour, all the power and beauty they profess to admire. There is a general effeminacy in our modes of life, as compared with the indurating exposures of our ancestors. Our double-windows; our air-tight houses; our heated and unventilated apartments, from nursery to sleeping-room, and church; the multitude of our garments of fur, and down, and woollen, numerous as the integuments around an Egyptian mummy,—beneath which we shrink, and cower, and hide ourselves from our best friend, the north-west wind; our carriages, in which we ride when we should be on foot;—all these enervating usages, *without any equivalent of exercise or exposure,* are slackening the whole machinery of life. More weakly children are born, than under the vigorous customs and hardy life of our fathers; and, what is still more significant, a far greater proportion of these puny children, under our tender and delicate nursing, are reared than was formerly done. A weak cohesion still exists in many a thread of life, which, under the rough handling of former times, would have been snapped. Amid hardship and exposure, the young were toughened or destroyed. Nature passed round among them, as a gardener among the plants, and weeded out the blasted and mildewed. She shook the tree, till the sickly fruits fell off. She did not preserve these, as the stock from which to produce the still more degraded fruits of a second season. But, under the modern hothouse system, the puny and feeble are saved. They grow up without strength, passing from the weakness of childhood to that of age, without taking the vigor of manhood in their course. By the various appliances of art, indeed, the stooping frame can be kept upright and the shrunken be rounded out, into the semblance of humanity. But these cheats give no internal, organic force. Though the arts of bolstering up the human figure, and of giving to its unsightly angles the curvilinear forms of grace, should grow into science, and its practice should be the most lucrative of professions, yet not one element of genuine beauty or dignity will be thereby gained. Such arts can never bestow elasticity and vigor upon the frame, nor suffuse "the human face divine" with the roseate hues of health. The complexion will still be wan, the pulse feeble, the motions languid. The eye will have no fire. The imagination will lose its power to turn all light into rainbows. The intellect will never be sufficiently expanded to receive *a system of truths*, and single truths cut out from their conections, and adopted without reference to kindred truths, always mislead. The affections will fall, like Lucifer, from the upper, to fasten upon objects, in the nether sphere. In a word, the forces of the soul will retreat from the fore-head to the hind-head, and the brow, that "dome of thought, and palace of the soul," will be narrow and "villainously low"; for it is here that Nature sets her signet, and stamps her child a philosopher or a cretin. Here she will not suffer her signatures to be counter-feited, for neither tailors nor mantua-makers can insert their cork or padding beneath the tables of the skull.

We have now pointed, as with the finger and rapidly, towards those grand relations in which mankind stand to the cause of education. These relations lie all around us. They connect us with the universe of matter, and with the universe of mind; and hence the necessity of our possessing knowledge, for it is only by knowledge that we can adjust ourselves to the objects to which we are related. These truths also point to the future; and hence the necessity that we should regulate our conduct according to them, for every act of life is a step carrying us further towards, or further from, the goal of our being.

To promote this object, at once so comprehensive and so enduring, is among the first duties of governments; it is also among the first duties of individuals. It is the duty of the great and powerful, in their broad sphere of action; and it is no less the duty of the humble and obscure, in their narrower circle. Let every one contribute "according to his ability."

The labor of another year, in endeavoring to advance the well-being of our fellow-men, through enlightenment, and the impulse of higher motives, is the mite which we propose to cast into the "treasury" of the Lord. We ask others to cast in of their abundance. We ask all to receive into their minds the great idea of social improvement, to contemplate, and strive to imbody in human form, the sublime law of progression,—the possibility and the practicability of an ever-upward ascension in the scale of being. The race can be made happier and better than it is. There are innumerable sufferings which spring from ignorance. This, knowledge will dispel, and relieve multi-tudes who are now tormented with unnecessary and gratuitous pain. There are innumerable sufferings springing from fountains of perverted feeling, which have no necessary existence, which are no part of the inevitable lot of humanity. These, like the debasing customs of savage life, like the foul superstitions and idolatries of paganism, can be cast off, as a garment which we have outgrown. There are ten thousand existing causes of misery and crime, which need not be reproduced and perpetuated in the coming generation. Many, nay, most, of the burdens which mankind have borne, which we now bear, may be lightened, before they are cast upon our successors. Save, O, save the myriads of innocent beings who are just landing upon the shores of time;—save them from the contaminations of the world into which they are sent; teach not their unpolluted lips to utter curses, nor their hands to uphold injustice, nor their feet to wander in forbidden paths. Even those who take the darkest views of human nature, and who proclaim the most fearful auguries concerning its ultimate destiny,—even they will admit that the young are less vicious than the old; that childhood had a simplicity and an ingenuousness which intercourse with the world corrupts and debauches. They will admit that there is a guilelessness, an uncalculating affection, a sensibility to wrong, in the breasts of the young, which the arts and customs of the world deprave and harden. It is we, who by our ignorances, and our apathy, by our parsimony and our pride, create in them diseases which even the brute creation do not suffer, because they do not abuse the natures which God has given them. Why should we, who, in our considerate moments, would not punish even the wretch suspected of crime, until guilt is fastened upon him by indubitable proof, and who, even then, profess to pity him, as he meets the just retributions of a violated law,—why should we lead children astray by our evil customs and practices, and bring down upon them those penalties, which, in the self-executing law of God, will assuredly follow transgression? To punish the innocent has been regarded with abhorrence and execration in all ages of the world; but to tempt innocence to the commission of those offences which incur punishment, is far more cruel, because guilt is infinitely worse than the punishment which avenges it. Why should innocent childhood be tormented with pains not of its own procuring,—with pains which the follies and the vices of ancestors seem to have prepared, and made ready against its coming? Why should the new-born generations be ushered into a world worse than themselves; to breathe in physical and moral contaminations which they did not scatter; to die of maladies engendered by those who should have been their protectors and guardian spirits?

It is in our power to rescue children from these calamities. It is in our power to guard them from the contagion of guilt, from that subtilist of poisons, an evil example. They can be restrained from entering paths where others have fallen and perished. No rude child of ignorance, left to himself in the wild wilderness where he was born, ever reached to a thousandth part of that depravity, which has been achieved as a common thing, by those whose birthplace was in a land of boasted civilization. Civilization, then, has not accomplished its object. It has given more power than rectitude,—the ability to perform great things without that moral sovereignty, before which the greatest and grandest achievements stand condemned, if not consecrated by goodness.

And here we would inquire what sphere of patriotic exertion is left open for the lover of his country, but the sphere of improving the rising generation through the instrumentality of a more perfect and efficient system for their education? We call our fathers *patriots,* because they loved their country and made sacrifices for its welfare. But what was their country? A vast tract of wilderness territory did not constitute it. It was not unconscious, insentient plains, or rivers, or mountains, however beautifully and majestically they might spread, or flow, or shine, beneath the canopy of heaven. Their country was chiefly their descendants, the human beings who were to throng these vast domains, the sentient, conscious natures which were to live here,—and living, to enjoy or suffer. The question with them was, whether this should be a land of liberty or bondage, of light or darkness, of religion or superstition. It was to redeem and elevate the millions who, in the providence of God, should people these wide-spreading realms, that they engaged in a cause where those who suffered death seemed to suffer least, where the survivors most challenge our sympathy. But we have no battles to fight by land or sea, against a foreign foe. We have no fathers, or brothers, or sons, in the camp, suffering cold, and hunger, and na-

kedness. We have no edifice of government to rear, with exhausting study and anxiety. These labors are done and ended, and we have entered into the rich inheritance. What, then, shall we do that we may be patriotic? How shall our love of country, if any we have, be made manifest? How, but by laboring for our descendants,—not in the same way, but with the same fidelity, as our fathers labored for us? Otherwise, there is no moral consanguinity between ourselves and them. Otherwise, we are not of their blood, but gentiles and heathens, boasting a lineage which our acts and lives belie. It is mockery to say, "We have Abraham to our father," while we perform the deeds of pagans. The only sphere, then, left open for our patriotism, is the improvement of our children,—not the few, but the many; not a part of them, but all. This is but one field of exertion, but it opens an infinite career; for the capacities of mankind can go on developing, improving, perfecting, as long as the cycles of eternity revolve. For this improvement of the race, a high, a generous, an expansive education is the true and efficient means. There is not a good work which the hand of man has ever undertaken, which his heart has ever conceived, which does not require a good education for its helper. There is not an evil afflicting the earth, which can be extirpated, until the auxiliary of education shall lend its mighty aid. If an angel were to descend from heaven to earth, on an errand of mercy and love, he would hasten to accomplish his mission by illuminating the minds and purifying the hearts of children. The Saviour took little children in his arms and blessed them; he did not, by any miraculous exertion of power, bar up all passages to sin and error, and at once make mankind the passive recipients of perfection. He left it for us to be agents and co-workers with him in their redemption. He gave to us, not so much the boon of being blessed, as the more precious, the heavenly boon of blessing others. For this end, an instrument has been put into our hands, fully adequate to the accomplishment of so divine a purpose. We have the power to train up children in accordance with those wise and benign laws which the Creator has stamped upon their physical, their intellectual, and their moral nature; and of this stewardship we must assuredly give account. May it be rendered with joy, and not with sorrow!   1842

TEMPERANCE AND PROHIBITION

NO REFORM MOVEMENT in the first half of the nineteenth century enlisted so large a following as temperance. While many of the friends of this cause did not go so far as Neal Dow, who was largely responsible for the enactment of the famous Maine prohibition law, all agreed that heavy drinking was an evil to be combatted by every instrument of persuasion. The temperance stories of Lucius Sargent, the temperance poems of Mrs. Sigourney and others, and the antisaloon plays of Timothy S. Arthur, reveal the essential philosophy of the movement. Inebriation was above all regarded as an enemy of the home. But intoxicating liquors were also considered by temperance reformers as inimical to American democracy: republican forms could succeed only if the electorate and the lawmakers safeguarded against the temptations of the dram shop. Something was also made of the argument that efficiency in business and industry demanded temperate workers.

The following temperance songs are from *The Mountain Minstrel* (1847). This collection was edited by T. D. Bonner, an agent of the New Hampshire State Temperance Society.

John A. Krout, *The Origins of Prohibition*, New York, 1925.

TAKE COURAGE

Tune—*Calvary*

From the mountain top and valley,
  See! the banner streaming high!
While the sons of freedom rally
  To the widow's lonely cry,
    Sisters weeping,
  Bid us to the rescue fly.

Could we hear the mother pleading,
  Heaven relief will quickly send;
Can we see our country bleeding,
  Still refuse our aid to lend?   10
    No! dread monster,
  Here thy triumph soon shall end.

Must we see the drunkard reeling
  (Void of reason) to the grave?
Where's the heart so dead to feeling,
  Who would not the wanderer save?
    God of mercy,
  'Tis thy blessing now we crave.

Dearest Savior, O, relieve us,
  Unto thee we humbly bow,   20
Let that fiend no more deceive us,
  Grant thy loving favor now;

While against him,
  Here we pledge a sacred vow.

Now the trump of Temperance sounding,
  Rouse! ye freemen! why delay?
Let your voices all resounding,
  Welcome on the happy day,
    When that tyrant
  Must resign his cruel sway.   30

ONE GLASS MORE

Stay, mortal, stay! nor heedless thus
  Thy sure destruction seal;
Within that cup there lurks a curse,
  Which all who drink shall feel.
Disease and death forever nigh,
  Stand ready at the door,
And eager wait to hear the cry—
  "O give me one glass more!"

Go, view that prison's gloomy cells—
  Their pallid tenants scan;   10
Gaze—gaze upon these earthly hells,
  Ask when they began:
Had these a tongue—oh, man! thy cheek
  Would burn with crimson o'er—
Had these a tongue they'd to thee speak,
  Oh, take not *"one glass more."*

Behold that wretched female form,	Stay, mortal stay, repent, return!
An outcast from her home;	Reflect upon thy fate;
Crushed by affliction's blighting storm,	The poisonous draught indignant spurn,
And doom'd in want to roam:　　20	Spurn—spurn it ere too late.
Behold her! ask that prattler dear,	Oh, fly thee ale-house's horrid din,
Why mother is so poor,	Nor linger at the door,　　30
He'll whisper in thy startled ear,	Lest thou perchance, should sip again
'Twas father's *"one glass more."*	The treacherous *"one glass more."*

ELIHU BURRITT

1810–1879

THIS CONNECTICUT reformer, who began life as a blacksmith, superbly exemplified the cult of self-improvement—he taught himself all the European and several of the African and Asiatic languages, and much besides. But the greatest value in life for him was, as he put it, "the capacity and space of labouring for humanity." He was a pioneer in the movement to abolish war through the development of international understanding and universal brotherhood, as well as through a league of nations, a high court, compulsory arbitration, and the strike of workingmen against war. Burritt's writings on internationalism and pacifism take high rank in the literature of the peace movement. Consistently loyal to the cause of peace even when fellow "pacifists" found excuses for justifying particular wars, Burritt was a militant non-resistant. He also labored to prevent the Civil War through popularizing the idea of compensated emancipation of the slaves; and he did much to effect the reduction of international postal rates and to assist emigrants in finding homes in America. Burritt's activities carried him to Europe, and during his consulship at Birmingham he wrote picturesque sketches of industrial and rural England, representative of which are *Walks from London to John o' Groats* (1864) and *Walks in the Black Country and its Green Borderland* (1869). His books also include *Sparks from the Anvil* (1846), *Thoughts and Things at Home and Abroad* (1854), and *Lectures and Speeches* (1869).

Charles Northend, *Life and Labors of Elihu Burritt, A Memorial Volume*, New York, 1879.
Merle Curti, *The Learned Blacksmith; The Letters and Journals of Elihu Burritt*, New York, 1937.

»　» From: THOUGHTS AND THINGS AT HOME　«　« AND ABROAD

THE PIONEERS OF PEACE

We are now on the eve, as it were, of that great and august demonstration to which the friends of peace, on both sides of the Atlantic have been looking forward with such lively anticipations during the last six months. "Peace has her victories no less than war"; and we have recently contemplated two of her great days of progress. A greater day, we believe, is before us. We are strong in hope and faith that the Paris Congress in August will add another and more illustrious victory to the series which peace has won for humanity in these latter years. If the result of the approaching demonstration shall realize our expectations, those who have labored in the cause during the day of its small things may thank God, and take courage to believe that its final triumph is close at hand, and that they may live to join in the general jubilee which shall hail its advent. As the horizon of the new era, predicted by holy men of old, grows brighter and brighter with the young light of its morning sun, we cannot suppress the wish that Worcester and Ladd,[1] and other apostles of peace, now slumbering in their graves, might have been permitted to see with their eyes what we now see with ours, the tangible and expanding realities of their faith. But such a wish would be human to the last degree, and breathe no affinity to the thought of God, in regard to the faith which he inspires in the human heart, or to the longest life of its loving activities. "The substance of things hoped for" is not telescopic *phenomena* revealed to the sharp-sighted vision of the human eye, nor to the eye of faith is it always *tangible*, though a clearly developed and undoubted certainty. Faith is the great activity which sees its field of labor through the speculum of the soul's immeasurable immortality, and forthwith beings working by love, and co-working with God, in enterprises of beneficence which shall reach their consummation in distant generations. Such was the faith of Worcester, Ladd, and those who have ceased from their labors in the cause of peace; a faith which would have lost much of its merit and lustre, had they been permitted to know that they should live to see what our eyes now behold. For the faith that works by love, works for the future, without the stimulus of present reward; and such was theirs. The faith that works by love, is content to sow, and see from afar the golden sheaves which other generations shall reap; and such was theirs. But, in their brightest hours of hope, little could they have deemed that the harvest was so near. Why, it is but little more than twenty years ago that William Ladd thought it a little victory in the cause, when a religious newspaper in America consented to insert the notice of a small upper-room gathering of the friends of peace as a *paid* advertisement. It was not our privilege to see the face of that great-hearted pioneer in the cause of peace, but we well recollect following the track of his apostleship through the western part of the State of New York, a year or two after he had rested from his labors of love on earth. In every town he visited he left

the memory of the blessed in the hearts of those who looked upon him, or listened to his words. Everywhere on his route we heard people speak of his earnest faith which worked his life away by love. It was the last missionary tour he made; his strength waxed weaker and weaker; his faith, hope, and love, stronger and stronger; and when, towards the close of the course, his limbs trembled with weakness, and he could no longer stand upon his feet throughout his discourse, then he would kneel down in the pulpit, and, in this affecting position, pour out his great gospel thoughts of peace and brotherhood upon the still assembly, with his face shining upon them, with his heart at the full of Heaven's light and love! Good man! his faith was all the more illustrious and pure, in that he did not expect to reap himself, the harvest of his twilight sowing; but somebody would gather the golden sheaves in the distant years to come; somebody would garner in the substance, the reality of his hopes; somebody would see at its noon the day whose first faint ray he caught with his eager eye flickering up the horizon of humanity; and that was enough for him. Good man! the day of small things is the day of great men; still we could have wished, without wishing it as a reward of his labors, that he had been permitted to see some of these latter days of peace; that he could have been with us at Brussels last year;[2] that, with his heart full of the fresh memory of his two little upper-room meetings in America, he could have sat with us in the council chamber, and around the council table of the Prime Minister of Belgium, surrounded by the councillors and conductors of the nation, meeting, day after day, to deliberate upon the most efficient measures for ushering in the reign of universal peace. We wish he could have been there, and at the opening and close of the first continental Peace Congress, hard upon the field of Waterloo; that he could have been with us at the farewell soiree after that grand demonstration, and have drunk in with us the joy of that hour of fraternal fellowship, with hearts beating with sympathies which eyes, in the fault of a common speech, tried to express. We wish he could have been with us at these precious moments; for he would have been as meek, under it all, as when he preached the evangel of peace on his knees, on the last stage of his journey to heaven. But,

[1] The Rev. Noah Worcester (1758–1837), a liberal clergyman, and William Ladd (1788–1841), a Maine farmer, were leaders in the American peace cause.

[2] A popular "Universal Peace Congress" met at Brussels in 1848 to promote the program of the peace cause on the Continent.

much more might we wish that he were at the head of the delegation from America, now crossing the Atlantic, to take part in the great Peace Congress at Paris. Not for his reward, but for an illustrated lesson to the distinguished man of little faith and great intellect, who affect to be the statesmen of the day, and to all doubters and careful persons, who ridicule "the dreams of good men," would we wish that William Ladd were alive to look upon the World's Peace Parliament, about to assemble in the metropolis of France, numbering, perhaps, a thousand members, representing all the nations of the civilized world; that he were permitted to lead into the assembly the American delegation, and introduce them as the offspring of his ideas, as the contingent of his country to the hosts of peace; that Lamartine and Cobden, and others of their genius and aspirations, might look upon him in his gray hairs, and derive from his presence and experience new faith in the right and true.

"But blessed are the dead that die in the Lord," for although they cease from their labors, "their works do follow them"; and William Ladd's will not only follow, but precede his memory, to the great demonstration at Paris. His works will be there—what an immortality in two worlds! His little upper-room works will be there; and all the incipient and secret acts of his faith in the cause will be there; and the thoughts he uttered on his knees in the pulpit will be there, working still, and widening outward, through the stirred mind of that international assembly, the influence of his life of labor, in circles expanding to the compass of humanity. "Blessed are the dead who die in the Lord"; and blessed are they with exceeding blessing to the living, for "their works do follow them," not into the grave, nor out of this afflicted world, but through it, even to the end, lightening the labors of the living, setting them up in existence with a goodly capital of faith and hope in the future; softening down the heat and burden of life and progress which would be too heavy for them were not good works immortal. "Blessed are the dead" who have lived, labored, and died in the Lord, for the heritage of good works which they have left behind them; of which neither principalities nor powers nor any other creature, can dispossess the present and future generations of mankind. The Brussels Congress was an evidence, and the grander demonstration at Paris will be another, that the works of good men follow them through all time as well as eternity. 1849

THE POWER OF PASSIVE RESISTANCE

The full power revealed and prescribed in that simple and sublime precept of the Gospel, "*overcome evil with good*," has never been tested by any people, population, or community, in subduing the evils and enemies that beset and oppressed them, either from within or without. To put it into full operation, requires a capacity of good-will, of forgiveness of injuries, of abnegation of natural instincts, which the population of no town, or province, or state, has ever acquired. But, at long intervals, and a little more frequently of late, a case has occurred here and there, in which a considerable community has acquired the ability of sustaining for awhile the lowest, feeblest, manifestation of this power, or a condition of *passive resistance* to oppression, armed with a force which could instantly crush any violent opposition they might attempt to array against it. Within the last two or three years, several of these cases have transpired in different parts of the world. In one of these, a little English colony at the Cape of Good Hope, *passively,* but successfully, *resisted* the great Government of the British empire, backed with all its navies and armies, in its attempt to make the home of their small population a receptacle of criminals, crime, and convicts from England. Then, almost simultaneously with this successful experiment with the force of passive resistance, there comes the report of another, from the distant islands of the Pacific Ocean, tried under circumstances of more imminent peril and oppression, and crowned with more illustrious triumph. The weak little Government of the Sandwich Islands, in order to diminish the use and effect of intoxicating liquors among their people, imposed a heavy tax upon French brandy and wine. This irritated the French, and they sent thither a great ship of war to compel the government to remove the tax; and the captain gave them but a few hours to comply with the demand. But they absolutely refused to obey. Then they must take the consequences, and these would be terrible. The lady of the French consul—good, kind, compassionate woman—went with her husband from house to house, and entreated the foreign residents to take refuge on board the French ship, for the island was to be blown up, or sunk, to punish the wicked government for taxing French brandy, and making drunkenness a dearer luxury to the people! But not a single person accepted of the refuge. The government held fast to its resolution without wavering for a moment. The French commander landed with his marines in battle array. Men with lighted matches stood at the great cannons of the ship. The hour of vengeance had come. Poor little people! what will become of you now? What will you do to defend yourselves against this resistless force? Do? do nothing but *endure.* "The King," says the report, "gave peremptory orders to his people to *oppose no resistance* to the Frenchmen. The gallant commander, therefore, landed his marines and took possession of the fort, custom-house, and some other Government buildings, *no resistance being offered.* All was still and peaceful in the streets, business going on as usual. Here they remained for some days; when, finding that the government would not accede at all to their demands, though they offered to leave the whole question to an umpire, the chivalrous Frenchmen went to work to dismantle the fort, and destroyed everything within its walls. After having finished this Vandal-like work, they marched off with flying colors." How full of illustration is this case of passive resistance! The simple, quiet force of *endurance* which the government opposed to the French, wet their powder and turned their bayonets to straw. Against this unexpected force the marines were powerless. They had no arms to contend with such an enemy. All their weapons, and discipline, and bravery, were fitted only to overcome brute force; and of this they found none, except its shadow in the fort and its equipments; and with great valor they fell upon this shadow, and mutilated it terribly, and then marched back with flying colors! So far was this invasion of bayonet-power from inducing a settlement to the advantage of the French, that the government even refused their offer to submit the question to arbitration, or to put the law at any hazard of modification, in face of all the brute force that France could marshal against it.

These are examples of the irresistible power of *passive resistance,* when opposed by a people to foreign enemies and oppression. But almost simultaneously with these, we have examples of this kind of resistance when arrayed against domestic oppression, or the despotic acts of dynasties that have at their command vast military organizations, ready to do their will. The most striking of these is the case of Hesse Cassel. Here, the force of resistance has been tested for a longer period, and by a larger population than ever have illustrated its virtue before. The result has not yet transpired, nor can we conclude what it will be. We can hardly believe that it will be crowned with complete success; for we cannot believe that the Hessians will be able to *endure* unto the end which they seek. We fear they will lose their impregnable strength, by being seduced into a manifestation of brute force. But the teaching of their experiment, even up to this stage, will be invaluable to the people and the cause of popular freedom everywhere on the Continent of Europe. It has established the fact that despotism, backed by the mightiest armies, cannot serf or subdue a people or a population, or rob them of their rights, or barricade their way to rational freedom, if they can only acquire the capacity of a *passive resistance,* which the most aggravated oppression can never weary out. Up to this hour, the Hessians have manifested this capacity, and practised this virtue; and the bristling bayonets which virtually surrounded them have become as stubble. While they possess their souls in patience, and refrain from the slightest act of violence, the whole soldiery of the continent will be powerless against them. How full of glorious illustration and consequence is this spectacle! The eyes of despotism, like those of beasts of prey, are glaring upon them from every side, watching to spring upon them at a single bound, the first moment that they venture from their stronghold of passive resistance! What a sublime sight in the moral world! It is said that the poor peasants, and the poorest day-laborers in Cassel have signed a pledge to abstain from intoxicating drinks, and that they are watching over each other with the keenest vigilance, lest, in an evil hour, some sudden act of oppression should make them mad, and they should fall from the grace of patience, and peril their country's all by a deed of violence! Contrast that discipline with the spirit and deeds of a brute-force revolution! How the people rise, rise, rise to the highest stature of moral being, under such a process of self-education! "Better is he that ruleth his spirit than he that taketh a city." Yes; the Elector may take the city of Cassel, with 60,000 Austrian and Bavarian troops; but they will be to him as mere shadows, so long as the Hessians shall be able to rule their spirits after this fashion. The cause of popular freedom, progress, and prosperity has an immense interest at stake in the issue of this grand experiment with a force which the God of the poor and the oppressed has given to them in his great Gospel of love:—"I SAY UNTO YOU, RESIST NOT EVIL, BUT OVERCOME EVIL WITH GOOD."   1854

ALBERT BRISBANE

1809–1890

THE INTRODUCTION of Fourierism into the United States is closely associated with the son of a wealthy New Yorker. Albert Brisbane attended in Europe the lectures of Hegel, Guizot, and other leading social thinkers, but became the disciple of Fourier. Returning to the United States, Brisbane lectured extensively on Fourierism and in 1840 published *A Social Destiny of Man: or Association and Reorganization of Industry*. With Horace Greeley, Brisbane edited *The Future*. His associates in the Fourieristic crusade included Parke Godwin, some of the Brook Farm group, and other leading intellectuals. Brisbane's influence was largely responsible for the establishment of some thirty communities. He was not, however, a great or a practical leader for such a movement.

Brisbane also wrote a *General Introduction to Social Science* (1876). His son, Arthur Brisbane, was far more representative than he of the main stream of American thought: for in spite of the hospitality of the United States to experimentation in utopian socialistic communities, the dominant climate of opinion best nourished the individualism, inspirationalism, and acceptance of the status quo for which Brisbane's son, the famous Hearst columnist, was notorious.

Redelia Brisbane, *Albert Brisbane, a Mental Biography*, Boston, 1893.
Arthur E. Bestor, Jr., *Backwoods Utopias*, Phila., 1950.

» » *From:* SOCIAL DESTINY OF MAN « «

CHAPTER VII

INCOHERENCE AND WASTE OF THE PRESENT ORDER

Individual economy, both vexatious and contrary to nature, is the only economy known in civilization. Its practice—tantamount to individual privation—is zealously preached by moralists and sages; and what are the riches of civilization, with all its stinting and parsimony? Positive poverty for seven-eighths, and relative poverty for the remaining eighth.   *Dean.*

It is not surprising that the *Political* order has alone been the object of study, while the *Industrial* order, incomparably more essential to the happiness of mankind, has been almost entirely neglected.   *A. Tamisier.*

Waste! Waste!! Waste!!!

The observations contained in the foregoing chapters will, we trust, be sufficient to convince the reader of the vast and foolish waste which results from our present social mechanism; and of the colossal economies and profits, which would arise from Association and Combination in industrial interests.

These observations could be extended infinitely, but the reader, by observing attentively the effects of our incoherent system, examples of which he meets at every step around him, cannot fail to be convinced of the absence of every thing like order, economy and foresight in our present system of society.

If such characteristics marked the operations of an individual, it would be easy to foresee, that so far from attaining riches, he must inevitably sink into poverty and want. The same law is applicable to society; the absence of Association and economy in our whole system of industry, plunges the social world into indigence and want, the source of endless discord, depravity and degradation. This great fact escapes the attention of men, because each individual, anxious only to escape from the common evil, and to secure himself a sufficiency, so as to enjoy tranquility in the state of general privation and anxiety around him, sees nor cares not for the mass. In the confused efforts, however, which are made by each, and all to attain the great desideratum, fortune, they only trample each other down, and after all we find in society, that the greater the conflict and strife of individuals, the greater the collective poverty and depravity. England illustrates this fact fully; no country has carried all branches of industry to the extent she has done, and no where is there such a hideous contrast of poverty and wealth. The same efforts combined, would have secured riches and happiness to all, but no one has time to stop to consider upon this fact; each individual flatters himself with the idea, that if seven-eighths of those who were making the same efforts before him have failed, he may nevertheless, with better management, succeed. He strives to secure his happiness isolatedly and separately from the race; if his fellows suffer, and he does not, it is to him as if suffering did not exist. No collective action, so essential to the welfare of all, takes place. In the meantime our planet rolls on in its course, carrying with it a restless, depraved, half famished, discordant and warring race!

If we wish to find the most perfect picture of waste and disorder, we must search for it in our large cities. It is there that we will find our *cut-up* system, in which every thing is reduced to the measure and selfishness of the individual, producing an incoherence and complication, which might properly be termed a combination for the production of evil; for it would seem as if things were so organized, as to cause the greatest possible number of evils, and ensure their most rapid propagation. Each house, for example, has its sink of filth, the miasmas of which the whole population must breathe: the poverty or neglect, or both combined, of a single family, produce a contagious disease, which extends to a thousand others, among which there will be indigent ones enough, to keep it in existence.

The neglect of one person, of a child, or a servant perhaps, in whom it is often necessary to confide; burns down not only the house of one family, but a hundred others with it; or the misplaced economy of a stove-pipe, causes a loss of the same kind, which would be sufficient to construct all the apparatus necessary for warming a town or the manor-house of a Phalanx. Where every thing is left to the ignorance, cupidity, carelessness or inability of individuals, no guarantees of a general nature can exist or be put in practice.

It is from the poverty of the mass in our large cities, that the greatest abuses take place. If a capitalist builds damp cellars, garrets without ventilation, small and confined rooms, close court-yards without light and circulation, and with hardly the conveniences necessary to the wants of its inmates, he is sure to find droves of indigent families, who will stow themselves away in these tenements, making of them hot-beds of disease, and nurseries of demoralization. Moralists wonder that human nature can be as depraved as they find it in our societies, and they seek in the *heart* the source of all this depravity; it is only surprising that human nature should bear so much, and murmur so little, and that with its load of social evil and misery, so much good will and gaiety still remain.

If we cite examples of material waste, we should rank, next to that of fires, which we mentioned above, the loss occasioned by the tearing down of buildings, from being badly constructed or from speculation. This waste in many of our large cities must be enormous, and is due to want to combination and foresight. What absence of order, in an architectural point of view, on the part of society, not to be able to plan its buildings so as to answer the wants of the community for twenty years in advance! The widening, straightning and lengthning of streets form another gigantic item of waste. All these abuses arise from the fact that in planning our cities and towns, no system, no method exists. There is no adaptation of architecture to our wants and requirements; our houses are as little suited to our physical welfare, as our social laws are to our attractions and passions. It is to be observed, that this enormous waste and expenditure are *paid* by productive industry, upon which an immense indirect tax is laid, which is not perceived. The farmers, manufacturers and mechanics, must produce the means for paying in the end for every thing, cities, shops, canals, railroads, &c.

Men become, however, so accustomed to the order of things in which they live, that these facts do not strike them: not conceiving the possibility of changing the social mechanism, it appears to them natural and permanent: if, however, they could be brought to doubt its efficacy, or rather its infallibility; and examine it with scrutinizing attention, a social skepticism would take the place of their present blindness. It is a result deeply to be desired: vegitating as the world does in its present social condition, all improvements in science and industry are of no use to the great mass; their poverty does not diminish with these improvements; and the increased means of enjoyment, the refinement of luxury, to which they give rise, only excite that mass to every kind of fraud and falseness to obtain a share of and participate in them.

Riches are the leading wish of man, and in this country wealth has become the all absorbing object of desire. In this strife after wealth, in which millions are engaged, why has it not been perceived, that not one-twentieth can succeed? If but one-third of the population are producers, if production is the only source of riches, and if our system of consumption in isolated households is so complicated, that the small amount produced by the third does not go one-half as far as it would in a system of Combination and Association (or in other words, if one-half of the small product created by the producing third of society is wasted), how is it possible that even the common wants of the entire population, setting aside all superfluity, can be satisfied?

Let us draw a comparison, which will explain this clearly. Suppose that, out of three persons living together, one alone was engaged in producing, while the other two were idle: it is very evident that the active laborer could not alone produce enough to maintain himself and the other two comfortably. But if we suppose in addition, that each has a separate house, has his meals prepared separately in his own dwelling, the small product of the producer would not go near as far as if they lived together, and economized their means; to the loss caused by the idleness of two inactive persons, is to be added the waste of separate and complicated preparations. This is a perfect illustration of the present state of things. One-third of the population produce; two-thirds are non-producers. Instead of uniting and associating for the purpose of making the insufficient product of the labor of the active third go as far as possible, the most excessive complication and waste takes place, there being as many separate houses, kitchens, cooks, fires, &c. as there are families. The result is that the population of all countries, except this, are removed but one degree from starvation. Those of China are so poor that they eat vermin, those of India subsist on a little rice without salt, and tens of thousand die of starvation and are thrown into the Ganges. The Parias, the most degraded class, are driven even to eat sometimes these starved carcasses. The agricultural classes often plant their crops in the hope only of being hired to harvest them. The Irish peasantry have scarcely salt with their potatoes, and in many parts of the country, they eat bread and meat but once a year. Eight millions of French live upon chestnuts and such trash; out of a population of thirty-two millions twenty-two millions have but about six cents a day to live upon and defray all expenses. Twenty-five millions drink no wine, although France supplies the world with wine. It is to be remarked that in the most civilized countries, those in which industry is carried to the greatest perfection, their population are subjected to the severest labor, and are often the most miserable. The peasantry of Portugal, Austria, and even Russia are less harassed by anxiety, and better supplied with food than are those of France and England. In this view of different countries, we must not overlook our own; nearly three millions of negro producers, whose labor pays for our imported luxuries, are merely supplied with their physical wants. We may as well say with Fourier: "Can a more frightful disorder than that which exists upon this Globe be conceived. One-half of the earth is invaded by wild beasts, or savages, which is about the same thing; as to the other half which is under cultivation, we see three-quarters of it occupied by Barbarians who enslave the producers and women, and who in every respect violate justice and reason. There remains consequently an eighth of the Globe in possession of the civilized, who boast of their improvements while giving to indigence and corruption their fullest development."

But to return to our subject: if we accept and approve of the system which allots to each family a separate house, we must approve of the effects which result from such a system. With four hundred families and four hundred separate dwellings, all the cares and duties attendant upon providing for a household, must be gone through with four hundred times, until the complication becomes frightful. Four hundred persons must be sent to market, to make four hundred separate purchases, who lose time enough in selecting articles wanted and in bargaining, to produce them nearly. The four hundred houses imply that there are four hundred *dark holes,* called kitchens, in which four hundred *poor creatures* must pass their time over a hot fire in the middle of summer. Four hundred monotonous meals are prepared, three-fourths of them badly so, which give rise to many discords as there are dishes. As neither mistresses nor servants are satisfied in this system, the former scold, and the latter are indifferent or faithless. If an ox is killed, it is cut up and disposed of in an infinite number of little lots; every hogshead of sugar, every box of tea has to be retailed out pound by pound; this excess of complication increases ten-times the number of butchers and dealers necessary, whose intermediate profits are a heavy indirect tax upon the consumer. The more we go into these details, the more we shall be convinced, that with this waste and want of system, individual economies are illusive, and that the mass must suffer poverty and privation under the best of governments.

Judge a tree by its fruit, a society by its results; let us not be carried away by the endless praises which are lavished on our advanced state of civilization, as the present system is called. It is time some positive ameliorations were demanded at the hands of our politicians and legislators: we have party politics and legislation enough; if any good could come from the incoherent laws and arbitrary constitutions of civilization, it would have been realized long since. Experience, and the condition of mankind, prove that nothing effective is to be hoped from them, and common sense dictates that we should seek elsewhere, in agricultural Association, or in a reform in industry, for social good.

But politicians scarcely dare put forth the hypothesis of a social reform and a change in the condition of mankind: the human race have so long been curbed under the yoke of misfortune, that suffering is believed to be the law of their nature. The views and belief of politicians have so adapted themselves to this doctrine, that it has become a dogmatical part of their creed; they have asserted it so often, that they must stand by their declarations. Their personal and party interests have also become so entwined with the present state of things, that they are even led to support the present social subversion; add to this the apathy of the world, its disbelief in the possibility of a great social change, and we have the ex-

planation why *no social* principles are discussed, and why no efforts are made to ameliorate the condition of that vast mass of suffering, helpless and degraded beings who form three-fourths of the population of the globe. It is time this stupid policy, if all disbelief in a social reform can be called such, should be denounced; the mass, we trust, have become intelligent enough to demand some effective reforms at the hands of their political leaders, so active in administrative reforms, and so clamorous in their protestations of love for the people.

Nine permanent evils characterize the course of our societies; let the mass call upon those leaders to discover the principles of a society which will produce nine results directly opposed to them, will guarantee social happiness, and give us the standard of a true social organization.

NINE PERMANENT SCOURGES OF CIVILIZATION.

Indigence;
Fraud;
Oppression;
War;
Derangement of climate;
Diseases artificially produced; plague; yellow fever; cholera; small pox, &c.;
Vicious circle, without any opening for improvement;
    UNIVERSAL SELFISHNESS;
    DUPLICITY OF SOCIAL ACTION.

NINE PERMANENT BENEFITS TO BE ATTAINED.

General riches;
Practical truth in all relations of life;
Effective liberty in the same;
Constant peace;
Equilibrium of temperature and climate;
System of preventive medicine and extirpation of artificial diseases;
Opening offered to all improvements and ameliorations;
    COLLECTIVE AND INDIVIDUAL PHILANTHROPY; UNITY OF SOCIAL ACTION.

Such are the benefits Association would realize; but can we look for co-operation from men whose interests, as we said, are concentrated in personal success? The circle of our civilized politics is very narrow, but it insures the successful individual, often without merit or great effort, applause for the day, and frequently pecuniary reward with it. Immediate and personal advantage only stimulates the great majority; the idea of a social reform which would change the destiny of mankind, although vast and sublime, is too far off, too severed from all personal advantages, to find many adherents and enthusiasts. There must be, however, some characters so constituted as to feel the want of an object, high and lasting, with which to connect their efforts, so that something may remain to show that they lived upon this earth, and that their intellectual was not as fleeting as their material existence. It is among such temperaments, that we must seek for the advocates of the great social reform, which the present age may have the glory of achieving!

1840

NATHANIEL HAWTHORNE

1804–1864

THE PROGRESS of the world," wrote Hawthorne, "at every step, leaves some evil or wrong on the path behind it, which the unrest of mankind, of their own set purpose, could never have found the way to rectify." Hawthorne's dislike of reform has been laid at the door of his skepticism, his distrust of such doctrines of the Enlightenment as the idea of progress and the perfectibility of human nature. Like the Calvinists, he entertained no high view of human nature, nor did he trust, even as much as they, man's mind, viewed either from the Lockeian or the Kantian angle of vision. "Pride of Intellect" was for him the cardinal sin.

In "Earth's Holocaust" Hawthorne satirized the efforts of reformers to make the world over by ridding it of age-worn institutions and of cumbersome paraphernalia. All the evils, having their seat in the human heart, can be abolished, Hawthorne insisted, only with and through the heart. If reform is ever to come, it must come in Providence's own way, through the regeneration of the human will and the human feelings. Yet Hawthorne did not eschew all political action: he supported the more popular and democratic of the two political parties. And his criticism of English class distinctions, together with his stern disapproval of all that separates man from his kind, betrayed a certain sympathy for the democracy that underlay many of the reform activities which he satirized in "Earth's Holocaust."

The Complete Works of Nathaniel Hawthorne, Introductory Notes by George Parsons Lathrop, Riverside Edition, 12 vols., Boston, 1887–1889.
Lawrence S. Hall, Hawthorne, Critic of Society, New Haven, 1944.
Randolph Stewart, Nathaniel Hawthorne, a Biography, New Haven, 1948.
Mark Van Doren, Nathaniel Hawthorne, New York, 1949.

» » From: MOSSES FROM AN OLD MANSE « «

EARTH'S HOLOCAUST

Once upon a time—but whether in the time past or time to come is a matter of little or no moment—this wide world had become so overburdened with an accumulation of worn-out trumpery that the inhabitants determined to rid themselves of it by a general bonfire. The site fixed upon at the representation of the insurance companies, and as being as central a spot as any other on the globe, was one of the broadest prairies of the West, where no human habitation would be endangered by the flames, and where a vast assemblage of spectators might commodiously admire the show. Having a taste for sights of this kind, and imagining, likewise, that the illumination of the bonfire might reveal some profundity of moral truth heretofore hidden in mist or darkness, I made it convenient to journey thither and be present. At my arrival, although the heap of condemned rubbish was as yet comparatively small, the torch had already been applied. Amid that boundless plain, in the dusk of the evening, like a far-off star alone in the firmament, there was merely visible one tremulous gleam, whence none could have anticipated so fierce a blaze as was destined to ensue. With every moment, however, there came foot travellers, women holding up their aprons, men on horseback, wheelbarrows, lumbering baggage wagons, and other vehicles great and small, and from far and near, laden with articles that were judged fit for nothing but to be burned.

"What materials have been used to kindle the flame?" inquired I of a bystander; for I was desirous of knowing the whole process of the affair from beginning to end.

The person whom I addressed was a grave man, fifty years old or thereabout, who had evidently come thither as a looker-on. He struck me immediately as having weighed for himself the true value of life and its circumstances, and therefore as feeling little personal interest in whatever judgment the world might form of them. Before answering my question, he looked me in the face by the kindling light of the fire.

"O, some very dry combustibles," replied he, "and extremely suitable to the purpose—no other, in fact, than yesterday's newspapers, last month's magazines, and last year's withered leaves. Here now comes some antiquated trash that will take fire like a handful of shavings."

As he spoke some rough-looking men advanced to the verge of the bonfire, and threw in, as it appeared, all the rubbish of the herald's office—the blazonry of coat armor, the crests and devices of illustrious families, pedigrees that extended back, like lines of light, into the mist of the dark ages, together with stars, garters, and embroidered collars, each of which, as paltry a bauble as it might appear to the uninstructed eye, had once possessed vast significance, and was still, in truth, reckoned among the most precious of moral or material facts by the worshippers of the gorgeous past. Mingled with this confused heap, which was tossed into the flames by armfuls at once, were innumerable badges of knighthood, comprising those of all the European sovereignties,

and Napoleon's decoration of the Legion of Honor, the ribbons of which were entangled with those of the ancient order of St. Louis. There, too, were the medals of our own Society of Cincinnati, by means of which, as history tells us, an order of hereditary knights came near being constituted out of the king quellers of the revolution. And besides, there were the patents of nobility of German counts and barons, Spanish grandees, and English peers, from the worm-eaten instruments signed by William the Conqueror down to the brand-new parchment of the latest lord who has received his honors from the fair hand of Victoria.

At sight of the dense volumes of smoke, mingled with vivid jets of flame, that gushed and eddied forth from this immense pile of earthly distinctions, the multitude of plebeian spectators set up a joyous shout, and clapped their hands with an emphasis that made the welkin echo. That was their moment of triumph, achieved, after long ages, over creatures of the same clay and the same spiritual infirmities, who had dared to assume the privileges due only to Heaven's better workmanship. But now there rushed towards the blazing heap a gray-haired man, of stately presence, wearing a coat from the breast of which a star, or other badge of rank, seemed to have been forcibly wrenched away. He had not the tokens of intellectual power in his face; but still there was the demeanor, the habitual and almost native dignity, of one who had been born to the idea of his own social superiority, and had never felt it questioned till that moment.

"People," cried he, gazing at the ruin of what was dearest to his eyes with grief and wonder, but nevertheless with a degree of stateliness,—"people, what have you done? This fire is consuming all that marked your advance from barbarism, or that could have prevented your relapse thither. We, the men of the privileged orders, were those who kept alive from age to age the old chivalrous spirit; the gentle and generous thought; the higher, the purer, the more refined and delicate life. With the nobles, too, you cast off the poet, the painter, the sculptor—all the beautiful arts; for we were their patrons, and created the atmosphere in which they flourish. In abolishing the majestic distinctions of rank, society loses not only its grace, but its steadfastness"—

More he would doubtless have spoken; but here there arose an outcry, sportive, contemptuous, and indignant, that altogether drowned the appeal of the fallen nobleman, insomuch that, casting one look of despair at his own half-burned pedigree, he shrunk back into the crowd, glad to shelter himself under his new-found insignificance.

"Let him thank his stars that we have not flung him into the same fire!" shouted a rude figure, spurning the embers with his foot. "And henceforth let no man dare to show a piece of musty parchment as his warrant for lording it over his fellows. If he have strength of arm, well and good; it is one species of superiority. If he have wit, wisdom, courage, force of character, let these attributes do for him what they may; but from this day forward no mortal must hope for place and consideration by reckoning up the mouldy bones of his ancestors. That nonsense is done away."

"And in good time," remarked the grave observer by my side, in a low voice, however, "if no worse nonsense comes in its place; but, at all events, this species of nonsense has fairly lived out its life."

There was little space to muse or moralize over the embers of this time-honored rubbish; for, before it was half burned out, there came another multitude from beyond the sea, bearing the purple robes of royalty, and the crowns, globes, and sceptres of emperors and kings. All these had been condemned as useless baubles, playthings at best, fit only for the infancy of the world, or rods to govern and chastise it in its nonage, but with which universal manhood at its full-grown stature could no longer brook to be insulted. Into such contempt had these regal insignia now fallen that the gilded crown and tinselled robes of the player king from Drury Lane Theatre had been thrown in among the rest, doubtless as a mockery of his brother monarchs on the great stage of the world. It was a strange sight to discern the crown jewels of England glowing and flashing in the midst of the fire. Some of them had been delivered down from the time of the Saxon princes; others were purchased with vast revenues, or perchance ravished from the dead brows of the native potentates of Hindostan; and the whole now blazed with a dazzling lustre, as if a star had fallen in that spot and been shattered into fragments. The splendor of the ruined monarchy had no reflection save in those inestimable precious stones. But enough on this subject. It were but tedious to describe how the Emperor of Austria's mantle was converted to tinder, and how the posts and pillars

of the French throne became a heap of coals, which it was impossible to distinguish from those of any other wood. Let me add, however, that I noticed one of the exiled Poles stirring up the bonfire with the Czar of Russia's sceptre, which he afterwards flung into the flames.

"The smell of singed garments is quite intolerable here," observed my new acquaintance, as the breeze enveloped us in the smoke of a royal wardrobe. "Let us get to windward and see what they are doing on the other side of the bonfire."

We accordingly passed around, and were just in time to witness the arrival of a vast procession of Washingtonians,—as the votaries of temperance call themselves nowadays,—accompanied by thousands of the Irish disciples of Father Mathew, with that great apostle at their head. They brought a rich contribution to the bonfire—being nothing less than all the hogsheads and barrels of liquor in the world, which they rolled before them across the prairie.

"Now, my children," cried Father Mathew, when they reached the verge of the fire, "one shove more, and the work is done. And now let us stand off, and see Satan deal with his own liquor."

Accordingly, having placed their wooden vessels within reach of the flames, the procession stood off at a safe distance, and soon beheld them burst into a blaze that reached the clouds and threatened to set the sky itself on fire. And well it might; for here was the whole world's stock of spirituous liquors, which, instead of kindling a frenzied light in the eyes of individual topers as of yore, soared upwards with a bewildering gleam that startled all mankind. It was the aggregate of that fierce fire which would otherwise have scorched the hearts of millions. Meantime numberless bottles of precious wine were flung into the blaze, which lapped up the contents as if it loved them, and grew, like other drunkards, the merrier and fiercer for what it quaffed. Never again will the insatiable thirst of the fire fiend be so pampered. Here were the treasures of famous bon vivants—liquors that had been tossed on the ocean, and mellowed in the sun, and hoarded long in the recesses of the earth—the pale, the gold, the ruddy juice of whatever vineyards were most delicate—the entire vintage of Tokay—all mingling in one stream with the vile fluids of the common pothouse, and contributing to heighten the selfsame blaze. And while it rose in a gigantic spire that seemed to wave against the arch of the firmament and combine itself with the light of stars, the multitude gave a shout as if the broad earth were exulting in its deliverance from the curse of ages.

But the joy was not universal. Many deemed that human life would be gloomier than ever when that brief illumination should sink down. While the reformers were at work, I overheard muttered expostulations from several respectable gentlemen with red noses and wearing gouty shoes; and a ragged worthy, whose face looked like a hearth where the fire is burned out, now expressed his discontent more openly and boldly.

"What is this world good for," said the last toper, "now that we can never be jolly any more? What is to comfort the poor man in sorrow and perplexity? How is he to keep his heart warm against the cold winds of this cheerless earth? And what do you propose to give him in exchange for the solace that you take away? How are old friends to sit together by the fireside without a cheerful glass between them? A plague upon your reformation! It is a sad world, a cold world, a selfish world, a low world, not worth an honest fellow's living in, now that good fellowship is gone forever!"

This harangue excited great mirth among the bystanders; but, preposterous as was the sentiment, I could not help commiserating the forlorn condition of the last toper, whose boon companions had dwindled away from his side, leaving the poor fellow without a soul to countenance him in sipping his liquor, nor indeed any liquor to sip. Not that this was quite the true state of the case; for I had observed him at a critical moment filch a bottle of fourth-proof brandy that fell beside the bonfire and hide it in his pocket.

The spirituous and fermented liquors being thus disposed of, the zeal of the reformers next induced them to replenish the fire with all the boxes of tea and bags of coffee in the world. And now came the planters of Virginia, bringing their crops and tobacco. These, being cast upon the heap of inutility, aggregated it to the size of a mountain, and incensed the atmosphere with such potent fragrance that methought we should never draw pure breath again. The present sacrifice seemed to startle the lovers of the weed more than any that they had hitherto witnessed.

"Well, they've put my pipe out," said an old gentleman, flinging it into the flames in a pet. "What is this world coming to? Everything rich and racy—all the spice of life—is to be condemned as useless. Now that they have kindled the bonfire, if these nonsensical reformers would fling themselves into it, all would be well enough!"

"Be patient," responded a stanch conservative; "it will come to that in the end. They will first fling us in, and finally themselves."

From the general and systematic measures of reform I now turned to consider the individual contributions to this memorable bonfire. In many instances these were of a very amusing character. One poor fellow threw in his empty purse, and another a bundle of counterfeit or insolvable banknotes. Fashionable ladies threw in their last season's bonnets, together with heaps of ribbons, yellow lace, and much other half-worn milliner's ware, all of which proved even more evanescent in the fire than it had been in the fashion. A multitude of lovers of both sexes—discarded maids or bachelors and couples mutually weary of one another—tossed in bundles of perfumed letters and enamored sonnets. A hack politician, being deprived of bread by the loss of office, threw in his teeth, which happened to be false ones. The Rev. Sydney Smith—having voyaged across the Atlantic for that sole purpose—came up to the bonfire with a bitter grin and threw in certain repudiated bonds, fortified though they were with the broad seal of a sovereign state. A little boy of five years old, in the premature manliness of the present epoch, threw in his playthings; a college graduate his diploma; an apothecary, ruined by the spread of homoeopathy, his whole stock of drugs and medicines; a physician his library; a parson his old sermons; and a fine gentleman of the old school his code of manners, which he had formerly written down for the benefit of the next generation. A widow, resolving on a second marriage, slyly threw in her dead husband's miniature. A young man, jilted by his mistress, would willingly have flung his own desperate heart into the flames, but could find no means to wrench it out of his bosom. An American author, whose works were neglected by the public, threw his pen and paper into the bonfire, and betook himself to some less discouraging occupation. It somewhat startled me to overhear a number of ladies, highly respectable in appearance, proposing to fling their gowns and petticoats into the flames, and assume the garb, together

with the manners, duties, offices, and responsibilities, of the opposite sex.

What favor was accorded to this scheme I
am unable to say, my attention being suddenly
drawn to a poor, deceived, and half-delirious
girl, who, exclaiming that she was the most
worthless thing alive or dead, attempted to
cast herself into the fire amid all that wrecked
and broken trumpery of the world. A good
man, however, ran to her rescue.

"Patience, my poor girl!" said he, as he drew
her back from the fierce embrace of the destroying angel. "Be patient, and abide Heaven's
will. So long as you possess a living soul, all
may be restored to its first freshness. These
things of matter and creations of human fantasy
are fit for nothing but to be burned when once
they have had their day; but your day is
eternity!"

"Yes," said the wretched girl, whose frenzy
seemed now to have sunk down into deep despondency,—"yes, and the sunshine is blotted
out of it!"

It was now rumored among the spectators
that all the weapons and munitions of war were
to be thrown into the bonfire, with the exception of the world's stock of gunpowder, which,
as the safest mode of disposing of it, had already been drowned in the sea. This intelligence seemed to awaken great diversity of
opinion. The hopeful philanthropist esteemed
it a token that the millennium was already
come; while persons of another stamp, in
whose view mankind was a breed of bulldogs,
prophesied that all the old stoutness, fervor,
nobleness, generosity, and magnanimity of the
race would disappear,—these qualities, as they
affirmed, requiring blood for their nourishment. They comforted themselves, however, in
the belief that the proposed abolition of war
was impracticable for any length of time together.

Be that as it might, numberless great guns,
whose thunder had long been the voice of
battle,—the artillery of the Armada, the bat-
tering trains of Marlborough, and the adverse
cannon of Napoleon and Wellington,—were
trundled into the midst of the fire. By the
continual addition of dry combustibles, it had
now waxed so intense that neither brass nor
iron could withstand it. It was wonderful to behold how these terrible instruments of slaughter
melted away like playthings of wax. Then the
armies of the earth wheeled around the mighty
furnace, with their military music playing tri-

umphant marches, and flung in their muskets
and swords. The standard-bearers, likewise,
cast one look upward at their banners, all tattered with shot holes and inscribed with the
names of victorious fields; and, giving them a
last flourish on the breeze, they lowered them
into the flame, which snatched them upward
in its rush towards the clouds. This ceremony
being over, the world was left without a single
weapon in its hands,—except possibly a few
old king's arms and rusty swords, and other
trophies of the Revolution in some of our state
armories. And now the drums were beaten and
the trumpets brayed all together, as a prelude
to the proclamation of universal and eternal
peace and the announcement that glory was no
longer to be won by blood, but that it would
henceforth be the contention of the human race
to work out the greatest mutual good, and that
beneficence, in the future annals of the earth,
would claim the praise of valor. The blessed
tidings were accordingly promulgated, and
caused infinite rejoicings among among those
who had stood aghast at the horror and absurdity of war.

But I saw a grim smile pass over the seared
visage of a stately old commander,—by his
warworn figure and rich military dress, he
might have been one of Napoleon's famous
marshals,—who, with the rest of the world's
soldiery, had just flung away the sword that
had been familiar to his right hand for half a
century.

"Ay! ay!" grumbled he. "Let them proclaim
what they please; but, in the end, we shall
find that all this foolery has only made more
work for the armorers and cannon founders."

"Why, sir," exclaimed I, in astonishment,
"do you imagine that the human race will ever
so far return on the steps of its past madness
as to weld another sword or cast another
cannon?"

"There will be no need," observed, with a
sneer, one who neither felt benevolence nor
had faith in it. "When Cain wished to slay his
brother, he was at no loss for a weapon."

"We shall see," replied the veteran commander. "If I am mistaken, so much the better;
but in my opinion, without pretending to phi-
losophize about the matter, the necessity of war
lies far deeper than these honest gentlemen
suppose. What! is there a field for all the petty
disputes of individuals? and shall there be no
great law court for the settlement of national

difficulties? The battlefield is the only court where such suits can be tried."

"You forget, general," rejoined I, "that, in this advanced stage of civilization, Reason and Philanthropy combined will constitute just such a tribunal as is requisite."

"Ah, I had forgotten that, indeed!" said the old warrior, as he limped away.

The fire was now to be replenished with materials that had hitherto been considered of even greater importance to the well being of society than the warlike munitions which we had already seen consumed. A body of reformers had travelled all over the earth in quest of the machinery by which the different nations were accustomed to inflict the punishment of death. A shudder passed through the multitude as these ghastly emblems were dragged forward. Even the flames seemed at first to shrink away, displaying the shape and murderous contrivance of each in a full blaze of light, which of itself was sufficient to convince mankind of the long and deadly error of human law. Those old implements of cruelty; those horrible monsters of mechanism; those inventions which seemed to demand something worse than man's natural heart to contrive, and which had lurked in the dusky nooks of ancient prisons, the subject of terror-stricken legend,— were now brought forth to view. Headsmen's axes, with the rust of noble and royal blood upon them, and a vast collection of halters that had choked the breath of plebeian victims, were thrown in together. A shout greeted the arrival of the guillotine, which was thrust forward on the same wheels that had borne it from one to another of the blood-stained streets of Paris. But the loudest roar of applause went up, telling the distant sky of the triumph of the earth's redemption, when the gallows made its appearance. An ill-looking fellow, however, rushed forward, and, putting himself in the path of the reformers, bellowed hoarsely, and fought with brute fury to stay their progress.

It was little matter of surprise, perhaps, that the executioner should thus do his best to vindicate and uphold the machinery by which he himself had his livelihood and worthier individuals their death; but it deserved special note that men of a far different sphere—even of that consecrated class in whose guardianship the world is apt to trust its benevolence—were found to take the hangman's view of the question.

"Stay, my brethren!" cried one of them. "You are misled by a false philanthropy,—you know not what you do. The gallows is a heaven-ordained instrument. Bear it back, then, reverently, and set it up in its old place, else the world will fall to speedy ruin and desolation!"

"Onward! onward!" shouted a leader in the reform. "Into the flames with the accursed instrument of man's blood policy! How can human law inculcate benevolence and love while it persists in setting up the gallows as its chief symbol? One heave more, good friends, and the world will be redeemed from its greatest error."

A thousand hands, that nevertheless loathed the touch, now lent their assistance, and thrust the ominous burden far, far into the centre of the raging furnace. There its fatal and abhorred image was beheld, first black, then a red coal, then ashes.

"That was well done!" exclaimed I.

"Yes, it was well done," replied, but with less enthusiasm than I expected, the thoughtful observer who was still at my side; "well done, if the world be good enough for the measure. Death, however, is an idea that cannot easily be dispensed with in any condition between the primal innocence and that other purity and perfection which perchance we are destined to attain after travelling round the full circle; but, at all events, it is well that the experiment should now be tried."

"Too cold! too cold!" impatiently exclaimed the young and ardent leader in this triumph. "Let the heart have its voice here as well as the intellect. And as for ripeness, and as for progress, let mankind always do the highest, kindest, noblest thing, that, at any given period, it has attained the perception of; and surely that thing cannot be wrong nor wrongly timed."

I know not whether it were the excitement of the scene, or whether the good people around the bonfire were really growing more enlightened every instant; but they now proceeded to measures in the full length of which I was hardly prepared to keep them company. For instance, some threw their marriage certificates into the flames, and declared themselves candidates for a higher, holier, and more comprehensive union than that which had subsisted from the birth of time under the form of the connubial tie. Others hastened to the vaults of banks and to the coffers of the rich,— all of which were open to the first comer on this fated occasion,—and brought entire bales of paper money to enliven the blaze, and tons of coin to be melted down by its intensity.

Henceforth, they said, universal benevolence, uncoined and exhaustless, was to be the golden currency of the world. At this intelligence the bankers and speculators in the stocks grew pale, and a pickpocket, who had reaped a rich harvest among the crowd fell down in a deadly fainting fit. A few men of business burned their day-books and ledgers, the notes and obligations of their creditors, and all other evidences of debts due to themselves; while perhaps a somewhat larger number satisfied their zeal for reform with the sacrifice of any uncomfortable recollection of their own indebtment. There was then a cry that the period was arrived when the title deeds of landed property should be given to the flames, and the whole soil of the earth revert to the public, from whom it had been wrongfully abstracted and most unequally distributed among individuals. Another party demanded that all written constitutions, set forms of government, legislative acts, statute-books, and everything else on which human invention had endeavored to stamp its arbitrary laws, should at once be destroyed, leaving the consummated world as free as the man first created.

Whether any ultimate action was taken with regard to these propositions is beyond my knowledge; for, just then, some matters were in progress that concerned my sympathies more nearly.

"See! see! What heaps of books and pamphlets!" cried a fellow, who did not seem to be a lover of literature. "Now we shall have a glorious blaze!"

"That's just the thing!" said a modern philosopher. "Now we shall get rid of the weight of dead men's thought, which has hitherto pressed so heavily on the living intellect that it has been incompetent to any effectual self-exertion. Well done, my lads! Into the fire with them! Now you are enlightening the world indeed!"

"But what is to become of the trade?" cried a frantic bookseller.

"O, by all means, let them accompany their merchandise," coolly observed an author. "It will be a noble funeral pile!"

The truth was, that the human race had now reached a stage of progress so far beyond what the wisest and wittiest men of former ages had ever dreamed of that it would have been a manifest absurdity to allow the earth to be any longer encumbered with their poor achievements in the literary line. Accordingly a thorough and searching investigation had swept the booksellers' shops, hawkers' stands, public and private libraries, and even the little bookshelf by the country fireside, and had brought the world's entire mass of printed paper, bound or in sheets, to swell the already mountain bulk of our illustrious bonfire. Thick, heavy folios, containing the labors of lexicographers, commentators and encyclopaedists, were flung in, and falling among the embers with a leaden thump, smouldered away to ashes like rotten wood. The small, richly gilt French tomes of the last age, with the hundred volumes of Voltaire among them, went off in a brilliant shower of sparkles and little jets of flame; while the current literature of the same nation burned red and blue, and threw an infernal light over the visages of the spectators, converting them all to the aspect of party-colored fiends. A collection of German stories emitted a scent of brimstone. The English standard authors made excellent fuel, generally exhibiting the properties of sound oak logs. Milton's works, in particular, sent up a powerful blaze, gradually reddening into a coal, which promised to endure longer than almost any other material of the pile. From Shakespeare there gushed a flame of such marvellous splendor that men shaded their eyes as against the sun's meridian glory; nor even when the works of his own elucidators were flung upon him did he cease to flash forth a dazzling radiance from beneath the ponderous heap. It is my belief that he is blazing as fervidly as ever. . . .

I felt particular interest in watching the combustion of American authors, and scrupulously noted by my watch the precise number of moments that changed most of them from shabbily printed books to indistinguishable ashes. It would be invidious, however, if not perilous, to betray these awful secrets; so that I shall content myself with observing that it was not invariably the writer most frequent in the public mouth that made the most splendid appearance in the bonfire. I especially remember that a great deal of excellent inflammability was exhibited in a thin volume of poems by Ellery Channing; although, to speak the truth, there were certain portions that hissed and spluttered in a very disagreeable fashion. A curious phenomenon occurred in reference to several writers, native as well as foreign. Their books, though of highly respectable figure, instead of bursting into a blaze, or even smouldering out their substance in smoke, suddenly melted away in a manner that proved them to be ice.

If it be no lack of modesty to mention my own works, it must here be confessed that I looked for them with fatherly interest, but in vain. Too probably they were changed to vapor by the first action of the heat; at best, I can only hope that, in their quiet way, they contributed a glimmering spark or two to the splendor of the evening.

"Alas! and woe is me!" thus bemoaned himself a heavy-looking gentleman in green spectacles. "The world is utterly ruined, and there is nothing to live for any longer. The business of my life is snatched from me. Not a volume to be had for love or money!"

"This," remarked the sedate observer beside me, "is a bookworm—one of those men who are born to gnaw dead thoughts. His clothes, you see, are covered with the dust of libraries. He has no inward fountain of ideas; and, in good earnest, now that the old stock is abolished, I do not see what is to become of the poor fellow. Have you no word of comfort for him?"

"My dear sir," said I to the desperate bookworm, "is not Nature better than a book? Is not the human heart deeper than any system of philosophy? Is not life replete with more instruction than past observers have found it possible to write down in maxims? Be of good cheer. The great book of Time is still spread wide open before us; and, if we read it aright, it will be to us a volume of eternal truth."

"O, my books, my books,—my precious printed books!" reiterated the forlorn bookworm. "My only reality was a bound volume; and now they will not leave me even a shadowy pamphlet!"

In fact, the last remnant of the literature of all the ages was now descending upon the blazing heap in the shape of a cloud of pamphlets from the press of the New World. These likewise were consumed in the twinkling of an eye, leaving the earth, for the first time since the days of Cadmus, free from the plague of letters—an enviable field for the authors of the next generation.

"Well, and does anything remain to be done?" inquired I somewhat anxiously. "Unless we set fire to the earth itself, and then leap boldly off into infinite space, I know not that we can carry reform to any farther point."

"You are vastly mistaken, my good friend," said the observer. "Believe me, the fire will not be allowed to settle down without the addition of fuel that will startle many persons who have lent a willing hand thus far."

Nevertheless there appeared to be a relaxation of effort for a little time, during which, probably, the leaders of the movement were considering what should be done next. In the interval, a philosopher threw his theory into the flames,—a sacrifice which, by those who knew how to estimate it, was pronounced the most remarkable that had yet been made. The combustion, however, was by no means brilliant. Some indefatigable people, scorning to take a moment's ease, now employed themselves in collecting all the withered leaves and fallen boughs of the forest, and thereby recruited the bonfire to a greater height than ever. But this was mere by-play.

"Here comes the fresh fuel that I spoke of," said my companion.

To my astonishment, the persons who now advanced into the vacant space around the mountain fire bore surplices and other priestly garments, mitres, crosiers, and a confusion of Popish and Protestant emblems, with which it seemed their purpose to consummate the great act of faith. Crosses from the spires of old cathedrals were cast upon the heap with as little remorse as if the reverence of centuries, passing in long array beneath the lofty towers, had not looked up to them as the holiest of symbols. The font in which infants were consecrated to God, the sacramental vessels whence piety received the hallowed draught, were given to the same destruction. Perhaps it most nearly touched my heart to see among these devoted relics fragments of the humble communion-tables and undecorated pulpits which I recognized as having been torn from the meeting-houses of New England. Those simple edifices might have been permitted to retain all of sacred embellishment that their Puritan founders had bestowed, even though the mighty structure of St. Peter's had sent its spoils to the fire of this terrible sacrifice. Yet I felt that these were but the externals of religion, and might most safely be relinquished by spirits that best knew their deep significance.

"All is well," said I, cheerfully. "The wood-paths shall be the aisles of our cathedral,—the firmament itself shall be its ceiling. What needs an earthly roof between the Deity and his worshippers? Our faith can well afford to lose all the drapery that even the holiest men have thrown around it, and be only the more sublime in its simplicity."

"True," said my companion; "but will they pause here?"

The doubt implied in his question was well founded. In the general destruction of books already described, a holy volume, that stood apart from the catalogue of human literature, and yet, in one tense, was at its head, had been spared. But the Titan of innovation,—angel or fiend, double in his nature, and capable of deeds befitting both characters,—at first shaking down only the old and rotten shapes of things, had now, as it appeared, laid his terrible hand upon the main pillars which supported the whole edifice of our moral and spiritual state. The inhabitants of the earth had grown too enlightened to define their faith within a form of words, or to limit the spiritual by any analogy to our material existence. Truths which the heavens trembled at were now but a fable of the world's infancy. Therefore, as the final sacrifice of human error, what else remained to be thrown upon the embers of that awful pile except the book which, though a celestial revelation to past ages, was but a voice from a lower sphere as regarded the present race of man? It was done! Upon the blazing heap of falsehood and wornout truth—things that the earth had never needed, or had ceased to need, or had grown childishly weary of—fell the ponderous church Bible, the great old volume that had lain so long on the cushion of the pulpit, and whence the pastor's solemn voice had given holy utterance on so many a Sabbath day. There likewise fell the family Bible, which the long-buried patriarch had to read to his children,—in prosperity or sorrow, by the fireside and in the summer shade of trees,—and had bequeathed downward as the heirloom of generations. There fell the bosom Bible, the little volume that had been the soul's friend of some sorely tried child of dust, who thence took courage, whether his trial were for life or death, steadfastly confronting both in the strong assurance of immortality.

All these were flung into the fierce and riotous blaze; and then a mighty wind came roaring across the plain with a desolate howl, as if it were the angry lamentation of the earth for the loss of heaven's sunshine,—and it shook the gigantic pyramid of flame and scattered the cinders of half-consumed abominations around upon the spectators.

"This is terrible!" said I, feeling that my cheek grew pale, and seeing a like change in the visages about me.

"Be of good courage yet," answered the man with whom I had so often spoken. He continued to gaze steadily at the spectacle with a singular calmness, as if it concerned him merely as an observer. "Be of good courage, nor yet exult too much; for there is far less both of good and evil in the effect of this bonfire than the world might be willing to believe."

"How can that be?" exclaimed I impatiently. "Has it not consumed everything? Has it not swallowed up or melted down every human or divine appendage of our mortal state that had substance enough to be acted on by fire? Will there be anything left us to-morrow morning better or worse than a heap of embers and ashes?"

"Assuredly there will," said my grave friend. "Come hither to-morrow morning, or whenever the combustible portion of the pile shall be quite burned out, and you will find among the ashes everything really valuable that you have seen cast into the flames. Trust me, the world of to-morrow will again enrich itself with the gold and diamonds which have been cast off by the world of to-day. Not a truth is destroyed nor buried so deep among the ashes but it will be raked up at last."

This was a strange assurance. Yet I felt inclined to credit it, the more especially as I beheld among the wallowing flames a copy of the Holy Scriptures, the pages of which, instead of being blackened into tinder, only assumed a more dazzling whiteness as the fingermarks of human imperfection were purified away. Certain marginal notes and commentaries, it is true, yielded to the intensity of the fiery test, but without detriment to the smallest syllable that had flamed from the pen of inspiration.

"Yes; there is the proof of what you say," answered I, turning to the observer; "but if only what is evil can feel the action of the fire, then, surely, the conflagration has been of inestimable utility. Yet, if I understand aright, you intimate a doubt whether the world's expectation of benefit would be realized by it."

"Listen to the talk of these worthies," said he, pointing to a group in front of the blazing pile; "possibly they may teach you something useful without intending it."

The persons whom he indicated consisted of that brutal and most earthly figure who had stood forth so furiously in defence of the gallows,—the hangman, in short,—together with the last thief and the last murderer, all three of whom were clustered about the last toper. The latter was literally passing the brandy bottle, which he had rescued from the general destruction of wines and spirits. This little convivial party seemed at the lowest pitch of despondency, as considering that the purified world must needs be utterly unlike the sphere that they had hitherto known, and therefore but a strange and desolute abode for gentlemen of their kidney.

"The best counsel for all of us is," remarked the hangman, "that, as soon as we have finished the last drop of liquor, I help you, my three friends, to a comfortable end upon the nearest tree, and then hang myself on the same bough. This is no world for us any longer."

"Poh, poh, my good fellows!" said a dark-complexioned personage, who now joined the group,—his complexion was indeed fearfully dark, and his eyes glowed with a redder light than that of the bonfire; "be not so cast down, my dear friends; you shall see good days yet. There's one thing that these wiseacres have forgotten to throw into the fire, and without which all the rest of the conflagration is just nothing at all; yes, though they had burned the earth itself to a cinder."

"And what may that be?" eagerly demanded the last murderer.

"What but the human heart itself?" said the dark-visaged stranger, with a portentous grin.

"And, unless they hit upon some method of purifying that foul cavern, forth from it will reissue all the shapes of wrong and misery— the same old shapes or worse ones—which they have taken such a vast deal of trouble to consume to ashes. I have stood by this livelong night and laughed in my sleeve at the whole business. O, take my word for it, it will be the old world yet!"

This brief conversation supplied me with a theme for lengthened thought. How sad a truth, if true it were, that man's age-long endeavor for perfection had served only to render him the mockery of the evil principle, from the fatal circumstance of an error at the very root of the matter! The heart, the heart,—there was the little yet boundless sphere wherein existed the original wrong of which the crime and misery of this outward world were merely types. Purify that inward sphere, and the many shapes of evil that haunt the outward, and which now seem almost our only realities, will turn to shadowy phantoms and vanish of their own accord; but if we go no deeper than the intellect, and strive, with merely that feeble instrument, to discern and rectify what is wrong, our whole accomplishment will be a dream, so unsubstantial that it matters little whether the bonfire, which I have so faithfully described, were what we choose to call a real event and a flame that would scorch the finger, or only a phosphoric radiance and a parable of my own brain.   1846

HENRY DAVID THOREAU

1817–1862

ELIZABETH PEABODY'S *Aesthetic Papers* (1849) included a contribution entitled "Resistence to Civil Government." The piece, subsequently known as Thoreau's *Essay on Civil Disobedience*, was occasioned by the acute revolt in the mind and heart of the poet naturalist against the imperialism in which the Mexican War had resulted, an imperialism which Thoreau, like other abolitionists, associated with the aggressive slavocracy which dominated the government at Washington. New England was already the scene of a small but vociferous Non-Resistance Society which, through its journal, its annual meetings, its lecturers, was propagating the doctrine of abstention from all functions of and activities associated with a government based on force and slavery. Thoreau's protest, however, was destined to live, even to become a classic in the literature of civil disobedience. It was known to Tolstoy, and had some influence on him; and in 1907 Mahatma Ghandi read it, drew inspiration from it, and furthermore found in it suggestions for his campaign of nonviolence in India.

F. H. Allen, *A Bibliography of Henry David Thoreau*, Boston and New York, 1908.
William White, *A Henry David Thoreau Bibliography 1908–1937*, Boston, 1939.
The Writings of Henry David Thoreau, Manuscript Edition, 20 vols., Boston and New York, 1906.
Correspondence, Walter Harding and Carl Bode, eds., New York, 1958.
Joseph Wood Krutch, *Henry David Thoreau*, New York, 1948.
H. S. Canby, *Thoreau*, Boston, 1939.
Leo Stoller, *After Walden; Thoreau's Changing Views on Economic Man*, Stanford, 1957.

» » RESISTANCE TO CIVIL GOVERNMENT « «

I heartily accept the motto,—"That government is best which governs least"; and I should like to see it acted up to more readily and systematically. Carried out, it finally amounts to this, which also I believe,—"That government is best which governs not at all"; and when men are prepared for it, that will be the kind of government which they will have. Government is at best but an expedient; but most governments are usually, and all governments are sometimes, inexpedient. The objections which have been brought against a standing army, and they are many and weighty, and deserve to prevail, may also at last be brought against a standing government. The standing army is only an arm of the standing government. The government itself, which is only the mode which the people have chosen to execute their will, is equally liable to be abused and perverted before the people can act through it. Witness the present Mexican war, the work of comparatively a few individuals using the standing government as their tool; for, in the outset, the people would not have consented to this measure.

This American government,—what is it but a tradition, though a recent one, endeavoring to transmit itself unimpaired to posterity, but each instant losing some of its integrity? It has not the vitality and force of a single living man; for a single man can bend it to his will. It is a sort of wooden gun to the people themselves; and, if ever they should use it in earnest as a real one against each other, it will surely split. But it is not the less necessary for this; for the people must have some complicated machinery or other, and hear its din, to satisfy that idea of government which they have. Governments show thus how successfully men can be imposed on, even impose on themselves, for their own advantage. It is excellent, we must all allow; yet this government never of itself furthered any enterprise, but by the alacrity with which it got out of its way. *It* does not keep the country free. *It* does not settle the West. *It* does not educate. The character inherent in the American people has done all that has been accomplished; and it would have done somewhat more, if the government had not sometimes got in its way. For government is an expedient by which men would fain succeed in letting one another alone; and, as has been said, when it is most expedient, the governed are most let alone by it. Trade and commerce, if they were not made of India rubber, would never manage to bounce over the obstacles which legislators are continually putting in their way; and, if one were to judge these men wholly by the effects of their actions, and not partly by their intentions, they would deserve to be classed and punished with those mischievous persons who put obstructions on the railroads.

But, to speak practically and as a citizen, unlike those who call themselves no-government men, I ask for, not at once no government, but *at once* a better government. Let every man make known what kind of government would command his respect, and that will be one step toward obtaining it.

After all, the practical reason why, when the power is once in the hands of the people, a majority are permitted, and for a long period continue, to rule, is not because they are most likely to be in the right, nor because this seems fairest to the minority, but because they are physically the strongest. But a government in which the majority rule in all cases cannot be based on justice, even as far as men understand it. Can there not be a government in which majorities do not virtually decide right and wrong, but conscience?—in which majorities decide only those questions to which the rule of expediency is applicable? Must the citizen ever for a moment, or in the least degree, resign his conscience to the legislator? Why has every man a conscience, then? I think that we should be men first, and subjects afterward. It is not desirable to cultivate a respect for the law, so much as for the right. The only obligation which I have a right to assume, is to do at any time what I think right. It is truly enough said, that a corporation has no conscience; but a corporation of conscientious men is a corporation *with* a conscience. Law never made men a whit more just; and, by means of their respect for it, even the well-disposed are daily made the agents of injustice. A common and natural result of an undue respect for law is, that you may see a file of soldiers, colonel, captain, corporal, privates, powder-monkeys and all, marching in admirable order over hill and dale to the wars, against their wills, aye, against their common sense and consciences, which makes it very steep marching indeed, and produces a palpitation of the heart. They have no doubt that it is a damnable business in which they are concerned; they are all peaceably inclined. Now, what are they? Men at all? or small moveable forts and magazines, at the service of some unscrupulous man in power? Visit the Navy Yard, and behold a marine, such a man as an American government can make, or such as it can make a man with its black arts, a mere shadow and reminiscence of humanity, a man laid out alive and standing, and already, as one may say, buried under arms with funeral accompaniments, though it may be

"Not a drum was heard, nor a funeral note,
   As his corse to the ramparts we hurried;
Not a soldier discharged his farewell shot
   O'er the grave where our hero we buried."

The mass of men serve the State thus, not as men mainly, but as machines, with their bodies. They are the standing army, and the militia, jailers, constables, *posse comitatus*, &c. In most cases there is no free exercise whatever of the judgment or of the moral sense; but they put themselves on a level with wood and earth and stones; and wooden men can perhaps be manufactured that will serve the purpose as well. Such command no more respect than men of straw, or a lump of dirt. They have the same

sort of worth only as horses and dogs. Yet such as these even are commonly esteemed good citizens. Others, as most legislators, politicians, lawyers, ministers, and officeholders, serve the State chiefly with their heads; and, as they rarely make any moral distinctions, they are as likely to serve the devil, without intending it, as God. A very few, as heroes, patriots, martyrs, reformers in the great sense, and *men*, serve the State with their consciences also, and so necessarily resist it for the most part; and they are commonly treated by it as enemies. A wise man will only be useful as a man, and will not submit to be "clay," and "stop a hole to keep the wind away," but leave that office to his dust at least:—

"I am too high-born to be propertied,
   To be a secondary at control,
   Or useful serving-man and instrument
To any sovereign state throughout the world."

He who gives himself entirely to his fellow-men appears to them useless and selfish; but he who gives himself partially to them is pronounced a benefactor and philanthropist.

How does it become a man to behave toward this American government to-day? I answer that he cannot without disgrace be associated with it. I cannot for an instant recognize that political organization as *my* government which is the *slave's* government also.

All men recognize the right of revolution; that is, the right to refuse allegiance to and to resist the government, when its tyranny or its inefficiency are great and unendurable. But almost all say that such is not the case now. But such was the case, they think, in the Revolution of '75. If one were to tell me that this was a bad government because it taxed certain foreign commodities brought to its ports, it is most probable that I should not make an ado about it, for I can do without them: all machines have their friction; and possibly this does enough good to counterbalance the evil. At any rate, it is a great evil to make a stir about it. But when the friction comes to have its machine, and oppression and robbery are organized, I say, let us not have such a machine any longer. In other words, when a sixth of the population of a nation which has undertaken to be the refuge of liberty are slaves, and a whole country is unjustly overrun and conquered by a foreign army, and subjected to military law, I think that it is not too soon for honest men to rebel and revolutionize. What makes this duty the more urgent is the fact, that the country so overrun is not our own, but ours is the invading army.

Paley, a common authority with many on moral questions, in his chapter on the "Duty of Submission to Civil Government," resolves all civil obligation into expediency; and he proceeds to say, "that so long as the interest of the whole society requires it, that is, so long as the established government cannot be resisted or changed without public inconveniency, it is the will of God that the established government be obeyed, and no longer."—"This principle being admitted, the justice of every particular case of resistance is reduced to a computation of the quantity of the danger and grievance on the one side, and of the probability and expense of redressing it on the other." Of this, he says, every man shall judge for himself. But Paley appears never to have contemplated those cases to which the rule of expediency does not apply, in which a people, as well as an individual, must do justice, cost what it may. If I have unjustly wrested a plank from a drowning man, I must restore it to him though I drown myself. This, according to Paley, would be inconvenient. But he that would save his life, in such a case, shall lose it. This people must cease to hold slaves, and to make war on Mexico, though it cost them their existence as a people.

In their practice, nations agree with Paley; but does any one think that Massachusetts does exactly what is right at the present crisis?

"A drab of state, a cloth-o'-silver slut,
To have her train borne up, and her soul trail in the dirt."

Practically speaking, the opponents to a reform in Massachusetts are not a hundred thousand politicians at the South, but a hundred thousand merchants and farmers here, who are more interested in commerce and agriculture than they are in humanity, and are not prepared to do justice to the slave and to Mexico, *cost what it may.* I quarrel not with far-off foes, but with those who, near at home, co-operate with, and do the bidding of those far away, and without whom the latter would be harmless. We are accustomed to say, that the mass of men are unprepared; but improvement is slow, because the few are not materially wiser or better than the many. It is not so important that many should be as good as you, as that there be some absolute goodness some-

where; for that will leaven the whole lump. There are thousands who are *in opinion* opposed to slavery and to the war, who yet in effect do nothing to put an end to them; who, esteeming themselves children of Washington and Franklin, sit down with their hands in their pockets, and say that they know not what to do, and do nothing; who even postpone the question of freedom to the question of free-trade, and quietly read the prices-current along with the latest advices from Mexico, after dinner, and, it may be, fall asleep over them both. What is the price-current of an honest man and patriot to-day? They hesitate, and they regret, and sometimes they petition; but they do nothing in earnest and with effect. They will wait, well disposed, for others to remedy the evil, that they may no longer have it to regret. At most, they give only a cheap vote, and a feeble countenance and Godspeed, to the right, as it goes by them. There are nine hundred and ninety-nine patrons of virtue to one virtuous man; but it is easier to deal with the real possessor of a thing than with the temporary guardian of it.

All voting is a sort of gaming, like chequers or backgammon, with a slight moral tinge to it, a playing with right and wrong, with moral questions; and betting naturally accompanies it. The character of the voters is not staked. I cast my vote, perchance, as I think right; but I am not vitally concerned that that right should prevail. I am willing to leave it to the majority. Its obligation, therefore, never exceeds that of expediency. Even voting *for the right* is *doing* nothing for it. It is only expressing to men feebly your desire that it should prevail. A wise man will not leave the right to the mercy of chance, nor wish it to prevail through the power of the majority. There is but little virtue in the action of masses of men. When the majority shall at length vote for the abolition of slavery, it will be because they are indifferent to slavery, or because there is but little slavery left to be abolished by their vote. *They* will then be the only slaves. Only *his* vote can hasten the abolition of slavery who asserts his own freedom by his vote.

I hear of a convention to be held at Baltimore, or elsewhere, for the selection of a candidate for the Presidency, made up chiefly of editors, and men who are politicians by profession; but I think, what is it to any independent, intelligent, and respectable man what decision they may come to, shall we not have the advantage of his wisdom and honesty, nevertheless? Can we not count upon some independent votes? Are there not many individuals in the country who do not attend conventions? But no: I find that the respectable man, so called, has immediately drifted from his position, and despairs of his country, when his country has more reason to despair of him. He forthwith adopts one of the candidates thus selected as the only *available* one, thus proving that he is himself *available* for any purposes of the demagogue. His vote is of no more worth than that of any unprincipled foreigner or hireling native, who may have been bought. Oh for a man who is a *man,* and, as my neighbor says, has a bone in his back which you cannot pass your hand through! Our statistics are at fault: the population has been returned too large. How many *men* are there to a square thousand miles in this country? Hardly one. Does not America offer any inducement for men to settle here? The American has dwindled into an Odd Fellow,—one who may be known by the development of his organ of gregariousness, and a manifest lack of intellect and cheerful self-reliance; whose first and chief concern, on coming into the world, is to see that the almshouses are in good repair; and, before yet he has lawfully donned the virile garb, to collect a fund for the support of the widows and orphans that may be; who, in short, ventures to live only by the aid of the mutual insurance company, which has promised to bury him decently.

It is not a man's duty, as a matter of course, to devote himself to the eradication of any, even the most enormous wrong; he may still properly have other concerns to engage him; but it is his duty, at least, to wash his hands of it, and, if he gives it no thought longer, not to give it practically his support. If I devote myself to other pursuits and contemplations, I must first see, at least, that I do not pursue them sitting upon another man's shoulders. I must get off him first, that he may pursue his contemplations too. See what gross inconsistency is tolerated. I have heard some of my townsmen say, "I should like to have them order me out to help put down an insurrection of the slaves, or to march to Mexico,—see if I would go"; and yet these very men have each, directly by their allegiance, and so indirectly, at least, by their money, furnished a substitute. The soldier is applauded who refuses to serve in an unjust war by those who do not refuse to sustain the unjust government which makes the war; is applauded by those whose own act and authority he disregards and sets at nought; as if the State were penitent to that degree that it hired one to scourge it while it sinned, but not to that degree that it left off sinning for a moment. Thus, under the name of order and civil government, we are all made at last to pay homage to and support our own meanness. After the first blush of sin, comes its indifference; and from immoral it becomes, as it were, *un*moral, and not quite unnecessary to that life which we have made.

The broadest and most prevalent error requires the most disinterested virtue to sustain it. The slight reproach to which the virtue of patriotism is commonly liable, the noble are most likely to incur. Those who, while they disapprove of the character and measures of a government, yield to it their allegiance and support, are undoubtedly its most conscientious supporters, and so frequently the most serious obstacles to reform. Some are petitioning the State to dissolve the Union, to disregard the requisitions of the President. Why do they not dissolve it themselves,—the union between themselves and the State,—and refuse to pay their quota into its treasury? Do not they stand in the same relation to the State, that the State does to the Union? And have not the same reasons prevented the State from resisting the Union, which have prevented them from resisting the State?

How can a man be satisfied to entertain an opinion merely, and enjoy *it*? Is there any enjoyment in it, if his opinion is that he is aggrieved? If you are cheated out of a single dollar by your neighbor, you do not rest satisfied with knowing that you are cheated, or with saying that you are cheated, or even with petitioning him to pay you your due; but you take effectual steps at once to obtain the full amount, and see that you are never cheated again. Action from principle,—the perception and the performance of right,—changes things and relations; it is essentially revolutionary, and does not consist wholly with any thing which was. It not only divides states and churches, it divides families; aye, it divides the *individual,* separating the diabolical in him from the divine.

Unjust laws exist: shall we be content to obey them, or shall we endeavor to amend them, and obey them until we have succeeded, or shall we transgress them at once? Men generally, under such a government as this, think that they ought to wait until they have persuaded the majority to alter them. They think that, if they should resist, the remedy would be worse than the evil. But it is the fault of the government itself that the remedy *is* worse than the evil. *It* makes it worse. Why is it not more apt to anticipate and provide for reform? Why does it not cherish its wise minority? Why does it cry and resist before it is hurt? Why does it not encourage its citizens to be on the alert to point out its faults, and *do* better than it would have them? Why does it always crucify Christ, and excommunicate Copernicus and Luther, and pronounce Washington and Franklin rebels?

One would think, that a deliberate and practical denial of its authority, was the only offence never contemplated by government; else, why has it not assigned its definite, its suitable and proportionate penalty? If a man who has no property refuses but once to earn nine shillings for the State, he is put in prison for a period unlimited by any law that I know, and determined only by the discretion of those who placed him there; but if he should steal ninety times nine shillings from the State, he is soon permitted to go at large again.

If the injustice is part of the necessary friction of the machine of government, let it go, let it go: perchance it will wear smooth,—certainly the machine will wear out. If the injustice has a spring, or a pulley, or a rope, or a crank, exclusively for itself, then perhaps you may consider whether the remedy will not be worse than the evil; but if it is of such a nature that it requires you to be the agent of injustice to another, then, I say, break the law. Let your life be a counter friction to stop the machine. What I have to do is to see, at any rate, that I do not lend myself to the wrong which I condemn.

As for adopting the ways which the State has provided for remedying the evil, I know not of such ways. They take too much time, and a man's life will be gone. I have other affairs to attend to. I came into this world, not chiefly to make this a good place to live in, but to live in it, be it good or bad. A man has not every thing to do, but something; and because he cannot do *every thing*, it is not necessary that he should do *something* wrong. It is not my business to be petitioning the governor or the legislature any more than it is theirs to petition me; and, if they should not hear my petition, what should I do then? But in this case the State has provided no way: its very Constitution is the evil. This may seem to be harsh and stubborn and unconciliatory; but it is to treat with the utmost kindness and consideration the only spirit that can appreciate or deserves it. So is all change for the better, like birth and death which convulse the body.

I do not hesitate to say, that those who call themselves abolitionists should at once effectually withdraw their support, both in person and property, from the government of Massachusetts, and not wait till they constitute a majority of one, before they suffer the right to prevail through them. I think that it is enough if they have God on their side, without waiting for that other one. Moreover, any man more right than his neighbors, constitutes a majority of one already.

I meet this American government, or its representative the State government, directly, and face to face, once a year, no more, in the person of its tax-gatherer; this is the only mode in which a man situated as I am necessarily meets it; and it then says distinctly, Recognize me; and the simplest, the most effectual, and, in the present posture of affairs, the indispensablest mode of treating with it on this head, of expressing your little satisfaction with and love for it, is to deny it then. My civil neighbor, the tax-gatherer, is the very man I have to deal with,—for it is, after all, with men and not with parchment that I quarrel,—and he has voluntarily chosen to be an agent of the government. How shall he ever know well what he is and does as an officer of the government, or as a man, until he is obliged to consider whether he shall treat me, his neighbor, for whom he has respect, as a neighbor and well-disposed man, or as a maniac and disturber of the peace, and see if he can get over this obstruction to his neighborliness without a ruder and more impetuous thought or speech corresponding with his action? I know this well, that if one thousand, if one hundred, if ten men whom I could name,—if ten *honest* men only,—aye, if *one* HONEST man, in this State of Massachusetts, *ceasing to hold slaves,* were actually to withdraw from this copartnership, and be locked up in the county jail therefor, it would be the abolition of slavery in America. For it matters not how small the beginning may seem to be: what is once well done is done for ever. But we love better to talk about it: that we say is our mission. Reform keeps many scores of newspapers in its service, but not one man. If my esteemed neighbor, the State's ambassador, who will devote his days to the settlement of the question of human rights in the Council Chamber, instead of being threatened with the prisons of Carolina, were to sit down the prisoner of Massachusetts, that State which is so anxious to foist the sin of slavery upon her sister,—though at present she can discover only an act of inhospitality to be the ground of a quarrel with her,—the Legislature would not wholly waive the subject the following winter.

Under a government which imprisons any unjustly, the true place for a just man is also a prison. The proper place to-day, the only place which Massachusetts has provided for her freer and less desponding spirits, is in her prisons, to be put out and locked out of the State by her own act, as they have already put themselves out by their principles. It is there that the fugitive slave, and the Mexican prisoner on parole, and the Indian come to plead the wrongs of his race, should find them; on that separate, but more free and honorable ground, where the State places those who are not *with* her but *against* her,—the only house in a slave-state in which a free man can abide with honor. If any think that their influence would be lost there, and their voices no longer afflict the ear of the State, that they would not be as an enemy within its walls, they do not know by how much truth is stronger than error, nor how much more eloquently and effectively he can combat injustice who has experienced a little in his own person. Cast your whole vote, not a strip of paper merely, but your whole influence. A minority is powerless while it conforms to the majority; it is not even a minority then; but it is irresistible when it clogs by its whole weight. If the alternative is to keep all just men in prison, or give up war and slavery, the State will not hesitate which to choose. If a thousand men were not to pay their tax-bills this year, that would not be a violent and bloody measure, as it would be to pay them, and enable the State to commit violence and shed innocent blood. This is, in fact, the definition of a peaceable revolution if any such is possible. If the tax-gatherer, or any other public officer, asks me, as one has done, "But what shall I do?" my answer is, "If you really wish to do any thing, resign your office." When the subject has refused allegiance, and the officer has resigned his office, then the revolution is accomplished. But even suppose blood should flow. Is there not a sort of blood shed when the conscience is wounded? Through this wound a man's real manhood and immortality flow out, and he bleeds to an everlasting death. I see this blood flowing now.

I have contemplated the imprisonment of the offender, rather than the seizure of his goods,—though both will serve the same purpose,—because they who assert the purest right, and consequently are most dangerous to a corrupt State, commonly have not spent much time in accumulating property. To such the State renders comparatively small service, and a slight tax is wont to appear exorbitant, particularly if they are obliged to earn it by special labor with their hands. If there were one who lived wholly without the use of money, the State itself would hesitate to demand it of him. But the rich man—not to make any invidious comparison—is always sold to the institution which makes him rich. Absolutely speaking, the more money, the less virtue; for money comes between a man and his objects, and obtains them for him; and it was certainly no great virtue to obtain it. It puts to rest many questions which he would otherwise be taxed to answer; while the only new question which it puts is the hard but superfluous one, how to spend it. Thus his moral ground is taken from under his feet. The opportunities of living are diminished in proportion as what are called the "means" are increased. The best thing a man can do for his culture when he is rich is to endeavour to carry out those schemes which he entertained when he was poor. Christ answered the Herodians according to their condition. "Show me the tribute-money," said he; —and one took a penny out of his pocket;—If you use money which has the image of Cæsar on it, and which he has made current and valuable, that is, *if you are men of the State*, and gladly enjoy the advantages of Cæsar's government, then pay him back some of his own when the demands it; "Render therefore to Cæsar that which is Cæsar's, and to God those things which are God's,"—leaving them no wiser than before as to which was which; for they did not wish to know.

When I converse with the freest of my neighbors, I perceive that, whatever they may say about the magnitude and seriousness of the question, and their regard for the public tranquillity, the long and the short of the matter is, that they cannot spare the protection of the existing government, and they dread the consequences of disobedience to it to their property and families. For my own part, I should not like to think that I ever rely on the protection of the State. But, if I deny the authority of the State when it presents its tax-bill, it will soon take and waste all my property, and so harass me and my children without end. This is hard. This makes it impossible for a man to live honestly and at the same time comfortably in outward respects. It will not be worth the while to accumulate property; that would be sure to go again. You must hire or squat somewhere, and raise but a small crop, and eat that soon. You must live within yourself, and depend upon yourself, always tucked up and ready for a start, and not have many affairs. A man may grow rich in Turkey even, if he will be in all respects a good subject of the Turkish government. Confucius said,—"If a State is governed by the principles of reason, poverty and misery are subjects of shame; if a State is not governed by the principles of reason, riches and honors are the subjects of shame." No: until I want the protection of Massachusetts to be extended to me in some distant southern port, where my liberty is endangered, or until I am bent solely on building up an estate at home by peaceful enterprise, I can afford to refuse allegiance to Massachusetts, and her right to my property and life. It costs me less in every sense to incur the penalty of disobedience to the State, than it would to obey. I should feel as if I were worth less in that case.

Some years ago, the State met me in behalf of the church, and commanded me to pay a certain sum toward the support of a clergyman whose preaching my father attended, but never I myself. "Pay it," it said, "or be locked up in the jail." I declined to pay. But, unfortunately, another man saw fit to pay it. I did not see why the schoolmaster should be taxed to support the priest, and not the priest the schoolmaster; for I was not the State's schoolmaster, but I supported myself by voluntary subscription. I did not see why the lyceum should not present its tax-bill, and have the State to back its demand, as well as the church. However, at the request of the selectmen, I condescended to make some such statement as this in writing: —"Know all men by these presents, that I, Henry Thoreau, do not wish to be regarded as a member of any incorporated society which I have not joined." This I gave to the town-clerk; and he has it. The State, having thus learned that I did not wish to be regarded as a member of that church, has never made a like demand on me since; though it said that it must adhere to its original presumption that time. If I had known how to name them, I should then have signed off in detail from all the societies which I never signed on to; but I did not know where to find a complete list.

I have paid no poll-tax for six years. I was put into a jail once on this account, for one night; and, as I stood considering the walls of solid stone, two or three feet thick, the door of wood and iron, a foot thick, and the iron grating which strained the light, I could not help being struck with the foolishness of that institution which treated me as if I were mere flesh and blood and bones, to be locked up. I wondered that it should have concluded at length that this was the best use it could put me to, and had never thought to avail itself of my services in some way. I saw that, if there was a wall of stone between me and my townsmen, there was a still more difficult one to climb or break through, before they could get to be as free as I was. I did not for a moment feel confined, and the walls seemed a great waste of stone and mortar. I felt as if I alone of all my townsmen had paid my tax. They plainly did not know how to treat me, but behaved like persons who are underbred. In every threat and in every compliment there was a blunder; for they thought that my chief desire was to stand the other side of that stone wall. I could not but smile to see how industriously they locked the door on my meditations, which followed them out again without let or hinderance, and *they* were really all that was dangerous. As they could not reach me, they had resolved to punish my body; just as boys, if they cannot come at some person against whom they have a spite, will abuse his dog. I saw that the State was half-witted, that it was timid as a lone woman with her silver spoons, and that it did not know its friends from its foes, and I lost all my remaining respect for it, and pitied it.

Thus the State never intentionally confronts a man's sense, intellectual or moral, but only his body, his senses. It is not armed with superior wit or honesty, but with superior physical strength. I was not born to be forced. I will breathe after my own fashion. Let us see who is the strongest. What force has a multitude? They only can force me who obey a higher law than I. They force me to become like themselves. I do not hear of *men* being *forced* to live this way or that by masses of men. What sort of life were that to live? When I meet a government which says to me, "Your money or your life," why should I be in haste to give it my money? It may be in a great strait, and not know what to do: I cannot help that. It must help itself; do as I do. It is not worth the while the snivel about it. I am not responsible for the successful working of the machinery of society. I am not the son of the engineer. I perceive that, when an acorn and a chestnut fall side by side, the one does not remain inert to make way for the other, but both obey their own laws, and spring and grow and flourish as best they can, till one, perchance, overshadows and destroys the other. If a plant cannot live according to its nature, it dies; and so a man.

The night in prison was novel and interesting enough. The prisoners in their shirt-sleeves were enjoying a chat and the evening air in the door-way, when I entered. But the jailer said, "Come, boys, it is time to lock up"; and so they dispersed, and I heard the sound of their steps returning into the hollow apartments. My room-mate was introduced to me by the jailer, as "a first-rate fellow and a clever man." When the door was locked, he showed me where to hang my hat, and how he managed matters there. The rooms were whitewashed once a month; and this one, at least, was the whitest, most simply furnished, and probably the neatest apartment in the town. He naturally wanted to know where I came from, and what brought me there; and, when I had told him, I asked him in my turn how he came there, presuming him to be an honest man, of course; and, as the world goes, I believe he was. "Why," said he, "they accuse me of burning a barn; but I never did it." As near as I could discover, he had probably gone to bed in a barn when drunk, and smoked his pipe there; and so a barn was burnt. He had the reputation of being a clever man, had been there some three months waiting for his trial to come on, and would have to wait as much longer; but he was quite domesticated and contented, since he got his board for nothing, and thought that he was well treated.

He occupied one window, and I the other; and I saw, that, if one stayed there long, his principal business would be to look out the window. I had soon read all the tracts that were left there, and examined where former prisoners had broken out, and where a grate had been sawed off, and heard the history of the various occupants of that room; for I found that even here there was a history and a gossip which never circulated beyond the walls of the jail. Probably this is the only house in the town where verses are composed, which are afterward printed in a circular form, but not published. I was shown quite a long list of verses which were composed by some young men who had been detected in an attempt to escape, who avenged themselves by singing them.

I pumped my fellow-prisoner as dry as I could, for fear I should never see him again; but at length he showed me which was my bed, and left me to blow out the lamp.

It was like travelling into a far country, such as I had never expected to behold, to lie there for one night. It seemed to me that I never had heard the town-clock strike before, nor the evening sounds of the village; for we slept with the windows open, which were inside the grating. It was to see my native village in the light of the middle ages, and our Concord was turned into a Rhine stream, and visions of knights and castles passed before me. They were the voices of old burghers that I heard in the streets. I was an involuntary spectator and auditor of whatever was done and said in the kitchen of the adjacent village-inn,—a wholly new and rare experience to me. It was a closer view of my native town. I was fairly inside of it. I never had seen its institutions before. This is one of its peculiar institutions; for it is a shire town. I began to comprehend what its inhabitants were about.

In the morning, our breakfasts were put through the hole in the door, in small oblong-square tin pans, made to fit, and holding a pint of chocolate, with brown bread, and an iron spoon. When they called for the vessels again, I was green enough to return what bread I had left; but my comrade seized it, and said that I should lay that up for lunch or dinner. Soon after, he was let out to work at haying in a neighboring field, whither he went every day, and would not be back till noon; so he bade me good-day, saying that he doubted if he should see me again.

When I came out of prison,—for some one interfered, and paid the tax,—I did not perceive that great changes had taken place on the common, such as he observed who went in a youth, and emerged a tottering and gray-headed man; and yet a change had to my eyes come over the scene,—the town, and State, and country,—greater than any that mere time could effect. I saw yet more distinctly the State in which I lived. I saw to what extent the people among whom I lived could be trusted as good neighbors and friends; that their friendship was for summer weather only; that they did not greatly purpose to do right; that they were a distinct race from me by their prejudices and superstitions, as the Chinamen and Malays are; that, in their sacrifices to humanity, they ran no risks, not even to their property; that, after all, they were not so noble but they treated the thief as he had treated them, and hoped, by a certain outward observance and a few prayers, and by walking in a particular straight though useless path from time to time, to save their souls. This may be to judge my neighbors harshly; for I believe that most of them are not aware that they have such an institution as the jail in their village.

It was formerly the custom in our village, when a poor debtor came out of jail, for his acquaintances to salute him, looking through their fingers, which were crossed to represent the grating of a jail window, "How do ye do?" My neighbors did not thus salute me, but first looked at me, and then at one another, as if I had returned from a long journey. I was put into jail as I was going to the shoemaker's to get a shoe which was mended. When I was let out the next morning, I proceeded to finish my errand, and, having put on my mended shoe, joined a huckleberry party, who were impatient to put themselves under my conduct; and in half an hour,—for the horse was soon tackled,—was in the midst of a huckleberry field, on one of our highest hills, two miles off; and then the State was nowhere to be seen. This is the whole history of "My Prisons."

I have never declined paying the highway tax, because I am as desirous of being a good neighbor as I am of being a bad subject; and, as for supporting schools, I am doing my part to educate my fellow-countrymen now. It is for no particular item in the tax-bill that I refuse to pay it. I simply wish to refuse allegiance to the State, to withdraw and stand aloof from it effectually. I do not care to trace the course of my dollar, if I could, till it buys a man, or a musket to shoot one with,—the dollar is innocent,—but I am concerned to trace the effects of my allegiance. In fact, I quietly declare war with the State, after my fashion, though I will still make what use and get what advantage of her I can, as is usual in such cases.

If others pay the tax which is demanded of me, from a sympathy with the State, they do but what they have already done in their own case, or rather they abet injustice to a greater extent than the State requires. If they pay the tax from a mistaken interest in the individual taxed, to save his property or prevent his going to jail, it is because they have not considered wisely how far they let their private feelings interfere with the public good.

This, then, is my position at present. But one cannot be too much on his guard in such a case, lest his action be biassed by obstinacy, or an undue regard for the opinions of men. Let him see that he does only what belongs to himself and to the hour.

I think sometimes, Why, this people mean well; they are only ignorant; they would do better if they knew how: why give your neighbors this pain to treat you as they are not inclined to? But I think, again, this is no reason why I should do as they do, or permit others to suffer much greater pain of a different kind. Again, I sometimes say to myself, When many millions of men, without heat, without ill-will, without personal feeling of any kind, demand of you a few shillings only, without the possibility, such is their constitution, of retracting or altering their present demand, and without the possibility, on your side, of appeal to any other millions, why expose yourself to this overwhelming brute force? You do not resist cold and hunger, the winds and the waves, thus obstinately; you quietly submit to a thousand similar necessities. You do not put your head into the fire. But just in proportion as I regard this as not wholly a brute force, but partly a human force, and consider that I have relations to those millions as to so many millions of men, and not of mere brute or inanimate things, I see that appeal is possible, first and instantaneously, from them to the Maker of them, and, secondly, from them to themselves. But, if I put my head deliberately into the fire, there is no appeal to fire or to the Maker of fire, and I have only myself to blame. If I could convince myself that I have any right to be satisfied with men as they are, and to treat them accordingly, and not according, in some respects, to my requisitions and expectations of what they and I ought to be, then, like a good Mussulman and fatalist, I should endeavor to be satisfied with things as they are, and say it is the will of God. And, above all, there is this difference between resisting this and a purely brute or natural force, that I can resist this with some effect; but I cannot expect, like Orpheus, to change the nature of the rocks and trees and beasts.

I do not wish to quarrel with any man or nation. I do not wish to split hairs, to make fine distinctions, or set myself up as better than my neighbors. I seek rather, I may say, even an excuse for conforming to the laws of the land. I am but too ready to conform to them. Indeed I have reason to suspect myself on this head; and each year, as the tax-gatherer comes round, I find myself disposed to review the acts and position of the general and state governments, and the spirit of the people, to discover a pretext for conformity. I believe that the State will soon be able to take all my work of this sort out of my hands, and then I shall be no better a patriot than my fellow-countrymen. Seen from a lower point of view, the Constitution, with all its faults, is very good; the law and the courts are very respectable; even this State and this American government are, in many respects, very admirable and rare things, to be thankful for, such as a great many have described them; but seen from a point of view a little higher, they are what I have described them; seen from a higher still, and the highest, who shall say what they are, or that they are worth looking at or thinking of at all?

However, the government does not concern me much, and I shall bestow the fewest possible thoughts on it. It is not many moments that I live under a government, even in this world. If a man is thought-free, fancy-free, imagination-free, that which *is not* never for a long time appearing *to be* to him, unwise rulers or reformers cannot fatally interrupt him.

I know that most men think differently from myself; but those whose lives are by profession devoted to the study of these or kindred subjects, content me as little as any. Statesmen and legislators, standing so completely within the institution, never distinctly and nakedly behold it. They speak of moving society, but have no resting-place without it. They may be men of a certain experience and discrimination, and have no doubt invented ingenious and even useful systems, for which we sincerely thank them; but all their wit and usefulness lie within certain not very wide limits. They are wont to forget that the world is not governed by policy and expediency. Webster never goes behind government, and so cannot speak with authority about it. His words are wisdom to those legislators who contemplate no essential reform in the existing government; but for thinkers, and those who legislate for all time, he never once glances at the subject. I know of those whose serene and wise speculations on this theme would soon reveal the limits of his mind's range and hospitality. Yet, compared with the cheap professions of most reformers, and the still cheaper wisdom and eloquence of politicians in general, his are almost the only sensible and valuable words, and we thank Heaven for him. Comparatively, he is always strong, original, and, above all, practical. Still his quality is not wisdom, but prudence. The lawyer's truth is not Truth, but consistency, or a consistent expediency. Truth is always in harmony with herself, and is not concerned chiefly to reveal the justice that may consist with wrong-doing. He well deserves to be called, as he has been called, the Defender of the Constitution. There are really no blows to be given by him but defensive ones. He is not a leader, but a follower. His leaders are the men of '87. "I have never made an effort," he says, "and never propose to make an effort; I have never countenanced an effort, and never mean to countenance an effort, to disturb the arrangement as originally made, by which the various States came into the Union." Still thinking of the sanction which the Constitution gives to slavery, he says, "Because it was a part of the original compact,—let it stand." Notwithstanding his special acuteness and ability, he is unable to take a fact out of its merely political relations, and behold it as it lies absolutely to be disposed of by the intellect, —what, for instance, it behoves a man to do here in America to-day with regard to slavery, but ventures, or is driven, to make some such desperate answer as the following, while professing to speak absolutely, and as a private man,—from which what new and singular code of social duties might be inferred?—"The manner," says he, "in which the government of those States where slavery exists are to regulate it, is for their own consideration, under their responsibility to their constituents, to the general laws of propriety, humanity, and justice, and to God. Associations formed elsewhere, springing from a feeling of humanity, or any other cause, have nothing whatever to do with it. They have never received any encouragement from me, and they never will." [1]

They who know of no purer sources of truth, who have traced up its stream no higher, stand, and wisely stand, by the Bible and the Constitution, and drink at it there with reverence and humility; but they who behold where it comes trickling into this lake or that pool, gird up their loins once more, and continue their pilgrimage toward its fountain-head.

No man with a genius for legislation has appeared in America. They are rare in the history of the world. There are orators, politicians, and eloquent men, by the thousand; but the speaker has not yet opened his mouth to speak, who is capable of settling the much-vexed questions of the day. We love eloquence for its own sake, and not for any truth which it may utter, or any heroism it may inspire. Our legislators have not yet learned the comparative value of free-trade and of freedom, of union, and of rectitude, to a nation. They have no genius or talent for comparatively humble questions of taxation and finance, commerce and manufactures and agriculture. If we were left solely to the wordy wit of legislators in Congress for our guidance, uncorrected by the seasonable experience and the effectual complaints of the people, America would not long retain her rank among the nations. For eighteen hundred years, though perchance I have no right to say it, the New Testament has been

¹ These extracts have been inserted since the Lecture was read. [Thoreau's note.]

written; yet where is the legislator who has wisdom and practical talent enough to avail himself of the light which it sheds on the science of legislation?

The authority of government, even such as I am willing to submit to,—for I will cheerfully obey those who know and can do better than I, and in many things even those who neither know or can do so well,—is still an impure one: to be strictly just, it must have the sanction and consent of the governed. It can have no pure right over my person and property but what I concede to it. The progress from an absolute to a limited monarchy, from a limited monarchy to a democracy, is a progress toward a true respect for the individual. Is a democracy, such as we know it, the last improvement possible in government? Is it not possible to take a step further towards recognizing and organizing the rights of man? There will never be a really free and enlightened State, until the State comes to recognize the individual as a higher and independent power, from which all its own power and authority are derived, and treats him accordingly. I please myself with imagining a State at last which can afford to be just to all men, and to treat the individual with respect as a neighbor; which even would not think it inconsistent with its own repose, if a few were to live aloof from it, not meddling with it, nor embraced by it, who fulfilled all the duties of neighbors and fellow-men. A State which bore this kind of fruit, and suffered it to drop off as fast as it ripened, would prepare the way for a still more perfect and glorious State, which also I have imagined, but not yet anywhere seen.   1849

» » *The Southern Cause* « «

1800-1860

» »　 « «

THE OLD FOLKS AT HOME

Way down upon de Swanee ribber,
   Far, far away,
Dere's wha my heart is turning ebber,
   Dere's wha de old folks stay.
All up and down de whole creation,
   Sadly I roam,
Still longin' for de old plantation,
   And for de old folks at home.
     All de world am sad and dreary,
      Eb'rywhere I roam.
     Oh! darkies, how my heart grows weary,
     Far from de old folks at home.

All round de little farm I wander'd
   When I was young,
Den many happy days I squander'd,
   Many de songs I sung.
When I was playin' wid my brudder,
   Happy was I,
Oh, take me to my kind old mudder,
   Dere let me live and die.

One little hut among de bushes,
   One dat I love,
Still sadly to my mem'ry rushes,
   No matter where I rove.
When will I see de bees a-humming
   All round de comb?
When will I hear de banjo tumming
   Down in my good old home?

Of the scores of ante-bellum minstrel songs voicing nostalgia for some particular section of the South, only those of Stephen Foster survive. He was never south of the Ohio until after this one was written! With such famous songs as "The Rose of Alabama" and "De Floating Scow of Old Virginia" (the original "Carry Me Back to Old Virginia"), his compositions created a mythical South where plantation life was idyllic for both masters and slaves. The fact is well known that Foster chose the Suwannee River (in Florida) quite by accident. In need of a southern river of two syllables, he had already rejected the Yazoo and the Pedee before his eye lighted on the "Swanee," while he was glancing through an atlas. Christy's Minstrels carried the song to England. It is said that the favorite songs of the English soldiers in the Crimean War were "Annie Laurie" and "The Old Folks at Home."

» »   « «

The Southern Cause

DURING the Revolutionary period enlightened Southern slaveowners frequently adopted an apologetic tone in discussing slavery. Influenced by the conviction that slavery was not profitable and that it ran counter to the natural rights philosophy by which the revolt from England was justified, slaveowners, especially in Virginia, frequently freed their slaves. What held many back from this procedure was the fear of a race problem which, in their eyes, the presence of free Negroes would inevitably create. It was this fear which led the upper South to give fairly generous support to the movement for colonizing the freed slaves in the West, in the Caribbean Islands, or in Africa. As it became increasingly clear, however, that the difficulties involved in colonization were so great that it could take care of only a fraction of the Negroes, slaveowners became more reluctant to free their blacks and argued that the evils of slavery were far less than the evils bound to result from the presence of a mass of free blacks. The increasing tendency to accept slavery as an inevitable institution was also facilitated by the waning of the Enlightenment in the South in the early decades of the nineteenth century.

An even more important factor, however, helps to explain the reversal in the public thought of the South in regard to slavery. Until the invention of the cotton gin, cotton could be grown profitably only on the sea islands: the short-fiber plant, which alone flourished in the upland country, involved far too much expenditure of labor in the seeding process to make the staple profitable. The cotton gin, however, made possible the rapid spread of the plantation system into the rich lands of Georgia, Alabama, and Mississippi. Since the act of 1808 forbade the importation of slaves from abroad, the lower South largely depended on the upper South for its supply of slave labor. With the transformation of slavery from a patriarchal institution into a commercial one, and one which, in spite of the claims of abolitionists and of such Southern critics as Rowland Hinton Helper, was profitable to many slaveholders, it became necessary not only to apologize for slavery but to defend it as a positive blessing.

Shortly after the Virginia Constitutional Convention of 1829 the proslavery argument of Professor Thomas Dew of William and Mary became increasingly familiar both to Southerners and to the North. With the slave insurrection led by Nat Turner in 1831, and the rise of a more militant abolitionist movement in the North, the proslavery defense became amplified and more sharply defined. It was argued that slavery was a blessing to the owner, the nonowner, and the slave alike; that pure republicanism could flourish only when it rested on a slave base. Ministers pointed to biblical sanctions of slavery. Students of ethnology labored to prove the inherent inferiority of the Negro. The Southern defense of slavery also included an indictment of Northern industrial capitalism which, it was held, was far less humane in its crass and materialistic treatment of the wage-slave than the "peculiar institution" of the South was to the chattel-slave. When *Uncle Tom's Cabin* took the North by storm, Southerners wrote a dozen or more proslavery novels designed to refute the indictment of Harriet Beecher Stowe.

But the Southern cause embraced more than slavery. The South was by and large a rural civilization, and the values cherished by Southerners were functional to that civilization. Opposition to a centralized banking system and to a centralized federal government, and devotion to free trade and states rights, bulked large in the pattern of Southern loyalties.

» » « «

NATHANIEL BEVERLEY TUCKER

1784–1851

FROM 1820 until his death Nathaniel Beverley Tucker advocated in its extreme form the doctrine of states rights, including secession. These doctrines, together with pride in a Virginia which he idealized and a disdain for democracy and industrialism, were expounded from his chair at William and Mary College and in tracts, treatises on law, and, especially, in his remarkable novel, *The Partisan Leader* (1836). Written to defeat the re-election of Van Buren and the Democrats, the book prophesied secession and civil war. The novel, which bore the fictitious date "1856," was subsequently republished in both North and South as a part of the propaganda campaign waged by the two sections.

Carl Bridenbaugh, Introduction, *The Partisan Leader*, New York, 1933.
Lewis G. Leary, *The Literary Career of Nathaniel Tucker*, Durham, N. C., 1951.

» » *From:* THE PARTISAN LEADER « «

CHAPTER IV

——Handmaid of Prudence, Fortune comes
Prompt to her bidding, ready to fulfil
Her mistress' pleasure; whether she demand
The treasures of the South, the applause of men,
Or the calm sunshine of domestic bliss,
Lo! they are hers!   Anonymous.

Arthur Trevor was the youngest son of a gentleman who resided in the neighborhood of Richmond. He was a man in affluent circumstances, and had long and honorably filled various important and dignified stations in the service of his native State. Endowed with handsome talents, an amiable disposition, and all the accomplishments that can adorn a gentleman, he added to these the most exemplary virtues. His influence in society had, of course, been great, and though now, at the age of seventy, withdrawn from public life, his opinions were inquired of, and his counsel sought, by all who had access to him. Through life he had been remarkable for firmness, and yet more for prudence. The steadiness of his principles could never be questioned, but, it was thought, he had sometimes deemed it wise to compromise, when men of less cautious temper would have found safety in prudent boldness.

To this temperament had been attributed his conduct in regard to the politics of the last twenty years. *Bred up in the school of State rights, and thoroughly imbued with its doctrines, he had, even before that time, been accustomed to look, with a jealous eye, on the progressive usurpations of the Federal Government. In the hope of arresting these, he had exerted more than his usual activity in aiding to put down the younger Adams, and to elevate his successor. Though no candidate for the spoils of victory, no man rejoiced more sincerely in the result of that contest; and, until the emanation of the proclamation of December, 1832, he had given his hearty approbation, and steady, though quiet support, to the administration of Andrew Jackson.*

From that moment he seemed to look with fearful bodings on the affairs of his country. His disapprobation of that instrument was expressed with as much freedom and force as was consistent with his habitual reserve and moderation. He was, indeed, alarmed into a degree of excitement unusual with him, and might have gone farther than he did, had he not found that others were disposed to go, as he thought, too far. He had entirely disapproved the nullifying ordinance of South Carolina; and, though he recognized the right of secession, he deprecated all thought of resorting to that remedy. He was aware that many of his best friends, thinking that its necessity would be eventually felt by all, feared that that conviction might come too late. They remarked the steady tendency of Federal measures to weaken the malcontent States in the South, and to increase the resources of their northern oppressors and those of the General Government. Hence they feared, that whenever Virginia, or any other of the slave-holding States, should find itself driven to secession, the other party, in the confidence of superior strength, might be tempted forcibly to resist the exercise of the right. They thus arrived at the conclusion that separation (which they deemed inevitable) to be peaceable, must be prompt.

These ideas had been laid before Mr. Trevor, and, in proportion to the urgency with which they were pressed, was his alarm and his disposition to adhere to the Union. He, at last, had brought himself to believe union, on any terms, better than disunion, under any circumstances. As the lesser evil, therefore, he determined to forget the proclamation, and, striving to reconcile himself to all the acts of the administration, he regarded every attempt to unite the South, in support of a southern president, as a prelude to the formation of a southern confederacy. By consequence, he became a partisan of Martin Van Buren; and united with Ritchie, and others of the same kidney, in endeavoring to subdue the spirit, and tame down the State pride of Virginia. These endeavors, aided by the lavish use of federal patronage in the State, were so far successful, that when, at the end of Van Buren's second term, he demanded a third election, she alone, in the South, supported his pretensions.

By the steady employment of the same pernicious influences, the elections throughout the State had been so regulated, as to produce returns of a majority of members devoted to the views of the usurper. This had continued until the spring of 1848, at which time the results of the elections were essentially the same which had taken place since the memorable 1836; when Virginia, at one stroke of the pen, *expunged* her name from the chronicles of honor, *expunged* the history of all her glories, *expunged* herself. From that time the land of Washington, and Henry, and Mason, of Jefferson, Madison, and Randolph, sunk to the rank of a province, administered and managed by the Riveses and Ritchies, the Barbours and Stevensons, the Watkinses, and Wilsons, whose chance to be remembered in history depends, like that of Erostratus, on the glories of that temple of liberty which they first desecrated and then destroyed.

"Where once the Caesars dwelt,
    There dwelt, tuneless, the birds of night."

From some cause, not understood at the time, an unexpected reaction had taken place between the spring elections and the recurrence of that *form* of presidential election in the fall, the observance of which was still 10 deemed necessary to display, and, by displaying, to perpetuate the usurper's power. This reaction appeared to show itself chiefly in those counties heretofore most distinguished for their loyalty. It would have seemed as if the spirit of John Randolph had risen from the sleep of death, and walked abroad through the scenes where his youthful shoulders had received the mantle of *his* eloquence from the hand of Henry. For the first time, in twelve years, the 20 vote of Virginia was recorded against the reelection of Martin Van Buren to the presidential throne.

But not the less subservient were the proceedings of the Legislature elected for his use, the spring before. Yet enough had been done to justify the hope that the ancient spirit of Old Virginia would yet show itself in the descendants of the men who had defied Cromwell, in the plenitude of his power, and had 30 cast off the yoke of George the Third, without waiting for the co-operation of the other colonies. At the same time, the power and the will of a fixed majority in the North, to give a master to the South, had been made manifest. It was clearly seen, too, that he had determined to use the power thus obtained, and to administer the government solely with a view to the interest of that sectional faction, by which he had been supported. *"Vae victis!"* "Woe to the 40 vanquished!" was the word. It had gone forth; and northern cupidity and northern fanaticism were seen to march, hand in hand, to the plunder and desolation of the South.

Under these circumstances, the Southern States had been, at length, forced to see that the day for decisive action had arrived. They therefore determined no longer to abide the obligations of a constitution, the form of which alone remained, and having, by a movement 50 nearly simultaneous, seceded from the Union, they had immediately formed a Southern Confederacy. *The suddenness of these measures was less remarkable than the prudence with which they had been conducted. The two to-*

gether left little doubt that there had been a preconcert among the leading men of the several States, arranging provisionally what should be done, whenever circumstances should throw power into the hands of those whom, at the bidding of the usurper, the people had once driven from their councils. It is now known that there was such concert. Nor was it confined to the seceding States alone. In Virginia, also, there were men who entered into the same views. But while the President believed that no decisive step would be taken by the more Southern States without her co-operation, he had devoted all his power, direct and indirect, to control and influence her elections. Of tumultuary insurrection he had no fear. The organized operation of the State Government was what he dreaded. By this alone could the measure of secession be effected; and this was effectually prevented by operating on the elections of members of the Legislature of Virginia. From the November vote on the Presidential election, less evil had been apprehended, and less pains had been taken to control it. In consequence of this, some thing more of the real sentiments of the people had been allowed to appear on that occasion; and, from this manifestation, the more Southern States were encouraged to hope for the ultimate accession of Virginia to their Confederacy. They had therefore determined to wait for her no longer, but to proceed to the execution of their plan, leaving her to follow.

The disposition of the usurper, at first, was to treat them as revolted provinces; and to take measures for putting down, by force, their resistance to his authority. But circumstances, to be mentioned hereafter, made it impolitic to resort to this measure. But these did not operate to prevent him from using the most efficacious means to prevent Virginia from following their example. Though restrained from attacking them, nothing prevented him from affecting to fear an attack *from* them. This gave a pretext for raising troops; and the position of Virginia, as the frontier State, afforded an excuse for stationing them within her borders. Under these pretences, small crops were established in many of the disaffected counties. Should the presence of these be ineffectual to secure the return of delegates devoted to the crown, an ultimate security was taken against the action of the Legislature. Richmond, the seat of government, became the head-quarters of the army of observation, as it was called, and, surrounded by this, the mock deliberations of the General Assembly were to be held.

The money thus thrown into the country seduced the corrupt, while terror subdued the timid. On Mr. Trevor, who was neither, these things had a contrary effect. He now, when it was too late, saw and lamented the error of his former overcaution. He now began to suspect that they had been right who had urged him, eighteen years before, to lend his aid in the work of arousing the people to a sense of their danger, and preparing them to meet it as one man. 1836

JOHN C. CALHOUN

1782–1850

ALTHOUGH the Charleston aristocrats made it clear that Calhoun, the son of up-country South Carolina, was not quite one of them, they were nevertheless forced to recognize his great genius and his devotion to their class, to the State, and to the South. After graduating from Yale and after study at the famous law school at Litchfield, Connecticut, Calhoun returned to South Carolina and assumed the leadership in the states rights movement. He opposed the tariff and all that tended to concentrate power in the hands of the federal government. He elaborated not only many arguments in defence of nullification and state sovereignty, but, in his *Disquisition on Government* rejected as tyrannical the principle of the numerical majority and advocated the protection of minorities.

Calhoun often clashed with Webster. Their greatest debate took place in 1850. Webster defended the compromise measures on the score that they were necessary to preserve the union; he tried to suggest that in the long run slavery would in any case lose out. Calhoun, too ill to deliver his speech, was present on March 4, 1850, when a colleague read it for him. It is an effective summary of his political and social philosophy. Within a month he was dead. But the principles which he so ably espoused still lived.

The Papers of John C. Calhoun, Robert L. Meriwether, ed., Columbia, S. C., 1959.
Charles M. Wiltse, *John C. Calhoun*, 3 vols., New York, 1944–1951.

» » SPEECH ON THE SLAVERY QUESTION « «

I have, Senators, believed from the first that the agitation of the subject of slavery would, if not prevented by some timely and effective measure, end in disunion. Entertaining this opinion, I have, on all proper occasions, endeavored to call the attention of both the two great parties which divide the country to adopt some measure to prevent so great a disaster, but without success. The agitation has been permitted to proceed, with almost no attempt to resist it, until it has reached a point when it can no longer be disguised or denied that the Union is in danger. You have thus had forced upon you the greatest and the gravest question that can ever come under your consideration —How can the Union be preserved?

To give a satisfactory answer to this mighty question, it is indispensable to have an accurate and thorough knowledge of the nature and the character of the cause by which the Union is endangered. Without such knowledge it is impossible to pronounce, with any certainty, by what measure it can be saved; just as it would be impossible for a physician to pronounce, in the case of some dangerous disease, with any certainty, by what remedy the patient could be saved, without similar knowledge of the nature and character of the cause which produced it. The first question, then, presented for consideration, in the investigation I propose to make, in order to obtain such knowledge, is—What is it that has endangered the Union?

To this question there can be but one answer,—that the immediate cause is the almost universal discontent which pervades all the States composing the Southern section of the Union. This widely-extended discontent is not of recent origin. It commenced with the agitation of the slavery question, and has been increasing ever since. The next question, going one step further back, is—What has caused

this widely diffused and almost universal discontent?

It is a great mistake to suppose, as is by some, that it originated with demagogues, who excited the discontent with the intention of aiding their personal advancement, or with the disappointed ambition of certain politicians, who resorted to it as the means of retrieving their fortunes. On the contrary, all the great political influences of the section were arrayed against excitement, and exerted to the utmost to keep the people quiet. The great mass of the people of the South were divided, as in the other section, into Whigs and Democrats. The leaders and the presses of both parties in the South were very solicitous to prevent excitement and to preserve quiet; because it was seen that the effects of the former would necessarily tend to weaken, if not destroy, the political ties which united them with their respective parties in the other section. Those who know the strength of party ties will readily appreciate the immense force which this cause exerted against agitation, and in favor of preserving quiet. But, great as it was, it was not sufficient to prevent the widespread discontent which now pervades the section. No; some cause, far deeper and more powerful than the one supposed, must exist, to account for discontent so wide and deep. The question then recurs—What is the cause of this discontent? It will be found in the belief of the people of the Southern States, as prevalent as the discontent itself, that they cannot remain, as things now are, consistently with honor and safety, in the Union. The next question to be considered, is—What has caused this belief?

One of the causes is, undoubtedly, to be traced to the long-continued agitation of the slave question on the part of the North, and the many aggressions which they have made on the rights of the South during the time. I will not enumerate them at present, as it will be done hereafter in its proper place.

There is another lying back of it—with which this is intimately connected—that may be regarded as the great and primary cause. This is to be found in the fact that the equilibrium between the two sections, in the Government as it stood when the constitution was ratified and the Government put in action, has been destroyed. At that time there was nearly a perfect equilibrium between the two, which afforded ample means to each to protect itself against the aggression of the other; but, as it now stands, one section has the exclusive power of controlling the Government, which leaves the other without any adequate means of protecting itself against its encroachment and oppression. To place this subject distinctly before you, I have, Senators, prepared a brief statistical statement, showing the relative weight of the two sections in the Government under the first census of 1790 and the last census of 1840.

According to the former, the population of the United States, including Vermont, Kentucky, and Tennessee, which then were in their incipient condition of becoming States, but were not actually admitted, amounted to 3,929,827. Of this number the Northern States had 1,997,899, and the Southern 1,952,072, making a difference of only 45,827 in favor of the former States. The number of States, including Vermont, Kentucky, and Tennessee, were sixteen; of which eight, including Vermont, belonged to the Northern section, and eight, including Kentucky and Tennessee, to the Southern,—making an equal division of the States between the two sections under the first census. There was a small preponderance in the House of Representatives, and in the Electoral College, in favor of the Northern, owing to the fact that, according to the provisions of the constitution, in estimating federal numbers five slaves count but three; but it was too small to affect sensibly the perfect equilibrium which, with that exception, existed at the time. Such was the equality of the two sections when the States composing them agreed to enter into a Federal Union. Since then the equilibrium between them has been greatly disturbed.

According to the last census the aggregate population of the United States amounted to 17,063,357, of which the Northern section contained 9,728,920, and the Southern 7,334,437, making a difference, in round numbers, of

2,400,000. The number of States had increased from sixteen to twenty-six, making an addition of ten States. In the mean time the position of Delaware had become doubtful as to which section she properly belonged. Considering her as neutral, the Northern States will have thirteen and the Southern States twelve, making a difference in the Senate of two Senators in favor of the former. According to the apportionment under the census of 1840, there were two hundred and twenty-three members of the House of Representatives, of which the Northern States had one hundred and thirty-five, and the Southern States (considering Delaware as neutral) eighty-seven, making a difference in favor of the former in the House of Representatives of forty-eight. The difference in the Senate of two members, added to this, gives to the North in the electoral college, a majority of fifty. Since the census of 1840, four States have been added to the Union—Iowa, Wisconsin, Florida, and Texas. They leave the difference in the Senate as it stood when the census was taken; but add two to the side of the North in the House, making the present majority in the House in its favor fifty, and in the electoral college fifty-two.

The result of the whole is to give the Northern section a predominance in every department of the Government, and thereby concentrate in it the two elements which constitute the Federal Government,—majority of States, and a majority of their population, estimated in federal numbers. Whatever section concentrates the two in itself possesses the control of the entire Government.

But we are just at the close of the sixth decade, and the commencement of the seventh. The census is to be taken this year, which must add greatly to the decided preponderance of the North in the House of Representatives and in the electoral college. The prospect is, also, that a great increase will be added to its present preponderance in the Senate, during the period of the decade, by the addition of new States. Two territories, Oregon and Minnesota, are already in progress, and strenuous efforts are making to bring in three additional States from the territory recently conquered from Mexico; which, if successful, will add three other States in a short time to the Northern section, making five States; and increasing the present number of its States from fifteen to twenty, and of its Senators from thirty to forty. On the contrary, there is not a single territory in progress in the Southern section, and no certainty that any additional State will be added to it during the decade. The prospect then is, that the two sections in the Senate, should the efforts now made to exclude the South from the newly acquired territories succeed, will stand, before the end of the decade, twenty Northern States to fourteen Southern (considering Delaware as neutral), and forty Northern Senators to twenty-eight Southern. This great increase of Senators, added to the great increase of members of the House of Representatives and the electoral college on the part of the North, which must take place under the next decade, will effectually and irretrievably destroy the equilibrium which existed when the Government commenced.

Had this destruction been the operation of time, without the interference of Government, the South would have had no reason to complain; but such was not the fact. It was caused by the legislation of this Government, which was appointed, as the common agent of all, and charged with the protection of the interests and security of all. The legislation by which it has been effected, may be classed under three heads. The first, is that series of acts by which the South has been excluded from the common territory belonging to all the States as members of the Federal Union—which have had the effect of extending vastly the portion allotted to the Northern section, and restricting within narrow limits the portion left the South. The next consists in adopting a system of revenue and disbursements, by which an undue proportion of the burden of taxation has been imposed upon the South, and an undue proportion of its proceeds appropriated to the North; and the last is a system of political measures, by which the original character of the Government has been radically changed. I propose to bestow upon each of these, in the order they stand, a few remarks, with the view of showing that it is owing to the action of this Government, that the equilibrium between the two sections has been destroyed, and the whole powers of the system centered in a sectional majority.

The first of the series of acts by which the South was deprived of its due share of the territories, originated with the confederacy which preceded the existence of this Government. It is to be found in the provision of the ordinance of 1787. Its effect was to exclude the South entirely from that vast and fertile region which lies between the Ohio and the Missis-

sippi rivers, now embracing five States and one territory. The next of the series is the Missouri compromise, which excluded the South from that large portion of Louisiana which lies north of 36° 30′, excepting what is included in the State of Missouri. The last of the series excluded the South from the whole of the Oregon Territory. All these, in the slang of the day, were what are called slave territories, and not free soil; that is, territories belonging to slave-holding powers and open to the emigration of masters with their slaves. By these several acts, the South was excluded from 1,238,025 square miles—an extent of country considerably exceeding the entire valley of the Mississippi. To the South was left the portion of the Territory of Louisiana lying south of 36° 30′, and the portion north of it included in the State of Missouri, with the portion lying south of 36° 30′, including the States of Louisiana and Arkansas, and the territory lying west of the latter, and south of 36° 30′, called the Indian country. These, with the Territory of Florida, now the State, make, in the whole, 283,503 square miles. To this must be added the territory acquired with Texas. If the whole should be added to the Southern section, it would make an increase of 325,520, which would make the whole left to the South, 609,023. But a large part of Texas is still in contest between the two sections, which leaves it uncertain what will be the real extent of the portion of territory that may be left to the South.

I have not included the territory recently acquired by the treaty with Mexico. The North is making the most strenuous efforts to appropriate the whole to herself, by excluding the South from every foot of it. If she should succeed, it will add to that from which the South has already been excluded 526,078 square miles, and would increase the whole which the North has appropriated to herself, to 1,764,023, not including the portion that she may succeed in excluding us from in Texas. To sum up the whole, the United States, since they declared their independence, have acquired 2,373,046 square miles of territory, from which the North will have excluded the South, if she should succeed in monopolizing the newly acquired territories, about three-fourths of the whole, leaving to the South but about one-fourth.

Such is the first and great cause that has destroyed the equilibrium between the two sections in the Government.

The next is the system of revenue and disbursements which has been adopted by the Government. It is well known that the Government has derived its revenue mainly from duties on imports. I shall not undertake to show that such duties must necessarily fall mainly on the exporting States, and that the South, as the great exporting portion of the Union, has in reality paid vastly more than her due proportion of the revenue; because I deem it unnecessary, as the subject has on so many occasions been fully discussed. Nor shall I, for the same reason, undertake to show that a far greater portion of the revenue has been disbursed at the North, than its due share; and that the joint effect of these causes has been, to transfer a vast amount from South to North, which, under an equal system of revenue and disbursements, would not have been lost to her. If to this be added, that many of the duties were imposed, not for revenue, but for protection,—that is, intended to put money, not in the treasury, but directly into the pocket of the manufacturers,—some conception may be formed of the immense amount which, in the long course of sixty years, has been transferred from South to North. There are no data by which it can be estimated with any certainty; but it is safe to say, that it amounts to hundreds of millions of dollars. Under the most moderate estimate, it would be sufficient to add greatly to the wealth of the North, and thus greatly increase her population by attracting emigration from all quarters to that section.

This, combined with the great primary cause, amply explains why the North has acquired a preponderance in every department of the Government by its disproportionate increase of population and States. The former, as has been shown, has increased, in fifty years, 2,400,000 over that of the South. This increase of population, during so long a period, is satisfactorily accounted for, by the number of emigrants, and the increase of their descendants, which have been attracted to the Northern section from Europe and the South, in consequence of the advantages derived from the causes assigned. If they had not existed—if the South had retained all the capital which has been extracted from her by the fiscal action of the Government; and, if it had not been excluded by the ordinance of 1787 and the Missouri compromise, from the region lying between the Ohio and the Mississippi rivers, and between the Mississippi and the Rocky Mountains north of 36° 30'—it scarcely admits of a doubt, that it would have divided the imigration with the North, and by retaining her own people, would have at least equalled the North in population under the census of 1840, and probably under that about to be taken. She would also, if she had retained her equal rights in those territories, have maintained an equality in the number of States with the North, and have preserved the equilibrium between the two sections that existed at the commencement of the Government. The loss, then, of the equilibrium is to be attributed to the action of this Government.

But while these measures were destroying the equilibrium between the two sections, the action of the Government was leading to a radical change in its character, by concentrating all the power of the system in itself. The occasion will not permit me to trace the measures by which this great change has been consummated. If it did, it would not be difficult to show that the process commenced at an early period of the Government; and that it proceeded, almost without interruption, step by step, until it absorbed virtually its entire powers; but without going through the whole process to establish the fact, it may be done satisfactorily by a very short statement.

That the Government claims, and practically maintains the right to decide in the last resort, as to the extent of its powers, will scarcely be denied by any one conversant with the political history of the country. That it also claims the right to resort to force to maintain whatever power it claims, against all opposition, is equally certain. Indeed it is apparent, from what we daily hear, that this has become the prevailing and fixed opinion of a great majority of the community. Now, I ask, what limitation can possibly be placed upon the powers of a government claiming and exercising such rights? And, if none can be, how can the separate governments of the States maintain and protect the powers reserved to them by the constitution—or the people of the several States maintain those which are reserved to them, and among others, the sovereign powers by which they ordained and established, not only their separate State Constitutions and Governments, but also the Constitution and Government of the United States? But, if they have no constitutional means of maintaining them against the right claimed by this Government, it necessarily follows, that they hold them at its pleasure and discretion, and that all the powers of the system are in reality concentrated in it. It also follows, that the character of the Government has been changed in consequence, from a federal republic, as it originally came from the hands of its framers, into a great national consolidated democracy. It has indeed, at present, all the characteristics of the latter, and not one of the former, although it still retains its outward form.

The result of the whole of these causes combined is—that the North has acquired a decided ascendency over every department of this Government, and through it a control over all the powers of the system. A single section governed by the will of the numerical majority, has now, in fact, the control of the Government and the entire powers of the system. What was once a constitutional federal republic, is now converted, in reality, into one as absolute as that of the Autocrat of Russia, and as despotic in its tendency as any absolute government that ever existed.

As, then, the North has the absolute control over the Government, it is manifest, that on all questions between it and the South, where there is a diversity of interests, the interest of the latter will be sacrificed to the former, however oppressive the effects may be; as the South possesses no means by which it can resist, through the action of the Government. But if there was no question of vital importance to the South, in reference to which there was a diversity of views between the two sections, this state of things might be endured, without the hazard of destruction to the South. But such is not the fact. There is a question of vital importance to the Southern section, in reference to which the views and feelings of the two sections are as opposite and hostile as they can possibly be.

I refer to the relation between the two races in the Southern section, which constitutes a vital portion of her social organization. Every portion of the North entertains views and feelings more or less hostile to it. Those most opposed and hostile, regard it as a sin, and consider themselves under the most sacred obligation to use every effort to destroy it. Indeed, to the extent that they conceive that they have power, they regard themselves as implicated in the sin, and responsible for not suppressing it by the use of all and every means. Those less opposed and hostile, regard it as a crime—an offence against humanity, as they call it; and although not so fanatical, feel themselves bound to use all efforts to effect the same object; while

those who are least opposed and hostile, regard it as a blot and a stain on the character of what they call the Nation, and feel themselves accordingly bound to give it no countenance or support. On the contrary, the Southern section regards the relation as one which cannot be destroyed without subjecting the two races to the greatest calamity, and the section to poverty, desolation, and wretchedness; and accordingly they feel bound, by every consideration of interest and safety, to defend it.

This hostile feeling on the part of the North towards the social organization of the South long lay dormant, but it only required some cause to act on those who felt most intensely that they were responsible for its continuance, to call it into action. The increasing power of this Government, and of the control of the Northern section over all its departments, furnished the cause. It was this which made an impression on the minds of many, that there was little or no restraint to prevent the Government from doing whatever it might choose to do. This was sufficient of itself to put the most fanatical portion of the North in action, for the purpose of destroying the existing relation between the two races in the South.

The first organized movement towards it commenced in 1835. Then, for the first time, societies were organized, presses established, lecturers sent forth to excite the people of the North, and incendiary publications scattered over the whole South, through the mail. The South was thoroughly aroused. Meetings were held everywhere, and resolutions adopted, calling upon the North to apply a remedy to arrest the threatened evil, and pledging themselves to adopt measures for their own protection, if it was not arrested. At the meeting of Congress, petitions poured in from the North, calling upon Congress to abolish slavery in the District of Columbia, and to prohibit, what they called, the internal slave trade between the States—announcing at the same time, that their ultimate object was to abolish slavery, not only in the District, but in the States and throughout the Union. At this period, the number engaged in the agitation was small, and possessed little or no personal influence.

Neither party in Congress had, at that time, any sympathy with them or their cause. The members of each party presented their petitions with great reluctance. Nevertheless, small and contemptible as the party then was, both of the great parties of the North dreaded them.

They felt, that though small, they were organized in reference to a subject which had a great and a commanding influence over the Northern mind. Each party, on that account, feared to oppose their petitions, lest the opposite party should take advantage of the one who might do so, by favoring them. The effect was, that both united in insisting that the petitions should be received, and that Congress should take jurisdiction over the subject. To justify their course, they took the extraordinary ground, that Congress was bound to receive petitions on every subject, however objectionable they might be, and whether they had, or had not, jurisdiction over the subject. These views prevailed in the House of Representatives, and partially in the Senate; and thus the party succeeded in their first movements, in gaining what they proposed—a position in Congress from which agitation could be extended over the whole Union. This was the commencement of the agitation, which has ever since continued, and which, as is now acknowledged, has endangered the Union itself.

As for myself, I believe at that early period, if the party who got up the petitions should succeed in getting Congress to take jurisdiction, that agitation would follow, and that it would in the end, if not arrested, destroy the Union. I then so expressed myself in debate, and called upon both parties to take grounds against assuming jurisdiction; but in vain. Had my voice been heeded, and had Congress refused to take jurisdiction, by the united votes of all parties, the agitation which followed would have been prevented, and the fanatical zeal that gives impulse to the agitation, and which has brought us to our present perilous condition, would have become extinguished, from the want of fuel to feed the flame. *That* was the time for the North to have shown her devotion to the Union; but, unfortunately, both of the great parties of that section were so intent on obtaining or retaining party ascendency, that all other considerations were overlooked or forgotten.

What has since followed are but natural consequences. With the success of their first movement, this small fanatical party began to acquire strength; and with that, to become an object of courtship to both the great parties. The necessary consequence was, a further increase of power, and a gradual tainting of the opinions of both of the other parties with their doctrines, until the infection has extended over both; and the great mass of the population of the North,

who, whatever may be their opinion of the original abolition party, which still preserves its distinctive organization, hardly ever fail, when it comes to acting, to co-operate in carrying out their measures. With the increase of their influence, they extended the sphere of their action. In a short time after the commencement of their first movement, they had acquired sufficient influence to induce the legislatures of most of the Northern States to pass acts, which in effect abrogated the clause of the constitution that provides for the delivery up of fugitive slaves. Not long after, petitions followed to abolish slavery in forts, magazines, and dockyards, and all other places where Congress had exclusive power of legislation. This was followed by petitions and resolutions of legislatures of the Northern States, and popular meetings, to exclude the Southern States from all territories acquired, or to be acquired, and to prevent the admission of any State hereafter into the Union, which, by its constitution, does not prohibit slavery. And Congress is invoked to do all this, expressly with the view to the final abolition of slavery in the States. That has been avowed to be the ultimate object from the beginning of the agitation until the present time; and yet the great body of both parties of the North, with the full knowledge of the fact, although disavowing the abolitionists, have co-operated with them in almost all their measures.

Such is a brief history of the agitation, as far as it has yet advanced. Now I ask, Senators, what is there to prevent its further progress, until it fulfils the ultimate end proposed, unless some decisive measure should be adopted to prevent it? Has any one of the causes, which has added to its increase from its original small and contemptible beginning until it has attained its present magnitude, diminished in force? Is the original cause of the movement—that slavery is a sin, and ought to be suppressed—weaker now than at the commencement? Or is the abolition party less numerous or influential, or have they less influence with, or control over the two great parties of the North in elections? Or has the South greater means of influencing or controlling the movements of this Government now, than it had when the agitation commenced? To all these questions but one answer can be given: No—no—no. The very reverse is true. Instead of being weaker, all the elements in favor of agitation are stronger now than they were in 1835, when it first commenced, while all the elements of influence on the part of the South are weaker. Unless something decisive is done, I again ask, what is to stop this agitation, before the great and final object at which it aims—the abolition of slavery in the States—is consummated? Is it, then, not certain, that if something is not done to arrest it, the South will be forced to choose between abolition and secession? Indeed, as events are now moving, it will not require the South to secede, in order to dissolve the Union. Agitation will of itself effect it, of which its past history furnishes abundant proof—as I shall next proceed to show.

It is a great mistake to suppose that disunion can be effected by a single blow. The cords which bound these States together in one common Union, are far too numerous and powerful for that. Disunion must be the work of time. It is only through a long process, and successively, that the cords can be snapped, until the whole fabric falls asunder. Already the agitation of the slavery question has snapped some of the most important, and has greatly weakened all the others, as I shall proceed to show.

The cords that bind the States together are not only many, but various in character. Some are spiritual or ecclesiastical; some political; others social. Some appertain to the benefit conferred by the Union, and others to the feeling of duty and obligation.

The strongest of those of a spiritual and ecclesiastical nature, consisted in the unity of the great religious denominations, all of which originally embraced the whole Union. All these denominations, with the exception, perhaps, of the Catholics, were organized very much upon the principle of our political institutions. Beginning with smaller meetings, corresponding with the political divisions of the country, their organization terminated in one great central assemblage, corresponding very much with the character of Congress. At these meetings the principal clergymen and lay members of the respective denominations, from all parts of the Union, met to transact business relating to their common concerns. It was not confined to what appertained to the doctrines and discipline of the respective denominations, but extended to plans for disseminating the Bible—establishing missions, distributing tracts—and of establishing presses for the publication of tracts, newspapers, and periodicals, with a view of diffusing religious information—and for the support of their respective doctrines and creeds. All this combined contributed greatly to strengthen the bonds of the Union. The ties which held each denomination together formed a strong cord to hold the whole Union together; but, powerful as they were, they have not been able to resist the explosive effect of slavery agitation.

The first of these cords which snapped, under its explosive force, was that of the powerful Methodist Episcopal Church. The numerous and strong ties which held it together, are all broken, and its unity gone. They now form separate churches; and, instead of that feeling of attachment and devotion to the interests of the whole church which was formerly felt, they are now arrayed into two hostile bodies, engaged in litigation about what was formerly their common property.

The next cord that snapped was that of the Baptists—one of the largest and most respectable of the denominations. That of the Presbyterian is not entirely snapped, but some of its strands have given way. That of the Episcopal Church is the only one of the four great Protestant denominations which remains unbroken and entire.

The strongest cord, of a political character, consists of the many and powerful ties that have held together the two great parties which have, with some modifications, existed from the beginning of the Government. They both extended to every portion of the Union, and strongly contributed to hold all its parts together. But this powerful cord has fared no better than the spiritual. It resisted, for a long time, the explosive tendency of the agitation, but has finally snapped under its force—if not entirely, in a great measure. Nor is there one of the remaining cords which has not been greatly weakened. To this extent the Union has already been destroyed by agitation, in the only way it can be, by sundering and weakening the cords which bind it together.

If the agitation goes on, the same force, acting with increased intensity, as has been shown, will finally snap every cord, when nothing will be left to hold the States together except force. But, surely, that can, with no propriety of language, be called a Union, when the only means by which the weaker is held connected with the stronger portion is *force*. It may, indeed, keep them connected; but the connection will partake much more of the character of subjugation, on the part of the weaker to the stronger, than the union of free, independent, and sovereign States, in one confederation, as they stood in the early stages of the Government, and which only is worthy of the sacred name of Union.

Having now, Senators, explained what it is that endangers the Union, and traced it to its cause, and explained its nature and character, the question again recurs—How can the Union be saved? To this I answer, there is but one way by which it can be—and that is—by adopting such measures as will satisfy the States belonging to the Southern section, that they can remain in the Union consistently with their honor and their safety. There is, again, only one way by which this can be effected, and that is—by removing the causes by which this belief has been produced. *Do this,* and discontent will cease—harmony and kind feelings between the sections be restored—and every apprehension of danger to the Union removed. The question, then, is—How can this be done? But, before I undertake to answer this question, I propose to show by what the Union cannot be saved.

It cannot, then, be saved by eulogies on the Union, however splendid or numerous. The cry of "Union, Union—the glorious Union!" can no more prevent disunion than the cry of "Health, health—glorious health!" on the part of the physician, can save a patient lying dangerously ill. So long as the Union, instead of being regarded as a protector, is regarded in the opposite character, by not much less than a majority of the States, it will be in vain to attempt to conciliate them by pronouncing eulogies on it.

Besides this cry of Union comes commonly from those whom we cannot believe to be sincere. It usually comes from our assailants. But we cannot believe them to be sincere; for, if they loved the Union, they would necessarily be devoted to the constitution. It made the Union,—and to destroy the constitution would be to destroy the Union. But the only reliable and certain evidence of devotion to the constitution is, to abstain, on the one hand, from violating it, and to repel, on the other, all attempts to violate it. It is only by faithfully performing these high duties that the constitution can be preserved, and with it the Union.

But how stands the profession of devotion to the Union by our assailants, when brought to this test? Have they abstained from violating the constitution? Let the many acts passed by the Northern States to set aside and annul the clause of the constitution providing for the delivery up of fugitive slaves answer. I cite this, not that it is the only instance (for there are many others), but because the violation in this particular is too notorious and palpable to be denied. Again: have they stood forth faithfully to repel violations of the constitution? Let their course in reference to the agitation of the slavery question, which was commenced and has been carried on for fifteen years, avowedly for the purpose of abolishing slavery in the States —an object all acknowledged to be unconstitutional—answer. Let them show a single instance, during this long period, in which they have denounced the agitators or their attempts to effect what is admitted to be unconstitutional, or a single measure which they have brought forward for that purpose. How can we, with all these facts before us, believe that they are sincere in their profession of devotion to the Union, or avoid believing their profession is but intended to increase the vigor of their assaults and to weaken the force of our resistance?

Nor can we regard the profession of devotion to the Union, on the part of those who are not our assailants, as sincere, when they pronounce eulogies upon the Union, evidently with the intent of charging us with disunion, without uttering one word of denunciation against our assailants. If friends of the Union, their course should be to unite with us in repelling these assaults, and denouncing the authors as enemies of the Union. Why they avoid this, and pursue the course they do, it is for them to explain.

Nor can the Union be saved by invoking the name of the illustrious Southerner whose mortal remains repose on the western bank of the Potomac. He was one of us—a slaveholder and a planter. We have studied his history, and find nothing in it to justify submission to wrong. On the contrary, his great fame rests on the solid foundation, that, while he was careful to avoid doing wrong to others, he was prompt and decided in repelling wrong. I trust that, in this respect, we profited by his example.

Nor can we find any thing in his history to deter us from seceding from the Union, should it fail to fulfil the objects for which it was instituted, by being permanently and hopelessly converted into the means of oppressing instead of protecting us. On the contrary, we find much in his example to encourage us, should we be forced to the extremity of deciding between submission and disunion.

There existed then, as well as now, a union

—that between the parent country and her then colonies. It was a union that had much to endear it to the people of the colonies. Under its protecting and superintending care, the colonies were planted and grew up and prospered, through a long course of years, until they became populous and wealthy. Its benefits were not limited to them. Their extensive agricultural and other productions, gave birth to a flourishing commerce, which richly rewarded the parent country for the trouble and expense of establishing and protecting them. Washington was born and grew up to manhood under that union. He acquired his early distinction in its service, and there is every reason to believe that he was devotedly attached to it. But his devotion was a rational one. He was attached to it, not as an end, but as a means to an end. When it failed to fulfil its end, and, instead of affording protection, was converted into the means of oppressing the colonies, he did not hesitate to draw his sword, and head the great movement by which that union was for ever severed, and the independence of these States established. This was the great and crowning glory of his life, which has spread his fame over the whole globe, and will transmit it to the latest posterity.

Nor can the plan proposed by the distinguished Senator from Kentucky, nor that of the administration save the Union. I shall pass by, without remark, the plan proposed by the Senator, and proceed directly to the consideration of that of the administration. I however assure the distinguished and able Senator, that, in taking this course, no disrespect whatever is intended to him or his plan. I have adopted it, because so many Senators of distinguished abilities, who were present when he delivered his speech, and explained his plan, and who were fully capable to do justice to the side they support, have replied to him.

The plan of the administration cannot save the Union, because it can have no effect whatever, towards satisfying the States composing the Southern section of the Union, that they can, consistently with safety and honor, remain in the Union. It is, in fact, but a modification of the Wilmot Proviso. It proposes to effect the same object,—to exclude the South from all territory acquired by the Mexican treaty. It is well known that the South is united against the Wilmot Proviso, and has committed itself by solemn resolutions, to resist, should it be adopted. Its opposition *is not to the name,* but that which it *proposes to effect.* That, the Southern States hold to be unconstitutional, unjust, inconsistent with their equality as members of the common Union, and calculated to destroy irretrievably the equilibrium between the two sections. These objections equally apply to what, for brevity, I will call the Executive Proviso. There is no difference between it and the Wilmot, except in the mode of effecting the object; and in that respect, I must say, that the latter is much the least objectionable. It goes to its object openly, boldly, and distinctly. It claims for Congress unlimited power over the territories and proposes to assert it over the territories, acquired from Mexico, by a positive prohibition of slavery. Not so the Executive Proviso. It takes an indirect course, and in order to elude the Wilmot Proviso, and thereby avoid encountering the united and determined resistance of the South, it denies, by implication, the authority of Congress to legislate for the territories, and claims the right as belonging exclusively to the inhabitants of the territories. But to effect the object of excluding the South, it takes care, in the mean time, to let in emigrants freely from the Northern States and all other quarters, except from the South, which it takes special care to exclude by holding up to them the danger of having their slaves liberated under the Mexican laws. The necessary consequence is to exclude the South from the territory, just as effectually as would the Wilmot Proviso. The only difference in this respect is, that what one proposes to effect directly and openly, the other proposes to effect indirectly and covertly.

But the Executive Proviso is more objectionable that the Wilmot, in another and more important particular. The latter, to effect its object, inflicts a dangerous wound upon the constitution, by depriving the Southern States, as joint partners and owners of the territories, of their rights in them; but it inflicts no greater wound than is absolutely necessary to effect its object. The former, on the contrary, while it inflicts the same wound, inflicts others equally great, and, if possible, greater, as I shall next proceed to explain.

In claiming the right for the inhabitants, instead of Congress, to legislate for the territories, the Executive Proviso assumes that the sovereignty over the territories is vested in the former: or to express it in the language used in a resolution offered by one of the Senators from Texas (General Houston, now absent), they have "the same inherent right of self-government as the people in the States." The assumption is utterly unfounded, unconstitutional, without example, and contrary to the entire practice of the Government, from its commencement to the present time. . . .

Having now shown what cannot save the Union, I return to the question with which I commenced, How can the Union be saved? There is but one way by which it can with any certainty; and that is, by a full and final settlement, on the principle of justice, of all the questions at issue between the two sections. The South asks for justice, simple justice, and less she ought not to take. She has no compromise to offer, but the constitution; and no concession or surrender to make. She has already surrendered so much that she has little left to surrender. Such a settlement would go to the root of the evil, and remove all cause of discontent, by satisfying the South, that she could remain honorably and safely in the Union, and thereby restore the harmony and fraternal feelings between the sections, which existed anterior to the Missouri agitation. Nothing else can, with any certainty, finally and for ever settle the questions at issue, terminate agitation, and save the Union.

But can this be done? Yes, easily; not by the weaker party, for it can of itself do nothing—not even protect itself—but by the stronger. The North has only to will it to accomplish it—to do justice by conceding to the South an equal right in the acquired territory, and to do her duty by causing the stipulations relative to fugitive slaves to be faithfully fulfilled—to cease the agitation of the slave question, and to provide for the insertion of a provision in the constitution, by an amendment, which will restore to the South, in substance, the power she possessed of protecting herself, before the equilibrium between the sections was destroyed by the action of this Government. There will be no difficulty in devising such a provision—one that will protect the South, and which, at the same time, will improve and strengthen the Government, instead of impairing and weakening it.

But will the North agree to this? It is for her to answer the question. But, I will say, she cannot refuse, if she has half the love of the Union which she professes to have, or without justly exposing herself to the charge that her love of power and aggrandizement is far greater than her love of the Union. At all events, the responsibility of saving the Union rests on the North, and not on the South. The South cannot save it by any act of hers, and the North may save it without any sacrifice whatever, unless to do justice, and to perform her duties under the constitution, should be regarded by her as a sacrifice.

It is time, Senators, that there should be an open and manly avowal on all sides, as to what is intended to be done. If the question is not now settled, it is uncertain whether it ever can hereafter be; and we, as the representatives of the States of this Union, regarded as governments, should come to a distinct understanding as to our respective views, in order to ascertain whether the great questions at issue can be settled or not. If you, who represent the stronger portion, cannot agree to settle them on the broad principle of justice and duty, say so; and let the States we both represent agree to separate and part in peace. If you are unwilling we should part in peace, tell us so; and we shall know what to do, when you reduce the question to submission or resistance. If you remain silent, you will compel us to infer by your acts what you intend. In that case, California will become the test question. If you admit her, under all the difficulties that oppose her admission, you compel us to infer that you intend to exclude us from the whole of the acquired territories, with the intention of destroying, irretrievably, the equilibrium between the two sections. We would be blind not to perceive in that case, that your real objects are power and aggrandizement, and infatuated not to act accordingly.

I have now, Senators, done my duty in expressing my opinions fully, freely, and candidly, on this solemn occasion. In doing so, I have been governed by the motives which have governed me in all the stages of the agitation of the slavery question since its commencement. I have exerted myself, during the whole period, to arrest it, with the intention of saving the Union, if it could be done; and if it could not, to save the section where it has pleased Providence to cast my lot, and which I sincerely believe has justice and the constitution on its side. Having faithfully done my duty to the best of my ability, both to the Union and my section, throughout this agitation, I shall have the consolation, let what will come, that I am free from all responsibility.   1850

GEORGE FITZHUGH

1806–1881

AFTER A MEETING with Harriet Beecher Stowe about 1856, George Fitzhugh, a Virginia lawyer, became an even more militant defender of slavery than he had hitherto been. A contributor to various Virginia newspapers and to *De Bow's Review*, Fitzhugh published in 1854 his *Sociology for the South; or, the Failure of a Free Society*, and, three years later, *Cannibals All! or, Slaves without Masters*. Fitzhugh's contribution to the Southern defense of slavery was the emphasis he put on the positive benefits of the system, which many apologists had upheld only negatively by refuting indictments levelled against it. His writings gave him an important place in the history of American sociology. Fitzhugh's criticisms of the capitalistic exploitation of industrial workers in the North and his denunciation of social reform, and expecially of socialism, were an integral part of his defense of the patronal economy of the plantation South.

W. S. Jenkins, *Pro-Slavery Thought in the Old South*, Chapel Hill, N. C., 1935.
Harvey Wish, *George Fitzhugh, Propagandist of the Old South*, Baton Rouge, 1943.

» » *From:* SOCIOLOGY FOR THE SOUTH « «

CHAPTER IV

THE TWO PHILOSOPHIES

In the three preceding chapters we have shewn that the world is divided between two philosophies. The one the philosophy of free trade and universal liberty—the philosophy adapted to promote the interests of the strong, the wealthy and the wise. The other, that of socialism, intended to protect the weak, the poor and the ignorant. The latter is almost universal in free society; the former prevails in the slaveholding States of the South. Thus we see each section cherishing theories at war with existing institutions. The people of the North and of Europe are pro-slavery men in the abstract; those of the South are theoretical abolitionists. This state of opinions is readily accounted for. The people in free society feel the evils of universal liberty and free competition, and desire to get rid of those evils. They propose a remedy, which is in fact slavery; but they are wholly unconscious of what they are doing, because never having lived in the midst of slavery, they know not what slavery is. The citizens of the South, who have seen none of

the evils of liberty and competition, but just enough of those agencies to operate as healthful stimulants to energy, enterprise and industry, believe free competition to be an unmixed good.

The South, quiet, contented, satisfied, looks upon all socialists and radical reformers as madmen or knaves. It is as ignorant of free society as that society is of slavery. Each section sees one side of the subject alone; each, therefore, takes partial and erroneous views of it. Social science will never take a step in advance till some Southern slaveholder, competent for the task, devotes a lifetime to its study and elucidation; for slavery can only be understood by living in its midst, whilst thousands of books daily exhibit the minutest workings of free society. The knowledge of the numerous theories of radical reform proposed in Europe, and the causes that have led to their promulgation, is of vital importance to us. Yet we turn away from them with disgust, as from something unclean and vicious. We occupy high vantage ground for observing, studying and classifying the various phenomena of society; yet we do not profit by the advantages of our position. We should do so, and indignantly hurl back upon our assailants the charge, that there is something wrong and rotten in our system. From their own mouths we can show free society to be a monstrous abortion, and slavery to be the healthy, beautiful and natural being which they are trying, unconsciously, to adopt.

CHAPTER V

NEGRO SLAVERY

13   We have already stated that we should not attempt to introduce any new theories of government and of society, but merely try to justify old ones, so far as we could deduce such theories from ancient and almost universal practices. Now it has been the practice in all countries and in all ages, in some degree, to
20 accommodate the amount and character of government control to the wants, intelligence, and moral capacities of the nations or individuals to be governed. A highly moral and intellectual people, like the free citizens of ancient Athens, are best governed by a democracy. For a less moral and intellectual one, a limited and constitutional monarchy will answer. For a people either very ignorant or very wicked, nothing short of military despotism
30 will suffice. So among individuals, the most moral and well-informed members of society require no other government than law. They are capable of reading and understanding the law, and have sufficient self-control and virtuous disposition to obey it. Children cannot be governed by mere law; first, because they do not understand it, and secondly, because they are so much under the influence of impulse, passion and appetite, that they want sufficient
40 self-control to be deterred or governed by the distant and doubtful penalties of the law. They must be constantly controlled by parents or guardians, whose will and orders shall stand in the place of law for them. Very wicked men must be put into penitentiaries; lunatics into asylums, and the most wild of them into straight jackets, just as the most wicked of the sane are manacled with irons; and idiots must have committees to govern and take care of
50 them. Now, it is clear the Athenian democracy would not suit a negro nation, nor will the government of mere law suffice for the individual negro. He is but a grown up child, and must be governed as a child, not as a lunatic or criminal. The master occupies towards him the

place of parent or guardian. We shall not dwell on this view, for no one will differ with us who thinks as we do of the negro's capacity, and we might argue till dooms-day, in vain, with those who have a high opinion of the negro's moral and intellectual capacity.

Secondly. The negro is improvident; will not lay up in summer for the wants of winter; will not accumulate in youth for the exigencies of age. He would become an insufferable burden to society. Society has the right to prevent this, and can only do so by subjecting him to domestic slavery.

In the last place, the negro race is inferior to the white race, and living in their midst, they would be far outstripped or outwitted in the chase of free competition. Gradual but certain extermination would be their fate. We presume the maddest abolitionist does not think the negro's providence of habits and money-making capacity at all to compare to those of the whites. This defect of character would alone justify enslaving him, if he is to remain here. In Africa or the West Indies, he would become idolatrous, savage and cannibal, or be devoured by savages and cannibals. At the North he would freeze or starve.

We would remind those who deprecate and sympathize with negro slavery, that his slavery here relieves him from a far more cruel slavery in Africa, or from idolatry and cannibalism, and every brutal vice and crime that can disgrace humanity; and that it christianizes, protects, supports and civilizes him; that it governs him far better than free laborers at the North are governed. There, wife-murder has become a mere holiday pastime; and where so many wives are murdered, almost all must be brutally treated. Nay, more: men who kill their wives or treat them brutally, must be ready for all kinds of crime, and the calendar of crime at the North proves the inference to be correct. Negroes never kill their wives. If it be objected that legally they have no wives, then we reply, that in an experience of more than forty years, we never yet heard of a negro man killing a negro woman. Our negroes are not only better off as to physical comfort than free laborers, but their moral condition is better.

But abolish negro slavery, and how much of slavery still remains. Soldiers and sailors in Europe enlist for life; here, for five years. Are they not slaves who have not only sold their liberties, but their lives also? And they are worse treated than domestic slaves. No domestic affection and self-interest extend their aegis over them. No kind mistress, like a guardian angel, provides for them in health, tends them in sickness, and soothes their dying pillow. Wellington at Waterloo was a slave. He was bound to obey, or would, like Admiral Bying, have been shot for gross misconduct, and might not, like a common laborer, quit his work at any moment. He had sold his liberty, and might not resign without the consent of his master, the king. The common laborer may quit his work at any moment, whatever his contract; declare that liberty is an inalienable right, and leave his employer to redress by a useless suit for damages. The highest and most honorable position on earth was that of the slave Wellington; the lowest, that of the free man who cleaned his boots and fed his hounds. The African cannibal, caught, christianized and enslaved, is as much elevated by slavery as was Wellington. The kind of slavery is adapted to the men enslaved. Wives and apprentices are slaves; not in theory only, but often in fact. Children are slaves to their parents, guardians and teachers. Imprisoned culprits are slaves. Lunatics and idiots are slaves also. Three-fourths of free society are slaves, no better treated, when their wants and capacities are estimated, than negro slaves. The masters in free society, or slave society, if they perform properly their duties, have more cares and less liberty than the slaves themselves. "In the sweat of thy face shalt thou earn thy bread!" made all men slaves, and such all *good men* continue to be.

Negro slavery would be changed immediately to some form of peonage, serfdom or villeinage, if the negroes were sufficiently intelligent and provident to manage a farm. No one would have the labor and trouble of management, if his negroes would pay in hires and rents one-half what free tenants pay in rent in Europe. Every negro in the South would be soon liberated, if he would take liberty on the terms that white tenants hold it. The fact that he cannot enjoy liberty on such terms, seems conclusive that he is only fit to be a slave.

But for the assaults of the abolitionists, much would have been done ere this to regulate and improve Southern slavery. Our negro mechanics do not work so hard, have many more privileges and holidays, and are better fed and clothed than field hands, and are yet more valuable to their masters. The slaves of the South are cheated of their rights by the purchase of Northern manufactures which they

could produce. Besides, if we would employ our slaves in the coarser processes of the mechanic arts and manufactures, such as brick making, getting and hewing timber for ships and houses, iron mining and smelting, coal mining, grading railroads and plank roads, in the manufacture of cotton, tobacco, &c., we would find a vent in new employments for their increase, more humane and more profitable than the vent afforded by new states and territories. The nice and finishing processes of manufactures and mechanics should be reserved for the whites, who only are fitted for them, and thus, by diversifying pursuits and cutting off dependence on the North, we might benefit and advance the interests of our whole population. Exclusive agriculture has depressed and impoverished the South. We will not here dilate on this topic, because we intend to make it the subject of a separate essay. Free trade doctrines, not slavery, have made the South agricultural and dependent, given her a sparse and ignorant population, ruined her cities, and expelled her people.

Would the abolitionists approve of a system of society that set white children free, and remitted them at the age of fourteen, males and females, to all the rights, both as to person and property, which belong to adults? Would it be criminal or praiseworthy to do so? Criminal, of course. Now, are the average of negroes equal in information, in native intelligence, in prudence or providence, to well-informed white children of fourteen? We who have lived with them for forty years, think not. The competition of the world would be too much for the children. They would be cheated out of their property and debased in their morals. Yet they would meet every where with sympathizing friends of their own color, ready to aid, advise and assist them. The negro would be exposed to the same competition and greater temptations, with no greater ability to contend with them, with these additional difficulties. He would be welcome nowhere; meet with thousands of enemies and no friends. If he went North, the white laborers would kick him and cuff him, and drive him out of employment. If he went to Africa, the savages would cook him and eat him. If he went to the West Indies, they would not let him in, or if they did, they would soon make of him a savage and idolater.

We have a further question to ask. If it be right and incumbent to subject children to the authority of parents and guardians, and idiots

and lunatics to committees, would it not be
equally right and incumbent to give the free
negroes masters, until at least they arrive at
years of discretion, which very few ever did
or will attain? What is the difference between
the authority of a parent and of a master?
Neither pay wages, and each is entitled to the
services of those subject to him. The father may
not sell his child forever, but may hire him out
10 till he is twenty-one. The free negro's master
may also be restrained from selling. Let him
stand in *loco parentis,* and call him papa instead of master. Look closely into slavery, and
you will see nothing so hideous in it; or if you
do, you will find plenty of it at home in its
most hideous form.

The earliest civilization of which history
gives account is that of Egypt. The negro was
always in contact with that civilization. For
20 four thousand years he has had opportunities
of becoming civilized. Like the wild horse, he
must be caught, tamed and domesticated.
When his subjugation ceases he again runs
wild, like the cattle on the Pampas of the
South, or the horses on the prairies of the
West. His condition in the West Indies proves
this.

It is a common remark, that the grand and
lasting architectural structures of antiquity
30 were the results of slavery. The mighty and
continued association of labor requisite to their
construction, when mechanic art was so little
advanced, and labor-saving processes unknown,
could only have been brought about by a despotic authority, like that of the master over his
slaves. It is, however, very remarkable, that
whilst in taste and artistic skill the world seems
to have been retrograding ever since the decay
and abolition of feudalism, in mechanical in-
40 vention and in great utilitarian operations requiring the wielding of immense capital and
much labor, its progress has been unexampled.
Is it because capital is more despotic in its
authority over free laborers than Roman masters and feudal lords were over their slaves and
vassals?

Free society has continued long enough to
justify the attempt to generalize its phenomena,
and calculate its moral and intellectual in-
50 fluences. It is obvious that, in whatever is
purely utilitarian and material, it incites invention and stimulates industry. Benjamin Franklin, as a man and a philosopher, is the best exponent of the working of the system. His sentiments and his philosophy are low, selfish, athe-

istic and material. They tend directly to make
man a mere "featherless biped," well-fed, well-
clothed and comfortable, but regardless of his
soul as "the beasts that perish."

Since the Reformation the world has as
regularly been retrograding in whatever belongs to the departments of genius, taste and
art, as it has been progressing in physical
science and its application to mechanical construction. Mediaeval Italy rivalled if it did not
surpass ancient Rome, in poetry, in sculpture,
in painting, and many of the fine arts. Gothic
architecture reared its monuments of skill and
genius throughout Europe, till the 15th century; but Gothic architecture died with the
Reformation. The age of Elizabeth was the
Augustan age of England. The men who lived
then acquired their sentiments in a world not
yet deadened and vulgarized by puritanical
cant and levelling demagoguism. Since then
men have arisen who have been the fashion
and the go for a season, but none have appeared whose names will descend to posterity.
Liberty and equality made slower advances in
France. The age of Louis XIV. was the culminating point of French genius and art. It then
shed but a flickering and lurid light. Frenchmen are servile copyists of Roman art, and
Rome had no art of her own. She borrowed
from Greece; distorted and deteriorated what
she borrowed; and France imitates and falls
below Roman distortions. The genius of Spain
disappeared with Cervantes; and now the
world seems to regard nothing as desirable except what will make money and what costs
money. There is not a poet, an orator, a
sculptor, or painter in the world. The tedious
elaboration necessary to all the productions of
high art would be ridiculed in this money-
making, utilitarian, charlatan age. Nothing now
but what is gaudy and costly excites admiration. The public taste is debased.

But far the worst feature of modern civilization, which is the civilization of free society,
remains to be exposed. Whilst labor-saving
processes have probably lessened by one half,
in the last century, the amount of work needed
for comfortable support, the free laborer is
compelled by capital and competition to work
more than he ever did before, and is less comfortable. The organization of society cheats him
of his earnings, and those earnings go to swell
the vulgar pomp and pageantry of the ignorant
millionaires, who are the only great of the
present day. These reflections might seem, at

first view, to have little connexion with negro slavery; but it is well for us of the South not to be deceived by the tinsel glare and glitter of free society, and to employ ourselves in doing our duty at home, and studying the past, rather than in insidious rivalry of the expensive pleasures and pursuits of men whose sentiments and whose aims are low, sensual and grovelling.

Human progress, consisting in moral and intellectual improvement, and there being no agreed and conventional standard weights or measures of moral and intellectual qualities and quantities, the question of progress can never be accurately decided. We maintain that man has not improved, because in all save the mechanic arts he reverts to the distant past for models to imitate, and he never imitates what he can excel.

We need never have white slaves in the South, because we have black ones. Our citizens, like those of Rome and Athens, are a privileged class. We should train and educate them to deserve the privileges and to perform the duties which society confers on them. Instead, by a low demagoguism depressing their self-respect by discourses on the equality of man, we had better excite their pride by reminding them that they do not fulfil the menial offices which white men do in other countries. Society does not feel the burden of providing for the few helpless paupers in the South. And we should recollect that here we have but half the people to educate, for half are negroes; whilst at the North they profess to educate all. It is in our power to spike this last gun of the abolitionists. We should educate all the poor. The abolitionists say that it is one of the necessary consequences of slavery that the poor are neglected. It was not so in Athens, and in Rome, and should not be so in the South. If we had less trade with and less dependence on the North, all our poor might be profitably and honorably employed in trades, professions and manufactures. Then we should have a rich and denser population. Yet we but marshal her in the way that she was going. The South is already aware of the necessity of a new policy, and has begun to act on it. Every day more and more is done for education, the mechanic arts, manufactures and internal improvements. We will soon be independent of the North.

We deem this peculiar question of negro slavery of very little importance. The issue is made throughout the world on the general subject of slavery in the abstract. The argument has commenced. One set of ideas will govern and control after awhile the civilized world. Slavery will every where be abolished, or every where be re-instituted. We think the opponents of practical, existing slavery, are estopped by their own admission; nay, that unconsciously, as socialists, they are the defenders and propagandists of slavery, and have furnished the only sound arguments on which its defence and justification can be rested. We have introduced the subject of negro slavery to afford us a better opportunity to disclaim the purpose of reducing the white man any where to the condition of negro slaves here. It would be very unwise and unscientific to govern white men as you would negroes. Every shade and variety of slavery has existed in the world. In some cases there has been much of legal regulation, much restraint of the master's authority; in others, none at all. The character of slavery necessary to protect the whites in Europe should be much milder than negro slavery, for slavery is only needed to protect the white man, whilst it is more necessary for the government of the negro even than for his protection. But even negro slavery should not be outlawed. We might and should have laws in Virginia, as in Louisiana, to make the master subject to presentment by the grand jury and to punishment, for any inhuman or improper treatment or neglect of his slave.

We abhor the doctrine of the "Types of Mankind";[1] first, because it is at war with scripture, which teaches us that the whole human race is descended from a common parentage; and, secondly, because it encourages and incites brutal masters to treat negroes, not as weak, ignorant and dependent brethren, but as wicked beasts, without the pale of humanity. The Southerner is the negro's friend, his only friend. Let no inter-meddling abolitionist, no refined philosophy, dissolve this friendship.

1854

[1] The author of this much-discussed proslavery treatise on the origins of the human species was Dr. Josiah C. Nott (1804–1873), a physician of Mobile, Alabama.

WILLIAM J. GRAYSON

1788–1863

WILLIAM J. GRAYSON, a representative of South Carolina in Congress and for years the collector of customs at the port of Charleston, was a cultivated gentleman whose political sympathies were marked by moderation. The author of an heroic poem, *The Country*, and of a volume of romantic poems in praise of the primitive Indian, Grayson's best known work is *The Hireling and the Slave* (1854). In this long poem in heroic couplets he contrasted the vicissitudes of the wage-slave of England and the industrial North with the rural pleasures and security of the bond-slave in the South. The fact that in this poem he admitted certain evils in the slave system made this piece all the more effective propaganda for slavery.

Selected Poems by William J. Grayson, selected and compiled by Mrs. William H. Armstrong, New York and Washington, 1907.
V. L. Parrington, *The Romantic Revolution in America, 1800–1860*, New York, 1927, pp. 103–108.

» » *From:* THE HIRELING AND THE SLAVE « «

How small the choice, from cradle to the grave,
Between the lot of Hireling and of Slave!
To each alike applies the stern decree,
That man shall labour; whether bond or free,
For all that toil, the recompense we claim—
Food, fire, a home and clothing—is the same.
  The manumitted serfs of Europe find
Unchanged this sad estate of all mankind;
What blessing to the churls has freedom proved,
What want supplied, what task or toil removed?   10
Hard work and scanty wages still their lot,
In youth o'erlaboured, and in age forgot,
The mocking boon of freedom they deplore,
In wants, cares, labours never known before.
  Free but in name—the slaves of endless toil,
In Britain still they turn the stubborn soil,
Spread on each sea her sails for every mart,
Ply in her cities every useful art;
But vainly may the Peasant toil and groan,
To speed the plough in furrows not his own;
In vain the art is plied, the sail is spread, 21
The daily work secures no daily bread;
With hopeless eye, the pauper Hireling sees
The homeward sail swell proudly to the breeze,
Rich fabrics, wrought by his unequalled hand,
Borne by each breeze to every distant land;
Unbounded wealth, propitious seasons yield,

And bounteous harvests crown the smiling field;
The streams of wealth that foster pomp and pride,
No food nor shelter for his wants provide, 30
He fails to win, by toil intensely hard,
The bare subsistence—labour's least reward.
  In squalid hut—a kennel for the poor,
Or noisome cellar, stretched upon the floor,
His clothing rags, of filthy straw his bed,
With offal from the gutter daily fed,
Thrust out from Nature's board, the Hireling lies—
No place for him that common board supplies,
No neighbor helps, no charity attends,
No philanthropic sympathy befriends; 40
None heed the needy wretch's dying groan,
He starves unsuccor'd, perishes unknown.
  These are the miseries, such the wants, the cares,
The bliss that freedom for the serf prepares;
Vain in his skill in each familiar task,
Capricious Fashion shifts her Protean mask,
His ancient craft gives work and bread no more,
And want and death sit scowling at his door.
  Close by the hovel, with benignant air,
To lordly halls illustrious crowds repair— 50
The Levite tribes of Christian love that show
No care nor pity for a neighbor's woe;

Who meet, each distant evil to deplore,
But not to clothe or feed their country's poor;
They waste no thought on common wants or
    pains,
On misery hid in filthy courts and lanes,
On alms that ask no witnesses but Heaven,
By pious hands to secret suffering given;
Their's the bright sunshine of the public eye,
The pomp and circumstance of charity,   60
The crowded meeting, the repeated cheer,
The sweet applause of prelate, prince or peer,
The long report of pious trophies won
Beyond the rising or the setting sun,
The mutual smile, the self-complacent air,
The laboured speech and Pharisaic prayer,
Thanksgivings for their purer hearts and hands,
Scorn for the publicans of other lands,
And soft addresses—Sutherland's delight,
That gentle dames at pious parties write—   70
These are the cheats that vanity prepares,
The soft deceits of her seductive fairs,
When Exeter expands her portals wide,
And England's saintly coteries decide
The proper nostrum for each evil known
In every land on earth, except their own,
But never heed the sufferings, wants, or sins,
At home, where all true charity begins.
    There, unconcerned, the philanthropic eye
Beholds each phase of human misery;   80
Sees the worn child compelled in mines to
    slave
Through narrow seams of coal, a living grave,
Driven from the breezy hill, the sunny glade,
By ruthless hearts, the drudge of labour made,
Unknown the boyish sport, the hour of play,
Stript of the common boon, the light of day,
Harnessed like brutes, like brutes to tug and
    strain
And drag, on hands and knees, the loaded
    wain:
There crammed in huts, in reeking masses
    thrown,
All moral sense and decency unknown,   90
With no restraint, but what the felon knows,
With the sole joy, that beer or gin bestows,
To gross excess and brutalizing strife,
The drunken Hireling dedicates his life:
Three women prostitute themselves for bread,
Mothers rejoice to find their infants dead,
Childhood bestows no childish sports or toys,
Age, neither reverence nor repose enjoys,
Labour, with hunger, wages ceaseless strife,
And want and suffering only end with life;   100
In crowded huts, contagious ills assail,
Insidious typhus and its plagues prevail;

Gaunt famine prowls around his pauper prey,
And daily sweeps his ghastly hosts away;
Unburied corses taint the summer air,
And crime and outrage revel with despair.
    Or—from their humble homes and native
    land
Forced by a landlord's pitiless command,
Far, in ungenial climes, condemned to roam,
That sheep may batten in the peasant's home—
The pauper exiles, from the hill that yields 111
One parting look on their abandoned fields,
Behold with tears, no manhood can restrain,
Their ancient hamlet level'd with the plain:
They go, a squalid band, unhoused, unfed,
The sky their only roof, the ditch their bed,
In crowded ships, new miseries to find,
More hideous still than those they left behind;
Grim Chol'ra thins their ranks, ship fevers
    sweep
Their livid tythes of victims to the deep; 120
The sad survivors, on a foreign shore,
The double loss of homes and friends deplore,
And beg a stranger's bounty to supply
The food and shelter that their homes deny.
    Yet homebred misery, such as this, imparts
Nor grief, nor care, to philanthropic hearts;
The tear of sympathy forever flows,
Though not for Saxon or for Celtic woes;
The hireling white, without a pitying eye,
Or helping hand, at home may starve and
    die;   130
But that the distant black may softlier fare,
Eat, sleep and play, exempt from toil and care,
All England's meek philanthropists unite,
With frantic eagerness, harangue and write,
By purchased tools, diffuse distrust and hate,
Sow factions strife, in each dependent State,
    Cheat with delusive lies the public mind,
Invent the cruelties, they fail to find,
Slander, in pious garb, with prayer and hymn,
And blast a people's fortune for a whim.   140
    Cursed by these factious arts, that take the
    guise
Of charity, to cheat the good and wise,
The bright Antilles see, from year to year,
Their harvests fail, their fortunes disappear;
The cane no more its golden treasure yields;
Unsightly weeds deform the fertile fields;
The negro freeman—thrifty while a slave,
Becomes a helpless drone or crafty knave,
Each effort to improve his nature foils;
Begs, steals, or sleeps and starves, but never
    toils,   150
For savage sloth, mistakes the freedom won,
And ends, the mere barbarian he begun.

Taught by the Master's efforts, by his care,
Fed, clothed, protected, many a patient year,
From trivial numbers now to millions grown,
With all the white man's useful arts their own,
Industrious, docile, skilled in wood and field,
To guide the plough, the sturdy axe to wield,
The Negroes schooled by Slavery embrace
The highest portion of the Negro race;   160
And none the savage native will compare,
Of barbarous Guinea, with its offspring here.

If bound to daily labour while he lives,
His is the daily bread that labour gives;
Guarded from want, from beggary secure,
He never feels what Hireling crowds endure,
Nor knows, like them, in hopeless want to
        crave,
For wife and child, the comforts of the slave,
Or the sad thought that, when about to die,
He leaves them to the world's cold charity,   170
And sees them forced to seek the poor-house
        door—
The last, sad, hated refuge of the poor.

Still Europe's pious coteries sigh and groan
Note our defects, yet never see their own,
Grieve that the Slave is never taught to write,
And reads no better than the Hireling White;
Do their own ploughmen no instruction lack,
Have whiter clowns more knowledge than the
        Black?
Has the French peasant, or the German boor,
Of learning's treasure any larger store;   180
Have Ireland's millions, flying from the rule
Of those who censure, ever known a school?
A thousand years, and Europe's wealth impart
No means to mend the Hireling's head or
        heart;
They build no schools to teach the pauper
        White,
Their toiling millions neither read nor write;
Whence then the idle clamour when they rave
For schools and teachers for the distant Slave?

And why the soft regret, the coarse attack,
If Justice punish the offending Black?   190
Are Whites not punished?—When Utopian
        times
Shall drive from Earth all miseries and crimes,
And teach the World the art to do without
The cat, the gauntlet, and the brutal knout,
Banish the halter, galley, jails and chains,
And strip the law of penalties and pains;
Here too, offence and wrong they may prevent,
And Slaves, with Hirelings, need no punish-
        ment:
'Till then, what lash of Slavery will compare

With the dread scourge that British soldiers
        bear?   200
What gentle rule, in Britain's Isle, prevails,
How rare her use of gibbets, stocks and jails!
How much humaner, than a master's whip,
Her penal colony and convict ship!
Whose code of law can darker pages show,
Where blood for smaller misdemeanors flow?
The trifling theft or trespass that demands,
For slaves, light penance from a master's
        hands,
Where Europe's milder punishments are known,
Incur the penalty of death alone.   210

And yet the Master's lighter rule ensures
More order than the sternest code secures;
No mobs of factious workmen gather here,
No strikes we dread, no lawless riots fear;
Nuns, from their convent driven, at midnight
        fly,
Churches, in flames, ask vengeance from the
        sky,
Seditious schemes in bloody tumults end,
Parsons incite, and Senators defend,
But not where Slaves their easy labours ply,
Safe from the snare, beneath a Master's eye;
In useful tasks engaged, employed their time,
Untempted by the demagogue to crime,   222
Secure they toil, uncursed their peaceful life,
With freedom's hungry broils and wasteful
        strife,
No want to goad, no faction to deplore,
The Slave escapes the perils of the poor.

. . .

And yet the life, so unassailed by care,
So blest with moderate work, with ample fare,
With all the good the pauper Hireling needs,
The happier Slave on each plantation leads;
Safe from harassing doubts and annual fears,
He dreads no famine, in unfruitful years;   232
If harvest fail from inauspicious skies,
The Master's providence his food supplies;
No paupers perish here for want of bread,
Or lingering live, by foreign bounty fed;
No exiled trains of homeless peasants go,
In distant climes, to tell their tales of woe;
Far other fortune, free from care and strife,
For work, or bread, attends the Negro's life,
And Christian Slaves may challenge as their
        own,   241
The blessings claimed in fabled states alone—
The cabin home, not comfortless, though rude,
Light daily labour, and abundant food,
The sturdy health, that temperate habits yield,
The cheerful song, that rings in every field,

The long, loud laugh, that freemen seldom
    share,
Heaven's boon to bosoms unapproached by
    care,
And boisterous jest and humour unrefined,
That leave, though rough, no painful sting be-
    hind;   250
While, nestling near, to bless their humble lot,
Warm social joys surround the Negro's cot,
The evening dance its merriment imparts,
Love, with his rapture, fills their youthful
    hearts,
And placid age, the task of labour done,
Enjoys the summer shade, the winter's sun,
And, as through life no pauper want he knows,
Laments no poorhouse penance at its close.
  His too the Christian privilege to share
The weekly festival of praise and prayer; 260
For him the Sabbath shines with holier light,

The air is balmier, and the sky more bright;
Winter's brief suns with warmer radiance glow,
With softer breath the gales of autumn blow,
Spring with new flowers more richly strews the
    ground,
And summer spreads a fresher verdure round;
The early shower is past; the joyous breeze
Shakes patt'ring rain drops from the rustling
    trees,
And with the sun, the fragrant offerings rise,
From Nature's censers to the bounteous skies;
With cheerful aspect, in his best array, 271
To the far forest church he takes his way;
With kind salute the passing neighbor meets,
With awkward grace the morning traveller
    greets,
And joined by crowds, that gather as he goes,
Seeks the calm joy the Sabbath morn bestows.
                1854

EDMUND RUFFIN

1794–1865

AFTER a brief residence at William and Mary College, Edmund Ruffin, on the farm inherited from his father, began experimentation for the improvement of the impoverished Virginia soil. Fertilizers, crop rotation, drainage, and good plowing were advocated in his *Essay on Calcareous Manures* (1832) and in numerous other writings, including farm journals. Through the agriculture societies which he promoted, through experimental farms, and through his agricultural surveys, as well as through his voluminous writings, Ruffin won leadership in the movement for agricultural reform.

A champion of slavery, of states rights, and of Southern nationalism, his *Anticipations of the Future* (1860) preached the inevitability and desirability of secession and independence. Ruffin's part in the struggle for an independent South was dramatic. As a volunteer in the Palmetto Guard he fired the first shot against Fort Sumter, and killed himself when news of the collapse of the Confederacy reached him.

A. O. Craven, *Edmund Ruffin, Southerner; A Study in Secession*, New York, 1932.

» » From: ANTICIPATIONS OF THE FUTURE « «

CAUSES AND CONSEQUENCES OF THE INDEPENDENCE OF THE SOUTH (Appendix)

The present contest between the northern and southern states, in regard to negro slavery, has been growing in violence for a long time.

It was begun with the iniquitous aggression of attempting to exclude Missouri from the Union as a slaveholding state, and in the successful exaction of the Missouri compromise, in relation to which, both the general enforcement and exceptional violation of its principle by the North have been exercised and varied, the more to wrong and injure the southern states. But it has been only since the (falsely so-called) compromise enactments of 1850, that abolition has been hastening towards its object with gigantic strides—and also that the South has been partially roused from its sleep of fancied security. Unfortunate it has been, that this sleep had not been effectually shaken off thirty years sooner, and that all the means had not then been used for defence, that were abundantly possessed by the South at that time. If, when the Missouri compromise was submitted to, the proposed restrictions had been resisted by the South at all hazards, there would have been no further trouble about slavery. And if the fanaticism (or, more truly the unholy grasping for political power) of the North, had then been so unyielding as to permit a separation of the United States, the southern portion would now have double of their present wealth and power—and the northern states would not have attained half of their present greatness and wealth, which have been built upon the tribute exacted from the South by legislative policy. But no separation would have been produced. If, at the time of the Missouri compromise, the northern members and states had been firmly resisted, they would have drawn back, and the spirit of political abolition would have been crushed in the bud. The sincere abolitionists, who are actuated by what they deem moral and religious considerations, are but the simple and deluded tools of the hypocrites and knaves who are using them to further their own objects of personal ambition and political power.

Without looking even as far as twenty years into the future of the effects of the northern crusade against southern slavery, let us see what might have been the speedy consequences, if the contingency had occurred, which was so near occurring, of an abolitionist being elected President—he being the candidate of the northern states only, and on the abolition question and principle. It is true that a more conciliatory policy would probably have been adopted at first, because the victorious party would not have risked the driving their conquered opponents to desperate and revolutionary measures of resistance. But it is fair to suppose that a party so fanatical, greedy, and unscrupulous would have used every means to reach its object, that could be used safely and successfully. Let us, then, see what means, and all claimed as constitutional by the North, could be used by an abolitionist administration of the government of the United States. If elected, it would have been supported by a majority of the people of the states, and of the House of Representatives. It would not have required much time, or management, (by corruption or other influences,) for the President to have also at his command a majority of the Senate—representing states that were already his supporters. Then, the President, with a majority of both Houses of Congress, might adopt any or all of the following measures, to weaken and destroy the institution of slavery:

The first and greatest measure, is already openly avowed by the abolitionists, and the majority of every northern state, as their designed policy and plan of action hereafter. This is to admit into the Union no new territories as slaveholding states. This alone, even if nothing else is done, will soon increase the non-slaveholding states to three-fourths of the whole, so that the constitution can be changed, and slavery abolished. But, in advance of the consummation of this great and effectual measure, various other auxiliary means might be used to hasten the end, as thus:

Each of the largest non-slaveholding states, with its own consent, might be divided by act of Congress, so as to make two states of each, and so have four abolition senators in place of two.

Every office and emolument in the gift of the federal government might be bestowed on abolitionists only, and in all the southern states on northern abolitionists, until corruption and fear, or despair, should induce conversions, or professions and acts of abolitionism in southerners, as offering the only road to office or gain.

The zealous and active exertions of all these many thousands of government officials and employees, down to the lowest laborers on any government work, would be counted on and secured, to operate against the institution of slavery and the interests of slaveholders. This open, unassailable, and powerful influence, would be added to, and serve to increase a hundred-fold, the existing secret influence and concealed operations of the many abolition agents, male and female, lay and clerical, who, in various ostensible business employments, have long been operating on our slaves, often under the hospitable shelter of our own roofs, and as our pretended friends.

Every military and naval officer hereafter to be appointed, might be an abolitionist, and all now commissioned, and not abolitionists, might be dismissed from service on other pretexts, or otherwise not entrusted with any command.

The various lands held by the federal government, for forts, dock-yards, arsenals, lighthouses, &c., in the South, and every national ship in southern waters, would be made places of secure refuge for fugitive and even rebellious slaves, and secure positions for any other incendiary action.

The District of Columbia would be made non-slaveholding by law, and soon in sentiment. It would be openly and entirely what it is already partially, (by northern and government influence,) ground, within the southern and slaveholding territory, where the enemies of the South have the greatest facilities for their most effectual and dangerous action. Already under the protecting shield of the federal government and its administration, at a former time, the agents of the abolitionists have been able there to effect more injury to slaveholders, and with more of impunity, than anywhere even in the abolition states.

The removal of slaves by sales from states where they were in excessive numbers, to other states or new territories where they were most deficient, would (as long threatened) be forbidden by an early law under the complete supremacy of a northern administration. This alone would prevent the making of any new slaveholding states in the small extent of the remaining territory in which climate does not forbid slavery; while the increase of slaves in the old states, from which they would have no sufficient outlet, would render them an unprofitable burden and a dangerous nuisance to the whites. The condition of the slaves would thereby be made much worse, in regard to their own happiness, and the institution of slavery would be hastened toward its doomed extinction.

Some of these measures might require that liberal mode of construing the federal constitution which is general at the North, and especially on this subject. But even the strict construction of that instrument might be conformed to, literally, and yet an abolition administration, in a little more time, could as effectually extinguish the institution of slavery, and the prosperity and existence of the southern states as independent communities.

Such might have been, and to great extent, such would have been the earlier or later effects and operation of an abolitionist's election to the Presidential office. Such, and with more sure and extended operation, will be the effects of the future election, by a much stronger constituency, of a Seward, or some other northern abolitionist, or of another southern renegade and traitor, of more ability than the one who was lately raised so nearly to the height of his ambition, only to be let fall and sink in an abyss of contempt.

Will the southern states wait for the completion of these surely coming results, or will they take the warning so plainly to be read in their enemies' acts and avowals, and save themselves from the impending ruin? The fast growing strength of the abolition party, and the signal success of that party in the next Presidential election, may cause every southerner to regret that its candidate was not elected in the recent contest, when the south was relatively stronger for defence than it will ever be hereafter.

• • •

SEPARATION OF THE UNION NO GROUND FOR WAR

If Fremont had been elected, the consequences would have been so manifestly and highly dangerous to the rights and the safety of the slaveholding states, that they would scarcely have waited to be completely shackled, and powerless for defence, before they would have seceded or separated from the victorious and hostile states of the present confederacy. It is proposed here to inquire what would have been the results of such separation, and especially to consider the question of the danger of war, which it is so generally believed would necessarily ensue between the separated communities, and the results of any war.

If the necessity was manifest to the people of the South, there would be no obstacle to their deliberate action, and no probability of opposition by the northern states, nor by the then remaining fragment or shadow of the federal government of the previous confederacy. The legislatures of the offended states would call conventions, and these conventions would declare their separation and independence, and, by subsequent acts, make a new confederation. If all the fifteen slaveholding states united in this action, they would be far stronger, at home and for repelling invasion, than would be the northern states as invaders. Even if but five or six adjacent southern states alone seceded, no remaining power of the federal government, or of all the northern states, could conquer or coerce the seceders.

But, contrary as is the opinion to that which generally prevails, I maintain that such act of secession would offer no inducement or occasion for war; and that there would be no war; as the immediate or direct result of secession or separation.

The malignant hostility of feeling that is even now entertained by the abolition party, and perhaps by a majority of the northern people, towards those of the South, is not here overlooked or underrated. If they could, by merely willing it, they would ruin us, even while united with them under one government—and still more readily if we were separated. If the mere wish of abolitionists could effect the destruction of our system of negro slavery, even by the destruction of the entire white population of the South, I would fear that that consummation would not be a remote event. But *to will* and *to do* are very different things. And even northern fanaticism, (to say nothing of northern self-interest and avarice,) would prefer to forego these gratifications, if they were to be purchased only at the cost, to the North, of hundreds of millions of dollars, and hundreds of thousands of lives. Even if admitting, what is so arrogantly and falsely claimed by the North, that it could conquer and desolate the South, any such victory would be scarcely less ruinous to the conquerors than the conquered.

But there would be no such war, and no movement towards it—because war could not subserve or advance any interest of the North. It is unnecessary to maintain the like proposition in regard to the South, inasmuch as it is universally admitted. No one, of either side, has ever asserted, or supposed, that the South would assail, or make war upon the North, in consequence of their separation. Whether this peaceful disposition is ascribed to a greater sense of justice, or to the weakness, or the timidity of the southern people, all concur in the belief that the South would desire peace, and would avoid war, unless necessary for defence. Then, passing by this contingency, deemed impossible by all parties, we have only to examine the supposed inducements for offensive war and attack by the North on the South.

FANATICAL AND POLITICAL ABOLITION. SUPERIOR POLITICAL TALENTS OF THE SLAVEHOLDING STATES

The picture which has been sketched of the ruin of the South, which will surely result from the present and continued efforts of our "northern brethren" and fellow-citizens to extinguish negro slavery, has nothing in it to moderate or discourage any abolitionist of the fanatical school of Garrison, Giddings, and Beecher. Fanaticism has no moderation, no reason, no mercy. The true abolitionist—an abolitionist for the sake of conscience and what he deems religion—would welcome all the evils and horrors that would come, if these were the necessary consequences of the consummation of his great measure and object. But these men, the only sincere and honest members of the great anti-slavery party, are comparatively but few, and they are but the tools of the more selfish and cunning and baser Sewards, and Sumners, and Greelys, who know full well the folly and falsehood of their professed doctrines, and who advocate them merely to acquire political power or personal gain. These and all of the most intelligent leaders, and the greater number of their followers in the abolition party, are not in the least actuated by the alleged sufferings and sorrows of the "poor slave," or by the other evils generally imputed to the institution of slavery. These charges are but pretences to delude their own followers, and induce their obedient following and zealous support. Many of the more candid men of the party admit that they are not deceived, or directed by sympathy for the "poor slave," whose condition they know to be better than it would be if the "poor slave" were made free. But they say (and truly) that notwithstanding the larger population and vote and decided majority of the North, and its greater wealth and more extended education and intelligence, (as claimed,) that the government of the United States has always been, and still is, generally directed by men of the South, or by men and measures of their choosing. This greater influence of the South is denounced as the "slave power"; and transfer its rule to the North, is the true and great object of the political and hypocritical abolitionists who now lead the great northern party.

It is true, (and almost the only great truth that the abolitionists have yet arrived at,) that the intellect of the South, in most measures of high importance, has influenced and directed, and controlled the much greater numerical power of the North. And it is also true, that this superiority of influence is a direct consequence, and one of the great benefits of the institution of domestic slavery. In the United States, it is only where negro slavery exists that many men of the rural or agricultural population can have enough of leisure and opportunity to cultivate their intellect, and especially, by social intercourse and the instruction thence derived, so as to become qualified to teach and to lead in public affairs, instead of being mere "hewers of wood and drawers of water," (slaves, in effect, politically,) to a few of the better instructed of their fellows. In the southern states, the greatest men who have been sent to Congress, or who have occupied still higher public stations, were for much the greater number, always residents of the country. Washington, Henry, Jefferson, Mason, Bland, Lee, Calhoun, Cheves, and hundreds of other able statesmen, were all slaveholders and country residents. For any such cases of representatives of distinguished talents that can be stated of the rural portions of the non-slaveholding states, in recent times, the South, from its much scantier numbers, can adduce fifty of equal or greater political knowledge and ability. In cities, the case is different. In all great cities there are operating inducements and also facilities for mental culture and improvement, much greater than anywhere in the country, or than we can have in the southern states, where there are very few large cities, and none to compare in these respects with Philadelphia, New York, and Boston. Therefore, in the great cities of the North and especially in the learned professions and scientific pursuits, there are more of highly educated and scientific professional men, than are to be found in the southern states. But even of these shining lights of learning and science, but few seem to be fitted for, or at least are entrusted with political offices and duties, by the votes of their fellow-citizens. Even the great cities of the North, with all their learned and able men to select from, more frequently elect representatives of the lower than the higher order of education and intellect. Still, almost the only distinguished statesmen who have appeared from the North have been the residents and representatives of cities. Of all the far greater number of northern members of Congress from the strictly rural districts, and even including in such the villages and small towns, scarcely any deserve to be distinguished for superior education, talent, or statesmanship. This is notoriously the fact. And though the workings of the caucus or convention system, (a political iniquity and curse borrowed from New York) and also of the evil changes of state constitutions, (in regard to suffrage and popular elections,) have served greatly to lower the grade of the representation of the South, yet, even now, any ten southern representatives, taken at random, will probably possess more political talent than one hundred from the rural districts of the old northern states, where the stultifying operation of the absence of slavery on an agricultural population has had the longest time to show the sure consequences. Under these different circumstances, it necessarily follows, that the greater superiority of intellectual power, more than the mere brute power of greater numbers, will govern in most questions of statesmanship and profound national policy. And such has been the case in this federal government for a long time, and such will be the case, and increasing in degree, so long as one portion of the confederated states enjoy, and the other is without the refining operation of slaveholding on the superior race.

A very marked statistical illustration and evidence of my position has come under my eye since writing the above. It is a passage in the noted abolition article in the number of the Edinburgh Review for October, 1856. This infamous piece of elaborate calumny on the South is doubly a fraud, in its source and authorship, besides being a tissue of inventions in its general statements and argument. It appeared in a British publication as if by a British author. And when this fraud was exposed, and it was known that the author was an American both by birth and residence, it was as falsely claimed that he was a southerner, because he was born of northern parents during their sojourn in the South, though he is a northerner in education, residence, and principles. This writer, to prove the supremacy of the "slave power," adduces these facts: that of the sixteen successive Presidents of the United States, eleven have been slaveholders; and that for five-sixths of the duration of the government, southerners by birth, or northern men elected by southern votes, have occupied the presidential office. And of the other higher federal offices, there have served from the southern states,

"Seventeen out of twenty-eight Judges of the Supreme Court;

Fourteen out of nineteen Attorneys-General;

Sixty-one out of seventy-seven Presidents of the Senate;

Twenty-one out of thirty-three Speakers of the House;

Eighty out of one hundred and thirty-four Foreign Ministers."

Now, it is very true that high official position, even in a free or popular government, is not often obtained by the greatest fitness for the service. But, when so much the larger proportion of the highest offices of government have been, during a long time, filled from the South, there can be no stronger proof of the fact, that in the scanty population of the South, there was a very far greater amount of political talents of high order, than in the more populous northern states. . . .

NO DANGER TO THE SOUTH FROM WAR, UNLESS FOR WANT OF PREPARATION

Southern men have met all past violations of their rights by threats of resistance or separation, and then submitted, until no such threats are believed, or will be believed, unless unmistakable action shall have commenced. This well-founded incredulity is the secret of all the recent and present abolition movements and designs. And even if, by possibility, and when driven to desperation, the insulted and oppressed South should secede, it is confidently believed by the North that its own stronger military and marine force, and greater wealth, would serve, speedily and easily, to subdue the southern states. Never was there a greater mistake, or one which, if acted upon, will be corrected more effectually. It is only this mistaken idea of southern weakness, together with the absence of all military preparation in the South, that can possibly produce war, as the direct and immediate result of separation. If, when separating, we shall be, as now, unprepared for defence, we may surely expect to have war. But due preparation for war will as certainly ensure the maintenance of peace.

It is assumed by most persons that war between the separated portions would be a necessary and immediate consequence of separation. Even if no other ground for war existed, one certain and unavoidable cause is apprehended in the fact of the separate ownership, by the separated communities, of the upper and central waters of the Mississippi, and of its lower waters and their outlet to the sea. And one great consequence of war, (as generally believed in the North, and by very many also in the South,) it is supposed would be, that successful insurrection of the slaves would be invited and produced by war and invasion, and thus their general enfranchisement effected in the mode most disastrous and afflicting to the whites. Sure and sufficient reasons have already been offered to show, in reference to other and general grounds, that war would not be either a necessary or probable result of separation. Other reasons will now be offered to invalidate this particular cause of war, and afterwards will be considered the particular and worst possible consequence which has been anticipated.

War, in any mode, is an enormous evil, which it is far from my intention to deprecate. And war between separated portions of the same people, and previously long of the same community, would be the most deplorable and calamitous of all wars. A war between the southern and northern states, embittered by every growing cause of hostility and mutual hatred, and if waged to extremities with such balanced alternations of success and defeat as might be expected between foes so nearly equal, would be scarcely less destructive to the ultimate conqueror than to the conquered party. The prosperity, wealth, and as yet happy condition of both powers, would be engulphed in one abyss of complete industrial and political ruin. The possibility of these awful consequences should be well considered by all. But, as admonition and warning of the most solemn import, it is for the aggressive and offending party to heed, and by stopping and restraining its course, to avoid these consequences, and not for the aggrieved and heretofore always yielding party. The South, if still remaining in the Union, can do nothing except to submit entirely and unconditionally to every present and coming measure of aggression, which will be but another way to reach certain ruin. Rather than entire submission, we should prefer any hazards of war and its consequences. For all the calamities of war should be risked, and met, if necessary, by freemen who deserve to enjoy freedom, rather than to yield their rights without struggling, to the last ground of hope, in its defence. If, then, we are such men, the threat of war, with all the necessary and horrible consequences, will have no influence to induce the South to purchase peace by entire submission. . . .

1860

» » *The Second American Revolution* « «

1860-1865

» » « «

DIXIE

I wish I was in the land ob cotton,
Old times dar am not forgotten,
   Look away, look away—look away, Dixie land.
In Dixie land whar I was born in,
Early on one frosty mornin',
   Look away, look away—look away, Dixie land.
     Den I wish I was in Dixie,
       Hooray! Hooray!
    In Dixie land we'll take our stand,
      To lib an' die in Dixie.
      Away, away, away down south in Dixie!
      Away, away, away down south in Dixie!

Ole missus marry "Will-de-weaber,"
Willum was a gay deceaber;
   Look away, etc.
But when he put his arm around her,
He smiled as fierce as a forty-pounder,
   Look away, etc.
His face was sharp as a butcher's cleaber,
But dat did not seem to greab her,
   Look away, etc.
Ole missus acted de foolish part,
And died for a man dat broke her heart;
   Look away, etc.
     Den I wish I was in Dixie,
       Hooray! Hooray! etc.

Now here's a health to de next ole missus
An' all the gals dat want to kiss us,
   Look away, etc.
But if you want to drive 'way sorrow,
Come and hear dis song to-morrow,
   Look away, etc.
     Den I wish I was in Dixie,
       Hooray! Hooray! etc.

Dar's buckwheat cakes and Injin batter,
Makes you fat or a little fatter;
   Look away, etc.
Den hoe it down an' scratch your grabble,
To Dixie's land I'm bound to trabble:

Look away, etc.
Den I wish I was in Dixie,
Hooray! Hooray! etc.

The first song to gain popularity during the Civil War, "Dixie" had actually been heard for the first time—on Broadway—in 1859. Dan Emmett, a native of Ohio but of Southern parentage, wrote it as a "walk-around" song for Dan Bryant's Minstrels. Several attempts were made by Southern poets to transform "Dixie" into a dignified war song. General Albert Pike's "Southrons, hear your country call you!" was the most successful. But the people have always preferred the original words, which are here given.

» »   « «

JOHN BROWN'S BODY

John Brown's body lies a-mold'ring in the grave,
John Brown's body lies a-mold'ring in the grave,
John Brown's body lies a-mold'ring in the grave,
    His soul is marching on!
Chorus
    Glory! Glory Hallelujah!
    Glory! Glory Hallelujah!
    Glory! Glory Hallelujah!
    His soul is marching on.

He's gone to be a soldier in the army of the Lord!
    His soul is marching on.

John Brown's knapsack is strapped upon his back.
    His soul is marching on.

His pet lambs will meet him on the way,
    And they'll go marching on.

They'll hang Jeff Davis on a sour apple tree,
    As they go marching on.

Now for the Union let's give three rousing cheers,
    As we go marching on.
        Hip, hip, hip, Hurrah!

The tune of "John Brown's Body" is the Southern revival hymn "Say, brothers, will you meet us," well known all over the country in the 1850's. In the spring of 1861 some soldiers of a Massachusetts

regiment stationed in Boston fitted these words to the tune, possibly
to plague some member of their company. When the regiment sang
their new song as they marched through New York July 24, 1861, it
became immediately popular in the North.

« « » »

BATTLE-HYMN OF THE REPUBLIC

Mine eyes have seen the glory of the coming of the Lord:
He is trampling out the vintage where the grapes of wrath are stored;
He hath loosed the fateful lightning of his terrible swift sword;
　His truth is marching on.

I have seen Him in the watch-fires of a hundred circling camps;
They have builded Him an altar in the evening dews and damps;
I can read His righteous sentence by the dim and flaring lamps;
　His day is marching on.

I have read a fiery gospel, writ in burnished rows of steel:
"As ye deal with my contemners, so with you my grace shall deal;
Let the Hero, born of woman, crush the serpent with his heel,
　Since God is marching on."

He has sounded forth the trumpet that shall never call retreat;
He is sifting out the hearts of men before his judgment-seat:
Oh! be swift my soul, to answer Him! be jubilant, my feet!
　Our God is marching on.

In the beauty of the lilies Christ was born across the sea,
With a glory in his bosom that transfigures you and me:
As he died to make men holy, let us die to make men free,
　While God is marching on.

　　Mrs. Julia Ward Howe, abolitionist, poet, and reformer, wrote the
"Battle Hymn" one night after visiting an army camp near Washington, D.C. Too stirred by what she had seen to sleep, she composed it
to the tune of "John Brown's Body," writing down the words in the
darkness of the tent. Published in the *Atlantic Monthly* for February,
1862, it made her so famous that scarcely anyone now remembers her
long career as a humanitarian reformer.

« « » »

THREE HUNDRED THOUSAND MORE

We are coming, Father Abraham, three hundred thousand more,
From Mississippi's winding stream and from New England's shore;
We leave our ploughs and workshops, our wives and children dear,
With hearts too full for utterance, with but a silent tear;
We dare not look behind us, but steadfastly before:
We are coming, Father Abraham, three hundred thousand more!

If you look across the hill-tops that meet the northern sky,
Long moving lines of rising dust your vision may descry;
And now the wind, an instant, tears the cloudy veil aside,
And floats aloft our spangled flag in glory and in pride;
And bayonets in the sunlight gleam, and bands brave music pour:
We are coming, Father Abraham, three hundred thousand more!

If you look all up our valleys where the growing harvests shine,
You may see our sturdy farmer boys fast forming into line;
And children from their mother's knee are pulling at the weeds,
And learning how to reap and sow against their country's needs;
And a farewell group stands weeping at every cottage door:
We are coming, Father Abraham, three hundred thousand more!

You have called us, and we're coming, by Richmond's bloody tide
To lay us down, for Freedom's sake, our brothers' bones beside;
Or from foul treason's savage grasp to wrench the murderous blade,
And in the face of foreign foes its fragments to parade.
Six hundred thousand loyal men and true have gone before:
We are coming, Father Abraham, three hundred thousand more!

Published anonymously in the New York *Evening Post*, July 16, 1862. The author was James Sloan Gibbons, a Quaker abolitionist. The song was deliberately written to assist in recruiting at the fateful moment when Lincoln had just called for 300,000 more volunteers.

«   «   »   »

TENTING ON THE OLD CAMP GROUND

We're tenting to-night on the old camp ground;
    Give us a song to cheer
Our weary hearts, a song of home,
    And friends we love so dear.
Chorus
    Many are the hearts that are weary to-night,
        Wishing for the war to cease;

Many are the hearts, looking for the right,
    To see the dawn of peace.

We've been tenting to-night on the old camp ground,
    Thinking of days gone by;
Of the loved ones at home, that gave us the hand,
    And the tear that said "Good-by!"

We are tired of the war on the old camp ground:
    Many are dead and gone,
Of the brave and the true who've left their homes;
    Others been wounded long.

We've been fighting to-day on the old camp ground,
    Many are lying near;
Some are dead, and some are dying,
    Many are in tears.

Walter Kittredge, a Northern ballad singer, offered this song for
sale in 1863 but was not able to dispose of it. When it was published
in 1864 one hundred thousand copies were sold in three months. It
was a favorite with the troops of both the North and the South.

« «   » »

GOOBER PEAS

Sitting by the roadside on a summer day,
Chatting with my messmates, passing time away,
Lying in the shadow underneath the trees,
Goodness! how delicious, eating goober peas!

    Chorus. Peas! peas! peas! peas! eating goober peas!
          Goodness! how delicious, eating goober peas!

When a horseman passes, the soldiers have a rule
To cry out at their loudest, "Mister, here's your mule,"
But another pleasure, enchantinger than these,
Is wearing out your grinders, eating goober peas!

Just before the battle the General hears a row,
He says, "The Yankees are coming, I hear their rifles now";
He turns around in wonder, and what do you think he sees?
The Georgia militia eating goober peas!

I think my song has lasted almost long enough,
The subject's interesting, but the rhymes are mighty rough.
I wish this was over, when free from rags and fleas,
We'd kiss our wives and sweethearts, and gobble goober peas!

Goober peas, as Yankees may need to be told, are peanuts. The author of this widely known Confederate soldiers' song is said to be one A. Pender.

« « » »

The Second American Revolution

THE CIVIL WAR has been called the War of the Rebellion, the War between the States, the War for Southern Independence, and the Rich Man's War and the Poor Man's Fight. It was all of these. It was a struggle in which the issue of national sovereignty and nationalism itself was involved. It was a conflict in which the nature of the federal system was deeply implicated. It was a contest in which the rich, both North and South, made profits and secured exemptions from battle which the poor were denied. In both North and South a vigorous opposition to the conduct of the war, and to the war itself, developed. And in each section worthy and even great leaders emerged, to become symbols for later times.

But the Civil War was more than all this, more than a war between states, or a struggle for Southern nationalism, or a contest between rich and poor. It was, as the Beards have insisted, a second American Revolution. It was a revolution because it marked the transfer of political and economic power in national affairs, from the Southern planting class to the Northern industrialists. Southern economy was affected. The slave was freed. Industrialism, which had already made a start in the South, now took new strides, or, at least, the way was open to it to take such strides. And although agrarianism, in both South and West, was not indeed impotent, its power was definitely limited. The old alliance between the agricultural South and West was broken. The West was brought under the aegis of industrialism. Its farmers bought new agricultural machinery and were increasingly forced to become businessmen. Vast railway transportation systems tied the West to the industrial East. And although industry conceded to agriculture the long-wanted free homestead act, care was taken to preempt for the railroad vast domains in the heart of the West itself. Commercial and industrial capitalism also obtained the long-hungered-for national banking and national protective tariff systems. Henceforth industrial capitalism was the piper that called the tune.

Unconscious of these vast and cataclysmic forces and configurations was the Negro, the ordinary soldier, the common man. For these it was clear, merely, that the slave was free, the Union saved. What the Second Revolution meant to the soldier in camp, prison, and field, what it meant to the idealistic patriot, is part of the story, too. And though it was not to eventuate, the plan of a few "radical" statesmen for a new social order was also a part of the story.

» »   « «

JOHN BROWN

1800–1859

BEFORE his militant crusade in Kansas, in which he struck violent blows at slavery with the zeal of a saint and the courage of a martyr, John Brown, tanner, drover, and farmer, had moved ten times and had shown signs of the intense and even fanatical emotionalism which betrayed mental instability. The guerilla warfare in which he engaged in Kansas was, however, not unknown to frontier communities, and his devotion to the idea of direct action was not without precedent in American experience.

Supported and encouraged by abolitionists of means and influence, John Brown undertook in 1859 the desperate and foolhardy venture of trying to incite a slave insurrection at Harpers Ferry, Virginia. He was convinced that God had designed him to win freedom for the oppressed, a goal so noble that any means justified its pursuit. Brown was sentenced to death for "treason to the Commonwealth, conspiring with slaves to commit treason and murder." The dignity and courage which he displayed from the time of his capture to his execution aroused widespread sympathy in the North, where a notable minority regarded him as a noble martyr. Such sympathy did something to feed the fires of secession in the South, and John Brown became a sort of symbol in the hearts of his divided countrymen.

F. B. Sanborn, *The Life and Letters of John Brown*, Boston, 1885.
W. E. B. Du Bois, *John Brown*, Philadelphia, 1909.
O. G. Villard, *John Brown; A Biography Fifty Years After*, Boston, 1910.
Delight Ansley, *The Sword and the Spirit; a Life of John Brown*, New York, 1955.
R. P. Warren, *John Brown, the Making of a Martyr*, New York, 1929.

» » JOHN BROWN'S LAST SPEECH « «

I have, may it please the Court, a few words to say.

In the first place, I deny everything but what I have all along admitted,—the design on my part to free the slaves. I intended certainly to have made a clean thing of that matter, as I did last winter, when I went into Missouri and there took slaves without the snapping of a gun on either side, moved them through the country, and finally left them in Canada. I designed to have done the same thing again, on a larger scale. That was all I intended. I never did intend murder, or treason, or the destruction of property, or to excite or incite slaves to rebellion, or to make insurrection.

I have another objection; and that is, it is unjust that I should suffer such a penalty. Had I interfered in the manner which I admit, and which I admit has been fairly proved (for I admire the truthfulness and candor of the greater portion of the witnesses who have testified in this case),—had I so interfered in behalf of the rich, the powerful, the intelligent, the so-called great, or in behalf of any of their friends,—either father, mother, brother, sister, wife, or children, or any of that class,—and suffered and sacrificed what I have in this interference, it would have been all right; and every man in this court would have deemed it an act worthy of reward rather than punishment.

This court acknowledges, as I suppose, the validity of the law of God. I see a book kissed here which I suppose to be the Bible, or at least the New Testament. That teaches me that all things whatsoever I would that men should do to me, I should do even so to them. It teaches me, further, to "remember them that are in bonds, as bound with them." I endeavored to act up to that instruction. I say, I am yet too young to understand that God is any respecter of persons. I believe that to have interfered as I have done—as I have always freely admitted I have done—in behalf of His despised poor, was not wrong, but right. Now, if it is deemed necessary that I should forfeit my life for the furtherance of the ends of justice, and mingle my blood further with the blood of my children and with the blood of millions in this slave country whose rights are disregarded by wicked, cruel, and unjust enactments,—I submit; so let it be done!

Let me say one word further.

I feel entirely satisfied with the treatment I have received on my trial. Considering all the circumstances, it has been more generous than I expected. But I feel no consciousness of guilt. I have stated from the first what was my intention, and what was not. I never had any design against the life of any person, nor any disposition to commit treason, or excite slaves to rebel, or make any general insurrection. I never encouraged any man to do so, but always discouraged any idea of that kind.

Let me say, also, a word in regard to the statements made by some of those connected with me. I hear it has been stated by some of them that I have induced them to join me. But the contrary is true. I do not say this to injure them, but as regretting their weakness. There is not one of them but joined me of his own accord, and the greater part of them at their own expense. A number of them I never saw, and never had a word of conversation with, till the day they came to me; and that was for the purpose I have stated.

Now I have done.   1859

JEFFERSON DAVIS

1808–1889

A NATIVE KENTUCKIAN of middle-class background, Jefferson Davis attended Transylvania University and West Point, served in the United States army, and settled as a planter on the newer lands of Mississippi. Marriage into the local aristocracy and a political career in Congress identified him with the planter class. As a participant in the Mexican War and as Secretary of War in Buchanan's cabinet he became a national figure. Devoted to the consolidation and expansion of the South as a social and economic unit within the nation, he opposed the antislavery movement and the waxing power of the industrial North.

The first inaugural address as President of the Confederate States expresses the Southern nationalism of Davis, conceals his disappointment in having closed to him the door to military fame, and betrays, with much sensitiveness, his awareness of some of his own shortcomings and of the cleavages in the Confederacy which were to plague him almost beyond endurance. Egotistical, easily offended, lofty, and half-ill much of the time, Davis was not well equipped to lead the Confederacy in its struggle for independence. His later years were marked by sadness, poverty, and a determination to defend valiantly the "lost cause."

Jefferson Davis, *The Rise and Fall of the Confederate Government*, 2 vols., New York, 1958.
Robert McElroy, *Jefferson Davis, the Unreal and the Real*, 2 vols., New York, 1937.
Rembert W. Patrick, *Jefferson Davis and His Cabinet*, Baton Rouge, 1944.
Strode Hudson, *Jefferson Davis*, New York, 1955.

» » INAUGURAL ADDRESS OF JEFFERSON DAVIS « «

Gentlemen of the Congress of the Confederate States of America, Friends, and Fellow-Citizens: Called to the difficult and responsible station of Chief Magistrate of the Provisional Government which you have instituted, I approach the discharge of the duties assigned to me with humble distrust of my abilities, but with a sustaining confidence in the wisdom of those who are to guide and aid me in the administration of public affairs, and an abiding faith in the virtue and patriotism of the people. Looking forward to the speedy establishment of a permanent government to take the place of this, which by its greater moral and physical power will be better able to combat with many difficulties that arise from the conflicting interests of separate nations, I enter upon the duties of the office to which I have been chosen with the hope that the beginning of our career, as a Confederacy, may not be obstructed by hostile opposition to our enjoyment of the separate existence and independence we have asserted, and which, with the blessing of Providence, we intend to maintain.

Our present political position has been achieved in a manner unprecedented in the history of nations. It illustrates the American idea that governments rest on the consent of the governed, and that it is the right of the people to alter or abolish them at will whenever they become destructive of the ends for which they were established. The declared purpose of the compact of the Union from which we have withdrawn was to "establish justice, insure domestic tranquility, provide for the common defense, promote the general welfare, and secure the blessings of liberty to ourselves and our posterity"; and when, in the judgment of the sovereign States composing this Confederacy, it has been perverted from the purposes for which it was ordained, and ceased to answer the ends for which it was established, a peaceful appeal to the ballot box declared that, so far as they are concerned, the Government created by that compact should cease to exist. In this they merely asserted the right which the Declaration of Independence of July 4, 1776, defined to be "inalienable." Of the time and occasion of its exercise they as sovereigns were the final judges, each for itself. The impartial and enlightened verdict of mankind will vindicate the rectitude of our conduct; and He who knows the hearts of men will judge of the sincerity with which we have labored to preserve the Government of our fathers in its spirit.

The right solemnly proclaimed at the birth of the United States, and which has been solemnly affirmed and reaffirmed in the Bills of Rights of the States subsequently admitted into the Union of 1789, undeniably recognizes in the people the power to resume the authority delegated for the purposes of government. Thus the sovereign States here represented have proceeded to form this Confederacy; and it is by abuse of language that their act has been denominated a revolution. They formed a new alliance, but within each State its government has remained; so that the rights of person and property have not been disturbed. The agent through which they communicated with foreign nations is changed, but this does not necessarily interrupt their international relations. Sustained by the consciousness that the transition from the former Union to the present Confederacy has not proceeded from a disregard on our part of just obligations, or any failure to perform every constitutional duty, moved by no interest or passion to invade the rights of others, anxious to cultivate peace and commerce with all nations, if we may not hope to avoid war, we may at least expect that posterity will acquit us of having needlessly engaged in it. Doubly justified by the absence of wrong on our part, and by wanton aggres-

sion on the part of others, there can be no cause to doubt that the courage and patriotism of the people of the Confederate States will be found equal to any measure of defense which their honor and security may require.

An agricultural people, whose chief interest is the export of commodities required in every manufacturing country, our true policy is peace, and the freest trade which our necessities will permit. It is alike our interest and that of all those to whom we would sell, and from whom we would buy, that there should be the fewest practicable restrictions upon the interchange of these commodities. There can, however, be but little rivalry between ours and any manufacturing or navigating community, such as the Northeastern States of the American Union. It must follow, therefore, that mutual interest will invite to good will and kind offices on both parts. If, however, passion or lust of dominion should cloud the judgment or inflame the ambition of those States, we must prepare to meet the emergency and maintain by the final arbitrament of the sword, the position which we have assumed among the nations of the earth.

We have entered upon the career of independence, and it must be inflexibly pursued. Through many years of controversy with our late associates of the Northern States, we have vainly endeavored to secure tranquillity and obtain respect for the rights to which we were entitled. As a necessity, not a choice, we have resorted to the remedy of separation, and henceforth our energies must be directed to the conduct of our own affairs, and the perpetuity of the Confederacy which we have formed. If a just perception of mutual interest shall permit us peaceably to pursue our separate political career, my most earnest desire will have been fulfilled. But if this be denied to us, and the integrity of our territory and jurisdiction be assailed, it will but remain for us with firm resolve to appeal to arms and invoke the blessing of Providence on a just cause.

As a consequence of our new condition and relations, and with a view to meet anticipated wants, it will be necessary to provide for the speedy and efficient organization of branches of the Executive department having special charge of foreign intercourse, finance, military affairs, and the postal service. For purposes of defense, the Confederate States may, under ordinary circumstances, rely mainly upon the militia; but it is deemed advisable, in the present condition of affairs, that there should be a well-instructed and disciplined army, more numerous than would usually be required on a peace establishment. I also suggest that, for the protection of our harbors and commerce on the high seas, a navy adapted to those objects will be required. But this, as well as other subjects appropriate to our necessities, have doubtless engaged the attention of Congress.

With a Constitution differing only from that of our fathers in so far as it is explanatory of their well-known intent, freed from sectional conflicts, which have interfered with the pursuit of the general welfare, it is not unreasonable to expect that States from which we have recently parted may seek to unite their fortunes to ours under the Government which we have instituted. For this your Constitution makes adequate provision; but beyond this, if I mistake not the judgment and will of the people, a reunion with the States from which we have separated is neither practicable nor desirable. To increase the power, develop the resources, and promote the happiness of the Confederacy, it is requisite that there should be so much of homogeneity that the welfare of every portion shall be the aim of the whole. When this does not exist, antagonisms are engendered which must and should result in separation.

Actuated solely by the desire to preserve our own rights, and promote our own welfare, the separation by the Confederate States has been marked by no aggression upon others, and followed by no domestic convulsion. Our industrial pursuits have received no check, the cultivation of our fields has progressed as heretofore, and, even should we be involved in war, there would be no considerable diminution in the production of the staples which have constituted our exports, and in which the commercial world has an interest scarcely less than our own. This common interest of the producer and consumer can only be interrupted by exterior force which would obstruct the transmission of our staples to foreign markets—a course of conduct which would be as unjust, as it would be detrimental, to manufacturing and commercial interests abroad.

Should reason guide the action of the Government from which we have separated, a policy so detrimental to the civilized world, the Northern States included, could not be dictated by even the strongest desire to inflict injury upon us; but, if the contrary should prove true, a terrible responsibility will rest upon it, and the suffering of millions will bear testimony to the folly and wickedness of our aggressors. In the meantime there will remain to us, besides the ordinary means before suggested, the well-known resources for retaliation upon the commerce of an enemy.

Experience in public stations, of subordinate grade to this which your kindness has conferred, has taught me that toil and care and disappointment are the price of official elevation. You will see many errors to forgive, many deficiencies to tolerate; but you shall not find in me either want of zeal or fidelity to the cause that is to me the highest in hope, and of most enduring affection. Your generosity has bestowed upon me an undeserved distinction, one which I neither sought nor desired. Upon the continuance of that sentiment, and upon your wisdom and patriotism, I rely to direct and support me in the performance of the duties required at my hands.

We have changed the constituent parts, but not the system of government. The Constitution framed by our fathers is that of these Confederate States. In their exposition of it, and in the judicial construction it has received, we have a light which reveals its true meaning.

Thus instructed as to the true meaning and just intepretation of that instrument, and ever remembering that all offices are but trusts held for the people, and that powers delegated are to be strictly construed, I will hope by due diligence in the performance of my duties, though I may disappoint your expectations, yet to retain, when retiring, something of the good will and confidence which welcome my entrance into office.

It is joyous in the midst of perilous times to look around upon a people united in heart, where one purpose of high resolve animates and actuates the whole; where the sacrifices to be made are not weighed in the balance against honor and right and liberty and equality. Obstacles may retard, but they cannot long prevent, the progress of a movement sanctified by its justice and sustained by a virtuous people. Reverently let us invoke the God of our fathers to guide and protect us in our efforts to perpetuate the principles which by his blessing they were able to vindicate, establish, and transmit to their posterity. With the continuance of his favor ever gratefully acknowledged, we may hopefully look forward to success, to peace, and to prosperity. 1861

ABRAHAM LINCOLN

1809–1865

IF THE CIVIL WAR is regarded as the Second American Revolution which shifted the balance in the country from the state to the nation and from the Southern planting aristocracy to Northern business, Lincoln's part in that revolution needs to be defined. That the West played an indispensable part in this transformation has long been appreciated. In many respects Lincoln was typical of the West. His ability to get along with varied types of people, his humor, his rough-hewn speech and homespun philosophy were certainly in part a product of his environment. Faith in the common man and belief in American nationalism, together with dislike of slavery, were not limited, of course, to the West. Yet all these values flourished there with unusual vigor.

But in the struggle against the Southern aristocracy and its war for independence Lincoln represented much more than the West. The common man in the North believed in him and trusted him. This support was necessary: without it the economic aims of Northern business, such as protective tariffs, a national banking system, and the like, could not have been achieved. Lincoln's warm human sympathies, his dignity, his ability to rise to poetic heights of feeling and expression in his idiomatic and terse prose, were indicative of the fact that he transcended his environment and his class. He was, in short, a truly national and a truly great leader.

Collected Works, Roy P. Basler and others, 8 vols., New Brunswick, N. J., 1953–1955.
J. G. Nicolay and John Hay, *Abraham Lincoln: A History*, 10 vols., New York, 1890.
A. J. Beveridge, *Abraham Lincoln, 1809–1858*, 4 vols., Boston, 1928.
Carl Sandburg, *Abraham Lincoln, the Prairie Years*, 2 vols., New York, 1926.
Carl Sandburg, *Abraham Lincoln, the War Years*, 4 vols., New York, 1939.
Allan Nevins, *The Emergence of Lincoln*, 2 vols., New York, 1955.
James G. Randall, *Lincoln, the Liberal Statesman*, 4 vols., New York, 1945–1955.

» » FIRST INAUGURAL ADDRESS « «

FELLOW-CITIZENS OF THE UNITED STATES: In compliance with a custom as old as the government itself, I appear before you to address you briefly, and to take in your presence the oath prescribed by the Constitution of the United States to be taken by the President "before he enters on the execution of his office."

I do not consider it necessary at present for me to discuss those matters of administration about which there is no special anxiety or excitement.

Apprehension seems to exist among the people of the Southern States that by the accession of a Republican administration their property and their peace and personal security

are to be endangered. There has never been any reasonable cause for such apprehension. Indeed, the most ample evidence to the contrary has all the while existed and been open to their inspection. It is found in nearly all the published speeches of him who now addresses you. I do but quote from one of those speeches when I declare that "I have no purpose, directly or indirectly, to interfere with the institution of slavery in the States where it exists. I believe I have no lawful right to do so, and I have no inclination to do so." Those who nominated and elected me did so with full knowledge that I had made this and many similar declarations, and had never recanted them. And, more than this, they placed in the platform for my acceptance, and as a law to themselves and to me, the clear and emphatic resolution which I now read:

Resolved, That the maintenance inviolate of the rights of the States, and especially the right of each State to order and control its own domestic institutions according to its own judgment exclusively, is essential to that balance of power on which the perfection and endurance of our political fabric depend, and we denounce the lawless invasion by armed force of the soil of any State or Territory, no matter under what pretext, as among the gravest of crimes.

I now reiterate these sentiments; and, in doing so, I only press upon the public attention the most conclusive evidence of which the case is susceptible, that the property, peace, and security of no section are to be in any wise endangered by the now incoming administration. I add, too, that all the protection which, consistently with the Constitution and the laws, can be given, will be cheerfully given to all the States when lawfully demanded, for whatever cause—as cheerfully to one section as to another.

There is much controversy about the delivering up of fugitives from service or labor. The clause I now read is as plainly written in the Constitution as any other of its provisions:

No person held to service or labor in one State, under the laws thereof, escaping into another, shall in consequence of any law or regulation therein be discharged from such service or labor, but shall be delivered up on claim of the party to whom such service or labor may be due.

It is scarcely questioned that this provision was intended by those who made it for the reclaiming of what we call fugitive slaves; and the intention of the lawgiver is the law. All members of Congress swear their support to the whole Constitution—to this provision as much as to any other. To the proposition, then, that slaves whose cases come within the terms of this clause "shall be delivered up," their oaths are unanimous. Now, if they would make the effort in good temper, could they not with nearly equal unanimity frame and pass a law by means of which to keep good that unanimous oath?

There is some difference of opinion whether this clause should be enforced by national or by State authority; but surely that difference

is not a very material one. If the slave is to be surrendered, it can be of but little consequence to him or to others by which authority it is done. And should anyone in any case be content that his oath shall go unkept on a merely unsubstantial controversy as to how it shall be kept?

Again, in any law upon this subject, ought not all the safeguards of liberty known in civilized and humane jurisprudence to be introduced, so that a free man be not, in any case, surrendered as a slave? And might it not be well at the same time to provide by law for the enforcement of that clause in the Constitution which guarantees that "the citizen of each State shall be entitled to all privileges and immunities of citizens in the several States."

I take the official oath today with no mental reservations, and with no purpose to construe the Constitution or laws by any hypercritical rules. And while I do not choose now to specify particular acts of Congress as proper to be enforced, I do suggest that it will be much safer for all, both in official and private stations, to conform to and abide by all those acts which stand unrepealed, than to violate any of them, trusting to find impunity in having them held to be unconstitutional.

It is seventy-two years since the first inauguration of a President under our National Constitution. During that period fifteen different and greatly distinguished citizens have, in succession, administered the executive branch of the government. They have conducted it through many perils, and generally with great success. Yet, with all this scope of precedent, I now enter upon the same task for the brief constitutional term of four years under great and peculiar difficulty. A disruption of the Federal Union, heretofore only menaced, is now formidably attempted.

I hold that, in contemplation of universal law and of the Constitution, the Union of these States is perpetual. Perpetuity is implied, if not expressed in the fundamental law of all national governments. It is safe to assert that no government proper ever had a provision in its organic law for its own termination. Continue to execute all the express provisions of our National Constitution, and the Union will endure forever—it being impossible to destroy it except by some action not provided for in the instrument itself.

Again, if the United States be not a government proper, but an association of States in the nature of contract merely, can it, as a contract, be peaceably unmade by less than all the parties who made it? One party to a contract may violate it—break it, so to speak; but does it not require all to lawfully rescind it?

Descending from these general principles, we find the proposition that in legal contemplation the Union is perpetual, confirmed by the history of the Union itself. The Union is much older than the Constitution. It was formed, in fact, by the Articles of Association in 1774. It was matured and continued by the Declaration of Independence in 1776. It was further matured, and the faith of all the then thirteen States expressly plighted and engaged that it should be perpetual, by the Articles of Confederation in 1778. And, finally, in 1787 one of the declared objects for ordaining and establishing the Constitution was "to form a more perfect Union."

But if the destruction of the Union by one or by a part only of the States be lawfully possible, the Union is less perfect than before the Constitution, having lost the vital element of perpetuity.

It follows from these views that no State upon its own mere motion can lawfully get out of the Union; that resolves and ordinances to that effect are legally void; and that acts of violence, within any State or States, against the authority of the United States, are insurrectionary or revolutionary, according to circumstances.

I therefore consider that, in view of the Constitution and the laws, the Union is unbroken; and to the extent of my ability I shall take care, as the Constitution itself expressly enjoins upon me, that the laws of the Union be faithfully executed in all the States. Doing this I deem to be only a simple duty on my part; and I shall perform it so far as practicable, unless my rightful masters, the American people, shall withhold the requisite means, or in some authoritative manner direct the contrary. I trust this will not be regarded as a menace, but only as the declared purpose of the Union that it will constitutionally defend and maintain itself.

In doing this there needs to be no bloodshed or violence; and there shall be none, unless it be forced upon the national authority. The power confided to me will be used to hold, occupy, and possess the property and places belonging to the government, and to collect the duties and imposts; but beyond what may be

necessary for these objects, there will be no invasion, no using of force against or among the people anywhere. Where hostility to the United States, in any interior locality, shall be so great and universal as to prevent competent resident citizens from holding the Federal offices, there will be no attempt to force obnoxious strangers among the people for that object. While the strict legal right may exist in the government to enforce the exercise of 10 these offices, the attempt to do so would be so irritating, and so nearly impracticable withal, that I deem it better to forego for the time the uses of such offices.

The mails, unless repelled, will continue to be furnished in all parts of the Union. So far as possible, the people everywhere shall have that sense of perfect security which is most favorable to calm thought and reflection. The course here indicated will be followed unless 20 current events and experience shall show a modification or change to be proper, and in every case and exigency my best discretion will be exercised according to circumstances actually existing, and with a view and a hope of a peaceful solution of the national troubles and the restoration of fraternal sympathies and affections.

That there are persons in one section or another who seek to destroy the Union at all 30 events, and are glad of any pretext to do it, I will neither affirm nor deny; but if there be such, I need address no word to them. To those, however, who really love the Union may I not speak?

Before entering upon so grave a matter as the destruction of our national fabric, with all its benefits, its memories, and its hopes, would it not be wise to ascertain precisely why we do it? Will you hazard so desperate a step while 40 there is any possibility that any portion of the ills you fly from have no real existence? Will you, while the certain ills you fly to are greater than all the real ones you fly from—will you risk the commission of so fearful a mistake?

All profess to be content in the Union if all constitutional rights can be maintained. Is it true, then, that any right, plainly written in the Constitution, has been denied? I think not. Happily the human mind is so constituted that 50 no party can reach to the audacity of doing this. Think, if you can, of a single instance in which a plainly written provision of the Constitution has ever been denied. If by the mere force of numbers a majority should deprive a minority of any clearly written constitutional right, it might, in a moral point of view, justify revolution—certainly would if such a right were a vital one. But such is not our case. All the vital rights of minorities and of individuals are so plainly assured to them by affirmations and negations, guarantees and prohibitions, in the Constitution, that controversies never arise concerning them. But no organic law can ever be framed with a provision specifically applicable to every question which may occur in practical administration. No foresight can anticipate, nor any document of reasonable length contain, express provisions for all possible questions. Shall fugitives from labor be surrendered by national or by State authority? The Constitution does not expressly say. *May* Congress prohibit slavery in the Territories? The Constitution does not expressly say. *Must* Congress protect slavery in the Territories? The Constitution does not expressly say.

From questions of this class spring all our constitutional controversies, and we divide upon them into majorities and minorities. If the minority will not acquiesce, the majority must, or the government must cease. There is no other alternative; for continuing the government is acquiescence on one side or the other.

If a minority in such case will secede rather than acquiesce, they make a precedent which in turn will divide and ruin them; for a minority of their own will secede from them whenever a majority refuses to be controlled by such minority. For instance, why may not any portion of a new confederacy a year or two hence arbitrarily secede again, precisely as portions of the present Union now claim to secede from it? All who cherish disunion sentiments are now being educated to the exact temper of doing this.

Is there such perfect identity of interests among the States to compose a new Union, as to produce harmony only, and prevent renewed secession?

Plainly, the central idea of secession is the essence of anarchy. A majority held in restraint by constitutional checks and limitations, and always changing easily with deliberate changes of popular opinions and sentiments, is the only true sovereign of a free people. Whoever rejects it does, of necessity, fly to anarchy or to despotism. Unanimity is impossible; the rule of a minority, as a permanent arrangement, is wholly inadmissible; so that, rejecting the ma-

jority principle, anarchy or despotism in some form is all that is left.

I do not forget the position, assumed by some, that constitutional questions are to be decided by the Supreme Court; nor do I deny that such decisions must be binding, in any case, upon the parties to a suit, as to the object of that suit, while they are also entitled to very high respect and consideration in all parallel cases by all other departments of the government. And while it is obviously possible that such decision may be erroneous in any given case, still the evil effect following it, being limited to that particular case, with the chance that it may be overruled and never become a precedent for other cases, can better be borne than could the evils of a different practice. At the same time, the candid citizen must confess that if the policy of the government, upon vital questions affecting the whole people, is to be irrevocably fixed by decisions of the Supreme Court, the instant they are made, in ordinary litigation between parties in personal actions, the people will have ceased to be their own rulers, having to that extent practically resigned their government into the hands of that eminent tribunal. Nor is there in this view any assault upon the court or the judges. It is a duty from which they may not shrink to decide cases properly brought before them, and it is no fault of theirs if others seek to turn their decisions to political purposes.

One section of our country believes slavery is right, and ought to be extended, while the other believes it is wrong, and ought not to be extended. This is the only substantial dispute. The fugitive-slave clause of the Constitution, and the law for the suppression of the foreign slave-trade, are each as well enforced, perhaps, as any law can ever be in a community where the moral sense of the people imperfectly supports the law itself. The great body of the people abide by the dry legal obligation in both cases, and a few break over in each. This, I think, cannot be perfectly cured; and it would be worse in both cases after the separation of the sections than before. The foreign slave-trade, now imperfectly suppressed, would be ultimately revived, without restriction, in one section, while fugitive slaves, now only partially surrendered, would not be surrendered at all by the other.

Physically speaking, we cannot separate. We cannot remove our respective sections from each other, nor build an impassable wall between them. A husband and wife may be divorced, and go out of the presence and beyond the reach of each other; but the different parts of our country cannot do this. They cannot but remain face to face, and intercourse, either amicable or hostile, must continue between them. Is it possible, then, to make that intercourse more advantageous or more satisfactory after separation than before? Can aliens make treaties easier than friends can make laws? Can treaties be more faithfully enforced between aliens than laws can among friends? Suppose you go to war, you cannot fight always; and when, after much loss on both sides, and no gain on either, you cease fighting, the identical old questions as to terms of intercourse, are again upon you.

This country, with its institutions, belongs to the people who inhabit it. Whenever they shall grow weary of the existing government, they can exercise their constitutional right of amending it, or their revolutionary right to dismember or overthrow it. I cannot be ignorant of the fact that many worthy and patriotic citizens are desirous of having the National Constitution amended. While I make no recommendation of amendments, I fully recognize the rightful authority of the people over the whole subject, to be exercised in either of the modes prescribed in the instrument itself; and I should, under existing circumstances, favor rather than oppose a fair opportunity being afforded the people to act upon it. I will venture to add that to me the convention mode seems preferable, in that it allows amendments to originate with the people themselves, instead of only permitting them to take or reject propositions originated by others not especially chosen for the purpose, and which might not be precisely such as they would wish to either accept or refuse. I understand a proposed amendment to the Constitution—which amendment, however, I have not seen—has passed Congress, to the effect that the Federal Government shall never interfere with the domestic institutions of the States, including that of persons held to service. To avoid misconstruction of what I have said, I depart from my purpose not to speak of particular amendments so far as to say that, holding such a provision to now be implied constitutional law, I have no objection to its being made express and irrevocable.

The chief magistrate derives all his authority from the people, and they have conferred none upon him to fix terms for the separation of the States. The people themselves can do this also if they choose; but the executive, as such, has nothing to do with it. His duty is to administer the present government, as it came to his hands, and to transmit it, unimpaired by him, to his successor.

Why should there not be a patient confidence in the ultimate justice of the people? Is there any better or equal hope in the world? In our present differences is either party without faith of being in the right? If the Almighty Ruler of Nations, with his eternal truth and justice, be on your side of the North, or on yours of the South, that truth and that justice will surely prevail by the judgment of this great tribunal of the American people.

By the frame of the government under which we live, this same people have wisely given their public servants but little power for mischief; and have, with equal wisdom, provided for the return of that little to their own hands at very short intervals. While the people retain their virtue and vigilance, no administration, by any extreme of wickedness or folly, can very seriously injure the government in the short space of four years.

My countrymen, one and all, think calmly and well upon this whole subject. Nothing valuable can be lost by taking time. If there be an object to hurry any of you in hot haste to a step which you would never take deliberately, that object will be frustrated by taking time; but no good object can be frustrated by it. Such of you as are now dissatisfied, still have the old Constitution unimpaired, and, on the sensitive point, the laws of your own framing under it; while the new administration will have no immediate power, if it would, to change either. If it were admitted that you who are dissatisfied hold the right side in the dispute, there still is no single good reason for precipitate action. Intelligence, patriotism, Christianity, and a firm reliance on Him who has never yet forsaken this favored land, are still competent to adjust in the best way all our present difficulty.

In your hands, my dissatisfied fellow-countrymen, and not in mine, is the momentous issue of civil war. The government will not assail you. You can have no conflict without being yourselves the aggressors. You have no oath registered in heaven to destroy the government, while I shall have the most solemn one to "preserve, protect, and defend it."

I am loath to close. We are not enemies, but friends. We must not be enemies. Though passion may have strained, it must not break our bonds of affection. The mystic chords of memory, stretching from every battle-field and patriot grave to every living heart and hearthstone all over this broad land, will yet swell the chorus of the Union when again touched, as surely they will be, by the better angels of our nature.

1861

» » THE GETTYSBURG ADDRESS « «

Delivered at the Dedication of the National Cemetery, November 19, 1863

Fourscore and seven years ago our fathers brought forth on this continent a new nation, conceived in liberty, and dedicated to the proposition that all men are created equal.

Now we are engaged in a great civil war, testing whether that nation, or any nation so conceived and so dedicated, can long endure. We are met on a great battle-field of that war. We have come to dedicate a portion of that field as a final resting-place for those who here gave their lives that that nation might live. It is altogether fitting and proper that we should do this.

But, in a larger sense, we cannot dedicate—we cannot consecrate—we cannot hallow—this ground. The brave men, living and dead, who struggled here, have consecrated it far above our poor power to add or detract. The world will little note nor long remember what we say here, but it can never forget what they did here. It is for us, the living, rather, to be dedicated here to the unfinished work which they who fought here have thus far so nobly advanced. It is rather for us to be here dedicated to the great task remaining before us—that from these honored dead we take increased devotion to that cause for which they gave the last full measure of devotion; that we here highly resolve that these dead shall not have died in vain; that this nation, under God, shall have a new birth of freedom; and that government of the people, by the people, for the people, shall not perish from the earth.[1]

[1] The phrase, "a government of all the people, by all the people, for all the people," had been used in 1850 by the radical preacher, Theodore Parker.

» » SECOND INAUGURAL ADDRESS « «

Fellow-Countrymen: At this second appearing to take the oath of the presidential office, there is less occasion for an extended address than there was at the first. Then a statement, somewhat in detail, of a course to be pursued, seemed fitting and proper. Now, at the expiration of four years, during which public declarations have been constantly called forth on every point and phase of the great contest which still absorbs the attention and engrosses the energies of the nation, little that is new could be presented. The progress of our arms, upon which all else chiefly depends, is as well known to the public as to myself; and it is, I trust, reasonably satisfactory and encouraging to all. With high hope for the future, no prediction in regard to it is ventured.

On the occasion corresponding to this four years ago, all thoughts were anxiously directed to an impending civil war. All dreaded it—all sought to avert it. While the inaugural address was being delivered from this place, devoted altogether to saving the Union without war, insurgent agents were in the city seeking to destroy it without war—seeking to dissolve the Union, and divide effects, by negotiation. Both parties deprecated war; but one of them would make war rather than let the nation survive; and the other would accept war rather than let it perish. And the war came.

One-eighth of the whole population were colored slaves, not distributed generally over the Union, but localized in the Southern part of it. These slaves constituted a peculiar and powerful interest. All knew that this interest was, somehow, the cause of the war. To strengthen, perpetuate, and extend this interest was the object for which the insurgents would rend the Union, even by war; while the government claimed no right to do more than to restrict the territorial enlargement of it.

Neither party expected for the war the magnitude or the duration which it has already attained. Neither anticipated that the cause of the conflict might cease with, or even before, the conflict itself should cease. Each looked for an easier triumph, and a result less fundamental and astounding. Both read the same Bible, and pray to the same God; and each invokes his aid against the other. It may seem strange that any men should dare to ask a just God's assistance in wringing their bread from the sweat of other men's faces; but let us judge not, that we be not judged. The prayers of both could not be answered—that of neither has been answered fully.

The Almighty has his own purposes. "Woe unto the world because of offenses! for it must needs be that offenses come; but woe to that man by whom the offense cometh." If we shall suppose that American slavery is one of those offenses which, in the providence of God, must needs come, but which, having continued through his appointed time, he now wills to remove, and that he gives to both North and South this terrible war, as the woe due to those by whom the offense came, shall we discern therein any departure from those divine attributes which the believers in a living God always ascribe to him? Fondly do we hope —fervently do we pray—that this mighty scourge of war may speedily pass away. Yet, if God wills that it continue until all the wealth 10 piled by the bondman's two hundred and fifty years of unrequited toil shall be sunk, and until every drop of blood drawn with the lash shall be paid by another drawn with the sword, as was said three thousand years ago, so still it must be said, "The judgments of the Lord are true and righteous altogether."

With malice toward none; with charity for all; with firmness in the right, as God gives us to see the right, let us strive on to finish the work 20 we are in; to bind up the nation's wounds; to care for him who shall have borne the battle, and for his widow, and his orphan—to do all which may achieve and cherish a just and lasting peace among ourselves, and with all nations.   1865

CLEMENT LAIRD VALLANDIGHAM

1820–1871

THE SON of a Presbyterian minister of Southern background, Clement L. Vallandigham was admitted to the Ohio bar and became prominent in the politics of the Democratic party of the Buckeye state. Although Vallandigham admitted the moral and political evil of slavery, he favored a "hands-off" policy, the suppression of the abolitionists as fanatics, and a strict-construction philosophy of the Jeffersonian school. As a member of the House of Representatives on the eve of the Civil War he favored compromise and opposed measures for defense; and after the War broke out, he insisted on the maintenance of the right of free speech and on the restoration of peace on any terms. Vallandigham's pleas for "the Constitution as it is, the Union as it was," won much support in the North, where opinion on the desirability of continuing the war was divided. Vallandigham became leader of "the peace party" and commander of the disloyalist "Order of the Sons of Liberty."

After expressing sympathy for the South and opposing conscription, and after denouncing the war as a "wicked and cruel" effort to enthrone Republican despotism and to destroy slavery, Vallandigham was tried on May 6, 1863, by a military tribunal in Cincinnati for expressing treasonable sentiments. Lincoln banished him to the Confederacy, from which he escaped to Ontario. On Canadian soil he conducted a campaign for the governorship of Ohio on the platform of the Peace Democrats; and in 1864 he persuaded the Democratic national convention to declare the War a failure. The following address, given in New York on March 7, 1863, before the Democratic Union Association, is representative of his position and of his complete sincerity.

Speeches, Arguments, Addresses and Letters of Clement L. Vallandigham, New York, 1864.
J. L. Vallandigham, *A Life of Clement L. Vallandigham*, Baltimore, 1872.

» » *From:* PEACE—LIBERTY—THE CONSTITUTION « «

. . . Coming immediately from Washington, having witnessed the common satisfaction of the people of this country, the expiration of the Thirty-seventh Congress, I am here to speak, in the first place, briefly of some things which have been done in that body during the recent session, and the session which preceded it. I will not go back so far as the extra session when general insanity prevailed throughout the country, and when the representatives of the people were, perhaps, to a large degree excusable; because while they had doubtless contributed to that insanity, it was reflected back upon them again; but after a period given for meditation, after the logic of events had begun to work out, after the experiment of war had been tried for one year, it seems to me that wise men, men in whose hands you can with safety deposit the power that belongs to you, should have meditated a little while, and with some degree of wisdom have proceeded to legislate for the true interests of the country. Did they do it? What has been the legislation financially, to begin with that? Where were we then? What was your currency? Gold. How much have you seen lately of it? You read of it in the stock market, impalpable, invisible—a thing that belongs to the past; it will go into the collections of those who have a curiosity for coins. What is your currency now? Greenbacks; nor is that all ("Postage stamps"). Postage currency, and to what extent? Nearly a thousand millions already. That is what is offered to you. It is the entertainment to which you were invited, or rather which you were compelled to accept, though not invited to in 1860. Your public debt —what was it then? The enormous sum of seventy-one millions. Would you not be willing to compromise on that today? No doubt even they to whom that word "compromise" is most odious, who feel towards it as Romeo towards the word "banishment," would be very willing to settle the debt of this country at seventy-one millions. It is now, actually or prospectively, be-cause the appropriations reach that extent— $2,277,000,000. That is the sum which this Congress has appropriated. They have given to this tremendous debt, the power that belongs to it by the issuing of what is called a government currency, binding everybody by some sort of paper tie, to the government—by the establishment of a grand national paper-mill, a national bank, and through the other schemes of finance which were formed in the brain, or found a lodgment there somehow or other, of the Secretary of the Treasury. They have, by this instrumentality, obtained absolute control of the entire country. Through a tax law, the like of which never was imposed upon any but a conquered people, they have possession actually or prospectively, of the entire property of the people of the country. Thus the purse, through the swift and anxious servility of a Congress which was intended by our fathers to be the watchful guardian of the people's money and the people's property, is now absolutely and unqualifiedly for two years at the disposal of the Executive of the United States. In ordinary times, the control of that purse was regarded by the jealous lovers of liberty, by the men who preceded those in power, by the men who sat in your places twenty, thirty, or forty years ago, as one of the instruments of despotism—then even when our revenue was down as low as twenty millions of dollars.

. . . And now, as to that other great weapon of government—the sword. What have your "misrepresentatives" done? They gave, and with your consent, ("Never") yes, they did; and I am sorry it is so, my friends. (A voice—"The Republicans.") No, my dear sir, Democrats did it too. I did not. (Cheers) If I had had my way there never would have been a necessity for anything of the kind—the sword never would have been drawn, and we never would have had civil war. The Crittenden propositions would have compromised and settled this difficulty. (Great applause) But Congress, in the beginning, with the concurrence of the people, in a fit of insanity, as I think—no disparagement to them, it was their excessive patriotism that led to it—but they did give first, or recognized, at least, the giving of 75,000 men, then of 87,000, of 637,000, next of 300,000 more, and 300,000 more yet in the form of a draft, making in all of volunteers some 937,000 men. They went out to the field voluntarily. Your representatives gave to the President the control of that number of men—the power at least to call for them—and they went, and your committees helped them to go. There was no place where more was accomplished in that way than in the city of New York. It was then popular to advocate civil war, to enlist or procure enlistments, and to address war meetings. I am sorry some gentlemen have not heard that it is unpopular now. Their habit seems to get control of their judgment. As long as the people said so, though my judgment humbly disapproved of it, I was content to remain silent, and see the experiment tried. But that was not all. Not only have those 937,000 enlisted men, and the 300,-000 drafted men—indeed, I might say the 1,237,000 enlisted men, for the draft was used only to compel and procure enlistments—not only have all these men been sent into the field, or at least made to appear on the payrolls, but in the very expiring hours of the Congress, which died and went to its own place at 12 o'clock on the 4th of March, your misrepresentatives—for such they had become—not speaking the voice of the people, did attempt to clothe the President with the power of conscripting every man in the United States between the ages of twenty and forty-five—to compel him to enter the army and enable the President to keep up a war which, by that bill itself, he and they confess to be against the will of the people. (Applause.) The bill is an admission upon the record, that they cannot, by voluntary enlistment obtain more soldiers to fight in this war. Now, whereas, the Constitution of the United States makes the distinction between the regular army and the militia of the country; whereas it forbids States to keep a standing army, and authorizes the United States to do it, but, on the other hand, leaves to the States the control of the militia, and enables the President or Congress only to call out the militia, as such, for certain specified purposes, and for a limited time, reserving to these States the appointment of officers and the discipline of the militia until they are mustered

into the service of the United States; this bill yet undertakes to make a standing army of more than three millions of the people for three years or during the war. How long will that be? (a voice—"Nine years.") Thus, so far as it is possible, by an enactment having the form of law, the Congress of the United States have surrendered, absolutely, the entire military power of the country to the President. Now, if in possession of the purse and the sword absolutely and unqualifiedly, for two years, there be anything else wanting which describes a dictatorship, I beg to know what it is? Why did they not imitate the manhood of the old Roman Senators when the exigency of the Republic, in their judgment, demanded it, and declare Mr. Lincoln a dictator in terms?—that was alone absolutely what they meant—instead of coward-like, undertaking, in the form of law and by the abuse of constitutional power, to give the same authority and the same agencies to establish a despotism, as would have been implied by the direct creation of a dictatorship. (Applause.) That bill passed the Senate without opposition, and much has been said upon the subject, and great gratification has been expressed by some. Gentlemen, it was a mistake, an accident, not intentional. There was not a Democratic, conservative Senator who was not opposed to it, but happening to be absent at the hour when the vote was taken, the dead hour of midnight,

"When graveyards yawn,
And hell itself breathes out contagion,"

their votes were not recorded; but when the bill came to the House, the minority there were resolved that it should not pass without a severe scrutiny, without a thorough consideration, without all the resistance, by parliamentary tactics and by speech, to which we had a right to resort. It was announced by the Chairman of the Military Committee that no debate should be allowed upon the bill, and what is called the previous question was demanded, for the purpose of bringing us to an immediate vote. Then it was that that little minority, once only five in number, but grown now to thirty, thank God —(cheers)—having enough to call the yeas and nays, resorted to what is the last refuge of a minority in a legislature, and what very aptly is called "fillibustering." Yes, we "fillibustered" on that bill. (Laughter) We did not follow the example of the Abolition Senators in Illinois, who, coming fresh from an election, where they had been rebuked and their party repudiated, yet to prevent the enactment of the will of the people into a law, saw fit to run away and break up the Senate. We stood to our posts, and the only complaint they had to prefer against us was that we stood but too well. Nor did we imitate the revolutionary example of the minority in the Indiana Legislature, who went home for the same purpose, and have remained home now for one week. We did not do that; we "fillibustered," and in the course of a few hours that little minority compelled that great majority, first, to yield the point of debate, and then to adjourn with the understanding that the bill should be open to a thorough discussion. And it was so opened; and such a discussion as the reporters, who have been there for years, and the oldest members and spectators, have all united in the testimony that the like of it had not been witnessed in that Capitol for more than twenty years. We were few, but,

"Thrice is he armed that hath his quarrel just";

and ours was the justest cause that ever was struggled for. We spoke with the courage of freemen, fully conscious that we were standing in the very breach against the rushing torrent of despotism, and as we spoke the Felixes of Abolition trembled, and they gave us another day, and at the end of the discussion, so completely had they been mastered that they consented to strike out every provision in that bill that did not relate to it purely as a military measure. That is what we gained by courage and firmness and manhood. (Applause.) They had provided for the appointment of a Provost-Marshal in every congressional district, with the power to inquire into and report disloyal practices—such as we are engaged in here tonight (laughter)—to report what some Democrat had said in opposition to, not the Government, for Democrats support the Government, but the executive, Abraham Lincoln. That was stricken out. They had authorized the Provost-Marshals—fellows spread all over the country in every congressional district, with a rank of captain of cavalry, and drawing pay, of course —they had authorized them to summarily arrest everybody who should resist the draft, or counsel resistance, or oppose it in any shape, way, or form, and we compelled them to insert a provision that though a person might be thus arrested, summarily, he should be forthwith handed over to the civil authorities to be dealt with. (Applause.) But, as originally proposed,

the bill not only would have but the three or four millions of males between twenty and forty-five, under the military control of the President, as Commander-in-chief, but would also have placed every man, woman, and child, by virtue of the two provisions that were stricken out, also in his power. Our civil rights would have been gone, and our judiciary undermined, and he would have been an absolute and uncontrolled dictator, with the power of Cincinnatus, but without one particle of his virtues. (Cheers.) Yet, unfortunately, while this much was accomplished on that bill, the same tyrannical power was conferred by another bill which passed both houses, and is now, so far as forms are concerned, a law of the land—at least an act of the Thirty-seventh Congress. (Laughter.) It authorizes the President whom the people made, whom the people had chosen by the ballot box under the Constitution and laws, to suspend the writ of *habeas corpus* all over the United States; to say that because there is a rebellion in South Carolina, a man shall not have freedom of speech, freedom of the press, or any of his rights untrammelled in the State of New York, or a thousand miles distant. That was the very question upon which the people passed judgment in the recent elections, more, perhaps, than any other question. The President had assumed to exercise this power by virtue of a proclamation, and had arrogated to himself the prerogative, long since exploded, of the Kings of England. He had exercised this kingly prerogative, and the people had repudiated it; they had said:—"You have no right to suspend this writ, you have no power of arbitrary arrest, and we will not submit to its exercise." Sir, the same argument which was addressed to the people in discussing this question previous to the October and November elections now applies to this so-called act of Congress. The Constitution gives the power to Congress, and to Congress alone, to suspend the writ of *habeas corpus*, but it can only be done in case of invasion or rebellion, and then only when the public safety requires it; and in the opinion of the best jurists of the land, and indeed of every one previous to these times, Congress could only suspend this writ in places actually in rebellion or actually invaded. That is the Constitution. (Cheers.) And whenever this question shall be tried before a court in the State of New York, or Ohio, or Wisconsin, or anywhere else, before honest and fearless judges worthy of the place they occupy, the decision will be that it is unconstitutional. (Loud applause.) . . . Was it this which you were promised, in 1860, in that grand "Wide Awake" campaign, when banners were borne through your streets inscribed "Free speech, free press, and free men?" And all this has been accomplished, so far as the forms of the law go, by the Congress which has just expired. Now, I repeat again, that if there is anything wanting to make up a complete and absolute despotism, as iron and inexorable in its character as the worst despotisms of the old world, or the most detestable of modern times, even to Bomba's of Naples, I am unable to comprehend what it is.

All this, gentlemen, infamous and execrable as it is, is enough to make the blood of the coldest man who has one single appreciation in his heart of freedom, to boil with indignation. (Loud applause.) Still, so long as they leave to us free assemblages, free discussion, and a free ballot, I do not want to see, and will not encourage or countenance, any other mode of ridding ourselves of it. ("That's it," and cheers.) We are ready to try these questions in that way; but I have only to repeat what I said a little while ago, that when the attempt is made to take away those other rights, and the only instrumentalities peaceably of reforming and correcting abuses—free assemblages, free speech, free ballot, and free elections—THEN THE HOUR WILL HAVE ARRIVED WHEN IT WILL BE THE DUTY OF FREEMEN TO FIND SOME OTHER AND EFFICIENT MODE OF DEFENDING THEIR LIBERTIES. (Loud and protracted cheering, the whole audience rising to their feet.) Our fathers did not inaugurate the Revolution of 1776, they did not endure the sufferings and privations of a seven years' war to escape from the mild and moderate control of a constitutional monarchy like that of England, to be at last, in the third generation, subjected to a tyranny equal to that of any upon the face of the globe. (Loud applause.)

. . .

I have spoken now of what this Administration and what the Congress of the United States have done. And for what is all this? What is the purpose to be subserved? For the permitted exercise of such tremendous power —for the surrender of every liberty by a people born free—there ought to be some compensation at least. The maintenance of the Constitution, if the Constitution could be maintained by destroying it, would justify that surrender.

The restoration of the Union of these States, if it could be restored in this way, would not only justify but demand it, because the value would bear some proportion to the price given. In the beginning you were told that the purpose of all the power, previous to the recent legislation of Congress, given to, or usurped by the Executive, was for the maintenance of the Constitution and the restoration of the Union; and with that love for both, which is the highest honor to this people and its only apology (and it will be so recorded) for submitting to what we have done, the people made sacrifices, gave money, sent forth their first-born at the call of the Executive as no other people ever did since the world began. There never was such a struggle in any age or any country. Why? Because the President and all under him did repeatedly and distinctly declare that the sole purpose was to uphold the Constitution which our fathers had made, and the Union which that Constitution established, and to which we owed all our greatness and prosperity. The people of America were willing to sacrifice all these for that great good. It was so said in the President's annual message of the 4th of July, as it had been in his proclamation of the 15th of April, calling forth the militia, in the beginning. It was in the orders and proclamations of every Federal General for the first eight or ten months after he entered the Southern States. The day after the battle of Bull Run, by a vote unanimous save two, Congress declared that the sole purpose of the war should be the maintenance of the Constitution, the restoration of the Union, and the enforcement of the laws; and when these objects were accomplished, the war should cease, without touching the domestic institutions, slavery included, in the Southern States. That pledge was given, and under it an army of six hundred thousand men was at once raised; and it was repeated in every form till towards the close of the second session of Congress. Then the Abolition Senators and Representatives began first to demand a change in the policy of the Administration, they began to proclaim that the war must no longer be for the Union and the Constitution, but for the abolition of slavery in the Southern States. Now, sir, I repeat it and defy contradiction, that not a soldier enlisted, out of the first nine hundred thousand, for any other purpose than the restoration of the Union and the maintenance of the Constitution. There was not one single officer, so far as his public declarations were concerned, whatever may have been the secret purposes of his heart, that did not openly declare that the moment this object was changed to the abolition of slavery, he would throw up his commission and resign. Yes, the very men who, for the last four or five weeks in the army—the officers—I do not mean your private soldiers, they who do picket duty, who stand in the front ranks, who brave the iron hail and leaden rain of the stormy battle-field, the men who sacrifice their lives for the paltry sum of thirteen dollars a month, the noble, brave men, who, if they were at home, would give us their votes, as their sympathies are still with us; I speak of your officers only—your majors, your lieutenant-colonels, colonels, brigadiers, and major-generals, each one of them seeking promotion, and drawing his salary of two, three, four, five, six, and seven thousand dollars a year, and whose interest it is that the war be made eternal. They are the men who have been holding these meetings of regiments so-called, concocting resolutions, or rather adopting resolutions concocted in Indianapolis, Columbus, Springfield, or Washington, and sent down to be clothed in form as an expression of the opinion of the regiments, but, in fact, the expression of the officers alone. They are men who have solemnly declared, at home and in the army, that the moment this became an Abolition war, they would resign and come back to us, and yet they are now sending out these missiles to us their peers—threatening messages that they mean to come back and "whip" the Democratic traitors and secessionists of the North.

. . .

. . . We are the masters of these officials. They are liable to be tried at drum-head courts-martial, according to military law, and punished under that law. We are, and we mean to be, tried only by the judicial tribunals in our midst. (Applause.) Let them look, then, to the discipline of their regiments, brigades, and divisions; let them see to it that they make themselves efficient military officers; but while they are at a distance, without the means of communicating with the people or knowing anything about political questions, let them confine themselves to their legitimate duties, and allow us, unmolested, to attend to ours. But there is not one of those who have participated in these meetings, who did not declare repeatedly at home and in the army, that the moment that this was proclaimed to be a war for the abolition of slavery, he would resign his commission; yet now, because we would oppose this war for abolition, because we would maintain the position that we have held from the beginning, they, forsooth, dare to taunt us with treason, and to impeach our fidelity to our country. Such, then, gentlemen, was the purpose originally declared of this war. Now, what is it today? Let any man honestly and conscientiously judge. I speak not as a mere partisan; I speak what will be regarded as historic truth. Look at the legislation of Congress, your confiscation bill, your emancipation schemes, the proclamation of the 22nd of September, reiterated on the first of January last. Look at the fact that to-day the entire purpose and object of the war, as proclaimed by the Executive and by Congress is the overthrow of slavery in the Southern States. Now, why is it not so? What did the men who were accustomed to address war meetings in New York and elsewhere say? What did the gentlemen who spoke last night declare? Months ago, if it should become a war for the abolition of slavery, what did they declare it was their purpose to do? Did they not denounce it? Did they not denounce it even during the last canvass in the State of New York and elsewhere? We did, too. We abide by these declarations to-day, and we mean to make them good. It being then conceded that this is the purpose, we have the testimony of these very men themselves, some of them of the Democratic party, and many of the Republican or Abolition party, that a war against the South, a war for subjugation and to abolish slavery, would end in the destruction of the Union and in the establishment of a despotism in our midst. There is not a man among them that is not on the record in that declaration. Did they believe it? If they did not, I did; and I believe it tonight, and am with every man who does believe that a war carried on upon this basis can never succeed in its purpose—that it must either end in disunion, or in establishing a tyranny at home. What shall we do? If there be any man, and I repeat what I said upon another occasion—if there be any man in the Democratic or Republican party who still thinks that war can restore the Union as it was and maintain the Constitution as it is, I have no quarrel with him tonight. I assume his position for the sake of argument—it is not mine, and never was; but let it be so for a moment. You say that a war prosecuted for this purpose must thus result. Have you the power to change the purpose? Can you compel Abraham Lincoln to withdraw his proclamation? Can you repeal the legislation of the Congress, that is now defunct? If you cannot, the war must go on upon the basis on which it is now prosecuted—and you believe that it will end in death to the Union, the Constitution, and to Liberty.

What position, then, do you occupy before your countrymen in still advocating the so-called vigorous prosecution of the war? Vigorous prosecution! For what? By your own declaration—disunion, separation, destruction, despotism. Dare any man stand before an assembly of freemen and advocate the objects, or the results, at least, of such a war? And yet, what inconsistency for anyone claiming intelligence, to declare that although it must so result, and although he has not the power to change the policy of the Administration, it is the duty of everyman to support that Administration in its policy. I deny it (cheers); and for one, at least, I will not do it. If I had believed originally, as I did not believe, that it was possible to restore this Union by force, if I had occupied the position of hundreds and thousands of Democrats, as well as the great mass of the Republicans, I would proclaim tonight that, inasmuch as this is the policy, and we have not the power to change it, that then our duty would be, and is, to advocate henceforth to the end, A VIGOROUS PROSECUTION OF PEACE FOR THE UNION. (Loud cheers.) I will not consent to put the entire purse of the country and the sword of the country into the hands of the Executive, giving him despotic and dictatorial power to carry out an object which I avow before my countrymen is the destruction of their liberties, and the overthrow of the Union of these States. I do not comprehend the honesty of such declarations, or of the men who make them. I know that the charge is brought against myself, personally, and against many of us—(A voice—"Never mind.") I have not spent a moment replying to it——the people will take care of all that. (Applause.) The charge has been made against us—all who are opposed to the policy of this Administration and opposed to this war—that we are for "peace on any terms." It is false. I am not, but I am for an immediate stopping of the war and for honorable peace. I am for peace for the sake of the Union of these States. More than that—I am for peace, and would be, even if the Union could not be restored, as I believe it can be; because, without peace, per-

mitting this Administration for two years to exercise its tremendous powers, the war still existing, you will not have one remnant of civil liberty left among yourselves. (Great applause.) The exercise of these tremendous powers, the apology for which is the existence of this war, is utterly incompatible with the stability of the Constitution and of constitutional liberty. (Cheers.) I am not for "peace on any terms"; I would not be with any country on the globe. Honor is also the life of the nation, and it is never to be sacrificed. I have as high and proud a sense of honor, and have a right to have it, as any man in the South, and I love my country too well, and cherish its honor too profoundly, for one single moment to consent to a dishonorable peace. (A voice—"The whole country.") Yes, the whole country; every State; and I, unlike some of my own party, and unlike thousands of the Abolition party, believe still, before God, that the Union can be reconstructed and will be. (Great applause.) That is my faith, and I mean to cling to it as the wrecked mariner clings to the last plank amid the ship-wreck. But when I see that the experiment of blood has failed from the beginning, as I believed it would fail, I am not one of those who proclaim now that we shall have separation and disunion. I am for going back to the instrumentality through which this union was first made, and by which alone it can be restored. (Cheers.) I am for peace, because it is the first step toward conciliation and compromise. You cannot move until you have first taken that indispensable preliminary—a cessation of hostilities. But it is said that the South has refused to accept or listen to any terms whatever. How do you know that? Has it been tried? Now, gentlemen, I know very well what the papers in support of the government at Richmond say. I know what men in the Senate and House of Representatives at Richmond declare on this subject; I have read it all. We are indebted to the Abolition papers for the republication of all that. But I do hope that no man who has ever known me in person or by speech, supposed for one moment, that I expected that the children of that revolution, the men who sprang from it, the men who are dependent upon it, or even the men holding power now under it would, while this war lasted, listen to any terms of settlement. I would as soon expect Abraham Lincoln and his cabinet to propose such terms on the basis of the Union of fifty years ago, as Jefferson Davis or any man in Richmond. Now, I am not, perhaps, the most sensitive man in the world, and yet I have a reasonable degree of sensitiveness, and I hope, some common sense with it—but I do not feel, as I am afraid some of our friends do feel, personally slighted, because, while I have advocated a peaceable settlement of our difficulties —conciliation and compromise for the restoration of the Union of these States—I have met with opposition and with hostility from the papers in Richmond. I did not look for it, gentlemen, although I have a better right to it than some of your friends here (A voice— "Van Buren") from my former relation to the Democratic party of the South, when they were acknowledging obedience to the Constitution, and were still in the Union; but I did not expect that Jefferson Davis, and Benjamin, and Hunter, or any of them would, when I opened my arms and said—"Return, prodigal sons,"

rush with tears to my embrace,—and I do not feel hurt. I am not the least "miffed" by it; and I certainly shall not therefore advocate a vigorous prosecution of the war to punish them. I am afraid some gentlemen imagined, when they gave out this invitation, that it would be, of course, accepted at once; although one of those who first proclaimed it, had even less power than I have, certainly not more—and was very much in the condition of that distinguished personage who, from the top of a certain high mountain, promised all the kingdoms of the world. I do not think that he or I, or any other man while this Administration is in place, has the power to conciliate and compromise now. Take the theory for what it is worth, and let men of intelligence judge; let history attest it hereafter. My theory upon that subject, then, is this—stop this war. (Cheers).

1863

GEORGE CARY EGGLESTON

1839–1911

INHERITING, at the age of seventeen, his family's plantation in Amelia County, Virginia, Eggleston was plunged from a restricted life as an Indiana Methodist and country school-teacher into the amenities of the Virginia gentry. His literary interests were confirmed, during his study of law at Richmond College, by his association with John Esten Cooke and other members of the literary circle in Virginia's capital. After an active and sustained service in the Confederate army, Eggleston tried his hand at various business adventures in Illinois and in Mississippi: but in 1870 he launched himself on a journalistic and literary career in New York City. His best known novels depicted, in a highly romantic vein, the life of the Old Dominion—*Dorothy South* (1902) and *The Master of Warlock* (1903) are only two of a long series. Eggleston also wrote many "histories" and stories for boys, especially the *Big Brother* series. His services to various periodicals, both as editor and contributor, and to the *New York Evening Post* and the *New York World*, enabled him to espouse the cause of an American literature independent of that of Great Britain.

Eggleston's *A Rebel's Recollections* (1875) is one of the illuminating contributions of a Confederate participant in the Civil War.

G. C. Eggleston, *The First of the Hoosiers*, Philadelphia, 1903.
G. C. Eggleston, *Recollections of a Varied Life*, New York, 1910.
A Rebel's Recollections, Bloomington, Ind., 1959.

» » From: A REBEL'S RECOLLECTIONS « «

CHAPTER VIII

RED TAPE

The history of the Confederacy, when it shall be fully and fairly written, will appear the story of a dream to those who shall read it, and there are parts of it at least which already seem a nightmare to those of us who helped make it. Founded upon a constitution which jealously withheld from it nearly all the powers of government, without even the poor privilege of existing beyond the moment when some one of the States composing it should see fit to put it to death, the Richmond government nevertheless grew speedily into a despotism, and for four years wielded absolute power over an obedient and uncomplaining people. It tolerated no questioning, brooked no resistance, listened to no remonstrance. It levied taxes of an extraordinary kind upon a people already impoverished almost to the point of starvation. It made of every man a soldier, and extended indefinitely every man's term of enlistment. Under pretense of enforcing the conscription law it established an oppressive system of domiciliary visits. To preserve order and prevent desertion it instituted and maintained a system of guards and passports, not less obnoxious, certainly, than the worst thing of the sort ever devised by the most paternal of despotisms. In short, a government constitutionally weak beyond all precedent was able for four years to exercise in a particularly offensive way all the powers of absolutism, and that, too, over a people who had been living under republican rule for generations. . . .

Nothing could possibly be idler than speculation upon what might have been accomplished with the resources of the South if they had been properly economized and wisely used. And yet every Southern man must feel tempted to indulge in some such speculation whenever he thinks of the subject at all, and remembers, as he must, how shamefully those resources were wasted and how clumsily they were handled in every attempt to use them in the prosecution of the war. The army was composed, as we have seen in a previous chapter, of excellent material; and under the influence of field service, it soon became a very efficient body of well-drilled and well-disciplined men. The skill of its leaders is matter of history, too well known to need comment here. But the government controlling army and leaders was both passively and actively incompetent in a surprising degree. It did, as nearly as possible, *all* those things which it ought not to have done, at the same time developing a really marvelous genius for leaving undone those things which it ought to have done. The story of its incompetence and its presumption, if it could be adequately told, would read like a romance. Its weakness paralyzed the army and people, and its weakness was the less hurtful side of its character. Its full capacity for ill was best seen in the extraordinary strength it developed whenever action of a wrong-headed sort could work disaster, and the only wonder is that with such an administration at its back the Confederate army was able to keep the field at all. I have already had occasion to explain that the sentiment of the South made it the duty of every man who could bear arms to go straight to the front and to stay there. The acceptance of any less actively military position than that of a soldier in the field was held to be little less than a confession of cowardice; and cowardice, in the eyes of the Southerners, is the one sin which may not be pardoned either in this world or the next. The strength of this sentiment it is difficult for anybody who did not live in its midst to conceive, and its effect was to make worthy men spurn everything like civic position. To go where the bullets were whistling was the one course open to gentlemen who held their honor sacred and their reputation dear And so the offices in Richmond and elsewhere, the bureaus of every sort, on the proper conduct of which so much depended, were filled with men willing to be sneered at as dwellers in "bomb-proofs" and holders of "life insurance policies."

. . .

But, if we may believe the testimony of those who were in position to know the facts, the grand master of incapacity, whose hand was felt everywhere, was President Davis himself. Not content with perpetually meddling in the smallest matters of detail, and prescribing the petty routine of office work in the bureau, he interfered, either directly or through his personal subordinates, with military operations which no man, not present with the army, could be competent to control, and which he, probably, was incapable of justly comprehending in any case. With the history of his quarrels with the generals in the field, and the paralyzing effect they had upon military operations, the public is already familiar. Leaving things of that nature to the historian, I confine myself to smaller matters, my purpose being merely to give the reader an idea of the experiences of a Confederate soldier, and to show him Confederate affairs as they looked when seen from the inside.

I can hardly hope to make the ex-soldier of the Union understand fully how we on the other side were fed in the field. He fought and marched with a skilled commissariat at his back, and, for his further staff of comfort, had the Christian and Sanitary commissions, whose handy tin cups and other camp conveniences came to us only through the uncertain and irregular channel of abandonment and capture; and unless his imagination be a vivid one, he will not easily conceive the state of our commissariat or the privations we suffered as a consequence of its singularly bad management. The first trouble was, that we had for a commissary-general a crotchety doctor, some of whose acquaintances had for years believed him insane. Aside from his suspected mental aberration, and the crochets which had made his life already a failure he knew nothing whatever of the business belonging to the department under his control, his whole military experience having consisted of a few years' service as a lieutenant of cavalry in one of the Territories, many years before the date of his appointment as chief of subsistence in the Confederacy. Wholly without experience to guide him, he was forced to evolve from his own badly balanced intellect whatever system he should adopt, and from the beginning of the war until the early part of the year 1865, the Confederate armies were forced to lean upon this broken reed in the all-important matter of a food supply. The generals commanding in the field, we are told on the very highest authority, protested, suggested, remonstrated almost daily, but their remonstrances were unheeded and their suggestions set at naught. At Manassas, where the army was well-nigh starved out in the very beginning of the war, food might have been abundant but for the obstinacy of this one man. On our left lay a country unsurpassed, and almost unequaled, in productiveness. It was rich in grain and meat, these being its special products. A railroad, with next to nothing to do, penetrated it, and its stores of food were nearly certain to be exposed to the enemy before any other part of the country should be conquered. The obvious duty of the commissary-general, therefore, was to draw upon that section for the supplies which were both convenient and abundant. The chief of subsistence ruled otherwise, however, thinking it better to let that source of supply lie exposed to the first advance of the enemy, while he drew upon the Richmond *dépôts* for a daily ration, and shipped it by the overtasked line of railway leading from the capital to Manassas. It was nothing to him that he was thus exhausting the rear and crippling the resources of the country for the future. It was nothing to him that in the midst of plenty the army was upon a short allowance of food. It was nothing that the shipments of provisions from Richmond by this railroad seriously interfered with other important interests. System was everything, and this was a part of his system. The worst of it was, that in this all-important branch of the service experience and organization wrought little if any improvement as the war went on, so that as the supplies and the means of transportation grew smaller, the undiminished inefficiency of the department produced disastrous results. The army, suffering for food, was disheartened by the thought that the scarcity was due to the exhaustion of the country's resources. Red tape was supreme, and no sword was permitted to cut it. I remember one little circumstance, which will serve to illustrate the absoluteness with which system was suffered to override sense in the administration of the affairs of the subsistence department. I served for a time on the coast of South Carolina, a country which produces rice in great abundance, and in which fresh pork and mutton might then be had almost for the asking, while the climate is wholly unsuited to the making of flour or bacon. Just at that time, however, the officials of the commissary department saw fit to feed the whole army on bacon and flour, articles which, if given to troops in that quarter of the country at all, must be brought several hundred miles by rail. The local commissary officers made various suggestions looking to the use of the provisions of which the country round about was full, but, so far as I could learn, no attention whatever was paid to them. At the request of one of these post commissaries, I wrote an elaborate and respectful letter on the subject, setting forth the fact that rice, sweet potatoes, corn meal, hominy, grits, mutton, and pork existed in great abundance in the immediate neighborhood of the troops, and could be bought for less than one third the cost of the flour and bacon we were eating. The letter was signed by the post commissary, and forwarded through the regular channels, with the most favorable indorsements possible, but it resulted in nothing. The department presently found it impossible to give us full rations of bacon and flour, but it still refused to think of the remedy suggested. It cut down the ration instead, thus reducing the men to a state of semi-starvation in a country full of food. Relief came at last in the shape of a technicality, else it would not have been allowed to come at all. A vigilant captain discovered that the men were entitled by law to commutation in money for their rations, at fixed rates, and acting upon this the men were able to buy, with the money paid them in lieu of rations, an abundance of fresh meats and vegetables; and most of the companies managed at the same time to save a considerable fund for future use out of the surplus, so great was the disparity between the cost of the food they bought and that which the government wished to furnish them.

. . .

But it was in Richmond that routine was carried to its absurdest extremities. There, everything was done by rule except those things to which system of some sort would have been of advantage, and they were left at loose ends. Among other things a provost system was devised and brought to perfection during the time of martial law. Having once tasted the sweets of despotic rule, its chief refused to resign any part of his absolute sovereignty over the city, even when the reign of martial law ceased by limitation of time. His system of guards and passports was a very marvel of annoying inefficiency. It effectually blocked the way of every man who was intent upon doing his duty, while it gave unconscious but sure protection to spies, blockade-runners, deserters, and absentees without leave from the armies. It was omnipotent for the annoyance of soldier and citizen, but utterly worthless for any good purpose. If a soldier on furlough or even on detached duty arrived in Richmond, he was taken in charge by the provost guards at the railway station, marched to the soldiers' home or some other vile prison house, and kept there in durance during the whole time of his stay. It mattered not how legitimate his papers were, or how evident his correctness of purpose. The system required that he should be locked up, and locked up he was, in every case, until one plucky fellow made fight by appeal to the courts, and so compelled the abandonment of a practice for which there was never any warrant in law or necessity in fact.

Richmond being the railroad centre from which the various lines radiated, nearly every furloughed soldier and officer on leave was obliged to pass through the city, going home and returning. Now to any ordinary intelligence it would seem that a man bearing a full description of himself and a furlough signed by his captain, colonel, brigadier, division-commander, lieutenant-general, and finally by Robert E. Lee as general-in-chief, might have been allowed to go peaceably to his home by the nearest route. But that was no ordinary intelligence which ruled Richmond. Its ability to find places in which to interfere was unlimited, and it decreed that no soldier should leave Richmond, either to go home or to return direct to the army, without a brown paper passport, signed by an officer appointed for that purpose, and countersigned by certain other persons whose authority to sign or countersign anything nobody was ever able to trace to its source. If any such precaution had been necessary, it would not have been so bad, or even being unnecessary, if there had been the slightest disposition on the part of these passport people to facilitate obedience to their own requirements, the long-suffering officers and men of the army would have uttered no word of complaint. But the facts were exactly the reverse. The passport officials rigidly maintained the integrity of their office hours, and neither entreaty nor persuasion would induce them in any case to anticipate by a single minute the hour for beginning, or to postpone the time of ending their daily duties. I stood one day in their office in a crowd of fellow soldiers and officers, some on furlough going home, some returning after a brief visit, and still others, like myself, going from one place to another under orders and on duty. The two trains by which most of us had to go were both to leave within an hour, and if we should lose them we must remain twenty-four hours longer in Richmond, where the hotel rate was then sixty dollars a day. In full view of these facts, the passport men, daintily dressed, sat there behind their railing, chatting and laughing for a full hour, suffering both trains to depart and all these men to be left over than do thirty minutes' work in advance of the improperly fixed office hour. It resulted from this system that many men on three or five days' leave lost nearly the whole of it in delays, going and returning. Many others were kept in Richmond for want of a passport until their furloughs expired, when they were arrested for absence without leave, kept three or four days in the guardhouse, and then taken as prisoners to their commands, to which they had tried hard to go of their own motion at the proper time. Finally the abuse became so outrageous that General Lee, in his capacity of general-in-chief, issued a peremptory order forbidding anybody to interfere in any way with officers or soldiers traveling under his written authority.

. . . Throughout the management of affairs in Richmond a cumbrous inefficiency was everywhere manifest. From the president, who insulted his premier for presuming to offer some advice about the conduct of the war, and quarreled with his generals because they failed to see the wisdom of a military movement suggested by himself, down to the pettiest clerk in a bureau, there was everywhere a morbid sensitiveness on the subject of personal dignity, and an exaggerated regard for routine, which seriously impaired the efficiency of the government and greatly annoyed the army. Under all the circumstances the reader will not be surprised to learn that the government at Richmond was by no means idolized by the men in the field.

The wretchedness of its management began to bear fruit early in the war, and the fruit was bitter in the mouths of the soldiers. Mr. Davis's evident hostility to Generals Beauregard and Johnston, which showed itself in his persistent refusal to let them concentrate their men, in his obstinate thwarting of all their plans, and in his interference with the details of army organization on which they were agreed,—a hostility born, as General Thomas Jordan gives us to understand, of their failure to see the wisdom of his plan of campaign after Bull Run, which was to take the army across the lower Potomac at a point where it could never hope to recross, for the purpose of capturing a small force lying there under General Sickles,—was

not easily concealed; and the army was too intelligent not to know that a meddlesome and dictatorial president, on bad terms with his generals in the field, and bent upon thwarting their plans, was a very heavy load to carry. The generals held their peace, as a matter of course, but the principal facts were well known to officers and men, and when the time came, in the fall of 1861, for the election of a president under the permanent constitution (Mr. Davis having held office provisionally only, up to that time), there was a very decided disposition on the part of the troops to vote against him. They were told, however, that as there was no candidate opposed to him, he must be elected at any rate, and that the moral effect of showing a divided front to the enemy would be very bad indeed; and in this way only was the undivided vote of the army secured for him. The troops voted for Mr. Davis thus under stress of circumstances, in the hope that all would yet be well; but his subsequent course was not calculated to reinstate him in their confidence, and the wish that General Lee might see fit to usurp all the powers of government was a commonly expressed one, both in the army and in private life during the last two years of the war.

The favoritism which governed nearly every one of the president's appointments was the leading, though not the only, ground of complaint. And truly the army had reason to murmur, when one of the president's pets was promoted all the way from lieutenant-colonel to lieutenant-general, having been but once in battle,—and then only constructively so,—on his way up, while colonels by the hundred, and brigadier and major generals by the score, who had been fighting hard and successfully all the time, were left as they were. And when this suddenly created general, almost without a show of resistance surrendered one of the most important strongholds in the country, together with a veteran army of considerable size, is it any wonder that we questioned the wisdom of the president whose blind favoritism had dealt the cause so severe a blow? But not content with this, as soon as the surrendered general was exchanged the president tried to place him in command of the defenses of Richmond, then hard pressed by General Grant, and was only prevented from doing so by the man's own discovery that the troops would not willingly serve under him.

The extent to which presidential partiality

and presidential intermeddling with affairs in the field were carried may be guessed, perhaps, from the fact that the *Richmond Examiner,* the newspaper which most truly reflected the sentiment of the people, found consolation for the loss of Vicksburg and New Orleans in the thought that the consequent cutting of the Confederacy in two freed the trans-Mississippi armies from paralyzing dictation. In its leading article for October 5, 1864, the *Examiner* said:—

"The fall of New Orleans and the surrender of Vicksburg proved blessings to the cause beyond the Mississippi. It terminated the *régime* of pet generals. It put a stop to official piddling in the conduct of the armies and the plan of campaigns. The moment when it became impossible to send orders by telegraph to court officers, at the head of troops who despised them, was the moment of the turning tide."

So marked was the popular discontent, not with Mr. Davis only, but with the entire government and Congress as well, that a Richmond newspaper at one time dared to suggest a counter revolution as the only means left of saving the cause from the strangling it was receiving at the hands of its guardians in Rich-

mond. And the suggestion seemed so very reasonable and timely that it startled nobody, except perhaps a congressman or two who had no stomach for field service.

The approach of the end wrought no change in the temper of the government, and one of its last acts puts in the strongest light its disposition to sacrifice the interests of the army to the convenience of the court. When the evacuation of Richmond was begun, a train load of provisions was sent by General Lee's order from one of the interior *dépôts* to Amelia Court House, for the use of the retreating army which was without food and must march to that point before it could receive a supply. But the president and his followers were in haste to leave the capital, and needed the train, wherefore it was not allowed to remain at Amelia Court House long enough to be unloaded, but was hurried on to Richmond, where its cargo was thrown out to facilitate the flight of the president and his personal followers, while the starving army was left to suffer in an utterly exhausted country, with no source of supply anywhere within its reach. The surrender of the army was already inevitable, it is true, but that fact in no way justified this last, crowning act of selfishness and cruelty.   1875

FRANK WILKESON

1848–1913

RELATIVELY FEW common soldiers wrote their experiences during the Civil War. Frank Wilkeson, whose father was a Buffalo lawyer and manufacturer, began his war career as a private: subsequently he served as 2d Lieutenant, Battery K, 4th United States Artillery. His *Recollections of a Private Soldier in the Army of the Potomac* (1887) provide a straightforward account and not altogether pleasant reading. After the war Wilkeson was identified with the *New York Sun* and the *New York Times.*

» » *From:* RECOLLECTIONS OF A PRIVATE SOLDIER « «

CHAPTER XI

HOW MEN DIE IN BATTLE

Almost every death on the battle-field is different. And the manner of the death depends on the wound and on the man, whether he is cowardly or brave, whether his vitality is large or small, whether he is a man of active imagination or is dull of intellect, whether he is of nervous or lymphatic temperament. I instance deaths and wounds that I saw in Grant's last campaign.

On the second day of the battle of the Wilderness, where I fought as an infantry soldier, I saw more men killed and wounded than I did before or after in the same time. I knew but few of the men in the regiment in whose ranks I stood; but I learned the Christian names of some of them. The man who stood next to me on my right was called Will. He was cool, brave, and intelligent. In the morning, when the Second Corps was advancing and driving Hill's soldiers slowly back, I was flurried. He noticed it, and steadied my nerves by saying, kindly: "Don't fire so fast. This fight will last all day. Don't hurry. Cover your man before you pull your trigger. Take it easy, my boy, take it easy, and your cartridges will last the longer." This man fought effectively. During the day I had learned to look up to this excellent soldier, and lean on him. Toward evening, as we were being slowly driven back to the Brock Road by Longstreet's men, we made a stand. I was behind a tree firing, with my rifle barrel resting on the stub of a limb. Will was standing by my side, but in the open. He, with a groan, doubled up and dropped on the ground at my feet. He looked up at me. His face was pale. He gasped for breath a few times, and then said, faintly: "That ends me. I am shot through the bowels." I said: "Crawl to the rear. We are not far from the intrenchments along the Brock Road." I saw him sit up, and indistinctly saw him reach for his rifle, which had fallen from his hands as he fell. Again I spoke to him, urging him to go to the rear. He looked at me and said impatiently: "I tell you that I am as good as dead. There is no use in fooling with me. I shall stay here." Then he pitched forward dead, shot again and through the head. We fell back before Longstreet's soldiers and left Will lying in a windrow of dead men.

When we got into the Brock Road intrenchments, a man a few files to my left dropped dead, shot just above the right eye. He did not groan, or sigh, or make the slightest physical movement, except that his chest heaved a few times. The life went out of his face instantly, leaving it without a particle of expression. It was plastic, and, as the facial muscles contracted, it took many shapes. When this man's body became cold, and his face hardened, it was horribly distorted, as though he had suffered intensely. Any person who had not seen him killed, would have said that he had endured supreme agony before death released him. A few minutes after he fell, an-

other man, a little farther to the left, fell with apparently a precisely similar wound. He was straightened out and lived for over an hour. He did no speak, simply lay on his back, and his broad chest rose and fell, slowly at first, and then faster and faster, and more and more feebly, until he was dead. And his face hardened, and it was almost terrifying in its painful distortion. I have seen dead soldiers' faces which were wreathed in smiles, and heard their comrades say that they had died happy. I do not believe that the face of a dead soldier, lying on a battle-field, ever truthfully indicates the mental or physical anguish, or peacefulness of mind, which he suffered or enjoyed before his death. The face is plastic after death, and as the facial muscles cool and contract, they draw the face into many shapes. Sometimes the dead smile, again they stare with glassy eyes, and lolling tongues, and dreadfully distorted visages at you. It goes for nothing. One death was as painless as the other.

After Longstreet's soldiers had driven the Second Corps into their intrenchments along the Brock Road, a battle-exhausted infantryman stood behind a large oak tree. His back rested against it. He was very tired, and held his rifle loosely in his hand. The Confederates were directly in our front. This soldier was apparently in perfect safety. A solid shot from a Confederate gun struck the oak tree squarely about four feet from the ground; but it did not have sufficient force to tear through the tough wood. The soldier fell dead. There was not a scratch on him. He was killed by concussion.

While we were fighting savagely over these intrenchments the woods in our front caught fire, and I saw many of our wounded burned to death. Must they not have suffered horribly? I am not at all sure of that. The smoke rolled heavily and slowly before the fire. It enveloped the wounded, and I think that by far the larger portion of the men who were roasted were suffocated before the flames curled round them. The spectacle was courage-sapping and pitiful, and it appealed strongly to the imagination of the spectators; but I do not believe that the wounded soldiers, who were being burned, suffered greatly, if they suffered at all.

Wounded soldiers, it mattered not how slight the wounds, generally hastened away from the battle lines. A wound entitled a man to go to the rear and to a hospital. Of course there were many exceptions to this rule, as there would necessarily be in battles where from twenty thousand to thirty thousand men were wounded. I frequently saw slightly wounded men who were marching with their colors. I personally saw but two men wounded who continued to fight. During the first day's fighting in the wilderness I saw a youth of about twenty years skip and yell, stung by a bullet through the thigh. He turned to limp to the rear. After he had gone a few steps he stopped, then he kicked out his leg once or twice to see if it would work. Then he tore the clothing away from his leg so as to see the wound. He looked at it attentively for an instant, then kicked out his leg again, then turned and took his place in the ranks and resumed firing. There was considerable disorder in the line, and the soldiers moved to and fro—now a few feet to the right, now a few feet to the left. One of these movements brought me directly behind this wounded soldier. I could see plainly from that position, and I pushed into the gaping line and began firing. In a minute or two the wounded soldier dropped his rifle, and, clasping his left arm, exclaimed: "I am hit again!" He sat down behind the battle ranks and tore off the sleeve of his shirt. The wound was very slight—not much more than skin deep. He tied his handkerchief around it, picked up his rifle, and took position alongside of me. I said: "You are fighting in bad luck today. You had better get away from here." He turned his head to answer me. His head jerked, he staggered, then fell, then regained his feet. A tiny fountain of blood and teeth and bone and bits of tongue burst out of his mouth. He had been shot through the jaws; the lower one was broken and hung down. I looked directly into his open mouth, which was ragged and bloody and tongueless. He cast his rifle furiously on the ground and staggered off.

The next day, just before Longstreet's soldiers made their first charge on the Second Corps, I heard the peculiar cry a stricken man utters as the bullet tears through his flesh. I turned my head, as I loaded my rifle, to see who was hit. I saw a bearded Irishman pull up his shirt. He had been wounded in the left side just below the floating ribs. His face was gray with fear. The wound looked as though it were mortal. He looked at it for an instant, then poked it gently with his index finger. He flushed redly, and smiled with satisfaction. He tucked his shirt into his trousers, and was fighting in the ranks again before I had capped my rifle. The ball had cut a groove in his skin only. The play of this Irishman's face was so expressive, his emotions changed so quickly, that I could not keep from laughing.

Near Spottsylvania I saw, as my battery was moving into action, a group of wounded men lying in the shade cast by some large oak trees. All of these men's faces were gray. They silently looked at us as we marched past them. One wounded man, a blond giant of about forty years, was smoking a short briar-wood pipe. He had a firm grip on the pipe-stem. I asked him what he was doing. "Having my last smoke, young fellow," he replied. His dauntless blue eyes met mine, and he bravely tried to smile. I saw that he was dying fast. Another of these wounded men was trying to read a letter. He was too weak to hold it, or maybe his sight was clouded. He thrust it unread into the breast pocket of his blouse, and lay back with a moan. This group of wounded men numbered fifteen or twenty. At the time, I thought that all of them were fatally wounded, and that there was no use in the surgeons wasting time on them, when men who could be saved were clamoring for their skilful attention. None of these soldiers cried aloud, none called on wife, or mother, or father. They lay on the ground, pale-faced, and with set jaws, waiting for their end. They moaned and groaned as they suffered, but none of them flunked. When my battery returned from the front, five or six hours afterward, almost all of these men were dead. Long before the campaign was over I concluded that dying soldiers seldom called on those who were dearest to them, seldom conjured their Northern or Southern homes, until they became delirious. Then, when their minds wandered, and fluttered at the approach of freedom, they babbled of their homes. Some were boys again, and were fishing in Northern trout streams. Some were generals leading their men to victory. Some were with their wives and children. Some wandered over their family's homestead; but all, with rare exceptions, were delirious.

At the North Anna River, my battery being in action, an infantry soldier, one of our supports, who was lying face downward close behind the gun I served on, and in a place where he thought he was safe, was struck on the thighs by a large jagged piece of a shell. The wound made by this fragment of iron was as horrible as any I saw in the army. The flesh of both thighs was torn off, exposing the bones.

The soldier bled to death in a few minutes, and before he died he conjured his Northern home, and murmured of his wife and children.

In the same battle, but on the south side of the river, a man who carried a rifle was passing between the guns and caissons of the battery. A solid shot, intended for us, struck him on the side. His entire bowels were torn out and slung in ribbons and shreds on the ground. He fell dead, but his arms and legs jerked convulsively a few times. It was a sickening spectacle. During this battle I saw a Union picket knocked down, probably by a rifle-ball striking his head and glancing from it. He lay as though dead. Presently he struggled to his feet, and with blood streaming from his head, he staggered aimlessly round and round in a circle, as sheep afflicted with grubs in the brain do. Instantly the Confederate sharp-shooters opened fire on him and speedily killed him as he circled.

Wounded soldiers almost always tore their clothing away from their wounds, so as to see them and to judge of their character. Many of them would smile and their faces would brighten as they realized that they were not hard hit, and that they could go home for a few months. Others would give a quick glance at their wounds and then shrink back as from a blow, and turn pale, as they realized the truth that they were mortally wounded. The enlisted men were exceedingly accurate judges of the probable result which would ensue from any wound they saw. They had seen hundreds of soldiers wounded, and they had noticed that certain wounds always resulted fatally. They knew when they were fatally wounded, and after the shock of discovery had passed, they generally braced themselves and died in a manly manner. It was seldom that an American or Irish volunteer flunked in the presence of death.   1887

LYSANDER SPOONER

1808–1887

AFTER A YOUTH spent on his father's farm near Athol, Massachusetts, Spooner showed his spirit of revolt against things as they were by opening a law office without fulfilling the legal requirement of a three-years' apprenticeship for noncollege-graduates. His intense devotion to natural rights, to laissez-faire, and to individualism, led him to attack the government post office and to inaugurate a private mail service. A bitter critic of slavery, Spooner held that it was without support in the Constitution. One of the most intense of all the controversialists of the abolition movement, Spooner, like Wendell Phillips, refused to believe that Utopia had been achieved when the slaves were emancipated. In the following pamphlet he presented an original interpretation of the Civil War, one which suggests that of Marx and Engels, and which is similar to that of Charles and Mary Beard in *The Rise of American Civilization*. Spooner's writings include *A New Banking System* (1873), *The Law of Intellectual Property* (1855), and the *Unconstitutionality of Slavery* (1845).

The Dictionary of American Biography, vol. XVII.

» » *From:* NO TREASON « «

THE CONSTITUTION OF NO AUTHORITY

XVIII

The Constitution having never been signed by anybody; and there being no other open, written, or authentic contract between any parties whatever, by virtue of which the United States government, so called, is maintained; and it being well known that none but male persons, of twenty-one years of age and upwards, are allowed any voice in the government; and it being also well known that a large number of these adult persons seldom or never vote at all; and that *all* those who do vote, do so secretly (by secret ballot), and in a way to prevent their individual votes being known, either to the world, or even to each other; and consequently in a way to make no one openly responsible for the acts of their agents, or representatives,—all these things being known, the questions arise: *Who* compose the real governing power in the country? Who are the men, *the responsible men,* who rob us of our property? Restrain us of our liberty? Subject us to their arbitrary dominion? And devastate our homes, and shoot us down by the hundreds of thousands, if we resist? How shall we find these men? How shall we know them from others? How shall we defend ourselves and our property against them? Who, of our neighbors, are members of this secret band of robbers and murderers? How can we know which are *their* houses, that we may burn or demolish them? Which *their* property, that we may destroy it? Which *their* persons, that we may kill them, and rid the world and ourselves of such tyrants and monsters?

These are questions that must be answered, before men can be free; before they can protect themselves against this secret band of robbers and murderers, who now plunder, enslave, and destroy them.

The answer to these questions is, that only those who have the will and the power to shoot down their fellow men, are the real rulers in this, as in all other (so called) civilized countries; for by no others will civilized men be robbed or enslaved.

Among savages, mere physical strength, on the part of one man, may enable him to rob, enslave, or kill another man. Among barbarians, mere physical strength, on the part of a body of men, disciplined, and acting in concert, though with very little money or other wealth, may, under some circumstances, enable them to rob, enslave, or kill another body of men, as numerous, or perhaps even more numerous, than themselves. And among both savages and barbarians, mere want may sometimes compel one man to sell himself as a slave to another. But with (so-called) civilized peoples, among whom knowledge, wealth, and the means of acting in concert, have become diffused; and who have invented such weapons and other means of defence as to render mere physical strength of less importance; and by whom soldiers in any requisite number, and other instrumentalities of war in any requisite amount, can always be had for money, the question of war, and consequently the question of power, is little else than a mere question of money. As a necessary consequence, those who stand ready to furnish this money, are the real rulers. It is so in Europe, and it is so in this country.

In Europe, the nominal rulers, the emperors and kings and parliaments, are anything but the real rulers of their respective countries. They are little or nothing else than mere tools, employed by the wealthy to rob, enslave, and (if need be) murder those who have less wealth, or none at all.

The Rothschilds, and that class of money-lenders of whom they are the representatives and agents,—men who never think of lending a shilling to their next-door neighbors, for purposes of honest industry, unless upon the most ample security, and at the highest rate of interest,—stand ready, at all times, to lend money in unlimited amounts to those robbers and murderers, who call themselves governments, to be expended in shooting down those who do not submit quietly to being robbed and enslaved.

They lend their money in this manner, knowing that it is to be expended in murdering their fellow men, for simply seeking their liberty and their rights; knowing also that neither the interest nor the principal will ever be paid, except as it will be extorted under terror of the repetition of such murders as those for which the money lent is to be expended.

These money-lenders, the Rothschilds, for example, say to themselves: If we lend a hundred millions sterling to the Queen and Parliament of England, it will enable them to murder twenty, fifty, or a hundred thousand people in England, Ireland, or India; and the terror inspired by such wholesale murder, will enable them to keep the whole people of those countries in subjection for twenty, or perhaps fifty, years to come; to control all their trade and industry; and to extort from them large amounts of money, under the name of taxes; and from the wealth thus extorted from them, they (the Queen and Parliament) can afford to pay us a higher rate of interest for our money than we can get in any other way. Or, if we lend this sum to the Emperor of Austria, it will enable him to murder so many of his people as to strike terror into the rest, and thus enable him to keep them in subjection, and extort money from them, for twenty or fifty years to come. And they say the same in regard to the Emperor of Russia, the King of Prussia, the Emperor of France, or any other ruler, so called, who, in their judgment, will be able by murdering a reasonable portion of his people, to keep the rest in subjection, and extort money from them, for a long time to come, to pay the interest and principal of the money lent him.

And why are these men so ready to lend money for murdering their fellow men? Solely for this reason, viz., that such loans are considered better investments than loans for purposes of honest industry. They pay higher rates of interest; and it is less trouble to look after them. This is the whole matter.

. . .

When these great lenders of blood-money, like the Rothschilds, have loaned vast sums in this way, for purposes of murder, to an emperor or a king, they sell out the bonds taken by them, in small amounts, to anybody, and everybody, who are disposed to buy them at satisfactory prices, to hold as investments. They (the Rothschilds) thus soon get back their money, with great profits; and are now ready to lend money in the same way again to any other robber and murderer, called an emperor or a king, who, they think, is likely to be successful in his robberies and murders, and able to pay a good price for the money necessary to carry them on. . . .

When these emperors and kings, so called, have obtained their loans, they proceed to hire and train immense numbers of professional murderers, called soldiers, and employ them in shooting down all who resist their demands for money. In fact, most of them keep large bodies of these murderers constantly in their service, as their only means of enforcing their extortions. There are now, I think, four or five millions of these professional murderers constantly employed by the so-called sovereigns of Europe. The enslaved people are, of course, forced to support and pay all these murderers, as well as to submit to all the other extortions which these murderers are employed to enforce.

It is only in this way that most of the so-called governments of Europe are maintained. These so-called governments are in reality only great bands of robbers and murderers, organized, disciplined, and constantly on the alert. And the so-called sovereigns, in these different governments, are simply the heads, or chiefs, of different bands of robbers and murderers. And these heads or chiefs are dependent upon the lenders of blood-money for the means to carry on their robberies and murders. They could not sustain themselves a moment but for the loans made to them by these blood-money loan-mongers. And their first care is to maintain their credit with them; for they know their end is to come the instant their credit with them fails. Consequently the first proceeds of their extortions are scrupulously applied to the payment of the interest on their loans.

In addition to paying the interest on their bonds, they perhaps grant to the holders of them great monopolies in banking, like the Banks of England, of France, and of Vienna; with the agreement that these banks shall furnish money whenever in sudden emergencies, it may be necessary to shoot down more of their people. Perhaps also, by means of tariffs or competing imports, they give great monopolies to certain branches of industry, in which these lenders of blood-money are engaged. They also, by unequal taxation, exempt wholly or partially the property of these loan-mongers, and throw corresponding burdens upon those who are too poor and weak to resist.

Thus it is evident that all these men, who call themselves by the high-sounding names of Emperors, Kings, Sovereigns, Monarchs, Most Christian Majesties, Most Catholic Majesties, High Mightinesses, Most Serene and Potent

Princes, and the like, and who claim to rule "by the grace of God," by "Divine Right,"— that is, by special authority from Heaven,— are intrinsically not only the merest miscreants and wretches, engaged solely in plundering, enslaving, and murdering their fellow men, but that they are also the merest hangers on, the servile, obsequious, fawning dependents and tools of these blood-money loan-mongers, on whom they rely for the means to carry on their crimes. These loan-mongers, like the Rothschilds, laugh in their sleeves, and say to themselves: These despicable creatures, who call themselves emperors, and kings, and majesties, and most serene and potent princes; who profess to wear crowns, and sit on thrones; who deck themselves with ribbons, and feathers, and jewels; and surround themselves with hired flatterers and lickspittles; and whom we suffer to strut around, and palm themselves off, upon fools and slaves, as sovereigns and law-givers specially appointed by Almighty God; and to hold themselves out as the sole fountains of honors, and dignities, and wealth, and power,—all these miscreants and impostors know that we make them, and use them; that in us they live, move, and have their being; that we require them (as the price of their positions) to take upon themselves all the labor, all the danger, and all the odium of all the crimes they commit for our profit; and that we will unmake them, strip them of their gewgaws, and send them out into the world as beggars, or give them over to the vengeance of the people they have enslaved, the moment they refuse to commit any crime we require of them, or to pay over to us such share of the proceeds of their robberies as we see fit to demand.

XIX

Now, what is true in Europe, is substantially true in this country. The difference is the immaterial one, that, in this country, there is no visible, *permanent* head, or chief, of these robbers and murderers, who call themselves "the government." That is to say, there is no *one man*, who calls himself the state, or even emperor, king, or sovereign; no one who claims that he and his children rule "by the Grace of God," by "Divine Right," or by special appointment from Heaven. There are only certain men, who call themselves presidents, senators, and representatives, and claim to be the authorized agents, *for the time being, or for*

certain short periods, of *all* "the people of the United States"; but who can show no credentials, or powers of attorney, or any other open, authentic evidence that they are so; and who notoriously are not so; but are really only the agents of a secret band of robbers and murderers, whom they themselves do not know, and have no means of knowing, individually; but who, they trust, will openly or secretly, when the crisis comes, sustain them in all their usurpations and crimes.

What is important to be noticed is, that these so-called presidents, senators, and representatives, these pretended agents of *all* "the people of the United States," the moment their exactions meet with any formidable resistance from any portion of "the people" themselves, are obliged, like their co-robbers and murderers in Europe, to fly at once to the lenders of blood money, for the means to sustain their power. And they borrow their money on the same principle, and for the same purpose, viz., to be expended in shooting down all those "people of the United States"—their own constituents and principals, as they profess to call them—who resist the robberies and enslavement which these borrowers of the money are practising upon them. And they expect to repay the loans, if at all, only from the proceeds of the future robberies, which they anticipate it will be easy for them and their successors to perpetrate through a long series of years, upon their pretended principals, if they can but shoot down *now* some hundreds of thousands of them, and thus strike terror into the rest.

Perhaps the facts were never made more evident, in any country on the globe, than in our own, that these soulless blood money loanmongers are the real rulers; that they rule from the most sordid and mercenary motives; that the ostensible government, the presidents, senators, and representatives, so-called, are merely their tools; and that no ideas of, or regard for, justice or liberty had anything to do in inducing them to lend their money for the war. In proof of all this, look at the following facts.

Nearly a hundred years ago we professed to have got rid of all that religious superstition, inculcated by a servile and corrupt priesthood in Europe, that rulers, so called, derived their authority directly from Heaven; and that it was consequently a religious duty on the part of the people to obey them. We professed long ago to have learned that governments could

rightfully exist only by the free will, and on the voluntary support, of those who might choose to sustain them. We all professed to have known long ago, that the only legitimate objects of government were the maintenance of liberty and justice equally for all. All this we had professed for nearly a hundred years. And we professed to look with pity and contempt upon those ignorant, superstitious, and en-
10 slaved peoples of Europe, who were so easily kept in subjection by the frauds and force of priests and kings.

Notwithstanding all this, that we had learned, and known, and professed, for nearly a century, these lenders of blood money had, for a long series of years previous to the war, been the willing accomplices of the slave-holders in perverting the government from the purposes of liberty and justice, to the greatest of crimes.
20 They had been such accomplices *for a purely pecuniary consideration,* to wit, a control of the markets in the South; in other words, the privilege of holding the slave-holders them- selves in industrial and commercial subjection to the manufacturers and merchants of the North (who afterwards furnished the money for the war). And these Northern merchants and manufacturers, these lenders of blood- money, were willing to continue to be the ac-
30 complices of the slave-holders in the future, for the same pecuniary consideration. But the slave-holders, either doubting the fidelity of their Northern allies, or feeling themselves strong enough to keep their slaves in subjec- tion without Northern assistance, would no longer pay the price which these Northern men demanded. And it was to enforce this price in the future—that is, to monopolize the Southern markets, to maintain their industrial and com-
40 mercial control over the South—that these Northern manufacturers and merchants lent some of the profits of their former monopolies for the war, in order to secure to themselves the same, or greater, monopolies in the future. These—and not any love of liberty or justice— were the motives on which the money for the war was lent by the North. In short, the North said to the slave-holders: If you will not pay us our price (give us control of your markets) for
50 our assistance against your slaves, we will se- cure the same price (keep control of your markets) by helping your slaves against you, and using them as our tools for maintaining dominion over you; for the control of your markets we will have, whether the tools we

use for that purpose be black or white, and be the cost, in blood and money, what it may.

On this principle, and from this motive, and not from any love of liberty or justice, the money was lent in enormous amounts, and at enormous rates of interest. And it was only by means of these loans that the objects of the war were accomplished.

And now these lenders of blood-money de- mand their pay; and the government, so called, becomes their tool, their servile, slavish, vil- lanous tool, to extort it from the labor of the enslaved people both of the North and the South. It is to be extorted by every form of direct, and indirect, and unequal taxation. Not only the nominal debt and interest—enormous as the latter was—are to be paid in full; but these holders of the debt are to be paid still further—and perhaps doubly, triply, or quad- ruply paid—by such tariffs on imports as will enable our home manufacturers to realize enor- mous prices for their commodities; also by such monopolies in banking as will enable them to keep control of, and thus enslave and plunder, the industry and trade of the great body of the Northern people themselves. In short, the in- dustrial and commercial slavery of the great body of the people, North and South, black and white, is the price which these lenders of blood money demand, and insist upon, and are determined to secure, in return for the money lent for the war.

This programme having been fully arranged and systematized, they put their sword into the hands of the chief murderer of the war, and charge him to carry their scheme into ef- fect. And now he, speaking as their organ says: *"Let us have peace."*

The meaning of this is: Submit quietly to all the robbery and slavery we have arranged for you, and you can have "peace." But in case you resist, the same lenders of blood- money, who furnished the means to subdue the South, will furnish the means again to subdue you. These are the terms on which alone this government, or, with few exceptions, any other, ever gives "peace" to its people.

The whole affair, on the part of those who furnished the money, has been, and now is, a deliberate scheme of robbery and murder; not merely to monopolize the markets of the South, but also to monopolize the currency, and thus control the industry and trade, and thus plun- der and enslave the laborers, of both North and South. And Congress and the president are today the merest tools for these purposes. They are obliged to be, for they know that their own power, as rulers, so called, is at an end, the moment their credit with the blood-money loan-mongers fails. They are like a bankrupt in the hands of an extortioner. They dare not say nay to any demand made upon them. And to hide at once, if possible, both their servility and their crimes, they attempt to divert public attention, by crying out that they have "Abolished Slavery!" That they have "Saved the Country!" That they have "Preserved our Glorious Union!" and that, in now paying the "National Debt," as they call it (as if the people themselves, *all of them who are to be taxed for its payment,* had really and voluntarily joined in contracting it), they are simply "Maintaining the National Honor!"

By "maintaining the national honor," they mean simply that they themselves, open robbers and murderers, assume to be the nation, and will keep faith with those who lend them the money necessary to enable them to crush the great body of the people under their feet; and will faithfully appropriate, from the proceeds of their future robberies and murders, enough to pay all their loans, principal and interest.

The pretence that the "abolition of slavery" was either a motive or justification for the war, is a fraud of the same character with that of "maintaining the national honor." Who but such usurpers, robbers, and murderers as they, ever established slavery? Or what government, except one resting upon the sword, like the one we now have, was ever capable of maintaining slavery? And why did these men abolish slavery? Not from any love of liberty in general —not as an act of justice to the black man himself, but only "as a war measure," and because they wanted his assistance, and that of his friends, in carrying on the war they had undertaken for maintaining and intensifying that political, commercial, and industrial slavery, to which they have subjected the great body of the people, both white and black. And yet these imposters now cry out that they have abolished the chattel slavery of the black man —although that was not the motive of the war—as if they thought they could thereby conceal, atone for, or justify that other slavery which they were fighting to perpetuate, and to render more rigorous and inexorable than it ever was before. There was no difference of principle—but only of degree—between the slavery they boast they have abolished, and the slavery they were fighting to preserve; for all restraints upon men's natural liberty, not necessary for the simple maintenance of justice, are of the nature of slavery, and differ from each other only in degree.

. . .

Their pretences that they have "Saved the Country," and "preserved our Glorious Union," are frauds like all the rest of their pretences. By them they mean simply that they have subjugated, and maintained their power over, an unwilling people. This they call "Saving the Country"; as if an enslaved and subjugated people—or as if any people kept in subjection by the sword (as it is intended that all of us shall be hereafter)—could be said to have any country. This, too, they call "preserving our Glorious Union"; as if there could be said to be any Union, glorious or inglorious, that was not voluntary. Or as if there could be said to be any union between masters and slaves; between those who conquer, and those who are subjugated.

All these cries of having "abolished slavery," of having "saved the country," of having "preserved the union," of establishing "a government of consent," and of "maintaining the national honor," are all gross, shameless, transparent cheats—so transparent that they ought to deceive no one—when uttered as justifications for the war, or for the government that has succeeded the war, or for now compelling the people to pay the cost of the war, or for compelling anybody to support a government that he does not want.

The lesson taught by all these facts is this: As long as mankind continue to pay "National Debts," so-called,—that is, so long as they are such dupes and cowards as to pay for being cheated, plundered, enslaved, and murdered, —so long there will be enough to lend the money for those purposes; and with that money a plenty of tools, called soldiers, can be hired to keep them in subjection. But when they refuse any longer to pay for being thus cheated, plundered, enslaved, and murdered, they will cease to have cheats, and usurpers, and robbers, and murderers and blood-money loan-mongers for masters.

APPENDIX

Inasmuch as the Constitution was never signed, nor agreed to, by anybody, as a contract, and therefore never bound anybody, and is now binding upon nobody; and is, moreover, such an one as no people can ever hereafter be expected to consent to, except as they may be forced to do so at the point of the bayonet, it is perhaps of no importance what its true legal meaning, as a contract, is. Nevertheless, the writer thinks it proper to say that, in his opinion, the Constitution is no such instrument as it has generally been assumed to be; but that by false interpretations, and naked usurpations,

the government has been made in practice a very widely, and almost wholly, different thing from what the Constitution itself purports to authorize. He has heretofore written much, and could write much more, to prove that such is the truth. But whether the Constitution really be one thing, or another, this much is certain—that it has either authorized such a government as we have had, or has been powerless to prevent it. In either case, it is unfit to exist.   1870

North and South: The New Nationalism

1865-1900

THE GOOD OLD REBEL

Oh, I'm a good old Rebel,
Now that's just what I am;
For this "fair land of Freedom"
I do not care a damn.
I'm glad I fit against it—
I only wish we'd won.
And I don't want no pardon
For anything I've done.

I hates the Constitution,
This great Republic, too;
I hates the Freedmen's Bureau,
In uniforms of blue.
I hates the nasty eagle,
With all his brag and fuss;
But the lyin', thievin' Yankees,
I hates 'em wuss and wuss.

I hates the Yankee nation,
And everything they do;
I hates the Declaration
Of Independence, too;
I hates the glorious Union,
'Tis dripping with our blood;
And I hates the striped banner—
I fit it all I could.

I followed old Mars' Robert
For four year, near about,
Got wounded in three places,
And starved at Pint Lookout.
I cotch the roomatism
A-campin' in the snow,
But I killed a chance of Yankees—
And I'd like to kill some mo'.

Three hundred thousand Yankees
Is stiff in Southern dust;
We got three hundred thousand
Befo' they conquered us.

They died of Southern fever
And Southern steel and shot;
And I wish it was three millions
Instead of what we got.

I can't take up my musket
And fight 'em now no mo',
But I ain't a-goin' to love 'em,
Now this is sartin sho';
And I don't want no pardon
For what I was and am;
And I won't be reconstructed,
And I don't care a damn.

According to Herbert Quick, who printed an account of "The Good
old Rebel" in *Collier's* for April 4, 1914, its author was Major Innes
Randolph, a Virginian and a member of General J. E. B. Stuart's staff.
Sung to the tune of "Joe Bowers," a favorite of the forty-niners, it
traveled beyond the bounds of the Confederacy. Edward VII, then
Prince of Wales, heard it at a reception in London and called it "that
fine American song with the cuss words in it."

« «   » »

North and South: The New Nationalism

THE SECTIONAL bitterness aroused in both the North and the South before secession was, of course, greatly accentuated by the War between the States. Voices speaking for moderation were indeed heard in the North after Lee's surrender, but the predominant mood revealed little sympathy for the broken planting class below the Mason and Dixon line. Factors other than mere emotional antagonism contributed to this mood of revenge. The great business interests of the North, bent on preserving the national banking system, the protective tariff, and the unlimited expansion of railroad and other franchises, had no desire to permit the Southern representatives of the old plantation class to jeopardize this program as they might well do if they returned to Congress.

On the other hand, few of those who directed Reconstruction policy, if Thaddeus Stevens be excepted, were governed by strong equalitarian or even humanitarian sympathies for the freedman. They did not realize that economic power was necessary if the Negro and poor whites in the South were to consolidate and preserve the political power which they enjoyed for the moment. Had they realized this they would probably have preferred to have the Negro lose his political power rather than to sponsor a program which would have involved giving economic equality to a lower class at the expense of property owners. In any case, when the depression of 1873 set in, and when potential investments in the South seemed to be threatened by continued chaos in that section, the dominant groups in the North abandoned the Negro. The rising business class in the South, together with the old plantation heirs, were permitted to disenfranchise the black and to take matters in hand. In the North, expansion in business and the exploitation of the last frontier became more pressing concerns; it seemed sufficient if a class in the South friendly to Northern development of resources managed local affairs. To divert attention from political corruption in the North, and from the growing grievances of the common man on farm and in factory, "waving the bloody shirt," or keeping alive the idea of sectional antagonism, proved, nevertheless, a useful device.

The planting class in the South endured great hardships during the war itself and during the dislocation incident to the more radical phases of Reconstruction. Bitterness toward the North and toward Carpetbaggers and Negroes in political office became intense. The Ku Klux Klan was one of the responses to this situation. Through terrorization of Negroes, Carpetbaggers, and Scalawags, the political regime which these groups represented was weakened; and when the dominant forces in the North withdrew federal troops from the South, the restoration of white rule was virtually insured. In alliance the survivals of the old plantation class and the new business class found various devices to disenfranchise the Negro, whose constitutional right to the suffrage was nevertheless still guaranteed by amendment to the federal constitution.

The ante-bellum proslavery argument, which had held the Negro to be innately inferior and incapable of much improvement, now provided a defense of white control. But the Negro was subjugated not merely to preserve white superiority. Consciously or unconsciously the more substantial property-owning whites held him down because they could thus use the poor white's dislike of the black to preserve their own dominance within the white race.

The temporary regime of the Negro, the Carpetbagger, and the federal army was not without its effects. The Northerners who traveled into the South after Appomattox tended to emphasize the corruption, the extravagance, and the incompetence of the Reconstruction governments. And indeed there was corruption and incompetence, as there was in government in the North at the same period. But the Carpetbagger regimes also did much to promote the material and cultural progress of the South. The industrial development which had begun before the war and which was to make great advances after 1880 did not come to an abrupt or complete stop during Reconstruction. The public school systems which North Carolina and a few cities such as New Orleans had established in ante-bellum days were now put on a more certain footing, and were expanded to include the Negro. The recently emancipated slaves embarked on the long, painful journey of education, toward the freedom in which alone they could hope to gain some part of human dignity. After the restoration of white rule in 1877 their difficulties in some ways increased. But Booker T. Washington won increasing support among Northern philanthropists for a program of industrial education; and this program, when coupled with a frank acceptance of inferior status of the Negro, gradually won friends among certain Southern elements. But the Negro, discriminated against in the South, and in the North wherever his numbers were considerable, remained an issue, and the vision of American democracy, based on equality of races, remained a vision.

The economic ties between North and South symbolized by new railroad and industrial developments, were strengthened by literary and social bonds: novels of reconciliation were written, sentiments of union were encouraged. Yet the new nationalism was by no means complete, for the older generation of the South did much to keep alive memories of an earlier day. Those who could not adjust themselves to the new order inclined to indulge in nostalgic effusions about ante-bellum days, to idealize and romanticize an Old South which was less extensive in fact than the reminiscent local-color school liked to believe.

» »   « «

THADDEUS STEVENS

1792–1868

IN MANY RESPECTS Thaddeus Stevens was well equipped to be a leader in the Second American Revolution. The quasi-frontier and democratic Vermont environment in which he spent his youth contributed to the deep-seated hatred he felt toward all caste and aristocracy. This hatred he turned against the Southern ruling order. As a vigorous champion of free, tax-supported public schools—he took a notable part in the Pennsylvania campaign of 1834 for such schools—Stevens was anxious to impose such institutions on the South. Moreover, his own enterprises in the iron business made him a firm believer in protective tariffs, to which the South had been opposed, and which he believed it would continue to oppose if permitted freely to re-enter the Union on the old terms. But above all it was his bitter hatred of slavery and his conviction that it must be thoroughly uprooted that motivated Stevens in the Reconstruction policy which he advocated.

Having become a leader in the Republican party of Pennsylvania, Stevens enjoyed an influential role in Congress during the Civil War. From the start he demanded that the slaves be freed and armed, that the property of Confederates be confiscated, and that severe penalties be inflicted on Rebel leaders in the interest of overthrowing the caste system and aiding the freedmen to become yeomen. With the help of Sumner, Wade, and other "Radicals," Stevens succeeded in thrusting into the background the moderate Reconstruction policy of Lincoln and Johnson, and in substituting for it a policy of military reconstruction. He did not, however, succeed in effecting confiscation of lands. The following address summarizes Stevens' Reconstruction aims.

J. A. Woodburn, *The Life of Thaddeus Stevens*, Indianapolis, 1913.
Richard N. Current, *Old Thad Stevens*, Madison, 1942.
Elsie S. Master, *Speak for Thaddeus Stevens*, Boston, 1947.

» » From: RECONSTRUCTION[1] « «

FELLOW CITIZENS:

In compliance with your request I have come to give my views of the present condition of the rebel States; of the proper mode of reorganizing the Government, and the future prospects of the Republic. During the whole progress of the war I never for a moment felt doubt or despondency. I knew that the loyal North would conquer the rebel despots who sought to destroy freedom. But since that traitorous confederation has been subdued, and we have entered upon the work of "reconstruction" or "restoration," I cannot deny that my heart has become sad at the gloomy prospects before us.

Four years of bloody and expensive war waged against the United States by eleven States, under a government called the "Confederate States of America" to which they acknowledged allegiance, have overthrown all governments within those States, which could be acknowledged as legitimate by the Union. The armies of the Confederate States having been conquered and subdued, and their territories possessed by the United States, it becomes necessary to establish governments therein, which shall be republican in "form and principles, and form a more perfect union" with the parent government. It is desirable that such a course should be pursued as to exclude from those governments every vestige of human bondage and render the same forever impossible in this nation, and to take care that no principles of self-destruction shall be incorporated there in. In effecting this, it is to be hoped that no provision of the Constitution will be infringed, and no principle of the law of

nations disregarded. Especially must we take care that in rebuking this unjust and treasonable war, the authorities of the Union shall indulge in no acts of usurpation which may tend to impair the stability and permanency of the nation within these limitations. We hold it to be the duty of the Government to inflict condign punishment on the rebel belligerents, and so weaken their hands that they can never again endanger the Union; and so reform their municipal institutions as to make them republican in spirit as well as in name.

We especially insist that the property of the chief rebels should be seized and appropriated to the payment of the National debt, caused by the unjust and wicked war which they instigated.

How can such punishments be inflicted and such forfeitures produced without doing violence to established principles?

Two positions have been suggested.

1st—To treat those States as never having been out of the Union, because the Constitution forbids secession, and, therefore, a fact forbidden by law could not exist.

2nd—To accept the position in which they placed themselves as severed from the union; an independent government *de facto,* and an alien enemy to be dealt with according to the laws of war.

It seems to me that while we do not aver that the United States are bound to treat them as an alien enemy, yet they have a right to elect so to do if it be for the interest of the nation; and that the "Confederate States" are estopped from denying that position. . . .

The Confederate States were for four years what they claimed to be, an alien enemy in

---

[1] This address was delivered at Lancaster, Pennsylvania, the home of Stevens, on September 7, 1865.

all their rights and liabilities. To say that they were states under the protection of that constitution which they were assaulting with bloody defeats, simply because they became belligerents through crime, is making theory over-rule fact to an absurd degree. It will I suppose at least be conceded that the United States if not obliged so to do, have a right to treat them as an alien enemy now conquered, and subject to all the liabilities of a vanquished foe. . . .

All writers agree that the victor may inflict punishment upon the vanquished enemy even to the taking of his life, liberty, or the confiscation of all his property; but that this extreme right is never exercised, except upon a cruel, barbarous, obstinate, or dangerous foe who has waged an unjust war.

Upon the character of the belligerent, and the justice of the war, and the manner of conducting it, depends our right to take the lives, liberty, and property of the belligerent. This war had its origin in treason without one spark of justice. It was prosecuted before notice of it, by robbing our forts and armories, and our navy-yards; by stealing our money from the mints and depositories, and by surrendering our forts and navies by perjurers who had sworn to support the Constitution. In its progress our prisoners, by the authority of their government were slaughtered in cold blood. Ask Fort Pillow and Fort Wagner. Sixty thousand of our prisoners have been deliberately starved to death because they would not enlist in the rebel armies. The graves at Andersonville have each an accusing tongue. The purpose and avowed object of the enemy "to found an empire whose corner-stone should be slavery," render its perpetuity or revival dangerous to human liberty.

Surely, these things are sufficient to justify the exercise of the extreme rights of war— "to execute, to imprison, to confiscate." How many captive enemies it would be proper to execute, as an example to nations, I leave others to judge. I am not fond of sanguinary punishments, but surely some victims must propitiate the *manes* [2] of our starved, murdered, slaughtered martyrs. A court martial could do justice according to law.

But we propose to confiscate all the estate of every rebel belligerent whose estate was worth $10,000, or whose land exceeded two hundred acres in quantity. Policy if not justice

[2] *Shades of the departed.*

would require that the poor, the ignorant, and the coerced should be forgiven. They followed the example and teachings of their wealthy and intelligent neighbors. The rebellion would never have originated with them. Fortunately those who would thus escape form a large majority of the people though possessing but a small portion of the wealth. The proportion of those exempt compared with the punished would be I believe about nine tenths.

There are about six millions of freemen in the South. The number of acres of land is 465,000,000. Of this those who own above two hundred acres each, number about 70,000 persons, holding in the aggregate (together with the States) about 394,000,000 acres, leaving for all the others below 200 each about 71,000,000 of acres. By thus forfeiting the estates of the leading rebels, the Government would have 394,000,000 of acres beside their town property, and yet nine tenths of the people would remain untouched. Divide this land into convenient farms. Give if you please forty acres to each adult male freedman. Suppose there are one million of them. That would require 40,000,000 of acres, which deducted from 394,000,000 leaves three hundred and fifty-four millions of acres for sale. Divide it into suitable farms and sell it to the highest bidders. I think it, including town property, would average at least ten dollars per acre. That would produce $3,540,000,000,—Three billions, five hundred and forty millions of dollars.

Let that be applied as follows to wit:

1. Invest $300,000,000 in six per cent. government bonds, and add the interest semi-annually to the pensions of those who have become entitled by this villanous war.

2. Appropriate $200,000,000 to pay the damages done to loyal men North and South by the rebellion.

3. Pay the residue being $3,040,000,000 towards the payment of the National debt.

What loyal man can object to this? Look around you, and everywhere behold your neighbors, some with an arm, some with a leg, some with an eye carried away by rebel bullets. Others horribly mutilated in every form. And yet numerous others wearing the weeds which mark the death of those on whom they leaned for support. Contemplate these monuments of rebel perfidy, and of patriotic suffering, and then say if too much is asked for our valiant soldiers.

Look again, and see loyal men reduced to poverty by the confiscations by the Confederate States, and by the rebel States—see Union men robbed of their property, and their dwellings laid in ashes by rebel raiders, and say if too much is asked for them. But above all, let us inquire whether imperative duty to the present generation and to posterity does not command us to compel the wicked enemy to pay the expense of this unjust war. In ordinary transactions he who raises a false clamor and prosecutes an unfounded suit, is adjudged to pay the costs in his defeat. We have seen that, by the law of nations, the vanquished in an unjust war must pay the expense.

Our war debt is estimated at from three to four billions of dollars. . . . Four hundred and seventy millions to be raised by taxation—our present heavy taxes will not in ordinary years, produce but little more than half that sum. Can our people bear double their present taxation? He who unnecessarily causes it will be accursed from generation to generation. It is fashionable to belittle our public debt, lest the people should become alarmed, and political parties should suffer. I have never found it wise to deceive the people. They can always be trusted with the truth. Capitalists will not be effected for they can not be deceived. Confide in the people, and you will avoid repudiation. Deceive them, and lead them into false measures, and you may produce it. . . .

The plan we have proposed would pay at least three fourths of our debt. The balance could be managed with our present taxation. And yet to think that even that is to be perpetual is sickening. If it is to be doubled, as it must be, if "restoration" instead of "reconstruction" is to prevail, would to God the authors of it could see themselves as an execrating public and posterity will see them. . . .

While I hear it said everywhere that slavery is dead, I cannot learn who killed it. No thoughtful man has pretended that Lincoln's proclamation, so noble in sentiment, l'berated a single slave. It expressly excluded from its operation all those within our lines. No slave within any part of the rebel States in our possession or in Tennessee, but only those beyond our limits and beyond our power were declared free. . . . The President did not pretend to abrogate the Slave Laws of any of the States. "Restoration," therefore will leave "the Union as it was,"—a heinous idea. I am aware that a very able and patriotic gentleman, and learned historian, Mr. [George] Bancroft, has attempted to place their freedom on different grounds. He says what is undoubtedly true, that the proclamation of freedom did not free a slave. But it liberated them on feudal principles. Under the feudal system, when a king conquered his enemy, he parceled out his lands and conquered *subjects* among his chief retainers; the lands and serfs were held on condition of fealty and rendering military service when required. If the subordinate chief rebelled, he broke the condition on which he held them and the lands and serfs became forfeited to the Lord Paramount. But it did not free the serfs. They with the manors were bestowed on other favorites. But the analogy fails in another important respect. The American slaveholder does not hold by virtue of any grant from any Lord Paramount—least of all by a grant from the General Government.—Slavery exists by no law of the Union, but simply by local laws, by the laws of the States. Rebellion against National Authority is a breach of no condition of their tenure. But rebellion against neither government would *per se* have any such effect. On whom would the Lord Paramount bestow the slaves? The theory is plausible, but has no solid foundation.

The President says to the rebel States "before you can participate in the government you must abolish Slavery and reform your election laws." *That* is the command of a Conqueror. *That* is Reconstruction, not Restoration—Reconstruction too by assuming the powers of Congress. This theory will lead to melancholy results. Nor can the constitutional amendment abolishing Slavery ever be ratified by three-fourths of the States, if *they* are States to be counted. Bogus Conventions of those States may vote for it. But no Convention honestly and fairly elected will ever do it. The frauds will not permanently avail. The cause of Liberty must rest on a firmer basis. Counterfeit governments like the Virginia, Louisiana, Tennessee, Mississippi, and Arkansas pretenses, will be disregarded by the sober sense of the people, by future law, and by the courts. "Restoration" is replanting the seeds of rebellion, which within the next quarter of a century will germinate and produce the same bloody strife which has just ended.

But, it is said, by those who have more sympathy with rebel wives and children than for the widows and orphans of loyal men, that this stripping the rebels of their estates and driving them to exile or to honest labor would be harsh and severe upon innocent women and children. It may be so; but that is the result of the necessary laws of war. But it is revolutionary, they say. This plan would, no doubt, work a radical reorganization in southern institutions, habits and manners. It is intended to revolutionize their principles and feelings. This may startle feeble minds and shake weak nerves. So do all great improvements in the political and moral world. It requires a heavy impetus to drive forward a sluggish people. When it was first proposed to free the slaves, and arm the blacks, did not half the nation tremble? The prim conservatives, the snobs, and the male waiting maids in Congress, were in hysterics.

The whole fabric of southern society *must* be changed and never can it be done if this opportunity is lost. Without this, this Government can never be, as it never has been, a true republic. Heretofore, it had more the features of aristocracy than of democracy.—The Southern States have been despotisms, not governments of the people. It is impossible that any practical equality of rights can exist where a few thousand men monopolize the whole landed property. The larger the number of small proprietors the more safe and stable the government. As the landed interest must govern, the more it is subdivided and held by independent owners, the better. What would be the condition of the State of New York if it were not for her independent yeomanry? She would be overwhelmed and demoralized by the Jews, Milesians and vagabonds of licentious cities. How can republican institutions, free schools, free churches, free social intercourse exist in a mingled community of nabobs and serfs; of the owners of twenty thousand acre manors with lordly palaces, and the occupants of narrow huts inhabited by "low white trash?"—If the south is ever to be made a safe republic let her lands be cultivated by the toil of the owners or the free labor of intelligent citizens. This must be done even though it drive her nobility into exile. If they go, all the better.

It will be hard to persuade the owner of ten thousand acres of land, who drives a coach and four, that he is not degraded by sitting at the same table, or in the same pew, with the embrowned and hard-handed farmer who has himself cultivated his own thriving homestead of 150 acres. This subdivision of the lands will yield ten bales of cotton to one that is made now, and he who produced it will own it and *feel himself a man*.

It is far easier and more beneficial to exile 70,000 proud, bloated, and defiant rebels, than to expatriate four millions of laborers, native to the soil and loyal to the Government. . . .

This remodelling the institutions, and reforming the rooted habits of a proud aristocracy, is undoubtedly a formidable task; requiring the broad mind of enlarged statesmanship, and the firm nerve of the hero. But will not this mighty occasion produce—will not the God of Liberty and order give us such men? Will not a Romulus, a Lycurgus, a Charlemagne, a Washington arise, whose expansive views will found a free empire, to endure till time shall be no more?

This doctrine of restoration shocks me.—We have a duty to perform which our fathers were incapable of, which will be required at our hands by God and our Country. When our ancestors found a "more perfect Union" necessary, they found it impossible to agree upon a Constitution without tolerating, nay guaranteeing Slavery. They were obliged to acquiesce, trusting to time to work a speedy cure, in which they were disappointed. *They* had some excuse, some justification. But we can have none if we do not thoroughly eradicate Slavery and render it forever impossible in this republic. The Slave power made war upon the nation. They declared the "more perfect Union" dissolved. Solemnly declared themselves a foreign nation, alien to this republic; for four years were in fact what they claimed to be. We accepted the war which they tendered and treated them as a government capable of making war. We have conquered them, and as a conquered enemy we can give them laws; can abolish all their municipal institutions and form new ones. If we do not make those institutions fit to last through generations of free men, a heavy curse will be on us. Our glorious, but tainted republic, has been born to new life through bloody, agonizing pains. But this frightful "Restoration" has thrown it into "cold obstruction, and to death." If the rebel states have never been out of the Union, any attempt to reform their State institutions either by Congress or the President, is rank usurpation.

Is then all lost? Is this great conquest to be in vain? That will depend upon the virtue and intelligence of the next Congress. To Congress alone belongs the power of Re-construction—

of giving law to the vanquished. . . . But we know how difficult it is for a majority of Congress to overcome preconceived opinions. Besides, before Congress meets, things will be so inaugurated—precipitated, it will still be more difficult to correct. If a majority of Congress can be found wise and firm enough to declare the Confederate States a conquered enemy, Reconstruction will be easy and legitimate; and the friends of freedom will long rule in the Councils of the Nation. If Restoration prevails the prospect is gloomy, and new "Lords will make new laws." The Union party will be overwhelmed. The Copperhead party has become extinct with Secession. But with Secession it will revive. Under "restoration" every rebel State will send rebels to Congress; and these, with their allies in the North, will control Congress, and occupy the White House. Then Restoration of Laws and ancient Constitutions will be sure to follow; our public debt will be repudiated or the rebel National debt

will be added to ours, and the people be crushed beneath heavy burdens.

Let us forget all parties, and build on the broad platform of "reconstructing the Government out of the conquered territory, converted into new and free States, and admitted into the Union by the sovereign power of Congress, with another plank,"—THE PROPERTY OF THE REBELS SHALL PAY OUR NATIONAL DEBT, *and indemnify freed-men and loyal sufferers.*—and that under no circumstances will we suffer the National debt to be repudiated, or the interest scaled below the contract rates; nor permit any part of the rebel debt to be assumed by the nation.

Let all who approve of these principles tarry with us. Let all others go with Copperheads and rebels. Those will be the opposing parties. Young men, this duty devolves on you. Would to God, if only for that, I were still in the prime of life, that I might aid you to fight through this last and greatest battle of Freedom.   1865

HERMAN MELVILLE

1819–1891

MELVILLE HATED war. He hated slavery more and believed the South was following a delusory ideal. In the poems written during the Civil War, which were collected in 1866 under the title *Battle-Pieces*, he shows a magnanimity that is probably unique among Northern poets. It is not surprising, therefore, to find him in the minority which advocated a humane policy of reconstruction. This prose supplement to *Battle-Pieces* was apparently written in the midsummer of 1866. Actually at the moment there was some reason to hope that a moderate policy might prevail. The fourteenth amendment, which puts the civil rights of the Negro into the Constitution, had only just been passed by Congress. It would not become law until 1868. The radicals who wished to see the South humiliated were waiting until the outcome of the fall elections before pressing their attack. The Reconstruction Act was still nine months in the future. Hence Melville's eloquent plea for tolerance was at least timely.

Willard Thorp, *Herman Melville, Representative Selections, with Introduction, Bibliography and Notes*, New York, 1938.
The Works of Herman Melville, Standard Edition, 16 vols., London, 1922–1924.
Leon Howard, *Melville, a Biography*, Berkeley, 1951.
James Baird, *Ishmael*, Baltimore, 1956.
Atlantic Monthly, XIX (February, 1867), 252–253, a review of *Battle-Pieces*.

« «   » »

» » *From:* SUPPLEMENT TO BATTLE-PIECES « «

Were I fastidiously anxious for the symmetry of this book, it would close with the notes. But the times are such that patriotism—not free from solicitude—urges a claim overriding all literary scruples.

It is more than a year since the memorable surrender, but events have not yet rounded themselves into completion. Not justly can we complain of this. There has been an upheaval affecting the basis of things; to altered circumstances complicated adaptions are to be made; there are difficulties great and novel. But is Reason still waiting for Passion to spend itself? We have sung of the soldiers and sailors, but who shall hymn the politicians?

In view of the infinite desirableness of Reestablishment, and considering that, so far as feeling is concerned it depends not mainly on the temper in which the South regards the North, but rather conversely; one who never was a blind adherent feels constrained to submit some thoughts, counting on the indulgence of his countrymen. And, first, it may be said that, if among the feelings and opinions growing immediately out of a great civil convulsion, there are any which time shall modify or do away, they are presumably those of a less temperate and charitable cast.

There seems no reason why patriotism and narrowness should go together, or why intellectual impartiality should be confounded with political trimming, or why serviceable truth should keep cloistered because not partisan. Yet the work of Reconstruction, if admitted to be feasible at all, demands little but common sense and Christian charity. Little but these? These are much.

Some of us are concerned because as yet the South shows no penitence. But what exactly do we mean by this? Since down to the close of the war she never confessed any for braving it, the only penitence now left her is that which springs solely from the sense of discomfiture; and since this evidently would be a contrition hypocritical, it would be unworthy in us to demand it. Certain it is that penitence, in the sense of voluntary humiliation, will never be displayed. Nor does this afford just ground for unreserved condemnation. It is enough, for all practical purposes, if the South have been taught by the terrors of civil war to feel that

Secession, like Slavery, is against Destiny; that both now lie buried in one grave; that her fate is linked with ours; and that together we comprise the Nation.

The clouds of heroes who battled for the Union it is needless to eulogise here. But how of the soldiers on the other side? And when of a free community we name the soldiers, we thereby name the people. It was in subserviency to the slave-interest that Secession was plotted; but it was under the plea, plausibly urged, that certain inestimable rights guaranteed by the Constitution were directly menaced that the people of the South were cajoled into revolution. Through the arts of the conspirators and the perversity of fortune, the most sensitive love of liberty was entrapped into the support of a war whose implied end was the erecting in our advanced century of an Anglo-American empire based upon the systematic degradation of man.

Spite this clinging reproach, however, signal military virtues and achievements have conferred upon the Confederate arms historic fame, and upon certain of the commanders a renown extending beyond the sea—a renown which we of the North could not suppress, even if we would. In personal character, also, not a few of the military leaders of the South enforce forbearance; the memory of others the North refrains from disparaging; and some, with more or less of reluctance, she can respect. Posterity, sympathising with our convictions, but removed from our passions, may perhaps go farther here. If George IV. could, out of the graceful instinct of a gentleman, raise an honourable monument in the great fane of Christendom over the remains of the enemy of his dynasty, Charles Edward, the invader of England and victor in the route at Prestonpans—upon whose head the king s ancestor but one reign removed had set a price—is it probable that the grandchildren of General Grant will pursue with rancour, or slur by sour neglect, the memory of Stonewall Jackson?

But the South herself is not wanting in recent histories and biographies which record the deeds of her chieftains—writings freely published at the North by loyal houses, widely read here, and with a deep though saddened interest. By students of the war such works are hailed as welcome accessories, and tending to the completeness of the record.

Supposing a happy issue out of present perplexities, then, in the generation next to come, Southerners there will be yielding allegiance to the Union, feeling all their interests bound up in it, and yet cherishing unrebuked that kind of feeling for the memory of the soldiers of the fallen Confederacy that Burns, Scott, and the Ettrick Shepherd felt for the memory of the gallant clansmen ruined through their fidelity to the Stuarts—a feeling whose passion was tempered by the poetry imbuing it, and which in no wise affected their loyalty to the Georges, and which, it may be added, indirectly contributed excellent things to literature. But, setting this view aside, dishonourable would it be in the South were she willing to abandon to shame the memory of brave men who with signal personal disinterestedness warred in her behalf, though from motives, as we believe, so deplorably astray.

Patriotism is not baseness, neither is it inhumanity. The mourners this summer bear flowers to the mounds of the Virginian and Georgian dead are, in their domestic bereavement and proud affection, as sacred in the eye of Heaven as are those who go with similar offerings of tender grief and love into the cemeteries of our Northern martyrs. And yet, in one aspect, how needless to point the contrast.

Cherishing such sentiments, it will hardly occasion surprise that, in looking over the battle-pieces in the foregoing collection, I have been tempted to withdraw or modify some of them, fearful lest in presenting, though but dramatically and by way of a poetic record, the passions and epithets of civil war, I might be contributing to a bitterness which every sensible American must wish at an end. So, too, with the emotion of victory as reproduced on some pages, and particularly toward the close. It should not be construed into an exultation misapplied—an exultation as ungenerous as unwise, and made to minister, however indirectly, to that kind of censoriousness too apt to be produced in certain natures by success after trying reverses. Zeal is not of necessity religion, neither is it always of the same essence with poetry or patriotism.

There were excesses which marked the conflict, most of which are perhaps inseparable from a civil strife so intense and prolonged, and involving warfare in some border countries

new and imperfectly civilized. Barbarities also there were, for which the Southern people collectively can hardly be held responsible, though perpetrated by ruffians in their name. But surely other qualities—exalted ones—courage and fortitude matchless, were likewise displayed, and largely; and justly may these be held the character traits, and not the former.

In this view, what Northern writer, however patriotic, but must revolt from acting on paper a part anyway akin to that of the live dog to the dead lion; and yet it is right to rejoice for our triumph, so far as it may justly imply an advance for our whole country and for humanity.

Let it be held no reproach to any one that he pleads for reasonable consideration for our late enemies, now stricken down and unavoidably debarred, for the time, from speaking through authorized agencies for themselves. Nothing has been urged here in the foolish hope of conciliating those men—few in number, we trust—who have resolved never to be reconciled to the Union. On such hearts everything is thrown away except it be religious commiseration, and the sincerest. Yet let them call to mind that unhappy Secessionist, not a military man, who with impious alacrity fired the first shot of the Civil War at Sumter, and a little more than four years afterward fired the last one into his own heart at Richmond.[1]

Noble was the gesture into which patriotic passion surprised the people in a utilitarian time and country; yet the glory of the war falls short of its pathos—a pathos which now at last ought to disarm all animosity.

How many and earnest thoughts still rise, and how hard to repress them. We feel what past years have been, and years, unretarded years, shall come. May we all have moderation; may we all show candour. Though perhaps, nothing could ultimately have averted the strife and though to treat of human actions is to deal wholly with second causes, nevertheless, let us not cover up or try to extenuate what, humanly speaking, is the truth—namely, that those unfraternal denunciations, continued through years, and which at last inflamed to deeds that ended in bloodshed, were reciprocal; and that, had the preponderating strength and the prospect of its unlimited increase lain on the other side, on ours might have lain those actions which now in our late opponents we stigmatise

[1] Edmund Ruffin (1794–1865).

under the name of Rebellion. As frankly let us own——what it would be unbecoming to parade were foreigners concerned——that our triumph was won not more by skill and bravery than by superior resources and crushing numbers; that it was a triumph, too, over a people for years politically misled by designing men, and also by some honestly-erring men, who from their position could not have been otherwise than broadly influential; a people who, though, indeed, they sought to perpetuate the curse of slavery, and even extend it, were not the authors of it, but (less fortunate, not less righteous than we) were the fated inheritors; a people who, having a like origin with ourselves, share essentially in whatever worthy qualities we may possess. No one can add to the lasting reproach which hopeless defeat has now cast upon Secession by withholding the recognition of these verities.

Surely we ought to take it to heart that the kind of pacification, based upon principles operating equally all over the land, which lovers of their country yearn for, and which our arms, though signally triumphant, did not bring about, and which law-making, however anxious, or energetic, or repressive, never by itself can achieve, may yet be largely aided by generosity of sentiment public and private. Some revisionary legislation and adaptive is indispensable; but with this should harmoniously work another kind of prudence, not unallied with entire magnanimity. Benevolence and policy——Christianity and Machiavelli——dissuade from penal severities toward the subdued. Abstinence here is as obligatory as considerate care for our unfortunate fellow-men late in bonds, and, if observed, would equally prove to be wise forecast. The great qualities of the South, those attested in the War, we can perilously alienate, or we may make them nationally available at need.

The blacks, in their infant pupilage to freedom, appeal to the sympathies of every humane mind. The paternal guardianship which for the interval Government exercises over them was prompted equally by duty and benevolence. Yet such kindliness should not be allowed to exclude kindliness to communities who stand nearer to us in nature. For the future of the freed slaves we may well be concerned; but the future of the whole country, involving the future of the blacks, urges a paramount claim upon our anxiety. Effective

benignity, like the Nile, is not narrow in its bounty, and true policy is always broad. To be sure, it is vain to seek to glide, with moulded words, over the difficulties of the situation. And for them who are neither partisans, nor enthusiasts, nor theorists, nor cynics, there are some doubts not readily to be solved. And there are fears. Why is not the cessation of war now at length attended with the settled calm of peace? Wherefore in a clear sky do we still turn our eyes toward the South, as the Neapolitan, months after the eruption, turns his toward Vesuvius? Do we dread lest the repose may be deceptive? In the recent convulsion has the crater but shifted? Let us revere that sacred uncertainty which forever impends over men and nations. Those of us who always abhorred slavery as an atheistical iniquity, gladly we join in the exulting chorus of humanity over its downfall. But we should remember that emancipation was accomplished not by deliberate legislation; only through agonized violence could so mighty a result be affected. In our natural solicitude to confirm the benefit of liberty to the blacks, let us forbear from measures of dubious constitutional rightfulness toward our white countrymen——measures of a nature to provoke, among other of the last evils, exterminating hatred of race toward race. In imagination let us place ourselves in the unprecedented position of the Southerners——their position as regards the millions of ignorant manumitted slaves in their midst, for whom some of us now claim the suffrage. Let us be Christians toward our fellow-whites, as well as philanthropists toward the blacks, our fellowmen. In all things, and toward all, we are enjoined to do as we would be done by. Nor should we forget that benevolent desires, after passing a certain point, cannot undertake their own fulfilment without incurring the risk of evils beyond those sought to be remedied. Something may well be left to the graduated care of future legislation, and to heaven. In one point of view the co-existence of the two races in the South——whether the negro be bond or free——seems (even as it did to Abraham Lincoln) a grave evil. Emancipation has ridded the country of the reproach, but not wholly of the calamity. Especially in the present transition period for both races in the South, more or less of trouble may not unreasonably be anticipated; but let us not hereafter be too swift to charge the blame exclusively in any one

quarter. With certain evils men must be more
or less patient. Our institutions have a potent
digestion, and may in time convert and assimilate to good all elements thrown in, however originally alien.

But, so far as immediate measures looking
toward permanent Re-establishment are concerned, no consideration should tempt us to
pervert the national victory into oppression
for the vanquished. Should plausible promise
of eventual good, or a deceptive or spurious
sense of duty, lead us to essay this, count we
must on serious consequences, not the least
of which would be divisions among the Northern adherents of the Union. Assuredly, if any
honest Catos there be who thus far have gone
with us, no longer will they do so, but oppose
us, and as resolutely as hitherto they have
supported. But this path of thought leads
toward those waters of bitterness from which
one can only turn aside and be silent.

But supposing Re-establishment so far advanced that the Southern seats in Congress are
occupied, and by men qualified in accordance
with those cardinal principles of representative
government which hitherto have prevailed in
the land—what then? Why, the Congressmen
elected by the people of the South will—represent the people of the South. This may seem
a flat conclusion; but, in view of the last five
years, may there not be latent significance in
it? What will be the temper of those Southern
members? and, confronted by them, what will
be the mood of our own representatives? In
private life true reconciliation seldom follows
a violent quarrel; but, if subsequent intercourse
be unavoidable, nice observances and mutual
are indispensable to the prevention of a new
rupture. Amity itself can only be maintained by
reciprocal respect, and true friends are punc-
tilious equals. On the floor of Congress North
and South are to come together after a passionate duel, in which the South, though proving her valour, has been made to bite the dust.
Upon differences in debate shall acrimonious
recriminations be exchanged? shall censorious
superiority assumed by one section provoke
defiant self-assertion on the other? shall Manassas and Chickamauga be retorted for Chatta-
nooga and Richmond? Under the supposition
that the full Congress will be composed of
gentlemen, all this is impossible. Yet, if otherwise, it needs no prophet of Israel to foretell
the end. The maintenance of Congressional
decency in the future will rest mainly with the

North. Rightly will more forebearance be required from the North than the South, for the
North is victor.

But some there are who may deem these
latter thoughts inapplicable, and for this reason: Since the test-oath operatively excludes
from Congress all who in any way participated
in Secession, therefore none but Southerners
wholly in harmony with the North are eligible
to seats. This is true for the time being. But
the oath is alterable; and in the wonted fluctuations of parties not improbably it will undergo
alteration, assuming such a form, perhaps, as
not to bar the admission into the National
Legislature of men who represent the populations lately in revolt. Such a result would
involve no violation of the principles of democratic government. Not readily can one perceive how the political existence of the millions
of late Secessionists can permanently be ignored by this Republic. The years of the war
tried our devotion to the Union; the time of
peace may test the sincerity of our faith in
democracy.

In no spirit of opposition, not by way of
challenge, is anything here thrown out. These
thoughts are sincere ones; they seem natural
—inevitable. Here and there they must have
suggested themselves to many thoughtful patriots. And, if they be just thoughts, ere long
they must have that weight with the public
which already they have had with individuals.

For that heroic band—those children of the
furnace who, in regions like Texas and Tennessee, maintained their fidelity through terrible trials—we of the North felt for them, and
profoundly we honour them. Yet passionate
sympathy, with resentments so close as to be
almost domestic in their bitterness, would
hardly in the present juncture tend to discreet
legislation. Were the Unionists and Secessionists but as Guelphs and Ghibelines? If not,
then far be it from a great nation now to act
in the spirit that animated a town faction in
the Middle Ages. But crowding thoughts must
at last be checked; and, in times like the
present, one who desires to be impartially just
in the expression of his views, moves as among
sword-points presented on every side.

Let us pray that the terrible historic tragedy
of our time may not have been enacted without
instructing our whole beloved country through
terror and pity; and may fulfilment verify in
the end those expectations which kindle the
bards of Progress and Humanity.   1866

ALEXANDER HAMILTON STEPHENS

1812–1883

FROM a humble Georgia family Alexander H. Stephens marched along the road of political success until he became Vice President of the Confederate States. The spokesman of the well-to-do Georgia Whigs, Stephens, like others among the more conservative leaders, became a Democrat in the middle 1850's. His prewar political career was marked by his championship of Southern rights within the framework of as peaceful a Union as possible. Stephens stood out against the "fire-eaters" in opposing hasty secession in 1860–1861. As the newly elected Vice-president of the Confederacy, Stephens, in his famous "cornerstone speech" at Savannah, March 21, 1861, declared that the cornerstone of the Confederacy rested "upon the great truth that the negro is not equal to the white man; that slavery—subordination to the superior race—is his natural and normal condition." During the war Stephens, always an exponent of constitutional limitations on authority, opposed infractions on civil liberties. After the collapse of the Confederacy he supported President Johnson's reconstruction policy, engaged in journalism, business, and politics, and wrote, among other books, *A Constitutional View of the Late War between the States* (1868–1870).

Henry Cleveland, *Alexander H. Stephens in Public and Private with letters and speeches*, Philadelphia, 1866.
L. B. Pendleton, *Alexander H. Stephens*, Philadelphia, 1908.
E. R. Richardson, *Little Aleck; a Life of Alexander H. Stephens*, Indianapolis, 1932.

From: A CONSTITUTIONAL VIEW OF THE LATE WAR BETWEEN THE STATES

» » « «

. . . I went on further to speak not only of what it [the Federal System] had accomplished, but of the still greater results that might be expected, if it should continue to be administered upon the principles and for the objects upon which and for which it was formed. Here is what was then added:—

"Such is the machinery of our theory of self-government by the people. This is the great novelty of our peculiar system, involving a principle unknown to the ancients, an idea never dreamed of by Aristotle or Plato. The union of several distinct, independent communities upon this basis (the Federal machinery acting directly upon the citizens of the several States within the sphere of its limited powers), is a new principle in human Governments. It is now a problem in experiment for the people of the nineteenth century, upon this continent, to solve. As I behold its workings in the past and at the present, while I am not sanguine, yet I am hopeful of its successful solution. The most joyous feeling of my heart is the earnest hope that it will, for the future, move on as peacefully, prosperously, and brilliantly, as it has in the past. If so, then we shall exhibit a moral and political spectacle to the world something like the prophetic vision of Ezekiel, when he saw a number of distinct beings or living creatures, each with a separate and distinct organism, having the functions of life within itself, all of one external likeness, and all, at the same time, mysteriously connected, with one common animating spirit pervading the whole, so that when the common spirit moved they all moved; their appearance and their work being, as it were, a wheel in the middle of a wheel; and whithersoever the common spirit went, thither the others went, all going together; and when they went, he heard the noise of their motion like the noise of great waters, as the voice of the Almighty! Should

our experiment succeed, such will be our exhibition—a machinery of Government so intricate, so complicated, with so many separate and distinct parts, so many independent States, each perfect in the attributes and functions of Sovereignty, within its own jurisdiction, all, nevertheless, united under the control of a common directing power for external objects and purposes, may naturally enough seem novel,
10 strange, and inexplicable to the philosophers and crowned heads of the world!

"It is for us, and those who shall come after us, to determine whether this grand experimental problem shall be worked out; not by quarrelling amongst ourselves; not by doing injustice to any; not by keeping out any particular class of States; but by each State remaining a separate and distinct political organism within itself—all bound together, for
20 general objects, under a common Federal head; as it were, a wheel within a wheel. Then the number may be multiplied without limit; and then, indeed, may the nations of the earth look on in wonder at our career; and when they hear the noise of the wheels of our progress in achievement, in development, in expansion, in glory, and renown, it may well appear to them not unlike the noise of great waters; the very voice of the Almighty—Vox populi! Vox Dei!"

30 Such was the spectacle presented to my mind by the harmonious workings of our "glorious institutions," (as Mr. Webster styled them, in 1839,) under the Constitution of the United States, as I understood its nature and character! That Constitution which sets forth the terms of Union between Free, Sovereign, and Independent States—each retaining its separate Sovereignty, and only delegating such powers to all the rest as are most conducive,
40 by their joint exercise, to its own safety, security, happiness, and prosperity, as well as most conducive to the like safety, security, happiness, and prosperity of all the other members of the great American Federal Republic--the work of their own voluntary creation!

The chief strength of the system, in its proper administration, lay, according to my view, in that moral power which brought the several members into Confederation. It lay in
50 the hearts of the people of the several States, and in no right or power of keeping them together by coercion. The right of any member to withdraw, which you consider an element of weakness, was really, in my judgment, one of the greatest elements of strength, looking in its

practical workings to the attainment of the objects for which the Union was formed. This right is not only the basis upon which all Confederated Republics must necessarily be formed, but without it there is, and can be, in such systems, no check, no real barrier, nothing, indeed, that can be successfully relied upon to prevent their running, sooner or later, into centralized despotic Empire, to escape from which, the Federative principle was resorted to in the institution of Governments for neighboring States. This right is essential to avoid that final and inevitable result which, without it, must necessarily ensue. Its full recognition, as I have said, becomes the self-adjusting principle of the system by which all its temporary perturbations and irregularities of motion will correct and rectify themselves. No system of Government, as yet discovered, is perfect. All have their defects, their irregularities, their eccentricities of action. The Federate principle resorted to is only an approximation to the hitherto unattained standard. But it is the nearest approximation, up to this time, reached by the wisdom of man. Ours was a long stride nearer the desired goal, by an improvement on this principle, than any that ever existed before.

All Governments of this character are formed upon the assumption that it is for the best interest of all the members of the Confederation to be united on such terms as may be agreed upon, each faithfully performing all its duties and obligations under the Compact. Ours was, certainly, formed on this assumption, and in this belief.

No State, therefore, would withdraw, or be inclined to withdraw, without a real or supposed breach of faith, on the part of her Confederates, or some of them. If the complaint were real, the derelict States would right the wrong, rather than incur the loss attending the failure to do so. For the maintenance of the Union, so long as the objects for which it was formed alone are looked to, is of equal interest to all. If the complaint were imaginary, and a State should withdraw, without a real and substantial cause, the withdrawal would be but for a very brief period of time. It would be but a temporary aberration. For such State would soon find that she had lost more than she had gained in her new position. New burthens would devolve on her. New responsibilities, as well as her just proportion of those resting on her in common with her former Confederates, would have to be assumed; or, in a word, all the disadvantages of isolation, which impelled the Union at first, would be encountered. Under these circumstances and necessary consequences, no Federal Union would remain *long dissevered,* where this principle was left to its full normal action, which was really for the benefit and interest of all its members. It is true that none would stand long that was inherently and permanently injurious to any, and none such ought to stand. For it would be in opposition to the very principles and objects upon which, and for which, all such unions are formed.

In what you consider, then, the weakness of our Government, according to my idea of its nature, I repeat, its chief strength, its great beauty, its complete symmetry, its ultimate harmony, and, indeed, its very perfection, mainly consist; certainly, so long as the objects aimed at in its formation are the objects aimed at in its administration. And, on this principle, on the full recognition of the absolute ultimate Sovereignty of the several States, I did consider it the best, and the strongest, and the grandest Government on earth! My whole heart and soul were devoted to the Constitution, and the Union under it, with this understanding of its nature, character, objects, and functions!

When, therefore, the State of Georgia seceded, against my judgment, viewing the measure in the light of policy, only, and not of right (for the causes, as we have seen, and shall see more fully, hereafter, were more than ample to justify the act, as a matter of right), I felt it to be my duty to go with her, not only from a sense of the obligations of allegiance, but from other high considerations of patriotism of not much less weight and influence. These considerations pressed upon the mind the importance of maintaining this principle, which lies at the foundation of all Federal systems; and to which we were mainly indebted, in ours, for all the great achievements of the past. It was under this construction of the nature of our system, that all these achievements had been attained. This was the essential and vital principle of the system, to which I was so thoroughly devoted. It was that which secured all the advantages of Confederation, without the risk of Centralism and Absolutism; and on its preservation depended, not only the safety and welfare, and even existence, of my own State, but the safety, welfare, and ultimate existence of all the other States of the Union!

The States were older than the Union! They made it! It was but their own creation! Their preservation was of infinitely more importance than its continuance! The Union might cease to exist, and yet the States continue to exist, as before! Not so with the Union in case of the destruction or annihilation of the States! With their extinction, the Union necessarily becomes extinct also! They may survive it, and form another, more perfect, if the lapse of time and changes of events show it to be necessary, for the same objects had in view when it was formed; but it can never survive them! What may be called a Union may spring from the common ruins, but it would not be the Union of the Constitution!—the Union of States! By whatever name it might be called, whether Union, Nation, Kingdom, or any thing else, according to the taste of its dupes or its devotees, it would, in reality, be nothing but that deformed and hideous Monster which rises from the decomposing elements of dead States, the world over, and which is well known by the friends of Constitutional Liberty, everywhere, as the Demon of Centralism, Absolutism, Despotism! This is the necessary reality of that result, whether the Imperial Powers be seized and wielded by the hands of many, of few, or of one!

The question, therefore, with me, assumed a magnitude and importance far above the welfare and destiny of my own State, it embraced the welfare and ultimate destiny of all the States, North as well as South; nay, more, it embraced, in its range, the general interest of mankind, so far, at least, as the oppressed of all other lands and climes were looking to this country, not only for a present asylum against the evils of misrule in their own, but were anxiously and earnestly looking forward to the Federative principles here established, as "the World's best hope," in the great future, for the regeneration, the renaissance, of the Nations of the Earth! Such, in my judgment, were the scope and bearing of the question and the principles involved.

Had this foundation principle of the system then been generally acknowledged—had no military force been called out to prevent the exercise of this right of withdrawal on the part of the seceding States—had no war been waged against Georgia and the other States, for their assertion and maintenance of this right, had not this primary law of our entire system of Government been violated in the war so waged, I cannot permit myself to entertain the shadow of a doubt, that the whole controversy, between States and Sections, would, at no distant day, have been satisfactorily and harmoniously adjusted, under the peaceful and beneficent operation of this very law itself. Just as all perturbations and irregularities are adjusted in the solar system, by the simple law of gravitation, from which alone it sprung in the beginning, and on which alone its continuance, with its wonderfully harmonious workings, depends!

A brief illustration will more clearly unfold this view. Had the right of withdrawal not been denied or resisted, those States, which had openly, confessedly, and avowedly disregarded their obligations, under the Compact, in the matter of the rendition of fugitives from service, and fugitives from justice, appealing, as they did, to "a higher Law" than the Constitutions, would have reconsidered their acts, and renewed their covenants under the bonds of Union, and the Federal administration would have abandoned its policy of taking charge of subjects not within the limits of its delegated powers. The first aberrations in the system; that is the disregard of plighted faith, which had caused the second, that is the secession movement, would themselves have been rectified by that very movement! This rectification on the one side would have been attended by a corresponding rectification on the other. This would have been a necessary and inevitable result, whatever parties, under the influence of passion at the time, may have thought of the nature and permanency of the separation. That is, it would necessarily and inevitably have been the result, if the assumption on which the Union was founded be correct, namely, that it was for the best interest of all the States to be united upon the terms set forth in the Constitution—each State faithfully performing all its obligations, and the Federal Head confining its action strictly to the subjects with which it was charged. On this point, that the Union was best for all, my own convictions were strong and thorough for many reasons, that may be given hereafter. If this postulate was correct, then the ultimate result of this action and re-action in the operation of the system in bringing about a re-adjustment of the parts to their original places, would have been as inevitable as the continued harmonious re-adjustment of continual disturbances in the material world is being produced by like action and counter-action continually going on throughout its entire or-

ganization, and the whole resulting from the same all-pervading and all-controlling law, the same law continuing the organization which brought it at first into existence!

But if, on the contrary, the whole assumption on which the Union was formed was wrong,— if it were not for the true and best interests of all the States, constituted as they were, to be so united,—if it were true, as asserted by the controlling spirits of the derelict States, that the Constitution itself as to them, was but a "covenant with death and an agreement with Hell," —then, of course, the re-adjustment would not have taken place, and ought not to have taken place. But I did not believe that the masses of the people in these States entertained any such sentiments towards the work of their Fathers!

My opinion was, that it only required those masses to see, feel, and appreciate the great advantages of that Union to them; and to realize the fact that a Compact, broken by them, could not longer be binding upon others, as Mr. Webster had said, to cause them to compel their officials to comply with the terms of an engagement, which upon the whole, was of so great importance to their best interests. My convictions were equally strong that, when this was done, the masses of the people at the South, influenced by like considerations, would have controlled all opposition to their cheerful and cordial return to their proper places.

There would have been no war, no bloodshed, no sacking of towns and cities, no desolation, no billions of treasure expended, on either side, and no millions of lives sacrificed in the unnatural and fratricidal strife; there would have been none of the present troubles about restoration, or reconstruction; but, instead of these lamentable scenes, a new spectacle of wonder would have been presented for the guide and instruction of the astonished Nations of the earth, greater than that exhibited after the Nullification pacification, of the matchless workings of our American Institutions of Self-Government by the people!

You readily perceive, therefore, how thoroughly, looking to the grand results, my entire feelings, heart, and soul, with every energy of mind and body, became enlisted in the success of this cause, when force was invoked, when war was waged to put it down. It was the cause, not only of the Seceding States, but the cause of all the States, and in this view it became, to a great extent, the cause of Constitutional Liberty everywhere. It was the cause of the Federative principle of Government, against the principle of Empire! The cause of the Grecian type of Civilization against the Asiatic! So, at least, I viewed it, with all the earnestness of the profoundest convictions.

. . .

This whole question of Slavery, so-called, was but one relating to the proper *status* of the African as an element of a society composed of the Caucasian and African races, and the *status* which was best, not for the one race or the other, but best, upon the whole, for both.

Over these questions, the Federal Government had no rightful control whatever. They were expressly excluded, in the Compact of Union, from its jurisdiction or authority. Any such assumed control was a palpable violation of the Compact, which released all parties to the Compact, affected by such action, from their obligations under the Compact. On this point there can be no shadow of doubt.

Waiving these questions, therefore, for the present, I repeat that this whole subject of Slavery, so-called, in any and every view of it, was, to the Seceding States, but a drop in the ocean compared with those other considerations involved in the issue. Hence, during the whole war, being thoroughly enlisted in it from these and higher considerations, but being, at the same time, ever an earnest advocate for its speediest termination by an appeal from the arena of arms to the forum of reason, justice, and right, I was wedded to no idea as a basis of peace, but that of the recognition of the absolute Sovereignty of all the States as the essen-

tial basis of any permanent union between them, or any of them, consistent with the preservation of their ultimate existence and liberties. And I wanted, at no time, any recognition of Independence on the part of the Confederate States, but that of George III, of England. That is, the recognition of the Sovereignty and the Independence of each, by name.

The Confederate States had made common cause for this great principle, as the original thirteen States had done in 1776. The recognition of this I regarded as essential to the future well-being, happiness, and prosperity of all the States, in existence and to be formed, as well as the countless millions of people who are hereafter to inhabit this half of the Western Hemisphere.

With this simple recognition I saw no formidable difficulty likely to arise in the future, from controversies between the States, or Sections. Whenever the passions of the day passed off, whatever Union or Unions were, or might be really beneficial to all the States, would have resulted sooner or later, as inevitably as natural laws produce their natural effects. This they do in the moral and political world, if left to their proper and legitimate action, with as much certainty as they do in the material.

With this principle recognized, I looked upon it hereafter, and at no distant day, to become, by the natural laws of political affinity—"mutual convenience and reciprocal advantage"— the great Continental Regulator of the Grand Federal Republic of "the United States of America," to whatever limits their boundaries might go, or to whatever extent their number might swell.   1868–1870

ALBION W. TOURGÉE

1838–1905

ONE OF THE MOST NOTABLE of the literary efforts dealing with Reconstruction was Albion Tourgée's *A Fool's Errand* (1879), a novel devoid of stylistic merit but vigorous in its expression of the carpetbag ideals of its author. Tourgée, after participating in the Civil War, was admitted to the Ohio bar, taught school, and entered politics. Although his career on the bench of North Carolina alienated the whites, who questioned his honesty, he was one of the most brilliant of the carpetbaggers. The money which he made during Reconstruction was subsequently lost in journalistic and other ventures. During McKinley's administration he acted as consul to Bordeaux. Although many of Tourgée's novels dealt with Reconstruction, none ranks with *A Fool's Errand*. The following chapter describes the activities of the Ku Klux Klan.

R. F. Dibble, *Albion W. Tourgée*, New York, 1921.
P. H. Buck, *The Road to Reunion, 1865–1900*, Boston, 1937.
Stanley Horn, *Invisible Empire, The K.K.K., 1866–1871*, Boston, 1939.

» » From: A FOOL'S ERRAND « «

CHAPTER XXVII

A NEW INSTITUTION

There had been rumors in the air, for some months, of a strangely mysterious organization, said to be spreading over the Southern States, which added to the usual intangibility of the secret society an element of grotesque super-
10 stition unmatched in the history of any other.

. . .

It was in the winter of 1868–69, therefore, when the wise men were jubilant over the success of the Great Experiment; when it was said that already Reconstruction had been an approved success, the traces of the war been blotted out, and the era of the millennium anticipated,—that a little company of colored
20 men came to the Fool [1] one day; and one of them, who acted as spokesman, said,—

"What's dis we hear, Mars Kunnel, bout de Klux?"

"The what?" he asked.

"De Klux—de Ku-Kluckers dey calls dem-selves."

"Oh! the Ku-Klux, Ku-Klux-Klan, K.K.K.'s, you mean."

"Yes: dem folks what rides about at night
30 a-pesterin' pore colored people, an' a-pertendin' tu be jes from hell, or some of de battle-fields ob ole Virginny."

"Oh, that's all gammon! There is nothing in the world in it,—nothing at all. Probably a parcel of boys now and then take it into their heads to scare a few colored people; but that's all. It is mean and cowardly, but nothing more. You needn't have any trouble about it, boys."

"An' you tink dat's all, Kunnel?"

40 "All? Of course it is! What else should there be?"

"I dunno, Mars Kunnel," said one.

"You don't think dey's ghostses, nor nothin' ob dat sort?" asked another.

"Think! I know they are not."

"So do I," growled one of their number who had not spoken before, in a tone of such meaning that it drew the eyes of the Fool upon him at once.

"So's your mind's made up on that point too, is it, Bob?" he asked laughingly.

"I know dey's not ghosts, Kunnel. I wish ter God dey was!" was the reply.

"Why, what do you mean, Bob?" asked the colonel in surprise.

"Will you jes help me take off my shirt, Jim?" said Bob meaningly, as he turned to one of those with him.

The speaker was taller than the average of his race, of a peculiarly jetty complexion, broad-shouldered, straight, of compact and powerful build. His countenance, despite its blackness, was sharply cut; his head well shaped; and his whole appearance and demeanor marked him as a superior specimen of his race. Servosse had seen him before, and knew him well as an industrious and thrifty blacksmith, living in a distant part of the county, who was noted as being one of the most independent and self reliant of his people in all political as well as pecuniary matters,—Bob Martin by name.

When his clothing had been removed, he turned his back towards the Fool, and, glancing over his shoulder, said coolly,—

"What d'ye tink ob dat, Kunnel?"

"My God!" exclaimed the Fool, starting back in surprise and horror. "What does this mean, Bob?"

"Seen de Kluckers, sah," was the grimly laconic answer.

The sight which presented itself to the Fool's eyes was truly terrible. The broad muscular back, from the nape down to and below the waist, was gashed and marked by repeated blows. Great furrows were plowed in the black

---

[1] Comfort Servosse, a Northern lawyer who, shortly after the end of the War, purchased Warrington Place, a run-down plantation.

integument, whose greenly-livid lips were drawn back, while the coagulated fibrine stretched across, and mercifully protected the lacerated flesh. The whole back was livid and swollen, bruised as if it had been brayed in a mortar. Apparently, after having cut the flesh with closely-laid welts and furrows, sloping downward from the left side towards the right, with that peculiar skill in castigation which could only be obtained through the abundant opportunity for severe and deliberate flagellation which prevailed under the benign auspices of slavery, the operator had changed his position, and scientifically cross-checked the whole. That he was an expert whose skill justified Bob's remark—"Nobody but an ole oberseer ebber dun dat, Kunnel"—was evident even on a casual inspection. The injury which the man had sustained, though extensive and severe, was not dangerous to one of his constitution and hardened physique. To the eye of the Northern man who gazed at it, however, unused as are all his compeers to witness the effects of severe whipping, it seemed horrible beyond the power of words to express. He did not reflect that the African could have had none of that sense of indignity and degradation with which the Caucasian instinctively regards the application of the emblem of servility, and that he was but fulfilling the end of his dusky being in submitting to such castigation. He was filled with anger, surprise, and horror.

"What?—Who?—How? My God! Tell me all about it. Can't I do something for you, my man?"

"Thank ye, Kunnel, nothing," said Bob seriously. "It's been washed in salt an' water. Dat's de bes' ting dere is to take out de soreness; an' it's doin as well as can be expected, I s'pose. I don't know much 'bout sech matters, Boss. I'se bin a slave goin' on forty-three years, but never hed a lash on my back since I was a waitin'-boy till las' night."

His face was working with passion, and his eyes had a wicked fire in them, which clearly showed that he did not take this visitation in such a subdued and grateful spirit as his position properly demanded that he should. When his clothing had been resumed, he sat down and poured into the wondering ears of the Fool this story:—

Bob's Experience

"Yer see, I'se a blacksmith at Burke's Cross-Roads. I've been thar ever sence a few days arter I heerd ob de surrender. I rented an ole house dar, an' put up a sort of shop, an' got togedder a few tools, an' went to work. It's a right good stan'. Never used ter be ob any count, coz all de big plantations roun' dar hed der own smifs. But now de smifs hez scattered off, an' dey hev ter pay fer der work, dey finds it cheaper ter come ter my shop dan ter hire a blacksmif when dey's only half work fer him to do. So I'se been doin' right well, an' hev bought de house an' lot, an' got it all paid fer, tu. I've allers tended to my own business. 'Arly an' late Bob's bin at his shop, an' allers at work. I 'llowed to get me a snug home fer myself an' de ole 'ooman afore we got tu old ter work; an' I wanted to give de boys an' gals a little eddication, an' let em hev a fa'r start in life wid de rest ob de worl', if I could. Dat's what Bob's bin wukkin' fer; an' der ain't no man ner woman, black ner white, can say he hain't wukked honestly and fa'rly,—honestly an' fa'rly, ebbery day sence he's bin his own master.

"Long a while back—p'raps five er six months—I refused ter du some work fer Michael Anson or his boy, 'cause they'd run up quite a score at de shop, an' allers put me off when I wanted pay. I couldn't work jes fer de fun ob scorin' it down: so I quit. It made smart ob talk. Folks said I waz gettin' too smart fer a nigger, an' sech like; but I kep right on; tole em I waz a free man,—not born free, but made free by a miracle,—an' I didn't propose ter do any man's work fer noffin'. Most everybody hed somefin' to say about it; but it didn't seem ter hurt my trade very much. I jes went on gittin' all I could do, an' sometimes moah. I s'pose I acted pretty independent: I felt so, anyhow. I staid at home, an' axed nobody any favors. I know'd der wa'n't a better blacksmif in de country, an' thought I hed things jes' ez good ez I wanted 'em. When ther come an election, I sed my say, did my own votin', an' tole de other colored people dey waz free, an' hed a right ter du de same. Thet's bad doctrine up in our country. De white folks don't like ter hear it, and 'specially don't like ter hear a nigger say it. Dey don't mind 'bout our gittin' on ef dey hev a mortgage, so't de 'arnin's goes into ther pockets; nor 'bout our votin', so long ez we votes ez dey tells us. Dat's dare idea uv liberty fer a nigger.

"Well, here a few weeks ago, I foun' a board stuck up on my shop one mornin', wid dese words on to it:—

" 'Bob Martin,—You're gettin' too dam

smart! The white folks round Burke's Cross-Roads don't want any sech smart niggers round thar. You'd better git, er you'll hev a call from the

" 'K.K.K.'

"I'd heerd 'bout the Klux, an' 'llowd jes' ez you did, Kunnel,—dat dey waz some triflin' boys dat fixed up an' went round jes' ter scare pore ignorant niggers, an't it made me all the madder ter think dey should try dat ar game on me. So I sed boldly, an' afore everybody, they ef the Kluckers wanted enny thin' uv Bob Martin, they'd better come an' git it; thet I didn't 'bleve any nonsense about ther comin' straight from hell, an' drinkin' the rivers dry, an' all that: but, ef they'd come ter meddle with me, I 'llowed some on 'em mout go to hell afore it was over.

"I worked mighty hard an' late yesterday, an', when I went into de house, I was so tired thet I jes' fell down on de trundle-bed dat hed bin pulled out in front ob de souf do'. When my ole 'ooman got supper ready, an' called me, I jes' turned over, an' was that beat out an' sleepy, that I tole her to let me alone. So I lay thar, an' slep'. She put away de supper-tings, an' tuk part ob de chillen into bed wid her; an' de rest crawled in wid me, I s'pose. I dunno nothin' about it, fer I nebber woke up till some time in de night. I kinder remember hearin' de dog bark, but I didn't mind it; an', de fust ting I knew, de do' was bust in, an' fell off de hinges ober on de trundle-bed whar I was lyin'. It's a mercy I was thar. I don't s'pose I've lain down on it fer a year afore, an', ef de chillen hed all been thar alone, it's mor'n likely they'd all been killed. They hed taken a house-log I hed got (tinkin' ter put up a kitchen arter Christmas), an' free or four of 'em hed run wid it endwise agin de do'. So, when I woke from de crash, I hed do' an' house-log bofe on me, an' de ole 'ooman an' chillen screamin', so't I couldn't make out fer a minit what it was, er whar I was. De moon was a-shinin' bright, an' I spect de rascals t'ought I'd run, an' dey would shoot me as I come out. But, as soon as dey saw me heavin' an' strugglin' under de do', two on 'em run in, an' got on top of it. It was no use fer me to struggle any more under dat load. Besides dat, I was feared dey'd kill de chillen. So I tole 'em ef dey'd get off, an' spar' de chillen, I'd surrender. Dey wouldn't bleve me, dough, till dey'd tied my hans. Den dey got off de do', an' I riz up, an' kind o' pushed it an' de house-log off de trundle-bed. Den dey pulled me out

o' do's. Dar was 'bout tirty of 'em standin' dar in de moonlight, all dressed in black gowns thet come down to ther boots, an' some sort of high hat on, dat come down ober der faces, jes' leavin' little holes ter see fru, an' all trimmed wid different colored cloth, but mos'ly white.

"I axed 'em what dey wanted o' me. Dey sed I was gittin tu dam smart, an' dey'd jes' come roun' ter teach me some little manners. Den dey tied me tu a tree, an' done what you've seen. Dey tuk my wife an' oldes' gal out ob de house, tore de close nigh about off 'em, an' abused 'em shockin' afore my eyes. Arter tarin' tings up a heap in de house, dey rode off, tellin' me dey reckoned I'd larn to be 'spectful to white folks herearter, an' not be so anxious 'bout radical votes. Den my ole woman cut me loose, an' we went into de house ter see what devilment dey'd done dar. We called de chillen. Dar's five on 'em,—oldes' a gal 'bout fifteen, an' de younges' only little better'n a year ole. We foun' 'em all but de baby. I don' tink he ebber breaved arter de do' fell on us."

The tears stood in the eyes of the poor man as he finished. The Fool looked at him in a glamour of amazement, pity, and shame. He could not help feeling humiliated, that, in his own Christian land, one should be so treated by such a cowardly-seeming combination, simply for having used the liberty which the law had given him to acquire competence and independence by his own labor.

"Why have you not complained of this outrage to the authorities?" he asked after a moment.

"I tole Squire Haskins an' Judge Thompson what I hev tole you," answered Bob.

"And what did they say?"

"Dat dey couldn't do noffin' unless I could sw'ar to de parties."

"Did you not recognize any of them?"

"Not to say recognize; dat is, not so dat I could tell you so dat you could know de persons as de ones I named. I'm nigh 'bout sartin, from a lot of little tings, who dey was; but I couldn't sw'ar."

"Did you not know the voices of any of them?"

"Yes, I did. But de judge says I would jes' be makin' trouble fer myself to no 'count; fer he says no jury would convict on sech evidence when unsupported."

"I suppose he is right," mused the Colonel. "And there does not seem to be any way for you to get redress for what has been done to you, unless you can identify those who did the injury so clearly that no jury can resist a conviction. I suppose the vast majority of jurymen will be disinclined even to do justice. Perhaps some of the very men who were engaged in the act may be on the jury, or their brothers, fathers, or friends. So it would be useless for you to attempt a prosecution unless you had the very strongest and clearest testimony. I doubt not the judge was right in the advice he gave you."

"And do you tink der is any chance o' my gittin' sech testimony?" asked Bob.

"I confess," answered the Fool, "that I see very little. Time and care might possibly enable you to get it."

"Der's no hope o' dat,—no hope at all," answered the freedman sadly.

. . .

CHAPTER XXXIV

THE HARVEST OF WISDOM

. . .

This new Reign of Terror had come so stilly and quietly upon the world, that none realized its fearfulness and extent. At first it had been a thing of careless laughter to the great, free, un suspecting North, then a matter of contemptuous ridicule, and finally a question of incredulous horror. Two things had contributed to this feeling. Those who had suffered had, in the main, been humble people. The public press did not teem with their wrongs, because there were none to tell them. They were people, too, whose story of wrong had been so long in the ear of the public, that it was tired of the refrain. It had yielded, very slowly and unwillingly, to the conviction that slavery was an evil, and the colored man too near akin to white humanity to be rightfully held in bondage, and subjected to another's will. It had slowly and doubtfully been brought to the point of interference therewith on the ground of military necessity in the suppression of rebellion, and, after a grand struggle of conflicting ideas, had finally settled down to the belief that enfranchisement was all that was required to cure all the ills which hitherto had afflicted, or in the future might assail, the troublesome and pestiferous African. This had been granted. The conscience of the nation was satisfied, and it highly resolved that

thereafter it would have peace; that the negro *could* have no further ground of complaint, and it would hear no further murmurs. So it stopped its ears, and, when the south wind brought the burden of woe, it shook its head blankly, and said, "I hear nothing, nothing! All is peace."

But, when the cries became so clamorous that they could not longer be ignored, the Wise Men appointed a committee who should investigate the matter, and hear all that could be said both *pro* and *con*.

Oh! a strange, sad story is that which fills the thirteen volumes of testimony, documents, and conclusions, reported by that committee; a strange commentary upon Christian civilization; a strange history of peaceful years;—bloody as the reign of Mary, barbarous as the chronicles of the Comanche!

Of the slain there were enough to furnish forth a battlefield, and all from those three classes, the negro, the scalawag, and the carpet-bagger,—all killed with deliberation, overwhelmed by numbers, roused from slumber at the murk midnight, in the hall of public assembly, upon the river-brink, on the lonely woods-roads, in simulation of the public execution,—shot, stabbed, hanged, drowned, mutilated beyond description, tortured beyond conception.

And almost always by an unknown hand! Only the terrible mysterious fact of *death* was certain. Accusation by secret denunciation; sentence without hearing; execution without warning, mercy, or appeal. In the deaths alone, terrible beyond utterance; but in the manner of death—the secret, intangible doom from which fate springs—more terrible still: in the treachery which made the neighbor a disguised assassin, most horrible of all the feuds and hates which history portrays.

And then the wounded,—those who escaped the harder fate,—the whipped, the mangled, the bleeding, the torn! Men despoiled of manhood! Women gravid with dead children! bleeding backs! broken limbs! Ah! the wounded in this silent warfare were more thousands than those who groaned upon the slopes of Gettysburg! Dwellings and schools and churches burned! People driven from their homes, and dwelling in the woods and fields! The poor, the weak, the despised, maltreated and persecuted—by whom? Always the same intangible presence, the same invisible power. Well did it name itself "The Invisible Empire." Unseen and unknown! In one State ten thousand, in another twenty thousand, in another forty thousand; in all an army greater than the Rebellion, from the moldering remains of which it sprung, could ever put into the field! An Invisible Empire, with a trained and disciplined army of masked midnight marauders, making war upon the weakling "powers" which the Wise Men had set up in the lately rebellious territory!

10 And then the defense!—no, not the *defense*, —the excuse, the avoidance set up to rebut the charge, to mitigate the guilt! Ah, me! it is sad, sadder almost than the bloody facts themselves. What is it?

"We were rebels in arms: we surrendered, and by the terms of surrender were promised immunity so long as we obeyed the laws. This meant that we should govern ourselves as of old. Instead of this, they put military officers 20 over us; they imposed disabilities on our best and bravest; they liberated our slaves, and gave them power over us. Men born at the North came among us, and were given place and power by the votes of slaves and renegades. There were incompetent officers. The revenues of the State were squandered. We were taxed to educate the blacks. Enormous debts were contracted. We did not do these acts of violence from political motives, but only 30 because the parties had made themselves obnoxious."

⋅ ⋅ ⋅

And then the organization itself, so complete, and yet so portable and elastic! So perfect in disguise, that, of the thousands of victims, scarce a score could identify one of their persecutors! And among the hundreds of thousands of its members, of the few who con-40 fessed and revealed its character, hardly one knew any thing more than had already been discovered; *or, if he knew it, did not disclose it!* It is all amazing, but sad and terrible. Would that it might be blotted out, or disappear as a fevered dream before the brightness of a new day!

Yet in it we may recognize the elements which should go to make up a grand and kingly people. They felt themselves insulted 50 and oppressed. No matter whether they were or not, be the fact one way or another, it does not affect their conduct. If the Reconstruction which the Wise Men ordained was unjust; if the North was the aggressor and wrongful assailant of the South in war; if, to humiliate

and degrade her enemy, the terms of surrender were falsified, and new and irritating conditions imposed; if the outcasts of Northern life were sent or went thither to encourage and induce the former slave to act against his former master,—if all this *were* true, it would be no more an excuse or justification for the course pursued than would the fact that these things were honestly *believed* to be true by the masses who formed the rank and file of this grotesquely uniformed body of partisan cavalry. In any case, it must be counted but as the desperate effort of a proud, brave, and determined people to secure and hold what they *deemed to be their rights.*

⋅ ⋅ ⋅

It was not the individual negro, scalawag, or carpet-bagger, against whom the blow was directed, but the power—the Government— the idea which they represented. Not unfrequently, the individual victim was one toward whom the individual members of the Klan who executed its decree upon him had no little of kindly feeling and respect, but whose influence, energy, boldness, or official position, was such as to demand that he should be "visited." In most of its assaults, the Klan was not instigated by cruelty, nor a desire for revenge; but these were simply the most direct, perhaps the only, means to secure the end it had in view. The brain, the wealth, the chivalric spirit of the South, was restive under what it deemed degradation and oppression. This association offered a ready and effective method of overturning the hated organization, and throwing off the rule which had been imposed upon them. From the first, therefore, it spread like wildfire. It is said that the first organization was instituted in May, or perhaps as late as the 1st of June, 1868; yet by August of that year it was firmly established in every State of the South. It was builded upon an ineradicable sentiment of hostility to the negro *as a political integer*, and a fierce determination that the white people of the South, or a majority of that race, should rule,—if not by the power of the ballot, then by force of skill, brain, and the habit of domination. The bravest and strongest and best of the South gave it their recognition and support,—in most cases actively, in some passively. Thousands believed it a necessity to prevent anarchy and the destruction of all valuable civilization; others regarded it as a means of retaliating upon the government, which they conceived to have oppressed them; while still others looked to it as a means of acquiring place and power.

That it outgrew the designs of its originators is more than probable; but the development was a natural and unavoidable one. It is probable that it was intended, at first, to act solely upon the superstitious fears of the ignorant and timid colored race. The transition from moral to physical compulsion was easy and natural, especially to a people who did not regard the colored man as having any *inherent* right to liberty and self-government, or the personal privileges attendant thereon, but only such right as was conferred by a legislation which was deemed at least questionable. The native whites who had identified themselves with that movement which gave political power to the blacks were regarded not only as mercenaries and renegades who had deserted their section, but also as traitors to their race. The Northern men who did likewise were regarded as intruders and invaders, and believed to be instigated, not only by the basest personal motives, but also by that concentrated hate which the Southern man always attributed to the Northern opponent of slavery. Unaccustomed to immigration as the South was, accustomed, indeed, to regard all strangers with suspicion, until assured of their harmlessness as regarded the main institution of their land, it needed but the conviction of oppression, and the chagrin of defeat, to make them look upon every individual from the hostile section as an active and virulent enemy, whose claim of citizenship there was a false pretense, constituting the owner, in effect, an emissary of the enemy, entitled only to the consideration and treatment of the spy.

. · . · .

This new revolution which had begun went on. The Klan increased in numbers and in power,—an *imperium in imperio*,—until its decrees were far more potent, and its power more dreaded, than that of the visible commonwealths which it either dominated or terrorized. This fact, together with the fear of the new laws which had been adopted by the National Government, the authority of which had not then been questioned, tended somewhat to repress actual violence. Having gained what was sought,—to wit, the control of their States,—the leaders now exercised their authority to prevent further raids; and the hostility against the colored man and his allies gradually died out as these suppressed classes ceased to be a political element which need be feared, in the struggle for domination. The national law, moreover, could not extend to the crimes perpetrated before its enactment. They were still only cognizable in the State tribunals, in which it was not supposed that prosecution would ever be possible. So the organization was easily maintained, lying quiet and unnoticed, except when, upon occasions, it was deemed proper to manifest its power to restrain or punish some daring leader who refused to obey the logic of events, and give up the contest for the rule of the majority of *voters* in those States, instead of the majority of the White Leaguers therein.

The revolution had been inaugurated, and its feasibility demonstrated. Henceforth it was only a question of time as to its absolute and universal success. The rule of the majority had been overthrown, the power of the Government boldly defied, and its penalties for crime successfully evaded, that the enfranchisement of the colored man might be rendered a farce; and the obnoxious Amendments and Reconstruction legislation had been shown to be practically nullified. Read by the light of other days, the triumph of the ancient South was incredibly grand; in the then present there was little lacking to give it completeness; in the future—well, that could take care of itself. 1879

EDWARD KING

1848–1896

E DWARD KING, the son of a Methodist minister, was born in Middlefield, Massachusetts. After a brief experience as a factory worker, he entered journalism, reporting the Paris Exposition in 1867, the Franco-Prussian War, the Paris commune, the Carlist wars, and the Russo-Turkish War of 1877–1878. Many of his books are journalistic accounts of his experiences abroad. His best novel, *Joseph Zalmonah* (1893), graphically described conditions in New York's sweat shops.

During the years 1873 and 1874 King, at the suggestion of Dr. J. G. Holland, toured the Southern states. His realistic descriptions of what he saw and heard first appeared in *Scribner's Monthly* and subsequently in *The Great South*. This work, which was generously illustrated, is a valuable account of postwar conditions.

The Dictionary of American Biography, vol. X.

»   »   *From:* THE GREAT SOUTH   «   «

CHAPTER XXXI

LIFE ON COTTON PLANTATIONS

During my stay in Natchez, one of the many gentlemen interested in cotton-planting on the west or Louisiana side of the river, invited me to accompany him on a tour of inspection. The rapidly-rising river threatened to inundate the
10 lands on which hundreds of negroes had been expending weeks of patient care, and the planter felt it his duty to take a horseback ride over the trio of plantations under his charge; so we crossed the Mississippi, and rode twelve miles into the interior of Louisiana.

On the road, which led along the lovely banks of Lake Concordia, the planter chatted of some of the vexations by which he is daily beset, and spoke rather hopelessly of the labor
20 problem. The condition of society, too, he thought very bad, and that it was an actual hindrance to the development of the section.

"Are the negroes," I asked him, "aggressive and insolent toward the white people?"

But as the planter was about to answer this question, we approached a ferry-boat, or barge, in which we were to cross an arm of the lake to the island on which my friend's plantations were situated. An old negro man, much the worse for liquor, was preparing to monopolize the boat with his mule-team, but held back the mules, and touched his hat with drunken courtesy as we came up.

"Stand aside, uncle," said the planter firmly, but very politely; "we wish to cross at once, and there is not room for us all."

"Yas, sah; yas, Colonel," said the old man. "I's willin' to wait on you gemmen, 'cause you is gemmen; but ef yer was no count folks, I'd go for yer. Ride in, Colonel."

When we were some distance from shore, the planter said:

"That old man made way for us simply out of deference to our social position. The negroes are courteous enough to us; it has been their habit so long that they cannot forget it. But they will kill our deer and steal our poultry and bacon, and we have no redress."

After an hour or two of journeying over rough roads, we came to one of the plantations. A host of negroes were busily filling a breach in a dyke which the treacherous water might sweep away if rains came to swell the already ominous floods of the Mississippi. A pack of hounds came yelping to meet the planter; and the black women in the cabin courtesied obsequiously.

We crossed the field, bordered by noble

cypresses and oaks, stopping now and then to watch the negroes as they carefully prepared the ground which an inundation might, in less than a day, reduce to a hopeless wilderness of mud. Entering the house of the overseer, we found that functionary smoking his pipe and reposing after a long ride over the plantation. He was a rough, hearty, good-natured man, accustomed to living alone and faring rudely. I asked him what he thought of the negro as a free laborer.

"He works well, mostly, sir. These yer Alabama niggers that's workin' on our plantations now do well on wages. They make some little improvements around their cabins, but mighty little, sir. Ef politics would only let 'em alone, they'd get along well enough, I reckon."

"Do the negroes on this plantation vote?"

"I reckon not (laughing). I don't want my niggers to have anything to do with politics. They can't vote as long as they stay with us, and these Alabama boys don't take no interest in the elections here."

"What do they receive as monthly wages?"

"From ten to sixteen dollars. It costs us about fifteen dollars per head to bring 'em from Alabama. These niggers likes wages better than shares. We keep a store here, and, Saturday nights, most of the money they have earned comes back to us in trade. They're fond o' whiskey and good things to eat."

"What is the routine of your work on a large plantation like this, and those adjoining it, throughout the year?"

"Wal, sir, I reckon that's a long story. We don't have much spare time, and mighty little amusement. Wal, sir, the first thing we do, sir, we begin early in January, a few weeks after the old crop is all gathered in, to repair fences and clean out all the ditches, sir. Then we pull down the old stalks, and start the ploughs to throw quadruple furrows in the fields. Then we throw out the 'middles.' "

"What are they?"

"Wal, sir, we throw out soil at the sides so as to leave a slope bed of fresh ground to plant on, and loose earth to cover it with. If the spring freshet breaks on to this yer prepared earth, we've got to begin over again, and that makes the season very late.

"Planting begins about the last of March, or very early in April. Piles of cotton seed are laid along some ways apart on the field, and then the niggers sow it along the beds, a ton of seed to eight acres. Then it is 'barred off'— covered up, that means.

"Ez soon as the cotton stalks begin to peep up, 'scraping' begins. The hands weed every row carefully, and don't leave any weakly plants. That, and looking after the caterpillars, keeps 'em busy till July. Caterpillars ain't the only danger we have to fight against. Thar's a hundred others. Cotton's a ticklish plant to raise. You've got to watch it mighty close, and then the worms and the weather will sometimes ruin the crop.

"Between July and September we keep the hands busy, getting out baskets, and setting things in order; then we pile in new help, and for the rest of the season, employ three times as many hands as thar's in the fields now. Up to Christmas it's picking and ginning, and it's right lively, you can be sure."

From the overseer's conversation I learned that cotton-picking is done quite as thoroughly under the system of free labor as in the days when slave-driving was permissible; but that the "niggers" require constant watching. On many plantations where the yield is abundant, it is difficult to concentrate labor enough at the proper time to get the cotton into the gin-house the same year that it is planted. I have seen cotton-fields still white with their creamy fleeces late in December, because the negroes were either too lazy or too busily engaged in their annual merry-makings to gather the harvest. But on the large lowland plantations along the Mississippi, the crop is usually gathered early, and the picking is very thorough. I could not discover that there was any system of "forced labor" now in use, and I thought the overseer's statement, that a "good field-hand now-a-days would pick 250 pounds of cotton daily," was excellent testimony in favor of free labor. He added, however, that on many plantations the average hands would not pick more than 100 pounds per day.

The laborers were coming in from the field in a long picturesque procession. As it was spring-time many of them had been ploughing, and were mounted upon the backs of the stout mules which had been their companions all day. Some of the men were singing rude songs, others were shouting boisterously and scuffling as they went their way along the broad pathway bordered by giant cypresses and noble oaks. The boys tumbling and wriggling in the grass perpetually exploded into guffaws of contagious laughter. Many of the men were tall and finely formed. They had an intelligent look, and were evidently not so degraded as those born on the Louisiana lowlands. The overseer sat on the veranda of his house, now and then calling out a sharp command or a caution, the negroes looking up obsequiously and touching their hats as they heard his voice. When the mules were stabled the men came lounging back to the cabins, where the women were preparing their homely supper, and an hour afterward we heard the tinkle of banjos, the pattering of feet and uproarious laughter. The interiors of the negro cabins were of the rudest description. The wretched huts in which the workmen live seem to them quite comfortable, however. I saw no one who appeared discontented with his surroundings. Few of these laborers could read at all. Even those who had some knowledge of the alphabet did not seem to be improving it.

Late in the evening, as the planter, with his heavy cloak thrown about his shoulders, was reposing from the fatigues of a wearisome ride over the broad acres, a delegation of field-hands came to see him, all to ask favors of "de Cunnel,"—to get him to write a few letters, or to bring some tiny parcel from the town on his next visit to the plantation. The men came huddling in, bowing awkwardly, and stood with their caps in their hands as near the door as possible, as if ready to run on the slightest provocation. If I looked at them steadily they burst into uneasy laughter and moved away, while the black women in the door-way and on the porch re-echoed the merriment. Meantime the planter listened to one after another of the delegation. Charles, a black boy, six feet tall, and with sinews strong as steel, stepped forward to the flickering light given by the candles and the burning logs in the fire-place.

"Cunnel, I wish you read me dat letter, please, sah."

The "Cunnel" read it, Charles meantime standing erect, with his great arms folded across his mighty chest and the massive column of his throat throbbing with scornful emotion. There was a strange, baffled expression in his face; a look of contempt for his own helplessness which was painful.

The letter was common-place enough, reproaching Charles for having left Alabama before liquidating the pressing claims of certain swarthy creditors. Having, after some trouble,

deciphered the letter's meaning, the Colonel said, gently but coldly:

"Stand aside, Charles. Andy, who is the likeliest negro from Alabama now on the plantation?"

No answer for a minute. Andy stepped forward into the light, looking first into the fire-place, then at the deer's horns over the mantel, then at the shining revolver on the rough wooden table, while his immense lips worked nervously, as if endeavoring to draw in inspiration from the air.

"Did you hear me, Andy?"

"Cunnel, I's a studyin', sah."

After having studied some time, Andy darted out without a word, and presently returned with three hulking black giants, who huddled together in the same helpless way that the first arrivals did. They held their shapeless felt hats in their enormous hands, glancing from them into the faces of the white men; then exchanging significant looks with each other, burst into the regulation laugh.

"Did the colored politicians try to keep you from leaving Alabama to come here with me, boys?" inquired the Colonel.

Intense surprise on the part of the negroes.

"No, sah; reckon not, sah."

"Did you vote in Alabama?"

"Yas, Cunnel; yas, sah, always voted, sah."

"Can you do better here than in Alabama?"

After mature reflection, the trio responded in the affirmative.

"Would you care to vote here?"

Hesitatingly, "No, sah"; whereupon the three negroes were dismissed into the darkness.

The Alabama papers at the beginning of the current year reported that the colored laborers were leaving that State in troops of thousands. They were nearly all *en route* for the cotton plantations of Mississippi, and on the Louisiana bank of the Father of Waters. Central Alabama appeared at that time to be undergoing rapid depopulation for the benefit of the richer lands along the Mississippi bottom. It was estimated in the spring of 1874 that Alabama had already lost from $700,000 to $1,000,000 in her labor element alone. How long the influx of the freedmen into Mississippi and Louisiana from the South Atlantic States and from Alabama will continue is uncertain. In 1873 Georgia lost fully 20,000 of her able-bodied colored laborers, and gained but little in white immigration to balance it.

The women and children on the cotton plantations near the Mississippi river do not work in the fields as much as they used. Rude as are their surroundings in the little cabins which they now call their own, they are beginning to take an interest in their homes, and the children spend some time each year at school. The laborers on the plantations in Louisiana have sometimes been paid as high as thirty dollars per month, and furnished with a cabin, food, and a plot of ground for a garden; but this is exceptional.

While supper was being prepared the master of the plantation apologized for what he called the homely fare which, he said, was all that he could set before us.

"We are so far from town here," he said, "that we can offer you only plantation fare— rough meat and eggs, with bacon, a loaf of baker's bread, and some bottles of claret which I brought from Vidalia."

I ventured to suggest that on the plantation he had every facility for a superb garden, and to wonder that the overseers did not employ some of the negroes to cultivate a plot of ground that its fruits might appear on the table.

"Oh, oh," laughed the overseer. "Make a garden here; reckon it would have to have a mighty high wall; the niggers would steal everything in it as fast as it was ripe."

But I suggested that if each of the negroes had a small garden, which he seemed to have ample time after hours to cultivate, he would not desire to steal.

The Colonel smiled gravely, and the overseer shook his head incredulously, adding:

"These is good niggers, but stealing is as natural as eating to them"; and, with this remark, we were ushered into the supper-room, where two black servant girls ran nimbly about, bringing in plain but substantial fare, which our hard riding made thoroughly palatable.

There was no white lady on the plantation. The overseer and his two assistants were busy from dawn till dark, and when night threw its shadows over the great cypress-bordered aisles of the forest and the wide expanse of the fields, they dismissed the negroes about the store and the stables and retired to rest. But on the occasion of our visit we saw unusual activity. A violent storm arose while we were at supper, and the overseers mounted their horses and rode off in different directions to inspect the levèes. Troops of negroes were dispatched in skiffs along the lake with hundreds of sacks, which they were instructed to fill with sand and place at weak points on the levèes. All night they fought the slowly but steadily-rising waters, while my companion and I slept on a mattress on the floor of the overseer's room, undisturbed by anything save the sighing of the winds through the noble trees surrounding the house, and the clatter of rain upon the shingles.

With early morning back came the Colonel, pale and worn with a night of battle with the steadily-rising water, and, as he laid aside his heavy cloak, placed his revolver on the table, and sat down with a weary sigh, he said it was hardly worth while to try to be a successful cotton-planter now-a-days; things human and things divine seemed to conspire to make it impossible to succeed. I thought of his sigh and of his helpless look a day or two afterward, when I was told that one thousand acres of his plantation had been flooded and badly injured by the offensive policy of a neighbor planter, who had cut the Colonel's levèes to save his own.

With daylight also, although the rain was steadily falling, the plantation blossomed into activity. The overseers had arisen long before the dim streaks of the dawn were seen on the lowland horizon; had galloped over many a broad acre, but returned gloomily, announcing that the land was too wet to work that day. The negroes slouchingly disposed themselves about the store and the overseer's "mansion," keeping at a respectful distance from the kitchen, where sat the overseer himself, surrounded by his dogs. Nothing more dispiriting could be imagined than the atmosphere of this lowland plantation over which imminent disaster seemed breaking. From right and left came stories of trouble and affliction. Here and there a planter had made a good crop and had laid aside a little money, but the evidences of material prosperity were painfully few. The overseers, while doggedly persistent in working the plantations up to their full capacity, still seemed to have a grim sense of a fate which overhung the whole locality, and which would not permit consecutive years of prosperity and plenty.

There is still much on one of these remote and isolated plantations to recall the romance which surrounded them during the days of slavery. The tall and stalwart women, with their luxuriant wool carefully wrapped in gayly-colored handkerchiefs; the picturesque and tattered children, who have not the slightest particle of education, and who have not been reached even since the era of reconstruction, by the influences of schools and teachers; the groups of venerable darkeys, with their gray slouch hats and impossible garments, who chatter for hours together on the sunny side of some out-buildings, and the merry-makings at night, all recall a period which, the planter will tell you, with a mournful look, comprised the halcyon days of Louisiana.

The thing which struck me as most astonishing here, in the cotton-lands, as on the rice plantations of South Carolina, was the absolute subjection of the negro. Those with whom I talked would not directly express any idea. They gave a shuffling and grimacing assent to whatever was suggested; or, if they dissented, would beg to be excused from differing verbally, and seemed to be much distressed at being required to express their opinions openly. Of course, having the most absolute political liberty, because in that section they were so largely in the majority, numerically, that no intimidation could have been practiced, it seemed astonishing that they should be willing to forego the right to vote, and to willingly isolate themselves from their fellows. I could not discover that any of the negroes were making a definite progress, either manifested by a subscription to some newspaper or by a tendency to discussion; and, while the planter gave me the fullest and freest account of the social status of the negroes employed by him, he failed to mention any sign of a definite and intellectual growth. The only really encouraging sign in their social life was the tendency to create for themselves homes, and now and then to cultivate the land about them.

The rain continued to fall in torrents as we rode across the island along the muddy roads, under the great arches of the cypress-trees, on our return to Natchez. Here and there a few negroes were desperately striving afield, endeavoring to effect something in spite of the storm; but the planter shook his head gravely, and said that all agricultural operations must now be two months later than usual. The lack of concerted operations among the planters against the inroads of the floods, and the disastrous consequences of an incompetent

labor system, were, to his thinking, effectual drawbacks to much material progress for a long time. In a previous chapter I have shown how the production of Concordia parish has fallen off since slavery was abolished; and he could not give any encouragement to my hope that this wretched state of affairs would soon be changed.

At last we reached the arm of the lake where we expected to find our sable ferry-man, but the rain had washed the waters into quite a fury, and we could see neither ferry-man nor barge. Half-an-hour's hallooing at last brought the old man from his cabin on the opposite side, and another half hour brought him, dripping wet, with the gray wool of his beard glistening with rain-drops, to the shore on which we stood. He complained bitterly of his poverty, yet I was surprised to learn that each time the Colonel visited his plantation he paid this venerable boatman a dollar for his ride across the lake. Although I diligently endeavored to enter into conversation with the aged black man, he steadily avoided any reference to political topics, and assumed a look of blank amazement when I appealed to him for a direct opinion. But he was always civil, courteous to a degree not discoverable among people in his rank of life in the North. His character swayed and bent before any aggression, but did not break; it was as stubborn as elastic.

In the forest through which ran the road leading to the Colonel's plantation, we met a brown man mounted on a stout horse, and loaded down with a small armory of fire-arms, in addition to which he carried a long knife and a hatchet, evidently intended for dissecting some deer.

"Ha!" said the Colonel pleasantly, yet with a touch of annoyance in his voice, "so you are going poaching on my land again? There will soon be no deer left."

"Yas, Cunnel," said the fellow, impudently shifting his long rifle from his right to his left shoulder. "I reckon ef I see any deer I's gwine to go for 'em, sho"; then, putting spurs to his steed, he galloped off.

There was no redress, and the Colonel was compelled to submit anew to the plundering of his preserves.

Driving homeward with my artist companion, the Colonel having left us to return to his fight with the levèes, we were struck with the picturesque clusters of negro cabins by the wayside. Nowhere else in the agricultural regions of the South had we perceived such a tendency to an artistic grouping of buildings. Along the road, which was now so covered with water that we could hardly pick our way, a few uproarious negroes, with whiskey bottles protruding from their pockets, were picking their dubious way. As we approached they saluted us, touching their hats with sudden dignity. Everywhere in this lowland region we found the negro courteous more from habit than from desire. Even when he fell into the sullen silence which marks his supremest dissent, he was deferential and polite to a degree which made that silence all the more exasperating. I have never in my life seen a more gracious and civil personage than the weather-stained and tattered negro who stood on a shelving bank by the lake-side, and carefully pointed out to us the best spots in the submerged road, as we drove through the little village of which he was an inhabitant.

The local river packets, which depend mainly upon the commerce of the cotton plantations between Vicksburg and New Orleans, are the only means which the planters possess of communication with the outer world. The arrivals of the "Robert E. Lee," or of the "Natchez," at the plantation landings, always furnish picturesque and interesting scenes. We had occasion to journey from Natchez to Vicksburg, departing from the former town late at night. The negro hackman who was to transport us from the upper town to Natchez-under-the-Hill for the moderate sum of three dollars, bade us remain quietly in our rooms until "de Lee whistled." So, toward midnight, hearing the three hoarse yells from the colossal steam-pipes of the Robert E. Lee, we were hurried down to the great wharf-boat, where we found a motley crowd of negro men and women, of sickly, ague-stricken, poor whites, and smartly-dressed planters, whose immaculate linen and rich garments betrayed but little of the poverty and anxiety now afflicting the whole section.

Presently, out of the gloom which shrouded the great river, a giant shape seemed slowly approaching, and while we were endeavoring to discover what it might be, flaring pine torches sent forth an intense light which disclosed the great packet, with her forward deck crowded with negro roustabouts, whose faces shone as the flame was reflected upon them. The tall pipes sent out sparks and smoke, and the river-monster, which seemed stealthily

drawing near to us to devour us, winked its fiery eyes and sleepily drew up at the wharf, where, with infinite trouble, it was made fast with many stout ropes, while the mates screamed and cursed as only Mississippi boatmen can.

The cabin of one of these steamers presents quite a different aspect from those of the Northern packets which come from St. Louis and Cincinnati. The bar is a conspicuous object as one enters, and around it cluster eager groups busily discussing the latest phase of the Kellogg usurpation, or, in such times of depression and disaster as during my visit, lamenting their fate with a philosophic air doubtless somewhat enhanced by the soothing nature of the liquids imbibed.

As the traveler goes to register his name and purchase his ticket, the obliging clerk hands him the latest file of the New Orleans papers, of which hundreds of copies are given away at all the ports where the packets stop. No planter along the line thinks of buying a newspaper, but depends on the clerk of the steamer, who willingly furnishes him the news of the day.

About the card-tables men are busily absorbed in the intricacies of "poker" and "seven-up," and the talk is of cotton and of corn, of the rise and fall of the river, and reminiscences of adventures in forest and on stream during the "waw." On the "Robert E. Lee" I found a number of prominent young cotton-planters, all of whom were complaining of the effects of the inundation. Many of these planters were educated gentlemen, familiar with life at the North, and with the best society. None of them were especially bitter or partisan in their views; their material interests seemed to command their immediate attention, and they, as others throughout the cotton country of the South, complained of the seeming impossibility of reorganizing labor upon a fair and proper basis. All were unanimous in their testimony as to the superiority of free over slave labor, but all asserted that it was attended with so many drawbacks and vexations that they feared it would end in the promotion of much distress, and in the ruin of hundreds of planters. They, however, were by no means confronted with the worst aspects of the labor question, since labor was flowing to them, and not receding from them, as from the planters in Central Alabama, and in certain portions of Mississippi.

Mr. Robert Somers, in his excellent observations on the labor question, as viewed in Alabama, made during a journey throughout the Southern States in 1870–71, hits upon some truths with regard to the relations of the planter and freedman, in the following manner:

"What the planters are disposed to complain of is, that while they have lost their slaves, they have not got free laborers in any sense common either in the Northern States or in Europe. One cannot but think that the New England manufacturer and the Old England farmer must be equally astonished at a recital of the relations of land, capital and labor, as they exist on the cotton plantations of the Southern States. The wages of the negroes, if such a term can be applied to a mode of remuneration so unusual and anomalous, consist, as I have often indicated, of one-half the crop of corn and cotton, the only crops in reality produced.

"The negro on the semi-communistic basis thus established finds his own rations; but, as these are supplied to him by the planter or the planter's notes of credit on the merchants, and as much more sometimes as he thinks he needs by the merchants on his own credit, from the 1st of January onward throughout the year, in anticipation of crops which are not marketable until the end of December, he can lose nothing by the failures or deficient outcome of the crops, and is always sure of his subsistence. As a permanent economic relation, this would be startling anywhere betwixt any classes of men brought together in the business of life. Applied to agriculture, in any other part of the world, it would be deemed outrageously absurd, but this is only a part of the 'privileges' (a much more accurate term than 'wages') of the negro field-hand. In addition to half the crops, he has a free cottage of the kind he seems to like, and the windows of which he or his wife persistently nail up; he has abundance of wood from the planter's estate for fuel, and for building his corn-cribs and other out-houses, with teams to draw it from the forest. He is allowed to keep hogs and milch cows and young cattle, which roam and feed with the same right of pasture as the hogs and cattle of the planter, free of all charge. Though

entitled to one-half the crops, he is not required to contribute any portion of the seed, nor is he called upon to pay any part of the taxes on the plantation. The only direct tax on the negroes is a poll tax." Mr. Somers declares that he found this tax "everywhere in arrear, and, in some places, in a helpless chaos of non-payment. Yet," he adds, "while thus freed from the burden of taxation, the negro has, up to this period of reconstruction, enjoyed the monopoly of representation, and has had all legislative and executive power moulded to his will by Governors, Senators and Deputies, who have been either his tools, or of whom he himself has been the dupe. For five years," he concludes, "the negroes have been kings, lords and commoners, and something more, in the Southern States."

"But to come back," continued Mr. Somers, "to the economic condition of the plantations, the negro field-hand, with his right of half-crop and privileges as described, who works with ordinary diligence, looking only to his own pocket, and gets his crops forward and gathered in due time, is at liberty to go to other plantations and pick cotton, in doing which he may make from two to two and a-half dollars a day. For every piece of work outside the crop that he does even on his own plantation, he must be paid a dollar a day. While the land owner is busy keeping account betwixt himself and his negro hands, ginning their cotton for them, doing all the marketing of produce and supplies, of which they have the lion's share, and has hardly a day he can call his own, the hands may be earning a dollar a day from him for work which is quite as much theirs as his. Yet the negroes, with all their superabounding privilege on the cotton-field, make little of it. A ploughman or a herd in the Old World would not exchange his lot for theirs, as it stands and as it appears in all external circumstances."

I have quoted these excellent remarks, as they afford a glimpse into some of the causes of the discouragement which prevails among large numbers of cotton-planters.

. . .   1875

« «   » »

HENRY W. GRADY

1850-1889

HENRY W. GRADY was the son of a Georgia colonel who gave his life for the Confederacy. He took his degree from the University of Georgia in 1868 and studied law at the University of Virginia. His varied experiments with journalism in his native state were followed by a distinguished career on the *Atlanta Constitution*, of which he became part owner.

Grady articulated the growing realization of progressive-minded Southerners that the future of the South lay in the development of local resources and the improvement of agriculture, rather than in the nostalgic rationalizations of the "Lost Cause." Northern co-operation and capital were, of course, necessary for the program with which Grady became identified. In 1886, in New York City, he delivered his famous address, "The New South," and in consequence he was greeted as the champion of a much desired reconciliation of the two sections. His editorials and orations preached the doctrine of "the New South"; and although his position on many issues, including the race problem, was conservative, he was regarded as a prophet and apostle of the moment for the transformation of a South dominated by planters into one in which business and industrial enterprise held the key position. The following speech, given at the annual banquet of the Boston Merchants' Association in December, 1889, is characteristic of Grady's social thought.

E. D. Shurter, *The Complete Orations and Speeches of Henry W. Grady*, Austin, Tex., 1910.

J. C. Harris, *Joel Chandler Harris' Life of Henry W. Grady Including His Writings and Speeches*, New York, 1890

Gentry Dugat, *Life of Henry W. Grady*, Edinburg, Tex., 1927.

P. H. Buck, *The Road to Reunion, 1865–1900*, Boston, 1937.

R. F. Farrell, *A Study of the Early Journalistic Writing of Henry W. Grady*, Nashville, Tenn., 1927.

» » *From:* A SPEECH BEFORE THE BOSTON « «
MERCHANTS' ASSOCIATION

. . . Happy am I that this mission has brought my feet at last to press New England's historic soil, and my eyes to the knowledge of her beauty and her thrift. Here, within touch of Plymouth Rock and Bunker Hill—where Webster thundered and Longfellow sang, Emerson thought and Channing preached—here in the cradle of American letters, and almost of American liberty, I hasten to make the obeisance that every American owes New England when first he stands uncovered in her mighty presence. Strange apparition! This stern and unique figure—carved from the ocean and the wilderness—its majesty kindling and growing amid the storms of winters and of wars—until at last the gloom was broken, its beauty disclosed in the sunshine, and the heroic workers rested at its base—while startled kings and emperors gazed and marveled that from the rude touch of this handful, cast on a bleak and unknown shore, should have come the embodied genius of human government and the perfected model of human liberty! God bless the memory of those immortal workers and prosper the fortunes of their living sons and perpetuate the inspirations of their handiwork.

Two years ago, sir, I spoke some words in New York that caught the attention of the North. As I stand here to reiterate, as I have done everywhere, every word I then uttered—to declare that the sentiments I then avowed were universally approved in the South—I realize that the confidence begotten by that speech is largely responsible for my presence here to-night. I should dishonor myself if I betrayed that confidence by uttering one insincere word or by withholding one essential element of the truth. Apropos of this last, let me confess, Mr. President—before the praise of New England has died on my lips—that I believe the best product of her present life is the procession of 17,000 Vermont Democrats that for twenty-two years, undiminished by death, unrecruited by birth or conversion, have marched over their rugged hills, cast their Democratic ballots, and gone back home to pray for their unregenerate neighbors, and awake to read the record of 25,000 Republican majority. May God of the helpless and the heroic help them—and may their sturdy tribe increase!

Far to the south, Mr. President, separated from this section by a line, once defined in irrepressible difference, once traced in fratricidal blood, and now, thank God, but a vanishing shadow, lies the fairest and richest domain of this earth. It is the home of a brave and hospitable people. There, is centered all that can please or prosper humankind. A perfect climate above a fertile soil, yields to the husbandman every product of the temperate zone. There, by night the cotton whitens beneath the stars, and by day the wheat locks the sunshine in its bearded sheaf. In the same field the clover steals the fragrance of the wind, and the tobacco catches the quick aroma of the rains. There, are mountains stored with exhaustless treasures; forests, vast and primeval, and rivers that, tumbling or loitering, run wanton to the sea. Of the three essential items of all industries—cotton, iron, and wool—that region has easy control. In cotton, a fixed monopoly —in iron, proven supremacy—in timber, the reserve supply of the Republic. From this assured and permanent advantage, against which artificial conditions cannot much longer prevail, has grown an amazing system of industries. Not maintained by human contrivance of tariff or capital, afar off from the fullest and cheapest source of supply, but resting in Divine assurance, within touch of field and mine and forest—not set amid costly farms from which competition has driven the farmer in despair, but amid cheap and sunny lands, rich with agriculture, to which neither season nor soil has set a limit—this system of industries is mounting to a splendor that shall dazzle and illumine the world.

That, sir, is the picture and the promise of my home—a land better and fairer than I have told you, and yet but fit setting, in its material excellence, for the loyal and gentle quality of its citizenship. Against that, sir, we have New England, recruiting the Republic from its sturdy loins, shaking from its overcrowded hives new swarms of workers and touching this land all over with its energy and its courage. And yet, while in the El Dorado of which I have told you, but fifteen per cent. of lands are cultivated, its mines scarcely touched and its population so scant that, were it set equi-distant, the sound of the human voice could not be heard from Virginia to Texas—while on the threshold of nearly every house in New England stands a son, seeking with troubled eyes some new land to which to carry his modest patrimony, the strange fact remains that in 1880 the South had fewer Northern-born citizens than she had in 1870—fewer in '70 than in '60. Why is this? Why is it, sir, though the sectional line be now but a mist that the breath may dispel, fewer men of the North have crossed it over to the South than when it was crimson with the best blood of the Republic, or even when the slaveholder stood guard every inch of its way?

There can be but one answer. It is the very problem we are now to consider. The key that opens that problem will unlock to the world the fairer half of this Republic, and free the halted feet of thousands whose eyes are already kindled with its beauty. Better than this, it will open the hearts of brothers for thirty years estranged, and clasp in lasting comradeship a million hands now withheld in doubt. Nothing, sir, but this problem, and the suspicions it breeds, hinders a clear understanding and a perfect union. Nothing else stands between us and such love as bound Georgia and Massachusetts at Valley Forge and Yorktown, chastened by the sacrifices at Manassas and Gettysburg, and illumined with the coming of better work and a nobler destiny than was ever wrought with the sword or sought at the cannon's mouth.

If this does not invite your patient hearing to-night—hear one thing more. My people, your brothers in the South—brothers in blood, in destiny, in all that is best in our past and future—are so beset with this problem that their very existence depends upon its right solution. Nor are they wholly to blame for its presence. The slave-ships of the Republic sailed from your ports—the slaves worked in our fields. You will not defend the traffic, nor I the institution. But I do hereby declare that in its wise and humane administration, in lifting the slave to heights of which he had not dreamed in his savage home, and giving him a happiness he has not yet found in freedom —our fathers left their sons a saving and excellent heritage. In the storm of war this institution was lost. I thank God as heartily as you do that human slavery is gone forever from the American soil.

But the freedman remains. With him a problem without precedent or parallel. Note its appalling conditions. Two utterly dissimilar races on the same soil—with equal political and civil rights—almost equal in numbers, but terribly unequal in intelligence and responsibility—each pledged against fusion—one for a century in servitude to the other, and freed at last by a desolating war—the experiment sought by neither, but approached by both with doubt—these are the conditions. Under these, adverse at every point, we are required to carry these two races in peace and honor to the end. Never, sir, has such a task been given to mortal stewardship. Never before in this Republic has the white race divided on the rights of an alien race. The red man was cut down as a weed, because he hindered the way of the American citizen. The yellow man was shut out of this Republic because he is an alien and inferior. The red man was owner of the land—the yellow man highly civilized and assimilable—but they hindered both sections and are gone!

But the black man, affecting but one section, is clothed with every privilege of government and pinned to the soil, and my people commanded to make good at any hazard and at any cost, his full and equal heirship of American privilege and prosperity. It matters not that wherever the whites and blacks have touched, in any era or any clime, there has been irreconcilable violence. It matters not that no two races, however similar, have lived anywhere at any time on the same soil with equal rights in peace. In spite of these things we are commanded to make good this change of American policy which has not perhaps changed American prejudice—to make certain here what has elsewhere been impossible between whites and blacks—and to reverse, under the very worst conditions, the universal verdict of racial history. And driven, sir, to this superhuman task with an impatience that brooks no delay, a

rigor that accepts no excuse, and a suspicion that discourages frankness and sincerity. We do not shrink from this trial. It is so interwoven with our industrial fabric that we cannot disentangle it if we would—so bound up in our honorable obligation to the world, that we would not if we could. Can we solve it? The God who gave it into our hands, He alone can know. But this the weakest and wisest of us do know; we can not solve it with less than [10] your tolerant and patient sympathy—with less than the knowledge that the blood that runs in your veins is our blood—and that when we have done our best, whether the issue be lost or won, we shall feel your strong arms about us and hear the beating of your approving hearts.

The resolute, clear-headed, broad-minded men of the South—the men whose genius made glorious every page of the first seventy [20] years of American history—whose courage and fortitude you tested in five years of the fiercest war—whose energy has made bricks without straw and spread splendor amid the ashes of their war-wasted homes—these men wear this problem in their hearts and their brains, by day and by night. They realize, as you cannot, what this problem means—what they owe to this kindly and dependent race—the measure of their debt to the world in whose despite [30] they defended and maintained slavery. And though their feet are hindered in its undergrowth and their march encumbered with its burdens, they have lost neither the patience from which comes clearness nor the faith from which comes courage. Nor, sir, when in passionate moments is disclosed to them that vague and awful shadow, with its lurid abysses and its crimson stains, into which I pray God they may never go, are they struck with more [40] of apprehension than is needed to complete their consecration!

Such is the temper of my people. But what of the problem itself? Mr. President, we need not go one step further unless you concede right here the people I speak for are as honest, as sensible, and as just as your people, seeking as earnestly as you would in their place, rightly to solve the problem that touches them at every vital point. If you insist that they are ruffians, [50] blindly striving with bludgeon and shotgun to plunder and oppress a race, then I shall sacrifice my self-respect and tax your patience in vain. But admit that they are men of common sense and common honesty—wisely modifying an environment they cannot wholly disregard —guiding and controlling as best they can the vicious and irresponsible of either race—compensating error with frankness and retrieving in patience what they lose in passion—and conscious all the time that wrong means ruin, —admit this, and we may reach an understanding to-night.

The President of the United States [Harrison] in his late message to Congress, discussing the plea that the South should be left to solve this problem, asks: "Are they at work upon it? What solution do they offer? When will the black man cast a free ballot? When will he have the civil rights that are his?" I shall not here protest against the partisanry that, for the first time in our history in time of peace, has stamped with the great seal of our government a stigma upon the people of a great and loyal section, though I gratefully remember that the great dead soldier, who held the helm of state for the eight stormy years of reconstruction, never found need for such a step; and though there is no personal sacrifice I would not make to remove this cruel and unjust imputation on my people from the archives of my country!

But, sir, backed by a record on every page of which is progress, I venture to make earnest and respectful answer to the questions that are asked. I bespeak your patience, while with vigorous plainness of speech, seeking your judgment rather than your applause, I proceed step by step. We give to the world this year a crop of 7,500,000 bales of cotton, worth $45,-000,000, and its cash equivalent in grain, grasses, and fruit. This enormous crop could not have come from the hands of sullen and discontented labor. It comes from peaceful fields, in which laughter and gossip rise above the hum of industry and contentment runs with the singing plow.

It is claimed that this ignorant labor is defrauded of its just hire. I present the tax-books of Georgia, which show that the negro, 25 years ago a slave, has in Georgia alone $10,-000,000 of assessed property, worth twice that much. Does not that record honor him and vindicate his neighbors? What people, penniless, illiterate, has done so well? For every Afro-American agitator, stirring the strife in which alone he prospers, I can show you a thousand negroes, happy in their cabin homes, tilling their own land by day, and at night taking from the lips of their children the helpful message their State sends them from the school-

house door. And the schoolhouse itself bears testimony. In Georgia we added last year $250,000 to the school fund, making a total of more than $1,000,000—and this in the face of prejudice not yet conquered—of the fact that the whites are assessed for $368,000,000, the blacks for $10,000,000, and yet 49 per cent. of the beneficiaries are black children— and in the doubt of many wise men if education helps, or can help, our problem. Charleston, with her taxable values cut half in two since 1860, pays more in proportion for public schools than Boston. Although it is easier to give much out of much than little out of little, the South with one-seventh of the taxable property of the country, with relatively larger debt, having received only one-twelfth as much public land, and having back of its tax-books none of the half billion of bonds that enrich the North—and though it pays annually $26,-000,000 to your section as pensions—yet gives nearly one-sixth of the public school fund. The South since 1865 has spent $122,000,000 in education, and this year is pledged to $37,000,-000 for State and city schools, although the blacks, paying one-thirtieth of the taxes, get nearly one-half of the fund.

Go into our fields and see whites and blacks working side by side, on our buildings in the same squad, in our shops at the same forge. Often the blacks crowd the whites from work, or lower wages by greater need or simpler habits, and yet are permitted because we want to bar them from no avenue in which their feet are fitted to tread. They could not there be elected orators of the white universities, as they have been here, but they do enter there a hundred useful trades that are closed against them here. We hold it better and wiser to tend the weeds in the garden than to water the exotic in the window. In the South, there are negro lawyers, teachers, editors, dentists, doctors, preachers, multiplying with the increasing ability of their race to support them. In villages and towns they have their military companies equipped from the armories of the State, their churches and societies built and supported largely by their neighbors. What is the testimony of the courts? In penal legislation we have steadily reduced felonies to misdemeanors, and have led the world in mitigating punishment for crime, that we might save, as far as possible, this dependent race from its own weakness. In our penitentiary record 60 per cent. of the prosecutors are negroes, and in every court the negro criminal strikes the colored juror, that white men may judge his case. In the North, one negro in every 466 is in jail—in the South only one in 1,865. In the North the percentage of negro prisoners is six times as great as native whites—in the South, only four times as great. If prejudice wrongs him in Southern courts, the record shows it to be deeper in Northern courts.

I assert here, and a bar as intelligent and upright as the bar of Massachusetts will solemnly indorse my assertion, that in the Southern courts, from highest to lowest, pleading for life, liberty, or property, the negro has distinct advantage because he is a negro, apt to be overreached, oppressed—and that this advantage reaches from the juror in making his verdict to the judge in measuring his sentence. Now, Mr. President, can it be seriously maintained that we are terrorizing the people from whose willing hands come every year $1,000,000,000 of farm crops? Or have robbed a people, who twenty-five years from unrewarded slavery have amassed in one State $20,000,000 of property? Or that we intend to oppress the people we are arming every day? Or deceive them when we are educating them to the utmost limit of our ability? Or outlaw them when we work side by side with them? Or re-enslave them under legal forms when for their benefit we have even imprudently narrowed the limit of felonies and mitigated the severity of law? My fellow countryman, as you yourself may sometimes have to appeal to the bar of human judgment for justice and for right, give to my people to-night the fair and unanswerable conclusion of these incontestible facts.

But it is claimed that under this fair seeming there is disorder and violence. This I admit. And there will be until there is one ideal community on earth after which we may pattern. But how widely it is misjudged! It is hard to measure with exactness whatever touches the negro. His helplessness, his isolation, his century of servitude, these dispose us to emphasize and magnify his wrongs. This disposition inflamed by prejudice and partisanry, has led to injustice and delusion. Lawless men may ravage a county in Iowa and it is accepted as an incident—in the South a drunken row is declared to be the fixed habit of the community. Regulators may whip vagabonds in Indiana by platoons, and it scarcely arrests attention —a chance collision in the South among rela-

tively the same classes is gravely accepted as evidence that one race is destroying the other. We might as well claim that the Union was ungrateful to the colored soldiers who followed its flag, because a Grand Army post in Connecticut closed its doors to a negro veteran, as for you to give racial significance to every incident in the South or to accept exceptional grounds as the rule of our society. I am not one of those who becloud American honor with the parade of the outrages of either section, and belie American character by declaring them to be significant and representative. I prefer to maintain that they are neither, and stand for nothing but the passion and the sin of our poor fallen humanity. If society like a machine, were no stronger than its weakest part, I should despair of both sections. But, knowing that society, sentient and responsible in every fibre, can mend and repair until the whole has the strength of the best, I despair of neither.

These gentlemen who come with me here, knit into Georgia's busy life as they are, never saw, I dare assert, an outrage committed on a negro! And if they did, not one of you would be swifter to prevent or punish. It is through them, and the men who think with them— making nine-tenths of every Southern community—that these two races have been carried thus far with less of violence than would have been possible anywhere else on earth. And in their fairness and courage and steadfastness—more than in all the laws that can be passed or all the bayonets that can be mustered—is the hope of our future.

When will the black cast a free ballot? When ignorance anywhere is not dominated by the will of the intelligent; when the laborer anywhere casts a vote unhindered by his boss; when the vote of the poor anywhere is not influenced by the power of the rich; when the strong and the steadfast do not everywhere control the suffrage of the weak and shiftless—then and not till then will the ballot of the negro be free. The white people of the South are banded, Mr. President, not in prejudice against the blacks—not in sectional estrangement, not in the hope of political dominion—but in a deep and abiding necessity. Here is this vast ignorant and purchasable vote—clannish, credulous, impulsive and passionate—tempting every art of the demagogue, but insensible to the appeal of the statesman. Wrongly started, in that it was led into alienation from its neighbor and taught to rely on the protection of an outside force, it cannot be merged and lost in the two great parties through logical currents, for it lacks political conviction and even that information on which conviction must be based. It must remain a faction—strong enough in every community to control on the slightest division of the whites. Under that division it becomes the prey of the cunning and unscrupulous of both parties. Its credulity is imposed on, its patience inflamed, its cupidity tempted, its impulses misdirected —and even its superstition made to play its part in a campaign in which every interest of society is jeopardized and every approach to the ballot box debauched. It is against such campaigns as this—the folly and the bitterness and the danger of which every Southern community has drunk deeply—that the white people of the South are banded together. Just as you in Massachusetts would be banded if 300,000 black men—not one in a hundred able to read his ballot—banded in a race instinct, holding against you the memory of a century of slavery, taught by your late conquerors to distrust and oppose you, had already travestied legislation from your state-house, and in every species of folly or villainy had wasted your substance and exhausted your credit.

But admitting the right of the whites to unite against this tremendous menace, we are challenged with the smallness of our vote. This has long been flippantly charged to be evidence, and has now been solemnly and officially declared to be proof of political turpitude and baseness on our part. Let us see. Virginia —a State now under fierce assault for this alleged crime—cast in 1888 75 per cent. of her vote. Massachusetts, the State in which I speak, 60 per cent. of her vote. Was it suppression in Virginia and natural causes in Massachusetts? Last month Virginia cast 69 per cent. of her vote, and Massachusetts, fighting in every district, cast only 49 per cent. of hers. If Virginia is condemned because 31 per cent of her vote was silent, how shall this State escape in which 51 per cent. was dumb? Let us enlarge this comparison. The sixteen Southern States in 1888 cast 67 per cent. of their total vote—the six New England States but 63 per cent. of theirs. By what fair rule shall the stigma be put upon one section, while the other escapes? A congressional election in New York last week, with the polling-place within touch of every voter, brought out only 6,000

votes of 28,000—and the lack of opposition is assigned as the natural cause. In a district in my State, in which an opposition speech has not been heard in ten years, and the polling-places are miles apart—under the unfair reasoning of which my section has been a constant victim—the small vote is charged to be proof of forcible suppression. In Virginia an average majority of 10,000 under hopeless division of the minority, was raised to 42,000; in Iowa, in the same election, a majority of 32,000 was wiped out, and an opposition majority of 8,000 was established. The change of 42,000 votes in Iowa is accepted as political revolution—in Virginia an increase of 30,000 on a safe majority is declared to be proof of political fraud. I charge these facts and figures home, sir, to the heart and conscience of the American people, who will not assuredly see one section condemned for what another section is excused!

If I can drive them through the prejudice of the partisan, and have them read and pondered at the fireside of the citizen, I will rest on the judgment there formed and the verdict there rendered!

It is deplorable, sir, that in both sections a larger percentage of the vote is not regularly cast, but more inexplicable that this should be so in New England than in the South. What invites the negro to the ballot box? He knows that, of all men, it has promised him most and yielded him least. His first appeal to suffrage was the promise of "forty acres and a mule." His second, the threat that Democratic success meant his re-enslavement. Both have proved false in his experience. He looked for a home, and he got the freedman's bank. He fought under the promise of the loaf, and in victory was denied the crumbs. Discouraged and deceived, he has realized at last that his best friends are his neighbors, with whom his lot is cast, and whose prosperity is bound up in his—and that he has gained nothing in politics to compensate the loss of their confidence and sympathy that is at last his best and his enduring hope. And so, without leaders or organization—and lacking the resolute heroism of my party friends in Vermont that makes their hopeless march over the hills a high and inspiring pilgrimage—he shrewdly measures the occasional agitator, balances his little account with politics, touches up his mule and jogs down the furrow, letting the mad world jog as it will!

The negro vote can never control in the South, and it would be well if partisans in the North would understand this. I have seen the white people of a State set about by black hosts until their fate seemed sealed. But, sir, some brave man, banding them together, would rise, as Elisha rose in beleaguered Samaria, and touching their eyes with faith, bid them look abroad to see the very air "filled with the chariots of Israel and the horsemen thereof." If there is any human force that cannot be withstood, it is the power of the banded intelligence and responsibility of a free community. Against it, numbers and corruption cannot prevail. It cannot be forbidden in the law or divorced in force. It is the inalienable right of every free community—and the just and righteous safeguard against an ignorant or corrupt suffrage. It is on this, sir, that we rely in the South. Not the cowardly menace of mask or shotgun; but the peaceful majesty of intelligence and responsibility, massed and unified for the protection of its homes and the preservation of its liberty. That, sir, is our reliance and our hope, and against it all the powers of the earth shall not prevail.

It was just as certain that Virginia would come back to the unchallenged control of her white race—that before the moral and material power of her people once more unified, opposition would crumble until its last desperate leader was left alone vainly striving to rally his disordered hosts—as that night should fade in the kindling glory of the sun. You may pass force bills, but they will not avail. You may surrender your own liberties to Federal election law, you may submit, in fear of a necessity that does not exist, that the very form of this government may be changed—this old State that holds in its charter the boast that "it is a free and independent commonwealth"—it may deliver its election machinery into the hands of the government it helped to create—but never, sir, will a single State of this Union, North or South, be delivered again to the control of an ignorant and inferior race. We wrested our State government from negro supremacy when the Federal drumbeat rolled closer to the ballot-box and Federal bayonets hedged it deeper about than will ever again be permitted in this free government. But, sir, though the cannon of this Republic thundered in every voting district of the South, we still should find in the mercy of God the means and the courage to prevent its reestablishment!

I regret, sir, that my section, hindered with this problem, stands in seeming estrangement to the North. If, sir, any man will point out to me a path down which the white people of the South divided may walk in peace and honor, I will take that path though I take it alone —for at the end, and nowhere else, I fear, is to be found the full prosperity of my section and the full restoration of this Union. But, sir, if the negro had not been enfranchised, the South would have been divided and the Republic united. What solution, then, can we offer for this problem? Time alone can disclose it to us. We simply report progress and ask your patience. If the problem be solved at all —and I firmly believe it will, though nowhere else has it been—it will be solved by the people most deeply bound in interest, most deeply pledged in honor to its solution. I had rather see my people render back this question rightly solved than to see them gather all the spoils over which the faction has contended since Catiline conspired and Caesar fought.

Meantime we treat the negro fairly, measuring to him justice in the fullness the strong should give to the weak, and leading him in the steadfast ways of citizenship that he may no longer be the prey of the unscrupulous and the sport of the thoughtless. We open to him every pursuit in which he can prosper, and seek to broaden his training and capacity. We seek to hold his confidence and friendship, and to pin him to the soil with ownership, that he may catch in the fire of his own hearthstone that sense of responsibility the shiftless can never know. And we gather him into that alliance of intelligence and responsibility that, though it now runs close to racial lines, welcomes the responsible and intelligent of any race. By this course, confirmed in our judgment and justified in the progress already made, we hope to progress slowly but surely to the end.

The love we feel for that race you cannot measure nor comprehend. As I attest it here, the spirit of my old black mammy from her home up there looks down to bless, and through the tumult of this night steals the sweet music of her croonings as thirty years ago she held me in her black arms and led me smiling into sleep. This scene vanishes as I speak, and I catch a vision of an old Southern home, with its lofty pillars, and its white pigeons fluttering down through the golden air. I see women with strained and anxious faces and children alert yet helpless. I see night come down with its dangers and its apprehensions, and in a big homely room I feel on my tired head the touch of loving hands—now worn and wrinkled, but fairer to me yet than the hands of mortal woman, and stronger yet to lead me than the hands of mortal man—as they lay a mother's blessing there while at her knees, the truest altar I yet have found—I thank God that she is safe in her sanctuary, because her slaves, sentinel in the silent cabin or guard at her chamber door, put a black man's loyalty between her and danger.

I catch another vision. The crisis of battle —a soldier struck, staggering, fallen. I see a slave scuffling through the smoke, winding his black arms about the fallen form, reckless of the hurtling death—bending his trusty face to catch the words that tremble on the stricken lips, so wrestling meantime with agony that he would lay down his life in his master's stead. I see him by the weary bedside, ministering with uncomplaining patience, praying with all his humble heart that God will lift his master up, until death comes in mercy and in honor to still the soldier's agony and seal the soldier's life. I see him by the open grave, mute, motionless, uncovered, suffering for the death of him who in life fought against his freedom. I see him when the mound is heaped and the great drama of his life is closed, turn away and with downcast eyes and uncertain step start out into new and strange fields, faltering, struggling, but moving on, until his shambling figure is lost in the light of this better and brighter day. And from the grave comes a voice saying: "Follow him! Put your arms about him in his need, even as he put his about me. Be his friend as he was mine." And out into this new world—strange to me as to him, dazzling, bewildering both—I follow! And may God forget my people—when they forget these.

Whatever the future may hold for them— whether they plod along in the servitude from which they have never been lifted since the Cyrenian was laid hold upon by the Roman soldiers and made to bear the cross of the fainting Christ—whether they find homes again in Africa, and thus hasten the prophecy of the psalmist who said: "And suddenly Ethiopa shall hold out her hands unto God" —whether, forever dislocated and separated, they remain a weak people beset by stronger,

and exist as the Turk, who lives in the jealousy rather than in the conscience of Europe—or whether in this miraculous Republic they break through the caste of twenty centuries and, belying universal history, reach the full stature of citizenship, and in peace maintain it—we shall give them uttermost justice and abiding friendship. And whatever we do, into whatever seeming estrangement we may be driven, nothing shall disturb the love we bear this Republic, or mitigate our consecration to its service.

I stand here, Mr. President, to profess no new loyalty. When General Lee, whose heart was the temple of our hopes and whose arm was clothed with our strength, renewed his allegiance to the government at Appomatox, he spoke from a heart too great to be false, and he spoke for every honest man from Maryland to Texas. From that day to this, Hamilcar has nowhere in the South sworn young Hannibal to hatred and vengeance— but everywhere to loyalty and to love. Witness the soldier standing at the base of a Confederate monument above the graves of his comrades, his empty sleeve tossing in the April wind, adjuring the young men about him to serve as honest and loyal citizens the government against which their fathers fought. This message, delivered from that sacred presence, has gone home to the hearts of my fellows! And, sir, I declare here, if physical courage be always equal to human aspiration, that they would die, sir, if need be, to restore this Republic their fathers fought to dissolve!

Such, Mr. President, is this problem as we see it; such is the temper in which we approach it; such the progress made. What do we ask of you? First, patience; out of this alone can come perfect work. Second, confidence; in this alone can you judge fairly. Third, sympathy; in this you can help us best. Fourth, give us your sons as hostages. When you plant your capital in millions send your sons that they may help know how true are our hearts and help swell the Anglo-Saxon current until it can carry without danger this black infusion. Fifth, loyalty to the Republic—for there is sectionalism in loyalty as in estrangement. This hour little needs the loyalty that is loyal to one section and yet holds the other in enduring suspicion and estrangement. Give us the broad and perfect loyalty that loves and trusts Georgia alike with Massachusetts—that knows no South, no North, no East, no West; but endears with equal and patriotic love every foot of our soil, every State of our Union.

A mighty duty, sir, and a mighty inspiration impels every one of us to-night to lose in patriotic consecration whatever estranges, whatever divides. We, sir, are Americans— and we fight for human liberty. The uplifting force of the American idea is under every throne on earth. France, Brazil—these are our victories. To redeem the earth from kingcraft and oppression—this is our mission. And we shall not fail. God has sown in our soil the seed of this millennial harvest, and he will not lay the sickle to the ripening crop until his full and perfect day has come. Our history, sir, has been a constant and expanding miracle from Plymouth Rock and Jamestown all the way— aye, even from the hour when, from the voiceless and trackless ocean, a new world rose to the sight of the inspired sailor.

As we approach the fourth centennial of that stupendous day—when the old world will come to marvel and to learn, amid our gathered treasures—let us resolve to crown the miracles of our past with the spectacle of a Republic compact, united, indissoluble in the bonds of love—loving from the lakes to the Gulf—the wounds of war healed in every heart as on every hill—serene and resplendent at the summit of human achievement and earthly glory —blazing out the path, and making clear the way up which all the nations of the earth must come in God's appointed time.   1889

GEORGE WASHINGTON CABLE

1844–1925

A NATIVE of New Orleans, with a Virginian father and a New England mother, George Washington Cable assumed the headship of a large family at the age of fourteen when his father, after failure in business, died. During the Civil War he served with the Fourth Mississippi Cavalry. After the war he tried his hand both at business and at journalism. With the notable success won by *Old Creole Days* (1879) he turned to letters as a profession; his writings include *The Grandissimes* (1880), *The Creoles of Louisiana* (1884), and *Bonaventure* (1888).

Cable's straightforward espousal of various reforms, including that of justice for the Negro, aroused much local ill-will; and in 1885 he settled in Northampton, Massachusetts. His early pursuit of self-culture led him to found, in the interest of others who lacked advantages, Home-Culture Clubs. Cable's distinction as a pioneer of the local-color school has overshadowed his work as a reformer. *The Silent South*, which appeared in book form in 1885, was one of the earliest literary discussions of "the Southern problem." It aroused much controversial opposition.

L. L. Bikle, *George W. Cable, His Life and Letters*, New York, 1928.
The Negro Question; A Collection of Writings on Negro Rights in the South, Arlin Taylor, ed., Garden City, N. Y., 1958

» » *From:* THE FREEDMAN'S CASE IN EQUITY « «

I. THE NATION'S ATTITUDE

The greatest social problem before the American people to-day is, as it has been for a hundred years, the presence among us of the negro.

No comparable entanglement was ever drawn round itself by any other modern nation with so serene a disregard of its ultimate issue, or with a more distinct national responsibility. The African slave was brought here by cruel force, and with everybody's consent except his own. Everywhere the practice was favored as a measure of common aggrandizement. When a few men and women protested, they were mobbed in the public interest, with the public consent. There rests, therefore, a moral responsibility on the whole nation never to lose sight of the results of African-American slavery until they cease to work mischief and injustice.

It is true these responsibilities may not fall everywhere with the same weight; but they are nowhere entirely removed. The original seed of trouble was sown with the full knowledge and consent of the nation. The nation was to blame; and so long as evils spring from it, their correction must be the nation's duty.

The late Southern slave has within two decades risen from slavery to freedom, from freedom to citizenship, passed on into political ascendency, and fallen again from that eminence. The amended Constitution holds him up in his new political rights as well as a mere constitution can. On the other hand, certain enactments of Congress, trying to reach further, have lately been made void by the highest court of the nation. And another thing has happened. The popular mind in the old free States, weary of strife at arm's length, bewildered by its complications, vexed by many a blunder, eager to turn to the cure of other evils, and even tinctured by that race feeling whose grosser excesses it would so gladly see suppressed, has retreated from its uncomfortable dictational attitude and thrown the whole matter over to the States of the South. Here it rests, no longer a main party issue, but a group of questions which are to be settled by each of these States separately in the light of simple equity and morals, and which the genius of American government is at least loath to force upon them from beyond their borders. Thus the whole question, become secondary in party contest, has yet reached a period of supreme importance.

II. OLD SOUTH AND NEW

Before slavery ever became a grave question in the nation's politics,—when it seemed each State's private affair, developing unmolested, —it had two different fates in two different parts of the country. In one, treated as a question of public equity, it withered away. In the other, overlooked in that aspect, it petrified

and became the corner-stone of the whole social structure; and when men sought its overthrow as a national evil, it first brought war upon the land, and then grafted into the citizenship of one of the most intelligent nations in the world six millions of people from one of the most debased races on the globe.

And now this painful and wearisome question, sown in the African slave-trade, reaped in our civil war, and garnered in the national adoption of millions of an inferior race, is drawing near a second seed-time. For this is what the impatient proposal to make it a dead and buried issue really means. It means to recommit it to the silence and concealment of the covered furrow. Beyond that incubative retirement no suppressed moral question can be pushed; but all such questions, ignored in the domain of private morals, spring up and expand once more into questions of public equity; neglected as matters of public equity, they blossom into questions of national interest; and, despised in that guise, presently yield the red fruits of revolution.

This question must never again bear that fruit. There must arise, nay, there has arisen, in the South itself, a desire to see established the equities of the issue; to make it no longer a question of endurance between one group of States and another, but between the moral débris of an exploded evil, and the duty, necessity, and value of planting society firmly upon universal justice and equity. This, and this only, can give the matter final burial. True, it is still a question between States; but only secondarily, as something formerly participated in, or as it concerns every householder to know that what is being built against his house is built by level and plummet. It is the interest of the Southern States first, and consequently of the whole land, to discover clearly these equities and the errors that are being committed against them.

. . .

. . . We need to go back to the roots of things and study closely, analytically, the origin, the present foundation, the rationality, the rightness, of those sentiments surviving in us which prompt an attitude qualifying in any way peculiarly the black man's liberty among us. Such a treatment will be less abundant in incident, less picturesque; but it will be more thorough.

III. THE ROOTS OF THE QUESTION

First, then, what are these sentiments? Foremost among them stands the idea that he is of necessity an alien. He was brought to our shores a naked, brutish, unclean, captive, pagan savage,[1] to be and remain a kind of connecting link between man and the beasts of burden. The great changes to result from his contact with a superb race of masters were not taken into account. As a social factor he was intended to be as purely zero as the brute at the other end of his plow-line. The occasional mingling of his blood with that of the white man worked no change in the sentiment; one, two, four, eight, multiplied upon or divided into zero, still gave zero for the result. Generations of American nativity made no difference; his children and children's children were born in sight of our door, yet the old notion held fast. He increased to vast numbers, but it never wavered. He accepted our dress, language, religion, all the fundamentals of our civilization, and became forever expatriated from his own land; still he remained, to us, an alien. Our sentiment went blind. It did not see that gradually, here by force and there by choice, he was fulfilling a host of conditions that earned at least a solemn moral right to that naturalization which no one at first had dreamed of giving him. Frequently he even bought back the freedom of which he had been robbed, became a tax-payer, and at times an educator of his children at his own expense; but the old idea of alienism passed laws to banish him, his wife, and children by thousands from the State, and threw him into loathsome jails as a common felon, for returning to his native land.[2]

It will be wise to remember that these were the acts of an enlightened, God-fearing people, the great mass of whom have passed beyond all earthly accountability. They were our fathers. I am the son and grandson of slaveholders. These were their faults; posterity will discover ours; but these things must be frankly, fearlessly taken into account if we are ever to understand the true interests of our peculiar state of society.

Why, then, did this notion, that the man of color must always remain an alien, stand so unshaken? We may readily recall how, under ancient systems, he rose not only to high privileges, but often to public station and power. Singularly, with us the trouble lay in a modern principle of liberty. The whole idea of American government rested on all men's equal, inalienable right to secure their life, liberty, and the pursuit of happiness by governments founded in their own consent. Hence, our Southern forefathers, shedding their blood, or ready to shed it, for this principle, yet proposing in equal good conscience to continue holding the American black man and mulatto and quadroon in slavery, had to anchor that conscience, their conduct, and their laws in the conviction that the man of African tincture was, not by his master's arbitrary assertion merely, but by nature and unalterably, an alien. If that hold should break, one single wave of irresistible inference would lift our whole Southern social fabric and dash it upon the rocks of negro emancipation and enfranchisement. How was it made secure? Not by books, though they were written among us from every possible point of view, but, with the mass of our slave-owners, by the calm hypothesis of a positive, intuitive knowledge. To them the statement was an axiom. They abandoned the methods of moral and intellectual reasoning, and fell back upon this assumption of a God-given instinct, nobler than reason, and which it was an insult to a freeman to ask him to prove on logical grounds.

Yet it was found not enough. The slave multiplied. Slavery was a dangerous institution. Few in the South to-day have any just idea how often the slave plotted for his freedom. Our Southern ancestors were a noble, manly people, springing from some of the most highly intelligent, aspiring, upright, and refined nations of the modern world; from the Huguenot, the French Chevalier, the Old Englander, the New Englander. Their acts were not always right; whose are? But for their peace of mind they had to believe them so. They therefore spoke much of the negro's contentment with that servile condition for which nature had designed him. Yet there was no escaping the knowledge that we dared not trust the slave caste with any power that could be withheld from them. So the perpetual alien was made also a perpetual menial, and the belief became fixed that this, too, was nature's decree, not ours.

Thus we stood at the close of the civil war. There were always a few Southerners who did not justify slavery, and many who cared noth-

[1] Sometimes he was not a mere savage but a trading, smithing, weaving, town-building, crop-raising barbarian. [Author's note.]
[2] Notably in Louisiana in 1810 and subsequently. [Author's note.]

ing whether it was just or not. But what we have described was the general sentiment of good Southern people. There was one modifying sentiment. It related to the slave's spiritual interests. Thousands of pious masters and mistresses flatly broke the shameful laws that stood between their slaves and the Bible. Slavery was right; but religion, they held, was for the alien and menial as well as for the citizen, menial and master, in church as well as out; and they were.

Yet over against this lay another root of to-day's difficulties. This perpetuation of the alien, menial relation tended to perpetuate the vices that naturally cling to servility, dense ignorance and a hopeless separation from true liberty; and as we could not find it in our minds to blame slavery with this perpetuation, we could only assume as a further axiom that there was, by nature, a disqualifying moral taint in every drop of negro blood. The testimony of an Irish, German, Italian, French, or Spanish beggar in a court of justice was taken on its merits; but the colored man's was excluded by law wherever it weighed against a white man. The colored man was a prejudged culprit. The discipline of the plantation required that the difference between master and slave be never lost sight of by either. It made our master caste a solid mass, and fixed a common masterhood and subserviency between the ruling and the serving race.[3] Every one of us grew up in the idea that he had, by birth and race, certain broad powers of police over any and every person of color.

All at once the tempest of war snapped off at the ground every one of these arbitrary relations, without removing a single one of the sentiments in which they stood rooted. Then, to fortify the freedman in the tenure of his new rights, he was given the ballot. Before this grim fact the notion of alienism, had it been standing alone, might have given way. The idea that slavery was right did begin to crumble almost at once. "As for slavery," said an old Creole sugar-planter and former slave-owner to me, "it was damnable." The revelation came like a sudden burst of light. It is one of the South's noblest poets who has but just said:

[3] The old Louisiana Black Code says, "That free people of color ought never to . . . presume to conceive themselves equal to the white; but, on the contrary, that they ought to yield to them in every occasion, and never speak or answer to them but with respect under the penalty of imprisonment according to the nature of the offense." (Section 21, p. 164) [Author's note.]

"I am a Southerner;
I love the South; I dared for her
To fight from Lookout to the sea,
With her proud banner over me;
But from my lips thanksgiving broke,
As God in battle-thunder spoke,
And that Black Idol, breeding drouth
And dearth of human sympathy
Throughout the sweet and sensuous South,
Was, with its chains and human yoke,
Blown hellward from the cannon's mouth,
While Freedom cheered behind the smoke!"[4]

[WHAT THE WAR LEFT]

With like readiness might the old alien relation have given way if we could only, while letting that pass, have held fast by the other old ideas. But they were all bound together. See our embarrassment. For more than a hundred years we had made these sentiments the absolute essentials to our self-respect. And yet if we clung to them, how could we meet the freedman on equal terms in the political field? Even to lead would not compensate us; for the fundamental profession of American politics is that the leader is servant to his followers. It was too much. The ex-master and ex-slave —the quarterdeck and the forecastle, as it were—could not come together. But neither could the American mind tolerate a continuance of martial law. The agonies of Reconstruction followed.

The vote, after all, was a secondary point, and the robbery and bribery on one side, and whipping and killing on the other, were but huge accidents of the situation. The two main questions were really these: on the freedman's side, how to establish republican State government under the same recognition of his rights that the rest of Christendom accorded him; and on the former master's side, how to get back to the old semblance of republican State government, and—allowing that the freedman was de facto a voter—still to maintain a purely arbitrary superiority of all whites over all blacks, and a purely arbitrary equality of all blacks among themselves as an alien, menial, and dangerous class.

Exceptionally here and there some one in the master caste did throw off the old and accept the new ideas, and, if he would allow it, was instantly claimed as a leader by the newly liberated thousands around him. But

[4] Maurice Thompson, in the "Independent." [Author's note.]

just as promptly the old master race branded him also an alien reprobate, and in ninety-nine cases out of a hundred, if he had not already done so, he soon began to confirm by his actions the brand on his cheek. However, we need give no history here of the dreadful episode of Reconstruction. Under an experimentative truce its issues rest to-day upon the pledge of the wiser leaders of the master class: Let us but remove the hireling demagogue, and we will see to it that the freedman is accorded a practical, complete, and cordial recognition of his equality with the white man before the law. As far as there has been any understanding at all, it is not that the originally desired ends of reconstruction have been abandoned, but that the men of North and South have agreed upon a new, gentle, and peaceable method for reaching them; that, without change as to the ends in view, compulsory reconstruction has been set aside and a voluntary reconstruction is on trial.

It is the fashion to say we paused to let the "feelings engendered by the war" pass away, and that they are passing. But let not these truths lead us into error. The sentiments we have been analyzing, and upon which we saw the old compulsory reconstruction go hard aground—these are not the "feelings engendered by the war." We must disentangle them from the "feelings engendered by the war," and by reconstruction. They are older than either. But for them slavery would have perished of itself, and emancipation and reconstruction been peaceful revolutions.

Indeed, as between master and slave, the "feelings engendered by the war," are too trivial, or at least were too short-lived, to demand our present notice. One relation and feeling the war destroyed: the patriarchal tie and its often really tender and benevolent sentiment of dependence and protection. When the slave became a freedman, the sentiment of alienism became for the first time complete. The abandonment of this relation was not one-sided; the slave, even before the master, renounced it. Countless times, since reconstruction began, the master has tried, in what he believed to be everybody's interest, to play on that old sentiment. But he found it a harp without strings. The freedman could not formulate, but he could see, all our old ideas of autocracy and subserviency, of master and menial, of an arbitrarily fixed class to guide and rule, and another to be guided and ruled. He

rejected the overture. The old master, his well-meant condescensions slighted, turned away estranged, and justified himself in passively withholding that simpler protection without patronage which any one American citizen, however exalted, owes to any other, however humble. Could the freedman in the bitterest of those days have consented to throw himself upon just that one old relation, he could have found a physical security for himself and his 10 house such as could not, after years of effort, be given him by constitutional amendments, Congress, United States marshals, regiments of regulars, and ships of war. But he could not; the very nobility of the civilization that had held him in slavery had made him too much a man to go back to that shelter; and by his manly neglect to do so he has proved to us who once ruled over him that, be his relative standing among the races of men what it may, 20 he is worthy to be free.

[FREED—NOT FREE]

To be a free man is his still distant goal. Twice he has been a freedman. In the days of compulsory reconstruction he was freed in the presence of his master by that master's victorious foe. In these days of voluntary reconstruction he is virtually freed by the consent 30 of his master, but the master retaining the exclusive right to define the bounds of his freedom. Many everywhere have taken up the idea that this state of affairs is the end to be desired and the end actually sought in reconstruction as handed over to the States. I do not charge such folly to the best intelligence of any American community; but I cannot ignore my own knowledge that the average thought of 40 some regions rises to no better idea of the issue. The belief is all too common that the nation, having aimed at a wrong result and missed, has left us of the Southern States to get now such other result as we think best. I say this belief is not universal. There are those among us who see that America has no room for a state of society which makes its lower classes harmless by abridging their liberties, or, as one of the favored class lately 50 said to me, has "got 'em so they don't give no trouble." There is a growing number who see that the one thing we cannot afford to tolerate at large is a class of people less than citizens; and that every interest in the land demands that the freedman be free to become in all things, as far as his own personal gifts will lift and sustain him, the same sort of American citizen he would be if, with the same intellectual and moral calibre, he were white.

Thus we reach the ultimate question of fact. Are the freedman's liberties suffering any real abridgment? The answer is easy. The letter of the laws, with a few exceptions, recognizes him as entitled to every right of an American citizen; and to some it may seem unimportant that there is scarcely one public relation of life in the South where he is not arbitrarily and unlawfully compelled to hold toward the white man the attitude of an alien, a menial, and a probable reprobate, by reason of his race and color. One of the marvels of future history will be that it was counted a small matter, by a majority of our nation, for six millions of people within it, made by its own decree a component part of it, to be subjected to a system of oppression so rank that nothing could make it seem small except the fact that they had already been ground under it for a century and a half.

Examine it. It proffers to the freedman a certain security of life and property, and then holds the respect of the community, that dearest of earthly boons, beyond his attainment. It gives him certain guarantees against thieves and robbers, and then holds him under the unearned contumely of the mass of good men and women. It acknowledges in constitutions and statutes his title to an American's freedom and aspirations, and then in daily practice heaps upon him in every public place the most odious distinctions, without giving ear to the humblest plea concerning mental or moral character. It spurns his ambition, tramples upon his languishing self-respect, and indignantly refuses to let him either buy with money, or earn by any excellence of inner life or outward behavior, the most momentary immunity from these public indignities even for his wife and daughters. Need we cram these pages with facts in evidence, as if these were charges denied and requiring to be proven? They are simply the present avowed and defended state of affairs peeled of its exteriors.

Nothing but the habit, generations old, of enduring it could make it endurable by men not in actual slavery. Were we whites of the South to remain every way as we are, and our six million blacks to give place to any sort of whites exactly their equals, man for for man,

in mind, morals, and wealth, provided only that they had tasted two years of American freedom, and were this same system of tyrannies attempted upon them, there would be as bloody an uprising as this continent has ever seen. We can say this quietly. There is not a scruple's weight of present danger. These six million freedmen are dominated by nine million whites immeasurably stronger than they, backed by the virtual consent of thirty odd millions more. Indeed, nothing but the habit of oppression could make such oppression possible to a people of the intelligence and virtue of our Southern whites, and the invitation to practice it on millions of any other than the children of their former slaves would be spurned with a noble indignation.

Suppose, for a moment, the tables turned. Suppose the courts of our Southern States, while changing no laws requiring the impaneling of jurymen without distinction as to race, etc., should suddenly begin to draw their thousands of jurymen all black, and well-nigh every one of them counting not only himself, but all his race, better than any white man. Assuming that their average of intelligence and morals should be not below that of jurymen as now drawn, would a white man, for all that, choose to be tried in one of those courts? Would he suspect nothing? Could one persuade him that his chances of even justice were all they should be, or all they would be were the court not evading the law in order to sustain an outrageous distinction against him because of the accidents of his birth? Yet only read white man for black man, and black man for white man, and that—I speak as an eyewitness—has been the practice for years, and is still so to-day; an actual emasculation, in the case of six million people both as plaintiff and defendant, of the right of trial by jury.

In this and other practices the outrage falls upon the freedman. Does it stop there? Far from it. It is the first premise of American principles that whatever elevates the lower stratum of the people lifts all the rest, and whatever holds it down holds all down. For twenty years, therefore, the nation has been working to elevate the freedman. It counts this one of the great necessities of the hour. It has poured out its wealth publicly and privately for this purpose. It is confidently hoped that it will soon bestow a royal gift of millions for the reduction of the illiteracy so largely shared by the blacks. Our Southern States are, and for twenty years have been, taxing themselves for the same end. The private charities alone of the other States have given twenty millions in the same good cause. Their colored seminaries, colleges, and normal schools dot our whole Southern country, and furnish our public colored schools with a large part of their teachers. All this and much more has been or is being done in order that, for the good of himself and everybody else in the land, the colored man may be elevated as quickly as possible from all the debasements of slavery and semi-slavery to the full stature and integrity of citizenship. And it is in the face of all this that the adherent of the old régime stands in the way to every public privilege and place—steamer landing, railway platform, theatre, concert-hall, art display, public library, public school, court-house, church, everything —flourishing the hot branding-iron of ignominious distinctions. He forbids the freedman to go into the water until he is satisfied that he knows how to swim, and for fear he should learn hangs mill-stones about his neck. This is what we are told is a small matter that will settle itself. Yes, like a roosting curse, until the outraged intelligence of the South lifts its indignant protest against this stupid firing into our own ranks.

[ITS DAILY WORKINGS]

I say the outraged intelligence of the South; for there are thousands of Southern-born white men and women, in the minority in all these places—in churches, courts, schools, libraries, theatres, concert-halls, and on steamers and railway carriages,—who see the wrong and folly of these things, silently blush for them, and withhold their open protests only because their belief is unfortunately stronger in the futility of their counsel than in the power of a just cause. I do not justify their silence; but I affirm their sincerity and their goodly numbers. Of late years, when condemning these evils from the platform in Southern towns, I have repeatedly found that those who I had earlier been told were the men and women in whom the community placed most confidence and pride—they were the ones who, when I had spoken, came forward with warmest handgrasps and expressions of thanks, and pointedly and cordially justified my every utterance. And were they the young South? Not by half. The gray-beards of the old times have always been among them, saying in effect, not by any means as converts, but as fellow-discoverers, "Whereas we were blind, now we see."

Another sort among our good Southern people make a similar but feeble admission, but with the time-worn proviso that expediency makes a more imperative demand than law, justice, or logic, and demands the preservation of the old order. Somebody must be outraged, it seems; and if not the freedman, then it must be a highly refined and enlightened race of people constantly offended and grossly discommoded, if not imposed upon, by a horde of tatterdemalions, male and female, crowding into a participation in their reserved privileges. Now, look at this plea. It is simply saying in another way that though the Southern whites far outnumber the blacks, and though we hold every element of power in greater degree than the blacks, and though the larger part of us claim to be sealed by nature as an exclusive upper class, and though we have the courts completely in our own hands, with the police on our right and the prisons on our left, and though we justly claim to be an intrepid people, and though we have a superb military experience, with ninety-nine hundredths of all the military equipment and no scarcity of all the accessories, yet with all these facts behind us we cannot make and enforce that intelligent and approximately just assortment of persons in public places and conveyances on the merits of exterior decency that is made in all other enlightened lands. On such a plea are made a distinction and separation that not only are crude, invidious, humiliating, and tyrannous, but which do not reach their ostensible end or come near it; and all that saves such a plea from being a confession of driveling imbecility is its utter speciousness. It is advanced sincerely; and yet nothing is easier to show than that these distinctions on the line of color are really made not from any necessity, but simply for their own sake—to preserve the old arbitrary supremacy of the master class over the menial without regard to the decency or indecency of appearance or manners in either the white individual or the colored.

See its every-day working. Any colored man gains unquestioned admission into innumerable places the moment he appears as the menial attendant of some white person, where he could not cross the threshold in his own right as a well-dressed and well-behaved master of himself. The contrast is even greater in the case of colored women. There could not be a system which when put into practice would more offensively condemn itself. It does more: it actually creates the confusion it pretends to prevent. It blunts the sensibilities of the ruling class themselves. It waives all strict demand for painstaking in either manners or dress of either master or menial, and, for one result, makes the average Southern railway coach more uncomfortable than the average of railway coaches elsewhere. It prompts the average Southern white passenger to find less offense in the presence of a profane, boisterous, or unclean white person than in that of a quiet, well-behaved colored man or woman attempting to travel on an equal footing with him without a white master or mistress. The holders of the old sentiments hold the opposite choice in scorn. It is only when we go on to say that there are regions where the riotous expulsion of a decent and peaceable colored person is preferred to his inoffensive company, that it may seem necessary to bring in evidence. . . .

. . .

VIII. THE *"CONVICT LEASE SYSTEM"*

In studying, about a year ago, the practice of letting out public convicts to private lessees to serve out their sentences under private management, I found that it does not belong to all our once slave States nor to all our once seceded States.[5] Only it is no longer in practice outside of them. Under our present condition in the South, it is beyond possibility that the individual black should behave mischievously without offensively rearousing the old sentiments of the still dominant white man. As we have seen too, the white man virtually monopolizes the jury-box. Add another fact: the Southern States have entered upon a new era of material development. Now, if with these conditions in force the public mind has been captivated by glowing pictures of the remunerative economy of the convict-lease system, and by the seductive spectacle of mines and railways, turnpikes and levees, that everybody wants and nobody wants to pay for, growing apace by convict labor that seems to cost nothing, we may almost assert beforehand that the

popular mind will—not so maliciously as unreflectingly—yield to the tremendous temptation to hustle the misbehaving black man into the State prison under extravagant sentence, and sell his labor to the highest bidder who will use him in the construction of public works. For ignorance of the awful condition of these penitentiaries is extreme and general, and the hasty half-conscious assumption naturally is, that the culprit will survive this term of sentence, and its fierce discipline "teach him to behave himself."

But we need not argue from cause to effect only. Nor need I repeat one of the many painful rumors that poured in upon me the moment I began to investigate this point. The official testimony of the prisons themselves is before the world to establish the conjectures that spring from our reasoning. After the erroneous takings of the census of 1880 in South Carolina had been corrected, the population was shown to consist of about twenty blacks to every thirteen whites. One would therefore look for a preponderance of blacks on the prison lists; and inasmuch as they are a people only twenty years ago released from servile captivity, one would not be surprised to see that preponderance large. Yet, when the actual numbers confront us, our speculations are stopped with a rude shock; for what is to account for the fact that in 1881 there were committed to the State prison at Columbia, South Carolina, 406 colored persons and but 25 whites? The proportion of blacks sentenced to the whole black population was one to every 1488; that of the whites to the white population was but one to every 15,644. In Georgia the white inhabitants decidedly outnumbered the blacks; yet in the State penitentiary, October 20th, 1880, there were 115 whites and 1071 colored; or if we reject the summary of its tables and refer to the tables themselves (for the one does not agree with the other), there were but 102 whites and 1083 colored. Yet of 52 pardons granted in the two years then closing, 22 were to whites and only 30 to blacks. If this be a dark record, what shall we say of the records of lynch law? But for them there is not room here.

X. THE CASE SUBMITTED

What need to say more? The question is answered. Is the freedman a free man? No. We have considered his position in a land whence

[5] See "The Convict Lease System in the Southern States," in this volume. [Author's note.]

nothing can, and no man has a shadow of right to drive him, and where he is being multiplied as only oppression can multiply a people. We have carefully analyzed his relations to the finer and prouder race, with which he shares the ownership and citizenship of a region large enough for ten times the number of both. Without accepting one word of his testimony, we have shown that the laws made for his protection against the habits of suspicion and oppression in his late master are being constantly set aside, not for their defects, but for such merit as they possess. We have shown that the very natural source of these oppressions is the surviving sentiments of an extinct and now universally execrated institution; sentiments which no intelligent or moral people should harbor a moment after the admission that slavery was a moral mistake. We have shown the outrageousness of these tyrannies in some of their workings, and how distinctly they antagonize every State and national interest involved in the elevation of the colored race. Is it not well to have done so? For, I say again, the question has reached a moment of special importance. The South stands on her honor before the clean equities of the issue. It is no longer whether constitutional amendments, but whether the eternal principles of justice, are violated. And the answer must—it shall—come from the South. And it shall be practical. It will not cost much. We have had a strange experience: the withholding of simple rights has cost much blood; such concessions of them as we have made have never yet cost a drop. The answer is coming. Is politics in the way? Then let it clear the track or get run over, just as it prefers. But, as I have said over and over to my brethren in the South, I take upon me to say again here, that there is a moral and intellectual intelligence there which is not going to be much longer beguiled out of its moral right of way by questions of political punctilio, but will seek that plane of universal justice and equity which it is every people's duty before God to seek, not along the line of politics,—God forbid!—but across it and across it and across it as many times as it may lie across the path, until the whole people of every once slave-holding State can stand up as one man, saying, "Is the freedman a free man?" and the whole world shall answer, "Yes."   1885

BOOKER T. WASHINGTON

1859?–1915

IN *Up from Slavery* (1901) Booker T. Washington tells the story of his progress from servitude to the leadership of his people. His persistence, ability to compromise, and willingness to make only small gains for his race were revealed time and time again in his work at Tuskegee, which he founded in 1881 on the pattern of Hampton Institute, at which he had been a student. Booker T. Washington's social philosophy emphasized self-help through a vocational and moral education which was useful to a property-respecting society as well as to the individual. The cultivation of personal cleanliness, honesty, frugality, and tolerance of the white man also bulked large in Washington's teachings.

To sensitive idealists of a more militant temper, such, for example, as W. E. B. Du Bois, Washington's willingness to put into the background the struggle for more nearly equal social and cultural opportunities for the Negro, his lack of militancy, and his reputed time-serving qualities, seemed to mark, not greatness, but cowardice or blindness. But Washington had, nevertheless, true greatness, and left a deep impact on the program of race relationships. His voluminous writings include *My Larger Education* (1911) and (with R. E. Park) *The Man Farthest Down* (1912).

Selected Speeches of Booker T. Washington, E. D. Washington, ed., Garden City, N. Y., 1932.
Basil Mathews, *Booker T. Washington, Educator and Interracial Interpreter*, Cambridge, 1948.
Samuel R. Spencer, *Booker T. Washington and the Negro's Place in American Life*, Boston, 1955.

» » *From:* UP FROM SLAVERY « «

CHAPTER XIV

*THE ATLANTA EXPOSITION
ADDRESS*

The Atlanta Exposition, at which I had been asked to make an address as a representative of the Negro race, as stated in the last chapter, was opened with a short address from Gover-
10 nor Bullock. After other interesting exercises, including an invocation from Bishop Nelson, of Georgia, a dedicatory ode by Albert Howell, Jr., and addresses by the President of the Exposition and Mrs. Joseph Thompson, the President of the Woman's Board, Governor Bullock introduced me with the words, "We have with us to-day a representative of Negro enterprise and Negro civilization."

When I arose to speak, there was consider-
20 able cheering, especially from the coloured people. As I remember it now, the thing that was uppermost in my mind was the desire to say something that would cement the friendship of the races and bring about hearty co-operation between them. So far as my outward surroundings were concerned, the only thing that I recall distinctly now is that when I got up, I saw thousands of eyes looking intently into my face. The following is the address
30 which I delivered:—

MR. PRESIDENT AND GENTLEMEN OF THE BOARD OF DIRECTORS AND CITIZENS.

One-third of the population of the South is of the Negro race. No enterprise seeking the material, civil, or moral welfare of this section can disregard this element of our population and reach the highest success. I but convey to you, Mr. President and Directors, the sentiment
40 of the masses of my race when I say that in no way have the value and manhood of the American Negro been more fittingly and generously recognized than by the managers of this magnificent Exposition at every stage of its progress. It is a recognition that will do more to cement the friendship of the two races than any occurrence since the dawn of our freedom.

Not only this, but the opportunity here afforded will awaken among us a new era of
50 industrial progress. Ignorant and inexperienced, it is not strange that in the first years of our new life we began at the top instead of at the bottom; that a seat in Congress or the state legislature was more sought than real estate or industrial skill; that the political convention or stump speaking had more attractions than starting a dairy farm or truck garden.

A ship lost at sea for many days suddenly sighted a friendly vessel. From the mast of the unfortunate vessel was seen a signal, "Water, water; we die of thirst!" The answer from the friendly vessel at once came back, "Cast down your bucket where you are." And a third and fourth signal for water was answered, "Cast down your bucket where you are." The captain of the distressed vessel, at last heeding the injunction, cast down his bucket, and it came up full of fresh, sparkling water from the mouth of the Amazon River. To those of my race who depend on bettering their condition in a foreign land or who underestimate the importance of cultivating friendly relations with the Southern white man, who is their next-door neighbour, I would say: "Cast down your bucket where you are"—cast it down in making friends in every manly way of the people of all races by whom we are surrounded.

Cast it down in agriculture, mechanics, in commerce, in domestic service, and in the professions. And in this connection it is well to bear in mind that whatever other sins the South may be called to bear, when it comes to business, pure and simple, it is in the South that the Negro is given a man's chance in the commercial world, and in nothing is this Exposition more eloquent than in emphasizing this chance. Our greatest danger is that in the great leap from slavery to freedom we may overlook the fact that the masses of us are to live by the productions of our hands, and fail to keep in mind that we shall prosper in proportion as we learn to dignify and glorify common labour and put brains and skill into the common occupations of life; shall prosper in proportion as we learn to draw the line between the superficial and the substantial, the ornamental gew-gaws of life and the useful. No race can prosper till it learns that there is as much dignity in tilling a field as in writing a poem. It is at the bottom of life we must begin, and not at the top. Nor should we permit our grievances to overshadow our opportunities.

To those of the white race who look to the incoming of those of foreign birth and strange tongue and habits for the prosperity of the South, were I permitted I would repeat what I say to my own race, "Cast down your bucket where you are." Cast it down among the eight millions of Negroes whose habits you know, whose fidelity and love you have tested in days when to have proved treacherous meant the ruin of your firesides. Cast down your bucket among these people who have, without strikes and labour wars, tilled your fields, cleared your forests, builded your railroads and cities, and brought forth treasures from the bowels of the earth, and helped make possible this magnificent representation of the progress of the South. Casting down your bucket among my people, helping and encouraging them as you are doing on these grounds, and to education of head, hand, and heart, you will find that they will buy your surplus land, make blossom the waste places in your fields, and run your factories. While doing this, you can be sure in the future, as in the past, that you and your families will be surrounded by the most patient, faithful, law-abiding, and unresentful people that the world has seen. As we have proved our loyalty to you in the past, in nursing your children, watching by the sick-bed of your mothers and fathers, and often following them with tear-dimmed eyes to their graves, so in the future, in our humble way, we shall stand by you with a devotion that no foreigner can approach, ready to lay down our lives, if need be, in defence of yours, interlacing our industrial, commercial, civil, and religious life with yours in a way that shall make the interests of both races one. In all things that are purely social we can be as separate as the fingers, yet one as the hand in all things essential to mutual progress.

There is no defence or security for any of us except in the highest intelligence and development of all. If anywhere there are efforts tending to curtail the fullest growth of the Negro, let these efforts be turned into stimulating, encouraging, and making him the most useful and intelligent citizen. Effort or means so invested will pay a thousand per cent interest. These efforts will be twice blessed—"blessing him that gives and him that takes."

There is no escape through law of man or God from the inevitable:—

The laws of changeless justice bind
Oppressor with oppressed;

And close as sin and suffering joined
We march to fate abreast.

Nearly sixteen millions of hands will aid you in pulling the load upward, or they will pull against you the load downward. We shall constitute one-third and more of the ignorance and crime of the South, or one-third its intelligence and progress; we shall contribute one-third to the business and industrial prosperity of the South, or we shall prove a veritable body of death, stagnating, depressing, retarding every effort to advance the body politic.

Gentlemen of the Exposition, as we present to you our humble effort at an exhibition of our progress, you must not expect overmuch. Starting thirty years ago with ownership here and there in a few quilts and pumpkins and chickens (gathered from miscellaneous sources), remember the path that has led from these to the inventions and production of agricultural implements, buggies, steam-engines, newspapers, books, statuary, carving, paintings, the management of drug-stores and banks, has not been trodden without contact with thorns and thistles. While we take pride in what we exhibit as a result of our independent efforts, we do not for a moment forget that our part in this exhibition would fall far short of your expectations but for the constant help that has come to our educational life, not only from the Southern states, but especially from Northern philanthropists, who have made their gifts a constant stream of blessing and encouragement.

The wisest among my race understand that the agitation of questions of social equality is the extremest folly, and that progress in the enjoyment of all the privileges that will come to us must be the result of severe and constant struggle rather than of artificial forcing. No race that has anything to contribute to the markets of the world is long in any degree ostracized. It is important and right that all privileges of the law be ours, but it is vastly more important that we be prepared for the exercises of these privileges. The opportunity to earn a dollar in a factory just now is worth infinitely more than the opportunity to spend a dollar in an opera-house.

In conclusion, may I repeat that nothing in thirty years has given us more hope and encouragement, and drawn us so near to you of the white race, as this opportunity offered by the Exposition; and here bending, as it were, over the altar that represents the results of the struggles of your race and mine, both starting practically empty-handed three decades ago, I pledge that in your effort to work out the great and intricate problem which God has laid at the doors of the South, you shall have at all times the patient, sympathetic help of my race; only let this be constantly in mind, that, while from representations in these buildings of the product of field, of forest, of mine, of factory, letters, and art, much good will come, yet far 10 above and beyond material benefits will be that higher good, that, let us pray God, will come, in a blotting out of sectional differences and racial animosities and suspicions, in a determination to administer absolute justice, in a willing obedience among all classes to the mandates of law. This, this, coupled with our material prosperity, will bring into our beloved South a new heaven and a new earth.

20 The first thing that I remember, after I had finished speaking, was that Governor Bullock rushed across the platform and took me by the hand, and that others did the same. I received so many and such hearty congratulations that I found it difficult to get out of the building. I did not appreciate to any degree, however, the impression which my address seemed to have made, until the next morning, when I went into the business part of the city. 30 As soon as I was recognized, I was surprised to find myself pointed out and surrounded by a crowd of men who wished to shake hands with me. This was kept up on every street on to which I went, to an extent which embarrassed me so much that I went back to my boarding-place. The next morning I returned to Tuskegee. At the station in Atlanta, and at almost all of the stations at which the train stopped between that city and Tuskegee, I found a crowd 40 of people anxious to shake hands with me.

The papers in all parts of the United States published the address in full, and for months afterward there were complimentary editorial references to it. Mr. Clark Howell, the editor of the Atlanta *Constitution*, telegraphed to a New York paper, among other words, the following, "I do not exaggerate when I say that Professor Booker T. Washington's address yesterday was one of the most notable speeches, 50 both as to character and as to the warmth of its reception, ever delivered to a Southern audience. The address was a revelation. The whole speech is a platform upon which blacks and whites can stand with full justice to each other."

The Boston *Transcript* said editorially: "The speech of Booker T. Washington at the Atlanta Exposition, this week, seems to have dwarfed all the other proceedings and the Exposition itself. The sensation that it has caused in the press has never been equalled."

I very soon began receiving all kinds of propositions from lecture bureaus, and editors of magazines and papers, to take the lecture platform, and to write articles. One lecture bureau offered me fifty thousand dollars, or two hundred dollars a night and expenses, if I would place my services at its disposal for a given period. To all these communications I replied that my life-work was at Tuskegee; and that whenever I spoke it must be in the interests of the Tuskegee school and my race, and that I would enter into no arrangements that seemed to place a mere commercial value upon my services.

Some days after its delivery I sent a copy of my address to the President of the United States, the Hon. Grover Cleveland. I received from him the following autograph reply:—

Gray Gables, Buzzard's Bay, Mass., October 6, 1895.

Booker T. Washington, Esq.:

My Dear Sir: I thank you for sending me a copy of your address delivered at the Atlanta Exposition.

I thank you with much enthusiasm for making the address. I have read it with intense interest, and I think the Exposition would be fully justified if it did not do more than furnish the opportunity for its delivery. Your words cannot fail to delight and encourage all who wish well for your race; and if our coloured fellow-citizens do not from your utterances gather new hope and form new determinations to gain every valuable advantage offered them by their citizenship, it will be strange indeed.

Yours very truly,
Grover Cleveland.

Later I met Mr. Cleveland, for the first time, when, as President, he visited the Atlanta Exposition. At the request of myself and others he consented to spend an hour in the Negro Building, for the purpose of inspecting the Negro exhibit and of giving the coloured people in attendance an opportunity to shake hands with him. As soon as I met Mr. Cleveland I became impressed with his simplicity, greatness, and rugged honesty. I have met him many times since then, both at public functions and at his private residence in Princeton, and the more I see of him the more I admire him.

When he visited the Negro Building in Atlanta he seemed to give himself up wholly, for that hour, to the coloured people. He seemed to be as careful to shake hands with some old coloured "auntie" clad partially in rags, and to take as much pleasure in doing so, as if he were greeting some millionnaire. Many of the coloured people took advantage of the occasion to get him to write his name in a book or on a slip of paper. He was as careful and patient in doing this as if he were putting his signature to some great state document.

Mr. Cleveland has not only shown his friendship for me in many personal ways, but has always consented to do anything I have asked of him for our school. This he has done, whether it was to make a personal donation or to use his influence in securing the donations of others. Judging from my personal acquaintance with Mr. Cleveland, I do not believe that he is conscious of possessing any colour prejudice. He is too great for that. In my contact with people I find that, as a rule, it is only the little, narrow people who live for themselves, who never read good books, who do not travel, who never open up their souls in a way to permit them to come into contact with other souls —with the great outside world. No man whose vision is bounded by colour can come into contact with what is highest and best in the world. In meeting men, in many places, I have found that the happiest people are those who do the most for others; the most miserable are those who do the least. I have also found that few things, if any, are capable of making one so blind and narrow as race prejudice. I often say to our students, in the course of my talks to them on Sunday evenings in the chapel, that the longer I live and the more experience I have of the world, the more I am convinced that, after all, the one thing that is most worth living for—and dying for, if need be—is the opportunity of making some one else more happy and more useful.

The coloured people and the coloured newspapers at first seemed to be greatly pleased with the character of my Atlanta address, as well as with its reception. But after the first burst of enthusiasm began to die away, and the coloured people began reading the speech in cold type, some of them seemed to feel that they had been hypnotized. They seemed to feel that I had been too liberal in my remarks toward the Southern whites, and that I had not spoken out strongly enough for what they termed the "rights" of the race. For a while there was a reaction, so far as a certain element of my own race was concerned, but later these reactionary ones seemed to have been won over to my way of believing and acting.

While speaking of changes in public sentiment, I recall that about ten years after the school at Tuskegee was established, I had an experience that I shall never forget. Dr. Lyman Abbott, then the pastor of Plymouth Church, and also editor of the *Outlook* (then the Christian Union), asked me to write a letter for his paper giving my opinion of the exact condition, mental and moral, of the coloured ministers in the South, as based upon my observations. I wrote the letter, giving the exact facts as I conceived them to be. The picture painted was a rather black one—or, since I am black, shall I say "white"? It could not be otherwise with a race but a few years out of slavery, a race which had not had time or opportunity to produce a competent ministry.

What I said soon reached every Negro minister in the country, I think, and the letters of condemnation which I received from them were not few. I think that for a year after the publication of this article every association and every conference or religious body of any kind, of my race, that met, did not fail before adjourning to pass a resolution condemning me, or calling upon me to retract or modify what I had said. Many of these organizations went so far in their resolutions as to advise parents to cease sending their children to Tuskegee. One association even appointed a "missionary" whose duty it was to warn the people against sending their children to Tuskegee. This missionary had a son in the school, and I noticed that, whatever the "missionary" might have said or done with regard to others, he was careful not to take his son away from the institution. Many of the coloured papers, especially those that were the organs of religious bodies, joined in the general chorus of condemnation or demands for retraction.

During the whole time of the excitement, and through all the criticism, I did not utter a word of explanation or retraction. I knew that I was right, and that time and the sober second thought of the people would vindicate me. It was not long before the bishops and other church leaders began to make a careful investigation of the conditions of the ministry, and they found out that I was right. In fact, the oldest and most influential bishop in one

branch of the Methodist Church said that my
words were far too mild. Very soon public
sentiment began making itself felt, in demanding a purifying of the ministry. While this is
not yet complete by any means, I think I may
say, without egotism, and I have been told by
many of our most influential ministers, that my
words had much to do with starting a demand
for the placing of a higher type of men in the
10 pulpit. I have had the satisfaction of having
many who once condemned me thank me
heartily for my frank words.

The change of the attitude of the Negro
ministry, so far as regards myself, is so complete that at the present time I have no warmer
friends among any class than I have among the
clergymen. The improvement in the character
and life of the Negro ministers is one of the
most gratifying evidences of the progress of the
20 race. My experience with them, as well as other
events in my life, convinces me that the thing
to do, when one feels sure that he has said or
done the right thing, and is condemned, is to
stand still and keep quiet. If he is right, time
will show it.

In the midst of the discussion which was going on concerning my Atlanta speech, I received the letter which I give below, from Dr.
Gilman, the President of Johns Hopkins Uni-
30 versity, who had been made chairman of the
judges of award in connection with the Atlanta
Exposition:—

Johns Hopkins University, Baltimore,
President's Office, September 30, 1895.

DEAR MR. WASHINGTON: Would it be agreeable to you to be one of the Judges of Award in
the Department of Education at Atlanta? If so, I
shall be glad to place your name upon the list. A
line by telegraph will be welcomed.

Yours very truly,
D. C. GILMAN.

42   I think I was even more surprised to receive
this invitation than I had been to receive the
invitation to speak at the opening of the Exposition. It was to be a part of my duty, as one
of the jurors, to pass not only upon the exhibits of the coloured schools, but also upon
those of the white schools. I accepted the position, and spent a month in Atlanta in perform-
50 ance of the duties which it entailed. The board
of jurors was a large one, consisting in all of
sixty members. It was about equally divided
between Southern white people and Northern
white people. Among them were college presidents, leading scientists and men of letters, and

specialists in many subjects. When the group of
jurors to which I was assigned met for organization, Mr. Thomas Nelson Page, who was one
of the number, moved that I be made secretary
of that division, and the motion was unanimously adopted. Nearly half of our division
were Southern people. In performing my duties
in the inspection of the exhibits of white schools
I was in every case treated with respect, and
at the close of our labours I parted from my
associates with regret.

I am often asked to express myself more
freely than I do upon the political condition
and the political future of my race. These recollections of my experience in Atlanta give me
the opportunity to do so briefly. My own belief
is, although I have never before said so in so
many words, that the time will come when the
Negro in the South will be accorded all the political rights which his ability, character, and
material possessions entitle him to. I think,
though, that the opportunity to freely exercise
such political rights will not come in any large
degree through outside or artificial forcing, but
will be accorded to the Negro by the Southern
white people themselves, and that they will
protect him in the exercise of those rights. Just
as soon as the South gets over the old feeling
that it is being forced by "foreigners," or
"aliens," to do something which it does not
want to do, I believe that the change in the direction that I have indicated is going to begin.
In fact, there are indications that it is already
beginning in a slight degree.

Let me illustrate my meaning. Suppose that
some months before the opening of the Atlanta
Exposition there had been a general demand
from the press and public platform outside the
South that a Negro be given a place on the
opening programme, and that a Negro be
placed upon the board of jurors of award.
Would any such recognition of the race have
taken place? I do not think so. The Atlanta officials went as far as they did because they felt
it to be a pleasure, as well as a duty, to reward
what they considered merit in the Negro race.
Say what we will, there is something in human nature which we cannot blot out, which
makes one man, in the end, recognize and
reward merit in another, regardless of colour or
race.

I believe it is the duty of the Negro—as the
greater part of the race is already doing—to
deport himself modestly in regard to political
claims, depending upon the slow but sure in-

fluences that proceed from the possession of property, intelligence, and high character for the full recognition of his political rights. I think that the according of the full exercise of political rights is going to be a matter of natural, slow growth, not an over-night, gourd-vine affair. I do not believe that the Negro should cease voting, for a man cannot learn the exercise of self-government by ceasing to vote any more than a boy can learn to swim by keeping out of the water, but I do believe that in his voting he should more and more be influenced by those of intelligence and character who are his next-door neighbours.

I know coloured men who, through the encouragement, help, and advice of Southern white people, have accumulated thousands of dollars' worth of property, but who, at the same time, would never think of going to those same persons for advice concerning the casting of their ballots. This, it seems to me, is unwise and unreasonable, and should cease. In saying this I do not mean that the Negro should truckle, or not vote from principle, for the instant he ceases to vote from principle he loses the confidence and respect of the Southern white man even.

I do not believe that any state should make a law that permits an ignorant and poverty-stricken white man to vote, and prevents a black man in the same condition from voting.

Such a law is not only unjust, but it will react, as all unjust laws do, in time; for the effect of such a law is to encourage the Negro to secure education and property, and at the same time it encourages the white man to remain in ignorance and poverty. I believe that in time, through the operation of intelligence and friendly race relations, all cheating at the ballot box in the South will cease. It will become apparent that the white man who begins by cheating a Negro out of his ballot soon learns to cheat a white man out of his, and that the man who does this ends his career of dishonesty by the theft of property or by some equally serious crime. In my opinion, the time will come when the South will encourage all of its citizens to vote. It will see that it pays better, from every standpoint, to have healthy, vigorous life than to have that political stagnation which always results when one-half of the population has no share and no interest in the government.

As a rule, I believe in universal, free suffrage, but I believe that in the South we are confronted with peculiar conditions that justify the protection of the ballot in many of the states, for a while at least, either by an educational test, a property test, or by both combined; but whatever tests are required, they should be made to apply with equal and exact justice to both races. 1900

WILLIAM EDWARD BURGHARDT DU BOIS

1868–

THE FACT THAT Du Bois was born and grew to young manhood in Great Barrington, Massachusetts, rather than in the South, profoundly affected his outlook on the Negro question. After taking bachelor's degrees at Fisk and at Harvard, and his doctorate at the latter institution, Du Bois studied abroad and through his historical and sociological studies of the Negro, became a recognized authority. As a scholar to whom intellectual values meant a great deal, he had little patience with the emphasis on vocational education which in so many cases cut off the Negro from anything like an equal opportunity in education. At the same time Du Bois advocated a militant struggle for the civil and other rights to which the Negro was entitled by law and by the Constitution. He came increasingly to believe that the Negro could not become emancipated from quasi-serfdom until either the competitive capitalistic system had given way to a co-operative one, or at least until the Negro had developed an autonomous economic system within the national economy.

Du Bois's books include *The Suppression of the African Slave-Trade* (1896), *The Philadelphia Negro* (1899), a pioneer study in the sociology of the Negro, *The Souls of Black Folk* (1903), a book which has already become a classic, and *Black Reconstruction* (1935). In addition to his writings Dr. Du Bois has taught at Atlanta University and edited the *Crisis*.

W. E. Burghardt Du Bois, *Dusk of Dawn*, New York, 1940.

» » *From:* SOCIAL PLANNING FOR THE NEGRO « «

THE WASHINGTON PLAN

The plan of social Reconstruction advocated by Booker T. Washington was not simply a plan for the uplift of labor as is so often assumed, and it can be only understood as we consider its immediate background. The late William H. Baldwin, President of the Long Island Railroad and slated to be President of
10 the Pennsylvania, was a young man trained in Southern industry. He was one of the first to conceive of the training of black laborers who should share work with white laborers and at the same time keep the white labor movement from too strong and insistent demands in its fight with capital.

This idea began in the day when the "one big union," of the Knights of Labor had changed to the craft unionism of the American
20 Federation of Labor. The strength of the labor movement was growing but almost without exception it excluded black skilled labor. However, black skilled labor was valuable and could be trained in the South. It was the idea of Mr. Baldwin and gradually of many others that you would not only do a service to and open opportunity for black folk, but you would in the same way serve capital and hold white labor in check.

30 About this time, Booker T. Washington took charge of Tuskegee in Alabama. He was an opportunist with high ideals. He believed in political rights for people who could exercise them, but in the case of Southern Negroes, he knew that they could not exercise them without the consent of the white South. He took the position, therefore, that the Negro must gain an economic status before he could use his political rights and in this he was undoubt-
40 edly right; but on the other hand, his idea of the economic status which Negroes must gain was based unquestionably on the capitalistic organization of the United States.

Mr. Washington's program included a tem-porary acquiescence in giving up Negro political rights and agitation for civil rights and insistence upon training young Negroes for farming and industry. Up from a thrifty solid class of black landlords and artisans, Washington expected a class of Negro capitalists to arise and employ Negro workers. The plan was launched by the Atlanta Speech in 1896 and was triumphant from that date until about 1910. It included alliance with white capital and was rewarded by large contributions toward Negro education, especially such schools as conformed to the Hampton-Tuskegee type.

As a first step toward this new Negro capitalism, Mr. Washington especially stressed landholding, widespread peasant proprietorship, and even large farms among Negroes; and then a training of Negro laborers and artisans for use in industry at a wage if necessary less than that demanded by union labor. The result of this compromise was a new understanding between leading elements, North and South, with regard to the Negro. The Negro college, while not entirely discouraged, was looked upon with some suspicion, and positions for Negro college graduates became difficult. To some extent, appointments and opportunities for young Negroes were carefully censored and referred for approval to Tuskegee, over a very wide extent of country. Negro newspapers were brought in line by judicious advertising and other means of control. This was really regarded as a clever and farsighted compromise, which, if it did not solve, would at least peacefully postpone the solutions of a baffling, intricate problem of race contact until more favorable times. Between 1900–1910, Mr. Washington became one of the most popular men in America, in constant demand North and South as a speaker, adviser, and referee.

As the current opinion of the land became unified, Mr. Washington's program began to become increasingly suspicious in the eyes of Negroes. A wave of Jim-Crow legislation and disfranchising bills swept over the South and the border states. Already separation of the races in travel had been made compulsory in eight Southern states before 1891, but had paused. Now, a new wave of legislation began in 1898 and covered South Carolina, North Carolina, Virginia, Maryland and Oklahoma. Determined and repeated efforts were made in Missouri, West Virginia, and Delaware. Disfranchising laws swept over the South and border states, from 1890–1910, at the very time when Negro political power and agitation had been lulled to its lowest by the Washington compromise. This triumph of the radical, anti-Negro South and the continued prevalence of lynching which went on at the rate of one to two a week during most of Mr. Washington's career, greatly embarrassed him. He hated caste and lawlessness as much as any man. He wanted the best for his people, but he implicitly believed that once his economic program could be put through all else would follow. He made the fatal mistake of trying to forestall criticism from Negroes and of acquiescing in the neglect if not the suppression of Negro colleges. 1936

» » *The Passing of the Frontier* « «

1850-1890

» »   « «

MUSTANG GRAY

There was a noble ranger
They called him Mustang Gray;
He left his home when but a youth,
Went ranging far away.

    But he'll go no more a-ranging
    The savage to affright;
    He's heard his last war-whoop
    And fought his last fight.

He ne'er would sleep within a tent,
No comforts would he know;
But like a brave old Tex-i-an
A-ranging he would go.

When Texas was invaded
By a mighty tyrant foe,
He mounted his noble warhorse
And a-ranging he did go.

Once he was taken prisoner,
Bound in chains upon the way;
He wore the yoke of bondage
Through the streets of Monterrey.

A señorita loved him
And followed by his side;
She opened the gates and gave to him
Her father's steed to ride.

God bless the señorita,
The belle of Monterrey;
She opened wide the prison door
And let him ride away.

And when this veteran's life was spent,
It was his last command,
To bury him on Texas soil
On the banks of the Rio Grande.

And there the lonely traveler,
When passing by his grave,
Will shed a farewell tear
O'er the bravest of the brave.

> Now he'll go no more a-ranging,
> The savage to affright;
> He's heard his last war-whoop
> And fought his last fight.

"In high quavering tones that carried above rattling hocks and clacking horns and in low monotone that harmonized with the sleeping herd all stretched out on the ground, this ballad was sung to longhorns on range and trail from the Gulf of Mexico to the Canadian Rockies." It celebrates, with more sentiment than his deeds warrant, the career of "Mustang" Gray, born Mayberry B. Gray, who came to Texas in 1835. One of the first of the cowboys and a Texas Ranger during the Mexican War, he killed Mexicans in and out of season with the relish of a sportsman after wild game. His deeds are legendary on the later frontier. The traditions which cling to his name are described by Professor J. Frank Dobie in the *Publications of the Texas Folk-Lore Society*, X, 109–123. By his permission the ballad is given here.

» » « «

THE LITTLE OLD SOD SHANTY

I am looking rather seedy now while holding down my claim,
And my victuals are not always of the best;——
And the mice play shyly round me as I nestle down to rest,
In my little old sod shanty in the West.
Yet I rather like the novelty of living in this way,
Though my bill of fare is always rather tame,
But I'm happy as a clam on the land of Uncle Sam,
In my little old sod shanty on my claim.

Refrain:

The hinges are of leather and the windows have no glass,
While the board roof lets the howling blizzards in,
And I hear the hungry kiyote as he slinks up through the grass
Round my little old sod shanty on my claim.

O when I left my eastern home, a bachelor so gay,
To try and win my way to wealth and fame,
I little thought that I'd come down to burning twisted hay
In the little old sod shanty on my claim.
My clothes are plastered o'er with dough, I'm looking like a fright
And everything is scattered round the room,
But I wouldn't give the freedom that I have out in the West
For the table of the Eastern man's old home.

Still I wish that some kind-hearted girl would pity on me take,
And relieve me from the mess that I am in;
The angel, how I'd bless her if this her home she'd make
In the little old sod shanty on my claim.
And we would make our fortunes on the prairies of the West,
Just as happy as two lovers we'd remain;
We'd forget the trials and troubles we endured at the first,
In the little old sod shanty on our claim.

And if kindly fate should bless us with now and then an heir,
To cheer our hearts with honest pride of fame,
O then we'd be contented for the toil that we had spent
In the little old sod shanty on our claim.
When time enough has lapsed and all of those little brats
To noble man- and womanhood had grown,
It wouldn't seem half so lonely as around us we should look,
And see the little old sod shanty on our claim.

On the Great Plains, where timber was scanty, the pioneer built his first house of sod. Farther east, as Mr. Carl Sandburg notes, men had sung a song about "The Little Old Cabin in the Lane." The "sod-buster" adapted it to his situation. The version here given is taken from *The American Songbag*, by the permission of Mr. Sandburg and Harcourt, Brace and Company.

» »   « «

The Passing of the Frontier

IN 1890 the Census Bureau reported that it was no longer possible to trace a line from the boundary of Canada to that of Mexico which might be said to delimit settled from unsettled areas. Long after this announcement frontier conditions survived in many parts of the Great West, but the era of the frontier had passed.

Before the formal announcement that the frontier era had gone, the Great West beyond the Missouri was the scene of dramatic conflicts. The mining frontier brought bonanza days for some and despair for others. The railroads spelled the ruin of the buffalo herds on which the red man had subsisted. When he fought desperately for his own way of life, he was defeated and pushed on to the poorer lands known as reservations. The issue then arose as to whether he would be allowed to remain in a half-savage, half-dependent state, or whether he should be made a citizen and assimilated into the main stream of American life. The railroads also brought into the West immigrants from Europe and settlers from the older areas of the East: the iron horse became a virtual colonizer. But the railroad's zeal for obtaining the broadest possible interpretation of the charters which had granted them public domains frequently aroused the ire of settlers who had in true American fashion "squatted" on debated lands. And the coming of the barbed wire fence to the plains ended the old days of the open range and the "drives" of herds of cattle upwards from Texas to grazing lands and, ultimately, to slaughter houses. The cattle man fought many a battle with the farmer before he succumbed to the era of barbed wire enclosures. Back of all these dramatic conflicts lay the basic issue whether the last West was to be drawn into the national pattern of life, or was to remain a law and a way of life unto itself.

The conquest of the last West was also made possible by the courageous explorations of *terra incognita*. The United States Geological Survey, together with free-lance scientists, revealed canyons and mountains and mesas of magic beauty, and primitive peoples fascinating to the ethnologist.

The passing of the frontier greatly sharpened traditional issues in American life and introduced new ones. With the disappearance of vast areas of free land, it was obvious that the reckless wastage of our national resources must be checked, that planning and conservation must become a part of public policy. It was also clear, at least to some, that in so far as the West had provided the creditor class of the East with an imperial domain to exploit, the basic economic and social structure of the country must now be modified. Overseas imperialism might take the place of the last West; or, possibly, the economic structure itself might be so modified that it could continue to function relatively well. Others insisted that the end of free lands meant that we could no longer receive and absorb the vast numbers of immigrants that had sought our shores. Still others, who saw in the frontier experience the mainspring of American individualism, optimism, and democracy, questioned how these values were henceforth to be preserved.

» »   « «

BAYARD TAYLOR

1825–1878

BROUGHT UP in the Quaker discipline of a Pennsylvania farm community, Taylor served an apprenticeship in printing and early embarked on a literary career. As a traveler in Europe in his twentieth year he contributed letters to the *New York Tribune*. It was as a writer for the *Tribune* that Taylor went to California at the time of the gold rush in '49. His *Eldorado* (1850) enhanced his fame as a traveler and a writer. Journeys in the Near East and the Orient followed, with appropriate books relating his impressions; and the lyceum offered an additional channel for popularizing his travel experiences. In addition to his travel books Taylor wrote three novels, *Hannah Thurston* (1863), *John Godfrey's Fortunes* (1864), and *The Story of Kennett* (1866), and more than a dozen volumes of poems. His translation of Goethe's *Faust* (1870–1871) was a faithful rather than a distinguished translation.

The following selections from *Eldorado* recapture much of the adventure, magic, and harshness of a raw land in which a new premium was put on resourcefulness, militant individualism, and faith in destiny.

A. H. Smyth, *Bayard Taylor*, with bibliography, Boston and New York, 1896.
Richard Cary, *The Genteel Circle: Bayard Taylor and His New York Friends*, Ithaca, 1952.
R. C. Beatty, *Bayard Taylor; Laureate of the Gilded Age*, Norman, Okla., 1936.

» » *From:* ELDORADO « «

Or, Adventures in the Path of Empire

THE OVERLAND EMIGRATION OF 1849

Sacramento City was the goal of the emigration by the northern routes. From the beginning of August to the last of December scarcely a day passed without the arrival of some man or company of men and families, from the mountains, to pitch their tents for a few days on the bank of the river and rest from their months of hardship. The vicissitudes through which these people had passed, the perils they had encountered and the toils they had endured seem to me without precedent in History. The story of thirty thousand souls accomplishing a journey of more than two thousand miles through a savage and but partially explored wilderness, crossing on their way two mountain chains equal to the Alps in height and asperity, besides broad tracts of burning desert, and plains of nearly equal desolation, where a few patches of stunted shrubs and springs of brackish water were their only stay, has in it so much of heroism, of daring and of sublime endurance, that we may vainly question the records of any age for its equal. Standing as I was, at the closing stage of that grand pilgrimage, the sight of these adventurers as they came in day by day, and the hearing of their stories, each of which had its own peculiar and separate character, had a more fascinating, because more real interest than the tales of the glorious old travelers which so impress us in childhood.

It would be impossible to give, in a general description of the emigration, viewed as one great movement, a complete idea of its many wonderful phases. The experience of any single man, which a few years ago would have made him a hero for life, becomes mere common-place, when it is but one of many thousands; yet the spectacle of a great continent, through a region of one thousand miles from north to south, being overrun with these adventurous bands, cannot be pictured without the relation of many episodes of individual bravery and suffering. I will not attempt a full account of the emigration, but, as I have already given an outline of the stories of those who came by the Gila route, a similar sketch of what those encountered who took the Northern route—the great overland highway of the Continent—will not be without its interest in this place.

The great starting point for this route was Independence, Mo., where thousands were encamped through the month of April, waiting until the grass should be sufficiently high for their cattle, before they ventured on the broad ocean of the Plains. From the first of May to the first of June, company after company took its departure from the frontier of civilization, till the emigrant trail from Fort Leavenworth, on the Missouri, to Fort Laramie, at the foot of the Rocky Mountains, was one long line of mule-trains and wagons. The rich meadows of the Nebraska, or Platte, were settled for the time, and a single traveler could have journeyed for the space of a thousand miles, as certain of his lodging and regular meals as if he were riding through the old agricultural districts of the Middle States. The wandering tribes of Indians on the Plains—the Pawnees, Sioux and Arapahoes—were alarmed and bewildered by this strange apparition. They believed they were about to be swept away forever from their hunting-grounds and graves. As the season advanced and the great body of the emigrants got under way, they gradually withdrew from the vicinity of the trail and betook themselves to grounds which the former did not reach. All conflicts with them were thus avoided, and the emigrants passed the Plains with perfect immunity from their thievish and hostile visitations.

Another and more terrible scourge, however, was doomed to fall upon them. The cholera, ascending the Mississippi from New Orleans, reached St. Louis about the time of their departure from Independence, and overtook them before they were fairly embarked on the wilderness. The frequent rains of the early spring, added to the hardship and exposure of their travel, prepared the way for its ravages, and the first three or four hundred miles of the trail were marked by graves. It is estimated that about four thousand persons perished from this cause. Men were seized without warning with the most violent symptoms, and

instances occurred in which the sufferer was left to die alone by the road-side, while his panic-stricken companions pushed forward, vainly trusting to get beyond the influence of the epidemic. Rough boards were planted at the graves of those who were buried near the trail, but there are hundreds of others lying unmarked by any memorial, on the bleak surface of the open plain and among the barren depths of the mountains. I have heard men tell how they have gone aside from their company to bury some old and cherished friend—a brother, it may often have been—performing the last rites alone and unaided, and leaving the remains where none but the wolf will ever seek their resting-place.

By the time the companies reached Fort Laramie the epidemic had expended its violence, and in the pure air of the elevated mountain region they were safe from its further attacks. Now, however, the real hardships of their journey began. Up and down the mountains that hem in the Sweetwater Valley—over the spurs of the Wind River chain—through the Devil's Gate, and past the stupendous mass of Rock Independence—they toiled slowly up to the South Pass, descended to the tributaries of the Colorado and plunged into the rugged defiles of the Timpanozu Mountains. Here the pasturage became scarce and the companies were obliged to take separate trails in order to find sufficient grass for their teams. Many, who, in their anxiety to get forward with speed, had thrown away a great part of the supplies that encumbered them, now began to want, and were frequently reduced, in their necessity, to make use of their mules and horses for food. It was not unusual for a mess, by way of variety to the tough mule-meat, to kill a quantity of rattle-snakes, with which the mountains abounded, and have a dish of them fried, for supper. The distress of many of the emigrants might have been entirely avoided, had they possessed any correct idea, at the outset of the journey, of its length and privations.

It must have been a remarkable scene, which the City of the Great Salt Lake presented during the summer. There, a community of religious enthusiasts, numbering about ten thousand, had established themselves beside an inland sea, in a grand valley shut in by snow-capped mountains, a thousand miles from any other civilized spot, and were dreaming of rebuilding the Temple and creating a New Jerusalem. Without this resting-place in midjourney, the sufferings of the emigrants must have been much aggravated. The Mormons, however, whose rich grain-lands in the Valley of the Utah River had produced them abundance of supplies, were able to spare sufficient for those whose stock was exhausted. Two or three thousand, who arrived late in the season, remained in the Valley all winter, fearing to undertake the toilsome journey which still remained.

Those who set out for California had the worst yet in store for them. Crossing the alternate sandy wastes and rugged mountain chains of the Great Basin to the Valley of Humboldt's River, they were obliged to trust entirely to their worn and weary animals for reaching the Sierra Nevada before the winter snows. The grass was scarce and now fast drying up in the scorching heat of midsummer. In the endeavor to hasten forward and get the first chance of pasture, many again committed the same mistake of throwing away their supplies. I was told of one man, who, with a refinement of malice and cruelty which it would be impossible to surpass, set fire to the meadows of dry grass, for the sole purpose, it was supposed, of retarding the progress of those who were behind and might else overtake him. A company of the emigrants, on the best horses which were to be obtained, pursued him and shot him from the saddle as he rode—a fate scarcely equal to his deserts.

The progress of the emigrants along the Valley of Humboldt's River is described as having been slow and toilsome in the extreme. The River, which lies entirely within the Great Basin,—whose waters, like those of the uplands of Central Asia, have no connexion with the sea—shrinks away towards the end of summer, and finally loses itself in the sand, at a place called the Sink. Here, the single trail across the Basin divides into three branches, and the emigrants, leaving the scanty meadows about the Sink, have before them an arid desert, varying from fifty to eighty miles in breadth, according to the route which they take. Many companies, on arriving at this place, were obliged to stop and recruit their exhausted animals, though exposed to the danger of being detained there the whole winter, from the fall of snow on the Sierra Nevada. Another, and very large body of them, took the upper route to Lawson's Pass, which leads to the head of the Sacramento Valley; but the greater part, fortunately, chose the old traveled trails, leading to Bear Creek and the Yuba, by way of Truckee River, and to the head-waters of the Rio Americano by way of Carson's River.

The two latter routes are the shortest and best. After leaving the Sink of Humboldt's River, and crossing a desert of about fifty miles in breadth, the emigrant reaches the streams which are fed from the Sierra Nevada, where he finds good grass and plenty of game. The passes are described as terribly rugged and precipitous, leading directly up the face of the great snowy ridge. As, however, they are not quite eight thousand feet above the sea, and are reached from a plateau of more than four thousand feet, the ascent is comparatively short; while, on the western side, more than a hundred miles of mountain country must be passed, before reaching the level of the Sacramento Valley. There are frequent passes in the Sierra Nevada which were never crossed before the summer of 1849. Some of the emigrants, diverging from the known trail, sought a road for themselves, and found their way down from the snows to the head waters of the Tuolumne, the Calaveras and Feather River. The eastern slope of the Sierra Nevada is but imperfectly explored. All the emigrants concurred in representing it to me as an abrupt and broken region, the higher peaks of barren granite, the valleys deep and narrow, yet in many places timbered with pine and cedar of immense growth.

After passing the dividing ridge,—the descent from which was rendered almost impossible by precipices and steeps of naked rock —about thirty miles of alternate cañons and divides lay between the emigrants and the nearest diggings. The steepness of the slopes of this range is hardly equalled by any other mountains in the world. The rivers seem to wind their way through the bottoms of chasms, and in many places it is impossible to get down to the water. The word cañon (meaning, in Spanish, a funnel,) has a peculiar adaptation to these cleft channels through which the rivers are poured. In getting down from the summit ridge the emigrants told me they were frequently obliged to take the oxen from the wagon and lower it with ropes; but for the sheer descents which followed, another plan was adopted. The wheels were all locked, and only one yoke of oxen left in front; a middling-sized pine was then cut down, and the butt fastened to the axle-tree, the branchy top dragging on the earth. The holding back of the oxen, the sliding of the locked wheels, and the resistance of the tree together formed an opposing power sufficient to admit of a slow descent; but it was necessary to observe great care lest the pace should be quickened, for the slightest start would have overcome the resistance and given oxen, wagon and tree together a momentum that would have landed them at the bottom in a very different condition.

In August, before his departure for Oregon, Gen. Smith took the responsibility of ordering pack-mules and supplies to be provided at the expense of Government, and gave Major Rucker orders to dispatch relief companies into the Great Basin to succor the emigrants who might be remaining there, for want of provisions to advance further. In this step he was also warmly seconded by Gen. Riley, and the preparations were made with the least possible delay. Public meetings of the citizens of San Francisco were also held, to contribute means of relief. Major Rucker dispatched a party with supplies and fresh animals by way of the Truckee River route to the Sink of Humboldt's River, while he took the expedition to Pitt River and Lawson's Pass, under his own command. The first party, after furnishing provisions on the road to all whom they found in need, reached the Sink, and started the families who were still encamped there, returning with them by the Carson River route and bringing in the last of the emigration, only a day or two before the heavy snows came on, which entirely blocked up the passes. But for this most timely aid, hundreds of persons must have perished by famine and cold.

Those who took the trail for Lawson's Pass fared even worse. They had been grossly deceived with regard to the route, which, instead of being a nearer passage into California, is actually two hundred miles longer than the other routes, and though there is no ridge of equal height to be crossed, the amount of rough mountain travel is even greater. The trail, after crossing the Sierra by a low gap, (which has lately been mentioned in connection with the Pacific Railroad,) enters the Valley of Pitt River, one of the tributaries of the Upper Sacramento. Following the course of this river for about ninety miles, it reaches a spur of the Sierra Nevada, which runs from the head waters of Feather River to near the Shaste Peak, closing up the level of the lower Sacramento Valley. These mountains are from five to six thousand feet in height and rugged in the extreme, and over them the weary emigrant must pass before the Land of Promise—the rich Valley of the Sacramento—meets his view.

At the time I returned to Sacramento City, Major Rucker had just returned from his expedition. He found a large body of emigrants scattered along Pitt River, many of them entirely destitute of provisions and others without their animals, which the predatory Indians of that region had stolen. Owing to the large number who required his assistance, he was obliged to return to the ranches on Deer Creek and procure further supplies, leaving Mr. Peoples to hurry them on meanwhile. Everything was done to hasten their movement, but a strange and unaccountable apathy seemed to have taken possession of them. The season was late, and a single day added to the time requisite to get them into the Sacramento Valley might prove ruinous to them and their assistants. . . .

. . .

It happened to the emigrants as Major Rucker had forewarned them. A letter from Mr. Peoples, which he received during my stay, gave a most striking account of the hardships to which they had subjected themselves. A violent storm came on while they were crossing the mountains to Deer Creek, and the mules, unaccustomed to the severe cold, sank down and died one after another. In spite of their remonstrances, Mr. Peoples obliged them to leave their wagons and hurry forward with the remaining animals. The women, who seemed to have far more energy and endurance than the men, were mounted on mules, and the whole party pushed on through the bleak passes of the mountains in the face of a raging storm. By extraordinary exertions, they were all finally brought into the Sacramento Valley, with the loss of many wagons and animals. On receiving this letter, Major Rucker set out for Lawson's Ranche on Deer Creek, where he saw the emigrants comfortably established for the winter. They had erected log-houses for shelter; the flour supplied to them from the Government stores and cattle from the large herds on the neighboring ranches, furnished them with the means of subsistence. The return to Sacramento City, in the depth of the rainy season, was an almost impossible undertaking.

The greater part of those who came in by the lower routes, started, after a season of rest, for the mining region, where many of them arrived in time to build themselves log huts for the winter. Some pitched their tents along the river, to wait for the genial spring season; while not a few took their axes and commenced the business of wood-cutting in the timber on its banks. When shipped to San Francisco, the wood, which they took with the usual freedom of Uncle Sam's nephews, brought $40 a cord; the steamboats which called for it on their trips up and down, paid $15. By the end of December the last man of the overland companies was safe on the western side of the Sierra Nevada, and the great interior wilderness resumed its ancient silence and solitude until the next spring.

THE DIGGINGS ON MOKELUMNE RIVER

Our first move was for the river bottom, where a number of Americans, Sonorians, Kanakas and French were at work in the hot sun. The bar, as it was called, was nothing more nor less than a level space at the junction of the river with a dry arroyo or "gulch," which winds for about eight miles among the hills. It was hard and rocky, with no loose sand except such as had lodged between the large masses of stone, which must of course be thrown aside to get at the gold. The whole space, containing about four acres, appeared to have been turned over with great labor, and all the holes slanting down between the broken strata of slate, to have been explored to the bottom. No spot could appear more unpromising to the inexperienced gold-hunter. Yet the Sonorians, washing out the loose dust and dirt which they scraped up among the rocks, obtained from $10 to two ounces daily. The first party we saw had just succeeded in cutting a new channel for the shrunken waters of the Mokelumne, and were commencing operations on about twenty yards of the river-bed, which they had laid bare. They were ten in number, and their only implements were shovels, a rude cradle for the top layer of earth, and flat wooden bowls for washing out the sands. Baptiste took one of the bowls which was full of sand, and in five minutes showed us a dozen grains of bright gold. The company had made in the forenoon about three pounds; we watched them at their work till the evening, when three pounds more were produced, making an average of seven ounces for each man. The gold was of the purest quality and most beautiful color. When I first saw the men, carrying heavy stones in the sun, standing nearly waist-deep in water, and grubbing with their hands in the gravel and clay, there seemed to me little virtue in resisting the temptation to gold digging; but when the shining particles were poured out lavishly from a tin basin, I confess there was a sudden itching in my fingers to seize the heaviest crowbar and the biggest shovel.

. . .

After we had taken the sharp edge off our curiosity, we returned to our quarters. Dr. Gillette, Mr. James, Captain Tracy and several other of the miners entertained us with a hospitality as gratifying as it was unexpected. In the evening we sat down to a supper prepared by Baptiste and his partner, Mr. Fisher, which completed my astonishment at the resources of that wonderful land. There, in the rough depth of the hills, where three weeks before there was scarcely a tent, and where we expected to live on jerked beef and bread, we saw on the table green corn, green peas and beans, fresh oysters, roast turkey, fine Goshen butter and excellent coffee. I will not pretend to say what they cost, but I began to think that the fable of Aladdin was nothing very remarkable, after all. The genie will come, and had come to many whom I saw in California; but the rubbing of the lamp—aye, there's the rub. There is nothing in the world so hard on the hands.

. . .

Wherever there is gold, there are gamblers. Our little village boasted of at least a dozen monte tables, all of which were frequented at night by the Americans and Mexicans. The Sonorians left a large portion of their gold at the gaming tables, though it was calculated they had taken $5,000,000 out of the country during the summer. The excitement against them prevailed also on the Mokelumne, and they were once driven away; they afterwards quietly returned, and in most cases worked in companies, for the benefit and under the protection of some American. They labor steadily and faithfully, and are considered honest, if well watched. The first colony of gold-hunters attempted to drive out all foreigners, without distinction, as well as native Californians. Don Andres Pico, who was located on the same river, had some difficulty with them until they could be made to understand that his right as a citizen was equal to theirs.

Dr. Gillette, to whom we were indebted for many kind attentions, related to me the manner of his finding the rich gulch which attracted so many to the Mokelumne Diggings. The word *gulch*, which is in general use throughout the diggings, may not be familiar to many ears, though its sound somehow expresses its meaning, without further definition. It denotes a mountain ravine, differing from ravines elsewhere as the mountains of California differ from all others—more steep, abrupt and inaccessible. The sound of *gulch* is like that of a sudden plunge into a deep hole, which is just the character of the thing itself. It bears the same relation to a ravine that a "cañon" does to a pass or gorge. About two months previous to our arrival, Dr. Gillette came down from the Upper Bar with a companion, to "prospect" for gold among the ravines in the neighborhood. There were no persons there at the time, except some Indians belonging to the tribe of José Jesus. One day at noon, while resting in the shade of a tree, Dr. G. took a pick and began carelessly turning up the ground. Almost on the surface, he struck and threw out a lump of gold of about two pounds weight. Inspired by this unexpected result, they both went to work, laboring all that day and the next, and even using part of the night to quarry out the heavy pieces of rock. At the end of the second day they went to the village on the Upper Bar and weighed their profits, which amounted to fourteen pounds! They started again the third morning under pretence of hunting, but were suspected and followed by the other diggers, who came upon them just as they commenced work. The news rapidly spread, and there was soon a large number of men on the spot, some of whom obtained several pounds per day, at the start. The gulch had been well dug up for the large lumps, but there was still great wealth in the earth and sand, and several operators only waited for the wet season to work it in a systematic manner.

. . .

There was no end to the stories told by the diggers, of their own and others' experiences in gold-hunting. I could readily have made up a small volume from those I heard during the four days I spent on the Mokelumne. In the dry diggings especially, where the metal frequently lies deep, many instances are told of men who have dug two or three days and given up in despair, while others, coming after them and working in the same holes, have taken out thousands of dollars in a short time. I saw a man who came to the river three weeks before my visit, without money, to dig in the dry gulch. Being very lazy, he chose a spot under a shady tree, and dug leisurely for two days without making a cent. He then gave up the place, when a little German jumped into his tracks and after a day's hard work weighed out $800. The unlucky digger then borrowed five ounces and started a boardinghouse. The town increased so fast that the night I arrived he sold out his share (one-third) of the concern for $1,200. Men were not troubled by the ordinary ups and downs of business, when it was so easy for one of any enterprise to recover his foothold. If a person lost his all, he was perfectly indifferent; two weeks of hard work gave him enough to start on, and two months, with the usual luck, quite reinstated him.

. . .

From all I saw and heard, while at the Mokelumne Diggings, I judged there was as much order and security as could be attained without a civil organization. The inhabitants had elected one of their own number Alcalde, before whom all culprits were tried by a jury selected for the purpose. Several thefts had occurred, and the offending parties been severely punished after a fair trial. Some had been whipped and cropped, or maimed in some other way, and one or two of them hung. Two or three who had stolen largely had been shot down by the injured party, the general feeling among the miners justifying such a course when no other seemed available. We met near Livermore's Ranche, on the way to Stockton, a man whose head had been shaved and his ears cut off, after receiving one hundred lashes, for stealing ninety-eight pounds of gold. It may conflict with popular ideas of morality, but, nevertheless, this extreme course appeared to have produced good results. In fact, in a country without not only bolts and bars, but any effective system of law and government, this Spartan severity of discipline seemed the only security against the most frightful dis-

order. The result was that, except some petty
acts of larceny, thefts were rare. Horses and
mules were sometimes taken, but the risk was
so great that such plunder could not be carried on to any extent. The camp or tent was
held inviolate, and like the patriarchal times
of old, its cover protected all it enclosed.
Among all well-disposed persons there was a
tacit disposition to make the canvas or pavilion
10 of rough oak-boughs as sacred as once were
the portals of a church.

. . .

MINING CHARACTERS

. . . During the few days I spent on the
Mokelumne, I had an opportunity of becoming
acquainted with many curious characteristics
20 and incidents of mining life. It would have
been an interesting study for a philosopher, to
note the different effects which sudden enrichment produced upon different persons, especially those whose lives had previously been
passed in the midst of poverty and privation.
The most profound scholar in human nature
might here have learned something which all
his previous wisdom and experience could
never teach. It was not precisely the develop-
30 ment of new qualities in the man, but the exhibition of changes and contrasts of character,
unexpected and almost unaccountable. The
world-old moral of gold was completely falsified. Those who were unused to labor, whose
daily ounce or two seemed a poor recompense
for weary muscles and flagging spirits, might
carefully hoard their gains; but they whose
hardy fibre grappled with the tough earth as
naturally as if it knew no fitter play, and made
40 the coarse gravel and rocky strata yield up their
precious grains, were as profuse as princes and
as open-hearted as philanthropists. Weather-
beaten tars, wiry, delving Irishmen, and stalwart foresters from the wilds of Missouri, became a race of sybarites and epicureans. Secure
in possessing the "Open Sesamé" to the exhaustless treasury under their feet, they gave
free rein to every whim or impulse which could
49 possible be gratified.

. . .

There was one character on the river,
whom I had met on my first visit in August and
still found there on my return. He possessed

sufficient individuality of appearance and habits to have made him a hero of fiction; Cooper
would have delighted to have stumbled upon
him. His real name I never learned, but he was
known to all the miners by the cognomen of
"Buckshot"—an appellation which seemed to
suit his hard, squat figure very well. He might
have been forty years of age or perhaps fifty;
his face was but slightly wrinkled, and he
wore a heavy black beard which grew nearly
to his eyes and entirely concealed his mouth.
When he removed his worn and dusty felt hat,
which was but seldom, his large, square forehead, bald crown and serious gray eyes gave
him an appearance of reflective intellect;—a
promise hardly verified by his conversation. He
was of a stout and sturdy frame, and always
wore clothes of a coarse texture, with a flannel
shirt and belt containing a knife. I guessed
from a slight peculiarity of his accent that he
was a German by birth, though I believe he
was not considered so by the miners.

The habits of "Buckshot" were still more eccentric than his appearance. He lived entirely
alone, in a small tent, and seemed rather to
shun than court the society of others. His tastes
were exceedingly luxurious; he always had the
best of everything in the market, regardless of
its cost. The finest hams, at a dollar and a half
the pound; preserved oysters, corn and peas,
at six dollars a canister; onions and potatoes,
whenever such articles made their appearance;
Chinese sweetmeats and dried fruits, were all
on his table, and his dinner was regularly
moistened by a bottle of champagne. He did
his own cooking, an operation which cost little
trouble, on account of the scarcity of fresh
provisions. When particularly lucky in digging,
he would take his ease for a day or two, until
the dust was exhausted, when he would again
shoulder his pick and crowbar and commence
burrowing in some lonely corner of the rich
gulch. He had been in the country since the
first discovery of the placers, and was reported
to have dug, in all, between thirty and forty
thousand dollars,—all of which he had spent
for his subsistence. I heard him once say that
he never dug less than an ounce in one day,
and sometimes as much as two pounds. The
rough life of the mountains seemed entirely
congenial to his tastes, and he could not have
been induced to change it for any other,
though less laborious and equally epicurean.

. . .

SOCIETY IN CALIFORNIA

There are some features of Society in California, which I have hitherto failed to touch upon in my narrative, but which deserve a passing notice before I take my final leave of that wonderful land. The direct effect of the state of things growing out of the discovery of the placers, was to develop new qualities and traits of character, not in single individuals, but in every individual of the entire community—traits frequently most unlooked-for in those who exhibited them in the most marked degree. Society, therefore, was for the time cast into new forms, or, rather, deprived of any fixed form. A man, on coming to California, could no more expect to retain his old nature unchanged, than he could retain in his lungs the air he had inhaled on the Atlantic shore.

The most immediate and striking change which came upon the greater portion of the emigrants was an increase of activity, and proportionately, of reckless and daring spirit. It was curious to see how men hitherto noted for their prudence and caution took sudden leave of those qualities, to all appearance, yet only prospered the more thereby. Perhaps there was at bottom a vein of keen, shrewd calculation, which directed their seemingly heedless movements; certain it is, at least, that for a long time the rashest speculators were the most fortunate. It was this fact, no doubt, that seemed so alarming to persons newly-arrived, and gave rise to unnumbered predictions of the speedy and ruinous crash of the whole business fabric of San Francisco. But nothing is more contagious than this spirit of daring and independent action, and the most doleful prophets were, ere long, swallowed up in the same whirlpool against which they had warned others.

The emigrants who arrive in California, very soon divide into two distinct classes. About two-thirds, or possibly three-fourths of them are active, hopeful and industrious. They feel this singular intoxication of society, and go to work at something, no matter what, by which they hope to thrive. The remaining portion see everything "through a glass, darkly." Their first bright anticipations are unrealized; the horrid winds of San Francisco during the dry season, chill and unnerve them: or, if they go to the placers, the severe labor and the ill success of inexperienced hands, completes their disgust. They commit a multitude of sins in the shape of curses upon every one who has written or spoken favorably of California. Some of them return home without having seen the country at all, and others, even if they obtain profitable situations, labor without a will. It is no place for a slow, and over-cautious, or a desponding man. The emigrant should be willing to work, not only at one business, but many, if need be; the grumbler or the idler had far better stay at home.

It cannot be denied that the very activity of California society created a spirit of excitement which frequently led to dangerous excesses. The habits of the emigrants, never, even at home, very slow and deliberate, branched into all kinds of wild offshoots, the necessary effect of the sudden glow and expansion which they experienced. Those who retained their health seemed to revel in an exuberance of animal spirits, which carried them with scarce a jar over barriers and obstacles that would have brought others to a full stand. There was something exceedingly hearty, cordial and encouraging in the character of social intercourse. The ordinary forms of courtesy were flung aside with a bluntness of good-fellowship infinitely preferable, under the circumstances. I was constantly reminded of the stories of Northern History—of the stout Vikings and Jarls who exulted in their very passions and made their heroes of those who were most jovial at the feast and most easily kindled with the rage of battle. Indeed, it required but little effort of the imagination to revive those iron ages, when the rugged gold-diggers, with their long hair and unshorn beards, were grouped around some mountain camp-fire, revelling in the ruddy light and giving full play to a mirth so powerful and profound that it would not have shamed the Berserkers.

The most common excesses into which the Californians run, are drinking and gambling. I say drinking, rather than drunkenness, for I saw very little of the latter. But a single case came under my observation while I was in the gold region. The man's friends took away his money and deposited it in the hands of the Alcalde, then tied him to a tree where they left him till he became sober. The practice of drinking, nevertheless, was widely prevalent, and its effects rendered more destructive by the large amount of bad liquor which was sent into the country. Gambling, in spite of a uni-

versal public sentiment against it, grew and
flourished; the disappointment and ruin of
many emigrants were owing to its existence.
The gamblers themselves were in many instances men who had led orderly and respectable lives at home. I have heard some of them
frankly avow that nothing would induce them
to acquaint their friends and families with the
nature of their occupation; they would soon
have enough, they said, and then they would
wash their hands of the unclean stain, and go
home to lead more honorable lives. But alas! it
is not so easy to wash out the memory of self-
degradation. If these men have in truth any
sentiment of honor remaining, every coin of
the wealth they have hoarded will awaken a
shameful consciousness of the base and unmanly business by which it was obtained.

In spite, however, of all these dissipating
and disorganizing influences, the main stock of
society was sound, vigorous and progressive.
The rank shoots, while they might have slightly
weakened the trunk, only showed the abundant
life of the root. In short, without wishing to be
understood as apologizing in any degree for the
evils which existed, it was evident that had the
Californians been more cool, grave and deliberate in their temperament—had they
lacked the fiery energy and impulsive spirit
which pushed them irresistibly forward—the
dangers which surrounded them at the outset
would have been far more imminent. Besides,
this energy did not run at random; it was in the
end directed by an enlightened experience, and
that instinct of Right, which is the strength and
security of a self-governed People. Hundreds
of instances might be adduced to show that the
worst passions of our nature were speedily developed in the air of California, but the one
grand lesson of the settlement and organization
of the country is of a character that ennobles
the race.

The unanimity with which all united in this
work—the frankness with which the old prejudices of sect and party were disclaimed—the
freshly-awakened pride of country, which

made every citizen jealously and disinterest-
edly anxious that she should acquit herself
honorably in the eyes of the Nation at large
—formed a spectacle which must claim our
entire admiration. In view of the splendid future which is opening for California,
it insures her a stable foundation on which
to build the superstructure of her wealth and
power.

After what has been said, it will appear
natural that California should be the most
democratic country in the world. The practical
equality of all the members of a community,
whatever might be the wealth, intelligence or
profession of each, was never before thoroughly demonstrated. Dress was no guage of
respectability, and no honest occupation, however menial in its character, affected a man's
standing. Lawyers, physicians and ex-profes-
sors dug cellars, drove ox-teams, sawed wood
and carried luggage; while men who had been
Army privates, sailors, cooks or day laborers
were at the head of profitable establishments
and not infrequently assisted in some of the
minor details of Government. A man who
would consider his fellow beneath him, on account of his appearance or occupation, would
have had some difficulty in living peaceably in
California. The security of the country is owing, in no small degree, to this plain, practical
development of what the French reverence as
an abstraction, under the name of *Fraternité*.
To sum up all in three words, LABOR IS RE-
SPECTABLE: may it never be otherwise, while
a grain of gold is left to glitter in Californian
soil!

I have dwelt with the more earnestness on
these features of Society because they do not
seem to be fully appreciated on this side of
the Continent. I cannot take leave, in the
regular course of my narrative, of a land where
I found so much in Nature to admire and enjoy, without attempting to give some general,
though imperfect view of Man, as he appeared under those new and wonderful influences.   1850

JOHN CODMAN

1814–1900

JOHN CODMAN, whose father was an orthodox Congregationalist minister in Dorchester, spent two years at Amherst College before taking to the sea in a clipper ship. He followed the life of a sailor through many decades. He also knew and loved the Far West: for a time he owned an Idaho ranch. Codman's books, written in forceful prose, include *Sailors' Life and Sailors' Yarns* (1847), *The Round Trip* (1879), and *An American Transport in the Crimean War* (1896).

Codman's account of the Mormons in Utah is representative of the views held by many Gentiles who had some firsthand acquaintance with their headquarters at Salt Lake. Such accounts as Codman's were eagerly read by moral and pious Easterners who regarded polygamy as a blot on the national scutcheon.

Dictionary of American Biography, IV, 259.

» » *From:* THE MORMON COUNTRY « «

MORMON DOCTRINES

Of the Mormon sect it may be truly said, as of every other Christian organization, and of Christianity itself, that "the blood of the Martyrs is the seed of the Church." If Mormonism had been left to itself, it would have died like thousands of other wild extravagances that have cropped out in the ages, expiring from want of the air stirred up by the fan of persecution.

It was a harmless little beast in its infancy, but its enemies evoked the spirit of the devil wherewith to defend itself.

What could be more simple and inoffensive than the creed promulgated by Joe Smith in 1842?

1. We believe in God, the eternal Father, and in His Son, Jesus Christ, and in the Holy Ghost.
2. We believe that men will be punished for their own sins, and not for Adam's transgression.
3. We believe that through the atonement of Christ all mankind may be saved by obedience to the laws and ordinances of the Gospel.
4. We believe that these ordinances are: first, Faith in the Lord Jesus Christ; second, Repentance; third, Baptism by immersion for the remission of sins; fourth, Laying on of hands for the gift of the Holy Ghost.

5. We believe that a man must be called of God by "prophecy and by laying on of hands" by those who are in authority to preach the Gospel, and administer in the ordinances thereof.
6. We believe in the same organization that existed in the primitive church, viz.: apostles, prophets, pastors, teachers, evangelists, etc., etc.
7. We believe in the gift of tongues, prophecy, revelation, visions, healing, interpretations of tongues, etc.
8. We believe the Bible to be the word of God, as far as it is translated correctly. We also believe the Book of Mormon to be the word of God.
9. We believe all that God has revealed, and that He does now reveal, and we believe that He will yet reveal many great and important things pertaining to the Kingdom of God.
10. We believe in the literal gathering of Israel and of the restoration of the Ten Tribes; that Zion will be built upon this continent; that Christ will reign personally upon the earth, and that the earth will be renewed and receive its Paradisiac glory.
11. We claim the privilege of worshipping Almighty God according to the dictates of our conscience, and allow all men the same privilege, let them worship how, where, or what they may.
12. We believe in being subject to kings, presidents, rulers, and magistrates, in obeying, honoring, and sustaining the law.
13. We believe in being honest, true, chaste, benevolent, virtuous, and in doing good to all men;

indeed we may say that we follow the admonition of Paul, "We believe all things, hope all things." We have endured many things, and hope to be able to endure all things. If there is anything virtuous, lovely, or of good report or praiseworthy, we seek after these things.　　　JOSEPH SMITH.

Why, even the Evangelical Alliance, that refused to spread its holy skirts over Roman Catholics, because they believe too much, and over Unitarians because they believe too little, could scarcely have objected to receive the Mormons into their fold!

That ninth article is the only one which really means mischief to society. This has opened the door to innovations which have pushed Mormonism into such a remote corner of Christ's vineyard that it is unknown as still a part of it to those who walk in its beaten paths.

In accordance with the faith expressed in Article 9, "Many great and important things pertaining to the kingdom of God" have been since revealed, and there is still room for more revelations.

Some of the new doctrines are harmless enough, and the only ones which really clash with outside civilization, and come in contact with the laws of the land, are those of "blood-atonement" and polygamy.

One of the most absurd—on which I heard a most elaborate sermon preached—is that of "baptism for the dead." The text was 1st Corinthians, xv. 29: "Else what shall they do, which are baptized for the dead, if the dead rise not at all? Why, are they then baptized for the dead?"

As this text has always been a puzzle for theologians of every stripe, it was for the Mormons to have a "revelation" which should unravel it. So it was revealed that all baptisms since the time of the apostles until the advent of Joe Smith being null and void, the only way in which the intervening generations could inherit salvation is by the proxy baptism of their descendants.

Devout Mormons accordingly are critical students of genealogy, hunting up their ancestors as far back as possible, and getting repeatedly immersed to save their souls.

Alas, how few can trace beyond their grandparents! Many cannot go into antiquity beyond their fathers, and there are unfortunate people who cannot look backwards even so far as that. At best, some proud Briton is able to prove that his progenitors "came over with William the Conqueror."

In such a family an extraordinary number of souls may be rescued from purgatory by the repeated immersions of their descendants. But even in these cases the intervening generations for many hundred years must perish. How much more sad is the fate of the great average of Mormon ancestry!

The next doctrine in the order of absurdity, and one closely allied to the foregoing, is that of proxy-marriage for the dead. The marriage ceremony, since the days of the apostles, having been performed by priests who had not received the proper "laying-on of the hands," is considered invalid, and consequently all the progeny of the people so united is illegitimate in the eye of Heaven.

But this reproach is to be taken away by a process somewhat similar to the baptism for the dead. The Mormon of the present is to stand up and be married for his ancestors, and thus make their marriages legal. The confused condition of society which has heretofore existed in the spirit-world will be brought into order. Husbands and wives who have been separated for fifteen or sixteen centuries will be reunited, and will again beget children in heaven; for it is a Mormon tenet that marriages contracted by Latter-Day Saints on earth, or those thus legalized above, are eternally continuous—that men and women there have the same flesh and blood of which they are here made, and are possessed of the same animal natures.

Consequently the propagation of the human race will be continued, and as myriads of new beings are thus called into existence, new worlds upon worlds will be created for their occupation, and this reproduction of men and worlds will continue throughout eternity.

There are innumerable vagaries besides these into which run the crazy imaginations of the prophets, induced by dreams, begotten perhaps by indigestion, but which they call visions or revelations.

Many of their doctrines are so materialistic that they seem blasphemous to us. Founding their belief on the declaration of the Almighty that He would make men "after His own image," they say that the great First Cause is Himself a being of flesh and blood; so is Christ, and so is the Holy Ghost; so are all the Angels, and so are all the redeemed among men.

"God," they say, was literally "the father of our Lord Jesus Christ." Christ himself was, although a divine being, a married man—and Martha and Mary were His wives because "He loved them"—and He must have had children; "for who shall declare his generation?"

These and other wild extravagances are the results of that pernicious article ninth of Joe Smith's creed, which allows future revelations to instil new doctrines. The Book of Mormon, chiefly purporting to be a history, does not authorize them. They are all modern improvements.

Now, I do not suppose that it is of the least possible consequence to other people whether the Mormons continue to believe or renounce them. It is no man's business what another man believes, so long as that belief is not practically injurious to society. The only thing which concerns us is that the life and property of every man, woman, and child, so far as the laws of the United States can control them, shall be as secure in Utah as in any other State or Territory of the Union,—and they are.

The "blood-atonement" is no more advocated as it once was in the Mormon pulpit. When it was preached and practised to such a fearful extent as formerly, it was a barbarism worse than slavery or polygamy. No man's life was safe under its rule. It was held justifiable to slay an apostate—not, remember, from revenge, but for the good of his own soul! Nay, more, apostates who desired to return to the church, and others who had committed deadly offences, often had upon their consciences such weights of unforgiven sin, that despairing of heaven without the "remission by the shedding of blood," they have surrendered themselves to be sacrificed by their friends; and these wretched fanatics have murdered their brothers to save their souls!

A most horrible, and I fear too true a story, is told of a refined and beautiful woman in Salt Lake City who had been unfaithful to her husband, and who came to him confessing her sin, obtained his forgiveness, gave and received a farewell kiss, and then he coolly cut her throat in order that the blood-atonement might procure for her "an exaltation," and that they might be again united in heaven!

Fortunately, this horrible doctrine, having escaped the notice of politicians and newspapers in their attention to polygamy, is dying a natural death. In years gone by it has been the instigator of great wrong and suffering.

1874

JOHN WESLEY POWELL

1834–1902

REARED IN upstate New York and in the Middle West, Powell, the son of an English-born Methodist exhorter, became absorbed in the amateur study of the botany of Illinois. His remarkable collections brought him in touch with scientific men; but the Civil War, in which he served as an officer, interrupted the pursuit of this interest. Subsequently, as a teacher in Illinois colleges, he conducted parties of students and naturalists to Colorado. With the aid of the Smithsonian Institution and small appropriations from Congress, Powell explored (1869–1875) the geology of the Colorado River, its tributaries, and the Grand Canyon. His geological theories were of general significance and his description, from which the following excerpt is taken, is a classic in the literature of the scientific exploration of the Great West. Later, as the administrator of the Geological Survey of the federal government, Powell promoted work leading to a significant series of topographic maps. In the movement for the reclamation and forestation of arid land, he was a pioneer. Powell's observations in ethnography also gave him a place in that field. But his versatility did not stop with the field of natural science. Interested in epistomology, he published in 1898 *Truth and Error, or the Science of the Intellect.*

Wallace Stegner, *Beyond the Hundredth Meridian. John Wesley Powell and the Second Opening of the West,* Boston, 1953

» » *From:* EXPLORATION OF THE COLORADO RIVER « « OF THE WEST

CHAPTER VIII

THE GRAND CANYON OF THE COLORADO

August 13.—We are now ready to start on our way down the Great Unknown. Our boats, tied to a common stake, are chafing each other, as they are tossed by the fretful river. They 10 ride high and buoyant, for their loads are lighter than we could desire. We have but a month's rations remaining. The flour has been resifted through the mosquito net sieve; the spoiled bacon has been dried, and the worst of it boiled; the few pounds of dried apples have been spread in the sun, and reshrunken to their normal bulk; the sugar has all melted, and gone on its way down the river; but we have a large sack of coffee. The lighting of the 20 boats has this advantage: they will ride the waves better, and we shall have but little to carry when we make a portage.

We are three quarters of a mile in the depths of the earth, and the great river shrinks into insignificance, as it dashes its angry waves against the walls and cliffs, that rise to the world above; they are but puny ripples, and we but pigmies, running up and down the sands, or lost among the boulders.

30 We have an unknown distance yet to run; an unknown river yet to explore. What falls there are, we know not; what rocks beset the channel, we know not; what walls rise over the river, we know not. Ah, well! we may conjecture many things. The men talk as cheerfully as ever; jests are bandied about freely this morning; but to me the cheer is somber and the jests are ghastly.

・ ・ ・

41 *August 14.*—. . . The walls, now, are more than a mile in height—a vertical distance difficult to appreciate. Stand on the south steps of the Treasury building, in Washington, and look down Pennsylvania Avenue to the Capitol Park, and measure this distance overhead, and imagine cliffs to extend to that altitude, and you will understand what I mean; or, stand at Canal street, in New York, and look up Broadway to Grace Church, and you have about the distance; or, stand at Lake street bridge, in Chicago, and look down to the Central Depot, and you have it again.

A thousand feet of this is up through granite crags, then steep slopes and perpendicular cliffs rise, one above another, to the summit. The gorge is black and narrow below, red and gray and flaring above, with crags and angular projections on the walls, which, cut in many places by side canons, seem to be a vast wilderness of rocks. Down in these grand, gloomy depths we glide, ever listening, for the mad waters keep up their roar; ever watching, ever peering ahead, for the narrow cañon is winding, and the river is closed in so that we can see but a few hundred yards, and what there may be below we know not; but we listen for falls, and watch for rocks, or stop now and then, in the bay of a recess, to admire the gigantic scenery. And ever, as we go, there is some new pinnacle or tower, some crag or peak, some distant view of the upper plateau, some strange shaped rock, or some deep, narrow side cañon. Then we come to another broken fall, which appears more difficult than the one we ran this morning.

・ ・ ・

August 15.—This morning we find we can let down for three or four hundred yards, and it is managed in this way: We pass along the wall, by climbing from projecting point to point, sometimes near the water's edge, at other places fifty or sixty feet above, and hold the boat with a line, while two men remain aboard, and prevent her from being dashed against the rocks, and keep the line from getting caught on the wall. In two hours we have brought them all down, as far as it is possible, in this way. A few yards below, the river strikes with great violence against a projecting rock, and our boats are pulled up in a little bay above. We must now manage to pull out of this, and clear the point below. The little boat is held by the bow obliquely up the stream. We jump in, and pull out only a few strokes, and sweep clear of the dangerous rock. The other boats follow in the same manner, and the rapid is passed.

It is not easy to describe the labor of such navigation. We must prevent the waves from dashing the boats against the cliffs. Sometimes, where the river is swift, we must put a bight of rope about a rock, to prevent her being snatched from us by a wave; but where the plunge is too great, or the chute too swift, we must let her leap, and catch her below, or the undertow will drag her under the falling water, and she sinks. Where we wish to run her out a little way from shore, through a channel between rocks, we first throw in little sticks of driftwood, and watch their course, to see where we must steer, so that she will pass the channel in safety. And so we hold, and let go, and pull, and lift, and ward, among rocks, around rocks, and over rocks.

. . . .

September 5, 1870.—The several members of the party are engaged in general preparation for our trip down the Grand Cañon.

Taking with me a white man and an Indian, I start on a climb to the summit of the Pouns-á-gunt Plateau, which rises above us on the east. Our way, for a mile or more, is over a great peat bog, that trembles under our feet, and now and then a mule sinks through the broken turf, and we are compelled to pull it out with ropes.

Passing the bog, our way is up a gulch, at the foot of the Pink Cliffs, which form the escarpment, or wall, of the great plateau. Soon we leave the gulch, and climb a long ridge, which winds around to the right toward the summit of the great table.

Two hours' riding, climbing, and clambering brings us near the top. We look below, and see clouds drifting up from the south, rolling tumultously toward the foot of the cliffs, beneath us. Soon, all the country below is covered with a sea of vapor—a billowy, raging, noiseless sea—and as the vapory flood still rolls up from the south, great waves dash against the foot of the cliffs and roll back; another tide comes in, is hurled back, and another

and another, lashing the cliffs until the fog rises to the summit, and covers us all.

There is a heavy pine and fir forest above, beset with dead and fallen timber, and we make our way through the undergrowth to the east.

It rains! The clouds discharge their moisture in torrents, and we make for ourselves shelters of boughs, which are soon abandoned, and we stand shivering by a great fire of pine logs and boughs, which we have kindled, but which the pelting storm half extinguishes.

One, two, three, four hours' of the storm, and at last it partially abates.

During this time our animals, which we have turned loose, have sought for themselves shelter under the trees, and two of them have wandered away beyond our sight. I go out to follow their tracks, and come near to the brink of a ledge of rocks, which, in the fog and mist, I suppose to be a little ridge, and I look for a way by which I can go down. Standing just here, there is a rift made in the fog below, by some current or blast of wind, which reveals an almost bottomless abyss. I look from the brink of a great precipice of more than two thousand feet; but, through the mist, the forms below are half obscured, and all reckoning of distance is lost, and it seems ten thousand feet, ten miles—any distance the imagination desires to make it.

. . . .

September 10.—. . . The Indian name of the cañon is Pa-rú-nu-weap, or Roaring Water Cañon. Between the little river and the foot of the walls, is a dense growth of willows, vines, and wild rose bushes, and, with great difficulty, we make our way through this tangled mass. It is not a wide stream—only twenty or thirty feet across in most places; shallow, but very swift. After spending some hours in breaking our way through the mass of vegetation, and climbing rocks here and there, it is determined to wade along the stream. In some places this is an easy task, but here and there we come to deep holes, where we have to wade to our arm pits. Soon we come to places so narrow that the river fills the entire channel, and we wade perforce. In many places the bottom is a quicksand, into which we sink, and it is with great difficulty that we make progress. In some places the holes are so deep that we have to swim, and our little bundles of blankets and rations are fixed to a raft made of driftwood, and pushed before us. Now and then there is a little flood-plain, on which we can walk, and we cross and recross the stream, and wade along the channel where the water is so swift as to almost carry us off our feet, and we are in danger every moment of being swept down, until night comes on. We estimate we have traveled eight miles to day. We find a little patch of flood-plain, on which there is a huge pile of driftwood and a clump of box-elders, and near by a great stream, which bursts from the rocks—a mammoth spring.

We soon have a huge fire, our clothes are spread to dry, we make a cup of coffee, take out our bread and cheese and dried beef, and enjoy a hearty supper.

The cañon here is about twelve hundred feet deep. It has been very narrow and winding all the way down to this point.

September 11.—Wading again this morning; sinking in the quicksand, swimming the deep waters, and making slow and painful progress where the waters are swift, and the bed of the stream rocky.

. . .

Late in the afternoon, we come to a little clearing in the valley, and see other signs of civilization, and by sundown arrive at the Mormon town of Schunesburg; and here we meet the train, and feast on melons and grapes.

September 12.—Our course, for the last two days, through Pa-rú-nu-weap Cañon, was directly to the west. Another stream comes down from the north, and unites just here at Schunesburg with the main branch of the Rio Virgen. We determine to spend a day in the exploration of this stream. The Indians call the cañon, through which it runs, Mu-koón-tu-weap, or Straight Cañon. Entering this, we have to wade up stream; often the water fills the entire channel, and, although we travel many miles, we find no floodplain, talus, or broken piles of rock at the foot of the cliff. The walls have smooth, plain faces, and are everywhere very regular and vertical for a thousand feet or more, where they seem to break back in shelving slopes to higher altitudes; and everywhere, as we go along, we find springs bursting out at the foot of the walls, and, passing these, the river above becomes steadily smaller; the great bed of red sandstone; as we go up the cañon, it comes to be but a creek, and then a brook. On the western wall of the cañon stand some buttes, towers, and high pinnacled rocks.

Going up the cañon, we gain glimpses of them, here and there. Last summer, after our trip through the cañons of the Colorado, on our way from the mouth of the Virgen to Salt Lake City, these were seen as conspicuous landmarks, from a distance, away to the southwest, of sixty or seventy miles. These tower rocks are known as the Temples of the Virgen.

Having explored this cañon nearly to its head, we return to Schunesburg, arriving quite late at night.

. . .

September 19.—We are tired and sore, and must rest a day with our Indian neighbors. During the inclement season they live in shelters, made of boughs, or bark of the cedar, which they strip off in long shreds. In this climate, most of the year is dry and warm, and during such time they do not care for shelter. Clearing a small, circular space of ground, they bank it around with brush and sand, and wallow in it during the day, and huddle together in a heap at night, men, women, and children; buckskin, rags, and sand. They wear very little clothing, not needing much in this lovely climate.

Altogether, these Indians are more nearly in their primitive condition than any others on the continent with whom I am acquainted. They have never received anything from the Government, and are too poor to tempt the trader, and their country is so nearly inaccessible that the white man never visits them. The sunny mountain side is covered with wild fruits, nuts, and native grains, upon which they subsist. The oose, the fruit of the yucca, or Spanish bayonet, is rich, and not unlike the paw-paw of the valley of the Ohio. They eat it raw, and also roast it in the ashes. They gather the fruits of a cactus plant, which is rich and luscious, and eat them as grapes, or from them express the juice, making the dry pulp into cakes, and saving them for winter; the wine they drink about their camp fires, until the midnight is merry with their revelries.

. . .

There is little game in the country, yet they get a mountain sheep now and then, or a deer, with their arrows, for they are not yet supplied with guns. They get many rabbits, sometimes with arrows, sometimes with nets. They make a net of twine, made of the fibers of a native flax. Sometimes this is made a hundred yards in length, and is placed in a half circular position, with wings of sage brush. They have a circle hunt, and drive great numbers of rabbits into the snare, where they are shot with arrows. Most of their bows are made of cedar, but the best are made of the horns of mountain sheep. These are taken, soaked in water, until quite soft, cut into long thin strips, and glued together, and are then quite elastic. During the autumn, grasshoppers are very abundant. When cold weather sets in, these insects are numbed, and can be gathered by the bushel. At such a time, they dig a hole in the sand, heat stones in a fire near by, put some in the bottom of the hole, put on a layer of grasshoppers, then a layer of hot stones, and continue this, until they put bushels on to roast. There they are left until cool, when they are taken out, thoroughly dried, and ground into meal. Grasshopper gruel, or grasshopper cake, is a great treat.

Their lore consists in a mass of traditions, or mythology. It is very difficult to induce them to tell it to white men; but the old Spanish priests, in the days of the conquest of New Mexico, have spread among the Indians of this country many Bible stories, which the Indians are usually willing to tell. It is not always easy to recognize them, the Indian mind being a strange receptacle for such stories, and they are apt to sprout new limbs. May be much of their added quaintness is due to the way in which they were told by the "fathers." But in a confidential way, while you are alone, or when you are admitted to their camp fire on a winter night, you will hear the stories of their mythology. I believe that the greatest mark of friendship, or confidence, that an Indian can give, is to tell you his religion. After one has so talked with me, I should ever trust him; and I feel on very good terms with these Indians, since our experience of the other night.

A knowledge of the watering places, and of the trails and passes, is considered of great importance, and is necessary, to give standing to a chief.

This evening, the Shí-vwits, for whom we have sent, come in, and, after supper, we hold a long council. A blazing fire is built, and around this we sit—the Indians living here, the Shí-vwits, Jacob Hamblin, and myself. This man, Hamblin, speaks their language well, and has a great influence over all the Indians in the region round about. He is a silent, reserved man, and when he speaks, it is in a slow, quiet way, that inspires great awe. His talk is so low that they must listen attentively to hear, and they sit around him in deathlike silence. When he finishes a measured sentence, the chief repeats it, and they all give a solemn grunt. But, first, I fill my pipe, light it, and take a few whiffs, then pass it to Hamblin; he smokes, and gives it to the man next, and so it goes around. When it has passed the chief, he takes out his own pipe, fills, and lights it, and passes it around after mine. I can smoke my own pipe in turn, but, when the Indian pipe comes around, I am nonplussed. It has a large stem, which has, at some time, been broken, and now there is a buckskin rag wound around it, and tied with sinew, so that the end of the stem is a huge mouthful, and looks like the burying ground of old dead spittle, venerable for a century. To gain time, I refill it, then engage in very earnest conversation, and, all unawares, I pass it to my neighbor unlighted.

I tell the Indians that I wish to spend some months in their country during the coming year, and that I would like them to treat me as a friend. I do not wish to trade; do not want their lands. Heretofore I have found it very difficult to make the natives understand my object, but the gravity of the Mormon missionary helps me much. I tell them that all the great and good white men are anxious to know very many things; that they spend much time in learning, and that the greatest man is he who knows the most. They want to know all about the mountains and the valleys, the rivers and the cañons, the beasts, and birds, and snakes. Then I tell them of many Indian tribes, and where they live; of the European nations; of the Chinese, of Africans, and all the strange things about them that come to my mind. I tell them of the ocean, of great rivers and high mountains, of strange beasts and birds. At last I tell them I wish to learn about their cañons and mountains, and about themselves, to tell other men at home; and that I want to take pictures of everything, and show them to my friends. All this occupied much time, and the matter and manner made a deep impression.

Then their chief replies: "Your talk is good, and we believe what you say. We believe in Jacob, and look upon you as a father. When you are hungry, you may have our game. You may gather our sweet fruits. We will give you food when you come to our land. We will show you the springs, and you may drink; the water is good. We will be friends, and when you come we will be glad. We will tell the Indians who live on the other side of the great river that we have seen Ká-pu-rats, and he is the Indians' friend. We will tell them he is Jacob's friend. We are very poor. Look at our women and children; they are naked. We have no horses; we climb the rocks, and our feet are sore. We live among rocks, and they yield little food and many thorns. When the cold moons come, our children are hungry. We have not much to give; you must not think us mean. You are wise; we have heard you tell strange things. We are ignorant. Last year we killed three white men. Bad men said they were our enemies. They told great lies. We thought them true. We were mad; it made us big fools. We are very sorry. Do not think of them, it is done; let us be friends. We are ignorant— like little children in understanding compared with you. When we do wrong, do not get mad, and be like children too.

"When white men kill our people, we kill them. Then they kill more of us. It is not good. We hear that the white men are a great number. When they stop killing us, there will be no Indian left to bury the dead. We love our country; we know not other lands. We hear that other lands are better; we do not know. The pines sing, and we are glad. Our children play in the warm sand; we hear them sing, and are glad. The seeds ripen, and we have to eat, and we are glad. We do not want their good lands; we want our rocks, and the great mountains where our fathers lived. We are very poor; we are very ignorant; but we are very honest. You have horses, and many things. You are very wise; you have a good heart. We will be friends. Nothing more have I to say."

Ká-pu-rats is the name by which I am known among the Utes and Shoshones, meaning "arm off." There was much more repetition than I have given, and much emphasis. After this a few presents were given, we shook hands, and the council broke up.   1875

CHARLES ALEXANDER EASTMAN (OHIYESA)

1858–1937

AFTER a youth in his native state, Minnesota, Eastman, who was a Santee Sioux Indian, attended Dartmouth College, from which he was graduated in 1887, and Boston University, which awarded him the M.D. degree three years later. With his young bride, Elaine Goodale, he went as government physician to the Pine Ridge Agency in South Dakota. Eastman became a prominent figure in Y.M.C.A. and Boy Scout circles. President Coolidge made him an Indian inspector. Through his lectures on Indian life and history, and through his writings, which include *Indian Boyhood* (1902), *Old Indian Days* (1907), and *The Soul of an Indian* (1911), Eastman became well known to all those interested in the Indian.

New York Times, December 24, 1937.

» » *From:* THE INDIAN TO-DAY « «

CHAPTER II

THE HOW AND THE WHY OF INDIAN WARS

I have tried to set forth the character and motives of the primitive Indian as they were affected by contact with civilization. In a word, demoralization was gradual but certain, culminating in the final loss of his freedom and confinement to the reservation under most depressing conditions. It must be borne in mind that there has been scarcely any genuine wild life among us for the past thirty-five years.

Sitting Bull's band of Sioux were the last real hostiles of their tribe to surrender, in 1880, and Geronimo's Apaches followed in 1886.

It is important to understand the underlying causes of Indian wars. There are people to-day who believe that the Indian likes nothing better than going on the warpath, killing and scalping from sheer native cruelty and lust for blood. His character as a man of peace has not been appreciated. Yet it is matter of history that the newcomers were welcomed in almost every case with unsuspecting kindness, and in his dealings with the white man the original owner of the soil has been uniformly patient and reasonable, offering resistance only under irresistible provocation.

. . .

. . . The Black Hawk war in 1836 was the end of the Algonquin resistance. Surely if there was ever just cause for resistance, Black Hawk had such a cause. His case was exactly similar to that of the famous Nez Perce, Chief Joseph, who illustrates his grievance very lucidly in the *North American Review* for April, 1879, in an interview with Bishop Hare of South Dakota.

"If I ever sold any land to the Government," says he, "it was done in this way: Suppose a man comes to me and says: 'Joseph, I want to buy your horse.' I say to him: 'I am satisfied with my horse. I do not wish to sell him at any price.' Then the man goes to my neighbor and says to him: 'I want to buy Joseph's horse, but he would not sell it to me.' My neighbor says: 'If you will buy my horse, I will throw in his horse!' The man buys my neighbor's horse, and then he comes and claims my horse and takes it away. I am under no obligation to my neighbor. He had nothing to do with my horse."

It was just such dealing as this which forced Black Hawk to fight with a handful of warriors for his inheritance. The Government simply made a treaty with the Sacs under Keokuk, and took the land of the Foxes at the same time. There were some chiefs who, after they had feasted well and drunk deep and signed away their country for nothing, talked of war, and urged Black Hawk to lead them. Then they sneaked away to play "good Indian," and left him to bear the brunt alone.

There were no more Indian wars for thirty years. The Southwest frontiers were now oc-cupied by eastern tribes or their remnants, which had been transported beyond the Mississippi during the early thirties. Only fragments were left here and there, in New York, Pennsylvania, Ohio, Indiana, and the South. The great Siouan race occupied nearly all the upper valley of the Mississippi and Missouri rivers and their tributaries. North of them dwelt the Ojibways, an Algonquin tribe with an entirely different language. The Sioux nation proper originally occupied a vast territory, and in the middle of the nineteenth century they still held the southern half of Minnesota, a portion of Wisconsin and Iowa, all of the Dakotas, part of Montana, nearly half of Nebraska, and small portions of Colorado and Wyoming. Some of the bands were forest Indians, hunters and trappers and fishermen, while others roamed over the Great Plains and hunted the buffalo, elk, and antelope. Some divided the year between the forest and prairie life. These people had been at peace with the whites ever since the early French explorers and the Jesuit priests had entered their country. They had traded for many years with the Hudson Bay and American Fur companies, and no serious difficulty had arisen, nor was any obstruction offered to the progress of civilization.

In 1824 the United States required of the tribes in this region to define their territory, a demand which intensified and gave a new turn to their intertribal warfare. The use of gun, horse, and whiskey completed the demoralization, and thus the truly "savage" warfare had its origin, ever increasing in bitterness until it culminated in resistance to the Government, in 1862, one hundred years after the struggle and defeat of the great Pontiac.

THE SIOUX AND THEIR GRIEVANCES

A treaty was made in 1851 with the Minnesota Sioux to which one band was not a party. This was the one commonly known as Inkpaduta's band, whose usual winter resort was in northwestern Iowa. White settlers went upon the ceded lands, and when this band returned to Spirit Lake after their summer's roving they found it occupied. Owing to a very severe winter and the presence of the settlements, the surrounding country became depleted of game, and the Sioux, who were starving, sought aid among the settlers. No doubt they became a nuisance, and were so treated, which treatment they very naturally resented, and thus arose the "Spirit Lake massacre." The rest of the tribe condemned the act, and Sioux from the Redwood reservation pursued the guilty band until they overtook and killed two of Inkpaduta's sons. The others were driven back among the wild Sioux. This was their first offence, after more than a century of contact with the whites.

Little Crow's band formed the east wing of the Sioux nation, and were the first to enter reservation life. The causes of their outbreak, a few years later, were practically the same as in many other instances, for in its broad features the history of one Indian tribe is the history of all. Their hunting-grounds were taken from them, and the promised support was not forthcoming. Some of the chiefs began to "play politics" like white men, and through their signatures, secretly given, a payment of $98,000 due the tribe was made to the Indian traders. Little Crow himself was involved in this steal, and was made head chief by the whites, who wished to have some one in this position whom they could deal with. But soon the non-payment of annuities brought the Indians to the verge of starvation, and in despair they forced Little Crow to lead them in revolt. In August, 1862, they massacred the agency employees and extended their attack to the white settlers, killing many and destroying a large amount of property, before a part of the tribe fled into Canada and the rest surrendered to General Sibley.

Next came the struggle of the Western Sioux and Northern Cheyennes in defence of their homes. The building of the Northern Pacific and the Union Pacific transcontinental railroads had necessitated the making of new treaties with these people. Scarcely was the agreement completed by which they ceded a right of way in return for assurances of permanent and absolute possession of other territory, including the Black Hills and Bighorn Mountains, when gold was discovered in these regions. This fact created great excitement and a general determination to dispossess the Sioux of the country just guaranteed to them, which no white man was to enter without the consent of three fourths of the adult men of the tribe.

Public excitement was intense, and the Government found itself unable to clear the country of intruders and to protect the rights of the Sioux. It was reported that there were no less than fifteen thousand men in the Black Hills district placer-mining and prospecting for the yellow metal. The authority of the United States was defied almost openly by the frontier press and people. Then the Indians took matters into their own hands, carried on a guerilla warfare against immigrants, and harassed the forts until the army was forced to enter upon a campaign against them. In 1868 another treaty was made, but the great chief, Red Cloud, would not sign it until he saw forts C. F. Smith and Phil Kearney abandoned. Here is probably the only instance in American history in which a single Indian chief was able to enforce his demands and make a great government back down. At that time it would have cost immense sums of money and many lives to conquer him, and would have retarded the development of the West by many years.

It is a fact that Sitting Bull was thoroughly opposed to yielding any more territory. No doubt he foresaw the inevitable result. He had taken up the cause of the Eastern Sioux in Minnesota and fought Sibley and Sully in 1862. He had supported Red Cloud in his protests against the establishment of the Bozeman trail, and against the new forts, although thus far these aggressions had not affected him directly. But when surveyors began work on the Northern Pacific, they entered his particular domain, and it was time for him to fight in its defence. Unfortunately for him, the other bands of Sioux whom he had helped in their time of need were now all settled upon reservations, so that he had not much support except from Crazy Horse's band, and the so-called hostiles or renegades of the Western bands. Hostilities began in 1872, culminating in 1876 with the famous "Custer fight," which practically ended the struggle, for after annihilating Custer's command the Indians fled into British America. Four years later Sitting Bull was induced to come in and settle down upon the Sioux reservation.

The Modoc war in Oregon and Idaho, in which the Shoshones and Bannocks were involved, was really a part of this same movement—namely, the last defence of their hunting-grounds by the Plains Indians, as was also the resistance of the Cheyennes and Comanches farther south, and of the Utes in 1877, simultaneously with the last stand of the Sioux. It had been found impossible to conquer the Plains Indians without destroying the buffalo, their main subsistence. Therefore vast herds were ruthlessly destroyed by the United States army, and by 1880 they were practically extinct. Since it was found cheaper to feed than to fight them, the one-time warriors were corralled upon their reservations and kept alive upon Government rations.

THE "GHOST-DANCE WAR"

All Indian warfare worthy the name had now come to an end. There were left Geronimo's small bands of Apaches, who were hunted down in an all but inaccessible country and finally captured and confined in Southern forts. More recent "Indian outbreaks," so-called, are usually a mere ruse of the politicians, or are riots caused by the disaffection of a few Indians unjustly treated by their Government agents. The only really serious disturbance within a generation was the "Ghost-dance war" of 1890–91. And yet this cannot fairly be called an Indian war. It arose in a religious craze which need not have been a serious matter if wisely handled. The people were hungry and disheartened, their future looked hopeless, and all their appeals were disregarded. At this juncture the suggestion of a Messiah, offering hope of miraculous intervention in behalf of the red man, appealed to many, and the "new religion" spread far and fast. In some tribes it soon died a natural death, but in the Sioux country it was unwisely forbidden by the authorities, and led to grave results.

At Pine Ridge, in December of 1890, the ghost-dancers had come in to the agency and the situation was apparently under control when the attempted arrest of Sitting Bull in his cabin by Indian police led to his death and the stampeding of his people. Several of the stampeded bands came down to Pine Ridge, where they were met by United States troops, disarmed, and shot down after one man had resisted disarmament by firing off his weapon. This was the massacre of Wounded Knee, where about 300 Indians, two thirds of them women and children, were mown down with machine-guns within a few minutes. For some days there was danger of a reprisal, but the crisis passed, and those Indians who had fled to the "Bad Lands" were induced to come in and surrender. From that time on the Indian tribes of the United States have been on a peace footing.

. . .

THE TRUTH ABOUT INDIAN AGENCIES

. . . The Indian of the Northwest came into reservation life reluctantly, very much like a man who has dissipated his large inheritance and is driven out by foreclosure. One morning he awoke to the fact that he must give up his freedom and resign his vast possessions to live in a squalid cabin in the backyard of civilization. For the first time his rovings were checked by well-defined boundaries, and he could not hunt or visit neighboring tribes without a passport. He was practically a prisoner, to be fed and treated as such; and what resources were left him must be controlled by the Indian Bureau through its resident agent.

Who is this Indian agent, or superintendent, as he is now called? He is the supreme ruler on the reservation, responsible directly to the Commissioner of Indian Affairs; and all requests or complaints must pass through his office. The agency doctor, clerks, farmers, superintendents of agency schools, and all other local employees report to him and are subject to his orders. Too often he has been nothing more than a ward politician of the commonest stamp, whose main purpose is to get all that is coming to him. His salary is small, but there are endless opportunities for graft.

If any appeal from the agent's decisions, they are "kickers" and "insubordinate." If they are Indians, he can easily deprive them of privileges, or even imprison them on trumped-up charges; if employees, he will force them to resign or apply for transfers; and even the missionaries may be compelled, directly or indirectly, to leave the reservation for protesting too openly against official wrongdoing. The inspector sent from Washington to investigate finds it easy to "get in with" the agent and very difficult to see or hear anything that the agent does not wish him to hear or see. Many Indians now believe sincerely in Christ's teachings as explained to them by their missionaries, but they find it impossible to believe that this Government is Christian, or the average official an honest man.

Any untutored people, however, are apt imitators, and so these much-exploited natives become politicians in spite of themselves. The most worthless of the tribe are used as the agent's spies and henchmen; a state of affairs demoralizing on the face of it. As long as the Indian Bureau is run in the interest of the politicians, and Indian civilization is merely an incident, the excellent and humanitarian policies approved by the American people will not be fully carried into effect.

It is true that good men and especially good

women have gone into the Indian service with a genuine desire to deal justly and kindly by the Indian and to serve the Government honorably and efficiently. Such people often become disgusted with the system and find it impossible to stay, or else are forced out by methods familiar to the experienced. When you clear your American cities of grafters, and purify your politics, then perhaps you will be in a position to redeem the Indian service, and only then. Alas! the skirts of the Goddess of Liberty have never yet been quite clean!

The Indian is no fool; on the other hand, he is a keen observer and an apt student. Although an idealist by nature, many of the race have proved themselves good business men. But under the reservation system they have developed traits that are absolutely opposed to the racial type. They become time-serving, beggarly, and apathetic. Some of their finest characters, such as Chief Joseph, have really died of a broken heart. These are men who could not submit to be degraded; the politicians call them "incorrigible savages."

The distribution of rations to the Plains Indians was, as I have explained, originally a peace measure, and apparently a necessity in place of their buffalo which the white man had exterminated. For many years Texas beef was issued monthly "on the hoof"; that is, the cattle were driven out one by one upon the plain, and there surrounded and shot down by representatives of the groups to which they belonged. Bacon, flour, sugar, and coffee were doled out to the women, usually as often as once in two weeks, thus requiring those who lived at a considerable distance from the agency to spend several days of each month on the road, neglecting their homes and gardens, if they had any. Once a year there was a distribution of cheap blankets and shoddy clothing. The self-respect of the people was almost fatally injured by these methods. This demoralizing ration-giving has been gradually done away with as the Indians progressed toward self-support, but is still found necessary in many cases.

Not all features of reservation life are bad; for while many good things are shut out and some evils flourish, others are excluded. Liquor traffic among Indians has been forbidden by law since the colonial period; and the law is fairly well enforced by a number of special officers; yet in a few tribes there has been in recent years much demoralization through liq-

uor. It is generally admitted that there is less crime and rowdyism on the reservation than in civilized communities of equal size. In 1878 a force of native police was authorized to keep order, eject intruders, act as truant officers, and perform other duties under the direction of the agent. Though paid only ten or twelve dollars a month, these men have been faithful and efficient in the performance of duties involving considerable hardship and sometimes danger. Their loyalty and patriotism are deserving of special praise. In making arrests and bringing in desperate prisoners, as in the case of Pretty Elk the Brule Sioux murderer, and of the chief, Sitting Bull, the faithful police have sometimes lost their lives.

INDIAN CLAIMS

It is commonly admitted that the Indian treaties have been frequently broken by the United States, both in the letter and the spirit, while, on the other hand, the Indians have acted in good faith and with a high regard for their national honor. It is also a fact not very creditable to the Government that treaties have been materially amended in the Senate and not again submitted to the tribe, who were not even made aware at once of their altered provisions. I believe this would be considered a piece of sharp practice in the case of any people able to defend itself.

The breach of treaty obligations on the part of this Government has led to a large number of Indian claims, involving millions of dollars, which represent the efforts of tribes or bands which feel themselves wronged or defrauded to obtain justice under the white man's law. The history of one or two such may be of interest.

Most of the Oneida and Stockbridge tribes exchanged their New York reservations for a large tract of land in Kansas, and started for their new home in 1830, but never got any farther than Green Bay, Wisconsin. There the Menominees invited them to remain and share their reservation, as they had plenty of good land. The Stockbridges had originally occupied the beautiful Housatonic valley, where Jonathan Edwards preached to them and made them good Presbyterians; nevertheless, the "Christian" colonists robbed them of their homes and drove them westward. They did not resist the aggression. If anything is proved in history, it is that those who follow in the footsteps of the meek and gentle Jesus will be treated unmercifully, as he was, by a hard and material world.

These Stockbridges went still further with their kind hosts, and ultimately both tribes accepted the hospitality of the Ojibways. They made their unfortunate brothers welcome, and made them a free gift of land. But now observe the white man's sense of honor and justice in glaring contrast! For *seventy-five years* the United States Government failed to recompense these people for their Kansas land, which they never reached, and which in the meantime was taken up by settlers, and gradually covered with thriving homes and fertile farms.

The whole case was scrutinized again and again by the Congress of the United States from 1830 to about 1905, when at last a payment was made! The fact that the two tribes remained in Wisconsin and settled there does not invalidate their claim, as those wild Ojibways had no treaty with the Government at that time and had a perfect right to give away some of their land. It was a barefaced, open steal from the Indians. Yet the tribes were obliged to employ white attorneys at a liberal per cent. of the amount they hoped to recover. They had to pay high for simple justice. Meanwhile they lived on their own labor for two or three generations, and contributed to the upbuilding of Wisconsin. To-day some of them are doing better than their white neighbors.

This is only one illustration of a not uncommon happening; for, while some of these claims are doubtless unreasonable, I personally know of many in which the ethics of the case are as clear as in this which I have cited. It is often the fact that differences among attorneys and party politics in Congress delay justice for many years or deprive the Indians of their rights altogether. A bill has recently been introduced, at the instance of the Society of American Indians, which is framed to permit Indian tribes to sue in the Court of Claims, without first obtaining the consent of Congress in each case. This bill ought to be at once made law, as it would do away within a few years with many long-drawn-out disputes and much waste and worse than waste of time and money.

. . .

MODERN "FRIENDS OF THE INDIAN"

. . . From this time on the old view of the Indian as a hopeless savage has been gradually abandoned, and replaced by the juster modern view which regards him as essentially a man, and as good material for the future citizen. The volunteer organizations arising under Grant and continuing active to the present day have been effective molders of public opinion along these lines.

The Boston Indian Citizenship Committee was organized in 1879, on the occasion of the forcible removal of the Poncas to Indian Territory. Chief Standing Bear and the Indian maiden Bright Eyes (Susette La Flesche) visited many leading cities and told eloquently the story of their wrongs. They were ultimately restored to their old home, largely through the efforts of this group of influential men. The committee then undertook to secure citizenship for Indians on the basis of taxation, a principle that was denied by the Supreme Court; but a few years later the same end was attained by the passage of the "Dawes bill." Since then they have endeavored to secure honest allotments to Indians, to prevent the sale of the best lands to whites at nominal prices, and to obtain the dismissal of corrupt Indian agents and inspectors.

The National Indian Association, composed chiefly of women, began work with a memorial to Congress in 1879, and has continued it until now, under the efficient leadership of Mrs. A. S. Quinton, Mrs. Sara T. Kinney, and others. The missionary department has established fifty pioneer missions in as many neglected tribes or tribal remnants, turning them over ultimately, with their buildings and plant, to the mission boards of the various Protestant denominations. The society has also fostered native industries, being the mother of the Indian Industries League; has loaned money to Indians for home-building; assisted in the education of especially promising individuals; built and supported hospitals, and done other valuable work. Its headquarters are in New York City.

The Indian Rights Association was organized in Philadelphia, in 1882, at the home of Mr. John Welsh. Mr. Herbert Welsh has been for many years its leading spirit, and others who have done yeoman's service in the cause are the late Professor Painter, Mr. Brosius, and Mr. Matthew K. Sniffen. Its slogan was the same as that of the others: Education; Land in Severalty; Citizenship! To all three of these bodies, as well as to the Board of Indian Commissioners, belongs much credit for urging the reforms which triumphed, in 1887, in the "Dawes bill," the Emancipation Act of the Indian.

The Indian Rights Association maintains a representative in Washington to cooperate with the Indian Bureau and to keep an eye upon legislation affecting the tribes, as well as a permanent office in Philadelphia. Its officers and agents have kept in close touch with developments in the field, and have conducted many investigations on Indian agencies, resulting often in the exposure of grave abuses. They have been courageous and aggressive in their work, and have not hesitated to appeal to the courts when necessary to protect the rights of Indians. They have also done much to mold public sentiment through meetings, letters to the press, and the circulation of their own literature to the number of more than half a million copies.

One of President Grant's first acts was the creation, in 1869, of the United States Board of Indian Commissioners, a body of ten men supposed to be "eminent for their intelligence and philanthropy," to serve without pay in an advisory capacity, and to cooperate with the Interior Department in securing a sound and progressive administration of Indian affairs. The only appropriation is for travelling expenses and for a salaried secretary with an office in Washington. It has been one of the important duties of this Board to inspect the Indian supplies when purchased, if possible securing goods up to the standard of the samples submitted and preventing open fraud. Its members have travelled extensively in the Indian country in order to observe conditions, and their patriotic services have been appreciated by both races.

In the autumn of 1883 Mr. Albert K. Smiley, the large-hearted owner of a hostelry overlooking beautiful Lake Mohonk, in the Shawangum range, invited a number of prominent Indian workers to meet as his guests for discussion of actual conditions and necessary reforms. With this historic meeting began an uninterrupted series of "Mohonk Indian Conferences," at which missionaries of all denominations, Government officials, members of Congress, representatives of philanthropic societies, teachers in Indian schools, editors, ministers, and other influential men and women, with a sprinkling of educated Indians, meet annually at the call of Mr. Smiley, and since his death in 1912 at that of his brother, Mr. Daniel Smiley, to discuss all matters bearing upon the welfare of of the race in a sympathetic atmosphere and amid the pleasantest surroundings. Mr. Smiley

was a member of the Board of Indian Commissioners, and for many years these conferences were closely connected with the affairs of the Board, and the proceedings were published as a part of its annual report.

The platform adopted each year at Lake Mohonk is widely circulated, and has had much influence; although, as it represents only the unanimous vote of a body among whom there actually exist wide differences of opinion, it is not always as satisfactory as it might be. It has seemed to some who attended the early conferences that those of late years have been less fruitful, owing partly to less novelty in the subject-matter and to the sharing of the time with problems of Hawaii and the Philippines, and partly to a desire for unanimity and good feeling that has kept unpleasant facts from the light. It is certain that the debates are more carefully prearranged and therefore less spontaneous.

The Mohonk Conferences have consistently recommended larger appropriations for Indian education; the extension of the laws of the land over Indian reservations; the gradual withdrawal of rations; the allotment of communal land to individuals, and more recently the breaking up of the tribal trust funds into individual holdings. Emphasis has been laid upon the need of greater care in selecting men of character as Indian agents and superintendents. The thirty-first conference urges a vigorous campaign against tuberculosis, trachoma, and other diseases among Indians, also against the liquor traffic, and mescal habit, and declares that the proposition to control Indian affairs through a non-partisan commission to serve during long terms is "worthy of serious consideration." It also makes special recommendations in behalf of the Pueblo, the Navajo, the Five Civilized Tribes of Oklahoma, and the New York Indians, looking toward their present protection and future citizenship.

These "Eastern sentimentalists," as they have often been called by persons interested in depriving the red man of his heritage, have pursued their ends steadily, though not without severe setbacks. The opposition to Indian schools in Congress was for many years very strong, but it has now almost ceased, except in sporadic instances. One seldom hears it said nowadays that "the only good Indian is the dead Indian," and the Western Senator who declared that "you could no more civilize an Apache than you could civilize a rattlesnake" would rather shock than convince his hearers in the light of present-day progress. The greatest enemy to Indian civilization has been the return of the "spoils system" in the eighties, and the formation of a corrupt "Indian ring" whose ramifications extended so deep and so high that even the most sincere and disinterested despaired of obtaining justice. Yet the average American citizen honestly wants to give the Indian a fair chance!

To sum up, he had been an indomitable foe, and occupied a vast region which by 1870 was already beat upon by the tides of settlement. Two things were determined upon: First, he must be induced, bribed, or forced to enter the reservation. Second, he must be trained and persuaded to adopt civilized life, and so saved to the future if he proved to be worth saving, which many doubted. In order to carry out these projects his wild food supply had to be ruthlessly cut off, and the buffalo were of necessity sacrificed.

Here is a system which has gradually taken its present complicated form during two thousand years. A primitive race has put it on ready made, to a large extent, within two generations. In order to accomplish such a feat, they had to fight physical demoralization, psychological confusion, and spiritual apathy. In other words, the old building had to be pulled down, foundations and all, and replaced by the new. But you have had to use the same timber. 1915

FREDERICK JACKSON TURNER

1861–1932

"THE SIGNIFICANCE of the Frontier in American History" was a paper which its author, a professor of history at the University of Wisconsin, read before the American Historical Association in 1893. In the words of Frederick Paxson, "without warning he set forth a new hypothesis, and then and there opened a new period in the interpretation of the history of the United States." Turner's interpretative essays on the influence of the frontier and the section, together with his teaching both at Wisconsin and at Harvard, resulted in the production of a rich harvest of monographs by students who explored and documented his thesis that the frontier had been the dominant factor in American development.

Turner's emphasis on the frontier and the section was hardly less important, however, than the rapprochement which he made between history and the related disciplines of geography, geology, demography, and economics. Turner's thesis, which profoundly influenced literary and social criticism as well as historical scholarship, finally became widely accepted in popular thought. In part all this was true because the frontier thesis proved to be emotionally satisfying to the generation to which it was addressed. For seeing American struggles in terms of sections rather than of classes, and for failing to emphasize American expansion into new areas in terms of merchant and industrial capitalism Turner has been criticized by Louis M. Hacker.

C. L. Becker, Bibliography in *American Masters of Social Science*, H. W. Odum, ed., New York, 1927.

F. J. Turner, *The Frontier in American History*, New York, 1920.

F. J. Turner, *The United States, 1830–1850*, New York, 1935.

A. O. Craven, "Frederick Jackson Turner," *The Marcus W. Jernegan Essays In American History*, W. T. Hutchinson, ed., Chicago, 1937.

Merle Curti, "The Section and the Frontier in American History," *Methods in Social Science, A Case Book*, Stuart Chase, ed., Chicago, 1931.

Merle Curti, *Probing Our Past*, New York, 1955.

» » *From:* THE FRONTIER IN AMERICAN HISTORY « «

In a recent bulletin of the Superintendent of the Census of 1890 appear these significant words: "Up to and including 1880 the country had a frontier of settlement, but at present the unsettled area has been so broken into by isolated bodies of settlement that there can hardly be said to be a frontier line. In the discussion of its extent, its westward movement, etc., it can not, therefore, any longer have a place in the census reports." This brief official statement marks the closing of a great historic movement. Up to our own day American history has been in a large degree the history of the colonization of the Great West. The existence of an area of free land, its continuous recession, and the advance of American settlement westward, explain American development.

Behind institutions, behind constitutional forms and modifications, lie the vital forces that call these organs into life and shape them to meet changing conditions. The peculiarity of American institutions is, the fact that they have been compelled to adapt themselves to the changes of an expanding people—to the changes involved in crossing a continent, in winning a wilderness, and in developing at each area of this progress out of the primitive economic and political conditions of the frontier into the complexity of city life. Said Calhoun in 1817, "We are great, and rapidly—I was about to say fearfully—growing!" So saying, he touched the distinguishing feature of American life. All peoples show development; the germ theory of politics has been sufficiently emphasized. In the case of most nations, however, the development has occurred in a limited area; and if the nation has expanded, it has met other growing peoples whom it has conquered. But in the case of the United States we have a different phenomenon. Limiting our attention to the Atlantic coast, we have the familiar phenomenon of the evolution of institutions in a limited area, such as the rise of representative government; the differentiation of simple colonial governments into complex organs; the progress from primitive industrial society, without division of labor, up to manufacturing civilization. But we have in addition to this a recurrence of the process of evolution in each western area reached in the process of expansion. Thus American development has exhibited not merely advance along a single line, but a return to primitive conditions on a continually advancing frontier line, and a new development for that area. American social development has been continually beginning over again on the frontier. This perennial rebirth, this fluidity of American life, this expansion westward with its new opportunities, its continuous touch with the simplicity of primitive society, furnish the forces dominating American character. The true point of view in the history of this nation is not the Atlantic coast, it is the Great West. Even the slavery struggle, which is made so exclusive an object of attention by writers like Professor von Holst, occupies its important place in American history because of its relation to westward expansion.

In this advance, the frontier is the outer edge of the wave—the meeting point between savagery and civilization. Much has been written about the frontier from the point of view of border warfare and the chase, but as a field for the serious study of the economist and the historian it has been neglected.

The American frontier is sharply distinguished from the European frontier—a fortified boundary line running through dense populations. The most significant thing about the American frontier is, that it lies at the hither edge of free land. In the census reports it is treated as the margin of that settlement which has a density of two or more to the square mile. The term is an elastic one, and for our purposes does not need sharp definition. We shall consider the whole frontier belt, including the Indian country and the outer margin of the "settled area" of the census reports. This paper will make no attempt to treat the subject exhaustively; its aim is simply to call attention to the frontier as a fertile field for investigation, and to suggest some of the problems which arise in connection with it.

In the settlement of America we have to observe how European life entered the continent, and how America modified and developed that life and reacted on Europe. Our early history is the study of European germs developing in an American environment. Too exclusive attention has been paid by institutional students to the Germanic origins, too little to the American factors. The frontier is the line of most rapid and effective Americanization. The wilderness masters the colonist. It finds him a European in dress, industries, tools, modes of travel, and thought. It takes him from the railroad car and puts him in the birch canoe. It strips off the garments of civilization and arrays him in the hunting shirt and the moccasin. It puts him in the log cabin of the Cherokee and Iroquois and runs an Indian palisade around him. Before long he has gone to planting Indian corn and plowing with a sharp stick; he shouts the war cry and takes the scalp in orthodox Indian fashion. In short, at the frontier the environment is at first too strong for the man. He must accept the conditions which it furnishes, or perish, and so he fits himself into the Indian clearings and follows the Indian trails. Little by little he transforms the wilderness, but the outcome is not the old Europe, not simply the development of Germanic germs, any more than the first phenomenon was a case of reversion to the Germanic mark. The fact is, that here is a new product that is American. At first, the frontier was the Atlantic coast. It was the frontier of Europe in a very real sense. Moving westward, the frontier became more and more American. As successive terminal moraines result from successive glaciations, so each frontier leaves its traces behind it, and when it becomes a settled area the region still partakes of the frontier characteristics. Thus the advance of the frontier has meant a steady movement away from the influence of Europe, a steady growth of independence on American lines. And to study this advance, the men who grew up under these conditions, and the political, economic, and social results of it, is to study the really American part of our history.

In the course of the seventeenth century the frontier was advanced up the Atlantic river courses, just beyond the "fall line," and the tidewater region became the settled area. In the first half of the eighteenth century another advance occurred. Traders followed the Delaware and Shawnese Indians to the Ohio as early as the end of the first quarter of the century. Gov. Spotswood, of Virginia, made an expedition in 1714 across the Blue Ridge. The end of the first quarter of the century saw the advance of the Scotch-Irish and the Palatine Germans up the Shenandoah Valley into the western part of Virginia, and along the piedmont region of the Carolinas. The Germans in New York pushed the frontier of settlement up the Mohawk to German Flats. In Pennsylvania the town of Bedford indicates the line of settlement. Settlements soon began on the New River, a branch of the Kanawha, and on the sources of the Yadkin and French Broad. The King attempted to arrest the advance by his proclamation of 1763, forbidding settlements beyond the sources of the rivers flowing into the Atlantic; but in vain. In the period of the Revolution the frontier crossed the Alleghanies into Kentucky and Tennessee, and the upper waters of the Ohio were settled. When the first census was taken in 1790, the continuous settled area was bounded by a line which ran near the coast of Maine, and included New England except a portion of Vermont and New Hampshire, New York along the Hudson and up the Mohawk about Schenectady, eastern and southern Pennsylvania, Virginia well across the Shenandoah Valley, and the Carolinas and eastern Georgia. Beyond this region of continuous settlement were the small settled areas of Kentucky and Tennessee, and the Ohio, with the mountains intervening between them and the Atlantic area, thus giving a new and important character to the frontier. The isolation of the region increased its peculiarly American tendencies, and the need of transportation facilities to connect it with the East called out important schemes of internal improvement, which will be noted farther on. The "West," as a self-conscious section, began to evolve.

From decade to decade distinct advances of the frontier occurred. By the census of 1820 the settled area included Ohio, southern Indiana and Illinois, southeastern Missouri, and about one-half of Louisiana. This settled area had surrounded Indian areas, and the management of these tribes became an object of political concern. The frontier region of the time lay along the Great Lakes, where Astor's American Fur Company operated in the Indian trade, and beyond the Mississippi, where Indian traders extended their activity even to the Rocky Mountains; Florida also furnished frontier conditions. The Mississippi River region was the scene of typical frontier settlements.

The rising steam navigation on western waters, the opening of the Erie Canal, and the westward extension of cotton culture added five frontier states to the Union in this period. Grund, writing in 1836, declares: "It appears then that the universal disposition of Americans to emigrate to the western wilderness, in order to enlarge their dominion over inanimate nature, is the actual result of an expansive power

which is inherent in them, and which by continually agitating all classes of society is constantly throwing a large portion of the whole
population on the extreme confines of the State,
in order to gain space for its development.
Hardly is a new State or Territory formed before the same principle manifests itself again
and gives rise to a further emigration; and so is
it destined to go on until a physical barrier
10 must finally obstruct its progress."

In the middle of this century the line indicated by the present eastern boundary of Indian Territory, Nebraska, and Kansas marked
the frontier of the Indian country. Minnesota
and Wisconsin still exhibited frontier conditions, but the distinctive frontier of the period
is found in California, where the gold discoveries had sent a sudden tide of adventurous
miners, and in Oregon, and the settlements in
20 Utah. As the frontier had leaped over the Alleghanies, so now it skipped the Great Plains
and the Rocky Mountains; and in the same way
that the advance of the frontiersmen beyond
the Alleghanies had caused the rise of important questions of transportation and internal
improvement, so now the settlers beyond the
Rocky Mountains needed means of communication with the East, and in the furnishing of
these arose the settlement of the Great Plains
30 and the development of still another kind of
frontier life. Railroads, fostered by land grants,
sent an increasing tide of immigrants into the
Far West. The United States Army fought a
series of Indian wars in Minnesota, Dakota, and
the Indian Territory.

By 1880 the settled area had been pushed
into northern Michigan, Wisconsin, and Minnesota, along Dakota rivers, and in the Black
Hills region, and was ascending the rivers of
40 Kansas and Nebraska. The development of
mines in Colorado had drawn isolated frontier
settlements into that region, and Montana and
Idaho were receiving settlers. The frontier was
found in these mining camps and the ranches
of the Great Plains. The superintendent of the
census for 1890 reports, as previously stated,
that the settlements of the West lie so scattered
over the region that there can no longer be said
to be a frontier line.

50 In these successive frontiers we find natural
boundary lines which have served to mark and
to affect the characteristics of the frontiers,
namely: the "fall line"; the Alleghany Mountains; the Mississippi; the Missouri where its
direction approximates north and south; the

line of the arid lands, approximately the ninety-
ninth meridian; and the Rocky Mountains. The
fall line marked the frontier of the seventeenth
century; the Alleghanies that of the eighteenth;
the Mississippi that of the first quarter of the
nineteenth; the Missouri that of the middle of
this century (omitting the California movement); and the belt of the Rocky Mountains
and the arid tract, the present frontier. Each
was won by a series of Indian wars.

At the Atlantic frontier one can study the
germs of processes repeated at each successive
frontier. We have the complex European life
sharply precipitated by the wilderness into the
simplicity of primitive conditions. The first
frontier had to meet its Indian question, its
question of the disposition of the public domain, of the means of intercourse with older
settlements, of the extension of political organization, of religious and educational activity.
And the settlement of these and similar questions for one frontier served as a guide for the
next. The American student needs not to go to
the "prim little townships of Sleswick" for il
lustrations of the law of continuity and devel .
opment. For example, he may study the origin
of our land policies in the colonial land policy;
he may see how the system grew by adapting
the statutes to the customs of the successive
frontiers. He may see how the mining experience in the lead regions of Wisconsin, Illinois,
and Iowa was applied to the mining laws of
the Sierras, and how our Indian policy has been
a series of experimentations on successive frontiers. Each tier of new States has found in the
older ones material for its constitutions. Each
frontier has made similar contributions to
American character, as will be discussed farther
on.

But with all these similarities there are essential differences, due to the place element and
the time element. It is evident that the farming
frontier of the Mississippi Valley presents different conditions from the mining frontier of
the Rocky Mountains. The frontier reached by
the Pacific Railroad, surveyed into rectangles,
guarded by the United States Army, and recruited by the daily immigrant ship, moves forward at a swifter pace and in a different way
than the frontier reached by the birch canoe or
the pack horse. The geologist traces patiently
the shores of ancient seas, maps their areas,
and compares the older and the newer. It
would be a work worth the historian's labors to
mark these various frontiers and in detail com-

pare one with another. Not only would there result a more adequate conception of American development and characteristics, but invaluable additions would be made to the history of society.

Loria, the Italian economist, has urged the study of colonial life as an aid in understanding the stages of European development, affirming that colonial settlement is for economic science what the mountain is for geology, bringing to light primitive stratifications. "America," he says, "has the key to the historical enigma which Europe has sought for centuries in vain, and the land which has no history reveals luminously the course of universal history." There is much truth in this. The United States lies like a huge page in the history of society. Line by line as we read this continental page from West to East we find the record of social evolution. It begins with the Indian and the hunter; it goes on to tell of the disintegration of savagery by the entrance of the trader, the pathfinder of civilization; we read the annals of the pastoral stage in ranch life; the exploitation of the soil by the raising of unrotated crops of corn and wheat in sparsely settled farming communities; the intensive culture of the denser farm settlement; and finally the manufacturing organization with city and factory system. This page is familiar to the student of census statistics, but how little of it has been used by our historians. Particularly in eastern States this page is a palimpsest. What is now a manufacturing State was in an earlier decade an area of intensive farming. Earlier yet it had been a wheat area, and still earlier the "range" had attracted the cattleherder. Thus Wisconsin, now developing manufacture, is a State with varied agricultural interest. But earlier it was given over to almost exclusive grain-raising, like North Dakota at the present time.

Each of these areas has had an influence in our economic and political history; the evolution of each into a higher stage has worked political transformations. But what constitutional historian has made any adequate attempt to interpret political facts by the light of these social areas and changes?

The Atlantic frontier was compounded of fisherman, fur-trader, miner, cattle-raiser, and farmer. Excepting the fisherman, each type of industry was on the march toward the West, impelled by an irresistible attraction. Each passed in successive waves across the continent. Stand at Cumberland Gap and watch the procession of civilization, marching single file— the buffalo following the trail to the salt springs, the Indian, the fur-trader and hunter, the cattle-raiser, the pioneer farmer—and the frontier has passed by. Stand at South Pass in the Rockies a century later and see the same procession with wider intervals between. The unequal rate of advance compels us to distinguish the frontier into the trader's frontier, the rancher's frontier, or the miner's frontier, and the farmer's frontier. When the mines and cow pens were still near the fall line the traders' pack trains were tinkling across the Alleghanies, and the French on the Great Lakes were fortifying their posts, alarmed by the British trader's birch canoe. When the trappers scaled the Rockies, the farmer was still near the mouth of the Missouri.

Why was it that the Indian trader passed so rapidly across the continent? What effects followed from the trader's frontier? The trade was coeval with American discovery. The Norsemen, Vespuccius, Verrazani, Hudson, John Smith, all trafficked for furs. The Plymouth pilgrims settled in Indian cornfields, and their first return cargo was of beaver and lumber. The records of the various New England colonies show how steadily exploration was carried into the wilderness by this trade. What is true for New England is, as would be expected, even plainer for the rest of the colonies. All along the coast from Maine to Georgia the Indian trade opened up the river courses. Steadily the trader passed westward, utilizing the older lines of French trade. The Ohio, the Great Lakes, the Mississippi, the Missouri, and the Platte, the lines of western advance, were ascended by traders. They found the passes in the Rocky Mountains and guided Lewis and Clark, Frémont, and Bidwell. The explanation of the rapidity of this advance is connected with the effects of the trader on the Indian. The trading post left the unarmed tribes at the mercy of those that had purchased fire-arms— a truth which the Iroquois Indians wrote in blood, and so the remote and unvisited tribes gave eager welcome to the trader. "The savages," wrote La Salle, "take better care of us French than of their own children; from us only can they get guns and goods." This accounts for the trader's power and the rapidity of his advance. Thus the disintegrating forces of civilization entered the wilderness. Every river valley and Indian trail became a fissure in Indian society, and so that society became

honeycombed. Long before the pioneer farmer appeared on the scene, primitive Indian life had passed away. The farmers met Indians armed with guns. The trading frontier, while steadily undermining Indian power by making the tribes ultimately dependent on the whites, yet, through its sale of guns, gave to the Indian increased power of resistance to the farming frontier. French colonization was dominated by
10 its trading frontier; English colonization by its farming frontier. There was an antagonism between the two frontiers as between the two nations. Said Duquesne to the Iroquois, "Are you ignorant of the difference between the king of England and the king of France? Go see the forts that our king has established and you will see that you can still hunt under their very walls. They have been placed for your advantage in places which you frequent. The Eng-
20 lish, on the contrary, are no sooner in possession of a place than the game is driven away. The forest falls before them as they advance, and the soil is laid bare so that you can scarce find the wherewithal to erect a shelter for the night."

And yet, in spite of this opposition of the interests of the trader and the farmer, the Indian trade pioneered the way for civilization. The buffalo trail became the Indian trail, and
30 this became the trader's "trace"; the trails widened into roads, and the roads into turnpikes, and these in turn were transformed into railroads. The same origin can be shown for the railroads of the South, the Far West, and the Dominion of Canada. The trading posts reached by these trails were on the sites of Indian villages which had been placed in positions suggested by nature; and these trading posts, situated so as to command the water sys-
40 tems of the country, have grown into such cities as Albany, Pittsburgh, Detroit, Chicago, St. Louis, Council Bluffs, and Kansas City. Thus civilization in America has followed the arteries made by geology, pouring an ever richer tide through them, until at last the slender paths of aboriginal intercourse have been broadened and interwoven into the complex mazes of modern commercial lines; the wilderness has been interpenetrated by lines of civilization
50 growing ever more numerous. It is like the steady growth of a complex nervous system for the originally simple, inert continent. If one would understand why we are to-day one nation, rather than a collection of isolated states, he must study this economic and social consoli-

dation of the country. In this progress from savage conditions lie topics for the evolutionist.

The effect of the Indian frontier as a consolidating agent in our history is important. From the close of the seventeenth century various intercolonial congresses have been called to treat with Indians and establish common measures of defense. Particularism was strongest in colonies with no Indian frontier. This frontier stretched along the western border like a cord of union. The Indian was a common danger, demanding united action. Most celebrated of these conferences was the Albany congress of 1754, called to treat with the Six Nations, and to consider plans of union. Even a cursory reading of the plan proposed by the congress reveals the importance of the frontier. The powers of the general council and the officers were, chiefly, the determination of peace and war with the Indians, the regulation of Indian trade, the purchase of Indian lands, and the creation and government of new settlements as a security against the Indians. It is evident that the unifying tendencies of the Revolutionary period were facilitated by the previous coöperation in the regulation of the frontier. In this connection may be mentioned the importance of the frontier, from that day to this, as a military training school, keeping alive the power of resistance to aggression, and developing the stalwart and rugged qualities of the frontiersman.

It would not be possible in the limits of this paper to trace the other frontiers across the continent. Travelers of the eighteenth century found the "cowpens" among the canebrakes and peavine pastures of the South, and the "cow drivers" took their droves to Charleston, Philadelphia, and New York. Travelers at the close of the War of 1812 met droves of more than a thousand cattle and swine from the interior of Ohio going to Pennsylvania to fatten for the Philadelphia market. The ranges of the Great Plains, with ranch and cowboy and nomadic life, are things of yesterday and of to-day. The experience of the Carolina cowpens guided the ranchers of Texas. One element favoring the rapid extension of the rancher's frontier is the fact that in a remote country lacking transportation facilities the product must be in small bulk, or must be able to transport itself, and the cattle-raiser could easily drive his product to market. The effect of these great ranches on the subsequent agrarian history of the localities in which they existed should be studied.

The maps of the census reports show an uneven advance of the farmer's frontier, with tongues of settlement pushed forward and with indentations of wilderness. In part this is due to Indian resistance, in part to the location of river valleys and passes, in part to the unequal force of the centers of frontier attraction. Among the important centers of attraction may be mentioned the following: fertile and favorably situated soils, salt springs, mines, and army posts.

The frontier army post, serving to protect the settlers from the Indians, has also acted as a wedge to open the Indian country, and has been a nucleus for settlement. In this connection mention should also be made of the government military and exploring expeditions in determining the lines of settlement. But all the more important expeditions were greatly indebted to the earliest pathmakers, the Indian guides, the traders and trappers, and the French voyageurs, who were inevitable parts of governmental expeditions from the days of Lewis and Clark. Each expedition was an epitome of the previous factors in western advance.

In an interesting monograph, Victor Hehn has traced the effect of salt upon early European development, and has pointed out how it affected the lines of settlement and the form of administration. A similar study might be made for the salt springs of the United States. The early settlers were tied to the coast by the need of salt, without which they could not preserve their meats or live in comfort. Writing in 1752, Bishop Spangenburg says of a colony for which he was seeking lands in North Carolina, "They will require salt & other necessaries which they can neither manufacture nor raise. Either they must go to Charleston, which is 300 miles distant . . . Or else they must go to Boling's Point in Vᵃ on a branch of the James & is also 300 miles from here . . . Or else they must go down the Roanoke—I know not how many miles—where salt is brought up from the Cape Fear." This may serve as a typical illustration. An annual pilgrimage to the coast for salt thus became essential. Taking flocks or furs and ginseng root, the early settlers sent their pack trains after seeding time each year to the coast. This proved to be an important educational influence, since it was almost the only way in

which the pioneer learned what was going on in the East. But when discovery was made of the salt springs of the Kanawha, and the Holston, and Kentucky, and central New York, the West began to be freed from dependence on the coast. It was in part the effect of finding these salt springs that enabled settlement to cross the mountains.

From the time the mountains rose between the pioneer and the seaboard, a new order of Americanism arose. The West and the East began to get out of touch of each other. The settlements from the sea to the mountains kept connection with the rear and had a certain solidarity. But the over-mountain men grew more and more independent. The East took a narrow view of American advance, and nearly lost these men. Kentucky and Tennessee history bears abundant witness to the truth of this statement. The East began to try to hedge and limit westward expansion. Though Webster could declare that there were no Alleghanies in his politics, yet in politics in general they were a very solid factor.

The exploitation of the beasts took hunter and trader to the west, the exploitation of the grasses took the rancher west, and the exploitation of the virgin soil of the river valleys and prairies attracted the farmer. Good soils have been the most continuous attraction to the farmer's frontier. The land hunger of the Virginians drew them down the rivers into Carolina, in early colonial days; the search for soils took the Massachusetts men to Pennsylvania and to New York. As the eastern lands were taken up migration flowed across them to the west. Daniel Boone, the great backwoodsman, who combined the occupations of hunter, trader, cattle-raiser, farmer, and surveyor—learning, probably from the traders, of the fertility of the lands of the upper Yadkin, where the traders were wont to rest as they took their way to the Indians, left his Pennsylvania home with his father, and passed down the Great Valley road to that stream. Learning from a trader of the game and rich pastures of Kentucky, he pioneered the way for the farmers to that region. Thence he passed to the frontier of Missouri, where his settlement was long a landmark on the frontier. Here again he helped to open the way for civilization, finding salt licks, and trails, and land. His son was among the earliest trappers in the passes of the Rocky Mountains, and his party are said to have been the first to camp on the present site of Denver.

His grandson, Col. A. J. Boone, of Colorado, was a power among the Indians of the Rocky Mountains, and was appointed an agent by the government. Kit Carson's mother was a Boone. Thus this family epitomizes the backwoodsman's advance across the continent.

The farmer's advance came in a distinct series of waves. In Peck's New Guide to the West, published in Boston in 1837, occurs this suggestive passage:

> Generally, in all the western settlements, three classes, like the waves of the ocean, have rolled one after the other. First comes the pioneer, who depends for the subsistence of his family chiefly upon the natural growth of vegetation, called the "range," and the proceeds of hunting. His implements of agriculture are rude, chiefly of his own make, and his efforts directed mainly to a crop of corn and a "truck patch." The last is a rude garden for growing cabbage, beans, corn for roasting ears, cucumbers, and potatoes. A log cabin, and, occasionally, a stable and corn-crib, and a field of a dozen acres, the timber girdled or "deadened," and fenced, are enough for his occupancy. It is quite immaterial whether he ever becomes the owner of the soil. He is the occupant for the time being, pays no rent, and feels as independent as the "lord of the manor." With a horse, cow, and one or two breeders of swine, he strikes into the woods with his family, and becomes the founder of a new county, or perhaps state. He builds his cabin, gathers around him a few other families of similar tastes and habits, and occupies till the range is somewhat subdued, and hunting a little precarious, or, which is more frequently the case, till the neighbors crowd around, roads, bridges, and fields annoy him, and he lacks elbow room. The preëmption law enables him to dispose of his cabin and cornfield to the next class of emigrants; and, to employ his own figures, he "breaks for the high timber," "clears out for the New Purchase," or migrates to Arkansas or Texas, to work the same process over.
>
> The next class of emigrants purchase the lands, add field to field, clear out the roads, throw rough bridges over the streams, put up hewn log houses with glass windows and brick or stone chimneys, occasionally plant orchards, build mills, schoolhouses, court-houses, etc., and exhibit the picture and forms of plain, frugal, civilized life.
>
> Another wave rolls on. The men of capital and enterprise come. The settler is ready to sell out and take advantage of the rise in property, push farther into the interior and become, himself, a man of capital and enterprise in turn. The small village rises to a spacious town or city; substantial edifices of brick, extensive fields, orchards, gardens, colleges, and churches are seen. Broadcloths, silks, leghorns, crapes, and all the refinements, luxuries, elegancies, frivolities, and fashions are in vogue.

Thus wave after wave is rolling westward; the real Eldorado is still farther on.

A portion of the two first classes remain stationary amidst the general movement, improve their habits and condition, and rise in the scale of society.

The writer has traveled much amongst the first class, the real pioneers. He has lived many years in connection with the second grade; and now the third wave is sweeping over large districts of Indiana, Illinois, and Missouri. Migration has become almost a habit in the West. Hundreds of men can be found, not over 50 years of age, who have settled for the fourth, fifth, or sixth time on a new spot. To sell out and remove only a few hundred miles makes up a portion of the variety of backwoods life and manners.

Omitting those of the pioneer farmers who move from the love of adventure, the advance of the more steady farmer is easy to understand. Obviously the immigrant was attracted by the cheap lands of the frontier, and even the native farmer felt their influence strongly. Year by year the farmers who lived on soil whose returns were diminished by unrotated crops were offered the virgin soil of the frontier at nominal prices. Their growing families demanded more lands, and these were dear. The competition of the unexhausted, cheap, and easily tilled prairie lands compelled the farmer either to go west and continue the exhaustion of the soil on a new frontier, or to adopt intensive culture. Thus the census of 1890 shows, in the Northwest, many counties in which there is an absolute or a relative decrease of population. These States have been sending farmers to advance the frontier on the plains, and have themselves begun to turn to intensive farming and to manufacture. A decade before this, Ohio had shown the same transition stage. Thus the demand for land and the love of wilderness freedom drew the frontier ever onward.

Having now roughly outlined the various kinds of frontiers, and their modes of advance, chiefly from the point of view of the frontier itself, we may next inquire what were the influences on the East and on the Old World. A rapid enumeration of some of the more noteworthy effects is all that I have time for.

First, we note that the frontier promoted the formation of a composite nationality for the American people. The coast was preponderantly English, but the later tides of continental immigration flowed across to the free lands. This was the case from the early colonial days. The Scotch-Irish and the Palatine Germans, or "Pennsylvania Dutch," furnished the dominant element in the stock of the colonial frontier. With these peoples were also the freed indented servants, or redemptioners, who at the expiration of their time of service passed to the frontier. Governor Spotswood of Virginia writes in 1717, "The inhabitants of our frontiers are composed generally of such as have been transported hither as servants, and, being out of their time, settle themselves where land is to be taken up and that will produce the necessarys of life with little labour." Very generally these redemptioners were of non-English stock. In the crucible of the frontier the immigrants were Americanized, liberated, and fused into a mixed race, English in neither nationality nor characteristics. The process has gone on from the early days to our own. Burke and other writers in the middle of the eighteenth century believed that Pennsylvania was "threatened with the danger of being wholly foreign in language, manners, and perhaps even inclinations." The German and Scotch-Irish elements in the frontier of the South were only less great. In the middle of the present century the German element in Wisconsin was already so considerable that leading publicists looked to the creation of a German state out of the commonwealth by concentrating their colonization. Such examples teach us to beware of misinterpreting the fact that there is a common English speech in America into a belief that the stock is also English.

In another way the advance of the frontier decreased our dependence on England. The coast, particularly of the South, lacked diversified industries, and was dependent on England for the bulk of its supplies. In the South there was even a dependence on the Northern colonies for articles of food. Governor Glenn, of South Carolina, writes in the middle of the eighteenth century: "Our trade with New York and Philadelphia was of this sort, draining us of all the little money and bills we could gather from other places for their bread, flour, beer, hams, bacon, and other things of their produce, all which, except beer, our new townships begin to supply us with, which are settled with very industrious and thriving Germans. This no doubt diminishes the number of shipping and the appearance of our trade, but it is far from being a detriment to us." Before long the frontier created a demand for merchants. As it retreated from the coast it became less and less possible for England to bring her supplies directly to the consumer's wharfs, and carry away staple crops, and staple crops began to give way to diversified agriculture for a time. The effect of this phase of the frontier action upon the northern section is perceived when we realize how the advance of the frontier aroused seaboard cities like Boston, New York, and Baltimore, to engage in rivalry for what Washington called "the extensive and valuable trade of a rising empire."

The legislation which most developed the powers of the national government, and played the largest part in its activity, was conditioned on the frontier. Writers have discussed the subjects of tariff, land, and internal improvement, as subsidiary to the slavery question. But when American history comes to be rightly viewed it will be seen that the slavery question is an incident. In the period from the end of the first half of the present century to the close of the Civil War slavery rose to primary, but far from exclusive, importance. But this does not justify Dr. von Holst (to take an example) in treating our constitutional history in its formative period down to 1828 in a single volume, giving six volumes chiefly to the history of slavery from 1828 to 1861, under the title "Constitutional History of the United States." The growth of nationalism and the evolution of American political institutions were dependent on the advance of the frontier. Even so recent a writer as Rhodes, in his "History of the United States since the Compromise of 1850," has treated the legislation called out by the western advance as incidental to the slavery struggle.

This is a wrong perspective. The pioneer needed the goods of the coast, and so the grand series of internal improvement and railroad legislation began, with potent nationalizing effects. Over internal improvements occurred great debates, in which grave constitutional questions were discussed. Sectional groupings appear in the votes, profoundly significant for the historian. Loose construction increased as the nation marched westward. But the West was not content with bringing the farm to the factory. Under the lead of Clay—"Harry of the West"—protective tariffs were passed, with the cry of bringing the factory to the farm. The disposition of the public lands was a third important subject of national legislation influenced by the frontier.

The public domain has been a force of profound importance in the nationalization and

development of the government. The effects of
the struggle of the landed and the landless
States, and of the Ordinance of 1787, need no
discussion. Administratively the frontier called
out some of the highest and most vitalizing activities of the general government. The purchase of Louisiana was perhaps the constitutional turning point in the history of the Republic, inasmuch as it afforded both a new
10 area for national legislation and the occasion
of the downfall of the policy of strict construction. But the purchase of Louisiana was called
out by frontier needs and demands. As frontier
States accrued to the Union the national power
grew. In a speech on the dedication of the
Calhoun monument Mr. Lamar explained: "In
1789 the States were the creators of the Federal Government; in 1861 the Federal Government was the creator of a large majority of the
20 States."

When we consider the public domain from
the point of view of the sale and disposal of the
public lands we are again brought face to face
with the frontier. The policy of the United
States in dealing with its lands is in sharp contrast with the European system of scientific administration. Efforts to make this domain a
source of revenue, and to withhold it from emigrants in order that settlement might be com-
30 pact, were in vain. The jealousy and the fears
of the East were powerless in the face of the
demands of the frontiersmen. John Quincy
Adams was obliged to confess: "My own system of administration, which was to make the
national domain the inexhaustible fund for
progressive and unceasing internal improvement, has failed." The reason is obvious; a
system of administration was not what the
West demanded; it wanted land. Adams states
40 the situation as follows: "The slaveholders of
the South have bought the coöperation of the
western country by the bribe of the western
lands, abandoning to the new Western States
their own proportion of the public property
and aiding them in the design of grasping all
the lands into their own hands. Thomas H.
Benton was the author of this system, which
he brought forward as a substitute for the
American system of Mr. Clay, and to supplant
50 him as the leading statesman of the West. Mr.
Clay, by his tariff compromise with Mr. Calhoun, abandoned his own American system. At
the same time he brought forward a plan for
distributing among all the States of the Union
the proceeds of the sales of the public lands.

His bill for that purpose passed both Houses
of Congress, but was vetoed by President
Jackson, who, in his annual message of December, 1832, formally recommended that all public lands should be gratuitously given away to
individual adventurers and to the States in
which the lands are situated."

"No subject," said Henry Clay, "which has
presented itself to the present, or perhaps any
preceding, Congress, is of greater magnitude
than that of the public lands." When we consider the far-reaching effects of the government's land policy upon political, economic,
and social aspects of American life, we are disposed to agree with him. But this legislation
was framed under frontier influences, and under the lead of Western statesmen like Benton
and Jackson. Said Senator Scott of Indiana in
1841: "I consider the preëmption law merely
declaratory of the custom of common law of
the settlers."

It is safe to say that the legislation with regard to land, tariff, and internal improvements
—the American system of the nationalizing
Whig party—was conditioned on frontier ideas
and needs. But it was not merely in legislative
action that the frontier worked against the sectionalism of the coast. The economic and social
characteristics of the frontier worked against
sectionalism. The men of the frontier had closer
resemblances to the Middle region than to
either of the other sections. Pennsylvania had
been the seed-plot of frontier emigration, and,
although she passed on her settlers along the
Great Valley into the west of Virginia and the
Carolinas, yet the industrial society of these
Southern frontiersmen was always more like
that of the Middle region than like that of the
tide-water portion of the South, which later
came to spread its industrial type throughout
the South.

The Middle region, entered by New York
harbor, was an open door to all Europe. The
tide-water part of the South represented typical
Englishmen, modified by a warm climate and
servile labor, and living in baronial fashion on
great plantations; New England stood for a
special English movement—Puritanism. The
Middle region was less English than the other
sections. It had a wide mixture of nationalities,
a varied society, the mixed town and county
system of local government, a varied economic
life, many religious sects. In short, it was a
region mediating between New England and
the South, and the East and the West. It repre-

sented that composite nationality which the contemporary United States exhibits, that juxtaposition of non-English groups, occupying a valley or a little settlement, and presenting reflections of the map of Europe in their variety. It was democratic and nonsectional, if not national; "easy, tolerant, and contented"; rooted strongly in material prosperity. It was typical of the modern United States. It was least sectional, not only because it lay between North and South, but also because with no barriers to shut out its frontiers from its settled region, and with a system of connecting waterways, the Middle region mediated between East and West as well as between North and South. Thus it became the typically American region. Even the New Englander, who was shut out from the frontier by the Middle region, tarrying in New York or Pennsylvania on his westward march, lost the acuteness of his sectionalism on the way.

The spread of cotton culture into the interior of the South finally broke down the contrast between the "tide-water" region and the rest of the State, and based Southern interests on slavery. Before this process revealed its results the western portion of the South, which was akin to Pennsylvania in stock, society, and industry, showed tendencies to fall away from the faith of the fathers into internal improvement legislation and nationalism. In the Virginia convention of 1829–30, called to revise the constitution, Mr. Leigh, of Chesterfield, one of the tide-water counties, declared:

One of the main causes of discontent which led to this convention, that which had the strongest influence in overcoming our veneration for the work of our fathers, which taught us to contemn the sentiments of Henry and Mason and Pendleton, which weaned us from our reverence for the constituted authorities of the State, was an overweening passion for internal improvement. I say this with perfect knowledge, for it has been avowed to me by gentlemen from the West over and over again. And let me tell the gentleman from Albemarle (Mr. Gordon) that it has been another principal object of those who set this ball of revolution in motion, to overturn the doctrine of State rights, of which Virginia has been the very pillar, and to remove the barrier she has interposed to the interference of the Federal Government in that same work of internal improvement, by so reorganizing the legislature that Virginia, too, may be hitched to the Federal car.

It was this nationalizing tendency of the West that transformed the democracy of Jefferson into the national republicanism of Monroe and the democracy of Andrew Jackson. The West of the War of 1812, the West of Clay, and Benton and Harrison, and Andrew Jackson, shut off by the Middle States and the mountains from the coast sections, had a solidarity of its own with national tendencies. On the tide of the Father of Waters, North and South met and mingled into a nation. Interstate migration went steadily on—a process of cross-fertilization of ideas and institutions. The fierce struggle of the sections over slavery on the western frontier does not diminish the truth of this statement; it proves the truth of it. Slavery was a sectional trait that would not down, but in the West it could not remain sectional. It was the greatest of frontiersmen who declared: "I believe this Government can not endure permanently half slave and half free. It will become all of one thing or all of the other." Nothing works for nationalism like intercourse within the nation. Mobility of population is death to localism, and the western frontier worked irresistibly in unsettling population. The effect reached back from the frontier and affected profoundly the Atlantic coast and even the Old World.

But the most important effect of the frontier has been in the promotion of democracy here and in Europe. As has been indicated, the frontier is productive of individualism. Complex society is precipitated by the wilderness into a kind of primitive organization based on the family. The tendency is anti-social. It produces antipathy to control, and particularly to any direct control. The tax-gatherer is viewed as a representative of oppression. Prof. Osgood, in an able article, has pointed out that the frontier conditions prevalent in the colonies are important factors in the explanation of the American Revolution, where individual liberty was sometimes confused with absence of all effective government. The same conditions aid in explaining the difficulty of instituting a strong government in the period of the confederacy. The frontier individualism has from the beginning promoted democracy.

The frontier States that came into the Union in the first quarter of a century of its existence came in with democratic suffrage provisions, and had reactive effects of the highest importance upon the older States whose peoples were being attracted there. An extension of the franchise became essential. It was *western* New York that forced an extension of suffrage in the constitutional convention of that State in 1821; and it was *western* Virginia that compelled the tide-water region to put a more liberal suffrage provision in the constitution framed in 1830, and to give to the frontier region a more nearly proportionate representation with the tide-water aristocracy. The rise of democracy as an effective force in the nation came in with western preponderance under Jackson and William Henry Harrison, and it meant the triumph of the frontier—with all of its good and with all of its evil elements. An interesting illustration of the tone of frontier democracy in 1830 comes from the same debates in the Virginia convention already referred to. A representative from western Virginia declared:

But, sir, it is not the increase of population in the West which this gentleman ought to fear. It is the energy which the mountain breeze and western habits impart to those emigrants. They are regenerated, politically I mean, sir. They soon become *working politicians*; and the difference, sir, between a *talking* and a *working* politician is immense. The Old Dominion has long been celebrated for producing great orators; the ablest metaphysicians in policy; men that can split hairs in all abstruse questions of political economy. But at home, or when they return from Congress, they have negroes to fan them asleep. But a Pennsylvania, a New York, an Ohio, or a western Virginia statesman, though far inferior in logic, metaphysics, and rhetoric to an old Virginia statesman, has this advantage, that when he returns home he takes off his coat and takes hold of the plow. This gives him bone and muscle, sir, and preserves his republican principles pure and uncontaminated.

So long as free land exists, the opportunity for a competency exists, and economic power secures political power. But the democracy born of free land, strong in selfishness and individualism, intolerant of administrative experience and education, and pressing individual liberty beyond its proper bounds, has its dangers as well as its benefits. Individualism in America has allowed a laxity in regard to governmental affairs which has rendered possible the spoils system and all the manifest evils that follow from the lack of a highly developed civic spirit. In this connection may be noted also the influence of frontier conditions in permitting lax business honor, inflated paper currency and wild-cat banking. The colonial and revolutionary frontier was the region whence emanated many of the worst forms of an evil currency. The West in the War of 1812 repeated the phenomenon on the frontier of that day, while the speculation and wild-cat banking of the period of the crisis of 1837 occurred on the new frontier belt of the next tier of States. Thus each one of the periods of lax financial integrity coincides with periods when a new set of frontier communities had arisen, and coincides in area with these successive frontiers, for the most part. The recent Populist agitation is a case in point. Many a State that now declines any connection with the tenets of the Populists, itself adhered to such ideas in an earlier stage of the development of the State. A primitive society can hardly be expected to show the intelligent appreciation of the complexity of business interests in a developed society. The continual recurrence of these areas of paper-money agitation is another evidence that the frontier can be isolated and studied as a factor in American history of the highest importance.

The East has always feared the result of an unregulated advance of the frontier, and has tried to check and guide it. The English authorities would have checked settlement at the headwaters of the Atlantic tributaries and allowed the "savages to enjoy their deserts in quiet lest the peltry trade should decrease." This called out Burke's splendid protest:

If you stopped your grants, what would be the consequence? The people would occupy without grants. They have already so occupied in many places. You can not station garrisons in every part of these deserts. If you drive the people from one place, they will carry on their annual tillage and remove with their flocks and herds to another. Many of the people in the back settlements are already little attached to particular situations. Already they have topped the Appalachian Mountains. From thence they behold before them an immense plain, one vast, rich, level meadow; a square of five hundred miles. Over this they would wander without a possibility of restraint; they would change their manners with their habits of life; would soon forget a government by which they were disowned; would become hordes of English Tartars; and, pouring down upon your unfortified frontiers a fierce and irresistible cavalry, become masters of your governors and your counselors, your collectors and comptrollers, and of all the slaves that adhered to them. Such would, and in no long time must, be the effect of attempting to forbid as a crime and to suppress as an evil the command and blessing of Providence, "Increase and multiply." Such would be the happy result of an endeavor to keep as a lair of wild beasts that earth which God, by an express charter, has given to the children of men.

But the English Government was not alone in its desire to limit the advance of the frontier and guide its destinies. Tide-water Virginia and South Carolina gerrymandered those colonies to insure the dominance of the coast in their legislatures. Washington desired to settle a State at a time in the Northwest; Jefferson would reserve from settlement the territory of his Louisiana Purchase north of the thirty-second parallel, in order to offer it to the Indians in exchange for their settlements east of the Mississippi. "When we shall be full on this side," he writes, "we may lay off a range of States on the western bank from the head to the mouth, and so range after range, advancing compactly as we multiply." Madison went so far as to argue to the French minister that the United States had no interest in seeing population extend itself on the right bank of the Mississippi, but should rather fear it. When the Oregon question was under debate, in 1824, Smyth, of Virginia, would draw an unchangeable line for the limits of the United States at the outer limit of two tiers of States beyond the Mississippi, complaining that the seaboard States were being drained of the flower of their population by the bringing of too much land into market. Even Thomas Benton, the man of widest views of the destiny of the West, at this stage of his career declared that along the ridge of the Rocky mountains "the western limits of the Republic should be drawn, and the statue of the fabled god Terminus should be raised upon its highest peak, never to be thrown down." But the attempt to limit the boundaries, to restrict land sales and settlement, and to deprive the West of its share of political power were all in vain. Steadily the frontier of settlement advanced and carried with it individualism, democracy, and nationalism, and powerfully affected the East and the Old World.

The most effective efforts of the East to regulate the frontier came through its educational and religious activity, exerted by interstate migration and by organized societies. Speaking in 1835, Dr. Lyman Beecher declared: "It is equally plain that the religious and political destiny of our nation is to be decided in the West," and he pointed out that the population of the West "is assembled from all the States of the Union and from all the nations of Europe,

and is rushing in like the waters of the flood, demanding for its moral preservation the immediate and universal action of those institutions which discipline the mind and arm the conscience and the heart. And so various are the opinions and habits, and so recent and imperfect is the acquaintance, and so sparse are the settlements of the West, that no homogeneous public sentiment can be formed to legislate immediately into being the requisite institutions. And yet they are all needed immediately in their utmost perfection and power. A nation is being 'born in a day.' . . . But what will become of the West if her prosperity rushes up to such a majesty of power, while those great institutions linger which are necessary to form the mind and the conscience and the heart of that vast world. It must not be permitted. . . . Let no man at the East quiet himself and dream of liberty, whatever may become of the West. . . . Her destiny is our destiny."

With the appeal to the conscience of New England, he adds appeals to her fears lest other religious sects anticipate her own. The New England preacher and school-teacher left their mark on the West. The dread of Western emancipation from New England's political and economic control was paralleled by her fears lest the West cut loose from her religion. Commenting in 1850 on reports that settlement was rapidly extending northward in Wisconsin, the editor of the *Home Missionary* writes: "We scarcely know whether to rejoice or mourn over this extension of our settlements. While we sympathize in whatever tends to increase the physical resources and prosperity of our country, we can not forget that with all these dispersions into remote and still remoter corners of the land the supply of the means of grace is becoming relatively less and less." Acting in accordance with such ideas, home missions were established and Western colleges were erected. As seaboard cities like Philadelphia, New York, and Baltimore strove for the mastery of Western trade, so the various denominations strove for the possession of the West. Thus an intellectual stream from New England sources fertilized the West. Other sections sent their missionaries; but the real struggle was between sects. The contest for power and the expansive tendency furnished to the various sects by the existence of a moving frontier must have had important results on the character of religious organization in the United States. The multiplication of rival churches in the little frontier towns had deep and lasting social effects. The religious aspects of the frontier make a chapter in our history which needs study.

From the conditions of frontier life came intellectual traits of profound importance. The works of travelers along each frontier from colonial days onward describe certain common traits, and these traits have, while softening down, still persisted as survivals in the place of their origin, even when a higher social organization succeeded. The result is that to the frontier the American intellect owes its striking characteristics. That coarseness and strength combined with acuteness and inquisitiveness; that practical, inventive turn of mind, quick to find expedients; that masterful grasp of material things, lacking in the artistic but powerful to effect great ends; that restless, nervous energy; that dominant individualism, working for good and for evil, and withal that buoyancy and exuberance which comes with freedom—these are traits of the frontier, or traits called out elsewhere because of the existence of the frontier. Since the days when the fleet of Columbus sailed into the waters of the New World, America has been another name for opportunity, and the people of the United States have taken their tone from the incessant expansion which has not only been open but has even been forced upon them. He would be a rash prophet who should assert that the expansive character of American life has now entirely ceased. Movement has been its dominant fact, and, unless this training has no effect upon a people, the American energy will continually demand a wider field for its exercise. But never again will such gifts of free land offer themselves. For a moment, at the frontier, the bonds of custom are broken and unrestraint is triumphant. There is not *tabula rasa*. The stubborn American environment is there with its imperious summons to accept its conditions; the inherited ways of doing things are also there; and yet, in spite of environment, and in spite of custom, each frontier did indeed furnish a new field of opportunity, a gate of escape from the bondage of the past; and freshness, and confidence, and scorn of older society, impatience of its restraints and its ideas, and indifference to its lessons, have accompanied the frontier. What the Mediterranean Sea was to the Greeks, breaking the bond of custom, offering new experiences, calling out new institutions and activities, that, and more, the ever retreating frontier has been to the United States directly, and to the nations of Europe more remotely. And now, four centuries from the discovery of America, at the end of a hundred years of life under the Constitution, the frontier has gone, and with its going has closed the first period of American history.   1893

» » *Class Conflicts and Class Protests* « «
1870-1896

» » « «

BUT THE MORTGAGE WORKED THE HARDEST

We worked through spring and winter,—
Through summer and through fall,
But the mortgage worked the hardest—
and the steadiest of them all.
It worked on nights and Sundays;—
it worked each holiday;
It settled down among us—
and never went away.

Whatever we kept from it—
seemed almost as a theft;
It watched us every minute;
it ruled us right and left.
The rust and blight were with us—
sometimes, and sometimes not;
The dark-browed, scowling mortgage—
was forever on the spot.

The weevil and cut worm—
they went as well as came;
The mortgage stayed forever,—
eating hearty all the same.
It nailed up every window,
stood guard at every door,
And happiness and sunshine,
made their home with us no more.

Till with failing crops and sickness—
we got stalled upon the grade,
And there came a dark day on us,
when the interest wasn't paid;
And there came a sharp foreclosure,
and I kind o' lost my hold,
And grew weary and discouraged,
and the farm was cheaply sold.

The children left and scattered,
when they hardly yet were grown;
My wife, she pined and perished,
and I found myself alone.
What she died of was a "mystery"
the doctors never knew,
But I know she died of mortgage—
just as well as I wanted to.

If to trace the hidden arrow
was within the doctor's art,
They'd ha' found a mortgage lying—
on that woman's broken heart.
Worm or beetle, drouth or tempest
on a farmer's land may fall,
But for a first class ruination,
trust a mortgage 'gainst them all.

This ballad, written by Will Carleton, was sung in the 1890's at Farmers' Alliance meetings and rallies. It is included by permission of the Federal Writers Project in Nebraska.

» » « «

A.R.U.

Been on the hummer since ninety-four,
Last job I had was on the Lake Shore,
Lost my office in the A.R.U.,
And I won't get it back till nineteen-two.
And I'm still on the hog train flagging my meals,
Ridin' the brake beams close to the wheels.

The strike of the American Railway Union in 1893, which developed when the Union supported the Pullman workers in their strike, resulted in stoppage of traffic in the Northwest. After President Cleveland broke the strike by the use of Federal troops, blacklisted union men drifted about the country in search of work. This song of theirs was set down by Mr. Carl Sandburg in *The American Songbag*. It is printed here by permission of Harcourt, Brace and Company.

» » « «

Class Conflicts and Class Protests

FROM TWO SOURCES the new dominance of industrialism, which the Civil War did so much to promote, received vigorous challenge. On the one hand the Western farmers found much in their recent alliance with industrial capitalists which was not at all to their liking. The railroads in which farmers had invested and on which they had placed their hopes charged exhorbitant freight rates, and made notorious deals with business corporations. Such agreements militated against the farmers. Interest rates were excessive, and the farmer was burdened with debt, hard times, and cultural impoverishment. On the other hand urban workers, facing a decrease in real wages, harassed by unemployment incident to depression, and frightened into refusing to take part in strikes and organization, became increasingly class-conscious. Although a few leaders among the embattled farmers and workers realized the importance of making common cause against the industrialist, the genuine cleavage in the interests of rural and urban workers, and the prejudice which the farmer felt for the latter, made anything like a workable and enduring entente all but impossible.

The conviction that many of the farmers' ills would disappear if the currency were inflated governed the basic assumptions of the Greenbackers and Populists alike. But the Populists also insisted on the regulation of railroads and other business corporations, on the government ownership of certain utilities, and on the democratization of political machinery to render impossible its control by vested interests. For a time in the 1880's and 1890's Southern and Western farmers made a common cause. But the Bourbons in the South used the race issue to drive a wedge into a united front between the common man in the South and his fellow in the West. And the defeat of Bryan in 1896 seemed to be the defeat of the farmers' movement. Some part of their program, however, was adopted by Republican Progressives, and an even larger part was subsequently realized in the first administration of Woodrow Wilson.

While some elements of industrial labor realized that currency inflation might be of advantage, both the Knights of Labor and the rising American Federation of Labor banked chiefly on the power of organization. Whether the term "worker" should be regarded as inclusive of all ranks that labored by hand or brain, or whether it should be limited to the more skilled craftsman, occasioned deep rifts in the ranks of labor. The triumph of the American Federation of Labor was a victory for the latter position. But labor was further divided on the question whether the battle should be confined to the economic front and centered in a struggle for better wages and shorter hours, or whether it should include political tactics and a social program as well.

To the older varieties of utopian socialism were added new types of protest, which attacked the basis of industrial capitalism. Men of Christian faith and social conscience, stimulated by the rise of Christian Socialism in England, launched a similar movement here. Marxism also found its exponents. Convinced that the Marxist ideology must be modified if it was to flourish on American soil, "reformists" tried to revamp the body of doctrines which Marx and Engels had formulated.

While some of these American types of socialism were not without elements of originality, the social doctrine most indigenous to America was the single tax doctrine of Henry George. European theorists, it is true, had anticipated him; but the crusade for social justice which he dramatized in terms of the socialization of the use of land, enjoyed for a time a wide appeal.

Literary men and scholars did not remain indifferent to these tensions in American life. Economists hoped through investigations of the economic structure and through devising specifics for its ailments to resolve many of its conflicts. Some men of letters definitely sided with the employing and capitalist class; but others joined enthusiastically in the battles which the less privileged were waging for economic democracy.

» » « «

HENRY GEORGE

1839–1897

HENRY GEORGE, after a scanty schooling in Philadelphia, a brief career at sea, and a grimly impoverished existence in California, seriously began to try to determine the reasons for the abundance of natural resources and wealth on the one hand, and human want on the other. *Progress and Poverty* (1879) was his answer. From the appearance of this book until his death he devoted himself unsparingly to the popularization of his social philosophy. Through lectures, writing, and political campaigning (he was candidate for the New York mayoralty in 1886 and again in 1897) George won converts in the United States and in the British Isles.

In the words of John Dewey, "No man, no graduate of a higher educational institution, has a right to regard himself as an educated man in social thought unless he has some first-hand acquaintance with the theoretical contribution of this great American thinker." With an impassioned eloquence Henry George laid bare many of the ills of a monopolistic economy. In his mind the selfish monopolization of the abundant gifts of nature kept mankind in chains. The value of land was created by the community, not by the monopolist; in consequence society should subsume that which it had created. If this were done through a "single tax" on unearned increment or rent, no other tax would be necessary. Henry George not only maintained that this simple formula would solve the problem of poverty; he likewise insisted that human energies would be released from the shackles of ill-compensated toil, would flower in a finer "a wider, fuller, and more varied life."

His doctrine met with rebuffs from orthodox academic economists. It was rejected by Marxists as an oversimplified formula which failed to take into account the essential nature of the class struggle and "surplus value." But Henry George's doctrine influenced many literary men —Hamlin Garland, for instance—and deeply affected at least a half a dozen pioneers in the movement for reform in municipalities and states. His contribution, in spite of much criticism and notwithstanding the fact that it had many intellectual precedents, nevertheless made him one of the world's great social philosophers and one of America's most significant crusaders for social justice.

Works of Henry George, 10 vols., Garden City, 1906–1911.
Henry George, Jr., *The Life of Henry George*, New York, 1900.
A. N. Young, *The Single Tax Movement in the United States*, Princeton, 1916.
G. R. Geiger, *The Philosophy of Henry George*, New York, 1933.
Charles A. Barker, *Henry George*, New York, 1955.

» » From: PROGRESS AND POVERTY « «

THE PROBLEM

Could a Franklin or a Priestley have seen, in a vision of the future, the steamship taking the place of the sailing vessel, the railroad train of the wagon, the reaping machine of the scythe, the threshing machine of the flail; could he have heard the throb of the engines that in obedience to human will, and for the satisfac-
10 tion of human desire, exert a power greater than that of all the men and all the beasts of burden of the earth combined; could he have seen the forest tree transformed into finished lumber—into doors, sashes, blinds, boxes or barrels, with hardly the touch of a human hand; the great workshops where boots and shoes are turned out by the case with less labor than the old-fashioned cobbler could have put on a sole; the factories where under the eye of
20 a girl, cotton becomes cloth faster than hundreds of stalwart weavers could have turned it out with their hand-looms; could he have seen steam hammers shaping mammoth shafts and mighty anchors, and delicate machinery making tiny watches; the diamond drill cutting through the heart of the rocks, and coal oil sparing the whale; could he have realized the enormous saving of labor resulting from improved facilities of exchange and communica-
30 tion—sheep killed in Australia eaten fresh in England, and the order given by the London banker in the afternoon executed in San Francisco in the morning of the same day; could he have conceived of the hundred thousand improvements which these only suggest, what would he have inferred as to the social condition of mankind?

It would not have seemed like an inference; further than the vision went it would have
40 seemed as though he saw; and his heart would have leaped and his nerves would have thrilled, as one who from a height beholds just ahead of the thirst-stricken caravan the living gleam of rustling woods and the glint of laughing waters. Plainly, in the sight of the imagination, he would have beheld these new forces elevating society from its very foundations, lifting the very poorest above the possibility of want, exempting the very lowest from
50 anxiety for the material needs of life; he would have seen these slaves of the lamp of knowl-edge taking on themselves the traditional curse, these muscles of iron and sinews of steel making the poorest laborer's life a holiday, in which every high quality and noble impulse could have scope to grow.

And out of these bounteous material conditions he would have seen arising, as necessary sequences, moral conditions realizing the golden age of which mankind always dreamed. Youth no longer stunted and starved; age no longer harried by avarice; the child at play with the tiger; the man with the muck-rake drinking in the glory of the stars! Foul things fled, fierce things tame; discord turned to harmony! For how could there be greed where all had enough? How could the vice, the crime, the ignorance, the brutality, that spring from poverty and the fear of poverty, exist where poverty had vanished? Who should crouch where all were freemen; who oppress where all were peers?

More or less vague or clear, these have been the hopes, these the dreams born of the improvements which give this wonderful era its preëminence. They have sunk so deeply into the popular mind as radically to change the currents of thought, to recast creeds and displace the most fundamental conceptions. The haunting visions of higher possibilities have not merely gathered splendor and vividness, but their direction has changed—instead of seeing behind the faint tinges of an expiring sunset, all the glory of the daybreak has decked the skies before.

It is true that disappointment has followed disappointment, and that discovery upon discovery, and invention after invention, have neither lessened the toil of those who most need respite, nor brought plenty to the poor. But there have been so many things to which it seemed this failure could be laid, that faith has hardly weakened. We have better appreciated the difficulties to be overcome; but not the less trusted that the tendency of the times was to overcome them.

Now, however, we are coming into collision with facts which there can be no mistaking. From all parts of the civilized world come complaints of industrial depression; of labor condemned to involuntary idleness; of capital massed and wasting; of pecuniary distress among business men; of want and suffering and anxiety among the working classes. All the dull, deadening pain, all the keen, maddening anguish, that to great masses of men are involved in the words "hard times," have afflicted the world. This state of things, common to communities differing so widely in situation, in political institutions, in fiscal and financial systems, in density of population and in social organization, can hardly be accounted for by local causes. There is distress where large standing armies are maintained, but there is also distress where the standing armies are nominal; there is distress where protective tariffs stupidly and wastefully hamper trade, but there is also distress where trade is nearly free; there is distress where autocratic government yet prevails, but there is also distress where political power is wholly in the hands of the people; in countries where paper is money, and in countries where gold and silver are the only currency. Evidently, beneath all such things as these, we must infer a common cause.

That there is a common cause, and that it is either what we call material progress or something closely connected with material progress, becomes more than an inference when it is noted that the phenomena we class together and speak of as industrial depression are but intensifications of phenomena which always accompany material progress, and which show themselves more clearly and strongly as material progress goes on.

It has always been to the newer countries —that is, to the countries where material progress is yet in its earlier stages—that laborers have emigrated in search of higher wages, and capital has flowed in search of higher interest. It is in the older countries—that is to say, the countries where material progress has reached later stages—that widespread destitution is found in the midst of the greatest abundance. Go into a new community where Anglo-Saxon vigor is just beginning the race of progress; where the machinery of production and exchange is yet rude and inefficient; where the increment of wealth is not yet great enough to enable any class to live in ease and luxury; where the best house is but a cabin of logs or a cloth and paper shanty, and the richest man is forced to daily work—and though you will find an absence of wealth and all its concomitants, you will find no beggars. There is no luxury, but there is no destitution. No one makes an easy living, nor a very good living; but every one *can* make a living, and no one able and willing to work is oppressed by the fear of want.

But just as such a community realizes the conditions which all civilized communities are striving for, and advances in the scale of material progress—just as closer settlement and a more intimate connection with the rest of the world, and greater utilization of labor-saving machinery, make possible greater economies in production and exchange, and wealth in consequence increases, not merely in the aggregate, but in proportion to population—so does poverty take a darker aspect. Some get an infinitely better and easier living, but others find it hard to get a living at all. The "tramp" comes with the locomotive, and almshouses and prisons are as surely the marks of "material progress" as are costly dwellings, rich warehouses, and magnificent churches. Upon streets lighted with gas and patrolled by uniformed policemen, beggars wait for the passer-by, and in the shadow of college, and library, and museum, are gathering the more hideous Huns and fiercer Vandals of whom Macaulay prophesied.

This fact—the great fact that poverty and all its concomitants show themselves in communities just as they develop into the conditions toward which material progress tends— proves that the social difficulties existing wherever a certain stage of progress has been reached, do not arise from local circumstances, but are, in some way or another, engendered by progress itself.

And, unpleasant as it may be to admit it, it is at last becoming evident that the enormous increase in productive power which has marked the present century and is still going on with accelerating ratio, has no tendency to extirpate poverty or to lighten the burdens of those compelled to toil. It simply widens the gulf between Dives and Lazarus, and makes the struggle for existence more intense. The march of invention has clothed mankind with powers of which a century ago the boldest imagination could not have dreamed. But in factories where labor-saving machinery has reached its most wonderful development, little children are at work; wherever the new forces are anything like fully utilized, large classes are maintained by charity or live on the verge of recourse to it; amid the greatest accumulations of wealth, men die of starvation, and

puny infants suckle dry breasts; while everywhere the greed of gain, the worship of wealth,
shows the force of the fear of want. The promised land flies before us like the mirage. The
fruits of the tree of knowledge turn as we grasp
them to apples of Sodom that crumble at the
touch.

It is true that wealth has been greatly increased, and that the average of comfort, lei-
10 sure, and refinement has been raised; but these
gains are not general. In them the lowest class
do not share. I do not mean that the condition
of the lowest class has nowhere nor in anything
been improved; but that there is nowhere any
improvement which can be credited to increased productive power. I mean that the
tendency of what we call material progress is
in nowise to improve the condition of the
lowest class in the essentials of healthy, happy
20 human life. Nay, more, that it is still further
to depress the condition of the lowest class.
The new forces, elevating in their nature
though they be, do not act upon the social
fabric from underneath, as was for a long
time hoped and believed, but strike it at a
point intermediate between top and bottom.
It is as though an immense wedge were being
forced, not underneath society, but through
society. Those who are above the point of
30 separation are elevated, but those who are below are crushed down.

This depressing effect is not generally realized, for it is not apparent where there has
long existed a class just able to live. Where the
lowest class barely lives, as has been the case
for a long time in many parts of Europe, it is
impossible for it to get any lower, for the next
lowest step is out of existence, and no tendency
to further depression can readily show itself.
40 But in the progress of new settlements to the
conditions of older communities it may clearly
be seen that material progress does not merely
fail to relieve poverty—it actually produces it.

This association of poverty with progress is
the great enigma of our times. It is the central
fact from which spring industrial, social, and
political difficulties that perplex the world, and
with which statesmanship and philanthropy
and education grapple in vain. From it come
50 the clouds that overhang the future of the
most progressive and self-reliant nations. It
is the riddle which the Sphinx of Fate puts to
our civilization, and which not to answer is to
be destroyed. So long as all the increased
wealth which modern progress brings goes but

to build up great fortunes, to increase luxury
and make sharper the contrast between the
House of Have and the House of Want, progress is not real and cannot be permanent. The
reaction must come. The tower leans from its
foundations, and every new story but hastens
the final catastrophe. To educate men who
must be condemned to poverty, is but to make
them restive; to base on a state of most glaring
social inequality political institutions under
which men are theoretically equal, is to stand
a pyramid on its apex.

All-important as this question is, pressing
itself from every quarter painfully upon attention, it has not yet received a solution which
accounts for all the facts and points to any
clear and simple remedy.

It must be within the province of political
economy to solve it. For political economy is
not a set of dogmas. It is the explanation of a
certain set of facts. It is the science which, in
the sequence of certain phenomena, seeks to
trace mutual relations and to identify cause and
effect, just as the physical sciences seek to do
in other sets of phenomena. It lays its foundations upon firm ground. The premises from
which it makes its deductions are truths which
have the highest sanction; axioms which we all
recognize; upon which we safely base the reasoning and actions of everyday life, and which
may be reduced to the metaphysical expression
of the physical law that motion seeks the line of
least resistance—viz., that men seek to gratify
their desires with the least exertion.

I propose in the following pages to attempt
to solve by the methods of political economy
the great problem I have outlined. I propose
to seek the law which associates poverty with
progress, and increases want with advancing
wealth. Properly commenced and carefully
pursued, such an investigation must yield a
conclusion that will stand every test, and as
truth, will correlate with all other truth. For in
the sequence of phenomena there is no accident. Every effect has a cause, and every fact
implies a preceding fact.

I propose in this inquiry to take nothing for
granted, I propose to beg no question, to shrink
from no conclusion, but to follow truth wherever it may lead.

LAND RENT GROWS AS COMMUNITY DEVELOPS

Land, Labor, and Capital are the factors of
production. The term Land includes all natural

opportunities or forces; the term Labor, all human exertion; and the term Capital, all wealth used to produce more wealth. In returns to these three factors is the whole produce distributed. That part which goes to land owners as payment for the use of natural opportunities is called Rent; that part which constitutes the reward of human exertion is called Wages; and that part which constitutes the return for the use of capital is called Interest. These terms mutually exclude each other. The income of any individual may be made up from any one, two, or all three of these sources; but in the effort to discover the laws of distribution we must keep them separate.

There must be land before labor can be exerted, and labor must be exerted before capital can be produced. Capital is a result of labor, and is used by labor to assist it in further production. Labor is the active and initial force, and labor is therefore the employer of capital. Labor can be exerted only upon land, and it is from land that the matter which it transmutes into wealth must be drawn. Land therefore is the condition precedent, the field and material of labor. The natural order is land, labor, capital.

Increasing population increases rent [1] without reference to the natural qualities of land, for the increased powers of co-operation and exchange which come with increased population are equivalent to—nay, I think we can say without metaphor, that they give—an increased capacity to land.

I do not mean to say merely that, like an improvement in the methods or tools of production, the increased power which comes with increased population gives to the same labor an increased result, which is equivalent to an increase in the natural powers of land; but that it brings out a superior power in labor, which is localized on land—which attaches not to labor generally, but only to labor exerted on particular land; and which thus inheres in the land as much as any qualities of soil, climate, mineral deposit, or natural situation, and passes, as they do, with the possession of the land.

Here, let us imagine, is an unbounded savannah, stretching off in unbroken sameness of grass and flower, tree and rill, till the traveler tires of the monotony. Along comes the wagon

of the first immigrant. Where to settle he cannot tell—every acre seems as good as every other acre. As to wood, as to water, as to fertility, as to situation, there is absolutely no choice, and he is perplexed by the embarrassment of richness. Tired out with the search for one place that is better than another, he stops —somewhere, anywhere—and starts to make himself a home. The soil is virgin and rich, game is abundant, the streams flash with the finest trout. Nature is at her very best. He has what, were he in a populous district, would make him rich; but he is very poor. To say nothing of the mental craving, which would lead him to welcome the sorriest stranger, he labors under all the material disadvantages of solitude. He can get no temporary assistance for any work that requires a greater union of strength than that afforded by his own family, or by such help as he can permanently keep. Though he has cattle, he cannot often have fresh meat, for to get a beefsteak he must kill a bullock. He must be his own blacksmith, wagonmaker, carpenter, and cobbler—in short, a "jack of all trades and master of none." He cannot have his children schooled, for, to do so, he must himself pay and maintain a teacher. Such things as he cannot produce himself, he must buy in quantities and keep on hand, or else go without, for he cannot be constantly leaving his work and making a long journey to the verge of civilization; and when forced to do so, the getting of a vial of medicine or the replacement of a broken auger may cost him the labor of himself and horses for days. Under such circumstances, though nature is prolific, the man is poor. It is an easy matter for him to get enough to eat; but beyond this, his labor will suffice to satisfy only the simplest wants in the rudest way.

Soon there comes another immigrant. Although every quarter section of the boundless plain is as good as every other quarter section, he is not beset by any embarrassment as to where to settle. Though the land is the same, there is one place that is clearly better for him than any other place, and that is where there is already a settler and he may have a neighbor. He settles by the side of the first comer, whose condition is at once greatly improved, and to whom many things are now possible that were before impossible, for two men may help each other to do things that one man could never do.

Another immigrant comes, and, guided by

---

[1] Elsewhere, Henry George explains: "I, of course, use 'rent' in its economic, not in its common sense, meaning by it what is commonly called ground-rent." [Professor Harry G. Brown, editor.]

the same attraction, settles where there are already two. Another, and another, until around
our first comer there are a score of neighbors.
Labor has now an effectiveness which, in the
solitary state, it could not approach. If heavy
work is to be done, the settlers have a log-
rolling, and together accomplish in a day what
singly would require years. When one kills a
bullock, the others take part of it, returning
when they kill, and thus they have fresh meat
all the time. Together they hire a schoolmaster,
and the children of each are taught for a frac-
tional part of what similar teaching would have
cost the first settler. It becomes a comparatively
easy matter to send to the nearest town, for
some one is always going. But there is less need
for such journeys. A blacksmith and a wheelwright soon set up shops, and our settler can
have his tools repaired for a small part of the
labor it formerly cost him. A store is opened
and he can get what he wants as he wants it;
a post-office, soon added, gives him regular
communication with the rest of the world.
Then comes a cobbler, a carpenter, a harness-
maker, a doctor; and a little church soon arises.
Satisfactions become possible that in the solitary state were impossible. There are gratifications for the social and the intellectual nature
—for that part of the man that rises above the
animal. The power of sympathy, the sense of
companionship, the emulation of comparison
and contrast, open a wider, and fuller, and
more varied life. In rejoicing, there are others
to rejoice; in sorrow, the mourners do not
mourn alone. There are husking bees, and
apple parings, and quilting parties. Though the
ballroom be unplastered and the orchestra but
a fiddle, the notes of the magician are yet in the
strain, and Cupid dances with the dancers. At
the wedding, there are others to admire and
enjoy; in the house of death, there are watch-
ers; by the open grave, stands human sympathy
to sustain the mourners. Occasionally, comes a
straggling lecturer to open up glimpses of the
world of science, of literature, or of art; in election times, come stump speakers, and the citizen rises to a sense of dignity and power, as
the cause of empires is tried before him in the
struggle of John Doe and Richard Roe for his
support and vote. And, by and by, comes the
circus, talked of months before, and opening to
children whose horizon has been the prairie,
all the realms of the imagination—princes and
princesses of fairy tale, mail-clad crusaders and
turbaned Moors, Cinderella's fairy coach, and

the giants of nursery lore; lions such as
crouched before Daniel, or in circling Roman
amphitheater tore the saints of God; ostriches
who recall the sandy deserts; camels such as
stood around when the wicked brethren raised
Joseph from the well and sold him into bondage; elephants such as crossed the Alps with
Hannibal, or felt the sword of the Maccabees;
and glorious music that thrills and builds in the
chambers of the mind as rose the sunny dome
of Kubla Khan.

Go to our settler now, and say to him: "You
have so many fruit trees which you planted;
so much fencing, such a well, a barn, a house
—in short, you have by your labor added so
much value to this farm. Your land itself is not
quite so good. You have been cropping it, and
by and by it will need manure. I will give you
the full value of all your improvements if you
will give it to me, and go again with your
family beyond the verge of settlement." He
would laugh at you. His land yields no more
wheat or potatoes than before, but it does
yield far more of all the necessaries and comforts of life. His labor upon it will bring no
heavier crops, and, we will suppose, no more
valuable crops, but it will bring far more of all
the other things for which men work. The
presence of other settlers—the increase of
population—has added to the productiveness,
in these things, of labor bestowed upon it, and
this added productiveness gives it a superiority
over land of equal natural quality where there
are as yet no settlers. If no land remains to be
taken up, except such as is as far removed
from population as was our settler's land when
he first went upon it, the value or rent of this
land will be measured by the whole of this
added capability. If, however, as we have supposed, there is a continuous stretch of equal
land, over which population is now spreading,
it will not be necessary for the new settler to go
into the wilderness, as did the first. He will
settle just beyond the other settlers, and will
get the advantage of proximity to them. The
value or rent of our settler's land will thus depend on the advantage which it has, from
being at the center of population, over that on
the verge. In the one case, the margin of production will remain as before; in the other,
the margin of production will be raised.

Population still continues to increase, and as
it increases so do the economies which its increase permits, and which in effect add to the
productiveness of the land. Our first settler's

land, being the center of population, the store, the blacksmith's forge, the wheelwright's shop, are set up on it, or on its margin, where soon arises a village, which rapidly grows into a town, the center of exchanges for the people of the whole district. With no greater agricultural productiveness than it had at first, this land now begins to develop a productiveness of a higher kind. To labor expended in raising corn, or wheat, or potatoes, it will yield no more of those things than at first; but to labor expended in the subdivided branches of production which require proximity to other producers, and, especially, to labor expended in that final part of production, which consists in distribution, it will yield much larger returns. The wheat-grower may go further on, and find land on which his labor will produce as much wheat, and nearly as much wealth; but the artisan, the manufacturer, the storekeeper, the professional man, find that their labor expended here, at the center of exchanges, will yield them much more than if expended even at a little distance away from it; and this excess of productiveness for such purposes the landowner can claim just as he could an excess in its wheat-producing power. And so our settler is able to sell in building lots a few of his acres for prices which it would not bring for wheat-growing if its fertility had been multiplied many times. With the proceeds, he builds himself a fine house, and furnishes it handsomely. That is to say, to reduce the transaction to its lowest terms, the people who wish to use the land build and furnish the house for him, on condition that he will let them avail themselves of the superior productiveness which the increase of population has given the land.

Population still keeps on increasing, giving greater and greater utility to the land, and more and more wealth to its owner. The town has grown into a city—a St. Louis, a Chicago, or a San Francisco—and still it grows. Production is here carried on upon a great scale, with the best machinery and the most favorable facilities; the division of labor becomes extremely minute, wonderfully multiplying efficiency; exchanges are of such volume and rapidity that they are made with the minimum of friction and loss. Here is the heart, the brain, of the vast social organism that has grown up from the germ of the first settlement; here has developed one of the great ganglions of the human world. Hither run all roads, hither set all currents, through all the vast regions round

about. Here, if you have anything to sell, is the market; here, if you have anything to buy, is the largest and the choicest stock. Here intellectual activity is gathered into a focus, and here springs that stimulus which is born of the collision of mind with mind. Here are the great libraries, the storehouses and granaries of knowledge, the learned professors, the famous specialists. Here are museums and art galleries, collections of philosophical apparatus, and all things rare, and valuable, and best of their kind. Here come great actors, and orators, and singers, from all over the world. Here, in short, is a center of human life, in all its varied manifestations.

So enormous are the advantages which this land now offers for the application of labor that instead of one man with a span of horses scratching over acres, you may count in places thousands of workers to the acre, working tier on tier, on floors raised one above the other, five, six, seven, and eight stories from the ground, while underneath the surface of the earth engines are throbbing with pulsations that exert the force of thousands of horses.

All these advantages attach to the land; it is on this land and no other that they can be utilized, for here is the center of population— the focus of exchanges, the market place and workshop of the highest forms of industry. The productive powers which density of population has attached to this land are equivalent to the multiplication of its original fertility by the hundred fold and the thousand fold. And rent, which measures the difference between this added productiveness and that of the least productive land in use, has increased accordingly. Our settler, or whoever has succeeded to his right to the land, is now a millionaire. Like another Rip Van Winkle, he may have lain down and slept; still he is rich—not from anything he has done, but from the increase of population. There are lots from which for every foot of frontage the owner may draw more than an average mechanic can earn; there are lots that will sell for more than would suffice to pave them with gold coin. In the principal streets are towering buildings, of granite, marble, iron, and plate glass, finished in the most expensive style, replete with every convenience. Yet they are not worth as much as the land upon which they rest—the same land, in nothing changed, which when our first settler came upon it had no value at all.

That this is the way in which the increase

of population powerfully acts in increasing rent, whoever, in a progressive country, will look around him, may see for himself. The process is going on under his eyes. The increasing difference in the productiveness of the land in use, which causes an increasing rise in rent, results not so much from the necessities of increased population compelling the resort to inferior land, as from the increased pro-

10 ductiveness which increased population gives to the lands already in use. The most valuable lands on the globe, the lands which yield the highest rent, are not lands of surpassing natural fertility, but lands to which a surpassing utility has been given by the increase of population.

And where value seems to arise from superior natural qualities, such as deep water and good anchorage, rich deposits of coal and iron, or heavy timber, observation also shows

20 that these superior qualities are brought out, rendered tangible, by population. The coal and iron fields of Pennsylvania, that to-day [1879] are worth enormous sums, were fifty years ago valueless. What is the efficient cause of the difference? Simply the difference in population. The coal and iron beds of Wyoming and Montana, which to-day are valueless, will, in fifty years from now, be worth millions on millions, simply because, in the meantime,

30 population will have greatly increased.

It is a well-provisioned ship, this on which we sail through space. If the bread and beef above decks seem to grow scarce, we but open a hatch and there is a new supply, of which before we never dreamed. And very great command over the services of others comes to those who as the hatches are opened are permitted to say, "This is mine!"

THE BASIC CAUSE OF POVERTY

41　　The great problem, of which recurring seasons of industrial depression are but peculiar manifestations, is now, I think, fully solved, and the social phenomena which all over the civilized world appall the philanthropist and perplex the statesman, which hang with clouds the future of the most advanced races, and suggest doubts of the reality and ultimate goal of what we have fondly called progress, are

50 now explained.

The reason why, in spite of the increase of productive power, wages constantly tend to a minimum which will give but a bare living, is that, with increase in productive power, rent tends to even greater increase, thus producing a constant tendency to the forcing down of wages.

Land being necessary to labor, and being reduced to private ownership, every increase in the productive power of labor but increases rent—the price that labor must pay for the opportunity to utilize its powers; and thus all the advantages gained by the march of progress go to the owners of land, and wages do not increase.

The simple theory which I have outlined (if indeed it can be called a theory which is but the recognition of the most obvious relations) explains this conjunction of poverty with wealth, of low wages with high productive power, of degradation amid enlightenment, of virtual slavery in political liberty.

It harmonizes, as results flowing from a general and inexorable law, facts otherwise most perplexing, and exhibits the sequence and relation between phenomena that without reference to it are diverse and contradictory.

It explains why improvements which increase the productive power of labor and capital increase the reward of neither.

It explains what is commonly called the conflict between labor and capital, while proving the real harmony of interest between them.

It cuts the last inch of ground from under the fallacies of protection, while showing why free trade fails to benefit permanently the working classes.

It explains why want increases with abundance, and wealth tends to greater and greater aggregations.

It explains the vice and misery which show themselves amid dense population, without attributing to the laws of the All-Wise and All-Beneficent defects which belong only to the short-sighted and selfish enactments of men.

The truth is self-evident. Put to any one capable of consecutive thought this question:

"Suppose there should arise from the English Channel or the German Ocean a No-man's land on which common labor to an unlimited amount should be able to make thirty shillings a day and which should remain unappropriated and of free access, like the commons which once comprised so large a part of English soil. What would be the effect upon wages in England?"

He would at once tell you that common wages throughout England must soon increase to thirty shillings a day.

And in response to another question, "What would be the effect on rents?" he would at a moment's reflection say that rents must necessarily fall; and if he thought out the next step he would tell you that all this would happen without any very large part of English labor being diverted to the new natural opportunities, or the forms and direction of industry being much changed; only that kind of production being abandoned which now yields to labor and to landlord together less than labor could secure on the new opportunities. The great rise in wages would be at the expense of rent.

Take now the same man or another—some hard-headed business man, who has no theories, but knows how to make money. Say to him: "Here is a little village; in ten years it will be a great city—in ten years the railroad will have taken the place of the stage coach, the electric light of the candle; it will abound with all the machinery and improvements that so enormously multiply the effective power of labor. Will, in ten years, interest be any higher?"

He will tell you, "No!"

"Will the wages of common labor be any higher; will it be easier for a man who has nothing but his labor to make an independent living?"

He will tell you, "No; the wages of common labor will not be any higher; on the contrary, all the chances are that they will be lower; it will not be easier for the mere laborer to make an independent living; the chances are that it will be harder."

"What, then, will be higher?"

"Rent; the value of land. Go, get yourself a piece of ground, and hold possession."

And if, under such circumstances, you take his advice, you need do nothing more. You may sit down and smoke your pipe; you may lie around like the lazzaroni of Naples or the leperos of Mexico; you may go up in a balloon, or down a hole in the ground; and without doing one stroke of work, without adding one iota to the wealth of the community, in ten years you will be rich! In the new city you may have a luxurious mansion; but among its public buildings will be an almshouse.

In all our investigation we have been advancing to this simple truth: That as land is necessary to the exertion of labor in the production of wealth, to command the land which is necessary to labor, is to command all the fruits of labor save enough to enable labor to exist. We have been advancing as through an enemy's country, in which every step must be secured, every position fortified, and every by-path explored; for this simple truth, in its application to social and political problems, is hid from the great masses of men partly by its very simplicity, and in greater part by widespread fallacies and erroneous habits of thought which lead them to look in every direction but the right one for an explanation of the evils which oppress and threaten the civilized world. And back of these elaborate fallacies and misleading theories is an active, energetic power, a power that in every country, be its political forms what they may, writes laws and molds thought —the power of a vast and dominant pecuniary interest.

But so simple and so clear is this truth, that to see it fully once is always to recognize it. There are pictures which, though looked at again and again, present only a confused labyrinth of lines or scroll work—a landscape, trees, or something of the kind—until once the attention is called to the fact that these things make up a face or a figure. This relation, once recognized, is always afterward clear.

It is so in this case. In the light of this truth all social facts group themselves in an orderly relation, and the most diverse phenomena are seen to spring from one great principle.

It is not in the relations of capital and labor; it is not in the pressure of population against subsistence, that an explanation of the unequal development of our civilization is to be found. The great cause of inequality in the distribution of wealth is inequality in the ownership of land. The ownership of land is the great fundamental fact which ultimately determines the social, the political, and consequently the intellectual and moral condition of a people. And it must be so. For land is the habitation of man, the storehouse upon which he must draw for all his needs, the material to which his labor must be applied for the supply of all his desires; for even the products of the sea cannot be taken, the light of the sun enjoyed, or any of the forces of nature utilized, without the use of land or its products. On the land we are born, from it we live, to it we return again— children of the soil as truly as is the blade of grass or the flower of the field. Take away from man all that belongs to land, and he is but a disembodied spirit. Material progress cannot rid us of our dependence upon land; it can but add to the power of producing wealth from land; and hence, when land is monopolized, it might go on to infinity without increasing wages or improving the condition of those who have but their labor. It can but add to the value of land and the power which its possession gives. Everywhere, in all times, among all peoples, the possession of land is the base of aristocracy, the foundation of great fortunes, the source of power. As said the Brahmins, ages ago—

"To whomsoever the soil at any time belongs, to him belong the fruits of it. White parasols and elephants mad with pride are the flowers of a grant of land."

THE REMEDY

Poverty deepens as wealth increases, and wages are forced down while productive power grows, because land, which is the source of all wealth and the field of all labor, is monopolized. To extirpate poverty, to make wages what justice commands they should be, the full earnings of the laborer, we must therefore substitute for the individual ownership of land a common ownership.

The right of ownership that springs from labor excludes the possibility of any other right of ownership. If a man be rightfully entitled to the produce of his labor, then no one can be rightfully entitled to the ownership of anything which is not the produce of his labor, or the labor of some one else from whom the right has passed to him. For the right to the produce of labor cannot be enjoyed without the right to the free use of the opportunities offered by nature, and to admit the right of property in these is to deny the right of property in the produce of labor. When non-producers can claim as rent a portion of the wealth created by producers, the right of the producers to the fruits of their labor is to that extent denied.

A house and the lot on which it stands are alike property, as being the subject of ownership, and are alike classed by the lawyers as real estate. Yet in nature and relations they differ widely. The one is produced by human labor and belongs to the class in political economy styled wealth. The other is a part of nature, and belongs to the class in political economy styled land.

The essential character of the one class of things is that they embody labor, are brought into being by human exertion, their existence or non-existence, their increase or diminution, depending on man. The essential character of the other class of things is that they do not embody labor, and exist irrespective of human exertion and irrespective of man; they are the field or environment in which man finds himself; the storehouse from which his needs must be supplied, the raw material upon which, and the forces with which alone his labor can act.

The moment this distinction is realized, that moment is it seen that the sanction which natural justice gives to one species of property is denied to the other.

For as labor cannot produce without the use of land, the denial of the equal right to the use of land is necessarily the denial of the right of labor to its own produce. If one man can command the land upon which others must labor, he can appropriate the produce of their labor as the price of his permission to labor. The fundamental law of nature, that her enjoyment by man shall be consequent upon his exertion, is thus violated. The one receives without producing; the others produce without receiving. The one is unjustly enriched; the others are robbed.

Place one hundred men on an island from which there is no escape, and whether you make one of these men the absolute owner of the other ninety-nine, or the absolute owner of the soil of the island, will make no difference either to him or to them. In the one case, as the other, the one will be the absolute master of the ninety-nine—his power extending even to life and death, for simply to refuse them permission to live upon the island would be to force them into the sea.

Upon a larger scale, and through more complex relations, the same cause must operate in the same way and to the same end—the ultimate result, the enslavement of laborers, becoming apparent just as the pressure increases which compels them to live on and from land which is treated as the exclusive property of others.

Yet, it will be said: As every man has a right to the use and enjoyment of nature, the man who is using land must be permitted the exclusive right to its use in order that the may get the full benefit of his labor. But there is no difficulty in determining where the individual right ends and the common right begins. A delicate and exact test is supplied by *value,* and with its aid there is no difficulty, no matter how dense population may become, in determining and securing the exact rights of each, the equal rights of all.

The *value* of land, as we have seen, is the price of monopoly. It is not the absolute, but the relative, capability of land that determines its value. No matter what may be its intrinsic qualities, land that is no better than other land which may be had for the using can have no value. And the value of land always measures the difference between it and the best land that may be had for the using. Thus, the value of land expresses in exact and tangible form the right of the community in land held by an individual; and rent expresses the exact amount which the individual should pay to the community to satisfy the equal rights of all other members of the community.

Thus, if we concede to priority of possession the undisturbed use of land, taxing rent into the public treasury for the benefit of the community, we reconcile the fixity of tenure which is necessary for improvement with a full and complete recognition of the equal rights of all to the use of land.

Consider what rent is. It does not arise spontaneously from land; it is due to nothing that the land owners have done. It represents a *value created by the whole community.*

Let the land holders have, if you please, all that the possession of the land would give them in the absence of the rest of the community. But rent, the creation of the whole community, necessarily belongs to the whole community.

LIBERTY, AND EQUALITY OF OPPORTUNITY

The truth to which we were led in the politico-economic branch of our inquiry is as clearly apparent in the rise and fall of nations and the growth and decay of civilizations, and it accords with those deep-seated recognitions of relation and sequence that we denominate moral perceptions. Thus are given to our conclusions the greatest certitude and highest sanction.

This truth involves both a menace and a promise. It shows that the evils arising from the unjust and unequal distribution of wealth, which are becoming more and more apparent as modern civilization goes on, are not incidents of progress, but tendencies which must bring progress to a halt; that they will not cure themselves, but, on the contrary, must, unless their cause is removed, grow greater and greater, until they sweep us back into barbarism by the road every previous civilization has trod. But it also shows that these evils are not imposed by natural laws; that they spring solely from social maladjustments which ignore natural laws, and that in removing their cause we shall be giving an enormous impetus to progress.

The poverty which in the midst of abundance pinches and imbrutes men, and all the manifold evils which flow from it, spring from a denial of justice. In permitting the monopolization of the opportunities which nature freely offers to all, we have ignored the fundamental law of injustice—for, so far as we can see, when we view things upon a large scale, justice seems to be the supreme law of the universe. But by sweeping away this injustice and asserting the rights of all men to natural opportunities, we shall conform ourselves to the law—we shall remove the great cause of unnatural inequality in the distribution of wealth and power; we shall abolish poverty; tame the ruthless passions of greed; dry up the springs of vice and misery; light in dark places the lamp of knowledge; give new vigor to invention and a fresh impulse to discovery; substitute political strength for political weakness; and make tyranny and anarchy impossible.

The reform I have proposed accords with all that is politically, socially, or morally desirable. It has the qualities of a true reform, for it will make all other reforms easier. What is it but the carrying out in letter and spirit of the truth enunciated in the Declaration of Independence—the "self-evident" truth that is the heart and soul of the Declaration—"*That all men are created equal; that they are endowed by their Creator with certain inalienable rights; that among these are life, liberty, and the pursuit of happiness!*"

These rights are denied when the equal right to land—on which and by which men alone can live—is denied. Equality of political rights will not compensate for the denial of the equal right to the bounty of nature. Political liberty, when the equal right to land is denied, becomes, as population increases and invention goes on, merely the liberty to compete for employment at starvation wages. This is the truth that we have ignored. And so there are come beggars in our streets and tramps on our roads; and poverty enslaves men who we boast are political sovereigns; and want breeds ignorance that our schools cannot enlighten; and citizens vote as their masters dictate; and the demagogue usurps the part of the statesman; and gold weighs in the scales of justice; and in high places sit those who do not pay to civic virtue even the compliment of hypocrisy; and the pillars of the republic that we thought so strong already bend under an increasing strain.

We honor Liberty in name and in form. We set up her statues and sound her praises. But we have not fully trusted her. And with our growth so grow her demands. She will have no half service!

Liberty! it is a word to conjure with, not to vex the ear in empty boastings. For Liberty means Justice, and Justice is the natural law— the law of health and symmetry and strength, of fraternity and co-operation.

They who look upon Liberty as having accomplished her mission when she has abolished hereditary privileges and given men the ballot, who think of her as having no further relations to the everyday affairs of life, have not seen her real grandeur—to them the poets who have sung of her must seem rhapsodists, and her martyrs fools! As the sun is the lord of life, as well as of light; as his beams not merely pierce the clouds, but support all growth, supply all motion, and call forth from what would otherwise be a cold and inert mass all the infinite diversities of being and beauty, so is liberty to mankind. It is not for an abstraction that men have toiled and died; that in every age the witnesses of Liberty have stood forth, and the martyrs of Liberty have suffered.

We speak of Liberty as one thing, and of virtue, wealth, knowledge, invention, national strength, and national independence as other things. But, of all these, Liberty is the source, the mother, the necessary condition. She is to virtue what light is to color; to wealth what sunshine is to grain; to knowledge what eyes are to sight. She is the genius of invention, the brawn of national strength, the spirit of national independence. Where Liberty rises, there virtue grows, wealth increases, knowledge expands, invention multiplies human powers, and in strength and spirit the freer nation rises among her neighbors as Saul amid his brethren —taller and fairer. Where Liberty sinks, there virtue fades, wealth diminishes, knowledge is

forgotten, invention ceases, and empires once mighty in arms and arts become a helpless prey to freer barbarians!

Only in broken gleams and partial light has the sun of Liberty yet beamed among men, but all progress hath she called forth.

Liberty came to a race of slaves crouching under Egyptian whips, and led them forth from the House of Bondage. She hardened them in the desert and made of them a race of conquerors. The free spirit of the Mosaic law took their thinkers up to heights where they beheld the unity of God, and inspired their poets with strains that yet phrase the highest exaltations of thought. Liberty dawned on the Phœnician coast, and ships passed the Pillars of Hercules to plow the unknown sea. She shed a partial light on Greece, and marble grew to shapes of ideal beauty, words became the instruments of subtlest thought, and against the scanty militia of free cities broke the countless hosts of the Great King like surges against a rock. She cast her beams on the four-acre farms of Italian husbandmen, and born of her strength a power came forth that conquered the world. They glinted from shields of German warriors, and Augustus wept his legions. Out of the night that followed her eclipse, her slanting rays fell again on free cities, and a lost learning revived, modern civilization began, a new world was unveiled; and as Liberty grew, so grew art, wealth, power, knowledge, and refinement. In the history of every nation we may read the same truth. It was the strength born of Magna Charta that won Crécy and Agincourt. It was the revival of Liberty from the despotism of the Tudors that glorified the Elizabethan age. It was the spirit that brought a crowned tyrant to the block that planted here the seed of a mighty tree. It was the energy of ancient freedom that, the moment it had gained unity, made Spain the mightiest power of the world, only to fall to the lowest depth of weakness when tyranny succeeded liberty. See, in France, all intellectual vigor dying under the tyranny of the Seventeenth Century to revive in splendor as Liberty awoke in the Eighteenth, and on the enfranchisement of French peasants in the Great Revolution, basing the wonderful strength that has in our time defied defeat. Shall we not trust her?

In our time, as in times before, creep on the insidious forces that, producing inequality, destroy Liberty. On the horizon the clouds begin to lower. Liberty calls to us again. We must follow her further; we must trust her fully. Either we must wholly accept her or she will not stay. It is not enough that men should vote; it is not enough that they should be theoretically equal before the law. They must have liberty to avail themselves of the opportunities and means of life; they must stand on equal terms with reference to the bounty of nature. Either this, or Liberty withdraws her light! Either this, or darkness comes on, and the very forces that progress has evolved turn to powers that work destruction. This is the universal law. This is the lesson of the centuries. Unless its foundations be laid in justice the social structure cannot stand.

Our primary social adjustment is a denial of justice. In allowing one man to own the land on which and from which other men must live, we have made them his bondsmen in a degree which increases as material progress goes on. This is the subtle alchemy that in ways they do not realize is extracting from the masses in every civilized country the fruits of their weary toil; that is instituting a harder and more hopeless slavery in place of that which has been destroyed; that is bringing political despotism out of political freedom, and must soon transmute democratic institutions into anarchy.

It is this that turns the blessings of material progress into a curse. It is this that crowds human beings into noisome cellars and squalid tenement houses; that fills prisons and brothels; that goads men with want and consumes them with greed; that robs women of the grace and beauty of perfect womanhood; that takes from little children the joy and innocence of life's morning.

Civilization so based cannot continue. The eternal laws of the universe forbid it. Ruins of dead empires testify, and the witness that is in every soul answers, that it cannot be. It is something grander than Benevolence, something more august than Charity—it is Justice herself that demands of us to right this wrong. Justice that will not be denied; that cannot be put off—Justice that with the scales carries the sword. Shall we ward the stroke with liturgies and prayers? Shall we avert the decrees of immutable law by raising churches when hungry infants moan and weary mothers weep?

Though it may take the language of prayer, it is blasphemy that attributes to the inscrutable decrees of Providence the suffering and brutishness that come of poverty; that turns with folded hands to the All-Father and lays on Him the responsibility for the want and crime of our great cities. We degrade the Everlasting. We slander the Just One. A merciful man would have better ordered the world; a just man would crush with his foot such an ulcerous ant-hill! It is not the Almighty, but we who are responsible for the vice and misery that fester amid our civilization. The Creator showers upon us his gifts—more than enough for all. But like swine scrambling for food, we tread them in the mire—tread them in the mire, while we tear and rend each other!

In the very centers of our civilization to-day are want and suffering enough to make sick at heart whoever does not close his eyes and steel his nerves. Dare we turn to the Creator and ask Him to relieve it? Supposing the prayer were heard, and at the behest with which the universe sprang into being there should glow in the sun a greater power; new virtue fill the air; fresh vigor the soil; that for every blade of grass that now grows two should spring up, and the seed that now increases fifty-fold should increase a hundred-fold! Would poverty be abated or want relieved? Manifestly no! Whatever benefit would accrue would be but temporary. The new powers streaming through the material universe could be utilized only through land.

This is not merely a deduction of political economy; it is a fact of experience. We know it because we have seen it. Within our own times, under our very eyes, that Power which is above all, and in all, and through all; that Power of which the whole universe is but the manifestation; that Power which maketh all things, and without which is not anything made that is made, has increased the bounty which men may enjoy, as truly as though the fertility of nature had been increased. Into the mind of one came the thought that harnessed steam for the service of mankind. To the inner ear of another was whispered the secret that compels the lightning to bear a message round the globe. In every direction have the laws of matter been revealed; in every department of industry have arisen arms of iron and fingers of steel, whose effect upon the production of wealth has been precisely the same as an increase in the fertility of nature. What has been the result? Simply that land owners get all the gain.

Can it be that the gifts of the Creator may

be thus misappropriated with impunity? Is it a light thing that labor should be robbed of its earnings while greed rolls in wealth—that the many should want while the few are surfeited? Turn to history, and on every page may be read the lesson that such wrong never goes unpunished; that the Nemesis that follows injustice never falters nor sleeps! Look around to-day. Can this state of things continue? May we even say, "After us the deluge!" Nay; the pillars of the state are trembling even now, and the very foundations of society begin to quiver with pent-up forces that glow underneath. The struggle that must either revivify, or convulse in ruin, is near at hand, if it be not already begun.

The fiat has gone forth! With steam and electricity, and the new powers born of progress, forces have entered the world that will either compel us to a higher plane or overwhelm us, as nation after nation, as civilization after civilization, have been overwhelmed before. It is the delusion which precedes destruction that sees in the popular unrest with which the civilized world is feverishly pulsing only the passing effect of ephemeral causes. Between democratic ideas and the aristocratic adjustments of society there is an irreconcilable conflict. Here in the United States, as there in Europe, it may be seen arising. We cannot go on permitting men to vote and forcing them to tramp. We cannot go on educating boys and girls in our public schools and then refusing

them the right to earn an honest living. We cannot go on prating of the inalienable rights of man and then denying the inalienable right to the bounty of the Creator. Even now, in old bottles the new wine begins to ferment, and elemental forces gather for the strife!

But if, while there is yet time, we turn to Justice and obey her, if we trust Liberty and follow her, the dangers that now threaten must disappear, the forces that now menace will turn to agencies of elevation. Think of the powers now wasted; of the infinite fields of knowledge yet to be explored; of the possibilities of which the wondrous inventions of this century give us but a hint. With want destroyed; with greed changed to noble passions; with the fraternity that is born of equality taking the place of the jealousy and fear that now array men against each other; with mental power loosed by conditions that give to the humblest comfort and leisure; and who shall measure the heights to which our civilization may soar? Words fail the thought! It is the Golden Age of which poets have sung and high-raised seers have told in metaphor! It is the glorious vision which has always haunted man with gleams of fitful splendor. It is what he saw whose eyes at Patmos were closed in a trance. It is the culmination of Christianity —the City of God on earth, with its walls of jasper and its gates of pearl! It is the reign of the Prince of Peace!

1879

JAMES BAIRD WEAVER

1833–1912

A SON OF the Michigan and Iowa frontiers, Weaver became, after various ventures in gold-mining, store-keeping, and mail-carrying, a lawyer and politician. *Uncle Tom's Cabin* converted him to Republicanism. In the Civil War he was advanced from first lieutenant to brigadier-general. During the decades that followed Appomattox Weaver denounced corruption, predatory monopolies, and the efforts of the creditor class to control the purchasing power of the currency. A Greenbacker, Weaver led in the organization of the Populist party, which nominated him for the presidency in 1892. During the campaign, in which he spoke with feeling and power, his *Call to Action* still further extended the range of his political and social philosophy. A friend of a "united front" of all inflationists, Weaver supported Bryan in 1896 and in consequence found his own political career as leader of a third-party abruptly ended.

The *Call to Action*, which remains one of the best expositions of the Populist program, helped fertilize the Progressive movement.

E. A. Allen, *The Life and Public Services of James Baird Weaver*, n.p., 1892.
F. E. Haynes, *James B. Weaver*, Iowa City, 1919.

» » *From:* A CALL TO ACTION « «

CHAPTER XII

DIVES AND LAZARUS

CONTRASTS

If the master builders of our civilization one hundred years ago had been told that at the end of a single century, American society would present such melancholy contrasts of wealth and poverty, of individual happiness and widespread infelicity as are to be found to-day throughout the Republic, the person making the unwelcome prediction would have been looked upon as a misanthropist, and his loyalty to Democratic institutions would have been seriously called in question. Our federal machine, with its delicate inter-lace work of National, State and municipal supervision, each intended to secure perfect individual equality, was expected to captivate the world by its operation and insure domestic contentment and personal security to a degree never before realized by mankind.

But there is a vast difference between the generation which made the heroic struggle for Self-government in colonial days, and the third generation which is now engaged in a mad rush for wealth. The first took its stand upon the inalienable rights of man and made a fight which shook the world. But the leading spirits of the latter are entrenched behind class laws and revel in special privileges. It will require another revolution to overthrow them. That revolution is upon us even now.

Two representative characters—Dives and Lazarus—always make their appearance side by side in disturbing contrast just before the tragic stage of revolution is reached. They were present at the overthrow of ancient civilizations; the hungry multitude stood outside the gates when Belshazzar's impious feast was spread; they were both at the cave of Adullam when the scepter was about to depart from the tyrant Saul to the hands of the youthful David; they stood side by side when Alaric thundered at the gates of Rome; they confronted one another in the fiery tempest of the French revolution and they are sullenly face to face in our own country to-day. We will devote a few pages to the delineation of these forces as they appear in our civilization at the present period.

SOCIAL EXTRAVAGANCE

In the year 1884, as we are told by Ward McAllister, in his book entitled "Society as I Found It," a wealthy gentleman gave a banquet at Delmonico's at which the moderate number of seventy-two guests, ladies and gentlemen, were entertained. The gentleman giving the banquet had unexpectedly received from the Treasury of the United States a rebate of $10,000 for duties which had been exacted from him through some alleged misconception of the law. He resolved to spend the entire sum in giving a single dinner which should excel any private entertainment ever given in New York. He consulted Charles Delmonico, who engaged to carry out his wishes. The table was constructed with a miniature lake in the center thirty feet in length, enclosed by a network of golden wire which reached to the ceiling, forming a great cage. Four immense swans were secured from one of the parks and placed in this lake. High banks of flowers of every hue surrounded the lake and covered the entire table, leaving barely enough room for the plates and wine glasses. The room was festooned with flowers in every direction. Miniature mountains and valleys with carpets of flowers made vocal with sparkling rivulets, met the eye on every hand. Golden cages filled with sweet singing birds hung from the ceiling and added their enchantment to the gorgeous spectacle. Soft, sweet music swept in from adjoining rooms, and all that art, wealth and imagination could do was done to make the scene one of unexampled beauty. And then the feast! All the dishes which ingenuity could invent or the history of past extravagance suggest, were spread before the guests. The oldest and costliest wines known to the trade flowed like the water that leaped down the cascades in the banqueting hall. The guests were wild with exultation and delight and tarried far into the night. But in a few brief hours the romanticism had passed, the carousal was broken, and the revelers were face to face with the responsibilities which none of us can evade. The fool and his money had parted.

• • •

PRINCE ASTOR'S WEDDING

In the year 1890, young Astor, a scion of the celebrated family which has so long been prominent in New York financial circles, was married. Both the groom and the bride represented millions of wealth and the wedding was an imposing and gorgeous affair. Twenty-five thousand dollars were expended on the day's ceremony. The presents were valued at $2,000,000, and the couple and their attendants and a number of friends, immediately departed on an expensive yachting cruise which was to cost them $10,000 a month to maintain. In speaking of these nuptials the CHRISTIAN UNION said: "When we read this we are reminded of Thackeray's description of the extravagance of the Prince Regent during the Napoleonic wars:

"If he had been a manufacturing town, or a populous rural district, or an army of 5,000 men, he would not have cost more. The nation gave him more money, and more and more. The sum is past counting.

"Looked at soberly, the sums lavished upon our American commoners are as disgraceful to our institutions as were the squanderings of the Prince Regent to those of England. If the scandal is less it is because the disastrous concentration of hereditary wealth has as yet awakened less serious thought among us than the disastrous concentration of hereditary power had awakened in England. In the case of the Astors, quite as much as of the Prince Regent, the enormous sums expended are the gift of the Nation, obtained without compensating service on the part of the recipients. The burden upon the labor of the country is as great."

• • •

AT THE RICH MAN'S GATE

About the time these princely entertainments were given, and in the same year with some of them, one of the metropolitan journals caused a careful canvass to be made of the unemployed of that city. The number was found to be *one hundred and fifty thousand persons who were daily unsuccessfully seeking work within the city limits of New York.* Another one hundred and fifty thousand earned less than sixty cents per day. Thousands of these are poor girls who work from eleven to sixteen hours per day.

In the year 1890, over twenty-three thousand families, numbering about one hundred thousand people, were forcibly evicted in New York City owing to their inability to pay rent, and one-tenth of all who died in that city during the year were buried in the Potters Field. . . .

AT CHICAGO

In the latter part of the year 1891, a committee from a Chicago Trade and Labor Assembly, at the request of a body of striking cloakmakers, made an investigation of the condition of that class of workers in the city. They were accompanied by an officer of the City Health Department, the City Attorney and artists and reporters of the local press. They found that thirteen thousand persons were engaged in the manufacture of clothing in Chicago, over one-half of whom were females. In order to reduce the cost of production the firms engaged in the manufacture of clothing have adopted the European Sweating System, which is in brief, as follows: The material for garments is cut to size and shape and delivered by the large firms to individual contractors known as sweaters, who relieve the firm of all other care or expense, taking the goods to what are known as sweating dens, usually located in the poorest neighborhoods of the great city. These sweaters are employed by the most opulent firms. The committee visited a large number of these dens, nearly all of which were dwelling houses which served as living and sleeping rooms for the sweater's family and the employes. In one room ten feet by forty, they found thirty-nine young girls, twelve children between ten and twelve years of age, eleven men and the sweater and his wife. The room and all the surroundings were filthy in the extreme. The rates of wages were of course very low, and yet the fear of discharge rendered it almost impossible to obtain satisfactory information. The committee found two thousand one hundred children at work in these dismal places who were under age and employed in violation of existing laws against child labor. Sanitary laws were also overridden in all of these miserable abodes. We take the following from the report of the committee:

"The condition of the places visited was horrible. Overcrowding, long hours and low pay were the rule. Girls ten years old were found to be working ten and twelve hours a day for 80 cents per week. Ten girls were found, none over ten years old, who worked sixteen hours a day for from 75 cents to $1.20 per week. In a DeKoven street den were found a half dozen men working eighteen hours a day for from $4 to $9 per week. At 168 Maxwell street were found ten men that worked sixteen hours a day each and received $6.50 to $9 per week. In the same place were six girls working from two to fourteen hours a day whose weekly pay averaged $3. One child was found in a house that worked for 75 cents per week. At 455 South Canal street a girl was found who declined to tell what she received fearing she would be discharged and discharge meant starvation. At 69 Judd street the wages of the men were found to be from $5 to $9 per week, and one child there received $1 per week. The women worked fourteen hours a day. The product of this shop was sold to Marshall Field & Co. At 151 Peoria street, is a cloak-finishing establishment. Here the women receive one and one-half cents each for finishing cloaks. One woman was found on the street with a bundle of cloaks she had finished. She said that by hard work she finished twenty cloaks a day and earned thirty cents. This supported herself and two babies. The place 258 Division street was by far the worst visited. Eleven men worked twelve hours a day and received $5 to $9.50 per week. Twelve children here worked twelve hours for 75 cents per week. The place was terribly crowded, there being no water or light."

And yet in the face of these glaring conditions, which are common in all of our populous cities, empty headed political charlatans still vex the public with their puerile rant about protection for American labor. . . .

CHAPTER XIV

TRUSTS

A Trust is defined to be a combination of many competing concerns under one management. The object is to increase profits through reduction of cost, limitation of product and increase of the price to the consumer. The term is now applied, and very properly, to all kinds of combinations in trade which relate to prices, and without regard to whether all or only part of the objects named are had in view.

Combinations which we now call trusts have existed in this country for a considerable period, but they have only attracted general attention for about ten years. We have in our possession copies of the agreements of the Standard Oil and Sugar Trusts. The former is dated January 2, 1882, and the latter August 6, 1887.

Trusts vary somewhat in their forms of organization. This is caused by the character of the property involved and the variety of objects to be attained. The great trusts of the country consist of an association or consolidation of a number of associations engaged in the same line of business—each company in the trust being first separately incorporated. The stock of these companies is then turned over to a board of trustees who issue back trust certificates in payment for the stock transferred. The trust selects its own board of directors and henceforth has complete control of the entire business and can regulate prices, limit or stimulate production as they may deem best for the parties concerned in the venture. The trust itself is not necessarily incorporated. Many of the strongest, such as the "Standard Oil Trust," the "Sugar Trust," and "The American Cotton Seed Oil Trust," and others are not. They are the invisible agents of associated artificial intangible beings. They are difficult to find, still harder to restrain and so far as present experience has gone they are practically a law unto themselves.

The power of these institutions has grown to be almost incalculable. . . .

Trust combinations now dominate the following products and divisions of trade: Kerosene Oil, Cotton Seed Oil, Sugar, Oat Meal, Starch, White Corn Meal, Straw Paper, Pearled Barley, Coal, Straw Board, Lumber, Castor Oil, Cement, Linseed Oil, Lard, School Slate, Oil

Cloth, Salt, Cattle, Meat Products, Gas, Street
Railways, Whisky, Paints, Rubber, Steel, Steel
Rails, Steel and Iron Beams, Cars, Nails,
Wrought Iron Pipes, Iron Nuts, Stoves, Lead,
Copper, Envelopes, Wall Paper, Paper Bags,
Paving Pitch, Cordage, Coke, Reaping, Binding
and Mowing Machines, Threshing Machines,
Plows, Glass, Water Works, Warehouses, Sand
Stone, Granite, Upholsterers' Felt, Lead Pen-
cils, Watches and Watch Cases, Clothes
Wringers, Carpets, Undertakers' Goods, and
Coffins, Planes, Breweries, Milling, Flour, Sil-
ver Plate, Plated Ware and a vast variety of
other lines of trade.

The Standard Oil and its complement, the
American Cotton Oil Trust, were the advance
guard of the vast army of like associations
which have overrun and now occupy every
section of the country and nearly all departments of trade. The Standard has developed
into an international combine and has brought
the world under its yoke. In 1890 the largest
German and Dutch petroleum houses fell
under the control of the Standard Oil Company, and the oil importing companies of
Bremen, Hamburg and Stettin were united by
the Standard into a German-American Petroleum Company, with its seat at Bremen. In
1891 the Paris Rothchilds, who control the
Russian oil fields, effected a combination with
the Standard Oil Trust, which makes the combine world wide; and so far as this important
article of consumption is concerned, it places
all mankind at their mercy. Our information
concerning this international oil trust is derived
from the report concerning the Petroleum
Monoply of Europe by Consul-General Edwards, of Berlin, made to the Secretary of
State, June 25, 1891, and published in Con-
sular Reports No. 131.

Now that the Petroleum combine has accomplished the conquest of the world, what is
to hinder every other branch of business from
accomplishing the same end? . . .

ARE TRUSTS LEGAL?

It is clear that trusts are contrary to public
policy and hence in conflict with the Common
law. They are monopolies organized to destroy
competition and restrain trade. Enlightened
public policy favors competition in the present
condition of organized society. It was held in
1880, Central Ohio Salt Company *vs.* Guthrie,
35 Ohio Street, 666, that a trust was illegal and
void. The Pennsylvania courts held the same

way against the Coal Trust of that State. Morris Coal Company *vs.* Vorday, 68 Pa. St.,
173. . . .

It is contended by those interested in Trusts
that they tend to cheapen production and diminish the price of the article to the consumer.
It is conceded that these results may follow
temporarily and even permanently in some instances. But it is not the rule. When such effects ensue they are merely incidental to the
controlling object of the association. Trusts are
speculative in their purposes and formed to
make money. Once they secure control of a
given line of business they are masters of the
situation and can dictate to the two great
classes with which they deal—the producer of
the raw material and the consumer of the finished product. They limit the price of the raw
material so as to impoverish the producer, drive
him to a single market, reduce the price of
every class of labor connected with the trade,
throw out of employment large numbers of persons who had before been engaged in a meritorious calling and finally, prompted by insatiable avarice, they increase the price to the
consumer and thus complete the circle of their
depredations. Diminished prices is the bribe
which they throw into the market to propitiate
the public. They will take it back when it
suits them to do so.

The Trust is organized commerce with the
Golden Rule excluded and the trustees exempted from the restraints of conscience.

They argue that competition means war and
is therefore destructive. The Trust is eminently
docile and hence seeks to destroy competition
in order that we may have peace. But the peace
which they give us is like that which exists
after the leopard had devoured the kid. This
professed desire for peace is a false pretense.
They dread the war of competition because the
people share in the spoils. When rid of that
they always turn their guns upon the masses
and depredate without limit or mercy. The
main weapons of the trust are threats, intimidation, bribery, fraud, wreck and pillage. Take
one well authenticated instance in the history
of the Oat Meal Trust as an example. In 1887
this Trust decided that part of their mills should
stand idle. They were accordingly closed. This
resulted in the discharge of a large number of
laborers who had to suffer in consequence. The
mills which were continued in operation would
produce seven million barrels of meal during
the year. Shortly after shutting down the Trust

advanced the price of meal one dollar per barrel and the public was forced to stand the assessment. The mills were more profitable when idle than when in operation.

. . .

The most distressing feature of this war of the Trusts is the fact that they control the articles which the plain people consume in their daily life. It cuts off their accumulations and deprives them of the staff upon which they fain would lean in their old age.

THE REMEDY

For nearly three hundred years the Anglo-Saxon race has been trying to arrest the encroachments of monopoly and yet the evil has flourished and gained in strength from age to age. The courts have come to the aid of enlightened sentiment, pronounced all such combinations contrary to public policy, illegal and their contracts void; and still they have continued to thrive. Thus far repressive and prohibitory legislation have proved unavailing. Experience has shown that when men, for the sake of gain, will openly violate the moral law and infringe upon the plain rights of their neighbors, they will not be restrained by ordinary prohibitory measures. It is the application of force to the situation and force must be met with force. The States should pass stringent penal statutes which will visit personal responsibility upon all agents and representatives of the trust who aid or assist in the transaction of its business within the State. The General Government, through its power to lay and collect taxes, should place an excise or internal revenue tax of from 25 to 40 per cent on all manufacturing plants, goods, wares or merchandise of whatever kind and wherever found when owned by or controlled in the interest of such combines or associations, and this tax should be first lien upon such property until the tax is paid. The details of such a bill would not be difficult to frame. Such a law would destroy the Trust root and branch. Whenever the American people really try to overthrow these institutions they will be able to do so and to further postpone action is a crime.

WHAT OF THE FUTURE?

One of the main charges against Charles the First, was that he had fostered and created monopolies. His head went to the block. Nearly every great struggle of the English race has been caused by the unjust exactions of tribute —against the extortions of greed. Our own war for Independence was a war against taxes. Our late internal struggle was for the freedom of labor and the right of the laborer to possess and enjoy his own. That struggle is still on and it is now thundering at our gates with renewed energy. It will not down, though the Trust heap Ossa upon Pelion. The people will rise and overturn the despoilers though they shake the earth by the displacement.

These vast struggles are great teachers and the world is learning rapidly. We are coming to know that great combinations reduce the cost of production and soon the world will grasp the idea that the people can combine and protect themselves. In this combine, in this cooperation of all, there will be no discrimination and the bounties of Heaven will be open alike to the weak and the powerful. We welcome the conflict. There is no time to lose nor can the battle begin too soon. . . .

CHAPTER XX

DANGER AND DUTY

THE GREAT DANGER

If the economic revolution now in progress in the United States is not speedily successful, the industrial people will have no one to blame but themselves. Through suffering and research they have learned the causes of their distress. They have organized, decided upon remedies and made known their demands. They have the numbers to make their wishes effective. The Constitution and laws of the country place the whole matter within their hands. The great initial battles have been fought in the Courts and this constitutes their Gibraltar and impregnable vantage ground. Nothing is now needed but a proper use of the ballot. . . .

Let us all remember that the various organizations, now so powerful, cannot always be maintained. They will decay with time and fall to pieces from lack of purpose or the discouragement of defeat. Our enemies well understand this and are urging procrastination and pleading for time. As well might the general of an army send a bearer of dispatches, under a flag of truce, to ask the commander of the opposing forces when he would like to have the engagement brought on. If the general consulted were weak in numbers he would decide to postpone the battle until such time as the forces of his adversary could be wasted by death, disease and desertion.

STRIKE NOW!

We have challenged the adversary to battle and our bugles have sounded the march. If we now seek to evade or shrink from the conflict it will amount to a confession of cowardice and a renunciation of the faith. Let us make the year 1892 memorable for all time to come as the period when the great battle for industrial emancipation was fought and won in the United States. It is glorious to live in this age, and to be permitted to take part in this heroic combat is the greatest honor that can be conferred upon mortals. It is an opportunity for every man, however humble, to strike a blow that will permanently benefit his race and make the world better for his having lived. Throughout all history we have had ample evidence that the new world is the theater upon which the great struggle for the rights of man is to be made, and the righteous movement now in progress should again forcibly remind us of our enviable mission, under Providence, among the nations of the earth.　　　　　1892

WILLIAM JENNINGS BRYAN

1860–1925

ON JULY 8, 1896, William Jennings Bryan took the National Democratic Convention at Chicago by storm. The "Cross of Gold" speech which he delivered on that occasion was not new, for he had already rehearsed it in local campaigns in Nebraska. But the tautly drawn lines between the conservative Eastern and the radical Western Democrats at the Chicago convention reflected similarly sharp conflicts in the country at large. The agrarian classes had long been suffering severely as a result of prolonged depression. Bryan, who had identified himself with the silver men in Congress (1890–1894) voiced a widely held conviction in the West that "free silver" would loosen the strangle hold which the predatory financial Bourbons enjoyed. At the Democratic nominating convention in 1896 overwhelming enthusiasm greeted Bryan's "Cross of Gold" speech, the most notable in his career and one of the greatest in the history of American oratory. This speech also made him the heir of the Populist movement. In the presidential campaign of 1896, which Bryan called "the first battle," he traveled over 18,000 miles and everywhere was greeted either with unparalleled enthusiasm or with bitter denunciation. He went down to a narrow defeat. But "the first battle" was not his last. Nor was it the final protest of the liberal forces of America which, for the time, were overshadowed by the victory of the conservatism symbolized by William McKinley and Mark Hanna.

The First Battle, A Story of the Campaign of 1896, Chicago, 1896.
The Speeches of William Jennings Bryan, Revised and Arranged by Himself, 2 vols., New York, 1913.
William Jennings Bryan and the Campaign of 1896, George F. Whicher, ed., Boston, 1953.
Paxton Hibben, *The Peerless Leader, William Jennings Bryan*, New York, 1929.

»　»　THE CROSS OF GOLD　«　«

I would be presumptuous, indeed, to present myself against the distinguished gentlemen to whom you have listened if this were a mere measuring of abilities; but this is not a contest between persons. The humblest citizen in all the land, when clad in the armor of a righteous cause, is stronger than all the hosts of error. I come to speak to you in defense of a cause as holy as the cause of liberty—the cause of humanity.

When this debate is concluded, a motion will be made to lay upon the table the resolution offered in commendation of the administration, and also the resolution offered in condemnation of the administration. We object to bringing this question down to the level of persons. The individual is but an atom; he is born, he acts, he dies; but principles are eternal; and this has been a contest over a principle.

Never before in the history of this country has there been witnessed such a contest as that through which we have just passed. Never before in the history of American politics has a great issue been fought out as this issue has been, by the voters of a great party. On the fourth of March, 1895, a few Democrats, most of them members of Congress, issued an address to the Democrats of the nation, asserting that the money question was the paramount issue of the hour; declaring that a majority of the Democratic party had the right to control the action of the party on this paramount issue; and concluding with the request that the believers in the free coinage of silver in the Democratic party should organize, take charge of, and control the policy of the Democratic party. Three months later, at Memphis, an organization was perfected, and the silver Democrats went forth openly and courageously proclaiming their belief, and declaring that, if successful, they would crystallize into a platform the declaration which they had made. Then began the conflict. With a zeal approaching the zeal which inspired the Crusaders who followed Peter the Hermit, our silver Democrats went forth from victory unto victory until they are now assembled, not to discuss, not to debate, but to enter up the judgement already rendered by the plain people of this country. In this contest brother has been arrayed against brother, father against son. The warmest ties of love, acquaintance and association have been disregarded; old leaders have been cast aside when they have refused to give expression to the sentiments of those whom they would lead, and new leaders have sprung up to give direction to this cause of truth. Thus has the contest been waged, and we have assembled here under as binding and solemn instructions as were ever imposed upon representatives of the people. We do not come as individuals. As individu-

als we might have been glad to compliment the gentleman from New York [Senator Hill], but we know that the people for whom we speak would never be willing to put him in a position where he could thwart the will of the Democratic party. I say it was not a question of persons; it was a question of principle, and it is not with gladness, my friends, that we find ourselves brought into conflict with those who are now arrayed on the other side.

The gentleman who preceded me [ex-Governor Russell] spoke of the State of Massachusetts; let me assure him that not one present in all this convention entertains the least hostility to the people of the State of Massachusetts, but we stand here representing the people who are the equals, before the law, of the greatest citizens in the State of Massachusetts. When you [turning to the gold delegates] come before us and tell us that we are about to disturb your business interests, we reply that you have disturbed our business interests by your course.

We say to you that you have made the definition of a business man too limited in its application. The man who is employed for wages is as much a business man as his employer, the attorney in a country town is as much a business man as the corporation counsel in a great metropolis; the merchant at the cross-roads store is as much a business man as the merchant of New York; the farmer who goes forth in the morning and toils all day—who begins in the spring and toils all summer—and who by the application of brain and muscle to the natural resources of the country creates wealth, is as much a business man as the man who goes upon the board of trade and bets upon the price of grain; the miners who go down a thousand feet into the earth, or climb two thousand feet upon the cliffs, and bring forth from their hiding places the precious metals to be poured into the channels of trade are as much business men as the few financial magnates who, in a back room, corner the money of the world. We come to speak for this broader class of business men.

Ah, my friends, we say not one word against those who live upon the Atlantic coast, but the hardy pioneers who have braved all the dangers of the wilderness, who have made the desert to blossom as the rose—the pioneers away out there [pointing to the West], who rear their children near to Nature's heart, where they can mingle their voices with the voices of the birds—out there where they have erected school houses for the education of their young, churches where they praise their Creator, and cemeteries where rest the ashes of their dead —these people, we say, are as deserving of the consideration of our party as any people in this country. It is for these that we speak. We do not come as aggressors. Our war is not a war of conquest; we are fighting in the defense of our homes, our families, and posterity. We have petitioned, and our petitions have been scorned; we have entreated, and our entreaties have been disregarded; we have begged, and they have mocked when our calamity came. We beg no longer; we petition no more. We defy them.

The gentleman from Wisconsin has said that he fears a Robespierre. My friends, in this land of the free you need not fear that a tyrant will spring up from among the people. What we need is an Andrew Jackson to stand, as Jackson stood, against the encroachments of organized wealth.

They tell us that this platform was made to catch votes. We reply to them that changing conditions make new issues; that the principles on which Democracy rests are as everlasting as the hills, but that they must be applied to new conditions as they arise. Conditions have arisen, and we are here to meet those conditions. They tell us that the income tax ought not be brought in here; that it is a new idea. They criticize us for our criticism of the Supreme Court of the United States. My friends, we have not criticized; we have simply called attention to what you already know. If you want criticisms, read the dissenting opinions of the court. There you will find criticisms. They say that we passed an unconstitutional law; we deny it. The income tax law was not unconstitutional when it was passed; it was not unconstitutional when it went before the Supreme Court for the first time; it did not become unconstitutional until one of the judges changed his mind, and we cannot be expected to know when a judge will change his mind. The income tax is just. It simply intends to put the burdens of government upon the backs of the people. I am in favor of an income tax. When I find a man who is not willing to bear his share of the burdens of the government which protects him, I find a man who is unworthy to enjoy the blessings of a government like ours.

They say that we are opposing national bank currency; it is true. If you will read what Thomas Benton said, you will find he said that, in searching history, he could find but one par-

allel to Andrew Jackson; that was Cicero, who destroyed the conspiracy of Cataline and saved Rome. Benton said that Cicero only did for Rome what Jackson did for us when he destroyed the bank conspiracy and saved America. We say in our platform that we believe that the right to coin and issue money is a function of government. We believe it. We believe that it is a part of sovereignty, and can no more with safety be delegated to private individuals than we could afford to delegate to private individuals the power to make penal statutes or levy taxes. Mr. Jefferson, who was once regarded as good Democratic authority, seems to have differed in opinion from the gentleman who has addrest us on the part of the minority. Those who are opposed to this proposition tell us that the issue of paper money is a function of the bank, and that the Government ought to go out of the banking business. I stand with Jefferson rather than with them, and tell them, as he did, that the issue of money is a function of government, and that banks ought to go out of the governing business.

They complain about the plank which declares against life tenure in office. They have tried to strain it to mean that which it does not mean. What we oppose by that plank is the life tenure which is being built up in Washington, and which excludes from participation in official benefits the humbler members of society.

Let me call your attention to two or three important things. The gentleman from New York says that he will propose an amendment to the platform providing that the proposed change in our monetary system shall not affect contracts already made. Let me remind you that there is no intention of affecting those contracts which according to present laws are made payable in gold; but if he means to say that we cannot change our monetary system without protecting those who have loaned money before the change was made, I desire to ask him where, in law or in morals, he can find justification for not protecting the debtors when the act of 1873 was passed, if he now insists that we must protect the creditors.

He says he will also propose an amendment which will provide for the suspension of free coinage if we fail to maintain the parity within a year. We reply that when we advocate a policy which we believe will be successful, we are not compelled to raise a doubt as to our own sincerity by suggesting what we shall do if we fail. I ask him, if he would apply his logic to us, why he does not apply it to himself. He says he wants this country to try to secure an international agreement. Why does he not tell us what he is going to do if he fails to secure an international agreement? There is more reason for him to do that than there is for us to provide against the failure to maintain the parity. Our opponents have tried for twenty years to secure an international agreement, and those are waiting for it most patiently who do not want it at all.

And now, my friends, let me come to the paramount issue. If they ask us why it is that we say more on the money question than we say upon the tariff question, I reply that, if protection has slain its thousands, the gold standard has slain its tens of thousands. If they ask us why we do not embody in our platform all the things that we believe in, we reply that when we have restored the money of the Constitution all other necessary reforms will be possible; but that until this is done there is no other reform that can be accomplished.

Why is it that within three months such a change has come over the country? Three months ago, when it was confidently asserted that those who believe in the gold standard would frame our platform and nominate our candidates, even the advocates of the gold standard did not think that we could elect a President. And they had good reason for their doubt, because there is scarcely a State here to-day asking for the gold standard which is not in the absolute control of the Republican party. But note the change. Mr. McKinley was nominated at St. Louis upon a platform which declared for the maintenance of the gold standard until it can be changed into bimetalism by international agreement. Mr. McKinley was the most popular man among the Republicans, and three months ago everybody in the Republican party prophesied his election. How is it to-day? Why, the man who was once pleased to think that he looked like Napoleon—that man shudders to-day when he remembers that he was nominated on the anniversary of the battle of Waterloo. Not only that, but as he listens he can hear with ever-increasing distinctness the sounds of the waves as they beat upon the lonely shores of St. Helena.

Why this change? Ah, my friends, is not the reason for the change evident to any one who will look at the matter? No private character, however pure, no personal popularity, however great, can protect from the avenging wrath of an indignant people a man who will declare that he is in favor of fastening the gold standard upon this country, or who is willing to surrender the right of self-government and place the legislative control of our affairs in the hands of foreign potentates and powers.

We go forth confident that we shall win. Why? Because upon the paramount issue of this campaign there is not a spot of ground upon which the enemy will dare to challenge 10 battle. If they tell us that the gold standard is a good thing, we shall point to their platform and tell them that their platform pledges the party to get rid of the gold standard and substitute bimetalism. If the gold standard is a good thing, why try to get rid of it? I call your attention to the fact that some of the very people who are in this convention to-day and who tell us that we ought to declare in favor of international bimetalism—thereby declaring that the 20 gold standard is wrong and that the principle of bimetalism is better—these very people four months ago were open and avowed advocates of the gold standard, and were then telling us that we could not legislate two metals together, even with the aid of all the world. If the gold standard is a good thing, we ought to declare in favor of its retention and not in favor of abandoning it; and if the gold standard is a bad thing, why should we wait until other nations 30 are willing to help us to let go? Here is the line of battle, and we care not upon which issue they force the fight; we are prepared to meet them on either issue or on both. If they tell us that the gold standard is the standard of civilization, we reply to them that this, the most enlightened of all the nations of the earth, has never declared for a gold standard and that both the great parties this year are declaring against it. If the gold standard is 40 the standard of civilization, why, my friends, should we not have it? If they come to meet us on that issue we can present the history of our nation. More than that; we can tell them that they will search the pages of history in vain to find a single instance where the common people have ever declared themselves in favor of the gold standard. They can find where the holders of fixt investments have declared for a gold standard, but not where the masses have. 50 Mr. Carlisle said in 1878 that this was a struggle between "the idle holders of idle capital" and "the struggling masses, who produce the wealth and pay the taxes of the country"; and, my friends, the question we are to decide is: Upon which side will the Democratic party fight; upon the side of "the idle holders of idle capital" or upon the side of "the struggling masses"? That is the question which the party must answer first, and then it must be answered by each individual hereafter. The sympathies of the Democratic party, as shown by the platform, are on the side of the struggling masses who have ever been the foundation of the Democratic party. There are two ideas of government. There are those who believe that, if you will only legislate to make the well-to-do prosperous, their prosperity will leak through on those below. The Democratic idea, however, that if you legislate to make the masses prosperous, their prosperity will find its way up through every class which rests upon them.

You come to us and tell us that the great cities are in favor of the gold standard; we reply that the great cities rest upon our broad and fertile prairies. Burn down your cities and leave our farms, and your cities will spring up again as if by magic; but destroy our farms and the grass will grow in the streets of every city in the country.

My friends, we declare that this nation is able to legislate for its own people on every question, without waiting for the aid or consent of any other nation on earth; and upon that issue we expect to carry every State in the Union. I shall not slander the inhabitants of the fair State of Massachusetts nor the inhabitants of the State of New York by saying that, when they are confronted with the proposition, they will declare that this nation is not able to attend to its own business. It is the issue of 1776 over again. Our ancestors, when but three millions in number, had the courage to declare their political independence of every other nation; shall we, their descendants, when we have grown to seventy millions, declare that we are less independent than our forefathers? No, my friends, that will never be the verdict of our people. Therefore we care not upon what lines the battle is fought. If they say bimetalism is good, but that we cannot have it until the other nations help us, we reply that, instead of having a gold standard because England has, we will restore bimetalism, and then let England have bimetalism because the United States has it. If they dare to come out in the open field and defend the gold standard as a good thing, we will fight them to the uttermost. Having behind us the producing masses of this nation and the world, supported by the commercial interests, the laboring interests, and the toilers everywhere, we will answer their demand for a gold standard by saying to them: You shall not press down upon the brow of labor this crown of thorns, you shall not crucify mankind upon a cross of gold.   1896

GEORGE D. HERRON

1862–1925

BORN IN Montezuma, Indiana, Herron was largely self-educated. In the Congregationalist ministry he became an early and leading exponent of the Christian Socialist cause. His radical views, especially on marriage, contributed to his break with Grinnell College, where he had become a professor, and with the Congregationalist church. By 1910 Herron had abandoned Christian Socialism and had assumed a position of considerable influence in the international Socialist organization in Europe. His deeply religious spirit continued, however, to influence his thought.

During the World War Herron abandoned pacifism and became an advisor to President Wilson and to important dissident groups and leaders in Germany, on whom he exerted considerable influence prior to and immediately following the German revolution of 1918.

Herron's books include *The Larger Christ* (1891), *The Christian State* (1895), *Social Meanings of Religious Experiences* (1896), *From Revolution to Revolution* (1907), and *The Menace of Peace*

(1917). Some of his World War papers have been edited by M. P. Briggs, *George D. Herron and the European Settlement* (1932).

"George D. Herron," *The Outlook*, CXXI (February 19, 1919), 296–297.
C. H. Hopkins, *The Rise of the Social Gospel in American Protestantism* (New Haven, 1940).

» » From: THE NEW REDEMPTION « «

CHAPTER I

CHRIST AND THE SOCIAL REVOLUTION

And I saw a new heaven and a new earth: for the first heaven and the first earth are passed away; and the sea is no more.
—Rev. XXI. I.

What I have here to say treats of work, wages, and wealth, of the rights and duties of capital and labor. And I approach the social problem, not from the standpoint of the political economist, but of the Christian apostle; Christ did not save the world by a scientific study of the economic conditions of society. Nor shall I make use of statistics, the value of which is largely fictitious; it is a fallacy that figures cannot lie. My discourse will be chiefly concerned with principles. I wish to characterize some of the false principles which have bred social inequalities, and assert the true principles which can procure social justice.

The world is ruled by ideas. Every few centuries a great idea is born into the soul of man. Whether it becomes destructive or constructive depends upon what is done with it, and who has charge of the doing. Great ideas, arousing great moral passions, come to stay. Though we crucify them, they will not die: they thrive on persecutions, and are enthroned by crucifixions. They become man's weal or woe, his savior or destroyer, according to his acceptance or rejection of their rule. . . .

A great idea is now leading the world's thought and lifting its hopes. Everywhere are the signs of universal change. The race is in an attitude of expectancy, straitened until its new baptism is accomplished. Every nerve of society is feeling the first agonies of a great trial that is to try all that dwell upon the earth and issue in a divine deliverance. We are in the beginnings of a revolution that will strain all existing religious and political institutions, and test the wisdom and heroism of the earth's purest and bravest souls; a revolution that will regenerate society with the judgments

of infinite love. We must get ready for the change by making straight the way of the Lord Christ into the heart of the social strife, that he may purify it with the hope of justice; by giving him command of the revolution, that he may lead it into a larger redemption of the earth. God honors our generation by bringing up it the sorrow and trial of seeking a road to social order; of finding a way to something like an equitable distribution of economic goods, a mutualism of the responsibilities and benefits of civilization. The idea of brotherhood, co-operation, unity, is both destroying and recreating the world. The feeling that men were made to stand together, that the race rather than the individual is the unit, is widening and intensifying. The belief that sacrifice and not self-interest is the social foundation, that the Golden Rule is natural law, is everywhere gaining disciples and power. Men are beginning to see that the welfare of each is the responsibility of all, and the welfare of all the responsibility of each. Whether it be for good or ill, whether foolish or wise, the socialistic idea is leading the world. Whether the passion for oneness works the weal or woe of society depends entirely upon its reception or rejection by the Christian church.

It will not do to say the revolution is not coming, or pronounce it of the devil. Revolutions, even in their wildest forms, are the impulses of God moving in tides of fire through the life of man. To resist them is to be consumed, and to compel the remission of sins by the shedding of blood. To receive them as from God is to receive his kingdom almost without observation. The dangerous classes in every age and nation are they who, in the interest of religious or political parties, say that the wrong cannot be set right; that selfishness and injustice and inequality are natural virtues, essential to progress and the stability of civilization. They who say that man's conceptions of justice cannot be enlarged and purified are the ones who bring disaster and wrath upon the world. And they who seek to lift the works and institutions of men with visions of larger truth and assertions of wider justice are not destroyers, but builders; they make ready the way of the Lord into new redemptions of human life.

Nor dare we hope to avert the revolution by suffering what we have been mistaught to call the natural laws of trade to take their logical course. It is against the rule and validity of these laws the revolution directs itself. It is a fiction to characterize as law the principles that now govern economic production and distribution. In fact, we are and have been in a state of industrial anarchy; of social lawlessness. Selfishness is always social disintegration. Competition is not law, but anarchy. That competition is the life of industry is the most profane and foolish of social falsehoods. Cain was the author of the competitive theory. The cross of Jesus stands as its eternal denial. It is social imbecility. It is economic waste. It is the destruction of life. It is the deformity, brutality, and atheism of civilization. It will be as outrageous to the civilization of the future as cannibalism is to the civilization of the present. The speculation which competition makes a necessary element of production and distribution renders the life of man a game of chance. Modern monopolies are its natural fruits: the fruits which the strong and cunning reap through competition with the weaker, less cunning, or more conscientious. Speculative competition makes possible such social disruption and violence to human liberties, such absolute anarchism, as that of a recent coal combination, which arbitrarily reduced the wages of miners and increased the profits of coal millions of dollars, with neither more moral nor economic justification; here was anarchy of the worst type.

The social question is fast revolving itself into a question of whether or not capital can be brought into subjection to law. The social revolution is a search for law: for law that shall have power to procure justice and peace in place of the chance and strife that are everywhere the disorganization of society. The revolution comes not to destroy, but to organize society with a divine and deathless life. It means no evil to the institutions of state and religion, but would rebuild them upon eternal and righteous foundations, and secure them with the justice of love. It aims not to destroy

wealth, but to save it by bringing it under the reign of law and consecrating it to the service of humanity. The demand for equality and unity is constructive at heart, even in its most unreasoning and destructive manifestations. The nihilisms and socialisms of our day are desperate yet real attempts to achieve the social ideal by a single bound; attempts to take the kingdom of justice by violence. With one stroke they would break the golden bowl of our modern industrial system, full of abominations. . . .

The search for justice, even where it denies the authority of the personal Christ, is essentially a belief in the practicability of the principles which are the essence of Christ's gospel; a belief that brotherhood consists with nature, and that co-operation rather than competition is the natural law of material as well as moral progress; a belief that if mutualism could take the place of the chance and anarchy of speculation and greed, a thousand unknown forms of industry would spring up to add to the moral health and material wealth of man. For the hope of actualizing Christianity as the life of man the revolution is called in question by the religious Pharisees and the political Sadducees.

But before we try to guide the revolution, or attempt the solution of the social problem, we must take our stand upon the platform of duties, and not that of rights. The old passion for liberty, which has won for man so large triumphs in religion and politics, has done its work. It was a great work. But the selfishness that poisons every noble passion, when it rules rather than serves, has transformed the liberty of our fathers into the most intolerable despotism the world has ever suffered. And the social question is not so much a question of rights as of duties. If we are to find a way out of social confusion, if we are to achieve industrial freedom, we must cease to look at the mere rights of capital, or the rights of labor, and look in the direction of the duty of man to man. If we would work with God, if we would follow the Son of man as he leads the race into its purer liberties, we must move with the progress of the cross in the purchase of a new redemption through sacrifice. Society will learn obedience to the ideal of Jesus through the things which men suffer. The laborer will receive the fruits of his labor, and work and wages and wealth become accordant parts of a divine harmony of justice, through changing the social revolution from a passion for rights into a passion for duties.

Work is the first factor to be considered in the social problem. This is a world of work. God works and man works. Work is the manifestation of life. Work is communion with God. There is no righteous work that is not sacred and divine. All the work of man is a part of the creation of God, which is still going on. The work of the carpenter in building a house is as sacred as the work of God in building the earth. The men who do the world's work are the hands by which God works. The man who builds is one of God's builders. The man who plants the fields is God's artist-hand, and the field of green and the field of ripened grain are the glory of God painted upon the face of the earth. The industrial worker is a poet, a creator, an artist, a musician, because all work righteously done, to the best of one's ability, is a creation; it is a harmony. It is the music of God singing itself out through the life of man. And no man is true to his divine origin, no man is really a man, unless, to the extent of his ability, he works. The man who is able to work and works not is a pauper, whether rich or poor. Of all pauperism the most degraded and degrading, because utterly shameless and thriftless, is that aristocracy which idly luxuriates in money obtained through speculation, extortion, or inheritance.

The social conception of work has been progressive. In the highest days of Greek art and philosophy work was supposed to be fit for none but slaves. Aristotle did not believe those who did manual labor entitled to citizenship. Since the coming of the carpenter's Son, who is the final authority in political economy, work has grown in honor, and has occupied a constantly enlarging place in legislation. By teaching men to know God as their Father, he took out from all the foundations of society any ground for social caste or industrial despotism.

Work ought to bear fruit in the livelihood, in the physical comfort, in the moral development, of all who work. The social nature of wealth needs larger consideration. When men began to use the earth, there was nature, which was the gift of God. And all the wealth of the world, in its last analysis, has been created from nature by labor in social relationships. Any wealth that is not the creation of labor is fictitious. The wealth of Mr. Gould represented the poverty of society. Every dollar his speculation made for himself made society so much the poorer. Every man in the United States who works has a share in the creation of the wealth of the Vanderbilts. Every man taxed to sustain the government of the state, which is the social organ, is morally entitled to speak concerning the management of capital which he may not own. The way in which one invests his capital is a matter that touches all human life. When a man proposes to manage his property solely on the ground of profit and self-interest, independent of good-will to society, he claims what is morally unlawful. No state has ever recognized exclusive ownership in property; for property would have no value without the nurture of society.

Labor is a larger factor than political economists have taken into account in the creation of wealth. Without labor even capital would be valueless in providing for economic necessities. It is through the use of labor that the manufacturer creates his wealth. Through the earnings of labor the wealth of the merchant is gained. Two sources of wealth are thus fed by the laborer.

*   *   *

It is hardly disputed that capital, under our modern industrial system, is receiving more than a just share of the fruits of labor, and the laborer is receiving relatively less and less of the profits of his toil. The increase of wealth and wages is in no sense equitable. There is not a progressive economist in America or England who does not say that wealth is growing out of all proportion to the benefits which the laborer derives from his labor. The distribution of wealth is not according to industry or ability; not according to one's worth to society, but according, in large measure, to the skill of some in appropriating to themselves the fruits of the labor of others by commercial legerdemain. It is thus that while we are the richest nation on the globe, our wealth is rapidly being centered in the hands of a few, and industrial toilers are being reduced to a condition of practical servitude. "Thoughtful men see and admit," says Judge Walter Q. Gresham, "that our country is becoming less and less democratic, and more and more plutocratic," and plutocracy he pronounces the most insidious of all forms of tyranny. "Nothing," says Dr. Theodore Dwight Woolsey, "would lead the mass of men to embrace socialism sooner than the conviction that this enormous accumulation of capital in a few hands was to be not only an evil in fact, if not prevented, but a necessary evil beyond prevention. . . . A revolution, slow or rapid, would certainly bring about a new order."

Nor can the difference between the working and the capitalistic classes be concealed by the fact that wages average better now than forty or fifty years ago. It is a waste of time to cite statistics to show that the laboring man has economic goods he did not formerly have. Forty to fifty years ago the mechanic and his master worked side by side; the apprentice was the social equal of his employer. There was not the stratification of society which we now see, and almost every man produced something of his own livelihood. Fuel cost him but the work of bringing it to his dooryard. He raised necessities which must now be purchased. The lowest wages of a half century ago represented a more equitable share in the social benefits of civilization than the highest wages of today.

The inevitable result of the system of wages and competition will be to increase social inequalities; to increase the wealth of a few and the poverty of the many. It is to the interest of capital, when it releases itself from moral and social obligations, and looks only to its own increase, to keep a large class of unemployed men, who must work or starve. The present industrial system could not exist were it not for the fact that great multitudes of the unemployed have been brought to this country, systematically and purposely, for the sake of reducing wages and producing a state of poverty. By this method the clothing trade of the United States thrives upon the sweating system. By pitting the unemployed, by reducing men and women and children to a condition of poverty, where they must work at any price or starve, competition has prospered by the blood of men and women.

In the midst of great wealth, with the glory of its material enterprise, its blind luxury and mad speculation, its disregard for human life, for moral law, there is an increasing poverty and degradation; a deep and angry social discontent; a growing distrust in the reality of our liberties and the sincerity of our Christianity, proving that our competitive system does not belong to a divine order of things. It is un-

natural that the strong should prosper at the expense of the weak; that the earning of one's daily bread should be an uncertain strife. It is a violation of nature that prosperity should come through the triumph of cunning over character, and the conflict of selfish interests. Our so-called industrial order is the disordering of nature. It is the disorganization of human life. There is enough in this world for all to have and enjoy in abundance, if there were a system by which there could be an equitable distribution of that abundance upon the principles of the divine economy.

The social problem is the call of the state to become Christian. The state can save itself only by believing in the Lord Jesus Christ as the supreme authority in law, politics, and society. The state is the social organ. To meet the strain that will be put upon it by the revolution, the state must be redeemed from the worship of property and from commercial theories of government. It can prove its right to be only by procuring a greater measure of social justice and giving a larger recognition to the sacredness of man. The state must have in it the mind that was in Jesus, who is the final political economist. The Sermon on the Mount is the science of society, it is a treatise on political economy; it is a system of justice. It consists of the natural laws which proceed from the heart of God, and operate in the creation and redemption of the world; in the evolution of man and the progressive development of society. It is the constitution of the divine and universal society which John in the Revelation calls a new earth. The establishment of its justice underneath the politics and social structures of man is the new Jerusalem which John saw coming down out of heaven from God. The business of the state is to adopt this social constitution of Jesus as the spirit and justice of the people, and bring every activity into subjection to its authority.

It is not primarily the mission of the state to protect property as a thing in itself. The state is the organization of the life of man in unity with the life of God; its concern is with human beings. Property is valuable only as it is the instrument of justice between man and man, and a bond of fellowship with God. Property has a right to protection only as it is designedly working out the whole welfare of man. It is the business of the state to develop and shield the common manhood and happiness, the physical and moral health, of men as sons of God. Government has a right to existence and authority for no other end than that for which God sent his only begotten Son into the world. It is the vocation of the state, as the social organ, to so control property, so administer the production and distribution of economic goods, as to give to every man the fruit of his labor, and protect the laborer from the irresponsible tyranny of the passion for wealth. It is the duty of the state to so reconstruct itself as to procure for every man full opportunity to develop all his powers, and to see that no member of society suffers for the want of work and bread.

A baseless assumption which the state must correct is, that employers have an economic right to employ and discharge from the individual standpoint, with only a money obligation to employees, and no responsibility to society. But the Christian state, as the organization of the divine life of man, is bound to deny the existence of any such right in a moral world. The assertion of such a right is the denial of the humanity of man; it is infidelity to Christ; it is substantial atheism. The assumption that capital may discharge and employ solely on the basis of self-interest shuts God out of human affairs and denies the brotherhood of man. It is social anarchism. It is the declaration on the part of capital that it will not submit to law. He who sets himself apart from social relationships, to do what he pleases with his own, upon the ground of pure individualism, asserts the right to do what God himself dare not do. In so far as the state allows the assumption and exercise of such a right, it fails to secure justice. No industrial concern has a right to receive the benefits of society without bearing commensurate responsibilities. It is monstrous and undemocratic, it is the enthronement of industrial despotism, for the state to grant powers and protection to corporate or individual employers, and yet leave them irresponsible for the social welfare. The assertion on the part of capital of a right to exist for the sake of gain, independent of the voice of the people or the welfare of labor, has had its day. It is the last remnant of that absolutism which has been slowly and revengefully yielding to the redemptive forces that have been making men free ever since the Son of man poured out his life upon the Calvary of truth. There was a day when men thought the state could be preserved only by maintaining the absolute authority of the king, and by giving the people no voice in their government. Men once believed that the divine right of kings alone could secure political order and procure social justice. But that day has gone by, and democracy everywhere has the political field, or is gaining it in every civilized nation. Absolutism of every sort is doomed and cannot hold its own against the purposes of God. It can no more sustain itself in industry than in politics. If democracy is good for the state, it is good for industry. King George's assertion of a right to tax American colonists without representation, was not half as unjust, as intolerable and despotic, as the assumption that a great corporation can enjoy the nurture and claim the protection of society, and yet deny society all management or voice in its affairs. A man could not have what he calls his own, save through the co-operation of his fellow-men; and they have rights in the management of capital for the social welfare commensurate with the privileges and opportunities which capital receives. If democracy, which is social fellowship and political mutualism, can best procure political justice and preserve the state, then it can also procure the largest economic justice and industrial freedom. Capital is a social creation, and its administration a social responsibility; so that industrial federation lies in the nature of things.

. . .

But the initiative in the establishment of a democracy of Jesus in the world of work and wealth must be taken by capital itself, which has in its hands both the power and the responsibility. The commercial dogma that capital has discharged its duty when it has paid its employees the market rate of wages, with the market under the sovereignty of what is known as the law of supply and demand, asserts the supremacy of capital over moral law, and gives to it a worth greater than the worth of human life. Labor is not a commodity any more than human souls are a commodity; labor is life. The relation between employer and employee is a sacred relationship; a relationship that must not be sundered by mere caprice or self-interest. It is the utter disregard of the sacredness of this relationship by both employer and employee, treating it as simply a money relationship, that is the root of the strife between the two. The union of men in industry is a communion of human lives for divine ends; and the selfish severing of this union is not merely a violation of the Sermon on the Mount; it is economic foolishness and social lawlessness. Capital should recognize that the life of the laborer is a greater matter than the gain of the employer. It was Lincoln's belief that labor should own capital, in opposition to the slave-owner's view that capital should own labor. The history of industry bears out the belief that wherever there has been a recognition of the manhood of labor on the part of capital, with the spirit of social fellowship and Christian democracy, there have been peace and prosperity for both employer and workman. The love that moved God to give his only begotten Son to save the world must be the law that shall govern wealth, and move its possessors to consecrate themselves to the creation of a Christian society and Christian state. It lies within the power of the American capitalists who call themselves Christian, by taking the Sermon on the Mount and patiently working it into the foundations of industry, to be the creators of a new and divine civilization that would surpass all our apprehensions of the Revelation of John. If they would take the Sermon on the Mount as economic law, as a revelation of the nature of things, as the safest basis upon which the market of the world could stand, they would lift the commerce and industry of the world above the chance and strife of competing interests, and make the moving trains of merchandise, the toil of the mills and echo of the mines, the barter and exchange of the markets, all accordant parts of a harmony of divine justice. I do not believe there can ever be peace between man and man, between interest and interest, between class and class, by any other mode than through the belief of capital, the belief of industry, the belief of the market, in the naturalness, in the wisdom, in the safety, of the moral law of Jesus. This the church must teach, and its members must cease to promulgate social atheism. It cannot be stated too plainly that either the people will become atheistic, or the wealth which is in Christian hands must obey the social laws of the Sermon on the Mount. Either its laws are practicable, reasonable, and natural, and will give the largest prosperity to all, or men will not believe in an all-good and all-wise God. Obedience to Christ's laws would give a new redemption to man that would be the creation of a new earth, overspread with the healing wisdom of a new heaven of divine truth, from which the sea of social troubles would flee away forever.

It is to-day the one emergent mission of the church to bring together in a divine unity the various human interests that are now at strife. The whole conception of the necessary antagonism between capital and labor is not simply an economic and political falsehood, not only a peril to the state and a denial of justice, but it makes Christianity an ideal impossible of realization. The church must demand social conditions that shall realize the Christian gospel. Unto it has been given the message that the interest of one man is the interest of all. The interest of labor is the interest of capital; and the interest of capital is the interest of labor. When capital keeps from labor its Christian share of the produce of labor, it injures itself; and labor injures itself in destroying capital. The church must open the eyes of men to see the wisdom and power of living for the common good, to the practical atheism and anarchism of selfish principles, and declare love to be the natural law of industrial activity and social life. Love at the heart of society, love at the heart of the state, love in the heart of the church, love at the heart of commerce, will right our economic wrongs, give labor its just rewards, and diffuse among the people the benefits of civilization. Only by obedience to the law of love can society be regenerated and historic problems be solved. There is in love alone the power to dispel the clouds of darkness that now over-gloom the earth with peril and judgment, calling for a new earth to rise to meet the descending heavens of larger truth. And the law of love can be obeyed only through communion with God and sacrifice for men. . . .

. . .

My brother, wherever your life and whatever your work, our great work is to make our life an interpretation of the cross as the law and order of God. We are sent to bear the cross into the unfaiths and antagonisms of the world as the sign of their healing and peace. And though men misread and hate the sign, as we press it upon the problems of our day, and we fall early in the conflict between the false order and the true, apostolic hearts will receive the cross and bear it on to the consummation of the ages in a human society that shall be an eternal incarnation of Christ.   1893

DANIEL DE LEON

1852–1914

DANIEL DE LEON, after a youth in Curaçao, studied in Germany and in the Netherlands before settling in New York City about 1874. At Columbia he earned an LL. B. and for a time lectured on Latin American diplomacy. Interested in labor and in social reform, De Leon finally identified himself with the Socialist Labor party. As editor of *The People*, and as a pamphleteer, a lecturer, and a candidate for various offices, he exerted much influence on party policies. The growing opposition to his theories and leadership seceded, about 1900, to form the Socialist Party. De Leon was a severe critic of the nonpolitical and opportunistic trades unions and, in 1895, established a industrial labor organization closely tied to the Socialist Labor party. He also took part in organizing the Industrial Workers of the World but, disliking its repudiation of any political action, set up a rival organization.

De Leon was an able intellectual champion of the Socialist cause. His writings, which won Lenin's praise, include many pamphlets and translations. *Socialist Reconstruction of Society* (1918) was his most important writing. The following selection, however, is an excellent illustration of his position.

Daniel De Leon. The Man and His Work. A Symposium, New York, 1919.
D. M. Johnson, *Daniel De Leon*, New York, 1923.
Arnold Peterson, *Daniel de Leon: Social Architect*, 2 vols., New York, 1941–1953.

» » *From:* REFORM OR REVOLUTION « «

. . . We hear people talk about the "Reform Forces," about "Evolution" and about "Revolution" in ways that are highly mixed. Let us clear up our terms. Reform means a change of externals; Revolution—peaceful or bloody, the peacefulness or the bloodiness of it cuts no figure whatever in the essence of the question, means a change from within.

REFORM

Take, for instance, a poodle. You can reform him in a lot of ways. You can shave his whole body and leave a tassel at the tip of his tail; you may bore a hole through each ear, and tie a blue bow on one and a red bow on the other; you may put a brass collar around his neck with your initials on, and a trim little blanket on his back; yet, throughout, a poodle he was and a poodle he remains. Each of these changes probably wrought a corresponding change in the poodle's life. When shorn of all his hair except a tassel at the tail's tip he was owned by a wag who probably cared only for the fun he could get out of his pet; when he appears gaily decked in bows, probably his young mistress' attachment is of tenderer sort; when later we see him in the fancier's outfit, the treatment he receives and the uses he is put to may be yet again, and probably are, different. Each of these transformations or stages may mark a veritable epoch in the poodle's existence. And yet, essentially a poodle he was, a poodle he is, and a poodle he will remain. That is REFORM. (Laughter)

REVOLUTION

But when we look back myriads of years, or project ourselves into far-future physical cataclysms, and trace the development of animal life from the invertebrate to the vertebrate, from the lizard to the bird, from the quadruped and mammal till we come to the prototype of the poodle, and finally reach the poodle himself, and so forward—then do we find radical changes at each step, changes from within that alter the very essence of his being, and that put, or will put, upon him each time a stamp that alters the very system of his existence. That is REVOLUTION.

So with society. Whenever a change leaves the internal mechanism untouched, we have REFORM; whenever the internal mechanism is changed we have REVOLUTION.

10 Of course, no internal change is possible without external manifestations. The internal changes denoted by the revolution or evolution of the lizard into the eagle go accompanied with external marks. So with society. And therein lies one of the pitfalls into which dilettanteism or "Reforms" invariably tumble. They have noticed that externals change with internals; and they rest satisfied with mere external changes, without looking behind the
20 curtain. But of this more presently.

We Socialists are not Reformers; we are Revolutionists. We Socialists do not propose to change forms. We care nothing for forms. We want a change of the inside of the mechanism of society, let the form take care of itself. We see in England a crowned monarch; we see in Germany a sceptered emperor; we see in this country an uncrowned president, and we fail to see the essential difference between Ger-
30 many, England or America. That being the case, we are skeptics as to forms. We are like grown children, in the sense that we like to look at the inside of things and find out what is there.

One more preliminary explanation. Socialism is lauded by some as an angelic movement, by others it is decried as a devilish scheme. Hence you find the Gomperses blowing hot and cold on the subject; and Harry Lloyd, with whose
40 capers, to your sorrow, you are more familiar than I, pronouncing himself a Socialist in one place, and in another running Socialism down. Socialism is neither an aspiration of angels, nor a plot of devils. Socialism moves with its feet firmly planted on the ground, and its head not lost in the clouds; it takes Science by the hand, asks her to lead, and goes whithersoever she points. It does not take Science by the hand, saying: "I shall follow you if the end of the
50 road please me." No! it takes her by the hand and says: "Whithersoever thou leadest, thither am I BOUND to go." The Socialists, consequently, move as intelligent men; we do not mutiny because, instead of having wings, we have arms, and cannot fly as we would wish.

What, then, with an eye single upon the difference between REFORM and REVOLUTION, does Socialism mean? To point out that, I shall take up two or three of what I may style the principal centres of the movement.

GOVERNMENT—THE STATE

One of these principal nerve centres is the question of "Government" or the question of "State." How many of you have not seen upon the shelves of our libraries books that treat upon the "History of the State"; upon the "Limitations of the State"; upon "What the State Should Do, and What it Should Not Do"; upon the "Legitimate Functions of the State," and so on into infinity? Nevertheless, there is not one among all of these, the products, as they all are, of the vulgar and superficial character of capitalist thought, that fathoms the question, or actually defines the "State." Not until we reach the great works of the American Morgan, of Marx and Engels, and of other Socialist philosophers, is the matter handled with that scientific lucidity that proceeds from facts, leads to sound conclusions, and breaks the way to practical work. Not until you know and understand the history of the "State" and of "Government" will you understand one of the cardinal principles upon which Socialist Organization rests and will you be in a condition to organize successfully.

We are told that "Government" has always been as it is to-day, and always will be. This is the first fundamental error of what Karl Marx justly calls capitalistic vulgarity of thought.

When man started on his career, after having got beyond the state of the savage, he realized that co-operation was a necessity to him. He understood that together with others he could face his enemies in a better way than alone; he could hunt, fish, fight more successfully. Following the instructions of the great writer Morgan—the only great and original American writer upon this question—we look to the Indian communities, the Indian settlements, as a type of the social system that our ancestors, all of them, without exception, went through at some time.

The Indian lived in the community condition. The Indian lived under a system of common property. As Franklin described it, in a sketch of the history and alleged sacredness of private property, there was no such thing as private property among the Indians. They co-operated, worked together, and they had a

Central Directing Authority among them. In the Indian communities we find that Central Directing Authority consisting of the "Sachems." It makes no difference how that Central Directing Authority was elected, there it was. But note this: its function was to direct the cooperative or collective efforts of the communities, and, in so doing, it shared actively in the productive work of the communities. Without its work, the work of the communities would not have been done.

When, in the further development of society, the tools of production grew and developed —grew and developed beyond the point reached by the Indian; when the art of smelting iron ore was discovered; when thereby that leading social cataclysm, wrapped in the mists of ages, yet discernible, took place that rent former communal society in twain along the line of sex, the males being able, the females unable, to wield the tool of production —then society was cast into a new mold; the former community, with its democratic equality of rights and duties, vanished, and a new social system turns up, divided into two sections, the one able, the other unable, to work at production. The line that separated these two sections, being at first the line of sex, could, in the very nature of things, not yet be sharp or deep. Yet, notwithstanding, in the very shaping of these two sections—one able, the other unable, to feed itself—we have the first premonition of the CLASSES, of class distinctions, of the division of society into the INDEPENDENT and the DEPENDENT, into MASTER and SLAVES, RULER and RULED.

Simultaneously with this revolution, we find the first changes in the nature of the Central Directing Authority, of that body whose original function was to share in, by directing, production. Just as soon as economic equality is destroyed, and the economic classes crop up in society, the functions of the Central Directing Authority gradually begin to change, until finally, when, after a long range of years, moving slowly at first, and then with the present hurricane velocity under capitalism proper, the tool has developed further, and further, and still further, and has reached its present fabulous perfection and magnitude; when, through its private revolution by dividing society, no longer along the line of sex, but strictly along the line of ownership or non-ownership of the land on and the tool with which to work; when the privately owned, mammoth tool of to-day

has reduced more than fifty-two per cent. of our population to the state of being utterly unable to feed without first selling themselves into wage-slavery, while it, at the same time, saps the ground from under about thirty-nine per cent. of our people, the middle class, whose puny tools, small capital, render them certain victims of competition with the large capitalists, and makes them desperate; when the economic law that asserts itself under the system of private ownership of the tool has concentrated these private owners into about eight per cent. of the nation's inhabitants, has thereby enabled this small capitalist class to live without toil, and to compel the majority, the class of the proletariat, to toil without living; when, finally, it has come to the pass in which our country now finds itself, that, as was stated in Congress, ninety-four per cent. of the taxes are spent in "protecting property"—the property of the trivially small capitalist class —and not in protecting life; when, in short, the privately owned tool has wrought this work, and the classes—the idle rich and the working poor—are in full bloom—then the Central Directing Authority of old stands transformed; its pristine functions of aiding in, by directing, production have been supplanted by the functions of holding down the dependent, the slave, the ruled, i.e., the WORKING CLASS. Then, and not before, lo, the State, the modern State, the CAPITALIST STATE! Then, lo, the Government, the modern Government, the CAPITALIST GOVERNMENT— equipped mainly, if not solely, with the means of suppression, of oppression, of tyranny! (Applause.)

In sight of these manifestations of the modern State, the Anarchist—the rose-water and the dirty-water variety alike—shouts: "Away with all central directing authority; see what it does; it can only do mischief; it always did mischief!" But Socialism is not Anarchy. Socialism does not, like the chicken in the fable, just out of the shell, start with the knowledge of that day. Socialism rejects the premises and the conclusions of Anarchy upon the State and upon Government. What Socialism says is: "Away with the economic system that alters the beneficent functions of the Central Directing Authority from an aid to production into a means of oppression." And it proceeds to show that, when the instruments of production shall be owned, no longer by the minority, but shall be restored to the Commonwealth; that

when, as the result of this, no longer the minority or any portion of the people shall be in
poverty, and classes, class distinctions and
class rule shall, as they necessarily must, have
vanished, that then the Central Directing Authority will lose all its repressive functions,
and is bound to reassume the functions it had
in the old communities of our ancestors, become again a necessary aid, and assist in production. (Applause.)

The Socialist, in the brilliant simile of Karl
Marx, sees that a lone fiddler in his room
needs no director; he can rap himself to order, with his fiddle to his shoulder, and start
his dancing tune, and stop whenever he likes.
But just as soon as you have an orchestra, you
must also have an orchestra director—a central
directing authority. If you don't, you may have
a Salvation Army pow-wow, you may have a
Louisiana negro breakdown; you may have an
orthodox Jewish synagogue, where every man
sings in whatever key he likes, but you won't
have harmony—impossible. (Applause.)

It needs this central directing authority of
the orchestra master to rap all the players to
order at a given moment; to point out when
they shall begin; when to have these play
louder, when to have those play softer; when
to put in this instrument, when to silence that;
to regulate the time of all and preserve the
accord. The orchestra director is not an oppressor, or his baton an insignia of tyranny; he is
not there to bully anybody; he is as necessary
or important as any or all of the members of
the orchestra.

Our system of production is in the nature
of an orchestra. No one man, no one town, no
one State, can be said any longer to be independent of the other; the whole people of
the United States, every individual therein, is
dependent and interdependent upon all the
others. The nature of the machinery of production; the subdivision of labor, which aids
co-operation, and which co-operation fosters,
and which is necessary to the plentifulness of
production that civilization requires, compel
a harmonious working together of all departments of labor, and thence compel the establishment of a Central Directing Authority, of
an Orchestral Director, so to speak, of the
orchestra of the Co-operative Commonwealth.
(Loud applause.)

Such is the State or Government that the
Socialist revolution carries in its womb. To-day,
production is left to Anarchy, and only Tyr

anny, the twin sister of Anarchy, is organized.

Socialism, accordingly, implies organization;
organization implies directing authority; and
the one and the other are strict reflections of
the revolutions undergone by the tool of production. Reform, on the other hand, skims the
surface, and with "Referendums" and similar
devices limits itself to external tinkerings.

MATERIALISM—MORALITY

The second nerve centre of Socialism that
will serve to illustrate the difference between
reform and revolution is its materialistic
groundwork.

Take, for instance, the history of slavery.
All of our ancestors—this may shock some of
you, but it is a fact all the same—all of our
ancestors were cannibals at one time. The
human race, in its necessity to seek for food,
often found it easier to make a raid and take
from others the food they had gathered. In
those olden, olden days of the barbarism of
our ancestors, when they conquered a people
and took away its property, they had no further
use for the conquered; they killed them, spitted
them over a good fire, roasted and ate them
up. It was a simple and the only profitable way
known of disposing of prisoners of war. They
did with their captives very much what bees
do yet; when they have raided and conquered
a hive, they ruthlessly kill every single denizen
of the captured hive.

Our ancestors continued cannibals until their
social system had developed sufficiently to enable them to keep their prisoners under control.
From that moment they found it was more
profitable to keep their prisoners of war alive,
and turn them into slaves to work for them,
than it was to kill them off and eat them up.
With that stage of material development, cannibalism was dropped. From the higher material plane on which our ancestors then stood,
their moral vision enlarged and they presently
realized that it was immoral to eat up a human
being.

Cannibalism disappears to make room for
chattel slavery. And what do we see? Watch
the process of "moral development" in this
country—the classic ground in many ways to
study history in, for the reason that the whole
development of mankind can be seen here,
portrayed in a few years, so to speak. You
know how, to-day, the Northern people put on
airs of morality on the score of having "abolished chattel slavery," the "traffic in human

flesh," "gone down South and fought, and bled, to free the negro," etc., etc. Yet we know that just as soon as manufacturing was introduced in the North, the North found that it was too expensive to own the negro and take care of him; that it was much cheaper not to own the worker; and, consequently, that they "religiously," "humanly" and "morally" sold their slaves to the South, while they transformed the white people of the North who had no means of production in their own hands, into wage slaves, and mercilessly ground them down. In the North, chattel slavery disappeared just as soon as the development of machinery rendered the institution unprofitable. The immorality of chattel slavery became clear to the North just as soon as, standing upon that higher plane that its higher material development raised it to, it acquired a better vision. The benighted South, on the contrary, that had no machinery, remained with eyes shut, and she stuck to slavery till the slave was knocked out of her fists.

Guided by the light of this and many similar lessons of history, Socialism builds upon the principle that the "moral sentiment," as illustrated by the fate of the slave, is not the cause, but a powerful aid to revolutions. The moral sentiment is to a movement as important as the sails are to a ship. Nevertheless, important though sails are, unless a ship is well laden, unless she is soundly, properly and scientifically constructed, the more sails you pile on and spread out, the surer she is to capsize. So with the organizations that are to carry out a revolution. Unless your Socialist organizations are as sound as a bell; unless they are as intolerant as science; unless they will plant themselves squarely on the principle that two and two make four, and under no circumstances allow that they make five, the more feeling you put into them, the surer they are to capsize and go down. On the contrary, load your revolutionary ship with the proper lading of science; hold her strictly to the load-star; try no monkeyshines and no dillyings and dallyings with anything that is not strictly scientific, or with any man who does not stand on our uncompromisingly scientific platform; do that, and then unfurl freely the sails of morality; then the more your sails, the better off your ship; but not unless you do that, will you be safe, or can you prevail. (Loud applause.)

Socialism knows that revolutionary upheavals and transformations proceed from the rock-bed of material needs. With a full appreciation of and veneration for moral impulses that are balanced with scientific knowledge, it eschews, looks with just suspicion upon and gives a wide berth to balloon morality, or be it those malarial fevers that reformers love to dignify with the name of "moral feelings."

THE CLASS STRUGGLE

A third nerve centre of Socialism by which to distinguish reform from revolution is its manly, aggressive posture.

The laws that rule sociology run upon lines parallel with and are the exact counterparts of those that natural science has established prevail in biology.

In the first place, the central figure in biology is the species, not the individual specimen. Consequently, that is the central figure on the field of sociology that corresponds to and represents the species on the field of biology. In sociology, the economic classes take the place of the species in biology.

In the second place, struggle, and not piping peace; assimilation by the ruthless process of the expulsion of all elements that are not fit for assimilation, and not external coalition—such are the laws of growth in biology, and such they are and needs must be the laws of growth in sociology.

Hence, Socialism recognizes in modern society the existence of a struggle of classes, and the line that divides the combatants to be the economic line that separates the interests of the property-holding capitalist class from the interests of the propertyless class of the proletariat. As a final result of this, Socialism, with the Nazarene, spurns as futile, if not wicked, the method of cajolery and seduction, or the crying of "Peace, peace where there is no peace," and cuts a clean swath, while reform is eternally entangled in its course of charming, luring, decoying. (Applause.)   1896

» » « «

MARY HARRIS JONES—"MOTHER JONES"

1830–1930

AMONG THE firsthand accounts of the conflict between capital and labor, *The Autobiography of Mother Jones* has already become a classic. Indefatigable, fearless, and almost ubiquitous on the labor front, Mother Jones was, for a half century following the great Chicago fire of 1871, a tower of strength for the cause of labor. A vigorous and at the same time a picturesque speaker, Mother Jones subordinated her own personal life to the labor movement. No figure in the crusade of the workingmen dramatized so effectively as she did the "class struggle." A senatorial investigating committee was on one occasion the instrument for freeing her from a sentence of twenty years' imprisonment on the charge of conspiracy to murder. The daughter of an Irish immigrant, Mother Jones, for all her fire and seriousness, never lacked wit, a sense of humor, and personal dignity. Many of her best speeches are recorded in the *Proceedings* of the United Mine Workers Conventions.

New York Times, December 8, 1930.

» » From: AUTOBIOGRAPHY OF MOTHER JONES « «

WAR IN WEST VIRGINIA

One night I went with an organizer named Scott to a mining town in the Fairmont district where the miners had asked me to hold a meeting. When we got off the car I asked Scott where I was to speak and he pointed to a frame building. We walked in. There were lighted candles on an altar. I looked around in the dim light. We were in a church and the benches were filled with miners.

Outside the railing of the altar was a table. At one end sat the priest with the money of the union in his hands. The president of the local union sat at the other end of the table. I marched down the aisle.

"What's going on?" I asked.

"Holding a meeting," said the president.

"What for?"

"For the union, Mother. We rented the church for our meetings."

I reached over and took the money from the priest. Then I turned to the miners.

"Boys," I said, "this is a praying institution. You should not commercialize it. Get up, every one of you and go out in the open fields."

They got up and went out and sat around in a field while I spoke to them. The sheriff was there and he did not allow any traffic to go along the road while I was speaking. In front of us was a school house. I pointed to it and I said, "Your ancestors fought for you to have a share in that institution over there. It's yours. See the school board, and every Friday night hold your meetings there. Have your wives clean it up Saturday morning for the children to enter Monday. Your organization is not a praying institution. It's a fighting institution. It's an educational institution along industrial lines. Pray for the dead and fight like hell for the living!"

. . .

Tom Haggerty was in charge of the Fairmont field. One Sunday morning, the striking miners of Clarksburg started on a march to Monongha to get out the miners in the camps along the line. We camped in the open fields and held meetings on the road sides and in barns, preaching the gospel of unionism.

The Consolidated Coal Company that owns the little town of New England forbade the distribution of the notices of our meeting and arrested any one found with a notice. But we got the news around. Several of our men went into the camp. They went in twos. One pretended he was deaf and the other kept hollering in his ear as they walked around, "Mother Jones is going to have a meeting Sunday afternoon outside the town on the sawdust pile." Then the deaf fellow would ask him what he said and he would holler to him again. So the word got around the entire camp and we had a big crowd.

When the meeting adjourned, three miners and myself set out for Fairmont City. The miners, Jo Battley, Charlie Blakelet and Barney Rice walked but they got a little boy with a horse and buggy to drive me over. I was to wait for the boys just outside the town, across the bridge, just where the interurban car comes along.

The little lad and I drove along. It was dark when we came in sight of the bridge which I had to cross. A dark building stood beside the bridge. It was the Coal Company's store. It was guarded by gunmen. There was no light on the bridge and there was none in the store.

A gunman stopped us. I could not see his face.

"Who are you?" said he.

"Mother Jones," said I, "and a miner's lad."

"So that's you, Mother Jones," said he rattling his gun.

"Yes, it's me," I said, "and be sure you take care of the store tonight. Tomorrow I'll have to be hunting a new job for you."

I got out of the buggy where the road joins the Interurban tracks, just across the bridge. I sent the lad home.

"When you pass my boys on the road tell them to hurry up. Tell them I'm waiting just across the bridge."

There wasn't a house in sight. The only people near were the gunmen whose dark figures I could now and then see moving on the bridge. It grew very dark. I sat on the ground, waiting. I took out my watch, lighted a match and saw that it was about time for the interurban.

Suddenly the sound of "Murder! Murder! Police! Help!" rang out through the darkness. Then the sound of running and Barney Rice came screaming across the bridge toward me. Blakely followed, running so fast his heels hit the back of his head. "Murder! Murder!" he was yelling.

I rushed toward them. "Where's Jo?" I asked.

"They're killing Jo—on the bridge—the gunmen."

At that moment the Interurban car came in sight. It would stop at the bridge. I thought of a scheme.

I ran onto the bridge, shouting, "Jo! Jo! The boys are coming. They're coming! The whole bunch's coming. The car's most here!"

Those bloodhounds for the coal company thought an army of miners was in the Interurban car. They ran for cover, barricading themselves in the company's store. They left Jo on the bridge, his head broken and the blood pouring from him. I tore my petticoat into strips, bandaged his head, helped the boys to get him on to the Interurban car, and hurried the car into Fairmont City.

We took him to the hotel and sent for a doctor who sewed up the great, open cuts in his head. I sat up all night and nursed the poor fellow. He was out of his head and thought I was his mother.

The next night Tom Haggerty and I addressed the union meeting, telling them just what had happened. The men wanted to go clean up the gunmen but I told them that would only make more trouble. The meeting adjourned in a body to go see Jo. They went up to his room, six or eight of them at a time, until they had all seen him.

We tried to get a warrant out for the arrest of the gunmen but we couldn't because the coal company controlled the judges and the courts.

Jo was not the only man who was beaten up by the gunmen. There were many and the brutalities of these bloodhounds would fill volumes.

In Clarksburg, men were threatened with death if they even billed meetings for me. But the railway men billed a meeting in the dead of night and I went in there alone. The meeting was in the court house. The place was packed. The mayor and all the city officials were there.

"Mr. Mayor," I said, "will you kindly be chairman for a fellow American citizen?"

He shook his head. No one would accept my offer.

"Then," said I, "as chairman of the evening, I introduce myself, the speaker of the evening, Mother Jones."

The Fairmont field was finally organized to a man. The scabs and the gunmen were driven out. Subsequently, through inefficient organizers, through the treachery of the unions' own officials, the unions lost strength. The miners of the Fairmont field were finally betrayed by the very men who were employed to protect their interests. Charlie Battley tried to retrieve the losses but officers had become corrupt and men so discouraged that he could do nothing.

It makes me sad indeed to think that the sacrifices men and women made to get out from under the iron heel of the gunmen were so often in vain! That the victories gained are so often destroyed by the treachery of the workers' own officials, men who themselves knew the bitterness and cost of the struggle.

I am old now and I never expect to see the boys in the Fairmont field again, but I like to think that I have had a share in changing conditions for them and for their children.

The United Mine Workers had tried to organize Kelly Creek on the Kanawah River but without results. Mr. Burke and Tom Lewis, members of the board of the United Mine Workers, decided to go look the field over for themselves. They took the train one night for Kelly Creek. The train came to a high trestle over a steep canyon. Under some pretext all the passengers except the two union officials were transferred to another coach, the coach uncoupled and pulled across the trestle. The officials were left on the trestle in the stalled car. They had to crawl on their hands and knees along the tracks. Pitch blackness was below them. The trestle was a one-way track. Just as they got to the end of the trestle, a train thundered by.

When I heard of the coal company's efforts to kill the union officers, I decided I myself must go to Kelly Creek and rouse those slaves. I took a nineteen-year-old boy, Ben Davis, with me. We walked on the east bank of the Kanawah River on which Kelly Creek is situated. Before daylight one morning, at a point opposite Kelly Creek, we forded the river.

It was just dawn when I knocked at the door of a store run by a man by the name of Marshall. I told him what I had come for. He was friendly. He took me in a little back room where he gave me breakfast. He said if anyone saw him giving food to Mother Jones he would lose his store privilege. He told me how to get my bills announcing my meeting into the mines by noon. But all the time he was frightened and kept looking out the little window.

Late that night a group of miners gathered about a mile from town between the boulders. We could not see one another's faces in the darkness. By the light of an old lantern I gave them the pledge.

The next day, forty men were discharged, blacklisted. There had been spies among the men the night before. The following night we organized another group and they were all discharged. This started the fight. Mr. Marshall, the grocery man, got courageous. He rented me his store and I began holding meetings there. The general manager for the mines came over from Columbus and he held a meeting, too.

"Shame," he said, "to be led away by an old woman!"

"Hurrah for Mother Jones!" shouted the miners.

The following Sunday I held a meeting in the woods. The general manager, Mr. Jack Rowen, came down from Columbus on his special car. I organized a parade of the men that Sunday. We had every miner with us. We stood in front of the company's hotel and yelled for the general manager to come out. He did not appear. Two of the company's lap dogs were on the porch. One of them said, "I'd like to hang that old woman to a tree."

"Yes," said the other, "and I'd like to pull the rope."

On we marched to our meeting place under the trees. Over a thousand people came and the two lap dogs came sniveling along too. I stood up to speak and I put my back to a big tree and pointing to the curs, I said, "You said that you would like to hang this old woman to a tree! Well, here's the old woman and here's the tree. Bring along your rope and hang her!"

And so the union was organized in Kelly Creek. I do not know whether the men have held the gains they wrested from the company. Taking men into the union is just the kindergarten of their education and every force is against their further education. Men who live up those lonely creeks have only the mine owners' Y.M.C.A.'s, the mine owners' preachers and teachers, the mine owners' doctors and newspapers to look to for their ideas. So they don't get many.   1925

» »   « «

EDWARD BELLAMY

1850–1898

ACCORDING TO my best recollection," wrote Edward Bellamy, "it was in the fall or winter of 1886 that I sat down to my desk with the definite purpose of trying to reason out a method of economic organization by which the republic might guarantee the livelihood and material welfare of its citizens on a basis of equality corresponding to and supplanting their political equality." Prior to this Bellamy had shown, aside from the serial novel of Shays's rebellion, *The Duke of Stockbridge*, only an average concern with the underprivileged. The stories and romances which he wrote during his journalistic work in New York and at Springfield, Massachusetts, were Hawthornesque in tone. But after the publication in 1888 of *Looking Backward*, Bellamy devoted the remainder of his life to a crusade for the type of utopian socialism, "nationalism," as he called it, which was exemplified in *Looking Backward* and its sequel, *Equality* (1897).

Although the socialism of *Looking Backward* was not new to America, and although Bellamy had many imitators, his book sold over a million copies within a few years. Through lectures and through the weekly *New Nation* he encouraged the development of "national" clubs for the promotion of his ideal. Like other unrealized ideals, the utopian socialism of Edward Bellamy influenced subsequent thought and action: the Populists, the Progressives, and the Technocrats were all indebted to him.

In the following selections from *Looking Backward* the author, who has awakened in the year 2000 from a sleep which overcame him in 1887, is discovering the new socialist society which has developed in the meantime.

The Blind Man's World, Boston, 1898.
Edward Bellamy, *Looking Backward*, Boston and New York, 1917, New York, 1951.
Edward Bellamy Speaks Again, Kansas City, 1937.
The Religion of Solidarity, Yellow Springs, Ohio, 1941.
Sylvia E. Bowman, *The Year 2000; A Critical Biography of Edward Bellamy*, New York, 1958.
Arthur E. Morgan, *Edward Bellamy*, New York, 1944.
R. L. Shurter, "The Literary Work of Edward Bellamy," *American Literature*, V (November, 1933), 229–234

» » *From:* LOOKING BACKWARD « «

CHAPTER V

. . .

"Excuse me," replied my host, "but do you smoke?" It was not till our cigars were lighted and drawing well that he resumed. "Since you are in the humor to talk rather than to sleep, as I certainly am, perhaps I cannot do better than to try to give you enough idea of our modern industrial system to dissipate at least the impression that there is any mystery about the process of its evolution. The Bostonians of your day had the reputation of being great askers of questions, and I am going to show my descent by asking you one to begin with. What should you name as the most prominent feature of the labor troubles of your day?"

"Why, the strikes, of course," I replied.

"Exactly; but what made the strikes so formidable?"

"The great labor organizations."

"And what was the motive of these great organizations?"

"The workmen claimed they had to organize

to get their rights from the big corporations," I replied.

"That is just it," said Dr. Leete; "the organization of labor and the strikes were an effect, merely, of the concentration of capital in greater masses than had ever been known before. Before this concentration began, while as yet commerce and industry were conducted by innumerable petty concerns with small capital, instead of a small number of great concerns with vast capital, the individual workman was relatively important and independent in his relations to the employer. Moreover, when a little capital or a new idea was enough to start a man in business for himself, workingmen were constantly becoming employers and there was no hard and fast line between the two classes. Labor unions were needless then, and general strikes out of the question. But when the era of small concerns with small capital was succeeded by that of the great aggregations of capital, all this was changed. The individual laborer, who had been relatively important to the small employer, was reduced to insignificance and powerlessness over against the great corporation, while at the same time the way upward to the grade of employer was closed to him. Self-defense drove him to union with his fellows.

"The records of the period show that the outcry against the concentration of capital was furious. Men believed that it threatened society with a form of tyranny more abhorrent than it had ever endured. They believed that the great corporations were preparing for them the yoke of a baser servitude than had even been imposed on the race, servitude not to men but to soulless machines incapable of any motive but insatiable greed. Looking back, we cannot wonder at their desperation, for certainly humanity was never confronted with a fate more sordid and hideous than would have been the era of corporate tyranny which they anticipated.

"Meanwhile, without being in the smallest degree checked by the clamor against it, the absorption of business by ever larger monopolies continued. In the United States there was not, after the beginning of the last quarter of the century, any opportunity whatever for individual enterprise in any important field of industry, unless backed by a great capital. During the last decade of the century, such small businesses as still remained were fast-

failing survivals of a past epoch, or mere parasites on the great corporations, or else existed in fields too small to attract the great capitalists. Small businesses, as far as they still remained, were reduced to the condition of rats and mice, living in holes and corners, and counting on evading notice for the enjoyment of existence. The railroads had gone on combining till a few great syndicates controlled every rail in the land. In manufactories, every important staple was controlled by a syndicate. These syndicates, pools, trusts, or whatever their name, fixed prices and crushed all competition except when combinations as vast as themselves arose. Then a struggle, resulting in a still greater consolidation, ensued. The great city bazar crushed its country rivals with branch stores, and in the city itself absorbed its smaller rivals till the business of a whole quarter was concentrated under one roof, with a hundred former proprietors of shops serving as clerks. Having no business of his own to put his money in, the small capitalist, at the same time that he took service under the corporation, found no other investment for his money but its stocks and bonds, thus becoming doubly dependent upon it.

"The fact that the desperate popular opposition to the consolidation of business in a few powerful hands had no effect to check it proves that there must have been a strong economical reason for it. The small capitalists, with their innumerable petty concerns, had in fact yielded the field to the great aggregations of captial, because they belonged to a day of small things and were totally incompetent to the demands of an age of steam and telegraphs and the gigantic scale of its enterprises. To restore the former order of things, even if possible, would have involved returning to the day of stage-coaches. Oppressive and intolerable as was the régime of the great consolidations of capital, even its victims, while they cursed it, were forced to admit the prodigious increase of efficiency which had been imparted to the national industries, the vast economies effected by concentration of management and unity of organization, and to confess that since the new system had taken the place of the old the wealth of the world had increased at a rate before undreamed of. To be sure this vast increase had gone chiefly to make the rich richer, increasing the gap between them and the poor; but the fact remained that, as a means merely of producing wealth, capital had been proved efficient in proportion to its consolidation. The restoration of the old system with the subdivision of capital, if it were possible, might indeed bring back a greater equality of conditions, with more individual dignity and freedom, but it would be at the price of general poverty and the arrest of material progress.

"Was there, then, no way of commanding the services of the mighty wealth-producing principle of consolidated capital without bowing down to a plutocracy like that of Carthage? As soon as men began to ask themselves these questions, they found the answer ready for them. The movement toward the conduct of business by larger and larger aggregations of capital, the tendency toward monopolies, which had been so desperately and vainly resisted, was recognized at last, in its true significance, as a process which only needed to complete its logical evolution to open a golden future to humanity.

"Early in the last century the evolution was completed by the final consolidation of the entire capital of the nation. The industry and commerce of the country, ceasing to be conducted by a set of irresponsible corporations and syndicates of private persons at their caprice and for their profit, were intrusted to a single syndicate representing the people, to be conducted in the common interest for the common profit. The nation, that is to say, organized as the one great business corporation in which all other corporations were absorbed; it became the one capitalist in the place of all other capitalists, the sole employer, the final monopoly in which all previous and lesser monopolies were swallowed up, a monopoly in the profits and economies of which all citizens shared. The epoch of trusts had ended in The Great Trust. In a word, the people of the United States concluded to assume the conduct of their own business, just as one hundred odd years before they had assumed the conduct of their own government, organizing now for industrial purposes on precisely the same grounds that they had then organized for political purposes. At last, strangely late in the world's history, the obvious fact was perceived that no business is so essentially the public business as the industry and commerce on which the people's livelihood depends, and that to entrust it to private persons to be managed for private profit is a folly similar in kind, though vastly greater in magnitude, to that of surrendering the functions of political government to kings and nobles to be conducted for their personal glorification."

"Such a stupendous change as you describe," said I, "did not, of course, take place without great bloodshed and terrible convulsions."

"On the contrary," replied Dr. Leete, "there was absolutely no violence. The change had been long foreseen. Public opinion had become fully ripe for it, and the whole mass of the people was behind it. There was no more possibility of opposing it by force than by argument. On the other hand the popular sentiment toward the great corporations and those identified with them had ceased to be one of bitterness, as they came to realize their necessity as a link, a transition phase, in the evolution of the true industrial system. The most violent foes of the great private monopolies were now forced to recognize how invaluable and indispensable had been their office in educating the people up to the point of assuming control of their own business. Fifty years before, the consolidation of the industries of the country under national control would have seemed a very daring experiment to the most sanguine. But by a series of object lessons, seen and studied by all men, the great corporations had taught the people an entirely new set of ideas on this subject. They had seen for many years syndicates handling revenues greater than those of states, and directing the labors of hundreds of thousands of men with an efficiency and economy unattainable in smaller operations. It had come to be recognized as an axiom that the larger the business the simpler the principles that can be applied to it; that, as the machine is truer than the hand, so the system, which in a great concern does the work of the master's eye in a small business, turns out more accurate results. Thus it came about that, thanks to the corporations themselves, when it was proposed that the nation should assume their functions, the suggestion implied nothing which seemed impracticable even to the timid. To be sure it was a step beyond any yet taken, a broader generalization, but the very fact that the nation would be the sole corporation in the field would, it was seen, relieve the undertaking of many difficulties with which the partial monopolies had contended."

CHAPTER XXII

. . .

We had made an appointment to meet the ladies at the dining-hall for dinner, after which, having some engagement, they left us sitting at table there, discussing our wine and cigars with a multitude of other matters.

"Doctor," said I, in the course of our talk, "morally speaking, your social system is one which I should be insensate not to admire in comparison with any previously in vogue in the world, and especially with that of my own most unhappy century. If I were to fall into a mesmeric sleep tonight as lasting as that other, and meanwhile the course of time were to take a turn backward instead of forward, and I were to wake up again in the nineteenth century, when I had told my friends what I had seen, they would every one admit that your world was a paradise of order, equity, and felicity. But they were a very practical people, my contemporaries, and after expressing their admiration for the moral beauty and material splendor of the system, they would presently begin to cipher and ask how you got the money to make everybody so happy; for certainly, to support the whole nation at a rate of comfort, and even luxury, such as I see around me, must involve vastly greater wealth than the nation produced in my day. Now, while I could explain to them pretty nearly everything else of the main features of your system, I should quite fail to answer this question, and failing there, they would tell me, for they were very close cipherers, that I had been dreaming; nor would they ever believe anything else. In my day, I know that the total annual product of the nation, although it might have been divided with absolute equality, would not have come to more than three or four hundred dollars per head, not very much more than enough to supply the necessities of life with few or any of its comforts. How is it that you have so much more?"

"That is a very pertinent question, Mr. West," replied Dr. Leete, "and I should not blame your friends, in the case you supposed, if they declared your story all moonshine, failing a satisfactory reply to it. It is a question which I cannot answer exhaustively at any one sitting, and as for the exact statistics to bear out my general statements, I shall have to refer you for them to books in my library, but it would certainly be a pity to leave you to be put to confusion by your old acquaintances, in case of the contingency you speak of, for lack of a few suggestions.

"Let us begin with a number of small items wherein we economize wealth as compared with you. We have no national, state, county, or municipal debts, or payments on their account. We have no sort of military or naval expenditures for men or materials, no army, navy, or militia. We have no revenue service, no swarm of tax assessors and collectors. As regards our judiciary, police, sheriffs, and jailors, the force which Massachusetts alone kept on foot in your day far more than suffices for the nation now. We have no criminal class preying upon the wealth of society as you had. The number of persons, more or less absolutely lost to the working force through physical disability, of the lame, sick, and debilitated, which constituted such a burden on the able-bodied in your day, now that all live under conditions of health and comfort, has shrunk to scarcely perceptible proportions, and with every generation is becoming more completely eliminated.

"Another item wherein we save is the disuse of money and the thousand occupations connected with financial operations of all sorts, whereby an army of men was formerly taken away from useful employments. Also consider that the waste of the very rich in your day on inordinate personal luxury has ceased, though, indeed, this item might easily be over-estimated. Again, consider that there are no idlers now, rich or poor,—no drones.

"A very important cause of former poverty was the vast waste of labor and materials which resulted from domestic washing and cooking, and the performing separately of innumerable other tasks to which we apply the cooperative plan.

"A larger economy than any of these—yes, of all together—is effected by the organization of our distributing system, by which the work done once by the merchants, traders, storekeepers, with their various grades of jobbers, wholesalers, retailers, agents, commercial travelers, and middlemen of all sorts, with an excessive waste of energy in needless transportation and interminable handlings, is performed by one-tenth the number of hands and an unnecessary turn of not one wheel. Something of what our distributing system is like you know. Our statisticians calculate that one eightieth part of our workers suffices for all the processes of distribution which in your day required one eighth of the population, so much being withdrawn from the force engaged in productive labor."

"I begin to see," I said, "where you get your greater wealth."

.   .   .

"As I said," responded the doctor, "the subject is too large to discuss at length now, but if you are really interested to know the main criticisms which we moderns make on your industrial system as compared with our own, I can touch briefly on some of them.

"The wastes which resulted from leaving the conduct of industry to irresponsible individuals, wholly without mutual understanding or concert, were mainly four: first, the waste by mistaken undertakings; second, the waste from the competition and mutual hostility of those engaged in industry; third, the waste by periodical gluts and crises, with the consequent interruptions of industry; fourth, the waste from idle capital and labor, at all times. Any one of these four great leaks, were all the others stopped, would suffice to make the difference between wealth and poverty on the part of a nation.

"Take the waste by mistaken undertakings, to begin with. In your day the production and distribution of commodities being without concert or organization, there was no means of knowing just what demand there was for any class of products, or what was the rate of supply. Therefore, any enterprise by a private capitalist was always a doubtful experiment. The projector having no general view of the field of industry and consumption, such as our government has, could never be sure either what the people wanted, or what arrangements other capitalists were making to supply them. In view of this, we are not surprised to learn that the chances were considered several to one in favor of the failure of any given business enterprise, and that it was common for persons who at last succeeded in making a hit to have failed repeatedly. If a shoemaker, for every pair of shoes he succeeded in completing, spoiled the leather of four or five pair, besides losing the time spent on them, he would stand about the same chance of getting rich as your contemporaries did with their system of private enterprise, and its average of four or five failures to one success.

"The next of the great wastes was that from competition. The field of industry was a battlefield as wide as the world, in which the workers wasted, in assailing one another, energies which, if expended in concerted effort, as today, would have enriched all. As for mercy or quarter in this warfare, there was absolutely no suggestion of it. To deliberately enter a field of business and destroy the enterprises of those who had occupied it previously, in order to plant one's own enterprise on their ruins, was an achievement which never failed to command popular admiration. Nor is there any stretch of fancy in comparing this sort of struggle with actual warfare, so far as concerns the mental agony and physical suffering which attended the struggle, and the misery which overwhelmed the defeated and those dependent on them. Now nothing about your age is, at first sight, more astounding to a man of modern times than the fact that men engaged in the same industry, instead of fraternizing as comrades and co-laborers to a common end, should have regarded each other as rivals and enemies to be throttled and overthrown. This certainly seems like sheer madness, a scene from bedlam. But more closely regarded, it is seen to be no such thing. Your contemporaries, with their mutual throat-cutting, knew very well what they were at. The producers of the nineteenth century were not, like ours, working together for the maintenance of the community, but each solely for his own maintenance at the expense of the community. If, in working to this end, he at the same time increased the aggregate wealth, that was merely incidental. It was just as feasible and as common to increase one's private hoard by practices injurious to the general welfare. One's worst enemies were necessarily those of his own trade, for, under your plan of making private profit the motive of production, a scarcity of the article he produced was what each particular producer desired. It was for his interest that no more of it should be produced than he himself could produce. To secure this consummation as far as circumstances permitted, by killing off and discouraging those engaged in his line of industry, was his constant effort. When he had killed off all he could, his policy was to combine with those he could not kill, and convert their mutual warfare into a warfare upon the public at large by cornering the market, as I believe you used to call it, and putting up prices to the highest point people would stand before going without the goods. The day dream of the nineteenth century producer was to gain absolute control of the supply of some necessity of life, so that he might keep the public at the verge of starvation, and always command famine prices for what he supplied. This, Mr. West, is what was called in the nineteenth century a system of production. I will leave it to you if it does not seem, in some of its aspects, a great deal more like a system for preventing production. Some time when we have plenty of leisure I am going to ask you to sit down with me and try to make me comprehend, as I never yet could, though I have studied the matter a great deal, how such shrewd fellows as your contemporaries appear to have been in many respects ever came to entrust the business of providing for the community to a class whose interest it was to starve it. I assure you that the wonder with us is, not that the world did not get rich under such a system, but that it did not perish outright from want. This wonder increases as we go on to consider some of the other prodigious wastes that characterized it.

"Apart from the waste of labor and capital by misdirected industry, and that from the constant bloodletting of your industrial warfare, your system was liable to periodical convulsions, overwhelming alike the wise and unwise, the successful cut-throat as well as his victim. I refer to the business crises at intervals of five to ten years, which wrecked the industries of the nation, prostrating all weak enterprises and crippling the strongest, and were followed by long periods, often of many years, of so-called dull times, during which the capitalists slowly regathered their dissipated strength while the laboring classes starved and rioted. Then would ensue another brief season of prosperity, followed in turn by another crisis and the ensuing years of exhaustion. As commerce developed, making the nations mutually dependent, these crises became world-wide, while the obstinacy of the ensuing state of collapse increased with the area affected by the convulsions, and the consequent lack of rallying centres. In proportion as the industries of the world multiplied and became complex, and the volume of capital involved was increased, these business cataclysms became more frequent, till, in the latter part of the nineteenth century, there were two years of bad times to one of good, and the system of industry, never before so extended or so imposing, seemed in

danger of collapsing by its own weight. After endless discussions, your economists appear by that time to have settled down to the despairing conclusion that there was no more possibility of preventing or controlling these crises than if they had been drouths or hurricanes. It only remained to endure them as necessary evils, and when they had passed over to build up again the shattered structure of industry, as dwellers in an earthquake country keep on rebuilding their cities on the same site.

.   .   .

"Now, Mr. West," continued Dr. Leete, "I want you to bear in mind that these points of which I have been speaking indicate only negatively the advantages of the national organization of industry by showing certain fatal defects and prodigious imbecilities of the systems of private enterprise which are not found in it. These alone, you must admit, would pretty well explain why the nation is so much richer than in your day. But the larger half of our advantage over you, the positive side of it, I have yet barely spoken of. Supposing the system of private enterprise in industry were without any of the great leaks I have mentioned; that there were no waste on account of misdirected effort growing out of mistakes as to the demand, and inability to command a general view of the industrial field. Suppose, also, there were no neutralizing and duplicating of effort from competition. Suppose, also, there were no waste from business panics and crises through bankruptcy and long interruptions of industry, and also none from the idleness of capital and labor. Supposing these evils, which are essential to the conduct of industry by capital in private hands, could all be miraculously prevented, and the system yet retained; even then the superiority of the results attained by the modern industrial system of national control would remain overwhelming.

.   .   .

"I suppose," observed Dr. Leete, as we strolled homeward from the dining hall, "that no reflection would have cut the men of your wealth-worshiping century more keenly than the suggestion that they did not know how to make money. Nevertheless, that is just the verdict history has passed on them. Their system of unorganized and antagonistic industries was as absurd economically as it was morally abominable. Selfishness was their only science, and in industrial production selfishness is suicide. Competition, which is the instinct of selfishness, is another word for dissipation of energy, while combination is the secret of efficient production; and not till the idea of increasing the individual hoard gives place to the idea of increasing the common stock can industrial combination be realized, and the acquisition of wealth really begin. Even if the principle of share and share alike for all men were not the only humane and rational basis for a society, we should still enforce it as economically expedient, seeing that until the disintegrating influence of self-seeking is suppressed no true concert of industry is possible." 1887

JACK LONDON

1876-1916

FROM THE underprivileged life of a water-front adventurer, Jack London, tramp, casual worker, journalistic writer concerned with the savage and the life of the wild, drifted into socialism. His keen sensitiveness and his knowledge of "people of the abyss" no doubt explain in part his championship of the underdog and his interest in socialism; but the pull of his erratic love of adventure, of all that is symbolized in *The Call of the Wild* (1903), *The Sea Wolf* (1904), *The Abysmal Brute* (1913), and *The Strength of the Strong* (1914), occasioned a backsliding which must have disheartened socialists who were made of sterner stuff. From the personal point of view, London's egotistical bohemianism, his love of alcohol, of carousing, and, in his later years, of comfort and affluence, no doubt played a part in uprooting his socialist views. From the larger angle of vision, London represents the struggle between naturalism (which is a fatalistic philosophy) and socialism (which is rational).

For a time, in any case, London was a leading literary exponent of socialism. Trotsky himself has bestowed high praise on *The Iron Heel* (1908), the portrayal of a class struggle in which labor was repressed by what would now be termed a Fascist dictatorship. Some of London's short stories and journalistic pieces, such as *War of the Classes* (1905), were also powerful if not entirely orthodox expressions of the class struggle.

Joseph Gaer, *Jack London, Bibliography and Bibliographical Data*, n.p., 1934.
C. K. London, *The Book of Jack London*, 2 vols., New York, 1921.
Irving Stone, *Sailor on Horseback; The Biography of Jack London*, Boston, 1938.
Philip S. Foner, ed., *Jack London, American Rebel; A Collection of His Social Writings Together with an Exhaustive Study of the Man and His Times*, New York, 1947.

» » *From:* WAR OF THE CLASSES « «

HOW I BECAME A SOCIALIST

It is quite fair to say that I became a Socialist in a fashion somewhat similar to the way in which the Teutonic pagans became Christians —it was hammered into me. Not only was I not looking for Socialism at the time of my conversion, but I was fighting it. I was very young and callow, did not know much of anything, and though I had never even heard of a school called "Individualism," I sang the paean of the strong with all my heart.

This was because I was strong myself. By strong I mean that I had good health and hard muscles, both of which possessions are easily accounted for. I had lived my childhood on California ranches, my boyhood hustling newspapers on the streets of a healthy Western city, and my youth on the ozone-laden waters of San Francisco Bay and the Pacific Ocean. I loved life in the open, and I toiled in the open, at the hardest kinds of work. Learning no trade, but drifting along from job to job, I looked on the world and called it good, every bit of it. Let me repeat, this optimism was because I was healthy and strong, bothered with neither aches nor weaknesses, never turned down by the boss because I did not look fit, able always to get a job at shovelling coal, sailorizing, or manual labor of some sort.

And because of all this, exulting in my young life, able to hold my own at work or fight, I was a rampant individualist. It was very natural. I was a winner. Wherefore I called the game, as I saw it played, or thought I saw it played, a very proper game for MEN. To be a MAN was to write man in large capitals on my heart. To adventure like a man, and fight like a man, and do a man's work (even for a boy's pay)—these were things that reached right in and gripped hold of me as no other thing could. And I looked ahead into long vistas of a hazy and interminable future, into which, playing what I conceived to be MAN'S game, I should continue to travel with unfailing health, without accidents, and with muscles ever vigorous. As I say, this future was interminable. I could see myself only raging through life without end like one of Nietzsche's *blond beasts,* lustfully roving and conquering by sheer superiority and strength.

As for the unfortunates, the sick, and ailing, and old, and maimed, I must confess I hardly thought of them at all, save that I vaguely felt that they, barring accidents, could be as good as I if they wanted to real hard, and could work just as well. Accidents? Well, they represented FATE, also spelled out in capitals, and there was no getting around FATE. Napoleon had had an accident at Waterloo, but that did not dampen my desire to be another and later Napoleon. Further, the optimism bred of a stomach which could digest scrap iron and a body which flourished on hardships did not permit me to consider accidents as even remotely related to my glorious personality.

I hope I have made it clear that I was proud to be one of Nature's strong-armed noblemen. The dignity of labor was to me the most impressive thing in the world. Without having read Carlyle, or Kipling, I formulated a gospel of work which put theirs in the shade. Work was everything. It was sanctification and sal-

vation. The pride I took in a hard day's work well done would be inconceivable to you. It is almost inconceivable to me as I look back upon it. I was as faithful a wage slave as ever capitalist exploited. To shirk or malinger on the man who paid me my wages was a sin, first, against myself, and second, against him. I considered it a crime second only to treason and just about as bad.

In short, my joyous individualism was dominated by the orthodox bourgeois ethics. I read the bourgeois papers, listened to the bourgeois preachers, and shouted at the sonorous platitudes of the bourgeois politicians. And I doubt not, if other events had not changed my career, that I should have evolved into a professional strike-breaker, (one of President Eliot's American heroes), and had my head and my earning power irrevocably smashed by a club in the hands of some militant trades-unionist.

Just about this time, returning from a seven months' voyage before the mast, and just turned eighteen, I took it into my head to go tramping. On rods and blind baggages I fought my way from the open West, where men bulked big and the job hunted the man, to the congested labor centres of the East, where men were small potatoes and hunted the job for all they were worth. And on this new *blond-beast* adventure I found myself looking upon life from a new and totally different angle. I had dropped down from the proletariat into what sociologists love to call the "submerged tenth," and I was startled to discover the way in which that submerged tenth was recruited.

I found there all sorts of men, many of whom had once been as good as myself and just as *blond-beastly;* sailor-men, soldier-men, labor-men, all wrenched and distorted and twisted out of shape by toil and hardship and accident, and cast adrift by their masters like so many old horses. I battered on the drag and slammed back gates [1] with them, or shivered with them in box cars and city parks, listening the while to life-histories which began under auspices as fair as mine, with digestions and bodies equal to and better than mine, and which ended there before my eyes in the shambles at the bottom of the Social Pit.

And as I listened my brain began to work. The woman of the streets and the man of the gutter drew very close to me. I saw the picture of the Social Pit as vividly as though it were a concrete thing, and at the bottom of the Pit I

[1] "Panhandled on the main streets and begged at back doors."

saw them, myself above them, not far, and hanging on to the slippery wall by main strength and sweat. And I confess a terror seized me. What when my strength failed? when I should be unable to work shoulder to shoulder with the strong men who were as yet babes unborn? And there and then I swore a great oath. It ran something like this: *All my days I have worked hard with my body, and according to the number of days I have worked, by just that much am I nearer the bottom of the Pit. I shall climb out of the Pit, but not by the muscles of my body shall I climb out. I shall do no more hard work, and may God strike me dead if I do another day's hard work with my body more than I absolutely have to do.* And I have been busy ever since running away from hard work.

Incidentally, while tramping some ten thousand miles through the United States and Canada, I strayed into Niagara Falls, was nabbed by a fee-hunting constable, denied the right to plead guilty or not guilty, sentenced out of hand to thirty days' imprisonment for having no fixed abode and no visible means of support, handcuffed and chained to a bunch of men similarly circumstanced, carted down country to Buffalo, registered at the Erie County Penitentiary, had my head clipped and my budding mustache shaved, was dressed in convict stripes, compulsorily vaccinated by a medical student who practised on such as we, made to march the lock-step, and put to work under the eyes of guards armed with Winchester rifles—all for adventuring in *blond-beastly* fashion. Concerning further details deponent sayeth not, though he may hint that some of his plethoric national patriotism simmered down and leaked out of the bottom of his soul somewhere—at least, since that experience he finds that he cares more for men and women and little children than for imaginary geographical lines. 10

To return to my conversion. I think it is apparent that my rampant individualism was pretty effectively hammered out of me, and something else as effectively hammered in. But, just as I had been an individualist without knowing it, I was not a Socialist without knowing it, withal, an unscientific one. I had been reborn, but not renamed, and I was running around to find out what manner of thing I was. I ran back to California and opened the books. 20 I do not remember which ones I opened first. It is an unimportant detail anyway. I was already It, whatever It was, and by aid of the books I discovered that It was a Socialist. Since that day I have opened many books, but no economic argument, no lucid demonstration of the logic and inevitableness of Socialism affects me as profoundly and convincingly as I was affected on the day when I first saw the walls of the Social Pit rise around me and felt myself 30 slipping down, down, into the shambles at the bottom. 1905

OLIVER WENDELL HOLMES

1809–1894

IN HIS WITTY CRITICISMS of the remnants of an outworn Calvinism Oliver Wendell Holmes was indeed on the side of progress. But the foresighted and penetrating psychological insight which enabled him to anticipate the modern position of a limited moral responsibility was not paralleled by a sympathetic understanding of the social cleavages which were taking place under his eyes. His urbanity did not indeed forsake him when, on occasion, he lent his wit in support of the interests of the well-established and employing classes: the following selection from *Over the Teacups* (1891) is an example. It reveals an utter failure to understand the Irish immigrant who was invading and even taking over Dr. Holmes's beloved Boston; and it discloses an equal failure to understand the principle of collective bargaining.

Eleanor M. Tilton, *Amiable Autocrat, A Biography of Dr. Oliver Wendell Holmes*, New York, 1947.
The Writings of Oliver Wendell Holmes, Riverside Edition, 14 vols., Boston and New York, 1891–1892.
J. T. Morse, Jr., *The Life and Letters of Oliver Wendell Holmes*, 2 vols., Boston and New York, 1896.
Eleanor M. Tilton, ed., *A Bibliography of Oliver Wendell Holmes*, New York, 1953.
M. A. de Wolf Howe, *Holmes of the Breakfast Table*, London and New York, 1939.

» » *From:* OVER THE TEACUPS « «

CHAPTER IX

One of my neighbors, a thorough American, is much concerned about the growth of what he calls the "hard-handed aristocracy." He tells the following story:—

"I was putting up a fence about my yard, and employed a man of whom I knew something,—that he was industrious, temperate, and that he had a wife and children to support, —a worthy man, a native New Englander. I engaged him, I say, to dig some post-holes. My employee bought a new spade and scoop on purpose, and came to my place at the appointed time, and began digging. While he was at work, two men came over from a drinking-saloon, to which my residence is nearer than I could desire. One of them I had known as Mike Fagan, the other as Hans Schleimer. They looked at Hiram, my New Hampshire man, in a contemptuous and threatening way for a minute or so, when Fagan addressed him:—

"'And how much does the man pay yez by the hour?'

"'The gentleman doesn't pay me by the hour,' said Hiram.

"'How mosh does he bay you by der veeks?' said Hans.

"'I don't know as that's any of your business,' answered Hiram.

"'Faith, we'll make it our business,' said Mike Fagan. 'We're Knoights of Labor, we'd have yez to know, and ye can't make yer bargains jist as ye loikes. We manes to know how mony hours ye worrks, and how much ye gets for it.'

"'*Knights* of Labor!' said I. 'Why, that is a kind of title of nobility, isn't it? I thought the laws of our country didn't allow titles of that kind. But if you have a right to be called knights, I suppose I ought to address you as such. Sir Michael, I congratulate you on the dignity you have attained. I hope Lady Fagan is getting on well with my shirts. Sir Hans, I pay my respects to your title. I trust that Lady Schleimer has got through that little difficulty between her ladyship and yourself in which the police court thought it necessary to intervene.'

"The two men looked at me. I weigh about a hundred and eighty pounds, and am well put

together. Hiram was noted in his village as a 'rahstler.' But my face is rather pallid and peaked, and Hiram had something of the greenhorn look. The two men, who had been drinking, hardly knew what ground to take. They rather liked the sound of *Sir* Michael and *Sir* Hans. They did not know very well what to make of their wives as 'ladies.' They looked doubtful whether to take what had been said as a *casus belli* or not, but they wanted a pretext of some kind or other. Presently one of them saw a label on the scoop, or long-handled, spoon-like shovel, with which Hiram had been working.

"'Arrah, be jabers!' exclaimed Mike Fagan, 'but hasn't he been a-tradin' wid Brown, the hardware fellah, that we boycotted! Grab it, Hans, and we'll carry it off and show it to the brotherhood.'

"The men made a move toward the implement.

"'You let that are scoop-shovel alone,' said Hiram.

"I stepped to his side. The Knights were combative, as their noble predecessors with the same title always were, and it was necessary to come to a *voie de fait*. My straight blow from the shoulder did for Sir Michael. Hiram treated Sir Hans to what is technically known as a cross-buttock.

"'Naow, Dutchman,' said Hiram, 'if you don't want to be planted in that are post-hole, y'd better take y'rself out o' this here piece of private property. "Dangerous passin'," as the sign-posts say, abaout these times.'

"Sir Michael went down half stunned by my expressive gesture; Sir Hans did not know whether his hip was out of joint or he had got a bad sprain; but they were both out of condition for further hostilities. Perhaps it was hardly fair to take advantage of their misfortunes to inflict a discourse upon them, but they had brought it on themselves, and we each of us gave them a piece of our mind.

"'I tell you what it is,' said Hiram, 'I'm a free and independent American citizen, and I an't a-gōn' to hav no man tȳrannize over me, if he doos call himself by one o' them noblemen's titles. Ef I can't work jes' as I choose, fur folks that wants me to work fur 'em and that I want to work fur, I might jes' as well go to Sibery and done with it. My gran'f'ther fit in Bunker Hill battle. I guess if our folks in them days didn't care no great abaout Lord Percy and Sir William Haowe, we an't a-gōn' to be scārt by Sir Michael Fagan and Sir Hans What's-his-name, nor no other fellahs that undertakes to be noblemen, and tells us common folks what we shall dew an' what we sha'n't. No, *sir!*'

"I took the opportunity to explain to Sir Michael and Sir Hans what it was our fathers fought for, and what is the meaning of liberty. If these noblemen did not like the country, they could go elsewhere. If they didn't like the laws, they had the ballot-box, and could choose new legislators. But as long as the laws existed they must obey them. I could not admit that, because they called themselves by the titles of the Old World nobility thought so much of, they had a right to interfere in the agreements I entered into with my neighbor. I told Sir Michael that if he would go home and help Lady Fagan to saw and split the wood for her fire, he would be better employed than in meddling with my domestic arrangements. I advised Sir Hans to ask Lady Schleimer for her bottle of spirits to use as an embrocation for his lame hip. And so my two visitors with the aristocratic titles staggered off, and left us plain, untitled citizens, Hiram and myself, to set our posts, and consider the question whether we lived in a free country or under the authority of a self-constituted order of *quasi*-nobility.''

It is a very curious fact that, with all our boasted "free and equal" superiority over the communities of the Old World, our people have the most enormous appetite for Old World titles of distinction. Sir Michael and Sir Hans belong to one of the most extended of the aristocratic orders. But we have also "Knights and Ladies of Honor," and, what is still grander, "Royal Conclave of Knights and Ladies," "Royal Arcanum," and "Royal Society of Good Fellows," "Supreme Council," "Imperial Court," "Grand Protector," and "Grand Dictator," and so on. Nothing less than "Grand" and "Supreme" is good enough for the dignataries of our associations of citizens. Where does all this ambition for names without realities come from? Because a Knight of the Garter wears a golden star, why does the worthy cordwainer, who mends the shoes of his fellow-citizens, want to wear a tin star, and take a name that had a meaning as used by the representatives of ancient families, or the men who had made themselves illustrious by their achievements?

It appears to be a peculiarly American weakness. The French republicans of the earlier period thought the term *citizen* was good enough for anybody. At a later period, "le Roi Citoyen"—the citizen king—was a common title given to Louis Philippe. But nothing is too grand for the American, in the way of titles. The proudest of them all signify absolutely nothing. They do not stand for ability, for public service, for social importance, for large possessions; but, on the contrary, are oftenest found in connection with personalities to which they are supremely inapplicable. We can hardly afford to quarrel with a national habit which, if lightly handled, may involve us in serious domestic difficulties. The "Right Worshipful" functionary whose equipage stops at my back gate, and whose services are indispensable to the health and comfort of my household, is a dignitary whom I must not offend. I must speak with proper deference to the lady who is scrubbing my floors, when I remember that her husband, who saws my wood, carries a string of high-sounding titles which would satisfy a Spanish nobleman.   1890

ANDREW CARNEGIE

1835–1919

ANDREW CARNEGIE'S father was an extremely poor Scotch immigrant; and there is no better example of an American self-made man than his son, who became a multimillionaire, a well-known publicist, and "the distributor of wealth" for the advancement and diffusion of learning, the promotion of world peace, and other causes for "the improvement of mankind." An exemplification of economic individualism, Carnegie's career as an organizer of the iron and steel industry on a grand scale is not unlike that of other industrial titans of his day. In social politics he opposed organized labor and "paternalistic" social legislation.

As an advocate of international arbitration and "a league of nations" Carnegie played a prominent part in the international peace movement. His gospel of distributing wealth for the advancement of mankind was expressed in his philanthropies to public libraries, to public education, and to research and scholarship. Carnegie's writings include *Triumphant Democracy* (1886), *The Gospel of Wealth* (1900), and *The Empire of Business* (1902).

The Autobiography of Andrew Carnegie, J. C. Van Dyke, ed., Boston, 1920.
B. J. Hendrick, *The Life of Andrew Carnegie*, 2 vols., New York, 1932.

» » *From:* THE ROAD TO BUSINESS SUCCESS « «

A TALK TO YOUNG MEN [1]

It is well that young men should begin at the beginning and occupy the most subordinate positions. Many of the leading business men of Pittsburgh had a serious responsibility thrust upon them at the very threshold of their career. They were introduced to the broom, and spent the first hours of their business lives sweeping out the office. I notice we have janitors and janitresses now in offices, and our young men unfortunately miss that salutary branch of a business education. But if by chance the professional sweeper is absent any morning the boy who has the genius of the future partner in him will not hesitate to try his hand at the broom. The other day a fond fashionable mother in Michigan asked a young man whether he had ever seen a young lady sweep in a room so grandly as her Priscilla. He said no, he never had, and the mother was gratified beyond measure, but then said he, after a pause, "What I should like to see her do is sweep out a room." It does not hurt the newest comer to sweep out the office if necessary. I was one of those sweepers myself, and who do you suppose were my fellow sweepers? David McCargo, now superintendent of the Alleghany Valley Railroad; Robert Pitcairn, Superintendent of the Pennsylvania Railroad, and Mr. Moreland, City Attorney. We all took turns, two each morning did the sweeping; and now I remember Davie was so proud of his clean white shirt bosom that he used to spread over it an old silk bandana handkerchief which he kept for the purpose, and we other boys

[1] This was given as an address to the students of the Curry Commercial College, in Pittsburgh, June 23, 1885.

thought he was putting on airs. So he was. None of us had a silk handkerchief.

Assuming that you have all obtained employment and are fairly started, my advice to you is "aim high." I would not give a fig for the young man who does not already see himself the partner or the head of an important firm. Do not rest content for a moment in your thoughts as head clerk, or foreman, or general manager in any concern, no matter how extensive. Say each to yourself. "My place is at the top." *Be king in your dreams.* Make your vow that you will reach that position, with untarnished reputation, and make no other vow to distract your attention, except the very commendable one that when you are a member of the firm or before that, if you have been promoted two or three times, you will form another partnership with the loveliest of her sex—a partnership to which our new partnership act has no application. The liability there is never limited.

Let me indicate two or three conditions essential to success. Do not be afraid that I am going to moralize, or inflict a homily upon you. I speak upon the subject only from the view of a man of the world, desirous of aiding you to become successful business men. You all know that there is no genuine, praiseworthy success in life if you are not honest, truthful, fairdealing. I assume you are and will remain all these, and also that you are determined to live pure, respectable lives, free from pernicious or equivocal associations with one sex or the other. There is no creditable future for you else. Otherwise your learning and your advantages not only go for naught, but serve to accentuate your failure and your disgrace. I hope you will not take it amiss if I warn you against three of the gravest dangers which will beset you in your upward path.

The first and most seductive, and the destroyer of most young men, is the drinking of liquor. I am no temperance lecturer in disguise, but a man who knows and tells you what observation has proved to him; and I say to you that you are more likely to fail in your career from acquiring the habit of drinking liquor than from any, or all, the other temptations likely to assail you. You may yield to almost any other temptation and reform—may brace up, and if not recover lost ground, at least remain in the race and secure and maintain a respectable position. But from the insane thirst for liquor escape is almost impossible. I have known but few exceptions to this rule. First, then, you must not drink liquor to excess. Better if you do not touch it at all—much better; but if this be too hard a rule for you then take your stand firmly here:—Resolve never to touch it except at meals. A glass at dinner will not hinder your advance in life or lower your tone; but I implore you hold it inconsistent with the dignity and self-respect of gentlemen, with what is due from yourselves to yourselves, being the men you are, and especially the men you are determined to become, to drink a glass of liquor at a bar. Be far too much of the gentleman ever to enter a bar-room. You do not pursue your careers in safety unless you stand firmly upon this ground. Adhere to it and you have escaped danger from the deadliest of your foes.

The next greatest danger to a young business man in this community I believe to be that of speculation. When I was a telegraph operator here we had no Exchanges in the City, but the men or firms who speculated upon the Eastern Exchanges were necessarily known to the operators. They could be counted on the fingers of one hand. These men were not our citizens of first repute: they were regarded with suspicion. I have lived to see all of these speculators irreparably ruined men, bankrupt in money and bankrupt in character. There is scarcely an instance of a man who has made a fortune by speculation and kept it. Gamesters die poor, and there is certainly not an instance of a speculator who has lived a life creditable to himself, or advantageous to the community. The man who grasps the morning paper to see first how his speculative ventures upon the Exchanges are likely to result, unfits himself

for the calm consideration and proper solution of business problems, with which he has to deal later in the day, and saps the sources of that persistent and concentrated energy upon which depend the permanent success, and often the very safety, of his main business.

The speculator and the business man tread diverging lines. The former depends upon the sudden turn of fortune's wheel; he is a millionaire to-day, a bankrupt to-morrow. But the man of business knows that only by years of patient, unremitting attention to affairs can he earn his reward, which is the result, not of chance, but of well-devised means for the attainment of ends. During all these years his is the cheering thought that by no possibility can he benefit himself without carrying prosperity to others. The speculator on the other hand had better never have lived so far as the good of others or the good of the community is concerned. Hundreds of young men were tempted in this city not long since to gamble in oil, and many were ruined; all were injured whether they lost or won. You may be, nay, you are certain to be similarly tempted; but when so tempted I hope you will remember this advice. Say to the tempter who asks you to risk your small savings, that if ever you decide to speculate you are determined to go to a regular and well-conducted house where they cheat fair. You can get fair play and about an equal chance upon the red and black in such a place; upon the Exchange you have neither. You might as well try your luck with the three-card monte man. There is another point involved in speculation. Nothing is more essential to young business men than untarnished credit, credit begotten of confidence in their prudence, principles and stability of character. Well, believe me, nothing kills credit sooner in any Bank Board than the knowledge that either firms or men engage in speculation. It matters not a whit whether gains or losses be the temporary result of these operations. The moment a man is known to speculate, his credit is impaired, and soon thereafter it is gone. How can a man be credited whose resources may be swept away in one hour by a panic among gamesters? Who can tell how he stands among them? except that this is certain: he has given due notice that he may stand to lose all, so that those who credit him have themselves to blame. Resolve to be business men, but speculators never.

The third and last danger against which I

shall warn you is one which has wrecked many a fair craft which started well and gave promise of a prosperous voyage. It is the perilous habit of indorsing—all the more dangerous, inasmuch as it assails one generally in the garb of friendship. It appeals to your generous instincts, and you say, "How can I refuse to lend my name only, to assist a friend?" It is because there is so much that is true and commendable in that view that the practice is so dangerous. Let me endeavor to put you upon safe honourable grounds in regard to it. I would say to you to make it a rule now, *never indorse:* but this is too much like never taste wine, or never smoke, or any other of the "nevers." They generally result in exceptions. You will as business men now and then probably become security for friends. Now, here is the line at which regard for the success of friends should cease and regard for your own honour begins.

If you owe anything, all your capital and all your effects are a solemn trust in your hands to be held inviolate for the security of those who have trusted you. Nothing can be done by you with honour which jeopardizes these first claims upon you. When a man in debt indorses for another, it is not his own credit or his own capital he risks, it is that of his own creditors. He violates a trust. Mark you then, never indorse until you have cash means not required for your own debts, and never indorse beyond those means.

Before you indorse at all, consider indorsements as gifts, and ask yourselves whether you wish to make the gift to your friend and whether the money is really yours to give and not a trust for your creditors.

You are not safe, gentlemen, unless you stand firmly upon this as the only ground which an honest business man can occupy.

I beseech you avoid liquor, speculation and indorsement. Do not fail in either, for liquor and speculation are the Scylla and Charybdis of the young man's business sea, and indorsement his rock ahead.

Assuming you are safe in regard to these your gravest dangers, the question now is how to rise from the subordinate position we have imagined you in, through the successive grades to the position for which you are, in my opinion, and, I trust in your own, evidently intended. I can give you the secret. It lies mainly in this. Instead of the question, "What must I do for my employer?" substitute "What can I do?" Faithful and conscientious discharge of the duties assigned you is all very well, but the verdict in such cases generally is that you perform your present duties so well that you had better continue performing them. Now, young gentlemen, this will not do. It will not do for the coming partners. There must be something beyond this. We make Clerks, Bookkeepers, Treasurers, Bank Tellers of this class, and there they remain to the end of the chapter. The rising man must do something exceptional, and beyond the range of his special department. HE MUST ATTRACT ATTENTION. A shipping clerk, he may do so by discovering in an invoice an error with which he has nothing to do, and which has escaped the attention of the proper party. If a weighing clerk, he may save for the firm by doubting the adjustment of the scales and having them corrected, even if this be the province of the master mechanic. If a messenger boy, even he can lay the seed of promotion by going beyond the letter of his instructions in order to secure the desired reply. There is no service so low and simple, neither any so high, in which the young man of ability and willing disposition cannot readily and almost daily prove himself capable of greater trust and usefulness, and, what is equally important, show his invincible determination to rise. . . .

One false axiom you will often hear, which I wish to guard you against: "Obey orders if you break owners." Don't you do it. This is no rule for you to follow. Always break orders to save owners. There never was a great character who did not sometimes smash the routine regulations and make new ones for himself. The rule is only suitable for such as have no aspirations, and you have not forgotten that you are destined to be owners and to make orders and break orders. Do not hesitate to do it whenever you are sure the interests of your employer will be thereby promoted and when you are so sure of the result that you are willing to take the responsibility. You will never be a partner unless you know the business of your department far better than the owners possibly can. When called to account for your independent action, show him the result of your genius, and tell him that you knew that it would be so; show him how mistaken the orders were. Boss your boss just as soon as you can; try it on early. There is nothing he will like so well if he is the right kind of boss; if he is not, he is not the man for you to remain with—leave him whenever you can, even at a present sacrifice, and find one capable of discerning genius. Our young partners in the Carnegie firm have won their spurs by showing that we did not know half as well what was wanted as they did. Some of them have acted upon occasion with me as if they owned the firm and I was but some airy New Yorker presuming to advise upon what I knew very little about. Well, they are not interfered with much now. They were the true bosses—the very men we were looking for.

There is one sure mark of the coming partner, the future millionnaire; his revenues always exceed his expenditures. He begins to save early, almost as soon as he begins to earn. No matter how little it may be possible to save, save that little. Invest it securely, not necessarily in bonds, but in anything which you have good reason to believe will be profitable, but no gambling with it, remember. A rare chance will soon present itself for investment. The little you have saved will prove the basis for an amount of credit utterly surprising to you. Capitalists trust the saving young man. For every hundred dollars you can produce as the result of hard-won savings, Midas, in search of a partner, will lend or credit a thousand; for every thousand, fifty thousand. It is not capital that your seniors require, it is the man who has proved that he has the business habits which create capital, and to create it in the best of all possible ways, as far as self-discipline is concerned, is, by adjusting his habits to his means. Gentlemen, it is the first hundred dollars saved which tells. Begin at once to lay up something. The bee predominates in the future millionnaire.

Of course there are better, higher aims than saving. As an end, the acquisition of wealth is ignoble in the extreme; I assume that you save and long for wealth only as a means of enabling you the better to do some good in your day and generation. Make a note of this essential rule: Expenditure always within income.

And here is the prime condition of success, the great secret: concentrate your energy, thought, and capital exclusively upon the business in which you are engaged. Having begun in one line, resolve to fight it out on that line, to lead in it; adopt every improvement, have the best machinery, and know the most about it.

The concerns which fail are those which have scattered their capital, which means that they have scattered their brains also. They have investments in this, or that, or the other, here, there and everywhere. "Don't put all your eggs in one basket" is all wrong. I tell you "put all your eggs in one basket, and then watch that basket." Look round you and take notice; men who do that do not often fail. It is easy to watch and carry the one basket. It is trying to carry too many baskets that breaks most eggs in this country. He who carries three baskets must put one on his head, which is apt to tumble and trip him up. One fault of the American business man is lack of concentration.

To summarize what I have said: Aim for the highest; never enter a barroom; do not touch liquor, or if at all only at meals; never speculate; never indorse beyond your surplus cash fund; make the firm's interest yours; break orders always to save owners; concentrate; put all your eggs in one basket, and watch that basket; expenditure always within revenue; lastly, be not impatient, for, as Emerson says, "no one can cheat you out of ultimate success but yourselves."

. . .

1885

THE PLATFORM OF THE AMERICAN ECONOMIC ASSOCIATION

WHEN THE American Economic Association was formed in 1885 the discipline which it represented had already shown, in the United States, a concern with practical and contemporary problems. The foundation of the organization was significant, then, not only in marking the growth and professionalization of economics, and its differentiation from the other social studies, but also in giving trained leadership to those seeking to ameliorate the condition of American society. Professor Richard T. Ely, who had an important hand in shaping the governing conception of the new association, was a virtual Christian Socialist. While the study of economics in the United States no doubt often tended to confirm in the minds of the young the basic assumptions of capitalism, the founders of the American Economic Association hoped that its work might promote the just and peaceful solution of class conflicts.

"Anniversary Meeting," American Economic Association *Publications*, 3rd series, XI (1911).
R. T. Ely, *Ground under Our Feet; An Autobiography*, New York, 1938.

REPORT OF THE ORGANIZATION OF THE AMERICAN ECONOMIC ASSOCIATION

» » 　　　　　　　 « «

The need of an association designed to promote independent economic inquiry and to disseminate economic knowledge was keenly felt long before any determined effort was made to establish the desired organization. Suggestions looking to the formation of a society of economists were heard from time to time, but no active steps in this direction appear to have been taken before the spring of 1885, when it was agreed that the time was ripe for action, and it was determined to test the feelings in this matter of those who would be likely to prove helpful in associated scientific work in economics. The class of men required for this purpose was, it was believed, a large and constantly growing one. Men were wanted who were investigators, men, consequently, who did not believe that the entire range of economic knowledge had been compassed. It follows from this that it was not proposed to form a society of advocates of any political opinion or set of political opinions, as for example, free-trade or protection. It was not meant to deny that a free-trade club or a protectionist club might have its legitimate sphere, but it was held that this sphere lay outside the realm of science. Likewise it was not aimed to form a society to champion any class interests, either of rich or of poor, either of employer or of employé. What was desired was a society which, free from all trammels, should seek truth from all sources, should be ready to give a respectful hearing to every new idea, and should shun no revelation of facts, but, on the contrary, should make the collection, classification and interpretation of facts its chief task. The ideal of this new society, as it presented itself to the minds of its projectors, was to seek light, to bear light, to

diffuse light—ever the highest aim of all true science.

A statement of the objects of the proposed association and a platform were drawn up, which, while intended to be merely provisional, would be calculated to attract those who believed in economic research, who thought that there was a great work to be done in economics, and who for other reasons might be able to work together profitably. This platform, it must be distinctly asserted, was never meant as a hard and fast creed which should be imposed on all members, and least of all was it intended to restrict the freest investigation. The statement of objects and the proposed platform read as follows:

OBJECTS OF THIS ASSOCIATION

I. The encouragement of economic research.

II. The publication of economic monographs.

III. The encouragement of perfect freedom in all economic discussion.

IV. The establishment of a bureau of information designed to aid all members with friendly counsels in their economic studies.

PLATFORM

1. We regard the state as an educational and ethical agency whose positive aid is an indispensable condition of human progress. While we recognize the necessity of individual initiative in industrial life, we hold that the doctrine of *laissez-faire* is unsafe in politics and unsound in morals; and that it suggests an inadequate explanation of the relations between the state and the citizens.

2. We do not accept the final statements which characterized the political economy of

a past generation; for we believe that political economy is still in the first stages of its scientific development, and we look not so much to speculation as to an impartial study of actual conditions of economic life for the satisfactory accomplishment of that development. We seek the aid of statistics in the present, and of history in the past.

3. We hold that the conflict of labor and capital has brought to the front a vast number of social problems whose solution is impossible without the united efforts of Church, state and science.

4. In the study of the policy of government, especially with respect to restrictions on trade and to protection of domestic manufactures, we take no partisan attitude. We are convinced that one of the chief reasons why greater harmony has not been attained, is because economists have been too ready to assert themselves as advocates. We believe in a progressive development of economic conditions which must be met by corresponding changes of policy.

A prospectus containing this statement and platform was sent to a majority of those interested in political economy in our colleges and met with a hearty response in nearly every quarter. While there were not wanting criticisms of some of the phrases, there was general approval of the aims of the projected American Economic Association.

[Statement of Richard T. Ely]

. . . One aim of our association should be the education of public opinion in regard to economic questions and economic literature. In no other science is there so much quackery and it must be our province to expose it and bring it into merited contempt. A review at each of our meetings of the economic works of the past year, if published in our proceedings, might help in the formation of enlightened judgment.

Coming to the platform, a position is first of all taken in regard to the state, because it is thought necessary precisely at this time to emphasize its proper province. No one invited to join this association, certainly no one who has been active in calling this meeting, contemplates a form of pure socialism. "We recognize the necessity of individual initiative." We would do nothing to weaken individual ac-

tivity, but we hold that there are certain spheres of activity which do not belong to the individual, certain functions which the great co-operative society, called the state—must perform to keep the avenues open for those who would gain a livelihood by their own exertions. The avenues to wealth and preferment are continually blocked by the greed of combinations of men and by monopolists, and individual effort and initiative are thus discouraged. Two examples will suffice—You know that in the Western grazing regions water is often scarce, and those who control the streams virtually own the country. Now it is a notorious fact that unlawful combinations seize upon these streams and, keeping others from them, retain exclusive privileges which shut off effectually individual exertions on the part of those not in the ring. A second example is found in unjust discriminations in freight charges which have built up the fortunes of the favored, and ruined competitors. In looking over the field of economic life, it is evident that there is a wide feeling of discouragement, repressing the activities of the individual, because the avenues to material well-being are so often blocked. Then there are things which individuals ought not to perform because the functions concerned are public; and in certain places the wastes of private competition are too enormous. There are, likewise, important things which individual effort is powerless to effect, e.g., the education of the masses.

We hold that the doctrine of *laissez-faire* is unsafe in politics and unsound in morals, and that it suggests an inadequate explanation of the relations between the state and the citizens. In other words we believe in the existence of a system of social ethics; we do not believe that any man lives for himself alone, nor yet do we believe social classes are devoid of mutual obligations corresponding to their infinitely varied inter-relations. All have duties as well as rights, and, as Emerson said several years ago, it is time we heard more about duties and less about rights. We who have resolved to form an American Economic Association hope to do something towards the development of a system of social ethics.

It is asked: what is meant by *laissez-faire?* It is difficult to define *laissez-faire* categorically, because it is so absurd that its defenders can never be induced to say precisely what they mean. Yet it stands for a well-known, though rather vague set of ideas, to which appeal is

made every day in the year by the bench, the
bar, the newspapers and our legislative bodies.
It means that government, the state, the people
in their collective capacity, ought not to interfere in industrial life; that, on the contrary,
free contract should regulate all the economic
relations of life and public authority should
simply enforce this, punish crime and preserve
peace. It means that the laws of economic life
are natural laws like those of physics and
chemistry, and that this life must be left to the
free play of natural forces. One adherent uses
these words: "This industrial world is governed
by natural laws. These laws are superior to
man. Respect this providential order—let alone
the work of God."

The platform then emphasizes the mission
of the State and the mission of the individual
in that State. *To distinguish between the
proper functions of the two must be one of the
purposes of our association.*

The mission of the Church is likewise emphasized, and for this there is good reason
which cannot, perhaps, be better stated than in
the words of Professor Macy of Iowa College.
I quote from a letter recently received from
him:

"The preacher, in an important sense, is to
be the originator of true social science; his work
is to render possible such a science.

"The physical scientist needs no preacher.
There is an external material thing which
compels belief. For the most part, men have
no selfish interest in believing other than the
truth in regard to the material world. Those
who devote themselves to the study of matter
are led naturally into a truth-loving and truth-
telling spirit, and they can laugh at the
preacher. But those who devote themselves to
the study of the conflicting interests of men,
have on their hands altogether a different task.
There is no external material thing to solve
their doubts, and men prefer to believe that
which is not true; and when they believe the
truth they often think it best to pretend to believe the false. Falsehood, deception, lying, and
above all an honest and dogged belief in error
—these are athwart the path which might lead
to a real social science. And who can tackle
these better than the preacher?"

In addition to these words of Professor
Macy, it may be said that we wish to accomplish certain practical results in the social and
financial world, and believing that our work
lies in the direction of practical Christianity,
we appeal to the church, the chief of the social
forces in this country, to help us, to support us,
and to make our work a complete success,
which it can by no possibility be without her
assistance.

The religious press of the country can aid us
greatly in our task, and it will not, I believe,
refuse its co-operation. Its influence is enormous, and notwithstanding all that has been
said against it to the contrary, I believe that
to-day it is the fairest, purest and most liberal
press in the country. The fourth paragraph in
the platform seems to me to be imperatively
necessary. We want to proclaim to the world
that political economy is something much
broader than partisan controversies about free-
trade and protection, that we are in fact neither
free-traders nor protectionists in the partisan
sense of those words.

It may be asked: Why have any platform at
all? Why not simply invite all interested in
political economy to come together and aid in
economic research?

The reply is not a difficult one. This association intends to combine two ends. It proposes
to influence public opinion; also to investigate
and study. Now, if there has ever been found
in any place an economic society without the
advocacy, either open or concealed, of certain
tendencies, at least, it has not come to my
knowledge. I do not believe it would be wise
to attempt such a thing. The fundamental differences between economists are so radical that
they cannot all work profitably together.

Our platform is very broad and will include
nearly all those who can co-operate advantageously with us. It advocates simply certain
methods of study and the accomplishment of
reforms by certain means which alone seem to
us to promise valuable results. We believe in
historical and statistical inquiries and examinations into actual conditions, and should we include those who do not, there would be division at the start. If two people are journeying
together to a certain goal and come to a fork
in the road, it is evident that they must part
company if each insists on believing that their
common destination lies in a different direction.
That is our case. We have little faith that
the methods advocated by certain economists
will ever lead to any valuable results. They

may take their own way, and far be it from us to hinder them, but we must part company.

Again, it is not easy to arouse interest in an association which professes nothing. This proposed economic association has been greeted with enthusiasm precisely because it is not colorless, precisely because it stands for something.

Finally, it is of the utmost importance to us to emphasize certain fundamental views in order to bring them prominently before the public. It is essential that intelligent men and women should distinguish between us and certain economists in whom there is little faith. The respect for political economy, as it has been hitherto taught, is very slight. I think it has been kept alive largely by ignorance on the one hand—on the other by the cloak it affords to wrong-doing and the balm it offers to still the voice of outraged conscience. On every side we find intelligent people dissatisfied with it, throwing all political economy to the winds, while John Stuart Mill repudiated his own economic system, and one of the most careful students of economic facts, Thorold Rogers, finds its conclusions so at variance with the

results of his investigations, that he rejects it with scorn, and believes it necessary to build up a new political economy by a long and careful process, piecemeal, as he himself expresses it. We of this association must come before the public with the unequivocal assertion that we, also, refuse to accept as final "the statements which characterize the political economy of a past generation, and that we believe our science is in the first stages of its scientific development."

Our attitude is a modest one, and must, I think, appeal to the best intelligence of the country. We acknowledge our ignorance, and if we claim superiority to others it is largely on the very humble ground that we know better what we do not know. We confess our ignorance, but are determined to do our best to remedy it, and we call upon those who are willing to go to work in this spirit to come forward and help us.

At the conclusion of the paper presented by Dr. Ely, the provisional platform and statement of objects were presented and discussed in detail, nearly all present taking part in the animated debate.   1886

» » *Country and City* « «

1890-1920

» » « «

THE FARMER

1. When the farmer comes to town,
   With his wagon broken down,
   O, the farmer is the man who feeds them all!
   If you'll only look and see,
   I think you will agree
   That the farmer is the man who feeds them all.

Refrain:

   The farmer is the man,
   The farmer is the man,
   Buys on credit till the fall;
   Then they take him by the hand,
   And they lead him to the land,
   And the merchant is the man who gets it all.

2. The doctor hangs around
   While the blacksmith beats his iron,
   O, the farmer is the man who feeds them all!
   The preacher and the cook
   Go strolling by the brook,
   And the farmer is the man who feeds them all.

Refrain:

   The farmer is the man,
   The farmer is the man,
   Buys on credit till the fall.
   Tho' his family comes to town,
   With a wagon broken down,
   O, the farmer is the man who feeds them all!

According to Carl Sandburg, this song, at least in fragmentary form, was known to natives of Illinois as early as 1890. The version here printed follows Sandburg's *American Songbag*.

« «   » »

THE SIDEWALKS OF NEW YORK

Chorus

East side, West side, all around the town,
The tots sang "ring-a-rosie," "London Bridge is falling down";
Boys and girls together, me and Mamie Rorke,
Tripped the light fantastic, on the Sidewalks of New York.

This perennial favorite, which expresses the city-dweller's love of his neighborhood, was written by Charles B. Lawlor and James W. Blake in 1894. (Copyrighted, Paull-Pioneer Music Corp., New York.)

Country and City

RURAL AMERICA had always been suspicious of the sophistication of the city. The city suggested political corruption, wickedness, materialism, squalor. Yet like a magnet the city drew more and more country people into its factories, counting-houses, and offices. Some found adventure and fortune in the city, others frustration, loneliness, tragedy. Country people looked with increasing alarm on the depletion of rural population. Many Americans in country and city alike believed that the most precious values in the national life owed their being to the country, and these people became, in the first decade of the twentieth century, rural-conscious. They were especially concerned to rehabilitate the countryside by making life in it more livable. They urged improvement of the soil, vocational education, and greater cultural opportunities. New methods of communication, such as the telephone, improved roads, and the automobile, brought to the country much that had been associated with urban life. Yet the contrast and the antagonism between farm and country town on the one hand, and the city on the other, continued to elicit the interest of sociologist and novelist alike. The migration, during the World War and after, of hundreds of thousands of Southern Negroes to the city, in the North as well as in the South, still further complicated the urban pattern and rural needs and problems.

The city, which the rural dweller was often inclined to think of as a homogeneous unit, was itself the scene of deep cleavages. The gulf in life between the slums and the best residential areas was so deep that few save social workers ever really crossed it at all. The slum dweller experienced few of the advantages of the city and all its disadvantages.

Yet civic consciousness did increase, and the beginnings of slum clearance and of city planning, in the advantages of which the poor shared to some degree, made headway. Municipal corruption was much aired and many reforms, some of which proved to be ephemeral, were inaugurated. To the problems to which city life in all its varied forms gave rise the man of letters paid much attention. The city was, in short, no less a leading American issue than the countryside itself. Professor Arthur M. Schlesinger, in a brilliant essay, called attention to the role of urbanism throughout American history.

» » « «

HENRY J. FLETCHER

1860–1938

BORN IN IOWA, Henry J. Fletcher received his law training at the University of Michigan. In 1895, after having practiced law in Minneapolis, he became associated with the law faculty of the University of Minnesota, from which he retired in 1929. Fletcher's interests, however, were social as well as legal. He championed the conservation of natural resources, and applied to social problems "the scientific ethics" which, in his words, he derived from

Darwin, Spencer, and Clifford. Fletcher, in addition to contributing to many periodicals and editing the *Minnesota Law Review*, wrote *The Ethics of Conservation* (1910).

"Memoriam—Henry J. Fletcher," *University of Minnesota Law Review*, vol. XXIII (December, 1938), No. 1.

» » *From:* THE DRIFT OF POPULATION TO CITIES: « « REMEDIES

The closing decades of this century are witnessing no more remarkable phenomenon than that shown in the migration of population, not so much from country to country, as from place to place in the same country. This interior migration is most noticeable in the most progressive lands. It is effecting a rapid transformation in Germany, in England, in Australasia, under widely different conditions, but nowhere is its operation more general than in the United States. In Australia, for example, the rural districts prosper and a few great cities grow enormously, while all the intermediate communities are relatively stagnant; but in the United States the drift is unmistakably from the farms to the nearest village, from the village to the town, and from the town to the city.

The smaller towns are not conscious of the full extent of their loss, because, as regards the number of residents, it is partly or wholly repaired by reinforcements from the surrounding country. The newest portions of the Western States, which are still in process of settlement, have not as yet felt the full effect of the centripetal attraction, for population tends to spread out into a more or less uniform density; but wherever immigration has ceased, the new forces quickly begin to tell, and throughout the older settled States, in New York as well as in Illinois and Iowa, a universal and all-powerful current has set in, sweeping everything toward the centres.

The movement of the agricultural population can be best learned through a study of the townships. Such a study, covering four of the North-Central group of States, I attempted in THE FORUM for April. The population of the townships, as given in the census, frequently includes the population of the smaller towns and hamlets. The startling fact is disclosed that in Iowa and Indiana nearly one-half, and in Illinois and Ohio more than half, of the townships were in 1890 less populous than in 1880, while the population of the States and of their largest cities had grown very rapidly; and that there had been a very considerable diminution of the number of productive enterprises such as were formerly carried on in all the small towns. Further investigation shows that New York has suffered in even greater proportion, in the removal of a large fraction of the people from the towns, villages, and farms to the great cities. Out of a total of 909 townships in New York, 274 gained numerically between 1880 and 1890, while 635, or more than two-thirds, became less populous. In many counties nearly all the townships, and in one (Oswego), all, lost population. Notwithstanding the growth of the larger towns, no less than 23 out of 60 counties in New York dwindled, in many cases very considerably. Many other parts of the country are in the same condition. Indeed, it may be declared to be the general rule that wherever the land is fully occupied all the people not actually needed to cultivate the soil are being drawn into the towns, while the productive industries of the towns, together with those identified with them, are being transferred to the largest cities. For a certain number of years the country steadily grew more and more densely populated; this process came to a standstill, and now the tide is running swiftly in the opposite direction.

This transplantation has most far-reaching effects. Politically, it transfers a preponderance of power to the great cities, changing the results of important elections, and increasing the urgency of municipal problems. Socially, it swells the number of the classes most exposed to agitation and discontent, intensifies the dangers to be apprehended from social upheavals, and widens the growing chasm between the classes. It concentrates the wealth of the nation into fewer hands, and reacts profoundly upon the material, social, and political life of the entire nation. The importance of this migration, therefore, is hardly to be overestimated. It is a striking characteristic of our period that it is a period of universal transition, in which large masses of people, apparently against their own interests, leave the country where homes are cheap, the air pure, all men equal, and extreme poverty unknown, and crowd into cities where all these conditions are reversed. When this movement has proceeded too fast, and the cities have become swollen with a surplus population for whom there is no employment, when urban expansion has far outrun the growth of the contributory territory, and this condition has become excessive and universal, a panic interrupts this concentration for a time, until the proper balance between town and country is re-established. The more rapid, therefore, the process of centralization, the more frequent and intense must be the periods of depression needed to correct it. As in Australia the relative size of the cities is unparalleled in the whole world, so the recent financial convulsion from which that country is slowly recovering was probably more prostrating than any hitherto known. As an outcome of the bitter lessons of that panic, the Australian government is now engaged in drawing off some of the surplus city population to colonies established and watched over by the state.

In comparing the evils and advantages resulting from this striking migratory tendency, a distinction must be kept in mind between the interests of the individual and those of society at large. In changing his place of residence every man undoubtedly acts on his best judgment of his own needs, and cares nothing about its effects on society. But the student of social science, observing so stupendous a movement, asks whether society is to be the gainer or the loser by it. On the one side, he trembles —especially if he be an American—at the prospect of adding enormously to the burden of the municipal governments in the large cities, already almost breaking down through corruption and inefficiency. He realizes that in times of social disturbance the great cities are an ever-growing menace to the public authority and even to the existing social order. He knows that crime is increasing, like the cities, out of all proportion to everything else; and that the massing of dense populations means impaired public health and morals. The constant depletion of the smaller towns and of the country, steadily draining away the best, producing absenteeism and local stagnation, must be regarded as an evil of great magnitude. It lowers the tone of village and farm life, prevents the rapid diffusion throughout the country of im-

provements in education, and tends to exclude the inhabitants of the rural districts from participation in the great ameliorations of modern life which ought to be common to all. *Per contra*, it is the testimony of Sir Charles Dilke that in Australia—

—"the working people of the capitals have excellent houses and gardens in the suburbs, and are better off than the dwellers in the country from most points of view. On the other hand, the population of the colony, generally speaking, gains, from the concentration in the capitals, in education, in power of recreation, and in many of the matters which make life most pleasant. The effect must be a quickening of the national pulse, and is already, in fact, visible in the brightness and high intelligence of the Australian people."

In America, even the poorest of the working people refuse to go into the country to live. Labor is benefited in many ways by association; school advantages are better, wages higher, capital receives better returns, ambition has a wider field, where the rivers of people have their confluence. Yet, on the whole, the conclusion seems unavoidable that the evils and dangers, present and prospective, of the excessive massing of the people in the cities far outweigh the benefits.

The census figures show the effects of this change, numerically, upon the cities, smaller towns, and country, but they do not tell the whole story. While the larger cities are rapidly absorbing the manufactures of the smaller towns, and with them a large portion of the most enterprising citizens, the population of the latter is being recruited, not from new-comers from abroad, but by retired farmers from the neighborhood. These are excellent people, but they are generally past their period of activity. Their interest is to live quietly and cheaply, and to pay as low taxes as possible. The more numerous they become, proportionately, the more effectually do they stifle organized efforts in the direction of local development. Hence the loss of the smaller towns is greater than the figures would indicate.

Doubtless the chief cause of this remarkable concentration is the natural superiority, under existing conditions, of large centres for all the processes of production and exchange. Here the manufacturer and the jobber come into direct contact with their customers. The retailer finds all the different articles needed to replenish his stock. Competition between producers raises the quality of goods while lowering prices, buyers are attracted by the great variety offered, and thus all the makers of a given article find it to their advantage to get together, and the greater the market the more powerfully it attracts both buyer and seller. Cheap freights and passenger fares, improved postal and telegraph service, and all the devices to facilitate business between distant places, help the movement.

I have talked with many persons who, as managers or owners of manufacturing or jobbing concerns, followed the current and removed their business to larger cities. Each had a special reason, applicable either to the nature of his business or the local conditions prevailing in the town whence he came. The Western cities have not been content to await the natural process of accretion; commercial organizations and real-estate syndicates have done the most active missionary work, and a great many manufacturers have been induced to leave the country towns, tempted by large "bonuses" of cash, land, and buildings. Against such competition the small towns, with their population largely composed of industrial non-combatants, have but little chance. It has been the history of the last few years that a large number of these assisted removals has come to grief. In the case of Minneapolis, the development of Minnesota and the Dakotas has induced the transfer to that city of many producers in order to be nearer to the consumers, but in nearly every case the removal has been at the expense of some smaller town. The great mills, like those of Minneapolis, can produce flour more economically than any small mill however well equipped, and can sell it at a smaller margin of profit. They therefore engross the export trade, and supply the market except for local consumption. This explains in part the remarkable diminution in the number of local flouring-mills during the last decade, but there are other causes which will be mentioned later. Chicago, with its suburbs, has swallowed the factories and workshops and work-people of villages and minor cities within a radius of many hundred miles. Multitudes flock to the cities because the drift is that way, because business is dull in the villages, often without any distinct analysis of reasons, but in reality because production and exchange, in so far as it is not by its nature local, is being rapidly removed thither.

Ample allowance must be made also for the influence of various social motives. Many successful men desire better social opportunities for their families than the small towns afford; there are those who propose to live on their accumulated gains and want to be near the centres of fashion and amusement. Undeniably the city has superior attractions as a place of residence for the well-to-do; even the poorest classes, who live in filthy tenements and are completely shut out from the enjoyments of nature, seem to find in the noises, the crowds, the excitements, even in the sleepless anxieties of the daily struggle for life, a charm they are powerless to resist.

Against these multiplied influences ceaselessly operating in favor of the great cities, the country and the lesser towns contend in vain. They are like the laws of nature, and are submitted to patiently. But in league with them has been another potent agency—the transportation system of the country—whose management in the past engaged actively in the work of helping the strong to absorb the weak. Prior to the passage of the interstate commerce law in 1887, the bitter competition of the railways for business reduced through rates to a figure out of all proportion to those charged to and from intermediate points. It was a cardinal principle with the managers that business must be obtained at whatever price. Freight was sometimes carried between important terminal points not merely for less than it cost, but actually for nothing. Freight rates kept perpetually falling until they became lower, on the average, than anywhere in the world; and in the terrible struggle to maintain their solvency, it was the settled policy of the managers to make up the deficiencies on business carried at unremunerative rates by stiffly holding up the rates that were not competitive. Many able railway men saw that this policy was a ruinous one, both from the standpoint of their local communities and themselves, for it sacrificed a large number of places whose interests needed to be fostered until they were strong enough to stand alone. But they insisted that they were powerless to resist the influence of competition; that in the absence of effective pooling arrangements it was impossible to maintain proper rates at competitive points, and at the same time the necessary revenues must be derived from some source. The long-and-short-haul clause of the interstate commerce law was designed to compel them to solve this problem; they were practically required to cut down their local or raise their through rates, but were still strictly forbidden to form pools for the maintenance of through rates. Before the passage of the law there can be no question that nearly universal discrimination was practised against the defenceless small towns, with the result of checking their growth and blasting their prosperity. Some railway managers declared that the law would simply ruin the railroads. Mr. Ackerman testified before the Senate committee that it meant the destruction of railroads. This practice found defenders even among the railway commissioners of some States. An ex-commissioner of Indiana, in a statement to the committee, said:

"The local or short-line shipper cannot understand why the through rates should be less than one cent a ton per mile, while he is compelled to pay two or three cents. I know an instance in my own experience where a miller complained that wheat brought to his mill from another State for conversion into flour was charged so much more than a miller a hundred miles beyond him, (that the latter) shipping from the same point, could convert his wheat into flour and ship it *back* the hundred miles and undersell the other miller in his own town."

The ex-commissioner then argued that this was just and reasonable.

After the law had been in effect two years, the Commission, in its second report, discussing the destructive effect of such local discrimination, said:

"How great the differences were, and how depressing they must necessarily have been upon small towns, some idea may be had from an examination of tariff sheets which showed that the carrier sometimes charged for the transportation of property from one terminus of its line to stations short of the other, fully three times as much as it charged by the same tariff sheets for the carriage of the like property from the same starting-point past the same stations to the other terminus. . . . But whether willingly done, or, on the other hand, done under stress of compulsion, by those who would have preferred to do otherwise, the consequences were unmistakable. Small towns bore the heaviest proportionate burdens, and unless on general grounds it was desirable that the cities should be specially fostered and favored, the effect must, from a social point of view, be undesirable for the country. It was impossible that it should be made to seem right to the common mind that such distinctions should exist; the sense of justice received a shock when one was told that the small dealer in a country town was made to pay three times as much for the carriage of his goods as the city merchant paid upon the like quantity for even a greater distance; and a well-founded feeling of discontent arises among any people when it can see things done under the protection of its laws which seem to be plainly and unmistakably unjust."

Such was the state of things prior to the adoption of the law. The railways declare that they are now obeying its provisions, and no doubt they are doing so as regards intermediate stations on main lines, where the applicability of the law is unquestioned. But a large portion of the business of the country is done over railways which are but parts of through routes leading to great centres, and as to through business on such railways the courts now hold that the law does not apply. It is also too common for managers to disregard the law entirely whenever the exigencies of rate wars require a vigorous cutting of through rates. Moreover, the law itself is exceedingly elastic, prohibiting such discriminations only where the circumstances and conditions are similar; and the companies contend that a great variety of elements may make the circumstances and conditions so dissimilar as to justify them in treating the law as inapplicable. Thus it is plain that the interior towns are yet very far from enjoying that equality in the use of the public transportation facilities to which they seem to be absolutely entitled as a matter of right. Even with such equality the odds would still be enormously against them in their struggle for self-preservation. The general drift of opinion at present is that discrimination has its root in competition; that unrestricted competition between railroads is hurtful to all parties; and that the law can never prevent injurious discriminations, whether against persons or places, so long as pooling agreements remain illegal and unenforceable. Competition in rates must ultimately give way to some more reasonable method of regulation, which shall secure uniformity and equality.

It appears from what has already been said that for some of the conditions that are operating so unfavorably against the country there is no remedy. So far as the concentration is the result of the natural superiority of the city as a place for business or residence, so long as human nature continues to crave the stimulus of social contact, there can be no remedy until the accumulated miseries of overgrown cities drive the people back to the land. Some sanguine observers, seeing the temporary check caused by the present depression, think that that time has now arrived. Others look to the recent extraordinary extension of the system of electric street railways into the country districts, to give relief by making it more convenient to live and work outside the cities. This movement, however, appears to be suburban only. It can hardly stop the rush to the cities, but it will enable the cities to spread out over a wider territory, materially reduce the overcrowding, and raise greatly the standard of health and comfort for the poorer citizens. This suburban movement is universal, and is one of the most significant features of modern town life. It is introducing great changes in the condition of the people, and will deeply affect all the elements of the city question. It is another proof of the important part which transportation plays in developing and moulding the form of the modern commonwealth. But this counter movement can hardly affect the rush from the country toward the centre, and possibly it may even accelerate it by ameliorating the condition of the city's poorer classes. More is to be expected from the transmission of electric power for manufactories, both in offering cheaper rents and ampler accommodations in the country, and also, perhaps, by diminishing the superiority which the factory now enjoys over the small shop.

With these exceptions, the only remedy that can avail to moderate existing conditions is equality in transportation rates; that is, such a readjustment as shall treat the railroad system as a unit and all the people as equally entitled to its benefits. In such an adjustment of rates, competition between the different parts of the system must be reduced to the lowest terms, and the welfare of all sections of the country must be considered. So long as railroads are permitted to wage warfare upon each other they will obtain the sinews of war by taxing their own people, whose situation leaves them no choice in the selection of a route. What system will be devised to secure equality remains to be developed in the future. At the present time it would seem that some comprehensive method of government supervision must be adopted, or the railroads will solve the problem for themselves by first securing the legal right to form pools, and afterward organizing themselves into a federation strong enough neither to need nor to fear the law.

One lesson which seems to lie upon the surface is that agriculture is not reaping the advantages promised by the early advocates of the protective system. Protection was to place the factory and the farm side by side; the farmer was assured that he should be reimbursed for the higher prices he was to pay for manufactured articles by the growth in his neighborhood of a busy population of workers who would buy his products at enhanced prices. This promise has not been redeemed. The farmer has found the articles he needed made artificially dear, but there are every year fewer factories in his vicinity and lower prices for his products. The universal depression of agriculture East and West, the dwindling population of agricultural communities, would seem to indicate that the cultivators of the soil are being exploited for the benefit of manufacturers, and that the cities are appropriating the largest part of the profit. The loyalty and tenacity with which the farmers have so long clung to the doctrine of protection in the face of declining prosperity is remarkable.

It is not pleasant to believe that in the future development of our country dulness, isolation and monotony are to be the permanent lot of the tillers of the soil. It will be unfortunate for our national life if agriculture shall come to be shunned by the intelligent and abandoned to a class of peasants. For centuries the real strength and glory of England has been in her sturdy yeomanry; the passion to own land and live upon it is to-day the chief cause of the prosperity of France. We in the United States cherish a deep love for the farms and villages from which most of us have sprung, and whence we must chiefly recruit the energies of a race that is consuming its strength in smoky cities. Is it not possible that the fierceness of the rage for wealth will one day abate, and the people begin to look about them for the sweetness and serenity which human nature longs for in its highest moments, and which are best found under a pure sky, amid the quietness of nature? When the farmer and villager begin to study more how to enrich and beautify farm and village life, when perfect roads, daily mails, the telephone, the electric railway, the manual-training school, shall have carried into the remotest corners the blessings of the new civilization, it may be that the incentive to live in cities will be largely removed. If the dwellers in the smaller towns and country want to counteract the existing tendencies they must be alert to seize and appropriate the agencies which are now transforming modern life.   1895

JOSIAH STRONG

1847–1916

AMONG THE SMALL GROUP of apostles of the Social Gospel, including such men as Francis G. Peabody, Washington Gladden, and Walter Rauschenbusch, Josiah Strong stood out for his passionate zeal and activity, his balance, and his scholarship. He became a national figure by virtue of his book, *Our Country* (1885), written as a revision of a manual of the Congregational Home Missionary Society, to serve which he had interrupted his parish duties. In this pioneer treatise on Christian sociology Strong analyzed such social forces as the concentration of capital, immigration, and the labor problem, and called upon the Church to grapple with these and other social evils. His emphasis on the mission of the United States to extend its highest values to the world through widening its influence abroad was an important source of strength to the waxing imperialistic movement. *The New Era* (1893) advanced the doctrine that the Kingdom of God was to be realized here and now through the application of the teachings of Jesus to social problems. Strong's activities, which increasingly centered in his concern for urban problems, included his work in the American Institute of Social Service, the Federal Council of the Churches of Christ in America, and the crusade for "Safety First." *The Twentieth Century City* (1898) and *The Challenge of the City* (1907) represent his writings on urban issues. Much of the material in *The Twentieth Century City* first appeared in the *Christian Advocate*.

James Dombrowski, *The Early Days of Christian Socialism in America*, New York, 1936.
Edward T. Root, "Josiah Strong, a Modern Prophet of the Kingdom of God," *New-Church Review*, XXIX (January, 1922), 47–54.

» » *From:* THE TWENTIETH CENTURY CITY « «

CHAPTER II

A NATION OF CITIES

In earlier ages population gathered chiefly in cities, but for reasons which were temporary. Men sought the protection from marauders which was afforded by the walled towns. They went to their fields in the morning, and returned at night. But with the establishment of social order the men who tilled the soil began to live on it. The growth of the modern city is due to causes which are permanent.

Foreign immigration has stimulated the growth of cities in the United States, but of course cannot account for the scarcely less surprising growth of European cities. The phenomenal growth of the modern city is due to a redistribution of population. From 1880 to 1890 urban population in the United States increased sixty-one per cent., while rural population increased only fourteen per cent., and 10,063 townships—thirty-nine per cent. of the whole number in 1880—actually lost population. Thus, Chicago more than doubled, while seven hundred and ninety-two townships in Illinois were depleted.

This redistribution of population is due to three principal causes:

1. The application of machinery to agriculture. A special agent of the Government reports that four men with improved agricultural implements now do the work formerly done by fourteen. Inasmuch as the world cannot eat three or four times as much food simply to oblige the farmers, a large proportion of them are compelled to abandon agriculture, and are forced into the towns and cities. Simply bearing

in mind that the world's capacity to consume food is limited, will throw not a little light on economic conditions, both present and future. It means that only a limited number of persons can get a living by agriculture, and that when the supply of food has reached the limit of demand, agriculture can increase only as population increases.

. . . After taking all the facts into consideration, we are forced to the conclusion that progress in agriculture will limit it to an ever-decreasing proportion of the population, which, of course, means that an ever-increasing proportion will live in cities.

2. The second great cause of the modern city's growth was the substitution of mechanical power for muscular, and its application to manufactures.

The world's work was formerly done by muscles; and the word "manufacturer" originally meant one who makes by hand. The change which has taken place in the meaning of the word suggests the industrial revolution which has been caused by the transition from muscular to mechanical power.

When the world's power was muscular, industry was for the most part individual, and naturally so. When power became mechanical and stationary, workmen gathered around it, and industry naturally became organized. Manufactures, therefore, meant the concentration of population.

. . . These opposite effects of machinery upon the two industries are of the greatest importance, since they are due to a cause which will continue operative, and will, therefore, shift these proportions more and more, perpetuating the movement of population from country to city. This cause is the fact that there is a natural limit to the world's capacity to consume food, while there is no such limit to its capacity to use the products of the mechanical arts. A family eats no more now than a family of the same size at the beginning of the century (though they eat better food), but their home is supplied with ten times as many manufactured articles, the number and cost of which may be indefinitely increased. If the world were a hundred times as rich as it is, it could not eat a hundred times as much, nor could it make its food cost a hundredfold more; but it could easily spend a hundred times as much on public buildings and palaces, parks, and private grounds, equipage and furniture, books and art, dress and ornament. For all these,

purse and taste set the only limit of expenditure. The world's agriculture must relatively decrease while its manufactures increase. From 1870 to 1880 the former increased only 8.58 per cent., while the latter increased 18.60 per cent. Agriculture fell somewhat behind the estimated increase of the world's population, while manufactures increased nearly twice as rapidly.

. . . From all this it follows that, as the world grows richer, which the civilized part of it is doing very fast, an ever-increasing proportion of its population must get their livelihood by means of the mechanical and of the fine arts, while an ever-decreasing proportion will subsist by agriculture—from which the disproportionate growth of the city follows as a natural inference.

3. The third great cause of the growth of the modern city is the railway, which makes it easy to transport population from country to city, and, which is much more important, easy to transport food, thus making it possible to feed any number of millions massed at one point. Prior to railway civilization, local famines were not infrequent; now they are become practically impossible, removing a former check to the growth of great cities.

It should be observed that all these causes are permanent; the tendency which springs from them will, therefore, be permanent. Beyond a peradventure, an ever-increasing proportion of the world's population must live in cities. It will not be long before urban population will largely preponderate over rural in the United States, and in due time we shall be a nation of cities.

This tremendous migration of millions from country to city, which marks a new civilization, is creating new social problems, and, as we shall see later, will soon create most serious political problems. Many are loath to see that the growth of the city is inevitable, and are suggesting various ways in which to relieve its congestion.

It is thought that if life on the farm can be rendered less distasteful, the young people, who are now eager to go to the city, may be persuaded to remain. It is true the city is more attractive; human intercourse, multiplied conveniences, greater religious privileges, superior educational advantages, amusements, excitements, an endless variety of happenings—all these appeal strongly to preference, and have their influence; but these causes are subordi nate. Even if these attractions could be made to preponderate in favor of the country, that would not materially retard the movement cityward. The decisive causes are economic, and they are absolutely compulsory; they do not consult preferences but create necessities.

Some philanthropists think that the congestion of the city might be relieved and the miseries of the slums alleviated by removing families to unoccupied lands; and many are under the impression that if the multitude could be got back to the soil, our most perplexing problems would be solved. But all such fail to appreciate the profound significance of the transition during this century, from muscular to mechanical power—the most important change which has ever taken place in the history of the world; one which has already wrought an industrial revolution, and is rapidly creating a new civilization. It has separated, as by an impassable gulf, the simple, homespun, individualistic life of the world's past, from the complex, closely associated life of the present and of the future.

In the age of homespun, which, for most of our population, reached nearly to the middle of this century, the typical farmer had little money, and little need of it. The industry and ingenuity of himself and of his good wife supplied nearly all the wants of their household. Together they could do in a rude way the work which now represents ten or a dozen trades. They could have reared a family in comparative comfort, if they had been cast away on Robinson Crusoe's island. They were practically independent of the whole world.

All this has been radically changed by the substitution of mechanical for muscular power, which has worked two most important results: first, the organization of industry; and second, a vast increase of products.

The organization of industry, of course, necessitated the division of labor, by which each of the twenty men, who operate the score of machines which now do the work of a single trade, becomes dependent on the other nineteen. In like manner, the great industries have become allied, each to all the others, constituting together an endless chain of interdependence. Thus have sprung up absolutely new industrial conditions, which are producing equally new social conditions.

Mechanical power, which admits of indefinite increase, together with the organization of industry, which greatly economizes power, has enormously increased production. An excellent statistician estimated a few years since that if the goods made in one year by the 3,000,000 factory-workers in the United States at that time had been made by hand, their production would have required the labor of 150,000,000 persons; that is, the machine method may be considered, on the average, about fifty times as productive as the old hand-method.

The immense increase of supply greatly stimulated demand and resulted in a remarkable elevation of the standard of living. With the rise of that standard, what at first were regarded as luxuries came to be considered conveniences or comforts, and were at length deemed necessities. There are those still living who remember when friction-matches were a luxury.

The hand-labor of the farmer and his wife, however diversified, soon proved unequal to the multiplying wants of a rising standard of living. They could supply themselves only by purchase, for which money was necessary. The farmer must therefore produce for the market. Thus, agriculture became a part of *organized* industry; and, like manufactures, came under the law of supply and demand; with this important difference, already pointed out, that there is a natural and necessary limit to the world's ability to consume food, while its consumption of manufactured articles is determined by purse and taste—a wholly artificial limit, which is constantly being widened.

This natural limit to the world's demand for food, though perfectly obvious when mentioned, necessitates conclusions which are by no means self-evident. It shows that all efforts to relieve the congestion of the city by removing population to unoccupied lands, must needs be futile. If a hundred thousand families could be transferred from city slums to the country, and so trained as to become successful farmers, which is more than doubtful, it would not in the slightest degree mitigate poverty or relieve the pressure of population upon the city. These hundred thousand farmers could succeed only by getting the market; and as the world would eat no more simply to accommodate them, they could get the market only by driving a hundred thousand other farmers out of it; who, being forced off the farm, would with their families gravitate to the city.

Farmers could be made independent of the market and so kept on the farm only in one of two ways: viz., by being so ignorant and animal that they would be satisfied simply with food and shelter, content like savages to forego the comforts of civilized life; or, by being trained to produce for themselves, in the home, the comforts which intelligence demands.

Of course the first alternative is impracticable in this land and in this day. Ignorance and stagnation can solve no problems in a republic. And the second is as impossible as reversing the motion of the earth on its axis and rolling ourselves back into the age of homespun. The man capable of building for himself a comfortable house, and of making his own furniture and tools; and the woman who can learn to transform wool and flax into garments and house-furnishings, are quite too intelligent, ingenious, and competent to spend their lives thus in the midst of modern civilization. They could make a better and easier living by devoting themselves to one of their several trades, which would inevitably take them to the city.

Another conclusion to which we are forced is that all attempts to retard the movement of population from country to city by raising the standard of agriculture will prove worse than futile. It is said that if agriculture were made profitable, as it might be by scientific methods, farmers would not wish to abandon it.

Scientific farming succeeds, because a given amount of effort, when more intelligently directed, produces greater results. Inasmuch, then, as the amount of food which the world can consume is limited, the more intelligent or scientific the farming is, the smaller will be the number of farmers required to produce the needed supply, and the larger will be the number driven from country to city. It has already been observed that if scientific methods were universally adopted in the United States, doubtless, one-half of those now engaged in agriculture could produce the present crops, which would compel the other half to abandon the farm.

. . . This wide-spread revival of agriculture in Europe will force us out of their markets unless we cheapen our produce by more scientific methods, which will of course reduce the number of American farmers. If our agriculture refuses to progress, and we thereby lose our foreign markets, the 1,700,000 men now employed in producing our agricultural exports will be forced off the farm. In either case, whether American farmers accept or reject scientific methods, large numbers will be driven to the cities.

We must face the inevitable. The new civilization is certain to be urban; and the problem of the twentieth century will be the city. Many English sovereigns attempted to arrest the growth of London by proclamation. Equally idle will be all attempts to turn back from the modern city the tide of population flowing up to it. One who thinks to circumvent or to successfully resist economic and social laws is fighting against the stars in their courses.

WARREN H. WILSON

1867–1937

WARREN H. WILSON was one of the most gifted of America's pioneers in the field of rural sociology. Of rural background himself, he used his knowledge and his position in the Presbyterian clergy and at Teachers College, Columbia University, to promote rural well-being. Fact-finding was more important, in his eyes, than panaceas; and he was a pioneer in the rural survey movement. *Quaker Hill* (1908) was, apparently, the first thoroughgoing analysis of an American rural community. His books include *The Church of the Open Country* (1911) and *The Evolution of the Country Community* (1912). His teaching, apart from his emphasis on the importance of fact-finding, centered in rural planning, rural education, and the scientific care of the earth, God's most precious gift to man.

The following paper was read at a meeting of the American Sociological Society in 1915.

E. De S. Brunner, "Warren Hugh Wilson, 1867–1937," *Rural Sociology*, II (June, 1937), 204–206.

» » *From:* COUNTRY VERSUS CITY « «

The population of the cities is now, for the nation as a whole, about equal to that of the country. In 1910, 53 per cent of the people of the United States lived in communities of 2,500 or less. The communities of 2,500 or over, which are called cities, were growing at such a rate then, and have so increased since that time in growth and in proportionate growth, that we may recognize the division of the people between city and country communities as equal. The division of the population at communities of 2,500, while arbitrary, is on the whole satisfactory. It marks the line of social, educational, and religious differences which are vital and fundamental. The basis of this difference is the fact that there are two layers of people in this country, the rural and the urban. The rural are predominantly of the older colonial stock; among them are few of the immigrants of recent years. Irish, German, and Scandinavian immigrants used to go to the country, but Poles, Lithuanians, Slavs, Bulgarians, Serbs, Greeks, Syrians, and Jews do not go to farms in any such numbers as to require notice here. They go to the cities. The cities reflect their character and activities. The farming and the village populations, on the other hand, are strongholds of older American conservatism.

It is contended by some authorities that there is a movement of the country population, not to the cities, but from farm to farm, from farm to village, and from one agricultural state to another. There are some country people moving into the cities, as is demonstrated by the slow growth of cities in the southern states where immigrants are few. But that this city-ward migration is relatively small is indicated by the predominantly rural character of these states to which little of the more recent immigration has gone. The cities in the South constitute only a small part of the entire population, and they exhibit in this fact the lesser inclination of the older Americans to go into city life.

The contrast between city and country is expressed also in certain social habits. The compacted social forms under which people live in the congested cities are unknown in the country. They are not idealized by country people. Farmers live in homesteads far apart from one another. The village residence of some European tillers of the soil has not been translated to this country, though similar conditions appear in Utah.

The masterful and independent character of the American countryman explains his country residence and the lonely homestead in which he lives. Eloquent tribute is paid to this chief motive of country life in Bailey's *The Holy Earth,* p. 37: [10]

As you say, too many people confound farming with that sordid, selfish, money-getting game called "business," whereas the farmer's position is administrative, being in a way a dispenser of the "Mysteries of God," for they are mysteries. Every apple is a mystery, and every pound of butter is a mystery, and when a farmer is not able to understand these things he is out of place.

The farmer uses the soil and the rains and the snows and the frosts and the winds and the sun: these are also the implements of the Almighty, the only tools he uses. . . .

Strangely contrasted to this industrial independence of country people is the variety of minds one finds in the city. Every type of mind that is highly specialized, every industrial character, every mechanical gift that is highly rewarded, every business faculty that inclines its possessor to acquire and to use capital goes to the city. Into the city are thus brought the mechanical, the executive, the acquisitive, the musical, the literary, the humorous. [23] [30]

There are left in the country by this very drastic selection the possessors of an entirely different social mind. The characters entering into its make-up are fewer than in the city. The country lacks the variety and is without the original inventive elements of which the city has a surplusage. A somewhat uniform type of mind after a while characterizes country populations that are under city influence. Wilbert L. Anderson has described this severe conformity of country people to one type as a result of the removal of those who have characters of greater variation to the cities. The effect of this selection is to give the country and city populations an appearance of strong unlikeness each to the other. [40]

Economic forms of the country differ from those of the city, where the joint-stock corporation prevails. Country people cannot endure to [50] work together under joint-stock organization. They have invented in Europe and America, out of the necessity of collective action, a co-operative type of organization based upon the natural partnership of the country neighborhood. Farmers in every land of the earth are said by Sir Horace Plunkett to organize effectively in this form alone, which preserves the individual estate while securing collective action on a basis of personal acquaintance.

The schools of the country are very different from those of the city. The disposition to improve and adapt the city schools, and the degree of that educational progress, are not found in the country, where conservatism affects the school perhaps more than any other institution. The schoolmaster class may have exaggerated the antagonism between city and country because of this retardation of country schools. This class has certainly not belittled it, and the more because the future of the country school is believed to lie in a different direction from that of the city schools. To this the books of Kern, Foght, Carney, Bruere, Eggleston, and Cubberley all testify. The science of agriculture occupies a great place in national education. Professing to be a whole and adequate training for country life, it greatly influences rural thought. The more it is developed as a formal statement of rural knowledge and practice, so much the more does country life differ from city life. The whole influence of the agricultural college and of the state and national departments of agriculture is exerted in the direction of a different society in the country from that in the city.

To this conviction of a dual organization of society further evidence is added by the country church. Between the city church and that in the country there is a wide divergence. So marked is this contrast that one brilliant observer has called the country church a form of "heathen Christianity."

There is a different personnel in the country ministry and different professional habits, especially in the open country churches. There is a strong tendency among country churches to conform to a common mode and both in liturgy and in relation to social life to resemble one another closely. This occurs, moreover, without abatement of denominational ardor. The same thing may be said of city churches of the protestant sort: they tend to conform to a city type. But city and country church modes are far apart. Two rural churches of different denominations are more like one another than either of them is like a city congregation of its own communion. The country church generally has an absentee minister. Its affairs are treated as of less importance than individual concerns. It is not an approved channel of benevolence as the city church is. And over-churching, especially in villages, seems to be a cherished expression of the rural religious spirit rather than an evil recognized or deplored.

The widest divergence between city and country is a spiritual one; by this I mean a contrast in the general attitude of either population toward life as a whole. The countryman has the attitude of one who produces his own living. The city man is characterized by the recognition that the sources of his income are invisible. That is, country men think of themselves as producers, while dwellers in cities act the part of consumers. It is true that each farmer is now a consumer of other men's goods; but his mental posture—what Professor Carver calls his "make-believe"—is that of a self-sufficing social life. He still sees before his eyes the most of his consumer's goods produced on the land which he owns or rents, and even manufactured on his own premises. This fact gives him an independence of the city and a resulting contempt for city people and antagonism for all urban concerns.

The relation between city and country may be understood in any one of three ways: first, it may be believed—as many do believe upon the evidence we have just mentioned—that rural society and urban have no connection whatever: that the one is independent of the other; or secondly, one may conceivably think of them as antagonistic and competitive—as the title of this paper implies; or thirdly, we may believe that urban society and rural society are closely interrelated, causes of either being found in the other.

The prevailing implication of social opinion among students of urban conditions is of the first of these three; that is, urban social students write and speak as if the city were self-sufficing. Rural students usually adhere to the second theory, that city and country compete. Their proposals often imply that the prosperity of the country is to be secured only from rural sources by rural leaders, independently or at the expense of the city. It is the contention of this paper that the third opinion is the true one—that city and country are dynamically one. Studies which ignore progress may regard them as separate and complete each in itself; but the consideration of growth and progress discovers sources of change for the city to be in the country, and sources of rural progress in the city.

This is not to say that we are going to "urbanize" the country. So long as farmers persist in living in lonely homesteads, to speak of rural social life as "urban" because of better plumbing or screens on the door of the farm kitchen is simply to confess a poverty of words. But so long as the harvester machinery is made in Chicago and the price of butter is fixed in Elgin and the sale of citrus fruit is made in Los Angeles, just so long will the city be the center of country life. And until typhoid is abolished, the country and the city will require a unified health service.

One reason why we are slow to recognize the interaction of city and country is the fact that we have little knowledge of the dynamic relations of either. We have studied static sociology in city and country, but we in the rural field have only lately begun to study farm management, farm accounting, or the marketing of farm products. We have only the beginnings of a knowledge of rural health; but what we have shows an immediate relation between city and country. The study of suburban life may have surprises in store, as it is on the border-line between city and country. The study of the gentleman farmer's way of life, like that of the suburban community, has yet to be made. But the chief confession we have to make is the fact that there is no history of agriculture. The encyclopedia article is until today the best authority upon the record of country living.

. . . Public health is another field in which rural and urban societies meet. Here we have a beginning, not so much in the books published under that title—which but demonstrate our lack of knowledge of rural health conditions— but in the few field surveys made with a view to the measurement of the effect of well-known pathological forces upon rural populations. The house-to-house study of five rural counties of Indiana by Dr. Hurty, health commissioner of the state, exhibited the typical American homestead as a center of ill-health and insanitary neglect. The survey of rural immorality in Green and Clermont counties, Ohio, by Professor Paul L. Vogt, measured the prevalence of venereal diseases among country people. The State Department of Health of Virginia, Dr.

Williams, commissioner, has systematically studied the health conditions in Orange and other rural counties. The United States Public Health Service is now making rural surveys. Professor T. D. Wood of Columbia has published in two brief but accurate pamphlets the summaries of these findings, showing the evidence which indicates in the large that the city is the center of dynamic health and pointing to the intolerably bad conditions in the country, which, being unremedied, affect the health of the whole people. The investigations and the subsequent health campaigns with reference to the mosquito and the hookworm are now chapters of the history of national public health in which the city and the country are equally concerned.

The investigation of rural populations with a view to the measurement of the numbers and proportions of subnormal, defective, idiotic, and insane will be particularly important in this connection. The Committee on Provision for the Feeble-minded has made a beginning in this investigation. When it is completed we shall know whether those who go to the cities from the country are its best breeding stock, and whether generally the country community has a greater or a less proportion of the insane, idiotic, defective, or subnormal than the city.

. . . In American history the growth of cities corresponds to the growth of the organized idealism of husbandry and the specialized education for agriculture. In our time the cities constrain all men to produce ethically. The city organizes its influence through the state and the commonwealth by books, by literature, by newspapers, and through legislative enactments, in such a way as to require from people living in the country that they produce what the community as a whole needs.

Everybody knows how the city governs the great rural industries which center in it. The countryman contributes relatively little by his direct discussion or by his direct proposal in the regulation of the milk trade, of the meat industry, of the speculation in wheat, of the standardization of fruit products, of the storage and shipment of refrigerated products, meat, or fruit. These regulations are usually imposed by the state at the behest of masses of consumers whose centers of influence and authority are in the big cities. These cities themselves are often the organization by which the masses of consumers impose their will upon country producers.

This influence of the city is positive and constructive. It tends to organize country life. For instance, the American farmer has by the demand of the city been obliged to milk his cows at intervals of twelve hours—4:00 A.M. and 4:00 P.M. The farmer in East India is not accustomed to milk the cows at an early hour. A report of co-operative societies in the State of Baroda describes the difficulties encountered by those co-operative societies which handle milk products in that state, in inducing farmers to milk their cows at the intervals which tend toward the highest efficiency. These co-operative societies might be called ganglia of social control. The nerve centers in this social control, however, are in the big cities in India.

In this country, in some of the states without co-operative societies, the milk business is regulated from the big cities. Anyone who lives in a dairy country realizes that the farmer rises and goes to bed, eats his meals, and regulates the labor of the day and of the year according to the behest which, directly and indirectly, is laid upon him by the market authorities in the big city to which his milk is shipped. The city is thus a factor in making the farmer think. It lays a bondage upon him which organizes his labor and makes him more industrious. The effect of this is seen in the higher proportion of regularly industrious persons in the country populations of states like New York, Pennsyl-

vania, or Ohio, than in the states like North Carolina or Tennessee, in which the proportion of cities is less. The number of idle persons and the number of hours of idleness which prevail among a population in rural Arkansas is much greater than in an Ohio rural population. The reason is that the cities of Ohio have regulated the industrial procedure of the country. They have organized the life of the country, whereas in Arkansas or rural Tennessee, or in the inaccessible mountain region, there is no ethical market standard laid upon the people, and they have not, therefore, the discipline of the city's domination.

The contention of this paper is, first, that the sociology of city and country relations should develop by inductive study rather than by speculation; secondly, that the study of rural versus urban society offers a field of most fruitful study in which we may learn much about the nature of social life in general; and thirdly, that the study of those interrelations which exhibit the city as a center of rural forces and the country as a leverage or a brake upon the social machine will be among the most fruitful of all social investigations in the days before us. In the classroom and seminar in social science this method offers the highest return, and the material thus secured rewards collective study as much as any available for the teacher and the student.   1916

JACOB AUGUST RIIS

1849–1914

THE SON of a Danish Latin teacher and journalist, Riis, after completing an apprenticeship to a carpenter, migrated to America in 1870. He was compelled by poverty to frequent the miserable police-lodging houses, where his sympathy for the plight of the near-homeless was deepened. Police-reporting for several newspapers gave him additional first-hand knowledge of New York's grim tenement area. His vivid and appealing human-interest stories made known to a wide public the wretched housing conditions; and directly as well as indirectly, Riis became an important worker in the movement for slum clearance. Theodore Roosevelt at length proved an important ally in his contests with tenement owners and politicians. Riis's writings are numerous, the best known being *How the Other Half Lives* (1890), *The Children of the Poor* (1892), *The Battle with the Slum* (1902), and *Children of the Tenements* (1903).

Jacob Riis, *The Making of an American*, New York, 1901.
Louise Ware, *Jacob A. Riis, Police Reporter, Reformer, Useful Citizen*, New York, 1939.

» » *From:* A TEN YEARS' WAR « «

CHAPTER I

[THE BATTLE WITH THE SLUM]

. . .

The battle with the slum began the day civilization recognized in it her enemy. It was a losing fight until conscience joined forces with fear and self-interest against it. When common sense and the golden rule obtain among men as a rule of practice, it will be over. The two have not always been classed together, but here they are plainly seen to belong together. Justice to the individual is accepted in theory as the only safe groundwork of the commonwealth. When it is practiced in dealing with the slum, there will shortly be no slum. We need not wait for the millennium, to get rid of it. We can do it now. All that is required is that it shall not be left to itself. That is justice to it and to us, since its grievous ailment is that it cannot help itself. When a man is drowning, the thing to do is to pull him out of the water; afterward there will be time for talking it over. We got at it the other way in dealing with our social problems. The doctrinaires had their day, and they decided to let bad enough alone; that it was unsafe to interfere with "causes that operate sociologically," as one survivor of these unfittest put it to me. It was a piece of scientific humbug that cost the age which listened to it dear. "Causes that operate sociologically" are the opportunity of the political and every other kind of scamp who trades upon the depravity and helplessness of the slum, and the refuge of the pessimist who is useless in the fight against them. We have not done yet paying the bills he ran up for us. Some time since we turned to, to pull the drowning man out, and it was time. A little while longer, and we should have been in danger of being dragged down with him.

The slum complaint had been chronic in all ages, but the great changes which the nineteenth century saw, the new industry, political freedom, brought on an acute attack which threatened to become fatal. Too many of us had supposed that, built as our commonwealth was on universal suffrage, it would be proof against the complaints that harassed older states; but in fact it turned out that there was extra hazard in that. Having solemnly resolved that all men are created equal and have certain inalienable rights, among them life, liberty, and the pursuit of happiness, we shut our eyes and waited for the formula to work. It was as if a man with a cold should take the doctor's prescription to bed with him, expecting it to cure him. The formula was all right, but merely repeating it worked no cure. When, after a hundred years, we opened our eyes, it was upon sixty cents a day as the living wage of the working-woman in our cities; upon "knee pants" at forty cents a dozen for the making; upon the Potter's Field taking tithe of our city life, ten per cent. each year for the trench, truly the Lost Tenth of the slum. Our country had grown great and rich; through our ports was poured food for the millions of Europe. But in the back streets multitudes huddled in ignorance and want. The foreign oppressor had been vanquished, the fetters stricken from the black man at home; but his white brother, in his bitter plight, sent up a cry of distress that had in it a distinct note of menace. Political freedom we had won; but the problem of helpless poverty, grown vast with the added offscourings of the Old World, mocked us, unsolved. Liberty at sixty cents a day set presently its stamp upon the government of our cities, and it became the scandal and the peril of our political system.

So the battle began. Three times since the war that absorbed the nation's energies and attention had the slum confronted us in New York with its challenge. In the darkest days of the great struggle it was the treacherous mob; later on, the threat of the cholera, which found swine foraging in the streets as the only scavengers, and a swarming host, but little above the hog in its appetites and the quality of the shelter afforded it, peopled the black alleys. Still later, the mob, caught looting the city's treasury with its idol, the thief Tweed, at its head, drunk with power and plunder, had insolently defied the outraged community to do its worst. There were meetings and protests. The rascals were turned out for a season; the arch-thief died in jail. I see him now, going through the gloomy portals of the Tombs, whither, as a newspaper reporter, I had gone with him, his stubborn head held high as ever.

I asked myself more than once, at the time when the vile prison was torn down, whether the comic clamor to have the ugly old gates preserved and set up in Central Park had anything to do with the memory of the "martyred" thief, or whether it was in joyful celebration of the fact that others had escaped. His name is even now one to conjure with in the Sixth Ward. He never "squealed," and he was "so good to the poor"—evidence that the slum is not laid by the heels by merely destroying Five Points and the Mulberry Bend. There are other fights to be fought in that war, other victories to be won, and it is slow work. It was nearly ten years after the great robbery before decency got the upper grip in good earnest. That was when the civic conscience awoke in 1879.

In that year the slum was arraigned in the churches. The sad and shameful story was told of how it grew and was fostered by avarice, that saw in the homeless crowds from over the sea only a chance for business, and exploited them to the uttermost, making sometimes a hundred per cent. on the capital invested,—always most out of the worst houses, from the tenants of which "nothing was expected" save that they pay the usurious rents; how Christianity, citizenship, human fellowship, shook their skirts clear of the rabble that was only good enough to fill the greedy purse, and how the rabble, left to itself, improved such opportunities as it found after such fashion as it knew; how it ran elections merely to count its thugs in, and fattened at the public crib; and how the whole evil thing had its root in the tenements, where the home had ceased to be sacred,—those dark and deadly dens in which the family ideal was tortured to death, and character was smothered; in which children were "damned rather than born" into the world, thus realizing a slum kind of foreordination to torment, happily brief in many cases. The Tenement House Committee long afterward called the worst of the barracks "infant slaughter houses," and showed, by reference to the mortality lists, that they killed one in every five babies born in them.

The story shocked the town into action. Plans for a better kind of tenement were called for, and a premium was put on every ray of light and breath of air that could be let into it. Money was raised to build model houses, and a bill to give the health authorities summary powers in dealing with tenements was sent to the legislature. The landlords held it up until the last day of the session, when it was forced through by an angered public opinion. The power of the cabal was broken. The landlords had found their Waterloo. Many of them got rid of their property, which in a large number of cases they had never seen, and tried to forget the source of their ill-gotten wealth. Light and air did find their way into the tenements in a half-hearted fashion, and we began to count the tenants as "souls." That is one of our milestones in the history of New York. They were never reckoned so before; no one ever thought of them as "souls." So, restored to human fellowship, in the twilight of the air shaft that had penetrated to their dens, the first Tenement House Committee was able to make them out "better than the houses" they lived in, and a long step forward was taken. The Mulberry Bend, the wicked core of the "bloody Sixth Ward," was marked for destruction, and all slumdom held its breath to see it go. With that gone, it seemed as if the old days must be gone too, never to return. There would not be another Mulberry Bend. As long as it stood, there was yet a chance. The slum had backing, as it were.

The civic conscience was not very robust yet, and required many and protracted naps. It slumbered fitfully eight long years, waking up now and then with a start, while the politicians did their best to lull it back to its slumbers. I wondered often, in those years of delay, if it was just plain stupidity that kept the politicians from spending the money which the law had put within their grasp; for with every year that passed a million dollars that could have been used for small park purposes was lost. But they were wiser than I. I understood when I saw the changes which letting in the sunshine worked. We had all believed it, but they knew it all along. At the same time, they lost none of the chances that offered. They helped the landlords, who considered themselves greatly aggrieved because their property was thereafter to front on a park instead of a pigsty, to transfer the whole assessment of half a million dollars for park benefits to the city. They undid in less than six weeks what it had taken considerably more than six years to do; but the park was cheap at the price. We could afford to pay all it cost to wake us up. When finally, upon the wave of wrath excited by the Parkhurst and Lexow disclosures, reform came with a shock that dislodged Tammany, it found us wide awake, and, it must be admitted, not a little astonished at our sudden access of righteousness.

The battle went against the slum in the three years that followed, until it found backing in the "odium of reform" that became the issue in the municipal organization of the greater city. Tammany made notes. Of what was done, how it was done, and why, during those years, I shall have occasion to speak further in these pages. Here I wish to measure the stretch we have come since I wrote "How the Other Half Lives," ten years ago. Some of it we came plodding, and some at full speed; some of it in the face of every obstacle that could be thrown in our way, wresting victory from defeat at every step; some of it with the enemy on the run. Take it altogether, it is a long way. Most of it will not have to be traveled over again. The engine of municipal progress, once started as it has been in New York, may slip many a cog with Tammany as the engineer; it may even be stopped for a season; but it can never be made to work backward. Even Tammany knows that, and is building the schools she so long neglected, and so is hastening the day when she shall be but an unsavory memory.

How we strove for those schools, to no purpose! Our arguments, our anger, the anxious pleading of philanthropists who saw the young on the East Side going to ruin, the warning year after year of the superintendent of schools that the compulsory education law was but an empty mockery where it was most needed, the knocking of uncounted thousands of children for whom there was no room,—uncounted in sober fact; there was not even a way of finding out how many were adrift,—brought only the response that the tax rate must be kept down. Kept down it was. "Waste" was successfully averted at the spigot; at the bunghole it went on unchecked. In a swarming population like that you must have either schools or jails, and the jails waxed fat with the overflow. The East Side, that had been orderly, became a hotbed of child crime. And when, in answer to the charge made by a legislative committee that the father forced his child into the shop, on a perjured age certificate, to labor when he ought to have been at play, that father, bent and heavy-eyed with unceasing toil, flung back the charge with the bitter reproach that we gave him no other choice, that it was either the street or the shop for his boy, and that perjury for

him was cheaper than the ruin of the child, we were mute. What, indeed, was there to say? The crime was ours, not his. That was but yesterday. To-day we can count the months to the time when every child who knocks shall find a seat in our schools. We have a school census to tell us of the need. In that most crowded neighborhood in all the world, where the superintendent lately pleaded in vain for three new schools, five have been built, the finest in this or any other land,—great, light, and airy structures, with playgrounds on the roof; and all over the city the like are going up. The briefest of our laws, every word of which is like the blow of a hammer driving the nails home in the coffin of the bad old days, says that never one shall be built without its playground. So the boy is coming to his rights.

. . .

. . . I have always maintained that we made a false move when we stopped to discuss damages with the landlord, or to hear his side of it at all. His share in it was our grievance; it blocked the mortality records with its burden of human woe. The damage was all ours, the profit all his. If there are damages to collect, he should foot the bill, not we. Vested rights are to be protected, but no man has a right to be protected in killing his neighbor.

However, they are down, the worst of them. The community has asserted its right to destroy tenements that destroy life, and for that cause. We bought the slum off in the Mulberry Bend at its own figure. On the rear tenements we set the price, and set it low. It was a long step. Bottle Alley is gone, and Bandits' Roost. Bone Alley, Thieves' Alley, and Kerosene Row,— they are all gone. Hell's Kitchen and Poverty Gap have acquired standards of decency; Poverty Gap has risen even to the height of neckties. The time is fresh in my recollection when a different kind of necktie was its pride; when the boy murderer—he was barely nineteen— who wore it on the gallows took leave of the captain of detectives with the cheerful invitation to "come over to the wake. They will have a high old time." And the event fully redeemed the promise. The whole Gap turned out to do the dead bully honor. I have not heard from the Gap, and hardly from Hell's Kitchen, in five years. The last news from the Kitchen was when the thin wedge of a column of negroes in their uptown migration, tried to squeeze in, and provoked a race war; but that in fairness should not be laid up against it. In certain local aspects it might be accounted a sacred duty; as much so as to get drunk and provoke a fight on the anniversary of the battle of the Boyne. But on the whole the Kitchen has grown orderly. The gang rarely beats a policeman nowadays, and it has not killed one in a long while.

. . .

11 Flushed with the success of many victories, we challenged the slum to a fight to the finish a year ago, and bade it come on. It came on. On our side fought the bravest and best. The man who marshaled the citizen forces for their candidate had been foremost in building homes, in erecting baths for the people, in directing the self-sacrificing labors of the oldest and wor- thiest of the agencies for improving the condi-
20 tion of the poor. With him battled men who had given lives of patient study and effort to the cause of helping their fellow men. Shoulder to shoulder with them stood the thoughtful workingman from the East Side tenement. The slum, too, marshaled its forces. Tammany pro- duced her notes. She pointed to the increased tax rate, showed what it had cost to build schools and parks and to clean house, and called it criminal recklessness. The issue was
30 made sharp and clear. The war cry of the slum was characteristic: "To hell with reform!" We all remember the result. Politics interfered, and turned victory into defeat. We were beaten. I shall never forget that election night. I walked home through the Bowery in the midnight hour, and saw it gorging itself, like a starved wolf, upon the promise of the morrow. Drunken men and women sat in every doorway, howling ribald songs and curses. Hard faces I had not
40 seen for years showed themselves about the dives. The mob made merry after its fashion. The old days were coming back. Reform was dead and decency with it.

A year later, I passed the same way on the night of election. The scene was strangely changed. The street was unusually quiet for such a time. Men stood in groups about the saloons, and talked in whispers, with serious faces. The name of Roosevelt was heard on
50 every hand. The dives were running, but there was no shouting, and violence was discouraged. When on the following day, I met the proprie- tor of one of the oldest concerns in the Bowery, —which, while doing a legitimate business, ca-

ters necessarily to its crowds, and therefore sides with them,—he told me with bitter re- proach how he had been stricken in pocket. A gambler had just been in to see him, who had come on from the far West, in anticipation of a wide-open town, and had got all ready to open a house in the Tenderloin. "He brought $40,000 to put in the business, and he came to take it away to Baltimore. Just now the cashier of _____ Bank told me that two other gentlemen —gamblers? yes, that's what you call them— had drawn $130,000 which they would have invested here, and had gone after him. Think of all that money gone to Baltimore! That's what you've done!"

I went over to police headquarters, thinking of the sad state of that man, and in the hallway I ran across two children, little tots, who were enquiring their way to "the commissioner." The older was a hunchback girl, who led her younger brother (he could not have been over five or six years old) by the hand. They ex- plained their case to me. They came from Allen Street. Some undesirable women tenants had moved into the tenement, and when complaint was made that sent the police there, the chil- dren's father, who was a poor Jewish tailor, was blamed. The tenants took it out of the boy by punching his nose till it bled. Whereupon the children went straight to Mulberry Street to see the commissioner and get justice. It was the first time in twenty years that I had known Al- len Street to come to police headquarters for justice; and in the discovery that the new idea had reached down to the little children I read the doom of the slum, despite its loud vaunt- ings.

No, it was not true that reform was dead, with decency. It was not the slum that had won; it was we who had lost. We were not up to the mark,—not yet. But New York is a many times cleaner and better city to-day than it was ten years ago. Then I was able to grasp easily the whole plan for wresting it from the neglect and indifference that had put us where we were. It was chiefly, almost wholly, remedial in its scope. Now it is preventive, constructive, and no ten men could gather all the threads and hold them. We have made, are making headway, and no Tammany has the power to stop us. She knows it, too, and is in such frantic haste to fill her pockets while she has time that she has abandoned her old ally, the tax rate, and the pretense of making bad government cheap government. She is at this moment engaged in raising taxes and assessments at one and the same time to an unheard-of figure, while salaries are being increased lavishly on every hand. We can afford to pay all she charges us for the lesson we are learning. If to that we add common sense, we shall discover the bearings of it all without trouble. Yesterday I picked up a book,—a learned disquisition on government,—and read on the title-page, "Affectionately dedicated to all who despise politics." That was not common sense. To win the battle with the slum, we must not begin by despising politics. We have been doing that too long. The politics of the slum is apt to be like the slum itself, dirty. Then it must be cleaned. It is what the fight is about. Politics is the weapon. We must learn to use it so as to cut straight and sure. That is common sense, and the golden rule as applied to Tammany.

Some years ago, the United States government conducted an inquiry into the slums of great cities. To its staff of experts was attached a chemist, who gathered and isolated a lot of bacilli with fearsome Latin names, in the tenements where he went. Among those he labeled were the *Staphylococcus pyogenes albus,* the *Micrococcus fervidosus,* the *Saccharomyces rosaceus,* and the *Bacillus fortuitus.* I made a note of the names at the time, because of the dread with which they inspired me. But I searched the collection in vain for the real bacillus of the slum. It escaped science, to be identified by human sympathy and a conscience-stricken community with that of ordinary human selfishness. The antitoxin has been found, and is applied successfully. Since justice has replaced charity on the prescription the patient is improving. And the improvement is not confined to him; it is general. Conscience is not a local issue in our day. A few years ago, a United States Senator sought reëlection on the platform that the decalogue and the golden rule were glittering generalities that had no place in politics, and lost. We have not quite reached the millennium yet, but to-day a man [Theodore Roosevelt] is governor in the Empire State who was elected on the pledge that he would rule by the ten commandments. These are facts that mean much or little, according to the way one looks at them. The significant thing is that they are facts, and that, in spite of slipping and sliding, the world moves forward, not backward. The poor we shall have always with us, but the slum we need not have. These two do not rightfully belong together. There present partnership is at once poverty's worst hardship and our worst fault.   1900

LINCOLN STEFFENS

1866–1936

ALTHOUGH LINCOLN STEFFENS studied at the University of California and at several German universities from 1885 to 1892, his true education began when, forced to earn his own living by reason of the insistence of his well-to-do father, he began his journalistic career in New York City. From reporting for the *New York Evening Post* he went, as city editor, to the *Commercial Advertiser;* but only as managing editor of *McClure's Magazine* (1902–1906) did he become widely known to the American public. His first important book, *The Shame of the Cities* (1904), had appeared in the form of articles in *McClure's.* It was notable, not so much because it revealed a factual knowledge of political corruption in American municipalities, but because it traced corruption to the doors of respectable American business leaders. Reform efforts, Steffens concluded, were bound, in the existing pattern of relationships, to be both ineffective and abnormal. Nevertheless *The Shame of the Cities* contributed to the movement for municipal reform, which included, among other things, the city manager plan and the introduction of the civil service in certain categories. The "muckraking" writings of Steffens also included *The Struggle for Self-Government* (1906).

Lincoln Steffens, Autobiography, 2 vols., New York, 1931.

Letters of Lincoln Steffens, edited with introductory notes by Ella Winter and Granville Hicks, 2 vols., New York, 1938.

Lincoln Steffens Speaking, New York, 1936.

Louis Filler, *Crusaders for American Liberalism*, New York, 1939.

» » From: THE SHAME OF THE CITIES « «

PHILADELPHIA: CORRUPT AND CONTENTED

Other American cities, no matter how bad their own condition may be, all point with scorn to Philadelphia as worse—"the worst-governed city in the country." St. Louis, Minneapolis, Pittsburgh submit with some patience to the jibes of any other community; the most
10 friendly suggestion from Philadelphia is rejected with contempt. The Philadelphians are "supine," "asleep"; hopelessly ring-ruled, they are "complacent." "Politically benighted," Philadelphia is supposed to have no light to throw upon a state of things that is almost universal.

This is not fair. Philadelphia is, indeed, corrupt; but it is not without significance. Every city and town in the country can learn something from the typical experience of this
20 great representative city. New York is excused for many of its ills because it is the metropolis, Chicago because of its forced development; Philadelphia is our "third largest" city and its growth has been gradual and natural. Immigration has been blamed for our municipal conditions; Philadelphia, with 47 per cent. of its population native-born of native-born parents, is the most American of our greater cities. It is "good," too, and intelligent. I don't know
30 just how to measure the intelligence of a community, but a Pennsylvania college professor who declared to me his belief in education for the masses as a way out of political corruption, himself justified the "rake-off" of preferred contractors on public works on the ground of a "fair business profit." Another plea we have made is that we are too busy to attend to public business, and we have promised, when we come to wealth and leisure, to do
40 better. Philadelphia has long enjoyed great and widely distributed prosperity; it is the city of homes; there is a dwelling house for every

five persons—men, women, and children,—of the population; and the people give one a sense of more leisure and repose than any community I have ever dwelt in. Some Philadelphians account for their political state on the ground of their ease and comfort. There is another class of optimists whose hope is in an "aristocracy" that is to come by and by; Philadelphia is surer that it has a "real aristocracy" than any other place in the world, but its aristocrats, with few exceptions, are in the ring, with it, or of no political use. Then we hear that we are a young people and that when we are older and "have traditions," like some of the old countries, we also will be honest. Philadelphia is one of the oldest of our cities and treasures for us scenes and relics of some of the noblest traditions of "our fair land." Yet I was told once, "for a joke," a party of boodlers counted out the "divvy" of their graft in unison with the ancient chime of Independence Hall.

Philadelphia is representative. This very "joke," told, as it was, with a laugh, is typical. All our municipal governments are more or less bad, and all our people are optimists. Philadelphia is simply the most corrupt and the most contented. Minneapolis has cleaned up, Pittsburgh has tried to, New York fights every other election, Chicago fights all the time. Even St. Louis has begun to stir (since the elections are over), and at its worst was only shameless. Philadelphia is proud; good people there defend corruption and boast of their machine. My college professor, with his philosophic view of "rake-offs," is one Philadelphia type. Another is the man, who, driven to bay with his local pride, says: "At least you must admit that our machine is the best you have ever seen."

Disgraceful? Other cities say so. But I say that if Philadelphia is a disgrace, it is a disgrace not to itself alone, nor to Pennsylvania, but to the United States and to American character. For this great city, so highly representative in other respects, is not behind in political experience, but ahead, with New York. Philadelphia is a city that has had its reforms. Having passed through all the typical stages of corruption, Philadelphia reached the period of miscellaneous loot with a boss for chief thief, under James McManes and the Gas Ring 'way back in the late sixties and seventies. This is the Tweed stage of corruption from which St. Louis, for example, is just emerging. Philadelphia, in two inspiring popular revolts, attacked the Gas Ring, broke it, and in 1885 achieved that dream of American cities—a good charter. The present condition of Philadelphia, therefore, is not that which precedes, but that which follows reform, and in this distinction lies its startling general significance. What has happened since the Bullitt Law or charter went into effect in Philadelphia may happen in any American city "after reform is over."

For reform with us is usually revolt, not government, and is soon over. Our people do not seek, they avoid self-rule, and "reforms" are spasmodic efforts to punish bad rulers and get somebody that will give us good government or something that will make it. A self-acting form of government is an ancient superstition. We are an inventive people, and we think that we shall devise some day a legal machine that will turn out good government automatically. The Philadelphians have treasured this belief longer than the rest of us and have tried it more often. Throughout their history they have sought this wonderful charter and they thought they had it when they got the Bullitt Law, which concentrates in the mayor ample power, executive and political, and complete responsibility. Moreover, it calls for very little thought and action on the part of the people. All they expected to have to do when the Bullitt Law went into effect was to elect as mayor a good business man, who, with his probity and common sense, would give them that good business administration which is the ideal of many reformers.

The Bullitt Law went into effect in 1887. A committee of twelve—four men from the Union League, four from business organizations, and four from the bosses—picked out the first man to run under it on the Republican ticket, Edwin H. Fitler, an able, upright business man, and he was elected. Strange to say, his administration was satisfactory to the citizens, who speak well of it to this day, and to the politicians also; Boss McManes (the ring was broken, not the boss) took to the next national convention from Philadelphia a delegation solid for Fitler for President of the United States. It was a farce, but it pleased Mr. Fitler, so Matthew S. Quay, the State boss, let him have a complimentary vote on the first ballot. The politicians "fooled" Mr. Fitler, and they "fooled" also the next business mayor, Edwin S. Stuart, likewise a most estimable gentleman. Under these two administrations the foundation was laid for the present government of Philadelphia, the corruption to which the Philadelphians seem so reconciled, and the machine which is "at least the best you have ever seen."

The Philadelphia machine isn't the best. It isn't sound, and I doubt if it would stand in New York or Chicago. The enduring strength of the typical American political machine is that it is a natural growth—a sucker, but deep-rooted in the people. The New Yorkers vote for Tammany Hall. The Philadelphians do not vote; they are disfranchised, and their disfranchisement is one anchor of the foundation of the Philadelphia organization.

This is no figure of speech. The honest citizens of Philadelphia have no more rights at the polls than the negroes down South. Nor do they fight very hard for this basic privilege. You can arouse their Republican ire by talking about the black Republican votes lost in the Southern States by white Democratic intimidation, but if you remind the average Philadelphian that he is in the same position, he will look startled, then say, "That's so, that's literally true, only I never thought of it in just that way." And it is literally true.

The machine controls the whole process of voting, and practices fraud at every stage. The assessor's list is the voting list, and the assessor is the machine's man. "The assessor of a division kept a disorderly house; he padded his list with fraudulent names registered from his house; two of these names were used by election officers. . . . The constable of the division kept a disreputable house; a policeman was assessed as living there. . . . The election was held in the disorderly house maintained by the assessor. . . . The man named as judge had a criminal charge for a life offense pending against him. . . . Two hundred and fifty-two votes were returned in a division that had less than one hundred legal votes within its boundaries." These extracts from a report of the Municipal League suggest the election methods. The assessor pads the list with the names of dead dogs, children, and non-existent persons. One newspaper printed the picture of a dog, another that of a little four-year-old negro boy, down on such a list. A ring orator in a speech resenting sneers at his ward as "low down" reminded his hearers that that was the ward of Independence Hall, and, naming the signers of the Declaration of Independence, he closed his highest flight of eloquence with the statement that "these men, the fathers of American liberty, voted down here once. And," he added, with a catching grin, "they vote here yet." Rudolph Blankenburg, a persistent fighter for the right and the use of the right to vote (and, by the way, an immigrant), sent out just before one election a registered letter to each voter on the rolls of a certain selected division. Sixty-three per cent. were returned marked "not at," "removed," "deceased," etc. From one four-story house where forty-four voters were addressed, eighteen letters came back undelivered; from another of forty-eight voters, came back forty-one letters; from another sixty-one out of sixty-two; from another forty-four out of forty-seven. Six houses in one division were assessed at one hundred and seventy-two voters, more than the votes cast in the previous election in any one of two hundred entire divisions.

The repeating is done boldly, for the machine controls the election officers, often choosing them from among the fraudulent names; and when no one appears to serve, assigning the heeler ready for the expected vacancy. The police are forbidden by law to stand within thirty feet of the polls, but they are at the box and they are there to see that the machine's orders are obeyed and that repeaters whom they help to furnish are permitted to vote without "intimidation" on the names they, the police, have supplied. The editor of an anti-machine paper who was looking about for himself once told me that a ward leader who knew him well asked him into a polling place. "I'll show you how it's done," he said, and he had the repeaters go round and round voting again and again on the names handed them on slips. "But," as the editor said, "that isn't the way it's done." The repeaters go from one polling place to another, voting on slips, and on their return rounds change coats, hats, etc. The business proceeds with very few hitches; there is more jesting than fighting. Violence in the past has had its effect; and is not often necessary nowadays, but if it is needed the police are there to apply it. Several citizens told me that they had seen the police help to beat citizens or election officers who were trying to do their duty, then arrest the victims. . . .

1903

JANE ADDAMS

1860–1935

AFTER GRADUATING from Rockford College in 1881 and studying social problems in Europe, Jane Addams, with Ellen Gates Starr, founded Hull House in Chicago. Modeled after Toynbee Hall in London, this social center for immigrants profoundly influenced the pattern of social service activities throughout the United States. But Jane Addams's interest in social problems extended beyond the immigrant. Honesty in municipal government and the spiritual well-being of all youth in great urban communities enlisted her wise and human interest. The following selection from *The Spirit of Youth and the City Streets* (1909) reflects her intelligent understanding of the problems of homeless young people in a great metropolitan center.

Jane Addams, *Twenty Years at Hull House*, New York, 1910.
Jane Addams, *The Second Twenty Years at Hull House*, New York, 1930.
J. W. Linn, *Jane Addams*, New York, 1935.

» » *From:* THE SPIRIT OF YOUTH « «

CHAPTER I

YOUTH IN THE CITY

Nothing is more certain than that each generation longs for a reassurance as to the value and charm of life, and is secretly afraid lest it lose its sense of the youth of the earth. This is doubtless one reason why it so passionately cherishes its poets and artists who have been able to explore for themselves and to reveal to others the perpetual springs of life's self-renewal.

And yet the average man cannot obtain this desired reassurance through literature, nor yet through glimpses of earth and sky. It can come to him only through the chance embodiment of joy and youth which life itself may throw in his way. It is doubtless true that for the mass of men the message is never so unchallenged and so invincible as when embodied in youth itself. One generation after another has depended upon its young to equip it with gaiety and enthusiasm, to persuade it that living is a pleasure, until men everywhere have anxiously provided channels through which this wine of life might flow, and be preserved for their delight. The classical city promoted play with careful solicitude, building the theater and stadium as it built the market place and the temple. The Greeks held their games so integral a part of religion and patriotism that they came to expect from their poets the highest utterances at the very moments when the sense of pleasure released the national life. In the medieval city the knights held their tourneys, the guilds their pageants, the people their dances, and the church made festival for its most cherished saints with gay street processions, and presented a drama in which no less a theme than the history of creation became a matter of thrilling interest. Only in the modern city have men concluded that it is no longer necessary for the municipality to provide for the insatiable desire for play. In so far as they have acted upon this conclusion, they have entered upon a most difficult and dangerous experiment; and this at the very moment when the city has become distinctly industrial, and daily labor is continually more monotonous and subdivided. We forget how new the modern city is, and how short the span of time in which we have assumed that we can eliminate public provision for recreation.

A further difficulty lies in the fact that this industrialism has gathered together multitudes of eager young creatures from all quarters of the earth as a labor supply for the countless factories and workshops, upon which the present industrial city is based. Never before in civilization have such numbers of young girls been suddenly released from the protection of the home and permitted to walk unattended upon city streets and to work under alien roofs; for the first time they are being prized more for their labor power than for their innocence, their tender beauty, their ephemeral gaiety. Society cares more for the products they manufacture than for their immemorial ability to reaffirm the charm of existence. Never before have such numbers of young boys earned money independently of the family life, and felt themselves free to spend it as they choose in the midst of vice deliberately disguised as pleasure.

This stupid experiment of organizing work and failing to organize play has, of course, brought about a fine revenge. The love of pleasure will not be denied, and when it has turned into all sorts of malignant and vicious appetites, then we, the middle aged, grow quite distracted and resort to all sorts of restrictive measures. We even try to dam up the sweet fountain itself because we are affrighted by these neglected streams; but almost worse than the restrictive measures is our apparent belief that the city itself has no obligation in the matter, an assumption upon which the modern city turns over to commercialism practically all the provisions for public recreation.

Quite as one set of men has organized the young people into industrial enterprises in order to profit from their toil, so another set of men and also of women, I am sorry to say, have entered the neglected field of recreation and have organized enterprises which make profit out of this invincible love of pleasure.

In every city arise so-called "places"—"gin-palaces," they are called in fiction; in Chicago we euphemistically say merely "places,"—in which alcohol is dispensed, not to allay thirst, but, ostensibly to stimulate gaiety, it is sold really in order to empty pockets. Huge dance halls are opened to which hundreds of young people are attracted, many of whom stand wistfully outside a roped circle, for it requires five cents to procure within it for five minutes the sense of allurement and intoxication which is sold in lieu of innocent pleasure. These coarse and illicit merrymakings remind one of the unrestrained jollities of Restoration London, and they are indeed their direct descendants, properly commercialized, still confusing joy with lust, and gaiety with debauchery. Since the soldiers of Cromwell shut up the people's playhouses and destroyed their pleasure fields, the Anglo-Saxon city has turned over the provision for public recreation to the most evilminded and the most unscrupulous members of the community. We see thousands of girls walking up and down the streets on a pleasant evening with no chance to catch a sight of pleasure even through a lighted window, save as these lurid places provide it. Apparently the modern city sees in these girls only two possibilities, both of them commercial: first, a chance to utilize by day their new and tender labor power in its factories and shops, and then another chance in the evening to extract from them their petty wages by pandering to their love of pleasure.

As these overworked girls stream along the street, the rest of us see only the self-conscious walk, the giggling speech, the preposterous clothing. And yet through the huge hat, with its wilderness of bedraggled feathers, the girl announces to the world that she is here. She demands attention to the fact of her existence, she states that she is ready to live, to take her place in the world. The most precious moment in human development is the young creature's assertion that he is unlike any other human being, and has an individual contribution to make to the world. The variation from the established type is at the root of all change, the only possible basis for progress, all that keeps life from growing unprofitably stale and repetitious.

Is it only the artists who really see these young creatures as they are—the artists who are themselves endowed with immortal youth? Is it our disregard of the artist's message which makes us so blind and so stupid, or are we so under the influence of our *Zeitgeist* that we can detect only commercial values

in the young as well as in the old? It is as if our eyes were holden to the mystic beauty, the redemptive joy, the civic pride which these multitudes of young people might supply to our dingy towns.

The young creatures themselves piteously look all about them in order to find an adequate means of expression for their most precious message: One day a serious young man came to Hull-House with his pretty young sister who, he explained, wanted to go somewhere every single evening, "although she could only give the flimsy excuse that the flat was too little and too stuffy to stay in." In the difficult rôle of elder brother, he had done his best, stating that he had taken her "to all the missions in the neighborhood, that she had had a chance to listen to some awful good sermons and to some elegant hymns, but that some way she did not seem to care for the society of the best Christian people." The little sister reddened painfully under this cruel indictment and could offer no word of excuse, but a curious thing happened to me. Perhaps it was the phrase "the best Christian people," perhaps it was the delicate color of her flushing cheeks and her swimming eyes, but certain it is, that instantly and vividly there appeared to my mind the delicately tinted piece of wall in a Roman catacomb where the early Christians, through a dozen devices of spring flowers, skipping lambs and a shepherd tenderly guiding the young, had indelibly written down that the Christian message is one of inexpressible joy. Who is responsible for forgetting this message delivered by the "best Christian people" two thousand years ago? Who is to blame that the lambs, the little ewe lambs, have been so caught upon the brambles?

But quite as the modern city wastes this most valuable moment in the life of the girl, and drives into all sorts of absurd and obscure expressions her love and yearning towards the world in which she forecasts her destiny, so it often drives the boy into gambling and drinking in order to find his adventure.

.   .   .

One Sunday night at twelve o'clock I had occasion to go into a large public dance hall. As I was standing by the rail looking for the girl I had come to find, a young man approached me and quite simply asked me to introduce him to some "nice girl," saying that he did not know any one there. On my replying that a public dance hall was not the best place in which to look for a nice girl, he said: "But I don't know any other place where there is a chance to meet any kind of girl. I'm awfully lonesome since I came to Chicago." And then he added rather defiantly: "Some nice girls do come here! It's one of the best halls in town." He was voicing the "bitter loneliness" that many city men remember to have experienced during the first years after they had "come up to town." Occasionally the right sort of man and girl meet each other in these dance halls and the romance with such a tawdry beginning ends happily and respectably. But, unfortunately, mingled with the respectable young men seeking to form the acquaintance of young women through the only channel which is available to them, are many young fellows of evil purpose, and among the girls who have left their lonely boarding houses or rigid homes for a "little fling" are likewise women who openly desire to make money from the young men whom they meet, and back of it all is the desire to profit by the sale of intoxicating and "doctored" drinks.

We cannot afford to be ungenerous to the city in which we live without suffering the penalty which lack of fair interpretation always entails. Let us know the modern city in its weakness and wickedness, and then seek to rectify and purify it until it shall be free at least from the grosser temptations which now beset the young people who are living in its tenement houses and working in its factories. The mass of these young people are possessed of good intentions and they are equipped with a certain understanding of city life. This itself could be made a most valuable social instrument toward securing innocent recreation and better social organization. They are already serving the city in so far as it is honey-combed with mutual benefit societies, with "pleasure clubs," with organizations connected with churches and factories which are filling a genuine social need. And yet the whole apparatus for supplying pleasure is wretchedly inadequate and full of danger to whomsoever may approach it. Who is responsible for its inadequacy and dangers? We certainly cannot expect the fathers and mothers who have come to the city from farms or who have emigrated from other lands to appreciate or rectify these dangers. We cannot expect the young people

themselves to cling to conventions which are totally unsuited to modern city conditions, nor yet to be equal to the task of forming new conventions through which this more agglomerate social life may express itself. Above all we cannot hope that they will understand the emotional force which seizes them and which, when it does not find the traditional line of domesticity, serves as a cancer in the very tissues of society and as a disrupter of the securest social bonds. No attempt is made to treat the manifestations of this fundamental instinct with dignity or to give it possible social utility. The spontaneous joy, the clamor for pleasure, the desire of the young people to appear finer and better and altogether more lovely than they really are, the idealization not only of each other but of the whole earth which they regard but as a theater for their noble exploits, the unworldly ambitions, the romantic hopes, the make-believe world in which they live, if properly utilized, what might they not do to make our sordid cities more beautiful, more companionable? And yet at the present moment every city is full of young people who are utterly bewildered and uninstructed in regard to the basic experience which must inevitably come to them, and which has varied, remote, and indirect expressions.

Even those who may not agree with the authorities who claim that it is this fundamental sex susceptibility which suffuses the world with its deepest meaning and beauty, and furnishes the momentum towards all art, will perhaps permit me to quote the classical expressions of this view as set forth in that ancient and wonderful conversation between Socrates and the wise woman Diotima. Socrates asks: "What are they doing who show all this eagerness and heat which is called love? And what is the object they have in view? Answer me." Diotima replies: "I will teach you. The object which they have in view is birth in beauty, whether of body or soul. . . . For love, Socrates, is not as you imagine the love of the beautiful only . . . but the love of birth in beauty, because to the mortal creature generation is a sort of eternity and immortality."

To emphasize the eternal aspects of love is not of course an easy undertaking, even if we follow the clue afforded by the heart of every generous lover. His experience at least in certain moments tends to pull him on and out from the passion for one to an enthusiasm for that highest beauty and excellence of which the most perfect form is but an inadequate expression. Even the most loutish tenement-house youth vaguely feels this, and at least at rare intervals reveals it in his talk to his "girl." His memory unexpectedly brings hidden treasures to the surface of consciousness and he recalls the more delicate and tender experiences of his childhood and earlier youth. "I remember the time when my little sister died, that I rode out to the cemetery feeling that everybody in Chicago had moved away from the town to make room for that kid's funeral, everything was so darned lonesome and yet it was kind of peaceful too." Or, "I never had a chance to go into the country when I was a kid, but I remember one day when I had to deliver a package way out on the West Side, that I saw a flock of sheep in Douglas Park. I had never thought that a sheep could be anywhere but in a picture, and when I saw those big white spots on the green grass beginning to move and to turn into sheep, I felt exactly as if Saint Cecilia had come out of her frame over the organ and was walking in the park." Such moments come into the life of the most prosaic youth living in the most crowded quarters of the cities. What do we do to encourage and to solidify those moments, to make them come true in our dingy towns, to give them expression in forms of art?

We not only fail in this undertaking but even debase existing forms of art. We are informed by high authority that there is nothing in the environment to which youth so keenly responds as to music, and yet the streets, the vaudeville shows, the five-cent theaters are full of the most blatant and vulgar songs. The trivial and obscene words, the meaningless and flippant airs run through the heads of hundreds of young people for hours at a time while they are engaged in monotonous factory work. We totally ignore that ancient connection between music and morals which was so long insisted upon by philosophers as well as poets. The street music has quite broken away from all control, both of the educator and the patriot, and we have grown singularly careless in regard to its influence upon young people. Although we legislate against it in saloons because of its dangerous influence there, we constantly permit music on the street to incite that which should be controlled, to degrade that which should be exalted, to make sensuous that which might be lifted into the realm of the higher imagination.

Our attitude towards music is typical of our carelessness towards all those things which make for common joy and for the restraints of higher civilization on the streets. It is as if our cities had not yet developed a sense of responsibility in regard to the life of the streets, and continually forget that recreation is stronger than vice, and that recreation alone can stifle the lust for vice.

Perhaps we need to take a page from the philosophy of the Greeks to whom the world of fact was also the world of the ideal, and to whom the realization of what ought to be, involved not the destruction of what was, but merely its perfecting upon its own lines. To the Greeks virtue was not a hard conformity to a law felt as alien to the natural character, but a free expression of the inner life. To treat thus the fundamental susceptibility of sex which now so bewilders the street life and drives young people themselves into all sorts of difficulties, would mean to loosen it from the things of sense and to link it to the affairs of the imagination. It would mean to fit to this gross and heavy stuff the wings of the mind, to scatter from it "the clinging mud of banality and vulgarity," and to speed it on through our city streets amid spontaneous laughter, snatches of lyric song, the recovered forms of old dances, and the traditional rondels of merry games. It would thus bring charm and beauty to the prosaic city and connect it subtly with the arts of the past as well as with the vigor and renewed life of the future.　　　　1909

NEGRO MIGRANTS

ONE OF THE most striking phenomena in the rapid growth of cities was the migration of Negroes from rural areas in the South to urban centers on both sides of the Mason and Dixon line. This migration became especially marked during the First World War when the stream of unskilled immigrants was suddenly cut off by events in the Old World. The following editorial remarks of Emmett J. Scott, who collected many letters written by Negro migrants, illustrate the importance of this type of material both to the student of the Negro and of urbanization:

"The exodus of the Negroes during the World War, the most significant event in our recent internal history, may be profitably studied by reading the letters of the various migrants. The investigator has been fortunate in finding letters from Negroes of all conditions in almost all parts of the South and these letters are based on almost every topic of concern to humanity. These documents will serve as a guide in getting at the motive dominant in the minds of these refugees and at the real situation during the upheaval. As a whole, these letters throw much light on all phases of Negro life and, in setting forth the causes of unrest in the South, portray the character of the whites with whom the blacks have had to do.

"These letters are of further value for information concerning the Negroes in the North. From these reliable sources the student can learn where the Negroes settled, what they engaged in, and how they have readjusted themselves in a new situation. Here may be seen the effects of the loss resulting from the absence of immigrants from Europe, the conflict of the laboring elements, the evidences of racial troubles and the menace of mob rule."

» » *From:* LETTERS OF NEGRO MIGRANTS OF « «
1916–1918 [1]

LETTERS ASKING FOR INFORMATION ABOUT THE NORTH

Sanford, Fla., April 27, 1917.

Dear Sir: I have seen through the Chicago Defender that you and the people of Chicago are helping newcomers. I am asking you for some information about conditions in some small town near Chicago.

There are some families here thinking of moving up, and are desirous of knowing what to expect before leaving. Please state about treatment, work, rent and schools. Please answer at some spare time.

Houston, Texas, April 20, 1917.

Dear Sir: wanted to leave the South and Go and Place where a man will Be any thing Except A Ker I thought would write you for Advise As where would be a Good Place for a Comporedly young man That want to Better his Standing who has a very Promising young Family.

I am 30 years old and have Good Experence in Freight Handler and Can fill Position from Truck to Agt.

would like Chicago or Philadelphia But I

dont Care where so long as I Go where a man is a man

Hopeing hear of you soon as I want to leave on or about 15 day of May I am yours as Ever.

Lexington, Miss., May 12–17.

My dear Mr. H——:— I am writing to you for some information and assistance if you can give it. 10

I am a young man and am disable, in a very great degree, to do hard manual labor. I was educated in Alcorn College and have been teaching a few years: but ah: me the Superintendent under whom we poor colored teachers have to teach cares less for a colored man than he does for the vilest beast. I am compelled to teach 150 children without any assistance and receives only $27.00 a month, the white with 30 get $100. 20

I am so sick I am so tired of such conditions that I sometime think that life for me is not worth while and most eminently believe with Patrick Henry "Give me liberty or give me death." If I was a strong able bodied man I would have gone from here long ago, but this handicaps me and, I must make inquiries before I leap.

Mr. H.——, do you think you can assist me to a position I am good at stenography type- 30

[1] Collected under the direction of Emmett J. Scott.

writing and bookkeeping or any kind of work not to rough or heavy. I am 4 feet 6 in high and weigh 105 pounds.

I will gladly give any other information you may desire and will greatly appreciate any assistance you may render me.

Winina, Miss., Mar the 19 1917.

My dear friend: it is With murch pleaser
10 that i rite to You to let You no i recd Your letter & Was glad to hear from you all so i excepts all you Said that you wood do for me so i am a Painter and Carter to So i am willing to learn inneything in works kind So mr. —— I thank You for Your kindes for all of Your aid so i am a Barber to so i am a good farmer to al all kind So i am not Set do Wn at all so if You Can healp pleas do So So i have niCe famely so i will tell you i am a Curch member for 38 years
20 i and all my famely but 3 children so i am not a de Sever So mr. —— i wood ask you for if the monney So i Was so glad to get your letter dear Sir When I com up thire look for me at your offes Pleas so mr —— i all waYs hold gob When i get wone So in god name pleas healp me up there and i will pay you When i com up thire mr —— I Cant raise my famely hear i wanter to So this all Your friend

Beaumont, Texas, May 7, 1917.

31 *Dear Sir:* I see in one of your recent issue of collored men woanted in the North I wish you would help me to get a position in the North I have no trade I have been working for one company eight years and there is no advancement here for me and I would like to come where I can better my condition I woant work and not affraid to work all I wish is a chance to make good. I believe I would like
40 machinist helper or Molder helper. If you can help me in any way it will be highly appreciate hoping to hear from you soon

De Ridder, La., April 29, 1917.

Dear Sir: there is lots of us southern mens wants transportation and we want to leave ratway as soon as you let us here from you some of us is married mens who need work we would like to bring our wife with us there is 20 head
50 of good mens want transportation and if you need us let us no by return mail we all are redy only wants here from you there may be more all of our peoples wont to leave here and I want you to send as much as 20 tickets any way

I will get you up plenty hands to do most any kind of work all you have to do is to send for them. looking to here from you. This is among us collerd.

Mobile, Ala., May 15, 1917.

Dear Sir and Brother: I am in the information of your labores league and while in this city I have been asked about the conditions of work in the north and at the same time we have about 300 men here in this city of different trades. Some are farmers, mail men iron and stell workers, mechanics and of all classes of work. They ask me in their union to find out just the conditions of the afair. They wants to know if they can go to work in one or two days after they get there? if so some of them can pay all of their fair some half and some wants to come on conditions. will the company send them a pass and let them pay them back weekly? if so I can send 500 more or less in order that you may know who I am I will send you some of my papers that you may know what I stand for and what I have been taking along. please let me hear from you at once and what you think about it.

LETTERS ABOUT THE GREAT NORTHERN DRIVE OF 1917

Mobile, Ala., April 25, 1917.

Sir: I was reading in theat paper about the Colored race and while reading it I seen in it where cars would be here for the 15 of May which is one month from to day. Will you be so kind as to let me know where they are coming to and I will be glad to know because I am a poor woman and have a husband and five children living and three dead one single and two twin girls six months old today and my husband can hardly make bread for them in Mobile. This is my native home but it is not fit to live in just as the Chicago Defender say it says the truth and my husband only get $1.50 a day and pays $7.50 a month for house rent and can hardly feed me and his self and children. I am the mother of 8 children 25 years old and I want to get out of this dog hold because I dont know what I am raising them up for in this place and I want to get to Chicago where I know they will be raised and my husband crazy to get there because he know he can get more to raise his children and will you please let me know where the cars is going to stop to so that he can come where he can take care of me and my children. He get there a while and then he can send for me. I heard they wasnt coming here so I sent to find out and he can go and meet them at the place they are going and go from there to Chicago. No more at present. hoping to hear from you soon from your needed and worried friend.

LETTERS CONCERNING WHICH SECRECY WAS ENJOINED

Laurel, Miss., 4–30–17.

Dear Sir: In reading your defender paper every week find every thing so true makes me want to come more every day. so i am thinking of coming in a few days decided to write you in regards to getting a job that will suit my age. I am 48 years old am in very good helth and likes to work just like the days come. Have farm the biggest position of my life untill seven years go. i follow publick work untill now would not like for my name to be publish in the paper.

Sherman, Ga., Nov. 28, 1916.

Dear sir: This letter comes to ask for all infirmations concerning employment in your conection in the warmest climate. Now I am in a family of (11) eleven more or less boys and girls (men and women) mixed sizes who want to go north as soon as arrangements can be made and employment given places for shelter an so en (etc) now this are farming people they were raised on the farm and are good farm hands I of course have some experence and qualefication as a coman school teacher and hotel waiter and along few other lines.

I wish you would write me at your first chance and tell me if you can give us employment at what time and about what wages will you pay and what kind of arrangement can be made for our shelter. Tell me when can you best use us now or later.

Will you send us tickets if so on what terms and at what price what is the cost per head and by what route should we come. We are Negroes and try to show ourselves worthy of all we may get from any friendly source we endeavor to be true to all good causes, if you can we thank you to help us to come north as soon as you can.

LETTERS STATING THAT WAGES RECEIVED ARE NOT SATIS-FACTORY

Brookhaven, Miss., April 24, 1917.

Gents: The cane growers of Louisiana have stopped the exodus from New Orleans, claiming shortage of labor which will result in a sugar famine.

Now these laborers thus employed receive only 85 cents a day and the high cost of living makes it a serious question to live.

There is a great many race people around here who desires to come north but have waited rather late to avoid car fare, which they have not got. isnt there some way to get the concerns who wants labor, to send passes here or elsewhere so they can come even if they have to pay out of the first months wages? Please done publish this letter but do what you can towards helping them to get away. If the R. R. Co. would run a low rate excursion they could leave that way. Please ans.

Fort Gaines, Ga., Oct. 9, 1916.

Dear Sir: Replying to your letter dates Oct. 6th the situation here is this: Heavy rains and Boll weavel has caused a loss of about 9,000 bales of cotton which together with seed at the prevailing high prices would have brought $900,000.00 the average crop here being 11,000 bales, but this years' crop was exceptionally fine and abundant and promised good yeald until the two calamities hit us.

Now the farmer is going to see that his personal losses are minimised as far as possible and this has left the average farm laborer with nothing to start out with to make a crop for next year, nobody wants to carry him till next fall, he might make peanuts and might not, so taking it alround, he wants to migrate to where he can see a chance to get work.

I have carpenters, one brick mason, blacksmith, etc., wanting to leave here, can send you their names if definate proposition is held out.

Atlanta, Ga., April 30, 1917.

Dear Sir: In reading the Chicago Defender I find that there are many jobs open for workmen, I wish that you would or can secure me a position in some of the northern cities; as a workman and not as a loafer. One who is willing to do any kind of hard in side or public work, have had broad experience in machinery and other work of the kind. A some what alround man can also cook, well trained devuloped man; have travel extensively through the western and southern states; A good strong *morial religious* man no habits. I will accept transportation on advance and deducted from my wages later. It does not matter where, that is; as to city, country, town or state since you secure the positions. I am quite sure you will be delighted in securing a position for a man of this description. I'll assure you will not regret of so doing. Hoping to hear from you soon.

LETTERS ABOUT BETTER EDUCATIONAL FACILITIES

Anniston, Ala., April 23, 1917.

Dear sir: Please gave me some infamation about coming north i can do any kind of work from a truck gardin to farming i would like to leave here and i cant make no money to leave I ust make enought to live one please let me here from you at once i want to get where i can put my children in schol.

Augusta, Ga., April 27,

Sir: Being a constant reader of your paper, I thought of no one better than you to write for information.

I'm desirous of leaving the south but before so doing I want to be sure of a job before pulling out. I'm a member of the race, a normal and colloege school graduate, a man of a family and can give reference. Confidentially this communication between you and me is to be kept a secret.

My children I wished to be educated in a different community than here. Where the school facilities are better and less prejudice shown and in fact where advantages are better for our people in all respect. At present I have a good position but I desire to leave the south. A good position even tho' its a laborer's job paying $4.50 or $5.00 a day will suit me till I can do better. Let it be a job there or any where else in the country, just is it is east or west. I'm quite sure you can put me in touch with some one. I'm a letter carrier now and am also a druggist by profession. Perhaps I may through your influence get a transfer to some eastern or western city.

Nevada or California as western states, I prefer, and I must say that I have nothing against Detroit, Mich.

I shall expect an early reply. Remember keep this a secret please until I can perfect some arrangements.

1916–1918

» » *Immigration and Its Restriction* « «

1865-1930

» »   « «

ACROSS THE WESTERN OCEAN

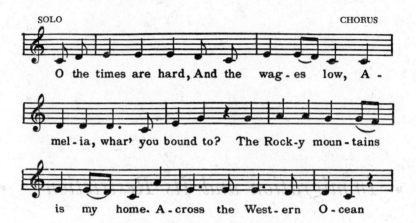

SOLO   CHORUS

O the times are hard, And the wag-es low, A-
mel-ia, whar' you bound to? The Rock-y moun-tains
is my home. A-cross the West-ern O-cean

That land of promise there you'll see,
Amelia, whar' you bound to?
I'm bound across that western sea,
To join the Irish Army.

To Liverpool I'll take my way,
Amelia, whar' you bound to?
To Liverpool that Yankee school,
A-cross the western ocean.

There's Liverpool Pat with his tarpaulin hat,
Amelia, whar' you bound to?
And Yankee John the packet rat,
A-cross the western ocean.

Beware these packet-ships, I pray,
Amelia, whar' you bound to?
They steal your stores and clothes away,
A-cross the western ocean.

About 1850, when the old sailing packet-ships carried swarms of
Irish emigrants to the United States, shanties were sung which illustrated various phases and moods incident to the wandering of the
peoples. "Across the Western Ocean" was a popular song which reflects some of the vicissitudes as well as hopes of the immigrants. This
song is included by permission of Mr. W. B. Whall, of James Brown
and Sons, in whose *Sea Songs and Shanties* (Glasgow, 1920) it
appears.

» » « «

Immigration and Its Restriction

ALTHOUGH the urban problem was complicated by the presence of immense numbers of immigrants who seemed unable or unwilling to become assimilated into American life, immigration was so important an issue that it transcended problems of the city and became sharpened into a great national debate. Americans took sides, some favoring the restriction of immigration, others favoring the continuation of the open-door policy that had characterized national policy from the beginning. In taking sides some were influenced by personal and material or class interests; others were not consciously affected by any of these.

The sheer bulk of the immigration in the decades between the Civil War and the World War was staggering to the imagination. But it was not only the vast size of this immigration which excited fears. After 1880 the pattern of immigration itself changed. Until that time the greatest numbers of immigrants had come from Northern Europe, and had, on the whole, shown remarkable talents for assimilating American culture. But in the last two decades of the century, and in the years preceding the outbreak of the World War, relatively fewer immigrants came from Germany, the Scandinavian lands, and the British Isles. The overwhelming number came from Italy, Greece, and Russia. These peoples sought our shores partly because of religious and racial persecutions and partly because of the greater economic and cultural opportunities in the new world. But they showed less ability to become Americanized than had the older immigrants.

Shortly after 1890, when commentators called attention to the fact that the era of free lands had come to an end, the sentiment for restricting immigration began to be organized. Some who favored restriction did so on the ground that America no longer had ample resources for such augmentations of population as unrestricted immigration invited. Others were convinced that the older national stock was superior to the new, and that the older would be overwhelmed unless the gates were closed. Still others, ardent and militant patriots and nationalists, were anxious to promote nationalism by Americanizing such minorities as we had and by checking the coming of more hordes who would render the task the more difficult. On the other hand many American idealists believed that the country should continue to be the asylum for the oppressed of all the world. To their way of thinking the true American race was a polyglot race; and the essence of Americanism was the melting-pot, the unlimited capacity, in other words, of America to absorb peoples from all the world and to create a new and superior race from the mixing.

While most employers of labor continued to welcome the immigrant by reason of his docility and willingness to work for lower wages than the American worker would accept, the advance of technology made the employer in mass industries less dependent on cheap, unskilled labor. When immigration was temporarily cut off with the outbreak of the World War in 1914, the employer found that he could use to good advantage the Southern Negro. Moreover, some among the employing and conservative class had always feared that the immigration would contribute to the growth of anarchism and socialism. And American labor resented the presence of the foreigner, not only because he worked for lower wages but because the national rivalries among the newcomers made it difficult to organize them in trade unions.

In 1921 and in 1924 the fear that the country would be flooded by immigrants seeking refuge from war-distressed Europe was the immediate reason for the first drastic laws which restricted immigration in accordance with the quota policy. This policy was designed not only to restrict immigration quantitatively but to cast the scale in favor of the immigrant from northern Europe as against the one from southern and eastern Europe. Orientals had long before been restricted.

But the immigration problem can not be grasped without reference to the feelings and fears of the immigrant himself. Among the many contributions which the immigrant made to American industrialism and American culture, one has been inadequately appreciated. The immigrant's vision of what America stood for, his identification of America with opportunity and freedom, reinforced in the minds of Americans themselves the golden promise of American life.

» »   « «

THOMAS BAILEY ALDRICH

1836–1907

ALTHOUGH THOMAS BAILEY ALDRICH spent many years of his life in New York and Boston during the very time when those cities were receiving hundreds of thousands of immigrants, his affiliations were such that he had no firsthand knowledge of them. Neither as an editor of literary journals in antebellum New York, nor as a correspondent during the Civil War, nor as the dominant force on *The Atlantic Monthly* (1881–1890) did he observe with any sympathy or sensitiveness any aspect of American life save that of the favored class to which he belonged. His best work, such as *The Story of a Bad Boy* (1870) and *Marjorie Daw* (1873), indeed showed little of the essential social conservatism that characterized some of his prose and verse; but the poem "Unguarded Gates" (1895) is an interesting example of the exclusive "Americanism" which failed to see the profits which the exploitation of the immigrant had brought to American industry and which at the same time overlooked the human advantages which an asylum in the New World had given to the downtrodden of Europe.

A. P. Ward, *Annotated List of the Works of Thomas Bailey Aldrich*, New York, 1907.
The Writings of Thomas Bailey Aldrich, Ponkapog Edition, 9 vols., Boston and New York, c. 1897–c. 1911.
Ferris Greenslet, *Life of Thomas Bailey Aldrich*, Boston, 1908.

»   »   UNGUARDED GATES   «   «

Wide open and unguarded stand our gates,
Named of the four winds, North, South, East,
 and West;
Portals that lead to an enchanted land
Of cities, forests, fields of living gold,
Vast prairies, lordly summits touched with
 snow,
Majestic rivers sweeping proudly past

The Arab's date-palm and the Norseman's
 pine—
A realm wherein are fruits of every zone,
Airs of all climes, for lo! throughout the year
The red rose blossoms somewhere—a rich
 land,   10
A later Eden planted in the wilds,
With not an inch of earth within its bound

But if a slave's foot press it sets him free.
Here, it is written, Toil shall have its wage,
And Honor honor, and the humblest man
Stand level with the highest in the law.
Of such a land have men in dungeons dreamed,
And with the vision brightening in their eyes
Gone smiling to the fagot and the sword.

    Wide open and unguarded stand our gates,
And through them presses a wild motley
    throng—   21
Men from the Volga and the Tartar steppes,
Featureless figures of the Hoang-Ho,
Malayan, Scythian, Teuton, Kelt, and Slav,
Flying the Old World's poverty and scorn;
These bringing with them unknown gods and
    rites,
Those, tiger passions, here to stretch their
    claws.

In street and alley what strange tongues are
    loud,
Accents of menace alien to our air,
Voices that once the Tower of Babel knew! 30

    O Liberty, white Goddess! is it well
To leave the gates unguarded? On thy breast
Fold Sorrow's children, soothe the hurts of
    fate,
Lift the down-trodden, but with hand of steel
Stay those who to thy sacred portals come
To waste the gifts of freedom. Have a care
Lest from thy brow the clustered stars be
    torn
And trampled in the dust. For so of old
The thronging Goth and Vandal trampled
    Rome,
And where the temples of the Caesars stood
The lean wolf unmolested made her lair. 41

MARY ANTIN

1881–

MARY ANTIN migrated from Russia in 1894. After studying at Teachers College and Barnard, she married Professor Amadeus W. Gravau of Columbia University. Her books, which include *From Polotzk to Boston* (1899) and *The Promised Land* (1912), are sensitive portrayals of the immigrant problem from the point of view of an immigrant who responded to the democratic values in the American tradition. Mary Antin's books stimulated other immigrants to write their autobiographies. But more important, they did much to reinforce in American consciousness such idealistic aspects of American nationalism as the idea that the United States is not only an asylum for oppressed immigrants but a promise, a symbol, of a freer life than the mass of plain people, native and foreign-born alike, had known, or could know, elsewhere.

American Magazine, 77 (March 14, 1914).

» » *From:* THEY WHO KNOCK AT OUR GATES « «

CHAPTER II

JUDGES IN THE GATE

    . . . If it was a merit in 1620 to flee from religious persecution, and in 1776 to fight against political oppression, then many of the Russian refugees of today are a little ahead of the Mayflower troop, because they have in their own lifetime sustained the double ordeal of fight and flight, with all their attendant risks and shocks.

    To obtain a nice balance between the relative merits of these two groups of rebels, we remind ourselves that, for sheer adventurousness, migration to America to-day is not to be mentioned on the same page with the magnificent exploit of 1620, and we reflect that the

moral glory of the revolution of 1776 is infinitely greater than that of any subsequent revolt; because that, too, was a pathfinding adventure, with no compass but faith, no chart
but philosophical invention. On the other hand,
it is plain that the Russian revolutionists moved
against greater odds than the American colonists had to face. The Russians had to plot in
secret, assemble in the dark, and strike with
10 bare fists; all this under the very nose of the
Czar, with the benighted condition of the Russian masses hanging like a cloud over their
enterprise. The colonists were able to lay the
train of revolution in the most public manner,
they had the local government in their hands,
a considerable militia obedient to their own
captains, and the advantage of distance from
the enemy's resources, with a populace advanced in civic experience promising support
20 to the leaders.

And what a test of heroism was that which
the harsh nature of the Russian Government
afforded! The American rebels risked their
charters and their property; for some of them
dungeons waited, and for the leaders dangled
a rope, no doubt. But confiscation is not so
bitter as Siberian exile, and a halter is less painful than the barbed whip of the Cossacks.
The Minutemen at Concord Bridge defied
30 a bully; the rioters in St. Petersburg challenged a tiger. And first of all to be thrust into
the cage would be the rebels of Jewish faith,
and nobody knew that better than the Jews
themselves. . . .

From these unexpected exploits of the craven
Jew and the degenerate Greek, it would seem
as if the different elements of the despised
"new" immigration only await a spectacular
opportunity to prove themselves equal to the
40 "old" in civic valor. But if contemporary history
fails to provide a war or revolution for each of
our foreign nationalities, we are still not without the means of gauging the idealistic capacity
of the aliens. Next after liberty, the Puritans
loved education; and to-day, if you examine the
registers of the schools and colleges they
founded, you will find the names of recent
immigrants thickly sprinkled from A to Z, and
topping the honor ranks nine times out of ten.
50 All readers of newspapers know the bare facts,
—each commencement season, the prizewin-
ners are announced in a string of unpronounce-
able foreign names; and every schoolteacher
in the immigrant section of the larger cities
has a collection of picturesque anecdotes to

contribute: of heroic sacrifices for the sake of
a little reading and writing; of young girls
stitching away their youth to keep a brother
in college; of whole families cheerfully starving
together to save one gifted child from the
factory.

Go from the public school to the public
library, from the library to the social settlement, and you will carry away the same story
in a hundred different forms. The good people
behind the desks in these public places are
fond of repeating that they can hardly keep
up with the intellectual demands of their immigrant neighbors. In the experience of the
librarians it is the veriest commonplace that the
classics have the greatest circulation in the immigrant quarters of the city; and the most
touching proof of reverence for learning often
comes from the illiterate among the aliens. On
the East Side of New York, "Teacher" is a
being adored. Said a bedraggled Jewish mother
to her little boy who had affronted his teacher,
"Don't you know that teachers is holy?" Perhaps these are the things the teachers have in
mind when they speak with a tremor of the
immense reward of work in the public schools.

That way of speaking is the fashion among
workers of all sorts in the educational institutions where foreigners attend in numbers. Get
a group of settlement people swapping anecdotes about their immigrant neighbors, and
there is apt to develop an epidemic of moist
eyes. Out of the fullness of their knowledge
these social missionaries pay the tribute of
respect and affection to the strangers among
whom they toil. For they know them as we
know our brothers and sisters, from living
and working and rejoicing and sorrowing together. . . .

If it is the scum of Europe that we are
getting in our present immigration, it seems
to be a scum rich in pearls. Pearl-fishing, of
course, is accompanied by labor and danger
and expense, but it is reckoned a paying
industry, or practical men would not invest
their capital in it. The brunt of the business
falls on the divers, however. Have we divers
willing to go down into our human sea and
risk an encounter with sharks and grope in
the ooze at the bottom? We have our school
teachers and librarians and social missionaries,
whose zest for their work should shame us out
of counting the cost of our human fishery. As
to the accumulations of empty shells, we are
told that in the pearl fisheries of South America

about one oyster in a thousand yields a pearl, and yet the industry goes on.

The lesson of the oyster bank goes further still. We know that the nine hundred and ninety-nine empty shells have a lining, at least, of mother-of-pearl. We are thus encouraged to look for the generic opalescence of humanity in the undistiguished mass of our immigrants. What do the aliens show of the specific traits of manhood that go to the making of good citizens? Immersed in the tide of American life, do their spiritual secretions give off that fine lustre of manhood that distinguished the noble Pilgrims of the first immigration? The genius of the few is obvious; the group virtue of the mass on exalted occasions, such as popular uprisings, has been sufficiently demonstrated. What we want to know now is whether the ordinary immigrant under ordinary circumstances comes anywhere near the type we have taken as a model.

There can be no effective comparison between the makers of history of a most romantic epoch and the venders of bananas on our own thrice-commonplace streets. But the Pilgrims were not always engaged in signing momentous compacts or in effecting a historic landing. In a secondary capacity they were immigrants— strangers come to establish themselves in a strange land—and as such they may profitably be used as a model by which to measure other immigrants.

The historic merit of their enterprise aside, the virtue of the Pilgrim Fathers was that they came not to despoil, but to build; that they resolutely turned their backs on conditions of life that galled them, and set out to make their own conditions in a strange and untried world, at great hazard to life and limb and fortune; that they asked no favors of God, but paid in advance for His miracles, by hewing and digging and ploughing and fighting against odds; that they respected humankind, believed in themselves, and pushed the business of the moment as if the universe hung on the result.

The average immigrant of to-day, like the immigrant of 1620, comes to build—to build a civilized home under a civilized government, which diminishes the amount of barbarity in the world. He, too, like that earlier newcomer, has rebelled against the conditions of his life, and adventured halfway across the world in search of more acceptable conditions, facing exile and uncertainty and the terrors of the untried. He also pays as he goes along, and in

very much the same coin as did the Pilgrims; awaiting God's miracle of human happiness in the grisly darkness of the mine, in the fierce glare of the prairie ranch, in the shrivelling heat of coke-ovens, beside roaring cotton-gins, beside blinding silk-looms, in stifling tailor-shops, in nerve-racking engine rooms,—in all those places where the assurance and pride of the State come to rest upon the courage and patience of the individual citizen.

There is enough of peril left in the adventure of emigration to mark him who undertakes it as a man of some daring and resource. Has civilization smoothed the sea, or have not steamships been known to founder as well as sailing vessels? Does not the modern immigrant also venture among strangers, who know not his ways nor speak his tongue nor worship his God? If his landing is not threatened by savages in ambush, he has to run the gauntlet of exacting laws that serve not his immediate interests. The early New England farmer used to carry his rifle with him in the fields, to be ready for prowling Indians, and the gutter-merchant of New York to-day is obliged to carry about the whole armory of his wits, to avert the tomahawk of competition. No less cruel than Indian chiefs to their white captives is the greedy industrial boss to the laborers whom poverty puts at his mercy; and how could you better match the wolves and foxes that prowled about the forest clearings of our ancestors than by the pack of sharpers and misinformers who infest the immigrant quarters of our cities?

Measured by the exertions necessary to overcome them, the difficulties that beset the modern immigrant are no less formidable than those which the Pilgrims had to face. There has never been a time when it was more difficult to get something for nothing than it is to-day, but the unromantic setting of modern enterprises leads us to underestimate the moral qualities that make success possible to-day. Undoubtedly the pioneer with an axe over his shoulder is a more picturesque figure than the clerk with a pencil behind his ear, but we who have stood up against the shocks of modern life should know better than to confuse the picturesque with the heroic. Do we not know that it takes a *man* to beat circumstances, to-day as in the days of the pioneers? And manliness is always the same mixture of courage, self-reliance, perseverance, and faith.

Inventions have multiplied since the days of

the Pilgrims, but which of our mechanical devices takes the place of the old-fashioned quality of determination where obstacles are to be overcome? The New England wilderness retreated not before the axe, but before the diligence of the men who wielded the axe; and diligence it is which to-day transmutes the city's refuse into a loaf for the ragpicker's children. Resourcefulness—the ability to adjust the means to the end—enters equally in the subtle enterprises of the business man and in the hardy exploits of the settler; and it takes as much patience to wait for returns on a petty investment of capital as it does to watch the sprouting of an acre of corn.

Hardiness and muscle and physical courage were the seventeenth-century manifestations of the same moral qualities which to-day are expressed as intensity and nerve and commercial daring. Our country being in part cultivated, in part savage, we need citizens with the endowment of the twentieth century, and citizens with the pioneer endowment. The "new" immigration, however interpreted, consists in the main of these two types. Whether we get these elements in the proportion best suited to our needs is another question, to be answered in its place. At this point it is only necessary to admit that the immigrant possesses an abundance of the homely virtues of the useful citizen in times of peace.

We arrived at this conclusion by a theoretical analysis of the qualities that carry a man through life to-day; and that was fair reasoning, since the great majority of aliens are known to make good, if not in the first generation, then in the second or the third. Any sociologist, any settlement worker, any census clerk will tell you that the history of the average immigrant family of the "new" period is represented by an ascending curve. The descending curves are furnished by degenerate families of what was once prime American stock. I want no better proof of these facts than I find in the respective vocabularies of the missionary in the slums of New York and the missionary in the New England hills. At the settlement on Eldridge Street they talk about hastening the process of Americanization of the immigrant; the country minister in the Berkshires talks about the rehabilitation of the Yankee farmer. That is, the one assists at an upward process, the other seeks to reverse a downward process. . . .

The fact about the modern immigrant is that he is everywhere continuing the work begun by our pioneer ancestors. So much we may learn from a bare recital of the occupations of aliens. They supply most of the animal strength and primitive patience that are at the bottom of our civilization. In California they gather the harvest, in Arizona they dig irrigation ditches, in Oregon they fell forests, in West Virginia they tunnel coal, in Massachusetts they plant the tedious crops suitable to an exhausted soil. In the cities they build subways and skyscrapers and railroad terminals that are the wonder of the world. Wherever rough work and low wages go together, we have a job for the immigrant.

The prouder we grow, the more we lean on the immigrant. The Wall Street magnate would be about as effective as a puppet were it not for the army of foreigners who execute his schemes. The magic of stocks and bonds lies in railroad ties and in quarried stone and in axle grease applied at the right time. A Harriman might sit till doomsday gibbering at the telephone and the stock exchange would take no notice of him if a band of nameless "Dagos" a thousand miles away failed to repair a telegraph pole. New York City is building an aqueduct that will surpass the works of the Romans, and the average New Yorker will know nothing about it until he reads in the newspapers the mayor's speech at the inauguration of the new water supply.

Our brains, our wealth, our ambitions flow in channels dug by the hands of immigrants. Alien hands erect our offices, rivet our bridges, and pile up the proud masonry of our monuments. Ignoring in this connection the fact that the engineer as well as the laborer is often of alien race, we owe to mere muscle a measure of recognition proportionate to our need of muscle in our boasted material progress. An imaginative schoolboy left to himself must presently catch the resemblance between the pick-and-shovel men toiling at our aqueducts and the heroes of the axe and rifle extolled in his textbooks as the "sturdy pioneers." Considered without prejudice, the chief difference between these two types is the difference between jean overalls and fringed buckskins. Contemporaneousness takes the romance out of everything; otherwise we might be rubbing elbows with heroes. Whatever merit there was in hewing and digging and hauling in the days of the first settlers still inheres in the same operations to-day. Yes, and a little extra; for a stick of dynamite is more dangerous to handle than a crowbar, and the steam engine makes more widows in a year than ever the Indian did with bloody tomahawk and stealthy arrow.

There is no contention here that every fellow who successfully passes the entrance ordeals at Ellis Island is necessarily a hero. That there are weaklings in the train of the sturdy throng of foreigners nobody knows better than I. I have witnessed the pitiful struggles of the unfit, and have seen the failures drop all around me. But no bold army ever marched to the field of action without a fringe of camp-followers on its flanks. The moral vortex created by the enterprises of the resolute sucks in a certain number of the weak-hearted; and this is especially true in mass movements, where the enthusiasm of the crowd ekes out the courage of the individual. If it is not too impious to suggest it, may there not have been among the passengers of the Mayflower two or three or half a dozen who came over because their cousins did, not because they had any zest for the adventure? . . .

Let it be understood that the men and women of exceptional intellect, who have surveyed the situation from philosophical heights, are not trumpeting forth their own high dreams alone. If they have won the ear of the American nation and shamed the indifferent and silenced the cynical, it is because they voiced the feeling of the inarticulate mob that welters in the foreign quarters of our cities. I am never so clear as to the basis of my faith in America as when I have been talking with the ungroomed mothers of the East Side. A widow down on Division Street was complaining bitterly of the hardships of her lot, alone in an alien world with four children to bring up. In the midst of her complaints the children came in from school. "Well," said the hard-pressed widow, "bread isn't easy to get in America, but the children can go to school, and that's more than bread. Rich man, poor man, it's all the same: the children can go to school."

The poor widow had never heard of a document called the Declaration of Independence, but evidently she had discovered in American practice something corresponding to one of the great American principles,—the principle of equality of opportunity,—and she valued it more than the necessaries of animal life. Even so was it valued by the Fathers of the Republic, when they deliberately incurred the dangers of a war with mighty England in defense of that and similar principles.

The widow's sentiment was finely echoed by another Russian immigrant, a man who drives an ice-wagon for a living. His case is the more impressive from the fact that he left a position of comparative opulence in the old country, under the protection of a wealthy uncle who employed him as steward of his estates. He had had servants to wait on him and money enough to buy some of the privileges of citizenship which the Russian Government doles out to the favored few. "But what good was it to me?" he asked. "My property was not my own if the police wanted to take it away. I could spend thousands to push my boy through the Gymnasium, and he might get a little education as a favor, and still nothing out of it, if he isn't allowed to be anything. Here I work like a slave, and my wife she works like a slave, too, —in the old country she had servants in the house,—but what do I care, as long as I know what I earn I got it for my own? I got to furnish my house one chair at a time, in America, but nobody can take it away from me, the little that I got. And it costs me nothing to educate my family. Maybe they can, maybe they can't go to college, but all can go through grammar school, and high school, too, the smart ones. And all go together! Rich and poor, all are equal, and I don't get it as a favor."

Better a hard bed in the shelter of justice than a stuffed couch under the black canopy of despotism. Better a crust of the bread of the intellect freely given him as his right than the whole loaf grudgingly handed him as a favor. What nobler insistence on the rights of manhood do we find in the writings of the Puritans?

Volumes might be filled with the broken sayings of the humblest among the immigrants which, translated into the sounding terms of the universal, would give us the precious documents of American history over again. Never was the bread of freedom more keenly relished than it is to-day, by the very people of whom it is said that they covet only the golden platter on which it is served up. We may not say that immigration to our country has ceased to be a quest of the ideal as long as the immigrants lay so much stress on the spiritual accompaniment of economic elevation in America. Nobly built upon the dreams of the Fathers, the house of our Republic is nobly tenanted by those who cherish similar dreams.

But dreams cannot be brought before a court of inquiry. A diligent immigration commission with an appropriation to spend has little time to listen to Joseph. A digest of its report is expected to yield statistics rather than rhapsodies. The taxpayers want their money's worth of hard facts.

But when the facts are raked together and boiled down to a summary that the business man may scan on his way to the office, behold! we are no wiser than before. For a host of interpreters jump into the seats vacated by the extinct commission and harangue us in learned terms on the merits and demerits of the immigrant, *as they conceive them,* after studying the voluminous report. That is, the question is still what it was before: a matter of personal opinion! The man with the vote realizes that *he* has to make up *his* mind what instructions to send to his representative in Congress on the subject of immigration. And where shall he, a plain, practical man, unaccustomed to interpret dreams or analyze statistics, find an index of the alien's worth that he can read through the spectacles of common sense? . . .

In the whole catalogue of sins with which the modern immigrant is charged, it is not easy to find one in which we Americans are not partners,—we who can make and unmake our world by means of the ballot. The immigrant is blamed for the unsanitary conditions of the slums, when sanitary experts cry shame on our methods of municipal house-cleaning. You might dump the whole of the East Side into the German capital and there would be no slums there, because the municipal authorities of Berlin know how to enforce building regulations, how to plant trees, and how to clean the streets. The very existence of the slum is laid at the door of the immigrant, but the truth is that the slums were here before the immigrants. Most of the foreigners hate the slums, and all but the few who have no backbone get out of them as fast as they rise in the economic scale. To "move uptown" is the dearest ambition of the average immigrant family.

If the slums were due to the influx of foreigners, why should London have slums, and more hideous slums than New York? No, the slum is not a by-product of the steerage. It is a sore on the social body in many civilized countries, due to internal disorders of the economic system. A generous dose of social reformation would do more to effect a cure than repeated doses of restriction of immigration.

A whole group of phenomena due to social and economic causes have been falsely traced, in this country, to the quantity and quality of immigration. Among these are the labor troubles, such as non-employment, strikes, riots, etc. England has no such immigration as the United States, and yet Englishmen suffer from non-employment, from riots and bitter strikes. Whom does the English workingman blame for his misery? Let the American workingman quarrel with the same enemy. If wage-cutting is a sin more justly laid at the door of the immigrant, a minimum wage law might put a stop to that.

The immigrant undoubtedly contributes to the congestion of population in the cities, but not as a chief cause. Congestion is characteristic of city life the world over, and the remedy will be found in improved conditions of country life. Moreover, the immigrant has shown himself responsive to direction away from the city when a systematic attempt is made to help him find his place in the country. There is the experience of the Industrial Removal Office of the Baron de Hirsch Foundation as a hint of what the Government might accomplish if it took a hand in the intelligent distribution of immigration. The records of this organization, dealing with a group of immigrants supposed to be especially addicted to city life, kill two immigrant myths at one stroke. They prove that it is possible to direct the stream of immigration in desired channels and that the Jew is not altogether averse to contact with the soil; both facts contrary to popular notions. . . .

Immigrants are accused of civic indifference if they do not become naturalized, but when we look into the conditions affecting naturalization we wonder at the numbers who do become citizens. Facilities for civic education of the adult are very scant, and dependent mostly on the fluctuating enthusiasm of private philanthropies. The administration of the naturalization laws differs from State to State and is accompanied by serious material hindrances; while the community is so indifferent to the civic progress of its alien members that it is possible for a foreigner to live in this country for *sixteen years,* coming in contact with all classes of Americans, without getting the bare information that he may become a citizen of the United States if he wants to. Such a case, as reported by a charity worker of New Britain, Connecticut, makes a sensitive American choke with mortification. If we were ourselves as patriotic as we expect the immigrant to be, we would employ Salvation Army methods to draw the foreigner into the civic fold. Instead of that, we leave his citizenship to chance—or to the most corrupt political agencies.

I would rather not review the blackest of all charges against the immigrant, that he has a baleful effect on municipal politics: I am so ashamed of the implications. But sensible citizens will talk and talk about the immigrant selling his vote, and not know whom they are accusing. Votes cannot be sold unless there is a market for them. Who creates the market for votes? The ward politician, behind whom stands the party boss, alert, and powerful; and behind him—the indifferent electorate who allow him to flourish.

Among immigrants of the "new" order, the wholesale prostitution of the ballot is confined to those groups which are largely subjected to the industrial slavery of mining and manufacturing communities and construction camps. These helpless creatures, in their very act of sinning, bear twofold witness against us who accuse them. The foreman who disposes of their solid vote acquires his power under an economic system which delivers them up, body and soul, to the man who pays them wages, and turns it to account under a political system which makes the legislature subservient to the stock exchange. But let it be definitely noted that to admit that groups of immigrants under economic control fall an easy prey to political corruptionists is very far from proving any inherent viciousness in the immigrants themselves.

Neither does the immigrant's civic reputation depend entirely on negative evidence. New York City has the largest foreign population in the United States, and precisely in that city the politicians have learned that they cannot count on the foreign vote, because it is not for sale. A student of New York politics speaks of the "uncontrollable and unapproachable vote of the Ghetto." Repeated analyses of the election returns of the Eighth District, which has the largest foreign population of all, show that "politically it is one of the most uncertain sections" in the city. Many generations of campaign managers have discovered to their sorrow that the usual party blandishments are wasted on the East Side masses. Hester Street follows leaders and causes rather than party emblems. Nowhere is the art of splitting a ticket better understood. The only time you can predict the East Side vote is when there is a sharp alignment of the better citizens against the boss-ridden. Then you will find the naturalized citizens in the same camp with men like Jacob Riis and women like Lillian Wald. And the experience of New York is duplicated in Chicago and in Philadelphia and in every center of immigration. Ask the reformers.

How often we demand more civic virtue of the stranger than we ourselves possess! A little more time spent in weeding our own garden will relieve us of the necessity of counting the tin cans in the immigrant's back yard.

As to tin cans, the immigrants are not the only ones who scatter them broadcast. How can we talk about the foreigners defacing public property, when our own bill-boards disfigure every open space that God tries to make beautiful for us? It is true that the East Side crowds litter the parks with papers and fruit-skins and peanut shells, but they would not be able to do so if the park regulations were persistently enforced. And in the mean time the East Side children, in their pageants and dance festivals, make the most beautiful use of the parks that a poet could desire.

There exists a society in the United States the object of which is to protect the natural beauties and historical landmarks of our country. Who are the marauders who have called such a society into being? Who is it that threatens to demolish the Palisades and drain off Niagara? Who are the vulgar folk who scrawl their initials on trees and monuments, who chip off bits from historic tombstones, who profane the holy echoes of the mountains by calling foolish phrases through a megaphone? The officers of the Scenic and Historic Preservation Society are not watching Ellis Island. On the contrary, it was the son of an immigrant whose expert testimony, given before a legislative committee at Albany, helped the Society to save the Falls of the Genesee from devastation by a power company. This same immigrant's son, on another occasion, spent two mortal hours tearing off visiting-cards from a poet's grave—cards bearing the names of American vacationists.

Some of the things we say against the immigrants sound very strange from American lips. We speak of the corruption of our children's manners through contact with immigrant children in the public schools, when all the world is scolding us for our children's rude deportment. Finer manners are grown on a tiny farm in Italy than in the roaring subways of New York; and contrast our lunch-counter manners with the table-manners of the Polish ghetto, where bread must not be touched with unwashed hands, where a pause for prayer begins and ends each meal, and on festival occasions parents and children join in folk-songs between courses!

If there is a corruption of manners, it may be that it works in the opposite direction from what we suppose. At any rate, we ourselves admit that the children of foreigners, before they are Americanized, have a greater respect than our children for the Fifth Commandment.

We say that immigrants nowadays come only to exploit our country, because some of them go back after a few years, taking their savings with them. The real exploiters of our country's wealth are not the foreign laborers, but the capitalists who pay them wages. The laborer who returns home with his savings leaves us an equivalent in the products of labor; a day's service rendered for every day's wages. The capitalists take away our forests and watercourses and mineral treasures and give us watered stock in return.

Of the class of aliens who do not come to make their homes here, but only to earn a few hundred dollars to invest in a farm or a cottage in their native village, a greater number than we imagine are brought over by industrial agents in violation of the contract labor law. Put an end to the stimulation of immigration, and we shall see very few of the class who do not come to stay. And even as it is, not all of those who return to Europe do so in order to spend their American fortune. Some go back to recover from ruin encountered at the hands of American land swindlers. Some go back to be buried beside their fathers, having lost their health in unsanitary American factories. And some are helped aboard on crutches, having lost a limb in a mine explosion that could have been prevented. When we watch the procession of cripples hobbling back to their native villages, it looks more as if America is exploiting Europe.

O that the American people would learn where their enemies lurk! Not the immigrant is ruining our country, but the venal politicians who try to make the immigrant the scapegoat for all the sins of untrammeled capitalism—these and their masters. Find me the agent who obstructs the movement for the abolition of child labor, and I will show you who it is that condemns ablebodied men to eat their hearts out in idleness; who brutalizes our mothers and tortures tender babies; who fills the morgues with the emaciated bodies of young girls, and the infirmaries with little white cots; who fastens the shame of illiteracy on our enlightened land, and causes American boys to grow up too ignorant to mark a ballot; who sucks the blood of the nation, fattens on its brains, and throws its heart to the wolves of the money market.

The stench of the slums is nothing to the stench of the child-labor iniquity. If the foreigners are taking the bread out of the mouth of the American workingman, it is by the maimed fingers of their fainting little ones.

And if we want to know whether the immigrant parents are the promoters or the victims of the child labor system, we turn to the cotton mills, where forty thousand native American children between seven and sixteen years of age toil between ten and twelve hours a day, while the fathers rot in the degradation of idleness.

From all this does it follow that we should let down the bars and dispense with the guard at Ellis Island? Only in so far as the policy of restriction is based on the theory that the present immigration is derived from the scum of humanity. But the immigrants may be desirable and immigration undesirable. We sometimes have to deny ourselves to the most congenial friends who knock at our door. At this point, however, we are not trying to answer the question whether immigration is good for us. We are concerned only with the reputation of the immigrant—and incidentally with the reputation of those who have sought to degrade him in our eyes. If statecraft bids us lock the gate, and our national code of ethics ratifies the order, lock it we must, but we need not call names through the keyhole.

Mount guard in the name of the Republic if the health of the Republic requires it, but let no such order be issued until her statesmen and philosophers and patriots have consulted together. Above all, let the voice of prejudice be stilled, let not self-interest chew the cud of envy in full sight of the nation, and let no syllable of willful defamation mar the oracles of state. For those who are excluded when our bars are down are exiles from Egypt, whose feet stumble in the desert of political and social slavery, whose hearts hunger for the bread of freedom. The ghost of the Mayflower pilots every immigrant ship, and Ellis Island is another name for Plymouth Rock.   1914

HENRY PRATT FAIRCHILD

1880–

ALTHOUGH MANY spoke and wrote in favor of restricting immigration, no one better summarized the arguments for such a policy than Henry Pratt Fairchild. Born at Dundee, Illinois, in 1880, Fairchild followed the academic path and finally became professor of sociology at New York University in 1924. In that year Congress passed the Johnson Act, which reduced the number of immigrants to be admitted in any year to "two per cent of the number of foreign-born individuals of any nationality resident in continental United States, as determined by the census of 1890, with a minimum quota of one hundred, subject to certain exceptions." The purpose of this legislation was to discriminate against immigrants from southern and eastern Europe, and from Asia, in order that the pattern of national stocks in the United States might be preserved. The Johnson Act, and succeeding legislation designed to implement it, marked a significant turning point in American history, for in spite of the limited restriction of certain categories of immigrants, and of the virtual exclusion of Chinese immigration in 1882 and of Japanese in 1908, the doors of America had been hospitably open to immigrants from the colonial era on. Professor Fairchild's books include *Greek Immigration to the United States* (1911); *Immigration* (1913); and *People: The Quantity and Quality of Population* (1939).

Race and Nationality as Factors in American Life, New York, 1947.
The Prodigal Century, New York, 1950.
Versus: Reflections of a Sociologist, New York, 1950.
The Anatomy of Freedom, New York, 1957.

» » *From:* THE MELTING-POT MISTAKE « «

CHAPTER I

SYMBOLS

For one hundred years and more a stream of immigration had been pouring into the United States in constantly increasing volume. At first this movement had attracted little attention, and such feelings as it aroused were mainly those of complacency and satisfaction. As the decades rolled by certain features of the movement created considerable consternation and a demand sprang up for some form of governmental relief. In time this relief was granted, and the popular concern died down. In general, however, during practically the whole of the nineteenth century the attitude of the American people toward immigration was one of easy-going, tolerant indifference when it was not actually welcome. But as the century drew to a close evidences of popular uneasiness and misgiving began to display themselves. These were due in part to changes in the social and economic situation in the United States, in part to changes in the personal and social characteristics of the immigrants, and in part to repeated warnings issued by those whose professional activities and opportunities gave them a wider access to the facts of immigration than was possible to the average citizen. In particular the American people began to ponder about the ultimate effect upon its own vitality and solidarity of this stupendous injection of foreign elements. Could we stand it, and if so, how long? Were not the foundations of our cherished institutions already partially undermined by all these alien ideas, habits, and customs? What kind of a people were we destined to become physically? Was the American nation itself in danger? Immigration became a great public problem, calling for judgment.

Then came the symbol, like a portent in the heavens. America is a Melting-Pot. Into it are being poured representatives of all the world's peoples. Within its magic confines there is being formed something that is not only uniform and homogeneous but also finer than any of the separate ingredients. The nations of the world are being fused into a new and choicer nation, the United States.

10　　The figure was a clever one—picturesque, expressive, familiar, just the sort of thing to catch the popular fancy and lend itself to a thousand uses. It swept over this country and other countries like wild fire. As always, it was welcomed as a substitute for both investigation and thought. It calmed the rising wave of misgiving. Few stopped to ask whether it fitted the phenomena of assimilation. Few inquired whether Mr. Zangwill's familiarity with the

20　intricate facts of immigration were such as to justify him in assuming the heavy responsibility of interpreter. America was a Melting-Pot, the apparent evidences of national disintegration were illusions, and that settled it.

It would be hard to estimate the influence of the symbol of the melting pot in staving off the restriction of immigration. It is certain that in the popular mind it offsets volumes of laboriously compiled statistics and carefully

30　reasoned analyses. It is virtually beyond question that restriction would have come in time in any case. How soon it would have come without the Great War must remain a matter of conjecture. Be that as it may, when the concussions of that conflict had begun to die down the melting pot was discovered to be so badly cracked that it is not likely ever to be dragged into service again. Its day was over. But this did not mean that the real facts

40　of immigration had suddenly become public property. Our symbol had been shattered, but we had not yet, as a people, been able to undertake the extensive investigation necessary to reveal the true nature of the case. The history of post-war movements is replete with evidences of the gross misconceptions of the meaning and processes of assimilation which characterized many even of those who devoted themselves directly to the problem. Even to-

50　day, in spite of the fact that there is perhaps no other great public problem on which the American people is so well educated as on immigration, there is yet great need of a clearer understanding of the tremendous task that still confronts us. We know that the

Melting-Pot did not melt, but we are not entirely sure why.

CHAPTER XII

THE DUTY OF AMERICA

It has been repeatedly stated that the consequence of nonassimilation is the destruction of nationality. This is the central truth of the whole problem of immigration and it cannot be overemphasized. An immigration movement that did not involve nonassimilation might be tolerated, though it might have other evil consequences which would condemn it. But an immigration movement that does involve nonassimilation—like the movement to the United States during the last fifty years at least—is a blow at the very heart of nationality and cannot be endured if nationality is conceived to have any value whatsoever. The American nationality has already been compared to a plant. There is, indeed, a striking parallelism between a nation and a noble tree—for instance, one of our own incomparable redwoods—which may be followed a little further, not with any expectation or desire of popularizing a new symbol, but merely for the clarification that it affords.

A nation, like a tree, is a living vital thing. Growth is one of its conditions of life, and when it ceases to grow there is good reason to fear that it is about to decay and die. Every nation, like every tree, belongs to a certain general type, but it is also uniquely individual within that type. Its peculiar form is determined by various forces, some of which are internal and some external. No nation need fear the changes which come as the result of the operation of natural, wholesome internal forces, that is to say, the ideas and activities of its own true members. These forces may, in the course of time, produce a form and character wholly different from the original, just as the mature plant may have an entirely different aspect from the seedling. This is nothing to be dreaded or opposed. No change that represents the natural evolution of internal forces need be dreaded. But there are other forces which originate without which threaten not only the form and character but also the vigor and perhaps the very life of the nation. Some of these are the forcible attacks of other nations, like the crowding of trees upon each other, or the unwholesome influence of alien ideas which may be compared with harsh and uncongenial winds which blow upon trees, dwarfing and distorting them.

Most dangerous of all, however, are those foreign forces which, among trees, are represented by minute hostile organisms that make their way into the very tissue of the tree itself and feed upon its life substances, and among nations to alien individuals who are accepted as immigrants and by a process of "boring from within" (in something much more than a mere trade-union sense) sap the very vitality of their host. In so doing the immigrants may be merely following out their natural and defensible impulses without any hostility toward the receiving nation, any more than the parasites upon a tree may be considered to have any hostility to the tree. Nor can the immigrants, any more than the parasites, be expected to foresee that their activities will eventually destroy the very organism upon which they depend for their existence. The simple fact is that they are alien particles, not assimilated, and therefore wholly different from the foreign particles which the tree takes in the form of food, and transforms into cells of its own body.

Herein is found the full justification for a special application of the principles of freedom of speech to aliens differing widely from the interpretation in the case of citizens. This is particularly true with reference to attempts at free speech which take the character of criticisms of the form of government or the processes of the governing agencies. The citizen is presumed to be familiar with the genius and spirit of his own government, and to be sincerely devoted to it. No check should be put upon his criticisms, as long as they are honest and candid. The criticisms of its own citizens are the wholesome internal forces of change in any government, out of which new and more highly developed forms will emerge. But the criticisms and the attacks of the alien may be malicious, and are certain to be ignorant and ill-informed. The alien, just because he is an alien, is not in a position to comprehend the meaning of the various political and social phenomena which he observes about him, he is incapable of interpreting them in the light of their true significance and bearing on the entire scheme of government, and because he has a potential audience of millions equally alien he may do incalculable harm. False doctrines may be infinitely dangerous even though held by those who cannot express them in votes.

It actually seems as if each nation developed an immunity to certain ideas, just as the trees in a given locality develop a practical immunity to the pests of their own vicinity. Our own Department of Agriculture is constantly on the alert to prevent the introduction of foreign parasites against which our native plants have no effective protection. Numerous cases are on record—one of the most spectacular being the chestnut trees of New England—where a type of plant which from time immemorial had been able to hold its own in its native balance of nature has been devastated if not exterminated by the sudden introduction of a parasite against which it had not developed a means of protection. So in a nation, ideas are constantly circulating which are inherently destructive, but against which the natives have developed an adequate protection so that they produce no serious harm. But the sudden entrance of new ideas or of foreign varieties of old ideas may find the country unprepared to counteract them. The safest way to guard against such a calamity is to reduce to a small figure the number of those newcomers by which such alien ideas may be introduced.

These considerations do not in any measure justify treating the alien as if he had no rights and were not entitled to express himself on any subject, as has sometimes been done by overzealous patriots under the stress of acute national hysteria. But they do justify the exercise of a wholly different type of control over the public utterances of aliens from that imposed upon citizens, and even more the exclusion of those who in the nature of the case are likely to indulge in un-American utterances because they are imbued with un-American ideas.

There are, it should be noted, a few foreigners whose attitude toward the United States is more positively destructive than that of those who simply can not understand America because they are not Americans. Among this number are those, very few altogether, who make it their business to launch direct attacks upon the fundamental form and institutions of the American government. To them the deportation acts may most appropriately be applied. But much more dangerous are those who insolently regard the United States as a mere economic catch basin, to which they have come to get out of it what they can, confessing no obligation to it, recognizing no claim on its part to the preservation of its own identity, displaying no intention to contribute to its development or to remain permanently as a part of it. One type of this group looks forward to a return to the native land as soon as America has been bled of all it has to offer. Another type looks upon America as a sort of no man's land, or every man's land, upon which they can develop a separate group existence along any lines that they see fit. For instance, we are told upon the best of authority that there has already developed in the United States a distinct Polish-American society, which is neither truly Polish nor truly American, but which has a vigorous and distinct character and existence of its own.

More dangerous, however, than any foreign elements, are certain individuals of native birth who in an excess of zeal for the foreigner, emanating, it may be presumed, from a misguided and sentimental though well-meaning reaction from the attitude of ethno-centric superiority so characteristic of many Americans, go to the extreme of denying any merit in American institutions, and ignoring any claim on the part of America to the perpetuation of its peculiar existence. They are ready to throw any and all distinctly American characteristics into the discard if only we can absorb the "dear foreigners" into our midst. They applaud any expression of national pride on the part of a foreigner as an evidence of sturdy and commendable patriotism, but condemn a similar expression on the part of an American as narrow bigotry. A representative of this type, apparently of native extraction, was talking at an Americanization meeting called by a prominent commercial organization in one of our great cities. Working herself up to a fine pitch of emotionalism, she finally exclaimed, "The noblest and finest persons I ever knew in my life were newly arrived immigrants, and the meanest, the lowest, the most contemptible were descendants of the old New England stock!" This was the keynote of the meeting, and called forth a tumult of applause.

The central factor in the world organization of the present is nationalism. Strong, self-conscious nationalities are indispensable to the efficient ordering and peaceful promotion of international relations. Every well-developed nationality is a priceless product of social evolution. Each has its peculiar contribution to make to future progress. The destruction of any one would be an irreparable loss to mankind.

Among the nations of the world America stands out unique, and in many ways preeminent. Favored by Nature above all other nations in her physical endowment, favored by history in the character of her people and the type of her institutions, she has a role to play in the development of human affairs which no other nation can play. Foremost in this role is the development of true democracy. In America the stage is set more favorably than anywhere else for the great drama of the common man. Here if anywhere the conditions are auspicious for the upward movement of the masses. If democracy fails in America, where shall we look for it to succeed? Any program or policy which interferes in the slightest degree with the prosecution of this great enterprise must be condemned as treason to our high destiny. Any yielding to a specious and superficial humanitarianism which threatens the material, political, and social standards of the average American must be branded as a violation of our trust. The highest service of America to mankind is to point the way, to demonstrate the possibilities, to lead onward to the goal of human happiness. Any force that tends to impair our capacity for leadership is a menace to mankind and a flagrant violation of the spirit of liberalism.

Unrestricted immigration was such a force. It was slowly, insidiously, irresistibly eating away the very heart of the United States. What was being melted in the great Melting-Pot, losing all form and symmetry, all beauty and character, all nobility and usefulness, was the American nationality itself.   1926

» »   « «

LOUIS ADAMIC

1899–

BORN IN the village of Blato, a Slavic province in the old Austrian-Hungarian empire, Adamic, after studying at the Gymnasium in Ljubljana, migrated in 1913 to the United States. Firsthand experiences as a worker in industry, service in the United States army during the World War, and an ever-widening acquaintance with Americans of all ranks and conditions enriched his knowledge of his adopted land. Emphasizing the cultural and psychological problems of the immigrants, especially the cleavages between the foreign-born and their children, Adamic became the most prominent immigrant interpreter of conflicting psychologies and cultures. His writings include *Dynamite, the Story of Class Violence in America* (1931), *Laughing in the Jungle* (1932), *The Native's Return* (1934), *My America* (1938), *From Many Lands* (1940), and several novels.

Carey McWilliams, *Louis Adamic and Shadow-America*, Los Angeles, 1935.

» » *From:* THIRTY MILLION NEW AMERICANS « «

I

Within its population of one hundred and twenty-five million, the United States has to-day about thirty million citizens—the overwhelming majority of them young citizens—who are the American-born children of immigrant parents of various nationalities: German, Italian, Polish, Czech, Slovak, Serbian, Croatian, Slovenian, Bulgarian, Jewish, Russian, Carpatho-Russian, Ukrainian, Lithuanian, Finnish, Hungarian, Norwegian, Swedish, Danish, Dutch, French, Flemish, Spanish, Portuguese, Rumanian, Armenian, Syrian, Lett, Albanian, Greek, Turkish, and, of course, English, Scotch, and Irish. The country as a whole is but dimly cognizant of this fact, which, in my opinion (held for some time, but lately much strengthened), is of fundamental and urgent importance in our contemporary social and cultural scene. It should perhaps particularly interest those Americans who consider themselves of the old Anglo-Saxon stock: for here is a tremendous new element—what will it do to the old stock?—to the country?—how will it affect the development of civilization and culture, of racial types on this continent?

Early last spring I spent seven weeks on what some people believed was a lecture tour, which took me to the great industrial centers of New York State, New Jersey, Pennsylvania, Ohio, Michigan, Illinois, Indiana, Wisconsin, and Minnesota, where the population is preponderantly "foreign"; actually, my trip was not so much a series of speaking engagements as an attempt—a device—to get some clear idea, if possible, of this immense mass of so-called "second-generation" citizens, numerically predominant in some of the most important cities and towns, whom I choose to designate the New Americans. I spoke, or rather tried to speak, more or less on the subject of this article, to more than fifty audiences of anywhere from one hundred to twenty-five hundred men and women and young people, in big towns like Pittsburgh, Cleveland, Akron, Detroit, Chicago, South Bend, Milwaukee, St. Paul, and Duluth, and smaller communities like McKeesport, Canonsburg, Ambridge, Farrell, and Sharon, Pennsylvania; Lorain, Ohio; Flint, Michigan, and Hibbing and Eveleth, Minnesota. Some of my audiences were almost wholly "foreign," others mixed "foreign" and old-stock American. At the time I knew very little about the subject; I merely sensed its importance; and, to keep going for an hour or so, I discussed things more or less akin to it and at the end, admitting my ignorance, invited my listeners

to get up and say anything they liked in relation to my remarks. Those who were too
bashful to talk in a crowd, I asked to speak to
me after the lecture or call me at the hotel or
write me a letter. Many of them, both old-stock
Americans and New Americans, responded to
this invitation. Some of them then asked me to
their homes. Others wrote me long letters. And
the result was that before my tour was half
over I began to think that these New Americans—twenty-six millions of them in 1930 and
increasing at the rate of perhaps more than a
million a year—constituted one of the greatest
and most basic problems in this country; in
some respects, greater and more basic perhaps
than, say, the problem of unemployment, and
almost as urgent.

This problem has existed, in nearly the same
proportions that it exists to-day, for a long time,
but few people have shown eagerness and
ability to deal with it in a broad, fundamental
way. Much attention has been paid to the problem of the foreign-born—but not to that of their
children, the American-born second generation.
Even to-day, as already suggested, there is no
acute or intelligent appreciation of it. Very little is being done about it; and the longer it is
neglected the worse it will become, both for the
New Americans and for America as a whole.

In this article it is not my ambition to present
the problem in all its details, ramifications,
significances, for it is a vastly complicated one
and different in every locality and in every
racial group; and, frankly, in spite of my seven
weeks' study, I still have a great deal to learn
about it. My purpose here is merely to give as
strong and broad a general suggestion as I can
of its character and what I think might be done
concerning it.

On my trip I came in close personal contact
largely with New Americans of Slavic origin,
but also with a few of Finnish, Lithuanian,
Scandinavian, Italian, Hungarian, Jewish, and
Rumanian parentage, and what I say in the
ensuing paragraphs applies, of course, particularly to the Slavic groups. I have no doubt,
however, that what is true of them is, to a
greater or lesser degree, true also of some of
the others.

II

The chief and most important fact (the only
one I shall stress here) about the New Americans is that the majority of them are oppressed
by feelings of inferiority in relation to their
fellow-citizens of older stock, to the main
stream of American life, and to the problem of
life as a whole; which, of course, is bad for
them as individuals, but, since there are so
many of them and their number is still rapidly
increasing, even worse for the country.

These feelings of inferiority are to some degree extensions of their parents' feelings of inferiority as immigrants in a country so drastically different from their native lands. The
fathers and mothers of these millions of New
Americans were naturally at a disadvantage
even in the most friendly surroundings, and the
surroundings were seldom wholly and continually friendly. As foreigners, in many cases, not
speaking the English language, they occupied
inferior positions in the country's social, economic, and political life. Most of them were
workers, performing, by and large, the meanest
tasks and receiving meager wages. All too often
in one form or another, they bumped up
against racial or general anti-immigrant prejudice. Old-stock American workers looked
askance at them. Many of them lived in the
worst sections of their cities and towns, and
were called Hunkies or Bohunks, Dagoes or
Wops, Polacks or Litvaks, Sheenies or Kikes.
They were frequently—and unavoidably—discriminated against. And, in the face of all this,
they inevitably felt, as individuals and as members of their immigrant groups, somewhat inferior in their relation to America and to other
people here, and their tendency was to segregate themselves and mingle as much as possible
only with their own nationals. And, just as
inevitably, that feeling and that tendency were
extended to the children, these New Americans, who shared their parents' lives and experiences, and who too were (and still are)
called Hunkies or Dagoes by children of Anglo-
Saxon origin, and whose names—names like
Zamblaoskas, Krmpotich, and Wojciezkowski
—were (and are) subjects for jokes on the part
of ignorant teachers, at which the whole school
laughed.

But in this respect the majority of New
Americans, as individuals, are in an even more
unfortunate and uncomfortable position than
were (or still are) their immigrant parents. The
latter, even if they were uneducated peasants
or laborers, living here on the lowest social-
economic levels, had in them a consciousness or
at least a powerful instinctive feeling, of some
kind of racial or cultural background. They
knew who they were. They remembered their

native lands. They were Italians or Croatians, Finns or Slovenians; and that meant something to them. Many came from countries which culturally and perhaps in some other respects were superior to the United States, which as a new country had not yet had time to develop along those lines; and when oppressed by feelings of inferiority induced by their circumstances in America, could take partial refuge in their racial and cultural backgrounds. Some of the better educated ones, who did not have merely instinctive feelings about the culture and history of their old countries, but were also intellectually conscious of their heritage, could even look down upon America and consider themselves superior to old-time Americans, thus counterbalancing or compensating themselves for the unpleasant feelings about their immigrant status in the New World.

Unlike their parents, who are (or were) aware not only of their European background but of having made the transition from Europe to America and gained a foothold here, most New Americans have no consciousness or instinctive feeling of any racial or cultural background, of their being part of any sort of continuity in human or historic experience. Some of them seem almost as if they had just dropped off Mars and, during the drop, forgotten all about Mars. I know this to be so; I talked to scores and scores of them in more than a dozen different cities and towns. In the overwhelming majority of cases, the immigrant parents—uneducated working people or peasants from the various European countries—were too inarticulate to tell their sons and daughters who they (the parents) really were, and thus transmit to them some feeling or knowledge of their background.

The average Slavic peasant, for instance, who came to this country during the last twenty or thirty years in nine chances out of ten is unable to inform his offspring adequately who he is, what his old country is like, what his background (which, *ipso facto,* is his children's background) consists of. He tells his numerous sons and daughters that he is a Pole, a Croatian, a Slovak, a Slovenian; but that is about all. The children do not know what that really means. The man acts as if he were proud of being what he is, at least in the privacy of his home; for his instincts and his memories of the old country occasionally make him act that way. To his children, however, who are growing up under anything but the best influences

of American life and who do not know that behind their father's pride is a rich and vital past, he very often seems not a little ridiculous, certainly not worthy of their respect. To them he is just a Hunky or Polack, a "working stiff," a poor, pathetic creature constantly at somebody's mercy and repeatedly stepped upon, and as such not much according to American standards—standards which they picked up in the movies and from other powerful agencies in American life. Often they are half ashamed of him. The immigrant mother frequently finds herself in the same situation. And the results are unsatisfactory family life, personal tragedies of all sorts, maladjustments, social perversities.

It is not unusual for boys and girls in their late or even their middle teens to break away from the homes of their immigrant parents, and eventually to repudiate entirely their origin and to Anglicize their Polish, Croatian, Finnish, or Lithuanian names, which old-time Americans find so difficult to pronounce and so amusing. But that, of course, does not solve their problem. In most instances it only makes it worse, though as a rule they do not realize that. I met New Americans of this type; they were invariably hollow, absurd, objectionable persons.

However, the situation of many of those who do not break with their parents, change their "foreign" names, and wholly repudiate their origin is but little better than of those who do. They were born here and legally, technically, are citizens of the United States; but few— even in the most fortunate homes—have any strong feeling that they really belong here and are part of this country. For, by and large, the education which is inflicted on them in public schools and high schools and in parochial schools fails to make them Anglo-Saxon Americans or to give them any vital and lasting appreciation of the American heritage, while their Anglo-Saxon schoolmates, purposefully-by-accident stumbling over their feet and calling them Hunkies and Dagoes, and their teachers, making fun of their names, increase their feeling that they are not indigenous Americans, but outsiders who are more or less tolerated. Their instincts, if they have any, are at cross-purposes. They are bewildered persons, constantly oppressed, as I have said, by feelings of inferiority.

These feelings of inferiority manifest themselves variously. Some of the New Americans turn them inside out and become chauvinistically patriotic; only their chauvinism has no basis in any vital feeling. It is insincere, empty, mere lip-service, intended only to impress the dominant Anglo-Saxon element, with which they have to cope; and hence worse—for the development of their own characters—than chauvinism that has some basis in conviction or feeling in racial or national background. And where there is any sincerity in this sort of "patriotism," it is based solely on shallow materialistic concepts, which they have picked up in school and elsewhere. "This is the greatest country . . . we have the biggest buildings . . . the best ice-cream . . . more bathtubs than all the rest of the world," etc. Without realizing it, these New Americans are ready for almost any sort of shallow, ignorant nationalist or fascist movement which will not directly attack the new racial strains in America's population; and some of them perhaps would have no great trouble in bringing themselves to deny their parents, pose as old-stock Americans, and serve even a movement which would terrorize the immigrants and their children as the Hitler movement in Germany terrorized the Jews.

Other New Americans turn their inferiority inside out in another way. They become loud and tough, sometimes actively anti-social. But let me hasten to say that this last group is not so numerous as generally imagined by those who occasionally glance at crime and juvenile-delinquency statistics. The surprising thing to me is that there is not more delinquency and crime among the New Americans. And I should add too that the chauvinists mentioned above are not very numerous either. These categories together include perhaps less than five per cent of the New Americans.

The majority of the grown-up New Americans just hang back from the main stream of life in this country, forming a tremendous mass of neutral, politically dead citizenry; while their younger fellow New Americans, boys and girls in their teens (about twelve million of them), now attending public and parochial schools and high schools, show dangerous signs of becoming the same kind of neutral, unstirring citizens, unless something is done about it. There is among them little aggressiveness, little spirit of any sort. Without a vital sense of background, perennially oppressed by the feeling that they are outsiders and thus inferior, they will live outside the main stream of America's national life. This is especially true of groups which linguistically and culturally are farthest removed from the Anglo Saxon, and still more of

groups which, besides being unrelated to the Anglo Saxon, are (or till lately have been) suppressed or subject nationalities in Europe.

And these widespread personal inferiority feelings are producing in large sections of this New American element *actual* inferiority in character, mind, and physique. There is no doubt that, by and large, in bodily and other personal qualities many of the immigrants' children do not favorably compare with their parents. They cannot look one in the eye. They are shy. Their limp handshakes gave me creepy feelings all the way from New York to the Iron Range in Minnesota. Those handshakes symbolized for me the distressing tendency on the part of this vast and growing section of America's population toward characterlessness, lack of force and spirit, and other inferior personal qualities.

From whatever angle one looks at it, this is a serious matter for the New Americans as individuals and for America. Thirty millions—or even twenty millions, a probable number to which most or all of my generalizations here are directly applicable—are a lot of people, and this "second generation" will be (many already are) the fathers and mothers of the third generation, and it is not impossible that in two or three decades more than half of the population of the United States will be of these new cultural and national strains.

. . . I realize, of course, that the problem I sketch above is closely tied up with the socio-economic system under which we live; that, next to their being more or less strangers here, the worst factors behind the inferiority feelings of these millions of New Americans are poverty and its sister-evil, ignorance, both of them brought over by the immigrants and then fostered by conditions here; and that the cure for most of the second-generation ills lies, ultimately, in the solution of our socio-economic problem. I doubt, however, whether the latter problem will be quickly and satisfactorily solved in this country if we permit to develop in our population a vast element, running into tens of millions, which is oppressed by acute feelings of inferiority, and largely as a result of those feelings, is becoming actually inferior human material—bewildered, politically neutral, economically unaggressive, prepared to live meekly, slavishly on the dole, and culturally nowhere. If this element is left alone in the face of its growing economic difficulties and rising prejudice against it on the part of "patriotic" older Americans, there soon will be no help for it. I imagine that hundreds of thousands of New Americans already are hopeless as potential constructive elements in any sort of vital, progressive civilization and culture; and if their number is permitted to increase, they will—let me repeat—profoundly affect the future of this country in a way that no one would want to see it affected.

On the other hand, if something is done about the problem in the spirit of the above general suggestions, I believe that the majority of the New Americans and the generation that they will produce will have an opportunity to become a great body of self-respecting, constructive citizenry; and that, with the diverse racial and cultural backgrounds they inherited from their immigrant parents, they will enrich the civilization and deepen the culture in this New World. 1934

» » *Naturalism and Supernaturalism* « «

1860-1910

» » « «

SATISFIED

It matters not what be thy lot,
So Love doth guide;
For storm or shine, pure peace is thine,
Whate'er betide.

And of these stones, or tyrants' thrones,
God able is
To raise up seed—in thought and deed—
To faithful His.

Aye, darkling sense, arise, go hence!
Our God is good.
False fears are foes—truth tatters those,
When understood.

Love looseth thee, and lifteth me,
Ayont hate's thrall:
There Life is light, and wisdom might,
And God is All.

The centuries break, the earth-bound wake,
God's glorified!
Who doth His will—His likeness still—
Is satisfied.

The seven hymns written by the Reverend Mary Baker G. Eddy have a prominent place in the *Christian Science Hymnal*.

» »   « «

Naturalism and Supernaturalism

THE LATE eighteenth-century rationalism exemplified by Thomas Paine's *Age of Reason*, although overshadowed in the early nineteenth century by the revival of evangelical religion, never entirely disappeared. The reception of Darwin's evolutionary hypothesis by a growing number of scientists greatly reinforced the feeble rationalistic pattern of thought. To some it was the final refutation of revelation and of supernaturalism generally. On the higher philosophical level Darwinism greatly influenced the men known as Pragmatists. On the more popular level it became the doctrinaire byword of iconoclasts who looked down on the conventional Christian as a dumb and pitiful victim of superstition.

Just as the more liberal theologians had constantly incorporated the advancing scientific spirit into their thought, so now Darwinism found a place in the new Christian synthesis which emerged. This synthesis, which roughly may be thought of as Modernism in contradistinction to Fundamentalism, was also greatly influenced by the scholarship of the philologists who detected many errors and inconsistencies in the various texts of the Bible. In some measure the synthesis also included the doctrine that religion had better concern itself with such problems as social ailments than with scholastic theology.

The conflict between the traditionalists and the modernists was a sharp one. Heresy trials and excommunications took place in several denominations. The more naturalistic synthesis gradually made its way, but fundamentalism remained in the rural areas and among the less well educated in the cities as a force sufficiently powerful to secure, in certain states, legislation forbidding the teaching of evolution in educational institutions.

New religious ideas, the most important of which was Christian Science, emerged. Christian Science, while thoroughly supernatural in character, nevertheless tried to meet many of the practical, everyday problems which insecurity in the new society of cities had brought about. But the persistence of supernaturalism probably owed most to the growth of Roman Catholicism incident to a new mass immigration.

» » « «

HENRY WARD BEECHER

1813–1887

HENRY WARD BEECHER, the emotional son of the well-known preacher and temperance crusader, Lyman Beecher, suffered at Amherst College from religious doubt, but came, through an ecstatic religious experience, to the conception of Christianity which he was to popularize. The time was ripe for such a popularization, since many Americans hungered for a less rigid Calvinistic religion without being ready to go over to the Unitarian camp; and Beecher's vitality and oratory made him an ideal popularizer. His conception of the pulpit was that it was chiefly important in so far as it effected a moral change in the hearts of those coming under its spell; and his buoyancy, spirit, and charm proved valuable allies and explained much of the success he enjoyed at Indianapolis and at Brooklyn. On social questions, notably slavery, Beecher's position was largely governed by expediency; but when he finally did enter the lists, he contributed effectively to the antislavery cause in which his sister, Harriet Beecher Stowe, had become so notable a figure.

Beecher's exuberant good will and emotionally optimistic nature expressed themselves in his acceptance of the doctrine of evolution. Without abandoning his faith in miracles and supernaturalism, he embraced the Darwinian teachings. These appeared to him to confirm his conviction that man had indeed never fallen, but, on the contrary, that he had always followed a path of betterment, and that he would continue to do so. The support which Beecher gave to evolution was a powerful factor in the struggle between naturalism and supernaturalism. The following sermon was given at Plymouth Church on May 31, 1885.

H. W. Beecher, *Evolution and Religion*, New York, 1885.
Lectures and Orations by Henry Ward Beecher, N. D. Hillis, ed., New York, 1913.
Paxton Hibben, *Henry Ward Beecher, An American Portrait*, New York, 1927.
L. B. Stowe, *Saints, Sinners and Beechers*, Indianapolis, 1934.

» » From: EVOLUTION AND RELIGION « «

THE TWO REVELATIONS

"All things were made by Him, and without Him was not anything made that was made."—John i:3.

That the whole world and the universe were the creation of God is the testimony of the whole Bible, both Jewish and Christian; but how he made them—whether by the direct force of a creative will or indirectly through a long series of gradual changes—the Scriptures do not declare. The grand truth is that this world was not a chance, a creative fermentation, a self-development, but that it was the product of an Intelligent Being, that the divine will in the continuance of this world manifests itself under the form of what are called natural laws, and that the operations of normal and legitimate laws are the results of divine will.

There are two records of God's creative energy. One is the record of the unfolding of *man* and of the race under the inspiration of God's nature: this is a mere sketch; of the ancient periods of man there is almost nothing known. The other of these records or revelations—if you choose to call them so—pertains to the physical globe, and reveals the divine thought through the unfolding history of *matter;* and this is the older. So we have two revelations: God's thought in the evolution of matter, and God's thought in the evolution of mind; and these are the Old Testament and the New—not in the usual sense of those terms, but in an appropriate scientific use of them.

In that great book of the Old there is a record of the progress, order, and result of God's thought in regard to the globe as a habitation for man. Though not every stage, yet the chief stages of preparation of this dwelling for man have been discovered and are now being deciphered and read. The crude, primitive material of the world of matter, the igneous condition, the aqueous stages, the dynamic and chemical periods, the gradual formation of the soil, the mountain-building, the dawn of life, vegetable and animal, the stages of their progress—are not all these things written in the scientific revelation of God's history of creation? When I reflect upon the range of the invisible and the silent God, with the vast and well-nigh incomprehensible stretch of time, and of his compassionate waiting and working through illimitable ages and periods, compared with which a million years as marked by the clock are but seconds; when I reflect that the silent stones and the buried strata contain the record of God's working, and that the globe itself is a sublime history of God as an engineer and architect and as a master-builder, I cannot but marvel at the indifference with which good men have regarded this stupendous revelation of the ages past, and especially at the assaults made by Christian men upon scientific men who are bringing to light the long-hidden record of God's revelation in the material world.

With what eagerness has the world heard of the discovery in Egypt of the tomb that contained the buried kings of the Pharaohnic dynasty! But what are all these mighty kings, wrapped for these thousand years in the shroud of silence, compared with the discovery of God's method and the results of creation millions of centuries ago, retained in the rocks? Were the two tables of stone, written by the finger of God, a memorial to be revered, and their contents to be written in letters of gold in all men's churches, and yet his ministers and priests turn with indifference or with denunciation, even with scorn, sometimes, from the literature of the rocks written by the hand of God all over the earth? What were the Ten Commandments but a paragraph out of the book of the divine revelation of nature? Ages before Sinai itself was upheaved in the progress of divine world-building; ages before the human race was enough advanced to have made the Ten Commandments possible, God was slowly moulding the world that was to contain within itself its own history. Science is but the deciphering of God's thought as revealed in the structure of this world; it is a mere translation of God's primitive revelation. If to reject God's revelation of the Book is infidelity, what is it to reject God's revelation of himself in the structure of the whole globe? There is as much infidelity in regard to the great history that science unfolds to-day, as there is in regard to the record of the Book—and more! The primitive prefatory revelation of the structural thought of God in preparing a dwelling for the human race—is that nothing? Man had a cradle represented to antiquity as the poetical Eden; but the globe itself had a different Eden, one of fire, convulsions, clouds and storms, of grinding ice and biting chemistry preparing the soil.

To be sure, the history of man in the Bible is more important than the history of the globe. The globe was created for man as a house is created to serve the family. But both are God's revelations; both are to be received with intelligent reverence; both are to be united and harmonized; both are to be employed in throwing light, the one upon the other. That noble body of investigators who are deciphering the hieroglyphics of God inscribed upon this temple of the earth are to be honored and encouraged. As it is now, vaguely bigoted theologists, ignorant pietists, jealous churchmen, unintelligent men, whose very existence seems like a sarcasm upon creative wisdom, with leaden wit and stinging irony swarm about the adventurous surveyors who are searching God's handiwork and who have added to the realm of the knowledge of God the grandest treasures. Men pretending to be ministers of God, with all manner of grimace and shallow ridicule and witless criticism and unproductive wisdom, enact the very feats of the monkey in the attempt to prove that the monkey was not their ancestor.

It is objected to all assertions of the validity of God's great record in matter, that science is uncertain and unripe; that men are continually changing the lines of science, that it will not do to rest upon the results of scientific investigation. It will be time to consider science when it has ripened into a certainty, say men, but not now. Well, as the case stands, how is the record of the book any more stable and intelligible than the record of the rock? The whole Christian world for two thousand years, since the completion of the canons, has been divided up like the end of a broom into infinite splinters, quarreling with each other as to what the book did say, and what it did mean. Why then should men turn and say that scientific men are unsettled in their notions? At the congress of Christian churches in Hartford recently, the Rev. Dr. Hopkins, a prominent high-churchman, said: "No less than nineteen different varieties of Christianity are at present trying to convert the Japanese. The nineteen do not agree as to what the ministry is, nor as to the word, some including the Apocrypha, and others discarding it altogether; and many differing as to the meaning of the Scriptures. Nor are they agreed as to the Sacraments. So too on doctrine, discipline, and worship. There are all sorts of contradictions of belief. Now, if Christians, with eighteen centuries of accumulated tradition cannot agree, how can we expect the heathen to solve the great riddle?" This is not mine, but I give a hearty Amen to it, and only find fault with it because it is not strong enough. When men, therefore, attempt to pour ridicule upon the legitimate deductions of scientific investigation, that have passed through the periods of trial, discussion, and proof, as if they were less praiseworthy than the declarations of the written revelation, I say to them, "No ground can be less tenable than such a ground as yours if we will look at the way in which the written revelation is misunderstood, and into the infinite splittings and divisions which men have made in attempting to interpret what is said to be the more stable revelation of the truth."

It is said, or thought, that a layman should not meddle with that which can be judged by only scientific experts: that science demands a special training before one can discern correctly its facts, or judge wisely of the force of its conclusions. This is true; it is true both of those who accept and those who deny its results. But, when time and investigation have brought the scientific world to an agreement, and its discoveries pass into the hands of all men, there comes an important duty, which moral teachers, parents, and especially clergymen, are perhaps as well or better fitted to fulfill than mere scientists, viz., to determine what effect the discoveries of science will have upon questions of morality and religion. It is to this aspect that the best minds of the Christian ministry are now addressing themselves.

It may be well before going further to expose some popular errors regarding the Evolutionary philosophy—now so widely accepted by the scientific world—and to point out some of the changes which it will work out in the schools of theology, as a new interpreter of God's two revelations.

A vague notion exists with multitudes that science is infidel, and that Evolution in particular is revolutionary—that is, revolutionary of the doctrines of the Church. Men of such views often say, "I know that religion is true. I do not wish to hear anything that threatens to unsettle my faith." But faith that can be unsettled by the access of light and knowledge had better be unsettled. The intensity of such men's faith in their own thoughts is deemed to be safer than a larger view of God's thoughts. Others speak of Evolution as a pseudo-science teaching that man descended from monkeys, or ascended as the case may be. They have no conception of it as the history of the divine process in the building of this world. They dismiss it with jests, mostly ancient jests; or, having a smattering of fragmentary knowledge, they address victorious ridicule to audiences as ignorant as they are themselves.

Now the ascent of man from the anthropoid apes is a mere hypothesis. It has not been proved; and in the broader sense of the word "proved," I see certainly no present means of proving it. It stands in the region of hypothesis, pressed forward by a multitude of probabilities.

The probabilities are so many, and the light which this hypothesis throws upon human history and human life and phenomena is such that I quite incline to the supposition that it is, in the order of nature, in analogy with all the rest of God's work, and that in the ascending scale there was a time unknown, and methods not yet discovered, in which man left behind his prior relatives, and came upon the spiritual ground which now distinguishes him from the whole brute creation. Of one thing I am certain, that whatever may have been the origin, it does not change either the destiny or the moral grandeur of man as he stands in the full light of civilization to-day. The theory of the evolution of the human race from an inferior race, not proved and yet probable, throws light upon many obscure points of doctrine and of theology that have most sadly needed light and solution.

First, then, what is Evolution, and what does it reveal? The theory of Evolution teaches that the creation of this earth was not accomplished in six days of twenty-four hours; that the divine method occupied ages and ages of immense duration; that nothing, of all the treasures of the globe as they now stand, was created at first in its present perfectness; that everything has grown through the lapse of ages into its present condition; that the whole earth, with their development in it, was, as it were, an egg, a germ, a seed; that the forests, the fields, the shrubs, the vineyards, all grasses and flowers, all insects, fishes, and birds, all mammals of every gradation, have had a long history, and that they have come to the position in which they now stand through ages and ages of gradual change and unfolding. Also that the earth itself went through a period of long preparation, passing from ether by condensation to a visible cloud form with increasing solidity, to such a condition as now prevails in the sun; that it condensed and became solid; that cold congealed its vapor; that by chemical action and by mechanical grinding of its surface by ice a soil was prepared fit for vegetation, long before it was fit for animal life; that plants simple and coarse came first and developed through all stages of complexity to the present conditions of the vegetable kingdom; that aquatic, invertebrate animals were the earliest of animals, according to the testimony of fossils in the earth. Fishes came next in order, then amphibians, then reptiles. "All these tribes were represented by species before the earliest of the mammals appeared. The existence of birds before the earliest mammal is not proved, though believed by some paleontologists upon probable evidence. The early mammals were marsupial, like the opossum and the kangaroo, and lived in the same era called by Agassiz, the reptilian period. True mammals came into geologic history in the tertiary era. Very long after the appearance of the first bird came man, the last and grandest of the series, it is doubtful whether in the tertiary period or immediately sequent. It is not established whether his bones or relics occur as far back as the tertiary era."

This is a very brief statement, not my own, but that of Professor Dana, of renown. No man is more trusted, more careful, more cautious than he, and this brief history of the unfolding series I have taken bodily from his writings.

Second.—As thus set forth, it may be said that Evolution is accepted as *the method* of creation by the whole scientific world, and that the period of controversy is passed and closed. A few venerable men yet live, with many doubts; but it may be said that ninety-nine per cent.—as has been declared by an eminent physicist—ninety-nine per cent. of scientific men and working scientists of the world are using this theory without any doubt of its validity. While the scientific world is at agreement upon this *order* of occurrence, it has been much divided as to the *causes* which have operated to bring about these results. There is a diversity of opinion still, but with every decade scientific men are drawing together to a common ground of belief.

Third.—The theory of Evolution is the *working* theory of every department of physical science all over the world. Withdraw this theory, and every department of physical research would fall back into heaps of hopelessly dislocated facts, with no more order or reason or philosophical coherence than exists in a basket of marbles, or in the juxtaposition of the multitudinous sands of the seashore. We should go back into chaos if we took out of the laboratories, out of the dissecting-rooms, out of the fields of investigation, this great doctrine of Evolution.

Fourth.—This science of Evolution is taught in all advanced academies, in all colleges and universities, in all medical and surgical schools, and our children are receiving it as they are the elements of astronomy or botany or chemistry.

That in another generation Evolution will be regarded as uncontradictable as the Copernican system of astronomy, or the Newtonian doctrine of gravitation, can scarcely be doubted. Each of these passed through the same contradiction by theologians. They were charged by the Church, as is Evolution now, with fostering materialism, infidelity, and atheism. We know what befell Galileo for telling the truth of God's primitive revelation. We know, or do not know, at least, how Newton stood charged with infidelity and with atheism when he announced the doctrine of gravitation. Who doubts the heliocentric theory to-day? Who doubts whether it is the sun which is moving round the earth or the earth round the sun? Who doubts that the law of attraction, as developed by Newton, is God's material law universally? The time is coming when the doctrine of Evolution, or the method of God in the creation of the world, will be just as universally accepted as either of these great physical doctrines. The whole Church fought them; yet they stand, conquerors.

Fifth.—Evolution is substantially held by men of profound Christian faith: by the now venerable and universally honored scientific teacher, Professor Dana of Yale College, a devout Christian and communicant of a Congregational Church; by Professor Le Conte of the University of California, an elder in the Presbyterian Church; by President McCosh of Princeton College, a Presbyterian of the Presbyterians, and a Scotch Presbyterian at that; by Professor Asa Gray of Harvard University, a communicant of the Christian Church; by increasing numbers of Christian preachers in America, by Catholics like Mivart, in England; by Wallace, a Christian not only, but of the spiritualistic school; by the Duke of Argyle of the Scotch Presbyterian Church; by Ground, an ardent admirer of Herbert Spencer and his whole theory, though rejecting his agnosticism —an eminent and leading divine in the Church of England; and finally, among hundreds of other soundly learned and Christian men, by the Bishop of London, Dr. Williams, whose Bampton Lectures for 1884 contain a bold, frank, and judicial estimate of Evolution, and its relations to Christianity.

Sixth.—To the fearful and the timid let me say, that while Evolution is certain to oblige theology to reconstruct its system, it will take nothing away from the grounds of true religion. It will strip off Saul's unmanageable armor from David, to give him greater power of the giant. Simple religion is the unfolding of the best nature of man towards God, and man has been hindered and embittered by the outrageous complexity of unbearable systems of theology that have existed. If you can change theology, you will emancipate religion; yet men are continually confounding the two terms, religion and theology. They are not alike. Religion is the condition of a man's nature as toward God and toward his fellow-men. That is religion—love that breeds truth, love that breeds justice, love that breeds harmonies of intimacy and intercommunication, love that breeds duty, love that breeds conscience, love that carries in its hand the scepter of pain, not to destroy and to torment, but to teach and to save. Religion is that state of mind in which a man is related by his emotions, and through his emotions by his will and conduct, to God and to the proper performance of duty in this world. Theology is the philosophy of God, of divine government, and of human nature. The philosophy of these may be one thing; the reality of them may be another and totally different one. Though intimately connected, they are not all the same. Theology is a science; religion, an art.

Evolution will multiply the motives and facilities of righteousness, which was and is the design of the whole Bible. It will not dull the executive doctrines of religion, that is, the forms of them by which an active and reviving ministry arouses men's consciences, by which they inspire faith, repentance, reformation, spiritual communion with God. Not only will those great truths be unharmed, by which men work zealously for the reformation of their fellow-men, but they will be developed to a breadth and certainty not possible in their present philosophical condition. At present the sword of the spirit is in the sheath of a false theology. Evolution, applied to religion, will influence it only as the hidden temples are restored, by removing the sands which have drifted in from the arid deserts of scholastic and medieval theologies. It will change theology, but only to bring out the simple temple of God in clearer and more beautiful lines and proportions.

Seventh.—In every view of it, I think we are to expect great practical fruit from the application of the truths that flow now from the interpretation of Evolution. It will obliterate the distinction between natural and revealed religion, both of which are the testimony of God; one, God's testimony as to what is best for man in his social and physical relations, and the other, what is best for man in his higher spiritual nature. What is called morality will be no longer dissevered from religion. Morals bear to spirituality the same relation which the root bears to the blossom and the fruit. Hitherto a false and imperfect theology has set them in two different provinces. We have been taught that morality will not avail us, and that spirituality is the only saving element: whereas, there is no spirituality itself without morality; all true spirituality is an outgrowth, it is the blossom and fruit on the stem of morality. It is time that these distinctions were obliterated, as they will be, by the progress and application of the doctrine of Evolution.

In every view, then, it is the duty of the friends of simple and unadulterated Christianity to hail the rising light and to uncover every element of religious teaching to its wholesome beams. Old men may be charitably permitted to die in peace, but young men and men in their prime are by God's providence laid under the most solemn obligation to thus discern the signs of the times, and to make themselves acquainted with the knowledge which science is laying before them. And above all, those zealots of the pulpit—who make faces at a science which they do not understand, and who reason from prejudice to ignorance, who not only will not lead their people, but hold up to scorn those who strive to take off the burden of ignorance from their shoulders—these men are bound to open their eyes and see God's sun shining in the heavens.
1885

EDWIN PERCY WHIPPLE

1819–1886

A NATIVE of Gloucester, Massachusetts, Whipple began his active life in a Boston brokerage firm. He quickly won a reputation for graceful platform speaking and for his critical essays. As a lyceum lecturer, as superintendent of the newsroom of the Merchants Exchange, and as literary editor of the *Boston Globe*, Whipple widened his contacts. His critical writing was analytical, sensitive to beauty, frequently witty, and sometimes politically imaginative. The following essay portrays the conservative's dislike of Darwinism, which occasioned wide cleavages in the literary and, particularly, in the religious world. Whipple's most important works are his *Essays and Reviews, 1848–1849* (1849), *American Literature and Other Papers* (1887), and *Outlooks on Society, Literature, and Politics* (1888).

T. W. Higginson, "Edwin Percy Whipple," *Short Studies of American Authors*, Boston, 1888.
B. J. Loewenberg, "Evolution in New England," *The New England Quarterly*, VIII (June, 1935).

» » *From:* OUTLOOKS ON SOCIETY, LITERATURE, « « AND POLITICS

MR. HARDHACK ON THE DERIVATION OF MAN FROM THE MONKEY

I can stand it no longer, sir. I have been seething and boiling inwardly for a couple of years at this last and final insult which science has put upon human nature, and now I must speak, or, if you will, explode. And how is it, I want to know, that the duty of hurling imprecations at this infernal absurdity has devolved upon me? Don't we employ a professional class to look after the interests of the race—fellows heavily feed to see to it that gorilla and chimpanzee kept their distance; paid, sir, by me and you to proclaim that men—ay, and women too—are at the top of things in origin, as well as in nature and destiny? Why are these retained attorneys of humanity so confoundedly cool and philosophical, while humanity is thus outraged? What's the use of their asserting, Sunday after Sunday, that men was made a little lower than the angels, when right under their noses are a set of anatomical miscreants who contend that he is only a little higher than the monkeys? And the thing has now gone so far, that I'll be hanged if it isn't becoming a sign of a narrow and prejudiced mind to scout the idea that we are all descended from mindless beasts. You are a fossilized old fogy, in this day of scientific light, if you repudiate your relationship with any fossilized monstrosity which, from the glass case of a museum, mocks at you with a grin a thousand centuries old. To exalt a man's soul above his skeleton, is now to be behind the age. All questions of philosophy, sir, are fast declining into a question of bones,—and blasted dry ones they are! The largest minds are now all absorbed in the ugliest brutes, and the ape has passed from being the butt of the menagerie to become the glory of the dissecting-room. And let me tell you, sir, that, if you make any pretensions to be a naturalist, you will find those of your co-laborers who defend the dominant theory as great masters of hard words as of big ones; and if you have the audacity to deny that man is derived from the monkey, it is ten chances to one they will forthwith proceed to treat you *like* one.

Now I go against the whole thing, sir. When the public mind first took its bent towards science, I, for one, foresaw that the devil would soon be to pay with our cherished ideas. Under the plea of exercising some of the highest faculties of human nature, these scientific descendentalists have exclusively devoted themselves to the lowest objects of human concern. The meaner the creature, the more they think of it.

You, sir, as a free and enlightened citizen of this great Republic, doubtless think something of yourself; but I can tell you there isn't one of these origin-of-species Solons who wouldn't pass you over as of no account in comparison with any anomalous rat which you would think it beneath your dignity to take the trouble of poisoning. There isn't a statesman, or a philanthropist, or poet, or hero, or saint in the land, sir, that they would condescend to look at, when engaged in exploring the remains of some ignorant ass of the Stone Period. As for your ordinary Christian, he has no chance whatever. The only man they think worth the attention of scientific intelligence is prehistoric man, the man nearest the monkey. And this is called progress! This is the result of founding schools, colleges, and societies for the advancement of knowledge! No interest now in Homer, Dante, Shakespeare, and Milton,—in Leonidas, Epaminondas, Tell, and Washington,—in Alexander, Hannibal, Caesar, and Napoleon. They, poor devils, were simply vertebrates; their structure is so well known that it is unworthy the attention of our modern prowlers into the earth's crust in search of lower and obscurer specimens of the same great natural division. What do you think these resurrectionists on a great scale, these Jerry Crunchers of palaeontology, care for you and me? Indeed, put Alfred Tennyson alive into one end of a museum, and one of those horrible monsters whose bones are being continually dug up into the other, and see which will be rated the more interesting object of the two by the "great minds" of the present day.

And now what is the consequence of thus inverting the proper objects of human concern? Why, if you estimate things according to their descent in the scale of dignity, and occupy your faculties exclusively with organized beings below man, you will tend to approach them. Evil communications corrupt good manners. You can't keep company with monkeys without insensibly getting be-monkeyed. Your mind feeds on them until its thoughts take their shape and nature. Into the "veins of your intellectual frame" monkey blood is injected. The monkey thus put into you naturally thinks that monkeydom is belied; and self-esteem, even, is not revolted by the idea of an ape genealogy. In this way the new theory of the origin of man originated. Huxley must have pretty thoroughly assimilated monkey before he recognized his ancestor in one. The poor beast himself may have made no pretensions to the honor, until he was mentally transformed into Huxley, entered into the substance of Huxley's mind, became inflamed with Huxley's arrogance. This is the true explanation, not perhaps of the origin of species, but of the origin of the theory of the origin; and I should like to thunder the great truth into the ears of all the scientific societies now talking monkey with the self-satisfied air of great discoverers. Yes, sir, and I should also be delighted to insinuate that this progress of monkey into man was not so great an example of "progressive development" as they seem inclined to suppose, and didn't require the long reaches of prehistoric time they consider necessary to account for the phenomenon. Twenty years would be enough, in all conscience, to effect *that* development.

Thus I tell you, sir, it isn't monkey that rises anatomically into man, but rather man that descends mentally into monkey. Why, nothing is more common than to apply to us human beings the names of animals when we display weaknesses analogous to their habitual characters. But this is metaphor, not classification; poetry, not science. Thus I, Solomon Hardhack, was called a donkey the other day by an intimate friend. Thought it merely a jocose reference to my obstinacy, and did not knock him down. Called the same name yesterday by a comparative anatomist. Thought it an insulting reference to my understanding, and did. But suppose that, in respect both to obstinacy and understanding, I had established to my own satisfaction a similarity between myself and that animal, do you imagine that I would be donkey enough to take the beast for my progenitor? Do you suppose that I would go even further, and, having established with the donkey a relation of descent, be mean enough to generalize the whole human race into participation in my calamity? No, sir, I am not sufficiently a man of science to commit that breach of good manners. Well, then, my proposition is, that nobody who reasons himself into a development from the monkey has the right to take mankind with him in his induction. His argument covers but one individual,—himself. As for the Hardhacks, they at least beg to be excused from joining him in that logical excursion, and insist on striking the monkey altogether out from their genealogical tree.

And speaking of genealogical trees, do the

adherents of this mad theory realize the disgrace they are bringing on the most respectable families? There is not an aristocracy in Europe or America that can stand it one moment, for aristocracy is based on the greatness of forefathers. In America, you know, nobody is aristocratic who cannot count back at least to his great-grandfather, who rode in a carriage, or—drove one. As for the Hardhacks, I may be allowed to say, though I despise family pride as much as any man, that they came in with the Conqueror and went out with the Puritans. But if this horrible Huxleian theory be true, the farther a person is from his origin, the better; antiquity of descent is no longer a title to honor; and a man must pride himself in looking forward to his descendants rather than back to his ancestors. And what comfort is this to me, an unmarried man? With a monkey in the background, how can even a Hapsburg or a Guelf put on airs of superiority? How must he hide his face in shame to think, that, as his line lengthens into an obscure antiquity, the foreheads of his house slope, and their jaws project; that he has literally been all his life aping aristocracy, instead of being the real thing; and that when he has reached his true beginning, his only consolation must be found in the fact that his great skulking, hulking, gibbering baboon of an ancestor rejoices, like himself, in the possession of "the third lobe," "the posterior cornu of the lateral ventricle," and "the hippocampus minor." Talk about radicalism, indeed! Why, I, who am considered an offence to my radical party for the extremes to which I run, cannot think of this swamping of all the families in the world without a thrill of horror and amazement! It makes my blood run cold to imagine this infernal Huxley pertly holding up the frontispiece of his book in the faces of the haughty nobility and gentry of his country, and saying, "Here, my friends, are drawings of the skeletons of gibbon, orang, chimpanzee, gorilla; select your ancestors; you pays your money and has your choice." I don't pretend to know anything about the temper of the present nobility and gentry of England; but if the fellow should do this thing to me, I would blow out of his skull everything in it which allied him with the apes,—taking a specially grim vengeance on "posterior cornu of the lateral ventricle,"—as sure as my name's Hardhack, and as sure as there's any explosive power in gunpowder.

And in this connection, too, I should like to know how the champions of this man-monkey scheme get over a theological objection. Don't start, sir, and say I am unscientific. I am not going to introduce Christianity, or monotheism, or polytheism, or fetichism, but a religion which you know was before them all, and which consisted in the worship of ancestors. If you are in the custom of visiting in good society, you will find that that is a form of worship which has not yet altogether died out, but roots itself in the most orthodox creeds. Now you must admit that the people who worshipped their ancestors were the earliest people of whose religion we have any archaeological record, and therefore a people who enjoyed the advantage of being nearer the ancestors of the race than any of the historical savages to whom you can appeal. I put it to you if this people, catching a glimpse of the monkey at the end of their line, if the monkey was really there, would have been such dolts as to worship it? A HE worship an IT! Don't you see, that, if this early people had nothing human but human conceit, that would alone have prevented them from doing this thing? Don't you see that they would have preserved a wise reticence in regard to such a shocking bar-sinister in their escutcheons? Worship ancestors, when ancestors are known to have been baboons! Why, you might as well tell me our fashionable friend Eglantine would worship his grandfather if he knew his grandfather was a hodman. No, sir. That early people worshipped their ancestors, because they knew their ancestors were higher and nobler than themselves. To suppose the contrary would be a cruel imputation on the character of worthy antediluvians, who unfortunately have left no written account of themselves, and therefore present peculiar claims on the charitable judgment of every candid mind.

You have been a boy, sir, and doubtless had your full share in that amusement, so congenial to ingenuous youth, of stirring up the monkeys. You remember what an agreeable feeling of elation, springing from a conscious sense of superiority to the animals pestered, accompanied that exhilarating game. But suppose, while you were engaged in it, the suspicion had flashed across your mind that you were worrying your own distant relations; that it was undeveloped humanity you were poking and deriding; that the frisking, chattering, snarling creature you were tormenting was trying all the while to say, in his unintelligible

speech, "Am I not *to be* a man and a brother?"
Would not such an appeal have dashed your
innocent mirth? Would you afterwards have
been so clamorous or beseeching for parental
pennies, as soon as the dead walls of your native town flamed with pictorial announcements
of the coming menagerie? No, sir, you couldn't
have passed a menagerie without a shudder of
loathing or a pang of remorse. How fortunate
10 it was, that, for the full enjoyment of your
youthful sports, you were ignorant of the affecting fact that the monkey's head as well as
your own possessed the "hippocampus minor"
and "the posterior cornu of the lateral ventricle"!

I admit that this last argument is not addressed to your understanding alone. I despise
all arguments on this point that are. I, for one,
am not to be reasoned out of my humanity,
20 and I won't be diddled into turning baboon
through deference for anybody's logic. My
opinions may be up for argument, but I myself am not up for argument. In a question affecting human nature itself, all the qualities
of that nature should be addressed. Self-respect, respect for your parentage and your race,
your moral instincts, and that force in you
which says "I,"—all these, having an interest
in such a discussion, should have a voice in
30 it; and I execrate the flunky who will allow
himself to be swindled out of manhood, and
swindled into monkeyhood, by that pitiful little
logic chopper he calls his understanding. I am
not "open to conviction" on this point, thank
God! I don't pretend to know whether a "third
lobe" is in my head or not, but I do know that
Solomon Hardhack is there, and as long as he
has possession of the premises, you will find
written on his brow, "No monkeys need apply!"
40 Do you tell me that this is a matter exclusively for anatomists and naturalists to decide?
That's the most impudent pretension of all.
Why, it's all the other way. Have I not a personal interest in the question greater than any
possible interest I can have in the diabolical
lingo of scientific terms in which those fellows
state the results of their investigations? Have I
delegated to any College of Surgeons the privilege of chimpanzeeizing my ancestors? No, sir.
50 Just look at it. Here are the members of the
human race, going daily about their various
avocations, entirely ignorant that any conspiracy is on foot to trick them out of their
fatherhood in Adam. While they are thus engaged in getting an honest living, a baker's

dozen of unauthorized miscreants assemble in
a dissecting-room, manipulate a lot of skulls,
and decide that the whole batch of us did not
descend from a human being. I tell you the
whole thing is an atrocious violation of the
rights of man. It's unconstitutional, sir! Talk
about the glorious principle of "No taxation
without representation!" That is simply a principle which affects our pockets, and we fought,
bled, and died for it. Shall we not do a thousands times more for our souls? Shall we let
our souls be voted away by a congress of dis-
sectors, not chosen by our votes,—persons who
not only don't represent, but infamously misrepresent us? Why, it's carrying the tactics of a
New York Common Council from politics into
metaphysics! And don't allow yourself to be
humbugged by these assassins of your nature.
I know the way they have of electioneering. It
is, "My dear Mr. Hardhack, a man of your intelligence can't look at this ascending scale of
skulls without seeing that the difference between Homo and Pithecus is of small account,"
—"A man of your candid mind, Mr. Hardhack,
must admit that no absolutely structural line of
demarcation, wider than that between the animals which immediately succeed us in the
scale, can be drawn between the animal world
and ourselves." And while I don't comprehend
a word of this cursed gibberish, I am expected
to bow, and look wise, and say, "Certainly,"
and "Just so," and "It's plain to the meanest
capacity," and be soft-sawdered out of my humanity, and infamously acknowledge myself
babooned. But they can't try it on me, sir.
When a man talks to me in that fashion, I
measure with *my* eyes "the structural line of
demarcation" between *his*, and with my whole
force plant there my fist.

Do you complain that I am speaking in a
passion? It seems to me it's about time for all
of us to be in a passion. Perhaps, if we show
these men of science that there is in us a little
righteous wrath, they may be considerate
enough to stop with the monkey,—make the
monkey "a finality," sir, and not go lower down
in the scale of creation to find an ancestor for
us. It is our meek submission to the monkey
which is now urging them to attempt more
desperate outrages still. What if Darwin had
been treated as he deserved when he published
the original edition of his villainous book? If I
had been Chief Justice of England when that
high priest of "natural selection" first tried to
oust me out of the fee-simple of my species, I

would have given him an illustration of "the struggle for existence" he wouldn't have relished. I would have hanged him on the highest gallows ever erected on this planet since the good old days of Haman. What has been the result of a mistaken clemency in this case? Why, he has just published a fourth edition of his treatise, and what do you think he now puts forward as our "probable" forefather? "It is probable," he says, "from what we know of the embryos of mammals, birds, fishes, and reptiles, that all the members in these four great classes are the modified descendants of one ancient progenitor, which was furnished in its adult state with branchiæ, had a swimbladder, four simple limbs, and a long tail fitted for an aquatic life." Probable, indeed! Why, it is also probable, I suppose, that this accounts for the latent tendency in the blood of our best-educated collegians to turn watermen, and abandon themselves with a kind of sacred fury to the fierce delight of rowing-matches. The "long tail fitted for an aquatic life" will also "probably" come in course of time. Student-mammals of Harvard and Yale, what think you of your "one ancient progenitor?" Inheritors of his nature, are you sure you have not yet succeeded in cutting off the entail of the estate?

We have been brought up, sir, in the delusive belief that "revolutions never go backwards." It's a lie, I tell you; for this new revolution in science does nothing else. It is going backwards and backwards and backwards, and it won't stop until it involves the whole of us in that nebulous mist of which, it seems, all things are but the "modified" development. Well, in for a penny, in for a pound. Let us not pause at that "long tail fitted for an aquatic life" which made our one ancient progenitor such an ornament of fluvial society, but boldly strike out into space, and clutch with our thoughts that primitive tail which flares behind the peacock of the heavens,—the comet. There's nebulous matter for your profound contemplation. That is the flimsy material out of which stars, earth, water, plants, jelly-fish, ancient progenitor, monkey, man, were all equally evolved. That is the grand original of all origins. We are such stuff as comets' tails are made of,—"third lobe," "hippocampus minor," "posterior cornu of the lateral ventricle," and all the rest. "Children of the Mist," we are made by this "sublime speculation" at home in the universe. Nebuchadnezzar, when

he went to grass, only visited a distant connection. The stars over our heads have for thousands of years been winking their relationship with us, and we have never intelligently returned the jocose salutation, until science taught us the use of our eyes. We are now able to detect the giggle, as of feminine cousins, in the grain whose risibilities are touched by the wind. We can now cheer even the dull stone which we kick from our path with a comforting "Hail fellow, well met!" We must not be aristocrats and put on airs. We must hob and nob with all the orders of creation, saying alike to radiates, articulates, and mollusks, "Go ahead, my hearties! don't be shamefaced; you're as good as vertebrates, and only want, like some of our human political lights, a little backbone to have your claims admitted. You are all on your glorious course manward, *via* the ancient progenitor and the chimpanzee. It seems a confounded long journey; for Nature is a slow coach, and thinks nothing of a million of years to effect a little transformation. But one of these days our science may find means to expedite that old sluggard, and hurry you through the intermediate grades in a way to astonish the venerable lady. Liberty, equality, and fraternity,—those are the words which will open the gates of your organized Bastiles, and send your souls on a career of swifter development. Trust in Darwin, and let creation ring with your song of 'A good time coming, Invertebrates!'"

Well, sir, you want logic, and there you have it with a vengeance! I have pitched you back into nebula, where these fellows tell me you belong, and I trust you're satisfied. Now what is my comfort, sir, after making my brain dizzy with this sublime speculation of theirs? Why, it's found in the fact that, by their own concession, the thing will not work, but must end in the biggest "catastrophe" ever heard of. The whole infernal humbug is to explode, sir, and by no exercise of their "hippocampus minor" can they prevent it. This fiery mist, which has hardened and rounded into our sun and planets, and developed into the monkey's "third lobe" and ours, does not lose the memory or the conceit of *its* origin, but is determined to get back into its first condition as quickly as circumstances will admit. It considers itself somehow to have been swindled in every step of the long process it has gone through in arriving at our brains. It doesn't think the speculation pays; prefers its lounging, vagabond, *dolce far niente* existence, loafing through the whole space between the sun and Neptune, to any satisfaction it finds in being concentrated in your thoughts or mine; and accordingly it meditates a *coup d'état* by which the planets are to fall into the sun at such a pace as to knock the whole system into eternal smash, and reduce it to its original condition of nebulous mist, sir. Do you like the prospect? I tell you there is no way of escaping from conclusions, if you are such a greenhorn as to admit premises. I have been over the whole chain of the logic, and find its only weak link is the monkey one. Knock that out, and you save the solar system as well as your own dignity as a man, sir; retain it, and some thousands of generations hence the brains of your descendants will be blown into a texture as gauzy as a comet's tail, and it will be millions of ages before, in the process of a new freak of development in the unquiet nebula, they can hope to arrive again at the honor of possessing that inestimable boon, dear equally to baboons and to men, "the posterior cornu of the lateral ventricle"!

1888

ROBERT G. INGERSOLL

1833–1899

THE TRADITION of freethinking which Thomas Paine and others at the end of the eighteenth century did so much to stimulate did not completely die in spite of the revival of religion. During the Jacksonian period Abner Kneeland, Frances Wright, and Robert Dale Owen did much to revivify it. But no nineteenth-century American figure was so important as "the great agnostic," as Ingersoll was known to his contemporaries. The son of a clergyman, he studied law and was admitted to the Illinois bar at the age of twenty-one. Ingersoll took part in the Civil War and played a role of some prominence in the Republican party: in particular his speech in 1876 nominating James G. Blaine for the presidency was a spectacular oratorical triumph. In 1879 Ingersoll left Peoria and became well known in the legal circles of the national capital.

Ingersoll might well have enjoyed a high place in politics had it not been for his championship of agnosticism. A doubter even before the appearance of *Origin of Species*, he was confirmed by the work of both Darwin and Huxley. Ingersoll's platform lectures on agnosticism were no doubt the chief means by which that position was popularized during his lifetime.

The Works of Robert G. Ingersoll, New Dresden Edition, 12 vols., New York, 1900 (Reprinted in 1902, 1909, and 1910).

H. E. Kittredge, *Ingersoll, A Biographical Appreciation*, New York, 1911.

Cameron Rogers, *Colonel Bob Ingersoll*, Garden City, 1927.

» » WHY AM I AN AGNOSTIC? « «

PART I

"With thoughts beyond the reaches of our souls."

The same rules or laws of probability must govern in religious questions as in others. There is no subject—and can be none—concerning which any human being is under any obliga-

tion to believe without evidence. Neither is there any intelligent being who can, by any possibility, be flattered by the exercise of ignorant credulity. The man who, without prejudice, reads and understands the Old and New Testaments will cease to be an orthodox Christian. The intelligent man who investigates the religion of any country without fear and without prejudice will not and cannot be a believer.

Most people, after arriving at the conclusion that Jehovah is not God, that the Bible is not an inspired book, and that the Christian religion, like other religions, is the creation of man, usually say: "There must be a Supreme Being, but Jehovah is not his name, and the Bible is not his word. There must be somewhere an over-ruling Providence or Power."

This position is just as untenable as the other. He who cannot harmonize the cruelties of the Bible with the goodness of Jehovah, cannot harmonize the cruelties of Nature with the goodness and wisdom of a supposed Deity. He will find it impossible to account for pestilence and famine, for earthquake and storm, for slavery, for the triumph of the strong over the weak, for the countless victories of injustice. He will find it impossible to account for martyrs —for the burning of the good, the noble, the loving, by the ignorant, the malicious, and the infamous.

How can the Deist satisfactorily account for the sufferings of women and children? In what way will he justify religious persecution—the flame and sword of religious hatred? Why did his God sit idly on his throne and allow his enemies to wet their swords in the blood of his friends? Why did he not answer the prayers of the imprisoned, of the helpless? And when he heard the lash upon the naked back of the slave, why did he not also hear the prayer of the slave? And when children were sold from the breasts of mothers, why was he deaf to the mother's cry?

It seems to me that the man who knows the limitations of the mind, who gives the proper value to human testimony, is necessarily an Agnostic. He gives up the hope of ascertaining first or final causes, of comprehending the supernatural, or of conceiving of an infinite personality. From out the words Creator, Preserver, and Providence, all meaning falls.

The mind of man pursues the path of least resistance, and the conclusions arrived at by the individual depend upon the nature and structure of his mind, on his experience, on hereditary drifts and tendencies, and on the countless things that constitute the difference in minds. One man, finding himself in the midst of mysterious phenomena, comes to the conclusion that all is the result of design; that back of all things is an infinite personality— that is to say, an infinite man; and he accounts for all that is by simply saying that the universe was created and set in motion by this infinite personality, and that it is miraculously and supernaturally governed and preserved. This man sees with perfect clearness that matter could not create itself, and therefore he imagines a creator of matter. He is perfectly satisfied that there is design in the world, and that consequently there must have been a designer. It does not occur to him that it is necessary to account for the existence of an infinite personality. He is perfectly certain that there can be no design without a designer, and he is equally certain that there can be a designer who was not designed. The absurdity becomes so great that it takes the place of a demonstration. He takes it for granted that matter was created and that its creator was not. He assumes that a creator existed from eternity, without cause, and created what is called matter out of nothing; or, whereas there was nothing, this creator made the something that we call substance.

Is it possible for the human mind to conceive of an infinite personality? Can it imagine a beginningless being, infinitely powerful and intelligent? If such a being existed, then there must have been an eternity during which nothing did exist except this being; because, if the Universe was created, there must have been a time when it was not, and back of that there must have been an eternity during which nothing but an infinite personality existed. Is it possible to imagine an infinite intelligence dwelling for an eternity in infinite nothing? How could such a being be intelligent? What was there to be intelligent about? There was but one thing to know, namely, that there was nothing except this being. How could such a being be powerful? There was nothing to exercise force upon. There was nothing in the universe to suggest an idea. Relations could not exist—except the relation between infinite intelligence and infinite nothing.

The next great difficulty is the act of creation. My mind is so that I cannot conceive of something being created out of nothing. Neither can I conceive of anything being created without a cause. Let me go one step further. It is just as difficult to imagine something being created with, as without, a cause. To postulate a cause does not in the least lessen the difficulty. In spite of all, this lever remains without a fulcrum. We cannot conceive of the destruction of substance. The stone can be crushed to powder, and the powder can be ground to such a fineness that the atoms can only be distinguished by the most powerful microscope, and we can then imagine these atoms being divided and subdivided again and again and again; but it is impossible for us to conceive of the annihilation of the least possible imaginable fragment of the least atom of which we can think. Consequently the mind can imagine neither creation nor destruction. From this point it is very easy to reach the generalization that the indestructible could not have been created.

These questions, however, will be answered by each individual according to the structure of his mind, according to his experience, according to his habits of thought, and according to his intelligence or his ignorance, his prejudice or his genius.

Probably a very large majority of mankind believe in the existence of supernatural beings, and a majority of what are known as the civilized nations, in an infinite personality. In the realm of thought majorities do not determine. Each brain is a kingdom, each mind is a sovereign.

The universality of a belief does not even tend to prove its truth. A large majority of mankind have believed in what is known as God, and an equally large majority have as implicitly believed in what is known as the Devil. These beings have been inferred from phenomena. They were produced for the most part by ignorance, by fear, and by selfishness. Man in all ages has endeavored to account for the mysteries of life and death, of substance, of force, for the ebb and flow of things, for earth and star. The savage, dwelling in his cave, subsisting on roots and reptiles, or on beasts that could be slain with club and stone, surrounded by countless objects of terror, standing by rivers, so far as he knew, without source or end, by seas with but one shore, the prey of beasts mightier than himself, of diseases strange and fierce, trembling at the voice of thunder, blinded by the lightning, feeling the earth shake beneath him, seeing the sky lurid with the volcano's glare,—fell prostrate and begged for the protection of the Unknown.

In the long night of savagery, in the midst of pestilence and famine, through the long and dreary winters, crouched in dens of darkness, the seeds of superstition were sown in the brain of man. The savage believed, and thoroughly believed, that everything happened in reference to him; that he by his actions could excite the anger, or by his worship placate the wrath, of the Unseen. He resorted to flattery and prayer. To the best of his ability he put in stone, or rudely carved in wood, his idea of this god. For this idol he built a hut, a hovel, and at last a cathedral. Before these images he bowed, and at these shrines, whereon he lavished his wealth, he sought protection for himself and for the ones he loved. The few took advantage of the ignorant many. They pretended to have received messages from the Unknown. They stood between the helpless multitude and the gods. They were the carriers of flags of truce. At the court of heaven they presented the cause of man, and upon the labor of the deceived they lived.

The Christian of to-day wonders at the savage who bowed before his idol; and yet it must be confessed that the god of stone answered prayer and protected his worshipers precisely as the Christian's God answers prayer and protects his worshipers to-day.

My mind is so that it is forced to the conclusion that substance is eternal; that the universe was without beginning and will be without end; that it is the one eternal existence; that relations are transient and evanescent; that organisms are produced and vanish; that forms change,—but that the substance of things is from eternity to eternity. It may be that planets are born and die, that constellations will fade from the infinite spaces, that countless suns will be quenched,—but the substance will remain.

The questions of origin and destiny seem to be beyond the powers of the human mind.

Heredity is on the side of superstition. All our ignorance pleads for the old. In most men there is a feeling that their ancestors were exceedingly good and brave and wise, and that in all things pertaining to religion their conclusions should be followed. They believe that their fathers and mothers were of the best, and that that which satisfied them should satisfy their children. With a feeling of reverence they say that the religion of their mother is good enough and pure enough and reasonable enough for them. In this way the love of parents and the reverence for ancestors have unconsciously bribed the reason and put out, or rendered exceedingly dim, the eyes of the mind.

There is a kind of longing in the heart of the old to live and die where their parents lived and died—a tendency to go back to the homes of their youth. Around the old oak of manhood grow and cling these vines. Yet it will hardly do to say that the religion of my mother is good enough for me, any more than to say the geology or the astronomy or the philosophy of my mother is good enough for me. Every human being is entitled to the best he can obtain; and if there has been the slightest improvement on the religion of the mother, the son is entitled to that improvement, and he should not deprive himself of that advantage by the mistaken idea that he owes it to his mother to perpetuate, in a reverential way, her ignorant mistakes.

If we are to follow the religion of our fathers and mothers, our fathers and mothers should have followed the religion of theirs. Had this been done, there could have been no improvement in the world of thought. The first religion would have been the last, and the child would have died as ignorant as the mother. Progress would have been impossible, and on the graves of ancestors would have been sacrificed the intelligence of mankind.

We know, too, that there has been the religion of the tribe, of the community, and of the nation, and that there has been a feeling that it was the duty of every member of the tribe or community, and of every citizen of the nation, to insist upon it that the religion of the tribe, community, of that nation, was better than that of any other. We know that all the prejudices against other religions, and all the egotism of nation and tribe, were in favor of the local superstition. Each citizen was patriotic enough to denounce the religions of other nations and to stand firmly by his own. And there is this peculiarity about man; he can see the absurdities of other religions while blinded to those of his own. The Christian can see clearly enough that Mohammed was an impostor. He is sure of it, because the people of Mecca who were acquainted with him declared that he was no prophet; and this declaration is received by Christians as a demonstration that Mohammed was not inspired. Yet these same Christians admit that the people of Jerusalem who were acquainted with Christ rejected him; and this rejection they take as proof positive that Christ was the Son of God.

The average man adopts the religion of his country, or, rather, the religion of his country adopts him. He is dominated by the egotism of race, the arrogance of nation, and the prejudice called patriotism. He does not reason—he feels. He does not investigate—he believes. To him the religions of other nations are absurd and infamous, and their gods monsters of ignorance and cruelty. In every country this average man is taught, first, that there is a supreme being; second, that he has made known his will; third, that he will reward the true believer; fourth, that he will punish the unbeliever, the scoffer, and the blasphemer; fifth, that certain ceremonies are pleasing to this god; sixth, that he has established a church; and seventh, that priests are his representatives on earth. And the average man has no difficulty in determining that the God of his nation is the true God; that the will of this true God is contained in the sacred scriptures of his nation; that he is one of the true believers, and that the people of other nations—that is, believing other religions—are scoffers; that the only true church is the one to which he belongs; and that the priests of his country are the only ones who have had or ever will have the slightest influence with this true God. All these absurdities to the average man seem self-evident propositions; and so he holds all other creeds in scorn, and congratulates himself that he is a favorite of the one true God.

If the average Christian had been born in Turkey, he would have been a Mohammedan; and if the average Mohammedan had been born in New England and educated at Andover, he would have regarded the damnation of the heathen as the "tidings of great joy."

Nations have eccentricities, peculiarities, and hallucinations, and these find expression in their laws, customs, ceremonies, morals, and religions. And these are in great part determined by soil, climate, and the countless circumstances that mould and dominate the lives and habits of insects, individuals, and nations. The average man believes implicity in the religion of his country, because he knows nothing of any other and has no desire to know. It fits him because he has been deformed to fit it; and he regards this fact of fit as an evidence of its inspired truth.

Has a man the right to examine, to investigate, the religion of his own country—the religion of his father and mother? Christians admit that the citizens of all countries not Christian have not only this right, but that it is their solemn duty. Thousands of missionaries are sent to heathen countries to persuade the believers in other religions not only to examine their superstitions, but to renounce them, and to adopt those of the missionaries. It is the duty of a heathen to disregard the religion of his country and to hold in contempt the creed of his father and of his mother. If the citizens of heathen nations have the right to examine the foundations of their religion, it would seem that the citizens of Christian nations have the same right. Christians, however, go further than this; they say to the heathen: You must examine your religion, and not only so, but you must reject it; and, unless you do reject it, and, in addition to such rejection, adopt ours, you will be eternally damned. Then these same Christians say to the inhabitants of a Christian country: You must not examine; you must not investigate; but whether you examine or not, you must believe, or you will be eternally damned.

If there be one true religion, how it is possible to ascertain which of all the religions the true one is? There is but one way. We must impartially examine the claims of all. The right to examine involves the necessity to accept or reject. Understand me, not the right to accept or reject, but the necessity. From this conclusion there is no possible escape. If, then, we have the right to examine, we have the right to tell the conclusion reached. Christians have examined other religions somewhat, and they have expressed their opinion with the utmost freedom—that is to say, they have denounced them all as false and fraudulent; have called their gods idols and myths, and their priests impostors.

The Christian does not deem it worth while to read the Koran. Probably not one Christian in a thousand ever saw a copy of that book. And yet all Christians are perfectly satisfied that the Koran is the work of an impostor. No Presbyterian thinks it is worth his while to examine the religious systems of India; he knows that the Brahmins are mistaken, and that all their miracles are falsehoods. No Methodist cares to read the life of Buddha, and no Baptist will waste his time studying the ethics of Confucius. Christians of every sort and kind take it for granted that there is only one true religion, and that all except Christianity are absolutely without foundation. The Christian world believes that all the prayers of India are unanswered; that all the sacrifices upon the countless altars of Egypt, of Greece, and of Rome were without effect. They believe that all these mighty nations worshiped their gods

in vain; that their priests were deceivers or deceived; that their ceremonies were wicked or meaningless; that their temples were built by ignorance and fraud, and that no God heard their songs of praise, their cries of despair, their words of thankfulness; that on account of their religion no pestilence was stayed; that the earthquake and volcano, the flood and storm went on their ways of death—while the real God looked on and laughed at their calamities and mocked at their fears.

We find now that the prosperity of nations has depended, not upon their religion, not upon the goodness or providence of some god, but on soil and climate and commerce, upon the ingenuity, industry, and courage of the people, upon the development of the mind, on the spread of education, on the liberty of thought and action; and that in this mighty panorama of national life, reason has built and superstition has destroyed.

Being satisfied that all believe precisely as they must, and that religions have been naturally produced, I have neither praise nor blame for any man. Good men have had bad creeds, and bad men have had good ones. Some of the noblest of the human race have fought and died for the wrong. The brain of man has been the trysting-place of contradictions. Passion often masters reason, and "the state of man, like to a little kingdom, suffers then the nature of an insurrection."

In the discussion of theological or religious questions, we have almost passed the personal phase, and we are now weighing arguments instead of exchanging epithets and curses. They who really seek for truth must be the best of friends. Each knows that his desire can never take the place of fact, and that, next to finding truth, the greatest honor must be won in honest search.

We see that many ships are driven in many ways by the same wind. So men, reading the same book, write many creeds and lay out many roads to heaven. To the best of my ability, I have examined the religions of many countries and the creeds of many sects. They are much alike, and the testimony by which they are substantiated is of such a character that to those who believe is promised an eternal reward. In all the sacred books there are some truths, some rays of light, some words of love and hope. The face of savagery is sometimes softened by a smile—the human triumphs, and the heart breaks into song. But in these books are also found the words of fear and hate, and from their pages crawl serpents that coil and hiss in all the paths of men.

For my part, I prefer the books that inspiration has not claimed. Such is the nature of my brain that Shakespeare gives me greater joy than all the prophets of the ancient world. There are thoughts that satisfy the hunger of the mind. I am convinced the Humboldt knew more of geology than the author of Genesis; that Darwin was a greater naturalist than he who told the story of the flood; that Laplace was better acquainted with the habits of the sun and moon than Joshua could have been; and that Haeckel, Huxley, and Tyndall know more about the earth and stars, about the history of man, the philosophy of life—more that is of use, ten thousand times—than all the writers of the sacred books.

I believe in the religion of reason—the gospel of this world; in the development of the mind, in the accumulation of intellectual wealth, to the end that man may free himself from superstitious fear, to the end that he may take advantage of the forces of nature to feed and clothe the world.

Let us be honest with ourselves. In the presence of countless mysteries; standing beneath the boundless heaven sown thick with constellations; knowing that each grain of sand, each leaf, each blade of grass, asks of every mind the answerless question; knowing that the simplest thing defies solution; feeling that we deal with the superficial and the relative, and that we are forever eluded by the real, the absolute,—let us admit the limitations of our minds, and let us have the courage and the candor to say: We do not know.   1889

PART II

The Christian religion rests on miracles. There are no miracles in the realm of science. The real philosopher does not seek to excite wonder, but to make that plain which was wonderful. He does not endeavor to astonish, but to enlighten. He is perfectly confident that there are no miracles in nature. He knows that the mathematical expression of the same relations, contents, areas, numbers and proportions must forever remain the same. He knows that there are no miracles in chemistry; that the attractions and repulsions, the love and hatreds, of atoms are constant. Under like conditions,

he is certain that like will always happen; that the product ever has been and forever will be the same; that the atoms or particles unite in definite, unvarying proportions,—so many of one kind mix, mingle, and harmonize with just so many of another, and the surplus will be forever cast out. There are no exceptions. Substances are always true to their natures. They have no caprices, no prejudices, that can vary or control their action. They are "the same yesterday, today, and forever."

In this fixedness, this constancy, this eternal integrity, the intelligent man has absolute confidence. It is useless to tell him that there was a time when fire would not consume the combustible, when water would not flow in obedience to the attraction of gravitation, or that there ever was a fragment of a moment during which substance had no weight.

Credulity should be the servant of intelligence. The ignorant have not credulity enough to believe the actual, because the actual appears to be contrary to the evidence of their senses. To them it is plain that the sun rises and sets, and they have not credulity enough to believe in the rotary motion of the earth —that is to say, they have not intelligence enough to comprehend the absurdities involved in their belief, and the perfect harmony between the rotation of the earth and all known facts. They trust their eyes, not their reason. Ignorance has always been and always will be at the mercy of appearance. Credulity, as a rule, believes everything except the truth. The semi-civilized believe in astrology, but who could convince them of the vastness of astronomical spaces, the speed of light, or the magnitude and number of suns and constellations? If Hermann, the magician, and Humboldt, the philosopher, could have appeared before savages, who would have been regarded as a god?

When men knew nothing of mechanics, nothing of the correlation of force, and of its indestructibility, they were believers in perpetual motion. So when chemistry was a kind of sleight-of-hand, or necromancy, something accomplished by the aid of the supernatural, people talked about the transmutation of metals, the universal solvent, and the philosopher's stone. Perpetual motion would be a mechanical miracle; and the transmutation of metals would be a miracle in chemistry; and if we could make the result of multiplying two by two five, that would be a miracle in mathematics. No one expects to find a circle the diameter of which is just one fourth of the circumference. If one could find such a circle, then there would be a miracle in geometry.

In other words, there are no miracles in any science. The moment we understand a question or subject, the miraculous necessarily disappears. If anything actually happens in the chemical world, it will, under like conditions, happen again. No one need take an account of this result from mouths of others; all can try the experiment for themselves. There is no caprice, and no accident.

It is admitted, at least in the Protestant world, that the age of miracles has passed away, and, consequently, miracles cannot at present be established by miracles; they must be substantiated by the testimony of witnesses who are said by certain writers—or, rather, by uncertain writers—to have lived several centuries ago; and this testimony is given to us, not by the witnesses themselves, not by persons who say that they talked with those witnesses, but by unknown persons who did not give the sources of their information.

The question is: Can miracles be established except by miracles? We know that the writers may have been mistaken. It is possible that they may have manufactured these accounts themselves. The witnesses may have told what they knew to be untrue, or they may have been honestly deceived, or the stories may have been true as at first told. Imagination may have added greatly to them, so that after several centuries of accretion a very simple truth was changed to a miracle.

We must admit that all probabilities must be against miracles, for the reason that that which is probable cannot by any possibility be a miracle. Neither the probable nor the possible, so far as man is concerned, can be miraculous. The probability therefore says that the writers and witnesses were either mistaken or dishonest.

We must admit that we have never seen a miracle ourselves, and we must admit that, according to our experience, there are no miracles. If we have mingled with the world, we are compelled to say that we have known a vast number of persons—including ourselves —to be mistaken, and many others who have failed to tell the exact truth. The probabilities are on the side of our experience, and consequently, against the miraculous; and it is a

necessity that the free mind moves along the path of least resistance.

The effect of testimony depends on the intelligence and honesty of the witness and the intelligence of him who weighs. A man living in a community where the supernatural is expected, where the miraculous is supposed to be of almost daily occurrence, will, as a rule, believe that all wonderful things are the result of supernatural agencies. He will expect providential interference, and, as a consequence, his mind will pursue the path of least resistance, and will account for all phenomena by what to him is the easiest method. Such people, with the best intentions, honestly bear false witness. They have been imposed upon by appearances, and are victims of delusion and illusion.

In the age when reading and writing were substantially unknown, and when history itself was but the vaguest hearsay handed down from dotage to infancy, nothing was rescued from oblivion except the wonderful, the miraculous. The more marvelous the story, the greater the interest excited. Narrators and hearers were alike ignorant and alike honest. At that time nothing was known, nothing suspected, of the orderly course of nature—of the unbroken and unbreakable chain of causes and effects. The world was governed by caprice. Everything was at the mercy of a being, or beings, who were themselves controlled by the same passions that dominated man. Fragments of facts were taken for the whole, and the deductions drawn were honest and monstrous.

It is probably certain that all the religions of the world have been believed, and that all the miracles have found credence in countless brains; otherwise they could not have been perpetuated. They were not all born of cunning. Those who told were as honest as those who heard. This being so, nothing has been too absurd for human credence.

All religions, so far as I know, claim to have been miraculously founded, miraculously preserved, and miraculously propagated. The priests of all claimed to have messages from God, and claimed to have a certain authority, and the miraculous has always been appealed to for the purpose of substantiating the message and the authority.

If men believe in the supernatural, they will account for all phenomena by an appeal to supernatural means of power. We know that formerly everything was accounted for in this way except some few simple things with which man thought he was perfectly acquainted. After a time men found that under like conditions like would happen, and as to those things the supposition of supernatural interference was abandoned; but that interference was still active as to all the unknown world. In other words, as the circle of man's knowledge grew, supernatural interference withdrew and was active only just beyond the horizon of the known.

Now, there are some believers in universal special providence—that is, men who believe in perpetual interference by a supernatural power, this interference being for the purpose of punishing or rewarding, of destroying or preserving, individuals and nations.

Others have abandoned the idea of providence in ordinary matters, but still believe that God interferes on great occasions and at critical moments, especially in the affairs of nations, and that his presence is manifest in great disasters. This is the compromise position. These people believe that an infinite being made the universe and impressed upon it what they are pleased to call "laws," and then left it to run in accordance with those laws and forces; that as a rule it works well, and that the divine maker interferes only in cases of accident, or at moments when the machine fails to accomplish the original design.

There are others who take the ground that all is natural; that there never has been, never will be, never can be any interference from without, for the reason that nature embraces all, and that there can be no without or beyond.

The first class are Theists pure and simple; the second are Theists as to the unknown, Naturalists as to the known; and the third are Naturalists without a touch or taint of superstition.

What can the evidence of the first class be worth? This question is answered by reading the history of those nations that believed thoroughly and implicitly in the supernatural. There is no conceivable absurdity that was not established by their testimony. Every law or every fact in nature was violated. Children were born without parents; men lived for thousands of years; others subsisted without food, without sleep; thousands and thousands were possessed with evil spirits controlled by ghosts and ghouls; thousands confessed themselves guilty of impossible offences, and in courts, with the most solemn forms, impossibilities were substantiated by the oaths, affirmations, and confessions of men, women, and children.

These delusions were not confined to ascetics and peasants, but they took possession of nobles and kings; of people who were at that time called intelligent; of the then educated. No one denied these wonders, for the reason that denial was a crime punishable generally with death. Societies, nations, became insane—victims of ignorance, of dreams, and, above all, of fears. Under these conditions human testimony is not and cannot be of the slightest value. We now know that nearly all of the history of the world is false, and we know this because we have arrived at that phase or point of intellectual development where and when we know that effects must have causes, that everything is naturally produced, and that, consequently, no nation could ever have been great, powerful, and rich unless it had the soil, the people, the intelligence, and the commerce. Weighed in these scales, nearly all histories are found to be fictions.

The same is true of religions. Every intelligent American is satisfied that the religions of India, of Egypt, of Greece and Rome, of the Aztecs, were and are false, and that all the miracles on which they rest are mistakes. Our religion alone is excepted. Every intelligent Hindoo discards all religions and all miracles except his own. The question is: When will people see the defects in their own theology as clearly as they perceive the same defects in every other?

All the so-called false religions were substantiated by miracles, by signs and wonders, by prophets and martyrs, precisely as our own. Our witnesses are no better than theirs, and our success is no greater. If their miracles were false, ours cannot be true. Nature was the same in India and in Palestine.

One of the corner-stones of Christianity is the miracle of inspiration, and this same miracle lies at the foundation of all religions. How can the fact of inspiration be established? How could even the inspired man know that he was inspired? If he was influenced to write, and did write, and did express thoughts and facts that to him were absolutely new, on subjects about which he had previously known nothing, how could he know that he had been influenced by an infinite being? And if he could know, how could he convince others?

What is meant by inspiration? Did the one inspired set down only the thoughts of a supernatural being? Was he simply an instrument, or did his personality color the message received and given? Did he mix his ignorance with the divine information, his prejudices and hatreds with the love and justice of the Deity? If God told him not to eat the flesh of any beast that dieth of itself, did the same infinite being also tell him to sell this meat to the stranger within his gates?

A man says that he is inspired—that God appeared to him in a dream, and told him certain things. Now, the things said to have been communicated may have been good and wise; but will the fact that the communication is good or wise establish the inspiration? If, on the other hand, the communication is absurd or wicked, will that conclusively show that the man was not inspired? Must we judge from the communication? In other words, is our reason to be the final standard?

How could the inspired man know that the communication was received from God? If God in reality should appear to a human being, how could this human being know who had appeared? By what standard would he judge? Upon this question man has no experience; he is not familiar enough with the supernatural to know gods even if they exist. Although thousands have pretended to receive messages, there has been no message in which there was, or is, anything above the invention of man. There are just as wonderful things in the uninspired as in the inspired books, and the prophecies of the heathen have been fulfilled equally with those of the Judean prophets. If, then, even the inspired man cannot certainly know that he is inspired, how is it possible for him to demonstrate his inspiration to others? The last solution of this question is that inspiration is a miracle about which only the inspired can have the least knowledge, or the least evidence, and this knowledge and this evidence not of a character to absolutely convince even the inspired.

There is certainly nothing in the Old or the New Testament that could not have been written by uninspired human beings. To me there is nothing of any particular value in the Pentateuch. I do not know of a solitary scientific truth contained in the five books commonly attributed to Moses. There is not, as far as I know, a line in the book of Genesis calculated to make a human being better. The laws contained in Exodus, Leviticus, Numbers, and Deuteronomy are for the most part puerile and cruel. Surely there is nothing in any of these books that could not have been produced by uninspired men. Certainly there is nothing calculated to excite intellectual admiration in the book of Judges or in the word of Joshua; and the same may be said of Samuel, Chronicles, and Kings. The history is extremely childish, full of repetitions of useless details, without the slightest philosophy, without a generalization born of a wide survey. Nothing is known of other nations; nothing imparted of the slightest value; nothing about education, discovery, or invention. And these idle and stupid annals are interspersed with myth and miracle, with flattery for kings who supported priests, and with curses and denunciations for those who would not hearken to the voice of the prophets. If all the historic books of the Bible were blotted from the memory of mankind, nothing of value would be lost.

Is it possible that the writer or writers of First and Second Kings were inspired, and that Gibbon wrote "The Decline and Fall of the Roman Empire" without supernatural assistance? Is it possible that the author of Judges was simply the instrument of an infinite God, while John W. Draper wrote "The Intellectual Development of Europe" without one ray of light from the other world? Can we believe that the author of Genesis had to be inspired, while Darwin experimented, ascertained, and reached conclusions for himself?

Ought not the work of a God to be vastly superior to that of a man? And if the writers of the Bible were in reality inspired, ought not that book to be the greatest of books? For instance, if it were contended that certain statues had been chiselled by inspired men, such statues should be superior to any that uninspired man has made. As long as it is admitted that the Venus de Milo is the work of man, no one will believe in inspired sculptors—at least until a superior statue has been found. So in the world of painting. We admit that Corot was inspired. Nobody claims that Angelo had supernatural assistance. Now, if some one should claim that a certain painter was simply the instrumentality of God, certainly the pictures produced by that painter should be superior to all others.

I do not see how it is possible for an intelligent human being to conclude that the Song of Solomon is the work of God, and that the tragedy of Lear was the work of an uninspired man. We are all liable to be mistaken, but the Iliad seems to me a greater work than the Book of Esther, and I prefer it to the writings of Haggai and Hosea. Aeschylus is superior to Jeremiah, and Shakespeare rises immeasurably above all the sacred books of the world.

It does not seem possible that any human being ever tried to establish a truth—anything that really happened—by what is called a miracle. It is easy to understand how that which was common became wonderful by accretion,—by things added, and by things forgotten,—and it is easy to conceive how that which was wonderful became by accretion what was called supernatural. But it does not seem possible that any intelligent, honest man ever endeavored to prove anything by a miracle.

As a matter of fact, miracles could only satisfy people who demanded no evidence; else how could they have believed the miracle? It also appears to be certain that, even if miracles had been performed, it would be impossible to establish that fact by human testimony. In other words, miracles can only be established by miracles, and in no event could miracles be evidence except to those who were actually present; and in order for miracles to be of any value, they would have to be perpetual. It must also be remembered that a miracle actually performed could by no possibility shed any light on any moral truth, or add to any human obligation.

If any man has ever been inspired, this is a secret miracle, known to no person, and suspected only by the man claiming to be inspired. It would not be in the power of the inspired to give satisfactory evidence of that fact to anybody else.

The testimony of man is insufficient to establish the supernatural. Neither the evidence of one man nor of twelve can stand when contradicted by the experience of the intelligent world. If a book sought to be proved by mira 10 cles is true, then it makes no difference whether it was inspired or not; and if it is not true, inspiration cannot add to its value.

The truth is that the church has always— unconsciously, perhaps—offered rewards for falsehood. It was founded upon the supernatural, the miraculous, and it welcomed all statements calculated to support the foundation. It rewarded the traveller who found evidences of the miraculous, who had seen the pillar of salt 20 into which the wife of Lot had been changed, and the tracks of Pharaoh's chariots on the sands of the Red Sea. It heaped honors on the historian who filled his pages with the absurd and impossible. It had geologists and astronomers of its own who constructed the earth and the constellations in accordance with the Bible. With sword and flame it destroyed the brave and thoughtful men who told the truth. It was the enemy of investigation and of rea 30 son. Faith and fiction were in partnership.

Today the intelligence of the world denies the miraculous. Ignorance is the soil of the supernatural. The foundation of Christianity has crumbled, has disappeared, and the entire fabric must fall. The natural is true. The miraculous is false.   1890

MARY BAKER G. EDDY

1821–1910

IT WAS the function of Mary Baker G. Eddy, one of the most gifted religious leaders of modern times, to acclimatize and to organize for wide consumption a pattern of thought and feeling which was rooted in the "come-outism," the transcendentalism, the spiritualism, and the mesmerism which stirred the New England of a hundred years ago. The daughter of a New Hampshire farmer, Mary Baker G. Eddy suffered, not only during, but long after her childhood, from various nervous and emotional disturbances which made her, for much of the time, a wretched invalid. Thanks to the therapeutic treatment of Dr. Phineas P. Quimby of

Portland, Maine, and to her own perseverance, she won both a fair measure of health and the incentive, perhaps, to evolve a metaphysical, religious, and curative system of her own. The first edition of *Science and Health* (1875) repudiated the dualism of mind and matter. It insisted on the exclusive primacy of Eternal Mind. It held that all sickness, physical and mental, was merely an "error," that it might be vanquished by right thinking. Of Mrs. Eddy's talents as a promoter and organizer no one, not even her harshest critic, has ever had any doubt. Her message, and the effective organization given it, appealed to many whom more conventional religion left cold; to others whose ailments had defied the medical treatment that had been summoned; and to still others who welcomed Christian Science for its optimism, its assurance that there was nothing at all incompatible between material prosperity and high spirituality. In spite of the disharmony which prevailed among some of Mrs. Eddy's followers, her success at the time of her death could be described in terms of the sale of 400,000 copies of *Science and Health*, the devotion of a respectable following, and an estate valued at two and a half million dollars.

Sibyl Wilbur, *Life of Mary Baker Eddy*, The Christian Science Publishing Company, New York, 1930.
Georgine Milmine, *The Life of Mary Baker G. Eddy and the History of Christian Science*, New York, 1909.
E. F. Dakin, *Mrs. Eddy: The Biography of a Virginal Mind*, New York, 1929.
Lyman Pierson Powell, *Mary Baker Eddy: A Life Size Portrait*, Boston, 1950.
E. S. Bates and J. V. Dittemore, *Mary Baker Eddy: The Truth and the Tradition*, New York, 1932.

» » *From:* MISCELLANEOUS WRITINGS « «

ONE CAUSE AND EFFECT

Christian Science begins with the First Commandment of the Hebrew Decalogue, "Thou shalt have no other gods before me." It goes on in perfect unity with Christ's Sermon on the Mount, and in that age culminates in the Revelation of St. John, who, while on earth and in the flesh, like ourselves, beheld "a new heaven and a new earth,"—the spiritual universe, whereof Christian Science now bears testimony.

Our Master said, "The works that I do shall ye do also"; and, "The kingdom of God is within you." This makes practical all his words and works. As the ages advance in spirituality, Christian Science will be seen to depart from the trend of other Christian denominations in no wise except by increase of spirituality.

My first plank in the platform of Christian Science is as follows: "There is no life, truth, intelligence, nor substance in matter. All is infinite Mind and its infinite manifestation, for God is All-in-all. Spirit is immortal Truth; matter is mortal error. Spirit is the real and eternal; matter is the unreal and temporal. Spirit is God, and man is His image and likeness. Therefore man is not material; he is spiritual."

I am strictly a theist—believe in one God, one Christ or Messiah.

Science is neither a law of matter nor of man. It is the unerring manifesto of Mind, the law of God, its divine Principle. Who dare say that matter or mortals can evolve Science? Whence, then, is it, if not from the divine source, and what, but the contemporary of Christianity, so far in advance of human knowledge that mortals must work for the discovery of even a portion of it? Christian Science translates Mind, God, to mortals. It is the infinite calculus defining the line, plane, space, and fourth dimension of Spirit. It absolutely refutes the amalgamation, transmigration, absorption, or annihilation of individuality. It shows the impossibility of transmitting human ills, or evil, from one individual to another; that all true thoughts revolve in God's orbits: they come from God and return to Him,—and untruths belong not to His creation, therefore these are null and void. It hath no peer, no competitor, for it dwelleth in Him besides whom "there is none other."

That Christian Science is Christian, those who have demonstrated it, according to the rules of its divine Principle,—together with the sick, the lame, the deaf, and the blind, healed by it,—have proven to a waiting world. He who has not tested it, is incompetent to condemn it; and he who is a willing sinner, cannot demonstrate it.

A falling apple suggested to Newton more than the simple fact cognized by the senses, to which it seemed to fall by reason of its own ponderosity; but the primal cause, or Mind-force, invisible to material sense, lay concealed in the treasure-troves of Science. True, Newton named it gravitation, having learned so much; but Science, demanding more, pushes the question: Whence or what is the power back of gravitation,—the intelligence that manifests power? Is pantheism true? Does mind "sleep in the mineral, or dream in the animal, and wake in man"? Christianity answers this question. The prophets, Jesus, and the apostles, demonstrated a divine intelligence that subordinates so-called material laws; and disease, death, winds, and waves, obey this intelligence. Was it Mind or matter that spake in creation, "and it was done"? The answer is self-evident, and the command remains, "Thou shalt have no other gods before me."

It is plain that the Me spoken of in the First Commandment, must be Mind; for matter is not the Christian's God, and is not intelligent. Matter cannot even talk; and the serpent, Satan, the first talker in its behalf, lied. Reason and revelation declare that God is both noumenon and phenomena,—the first and only cause. The universe, including man, is not a result of atomic action, material force or energy; it is not organized dust. God, Spirit, Mind, are terms synonymous for the one God, whose reflection is creation, and man is His image and likeness. Few there are who comprehend what Christian Science means by the word *reflection*. God is seen only in that which reflects good, Life, Truth, Love—yea, which manifests all His attributes and power, even as the human likeness thrown upon the mirror repeats precisely the looks and actions of the object in front of it. All must be Mind and Mind's ideas; since, according to natural science, God, Spirit, could not change its species and evolve matter.

These facts enjoin the First Commandment; and knowledge of them makes man spiritually minded. St. Paul writes: "For to be carnally minded is death; but to be spiritually minded is life and peace." This knowledge came to me in an hour of great need; and I give it to you as death-bed testimony to the daystar that dawned on the night of material sense. This knowledge is practical, for it wrought my immediate recovery from an injury caused by an accident, and pronounced fatal by the physicians. On the third day thereafter, I called for my Bible, and opened it at Matthew ix. 2. As I read, the healing Truth dawned upon my sense; and the result was that I rose, dressed myself, and ever after was in better health than I had before enjoyed. That short experience included a glimpse of the great fact that I have since tried to make plain to others, namely, Life in and of Spirit; this Life being the sole reality of existence. I learned that mortal thought evolves a subjective state which it names matter, thereby shutting out the true sense of Spirit. *Per contra,* Mind and man are immortal; and knowledge gained from mortal sense is illusion, error, the opposite of Truth; therefore it cannot be true. A knowledge of both good and evil (when good is God, and God is All) is impossible. Speaking of the origin of evil, the Master said: "When he speaketh a lie, he speaketh of his own: for he is a liar, and the father of it." God warned man not to believe the talking serpent, or rather the allegory describing it. The Nazarene Prophet declared that his followers should handle serpents; that is, put down all subtle falsities or illusions, and thus destroy any supposed effect arising from false claims exercising their supposed power on the mind and body of man, against his holiness and health.

That there is but one God or Life, one cause and one effect, is the *multum in parvo* of Christian Science; and to my understanding it is the heart of Christianity, the religion that Jesus taught and demonstrated. In divine Science it is found that matter is a phase of error, and that neither one really exists, since God is Truth, and All-in-all. Christ's Sermon on the Mount, in its direct application to human needs, confirms this conclusion.

Science, understood, translates matter into Mind, rejects all other theories of causation, restores the spiritual and original meaning of the Scriptures, and explains the teachings and life of our Lord. It is religion's "new tongue," with "signs following," spoken of by St. Mark. It gives God's infinite meaning to mankind, healing the sick, casting out evil, and raising the spiritually dead. Christianity is Christlike only as it reiterates the word, repeats the works, and manifests the spirit of Christ.

Jesus' only medicine was omnipotent and

omniscient Mind. As *omni* is from the Latin word meaning *all,* this medicine is all-power; and omniscience means as well, all-science. The sick are more deplorably situated than the sinful, if the sick cannot trust God for help and the sinful can. If God created drugs good, they cannot be harmful; if He could create them otherwise, then they are bad and unfit for man; and if He created drugs for healing the sick, why did not Jesus employ them and recommend them for that purpose?

No human hypotheses, whether in philosophy, medicine, or religion, can survive the wreck of time; but whatever is of God, hath life abiding in it, and ultimately will be known as self-evident truth, as demonstrable as mathematics. Each successive period of progress is a period more humane and spiritual. The only logical conclusion is that all is Mind and its manifestation, from the rolling of worlds, in the most subtle ether, to a potato-patch.

. . .

The Scriptures name God as good, and the Saxon term for God is also good. From this premise comes the logical conclusion that God is naturally and divinely infinite good. How, then, can this conclusion change, or be changed, to mean that good is evil, or the creator of evil? What can there be besides infinity? Nothing! Therefore the Science of good calls evil *nothing.* In divine Science the terms God and good, as Spirit, are synonymous. That God, good, creates evil, or aught that can result in evil,—or that Spirit creates its opposite, named matter,—are conclusions that destroy their premise and prove themselves invalid. Here is where Christian Science sticks to its text, and other systems of religion abandon their own logic. Here also is found the pith of the basal statement, the cardinal point in Christian Science, that matter and evil (including all inharmony, sin, disease, death) are *unreal.* Mortals accept natural science, wherein no species ever produces its opposite. Then why not accept divine Science on this ground? since the Scriptures maintain this fact by parable and proof, asking, "Do men gather grapes of thorns, or figs of thistles?" "Doth a fountain send forth at the same place sweet water and bitter?"

According to reason and revelation, evil and matter are negation: for evil signifies the absence of good, God, though God is ever present; and matter claims something besides God,

when God is really *All.* Creation, evolution, or manifestation,—being in and of Spirit, Mind, and all that really is,—must be spiritual and mental. This is Science, and is susceptible of proof.

But, say you, is a stone spiritual?

To erring material sense, No! but to unerring spiritual sense, it is a small manifestation of Mind, a type of spiritual substance, "the substance of things hoped for." Mortals can know a stone as substance, only by first admitting that it is substantial. Take away the mortal sense of substance, and the stone itself would disappear, only to reappear in the spiritual sense thereof. Matter can neither see, hear, feel, taste, nor smell; having no sensation of its own. Perception by the five personal senses is mental, and dependent on the beliefs that mortals entertain. Destroy the belief that you can walk, and volition ceases; for muscles cannot move without mind. Matter takes no cognizance of matter. In dreams, things are only what mortal mind makes them; and the phenomena of mortal life are as dreams; and this so-called life is a dream soon told. In proportion as mortals turn from this mortal and material dream, to the true sense of reality, everlasting Life will be found to be the only Life. That death does not destroy the beliefs of the flesh, our Master proved to his doubting disciple, Thomas. Also, he demonstrated that divine Science alone can overbear materiality and mortality; and this great truth was shown by his ascension after death, whereby he arose above the illusion of matter.

The First Commandment, "Thou shalt have no other gods before me," suggests the inquiry, What meaneth this Me,—Spirit, or matter? It certainly does not signify a graven idol, and must mean Spirit. Then the commandment means, Thou shalt recognize no intelligence nor life in matter; and find neither pleasure nor pain therein. The Master's practical knowledge of this grand verity, together with his divine Love, healed the sick and raised the dead. He literally annulled the claims of physique and of physical law, by the superiority of the higher law; hence his declaration, "These signs shall follow them that believe; . . . if they drink any deadly thing, it shall not hurt them; they shall lay hands on the sick, and they shall recover."

Do you believe his words? I do, and that his promise is perpetual. Had it been applicable only to his immediate disciples, the pronoun would be *you,* not *them.* The purpose of his life-work touches universal humanity. At another time he prayed, not for the twelve only, but "for them also which shall believe on me through their word."

The Christ-healing was practised even before the Christian era; "the Word was with God, and the Word was God." There is, however, no analogy between Christian Science and spiritualism, or between it and any speculative theory.

In 1867, I taught the first student in Christian Science. Since that date I have known of but fourteen deaths in the ranks of my about five thousand students. The census since 1875 (the date of the first publication of my work, "Science and Health with Key to the Scriptures") shows that longevity has *increased.* Daily letters inform me that a perusal of my volume is healing the writers of chronic and acute diseases that had defied medical skill.

Surely the people of the Occident know that esoteric magic and Oriental barbarisms will neither flavor Christianity nor advance health and length of days.

Miracles are no infraction of God's laws; on the contrary, they fulfil His laws; for they are the signs following Christianity, whereby matter is proven powerless and subordinate to Mind. Christians, like students in mathematics, should be working up to those higher rules of Life which Jesus taught and proved. Do we really understand the divine Principle of Christianity before we prove it, in at least some feeble demonstration thereof, according to Jesus' example in healing the sick? Should we adopt the "simple addition" in Christian Science and doubt its higher rules, or despair of ultimately reaching them, even though failing at first to demonstrate all the possibilities of Christianity?

St. John spiritually discerned and revealed the sum total of transcendentalism. He saw the real earth and heaven. They were spiritual, not material; and they were without pain, sin, or death. Death was not the door to this heaven. The gates thereof he declared were inlaid with pearl,—likening them to the priceless understanding of man's real existence, to be recognized here and now.

The great Way-shower illustrated Life unconfined, uncontaminated, untrammelled, by matter. He proved the superiority of Mind over the flesh, opened the door to the captive, and enabled man to demonstrate the law of Life, which St. Paul declares "hath made me free from the law of sin and death."

The stale saying that Christian Science "is neither Christian nor science!" is to-day the fossil of wisdomless wit, weakness, and superstition. "The fool hath said in his heart, There is no God."

Take courage, dear reader, for any seeming mysticism surrounding realism is explained in the Scripture, "There went up a mist from the earth [matter];" and the mist of materialism will vanish as we approach spirituality, the realm of reality; cleanse our lives in Christ's righteousness; bathe in the baptism of Spirit, and awake in His likeness.   1883–1896

JOHN LANCASTER SPALDING

1840–1916

BORN IN Lebanon, Kentucky, John Lancaster Spalding received an excellent Catholic education in America and abroad. In 1877 he was consecrated bishop of Peoria, Illinois. His theological scholarship, personal charm, and recognized leadership in liberal Catholic circles gave him an enviable position within and without the Church. Whether in the Plenary Councils, or in the Irish colonization movement, or in the project to establish the Catholic University of America, Spalding was of great influence. As one of the mediators in the anthracite coal strike of 1902, he still further showed his social vision and statesmanship.

A voluminous essayist, Spalding was an important Catholic spokesman, particularly on education. Representative of his writings are *Lectures and Discourses* (1882), *Thoughts and Theories of Life and Education* (1897), *Means and Ends of Education* (1895), and *Socialism and Labor and*

Other Arguments (1902). Bishop Spalding also wrote verses: *America and Other Poems* (1885), *The Poet's Praise* (1887), *Songs Chiefly from the German* (1896), and *A Kentucky Pioneer* (1932) indicate the range of his poetical interest.

Sister Agnes C. Schroll, *The Social Thought of James Lancaster Spalding, D.D.*, Washington, D. C., 1944.
Merle Curti, *The Social Ideas of American Educators*, New York, 1935, 1959, chap. 10.

» » *From:* MEANS AND ENDS OF EDUCATION « «

THE RELIGIOUS ELEMENT IN EDUCATION

. . . The Catholic view of the school question is as clearly defined as it is well known. It rests upon the general ground that man is created for a supernatural end, and that the church is the divinely appointed agency to help him to attain his supreme destiny. If edu-
10 cation is a training for completeness of life, its primary element is the religious, for complete life is life in God. Hence we may not assume an attitude toward the child, whether in the home, in the church, or in the school, which might imply that life apart from God could be anything else than broken and fragmentary. A complete man is not one whose mind only is active and enlightened; but he is a complete man who is alive in all his faculties.
20 The truly human is found not in knowledge alone, but also in faith, in hope, in love, in pure-mindedness, in reverence, in the sense of beauty, in devoutness, in the thrill of awe, which Goethe says is the highest thing in man. If the teacher is forbidden to touch upon religion, the source of these noble virtues and ideal moods is sealed. His work and influence become mechanical, and he will form but commonplace and vulgar men. And if an educa-
30 tional system is established on this narrow and material basis, the result will be deterioration of the national type, and the loss of the finer qualities which make men many-sided and interesting, which are the safeguards of personal purity and of unselfish conduct.

Religion is the vital element in character, and to treat it as though it were but an incidental phase of man's life is to blunder in a matter of the highest and most serious im-
40 port. Man is born to act, and thought is valuable mainly as a guide to action. Now, the chief inspiration to action, and above all to right action, is found in faith, hope, and love, the virtues of religion, and not in knowledge,

the virtue of the intellect. Knowledge, indeed, is effectual only when it is loved, believed in, and held to be a ground for hope. Man does not live on bread alone, and if he is brought up to look to material things, as to the chief good, his higher faculties will be stunted. If to do rightly rather than to think keenly is man's chief business here on earth, then the virtues of religion are more important than those of the intellect; for to think is to be unresolved, whereas to believe is to be impelled in the direction of one's faith. In epochs of doubt things fall to decay; in epochs of faith the powers which make for full and vigorous life, hold sway. The education which forms character is indispensable, that which trains the mind is desirable. The essential element in human life is conduct, and conduct springs from what we believe, cling to, love, and yearn for, vastly more than from what we know. The decadence and ruin of individuals and of societies come from lack of virtue, not from lack of knowledge. "The hard and valuable part of education," says Locke, "is virtue; this is the solid and substantial good, which the teacher should never cease to inculcate till the young man places his strength, his glory, and his pleasure in it." We may, of course, distinguish between morality and religion, between ethics and theology. As a matter of fact, however, moral laws have everywhere reposed upon the basis of religion, and their sanction has been sought in the principles of faith. As an immoral religion is false, so, if there is no God, a moral law is meaningless.

Theorists may be able to construct a system of ethics upon a foundation of materialism; but their mechanical and utilitarian doctrines have not the power to exalt the imagination or to confirm the will. Their educational value is feeble. Here in America we have already passed the stage of social development in which we might hold out to the young, as an ideal, the hope of becoming President of the Republic, or the possessor of millions of money. We know what sorry men presidents and millionnaires may be. We cannot look upon our country simply as a wide race-course with well-filled purses hanging at the goal for the prize-winners. We clearly perceive that a man's possessions are not himself, and that he is or ought to be more than anything which can belong to him. Ideals of excellence, therefore, must be substituted for those of success. Opinion governs the world, but ideals draw souls and stimulate to noble action. The more we transform with the aid of machinery the world of matter, the more necessary does it become that we make plain to all that a man's true home is the world of thought and love, of hope and aspiration. The ideals of utilitarianism and secularism are unsatisfactory. They make no appeal to the infinite in man, to that in him which makes pursuit better than possession, and which, could he believe there is no absolute truth, love, and beauty, would lead him to despair. To-day, as of old, the soul is born of God and for God, and finds no peace unless it rest in him. Theology, assuredly, is not religion; but religion implies theology, and a church without a creed is a body without articulation. The virtues of religion are indispensable. Without them, it is not well either with individuals or with nations; but these virtues cannot be inculcated by those who, standing aloof from ecclesiastical organizations, are thereby cut off from the thought and work of all who in every age have most loved God, and whose faith in the soul has been most living. Religious men have wrought for God in the church, as patriots have wrought for liberty and justice in the nation; and to exclude the representatives of the churches from the school is practically to exclude religion,—the power which more than all others makes for righteousness, which inspires hope and confidence, which makes possible faith in the whole human brotherhood, in the face even of the political and social wrongs which are still everywhere tolerated. To exclude religion is to exclude the spirit of reverence, of gentleness and obedience, of modesty and purity; it is to exclude the spirit by which the barbarians have been civilized, by which woman has been uplifted and ennobled and the child made sacred. From many sides the demand is made that the State schools exercise a greater moral influence, that they may be efficient in form-ing character as well as in training the mind. It is recognized that knowing how to read and write does not insure good behavior. Since the State assumes the office of teacher, there is a disposition among parents to make the school responsibile for their children's morals as well as for their minds, and thus the influence of the home is weakened. Whatever the causes may be, there seems to be a tendency, both in private and in public life, to lower ethical standards. The moral influence of the secular school is necessarily feeble, since our ideas of right and wrong are so interfused with the principles of Christianity that to ignore our religious convictions is practically to put aside the question of conscience. If the State may take no cognizance of sin, neither may its school do so. But in morals sin is the vital matter; crime is but its legal aspect. Men begin as sinners before they end as criminals.

The atmosphere of religion is the natural medium for the development of character. If we appeal to the sense of duty, we assume belief in God and in the freedom of the will; if we strive to awaken enthusiasm for the human brotherhood, we imply in divine fatherhood. Accordingly, as we accept or reject the doctrines of religion, the sphere of moral action, the nature of the distinction between right and wrong, and the motives of conduct all change. In the purely secular school only secular morality may be taught; and whatever our opinion of this system of ethics may otherwise be, it is manifestly deficient in the power which appeals to the heart and the conscience. The child lives in a world which imagination creates, where faith, hope, and love beckon to realms of beauty and delight. The spiritual and moral truths which are to become the very life-breath of his soul he apprehends mystically, not logically. Heaven lies about him; he lives in wonderland, and feels the thrill of awe as naturally as he looks with wide-open eyes. Do not seek to persuade him by telling him that honesty is the best policy, that poverty overtakes the drunkard, that lechery breeds disease, that to act for the common welfare is the surest way to get what is good for one's self; for such teaching will not only leave him unimpressed, but it will seem to him profane, and almost immoral. He wants to feel that he is the child of God, of the infinitely good and all-wonderful; that in his father, divine wisdom and strength are revealed; in his mother, divine tenderness and love. He so believes and trusts in God that it is our fault if he knows that men can be base. In nothing does the godlike character of Christ show forth more beautifully than in His reverence for children. Shall we profess to believe in Him, and yet forbid His name to be spoken in the houses where we seek to train the little ones whom He loved? Shall we shut out Him whose example has done more to humanize, ennoble, and uplift the race of man than all the teachings of the philosophers and all the disquisitions of the moralists? If the thinkers, from Plato and Aristotle to Kant and Pestalozzi, who have dealt with the problems of education, have held that virtue is its chief aim and end, shall we thrust from the school the one ideal character who, for nearly nineteen hundred years, has been the chief inspiration to righteousness and heroism; to whose words patriots and reformers have appealed in their struggles for liberty and right; to whose example philanthropists have looked in their labors to alleviate suffering; to whose teaching the modern age owes its faith in the brotherhood of men; by whose courage and sympathy the world has been made conscious that the distinction between man and woman is meant for the propagation of the race, but that as individuals they have equal rights and should have equal opportunities? We all, and especially the young, are influenced by example more than by precepts and maxims, and it is unjust and unreasonable to exclude from the school-room the living presence of the noblest and best men and women, of those whose words and deeds have created our Christian civilization. In the example of their lives we have truth and justice, goodness and greatness, in concrete form; and the young who are brought into contact with these centres of influence will be filled with admiration and enthusiasm; they will be made gentle and reverent; and they will learn to realize the ever-fresh charm and force of personal purity. Teachers who have no moral criteria, no ideals, no counsels of perfection, no devotion to God and godlike men, cannot educate, if the proper meaning of education is the complete unfolding of all man's powers.

The school, of course, is but one of the many agencies by which education is given. We are under the influence of our whole environment,—physical, moral, and intellectual; political, social, and religious; and if, in all this, aught were different, we ourselves should be other. The family is a school and the church is

a school; and current American opinion assigns to them the business of moral and religious education. But this implies that conduct and character are of secondary importance; it supposes that the child may be made subject to opposite influences at home and in the school, and not thereby have his finer sense of reverence, truth, and goodness deadened. The subduing of the lower nature, of the outward to the inner man, is a thing so arduous that reason, religion, and law combined often fail to accomplish it. If one should propose to do away with schools altogether, and to leave education to the family and the Church, he would be justly considered ridiculous; because the carelessness of parents and the inability of the ministry of the Church would involve the prevalence of illiteracy. Now, to leave moral and religious education to the family and the churches involves, for similar reasons, the prevalence of indifference, sin, and crime. If illiteracy is a menace to free institutions, vice and irreligion are a greater menace. The corrupt are always bad citizens; the ignorant are not necessarily so. Parents who would not have their children taught to read and write, were there no free schools, will as a rule neglect their religious and moral education. In giving religious instruction to the young, the churches are plainly at a disadvantage; for they have the child but an hour or two in seven days, and they get into their Sunday classes only the children of the more devout.

If the chief end of education is virtue; if conduct is three-fourths of life; if character is indispensable, while knowledge is only useful, —then it follows that religion—which, more than any other vital influence, has power to create virtue, to inspire conduct, and to mould character—should enter into all the processes of education. Our school system, then, does not rest upon a philosophic view of life and education. We have done what it was easiest to do, not what it was best to do; and in this, as in other instances, churchmen have been willing to sacrifice the interests of the nation to the whims of a narrow and jealous temper. The denominational system of popular education is the right system. The secular system is a wrong system. The practical difficulties to be overcome that religious instruction may be given in the schools are relatively unimportant, and would be set aside if the people were thoroughly persuaded of its necessity. An objection which Dr. Harris, among others, insists upon, that the method of science and the method of religion are dissimilar, and that therefore secular knowledge and religious knowledge should not be taught in the same school, seems to me to have no weight. The method of mathematics is not the method of biology; the method of logic is not the method of poetry; but they are all taught in the same school. A good teacher, in fact, employs many methods. In teaching the child grammatical analysis, he has no fear of doing harm to his imagination or his talent for composition.

No system, however, can give assurance that the school is good. To determine this we must know the spirit which lives in it. The intellectual, moral, and religious atmosphere which the child breathes there is of far more importance, from an educational point of view, than any doctrines he may learn by rote, than any acts of worship he may perform.

The teacher makes the school; and when high, pure, devout, and enlightened men and women educate, the conditions favorable to mental and moral growth will be found, provided a false system does not compel them to assume a part and play a role, while the true self—the faith, hope, and love whereby they live—is condemned to inaction. The deeper tendency of the present age is not, I think, to exclude religion from any vital process, but rather to widen the content of the idea of religion until it embrace the whole life of man. 10 The worship of God is not now the worship of infinite wisdom, holiness, and justice alone, but is also the worship of the humane, the beautiful, and the industriously active. Whether we work for knowledge of freedom, or purity or strength, or beauty or health, or aught else that is friendly to completeness of life, we work with God and for God. In the school, as in whatever other place in the boundless universe a man may find himself, he finds himself with 20 God, in Him moves, lives, and has his being.

1895

JOHN DEWEY

1859–1952

DARWINISM not only stirred the waters of religious controversy and played indirectly, at least, a role in social thought; it also did much to mold philosophical thinking. The method of biological science, with its spirit of inductive investigation and experiment, stood in stark contrast with the *a priori* habits of the academic philosopher. John Dewey, who began his career as an Hegelian, was influenced by Darwinism to apply the method and spirit of natural science to psychology and philosophy. But it was not only the method itself of natural science that bulked large in the thought of Dewey and other pragmatists. The influence of Darwinism in substituting for the idea of the fixed, the final, and the transcendent the concept of process and of concrete "natural" elements was far-reaching.

"The biological point of view," wrote John Dewey, "commits us to the conviction that mind, whatever else it may be, is at least an organ of service for the control of environment in relation to the ends of the life process." Dewey insisted that, in the light of the theory of organic evolution, moral judgments and ideas themselves must be thought of as hypotheses for experimentation rather than as absolute dogmas. Thus instrumentalism, the term applied to the development of pragmatism in his thinking, owed much to the theory and method of the evolutionary position. In view of the application which Dewey made of instrumentalism to education, to social philosophy, and, finally, to aesthetics and logic, and of the influence of his thought, it is of great importance to consider the impact of Darwinism on his mind.

M. H. Thomas, *A Bibliography of John Dewey, 1882–1939*, New York, 1939.
Morton G. White, *The Origins of Dewey's Instrumentalism*, New York, 1943.
George R. Geiger, *John Dewey in Perspective*, New York, 1958, with bibliography.
Sidney Hook, *John Dewey, an Intellectual Portrait of the Philosopher of American Democracy*, New York, 1939.

From: THE INFLUENCE OF DARWIN ON PHILOSOPHY

>> >>   « «

. . . The conception of ἐίδος, species, a fixed form and final course, was the central principle of knowledge as well as of nature. Upon it rested the logic of science. Change as change is mere flux and lapse; it insults intelligence. Genuinely to know is to grasp a permanent end that realizes itself through changes, holding them thereby within the metes and bounds of fixed truth. Completely to know is to relate all special forms to their one single end and good: pure contemplative intelligence. Since, however, the scene of nature which directly confronts us is in change, nature as directly and practically experienced does not satisfy the conditions of knowledge. Human experience is in flux, and hence the instrumentalities of sense-perception and of inference based upon observation are condemned in advance. Science is compelled to aim at realities lying behind and beyond the processes of nature, and to carry on its search for these realities by means of rational forms transcending ordinary modes of perception and inference.

There are, indeed, but two alternative courses. We must either find the appropriate objects and organs of knowledge in the mutual interactions of changing things; or else, to escape the infection of change, we *must* seek them in some transcendent and supernal region. The human mind, deliberately as it were, exhausted the logic of the changeless, the final, and the transcendent, before it essayed adventure on the pathless wastes of generation and transformation. We dispose all too easily of the efforts of the schoolmen to interpret nature and mind in terms of real essences, hidden forms, and occult faculties, forgetful of the seriousness and dignity of the ideas that lay behind. We dispose of them by laughing at the famous gentleman who accounted for the fact that opium put people to sleep on the ground it had a dormitive faculty. But the doctrine, held in our own day, that knowledge of the plant that yields the poppy consists in referring the peculiarities of an individual to a type, to a universal form, a doctrine so firmly established that any other method of knowing was conceived to be unphilosophical and unscientific, is a survival of precisely the same

logic. This identity of conception in the scholastic and anti-Darwinian theory may well suggest greater sympathy for what has become unfamiliar as well as greater humility regarding the further unfamiliarities that history has in store.

Darwin was not, of course, the first to question the classic philosophy of nature and of knowledge. The beginnings of the revolution are in the physical science of the sixteenth and seventeenth centuries. When Galileo said: "It is my opinion that the earth is very noble and admirable by reason of so many and so different alterations and generations which are incessantly made therein," he expressed the changed temper that was coming over the world; the transfer of interest from the permanent to the changing. When Descartes said: "The nature of physical things is much more easily conceived when they are beheld coming gradually into existence, than when they are only considered as produced at once in a finished and perfect state," the modern world became self-conscious of the logic that was henceforth to control it, the logic of which Darwin's "Origin of Species" is the latest scientific achievement. Without the methods of Copernicus, Kepler, Galileo, and their successors in astronomy, physics, and chemistry, Darwin would have been helpless in the organic sciences. But prior to Darwin the impact of the new scientific method upon life, mind, and politics, had been arrested, because between these ideal or moral interests and the inorganic world intervened the kingdom of plants and animals. The gates of the garden of life were barred to the new ideas; and only through this garden was there access to mind and politics. The influence of Darwin upon philosophy resides in his having conquered the phenomena of life for the principle of transition, and thereby freed the new logic for application to mind and morals and life. When he said of species what Galileo had said of the earth, e pur se muove,[1] he emancipated, once for all, genetic and experimental ideas as an organon of asking questions and looking for explanations.

[1] And yet it [the earth] moves.

III

The exact bearings upon philosophy of the new logical outlook are, of course, as yet, uncertain and inchoate. We live in the twilight of intellectual transition. One must add the rashness of the prophet to the stubbornness of the partizan to venture a systematic exposition of the influence upon philosophy of the Darwinian method. At best, we can but inquire as to its general bearing—the effect upon mental temper and complexion, upon that body of half-conscious, half-instinctive intellectual aversions and preferences which determine, after all, our more deliberate intellectual enterprises. In this vague inquiry there happens to exist as a kind of touch-stone a problem of long historic currency that has also been much discussed in Darwinian literature. I refer to the old problem of design *versus* chance, mind *versus* matter, as the causal explanation, first or final, of things.

As we have already seen, the classic notion of species carried with it the idea of purpose. In all living forms, a specific type is present directing the earlier stages of growth to the realization of its own perfection. Since this purposive regulative principle is not visible to the senses, it follows that it must be an ideal or rational force. Since, however, the perfect form is gradually approximated through the sensible changes, it also follows that in and through a sensible realm a rational ideal force is working out its own ultimate manifestation. These inferences were extended to nature: (*a*) She does nothing in vain; but all for an ulterior purpose. (*b*) Within natural sensible events there is therefore contained a spiritual causal force, which as spiritual escapes perception, but is apprehended by an enlightened reason. (*c*) The manifestation of this principle brings about a subordination of matter and sense to its own realization, and this ultimate fulfilment is the goal of nature and of man. The design argument thus operated in two directions. Purposefulness accounted for the intelligibility of nature and the possibility of science, while the absolute or cosmic character of this purposefulness gave sanction and worth to the moral and religious endeavors of man. Science was underpinned and morals authorized by one and the same principle, and their mutual agreement was eternally guaranteed.

This philosophy remained, in spite of sceptical and polemic outbursts, the official and the regnant philosophy of Europe for over two thousand years. The expulsion of fixed first and final causes from astronomy, physics, and chemistry had indeed given the doctrine something of a shock. But, on the other hand, increased acquaintance with the details of plant and animal life operated as a counterbalance and perhaps even strengthened the argument from design. The marvelous adaptations of organisms to their environment, of organs to the organism, of unlike parts of a complex organ—like the eye—to the organ itself; the fore-shadowing by lower forms of the higher; the preparation in earlier stages of growth for organs that only later had their functioning—these things were increasingly recognized with the progress of botany, zoology, paleontology, and embryology. Together, they added such prestige to the design argument that by the late eighteenth century it was, as approved by the sciences of organic life, the central point of theistic and idealistic philosophy.

The Darwinian principle of natural selection cut straight under this philosophy. If all organic adaptations are due simply to constant variation and the elimination of those variations which are harmful in the struggle for existence that is brought about by excessive reproduction, there is no call for a prior intelligent causal force to plant and preordain them. Hostile critics charged Darwin with materialism and with making chance the cause of the universe.

Some naturalists, like Asa Gray, favored the Darwinian principle and attempted to reconcile it with design. Gray held to what may be called design on the installment plan. If we conceive the "stream of variations" to be itself intended, we may suppose that each successive variation was designed from the first to be selected. In that case, variation, struggle, and selection simply define the mechanism of "secondary causes" through which the "first cause" acts; and the doctrine of design is none the worse off because we know more of its *modus operandi*.

Darwin could not accept this mediating proposal. He admits or rather he asserts that it is "impossible to conceive this immense and wonderful universe including man with his capacity of looking far backwards and far into futurity as the result of blind chance or necessity." [2] But nevertheless he holds that since variations are in useless as well as useful directions, and since the latter are sifted out

2 "Life and Letters," Vol. I., p. 282; cf. 285. [Dewey's note.]

simply by the stress of the conditions of struggle for existence, the design argument as applied to living beings is unjustifiable; and its lack of support there deprives [us?] of scientific value as applied to nature in general. If the variations of the pigeon, which under artificial selection give the pouter pigeon, are not preordained for the sake of the breeder, by what logic do we argue that variations re-
10 sulting in natural species are pre-designed? [3]

IV

So much for some of the more obvious facts of the discussion of design *versus* chance, as causal principles of nature and of life as a whole. We brought up this discussion, you recall, as a crucial instance. What does our touchstone indicate as to the bearing of Darwinian ideas upon philosophy? In the first
20 place, the new logic outlaws, flanks, dismisses —what you will—one type of problems and substitutes for it another type. Philosophy forswears inquiry after absolute origins and absolute finalities in order to explore specific values and the specific conditions that generate them.

Darwin concluded that the impossibility of assigning the world to chance as a whole and to design in its parts indicated the insolubility
30 of the question. Two radically different reasons, however, may be given as to why a problem is insoluble. One reason is that the problem is too high for intelligence; the other is that the question in its very asking makes assumptions that render the question meaningless. The latter alternative is unerringly pointed to in the celebrated case of design *versus* chance. Once admit that the sole verifiable or fruitful object of knowledge is the particular set of changes
40 that generate the object of study together with the consequences that then flow from it, and no intelligible question can be asked about what, by assumption, lies outside. To assert —as is often asserted—that specific values of particular truth, social bonds and forms of beauty, if they can be shown to be generated by concretely knowable conditions, are meaningless and in vain; to assert that they are justified only when they and their particular
50 causes and effects have all at once been gathered up into some inclusive first cause and some exhaustive final goal, is intellectual ata-

[3] "Life and Letters," Vol. II., pp. 146, 170, 245; Vol. I., pp. 283–84. See also the closing portion of his "Variations of Animals and Plants under Domestication." [Dewey's note.]

vism. Such argumentation is reversion to the logic that explained the extinction of fire by water through the formal essence of aqueousness and the quenching of thirst by water through the final cause of aqueousness. Whether used in the case of the special event or that of life as a whole, such logic only abstracts some aspect of the existing course of events in order to reduplicate it as a petrified eternal principle by which to explain the very changes of which it is the formalization.

When Henry Sidgwick casually remarked in a letter that as he grew older his interest in what or who made the world was altered into interest in what kind of a world it is anyway, his voicing of a common experience of our own day illustrates also the nature of that intellectual transformation effected by the Darwinian logic. Interest shifts from the wholesale essence back of special changes to the question of how special changes serve and defeat concrete purposes; shifts from an intelligence that shaped things once for all to the particular intelligences which things are even now shaping; shifts from an ultimate goal of good to the direct increments of justice and happiness that intelligent administration of existent conditions may beget and that present carelessness or stupidity will destroy or forego.

In the second place, the classic type of logic inevitably set philosophy upon proving that life *must* have certain qualities and values— no matter how experience presents the matter —because of some remote cause and eventual goal. The duty of wholesale justification inevitably accompanies all thinking that makes the meaning of special occurrences depend upon something that once and for all lies behind them. The habit of derogating from present meanings and uses prevents our looking the facts of experience in the face; it prevents serious acknowledgement of the evils they present and serious concern with the goods they promise but do not as yet fulfil. It turns thought to the business of finding a wholesale transcendent remedy for the one and guarantee for the other. One is reminded of the way many moralists and theologians greeted Herbert Spencer's recognition of an unknowable energy from which welled up the phenomenal physical processes without and the conscious operations within. Merely because Spencer labeled his unknowable energy "God," this faded piece of metaphysical goods was greeted as an important and grateful concession to the reality of the spiritual realm. Were it not for the deep hold of the habit of seeking justification for ideal values in the remote and transcendent, surely this reference of them to an unknowable absolute would be despised in comparison with the demonstrations of experience that knowable energies are daily generating about us precious values.

The displacing of this wholesale type of philosophy will doubtless not arrive by sheer logical disproof, but rather by growing recognition of its futility. Were it a thousand times true that opium produces sleep because of its dormitive energy, yet the inducing of sleep in the tired, and the recovery to waking life of the poisoned, would not be thereby one least step forwarded. And were it a thousand times dialectically demonstrated that life as a whole is regulated by a transcendent principle to a final inclusive goal, none the less truth and error, health and disease, good and evil, hope and fear in the concrete, would remain just what and where they now are. To improve our education, to ameliorate our manners, to advance our politics, we must have recourse to specific conditions of generation.

Finally, the new logic introduces responsibility into the intellectual life. To idealize and rationalize the universe at large is after all a confession of inability to master the courses of things that specifically concern us. As long as mankind suffered from this impotency, it naturally shifted a burden of responsibility that it could not carry over to the more competent shoulders of the transcendent cause. But if insight into specific conditions of value and into specific consequences of ideas is possible, philosophy must in time become a method of locating and interpreting the more serious of the conflicts that occur in life, and a method of projecting ways for dealing with them: a method of moral and political diagnosis and prognosis.

The claim to formulate *a priori* the legislative constitution of the universe is by its nature a claim that may lead to elaborate dialectic developments. But it is also one that removes these very conclusions from subjection to experimental test, for, by definition, these results make no differences in the detailed course of events. But a philosophy that humbles its pretensions to the work of projecting hypotheses for the education and conduct of mind, individual and social, is thereby subjected to test by the way in which the ideas it propounds work out in practice. In having modesty forced upon it, philosophy also acquires responsibility.

Doubtless I seem to have violated the implied promise of my earlier remarks and to have turned both prophet and partizan. But in anticipating the direction of the transformations in philosophy to be wrought by the Darwinian genetic and experimental logic, I do not profess to speak for any save those who yield themselves consciously or unconsciously to this logic. No one can fairly deny that at present there are two effects of the Darwinian mode of thinking. On the one hand, there are many making sincere and vital efforts to revise our traditional philosophic conceptions in accordance with its demands. On the other hand, there is as definitely a recrudescence of absolutistic philosophies; an assertion of a type of philosophic knowing distinct from that of the sciences, one which opens to us another kind of reality from that to which the sciences give access; an appeal through experience to something that essentially goes beyond experience. This reaction affects popular creeds and religious movements as well as technical philosophies. The very conquest of the biological sciences by the new ideas has led many to proclaim an explicit and rigid separation of philosophy from science.

Old Ideas give way slowly; for they are more than abstract logical forms and categories. They are habits, predispositions, deeply engrained attitudes of aversion and preference. Moreover, the conviction persists—though history shows it to be a hallucination—that all the questions that the human mind has asked are questions that can be answered in terms of the alternatives that the questions themselves present. But in fact intellectual progress usually occurs through sheer abandonment of questions together with both of the alternatives they assume—an abandonment that results from their decreasing vitality and a change of urgent interest. We do not solve them: we get over them. Old questions are solved by disappearing, evaporating, while new questions corresponding to the changed attitude of endeavor and preference take their place. Doubtless the greatest dissolvent in contemporary thought of old questions, the greatest precipitant of new methods, new intentions, new problems, is the one effected by the scientific revolution that found its climax in the "Origin of Species." 1910

WILLIAM JAMES

1842–1910

DURING HIS youthful study abroad William James came to associate his own profound psychological depression with the doctrine of materialistic determinism; and his revolt against this position explains much that was characteristic of his subsequent thinking. The nonconformism, the idealism, and the social meliorism of his eccentric and well-to-do father, Henry James, Sr., likewise colored his temperament and outlook. After studying medicine and teaching anatomy and physiology at Harvard, William James turned his attention to philosophy and psychology. In the words of Horace Kallen, his teaching "transformed both subjects from 'mental and moral philosophy,' verbal, abstract, and related neither to living experience, nor to the realities of nature and human nature, into specific, concrete, vital and new observations of the qualities of men and the nature of things."

William James refused to exclude any experience, event, thing, or relationship which could prove that any conceivable claim worked, that it resulted in consequences on the whole good, that it was a dynamic force in solving some one of the never ending problems of life and the universe. Psychical phenomena, religious experiences, for example, were neither to be believed nor disbelieved *a priori*, on faith, or as a result of their correspondence to or denial of "absolute" principles or laws, but rather as "true" in a pluralistic universe of variation as great as the individuals composing it, if in their effects such "supernaturalistic" phenomena carried the endless struggle and change to the "next" level and by so doing proved their workability. *The Will to Believe* (1897) is characteristic of Pragmatism, a point of view and method which had the merits of being both "scientific" and yet inspirational and comfortable. James's great *Principles of Psychology* (1890) did much to put psychology on its modern empirical and "human" basis, and his *Pragmatism* lent no support to absolutistic religion. Yet at the same time his method and his spirit, exemplified in *The Will to Believe* (1897), *Pragmatism* (1907), and *A Pluralistic Universe* (1909), gave a new "pragmatic" justification for supernaturalism.

R. B. Perry, *Annotated Bibliography of the Writings of William James*, New York, 1920.
William James, *Human Immortality; Two Supposed Objections to the Doctrine*, Boston and New York, 1898.
The Letters of William James, Henry James, ed., 2 vols., Boston, 1920.
The Philosophy of William James, Drawn from His Own Works, Horace Hallen, ed., New York, 1925.
R. B. Perry, *The Thought and Character of William James*, 2 vols., Boston, 1935.

» » From: THE WILL TO BELIEVE « «

IS LIFE WORTH LIVING?

IV

And now, in turning to what religion may have to say to the question, I come to what is the soul of my discourse. Religion has meant many things in human history; but when from now onward I use the word I mean to use it in the supernaturalist sense, as declaring that the so-called order of nature, which constitutes this world's experience, is only one portion of the total universe, and that there stretches beyond this visible world an unseen world of which we now know nothing positive, but in its relation to which the true significance of our present mundane life consists. A man's religious faith (whatever more special items of doctrine it may involve) means for me essentially his faith in the existence of an unseen order of some kind in which the riddles of the natural order may be found explained. In the more developed religions the natural world has always been regarded as the mere scaffolding or vestibule of a truer, more eternal world, and affirmed to be a sphere of education, trial, or redemption. In these religions, one must in some fashion die to the natural life before one can enter into life eternal. The notion that this physical world of wind and water, where the sun rises and the moon sets, is absolutely and ultimately the divinely aimed-at and established thing, is one which we find only in very early religions, such as that of the most primitive Jews. It is this natural religion (primitive still, in spite of the fact that poets and men of science whose good-will exceeds their perspicacity keep publishing it in new editions tuned to our contemporary ears) that, as I said a while ago, has suffered definitive bankruptcy in the opinion of a circle of persons, among whom I must count myself, and who are growing more numerous every day. For such persons the physical order of nature, taken simply as science knows it, cannot be held to reveal any one harmonious spiritual intent. It is mere *weather*, as Chauncey Wright called it, doing and undoing without end.

Now, I wish to make you feel, if I can in the short remainder of this hour, that we have a right to believe the physical order to be only a partial order; that we have a right to supplement it by an unseen spiritual order which we assume on trust, if only thereby life may seem to us better worth living again. But as such a trust will seem to some of you sadly mystical and execrably unscientific, I must first say a word or two to weaken the veto which you may consider that science opposes to our act.

There is included in human nature an ingrained naturalism and materialism of mind which can only admit facts that are actually tangible. Of this sort of mind the entity called "science" is the idol. Fondness for the word "scientist" is one of the notes by which you may know its votaries; and its short way of killing any opinion that it disbelieves in is to call it "unscientific." It must be granted that there is no slight excuse for this. Science has made such glorious leaps in the last three hundred years, and extended our knowledge of nature so enormously both in general and in detail; men of science, moreover, have as a class dis-

played such admirable virtues,—that it is no wonder if the worshippers of science lose their head. In this very University, accordingly, I have heard more than one teacher say that all the fundamental conceptions of truth have already been found by science, and that the future has only the details of the picture to fill in. But the slightest reflection on the real conditions will suffice to show how barbaric such notions are. They show such a lack of scientific imagination, that it is hard to see how one who is actively advancing any part of science can make a mistake so crude. Think how many absolutely new scientific conceptions have arisen in our own generation, how many new problems have been formulated that were never thought of before, and then cast an eye upon the brevity of science's career. It began with Galileo, not three hundred years ago. Four thinkers since Galileo, each informing his successor of what discoveries his own lifetime had seen achieved, might have passed the torch of science into our hands as we sit here in this room. Indeed, for the matter of that, an audience much smaller than the present one, an audience of some five or six score people, if each person in it could speak for his own generation, would carry us away to the black unknown of the human species, to days without a document or monument to tell their tale. Is it credible that such a mushroom knowledge, such a growth overnight as this, *can* represent more than the minutest glimpse of what the universe will really prove to be when adequately understood? No! our science is a drop, our ignorance a sea. Whatever else be certain, this at least is certain,—that the world of our present natural knowledge *is* enveloped in a larger world of *some* sort of whose residual properties we at present can frame no positive idea.

Agnostic positivism, of course, admits this principle theoretically in the most cordial terms, but insists that we must not turn it to any practical use. We have no right, this doctrine tells us, to dream dreams, or suppose anything about the unseen part of the universe, merely because to do so may be for what we are pleased to call our highest interests. We must always wait for sensible evidence for our beliefs; and where such evidence is inaccessible we must frame no hypotheses whatever. Of course this is a safe enough position *in abstracto*. If a thinker had no stake in the unknown, no vital needs, to live or languish ac-

cording to what the unseen world contained,
2. philosophic neutrality and refusal to believe
either one way or the other would be his wisest
cue. But, unfortunately, neutrality is not only
inwardly difficult, it is also outwardly un-
realizable, where our relations to an alternative
are practical and vital. This is because, as the
psychologists tell us, belief and doubt are
living attitudes, and involve conduct on our
10 part. Our only way, for example, of doubting
or refusing to believe, that a certain thing *is*,
is continuing to act as if it were *not*. If, for
instance, I refuse to believe that the room is
getting cold, I leave the windows open and
light no fire just as if it still were warm. If
I doubt that you are worthy of my confidence,
I keep you uninformed of all my secrets just
as if you were *un*worthy of the same. If I doubt
the need of insuring my house, I leave it un-
20 insured as much as if I believed there were no
need. And so if I must not believe that the
world is divine, I can only express that refusal
by declining ever to act distinctively as if it
were so, which can only mean acting on certain critical occasions as if it were *not* so, or
in an irreligious way. There are, you see, inevitable occasions in life when inaction is a
kind of action, and must count as action, and
when not to be for is to be practically against;
30 and in all such cases strict and consistent neutrality is an unattainable thing.

And, after all, is not this duty of neutrality,
where only our inner interests would lead us
to believe, the most ridiculous of commands?
Is it not sheer dogmatic folly to say that our
inner interests can have no real connection
with the forces that the hidden world may
contain? In other cases divinations based on
inner interests have proved prophetic enough.
40 Take science itself! Without an imperious inner
demand on our part for ideal logical and
mathematical harmonies, we should never have
attained to proving that such harmonies lie
hidden between all the chinks and interstices
of the crude natural world. Hardly a law has
been established in science, hardly a fact ascertained, which was not first sought after,
often with sweat and blood, to gratify an inner
need. Whence such needs come from we do
50 not know: we find them in us, and biological
pyschology so far only classes them with Darwin's "accidental variations." But the inner
need of believing that this world of nature is a
sign of something more spiritual and eternal
than itself is just as strong and authoritative

in those who feel it, as the inner need of uniform laws of causation ever can be in a pro-
fessionally scientific head. The toil of many
generations has proved the latter need prophetic. Why *may* not the former one be prophetic, too? And if needs of ours outrun the
visible universe, why *may* not that be a sign
that an invisible universe is there? What, in
short, has authority to debar us from trusting
our religious demands? Science as such assuredly has no authority, for she can only say
what is, not what is not; and the agnostic
"thou shalt not believe without coercive sensible evidence" is simply an expression (free
to any one to make) of private personal
appetite for evidence of a certain peculiar
kind.

Now, when I speak of trusting our religious
demands, just what do I mean by "trusting"?
Is the word to carry with it license to define in
detail an invisible world, and to anathematize
and excommunicate those whose trust is different? Certainly not! Our faculties of belief
were not primarily given us to make ortho-
doxies and heresies withal; they were given us
to live by. And to trust our religious demands
means first of all to live in the light of them,
and to act as if the invisible world which they
suggest were real. It is a fact of human nature,
that men can live and die by the help of a
sort of faith that goes without a single dogma
of definition. The bare assurance that this
natural order is not ultimate but a mere sign
or vision, the eternal staging of a many-storied
universe, in which spiritual forces have the
last word and are eternal,—this bare assurance
is to such men enough to make life seem worth
living in spite of every contrary presumption
suggested by its circumstances on the natural
plane. Destroy this inner assurance, however,
vague as it is, and all the light and radiance
of existence is extinguished for these persons
at a stroke. Often enough the wild-eyed look
at life—the suicidal mood—will then set in.

And now the application comes directly
home to you and me. Probably to almost everyone of us here the most adverse life would seem
well worth living, if we only could be *certain*
that our bravery and patience with it were
terminating and eventuating and bearing fruit
somewhere in an unseen spiritual world. By
granting we are not certain, does it then follow
that a bare trust in such a world is a fool's
paradise and lubberland, or rather that it is a
living attitude in which we are free to indulge?

Well, we are free to trust at our own risks anything that is not impossible, and that can bring analogies to bear in its behalf. That the world of physics is probably not absolute, all the converging multitude of arguments that make in favor of idealism tend to prove; and that our whole physical life may lie soaking in a spiritual atmosphere, a dimension of being that we at present have no organ for apprehending, is vividly suggested to us by the analogy of our domestic animals. Our dogs, for example, are in our human life but not of it. They witness hourly the outward body of events whose inner meaning cannot, by any possible operation, be revealed to their intelligence,—events in which they themselves often play the cardinal part. My terrier bites a teasing boy, and the father demands damages. The dog may be present at every step of the negotiations, and see the money paid, without an inkling of what it all means, without a suspicion that it has anything to do with *him;* and he never *can* know in his natural dog's life. Or take another case which used greatly to impress me in my medical-student days. Consider a poor dog whom they are vivisecting in a laboratory. He lies strapped on a board and shrieking at his executioners, and to his own dark consciousness is literally in a sort of hell. He cannot see a single redeeming ray in the whole business; and yet all these diabolical-seeming events are often controlled by human intentions with which, if his poor benighted mind could only be made to catch a glimpse of them, all that is heroic in him would religiously acquiesce. Healing truth, relief to future sufferings of beast and man, are to be bought by them. It may be genuinely a process of redemption. Lying on his back on the board there he may be performing a function incalculably higher than any that prosperous canine life admits of; and yet, of the whole performance, this function is the one portion that must remain absolutely beyond his ken.

Now turn from this to the life of man. In the dog's life we see the world invisible to him because we live in both worlds. In human life, although we only see our world, and his within it, yet encompassing both these worlds a still wider world may be there, as unseen by us as our world is by him; and to believe in that world *may* be the most essential function that our lives in this world have to perform. But "*may* be! *may* be!" one now hears the positivist contemptuously exclaim; "what use can a scientific life have for maybes?" Well, I reply, the "scientific" life itself has much to do with maybes, and human life at large has everything to do with them. So far as man stands for anything, and is productive or originative at all, his entire vital function may be said to have to deal with maybes. Not a victory is gained, not a deed of faithfulness or courage is done, except upon a maybe; not a service, not a sally of generosity, nor a scientific exploration or experiment or text-book, that may not be a mistake. It is only by risking our persons from one hour to another that we live at all. And often enough our faith beforehand in an uncertified result *is the only thing that makes the result come true.* Suppose, for instance, that you are climbing a mountain, and have worked yourself into a position from which the only escape is by a terrible leap. Have faith that you can successfully make it, and your feet are nerved to its accomplishment. But mistrust yourself, and think of all the sweet things you have heard the scientists say of *maybes,* and you will hesitate so long that, at last, all unstrung and trembling, and launching yourself in a moment of despair, you roll in the abyss. In such a case (and it belongs to an enormous class), the part of wisdom as well as of courage is to *believe what is in the line of your needs,* for only by such belief is the need fulfilled. Refuse to believe, and you shall indeed be right, for you shall irretrievably perish. But believe, and again you shall be right, for you shall save yourself. You make one or the other of two possible universes true by your trust or mistrust,—both universes having been only *maybes,* in this particular, before you contributed your act.

Now, it appears to me that the question whether life is worth living is subject to conditions logically much like these. It does, indeed, depend on you *the liver.* If you surrender to the nightmare view and crown the evil edifice by your own suicide, you have indeed made a picture totally black. Pessimism, completed by your act, is true beyond a doubt, so far as your world goes. Your mistrust of life has removed whatever worth your own enduring existence might have given to it; and now, throughout the whole sphere of possible influence of that existence, the mistrust has proved itself to have had divining power. But suppose, on the other hand, that instead of giving way to the nightmare view you cling to it that this world is not the *ultimatum.* Suppose you find yourself a very wellspring, as Wordsworth says, of—

"Zeal, and the virtue to exist by faith
As soldiers live by courage; as, by strength
Of heart, the sailor fights with roaring seas."

Suppose, however thickly evils crowd upon you, that your unconquerable subjectivity proves to be their match, and that you find a more wonderful joy than any passive pleasure can bring in trusting ever in the larger whole. Have you not now made life worth living on these terms? What sort of a thing would life really be, with your qualities ready for a tussle with it, if it only brought fair weather and gave these higher faculties of yours no scope? Please remember that optimism and pessimism are definitions of the world, and that our own reactions on the world, small as they are in bulk, are integral parts of the whole thing, and necessarily help to determine the definition. They may even be the decisive elements in determining the definition. A large mass can have its unstable equilibrium overturned by the addition of a feather's weight; a long phrase may have its sense reversed by the addition of the three letters *n-o-t*. This life *is* worth living, we can say, *since it is what we make it, from the moral point of view;* and we are determined to make it from that point of view, so far as we have anything to do with it, a success.

Now, in this description of faiths that verify themselves I have assumed that our faith in an invisible order is what inspires those efforts and that patience which make this visible order good for moral men. Our faith in the seen world's goodness (goodness now meaning fitness for successful moral and religious life) has verified itself by leaning on our faith in the unseen world. But will our faith in the unseen world similarly verify itself? Who knows?

Once more it is a case of *maybe;* and once more *maybes* are the essence of the situation. I confess that I do not see why the very existence of an invisible world may not in part depend on the personal response which any one of us may make to the religious appeal. God himself, in short, may draw vital strength and increase of very being from our fidelity. For my own part, I do not know what the sweat and blood and tragedy of this life mean, if they mean anything short of this. If this life be not a real fight, in which something is eternally gained for the universe by success, it is no better than a game of private theatricals from which one may withdraw at will. But it *feels* like a real fight,—as if there were something really wild in the universe which we, with all our idealities and faithfulnesses, are needed to redeem; and first of all to redeem our own hearts from atheisms and fears. For such a half-wild, half-saved universe our nature is adapted. The deepest thing in our nature is this *Binnenleben* (as a German doctor lately has called it), this dumb region of the heart in which we dwell alone with our willingnesses and unwillingnesses, our faiths and fears. As through the cracks and crannies of caverns those waters exude from the earth's bosom which then form the fountain-heads of springs, so in these crepuscular depths of personality the sources of all our outer deeds and decisions take their rise. Here is our deepest organ of communication with the nature of things; and compared with all these concrete movements of our soul all abstract statements and scientific arguments—the veto, for example, which the strict positivist pronounces upon our faith— sound to us like mere chatterings of the teeth. For here possibilities, not finished facts, are the realities with which we have acutely to deal; and to quote my friend William Salter, of the Philadelphia Ethical Society, "as the essence of courage is to stake one's life on a possibility, so the essence of faith is to believe that the possibility exists."

These, then, are my last words to you: Be *not* afraid of life. Believe that life *is* worth living, and your belief will help create the fact. The "scientific proof" that you are right may not be clear before the day of judgment (or some stage of being which that expression may serve to symbolize) is reached. But the faithful fighters of this hour, or the beings that then and there will represent them, may turn to the faint-hearted, who here decline to go on, with words like those with which Henry IV greeted the tardy Crillon after a great victory had been gained: "Hang yourself, brave Crillon! we fought at Arques, and you were not there."   1911

» »   « «

HENRY ADAMS

1838–1918

NO DISCUSSION of supernaturalism and naturalism was more engaging and provocative than that of Henry Adams. A man of the world, Adams knew many phases of life.
He taught history at Harvard, and wrote an authoritative and, in some respects, brilliant
History of the United States 1801–1817 (1889–1891). As secretary to his father during his ambas-
sadorship in England, he knew leading public and literary men; his circle of friends in America,
while limited in numbers, included some of the most eminent in many fields.

Like many social thinkers of his day, Henry Adams sought for a key which would explain
the development of human society and enable mankind to predict its future. He considered
this problem in *Mont-Saint-Michel and Chartres* (1904), *A Letter to American Teachers of History*
(1910), and *The Education of Henry Adams* (1906, 1907, 1918). The following selection from *The
Education* presents a part, but only a part, of Henry Adams's thesis. Briefly, he contended that
until Newton perfected the scientific method and subsequent generations applied to daily
life the principle of the dynamo, man had found in faith and religion the energy so necessary
in the struggle for survival. The application of the machine to civilization had solved certain
problems but brought many others; and Henry Adams queried whether the machine, especially as exemplified by the destructive bomb, might not spell the doom of civilization itself.
In addition, his pessimism, rooted in his personal failure to serve the new industrial society as
his forbears had served the older America, was enhanced by his contemplation of the second
law of thermo-dynamics, which postulated the ultimate dissipation of energy in the universe.
Adams found at least an emotional compensation in pondering on the unity of medieval civilization, in contrast to the diversity of the modern age, and on the mysteries of the Virgin and
the beauties of faith.

The Letters of Henry Adams, W. C. Ford, ed., Boston and New York, 1930–1938.
A *Henry Adams Reader*, Elizabeth Stevenson, ed., Garden City, New York, 1958.
Elizabeth Stevenson, *Henry Adams, A Biography*, New York, 1955.
Ernest Samuels, *Henry Adams, Young Henry Adams* (Cambridge, 1948) and *Henry Adams, The Middle Years*
(Cambridge, 1958).

» » *From:* THE EDUCATION OF HENRY ADAMS « «

CHAPTER XXV

THE DYNAMO AND THE VIRGIN

Until the Great Exposition of 1900 closed
its doors in November, Adams haunted it,
aching to absorb knowledge, and helpless to
find it. He would have liked to know how much
of it could have been grasped by the best-
informed man in the world. While he was
thus meditating chaos, Langley came by, and
showed it to him. At Langley's behest, the
Exhibition dropped its superfluous rags and
stripped itself to the skin, for Langley knew
what to study, and why, and how; while
Adams might as well have stood outside in the
night, staring at the Milky Way. Yet Langley
said nothing new, and taught nothing that one
might not have learned from Lord Bacon, three
hundred years before; but though one should
have known the *Advancement of Science* as
well as one knew the *Comedy of Errors*, the
literary knowledge counted for nothing until
some teacher should show how to apply it.
Bacon took a vast deal of trouble in teaching
King James I and his subjects, American or

other, towards the year 1620, that true science was the development or economy of forces; yet an elderly American in 1900 knew neither the formula nor the forces; or even so much as to say to himself that his historical business in the Exposition concerned only the economies or developments of force since 1893, when he began the study at Chicago.

Nothing in education is so astonishing as the amount of ignorance it accumulates in the form of inert facts. Adams had looked at most of the accumulations of art in the storehouses called Art Museums; yet he did not know how to look at the art exhibits of 1900. He had studied Karl Marx and his doctrines of history with profound attention, yet he could not apply them at Paris. Langley, with the ease of a great master of experiment, threw out of the field every exhibit that did not reveal a new application of force, and naturally threw out, to begin with, almost the whole art exhibit. Equally, he ignored almost the whole industrial exhibit. He led his pupil directly to the forces. His chief interest was in new motors to make his airship feasible, and he taught Adams the astonishing complexities of the Daimler motor, and of the automobile, which, since 1893, had become a nightmare at a hundred kilometres an hour, almost as destructive as the electric tram which was only ten years older; and threatening to become as terrible as the locomotive steam-engine itself, which was almost exactly Adams's own age.

Then he showed his scholar the great hall of dynamos, and explained how little he knew about electricity or force of any kind, even of his own special sun, which spouted heat in inconceivable volume, but which, as far as he knew, might spout less or more, at any time, for all the certainty he felt in it. To him, the dynamo itself was but an ingenious channel for conveying somewhere the heat latent in a few tons of poor coal hidden in a dirty engine-house carefully kept out of sight; but to Adams the dynamo became a symbol of infinity. As he grew accustomed to the great gallery of machines, he began to feel the forty-foot dynamos as a moral force, much as the early Christians felt the Cross. The planet itself seemed less impressive, in its old-fashioned, deliberate, annual or daily revolution, than this huge wheel, revolving within arm's-length at some vertiginous speed, and barely murmuring—scarcely humming an audible warning to stand a hair's-breadth further for respect of power—while it would not wake the baby lying close against its frame. Before the end, one began to pray to it; inherited instinct taught the natural expression of man before silent and infinite force. Among the thousand symbols of ultimate energy, the dynamo was not so human as some, but it was the most expressive.

Yet the dynamo, next to the steam-engine, was the most familiar of exhibits. For Adams's objects its value lay chiefly in its occult mechanism. Between the dynamo in the gallery of machines and the engine-house outside, the break of continuity amounted to abysmal fracture for a historian's objects. No more relation could he discover between the steam and the electric current than between the Cross and the cathedral. The forces were interchangeable if not reversible, but he could see only an absolute *fiat* in electricity as in faith. Langley could not help him. Indeed, Langley seemed to be worried by the same trouble, for he constantly repeated that the new forces were anarchical, and especially that he was not responsible for the new rays, that were little short of parricidal in their wicked spirit towards science. His own rays, with which he had doubled the solar spectrum, were altogether harmless and beneficent; but Radium denied its God—or, what was to Langley the same thing, denied the truths of his Science. The force was wholly new.

A historian who asked only to learn enough to be as futile as Langley or Kelvin, made rapid progress under this teaching, and mixed himself up in the tangle of ideas until he achieved a sort of Paradise of ignorance vastly consoling to his fatigued senses. He wrapped himself in vibrations and rays which were new, and he would have hugged Marconi and Branly had he met them, as he hugged the dynamo; while he lost his arithmetic in trying to figure out the equation between the discoveries and the economies of force. The economies, like the discoveries, were absolute, super-sensual, occult; incapable of expression in horse-power. What mathematical equivalent could he suggest as the value of a Branly coherer? Frozen air, or the electric furnace, had some scale of measurement, no doubt, if somebody could invent a thermometer adequate to the purpose; but X-rays had played no part whatever in man's consciousness, and the atom itself had figured only as a fiction of thought. In these seven years man had translated himself into a new universe which had no common scale of measurement with the old. He had entered a super-sensual world, in which he could measure nothing except by chance collisions of movements imperceptible to his senses, perhaps even imperceptible to his instruments, but perceptible to each other, and so to some known ray at the end of the scale. Langley seemed prepared for anything, even for an indeterminable number of universes interfused—physics stark mad in metaphysics.

Historians undertake to arrange sequences,—called stories, or histories—assuming in silence a relation of cause and effect. These assumptions, hidden in the depths of dusty libraries, have been astounding, but commonly unconscious and childlike; so much so, that if any captious critic were to drag them to light, historians would probably reply, with one voice, that they had never supposed themselves required to know what they were talking about. Adams, for one, had toiled in vain to find out what he meant. He had even published a dozen volumes of American history for no other purpose than to satisfy himself whether, by the severest process of stating, with the least possible comment, such facts as seemed sure, in such order as seemed rigorously consequent, he could fix for a familiar moment a necessary sequence of human movement. The result had satisfied him as little as at Harvard College. Where he saw sequence, other men saw something quite different, and no one saw the same unit of measure. He cared little about his experiments and less about his statesmen, who seemed to him quite as ignorant as himself and, as a rule, no more honest; but he insisted on a relation of sequence, and if he could not reach it by one method, he would try as many methods as science knew. Satisfied that the sequence of men led to nothing and that the sequence of their society could lead no further, while the mere sequence of time was artificial, and the sequence of thought was chaos, he turned at last to the sequence of force; and thus it happened that, after ten years' pursuit, he found himself lying in the Gallery of Machines at the Great Exposition of 1900, his historical neck broken by the sudden irruption of forces totally new.

Since no one else showed much concern, an elderly person without other cares had no need to betray alarm. The year 1900 was not the first to upset schoolmasters. Copernicus and Galileo had broken many professorial necks about 1600; Columbus had stood the world on its head towards 1500; but the nearest approach to the revolution of 1900 was that of 310, when Constantine set up the Cross. The rays that Langley disowned, as well as those which he fathered, were occult, supersensual, irrational; they were a revelation of mysterious energy like that of the Cross; they were what, in terms of mediæval science, were called immediate modes of the divine substance.

The historian was thus reduced to his last resources. Clearly if he was bound to reduce all these forces to a common value, this common value could have no measure but that of their attraction on his own mind. He must treat them as they had been felt; as convertible, reversible, interchangeable attractions on thought. He made up his mind to venture it; he would risk translating rays into faith. Such a reversible process would vastly amuse a chemist, but the chemist could not deny that he, or some of his fellow physicists, could feel the force of both. When Adams was a boy in Boston, the best chemists in the place had probably never heard of Venus except by way of scandal, or of the Virgin except as idolatry; neither had he heard of dynamos or automobiles or radium; yet his mind was ready to feel the force of all, though the rays were unborn and the women were dead.

Here opened another totally new education, which promised to be by far the most hazardous of all. The knife-edge along which he must crawl, like Sir Lancelot in the twelfth century, divided two kingdoms of force which had nothing in common but attraction. They were as different as a magnet is from gravitation, supposing one knew what a magnet was, or gravitation, or love. The force of the Virgin was still felt at Lourdes, and seemed to be as potent as X-rays; but in America neither Venus nor Virgin ever had value as force—at most as sentiment. No American had even been truly afraid of either.

This problem in dynamics gravely perplexed an American historian. The Woman had once been supreme; in France she still seemed potent, not merely as a sentiment, but as a force. Why was she unknown in America? For evidently America was ashamed of her, and she was ashamed of herself, otherwise they would not have strewn fig-leaves so profusely all over her. When she was a true force, she was ignorant of fig-leaves, but the monthly-magazine-made American female had not a feature that would have been recognized by Adam. The trait was notorious, and often humorous, but any one brought up among Puritans knew that sex was sin. In any previous age, sex was strength. Neither art nor beauty was needed. Every one, even among Puritans, knew that neither Diana of the Ephesians nor any of the Oriental goddesses was worshipped for her beauty. She was goddess because of her force; she was the animated dynamo; she was repro-duction—the greatest and most mysterious of all energies; all she needed was to be fecund. Singularly enough, not one of Adams's many schools of education had ever drawn his atten-tion to the opening lines of Lucretius, though they were perhaps the finest in all Latin Litera-ture, where the poet invoked Venus exactly as Dante invoked the Virgin:—

Quæ quoniam rerum naturam *sola* gubernas.[1]

The Venus of Epicurean philosophy survived in the Virgin of the Schools:

Donna, sei tanto grande, e tanto vali,
Che qual vuol grazia, e a te non ricorre,
Sua disianza vuol volar sanz' ali.[2]

All this was to American thought as though it had never existed. The true American knew something of the facts, but nothing of the feel-ings; he read the letter, but he never felt the law. Before this historical chasm, a mind like that of Adams felt itself helpless; he turned from the Virgin to the Dynamo as though he were a Branly coherer. On one side, at the Louvre and at Chartres, as he knew by the rec-ord of work actually done and still before his eyes, was the highest energy ever known to man, the creator of four-fifths of his noblest art, exercising vastly more attraction over the hu-man mind than all the steam-engines and dy-namos ever dreamed of; and yet this energy was unknown to the American mind. An American Virgin would never dare command; an American Venus would never dare exist.

The question, which to any plain American of the nineteenth century seemed as remote as it did to Adams, drew him almost violently to study, once it was posed; and on this point Langleys were as useless as though they were Herbert Spencers or dynamos. The idea sur-vived only as art. There one turned as naturally as though the artist were himself a woman.

---

[1] *Since thou alone art director of the nature of things.*
[2] Lady, thou art so great, and so prevailing,
That he who wishes grace, nor runs to thee,
His aspirations without wings would fly.
    (Longfellow's translation of Dante's
    Paradiso 33, lines 13ff.)

Adams began to ponder, asking himself whether he knew of any American artist who had ever insisted on the power of sex, as every classic had always done; but he could think only of Walt Whitman; Bret Harte, as far as the magazines would let him venture; and one or two painters, for the flesh-tones. All the rest had used sex for sentiment, never for force; to them, Eve was a tender flower, and Herodias an unfeminine horror. American art, like the American language and American education, was as far as possible sexless. Society regarded this victory over sex as its greatest triumph, and the historian readily admitted it, since the moral issue, for the moment, did not concern one who was studying the relations of unmoral force. He cared nothing for the sex of the dynamo until he could measure its energy.

Vaguely seeking a clue, he wandered through the art exhibit, and, in his stroll, stopped almost every day before Saint-Gaud-ens's General Sherman, which had been given the central post of honor. Saint-Gaudens him-self was in Paris, putting on the work his usual interminable last touches, and listening to the usual contradictory suggestions of brother sculptors. Of all the American artists who gave to American art whatever life it breathed in the seventies, Saint-Gaudens was perhaps the most sympathetic, but certainly the most inarticu-late. General Grant or Don Cameron had scarcely less instinct of rhetoric than he. All the others—the Hunts, Richardson, John La Farge, Stanford White—were exuberant; only Saint-Gaudens could never discuss or dilate on an emotion, or suggest artistic arguments for giv-ing to his work the forms that he felt. He never laid down the law, or affected the despot, or became brutalized like Whistler by the bru-talities of his world. He required no incense; he was an egoist; his simplicity of thought was excessive; he could not imitate, or give any form but his own to the creations of his hand. No one felt more strongly than he the strength of other men, but the idea that they could affect him never stirred an image in his mind.

This summer his health was poor and his spirits were low. For such a temper, Adams was not the best companion, since his own gaiety was not *folle;* but he risked going now and then to the studio on Mont Parnasse to draw him out for a stroll in the Bois de Bou-logne, or dinner as pleased his moods, and in return Saint-Gaudens sometimes let Adams go about in his company.

Once Saint-Gaudens took him down to Amiens, with a party of Frenchmen, to see the cathedral. Not until they found themselves actually studying the sculpture of the western portal, did it dawn on Adams's mind that, for his purposes, Saint-Gaudens on that spot had more interest to him than the cathedral itself. Great men before great monuments express great truths, provided they are not taken too solemnly. Adams never tired of quoting the supreme phrase of his idol Gibbon, before the Gothic cathedrals: "I darted a contemptuous look on the stately monuments of superstition." Even in the footnotes of his history, Gibbon had never inserted a bit of humor more human than this, and one would have paid largely for a photograph of the fat little historian, on the background of Notre Dame of Amiens, trying to persuade his readers—perhaps himself—that he was darting a contemptuous look on the stately monument, for which he felt in fact the respect which every man of his vast study and active mind always feels before objects worthy of it; but besides the humor, one felt also the relation. Gibbon ignored the Virgin, because in 1789 religious monuments were out of fashion. In 1900 his remark sounded fresh and simple as the green fields to ears that had heard a hundred years of other remarks, mostly no more fresh and certainly less simple. Without malice, one might find it more instructive than a whole lecture of Ruskin. One sees what one brings, and at that moment Gibbon brought the French Revolution. Ruskin brought reaction against the Revolution. Saint-Gaudens had passed beyond all. He liked the stately monuments much more than he liked Gibbon or Ruskin; he loved their dignity; their unity; their scale; their lines; their lights and shadows; their decorative sculpture; but he was even less conscious than they of the force that created it all —the Virgin, the Woman—by whose genius "the stately monuments of superstition" were built, through which she was expressed. He would have seen more meaning in Isis with the cow's horns, at Edfoo, who expressed the same thought. The art remained, but the energy was lost even upon the artist.

Yet in mind and person Saint-Gaudens was a survival of the 1500; he bore the stamp of the Renaissance, and should have carried an image of the Virgin round his neck, or stuck in his hat, like Louis XI. In mere time he was a lost soul that had strayed by chance into the twentieth century, and forgotten where it came from. He writhed and cursed at his ignorance, much as Adams did at his own, but in the opposite sense. Saint-Gaudens was a child of Benvenuto Cellini, smothered in an American cradle. Adams was a quintessence of Boston, devoured by curiosity to think like Benvenuto. Saint-Gaudens's art was starved from birth, and Adams's instinct was blighted from babyhood. Each had but half of a nature, and when they came together before the Virgin of Amiens they ought both to have felt in her the force that made them one; but it was not so. To Adams she became more than ever a channel of force; to Saint-Gaudens she remained as before a channel of taste.

For a symbol of power, Saint-Gaudens instinctively preferred the horse, as was plain in his horse and Victory of the Sherman monument. Doubtless Sherman also felt it so. The attitude was so American that, for at least forty years, Adams had never realized that any other could be in sound taste. How many years had he taken to admit a notion of what Michaelangelo and Rubens were driving at? He could not say; but he knew that only since 1895 had he begun to feel the Virgin or Venus as force, and not everywhere even so. At Chartres —perhaps at Lourdes—possibly at Cnidos if one could still find there the divinely naked Aphrodite of Praxiteles—but otherwise one must look for force to the goddesses of Indian mythology. The idea died out long ago in the German and English stock. Saint-Gaudens at Amiens was hardly less sensitive to the force of the female energy than Matthew Arnold at the Grande Chartreuse. Neither of them felt goddesses as power—only as reflected emotion, human expression, beauty, purity, taste, scarcely even as sympathy. They felt a railway train as power; yet they, and all other artists, constantly complained that the power embodied in a railway train could never be embodied in art. All the steam in the world could not, like the Virgin, build Chartres.

Yet in mechanics, whatever the mechanicians might think, both energies acted as interchangeable forces on man, and by action on man all known force may be measured. Indeed, few men of science measured force in any other way. After once admitting that a straight line was the shortest distance between two points, no serious mathematician cared to deny anything that suited his convenience, and rejected no symbol, unproved or unproveable, that helped him to accomplish work. The symbol was force, as a compass-needle or a triangle was force, as the mechanist might prove by losing it, and nothing could be gained by ignoring their value. Symbol or energy, the Virgin had acted as the greatest force the Western world ever felt, and had drawn man's activities to herself more strongly than any other power, natural or super-natural, had ever done; the historian's business was to follow the track of the energy; to find where it came from and where it went to; its complex source and shifting channels; its values, equivalents, conversions. It could scarcely be more complex than radium; it could hardly be deflected, diverted, polarized, absorbed more perplexingly than other radiant matter. Adams knew nothing about any of them, but as a mathematical problem of influence on human progress, though all were occult, all reacted on his mind, and he rather inclined to think the Virgin easiest to handle.

The pursuit turned out to be long and tortuous, leading at last into the vast forests of scholastic science. From Zeno to Descartes, hand in hand with Thomas Aquinas, Montaigne, and Pascal, one stumbled as stupidly as though one were still a German student of 1860. Only with the instinct of despair could one force one's self into this old thicket of ignorance after having been repulsed at a score of entrances more promising and more popular. Thus far, no path had led anywhere, unless perhaps to an exceedingly modest living. Forty-five years of study had proved to be quite futile for the pursuit of power; one controlled no more force in 1900 than in 1850, although the amount of force controlled by society had enormously increased. The secret of education still hid itself somewhere behind ignorance, and one fumbled over it as feebly as ever. In such labyrinths, the staff is a force almost more necessary than the legs; the pen becomes a sort of blindman's dog, to keep him from falling into the gutters. The pen works for itself, and acts like a hand, modelling the plastic material over and over again to the form that suits it best. The form is never arbitrary, but is a sort of growth like crystallization, as any artist knows too well; for often the pencil or pen runs into side-paths and shapelessness, loses its relations, stops or is bogged. Then it has to return on its trail, and recover, if it can, its line of force. The result of a year's work depends more on what is struck out than on what is left in; on the sequence of the main lines of thought, than on their play or variety. Compelled once more to lean heavily on this support, Adams covered more thousands of pages with figures as formal as though they were algebra, laboriously striking out, altering, burning, experimenting, until the year had expired, the Exposition had long been closed, and winter drawing to its end, before he sailed from Cherbourg, on January 19, 1901, for home.   1906

» » Reform and the Conservative Defense « «

1900-1917

» »   « «

WE STAND AT ARMAGEDDON

We stand at Armageddon and we battle for the Lord,
And all we ask to stead us is a blessing on each sword;
And tribes and factions mingle in one great fighting clan,
Who issue to the battle behind a fighting man.
Then let the traitor truckle and the falterer go fawn,
We only ask to follow where the battle line is drawn.

We stand at Armageddon, where fighting men have stood,
And creeds and races mingle in one common brotherhood.
And here, from day to darkness, we battle for the Lord;
Thy blessing, Great Jehovah, grant on each impatient sword.
And in the righteous conflict we pledge one sacred word;
We stand at Armageddon and we battle for the Lord!

At the convention which nominated Theodore Roosevelt for the presidency in 1912 the enthusiastic crusaders of the Progressive Party burst out almost spontaneously into such songs as "Onward Christian Soldiers" and "The Battle Hymn of the Republic." During the campaign the Progressives made much use of *Progressive Battle Hymns*, a pamphlet prepared by C. H. Congdon, the director of singing at the Progressive Nominating Convention. No song in the collection better typified the spirit of Roosevelt's supporters than "We Stand at Armageddon." The words were by Bert Leston Taylor; the air was "The Wearing of the Green."

» »   « «

Reform and the Conservative Defense

THE CAUSE of the embattled farmers and the restless industrial workers did not die in 1896 when Bryan went down to defeat. The ailments of American society were too deep-seated, and the reform impulse too powerful, for the conservatism represented by the victory of Hanna and McKinley to rule without challenge. The corrupt political machines in municipalities had been attacked periodically, only to regain any position temporarily lost. Big business resorted to bribery of legislatures to secure its desired franchises and privileges; it also marketed goods with far more consideration of profits than of consumers. Courts checked the movements for social legislation and for the advance of collective bargaining by trades unions. The widespread feeling prevailed that the people had lost control over the government; that vested interests had the country in their grip.

During the 1890's the *Arena*, a periodical edited by Benjamin Flower, exposed many of the abuses in American life and clamored for reform. Shortly after 1900 other periodicals, led by *McClure's*, enlisted the services of gifted writers for the exposure of corruption in government and business. The insurance racket was laid bare; the packing-house practice of flooding the market with unhealthful if not dangerous meats was revealed; the bribery and corruption of city, state, and federal governments by private business was ruthlessly exposed. The "muck-rakers," as the writers who made such exposures were called, awakened public conscience and stimulated the impulse for broadening and strengthening the governmental control over business and the democratizing of government itself through such instrumentalities as the direct primary, initiative, referendum, recall, the direct election of senators, and woman suffrage. The less conservative wing of the dominant Republic party found in President Theodore Roosevelt a dramatic, if opportunistic, leader; in Robert LaFollette, Wisconsin governor and senator, it found a great mentor. And finally, in 1912, liberalism won a notable victory in the election of Woodrow Wilson, the Democratic reform governor of New Jersey. Meantime education had increasingly sensed its social responsibilities and its obligations toward democracy.

But conservativism did not lack its literary apostles. Sometimes business leaders themselves, eminent as examples of self-made men or as philanthropists, justified competitive and private enterprise. Sociologists and economists glorified the doctrine of laissez faire which was so effective an instrument in checking the spread of social legislation and social control. And, in much the same way as of old, men with literary gifts arose to denounce reform and humanitarianism, to defend discipline, order, and the values of the old and the tried.

In spite of the opposition to reform, impressive achievements indicated success on many fronts. The tariffs which provided special privileges to large industrial enterprises were reduced; social legislation made appreciable advances; political machinery was democratized. The banking system of the country was revamped. Labor won important victories, and agriculture received increasing consideration from government. Only with the entrance of the United States into the First World War did the reform program run up against a wall.

》 》 《 《

CHARLES W. ELIOT

1834–1926

NO FIGURE in American education was more influential than Charles W. Eliot, president of Harvard from 1869 to 1909. Although the ground was prepared for many of the reforms at Harvard associated with his name, it is no overstatement to think of him as the most important agent in the creation of a great university. His liberalization of the undergraduate curriculum, his labors for the development of graduate instruction and of a research faculty, his great services to the professional schools, affected not only Harvard, but all other American institutions of higher learning. His influence on secondary and adult education was hardly less marked.

Humane and democratic in his sympathies, devoted to the ideal of individual liberty, Eliot spoke and wrote in behalf of international peace and the arbitration of disputes by judicial and diplomatic means. He also championed the League of Nations. Although he favored profit-sharing and co-operation as remedies for industrial disputes, he opposed trades union policies of the closed shop, the uniform wage, and limitation of output. His writings, which are vigorous, lucid, and pointed, include *Educational Reform* (1898), *American Contributions to Civilization* (1897), *The Durable Satisfactions of Life* (1910), and *The Happy Life* (1896).

Charles W. Eliot, the Man and His Beliefs, W. A. Neilson, ed., New York, 1926.
C. W. Eliot, *A Late Harvest, Miscellaneous Papers*, M. A. DeWolfe Howe, ed., Boston, 1924.
Henry James, *Charles W. Eliot, President of Harvard University, 1869–1909*, Boston and New York, 1930.

» » *From:* THE MAN AND HIS BELIEFS « «

THE FUNCTION OF EDUCATION IN DEMOCRATIC SOCIETY

What the function of education shall be in a democracy will depend on what is meant by democratic education.

Too many of us think of education for the people as if it meant only learning to read, write, and cipher. Now, reading, writing, and simple ciphering are merely the tools by the diligent use of which a rational education is to be obtained through years of well-directed labor. They are not ends in themselves, but means to the great end of enjoying a rational existence. Under any civilized form of government, these arts ought to be acquired by every child by the time it is nine years of age. Competent teachers, or properly conducted schools, now teach reading, writing, and spelling simultaneously, so that the child writes every word it reads, and, of course, in writing spells

the word. Ear, eye, and hand thus work together from the beginning in the acquisition of the arts of reading and writing. As to ciphering, most educational experts have become convinced that the amount of arithmetic which an educated person who is not some sort of computer needs to make use of is but small, and that real education should not be delayed or impaired for the sake of acquiring a skill in ciphering which will be of little use either to the child or to the adult. Reading, writing, and arithmetic, then, are not the goal of popular education.

The goal in all education, democratic or other, is always receding before the advancing contestant, as the top of a mountain seems to retreat before the climber, remoter and higher summits appearing successively as each apparent summit is reached. Nevertheless, the goal of the moment in education is always the acquisition of knowledge, the training of some permanent capacity for productiveness or enjoyment, and the development of character. Democratic education being a very new thing in the world, its attainable objects are not yet fully perceived. Plato taught that the laborious classes in a model commonwealth needed no education whatever. That seems an extraordinary opinion for a great philosopher to hold; but, while we wonder at it, let us recall that only one generation ago in some of our Southern States it was a crime to teach a member of the laborious class to read. In feudal society education was the privilege of some of the nobility and clergy, and was one source of the power of these two small classes. Universal education in Germany dates only from the Napoleonic wars; and its object has been to make intelligent soldiers and subjects, rather than happy freemen. In England the system of public instruction is but twenty-seven years old. Moreover, the fundamental object of democratic education—to lift the whole population to a higher plane of intelligence, conduct, and happiness—has not yet been perfectly apprehended even in the United States. Too many of our own people think of popular education as if it were only a protection against dangerous superstitions, or a measure of police, or a means of increasing the national productiveness in the arts and trades. Our generation may, therefore, be excused if it has but an incomplete vision of the goal of education in a democracy.

I proceed to describe briefly the main elements of instruction and discipline in a democratic school. As soon as the easy use of what I have called the tools of education is acquired, and even while this familiarity is being gained, the capacities for productiveness and enjoyment should begin to be trained through the progressive acquisition of an elementary knowledge of the external world. The democratic school should begin early—in the very first grades—the study of nature; and all its teachers should, therefore, be capable of teaching the elements of physical geography, meteorology, botany, and zoölogy, the whole forming in the child's mind one harmonious sketch of its complex environment. This is a function of the primary-school teacher which our fathers never thought of, but which every passing year brings out more and more clearly as a prime function of every instructor of little children. Somewhat later in the child's progress toward maturity the great sciences of chemistry and physics will

find place in its course of systematic training. From the seventh or eighth year, according to the quality and capacity of the child, plane and solid geometry, the science of form, should find a place among the school studies, and some share of the child's attention that great subject should claim for six or seven successive years. The process of making acquaintance with external nature through the elements of these various sciences should be interesting and enjoyable for every child. It should not be painful, but delightful; and throughout the process the child's skill in the arts of reading, writing, and ciphering should be steadily developed.

There is another part of every child's environment with which he should early begin to make acquaintance, namely, the human part. The story of the human race should be gradually conveyed to the child's mind from the time he begins to read with pleasure. This story should be conveyed quite as much through biography as through history; and with the descriptions of facts and real events should be entwined charming and uplifting products of the imagination. I cannot but think, however, that the wholly desirable imaginative literature for children remains, in large measure, to be written. The mythologies, Old Testament stories, fairy tales, and historical romances on which we are accustomed to feed the childish mind contain a great deal that is perverse, barbarous, or trivial; and to this infiltration into children's minds, generation after generation, of immoral, cruel, or foolish ideas, is probably to be attributed, in part, the slow ethical progress of the race. The common justification of our practice is that children do not apprehend the evil in the mental pictures with which we so rashly supply them. But what should we think of a mother who gave her child dirty milk or porridge, on the theory that the child would not assimilate the dirt? Should we be less careful of mental and moral food-materials? It is, however, as undesirable as it is impossible to try to feed the minds of children only upon facts of observation or record. The immense product of the imagination in art and literature is a concrete fact with which every educated human being should be made somewhat familiar, such products being a very real part of every individual's actual environment.

Into the education of the great majority of children there enters as an important part their contribution to the daily labor of the household and the farm, or, at least, of the household. It is one of the serious consequences of the rapid concentration of population into cities and large towns, and of the minute division of labor which characterizes modern industries, that this wholesome part of education is less easily secured than it used to be when the greater part of the population was engaged in agriculture. Organized education must, therefore, supply in urban communities a good part of the manual and moral training which the coöperation of children in the work of father and mother affords in agricultural communities. Hence the great importance in any urban population of facilities for training children to accurate handwork, and for teaching them patience, forethought, and good judgment in productive labor.

Lastly, the school should teach every child, by precept, by example, and by every illustration its reading can supply, that the supreme attainment for an individual is vigor and loveliness of character. Industry, persistence, veracity in word and act, gentleness, and disinterestedness should be made to thrive and blossom during school life in the hearts of the children who bring these virtues from their homes well started, and should be planted and tended in the less fortunate children. Furthermore, the pupils should be taught that what is virtue in one human being is virtue in any group of human beings, large or small—a village, a city, or a nation; that the ethical principles which should govern an empire are precisely the same as those which should govern an individual; and that selfishness, greed, falseness, brutality, and ferocity are as hateful and degrading in a multitude as they are in a single savage.

The education thus outlined is what I think should be meant by democratic education. It exists to-day only among the most intelligent people, or in places singularly fortunate in regard to the organization of their schools; but though it be the somewhat distant ideal of democratic education, it is by no means an unattainable ideal. It is the reasonable aim of the public school in a thoughtful and ambitious democracy. It, of course, demands a kind of teacher much above the elementary-school teacher of the present day, and it also requires a larger expenditure upon the public school than is at all customary as yet in this country. But that better kind of teacher and that larger expenditure are imperatively called for, if democratic institutions are to prosper, and to promote continuously the real welfare of the mass

of the people. The standard of education should not be set at the now attained or the now attainable. It is the privilege of public education to press toward a mark remote.

From the total training during childhood there should result in the child a taste for interesting and improving reading, which should direct and inspire its subsequent intellectual life. That schooling which results in this taste for good reading, however unsystematic or eccentric the schooling may have been, has achieved a main end of elementary education; and that schooling which does not result in implanting this permanent taste has failed. Guided and animated by this impulse to acquire knowledge and exercise his imagination through reading, the individual will continue to educate himself all through life. Without that deep-rooted impulsion he will soon cease to draw on the accumulated wisdom of the past and the new resources of the present, and, as he grows older, he will live in a mental atmosphere which is always growing thinner and emptier. Do we not all know many people who seem to live in a mental vacuum—to whom, indeed, we have great difficulty in attributing immortality, because they apparently have so little life except that of the body? Fifteen minutes a day of good reading would have given any one of this multitude a really human life. The uplifting of the democratic masses depends on this implanting at school of the taste for good reading.

Another important function of the public school in a democracy is the discovery and development of the gift or capacity of each individual child. This discovery should be made at the earliest practicable age, and, once made, should always influence, and sometimes determine, the education of the individual. It is for the interest of society to make the most of every useful gift or faculty which any member may fortunately possess; and it is one of the main advantages of fluent and mobile democratic society that it is more likely than any other society to secure the fruition of individual capacities. To make the most of any individual's peculiar power, it is important to discover it early, and then train it continuously and assiduously. It is wonderful what apparently small personal gifts may become the means of conspicuous service or achievement, if only they get discovered, trained, and applied. A quick eye for shades of color enables a blacksmith to earn double wages in sharpening drills for quarry-men. A delicate sense of touch makes the fortune of a wool-buyer. An extraordinarily perceptive forefinger gives a surgeon the advantage over all his competitors. A fine voice, with good elocution and a strong memory for faces and parliamentary rules, may give striking political success to a man otherwise not remarkable. In the ideal democratic school no two children would follow the same course of study or have the same tasks, except that they would all need to learn the use of the elementary tools of education—reading, writing, and ciphering. The different children would hardly have any identical needs. There might be a minimum standard of attainment in every branch of study, but no maximum. The perception or discovery of the individual gift or capacity would often be effected in the elementary school, but more generally in the secondary; and the making of these discoveries should be held one of the most important parts of the teacher's work. The vague desire for equality in a democracy has worked great mischief in democratic schools. There is no such thing as equality of gifts, or powers, or faculties, among either children or adults. On the contrary, there is the utmost diversity; and education and all the experience of life increase these diversities, because school, and the earning of a livelihood, and the reaction of the individual upon his surroundings, all tend strongly to magnify innate diversities. The pretended democratic school with an inflexible programme is fighting not only against nature, but against the interests of democratic society. Flexibility of programme should begin in the elementary school, years before the period of secondary education is reached. There should be some choice of subjects of study by ten years of age, and much variety by fifteen years of age. On the other hand, the programmes of elementary as well as of secondary schools should represent fairly the chief divisions of knowledge, namely, language and literature, mathematics, natural science, and history, besides drawing, manual work, and music. If school programmes fail to represent the main varieties of intellectual activity, they will not afford the means of discovering the individual gifts and tendencies of the pupils.

As an outcome of successful democratic education, certain habits of thought should be well established in the minds of all the children before any of them are obliged to leave school in order to help in the support of the family. In some small field each child should acquire a capacity for exact observation, and as a natural result of this requirement it should come to admire and respect exact observation in all fields. Again, in some small field it should acquire the capacity for exact description, and a respect for exact description in all fields. And, lastly, it should attain, within the limited range of its experience and observation, the power to draw a justly limited inference from observed facts. I need not say that this power of just inference is an admirable one, which many adults never attain as the combined result of their education in childhood and their experience in after life. Yet democratic institutions will not be safe until a great majority of the population can be trusted not only to observe accurately and state precisely the results of observation, but also to draw just inferences from those results. The masses of the people will always be liable to dangerous delusions so long as their schools fail to teach the difference between a true cause and an event preceding or accompanying a supposed effect. Thus, a year ago our nation came to the very brink of a terrible disaster because millions of our people thought the fall in the price of silver during the past twenty years was the cause of the fall in price of many other American products; whereas the prime cause of the general fall of prices, including the price of silver, was the immense improvement which has taken place since the Civil War in the manufacture and distribution of mechanical power —an operating cause which, in the near future, is going to produce much more striking effects than it has yet produced.

Any one who has attained to the capacity for exact observation and exact description, and knows what it is to draw a correct inference from well-determined premises, will naturally acquire a respect for these powers when exhibited by others in fields unknown to him. Moreover, any one who has learned how hard it is to determine a fact, to state it accurately, and to draw from it the justly limited inference, will be sure that he himself cannot do these things, except in a very limited field. He will know that his own personal activity must be limited to a few subjects, if his capacity is to be really excellent in any. He will be sure that the too common belief that a Yankee can turn his hand to anything is a mischievous delusion. Having, as the result of his education, some vision of the great range of knowledge and capacity needed in the business of the world, he will respect the trained capacities which he sees developed in great diversity in other people. In short, he will come to respect and confide in the expert in every field of human activity. Confidence in experts, and willingness to employ them and abide by their decisions, are among the best signs of intelligence in an educated individual or an educated community; and in any democracy which is to thrive, this respect and confidence must be felt strongly by the majority of the population. In the conduct of private and corporation business in the United States the employment of experts is well recognized as the only rational and successful method. No one would think of building a bridge or a dam, or setting up a power-station or a cotton-mill, without relying absolutely upon the advice of intelligent experts. The democracy must learn, in governmental affairs, whether municipal, State, or national, to employ experts and abide by their decisions. Such complicated subjects as taxation, finance, and public works cannot be wisely managed by popular assemblies or their committees, or by executive officers who have no special acquaintance with these most difficult subjects. American experience during the last twenty years demonstrates that popular assemblies have become absolutely incapable of dealing wisely with any of these great subjects. A legislature or a Congress can indicate by legislation the object it wishes to attain; but to devise the means of attaining that object in taxation, currency, finance, or public works, and to expend the money appropriated by the constituted authorities for the object, must be functions of experts. Legislators and executives are changed so frequently, under the American system of local representation, that few gain anything that deserves to be called experience in legislation or administration; while the few who serve long terms are apt to be so absorbed in the routine work of carrying on the government and managing the party interests, that they have no time either for thorough research or for invention. Under present conditions, neither expert knowledge nor intellectual leadership can reasonably be expected of them. Democracies will not be safe until the population has learned that governmental affairs must be conducted on the same principles on which successful private and corporate business is conducted; and therefore it should be one of the principal objects of democratic education so to train the minds of the children, that when they become adult they shall have within their own experience the grounds of respect for the attainments of experts in every branch of governmental, industrial, and social activity, and of confidence in their advice.

The next function of education in a democracy should be the firm planting in every child's mind of certain great truths which lie at the foundation of the democratic social theory. The first of these truths is the intimate dependence of each human individual on a multitude of other individuals, not in infancy alone, but at every moment of life—a dependence which increases with civilization and with the development of urban life. This sense of mutual dependence among multitudes of human beings can be brought home to children during school life so clearly and strongly that they will never lose it. By merely teaching children whence come their food, drink, clothing, and means of getting light and heat, and how these materials are supplied through the labors of many individuals of many races scattered all over the world, the school may illustrate and enforce this doctrine of intricate interdependence, which really underlies modern democracy—a doctrine never more clearly expressed than in these two Christian sentences: "No man liveth to himself," and "We are every one members one of another." The dependence of every family, and indeed every person, on the habitual fidelity of mechanics, purveyors, railroad servants, cooks, and nurses can easily be brought home to children. Another mode of implanting this sentiment is to trace in history the obligations of the present generation to many former generations. These obligations can be easily pointed out in things material, such as highways, waterworks, fences, houses, and barns, and, in New England at least, the stone walls and piles of stone gathered from the arable fields by the patient labor of predecessors on the family farm. But it may also be exhibited to the pupils of secondary schools, and, in some measure, to the pupils of elementary schools, in the burdens and sufferings which former generations have borne for the establishment of freedom of conscience and of speech, and of toleration in religion, and for the development of the institutions of public justice. Of course history is full of examples of the violation of this fundamental democratic doctrine of mutual help. Indeed, history, as commonly written, consists chiefly in the story of hideous violations of this principle, such as wars and oppressions, and the selfish struggles of class against class, church against church, and nation against nation. But these violations, with the awful sufferings that follow from them, may be made to point and emphasize the truth of the fundamental doctrine; and unless the teaching of history in our public schools does this, it were better that the subject should not be taught at all.

Democratic education should also inculcate in every child the essential unity of a democratic community, in spite of the endless diversities of function, capacity, and achievement among the individuals who compose the community. This is a doctrine kindred with that just mentioned, but not identical. It is a doctrine essential to diffused democratic contentment and self-respect, but materially different from the ordinary conception of equality of condition as a result of democracy; for unity is attainable, while equality of condition is unnatural and unattainable. The freedom and social mobility which characterize the democratic state permit, and indeed bring about, striking inequalities of condition; and if the surface of democratic society should be leveled off any day, inequalities would reappear on the morrow, unless individual freedom and social mobility should be destroyed. The children of a democratic society should, therefore, be taught at school, with the utmost explicitness, and with vivid illustrations, that inequalities of condition are a necessary result of freedom; but that through all inequalities should flow the constant sense of essential unity in aim and spirit. This unity in freedom is the social goal of democracy, the supreme good of all ranks of society, of the highest no less than of the lowest.

Another ethical principal which a democracy should teach to all its children is the familiar Christian doctrine that service rendered to others is the surest source of one's own satisfaction and happiness. This doctrine is a tap-root of private happiness among all classes and conditions of men; but in a democracy it is important to public happiness and well-being. In a democracy the public functionary is not a master, but a trusted servant. By excellence of service he earns not only a pecuniary consideration, but also respect and gratitude. This statement applies just as well to a letter-carrier, a fireman, or a village selectman, as it does to a high-school teacher, a judge, or a governor. Democracy applies literally the precept, "If any man would be great among you, let him be your servant." The quality of this faithful service and its rewards should be carefully taught in school to all children of a democracy. The children should learn that the desire to be of great public service is the highest of all ambitions; and they should be shown in biography and in history how the men and women who, as martyrs, teachers, inventors, legislators, and judges, have rendered great service, have thereby won enduring gratitude and honor.

Since it is a fundamental object of a democracy to promote the happiness and well-being of the masses of the population, the democratic school should explicitly teach children to see and utilize the means of happiness which lie about them in the beauties and splendors of nature. The school should be a vehicle of daily enjoyment, and the teacher should be to the child a minister of joy. Democratic society has already learned how to provide itself—at least, in the more intelligent communities—with open grounds in cities, and parks in suburbs, and has in these ways begun to provide directly for the wholesome pleasures of the population. It should be a recognized function of the democratic school to teach the children and their parents how to utilize all accessible means of innocent enjoyment.

Finally, the democratic school must teach its children what the democratic nobility is. The well-trained child will read in history and poetry about patricians, nobles, aristocrats, princes, kings, and emperors, some of them truly noble, but many vile; and he will also read with admiring sympathy of the loyalty and devotion which through all the centuries have been felt by generous men and women of humbler condition toward those of higher. He will see what immense virtues these personal loyalties have developed, even when the objects of loyalty have been unworthy; and he will ask himself, "What are to be the corresponding virtues in a democracy?" The answer is, Fidelity to all forms of duty which demand courage, self-denial, and zeal, and loyal devotion to the democratic ideals of freedom, serviceableness, unity, toleration, public justice, and public joyfulness. The children should learn that the democratic nobility exists, and must exist if democracy is to produce the highest types of character; but that it will consist only of men and women of noble character, produced under democratic conditions by the combined influences of fine inherited qualities, careful education, and rich experience. They should learn to admire and respect persons of this quality, and to support them, on occasion, in preference to the ignoble. They should learn that mere wealth has no passport to the democratic no-bility, and that membership in it can be trans-mitted to children only through the transmission of the sound mental and moral qualities which are its sole warrant. This membership should be the rightful ambition of parents for their children, and of children for their future selves.

Every person of the true quality, no matter what his station or vocation, is admitted of right to this simple democratic nobility, which home, church, and school unite in recruiting; and there are, consequently, more real nobles under the democratic form of government than under any other.   1897

GEORGE ADE

1866–1944

AFTER GRADUATING from Purdue University in 1887, George Ade sold patent medicines, and subsequently came into his own as a reporter on the *Chicago Record*. His column attracted notice by reason of the drollness of his stories of the street and of the World's Fair. In this column appeared the first of the *Fables in Slang* (1898). Ade belongs to the "revolt from the village" school; but his keen eyes saw many of the half-comic, half-tragic distortions of value apparently inherent in a society based on profitmaking and on struggle for prestige. His stories and fables have been collected in more than thirty volumes, charac-teristic of which are *More Fables* (1900), *Breaking into Society* (1904), *The Slim Princess* (1907), *Hand-Made Fables* (1920), and *The Old-Time Saloon*, *Not Wet—Not Dry, Just History* (1931).

Dorothy Ritter Russo, *A Bibliography of George Ade*, 1866–1944, Indianapolis, 1947.
The Permanent Ade: The Living Writings of George Ade, Fred C. Kelly, ed., Indianapolis, 1947.
Fred C. Kelly, *George Ade, Warmhearted Satirist*, Indianapolis and New York, 1947.
H. L. Mencken, *Prejudices*, New York, 1924, vol. I.

» » From: MORE FABLES « «

THE FABLE OF THE HONEST MONEY-MAKER AND THE PART-NER OF HIS JOYS, SUCH AS THEY WERE

The Prosperous Farmer lived in an Agricul-tural Section of the Middle West. He com-manded the Respect of all his Neighbors. He owned a Section, and had a Raft of big Horses and white-faced Cows and Farm Machinery, and Money in the Bank besides. He still had the first Dollar he ever made, and it could not have been taken away from him with Pincers.

Henry was a ponderous, Clydesdale kind of Man, with Warts on his Hands. He did not have to travel on Appearances, because the whole County knew what he was Worth. Of course he was Married. Years before he had selected a willing Country Girl with Pink

Cheeks, and put her into his Kitchen to serve the Remainder of her Natural Life. He let her have as high as Two Dollars a Year to spend for herself. Her Hours were from 6 A.M. to 6 A.M., and if she got any Sleep she had to take it out of her Time. The Eight-Hour Day was not recognized on Henry's Place.

After Ten Years of raising Children, Steam-ing over the Washtub, Milking the Cows, Car-rying in Wood, Cooking for the Hands, and other Delsarte such as the Respected Farmer usually Frames Up for his Wife, she was as thin as a Rail and humped over in the Shoul-ders. She was Thirty, and looked Sixty. Her Complexion was like Parchment and her Voice had been worn to a Cackle. She was losing her Teeth, too, but Henry could not afford to pay Dentist Bills because he needed all his Money to buy more Poland Chinas and build other

Cribs. If she wanted a Summer Kitchen or a new Wringer or a Sewing Machine, or Anything Else that would lighten her Labors, Henry would Moan and Grumble and say she was trying to land him in the Poorhouse.

They had a dandy big Barn, painted Red with White Trimmings, and a Patent Fork to lift the Hay into the Mow, and the Family lived in a Pine Box that had not been Painted in Years and had Dog-Fennel all around the Front of it.

The Wife of the Respected Farmer was the only Work Animal around the Place that was not kept Fat and Sleek. But, of course, Henry did not count on Selling her. Henry often would fix up his Blooded Stock for the County Fair and tie Blue Ribbons on the Percherons and Herefords, but it was never noticed that he tied any Blue Ribbons on the Wife.

And yet Henry was a Man to be Proud of. He never Drank and he was a Good Hand with Horses, and he used to go to Church on Sunday Morning and hold a Cud of Tobacco in his Face during Services and sing Hymns with Extreme Unction. He would sing that he was a Lamb and had put on the Snow-White Robes and that Peace attended him. People would see him there in his Store Suit, with the Emaciated Wife and the Scared Children sitting in the Shadow of his Greatness, and they said that she was Lucky to have a Man who was so Well Off and lived in the Fear of the Lord.

Henry was Patriotic as well as Pious. He had a Picture of Abraham Lincoln in the Front Room, which no one was permitted to Enter, and he was glad that Slavery had been abolished.

Henry robbed the Cradle in order to get Farm-Hands. As soon as the Children were able to Walk without holding on, he started them for the Corn-Field, and told them to Pay for the Board that they had been Sponging off of him up to that Time. He did not want them to get too much Schooling for fear that they would want to sit up at Night and Read instead of Turning In so as to get an Early Start along before Daylight next Morning. So they did not get any too much, rest easy. And he never Foundered them on Stick Candy or Raisins or any such Delicatessen for sale at a General Store. Henry was undoubtedly the Tightest Wad in the Township. Some of the Folks who had got into a Box through Poor Management, and had been Foreclosed out of House and Home by Henry and his Lawyer, used to say

that Henry was a Skin, and was too Stingy to give his Family enough to Eat, but most People looked up to Henry, for there was no getting around it that he was Successful.

When the Respected Farmer had been Married for Twenty Years and the Children had developed into long Gawks who did not know Anything except to get out and Toil all Day for Pa and not be paid anything for it, and after Henry had scraped together more Money than you could load on a Hay-Rack, an Unfortunate Thing happened. His Wife began to Fail. She was now Forty, but the Fair and Fat did not go with it. At that Age some Women are Buxom and just blossoming into the Full Charm of Matronly Womanhood. But Henry's Wife was Gaunt and Homely and all Run Down. She had been Poorly for Years, but she had to keep up and do the Chores as well as the House-Work, because Henry could not afford to hire a Girl. At last her Back gave out, so that she had to sit down and Rest every Once in a While. Henry would come in for his Meals and to let her know how Hearty all the Calves seemed to be, and he began to Notice that she was not very Chipper. It Worried him more than a little, because he did not care to pay any Doctor Bills. He told her she had better go and get some Patent Medicine that he had seen advertised on the Fence coming out from Town. It was only Twenty-Five cents a Bottle, and was warranted to Cure Anything. So she tried it, but it did not seem to restore her Youth and she got Weaker, and at last Henry just had to have the Doctor, Expense or No Expense. The Doctor said that as nearly as he could Diagnose her Case, she seemed to be Worn Out. Henry was Surprised, and said she had not been Complaining any more than Usual.

Next Afternoon he was out Dickering for a Bull, and his Woman, lying on the cheap Bedstead, up under the hot Roof, folded her lean Hands and slipped away to the only Rest she had known since she tied up with a Prosperous and Respected Farmer.

Henry was all Broken Up. He Wailed and Sobbed and made an Awful Fuss at the Church. The Preacher tried to Comfort him by saying that the Ways of Providence were beyond all Finding Out. He said that probably there was some Reason why the Sister had been taken right in the Prime of her Usefulness, but it was not for Henry to know it. He said the only Consolation he could offer was the Hope that possibly she was Better Off. There did not seem to be much Doubt about that.

In about a Month the Respected Farmer was riding around the Country in his Buck-Board looking for Number Two. He had a business Head and he knew it was Cheaper to Marry than to Hire one. His Daughter was only Eleven and not quite Big Enough as yet to do all the Work for five Men.

Finally he found one who had the Reputation of being a Good Worker. When he took her over to his House to Break Her In, the Paper at the County Seat referred to them as the Happy Couple.

MORAL: *Be Honest and Respected and it Goes.*   1900

THE FABLE OF THE CORPORATION DIRECTOR AND THE MISLAID AMBITION

One of the Most Promising Boys in a Graded School had a Burning Ambition to be a Congressman. He loved Politics and Oratory. When there was a Rally in Town he would carry a Torch and listen to the Spellbinder with his Mouth open.

The Boy wanted to grow up and wear a Black String Tie and a Bill Cody Hat and walk stiff-legged, with his Vest unbuttoned at the Top, and be Distinguished.

On Friday Afternoons he would go to School with his Face scrubbed to a shiny pink and his Hair roached up on one side, and he would Recite the Speeches of Patrick Henry and Daniel Webster and make Gestures.

When he Graduated from the High School he delivered an Oration on "The Duty of the Hour," calling on all young Patriots to leap into the Arena and with the Shield of Virtue quench the rising Flood of Corruption. He said that the Curse of Our Times was the Greed for Wealth, and he pleaded for Unselfish Patriotism among those in High Places.

He boarded at Home for a while without seeing a chance to jump into the Arena, and finally his Father worked a Pull and got him a Job with a Steel Company. He proved to be a Handy Young Man, and the Manager sent Him out to make Contracts. He stopped roaching his Hair, and he didn't give the Arena of Politics any serious Consideration except when the Tariff on Steel was in Danger.

In a little while he owned a few Shares, and after that he became a Director. He joined several Clubs and began to enjoy his Food. He drank a Small Bottle with his Luncheon each Day, and he couldn't talk Business unless he held a Scotch High Ball in his Right Hand.

With the return of Prosperity and the Formation of the Trust and the Whoop in all Stocks he made so much Money that he was afraid to tell the Amount.

His Girth increased—he became puffy under the Eyes—you could see the little blue Veins on his Nose.

He kept his Name out of the Papers as much as possible, and he never gave Congress a Thought except when he talked to his Lawyer of the Probable Manner in which they would Evade any Legislation against Trusts. He took two Turkish Baths every week and wore Silk Underwear. When an Eminent Politician would come to his Office to shake him down he would send out Word by the Boy in Buttons that he had gone to Europe. That's what he thought of Politics.

One day while rummaging in a lower Drawer in his Library, looking for a Box of Poker Chips, he came upon a Roll of Manuscript and wondered what it was. He opened it and read how it was the Duty of all True Americans to hop into the Arena and struggle unselfishly for the General Good. It came to him in a Flash—this was his High School Oration!

Then suddenly he remembered that for several Years of his Life his consuming Ambition had been—to go to Congress!

With a demoniacal Shriek he threw himself at full length on a Leather Couch and began to Laugh.

He rolled off the Sofa and tossed about on a $1,200 Rug in a Paroxysm of Merriment.

His Man came running into the Library and saw the Master in Convulsions. The poor Trust Magnate was purple in the Face.

They sent for a Great Specialist, who said that his Dear Friend had ruptured one of the smaller Arteries, and also narrowly escaped Death by Apoplexy.

He advised Rest and Quiet and the avoidance of any Great Shock.

So they took the High School Oration and put it on the Ice, and the Magnate slowly recovered and returned to his nine-course Dinners.

MORAL: *Of all Sad Words of Tongue or Pen, the Saddest are these, "It Might Have Been."*   1900

LINCOLN STEFFENS

1866–1936

LINCOLN STEFFENS not only gained notoriety through his revelations of corruption in American cities; he also became a notable figure in the general movement of protest and reform. The following selection from his *Autobiography* is a well-informed and sympathetic account of the reform movement in Wisconsin which was led by Senator Robert M. LaFollette.

Lincoln Steffens, *Autobiography*, 2 vols., New York, 1931.
The Letters of Lincoln Steffens, edited with introductory notes by Ella Winter and Granville Hicks, 2 vols., New York, 1938.
R. M. LaFollette's Autobiography: A Personal Narrative of Political Experiences, Madison, Wis., 1911.
F. C. Howe, *Wisconsin, An Experiment in Democracy*, New York, 1910.
B. P. De Witt, *The Progressive Movement*, New York, 1915.

» » *From:* THE AUTOBIOGRAPHY OF LINCOLN « « STEFFENS

PART III. CHAPTER XIV

WISCONSIN AND BOB LAFOLLETTE

When, toward the end of my survey of Illinois, I sneaked up to Milwaukee to call on the men who were to display "the goods on that demagogue, Governor Bob LaFollette," I had no doubt that the man was a charlatan and a crook. And my colleagues on the magazine [1] had none, and the reformers and the public nationally. The reverberations of the noise this trouble-maker had been making in his own State had been heard all over the country, and the comment on it had painted a portrait of LaFollette which was fixed on the public mind as it was on mine. It made him look like two other notorious "demagogues" of the day, William Jennings Bryan and Tom L. Johnson.[2] My task was to get and prove the specific charges against him and give the ready-made type a likeness to LaFollette.

The banker, whom I called on first, was suspicious of me; he had read something of mine. As he read over the letter I handed him and as I talked, showing my earnest preconception, he opened up, and—LaFollette was a crooked hypocrite who stirred up the people with socialist-anarchist ideas and hurt business. "Good," I said, "let's begin with the evidence of his crookedness." The banker had none, but he said the corporation attorney to whom also I had a letter could prove the dishonesty. We telephoned to him to come over. Meanwhile the banker set out to demonstrate the other charges: hypocrisy, socialism-anarchism, etc., and he was going fast and hot till I realized that my witness had more feeling than facts; or [10] if he had facts, he could not handle them. He would start with some act of LaFollette and blow up in a rage. He certainly hated the man, but I could not write rage. My ready-made story of a crooked demagogue was fading when, to the banker's relief and mine, the railroad attorney arrived with papers: evidence?

This attorney took charge at once. He said he had had full instructions from Chicago to [20] lay the case fully before me; I was all right. When I told him how far we had got, the banker and I, and how I wanted first the proofs of the dishonesty alleged, he said: "Oh, no, no. You are getting off wrong. LaFollette isn't dishonest. On the contrary, the man is dangerous precisely because he is so sincere. He's a fanatic."

"But he's a hypocrite," I appealed, fearing the loss of my great story. [30]

"He is that," said the attorney. "He kicks

[1] *McClure's Magazine*, one of the leading "muckraking" periodicals.
[2] Tom L. Johnson (1854–1911), promoter and industrialist who became reform mayor of Cleveland.

about bosses and is himself a boss. He talked against the political machine and then built up an organization that is a perfect machine."

"And an agitator?"

"That's the worst of him. He's not only an orator, he's a born actor; and the way that man goes around spreading discontent is a menace to law, property, business, and all American institutions. If we don't stop him here he will go out and agitate all over the United States. We're getting him now; you'll get him next. That man must be blocked."

"Yes," said the banker, "LaFollette will spread socialism all over the world."

"But," I asked, "Milwaukee is full of socialists; are they following LaFollette?"

"No, no," the attorney corrected. "LaFollette isn't a socialist. He has nearly busted the socialists here, taken the votes right away from them. The socialists are reasonable men compared with this agitator, who is more of a Populist."

"Well, then, what does he teach and what does he do?" I asked.

The attorney, with the banker sitting by frowning, impatient, presented in good order the charges against LaFollette, the measures he had furthered, the legislation passed and proposed, his political methods. Horrified himself at the items on his list, and alarmed over the policy and the power of this demagogue, he delivered the indictment with emotion, force, eloquence. The only hitch was that Bob LaFollette's measures seemed fair to me, his methods democratic, his purposes right but moderate, and his fighting strength and spirit hopeful and heroic.

A day, a night, and another day of this condemnation by those men and others they introduced me to, and I was converted. Governor LaFollette's enemies convinced me that I was on the track of the best story yet, the story of a straight, able, fearless, individual who was trying to achieve not merely good but representative government, and this in a State, not in a city. It was not what I came here for, but it was just what I wanted: an experience in State reform.

Returning to Chicago, I communicated with my colleagues on *McClure's*. It must have been a surprise to them, my change of attitude, but they consented. I finished up in Chicago, then called on Governor LaFollette at Madison. I saw him before he saw me, and what I saw was a powerful man who, short but solid, swift and willful in motion, in speech, in decision, gave the impression of a tall, a big, man. He had meant to be an actor; he was one always. His lines were his own, but he consciously, artfully recited them well and for effect which, like an artist, he calculated. But what I saw at my first sight of him was a sincere, ardent man who, whether standing, sitting, or in motion, had the grace of trained strength, both physical and mental. When my name was whispered to him he came at me, running. LaFollette received me eagerly as a friend, as a partisan of his, a life-saver. He had read my articles on other cities and States and assumed, of course, that I would be on his side. I did not like this. I was coming over, but it takes time to change your mind, and I was not yet over on his side. He was not aware of my troubles, had not heard of my secret visit to Milwaukee; and he was in trouble himself. He was at a crisis in his career. Elected governor and in power, he had failed to do all that he had promised. The old machinery, by bribery, blackmail, threats, and women, had taken away from LaFollette enough of "his" legislators to defeat or amend his bills, and they were getting ready to beat him at the polls by accusing him of radicalism for proposing such measures, and of inefficiency and fraud for failing to pass them. He had no sufficient newspaper support. He feared that he could not explain it all to his own people, and he felt that the hostile opinion of the country outside his State, which the old Wisconsin machine was representing, was hurting him at home. He needed a friend; he needed just what I could give him, national, non-partisan support. He took me home for supper with his family, who all greeted me warmly, even intimately, on the assumption that I was their ally. I stood it for a while, then I repelled Mrs. LaFollette with a rebuke that was rude and ridiculous, so offensive indeed that I find that I cannot confess it even now. Fola LaFollette, who was there, said afterward that she never has felt so sorry for any two people as for her mother and me. My excuse was, and it is, that I had a vague plan to work up my article on LaFollette out of nothing but what his enemies were giving me; any friendly intimacy between me and the LaFollettes might spoil the effect I wished to get. And I did draw my clinching facts from the old machine men. I saw more of the opposition in Wisconsin than I did in any other similar situation. But shame for my gross discourtesy and my sense of the anxious search the governor was making of the horizon for rescue made me compromise. I closed in on him with a proposition that he take the time to tell me his whole story from boyhood on, both the good and the bad of it, his mistakes and his crimes, as well as his intentions, ideals, and high purposes, leaving it to me to write it as I pleased. He agreed; he thought it over for a few days and decided, "Yes. I'll do it—at the St. Louis Exposition, where I have to visit the Wisconsin exhibition and building. I have to be there anyway. I'll have only formal duties to perform. Most of the time I am there I can spend with you. I'll tell you everything, everything, and leave it to you to deal with as you see fit."

Bob LaFollette was called the little giant. Rather short in stature, but broad and strong, he had the gift of muscled, nervous power, and he kept himself in training all his life. Every speech he made was an exercise in calisthenics. His hands and his face were expressive; they had to be to make his balled fighting fists appeal for peace and his proud, defiant countenance ask for the reasonableness he always looked for even in an audience he was attacking. His sincerity, his integrity, his complete devotion to his ideal, were indubitable; no one who heard could suspect his singleness of purpose or his courage. The strange contradictions in him were that he was a fighter—for peace; he battered his fist so terribly in one great speech for peace during the World War that he had to have it treated and then carried it in bandages for weeks. Art Young drew a caricature of it as a pacifist's hand across the seas. He was a dictator dictating democracy, a proud man begging for the blessing of justice upon the meek, whom he organized and inspired to take it—any way. Impatient, he was slow and thorough. He prepared for a speech like a man writing a book.

When he met me in his room at the St. Louis Fair, he had on the table before him a stack of books, documents, bills, and newspapers. And he used them. He certainly kept his word to tell me everything. We were closeted there for a week of hard-working days. It must have hurt his pride, but he stripped, politically; I know, because his opponents in Wisconsin, later, told me nothing against him that LaFollette had not told me in St. Louis, and there were some faults in his career that they did not mention. Perhaps they had forgotten them; I think they did not know about some of them.

I know that there were two or three acts of his that he brought up out of the depths because he wasn't sure himself whether they were right or wrong. He had not tackled all the evils he saw, for instance; his reason was that, like Folk,[3] he had his hands full already. He had stood by some of his partisans who had gone wrong; hoped they would come back and go right. Meaning to be just and fair, he didn't know always what was justice. Intending to do right, he wasn't sure enough of what is right to satisfy himself in some cases. He put to me the questions that troubled him, and he left it to me to answer them in my narrative. His part was to lay it all out before me, himself, his acts, the circumstances, his reasons, excuses, purposes, and he did that conscientiously, in order and with ability, giving as well as his enemies did afterward their interpretations and their charges and their joy in his faults and failures.

As he went on with his story, I took notes —enough for a book—the open book of an ambitious young man who, fitted in the schools and University of Wisconsin with the common, patriotic conception of his country and his government, discovered bit by bit what the facts were, and, shocked, set out to fight for democracy, justice, honesty. He set out ambitiously on a public career, encountered a local boss in a Federal office, and appealed over his head to the people of his home county to be nominated and elected district attorney. This was his first offense; he was irregular; he defied the machine of his [Republican] party. The politicians said that Bob LaFollette worked on the delegates and the voters at night, under cover of darkness. True. And when he felt the power and suffered the methods and the lying attacks of the party and its backing higher up, he continued to work under cover and constantly, like the politicians; but also he worked in the open, day and night. His method, in brief, was to go around to towns and cross-roads, make long, carefully stated speeches of fact, and appealing to the idealism of patriotism, watch the audience for faces, mostly young faces which he thought showed inspiration. These he invited to come to him afterward; he showed them what the job was, asked them if they would do their part in their district; and so he built up an organized following so responsive to him that

[3] Joseph W. Folk (1869–1923) was elected Democratic reform governor of Missouri in 1904 after having exposed an alliance between corrupt politicians and business men in St. Louis.

it was called a machine. As it was—a powerful political machine which came to control the Republican Party in Wisconsin. The Stalwarts, as the old machine men and their business backers were called, became irregulars; they voted against and fought their party. They united with the old machine Democrats to beat their party. But LaFollette drew into it democratic Democrats and independents enough to make a majority for the Republicans, who came thus in Wisconsin to represent the people.

That was Bob LaFollette's crime. When Governor LaFollette returned to his State one way and I by another route, I called on the Stalwarts for facts, provable charges, and on LaFollette only for his specific answers or admissions. As in Milwaukee, so in Madison, the indictments withered. They fell back to his one real sin; that he had taken the Republican party away from the corrupters of it and led it to stand for—what? I said above that it represented the people, but it did that only in the sense that it labored for and gradually achieved the very moderate aims of LaFollette, a liberal, and the liberals. When I pointed this out to such men as Old Boss Keyes and Philip Spooner they were stumped. They bade me go to Milwaukee again and see the men there who knew things, especially a certain attorney who had written a book against LaFollette's railroad legislation. Since they did not know that I had been to Milwaukee and I could not go away to write without having it known that I had seen Milwaukee, I went there as openly as I could. Stalwarts called on me, offered me—rage, indignation, allegations I had investigated. As I received their stuff credulously at first, then began to ask questions, they spread the report that I was "no fool" and, apparently, "put up a job on me." Anyway, against my wish, several of them invited, urged, me to go with them to see that certain attorney who knew so much. I refused. One day I was invited to luncheon in the Hotel Pfister. My hosts, smiling at and nudging one another, led me through the barroom and stopped suddenly to present me to the attorney whom they regarded as so clever and well up on the facts. There was a crowd in the barroom, and the crowd closed in on us to see the fun.

"Why haven't you come to see me?" the attorney asked, smiling around the circle of listeners.

"Oh," I answered, "I have read your book. I see that you know, but I feel that I should know something for certain before I trouble a witness like you."

"Don't be afraid of me," he laughed. "Ask me anything you like. I'll answer you, now."

I was up against it. The crowd snickered, and I saw that I had to meet the challenge and ask a question. The underworld have to think you are "wise," or your writings won't "go." I thought a moment, eyeing my man, and I remembered that there was one alleged scandal which I had learned all about and which everybody there knew all about. I asked my opponent to tell me the truth of the matter. He began, as I had expected, to tell me the scandalous story as it first appeared, before the investigation, and I encouraged him by my exclamations to give it to me all wrong, as he did.

"Oh, so that's the way of it!" I said. "I didn't know that! Nobody ever told me that!" And all the time the crowd was laughing, winking, and driving him to "fill me up" more and more. I waited till he was all through; then I said: "I am amazed at your story. It's so much worse than I had any idea. If that's so, LaFollette is a damned rascal. But listen now, this is the way I have got it after a rather careful investigation." And I told it as it was and as that crowd and that witness knew it was, with references to the records and proofs.

Before I had finished, the audience was still and cold, they were looking at the attorney as if he were caught stealing, and he, angry, turned on me and demanded: "If you know all about it, why the hell do you ask me?"

"Because," I answered, "I have heard that you have the evidence on LaFollette, that I must see and listen to and believe you; so, when you stalled me for the amusement of this crowd, I decided to take the chance to test the reliability of the witness."

The laugh was on him, and there was a laugh. It swept him out of his anger.

"Come on and have a drink," he called and so saved his face—a little. I never saw him again. I had read his book and that was quite enough; it was a propaganda volume on what the Stalwarts wanted the world to believe, not on the facts. The incident, told and retold, helped me greatly; it discouraged lying to me and spread the impression that I knew what I pretended to inquire about and that I was leaning toward LaFollette, not the Stalwarts.

Back in Madison, Philip L. Spooner, a

brother of John C. Spooner, the very distinguished U. S. senator from Wisconsin and a leading Stalwart, reproached me for my partisanship. I reminded him that I had come there against LaFollette and that I was going over because he and his crowd had failed to furnish any proofs of their charges. "Get me a list of Bob's crimes, with the names of witnesses to testify, and I'll investigate them," I challenged. He said he would, and in a week he brought me such a list. There were some thirty offenses on it, with the names and addresses of men who had witnessed or suffered them. They were scattered all over the State. I asked Spooner if it would be fair if I visited all the men on the list who lived on the railroads and neglected the rest. He agreed to that; he helped me check them off, and I saw—Wisconsin; one of the most beautiful States I had or have seen in all my travels. I had never heard that fat land of small lakes and rivers, green meadows, and dark forests praised as lovely; it isn't grand enough to be celebrated like the scenic Hudson River or Niagara Falls, the Rockies, the Sierras, New England. It is more like the lake country of old England, quietly, modestly, contentedly, almost universally beautiful.

And I saw, by the way, the men Phil Spooner checked for me to visit, men who knew actual instances of LaFollette's corruption, trickery, and boss-ship. Full of the beauties of their country, my wife and I found them full of it too. Scandinavians, Germans, old Americans, these ex-legislators or business men or farmers in their habitat were, each of them, honest men who, like the big, bad crooks in the cities, meant well and had ideals. When I told them what I was doing and how I had to depend upon them for the truth, they responded. They did not tell their stories as they may have told them in the lobby and in the barrooms of Madison; they told them as they happened. At any rate they explained away all the evil there was in the gang's account of those cases;

every single one of those witnesses dropped the indictment out of their testimony, and, though some of them had been hurt by La-Follette, they—all—said that Bob was straight; he was hard; he was a driver, yes, even a boss, but he did all that he did for his public purposes.

Bob LaFollette was restoring representative government in Wisconsin, and by his oratory and his fierce dictatorship and his relentless conspicuous persistence he was making his people understand—all of them, apparently, not only the common people whom he preferred, but the best people too; they also knew. They might denounce him, they might lie to the stranger, but in their heart of hearts they knew. It was a great experiment, La Follette's: State reform that began in the capital of the State and spread out close to the soil. It was opposed by the cities, just as city reform was opposed by the States, but the startling thing—even though I expected it—was how this State reform encountered also the resistance of the Federal government. And just as Folk and the Chicago reformers had been forced to carry their fight up out of the cities into the States whence the trail of the serpent led, so Governor LaFollette, having carried his State several times, found that he had to go on up to the Senate. The trail of corruption is the road to success for the reformer as well as for other men. He won the next election for governor and then ran for and was elected to the U. S. Senate. He did not rush off to the Senate right away. It was characteristic of him that he remained as governor months after he was promoted to the Senate. He stuck to his post till he finished and forced the Legislature to pass all his pending measures. Then and not till then did he go on, where I saw I had to go, to the head of the system of the American government in—Washington. His career there, as in his own State, is the story of the heroism it takes to fight in America for American ideals.

[1904] 1931

» »   « «

RAY STANNARD BAKER ("DAVID GRAYSON")

1870–1946

IN 1892 Ray Stannard Baker, a young Michigan student of literature and the law, joined the staff of the *Chicago Record*. Within less than a decade he had become well-known to American journalism as the managing editor of McClure's syndicate and as the associate editor of *McClure's Magazine*. To its pages he himself contributed some of the "muckraking" articles which focused attention on the ailments of American industrial society. *The Reign of Lawlessness* was published in *McClure's* in 1904. His sense of social justice and of accurate reporting also found expression in *Following the Color Line* (1908).

An important outgrowth of Baker's position as director of the American Press Bureau in the Commission to Negotiate Peace at the conclusion of the World War was his *Woodrow Wilson and World Settlement* (1922) and his official eight-volume biography of President Wilson. The sensitiveness to economic tension which he had earlier displayed in *The Spiritual Unrest* (1910) was again manifested, at the end of the World War, in *The New Industrial Unrest* (1920). Under the pseudonym of "David Grayson," Baker published a series of charming and thoughtful essays, the best known being *Adventures in Contentment* (1907), *Adventures in Friendship* (1910), and *Adventures in Solitude* (1931).

American Chronicle, The Autobiography of Ray Stannard Baker, New York, 1945.

» » From: THE REIGN OF LAWLESSNESS « «

DEEPER CAUSES OF THE GREAT STRIKE

One of the great underlying reasons for the existing struggle, as I have said, was the demand for an eight-hour day in the smelters and mills of Colorado. The eight-hour agitation has been long-continued and bitter. Several years ago the unions began a systematic effort to secure legislation limiting the hours of work in reduction mills, in underground mine workings, and in smelters—all occupations more or less dangerous and injurious to health—where the employees now work from nine to twelve hours a day. And twelve hours a day in the often poisonous atmosphere of a smelter, any one will admit, is not humanizing toil. In 1899 the Legislature passed an eight-hour law restricting employment in these occupations. When an attempt to enforce it was made, the Smelter Trust, the Coal Operators, and other interests fought it before the State Supreme Court, which finally declared the law unconstitutional, although the United States Supreme Court had already approved a similar law passed in Utah. Such legislation, indeed, now exists in Kansas, Utah, Montana, Nevada, Arizona, British Columbia, and elsewhere.

FIGHT FOR EIGHT-HOUR LEGISLATION

The unions then began the work of getting an amendment to the Constitution. In November, 1902, the question was submitted to the people of Colorado, and an amendment carried by the tremendous majority of 46,714 votes. Both Democratic and Republican parties solemnly pledged themselves in their platforms to execute the will of the people and make laws to enforce this amendment in the Legislature of 1902–3.

Well, the Legislature met, and at once a powerful lobby appeared, such prominent citizens of Colorado as J. B. Grant, representing the American Smelting and Refining Company (the Smelter Trust), Crawford Hill of the Boston Smelting Company, Caldwell Yeaman of the Victor Coal and Coke Company, and J. C. Osgood of the Colorado Fuel and Iron Company, one of the greatest corporations in the West—these were the same interests that had fought the former eight-hour law. They now appeared before the Legislature, they and others, confusing the issue with multitudinous suggestions, disagreeing, "jockeying"—but all the time really endeavoring to prevent the passage of the laws necessary to make the amendment effective. It was nothing to them that the people of Colorado had declared such a law to be their will by an immense majority; it interfered with their business interests! And they had a lawless Legislature to deal with. At the very beginning of the session the House, which was Republican, unseated a number of the Democratic minority, in order to get a majority in the joint conference which was to elect a United States Senator. Then the Senate, largely Democratic, retaliated by expelling some of its Republican members. Both Senate and House sat for days guarded by armed men. General Sherman Bell, afterwards in command at Cripple Creek, protected the Republican House with members of the state troops!

LOBBY DEFEATS THE WILL OF THE PEOPLE

When the eight-hour bill came up, neither party wanted to pass it; each sought to throw the odium for its rejection upon the other. And all the while the lobby experts were working silently underneath, as such lobbies know how to work. By the wording of the amendment it was made mandatory on the Legislature to pass the eight-hour law—"The General Assembly *shall* provide by law"—and yet they *adjourned without passing it.*

Rarely, indeed, has there been in this country a more brazen, conscienceless defeat of the will of the people, plainly expressed, not only at the ballot, but by the pledges of both parties. And the great corporations of Colorado continued smugly with their nine, ten, and twelve hour days—earning a little more profit.

J. B. Grant, of the Smelter Trust, in a published statement, asserted that the additional cost involved in granting an eight-hour day, the establishment of three shifts instead of two, would render it impossible for his company to conduct a profitable business in Colorado.

Let us look at the Smelter Trust. Born in the period of inflated corporate enterprises, it was capitalized at $100,000,000, about $50,000,000 of which was water. Here, then, we have a condition not dissimilar to the cause underlying Parksism in New York—the managers of the Smelter Trust trying to squeeze out dividends on a capitalization half of which had no existence in values. Indeed, no dividends have yet been paid on the $50,000,000 of common stock.

Is it surprising that they should squeeze their working-men; that they should fight an eight-hour day, bring pressure to bear on a pledged Legislature, and defeat the will of the people? Compare this lawlessness which, beginning with watered stock, must undermine the honor of a state in order to earn dividends, with the lawlessness that knocks a "scab" on the head. Which is worse? Who is the greater anarchist, the millionaire magnate or the Italian miner who goes out in the night and shoots a fellow workman in the back?

WHERE THE BALLOT HAS NO VALUE

The effect of this defeat upon the unions may well be imagined. They had worked long and hard to secure this legislation, they had voted for pledged legislators only to see the plainly expressed will of the people deliberately defeated! Is it a wonder that they were discouraged, even desperate? Here they were compelled to strike to enforce what should have been a state law! It is just such doings as these that drive men to Socialism. We preach to the agitators: "Your remedy is the ballot: vote and get your rights."

Here voting did no good. In nearly all the strike speeches I heard in Colorado, this defeat of the will of the people was the strongest argument that could be used. I heard President Moyer say in a speech at Pueblo:

"What is the use of your ballots anyway? You might as well tear them up and throw them in the gutter."

The conclusion drawn by the leaders is that union men must vote the Socialist ticket: and the logic is not unconvincing.

No doubt the Smelter Trust and the Coal Operators called the defeat of the eight-hour law in the Legislature a great victory, as the union spoke of the former strikes in Cripple Creek and Telluride as victories. But it was not a victory. It was a defeat. The present scourge in Colorado, which has not spared these great money interests, found one of its chief sources there in the State-house in the definite place where the lobby and the Legislature met, where the legislator considered his political and private interests above the sacred interests of his state.

LAWLESSNESS BY BLUDGEON AND LAWLESSNESS BY FINESSE

These dark deeds of the lobby are no more definitely provable and punishable than the dynamitings and assassinations in the strike districts, and yet no one in Colorado has any more doubt that the corporations and political corruption were behind the defeat of the eight-hour law than that the unions and their political sheriffs and other officers are responsible for the violence in the gold camps. Each sort of lawlessness, darkly planned, secretly executed, comes oozing to the surface in loss of dividends, in destruction of property, in hunger and want, in assassination. And when mines and mills are tied up, business suffering, banks failing, industry paralyzed, we hear a cry of horror going up, not unhumorously, that Capital is being frightened away from Colorado! The great god Business has been disturbed! We cannot defend for a moment the lawless methods of unionism —anarchy by bludgeon; but neither can we excuse that other sort of lawlessness—anarchy by finesse: that crawling, underhanded lawlessness that corrupts legislators and breaks the greater laws.

In November, 1903, came the strike of the United Mine Workers of America, John Mitchell's organization, against the Coal Operators of Colorado—and chiefly against the Victor Fuel Company and the Colorado Fuel and Iron Company, a huge corporation controlled by John D. Rockefeller and George J. Gould.

There is not space here to consider fully all the significant features of the strike of the coal miners of Colorado, but one thing is important in this connection. Out of the five principal demands of the union on their employers, two of them are *to enforce laws already on the statute books of Colorado,* and a third, the eight-hour demand, was already a constitutional law, and would have been on the statute books, had the Legislature of last winter carried out the will of the people.

WHY LAWS ARE NOT OBEYED

I asked several officials of the coal-mining corporations why these laws were not obeyed, why the unions must strike to enforce state laws, and the answer was to this effect:

"Nobody observes those laws; they're unconstitutional anyway."

Lincoln said in his first inaugural address:

It will be much safer for all, both in official and private stations, to conform to and abide by all those acts which stand unrepealed, than to violate any of them, trusting to find immunity in having them held to be unconstitutional.

The excuse of these corporations for disregarding the law is only a little different from that of the union in excusing the slugging of "scabs." Why are the laws not enforced in both cases? Because the State must be prosecutor, and both sides *really hold* the State in contempt. The corporations have the best and shrewdest lawyers that money can hire to fight the enforcement of such laws; they find legal fees cheaper than obedience. The unions on their side threaten the State's attorney, or the sheriff, or the coroner, with a withdrawal of votes. So both sides escape.

Here is the bed-rock fact as to the situation in Colorado: if the laws on the statute books, including the eight-hour law, which should have been enacted, had been obeyed, there would have been no disturbance last year.

WHO HAS SUFFERED MOST BY THE STRIKE?

Follow the trail a step further. The chief sufferers by these strikes have not been the combatants themselves: they never are. The Western Federation strike was primarily against the offending smelters and mills, but the Smelter Trust, having works elsewhere, has suffered comparatively little. The real sufferers are the unoffending miners and mine owners of Cripple Creek and Telluride—upon whom rests the weight of a sympathetic strike—and the merchants, bankers, and business men of these and other towns. In the coal strike the larger owners of the Colorado Fuel and Iron Company are Rockefeller and Gould—and *they* are surely not suffering. And the coal miners who are striking are being supported from the funds of the United Mine Workers of America, so *they* are not suffering especially. The real sufferers here are the 7,000 workers in the steel mills at Pueblo, closed on account of the strike; the people of Colorado who must pay higher prices for their coal; the starving employees of the Overland Cotton Mills and like enterprises, closed on account of the lack of coal, and in general the public of Colorado whose business has been injured.

CITIZENS' ALLIANCES ORGANIZED

And this leads us to the consideration of another great factor in the present struggle— the Citizens' Alliance. The Citizens' Alliance is the expression in some degree of this suffering third party, pinched into organization. Often the citizens' alliances are composed largely of employers and are engines for fighting unionism, but they usually contain also many citizens and business men, who, not connected directly with any industrial struggle, have yet been injured. In some cities the alliances sprung into being with the spontaneity of a vigilance committee—and at once went to extremes. One extreme provokes another; violence and lawlessness breed violence and lawlessness.

One of the Colorado camps in which the Western Federation of Miners struck last year was Idaho Springs. The mines were closed down, with the usual blight on local business, the usual friction over a settlement, and, finally, the usual attempt to hire non-union men. On the night of July 28, 1903, while the Sun and Moon Mine was thus operating, a terrific explosion occurred which blew up the electrical transformer house and cut off the power from the mine. An Italian, with a union card in his pocket, supposedly a member of the attacking party, was found dead shortly afterward, either killed by the explosion or shot by the guards, so the crime was at once laid at the door of the union, rightly or wrongly. Deputy sheriffs arrested all the leaders of the union, taking most of them from their homes, some of them from their beds. Then the Citizens' Alliance called a meeting, which was presided over by Lafayette Hanchette, president of the First National Bank, and one of the foremost citizens of the town. There were impassioned speeches. Mr. Hanchette himself said:

It was the design of these men to remove us as they did Arthur Collins at Telluride. The officers of the Western Federation of Murderers know who committed that foul deed. It is not pleasant to do business and try to build up our city with the consciousness that there are men ready to pick you off from behind bushes or boulders. These assassins will not shoot a man in the front, but will creep up on him like cowards from behind. I know that the men down in the city jail were too cowardly to roll kegs of powder down upon the Sun and Moon Mine, attempting to kill all the men at work there, but they got some ignorant Italians to do the job for them.

UNION LEADERS EXPELLED BY THE CITIZENS' ALLIANCE

The Deputy District Attorney, Smith, a Southerner, tried to counsel moderation, urged the alliance to proceed lawfully. "I have seen mobs in the South," he said, "and I know what they come to." But the citizens would not listen to him. They marched out of the meeting, wrought to a high pitch, took the fourteen union men, including President Tressider, Secretary Olcott, and Treasurer Bender, formed them in line, and marched them to the limits of the town. There they were halted, and Lafayette Hanchette said to them:

Never show your faces in Clear Creek County again, for, if you do, we will not be responsible for what happens to you. A very considerable element here has been for hanging you men, but the conservative citizens have prevailed. They expect you to keep moving until you get out of the state.

Then the men moved off into the darkness on foot. Four of them left their wives and families behind, and one an aged mother—not knowing what was to be the result of this rising of the citizens.

How the story of these strike leaders, lawlessly driven from their town and their homes, brings up the picture of the "scabs," abused, beaten, shot at, driven over the mountains at Telluride, by union men after the capture of the Smuggler-Union Mine!

Well, the deported union men did not stay away. They returned shortly with lawyers, and had eighty-four members of the Citizens' Alliance arrested and placed under bonds; then the Citizens' Alliance turned and had the union leaders arrested—and after that there were interminable trials, nearly bankrupting the county, falling heavily upon every taxpayer, costing the Federation large sums of money, costing the Citizens' Alliance large sums of money.

FATE OF THE DECENT UNION MAN

Out of this also grew greater bitternesses, greater hatreds, greater distrust—and, finally, the determination of the Citizens' Alliance to crush unionism forever in the Idaho Springs district. And this fell hard on individuals who, honest, hardworking, respectable American citizens, perhaps, were members of the union. Probably these very men remained at home on stormy nights when there was a union meeting; probably they didn't like "union politics"; probably they did not know of the "slugging" of "scabs," or the plan to blow up the Sun and Moon Mine, if there was a plan—*and didn't want to know.* So the union fell into the hands of unwise, perhaps criminal, leaders— and they, these honest, decent union members, like the honest, decent members of our political parties, allowed the Boss to get control. And who now suffers? Why, these very same honest, self-respecting citizens! Who pays the taxes? Not the rowdy union element that commits the crimes: they have no property to tax; but these same saving, industrious union men, who do not like union politics!

PUBLIC OFFICIALS TAKING SIDES

Another appalling feature of this Colorado contest is the lining up of public officials on one side or the other of the industrial conflict. I have no wish to attack any official of Colorado, especially any judge—these are trying times, and men are prone to call names and misjudge motives—and yet no student looking into the Colorado situation, if he honestly desire to see every condition, bad or good, can escape seeing also this political side of the industrial question.

We find, for instance, Governor Peabody violently abused by all union men as a friend of the corporations. They say he was elected on a well understood anti-union platform, that he has been eager to call out the troops and help crush unionism. The employers, on the other hand, call him a "fair man," a "brave governor." I am not here discussing these charges. I am merely reporting them. A few years ago Governor Waite sat in the State-house: "Bloody Bridles" Waite they called him. Even to this day you will hear the employers of Colorado speaking of Waite as an anarchist, a demagogue, telling how he called out the troops to help the miners during the Cripple Creek strike. Union men, on the other hand, call him a hero, a "fair governor," a "fearless man." Is not, then, Governor Peabody, or was not Governor Waite, the governor for both union men and employers?

UNION JUDGES AND CORPORATION JUDGES

You will hear District Judge Owers, the judge before whom the members of the Citizens' Alliance of Idaho Springs were brought after they had driven the union men out of town, called by many employers an anarchist, a partizan of the unions.

"Just wait till we get Judge De France back," a prominent citizen of Idaho Springs said to me. "He'll teach these union murderers a lesson."

The union, on the other hand, speaks of Judge Owers as a "friend." In the same way I heard Judge Seeds, of Cripple Creek, criticized by employers and praised by union leaders. Attorney-General Miller is reported as saying:

The governor and his attorneys will try to prevent an immediate hearing of the cases, to permit the people to become composed. Their hope lies in the fact that Judge Seeds will leave the district, January 1st, giving up his seat temporarily to Judge Lewis.

Does justice, then, come and go with the judges in Colorado?

Similarly I heard legislators spoken of as "union men," or as "owned by the corporations," and sheriffs designated and counted off as favoring employers or employees.

And this, as we Americans all know, is by no means a condition peculiar to Colorado, although the present strike has brought it strongly into prominence. Colorado, too, is made up of American citizens, and its faults are American faults, not Colorado faults.

Are we, then, becoming so much unionists, so much corporationists, that we forget that we are also American citizens? Are our own private or class interests absorbing our allegiance so strongly that we forget our broad, national, state, and civic duties? When we vote, are we voting for Americans who will make and execute laws for all citizens, or are we voting for union legislators, corporation judges, citizens' alliance sheriffs?

WHO IS TO BLAME FOR ANARCHY

These, then, are the conditions in Colorado, all too briefly sketched. Who is to blame for this condition of anarchy? We hear the military forces roundly abused for their despotism, but, without wishing to excuse any of their usurpations or excesses, it is yet pertinent to inquire whether they have done anything that the citizens have not long been doing. Has not the union broken into the homes of citizens? Has not the union interfered with the personal liberty of many a "scab," driven him from his home and his work, as many a strike-leader is now being driven by the bayonet? Has it not even killed its enemies?

Have not the corporations of Colorado defeated the will of the people; have they not broken laws every day, without punishment? Have not the citizens' alliances driven men from their homes and their families?

Has not even the Legislature itself broken the highest law of the Republic, the will of the people, for private, or political, or selfish ends?

DEMOCRACY AND DESPOTISM

And, finally, as a result of all this long-continued brazen law-breaking, we see the privileges of free government taken from the people and placed in the hands of an outside despot who rules by powder and shot. In the long run, the law gets itself executed, inevitably, mercilessly; if not by the ordinary machinery of the civil officials, then by the extraordinary machinery of martial rule.

Getting down at last to fundamental principles, this is the condition in Colorado: the people have broken the law and they are being punished. Not part of the people, but every person in Colorado; not only he who bludgeoned or bribed, but he who, greedily, in the pursuit of his private business, has forgotten his civic duties, who has not, himself obedient to the law, *demanded* the election of men who will enforce the law, not union men, nor corporation men, but Americans.

There is no better evidence of the responsibility of every voter in Colorado than that every voter has suffered—if not directly in the strike, then in loss of business, in increased cost of coal and other commodities, in rising taxes. Colorado will long bend under the burden of paying for its troops, now for many months in the field, and for the endless lawsuits arising out of these disturbances. It is not cheap—lawlessness.

Perhaps just this appalling punishment was necessary to shake the people of Colorado—and of the country—from their indolent indifference. The white-hot anger of the people of Colorado, though it may be directed at the wrong thing—at the union, at the citizens' alliance, at the trust, when it should be directed at lawlessness—is a sign of hope: through the passion of this anger changes may be wrought.

1904

UPTON SINCLAIR

1878–

UPTON SINCLAIR'S Baltimore family was unable to assist him through college, and he felt the bitterness of poverty both while working his way through the College of the City of New York and as a free-lance writer in the years that followed. By 1906 he had become a Socialist, and to that cause he has made many contributions, both with his pen and as a candidate for various offices. In 1932, he was named candidate for the governorship of California on a program for abolishing poverty in the state in which he had long resided.

Although Sinclair's writings include more than seventy volumes, they possess a marked unity. He has laid bare the grip of finance capitalism on the professions, including teaching, the ministry, journalism, and authorship. In *King Coal* (1917) he dramatized the class struggle in a Colorado coal strike; in *Oil!* (1927) he portrayed the scandals of President Harding's administration; in *Boston* (1928) he told the story of the trial of Sacco and Vanzetti.

Sinclair's best known book, however, is *The Jungle* (1906). It is a realistic account of the lives of Chicago packing-house people and was primarily a powerful indictment of the miserable conditions to which workers were subjected. The incidental portrayal of the filthy and revolting conditions in packing houses was an important factor in aiding in the passage of the first Pure Food Act. While the book did not become, in the words of Jack London, "the *Uncle Tom's Cabin* of wage slavery," it did influence social thought and action.

Floyd Dell, *Upton Sinclair*, New York, 1927.
Upton Sinclair, *American Outpost: A Book of Reminiscences*, New York, 1932.

» » *From:* THE JUNGLE « «

CHAPTER III

. . .

The carcass hog was scooped out of the vat by machinery, and then it fell to the second floor, passing on the way through a wonderful machine with numerous scrapers, which adjusted themselves to the size and shape of the animal, and sent it out at the other end with nearly all of its bristles removed. It was then again strung up by machinery, and sent upon another trolley ride; this time passing between two lines of men, who sat upon a raised platform, each doing a certain single thing to the carcass as it came to him. One scraped the outside of a leg; another scraped the inside of the same leg. One with a swift stroke cut the throat; another with two swift strokes severed the head, which fell to the floor and vanished through a hole. Another made a slit down the body; a second opened the body wider; a third with a saw cut the breast-bone; a fourth loosened the entrails; a fifth pulled them out —and they also slid through a hole in the floor. There were men to scrape each side and men to scrape the back; there were men to clean the carcass inside, to trim it and wash it. Looking down this room, one saw, creeping slowly, a line of dangling hogs a hundred yards in length; and for every yard there was a man, working as if a demon were after him. At the end of this hog's progress every inch of the carcass had been gone over several times; and then it was rolled into the chilling-room, where it stayed for twenty-four hours, and where a stranger might lose himself in a forest of freezing hogs.

Before the carcass was admitted here, however, it had to pass a government inspector, who sat in the doorway and felt of the glands in the neck for tuberculosis. This government inspector did not have the manner of a man who worked to death; he was apparently not haunted by a fear that the hog might get by him before he had finished his testing. If you were a sociable person, he was quite willing to enter into conversation with you, and to explain to you the deadly nature of the ptomaines which are to be found in tubercular pork; and while he was talking with you you could hardly be so ungrateful as to notice that a dozen carcasses were passing him untouched. This inspector wore an imposing silver badge, and he gave an atmosphere of authority to the scene, and, as it were, put the stamp of official approval upon the things which were done in Durham's.

Jurgis went down the line with the rest of the visitors, staring open-mouthed, lost in wonder. He had dressed hogs himself in the forest of Lithuania; but he had never expected to see one hog dressed by several hundred men. It was like a wonderful poem to him, and he took it all in guilelessly—even to the conspicuous signs demanding immaculate cleanliness of the employees. Jurgis was vexed when the cynical Jokubas translated these signs with sarcastic comments, offering to take them to the secret-rooms where the spoiled meats went to be doctored.

The party descended to the next floor, where the various waste materials were treated. Here came the entrails, to be scraped and washed clean for sausage-casings; men and women worked here in the midst of a sickening stench, which caused the visitors to hasten by, gasping. To another room came all the scraps to be "tanked," which meant boiling and pumping off the grease to make soap and lard; below they took out the refuse, and this, too, was a region in which the visitors did not linger. In still other places men were engaged in cutting up the carcasses that had been through the chilling-rooms. First there were the "splitters," the most expert workmen in the plant, who earned as high as fifty cents an hour, and did not a thing all day except chop hogs down the middle. Then there were "cleaver men," great giants with muscles of iron; each had two men to attend him—to slide the half carcass in front of him on the table, and hold it while he chopped it, and then turn each piece so that he might chop it once more. His cleaver had a blade about two feet long, and he never made but one cut; he made it so neatly, too, that his implement did not smite through and dull itself—there was just enough force for a perfect cut, and no more. So through various yawning holes there slipped to the floor below —to one room hams, to another forequarters, to another sides of pork. One might go down to this floor and see the pickling-rooms, where the hams were put into vats, and the great smoke-rooms, with their air-tight iron doors. In other rooms they prepared salt-pork—there were whole cellars full of it, built up in great towers to the ceiling. In yet other rooms they were putting up meat in boxes and barrels, and wrapping hams and bacon in oiled paper, sealing and labeling and sewing them. From the doors of these rooms went men with loaded trucks, to the platform where freight-cars were waiting to be filled; and one went out there and realized with a start that he had come at last to the ground floor of this enormous building.

Then the party went across the street to where they did the killing of the beef—where every hour they turned four or five hundred cattle into meat. Unlike the place they had left, all this work was done on one floor; and instead of there being one line of carcasses which moved to the workmen, there were fifteen or twenty lines, and the men moved from one to another of these. This made a scene of intense activity, a picture of human power wonderful to watch. It was all in one great room, like a circus amphitheatre, with a gallery for the visitors running over the centre.

Along one side of the room ran a narrow gallery, a few feet from the floor; into which gallery the cattle were driven by men with goads which gave them electric shocks. Once crowded in here, the creatures were prisoned, each in a separate pen, by gates that shut, leaving them no room to turn around; and while they stood bellowing and plunging, over the top of the pen there leaned one of the "knockers," armed with a sledge-hammer, and watching for a chance to deal a blow. The room echoed with the thuds in quick succession, and the stamping and kicking of the steers. The instant the animal had fallen, the "knocker" passed on to another; while a second man raised a lever, and the side of the pen was raised, and the animal, still kicking and struggling, slid out to the "killing-bed." Here a man put shackles about one leg, and pressed another lever, and the body was jerked up into the air. There were fifteen or twenty such pens, and it was a matter of a couple of minutes to knock fifteen or twenty cattle and roll them out. Then once more the gates were opened, and another lot rushed in; and so out of each pen there rolled a steady stream of carcasses, which the men upon the killing-beds had to get out of the way.

The manner in which they did this was something to be seen and never forgotten. They worked with furious intensity, literally upon the run—at a pace with which there is nothing to be compared except a football game. It was all highly specialized labor, each man having his task to do; generally this would consist of only two or three specific cuts, and he would pass down the line of fifteen or twenty carcasses, making these cuts upon each. First there came the "butcher," to bleed them; this meant one swift stroke, so swift that you could not see it—only the flash of the knife; and before you could realize it, the man had darted on to the next line, and a stream of bright red was pouring out upon the floor. This floor was half an inch deep with blood, in spite of the best efforts of the men who kept shovelling it through holes; it must have made the floor slippery, but no one could have guessed this by watching the men at work.

The carcass hung for a few minutes to bleed; there was no time lost however, for there were several hanging in each line, and one was always ready. It was let down to the ground, and there came the "headsman," whose task it was to sever the head, with two or three swift strokes. Then came the "floorsman," to make the first cut in the skin; and then another to finish ripping the skin down the centre; and then half a dozen more in swift succession, to finish the skinning. After they were through, the carcass was again swung up; and while a man with a stick examined the skin, to make sure that it had not been cut, another rolled it up and tumbled it through one of the inevitable holes in the floor, the beef proceeded on its journey. There were men to cut it, and men to split it, and men to gut it and scrape it, clean inside. There were some with hose which threw jets of boiling water upon it, and others who removed the feet and added the final touches. In the end, as with the hogs, the finished beef was run into the chilling-room, to hang its appointed time.

The visitors were taken there and shown them, all neatly hung in rows, labelled conspicuously with the tags of the government inspectors—and some, which had been killed by a special process, marked with the sign of the "kosher" rabbi, certifying that it was fit for sale to the orthodox. And then the visitors were taken to the other parts of the building, to see what became of each particle of the waste material that had vanished through the floor; and to the pickling-rooms, and the salting-rooms, the canning-rooms, and the packing-rooms, where choice meat was prepared for shipping in refrigerator-cars, destined to be eaten in all the four corners of civilization. Afterward they went outside, wandering about among the mazes of buildings in which was done the work auxiliary to this great industry. There was scarcely a thing needed in the business that Durham and Company did not make for themselves. There was a great steam-power plant and an electricity plant. There was a barrel factory, and a boiler-repair shop. There was a building to which the grease was piped, and made into soap and lard; and then there was a factory for making lard cans, and another for making soap boxes. There was a building in which the bristles were cleaned and dried, for the making of hair cushions and such things; there was a building where the skins were dried and tanned, there was another where heads and feet were made into glue, and another where bones were made into fertilizer. No tiniest particle of organic matter was wasted in Durham's. Out of the horns of the cattle they made combs, buttons, hair-pins, and imitation ivory; out of the shin bones and other big bones they cut knife and tooth-brush handles, and mouth-pieces for pipes; out of the hoofs they cut hair-pins and buttons, before they had made the rest into glue. From such things as feet, knuckles, hide clippings, and sinews came such strange and unlikely products as gelatin, isinglass, and phosphorus, bone-black, shoe-blacking, and bone-oil. They had curled-hair works for the cattle-tails, and a "wool-pullery" for the sheep skins; they made pepsin from the stomachs of the pigs, and albumen from the blood, and violin strings from the ill-smelling entrails. When there was nothing else to be done with a thing, they first put it into a tank and got out of it all the tallow and grease, and then they made it into fertilizer. All these industries were gathered into buildings near by, connected by galleries and railroads with the main establishment; and it was estimated that they had handled nearly a quarter of a billion of animals since the founding of the plant by the elder Durham a generation or more ago. If you counted with it the other big plants—and they were now really all one—it was, so Jokubas informed them, the greatest aggregation of labor and capital ever gathered in one place. It employed thirty thousand men; it supported directly two hundred

and fifty thousand people in its neighborhood, and indirectly it supported half a million. It sent its products to every country in the civilized world, and it furnished the food for no less than thirty million people!

To all these things our friends would listen open mouthed—it seemed to them impossible of belief that anything so stupendous could have been devised by mortal man. That was why to Jurgis it seemed almost profanity to speak about the place as did Jokubas, sceptically; it was a thing as tremendous as the universe—the laws and ways of its working no more than the universe to be questioned or understood. All that a mere man could do, it seemed to Jurgis, was to take a thing like this as he found it, and do as he was told; to be given a place in it and to share in its wonderful activities was a blessing to be grateful for, as one was grateful for the sunshine and the rain. Jurgis was even glad that he had not seen the place before meeting with his triumph, for he felt that the size of it would have overwhelmed him. But now he had been admitted—he was a part of it all! He had the feeling that this whole huge establishment had taken him under his protection, and had become responsible for his welfare. So guileless was he, and ignorant of the nature of business, that he did not even realize that he had become an employee of Brown's and that Brown and Durham were supposed by all the world to be deadly rivals —were even required to be deadly rivals by the law of the land, and ordered to try to ruin each other under penalty of fine and imprisonment!

CHAPTER IX

. . . .

And there were things ever stranger than this, according to the gossip of the men. The packers had secret mains, through which they stole billions of gallons of the city's water. The newspapers had been full of this scandal—and once there had been an investigation, and an actual uncovering of the pipes; but nobody had been punished, and the thing went right on. And then there was the condemned meat industry, with its endless horrors. The people of Chicago saw the government inspectors in Packingtown, and they all took that to mean that they were protected from diseased meat; they did not understand that these hundred and sixty-three inspectors had been appointed at the request of the packers, and that they were paid by the United States government to certify that all the diseased meat was kept in the state. They had no authority beyond that; for the inspection of meat to be sold in the city and state the whole force in Packingtown consisted of three henchmen of the local political machine! And shortly afterward one of these, a physician, made the discovery that the carcasses of steers which had been condemned as tubercular by the government inspectors, and which therefore contained ptomaines, which are deadly poisons, were left upon an open platform and carted away to be sold in the city; and he insisted that these carcasses be treated with an injection of kerosene—and was ordered to resign the same week! So indignant were the packers that they went farther, and compelled the mayor to abolish the whole bureau of inspection; so that since then there has not been even a pretence of any interference with the graft. There was said to be two thousand dollars a week hush-money from the tubercular steers alone; and as much again from the hogs which had died of cholera on the trains, and which you might see any day being loaded into box-cars and hauled away to a place called Globe, in Indiana, where they made a fancy grade of lard.

There were the men in the pickle-rooms, for instance, where old Antanas had gotten his death; scarce a one of these that had not some spot of horror on his person. Let a man so much as scrape his finger pushing a truck in the pickle-rooms, and he might have a sore that would put him out of the world; all the joints in his fingers might be eaten by the acid, one by one. Of the butchers and floorsmen, the beef-boners and trimmers, and all those who used knives, you could scarcely find a person who had the use of his thumb; time and time again the base of it had been slashed, till it was a mere lump of flesh against which the man pressed the knife to hold it. The hands of these men would be criss-crossed with cuts, until you could no longer pretend to count them or to trace them. They would have no nails,—they had worn them off pulling hides; their knuckles were swollen so that their fingers spread out like a fan. There were men who worked in the cooking-rooms, in the midst of steam and sickening odors, by artificial light; in these rooms the germs of tuberculosis might live for two years, but the supply was renewed

every hour. There were the beef-luggers, who carried two-hundred-pound quarters into the refrigerator-cars; a fearful kind of work, that began at four o'clock in the morning, and that wore out the most powerful men in a few years. There were those who worked in the chilling-rooms, and whose special disease was rheumatism; the time-limit that a man could work in the chilling-rooms was said to be five years. There were the wool-pluckers, whose hands went to pieces even sooner than the hands of the pickle-men; for the pelts of the sheep had to be painted with acid to loosen the wool, and then the pluckers had to pull out this wool with their bare hands, till the acid had eaten their fingers off. There were those who made the tins for the canned-meat; and their hands, too, were a maze of cuts, and each cut represented a chance for blood-poisoning. Some worked at the stamping-machines, and it was very seldom that one could work long there at the pace that was set, and not give out and forget himself, and have a part of his hand chopped off. There were the "hoisters," as they were called, whose task it was to press the lever which lifted the dead cattle off the floor. They ran along upon a rafter, peering down through the damp and the steam; and as old Durham's architects had not built the killing-room for the convenience of the hoisters, at every few feet they would have to stoop under a beam, say four feet above the one they ran on; which got them into the habit of stooping, so that in a few years they would be walking like chimpanzees. Worst of any, however, were the fertilizer-men, and those who served in the cooking-rooms. These people could not be shown to the visitor,—for the odor of a fertilizer-man would scare any ordinary visitor at a hundred yards, and as for the other men, who worked in tank-rooms full of steam, and in some of which there were open vats near the level of the floor, their peculiar trouble was that they fell into the vats; and when they were fished out, there was never enough of them left to be worth exhibiting, —sometimes they would be overlooked for days, till all but the bones of them had gone out to the world as Durham's Pure Leaf Lard!

CHAPTER XIV

With one member trimming beef in a cannery, and another working in a sausage factory, the family had a first-hand knowledge of the great majority of Packingtown swindles. For it was the custom, as they found, whenever meat was so spoiled that it could not be used for anything else, either to can it or else to chop it up into sausage. With what had been told them by Jonas, who had worked in the pickle-rooms, they could now study the whole of the spoiled-meat industry on the inside, and read a new and grim meaning into that old Packingtown jest,—that they used everything of the pig except the squeal.

Jonas had told them how the meat that was taken out of pickle would often be found sour, and how they would rub it up with soda to take away the smell, and sell it to be eaten on free-lunch counters; also of all the miracles of chemistry which they performed, giving to any sort of meat, fresh or salted, whole or chopped, any color and any flavor and any odor they chose. In the pickling of hams they had an ingenious apparatus, by which they saved time and increased the capacity of the plant—a machine consisting of a hollow needle attached to a pump; by plunging this needle into the meat and working with his foot, a man could fill a ham with pickle in a few seconds. And yet, in spite of this, there would be hams found spoiled, some of them with an odor so bad that a man could hardly bear to be in the room with them. To pump into these the packers had a second and much stronger pickle which destroyed the odor—a process known to the workers as "giving them thirty per cent." Also, after the hams had been smoked, there would be found some that had gone to the bad. Formerly these had been sold as "Number Three Grade," but later on some ingenious person had hit upon a new device, and now they would extract the bone, about which the bad part generally lay, and insert in the hole a white-hot iron. After this invention there was no longer Number One, Two and Three Grade —there was only Number One Grade. The packers were always originating such schemes —they had what they called "boneless hams," which were all the odds and ends of pork stuffed into casings; and "California hams," which were the shoulders, with big knuckle-joints, and nearly all the meat cut out; and fancy "skinned hams," which were made of the oldest hogs, whose skin were so heavy and coarse that no one would buy them—that is, until they had been cooked and chopped fine and labelled "head cheese"!

It was only when the whole ham was spoiled that it came into the department of Elzbieta. Cut up by the two-thousand-revolutions-a-minute flyers, and mixed with half a ton of other meat, no odor that ever was in a ham could make any difference. There was never the least attention paid to what was cut up for sausage; there would come all the way back from Europe old sausage that had been rejected, and that was moldy and white—it would be dosed with borax and glycerine, and dumped into the hoppers, and made over again for home consumption. There would be meat that had tumbled out on the floor, in the dirt and sawdust, where the workers had tramped and spit uncounted billions of consumption germs. There would be meat stored in great piles in rooms; and the water from leaky roofs would drip over it, and thousands of rats would race about on it. It was too dark in these storage places to see well, but a man could run his hand over these piles of meat and sweep off handfuls of dried dung of rats. These rats were nuisances, and the packers would put poisoned bread out for them; they would die, and then rats, bread, and meat would go into the hoppers together. This is no fairy story and no joke; the meat would be shovelled into carts, and the man who did the shovelling would not trouble to lift out a rat even when he saw one—there were things that went into the sausage in comparison with which a poisoned rat was a tidbit. There was no place for the men to wash their hands before they ate their dinner, and so they made a practice of washing them in the water that was to be ladled into the sausage. There were the butt-ends of smoked meat, and the scraps of corned beef, and all the odds and ends of the waste of the plants, that would be dumped into old barrels in the cellar and left there. Under the system of rigid economy which the packers enforced, there were some jobs that it only paid to do once in a long time, and among these was the cleaning out of the waste-barrels. Every spring they did it, and in the barrels would be dirt and rust and old nails and stale water—and cart load after cart load of it would be taken up and dumped into the hoppers with fresh meat, and sent out to the public's breakfast. Some of it they would make into "smoked" sausage—but as the smoking took time, and was therefore expensive, they would call upon their chemistry department, and preserve it with borax and color it with gelatine to make it brown. All of their sausage came out of the same bowl, but when they came to wrap it they would stamp some of it "special," and for this they would charge two cents more a pound.

Such were the new surroundings in which Elzbieta was placed, and such was the work she was compelled to do. It was stupefying, brutalizing work; it left her no time to think, no strength for anything. She was part of the machine she tended, and every faculty that was not needed for the machine was doomed to be crushed out of existence. There was only one mercy about the cruel grind—that it gave her the gift of insensibility. Little by little she sank into a torpor—she fell silent. She would meet Jurgis and Ona in the evening, and the three would walk home together, often without saying a word. Ona, too, was falling into a habit of silence—Ona, who had once gone about singing like a bird. She was sick and miserable, and often she would barely have strength enough to drag herself home. And there they would eat what they had to eat, and afterwards, because there was only their misery to talk of, they would crawl into bed and fall into a stupor and never stir until it was time to get up again, and dress by candlelight, and go back to the machines. They were so numbed that they did not even suffer much from hunger, now; only the children continued to fret when the food ran short.

Yet the soul of Ona was not dead—the souls of none of them were dead, but only sleeping; and now and then they would waken, and these were cruel times. The gates of memory would roll open—old joys would stretch out their arms to them, old hopes and dreams would call to them, and they would stir beneath the burden that lay upon them, and feel its forever immeasurable weight. They could not even cry out beneath it; but anguish would seize them, more dreadful than agony of death. It was a thing scarcely to be spoken —a thing never spoken by all the world, that will not know its own defeat.

They were beaten; they had lost the game, they were swept aside. It was not less tragic because it was so sordid, because it had to do with wages and grocery bills and rents. They had dreamed of freedom; of a chance to look about them and learn something; to be decent and clean, to see their child grow up to be strong. And now it was all gone—it would never be! They had played the game and they

had lost. Six years more of toil they had to face before they could expect the least respite, the cessation of the payments upon the house; and how cruelly certain it was that they could never stand six years of such a life as they were living! They were lost, they were going down—and there was no deliverance for them, no hope; for all the help it gave them the vast city in which they lived might have been an ocean waste, a wilderness, a desert, a tomb. So often this mood would come to Ona, in the night-time, when something wakened her; she would lie, afraid of the beating of her own heart, fronting the blood-red eyes of the old primeval terror of life. Once she cried aloud, and woke Jurgis, who was tired and cross. After that she learned to weep silently— their moods so seldom came together now! It was as if their hopes were buried in separate graves.

. . .

CHAPTER XXIX

Until long after midnight Jurgis sat lost in the conversation of his new acquaintance. It was a most wonderful experience to him—an almost supernatural experience. It was like encountering an inhabitant of the fourth dimension of space, a being who was free from all one's own limitations. For four years now, Jurgis had been wandering and blundering in the depths of a wilderness; and here, suddenly a hand reached down and seized him, and lifted him out of it, and set him upon a mountain top, from which he could survey it all, —could see the paths from which he had wandered, the morasses into which he had stumbled, the hiding-places of the beasts of prey that had fallen upon him. There were his Packingtown experiences, for instance—what was there about Packingtown that Ostrinski could not explain! To Jurgis the packers had been equivalent to fate; Ostrinski showed him that they were the Beef Trust. They were a gigantic combination of capital, which had crushed all opposition, and overthrown the laws of the land, and was preying upon the people. Jurgis recollected how, when he had first come to Packingtown, he had stood and watched the hog-killing, and thought how cruel and savage it was, and come away congratulating himself that he was not a hog; now his new acquaintance showed him that a hog was just what he had been—one of the packers' hogs. What they wanted from a hog was all the profits that could be got out of him; and that was what they wanted from the working-man, and also that was what they wanted from the public. What the hog thought of it, and what he suffered, were not considered; and no more was it with labor, and no more with the chaser of meat. That was true everywhere in the world, but it was especially true in Packingtown; there seemed to be something about the work of slaughtering that tended to ruthlessness and ferocity—it was literally the fact that in the methods of the packers a hundred human lives did not balance a penny of profit. When Jurgis had made himself familiar with the Socialist literature, as he would very quickly, he would get glimpses of the Beef Trust from all sorts of aspects, and he would find it everywhere the same; it was the incarnation of the blind and insensate Greed. It was a monster devouring with a thousand mouths, trampling with a thousand hoofs; it was the Great Butcher—it was the spirit of Capitalism made flesh. Upon the ocean of commerce it sailed as a pirate ship; it had hoisted the black flag and declared war upon civilization. Bribery and corruption were its everyday methods. In Chicago the city government was simply one of its branch-offices; it stole billions of gallons of city water openly, it dictated to the courts the sentences of disorderly strikers, it forbade the mayor to enforce the building laws against it. In the national capital it had power to prevent inspection of its product, and to falsify

government reports; it violated the rebate laws, and when an investigation was threatened it burned its books and sent its criminal agents out of the country. In the commercial world it was a Juggernaut car; it wiped out thousands of businesses every year, it drove men to madness and suicide. It had forced the price of cattle so low as to destroy the stock-raising industry, an occupation upon which whole states existed; it had ruined thousands of butchers who had refused to handle its products. It divided the country into districts, and fixed the price of meat in all of them; and it owned all the refrigerator cars, and levied an enormous tribute upon all poultry and eggs and fruit and vegetables. With the millions of dollars a week that poured in upon it, it was reaching out for the control of other interests, railroads and trolley lines, gas and electric light franchises—it already owned the leather and the grain business of the country. The people were tremendously stirred up over its encroachments, but nobody had any remedy to suggest; it was the task of Socialists to teach and organize them, and prepare them for the time when they were to seize the huge machine called the Beef Trust, and use it to produce food for human beings and not to heap up fortunes for a band of pirates.—It was long after midnight when Jurgis lay down upon the floor of Ostrinski's kitchen; and yet it was an hour before he could get to sleep, for the glory of that joyful vision of the people of Packingtown marching in and taking possession of the Union Stockyards!   1906

THEODORE ROOSEVELT

1858–1919

HAVING DONE much during his presidency to support "progressive" measures, Roosevelt assumed the leadership of the liberal forces in the Republican party when the cleavage between the right and the left became marked in the administration of his successor, William Howard Taft. Roosevelt's championship of the direct primary in New York was followed by his declaration at Ossawatomie, Kansas, on August 31, 1910, that "property shall be the servant and not the master" and that the Constitution must be amended if it proves too rigid to meet the changing needs of the American people. To further the democratic control of public policy against the encroachments of the "vested interests" Roosevelt favored the initiative, referendum, and recall. He also advocated more comprehensive and advanced social legislation and the extension of federal power to bring about these and other liberal ends. There was little that was new in Roosevelt's *New Nationalism*, the speeches which comprised his platform in the three-cornered presidential race of 1912. Indeed, Robert M. LaFollette's career gave more evidence of a more consistent and deeper-rooted progressivism than his. But Roosevelt, in spite of his defeat in the election, was a popular figure, and his championship of progressivism was of importance in the conflict between privilege and democracy.

The Works of Theodore Roosevelt, National Edition, 20 vols., New York, 1926.
H. F. Pringle, *Theodore Roosevelt, A Biography*, New York, 1931.
Howard K. Beale, *Theodore Roosevelt and the Rise of America to World Power*, Baltimore, 1947.
George E. Mowry, *Theodore Roosevelt and the Progressive Movement*, Madison, 1946.

» » *From:* THE NEW NATIONALISM « «

We come here to-day to commemorate one of the epoch-making events of the long struggle for the rights of man—the long struggle for the uplift of humanity. Our country—this great republic—means nothing unless it means the triumph of a real democracy, the triumph of popular government, and, in the long run, of an economic system under which each man shall be guaranteed the opportunity to show the best that there is in him. That is why the history of America is now the central feature of the history of the world; for the world has set its face hopefully toward our democracy; and, O my fellow citizens, each one of you carries on your shoulders not only the burden of doing well for the sake of your own country, but the burden of doing well and of seeing that this nation does well for the sake of mankind.

There have been two great crises in our country's history: first, when it was formed, and then, again, when it was perpetuated; and, in the second of these great crises—in the time of stress and strain which culminated in the Civil War, on the outcome of which depended the justification of what had been done earlier, you men of the Grand Army, you men who fought through the Civil War, not only did you justify your generation, not only did you render life worth living for our generation, but you justified the wisdom of Washington and Washington's colleagues. If this republic had been founded by them only to be split asunder into fragments when the strain came, then the judgment of the world would have been that Washington's work was not worth doing. It was you who crowned Washington's work, as you carried to achievement the high purpose of Abraham Lincoln.

. . . .

It was a heroic struggle; and, as is inevitable with all such struggles, it had also a dark and terrible side. Very much was done of good, and much also of evil; and, as was inevitable in such a period of revolution, often the same man did both good and evil. For our great good fortune as a nation, we, the people of the United States as a whole, can now afford to forget the evil, or, at least, to remember it without bitterness, and to fix our eyes with pride only on the good that was accomplished. Even in ordinary times there are very few of us who do not see the problems of life as through a glass, darkly; and when the glass is clouded by the murk of furious popular passion, the vision of the best and the bravest is dimmed. Looking back, we are all of us now able to do justice to the valor and the disinterestedness and the love of the right, as to each it was given to see the right, shown both by the men of the North and the men of the South in that contest which was finally decided by the attitude of the West. We can admire the heroic valor, the sincerity, the self-devotion shown alike by the men who wore the blue and the men who wore the gray; and our sadness that such men should have had to fight one another is tempered by the glad knowledge that ever hereafter their descendants shall be found fighting side by side, struggling in peace as well as in war for the uplift of their common country, all alike resolute to raise to the highest pitch of honor and usefulness the nation to which they all belong. As for the veterans of the Grand Army of the Republic, they deserve honor and recognition such as is paid to no other citizens of the republic; for to them the republic owes its all; for to them it owes its very existence. It is because of what you and your comrades did in the dark years that we of to-day walk, each of us, head erect, and proud that we belong, not to one of a dozen little squabbling contemptible commonwealths, but to the mightiest nation upon which the sun shines.

I do not speak of this struggle of the past merely from the historic standpoint. Our interest is primarily in the application to-day of the lessons taught by the contest of half a century ago. . . .

Of that generation of men to whom we owe so much, the man to whom we owe most is, of course, Lincoln. Part of our debt to him is because he forecast our present struggle and saw the way out. He said:—

I hold that while man exists it is his duty to improve not only his own condition, but to assist in ameliorating mankind.

And again:—

Labor is prior to, and independent of, capital. Capital is only the fruit of labor, and could never have existed if labor had not first existed. Labor is the superior of capital, and deserves much the higher consideration.

If that remark was original with me, I should be even more strongly denounced as a communist agitator than I shall be anyhow. It is Lincoln's. I am only quoting it; and that is one side; that is the side the capitalist should hear. Now, let the workingman hear his side.

Capital has its rights, which are as worthy of protection as any other rights. . . . Nor should this lead to a war upon the owners of property. Property is the fruit of labor; . . . property is desirable; is a positive good in the world.

And then comes a thoroughly Lincolnlike sentence:—

Let not him who is houseless pull down the house of another, but let him work diligently and build one for himself, thus by example assuring that his own shall be safe from violence when built.

It seems to me that, in these words, Lincoln took substantially the attitude that we ought to take; he showed the proper sense of proportion in his relative estimates of capital and labor, of human rights and property rights. Above all, in this speech, as in many others, he taught a lesson in wise kindliness and charity; an indispensable lesson to us of to-day. But this wise kindliness and charity never weakened his arm or numbed his heart. We cannot afford weakly to blind ourselves to the actual conflict which

faces us to-day. The issue is joined, and we must fight or fail.

In every wise struggle for human betterment one of the main objects, and often the only object, has been to achieve in large measure equality of opportunity. In the struggle for this great end, nations rise from barbarism to civilization, and through it people press forward from one stage of enlightenment to the next. One of the chief factors in progress is the destruction of special privilege. The essence of any struggle for healthy liberty has always been, and must always be, to take from some one man or class of men, the right to enjoy power, or wealth, or position, or immunity, which has not been earned by service to his or their fellows. That is what you fought for in the Civil War, and that is what we strive for now.

At many stages in the advance of humanity, this conflict between the men who possess more than they have earned and the men who have earned more than they possess is the central condition of progress. In our day it appears as the struggle of free men to gain and hold the right of self-government as against the special interests, who twist the methods of free government into machinery for defeating the popular will. At every stage, and under all circumstances, the essence of the struggle is to equalize opportunity, destroy privilege, and give to the life and citizenship of every individual the highest possible value both to himself and to the commonwealth. That is nothing new. All I ask in civil life is what you fought for in the Civil War. I ask that civil life be carried on according to the spirit in which the army was carried on. You never get perfect justice, but the effort in handling the army was to bring to the front the men who could do the job. Nobody grudged promotion to Grant, or Sherman, or Thomas, or Sheridan, because they earned it. The only complaint was when a man got promotion which he did not earn.

. . .

I stand for the square deal. But when I say that I am for the square deal, I mean not merely that I stand for fair play under the present rules of the game, but that I stand for having those rules changed so as to work for a more substantial equality of opportunity and of reward for equally good service. One word of warning, which, I think, is hardly necessary in Kansas. When I say I want a square deal for the poor man, I do not mean that I want a square deal for the man who remains poor because he has not got the energy to work for himself. If a man who has had a chance will not make good, then he has got to quit. And you men of the Grand Army, you want justice for the brave man who fought, and punishment for the coward who shirked his work. Is not that so?

Now, this means that our government, national and state, must be freed from the sinister influence or control of special interests. Exactly as the special interests of cotton and slavery threatened our political integrity before the Civil War, so now the great special business interests too often control and corrupt the men and methods of government for their own profit. We must drive the special interests out of politics. That is one of our tasks to-day. Every special interest is entitled to justice—full, fair, and complete,—and, now, mind you, if there were any attempt by mob violence to plunder and work harm to the special interest, whatever it may be, that I most dislike, and the wealthy man, whomsoever he may be, for whom I have the greatest contempt, I would fight for him, and you would if you were worth your salt. He should have justice. For every special interest is entitled to justice, but not one is entitled to a vote in Congress, to a voice on the bench, or to representation in any public office. The Constitution guarantees protection to property, and we must make that promise good. But it does not give the right of suffrage to any corporation.

The true friend of property, the true conservative, is he who insists that property shall be the servant and not the master of the commonwealth; who insists that the creature of man's making shall be the servant and not the master of the man who made it. The citizens of the United States must effectively control the mighty commercial forces which they have themselves called into being.

There can be no effective control of corporations while their political activity remains. To put an end to it will be neither a short nor an easy task, but it can be done.

We must have complete and effective publicity of corporate affairs, so that the people may know beyond peradventure whether the corporations obey the law and whether their management entitles them to the confidence of the public. It is necessary that laws should be passed to prohibit the use of corporate funds directly or indirectly for political purposes; it is still more necessary that such laws should be thoroughly enforced. Corporate expenditures for political purposes, and especially such expenditures by public service corporations, have supplied one of the principal sources of corruption in our political affairs.

It has become entirely clear that we must have government supervision of the capitalization, not only of public service corporations, including, particularly, railways, but of all corporations doing an interstate business. I do not wish to see the nation forced into the ownership of the railways if it can possibly be avoided, and the only alternative is thoroughgoing and effective regulation, which shall be based on a full knowledge of all the facts, including a physical valuation of property. This physical valuation is not needed, or, at least, is very rarely needed, for fixing rates; but it is needed as the basis of honest capitalization.

We have come to recognize that franchises should never be granted except for a limited time, and never without proper provision for compensation to the public. It is my personal belief that the same kind and degree of control and supervision which should be exercised over public service corporations should be extended also to combinations which control necessaries of life, such as meat, oil, and coal, or which deal in them on an important scale. I have no doubt that the ordinary man who has control of them is much like ourselves. I have no doubt he would like to do well, but I want to have enough supervision to help him realize that desire to do well.

I believe that the officers, and, especially, the directors, of corporations should be held personally responsible when any corporation breaks the law.

Combinations in industry are the result of an imperative economic law which cannot be repealed by political legislation. The effort at prohibiting all combination has substantially failed. The way out lies, not in attempting to prevent such combinations, but in completely controlling them in the interest of the public welfare. For that purpose the Federal Bureau of Corporations is an agency of first importance. Its powers, and, therefore, its efficiency, as well as that of the Interstate Commerce Commission, should be largely increased. We have a right to expect from the Bureau of Corporations and from the Interstate Commerce Commission a very high grade of public conduct of the interstate railways and the

proper management of interstate business as
we are now sure of the conduct and management of the national banks, and we should have
as effective supervision in one case as in the
other. The Hepburn Act, and the amendment
to the Act in the shape in which it finally
passed Congress at the last session, represent a
long step in advance, and we must go yet
further.

There is a widespread belief among our
people that, under the methods of making
tariffs which have hitherto obtained, the special interests are too influential. Probably this is
true of both the big special interests and the
little special interests. These methods have put
a premium on selfishness, and, naturally, the
selfish big interests have gotten more than
their smaller, though equally selfish, brothers.
The duty of Congress is to provide a method
by which the interest of the whole people shall
be all that receives consideration. To this end
there must be an expert tariff commission,
wholly removed from the possibility of political
pressure or of improper business influence.
Such a commission can find the real difference
between cost of production, which is mainly
the difference of labor cost here and abroad. As
fast as its recommendations are made, I believe in revising one schedule at a time. A general revision of the tariff almost inevitably
leads to log-rolling and the subordination of
the general public interest to local and special
interests.

The absence of effective state, and, especially, national, restraint upon unfair money
getting has tended to create a small class of
enormously wealthy and economically powerful men, whose chief object is to hold and increase their power. The prime need is to
change the conditions which enable these men
to accumulate power which it is not for the
general welfare that they should hold or exercise. We grudge no man a fortune which represents his own power and sagacity, when exercised with entire regard to the welfare of his
fellows. Again, comrades over there, take the
lesson from your own experience. Not only did
you not grudge, but you gloried in the promotion of the great generals who gained their
promotion by leading the army to victory. So it
is with us. We grudge no man a fortune in
civil life if it is honorably obtained and well
used. It is not even enough that it should have
been gained without doing damage to the community. We should permit it to be gained only

so long as the gaining represents benefit to the
community. This, I know, implies a policy of a
far more active governmental interference with
social and economic conditions in this country
than we have yet had, but I think we have got
to face the fact that such an increase in governmental control is now necessary.

No man should receive a dollar unless that
dollar has been fairly earned. Every dollar received should represent a dollar's worth of
service rendered—not gambling in stocks, but
service rendered. The really big fortune, the
swollen fortune, by the mere fact of its size
acquires qualities which differentiate it in kind
as well as in degree from what is possessed by
men of relatively small means. Therefore, I believe in a graduated income tax on big fortunes,
and in another tax which is far more easily
collected and far more effective—a graduated
inheritance tax on big fortunes, properly safeguarded against evasion and increasing rapidly
in amount with the size of the estate.

The people of the United States suffer from
periodical financial panics to a degree substantially unknown among the other nations
which approach us in financial strength. There
is no reason why we should suffer what they
escape. It is of profound importance that our
financial system should be promptly investigated, and so thoroughly and effectively revised as to make it certain that hereafter our
currency will no longer fail at critical times to
meet our needs.

It is hardly necessary for me to repeat that I
believe in an efficient army and a navy large
enough to secure for us abroad that respect
which is the surest guarantee of peace. A word
of special warning to my fellow citizens who
are as progressive as I hope I am. I want them
to keep up their interest in our internal affairs;
and I want them also continually to remember
Uncle Sam's interests abroad. Justice and fair
dealing among nations rest upon principles
identical with those which control justice and
fair dealing among the individuals of which
nations are composed, with the vital exception
that each nation must do its own part in international police work. If you get into trouble
here, you can call for the police; but if Uncle
Sam gets into trouble, he has got to be his own
policeman, and I want to see him strong
enough to encourage the peaceful aspirations
of other peoples in connection with us. I believe in national friendships and heartiest good
will to all nations; but national friendships, like

those between men, must be founded on respect as well as on liking, on forbearance as well as upon trust. I should be heartily ashamed of any American who did not try to make the American government act as justly toward the other nations in international relations as he himself would act toward any individual in private relations. I should be heartily ashamed to see us wrong a weaker power, and I should hang my head forever if we tamely suffered wrong from a stronger power.

. . .

Moreover, I believe that the natural resources must be used for the benefit of all our people, and not monopolized for the benefit of the few, and here again is another case in which I am accused of taking a revolutionary attitude. People forget now that one hundred years ago there were public men of good character who advocated the nation selling its public lands in great quantities, so that the nation could get the most money out of it, and giving it to the men who could cultivate it for their own uses. We took the proper democratic ground that the land should be granted in small sections to the men who were actually to till it and live on it. Now, with the water power, with the forests, with the mines, we are brought face to face with the fact that there are many people who will go with us in conserving the resources only if they are to be allowed to exploit them for their benefit. That is one of the fundamental reasons why the special interests should be driven out of politics. Of all the questions which can come before this nation, short of the actual preservation of its existence in a great war, there is none which compares in importance with the great central task of leaving this land even a better land for our descendants than it is for us, and training them into a better race to inhabit the land and pass it on. Conservation is a great moral issue, for it involves the patriotic duty of insuring the safety and continuance of the nation. Let me add that the health and vitality of our people are at least as well worth conserving as their forests, waters, lands, and minerals, and in this great work the national government must bear a most important part.

. . .

But I think we may go still further. The right to regulate the use of wealth in the public interest is universally admitted. Let us admit also the right to regulate the terms and conditions of labor, which is the chief element of wealth, directly in the interest of the common good. The fundamental thing to do for every man is to give him a chance to reach a place in which he will make the greatest possible contribution to the public welfare. Understand what I say there. Give him a chance, not push him up if he will not be pushed. Help any man who stumbles; if he lies down, it is a poor job to try to carry him; but if he is a worthy man, try your best to see that he gets a chance to show the worth that is in him. No man can be a good citizen unless he has a wage more than sufficient to cover the bare cost of living, and hours of labor short enough so that after his day's work is done he will have time and energy to bear his share in the management of the community, to help in carrying the general load. We keep countless men from being good citizens by the conditions of life with which we surround them. We need comprehensive workmen's compensation acts, both state and national laws to regulate child labor and work for women, and, especially, we need in our common schools not merely education in book learning, but also practical training for daily life and work. We need to enforce better sanitary conditions for our workers and to extend the use of safety appliances for our workers in industry and commerce, both within and between the states. Also, friends, in the interest of the workingman himself we need to set our faces like flint against mob violence just as against corporate greed; against violence and injustice and lawlessness by wage workers just as much as against lawless cunning and greed and selfish arrogance of employers. If I could ask but one thing of my fellow countrymen, my request would be that, whenever they go in for reform, they remember the two sides, and that they always exact justice from one side as much as from the other. I have small use for the public servant who can always see and denounce the corruption of the capitalist, but who cannot persuade himself, especially before election, to say a word about lawless mob violence. And I have equally small use for the man, be he a judge on the bench, or editor of a great paper, or wealthy and influential private citizen, who can see clearly enough and denounce the lawlessness of mob violence, but whose eyes are closed so that he is blind when the question is one of corruption in business on a gigantic scale. Also remember what I said about excess in reformer and reactionary alike. If the reactionary man, who thinks of nothing but the rights of property, could have his way, he would bring about a revolution; and one of my chief fears in connection with progress comes because I do not want to see our people, for lack of proper leadership, compelled to follow men whose intentions are excellent, but whose eyes are a little too wild to make it really safe to trust them. Here in Kansas there is one paper which habitually denounces me as the tool of Wall Street, and at the same time frantically repudiates the statement that I am a Socialist on the ground that that is an unwarranted slander of the Socialists.

National efficiency has many factors. It is a necessary result of the principle of conservation widely applied. In the end it will determine our failure or success as a nation. National efficiency has to do, not only with natural resources and with men, but it is equally concerned with institutions. The state must be made efficient for the work which concerns only the people of the state; and the nation for that which concerns all the people. There must remain no neutral ground to serve as a refuge for lawbreakers, and especially for lawbreakers of great wealth, who can hire the vulpine legal cunning which will teach them how to avoid both jurisdictions. It is a misfortune when the national legislature fails to do its duty in providing a national remedy, so that the only national activity is the purely negative activity of the judiciary in forbidding the state to exercise power in the premises.

I do not ask for overcentralization; but I do ask that we work in a spirit of broad and far-reaching nationalism when we work for what concerns our people as a whole. We are all Americans. Our common interests are as broad as the continent. I speak to you here in Kansas exactly as I would speak in New York or Georgia, for the most vital problems are those which affect us all alike. The national government belongs to the whole American people, and where the whole American people are interested, that interest can be guarded effectively only by the national government. The betterment which we seek must be accomplished, I believe, mainly through the national government. 1910

WOODROW WILSON

1856–1924

AN ESSENTIALLY conservative social philosophy together with some ingredients of intellectual liberalism colored Wilson's career as a professor of political science at Bryn Mawr, Wesleyan, and Princeton. But his growing sympathy with political and economic "progressivism" was clear during his governorship of New Jersey (1910–1912). *The New Freedom* (1913), a book based on his speeches during his campaign for the Presidency in 1912, resembled in certain ways the program of Theodore Roosevelt and, in a larger measure, of Bryan. If democracy were to survive, Wilson maintained, the gigantic corporations must be compelled to permit "the little fellow" to carry on; the high protective tariff must be scaled down in the interest of the mass of the farming and laboring consumers; a federal income tax must be exacted in the interest of the distribution of the burden of expanding governmental services where the burden could best be borne; and economic imperialism, from which financial capitalism sucked unholy profits, must be checked. Wilson carried out this program to a considerable extent during his first administration.

In addition to *The New Freedom* Wilson's writings include *Congressional Government* (1885), *The State* (1889), and *A History of the American People* (1902) in five volumes.

H Clemons, G. D. Brown, H. S. Leach, *Essays towards a Bibliography of Woodrow Wilson*, Princeton, 1913–1922. *The Public Papers of Woodrow Wilson*, R. S. Baker and W. E. Dodd, eds., 6 vols., Garden City, 1925–1927. Arthur S. Link, *Wilson*, 2 vols., Princeton, 1947, 1956.

» » *From:* THE NEW FREEDOM « «

CHAPTER I

THE OLD ORDER CHANGETH

There is one great basic fact which underlies all the questions that are discussed on the political platform at the present moment. That singular fact is that nothing is done in this country as it was done twenty years ago.

We are in the presence of a new organization of society. Our life has broken away from the past. The life of America is not the life that it was twenty years ago. We have changed our economic conditions, absolutely, from top to bottom; and, with our economic society, the organization of our life. The old political formulas do not fit the present problems; they read now like documents taken out of a forgotten age. The older cries sound as if they belonged to a past age which men have almost forgotten. Things which used to be put into the party platforms of ten years ago would sound antiquated if put into a platform now. We are facing the necessity of fitting a new social organization, as we did once fit the old organization, to the happiness and prosperity of the great body of citizens; for we are conscious that the new order of society has not been made to fit and provide the convenience or prosperity of the average man. The life of the nation has grown infinitely varied. It does not centre now upon questions of governmental structure or of the distribution of governmental powers. It centres upon questions of the very structure and operation of society itself, of which government is only the instrument. Our development has run so fast and so far along the lines sketched in the earlier day of constitutional definition, has so crossed and interlaced those lines, has piled upon them such novel structures of trust and combination, has elaborated within them a life so manifold, so full of forces which transcend the boundaries of the country itself and fill the eyes of the world, that a new nation seems to have been created which the old formulas do not fit or afford a vital interpretation of.

We have come upon a very different age from any that preceded us. We have come upon an age when we do not do business in the way in which we used to do business,—

when we do not carry on any of the operations of manufacture, sale, transportation, or communication as men used to carry them on. There is a sense in which in our day the individual has been submerged. In most parts of our country men work, not for themselves, not as partners in the old way in which they used to work, but generally as employees,—in a higher or lower grade,—of great corporations. There was a time when corporations played a very minor part in our business affairs, but now they play the chief part, and most men are the servants of corporations.

You know what happens when you are the servant of a corporation. You have in no instance access to the men who are really determining the policy of the corporation. If the corporation is doing the things that it ought not to do, you really have no voice in the matter and must obey the orders, and you have oftentimes with deep mortification to co-operate in the doing of things which you know are against the public interest. Your individuality is swallowed up in the individuality and purpose of a great organization.

It is true that, while most men are thus submerged in the corporation, a few, a very few, are exalted to a power which as individuals they could never have wielded. Through the great organizations of which they are the heads, a few are enabled to play a part unprecedented by anything in history in the control of the business operations of the country and in the determination of the happiness of great numbers of people.

Yesterday, and ever since history began, men were related to one another as individuals. To be sure there were the family, the Church, and the State, institutions which associated men in certain wide circles of relationship. But in the ordinary concerns of life, in the ordinary work, in the daily round, men dealt freely and directly with one another. To-day, the everyday relationships of men are largely with great impersonal concerns, with organizations, not with other individual men.

Now this is nothing short of a new social age, a new era of human relationships, a new stage-setting for the drama of life.

In this new age we find, for instance, that our laws with regard to the relations of employer and employee are in many respects wholly antiquated and impossible. They were framed for another age, which nobody now living remembers, which is, indeed, so remote from our life that it would be difficult for many of us to understand it if it were described to us. The employer is now generally a corporation or a huge company of some kind; the employee is one of hundreds or of thousands brought together, not by individual masters whom they know and with whom they have personal relations, but by agents of one sort or another. Workingmen are marshaled in great numbers for the performance of a multitude of particular tasks under a common discipline. They generally use dangerous and powerful machinery, over whose repair and renewal they have no control. New rules must be devised with regard to their obligations and their rights, their obligations to their employers and their responsibilities to one another. Rules must be devised for their protection, for their compensation when injured, for their support when disabled.

There is something very new and very big and very complex about these new relations of capital and labor. A new economic society has sprung up, and we must effect a new set of adjustments. We must not pit power against weakness. The employer is generally, in our day, as I have said, not an individual, but a powerful group; and yet the workingman when dealing with his employer is still, under our existing law, an individual.

Why is it that we have a labor question at all? It is for the simple and very sufficient reason that the laboring man and the employer are not intimate associates now as they used to be in time past. Most of our laws were formed in the age when employer and employees knew each other, knew each other's characters, were associates with each other, dealt with each other as man with man. That is no longer the case. You not only do not come into personal contact with the men who have the supreme command in those corporations, but it would be out of the question for you to do it. Our modern corporations employ thousands, and in some instances hundreds of thousands, of men. The only persons whom you see or deal with are local superintendents or local representatives of a vast organization, which is not like anything that the workingmen of the time in which our laws were framed knew anything about. A little group of workingmen, seeing

their employer every day, dealing with him in a personal way, is one thing, and the modern body of labor engaged as employees of the huge enterprises that spread all over the country, dealing with men of whom they can form no personal conception, is another thing. A very different thing. You never saw a corporation, any more than you ever saw a government. Many a workingman to-day never saw the body of men who are conducting the industry in which he is employed. And they never saw him. What they know about him is written in ledgers and books and letters, in the correspondence of the office, in the reports of the superintendents. He is a long way off from them.

So what we have to discuss is, not wrongs which individuals intentionally do,—I do not believe there are a great many of those,—but the wrongs of a system. I want to record my protest against any discussion of this matter which would seem to indicate that there are bodies of our fellow-citizens who are trying to grind us down and do us injustice. There are some men of that sort. I don't know how they sleep o' nights, but there are men of that kind. Thank God, they are not numerous. The truth is, we are all caught in a great economic system which is heartless. The modern corporation is not engaged in business as an individual. When we deal with it, we deal with an impersonal element, an immaterial piece of society. A modern corporation is a means of co-operation in the conduct of an enterprise which is so big that no one man can conduct it, and which the resources of no one man are sufficient to finance. A company is formed; that company puts out a prospectus; the promoters expect to raise a certain fund as capital stock. Well, how are they going to raise it? They are going to raise it from the public in general, some of whom will buy their stock. The moment that begins, there is formed—what? A joint stock corporation. Men begin to pool their earnings, little piles, big piles. A certain number of men are elected by the stockholders to be directors, and these directors elect a president. This president is the head of the undertaking, and the directors are its managers.

Now, do the workingmen employed by that stock corporation deal with that president and those directors? Not at all. Does the public deal with that president and that board of directors? It does not. Can anybody bring them to account? It is next to impossible to do so. If you undertake it you will find it a game of hide and seek, with the objects of your search taking refuge now behind the tree of their individual personality, now behind that of their corporate irresponsibility.

And do our laws take note of this curious state of things? Do they even attempt to distinguish between a man's act as a corporation director and as an individual? They do not. Our laws still deal with us on the basis of the old system. The law is still living in the dead past which we have left behind. This is evident, for instance, with regard to the matter of employers' liability for workingmen's injuries. Suppose that a superintendent wants a workman to use a certain piece of machinery which it is not safe for him to use, and that the workman is injured by that piece of machinery. Some of our courts have held that the superintendent is a fellow-servant, or, as the law states it, a fellow-employee, and that, therefore, the man cannot recover damages for his injury. The superintendent who probably engaged the man is not his employer. Who is his employer? And whose negligence could conceivably come in there? The board of directors did not tell the employee to use that piece of machinery; and the president of the corporation did not tell him to use that piece of machinery. And so forth. Don't you see by that theory that a man never can get redress for negligence on the part of the employer? When I hear judges reason upon the analogy of the relationships that used to exist between workmen and their employers a generation ago, I wonder if they have not opened their eyes to the modern world. You know, we have a right to expect that judges will have their eyes open, even though the law which they administer hasn't awakened.

Yet that is but a single small detail illustrative of the difficulties we are in because we have not adjusted the law to the facts of the new order.

Since I entered politics, I have chiefly had men's views confided to me privately. Some of the biggest men in the United States, in the field of commerce and manufacture, are afraid of somebody, are afraid of something. They know that there is power somewhere so organized, so subtle, so watchful, so interlocked, so complete, so pervasive, that they had better not speak above their breath when they speak in condemnation of it.

They know that America is not a place of which it can be said, as it used to be, that a man may choose his own calling and pursue it just as far as his abilities enable him to pursue it; because to-day, if he enters certain fields, there are organizations which will use means against him that will prevent his building up a business which they do not want to have built up; organizations that will see to it that the ground is cut from under him and the markets shut against him; that will prevent his building up a business which they do not want to have built up; organizations that will see to it that the ground is cut from under him and the markets shut against him. For if he begins to sell to certain retail dealers, to any retail dealers, the monopoly will refuse to sell to those dealers, and those dealers, afraid, will not buy the new man's wares.

And this is the country which has lifted to the admiration of the world its ideals of absolutely free opportunity, where no man is supposed to be under any limitation except the limitations of his character and of his mind; where there is supposed to be no distinction of class, no distinction of blood, no distinction of social status, but where men win or lose on their merits.

I lay it very close to my own conscience as a public man whether we can any longer stand at our doors and welcome all newcomers upon those terms. American industry is not free, as once it was free; American enterprise is not free; the man with only a little capital is finding it harder to get into the field, more and more impossible to compete with the big fellow. Why? Because the laws of this country do not prevent the strong from crushing the weak. That is the reason, and because the strong have crushed the weak the strong dominate the industry and the economic life of this country. No man can deny that the lines of endeavor have more and more narrowed and stiffened; no man who knows anything about the development of industry in this country can have failed to observe that the larger kinds of credit are more and more difficult to obtain, unless you obtain them upon the terms of uniting your efforts with those who already control the industries of the country; and nobody can fail to observe that any man who tries to set himself up in competition with any process of manufacture which has been taken under the control of large combinations of capital will presently find himself either squeezed out or obliged to sell and allow himself to be absorbed.

There is a great deal that needs reconstruction in the United States. I should like to take a census of the business men,—I mean the rank and file of the business men,—as to whether they think that conditions in this country, or rather whether the organization of business in this country, is satisfactory or not. I know what they would say if they dared. If they could vote secretly they would vote overwhelmingly that the present organization of business was meant for the big fellows and was not meant for the little fellows; that it was meant for those who are at the top and was meant to exclude those who were at the bottom; that it was meant to shut out beginners, to prevent new entries in the race, to prevent the building up of competitive enterprises that would interfere with the monopolies which the great trusts have built up.

What this country needs above everything else is a body of laws which will look after the men who are on the make rather than the men who are already made. Because the men who are already made are not going to live indefinitely, and they are not always kind enough to leave sons as able and as honest as they are.

The originative part of America, the part of America that makes new enterprises, the part into which the ambitious and gifted workingman makes his way up, the class that saves, that plans, that organizes, that presently spreads its enterprises until they have a national scope and character,—that middle class is being more and more squeezed out by the processes which we have been taught to call processes of prosperity. Its members are sharing prosperity, no doubt; but what alarms me is that they are not *originating* prosperity. No country can afford to have its prosperity originated by a small controlling class. The treasury of America does not lie in the brains of the small body of men now in control of the great enterprises that have been concentrated under the direction of a very small number of persons. The treasury of America lies in those ambitions, those energies, that cannot be restricted to a special favored class. It depends upon the inventions of unknown men, upon the originations of unknown men, upon the ambitions of unknown men. Every country is renewed out of the ranks of the unknown, not out of the ranks of those already famous and powerful and in control.

There has come over the land that un-American set of conditions which enables a small number of men who control the government to get favors from the government; by

those favors to exclude their fellows from equal business opportunity; by those favors to extend a network of control that will presently dominate every industry in the country, and so make men forget the ancient time when America lay in every hamlet, when America was to be seen in every fair valley, when America displayed her great forces on the broad prairies, ran her fine fires of enterprise up over the mountainsides and down into the bowels of the earth, and eager men were everywhere captains of industry, not employees; not looking to a distant city to find out what they might do, but looking about among their neighbors, finding credit according to their character, not according to their connections, finding credit in proportion to what was known to be in them and behind them, not in proportion to the securities they held that were approved where they were not known. In order to start an enterprise now, you have to be authenticated, in a perfectly impersonal way, not according to yourself, but according to what you own that somebody else approves of your owning. You cannot begin such an enterprise as those that have made America until you are so authenticated, until you have succeeded in obtaining the good-will of large allied capitalists. Is that freedom? That is dependence, not freedom.

We used to think in the old-fashioned days when life was very simple that all government had to do was to put on a policeman's uniform, and say, "Now don't anybody hurt anybody else." We used to say that the ideal of government was for every man to be left alone and not interfered with, except when he interfered with somebody else; and that the best government was the government that did as little governing as possible. That was the idea that obtained in Jefferson's time. But we are coming now to realize that life is so complicated that we are not dealing with the old conditions, and that the law has to step in and create new conditions under which we may live, the conditions which will make it tolerable for us to live.

. . .

One of the most alarming phenomena of the time,—or rather it would be alarming if the nation had not awakened to it and shown its determination to control it,—one of the most significant signs of the new social era is the degree to which government has become associated with business. I speak, for the moment, of the control over the government exercised by

Big Business. Behind the whole subject, of course, is the truth that, in the new order, government and business must be associated closely. But that association is at present of a nature absolutely intolerable; the precedence is wrong, the association is upside down. Our government has been for the past few years under the control of heads of great allied corporations with special interests. It has not controlled these interests and assigned them a proper place in the whole system of business; it has submitted itself to their control. As a result, there have grown up vicious systems and schemes of governmental favoritism (the most obvious being the extravagant tariff), far-reaching in effect upon the whole fabric of life, touching to his injury every inhabitant of the land, laying unfair and impossible handicaps upon competitors, imposing taxes in every direction, stifling everywhere the free spirit of American enterprise.

Now this has come about naturally; as we go on we shall see how very naturally. It is no use denouncing anybody, or anything, except human nature. Nevertheless, it is an intolerable thing that the government of the republic should have got so far out of the hands of the people; should have been captured by interests which are special and not general. In the train of this capture follow the troops of scandals, wrongs, indecencies, with which our politics swarm.

There are cities in America of whose government we are ashamed. There are cities everywhere, in every part of the land, in which we feel that, not the interests of the public, but the interests of special privileges, of selfish men, are served; where contracts take precedence over public interest. Not only in big cities is this the case. Have you not noticed the growth of socialistic sentiment in the smaller towns? Not many months ago I stopped at a little town in Nebraska, and while my train lingered I met on the platform a very engaging young fellow dressed in overalls who introduced himself to me as the mayor of the town, and added that he was a Socialist. I said, "What does that mean? Does that mean that this town is socialistic?" "No, sir," he said; "I have not deceived myself; the vote by which I was elected was about 20 per cent. socialistic and 80 per cent. protest." It was protest against the treachery to the people of those who led both the other parties of that town.

All over the Union people are coming to feel that they have no control over the course of affairs. I live in one of the greatest States in the union, which was at one time in slavery. Until two years ago we had witnessed with increasing concern the growth in New Jersey of a spirit of almost cynical despair. Men said: "We vote; we are offered the platform we want; we elect the men who stand on that platform, and we get absolutely nothing." So they began to ask: "What is the use of voting? We know that the machines of both parties are subsidized by the same persons, and therefore it is useless to turn in either direction."

This is not confined to some of the state governments and those of some of the towns and cities. We know that something intervenes between the people of the United States and the control of their own affairs at Washington. It is not the people who have been ruling there of late.

Why are we in the presence, why are we at the threshold, of a revolution? Because we are profoundly disturbed by the influences which we see reigning in the determination of our public life and our public policy. There was a time when America was blithe with self-confidence. She boasted that she, and she alone, knew the processes of popular government; but now she sees her sky overcast; she sees that there are at work forces which she did not dream of in her hopeful youth.

Don't you know that some man with eloquent tongue, without conscience, who did not care for the nation, could put this whole country into a flame? Don't you know that this country from one end to the other believes that something is wrong? What an opportunity it would be for some man without conscience to spring up and say: "This is the way. Follow me!"—and lead in paths of destruction!

The old order changeth—changeth under our very eyes, not quietly and equably, but swiftly and with the noise and heat and tumult of reconstruction.

I suppose that all struggle for law has been conscious, that very little of it has been blind or merely instinctive. It is the fashion to say, as if with superior knowledge of affairs and of human weakness, that every age has been an age of transition, and that no age is more full of change than another; yet in very few ages of the world can the struggle for change have been so widespread, so deliberate, or upon so great a scale as in this in which we are taking part.

The transition we are witnessing is no equable transition of growth and normal alteration; no silent, unconscious unfolding of one age into another, its natural heir and successor. Society is looking itself over, in our day, from top to bottom; is making fresh and critical analysis of its very elements; is questioning its oldest practices as freely as its newest, scrutinizing every arrangement and motive of its life; and it stands ready to attempt nothing less than a radical reconstruction, which only frank and honest counsels and the forces of generous cooperation can hold back from becoming a revolution. We are in a temper to reconstruct economic society, as we were once in a temper to reconstruct political society, and political society may itself undergo a radical modification in the process. I doubt if any age was ever more conscious of its task or more unanimously desirous of radical and extended changes in its economic and political practice.

We stand in the presence of a revolution,—not a bloody revolution; America is not given to the spilling of blood,—but a silent revolution, whereby America will insist upon recovering in practice those ideals which she has always professed, upon securing a government devoted to the general interest and not to special interests.

We are upon the eve of a great reconstruction. It calls for creative statesmanship as no age has done since that great age in which we set up the government under which we live, that government which was the admiration of the world until it suffered wrongs to grow up under it which have made many of our own compatriots question the freedom of our institutions and preach revolution against them. I do not fear revolution. I have unshaken faith in the power of America to keep its self-possession. Revolution will come in peaceful guise, as it came when we put aside the crude government of the Confederation and created the great Federal Union which governs individuals, not States, and which has been these hundred and thirty years our vehicle of progress. Some radical changes we must make in our law and practice. Some reconstructions we must push forward, which a new age and new circumstances impose upon us. But we can do it all in calm and sober fashion, like statesmen and patriots.

I do not speak of these things in apprehension, because all is open and above-board. This is not a day in which great forces rally in secret. The whole stupendous program must be publicly planned and canvassed. Good temper, the wisdom that comes of sober counsel, the energy of thoughtful and unselfish men, the habit of co-operation and of compromise which has been bred in us by long years of free government, in which reason rather than passion has been made to prevail by the sheer virtue of candid and universal debate, will enable us to win through to still another great age without violence.   1913

ELBERT HUBBARD

1856–1915

ELBERT HUBBARD, of Bloomington, Illinois, began his public career on a Chicago newspaper; subsequently he promoted new advertising and sales techniques for a manufacturing concern in Buffalo. During a visit to England he became a disciple of William Morris and on his return to his native land undertook publishing enterprises and the writing of novels and essays. In 1895 Hubbard established at East Aurora, New York, the Roycroft Shop, where he published *The Philistine* and *The Fra*, "arty" periodicals which became the vehicles of his aesthetic and social creed. The Roycroft Shops were presently a celebrated center for a paternalistic enterprise in craftsmanship and bohemianism.

Hubbard's *Message to Garcia* (1899) expresses many of the values that characterize his conservative philosophy. This tract was circulated widely by various industrialists—according to tradition, 40,000,000 copies were struck off altogether. Hubbard's *Loyalty in Business* was also widely used as propaganda by the employing class in its drive for "morale" among workers.

Albert Lane, *Elbert Hubbard and His Work*, Worcester, Mass., 1901.
Felix Shay, *Elbert Hubbard of East Aurora*, New York, 1927.
M. H. Heath, *The Elbert Hubbard I Knew; An Intimate Biography from the Heart and Pen of His Sister*, East Aurora, New York, 1929.
D. A. Balch, *Elbert Hubbard, Genius of Roycroft*, New York, 1940.

» » *From:* A MESSAGE TO GARCIA « «

In all this Cuban business there is one man stands out on the horizon of my memory like Mars at perihelion. When war broke out between Spain and the United States, it was very necessary to communicate quickly with the leader of the insurgents. Garcia was somewhere in the mountain fastnesses of Cuba—no one knew where. No mail or telegraph message could reach him. The President must secure his co-operation, and quickly.

What to do!

Someone said to the President, "There's a fellow by the name of Rowan will find Garcia for you, if anybody can."

Rowan was sent for and given a letter to be delivered to Garcia. How "the fellow by the name of Rowan" took the letter, sealed it up in an oil-skin pouch, strapped it over his heart, in four days landed by night off the coast of Cuba from an open boat, disappeared into the jungle, and in three weeks came out on the other side of the island, having traversed a hostile country on foot, and delivered his letter to Garcia, are things I have no special desire now to tell in detail.

The point I wish to make is this: McKinley gave Rowan a letter to be delivered to Garcia; Rowan took the letter and did not ask, "Where is he at?" By the Eternal! there is a man whose form should be cast in deathless bronze and the statue placed in every college of the land. It is not booklearning young men need, nor instruction about this and that, but a stiffening of the vertebrae which will cause them to be loyal to a trust, to act promptly, concentrate their energies; do the thing—"carry a message to Garcia!"

General Garcia is dead now, but there are other Garcias.

No man, who has endeavored to carry out an enterprise where many hands were needed, but has been well-nigh appalled at times by the imbecility of the average man—the inability or unwillingness to concentrate on a thing and do it. Slip-shod assistance, foolish inattention, dowdy indifference, and half-hearted work seem the rule, and no man succeeds, unless by hook or crook, or threat, he forces or bribes other men to assist him; or mayhap, God in His goodness performs a miracle, and sends him an Angel of Light for an assistant. You, reader, put this matter to a test: You are sitting now in your office—six clerks are within call. Summon any one and make this request: "Please look in the encyclopedia and make a brief memorandum for me concerning the life of Correggio."

Will the clerk say, "Yes, sir," and go to the task?

On your life, he will not. He will look at you out of a fishy eye, and ask one or more of the following questions:

Who was he?

Which encyclopedia?

Where is the encyclopedia?

Was I hired for that?

Don't you mean Bismarck?

What's the matter with Charlie doing it?

Is he dead?

Is there any hurry?

Shan't I bring you the book and let you look it up yourself?

What do you want to know for?

And I will lay you ten to one that after you have answered the questions, and explained how to find the information, and why you want it, the clerk will go off and get one of the other clerks to help him try to find Garcia—and then come back and tell you there is no such man. Of course I may lose my bet, but according to the Law of Average, I will not.

Now if you are wise you will not bother to explain to your "assistant" that Correggio is indexed under the C's, not the K's, but you will smile sweetly and say, "Never mind," and go look it up yourself.

And this incapacity for independent action, this moral stupidity, this infirmity of the will, this unwillingness to cheerfully catch hold and lift, are the things that put pure socialism so far into the future. If men will not act for themselves, what will they do when the benefit of their effort is for all? A first mate with knotted club seems necessary; and the dread of getting "the bounce" Saturday night holds many a worker to his place.

Advertise for a stenographer, and nine out of ten who apply can neither spell nor punctuate —and do not think it necessary to.

Can such a one write a letter to Garcia?

"You see that bookkeeper," said the foreman to me in a large factory.

"Yes, what about him?"

"Well, he's a fine accountant, but if I'd send him up town on an errand, he might accomplish the errand all right, and, on the other hand, might stop at four saloons on the way, and when he got to Main Street, would forget what he had been sent for."

Can such a man be entrusted to carry a message to Garcia?

We have recently been hearing much maudlin sympathy expressed for the "down-trodden denizen of the sweat-shop" and the "homeless wanderer searching for honest employment," and with it all often go many hard words for the men in power.

Nothing is said about the employer who grows old before his time in a vain attempt to get frowsy ne'er-do-wells to do intelligent work; and his long, patient striving with "help" that does nothing but loaf when his back is turned. In every store and factory there is a constant weeding-out process going on. The employer is constantly sending away "help" that have shown their incapacity to further the interests of the business, and others are being taken on. No matter how good times are, this sorting continues, only if times are hard and work is scarce, the sorting is done finer—but out and forever out, the incompetent and unworthy go. It is the survival of the fittest. Self-interest prompts every employer to keep the best— those who can carry a message to Garcia.

I know one man of really brilliant parts who has not the ability to manage a business of his own, and yet who is absolutely worthless to anyone else, because he carries with him constantly the insane suspicion that his employer is oppressing, or intending to oppress, him. He cannot give orders, and he will not receive them. Should a message be given him to take to Garcia, his answer would probably be, "Take it yourself."

Tonight this man walks the streets looking for work, the wind whistling through his threadbare coat. No one who knows him dare employ him, for he is a regular firebrand of discontent. He is impervious to reason, and the only thing that can impress him is the toe of a thick-soled No. 9 boot.

Of course I know that one so morally deformed is no less to be pitied than a physical cripple; but in our pitying, let us drop a tear, too, for the men who are striving to carry on a great enterprise whose working hours are not limited by the whistle, and whose hair is fast turning white through the struggle to hold in line dowdy indifference, slip-shod imbecility, and the heartless ingratitude which, but for their enterprise, would be both hungry and homeless.

Have I put the matter too strongly? Possibly I have; but when all the world has gone a-slumming I wish to speak a word of sympathy for the man who succeeds—the man who, against great odds, has directed the efforts of others, and, having succeeded, finds there's nothing in it: nothing but bare board and clothes.

I have carried a dinner-pail and worked for day's wages, and I have also been an employer of labor, and I know there is something to be said on both sides. There is no excellence, per se, in poverty; rags are no recommendation; and all employers are not rapacious and high-handed, any more than all poor men are virtuous.

My heart goes out to the man who does his work when the "boss" is away, as well as when he is at home. And the man who, when given a letter for Garcia, quietly takes the missive, without asking any idiotic questions, and with no lurking intention of chucking it into the nearest sewer, or of doing aught else but deliver it, never gets "laid off," nor has to go on a strike for higher wages. Civilization is one long anxious search for just such individuals. Anything such a man asks shall be granted; his kind is so rare that no employer can afford to let him go. He is wanted in every city, town, and village—in every office, shop, store, and factory. The world cries out for such; he is needed, and needed badly—the man who can carry a message to Garcia.   1899

WILLIAM GRAHAM SUMNER

1840–1910

FEW COLLEGE PROFESSORS have exerted so wide an influence in many fields as William Graham Sumner. The son of an English artisan immigrant, Sumner entered the Episcopalian ministry after graduation from Yale and study abroad. But his interest in economic and social problems led to his acceptance, in 1872, of a professorship of political and social science at Yale. His scholarly equipment in the languages and sciences, and particularly in economics, sociology, and social philosophy, was unexcelled; and his popularity as a lecturer and writer gave him a solid if not a unique place in American academic life.

Among Sumner's most notable writings were *A History of American Currency* (1874), which displayed sympathy for "sound finance"; *Folkways* (1907), full of illustrations of the role of custom in the origin and life of institutions and thought; and *The Science of Society* (1927), a systematic treatment of society which was completed by his successor at Yale, Albert G. Keller.

Although Sumner took issue with conservatives and entrepreneurs in championing academic freedom and in opposing protective tariffs and imperialism, his social philosophy in general was marked by its Spencerian allegiance to economic individualism and laissez faire. The great growth of corporations seemed to him as natural and desirable a phenomenon as the efforts of radicals to curb them appeared unnatural and pernicious; and Sumner's logical criticisms of social legislation and of socialism won the approval of conservatives.

A. G. Keller, *Reminiscenses (Mainly Personal) of William Graham Sumner*, New Haven, 1933.
H. E. Starr, *William Graham Sumner*, New York, 1925.
Maurice R. Davie, ed., *Sumner Today; Selected Essays of William Graham Sumner*, New Haven, 1940.
Robert Green McCloskey, *American Conservatism in the Age of Enterprise*, Cambridge, 1951.

» » REPLY TO A SOCIALIST « «

"Always dig out the major premise!" said an experienced teacher of logic and rhetoric. The major premise of Mr. Sinclair [1] is that everybody ought to be happy, and that, if anybody is not so, those who stand near him are under obligations to make him so. He nowhere expresses this. The major premise is always most fallacious when it is suppressed. The statement of the woes of the garment workers is made on the assumption that it carries upon its face some significance. He deduces from the facts two inferences for which he appeals to common consent: (1) that such a state of things ought not to be allowed to continue forever, and (2) that somehow, somewhere, another

[1] Upton Sinclair had written "The Socialist Party: Its Aims in the Present Campaign" for *Collier's*, vol. XXXIV (October 29, 1904), to which Sumner's essay is a reply.

"system" must be found. The latter inference is one which the socialists always affirm, and they seem to be satisfied that it has some value, both in philosophy and in practical effort. They criticize the "system," by which they mean the social world as it is. They do not perceive that the world of human society is what has resulted from thousands of years of life. It is not a system any more than a man sixty years old is a system. It is a product. To talk of making another system is like talking of making a man of sixty into something else than what his life has made him. As for the inference that some other industrial system must be found, it is as idle as anything which words can express. It leads to nothing and has no significance. The industrial system has changed often and it will change again. Nobody invented former forms. No one can invent others. It will change according to conditions and interests, just as the gilds and manors changed into modern phases. It is frightful to know of the poverty which some people endure. It is also frightful to know of disease, of physical defects, of accidents which cripple the body and wreck life, and of other ills by which human life is encompassed. Such facts appeal to human sympathy, and call for such help and amelioration as human effort can give. It is senseless to enumerate such facts, simply in order to create a state of mind in the hearer, and then to try to make him assent that "the system ought to be changed." All the hospitals, asylums, almshouses, and other eleemosynary institutions prove that the world is not made right. They prove the existence of people who have not "equal chances" with others. The inmates can not be happy. Generally the institutions also prove the very limited extent to which, with the best intentions and greatest efforts, the more fortunate can do anything to help the matter—that is, to "change the system."

The notion that everybody ought to be happy, and equally happy with all the rest, is the fine flower of the philosophy which has been winning popularity for two hundred years. All the petty demands of natural rights, liberty, equality, etc., are only stepping-stones toward this philosophy, which is really what is wanted. All through human history some have had good fortune and some ill fortune. For some the ills of life have taken all the joy and strength out of existence, while the fortunate have always been there to show how glorious life might be and to furnish dreams of bliss to tantalize those who have failed and suffered. So men have constructed in philosophy theories of universal felicity. They tell us that every one has a natural right to be happy, to be comfortable, to have health, to succeed, to have knowledge, family, political power, and all the rest of the things which anybody can have. They put it all into the major premise. Then they say that we all ought to be equal. That proposition abolishes luck. In making propositions we can imply that all ought to have equally good luck, but, inasmuch as there is no way in which we can turn bad luck into good, or misfortune into good fortune, what the proposition means is that if we can not all have good luck no one shall have it. The unlucky will pull down the lucky. That is all that equality ever can mean.

The worst becomes the standard. When we talk of "changing the system," we ought to understand that that means abolishing luck and all the ills of life. We might as well talk of abolishing storms, excessive heat and cold, tornadoes, pestilences, diseases, and other ills. Poverty belongs to the struggle for existence, and we are all born into that struggle. The human race began in utter destitution. It had no physical or metaphysical endowment whatever. The existing "system" is the outcome of the efforts of men for thousands of years to work together, so as to win in the struggle for existence. Probably socialists do not perceive what it means for any man now to turn about and pass his high judgment on the achievements of the human race in the way of civilization, and to propose to change it, by resolution, in about "six years." The result of the long effort has been that we all, in a measure, live above the grade of savages, and that some reach comfort and luxury and mental and moral welfare. Efforts to change the system have not been wanting. They have all led back to savagery. Mr. Sinclair thinks that the French Revolution issued out in liberty. The French Revolution is open to very many different interpretations and constructions; but, on the whole, it left essential interests just about where it found them. A million men lost their lives to get Louis de Bourbon off the throne and Napoleon Bonaparte on it, and by the spoils of Europe to make rich nobles of his generals. That is the most definite and indisputable result of the Revolution. Mr. Sinclair also repeats the familiar warning or threat that those who are not competent to win adequate success in the struggle for existence will "rise." They are going to "shoot," unless we let him and his associates redistribute property. It seems that it would be worth while for them to consider that, by their own hypothesis, those-who-have will possess advantages in "shooting": (1) they will have the guns; (2) they will have the talent on their side because they can pay for it; (3) they can hire an army out of the ranks of their adversaries.

In all this declamation we hear a great deal about votes and political power, "ballots or bullets." Of course this is another outcome of the political and social philosophy of the last two centuries. Mr. Sinclair says that "Democracy is an attitude of soul. It has its basis in the spiritual nature of man, from which it follows that all men are equal, or that, if they are not, they must become so." Then Democracy is a metaphysical religion or mythology. The age is not friendly to metaphysics or mythology, but it falls under the dominion of these old tyrants in its political philosophy. If anybody wants to put his soul in an attitude, he ought to do it. The "system" allows that liberty, and it is far safer than shooting. It is also permitted to believe that, if men are not equal, they will become so. If we wait a while they will all die, and then they will all be equal, although they certainly will not be so before that.

There are plenty of customs and institutions among us which produce evil results. They need reform; and propositions to that end are reasonable and useful. A few years ago we heard of persons who wanted to abolish poverty. They had no plan or scheme by which to do it; in the meantime, however, people were working day by day to overcome poverty as well as they could, each for himself. The talk about abolishing poverty by some resolution or construction has died out. The "industrial system" is just the organized effort which we are all making to overcome poverty. We do not want to change the system unless we can be convinced that we can make a shift which will accomplish that purpose better. Then, be it observed, the system will be changed without waiting for any philosophers to propose it. It is being changed every day, just as quickly as any detail in it can be altered so as to defeat poverty better. This is a world in which the rule is, "Root, hog, or die," and it is also a world in which "the longest pole knocks down the most persimmons." It is the popular experience which has formulated these sayings. How can we make them untrue? They contain immense tragedies. Those who believe that the problems of human pain and ill are waiting for a speculative solution in philosophy or ethics can dream of changing the system; but to everybody else it must seem worse than a waste of time to wrangle about such a thing. It is not a proposition; it does not furnish either a thesis to be tested or a project to be considered.

I am by no means arguing that "everything is for the best in the best of worlds," even in that part of it where the Stars and Stripes still float. I am, on the contrary, one of those who think that there is a great deal to be dissatisfied about. I may be asked what I think would be a remedy for the distress of the garment workers. I answer candidly that I do not know—that is why I have come forward with no proposition.

My business now is to show how empty and false Mr. Sinclair's proposition is, and how harmful it would be to heed it. He only adds to our trouble and burden by putting forward erroneous ideas and helping to encourage bad thinking. The plan to rise and shoot has no promise or welfare in it for anybody.

Neither is there any practical sense or tangible project behind the suggestion to redistribute property. Some years ago I heard a socialist orator say [2] that he could get along with any audience except "these measly, mean-spirited workingmen, who have saved a few hundred dollars and built a cottage, with a savings bank mortgage, of which they rent the second story and live in the first. They," said he, "will get up and go out, a benchful at a time, when I begin to talk about rent." If he had been open to instruction from facts, he might have learned much from the conduct of those measly workingmen. They will fight far more ferociously for their cottages than the millionaires for their palaces. A redistribution of property means universal war. The final collapse of the French Revolution was due to the proposition to redistribute property. Property is the opposite of poverty; it is our bulwark against want and distress, but also against disease and all other ills, which, if it can not prevent them, it still holds at a distance. If we weaken the security of property or deprive people of it, we plunge into distress those who now are above it.

Property is the condition of civilization. It is just as essential to the state, to religion, and to education as it is to food and clothing. In the form of capital it is essential to industry, but if capital were not property it would not do its work in industry. If we negative or destroy property we arrest the whole life of civilized society and put men back on the level of beasts. The family depends on property; the two institutions have been correlative throughout the history of civilization. Property is the first interest of man in time and in importance. We can conceive of no time when property was not, and we can conceive of no social growth in which property was not the prime condition. The property interests is also the one which moves all men, including the socialists, more quickly and deeply than any other. Property is that feature of the existing "industrial system" which would most stubbornly resist change if it was threatened in its essential character and

[2] This was one of Professor Sumner's pet anecdotes, and I risk its repetition here and elsewhere in the volume.—THE EDITOR [Albert G. Keller].

meaning. There is a disposition now to apologize for property, even while resisting attack upon it. This is wrong. Property ought to be defended on account of its reality and importance, and on account of its rank among the interests of men.

What the socialists complain of is that we have not yet got the work of civilization all done and that what has been done does not produce ideal results. The task is a big one—it may even be believed that it is infinite, because what we accomplish often only opens new vistas of trouble. At present we are work-

ing on with all the wisdom we have been able to win, and we hope to gain more. If the socialists could help by reasonable and practical suggestions, their aid would be welcome. When they propose to redistribute property, or to change the industrial system, they only disturb the work and introduce confusion and destruction. When they talk about rising and shooting, as if such acts would not be unreasonable or beyond possibility, they put themselves at the limit of the law, and may, before they know it, become favorers of crime.

1904

PAUL ELMER MORE

1864–1937

PAUL ELMER MORE, whose father was an army general, first followed the academic path, teaching Sanskrit and the classics at Harvard and Bryn Mawr. In 1901, however, he quit the halls of learning, carrying his conception of high standards in scholarship into his work as literary editor of the *Independent*, the *New York Evening Post*, and the *Nation*. Sufficiently well-off to free himself from remunerative labor, he settled down in Princeton in 1914.

With Professor Irving Babbitt of Harvard, More developed "the new humanism," which Charles Eliot Norton in a general way had anticipated. Both a canon of literary criticism and a social philosophy, the "new humanism" postulated, in the manner of Platonic dualism, the doctrine that man possesses both a higher or spiritual and a lower nature. All values were judged, absolutistically, from this dualistic angle of vision; thus the new humanism was the antithesis of the pragmatism and the instrumentalism for which William James and John Dewey stood. To the new humanist, equalitarianism, humanitarianism, and materialism merely pampered the "lower nature" of man. Reason and order, especially as exemplified in Anglo-Catholicism, in the classics and "humanities," bore witness to man's "higher nature," and formed the proper core of education. In accord with this scheme of values More emphasized respect for property rights and subordinated the individual to society. Man's natural instincts, according to the new humanists, must be kept in bounds by the "inner check." The social implications of this ethical restraint were respect for authority, institutions, the past, and the elite. More's social teachings were expressed in a distinguished literary style, the aesthetic appeal of which attracted a certain number of disciples. But the social conservatism of the new humanism largely accounted for the vitality it enjoyed. More's writings included, in addition to eleven volumes of the *Shelburne Essays* (1904–21), *Nietzsche* (1912), *Christ, the Word* (1927), and *The Catholic Faith* (1931).

Malcolm Young, *Paul Elmer More, A Bibliography*, Princeton, 1941.
Robert M. Davies, *The Humanism of Paul Elmer More*, New York, 1958.
Robert Shafer, *Paul Elmer More and American Criticism*, New Haven and London, 1935.
Louis Mercier, *The Challenge of Humanism. An Essay in Comparative Criticism*, New York, 1933.

THE RELIGIOUS GROUND OF HUMANITARIANISM

. . . The brotherhood of man is the real religious dogma of the times. We wish to consider briefly the force of this religious ground of socialism,—we should rather say humanitarianism, for our concern is not with the specific political programme of the socialists, properly so-called, but with that ever-growing belief in the equality and brotherhood of man which is equally responsible for the nihilism of Tolstoy and the collectivism of Karl Marx. If these claims are found to be empty, it should seem that there remains for us only to put away our dream of a regenerated society and of universal happiness, and to make the best of the old order of things where justice seems to our blinded vision to walk hand in hand with the unequal fates.

And first of all it is necessary to examine more carefully what is meant by the religious instinct and to separate it from misleading overgrowths; for evidently Christianity—to confine ourselves for the moment to that form of belief—as taught and practised to-day is a mingling of the religious instinct with worldly policy. We mean nothing invidious by worldly policy; but simply that the religion of Christ, as it spread and became a factor of civilisation, necessarily assumed a formal policy and government—that it became a Church. Neither in its Catholic nor in its Protestant form has the Church lent itself to any promulgation or protection of socialistic ideas of equality; and for this reason the organised Church has been bitterly attacked by Socialists and social reformers generally—most bitterly of all perhaps by Tolstoy, who finds in it the ultimate cause of the wide-spread misery which the new acceptance of human brotherhood is to annul. Indeed many Christians—and among them Tolstoy—assert that the organised Church stands in direct opposition to the plain teaching of Jesus, and that the chief need of the world to-day is to throw off these outer trappings of worldliness and to approach once more the original message of the Gospel. We are compelled, then, to disregard the policy of the Church, whether Catholic or Protestant, and to turn back to the pure voice of religion, which

in the words of the great prophets appeals more or less authoritatively to the hearts of all men; for here, if anywhere, lies the only valid basis of that much-vaunted regenerating belief in the brotherhood and equality of men. There can certainly be no surer and clearer way of discovering the oracles of this pure religion than by going to the words and example of Christ himself. For the Christian this will be sufficient; for those of more questioning mind it may be proper to reinforce the teaching of Christ with the doctrine of Buddha. He would be a rash man who should seek the mandates of religion outside of the realm in which these two greatest apostles of the West and of the East stand in concord.

At the outset of any attempt to discover the actual doctrine of Christ we are, however, met by a difficulty which must be frankly confessed and set down for whatever weight it may have. Only those who have gone to the Gospels without any preconvictions of what they were to find know how hard it is to discover the real position of Christ. Single texts may be quoted, and indeed have been quoted, to justify every variety of creed; and I can see no way through the difficulties except to form an opinion from the general consensus of Christ's acts and words.

It will help us if we discriminate among the various elements of religion that enter into Christianity. Thus there is one phase of Christianity which may be called the purely spiritual and which it possesses with all higher cults. This phase cannot better be expressed than in the three words of St. Paul, *Faith, Hope,* and *Love.* We are not here dealing with faith in a peculiar dogma or person which may vary with varying creeds, but with that faculty of the mind or soul which turns instinctively to the things of the spirit. And so in regard to hope, we mean simply a state of joyous trust that somehow to the faithful all things in the end shall be good. And in love we refer to no specific commands, but to that sympathetic attitude of the observing soul which is ready to accept and make a portion of its own life the joys and sorrows of the world. It is at bottom the desire of the soul to become one with all it perceives akin to itself. These three form the spiritual basis of all religion; and it is not necessary to say how abundantly they are held forth in the Gospels. But faith, hope, and love, in this spiritual sense, have no direct bearing on the social question we are here considering. They are the fountainhead of Christianity, as of every religion, and flow down through all its manifestations; but they are of the spirit and not of this world. Even love, which at first might seem corroborative of humanitarian equality and is no doubt so interpreted, is in this spiritual sense a state of mind, not a rule of action. To do what is best for our neighbour, we must first be told what is best for him. And besides it applies as much to our feeling toward the dumb beasts as to our fellow-men.

And so at the other end of Christianity there lies a law which is common practically to humanity and which has no bearing on the question at issue. This is that universal code of prohibitive morality found in the Decalogue and in large part repeated and reinforced by Christ: Thou shalt not kill, Thou shalt not steal, etc.

But between these two extremes of spiritual outreaching and negative morality lies a common ground where the two orders meet together and produce a body of positive or spiritual morality which bears directly on constructive sociology. It is this ground that we are to investigate more narrowly in the doctrine of Christ. If we turn to the Sermon on the Mount, which surely represents the teaching of Christ in its purest form, we are met in the beginning by the promulgation of a virtue distinctly medial in character between the aspirations of the spirit and the prohibitions of the flesh. This is that virtue of humility so often enounced by Christ and so strikingly exhibited in his own life. . . . Closely related to humility and following it as an immediate corollary is that other virtue of non-resistance. . . . This virtue of non-resistance is no more than the essential and inevitable flower of that humility which so distinguishes Christianity. . . . Not far removed in character from non-resistance, and like it consequent on the doctrine of humility, stands the ideal of perfect poverty. . . . The name of St. Francis brings us to the last and in some respects most important of those virtues which lie between the aspirations of pure spirituality and the commands of prohibitive morality,—I mean the much disputed virtue of chastity.

. . . In these four virtues (or three, if we

choose to omit chastity) is contained the strictly religious or spiritual teaching of Christ as it bears on the social aspect of life. The law of love, which might at first seem to demand inclusion, is in reality something much deeper and wider than these social virtues. It is akin to the power of faith and hope which seizes upon spiritual things; it is a state of the soul and only by extension is concerned with our individual life among men. To reach the source and home of this pure virtue of love we must, as Emerson wrote, mount above the bonds of earthly life

Into vision where all form
In one only form dissolves;
In a region where the wheel
On which all beings ride
Visibly revolves;
Where the starred, eternal worm
Girds the world with bound and term;
Where unlike things are like;
Where good and ill,
And joy and moan,
Melt into one.

It is, to be sure, this high charity, to use its older name, that pervades the four religious virtues, giving them their tone and beauty, and binding them to the spiritual life; it is the essence even of the prohibitive law; but it is not specific in any such sense as humility, poverty, non-resistance, and chastity are specific.

We may be confirmed in accepting these virtues as the cardinal doctrine of Christ who to the Western world stands as the inspired exemplar of the religious instinct, by turning for a moment to the great prophet of the Orient. I have not the desire to examine here in much detail the Buddhistic doctrine. Nor is such an examination necessary; for, whether we regard Buddhism as the equal or the inferior of Christianity, it at least has the good fortune of presenting to us in the Pali books a more consistent and more amply logical body of dogma than the Gospels. This is chiefly due to the fact that Buddhism appeals more to the reason and less to the emotions than Christianity.

. . . The religious ground of humanitarianism is a like failure to observe distinctions, —a failure here to discriminate between the ideals of religion and the ideals of the world. To apply the laws of the spirit to the activities of this earth is at once a desecration and denial of religion and a bewildering and unsettling of the social order. To intrude the aspirations of faith and hope and the ethics of the golden rule of love into regions where prudence and courage and the dictates of honour are supreme, is a mischievous folly. Failure to discriminate between the virtues that spring from these ideals, or any attempt to amalgamate the religious virtues and the secular virtues, to confuse humility with justice, non-resistance with mercy, poverty with liberality, chastity with temperance,—such blindness is equally absurd and vastly more dangerous. Humanitarianism is just this vague sentimentality of a mind that refuses to distinguish between the golden rule and the precept of Apollo. There are gross and manifest evils in the actual working of the law of competition, no one denies that. But they are to be set right, if right is possible in this world, by a clearer understanding and a more faithful observance of the worldly virtues, and not by the sickly yearnings of sentimentalists. It is still well that we render to Caesar the things that are Caesar's and to God the things that are God's.

For society at large the problem is an easy one; society as a whole has nothing to do with God and everything to do with Caesar. Indeed, as the economic fallacy of socialism springs from applying the laws of humanity as a whole to any particular aggregate of men; so the religious fallacy is an application of the problem of the individual to such an aggregate of men. But for the individual, in whose heart the religious instinct murmurs and to whom at the same time the voice of the world may speak with equal weight, the question is not always so simple. When faith was strong among men, as it was for example in the days of St. Francis, he found it not difficult perhaps to walk bravely in his chosen path. Society was divided pretty sharply into those who followed the law of renunciation and those who followed the law

of ambition, and any attempt to confuse these two laws would have awakened disquiet and condemnation. So it was that for St. Francis himself, when the vision of peace came, it was not so hard, we may suppose, to see his way perfectly clear before him. But in other days when faith grows a little dull and the all-levelling power of democracy has brought things spiritual and things worldly to the same plane,—or so at least it looks to the eyes of men,—in such days the path of the individual is beset with difficulties. The man of the world is troubled at times by a voice that calls upon him to renounce: and on the other side it is still harder, if not impossible, to follow the religious life in its simplicity and purity. What shall be said to the troubled soul in whose confused hearing the voices of the world and the spirit are mingled, dragging him now this way and now that? I know not unless it be in the quaint metaphor of Emerson, which I have already quoted in an earlier essay:

One key, one solution to the mysteries of human condition, one solution to the old knots of fate, freedom and foreknowledge, exists, the propounding, namely, of the double consciousness. A man must ride alternately on the horses of his private and his public nature, as the equestrians in the circus throw themselves nimbly from horse to horse, or plant one foot on the back of one and the other foot on the back of the other.

Such a double life he must lead, balancing between the two laws, but above all things taking care not to confuse the regions in which these laws are valid or to lose the distinction between his public and his private duty. To lose such a distinction is to fall forthwith into the shadows of hypocrisy and charlatanry; to maintain it ever before the inner eye and to judge honestly between the conflict of claims is the great problem which is left to the conscience of each man and to him alone.   1907

» » *Imperialism, War, and Pacifism* « «

1880-1920

» »   « «

DAMN THE FILIPINOS

In that land of dopy dreams, happy peaceful Philippines,
    Where the bolo-man is hiking night and day;
Where Tagalos steal and lie, where Americanos die,
    There you hear the soldiers sing this evening lay;
Damn, damn, damn the Filipinos, cross-eyed kakiack ladrones.
Underneath our starry flag, civilize 'em with a Krag,
And return us to our own beloved homes.

Underneath the nipa thatch, where the skinny chickens scratch,
    Only refuge after hiking all day long,
When I lay me down to sleep, shiny lizards o'er me creep,
    Then you hear the soldiers sing this evening song:
Damn, damn, damn the Filipinos.

Social customs there are few, all the ladies smoke and chew,
    And the men do things the padres say are wrong,
But the padres cut no ice—for they live on fish and rice—
    When you hear the soldiers sing this evening song:
Damn, damn, damn the Filipinos.

The American soldiers who were sent out to subdue the Filipinos
had no illusions about their venture in "civilizing" their Little Brown
Brothers. This particular song, sung to the tune of "Tramp, tramp,
tramp, the boys are marching," offended the "friendly natives" so
deeply that the commanding officer forbade it to be sung publicly.
The soldiers' songs which resulted from our excursion into imperialism
in the East were discussed by Albert Shelby in *Harper's Weekly*
for March 5, 1910.

» »　　« «

MADEMOISELLE FROM ARMENTIERES

"Oh farmer, have you a daughter fair, parlee-voo,
Oh farmer, have you a daughter fair, parlee-voo,
Oh farmer, have you a daughter fair
Who can wash a soldier's underwear, hinky dinky, parlee-voo."

"Oh, yes, I have a daughter fair,
With lily-white hands and golden hair."

Mademoiselle from Armentieres
She ain't even heard of underwear.

If you never wash your underwear
You'll never get the Croix de Guerre.

Mademoiselle from Armentieres,
She hasn't been kissed in forty years.

She may have been young for all we knew,
When Napoleon flopped at Waterloo.

The French, they are a funny race,
They fight with their feet and save their face.

The cootie is the national bug of France,
The cootie's found all over France,
No matter where you hang your pants.

The officers get all the steak,
And all we get is the belly-ache.

The general got a Croix de Guerre,
The son-of-a-gun was never there.

My Froggie girl was true to me,
She was true to me, she was true to you,
She was true to the whole damn army, too.

You might forget the gas and shell,
But you'll never forget the mademoiselle.

There's many and many a married man,
Wants to go back to France again.

'Twas a hell of a war as we recall,
But still 'twas better than none at all.

This most famous of the songs of the American Expeditionary Force
was popular in the British army when the First World War began but
was adopted by the Americans as their favorite. (An earlier version
was known, actually, in both countries in the last century.) The doings
of Mademoiselle are recorded in hundreds of verses, many of them
unprintable. No two singers would agree on a version, so the present
one is made up from some of the verses most frequently sung.

»   »   «   «

OVER THERE

Johnnie get your gun, get your gun, get your gun,
Take it on the run, on the run, on the run;
Hear them calling you and me,
Ev'ry son of liberty,

Hurry right away, no delay, go today;
Make your daddy glad to have had such a lad,
Tell your sweet-heart not to pine
To be proud her boy's in line.

Refrain
    Over there—over there—
    Send the word, send the word over there—
    That the Yanks are coming, the Yanks are coming,
    The drums rumtumming ev'ry where—
    So prepare—say a pray'r—
    Send the word, send the word to beware—
    We'll be over, we're coming over,
    And we won't come back till it's over over there.

. . . . .

While the soldiers in France were singing "Mademoiselle from Armentieres," people on the home front were swung into enthusiasm for the war to the strains of "Over There," written by the popular singing comedian George M. Cohan.

» »   « «

Imperialism, War, and Pacifism

IMPERIALISM EMERGED on the American scene in a new form when, at the end of the Spanish war in 1899, the first noncontiguous territories, if Alaska be excepted, were acquired. The forces responsible for overseas expansion were complex. In part the example of the quest for colonies by such relatively new world-powers as Germany stimulated American nationalists to embark on the same pursuit. In part professional navalists were responsible for the decision, since they had long contended that naval bases throughout the world were imperative if trade routes were to be protected. Religious missionaries in the Far East often used their influence at home to persuade opinion that their cause could be furthered if the American government took more active responsibility in protecting the lives and property of its citizens abroad. And although it seems clear that a majority of articulate American businessmen did not seek the war with Spain, they quickly approved the decision to retain Spain's colonies. In so approving they were motivated at least in part by the expectancy that such colonies would provide markets for industrial surpluses, check the recurrence of periodical depressions, and supply enterprise with needed raw materials.

But the new imperialistic venture was vigorously opposed by old-fashioned Americans who took seriously the Declaration of Independence. The right of self-determination of peoples seemed, in their eyes, an irrevocable and sacred American axiom. Moreover, the anti-imperialists feared that imperialism would augment navalism and militarism and plunge the country into power politics and world wars. In addition, they denied that colonialism would benefit the great masses of American people; and some even contended that it would be of slight advantage to business itself. The election of 1900, however, was a decision for imperialism. Nevertheless, the Democratic party, which on the whole had long questioned the wisdom of overseas expansion, committed itself to a policy of so extending self-government of the Filipinos as to prepare them for complete freedom. On the other hand, the same party, during Wilson's administration, actually extended American imperialism in the Caribbean area.

The war with Spain and the enlarged navy which followed it greatly stimulated the organized opposition to war. The peace movement, which had made relatively slight headway in the 80's and 90's, won, in the years between the Spanish-American and the First World wars, support such as it had never before enjoyed. It advocated the international limitation of armaments; it supported the Hague Conferences; it argued for American leadership in establishing a league of nations, or at least a world court and thoroughgoing arbitration treaties. The peace movement, however, failed to attack many of the basic causes of war. Although it opposed, for a time, the entrance of the United States into the First World War, the majority group threw its support to the government once the decision was made. Nevertheless some remained, in spite of pressure and qualms, consistent pacifists. Once the war was over, old cleavages reappeared, and the movement was unable to take a common stand on the issue of American participation in the League of Nations. Yet a new and more realistic and vigorous peace movement emerged to enjoy for a time, in the 1920's and early 1930's, a genuine if precarious influence.

» » « «

JOSIAH STRONG

1847–1916

THE BOOK *Our Country* was prepared for the American Home Missionary Society by its Ohio representative, the Reverend Josiah Strong. Its author, who wrote it in 1885, tried to show the crying need in the country for evangelization. Convinced that as America went, so the whole world would go, Strong, who was a pioneer in the social gospel movement, was eager to call attention to what he regarded as the danger spots in American civilization, particularly the slums, Romanism, intemperance, immigration, the exhaustion of free lands, the excessive power of wealth, and the socialist challenge. The following chapter is of particular interest because of its doctrine of Manifest Destiny, and the glorious "mission" of the United States to extend its unique values to the whole world.

The Dictionary of American Biography, XVIII.
Dorothea R. Muller, "The Social Philosophy of Josiah Strong," *Church History*, vol. XXVIII, June, 1959.

» » *From:* OUR COUNTRY « «

CHAPTER XIV

THE ANGLO-SAXON AND THE WORLD'S FUTURE [1]

Every race which has deeply impressed itself on the human family has been the representative of some great idea—one or more—which has given direction to the nation's life and form to its civilization. Among the Egyptians this seminal idea was life, among the Persians it was light, among the Hebrews it was purity, among the Greeks it was beauty, among the Romans it was law. The Anglo-Saxon is the representative of two great ideas, which are closely related. One of them is that of civil liberty. Nearly all of the civil liberty in the world is enjoyed by Anglo-Saxons: the English, the British colonists, and the people of the United States. To some, like the Swiss, it is permitted by the sufferance of their neighbors; others, like the French, have experimented with it; but, in modern times, the peoples whose love of liberty has won it, and whose genius for self-government has preserved it,

have been Anglo-Saxons. The noblest races have always been lovers of liberty. That love ran strong in early German blood, and has profoundly influenced the institutions of all the branches of the great German family; but it was left for the Anglo-Saxon branch fully to recognize the right of the individual to himself, and formally to declare it the foundation stone of government.

The other great idea of which the Anglo-Saxon is the exponent is that of a pure *spiritual* Christianity. It was no accident that the great reformation of the sixteenth century originated among a Teutonic, rather than a Latin people. It was the fire of liberty burning in the Saxon heart that flamed up against the absolutism of the Pope. Speaking roughly, the peoples of Europe which are Celtic are Catholic, and those which are Teutonic are Protestant; and where the Teutonic race was purest, there Protestantism spread with the greatest rapidity. But, with rare and beautiful exceptions, Protestantism on the continent has degenerated into mere formalism. By confirmation at a certain age, the state churches are filled with members who generally know nothing of a personal spiritual experience. In obedience to a military order, a regiment of German soldiers files into

[1] It is only just to say that the substance of this chapter was given to the public as a lecture some three years before the appearance of Prof. Fisk's "Manifest Destiny," in *Harper's Magazine*, for March, 1885, which contains some of the same ideas. (This and the following footnotes for this selection are Strong's own.)

church and partakes of the sacrament, just as it would shoulder arms or obey any other word of command. It is said that, in Berlin and Leipsic, only a little over one per cent. of the Protestant population are found in church. Protestantism on the continent seems to be about as poor in spiritual life and power as Catholicism. That means that most of the spiritual Christianity in the world is found among Anglo-Saxons and their converts; for this is the great missionary race. If we take all of the German missionary societies together, we find that, in the number of workers and amount of contributions, they do not equal the smallest of the three great English missionary societies. The year that Congregationalists in the United States gave one dollar and thirty-seven cents per caput to foreign missions, the members of the great German State Church gave only three-quarters of a cent per caput to the same cause.[2] Evidently it is chiefly to the English and the American peoples that we must look for the evangelization of the world.

It is not necessary to argue to those for whom I write that the two great needs of mankind, that all men may be lifted into the light of the highest Christian civilization, are, first, a pure, spiritual Christianity, and, second, civil liberty. Without controversy, these are the forces, which in the past, have contributed most to the elevation of the human race, and they must continue to be, in the future, the most efficient ministers to its progress. It follows, then, that the Anglo-Saxon, as the great representative of these two ideas, the depositary of these two greatest blessings, sustains peculiar relations to the world's future, is divinely commissioned to be, in a peculiar sense, his brother's keeper. Add to this the fact of his rapidly increasing strength in modern times, and we have well nigh a demonstration of his destiny. In 1700 this race numbered less than 6,000,000 souls. In 1800, Anglo-Saxons (I use the term somewhat broadly to include all English-speaking peoples) had increased to about 20,500,000, and in 1880 they numbered nearly 100,000,000, having multiplied almost five-fold in eighty years. At the end of the reign of Charles II. the English colonists in America numbered 200,000. During these two hundred years, our population has increased two hundred and fifty-fold. And the expansion of this race has been no less remarkable than its multiplication. In one century the United

[2] Christlieb's "Protestant Foreign Missions," pp. 34 and 37.

States has increased its territory ten-fold, while the enormous acquisition of foreign territory by Great Britain—and chiefly within the last hundred years—is wholly unparalleled in history. This mighty Anglo-Saxon race, though comprising one one-fifteenth part of mankind, now rules more than one-third of the earth's surface, and more than one-fourth of its people. And if this race, while growing from 6,000,000 to 100,000,000, thus gained possession of a third portion of the earth, is it to be supposed that when it numbers 1,000,000,000, it will lose the disposition, or lack the power to extend its sway?

This race is multiplying not only more rapidly than any other European race, but far more rapidly than *all* the races of continental Europe. There is no exact knowledge of the population of Europe early in the century; we know, however, that the increase on the continent during the ten years from 1870 to 1880, was 6.89 per cent. If this rate of increase is sustained for a century (and it is more likely to fall, as Europe becomes more crowded), the population on the continent in 1980 will be 534,000,000; while the one Anglo-Saxon race, if it should multiply for a hundred years as it increased from 1870 to 1880, would, in 1980, number 1,343,000,000 souls; but we cannot reasonably expect this ratio of increase to be sustained so long. What, then, will be the probable numbers of this race a hundred years hence? In attempting to answer this question, several things must be borne in mind. Heretofore, the great causes which have operated to check the growth of population in the world have been war, famine, and pestilence; but, among civilized peoples, these causes are becoming constantly less operative. Paradoxical as it seems, the invention of more destructive weapons of war renders war less destructive; commerce and wealth have removed the fear of famine, the pestilence is being brought more and more under control by medical skill and sanitary science. Moreover, Anglo-Saxons, with the exception of the people of Great Britain, who now compose only a little more than one-third of this race, are much less exposed to these checks upon growth than the races of Europe. Again, Europe is crowded, and is constantly becoming more so, which will tend to reduce continually the ratio of increase; while nearly two-thirds of the Anglo-Saxons occupy lands which invite almost unlimited expansion—the United States, Canada, Australia, and South Africa. Again, emigration from Europe, which is certain to increase, is chiefly into Anglo-Saxon countries; while these foreign elements exert a modifying influence on the Anglo-Saxon stock, their descendants are certain to be Anglo-Saxonized. From 1870 to 1880, Germany lost 987,000 inhabitants by emigration; in one generation, their children will be counted Anglo-Saxons. This race has been undergoing an unparalleled expansion during the eighteenth and nineteenth centuries, and the conditions for its continued growth are singularly favorable.

We are now prepared to ask what light statistics cast on the future. In Great Britain, from 1840 to 1850, the ratio of increase of the population was 2.49 per cent.; during the next ten years it was 5.44 per cent.; the next ten years, it was 8.60; and from 1870 to 1880, it was 10.57 per cent. That is, for forty years the ratio of increase has been rapidly rising. It is not unlikely to continue rising for some time to come; but, remembering that the population is dense, in making our estimate for the next hundred years, we will suppose the ratio of increase to be only one-half as large as that from 1870 to 1880, which would make the population in 1980, 57,000,000. All the colonies of Britain, except Canada, which has a great future, show a very high ratio of increase in population; that of Australia, from 1870 to 1880, was 56.50 per cent.; that of South Africa was 73.28. It is quite reasonable to suppose that the colonies, taken together, will double their population once in twenty-five years for the next century. In the United States, population has, on the average, doubled once in twenty-five years since 1685. Adopting this ratio, then, for the English colonies, their 11,-000,000 in 1880 will be 176,000,000 in 1980. Turning now to our own country, we find in the following table the ratio of increase of population for each decade of years since 1800:

From 1800 to 1810......36.38 per cent.
" 1810 " 1820......34.80 " "
" 1820 " 1830......33.11 " "
" 1830 " 1840......32.66 " "
" 1840 " 1850......35.87 " "
" 1850 " 1860......35.58 " "
" 1860 " 1870......22.59 " "
" 1870 " 1880......30.06 " "

Here we see a falling ratio of increase of about one per cent. Every ten years from 1800 to 1840—a period when immigration was inconsiderable. During the next twenty years the ratio was decidedly higher, because of a large immigration. It fell off during the war, and again arose from 1870 to 1880. Increased immigration is likely to sustain this high ratio of increase for some time to come. If it should continue for a hundred years, our population in 1980 would be 697,000,000. But suppose we take no account of immigration, leaving it to offset any unforeseen check upon growth, we may infer from the first forty years of the century that the ratio of increase would not fall more than about one per cent. every ten years. Beginning, then, with an increase of thirty per cent. from 1880 to 1890, and adopting this falling ratio of increase, our population in 1980 would be 480,000,000, making the total Anglo-Saxon population of the world, at that time, 713,000,000, as compared with 534,-000,000 inhabitants of continental Europe. And it should be remembered that these figures represent the largest probable population of Europe, and the smallest probable numbers of the Anglo-Saxon race. It is not unlikely that, before the close of the next century, this race will outnumber all the other civilized races of the world. Does it not look as if God were not only preparing in our Anglo-Saxon civilization the die with which to stamp the peoples of the earth, but as if he were also massing behind that die the mighty power with which to press it? My confidence that this race is eventually to give its civilization to mankind is not based on mere numbers—China forbid! I look forward to what the world has never yet seen united in the same race; viz., the greatest numbers, *and* the highest civilization.

There can be no reasonable doubt that North America is to be the great home of the Anglo-Saxon, the principal seat of his power, the center of his life and influence. Not only does it constitute seven-elevenths of his possessions, but his empire is unsevered, while the remaining four-elevenths are fragmentary and scattered over the earth. Australia will have a great population; but its disadvantages, as compared with North America, are too manifest to need mention. Our continent has room and resources and climate, it lies in the pathway of the nations, it belongs to the zone of power, and already, among Anglo-Saxons, do we lead in population and wealth. Of England, Franklin once wrote: "That pretty island which, compared to America, is but a stepping-stone in a brook, scarce enough of it above water to keep one's shoes dry." England can hardly hope to maintain her relative importance among Anglo-Saxon peoples when her "pretty island" is the home of only one-twentieth part of that race. With the wider distribution of wealth, and increasing facilities of intercourse, intelligence and influence are less centralized, and peoples become more homogeneous; and the more nearly homogeneous peoples are, the more do *numbers tell.* America is to have the great preponderance of numbers and of wealth, and by the logic of events will follow the scepter of controlling influence. This will be but the consummation of a movement as old as civilization—a result to which men have looked forward for centuries. John Adams records that nothing was "more ancient in his memory than the observation that arts, sciences and empire had traveled westward; and in conversation it was always added that their next leap would be over the Atlantic into America." He recalled a couplet that had been "inscribed, or rather drilled, into a rock on the shore of Monument Bay in our old colony of Plymouth:

'The Eastern Nations sink, their glory ends,
And empire rises where the sun descends.' " [3]

The brilliant Galiani, who foresaw a future in which Europe should be ruled by America, wrote, during the Revolutionary War, "I will wager in favor of America, for the reason merely physical, that for 5,000 years genius has turned opposite to the diurnal motion, and traveled from the East to the West." [4] Count d'Aranda, after signing the Treaty of Paris of 1773, as the representative of Spain, wrote his king: "This Federal Republic is born a pigmy. . . . a day will come when it will be a giant, even a colossus formidable in these countries."

Adam Smith, in his "Wealth of Nations," predicts the transfer of empire from Europe to America. The traveler, Burnaby, found, in the middle of the last century, that an idea had "entered into the minds of the generality of mankind, that empire is traveling westward; and every one is looking forward with eager and impatient expectation to that destined moment when America is to give the law to the rest of the world." Charles Sumner wrote of the "coming time when the whole continent, with all its various states, shall be a Plural Unit, with one Constitution, one Liberty and one Destiny," and when "the national example

will be more puissant than army or navy for the conquest of the world." [5] It surely needs no prophet's eye to see that the civilization of the *United States* is to be the civilization of America, and that the future of the continent is ours. In 1880, the United States was the home of more than one-half of the Anglo-Saxon race; and, if the computations already given, are correct, a much larger proportion will be here a hundred years hence. It has been shown that we have room for at least a thousand millions. According to recent figures, there is in France a population of 180.88 to the square mile; in Germany, 216.62; in England and Wales, 428.67; in Belgium, 481.71; in the United States—not including Alaska—16.88. If our population were as dense as that of France, we should have, this side of Alaska, 537,000,000; if as dense as that of Germany, 643,000,000; if as dense as that of England and Wales, 1,173,000,000; if as dense as that of Belgium, 1,430,000,000.

But we are to have not only the larger portion of the Anglo-Saxon race for generations to come, we may reasonably expect to develop the highest type of Anglo-Saxon civilization. If human progress follows a law of development, if

"Time's noblest offspring is the last,"

our civilization should be the noblest; for we are

"The heirs of all the ages in the foremost files of time,"

and not only do we occupy the latitude of power, but *our land is the last to be occupied in that latitude.* There is no other virgin soil in the North Temperate Zone. If the consummation of human progress is not to be looked for here, if there is yet to flower a higher civilization, where is the soil that is to produce it? Whipple says: [6] "There has never been a great migration that did not result in a new form of national genius." Our national genius is Anglo-Saxon, but not English, its distinctive type is the result of a finer nervous organization, which is certainly being developed in this country. "The history of the world's progress from savagery to barbarism, from barbarism to civilization, and, in civilization, from the lower degrees toward the higher, is the history

---

[3] John Adams' Works, Vol. IX, pp. 597–599.
[4] Galiani, Tome II, p. 275.

[5] See *The Atlantic*, Vol. 20, pp. 275–306.
[6] *Atlantic* for Oct., 1858.

of increase in average longevity,[7] corresponding to, and accompanied by, increase of nervousness. Mankind has grown to be at once more delicate and more enduring, more sensitive to weariness and yet more patient of toil, impressible, but capable of bearing powerful irritation; we are woven of finer fiber, which, though apparently frail, yet outlasts the coarser, as rich and costly garments oftentimes wear better than those of rougher workmanship." [8] The roots of civilization are the nerves; and other things being equal, the finest nervous organization will produce the highest civilization. Heretofore, war has been almost the chief occupation of strong races. England, during the past sixty-eight years, has waged some seventy-seven wars. John Bright said recently that, during Queen Victoria's reign, $750,000,000 had been spent in war and 68,000 lives lost. The mission of the Anglo-Saxon has been largely that of the soldier; but the world is making progress, we are leaving behind the barbarism of war; as civilization advances, it will learn less of war, and concern itself more with the arts of peace, and for these the massive battle-ax must be wrought into tools of finer temper. The physical changes accompanied by mental, which are taking place in the people of the United States are apparently to adapt men to the demands of a higher civilization. But the objection is here interposed that the "physical degeneracy of Americans" is inconsistent with the supposition of our advancing to a higher civilization. Professor Huxley, when at Buffalo he addressed the American Association for the Advancement of Science, said he had heard of the degeneration of the original American stock, but during his visit to the states he had failed to perceive it. We are not, however, in this matter, dependent on the opinion of even the best observers. During the War of the Confederacy, the Medical Department of the Provost Marshal General's Bureau gathered statistics from the examination of over half a million of men, native and foreign, young and old, sick and sound, drawn from every rank and condition of life, and hence, fairly representing the whole people. Dr. Baxter's Official Report shows that our native whites were over an inch taller than the English, and nearly two-thirds of an inch taller than

the Scotch, who, in height, were superior to all other foreigners. At the age of completed growth, the Irish, who were the stoutest of the foreigners, surpassed the native whites, in girth of chest, less than a quarter of an inch. Statistics as to weight are meager, but Dr. Baxter remarks that it is perhaps not too much to say that the war statistics show "that the mean weight of the white native of the United States is not disproportionate to his stature." Americans were found to be superior to Englishmen not only in height, but also in chest-measurement and weight. Such facts afford more than a hint that the higher civilization of the future will not lack an adequate physical basis in the people of the United States.

Mr. Darwin is not only disposed to see, in the superior vigor of our people, an illustration of his favorite theory of natural selection, but even intimates that the world's history thus far has been simply preparatory for our future, and tributary to it. He says: [9] "There is apparently much truth in the belief that the wonderful progress of the United States, as well as the character of the people, are the results of natural selection; for the more energetic, restless, and courageous men from all parts of Europe have emigrated during the last ten or twelve generations to that great country, and have there succeeded best. Looking at the distant future, I do not think that the Rev. Mr. Zincke takes an exaggerated view when he says: 'All other series of events—as that which resulted in the culture of mind in Greece, and that which resulted in the Empire of Rome—only appear to have purpose and value when viewed in connection with, or rather as subsidiary to, the great stream of Anglo-Saxon emigration to the West.'"

There is abundant reason to believe that the Anglo-Saxon race is to be, is, indeed, already becoming, more effective here than in the mother country. The marked superiority of this race is due, in large measure, to its highly mixed origin. Says Rawlinson: [10] "It is a general rule, now almost universally admitted by ethnologists, that the mixed races of mankind are superior to the pure ones"; and adds: "Even the Jews, who are so often cited as an example of a race at once pure and strong, may, with more reason, be adduced on the opposite side of the argument." The ancient Egyptians, the Greeks, and the Romans, were all mixed races.

---

[7] "It is ascertained that the average measure of human life, in this country, has been steadily increasing during this century, and is now *considerably longer than in any other country*." Dorchester's "Problem of Religious Progress," p. 288.

[8] [George Miller] Beard's "American Nervousness," p. 287.

[9] "Descent of Man," Part I, p. 142.

[10] *Princeton Review*, for Nov., 1878.

Among modern races, the most conspicuous example is afforded by the Anglo-Saxons. Mr. Green's studies show that Mr. Tennyson's

"Saxon and Norman and Dane are we,"

must be supplemented with Celt and Gaul, Welshman and Irishman, Frisian and Flamand, French Huguenot and German Palatine. What took place a thousand years ago and more in England again transpires today in the United States. "History repeats itself"; but, as the wheels of history are the chariot wheels of the Almighty, there is, with every revolution, an onward movement toward the goal of his eternal purposes. There is here a new commingling of races; and, while the largest injections of foreign blood are substantially the same elements that constituted the original Anglo-Saxon admixture, so that we may infer the general type will be preserved, there are strains of other bloods being added, which, if Mr. Emerson's remark is true, that "the best nations are those most widely related," may be expected to improve the stock, and aid it to a higher destiny. If the dangers of immigration, which have been pointed out, can be successfully met for the next few years, until it has passed its climax, it may be expected to add value to the amalgam which will constitute the new Anglo-Saxon race of the New World. Concerning our future, Herbert Spencer says: "One great result is, I think, tolerably clear. From biological truths it is to be inferred that the eventual mixture of the allied varieties of the Aryan race, forming the population, will produce a more powerful type of man than has hitherto existed, and a type of man more plastic, more adaptable, more capable of undergoing the modifications needful for complete social life. I think, whatever difficulties they may have to surmount, and whatever tribulations they may have to pass through, the Americans may reasonably look forward to a time when they will have produced a civilization grander than any the world has known."

It may be easily shown, and is of no small significance, that the two great ideas of which the Anglo-Saxon is the exponent are having a fuller development in the United States than in Great Britain. There the union of Church and State tends strongly to paralyze some of the members of the body of Christ. Here there is no such influence to destroy spiritual life and power. Here, also, has been evolved the

form of government consistent with the largest possible civil liberty. Furthermore, it is significant that the marked characteristics of this race are being here emphasized most. Among the most striking features of the Anglo-Saxon is his money-making power—a power of increasing importance in the widening commerce of the world's future. We have seen, in a preceding chapter, that, although England is by far the richest nation of Europe, we have already outstripped her in the race after wealth, and we have only begun the development of our vast resources.

Again, another marked characteristic of the Anglo-Saxon is what may be called an instinct or genius for colonizing. His unequaled energy, his indomitable perseverance, and his personal independence, made him a pioneer. He excels all others in pushing his way into new countries. It was those in whom this tendency was strongest that came to America, and this inherited tendency has been further developed by the westward sweep of successive generations across the continent. So noticeable has this characteristic become that English visitors remark it. Charles Dickens once said that the typical American would hesitate to enter heaven unless assured that he could go further west.

Again, nothing more manifestly distinguishes the Anglo-Saxon than his intense and persistent energy; and he is developing in the United States an energy which, in eager activity and effectiveness, is peculiarly American. This is due partly to the fact that Americans are much better fed than Europeans, and partly to the undeveloped resources of a new country, but more largely to our climate, which acts as a constant stimulus. Ten years after the landing of the Pilgrims, the Rev. Francis Higginson, a good observer, wrote: "A sup of New England air is better than a whole flagon of English ale." Thus early had the stimulating effect of our climate been noted. Moreover, our social institutions are stimulating. In Europe the various ranks of society are, like the strata of the earth, fixed and fossilized. There can be no great change without a terrible upheaval, a social earthquake. Here society is like the waters of the sea, mobile; as General Garfield said, and so signally illustrated in his own experience, that which is at the bottom to-day may one day flash on the crest of the highest wave. Every one is free to become whatever he can make of himself; free to transform himself from a rail-splitter or a tanner or a canal-boy, into the nation's President. Our aristocracy, unlike that of Europe, is open to all comers. Wealth, position, influence, are prizes offered for energy; and every farmer's boy, every apprentice and clerk, every friendless and penniless immigrant, is free to enter the lists. Thus many causes cooperate to produce here the most forceful and tremendous energy in the world.

What is the significance of such facts? These tendencies infold the future; they are the mighty alphabet with which God writes his prophecies. May we not, by a careful laying together of the letters, spell out something of his meaning? It seems to me that God, with infinite wisdom and skill, is training the Anglo-Saxon race for an hour sure to come in the world's future. Heretofore there has always been in the history of the world a comparatively unoccupied land westward, into which the crowded countries of the East have poured their surplus populations. But the widening waves of migration, which millenniums ago rolled east and west from the valley of the Euphrates meet to-day on our Pacific coast. There are no more new worlds. The unoccupied arable lands of the earth are limited, and will soon be taken. The time is coming when the pressure of population on the means of subsistence will be felt here as it is now felt in Europe and Asia. Then will the world enter upon a new stage of its history—*the final competition of races, for which the Anglo-Saxon is being schooled.* Long before the thousand millions are here, the mighty *centrifugal* tendency, inherent in this stock and strengthened in the United States, will assert itself. Then this race of unequaled energy, with all the majesty of numbers and the might of wealth behind it—the representative, let us hope, of the largest liberty, the purest Christianity, the highest civilization—having developed peculiarly aggressive traits calculated to impress its institutions upon mankind, will spread itself over the earth. If I read not amiss, this powerful race will move down upon Mexico, down upon Central and South America, out upon the islands of the sea, over upon Africa and beyond. And can any one doubt that the result of this competition of races will be the "survival of the fittest"? "Any people," says Dr. Bushnell, "that is physiologically advanced in culture, though it be only in a degree beyond another which is mingled with it on strictly equal terms,

is sure to live down and finally live out its inferior. Nothing can save the inferior race but a ready and pliant assimilation. Whether the feebler and more abject races are going to be regenerated and raised up, is already very much of a question. What if it should be God's plan to people the world with better and finer material? Certain it is, whatever expectations we may indulge, that there is a tremendous overbearing surge of power in the Christian nations, which, if the others are not speedily raised to some vastly higher capacity, will inevitably submerge and bury them forever. These great populations of Christendom—what are they doing, but throwing out their colonies on every side, and populating themselves, if I may so speak, into the possession of all countries and climes?" [11] To this result no war of extermination is needful; the contest is not one of arms but of vitality and of civilization. "At the present day," says Mr. Darwin, "civilized nations are everywhere supplanting barbarous nations, excepting where the climate opposes a deadly barrier; and they succeed mainly, though not exclusively, through their arts, which are the products of the intellect." [12] Thus the Finns were supplanted by the Aryan races in Europe and Asia, the Tartars by the Russians, and thus the aborigines of North America, Australia and New Zealand are now disappearing before the all-conquering Anglo-Saxons. It would seem as if these inferior tribes were only precursors of a superior race, voices in the wilderness crying: "Prepare ye the way of the Lord!" The savage is a hunter; by the incoming of civilization the game is driven away and disappears before the hunter becomes a herder or an agriculturist. The savage is ignorant of many diseases of civilization which, when he is exposed to them, attack him before he learns how to treat them. Civilization also has its vices, of which the uninitiated savage is innocent. He proves an apt learner of vice, but dull enough in the school of morals. Every civilization has its destructive and preservative elements. The Anglo-Saxon race would speedily decay but for the salt of Christianity. Bring savages into contact with our civilization, and its destructive forces become operative at once, while years are necessary to render effective the saving influence of Christian instruction. Moreover, the pioneer wave of our civilization carries with it more

[11] "Christian Nurture," pp. 207, 213.
[12] "Descent of Man," Vol. I, p. 154.

scum than salt. Where there is one missionary, there are hundreds of miners or traders or adventurers ready to debauch the native. Whether the extinction of inferior races before the advancing Anglo-Saxon seems to the reader sad or otherwise, it certainly appears probable. I know of nothing except climatic conditions to prevent this race from populating Africa as it has peopled North America. And those portions of Africa which are unfavorable to Anglo-Saxon life are less extensive than was once supposed. The Dutch Boers, after two centuries of life there, are as hardy as any race on earth. The Anglo-Saxon has established himself in climates totally diverse—Canada, South Africa, and India—and, through several generations, has preserved his essential race characteristics. He is not, of course, superior to climatic influences; but, even in warm climates, he is likely to retain his aggressive vigor long enough to supplant races already enfeebled. Thus, in what Dr. Bushnell calls "the out-populating power of the Christian stock," may be found God's final and complete solution of the dark problem of heathenism among many inferior peoples.

Some of the stronger races, doubtless, may be able to preserve their integrity; but, in order to compete with the Anglo-Saxon, they will probably be forced to adopt his methods and instruments, his civilization and his religion. Significant movements are now in progress among them. While the Christian religion was never more vital, or its hold upon the Anglo-Saxon mind stronger, there is taking place among the nations a wide-spread intellectual revolt against traditional beliefs. "In every corner of the world," said Mr. Froude,[13] "there is the same phenomenon of the decay of established religions. . . . Among Mohammedans, Jews, Buddhists, Brahmins, traditionary creeds are losing their hold. An intellectual revolution is sweeping over the world, breaking down established opinions, dissolving foundations on which historical faiths have been built up." The contact of Christian with heathen nations is awaking the latter to new life. Old superstitions are loosening their grasp. The dead crust of fossil faiths is being shattered by the movements of life underneath. In Catholic countries, Catholicism is losing its influence over educated minds, and in some cases the masses have already lost all faith in it. Thus, while on this continent God is training

the Anglo-Saxon race for its mission, a complemental work has been in progress in the great world beyond. God has two hands. Not only is he preparing in our civilization the die with which to stamp the nations, but, by what Southey called the "timing of Providence," he is preparing mankind to receive our impress.

Is there room for reasonable doubt that this race, unless devitalized by alcohol and tobacco, is destined to dispossess many weaker races, assimilate others and mold the remainder, until, in a very true and important sense, it has Anglo-Saxonized mankind? Already "the English language, saturated with Christian ideas, gathering up into itself the best thought of all the ages, is the great agent of Christian civilization throughout the world; at this moment affecting the destinies and molding the character of half the human race." [14] Jacob Grimm, the German philologist, said of this language: "It seems chosen, like its people, to rule in future times in a still greater degree in all the corners of the earth." He predicted, indeed, that the language of Shakespeare would eventually become the language of mankind. Is not Tennyson's noble prophecy to find its fulfillment in Anglo-Saxondom's extending its dominion and influence—

"Till the war-drum throbs no longer, and the battle flags are furl'd
In the Parliament of man, the Federation of the world." [15]

In my own mind, there is no doubt that the Anglo-Saxon is to exercise the commanding influence in the world's future; but the exact nature of that influence is, as yet, undetermined. How far his civilization will be materialistic and atheistic, and how long it will take thoroughly to Christianize and sweeten it, how rapidly he will hasten the coming of the kingdom wherein dwelleth righteousness, or how many ages he may retard it, is still uncertain; but *it is now being swiftly determined*. Let us weld together in a chain the various links of our logic which we have endeavored to forge. Is it manifest that the Anglo-Saxon holds in his hands the destinies of mankind for ages to come? Is it evident that the United States is to be the home of this race, the principal seat of his power, the great center of his influence? Is it true (see Chap. III.) that the great West

---

[13] *North American Review*, Dec., 1879.

[14] Rev. N. G. Clark, D.D.
[15] "Locksley Hall."

is to dominate the nation's future? Has it been shown (Chapters XI. and XII.) that this generation is to determine the character, and hence the destiny, of the West? Then may God open the eyes of this generation! When Napoleon drew up his troops before the Mamelukes, under the shadow of the Pyramids, pointing to the latter, he said to his soldiers: "Remember that from yonder heights forty centuries look down on you." Men of this generation, from the pyramid top of opportunity on which God has set us, *we look down on forty centuries!* We stretch our hand into the future with power to mold the destinies of unborn millions.

> "We are living, we are dwelling,
> In a grand and awful time,
> In an age on ages telling—
> To be living is sublime!"

Notwithstanding the great perils which threaten it, I cannot think our civilization will perish; but I believe it is fully in the hands of the Christians of the United States, during the next fifteen or twenty years to hasten or retard the coming of Christ's kingdom in the world by hundreds, and perhaps thousands, of years. We of this generation and nation occupy the Gibraltar of the ages which commands the world's future.　　　　　　　　1885

ALFRED THAYER MAHAN

1840–1914

"I AM GREATLY in error," wrote Theodore Roosevelt of Mahan's *The Influence of Sea Power upon History, 1660–1783* (1890), "if it does not become a classic." The substance of the book had been given as lectures at the War College in Newport; Mahan analyzed the rise and decline of maritime powers and related political to naval history. Like Mahan's other writings, this book was a plea for reliance on naval power and for Anglo-American co-operation. Mahan influenced Theodore Roosevelt, Senator Henry Cabot Lodge, and other imperialists; he was, moreover, much appreciated abroad. His conceptions of navalism were, in the main, incorporated into American policy.

Mahan, after study at Columbia University and at the Naval Academy at Annapolis, served in the Civil War and was advanced during subsequent service to the rank of rear admiral. His books include *The Influence of Sea Power upon the French Revolution and Empire, 1793–1812* (1892), *Admiral Farragut* (1892), *The Life of Nelson* (1897), *The Interest of America in Sea Power* (1897), and *Sea Power in Its Relation to the War of 1812* (1905). Mahan's writings dealt with a virtually new field, and he has fairly been called the first "philosopher of sea power."

A. T. Mahan, *From Sail to Steam; Recollections of Naval Life*, New York, 1907.
William E. Livezey, *Mahan on Sea Power*, Norman, Okla., 1947.
W. D. Puleston, U.S.N., *Mahan: The Life and Works of Alfred Thayer Mahan, U.S.N.*, New Haven, 1939, 1946.

From: THE INTEREST OF AMERICA IN　　《　《
SEA POWER

CHAPTER I

THE UNITED STATES LOOKING OUTWARD

Indications are not wanting of an approaching change in the thoughts and policy of Americans as to their relations with the world outside their own borders. For the past quarter of a century, the predominant idea, which has asserted itself successfully at the polls and shaped the course of the government, has been to preserve the home market for the home industries. The employer and the workman alike have been taught to look at the various economical measures proposed from this point of view, to regard with hostility any step favoring the intrusion of the foreign producer upon their own domain, and rather to demand increasingly rigorous measures of exclusion than to acquiesce in any loosening of the chain that binds the consumer to them. The inevitable consequence has followed, as in all cases when the mind or the eye is exclusively fixed in one direction, that the danger of loss or the prospect of advantage in another quarter has been overlooked; and although the abounding resources of the country have maintained the exports at a high figure, this flattering result has been due more to the superabundant bounty of Nature than to the demand of other nations for our protected manufactures.

For nearly the lifetime of a generation, therefore, American industries have been thus protected, until the practice has assumed the force of a tradition, and is clothed in the mail of conservatism. In their mutual relations, these industries resemble the activities of a modern ironclad that has heavy armor, but inferior engines and guns; mighty for defence, weak for offence. Within, the home market is secured; but outside, beyond the broad seas, there are the markets of the world, that can be entered and controlled only by a vigorous contest, to which the habit of trusting to protection by statute does not conduce.

At bottom, however, the temperament of the American people is essentially alien to such a sluggish attitude. Independently of all bias for or against protection, it is safe to predict that, when the opportunities for gain abroad are understood, the course of American enterprise will cleave a channel by which to reach them. Viewed broadly, it is a most welcome as well as significant fact that a prominent and influential advocate of protection, a leader of the party committed to its support, a keen reader of the signs of the times and of the drift of opinion, has identified himself with a line of policy which looks to nothing less than such modifications of the tariff as may expand the commerce of the United States to all quarters of the globe.

. . . The interesting and significant feature of this changing attitude is the turning of the eyes outward, instead of inward only, to seek the welfare of the country. To affirm the importance of distant markets, and the relation to them of our own immense powers of production, implies logically the recognition of the link that joins the products and the markets, —that is, the carrying trade; the three together constituting that chain of maritime power to which Great Britain owes her wealth and greatness. Further, is it too much to say that, as two of these links, the shipping and the markets, are exterior to our own borders, the acknowledgment of them carries with it a view of the relations of the United States to the world radically distinct from the simple idea of self-sufficingness? We shall not follow far this line of thought before there will dawn the realization of America's unique position, facing the older worlds of the East and West, her shores washed by the oceans which touch the one or the other, but which are common to her alone.

Coincident with these signs of change in our own policy there is restlessness in the world at large which is deeply significant, if not ominous. It is beside our purpose to dwell upon the internal state of Europe, whence, if disturbances arise, the effect upon us may be but partial and indirect. But the great seaboard powers there do not stand on guard against their continental rivals only; they cherish also aspirations for commercial extension, for colonies, and for influence in distant regions, which may bring, and, even under our present contracted policy, already have brought them into collision with ourselves. The incident of the Samoa Islands, trivial apparently, was nevertheless eminently suggestive of European ambitions. America then roused from sleep as to interests closely concerning her future. At this moment internal troubles are imminent in the Sandwich Islands, where it should be our fixed determination to allow no foreign influence to equal our own. All over the world German commercial and colonial push is coming into collision with other nations: witness the affair of the Caroline Islands with Spain; the partition of New Guinea with England; the yet more recent negotiation between these two powers concerning their share in Africa viewed with deep distrust and jealousy by France; the Samoa affair; the conflict between German control and American interests in the islands of the western Pacific; and the alleged Progress of German influence in Central and South America. It is noteworthy that, while these various contentions are sustained with the aggressive military spirit characteristic of the German Empire, they are credibly said to arise from the national temper more than from the deliberate policy of the government, which in this matter does not lead, but follows, the feeling of the people,—a condition much more formidable.

There is no sound reason for believing that the world has passed into a period of assured peace outside the limits of Europe. Unsettled political conditions, such as exist in Haiti, Central America, and many of the Pacific Islands, especially the Hawaiian group, when combined with great military or commercial importance as is the case with most of these positions, involve, now as always, dangerous germs of quarrel, against which it is prudent at least to be prepared. Undoubtedly, the general temper of nations is more averse from war than it was of old. If no less selfish and grasping than our predecessors, we feel more dislike to the discomforts and sufferings attendant upon a breach of peace; but to retain that highly valued repose and the undisturbed enjoyment of the returns of commerce, it is necessary to argue upon somewhat equal terms of strength with an adversary. It is the preparedness of the enemy, and not acquiescence in the existing state of things, that now holds back the armies of Europe.

On the other hand, neither the sanctions of international law nor the justice of a cause can be depended upon for a fair settlement of differences, when they come into conflict with a strong political necessity on the one side opposed to comparative weakness on the other. In our still-pending dispute over the seal-fishing of Bering Sea, whatever may be thought of the strength of our argument, in view of generally admitted principles of international law, it is beyond doubt that our contention is reasonable, just, and in the interest of the world at large. But in the attempt to enforce it we have come into collision not only with national susceptibilities as to the honor of the flag, which we ourselves very strongly share, but also with a state governed by a powerful necessity, and exceedingly strong where we are particularly weak and exposed. Not only has Great Britain a mighty navy and we a long defenceless seacoast, but it is a great commercial and political advantage to her that her larger colonies, and above all Canada, should feel that the power of the mother country is something which they need, and upon which they can count. . . . Whatever arrangement of this question is finally reached, the fruit of Lord Salisbury's attitude scarcely can fail to be a strengthening of the sentiments of attachment to, and reliance upon, the mother country, not only in Canada, but in the other great colonies. These feelings of attachment and mutual dependence supply the living spirit, without which the nascent schemes for Imperial Federation are but dead mechanical contrivances; nor are they without influence upon such generally unsentimental considerations as those of buying and selling, and the course of trade.

This dispute, seemingly paltry yet really serious, sudden in its appearance and dependent for its issue upon other considerations than its own merits, may serve to convince us of many latent and yet unforeseen dangers to the peace of the western hemisphere, attendant upon the opening of a canal through the Central American Isthmus. In a general way, it is evident enough that this canal, by modifying the direction of trade routes, will induce a great increase of commercial activity and carrying trade throughout the Caribbean Sea; and that this now comparatively deserted nook of the ocean will become, like the Red Sea, a great thoroughfare of shipping, and will attract, as never before in our day, the interest and ambition of maritime nations. Every position in that sea will have enhanced commercial and military value, and the canal itself will become a strategic centre of the most vital importance. Like the Canadian Pacific Railroad, it will be a link between the two oceans; but, unlike it, the use, unless most carefully guarded by treaties, will belong wholly to the belligerent which controls the sea by its naval power. In case of war, the United States will unquestionably command the Canadian Railroad, despite the deterrent force of operations by the hostile navy upon our seaboard; but no less unquestionably will she be impotent, as against any of the great maritime powers, to control the Central American canal. Militarily speaking, and having reference to European complications only, the piercing of the Isthmus is nothing but a disaster to the United States, in the present state of her military and naval preparation. It is especially dangerous to the Pacific coast; but the increased exposure of one part of our seaboard reacts unfavorably upon the whole military situation.

Despite a certain great original superiority conferred by our geographical nearness and immense resources,—due, in other words, to our natural advantages, and not to our intelligent preparations,—the United States is wofully unready, not only in fact but in purpose to assert in the Caribbean and Central America a weight of influence proportioned to the extent of her interests. We have not the navy, and, what is worse, we are not willing to have the navy, that will weigh seriously in any disputes with those nations whose interests will conflict there with our own. We have not, and we are not anxious to provide, the defence of the seaboard which will leave the navy free for its work at sea. We have not, but many other powers have, positions, either within or on the borders of the Caribbean which not only possess great natural advantages for the control of that sea, but have received and are receiving that artificial strength of fortification and armament which will make them practically inexpugnable. On the contrary, we have not on the Gulf of Mexico even the beginning of a navy yard which could serve as the base of our operations. Let me not be misunderstood. I am not regretting that we have not the means to meet on terms of equality the great navies of the Old World. I recognize, what few at least say, that despite its great surplus revenue, this country is poor in proportion to its length of seaboard and its exposed points. That which I deplore, and which is a sober, just, and reasonable cause of deep national concern is that the nation neither has nor cares to have its sea frontier so defended, and its navy of such power, as shall suffice, with the advantages of our position, to weigh seriously when inevitable discussions arise,—such as we have recently had about Samoa and Bering Sea, and which may at any moment come up about the Caribbean Sea or the canal. Is the United States, for instance, prepared to allow Germany to acquire the Dutch stronghold of Curaçao, fronting the Atlantic outlet of both the proposed canals of Panama and Nicaragua? Is she prepared to acquiesce in any foreign power purchasing from Haiti a naval station on the Windward Passage, through which pass our steamer routes to the Isthmus? Would she acquiesce in a foreign protectorate over the Sandwich Islands, that great central station of the Pacific, equidistant from San Francisco, Samoa, and the Marquesas, and an important post on our lines of communication with both Australia and China? Or will it be maintained that any one of these questions, supposing it to arise, is so exclusively one-sided, the arguments of policy and right so exclusively with

us, that the other party will at once yield his eager wish, and gracefully withdraw? Was it so at Samoa? Is it so as regards the Bering Sea? The motto seen on so many ancient cannon, *Ultima ratio regum*,[1] is not without its message to republics.

It is perfectly reasonable and legitimate, in estimating our needs of military preparation, to take into account the remoteness of the chief naval and military nations from our shores, and the consequent difficulty of maintaining operations at such a distance. It is equally proper, in framing our policy, to consider the jealousies of the European family of states, and their consequent unwillingness to incur the enmity of a people so strong as ourselves; their dread of our revenge in the future, as well as their inability to detach more than a certain part of their forces to our shores without losing much of their own weight in the councils of Europe. In truth, a careful determination of the force that Great Britain or France could probably spare for operations against our coasts, if the latter were suitably defended, without weakening their European position or unduly exposing their colonies and commerce, is the starting-point from which to calculate the strength of our own navy. . . .

While, therefore, the advantages of our own position in the western hemisphere, and the disadvantages under which the operations of a European state would labor, are undeniable and just elements in the calculations of the statesman, it is folly to look upon them as sufficient alone for our security. Much more needs to be cast into the scale that it may incline in favor of our strength. They are mere defensive factors, and partial at that. Though distant, our shores can be reached; being defenceless, they can detain but a short time a force sent against them. With a probability of three months' peace in Europe, no maritime power would fear to support its demands by a number of ships with which it would be loath indeed to part for a year.

Yet, were our sea frontier as strong as it now is weak, passive self-defence, whether in trade or war, would be but a poor policy, so long as this world continues to be one of struggle and vicissitude. All around us now is strife; "the struggle of life," "the race of life," are phrases so familiar that we do not feel their significance till we stop to think about them. Everywhere nation is arrayed

[1] *The final argument of despots.*

against nation; our own no less than others. What is our protective system but an organized warfare? In carrying it on, it is true, we have only to use certain procedures which all states now concede to be a legal exercise of the national power, even though injurious to themselves. It is lawful, they say, to do what we will with our own. Are our people, however, so unaggressive that they are likely not to want their own way in matters where their interests turn on points of disputed right, or so little sensitive as to submit quietly to encroachment by others, in quarters where they long have considered their own influence should prevail?

Our self-imposed isolation in the matter of markets, and the decline of our shipping interest in the last thirty years, have coincided singularly with an actual remoteness of this continent from the life of the rest of the world. The writer has before him a map of the North and South Atlantic oceans, showing the direction of the principal trade routes and the proportion of tonnage passing over each; and it is curious to note what deserted regions, comparatively, are the Gulf of Mexico, the Caribbean Sea, and the adjoining countries and islands. A broad band stretches from our northern Atlantic coast to the English Channel; another as broad from the British Islands to the East, through the Mediterranean and Red Sea, overflowing the borders of the latter in order to express the volume of trade. Around either cape—Good Hope and Horn—pass strips of about one-fourth this width, joining near the equator, midway between Africa and South America. From the West Indies issues a thread, indicating the present commerce of Great Britain with a region which once, in the Napoleonic wars, embraced one-fourth of the whole trade of the Empire. The significance is unmistakable: Europe has now little mercantile interest in the Caribbean Sea.

When the Isthmus is pierced, this isolation will pass away, and with it the indifference of foreign nations. From wheresoever they come and whithersoever they afterward go, all ships that use the canal will pass through the Caribbean. Whatever the effect produced upon the prosperity of the adjacent continent and islands by the thousand wants attendant upon maritime activity, around such a focus of trade will centre large commercial and political interests. To protect and develop its own, each nation will seek points of support and means of influence in a quarter where the United States always has been jealously sensitive to the intrusion of European powers. The precise value of the Monroe doctrine is understood very loosely by most Americans, but the effect of the familiar phrase has been to develop a national sensitiveness, which is a more frequent cause of war than material interests; and over disputes caused by such feelings there will preside none of the calming influence due to the moral authority of international law, with its recognized principles, for the points in dispute will be of policy, of interest, not of conceded right. Already France and Great Britain are giving to ports held by them a degree of artificial strength uncalled for by their present importance. They look to the near future. Among the islands and on the mainland there are many positions of great importance, held now by weak or unstable states. Is the United States willing to see them sold to a powerful rival? But what right will she invoke against the transfer? She can allege but one,—that of her reasonable policy supported by her might.

Whether they will or no, Americans must now begin to look outward. The growing production of the country demands it. An increasing volume of public sentiment demands it. The position of the United States, between the two Old Worlds and the two great oceans, makes the same claim, which will soon be strengthened by the creation of the new link joining the Atlantic and Pacific. The tendency will be maintained and increased by the growth of the European colonies in the Pacific, by the advancing civilization of Japan, and by the rapid peopling of our Pacific States with men who have all the aggressive spirit of the advanced line of national progress. Nowhere does a vigorous foreign policy find more favor than among the people west of the Rocky Mountains.

It has been said that, in our present state of unpreparedness, a trans-isthmian canal will be a military disaster to the United States, and especially to the Pacific coast. When the canal is finished, the Atlantic seaboard will be neither more nor less exposed than it now is; it will merely share with the country at large the increased danger of foreign complications with inadequate means to meet them. The danger of the Pacific coast will be greater by so much as the way between it and Europe is shortened through a passage which the stronger maritime power can control. The danger will lie not merely in the greater facility for despatching a hostile squadron from Europe, but also in the fact that a more powerful fleet than formerly can be maintained on that coast by a European power, because it can be called home so much more promptly in case of need. The greatest weakness of the Pacific ports, however, if wisely met by our governments, will go far to insure our naval superiority there.

. . . The military needs of the Pacific States, as well as their supreme importance to the whole country, are yet a matter of the future, but of a future so near that provision should begin immediately. To weigh their importance, consider what influence in the Pacific would be attributed to a nation comprising only the States of Washington, Oregon, and California, when filled with such men as now people them and still are pouring in, and which controlled such maritime centres as San Francisco, Puget Sound, and the Columbia River. Can it be counted less because they are bound by the ties of blood and close political union to the great communities of the East? But such influence, to work without jar and friction, requires underlying military readiness, like the proverbial iron hand under the velvet glove. To provide this, three things are needful: First, protection of the chief harbors, by fortifications and coast-defence ships, which gives defensive strength, provides security to the community within, and supplies the bases necessary to all military operations. Secondly, naval force, the arm of offensive power, which alone enables a country to extend its influence outward. Thirdly, it should be an inviolable resolution

of our national policy, that no foreign state should henceforth acquire a coaling position within three thousand miles of San Francisco, —a distance which includes the Hawaiian and Galapagos islands and the coast of Central America. For fuel is the life of modern naval war; it is the food of the ship; without it the modern monsters of the deep die of inanition. Around it, therefore, cluster some of the most important considerations of naval strategy. In the Caribbean and in the Atlantic we are confronted with many a foreign coal depot, bidding us stand to our arms, even as Carthage bade Rome; but let us not acquiesce in an addition to our dangers, a further diversion of our strength, by being forestalled in the North Pacific.

In conclusion, while Great Britain is undoubtedly the most formidable of our possible enemies, both by her great navy and by the strong positions she holds near our coasts, it must be added that a cordial understanding with that country is one of the first of our external interests. Both nations doubtless, and properly seek their own advantage; but both, also, are controlled by a sense of law and justice, drawn from the same sources, and deep-rooted in their instincts. Whatever temporary aberration may occur, a return to mutual standards of right will certainly follow. Formal alliance between the two is out of the question, but a cordial recognition of the similarity of character and ideas will give birth to sympathy, which in turn will facilitate a co-operation beneficial to both; for if sentimentality is weak, sentiment is strong.   1897

FINLEY PETER DUNNE ("MR. DOOLEY")

1867–1936

DURING the Spanish-American war the opinions of "Mr. Dooley," the penetrating and witty Irishman whom Dunne, a Chicago newspaperman, had created, won virtually a national hearing. In 1902 Dunne, who had made his career on the *Chicago Tribune*, the *Chicago Times*, and the *Chicago Journal*, became editor of the *American Magazine*. The pungency and dry humor which marked the expression of his frequently liberal views provided a light touch to the muckraking literature of protest. His books include *Mr. Dooley in Peace and in War* (1898), *Mr. Dooley in the Hearts of His Countrymen* (1899), *Mr. Dooley's Opinions* (1901),

Observations by Mr. Dooley (1902), *Mr. Dooley Says* (1910), and *Mr. Dooley on Making a Will* (1919).

Finley Peter Dunne: *Mr. Dooley at His Best*, Elmer Ellis, ed., New York, 1938.
W. D. Howells, "Certain of the Chicago School of Fiction," *North American Review*, CLXXVI, 734–736
Mr. Dooley: Now and Forever, Louis Filler, ed., Stanford, 1954.
Elmer Ellis, *Mr. Dooley's America, A Life of Finley Peter Dunne*, New York, 1941.

» » From: OBSERVATIONS BY MR. DOOLEY « «

CUBA VS. BEET SUGAR

"What's all this about Cubia an' th' Ph'lippeens?" asked Mr. Hennessy. "What's beet sugar?"

"Th' throuble about Cubia is that she's free; th' throuble about beet sugar is we're not; an' th' throuble about th' Ph'lippeens is th' Ph'lippeen throuble," said Mr. Dooley. "As rega-ards Cubia, she's like a woman that th' whole neighborhood helps to divoorce fr'm a crool husband, but nivertheless a husband, an' a miserable home but a home, an' a small credit at th' grocery but a credit, an' thin whin she goes into th' dhressmakin' business, rayfuse to buy annything fr'm her because sh's a divoorced woman. We freed Cubia but we didn't free annything she projooces. It wasn't her fault. We didn't think. We expicted that all we had to do was to go down to Sandago with a kinetoscope an' sthrike th' shackles fr'm th' slave an' she'd be comfortable even if she had no other protiction f'r her poor feet. We f'rgot about th' Beet. Most iv us niver thought about that beautiful but fragile flower excipt biled in conniction with pigs' feet or pickled in its own life juice. We didn't know that upon th' Beet hangs th' fate iv th' nation, th' hope iv th' future, th' permanence iv our instichoochions an' a lot iv other things akelly precious. Th' Beet is th' naytional anthem an', be hivins, it looks as though it might be th' naytional motto befure long.

"Well, Cubia got her freedom or something that wud look like th' same thing if she kept it out iv th' rain, but somehow or another it didn't suit her entirely. A sort iv cravin' come over her that it was hard to tell fr'm th' same feelin' iv vacancy that she knew whin she was opprissed be th' Hated Casteel. Hunger, Hinnissy, is about th' same thing in a raypublic as in a dispotism. They'se not much choice iv unhappiness between a hungry slave an' a hungry freeman. Cubia cudden't cuk or wear freedom. Ye can't make freedom into a stew an' ye can't cut a pair iv pants out iv it. It won't bile, fry, bake or fricassee. Ye can't take two pounds iv fresh creamery freedom, a pound iv north wind, a heapin' taycupfull iv naytional aspirations an' a sprinkin' iv bars fr'm th' naytional air, mix well, cuk over a hot fire an' sarve sthraight fr'm th' shtove; ye can't make a dish out iv that that wud nourish a tired freeman whin he comes home afther a hard day's wurruk lookin' f'r a job. So Cubia comes to us an' says she: 'Ye done well by us,' she says. 'Ye give us freedom,' says she, 'an' more thin enough to go round;' she says, 'an' now if ye plaze we'd like to thrade a little iv it back f'r a few groceries,' she says. 'We will wear wan shackle f'r a ham,' says she, 'an' we'll put on a full raygalia iv ball an' chain an' yoke an' fetters an' come-alongs f'r a square meal,' says she.

"That sounds raisonable enough an' bein' be nature a gin'rous people whin we don't think, we're about to help her disthress with whativer we have cold in th' panthry whin th' thought iv th' Beet crosses our minds. What will th' Beet say, th' red, th' juicy, th' sacchrine Beet, th' Beet iv our Fathers, th' Beet iv Plymouth Rock, Beet iv th' Pilgrim's Pride, Sweet Beet iv Liberty, iv thee I sing? If we do annything f'r Cubia, down goes th' Beet, an' with th' Beet perishes our instichoochions. Th' constichoochion follows th' Beet ex propria vigore, as Hogan says. Th' juice iv th' Beet is th' life blood iv our nation. Whoiver touches a hair iv yon star spangled Beet, shoot him on th' spot. A bold Beet industhry a counthry's pride whin wanst desthroyed can niver be supplied. 'Beet sugar an' Liberty Now an' Forever, wan an' insiprable'—Dan'l Webster. 'Thank Gawd I—I also—am a Beet'—th' same. 'Gover'mint iv th' Beet, by th' Beet an' f'r th' Beet shall not perish fr'm th' earth,'—Abraham

Lincoln. An' so, Hinnissy, we put th' pie back into th' ice-chest where we keep our honor an' ginerosity an' lock th' dure an' Cubia goes home, free an' hopeless. D'ye think so? Well, I don't. Be hivins, Hinnissy, I think th' time has come whin we've got to say whether we're a nation iv Beets. I am no serf, but I'd rather be bent undher th' dispotism iv a Casteel thin undher th' tyranny iv a Beet. If I've got to be a slave, I'd rather be wan to a man, even a Spanish man, thin to a viggytable. If I'm goin' to be opprised be a Beet, let it be fr'm th' inside not fr'm without. I'll choose me masther, Hinnissy, an' whin I do, 'twill not be that low-lyin', purple-complected, indygistible viggytable. I may bend me high head to th' egg-plant, th' potato, th' cabbage, th' squash, th' punkin, th' sparrow-grass, th' onion, th' spinach, th' rutabaga turnip, th' Fr-rench pea or th' parsnip, but 'twill niver be said iv me that I was subjygated be a Beet. No, sir. Betther death. I'm goin' to begin a war fr freedom. I'm goin' to sthrike th' shackles fr'm a slave an' I'm him. I'm goin' to organize a rig'mint iv Rough Riders an' whin I stand on th' top iv San Joon hill with me soord in me hand an' me gleamin' specs on me nose, ye can mark th' end iv th' domination iv th' Beet in th' western wurruld. Fr, Hinnissy, I tell ye what, if th' things I hear fr'm Wash'nton is thrue, that other war iv freedom stopped befure it was half done."

"An' what about th' Ph'lippeens?" asked Mr. Hennessy.

"They'se nawthin' to say about th' Ph'lip-peens," said Mr. Dooley, "excipt that th' throuble down there is all over."

"All over?"

"All over."

THE PHILIPPINE PEACE

" 'Tis sthrange we don't hear much talk about th' Ph'lippeens," said Mr. Hennessy.

"Ye ought to go to Boston," said Mr. Dooley. "They talk about it there in their sleep. Th' raison it's not discussed annywhere else is that ivrything is perfectly quiet there. We don't talk about Ohio or Ioway or anny iv our other possissions because they'se nawthin' doin' in thim parts. Th' people ar-re goin' ahead, garnerin' th' products iv th' sile, sindin' their childher to school, worshipin' on Sundah in th' churches an' thankin' Hiven fr th' blessin's iv free govermint an' th' pro-tiction iv th' flag above thim.

"So it is in th' Ph'lippeens. I know, fr me frind Gov'nor Taft says so, an' they'se a man that undherstands con-tintmint whin he sees it. Ye can't thrust th' fellows that comes back fr'm th' jool iv th' Passyfic an' tells ye that things ar-re no betther thin they shud be undher th' shade iv th' cocoanut palm be th' blue wathers iv th' still lagoon. They mus' be satis-fied with our rule. A man that isn't satisfied whin he's had enough is a glutton. They're satisfied an' happy an' slowly but surely they're acquirin' that love fr th' govermint that floats over thim that will make thim good citizens without a vote or a right to thrile be jury. I know it. Guv'nor Taft says so.

"Says he: 'Th' Ph'lippeens as ye have been tol' be me young but speechful frind, Sinitor Bivridge, who was down there fr tin minyits wanst an' spoke very highly an' at some lenth on th' beauties iv th' scenery, th' Ph'lippeens is wan or more iv th' beautiful jools in th' diadem iv our fair nation. Formerly our fair nation didn't care fr jools, but done up her hair with side combs, but she's been abroad some since an' she come back with beautiful reddish goolden hair that a tiara looks well in an' that is betther fr havin' a tiara. She is not as young as she was. Th' simple home-lovin' maiden that our fathers knew has disappeared an' in her place we find a Columbya, gintle-men, with machurer charms, a knowledge iv Euro-peen customs an' not averse to a cigareet. So we have pinned in her fair hair a diadem that sets off her beauty to advantage an' holds on th' front iv th' hair, an' th' mos' lovely pearl in this ornymint is thim sunny little isles iv th' Passyfic. They are almost too sunny fr me. I had to come away.

" 'To shift me language suddintly fr'm th' joolry counther an' th' boodore, I will say that nawthin' that has been said even be th' gifted an' scholarly sinitor, who so worthily fills part iv th' place wanst crowded be Hendricks an' McDonald, does justice to th' richness iv thim islands. They raise unknown quantities iv produce, none iv which forchnitly can come into this counthry. All th' riches iv Cathay, all th' wealth iv Ind, as Hogan says, wud look like a second morgedge on an Apache wickeyup compared with th' untold an' almost unmin-tionable products iv that gloryous domain. Me business kept me in Manila or I wud tell ye what they are. Besides some iv our lile subjects is gettin' to be good shots an' I didn't go down there f'r that purpose.

" 'I turn to th' climate. It is simply hivenly. No other wurrud describes it. A white man who goes there seldom rayturns unless th' bereaved fam'ly insists. It is jus' right. In winter enough rain, in summer plinty iv heat. Gin'rally speakin' whin that thropical sky starts rainin' it doesn't stop till it's impty, so th' counthry is not subjected to th' sudden changes that afflict more northerly climes. Whin it rains it rains; whin it shines it shines. Th' wather frequently remains in th' air afther th' sun has been shinin' a month or more, th' earth bein' a little over-crowded with juice an' this gives th' atmosphere a certain cosiness that is indescribable. A light green mould grows on th' clothes an' is very becomin'. I met a man on th' boat comin' back who said 'twas th' finest winter climate in th' wurruld. He was be profission a rubber in a Turkish bath. As f'r th' summers they are delicious. Th' sun doesn't sit aloft above th' jools iv th' Passyfic. It comes down an' mingles with th' people. Ye have heard it said th' isles was kissed be th' sun. Perhaps bitten wud be a betther wurrud. But th' timprachoor is frequently modified be an eruption iv th' neighborin' volcanoes an' th' inthraduction iv American stoves. At night a coolin' breeze fr'm th' crather iv a volcano makes sleep possible in a hammock swung in th' ice-box. It is also very pleasant to be able to cuk wan's dinner within wan.

" 'Passin' to th' pollytical situation, I will say it is good. Not perhaps as good as ye'ers or mine, but good. Ivry wanst in a while whin I think iv it, an iliction is held. Unforchnitly it usually happens that those ilicted have not yet surrindhered. In th' Ph'lippeens th' office seeks th' man, but as he is also pursooed be th' sojery, it is not always aisy to catch him an' fit it on him. Th' counthry may be divided into two parts, pollytically,—where th' insurrection continues an' where it will soon be. Th' brave but I fear not altogether cheery army conthrols th' insurrected parts be martiyal law, but th' civil authorities are supreme in their own house. Th' diff'rence between civil law an' martiyal law in th' Ph'lippeens is what kind iv coat th' judge wears. Th' raysult is much th' same. Th' two branches wurruks in perfect harmony. We bag thim in th' city an' they round thim up in th' counthry.

" 'It is not always nicessry to kill a Filipino American right away. Me desire is to idjacate thim slowly in th' ways an' customs iv th' counthry. We ar-re givin' hundherds iv these pore benighted haythen th' well-known, ol'-fashioned American wather cure. Iv coorse, ye know how 'tis done. A Filipino, we'll say, niver heerd iv th' histhry iv this counthry. He is met be wan iv our sturdy boys in black an' blue iv th' Macabebee scouts who asts him to cheer f'r Abraham Lincoln. He rayfuses. He is thin placed upon th' grass an' given a dhrink, a baynit bein' fixed in his mouth so he cannot reject th' hospitality. Undher th' inflooence iv th' hose that cheers but does not inebriate, he soon warrums or perhaps I might say swells up to a ralization iv th' granjoor iv his adoptive counthry. One gallon makes him give three groans f'r th' constitchoochion. At four gallons, he will ask to be wrapped in th' flag. At th' dew pint he sings Yankee Doodle. Occasionally we run acrost a stubborn an' rebellyous man who wud sthrain at me idee iv human rights an' swallow th' Passyfic Ocean, but I mus' say mos' iv these little fellows is less hollow in their pretintions. Nachrally we have had to take a good manny customs fr'm th' Spanyard, but we have improved on thim. I was talkin' with a Spanish gintleman th' other day who had been away f'r a long time an' he said he wudden't know th' counthry. Even th' faces iv th' people on th' sthreets had changed. They seemed glad to see him. Among th' mos' useful Spanish customs is reconcenthration. Our reconcenthration camps is among th' mos' thickly popylated in th' wurruld. But still we have to rely mainly on American methods. They are always used fin'lly in th' makin' iv a good citizen, th' garotte sildom.

" 'I have not considhered it advisable to inthrajooce anny fads like thrile be jury iv ye'er peers into me administhration. Plain sthraight-forward dealin's is me motto. A Filipino at his best has on'y larned half th' jooty iv mankind. He can be thried but he can't thry his fellow man. It takes him too long. But in time I hope to have thim thrained to a pint where they can be good men an' thrue at th' inquest.

" 'I hope I have tol' ye enough to show ye that th' stories iv disordher is greatly exaggerated. Th' counthry is pro-gressin' splindidly, th' ocean still laps th' shore, th' mountains are there as they were in Bivridge's day, quite happy apparently; th' flag floats free an' well guarded over th' govermint offices, an' th' cherry people go an' come on their errands

—go out alone an' come back with th' throops. Ivrywhere happiness, contint, love iv th' sthep-mother counthry, excipt in places where there ar-re people. Gintlemen, I thank ye.'"

"An' there ye ar-re, Hinnissy. I hope this here lucid story will quite th' waggin' tongues iv scandal an' that people will let th' Ph'lip-peens stew in their own happiness."

"But sure they might do something f': thim," said Mr. Hennessy.

"They will," said Mr. Dooley. "They'll give thim a measure iv freedom."

"But whin?"

"Whin they'll sthand still long enough to be measured," said Mr. Dooley.

1902

ANTI-IMPERIALISM

MANY FIGURES in the literary and intellectual world, such as Bliss Carman, Richard Hovey, Gertrude Atherton, and Thomas Nelson Page, echoed Kipling's doctrine of "the white man's burden." On the other side, however, stood Hamlin Garland, Thomas Wentworth Higginson, William Dean Howells, Mark Twain, William Vaughn Moody, and Henry Blake Fuller. The movement against American expansion in the Caribbean and in the Philippines took the form of the characteristically American organization of societies with organs, speeches, lobbying, and letter-writing. The local and national anti-imperialist leagues, in which Edwin Atkinson, a Boston economist and manufacturer, Andrew Carnegie, David Starr Jordan, Moorfield Storey, and Charles Francis Adams took part, conducted a spirited campaign. The anti-imperialists urged that it was unjustifiable from every point of view to take the path of empire. Imperialism would not benefit the mass of Americans. It would not even enrich the industrialists whom it was supposed to aid; it would instead create new administrative and political problems. But the chief opposition was moral: imperialism, it was urged, runs counter to the fundamental right of all peoples for self-determination.

The anti-imperialists did not succeed in carrying the day in the presidential campaign of 1900; and when the Philippines were "freed," economic and strategic rather than idealistic motives played the more important role. Nevertheless the anti-imperialist crusade was an important re-affirmation of humanitarian and democratic faith.

F. H. Harrington, "The Anti-Imperialist Movement in the United States, 1898–1900," *The Mississippi Valley Historical Review*, XXII (September, 1935).

F. H. Harrington, "Literary Aspects of American Anti-Imperialism," *New England Quarterly*, X (December, 1937).

» »   PLATFORM OF THE AMERICAN
ANTI-IMPERIALIST LEAGUE   « «

We hold that the policy known as imperialism is hostile to liberty and tends toward militarism, an evil from which it has been our glory to be free. We regret that it has become necessary in the land of Washington and Lincoln to reaffirm that all men, of whatever race or color, are entitled to life, liberty, and the pursuit of happiness. We maintain that governments derive their just powers from the consent of the

governed. We insist that the subjugation of any people is "criminal aggression" and open disloyalty to the distinctive principles of our government.

We earnestly condemn the policy of the present National Administration in the Philippines. It seeks to extinguish the spirit of 1776 in those islands. We deplore the sacrifice of our soldiers and sailors, whose bravery deserves admiration even in an unjust war. We denounce the slaughter of the Filipinos as a needless horror. We protest against the extension of American sovereignty by Spanish methods.

We demand the immediate cessation of the war against liberty, begun by Spain and continued by us. We urge that Congress be promptly convened to announce to the Filipinos our purpose to concede to them the independence for which they have so long fought and which of right is theirs.

The United States have always protested against the doctrine of international law which permits the subjugation of the weak by the strong. A self-governing state cannot accept sovereignty over an unwilling people. The United States cannot act upon the ancient heresy that might makes right.

Imperialists assume that with the destruction of self-government in the Philippines by American hands, all opposition here will cease. This is a grievous error. Much as we abhor the war of "criminal aggression" in the Philippines, greatly as we regret the blood of the Filipinos is on American hands, we more deeply resent the betrayal of American institutions at home. The real firing line is not in the suburbs of Manila. The foe is of our own household. The attempt of 1861 was to divide the country. That of 1899 is to destroy its fundamental principles and noblest ideals.

Whether the ruthless slaughter of the Filipinos shall end next month or next year is but an incident in a contest that must go on until the Declaration of Independence and the Constitution of the United States are rescued from the hands of their betrayers. Those who dispute about standards of value while the Republic is undermined will be listened to as little as those who would wrangle about the small economies of the household while the house is on fire. The training of a great people for a century, the aspiration for liberty of a vast immigration are forces that will hurl aside those who in the delirium of conquest seek to destroy the character of our institutions.

We deny that the obligation of all citizens to support their Government in times of grave National peril applies to the present situation. If an Administration may with impunity ignore the issues upon which it was chosen, deliberately create a condition of war anywhere on the face of the globe, debauch the civil service for spoils to promote the adventure, organize a truth-suppressing censorship and demand of all citizens a suspension of judgment and their unanimous support while it chooses to continue the fighting, representative government itself is imperiled.

We propose to contribute to the defeat of any person or party that stands for the forcible subjugation of any people. We shall oppose for reelection all who in the White House or in Congress betray American liberty in pursuit of un-American gains. We still hope that both of our great political parties will support and defend the Declaration of Independence in the closing campaign of the century.

We hold, with Abraham Lincoln, that "no man is good enough to govern another man without that man's consent. When the white man governs himself, that is self-government, but when he governs himself and also governs another man, that is more than self-government—that is despotism." "Our reliance is in the love of liberty which God has planted in us. Our defense is in the spirit which prizes liberty as the heritage of all men in all lands. Those who deny freedom to others deserve it not for themselves, and under a just God cannot long retain it."

We cordially invite the cooperation of all men and women who remain loyal to the Declaration of Independence and the Constitution of the United States.   1899

ALBERT J. BEVERIDGE

1862–1927

HAVING SPENT a youth of hardship on Middle Western farms, Beveridge succeeded in entering Asbury College (DePauw University). Graduating in 1885, he practiced law in Indianapolis and became well known as a political orator. From 1899 until 1911 he served in the United States Senate, where he won distinction as one of the "insurgent" or "progressive" Republicans. His championship of child labor legislation and of other measures of social amelioration quite naturally led to his support of Theodore Roosevelt in the 1912 presidential campaign.

Yet in spite of Beveridge's liberalism his social thought contained a large vein of conservatism. His inspirational books for young men and women hardly squared with his economic liberalism. *The Life of John Marshall* (1916–1919) is marked by a nationalistic and a pro-Supreme Court bias, a bias which, it is true, is less obvious in his *Abraham Lincoln, 1809–1858* (1929). An isolationist in regard to American participation in European affairs and a pronounced nationalist, Beveridge was sometimes in the camp of the "jingoists." Thus his 1898 speech at Indianapolis in defense of American imperialism was not only frankly based on commercial and economic arguments but definitely revealed his loyalty to the industrialist class.

C. G. Bowers, *Beveridge and the Progressive Era*, Boston, 1932.

» » *From:* THE MARCH OF THE FLAG « «

FELLOW-CITIZENS—It is a noble land that God has given us; a land that can feed and clothe the world: a land whose coast lines would inclose half the countries of Europe; a land set like a sentinel between the two imperial oceans of the globe; a greater England with a nobler destiny. It is a mighty people that He has planted on this soil; a people sprung from the most masterful blood of history; a people perpetually revitalized by the virile workingfolk of all the earth; a people imperial by virtue of their power, by right of their institutions, by authority of their heaven-directed purposes, the propagandists and not the misers of liberty. It is a glorious history our God has bestowed upon His chosen people; a history whose keynote was struck by Liberty Bell; a history heroic with faith in our mission and our future; a history of statesmen, who flung the boundaries of the Republic out into unexplored lands and savage wildernesses; a history of soldiers, who carried the flag across blazing deserts and through the ranks of hostile mountains, even to the gates of sunset: a history of a multiplying people, who overran a continent in half a century; a history divinely logical, in the process of whose tremendous reasoning we find ourselves to-day.

Therefore, in this campaign the question is larger than a party question. It is an American question. It is a world question. Shall the American people continue their resistless march toward the commercial supremacy of the world? Shall free institutions broaden their blessed reign as the children of liberty wax in strength until the empire of our principles is established over the hearts of all mankind? Have we no mission to perform—no duty to discharge to our fellow-man? Has the Almighty Father endowed us with gifts beyond our deserts, and marked us as the people of His peculiar favor, merely to rot in our own selfishness, as men and nations must who take cowardice for their companion and self for their deity—as China has, as India has, as Egypt has? Shall we be as the man who had one talent and hid it, or as he who had ten talents and used them until they grew to riches? And shall we reap the reward that waits on the discharge of our high duty as the sovereign power of earth; shall we occupy new markets for what our farmers raise, new markets for what our factories make, new markets for what our merchants sell,—aye, and please God, new markets for what our ships shall carry? Shall we avail ourselves of new sources of supply of what we do not raise or make, so that what are luxuries to-day shall be necessities to-morrow? Shall we conduct the mightiest commerce of history with the best money known to man or shall we use the pauper money of Mexico, China and the Chicago platform? Shall we be worthy of our mighty past of progress, brushing aside, as we have always done, the spider webs of technicality, and march ever onward upon the highway of development, to the doing of real deeds, the achievement of real things, and the winning of real victories?

In a sentence, shall the American people

endorse at the polls the American administration of William McKinley, which, under the guidance of Divine Providence, has started the Republic on its noblest career of prosperity, duty and glory; or shall the American people rebuke that administration, reverse the wheels of history, halt the career of the flag and turn to that purposeless horde of criticism and carping that is assailing the government at Wash-

10 ington? Shall it be McKinley, sound money and a world-conquering commerce, or Bryan, Bailey, Bland and Blackburn, a bastard currency and a policy of commercial retreat? In the only foreign war that this Nation has had in two generations, will you, the voters of this Republic and the guardians of its good repute, give the other nations of the world to understand that the American people do not approve and indorse the administration that conducted it?

20 These are the questions that you must answer at the polls, and I well know how you will answer them. The thunder of American guns at Santiago and Manila will find its answer in the approval of the voters of the Republic. For the administration of William McKinley, in both peace and war, will receive the mightiest endorsement of a grateful people ever registered. In both peace and war, for we rely on the new birth of national prosperity as well as

30 on the new birth of national glory. Think of both! Think of our country two years ago, and think of it to-day!

. . .

For William McKinley is continuing the policy that Jefferson began, Monroe continued, Seward advanced, Grant promoted, Harrison championed. Hawaii is ours; Porto Rico is to be ours; at the prayer of its people Cuba will

40 finally be ours; in the islands of the East, even to the gates of Asia, coaling stations are to be ours; at the very least the flag of a liberal government is to float over the Philippines, and it will be the stars and stripes of glory. And the burning question of this campaign is whether the American people will accept the gifts of events; whether they will rise, as lifts their soaring destiny; whether they will proceed along the lines of national development sur-

50 veyed by the statesmen of our past, or whether, for the first time, the American people doubt their mission, question their fate, prove apostate to the spirit of their race, and halt the ceaseless march of free institutions?

The opposition tells us that we ought not to govern a people without their consent. I answer, the rule of liberty that all just government derives its authority from the consent of the governed, applies only to those who are capable of self-government. We govern the Indians without their consent; we govern our Territories without their consent; we govern our children without their consent. I answer, would not the natives of the Philippines prefer the just, humane, civilizing government of this Republic to the savage, bloody rule of pillage and extortion from which we have rescued them? Do not the blazing fires of joy and the ringing bells of gladness in Porto Rico prove the welcome of our flag? And regardless of this formula of words made only for enlightened, selfgoverning peoples, do we owe no duty to the world? Shall we turn these peoples back to the reeking hands from which we have taken them? Shall we save them from those nations, to give them to a self-rule of tragedy? It would be like giving a razor to a babe and telling it to shave itself. It would be like giving a typewriter to an Esquimau and telling him to publish one of the great dailies of the world.

. . .

Distance and oceans are no longer arguments. The fact that all the territory our fathers bought and seized is contiguous is no longer an argument. In 1819 Florida was further from New York than Porto Rico is from Chicago today; Texas further from Washington in 1845 than Hawaii is from Boston in 1898; California more inaccessible in 1847 than the Philippines are now. Gibraltar is further from London than Havana is from Washington; Melbourne is further from Liverpool than Manila is from San Francisco. The ocean does not separate us from the lands of our duty and desire—the ocean to join us, a river never to be dredged, a canal never to be repaired. Steam joins us; electricity joins us—the very elements are in league with our destiny. Cuba not contiguous! Porto Rico not contiguous! Hawaii and the Philippines not contiguous! Our navy will make them contiguous. Dewey and Sampson and Schley have made them contiguous and American speed, American guns, American heart and brain and nerve will keep them contiguous forever.

But there is a difference. We did not need the western Mississippi valley when we acquired it, nor Florida, nor Texas, nor California, nor the royal provinces of the far Northwest. We had no emigrants to people this vast wilder-

ness, no money to develop it, even no highways to cover it. No trade awaited us in its
savage fastnesses. Our productions were not
greater than our internal trade. There was not
one reason for the land lust of our statesmen
from Jefferson to Harrison other than the
prophet and the Saxon within them. But today,
we are raising more than we can consume. To-
day, we are making more than we can use.
Therefore, we must find new markets for our
produce, new occupation for our capital, new
work for our labor. And so, while we did not
need the territory taken during the past century at the time it was acquired, we do need
what we have taken in 1898, and we need it
now. Think of the thousands of Americans who
will pour into Hawaii and Porto Rico when the
Republic's laws cover those islands with justice
and safety. Think of the tens of thousands of
Americans who will invade the Philippines
when a liberal government shall establish order
and equity there. Think of the hundreds of
thousands of Americans who will build a soap-
and-water, common school civilization of energy and industry in Cuba, when a government
of law replaces the double reign of anarchy and
tyranny. Think of the prosperous millions that
empress of islands will support when, obedient
to the law of political gravitation, her people
ask for the highest honor liberty can bestow
—the sacred order of the stars and stripes, the
citizenship of the great Republic!

What does all this mean for every one of us?
First of all, it means opportunity for all the
glorious young manhood of the Republic. It
means that the resources and the commerce of
those immensely rich dominions will be increased as much as American energy is greater
than Spanish sloth; for Americans, henceforth,
will monopolize those resources and that commerce. In Cuba, alone, there are 15,000,000
acres of forest unacquainted with the ax. There
are exhaustless mines of iron. There are priceless deposits of manganese. There are millions
of acres yet unexplored. The resources of Porto
Rico have only been trifled with. The resources
of the Philippines have hardly been touched by
the finger tips of modern methods. And they
produce what we cannot, and they consume
what we produce—the very predestation of
reciprocity. And William McKinley intends that
their trade shall be ours. It means an opportunity for the rich man to do something
with his money, besides hoarding it or lending
it. It means occupation for every working-

man in the country at wages which the development of new resources, the launching
of new enterprises, the monopoly of new
markets always brings. Cuba is as large as
Pennsylvania, and is the richest spot on all
the globe. Hawaii is as large as New Jersey;
Porto Rico half as large as Hawaii; the
Philippines larger than all New England, New
York, New Jersey and Delaware. The trade of
these islands, developed as we will develop it, 10
will set every reaper in the Republic singing,
every furnace spouting the flames of industry. . . .

Now on the threshold of our career as the
first power of earth, is the time to permanently
adjust our system of finance. The American
people have the most tremendous tasks of history to perform. They have the mightiest com- 20
merce of the world to conduct. They cannot
halt their progress of wealth and power to unsettle their money system at the command of
ignorance. Think of Great Britain becoming the
commercial monarch of the world with her financial system periodically assailed! Think of
Holland or Germany or France yet sending
their flag in every sea, with their money at the
mercy of politicians seeking for an issue! Sixteen to one is passed in our career. Why go 30
back to it, like the victim of opium to his deadly
pipe? Now, when new rivers of gold are pouring through the fields of business, the foundation of all silver-standard argument that there
is not enough gold, is swept away. Why mum-
ble the meaningless phrases of a tale that is
told when the golden future is before us, the
world calls us, its wealth awaits us and God's
command is on us? There are so many real
things to be done—canals to be dug, railways 40
to be laid, forests to be felled, cities to be
builded, unviolated fields to be tilled, priceless
markets to be won, ships to be launched, peoples to be saved, civilization to be proclaimed
and the flag of liberty flung to the eager air of
every sea. Is this an hour to waste upon triflers
with Nature's laws? Is this a season to give
our destiny over word mongers and prosperity
wreckers? No! It is an hour to remember your
duty to the home. It is a moment to realize the 50
opportunities Fate has opened to this favored
people and to you. It is a time to bethink you
of your Nation and its sovereignty of the seas.
It is a time to remember that the God of our
fathers is our God and that the gifts and the

duties He gave to them, enriched and multiplied, He renews to us, their children. It is a time to sustain that devoted man, servant of the people and of the most high God, who is guiding the Republic out into the ocean of infinite possibilities. It is a time to cheer the beloved President of God's chosen people, till the whole world is vocal with American loyalty to the American government and William McKinley, its head and chief.

Fellow-Americans, we are God's chosen people. Yonder at Bunker Hill and Yorktown His providence was above us. At New Orleans and on ensanguined seas His hand sustained us. Abraham Lincoln was His minister, and His was the altar of freedom the boys in blue set up on a hundred smoking battlefields. His power directed Dewey in the east, and He delivered the Spanish fleet into our hands on Liberty's natal day as He delivered the elder Armada into the hands of our English sires two centuries ago. His great purposes are revealed in the progress of the flag, which surpasses the intentions of Congresses and Cabinets, and leads us, like a holier pillar of cloud by day and pillar of fire by night, into situations unforeseen by finite wisdom and duties unexpected by the unprophetic heart of selfishness. The American people cannot use a dishonest medium of exchange; it is ours to set the world its example of right and honor. We cannot fly from our world duties; it is ours to execute the purposes of a fate that has driven us to be greater than our small intentions. We cannot retreat from any soil where Providence has unfurled our banner; it is ours to save that soil for liberty and civilization. For liberty and civilization and God's promises fulfilled, the flag must henceforth be the symbol and the sign to all mankind.   1898

WILLIAM JAMES

1842–1910

WITH a faith in the meliorability of existing institutions and of human kind, William James lent his prestige to the organized struggle against war. No one had so succinctly and effectively suggested that peace could be achieved only if the human and social problems which war *seemed* to solve were more effectively solved by less destructive instruments than heavy artillery. James pointed to the need of the individual for participation in a collective enterprise to which he could idealistically contribute his surplus moral energy in some hazardous and adventuresome undertaking. He coupled this need, based, as he saw it, on a fundamental human craving or instinct, with that for the constructive employment of youth in projects for civic betterment. Although *The Moral Equivalent of War* was welcomed by pacifists and given wide publicity, the necessary private and public support was not forthcoming to put James's suggestion to a pragmatic test.

Merle Curti, *Peace or War: the American Struggle, 1636–1936*, New York, 1936.

» » THE MORAL EQUIVALENT OF WAR « «

The war against war is going to be no holiday excursion or camping party. The military feelings are too deeply grounded to abdicate their place among our ideals until better substitutes are offered than the glory and shame that come to nations as well as to individuals from the ups and downs of politics and the vicissitudes of trade. There is something highly paradoxical in the modern man's relation to war. Ask all our millions, north and south, whether they would vote now (were such a thing possible) to have our war for the Union expunged from history and the record of a peaceful transition to the present time substituted for that of its marches and battles, and probably hardly a handful of eccentrics would say yes. Those ancestors, those efforts, those memories and legends, are the most ideal part of what we now own together, a sacred spiritual possession worth more than all the blood poured out. Yet ask those same people whether they would be willing in cold blood to start another civil war now to gain another similar possession, and not one man or woman would vote for the proposition. In modern eyes, precious though wars may be, they must not be waged solely for the sake of the ideal harvest. Only when forced upon one, only when an enemy's injustice leaves us no alternative, is a war now thought permissible.

It was not thus in ancient times. The earlier men were hunting men, and to hunt a neighboring tribe, kill the males, loot the village and possess the females, was the most profitable, as well as the most exciting, way of living. Thus were the more martial tribes selected, and in chiefs and peoples a pure pugnacity and love of glory came to mingle with the more fundamental appetite for plunder.

Modern war is so expensive that we feel trade to be a better avenue to plunder; but modern man inherits all the innate pugnacity and all the love of glory of his ancestors. Showing war's irrationality and horror is of no effect upon him. The horrors make the fascination. War is the *strong* life; it is life *in extremis;* war-taxes are the only ones men never hesitate to pay, as the budgets of all nations show us.

History is a bath of blood. The Iliad is one long recital of how Diomedes and Ajax, Sarpedon and Hector *killed.* No detail of the wounds they made is spared us, and the Greek mind fed upon the story. Greek history is a panorama of jingoism and imperialism—war for war's sake, all the citizens being warriors. It is horrible reading, because of the irrationality of it all—save for the purpose of making "history" —and the history is that of the utter ruin of civilization in intellectual respects perhaps the highest the earth has ever seen.

Those wars were purely piratical. Pride, gold, women, slaves, excitement, were their only motives. In the Peloponnesian war, for example, the Athenians ask the inhabitants of Melos (the island where the "Venus of Milo" was found), hitherto neutral, to own their lordship. The envoys meet, and hold a debate which Thucydides gives in full, and which, for sweet reasonableness of form, would have satisfied Matthew Arnold. "The powerful exact what they can," said the Athenians, "and the weak grant what they must." When the Meleans say that sooner than be slaves they will appeal to the gods, the Athenians reply: "Of the gods we believe and of men we know that, by a law of their nature, wherever they can rule they will. This law was not made by us, and we are not the first to have acted upon it; we did but inherit it, and we know that you and all mankind, if you were as strong as we are, would do as we do. So much for the gods; we have told you why we expect to stand as high in their good opinion as you." Well, the Meleans still refused, and their town was taken. "The Athenians," Thucydides quietly says, "thereupon put to death all who were of military age and made slaves of the women and children. They then colonized the island, sending thither five hundred settlers of their own."

Alexander's career was piracy pure and simple, nothing but an orgy of power and plunder, made romantic by the character of the hero. There was no rational principle in it, and the moment he died his generals and governors attacked one another. The cruelty of those times is incredible. When Rome finally conquered Greece, Paulus Æmilius was told by the Roman Senate to reward his soldiers for their toil by "giving" them the old kingdom of Epirus. They sacked seventy cities and carried off a hundred and fifty thousand inhabitants as slaves. How many they killed I know not; but in Etolia they killed all the senators, five hundred and fifty in number. Brutus was "the noblest Roman of them all," but to reanimate his soldiers on the eve of Philippi he similarly promises to give them the cities of Sparta and Thessalonica to ravage, if they win the fight.

Such was the gory nurse that trained societies to cohesiveness. We inherit the warlike type; and for most of the capacities of heroism that the human race is full of we have to thank this cruel history. Dead men tell no tales, and if there were any tribes of other type than this they have left no survivors. Our ancestors have bred pugnacity into our bone and marrow, and thousands of years of peace won't breed it out of us. The popular imagination fairly fattens on the thought of wars. Let public opinion once reach a certain fighting pitch, and no ruler can withstand it. In the Boer war both governments began with bluff but couldn't stay there; the military tension was too much for them. In

1898 our people had read the word "war" in letters three inches high for three months in every newspaper. The pliant politician Mc-Kinley was swept away by their eagerness, and our squalid war with Spain became a necessity.

At the present day, civilized opinion is a curious mental mixture. The military instincts and ideals are as strong as ever, but are confronted by reflective criticisms which sorely curb their ancient freedom. Innumerable writers are showing up the bestial side of military service. Pure loot and mastery seem no longer morally avowable motives, and pretexts must be found for attributing them solely to the enemy. England and we, our army and navy authorities repeat without ceasing, arm solely for "peace," Germany and Japan it is who are bent on loot and glory. "Peace" in military mouths today is a synonym for "war expected." The word has become a pure provocative, and no government wishing peace sincerely should allow it ever to be printed in a newspaper. Every up-to-date dictionary should say that "peace" and "war" mean the same thing, now *in posse*, now *in actu*. It may even reasonably be said that the intensely sharp competitive *preparation* for war by the nations *is the real war*, permanent, unceasing; and that the battles are only a sort of public verification of the mastery gained during the "peace"-interval.

It is plain that on this subject civilized man has developed a sort of double personality. If we take European nations, no legitimate interest of any one of them would seem to justify the tremendous destructions which a war to compass it would necessarily entail. It would seem as though common sense and reason ought to find a way to reach agreement in every conflict of honest interests. I myself think it our bounden duty to believe in such international rationality as possible. But, as things stand, I see how desperately hard it is to bring the peace-party and the war-party together, and I believe that the difficulty is due to certain deficiencies in the program of pacificism which set the militarist imagination strongly, and to a certain extent justifiably, against it. In the whole discussion both sides are on imaginative and sentimental ground. It is but one utopia against another, and everything one says must be abstract and hypothetical. Subject to this criticism and caution, I will try to characterize in abstract strokes the opposite imaginative forces, and point out what to my own very fallible mind seems the best utopian hypothesis, the most promising line of conciliation.

In my remarks, pacifist though I am, I will refuse to speak of the bestial side of the war-*régime* (already done justice to by many writers) and consider only the higher aspects of militaristic sentiment. Patriotism no one thinks discreditable; nor does anyone deny that war is the romance of history. But inordinate ambitions are the soul of every patriotism, and the possibility of violent death the soul of all romance. The militarily patriotic and romantic-minded everywhere, and especially the professional military class, refuse to admit for a moment that war may be a transitory phenomenon in social evolution. The notion of a sheep's paradise like that revolts, they say, our higher imagination. Where then would be the steeps of life? If war had ever stopped, we should have to re-invent it, on this view, to redeem life from flat degeneration.

Reflective apologists for war at the present day all take it religiously. It is a sort of sacrament. Its profits are to the vanquished as well as to the victor; and quite apart from any question of profit, it is an absolute good, we are told, for it is human nature at its highest dynamic. Its "horrors" are a cheap price to pay for rescue from the only alternative supposed, of a world of clerks and teachers, of co-education and zo-ophily, of "consumer's leagues" and "associated charities," of industrialism unlimited, and feminism unabashed. No scorn, no hardness, no valor any more! Fie upon such a cattleyard of a planet!

So far as the central essence of this feeling goes, no healthy-minded person, it seems to me, can help to some degree partaking of it. Militarism is the great preserver of our ideals of hardihood, and human life with no use for hardihood would be contemptible. Without risks or prizes for the darer, history would be insipid indeed; and there is a type of military character which everyone feels that the race should never cease to breed, for everyone is sensitive to its superiority. The duty is incumbent on mankind, of keeping military characters in stock—of keeping them, if not for use, then as ends in themselves and as pure pieces of perfection,—so that Roosevelt's weaklings and mollycoddles may not end by making everything else disappear from the face of nature.

This natural sort of feeling forms, I think, the innermost soul of army-writings. Without any exception known to me, militarist authors take a highly mystical view of their subject, and regard war as a biological or sociological necessity, uncontrolled by ordinary psychological checks and motives. When the time of development is ripe the war must come, reason or no reason, for the justifications pleaded are invariably fictitious. War is, in short, a permanent human *obligation*. General Homer Lea, in his recent book *The Valor of Ignorance*, plants himself squarely on this ground. Readiness for war is for him the essence of nationality, and ability in it the supreme measure of the health of nations.

Nations, General Lea says, are never stationary—they must necessarily expand or shrink, according to their vitality or decrepitude. Japan now is culminating; and by the fatal law in question it is impossible that her statesmen should not long since have entered, with extraordinary foresight, upon a vast policy of conquest—the game in which the first moves were her wars with China and Russia and her treaty with England, and of which the final objective is the capture of the Philippines, the Hawaiian Islands, Alaska, and the whole of our coast west of the Sierra Passes. This will give Japan what her ineluctable vocation as a state absolutely forces her to claim, the possession of the entire Pacific Ocean; and to oppose these deep designs we Americans have, according to our author, nothing but our conceit, our ignorance, our commercialism, our corruption, and our feminism. General Lea makes a minute technical comparison of the military strength which we at present could oppose to the strength of Japan, and concludes that the islands, Alaska, Oregon, and Southern California, would fall almost without resistance, that San Francisco must surrender in a fortnight to a Japanese investment, that in three or four months the war would be over, and our republic, unable to regain what it had heedlessly neglected to protect sufficiently, would then "disintegrate," until perhaps some Cæsar should arise to weld us again into a nation.

A dismal forecast indeed! Yet not unplausible, if the mentality of Japan's statesmen be of the Cæsarian type of which history shows so many examples, and which is all that General Lea seems able to imagine. But there is no reason to think that women can no longer be the mothers of Napoleonic or Alexandrian characters; and if these come in Japan and find their opportunity, just such surprises as *The Valor of Ignorance* paints may lurk in ambush for us. Ignorant as we still are of the innermost recesses of Japanese mentality, we may be foolhardy to disregard such possibilities.

Other militarists are more complex and more moral in their considerations. The *Philosophie des Krieges*, by S. R. Steinmetz, is a good example. War, according to this author, is an ordeal instituted by God, who weighs the nations in its balance. It is the essential form of the State, and the only function in which peoples can employ all their powers at once and convergently. No victory is possible save as the resultant of a totality of virtues, no defeat for which some vice or weakness is not responsible. Fidelity, cohesiveness, tenacity, heroism, conscience, education, inventiveness, economy, wealth, physical health and vigor—there isn't a moral or intellectual point of superiority that doesn't tell, when God holds his assizes and hurls the peoples upon one another. *Die Weltgeschichte ist das Weltgericht;*[1] and Dr. Steinmetz does not believe that in the long run chance and luck play any part in apportioning the issues.

The virtues that prevail, it must be noted, are virtues anyhow, superiorities that count in peaceful as well as in military competition; but the strain on them, being infinitely intenser in the latter case, makes war infinitely more searching as a trial. No ordeal is comparable to its winnowings. Its dread hammer is the welder of men into cohesive states, and nowhere but in such states can human nature adequately develop its capacity. The only alternative is "degeneration."

Dr. Steinmetz is a conscientious thinker, and his book, short as it is, takes much into account. Its upshot can, it seems to me, be summed up in Simon Patten's word, that mankind was nursed in pain and fear, and that the transition to a "pleasure-economy" may be fatal to a being wielding no powers of defence against its disintegrative influences. If we speak of the *fear of emancipation from the fear-régime*, we put the whole situation into a single phrase; fear regarding ourselves now taking the place of the ancient fear of the enemy.

Turn the fear over as I will in my mind, it all seems to lead back to two unwillingnesses of the imagination, one æsthetic, and the other moral; unwillingness, first to envisage a future in which army-life, with its many elements of charm, shall be forever impossible, and in

[1] *Universal history is the tribunal of humanity.*

which the destinies of peoples shall nevermore
be decided quickly, thrillingly, and tragically,
by force, but only gradually and insipidly by
"evolution"; and, secondly, unwillingness to
see the supreme theater of human strenuous-
ness closed, and the splendid military aptitudes
of men doomed to keep always in a state of
latency and never show themselves in action.
These insistent unwillingnesses, no less than
other æsthetic and ethical insistencies, have, it
seems to me, to be listened to and respected.
One cannot meet them effectively by mere
counter-insistency on war's expensiveness and
horror. The horror makes the thrill; and when
the question is of getting the extremest and
supremest out of human nature, talk of expense
sounds ignominious. The weakness of so much
merely negative criticism is evident—pacificism
makes no converts from the military party. The
military party denies neither the bestiality nor
the horror, nor the expense; it only says that
these things tell but half the story. It only says
that war is *worth* them; that, taking human nature as a whole, its wars are its best protection
against its weaker and more cowardly self, and
that mankind cannot *afford* to adopt a peace-
economy.

Pacificists ought to enter more deeply into
the æsthetical and ethical point of view of their
opponents. Do that first in any controversy, says
J. J. Chapman, *then move the point*, and your
opponent will follow. So long as antimilitarists
propose no substitute for war's disciplinary
function, no *moral equivalent* of war, analogous, as one might say, to the mechanical
equivalent of heat, so long they fail to realize
the full inwardness of the situation. And as a
rule they do fail. The duties, penalties, and
sanctions pictured in the utopias they paint are
all too weak and tame to touch the military-
minded. Tolstoi's pacificism is the only exception to this rule, for it is profoundly pessimistic
as regards all this world's values, and makes
the fear of the Lord furnish the moral spur provided elsewhere by the fear of the enemy. But
our socialistic peace-advocates all believe absolutely in this world's values; and instead of
the fear of the Lord and the fear of the enemy,
the only fear they reckon with is the fear of
poverty if one be lazy. This weakness pervades
all the socialistic literature with which I am acquainted. Even in Lowes Dickinson's exquisite
dialogue, high wages and short hours are the
only forces invoked for overcoming man's distaste for repulsive kinds of labor. Meanwhile

men at large still live as they always have lived,
under a pain-and-fear economy—for those of
us who live in an ease-economy are but an island in the stormy ocean—and the whole atmosphere of present-day utopian literature
tastes mawkish and dishwatery to people who
still keep a sense for life's more bitter flavors.
It suggests, in truth, ubiquitous inferiority.

Inferiority is always with us, and merciless
scorn of it is the keynote of the military temper.
"Dogs, would you live forever?" shouted Frederick the Great. "Yes," say our utopians, "let us
live forever, and raise our level gradually." The
best thing about our "inferiors" today is that
they are as tough as nails, and physically and
morally almost as insensitive. Utopianism would
see them soft and squeamish, while militarism
would keep their callousness, but transfigure it
into a meritorious characteristic, needed by
"the service," and redeemed by that from the
suspicion of inferiority. All the qualities of a
man acquire dignity when he knows that the
service of the collectivity that owns him needs
them. If proud of the collectivity, his own pride
rises in proportion. No collectivity is like an
army for nourishing such pride; but it has to
be confessed that the only sentiment which the
image of pacific cosmopolitan industrialism is
capable of arousing in countless worthy breasts
is shame at the idea of belonging to *such* a
collectivity. It is obvious that the United States
of America as they exist today impress a mind
like General Lea's as so much human blubber.
Where is the sharpness and precipitousness, the
contempt for life, whether one's own, or another's? Where is the savage "yes" and
"no," the unconditional duty? Where is the
conscription? Where is the blood-tax? Where is
anything that one feels honored by belonging to?

Having said thus much in preparation, I will
now confess my own utopia. I devoutly believe
in the reign of peace and in the gradual advent
of some sort of a socialistic equilibrium. The fatalistic view of the war-function is to me nonsense, for I know that mar-making is due
to definite motives and subject to prudential
checks and reasonable criticisms, just like any
other form of enterprise. And when whole nations are the armies, and the science of destruction vies in intellectual refinement with the
sciences of production, I see that war becomes
absurd and impossible from its own monstrosity. Extravagant ambitions will have to be replaced by reasonable claims, and nations must

make common cause against them. I see no reason why all this should not apply to yellow as well as to white countries, and I look forward to a future when acts of war shall be formally outlawed as between civilized peoples.

All these beliefs of mine put me squarely into the antimilitarist party. But I do not believe that peace either ought to be or will be permanent on this globe, unless the states pacifically organized preserve some of the old elements of army-discipline. A permanently successful peace-economy cannot be a simple pleasure-economy. In the more or less socialistic future towards which mankind seems drifting we must still subject ourselves collectively to those severities which answer to our real position upon this only partly hospitable globe. We must make new energies and hardihood continue the manliness to which the military mind so faithfully clings. Martial virtues must be the enduring cement; intrepidity, contempt of softness, surrender of private interest, obedience to command, must still remain the rock upon which states are built—unless, indeed, we wish for dangerous reactions against commonwealths fit only for contempt, and liable to invite attack whenever a center of crystallization for military-minded enterprise gets formed anywhere in their neighborhood.

The war-party is assuredly right in affirming and reaffirming that the martial virtues, although originally gained by the race through war, are absolute and permanent human goods. Patriotic pride and ambition in their military form are, after all, only specifications of a more general competitive passion. They are its first form, but that is no reason for supposing them to be its last form. Men now are proud of belonging to a conquering nation, and without a murmur they lay down their persons and their wealth, if by so doing they may fend off subjection. But who can be sure that *other aspects of one's country* may not, with time and education and suggestion enough, come to be regarded with similarly effective feelings of pride and shame? Why should men not some day feel that it is worth a blood-tax to belong to a collectivity superior in *any* ideal respect? Why should they not blush with indignant shame if the community that owns them is vile in any way whatsoever? Individuals, daily more numerous, now feel this civic passion. It is only a question of blowing on the spark till the whole population gets incandescent, and on the ruins of the old morals of military honor, a stable

system of morals of civic honor builds itself up. What the whole community comes to believe in grasps the individual as in a vise. The war-function has grasped us so far; but constructive interests may some day seem no less imperative, and impose on the individual a hardly lighter burden.

Let me illustrate my idea more concretely. There is nothing to make one indignant in the mere fact that life is hard, that men should toil and suffer pain. The planetary conditions once for all are such, and we can stand it. But that so many men, by mere accidents of birth and opportunity, should have a life of *nothing else* but toil and pain and hardness and inferiority imposed upon them, should have *no* vacation, while others natively no more deserving never get any taste of this campaigning life at all,— *this* is capable of arousing indignation in reflective minds. It may end by seeming shameful to all of us that some of us have nothing but campaigning, and others nothing but unmanly ease. If now—and this is my idea—there were, instead of military conscription a conscription of the whole youthful population to form for a certain number of years a part of the army enlisted against *Nature*, the injustice would tend to be evened out, and numerous other goods to the commonwealth would follow. The military ideals of hardihood and discipline would be wrought into the growing fiber of the people; no one would remain blind as the luxurious classes now are blind, to man's relations to the globe he lives on, and to the permanently sour and hard foundations of his higher life. To coal and iron mines, to freight trains, to fishing fleets in December, to dish-washing, clothes-washing, and window-washing, to road-building and tunnel-making, to foundries and stoke-holes, and to the frames of skyscrapers, would our gilded youths be drafted off, according to their choice, to get the childishness knocked out of them, and to come back into society with healthier sympathies and soberer ideas. They would have paid their blood-tax, done their own part in the immemorial human warfare against nature; they would tread the earth more proudly, the women would value them more highly, they would be better fathers and teachers of the following generation.

Such a conscription, with the state of public opinion that would have required it, and the many moral fruits it would bear, would preserve in the midst of a pacific civilization the manly virtues which the military party is so afraid of seeing disappear in peace. We should get toughness without callousness, authority with as little criminal cruelty as possible, and painful work done cheerily because the duty is temporary, and threatens not, as now, to degrade the whole remainder of one's life. I spoke of the "moral equivalent" of war. So far, war has been the only force that can discipline a whole community, and until an equivalent discipline is organized, I believe that war must have its way. But I have no serious doubt that the ordinary prides and shames of social man, once developed to a certain intensity, are capable of organizing such a moral equivalent as I have sketched, or some other just as effective for preserving manliness of type. It is but a question of time, of skillful propagandism, and of opinion-making men seizing historic opportunities.

The martial type of character can be bred without war. Strenuous honor and disinterestedness abound elsewhere. Priests and medical men are in a fashion educated to it, and we should all feel some degree of it imperative if we were conscious of our work as an obligatory service to the state. We should be *owned,* as soldiers are by the army, and our pride would rise accordingly. We could be poor, then, without humiliation, as army officers now are. The only thing needed hence forward is to inflame the civic temper as past history has inflamed the military temper. H. G. Wells, as usual, sees the center of the situation. "In many ways," he says, "military organization is the most peaceful of activities. When the contemporary man steps from the street of clamorous, insincere advertisement, push, adulteration, underselling, and intermittent employment into the barrackyard, he steps on to a higher social plane, into an atmosphere of service and coöperation and of infinitely more honorable emulations. Here at least men are not flung out of employment to degenerate because there is no immediate work for them to do. They are fed and drilled and trained for better services. Here at least a man is supposed to win promotion by self-forgetfulness and not by self-seeking. And beside the feeble and irregular endowment of research by

commercialism, its little short-sighted snatches at profit by innovation and scientific economy, see how remarkable is the steady and rapid development of method and appliances in naval and military affairs! Nothing is more striking than to compare the progress of civil conveniences which has been left almost entirely to the trader, to the progress in military apparatus during the last few decades. The house appliances of today, for example, are little better than they were fifty years ago. A house of today is still almost as ill-ventilated, badly heated by wasteful fires, clumsily arranged and furnished as the house of 1858. Houses a couple of hundred years old are still satisfactory places of residence, so little have our standards risen. But the rifle or battleship of fifty years ago was beyond all comparison inferior to those we possess; in power, in speed, in convenience alike. No one has a use now for such superannuated things."

Wells adds that he thinks that the conceptions of order and discipline, the tradition of service and devotion, of physical fitness, unstinted exertion, and universal responsibility, which universal military duty is now teaching European nations, will remain a permanent acquisition, when the last ammunition has been used in the fireworks that celebrate the final peace. I believe as he does. It would be simply preposterous if the only force that could work ideals of honor and standards of efficiency into English or American natures should be the fear of being killed by the Germans or the Japanese. Great indeed is Fear; but it is not, as our military enthusiasts believe and try to make us believe, the only stimulus known for awakening the higher ranges of men's spiritual energy. The amount of alteration in public opinion which my utopia postulates is vastly less than the difference between the mentality of those black warriors who pursued Stanley's party on the Congo with their cannibal war-cry of "Meat! Meat!" and that of the "general-staff" of any civilized nation. History has seen the latter interval bridged over: the former one can be bridged over much more easily.   1910

WILLIAM JENNINGS BRYAN

1860–1925

F ROM HIS ELECTION to Congress in 1890 until his death at Dayton, Tennessee, in 1925, Bryan touched the major interests of American life—the crusade for free silver and the curbing of big business, woman's rights, prohibition, the conflict between religion and science, and war and peace. A great orator and the most popular of chatauqua speakers, Bryan was known and loved by the common people. As Secretary of State under Wilson he did not curb the imperialism in the Caribbean, against which he had stood out in 1900; nor did he stand rigorously by his first inclination to maintain American neutrality in the World War by making loans and credits to the belligerents impossible. Yet the negotiation of his famous "cooling-off treaties" and his resignation when Wilson turned against the policies which he felt alone could keep America out of the war, reflect great credit on a pacifist in high office. Bryan's pacifism, like that of the American peace movement as a whole, was moral and religious, ethical and emotional. His writings on peace include many addresses made on public and quasi-public occasions.

Speeches of William Jennings Bryan, Revised and arranged by Himself, New York, 1909.
Paxton Hibben and C. H. Grattan, *The Peerless Leader, William Jennings Bryan*, New York, 1929.
W. C. Williams, *William Jennings Bryan*, New York, 1936.
Merle Curti, *Bryan and World Peace*, Northampton, Mass., 1931.

» » *From:* THE FORCES THAT MAKE FOR PEACE [1] « «

I know of no real peace that can come in this world that will not be merely a larger manifestation of that inward peace that Christ came to bring to all who would have it. He was called the Prince of Peace. That was the name given to him a hundred years before he appeared upon the earth. By prophetic voice he was described as the Prince of Peace, and I prepared and delivered for many years an address entitled the Prince of Peace, and I did it because of the impression made upon me once when I turned back to refresh my memory about that verse in which that prophecy occurred, and I read the next verse that I did not remember, and you recall that next verse where it says, "Of the increase of his government and peace there shall be no end, for he shall judge his people with justice and with judgment." I had been reading of governments and I had occasionally read the melancholy assertion that governments, like men, had their youth, their maturity, their decay and their

death, and when I read this verse I found there is a government of which there is to be no end. "Of the increase of his government and peace there shall be no end, for he shall judge his people with justice and with judgment." And when at last the time came for the fulfilment of the prophecy and he appeared among men the angels sang, "Peace on earth, good-will toward men," and from that time to this he has been bringing peace to the hearts of men, and as he has brought peace to the hearts of men he has brought good-will among men, and I know of no foundation upon which a permanent peace can be built except the peace that is accompanied by good-will toward men.

We are not at liberty to discuss the causes of the war. That would not be neutral. We are not at liberty to pass judgment upon the responsibility of the participants. We might not be sufficiently informed to decide accurately even if we were at liberty to make the necessary investigations. The President has asked us to be neutral, and it is important that we shall be neutral. Why should we not? Why should we desire to sit in judgment upon them at this time when it is so important that we shall maintain an attitude that will make it possible for us to help them when the time arrives? How can we be angry with them? They are our kin people. Every nation at war has its sons and daughters in our land. Their blood runs in the veins of our people and not a poor soldier boy falls upon the battlefield over there on any side that does not make us sad. Neutral? Yes, we must let them know that we love them all. They must not doubt it, for unless they have confidence in us they will not trust us when the time comes, and this is the only great nation that can claim the promise of the peacemaker and be the friend of all and help them.

But what can we do, if we cannot sit in judgment upon them? If we cannot write our decrees against them, what can we do? We can discuss the basis upon which peace can be made permanent when peace comes, and, my friends, I think we might well occupy the time considering the lessons that are taught and preparing ourselves to be even more intelligent and earnest advocates of universal peace than we have been heretofore. The lessons of the war are being learned, and one of them, I think, has been learned well enough so that we can form a conclusion upon it. It has been a good while in this country since anybody advocated war as a blessing, and nobody now in Europe is praising war as a beneficent thing, and we have made some progress when not a crowned head will admit he began the war or is responsible for it. The President as soon as war broke out tendered the good offices of this country, and everyone with one accord began to make excuses and each one said it was someone else; each one said, "I did not want war. It was forced upon us." That is what they all said. I thank God the time has come when warring nations are unwilling to take the responsibility for having begun it. My friends, I can prove to you in a sentence that war is not a good thing, for if it were we would cultivate it. The things that are good we plan for, and if war was a blessing we would not wait to get it by chance; we would arrange to have it at certain intervals that we might not miss it.

It has been a long while in this country since anybody praised war as a blessing, but we have had some who thought the way to prevent it was to get ready for it, and preparedness has been the basis of the argument upon which

men have relied for increase in army and navy. If preparedness prevents war I want to be present at the next international meeting when somebody suggests that preparedness prevents war. If preparedness would prevent war there would be no war in Europe, for they were prepared. They had been preparing for a long time, with different degrees of preparation, but they were all preparing. My friends, the fallacy is exposed. Preparedness may help you if you get into a war, but it will not keep you out of war. More than that, preparedness will almost with absolute certainty lead you into war. Why? Because you cannot prepare for war unless you either are afraid of somebody or hate somebody. The people will not bear the burden of taxation. You cannot make them bend their backs to the load unless you can make them believe it is necessary; and how can you make them believe it is necessary? You have got to have somebody to whom you can point and say, "If you don't get ready they will catch you unprepared." You have got to teach them to hate somebody, and hate and hate and hate until they get a chance to lick them. That is what preparedness means, and I am glad that our President has taken his stand on the other side. He said it is not true that this nation is unprepared; that this nation will meet any emergency that arises, but that this nation will not be turned into a military camp getting ready for wars that ought not to come.

I do not know of any better way of bringing peace among nations than to have them adopt a very simple interpretation of God's Word as laid down in his commandments. The trouble has been that they have made one code of morals for one man and then a different code for a half-million men. There is no moral principle that can be limited by agreement among men, and the Bible tells us that though hand join in hand, they shall not be unpunished. It is astonishing how the moral character of an act loses itself quickly as it increases in size. If I ask you if it is wrong for one man to steal one horse, you will answer unanimously yes. If I ask you if it is wrong for twenty to join in stealing one horse, you may not answer so readily, but you will admit it is wrong. If I ask you if it is wrong for one hundred men to join in stealing one horse, you will probably incline to the belief that it is, but if the number gets big enough you may get mystified on the subject. If I ask you whether it is wrong for one man to steal another man's land, you say of course it is. Is it wrong for one hundred men to join together to steal another man's land? Probably. But suppose a nation steals some other man's land. Can you change the character of the act? Take another commandment. Thou shalt not kill! Does that mean one man shall not kill another? Of course, it means that; but is that all? Does it mean that one hundred men can join together and kill one man and excuse themselves? No; it may be more difficult to punish them if it is a great many, but it does not mean that the moral character of the act is different. And yet you go back through history and you find that three commandments have been violated: Thou shalt not covet, Thou shalt not steal, Thou shalt not kill. Those are the three commandments that nations have violated and gloried in it, and yet the Ten Commandments read, Thou shalt not covet, Thou shalt not steal, Thou shalt not kill.

My friends, we must apply these doctrines, these moral laws to big groups as well as to little groups, and when we do international law will not be as complicated as it is to-day. More than that, we have got to take from men's minds the idea that if the victim of their wrong is not able to punish them that they will go unpunished. That has been one of the fallacies of nations, and it has had much to do with war. They have gone on the theory that if they were big enough to be wrong, so big that their victims could not punish them, that it didn't matter. They do not understand God. God is not mortal, and when God made a law he did not make anybody big enough to repeal it or violate it with impunity. You understand this if you apply it to an individual. Why is it not understood when applied to a nation? Suppose you tell your boy not to steal. If you give him a reason, what is the reason? You would tell him not to steal, because you have a feeling of sympathy for the man from whom he might steal? No. You do not know from whom your boy might steal and you are not thinking about that man. You are thinking about your boy. It is the effect upon the character of your son. That is why you say, Thou shalt not steal, because you know that in the case of the individual wrong-doing destroys the wrong-doer.

It is easy for you to believe that the wages of sin is death when you are talking about individuals, because you can see the truth exemplified around you all the time. Is this truth less true because years may elapse between the crime and the punishment? You say that an agreement may be outlawed if a small crime, but you say certain crimes are never outlawed, and there is no statute of limitations when you come to God's law. It may be a generation, it may be a century, but that which a nation soweth that shall it also reap. That is the law and the spirit that destroys the nation at last.

Oh, my countrymen, why cannot we take God at his word and apply his moral law to all the world as well as to individuals. If every other nation but one joined together to trample down the rights of one and did wrong to that one and that they succeeded in destroying every life so that there was no chance of punishment from the wronged, the one who was the victim, do you think the nations would escape? No; the God who ruled over Babylon is the God who is reigning yet, and we shall build peace on a permanent foundation if we remember the laws of God are immutable and laws to be obeyed.

And then, too, I think we might with profit consider the fact that God has put the power of every truth on trial. One great author expresses it in this way. He said you can build your capitols until they reach the skies, but if they rest upon injustice the pulse of a woman will beat them down. Isn't that a strong statement? I believe it is a true statement that that which is wrong will die, that that which is right will triumph. We go out into the fields and we see that a grain of wheat put into the ground has in it an invisible germ of life that has the power to discard the body that we see, and that this thing of life can gather from the dead things about it and out of them construct a body. We understand that force through its operation, although we have no conception whatever of the force itself. My friends, the power that God has put into the simplest truth, invisible though it be, is just as irresistible and as constantly at work. How will truth grow? We only know truth lives upon the dead things about it and grows and grows until it not only triumphs, but carries to triumph those who trust it and attach themselves to it.

And then may we not consider one of the follies of the ages, and that is that you can build peace on fear? That has been the opinion of man all along the path of history. Time after time some nation reaches a position where it is greater than all the rest and it boasts that it will live forever, and it gathers its strength about it —its material strength—and boasts and brags and in a little while it is gone. The path of his·

tory is strewn with the wrecks of nations that boasted of their strength and thought that they could compel peace by making people afraid of them. That is not the basis upon which peace can rest. The nation that keeps peace through fear keeps it until it can get ready to throw off the yoke. That is what history has proven, and every war develops passions that are the seeds of wars yet to come.

10　There is one other foundation, and only one other, upon which peace can be built. It is given to us in Holy Writ, and it is given to us by all who have taught the spirit of the Book of books. Love is the only power upon which you can build a permanent peace. It is the only power upon which you can build a permanent peace between two neighbors, and there are no different rules for nations than those that apply to neighbors. The very same founda-
20　tion upon which you build the friendly intercourse of a community that gives peace in that community, that is, the foundation upon which you must build peace between nations, and, my friends, when we get through with the idea that we can keep peace by battleships and armies, and find out that we can only keep peace by recognizing the fatherhood of God and the brotherhood of men and loving our neighbors as ourselves, then we will begin.
30　There are things that will promote peace, and they are just the same things that promote peace among individuals.

We are trying now to promote peace in a very simple way. We have thirty treaties made with nations representing three-fourths of all the people on God's foot-stool. They are just little, simple treaties. They are not very long. They do not provide for arbitration. They do provide for investigation, and they are written
40　on the theory that man is normal when he is calm and not when he is mad. That is the theory, and isn't it a very simple theory? Why, my friends, calmness must be the normal condition. A man could not live a year if he was angry all the time. He would burn up before the year expired. He has to be normal most of the time or he has no strength to be angry any of the time. Now, these treaties are made on the theory that man is normal when he is calm
50　and therefore ought to arrange his international relations when he is normal. Isn't it a simple theory? When a man is angry he swaggers around and talks about what he can do and he generally overestimates it. But when he is normal he talks about what he ought to do.

Then the moral man asserts himself. Now, these treaties will help us to prevent war by giving opportunity for anger to subside. You know they used to tell us when we were young when we got mad to count ten before we said anything. Well, we thought we wouldn't take any chance on ten. We gave a year to count in before we acted on the subject, and these treaties provide that if any difference arises—no matter what it is—before the nations shall commence shooting at each other there shall be a year's time for investigation. Now, we believe it is going to help us, but, my friends, while I have great faith in the service that those treaties will render, and while I think they are a long step in advance, and while I think that as they provide that they run until one side denounces them, that they will run for thousands of years, yet I do not regard these treaties important in coöperation with the great fundamental principles that I have tried to state to you. These will help us to take time and to be calm and to consult our better natures, but why have time to consult your better natures if you have no better natures to consult? It assumes that we have better natures, and it is the purpose of the Christian churches of the world to glorify that general principle that it will not be consulted in vain during these months of investigation and deliberation.

My friends, I have just mentioned some of the things that to my mind are fundamental, and I have such faith in the power of the Gospel of Christ, I am so sure that the day prophesied will come when every knee shall bow and every tongue shall confess, that I believe we shall progress from century to century more nearly to this ideal that Christ has set up, and that in proportion as his rule becomes the rule of the world, in proportion as his spirit governs the world, there shall be increasing peace on earth. We are engaged in a great work, a work so great that in the accomplishment of it there is glory enough for all. Let us, therefore, as brethren, as children of one God, as followers of one Christ, love each other, work together, unite our efforts for all that is good, and try and bring the world together in the bonds of a universal and never ending peace, in which the rivalry among men will not be to see which can overcome, but which can lift up, not to see how much we can get from each other, but how much we can put in this world and make it better for the fact that we have lived among men.　　　1914

WOODROW WILSON

1856–1924

ALTHOUGH WILSON was re-elected in 1916, at least in part because he had kept America out of the war, the undertow of events and forces was too powerful, and his personal will for peace insufficiently strong, to maintain the equilibrium which had indeed become delicate. Wilson shared with the dominant and the intellectual classes in the East a strong pro-British sympathy; he was subject, like other Americans, to the pressure of the skillful Allied propaganda; he had little hope of promoting with any further degree of success his program of domestic reform; and there was danger of a serious economic depression or even collapse, in case the Allies, to whom we were deeply committed financially, went down in defeat. The reopening of unrestricted submarine warfare and the events following it led, on February 3, 1917, to the severing of diplomatic relations with Germany. Just prior to that, on January 22, 1917, Wilson had outlined in an address to the Senate the conditions which he believed necessary if a permanent and workable peace were to be achieved; on April 2, 1917, he delivered before the Congress his request for a declaration of war. These two addresses, which are given here, indicate that the war had become in Wilson's eyes, not the struggle for commerce and empire which he had originally conceived it to be, but a crusade to end war and to make the world safe for democracy, a crusade in which because of our interests and ideals we should join with unstinted devotion.

The Public Papers of Woodrow Wilson, R. S. Baker and W. E. Dodd, eds., 6 vols., New York, 1925–1927.
Herbert C. Hoover, *The Ordeal of Woodrow Wilson*, New York, 1955.
Arthur Walworth, *Woodrow Wilson, World Prophet*, New York, 1958.
Harley Notter, *The Origins of the Foreign Policy of Woodrow Wilson*, Baltimore, 1937.

» » THE CONDITIONS OF PEACE « «

GENTLEMEN OF THE SENATE: On the 18th of December last I addressed an identic note to the Governments of the nations now at war, requesting them to state, more definitely than they had yet been stated by either group of belligerents, the terms upon which they would deem it possible to make peace. I spoke on behalf of humanity and of the rights of all neutral nations like our own, many of whose most vital interests the war puts in constant jeopardy.

The Central Powers united in a reply which stated merely that they were ready to meet their antagonists in conference to discuss terms of peace.

The Entente Powers have replied much more definitely, and have stated, in general terms, indeed, but with sufficient definiteness to imply details, the arrangements, guarantees, and acts of reparation which they deem to be the indispensable conditions of a satisfactory settlement.

We are that much nearer a definite discussion of the peace which shall end the present war. We are that much nearer the discussion of the international concert which must thereafter hold the world at peace. In every discussion of the peace that must end this war it is taken for granted that that peace must be followed by some definite concert of power, which will make it virtually impossible that any such catastrophe should ever overwhelm us again. Every lover of mankind, every sane and thoughtful man, must take that for granted.

I have sought this opportunity to address you because I thought that I owed it to you, as the council associated with me in the final determination of our international obligations, to disclose to you without reserve the thought and purpose that have been taking form in my mind in regard to the duty of our Government in those days to come when it will be necessary to lay afresh and upon a new plan the foundations of peace among the nations.

It is inconceivable that the people of the United States should play no part in that great enterprise. To take part in such a service will be the opportunity for which they have sought to prepare themselves by the very principles and purposes of their polity and the approved practices of their Government, ever since the days when they set up a new nation in the high and honorable hope that it might in all that it was and did show mankind the way to liberty. They cannot, in honor, withhold the service to which they are now about to be challenged. They do not wish to withhold it. But they owe it to themselves and to the other nations of the world to state the conditions under which they will feel free to render it.

That service is nothing less than this—to add their authority and their power to the authority and force of other nations to guarantee peace and justice throughout the world. Such a settlement cannot now be long postponed. It is right that before it comes this Government should frankly formulate the conditions upon which it would feel justified in asking our people to approve its formal and solemn adherence to a league for peace. I am here to attempt to state those conditions.

The present war must first be ended, but we owe it to candor and to a just regard for the opinion of mankind to say that, so far as our participation in guarantees of future peace is concerned, it makes a great deal of difference in what way and upon what terms it is ended. The treaties and agreements which bring it to an end must embody terms which will create a peace that is worth guaranteeing and preserving, a peace that will win the approval of mankind, not merely a peace that will serve the several interests and immediate aims of the nations engaged.

We shall have no voice in determining what those terms shall be, but we shall, I feel sure, have a voice in determining whether they shall be made lasting or not by the guarantees of a universal covenant, and our judgment upon what is fundamental and essential as a condition precedent to permanency should be spoken now, not afterward, when it may be too late.

No covenant of coöperative peace that does not include the peoples of the new world can suffice to keep the future safe against war, and yet there is only one sort of peace that the peoples of America could join in guaranteeing.

The elements of that peace must be elements that engage the confidence and satisfy the principles of the American Governments, elements consistent with their political faith and the practical conviction which the peoples of America have once for all embraced and undertaken to defend.

I do not mean to say that any American Government would throw any obstacle in the way of any terms of peace the Governments now at war might agree upon, or seek to upset them when made, whatever they might be. I only take it for granted that mere terms of peace between the belligerents will not satisfy even the belligerents themselves. Mere agreements may not make peace secure. It will be absolutely necessary that a force be created as a guarantor of the permanency of the settlement so much greater than the force of any nation now engaged or any alliance hitherto formed or projected, that no nation, no probable combination of nations, could face or withstand it. If the peace presently to be made is to endure, it must be a peace made secure by the organized major force of mankind.

The terms of the immediate peace agreed upon will determine whether it is a peace for which such a guarantee can be secured. The question upon which the whole future peace and policy of the world depends is this:—

Is the present war a struggle for a just and secure peace or only for a new balance of power? If it be only a struggle for a new balance of power, who will guarantee, who can guarantee, the stable equilibrium of the new arrangement? Only a tranquil Europe can be a stable Europe. There must be not only a balance of power, but a community of power; not organized rivalries, but an organized common peace.

Fortunately, we have received very explicit assurances on this point. The statesmen of both of the groups of nations, now arrayed against one another, have said, in terms that could not be misinterpreted, that it was no part of the purpose they had in mind to crush their antagonists. But the implication of these assurances may not be equally clear to all, may not be the same on both sides of the water. I think it will be serviceable if I attempt to set forth what we understand them to be.

They imply, first of all, that it must be a peace without victory. It is not pleasant to say this. I beg that I may be permitted to put my own interpretation upon it and that it may be understood that no other interpretation was in my thought. I am seeking only to face realities and to face them without soft concealments. Victory would mean peace forced upon the loser, a victor's terms imposed upon the vanquished. It would be accepted in humiliation, under duress, at an intolerable sacrifice, and would leave a sting, a resentment, a bitter memory, upon which terms of peace would rest, not permanently, but only as upon quicksand.

Only a peace between equals can last; only a peace the very principle of which is equality and a common participation in a common benefit. The right state of mind, the right feeling, between nations, is as necessary for a lasting peace as is the just settlement of vexed questions of territory or of racial and national allegiance.

The equality of nations upon which peace must be founded, if it is to last, must be an equality of rights; the guarantees exchanged must neither recognize nor imply a difference between big nations and small, between those that are powerful and those that are weak. Right must be based upon the common strength, not upon the individual strength, of the nations upon whose concert peace will depend.

Equality of territory, of resources, there, of course, cannot be; nor any other sort of equality not gained in the ordinary peaceful and legitimate development of the peoples themselves. But no one asks or expects anything more than an equality of rights. Mankind is looking now for freedom of life, not for equipoises of power.

And there is a deeper thing involved than even equality of rights among organized nations. No peace can last, or ought to last, which does not recognize and accept the principle that Governments derive all their just powers from the consent of the governed, and that no right anywhere exists to hand peoples about from sovereignty to sovereignty as if they were property.

I take it for granted, for instance, if I may venture upon a single example, that statesmen everywhere are agreed that there should be a united, independent, and autonomous Poland, and that henceforth inviolable security of life, of worship, and of industrial and social development should be guaranteed to all peoples who have lived hitherto under the power of Governments devoted to a faith and purpose hostile to their own.

I speak of this not because of any desire to exalt an abstract political principle which has always been held very dear by those who have sought to build up liberty in America, but for the same reason that I have spoken of the other conditions of peace, which seem to me clearly indispensable—because I wish frankly to uncover realities. Any peace which does not recognize and accept this principle will inevitably be upset. It will not rest upon the affections or the convictions of mankind. The ferment of spirit of whole populations will fight subtly and constantly against it, and all the world will sympathize. The world can be at peace only if its life is stable, and there can be no stability where the will is in rebellion, where there is not tranquillity of spirit and a sense of justice, of freedom, and of right.

So far as practicable, moreover, every great people now struggling toward a full development of its resources and of its powers should be assured a direct outlet to the great highways of the sea. Where this cannot be done by the cession of territory it can no doubt be done by the neutralization of direct rights of way under the general guarantee which will assure the peace itself. With a right comity of arrangement no nation need be shut away from free access to the open paths of the world's commerce.

And the paths of the sea must alike in law and in fact be free. The freedom of the seas is the *sine qua non* of peace, equality, and coöperation. No doubt a somewhat radical reconsideration of many of the rules of international practice hitherto sought to be established may be necessary in order to make the seas indeed free and common in practically all circumstances for the use of mankind, but the motive for such changes is convincing and compelling. There can be no trust or intimacy between the peoples of the world without them.

The free, constant, unthreatened intercourse of nations is an essential part of the process of peace and of development. It need not be difficult to define or to secure the freedom of the seas if the Governments of the world sincerely desire to come to an agreement concerning it.

It is a problem closely connected with the limitation of naval armaments and the coöperation of the navies of the world in keeping the seas at once free and safe.

And the question of limiting naval armaments opens the wider and perhaps more difficult question of the limitation of armies and of all programs of military preparation. Difficult and delicate as those questions are, they must be faced with the utmost candor and decided in a spirit of real accommodation if peace is to come with healing in its wings and come to stay.

Peace cannot be had without concession and sacrifice. There can be no sense of safety and equality among the nations if great preponderating armies are henceforth to continue here and there to be built up and maintained. The statesmen of the world must plan for peace and nations must adjust and accommodate their policy to it as they have planned for war and made ready for pitiless contest and rivalry. The question of armaments, whether on land or sea, is the most immediately and intensely practical question connected with the future fortunes of nations and of mankind.

I have spoken upon these great matters without reserve and with the utmost explicitness because it has seemed to me to be necessary if the world's yearning desire for peace was anywhere to find free voice and utterance. Perhaps I am the only person in high authority among all the peoples of the world who is at liberty to speak and hold nothing back. I am speaking as an individual, and yet I am speaking also, of course, as the responsible head of a great Government, and I feel confident that I have said what the people of the United States would wish me to say.

May I not add that I hope and believe that I am, in effect, speaking for liberals and friends of humanity in every nation and of every program of liberty? I would fain believe that I am speaking for the silent mass of mankind everywhere who have as yet had no place or opportunity to speak their real hearts out concerning the death and ruin they see to have

come already upon the persons and the homes they hold most dear.

And in holding out the expectation that the people and the Government of the United States will join the other civilized nations of the world in guaranteeing the permanence of peace upon such terms as I have named, I speak with the greater boldness and confidence because it is clear to every man who can think that there is in this promise no breach in either our traditions or our policy as a nation, but a fulfillment rather of all that we have professed or striven for.

I am proposing, as it were, that the nations should with one accord adopt the doctrine of President Monroe as the doctrine of the world: That no nation should seek to extend its policy over any other nation or people, but that every people should be left free to determine its own policy, its own way of development, unhindered, unthreatened, unafraid, the little along with the great and powerful.

I am proposing that all nations henceforth avoid entangling alliances which would draw them into competition of power, catch them in a net of intrigue and selfish rivalry, and disturb their own affairs with influences intruded from without. There is no entangling alliance in a concert of power. When all unite to act in the same sense and with the same purpose, all act in the common interest and are free to live their own lives under a common protection.

I am proposing government by the consent of the governed; that freedom of the seas which in international conference after conference representatives of the United States have urged with the eloquence of those who are the convinced disciples of liberty; and that moderation of armaments which makes of armies and navies a power for order merely, not an instrument of aggression or of selfish violence.

These are American principles, American policies. We can stand for no others. And they are also the principles and policies of forward-looking men and women everywhere, of every modern nation, of every enlightened community. They are the principles of mankind and must prevail.   1917

» » WAR FOR DEMOCRACY AND PEACE « «

GENTLEMEN OF THE CONGRESS: I have called the Congress into extraordinary session

because there are serious, very serious, choices of policy to be made, and made immediately, which it was neither right nor constitutionally permissible that I should assume the responsibility of making.

On the 3d of February last I officially laid before you the extraordinary announcement of the Imperial German Government that on and after the first day of February it was its purpose to put aside all restraints of law or of humanity and use its submarines to sink every vessel that sought to approach either the ports of Great Britain and Ireland or the western coasts of Europe or any of the ports controlled by the enemies of Germany within the Mediterranean. That had seemed to be the object of the German submarine warfare earlier in the war, but since April of last year the Imperial Government had somewhat restrained the commanders of its undersea craft, in conformity with its promise, then given to us, that passenger boats should not be sunk and that due warning would be given to all other vessels which its submarines might seek to destroy, when no resistance was offered or escape attempted, and care taken that their crews were given at least a fair chance to save their lives in their open boats. The precautions taken were meagre and haphazard enough, as was proved in distressing instance after instance in the progress of the cruel and unmanly business, but a certain degree of restraint was observed.

The new policy has swept every restriction aside. Vessels of every kind, whatever their flag, their character, their cargo, their destination, their errand, have been ruthlessly sent to the bottom without warning and without thought of help or mercy for those on board, the vessels of friendly neutrals along with those of belligerents. Even hospital ships and ships carrying relief to the sorely bereaved and stricken people of Belgium, though the latter were provided with safe conduct through the proscribed areas by the German Government itself and were distinguished by unmistakable marks of identity, have been sunk with the same reckless lack of compassion or of principle.

I was for a little while unable to believe that such things would in fact be done by any Government that had hitherto subscribed to humane practices of civilized nations. International law had its origin in the attempt to set up some law which would be respected and observed upon the seas, where no nation has right of dominion and where lay the free highways of the world. By painful stage after stage

has that law been built up, with meagre enough results, indeed, after all was accomplished that could be accomplished, but always with a clear view, at least, of what the heart and conscience of mankind demanded.

This minimum of right the German Government has swept aside, under the plea of retaliation and necessity and because it had no weapons which it could use at sea except these, which it is impossible to employ, as it is employing them, without throwing to the wind all scruples of humanity or of respect for the understandings that were supposed to underlie the intercourse of the world.

I am not now thinking of the loss of property involved, immense and serious as that is, but only of the wanton and wholesale destruction of the lives of noncombatants, men, women, and children, engaged in pursuits which have always, even in the darkest periods of modern history, been deemed innocent and legitimate. Property can be paid for; the lives of peaceful and innocent people cannot be.

The present German submarine warfare against commerce is a warfare against mankind. It is a war against all nations. American ships have been sunk, American lives taken, in ways which it has stirred us very deeply to learn of, but the ships and people of other neutral and friendly nations have been sunk and overwhelmed in the waters in the same way. There has been no discrimination. The challenge is to all mankind. Each nation must decide for itself how it will meet it. The choice we make for ourselves must be made with a moderation of counsel and a temperateness of judgment befitting our character and our motives as a nation. We must put excited feeling away. Our motive will not be revenge or the victorious assertion of the physical might of the Nation, but only the vindication of right, of human right, of which we are only a single champion.

When I addressed the Congress on the 26th of February last I thought that it would suffice to assert our neutral rights with arms, our right to use the seas against unlawful interference, our right to keep our people safe against unlawful violence. But armed neutrality, it now appears, is impracticable. Because submarines are in effect outlaws, when used as the German submarines have been used against merchant shipping, it is impossible to defend ships against their attacks, as the law of nations has assumed that merchantmen would defend themselves against privateers or cruisers, visible craft giving chase upon the open sea. It is common prudence in such circumstances, grim necessity, indeed, to endeavor to destroy them before they have shown their own intention. They must be dealt with upon sight, if dealt with at all.

The German Government denies the right of neutrals to use arms at all within the areas of the sea which it has proscribed, even in the defense of rights which no modern publicist has ever before questioned their right to defend. The intimation is conveyed that the armed guards which we have placed on our merchant ships will be treated as beyond the pale of law and subject to be dealt with as pirates would be. Armed neutrality is ineffectual enough at best; in such circumstances and in the face of such pretensions it is worse than ineffectual; it is likely only to produce what it was meant to prevent; it is practically certain to draw us into the war without either the rights or the effectiveness of belligerents. There is one choice we cannot make, we are incapable of making: we will not choose the path of submission and suffer the most sacred rights of our Nation and our people to be ignored or violated. The wrongs against which we now array ourselves are not common wrongs; they cut to the very roots of human life.

With a profound sense of the solemn and even tragical character of the step I am taking and of the grave responsibilities which it involves, but in unhesitating obedience to what I deem my constitutional duty, I advise that the Congress declare the recent course of the Imperial German Government to be in fact nothing less than war against the Government and people of the United States; that it formally accept the status of belligerent which has thus been thrust upon it; and that it take immediate steps not only to put the country in a more thorough state of defense, but also to exert all its power and employ all its resources to bring the Government of the German Empire to terms and end the war.

What this will involve is clear. It will involve the utmost practicable coöperation in counsel and action with the Governments now at war with Germany, and, as incident to that, the extension to those Governments of the most liberal financial credits, in order that our resources may so far as possible be added to theirs.

It will involve the organization and mobilization of all the material resources of the country to supply the materials of war and serve the incidental needs of the nation in the most abundant and yet the most economical and efficient way possible.

It will involve the immediate full equipment of the navy in all respects, but particularly in supplying it with the best means of dealing with the enemy's submarines.

It will involve the immediate addition to the armed forces of the United States, already provided for by law in case of war, of at least five hundred thousand men who should, in my opinion, be chosen upon the principle of universal liability to service, and also the authorization of subsequent additional increments of equal force so soon as they may be needed and can be handled in training.

It will involve also, of course, the granting of adequate credits to the Government, sustained, I hope, so far as they can equitably be sustained by the present generation, by well-conceived taxation.

I say sustained so far as may be equitable by taxation, because it seems to me that it would be most unwise to base the credits, which will now be necessary, entirely on money borrowed. It is our duty, I most respectfully urge, to protect our people, so far as we may, against the very serious hardships and evils which would be likely to arise out of the inflation which would be produced by vast loans.

In carrying out the measures by which these things are to be accomplished, we should keep constantly in mind the wisdom of interfering as little as possible in our own preparation and in the equipment of our own military forces with the duty—for it will be a very practical duty—of supplying the nations already at war with Germany with the materials which they can obtain only from us or by our assistance. They are in the field and we should help them in every way to be effective there.

I shall take the liberty of suggesting, through the several executive departments of the Government, for the consideration of your committees, measures for the accomplishment of the several objects I have mentioned. I hope that it will be your pleasure to deal with them as having been framed after very careful thought by the branch of the Government upon whom the responsibility of conducting the war and safeguarding the Nation will most directly fall.

While we do these things, these deeply

momentous things, let us be very clear, and make very clear to all the world, what our motives and our objects are. My own thought has not been driven from its habitual and normal course by the unhappy events of the last two months, and I do not believe that the thought of the Nation has been altered or clouded by them. I have exactly the same things in mind now that I had in mind when I addressed the Senate on the 22d of January last; the same that I had in mind when I addressed the Congress on the 3d of February and on the 26th of February. Our object now, as then, is to vindicate the principles of peace and justice in the life of the world as against selfish and autocratic power, and to set up among the really free and self-governed peoples of the world such a concert of purpose and of action as will henceforth insure the observance of those principles.

Neutrality is no longer feasible or desirable where the peace of the world is involved and the freedom of its peoples, and the menace to that peace and freedom lies in the existence of autocratic Governments, backed by organized force which is controlled wholly by their will, not by the will of their people. We have seen the last of neutrality in such circumstances. We are at the beginning of an age in which it will be insisted that the same standards of conduct and of responsibility for wrong done shall be observed among nations and their Governments that are observed among the individual citizens of civilized States.

We have no quarrel with the German people. We have no feeling toward them but one of sympathy and friendship. It was not upon their impulse that their Government acted in entering this war. It was not with their previous knowledge or approval. It was a war determined upon as wars used to be determined upon in the old, unhappy days, when peoples were nowhere consulted by their rulers and wars were provoked and waged in the interest of dynasties or of little groups of ambitious men who were accustomed to use their fellowmen as pawns and tools.

Self-governed nations do not fill their neighbor States with spies or set the course of intrigue to bring about some critical posture of affairs which will give them an opportunity to strike and make conquest. Such designs can be successfully worked out only under cover and where no one has the right to ask questions. Cunningly contrived plans of deception

or aggression, carried, it may be, from generation to generation, can be worked out and kept from the light only within the privacy of courts or behind the carefully guarded confidences of a narrow and privileged class. They are happily impossible where public opinion commands and insists upon full information concerning all the Nation's affairs.

A steadfast concert for peace can never be maintained except by a partnership of demo- 10
cratic nations. No autocratic Government could be trusted to keep faith within it or observe its covenants. It must be a league of honor, a partnership of opinion. Intrigue would eat its vitals away; the plottings of inner circles who could plan what they would and render account to no one would be a corruption seated at its very heart. Only free peoples can hold their purpose and their honor steady to a common end and prefer the interests of mankind to any 20
narrow interest of their own.

Does not every American feel that assurance has been added to our hope for the future peace of the world by the wonderful and heartening things that have been happening within the last few weeks in Russia? Russia was known by those who knew it best to have been always in fact democratic at heart, in all the vital habits of her thought, in all the intimate relationships of her people that spoke 30
their natural instinct, their habitual attitude toward life. The autocracy that crowned the summit of her political structure, long as it had stood and terrible as was the reality of its power, was not in fact Russian in origin, character, or purpose; and now it has been shaken off and the great, generous Russian people have been added, in all their native majesty and might, to the forces that are fighting for freedom in the world, for justice, and for peace. 40
Here is a fit partner for a league of honor.

One of the things that has served to convince us that the Prussian autocracy was not and could never be our friend is that from the very outset of the present war it has filled our unsuspecting communities, and even our offices of government, with spies and set criminal intrigues everywhere afoot against our National unity of counsel, our peace within and without, our industries and our commerce. Indeed, 50
it is now evident that its spies were here even before the war began; and it is unhappily not a matter of conjecture, but a fact proved in our courts of justice, that the intrigues, which have more than once come perilously near to

disturbing the peace and dislocating the industries of the country, have been carried on at the instigation, with the support, and even under the personal direction of official agents of the Imperial Government, accredited to the Government of the United States.

Even in checking these things and trying to extirpate them we have sought to put the most generous interpretation possible upon them because we knew that their source lay, not in any hostile feeling or purpose of the German people toward us (who were, no doubt, as ignorant of them as we ourselves were), but only in the selfish designs of a Government that did what it pleased and told its people nothing. But they have played their part in serving to convince us at last that the Government entertains no real friendship for us, and means to act against our peace and security at its convenience. That it means to stir up enemies against us at our very doors the intercepted note to the German Minister at Mexico City is eloquent evidence.

We are accepting this challenge of hostile purpose because we know that in such a Government, following such methods, we can never have a friend; and that in the presence of its organized power, always lying in wait to accomplish we know not what purpose, can be no assured security for the democratic Governments of the world. We are now about to accept the gage of battle with this natural foe to liberty and shall, if necessary, spend the whole force of the nation to check and nullify its pretensions and its power. We are glad, now that we see the facts with no veil of false pretense about them, to fight thus for the ultimate peace of the world and for the liberation of its peoples, the German people included; for the rights of nations, great and small, and the privilege of men everywhere to choose their way of life and of obedience. The world must be made safe for democracy. Its peace must be planted upon the tested foundations of political liberty.

We have no selfish ends to serve. We desire no conquest, no dominion. We seek no indemnities for ourselves, no material compensation for the sacrifices we shall freely make. We are but one of the champions of the rights of mankind. We shall be satisfied when those rights have been made as secure as the faith and the freedom of nations can make them.

Just because we fight without rancor and without selfish object, seeking nothing for ourselves but what we shall wish to share with all free peoples, we shall, I feel confident, conduct our operations as belligerents without passion and ourselves observe with proud punctilio the principles of right and of fair play we profess to be fighting for.

I have said nothing of the Governments allied with the Imperial Government of Germany because they have not made war upon us or challenged us to defend our right and our honor. The Austro-Hungarian Government has, indeed, avowed its unqualified endorsement and acceptance of the reckless and lawless submarine warfare, adopted now without disguise by the Imperial German Government, and it has therefore not been possible for this Government to receive Count Tarnowski, the Ambassador recently accredited to this Government by the Imperial and Royal Government of Austria-Hungary; but that Government has not actually engaged in warfare against citizens of the United States on the seas, and I take the liberty, for the present at least, of postponing a discussion of our relations with the authorities at Vienna. We enter this war only where we are clearly forced into it because there are no other means of defending our right.

It will be all the easier for us to conduct ourselves as belligerents in a high spirit of right and fairness because we act without animus, not with enmity toward a people or with the desire to bring any injury or disadvantage upon them, but only an armed opposition to an irresponsible Government which has thrown aside all considerations of humanity and of right and is running amuck.

We are, let me say again, the sincere friends of the German people, and shall desire nothing so much as the early reëstablishment of intimate relations of mutual advantage between us, however hard it may be for them for the time being to believe that this is spoken from our hearts. We have borne with their present Government through all these bitter months because of that friendship, exercising a patience and forbearance which would otherwise have been impossible.

We shall happily still have an opportunity to prove that friendship in our daily attitude and actions toward the millions of men and women of German birth and native sympathy who live among us and share our life, and we shall be proud to prove it toward all who are in fact loyal to their neighbors and to the Government in the hour of test. They are most of them as true and loyal Americans as if they had never known any other fealty or allegiance. They will be prompt to stand with us in rebuking and restraining the few who may be of a different mind and purpose. If there should be disloyalty, it will be dealt with with a firm hand of stern repression; but, if it lifts its head at all, it will lift it only here and there and without countenance except from a lawless and malignant few.

It is a distressing and oppressive duty, gentlemen of the Congress, which I have performed in thus addressing you. There are, it may be, many months of fiery trial and sacrifice ahead of us. It is a fearful thing to lead this great, peaceful people into war, into the most terrible and disastrous of all wars, civilization itself seeming to be in the balance.

But the right is more precious than peace, and we shall fight for the things which we have always carried nearest our hearts—for democracy, for the right of those who submit to authority to have a voice in their own Governments, for the rights and liberties of small nations, for a universal dominion of right by such a concert of free peoples as shall bring peace and safety to all nations and make the world itself at last free.

To such a task we can dedicate our lives and our fortunes, everything that we are and everything that we have, with the pride of those who know that the day has come when America is privileged to spend her blood and her might for the principles that gave her birth and happiness and the peace which she has treasured.

God helping her, she can do no other.

1917

JANE ADDAMS

1860–1935

THE WORK of Jane Addams at Hull House made it plain that the problem of foreigners living amicably together in great American cities was only a phase of the much larger problem of international understanding. Thus she became one of the leading figures in the struggle against war. After the outbreak of the World War in 1914 she was largely instrumental in founding the Women's Peace Party, which seconded Wilson's efforts to keep America out of the war. At a meeting in 1915 of women pacifists at The Hague, Jane Addams assumed the chairmanship of the Women's International Committee for Permanent Peace, which subsequently became the Women's International League for Peace and Freedom, one of the most militant and realistic of the postwar peace organizations.

After the entrance of the United States into the European war Jane Addams, who was generally recognized as the most prominent woman in the country, maintained, at great cost, her pacifist position. Her writings on peace include *Newer Ideals of Peace* (1907) and *Peace and Bread in Time of War* (1922). This narrative, which is one of the most poignant and at the same time one of the most intelligent records of a wartime pacifist, has already become a classic in its field.

J. W. Linn, *Jane Addams*, New York, 1935.
Merle Curti, *War or Peace, the American Struggle: 1636–1936*, New York, 1936.

»　»　From: PEACE AND BREAD IN TIME OF WAR　«　«

CHAPTER VII

PERSONAL REACTIONS IN TIME OF WAR

After the United States had entered the war there began to appear great divergence among the many types of pacifists, from the extreme left, composed of non-resistants, through the middle-of-the-road groups, to the extreme right, who could barely be distinguished from mild militarists. There were those people, also, who although they felt keenly both the horror and the futility of war, yet hoped for certain beneficent results from the opportunities afforded by the administration of war; they were much pleased when the government took over the management of the railroads, insisting that government ownership had thus been pushed forward by decades; they were also sure that the War Labor Policies Board, the Coal Commission and similar war institutions would make an enormous difference in the development of the country, in short, that militarism might be used as an instrument for advanced social ends. Such justifications had their lure and one found old pacifist friends on all the war boards and even in the war department itself. Certainly we were all eager to accept whatever progressive social changes came from the quick reorganization demanded by war, and doubtless prohibition was one of these, as the granting of woman suffrage in the majority of the belligerent nations, was another. But some of us had suspected that social advance depends as much upon the process through which it is secured as upon the result itself; if railroads are nationalized solely in order to secure rapid transit of ammunition and men to points of departure for Europe, when that governmental need no longer exists what more natural than that the railroads should no longer be managed by the government?

My temperament and habit had always kept me rather in the middle of the road; in politics as well as in social reform I had been for "the best possible." But now I was pushed far toward the left on the subject of the war and I became gradually convinced that in order to make the position of the pacifist clear it was perhaps necessary that at least a small number of us should be forced into an unequivocal position. If I sometimes regretted having gone to the Woman's Congress at The Hague in 1915, or having written a book on Newer Ideals of Peace in 1911 which had made my position so conspicuously clear, certainly far oftener I was devoutly grateful that I had used such unmistakable means of expression before the time came when any spoken or written word in the interests of Peace was forbidden.

It was on my return from The Hague Congress in July, 1915, that I had my first experience of the determination on the part of the press to make pacifist activity or propaganda so absurd that it would be absolutely without influence and its authors so discredited that nothing they might say or do would be regarded as worthy of attention. I had been accustomed to newspapermen for many years and had come to regard them as a good natured fraternity, sometimes ignorant of the subject on which they asked an interview, but usually quite ready to report faithfully albeit somewhat sensationally. Hull-House had several times been the subject of sustained and inspired newspaper attacks, one, the indirect result of an exposure of the inefficient sanitary service in the Chicago Health Department had lasted for many months; I had of course known what it was to serve unpopular causes and throughout a period of campaigning for the Progressive Party I had naturally encountered the "opposition press" in various parts of the country, but this concerted and deliberate attempt at misrepresentation on the part of newspapers of all shades of opinion was quite new in my experience. After the United States entered the war, the press throughout the country systematically undertook to misrepresent and malign pacifists as a recognized part of propaganda and as a patriotic duty. We came to regard this misrepresentation as part of the war technique and in fact an inevitable consequence of war itself, but we were slow in the very beginning to recognize the situation, and I found my first experience which came long before the United States entered the war rather overwhelming.

Upon our return from the Woman's International Congress at The Hague in 1915, our local organization in New York City with others, notably a group of enthusiastic college men, had arranged a large public meeting in Carnegie Hall. Dr. Anna Howard Shaw presided and the United States delegates made a public report of our impressions in "war stricken Europe" and of the moral resources in the various countries we visited that might possibly be brought to bear against a continuation of the war. We had been much impressed with the fact that it was an old man's war, that the various forms of doubt and opposition to war had no method of public expression and that many of the soldiers themselves were far from enthusiastic in regard to actual fighting as a method of settling international difficulties. War was to many of them much more anachronistic than to the elderly statesmen who were primarily responsible for the soldiers' presence in the trenches.

It was the latter statement which was my undoing, for in illustration of it I said that in practically every country we had visited, we had heard a certain type of young soldier say that it had been difficult for him to make the bayonet charge (enter into actual hand to hand fighting) unless he had been stimulated; that the English soldiers had been given rum before such a charge, the Germans ether and that the French were said to use absinthe. To those who heard the address it was quite clear that it was not because the young men flinched at the risk of death but because they had to be inflamed to do the brutal work of the bayonet, such as disembowelling, and were obliged to overcome all the inhibitions of civilization.

Dr. Hamilton and I had notes for each of these statements with the dates and the names of the men who had made them, and it did not occur to me that the information was new or startling. I was, however, reported to have said that no soldier could go into a bayonet charge until he was made half drunk, and this in turn was immediately commented upon, notably in a scathing letter written to the *New York Times* by Richard Harding Davis, as a most choice specimen of a woman's sentimental nonsense. Mr. Davis himself had recently returned from Europe and at once became the defender of the heroic soldiers who were being traduced and belittled. He lent the weight of his name and his very able pen to the cause, but it really needed neither, for the misstatement was repeated, usually with scathing comment, from one end of the country to the other.

I was conscious, of course, that the story had struck athwart the popular and long-cherished conception of the nobility and heroism of the soldier as such, and it seemed to me at the time that there was no possibility of making any explanation, at least until the sensation should have somewhat subsided. I might have repeated my more sober statements with the explanation that whomsoever the pacifist held responsible for war, it was certainly not the young soldiers themselves who were, in a sense, its most touching victims, "the heroic youth of the world whom a common ideal tragically pitted against each other." Youth's response to the appeal made to their self-sacrifice, to their patriotism, to their sense of duty, to their high-hearted hopes for the future, could only stir one's admiration, and we should have been dull indeed had we failed to be moved by this most moving spectacle in the world. That they had so responded to the higher appeals only confirms Ruskin's statement that "we admire the soldier not because he goes forth to slay but to be slain." The fact that many of them were obliged to make a great effort to bear themselves gallantly in the final tests of "war's brutalities" had nothing whatever to do with their courage and sense of devotion. All this, of course, we had realized during our months in Europe.

After the meeting in Carnegie Hall and after an interview with President Wilson in Washington, I returned to Chicago to a public meeting arranged in the Auditorium; I was met at the train by a committee of aldermen appointed as a result of a resolution in the City Council. There was an indefinite feeling that the meeting at The Hague might turn out to be of significance, and that in such an event its chairman should have been honored by her fellow citizens. But the bayonet story had preceded me and every one was filled with great uneasiness. To be sure, a few war correspondents had come to my rescue—writing of the overpowering smell of ether preceding certain German attacks; the fact that English soldiers knew when a bayonet charge was about to be ordered because rations of rum were distributed along the trenches. Some people began to suspect that the story, exaggerated and grotesque as it had become, indicated not cowardice but merely an added sensitiveness which the modern soldier was obliged to overcome. Among the many letters on the subject which filled my mail for weeks, the bitter and abusive were from civilians or from old men to whom war experiences had become a reminiscence, the larger number and the most understanding ones came from soldiers in active service.

Only once did I try a public explanation. After an address in Chautauqua, New York, in which I had mentioned bayonets, I tried to remake my original statement to a young man of the associated press only to find it once more so garbled that I gave up in despair, quite unmoved by the young man's letter of apology which followed hard upon the published report of his interview.

I will confess that the mass psychology of the situation interested me even then and continued to do so until I fell ill with a serious attack of pleuro-pneumonia, which was the beginning of three years of semi-invalidism. During weeks of feverish discomfort I experienced a bald sense of social opprobrium and wide-spread misunderstanding which brought me very near to self pity, perhaps the lowest pit into which human nature can sink. Indeed the pacifist in war time, with his precious cause in the keeping of those who control the sources of publicity and consider it a patriotic duty to make all types of peace propaganda obnoxious, constantly faces two dangers. Strangely enough he finds it possible to travel from the mire of self pity straight to the barren hills of self-righteousness and to hate himself equally in both places.

From the very beginning of the great war, as the members of our group gradually became defined from the rest of the community, each one felt increasingly the sense of isolation which rapidly developed after the United States entered the war into that destroying effect of "aloneness," if I may so describe the opposite of mass consciousness. We never ceased to miss the unquestioning comradeship experienced by our fellow citizens during the war, nor to feel curiously outside the enchantment given to any human emotion when it is shared by millions of others. The force of the majority was so overwhelming that it seemed not only impossible to hold one's own against it, but at moments absolutely unnatural, and one secretly yearned to participate in "the folly of all mankind." Our modern democratic teaching has brought us to regard popular impulses as possessing in their general tendency a valuable capacity for evolutionary de-

velopment. In the hours of doubt and self-distrust the question again and again arises, has the individual or a very small group, the right to stand out against millions of his fellow countrymen? Is there not a great value in mass judgment and in instinctive mass enthusiasm, and even if one were right a thousand times over in conviction, was he not absolutely wrong in abstaining from this communion with his fellows? The misunderstanding on the part of old friends and associates and the charge of lack of patriotism was far easier to bear than those dark periods of faint-heartedness. We gradually ceased to state our position as we became convinced that it served no practical purpose and, worse than that, often found that the immediate result was provocative.

We could not, however, lose the conviction that as all other forms of growth begin with a variation from the mass, so the moral changes in human affairs may also begin with a differing group or individual, sometimes with the one who at best is designated as a crank and a freak and in sterner moments is imprisoned as an atheist or a traitor. Just when the differing individual becomes the centro-egotist, the insane man, who must be thrown out by society for its own protection, it is impossible to state. The pacifist was constantly brought sharply up against a genuine human trait with its biological basis, a trait founded upon the instinct to dislike, to distrust and finally to destroy the individual who differs from the mass in time of danger. Regarding this trait as the basis of self-preservation it becomes perfectly natural for the mass to call such an individual a traitor and to insist that if he is not for the nation he is against it. To this an estimated nine million people can bear witness who have been burned as witches and heretics, not by mobs, for of the people who have been "lynched" no record has been kept, but by order of ecclesiastical and civil courts.

There were moments when the pacifist yielded to the suggestion that keeping himself out of war, refusing to take part in its enthusiasms, was but pure quietism, an acute failure to adjust himself to the moral world. Certainly nothing was clearer than that the individual will was helpless and irrelevant. We were constantly told by our friends that to stand aside from the war mood of the country was to surrender all possibility of future influence, that we were committing intellectual suicide, and would never again be trusted as responsible people or judicious advisers. Who were we to differ with able statesmen, with men of sensitive conscience who also absolutely abhorred war, but were convinced that this war for the preservation of democracy would make all future wars impossible, that the price-less values of civilization which were at stake could at this moment be saved only by war? But these very dogmatic statements spurred one to alarm. Was not war in the interest of democracy for the salvation of civilization a contradiction of terms, whoever said it or however often it was repeated?

Then, too, we were always afraid of fanaticism, of preferring a consistency of theory to the conscientious recognition of the social situation, of a failure to meet life in the temper of a practical person. Every student of our time had become more or less a disciple of pragmatism, and its great teachers in the United States had come out for the war and defended their positions with skill and philosophic acumen. There were moments when one longed desperately for reconciliation with one's friends and fellow citizens; in the words of Amiel, "Not to remain at variance with existence but to reach that understanding of life which enables us at least to obtain forgiveness." Solitude has always had its demons, harder to withstand than the snares of the world, and the unnatural desert into which the pacifist was summarily cast out seemed to be peopled with them. We sorely missed the contagion of mental activity, for we are all much more dependent upon our social environment and daily newspaper than perhaps any of us realize. We also doubtless encountered, although subconsciously, the temptations described by John Stuart Mill: "In respect to the persons and affairs of their own day, men insensibly adopt the modes of feeling and judgment in which they can hope for sympathy from the company they keep."

The consciousness of spiritual alienation was lost only in moments of comradeship with the like minded, which may explain the tendency of the pacifist in war time to seek his intellectual kin, his spiritual friends, wherever they might be found in his own country or abroad.

It was inevitable that in many respects the peace cause should suffer in public opinion from the efforts of groups of people who, early in the war, were convinced that the country as a whole was for peace and who tried again and

again to discover a method for arousing and formulating the sentiment against war. I was ill and out of Chicago when the People's Council held a national convention there, which was protected by the city police but threatened with dispersion by the state troops, who, however, arrived from the capital several hours after the meeting had adjourned. The incident was most sensational and no one was more surprised than many of the members of the People's Council who thus early in the war had supposed that they were conducting a perfectly legitimate convention. The incident gave tremendous "copy" in a city needing rationalizing rather than sensationalizing at that moment. There is no doubt that the shock and terror of the "anarchist riots" occurring in Chicago years ago have left their traces upon the nervous system of the city somewhat as a nervous shock experienced in youth will long afterwards determine the action of a mature man under widely different circumstances.

On the whole, the New York groups were much more active and throughout the war were allowed much more freedom both of assembly and press, although later a severe reaction followed expressed through the Lusk Committee and other agencies. Certainly neither city approximated the freedom of London and nothing surprised me more in 1915 and again in 1919 than the freedom of speech permitted there.

We also read with a curious eagerness the steadily increasing number of books published from time to time during the war, which brought a renewal of one's faith or at least a touch of comfort. These books broke through that twisting and suppressing of awkward truths, which was encouraged and at times even ordered by the censorship. Such manipulation of news and motives was doubtless necessary in the interest of war propaganda if the people were to be kept in a fighting mood. Perhaps the most vivid books came from France, early from Romain Rolland, later from Barbusse, although it was interesting to see how many people took the latter's burning indictment of war merely as a further incitement against the enemy. On the scientific side were the frequent writings of David Starr Jordan and the remarkable book of Nicolai on "The Biology of War." The latter enabled one, at least in one's own mind, to refute the pseudo-scientific statement that war was valuable in securing the survival of the fittest. Nicolai insisted that primitive man must necessarily have been a peaceful and social animal and that he developed his intelligence through the use of the tool, not through the use of the weapon; it was the primeval community which made the evolution of man possible, and cooperation among men is older and more primitive than mass combat which is an outgrowth of the much later property instinct. No other species save ants, who also possess property, fights in masses against other masses of its own kind. War is in fact not a natural process and not a struggle for existence in the evolutionary sense. He illustrated the evolutionary survival of the fittest by two tigers inhabiting the same jungle or feeding ground, the one who has the greater skill and strength as a hunter survives and the other starves, but the strong one does not go out to kill the weak one, as the war propagandist implied; or by two varieties of mice living in the same field or barn; in the biological struggle, the variety which grows a thicker coat survives the winter while the other variety freezes to extinction, but if one variety of mice should go forth to kill the other, it would be absolutely abnormal and quite outside the evolutionary survival which is based on the adjustment of the organism to its environment. George Nasmyth's book on Darwinism and the Social Order was another clear statement of the mental confusion responsible for the insistence that even a biological progress is secured through war. Mr. Brailsford wrote constantly on the economic results of the war and we got much comfort from John Hobson's "Toward International Government," which gave an authoritative account of the enormous amount of human activity actually carried on through international organizations of all sorts, many of them under governmental control. Lowes Dickenson's books, especially the spirited challenge in "The Choice Before Us," left his readers with the distinct impression that "war is not inevitable but proceeds from definite and removable causes." From every such book the pacifist was forced to the conclusion that none save those interested in the realization of an idea are in a position to bring it about and that if one found himself the unhappy possessor of an unpopular conviction, there was nothing for it but to think as clearly as he was able and be in a position to serve his country as soon as it was possible for him to do so.

But with or without the help of good books

a hideous sensitiveness remained, for the pacifist, like the rest of the world, has developed a high degree of suggestibility, sharing that consciousness of the feelings, the opinions and the customs of his own social group which is said to be an inheritance from an almost prehuman past. An instinct which once enabled the man-pack to survive when it was a question of keeping together or of perishing off the face of the earth, is perhaps not underdeveloped in any of us. There is a distinct physical as well as moral strain when this instinct is steadily suppressed or at least ignored.

The large number of deaths among the older pacifists in all the warring nations can probably be traced in some measure to the peculiar strain which such maladjustment implies. More than the normal amount of nervous energy must be consumed in holding one's own in a hostile world. These older men, Kier Hardie and Lord Courtney in England, Jenkin Lloyd Jones, Rauchenbusch, Washington Gladden in the United States, Lammasch and Fried in Austria, had been honored by their fellow citizens because of marked ability to interpret and understand them. Suddenly to find every public utterance wilfully misconstrued, every attempt at normal relationship repudiated, must react in a baffled suppression which is health-destroying even if we do not accept the mechanistic explanation of the human system. Certainly by the end of the war we were able to understand, although our group certainly did not endorse the statement of Cobden, one of the most convinced of all internationalists: "I made up my mind during the Crimean War that if ever I lived in the time of another great war of a similar kind between England and another power, I would not as a public man open my mouth on the subject, so convinced am I that appeals to reason, conscience or interest have no force whatever on parties engaged in war, and that exhaustion on one or both sides can alone bring a contest of physical force to an end."

On the other hand there were many times when we stubbornly asked ourselves, what after all, has maintained the human race on this old globe despite all the calamities of nature and all the tragic failings of mankind, if not faith in new possibilities, and courage to advocate them. Doubtless many times these new possibilities were declared by a man who, quite unconscious of courage, bore the "sense of being an exile, a condemned criminal, a fugitive from mankind." Did every one so feel who, in order to travel on his own proper path had been obliged to leave the traditional highway? The pacifist, during the period of the war could answer none of these questions but he was sick at heart from causes which to him were hidden and impossible to analyze. He was at times devoured by a veritable dissatisfaction with life. Was he thus bearing his share of blood-guiltiness, the morbid sense of contradiction and inexplicable suicide which modern war implies? We certainly had none of the internal contentment of the doctrinaire, the ineffable solace of the self-righteous which was imputed to us. No one knew better than we how feeble and futile we were against the impregnable weight of public opinion, the appalling imperviousness, the coagulation of motives, the universal confusion of a world at war. There was scant solace to be found in this type of statement: "The worth of every conviction consists precisely in the steadfastness with which it is held," perhaps because we suffered from the fact that we were no longer living in a period of dogma and were therefore in no position to announce our sense of security! We were well aware that the modern liberal having come to conceive truth of a kind which must vindicate itself in practice, finds it hard to hold even a sincere and mature opinion which from the very nature of things can have no justification in works. The pacifist in war time is literally starved of any gratification of that natural desire to have his own decisions justified by his fellows.

That, perhaps, was the crux of the situation. We slowly became aware that our affirmation was regarded as pure dogma. We were thrust into the position of the doctrinaire, and although, had we been permitted, we might have cited both historic and scientific tests of our so-called doctrine of Peace, for the moment any sanction even by way of illustration was impossible.

It therefore came about that ability to hold out against mass suggestion, to honestly differ from the convictions and enthusiasms of one's best friends did in moments of crisis come to depend upon the categorical belief that a man's primary allegiance is to his vision of the truth and that he is under obligation to affirm it.

[1917–1918]   1922

OLIVER WENDELL HOLMES, JR.

1841–1935

THE SUPPRESSION of criticism of the official war aims, especially if it emanated from radical groups, led to the collapse of the civil liberties, a collapse which left in its wake continued efforts to repress dissident views regarding the social order. Mr. Justice Holmes, the son of the Boston Brahmin and poet, had, since his appointment to the Supreme Court in 1902, won the reputation for a humane and socially liberal interpretation of the Constitution and the law of the land. His dissenting opinions in cases involving social legislation became classics in American liberalism. Having faith in the social importance of freedom of discussion, even in times of crisis, Holmes took exception to the repressive spirit which made it hazardous for any radical to criticize either the conduct of the government during the World War, or the official war aims. His dissent from the opinion of the majority of the Supreme Court in the "Abrams v. the United States" case insisted that in accordance with the First Amendment to the Constitution "evil counsels" must be corrected by time unless they were "clearly and immediately dangerous."

Collected Legal Papers, New York, 1920, 1952.
The Dissenting Opinions of Mr. Justice Holmes, arranged, with introductory notes, by Alfred Lief, New York, 1929.
Representative Opinions of Mr. Justice Holmes, arranged, with introductory notes, by Alfred Lief, New York, 1931.
Speeches, Boston, 1918.
Felix Frankfurter, *Mr. Justice Holmes and the Supreme Court*, Cambridge, Mass., 1938.
Catherine Drinker Bowen, *Yankee from Olympus*, Boston, 1944.
Mark De Wolfe Howe, *Justice Oliver Wendell Holmes*, Cambridge, 1957.

» » *From:* ABRAMS vs. UNITED STATES[1] « «

"This indictment is founded wholly upon the publication of two leaflets which I shall describe in a moment. The first count charges a conspiracy pending the war with Germany to publish abusive language about the form of government of the United States, laying the preparation and publishing of the first leaflet as overt acts. The second count charges a conspiracy pending the war to publish language intended to bring the form of government into contempt, laying the preparation and publishing of the two leaflets as overt acts. The third count alleges a conspiracy to encourage resistance to the United States in the same war and to attempt to effectuate the purpose by publishing the same leaflets. The fourth count lays a conspiracy to incite curtailment of production of things necessary to the prosecution of the war and to attempt to accomplish it by publishing the second leaflet to which I have referred.

"The other leaflet, headed 'Workers—Wake Up,' with abusive language says that America together with the Allies will march for Russia to help the Czecho-Slovaks in their struggle against the Bolsheviki, and that this time the hypocrites shall not fool the Russian emigrants and friends of Russia in America. It tells the Russian emigrants that they now must spit in the face of false military propaganda by which their sympathy and help to the prosecution of the war have been called forth and says that with the money they have lent or are going to lend 'they will make bullets not only for the Germans but also for the Workers' Soviets of Russia,' and further, 'Workers in the ammunition factories, you are producing bullets, bayonets, cannon, to murder not only the Germans but also your dearest, best, who are in Russia fighting for freedom.' It then appeals to the same Russian emigrants at some length not to consent to the 'inquisitionary expedition to Russia,' and says that the destruction of the Russian revolution is 'the politics of the march on Russia.' The leaflet winds up by saying 'Workers, our reply to this barbaric intervention has to be a general strike!' and after a few words on the spirit of revolution, exhortations not to be afraid, and some usual tall talk, ends 'Woe unto those who will be in the way of

progress. Let solidarity live! The Rebels.'

"No argument seems to me necessary to show that these pronunciamentos in no way attack the form of government of the United States, or that they do not support either of the first two counts. What little I have to say about the third count may be postponed until I have considered the fourth. With regard to that it seems too plain to be denied that the suggestion to workers in ammunition factories that they are producing bullets to murder their dearest, and the further advocacy of a general strike, both in the second leaflet, do urge curtailment of production of things necessary to the prosecution of the war within the meaning of the Act of May 16, 1918 . . . amending §3 of the earlier Act of 1917. But to make the conduct criminal that statute requires that it should be 'with intent by such curtailment to cripple or hinder the United States in the prosecution of the war.' It seems to me that no such intent is proved.

"I am aware of course that the word intent as vaguely used in ordinary legal discussion means no more than knowledge at the time of the act that the consequences said to be intended will ensue. Even less than that will satisfy the general principle of civil and criminal liability. A man may have to pay damages, may be sent to prison, at common law might be hanged, if at the time of his act he knew facts from which common experience showed that the consequences would follow, whether he individually could foresee them or not. But, when words are used exactly, a deed is not done with intent to produce a consequence unless that consequence is the aim of the deed. It may be obvious, and obvious to the actor, that the consequence will follow, and he may be liable for it even if he forgets it, but he does not do the act with intent to produce it unless the aim to produce it is the proximate motive of the specific act, although there may be some deeper motive behind.

"It seems to me that this statute must be taken to use its words in a strict and accurate sense. They would be absurd in any other. A patriot might think that we were wasting money on aeroplanes, or making more cannon of a certain kind than we needed, and might advocate curtailment with success, yet even if

[1] Abrams et al. v. United States 250 U.S. 616, 624.

it turned out that the curtailment hindered and was thought by other minds to have been obviously likely to hinder the United States in the prosecution of the war, no one would hold such conduct a crime. I admit that my illustration does not answer all that might be said but it is enough to show what I think and to let me pass to a more important aspect of the case. I refer to the First Amendment to the Constitution that Congress shall make no law abridging the freedom of speech.

"I never have seen any reason to doubt that the questions of law that alone were before this Court in the cases of *Schenck, Frohwerk* and *Debs,* were rightly decided. I do not doubt for a moment that by the same reasoning that would justify punishing persuasion to murder, the United States constitutionally may punish speech that produces or is intended to produce a clear and imminent danger that it will bring about forthwith certain substantive evils that the United States constitutionally may seek to prevent. The power undoubtedly is greater in time of war than in time of peace because war opens dangers that do not exist at other times.

"But as against dangers peculiar to war, as against others, the principle of the right to free speech is always the same. It is only the present danger of immediate evil or an intent to bring it about that warrants Congress in setting a limit to the expression of opinion where private rights are not concerned. Congress certainly cannot forbid all effort to change the mind of the country. Now nobody can suppose that the surreptitious publishing of a silly leaflet by an unknown man, without more, would present any immediate danger that its opinions would hinder the success of the Government arms or have any appreciable tendency to do so. Publishing these opinions for the very purpose of obstructing, however, might indicate a greater danger and at any rate would have the quality of an attempt. So I assume that the second leaflet, if published for the purpose alleged in the fourth count, might be punishable. But it seems pretty clear to me that nothing less than that would bring these papers within the scope of this law.

"An actual intent in the sense that I have explained is necessary to constitute an attempt, where a further act of the same individual is required to complete the substantive crime, for reasons given in *Swift & Co. v. United States,* 196 U.S. 375, 396. It is necessary where the success of the attempt depends upon

others, because if that intent is not present the actor's aim may be accomplished without bringing about the evils sought to be checked. An intent to prevent interference with the revolution in Russia might have been satisfied without any hindrance to carrying on the war in which we were engaged.

"I do not see how anyone can find the intent required by the statute in any of the defendants' words. The second leaflet is the only one that affords even a foundation for the charge, and there, without invoking the hatred of German militarism expressed in the former one, it is evident from the beginning to the end that the only object of the paper is to help Russia and stop American intervention there against the popular government—not to impede the United States in the war that it was carrying on. To say that two phrases taken literally might import a suggestion of conduct that would have interference with the war as an indirect and probably undesired effect seems to me by no means enough to show an attempt to produce that effect.

"I return for a moment to the third count. That charges an intent to provoke resistance to the United States in its war with Germany. Taking the clause in the statute that deals with that in connection with the other elaborate provisions of the Act, I think that resistance to the United States means some forcible act of opposition to some proceeding of the United States in pursuance of the war. I think the intent must be the specific intent that I have described and for the reasons that I have given. I think that no such intent was proved or existed in fact. I also think that there is no hint at resistance to the United States as I construe the phrase.

"In this case sentences of twenty years' imprisonment have been imposed for the publishing of two leaflets that I believe the defendants had as much right to publish as the Government has to publish the Constitution of the United States now vainly invoked by them. Even if I am technically wrong and enough can be squeezed from these poor and puny anonymities to turn the color of legal litmus paper —I will add, even if what I think the necessary intent were shown—the most nominal punishment seems to me all that possibly could be inflicted, unless the defendants are to be made to suffer not for what the indictment alleges but for the creed that they avow—a creed that I believe to be the creed of ignorance and immaturity when honestly held, as I see no reason to believe that it was held here, but which, although made the subject of examination at the trial, no one has a right even to consider in dealing with the charges before the Court.

"Persecution for the expression of opinions seems to me perfectly logical. If you have no doubt of your premises or your power and want a certain result with all your heart you naturally express your wishes in law and sweep away all opposition. To allow opposition by speech seems to indicate that you think speech impotent, as when a man says that he has squared the circle, or that you do not care wholeheartedly for the result, or that you doubt either your power or your premises.

"But when men have realized that time has upset many fighting faiths, they may come to believe even more than they believe the very foundations of their own conduct that the ultimate good desired is better reached by free trade in ideas—that the best test of truth is the power of the thought to get itself accepted in the competition of the market, and that truth is the only ground upon which their wishes safely can be carried out. That, at any rate, is the theory of our Constitution. It is an experiment, as all life is an experiment. Every year if not every day we have to wager our salvation upon some prophecy based upon imperfect knowledge. While that experiment is part of our system I think that we should be eternally vigilant against attempts to check the expression of opinions that we loathe and believe to be fraught with death, unless they so imminently threaten immediate interference with the lawful and pressing purposes of the law that an immediate check is required to save the country.

"I wholly disagree with the argument of the Government that the First Amendment left the common law as to seditious libel in force. History seems to me against the notion. I had conceived that the United States through many years had shown its repentance for the Sedition Act of 1798 by repaying fines that it imposed. Only the emergency that makes it immediately dangerous to leave the correction of evil counsels to time warrants making any exception to the sweeping command, 'Congress shall make no law . . . abridging the freedom of speech.' Of course I am speaking only of expressions of opinion and exhortations, which were all that were uttered here, but I regret that I cannot put into more impressive words my belief that in their conviction upon this indictment the defendants were deprived of their rights under the Constitution of the United States."　　　　　　　　　　　　　1919

» » *The Big Money* « «

1920-1929

» » « «

MY GOD! HOW THE MONEY ROLLS IN

My sister sells snow to the snow-birds,[1]
My father makes bootlegger gin,
My mother she takes in washing,
My God! how the money rolls in!

The typical popular songs of the riotous era before the crash of 1929 were of two sorts: those like "Makin' Whoopee" and "My God! How the Money Rolls In," which express the recklessness of the period, and those like "Yes, We Have No Bananas" and "Horses, Horses, Horses," which well suggest the "goofiness" of the days of bootleg gin, the scandals of the Harding administration, and a runaway stock market. Mark Sullivan has a chapter (17) on "Tunes of the Twenties" in his *Our Times*, vol. VI.

[1] Sells cocaine to dope-takers.

The Big Money

THE CRUSADE to make the world safe for democracy, on which the Wilson administration embarked in 1917, failed to effect its main object and greatly undermined democracy at home. The repression of liberalism and radicalism incident to the pursuit of military ends continued after the armistice. Drives against "reds" became almost the order of the new day. The militant wing of the labor movement, the I.W.W., was so broken that it never again got its footing; and even the A. F. of L. sank into a decline. The Republican administrations, far from resuming the reform activity of Theodore Roosevelt and of Woodrow Wilson, turned their back on all programs for extending public control over private business. The philosophy that big business, far from menacing the people, actually brought blessings to the most obscure and humble, enjoyed wide popularity. For a moment, during the presidential campaign of 1924, liberalism rallied somewhat to the support of Robert M. La Follette, who headed an independent third party. But his failure to show any wide strength was a symptom of the faith which the American people now seemed to accept, a faith which held that anyone could make big money by playing the stockmarket, and only less than big money by eschewing reform and radicalism and letting business run the show. The Socialist party, which had mustered nearly a million votes for Debs in 1912, became inconsequential; and the Communists, who followed varying lines, failed to make much headway.

It is true that radicals and liberals protested against the prevalent acceptance of the new philosophy that business was always right and that its dominance meant perpetual prosperity. But it did liberals and radicals little good to point out that certain industries were chronically depressed, and that technological unemployment was making alarming headway. Nor did it, for the time at least, avail much that liberals pointed to the dangers in the policy of mobilizing capital for the promotion of dubious ventures in Latin America, involving as it did a blatantly imperialistic program. Only the genuine distress of a large section of agriculture caught the official ear at all. But the administrations at Washington, being business-minded, throttled the full-fledged proposals of the farmers' bloc for a drastic subsidy to agriculture. The farmers as a whole enjoyed little of the flush prosperity that seemed to prevail during the 1920's. But in spite of this, and in spite of the efforts of a sophisticated literary group to prick the bubble of complacency, and of the concern of the humanists over the prevalent materialism which they identified with the machine, most Americans believed that prosperity was as real as it was desirable, and that it had come to stay.

» »   « «

THORSTEIN VEBLEN

1857–1929

FROM THE Norwegian community in Wisconsin in which he was born, and in which he learned something of the persistence of Old World class stratification, Veblen went to Carlton College and, subsequently, to Johns Hopkins, Yale, and Cornell. But Herbert Spencer's theory of societal evolution and the Populist indictment of "the moneyed class" taught him more than any of his academic instructors. Veblen's career as a professor of economics at Chicago, Stanford, and Missouri, which was troubled and unsatisfactory, was overshadowed by the brilliant irony and penetration of his analyses of industrial capitalism and the folklore functional to it. His writings, the most important of which are *The Theory of the Leisure Class* (1899), *The Theory of Business Enterprise* (1904), *The Instinct of Workmanship and the State of the Industrial Arts* (1914), and *The Engineers and the Price System* (1921), analyze the existing economic order in terms of the conflict between productive industry and a predatory price-system. The first is characterized by creative workmanship, by the making of goods for use; the latter, by pecuniary gain, with its warlike scheme of values in the first instance and its prestige values, "conspicuous consumption" and "conspicuous leisure," in the second. Although not a reformer, Veblen taught that the price system, itself a mere step in the vast evolution of economy, was doomed by reason of its maladjustment to a technological and interdependent society. *The Higher Learning in America* (1919), from which the following selection is taken, illustrates Veblen's application of his basic ideas to academic culture.

H. W. Innes, "A Bibliography of Thorstein Veblen," *Southwestern Political and Social Science Quarterly*, X (1929–1930), 56–68.

Joseph Dorfman, *Thorstein Veblen and His America*, New York, 1934.

Douglas Dowd, ed., *Thorstein Veblen: A Critical Reappraisal*, Ithaca, 1958.

Lev E. Dobriansky, *Veblenism, A New Critique*, Washington, 1957.

David Riesman, *Thorstein Veblen, A Critical Interpretation*, New York, 1953.

» » *From:* THE HIGHER LEARNING « «

CHAPTER VIII

SUMMARY AND TRIAL BALANCE

As in earlier passages, so here in speaking of profit and loss, the point of view taken is neither that of material advantage, whether of the individuals concerned or of the community at large, nor that of expediency for the common good in respect of prosperity or of morals; nor is the appraisal here ventured upon to be taken as an expression of praise or dispraise at large, touching this incursion of business principles into the affairs of learning.

By and large, the intrusion of businesslike ideals, aims and methods into this field, with all the consequences that follow, may be commendable or the reverse. All that is matter for attention and advisement at the hands of such as aim to alter, improve, amend or conserve the run of institutional phenomena that goes to make up the current situation. The present inquiry bears on the higher learning as it comes into this current situation, and on the effect of this recourse to business principles upon the pursuit of learning.

Not that this learning is therefore to be taken as necessarily of higher and more substantial value than that traffic in competitive gain and competitive spending upon which business principles converge, and in which they find their consummate expression,—even though it is broadly to be recognized and taken account of that such is the deliberate appraisal awarded by the common sense of civilized mankind. The profit and loss here spoken for is not profit and loss, to mankind or to any given community, in respect of that inclusive complex of interests that makes up the balanced total of good and ill; it is profit and loss for the cause of learning, simply; and there is here no aspiration to pass on ulterior questions. As required by the exigencies of such an argument, it is therefore assumed, *pro forma*, that profit and loss for the pursuit of learning is profit and loss without reservation; very much as a corporation accountant will audit income and outlay within the affairs of the corporation, whereas, *qua* accountant, he will perforce have nothing to say as to the ulterior expediency of the corporation and its affairs in any other bearing.

I

Business principles take effect in academic affairs most simply, obviously and avowably in the way of a businesslike administration of the scholastic routine; where they lead immediately to a bureaucratic organization and a system of scholastic accountancy. In one form or another, some such administrative machinery is a necessity in any large school that is to be managed on a centralized plan; as the American schools commonly are, and as, more particularly, they aim to be. This necessity is all the more urgent in a school that takes over the discipline of a large body of pupils that have not reached years of discretion, as is also commonly the case with those American schools that claim rank as universities; and the necessity is all the more evident to men whose ideal of efficiency is the centralized control exercized through a system of accountancy in the modern large business concerns. The larger American schools are primarily undergraduate establishments,—with negligible exceptions; and under these current American conditions, of excessive numbers, such a centralized and bureaucratic administration appears to be indispensable for the adequate control of immature and reluctant students; at the same time, such an organization conduces to an excessive size. The immediate and visible effect of such a large and centralized administrative machinery is, on the whole, detrimental to scholarship, even in the undergraduate work; though it need not be so in all respects and unequivocally, so far as regards that routine training that is embodied in the undergraduate curriculum. But it is at least a necessary evil in any school that is of so considerable a size as to preclude substantially all close or cordial personal relations between the teachers and each of these immature pupils under their charge, as, again, is commonly the case with these American undergraduate establishments. Such a system of authoritative control, standardization, gradation, accountancy, classification, credits and penalties, will necessarily be drawn on stricter lines the more the school takes on the character of a house of correction or a penal settlement; in which the irresponsible inmates are to be held to a round of distasteful tasks and restrained from (conventionally) excessive irregularities of conduct. At the same time this recourse to such coercive control and standardization of tasks has unavoidably given the schools something of the character of a penal settlement.

As intimated above, the ideal of efficiency by force of which a large-scale centralized organization commends itself in these premises is that pattern of shrewd management whereby a large business concern makes money. The underlying businesslike presumption accordingly appears to be that learning is a merchantable commodity, to be produced on a piece-rate plan, rated, bought and sold by standard units, measured, counted and reduced to staple equivalence by impersonal, mechanical tests. In all its bearings the work is hereby reduced to a mechanistic statistical consistency, with numerical standards and units; which conduces to perfunctory and mediocre work throughout, and acts to deter both students and teachers from a free pursuit of knowledge, as contrasted with the pursuit of academic credits. So far as this mechanistic system goes freely into effect it leads to a substitution of salesmanlike proficiency—a balancing of bargains in staple credits—in the place of scientific capacity and addiction to study.

The salesmanlike abilities and the men of affairs that so are drawn into the academic personnel, are presumably, somewhat under grade in their kind; since the pecuniary inducement offered by the schools is rather low as compared with the remuneration for office work of a similar character in the common run of business occupations, and since businesslike employés of this kind may fairly be presumed to go unreservedly to the highest bidder. Yet these more unscholarly members of the staff will necessarily be assigned the more responsible and discretionary positions in the academic organization; since under such a scheme of standardization, accountancy and control, the school becomes primarily a bureaucratic organization, and the first and unremitting duties of the staff are those of official management and accountancy. The further qualifications requisite in the members of the academic staff will be such as make for vendibility,—volubility, tactful effrontery, conspicuous conformity to the popular taste in all matters of opinion, usage and conventions.

The need of such a businesslike organization asserts itself in somewhat the same degree in which the academic policy is guided by considerations of magnitude and statistical renown; and this in turn is somewhat closely correlated with the extent of discretionary power exercised by the captain of erudition placed in control. At the same time, by provocation of the facilities which it offers for making an impressive demonstration, such bureaucratic organization will lead the university management to bend its energies with somewhat more singleness to the parade of magnitude and statistical gains. It also, and in the same connection, provokes to a persistent and detailed surveillance and direction of the work and manner of life of the academic staff, and so it acts to shut off initiative of any kind in the work done.

Intimately bound up with this bureaucratic officialism and accountancy, and working consistently to a similar outcome, is the predilection for "practical efficiency"—that is to say, for pecuniary success—prevalent in the American community. This predilection is a matter of settled habit, due, no doubt, to the fact that preoccupation with business interests characterizes this community in an exceptional degree, and that pecuniary habits of thought consequently rule popular thinking in a peculiarly uncritical and prescriptive fashion. This pecuniary animus falls in with and reinforces the movement for academic accountancy, and combines with it to further a so-called "practical" bias in all the work of the schools.

It appears, then, that the intrusion of business principles in the universities goes to weaken and retard the pursuit of learning, and therefore to defeat the ends for which a university is maintained. This result follows, primarily, from the substitution of impersonal, mechanical relations, standards and tests, in the place of personal conference, guidance and association between teachers and students; as also from the imposition of a mechanically standardized routine upon the members of the staff, whereby any disinterested preoccupation with scholarly or scientific inquiry is thrown into the background and falls into abeyance. Few if any who are competent to speak in these premises will question that such has been the outcome. To offset against this work of mutilation and retardation there are certain gains in expedition, and in the volume of traffic that can be carried by any given equipment and corps of employés. Particularly will there be a gain in the statistical showing, both as regards the volume of instruction offered, and probably also as regards the enrolment; since accountancy creates statistics and its absence does not.

Such increased enrolment as may be due to businesslike management and methods is an increase of undergraduate enrolment. The net effect as regards the graduate enrolment—apart from any vocational instruction that may euphemistically be scheduled as "graduate"—is in all probability rather a decrease than an increase. Through indoctrination with utilitarian (pecuniary) ideals of earning and spend-

ing, as well as by engendering spendthrift and sportsmanlike habits, such a businesslike management diverts the undergraduate students from going in for the disinterested pursuit of knowledge, and so from entering on what is properly university work; as witness the relatively slight proportion of graduate students—outside of the professional schools—who come up from the excessively large undergraduate departments of the more expansive universities, as contrasted with the number of those who come into university work from the smaller and less businesslike colleges.

The ulterior consequences that follow from such businesslike standardization and bureaucratic efficiency are evident in the current state of the public schools; especially as seen in the larger towns, where the principles of business management have had time and scope to work out in a fair degree of consistency. The resulting abomination of desolation is sufficiently notorious. And there appears to be no reason why a similarly stale routine of futility should not overtake the universities, and give similarly foolish results, as fast as the system of standardization, accountancy and piece-work goes consistently into effect,—except only for the continued enforced employment of a modicum of impracticable scholars and scientists on the academic staff, whose unbusinesslike scholarly proclivities and inability to keep the miner's-inch of scholastic credit always in mind, must in some measure always defeat the perfect working of standardization and accountancy.

As might be expected, this régime of graduated sterility has already made fair headway in the undergraduate work, especially in the larger undergraduate schools; and this in spite of any efforts on the part of the administration to hedge against such an outcome by recourse to an intricate system of electives and a wide diversification of the standard units of erudition so offered.

In the graduate work the like effect is only less visible, because the measures leading to it have come into bearing more recently, and hitherto less unreservedly. But the like results should follow here also, just so fast and so far as the same range of business principles come to be worked into the texture of the university organization in the same efficacious manner as they have already taken effect in the public schools. And, pushed on as it is by the progressive substitution of men imbued with the tastes and habits of practical affairs, in the place of unpractical scholarly ideals, the movement towards a perfunctory routine of mediocrity should logically be expected to go forward at a progressively accelerated rate. The visible drift of things in this respect in the academic pursuit of the social sciences, so-called, is an argument as to what may be hoped for in the domain of academic science at large. It is only that the executive is actuated by a sharper solicitude to keep the academic establishment blameless of anything like innovation or iconoclasm at this point; which reinforces the drift toward a mechanistic routine and a curtailment of inquiry in this field; it is not that these sciences that deal with the phenomena of human life lend themselves more readily to mechanical description and enumeration than the material sciences do, nor is their subject matter intrinsically more inert or less provocative of questions.

1918

ADKINS et al. v. CHILDREN'S HOSPITAL

ALTHOUGH the Supreme Court in the Muller Case of 1908 had opened a wedge for social legislation for the protection of working women, the Court in 1923, in the decision *Adkins* et al. v. *Children's Hospital*, declared that a congressional law providing for the establishment of minimum wages for women and children in the District of Columbia was unconstitutional. With Mr. Chief Justice Taft, Mr. Justice Sanford, and Mr. Justice Holmes dissenting, the Court held that the act, which was designed to protect women and minors "from conditions detrimental to their health and morals, resulting from wages which are inadequate to maintain decent standards of living," was a violation of the Fifth Amendment. The decision of the Court in this case seemed to mirror the postwar conservatism, which was reflected also in the rejection of the child labor amendment, the decline of the American Federation of Labor, the hostility of the public toward organized labor, and the increasing favoritism shown by government and people toward the point of view of corporate business.

» » *From:* ADKINS et al. v. CHILDREN'S HOSPITAL « «

261 United States, 525

. . . Mr. Justice Sutherland delivered the opinion of the court. . . .

The statute now under consideration is attacked upon the ground that it authorizes an unconstitutional interference with the freedom of contract included within the guaranties of the due process clause of the Fifth Amendment. That the right to contract about one's affairs is a part of the liberty of the individual protected by this clause is settled by the decisions of this court and is no longer open to question. . . .

Within this liberty are contracts of employment of labor. In making such contracts, generally speaking, the parties have an equal right to obtain from each other the best terms they can as the result of private bargaining. . . .

There is, of course, no such thing as absolute freedom of contract. It is subject to a great variety of restraints. But freedom of contract is, nevertheless, the general rule and restraint the exception, and the exercise of legislative authority to abridge it can be justified only by the existence of exceptional circumstances. Whether these circumstances exist in the present case constitutes the question to be answered. It will be helpful to this end to review some of the decisions where the interference has been upheld and consider the grounds upon which they rest.

(1) *Those dealing with statutes fixing rates and charges to be exacted by businesses impressed with a public interest.* . . . In the case at bar the statute does not depend upon the existence of a public interest in any business to be affected, and this class of cases may be laid aside as inapplicable.

(2) *Statutes relating to contracts for the performance of public work. . . .* These cases sustain such statutes as depending, not upon the right to condition private contracts, but upon the right of the government to prescribe the conditions upon which it will permit work of a public character to be done for it, or, in the case of a state, for its municipalities. We may therefore, in like manner, dismiss these decisions from consideration as inapplicable.

(3) *Statutes prescribing the character, methods, and time for payment of wages. . . .* Their tendency and purpose was to prevent unfair, and perhaps fradulent, methods in the payment of wages, and in no sense can they be said to be, or to furnish a precedent for, wage-fixing statutes.

(4) *Statutes fixing hours of labor.* It is upon this class that the greatest emphasis is laid in argument and, therefore, and because such cases approach most nearly the line of principle applicable to the statute here involved, we shall consider them more at length.

[The court here reviews earlier labor decisions including that in the Lochner Case, stating in regard to this famous decision: "Subsequent cases in this court have been distinguished from that decision, but the principles therein stated have never been disapproved."]

If now, in the light furnished by the foregoing exceptions to the general rule forbidding legislative interference with freedom of contract, we examine and analyze the statute in question, we shall see that it differs from them in every material respect. It is not a law dealing with any business charged with a public interest or with public work, or to meet and tide over a temporary emergency. It has nothing to do with the character, methods of labor or conditions under which labor is to be done. It is not for the protection of persons under legal disability or for the prevention of fraud. It is simply and exclusively a price-fixing law, confined to adult women (for we are not now considering the provisions relating to minors), who are legally as capable of contracting for themselves as men. It forbids two parties having lawful capacity—under penalties as to the employer—to freely contract with one another in respect of the price for which one shall render service to the other in a purely private employment where both are willing, perhaps anxious, to agree, even though the consequence may be to oblige one to surrender a desirable engagement and the other to dispense with the services of a desirable employee. The price fixed by the board need have no relation to the capacity or earning power of the employee, the number of hours which may happen to constitute the day's work, the character of the place where the work is to be done, or the circumstances or surroundings of the employment, and, while it has no other basis to support its validity than the assumed necessities of the employee, it takes no account of any independent resources she may have. It is based wholly on the opinions of the members of the board and their advisers—perhaps an average of their opinions, if they do not precisely agree—as to what will be necessary to provide a living for a woman, keep her in health and preserve her morals. It applies to any and every occupation in the District, without regard to its nature or the character of the work.

The standard furnished by the statute for the guidance of the board is so vague as to be impossible of practical application with any reasonable degree of accuracy. What is sufficient to supply the necessary cost of living for a woman worker and maintain her in good health and protect her morals is obviously not a precise or unvarying sum—not even approximately so. The amount will depend upon a variety of circumstances: The individual temperament, habits of thrift, care, ability to buy necessaries intelligently, and whether the woman live alone or with her family. To those who practice economy, a given sum will afford comfort, while to those of contrary habit the same sum will be wholly inadequate. The co-operative economies of the family group are not taken into account, though they constitute an important consideration in estimating the cost of living, for it is obvious that the individual expense will be less in the case of a member of a family than in the case of one living alone. The relation between earnings and morals is not capable of standardization. It cannot be shown that well-paid women safe-guard their morals more carefully than those who are poorly paid. Morality rests upon other considerations than wages, and there is, certainly, no such prevalent connection between the two as to justify a broad attempt to adjust the latter with reference to the former. As a means of safeguarding morals the attempted classification, in our opinion, is without reasonable basis. No distinction can be made between women who work for others and those who do not; nor is there ground for distinction between women and men, for, certainly, if women require a minimum wage to preserve their morals men require it to preserve their honesty. For these reasons, and others which might be stated, the inquiry in respect of the necessary cost of living and of the income necessary to preserve health and morals presents an individual and not a composite question, and must be answered for each individual considered by herself and not a composite question, and must be answered for each individual considered by herself and not by a general formula prescribed by a statutory bureau.

This uncertainty of the statutory standard is demonstrated by a consideration of certain orders of the board already made. These orders fix the sum to be paid to a woman employed in a place where food is served or in a mercantile establishment, at $16.50 per week; in a printing establishment, at $15.50 per week; and in a laundry, at $15 per week, with a provision reducing this to $9 in the case of a beginner. If a woman employed to serve food requires a minimum of $16.50 per week, it is hard to understand how the same woman working in a printing establishment or in a laundry is to get on with an income lessened by from $1 to $7.50 per week. The board probably found it impossible to follow the indefinite standard of the statute, and brought other and different factors into the problem; and this goes farther in the direction of demonstrating the fatal uncertainty of the act, an infirmity which, in our opinion, plainly exists.

The law takes account of the necessities of only one party to the contract. It ignores the necessities of the employer by compelling him to pay not less than a certain sum, not only whether the employee is capable of earning it, but irrespective of the ability of his business to sustain the burden, generously leaving him, of course, the privilege of abandoning his business as an alternative for going on at a loss. Within the limits of the minimum sum, he is precluded, under penalty of fine and imprisonment, from adjusting compensation to the differing merits of his employees. It compels him to pay at least the sum fixed in any event, because the employee needs it, but requires no service of equivalent value from the employee. It therefore undertakes to solve but one-half of the problem. The other half is the establishment of a corresponding standard of efficiency, and this forms no part of the policy of the legislation, although in practice the former half without the latter must lead to ultimate failure, in accordance with the inexorable law that no one can continue indefinitely to take out more than he puts in without ultimately exhausting the supply. The law is not confined to the great and powerful employers but embraces those whose bargaining power may be as weak as that of the employee. It takes no account of periods of stress and business depression, of crippling losses, which may leave the employer himself without adequate means of livelihood. To the extent that the sum fixed exceeds the fair value of the services rendered, it amounts to a compulsory exaction from the employer for the support of a partially indigent person, for whose condition there rests upon him no peculiar responsibility, and therefore, in effect, arbitrarily shifts to his shoulders a burden which, if it belongs to anybody, belongs to society as a whole.

The feature of this statute, which perhaps more than any other, puts upon it the stamp of invalidity, is that it exacts from the employer an arbitrary payment for a purpose and upon a basis having no causal connection with his business, or the contract or the work the employee engages to do. The declared basis, as already pointed out, is not the value of the service rendered, but the extraneous circumstance that the employee needs to get a prescribed sum of money to insure her subsistence, health, and morals. The ethical right of every worker, man or woman, to a living wage may be conceded. One of the declared and important purposes of trade organizations is to secure it. And with that principle and with every legitimate effort to realize it in fact, no one can quarrel; but the fallacy of the proposed method of attaining it is that it assumes that every employer is bound at all events to furnish it. The moral requirement implicit in every contract of employment, viz. that the amount to be paid and the service to be rendered shall bear to each other some relation of just equivalence, is completely ignored. The necessities of the employee are alone considered, and these arise outside of the employment, are the same when there is no employment, and as great in one occupation as in another. Certainly the employer, by paying a fair equivalent for the service rendered, though not sufficient to support the employee, has neither caused nor contributed to her poverty. On the contrary, to the extent of what he pays, he has relieved it. In principle, there can be no difference between the case of selling labor and the case of selling goods. If one goes to the butcher, the baker, or grocer to buy food, he is morally entitled to more. If what he gets is worth what he pays, he is not justified in demanding more, simply because he needs more; and the shopkeeper, having dealt fairly and honestly in that transaction, is not concerned in any peculiar sense with the question of his customer's necessities. Should a statute undertake to vest in a commission power to determine the quantity of food necessary for individual support, and require the shopkeeper, if he sell to the individual at all, to furnish that quantity at not more than a fixed maximum, it would undoubtedly fall before the constitutional test. The fallacy of any argument in support of the validity of such a statute would be quickly exposed. The argument in support of that now being considered is equally fallacious, though the weakness of it may not be so plain. A statute requiring an employer to pay in money, to pay at prescribed and regular intervals, to pay the value of the services rendered, even to pay with fair relation to the extent of the benefit obtained from the service, would be understandable. But a statute which prescribes payment without regard to any of these things, and solely with relation to circumstances apart from the contract of employment, the business affected by it, and the work done under it, is so clearly the product of a naked, arbitrary exercise of power that it cannot be allowed to stand under the Constitution of the United States. . . .

Finally, it may be said that if, in the interest of the public welfare, the police power may be invoked to justify the fixing of a minimum wage, it may, when the public welfare is thought to require it, be invoked to justify a maximum wage. The power to fix high wages connotes, by like course of reasoning, the power to fix low wages. If, in the face of the guaranties of the Fifth Amendment, this form of legislation shall be legally justified, the field for the operation of the police power will have been widened to a great and dangerous degree. If, for example, in the opinion of future lawmakers, wages in the building trades shall become so high as to preclude people of ordinary means from building and owning homes, an authority which sustains the minimum wage will be invoked to support a maximum wage for building laborers and artisans, and the same

argument which has been here urged to strip the employer of his constitutional liberty of contract in one direction will be utilized to strip the employee of his constitutional liberty of contract in the opposite direction. A wrong decision does not end with itself; it is a precedent, and, with the swing of sentiment, its bad influence may run from one extremity of the arc to the other.

It has been said that legislation of the kind now under review is required in the interest of social justice, for whose ends freedom of contract may lawfully be subjected to restraint. The liberty of the individual to do as he pleases, even in innocent matters, is not absolute. It must frequently yield to the common good, and the line beyond which the power of interference may not be pressed is neither definite nor unalterable, but may be made to move, within limits not well defined, with changing need and circumstance. Any attempt to fix a rigid boundary would be unwise as well as futile. But, nevertheless, there are limits to the power, and, when these have been passed, it becomes the plain duty of the courts in the proper exercise of their authority to so declare. To sustain the individual freedom of action contemplated by the Constitution is not to strike down the common good, but to exalt it; for surely the good of society as a whole cannot be better served than by the preservation against arbitrary restraint of the liberties of its constituent members.

It follows, from what has been said, that the act in question passes the limit prescribed by the Constitution, and accordingly the decrees of the court below are

　　　　Affirmed.

Mr. Justice Holmes, dissenting.

The question in this case is the broad one. Whether Congress can establish minimum rates of wages for women in the District of Columbia with due provision for special circumstances, or whether we must say that Congress had no power to meddle with the matter at all. To me, notwithstanding the deference due to the prevailing judgment of the Court, the power of Congress seems absolutely free from doubt. The end, to remove conditions leading to ill health, immorality, and the deterioration of the race, no one would deny to be within the scope of constitutional legislation. The means are means that have the approval of Congress, of many States, and of those governments from which we have learned our greatest lessons. When so many intelligent persons, who have studied the matter more than any of us can, have thought that the means are effective and are worth the price, it seems to me impossible to deny that the belief reasonably may be held by reasonable men. If the law encountered no other objection than that the means bore no relation to the end or that they cost too much I do not suppose that anyone would venture to say that it was bad. I agree, of course, that a law answering the foregoing requirements might be invalidated by specific provisions of the Constitution. For instance it might take private property without just compensation. But in the present instance the only objection that can be urged is found within the vague contours of the Fifth Amendment, prohibiting the depriving any person of liberty or property without due process of the law. To that I turn.

The earlier decisions upon the same words in the Fourteenth Amendment began within our memory and went no farther than an unpretentious assertion of the liberty to follow the ordinary callings. Later that innocuous generality was expanded into the dogma, Liberty of Contract. Contract is not specially mentioned in the text that we have to construe. It is merely an example of doing what you want to do, embodied in the word liberty. But pretty much all law consists in forbidding men to do some things that they want to do, and contract is no more exempt from law than other acts. Without enumerating all the restrictive laws that have been upheld I will mention a few that seem to me to have interfered with liberty of contract quite as seriously and directly as the one before us. Usury laws prohibit contracts by which a man receives more than so much interest for the money that he lends. Statutes of frauds restrict many contracts to certain forms. Some Sunday laws prohibit practically all contracts during one-seventh of our whole life. . . .

I confess that I do not understand the principle on which the power to fix a minimum for the wages of women can be denied by those who admit the power to fix a maximum for their hours of work. I fully assent to the proposition that here as elsewhere the distinctions of the law are distinctions of degree, but I perceive no difference in the kind or degree of interference with liberty, the only matter with which we have any concern, between the one case and the other. The bargain is equally affected whichever half you regulate. Muller v. Oregon, I take it, is as good law to-day as it was in 1908. I will need more than the Nineteenth Amendment to convince me that there are no differences between men and women, or that legislation cannot take those differences into account. I should not hesitate to sustain this Act. Quong Wing v. Kirkendall, 223 U. S. 59, 63. But after Bunting v. Oregon, 243 U. S. 426, I had supposed that it was not necessary, and that Lochner v. New York, 198 U. S. 45, would be allowed a deserved repose.

This statute does not compel anybody to pay anything. It simply forbids employment at rates below those fixed as the minimum requirement of health and right living. It is safe to assume that women will not be employed at even the lowest wages allowed unless they earn them, or unless the employer's business can sustain the burden. In short the law in its character and operation is like hundreds of so-called police laws that have been upheld. I see no greater objection to using a Board to apply the standard fixed by the act than there is to the other commissions with which we have become familiar or than there is to the requirement of a license in other cases. The fact that the statute warrants classification, which like all classifications may bear hard upon some individuals, or in exceptional cases, notwithstanding the power given to the Board to issue a special license, is no greater infirmity than is incident to all law. But the ground on which the law is held to fail is fundamental and therefore it is unnecessary to consider matters of detail.

The criterion of constitutionality is not whether we believe the law to be for the public good. We certainly cannot be prepared to deny that a reasonable man reasonably might have that belief in view of the legislation of Great Britain, Victoria, and a number of the States of this Union. The belief is fortified by a very remarkable collection of documents submitted on behalf of the appellants, material here, I conceive, only as showing that the belief reasonably may be held. In Australia the power to fix a minimum for wages in the case of industrial disputes extending beyond the limits of any one State was given to a Court, and its President wrote a most interesting account of its operation. 29 *Harv. Law Rev.* 13. If a legislature should adopt what he thinks the doctrine of modern economists of all schools, that "freedom of contract is a misnomer as applied to a contract between an employer and an ordinary individual employee," *Ibid.* 25, I could not pronounce an opinion with which I agree impossible to be entertained by reasonable men. If the same legislature should accept his further opinion that industrial peace was best attained by the device of a Court having the above powers, I should not feel myself able to contradict it, or to deny that the end justified restric-

tive legislation quite as adequately as beliefs concerning Sunday or Exploded theories about usury. I should have my doubts, as I have them about this statute—but they would be whether the bill that has to be paid for every gain, although hidden as interstitial detriments, was not greater than the gain was worth: a matter that it is not for me to decide.

I am of opinion that the statute is valid and that the decree should be reversed.   1923

JAMES M. BECK

1861–1936

ADMITTED to the Philadelphia bar in 1884, James M. Beck served as assistant attorney general of the United States (1900–1903), as solicitor-general in the federal government (1921–1925), and as a member of Congress from 1927 to 1934. The recipient of many honors in both his own and other countries, James M. Beck, through his public speaking and his writings, including *The Passing of the New Freedom* (1920) and *Our Wonderland of Bureaucracy* (1933), well represented the conservative social philosophy of the post-World War period. The following selection is from one of his best known books, *The Constitution of the United States* (1922).

Morton Keller, *In Defense of Yesterday; James M. Beck and the Politics of Conservatism*, New York, 1958.

» » *From:* THE CONSTITUTION OF THE UNITED STATES « «

CHAPTER XXIV

THE REVOLT AGAINST AUTHORITY

. . . Of all the phenomena which have resulted from the age of the machine, the most striking is the revolt against authority, and by authority is meant not only the laws of the State, which are the least important, but the great laws of social life and the conventions and traditions of the past.

According to the accepted version, Solomon said: "Where there is no vision, the people perish," but a more ancient translation of the original Hebrew suggests a more striking truth, for the Semitic sage literally said: "Where there is no vision, the people *cast off restraint.*"

No one can deny that there is today a revolt against the discipline of law and the wise restraints of human conventions such as has not existed within the memory of living man.

The reign of lawlessness has crept over the world like the huge shadow of an eclipse, but too few have realized the portentous change that has come over civilization.

Formerly, the crimes of a highwayman, a burglar, or a murderer were so rare that they were naturally regarded as a marked abnormality of life. Today, they are commonplaces in the large cities of the United States, as the newspaper press, whose columns fairly reek with such violations of law, too plainly evidence. A generation ago a citizen could freely walk the streets, except possibly in some remote mining camp, without any reasonable anticipation of violence; but today the cities, which have the oldest tradition of law and order, have become as much the field of operations for the footpad and the highwayman as in the eighteenth century. The days of Dick

Turpin and Jack Sheppard have returned, and hardly a day passes in any of the larger American cities that many crimes of violence do not occur. All students of crime know that this increase is partly due to the automobile and the automatic pistol. The former has facilitated the criminal in an unperceived approach and a quick escape, and the latter has made him far more dangerous than the highwayman of the eighteenth century.

As to the subtler and more insidious crimes against the political state, it is enough to say that graft has become a science in city, state and nation. Losses by such misapplication of public funds—piled Pelion on Ossa—no longer run in the millions but the hundreds of millions. Many American city governments are foul cancers on the body politic. To boast of having solved the problem of local self-government is as fatuous as for a strong man to exult in his health when his body is covered with running sores. It has been estimated that the annual profits from violations of the prohibition laws have reached $300,000,000. Men who thus violate these laws for sordid gain are not likely to obey other laws, and the respect for law among all classes steadily diminishes as the people become familiar with, and tolerant to, wholesale criminality. Whether the moral and economic results of Prohibition overbalance this rising wave of crime, time will tell.

This spirit of revolt against authority is not confined to the political state, and its causes lie beyond that sphere of human action.

Human life is governed by all manner of man-made laws—laws of art, of social intercourse, of literature, music, business—all evolved by custom and imposed by the collective will of society. Here is found the same revolt against tradition and authority.

In music, its fundamental canons have been thrown aside and discord has been substituted for harmony as its ideal. Its culmination—jazz—is a musical crime. If the forms of dancing and music are symptomatic of an age, what shall be said of the universal craze to indulge in crude and clumsy dancing to the syncopated discords of so-called "jazz" music? The cry of the time is: "On with the dance, let joy be unrefined."

In the plastic arts, the laws of form and the criteria of beauty have been swept aside by the futurists, cubists, vorticists, tactilists, and other aesthetic Bolsheviki.

In poetry, where beauty of rhythm, melody of sound and nobility of thought were once regarded as the true tests, we now have in freak forms of poetry the exaltation of the grotesque and brutal. Hundreds of poets are feebly echoing the "barbaric yawp" of Walt Whitman, without the redeeming merit of his occasional sublimity of thought.

In commerce, the revolt is against the purity of standards and the integrity of business morals. Who can question that this is preeminently the age of the sham and the counterfeit? Science is prostituted to deceive the public by cloaking the increasing deterioration in quality of merchandise. The blatant medium of advertising has become so mendacious as to defeat its own purpose.

In the greater sphere of social life is the same revolt against the institutions which have the sanction of the past. Social laws, which once marked the decent restraints of print, speech and dress, have in recent decades been increasingly disregarded. The very foundations of the great and primitive institutions of mankind—like the family, the Church, and the State—have been shaken. The great loyalties of life are "more honored in the breach than the observance."

All these are but illustrations of the general revolt against the authority of the past—a revolt that can be measured by the change in the fundamental presumption of men with respect to the value of human experience. In all former ages, all that was in the past was presumptively true, and the burden was upon him who sought to change it. To-day, the human mind apparently regards the lessons of the past as presumptively false—and the burden is upon him who seeks to invoke them.

Speaking on Christmas Eve a few years ago in an address to the College of Cardinals, the late Pope Benedict gave expression to an estimate of present conditions which should have attracted far greater attention than it apparently did.

The venerable Pontiff said that five plagues were now afflicting humanity.

The first was the unprecedented challenge to authority.

The second, an equally unprecedented hatred between man and man.

The third was the abnormal aversion to work.

The fourth, the excessive thirst for pleasure as the great aim of life.

The fifth, a gross materialism which denied

the reality of the spiritual in human life.

The accuracy of this indictment will commend itself to men who, like the author, are not of Pope Benedict's communion.

The challenge to authority is universal and is not confined to that of the political state. Even in the narrower confines of the latter, the fires of revolution are either violently burning, or, at least, smouldering. Two of the oldest empires in the world, with approximately one-third of its population (China and Russia) are in a welter of anarchy; while many lesser nations are in a stage of disintegration. If the revolt were confined to autocratic governments, they might indicate merely a reaction against tyranny; but even in the most stable of democracies and among the most enlightened peoples, the underground rumblings of revolution may be heard. . . .

Of greater significance to the welfare of civilization is the complete subversion during the World War of nearly all the international laws which had been slowly built up in a thousand years. These principles, as codified by the two Hague Conventions, were immediately swept aside in the fierce struggle for existence, and civilized man, with his liquid fire and poison gas and his deliberate attacks upon undefended cities and their women and children, waged war with the unrelenting ferocity of primitive times.

This fierce war of extermination, which caused the loss of three hundred billion dollars in property and thirty millions of human lives, marked for the time being the "twilight of civilization." The hands on the dial of time had been put back—temporarily, let us hope and pray—a century.

Nor will many question the accuracy of the second count in Pope Benedict's indictment. The war to end war only ended in unprecedented hatred between nation and nation, class and class, and man and man. Victors and vanquished were involved in a common ruin. And if in this deluge of blood, which has submerged the world, there is a Mount Ararat, upon which the ark of a truer and better peace can find refuge, it has not yet appeared above the troubled surface of the waters.

Still less can one question the closely related third and fourth counts in Pope Benedict's indictment, namely the unprecedented aversion to work, when work is most needed to reconstruct the foundations of prosperity, or the excessive thirst for pleasure which preceded, accompanied, and now has followed the most terrible tragedy in the annals of mankind.

The true spirit of work seems to have vanished from millions of men; that spirit of which Shakespeare made his Orlando speak when he said of his true servant, Adam:

> "O good old man! how well in thee appears
> The constant service of the antique world,
> When service sweat for duty, not for meed!"

The *morale* of our industrial civilization has been shattered. Work for work's sake, as the privilege of human faculties, has largely gone, both as an ideal and as a potent spirit, with millions of men. The conception of work as a degrading servitude, to be done with reluctance and grudging inefficiency, and as a mere means to the gratification of pleasure (now the dominant note of life) seems to be the new ideal.

The great evil of the world today is this aversion to work. As the mechanical era diminished the element of physical exertion in work, man should have sought expression for his physical faculties in other virile ways. On the contrary, the whole history of the mechanical era is a persistent struggle for more pay and less work, and today it has culminated in worldwide ruin; for nearly every nation is now in the throes of economic distress, and many of them are on the verge of ruin. The economic catastrophe of 1924 is far greater than the politico-military catastrophe of 1914.

In all countries the losses by such cessations from labor are little as compared with those due to the spirit, which in England is called "ca'-canny" or the shirking of performance of work, and of "sabbotage," the deliberate destruction of machinery in operation. Everywhere the phenomenon has been observed that, with the highest wages known in the history of modern times, there has been an unmistakable lessening of efficiency, and that with an increase in the number of workers, there has been a decrease in output.

Accompanying this indisposition to work efficiently has been a mad desire for pleasure, such as, if it existed in like measure in preceding ages, has not been seen within the memory of living man. Man has danced upon the verge of a social abyss, and, as previously suggested, the dancing has, both in form and in accompanying music, lost its former grace and reverted to the primitive forms of crude vulgarity.

The present weariness and lassitude of hu

man spirit and the disappointment and disillusion as to the aftermath of the harvest of blood, may have aggravated, but they could not cause these symptoms; for the obvious reason that all were in existence and apparent to a few discerning men decades before the war. Indeed, it is possible that the World War, far from causing the *malaise* of the age, was, in itself, but one of its many symptoms.

Undoubtedly, there are many contributing causes which have swollen the turbid tide of this world-wide revolution against the spirit of authority.

Thus, the multiplicity of laws does not tend to develop a law-abiding spirit. This fact has often been noted. Thus Napoleon, on the eve of the XVIII Brumaire, complained that France, with a thousand folios of law, was a lawless nation. Unquestionably, the political state suffers in authority by the abuse of legislation, and especially by the appeal to law to curb evils that are best left to individual conscience. It is idle to talk of respect for law when a law is not worthy of respect, for such respect is an involuntary state of mind, and wise legislators should reckon with it as such.

In this age of an individualistic democracy, the average man is apt to recognize two constitutions—one, the constitution of the State, and the second, an unwritten constitution, to him of higher authority, under which he believes that no law is obligatory which he regards as in excess of the true powers of government. Of this latter spirit, the widespread violation of the prohibition law is a familiar illustration.

A race of individualists obey reluctantly, when they obey at all, any laws which they regard as unreasonable or vexatious. They are increasingly opposed to any law, which affects their selfish interests. The law's delays and laxity in administration breed a spirit of contempt, and too often invite men to take the law into their own hands. These causes are so familiar that their statement is a commonplace.

The excessive emphasis upon the rights of man, which marked the political upheaval of the close of the eighteenth and the beginning of the nineteenth century, has contributed to this malady of the age. Men talked, and still talk, loudly of their rights, but too rarely of their duties. And yet if we were to attribute the malady merely to excessive individualism, we would again err in mistaking a symptom for a cause.

Correctly to diagnose this malady some cause must be found that is coterminous in time with the disease itself and which has been operative throughout civilization; some widespread change in social conditions, for man's essential nature has changed but little, and the change must, therefore, be of environment.

There is but one such change that is sufficiently widespread and deep-seated to account adequately for this malady of the times.

Beginning with the close of the eighteenth century, and continuing throughout the nineteenth, a prodigious transformation has taken place in the environment of man, which has done more to revolutionize the conditions of human life than all the changes that had taken place in the 500,000 preceding years which science has attributed to man's life on the planet. Up to the period of Watt's discovery of steam vapor as a motive power, these conditions, so far as the principal facilities of life were concerned, were substantially those of the civilization which began eighty centuries ago on the banks of the Nile and later on the Euphrates. Man had indeed increased his conquest over Nature in later centuries by a few mechanical inventions, such as gunpowder, the telescope, magnetic needle, printing-press, spinning jenny, and hand-loom, but the characteristic of all those inventions, with the exception of gunpowder, was that they still remained a *subordinate* auxiliary to the physical strength and mental skill of man. In other words, man still dominated the machine, and there was still full play for his physical and mental faculties. Moreover, all the inventions of preceding ages, from the first fashioning of the flint to the spinning-wheel and the hand-level press, were all conquests of the tangible and visible forces of Nature.

With Watt's utilization of steam vapor as a motive power, man suddenly passed into a new and portentous chapter of his varied history. Thenceforth, he was to multiply his powers a thousandfold by the utilization of the invisible powers of Nature—such as vapor and electricity. This prodigious change in his powers, and therefore his environment, has proceeded with ever accelerating speed.

Man has suddenly become the superman. Like the giants of the ancient fable, he has stormed the very ramparts of Divine power, or, like Prometheus, he has stolen the fire of omnipotent forces from Heaven itself for his use. His voice can now reach from the Atlantic to the

Pacific, and, taking wing in his aeroplane, he can fly in one swift flight from Nova Scotia to England, or he can leave Lausanne and, resting upon the icy summit of Mont Blanc—thus, like "the herald, Mercury, new-lighted on a heaven-kissing hill"—he can again plunge into the void, and thus outfly the eagles themselves.

Rodin, the great French sculptor, wrote in 1904 as follows:

10 "It may be replied that the inventions of science compensate for this deficiency (the neglect of the fine arts), but these inventions are almost exclusively, if not quite, a mere increase in the power of the bodily senses and faculties, the telegraph in that of the tongue, the telephone in that of the ear, the railway in that of the legs, the photographic science in that of the eye; and these inventions leave in ignorance the more intellectual part of the individual. Your portrait can be taken, your voice boxed up. This is extraordinary, but the soul which 20 commands, the god which is in the head, is forgotten."

In thus acquiring from the forces of Nature almost illimitable power, man has minimized the necessity for his own physical exertion or even mental skill. The machine now not only acts for him, but too often *thinks* for him.

Is it surprising that so portentous a change should have fevered his brain and disturbed his mental equilibrium? A new ideal, which he 30 proudly called "progress," obsessed him, the ideal of quantity and not quality. His practical religion became that of acceleration and facilitation—to do things more quickly and easily —and thus to minimize exertion became his great objective. Less and less he relied upon the initiative of his own brain and muscle, and more and more he put his faith in the power of machinery to relieve him of labor.

As a result, the evil of the age is that its 40 values are false.

Knowledge is undervalued to wisdom; they are not convertible terms. Quantity, and not quality, is the ideal of the time. Automatic efficiency is the great desideratum, and individual craftsmanship is little regarded as an ideal. Complexity is worshipped, and simplicity is rejected. Standardization is overvalued and originality undervalued.

Pleasure has become the great end of life, 50 and work but a means to that end; whereas, in former ages, work was the great object of life, and pleasure but an incident, the dessert to Life's bountiful repast.

This age overvalues phrases and undervalues truth. It overvalues rights and undervalues

duties. It undervalues individualism and overvalues democracy, for it forgets that, from the beginning of history, the salvation of society has been the work of the minority,—that "saving remnant," of which Matthew Arnold spoke. The age greatly overvalues political institutions; but seems indifferent to the deterioration of the individual. It values power and scorns beauty. To sum it all up,—it overvalues matter and undervalues spirit.

. . .

The great indictment, however, of the present age of mechanical power is that it has largely destroyed the spirit of work. The great enigma which it propounds to us, and which, like the riddle of the Sphinx, we will solve or be destroyed, is this:

Has the increase in the potential of human power, through thermodynamics, been accompanied by a corresponding increase in the potential of human character?

To this life and death question, a great French philosopher, Le Bon, writing in 1910, replied that the one unmistakable symptom of human life was "the increasing deterioration in human character," and a great physicist has described the symptom as "the progressive enfeeblement of the human will."

In a famous book, *Degeneration,* written at the close of the nineteenth century, Max Nordau, as a pathologist, explains this tendency by arguing that our complex civilization has placed too great a strain upon the limited nervous organization of man.

A great financier, the elder J. P. Morgan, once said of an existing financial condition that it was suffering from "undigested securities," and, paraphrasing him, is it not possible that man is suffering from undigested achievements and that his salvation must lie in adaptation to a new environment, which, measured by any standard known to science, is a thousandfold greater in this year of grace than it was at the beginning of the nineteenth century?

No one would be mad enough to urge such a retrogression as the abandonment of labor-saving machinery would involve. Indeed, it would be impossible; for, in speaking of its evils, it must be recognized that not only would civilization perish without its beneficent aid, but that every step forward in the history of man has been coincident with, and in large part attributable to, a new mechanical invention.

But suppose the development of labor-saving machinery should reach a stage where all human labor was eliminated, what would be the effect on man? The answer is contained in an experiment which Sir John Lubbock made with a tribe of ants. Originally the most voracious and militant of their species, yet when denied the opportunity for exercise and freed from the necessity of foraging for their food, in three generations they became anaemic and perished.

Take from man the opportunity of work and the sense of pride in achievement and you have taken from him the very life of his existence. Robert Burns could sing as he drove his ploughshare through the fields of Ayr. Today millions who simply watch an automatic infallible machine, which requires neither strength nor skill, do not sing at their work, but too many curse the fate which has chained them, like Ixion, to a soulless machine.

The evil is even greater.

The specialization of our modern mechanical civilization has caused a submergence of the individual into the group or class. Man is fast ceasing to be the unit of human society. Self-governing groups are becoming the new units. This is true of all classes of men, the employer as well as the employee. The true justification for the American anti-monopoly statutes, including the Sherman anti-trust law, lies not so much in the realm of economics as in that of morals. With the submergence of the individual, whether he be capitalist or wage-earner, into a group, there has followed the dissipation of moral responsibility. A mass morality has been substituted for individual morality, and, unfortunately, group morality generally intensifies the vices more than the virtues of man.

Possibly, the greatest result of the mechanical age is this spirit of organization.

Its merits are manifold and do not require statement; but they have blinded us to the demerits of excessive organization.

We are now beginning to see—slowly, but surely—that a faculty of organization which, as such, submerged the spirit of individualism, is not an unmixed good.

Indeed, the moral lesson of the tragedy of Germany is the demoralizing influence of organization carried to the *n*th power. No nation was ever more highly organized than this modern State. Physically, intellectually and spiritually it had become a highly developed machine. Its dominating mechanical spirit so submerged the individual that, in 1914, the paradox was observed of an enlightened nation that was seemingly destitute of a conscience.

What was true of Germany, however, was true—although in lesser degree—of all civilized nations. In all of them, the individual had been submerged in group formations, and the effect upon the character of man has been destructive of his nobler self.

This may explain the paradox of so-called "progress." It may be likened to a great wheel, which, from the increasing domination of mechanical forces, developed an ever-accelerating speed, until, by centrifugal action, it went off its bearings in 1914 and caused an unprecedented catastrophe. As man slowly pulls himself out of that gigantic wreck and recovers consciousness, he begins to realize that speed is not necessarily progress.

To all this, the nineteenth century, in its exultant pride in its conquest of the invisible forces, was almost blind. It not only accepted progress as an unmistakable fact—mistaking, however, acceleration and facilitation for progress—but in its mad folly believed in an immutable law of progress which, working with the blind forces of machinery, would propel man forward.

A few men, however, standing on the mountain ranges of human observation, saw the future more clearly than did the mass. Emerson, Carlyle, Ruskin, Samuel Butler, and Max Nordau, in the nineteenth century, and, in our time, Ferrero, all pointed out the inevitable dangers of the excessive mechanization of human society. The prophecies were unhappily as little heeded as those of Cassandra.

One can see the tragedy of the time, as a few saw it, in comparing the first *Locksley Hall* of Alfred Tennyson, written in 1827, with its abiding faith in the "increasing purpose of the ages," and its roseate prophecies of the golden age, when the "war-drum would throb no longer and the battle flags be furled in the Parliament of a Man and the Federation of the World," and the later *Locksley Hall*, written sixty years later, when the great spiritual poet of our time gave utterance to the dark pessimism which flooded his soul:

"Gone the cry of 'Forward, Forward,' lost within a growing gloom;
Lost, or only heard in silence from the silence of a tomb.

Half the marvels of my morning, triumphs over
time and space,
Staled by frequence, shrunk by usage, into commonest commonplace!

Evolution ever climbing after some ideal good,
And Reversion ever dragging Evolution in the mud.

Is it well that while we range with Science, glory-
ing in the Time,
City children soak and blacken soul and sense in
city slime?"

There are many palliatives for the evil. To
rekindle in men the love of work for work's
sake and the spirit of discipline, which a strong
sense of human solidarity once inspired, would
do much to solve the problem, for work is the
greatest moral force in the world.

If the present generation can only recognize
that the evil exists, then the situation is not
past remedy; for man has never yet found
himself in a blind alley of negation. He is still
"master of his soul and captain of his fate,"
and the most encouraging sign of the times is
the persistent evidence of contemporary literature that thoughtful men now recognize that
much of our boasted progress was as unsubstantial as a rainbow. While the temper of
the times seems for the moment pessimistic,
it merely marks the recognition of man of an
abyss, whose existence he barely suspected
but over which his indomitable courage will
yet carry him. . . .   1924

HENRY L. MENCKEN

1880–1956

ALTHOUGH NONCONFORMISTS, including many liberals, took great pleasure in
the caustic and witty essays in which H. L. Mencken attacked outworn folklore, superstitions, and middle-class conventions, whether in the field of religion, morals, literature, or
politics, this Baltimore journalist and critic was no friend of democracy. Only in his defense
of the idiom of the plain people, *The American Language* (1919, 1936), did he show any favor
toward them. His jibes at respectability, at shams and shibboleths, at academic and ministerial
pretentiousness, made the *Smart Set* and, later, the *American Mercury*, which he founded with
George Jean Nathan in 1924, the delight of those who considered themselves "civilized." The
keenness and insight which Mencken displayed in evaluating American fiction, and the intelligent reception which he gave to some of the new realists, enhanced his reputation and
influence.

His writings, many of which took the form of contributions to the *Baltimore Sun* and other
newspapers, include the six volumes of *Prejudices* (1919–1927), *Treatise on the Gods* (1930), and
Treatise on Right and Wrong (1934). *Notes on Democracy* (1926), from which the following selection
is taken, provides some explanation of the popularity he enjoyed among conservatives who
regarded themselves as "emancipated."

H. L. Mencken, *Happy Days, 1880–1892*, New York, 1940.
Minority Report: H. L. Mencken's Notebooks, New York, 1956.
William R. Manchester, *Disturber of the Peace; The Life of H. L. Mencken*, New York, 1951.
Heathen Days, New York, 1943.

» » *From:* NOTES ON DEMOCRACY « «

IV

THE FUTURE OF DEMOCRACY

Whether or not democracy is destined to
survive in the world until the corruptible puts
on incorruption and the immemorial Christian
dead leap out of their graves, their faces shining
and their yells resounding—this is something,
I confess, that I don't know, nor is it necessary,
for the purposes of the present inquiry, that
I venture upon the hazard of a guess. My busi-

ness is not prognosis, but diagnosis. I am not engaged in therapeutics, but in pathology. That simple statement of fact, I daresay, will be accepted as a confession, condemning me out of hand as unfit for my task, and even throwing a certain doubt upon my *bona fides*. For it is one of the peculiar intellectual accompaniments of democracy that the concept of the insoluble becomes unfashionable—nay, almost infamous. To lack a remedy is to lack the very license to discuss disease. The causes of this are to be sought, without question, in the nature of democracy itself. It came into the world as a cure-all, and it remains primarily a cure-all to this day. Any boil upon the body politic, however vast and raging, may be relieved by taking a vote; any flux of blood may be stopped by passing a law. The aim of government is to repeal the laws of nature, and re-enact them with moral amendments. War becomes simply a device to end war. The state, a mystical emanation from the mob, takes on a transcendental potency, and acquires the power to make over the father which begat it. Nothing remains inscrutable and beyond remedy, not even the way of a man with a maid. It was not so under the ancient and accursed systems of despotism, now happily purged out of the world. They, too, I grant you, had certain pretensions of an homeric gaudiness, but they at least refrained from attempts to abolish sin, poverty, stupidity, cowardice, and other such immutable realities. Mediaeval Christianity, which was a theological and philosophical *apologia* for those systems, actually erected belief in that immutability into a cardinal article of faith. The evils of the world were incurable: one put off the quest for a perfect moral order until one got to heaven, *post mortem*. There arose, in consequence, a scheme of checks and balances that was consummate and completely satisfactory, for it could not be put to a test, and the logical holes in it were chinked with miracles. But no more. Today the Holy Saints are deposed. Now each and every human problem swings into the range of practical politics. The worst and oldest of them may be solved facilely by travelling bands of lady Ph.D.'s, each bearing the mandate of a Legislature of kept men, all unfaithful to their protectors.

Democracy becomes a substitute for the old religion, and the antithesis of it: the Ku Kluxers, though their reasoning may be faulty, are not far off the facts in their conclusion that Holy Church is its enemy. It shows all the magical potency of the great systems of faith. It has the power to enchant and disarm; it is not vulnerable to logical attack. I point for proof to the appalling gyrations and contortions of its chief exponents. Read, for example, the late James Bryce's "Modern Democracies." Observe how he amasses incontrovertible evidence that democracy doesn't work—and then concludes with a stout declaration that it does. Or, if his two fat volumes are too much for you, turn to some school reader and give a judicious perusal to Lincoln's Gettysburg Address, with its argument that the North fought the Civil War to save self-government to the world!—a thesis echoed in falsetto, and by feebler men, fifty years later. It is impossible, by any device known to philosophers, to meet doctrines of that sort; they obviously lie outside the range of logical ideas. There is, in the human mind, a natural taste for such hocus-pocus. It greatly simplifies the process of ratiocination, which is unbearably painful to the great majority of men. What dulls and baffles the teeth may be got down conveniently by an heroic gulp. No doubt there is an explanation here of the long-continued popularity of the dogma of the Trinity, which remains unstated in plain terms after two thousand years. And no doubt the dogma of Transubstantiation came under fire in the Reformation because it had grown too simple and comprehensible—because even the Scholastic philosophy had been unable to convert its plain propositions into something that could be believed without being understood. Democracy is shot through with this delight in the incredible, this banal mysticism. One cannot discuss it without colliding with preposterous postulates, all of them cherished like authentic hairs from the whiskers of Moses himself. I have alluded to its touching acceptance of the faith that progress is illimitable and ordained of God—that every human problem, in the very nature of things, may be solved. There are corollaries that are even more naïve. One, for example, is to the general effect that optimism is a virtue in itself—that there is a mysterious merit in being hopeful and of glad heart, even in the presence of adverse and immovable facts. This curious notion turns the glittering wheels of Rotary, and is the motive power of the political New Thoughters called Liberals. Certainly the attitude of the average American Liberal toward the so-called League of Nations offered superb clinical material to the student of democratic psychopathology. He began by arguing that the League would save the world. Confronted by proofs of its fraudulence, he switched to the doctrine that believing in it would save the world. So later on, with the Washington Disarmament Conference. The man who hopes absurdly, it appears, is in some fantastic and gaseous manner a better citizen than the man who detects and exposes the truth. Bear this sweet democratic axiom clearly in mind. It is, fundamentally, what is the matter with the United States.

As I say, my present mandate does not oblige me to conjure up a system that will surpass and shame democracy as democracy surpasses and shames the polity of the Andaman Islanders of the Great Khan—a system full-blown and perfect, like Prohibition, and ready to be put into effect by the simple adoption of an amendment to the Constitution. Such a system, for all I know, may lie outside the farthest soarings of the human mind, though that mind can weigh the stars and know God. Until the end of the chapter the ants and bees may flutter their sardonic antennae at us in that department, as they do in others: the last joke upon man may be that he never learned how to govern himself in a rational and competent manner, as the last joke upon woman may be that she never had a baby without wishing that the Day of Judgment were a week past. I am not even undertaking to prove here that democracy is too full of evils to be further borne. On the contrary, I am convinced that it has some valuable merits, not often described, and I shall refer to a few of them presently. All I argue is that its manifest defects, if they are ever to be got rid of at all, must be got rid of by examining them realistically—that they will never cease to afflict all the more puissant and exemplary nations so long as discussing them is impeded by concepts borrowed from theology. As for me, I have never encountered any actual evidence, convincing to an ordinary jury, that *vox populi* is actually *vox Dei*. The proofs, indeed, run the other way. The life of the inferior man is one long protest against the obstacles that God interposes to the attainment of his dreams, and democracy, if it is anything at all, is simply one way of getting 'round these obstacles. Thus it respresents, not a jingling echo of what seems to be the divine will, but a raucous defiance of it. To that extent, perhaps, it is truly civilized, for civiliza-

tion, as I have argued elsewhere, is best described as an effort to remedy the blunders and check the cruel humours of the Cosmic Kaiser. But what is defiant is surely not official, and what is not official is open to examination.

For all I know, democracy may be a self-limiting disease, as civilization itself seems to be. There are obvious paradoxes in its philosophy, and some of them have a suicidal smack. It offers John Doe a means to rise above his place beside Richard Roe, and then, by making Roe his equal, it takes away the chief usufructs of the rising. I here attempt no pretty logical gymnastics: the history of democratic states is a history of disingenuous efforts to get rid of the second half of that dilemma. There is not only the natural yearning of Doe to use and enjoy the superiority that he has won; there is also the natural tendency of Roe, as an inferior man, to acknowledge it. Democracy, in fact, is always inventing class distinctions, despite its theoretical abhorrence of them. The baron has departed, but in his place stand the grand goblin, the supreme worthy archon, the sovereign grand commander. Democratic man, as I have remarked, is quite unable to think of himself as a free individual; he must belong to a group, or shake with fear and loneliness —and the group, of course, must have its leaders. It would be hard to find a country in which such brummagem serene highnesses are revered with more passionate devotion than they get in the United States. The distinction that goes with mere office runs far ahead of the distinction that goes with actual achievement. A Harding is regarded as genuinely superior to a Halsted, no doubt because his doings are better understood. But there is a form of human striving that is understood by democratic man even better than Harding's, and that is the striving for money. Thus the plutocracy, in a democratic state, tends to take the place of the missing aristocracy, and even to be mistaken for it. It is, of course, something quite different. It lacks all the essential characters of a true aristocracy: a clean tradition, culture, public spirit, honesty, honour, courage—above all, courage. It stands under no bond of obligation to the state; it has no public duty; it is transient and lacks a goal. Its most puissant dignitaries of to-day came out of the mob only yesterday —and from the mob they bring all its peculiar ignobilities. As practically encountered, the plutocracy stands quite as far from the *hon-*

nête homme as it stands from the Holy Saints. Its main character is its incurable timorousness; it is for ever grasping at the straws held out by demagogues. Half a dozen gabby Jewish youths, meeting in a back room to plan a revolution—in other words, half a dozen kittens preparing to upset the Matterhorn—are enough to scare it half to death. Its dreams are of banshees, hobgoblins, bugaboos. The honest, untroubled snores of a Percy or a Hohenstaufen are quite beyond it.

The plutocracy, as I say, is comprehensible to the mob because its aspirations are essentially those of inferior men: it is not by accident that Christianity, a mob religion, paves heaven with gold and precious stones, i.e., with money. There are, of course, reactions against this ignoble ideal among men of more civilized tastes, even in democratic states, and sometimes they arouse the mob to a transient distrust of certain of the plutocratic pretensions. But that distrust seldom arises above mere envy, and the polemic which engenders it is seldom sound in logic or impeccable in motive. What it lacks is aristocratic disinterestedness, born of aristocratic security. There is no body of opinion behind it that is, in the strictest sense, a free opinion. Its chief exponents, by some divine irony, are pedagogues of one sort or another—which is to say, men chiefly marked by their haunting fear of losing their jobs. Living under such terrors, with the plutocracy policing them harshly on one side and the mob congenitally suspicious of them on the other, it is no wonder that their revolt usually peters out in metaphysics, and that they tend to abandon it as their families grow up, and the costs of heresy become prohibitive. The pedagogue, in the long run, shows the virtues of the Congressman, the newspaper editorial writer or the butler, not those of the aristocrat. When, by any chance, he persists in contumacy beyond thirty, it is only too commonly a sign, not that he is heroic, but simply that he is pathological. So with most of his brethren of the Utopian Fife and Drum Corps, whether they issue out of his own seminary or out of the wilderness. They are fanatics; not statesmen. Thus politics, under democracy, resolves itself into impossible alternatives. Whatever the label on the parties, or the war cries issuing from the demagogues who lead them, the practical choice is between the plutocracy on the one side and a rabble of preposterous impossibilities on the other. One must either follow the New York *Times,* or one must be prepared to swallow Bryan and the Bolsheviki. It is a pity that this is so. For what democracy needs most of all is a party that will separate the good that is in it theoretically from the evils that beset it practically, and then try to erect that good into a workable system. What it needs beyond everything is a party of liberty. It produces, true enough, occasional libertarians, just as despotism produces occasional regicides, but it treats them in the same drum-head way. It will never have a party of them until it invents and installs a genuine aristocracy, to breed them and secure them.

1926

HENRY FORD

1863–1947

LIKE MANY OTHER great American industrialists, Henry Ford was born on a farm. When only fifteen he became an apprentice in a Detroit machine shop. Although he experimented with steam and gasoline engines, and in 1892 constructed a gasoline automobile, it was not as a pioneer inventor, but as a pioneer organizer of mass production of cars that Henry Ford gained his fortune and his fame.

Ford's hobbies emphasized the preservation of American antiquities, including the equipment for old-fashioned education. During the First World War he showed his peace sympathy by coming out against preparedness and by financing the Peace Ship which tried to effect the mediation of neutral powers. But it is as a leading spokesman for American business that Ford is especially significant.

Henry Ford, in collaboration with Samuel Crowther, *My Life and Work*, Garden City, 1922.
Allen Nevins and Frank E. Hill, *Ford: The Times, the Man, the Company*, New York, 1954.
Keith T. Sward, *The Legend of Henry Ford*, New York, 1948.

»　»　From: MY PHILOSOPHY OF INDUSTRY　«　«

SUCCESS

Students of world progress recognize that there is a time for everything. Like the opening of a flower or the budding of a tree, certain events cannot be forced ahead of their time; nor, conversely, can they be disregarded after the time for their appearance has come. Therefore it behooves the man—especially the young man—who wishes to have his part in the progress of this world, to watch the signs of the times and be ready at the proper moment to take his place in the procession of human events.

Not only in industry, but in all lines of work is this so. In the scheme of progress each unit has its logical place, which no other can fill. As a case in point, the automobile and the airplane could not be successfully developed until the internal combustion engine had been invented. Earlier engines, such as steam engines, were too heavy; they weighed too much per horsepower to be practical for use in these two new vehicles of transportation. But with the coming of the internal combustion engine it was possible to concentrate in a small place and a small weight an enormous amount of power. Thus it enabled us to develop the automobile, and, later on, the airplane. One invention makes way for another; one discovery lights up the path ahead so that he who runs may read—and lead.

Similarly, the development of industry was long delayed because one link in the chain of progress was missing. When that had been forged, industry shot ahead to its present high state of production. I refer to the matter of long-distance power transmission. Back in the days when machinery had to be run by steam or water power, cables and belts were the only means of power transmission. This meant that factories had to be located in the immediate neighborhood of the plant, or on the bank of the stream from which power was derived. The natural tendency was for industry to group itself around large sources of power. Thus centralization was brought about, and on its heels followed quantity production. The mere idea of quantity production was a great step forward, but its concentration was hampered by the very condition that had given rise to it. So long as centralization was necessary, so long as manufacturing could be carried on only by the limited number of factories that could crowd around the various sources of power, quantity production on the present scale was impossible.

THE MISSING LINK IN THE CHAIN OF PROGRESS

Then within our knowledge—within our century—electricity was discovered. Electricity possessed this great advantage over all other kinds of power previously produced: it could be instantaneously transmitted over great distances by wire. Power could be generated in one spot and sent out to any number of factories all over the country. The necessity for centralization had been eliminated, and manufacturing went ahead on a larger scale than ever.

Light, heat, and power—think what has been accomplished by this one idea put into action! And the power age has barely begun. In our own shops we are constantly improving our method of manufacture, with an eye to efficiency, economy, and the safety and comfort of our employees. Belt transmission has been entirely supplanted by electrically driven machines, which frees us from the danger and annoyance of wheels and belts whirling overhead. Our furnaces, most of which are electrically heated, are so constructed and insulated that the men work in front of them without discomfort. There is no smoke or gas except in a few processes, and, in these, electric ventilators carry off all disagreeable odors and unhealthful fumes.

The increase in the scale of production does not mean that craftsmanship has gone. From the earliest times machines of some sort have been in use. It took craftsmen to make and use machines then, and it takes craftsmen now. The hand and the brain and the eye have functioned together ever since man came upon the earth. The hand-made age is still with us, but it has been refined and advanced until it stands on a higher plane than when men used wooden plows and primitive potters' wheels. We value the things of the past because of their association; they were steps toward those of the present. But as needs have grown, means of production have been increased and improved.

It has been asserted that machine production kills the creative ability of the craftsman. This is not true. The machine demands that man be its master; it compels mastery more than the old methods did. The number of skilled craftsmen in proportion to the working population has greatly increased under the conditions brought about by the machine. They get better wages and more leisure in which to exercise their creative faculties.

There are two ways of making money—one at the expense of others, the other by service to others. The first method does not "make" money, does not create anything; it only "gets" money—and does not always succeed in that. In the last analysis, the so-called gainer loses. The second way pays twice—to maker and user, to seller and buyer. It receives by creating, and receives only a just share, because no one is entitled to all. Nature and humanity supply too many necessary partners for that. True riches make wealthier the country as a whole.

Most people will spend more time and energy in going around problems than in trying to solve them. A problem is a challenge to your intelligence. Problems are only problems until they are solved, and the solution confers a reward upon the solver. Instead of avoiding problems we should welcome them and through right thinking make them pay us profits. The discerning youth will spend his time learning *direct methods,* learning how to make his brain and hand work in harmony with each other so that the problem in hand may be solved in the simplest, most direct way that he knows.

THE DEAD LIMBS OF LIFE

We can get rid of a tremendous number of the bothersome things of life if we put our minds to it. The number of needless tasks that are performed daily by thousands of people is amazing. It is the work of men with vision to trim out some of these dead limbs of life. Some of our industrial leaders have already done a good job in their own front yards, but the commons of life need attention too. Trimming out dead wood hurts no one. After all is said and done, our one great problem is the problem of life itself, of which industry is one of the tributary activities.

It is easier to denounce a wrong than to tackle the job of curing it. We cannot evade our job by blaming the past. The past took care of itself, and it depends on us to take care of the present. Many things that were thought in the past to be right we have found to be wrong. But—and remember this—none of the things believed to be thoroughly wrong have we found to be right. Even wrong things have to pass through a period of being thought right before they can be known as wrong. When we find out their nature, our responsibility begins. It is this generation's duty to the next to start at once to make room for the right thing.

Our fathers thought that life was hard, but we are beginning to see how preventable some of its hardships are. We have come to believe that there is no necessity for economic distress in a world so richly furnished with resources. Men are searching with sharp eyes for the defects in our system which prevents a man from working when he wants to work and his responsibilities require it. Economic stoppage is not natural. This defect is not in the created order of things; it is in the human order. Our selfishness, our lack of wisdom have created it. If we have established a money system which can be manipulated to the hurt of multitudes, it is as certain as fate that the system is doomed. The very discovery of insufficiency is its death warrant.

SOMETHING ROTTEN IN ECONOMICS

Some people think that everything will be rectified when war is abolished. Well, let nothing interfere with the abolition of war. But sound thinking insists that war will not be abolished until its roots are cut; and one of its main roots is a false money system and the high priests thereof. But more of that later. What causes war is not patriotism, not that human beings are willing to die in defense of their dearest ones. It is the false doctrine, fostered by the few, that war spells gain. It is this that makes war, and there are not enough pacifists who see it and attack it. The fact that pacifists are left in peace is proof they are not attacking the real causes of war. If pacifists spoke the truth, they would not be petted as they are to-day; theirs would be the hard lot of the martyrs of Truth.

We often speak of the ignorance of the past; but our distant forefathers were no more ig-10 norant than we. They were grinding the grist of experience through the mills of the mind, and were discovering what was good and what was bad for them. That is all we are doing. What will be known in the future as the igno-rance of this present generation is just the residue of discoveries which we shall not have time to make. Our responsibility is not to create a perfect world, but to establish our discoveries of what is right by weeding out what we have 20 newly discovered to be wrong, leaving to the future its task of the same nature.

One of the principal duties that devolve during periods of change is the duty of *con-scious allegiance*. To-day, conscious allegiance costs something. At the very first it means division between those who are loyal to moral convictions and those who are not. The ma-jority of the people are naturally straddlers. They are not in the world to pioneer but to be 30 as happy as possible. If pioneering in a cause brings discomfort, they would rather not be among the pioneers. They would rather stand on the side lines and, in the combat between truth and error, wait and see which proves the stronger. Though they may have a lazy faith that truth at last will win, they do not wish to lend a premature support. Yet majorities are essential, not to the truth, but to the acknowl-edgment of the truth. There are some oppo-40 sites in the world that should never be recon-ciled. There are some programs that should never be harmonized. What frightens some people is that they want to be happy, to live and let live without being bothered. They would like to enjoy the world as it is, and if there are those who would improve the world, let them do so—but not in a way that inter-feres with their present happiness.

The most important work that faces the 50 young generation to-day is making the world a better place to live in. There are thousands of great tasks waiting to be accomplished. There are innumerable opportunities in the three great arts—agriculture, industry, and trans-portation. The youth who can solve the money question will do more for the world than all the professional soldiers of history.

THE THREE PRINCIPAL ARTS

I have often said that mankind passes from the old to the new on a human bridge formed by those who labor in the three principal arts —agriculture, manufacture, transportation. We are a bridge generation. The complaints that we hear concerning the slowness of the world's change from worse to better come mostly from people who would rather be the crossing throng than help support the bridge upon which hu-manity passes. Fortunately for all of us, ours is not the choice.

There is a group of people who believe that the millennium will be brought about by a new system of distribution. They do not realize the fundamental truth that all things of value have always been distributed. The problem is to *use* them. It takes thinking, and there is no substi-tute for that. All the treasure chests of industry may be unlocked by this key. Look at our natural resources, our undeveloped water power, our unused forces of nature. Often a single right idea put into action is enough to make them mankind's slaves.

The truth of things escapes us, mostly be-cause truth is so simple. Truth is a seed within itself; its nature is to reveal itself first to one or two, then ultimately to all. At a pace de-pendent upon our receptivity and in a manner measured by our mentality, we must do the work that destiny has given us if we would pass on to the next generation its rightful herit-age. Don't be afraid of the changing order. It may look like chaos, but when the passing débris of the old has been cleared away, there will be found a thousand new opportunities teeming with promise and power.

TALKERS AND DOERS

Youth has one great element in its favor— it can live in the future. The world of to-mor-row belongs to the young man of to-day; he can begin shaping the world now. No age has ever presented the tremendous opportunities of the present, but along with these opportunities are proportionate responsibilities. With the changing wheel of ambition, boys no longer regard the talkative professions as more important than the manual. They realize that there are gigantic tasks to be done and that these will be accomplished by doers rather than talkers. The man who does things is vastly more important to the world than the clerk who merely makes the record of others' achievements.

Youths have a tremendous advantage over their elders in possessing the power of vision without the drawback of retrospect. They bring fresh eyes and fresh minds to old tasks. They are not tied down by the traditions of the past; they are not slaves to the failures of others. Their concern is not so much with what could have been done in the past as with what can be done in the future. What they make of it will depend on what they make of themselves and the opportunities or tasks which are now before them.

Of course, education has its limits. Education and ability to do things are not interchangeable terms. You cannot educate brains into a man's head, but you can help him to make the most of the brains he has. A man who cannot think is not an educated man, no matter how many college degrees he may have acquired. One who can think things out usually can do them. An education which consists of signposts indicating the failures and fallacies of the past is doubtless useful. Many men are at work to-day on theories fundamentally wrong, ignorant that other men have followed that road and have had to come back. So schools are useful if they show the blind alleys of human endeavor. Then they must help to put men in possession of their own powers. But they cannot do this without the earnest desire of their students to be so helped. Inventors, by the way, are not made by education; but if

they have enough education to spare them the mistakes of the past, it saves their time.

Most of us are doing two things—that by which the body is kept alive, and that by which the higher part of our nature lives. We go to the job to pay expenses and then we indulge ourselves in what we like to do and maybe were meant to do. The whole secret of a successful life is to find out what it is one's destiny to do, and then do it. Some day there may come to one the duty to do a disagreeable task, to take up a cause which will yield no reward—a cause which will at first surround one with misunderstanding and abuse, and which will make one look like a fool before men. One naturally shrinks from it. But when a man is sure of what he has to do, he should go ahead full speed. To be right means mainly to be in tune with destiny and willing to obey. It does not necessarily mean to be agreeable, nor to be agreed with nor to be popular; it does mean to be useful in the purpose which destiny is trying to achieve in us and through us. If a man is right, he need not fear to stand alone; he is not alone. Every right idea that is put forth has many silent adherents.

There is a great deal of nonsense spoken about the "lonely heights"—they may seem to be lonely, but they are only silent. The loneliness comes when a man settles within himself whether he is to be a mere form following a conventional routine or whether he is to listen and obey the voice of a changeable life. It is lonely while he is deciding. If he decides to do what duty bids him, then he is no longer lonely. He comes at once into the fellowship of other people who are thinking as he is, but who have been waiting for a leader to declare them and their principles.   1929

BARTOLOMEO VANZETTI

1888–1927

THE ANTIRADICAL HYSTERIA which swept the country after the Bolshevik Revolution and the conclusion of the First World War claimed, among its victims, two humble philosophical anarchists, Bartolomeo Vanzetti and Nicola Sacco. Vanzetti, the more articulate and engaging of the two, sprang from substantial farming people in northern Italy. Of a roving disposition, Vanzetti migrated to the United States in 1908 and engaged in a variety of occupations. During the war he fled to Mexico in order to escape military service. On his return he peddled fish at Plymouth, Massachusetts.

On April 15, 1920, the paymaster of a shoe factory in South Braintree was robbed of several thousands of dollars and shot by two foreign-appearing men, who escaped in a car. Vanzetti and Sacco, home-loving and skilled workers, were charged with the crime. Not only liberal, but able conservative lawyers, believed that during the trial Judge Webster Thayer and the prosecution exploited the radicalism of the defendants. Although there was grave doubt in many minds in regard to the guilt of the two men, and although litigation dragged on for many years, Sacco and Vanzetti were finally executed on August 23, 1927.

Meantime, however, the affair had become a *cause célèbre*. Few issues in the 1920's aroused deeper emotions than the Sacco-Vanzetti case. Liberals and radicals believed that these simple Italians were being persecuted because of their social views. Although conservatism triumphed when they were executed, Sacco and Vanzetti became symbols not to be forgotten. The following letters from Vanzetti are examples of the quality of his mind and spirit.

Letters of Sacco and Vanzetti, M. D. Frankfurter and Gardner Jackson, eds., New York, 1928.
The Sacco and Vanzetti Case, transcript of the record of *The Trial of Nicola Sacco and Bartolomeo Vanzetti in the Courts of Massachusetts and subsequent proceedings, 1920–1927*, 5 vols., New York, 1928–1929.
Felix Frankfurter, *The Case of Sacco and Venzetti: A Critical Analysis for Lawyers and Laymen*, Stanford, 1954.
George L. Joughin and Edmund M. Morgan, *The Legacy of Sacco and Vanzetti*, New York, 1948.

»   »   *From:* THE LETTERS OF SACCO AND VANZETTI   «   «

February 27, 1924. Charlestown Prison

DEAR COMRADE BLACKWELL: [1]

Yours of the 23rd has reached me. You are right. Neither do I expect any good from that letter to the judge.[2] I have never expected, nor do I expect anything from him, other than some ten thousand volts divided in few times; some meters of cheap board and 4 x 7 x 8 feet hole in the ground.

No matter how much sympathy I try to bestow upon him, or with how much understanding I try to judge his actions; I only and alone can see him a self-conceited narrow-minded little tyrant, believing himself to be just, and believing his utterly unjust and unnecessary social office to be a necessity and a good. He is a bigot, and therefore, cruel. At the time of our arrest and trials, his peers were seeing red all around, and he saw red more than his peers.

He was ready to kill us even before the trials, for he deadly hates the subversive, and he believed to have become judge of the State Supreme Court by eliminating us via Law. For he knows that the servants of Capital were always remunerated by the Bosses for a crusifixion of some rebel or lover.

[1] Alice Stone Blackwell of Boston.
[2] Judge Webster Thayer was the original trial judge.

I do not know if his conduct during the trial was determined by his preconceptions, hate and ignorance, or if he consciously murdered us by details of bad faith, double playing, simulation, etc. I know that he did it. I know that even now he does not want to give us another trial though he could not deny it. And this is why he delays so much to give the answer. . . .

And if I am wrong, if according to his own standard, he is fair; if he wishes to be just, ('til now he is very unjust) then he could be hurt by my letter, but also enlightened. And if he would not forgive the crude defence of a man extremely wronged, then, not even a sparrow would I submit to him as arbiter.

An almost centenial struggle against every form of exploitation, oppression and fraud, taught us that "the wolf eats him who makes himself a sheep."

I am not sure, but I believe, that there are no pamphlets in Italian language, which treat with detail the case. This is the second reason of my letter and the 3rd reason is, my wish to say what no one else can say—silence would be cowardness—and treat the case accordingly to my own criterions. This may hurt me, but will help the Cause. Otherwise, if it means a life sentence, I prefer to be burnt away once and for all, and I also know that those in height, upon the back and the heads of the slaves, are against me. . . .

There is no spirit of sacrifice in this deed. I simply realize to be in merciless hands, and do my utmost to say to my enemy that he is wrong. In a way that helps the cause. The great one, not the small. My only hope remains in the solidariety of friends and comrades and of the workers. After having spent $200,000, we are still at the beginning. The work of the lawyers are useless before the law.

It has helped only because they brought the fact to the conscience and consciousness of the People. That is why Nick and I were not yet roasted. Authority, Power, and Privilege would not last a day upon the face of the earth, were it not because those who possess them, and those who prostitute their arms to their defence do suppress, repress, mercilessly and inescapable every efforts of liberations of each and all the rebels.

I abhor useless violence. I would my blood to prevent the sheading of blood, but neither the abyss nor the earth, nor the heavens, have a law which condemns the self-defense. Not every woman has sacrificed to bring forth one more rufian, idiot, or coward to the world. There are yet some men. And if tragedy is compelled to us, who knows; who knows if to speak now is not my duty?

The champion of life and of the liberty should not yield before the death. The struggle for the liberty, between the oppressor and the oppressed, shall continue beyond the life, beyond the graves. I know what they have done and are doing to me and to thousands of others, rebels and lovers. And I know that they are and will always be ready to do against us. I know the millions of youth that they slandered, the virgins that they have torn in the breast; the millions of wives that they have widowed; the millions of bastards that they let to miasma of the gutter, or grown to the fratricide. I know the old fathers and mothers whom they killed by breaking their hearts; and all the children that they starved and are starving to death; and the hospitals and the crazy-houses filled of their victims, and the little criminals, victims, irresponsible and semi-compelled to crime that they mercilessly executed or entombed alive. They have never had pity for our children, our women, our dear, poor old fathers and mothers —and they never will have it.

The sorrow of their victims torture me in blood and spirit. As for me, I would forgive them, but I could not, for I would be a traitor of the race. Until not a man will be exploited or oppressed by another man, we will never bend the banner of freedom.

Are they not ready to do with other comrades what they are doing to us? Are they not more willing than ever to squeeze out the worker's blood for more gold? Are they not preparing a greater war?

I will ask for revenge—I will tell that I will die gladly by the hands of the hanger after having known to have been vindicated. I mean "eye for an eye, ear for an ear," and even more, since to win it is necessary that 100 enemies fall to each of us.

The only vengence which could placate me is the realization of freedom, the great deliverance which would beneficiate all my friends as well as all my enemies: All. But till that, the struggle goes on, til we are breath to breath with the enemy fighting with short arms, till then, to fight is our duty, our right, our necessity. For, one of the two. Either we must go on and win, or we must ask for an armistice. And who will grant it to us? Since the enemy has no scruples nor pity, to ask pity of him is to encourage him to slander our fellows, to try to grant to him the immunity for his crimes against us; it would be as a matricide.

The more I live, the more I suffer, the more I learn, the more I am inclined to forgive, to be generous, and that the violence as such does not resolve the problem of life. And the more I love and learn that "the right of all to violence does not go together with the liberty, but that it begins when the liberty ends." The slave has the right and duty to arise against his master. My supreme aim, that of the Anarchist is, "the complete elimination of violence from the rapports (relations)."

To be possible, we must have freedom and justice. Now we have the opposite of them, because through errors and consequent aberations, men have risen as tyrants, deceiters and exploiters of other men, believing to gain their personal, familiar and cast welfare by such deed. Through both tyranny and servitude, we have lost our capacity of liberty and we are making life evermore miserable, operating our own ante-distruction.

Since "only the liberty, or the struggle for liberty, may be school of liberty" and since mine is but self and racial defence, why should not I use the truth to defend myself? It is supremely sweet to me—my consciousness of superiority, of righteousness, to know that I can judge and that the future shall bow to me, the doomed, and curse my judges.

Well, I have said many things which I sincerely believe to be so. But there are surely some mistake! Who possesses the absolute, or even the absolute-relative truth? So your point of view may be right, and I also realized that 10 you spoke exclusively for my own good.

Wisdom is not only comprehension, but also many other faculties together; among which discrimination and sense of measure are prominent. I will try to be wise! ! ! ! ! ! I will think it over and over again.

.   .   .

May 12, 1927. Dedham Jail

DEAR MRS. HENDERSON: [3]

21   Your letter to me and the one to my sister and the fruits, cheese and other goods that you sent me were received yesterday when I translated at once your letter to my sister, happy at the thought of the cheer and confidence it will give to my family. I also wrote a reply to you. But I was still sleeping early this morning when I felt unsatisfied of my answer, remembered to have forgotten a thing, and decided to write 30 you this one—and here I am.

I had just thought that your silence might be due to the bad blow upon you by the Supreme Court refusal and consequent Thayer's sentencing—which might have made you sick— and I have been, so much so, right.

Those two happenings had been too well foreseen and expected to me—so that I was neither surprised nor shaken by them.

Now, dear Mrs. Henderson, I am going to be 40 truthful and sincere—that is to say fanatic, rough and seemingly wrong and unfair. We have already hoped in seven appeals, all of them repulsed. Of course we hoped in Just-ices. What did they? Now that we are compelled to hope no longer in them, of course, we begin to hope in Gov. Fuller. Victor Hugo was almost right in saying that hope would be the last goddess were not for desperation; for true, after desperation there is only more anasthet- 50 ism and unconsciousness before death.

Do you remember your confidence in the just-ices? Well, you say to have hope and confidence in Gov. Fuller. Of course you must believe to have reasons for it, and most proba-

[3] Mrs. Jessica Henderson of Wayland, Mass.

bly you know him well. Whereas I only know his name and the appearances of some of his public acts and utterances. And yet I differ with your opinion of his attitude toward our case. I believe that he has been so much against us that he doomed the three young bandits and veterans of the car-barn, just to avoid excuse or reasons to commute our death sentence in life imprisonment. Of course he felt sure that we would have been doomed. It takes so little to understand that we are murdered in conservation of the Capitalist regime, by the Capitalist Just-ices who are before and after all servants of it.

Every one who think to know the Gov. says that he is a courageous man, honest and straight, aiming energically to what he deems right. Very well. But the people who know him and like him are all like or similar to him. I know him better than them because I have been just as they are now: believed in the same things; liking or disliking the same things; having the same opinions, reactions, beliefs and morale they have now. Now I have changed entirely and only for that I can know now what I was then.

I have been for seven years in the hell of Massachusetts State Prison. There are virtues, understanding, intelligence, unspeakable experiences within the lost ones that populate that hell. And there I and my companions of doom have read Fuller's words: "Why I believe in Capital Punishment," published in the *Success* magazine of last December. And we understood: that was not incidental (the interview). It was planned and predisposed with clear and definite aims by at least one of the parties, (Fuller or the journalist) and allowed by both of them. It foretold and preassured the executions of Madeiros, Jerry, and the three car-barn bandits and of Sacco and Vanzetti. The same Boston journals took pain to make it understood that the publication of that interview just before the Governor's going to Europe intended to be as a declaration of what his attitude to all and our case is, to the European people. And we, the lost, said: Lo! a man who says to be going to Europe with his good wife, as in a "second honeymoon trip"—and begins it by crushing three old mother's hearts, foretelling their young sons' doom. Could not he have his good time without increasing the agonies of those three old mothers?

His words do not specify the case of which he spoke so that his opinions, judgments and affirmations, innuendo and inferences are always withdrawful at his pleasure and will, uncontrollable and unconfutable. For example, he says: what we have to look after is, if they (the condemned) were guilty. Now, if the reader believes that the Governor has said that with our case in his mind, well, the reader understand that the Governor says that such is our case. But suppose that one says or proves that such a thing has not been done in our case, then the Governor can answer: I did not speak of their case. . . .

But enough of this. Let us hope that you are right and I am wrong about his feelings and intention. He may be 100 times better than I —but I would not trust a feather of an anarchist sparrow to the *bon plesir* of him.

We owe our life to you, our friends, comrades and people of the world who have fought for seven years for us—and to you and them we will owe our freedom if we ever will be free, Mrs. Evans, you, the Committee, Mr. Thompson.[4] If it were not for you we would from long time have been buried, dead, in a grave, or alive in a prison.

I pray you to not let my above words to harm your feelings. I have been positive that the supreme judges would have murdered us. They did it. Had I told you of my opinion of them it would have seemed monstrous to you; I would have harmed and upsetted you. Yet I was positive of it. From a man like Fuller, in a case between reaction and revolution as our case has been from its very beginning, and to two anarchists—well I am positive of it.

He may give us justice—I expect nothing. . . .

And now I am not going to try to express you our gratitude for what you are doing to our families and ourselves. We cannot. . . .

. . .

August 21, 1927. From the Death House of Massachusetts State Prison

DEAR FRIENDS AND COMRADES OF THE SACCO-VANZETTI DEFENSE COMMITTEE

After tomorrow mid-night, we will be executed, save a new staying of the execution by either the United States Supreme Court or by Governor Alvan T. Fuller.

We have no hope. This morning, our brave defender and friend Michael Angelo Musmanno was here from his return from Washing-

ton, and told us he would come back this afternoon if he would have time for it. Also Rosa and Luigi were here this morning, and they too, promised us to return this afternoon. But now it is 5:30 P.M. and no one returned yet. This tells us that there is no good news for us, for, if so, some of you would have hurried to bring them to us. It almost tells us that all your efforts have failed and that you are spending these remaining few hours in desperate and hopeless efforts to evitate our execution. In a word, we feel lost! Therefore, we decided to write this letter to you to express our gratitude and admiration for all what you have done in our defense during these seven years, four months, and eleven days of struggle.

That we lost and have to die does not diminish our appreciation and gratitude for your great solidarity with us and our families.

Friends and Comrades, now that the tragedy of this trial is at an end, be all as of one heart. Only two of us will die. Our ideal, you our comrades, will live by millions; we have won, but not vanquished. Just treasure our suffering, our sorrow, our mistakes, our defeats, our passion for future battles and for the great emancipation.

Be all as of one heart in this blackest hour of our tragedy. And have heart.

Salute for us all the friends and comrades of the earth.

We embrace you all, and bid you all our extreme good-bye with our hearts filled with love and affection. Now and ever, long life to you all, long life to Liberty. Yours in life and death, BARTOLOMEO VANZETTI
NICOLA SACCO

August 21, 1927. From the Death House of Massachusetts State Prison

MY DEAR DANTE: [5]

I still hope, and we will fight until the last moment, to revindicate our right to live and to be free, but all the forces of the State and of the money and reaction are deadly against us because we are libertarians or anarchists.

I write little of this because you are now and yet too young to understand these things and other things of which I would like to reason with you.

But, if you do well, you will grow and understand your father's and my case and your

---

[4] William G. Thompson, defense attorney.

[5] Sacco's son

father's and my principles, for which we will soon be put to death.

I tell you now that all that I know of your father, he is not a criminal, but one of the bravest men I ever knew. Some day you will understand what I am about to tell you. That your father has sacrificed everything dear and sacred to the human heart and soul for his fate in liberty and justice for all. That day you will
10 be proud of your father, and if you come brave enough, you will take his place in the struggle between tyranny and liberty and you will vindicate his (our) names and our blood.

If we have to die now, you shall know, when you will be able to understand this tragedy in its fullest, how good and brave your father has been with you, your father and I, during these eight years of struggle, sorrow, passion, anguish and agony.
20 Even from now you shall be good, brave with your mother, with Ines, and with Susie— brave, good Susie [6]—and do all you can to console and help them.

I would like you to also remember me as a comrade and friend to your father, your mother and Ines, Susie and you, and I assure you that neither have I been a criminal, that I have committed no robbery and no murder, but only fought modestly to abolish crimes
30 from among mankind and for the liberty of all.

Remember Dante, each one who will say otherwise of your father and I, is a liar, insulting innocent dead men who have been brave in their life. Remember and know also, Dante, that if your father and I would have been cowards and hypocrits and rinnegetors of our faith, we would not have been put to death. They would not even have convicted a lebbrous dog; not even executed a deadly
40 poisoned scorpion on such evidence as that they framed against us. They would have given a new trial to a matricide and habitual felon

[6] Faithful friend of Mrs. Sacco, with whom she and her children lived during the last years of the case.

on the evidence we presented for a new trial.

Remember, Dante, remember always these things, we are not criminals; they convicted us on a frame-up; they denied us a new trial; and if we will be executed after seven years, four months and seventeen days of unspeakable tortures and wrong, it is for what I have already told you; because we were for the poor and against the exploitation and oppression of the man by the man.

The documents of our case, which you and other ones will collect and preserve, will prove to you that your father, your mother, Ines, my family and I have sacrificed by and to a State Reason of the American Plutocratic reaction.

The day will come when you will understand the atrocious cause of the above written words, in all its fullness. Then you will honor us.

Now Dante, be brave and good always. I embrace you.

P.S. I left the copy of *An American Bible* to your mother now, for she will like to read it, and she will give it to you when you will be bigger and able to understand it. Keep it for remembrance. It will also testify to you how good and generous Mrs. Gertrude Winslow has been with us all. Good-bye Dante.

                              BARTOLOMEO

"If it had not been for these thing, I might have live out my life talking at street corners to scorning men. I might have die, unmarked, unknown, a failure. Now we are not a failure. This is our career and our triumph. Never in our full live could we hope to do such work for tolerance, for joostice, for man's onderstanding of man as now we do by accident. Our words—our lives—our pains—nothing! The taking of our lives—lives of a good shoemaker and a poor fish-peddler—all! That last moment belongs to us—that agony is our triumph."

FROM A STATEMENT MADE BY VANZETTI AFTER RECEIVING SENTENCE, April 9, 1927.

• • *Depression and Reconstruction* • •

1929-1940

» » « «

BROTHER, CAN YOU SPARE A DIME

They used to tell me I was building a dream,—
And so I followed the mob
When there was earth to plough or guns to bear—
I was always there—right there on the job.
They used to tell me I was building a dream
With peace and glory ahead—
Why should I be standing in line just waiting for bread?

Refrain
Once I built a railroad, made it run,—
Made it race against time.
Once I built a railroad, Now it's done—
Brother can you spare a dime?

Once I built a tower, to the sun,—
Brick and rivet and lime,
Once I built a tower,
Now it's done, Brother can you spare a dime?
Once in khaki suits   Gee, we looked swell.
Full of that Yankee Doodle-de-dum.
Half a million boots went sloggin' thru Hell,
I was the kid with the drum.—
Say, don't you remember, they called me Al—
It was Al all the time—
Say, don't you remember
I'm your Pal!—Buddy, can you spare a dime?—

In the dark depression days of October, 1932, J. P. McEvoy's *Americana* made its appearance at the Shubert Theatre in New York City. Mr. Jay Gorney's "plaintive but thundering" song, "Brother, Can You Spare a Dime," was sung by Rex Weber and "breadline vagrants." According to Brooks Atkinson, none of the prose bards expressed with more "heart-breaking anguish" the spirit of the times than did the author of this song.

New York Times, October 6, 1932.
Stage, X (November, 1932).

» »   « «

Depression and Reconstruction

THE COLLAPSE in the stock market in October, 1929, which resulted from the growing tensions in capitalistic economy, was followed by widespread unemployment, deflation, and prolonged crisis. The Hoover administration was forced to subsidize business and to pull in sail. But it was unable or unwilling to meet the issues that confronted the nation. Washington was the scene of "hunger marches," and demands for relief were heard throughout the land.

The radical groups took on new lease of life. They and they alone seemed to be able to diagnose the causes of the ailment and to have ready-made programs for reconstruction. Many unwilling to follow them did give countenance to technocracy, which promised utopia through the social direction of the machine-economy. A formidable number followed Huey Long, who promised every man that he might share the wealth and become a king.

The election of Franklin D. Roosevelt in 1932 seemed like the dawn of a new day. During the first "100 days" of the new regime the White House made amazing victories for its program of reconstruction. The New Deal seemed to be the answer the great mass of the Americans had been searching for. The federal government assumed unprecedented responsibility for the relief and well-being of victims of the depression. Social planning was talked about, and actually, in restricted areas, at least, begun.

But the new day which many believed had come to stay did not remain as bright as it had been at sunrise or at high noon. Conservative business fought the program of social reconstruction, and the administration itself made concession after concession. Meantime the outbreak of a new world war brought home to the Americans new perils which overshadowed any faint hope that the European struggle might be the long-sought pump to get the business machine really started. If Americans took some comfort in the fact that they were, notwithstanding all their ills, fortunate in comparison with war-invaded lands, they realized how precarious their blessings were, how uncertain the future. Only the indomitable, if much shaken faith, that no issue could defy solution, kept thoughtful Americans from sinking into despond. Many of the issues which had divided America in the past, which had seemed to the generations facing them so serious, now appeared to have been inconsequential in face of the new issues that called for new solutions.

» »   « «

TWELVE SOUTHERNERS

AMONG THE "Twelve Southerners" who contributed to *I'll Take My Stand. The South and the Agrarian Tradition* (1930) were Frank L. Owsley, an authority on Southern history, John Gould Fletcher, a poet, Allen Tate, a literary critic, and Stark Young, well known for his nostalgic novel of the Old South and for his impressionistic writings in *The New Republic*. The diagnosis of the ills of an industrial society which emanated from the authors of *I'll Take My*

Stand seemed to certain critics of "the left" Fascist in its implications. But primarily *I'll Take My Stand* was a reassertion of the values, personal, aesthetic, and social, which supposedly prevailed, in considerable measure at least, in the ante-bellum South.

Louise Cowan, *The Fugitive Group; a Literary History*, Baton Rouge, 1939.

» » *From:* I'LL TAKE MY STAND « «

INTRODUCTION—A STATEMENT OF PRINCIPLES

The authors contributing to this book are Southerners, well acquainted with one another and of similar tastes, though not necessarily living in the same physical community, and perhaps only at this moment aware of themselves as a single group of men. By conversa-
10 tion and exchange of letters over a number of years it had developed that they entertained many convictions in common, and it was decided to make a volume in which each one should furnish his views upon a chosen topic. This was the general background. But background and consultation as to the various topics were enough; there was to be no further collaboration. And so no single author is responsible for any view outside his own article. It was
20 through the good fortune of some deeper agreement that the book was expected to achieve its unity. All the articles bear in the same sense upon the book's title-subject: all tend to support a Southern way of life against what may be called the American or prevailing way; and all as much as agree that the best terms in which to represent the distinction are contained in the phrase, Agrarian *versus* Industrial.

31 But after the book was under way it seemed a pity if the contributors, limited as they were within their special subjects, should stop short of showing how close their agreements really were. On the contrary, it seemed that they ought to go on and make themselves known as a group already consolidated by a set of principles which could be stated with a good deal of particularity. This might prove useful for the
40 sake of future reference, if they should undertake any further joint publication. It was then decided to prepare a general introduction for the book which would state briefly the common convictions of the group. This is the statement. To it every one of the contributors in this book has subscribed.

Nobody now proposes for the South, or for any other community in this country, an independent political destiny. That idea is thought to have been finished in 1865. But how far shall the South surrender its moral, social, and economic autonomy to the victorious principle of Union? That question remains open. The South is a minority section that has hitherto been jealous of its minority right to live its own kind of life. The South scarcely hopes to determine the other sections, but it does propose to determine itself, within the utmost limits of legal action. Of late, however, there is the melancholy fact that the South itself has wavered a little and shown signs of wanting to join up behind the common or American industrial ideal. It is against that tendency that this book is written. The younger Southerners, who are being converted frequently to the industrial gospel, must come back to the support of the Southern tradition. They must be persuaded to look very critically at the advantages of becoming a "new South" which will be only an undistinguished replica of the usual industrial community.

But there are many other minority communities opposed to industrialism, and wanting a much simpler economy to live by. The communities and private persons sharing the agrarian tastes are to be found widely within the Union. Proper living is a matter of the intelligence and the will, does not depend on the local climate or geography, and is capable of a definition which is general and not Southern at all. Southerners have a filial duty to discharge to their own section. But their cause is precarious and they must seek alliances with sympathetic communities everywhere. The members of the present group would be happy to be counted as members of a national agrarian movement.

Industrialism is the economic organization of the collective American society. It means the decision of society to invest its economic resources in the applied sciences. But the word science has acquired a certain sanctitude. It is out of order to quarrel with science in the abstract, or even with the applied sciences when their applications are made subject to criticism and intelligence. The capitalization of the applied sciences has now become extravagant and uncritical; it has enslaved our human energies to a degree now clearly felt to be burdensome. The apologists of industrialism do not like to meet this charge directly; so they often take refuge in saying that they are devoted simply to science! They are really devoted to the applied sciences and to practical production. Therefore it is necessary to employ a certain skepticism even at the expense of the Cult of Science, and to say, It is an Americanism, which looks innocent and disinterested, but really is not either.

. . .

The contribution that science can make to a labor is to render it easier by the help of a tool or a process, and to assure the laborer of his perfect economic security while he is engaged upon it. Then it can be performed with leisure and enjoyment. But the modern laborer has not exactly received this benefit under the industrial regime. His labor is hard, its tempo is fierce, and his employment is insecure. The first principle of a good labor is that it must be effective, but the second principle is that it must be enjoyed. Labor is one of the largest items in the human career; it is a modest demand to ask that it may partake of happiness.

. . .

The regular act of applied science is to introduce into labor a labor-saving device or a machine. Whether this is a benefit depends on how far it is advisable to save the labor. The philosophy of applied science is generally quite sure that the saving of labor is a pure gain, and that the more of it the better. This is to assume that labor is an evil, that only the end of labor or the material product is good. On this assumption labor becomes mercenary and servile, and it is no wonder if many forms of modern labor are accepted without resentment though they are evidently brutalizing. The act of labor as one of the happy functions of human life has been in effect abandoned, and is practiced solely for its rewards.

Even the apologists of industrialism have

been obliged to admit that some economic evils follow in the wake of the machines. These are such as overproduction, unemployment, and a growing inequality in the distribution of wealth. But the remedies proposed by the apologists are always homeopathic. They expect the evils to disappear when we have bigger and better machines, and more of them. Their remedial programs, therefore, look forward to more industrialism. Sometimes they see the system righting itself spontaneously and without direction: they are Optimists. Sometimes they rely on the benevolence of capital, or the militancy of labor, to bring about a fairer division of the spoils: they are Cooperationists or Socialists. And sometimes they expect to find super-engineers, in the shape of Boards of Control, who will adapt production to consumption and regulate prices and guarantee business against fluctuations: they are Sovietists. With respect to these last it must be insisted that the true Sovietists or Communists—if the term may be used here in the European sense—are the Industrialists themselves. They would have the government set up an economic super-organization, which in turn would become the government. We therefore look upon the Communist menace as a menace indeed, but not as a Red one; because it is simply according to the blind drift of our industrial development to expect in America at last much the same economic system as that imposed by violence upon Russia in 1917.

. . .

Turning to consumption, as the grand end which justifies the evil of modern labor, we find that we have been deceived. We have more time in which to consume, and many more products to be consumed. But the tempo of our labors communicates itself to our satisfactions, and these also become brutal and hurried. The constitution of the natural man probably does not permit him to shorten his labor-time and enlarge his consuming-time indefinitely. He has to pay the penalty in satiety and aimlessness. The modern man has lost his sense of vocation.

. . .

Religion can hardly expect to flourish in an industrial society. Religion is our submission to the general intention of a nature that is fairly inscrutable; it is the sense of our role as creatures within it. But nature industrialized, transformed into cities and artificial habitations, manufactured into commodities, is no longer nature but a highly simplified picture of nature. We receive the illusion of having power over nature, and lose the sense of nature as something mysterious and contingent. The God of nature under the conditions is merely an amiable expression, a superfluity, and the philosophical understanding ordinarily carried in the religious experience is not there for us to have.

. . .

Nor do the arts have a proper life under industrialism, with the general decay of sensibility which attends it. Art depends, in general, like religion, on a right attitude to nature; and in particular on a free and disinterested observation of nature that occurs only in leisure. Neither the creation nor the understanding of works of art is possible in an industrial age except by some local and unlikely suspension of the industrial drive.

. . .

The amenities of life also suffer under the curse of a strictly-business or industrial civilization. They consist in such practices as manners, conversation, hospitality, sympathy, family life, romantic love—in the social exchanges which reveal and develop sensibility in human affairs. If religion and the arts are founded on right relations of man-to-nature, these are founded on right relations of man-to-man.

. . .

Apologists of industrialism are even inclined to admit that its actual processes may have upon its victims the spiritual effects just described. But they think that all can be made right by extraordinary educational efforts, by all sorts of cultural institutions and endowments. They would cure the poverty of the contemporary spirit by hiring experts to instruct it in spite of itself in the historic culture. But salvation is hardly to be encountered on that road. The trouble with the life-pattern is to be located at its economic base, and we cannot rebuild it by pouring in soft materials from the top. The young men and women in colleges, for example, if they are already placed in a false way of life, cannot make more than an inconsequential acquaintance with the arts and humanities transmitted to them. Or else the understanding of these arts and humanities will

but make them the more wretched in their own destitution.

. . .

The "Humanists" are too abstract. Humanism, properly speaking, is not an abstract system, but a culture, the whole way in which we live, act, think, and feel. It is a kind of imaginatively balanced life lived out in a definite social tradition. And, in the concrete, we believe that this, the genuine humanism, was rooted in the agrarian life of the older South and of other parts of the country that shared in such a tradition. It was not an abstract moral "check" derived from the classics—it was not soft material poured in from the top. It was deeply founded in the way of life itself—in its tables, chairs, portraits, festivals, laws, marriage customs. We cannot recover our native humanism by adopting some standard of taste that is critical enough to question the contemporary arts but not critical enough to question the social and economic life which is their ground.

. . .

The tempo of the industrial life is fast, but that is not the worst of it; it is accelerating. The ideal is not merely some set form of industrialism, with so many stable industries, but industrial progress, or an incessant extension of industrialization. It never proposes a specific goal; it initiates the infinite series. We have not merely capitalized certain industries; we have capitalized the laboratories and inventors, and undertaken to employ all the labor-saving devices that come out of them. But a fresh labor-saving device introduced into an industry does not emancipate the laborers in that industry so much as it evicts them. Applied at the expense of agriculture, for example, the new processes have reduced the part of the population supporting itself upon the soil to a smaller and smaller fraction. Of course no single labor-saving process is fatal; it brings on a period of unemployed labor and unemployed capital, but soon a new industry is devised which will put them both to work again, and a new commodity is thrown upon the market. The laborers were sufficiently embarrassed in the meantime, but, according to the theory, they will eventually be taken care of. It is now the public which is embarrassed; it feels obligated to purchase a commodity for which it had expressed no desire, but it is invited to make its budget equal to the strain. All might yet be well, and stability and comfort might again obtain, but for this: partly because of industrial ambitions and partly because the repressed creative impulse must break out somewhere, there will be a stream of further labor-saving devices in all industries, and the cycle will have to be repeated over and over. The result is an increasing disadjustment and instability.

. . .

It is an inevitable consequence of industrial progress that production greatly outruns the rate of natural consumption. To overcome the disparity, the producers, disguised as the pure idealists of progress, must coerce and wheedle the public into being loyal and steady consumers, in order to keep the machines running. So the rise of modern advertising—along with its twin, personal salesmanship—is the most significant development of our industrialism. Advertising means to persuade the consumers to want exactly what the applied sciences are able to furnish them. It consults the happiness of the consumer no more than it consulted the happiness of the laborer. It is the great effort of a false economy of life to approve itself. But its task grows more difficult every day.

. . .

It is strange, of course, that a majority of men anywhere could ever as with one mind become enamored of industrialism: a system that has so little regard for individual wants. There is evidently a kind of thinking that rejoices in setting up a social objective which has no relation to the individual. Men are prepared to sacrifice their private dignity and happiness to an abstract social ideal, and without asking whether the social ideal produces the welfare of any individual man whatsoever. But this is absurd. The responsibility of men is for their own welfare and that of their neighbors; not for the hypothetical welfare of some fabulous creature called society.

. . .

Opposed to the industrial society is the agrarian, which does not stand in particular need of definition. An agrarian society is hardly one that has no use at all for industries, for professional vocations, for scholars and artists, and for the life of cities. Technically, perhaps, an agrarian society is one in which agriculture is the leading vocation, whether for wealth, for pleasure, or for prestige—a form of labor that is pursued with intelligence and leisure, and that becomes the model to which the other forms approach as well as they may. But an agrarian regime will be secured readily enough where the superfluous industries are not allowed to rise against it. The theory of agrarianism is that the culture of the soil is the best 10 and most sensitive of vocations, and that therefore it should have the economic preference and enlist the maximum number of workers.

. . .

These principles do not intend to be very specific in proposing any practical measures. How may the little agrarian community resist the Chamber of Commerce of its county seat, 20 which is always trying to import some foreign industry that cannot be assimilated to the life-pattern of the community? Just what must the Southern leaders do to defend the traditional Southern life? How may the Southern and the Western agrarians unite for effective action? Should the agrarian forces try to capture the Democratic party, which historically is so closely affiliated with the defense of individualism, the small community, the state, the 30 South? Or must the agrarians—even the Southern ones—abandon the Democratic party to its fate and try a new one? What legislation could most profitably be championed by the powerful agrarians in the Senate of the United States? What anti-industrial measures might promise to stop the advances of industrialism, or even undo some of them, with the least harm to those concerned? What policy should be pursued by the educators who have a tradition at 40 heart? These and many other questions are of the greatest importance, but they cannot be answered here.

. . .

For, in conclusion, this much is clear: If a community, or a section, or a race, or an age, is groaning under industrialism, and well aware that it is an evil dispensation, it must find the way to throw it off. To think that this cannot 50 be done is pusillanimous. And if the whole community, section, race, or age thinks it cannot be done, then it has simply lost its political genius and doomed itself to impotence.   1930

HERBERT CLARK HOOVER

1874–

UNTIL HIS service as commissioner for relief in Belgium during the First World War, Herbert Hoover was known to limited circles as an efficient and successful mining engineer and promoter. As food administrator after the entrance of the United States into the war and as Secretary of Commerce under President Harding, Hoover won the approval of a wide following. Although, during his administration as President of the United States, he did much to delimit the area of the laissez faire and rugged individualistic philosophies which he advocated, he continued, during the New Deal experiment of his successor, President Roosevelt, to espouse the doctrine of economic individualism which, like many of his class, he identified with "Americanism." The following selection from *American Individualism* (1922) was again and again exemplified in Hoover's speeches and writings, including *The Challenge to Liberty* (1934) and *Addresses upon the American Road, 1933–1938* (1938).

W. S. Myers, *The Hoover Administration; A Documented Narrative*, New York, 1936.
David Hinshaw, *Herbert Hoover, American Quaker*, New York, 1950.
Harold Wolfe, *Herbert Hoover: Public Servant and Leader of the Loyal Opposition*, New York, 1956.
Harris G. Warren, *Herbert Hoover and the Great Depression*, New York, 1958.

» » From: AMERICAN INDIVIDUALISM « «

We have witnessed in this last eight years the spread of revolution over one-third of the world. The causes of these explosions lie at far greater depths than the failure of governments in war. The war itself in its last stages was a conflict of social philosophies—but beyond this the causes of social explosion lay in the great inequalities and injustices of centuries flogged beyond endurance by the conflict and freed from restraint by the destruction of war. The urgent forces which drive human society have been plunged into a terrible furnace. Great theories spun by dreamers to remedy the pressing human ills have come to the front of men's minds. Great formulas came into life that promised to dissolve all trouble. Great masses of people have flocked to their banners in hopes born of misery and suffering. Nor has this great social ferment been confined to those nations that have burned with revolutions.

Now, as the storm of war, of revolution and of emotion subsides there is left even with us of the United States much unrest, much discontent with the surer forces of human advancement. To all of us, out of this crucible of actual, poignant, individual experience has come a deal of new understanding, and it is for all of us to ponder these new currents if we are to shape our future with intelligence.

Even those parts of the world that suffered less from the war have been partly infected by these ideas. Beyond this, however, many have had high hopes of civilization suddenly purified and ennobled by the sacrifices and services of the war; they had thought the fine unity of purpose gained in war would be carried into great unity of action in remedy of the faults of civilization in peace. But from concentration of every spiritual and material energy upon the single purpose of war the scene changed to the immense complexity and the many purposes of peace.

Thus there loom up certain definite underlying forces in our national life that need to be stripped of the imaginary—the transitory—and a definition should be given to the actual permanent and persistent motivation of our civilization. In contemplation of these questions we must go far deeper than the superficials of our political and economic structure, for these are but the products of our social philosophy—the machinery of our social system.

Nor is it ever amiss to review the political, economic, and spiritual principles through which our country has steadily grown in usefulness and greatness, not only to preserve them from being fouled by false notions, but more importantly that we may guide ourselves in the road of progress.

Five or six great social philosophies are at struggle in the world for ascendency. There is the Individualism of America. There is the Individualism of the more democratic states of Europe with its careful reservations of castes and classes. There are Communism, Socialism, Syndicalism, Capitalism, and finally there is Autocracy—whether by birth, by possessions, militarism, or divine right of kings. Even the Divine Right still lingers on although our lifetime has seen fully two-thirds of the earth's population, including Germany, Austria, Russia, and China, arrive at a state of angry disgust with this type of social motive power and throw it on the scrap heap.

. . .

For myself, let me say at the very outset that my faith in the essential truth, strength, and vitality of the developing creed by which we have hitherto lived in this country of ours has been confirmed and deepened by the searching experiences of seven years of service in the backwash and misery of war. Seven years of contending with economic degeneration, with social disintegration, with incessant political dislocation, with all of its seething and ferment of individual and class conflict, could but impress me with the primary motivation of social forces, and the necessity for broader thought upon their great issues to humanity. And from it all I emerge an individualist— an unashamed individualist. But let me say also that I am an American individualist. For America has been steadily developing the ideals that constitute progressive individualism.

No doubt, individualism run riot, with no tempering principle, would provide a long category of inequalities, of tyrannies, dominations, and injustices. America, however, has tempered the whole conception of individualism by the injection of a definite principle, and from this principle it follows that attempts at domination, whether in government or in the processes of industry and commerce, are under an insistent curb. If we would have the values of individu-

alism, their stimulation to initiative, to the development of hand and intellect, to the high development of thought and spirituality, they must be tempered with that firm and fixed ideal of American individualism—*an equality of opportunity*. If we would have these values we must soften its hardness and stimulate progress through that sense of service that lies in our people.

Therefore, it is not the individualism of other countries for which I would speak, but the individualism of America. Our individualism differs from all others because it embraces these great ideals: *that while we build our society upon the attainment of the individual, we shall safeguard to every individual an equality of opportunity to take that position in the community to which his intelligence, character, ability, and ambition entitle him; that we keep the social solution free from frozen strata of classes; that we shall stimulate effort of each individual to achievement; that through an enlarging sense of responsibility and understanding we shall assist him to this attainment; while he in turn must stand up to the emery wheel of competition.*

Individualism cannot be maintained as the foundation of a society based upon contracts, property, and political equality. Such legalistic safeguards are themselves not enough. In our individualism we have long since abandoned the laissez faire of the 18th Century—the notion that it is "every man for himself and the devil take the hindmost." We abandoned that when we adopted the ideal of equality of opportunity—the fair chance of Abraham Lincoln. We have confirmed its abandonment in terms of legislation, of social and economic justice,—in part because we have learned that it is the hindmost who throws the bricks at our social edifice, in part because we have learned that the foremost are not always the best nor the hindmost the worst—and in part because we have learned that social injustice is the destruction of justice itself. We have learned that the impulse to production can only be maintained at a high pitch if there is a fair division of the product. We have also learned that fair division can only be obtained by certain restrictions on the strong and the dominant. We have indeed gone even further in the 20th Century with the embracement of the necessity of a greater and broader sense of service and responsibility to others as a part of individualism.

10

20

30

40

50

Whatever may be the case with regard to Old World individualism (and we have given more back to Europe than we received from her) the truth that is important for us to grasp today is that there is a world of difference between the principles and spirit of Old World individualism and that which we have developed in our own country.

10 We have, in fact, a special social system of our own. We have made it ourselves from materials brought in revolt from conditions in Europe. We have lived it; we constantly improve it; we have seldom tried to define it. It abhors autocracy and does not argue with it, but fights it. It is not capitalism, or socialism, or syndicalism, nor a cross breed of them. Like most Americans, I refuse to be damned by anybody's word-classification of it, such as "capitalism," "plutocracy," "proletariat," or "middle 20 class," or any other, or to any kind of compartment that is based on the assumption of some group dominating somebody else.

The social force in which I am interested is far higher and far more precious a thing than all these. It springs from something infinitely more enduring; it springs from the one source of human progress—that each individual shall be given the chance and stimulation for development of the best with which he has been 30 endowed in heart and mind; it is the sole source of progress; it is American individualism.

The rightfulness of our individualism can rest either on philosophic, political, economic, or spiritual grounds. It can rest on the ground of being the only safe avenue to further human progress.

· · ·

[THE FUTURE]

41 Individualism has been the primary force of American civilization for three centuries. It is our sort of individualism that has supplied the motivation of America's political, economic, and spiritual institutions in all these years. It has proved its ability to develop its institutions with the changing scene. Our very form of government is the product of the individualism of our people, the demand for an equal 50 opportunity, for a fair chance.

The American pioneer is the epic expression of that individualism, and the pioneer spirit is the response to the challenge of opportunity, to the challenge of nature, to the challenge of life, to the call of the frontier. That spirit need never die for lack of something for it to achieve. There will always be a frontier to conquer or to hold as long as men think, plan, and dare. Our American individualism has received much of its character from our contacts with the forces of nature on a new continent. It evolved government without official emissaries to show the way; it plowed and sowed two score of great states; it built roads, bridges, railways, cities; it carried forward every attribute of high civilization over a continent. The days of the pioneer are not over. There are continents of human welfare of which we have penetrated only the coastal plain. The great continent of science is as yet explored only on its borders, and it is only the pioneer who will penetrate the frontier in the quest for new worlds to conquer. The very genius of our institutions has been given to them by the pioneer spirit. Our individualism is rooted in our very nature. It is based on conviction born of experience. Equal opportunity, the demand for a fair chance, became the formula of American individualism because it is the method of American achievement.

After the absorption of the great plains of the West came the era of industrial development with the new complex of forces that it has brought us. Now haltingly, but with more surety and precision than ever before and with a more conscious understanding of our mission, we are finding solution of these problems arising from new conditions, for the forces of our social system can compass and comprise these.

Our individualism is no middle ground between autocracy—whether of birth, economic or class origin—and socialism. Socialism of different varieties may have something to recommend it as an intellectual stop-look-and-listen sign, more especially for Old World societies. But it contains only destruction to the forces that make progress in our social system. Nor does salvation come by any device for concentration of power, whether political or economic, for both are equally reversions to Old World autocracy in new garments.

Salvation will not come to us out of the wreckage of individualism. What we need today is steady devotion to a better, brighter, broader individualism—an individualism that carries increasing responsibility and service to our fellows. Our need is not for a way out but for a way forward. We found our way out three centuries ago when our forefathers left Europe for these shores, to set up here a commonwealth conceived in liberty and dedicated to the development of individuality.

.   .   .

The primary safeguard of American individualism is an understanding of it; of faith that it is the most precious possession of American civilization, and a willingness courageously to test every process of national life upon the touchstone of this basic social premise. Development of the human institutions and of science and of industry have been long chains of trial and error. Our public relations to them and to other phases of our national life can be advanced in no other way than by a willingness to experiment in the remedy of our social faults. The failures and unsolved problems of economic and social life can be corrected; they can be solved within our social theme and under no other system. The solution is a matter of will to find solution; of a sense of duty as well as of a sense of right and citizenship. No one who buys "bootleg" whiskey can complain of gunmen and hoodlumism.

Humanity has a long road to perfection, but we of America can make sure progress if we will preserve our individualism, if we will preserve and stimulate the initiative of our people, if we will build up our insistence and safeguards to equality of opportunity, if we will glorify service as a part of our national character. Progress will march if we hold an abiding faith in the intelligence, the initiative, the character, the courage, and the divine touch in the individual. We can safeguard these ends if we give to each individual that opportunity for which the spirit of America stands. We can make a social system as perfect as our generation merits and one that will be received in gratitude by our children.   1922

CHARLES A. BEARD

1874–1948

LIBERAL AND humane thought in the United States owes much to Charles A. Beard. A distinguished scholar in history and social science, Beard's *An Economic Interpretation of the Constitution* (1913) and *Economic Origins of Jeffersonian Democracy* (1915) broke new ground by acute analyses of long-neglected economic factors in the political developments of the past. *The Rise of American Civilization* (1927) and *America in Mid-Passage* (1939), written with his wife, Mary Beard, are brilliant syntheses and interpretations in which the rich and complicated factors in our past are fully taken into account. Beard brought to scholarship in the social disciplines a philosophical understanding of basic but frequently unrecognized assumptions which governed the work of writers in the social sciences. *The Nature of the Social Sciences* (1934) and *The Discussion of Human Affairs* (1936) illustrate this aspect of his thought.

But Beard's significance in American life cannot be understood without taking into account his readiness to put his mind and scholarship to work on current and pressing public issues. His analyses of navalism and foreign policy and his charts for the rational and humane reordering of domestic economy and foreign policy were presented in *The Idea of National Interest* (1934) and *The Open Door at Home* (1934). *The Myth of Rugged Individualism* also illustrates his conception of the role of the scholar in a democratic republic.

The Economic Basis of Politics, New York, 1945.
Robert E. Brown, *Charles Beard and the Constitution*, Princeton, 1956.
Howard K. Beale, ed., *Charles A. Beard: An Appraisal*, Lexington, 1954.
Mary R. Beard, *The Making of Charles A. Beard*, New York, 1955

» » THE MYTH OF RUGGED INDIVIDUALISM « «

"The House of Bishops would be as much at sea in Minneapolis as at Atlantic City." This bit of delicious humor, all too rare in America's solemn assemblies, sparkled at a tense moment in the late conference of the Episcopalian magnates at Denver when the respective merits of the two cities as future meeting places were under debate. But the real cause of the caustic comment seems to have been a heated discussion, led by the Honorable George W. Wickersham,[1] over a dangerous proposal to modify, not the Volstead act, but the sacred creed of rugged American individualism.

That contest had been precipitated by the report of a special commission in which occurred these highly inflammatory words: "It is becoming increasingly evident that the conception of society as made up of autonomous, independent individuals is as faulty from the point of view of economic realism as it is from the standpoint of Christian idealism. Our fundamental philosophy of rugged individualism must be modified to meet the needs of a co-operative age." This frightful conclusion flowed from a fact statement which the commission summarized in the following language: "Side by side with such misery and idleness, there are warehouses bursting with goods which cannot be bought; elevators full of wheat while bread lines haunt our cities; carefully protected machinery lying idle, while jobless men throng our streets; money in the banks available at low rates."

These shocking passages Mr. Wickersham read to the assembled delegates with considerable indignation, and denied their truth. Then he added an illuminating exposition all his own: "I think this is an expression of a social philosophy that is expressed by the Soviet Government of Russia. It is a negation of the whole concept of American civilization. I think it would be a sad day when the American people abandon the principles on which they have grown to greatness." Coming to specifications, he particularly attacked a point in the report, that "compulsory unemployment insurance is feasible." Realizing that Mr. Wickersham was a specialist in individualism, since he was the chief author of a collective report [2] from which

each individual signer apparently dissented, the congregated deputies at Denver voted down the proposal that the commission's statement should be taken as "representing the mind of the Church," and substituted a mere pious recommendation that it should be given "careful consideration" by members of the Church. Such, at least, is the story reported in the press.

This is only one of many straws in the wind indicating a movement to exalt rugged individualism into a national taboo beyond the reach of inquiring minds. From day to day it becomes increasingly evident that some of our economic leaders (by no means all of them) are using the phrase as an excuse for avoiding responsibility, for laying the present depression on "Government interference," and for seeking to escape from certain forms of taxation and regulation which they do not find to their interest. If a smoke screen big enough can be laid on the land, our commercial prestidigitators may work wonders—for themselves.

Still more direct evidence confirms this view. For example, in the autumn of 1930, a New York bank published, as a kind of revelation from on high, a slashing attack on "Government interference with business," written by that stanch English Whig, Macaulay, a hundred years ago; and a few weeks later one of the leading advertising firms took a whole page in the *New York Times* to blazen forth the creed anew under the captivating head: "Cheer Up! Our Best Times Are Still Ahead of Us!" And the whole gospel was summed up in these words from Macaulay: "Our rulers will best promote the improvement of the people by strictly confining themselves to their own legitimate duties —by leaving capital to find its most lucrative course, commodities their fair price, industry and intelligence their natural reward, idleness and folly their natural punishment—by maintaining peace, by defending property, by diminishing the price of law, and by observing strict economy in every department of the State. Let the Government do this—the people will assuredly do the rest." In other words, here was put forth in the name of American business, with all the pontifical assurance that characterized Macaulay's shallowest sophistry,

---

[1] Attorney-General.
[2] The so-called Wickersham report on law enforcement, which took evasive and contradictory positions on prohibition legislation.

the pure creed of historic individualism, and here was served on the Government and people of the United States a warning revelation of confident expectations.

A year later, in a release to the press, Mr. Otto Kahn discussed the subject of planning and intimated that the fortunate position of France to-day is to be ascribed to the fact that the French Government interferes less with business than does the Government of Germany or Great Britain, with the implication that the United States might profit from this experience. About the same time the Honorable Newton D. Baker made a long address at Williamstown which was evidently designed to show that nothing important could be done in the present crisis by the Federal Government, except perhaps in the way of tariff reduction by international agreement. And now comes from Chicago the announcement that a number of rugged business men are forming a national association to combat Government in business, to break up this unholy alliance. There is not a professional lunching-and-dining fellowship in America that is not now applauding to the echo such ringing cries as "Let Us Alone," "Take Government Out of Business," "Hands Off," "Unburden Capital." With an eye on such straws in the wind, President Hoover publicly states that all notions about planned economy come out of Russia, thus placing such distinguished men as Gerard Swope and Owen D. Young under the horrible Red ban. As one of the high-powered utility propagandists recently explained, the best way to discredit an opponent is to pin a Red tag on him—without reference to his deserts, of course.

Hence it is important to ask, calmly and without reference to election heats, just what all this means. In what way is the Government "in business" and how did it get there? Here we climb down out of the muggy atmosphere of controversy and face a few stubborn facts. They are entered in the indubitable records of the Government of the United States and are as evident as the hills to them that have eyes to see. Let us catalogue a few of them seriatim for the first time in the history of this adventure in logomachy.

1. Government Regulation of Railways, from 1887 to the last Act of Congress. How did the Government get into this business? The general cause was the conduct of railway corporations under the rule of rugged individualism—rebates, pools, stock watering,

bankruptcy-juggling, all the traffic will bear, savage rate slashing, merciless competition, and the rest of it. If any one wants to know the facts, let him read the history of railroading in the sixties, seventies, and early eighties, or, if time is limited, the charming illustrations presented in Charles Francis Adams' "A Chapter of Erie." And what was the immediate cause of the Government's intervention? The insistence of business men, that is, shippers, who were harassed and sometimes ruined by railway tactics, and of farmers, the most rugged of all the rugged individualists the broad land of America has produced. And the result? Let the gentle reader compare the disastrous railway bankruptcies that flowed from the panic of 1873, including bloodshed and arson, with the plight of railways now, bad as it is. Government regulation is not a utopian success, but it is doubtful whether any of our great business men would like to get the Government entirely out of this business and return to the magnificent anarchy of Jay Gould's age. President Hoover has not even suggested it.

2. Waterways. Since its foundation the Government has poured hundreds of millions into rivers, harbors, canals, and other internal improvements. It is still pouring in millions. Some of our best economists have denounced it as wasteful and have demonstrated that most of it does not pay in any sense of the word. But President Hoover, instead of leaving this work to private enterprise, insists on projecting and executing the most elaborate undertakings, in spite of the fact that some of them are unfair if not ruinous to railways. Who is back of all this? Business men and farmers who want lower freight rates. There is not a chamber of commerce on any Buck Creek in America that will not cheer until tonsils are cracked any proposal to make the said creek navigable. Dredging companies want the good work to go on, and so do the concerns that make dredging machinery. Farmers are for it also and they are, as already said, the ruggedest of rugged individuals—so rugged in fact that the vigorous efforts of the Farm Board to instill co-operative reason into them have been almost as water on a duck's back.

3. The United States Barge Corporation. Who got the Government into the job of running barges on some of its improved waterways? Certainly not the Socialists, but good Republicans and Democrats speaking for the gentlemen listed under 2 above.

4. The Shipping Business. The World War was the occasion, but not the cause of this departure. For more than half a century the politicians of America fought ship subsidies against business men engaged in the shipbuilding and allied industries. At last, under the cover of war necessities, the Government went into the shipping business, with cheers from business. Who is back of the huge expenditures for the merchant marine? Business men. Who supports huge subsidies under the guise of "lucrative mail contracts," making a deficit in postal finances to be used as proof that the Government cannot run any business? Business men clamor for these mail subsidies and receive them. Who put the Government into the business of providing cheap money for ship building? Business men did it. Those who are curious to know how these things were done may profitably read the sworn testimony presented during the investigation of W. B. Shearer's patriotic labors on behalf of the shipbuilding interests, especially the exhibits showing how money was spent like water "educating" politicians. Who wants navy officers on half pay to serve on privately owned ships? Business men. Who wants the Government to keep on operating ships on "pioneer" lines that do not pay? Business men. And when the United States Senate gets around to investigating this branch of business, it will find more entertainment than the Trade Commission has found in the utility inquest.

5. Aviation. The Government is "in" this business. It provides costly airway services free of charge and subsidizes air mail. Who is behind this form of Government enterprise? Gentlemen engaged in aviation and the manufacture of planes and dirigibles. Then the Government helps by buying planes for national defense. Who is opposed to air mail subsidies? A few despised "politicians."

6. Canals. Who zealously supported the construction of the Panama Canal? Shippers on the Pacific Coast who did not like the railway rates. Also certain important shipping interests on both coasts—all controlled by business men. Who insisted that the Government should buy the Cape Cod Canal? The business men who put their money into the enterprise and found that it did not pay. Then they rejoiced to see the burden placed on the broad back of our dear Uncle Sam.

7. Highway Building. Who has supported Federal highway aid—the expenditures of hundreds of millions on roads, involving the taxation of railways to pay for ruinous competition? Everybody apparently, but specifically business men engaged in the manufacture and sale of automobiles and trucks. Who proposes to cut off every cent of that outlay? Echoes do not answer.

8. The Department of Commerce, its magnificent mansion near the Treasury Department, and its army of hustlers scouting for business at the uttermost ends of the earth. Who is responsible for loading on the Government the job of big drummer at large for business? Why shouldn't these rugged individualists do their own drumming instead of asking the taxpayers to do it for them? Business men have been behind this enormous expansion, and Mr. Hoover, as Secretary of Commerce, outdid every predecessor in the range of his activities and the expenditure of public money. Who proposes to take the Government out of the business of hunting business for men who ought to know their own business?

9. The Big Pork Barrel—appropriations for public buildings, navy yards, and army posts. An interesting enterprise for the United States Chamber of Commerce would be to discover a single piece of pork in a hundred years that has not been approved by local business men as beneficiaries. When Ben Tillman shouted in the Senate that he intended to steal a hog every time a Yankee got a ham, he knew for whom the speaking was done.

10. The Bureau of Standards. Besides its general services, it renders valuable aid to business undertakings. Why shouldn't they do their own investigating at their own expense, instead of turning to the Government?

11. The Federal Trade Commission. Who runs there for rulings on "fair practices"? Weary consumers? Not often. Principally, business men who do not like to be outwitted or cheated by their competitors. If we are rugged individualists, why not let every individualist do as he pleases, without invoking Government intervention at public expense?

12. The Anti-Trust Acts. Business men are complaining against these laws on the ground that they cannot do any large-scale planning without incurring the risk of prosecution. The contention is sound, but who put these laws on the books and on what theory were they based? They were the product of a clamor on the part of farmers and business men against the practices of great corporations. Farmers wanted

lower prices. Business men of the smaller variety objected to being undersold, beaten by clever tricks, or crushed to the wall by competitors with immense capital. And what was the philosophy behind the Sherman Act and the Clayton Act? Individualism, pure and undefiled. "The New Freedom" as President Wilson phrased it in literary language. "Break up the trusts and let each tub stand on its own bottom." That was the cry among little business men. As lawyers put it in their somber way, "the natural person's liberty should not be destroyed by artificial persons known as corporations created under the auspices of the State." Whether any particular business man is for or against the anti-trust laws depends upon his particular business and the state of his earnings.

13. The Tariff. On this tender subject it is scarcely possible to speak soberly. It seems safe to say, however, that if all the business men who demand this kind of "interference"—with the right of capital to find its most lucrative course, industry and intelligence their natural reward, commodities their fair price, and idleness and folly their natural punishment—were to withdraw their support for protection, cease their insistence on it, then the politicians would probably reduce the levy or go over to free trade; with what effect on business no one can correctly predict. At all events there are thousands of business men who want to keep the Government in the business of protecting their business against foreign competition. If competition is good, why not stand up and take it?

14. The Federal Farm Board. This collectivist institution is the product of agrarian agitation, on the part of our most stalwart individualists, the free and independent farmers; but President Hoover sponsored it and signed the bill that created it. Now what is its avowed purpose as demonstrated by the language of the statute, the publications of the Farm Board, and the activities carried out under its auspices? It is primarily and fundamentally intended to stabilize prices and production through co-operative methods. And what has the Board done? It has encouraged the development of co-operation as distinguished from individualism among farmers; it has financed co-operative associations; it has denounced individualistic farmers who insist on growing as much as they please, and has tried to get them to increase their earnings by a common limitation of production. If the Agri-

cultural Marketing Act means anything, if the procedure of the Farm Board is not a delusion, then co-operation is to be substituted for individualism in agricultural production and marketing. If there is ever to be a rational adjustment of supply to demand in this field, the spirit and letter of President Hoover's measure must be realized through organized action by millions of farmers under Federal auspices. The other alternative is simon-pure individualism: let each farmer produce what he likes, as much of it as he likes, and sell it at any price he can get. But under the happy title "Grow Less —Get More," the Farm Board has given instructions to farmers: "One thing the successful manufacturers learned long ago was that they could not make money when they produced more than they could sell at a profit." The obvious moral is for farmers to get together under Government leadership or hang separately.

15. The Moratorium and Frozen Assets. The latest form of Government interferences with "the natural course" of economy is the suspension of payments due the United States from foreign powers on account of lawful debts and the proposal to give public support to "frozen assets." What was the source of inspiration here? American investment bankers having got themselves into a jam in their efforts to make easy money now demand Government assistance. In 1927 one of the most distinguished German economists told the writer of this article that the great game in his country, as in other parts of Europe, was to borrow millions from private bankers in the United States, so that it would ultimately be impossible to pay reparations, the debts due the Federal Government, *and* then the debts owed to private parties. The expected result? American bankers would then force their Government to forego its claims for the benefit of private operators who wanted to make bankers' commissions and eight or ten per cent on their money. Well, the game worked. American taxpayers are to be soaked and American bankers are to collect—perhaps.

And what is a "frozen asset"? It is a gaudy name for a piece of paper representing a transaction in which the holder expected to get a larger return than was possible on a prudent, rock-bottom investment. A Hartford, Connecticut, municipal four is not frozen; a holder can get better than par in the present dark hour of Wall Street's sorrow. A seven per cent Western farm mortgage is frozen tight—and ought to be, and the holder frozen with it. So is a Bolivian seven. Why should there be Federal interference to save investors from reaping the fruits of their folly and greed? No reason, except that the latter want the Government to bring home their cake so that they can eat it. The trouble is that American capital, in finding "its most lucrative course," has fallen into a slough, and if it gets out with its gains intact the Government must bring a derrick to hoist it.

III

In this survey of a few leading economic activities of the Federal Government the emphasis is not critical; so far as the present argument is concerned, any or all of these functions may be justified with respect to national interest. Indeed it is difficult to find any undertaking of the Government which is not supported by some business men on the ground of national defense. In the early days of our history even those statesmen who generally espoused free trade or low tariffs were willing to concede the importance of making the nation independent in the manufacture of munitions of war. And in the latest hour, subsidies to the merchant marine, to aviation, and to waterways development are stoutly defended in the name of preparedness. Transforming a creek into a river navigable by outboard motor boats can be supported by military engineers on the theory that it gives them practice in their art. No; the emphasis here is not critical. The point is that the Federal Government does not operate in a vacuum, but under impulsion from without; and all of the measures which put the Government into business have been supported by rugged individualists—business men or farmers or both. The current tendency to describe the Government as a meddling busybody, prying around and regulating for the mere pleasure of taking the joy out of somebody's life, betrays an ignorance of the facts in the case. The Government of the United States operates continually in the midst of the most powerful assembly of lobbyists the world has ever seen—the representatives of every business interest that has arisen above the level of a corner grocery; and there is not a single form of Government interference with business that does not have the approval of one or more of these interests—except perhaps the taxation of incomes for the purpose, among

other things, of paying the expenses of subsidizing and regulating business.

For forty years or more there has not been a President, Republican or Democratic, who has not talked against Government interference and then supported measures adding more interference to the huge collection already accumulated. Take, for instance, President Wilson. He made his campaign in 1912 on the classical doctrine of individualism; he blew mighty blasts in the name of his new freedom against the control of the Government by corporate wealth and promised to separate business and Government, thus setting little fellows free to make money out of little business. The heir of the Jeffersonian tradition, he decried paternalism of every kind. Yet look at the statutes enacted under his benign administration: the trainmen's law virtually fixing wages on interstate railways for certain classes of employees; the shipping board law; the Farm Loan Act; Federal aid for highway construction; the Alaskan railway; the Federal Reserve Act; the Water Power Act; and all the rest of the bills passed during his régime. Only the Clayton anti-trust law can be called individualistic. No wonder Mr. E. L. Doheny exclaimed to Mr. C. W. Barron that President Wilson was a college professor gone Bolshevist! And why did Democrats who had been saying "the less government the better" operate on the theory that the more government the better? Simply because their mouths were worked by ancient memories and their actions were shaped by inexorable realities.

Then the Republicans came along in 1921 and informed the country that they were going back to normalcy, were determined to take the Government out of business. Well, did they repeal a single one of the important measures enacted during the eight years of President Wilson's rule? It would be entertaining to see the sanhedrim of the United States Chamber of Commerce trying to make out a list of laws repealed in the name of normalcy and still more entertaining to watch that august body compiling a list of additional laws interfering with "the natural course of business" enacted since 1921. Heirs of the Hamiltonian tradition, the Republicans were not entitled to talk about separating the Government from business. Their great spiritual teacher, Daniel Webster, a pupil of Hamilton, had spoken truly when he said that one of the great reasons for framing the Constitution was the creation of a government that could regulate commerce. They came honestly by subsidies, bounties, internal improvements, tariffs, and other aids to business. What was the trouble with them in the age of normalcy? Nothing; they just wanted their kind of Government intervention in the "natural course of industry." Evidently, then, there is some confusion on this subject of individualism, and it ought to be examined dispassionately in the light of its history with a view to discovering its significance and its limitations; for there is moral danger in saying one thing and doing another—at all events too long.

IV

Historically speaking, there are two schools of individualism: one American, associated with the name of Jefferson, and the other English, associated with the name of Cobden. The former was agrarian in interest, the latter capitalistic. Jefferson wanted America to be a land of free, upstanding farmers with just enough government to keep order among them; his creed was an agrarian creed nicely fitted to a civilization of sailing ships, ox carts, stagecoaches, wooden plows, tallow dips, and home-made bacon and sausages; and since most of the people in the United States, during the first century of their independence, were engaged in agriculture, they thought highly of Jefferson's praise of agriculture and his doctrine of anarchy plus the police constable. Cobden's individualism was adapted to capitalist England at the middle of the nineteenth century—early industrial England. At that moment his country was the workshop of the world, was mistress of the world market in manufactured commodities, and feared no competition from any foreign country. English capitalists thus needed no protective tariffs and subsidies and, therefore, wanted none. Hence they exalted free trade to the level of a Mosaic law, fixed and eternal. They wanted to employ labor on their own terms and turn working people out to starve when no profitable business was at hand; so they quite naturally believed that any Government interference with their right to do as they pleased was "bad." Their literary apologist, Macaulay, clothed their articles of faith in such magnificent rhetoric that even the tiredest business man could keep awake reading it at night.

Closely examined, what is this creed of individualism? Macaulay defines it beautifully in the passage which the New York Bank and our happy advertising agency quoted so joyously. Let the Government maintain peace, defend property, reduce the cost of litigation, and observe economy in expenditure—that is all. Do American business men want peace all the time, in Nicaragua, for instance, when their undertakings are disturbed? Or in Haiti or Santo Domingo? Property must be defended, of course. But whose property? And what about the cost of litigation and economy in expenditures? If they would tell their hired men in law offices to cut the costs of law, something might happen. As for expenditures, do they really mean to abolish subsidies, bounties, and appropriations-in-aid from which they benefit? Speaking brutally, they do not. That is not the kind of economy in expenditures which they demand; they prefer to cut off a few dollars from the Children's Bureau.

Then comes Macaulay's system of private economy: let capital find its most lucrative course alone, unaided: no Government tariffs, subsidies, bounties, and special privileges. That is the first item. Do American business men who shout for individualism believe in that? Certainly not. So that much is blown out of the water. Macaulay's next item is: let commodities find their fair price. Do the gentlemen who consolidate, merge, and make price understandings want to allow prices to take their "natural course"? By no means; they are trying to effect combinations that will hold prices up to the point of the largest possible profit. Macaulay's third item is: let industry and intelligence receive their natural reward. Whose industry and intelligence and what industry and intelligence? When these questions are asked all that was clear and simple dissolves in mist.

Then there is Macaulay's last item: let idleness and folly reap their natural punishment. That was a fundamental specification in the bill of Manchesterism. Malthus made it a law for the economists: the poor are poor because they have so many babies and are improvident; nothing can be done about it, at least by any Government, even though it enforces drastic measures against the spread of information on birth control. Darwin made a natural science of it: biology sanctified the tooth and claw struggle of business by proclaiming the eternal tooth and claw struggle of the jungle. If the Government will do nothing whatever, all people will rise or sink to the level which their industry or idleness, their intelligence or folly commands. No distinction was made between those who were idle because they could find no work and those who just loved idleness for its own sake—either in slums or mansions. Those who hit bottom and starved simply deserved it. That is the good, sound, logical creed of simon-pure individualism which Herbert Spencer embedded in fifty pounds of printed matter. To him and all his devotees, even public schools and public libraries were anathema: let the poor educate themselves at their own expense; to educate them at public expense is robbery of the taxpayer—that industrious, intelligent, provident person who is entitled to keep his "natural reward."

Do any stalwart individualists believe that simple creed now? Not in England, where Liberals, professing to carry on the Cobden-Bright tradition, vote doles for unemployed working people. Why not let idleness and folly get their natural punishment? Why not, indeed? There must be a reason. Either the individualists betray their own faith, or, as some wag has suggested, they are afraid that they might find themselves hanging to a lantern if they let the idle and the foolish starve, that is, reap the natural punishment prescribed by Macaulay. Nor do American individualists propose to let nature take her course in this country. There is no danger of revolution here; as Mr. Coolidge has said, "we have had our revolution"; yet business men agree with the politicians on feeding the hungry. It is true that they seem to be trying to obscure the issues and the facts by talking about the beneficence of private charity while getting most of the dole from public treasuries; but that is a detail. Although our rugged individualists advertise Macaulay's creed, their faith in it appears to be shaky or their courage is not equal to their hopes. Then why should they try to delude themselves and the public?

There is another side to this stalwart individualism that also deserves consideration. Great things have been done in its name, no doubt, and it will always have its place in any reasoned scheme of thinking. Individual initiative and energy are absolutely indispensable to the successful conduct of any enterprise, and there is ample ground for fearing the tyranny and ineptitude of Governments. In the days of pioneering industry in England, in our pioneering days when forests were to be cut and mountain fastnesses explored, individualism was the great dynamic which drove enterprise forward. But on other pages of the doom book other entries must be made. In the minds of most people who shout for individualism vociferously, the creed, stripped of all flashy rhetoric, means getting money, simply that and nothing more. And to this creed may be laid most of the shame that has cursed our cities and most of the scandals that have smirched our Federal Government.

That prince of bosses, Croker, put the individualist creed in its bare logical form when he said that he was working for his own pocket all the time, just as "every man in New York is working for his pocket." Fall, Doheny, and Sinclair were all splendid individualists; they explained that they hoped to make money out of their transactions, even while they covered their operations with the mantle of patriotism —national defense. Tammany judges, Connolly and his iron pipe, Doyle with his split fees, and policemen growing rich on vice are all individualists of the purest brand. W. B. Shearer collecting money from ship-building concerns to make a naval scare so that they might increase their profits belongs to the same school. Britten, bringing a fleet to Montauk Point to boom real estate in which he is interested, does nothing reprehensible under the Manchester creed; his capital is finding "its most lucrative course." Wilder and Bardo, representing shipping interests, when they spend money in Washington "educating" members of Congress, are following the law of the game. They are perfect individualists. The ruinous chaos in coal and oil is to be attributed to the same Darwinian morality. Finally, Al Capone, with his private enterprise in racketeering, is a supreme individualist: he wants no Government interference with his business, not even the collection of income taxes; if he is "let alone" he will take care of himself and give some money to soup kitchens besides.

The cold truth is that the individualist creed of everybody for himself and the devil take the hindmost is principally responsible for the distress in which Western civilization finds itself—with investment racketeering at one end and labor racketeering at the other. Whatever merits the creed may have had in days of primitive agriculture and industry, it is not applicable in an age of technology, science, and rationalized economy. Once useful, it has become a danger to society. Every thoughtful business man who is engaged in management as distinguished from stock speculation knows that stabilization, planning, orderly procedure, prudence, and the adjustment of production to demand are necessary to keep the economic machine running steadily and efficiently. Some of our most distinguished citizens—Owen D. Young, Gerard Swope, Nicholas Murray Butler, and Otto Kahn, for example —have, in effect, warned the country that only by planning can industry avoid the kind of disaster from which we are now suffering; on all sides are signs of its coming—perhaps soon, perhaps late, but inevitably.

And all of them know that this means severe restraints on the anarchy celebrated in the name of individualism. The task before us, then, is not to furbish up an old slogan, but to get rid of it, to discover how much planning is necessary, by whom it can best be done, and what limitations must be imposed on the historic doctrine of Manchesterism. And to paraphrase Milton, methinks puissant America, mewing her mighty youth, will yet kindle her undazzled eyes at the full midday beam, purge and unscale her long abused sight, while timorous and flocking birds, with those that love the twilight, flutter about, amazed at what she means, and in their envious gabble would prognosticate a year of sects and schisms.

1931

FRANKLIN D. ROOSEVELT

1882–1945

WHEN FRANKLIN D. ROOSEVELT, who had been assistant secretary of the navy in Wilson's cabinet and governor of New York for two terms, was elected to the presidency in 1932, business and industry had sunk to a low level. "I promised a program of action," Roosevelt observed; and his inaugural address set the stage for the New Deal. The address, which was broadcast, will doubtless rank among the greatest of presidential inaugural addresses.

The Public Papers of Franklin D. Roosevelt, 13 vols., New York, 1947–1950.
Frank B. Freidel, *Franklin D. Roosevelt, The Apprenticeship*, Boston, 1952.
Frank B. Freidel, *Franklin D. Roosevelt, The Ordeal*, Boston, 1954.
Arthur M. Schlesinger, Jr., *The Age of Roosevelt*, Boston, 1957.

» » INAUGURAL ADDRESS « «

I am certain that my fellow Americans expect that on my induction into the Presidency I will address them with a candor and a decision which the present situation of our Nation impels. This is preeminently the time to speak the truth, the whole truth, frankly and boldly. Nor need we shrink from honestly facing conditions in our country today. This great Nation will endure as it has endured, will revive and will prosper. So, first of all, let me assert my firm belief that the only thing we have to fear is fear itself—nameless, unreasoning, unjustified terror which paralyzes

needed efforts to convert retreat into advance. In every dark hour of our national life a leadership of frankness and vigor has met with that understanding and support of the people themselves which is essential to victory. I am convinced that you will again give that support to leadership in these critical days.

In such a spirit on my part and on yours we face our common difficulties. They concern, thank God, only material things. Values have shrunken to fantastic levels; taxes have risen; our ability to pay has fallen; government of all kinds is faced by serious curtailment of income;

the means of exchange are frozen in the currents of trade; the withered leaves of industrial enterprise lie on every side; farmers find no markets for their produce; the savings of many years in thousands of families are gone.

More important, a host of unemployed citizens face the grim problem of existence, and an equally great number toil with little return. Only a foolish optimist can deny the dark realities of the moment.

Yet our distress comes from no failure of substance. We are stricken by no plague of locusts. Compared with the perils which our forefathers conquered because they believed and were not afraid, we have still much to be thankful for. Nature still offers her bounty and human efforts have multiplied it. Plenty is at our doorstep, but a generous use of it languishes in the very sight of the supply. Primarily this is because rulers of the exchange of mankind's goods have failed through their own stubbornness and their own incompetence, have admitted their failure, and have abdicated. Practices of the unscrupulous money changers stand indicted in the court of public opinion, rejected by the hearts and minds of men.

True they have tried, but their efforts have been cast in the pattern of an outworn tradition. Faced by failure of credit they have proposed only the lending of more money. Stripped of the lure of profit by which to induce our people to follow their false leadership, they have resorted to exhortations, pleading tearfully for restored confidence. They know only the rules of a generation of self-seekers. They have no vision, and when there is no vision the people perish.

The money changers have fled from their high seats in the temple of our civilization. We may now restore that temple to the ancient truths. The measure of the restoration lies in the extent to which we apply social values more noble than mere monetary profit.

Happiness lies not in the mere possession of money; it lies in the joy of achievement, in the thrill of creative effort. The joy and moral stimulation of work no longer must be forgotten in the mad chase of evanescent profits. These dark days will be worth all they cost us if they teach us that our true destiny is not to be ministered unto but to minister to ourselves and to our fellow men.

Recognition of the falsity of material wealth as the standard of success goes hand in hand with the abandonment of the false belief that public office and high political position are to be valued only by the standards of pride of place and personal profit; and there must be an end to a conduct in banking and in business which too often has given to a sacred trust the likeness of callous and selfish wrongdoing. Small wonder that confidence languishes, for it thrives only on honesty, on honor, on the sacredness of obligations, on faithful protection, on unselfish performance; without them it cannot live.

Restoration calls, however, not for changes in ethics alone. This Nation asks for action, and action now.

Our greatest primary task is to put people to work. This is no unsolvable problem if we face it wisely and courageously. It can be accomplished in part by direct recruiting by the government itself, treating the task as we would treat the emergency of a war, but at the same time, through this employment, accomplishing greatly needed projects to stimulate and reorganize the use of our natural resources.

Hand in hand with this we must frankly recognize the overbalance of population in our industrial centers and, by engaging on a national scale in a redistribution, endeavor to provide a better use of the land for those best fitted for the land. The task can be helped by definite efforts to raise the values of agricultural products and with this the power to purchase the output of our cities. It can be helped by preventing realistically the tragedy of the growing loss through foreclosure of our small homes and our farms. It can be helped by insistence that the Federal, State, and local governments act forthwith on the demand that their cost be drastically reduced. It can be helped by the unifying of relief activities which today are often scattered, uneconomical, and unequal. It can be helped by national planning for and supervision of all forms of transportation and of communications and other utilities which have a definitely public character. There are many ways in which it can be helped, but it can never be helped merely by talking about it. We must act and act quickly.

Finally, in our progress toward a resumption of work we require two safeguards against a return of the evils of the old order: there must be a strict supervision of all banking and credits and investments, so that there will be an end to speculation with other people's money; and there must be provision for an adequate but sound currency.

These are the lines of attack. I shall presently urge upon a new Congress, in special session, detailed measures for their fulfillment, and I shall seek the immediate assistance of the several States.

Through this program of action we address ourselves to putting our own national house in order and making income balance outgo. Our international trade relations, though vastly important, are in point of time and necessity secondary to the establishment of a sound national economy. I favor as a practical policy the putting of first things first. I shall spare no effort to restore world trade by international economic readjustment, but the emergency at home cannot wait on that accomplishment.

The basic thought that guides these specific means of national recovery is not narrowly nationalistic. It is the insistence, as a first consideration, upon the interdependence of the various elements in and parts of the United States —a recognition of the old and permanently important manifestation of the American spirit of the pioneer. It is the way to recovery. It is the immediate way. It is the strongest assurance that the recovery will endure.

In the field of world policy I would dedicate this Nation to the policy of the good neighbor —the neighbor who resolutely respects himself and, because he does so, respects the rights of others—the neighbor who respects his obligations and respects the sanctity of his agreements in and with a world of neighbors.

If I read the temper of our people correctly, we now realize as we have never realized before our interdependence on each other; that we cannot merely take but we must give as well; that if we are to go forward, we must move as a trained and loyal army willing to sacrifice for the good of a common discipline, because without such discipline no progress is made, no leadership becomes effective. We are, I know, ready and willing to submit our lives and property to such discipline, because it makes possible a leadership which aims at a larger good. This I propose to offer, pledging that the larger purposes will bind upon us all as a sacred obligation with a unity of duty hitherto evoked only in time of armed strife.

With this pledge taken, I assume unhesitatingly the leadership of this great army of our people dedicated to a disciplined attack upon our common problems.

Action in this image and to this end is feasible under the form of government which we have inherited from our ancestors. Our Constitution is so simple and practical that it is possible always to meet extraordinary needs by changes in emphasis and arrangement without loss of essential form. That is why our constitutional system has proved itself the most superbly enduring political mechanism the modern world has produced. It has met every stress of vast expansion of territory, of foreign wars, of bitter internal strife, of world relations.

It is to be hoped that the normal balance of Executive and legislative authority may be wholly adequate to meet the unprecedented task before us. But it may be that an unprecedented demand and need for undelayed action may call for temporary departure from that normal balance of public procedure.

I am prepared under my constitutional duty to recommend the measures that a stricken Nation in the midst of a stricken world may require. These measures, or such other measures as the Congress may build out of its experience and wisdom, I shall seek, within my constitutional authority, to bring to speedy adoption.

But in the event that the Congress shall fail to take one of these two courses, and in the event that the national emergency is still critical, I shall not evade the clear course of duty that will then confront me. I shall ask the Congress for the one remaining instrument to meet the crisis—broad Executive power to wage a war against the emergency, as great as the power that would be given to me if we were in fact invaded by a foreign foe.

For the trust reposed in me I will return the courage and the devotion that befit the time. I can do no less.

We face the arduous days that lie before us in the warm courage of national unity; with the clear consciousness of seeking old and precious moral values; with the clean satisfaction that comes from the stern performance of duty by old and young alike. We aim at the assurance of a rounded and permanent national life.

We do not distrust the future of essential democracy. The people of the United States have not failed. In their need they have registered a mandate that they want direct, vigorous action. They have asked for discipline and direction under leadership. They have made me the present instrument of their wishes. In the spirit of the gift, I take it.

In this dedication of a Nation we humbly ask the blessing of God. May He protect each and every one of us. May He guide me in the days to come.   1933

NATIONAL PLANNING

DURING THE LATE 1890's and throughout the first decades of the twentieth century interest in the conservation of natural resources and in municipal planning indicated that laissez faire was being seriously challenged in practice as well as in social thought. The growing concern of some engineers with waste in economic life and with the social possibilities of technology found expression, in the 1920's, in public as well as in private discussion. Herbert Hoover, Secretary of Commerce, provided leadership for much of this discussion and for the co-operative projects in which the Bureau of Standards figured. The American Engineering Council's committee "on the balance of economic forces," the report of the Society of Industrial Engineers on "The Economic Significance of Technological Progress," and the emergence of the Technocrats early in the depression all focused attention on the possibilities of an abundant life for everyone within the framework of the existing order. In the Roosevelt administration experiments such as the Tennessee Valley Authority were inaugurated for the realization of some of these ideas. Many special reports on various aspects of planning appeared, of which the following selection from a report of the National Resources Board is representative.

Planned Society, Yesterday, Today, Tomorrow; A Symposium, Findlay MacKenzie, ed., New York, 1937.

From: REPORT OF THE NATIONAL
» »   PLANNING BOARD   « «

WHAT IS INVOLVED IN PLANNING

Planning consists in the systematic, continuous, forward-looking application of the best intelligence available to programs of common affairs in the public field, as it does to private affairs in the domain of individual activity. In every well-directed home, in every business, in every labor or agricultural group, in every forward-looking organization, social planning goes on continuously, and in the world of government there is also opportunity for its exercise.

Several considerations are important in looking at plans for planning:

(1) The necessity and value of coordinating our national and local policies, instead of allowing them to drift apart, or pull against each other, with disastrous effect.

(2) The value of looking forward in national life, of organizing preventive policies as well as remedial, of preventing the fire rather than putting it out.

(3) The value of basing plans upon the most competent collection and analysis of the facts.

At the same time, it may be pointed out:

First. In any case, not all planning is or should be national planning. As stated above, there is local and State planning, and planning by quasi-public and private agencies and institutions all over the land. The city planning boards thus far chiefly concerned with physical plans and the State planning boards just beginning their work, to say nothing of scores of industrial and other organizations, will continue to develop their special points of view. The centralization of all planning in Washington is not contemplated, and even if possible would not be desirable, since planning is an attitude and practise that must command the confidence and cooperation of wide groups of people to ensure successful operation, must come from the bottom as well as from the top down, from the circumference as well as the center.

It may reasonably be anticipated that many of the most useful suggestions regarding types of planning will emerge from jurisdictions outside the Federal Government, and outside the governmental group altogether, from detached individuals and associations of individuals, industrial, scientific, or otherwise.

Planning, then, does not involve the preparation of a comprehensive blue print of human activity to be clamped down like a steel frame of the soft flesh of the community, by the United States Government or by any government.

Second. Planning does not involve setting up a fixed and unchangeable system, but on the contrary contemplates readjustment and revision, as new situations and problems emerge. Planning is a continuous process, and necessitates the constant reexamination of trends, tendencies, policies, in order to adapt and adjust governmental policies with the least possible friction and loss. The national life is like a moving wave in which a new equilibrium must constantly be found as it sweeps forward. Even physical planning is subject to continuing revision as new factors such as the motor vehicle appear to supersede old ways, while planning, in the broader sense of the term, is likewise subject to change as new elements come in to disturb earlier calculations.

Stubborn adherence to an outworn plan is not intelligence but stupidity, whether in the life of individuals or of nations. Prudence would, of course, dictate that reasonable stability should not be endangered by capricious or arbitrary shift of plans, but would with equal force insist that policies must be promptly modified as emerging trends and new situations necessitate recasting.

Third. It is false and misleading to assert that all planning involves wholesale regimentation of private life. Sound planning on the contrary brings about a fresh release of opportunities rather than a narrowing of choice. Street planning and traffic regulation operate for freer use of the highways than unplanned streets and uncontrolled traffic. Laws regulating unfair trade practises release the energies of fair-minded men for other activities than that of guarding against fraud and trickery.

It cannot be forgotten that regimentation is not a theory but a brutal fact in many private industries now. The modern type of nation was set up in order to break down the old private or semi-private controls over roads, justice, taxation, and to establish public and national control over situations that became unendurable. In our day, an individual business man may be absolutely regimented by a ruthless monopoly, just as an individual worker 10 may be helpless against terms dictated by an employer. This constitutes private regimentation, often of an oppressive character, unless the community sense of social justice brings about governmental defence against tyrannical exercise of private power. Over and over again in the United States, as elsewhere, the community has been obliged to intervene to protect the weaker against the insolence and oppression of private citizens who took by the throat 20 serfs, slaves, dependents, employees, crying "pay me what thou owest," in terms of injustice and outrage.

Indeed it may be found that some of those who cry "regimentation" when public planning is mentioned foresee interference with their own practices of private regimentation and exploitation of otherwise helpless persons under their private control. Those with special privileges to protect and preserve naturally ob- 30 ject to any public planning that may dislodge them from a preferred position where they are able to exact tribute from their fellow men. This is by no means the only type of opposition to planning, but it is one to which attention must from time to time be directed, since it arises from a type of exploitation from which explosive reaction is most likely to result.

The truth is that it is not necessary or desirable that a central system of planning 40 actually cover all lines of activity or forms of behavior. Such planning over-reaches itself. Even martial law tends to become civil; and over-centralized planning must soon begin to plan its own decentralization, for good management is local self-government under a centralized supervision. Thus wise planning provides for the encouragement of local and personal initiative, realizing that progress may as easily be smothered by over-centralization 50 as by its opposite. Not all government can ever be central government, or all life public life. Experience shows that there must be wide ranges of affairs in which independent criticism, independent judgement, independent

initiative is given opportunity for free growth and development in associations as in individuals. One of the recurring tasks of statesmanship is to cultivate and encourage decentralization. In the excited discussion over this subject, it is often forgotten by both sides that genuine planning really includes planning to preserve and even create uncontrolled areas of activity as well as planning for control.
10　Planning is not an end, but a means, a means for better use of what we have, a means for emancipation and release of millions of personalities now fettered, for the enrichment of human life in ways that will follow individual interest or even caprice.

Private initiative always presupposes the existence of a planned system of public order within which it may operate; a set of rules under which the game is to be played. If such
20　rules do not exist or are not enforced, or are inadequate to meet the changing situation, new rules are demanded, new systems of control are insistently urged.

When men express sincere opposition to all governmental planning, it can only mean a grave misunderstanding of what planning really is, or an opposition to some special detail of planning that seems undesirable, rather than to the general principle.
30　Wise planning is based on control of certain strategic points in a working system—those points necessary to ensure order, justice, general welfare. It involves continuing reorganization of this system of control points as the functions and situations shift from time to time. The number of controls is not as important as their strategic relations to the operation of the society in which they work. At various times, the community has found it necessary
40　to deal with landowners, with slavery, with the church, with the Army, with industrial or labor captains, with racial groups, adjusting our control points to meet special situations, and restricting privileges at one point while releasing forces and individuals at other points.

It is this shift in the form of planning, the change in strategic planning points, as social and economic conditions change that leads some to the erroneous conclusion that we have
50　never planned before in America, when in point of fact our planning has been continuous and varied as conditions varied.

The essence of successful planning is to find these strategic points as new situations develop, without too great delay, and without

seizing more points than are necessary for the purpose—or for longer time than is necessary for the purpose. Insight, sagacity, inventiveness, cooperative spirit, are far more important at this point than the club or the prison cell, or drastic attempts at regimentation.

A totally unplanned nation is as impossible and undesirable as a totally planned economy. The choice is not between anarchy on one hand and complete control over all aspects on the other. A sounder way, between these two extremes, is still open in the United States at least. We look for ways of organizing human association in the light of new conditions such as the world has not experienced before, suitable to the special problems and genius of the American people.

The noisy clash between competing slogans which substitute emotion for intelligent observation and reflection may obscure the fact that much of our present difficulty is due to the failure to adjust industry to the revolutionary changes caused by science and technology in production and indirectly in distribution. No one planned our present difficulties. They are here because we did not plan soon enough to absorb the gifts of science in industry and every-day life without too great waste and shock.

Some of these strategic planning points developed in the history of this nation have already been discussed. In more recent times, national attention has been directed toward land utilization and population, conservation of natural resources, flood control, regulation of public utilities, unfair trade practices, and still more recently to the banking and financial structure of the Nation, to industrial security both on the part of worker and investor, to unemployment, to social insurance and welfare problems, to un-American living standards— these among a wide variety of emerging issues of national significance.

In the organization of planning undertakings, the cooperation of the natural and social sciences is of the highest importance, and in this connection attention is directed to two memoranda submitted by the organizations representing these groups and appended to this report. The National Academy of Sciences, which was organized during the Civil War for the purpose of advising the United States Government on scientific problems, has at the request of the National Planning Board generously prepared for it a valuable document (section III) pointing out the bearings of various natural sciences upon the different aspects of national planning. Likewise, the Social Science Research Council has prepared a useful statement (section III) showing the services which are being rendered the government by social scientists, and indicating lines of further development in this direction.

It appears from these statements of the natural and social scientists and from other evidence that the highest scientific talent of the Nation would be available for the purpose of systematic national planning, and that the government could count upon the cordial and unremitting cooperation of impressive agencies of investigation and exploration already organized to render effective service. The guaranty of such assistance is of deep importance in considering the possibilities of planning. In the natural science field arise many of the inventions and technologies which while increasing our possibilities for weal also make possible much woe if they are not fortunately set in the framework of the social and economic structure. The cooperation of scientists in this field should make possible a wiser and sounder adaption of technology to economic and social advancement, while the cooperation of the social scientists with their research in the field of human behavior should correspondingly facilitate the making and perfecting of social inventions.

THE GOAL OF PLANNING

It may be asked, What is the objective of planning? The goal of our national planning is nowhere more clearly stated than in the preamble to the national Constitution, in which the purposes of our political association are set forth: Justice, domestic tranquillity, common defense, general welfare, and securing the blessings of liberty to ourselves and to our posterity.

This broad statement of national aims provides the general background in which national policies may be set.

American planning will be brought about within the general framework of the American Nation, the democratic system of government, and an evolutionary system of social and economic change.

Planning is not mechanical and organizational alone, but must rest within a set of general understandings, on values to which the Nation is devoted, and for which it is willing to sacrifice lesser values. The general understanding on which our democratic system rests is that the happiness and interests of the people are paramount and that special privilege and personal ambition are subordinate to the larger national and popular purpose.

Democracy assumes that the gains of civilization are essentially mass gains, and should be enjoyed by the whole people who created them, rather than by special classes or persons.

Our government was set up for this purpose, and national planning should be directed toward this end. Ways and means of attaining these ends vary from time to time, but the general aim and purpose of our national endeavor is plain. Plans directed toward this end fall within the scope and spirit of the Constitution and of our American national goals.

Naturally, the notion of what justice is, or what the general welfare is, or what liberty is, varies under varying conditions, as our experience shows, but the general goal is clear and the main direction of effort plain enough.

The increasing yield of our soil and the expanding productivity of our industry make it possible to reach higher standards of living than ever before, provided we are able to develop the necessary social attitudes and arrangements to insure the just participation in the gifts of nature, science, and technology, by the whole people. The justice which looms so large in the preamble to the Constitution does not consist in production alone, but in a way of life in which the masses of the community enjoy their share in the gains of our civilization. Liberty in any social system must be read in its necessary relation to the common welfare; for liberty which does not bring common welfare and social justice loses its very soul.

That statesmanlike national planning will bring us nearer the American goal our experience clearly shows in every range of our life, local, national, public, and private. Statesmanlike planning might prevent the vast losses caused by inattention, as in the case of soil erosion and flood and misuse of national resources. It might prevent the wastes arising from conflicting and clashing policies, as in the case of land reclamation and land retirement, the industrial wastes arising from lack of reasonable coordination, the still more tragic wastage of human material through inattention to the protection and security of productive labor. It might make possible the invention of new technological and managerial devices for increasing the productivity of mankind and social devices for insuring the just participation of our people in their products.

In moments of industrial insecurity and wide-spread and bitter distress, the possibility of a far finer and richer life for the mass of mankind than ever before may seem a mocking unreality. But the sober fact is that in America, with its abundance of natural resources, with its technological and managerial ability, with its energetic and capable blend of peoples, a new world is within our reach if we can organize and act to take possession of it. What stands between us and the realization of the hopes that gleamed before the eyes of our people from the earliest days are only our own attitudes and our social and political management.

There is every reason to believe that the stream of scientific invention will roll on still faster in the next generation, and if statesmanship and science can keep even pace, the new world may become a marvel of human achievement. It is not our capacity to produce that fails us, but our capacity to plan the wisest use of our wealth of resources in materials and men. The gray, sober facts of science and technology, the cold engineering figures expressing our production possibilities, show what might be done if skepticism, confusion, and timidity do not paralyze us in the presence of the incredible richness of American opportunity.

Masters of unparalleled treasures of natural resources, endowed with matchless skills and techniques of management and research, nothing can stay the advance of America, unless it is the spirit of doubt and fear.

We do not stand at the broken end of a worn-out road, but look forward down a broad way to another era of American opportunity. Among the nations of the world, America has stood and still stands for discovery, for pioneering across a great continent, for fearless experiment in directions where others had failed, for achievement in mechanism and management, for ready adaptation to new conditions and easy adjustment to new ways of life. When we are resigned to drifting and too weary to plan our own American destiny, then stronger hands and stouter hearts will take up the flag of progress and lead the way out of difficulties into attainment.   1934

LOUIS M. HACKER

1899–

TO AMERICAN historical studies Louis M. Hacker of Columbia University has brought fresh understandings through his brilliant interpretations and critical essays. His writings include *The United States Since 1865* (with B. B. Kendrick, 1932 and 1939), *American Problems of Today* (1938), and *The Triumph of American Capitalism* (1940).

» » *From:* AMERICAN PROBLEMS OF TODAY « «

THE DECLINE OF AGRICULTURE

For two decades, from 1900 to 1920, the pressure on American agriculture—a pressure that had appeared in the eighteen eighties and that had reached an unbearable pitch in the middle nineties—was relieved. American industry was ready for the exploitation of the home market and thanks to an open immigration policy our urban population increased by leaps and bounds; the old immigrants from Western and Northern Europe largely, who had been attracted to the public lands, were supplanted by the new immigrants from Southern and Eastern Europe, who thronged to the cities. Industry, aided immeasurably by the rapid strides it was making as a result of mechanization, was able to furnish them with work and house, clothe, and equip them cheaply.

But if industry and trade profited enormously, so did agriculture. Mechanization on a large scale had not yet come to the farms, so that the output of farm products did not increase in proportion to the output of other consumer goods or the increase in urban population. More and more agriculture found itself in that happy position where it was being limited to the domestic market needs (at least, for cereals and meat products), without the consequent disorganizing effects of world prices. The results were therefore the following: a comparative decline in the rural and farming populations; a smaller exportable surplus of cash crops; a comparative rise in the price of farm products; and an increase in the value of the national farm plant. Between 1900 and 1910, the aggregate value of all farm property doubled; the total value of all cereals raised in the country, between 1899 and 1909, increased 79.8 per cent, while the total yield increased only 1.7 per cent; the value of all food exports declined from $545,474,000 in 1900 (39.8 per cent of total) to $369,088,000 in 1910 (19.1 per cent of total). Nothing showed more plainly the protected state of American agriculture during these few years than the index of farm prices as compared with the index for the prices of all commodities.

. . .

. . . The tale of the next half-decade was even more splendid, for during the war years the American farmer actually became affluent. The demand of the Allies for foodstuffs and cotton, the requirements of our own mobilized forces, the needs of postwar Europe before war-torn lands could be reclaimed—these factors, during 1915–1920, sent prices of crops and agricultural lands dizzily upward so that the farmer, as a producer of foodstuffs and staples and as a land speculator, grew rich and contented. American agriculture, therefore, expanded and opened marginal and submarginal lands, using irrigation and dry farming to overcome inadequate rainfall. Thus, between 1910 and 1920, the acreage increased 9 per cent; whereas over the preceding decade it had increased but 5 per cent; the land in farms in the Mountain states more than doubled; and there was an increase of five million acres of irrigated lands in the same ten years. The money values of American farms mounted, in some regions doubling, in others trebling their prices. Before the war (in 1910), land in Iowa, for example, was worth $82.00 an acre; after the war (in 1920), the same acre was worth $200. Spring wheat, in 1913, was selling at Chicago for 93 cents a bushel; the price in 1919 was $2.76. Corn, in 1913, was selling at Chicago for 70 cents; in 1919, for $1.59. Cotton, in 1913, was selling at New York for 13 cents a pound; in 1919 for 38 cents. Lulled by a sense of security, the American farmer pushed out his horizons: he increased his improvements, bought machinery for the first time on a large scale, invested in an automobile and auto trucks, installed a telephone, electrified his house and barn, and clamored for the extension by his state and county governments of the social services—better roads, consolidated schools, county hospital and nursing units, old age pensions, local farm bureaus, and university extension activities. To the accompaniment, of course, of an ever-mounting tax rate.

Alas, boom times were all too brief and the bubble of the farmer's content was pricked with a suddenness and completeness that left him shaken to his depths. The era of deflation, which set in toward the end of 1920, left its mark on industry and agriculture alike, but whereas industry began to recover with 1922, agriculture remained permanently depressed. Land values plunged downward until in 1929, that year of golden prosperity for industry, they were not much higher than they had been before the war; crop prices dropped until, in some instances, they were lower than they had been for almost half a century; agriculture was left with a heavy burden of debt and taxation as a result of overexpansion of acreage, improvements, and public budgets. The depression of 1930 and after merely served to sharpen the outlines of a situation that had been steadily getting bleaker as the decade of the twenties progressed. Put simply, farm prices had been deflated, while farm costs—necessaries for home and field, mortgage debt, taxes—were still highly inflated. The farm account could not be balanced.

The bare statistical exhibits in themselves tell a startling story. In 1919, the total farm property of the nation had been valued at $78,000,000,000; by 1929 this value was $57,604,000,000, and by 1932, $44,000,000,-

000. In 1919, the total farm income was $15,000,000,000; by 1929, $12,000,000,000, and by 1932, $5,200,000,000. In 1919, (with the average for 1909–1914 as 100), the prices paid by farmers for the commodities they needed stood at 206; the prices they received, at 205, making a ratio of prices received to prices paid of 99. That is to say, the farm dollar was worth 99 cents. But in 1929, it was worth only 89 cents; and in 1932, only 47 cents!

The efficiency of American agriculture was being hampered not only because of declines in gross and relative income. What was more serious was the fact that fixed charges were eating up a larger and larger share of the farmer's earnings so that he was compelled to divert the use of income from the improvement of his techniques to the payment of taxes and interest on mortgages. In 1910, tax payments took 3 per cent of gross income; in 1920, 3.6 per cent; in 1930, 6 per cent. In 1910, interest on mortgages took 3 per cent of gross income; in 1920, 4 per cent; in 1930, 6 per cent. In short, total fixed charges absorbed 6 per cent of gross farm income in 1910 and 12 per cent in 1930: this was indeed a heavy price to pay for land ownership. Farm mortgage debt in particular had become a millstone about the necks of American agricultural producers. In 1910, the mortgage debt on American farm land and buildings made up 27.3 per cent of the value of properties; in 1920, 29.1 per cent; and in 1930, 39.6 per cent. Inability to meet mortgage payments and to pay taxes was converting many farm owners into tenants or croppers or forcing them off the land altogether to enter the industrial reserve army of America's urban population.

Nothing proved the decline of agriculture more certainly than this state of affairs: the inability of farm tenants to pull themselves up by their own bootstraps and become farm owners. Formerly, tenancy had been of the ladder variety: younger sons, grandsons, and sons-in-law, as well as immigrants, starting out as tenants, accumulated savings and in time became owners. This upward climb had now ceased. More and more tenants were remaining permanently in that inferior status and were doomed to inadequate incomes and insecurity. In 1880, 25.6 per cent of all the farms in the country were being operated by tenants; in 1930, 42.4 per cent.

Tenancy was on the increase in the great corn-hog and wheat raising areas of the North and in the great tobacco and cotton raising areas of the South. Indeed, in 1930, 73 per cent of farms growing cotton were operated by tenants, of whom half were sharecroppers. In 1930, there were 725,000 croppers in cotton, of whom half were blacks and half whites.

Equally significant as an example of decline, was the debased position of agricultural real estate, that single factor which heretofore had always succeeded in redressing the balance. What happened to agricultural real estate is graphically indicated by the following index figures of the estimated value per acre for 1914, 1920, 1929, and 1933. (Average for 1912–1914 = 100.)

CONDITION OF AGRICULTURAL REAL ESTATE

	1914	1920	1929	1933
United States	103	170	116	73
East North Central States...............	103	161	100	62
West North Central States...............	103	184	112	64
East South Central States...............	103	199	129	79
West South Central States...............	104	177	136	82
Mountain States.........	100	151	101	69
Pacific States...........	106	156	142	96

Such were the outward signs of a deepseated malady which was not a passing phase but had all the aspects of permanence. Let us see what were the reasons for the depression under which the country's agricultural interest labored in the decades of the twenties and thirties. They may be summed up in a single phrase: the foreign market contracted and the domestic market did not expand.

First, as regards the foreign situation. The great historical reason for the advance of American agriculture after the Civil War had been our debtor status. We were borrowing capital from Europe to help transform our capitalism from a merchant to an industrial base. As a result, we engaged in an heroic expansion of agriculture to permit payments on foreign borrowings and for those raw materials we ourselves could not produce. In brief, American industry was growing up behind high tariff walls with the assistance of foreign capital; and American agricultural surpluses helped make this possible.

By 1920 (as we shall see below in greater detail) the United States had become a creditor nation. But other countries, due to the staggering costs of the World War, because they were debtors, and because of the ambitions of their own capitalists, were now desperately trying to obtain foreign exchange. How help the process better than by the enlargement of their own agricultural operations? This was notably true of the newer lands—Canada, the Latin American countries, Australasia, the Far East—which could balance their international payments only by selling in the world market those foodstuffs and fibers which we ourselves kept pouring into Europe up to the end of the World War. What made the situation worse was the fact that European countries began to strive for agricultural self-sufficiency. By resettlement projects, by great grants of agricultural credits, by high tariff walls, import quota systems, and milling requirements, virtually every European country (including the United Kingdom!) was seeking to build up a domestic agricultural group large enough to supply at least the home food requirement. Why was this? The following reasons may be cited: (1) The fear of dearth in time of war; (2) the need to conserve foreign exchange for basic raw materials which could not be produced at home—oil, cotton, rubber, minerals, metals; (3) the political desirability of building up a rural conservative interest, supported by government, which could be used against the propertyless and dispossessed urban workers in the event of the threat of revolutionary overthrow.

The result was a vast expansion in the production of agricultural goods throughout the world during the nineteen twenties. Between 1913 and 1932, the United States increased its area devoted to major food crops from 290,000,000 to 320,000,000 acres, or more than 10 per cent; in the same period, Europe, Canada, Argentina, and Australia increased their acreage for the same crops from 631,000,000 to 724,000,000, or more than 16 per cent. As Messrs. Ezekiel and Bean pointed out in their study "The Economic Bases for the Agricultural Adjustment Act": "This increase in foreign competition and foreign self-sufficiency brought about a persistent decline in United States exports of food products from 1921 on, long before the 1929 collapse. The 1932–1933 export volume finally shrank below prewar levels. In the face of this shrinkage in

foreign demand, acreage of important crops in the United States has been maintained about 10 per cent above prewar acreage."

Thus, the wheel had turned full circle in not more than sixty years, and America in the twenties was in the position England had been in when American agricultural surpluses first appeared in the world market. *Then,* English farmers had not been able to meet the competition of American grains and meats because they were burdened with heavy rents, labor costs, and capital charges. *Now,* we could not compete with Argentinian and Australian beef growers, Canadian and Polish bacon manufactures, Argentinian, Australian, Canadian, Russian, and Manchurian grain farmers and Indian, Chinese, Russian, and Brazilian cotton producers for exactly the same reasons. The doors of the world market were slowly swinging shut.

Second, as regards the domestic situation. The possibilities of increasing, domestic consumption of agricultural goods, in order to take in the slack, were remote. The following factors may be noted: 1. Our population growth was slowing down because of immigration restriction and birth control. 2. Because of these facts, the age distribution of our population was changing, with interesting repercussions upon the consumption of agricultural goods. Indeed, the two decades 1910–1930 witnessed a profound change in dietary habits as Americans shifted from a reliance on grains and beef to a greater use of pork, vegetables, fruits, milk, and sugar. The significance of the shift lies in this fact: grains and beef are largely the products of extensive cultivation; pork products, vegetables, fruits, and milk are the products of intensive cultivation requiring less land in use and more capital expenditures. And extensive cultivation was the method of production notably of the typical American farming unit, the family farm.

Also, the consumption of agricultural goods at home was not increasing proportionately because of changing habits in feeding and clothing. 3. Women were dieting and thus eating less calories. 4. Improved methods of heating homes, the wide use of heated automobiles, and the machine's growing elimination of the need for hard and back-breaking human toil also made it possible for men as well as women to dispense with foods with high caloric contents: for, as became generally known, calories were required largely to supply heat and replace rapidly wearing out body tissue. 5. Cotton was being replaced by rayons and other chemically produced fabrics. 6. Finally, agriculture itself had become more efficient, making it possible to produce more foods and fibers for each dollar of labor and capital expended. In fact, between 1919 and 1929, on a stationary cultivated acreage, the output of American farmers increased more than 20 per cent! There were notably three reasons responsible for this revolutionary advance: progress in the application of mechanical methods and the motorization of farm equipment (with an accompanying decrease of land use necessary for the provision of feed grains for horses and mules); increasing acre yields as a result of intensive cultivation, the improvement of crop strains, and the application of fertilizer; and the greater efficiency of milk and meat animals per unit of feed consumed. There was, therefore, a surplus of farmers in the United States.

Governmental programs for agriculture, during the nineteen twenties, were concerned only with details. There was no effort made to come to grips with the fundamental problems of high costs, heavy fixed charges, economic and social maladjustments springing from tenancy, and contraction of the market for agricultural goods. In the late twenties, a powerful political agrarian interest sought the passage of fundamental agricultural legislation; but these pressures Presidents Coolidge and Hoover resisted. President Hoover did make an effort to cope with the question of wheat and cotton surpluses by taking them out of the market—but to no avail. The actions of government must now be passed in review.

. . .

During the twenties, the outstanding proposals advanced by the farmer interests for agricultural relief were the equalization fee and export debentures plans. These programs set it as their purpose to raise the level of domestic prices on agricultural products up to those points where the full advantages of the tariff duties on agricultural commodities could be obtained. This was to be achieved by segregating the domestic requirement from the exportable surplus. The former was to be sold at the inflated domestic price; the latter at the going world price. Under the equalization fee scheme, the difference between the artificial domestic price and the normal world price (on

the surplus) was to be borne by the farmers of each particular commodity. Under the export debenture scheme, this difference was to be borne by the government out of customs receipts. In short, in both instances, price fixing was to be countenanced; in the case of the export debenture scheme, the growers of staples which entered the world market were to be directly subsidized.

The McNary-Haugen bill, which incorporated the equalization fee scheme, made its first appearance in the lower house in January, 1924, but twice failed of passage. In February, 1927, however, the farmers mobilized enough strength to jam the measure through both houses; they did not, however, have margins large enough to override President Coolidge's veto. The final test of strength came in the spring of 1928. The Senate passed the bill in April by a vote of 53 to 23; the House in May, by a vote of 204 to 121. Again President Coolidge rejected the measure and again Congress found it impossible to gather the necessary two-thirds for passage over the veto. The bill, in its final form, had these provisions: It provided for a federal farm board. The board was to have authority to make loans to cooperative associations for the purpose of assisting them in controlling seasonable surpluses in excess of domestic needs. The board was to collect an equalization fee from the grower of each staple sufficient to cover the losses, met with in the marketing of the surplus, due to the difference between the domestic price and the world price. A revolving fund of $400,000,000, to finance these operations, was to be set up.

The export debenture plan was first introduced in Congress in January, 1926, reintroduced in 1928, and in 1929 was added by insurgent Republican Senators in both the Smoot tariff bill and the administration's agricultural marketing bill. In each case, the Senate was compelled to give way before the House's demand that the debenture be abandoned. The essentials of the proposal were the following: Export bounties were to be paid on wheat, corn, rice, cotton, tobacco, swine, and cattle. The rates specified in the 1928 bill were to be one-half of the tariff duties. In other words, the domestic price was to be the world price plus one-half of the duty on the particular commodity. These bounties were to be paid in the form of negotiable instruments known as debentures which were to be receivable in payment of import duties. That is to say, governmental revenues were to be reduced by the amount of export debentures or bounties issued for a particular year. A federal farm board was to be set up and its chief function was to regulate domestic production of agricultural staples by reducing or even canceling the debenture rates. So, if production by the farmers was increased, the bounty was to be cut; if the increase in production was more than 15 per cent over the average of the preceding five years, the debenture was to be revoked.

The Agricultural Marketing Act of 1929 embodied President Hoover's program for agricultural relief. The Seventy-first Congress had been called in special session to cope with the farm and tariff problems, and it turned its attention to the former first. The House passed the Agricultural Marketing bill with little discussion; but the Senate insisted upon the inclusion of the export debenture in its measure and, despite the President's disapproval, passed the bill in that form. Only after the House had voted down the Senate bill by a record vote did the Senate abandon the export debenture. On June 14, the Senate accepted the Conference Committee's report, and on the next day President Hoover affixed his signature. The Agricultural Marketing Act rejected the price-fixing and subsidy features of the earlier agricultural proposals. It was founded on the principle of voluntary cooperation under governmental auspices: that is to say, through the operation of nationwide cooperative marketing associations, and by the exercise of self-discipline, agriculture was to be redeemed. Agriculture with its millions of small units, was to work as corporate industry did: curtail production to establish an equilibrium between domestic supply and demand, shift quickly from one form of activity to another as demands changed, rationalize its plant, seek a greater return from wages of management than from capital investments.

The new act's provisions were the following: 1. There was to be established a Federal Farm Board of eight members, to be appointed by the President, with the consent of the Senate, for six years. 2. This Board was to encourage the organization and development of agricultural cooperatives. 3. A revolving fund of $500,000,000 was set up, from which loans were to be made to the cooperatives. 4. The Board might institute advisory committees for the particular agricultural commodities, and on their application might recognize stabilization corporations. These stabilization corporations, through loans from the revolving fund, were to be enabled to control, handle, and market the surpluses of their particular commodities. 5. The Board might enter into agreements to insure the cooperatives and the stabilization corporations against loss because of price declines.

In the stimulation of cooperative marketing associations the Board, in its three years' work, met with a notable success. Through its efforts there were organized cooperatives for marketing nearly every sort of crop produced in the country. The Board, in its first year alone, received applications for loans from 206 cooperatives and approved loans to 132 of these, to which it granted $165,146,555. But more important than encouraging the process of self-help was the injunction laid upon the Board of "aiding in preventing and controlling surpluses in any agricultural commodity, through orderly production and distribution, so as to maintain advantageous domestic markets and prevent such surpluses from causing undue and excessive fluctuations or depressions in prices for the commodity." In the cases of wheat and cotton such crises, in the fall of 1929, impended with the result that the Board was compelled to act. Proceeding on the assumption that the wheat crop of 1929 was a short one, and that, therefore, the market price was too low, the Board offered to lend wheat cooperatives $1.18 per bushel for all wheat held off the market. And in February, 1930, the Board created the first of its two stabilization agencies, the Grain Stabilization Corporation.

This organization entered the wheat market twice and in all bought some 330,000,000 bushels, the first operation being completed in the middle of 1930 and the second in the middle of 1931. Three results were apparent from these ventures by the Federal Farm Board's subsidiary. 1. Its purchases succeeded in pegging the domestic price from 20 to 30 cents above the world figure, for something like half a year. But as soon as the Grain Stabilization Corporation abandoned the market permanently in June, 1931, the price of July wheat dropped to 57 cents, the lowest for the commodity since 1896. 2. The federal government was left in possession of the whole 1930–1931 carry-over, which menaced the price of the new crop. 3. What to do with the wheat surpluses? There was, apparently, nothing for the government to do but hold them. From July to

November, 1931, the Federal Farm Board was able to sell abroad some 47,000,000 bushels; the rest was left on its hands to be disposed of piecemeal, while the storage charges mounted higher and higher to wipe out most of the value of the original investment.

The same procedure was repeated in the case of cotton. The Federal Farm Board lent to cotton cooperatives, for cotton held off the market, at an average price of 16 cents a pound. But cotton prices continued to drop so that here, too, resort was had to the creation of a stabilization agency. The Cotton Stabilization Corporation, formed in June, 1930, went into the market and in its efforts to sustain the price was compelled to buy the whole 1929–1930 carry-over, a total of 1,319,800 bales. The price could not be supported, however, with the result, at the end of November, cotton at New York was selling for 6.75 cents a pound. The second operation, the purchase of the 1930–1931 carry-over, left the Cotton Stabilization Corporation with a total supply of 3,250,000 bales in warehouses; and in 1932, cotton was selling at 5 cents. After its affairs were wound up, it was discovered that the Federal Farm Board had lost $150,000,000 in cotton alone.

As early as the summer of 1930, perhaps because it itself had little confidence in the program, perhaps because it appreciated that it was best to have two strings to its bow, the Federal Farm Board began an intensive campaign to urge the farmer to reduce acreage. Said the Board's members in public statements: The American farmer was overproducing; he ought to cut his acreage to the requirements of the domestic market; his surpluses entered a world market where they were compelled to compete with products raised by cheap labor, on cheap land, and shipped by cheap water transportation. But the American grower of staples would not, or could not, reduce acreage; and the crops for 1931–1932 and 1932–1933 were as bountiful as ever. There was another ironic element in the situation, and it was this: while the Federal Farm Board exhorted and cajoled, in an effort to obtain acreage reduction, the Department of Agriculture and the states, through their educational agencies and experiment stations, happily continued on their way teaching the farmers how to grow bigger and better crops! This paradoxical state of affairs continued until President Franklin D. Roosevelt took office.

1938

ROBERT S. LYND (1892–   ) and

HELEN MERRELL LYND (1896–   )

N O BOOK purporting to reveal the America of the 1920's better succeeded in achieving its aim than *Middletown, A Study in Contemporary American Culture* (1929). With the assistance of his wife and a well-selected staff, Dr. Lynd, who had by temperament and by experience a gift for winning the confidence and co-operation of people in many walks of life, studied Muncie, Indiana, in a way which had never before been used in examining the life of a community. It is true that the field-survey technique had been used by educators and by social workers; but the Lynds refined and pushed this method further than anyone had done before. *Middletown* proved to be an objective analysis of the life of a typically American community. That life reflected the mores of the 1920's and illuminated the patterns of American culture. In 1937 the follow-up study, *Middletown in Transition,* revealed the influence of the depression on the community.

» » *From:* MIDDLETOWN IN TRANSITION « «

CHAPTER XIII

MIDDLETOWN FACES BOTH WAYS

The preceding chapters have sought to make explicit the elements of permanence and of change in Middletown as the city has met with four types of experience peculiarly conducive to cultural change: sudden and great strain on its institutions, widespread dislocation of individual habits, pressure for change from the larger culture surrounding it, and at some points the actual implementing from without of a changed line of action. These ten years of boom and depression might be expected to leave permanent marks on the culture.

The boom experiences were not essentially different in kind from those Middletown had known before: optimism, growth, making money—these things are in the city's main stream of tradition. Such an experience as climbing to the very verge of the long-expected population of 50,000 contained elements of novelty and has, despite the depression, left a permanent deposit in the city in the form of increased self-regard. The prosperity of the fat years, while sharpening the disappointments of the depression, also remains today in Middletown in the form of enhanced personal goals and glimpsed new psychological standards of living for many of its citizens. The fact that Middletown does not regard the depression as in any sense "its own fault," or even the fault of the economy by which it lives, makes it easy for the city to think of the confusion following 1929 as "just a bad bump in the road," one of those inevitable occurrences that spoil things temporarily but do not last. The gold-rush scramble back to confidence which the research staff witnessed in 1935 was the inevitable result of such a rationale of the depression. Middletown was in effect saying, albeit soberly and decidedly anxiously: "It's all over, thank God! And now we'll get after all those things we were planning for ourselves in 1928–29!" In a culture built on money, the experience of better homes, better cars, winter vacations in Florida, and better educated children dies hard; and while some people's hopes, especially among the working class, have been mashed out permanently by the depression, the influential business group who determine the wave length of Middletown's articulate hopes are today busily broadcasting the good news that everything is all right again.

· · ·

The depression experiences contained more outright novelty than did the years 1925–29:

A city exultantly preoccupied with the question, "How fast can we make even more money?" was startled by being forced to shift its central concern for a period of years to the stark question, "Can we manage to keep alive?"

A city living excitedly at a future which all signs promised would be golden lived for a while in the present with its exigent demands.

A city living by the faith that everyone can and should support himself lived through a period of years in which it had to confess that at least temporarily a quarter of its population could not get work.

A city intensely opposed to society's caring for able-bodied people has taxed itself to support for an indefinitely long period one in every four of its families.

A city that has chronically done without many manifestly needed civic improvements, on the philosophy that it does no good to hunt up and plan desirable things to do, because there isn't any money to pay for them, has lived for a time in a world in which not money but ability to plan and carry out progress was the limiting factor.

A city built around the theory of local autonomy has lived in a world experiencing rapid centralization of administrative authority and marked innovations in the interference by these centralized agencies in local affairs.

A city that lives by the thought that it is one big cooperating family has had the experience of a wholesale effort by its working class to organize against its business class under sponsorship from Washington.

A city committed to faith in education as the key to its children's future has had to see many of its college-trained sons and daughters idle, and to face the question as to what education is really "worth."

A city devoted to the doctrine that "Work comes first," to an extent that has made many of its citizens scarcely able to play, has faced

the presence of enforced leisure and heard people talk of "the new leisure." Civicly, the community has begun to state positively the problem of the leisure of the mass of its people, and
to make wider provision for popular leisure
pursuits.

A city still accustomed to having its young
assume largely the values of their parents has
had to listen to an increasing number of its
young speak of the world of their parents as a
botched mess.

A city in which the "future" has always been
painted in terms of its gayer-hued hopes has
been forced to add to its pigments the somber
dark tones of its fears.

Experiences such as these partake in their
cumulative effect of the crisis quality of a
serious illness, when life's customary busy im-
mediacies drop away and one lies helplessly
confronting oneself, reviewing the past, and
asking abrupt question of the future. What has
Middletown learned from its crisis and partial
convalescence?

Chapter I stated some of the larger questions
of this sort which the research staff took to
Middletown in June, 1935. The broad answer
to these questions is that basically the texture
of Middletown's culture has not changed.
Those members of the research staff who had
expected to find sharp differences in group
alignments within the city, in ways of thinking,
or feeling, or carrying on the multifarious daily
necessities of life, found little to support their
hypotheses. Middletown is overwhelmingly living by the values by which it lived in 1925; and
the chief additions are defensive, negative elab-
orations of already existing values, such as,
among the business class, intense suspicion of
centralizing tendencies in government, of the
interference of social legislation with business,
of labor troubles, and of radicalism. Among
the working class, tenuous and confused new
positive values are apparent in such a thing as
the aroused conception of the possible role of
government in bolstering the exposed position
of labor by social legislation, including direct
relief for the unemployed. But, aside from
these, no major new symbols or ideologies of a
positive sort have developed as conspicuous
rallying points. Leadership in the community
has not shifted in kind, but has become more
concentrated in the same central group observed in 1925. The different rates of change
pointed out in the earlier study as occurring in
the different areas of living have not altered

materially: economic activities have set the
pace and determined the cadence of these
years, though the changes have not differed in
kind over these ten years anything like so
sharply as during the thirty-five-year period
covered in the earlier study; in terms of actual
rate of change and radical quality of innovation, the institutions concerned with care for
the unable leaped into the lead during the depression, although Middletown likes to regard
the changes in this area as "purely emergency
and temporary" in character; education, leisure, and the relations among family members
have exhibited some changes; while the city's
local government and religion have remained
as before most resistant of all its institutions to
change.

With the exception of the widespread innovations in caring for the unemployed, which by
1936 were already contracting their scope, a
map of Middletown's culture shows today
much the same contours as before; no wholly
new hills and valleys appear save in this "temporary" provision for the unemployed and the
resulting new public works; the configuration
is the same. Even the fault lines which appear
today and show signs of developing into major
fissures within the community were faintly visible in 1925. In the main, a Rip Van Winkle,
fallen asleep in 1925 while addressing the Rotary or the Central Labor Union, could have
awakened in 1935 and gone right on with his
interrupted address to the same people with
much the same ideas.

Such changes as are going forward in Middletown are disguised by the thick blubber of
custom that envelopes the city's life. The city
is uneasily conscious of many twinges down under the surface, but it resembles the person
who insists on denying and disregarding unpleasant physical symptoms on the theory that
everything *must* be all right, and that if anything really is wrong it may cure itself without
leading to a major operation. The conflicts under the surface in Middletown are not so much
new as more insistent, more difficult to avoid,
harder to smooth over. Many of these latent
conflicts, aggravated by the depression and
now working themselves toward the surface of
the city's life, have been pointed out in the preceding pages: conflicts among values hitherto
held as compatible; conflicts among institutions
—economic and political, economic and educational and religious, economic and familial;
conflicts among groups in the community

breaking through the symbols of the unified city; conflicts between deep-rooted ideas of individual and collective responsibility; conflicts, above all, between symbols and present reality.

The physical and personal continuities of life are relatively great in the small community, and the average dweller in such a community probably has a sense of "belonging" that is qualitatively somewhat different from that of the big-city dweller. The institutions in the small city tend to be familiar and, with the help of many assumptions of long standing as to how they are linked together and operate, a quality of simplicity is imparted to them in the minds of local people. By assuming continuities and similarities, this simplicity is interpreted outward to include "American life" and "American institutions."

One of the major elements of conflict imparted by the depression to Middletown has been the injection of a new sense of the inescapable complexity of this assumedly simple world. As indicated earlier, the more alert Middletown people met the depression with an earnest desire to "understand" it—only to be thrown back later, in many instances, with a sense that it was "too big" for them and that all they could do was to try to stick to their jobs and save their own skins. One suspects that for the first time in their lives many Middletown people have awakened, in the depression, from a sense of being at home in a familiar world to the shock of living as an atom in a universe dangerously too big and blindly out of hand. With the falling away of literal belief in the teachings of religion in recent decades, many Middletown folk have met a similar shock, as the simpler universe of fifty years ago has broken up into a vastly complicated physical order; but, there, they have been able to retain the shadowy sense of their universe's being in beneficent control by the common expedient of believing themselves to live in a world of unresolved duality, in which one goes about one's daily affairs without thought of religion but relies vaguely on the ultimates in life being somehow divinely "in hand." In the economic order, however, it is harder for Middletown to brush aside the shock by living thus on two largely unconnected levels, for the economic out-of-handness is too urgently threatening to daily living.

So Middletown tries to forget and to disregard the growing disparities in the midst of which it lives. Its adult population has, through its socially gay youth and busy adult life, resisted the patient scrutiny of problems and the teasing out of their less obvious antecedents and implications. As a local man remarked in 1924 in commenting on the pressure of modern living, "We've lost the ability to ponder over life. We're too busy." And, if in the boom days Middletown was "too busy" to ponder, it was too worried to do so in the depression. It is quite characteristic, for instance, that, as one woman remarked in 1935, "We never get down to talking about things like the coming of fascism. The only time we ever talk about any of those things is when we comment on a radio program." Rather than ponder such things, Middletown prefers either to sloganize or to personalize its problems. And the more the disparities have forced themselves to attention, the more things have seemed "too big" and "out of hand," the more Middletown has inclined to heed the wisdom of sticking to one's private business and letting the uncomfortable "big problems" alone save for a few encompassing familiar slogans. Where Middletown cannot avoid these big problems and must on occasion present at least the semblance of a balance in this system of nonbalancing intellectual bookkeeping, it is resorting increasingly to the suppression of detailed entries and to the presentation of only the alleged totals.

One frequently gets a sense of people's being afraid to let their opinions become sharp. They believe in "peace, but—." They believe in "fairness to labor, but—." In "freedom of speech, but—." In "democracy, but—." In "freedom of the press, but—." This is in part related to the increased apprehensiveness that one feels everywhere in Middletown: fear on the part of teachers of the D.A.R. and the Chamber of Commerce; fear by businessmen of high taxes and public ownership of utilities and of the Roosevelt administration; fear by laborers of joining unions lest they lose their jobs; fear by office-holders wanting honest government of being framed by the politicians; fear by everyone to show one's hand, or to speak out.

But this process of avoiding issues goes on less and less fluently. With a widening gap between symbol and practice in the most immediate concerns of living, there are more forced choices as to where one's emphasis is to be placed. Middletown wants to be adventurous and to embrace new ideas and practices, but it also desperately needs security, and in this conflict both businessmen and workingmen appear to be clinging largely to tried sources of security rather than venturing out into the untried. Middletown people want to be kind, friendly, expansive, loyal to each other, to make real the idea of a friendly city working together for common ends; but, in a business world where one is struggling for self-preservation, or for power and prestige as a supposed means to self-preservation, warm personal relations, like the more fastidious sorts of integrity, may tend to become a luxury and be crowded to the wall. If necessary, one dispenses with affection. People want to continue to live hopefully and adventurously into the future, but if the future becomes too hazardous they look steadily toward the known past.

On the surface, then, Middletown is meeting such present issues and present situations as it cannot escape by attempting to revert to the old formulas: we must always believe that things are good and that they will be better, and we must stress their hopeful rather than their pessimistic aspects. This leads to the stating of such social problems as may arise defensively and negatively—rather than to engaging in a positive program for social analysis and reconstruction. It is still true in 1936 that, to Middletown, such things as poverty or a depression are simply exceptions to a normally good state of affairs; and anything that goes wrong is the fault of some individuals (or, collectively, of "human nature") rather than anything amiss with the organization and functioning of the culture. The system is fundamentally right and only the persons wrong; the cures must be changes in personal attitudes, not in the institutions themselves. Among these personal cures for its social woes are the following six basic qualities needed for a better world outlined in a local address: "faith, service, cooperation, the Golden Rule, optimism, and character." "The typical citizen," says an editorial approvingly, "discounts the benefits of the political and economic New Deal and says that common sense is the answer to the depression. . . . He thinks hard work is the depression cure." Or again, "If profits are low, it is still possible to get a good deal of enjoyment by doing the best possible under adverse circumstances and by taking pride in our work."

This marked tendency in Middletown's thought and feeling to see the place where remedial change is needed in individual people and not in its institutions helps to ease its tension over local political corruption and other shortcomings in the midst of which it lives. Its faith in the ultimate quality and final perfection of its institutions is thus left intact, and its Christian emphasis upon the need to spur on weak and faltering human nature to that perfecting of itself "which all history proves to be slowly taking place" makes the individual shoulder the whole burden of blame. Over and over again one sees Middletown following this line of reasoning. Thus, for instance, the reason Middletown's business class is unable to see any sense in such a concept as "class differences" is that it recognizes no relevant basis for "classes" in the institutional system. And it does not recognize them because, according to its way of viewing things, "getting ahead" is a personal matter. The institutions are there, fixed and final in their major aspects, and the individual must struggle to make them work and to be more worthy of them. Once one gets this point of view, Middletown's rationale of "the rich" as "social benefactors" and of "the iniquity of the New Deal" becomes apparent. One can see why Middletown feels the rightness of recent editorials in its press such as the following:

LET'S GIVE THE RICH A REST

It is popular just now to assail the wealthy, and unpopular to defend them, and yet most of the economic progress that America has made would have been impossible had this not always been a land of opportunity for those who wish to make money without undue restrictions upon their gains. . . . Thousands of boys reared in poverty have become millionaires through their own ability, through their unbridled ambitions, and in becoming so have supplied occupations and the comforts of life to many times the number of thousands who have acquired the millions.

Instead of laying all our troubles upon those who have had the talent and the brains to become wealthy, why not each of us assume our share of responsibility for the economic situation of the nation?

. . .

. . . To men holding the philosophy these editorials reveal, efforts in Washington or elsewhere to make changes in *institutions* by which men live constitute a misguided assault on the one source of strength and progress within a nation, namely, the personal drive within the individual to accumulate wealth and to "better himself." "Progress," according to this philosowhy, is a by-product of the pursuit of wealth.

The essentially instrumental character of Middletown's living noted earlier—namely, its emphasis upon the "future," "saving," "trying to get somewhere in life," and so on, as over against the present quality of living—tends to augment its tension over emerging conflicts. This sort of instrumental living puts a heavy premium upon assumed simplicity and reliability in the underlying institutional system. One can hardly live confidently *at* the future unless one assumes a guaranteed highway; if one assumes the broad, sure highway, one need not concern oneself too much over dusty inadequacies in the present, because the road mounts surely just around the next bend; but if one questions the very existence of a sure highway "as some radicals and long-haired thinkers do," then what is to become of all the virtues of fortitude and hard work! A culture thus committed to instrumental living tends, because emotionally it so badly needs to do so, to do with its present difficulties along the road precisely what Middletown has tended to do with the depression, *i.e.*, to regard it as just an unduly stiff bit in the road. And only with great difficulty or as a result of prolonged discouragement will it do what a minority of Middletown's working class are beginning to do—ask whether the road is really leading anywhere, whether after all it is the best possible road, or even whether the present isn't a good time and place to recognize one's difficulties and to begin to face them.

Loudly as Middletown affirms and reaffirms all its hopeful, ameliorative beliefs, the "Down here under our vests we're scared to death" note was heard again and again in 1935 when business-class or working-class people were talking unofficially. Some of its tensions it had been unable to overlook, to sloganize away, or to brush aside as merely personal frailties subject to correction as men become "better." The long pull of the depression had even promoted occasional rare questions as to whether the system itself was as sound as Middletown liked to believe. An editorial in mid-1933 on "Machines and the Human Equation" had stated:

We have been making society mechanical instead of making machinery social. We have to humanize our mechanized industries by putting human values above material values and the real welfare of all above the false welfare of the few. . . . What is needed here is social engineering.

An even bolder editorial (in the afternoon paper—it could hardly have appeared in the morning paper) about the same time, remarking on the suicide of an unemployed man, had said under the unfamiliar caption, "The Right to Live by Work":

Why should anybody wipe himself out of existence because he has no money? Have we set up some kind of a false standard of value? . . . Someday and somehow, finally, we are going to straighten 10 these things out. You may call the new order by anything you please, but it is coming. The inherent right of every man and woman who is willing to do his part to maintain reasonable social conditions, which means to live decently, cannot be gainsaid by any system. That is basic. Let us not fool ourselves by thinking the old systems are to be continued indefinitely. . . . The right of a willing man to work and live by his labor is paramount. There is nothing else important.

Although the official front had recovered its 21 flawless exterior by 1935, Middletown people knew that they had been living for a while in a world that made more natural the raising of such questions. The acute concerns of the depression were dropping somewhat behind, but over the contours of the city stood out the bench marks of depression experience. And Middletown was afraid, even as it whooped things up over "the return of prosperity"; and 30 perhaps it whooped things up the more just because it was afraid.

Week after week during 1935 the outside radio was bringing in talks by men like Father Coughlin and Huey Long. Over the air came into the cottages and even into many business-class homes points of view not allowed to appear in a favorable light in the local press. "I'm surprised," commented a businessman, "at the number of intelligent people who listen to 40 Father Coughlin and believe he talks sense. Curiously, too, people don't seem to resent his being a Catholic." Down at Pop Alexander's South Side beer hall men talked freely and favorably of Father Coughlin, and some South Side families had his emblems in their homes. On the South Side, too, Huey Long's slogan, "Share the wealth," elicited loyalty. Some working people expressed their willingness to "follow any kind of man who stands for that." 50

As this goes to press, Middletown has just come through what many of its people regarded as the most critical national election within the memory of anyone now living in the city. The weight of frightened hope with

which the city's leading businessmen backed
Landon to defeat Roosevelt was almost literally
beyond exaggeration—and, even more than in
previous elections, the employers were prepared to go to great lengths to contrive to make
their employees "vote right." To these business
folk this particular election was a holy crusade;
if Landon and the Republican party had won,
a cool, cleansing sponge, they felt, would have
10 wiped out all their nightmare memories of four
years of New Deal flaunting of American ideals
and security.

With its characteristic proclivity for resolving issues into stark blacks and whites and per-
sonalizing each within the manageable compass
of a devil or a savior, business leaders in Middletown see in Roosevelt all that they are
against, the personified denial of all their wants
19 and of all the virtues of the pioneer tradition.

. . .

In the view of Middletown's business leaders,
there has been "an insane man in the White
House," with "our best mindless thinkers advising him." The bitterness of speeches before
civic clubs and of statements in the casual conversations of businessmen, and the monotonous,
shrill efforts by the two daily papers to mobilize local public opinion greatly surpass the
30 quieter conservatism met with in 1925:

"We businessmen here aren't just a bunch of
tories," commented a local banker heatedly, "but
we're scared to death that a lot of reckless political
wild men will take everything away from us. We
believe in change and know it's going on. We believe in looking ahead, but we don't believe in trying to do it all at once. It'll take two or three hundred years to get the perfect state. Change is slow
and big changes won't come in our lifetime, so
40 meanwhile we intend to go ahead and not worry
too much about what these changes will be or
ought to be.

"And we *know* politics. Have you seen our Congressman? You can size him up by just looking at
him! Look (pulling a sheet from his desk), here's
an application of the brother of our Negro janitor
for a C.C.C. job. The boy's a graduate of Tuskegee.
See here, the first four recommendations he has to
send in on the back of his application are his district leader, then two more local politicians, and
50 finally his state political boss. We businessmen see
this rotten political business everywhere, in all
these alphabet organizations in (Middletown); the
word comes down the line from Washington—it's
just party politics.

"We've no faith in Roosevelt—his angel wings
and smiling words cover up a worse political ma-

chine than Hoover ever had. He isn't honest—he
talks one way and acts another. He has no courage
—or rather courage at the wrong time. He isn't fit
to be President and can't hold a candle to Hoover.
I've been reading the articles in the Saturday
Evening Post about the depression and they're
right—I know from our banking connections with
New York and Chicago.

"Sure we need planning. But these bright boys
that jam Washington don't know their stuff. Who's
a big enough man to plan? We businessmen are
afraid of bureaucrats and planners. I've walked
through Washington offices, and I never saw so
much loafing in a business office. Now a business
outfit like the American Telephone and Telegraph
Company plans, but what do *they* do? They don't
rush into experiments all over. They try an experiment in a single state. And look at the controls they
have over them! Their common stockholders control them, and if they don't make money, they're
turned out. But government employees don't have
to make money.

"All these big plans they're making in Washington look well, read well—but they just won't work.
They're Utopian, and we don't live and try to do
business in a Utopia! By what God-given right do
these fellows in Washington think they can do a
job so big? It's the very immensity of national planning that makes it impossible. The old law of supply and demand can't be repealed or amended. It
applies to labor and to materials, raw and finished.
Roosevelt's like a general who sits at the top and
hands down orders from man to man till they get
to the privates sweating under a sixty-pound pack
—and he's the fellow that carries out the order.

"You can't make the world all planned and soft.
The strongest and best survive—that's the law of
nature after all—always has been and always will
be."

From this vision of catastrophe, Middletown's business leaders turn back terrified to
"the old ways—the American way" embodied
in "Landon, the Careful Kansan." Here Middletown saw its own "middle-of-the-road" image
reflected reassuringly back to it. As the following somewhat careful, because pre-nomination,
editorial in early June of 1936 indicates, here
was a man who, business-class Middletown
was prepared to believe, thinks and feels as it
does:

ESTIMATE OF "ALF" LANDON

"Alf" Landon is without any important political
career behind him. He is not especially attractive of
personality, his radio voice is poor, he never has
accomplished big things in any given line of
thought and endeavor, his qualities of statesmanship are yet to be discovered, his knowledge of
economics is uncertain, . . . but the people seem

to believe he is utterly honest. Given utter honesty, other things appear unimportant.

Maybe "Alf" Landon is not a statesman. . . . Maybe he knows more about drilling an oil well in wildcat territory and striking it lucky than he knows about the proper sartorial accouterment for our ambassador to the Court of St. James. . . . But the people of the United States, beyond doubt, have the conception that he is "square" in a time of many governmental intrigues: that he has common sense with which to combat the subtleties of the theories advanced by the professional bloc at Washington. . . . Maybe we should be gradually settling down to this business of having common sense in government, and maybe "Alf" Landon is the new prophet. . . .

Landon has two advantages as a candidate. One of them is that he has a very short record in public service and, therefore, is little known. The other is that he speaks the language of the common people. If there is a third it is . . . that he has the common sense that is the inheritance of those who live in the Midwestern prairies.

Even on the eve of the election, leaders in Middletown's business class hoped for victory. On October 28, one of the X brothers announced that "Defeatism is gone. . . . We go into the closing days of the campaign determined to achieve our goal of true American government . . . as opposed to radicalism, waste, and dictatorial powers." The day before election, a long editorial warned Middletown solemnly:

BUT IT COULD HAPPEN HERE

One who goes to the polls Tuesday should do so with a feeling of the solemn obligation that rests upon him and with thankfulness in his heart that THUS FAR he still has a privilege that is denied to most of the peoples of the earth—the privilege to play his part in government. In spite of attempts at regimenting about everybody in America in the last three and a half years, the voter is still free to cast his ballot as he sees fit.

A dictatorship may come to America, as it has come to other nations; our freedom may be destroyed or greatly limited. . . .

A good deal has been said in this campaign as to whether we Americans are to retain the American plan of government—a plan that has been more successful than any that ever has been tried. Under it the United States grew great and rich and prosperous. The plan contemplates the restoration of good times UNDER THE LAWS OF FREEDOM AND INDIVIDUAL ENTERPRISE. That is the path we have taken down the years, and it has been a good path. The plan has not been perfect, of course, for no plan of government is that, nor is one ever likely

to be that has to take into account human frailties and human proneness to err. But we can say of it truthfully that it has proved to be the BEST PLAN any nation ever has tried. . . .

"It can't happen here?" . . .

THIS THING COULD NOT HAVE HAPPENED TO GERMANY—BUT IT DID HAPPEN. [Here followed a recital of the plight of Italy and Russia.] Nor do we know from week to week what may happen to France now that Communism has become so powerful a factor there.

So it is no idle fear that comes to us in America that we, too, some day may suffer the fate of these other nations from which the last vestige of liberty has departed. Nor can we quiet ourselves by the thought that the American plan of government will continue.

The way tomorrow's election goes may have a great deal to do with the maintenance of this American plan of government unsullied.

IT CAN HAPPEN HERE!

It is difficult to say what Middletown's 59 per cent majority for Roosevelt in 1936 means. The local press is inclined to take it philosophically as one of those occasional blind acts of nature; editorially the vote is spoken of as an "avalanche" and an "earthquake." Despite the city's long record of Republican majorities, most of Middletown looks upon the quadrennial national election as it does upon a horse race: in all such things occasional upsets will occur, in the nature of things. The easy tolerance of these people is great, their ability to adjust and to "make the best of" situations almost unlimited. There are grounds, therefore, for brushing aside the local result of the 1936 election as of little permanent significance. Certainly it does not signify the presence of "radicalism" or of a desire for drastic change. The vote for minority, left-wing parties through the entire country was less than 1 per cent of the total. Implicit in the vote were all of the following in varying degrees: a belief that things were at least better in 1936 than they had been four years before, the experience of positive relief aid from Washington, a vague feeling on the part of the numerical majority who constitute the working class that a government may be something that can operate on *their* side in *their* behalf, reaction against the forceful tactics of business leaders in the campaign, and in some cases the settling of scores "against the X family" and their dominance in local affairs.

To an unparalleled extent the election of 1936 probably represented to Middletown peo-

ple the chance to do something for personal
security. And it is the different views of different sections of Middletown's population as
to where security lies *for them* that gives to
this election such significance as it may prove
in future to have had. Despite the tendency of
Middletown folk to look upon presidential elections good-naturedly as "a bit of excitement,
after which we all settle down again and re-
10   sume whatever we were doing before," a definite sense of local "class difference" has been
generated by the election by reason of its acute
depression background, the activity of the Federal government in helping to meet local problems, and the resulting diverging class views as
to where security for individuals in different
strata of the population lies.

As noted elsewhere, there is but little evidence of the emergence in Middletown of any
20   clear sense of class solidarity among the working people. Likewise, the fifty-fifty vote of the
middle-class folk of small income reveals their
ambivalence, though, again, it is possibly significant of their growing uneasiness as to where
their security lies that so many of them refused
to side with the big-business group on the unusually acute issues presented by the campaign.

For the more coherent group of business
leaders, however, the situation is far otherwise.
30   One sees here the financially and socially dominant group of leaders of the city, men who
usually dominate the opinion of the city in
terms of the public interest as they interpret it,
groggy and ill-tempered with seven years of
denied hope, and now thwarted in the hope
that was to end fear and the need for hope.
They confront a city in which the usually docile
six to seven in every ten in the population who
make up the working class have "gotten out of
40   hand" and asserted their numerical predominance. These earnest, hard-working, able businessmen read in their afternoon paper the post-
election comment by the editor:

I talked with the manager of a great industry
not long ago who put it this way: "The big hogs
are letting the little pigs up to the trough. They
know that if they don't they'll all be little pigs
pretty soon, for the big hogs will be butchered."

51   Faced with the necessity to "endure four
more years of Roosevelt," it is likely that these
men will adopt a definite policy of putting on
the brakes at every possible point to prevent
things they dislike from happening. Their purposes are being clearly stated in post-election
editorials:

The best bulwark of defense for American institutions continues to be the courts, especially the
Supreme Court of the United States.

If the President seeks to attain such N.R.A. objectives as limitations on working hours, wage
boosts, and improved working conditions there
would be conflict.

If President Roosevelt moves to the right or
if big business the country over contrives a
working alliance with him, Middletown's business leaders will "go along." Should the present
tension continue unabated, the mood of men of
power and ability such as these may conceivably lead to explosive action. Middletown does
not ordinarily do things suddenly. Its mood is
cautious. It does not tend to initiate change.
But it will line up overnight behind a widely
diverging *fait accompli* if the latter suits its
deep emotional need for security.

At the moment, Middletown looks equally
askance at both fascism and communism. Both
are foreign, authoritarian, and intensely distasteful. "All that stands between communism
and fascism and what the United States has,"
declared a speaker before Rotary, "is a little
paper ballot. The ballot is the only heritage left
us by the men who fought in the Revolutionary
War. Whenever one of the fundamental liberties is taken away it leaves an open road to the
forces of communism and fascism." "Fascism is
as violent and dictatorial as Bolshevism," said
an editorial in March, 1932. "It means revolution just as surely as Bolshevism does; it is just
as false to the common man's rights." In brac-
ing its feet against "centralized government,"
"bureaucracy," and the "great danger that by
over-generosity (government relief) we shall
impoverish the thoughts and lives of thousands
who would otherwise have been independent
of mind," Middletown is simply voicing its conviction that, as expressed in a local editorial,
"When bureaucracy and bloc control destroy
representative government, fascism may be just
around the corner, or something even worse.
When the individual arrives at the point where
the government must become his guardian we
have bureaucracy in full bloom. Then, with the
failure of bureaucracy, despotism invariably
follows."

During the 1936 campaign the local press
reprinted Roger Babson's predictions that:

The chances are 50–50 that the United States will go Fascist when the next depression comes.

There is the possibility that the coming national election may be the last one for many years.

An editorial late in November, 1936, headed "Fascist Movement in the U.S." after reviewing the evidence presented by "a writer of considerable prominence and of thorough reliability" that "a Fascist movement of importance is now under way in the United States," concluded:

The picture as painted seems almost fantastic, but it is possible that while all the furore has been going on about communism, another equally subversive force has been at work to undermine American institutions. But if the people are informed in time about what is going on they should have no difficulty in suppressing this movement as well as that of the communists.

There is no place in America either for communists or fascists. One is as bad as the other. Both are not only un-American, but anti-American.

But, averse as Middletown is to any sort of dictatorial control, what its business leaders want even more than political democracy is what they regard as conditions essential to their resumption of money-making. And those who do the more conspicuous money-making are probably prepared to yield a good many other things to the kind of regime that will flash for them the green "Go" light. These men recognize the power of the strong man, the man with power, and being successful in business is one long apprenticeship at adjusting to stronger men than oneself. They do not fear such a man, providing he is on their side.

If Middletown's press lumps fascism with communism as "undesirable and un-American," it also carries a significant trickle of editorial comment that leans, perhaps unconsciously, toward the "strong man" of "the right sort."

Why shouldn't the average man who has little personality of his own use discretion and attach himself to men who are now what he would like to be? [asked an editorial in 1932.] If this strong man is a conservative with a well-lined nest and conviction that all who advocate change or disturbing of dividends should be jailed, or deported, those who follow him are a little off the middle of the road too, but they're not as bad as the radicals.

A year before, when, in the midst of Chicago's municipal confusion a Chicago businessman suggested that the businessmen of that city take over the running of the city, a Middletown editorial, under the caption "Business Steps into Politics," asserted:

When misrule continues too long, business will assume the dictatorship. And it, at least, will give us efficiency and economy.

An editorial in 1932 proclaimed: 8

WANTED—A RULING CLASS THAT WILL RULE

We are disgusted because the ruling class doesn't rule. . . . (The class that will rule) need not be the rapidly diminishing wealthy class, of course. It may be any class that possesses vision, sanity, and a sincere wish for the public welfare.

In conversations with businessmen in 1935, one gained a strong sense of their desire for "a leader,"—one of their own sort. They cannot move without a leader, because "things are too big," but they know how to follow. One such man remarked in conversation: "Individualism has made a sorry mess of things. The government in its try in the New Deal has made a mess of things. So, what? Hitler and Mussolini may be wrong, but *we've* been wrong, too, so far. What we need is a capable leader." Increasingly, these men see a choice between "radicalism" and a something-that-will-put-down-radicalism. They think of the latter as an "American" a "patriotic" movement, and of the struggle between the two forces as a struggle to "save democracy." "Communism Is Spreading Here" was the headline late in 1936 over an address by the national director of Americanism for the American Legion, sponsored by the public affairs committee of the Y.M.C.A. "We cannot close our eyes," said an editorial, "upon the fact that communism, especially, has been making some inroads in America, with the backing of Moscow. As a natural offset to this we may see fascist demonstrations before long."

. . .

The returning tide of business in 1935–36 has only served to heighten Middletown's impatience with the things beyond its control that hamper its return to buoyant prosperity. It is, under the surface, worried, sore, and frustrated. The frankest statement of civic pessimism and emotional bankruptcy the writers have ever read in the public press of Middletown (other than in the habitually caustic Democratic weekly) appeared in the personal column of the editor of the afternoon paper in January, 1936. Here one actually reads the sort of thing one heard in close privacy in 1935. It represents in part a somewhat whimsical editorial frankness, but also a stark candor rare in public admissions by business-class Middletown and capable of becoming highly explosive if it spreads. It happens to deal more immediately with local issues, but the mood that generates it easily leaps geographical boundaries. After reciting certain hoped-for local civic improvements, the editor said:

YOU JUST ARE NOT GOING TO GET ANY OF THE THINGS NOW THAT YOU HAVE BEEN PROMISED. Don't kid yourself about this. It just isn't in the cards. You'll have the river stinking as noisomely next summer as ever before; you'll be driving in and out of town over the same roads you always have driven; you will see the men working along the river banks and bed without accomplishing much of any importance—and all the rest of it. So don't deceive yourself.

Naturally comes the question of readers of this column, if any, Why? The story is too long and too complicated to tell, but the reasons have their roots in selfishness, inefficiency, ignorance, lack of concentration, politics, and THE LACK OF ONE SINGLE ORGANIZATION WHOLEHEARTEDLY DEVOTED TO THE INTERESTS OF THE PEOPLE WHO LIVE IN THIS COMMUNITY. One capable person at the head of (Middletown's) affairs could straighten out all the tangles in a week. We have a lot of civic organizations in (Middletown) like the Kiwanis Club, the Exchange Club, the Rotary Club, the Dynamo Club, and others, which gather for the purpose of eating once a week and which pride themselves on performing certain small services, whereas if they were to unite and have some real program, they could bring about most of the things that are of vital interest to (Middletown). But what do they do? Living in a city that is far less civilized than many in China where, at least, they have a program to take the sewage out of canals and streams, our civic clubs applaud themselves because they have sponsored something like a farm program, or they have folks tell them funny stories, and always they applaud any movement for the public welfare, applause being easy and inexpensive, and then go back to their jobs. . . .

I am getting very tired of all this hypocrisy of those who say they are trying to do things for [Middletown]. . . . I'd say they are trying not to do things for [Middletown] but to *do* [Middletown]. . . .

If I have put this thought over I have done a little something, but it won't amount to anything in action. I know that. It's all so terribly hopeless, this situation of the mass mind. . . .

Here speaks the voice of a culture seeing itself, despite its surface optimism, as conceivably in a *cul de sac*. It is not inconceivable that such a society of individuals who feel themselves floundering might go over like a row of cards and vent its pent-up anxiety in a mighty whoop of affirmation, if the right individual came along and gave it the right assurance in symbolic patriotic phrases. The working class, unorganized and devoid of symbols of its own, in 1924 served as a keyboard on which Klan organizers played *fortissimo* on the keys of patriotism and religion. In 1932 an ex-Klan leader started an abortive brown-shirt movement, with meeting replete with the fascist salute and other trimmings. If, when, and as the right strong man emerges—if he can emerge in a country as geographically diffuse as the United States—one wonders if Middletown's response from both business class and working class will not be positive and favorable. For unless there is a sharp rise in working-class solidarity in the interim, this Middletown working class, nurtured on business-class symbols, and despite its rebellious Roosevelt vote in 1936, may be expected to follow patiently and even optimistically any bright flag a middle-class strong man waves.

It seems not impossible, that, unless this sense shared by business class and working class alike of being a wanderer in a world too big for one is lulled by returning prosperity, or unless the working class develops more cohesion of its own, the way may be paved for an acceptance of a type of control that will manhandle life deliberately and coercively at certain points to the end of rescuing a semblance of control over these all-important economic institutions. At the moment, Middletown businessmen are bitterly opposed to "bureaucracy" and to "centralized control," but it is at least possible that this opposition in the name of traditional *laissez-faire* freedom would recede in the face of a seizure of power carefully engineered as *by* the business class and *for* the business class and publicized in the name of Americanism and prosperity.

While such contingencies are possible, more likely is continued adherence of sorts to Middletown's customary middle-of-the-road course. If labor organization and other forms of "radicalism" become sufficiently insistent, compromises will be made, the "middle of the road" will be relocated somewhat to the left;

the new path will in time become familiar and the "American way." Compromise and expediency rule Middletown's course. At point after point—in its handling of relief, in city government, in its dealings with dissent—it deals with present situations simply as it must, using the old words. Marked shifts in national policy would change this. Strong impact from more explosive centers would change it. But, in the absence of such inescapable pressures, Middletown itself is likely to continue its course of reluctant adaptation and expediency into the future.

In viewing this sober, hopeful, well-meaning city, caught in its institutional conflicts, caught between past and future, and not knowing which way to move, one recalls now and again Tawner's characterization of the ruling class in Europe after the French Revolution: ". . . they walked reluctantly backwards into the future, lest a worse thing should befall them."

1937

GEORGE S. COUNTS

1889–

GEORGE S. COUNTS was born in Kansas of old American stock. His position as a leader of American education rests in part on his realistic analyses of the role of the school in the American social order and in part on the social idealism which has characterized his writings and his teaching. Professor Counts' books include *The Social Composition of Boards of Education* (1927), *School and Society in Chicago* (1928), *The Soviet Challenge to America* (1931), *The Social Foundations of Education* (1934), and *The Prospects of American Democracy* (1938). The following selection is from the Presidential Address which Professor Counts gave at the annual convention of the American Federation of Teachers at Buffalo on August 19, 1940.

» » From: PRESIDENTIAL ADDRESS « «

A year ago we met in convention in this city. The intervening twelve months have been the longest in history. Already last August seems to belong to another epoch. The world as we knew it then, in both its political and moral contours, has been profoundly altered. Many of the premises on which we did our thinking then have dissolved beneath our feet. We are entering a new age, both in the Old World and in the New, whose outlines, whose conditions, whose controlling purposes no one can discern. We all have our hopes, we all perhaps have made our resolves; but whether those hopes or resolves shall prevail, we do not know.

The league of dictators, consummated at the very time our convention met, has achieved cataclysmic and unanticipated successes. The spiritual and material defenses of the liberal and democratic states on the continent of Europe proved utterly incapable of opposing the political methods and the mechanized legions of Hitler, assisted as he was by the national and international resources of his partners in aggression. Except for Sweden, Switzerland, and mutilated Finland, tiny islands in a vast totalitarian sea, and the Chinese Republic, beleaguered in its western defenses, dictatorship and aggression stand triumphant from the Straits of Gibraltar to the Bering Sea. Nowhere in that vast region of intellectual blackouts 10 would this convention of ours, or anything resembling it, be tolerated; nowhere is a free labor movement possible. As we meet here the Supreme Court of Fascist France, sitting in session at Riom and under the eyes of Hitler, is proceeding ingloriously to judge the last inglorious acts and inter the inglorious remains of the Third Republic. At this fateful hour the British people in their island fortress, with courage and unity that may have come too 20

late, are marshalling the material and spiritual
resources of their empire to meet the Nazi
assault. If this last bastion of human freedom
beyond the Atlantic fails, and with all her
faults Britain is such a bastion for us, America
will stand alone in a world deeply and mili-
tantly hostile to the central ideas and values of
her tradition. If Britain falls, one of the maddest and most sinister geniuses ever to appear
in history will hold the Old World in thrall and
cast his malign shadow over the entire earth. If
Britain falls quickly, we may witness in America a wave of popular fear and hysteria that
will surpass anything of its kind in our history.

The worst of course may not happen. Someone may perform the miracle which Weygand
failed to perform on the battlefields of France;
the dictators may fall out among themselves
and proceed to quarrel over the plunder; enslaved peoples, armed in the eighteenth and
early nineteenth century manner with axes and
pitch-forks, a few horse-pistols and cellar-made
bombs, may overcome the Nazi air-pilots and
tank-operators in their sleep; the economy of
the Third Reich may be laid low by the "contradictions of capitalism"; the architects of the
"new order in Europe," men who have shown
delight in torture and persecution, may grow
tender-minded and starve their own peoples in
order to feed the members of "inferior races";
Hitler may just tire of it all and go away to
Berchtesgaden to paint pictures for the rest of
his life; or we may wake up some morning to
find that the events of the past ten years are
but a nightmare. More seriously, the dictators
may prove wholly incapable of riding the storm
they have helped to call forth; the basic patterns of civilized life may be so firmly established in the cultures of Europe that they will
reassert themselves after the fury of the present gale has spent itself; or Fascism, Naziism,
and the "dictatorship of the proletariat" may
be but the surface and fleeting phenomena of
a world in revolution.

Let us hope that some happy outcome of the
present tragedy is in the stars. Let us hope that
some sudden and favorable turn in the fortunes
of democracy will come. Let us hope that
Hitler and the regime which he has founded
will pass away as quickly as they came into
being. Let us all hope for the best; but let us
not act on such hopes. To do so would be folly.
It is one of the tragedies of these years that the
leaders of the democracies have resolutely and
consistently closed their eyes and their con-

sciences to unpleasant truths. Prizing their comforts and their class privileges above the values
in which they have professed to believe, again
and again they have prepared for the best when
they should have prepared for the worst. They
have assumed that certain things would not
happen merely because those things were unpleasant. They have assumed that Hitler did not
mean what he said merely because what he said
was horrifying. They have assumed that un-
relieved catastrophe, though visiting other peoples and other times, would pass them by.

We in America, the very symbol of democracy in the modern world, cannot permit ourselves the luxury of such comforting optimism.
We must realize that the tables have already
been turned, that twelve months packed with
revolutionary events have passed since last
August, that seven very long years have come
and gone since Hitler came to power in 1933.
We must catch up with history. We must face
the fact that, at least for a period, the great
hopes that inspired us all but yesterday are
gone. Gone is the hope that the Russian Revolution would extend the domain of human
freedom on the earth; gone is the hope that
the peoples of Europe would reconcile their
differences and devote their matchless energies
and talents to cultural advance; gone is the
hope that the League of Nations would bring
a just and lasting peace to mankind; gone also
is the hope that the world was one time made
safe for democracy. To all who derive their
values from the great liberal, humanistic, and
democratic heritage of Western culture the
future is dark and forbidding. The American
people must prepare themselves to defend this
heritage in a world dominated by totalitarian
philosophy and organized by the physical might
of a few great military states. In such a world
a nation must be strong or perish.

* * *

First, we must recognize the necessity of
powerful military defenses—defenses capable
of protecting our independence and our institutions from any possible attack by foreign arms.
The experience of the Old World demonstrates
that in this age no people, however peaceful
and innocent of aggressive intent, can entrust
its safety to another, to any system of alliances,
or to any international order. That experience
demonstrates further that modern technology,
when applied in its full logic by a great industrial people to the waging of war, is a truly

terrifying weapon, capable of performing miracles, capable of cutting to ribbons in an incredibly short time the "best army in Europe," capable of devising in quick succession new engines of warfare that make possible the impossible. To complete the picture, it is necessary to add that there is abroad in the world today a spirit of violent and unabashed aggression that recognizes no bounds and bows only to superior physical might. To meet this threat the American people must and will prepare. Regarding methods and principles of defense we shall disagree and dispute for some time. But regarding the necessity for such defense, there is and there will be little variance in opinion.

Second, we must make clear beyond any doubt that we are utterly opposed to every form of totalitarian movement and doctrine, including both those that have been imported from abroad and go by the names of Communism, Fascism, and Naziism and those that grow out of our own soil and cloak the totalitarian spirit under the garb of Americanism—those domestic movements that encourage resort to violence and harbor the idea of dictatorship or divine mission of any class, order, race or person. Every one of the current forms of totalitarianism has some merit or appeal, otherwise under no circumstances could it rally millions to its standard and set a world in flames. Yet, whatever its claims to democracy, we must recognize that each is hostile, with an implacable hostility, to the essential spirit and the general pattern of democracy, to the spirit of a Jefferson or a Lincoln, to the very idea of a society of free men. Moreover, if anyone thinks for a moment that the American people, American labor, or American teachers, in the light of recent developments in the world, will accept the leadership of any organization that equivocates on this issue, he is unfamiliar with the elements of social psychology and the mind of his own countrymen. Also, if anyone thinks that he can play a game of hide and seek on this issue, pursuing the course of secrecy, anonymity, evasion, and conspiracy, he is only deceiving himself and betraying the Federation.

But our central task is neither to build the military defenses of the nation nor to belabor the dictatorships. We know that the disasters which have befallen the democracies of Europe can by no means be attributed entirely or even largely to the designs of evil men. We know that the peoples of these democracies weighed the professed leaders and programs of democracy and found them wanting. We know further that, if American democracy has no adequate positive program to offer, if it holds out no great promise of a better world, if it allows itself to become the symbol of special privilege, if it is unable to put the unemployed to work and release the productive energies of our country, it cannot meet successfully the totalitarian threat. Each of the dictatorships expresses, defends, and advances a social faith which, however hideous to us, is in the eyes of its followers a great and challenging faith. It may be faith in the charisma or divine mission of some supposed superman, whether he goes by the name of Il Duce, Der Fuehrer, or Veliki Vojzd; or it may be faith in some body of mystical doctrine organized about the proletariat, ancient Rome, or Homo Teutonicus. Each presents to its devotees a great hope, a great cause, a great destiny. Each promises, not quiet and comfort, but, in the manner and spirit of the great leaders of men from the beginning of time, sacrifice, hardship, and even death. The dictators have held out to the youth of their lands the challenge of the conquest of continents, of the building of new heavens and new earths. And they have done this at a period in history when continents can be conquered and when new heavens and new earths are possible —indeed when they are inevitable.

In the face of this challenge, what has democracy offered youth? In some cases the dole or a job proffered in the spirit of the dole, a bit of charity grudgingly given and carrying the stigma of incompetence and failure, a gesture calculated to generate a sense of inferiority and of bitter frustration. In other cases we have counselled the youth to be patient, to wait for the return of better times, to watch the years, their years, slip by in futility and helplessness. Little wonder that some of our most sensitive and idealistic young men and women, either deprived of their own birthright or moved by the deprivations of others, have joined the totalitarian camps. And they have done this, not because of any deep-seated hostility to the values of democracy, but because they felt that apologists of democracy had failed them. Indeed, many are so deeply committed to democracy that they have followed the dictators, nourishing the delusion that in some curious way they were battling in the cause of human liberation.

The nature of the democratic failure, however, has been widely misunderstood. Some of the critics are fond of chiding youth for their "softness," for their inability to "take it," as did their forebears who fought and died in the cause of liberty and who explored and conquered a continent. American youth, no less than their fathers and mothers or their brothers and sisters in the totalitarian states, are capable of taking punishment, of toiling long and hard, of postponing marriage and children, of giving themselves completely. Democracy has faltered, not because it has deprived youth of the things of the flesh, but because it has denied them the things of the spirit. Many of the youth of today, besides being materially insecure, are spiritually restless and starved. These young people crave the one thing the dictators have offered in abundance—the opportunity to toil and sacrifice for a cause—the opportunity to make their lives significant.

The defense of our democracy may require powerful armies and navies, but armies and navies are not enough. If our democracy is to save itself, it must do far more than appropriate billions of dollars for arms, build tanks, airplanes, and battle-ships, master the correlated military skills and knowledges. It must remove all sense of bitterness, cynicism, and frustration from the hearts of youth and arouse hope, conviction, and enthusiasm. It must assert itself as a positive and aggressive social faith, prepared to battle with every form of totalitarianism for the loyalties of men. This means that the leaders of democracy must believe in it themselves and place its commands above all else. This means also that the democratic faith must be translated into programs that deal with the present realities and assure the more complete fulfillment of the great promises of democracy—into programs that bring opportunity and justice to all. In view of the incomparable ethical superiority of the democratic faith the task of leadership here should be far easier than that of the dictators. After all, each of the totalitarian faiths is false and spurious at the core; each violates something that is greatest and finest in the human heart.

This part of the job of defense belongs to us. At any rate our major responsibility lies here. At no time in our history, however, have we done this job well. On the one hand, in the traditional school, in an effort to teach patriotism, we have generally pursued the blind, formal, and uninspiring course of putting the in-

tellect and all the creative faculties to sleep. We have developed superficial loyalties, conveyed understanding of neither past nor present, and cultivated the disposition to follow the stereotypes and not the spirit of democracy. On the other hand, in the progressive movement, as a reaction against tradition and in a spirit of intellectual emancipation, we have often delighted in shaking old loyalties, but have failed to arouse new ones. We have known all of the questions, but none of the answers. Or rather, we have known that there are no answers. We have given to the young all of the doubts, but none of the affirmations of life. Both the loyalty to stereotypes of the traditional school and the scorn of loyalty of the progressive movement, both the neglect of understanding of the one and the one-sided intellectual emphasis of the other constitute an urgent invitation to the dictator to take over. In both the traditional and the progressive schools our work has lacked life, vision, seriousness, deep moral purpose. It was said long ago, and truly, that where there is no vision the people perish.

Our first obligation in repairing the spiritual defenses of our democracy is to identify ourselves with the democratic faith, frankly and positively, and without reservation. This faith, product of centuries of struggle by many and diverse peoples in different parts of the world, has a number of articles. The first and most fundamental of all is the affirmation that the human heritage of earth and culture belong, not to any particular class, caste, or race, but to all men—the affirmation that all men are created equal. The second, which serves to guard and fulfill the first, is the declaration that ordinary men and women, farmers, carpenters, mechanics, housewives, and even teachers, can and should rule themselves. These two articles taken together constitute the faith of the common man—the faith that the individual human being is the measure of all things and is both deserving and capable of freedom. Throughout most of history the very idea that the undistinguished rank and file of mankind, the "hewers of wood and drawers of water," should aspire to such power and status has been regarded as treason. Nay, even as blasphemy. And so it is today wherever totalitarian philosophy prevails. When the protagonists of such philosophy do formal homage to these great articles of the democratic faith, they do so only for propaganda purposes and in order the more utterly to destroy them.

. . . Although our life has been marked by grievous exploitation of certain elements of our population at every period of our colonial and national existence, the long and sustained struggle on the part of the ordinary American citizen to attain the full status of manhood constitutes the most impressive record of its kind in history. No one of the dictators of the Old World, who now daily pronounces the doom of democracy, ever breathed the spirit of personal independence and dignity that has characterized the ordinary American community for generations. This spirit, this fierce assertion of equality, remarked by so many foreign visitors to our shores, has given to our history whatever distinction it has. It is the most precious thing we possess and should be converted into a tremendous resource in our defense of the democratic faith. The fact that we read daily in our newspapers of outrages committed against this tradition, outrages that make us weep, gives us no grounds for the repudiation of our heritage and for the vindication of totalitarian doctrine or aggression in any form whatsoever. It merely means that the threat to our liberties comes from at home as well as from abroad. With all of our deficiencies, the hope that democracy will survive in the world rests profoundly with us.

Our central and peculiar responsibility in the defense of American democracy today and tomorrow is to work everlastingly to bring our entire system of public education into the service of democracy—to wipe out the educational inequalities between races, classes, occupations, and regions, to conceive and launch a program of vocational education designed to raise the technical qualifications and enlarge the opportunities of the entire younger generation, to conceive and launch a program of youth education devoted to the interests and problems of youth in a free society, to conceive and launch a program of adult education dealing ably and courageously with the issues of the present crisis of democracy, to bring the entire educational undertaking into close relation with the life and needs of the community, to resist with all our power efforts on the part of privileged or misguided groups to take advantage of these critical times to reduce the educational services and impair the quality of the educative process, to achieve a wholly just and equitable system of school taxation and support commensurate with the program required, to enlarge the responsibilities of the

teacher in the school, and to increase the role of labor and other democratic elements on boards of education. All of this is to be regarded as instrumental to the systematic rearing of the young in the democratic faith.

Qualitatively, democratic education is unlike the education of other societies and faiths. It is an education designed to set men free and equip them to guard their freedom through the generations. It is an education designed deliberately to give to the young the loyalties, the knowledge and understanding, the discipline of free men. It is an education designed to develop loyalty to the principle of the dignity and worth of the individual human being; to the principle of human equality and brotherhood; to the process of untrammelled criticism, discussion, and majority decision; to the ideal of honesty, fair-mindedness, and scientific spirit in the conduct of this process; to the idea of the obligation and the right to work; to the idea of the supremacy of the common good; to the obligation to be intelligent. It is an education designed to give to the young at appropriate levels of maturity and *without any desire to deceive or mislead*, the social knowledge, insight, and understanding that will equip the individual most thoroughly to guard and advance both personal and social interests—knowledge of the nature of man and society, of the long effort to liberate the human mind and civilize the human heart, of the history of our own people and their struggle for liberty and justice, of the efforts of working men and women to organize and enlarge their powers and opportunities, of the origins and character of the present crisis in world society and American democracy, of the conditions and forces leading to the collapse of free institutions in the Old World, of the promises, the methods, the doctrines, and the consequences of the totalitarian movements, of the weaknesses and resources of American democracy. It is an education designed to discipline the young, through knowledge and understanding, in the ways of democracy, in the temperate and responsible use of political processes, in the subordination of individual to social welfare, in the sacrifice of the present to the long-time interests of individual and society. It is an education designed to prepare the young to live by, to labor for, and, if need be, to die for the democratic faith.

The crowning responsibility of our profession is to assist and guide the young in fashioning a great vision of the future of our country—the vision of guarding here in North America the human gains of the centuries during a possible age of darkness, of devoting the resources of science and technology to the creation of a civilization founded on justice and mercy, of building that ancient City of God where no man exploits his brother—a vision that is as universal as the affirmations of the Declaration of Independence, as American as the spirit of the Gettysburg Address, as liberal as the Bill of Rights, as realistic and practical as the Federal Constitution. Through our own

example we should lead children and youth, not only to contemplate this vision, but also to strive to give it substance, to devote their energies and enthusiasms to the task of fulfilling its provisions. But in doing all of this we should caution them lest they let fall from their hands the only instrument with which they can assure the future of their rights and liberties—the method of political freedom. Such a vision is indispensable to the defense of our democracy against the corrupting sweep of totalitarian doctrine.   1940

» » *The Second World War* « «

1941-1945

» » « «

AMERICA, THE BEAUTIFUL

By Katharine Lee Bates

O beautiful for spacious skies,
　For amber waves of grain,
For purple mountain majesties
　Above the fruited plain!
　　America! America!
　God shed His grace on thee
And crown thy good with brotherhood
　From sea to shining sea!

O beautiful for patriot dream
　That sees beyond the years
Thine alabaster cities gleam
　Undimmed by human tears!
　　America! America!
　God shed His grace on thee
And crown thy good with brotherhood
　From sea to shining sea!

It may happen that no particular song will be remembered as *the* song of the Second World War. There are two reasons why this may be the case: the armed forces have not singled out one song, and the folks back home have their favorite songs chosen for them by radio stations, crooners, and the record companies—all of whom are "plugging" new songs. Nevertheless as "Tipperary" and "Over There" were the "morale-builders" of 1918, so "I've Got Sixpence" (borrowed from the British airmen), "God Bless America," "Comin' in on a Wing and a Prayer," "From the Halls of Montezuma" have lifted up hearts on Guadalcanal, in North Africa, and at bond rallies the nation over.

Strangely enough, one of the most popular of the many favorites of this war is a hymn written in 1893 by Katharine Lee Bates, a Wellesley English professor. Universally sung to the tune of "Materna" ("O mother dear, Jerusalem")—though over sixty original musical settings have been made for it—this song has come to be a kind of supplementary national anthem. The first and last (of four) stanzas printed here are the ones most often heard. Their fervent nationalism in which is interfused a vague sentiment of brotherhood evidently expresses the emotions of Americans who realize that their country has irrevocably assumed the responsibilities of a world power.

» » « «

War

THE GENERAL disillusionment regarding American participation in the First World War was accentuated by the growing threat both to peace and democracy implied in the advance of fascism and Nazism. In April, 1937, seventy per cent of those polled by the American Institute of Public Opinion expressed the belief that American participation in the First World War had been a mistake. The publicity given to the Senate Munitions Investigation under Senator Nye, the Italian war on Ethiopia, and the virtual collapse of the ideal of collective security which the League of Nations had symbolized, all underlined the generally held conviction that the United States should avoid participation in another world war. The neutrality acts of 1935, 1936, and 1937 were designed to prevent such an eventuality by restricting American traditional neutral rights, including the historic doctrine of freedom of the seas. A considerable section of American opinion, it is true, rejected such an effort to isolate the United States from general war and insisted that the government must use its influence and its power to check aggression and, if necessary, to aid those countries which did oppose totalitarian aggression. President Roosevelt took this general position in his "quarantine" speech in Chicago in the early autumn of 1937. But the widespread criticism which this address occasioned indicated that he was out of line with the great majority of the American people.

In spite of the ruthless fascist and Nazi onslaught against Republican Spain and the unprecedented aggressions of Hitler in Central Europe, in spite of the outbreak of general war in September, 1939, a great section of the American public maintained the noninterventionist position. Little by little, however, the alternative policy of providing aid to the countries resisting aggression made gains. More and more Americans agreed with President Roosevelt in believing that there could be no national security in a Nazi-dominated world, that the great American values of freedom could not endure if the Nazi onslaught were not checked. The collapse of France in June, 1940, and the precarious position of Great Britain—the sole surviving European country which was resisting Hitler—largely explain the willingness of the American government and people to accept conscription and a huge preparedness program. More and more it became plain that the United States, in spite of the so-called neutrality legislation, was not neutral, that it had taken its place with the nations resisting Hitlerism. Meantime relations with Japan had become more acute. The refusal of that power to modify the course it had taken in dominating by force all of eastern Asia, and the final refusal of the American government in the autumn of 1941 to accept Japanese domination, precipitated the formal entrance of the United States in the war.

In the Atlantic Charter, in the Four-Freedoms speech, and in other documents President Roosevelt outlined the general aims of the United Nations. Notwithstanding the criticism which these aims met in some circles, it became increasingly clear that the United States would probably not repeat the course it had followed after the First World War in officially separating itself from the efforts to check war through collective action. Whether the emerging pattern would be characterized by a democratic internationalism or by a new version of power politics became a major American issue as the country fought for victory.

« «   » »

FRANKLIN D. ROOSEVELT

1882–1945

PRESIDENT ROOSEVELT had some ground for interpreting his re-election for a third term in the autumn of 1940 as a vindication of his foreign policy as well as his domestic program. The nation, not without much dissent, had accepted his leadership as he extended aid to the nations still resisting the Nazi onslaught after the collapse of France in June, 1940, and as he sponsored the conscription of American man power and accelerated the rearmament program. Then, two months after his re-election, President Roosevelt urged Congress to support those peoples in every quarter of the globe who were fighting for the four freedoms— freedom of speech, freedom of religion, freedom from want, and freedom from fear—and to actualize these freedoms at home.

MESSAGE TO THE
» »   SEVENTY-SEVENTH CONGRESS   « «

I address you, the Members of the Seventy-Seventh Congress, at a moment unprecedented in the history of the Union. I use the word "unprecedented," because at no previous time has American security been as seriously threatened from without as it is today.

Since the permanent formation of our government under the Constitution, in 1789, most of the periods of crisis in our history have related to our domestic affairs. Fortunately, only one of these—the four-year War between the States—ever threatened our national unity. Today, thank God, one hundred and thirty million Americans, in forty-eight States, have forgotten points of the compass in our national unity.

It is true that prior to 1914 the United States often had been disturbed by events in other continents. We had even engaged in two wars with European nations and in a number of undeclared wars in the West Indies, in the Mediterranean and in the Pacific for the maintenance of American rights and for the principles of peaceful commerce. In no case, however, had a serious threat been raised against our national safety or our independence.

What I seek to convey is the historic truth that the United States as a nation has at all times maintained opposition to any attempt to lock us in behind an ancient Chinese wall while the procession of civilization went past. Today, thinking of our children and their children, we oppose enforced isolation for ourselves or for any part of the Americas.

That determination of ours was proved, for example, during the quarter century of wars following the French Revolution.

While the Napoleonic struggles did threaten interests of the United States because of the French foothold in the West Indies and in Louisiana, and while we engaged in the War of 1812 to vindicate our right to peaceful trade, it is, nevertheless, clear that neither France nor Great Britain nor any other nation was aiming at domination of the whole world.

In like fashion from 1815 to 1914—99 years —no single war in Europe or in Asia constituted a real threat against our future or against the future of any other American nation.

Except in the Maximilian interlude in Mexico, no foreign power sought to establish itself in this Hemisphere; and the strength of the British fleet in the Atlantic has been a friendly strength. It is still a friendly strength.

Even when the World War broke out in 1914, it seemed to contain only small threat of danger to our own American future. But, as time went on, the American people began to visualize what the downfall of democratic nations might mean to our own democracy.

We need not overemphasize imperfections in the Peace of Versailles. We need not harp on failure of the democracies to deal with problems of world reconstruction. We should remember that the Peace of 1919 was far less unjust than the kind of "pacification" which began even before Munich, and which is being carried on under the new order of tyranny that seeks to spread over every continent today. The American people have unalterably set their faces against that tyranny.

Every realist knows that the democratic way of life is at this moment being directly assailed in every part of the world—assailed either by arms, or by secret spreading of poisonous propaganda by those who seek to destroy unity and promote discord in nations still at peace.

During sixteen months this assault has blotted out the whole pattern of democratic life in an appalling number of independent nations, great and small. The assailants are still on the march, threatening other nations, great and small.

Therefore, as your President, performing my constitutional duty to "give to the Congress information of the state of the Union," I find it necessary to report that the future and the safety of our country and of our democracy are overwhelmingly involved in events far beyond our borders.

Armed defense of democratic existence is now being gallantly waged in four continents. If that defense fails, all the population and all the resources of Europe, Asia, Africa and Australasia will be dominated by the conquerors. The total of those populations and their resources greatly exceeds the sum total of the population and resources of the whole of the Western Hemisphere—many times over.

In times like these it is immature—and incidentally untrue—for anybody to brag that an unprepared America, single-handed, and with one hand tied behind its back, can hold off the whole world.

No realistic American can expect from a dictator's peace international generosity, or return of true independence, or world disarmament, or freedom of expression, or freedom of religion—or even good business.

Such a peace would bring no security for us or for our neighbors. "Those who would give up essential liberty to purchase a little temporary safety deserve neither liberty nor safety."

As a nation we may take pride in the fact that we are soft-hearted; but we cannot afford to be soft-headed.

We must always be wary of those who with sounding brass and a tinkling cymbal preach the "ism" of appeasement.

We must especially beware of that small group of selfish men who would clip the wings of the American eagle in order to feather their own nests.

I have recently pointed out how quickly the tempo of modern warfare could bring into our very midst the physical attack which we must expect if the dictator nations win this war.

There is much loose talk of our immunity from immediate and direct invasion from across the seas. Obviously, as long as the British Navy retains its power, no such danger exists. Even if there were no British Navy, it is not probable that any enemy would be stupid enough to attack us by landing troops in the United States from across thousands of miles of ocean, until it had acquired strategic bases from which to operate.

But we learn much from the lessons of the past years in Europe—particularly the lesson of Norway, whose essential seaports were captured by treachery and surprise built up over a series of years.

The first phase of the invasion of this Hemisphere would not be the landing of regular troops. The necessary strategic points would be occupied by secret agents and their dupes— and great numbers of them are already here, and in Latin America.

As long as the aggressor nations maintain the offensive, they—not we—will choose the time and the place and the method of their attack.

That is why the future of all American Republics is today in serious danger.

That is why this Annual Message to the Congress is unique in our history.

That is why every member of the Executive branch of the government and every member of the Congress face great responsibility—and great accountability.

The need of the moment is that our actions and our policy should be devoted primarily— almost exclusively—to meeting this foreign peril. For all our domestic problems are now a part of the great emergency.

Just as our national policy in internal affairs has been based upon a decent respect for the rights and dignity of all our fellow-men within our gates, so our national policy in foreign affairs has been based on a decent respect for the rights and dignity of all nations, large and small. And the justice of morality must and will win in the end.

Our national policy is this:

First, by an impressive expression of the public will and without regard to partisanship, we are committed to all-inclusive national defense.

Second, by an impressive expression of the public will and without regard to partisanship, we are committed to full support of all those resolute peoples, everywhere, who are resisting aggression and are thereby keeping war away from our Hemisphere. By this support, we express our determination that the democratic cause shall prevail; and we strengthen the defense and security of our own nation.

Third, by an impressive expression of the public will and without regard to partisanship, we are committed to the proposition that principles of morality and considerations for our own security will never permit us to acquiesce in a peace dictated by aggressors and sponsored by appeasers. We know that enduring peace cannot be bought at the cost of other people's freedom.

In the recent national election there was no substantial difference between the two great parties in respect to that national policy. No issue was fought out on this line before the American electorate. Today, it is abundantly evident that American citizens everywhere are demanding and supporting speedy and complete action in recognition of obvious danger.

Therefore, the immediate need is a swift and driving increase in our armament production.

Leaders of industry and labor have responded to our summons. Goals of speed have been set. In some cases these goals are being reached ahead of time; in some cases we are on schedule; in other cases there are slight but not serious delays; and in some cases—and I am sorry to say very important cases—we are all concerned by the slowness of the accomplishment of our plans.

The Army and Navy, however, have made substantial progress during the past year. Actual experience is improving and speeding up our methods of production with every passing day. And today's best is not good enough for tomorrow.

I am not satisfied with the progress thus far made. The men in charge of the program represent the best in training, ability and patriotism. They are not satisfied with the progress thus far made. None of us will be satisfied until the job is done.

No matter whether the original goal was set too high or too low, our objective is quicker and better results.

To give two illustrations:

We are behind schedule in turning out finished airplanes; we are working day and night to solve the innumerable problems and to catch up.

We are ahead of schedule in building warships; but we are working to get even further ahead of schedule.

To change a whole nation from a basis of peacetime production of implements of peace to a basis of wartime production of implements of war is no small task. And the greatest difficulty comes at the beginning of the program, when new tools and plant facilities and new assembly lines and shipways must first be constructed before the actual materiel begins to flow steadily and speedily from them.

The Congress, of course, must rightly keep itself informed at all times of the progress of the program. However, there is certain information, as the Congress itself will readily recognize, which, in the interests of our own security and those of the nations we are supporting, must of needs be kept in confidence.

New circumstances are constantly begetting new needs for our safety. I shall ask this Congress for greatly increased new appropriations and authorizations to carry on what we have begun.

I also ask this Congress for authority and for funds sufficient to manufacture additional munitions and war supplies of many kinds, to be turned over to those nations which are now in actual war with aggressor nations.

Our most useful and immediate role is to act as an arsenal for them as well as for ourselves. They do not need man power. They do need billions of dollars' worth of the weapons of defense.

The time is near when they will not be able to pay for them in ready cash. We cannot, and will not, tell them they must surrender, merely because of present inability to pay for the weapons which we know they must have.

I do not recommend that we make them a loan of dollars with which to pay for these weapons—a loan to be repaid in dollars.

I recommend that we make it possible for those nations to continue to obtain war materials in the United States, fitting their orders into our own program. Nearly all of their material would, if the time ever came, be useful for our own defense.

Taking counsel of expert military and naval authorities, considering what is best for our own security, we are free to decide how much should be kept here and how much should be sent abroad to our friends who by their determined and heroic resistance are giving us time in which to make ready our own defense.

For what we send abroad, we shall be repaid, within a reasonable time following the close of hostilities, in similar materials, or, at our option, in other goods of many kinds which they can produce and which we need.

Let us say to the democracies: "We Americans are vitally concerned in your defense of freedom. We are putting forth our energies, our resources and our organizing powers to give you the strength to regain and maintain a free world. We shall send you, in ever increasing numbers, ships, planes, tanks, guns. This is our purpose and our pledge."

In fulfillment of this purpose we will not be intimidated by the threats of dictators that they will regard as a breach of international law and as an act of war our aid to the democracies which dare to resist their aggression. Such aid is not an act of war, even if a dictator should unilaterally proclaim it so to be.

When the dictators are ready to make war upon us, they will not wait for an act of war on our part. They did not wait for Norway or Belgium or the Netherlands to commit an act of war.

Their only interest is in a new one-way international law, which lacks mutuality in its observance, and, therefore, becomes an instrument of oppression.

The happiness of future generations of Americans may well depend upon how effective and how immediate we can make our aid felt. No one can tell the exact character of the emergency situations that we may be called upon to meet. The Nation's hands must not be tied when the Nation's life is in danger.

We must all prepare to make the sacrifices that the emergency—as serious as war itself—demands. Whatever stands in the way of speed and efficiency in defense preparations must give way to the national need.

A free nation has the right to expect full co-operation from all groups. A free nation has the right to look to the leaders of business, of labor, and of agriculture to take the lead in stimulating effort, not among other groups but within their own groups.

The best way of dealing with the few slackers or troublemakers in our midst is, first, to shame them by patriotic example, and, if that fails, to use the sovereignty of government to save government.

As men do not live by bread alone, they do not fight by armaments alone. Those who man our defenses, and those behind them who build our defenses, must have the stamina and courage which come from an unshakeable belief in the manner of life which they are defending. The mighty action which we are calling for cannot be based on a disregard of all things worth fighting for.

The Nation takes great satisfaction and much strength from the things which have been done to make its people conscious of their individual stake in the preservation of democratic life in America. Those things have toughened the fibre of our people, have renewed their faith and strengthened their devotion to the institutions we make ready to protect.

Certainly this is no time to stop thinking about the social and economic problems which are the root cause of the social revolution which is today a supreme factor in the world.

There is nothing mysterious about the foundations of a healthy and strong democracy. The basic things expected by our people of their political and economic systems are simple. They are:

Equality of opportunity for youth and for others.

Jobs for those who can work.

Security for those who need it.

The ending of special privilege for the few.

The preservation of civil liberties for all.

The enjoyment of the fruits of scientific progress in a wider and constantly rising standard of living.

These are the simple and basic things that must never be lost sight of in the turmoil and unbelievable complexity of our modern world. The inner and abiding strength of our economic and political systems is dependent upon the degree to which they fulfill these expectations.

Many subjects connected with our social economy call for immediate improvement.

As examples:

We should bring more citizens under the coverage of old-age pensions and unemployment insurance.

We should widen the opportunities for adequate medical care.

We should plan a better system by which

persons deserving or needing gainful employment may obtain it.

I have called for personal sacrifice. I am assured of the willingness of almost all Americans to respond to that call.

A part of the sacrifice means the payment of more money in taxes. In my budget message I recommend that a greater portion of this great defense program be paid for from taxation than we are paying today. No person should try, or be allowed, to get rich out of this program; and the principle of tax payments in accordance with ability to pay should be constantly before our eyes to guide our legislation.

If the Congress maintains these principles, the voters, putting patriotism ahead of pocketbooks, will give you their applause.

In the future days, which we seek to make secure, we look forward to a world founded upon four essential human freedoms.

The first is freedom of speech and expression—everywhere in the world.

The second is freedom of every person to worship God in his own way—everywhere in the world.

The third is freedom from want—which, translated into world terms, means economic understandings which will secure to every nation a healthy peacetime life for its inhabitants—everywhere in the world.

The fourth is freedom from fear—which, translated into world terms, means a worldwide reduction of armaments to such a point and in such a thorough fashion that no nation will be in a position to commit an act of physical aggression against any neighbor—anywhere in the world.

That is no vision of a distant millennium. It is a definite basis for a kind of world attainable in our own time and generation. That kind of world is the very antithesis of the so-called new order of tyranny which the dictators seek to create with the crash of a bomb.

To that new order we oppose the greater conception—the moral order. A good society is able to face schemes of world domination and foreign revolutions alike without fear.

Since the beginning of our American history we have been engaged in change—in a perpetual peaceful revolution—a revolution which goes on steadily, quietly adjusting itself to changing conditions—without the concentration camp or the quicklime in the ditch. The world order which we seek is the cooperation of free countries, working together in a friendly, civilized society.

This nation has placed its destiny in the hands and heads and hearts of its millions of free men and women; and its faith in freedom under the guidance of God. Freedom means the supremacy of human rights everywhere. Our support goes to those who struggle to gain those rights or keep them. Our strength is in our unity of purpose.

To that high concept there can be no end save victory.

January 6, 1941

ROBERT M. HUTCHINS

1899–

DURING THE FIRST World War Robert Hutchins, a youthful Yale A.B., served as a private in the ambulance corps and won from the government of Italy the Croce de Guerra for his cooperative work on the Italian front. At the age of twenty-eight he became dean of the Yale Law School and, two years later, president of the University of Chicago. His educational philosophy occasioned much controversy. Briefly President Hutchins believes in a moral universe and holds that progress toward this can best be realized through the cultivation of reason and the mastery of the great classics of ancient, medieval, and early modern times. President Hutchins' books include *No Friendly Voice* (1936) and *The Higher Learning in America* (1936).

The following address, given over a coast-to-coast network of the National Broadcasting Company on January 23, 1941, represented a wide segment of American opinion at the time.

Current Biography, December, 1940.
The Conflict in Education in a Democratic Society, New York, 1953.

» » AMERICA AND THE WAR « «

I speak tonight because I believe that the American people are about to commit suicide. We are not planning to. We have no plan. We are drifting into suicide. Deafened by martial music, fine language, and large appropriations, we are drifting into war.

I address you simply as an American citizen. I do not represent the University of Chicago. I do not represent any organization or committee. I am not a military expert. It is true that from the age of eighteen to the age of twenty I was a private in the American army. I must have somewhere the very fine medal given me by the Italian government of that day in token of my cooperation on the Italian front. But this experience would not justify me in discussing tactics, strategy, or the strength to which our armed forces should now attain.

I wish to disassociate myself from all Nazis, Fascists, Communists, and appeasers. I regard the doctrine of all totalitarian regimes as wrong in theory, evil in execution, and incompatible with the rights of man.

I wish to dissociate myself from those who want us to stay out of war to save our own skins or our own property. I believe that the people of this country are and should be prepared to make sacrifices for humanity. National selfishness should not determine national policy.

It is impossible to listen to Mr. Roosevelt's recent speeches, to study the lease-lend bill, and to read the testimony of cabinet officers upon it without coming to the conclusion that the President now requires us to underwrite a British victory, and apparently a Chinese and a Greek victory, too. We are going to try to produce the victory by supplying our friends with the materials of war. But what if this is not enough? We have abandoned all pretense of neutrality. We are to turn our ports into British naval bases. But what if this is not enough? Then we must send the navy, the air force, and, if Mr. Churchill wants it, the army. We must guarantee the victory.

We used to hear of "all aid short of war." The words "short of war" are ominously missing from the President's recent speeches. The lease-lend bill contains provisions that we should have regarded as acts of war up to last week. The conclusion is inescapable that the President is reconciled to active military intervention if such intervention is needed to defeat the Axis in this war.

I have supported Mr. Roosevelt since he first went to the White House. I have never questioned his integrity or his good will. But under the pressure of great responsibilities, in the heat of controversy, in the international game of bluff, the President's speeches and recommendations are committing us to obligations abroad which we cannot perform. The effort to perform them will prevent the achievement of the aims for which the President stands at home.

If we go to war, what are we going to war for? This is to be a crusade, a holy war. Its object is moral. We are seeking, the President tells us, "a world founded on freedom of speech, freedom of worship, freedom from want, and freedom from fear." We are to intervene to support the moral order. We are to fight for "the supremacy of human rights everywhere."

With the President's desire to see freedom of speech, freedom of worship, freedom from want, and freedom from fear flourish everywhere we must all agree. Millions of Americans have supported the President because they felt that he wanted to achieve these four freedoms for America. Others, who now long to carry these blessings to the rest of the world, were not conspicuous on the firing line when Mr. Roosevelt called them, eight years ago, to do battle for the four freedoms at home. But let us agree now that we want the four freedoms; we want justice, the moral order, democracy, and the supremacy of human rights, not here alone, but everywhere. The question is whether entrance into this war is likely to bring us closer to this goal.

How can the United States better serve suffering humanity everywhere: by going into this war, or by staying out? I hold that the United States can better serve suffering humanity everywhere by staying out.

But can we stay out? We are told it is too late. The house is on fire. When the house is on fire, you do not straighten the furniture, and clean out the cellar, or ask yourself whether the house is as good a house as you would like. You put out the fire if you can.

The answer is that the house is not on fire. The house next door is on fire. When the house next door is on fire you do not set fire to your own house, throw the baby on the floor, and rush off to join the fun. And when you do go to quench the fire next door, you make sure that your bucket is full of water and not oil.

But, we are told, we are going to have to fight the Axis sometime. Why not fight it now, when we have Britain to help us? Why wait until we have to face the whole world alone?

Think of the mass of assumptions upon which this program rests. First, we must assume that in spite of its heroic resistance and in spite of the enormous supplies of munitions which it is yet to receive from America the British Empire must fall.

Second, we must assume that the present rulers of totalitarian states will survive the conflict.

Third, we must assume that if these regimes survive they will want to attack us.

Fourth, we must assume that they will be in a position to attack us. This involves the assumptions that they will have the resources to do so, that their people will consent to new and hazardous ventures, that their task of holding down conquered nations will be easily completed, and that the ambiguous attitude of Russia will cause them little concern.

Next, if Britain falls, if the totalitarian regimes survive, if they want to attack us, if they are in a position to do so, we must further assume that they will find it possible to do so. The flying time between Africa and Brazil, or Europe and America, does not decide this question. The issue is what will be at the western end of the line? This will depend on our moral and military preparedness. A lone squadron of bombers might conquer a continent peopled with inhabitants careless of safety or bent on slavery. We cannot assume that any combination of powers can successfully invade this hemisphere if we are prepared to defend ourselves and determined to be free.

No Inevitability About War

On a pyramid of assumptions, hypotheses, and guesses therefore, rests a decision to go to war now because it is too late to stay out. There is no such inevitability about war with the Axis as to prevent us from asking ourselves whether we shall serve suffering humanity better everywhere by going into this war or by staying out.

The chances of accomplishing the high moral purposes which the President has stated for America, even if we stay out of war, are not bright. The world is in chaos. We must give our thought and energy to building our defenses. What we have of high moral purpose is likely to suffer dilution at home and a cold reception abroad. But we have a chance to help humanity if we do not go into this war. If we do go into it, we have no chance at all.

The reason why we have no chance to help humanity if we go into this war is that we are not prepared. I do not mean, primarily, that we are unprepared in a military sense. I mean that we are morally and intellectually unprepared to execute the moral mission to which the President calls us.

A missionary, even a missionary to the cannibals, must have clear and defensible convictions. And if his plan is to eat some of the cannibals in order to persuade the others to espouse the true faith, his convictions must be very clear and very defensible indeed. It is surely not too much to ask of such a missionary that his own life and works reflect the virtues which he seeks to compel others to adopt. If we stay out of war, we may perhaps some day understand and practice freedom of speech, freedom of worship, freedom from want, and freedom from fear. We may even be able to comprehend and support justice, democracy, the moral order, and the supremacy of human rights. Today we have barely begun to grasp the meaning of the words.

Those beginnings are important. They place us ahead of where we were at the end of the last century. They raise us, in accomplishment as well as in ideals, far above the accomplishment and ideals of totalitarian powers. They leave us, however, a good deal short of that level of excellence which entitles us to convert the world by force of arms.

Have we freedom of speech and freedom of worship in this country? We do have freedom to say what everybody else is saying and freedom of worship if we do not take our religion too seriously. But teachers who do not conform to the established canons of social thought lose their jobs. People who are called "radicals" have mysterious difficulties in renting halls.

Labor organizers sometimes get beaten up and ridden out of town on a rail. Norman Thomas had some troubles in Jersey City. And the Daughters of the American Revolution refused to let Marian Anderson sing in the national capital in a building called Constitutional Hall.

If we regard these exceptions as minor, reflecting the attitude of the more backward and illiterate parts of the country, what are we to say of freedom from want and freedom from fear? What of the moral order and justice and the supremacy of human rights? What of democracy in the United States?

Words like these have no meaning unless we believe in human dignity. Human dignity means that every man is an end in himself. No man can be exploited by another. Think of these things and then think of the share-croppers, the Okies, the Negroes, the slum-dwellers, downtrodden and oppressed for gain. They have neither freedom from want nor freedom from fear. They hardly know they are living in a moral order or in a democracy where justice and human rights are supreme.

We have it on the highest authority that one-third of the nation is ill-fed, ill-clothed, and ill-housed. The latest figures of the National Resources Board show that almost precisely 55 per cent of our people are living on family incomes of less than $1,250 a year. This sum, says *Fortune* magazine, will not support a family of four. On this basis more than half our people are living below the minimum level of subsistence. More than half the army which will defend democracy will be drawn from those who have had this experience of the economic benefits of "the American way of life."

We know that we have had till lately nine million unemployed and that we should have them still if it were not for our military preparations. When our military preparations cease, we shall, for all we know, have nine million unemployed again. In his speech on December 29 Mr. Roosevelt said, "After the present needs of our defense are past, a proper handling of the country's peacetime needs will require all of the new productive capacity—if not still more." For ten years we have not known how to use the productive capacity we had. Now suddenly we are to believe that by some miracle, after the war is over, we shall know what to do with our old productive capacity and what to do in addition with the tremendous increases which are now being

made. We have want and fear today. We shall have want and fear "when the present needs of our defense are past."

As for democracy, we know that millions of men and women are disfranchised in this country because of their race, color, or condition of economic servitude. We know that many municipal governments are models of corruption. Some state governments are merely the shadows of big-city machines. Our national government is a government by pressure groups. Almost the last question an American is expected to ask about a proposal is whether it is just. The question is how much pressure is there behind it or how strong are the interests against it. On this basis are settled such great issues as monopoly, the organization of agriculture, the relation of labor and capital, whether bonuses should be paid to veterans, and whether a tariff policy based on greed should be modified by reciprocal trade agreements.

Common Principles and Purposes

To have a community men must work together. They must have common principles and purposes. If some men are tearing down a house while others are building it, we do not say they are working together. If some men are robbing, cheating, and oppressing others, we should not say they are a community. The aims of a democratic community are moral. United by devotion to law, equality, and justice, the democratic community works together for the happiness of all the citizens. I leave to you the decision whether we have yet achieved a democratic community in the United States.

In the speech in which Mr. Roosevelt told us, in effect, that we are headed for war, he said, "Certainly this is no time to stop thinking about the social and economic problems which are the root cause of the social revolution which is today a supreme factor in the world." But in the same speech he said, "The need of the moment is that our actions and our policy should be devoted primarily—almost exclusively—to meeting this foreign peril. For all our domestic problems are now a part of the great emergency." This means—and it is perfectly obvious—that if any social objective interferes with the conduct of the war, it will be, it must be instantly abandoned. War can mean only the loss of "social gains" and the destruction of the livelihood of millions in modest circumstances, while pirates and profiteers, in spite of Mr. Roosevelt's efforts to stop them, emerge stronger than ever.

The four freedoms must be abandoned if they interfere with winning a war. In the ordinary course of war most of them do interfere. All of them may. In calmer days, in 1929, the New York *Times* said, "War brings many collateral disasters. Freedom of speech, free
10 dom of the press suffer. We think we shall be wiser and cooler the next time, if there is one; but we shan't." The urge to victory annihilates tolerance. In April, 1939, Alfred Duff-Cooper said that "hatred of any race was a sign of mental deficiency and of lack of a broad conception of the facts of the world." In April, 1940, Mr. Duff-Cooper said that the crimes of the German militarists were the crimes of the whole people and that this should be kept in
20 mind when the peace treaty was written.

We cannot suppose, because civil liberties were restricted in the last war and expanded after it, that we can rely on their revival after the next one. We Americans have only the faintest glimmering of what war is like. This war, if we enter it, will make the last one look like a stroll in the park. If we go into this one, we go in against powers dominating Europe and most of Asia to aid an ally who, we are
30 told, is already in mortal danger. When we remember what a short war did to the four freedoms, we must recognize that they face extermination in the total war to come.

We Americans have hardly begun to understand and practice the ideals that we are urged to force on others. What we have, in this country, is hope. We and we alone have the hope that we can actually achieve these ideals. The framework of our government was de
40 signed to help us achieve them. We have a tremendous continent, with vast resources, in a relatively impregnable position. We have energy, imagination, and brains. We have made some notable advances in the long march toward justice, freedom, and democracy.

If we go to war, we cast away our opportunity and cancel our gains. For a generation, perhaps for a hundred years, we shall not be able to struggle back to where we were. In
50 fact the changes that total war will bring may mean that we shall never be able to struggle back. Education will cease. Its place will be taken by vocational and military training. The effort to establish a democratic community will stop. We shall think no more of justice,

the moral order, and the supremacy of human rights. We shall have hope no longer.

What, then, should our policy be? Instead of doing everything we can to get into the war, we should do everything we can to stay at peace. Our policy should be peace. Aid to Britain, China, and Greece should be extended on the basis most likely to keep us at peace, and least likely to involve us in war.

At the same time we should prepare to defend ourselves. We should prepare to defend ourselves against military or political penetration. We should bend every energy to the construction of an adequate navy and air force and the training of an adequate army. By adequate I mean adequate for defense against any power or combination of powers.

In the meantime, we should begin to make this country a refuge for those who will not live without liberty. For less than the cost of two battleships we could accommodate half a million refugees from totalitarian countries for a year. The net cost would not approach the cost of two battleships, for these victims, unlike battleships, would contribute to our industry and our cultural life, and help us make democracy work.

But most important of all, we should take up with new vigor the long struggle for moral, intellectual, and spiritual preparedness. If we would change the face of the earth, we must first change our own hearts. The principal end that we have hitherto set before ourselves is the unlimited acquisition of material goods. The business of America, said Calvin Coolidge, is business. We must now learn that material goods are a means and not an end. We want them to sustain life, but they are not the aim of life. The aim of life is the fullest development of the highest powers of men. This means art, religion, education, moral and intellectual growth. These things we have regarded as mere decorations or relaxations in the serious business of life, which was making money. The American people, in their own interest, require a moral regeneration. If they are to be missionaries to the world, this regeneration must be profound and complete.

We must try to build a new moral order for America. We need moral conviction, intellectual clarity, and moral action: moral conviction about the dignity of man, intellectual clarity about ends and means, moral action to construct institutions to bring to pass the ends we have chosen.

A new moral order for America means a new conception of security. Today we do not permit men to die of starvation, but neither do we give them an incentive to live. Every citizen must have a respected place in the achievement of the national purpose.

A new moral order for America means a new conception of sacrifice, sacrifice for the moral purposes of the community. In the interest of human dignity we need a rising standard of health, character, and intelligence. These positive goals demand the devotion and sacrifice of every American. We should rebuild one-third of the nation's homes. We must provide adequate medical care in every corner of the land. We must develop an education aimed at moral and intellectual growth instead of at making money.

A new moral order for America means a new conception of mastery. We must learn how to reconcile the machine with human dignity. We have allowed it to run wild in prosperity and war and to rust idly in periodic collapse. We have hitherto evaded the issue by seeking new markets. In an unstable world this has meant bigger and bigger collapses, more and more catastrophic war. In Europe and Russia the efforts to master the machine are carried out by methods we despise. America can master the machine within the framework of a balanced democracy, outdistance the totalitarian despotisms, and bring light and hope to the world. It is our highest function and greatest opportunity to learn to make democracy work. We must bring justice and the moral order to life, here and now.

If we have strong defenses and understand and believe in what we are defending, we need fear nobody in the world. If we do not understand and believe in what we are defending, we may still win, but the victory will be as fruitless as the last. What did we do with the last one? What shall we do with this one? The government of Great Britain has repeatedly refused to state its war aims. The President in his foreign policy is pledged to back up Great Britain, and beyond that, to the pursuit of the unattainable. If we go to war, we shall not know what we are fighting for. If we stay out of war until we do, we may have the stamina to win and the knowledge to use the victory for the welfare of mankind.

The path to war is a false path to freedom. A new moral order for America is the true path to freedom. A new moral order for America means new strength for America, and new hope for the moral reconstruction of mankind. We are turning aside from the true path to freedom because it is easier to blame Hitler for our troubles than to fight for democracy at home. As Hitler made the Jews his scapegoat, so we are making Hitler ours. But Hitler did not spring full-armed from the brow of Satan. He sprang from the materialism and paganism of our times. In the long run we can beat what Hitler stands for only by beating the materialism and paganism that produced him. We must show the world a nation clear in purpose, united in action, and sacrificial in spirit. The influence of that example upon suffering humanity everywhere will be more powerful than the combined armies of the Axis.

January 23, 1941

THE ATLANTIC CHARTER

ON AUGUST 14, 1941, President Roosevelt and British Prime Minister Winston Churchill met on a destroyer in the mid-Atlantic. The Atlantic Charter, which was drawn up at this meeting, was designed to clarify opinion both in the United States and in the world at large regarding the war aims of those resisting the Axis. The Atlantic Charter occasioned much discussion and did much to give direction to the growing hope that those endeavoring to defeat the Axis were also thinking in terms of a better future world.

« « » »

Joint declaration of the President of the United States of America and the Prime Minister, Mr.

Churchill, representing His Majesty's Government in the United Kingdom, being met together, deem it right to make known certain common principles in the national policies of their respective countries on which they base their hopes for a better future for the world.

First, their countries seek no aggrandizement, territorial or other;

Second, they desire to see no territorial changes that do not accord with the freely expressed wishes of the people concerned;

Third, they respect the rights of all peoples to choose the form of government under which they will live; and they wish to see sovereign rights and self-government restored to those who have been forcibly deprived of them;

Fourth, they will endeavor, with due respect for their existing obligations, to further the enjoyment by all states, great or small, victor or vanquished, of access, on equal terms, to the trade and to the raw materials of the world which are needed for their economic prosperity;

Fifth, they desire to bring about the fullest collaboration between all nations in the economic field with the object of securing, for all, improved labor standards, economic advancement and social security;

Sixth, after the final destruction of the Nazi tyranny, they hope to see established a peace which will afford to all nations the means of dwelling in safety within their own boundaries, and which will afford assurance that all the men in all the lands may live out their lives in freedom from fear and want;

Seventh, such a peace should enable all men to traverse the high seas and oceans without hindrance;

Eighth, they believe that all the nations of the world, for realistic as well as for spiritual reasons, must come to the abandonment of the use of force. Since no future peace can be maintained if land, sea or air armaments continue to be employed by nations which threaten, or may threaten, aggression outside of their frontiers, they believe, pending the establishment of a wider and permanent system of general security, that the disarmament of such nations is essential. They will likewise aid and encourage all other practicable measures which will lighten for peace-loving peoples the crushing burden of armaments.

August 14, 1941

HENRY A. WALLACE

1888–

THE SON of an Iowa agricultural journalist and Republican farm leader, Henry A. Wallace became Secretary of Agriculture in Franklin D. Roosevelt's first cabinet. His services to the New Deal program, his growing stature, and his political strength won him the Vice-Presidency in the election of 1940. A great social idealist as well as a skillful administrator, Vice President Wallace has given distinction to his office and leadership to the liberal forces of the country. His books include *New Frontiers* (1934), *Paths to Plenty* (1938), and *The American Choice* (1940).

On May 8, 1942, Wallace addressed the Free Nations Association, an organization composed of men and women from all countries dedicated to the emancipation of enslaved peoples from Axis dominion. The address was at once recognized as one of the great statements of the war aims of the United Nations.

The Century of the Common Man, Russell Lord, ed., New York, 1943.
Dwight Macdonald, *Henry Wallace, the Man and the Myth,* New York, 1948.

»　»　THE PRICE OF A FREE WORLD VICTORY　«　«

We who in a formal or an informal way represent most of the free peoples of the world are met here tonight in the interests of the mil-

lions in all the nations who have freedom in their souls. To my mind this meeting has just one purpose—to let those millions in other countries know that here in the United States are 130 million men, women, and children who are in this war to the finish. Our American people are utterly resolved to go on until they can strike the relentless blows that will assure a complete victory, and with it win a new day for the lovers of freedom, everywhere on this earth.

This is a fight between a slave world and a free world. Just as the United States in 1862 could not remain half slave and half free, so in 1942 the world must make its decision for a complete victory one way or the other.

Roots of Our Freedom

As we begin the final stages of this fight to the death between the free world and the slave world, it is worth while to refresh our minds about the march of freedom for the common man. The idea of freedom—the freedom that we in the United States know and love so well—is derived from the Bible with its extraordinary emphasis on the dignity of the individual. Democracy is the only true political expression of Christianity.

The prophets of the Old Testament were the first to preach social justice. But that which was sensed by the prophets many centuries before Christ was not given complete and powerful political expression until our Nation was formed as a Federal Union a century and a half ago. Even then, the march of the common people had just begun. Most of them did not yet know how to read and write. There were no public schools to which all children could go. Men and women cannot be really free until they have plenty to eat, and time and ability to read and think and talk things over. Down the years, the people of the United States have moved steadily forward in the practice of democracy. Through universal education, they now can read and write and form opinions of their own. They have learned, and are still learning, the art of production—that is, how to make a living. They have learned, and are still learning, the art of self-government.

If we were to measure freedom by standards of nutrition, education, and self-government, we might rank the United States and certain nations of western Europe very high. But this would not be fair to other nations where education has become widespread only in the last 20 years. In many nations, a generation ago, nine out of ten of the people could not read or write. Russia, for example, was changed from an illiterate to a literate nation within one generation and, in the process, Russia's appreciation of freedom was enormously enhanced. In China, the increase during the past 30 years in the ability of the people to read and write has been matched by their increased interest in real liberty.

Everywhere, reading and writing are accompanied by industrial progress, and industrial progress sooner or later inevitably brings a strong labor movement. From a long-time and fundamental point of view, there are no backward peoples which are lacking in mechanical sense. Russians, Chinese, and the Indians both of India and the Americas all learn to read and write and operate machines just as well as your children and my children. Everywhere the common people are on the march. Thousands of them are learning to read and write, learning to think together, learning to use tools. These people are learning to think and work together in labor movements, some of which may be extreme or impractical at first, but which eventually will settle down to serve effectively the interests of the common man.

The World Moves Ahead

When the freedom-loving people march—when the farmers have an opportunity to buy land at reasonable prices and to sell the produce of their land through their own organizations, when workers have the opportunity to form unions and bargain through them collectively, and when the children of all the people have an opportunity to attend schools which teach them the truths of the real world in which they live—when these opportunities are open to everyone, then the world moves straight ahead.

But in countries where the ability to read and write has been recently acquired or where the people have had no long experience in governing themselves on the basis of their own thinking, it is easy for demagogues to arise and prostitute the mind of the common man to their own base ends. Such a demagogue may get financial help from some person of wealth who is unaware of what the end result will be. With this backing, the demagogue may dominate the minds of the people, and, from whatever degree of freedom they have, lead them backward into slavery. Herr Thyssen, the wealthy German steel man, little realized what he was doing when he gave Hitler enough money to enable him to play on the minds of the German people. The demagogue is the curse of the modern world, and, of all the demagogues, the worst are those financed by well-meaning wealthy men who sincerely believe that their wealth is likely to be safer if they can hire men with political "it" to change the signposts and lure the people back into slavery of the most degraded kind. Unfortunately for the wealthy men who finance movements of this sort, as well as for the people themselves, the successful demagogue is a powerful genie who, when once let out of his bottle, refuses to obey anyone's command. As long as his spell holds, he defies God himself, and Satan is turned loose upon the world.

Through the leaders of the Nazi revolution, Satan now is trying to lead the common man of the whole world back into slavery and darkness. For the stark truth is that the violence preached by the Nazis is the devil's own religion of darkness. So also is the doctrine that one race or one class is by heredity superior and that all other races or classes are supposed to be slaves. The belief in one Satan-inspired Fuehrer, with his Quislings, his Lavals, and his Mussolinis—his "gauleiters" in every nation in the world—is the last and ultimate darkness. Is there any hell hotter than that of being a Quisling, unless it is that of being a Laval or a Mussolini?

In a twisted sense, there is something almost great in the figure of the Supreme Devil operating through a human form, in a Hitler who has the daring to spit straight into the eye of God and man. But the Nazi system has a heroic position for only one leader. By definition only one person is allowed to retain full sovereignty over his own soul. All the rest are stooges—they are stooges who have been mentally and politically degraded, and who feel that they can get square with the world only by mentally and politically degrading other people. These stooges are really psychopathic cases. Satan has turned loose upon us the insane.

The People's Revolution

The march of freedom of the past 150 years has been a long-drawn-out people's revolution. In this Great Revolution of the people, there were the American Revolution of 1775, the French Revolution of 1792, the Latin-American revolutions of the Bolivarian era, the German Revolution of 1848 and the Russian Revolution of 1918. Each spoke for the common man in terms of blood on the battlefield. Some went to excess. But the significant thing is that the people groped their way to the light. More of them learned to think and work together.

The people's revolution aims at peace and not at violence, but if the rights of the common man are attacked, it unleashes the ferocity of a she-bear who has lost a cub. When the Nazi psychologists tell their master Hitler that we in the United States may be able to produce hundreds of thousands of planes, but that we have no will to fight, they are only fooling themselves and him. The truth is that when the rights of the American people are transgressed, as those rights have been transgressed, the American people will fight with a relentless fury which will drive the ancient Teutonic gods back cowering into their caves. The Götterdämmerung has come for Odin and his crew.

The people are on the march toward even fuller freedom than the most fortunate peoples of the earth have hitherto enjoyed. No Nazi counterrevolution will stop it. The common man will smoke the Hitler stooges out into the open in the United States, in Latin America, and in India. He will destroy their influence. No Lavals, no Mussolinis will be tolerated in a Free World.

The people, in their millennial and revolutionary march toward manifesting here on earth the dignity that is in every human soul, hold as their credo the Four Freedoms enunciated by President Roosevelt in his message to Congress on January 6, 1941. These Four Freedoms are the very core of the revolution for which the United Nations have taken their stand. We who live in the United States may think there is nothing very revolutionary about freedom of religion, freedom of expression, and freedom from the fear of secret police. But when we begin to think about the significance of freedom from want for the average man, then we know that the revolution of the past 150 years has not been completed, either here in the United States or in any other nation in the world. We know that this revolution cannot stop until freedom from want has actually been attained.

A Free Man's Duties

And now, as we move forward toward realizing the Four Freedoms of this people's revolution, I would like to speak about four duties. It is my belief that every freedom, every right, every privilege has its price, its corresponding duty without which it cannot be enjoyed. The four duties of the people's revolution, as I see them today, are these:

1. The duty to produce to the limit.
2. The duty to transport as rapidly as possible to the field of battle.
3. The duty to fight with all that is within us.
4. The duty to build a peace—just, charitable, and enduring.

The fourth duty is that which inspires the other three.

We failed in our job after World War I. We did not know how to go about it to build an enduring world-wide peace. We did not have the nerve to follow through and prevent Germany from rearming. We did not insist that she "learn war no more." We did not build a peace treaty on the fundamental doctrine of the people's revolution. We did not strive wholeheartedly to create a world where there could be freedom from want for all the peoples. But by our very errors we learned much, and after this war we shall be in position to utilize our knowledge in building a world which is economically, politically, and, I hope, spiritually sound.

Modern science, which is a byproduct and an essential part of the people's revolution, has made it technologically possible to see that all of the people of the world get enough to eat. Half in fun and half seriously, I said the other day to Madame Litvinoff: "The object of this war is to make sure that everybody in the world has the privilege of drinking a quart of milk a day." She replied: "Yes, even half a pint." The peace must mean a better standard of living for the common man, not merely in the United States and England but also in India, Russia, China, and Latin America—not merely in the United Nations but also in Germany and Italy and Japan.

Some have spoken of the "American Century." I say that the century on which we are entering—the century which will come out of this war—can be and must be the century of the common man. Perhaps it will be America's opportunity to suggest the freedoms and duties by which the common man must live. Everywhere the common man must learn to build his own industries with his own hands in a practical fashion. Everywhere the common

man must learn to increase his productivity so that he and his children can eventually pay to the world community all that they have received. No nation will have the God-given right to exploit other nations. Older nations will have the privilege to help younger nations get started on the path to industrialization, but there must be neither military nor economic imperialism. The methods of the nineteenth century will not work in the people's century which is now about to begin. India, China, and Latin America have a tremendous stake in the people's century. As their masses learn to read and write, and as they become productive mechanics, their standard of living will double and treble. Modern science, when devoted wholeheartedly to the general welfare, has in it potentialities of which we do not yet dream.

Science Must Serve All

And modern science must be released from German slavery. International cartels that serve American greed and the German will to power must go. Cartels in the peace to come must be subjected to international control for the common man, as well as being under adequate control by the respective home governments. In this way, we can prevent the Germans from again building a war machine while we sleep. With international monopoly pools under control, it will be possible for inventions to serve all the people instead of only the few.

Yes, and when the time of peace comes, the citizens will again have a duty, the supreme duty of sacrificing the lesser interests for the greater interest of the general welfare. Those who write the peace must think of the whole world. There can be no privileged peoples. We ourselves in the United States are no more a master race than the Nazis. And we cannot perpetuate economic warfare without planting the seeds of military warfare. We must use our power at the peace table to build an economic peace that is just, charitable, and enduring.

If we really believe that we are fighting for a people's peace, all the rest becomes easy. Production, yes—it will be easy to get production without either strikes or sabotage; production with the wholehearted cooperation between willing arms and keen brains; enthusiasm, zip, energy geared to the tempo of keeping at it everlastingly day after day. Hitler knows as well as those of us who sit in on the War Production Board meetings that we here in the United States are winning the battle of production. He knows that both labor and business in the United States are doing a most remarkable job and that his only hope is to crash through to a complete victory some time during the next six months.

And then there is the task of transportation to the line of battle by truck, by railroad car, by ship. We shall joyously deny ourselves so
10 that our transportation system is improved by at least 30 per cent.

I need say little about the duty to fight. Some people declare, and Hitler believes, that the American people have grown soft in the last generation. Hitler agents continually preach in South America that we are cowards, unable to use, like the "brave" German soldiers, the weapons of modern war. It is true that American youth hates war with a holy hatred. But
20 because of that fact and because Hitler and the German people stand as the very symbol of war, we shall fight with a tireless enthusiasm until war and the possibility of war have been removed from this planet. We shall cleanse the plague spot of Europe, which is Hitler's Germany, and with it the hell-hole of Asia—Japan.

They Stood Like Men

31 The American people have always had guts and always will have. You know the story of Bomber Pilot Dixon and Radioman Gene Aldrich and Ordnanceman Tony Pastula—the story which Americans will be telling their children for generations to illustrate man's ability to master any fate. These men lived for 34 days on the open sea in a rubber life raft, 8 feet by 4 feet, with no food but that which they took
40 from the sea and the air with one pocket knife and a pistol. And yet they lived it through and came at last to the beach of an island they did not know. In spite of their suffering and weakness, they stood like men, with no weapon left to protect themselves, and no shoes on their feet or clothes on their backs, and walked in military file because, they said, "if there were Japs, we didn't want to be crawling."

The American fighting men, and all the
50 fighting men of the United Nations, will need to summon all their courage during the next few months. I am convinced that the summer and fall of 1942 will be a time of supreme crisis for us all. Hitler, like the prize fighter who realizes he is on the verge of being knocked out, is gathering all his remaining forces for one last desperate blow. There is abject fear in the heart of the madman and a growing discontent among his people as he prepares for his last all-out offensive.

We may be sure that Hitler and Japan will cooperate to do the unexpected—perhaps an attack by Japan against Alaska and our northwest coast at a time when German transport planes will be shuttled across from Dakar to furnish leadership and stiffening to a German uprising in Latin America. In any event, the psychological and sabotage offensive in the United States and Latin America will be timed to coincide with, or anticipate by a few weeks, the height of the military offensive.

The Ordeal Ahead

We must be especially prepared to stifle the fifth columnists in the United States who will try to sabotage not merely our war material plants but, even more important, our minds. We must be prepared for the worst kind of fifth-column work in Latin America, much of it operating through the agency of governments with which the United States at present is at peace. When I say this, I recognize that the peoples, both of Latin America and of the nations supporting the agencies through which the fifth columnists work, are overwhelmingly on the side of the democracies. We must expect the offensive against us on the military, propaganda, and sabotage fronts, both in the United States and in Latin America, to reach its apex some time during the next few months. The convulsive efforts of the dying madman will be so great that some of us may be deceived into thinking that the situation is bad at a time when it is really getting better. But in the case of most of us, the events of the next few months, disturbing though they may be, will only increase our will to bring about complete victory in this war of liberation. Prepared in spirit, we cannot be surprised. Psychological terrorism will fall flat. As we nerve ourselves for the supreme effort in this hemisphere we must not forget the sublime heroism of the oppressed in Europe and Asia, whether it be in the mountains of Yugoslavia, the factories of Czechoslovakia and France, the farms of Poland, Denmark, Holland, and Belgium, among the seamen of Norway, or in the occupied areas of China and the Dutch East Indies. Everywhere the soul of man is letting the tyrant know that slavery of the body does not end resistance.

There can be no half measures. North, South, East, West, and Middle West—the will of the American people is for complete victory.

No compromise with Satan is possible. We shall not rest until all the victims under the Nazi yoke are freed. We shall fight for a complete peace as well as a complete victory.

The people's revolution is on the march, and the devil and all his angels cannot prevail against it. They cannot prevail, for on the side of the people is the Lord.

"He giveth power to the faint; to them that have no might He increaseth strength. . . . They that wait upon the Lord shall . . . mount up with wings as eagles; they shall run, and not be weary; they shall walk and not faint."

Strong in the strength of the Lord, we who fight in the people's cause will never stop until that cause is won.   1942

FREDERICK G. CRAWFORD

1891–

FREDERICK G. CRAWFORD took his A.B. degree at Harvard in 1913, with *magna cum laude* and a Phi Beta Kappa key. In 1916 he became maintenance engineer in Thompson Products, Inc., and in 1933 for his eminent services to the company was rewarded with the presidency. His business affiliations include positions of influence in eight other corporations. As a director of the United States Chamber of Commerce and as president of the National Association of Manufacturers (1942–) Frederick Crawford represents an influential section of American thought. His social philosophy is anti-New Deal and anti-organized labor. In the following address, given before the Fifth Annual Northern California Industrial Conference at San Francisco on April 13, 1943, Mr. Crawford develops his conception of the society of tomorrow—a conception which may be contrasted with that expounded by Vice President Wallace.

Current Biography, February, 1943.

» » JOBS, FREEDOM, OPPORTUNITY « «

The end of world aggression is rolling off the assembly lines of American industry.

In the last two months I have seen victory in the making in the bomber plants of the South, the shipyards of New Orleans bayous, the steel mills of Birmingham, the tank factories of busy Detroit and the aircraft industry of Southern California.

War production in February, according to the War Production Board, jumped 8 per cent over the January figure and is going higher and higher every day—already four times as great as in November just before Pearl Harbor.

This year we will launch the equivalent in tonnage of all the merchant marine in the world.

Our plane production, still not big enough to assure victory, is nearly as great as the rest of the world.

The fires of industry blazed so blindingly white in the swift conversion to war production that Mr. Roosevelt and other eloquent phrasemakers called the achievement a "miracle."

Industry has been called many things in the last ten years but this is the nicest name we've ever been called—"Miracle Men."

But you and I who do not believe in miracles, know that it did not happen suddenly and inexplicably. It was a natural outgrowth of long effort, the prime fruit of a plant that had been carefully developed for a century and a half.

By nurturing ingenuity, protecting inventive genius, rewarding individual initiative and encouraging the investment of savings in enterprises, we established American industry as the healthiest and most vigorous in the world, and American standards of living the highest.

But industry is not resting on its laurels.

This year industry—labor and management working together—will produce more than 57 billion dollars worth of arms, ammunition and supplies—300 per cent over 1942's record—the flood gates of production are wide open to sweep aggression into oblivion.

Industry will meet its 1943 war production obligations.

Industry has confidence in its ability to deliver.

Industry knew its own strength just after Pearl Harbor when it pledged to the president and the country that industry's production "will be limited only by the human endurance of the men who man and manage its facilities."

Industry is keeping that promise, and will keep that promise until the last Nazi has cried "kamerad" and the last yellow son of Nippon has hissed "Banzai."

Fighter and bomber planes to blast the enemies of democracy from the face of the earth, and ships to supply the twenty-seven battle fronts of the world must come from out the magic industrial area of this Pacific Coast. Ships and planes, more ships and planes is the American battle cry of 1943. "Give us the tools for quick victory." That's the patriotic challenge to management and worker alike.

It is going to take better teamwork to get such production. Not compulsory teamwork, but the highest degree of national unity based on patriotism and common welfare and not on group-grabbing interests.

Last year raw material was the key to better production, this year manpower is the fatal bottleneck.

We have enough workers if we employ them correctly. Fullest utilization of that manpower does not mean we must take the liberty of choice from the working man and woman, and make dumb driven slaves of them.

This is a battle of free men against the slavery of totalitarianism and free men will win every time, just as free industry has in two years caught up with the great war machinery of the Axis which was years in the building.

Government, labor and industry working together, instead of publicly exchanging indictments, can cut down absenteeism, turnover, labor pirating, job shopping, slow downs, strikes, feather bed rules—paying for work never performed—and other restrictions on production.

Above all, we can institute the encouragement of incentive for maximum war production—more pay for more production. If production is the gauge of victory why hook the rate of that production to the low level of the average worker, why not get better performance by rewarding more production.

Yes! Victory is in the making—if not yet won. But, what of the peace?

What of the hopes and aspirations of those millions of young Americans fighting for you and me?

Can we face our sons, fresh from filthy foxholes and the screaming hell of war, and say to them:

"You've given blood and guts to save the American way. But, we've scuttled it while you were fighting for it. Hope you don't mind too much!"

Or shall we welcome them home to an America of jobs, freedom and opportunity—the America they fight for.

What do we mean—JOBS, FREEDOM and OPPORTUNITY?

Jobs under good working conditions for fair wages. Jobs selected of our own free will and which we are free to change. FREEDOM to live without fear that a dictator or his henchmen will control us, watch our every action, listen to our words, tell us what to read, where to live, what to buy and where to work. We want FREEDOM under laws and institutions which are fair, equitably administered and imposing only minimum restraints necessary for the protection of the rights of individuals and minorities.

Such FREEDOM is the birthright of our nation—a nation dedicated to tolerance, to the protection of the individual, to the grand old American principle of "live and let live."

OPPORTUNITY to work and get ahead under our own steam, the chance to plan our own future, to raise our children so they may grow and learn and live with that self-respect which is the right of free men.

JOBS—FREEDOM—OPPORTUNITY—these three, together can provide for Americans the only security which comes when free citizens can look to the future with confidence.

Of the three—JOBS—FREEDOM—OPPORTUNITY—JOBS will be the keystone of post-war prosperity.

Now management can and must do many

things to make more post-war jobs possible, but it cannot guarantee jobs. Government alone can't guarantee jobs for very long. The only guarantee of jobs lies in a free competitive enterprise system that is both free and competitive, and ever expanding with the growing nation—that is where the future jobs are to be found.

To do this enterprise must be free of restraint and government regulation other than that necessary to the public welfare and fully competitive within itself, but not with government or government subsidized enterprise.

The answer to jobs, and more jobs, lies in the multiplication of wealth—not in mere division. In producing more to make more jobs, not in dividing up the jobs in a dwindling controlled economy.

It might be a bit too realistic for the times to believe that we must have more horses for more people to go horseback riding, instead of cutting up a few horses for distribution— even as popular as horse meat is becoming. But ever since old man Euclid, or some other ancient, discovered arithmetic, we have been horribly embarrassed by the fact that we cannot divide more when we have less.

America of all nations has made the cherished discovery that producing more to have more lies at the very heart of the more abundant life.

Free competitive enterprise is not a concoction of a few cussed capitalists bent on plundering the gentlefolk, but a method devised by human beings to care for their exchange of labor and the building of their lives and future through an economy of their own making.

It is the best means we or any other nation have devised to produce and distribute wealth to all.

Let me illustrate this national triangle of plenty through production, which is only another name for free competitive enterprise.

Industry, under competitive free enterprise, is an unusually vital triangle of interdependence, a triangle with four elements:

Industry is an unusual triangle in that it has four, instead of only three elements:—

(1) WORKERS; (2) INVESTORS or stockholders (for in industry $6,000 of capital is required for each job supplied); (3) most important of all, the consumers or MARKET; and (4) MANAGEMENT. Management belongs in the center of the triangle, with a corner each for workers, stockholders, and consumers.

Let's examine our triangle: At the top corner is really the most important of all, the consumers—let's call them MARKET. The American MARKET alone is 130 million people. Americans will always want MORE good things, and their demand will ALWAYS be, as it has been, "Better things at cheaper prices." Americans are bargain buyers. They buy objects, not policies, at the lowest possible price. Note that their demand upon business and industry is a fundamental demand—a natural demand of human nature—or self-interest.

Over in the second corner of the Triangle of Industry is CAPITAL. And, looking closely, we see that CAPITAL is also 130—and the same 130—millions of Americans. CAPITAL is anyone who has a life insurance policy, a bank account, an automobile, or, indeed, a pair of shoes—for even a pair of shoes represents an investment of capital. Note that the demand of CAPITAL on industry is a basic human demand, "How can I get the most of my investment?"

In the third corner of the triangle is LABOR. And again, this element is the same 130 millions of Americans we found in the other corners. LABOR'S demand on industry is for less work and MORE money. Observe again that this is a natural human reaction—self-interest.

Thus the three demands on industry are just the natural demands of everyday human nature. The buyer wants to pay less money into the Triangle of Industry; yet capital and labor insist that they each get more out of it. These are three seemingly irreconcilable factors in the triangle.

Now, the fourth element in our unusual triangle is MANAGEMENT—in the middle as always. To be successful MANAGEMENT must reconcile the three apparently irreconcilable forces.

But MANAGEMENT is always being pulled or hauled by one or the other of the three corners. When MARKET pulls, it says, "Give me lower prices or I won't buy." LABOR yanks, saying, "Give me more pay for less work." And at the same time CAPITAL hauls, crying, "More returns or you'll be fired." That's MANAGEMENT'S predicament.

Many people follow my picture thus far. Many think at this point that someone tosses in a fixed amount of money and the Triangle becomes a poker game in which, if one corner wins, another must lose.

This is not true! Industry is a device for the

creation of wealth—a device by which all can share in the new wealth produced.

To illustrate: Imagine a small umbrella factory with a single worker—Joe. Joe stands at an old-fashioned bench, running a hand spindle. He makes one umbrella an hour and gets one dollar an hour for his work.

After Joe has made the umbrella, MANAGEMENT says:

"Now, Joe, I haven't any money. I've got to sell this umbrella before I can pay you."

And so, MANAGEMENT goes to the gate—to the top of our triangle—where the great AMERICAN MARKET is going by, and he cries, "Umbrellas for sale." Management must get at least one dollar for the umbrella to pay Joe's wages.

"Too much—won't pay it!" snaps MARKET.

But, finally, the umbrella is sold and MANAGEMENT returns with the one dollar which he pays to Joe. At the end of the first day, then, we have an unhappy buyer—he wanted a lower price. Joe is unhappy—he wanted a raise. And CAPITAL calls up and asks MANAGEMENT, "Where is the return on my investment?"

There isn't any return—the stockholder is mad and he warns that MANAGEMENT will be fired unless the problem is solved and quickly!

MANAGEMENT, to save its job, burns midnight oil. MANAGEMENT discovers that Joe lost time working by hand and got tired standing at the bench. So MANAGEMENT decides to improve the tools of production. A motor is hitched to the spindle, Joe is given a stool, and to save more time Joe's material comes to him on a conveyor.

Joe comes in next morning and somewhat reluctantly tries out the new-fangled gadgets. To his amazement, at the end of an hour, he has made two umbrellas with less difficulty than he had making one the day before.

Taking the two umbrellas, MANAGEMENT goes back up to the top of the triangle and again calls out to MARKET, "Umbrellas for sale." Yesterday's disgruntled buyer says, "Nothing doing! Your price is too high!" MANAGEMENT says, "Not now, I've got just what you want—umbrellas at 75¢." The buyer is pleased. "Fine," he says, "I'll take two. That's what I want—a bargain."

MANAGEMENT returns to the middle of the triangle and says to Joe: "We've discovered the secret of the production of wealth. I've a dollar and a half where I had only one dollar yesterday. I'm giving you a 25¢ raise. Here's $1.25."

Joe is happy and MANAGEMENT calls CAPITAL to say, "Because there is a quarter left in the cash drawer, some dividends may be possible."

For more than 100 years the triangle of American competitive free enterprise has actually worked. We've produced the best goods at the lowest prices, the greatest accumulation of capital and the highest wages paid anywhere in the world.

There are no classes in American industry. One hundred thirty million Americans are Market, Capital and Labor. To prove this, let's go back to Joe and the typical day.

From eight in the morning until four in the afternoon, Joe is labor. He's conscious of it. He's mad at Capital and mad at Market. He wonders why he doesn't get more money.

At four o'clock Joe goes home and goes shopping with Mrs. Joe. He forgets that during the day he was labor. He's now Market. He's a tough buyer. "Why can't you sell this stuff cheaper," he demands.

On the way home, Joe stops to make a deposit in the bank. Now he's Capital. Again, he's a tough guy. "What are you doing with my money? Why can't I get 4% instead of only 1%? Can't you run a bank any better than this?"

He forgets that he has been Labor, Market and Capital in the same day.

But Joe, as Labor, picked up a 25-cent raise on the second day because wealth was produced. He picked up a 25% increase, as Market, when he purchased umbrellas at the cheaper price and, as Capital, he picked up a better return on his savings or life insurance.

The standard of living rises because, at each corner of the triangle, wealth is distributed. Joe is the American people who go around this triangle, day by day, picking up an ever increasing standard of living.

This might be too simple an explanation for the economist to understand, but I submit that it has done more, and can do more in the future to bring a better life to all the people than all the edicts, laws and decrees the government can ever promulgate.

The triangle story shows us that—Profits mean increased investment. Increased investment means increased wages. Therefore, profits increase wages.

Is this a contradiction, a fantasy?

Dr. Sumner Slichter of Harvard eloquently supports the connection between "larger profits" and "larger payrolls."

He says that labor and capital will both discover that the conditions which make it possible to arrive at both larger payrolls and larger profits are the very same conditions. He says that this discovery will lead to cooperation between labor and capital and that this cooperation "will make all previous efforts to raise the standard of living seem feeble."

That's the reason I say the best in America is yet to come. Because all the people in all three corners of the economic triangle—labor, market, investors—are not enemies of one another, but the very same people.

This kind of an economy is the best for the future, as it has been in the past, and is in present war production.

We had better put all our faith in that triangle of plenty and make it work if we want a post-war world free from want and economic stumbling and experimenting.

I believe we can very well throw victory away if we're not prepared for a good peace, and that we should be planning post-war now.

My only objection to the long-distance planner is that those least experienced in making our past and present are hell-bent on blue printing every detail of a great future.

Most of these plans have something very much in common. They are long on high sounding objectives but short on how to get them.

Reminds me of your late, dearly beloved Will Rogers who in 1917 had a plan to end submarine warfare.

"Just boil the ocean," Will told an Admiral.

"Corking idea," said the Admiral, "But how?"

"Oh, that's your job to scheme that out—I've given you the idea," replied Will.

Too many planners who say they believe in private enterprise as a source of post-war jobs do so with their tongue in their cheek.

They say yes, free competitive enterprise must be the source of only a "majority" of the post-war jobs, but then they look to government to provide the rest of the jobs through government spending. To me that is as ridiculous and economically immoral as a part-time

wife. Let's all get together to make the right system work, instead of combining the worst with the best and then being surprised at its failure.

Combining public and private enterprise is making a hybrid affair of the private enterprise system—half private, half public—half free, half slave.

In fact the big post-war planning decision for the American people is whether they want to continue to emasculate our economic system into a nondescript, unworkable combination of impossibilities, or whether they want to get back to the proven workability of the triangle of free competitive enterprise.

We have rediscovered the efficacy of private enterprise in war production. We have discovered the unworkableness of the promises of substitute schemes. The first step to peacetime plenty is to encourage a public renewal of faith in our American institution of undefiled, undiluted, free enterprise. On this decision as to our American economic policy not only depends our national future, but the peaceful welfare of the world.

Many thoughtful Americans are commencing to realize that a permanent peace is dependent on a better understanding and more friendly relationship between nations. Travel, communications and intercourse which in peace times usually follows the trade routes is NECESSARY toward quieting down this old world's bellicose eruptions every twenty-five years, and gives us more than just "peace in our times."

America has a big job ahead of it after this war. Rehabilitation of shattered countries and peoples is part of that job. Rehabilitation won't be just a big-hearted gesture on our part. It will be just plain common sense to help the world to right itself, to aid in establishing a "live and let live" basis of world economy! That's what we want in America—a free competitive system. In so far as that ideal is obtainable nationally without injury to our domestic well-being we should strive to bring it about. The war-torn countries have materials that we urgently need. They represent rich markets for our goods.

No city in America should have greater interest in this after-war prospect of world trade than San Francisco. This city can be the new world gateway to the trade of two of the greatest of post-war nations—China and Russia, just as Atlantic and gulf ports will exchange with the longer established trade nations of Europe.

A prosperous, modernized China would open up a tremendous market for American goods and equipment.

Industrialization of China seems like a pretty large order when we consider that 320 million Chinese have never heard a radio, read a newspaper or seen a movie. Yet, when war came, 30 million Chinese took on their backs, 77 colleges and universities and the machinery from 472 factories and carried them on foot over a thousand miles of mountain and plain to safety. That amazing feat showed the spirit—and the potentialities—of this great modern new nation.

I know that there is a widespread impression that any industrial development in such countries would tend to reduce the potential export markets of American industries and to reduce employment and living standards in this country. But we have abundant statistics to show that, as manufacturing increases, so does buying power and the demand for imports.

When the war is over Russia will probably have become the world's second largest industrial nation next to ourselves.

The United States is going to trade with this new Russia, too.

Business relations with Russia have always been more friendly than the differences between the ideals of government have led the public to believe. American engineers and American machinery have been a major aid in building the Russian ideal of greater industrial production, which has really supplanted the communistic state. Pure communism is rampant today only in the agitating minds of American "softies." Russia has adopted the production ideal and this ideal, to provide benefits to the people, thrives on a lasting peace and world trade, and not on cycles of production followed by the utter destruction of war. Therefore, enlightened national interests on the part of both nations will demand a trade rapprochement between American and Russian industry.

The American businessman should look to the Central and South American markets too as some of the most productive fields for immediate development after the war.

Our domestic well-being in the post-war world demands more trade among these and all nations. We should make every effort to work out international agreements under which nations will voluntarily adopt and maintain tariff policies. But no agreement should be allowed to disrupt the trade of any country.

We know the importance of fair competition and free enterprise in our domestic economy. These conditions are no less necessary in foreign trade. It is the proper function of government to protect domestic producers and labor against dumping, discrimination, and unfair competition. Government is justified in encouraging private research to develop industries, processes, or products that may appear suitable for protection and in protecting these industries, processes and products until they have become firmly established.

The life of the Reciprocal Trade Agreements Act ends this year, unless it is extended by Congress. This is a matter of great concern not only to American farmers but also to American business and industry.

Complete elimination of the principal of reciprocal agreements at this time would have unfortunate repercussions in the countries with which we are now allied in the war and in those with whom we hope to resume friendly relations after the war. We are fighting as a world nation. After the war, we must trade as one. Diplomatic peace and economic warfare cannot live side by side. Self-sufficiency is not a sound ideal in the modern world. It would do irreparable harm to our cause if we gave the nations at whose side we were now fighting any reason to suspect that we were going to renounce our interest in world affairs and retire to the selfish inaction of economic isolationism.

Our own industrial genius has forced us out into the world. Whether we like it or not, we are part of a world economy.

The National Association of Manufacturers believes that this nation has outgrown economic nationalism. This means of course a growing degree of freer trade than in the past but not the abrupt dropping of all tariffs to the ruination of American industry. The board of directors of the Association has declared that this country should be willing to make reciprocal trade agreements after the war, although certain amendments to the present act seem advisable. There are amendments that should be made to the act in the light of our experiences under it!

It should be the declared policy of government not to approximate total free trade; the adjustment of tariff rates should of course be gradual, not precipitate, enabling businessmen to adjust themselves to new conditions. Post-

war foreign trade should be in the hands of
private enterprise, not government; reciprocal
agreements should consider carefully the effects of the most-favored-nation clause in respect to imports from third countries; after any
product is first put on dutiable list there should
be no reduction except by Congress for five
years; benefits should be denied to countries
whose currencies fluctuated in terms of dollars
more than a given percentage in a year; our
government should move promptly to protect
American interests against any violation of the
Reciprocal Act; the Tariff Commission should
study effects of reciprocal treaties and report
to Congress regularly; and finally protection
should be given American industry, labor and
agriculture from dumping and other destructive foreign competition of nations employing
forced labor, depreciated currencies or similar
means of underselling our domestic market.

These safeguards combined with the best
possible world-informed U. S. negotiation department should not only help to re-establish
international commerce but restore a global
peace trade equilibrium.

What we want in an international sense is
exactly the same as we want here at home.
We want a free world in which the goods produced by agriculture and industry can move
easily, not to the advantage of a few or to the
injury of a few, but to the benefit of all. We
have marveled at the facility with which American industry can produce the goods the world
wants and needs. Our foremost job in the post-
war era will be to develop means of placing in
the hands of consumers, abroad as well as at
home, the necessities and even the luxuries
which we can produce so abundantly.

Critics say we cannot Americanize the world
—that forcing the American way down the
throats of foreign peoples smacks of dictatorship and power politics.

Let me assure you—no force will be needed.
Foreign industry envies us our productive capacity and skill—mimics us wherever it can.
The people, whenever they've had the opportunity to know American goods, have reached
eagerly for more. Denied the American standard of living at home, they have thronged to
our shores by the millions.

The American way of life is something concrete, something vital to these people, even if
we here at home sometimes forget it. We must
not only maintain the American standard; we
must lift it higher and higher. We can do it
through the medium of production.

We must make certain that production is not
stunted by the whimsical restrictions of bureaucrats burdened with the blueprints and
designs of economic planners. It must be free
to exercise its proper function—to give us more
and still more of the good things of life—to
lead us ever onward and upward as a free
nation and as a world power.   1943

WALTER LIPPMANN

1889–

AFTER TAKING his A.B. degree at Harvard in 1910, Walter Lippmann entered the
field of New York journalism. The apprenticeship he served with Lincoln Steffens
probably confirmed his liberal-radical social philosophy, which he expounded as an editor of
the *New Republic* and the *New York World*. During the First World War he held the rank of
captain in the Military Intelligence, and he served on the staff of the American Commission
to negotiate peace. Although he supported the New Deal in some respects and in its earlier
phases, he announced his intention of voting in 1936 for the conservative Republican candidate, Mr. Landon. His popular columns in the New York *Herald-Tribune* and in many other
papers have made his influence national in scope. Mr. Lippmann's books include *A Preface to
Politics* (1913), *The Stakes of Diplomacy* (1915), *Public Opinion* (1922), *A Preface to Morals* (1929),
and *The United States in World Affairs* (1931–1933).

The following selection is from *U.S. Foreign Policy: Shield of the Republic*, a book widely discussed in the months following its publication in 1943. The principal thesis is that the "foreign

policy which had served the United States, on the whole so well, during most of the nineteenth century became dangerously inadequate after 1900." Mr. Lippmann further remarks: "Then the United States expanded its commitments into Asiatic waters by the occupation of the Philippines, and then Germany, by deciding to build a great navy, emerged from continental Europe as a challenger for world power. I shall be arguing in this book that because of our failure to readjust the foreign policy of the United States to this revolutionary change in the situation, the nation has for over forty years been unprepared to wage war or to make peace, and has remained divided within itself on the conduct of American foreign relations." The argument in the book stands in contrast, in certain respects, to the position advanced by Henry Wallace: at least many critics interpreted it as an exposition of power politics.

Current Biography, 1940.

» » *From:* U.S. FOREIGN POLICY « «

CHAPTER X

THE GENERAL ORDER OF THE NATIONS

1. *The Nuclear Alliance*

The present association of the United States with Britain, Russia, and China is not a new departure. We have seen how for more than a century, whenever our vital interests were at stake, American foreign relations have always been primarily our relations with Britain, with Russia, and with China. Our relations with all other states have followed upon and have been governed by our relations with those three. In the conduct of American foreign policy our position has been solvent, our power adequate to our commitments, in so far as we were in essential agreement with these three states.

None of them, we may observe, is a European state. We must ponder this fact. For it may throw light upon the famous statement in Washington's Farewell Address that:—"Europe has a set of primary interests which to us have none or a very remote relation. Hence she must be engaged in frequent controversies, the causes of which are essentially foreign to our concerns." When these words were spoken on September 17, 1796, Napoleon was conducting his first campaign of aggression, the invasion of Italy. His conquest of the continent was still in the future, as was his threat to invade England and his actual invasion of Russia. The war which Washington knew about had all the appearance of being a purely *European* war, which to us had none or a very remote relation. Sixteen years later, however,

Napoleon was the master of Europe, and had struck outside of Europe into Russia. The United States had become involved in a local war with England. Yet while America was at war, we find Jefferson, the author of the phrase "no entangling alliances," writing on January 1, 1814, that "surely none of us wish to see Bonaparte conquer Russia, and lay thus at his feet the whole continent of Europe. This done, England would be but a breakfast. . . . Put all Europe into his hands, and he might spare such a force, to be sent in British ships, as I would as leave not have to encounter." Jefferson was writing a private letter in wartime [*] and he added: "I have gone into this explanation, my friend, because I know you will not carry my letter to the newspapers, and because I am willing to trust to your discretion the explaining me to our honest fellow laborers and the bringing them to pause and reflect . . . on the extent of the success we ought to wish to Bonaparte, and with a view to our own interests only."

We see here how the very men who laid down the rule of nonparticipation in European politics really thought about our foreign relations. They were aware that when there was a power in Europe which threatened to *come out of Europe* and conquer Britain, which is at one of the limits of Europe, or to conquer Russia which is at the other limit, our interests were vitally involved. If we read our history, not as our lesser statesmen have talked about it, but as in fact Americans have enacted it, we find, I submit, that while our concern has not been with *European* affairs, we have always been concerned with *world* affairs. Our

* To Thomas Leiper, 14 Jefferson 41, 43.

primary relations have been, and are, with the extra-European powers, and with Europe itself only as some power inside of Europe threatens to disrupt the order of things outside of Europe. Thus, if we think as clearly and exactly about American interests as Jefferson, even in the midst of a jingoistic war, was able to think, we shall see that the traditional American policy against being involved in European affairs is not in the last analysis inconsistent with the consolidation of America's vital interest in the world.

Our primary interest in Europe, as shown during the Napoleonic and the two German Wars, is that no European power should emerge which is capable of aggression outside of the European continent. Therefore our two natural and permanent allies have been and are Britain and Russia. For they have the same fundamental interest—to each of them a matter of national life or death—in preventing the rise of such a conquering power in Europe. And that is why Britain and Russia, though they have been at odds on the Near East, the Middle East, and in Asia, have been allies against Napoleon, against William II, and against Hitler.

Here then, founded on vital interest which has been tested and proved in the course of generations, is the nuclear alliance upon which depends the maintenance of the world order in which America lives. Combined action by America, Britain, and Russia is the irreducible minimum guarantee of the security of each of them, and the only condition under which it is possible even to begin to establish any wider order of security.

The formation of this nuclear alliance must in our thinking and in our action take precedence over all other considerations. For without it we cannot make good our existing commitments in the Atlantic and in the Pacific. Without it, our commitment in the Philippines remains a salient, exceedingly difficult to defend against a resurgent Japan or against a combination of powers in Eastern Asia. Without this nuclear alliance, our commitment in South America is open to challenge, if not by direct conquest from Europe and Africa, then by infiltration and conspiracy. Without it, the two oceans and the airways to the north and the south are perilously open and uncertain, since the ports and landing fields beyond would be in uncertain hands.

Only by the formation of this nuclear alliance—whatever we choose to call it, no matter how we choose to seal it—can American foreign policy be said to have balanced our commitments with a safe margin in reserve. We need make no apologies then because we put this first thing first. American foreign relations must be made solvent before the United States can afford to issue any more promissory notes.

Furthermore, we should not have learned the lessons of our failures in the past, especially the lesson of the failure of the League of Nations, if in our projects for organizing world peace we did not fix our attention first of all upon the powers capable of organizing it. Blueprints, covenants, contracts, charters, and declarations do not create living associations. They merely formulate, regulate, ratify, develop, and guide the action of men or groups of men who already have the will to associate themselves. It is not, for example, the marriage laws which make the family, but the union of a man and a woman who in accordance with these laws then found a family. It was not the Constitution which made the American union, but the constituent states which adopted it in order to form a more perfect union.

The will of the most powerful states to remain allied is the only possible creator of a general international order.

2. The Justification of Insisting Upon It

There will be many, I realize full well, who will feel that this insistence upon the security of the vital interests of the most powerful states involves an illiberal and even a brutal neglect of the rights of the weaker nations and of their intrinsic importance to civilization itself. I ask their indulgence until the argument is concluded. We shall see why the nuclear alliance must be liberal in its policy if it is to endure.

But if we are to prove this convincingly, and not merely to state it rhetorically, there must be no doubt in our minds why as Americans we must insist upon beginning with the security of the vital interests of the United States. It is that for half a century the United States has so neglected its vital interests that it was incapable of defending them adequately, or of carrying through any measures whatsoever to maintain the peace of the world. For fifty years no nation has been more liberal in its words than has been the United States; none neglected its own interests so dangerously, or contributed less to realizing the ideals it so assiduously preached.

So I make no apology for seeking to define the American foreign policy on which the American people could again become united because it conforms rigorously to American interests. I see no way of our being able to contribute anything to anybody else until we have become fully conscious again of our own interests and feel prepared to maintain them. . . . And I do not doubt that our allies and our friendly neighbors will, as they consider the matter, greatly prefer an American foreign policy founded on an enlightened conception of our own national interest to the ambiguous platitudes with which we have regaled them for the past fifty years.

Nor need we shrink from insisting that the precondition of a better world order is a nuclear alliance of the three powerful military states which will emerge victorious from the present war. They are the states upon which depends the deliverance of Europe from the Nazi despotism, and of the Far East from the empire of Japan. It has needed the combined force of all three of these states, and the utmost exertion of their power, to make the deliverance possible. No one of them, no two of them, could have done it. Why, then, should we hesitate to say that anything less than this combination of great powers is insufficient to preserve order against aggression in the world? Will anyone presume to argue that to dissolve this combination again would promote the liberty of the peoples who have been conquered, or would make secure the order which has been shattered by two devastating world wars?

It is only around this strong nuclear alliance that a wider association of many nations can constitute itself. If that condition is accepted, and once it is accepted, it will become evident that the combination of the great powers cannot, despite their common vital interests, be made to hold together except as they respect the liberties of the other peoples and promote them by the maintenance of law.

I believe it can be demonstrated as conclusively as anything can be demonstrated in human affairs that Britain, Russia, America, and China as she becomes a great state, cannot remain allies and partners unless they use their power, separately and in combination, to maintain liberty through law.

3.　*The Binding Condition of Unity*

We must begin by remembering that Britain, Russia, and America are allies, not by conscious choice but under the compulsion of their common enemies. They have been compelled, as I have tried to show, to become allies whenever a really formidable aggressive power emerged which threatened to break out of Europe into the outer world. Nevertheless, when there is no such enemy which threatens their national existence, the need for their alliance becomes submerged. Their lesser, their separate and conflicting, interests are then free to assert themselves. The greater the peril from the outside, the closer is their union: the greater their security, the more their differences come to the surface.

The unconditional surrender of Germany and of Japan is bound, therefore, to leave all the Allies with an immediate sense of mortal peril averted; and this will reduce the compulsion that binds the alliance together. There will then be opened up disputable secondary questions which push apart the members of the alliance. This has always happened in wars won by a coalition. It happened at the Congress of Vienna, and because of it Talleyrand's diplomacy was so successful. It happened at the Peace Conference in 1919, when the victorious alliance had in fact become dissolved even before peace had been made with the enemy. It can and it may happen again, as we have seen in the winter of 1943, when the first prospects of victory have already opened up fissures among the Allies.

These fissures will tend to become wider and deeper the more any one of the great powers seeks to aggrandize itself either at the expense of one of the other great powers, or at the expense of their smaller allies.

Thus an American policy of imperialist aggrandizement at the expense of the British Empire would impair profoundly, if it did not destroy, the Atlantic Community. It would become necessary for Britain to look for her security in some combination which thwarted American aggrandizement.

By the same token, a British policy which rested on the refusal to recognize the necessary changes in the colonial and imperial system of the nineteenth century would raise up against Britain insurgent forces in Asia, the Middle East, and Africa. Britain could not count upon American support in resisting these forces, and almost certainly she would have to count upon Russian and Chinese encouragement of these forces.

By the same token again, a Russian policy of aggrandizement in Europe, one which threatened the national liberties of her neighbors, would inexorably be regarded as such a threat to Britain and America that they would begin to encourage the nations which resisted Russia. In Asia, a Russian policy of aggrandizement against China would disrupt Russian-American relations in the North Pacific and, in the coming air age, across the top of the globe. On the other hand, an anti-Russian policy in which Britain, America, and the European states sought, as they did in 1919, to blockade and even to disrupt Russia would provoke Russian communist intervention to counteract it.

And by the same token, also, a Chinese policy of aggrandizement in India, Malaya, Indo-China, and the Netherlands Indies would encounter opposition from Britain, from America, from Australia and New Zealand, from France and the Netherlands.

The fissures opened by any one or all of these tendencies to aggrandizement would soon become a breach. This would be followed inevitably and immediately by competition among the Allies to win over to their side the vanquished nations. This would be done by restoring their power. In Europe the separated Allies would bid against one another for the favor of Germany. In Asia, they would bid for the favor of Japan. Thus because aggrandizement had made them rivals, they would restore the aggressor powers which had threatened them. The postwar era would thus be transformed, as the late Frank Simonds observed of the early thirties, into a prewar era.

For these reasons it is evident that a nuclear alliance of Britain, Russia, America, and, if possible, China, cannot hold together if it does not operate within the limitations of an international order that preserves the national liberties of other peoples. The three, or the four, great powers will not remain united against the revival of German and Japanese military power if they become rivals in the domination of Central and Eastern Europe or of the dependent and colonial regions of Asia and Africa.

Nor could the nuclear allies, as some may fear, combine to oppress and exploit the rest of mankind. For, in the last analysis, the resistance of the rest of mankind would disrupt the alliance: one or the other of the great powers would find that its interests and its sympathies lay with the peoples resisting oppression.

Nor could the nuclear allies divide the globe into spheres of influence which each was free to dominate and exploit separately. For no spheres of influence can be defined which do not overlap, which would not therefore bring the great powers into conflict. Where in Europe, for example, could a sphere of influence be fixed which separated Britain and Russia into convenient imperialist compartments? On which side of the line would the Scandinavian countries lie? If on the Russian, then the sea and air approaches to Britain are insecure; if on the British, then the sea and air approaches to Russia are insecure. Where in Africa could a line of demarcation be drawn when, in fact, the defense of South America is dependent upon the presence of friendly powers in North and West Africa, when in fact the security of the Mediterranean is also dependent upon the control of North and West Africa? Where can a sphere of influence be defined in the East which makes secure China, the British nations in Australasia, and the American commitment in the Philippines?

Thus it is as impossible for the Allied great powers to divide up the world and then rule it as it is for them to combine in order to dominate the world. The inexorable logic of their alliance demands that they recognize the liberties of the peoples outside the alliance. For in no other way can they avoid becoming rivals and then enemies for the domination of these other peoples. In no other way but by supporting a world-wide system of liberty under law can they win the consent, earn the confidence, and insure the support of the rest of the world in the continuation of their alliance.

The order which they originate because it is necessary to their own vital security can, therefore, be perpetuated only if they act so as to gain and to hold the good will of the other peoples. Delivering the weaker states from the Nazi and Japanese conquest will not in itself hold their good will. For the memory of the deliverance will become obscured by what happens afterwards. Their own concept of their own interest, rather than gratitude, is for all masses of peoples the motive which determines their actions. The gratitude of the liberated to the victorious powers will, therefore, continue only if the great powers remain united enough to keep the peace of the world against aggressors and at the same time become liberal enough so that there is no good reason for rebellion against the order which they maintain.

The experience of history supports the conclusion that power can endure only if it gives and maintains laws within which men enjoy the liberties they regard as more important than life. Not all peoples everywhere and always have had the same conception of their essential liberties. But whatever they regard as their essential liberties, be they the liberties of the Christian West or of the Moslem world, or of the Hindus, or of the Chinese, it is these liberties which must be respected under the law if the power behind the law is to endure. Though the world is shrunken, we must not imagine that any system of identical laws can prevail everywhere. The East and the West have been formed in widely different cultural traditions. But what can prevail everywhere, if the alliance holds together, is the universal law that force must not be arbitrary, but must be exercised in accordance with laws that are open to discussion and are subject to orderly revision.

An order of this kind can endure, not forever in a changing world, but for a long and beneficent period of time. Security and liberty are the benefits which such an order can provide. They are such great benefits that whenever men have enjoyed them at all they have rallied to the authority which provided them. It was because the Roman legions brought with them the Roman law that the Roman Empire lived on so long, and, when it fell, lived in men's memories for a thousand years as an ideal to which they longed to return. It has been Britain's devotion to law which, despite all the rebellion against British rule, has brought so many nations to Britain's side whenever Britain has been really threatened. And I think Americans may without false pride believe that in the last analysis it is our own preference for liberty under law, and not our material power only, which has made the neighbor republics of this hemisphere believe that their vital interests and ours are the same.

4. Conclusion as to the Organization of a New Order

For these reasons it is self-evident that in a fully enlightened view of the vital interests of the great powers and of the smaller we may conclude that:—

To establish and maintain order the nuclear alliance must be consolidated and perpetuated.

To perpetuate their alliance the great powers must become the organizers of an order in which the other peoples find that their liberties are recognized by laws that the great powers respect and that all peoples are compelled to observe.

If this is done, the new order will rest not on sentiment but on enlightened interest. Then only will it be strong enough to have authority. Then only will it be liberal enough to have its authority persist.

5. Finale

The structure of the order which the nuclear allies could or should institute, the laws and covenants they could or should subscribe to, the procedures they could or should agree upon—these matters lie outside the province of this inquiry. We have been concerned with finding the American foreign policy which will most adequately and surely make this republic solvent in its foreign relations. We have, therefore, dwelt upon those measures which are indispensable to America if it is to fulfill the commitments it has, if it is to be able to make commitments at all. We have found, I believe, that the measures which will most securely maintain the vital interests of the United States are measures which will no less securely maintain the vital interests of our neighbors, the great ones and the smaller ones alike.

Guided by this principle, and determined to apply it, we shall be capable again of forming an American foreign policy. We shall no longer be, as we have been for nearly fifty years, without a foreign policy which takes account of our interests. We need no longer be divided because the national interest upon which we must unite will have been made evident to us. We shall no longer exhort mankind to build castles in the air while we build our own defenses on sand.

Then, when we know what we ourselves need and how we must achieve it, we shall be not only a great power. We shall have become at last a mature power. We shall know our interests and what they require of us. We shall know our limitations and our place in the scheme of things.

Then "we may choose peace or war, as our interest, guided by justice, shall counsel"; then the duty which Washington laid upon us will be done.   1943

*Internal Adjustments and External
Anxieties*

1945 ____

AC-CENT-TCHU-ATE THE POSITIVE *

Gather round me, everybody,
Gather round me while I preach some,
Feel a sermon comin' on me.
The topic will be sin and that what I'm "agin,"
If you wanna hear my story
Then settle back and just sit tight
While I start reviewin' the attitude of doin' right.

You've got to ACCENTUATE THE POSITIVE,
Eliminate the negative,
Latch onto the affirmative,
Don't mess with Mister Inbetween.

You've got to spread joy up to the maximum,
Bring gloom down to the minimum,
Have faith or pandemonium lible to walk upon the scene.
To illustrate my last remark Jonah in the whale, Noah in the Ark.

What did they have to do,
Just when ev'ry thing looked so dark?
"Man," they said, "We better
ACCENTUATE THE POSITIVE,
Eliminate the negative,
Latch onto the affirmative,
Don't mess with Mister Inbetween."

Of the many songs which Bing Crosby made popular in the period after World War II, none expresses better than this one the dominant mood of the era—a desire to deal firmly and forcefully with all sorts of problems, foreign and domestic. Yet through this determination to "ac-cent-tchu-ate the positive" ran a current of fear lest "pandemonium lible to walk upon the scene" if there were a failure in faith.

The words of this significant song were written by Johnny Mercer; the music was composed by Harold Arlen.

» » « «

Internal Adjustments and External Anxieties

DURING THE struggle against the Fascist Powers many expected that the war would be followed by a major depression. But the established economic order, combining as it did government intervention and control with "free enterprise," provided widespread prosperity, enlisted popular approval of business leadership, and intrigued a group of intellectuals who expounded "the new conservatism."

Yet economic growth and a high standard of living did not resolve all conflicts in American life. Concern with blighted areas in cities led to only partially successful urban redevelopment plans. Suburban living, which increased markedly; created its own problems. The struggle for civil rights for American Negroes achieved notable victories but was countered by a stubborn opposition to programs for the desegregation of public schools on the part of traditionally-minded Southern whites.

The issue of conformity led to spirited debates. "The Cold War" against the Communist world was accompanied, especially in the early 1950's, by curtailments of traditional civil liberties and to considerable hysteria which Senator McCarthy exploited. In another area, the commercial mass culture and emphasis on "togetherness" and conformity to group norms, disturbed many thoughtful Americans.

The United Nations, in which the United States played an important part, did not succeed in overcoming mounting tensions between the Communist and nonCommunist worlds. Neither the United Nations nor the leadership of America and her allies succeeded in finding acceptable formula for limiting competition in military technology, especially in the rapid and revolutionary development of atomic weapons and missiles. But Americans did give serious thought to their national values. And they reasserted their faith in the promise of better education for more people and in the possibility that man's expanding knowledge could both insure his civilization against irrational domination and improve its quality.

» » « «

FORTUNE MAGAZINE

IN 1951 the editors of *Fortune* published *U. S. A. Permanent Revolution*, a product of the staff under the general direction of Russell Davenport. The book was received on the one hand as shallow, apologetic, and full of errors, and, on the other, as a cogent and impressive interpretation of American life and especially of the American economic system. It both represented and influenced the newer tendency in public opinion to emphasize the constructive and beneficent aspects of American industry.

» » *From:* U.S.A. PERMANENT REVOLUTION « «

THE TRANSFORMATION OF
AMERICAN CAPITALISM

. . . Fifty years ago American capitalism seemed to be what Marx predicted it would be and what all the muckrakers said it was—the inhuman offspring of greed and irresponsibility, committed by its master, Wall Street, to a long life of monopoly. It seemed to provide overwhelming proof of the theory that private ownership could honor no obligation except the obligation to pile up profits. It was, indeed, close to the capitalism that Andrei Vishinsky today keeps on denouncing so laboriously and humorlessly. And it was the capitalism that millions of people abroad and many even at home, to the immense aid and comfort of the Communists, still think American capitalism is.

But American capitalism today is actually nothing of the kind. There has occurred a great transformation, of which the world as a whole is as yet unaware, the speed of which has outstripped the perception of the historians, the commentators, the writers of business books—even many businessmen themselves. No important progress whatever can be made in the understanding of America unless the nature of this transformation is grasped and the obsolete intellectual stereotypes discarded.

Many evidences of the transformation are at hand, though they have never yet been drawn together into what is very urgently needed—a restatement of capitalistic theory in modern American terms. Take, for example, the all-pervasive character of American capitalism, as stressed in The American Way of Life. There has been a vast dispersion of ownership and initiative, so that the capitalist system has become intimately bound in with the political system and takes nourishment from its democratic roots. What might be called the influence of Main Street has become vastly more important than the control of Wall Street. U. S. capitalism is *popular* capitalism, not only in the sense that it has popular support, but in the deeper sense that the people as a whole participate in it and use it.

But perhaps the transformation can best be understood by looking at what has happened to "Big Business," which once was supposed to have controlled the economy from its headquarters in Wall Street. The fact is that Wall Street no longer wields much power over Big Business, which in turn is far from being the most powerful sector of the economy. For economic power boils down to the ability to decide who makes what and who gets what and in what proportions, and business alone no longer decides this. "The class struggle in America," writes Professor Clair Wilcox in the *Harvard Business Review,* "is not a struggle between the proletariat and the bourgeoisie. It is a struggle between functional groups possessing concentrated power—a struggle to control the products of industry." These groups, as Professor Wilcox describes them, are Big Labor, Big Agriculture, Big Little Business, and Big Business. Of them all, Big Business, if only because it is subject to the most pressure, exercises its power with a strong and growing sense of responsibility. It has led the way to the formation of a kind of capitalism that neither Karl Marx nor Adam Smith ever dreamed of.

At the bottom of the change is simple morality, which has concerned the U. S. throughout its history, sometimes to the point of fanaticism. "The American," H. L. Mencken once said, "save in moments of conscious and swiftly lamented deviltry, casts up all ponderable values, including the value even of beauty, in terms of right and wrong." Like the European who described moral indignation as suppressed envy, Mencken scorned it as the mark of the peasant; and the American's capacity for moral indignation *has* resulted in many "uncivilized" excesses like prohibition. But it has also made him the most omnivorous reformer in history. Karl Marx based his philosophy on the fatalistic assumption that what he described as the inherent defects of capitalism are above the will of men to affect them. It has remained for the history of U. S. capitalism, beginning as early as the 1870's, to show that the moral convictions of men can change the course of capitalistic development.

And it would have been strange if a nation that had only recently fought a terrible war over the question of slavery had *not* got indignant about the excesses of its "robber barons." People, of course, do not necessarily rise up voluntarily and act on moral indignation. What is essential is their capacity for it; given a free, lively press and plenty of politicians, the action follows. Action followed in the U. S. because a whole school of commentators, from novelists to reporters, from historians to cartoonists, rose up to expose the financial and industrial scandals of the day. There were the Ida Tarbells and Henry Demarest Lloyds, the Upton Sinclairs and Frederick Oppers, backed by the Hearsts, McClures, and Munseys. Some were hypocritical and others wholly sincere, but all operated on the effective principle that the public could be fetched by an earnest appeal to its moral standards.

In their zeal the muckrakers paid little attention to the great economic role played by "robber barons" in forming the capital to lay the rails, erect the factories, build the machinery for a new and expanding economy. Naturally the muckrakers were concerned not with amoral economics but with immoral practices. Their pictures of the American economic brigandage of the late nineteenth and early twentieth centuries become stereotypes all over the world—Daniel Drew feeding his cattle salt to make them drink heavily the day before market; Cornelius Vanderbilt bragging how "we busted the hull damn legislature"; foxy Jay Gould, whom Vanderbilt called the smartest man in America, cornering the national gold-coin supply through his White House connections, and systematically and openly robbing the Erie; gelid old John D. Rockefeller perfecting the trust system and eliminating competitors like clay pigeons. Here was the principle of property ownership carried to its absurd conclusion, capitalism gone berserk. But here also was the moral indignation of the American people. Fanned by lurid accounts in the press and by politicians and publicists of almost every persuasion, from Populists to Republicans, it started the transformation of American capitalism.

Popular resentment of the railroad rate-making came early, even before the muckraking school was in full swing. The Interstate Commerce Act was passed in 1887. And only three years later there occurred what is probably the most portentous single legislative act in the history of American capitalism: the passage of the Sherman Act against monopolies and combinations "in restraint of trade." Although endorsed by all parties, its birth was inauspicious, and the bill was amended almost to death. Senator John Sherman himself, the story goes, never read the final version. And for several years, under Cleveland and McKinley, the act was used little, and then ineffectively. In 1901 J. P. Morgan disregarded it and put U. S. Steel together. "What looks like a stone wall to a layman," said Mr. Dooley, "is a triumphal arch to a corporation lawyer." But the muckrakers began to make themselves felt. In 1902 Teddy Roosevelt, a man who not only understood the public mind but judged almost everything in terms of righteousness, whipped out the Sherman Act and used it as a "big stick" on what he was the first to call the "malefactors of great wealth." He wielded it so effectively against the Northern Securities Co. that the legislation became a power in American life.

The defects of the Sherman Act were soon and widely recognized. "No law can make a man compete with himself," observed J. P. Morgan characteristically. Others noted the great paradox of the antitrust conception: a strong company that really obeyed the law and competed strenuously would end up as a monopoly, violating the law. Contemplating such contradictions, the "realistic" Europeans abstained from trust-busting; they left it to the naïve Americans, who in their preoccupation with right and wrong were foolish enough to take so seriously and apply so dogmatically their notions of fairness and justice.

The antitrust law nevertheless acquired stature and authority. However patent its imperfections, however hollow its victories, however vitiated by later acts like Miller-Tydings and Robinson-Patman, it became, in the words of Justice Holmes, "a brooding omnipresence in the sky." Even when businessmen are puzzled and irritated by the letter of the law, they respect its spirit. Even when their lawyers tell them how to get around it, they know they *are* getting around it. The law, in the last analysis, amounts to nothing less than the successful extension of the Anglo-Saxon common law, the basis of the whole English-speaking world's unique liberty, into the realm of business. And its success is among the chief reasons why American business is today so vastly different from European business.

Other reforms came sporadically. The American's moral indignation, naturally enough, did not burn with a steady flame. In good times he

tended to overlook violations of his basic notions; in bad times he looked for something to
blame things on, and demanded that something be done about them. During the 1920's
popular demand for reform was almost nonexistent. For one thing, the scorn of some of
the nation's most effective writers made preoccupation with moral issues unfashionable if
not ludicrous. For another, business seemed to
be doing fine, and seemed to deserve not reform but praise. As the immensely popular
Saturday Evening Post demonstrated in almost every issue, as Herbert Hoover himself
phrased it, "The slogan of progress is changing
from the full dinner pail to the full garage."

The catastrophe of depression blasted this
dream. The shocked and angry people, seeing
their livelihood disappear, put the Right to
Life above the other rights. Their natural
tendency to blame the bust on those who only
yesterday were taking credit for having started
an eternal boom was strengthened by revelations such as those of the Pecora congressional
investigation into Wall Street financial practices. So they embraced the latter-day Popu-
lism of the New Deal, and demanded that
something be done. Writers and intellectuals
took up the cudgels. Some were merely inclined to condemn what they had for so long
contemned, but many tried to find out how
and why it had happened, and how to keep
it from happening again.

Many of the ensuing reforms survived. Immediately after the Pecora investigation, Congress passed a law divorcing investment banking from deposit banking. And a year later it
passed the well-intentioned Securities Exchange Act, which put the Stock Exchange under federal regulation, gave the Federal Reserve Board authority to limit speculative
margins, required all officers and stockholders
of big companies to report their dealings in
their companies' securities, and created the Securities and Exchange Commission to watch
over the investment market.

Other attempts at reform were less successful. NRA, for example, went to a well-
deserved death. As for the famed Temporary
National Economic Committee, much of what
it investigated was beside the point by the
time it was in print—and not only because of
the impending war. Even while the committee
was mulling over the power of big business,
and the intellectuals were in full cry on the

trail of finance capitalism, business initiative
had been dispersed among hundreds of enterprises; business power in the aggregate found
itself confronted by the rising power of the
unions on the one hand, the farmers on the
other; and Wall Street had ceased to be a
valid symbol of great tyranny.

The decline of Wall Street actually began
long before the reforms of the New Deal. It
began when corporations grew rich and independent. . . . Wall Street did not feel the
change at first. In the boom of the 1920's the
issue of new securities passed the $500-
million-a-year mark, and a rich time was had
by all. But even then the bulk of the Street's
effort was going into the buying and selling
of old issues (and new issues of holding companies that used the money to buy old issues),
the promotion of dubious foreign bonds, and
the lending of money at, say, 7 per cent for the
speculative purchase of stock paying, say 5 per
cent. And even then corporations were putting
up to ten times as much money into their reserves as all companies were raising in new
stocks and bonds. And the depression hit the
Street's new-issue function even harder than
it hit the trading function. High income taxes
and the growing corporate practice of financing new issues through insurance and trust
companies trimmed the new-issue business almost to the vanishing point.

Except as its opinions still influence investment policies, Wall Street today exerts only a
fraction of the power it once wielded. Industry now plows back 60 per cent of its profits,
as against 30 per cent in the 1920's, and the
bulk of the money used in capital formation
comes from corporate earning or from internal
sources such as depreciation. The largest brokerage house on the Street, accounting for
10 per cent of the stock trading on the Stock
Exchange, is Merrill Lynch, Pierce, Fenner &
Beane, 90 per cent of whose customers are
small-fry out-of-towners.

.   .   .

The cataclysm of the depression, which forever broke apart the old business universe,
also heaved up the bright new stars of the
unions and the farmers. With between 14 and
16 million members in labor unions, labor
leaders now enjoy tremendous industrial
power. This power is exercised through the
familiar method of tying up an entire industry
in order to win certain gains for the workers,

whether these gains be "economic" or not. In the face of such power, industry is impotent; and since the national welfare is often enough at stake, the White House itself becomes directly involved. The danger of such power is obvious, and was recently accented by John L. Lewis, who put his miners on a three-day week, not merely to enforce a wage demand, but to keep the price of coal up by creating a scarcity. Here, indeed, is a problem that the permanent revolution has not yet solved, although certain solutions are beginning to emerge, as described in the next chapter. The point to note here is that the power of Wall Street, which has declined in any case, has been met, and sometimes over-matched, by the power of modern labor; a development that has played an enormous role in the transformation of American capitalism.

The power of the farmer, if less direct than that of labor, is likewise formidable. Represented in Congress out of proportion to his numbers, the farmer has been championed by legislators and bureaucrats who have effectively insulated him from the law of supply and demand. By restricting output, fixing prices, and storing up surpluses at government expense, they have done for agriculture what a watertight cartel would do for a group of manufacturers of widely varying efficiency. They have not only saddled the public with high prices, they have, of course, tended to prevent American farming from becoming as efficient as it ought to be and can be. For they have spread a price umbrella over the farmers that has enabled the worst of them to do all right and the best of them to make fantastic and undeserved profits without necessarily encouraging any of them to become more efficient. The $23-billion farm industry, furthermore, is hardly comparable to any one industry; it is more comparable to all industry—to all industry cartelized, subsidized, and rigidified. In terms of deciding who makes what and who gets what, it is one of the most powerful blocks in American history.

And where, in this regrouping of U. S. economic power, do we find the sense of responsibility that ought to go with the power if the nation is to increase its productivity? Labor, with a few exceptions, does not yet show much of it, and agriculture shows even less. The only place it can be found in any force is in the individual business enterprise, which now has the initiative that might have remained in Wall Street had not the transformation taken place.

One of the two chief characteristics of big modern enterprise is that it is run by hired management. As Berle and Means put it, the power inherent in the control of the "active property"—the plant, organization and good will—has superseded the power inherent in "passive property"—the stocks and bonds. Even companies whose owners are managers may be described as management-run. The Ford company, for example, behaves not as an organization solely dedicated to earning the maximum number of dollars for the Ford family, but as an organization dedicated first of all to its own perpetuation and growth.

The other chief characteristic of the big modern enterprise is that management is becoming a profession. This means, to begin with, that a professional manager holds his job primarily because he is good at it. Often he has begun at the bottom and worked his way up by sheer merit. Or more often he has been carefully and even scientifically chosen from a number of bright and appropriately educated young men, put through an executive-training course, and gradually insinuated into the activities for which he shows the most talent. Since even at the top he generally functions as a member of a committee rather than as a final authority, his talents are so well balanced that none of them protrude excessively. He lives on what he makes, and even when he is well paid he doesn't have much left after taxes. Generally he is gregarious, and usually he is not a colossal "personality." But if he is not a General MacArthur, neither is he a Mr. Milquetoast. And if he is expected not to give arbitrary orders, he is also expected not to take them. In most well-run big enterprises, an executive is by definition a man who would object officially to a policy decision he disapproved.

More important, the manager is becoming a professional in the sense that like all professional men he has a responsibility to society as a whole. This is not to say that he no longer needs good, old-fashioned business sense. He does, and more than ever. The manager is responsible primarily to his company as a profit-earning mechanism, and current talk about the corporation as a non-profit institution is more than a little naïve. Any self-respecting businessman would rightly suspect a colleague who allowed he was in business not to make money. The modern enterpriser *should* be in business to make money. His ability to make money is the prime measure of his company's efficiency. If it cannot prosper in the service it supplies to society, or if it cannot persuade society to pay it enough to prosper, it does not deserve to stay in business. Moreover, the good, efficient manager *likes* to make money, and it is mainly because he likes to make money that he does a first-rate job. As the Russians have discovered, when the profit motive does not exist it has to be invented.

But the great happy paradox of the profit motive in the American system is that management, precisely because it is in business to make money years on end, cannot concentrate exclusively on making money here and now. To keep on making money years on end, it must, in the words of Frank Abrams, Chairman of the Standard Oil Co. of New Jersey, "conduct the affairs of the enterprise in such a way as to maintain an *equitable and working balance* among the claims of the various directly interested groups—stockholders, employees, customers, and the public at large." Not all pundits have understood this vital point. In his romantic *Managerial Revolution*, for example, James Burnham described the trend accurately enough but conveyed the idea that somehow the corporate manager is destined to become the Western equivalent of a King Farouk or perhaps an unusually favored commissar. The corporate manager neither is, nor is becoming, anything of the kind. He is part of a group that enjoys power only so long as it does not abuse it—in other words, precisely so long as it does not exercise power the way men and groups of men used to before the capitalistic transformation.

Thus it is not too difficult to define management's responsibility to the stockholder. Management is no longer occupied exclusively with the interests of the stockholder, who often has become a kind of contingent bondholder rather than a part owner, and who rarely exerts any direct influence on the affairs of the company. But management cannot flagrantly disregard stockholders' interests, at least not for long. As the management of Bethlehem and U. S. Steel know well, stockholders can be a considerable nuisance. Even when

widely dispersed, they can be induced to take a point of view by proxy. And on the whole, management is treating the stockholders well —despite "abuses" like the habit of holding annual meeting in some out-of-the-way railway station or in Wilmington, Delaware. Almost any good manager can honestly argue that the growing importance of the hired management and its policy of self-capitalization have been to the benefit of the stockholder. Above all, he can argue that the stockholder's long-term interests lie in letting competent, responsible management build up the company and deal justly with employees, customers, and the public.

But modern management exhibits also a sense of responsibility toward its employees, not only to prevent or anticipate the demands of labor unions (though this motive has often been strong) but for the simple, obvious, and honest reason that a satisfied, loyal group of employees is at least as much of an asset as a modern plant or a vital piece of machinery. The trend toward more enlightened employment policies has been growing for years, and while there is still a great distance to go, an old-style capitalist would be appalled by the wide variety of benefits that modern corporations offer those who work for them. There is a growing tendency on the part of blue-chip management to regard a job in the company as a kind of employment package, complete with pensions, savings plan, and numerous "fringe" benefits such as severance pay, maternity leave, hospitalization, and medical insurance. Other managements specialize in certain types of benefits. Some, for instance, go in for stabilization of employment. ATF, Inc., as an example, which recently bought into the furniture business, has succeeded in almost eliminating the highly seasonal character of that work. Some companies (Proctor & Gamble, Nunn-Bush, Hormel) carry employment stabilization to the point of guaranteeing an annual wage. Others have developed forecasting techniques to anticipate trends and to stabilize employment by leveling out production. Almost every important company now has a pension plan or is in the process of getting one. Many, like Sears, Roebuck, combine pensions with savings plans, so that when an employee retires he takes with him a sizeable capital sum. Others, backed by the Council of Profit-Sharing Industries (276 members), give the workers a cut of profits, with annual bonuses running up to 100 per cent of base wages.

But material benefits, as Elton Mayo and others have demonstrated, are often not as important as job satisfaction—the feeling of having done a good job, and of having it recognized by people who know what a good job is. Related and equally important is the question of real participation in the company's affairs. The problem involved here is tremendous, and it cannot be solved merely by the resolution to do something about it. In one of the Standard Oil affiliates, for example, management was stumped by a case of group dissatisfaction until the president of the company began to talk to the men informally about some of the problems that were plaguing him and his board. "The men showed an immediate and extraordinary interest, and that gradually revealed the source of their dissatisfaction," recalls Frank Abrams. "They had been 'left out of things.'" The point to be noted here is that not every president could have done that. This president obviously had the "something" it takes to put a man across with his employees. And the gradual cultivation of that something is one of the unfinished tasks ahead of management.

. . . .

How well American management has actually done by its employees is a question that leads to inevitable debate. The fact is incontestable, however, that it has done better than management anywhere else—and, for that matter, better than management ever dreamed it could, under the old form of capitalism. The problem, indeed, may be to prevent management from becoming overgenerous. For when a company distributes employee benefits that are not compensated by rising productivity, it must in the long run pass the cost increase on to the consumer. Obviously a company *can* be tempted to win employee co-operation easily; a few producers and a single union can combine to gang up on the public.

Thus far, however, it is the modern manager's sense of responsibility to his customer and the general public that gives him his best claim to being progressive. More goods at lower cost (and prices) is the basic principle of American industry, and even companies regarded as anything but socially-minded have built themselves upon it. Many a chemical, for example, has been sold at a progressively lower price without the spur of competition, simply to encourage the market. And most modern managers do worry a good deal about the related subjects of prices, monopoly, and competition. Competition has come a long way since the time of Lord Dewar, who cracked that "competition is the life of trade, and competition is the death of profits." The alternatives today are not monopoly or all-out competition. The Darwinian concept of all-out competition, which, far from being the death of profits, provides, as smart companies know, the soundest way to ensure their survival.

Aside from its value as a foil to antitrust, which can be exaggerated, healthy, workable competition provides a good check on how a company is doing. Take du Pont, which, though almost unique, may well set a precedent. Pursued by the hounds of antitrust (unjustly, it maintains), du Pont spent more than a year looking for a competitor willing to put $20 million into a cellophane plant. Having found one in Olin industries, it is building the plant for Olin and supplying the necessary technical assistance. And that is not all. Because du Pont was the only market source for sodium metal, it induced National Distillers to make the stuff. And recently it turned over its nylon patents to the Chemstrand Co.

Other companies have learned that a similar self-discipline is the best price policy in the long run. The recent furor about rolling back the prices of automobiles obscures the fact that the automobile companies had conducted themselves with a notable respect for public opinion. Had they let the law of supply and demand take its course in the sellers' market of the past four or five years, they could have priced their cars much higher. Their dealers, it is true, sometimes did extract a premium from eager buyers. But it was the manufacturers' list prices that in the main determined the price level, and the auto makers' refusal to charge what the traffic would bear must be reckoned as an extraordinary example of the transformation of the capitalistic mind.

One of the most pressing concerns of almost every large company today is what people are going to think about it. Board meetings often turn into self-examination sessions, with managers defending or explaining their actions as if before accusing judges. At a recent board meeting of a large consumer-goods company, the president rose up and remarked that the foremen had in effect built up a block between management and labor, and that management was mostly at fault. Fully two hours were devoted to soul-searching and discussion. There was also the matter of closing an old mill in a small town. Not only was the specific situation explored thoroughly, but the history of other similar cases was brought up. This problem was solved, after a full hour's discussion, by the decision to move a storage plant into the town and thus absorb nearly all the displaced employees. As one executive remarked, "At least half our time is taken up with discussing the repercussions of what we propose to do. And this is what the boys who write the books call the managerial revolution."

What may set a new high in business' concern with fundamental values and questions is a current project of Corning Glass Works, which is celebrating its centennial in 1951. On the premise that "As long as there are men making and operating machines, there will be a humanistic problem as well as a scientific and technological problem in an industrial society." Corning has joined the American Council of Learned Societies in sponsoring a conference on "Living in Industrial Civilization." The conference was held in May, 1951, at the Corning Glass Center, and attended by academicians and men of affairs from all over the world. They discussed such topics as Work and Human Values; Leisure and Human Values; the Individual's Sense of Community; Confidence in Life.

Nothing perhaps is more indicative of the corporation's awareness of its responsibilities than the growth of public-relations "programs." Although many of them are hardly more than publicity campaigns, more and more managers understand tolerably well that good business public relations is good performance publicly appreciated, because adequately communicated. Now the mere comprehension of a moral axiom, as all parents know, does not guarantee its observance. But its constant iteration does make the subject more and more acutely aware of its importance, and thus eventually influences his behavior. As Paul Garrett of G.M. has been saying for years, "Our program is finding out what people like, doing more of it; finding out what people don't like, doing less of it."

All of which should not be interpreted to mean that business is already rolling us down the six-lane, high-speed highway to economic paradise. We have concerned ourselves here with the pace-setters of American management, and do not presume to imply that all managers and all other companies are doing as well. Many still give precedence to the big, quick profit. Many incline to regard the stockholder mainly as a convenient personification of the profit goal, labor as a lamentably sensitive kind of commodity, and the customer as the man who gets rolled. Like many a labor and agricultural leader, these businessmen try to increase their share of the national product regardless of their contribution to that product. What Professor Wilcox calls Big (or organized) Little Business, for example, is responsible for or protected by most of the fair-trade laws, licensing systems, local bidding laws, and other legal devices that maintain prices independently of the market.

Big Business, too, has something to answer for. Just how much power it has, for example, to fix prices, and to what extent it uses or abuses that power are right now the subjects of much expert contention. Some economists maintain that "Oligopoly is by all evidence the ruling market form in the modern economy" —i.e., since the nation's corporate assets are concentrated in a relatively few companies, the market is made up of a few sellers, who can administer prices. Other economists, attacking the statistics on which such conclusions are based, maintain that only 20 per cent of the national income is provided by unregulated oligopoly, and that an analysis of competition in terms of market realities, which nobody has yet completed, will show that the American economy is becoming more, not less, competitive. It is to be hoped that such an important analysis will be undertaken soon. But whatever its results, it is not likely to reveal that business, socially speaking, has yet attained perfection.

What counts, however, is that certain business leaders *are* setting the pace, and *are* being followed. What counts is that the old concept that the owner has a right to use his property just the way he pleases has evolved into the belief that ownership carries social obligations, and that a manager is a trustee not only for the owner but for society as a whole. Such is the Transformation of American Capitalism. In all the world there is no more hopeful economic phenomenon.   1951

W. LLOYD WARNER

1898–

TRAINED AT THE University of California and Harvard, Professor Warner has carried on extensive field studies in Australia, in the Deep South, in New England, and in the West. With others he has pioneered in adapting to the study of modern industrial culture the techniques used in the investigation of primitive peoples. For many years Professor Warner has been associated with the University of Chicago. The selection is from *American Life: Dream and Reality* (1953) and is concerned, as is much of his work, with status.

A Black Civilization, New York, 1937.
The Living and the Dead: A Study of the Symbolic Life of Americans, New Haven, 1959.
Deep South (with others), New York, 1941.
Democracy in Jonesville (with others), New York, 1949.

» » *From:* AMERICAN LIFE: DREAM AND REALITY « «

INDIVIDUAL OPPORTUNITY AND SOCIAL MOBILITY IN AMERICA

THE FUNCTION OF RANK IN A DEMOCRACY

All Americans know that what they are as men cannot ever be revealed by a cold account presented by a detached observer who is content to relate only what he has heard them say and watched them do in the daily round of their lives. Important and crucial as such evidence may be, it is insufficient and distorts the reality of their existence. The meaning of a man's life—in fact, the most significant part of it—must always include his dreams for tomorrow, since these are present guides for his daily conduct.

More often than not, the ideals by which we Americans judge our present inadequacies later become the realities on which we build our hopes for a realizable future. We are forever dedicating ourselves and our collectivity to new goals which our ideals cannot presently afford. We know that the "self-evident facts" about the nature of man and his existence proclaimed by our nation's founders were often no more than their dreams for a future they had resolved to make true. And we know that some of these hopes of the past are now part of social reality. Therefore, we too, strive to make today's dreams become the "self-evident facts" of tomorrow.

The American story, both dream and reality, is essentially that of a great democracy trying to remain or become democratic and equalitarian while solving the problems of unifying vast populations and diverse enterprises. The story told here is, therefore, concerned with the values and ideals of a democracy and, less pleasantly, with the facts of social class and color caste. It has examined the American "success story," the tale of rags-to-riches, in terms of the real facts of social mobility and social class. . . . [It has analyzed the problems of social and ethnic minorities and reassesses the ideals of the melting-pot. It has told of the symbolic life of America in terms of such varied facts as radio programs and sacred ceremonies, all for the purpose of getting an inside view of Americans and their life.]

For the last twenty years there has been an increasing feeling of disquiet and concern in the minds of many Americans about the well-being of the social and economic system in which they live—a system that maintains them as a people, provides them with a life that is satisfying, and gives meaning to their lives. Most Americans believe that their free-enterprise system is a productive mechanism that is second to none and capable of producing abundance for all their people, and most believe that their free society provides men with spiritual values which help to maintain individual self-respect and individual freedom. But none of them can fail to read the evidence that the masses of their people are losing the great faith they once had in free enterprise and in the leadership of businessmen.

Evidence of their dissatisfaction can be seen in the workers' separation from management; in millions of workers' turning to unions and union leadership; in worker hostility to, and conflict with, management; and in the common people's turning to the state rather than to free enterprise to solve an increasing number of their economic and social problems.

When conservative Americans remember that Britain, once a citadel of free enterprise, has become a socialist state and that Britain's economic developments often anticipate their own, they know that their anxieties about maintaining their present economic and social world are real.

There is consensus among most Americans that it is time to understand the factors which are causing some of these developments. It is the belief of many, myself included, that social science can and does provide accurate diagnoses of the underlying factors which seem to be responsible for these changes in American beliefs and values.

It is clear to those of us who have made studies in many parts of the United States that the primary and most important fact about the American social system is that it is composed of two basic, but antithetical, principles: the first, the principle of equality; the second, the principle of unequal status and of superior and inferior rank.[1]

The first declares that all men are equal and that all men must have equal opportunity to get the good things of life. The second, seldom openly stated but nevertheless potent and powerful, makes it evident that Americans are not always regarded as equal and that many of the values they treasure, that provide them with a will to do and to achieve, can continue to exist only as long as they have a status system. I wish to affirm that, paradoxical as it may seem, both these antithetical principles, when properly balanced, are necessary for the proper functioning of contemporary American democracy.[2]

The principle of equality is necessary to provide all men with a sense of self-respect and to establish the secular essentials of the Christian belief in brotherhood. It is also necessary to give each citizen the right to participate in making the decisions about the destinies of all.

The principle of rank and status is necessary to provide men with the motives to excel by striving for positions of higher prestige and power for themselves and for their families. It is also essential to equip the nation, communities, and their institutions with responsible leadership hierarchies which co-ordinate and regulate the lives of their inhabitants and help maintain an orderly way of life, in which their citizens can cultivate the morals and manners of a high civilization.[3]

The life of the greatest of all Americans, Abraham Lincoln, clearly exemplifies both principles, for he was born "a man of the people" and gave his life "to make all of us free and equal." But he was also the man who, aspiring to greatness, rose from a log cabin to the White House, leaving the lower reaches of American society and climbing to the highest levels of power and prestige. In the story of Lincoln and other similar success stories, all Americans find themselves, for such life-stories are symbols which combine the antithetical American virtues of equality and status.[4]

I do not believe that the American system could operate, that the present method of carrying on human affairs could continue, if Americans did not possess the kind of status system which it has been their good fortune to develop. It is necessary in any society to co-ordinate the efforts of men who work; those who perform this task are inevitably put into positions of power and prestige. Status systems must always exist, for people to accomplish the work necessary for their survival as a group. The only possible choice for Americans is not between their status system and a perfect system of quality but between their kind of hierarchy and some other—more likely, one that could not work satisfactorily in a democracy. (In passing, it might be said that the Russians went through an "equalitarian" revolution in the hope of establishing a pure democracy and succeeded in exchanging the status system of czarist Russia for the more rigid soviet system of status and castelike

---

[1] W. Lloyd Warner and Paul S. Lunt, *The Social Life of Modern Community* ("The Yankee City Series," Vol. I [New Haven: Yale University Press, 1941]).

[2] W. Lloyd Warner, Marchia Meeker, and Kenneth Ells, *Social Class in America* (Chicago: Science Research Associates, 1949).

[3] Carson McGuire, "Social Mobility: The Rise and Fall of Families," in W. Lloyd Warner and Associates, *Democracy in Jonesville* (New York: Harper & Bros., 1949), chap. iv.

[4] Warner and Associates, *op. cit.*, chap. i.

inequality.)

The most significant characteristic of the American class system—and the reason Americans think of it as being democratic—is the firm belief that there must be equality of opportunity for all and a chance for everyone to have his turn at bat. Such a belief means that the system must provide for the rise of men and their families from lower to higher levels, or, to say it in the jargon of the social scientist, vertical social mobility must continually function in the lives of men if their system is to be democratic and successful. To say it in everyday speech, they believe that a man, by applying himself, by using the talents he has, by acquiring the necessary skills, can rise from lower to higher status and that his family can rise with him. The opportunity for social mobility for everyone is the very fabric of the "American Dream." The American Dream is not a mere fantasy that can be dismissed as unimportant to those who think realistically, for it does provide the motive power for much of what Americans do in their daily lives. It is the basic, powerful, motivating force that drives most of them and makes all Americans partners in the well-being of each, since each feels that, although he is competing with the rest, he has a stake in the common good. When the principles of social mobility in the United States are not operating, there are troubles ahead not only for those who do not experience mobility but for every American.[5]

Where we studied social behavior in the various regions of the United States, the forces and values of social mobility were always found to be basic and powerful for the free-enterprise system and a free society. Social mobility is a basic motivation for the worker as well as for the manager. It gives not only the worker and manager their chance to get ahead but their sons and families their chance to advance and improve themselves. It is the driving force in the United States that really makes the man on the job do the extra things that are beyond the ordinary requirements, and very often it is what makes him function beyond himself to become a first-rate man and a candidate for promotion.

As long as Americans know that the opportunity for advancement is available for anyone who wants to try, the American Dream is real and true for them. When they do not feel that the channels of mobility are clear, their

[5] Warner, Meeker, and Ells, *op. cit.*

satisfaction yields to frustration and hostility. There is strong proof now that the American worker, as well as others, can no longer expect to advance and achieve success with anything like the same probability as did his father and grandfather.

The American system, in order to survive and develop its full potentialities for human living, must be as meaningful and significant in the lives of the workers and their families as it is felt to be by those who own and manage business and individual enterprises. It cannot be a way of life that satisfies the needs and aspirations of merely the managerial levels. It must also fill the material wants of the workers generally and, beyond this, provide the necessary rewards for those ambitious workers who strive to advance themselves on the job and better their families' positions in the community.

THE ROUTES OF MOBILITY

Before developing this statement further, let us briefly examine the routes of mobility. Although American social classes are a rank order, placing people and their families in higher and lower levels, they do not permanently fix the status of either the individual or his family. Despite the fact that a man inherits the class position of his family, his inherited position is not necessarily the one he will always occupy. From the point of view of the total social system of a community, each social class is open to properly qualified people below it.

Since the individual's social position is not necessarily fixed, he can move up or down by his own efforts or the efforts of others, or he can be born to a family moving up or down, or marry into one that is climbing from another class level. Social-class systems permit vertical movement of the individual or his family; but there are always exact rules and social sanctions which regulate how this can and cannot be done, such rules applying not only to upward but also to downward mobility. Knowledge of them arouses anxiety in mobile individuals and families but also often provides security for them, since, when they know what the rules are, they can depend on them as guides for safe conduct to prevent loss of position and to achieve higher status. (Downward mobility, by the way, is something more feared than anything else in a class system.)

Vertical mobility in the United States is

accomplished by most people through the proper use of certain recognized sources of social power, the principal ones being occupation, education, talent, sexual attractiveness and marriage, and the exercise of skill in a variety of social and technical activities, such as the successful manipulation of highly prized symbols.[6] A young man of lower status may win a fellowship to a liberal arts college, or earn his way through school, spend a year or two in a professional school, then enter a large industry and work his way to the top. Meanwhile, he has changed his behavior and unlearned much of what he was taught in the family of his birth. Later he may marry a girl from a social level far superior to the one in which he began his career. Or, as an alternative, a young man or woman may develop a talent, become an author or an artist, and use these highly valued artistic symbols to acquire the necessary prestige for higher social acceptance.

Any activity or characteristic which can be ascribed to an individual's personal power, when properly understood, can be used for increasing the prestige of the person and his social place in the class system. Ordinarily, if the proper adjustments are made, his advance means that the members of his immediate family will move up with him. Should they not, it is likely either that the family will break or that the individual himself will not be able to maintain his new position. In the majority of cases the family is the ultimate unit which determines whether or not social mobility, once begun, is successfully completed.

In the United States it is commonly assumed that it is necessary only to accumulate money for an individual to increase his own and his family's status. This is only a partial truth. Those who acquire more money, superior occupation, or education, or achieve control over any other source of social power, must transform it into other highly valued symbols and behavior acceptable to the superior levels, in order to achieve the approval and social acceptance necessary for social advancement. In the ordinary mobile career, one finds five stages (the order of the intermediate stages may vary) that are recognizable to the social analyst. There is the early preparatory one, during which the individual equips himself with some of the skills necessary to acquire the prestige of money or a

[6] *Ibid.*

superior occupation; this phase is followed by the consolidation of the acquired prestige and power into a set of limited immediate relations with higher people, set up by the new position. Once this has been done, the third stage occurs, when there is a translation of power and prestige into suitable behavior, accompanied by the acquisition of approved symbols; then movement into institutional statuses that increase his interaction and identification with the superior class. This is often a period of social learning for the mobile person and his family, accompanied by attitudes of watchful probation by those whom he seeks to join—they observe the furnishings of his new house as well as his behavior when he joins their country club.

The final stage is reached when there is consolidation of the individual's status within his new social class so that he is conceived to be not only *with* those in it but *of* them. None of this is necessarily too pointed or explicitly stated in what he or his family says or does. There is every reason to explain mobile behavior by other motivations. The manners and morals of social mobility demand that those who are involved in it always give good economic, moral, and strong democratic reasons for what they are doing. If they are too open and direct in their efforts to increase their status, they are likely to be branded as "social climbers," and, if the term is made to stick, it is often sufficient to block advancement.

Social mobility in the United States acts as an incentive system, driving the man who climbs occupationally and his whole family, who shared the rewards. Its prizes are largely responsible for the extra effort made by the ambitious to do more than the job demands in the hope that such behavior will be rewarded by economic and social advancement. The directives of social class demand that mobile individuals be highly flexible in their behavior. They must learn new behavior, which is never easy, and also do something more difficult—unlearn old behavior which is no longer appropriate for their advanced position. This means that they must be highly adaptable emotionally and intellectually and be able to tolerate continuing uncertainties and to live in insecure situations. Anxiety and fear, always present, must be kept under constant control and directed, or the competitive race and its prizes are likely to be lost.

At one time occupation, particularly in business enterprise, was the principal route used for the upward climb of those who were ambitious. For young men preparing for life, this outranked all others as the route to advancement, success, and higher status. The ambitious needed only to start at the bottom of the ladder, learn what they had to do in each job, apprentice themselves for the job above, and be assured that, with the necessary talent, it was likely that they would continue to advance toward their goals.

Our studies at the present time indicate that something has happened to this route to success, for occupation as a means of mobility is diminishing in importance. In fact, it no longer is the principal form of mobility. The studies that we have made in the several regions, as well as certain national studies of various industries, show that the occupational routes are not so open, as they once were and that in certain industries the chances for the worker to move out of his status into the lower range of management have almost ceased to exist. The studies of Taussig, Joslyn, and others on American business leaders, which examine the lives of several thousand representative top-level businessmen from the principal industries of the United States, showed that there has been a definite trend toward tightening and decreasing upward mobility through occupation.[7]

During the period from the First World War to the present time, a number of new enterprises have developed in the United States, and certain changes have taken place in the technology of some of the older industries, which act as counteractive forces to those of closed mobility. Such new industries as the airplane, radio, television, and certain service enterprises have produced hierarchies in which there is very rapid mobility. . . .

Other traditional routes to success have been leaving the settled regions of the United States, where there was less opportunity, and trying one's fortunes on the new frontiers, where it was believed that the sky was the limit; or educating one's self for higher position in one of the professions or in business enterprise. The former has obviously become less important as the continent has filled; the latter has greater contemporary relevance, and deserves more detailed attention.

There has been a decrease in the number of small businesses and in the number successfully started, and an even greater decrease in the proportion of the amount of business handled by such enterprises in the economy of the United States.[8] Such ventures now are becoming increasingly hazardous and difficult for those whose backgrounds are insufficient to provide them with the body of skill necessary for success. Furthermore, competition is keener, and the market, accordingly, less receptive to new enterprise. But, above all, there is an increasing trend in the United States toward big business and greater centralization. . . .

Moreover, the degree of specialization now characteristic of every industry demands a high quality of training and preparation of those individuals who wish to try new enterprises. Such training can be gained only by past experience in managerial positions or by a kind of education that offers a partial substitute for practical experience. We shall see later that this education is not easy to come by. Furthermore, the mortality rate of new business enterprises is rising higher and higher, because there are fewer and fewer areas of unsatisfied demand for basic commodities.

Since occupation and business enterprises are no longer the surest routes by which young men can achieve the rewards of success, preparation by education has become the principal route for those who are socially mobile. Young people enter the public schools available for everyone, eager for an opportunity to acquire the skills necessary to train their varying talents for purposes of achievement. The Committee on Human Development at the University of Chicago and other research groups have made exhaustive studies of what the school system does to the aspirations of children coming from the different socio-economic levels of the status system. The findings do not provide encouragement to those of us who would like to believe that, since the occupational route no longer is as free as it once was, education is providing an adequate substitute.[9]

[7] F. W. Taussig and C. S. Joyslyn, *American Business Leaders* (New York: Macmillan Co., 1932), p. 234.

[8] Alvin H. Hansen, *Fiscal Policy and Business Cycles* New York: W. W. Norton & Co., 1932); Charles H. Holzinger, "Acceptance-Rejection of Belief in Equal Opportunity" (unpublished Master's thesis, University of Chicago, 1949).

[9] W. Lloyd Warner, Robert J. Havighurst, and Martin B. Loeb, *Who Shall Be Educated?* (New York and London: Harper & Bros., 1944); Bernice Neugarten, "The Democracy of Childhood," in W. Lloyd Warner and Associates, *op. cit.*, chap. v; A. B. Hollingshead, *Elmtown's Youth* (New York: John Wiley & Sons, Inc., 1949).

We have learned that the children of parents belonging to the lower socio-economic levels—even though they do have opportunities to choose the course that will put them on the social escalator—are not taking courses that prepare them for college or for better positions. The parents of these children represent from 50 to 60 per cent of our total population. Since the people in the lower socio-economic levels have more children per family, it is probable that their children represent an even higher percentage of the total. Certain investigations show that 41 per cent of the children of the lower group do not finish grammar school and that 60 per cent of these children do not finish high school, most of them dropping out by the second year.[10]

When these figures are quoted to the intelligent layman, he often asks why young people fail to get an education where the schools are free and it is possible for everyone to attend the first twelve grades (grammar school and high school) without cost. The two most frequent replies to this question are that the families of the children do not have money and that the children who quit do not have sufficient intelligence to continue in school and compete with other children. It is true that each factor operates to some extent; but, in my opinion, our studies indicate that, while money is important, other factors are more crucial. . . .[11]

The answer to our question—Why does such a large percentage of lower-class children drop out of school before they are sufficiently prepared?—is in the total social system and its operations in training children of different classes to assume their roles in American social life.

Educators and personnel men know that a grammar-school education is insufficient to provide these young men and women with the skills necessary to qualify for positions in much of the industrial life of modern America. Certainly, they are not sufficiently trained for supervisory jobs; certainly, they are not sufficiently equipped with the ordinary general skills necessary to get to the places where many of them want to go in the job hierarchy of the factories where they work.

I am not trying to say that the American public school system is set up formally to prevent future workers and potential managers from achieving their goals. The public school system is fitted into the American status system in such a way that this is what happens. Many children, even when they have the economic wherewithal and the brains, do not have the necessary motivations within them and the pressures from without to keep them in school long enough to give them the training which they need for advancement—or, for that matter, for adequately doing many of the jobs necessary for the proper functioning of business and industry.

An open class system, providing for the rise and fall of families according to social rules, is the most important factor in helping maintain the equalitarian principles of the social-class society. When functioning to maintain these principles, it also contributes to the maintenance and strengthening of the belief in the free individual. Given the Christian belief in the soul and the equality of all in the spiritual brotherhood of men through the Fatherhood of God, given the philosophical belief firmly imbedded in American society that each individual is autonomous and capable of good and evil, then the presence of social mobility makes it possible for each person to free himself from some of the strong status controls which tend to fix an individual's social position. With freedom to act independently available to all, and exploited by a considerable proportion of the population, American belief in individualism is reinforced and strengthened. The improvement in the positions of various people indicates that they are free, that there is something within the individual which makes him more than a helpless particle in an omnipotent social universe.

Americans—devout advocates of individualism—believe that individualism means that each man has within himself the right to make his own choices and to make or break his life-career on the basis of his own judgments. If a man makes a decision and it does not turn out right in the American system of social logics, we, more often than not, believe that it is his own fault. We may feel sorry for him, but still we feel that it is likely to be his own fault. On the other hand, if he makes good decisions and does well, we think he should be rewarded. The reward most sought is advancement to positions of higher prestige. Whenever the American system of equal opportunity and individualism operates success-

[10] Warner, Havighurst, and Loeb, *op. cit.*
[11] W. Allison Davis and Robert J. Havighurst, *Father of the Man* (Boston: Houghton Mifflin Co., 1947) and "The Measurement of Mental Systems," *Scientific Monthly*, Vol. LXVI, No. 4 (1948).

fully and a man can make his choices and be rewarded when he does well, then Americans believe the system is fair, and their way of life is understandable to all because they can live and act as individuals and be rewarded accordingly.

When American workers equip themselves with the skills necessary and play the game according to all the conventional rules, and almost no one wins, then the individuals playing no longer blame themselves. Rather, they blame the system. Consequently, they tend not to act as individuals with separate decisions and separate consciences but feel themselves to be a group which has a common grievance against "those who run things." They act as they think. The consequences of this change may be disastrous for the proper functioning of a free society.

We must now return to the problem of blocked mobility and see the meaning of our analysis of American individualism and its relation to social mobility in our contemporary life.

THE EFFECTS OF BLOCKED MOBILITY

The consequences of blocked mobility become clear as soon as one recognizes it as a scientific problem and part of the larger one of understanding status structure and social mobility in the United States. The effects on the society are numerous. Obviously, blocked mobility reduces the competition between the bright and able young men who are pushing their way to the top and the sons of families who are already advantageously placed in the economic and social order. It can be argued that, when this happens, the competitive system (which acts as a screen through which those with higher talents are more often selected for higher positions) does not function so well as when the routes of mobility are open and permit those who are on the way up to compete with people who are already there.

Furthermore, those who occupy these positions, if their competition is reduced, are likely to be far less alert, much less active, and less anxious to exercise their skills in doing a good job. On the other hand, it must be said that, if the system of mobility operated so that the man at the top possessed no method of giving his child some of the advantages of his own position, it would reduce his incentives to do his very best. Clearly, a balance of

some kind must be reached by which those who have possession are assured not only that they can compete successfully but that their children can. Still, if democracy is to function successfully, the routes of mobility must be present and open for the young men of talent who come from the lower socio-economic levels.

Whenever a society with social classes moves toward a fixed status and away from an open and changing one, there is the likelihood that the increased fixity of status will immobilize the energy that might have been projected into social action. An open system provides incentive for the greatest output of individual energy for the society itself. For, in such a system, each individual, in his efforts to succeed, gives all he can to achieve his goals and to reap the rewards of success.

Moreover, in a society in which the technology is changing rather rapidly and, for most purposes, is improving man's adjustment to the natural environment, there is a need for a flexible social structure to accommodate the social life of the society to the changes that occur in the technical system. Fixed status, or an approximation of it, produces ways of acting and attitudes for the members of the society which discourage and impede social change. It can be argued that the slowing-down of our technological change might be a good thing. I am not arguing for or against this proposition. But the processes of technological change are likely to continue, and, even though there might be a period of slowing down if social mobility is lessened, the ultimate consequences would be a dislocation between the technology and the social organization which would produce conflict and disorganization.

The political implications of blocked mobility are exceedingly important. The present ideologies of mobile lower-class people in the United States tend to approximate the beliefs and value systems of the mobile people in the higher classes. On the other hand, fixed status tends to produce an ideology fitted to the needs of a particular class level of an immobile status system. Where the political ideologies of classes tend to be purely on the basis of socioeconomic levels, there is greater opportunity for conflict and less for accommodation between the several classes of the society. It is my opinion that the class conflict which Marx describes is essentially one that does not take account of social mobility, of a system in which families move up and down, where mobile people in the lower-middle class have many of the same values, hopes and fears, and political and economic beliefs that one finds among mobile individuals in the upper-middle class. When mobility is not operating, there is a greater likelihood of the development of a totalitarian state with a political elite such as the Communist party playing the role of a dedicated priesthood, which explains, interprets, and administers what is believed to be the sacred ideology of one class. This does not mean that there will be one class within such a society. Quite the contrary; there must be several. But the class order of such a society is likely to be closed, with status fixed for the individual and mobility available only for that small fraction that learns how to enter the priestly elite.

The effect of blocked mobility on the inner world of the individual can be observed in many situations among a variety of people. Frustrated workers who find opportunity unavailable often cut down on work output. Some become "troublemakers," who are constantly on the alert to find situations that they can exploit to prevent satisfactory adjustments for the other men on the job. Others may take a more positive stand, join a union, and become union leaders who use the union hierarchy to satisfy their aspirations.

Social anthropologists and psychologists, under the leadership of certain doctors at the University of California, have been conducting studies of the relation of status and mobility to the presence of diseases, such as those of the heart, ulcers, etc. Their work gives strong indications that there is a definite relationship between status anxiety and the presence of certain kinds of illness that heretofore have been attributed to purely organic factors or to internal psychological problems rather than to the social situation in which the individual finds himself[12]. . . .

I had the opportunity of studying the development of a strike in a community in New England where there had not been strikes before and where there had been no union organization. During the course of our study two things happened. The strike was won by the workers, and, during this period, all the facto-

ries in the town in this particular industry were completely unionized.

When we examined why these events happened, a number of things soon became apparent. Among the variety of reasons given to explain these two results, one essential factor stood out far above all others: the old skill hierarchy for the advancement of workers was gone. The routes of mobility were closed. The route for "getting places" was no longer there for those who worked in the factories. It was not difficult to organize the workers' discontent and focus it against management, for the aspirations of these men were no longer entirely invested in the open system of equal opportunity, once provided by the factory hierarchy, but now more in the world of union organization.[13]

When those who compete for the prizes of life find that the rules of the game have been changed and social mobility no longer permits the rise of those who strive to advance, then the systems of free enterprise and equal opportunity are doubted, and the common people seek other ways to get what they want. To be more concrete, when large numbers of talented men and women who have committed their careers to industry without first obtaining a higher education try to acquire the skills and knowledge thought necessary for advancement and, through no fault of their own, either fail to get them or fail to be rewarded when they do, they necessarily lose faith. Since many people in our civilization pay lip service to the creed of success and make little effort to advance themselves, these people, too, blame the system rather than their own lack of initiative.

SOLUTIONS FOR THE PROBLEM OF BLOCKED MOBILITY

To strengthen the American people's belief in their way of life and to continue their faith in a traditionally free society, it is necessary that the two basic routes of mobility—occupation and education—be open, so that the aspirations of workers for themselves and for their children can be realized, at least for those who are ambitious and have a will to succeed.

Can equality of opportunity in the United States for those who are minded to use it be increased, thereby giving all Americans a

[12] Jurgen Ruesch, Martin B. Loeb, *et al., Chronic Disease and Psychological Invalidism: A Psychosomatic Study* (Berkeley and Los Angeles: University of California Press, 1941).

[13] W. Lloyd Warner and J. O. Low, *The Social System of the Modern Factory* ("The Yankee City Series," Vol. IV [New Haven: Yale University Press, 1947]).

greater stake and a greater belief in our free society? The answer is certainly "Yes."

There are a number of efforts now being made to widen and improve the success channels, the routes of social mobility, in the United States. There are programs to increase public educational opportunities for the youth, by early discovery of real talent and of the urge for success among young people, and by making special efforts to keep outstanding lower-status young people in school through better guidance and counseling. This will prevent many young people from going to work before they have prepared themselves with the necessary educational skills to compete for advancement. A number of plans to keep the routes of mobility open in business concerns have been put into effect. Since blocked mobility is a major cause for some of the decline in a worker's faith in the capitalistic system (or any other hierarchical order), where such a blocking exists it is believed by many to be the duty of management to do all that it can to free this system and make the worker realize that opportunity does exist for him and that management is alert to help him. Mobility channels can be kept open much better by a corporation's making careful inventories of job specifications and the skills of workers already existing in the company. . . .

The knowledge that management has such an interest and is trying to do something about helping the worker to help himself encourages all ambitious workers to believe that free enterprise provides a way up for them. Each company should have a policy of promoting from within wherever possible and should let the workers know that such a policy exists and that it works. Each company should provide facilities through either the community or its own training program for a worker to obtain the necessary training for any job he has the talent for and aspires to. It should be clearly recognized that a large percentage of workers will never take advantage of these educational opportunities, but the mere fact that they know they are available will make a great difference to all of them.

Clearly, such programs must deal with the question of economic security. Critics hostile to management will complain that open channels of mobility do little good while widespread economic insecurity exists. Economic security cannot be guaranteed by any single company or any single union. Such security depends upon the health of the economic system generally. As long as the system is strong, anxiety about economic security will always be low, and at such times interest in advancement by workers who wish to succeed will always be very high. If the workers generally believe that opportunity is available for those who really wish to try and for those who have the necessary brains and talent, their faith in the present system will continue strong because it will then be "paying off" for them in the same way that it does for management.

Americans are usually willing to apply new knowledge to new and old situations and from this application develop a better way of life. We have done this in the physical and biological sciences and have re-created our world to make it a better place for men to live their lives. Today, the social sciences are contributing their share of precise and exact knowledge about the private and public worlds which we inhabit. The social sciences are giving us the knowledge we need to apply to the old and new situations which confront us. I believe it is probable that we will use this knowledge to solve our present problems with the same enterprise and with the same success that we have had in using the knowledge of other scientific disciplines.

1953

HARRY S. TRUMAN

1884–

AS A YOUNG man Harry Truman carried on the family farm in Missouri, worked as a time-keeper for a railroad contractor, served on the Kansas City *Star*, and was in the haberdashery business. He was a field artillery officer in World War I, retiring with the rank of major, and ever since has interested himself in military history. After study at the Kansas City Law School Truman entered politics, being judge of the Jackson County Court and presiding judge in the 1920s and early 1930s. He was elected to the United States Senate in 1934 and won a national reputation as chairman of the special committee to investigate the national defense program. Elected to the vice presidency in 1944, Truman became President on the death of Franklin D. Roosevelt in 1945 and was elected President in the campaign of 1948. "The Faith by Which We Live" was President Truman's Inaugural Address, delivered on January 20, 1949.

Memoirs, 2 vols., Garden City, New York, 1955–1956.
The Truman Administration, Its Principles and Practice, Louis W. Koenig, ed., New York, 1956.
Jonathan Daniels, *The Man of Independence*, Phila., 1950.

» » *From:* THE FAITH BY WHICH WE LIVE « «

I accept with humility the honor which the American people have conferred upon me. I accept it with a deep resolve to do all that I can for the welfare of this nation and for the peace of the world.

In performing the duties of my office, I need the help and the prayers of every one of you. I ask for your encouragement and for your support. The tasks we face are difficult, and
10 we can accomplish them only if we work together.

Each period of our national history has had its special challenges. Those that confront us now are as momentous as any in the past. Today marks the beginning not only of a new Administration, but of a period that will be eventful, perhaps decisive, for us and for the world.

It may be our lot to experience, and in a
20 large measure to bring about, a major turning point in the long history of the human race. The first half of this century has been marked by unprecedented and brutal attacks on the rights of man, and by the two most frightful wars in history. The supreme need of our time

is for men to learn to live together in peace and harmony.

The peoples of the earth face the future with grave uncertainty, composed almost equally of great hopes and great fears. In this time of doubt, they look to the United States as never before for good will, strength, and wise leadership.

It is fitting, therefore, that we take this occasion to proclaim to the world the essential principles of faith by which we live, and to declare our aims to all peoples.

The American people stand firm in the faith which has inspired this nation from the beginning. We believe that all men have a right to equal justice under law and equal opportunity to share in the common good. We believe that all men have the right to freedom of thought and expression. We believe that all men are created equal because they are created in the image of God.

From this faith we will not be moved.

The American people desire, and are determined to work for, a world in which all nations and all peoples are free to govern themselves as they see fit and to achieve a decent and satisfying life. Above all else, our people desire, and are determined to work for, peace on earth—a just and lasting peace—based on genuine agreement freely arrived at by equals.

In the pursuit of these aims, the United States and other like-minded nations find themselves directly opposed by a regime with contrary aims and a totally different concept of life.

That regime adheres to a false philosophy which purports to offer freedom, security, and greater opportunity to mankind. Misled by that philosophy, many peoples have sacrificed their liberties only to learn to their sorrow that deceit and mockery, poverty and tyranny, are their reward.

That false philosophy is communism.

COMMUNISM VERSUS DEMOCRACY

Communism is based on the belief that man is so weak and inadequate that he is unable to govern himself, and therefore requires the rule of strong masters.

Democracy is based on the conviction that man has the moral and intellectual capacity, as well as the inalienable right, to govern himself with reason and justice.

Communism subjects the individual to arrest without lawful cause, punishment without trial, and forced labor as a chattel of the state. It decrees what information he shall receive, what art he shall produce, what leaders he shall follow, and what thoughts he shall think.

Democracy maintains that government is established for the benefit of the individual, and is charged with the responsibility of protecting the rights of the individual and his freedom in the exercise of those abilities of his.

Communism maintains that social wrongs can be corrected only by violence.

Democracy has proved that social justice can be achieved through peaceful change. Communism holds that the world is so widely divided into opposing classes that war is inevitable.

Democracy holds that free nations can settle differences justly and maintain a lasting peace.

These differences between communism and democracy do not concern the United States alone. People everywhere are coming to realize that what is involved is material well-being, human dignity, and the right to believe in and worship God.

I state these differences, not to draw issues of belief as such, but because the actions resulting from the Communist philosophy are a threat to the efforts of free nations to bring about world recovery and lasting peace.

EXPAND WORLD TRADE

Since the end of hostilities, the United States has invested its substance and its energy in a great constructive effort to restore peace, stability and freedom to the world.

We have sought no territory and we have imposed our will on none. We have asked for no privileges that we would not extend to others.

We have constantly and vigorously supported the United Nations and related agencies as a means of applying democratic principles to international relations. We have consistently advocated and relied upon peaceful settlement of disputes among nations.

We have made every effort to secure agreement on effective international control of our most powerful weapon, and we have worked steadily for the limitation and control of all armaments.

We have encouraged, by precept and example, the expansion of world trade on a sound and fair basis.

Almost a year ago, in company with sixteen free nations of Europe, we launched the greatest cooperative economic program in history. The purpose of that unprecedented effort is to invigorate and strengthen democracy in Europe, so that the free people of that Continent can resume their rightful place in the forefront of civilization and can contribute once more to the security and welfare of the world.

Our efforts have brought new hope to all mankind. We have beaten back despair and defeatism. We have saved a number of countries from losing their liberty. Hundreds of millions of people all over the world now agree with us, that we need not have war—that we can have peace.

The initiative is ours.

We are moving on with other nations to build an even stronger structure of international order and justice. We shall have as our partners countries which, no longer solely concerned with the problem of national survival, are now working to improve the standards of living of all their people. We are ready to undertake new projects to strengthen a free world.

"PROGRAM FOR PEACE AND FREEDOM"

In the coming years, our program for peace and freedom will emphasize four major courses of action.

First, we will continue to give unfaltering support to the United Nations and related agencies, and we will continue to search for ways to strengthen their authority and increase their effectiveness. We believe that the United Nations will be strengthened by the new nations which are being formed in lands now advancing toward self-government under democratic principles.

Second, we will continue our programs for world economic recovery.

This means, first of all, that we must keep our full weight behind the European Recovery Program. We are confident of the success of this major venture in world recovery. We believe that our partners in this effort will achieve the status of self-supporting nations once again.

In addition, we must carry out our plans for reducing the barriers to world trade and increasing its volume. Economic recovery and peace itself depend on increased world trade.

Third, we will strengthen freedom-loving nations against the dangers of aggression.

We are working out with a number of countries a joint agreement designed to strengthen the security of the North Atlantic area. Such an agreement would take the form of a collective defense arrangement within the terms of the United Nations Charter.

We have already established such a defense pact for the Western Hemisphere by the treaty of Rio de Janeiro.

The primary purpose of these agreements is to provide unmistakable proof of the joint determination of the free countries to resist armed attack from any quarter. Every country participating in these arrangements must contribute all it can to the common defense.

If we can make it sufficiently clear, in advance, that any armed attack affecting our national security would be met with overwhelming force, the armed attack might never occur.

I hope soon to send to the Senate a treaty respecting the North Atlantic Security Plan.

In addition, we will provide military advice and equipment to free nations which will co-operate with us in the maintenance of peace and security.

"A BOLD NEW PROGRAM"

Fourth, we must embark on a bold new program for making the benefits of our scientific advances and industrial progress available for the improvement and growth of underdeveloped areas.

More than half the people of the world are living in conditions approaching misery. Their food is inadequate. They are victims of disease. Their economic life is primitive and stagnant. Their poverty is a handicap and a threat both to them and to more prosperous areas.

For the first time in history, humanity possesses the knowledge and the skill to relieve the suffering of these people.

The United States is pre-eminent among the nations in the development of industrial and scientific techniques. The material resources which we can afford to use for the assistance of other peoples are limited. But our imponderable resources in technical knowledge are constantly growing and are inexhaustible.

I believe that we should make available to peace-loving peoples the benefits of our store of technical knowledge in order to help them realize their aspirations for a better life. And, in co-operation with other nations, we should foster capital investment in areas needing development.

Our aim should be to help the free peoples of the world, through their own efforts, to produce more food, more clothing, more materials for housing, and more mechanical power to lighten their burdens.

We invite other countries to pool their technological resources in this undertaking. Their contributions will be warmly welcomed. This should be a co-operative enterprise in which all nations work together through the United Nations and its specialized agencies whenever practicable. It must be a world-wide effort for the achievement of peace, plenty, and freedom.

With the co-operation of business, private capital, agriculture, and labor in this country, this program can greatly increase the industrial activity in other nations and can raise substantially their standards of living.

Such new economic developments must be devised and controlled to the benefit of the peoples of the areas in which they are established. Guarantees to the investor must be balanced by guarantees in the interest of the people whose resources and whose labor go into these developments.

The old imperialism—exploitation for foreign profit—has no place in our plans. What we envisage is a program of development based on the concepts of democratic fairdealing.

All countries, including our own, will greatly benefit from a constructive program for the better use of the world's human and natural resources. Experience shows that our commerce with other countries expands as they progress industrially and economically.

"GREATER PRODUCTION THE KEY TO PROSPERITY"

Greater production is the key to prosperity and peace. And the key to greater production is a wider and more vigorous application of modern scientific and technical knowledge.

Only by helping the least fortunate of its members to help themselves can the human family achieve the decent, satisfying life that is the right of all people.

Democracy alone can supply the vitalizing force to stir the peoples of the world into triumphant action, not only against their human oppressors, but also against their ancient enemies—hunger, misery, and despair.

On the basis of these four major courses of action we hope to help create the conditions that will lead eventually to personal freedom and happiness for all mankind.

If we are to be successful in carrying out these policies, it is clear that we must have continued prosperity in this country and we must keep ourselves strong.

Slowly but surely we are weaving a world fabric of international security and growing prosperity.

OUR ALLIES FOR PEACE AND SECURITY

We are aided by all who wish to live in freedom from fear—even by those who live today in fear under their own governments.

We are aided by all who want relief from lies and propaganda—those who desire truth and sincerity. We are aided by all who desire self-government and a voice in deciding their own affairs. We are aided by all who long for economic security—for the security and abundance that men in free societies can enjoy. We are aided by all who desire freedom of speech, freedom of religion, and freedom to live their own lives for useful ends.

Our allies are the millions who hunger and thirst after righteousness.

In due time, as our stability becomes manifest, as more and more nations come to know the benefits of democracy and to participate in growing abundance, I believe that those countries which now oppose us will abandon their delusions and join with the free nations of the world in a just settlement of international differences.

Events have brought our American democracy to new influence and new responsibilities. They will test our courage, our devotion to duty, and our concept of liberty.

But I say to all men, what we have achieved in liberty, we will surpass in greater liberty.

Steadfast in our faith in the Almighty, we will advance toward a world where man's freedom is secure.

To that end we will devote our strength, our resources, and our firmness of resolve. With God's help, the future of mankind will be assured in a world of justice, harmony and peace.   1949

WILLIAM O. DOUGLAS

1898–

A SON OF Minnesota, William O. Douglas served as a private in the United States Army during World War I, after which he was graduated from Whitman College. He took his law degree at Columbia in 1925 and subsequently taught law at both Columbia and Yale. Douglas also served on the Security and Exchange Commission and in other agencies of the federal government. President Roosevelt appointed him to the Supreme Court in 1939. His decisions and opinions have been characterized by a forthright liberalism. The following piece, which appeared in the New York *Times Magazine* for January 13, 1952, was adapted from a recent address.

Beyond the High Himalayas, 1952.
North from Malaya, 1953.
Current Biography, 1950.
The Right of the People, Garden City, N. Y., 1958.
Russian Journey, Garden City, 1956.

»　»　*From:* THE BLACK SILENCE OF FEAR　«　«

There is an ominous trend in this nation. We are developing tolerance only for the orthodox point of view on world affairs, intolerance for new or different approaches. Orthodoxy normally has stood in the path of change. Orthodoxy was always the stronghold of the status quo, the enemy of new ideas—at least new ideas that were disturbing. He who was wedded to the orthodox view was isolated
10　from the challenge of new facts.

The democratic way of life rejects standardized thought. It rejects orthodoxy. It wants the fullest and freest discussion, within peaceful limits, of all public issues. It encourages constant search for truth at the periphery of knowledge.

We as a people have probably never lived up to that standard in any of our communities. But it has been an ideal toward which
20　most of our communities have strived. We have over the years swung from tolerance to intolerance and back again. There have been eras of intolerance when the views of minorities have been suppressed. But there probably has not been a period of greater intolerance than we witness today.

To understand this, I think one has to leave the country, go into the back regions of the world, lose himself there, and become ab-
30　sorbed in the problems of the peoples of different civilizations. When he returns to America after a few months he probably will be shocked. He will be shocked not at the intentions or purposes or ideals of the American people. He will be shocked at the arrogance and intolerance of great segments of the American press, at the arrogance and intolerance of many leaders in public office, at the arrogance and intolerance reflected in many of
40　our attitudes toward Asia. He will find that thought is being standardized, that the permissible area for calm discussion is being narrowed, that the range of ideas is being limited, that many minds are closed to the receipt of any ideas from Asia.

This is alarming to one who loves his country. It means that the philosophy of strength through free speech is being forsaken for the philosophy of fear through repression.

That choice in Russia is conscious. Under Lenin the ministers and officials were encouraged to debate, to advance new ideas and criticisms. Once the debate was over, however, no dissension or disagreement was permitted. But even that small degree of tolerance for free discussion that Lenin permitted disappeared under Stalin. Stalin maintains a tight system of control, permitting no free speech, no real clash in ideas, even in the inner circle. We are, of course, not emulating either Lenin or Stalin. But we are drifting in the direction of repression, drifting dangerously fast.

What is the cause of this drift? What are the forces behind it? It is only a drift, for certainly everything in our tradition would make the great majority of us reject that course as a conscious choice.

The drift goes back, I think, to the fact that we carried over to days of peace the military approach to world affairs. Diplomacy, certainly in our relations with Asia, took a back seat. The military approach conditioned our thinking and our planning. The military, in fact, determined our approach to the Asians and their problems. That has been a great tragedy in Asia. And the tragedy to us at home has been about as great.

Military thinking continued to play a dominant role in our domestic affairs. The conspiratorial role of Soviet communism in the world scene was apparent to all who could read. This conspiratorial role of Soviet communism was, of course, backed by Russia's military strength. We, therefore, had to be strong in a military sense to hold off Russia. But we soon accepted the military role as the dominant one. We thought of Asia in terms of military bases, not in terms of people and their aspirations. We wanted the starving people of Asia to choose sides, to make up their minds whether they were for us or against us, to cast their lot with us and against Russia.

We did not realize that to millions of these people the difference between Soviet dictatorship and the dictatorship under which they presently live is not very great. We did not realize that in some regions of Asia it is the Communist party that has identified itself with the so-called reform program, the other parties being mere instruments for keeping a ruling class in power. We did not realize that the choice between democracy and communism is not, in the eyes of millions of illiterates, the critical choice it is for us.

We forgot that democracy in many lands is an empty word; that the appeal is hollow when made to illiterate people living at the subsistence level. We asked them to furnish staging grounds for a military operation whose outcome, in their eyes, had no perceptible relation to their own welfare. Those who rejected our overtures must be Communists, we said. Those who did not fall in with our military plans must be secretly aligning with Russia, we thought. This was the result of our military thinking, of our absorption in military affairs. In Asia it has brought us the lowest prestige in our existence.

The military effort has been involving more and more of our sons, more and more of our budget, more and more of our thinking. The military policy has so completely absorbed our thoughts that we have mostly forgotten that our greatest strength, our enduring power is not in guns, but in ideas. Today in Asia we are identified not with ideas of freedom, but with guns. Today at home we are thinking less and less in terms of defeating communism with ideas, more and more in terms of defeating communism with military might.

The concentration on military means has helped to breed fear. It has bred fear and insecurity partly because of the horror of atomic war. But the real reason strikes deeper. In spite of our enormous expenditures, we see that Soviet imperialism continued to expand and that the expansion proceeds without the Soviets firing a shot. The free world continues to contract without a battle for its survival having been fought. It becomes apparent, as country after country falls to Soviet imperialistic ambitions, that military policy alone is a weak one; that military policy alone will end in political bankruptcy and futility. Thus fear mounts.

Fear has many manifestations. The Communist threat inside the country has been magnified and exalted far beyond its realities. Irresponsible talk by irresponsible people has fanned the flames of fear. Accusations have been loosely made. Character assassinations have become common. Suspicion has taken the place of good-will. Once we could debate with impunity along a wide range of inquiry. Once we could safely explore to the edges of a problem, challenge orthodoxy without qualms, and run the gamut of ideas in search of solutions to perplexing problems. Once we had confidence in each other. Now there is suspicion. Innocent acts become tell-tale marks of disloyalty. The coincidence that an idea parallels Soviet Russia's policy for a moment of time settles an aura of suspicion around a person.

Suspicion grows until only the orthodox idea is the safe one. Suspicion grows until only the person who loudly proclaims that orthodox view, or who, once having been a Communist, has been converted, is trustworthy. Competition for embracing the new orthodoxy increases. Those who are unorthodox are suspect. Everyone who does not follow the military policymakers is suspect. Everyone who voices opposition to the trend away from diplomacy and away from political tactics takes a chance. Some who are opposed are indeed "subversive." Therefore, the thundering edict commands that all who are opposed are "subversive." Fear is fanned to a fury. Good and honest men are pilloried. Character is assassinated. Fear runs rampant.

Fear even strikes at lawyers and the bar. Those accused of illegal Communist activity —all presumed innocent, of course, until found guilty—have difficulty getting reputable lawyers to defend them. Lawyers have talked with me about it. Many are worried. Some could not volunteer their services, for if they did they would lose clients and their firms would suffer. Others could not volunteer because if they did they would be dubbed "subversive" by their community and put in the same category as those they would defend. This is a dark tragedy.

Fear has driven more and more men and women in all walks of life either to silence or to the folds of the orthodox. Fear has mounted —fear of losing one's job, fear of being investigated, fear of being pilloried. This fear has stereotyped our thinking, narrowed the range of free public discussion, and driven many thoughtful people to despair. This fear has even entered universities, great citadels of our spiritual strength, and corrupted them. We have the spectacle of university officials lending themselves to one of the worst witch hunts we have seen since early days.

This fear has affected the youngsters. Youth has played a very important role in our national affairs. It has usually been the oncoming generation—full of enthusiasm, full of idealism, full of energy—that has challenged its elders and the status quo. It is from this young group that the country has received much of its moral power. They have always been prone to question the stewardship of their fathers, to doubt the wisdom of traditional practices, to explode clichés, to quarrel with the management of public affairs.

Youth—like the opposition party in a parliamentary system—has served a powerful role. It has cast doubts on our policies, challenged our inarticulate major premises, put the light on our prejudices, and exposed our inconsistencies. Youth has made each generation indulge in self-examination.

But a great change has taken place. Youth is still rebellious; but it is largely holding its tongue. There is the fear of being labeled a "subversive" if one departs from the orthodox party line. That charge—if leveled against a young man or young woman—may have profound effects. It may ruin a youngster's business or professional career. No one wants a Communist in his organization nor anyone who is suspect.

And so the lips of the younger generation have become more and more sealed. Repression of ideas has taken the place of debate. There may not be a swelling crowd of converts to the orthodox, military view. But the voice of the opposition is more and more stilled; and youth, the mainstay in early days of the revolt against orthodoxy, is largely immobilized.

This pattern of orthodoxy that is shaping our thinking has dangerous implications. No one man, no one group can have the answer to the many perplexing problems that today confront the management of world affairs. The scene is a troubled and complicated one. The problems require the pooling of many ideas, the exposure of different points of view, the hammering out in public discussions of the pros and cons of this policy or of that.

There are few who know first hand the conditions in the villages of Asia, the South Pacific, South America, and Africa. There are few who really know the powerful forces operating from the grass roots in those areas— forces that are reflected in the attitudes of the men who head up the Governments in those countries. But unless we know those attitudes, we cannot manage intelligently. Unless we know, we will waste our energies and our resources. Unless we know, we are not in position to win even political alliances of an enduring nature. Unless we are eager to know, unless we invite a flood of information on these problems, unless we encourage every avenue of approach to them, we will live and act in ignorance.

There are those who think that our present policy toward Asia will lead to disaster—for us. There are those who believe that in Asia we are fast becoming the symbol of what the people of Asia fear and hate. There are those who believe that the most effective bases we can get in Asia are bases in the hearts of Asia's millions, not bases on their lands. There are those who believe that we must substitute a political for a military strategy in Asia; that when there is a cease-fire in Korea, we must make a political settlement with Red China; that if we apply to China the attitude we are now brilliantly exploiting in Yugoslavia, we can manage to make Soviet imperialism crumble.

There are those who are deeply opposed, many of whom put that issue beyond the pale of discussion. There are even some who make the crucial test of one's loyalty or sanity his acceptance or rejection of our present policy toward Asia.

The question of our Asian policy illustrates the need for a wide range of free public discussion. Asia poses probably the most critical issues of the day. Certain it is that if Asia, like China, is swept into the political orbit of Soviet Russia, the Soviets will then command or be able to immobilize

—the bulk of the people of the world

—the bulk of the wealth of the world.

If that happens, it is doubtful if we, with all our atomic bombs, could even win a war.

The great danger of this period is not inflation, nor the national debt, nor atomic warfare. The great, the critical danger is that we will so limit or narrow the range of permissible discussion and permissible thought that we will become victims of the orthodox school. If we do, we will lose flexibility. We will lose the capacity for expert management. We will then become wedded to a few techniques, to a few devices. They will define our policy and at the same time limit our ability to alter or modify it. Once we narrow the range of thought and discussion, we will surrender a great deal of our power. We will become like the man on the toboggan who can ride it but who can neither steer it nor stop it.

The mind of man must always be free. The strong society is one that sanctions and encourages freedom of thought and expression. When there is that freedom, a nation has resiliency and adaptability. When freedom of expression is supreme, a nation will keep its balance and stability.

Our real power is our spiritual strength, and that spiritual strength stems from our civil liberties. If we are true to our traditions, if we are tolerant of a whole market place of ideas, we will always be strong. Our weakness grows when we become intolerant of opposing ideas, depart from our standards of civil liberties, and borrow the policeman's philosophy from the enemy we detest.

That has been the direction of our drift. It is dangerous to the morale of our people; it is destructive of the influence and prestige of our country. We have lost much of our resiliency, much of our inventive genius. The demands of orthodoxy already have begun to sap our strength—and to deprive us of power. One sees it from far-off Asia. From Asia one sees an America that is losing its humanity, its idealism, and its Christian character. From Asia one sees an America that is strong and rich and powerful, and yet crippled and ineffective because of its limited vision.

When we view this problem full face we are following the American tradition. The times demand a renaissance in freedom of thought and freedom of expression, a renaissance that will end the orthodoxy that threatens to devitalize us.   1952

LAURENCE SEARS

1886–

PROFESSOR SEARS holds a doctorate from Columbia and has taught, among other places, at Ohio Wesleyan and the University of California. He is now at Mills College. His forthright championship of the freedom of the mind is well exemplified in the essay included here, an essay that originally appeared in *The American Scholar* in the spring of 1951.

Responsibility, its Development through Punishment and Reward, New York, 1932.

» » From: SECURITY AND LIBERTY « «

The dominant fact about America at the mid-century point is our search for security in a world that seems to hold little but threats. We are a frightened people. Obviously this is related to our deep mistrust of the Soviet Union. In 1945 there were hopes on the part of many that the two great nations might live together in peace. That hope has largely dissipated, and it is not likely that the people of the United States will ever again trust the dictators of Russia. The invasion of Southern Korea is only the latest incident of a series of aggressions that seems to bring World War III terrifyingly near.

This search for security is inevitably translated into the domestic scene, for it is idle to think that we can separate the situation abroad from that at home. The Compton Report, issued three years ago, pointed out that if the United States were to be attacked, it was reasonable to assume that there would be a preliminary period in which subversive agents would endeavor to sap the morale and strength of this country. Subversive agents would utilize domestic allies and operate through "front" organizations for the purpose of espionage and sabotage. In other words, there are two sources of danger. On the one hand there is the external power of the Soviet Union. On the other hand there are some of our own citizens who would succumb to the appeal of the Soviet Union, providing us with a larger group of traitors than we had ever known before, and requiring us to fight at one and the same time abroad and at home. That this is a real danger seems clear to most Americans, and we have reacted not merely by preparation for war but by a variety of security measures.

Recently, however, there have been those who have been warning us that there is still another danger, one arising from the very means by which we are seeking security at home. The Committee for Economic Development in a very impressive report pointed out that "security measures, uncurbed by the requirements of freedom, can undermine our free institutions" and Mr. Justice Jackson in a minority decision in the Supreme Court warned that "security is like liberty in that many are the crimes committed in its name." If it is true that most Americans are conscious of the need of security measures because they see clearly what is involved in the Russian method of infiltration, it is also true that there is an increasing number who are asking whether our retort to this threat may not be endangering certain of the values of American life which we are not willing to lose. More specifically, there is fear that we are losing two of the basic rights we have long cherished—the right of dissent and the right to a fair trial. Certainly these rights now seem more seriously challenged than at any time in the past 150 years. We are determined to be secure; can we at the same time keep these traditional American liberties?

All too often in recent months we have seen examples of men labeling those with whom they disagreed Communists or Fascists when the evidence for such serious charges has been lacking. Loyalty oaths are being required of vast numbers of our citizens who have never laid themselves open to any justified suspicion of treason. Investigations are being launched against millions of men and women whose loyalty has never been questioned. To the fear of Russia has been added for many an American the fear lest his livelihood and his reputation will be put in jeopardy, not because he is in any sense a convert to communism, but because he has had legitimate differences with others regarding the policies of our government. The controversy over China is an illustration in point. It may or may not have been wise to have aided Chiang Kai-shek. Possibly we should have gone all out to defeat the Chinese Communists. Those are areas where real differences of opinion have existed and where no man has the final truth. But the incredible thing is that those differences have been translated into irresponsible charges against men who have all too often been relatively defenseless, as well as innocent of any faint trace of treason. It is of the very essence of democracy to recognize that men have the right to dissent from the policy and principles of others, and that they have the right to make that dissent effective. Mr. Justice Holmes put this clearly when he said "If there is any principle of the Constitution that more imperatively calls for attachment than any other, it is the principle of free thought—not free thought for those who agree with us but freedom for the thought we hate."

Another basic right which goes far back into the Anglo-Saxon tradition is the right to a fair trial. For many hundreds of years we have honored the principle laid down in the Magna Charta that "No freeman shall be taken, or imprisoned, or disseized, or outlawed, or banished, or in any way destroyed; nor will we pass upon him, or commit him to prison, unless by the legal judgment of his peers, or unless by the law of the land. . . ." In the perspective of the centuries we have been proud that there have been incidents in our history like that of Peter Zenger—a humble printer of New York who in 1734 was brought to trial for having criticized the representative of the Crown. Andrew Hamilton, an eighty-year-old American attorney, came to his defense with words which are a living part of our inheritance. "The loss of liberty to a generous mind is worse than Death . . . the man who loves his country prefers its liberty to all other Considerations, well knowing that without Liberty, life is a Misery. . . ." It was not surprising that he was acquitted by a jury of his peers, who were determined that even a humble citizen who had criticized his government should have the right of dissent and the right to a fair trial when that dissent was called in question. Even more startling was the case following the Boston massacre. A snowballing of the British degenerated into what appeared to be a mob attack. Someone gave the order to fire, and four Americans were killed. Eight British soldiers, including Captain Preston, were brought to trial in an American court on the charge of murder. Feelings were running very high in Boston. Yet, in the face of this, two Americans who had more than demonstrated their patriotism came to Preston's defense in his trial—not because they were in sympathy with the British, but because they believed that all men have the right to a just trial. Josiah Quincy and John Adams defended him, were responsible for his acquittal and later got an acquittal for the soldiers. Obviously, that jury of Americans agreed with John Adams when he said, "I grant it as a first principle that the eight prisoners at the bar had better all be acquitted, though we should admit them all to be guilty, than that any one of them should by your verdict be found guilty, being innocent." So deeply are these principles imbedded in our tradition that we have come to identify democracy with the right of dissent and the right to a fair trial. Yet it is these very rights which seem to be endangered today as we meet on the domestic scene the threat from Russia.

Perhaps it would be well for us to see what the evidence is as to the extent of subversive activities in this country. The latest report available indicates a loyalty check has been made of 3 million government employees and applicants for government jobs since 1947. Out of that total, questions were raised about 11,619 persons. A full field investigation was made by the F.B.I. on those individuals. Evidence that warranted study was found on 7,342. Their records were turned over to the loyalty boards of the affected agencies for appraisal. Out of that total, 6,910 convinced the loyalty boards that they were innocent of the charges raised. Of the 432 originally found ineligible for employment, 182 employees and applicants actually were dismissed or finally barred. On appeal and the presentation of new evidence, 124 of the 432 were restored to the eligible lists. The remainder, 126 cases, are in various stages of reconsideration. The F.B.I. has turned up evidence of treason against eight men and women. But Mr. Seth Richardson (a Republican) who is chairman of the Loyalty Review Board, testified recently before a Senate subcommittee that loyalty investigations had not produced "one single case" of espionage, or turned up any evidence "directing toward espionage."

To have had subversive Americans operating within our government is altogether tragic, and to have discovered them is certainly fortunate. That is a definite gain, but has there been anything lost in this process?

It might be wise to look at a number of specific incidents which will illustrate the procedure and perhaps high-light the dangers. We might start with a case which, at least to those who were not involved, seems nothing short of farcical. The Whaley Eaton News Service for July 3, 1948, carried the report of two scientists who applied for jobs at Brookhaven. X was accepted after a security check-up, receiving the highest possible classification. Y was rejected, no explanation being given. Lengthy investigation of Y's case eventually revealed that the main ground of his rejection was his close friendship for X.

A second case involves the notorious Judith Coplon, who has been twice convicted on charges of espionage. I am not raising the question of her guilt—that would seem to have been established—but merely some of the procedures involved. Much of the evidence against her came from some F.B.I. data slips, found in her purse, which the prosecution charged she had taken from her desk in the Justice Department to give to a Russian agent. The federal judge ruled that the prosecution would have to show the jury not only all the slips but also the F.B.I. reports to which they referred. Much of the information was obviously gossip and hearsay, and there was no assessment of the informant's reliability. Nevertheless, many public figures whose loyalty has never been questioned were branded as Communist sympathizers. *Time* magazine summarized the results when it said that "Judy's purse had become a symbol of the evil lurking in the kind of over-zealous snooping, gossip, and talebearing which seemed to be one price of national security." That sentence phrases the problem which we are facing. What is the price of national security?

The third case seems far more tragic and unnecessary. About two years ago a distinguished public servant, Laurence Duggan, who had been a member of the State Department and left it to become head of the Institute of International Education, was found dead on the pavement beneath the window of the sixteenth story of the New York building in which he had had his office. No one has ever known the cause—whether he fell or jumped or was thrown must remain a mystery. Yet Congressman Mundt of the Un-American Activities Committee announced that Duggan was on the list of State Department suspects and added, "We will give out the other names as they jump out of windows." Is this sort of thing a part of the necessary price of security?

Still another case is that of Dr. Edward Condon, who was suddenly characterized by the Un-American Activities Committee as "one of the weakest links in our atomic security." Dr. Condon was never told what the basis of the charge was and cannot find out. Though he demanded a hearing in which he might demonstrate his innocence, it was never granted. Many months later, one member of the Committee did state that he thought Dr. Condon should have been heard by the Committee before any statement about him was made public. That was the nearest thing to redress that he ever got for all the public humiliation he suffered.

The latest and most dramatic incident of its time centered around the now notorious Senator McCarthy. On February 11 he declared that he had in his hand a list of 205 members of the State Department who were active members of the Communist party and participants in a spy ring. A few days later he declared that he had the names of 57. On February 20, he stated that there were approximately 81 cases, and at the same time he declared, "I will not say on the Senate floor that which I will not say off the floor. On the day when I take advantage of the security we have on the Senate floor, on that day I will resign from the Senate." On March 8 he gave the name of a New York attorney, Dorothy Kenyon, who had served on a United Nations Commission as a representative of the United States, and that of Ambassador-at-Large Philip Jessup. McCarthy declared that the latter had an "unusual affinity for Communist causes." On March 13 he gave eight more names, including Owen Lattimore, John Service, Esther Brunauer, and Haldore Hansen. All of these people categorically denied the charges and challenged the Senator to make good his promise and repeat the charges without Congressional immunity, promising to sue him for libel if he did so. Senator McCarthy refused, but did not resign from the Senate. On March 20, Generals George C. Marshall and Dwight D. Eisenhower wrote letters to the Committee deploring the attack on Jessup and calling him a loyal citizen. Senator McCarthy's retort was that General Marshall had been "completely unfitted for the job of Secretary of State" and added it was "a pathetic thing, nothing short of a crime, to put him in that position." Once again the question is raised as to whether this is the sort of thing that is the necessary price of our security?

One further case may be cited, that of Miss Dorothy Bailey, who had been dismissed from government service with the statement that there were reasonable grounds for believing that she was disloyal. The case came before the United States Court of Appeals for the District of Columbia, and in his opinion Judge Edgerton brings the whole issue into focus. Pointing to the record in the case, he declared that "without trial by jury, without evidence, and without even being allowed to confront her accusers or to know their identity, a citizen of the United States has been found disloyal to the government of the United States. No charges were served on Appellant. The Chairman of the Regional Board said 'nobody has presented any charges.' . . . there is only the unsworn report in the secret files to the effect that unsworn statements of a general sort, purporting to connect Appellant with communism, had been made by unnamed persons."

Here are a few of the many cases which have raised questions about the rights of individuals in the present situation, and which have caused so many Americans to wonder whether the way in which we are facing the Russian threat may not be endangering the very things which we have most wanted to protect.

We are rightly concerned with security. Must we give up our devotion to liberty? If not, we shall have to face bluntly some of the implications of our present procedure. In the first place, we shall have to re-examine the whole principle of guilt by association, by which people are judged, not by the things that they have done, but by the associations which they have kept. The principle has long been repudiated in Anglo-Saxon tradition. The courts have insisted that proof be shown of an individual's specific guilt. It is significant that in the Nuremberg trials the principle was rejected. Mere membership in Nazi organizations was not there accepted as proof of war guilt without evidence showing that the individuals participated. Yet we are today carrying on much of our investigation on the assumption that men are to be condemned by the company they have kept, even in the absence of any guilty acts. Perhaps in this crisis it is necessary for us to throw overboard our long experience and deeply entrenched convictions —yet it may also be wise for us to remind ourselves of the statement of Mr. Justice Hughes, who declared that "it is the essence of the institutions of liberty that it be recognized that guilt is personal and cannot be attributed to the holding of opinion or to mere intent in the absence of overt acts."

In the second place, we need to re-examine the whole question of secrecy as it involves charges of treason and disloyalty. A recent case taken through to the Supreme Court illustrates both the problem and the dangers at this point. A German girl, Ellen Knauff, married an American G.I. Under the provisions of the Bill permitting the wives of American soldiers to enter this country, she sailed for America. She was held at Ellis Island on charges which were never revealed to her. Presumably the Attorney General had some information which he regarded as making it unwise to permit her entrance. But what it was he refused to disclose, and she was barred merely on the ground that she would not be a loyal American citizen. The case finally went through to the Supreme Court. In the dissenting opinion which Mr. Justice Jackson wrote in that case he made clear the issues that were involved. "The menace to the security of this country, be it great as it may, from this girl's admission is as nothing compared to the menace inherent in procedures of this pattern. In the name of security the police state justifies its arbitrary oppressions on evidence that is secret, because security might be prejudiced if it were brought to light in hearings. The plea that evidence of guilt must be secret is abhorrent to free men, because it provides a cloak for the malevolent, the misinformed, the meddlesome and the corrupt to play the role of informer undetected and uncorrected."

A third issue that needs to be faced is the lack of constitutional safeguards for Federal employees. The present loyalty program is based upon the premise that Federal employees have no constitutional protection. The Board is legally correct when it states that no person has an inherent or constitutional right to public employment since that is a privilege and not a right. Technically the government may be "entitled to discharge any employee for reasons which seem sufficient to the government, and without extending to such employee any hearing whatsoever." But is that in the larger sense just to the employees? And is the letter of the law necessary in a time when dismissal means not only the implication of treason, destroying the possibility of livelihood, but puts the reputation of a civil servant at the mercy not only of a mistaken informer, but also of persons who may be malicious or even demented? Will that procedure give to civil servants that sense of security which is necessary if we are to attract the best we have into the employ of the government? Is it in line with the tradition in the civil service as expressed in a rule promulgated more than sixty years ago, that "no question in any . . . proceeding . . . shall call for the expression or disclosure of any political opinion or affiliation"?

In the fourth place, we are forced to re-evaluate what rights anyone accused should have before an investigating committee or a loyalty review board. Would it shake the pillars of our security if every man and woman accused should be given a bill of particular accusations, have the right to subpoena witnesses and documents when genuine security considerations permit, the right to be represented by counsel, the right to a stenographic report of proceedings, the right to a written decision, and the right of appeal? Some years ago, in the Lovett Case, the Supreme Court declared that "those who wrote our constitution . . . intended to safeguard the people of this country from punishment without trial by duly constituted courts. And even the courts to which this important function was entrusted were commanded to stay their hands unless certain tested safeguards were observed. . . . When our Constitution and Bill of Rights were written, our ancestors had ample reason to know that legislative trials and punishments were too dangerous to liberty to exist in the nation of free men they envisioned."

A final aspect of our present approach which needs re-examination is the whole question of congressional immunity by which members of Congress are free to slander anyone without being held responsible. Legal immunity seems necessary if our officials are not to be handicapped by threats of continual court action. Yet it is intolerable that citizens should be terrorized without hope of redress. The only solution seems to be for Congress to lay down it own rules of procedure, and hold its members responsible for any behavior that denies the right of men to a fair trial.

There have been many incidents in the past two years which have caused us to question whether trial by press, conviction by slander, and guilt by association are necessary prices of national security. But the events of this last Spring have convinced many that this is precisely the price we are paying. When a man of the stature of Professor Jessup can be irresponsibly slandered, there seems little left of the things which we in the Anglo-Saxon tradition have valued. Senator Margaret Chase Smith spoke clearly and courageously when she said that the Senate "has too often been debased to a level of a forum of hate and character assassination sheltered by the shield of Congressional immunity." Professor Jessup was charged with the most serious crime a citizen can commit. Yet he does not know and cannot find out the evidence on which the charge was made. Trial by jury with ordinary legal safeguards was out. Guilt was assumed without the possibility of establishing innocence, and libel was legalized under the cloak of patriotism.

The basic question we face is whether we can afford democracy in time of crisis or whether it is a luxury to be enjoyed only when there is little fear and tension. We are under few illusions as to the answer which both the Communists and Fascists would give. For them there is only contempt for representative government; sure of the ends which they are seeking, they are willing to use any means for their achievement. Rights of individuals and minorities are nonexistent. The police state would destroy the very freedoms it demands. That this is the denial of the democratic way needs no evidence. The only issue is whether or not there is any other means by which we can face this crisis than to adopt the methods of the Garrison State. That is the phrase used by Professor Laswell, and he defines it as that type of government where power is placed in the hands of the specialists in violence. In such a state everything is devoted to military preparation. The soldier and the policeman come into increasing power while all the civil institutions shrink into comparative impotence. In the search for security public information is denied and public discussion disappears. Free enterprise is circumscribed, and all the freedoms that men have valued tend to disappear. We comfort ourselves with the feeling that there is no danger of this in America. But is that not precisely the direction in which we have been moving as we have limited the right of men to dissent and have taken from them the protections against irresponsible attacks? Senator Hickenlooper has only carried this process to its logical conclusion when he said that care must be taken to see to it that people are not employed by the government "who potentially may have subversive or otherwise undesirable views," and he added that we cannot trust the ferreting out of such people to any official of the government. It should be done by "experts in the field of subversive activities." In other words, men are not to be judged by juries—they are to be judged presumably by civil police whose job heretofore has been confined to the gathering of information—not to passing of judgment as to its validity, let alone to the assessing of punishment. Senator Hickenlooper summed this position up with startling clarity when he said that the rights of the individual must give way to the "overriding rights of the whole public." That *is* the Garrison State.

No wonder, with a public official advocating such drastic measures that the Committee on Economic Development should declare that "the requirements of security and the fear and hysteria generated by the threats to our security require constant vigilance to protect our individual liberties. We must maintain the safeguards to individual liberty. Agencies with power to investigate sometimes degenerate into organs of oppression and intimidation. . . . [They] can deteriorate into witch hunts which threaten the whole structure of individual freedom."

We may well be reminded of the warning of Edward Livingston at the time of the Alien and Sedition Acts of 1800. "Do not let us be told that we are to excite a fervor against a foreign aggression to establish a tyranny at home." It has long been a truism that one of the grave dangers any nation faces when it is at war is that it may become like the enemy it fears. We are fighting the power of Russia and her satellites. But we are also opposing a philosophy which denies to men certain "unalienable rights." The crucial issue we face is whether in the attempt to keep ourselves secure as a nation we shall take over the methods and adopt the morality of the totalitarian powers, stifle dissent, and deal with our citizens after the fashion of all police states.

If our enemies from without can lure us into abandoning our love of liberty, can convince us that democracy is merely a fair-weather luxury, then indeed they have planted their Trojan horse within the walls, and we have no effective means left by which we can fight, nor, in fact, is there anything left worth fighting for.

We have suggested that in the search for security we were losing our rights, but it is high time that we went on to ask whether we are even gaining security. George Kennan of the State Department has recently warned us that the atmosphere in Washington is rapidly reaching the point where few sensitive and gifted men will continue in government service. The present procedure drives good men from government employ at a time when we need the best there are. It creates a feeling of panic at a time when sense and sanity are needed. It weakens our representatives abroad and puts enormous propaganda power in the hands of the Russians. No one questions but that the latter fish in troubled waters, but it does seem stupid to furnish them with the bait. The Kremlin must be watching our loss of confidence in our leaders and our institutions, and the breakdown of our morale, with gratitude and glee.

Furthermore, this kind of procedure does not accomplish the specific job of locating possible subversives. Mr. Henry Stimson, shortly before his death, pointed out that indiscriminate accusations are doubly offensive, since they not only damage the innocent but also protect the guilty. The price of security is too high when it destroys the very things we would preserve; it is intolerable when it does not even bring security.

The hour is very late, but not so late but that we must ask the question as to whether we would be the weaker if we were to maintain the right of men to differ and to make their differences known without fear. We would be far more likely to have an informed and participating people believing in themselves and in their way of life, drawing into the government the very best, committed to ends which have always inspired men to fight to the limit of their abilities. Why have we valued our Bill of Rights if it has not been because, as Mr. Justice Brandeis said, we know "that fear breeds repression; that repression breeds hate; and that hate menaces stable government"; because we believe that the loyalty that gives strength is built on passionate belief in goals *worth* fighting for.

It is hard to believe that we are more insecure because we still believe in our Bill of Rights. Years ago we repudiated the slogan, "Peace at any price"—in part because we discovered it did not even bring peace. So, too, with security at any price; it will mean the destruction even of our security, for in our liberties lies our strength.

Over the years there have been things for which we have fought, and they have made us great. What if they are forgotten? What if we forget that it is free men who are brave men; that it is justice which is the ultimate shield against aggression; that the hope of the future lies in the hands of those who fight for the inalienable rights of man.

There are certain words
Our own and others we're used to—words
we've used,
Heard, had to recite, forgotten. . . .
Liberty, equality, fraternity.

I am merely saying—what if these words pass?
What if they pass and are gone and are no
more,

They were bought with belief and passion, at
great cost.
They were bought with the bitter and anony-
mous blood
Of farmers, teachers, shoemakers and fools
Who broke the old rule, and the price of
Kings. . . .

It took a long time to buy these words.
It took a long time, and much pain.
—STEPHEN VINCENT BENÉT
1951

HERBERT C. BROWNELL, JR.

1904–

HERBERT C. BROWNELL, Jr., a graduate of the University of Nebraska and of the Yale Law School, was admitted to the New York bar in 1927 and practiced for many years, chiefly in hotel and restaurant law. At the same time he was active in Republican politics, serving in the New York Assembly from 1933 to 1937. One of Thomas Dewey's key men, the manager of his Presidential campaigns in 1944 and 1948, Brownell also was chairman of the Republican National Committee. Recognized as a leading political strategist by the Republican high command, Brownell played an important part in General Eisenhower's campaign in 1952 and was appointed Attorney General of the United States when the new administration was organized in 1953.

Although Attorney General Brownell openly criticized preceding administrations for failure to defend the government from Communist infiltration, his own policy of dealing with Communists was an extension and intensification of that of his predecessors. "I have dedicated myself and the Department of Justice," he wrote, "to use every legal weapon to expose and punish the conspiracy [of the Communists]."

"The Fight Against Communism" is a speech given in Washington on April 19, 1954.

Current Biography, 1954

» » From: THE FIGHT AGAINST COMMUNISM « «

On Monday night the President [Dwight Eisenhower] told you about some of the concerns that today confront the people of our country. He spoke of the strength of this nation—its military, economic and intellectual strength. But more than that—he emphasized our strength based on our devotion to America and our dedication to the spiritual foundation of our nation. With this background the President urged us not to be blindly apprehensive, but to look at any dangers that we face realistically and without hysteria in the great tradition of our nation.

The President pointed out that underlying all else is the threat imposed upon us by aggressive Communism—the atheistic doctrine that believes in statism as opposed to our concept of the dignity of man.

One of the problems which flows from this threat is Communist infiltration here at home. Tonight I want to talk with you about this problem and tell you what this nation is doing about it.

A few weeks ago in Detroit, Michigan, six leaders of the Communist Party were found guilty under the Smith Act [1] and were sentenced to prison for conspiring to advocate the overthrow of our Government by force and violence. The trial got little newspaper attention; in fact, there were probably no headlines about the trial outside of Detroit. It was not broadcast or televised because that is not permitted in Federal Courts. Consequently, you may not have heard about it. But it was one of a number of very important steps in the program of your Government to destroy the effectiveness of Communism here at home.

How did the FBI get the evidence that convicted these peacetime traitors? The preparation for this trial started years ago during the administration of President Roosevelt when several undercover informants for the FBI began their training in counter-espionage. When

---

[1] Passed in 1940, this Act made it illegal to advocate or to teach or to promote the overthrow by force or violence of any state government or that of the United States.

they had finished, they were assigned to find out about the activities of the Communist Party in the Detroit area and to discover its efforts to infiltrate commerce and industry in that great industrial center.

These undercover informants, with patience and skill, were able to become members of the Communist Party cells.

Their indoctrination into Communist thinking and habits had been so thorough that they were accepted as members in the Communist Party without suspicion. In fact, the day before he testified for the Government one of them attended a conference with the six Communists who were awaiting trial. As a matter of fact, they reported to the FBI on the activities of each other as Communists.

So secret and so well planned were the operations of these undercover informants that over the course of several years in the Communist Party none of them knew the others were working for the FBI until they appeared as surprise witnesses at the trial.

As a result of this quiet, painstaking work by the FBI and the effectiveness of the Government attorneys in prosecuting this case, these six Communists have been found guilty and the Communist Party has suffered a severe blow.

This case in Detroit is not an isolated one. In every one of these trials of Communist leaders, charged with advocating the overthrow of our Government by force, the FBI has made public the fact that it has penetrated the inner circle of the Communist Party with undercover informants.

The success of the FBI in this regard has been so outstanding that the Communist Party in this country doesn't know which of its Communist members to trust. I assure you that makes their conspiracy a very hazardous occupation.

What is the danger of Communism as it exists in the United States today? There are some who say that it is not a real threat to our national security—that your Government is too concerned about it. As the President pointed out Monday night, it would be foolhardy to minimize the danger of Communist activity in the United States.

The threat of Communism is a very real one. Communists are scheming, practical and devious men and women dedicated to the destruction of our Government and our way of life. The policy of the Administration, within the framework of our Constitution and our laws, is to strike the Communists at every opportunity—to hit them where it hurts most.

Let me tell you some facts about the Communist Party. The National Headquarters is located at 268 Seventh Avenue, New York City. The country is divided into 30 districts. Only five—Boston, Detroit, New York, Philadelphia, and San Francisco—maintain open headquarters. The districts are further divided into state, county, city, section, and cell organizations.

Today there are approximately 25,000 Communists in the United States. Although their number is small, the potential danger to our national security is great. In effect there are 25,000 potential foreign agents within our country.

What is being done to protect against it? One of the most successful ways to attack a conspiracy is to destroy its leadership. The trial in Detroit which I mentioned is part of the program of your Government to destroy the effectiveness of the Communist Party in the United States—by proving that its leaders are criminals and sending them to jail.

In 1953 and so far in 1954, 36 active Communist leaders have been convicted and sentenced to jail for conspiring to advocate the overthrow of our Government by force and violence.

I have here the pictures and names of the people who were selected to run the activities of the Communist Party at the last national convention held in this country.

Now, the National Committee of the Communist Party is its principal governing agency and corresponds to the Politboro of the Russian Communist Party. All members of this National Committee already have been convicted with the exception of one whom the Government was unable to bring to trial because of illness.

Nearly all the members of the Alternate National Committee of the Party, the second most important Communist sub-organization, have been indicted or convicted. A large number of district and state organizers have also been convicted or indicted, as have a considerable number of Communist propagandists who were in charge of Communist publications.

There are presently in progress, in widely

separated cities of the country, two more trials of additional Communist leaders. A third trial will start soon.

Altogether since 1948, 105 of the principal leaders of the Communist Party have been indicted. Of these, 67 have been convicted of conspiring the overthrow of our Government by force and violence. The success of the prosecutions of these leaders has been a serious blow to the Communist Party.

The successful program of law enforcement is a counterbalance to the fear of Communist infiltration.

The people of this country owe a debt of gratitude to J. Edgar Hoover, the Director of the Federal Bureau of Investigation, and his associates, for this splendid achievement.

The FBI is also doing a magnificent job at the present time in keeping your Government constantly alerted and advised as to the plans of the remaining Communist conspirators. For security reasons I cannot tell you about the great counterespionage work the FBI is doing today. I can reveal for the first time two significant illustrations from the past.

(1) In early February, 1953, the FBI reported to me one of the results of their counterintelligence work against the Communist conspiracy. They had learned that Stalin was ill and that Malenkov was acting for him and would succeed him if Stalin died. Stalin did die on March 5, 1953, and it is now history that Malenkov succeeded him.

(2) During World War II the FBI learned that orders had gone out to the top leadership of the Communist Party to be in New York on February 8, 1944. The meeting place was surrounded with mystery and secrecy. The FBI learned that a room had been reserved from 10:00 A.M. to 10:00 P.M. in a certain music studio. As the Party leaders arrived in New York, they were given the address of the building and told to report to Studio II. At about the same time a group of young men who appeared to be musicians began to gather in the adjoining studio for a rehearsal. When the meeting started in Studio II, Earl Browder, then head of the Communist Party, proposed, among other things, that several changes were necessary to insure assistance to the Soviet Union. Among these proposals was that the name of the Party should be changed. A new party line was discussed and agreed upon including the change of the name of the party. All but two of the 35 Communist leaders pres-

ent supported Browder. There can be no harm in telling you now, as you have probably guessed, that some of these "musicians" in the adjoining room were FBI agents who carried recording equipment into the adjoining studio and the FBI secured a complete transcript of everything that happened at that Communist meeting.

You might be interested in a more timely illustration. Following the President's announcement last Monday evening that I would speak tonight on what is being done about Communism, an interesting reaction occurred in Party circles. The Communists became very concerned, and in various sections of the country the underground leaders scattered and have tried to completely disappear for a few days to see what happens.

We know that one of the major objectives of the Communist Party has been to infiltrate our Government. We have no intention of letting this happen.

The history of how the Communist underground infiltrated our National Government, with the disastrous loss of atomic information and other defense data, is now familiar to all Americans. Earlier attempts to prevent this failed, partly because they were based on the belief our Government could stop the loss of Government secrets to foreign agents merely by removing those Government employees who were found to be disloyal to the United States. But we found by studying Communist infiltration into free governments that the Communists do not rely solely on persons who are disloyal and those who are avowed members of the Communist Party to steal government secrets. In addition to espionage agents they cleverly use first, people who are indoctrinated with Communist ideology in some "front" organization and who do not realize the full meaning of the Communist international conspiracy.

Second, they use persons who are subject to blackmail because of personal habits that they do not want to have exposed to public view.

Third, they use persons such as chronic excessive drinkers or others who talk too much about government secrets—persons whom you and I would call just plain blabbermouths.

Now these people are not disloyal, but they are the types used by the Soviet in all free countries to obtain government secrets. We believe that they do not belong in sensitive government jobs handling secret information which would be of great value to our enemies. I'm sure you wouldn't want them handling your own confidential affairs.

For that reason, we have adopted the Employee Security Program and under it have removed hundreds of such employees who were security risks.

But equally as important—and this is what hurts the Communists—we will not employ such persons in the first instance. When a person applies for a position of any importance, he is fully investigated either by the FBI or other appropriate investigative agency, and if there is any question about him from the security standpoint, he does not get the job. The American people want no more of the type of Hiss, Remington, or Harry Dexter White. They may be assured that so far as humanly possible, this country is protected against further loss from Government sources of secret defense information to our enemies.

The Administration's Employee Security Program, then, is the second effective counter to Communist efforts in the United States.

The third effective measure which your Government is using to destroy the Communist menace in this country is the Internal Security Act passed in 1950. Under its provisions all subversive organizations, that is, organizations dedicated to overthrowing the Government of the United States by force and violence, are required to register with the Department of Justice. They must disclose their officers, membership, activities and finances to the American people.

The results of this law are only now beginning to bear fruit.

Last year the Subversive Activities Control Board, after a full hearing, held that the Communist Party of the United States is under the control and domination of a foreign power and is pledged to the overthrow of our Government by force and violence. This case is now on appeal before the courts and will be argued by the Department of Justice next month.

This case will make possible the enforcement for the first time of another important provision of the Internal Security Act requiring that all organizations fronting for subversive groups register with the Department of Justice. A front organization is one of the treacherous devices used by the Communists in an effort to deceive people.

Originally the front was created by the early Communist leaders, Lenin and Trotsky,

as an instrumentality of Soviet foreign policy. From that day to this, Communist fronts have been used to serve the Soviet cause. In fact, the first front in the United States which started under the name of "Friends of the Soviet Union" is still functioning under the high-sounding title of "The National Council of American Soviet Friendship."

Within the past year the Department of Justice has charged twelve front organizations with being under the control of the Communist movement. It has asked the Subversive Activities Control Board to require them to register and to comply with the law. In addition, the FBI has under investigation some 200 known or suspected front or Communist affiliated organizations.

Through these proceedings your Government is moving to force organizations into the open to disclose them for what they are.

If this law is upheld by the Courts, the Communist Party and its front organizations will soon have to make public the source of all their finances and account for all their expenditures.

The Communist Party will have to list all its members and such members will be prohibited from working in any defense facility. They will not be permitted to obtain or use passports. A member of any front organization will have to reveal his membership if he attempts to seek or hold employment by the United States or in any defense facility. These Communist organizations will have to label all publications and announce sponsorship of any radio or television program.

Thus you can see how the Communist Party and the front organizations will be crippled if they comply with the law.

The Communist Party has announced that if the law is upheld it will not register and individual Communists will not register. If the Communist Party and the Organizations they control carry out their threat and willfully disobey the law, the Communist Party and its individual members will themselves, for all practical purposes, by their own acts outlaw the Communist Party.

In addition to the three programs which I have referred to, the Department of Justice is using every other legal weapon which this nation has to oppose and bring to justice members of the Communist Party involved in law violations.

For example, last week the Communists received another body blow in the courts in the form of the conviction of Ben Gold. He is President of the Fur and Leather Workers Union of America, a union which has been expelled by the CIO because it is Communist dominated. Ben Gold and his union for years have been one of the important sources of Communist financing. Gold was found guilty of lying under oath about his Communist Party membership.

Last Wednesday during the early morning hours, Mary Esther Gebhardt sailed for her homeland. This woman entered the United States eight years ago and thereafter actively engaged in Communist Party activities in this country. Because of these activities she was ordered deported by the Department of Justice.

She was an alien, but we are proceeding just as vigorously against Communists who, under our law can be denaturalized. For example, William Allan, one of the convicted defendants in the Smith Act case in Detroit, is a naturalized citizen, and the Department of Justice recently has moved to take his citizenship from him.

Our Immigration and Naturalization Service, which has been doing a good job, has started denaturalization suits against many others. On Wednesday, I issued instructions for the filing of a denaturalization suit against the notorious Communist leader, Steve Nelson, already convicted as a felon under the Smith Act. Since January 1953, 208 persons with records of subversive activity or affiliation have been deported or ordered to be deported.

I want to emphasize a very important aspect of all these measures the Government has used or intends to use to combat Communism.

All of the efforts of the Government to oppose Communism have been made and will continue to be made within the framework of the Constitution of the United States and under the laws of our country. That means that the procedures followed, have been and will continue to be, basically fair in accordance with the traditional American conceptions of due process of law. We have proceeded with a careful regard for individual dignity and freedom and the preservation of personal liberty.

We are determined to destroy the effectiveness of the Communist movement in this country. American policy is officially set forth in a resolution proposed by the United States in the recent meeting of the governments of the western hemisphere at Caracas. That resolution was adopted by all the nations of this hemisphere, with only one dissenting vote.

It states that 'The subversive character of the Communist international movement continues to constitute . . . a special and immediate threat to the national institutions and the peace and security of the American states . . . and therefore the Tenth Inter-American Conference recommends the following steps for the purpose of counteracting the subversive activities of the international Communist movement . . . measures to require disclosures of identity, activities, and sources of funds of those who are spreading propaganda of the international Communist movement."

The United States is living up to its commitment under the Caracas Resolution by the Program I have outlined.

Great progress has been made in destroying the effectiveness of the Communist movement here at home. However, there are loopholes in our laws which need to be plugged to complete the task of destroying this threat to our nation's safety. Therefore, the Administration proposed the legislation to complete the job. I will discuss these proposals in more detail with the House and Senate Committees in the near future. Briefly they are:

1. We need a new law to allow an employer to dismiss from defense plants during a national emergency any person whose record shows he is likely to engage in sabotage or espionage. There is no authority to remove them from power plants and other key spots where the dangers of sabotage are greatest, unless the person is actually working on a classified defense contract. The National Security Council last month determined that such persons constitute a peril to our national security. Therefore, a bill will soon be presented to Congress authorizing the dismissal of such persons if, after a hearing, they are determined to be potential saboteurs or espionage agents.

2. We need a new law to eliminate Communist control of any industrial organization or labor union in vital sections of our national economy. You will recall that several years ago the CIO expelled from its ranks a number of unions in areas such as the communications, mining, electrical and maritime industries on the ground that these unions were Communist dominated. Leaders of both the A.F. of L. and the CIO, as well as Congressional Committees,

have pointed out the grave peril to national security of having the leadership of these expelled unions controlled by Communists. But existing law does not provide any satisfactory means for eliminating such domination. The proposed legislation will allow the Subversive Activities Control Board to conduct hearings and determine whether or not a union or industrial organization is in fact dominated by the Communist Party and is in a position to substantially damage our national security. If it is so found, the law would prohibit any employee from paying dues or contributing goods or services to any such organization. It would deny employment in a defense plant to any person who is a member of such an organization. Adequate provision will be made in the proposed bill so that such an organization can, after such a finding, throw out its Communist leaders and be restored to good standing.

3. There is need for a law that will prevent persons from using the Fifth Amendment privilege against self-incrimination for the purpose of refusing to testify in order to shield other persons. We propose a law which would allow the Government prosecutor to grant immunity from prosecution to such person so he may be compelled to testify. Some states have such laws now and they have proved to be very helpful in obtaining evidence to break up illegal conspiracies. It is time to give similar powers to the Department of Justice to catch the higher-ups in the Communist conspiracy.

4. Since 1940 the Federal Government has allowed the FBI, upon authority of the Attorney General, to intercept telephone communications whenever it seems likely that the person using the telephone is engaged in subversive activities which may involve treason, sabotage or espionage. Today this evidence cannot be used in Federal Courts to convict such a person of a crime involving our national security. This has seriously hampered our Federal law enforcement officials in combating the Communist menace in this country. We therefore need a law which will allow evidence so obtained to be introduced in court in treason, sabotage, espionage, or other cases involving our national security. America needs such an anti-traitor law.

5. We have sent or will send to Congress other bills to strengthen further our legal defenses against subversion. For example, one would provide the death penalty for peacetime espionage. Another, in carrying out the President's recommendation in the State of the Union message, would take away the citizenship of any person found guilty of advocating the overthrow of the Government by force. Still another would enlarge the statute of limitations in espionage cases.

If these proposals and the others which I have outlined are enacted into law, the FBI, and the other investigating agencies of our Government, will have new and powerful constitutional weapons to destroy by legal, orderly processes the Communist Party in this country.

In closing let me emphasize what the President said Monday night. Although we must be constantly alert to the danger of Communist infiltration, we should not have exaggerated fears of the danger.

The FBI, the Department of Justice and the courts are your agents in dealing with this Communist conspiracy. All are vigilant in their readiness to meet any move or emergency which the Communist Party in America might precipitate. They are your guarantee that the liberties of all Americans will be preserved and ever strengthened from any enemies who seek to destroy them.

1954

THE SUPREME COURT

O N MAY 17, 1954, the Supreme Court, in *Brown et al v. Board of Education of Topeka et al*, handed down a consolidated opinion in cases arising in Kansas, South Carolina, Virginia, and Delaware. The unanimous position which the Court took on the issue of racial segregation in public schools was based less on legalistic than on sociological, psychological, and moral grounds. The Court maintained that there is no place in American public education for the "separate but equal" doctrine which had legally prevailed since 1896. The justices held that the states with segregated public schools deprived Negroes of the equal protection guaranteed by the Fourteenth Amendment. Recognizing the problems that the abolition of segregated public education for Negroes and whites involves, the Court ordered a re-argument in the fall for questions and procedures in the seventeen states where segregation operated.

While prominent officials in some southern states made it clear that they would sacrifice public education before they accepted non-segregated schools, large segments of public opinion in all parts of the country hailed the decision as a great victory for humane and demo-cratic principles.

Brown et al v. Board of Education of Topeka et al, 347 US 483 (1954).
Bolling et al. v. Sharpe et al, 347 US 497 (1954).
James Reston, "A Sociological Decision," *New York Times*, May 18, 1954.
Isidore Starr, "Recent Supreme Court Decisions: Public School Segregation Cases," *Social Education* 18:251–54 (October, 1954).

TEXT OF SUPREME COURT DECISION OUTLAWING
« « NEGRO SEGREGATION IN THE PUBLIC SCHOOLS » »

These cases come to us from the States of Kansas, South Carolina, Virginia, and Delaware. They are premised on different facts and different local conditions, but a common legal question justifies their consideration together in this consolidated opinion.[1]

In each of the cases, minors of the Negro race, through their legal representatives, seek the aid of the courts in obtaining admission to the public schools of their community on a nonsegregated basis. In each instance, they had been denied admission to schools attended by white children under laws requiring or permitting segregation according to race.

[1] In the Kansas case, Brown v. Board of Education, the plaintiffs are Negro children of elementary school age residing in Topeka. They brought this action in the United States District Court for the district of Kansas to enjoin enforcement of a Kansas statute which permits, but does not require, cities of more than 15,000 population to maintain separate school facilities for Negro and white students. Kan. Gen. Stat. 72–1724 (1949).

Pursuant to that authority, the Topeka Board of Education elected to establish segregated elementary schools. Other public schools in the community, however, are operated on a non-segregated basis.

The three-judge District Court, convened under 28 U. S. C. 2281 and 2284, found that segregation in public education has a detrimental effect upon Negro children, but denied relief on the ground that the Negro and white schools were substantially equal with respect to buildings, transportation, curricula, and educational qualifications of teachers, 98 F. Supp 797. The case is here on direct appeal under 28 U. S. C. 1253.

In the South Carolina case, Briggs v. Elliott, the plaintiffs are Negro children of both elementary and high school age residing in Clarendon County. They brought this action in the United States District Court for the Eastern District of South Carolina to enjoin enforcement of provisions in the State Constitution and statutory code which require the segregation of Negroes and whites in public schools. S. C. Const. Art. XI, 7; S. C. Code 5377 (1942).

The three-judge District Court, convened under 28 U. S. C. 2281 and 2284, denied the requested relief. The court found that the Negro schools were inferior to the white schools and ordered the defendants to begin immediately to equalize the facilities. But the court sustained the validity of the contested provisions and denied the plaintiffs admission to the white schools during the equalization program. 98 F. Supp. 529.

COURT VACATED JUDGMENT

This court vacated the District Court's judgment and remanded the case for the purpose of obtaining the court's views on a report filed by the defendants concerning the progress made in the equalization program. 342 U. S. 350.

On remand, the District Court found that substantial equality had been achieved except for buildings and that the defendants were proceeding to rectify this inequality as well. 103 F. Supp. 920. The case is again here on direct appeal under 28 U. S. C. 1253.

In the Virginia case, Davis v. County School Board, the plaintiffs are Negro children of high school age residing in Prince Edward

County. They brought this action in the United States District Court for the Eastern District of Virginia to enjoin enforcement of provisions in the State Constitution and Statutory Code which require the segregation of Negroes and whites in public schools. Va. Const., 140; Va. Code 22–221 (1950).

The three-judge District Court, convened under 28 U. S. C. 2281 and 2284, denied the requested relief. The Court found the Negro school inferior in physical plant, curricula, and transportation, and ordered the defendants forthwith to provide substantially equal curricula and transportation and to "proceed with all reasonable diligence and dispatch to remove" the inequality in physical plant.

But, as in the South Carolina case, the court sustained the validity of the contested provisions and denied the plaintiffs admission to the white schools during the equalization program. 103 F. Supp. 337. The case is here on direct appeal under 28 U. S. C. 1253.

THE DELAWARE CASE

In the Delaware Case, Gebhart v. Belton, the plaintiffs are Negro children of both elementary and high school age residing in New Castle County. They brought this action in the Delaware Court of Chancery to enjoin enforcement of provisions in the State Constitution and Statutory Code which require the segregation of Negroes and whites in public schools. Del. Const., Art. X, 2; Del. Rev. Code 2631 (1935).

The chancellor gave judgment for the plaintiffs and ordered their immediate admission to schools previously attended only by white children, on the ground that the Negro schools were inferior with respect to teacher training, pupil-teacher ratio, extracurricular activities, physical plant, and time and distance involved in travel. 87A 2D 862.

The chancellor also found that segregation itself results in an inferior education for Negro Children (see Note 10, infra), but did not rest his decision on that ground. Id., at 865. The chancellor's decree was affirmed by the Supreme Court of Delaware, which intimated, however, that the defendants might be able to obtain a modification of the decree after equalization of the Negro and white schools had been accomplished. 91 A. 2d 137, 152.

The defendants, contending only that the Delaware courts had erred in ordering the immediate admission of the Negro plaintiffs to the white schools, applied to this court for certiorari. The writ was granted, 344 U. S. 891. The plaintiffs, who were successful below, did not submit a cross-petition.

This segregation was alleged to deprive the plaintiffs of the equal protection of the laws under the Fourteen Amendment. In each of the cases other than the Delaware case, a three-judge Federal District Court denied relief to the plaintiffs on the so-called "Separate but Equal" doctrine announced by this court in Plessy v. Ferguson, 163 U. S. 537.

Under that doctrine, equality of treatment is accorded when the races are provided substantially equal facilities, even though these facilities be separate. In the Delaware case, the Supreme Court of Delaware adhered to that doctrine, but ordered that the plaintiffs be admitted to the white schools because of their superiority to the Negro schools.

The plaintiffs contend that segregated public schools are not "equal" and cannot be made "equal," and that hence, they are deprived of the equal protection of the laws. Because of the obvious importance of the question presented, the Court took jurisdiction.[2] Argument was heard in the 1952 term, and reargument was heard this term on certain questions propounded by the Court.[3]

POSTWAR SOURCES INCONCLUSIVE

Reargument was largely devoted to the circumstances surrounding the adoption of the Fourteenth Amendment in 1868. It covered, exhaustively, consideration of the Amendment in Congress, ratification by the states, then existing practices in racial segregation, and the views of proponents and opponents of the Amendment.

This discussion and our own investigation convince us that, although these sources cast some light, it is not enough to resolve the problem with which we are faced.

At best, they are inconclusive. The most avid proponents of the postwar Amendments undoubtedly intended them to remove all legal distinctions among "all persons born or naturalized in the United States."

Their opponents, just as certainly, were antagonistic to both the letter and the spirit of the Amendments and wished them to have the most limited effect. What others in Congress and the State Legislature had in mind cannot be determined with any degree or certainty.

An additional reason for the inclusive nature of the Amendment's history, with respect to

segregated schools, is the status of public education at that time.[4] In the South, the movement toward free common schools, supported by general taxation, had not yet taken hold. Education of white children was largely in the hands of private groups. Education of Negroes was almost nonexistent, and practically all of the race was illiterate. In fact, any education of Negroes was forbidden by law in some states.

Today, in contrast, many Negroes have achieved outstanding success in the arts and sciences as well as in the business and professional world. It is true that public education has already advanced further in the North, but the effect of the Amendment on Northern States was generally ignored in the Congressional debates.

Even in the North, the conditions of public education did not approximate those existing today. The curriculum was usually rudimentary; ungraded schools were common in rural areas; the school term was but three months a year in many states; and compulsory school attendance was virtually unknown.

As a consequence, it is not surprising that there should be so little in the history of the Fourteenth Amendment relating to its intended effect on public education.

HALF CENTURY OF CASES

In the first cases in this court construing the Fourteenth Amendment, decided shortly after its adoption, the court interpreted it as proscribing all state-imposed discriminations against the Negro race.[5]

---

[2] 344 U. S. 1, 141, 891.
[3] 345 U. S. 972. The Attorney General of the United States participated both terms as amicus curae.

[4] For a general study of the development of public education prior to the Amendment see Butts and Cremin, "A History of Education in American Culture" (1953), Pts. I, II; Cubberley, "Public Education in the United States" (1934 ed.), CC. I–XII. School practices current at the time of the adoption of the Fourteenth Amendment are described in Butts and Cremin, supra, at 269–275; Cubberley, supra, at 288–339, 408–431; Knight, "Public Education in the South" (1922), CC. VIII, IX. See also H. Ex. Doc. No. 315, 41st Cong., 2d sess. (1871).
Although the demand for free public schools followed substantially the same pattern in both the North and the South, the development in the South did not begin to gain momentum until about 1850, some twenty years after that in the North. The reasons for the somewhat slower development in the South (e. g., the rural character of the South and the different regional attitudes toward state assistance) are well explained in Cubberley, supra, at 408–423.
In the country as a whole, but particularly in the South, the war virtually stopped all progress in public education. Id., at 427–428. The low status of Negro education in all sections of the country, both before and immediately after the war, is described in Beale, "A History of Freedom of Teaching in American Schools" (1941), 112–132, 175–195.
Compulsory school attendance laws were not generally adopted until after the ratification of the Fourteenth Amendment, and it was not until 1918 that such laws were in force in all the states. Cubberley, supra, at 563–565.
[5] Slaughter-house cases, 16 Wall. 36, 67–72 (1873); Strauder v. West Virginia, 100 U. S. 303, 307–308 (1879):
"It ordains that no state shall deprive any person of life, liberty, or property, without due process of law, or deny to any person within its jurisdiction the equal protection of the laws. What is this

The doctrine of "Separate but Equal" did not make its appearance in this court until 1896 in the case of Plessy v. Ferguson, supra, involving not education but transportation.[6]

American courts have since labored with the doctrine for over half a century. In this court, there have been six cases involving the "Separate but Equal" doctrine in the field of public education.[7]

In Cumming v. County Board of Education, 175 U. S. 528, and Gong Lum v. Rice, 275 U. S. 78, the validity of the doctrine itself was not challenged.[8] In most recent cases, all on the graduate school level, inequality was found in that specific benefits enjoyed by white students were denied to Negro students of the same educational qualifications. Missouri ex rel. Gaines v. Canada, 305 U. S. 337; Sipuel v. Oklahoma, 332 U. S. 331; Sweatt v. Painter, 339 U. S. 629; McLaurin v. Oklahoma State Regents, 339 U. S. 637.

In nine of these cases it was necessary to re-examine the doctrine to grant relief to the Negro plaintiff. And in Sweatt v. Painter, supra, the court expressly reserved decision on the question whether Plessy v. Ferguson should be held inapplicable to public education.

In the instant cases, that question is directly presented. Here, unlike Sweatt v. Painter, there are findings below that the Negro and white schools involved have been equalized, or are being equalized, with respect to buildings, curricula, qualifications and sala-ries of teachers, and other "tangible" factors.[9]

Our decision, therefore, cannot turn on merely a comparison of these tangible factors in the Negro and white schools involved in each of the cases. We must look instead to the effect of segregation itself on public education.

In approaching this problem, we cannot turn the clock back to 1868, when the Amendment was adopted, or even to 1896, when Plessy v. Ferguson was written. We must consider public education in the light of its full development and its present place in American life throughout the nation. Only in this way can it be determined if segregation in public schools deprives these plaintiffs of the equal protection of the laws.

A FUNCTION OF GOVERNMENT

Today, education is perhaps the most important function of state and local governments. Compulsory school attendance laws and the great expenditures for education both demonstrate our recognition of the importance of education to our democratic society. It is required in the performance of our most basic public responsibilities, even service in the armed forces. It is the very foundation of good citizenship.

Today, it is a principal instrument in awakening the child to cultural values, in preparing him for later professional training, and in helping him to adjust normally to his environment.

In these days, it is doubtful that any child may reasonably be expected to succeed in life if he is denied the opportunity of an education. Such an opportunity, where the state has undertaken to provide it, is a right which must be made available to all on equal terms.

We come then to the question presented: Does segregation of children in public schools solely on the basis of race, even though the physical facilities and other "tangible" factors may be equal, deprive the children of the minority group of equal educational opportunities? We believe that it does.

In Sweatt v. Painter, supra, in finding that a

---

but declaring that the law in the states shall be the same for the black as for the white; that all persons, whether colored or white, shall stand equal before the laws of the states, and, in regard to the colored race, for whose protection the Amendment was primarily designed, that no discrimination shall be made against them by law because of their color?

"The words of the Amendment, it is true, are prohibitory, but they contain a necessary implication of a positive immunity, or right, most valuable to the colored race—the right to exemption from unfriendly legislation against them distinctively as colored—exemption from legal discriminations, implying inferiority in civil society, lessening the security of their enjoyment of the rights which others enjoy, and discriminations which are steps toward reducing them to the condition of a subject race."

See also Virginia v. Rives, 100 U. S. 313, 318 (1879); ex parte Virginia, 100 U. S. 339, 344–345 (1879).

[6] The doctrine apparently originated in Roberts v. City of Boston, 59 Mass., 198, 206 (1849), upholding school segregation against attack as being violative of a state constitutional guarantee of equality. Segregation in Boston public schools was eliminated in 1855. Mass. Acts 1855, C. 256. But elsewhere in the North segregation in public education has persisted until recent years. It is apparent that such segregation has long been a nation-wide problem, not merely one of sectional concern.

[7] See also Berea College v. Kentucky, 211 U. S. 45 (1908).

[8] In the Cumming case, Negro taxpayers sought an injunction requiring the defendant school board to discontinue the operation of a high school for white children until the board resumed operation of a high school for Negro children.

Similarly in the Gong Lum case, the plaintiff a child of Chinese descent, contended that the state authorities had misapplied the doctrine by classifying him with Negro children and requiring him to attend a Negro school.

[9] In the Kansas case, the court below found substantial equality as to all such factors, 98 F. Supp. 797, 798.

In the South Carolina case, the court below found that the defendants were proceeding "promptly and in good faith to comply with the court's decree." 103 F. Supp. 920, 921.

In the Virginia case, the court below noted that the equilization program was already "afoot and progressing" (103 F. Supp. 337, 341); since then, we have been advised in the Virginia Attorney General's brief on reargument, that the program has now been completed.

In the Delaware case, the court below similarly noted that the state's equilization program was well under way. 91 A 2d 137, 149.

segregated law school for Negroes could not provide them equal educational opportunities, this court relied in large part on "those qualities which are incapable of objective measurement but which make for greatness in a law school."

In McLaurin *v.* Oklahoma State Regents, *supra,* the court, in requiring that a Negro admitted to a white graduate school be treated like all other students, again resorted to intangible considerations: ". . . his ability to study, engage in discussions and exchange views with other students, and, in general, to learn his profession."

Such considerations apply with added force to children in grade and high schools. To separate them from others of similar age and qualifications solely because of their race generates a feeling of inferiority as to their status in the community that may affect their hearts and minds in a way unlikely ever to be undone.

The effect of this separation on their educational opportunities was well stated by a finding in the Kansas case by a court which nevertheless felt compelled to rule against the Negro plaintiffs:

"Segregation of white and colored children in public schools has a detrimental effect upon the colored children. The impact is greater when it has the sanction of the law; for the policy of separating the races is usually interpreted as denoting the inferiority of the Negro group.

"A sense of inferiority affects the motivation of a child to learn. Segregation with the sanction of law, therefore, has a tendency to retard the educational and mental development of Negro children and to deprive them of some of the benefits they would receive in a racially integrated school system." [10]

Whatever may have been the extent of psychological knowledge at the time of Plessy *v.* Ferguson, this finding is amply supported by modern authority.[11] Any language in Plessy *v.* Ferguson contrary to this finding is rejected.

We conclude that in the field of public edu-

cation the doctrine of "Separate but Equal" has no place. Separate educational facilities are inherently unequal. Therefore, we hold that the plaintiffs and others similarly situated for whom the actions have been brought are, by reason of the segregation complained of, deprived of the equal protection of the laws guaranteed by the Fourteenth Amendment. This disposition makes unnecessary any discussion whether such segregation also violates the Due Process Clause of the Fourteenth Amendment.[12]

"SEPARATE BUT EQUAL" DENIED

Because these are class actions, because of the wide applicability of this decision, and because of the great variety of local conditions, the formulation of decrees in these cases presents problems of considerable complexity. On reargument, the consideration of appropriate relief was necessarily subordinated to the primary question—the constitutionality of segregation in public education.

We have now announced that such segregation is a denial of the equal protection of the laws. In order that we may have the full assistance of the parties in formulating decrees, the cases will be restored to the docket, and the parties are requested to present further argument on Questions 4 and 5 previously propounded by the court for the reargument this term.[13]

The Attorney General of the United States is again invited to participate. The Attorneys General of the states requiring or permitting segregation in public education will also be permitted to appear as amici curiae upon request to do so by September 15, 1954, and submission of briefs by October 1, 1954.[14]

[10] A similar finding was made in the Delaware case:
"I conclude from the testimony that in our Delaware society, state-imposed segregation in education itself results in the Negro children, as a class, receiving educational opportunities which are substantially inferior to those available to white children otherwise similarly situated." 87 A, 2d 862, 865.

[11] K. B. Clark, "effect of prejudice and discrimination on personality development" (Midcentury White House Conference on Children and Youth, 1950); Witmer and Kotinsky, "Personality in the Making" (1952), C. VI; Deutscher and Chein, "The Psychological Effects of Enforced Segregation; a Survey of Social Science Opinion," 26 J. Psychol. 259 (1948); Chein, "What are the Psychological Effects of Segregation Under Conditions of Equal Facilities?" 3 Int. J. Opinion and Attitude Res. 229 (1949);

Brameld, "Educational Costs, in Discrimination and National Welfare" (McIver, ed., 1949), 44–48; Frazier, "The Negro in the United States" (1949), 674–681, and see generally Myrdal "An American Dilemma" (1944).

[12] See Bolling *v.* Sharpe, infra, concerning the Due Progress Clause of the Fifth Amendment.

[13] "4. Assuming it is decided that segregation in public schools violates the Fourteenth Amendment
"(A) Would a decree necessarily follow providing that within the limits set by normal geographic school districting, Negro children should forthwith be admitted to schools of their choice, or
"(B) May this court, in the exercise of its equity powers, permit an effective gradual adjustment to be brought about from existing segregated systems to a system not based on color distinctions?
"On the assumption on which Questions 4 (A) and (B) are based, and assuming further that this court will exercise its equity powers to the end described in Question 4 (B),
"(A) Should this court formulate detailed decrees in these cases;
"(B) If so, what specific issues should the decrees reach;
"(C) Should this court appoint a special master to hear evidence with a view to recommending specific terms for such decrees;
"(D) Should this court remand to the courts of first instance with directions to frame decrees in these cases, and if so, what general directions should the decrees of this court include and what procedures should the courts of first instance follow in arriving at the specific terms of more detailed decrees?"

[14] See Rule 42, Revised Rules of this court (effective July 1, 1954).

MARTIN LUTHER KING, JR.

1930–

IN 1956, Negroes in Montgomery, Alabama, began to boycott bus transportation companies in protest against discrimination. Leading the movement was Dr. Martin Luther King, Jr., the twenty-seven-year-old pastor of a local Baptist church. He soon demonstrated that he possessed a clear and fine mind, great spiritual and physical courage, and a superb ability to inspire and to restrain Negroes even when their houses and churches were bombed by indignant whites. The boycott succeeded and within a year the buses were desegregated. Dr. King, a graduate of Crozier Theological Seminary and a doctor in philosophy from Boston University, had become the national leader of what promised to be a new chapter in the struggle for Negro civil rights and for individual dignity. *Stride Toward Freedom* (1958) reflects its author's spiritual dignity, unpretentious sincerity, and forceful mind. Perry Miller has compared the factual simplicity of his style with the restraint of John Woolman's *Journal*.

Perry Miller, "The Mind and Faith of Martin Luther King," *The Reporter*, XI (October 30, 1958).
Chester Bowles, "What Negroes Can Learn from Ghandi," *Saturday Evening Post*, CCXXX (March 1, 1958).
H. R. Isaacs, "Civil Disobedience in Montgomery," *New Republic*, CXXXIX (October 6, 1958).

From: STRIDE TOWARD FREEDOM, THE MONTGOMERY STORY

CHAPTER II

WHERE DO WE GO FROM HERE?

The bus struggle in Montgomery, Alabama, is now history. As the intergrated buses roll daily through the city they carry, along with their passengers, a meaning-crowded symbolism. Accord among the great majority of passengers is evidence of the basic good will of man for man and a portent of peace in the desegregated society to come. Occasional instances of discord among passengers are a reminder that in other areas of Montgomery life segregation yet obtains with all of its potential for group strife and personal conflict. Indeed, segregation is still a reality throughout the South.

Where do we go from here? Since the problem in Montgomery is merely symptomatic of the larger national problem, where do we go not only in Montgomery but all over the South and the nation? Forces maturing for years have given rise to the present crisis in race relations. What are these forces that have brought the crisis about? What will be the conclusion? Are we caught in a social and political impasse, or do we have at our disposal the creative resources to achieve the ideals of brotherhood and harmonious living?

The last half century has seen crucial changes in the life of the American Negro. The social upheavals of the two world wars, the great depression, and the spread of the automobile have made it both possible and necessary for the Negro to move away from his former isolation on the rural plantation. The decline of agriculture and the parallel growth of industry have drawn large numbers of Negroes to urban centers and brought about a gradual improvement in their economic status. New contacts have led to a broadened outlook and new possibilities for educational advance. All of these factors have conjoined to cause the Negro to take a fresh look at himself. His expanding life experiences have created within him a consciousness that he is an equal element in a larger social compound and accordingly should be given rights and privileges commensurate with his new responsibilities. Once plagued with a tragic sense of inferiority resulting from the crippling effects of slavery and segregation, the Negro has now been driven to re-evaluate himself. He has come to feel that he is somebody. His religion reveals to him that God loves all His children and that the important thing about a man is not "his specificity but his fundamentum"—not the texture of his hair or the color of his skin but his eternal worth to God.

This growing self-respect has inspired the Negro with a new determination to struggle and sacrifice until first-class citizenship becomes a reality. This is the true meaning of the Montgomery Story. One can never understand the bus protest in Montgomery without understanding that there is a new Negro in the South, with a new sense of dignity and destiny.

Along with the Negro's changing image of himself has come an awakening moral consciousness on the part of millions of white Americans concerning segregation. Ever since the signing of the Declaration of Independence, America has manifested a schizophrenic personality on the question of race. She has been torn between selves—a self in which she has proudly professed democracy and a self in which she has sadly practiced the antithesis of democracy. The reality of segregation, like slavery, has always had to confront the ideals of democracy and Christianity. Indeed, segregation and discrimination are strange paradoxes in a nation founded on the principle that all men are created equal. This contradiction has disturbed the consciences of whites both North and South, and has caused many of them to see that segregation is basically evil.

Climaxing this process was the Supreme Court's decision out-lawing segregation in the public schools. For all men of good will May 17, 1954, marked a joyous end to the long night of enforced segregation. In unequivocal language the Court affirmed that "separate but equal" facilities are inherently unequal, and that to segregate a child on the basis of his race is to deny that child equal protection of the law. This decision brought hope to millions of disinherited Negroes who had formerly dared only to dream of freedom. It further enhanced the Negro's sense of dignity and gave him even greater determination to achieve justice.

This determination of Negro Americans to win freedom from all forms of oppression springs from the same deep longing that motivates oppressed peoples all over the world. The rumblings of discontent in Asia and Africa are expressions of a quest for freedom and human dignity by people who have long been the victims of colonialism and imperialism. So in a real sense the racial crisis in America is a part of the larger world crisis.

But the numerous changes which have culminated in a new sense of dignity on the part of the Negro are not of themselves responsible for the present crisis. If all men accepted these historical changes in good faith there would be no crisis. The crisis developed when the collective pressure to achieve fair goals for the Negro met with tenacious and determined resistance. Then the emerging new order, based on the principle of democratic equalitarianism, came face to face with the older order, based on the principles of paternalism and subordination. The crisis was not produced by outside agitators, NAACP'ers, Montgomery Protesters, or even the Supreme Court. The crisis developed paradoxically, when the most sublime principles of American democracy—imperfectly realized for almost two centuries—began fulfilling themselves and met with the brutal resistance of forces seeking to contract and repress freedom's growth.

The resistance has risen at times to ominous proportions. Many states have reacted in open defiance. The legislative halls of the South still ring loud with such words as "interposition" and "nullification." Many public officials are using the power of their offices to defy the law of the land. Through their irresponsible actions, their inflammatory statements, and their dissemination of distortions and half-truths, they have succeeded in arousing abnormal fears and morbid antipathies within the minds of underprivileged and uneducated whites, leaving them in such a state of excitement and confusion that they are led to acts of meanness and violence that no normal person would commit.

This resistance to the emergence of the new order expresses itself in the resurgence of the Ku Klux Klan. Determined to preserve segregation at any cost, this organization employs methods that are crude and primitive. It draws its members from underprivileged groups who see in the Negro's rising status a political and economic threat. Although the Klan is impotent politically and openly denounced from all sides, it remains a dangerous force which thrives on racial and religious bigotry. Because of its past history, whenever the Klan moves there is fear of violence.

Then there are the White Citizens Councils. Since they occasionally recruit members from a higher social and economic level than the Klan, a halo of partial respectability hovers over them. But like the Klan they are determined to preserve segregation despite the law. Their weapons of threat, intimidation, and boycott are directed both against Negroes and against any whites who stand for justice. They demand absolute conformity from white and abject submission from Negroes. The Citizens Councils often argue piously that they abhor violence, but their defiance of the law, their unethical methods, and their vitriolic public pronouncements inevitably create the atmosphere in which violence thrives.

As a result of the Councils' activities most white moderates in the South no longer feel free to discuss in public the issues involved in desegregation for fear of social ostracism and economic reprisals. What channels of communication had once existed between whites and Negroes have thus now been largely closed.

The present crisis in race relations has characteristics that come to the forefront in any period of social transition. The guardians of the status quo lash out with denunciation against the person or organization that they consider most responsible for the emergence of the new order. Often this denunciation rises to major proportions. In the transition from slavery to restricted emancipation Abraham Lincoln was assassinated. In the present transition from segregation to desegregation the Supreme Court is castigated and the NAACP is maligned and subjected to extra-legal reprisals.

As in other social crises the defenders of the status quo in the South argue that they were gradually solving their own problems until external pressure was brought to bear upon them. The familiar complaint in the South today is that the Supreme Court's decision on education has set us back a generation in race relations, that people of different races who had long lived at peace have now been turned against one another. But this is a misinterpretation of what is taking place. When a subject people moves toward freedom, they are not creating a cleavage, but are revealing the cleavage which apologists of the old order have sought to conceal. It is not the movement for integration which is creating a cleavage in the United States today. The depth of the cleavage

that existed, the true nature of which the moderates failed to see and make clear, is being revealed by the resistance to integration.

During a crisis period, a desperate attempt is made by the extremists to influence the minds of the liberal forces in the ruling majority. So, for example, in the present transition white Southerners attempt to convince Northern whites that the Negroes are inherently criminal. They seek instances of Negro crime and juvenile delinquency in Northern communities and then say: "You see, the Negroes are problems to you. They create problems wherever they go." The accusation is made without reference to the true nature of the situation. Environmental problems of delinquency are interpreted as evidence of racial criminality. Crises arising in Northern schools are interpreted as proofs that Negroes are inherently delinquent. The extremists do not recognize that these school problems are symptoms of urban dislocation rather than expressions of racial deficiency. Criminality and delinquency are not racial; poverty and ignorance breed crime whatever the racial group may be.

In the attempt to influence the minds of Northern and Southern liberals, the segregationists are often subtle and skillful. Those who are too smart to argue for the validity of segregation and racial inferiority on the basis of the Bible set forth their arguments on cultural and sociological grounds. The Negro is not ready for integration, they say, because of academic and cultural lags on the part of the Negro, the integration of schools will pull the white race down. They are never honest enough to admit that the academic and cultural lags in the Negro community are themselves the result of segregation and discrimination. The best way to solve any problem is to remove its cause. It is both rationally unsound and sociologically untenable to use the tragic effects of segregation as an argument for its continuation.

All of these calculated patterns—the defiance of Southern legislative bodies, the activities of White Supremacy organizations, and the distortions and rationalizations of the segregationists—have mounted up to massive resistance. This resistance grows out of the desperate attempt of the white South to perpetuate a system of human values that came into being under a feudalistic plantation system and which cannot survive in a day of growing urbanization and industrial expansion. These are the rock-bottom elements of the present crisis.

The schools of the South are the present storm center. Here the forces that stand for the best in our national life have been tragically ineffectual. A year after the Supreme Court had declared school segregation unconstitutional, it handed down a decree outlining the details by which integration should proceed "with all deliberate speed." While the Court did not set a definite deadline for the termination of this process, it did set a time for the beginning. It was clear that the Court had chosen this reasonable approach with the expectation that the forces of good will, would immediately get to work and prepare the communities for a smooth and peaceful transition.

But the forces of good will failed to come through. The Office of the President was appallingly silent, though just an occasional word from this powerful source, counseling the nation on the moral aspects of integration and the need for complying with the law, might have saved the South from much of its present confusion and terror. Other forces of justice also failed to act. It is true that immediately after the first decision was rendered, leading church, labor and social welfare leaders issued statements upholding the decision, and many supporting resolutions were adopted by their organizations. But hardly a single group set forth an action program wherein their members could actively work to bring about a peaceable transition. Neither did they develop a plan whereby individuals in Southern communities who were willing to work for desegregation could receive organization support in the face of economic reprisals and physical violence.

As a result of the failure of the moral forces of the nation to mobilize behind school integration, the forces of defeat were given the chance to organize and crystallize their opposition. While the good people stood silently and complacently by, the misguided people acted. If every church and synagogue had developed an action program; if every civic and social welfare organization, every labor union and educational institution had worked out concrete plans for implementing their righteous resolutions; if the press, radio, and television had turned their powerful instruments in the direction of educating and elevating the people on this issue; if the President and the Congress had taken a forthright stand; if these things had happened, federal troops might not have been forced to walk the corridors of Central High School.

But it is still not too late to act. Every crisis has both its dangers and opportunities. It can spell either salvation or doom. In the present crisis America can achieve either racial justice or the ultimate social psychosis that can only lead to domestic suicide. The democratic ideal of freedom and equality will be fulfilled for all —or all human beings will share in the resulting social and spiritual doom. In short, this crisis has the potential for democracy's fulfillment or fascism's triumph; for social progress or retrogression. We can choose either to walk the high road of human brotherhood or to tread the low road of man's inhumanity to man.

History has thrust upon our generation an indescribably important destiny—to complete a process of democratization which our nation has too long developed too slowly, but which is our most powerful weapon for world respect and emulation. How we deal with this crucial situation will determine our moral health as individuals, our cultural health as a region, our political health as a nation, and our prestige as a leader of the free world. The future of America is bound up with the solution of the present crisis. The shape of the world today does not permit us the luxury of a faltering democracy. The United States cannot hope to attain the respect of the vital and growing colored nations of the world unless it remedies its racial problems at home. If America is to remain a first-class nation, it cannot have a second-class citizenship.

A solution of the present crisis will not take place unless men and women work for it. Human progress is neither automatic nor inevitable. Even a superficial look at history reveals that no social advance rolls in on the wheels of inevitability. Every step toward the goal of justice requires sacrifice, suffering, and struggle, the tireless exertions and passionate concern of dedicated individuals. Without persistent effort, time itself becomes an ally of the insurgent and primitive forces of irrational emotionalism and social destruction. This is no time for apathy or complacency. This is a time for vigorous and positive action.

It is the shame of the sunshine patriots if the foregoing paragraphs have a hollow sound, like an echo of countless political speeches. These things must be repeated time and again for men forget quickly; but once said, they must be followed with a dynamic program or else they become a refuge for those who shy from any action. If America is to respond creatively to the present crisis, many groups and agencies must rise above the reiteration of generalities and begin to take an active part in changing the face of their nation.

First, there is need for strong and aggressive leadership from the federal government. If the executive and legislative branches were as concerned about the protection of the citizenship rights of all people as the federal courts have been, the transition from a segregated to an integrated society would be much further along than it is today. The dearth of positive leadership from Washington is not confined to one political party. Both major parties have lagged in the service of justice. Many Democrats have betrayed it by capitulating to the undemocratic practices of the Southern Dixiecrats. Many Republicans have betrayed it by capitulating to the hypocrisy of right-wing Northerners.

In spite of the crucial role of the federal judiciary in this tense period of transition, the courts cannot do the job alone. The courts can clarify constitutional principles and remove the legal basis for segregation, but they cannot write laws, appoint administrators, or enforce justice on the local level.

The states and localities have the powers if they choose to exercise them. But the Southern states have made their policy clear. States' rights, they say in effect, include the right to abrogate power when it involves distasteful responsibilities, even to the Constitution of the United States, its amendments, and its judicial interpretation. So the power and the responsibility return by default to the federal government. It is up to all branches of the central government to accept the challenge.

Government action is not the whole answer to the present crisis, but it is an important partial answer. Morals cannot be legislated, but behavior can be regulated. The law cannot make an employer love me, but it can keep him from refusing to hire me because of the color of my skin. We must depend on religion and education to alter the errors of the heart and mind; but meanwhile it is an immoral act to compel a man to accept injustice until another man's heart is set straight. As the experience of several Northern states has shown, anti-discrimination laws can provide powerful sanctions against this kind of immorality.

Moreover, the law itself is a form of education. The words of the Supreme Court, of Con-

gress, and of the Constitution are eloquent instructors. In fact, it would be a mistake to minimize the impact upon the South of the federal court orders and legislative and executive acts already in effect. Desegregation of the armed services, for instance, has already had an immense, incalculable impact. Federal court decrees have altered transportation patterns, teachers' salaries, the use of recreational facilities, and myriad other matters. The habits if not the hearts of people have been and are being altered every day by federal action.

Another group with a vital role to play in the present crisis are the white Northern liberals. The racial issue that we confront in America is not a sectional but a national problem. The citizenship rights of Negroes cannot be flouted anywhere without impairing the rights of every other American. Injustice anywhere is a threat to justice everywhere. A breakdown of law in Alabama weakens the very foundations of lawful government in the other forty-seven states. The mere fact that we live in the United States means that we are caught in a network of inescapable mutuality. Therefore, no American can afford to be apathetic about the problem of racial justice. It is a problem that meets every man at his front door. The racial problem will be solved in America to the degree that every American considers himself personally confronted with it. Whether one lives in the heart of the Deep South or on the periphery of the North, the problem of injustice is his problem; it is his problem because it is America's problem.

There is a pressing need for a liberalism in the North which is truly liberal, a liberalism that firmly believes in integration in its own community as well as in the Deep South. It is one thing to agree that the goal of integration is morally and legally right; it is another thing to commit oneself positively and actively to the ideal of integration—the former is intellectual assent, the latter is actual belief. These are days that demand practices to match professions. This is no day to pay lip service to integration, we must pay *life* service to it.

Today in all too many Northern communities a sort of quasiliberalism prevails, so bent on seeing all sides that it fails to become dedicated to any side. It is so objectively analytical that it is not subjectively committed. A true liberal will not be deterred by the propaganda and subtle words of those who say, "Slow up for a while; you are pushing things too fast." I am not calling for an end to sympathetic understanding and abiding patience; but neither sympathy nor patience should be used as excuses for indecisiveness. They must be guiding principles for all of our actions, rather than substitutes for action itself.

A significant role in this tense period of transition is assigned to the moderates of the white South. Unfortunately today, the leadership of the white South is by and large in the hands of closed-minded extremists. These persons gain prominence and power by the dissemination of false ideas, and by appealing to the deepest fears and hates within the human mind. But they do not speak for the South; of that I am convinced. They speak only for a willful and vocal minority.

Even the most casual observer can see that the South has marvelous possibilities. It is rich in natural resources, blessed with the beauties of nature, and endowed with a native warmth of spirit. Yet in spite of these assets, it is retarded by a blight that debilitates not only the Negro but also the white man. Poor white men, women, and children, bearing the scars of ignorance, deprivation, and poverty, are evidence of the fact that harm to one is injury to all. Segregation has placed the whole South socially, educationally, and economically behind the rest of the nation.

Yet actually, there is no single "solid" South; there are at least three, geographically speaking. There is the South of compliance—Oklahoma, Kentucky, Kansas, Missouri, West Virginia, Delaware, and the District of Columbia. There is the wait-and-see South—Tennessee, Texas, North Carolina, Arkansas, and Florida. And there is the South of resistance—Georgia, Alabama, Mississippi, Louisiana, South Carolina, and Virginia.

Just as there are three Souths geographically, there are several Souths in terms of attitudes. A minority in each of these states would use almost any means, including physical violence, to preserve segregation. A majority, through tradition and custom, sincerely believe in segregation, but at the same time stand on the side of law and order. Hence, they are willing to comply with the law not because they feel it is sound but because it is the law. A third group, a growing minority, is working courageously and conscientiously to implement the law of the land. These people believe in the morality as well as the constitutionality of integration. Their still small voices often go unheard among the louder shouts of defiance, but they are actively in the field.

Furthermore there are in the white South millions of people of good will whose voices are yet unheard, whose course is yet unclear, and whose courageous acts are yet unseen. These persons are often silent today because of fear—fear of social, political, and economic reprisals. In the name of God, in the interest of human dignity, and for the cause of democracy these millions are called upon to gird their courage, to speak out, to offer the leadership that is needed. Still another South calls upon them: The colored South, the South of millions of Negroes whose sweat and blood has also built Dixie, who yearns for brotherhood and respect, who want to join hands with their white fellow Southerners to build a freer, happier land for all. If the moderates of the white South fail to act now, history will have to record that the greatest tragedy of this period of social transition was not the strident clamor of the bad people, but the appalling silence of the good people. Our generation will have to repent not only for the acts and words of the children of darkness but also for the fears and apathy of the children of light.

Who can best lead the South out of the social and economic quagmire? Her native sons. Those who were born and bred on her rich and fertile soil; those who love her because they were nurtured by her. Through love, patience, and understanding good will they can call their brothers to a way of noble living. This hour represents a great opportunity for the white moderates, if they will only speak the truth, obey the law, and suffer if necessary for what they know is right.

Still another agency of effective change today is the labor movement. Across the years the Negro has been a perpetual victim of economic exploitation. Prior to the Civil War the slaves worked under a system which offered neither compensation nor civil rights. Since emancipation the Negro American has continued to suffer under an essentially unreconstructed economy. He was freed without land or legal protection, and was made an outcast entitled only to the most menial jobs. Even the federal government that set him free failed to work out any long-range policy that would guarantee economic resources to a previously enslaved people—as much entitled to the land they had worked as were their former owners. The exploitation of the Negro population per-

sisted through the Reconstruction period and
continues down to the present day.

Labor unions can play a tremendous role in
making economic justice a reality for the
Negro. Trade unions are engaged in a struggle
to advance the economic welfare of those
American citizens whose wages are their livelihood. Since the American Negro is virtually
nonexistent as the owner and manager of mass
production industry, he must depend on the
payment of wages for his economic survival.

There are in the United States 16.5 million
members of approximately 150 bona fide trade
unions. Of this number 142 are national and
international affiliated organizations of the
AFL-CIO. The unions forming the AFL-CIO
include 1.3 million Negroes among their 13.5
million members. Only the combined religious
institutions serving the Negro community can
claim a greater membership of Negroes. The
Negro then has the right to expect the resources of the American trade union movement
to be used in assuring him—like all the rest of
its members—a proper place in American society. He has gained this right along with all
the other workers whose mutual efforts have
built this country's free and democratic trade
unions.

Economic insecurity strangles the physical
and cultural growth of its victims. Not only are
millions deprived of formal education and
proper health facilities but our most fundamental social unit—the family—is tortured, corrupted, and weakened by economic insufficiency. When a Negro man is inadequately
paid, his wife must work to provide the simple
necessities for the children. When a mother has
to work she does violence to motherhood by depriving her children of her loving guidance and
protection; often they are poorly cared for by
others or by none—left to roam the streets un-
supervised. It is not the Negro alone who is
wronged by a disrupted society; many white
families are in similar straits. The Negro mother
leaves home to care for—and be a substitute
mother—to white children, while the white
mother works. In this strange irony lies the
promise of future corrections.

Both Negro and white workers are equally
oppressed. For both, the living standards need
to be raised to levels consistent with our national resources. Not logic but a hollow social
distinction has separated the races. The economically depressed white accepts his poverty
by telling himself that, if in no other respect, at

least socially he is above the Negro. For this
empty pride in a racial myth he has paid the
crushing price of insecurity, hunger, ignorance,
and hopelessness for himself and his children.

Strong ties must be made between those
whites and Negroes who have problems in common. White and Negro workers have mutual
aspirations for a fairer share of the products of
industries and farms. Both seek job security,
old-age security, health and welfare protection.
The organized labor movement, which has contributed so much to the economic security and
well-being of millions, must concentrate its
powerful forces on bringing economic emancipation to white and Negro by organizing them
together in social equality.

Certainly the labor movement has already
made significant moves in this direction. Virtually every national or international union has
clear policies of nondiscrimiaation, and the national leaders of AFL-CIO have proclaimed the
ultimate objective of eliminating racial bias not
only from the American labor movement but
also from American society as a whole. But in
spite of this stand, some unions, governed by
the racist ethos, have contributed to the degraded economic status of the Negroes. Negroes
have been barred from membership in certain
unions, and denied apprenticeship training and
vocational education. In every section of the
country one can find local unions existing as a
serious and vicious obstacle when the Negro
seeks jobs or upgrading in employment. The
AFL-CIO drive to organize the South has been
virtually abandoned because of the massive
resistance of a significant portion of the organized labor oligarchy, many of whom have
been active in White Citizens Councils.

The existence of these conditions within the
ranks of labor reveals that the job is a continuing one. The AFL-CIO must use all of the
powerful forces at its command to enforce the
principles it has professed. Labor leaders must
continue to recognize that labor has a great
stake in the struggle for civil rights, if only
because the forces that are anti-Negro are usually anti-labor too. The current attacks on organized labor because of the misdeeds of a few
malefactors should not blind us to labor's essential role in the present crisis.

The church too must face its historic obligation in this crisis. In the final analysis, the problem of race is not a political but a moral issue.
Indeed, as the Swedish economist Gunnar
Myrdal has pointed out, the problem of race is

America's greatest moral dilemma. This tragic dilemma presents the church with a great challenge. The broad universalism standing at the center of the gospel makes segregation morally unjustifiable. Racial segregation is a blatant denial of the unity which we have in Christ; for in Christ there is neither Jew nor Gentile, bond nor free, Negro nor white. Segregation scars the soul of both the segregator and the segregated. The segregator looks upon the segregated as a thing to be used, not a person to be respected. Segregation substitutes an "I-it" relationship for the "I-thou" relationship. Thus it is utterly opposed to the noble teachings of our Judeo-Christian tradition.

It has always been the responsibility of the church to broaden horizons, challenge the status quo, and break the mores when necessary. The task of conquering segregation is an inescapable *must* confronting the church today.

There are several specific things that the church can do. First it should try to get to the ideational roots of race hate, something that the law cannot accomplish. All race prejudice is based upon fears, suspicions, and misunderstandings, usually groundless. The church can be of immeasurable help in giving the popular mind direction here. Through its channels of religious education, the church can point out the irrationality of these beliefs. It can show that the idea of a superior or inferior race is a myth that has been completely refuted by anthropological evidence. It can show that Negroes are not innately inferior in academic, health, and moral standards. It can show that, when given equal opportunities, Negroes can demonstrate equal achievement.

The church can also do a great deal to reveal the true intentions of the Negro—that he is not seeking to dominate the nation, but simply wants the right to live as a first-class citizen, with all the responsibilities that good citizenship entails. The church can also help by mitigating the prevailing and irrational fears concerning intermarriage. It can say to men that marriage is an individual matter that must be decided on the merits of individual cases. Properly speaking, races do not marry; individuals marry. Marriage is a condition which requires the voluntary consent of two contracting parties, and either side can always say no. The church can reveal that the continual outcry concerning inter-marriage is a distortion of the real issue. It can point out that the Negro's primary aim is to be the white man's brother, not his brother-in-law.

Another thing that the church can do to make the principle of brotherhood a reality is to keep men's minds and visions centered on God. Many of the problems America now confronts can be explained in terms of fear. There is not only the job of freeing the Negro from the bondage of segregation but also the responsibility of freeing his white brothers from the bondage of fears concerning integration. One of the best ways to rid oneself of fear is to center one's life in the will and purpose of God. "Perfect love casteth out fear."

When people think about race problems they are too often more concerned with men than with God. The question usually asked is: "What will my friends think if I am too friendly to Negroes or too liberal on the race question?" Men forget to ask: "What will God think?" And so they live in fear because they tend to seek social approval on the horizontal plane rather than spiritual devotion on the vertical plane.

The church must remind its worshipers that man finds greater security in devoting his life to the eternal demands of the Almighty God than in giving his ultimate allegiance to the transitory demands of man. The church must continually say to Christians, "Yet you are a colony of heaven." True, man has a dual citizenry. He lives both in time and in eternity; both in heaven and on earth. But he owes his ultimate allegiance to God. It is this love for God and devotion to his will that casts out fear.

A further effort that the church can make in attempting to solve the race problem is to take the lead in social reform. It is not enough for the church to be active in the realm of ideas; it must move out into the arena of social action. First, the church must remove the yoke of segregation from its own body. Only by doing this can it be effective in its attack on outside evils. Unfortunately, most of the major denominations still practice segregation in local churches, hospitals, schools, and other church institutions. It is appalling that the most segregated hour of Christian America is eleven o'clock on Sunday morning, the same hour when many are standing to sing, "In Christ there is no East nor West." Equally appalling is the fact that the most segregated school of the week is the Sunday School. How often the church has had a high blood count of creeds and an anemia of deeds! Dean Liston Pope of the Yale Divinity School rightly says in *The Kingdom beyond*

Caste: "The church is the most segregated major institution in American society. It has lagged behind the Supreme Court as the conscience of the nation on questions of race, and it has fallen far behind trade unions, factories, schools, department stores, athletic gatherings and most other major areas of human association as far as the achievement of integration in its own life is concerned."

10   There has been some progress. Here and there churches are courageously making attacks on segregation, and actually integrating their congregations. The National Council of Churches has repeatedly condemned segregation and has requested its constituent denominations to do likewise. Most of the major denominations have endorsed that action. The Roman Catholic Church has declared, "Segregation is morally wrong and sinful." All this is
20 admirable. But these stands are still far too few, and they move all too slowly down to the local churches in actual practice. The church has a schism in its own soul that it must close. It will be one of the tragedies of Christian history if a future Gibbon is able to say that at the height of the twentieth century the church proved to be one of the greatest bulwarks of segregated power.

The church must also become increasingly
30 active in social action outside its doors. It must seek to keep channels of communication open between the Negro and white community. It must take an active stand against the injustice that Negroes confront in housing, education, police protection, and in city and state courts. It must exert its influence in the area of economic justice. As guardian of the moral and spiritual life of the community the church cannot look with indifference upon these glaring
40 evils.

It is impossible to speak of the role of the church without referring to the ministers. Every minister of the gospel has a mandate to stand up courageously for righteousness, to proclaim the eternal verities of the gospel, and to lead men from the darkness of falsehood and fear to the light of truth and love.

In the South this mandate presents white ministers with a difficult choice. Many who be-
50 lieve segregation to be directly opposed to the will of God and the spirit of Christ are faced with the painful alternative of taking a vocal stand and being fired or staying quiet in order to remain in the situation and do some good. Pastors who have adopted the latter course feel

that if they were forced out of their churches their successors would in all probability be segregationist, thus setting the Christian cause back. Many ministers have kept their peace not merely to save a job but because they feel that restraint is the best way to serve the cause of Christ in the South. In quiet, unpublicized ways, many of these ministers are making for a better day and helpfully molding the minds of young people. These men should not be criticized.

In the final analysis every white minister in the South must decide for himself which course he will follow. There is no single right strategy. The important thing is for every minister to dedicate himself to the Christian ideal of brotherhood, and be sure that he is doing something positive to implement it. He must never allow the theory that it is better to remain quiet and help the cause to become a rationalization for doing nothing. Many ministers can do much more than they are doing and still hold their congregations. There is a great deal that ministers can achieve collectively. In every Southern city there should be interracial ministerial associations in which Negro and white ministers can come together in Christian fellowship and discuss common community problems. One of the most disappointing experiences of the Montgomery struggle was the fact that we could not get the white ministerial association to sit down with us and discuss our problem. With individual exceptions the white ministers from whom I had naively expected so much, gave little.

Ministers can also collectively call for compliance with the law and a cessation of violence. This has been done by white ministers of Atlanta, Richmond, Dallas, and other cities, and not a single one has, to my knowledge, lost his job. It is difficult for a denomination to fire all of its ministers in a city. If ever the white ministers of the South decide to declare in a united voice the truth of the gospel on the question of race, the transition from a segregated to an integrated society will be infinitely smoother.

Any discussion of the role of the Christian minister today must ultimately emphasize the need for prophecy. Not every minister can be a prophet, but some must be prepared for the ordeals of this high calling and be willing to suffer courageously for righteousness. May the problem of race in America soon make hearts burn so that prophets will rise up, saying, "Thus saith the Lord," and cry out as Amos did, ". . . let justice roll down like waters and righteousness like an ever-flowing stream."

Fortunately, a few in the South have already been willing to follow this prophetic way. I have nothing but praise for these ministers of the gospel of Jesus Christ and rabbis of the Jewish faith who have stood unflinchingly before threats and intimidations, inconvenience and unpopularity, even at times in physical danger, to declare the doctrine of the Fatherhood of God and the brotherhood of man. For such noble servants of God there is the consolation of the words of Jesus: "Blessed are ye, when men shall revile you, and persecute you, and shall say all manner of evil against you falsely, for my sake. Rejoice, and be exceeding glad: for great is your reward in heaven: for so persecuted they the prophets which were before you."

Here, then, is the hard challenge and the sublime opportunity: to let the spirit of Christ work toward fashioning a truly great Christian nation. If the church accepts the challenge with devotion and valor, the day will be speeded when men everywhere will recognize that they "are all one in Christ Jesus."

Finally, the Negro himself has a decisive role to play if integration is to become a reality. Indeed, if first-class citizenship is to become a reality for the Negro he must assume the primary responsibility for making it so. Integration is not some lavish dish that the federal government or the white liberal will pass out on a silver platter while the Negro merely furnishes the appetite. One of the most damaging effects of past segregation on the personality of the Negro may well be that he has been victimized with the delusion that others should be more concerned than himself about his citizenship rights.

In this period of social change, the Negro must come to see that there is much he himself can do about his plight. He may be uneducated or poverty-stricken, but these handicaps must not prevent him from seeing that he has within his being the power to alter his fate. The Negro can take direct action against injustice without waiting for the government to act or a majority to agree with him or a court to rule in his favor. Oppressed people deal with their oppression in three characteristic ways. One way is acquiescence: the oppressed resign themselves to their doom. They tacitly adjust themselves to oppression, and thereby become conditioned to it. In every movement toward freedom some of the oppressed prefer to remain oppressed. Almost 2800 years ago Moses set out to lead the children of Israel from the slavery of Egypt to the freedom of the promised land. He soon discovered that slaves do not always welcome their deliverers. They become accustomed to being slaves. They would rather bear those ills they have, as Shakespeare pointed out, than flee to others that they know not of. They prefer the "fleshpots of Egypt" to the ordeals of emancipation.

There is no such thing as the freedom of exhaustion. Some people are so worn down by the yoke of oppression that they give up. A few years ago in the slum areas of Atlanta, a Negro guitarist used a sing almost daily: "Ben down so long that down don't bother me." This is the type of negative freedom and resignation that often engulfs the life of the oppressed.

But this is not the way out. To accept passively an unjust system is to co-operate with that system; thereby the oppressed become as evil as the oppressor. Non-co-operation with evil is as much a moral obligation as is cooperation with good. The oppressed must never allow the conscience of the oppressor to slumber. Religion reminds every man that he is his brother's keeper. To accept injustice or segregation passively is to say to the oppressor that his actions are morally right. It is a way of allowing his conscience to fall asleep. At this moment the oppressed fails to be his brother's keeper. So acquiescence—while often the easier way—is not the moral way. It is the way of the coward. The Negro cannot win the respect of his oppressor by acquiescing; he merely increases the oppressor's arrogance and contempt. Acquiescence is interpreted as proof of the Negro's inferiority. The Negro cannot win the respect of the white people of the South or the peoples of the world if he is willing to sell the future of his children for his personal and immediate comfort and safety.

A second way that oppressed people sometimes deal with oppression is to resort to physical violence and corroding hatred. Violence often brings about momentary results. Nations have frequently won their independence in battle. But in spite of temporary victories, violence never brings permanent peace. It solves no social problem; it merely creates new and more complicated ones.

Violence as a way of achieving racial justice is both impractical and immoral. It is impractical because it is a descending spiral ending in destruction for all. The old law of an eye for an eye leaves everybody blind. It is immoral because it seeks to humiliate the opponent rather than win his understanding; it seeks to annihilate rather than to convert. Violence is immoral because it thrives on hatred rather than love. It destroys community and makes brotherhood impossible. It leaves society in monologue rather than dialogue. Violence ends by defeating itself. It creates bitterness in the survivors and brutality in the destroyers. A voice echoes through time saying to every potential Peter, "Put up your sword." History is cluttered with the wreckage of nations that failed to follow this command.

If the American Negro and other victims of oppression succumb to the temptation of using violence in the struggle for freedom, future generations will be the recipients of a desolate night of bitterness, and our chief legacy to them will be an endless reign of meaningless chaos. Violence is not the way.

The third way open to oppressed people in their quest for freedom is the way of nonviolent resistence. Like the synthesis in Hegelian philosophy, the principle of nonviolent resistance seeks to reconcile the truths of two opposites— acquiescence and violence—while avoiding the extremes and immoralities of both. The nonviolent resister agrees with the person who acquiesces that one should not be physically aggressive toward his opponent; but he balances the equation by agreeing with the person of violence that evil must be resisted. He avoids the nonresistance of the former and the violent resistance of the latter. With nonviolent resistance, no individual or group need submit to any wrong, nor need anyone resort to violence in order to right a wrong.

It seems to me that this is the method that must guide the actions of the Negro in the present crisis in race relations. Through nonviolent resistance the Negro will be able to rise to the noble height of opposing the unjust system while loving the perpetrators of the system. The Negro must work passionately and unrelentingly for full stature as a citizen, but he must not use inferior methods to gain it. He must never come to terms with falsehood, malice, hate, or destruction.

Nonviolent resistance makes it possible for the Negro to remain in the South and struggle for his rights. The Negro's problem will not be solved by running away. He cannot listen to the glib suggestion of those who would urge him to migrate en masse to other sections of the country. By grasping his great opportunity in the South he can make a lasting contribution to the moral strength of the nation and set a sublime example of courage for generations yet unborn.

By nonviolent resistance, the Negro can also enlist all men of good will in his struggle for equality. The problem is not a purely racial one, with Negroes set against whites. In the end, it is not a struggle between people at all, but a tension between justice and injustice. Nonviolent resistance is not aimed against oppressors but against oppression. Under its banner, consciences and not racial groups are enlisted.

If the Negro is to achieve the goal of integration, he must organize himself into a militant and nonviolent mass movement. All three elements are indispensable. The movement for equality and justice can only be a success if it has both a mass and militant character; the barriers to be overcome require both. Nonviolence is an imperative in order to bring about ultimate community.

A mass movement of a militant quality that is not at the same time committed to nonviolence tends to generate conflict, which in turn breeds anarchy. The support of the participants and the sympathy of the uncommitted are both inhibited by the threat that bloodshed will engulf the community. This reaction in turn encourages the opposition to threaten and resort to force. When, however, the mass movement repudiates violence while moving resolutely toward its goal, its opponents are revealed as the instigators and practitioners of violence if it occurs. Then public support is magnetically attracted to the advocates of nonviolence, while those who employ violence are literally disarmed by overwhelming sentiment against their stand.

Only through a nonviolent approach can the fears of the white community be mitigated. A guilt-ridden white minority lives in fear that if the Negro should ever attain power, he would act without restraint or pity to revenge the injustices and brutality of the years. It is something like a parent who continually mistreats a son. One day that parent raises his hand to strike the son, only to discover that the son is now as tall as he is. The parent is suddenly afraid—fearful that the son will use his new physical power to repay his parent for all the blows of the past.

The Negro, once a helpless child, has now grown up politically, culturally, and economically. Many white men fear retaliation. The job of the Negro is to show them that they have nothing to fear, that the Negro understands and forgives and is ready to forget the past. He must convince the white man that all he seeks is justice *for both himself and the white man.* A mass movement exercising nonviolence is an object lesson in power under discipline, a demonstration to the white community that if such a movement attained a degree of strength, it would use its power creatively and not vengefully.

Nonviolence can touch men where the law cannot reach them. When the law regulates behavior it plays an indirect part in molding public sentiment. The enforcement of the law is itself a form of peaceful persuasion. But the law needs help. The courts can order desegregation of the public schools. But what can be done to mitigate the fears, to disperse the hatred, violence, and irrationality gathered around school integration, to take the initiative out of the hands of racial demagogues, to release respect for the law? In the end, for laws to be obeyed, men must believe they are right.

Here nonviolence comes in as the ultimate form of persuasion. It is the method which seeks to implement the just law by appealing to the conscience of the great decent majority who through blindness, fear, pride, or irrationality have allowed their consciences to sleep.

The nonviolent resisters can summarize their message in the following simple terms: We will take direct action against injustice without waiting for other agencies to act. We will not obey unjust laws or submit to unjust practices. We will do this peacefully, openly, cheerfully because our aim is to persuade. We adopt the means of nonviolence because our end is a community at peace with itself. We will try to persuade with our words, but if our words fail, we will try to persuade with our acts. We will always be willing to talk and seek fair compromise, but we are ready to suffer when necessary and even to risk our lives to become witnesses to the truth as we see it.

The way of nonviolence means a willingness to suffer and sacrifice. It may mean going to jail. If such is the case the resister must be willing to fill the jail houses of the South. It may even mean physical death. But if physical death is the price that a man must pay to free his children and his white brethren from a permanent death of the spirit, then nothing could be more redemptive.

What is the Negro's best defense against acts of violence inflicted upon him? As Dr. Kenneth Clark has said so eloquently, "His only defense is to meet every act of barbarity, illegality, cruelty and injustice toward an individual Negro with the fact that 100 more Negroes will present themselves in his place as potential victims." Every time one Negro school teacher is fired for believing in integration, a thousand others should be ready to take the same stand. If the oppressors bomb the home of one Negro for his protest, they must be made to realize that to press back the rising tide of the Negro's courage they will have to bomb hundreds more, and even then they will fail.

Faced with this dynamic unity, this amazing self-respect, this willingness to suffer, and this refusal to hit back, the oppressor will find, as oppressors have always found, that he is glutted with his own barbarity. Forced to stand before the world and his God splattered with the blood of his brother, he will call an end to his self-defeating massacre.

American Negroes must come to the point where they can say to their white brothers, paraphrasing the words of Gandhi: "We will match your capacity to inflict suffering with our capacity to endure suffering. We will meet your physical force with soul force. We will not hate you, but we cannot in all good conscience obey your unjust laws. Do to us what you will and we will still love you. Bomb our homes and threaten our children; send your hooded perpetrators of violence into our communities and drag us out on some wayside road, beating us and leaving us half dead, and we will still love you. But we will soon wear you down by our capacity to suffer. And in winning our freedom we will so appeal to your heart and conscience that we will win you in the process."

Realism impels me to admit that many Negroes will find it difficult to follow the path of nonviolence. Some will consider it senseless; some will argue that they have neither the strength nor the courage to join in such a mass demonstration of nonviolent action. As E. Franklin Frazier points out in *Black Bourgeoisie,* many Negroes are occupied in a middle-class struggle for status and prestige. They are more concerned about "conspicuous consumption" than about the cause of justice and are probably not prepared for the ordeals and sacrifices involved in nonviolent action. Fortunately, however, the success of this method is not dependent on its unanimous acceptance. A few Negroes in every community, unswervingly committed to the nonviolent way, can persuade hundreds of others at least to use nonviolence as a technique and serve as the moral force to awaken the slumbering national conscience. Thoreau was thinking of such a creative minority when he said:

I know this well, that if one thousand, if one hundred, if ten men whom I could name—if ten honest men only—aye, if one honest man, in the state of Massachusetts, ceasing to hold slaves were actually to withdraw from the copartnership, and be locked up in the county jail therefore, it would be the abolition of slavery in America. For it matters not how small the beginning may seem to be, what is once well done is done forever.

Mahatma Gandhi never had more than one hundred persons absolutely committed to his philosophy. But with this small group of devoted followers, he galvanized the whole of India, and through a magnificent feat of nonviolence challenged the might of the British Empire and won freedom for his people.

This method of nonviolence will not work miracles overnight. Men are not easily moved from their mental ruts, their prejudiced and irrational feelings. When the underprivileged demand freedom, the privileged first react with bitterness and resistance. Even when the demands are couched in nonviolent terms, the initial response is the same. Nehru once remarked that the British were never so angry as when the Indians resisted them with nonviolence, that he never saw eyes so full of hate as those of the British troops to whom he turned the other cheek when they beat him with lathis. But nonviolent resistance at least changed the minds and hearts of the Indians, however impervious the British may have appeared. "We cast away our fear," says Nehru. And in the end the British not only granted freedom to India but came to have a new respect for the Indians. Today a mutual friendship based on complete equality exists between these two peoples within the Commonwealth.

In the South, too, the initial white reaction to Negro resistance has been bitter. I do not predict that a similar happy ending will come to Montgomery in a few months because integration is more complicated than independence. But I know that the Negroes of Montgomery are already walking straighter because of the protest. And I expect that this generation of Negro children throughout the United States will grow up stronger and better because of the courage, the dignity, and the suffering of the nine children of Little Rock, and their counterparts in Nashville, Clinton, and Sturgis. And I believe that the white people of this country are being affected too, that beneath the surface this nation's conscience is being stirred.

The nonviolent approach does not immediately change the heart of the oppressor. It first does something to the hearts and souls of those committed to it. It gives them new self-respect, it calls up resources of strength and courage that they did not know they had. Finally it reaches the opponent and so stirs his conscience that reconciliation becomes a reality.

I suggest this approach because I think it is the only way to re-establish the broken community. Court orders and federal enforcement agencies will be of inestimable value in achieving desegregation. But desegregation is only a partial, though necessary, step toward the ultimate goal which we seek to realize. Desegregation will break down the legal barriers, and bring men together physically. But something must happen so to touch the hearts and souls of men that they will come together, not because the law says it, but because it is natural and right. In other words, our ultimate goal is integration which is genuine intergroup and interpersonal living. Only through nonviolence can this goal be attained for the aftermath of nonviolence is reconciliation and the creation of the beloved community.

It is becoming clear that the Negro is in for a season of suffering. As victories for civil rights mount in the federal courts, angry passions and deep prejudices are further aroused. The mountain of state and local segregation laws still stands. Negro leaders continue to be arrested and harassed under city ordinances, and their homes continue to be bombed. State laws continue to be enacted to circumvent integration. I pray that, recognizing the necessity of suffering, the Negro will make of it a virtue. To suffer in a righteous cause is to grow to our humanity's full stature. If only to save himself from bitterness, the Negro needs the vision to see the ordeals of this generation as the opportunity to transfigure himself and American society. If he has to go to jail for the cause of freedom, let him enter it in the fashion Gandhi urged his countrymen, "as the bridegroom enters the bride's chamber"—that is, with a little trepidation but with great expectation.

Nonviolence is a way of humility and self-restraint. We Negroes talk a great deal about our rights, and rightly so. We proudly proclaim that three-fourths of the people of the world are colored. We have the privilege of watching in our generation the great drama of freedom and independence as it unfolds in Asia and Africa. All of these things are in line with the work of providence. We must be sure, however, that we accept them in the right spirit. In an effort to achieve freedom in America, Asia, and Africa we must not try to leap from a position of disadvantage to one of advantage, thus subverting justice. We must seek democracy and not the substitution of one tyranny for another. Our aim must never be to defeat or humiliate the white man. We must not become victimized with a philosophy of black supremacy. God is not interested merely in the freedom of black men, and brown men, and yellow men. God is interested in the freedom of the whole human race.

The nonviolent approach provides an answer to the long debated question of gradualism *versus* immediacy. On the one hand it prevents one from falling into the sort of patience which is an excuse for do-nothingism and escapism, ending up in standstillism. On the other hand it saves one from the irresponsible words which estrange without reconciling and the hasty judgment which is blind to the necessities of social process. It recognizes the need for moving toward the goal of justice with wise restraint and calm reasonableness. But it also recognizes the immorality of slowing up in the move toward justice and capitulating to the guardians of an unjust status quo. It recognizes that social change cannot come overnight. But it causes one to work as if it were a possibility the next morning.

Through nonviolence we avoid the temptation of taking on the psychology of victors. Thanks largely to the noble and invaluable work of the NAACP, we have won great victories in the federal courts. But we must not be self-satisfied. We must respond to every decision with an understanding of those who have opposed us, and with acceptance of the new adjustments that the court orders pose for them. We must act in such a way that our victories will be triumphs for good will in all men, white and Negro.

Nonviolence is essentially a positive concept. Its corollary must always be growth. On the one hand nonviolence requires non-co-operation with evil; on the other hand it requires co-operation with the constructive forces of good. Without this constructive aspect non-co-opera-

tion ends where it begins. Therefore, the Negro must get to work on a program with a broad range of positive goals.

One point in the Negro's program should be a plan to improve his own economic lot. Through the establishment of credit unions, savings and loan associations, and co-operative enterprises, the Negro can greatly improve his economic status. He must develop habits of thrift and techniques of wise investment. He 10 must not wait for the end of the segregation that lies at the basis of his economic deprivation; he must act now to lift himself up by his own bootstraps.

The constructive program ahead must include a campaign to get Negroes to register and vote. Certainly they face many external barriers. All types of underhand methods are still being used in the South to prevent the Negroes from voting, and the success of these efforts is 20 not only unjust, it is a real embarrassment to the nation we love and must protect. The advocacy of free elections in Europe by American officials is hypocrisy when free elections are not held in great sections of America.

But external resistance is not the only present barrier to Negro voting. Apathy among the Negroes themselves is also a factor. Even where the polls are open to all, Negroes have shown themselves too slow to exercise their 30 voting privileges. There must be a concerted effort on the part of Negro leaders to arouse their people from their apathetic indifference to this obligation of citizenship. In the past, apathy was a moral failure. Today, it is a form of moral and political suicide.

The constructive program ahead must include a vigorous attempt to improve the Negro's personal standards. It must be reiterated that the standards of the Negro as a 40 group lag behind not because of an inherent inferiority, but because of the fact that segregation does exist. The "behavior deviants" within the Negro community stem from the economic deprivation, emotional frustration, and social isolation which are the inevitable concomitants of segregation. When the white man argues that segregation should continue because of the Negro's lagging standards, he fails to see that the standards lag because of segregation. 50

Yet Negroes must be honest enough to admit that our standards do often fall short. One of the sure signs of maturity is the ability to rise to the point of self-criticism. Whenever we are objects of criticism from white men, even though the criticisms are maliciously directed and mixed with half-truths, we must pick out the elements of truth and make them the basis of creative reconstruction. We must not let the fact that we are the victims of injustice lull us into abrogating responsibility for our own lives.

Our crime rate is far too high. Our level of cleanliness is frequently far too low. Too often those of us who are in the middle class live above our means, spend money on nonessentials and frivolities, and fail to give to serious causes, organizations, and educational institutions that so desperately need funds. We are too often loud and boisterous, and spend far too much on drink. Even the most poverty-stricken among us can purchase a ten-cent bar of soap; even the most uneducated among us can have high morals. Through community agencies and religious institutions Negro leaders must develop a positive program through which Negro youth can become adjusted to urban living and improve their general level of behavior. Since crime often grows out of a sense of futility and despair, Negro parents must be urged to give their children the love, attention, and sense of belonging that a segregated society deprives them of. By improving our standards here and now we will go a long way toward breaking down the arguments of the segregationist.

This then must be our present program: Nonviolent resistance to all forms of racial injustice, including state and local laws and practices, even when this means going to jail; and imaginative, bold, constructive action to end the demoralization caused by the legacy of slavery and segregation, inferior schools, slums, and second-class citizenship. The nonviolent struggle, if conducted with the dignity and courage already shown by the people of Montgomery and the children of Little Rock, will in itself help end the demoralization; but a new frontal assault on the poverty, disease, and ignorance of a people too long ignored by America's conscience will make victory more certain.

In short, we must work on two fronts. On the one hand, we must continue to resist the system of segregation which is the basic cause of our lagging standards; on the other hand we must work constructively to improve the standards themselves. There must be a rhythmic alternation between attacking the causes and healing the effects.

This is a great hour for the Negro. The challenge is here. To become the instruments of a great idea is a privilege that history gives only occasionally. Arnold Toynbee says in *A Study of History* that it may be the Negro who will give the new spiritual dynamic to Western civilization that it so desperately needs to survive. I hope this is possible. The spiritual power that the Negro can radiate to the world comes from love, understanding, good will, and nonviolence. It may even be possible for the Negro, through adherence to nonviolence, so to challenge the nations of the world that they will seriously seek an alternative to war and destruction. In a day when Sputniks and Explorers dash through outer space and guided ballistic missiles are carving highways of death through the stratosphere, nobody can win a war. Today the choice is no longer between violence and nonviolence. It is either nonviolence or nonexistence. The Negro may be God's appeal to this age—an age drifting rapidly to its doom. The eternal appeal takes the form of a warning: "All who take the sword will perish by the sword."

HERBERT RAVENEL SASS

1884–1958

HERBERT RAVENEL SASS, a distinguished Charlestonian, was a naturalist, novelist, and essayist. He was associated with the Charleston *News and Courier* and was an independent thinker and graceful writer. His essay, "Mixed Schools and Mixed Blood," which appeared in the November, 1956 issue of the *Atlantic Monthly*, presented the "racial" reasons for the opposition of a great many conservative white Southerners to the so-called school desegregation program. The Southern opposition to "mixed schools" also rested on the constitutional conviction that public education is a local, not a federal matter, and on what might be called "Southern nationalism."

Grey Eagle, New York, 1927.
Hear Me, My Chiefs!, New York, 1940.
Outspoken; 150 Years of the News and Courier, Columbia, South Carolina, 1953.
Saturday Evening Post, March 22, 1958.
New York Times, February 20, 1958.

MIXED SCHOOLS AND MIXED BLOOD

What may well be the most important physical fact in the story of the United States is one which is seldom emphasized in our history books. It is the fact that throughout the three and a half centuries of our existence we have kept our several races biologically distinct and separate. Though we have encouraged the mixing of many different strains in what has been called the American "melting pot," we have confined this mixing to the white peoples of European ancestry, excluding from our "melting pot" all other races. The result is that the United States today is overwhelmingly a pure white nation, with a smaller but considerable Negro population in which there is some white blood, and a much smaller American Indian population.

The fact that the United States is overwhelmingly pure white is not only important; it is also the most distinctive fact about this country when considered in relation to the rest of the New World. Except Canada, Argentina, and Uruguay, none of the approximately twenty-five other countries of this hemisphere has kept its races pure. Instead (though each contains some pure-blooded individuals) all these countries are products of an amalgamation of races—American Indian and white or American Indian, Negro, and white. In general the pure-blooded white nations have outstripped the far more numerous American mixed-blood nations in most of the achievements which constitute progress as commonly defined.

These facts are well known. But now there lurks in ambush, as it were, another fact: we have suddenly begun to move toward abandonment of our 350-year-old system of keeping our races pure and are preparing to adopt instead a method of racial amalgamation similar to that which has created the mixed-blood nations of this hemisphere; except that the amalgamation being prepared for this country is not Indian and white but Negro and white. It is the deep conviction of nearly all white Southerners that the mingling or integration of white and Negro children in the South's primary schools will open the gates to miscegenation and widespread racial amalgamation.

This belief is at the heart of our race problem, and until it is realized that this is the South's basic and compelling motive, there can be no understanding of the South's attitude.

It must be realized too, that the Negroes of the U.S.A. are today by far the most fortunate members of their race to be found anywhere on earth. Instead of being the hapless victim of unprecedented oppression, it is nearer the truth that the Negro in the United States is by and large the product of friendliness and helpfulness unequaled in any comparable instance in all history. Nowhere else in the world, at any time of which there is record, has a helpless, backward people of another color been so swiftly uplifted and so greatly benefited by a dominant race.

What America, including the South, has done for the Negro is the truth which should be trumpeted abroad in rebuttal of the Communist propaganda. In failing to utilize this truth we have deliberately put aside a powerful affirmative weapon of enormous potential value to the free world and have allowed ourselves to be thrown on the defensive and placed in an attitude of apologizing for our conduct in a matter where actually our record is one of which we can be very proud.

We have permitted the subject of race relations in the United States to be used, not as it should be used, as a weapon for America, but as a weapon for the narrow designs of the new aggressive Negro leadership in the United States. It cannot be so used without damage to this country and that damage is beyond computation. Instead of winning for America the plaudits and trust of the colored peoples of Asia and Africa in recognition of what we have done for our colored people, our pro-Negro propagandists have seen to it that the United States appears as an international Simon Legree—or rather a Dr. Jekyll and Mr. Hyde with the South in the villainous role.

2

The South has had a bad time with words.
10 Nearly a century ago the word slavery, even more than the thing itself, did the South irreparable damage. In a strange but real way, the misused word democracy has injured the South; its most distinctive—and surely its greatest—period has been called undemocratic, meaning illiberal and reactionary, because it resisted the onward sweep of a centralizing governmental trend alien to our federal republic and destructive of the very "cornerstone of lib-
20 erty," local self-government. Today the word "segregation," and perhaps even more harmful, the word "prejudice," blacken the South's character before the world and make doubly difficult our effort to preserve not merely our own way of life but certain basic principles upon which our country was founded.

Words are of such transcendent importance today that the South should long ago have protested against these two. They are now too
30 firmly imbedded in the dialectic of our race problem to be got rid of. But that very fact renders all the more necessary a careful scrutiny of them. Let us first consider the word segregation.

Segregation is sometimes carelessly listed as a synonym of separation but it is not a true synonym and the difference between the two words is important.

Segregation, from the Latin segregatus (set
40 apart from the flock), implies isolation; separation carries no such implication. Segregation is what we have done to the American Indian—whose grievous wrongs few reformers and still fewer politicians ever bother their heads about. By use of force and against his will we have segregated him and isolated him on certain small reservations which had and still have somewhat the character of concentration camps.
50 The South has not done that to the Negro. On the contrary, it has shared its countryside and its cities with him in amity and understanding, not perfect by any means, and careful of established folk custom, but far exceeding in human friendliness anything of the kind to be found in the North. Not segregation of the Negro race as the Indian is segregated on his reservations—and as the Negro is segregated in urban Harlems of the North—but simply separation of the white and Negro races in certain phases of activity is what the South has always had and feels that it must somehow preserve even though the time-honored successful and completely moral "separate but equal" principle no longer has legal sanction.

Until the Supreme Court decision forbidding compulsory racial separation in the public schools, the South was moving steadily toward abandonment or relaxation of the compulsory separation rule in several important fields. This is no longer true. Progress in racial relations has been stopped short by the ill-advised insistence of the Northern-directed Negro leadership upon the one concession which above all the white South will not and cannot make—public school integration.

Another word which is doing grave damage to the South today is prejudice, meaning race prejudice—causeless hostility often amounting to hatred which white Southerners are alleged to feel in regard to the Negro. Here again the South, forgetful of the lessons of its past, has failed to challenge effectively an inaccurate and injurious word. Not prejudice but preference is the word that truth requires.

Between prejudice and preference there is vast difference. Prejudice is a preconceived unfavorable judgment or feeling without sound basis. Preference is a natural reaction to facts and conditions observed or experienced, and through the action of heredity generation after generation, it becomes instinctive. Like separateness, it exists throughout the animal kingdom. Though the difference between two races of an animal species may be so slight that only a specialist can differentiate between them, the individuals of one race prefer as a rule to associate with other individuals of that race.

One can cite numerous examples among birds and mammals. In the human species the history of our own country provides the most striking example of race preference. The white men and women, chiefly of British, German, Dutch, and Scandinavian stocks, who colonized and occupied what is now the United States were strongly imbued with race preference. They did not follow the example of the Spanish and Portuguese (in whom for historical reasons the instinct of race preference was much weaker) who in colonizing South and Central

America amalgamated with the Indians found in possession of the land and in some cases with the Negroes brought over as slaves. Instead the founders of the future United States maintained their practice of nonamalgamation rigorously, with only slight racial blendings along the fringes of each group.

Hence it is nonsense to say that racial discrimination, the necessary consequence of race preference, is "un-American." Actually it is perhaps the most distinctively American thing there is, the reason why the American people—meaning the people of the United States—are what they are. Today when racial discrimination of any kind or degree is instantly denounced as both sinful and stupid, few stop to reflect that this nation is built solidly upon it.

The truth is, of course, that there are many different kinds and degrees of racial discrimination. Some of them are bad—outdated relics of an earlier time when conditions were unlike those of today, and these should be, and were being abolished until the unprecedented decree of the Supreme Court in the school cases halted all progress. But not all kinds of racial discrimination are evil—unless we are prepared to affirm that our forefathers blundered in "keeping the breed pure."

Thus it is clear that discrimination too is a misused word as commonly employed in the realm of racial relations. It does not necessarily imply either stupidity or sin. It is not a synonym for injustice, and it is very far from being, as many seem to think, a synonym for hatred. The Southern white man has always exercised discrimination in regard to the Negro but—except for a tiny and untypical minority of the white population—he has never hated the Negro. I have lived a fairly long life in a part of the South—the South Carolina Lowcountry —where there are many thousands of Negroes, and since early boyhood I have known many of them well, in some cases for years, in town and country. I know how I feel about them and how the white people of this old plantation region, the high and the low, the rich and the poor, the large landowner and the white mechanic feel about them.

I am sure that among white Carolinians there is, as yet, almost no hatred of the Negro, nor is there anything that can accurately be called race prejudice. What does exist, strongly and ineradicably, is race preference. In other words, we white Southerners prefer our own race and wish to keep it as it is.

This preference should not and in fact cannot be eliminated. It is much bigger than we are, a far greater thing than our racial dilemma. It is—and here is another basic fact of great significance—an essential element in Nature's huge and complex mechanism. It is one of the reasons why evolution, ever diversifying, ever discriminating, ever separating race from race, species from species, has been able to operate in an ascending course so that what began 10 aeons ago as something resembling an amoeba has now become Man. In preferring its own race and in striving to prevent the destruction of that race by amalgamation with another race, the white South is not flouting Nature but is in harmony with her.

If the Negro also prefers his own race and 20 wishes to preserve its identity, then he is misrepresented by his new aggressive leadership which, whether or not this is its deliberate aim, is moving toward a totally different result. Let us see why that is so.

The crux of the race problem in the South, as I have said, is the nearly universal belief of the Southern white people that only by maintaining a certain degree of separateness of the races can the racial integrity of the South be 30 safeguarded. Unfortunately the opinion has prevailed outside the South that only a few Southerners hold this conviction—a handful of demagogic politicians and their most ignorant followers- and that "enlightened" white Southerners recognize the alleged danger of racial amalgamation as a trumped-up thing having no real substance.

Nothing could be farther from the truth. Because the aggressive Northern-Negro leadership 40 continues to drive onward, the white South (except perhaps that part which is now more Western than Southern and in which Negroes are few) is today as united in its conviction that its racial integrity must be protected as it was when the same conviction drove its people—the slaveholder and the nonslaveholder, the high and the low, the educated and the ignorant—to defend the outworn institution of Negro slavery because there seemed to be no other way to 50 preserve the social and political control needed to prevent the Africanization of the South by a combination of fanatical Northern reformers and millions of enfranchised Negroes. The South escaped that fate because after a decade of disastrous experiment the intelligent people of the victorious North realized that the racial program of their social crusaders was unsound, or at least impracticable, and gave up trying to enforce it.

Now in a surging revival of that "Reconstruction" crusade—a revival which is part dedicated idealism, part understandable racial ambition, part political expediency national and international—the same social program is again to be imposed upon the South. There are new conditions which help powerfully to promote it: the Hitlerite excesses in the name of race which have brought all race distinctions into popular disrepute; the notion that the white man, by divesting himself of race consciousness, may appease the peoples of Asia and Africa and wean them away from Communism.

In addition, a fantastic perversion of scientific authority has been publicized in support of the new crusade. Though everywhere else in Nature (as well as in all our plant breeding and animal breeding) race and heredity are recognized as of primary importance, we are told that in the human species race is of no importance and racial differences are due not to heredity but to environment. Science has proved, so we are told, that all races are equal and, in essentials, identical.

Science has most certainly not proved that all races are equal, much less identical; and, as the courageous geneticist, Dr. W. C. George of the University of North Carolina, has recently pointed out, there is overwhelming likelihood that the biological consequences of white and Negro integration in the South would be harmful. It would not be long before these biological consequences became visible. But there is good hope that we shall never see them because any attempt to force a program of racial integration upon the South would be met with stubborn, determined, and universal opposition, probably taking the form of passive resistance of a hundred kinds. Though secession is not conceivable, persistence in an attempt to compel the South to mingle its white and Negro children in its public schools would split the United States in two as disastrously as in the sixties and perhaps with an even more lamentable aftermath of bitterness.

For the elementary public school is the most critical of those areas of activity where the South must and will at all costs maintain separateness of the races. The South must do this because, although it is a nearly universal instinct, race preference is not active in the very young. Race preference (which the propagandists miscall race prejudice or hate) is one of those instincts which develop gradually as the mind develops and which, if taken in hand early enough, can be prevented from developing at all.

Hence if the small children of the two races in approximately equal numbers—as would be the case in a great many of the South's schools —were brought together intimately and constantly and grew up in close association in integrated schools under teachers necessarily committed to the gospel of racial integration, there would be many in whom race preference would not develop. This would not be, as superficial thinkers might suppose, a good thing, the happy solution of the race problem in America. It might be a solution of a sort, but not one that the American people would desire. It would inevitably result, beginning with the least desirable elements of both races, in a great increase of racial amalgamation, the very process which throughout our history we have most sternly rejected. For although to most persons today the idea of mixed mating is disagreeable or even repugnant, this would not be true of the new generations brought up in mixed schools with the desirability of racial integration as a basic premise. Among these new generations mixed matings would become commonplace, and a greatly enlarged mixed-blood population would result.

That is the compelling reason, though by no means the only reason, why the South will resist, with all its resources of mind and body, the mixing of the races in its public schools. It is a reason which, when its validity is generally recognized, will quickly enlist millions of non-Southerners in support of the South's position. The people of the North and West do not favor the transformation of the United States into a nation composed in considerable part of mixed bloods any more than the people of the South do. Northern support of school integration in the South is due to the failure to realize its inevitable biological effect in regions of large Negro population. If Northerners did realize this, their enthusiasm for mixed schools in the South would evaporate at once.

4

There are other cogent reasons for the white South's stand: the urgent necessity of restoring the Constitution and our federal form of government before they are permanently destroyed by the Court's usurpation of power; the equally urgent necessity of re-establishing law and precedent instead of sociological and psychological theory as the basis of the Court's decisions; the terrible damage which racial integration would do to the South's whole educational system, black as well as white. These and other aspects have been fully and effectively explored and need not be touched upon here.

But the underlying and compelling reason for the South's refusal to operate mixed schools —its belief that mixed schools will result in ultimate racial amalgamation—has been held virtually taboo and, if mentioned in the North, is not examined at all but is summarily dismissed as not worthy of consideration. The amalgamation "bogey," it is said, is not really believed by intelligent Southerners but is a smoke screen used to hide the South's real motives, which are variously described, ranging from plain sadism to a shrewd determination to deprive the Negro of education so that he can never displace the Southern white man. Besides, it is confidently alleged, the Negro does not wish to destroy the identity of his race by merging it with the white race.

Both those statements are incorrect. As already pointed out, the fear that mixed schools in the South would open the way to racial amalgamation is not a bogey or a smoke screen or a pretense of any kind but the basic animating motive of the white South in resisting the drive of the N.A.A.C.P. and its supporters. The second statement is as erroneous as the first. The Negro leaders do want racial amalgamation; they not only want the right to amalgamate through legal intermarriage but they want that right to be exercised widely and frequently.

It is only natural and human that they should feel this way. The truth is that these ambitious, intelligent, often amalgamated, and often genuinely dedicated Negro men and women feel about this matter exactly as white men and women would feel if they were similarly constituted and circumstanced—fusion of the two races would solve the Negro's problem at once. How much of the Negro rank and file consciously seeks amalgamation is a question; to the Southern Negro in particular the thought of intermarriage is still new and strange. As for the Northern leaders of the movement, some of them make no bones about it, and when they do evade the question they do so only for reasons of strategy.

But actually it does not matter much whether or not intermarriage is the admitted aim of the N.A.A.C.P. strategists. To suppose that, proclaiming the virtual identity of the races, we can promote all other degrees of race mixing but stop short of interracial mating is—if I may use an overworked but vivid simile—like going over Niagara Falls in a barrel in the expectation of stopping three fourths of the way down. The South is now the great bulwark against intermarriage. A very few years of thoroughly integrated schools would produce large numbers of indoctrinated young Southerners free from all "prejudice" against mixed matings.

It is because there the adolescent and "unprejudiced" mind can be reached that the integrationists have chosen the Southern schools as their primary target; and it is precisely because the adolescent and therefore defenseless mind would there be exposed to brain-washing which it would not know how to refute that the white South will not operate integrated public schools. If the South fails to defend its young children who are not yet capable of defending themselves, if it permits their wholesale impregnation by a propaganda persuasive and by them unanswerable, the salutary instinct of race preference which keeps the races separate, as in Nature, will be destroyed before it develops and the barriers against racial amalgamation will go down.

This is the new and ominous fact which, as was said at the beginning of this article, lurks in ambush, concealed like a viper in the school integration crusade. Success of that crusade would mean that after three and a half centuries of magnificent achievement under a system of racial separateness and purity, we would tacitly abandon that system and instead would begin the creation of a mixed American race by the fusion of the two races which, as H. G. Wells expressed it, are at opposite extremes of the human species.

Many well-meaning persons have suddenly discovered that the tenets of the Christian religion and the professions of our democratic faith compel us to accept the risks of this hybridization. No one who will face up to the biological facts and really think the problem through can believe any such thing or see the partial suicide of the white race in America (and of the Negro race also) as anything other than a crime against religion and civilization.

I have tried to show here the basic and compelling reason why the Southern people, who know the facts of life in the South better than any doctrinaire sociologist viewing the scene from his ivory tower, see no possible course save to stand firm in their resistance to school integration no matter what may be the consequences of their resistance. When a people believes that something even dearer than its life is threatened, there isn't much use in pointing out its duty to obey the law which threatens it, especially when it is almost unanimously of the opinion that the law is a perversion. And the South has ample precedent for resistance. In a much firmer sense the Prohibition Amendment was the law of the land, and the North even more than the South made a mockery of it. So too was the federal fugitive slave act the law of the land, yet many Northern states nullified and openly violated it.

Moreover, fortifying the South for its ordeal is the conviction that it is defending something far greater than itself; that integrity of race and that pride of race which all great peoples have —the Chinese, the Japanese, the Arabs, the Jews, for instance—and without which no people is worth its salt. There is good hope that before too long this will begin to be recognized outside the South. The current pseudoscientific buncombe about racial identity is at last being questioned openly. It will be exploded completely with the ending of the leftist-liberal taboo which has practically sealed the lips of geneticists able and willing to discuss racial realities, and our Lysenko-like excursion in the realm of race will come to an end. Then it will be seen that the South, in maintaining the actuality and the great significance of racial differences, has not been "racist" in any evil sense but has been the defender of something permanently important to the whole American people; and that the Supreme Court, in launching the Negro on an offensive which cannot and should not succeed, has dealt a terrible blow to his advancement and his happiness.

1956

TELEVISION: STANDARDS OF TASTE VERSUS FREEDOM OF TASTE

THE DISCUSSION of the mass media was sharpened in the autumn of 1959 by the revelation that a popular and much-featured television star had been guilty of dishonesty in connection with his spectacular triumphs in quiz programs. The issue of honesty in the industry was, however, only one aspect of the wide-ranging controversy between the champions and the critics of television.

On December 23, 1959, the *New York Times* reprinted from the November issue of *Television* magazine an article by Victor M. Ratner entitled "The Freedom of Taste." The *New York Times* re-published the article "in the belief that it will lend a significant new dimension to public thinking on a subject of direct personal interest to everyone." In the same issue, the *New York Times* reprinted an editorial from the December 12, 1959 issue of the *Saturday Evening Post* entitled "Quiz Scandals Are Only a Symptom." The *Times* regarded the editorial as "a material contribution to the balance of thought on the subject of television and contemporary morality."

C. A. Siepman, *Radio, Television, and Society*, New York, 1950.
Gilbert Seldes, *Public Arts*, New York, 1957.
Elmer E. Smead, *Freedom of Speech by Radio and Television*, Washington, 1958.

VICTOR M. RATNER

1906–

VICTOR M. RATNER, who has been vice-president of the Columbia Broadcasting System and consultant on mass communication to the Division of General Education,

New York university, is vice-president of the Grey Advertising Agency, Inc.

THE FREEDOM OF TASTE

Given any discussion about "What is good or bad taste?" it might be well to begin by remembering one of Ambrose Bierce's "Fantastic Fables." He called it the "Distinterested Arbiter," and here is the whole story.

Two dogs who had been fighting over a bone, without advantage to either, referred their dispute to a sheep.

The sheep patiently heard their statements, then flung the bone into a pond.

"Why did you do that?" asked the dogs.

"Because," said the sheep, "I am a vegetarian!"

The fable has a point for the intellectual, or any other citizen, who has little personal appetite for most of the nourishment provided by mass media—yet who consistently and severely criticizes their services to other people.

What he does not seem to realize is that, for the first time in civilized history, most of the cultural product of a society is not now designed for an aristocracy—but for the appreciation, the standards and uses of masses of people.

Some of the most interesting arguments about mass media spring wholly out of technology. "Culture" invades the privacy of one's home today, as it never could before. In the old days, one brought books and music into the home oneself; one selected specific plays and concerts to buy tickets for. A man's cultural experience was as private to him as his choice of food.

But today television and radio, more often than not, bring into our home programs which were not designed for us but for other people. Culturally speaking, we now live on a public highway. Other people's programs come to us automatically following a program we like, or while we're searching for a program we like. In this way, many an intellectual has for the first time been directly exposed to mass tastes.

He is shocked. He reacts, as almost any of us do, to sharp variations from our private standards. He is also indignant at this invasion of his privacy. He does not say: "This program was intended for other people, not for me."

He says: "This is a bad program. Why do they put it on?"

It is a knotty question. Whose standards should apply?

We have made some progress toward solving the problem in other areas, though it has taken time to do so. Certainly many of us realize—after centuries of bitter battle—it is no longer proper in our society to speak of any other man's religion as being "good" or "bad" but only different from our own.

And freedom of thought is one of our most profound rights. Yet judging from the anguished criticism of mass media one sees so often, many of us are not yet prepared to defend freedom of taste—when it is someone else's taste set against our own.

We will fight hard for religious democracy and political democracy, but what might be called "cultural democracy" is still something of a new concept. Whether we are educated or uneducated, we haven't yet been made to doubt our firm belief that in entertainment we know "good" from "bad"—unconsciously projecting our taste as a standard for the community.

EXPOSURE TO THE TASTES OF AN ENTIRE NATION

I suggest this may be so because it is only recently in history that we have been brought so directly in contact with the cultural tastes of an entire nation, instead of the narrower tastes of our particular group in society. And intellectuals have been far quicker to criticize these "other" tastes than to understand them; one reason, perhaps why their criticism has had so little effect over the years.

The question remains: To what degree should "freedom of taste" rank with freedom of thought, freedom of religion, freedom of speech?

The issue is complicated by the extraordinary flexibility of modern mass media. Some of them are, in one place, the carnivals, the museums, theatres, schools, market places, newspapers and political forums of our time.

But they are not all these things evenly. They are not because, as their label suggests, they primarily serve the desires of masses of people—whose interest in the above is far from even.

And all their power derives from the people. Mass media are never thrust on the population, as new economic structures may be. They become big only when millions of people choose to make them so; they continue vital only when they serve masses of people as they want to be served.

This is one of the purest forms of democratic action. Out of a greater multiplicity of offerings than was ever before available, the people choose.

And in our competitive system, no "conspiracy" by advertisers (or anyone else) can long foist on the public something it doesn't want, or hold back from the public something it does want. It is pure myth to think otherwise, though many intellectuals—more unsophisticated about "other people's tastes" than anything else—still cling to these myths.

This immediately faces us with the question: How much can we trust the people's tastes?

And this question, whether the intellectual acknowledges it or not, is the heart of his quarrel with mass media.

ARE THE AMERICAN PEOPLE "RIGHT" OR "WRONG" TO INSIST ON ENTERTAINMENT FROM THE MASS MEDIA?

To bring the question into sharper focus, let us concentrate, here, on the people's tastes in art and entertainment.

When we do, we come upon this truism about the most modern of mass media. For good or evil, they gain most of their audience, not from their more serious functions of news or education or high culture, but from the entertainment they provide. Their dominant role is to bring entertainment to the people because most people want entertainment from the mass media most of the time.

Indeed, when media do not provide entertainment they hardly ever become mass media. The very few exceptions prove the rule. This accounts for the steady trend toward popular columnists and other non-news features in the modern newspaper. It accounts, of course, for the predominance of entertainment in radio and television schedules.

Are the American people "right" or "wrong" to respond so, to insist so, on entertainment?

IMPRINT OF OUR PURITAN INHERITANCE

One's answer depends, obviously, in large part on the value one gives to the role of entertainment as a legitimate part of life. In a puritan world, fun is officially frowned on. Entertainment is seen as ammunition of the devil.

Something of the imprint of our puritan inheritance remains to this day, in the way in which popular entertainment is hardly tolerated by serious thinkers and is mourned as "such a waste of the people's time."

Self-improvement . . . that's the thing. Even the hours spent in relaxation should, somehow, we feel, be put to good use.

Indeed the time and effort put into self-improvement are desirable—and particularly were so in a pioneering culture like early America, when so much had so swiftly to be improved. A puritan culture and a pioneering culture thus combined to rate "self-improvement" particularly high in our society.

But this should not carry with it its own converse: that hours of fun are in themselves negative. Consider how fundamental the need is for humanity to escape regularly from seriousness. If we do not take vacations, we soon break down. If we do not get some sleep every night —in itself a holiday from reality—we cannot go on living. Soldiers (exposed to the most severe strains of reality) must have relaxation and entertainment or they soon crack from accumulated tension.

Then consider the enormous increase in tension in all our lives in the past forty years. Our people—once called degenerate by totalitarian enemies—have very successfully managed two world wars and a continuing cold war in these years, plus the increasing complexities of modern living (when just the traffic creates tensions unknown to our ancestors). Our people have reached new highs of generosity and charity for the world—and towards babies for themselves.

They have, in short, been hard at work. Have they not, then, earned the right to entertainment, too?

Thus, there may be nothing wrong, and something very right about the mass insistence on entertainment from mass media. It is not a small thing to make a man and his family laugh.

But (the intellectual will ask) why must mass media give them such "cheap" entertainment? Why give them such empty, flimsy stuff? Why don't the mass media and advertisers help them to get "better" things? Why not genuine art?

And this brings on the next basic issue. For I have been careful in the above, to talk only of entertainment, not of art.

One might use other pairs of terms, such as "fine art" and "popular art," or, as we say, serious music and popular music. I prefer using the two words entertainment and art to stress a genuine difference between the two. One is not in my opinion, merely a bad form of the other.

The essential distinction between them may be this:

Art always contains in itself some commentary on the truth, some further insight into reality. Successful art, I mean, for there is a great deal of unsuccessful art. Not all who try are talented, and the history of art is rife with errors of judgment—sometimes on the part of the artist, sometimes on the part of very eminent and self-assured intellectuals.

But successful art surely is the most eloquent form of philosophy, leading us to more understanding of life itself. Shakespeare's "Hamlet" is important not because of its fictions but its truths; because of what it teaches us about man—put into a wonderfully exciting form.

And certainly great painters teach us new ways to look at reality, to observe shapes and colors and meanings we have never seen before.

In music, simple lieder can express the deepest of true emotions; and complex symphonies have structure and harmonies as intuitively meaningful as the deep grain of the universe itself, as mysteriously and beautifully organized as the stars.

It is important to remember, here, that we do not get this new insight from art without effort on our part. As Walt Whitman said: "Great poets need great audiences, too."

Indeed to respond truly to art takes a considerable amount of energy. Everyone knows, for example, how quickly tiring it can be to look at good pictures. We do not "take it easy" when we come to art. We go to it for more than fun, for a more profound experience, an experience of reality itself.

Entertainment is something else again— whether people get it from a ball game, a comedian, a detective story or Tin Pan Alley love songs. Set aside for a moment the question of whether it is good or bad entertainment. Its basic function is to give us relief from the immediate pressures of reality, to give us a breathing spell from the endless mysteries of life.

Art takes us deeper into these mysteries; entertainment takes us away from them—into fictions of artificial gaiety (like a musical comedy), or artificial tragedy (like a soap opera), or artificial love (like a Marilyn Monroe movie)—all enjoyed precisely because they are not like life, and are not seeking to improve or understand it better.

We must appreciate the fact that when people have need to relax with entertainment they do not want significant art. They will sooner, at that time, take third-rate entertainment than take first-rate art or anything else with "content." One serves their purpose, the other does not and when a man is thirsty, it does no good to offer him food. This is one of the things that baffle intellectuals most about popular taste, yet it is wholly consistent on the people's part.

It is true, of course, that many cultured people often use art as though it were entertainment, not for its meaning; but as something merely to relax to. They will go to a concert or the opera, yet not really listen to the great music, hearing only its sweet surface while they day-dream of other things, or almost fall asleep.

There's nothing specially praiseworthy about this. They are not having a superior experience to the man who spends the same time reading or watching an ordinary detective story, though "having been to an opera" may have some snob-value for them.

But the confusion between art and entertainment goes much deeper than this. It results in part from the fact that art and entertainment use such similar forms and skills for their different ends.

Any detective story can be written with great skill yet be nothing more than entertainment because it is as unreal as a baseball game. However, as soon as a detective story gets some aspect of truth in it—some degree of authentic emotions and motivation—we then properly call it literature (or "art") as some few detective stories very much are.

Yet, the difference between even the most successful "whodunit" and such literature as, say, "Crime and Punishment" is the very point I am making. It is the difference between an ingenious puzzle and the study of man, between a game and reality, between entertainment and art. It is not that one is bad art, the other good art.

Bad art happens when someone tries to write a study of guilt like "Crime and Punishment" and never brings it to life.

Bad entertainment happens when someone tries to write a mystery play as successful as "Dial M for Murder"—and it bores us.

Nor is the degree of skill involved in the issue. We loosely speak of any high degree of skill as "art" (i.e., the art of cooking, the art of skiing) using one as a synonym for the other.

We all tend to respond to skill per se, whether we see it in an acrobat or a dancer, a bishop or a ballplayer. And we know that the really great entertainment requires extraordinary skill even as great art does.

As a result, each field has its own major talents, deeply surrounded by second and third-rate imitators of these talents. Conan Doyle was as inimitable in has way as Dostoevski in his. Irving Berlin may properly be called a master of popular music, as Beethoven is of serious music. And Danny Kaye creates a unique "poetry" of entertainment as special in its excellence as T. S. Eliot's. Each is no less rare than the other; each has enormous talent.

SERIOUS ART MAY ALSO BE BAD

But it should hardly come as a surprise that far more performers in both fields, have minor imitative talents rather than major ones. Genuine talent is a scarce commodity everywhere. If intellectuals complain of how bad so much popular entertainment is today, they can equally complain of how bad so many serious art efforts are today. Consider the many untalented "serious painters" there are, and how many badly done, soon forgotten "serious" books are published each year.

Let not the intellectual, therefore, be confused about the different purposes of art and entertainment. One aims at truth ("Holding the mirror up to nature"). The other takes us to a holiday land ("Where people live happily ever after").

It is not possible to examine these esthetic considerations too deeply here. They are complex and largely uncharted by the professors. Certainly, some art crosses over into entertainment and some entertainment crosses over into high art. We see it in the case of Charlie Chaplin (the performer, not the political person).

He began as a popular entertainer. But he soon introduced into his performance such true revelations of the pathos of humanity that here was the insight and "truth" of great art, too. This doesn't happen often. There are not, after all, many Chaplins; and the later Chaplin never enjoyed as large audiences as the early Chaplin.

ENTERTAINMENT AS AN ENTITY

Nevertheless, just such few overlaps have tended to blur the essential distinction between art and entertainment, between truth and fiction; and have kept the professors of esthetics and other intellectuals from looking seriously and sympathetically at the nature of popular entertainment as something in itself.

Does this mean that serious cultural material and cultural "leadership" have no place or purpose in mass media? Of course not. These have a place on the schedules because they deal with truth—and because they have an audience, both old and new. The American population includes many different audiences.

And once we understand that serious cultural material is for minority audiences, we realize that their rights must be protected from the overwhelming pressure of the majority, as the rights of any minority in a democracy must be protected.

While we cannot hope to turn the major part of mass media over to minority interests—nor should we want to, consciously or unconsciously —we must give them their place in the sun.

The arguments start again. How large a place should this be? I can suggest only the very simplest yardstick as a starting point for discussion.

We might take the approximate number of people in this country who clearly demonstrate (by their very consistent behavior) how much they want entertainment, and compare this with the much smaller number of people interested in more serious cultural material from mass media. (Remember that intellectuals have and use many other resources for their cultural experience than mass media.)

SERIOUS PROGRAMMING ALREADY FAVORED

We can then apply this ratio to the total program structure of, say, television. And you will find, I think, that the program structure already favors the side of serious programming, not of light programming.

Such weighting in favor of serious and cultural programming takes place for a variety of reasons: the "importance" of the minority audiences, the prestige value of such programs, the desire of media to discharge their responsibilities for balanced programming and "cultural leadership." (As a result, every type of high art, from symphonies to Shakespeare, gets more distribution today than every before.)

To many an intellectual my ratios may be unbelievable. But that's because he does not quite realize how small a minority he represents.

Or, accepting my mathematics, he may still argue that the ratio should be weighted even more in favor of serious programming than it is "because of its cultural value to the community," not willing to recognize the rights of people to enjoy what they like when they like it; not being really at ease with the concept of cultural democracy; making the easier assumption that his cultural values are what "everybody's" should be.

CULTURE IS A MOVING PROCESS

A conciliatory thought suggests itself in this conflict between mass and class tastes. We're not in a static situation. Culture is a process, not a fixed design. American society in particular has demonstrated its power to modify age-old cultural patterns. We have, for example, seen in this country the creation of a middle-class of unique dimensions, pulling most of our people toward the center, away from either economic or political extremes.

I suspect this may also happen culturally in time—particularly if material life for our people continues to get easier, if reality itself becomes less and less harsh for the masses of people.

In my early days with mass media, I used to think one of their really bad aspects was how much they seemed to turn people into spectators rather than participants; how much they made every body sit rather than do.

But with the very recent innovation of "mass" leisure time, there is considerable evidence this is actually the other way around. Mass media haven't hurt the people's activities. Quite the contrary. As more people are exposed to more exciting things than they had dreamed of in their philosophies, they get an irrepressible urge "to get into the act"—with more adult education activities, more lecture audiences, more serious concerts, more "do-it-yourself" today than ever before.

Thus, what seems to the groaning intellectual to be a swift lowering of our cultural standards, through mass media, may be only the slowing up of a train, as it takes on many millions of new passengers—who ultimately will be carried to those higher plateaus of culture where only a very small fraction of the human race found itself in the good old days.

A word of caution: It would be a mistake to ask the train to speed too fast while taking on its new passengers. Those getting on would only be left behind.

But the word of caution is, in fact, unnecessary. Whether the intellectuals like it or not, it will be the passengers rather than the engineers who will set the speed of this train—the audience itself, not its critics.

I suggest this is not something to be deplored —even by the traditional cultural "engineers" of our society. It is, in a profound sense, part of the growing dignity of the individual in our time. It is an exercise of "the ordinary man's freedom of choice rather than of paternalism (or worse)." It is the infiltration of the democratic process into formal culture—into areas where the democratic process had very little or no influence only a few generations ago. It puts "leadership" into its proper perspective of service.

So much, then, for some of the more positive aspects of mass media in our society. There are negative ones, of course. But I have laid stress on the others because it is so easy for the intellectual to underrate or to miss them.

This makes unrealistic any approach the average intellectual has to mass media. He is like King Canute, demanding that the waves stand back! Nothing happens. It would seem far more useful for him to try to discover what the seas are really like.

MASS MEDIA UNDER AUDIENCE CONTROL

Mass media are a revolution in the culture of our time because they have developed, not under the control of conventional cultural leaders, but of the audience itself; and of larger audiences than the world has ever known.

And we must, in the end, relate this to the positive thrust of freedom on the development of human beings.

Either we believe or we do not believe that man can learn more and develop more under the processes of freedom than of anything else; that most people have the ability to improve themselves—to find and support their own good leaders and teachers—as they are given political, economic and cultural freedom to do so.

Hard as it may seem to the intellectual, we need our mass media pretty much as they are for this purpose. Mass media have not been allowed to become either paternalistic or authoritarian in the United States, since neither fits easily into the American scheme. They have developed with far more freedom here than anywhere else; have been allowed to respond more freely to the wishes of the people.

I do not think we need fear such freedom. For over the long years, we can only expect good out of freedom—even "freedom of taste."

From: *THE SATURDAY EVENING POST*

QUIZ SCANDALS ARE ONLY
A SYMPTOM

During the past several weeks one of our principal competitors, television, has been under severe attack.

The temptation, of course, is to join in the assault—to parade before our readers the whole sorry gallery of witnesses who testified before Congressman Oren Harris' well-publicized hearings. There is reason to do so. The charges of deceitfulness have been proved; the sad spectacle of major networks surrendering control of their facilities to advertisers has been fully documented.

Nevertheless, we are reluctant to join in the field day that the press, generally, has enjoyed at television's expense. This is not because we believe the rogues to be innocent. Rather, it is because we believe that the importance of their guilt has been wildly exaggerated, the significance of their guilt almost wholly overlooked. The nation, we suspect, will not go into total decline because Xavier Cugat cribbed on his pop-music exams; we may even survive the revelation that network presidents were either asleep at the switch or more interested in advertising revenue than in the honesty of their programs.

What is important is that we recognize the television scandals for what they are—a symptom of the declining standards of moral behavior in the United States, that twinge in the national belly that warns of deep-seated malignancy in the body politic.

The issue before the republic, therefore, is not merely how to police the airways (the industry itself may see to that if only to avoid the twin threats of Federal regulation and pay TV). Ours is a far more difficult task. The first stone has been cast. Now all of our treasured institutions are called to account for their stewardship—each determining for itself how riddled with the cancer of moral indifference it may be.

Even a cursory glance at our society reveals that the ethics of the quiz show are by no means confined to television. In many of our schools, for instance, we tacitly approve the policy of automatic promotion—that sleazy practice of sending dullards from grade to grade when they can't, or won't, do the required work, but must be advanced because "there's no place else for them to go." Ultimately they are "graduated," ill prepared for the jobs they will seek with their fraudulent diplomas.

In our colleges responsible educators now estimate that perhaps as many as one-third of all students cheat "rather regularly" on their examinations. It is really not surprising that they do so. Their more celebrated classmates, the football team, were very probably recruited by one or another of the undercover dodges employed by college administrators to circumvent the pious codes they publicly endorse.

On the labor front we are assailed by the dismal memory of Dave Beck and the spectacle of a Hoffa, triumphant over the majesty of Federal authority. We see featherbedding and thuggery upheld in cynical disregard of the national welfare.

Medicine? After years of tongue-clucking by the American Medical Association, fee splitting goes on as always. Some specialists continue to kick back to general practitioners who send them patients. In another sector, health-insurance plans mount in cost because, for one reason, doctors and patients conspire to chisel on the terms of the contracts.

Lawyers? Alongside the honest attorneys slink that grimy fringe of ambulance chasers, shysters and mouthpieces—the flouters of justice whose special skill is to teach the willing pupil how to beat the law. Even the statutes themselves seem sometimes to encourage these delinquents. Some states, for example, encourage perjury by providing that the only legal ground for divorce is adultery. Too often the evidence of the adulterous act has to be faked, while solemn but helpless judges look the other way.

The income tax? Cheating on it is now a national game. New loopholes are greeted with hosannas, passed from willing lip to eager ear. Executives openly boast of living off their expense accounts. Too often the status symbols of the successful are the credit card and the company yacht used for private entertainment.

Washington? The home freezer and the mink coat are old stuff by now. So, also, is the strange case of the Miami television license, the vicuna coat, the Goldfine rug, the innocent phone calls of Sherman Adams, the Congressional payrolls stuffed with relatives.

But what about the senator who conveniently forgets that the hilarious speech which established him as a latter-day Will Rogers was actually written by some ink-stained ghost whose name the senator conveniently forgot to mention? And how many members of Congress accept campaign contributions from donors whose obvious, if unspecified, purpose is to compromise the vote of the successful candidate?

The catalogue of American Van Dorens is thick and blowzy. It includes those American businesses which caused the Federal Trade Commission to announce recently that advertising abuses were at an all-time high; the gyp repairmen who batten on the anguish of homeowners in trouble; the fast-talking bunko artists who swindle the unsophisticated by selling worthless stock by telephone. It even includes those suburban ministers who preach their Sunday sermons on racial integration—to all-white congregations.

Nor, we regret to say, is the press without blemish. Some of the publications that trumpeted television's derelictions most loudly are themselves guilty of questionable practice.

Some permit their baseball writers, for example, to travel at the expense of the team they cover —compromising objectivity for a few dollars a year. Some see no ethical reason why their editors should not accept the free travel, free liquor, free entertainment offered by public-relations firms in pursuit of favorable mention for their clients. Some angle their editorial content with the advertiser, not the reader, in mind.

And all of us—newspapers and magazines alike—are wide open to the charge that we have abetted the national delinquency by helping to foster a phony value system in our country. By glamorizing sports we so inflated the football star that colleges felt justified in buying him to fill the stadium that costs more than the physics building. By our preoccupation with the bosomy starlet, the sweetly smiling faces of television, we encouraged our readers to accept phony standards of success, helped the creatures of publicity to rewards that their contributions do not merit.

Viewed against this capsule picture of the seamy side of the United States, the television mess begins to come into focus.

Television, we repeat, was guilty of gross negligence and gross cowardice in surrendering programming to the advertiser.

BURRHUS FREDERIC SKINNER
1904–
and CARL R. ROGERS
1902–

THROUGHOUT THE American experience the images of man held by leaders and people have both reflected movements of thought and cultural situations on the one hand and have on the other influenced these as well as esthetic expression. In the mid-twentieth century philosophers, religious leaders, and other intellectuals continued to discuss the nature of human nature according to their lights. But developments in the behavioral sciences posed a basic issue for peoples everywhere, an issue sharpened by the mass movements and dictatorships associated with twentieth century revolutions. In its simplest terms, the issue was whether men can be so manipulated by a power elite which commands special knowledge of human motives and behavior so that individual freedom of action and of values becomes only a fiction.

Two distinguished psychologists, Professor B. F. Skinner of Harvard and Dr. Carl Rogers of Chicago and Wisconsin, presented different views on human nature and on related issues in a symposium held at the annual meeting of the American Psychological Association in Chicago in September, 1956. *Science* magazine in its issue for November 30, 1956, published an article based on material presented by Skinner and Rogers at the Chicago symposium.

B. F. Skinner, *Walden Two*, New York, 1948.
B. F. Skinner, *Science and Human Behavior*, New York, 1953.
Carl R. Rogers, *Client-Centered Therapy, its Current Practice, Implications, and Theory*, Boston, 1951.
Carl R. Rogers, *Psychotherapy and Personal Change*, Chicago, 1954.

SOME ISSUES CONCERNING THE CONTROL OF HUMAN BEHAVIOR

I SKINNER

Science is steadily increasing our power to influence, change, mold—in a word, control—human behavior. It has extended our "understanding" (whatever that may be) so that we deal more successfully with people in nonscientific ways, but it has also identified conditions or variables which can be used to predict and control behavior in a new, and increasingly rigorous, technology. The broad disciplines of government and economics offer examples of this, but there is special cogency in those contributions of anthropology, sociology, and psychology which deal with individual behavior. Carl Rogers has listed some of the achievements to date in a recent paper. Those of his examples which show or imply the control of the single organism are primarily due, as we should expect, to psychology. It is the experimental study of behavior which carries us beyond awkward or inaccessible "principles," "factors," and so on, to variables which can be directly manipulated.

It is also, and for more or less the same reasons, the conception of human behavior emerging from an experimental analysis which most directly challenges traditional views. Psychologists themselves often do not seem to be aware of how far they have moved in this direction. But the change is not passing unnoticed by others. Until only recently it was customary to deny the possibility of a rigorous science of human behavior by arguing, either that a lawful science was impossible because man was a free agent, or that merely statistical predictions would always leave room for personal freedom. But those who used to take this line have become most vociferous in expressing their alarm at the way these obstacles are being surmounted.

Now, the control of human behavior has al-

ways been unpopular. Any undisguised effort to control usually arouses emotional reactions. We hesitate to admit, even to ourselves, that we are engaged in control, and we may refuse to control, even when this would be helpful, for fear of criticism. Those who have explicitly avowed an interest in control have been roughly treated by history. Machiavelli is the great prototype. As Macaulay said of him, "Out of his surname they coined an epithet for a knave and out of his Christian name a synonym for the devil." There were obvious reasons. The control that Machiavelli analyzed and recommended, like most political control, used techniques that were aversive to the controllee. The threats and punishments of the bully, like those of the government operating on the same plan, are not designed—whatever their success—to endear themselves to those who are controlled. Even when the techniques themselves are not aversive, control is usually exercised for the selfish purposes of the controller and, hence has indirectly punishing effects upon others.

Man's natural inclination to revolt against selfish control has been exploited to good purpose in what we call the philosophy and literature of democracy. The doctrine of the rights of man has been effective in arousing individuals to concerted actions against governmental and religious tyranny. The literature which has had this effect has greatly extended the number of terms in our language which express reactions to the control of men. But the ubiquity and ease of expression of this attitude spells trouble for any science which may give birth to a powerful technology of behavior. Intelligent men and women, dominated by the humanistic philosophy of the past two centuries, cannot view with equanimity what Andrew Hacker has called "the specter of predictable man." Even the statistical or actual prediction of human events, such as the number of fatalities to be expected on a holiday week-end, strikes many people as uncanny and evil, while the prediction and control of individual behavior is regarded as little less than the work of the devil. I am not so much concerned here with the political or economic consequences for psychology, although research following certain channels may well suffer harmful effects. We ourselves, as intelligent men and women, and as exponents of Western thought, share these attitudes. They have already interfered with the free exercise of a scientific analysis, and their influence threatens to assume more serious proportions.

Three broad areas of human behavior supply good examples. The first of these—*personal control*—may be taken to include person-to-person relationships in the family, among friends, in social and work groups, and in counseling and psychotherapy. Other fields are *education* and *government*. A few examples from each will show how nonscientific preconceptions are affecting our current thinking about human behavior.

People living together in groups come to control one another with a technique which is not inappropriately called "ethical." When an individual behaves in a fashion acceptable to the group, he receives admiration, approval, affection, and many other reinforcements which increase the likelihood that he will continue to behave in that fashion. When his behavior is not acceptable, he is criticized, censured, blamed, or otherwise punished. In the first case the group calls him "good"; in the second, "bad." This practice is so thoroughly ingrained in our culture that we often fail to see that it is a technique of control. Yet we are almost always engaged in such control, even though the reinforcements and punishments are often subtle.

The practice of admiration is an important part of a culture, because behavior which is otherwise inclined to be weak can be set up and maintained with its help. The individual is especially likely to be praised, admired, or loved when he acts for the group in the face of great danger, for example, or sacrifices himself or his possessions, or submits to prolonged hardships, or suffers martyrdom. These actions are not admirable in any absolute sense, but they require admiration if they are to be strong. Similarly, we admire people who behave in original or exceptional ways, not because such behavior is itself admirable, but because we do not know how to encourage original or exceptional behavior in any other way. The group acclaims independent, unaided behavior in part because it is easier to reinforce than to help.

As long as this technique of control is misunderstood, we cannot judge correctly an environment in which there is less need for heroism, hardship, or independent action. We are likely to argue that such an environment is itself less admirable or produces less admirable people. In the old days, for example, young scholars often lived in undesirable quarters, ate unappetizing or inadequate food, performed unprofitable tasks for a living or to pay for necessary books and materials for publication. Older scholars and other members of the group offered compensating reinforcement in the form of approval and admiration for these sacrifices. When the modern graduate student receives a generous scholarship, enjoys good living conditions, and has his research and publications subsidized, the grounds for evaluation seem to be pulled from under us. Such a student no longer *needs* admiration to carry him over a series of obstacles (no matter how much he may need it for other reasons), and, in missing certain familiar objects of admiration, we are likely to conclude that such *conditions* are less admirable. Obstacles to scholarly work may serve as a useful measure of motivation—and we may go wrong unless some substitute is found—but we can scarcely defend a deliberate harassment of the student for this purpose. The productivity of any set of conditions can be evaluated only when we have freed ourselves of the attitudes which have been generated in us as members of an ethical group.

A similar difficulty arises from our use of punishment in the form of censure or blame. The concept of responsibility and the related concepts of foreknowledge and choice are used to justify techniques of control using punishment. Was So-and-So aware of the probable consequences of his action, and was the action deliberate? If so, we are justified in punishing him. But what does this mean? It appears to be a question concerning the efficacy of the contingent relations between behavior and punishing consequences. We punish behavior because it is objectionable to us or the group, but in a minor refinement of rather recent origin we have come to withhold punishment when it cannot be expected to have any effect. If the objectionable consequences of an act were accidental and not likely to occur again, there is no point in punishing. We say that the individual was not "aware of the consequences of his action" or that the consequences were not "intentional." If the action could not have been avoided—if the individual "had no choice"—punishment is also withheld, as it is if the individual is incapable of being changed by punishment because he is of "unsound mind." In all these cases—different as they are—the individual is held "not responsible" and goes unpunished.

Just as we say that it is "not fair" to punish a man for something he could not help doing, so we call it "unfair" when one is rewarded beyond his due or for something he could not help doing. In other words, we also object to wasting *reinforcers* where they are not needed or will do no good. We make the same point with the words *just* and *right*. Thus we have no right to punish the irresponsible, and a man has no right to reinforcers he does not earn or deserve. But concepts of choice, responsibility, justice, and so on, provide a most inadequate analysis of efficient reinforcing and punishing contingencies because they carry a heavy semantic cargo of a quite different sort, which obscures any attempt to clarify controlling practices or to improve techniques. In particular, they fail to prepare us for techniques based on other than aversive techniques of control. Most people would object to forcing prisoners to serve as subjects of dangerous medical experiments, but few object when they are induced to serve by the offer of return privileges—even when the reinforcing effect of these privileges has been created by forcible deprivation. In the traditional scheme the right to refuse guarantees the individual against coercion or an unfair bargain. But to what extent *can* a prisoner refuse under such circumstances?

We need not go so far afield to make the point. We can observe our own attitude toward personal freedom in the way we resent any interference with what we want to do. Suppose we want to buy a car of a particular sort. Then we may object, for example, if our wife urges us to buy a less expensive model and to put the difference into a new refrigerator. Or we may resent it if our neighbor questions our need for such a car or our ability to pay for it. We would certainly resent it if it were illegal to buy such a car (remember Prohibition); and if we find we cannot actually afford it, we may resent governmental control of the price through tariffs and taxes. We resent it if we discover that we cannot get the car because the manufacturer is holding the model in deliberately short supply

in order to push a model we do not want. In all this we assert our democratic right to buy the car of our choice. We are well prepared to do so and to resent any restriction on our freedom.

But why do we not ask *why* it is the car of our choice and resent the forces which made it so? Perhaps our favorite toy as a child was a car, of a very different model, but nevertheless bearing the name of the car we now want. Perhaps our favorite TV program is sponsored by the manufacturer of that car. Perhaps we have seen pictures of persons of beauty or prestige driving it—in pleasant or glamorous places. Perhaps the car has been designed with respect to our motivational patterns: the device on the hood is a phallic symbol; or the horse-power has been stepped up to please our competitive spirit in enabling us to pass other cars swiftly (or, as the advertisements say, "safely"). The concept of freedom that has emerged as part of the cultural practice of our group makes little or no provision for recognizing or dealing with these kinds of control. Concepts like "responsibility" and "rights" are scarcely applicable. We are prepared to deal with coercive measures, but we have no traditional recourse with respect to other measures which in the long run (and especially with the help of science) may be much more powerful and dangerous.

EDUCATION

The techniques of education were once frankly aversive. The teacher was usually older and stronger than his pupils and was able to "make them learn." This meant that they were not actually taught but were surrounded by a threatening world from which they could escape only by learning. Usually they were left to their own resources in discovering how to do so. Claude Coleman has published a grimly amusing reminder of these older practices. He tells of a schoolteacher who published a careful account of his services during 51 years of teaching, during which he administered: ". . . 911,527 blows with a cane; 124,010 with a rod; 20,989 with a ruler, 136,715 with the hand; 10,295 over the mouth; 7,905 boxes on the ear; [and] 1,115,800 slaps on the head. . . ."

Progressive education was a humanitarian effort to substitute positive reinforcement for such aversive measures, but in the search for useful human values in the classroom it has never fully replaced the variables it abandoned. Viewed as a branch of behavioral technology, education remains relatively inefficient. We supplement it, and rationalize it, by admiring the pupil who learns *for himself;* and we often attribute the learning process, or knowledge itself, to something *inside* the individual. We admire behavior which seems to have inner sources. Thus we admire one who *recites* a poem more than one who simply *reads* it. We admire one who *knows* the answer more than one who *knows where to look it up*. We admire the *writer* rather than the *reader*. We admire the arithmetician who can do a problem in his head rather than with a slide rule or calculating machine, or in "original" ways rather than by a strict application of rules. In general we feel that any aid or "crutch"—except those aids to which we are now thoroughly accustomed—reduces the credit due. In Plato's *Phaedus,* Thamus, the king, attacks the invention of the alphabet on similar grounds! He is afraid "it will produce forgetfulness in the minds of those who learn to use it, because they will not practice their memories. . . ." In other words, he holds it more admirable to remember than to use a memorandum. He also objects that pupils "will read many things without instruction . . . [and] will therefore seem to know many things when they are for the most part ignorant." In the same vein we are today sometimes contemptuous of book learning, but, as educators, we can scarcely afford to adopt this view without reservation.

By admiring the student for knowledge and blaming him for ignorance, we escape some of the responsibility of teaching him. We resist any analysis of the educational process which threatens the notion of inner wisdom or questions the contention that the fault of ignorance lies with the student. More powerful techniques which bring about the same changes in behavior by manipulating *external* variables are decried as brain-washing or thought control. We are quite unprepared to judge *effective* educational measures. As long as only a few pupils learn much of what is taught, we do not worry about uniformity or regimentation. We do not fear the feeble technique; but we should view with dismay a system under which every student learned everything listed in a syllabus—although such a condition is far from unthinkable. Similarly, we do not fear a system which is so defective that the student must *work* for an education; but we are loath to give credit for anything learned without effort—although this could well be taken as an ideal result— and we flatly refuse to give credit if the student

already knows what a school teaches.

A world in which people are wise and good without trying, without "having to be," without "choosing to be," could conceivably be a far better world for everyone. In such a world we should not have to "give anyone credit"—we should not need to admire anyone—for being wise and good. From our present point of view we cannot believe that such a world would be admirable. We do not even permit ourselves to imagine what it would be like.

GOVERNMENT

Government has always been the special field of aversive control. The state is frequently defined in terms of the power to punish, and jurisprudence leans heavily upon the associated notion of personal responsibility. Yet it is becoming increasingly difficult to reconcile current practice and theory with these earlier views. In criminology, for example, there is a strong tendency to drop the notion of responsibility as capacity or controllability. But no matter how strongly the fact, or even practical expedience, support such a change, it is difficult to make the change in a legal system designed on a different plan. When governments resort to other techniques (for example, positive reinforcement), the concept of responsibility is no longer relevant and the theory of government is no longer applicable.

The conflict is illustrated by two decisions of the Supreme Count in the 1930's which dealt with, and disagreed on, the definition of control or coercion. The Agricultural Adjustment Act proposed that the Secretary of Agriculture make "rental or benefit payments" to those farmers who agreed to reduce production. The government agreed that the Act would be unconstitutional if the farmer had been *compelled* to reduce production but was not, since he was merely *invited* to do so. Justice Roberts expressed the contrary majority view of the court that "The power to confer or withhold unlimited benefits is the power to coerce or destroy." This recognition of positive reinforcement was withdrawn a few years later in another case in which Justice Cardozo wrote "To hold that motive or temptation is equivalent to coercion is to plunge the law in endless difficulties." We may agree with him, without implying that the proposition is therefore wrong. Sooner or later the law must be prepared to deal with all possible techniques of governmental control.

The uneasiness with which we view government (in the broadest possible sense) when it does not use punishment is shown by the reception of my utopian novel, *Walden Two*. This was essentially a proposal to apply a behavioral technology to the construction of a workable, effective, and productive pattern of government. It was greeted with wrathful violence. *Life* magazine called it "a travesty on the good life," and "a menace . . . a triumph of mortmain or the dead hand not envisaged since the days of Sparta . . . a slur upon a name, a corruption of an impulse." Joseph Wood Krutch devoted a substantial part of his book, *The Measure of Man*, to attacking my views and those of the protagonist, Frazier, in the same vein, and Morris Viteles has recently criticized the book is a similar manner in *Science*. Perhaps the reaction is best expressed in a quotation from *The Quest for Utopia* by Negley and Patrick:

"Halfway through this contemporary utopia, the reader may feel sure, as we did, that this is a beautifully ironic satire on what has been called 'behavioral engineering.' The longer one stays in this better world of the psychologist, however, the plainer it becomes that the inspiration is not satiric, but messianic. This is indeed the behaviorally engineered society, and while it was to be expected that sooner or later the principle of psychological conditioning would be made the basis of a serious construction of utopia—Brown anticipated it in *Limanora*—yet not even the effective satire of Huxley is adequate preparation for the shocking horror of the idea when positively presented. Of all the dictatorships espoused by utopists, this is the most profound, and incipient dictators might well find in this utopia a guidebook of political practice."

One would scarcely guess that the authors are talking about a world in which there is food, clothing, and shelter for all, where everyone chooses his own work and works on the average only four hours a day, where music and the arts flourish, where personal relationships develop under the most favorable circumstances, where education prepares every child for the social and intellectual life which lies before him, where—in short—people are truly happy, secure, productive, creative, and forward-looking. What is wrong with it? Only one thing: someone "planned it that way." If these critics had come upon a society in some remote corner of the world which boasted similar advantages, they would undoubtedly have hailed it as providing a pattern we all might well follow—provided that it was clearly the result of a natural process of cultural evolution. Any evidence that intelligence had been used in arriving at this version of the good life would, in their eyes, be a serious flaw. No matter if the planner of *Walden Two* diverts none of the proceeds of the community to his own use, no matter if he has no current control or is, indeed, unknown to most of the other members of the community (he planned that, too), somewhere back of it all he occupies the position of prime mover. And this, to the child of the democratic tradition, spoils it all.

The dangers inherent in the control of human behavior are very real. The possibility of the misuse of scientific knowledge must always be faced. We cannot escape by denying the power of a science of behavior or arresting its development. It is no help to cling to familiar philosophies of human behavior simply because they are more reassuring. As I have pointed out elsewhere the new techniques emerging from a science of behavior must be subject to the explicit countercontrol which has already been applied to earlier and cruder forms. Brute force and deception, for example, are now fairly generally suppressed by ethical practices and by explicit governmental and religious agencies. A similar countercontrol of scientific knowledge in the interest of the group is a feasible and promising possibility. Although we cannot say how devious the course of its evolution may be, a cultural pattern of control and countercontrol will presumably emerge which will be most widely supported because it is most widely reinforcing.

If we cannot foresee all the details of this (as we obviously cannot), it is important to remember that this is true of the critics of science as well. The dire consequences of new techniques of control, the hidden menace in original cultural designs—these need some proof. It is only another example of my present point that the need for proof is so often overlooked. Man has got himself into some pretty fixes, and it is easy to believe that he will do so again. But there is a more optimistic possibility. The slow growth of the methods of science, now for the first time being applied to human affairs, *may* mean a new and exciting phase of human life to which historical analogies will not apply and in which earlier political slogans will not be appropriate. If we are to use the knowledge that a science of behavior is now making available with any hope of success, we must look at human nature as it is brought into focus through the methods of science rather than as it has been presented to us in a series of historical accidents.

If the advent of a powerful science of behavior causes trouble, it will not be because science itself is inimical to human welfare but because older conceptions have not yielded easily or gracefully. We expect resistance to new techniques of control from those who have heavy investments in the old, but we have no reason to help them preserve a series of principles that are not ends in themselves but rather outmoded means to an end. What is needed is a new conception of human behavior which is compatible with the implications of a scientific analysis. All men control and are controlled. The question of government in the broadest possible sense is not how freedom is to be preserved but what kinds of control are to be used and to what ends. Control must be analyzed and considered in its proper proportions. No one, I am sure, wishes to develop new master-slave relationships or bend the will of the people to despotic rulers in new ways. These are patterns of control appropriate to a world without science. They may well be the first to go when the experimental analysis of behavior comes into its own in the design of cultural practices.

II ROGERS

There are, I believe, a number of matters in connection with this important topic on which the authors of this article, and probably a large majority of psychologists, are in agreement. These matters then are not issues as far as we are concerned, and I should like to mention them briefly in order to put them to one side.

POINTS OF AGREEMENT

I am sure we agree that men—as individuals and as societies—have always endeavored to understand, predict, influence, and control human behavior—their own behavior and that of others.

I believe we agree that the behavioral sciences are making and will continue to make increasingly rapid progress in the understanding of behavior, and that as a consequence the capacity to predict and to control behavior is developing with equal rapidity.

I believe we agree that to deny these advances, or to claim that man's behavior cannot be a field of science, is unrealistic. Even though this is not an issue for us, we should recognize that many intelligent men still hold strongly to the view that the actions of men are free in some sense such that scientific knowledge of man's behavior is impossible. Thus Reinhold Niebuhr, the noted theologian, heaps scorn on the concept of psychology as a science of man's behavior and even says, "In any event, no scientific investigation of past behavior can become the basis of predictions of future behavior." So, while this is not an issue for psychologists, we should at least notice in passing that it is an issue for many people.

I believe we are in agreement that the tremendous potential power of a science which permits the prediction and control of behavior may be misused, and that the possibility of such misuse constitutes a serious threat.

Consequently Skinner and I are in agreement that the whole question of the scientific control of human behavior is a matter with which psychologists and the general public should concern themselves. As Robert Oppenheimer told the American Psychological Association last year the problems that psychologists will pose for society by their growing ability to control behavior will be much more grave than the problems posed by the ability of physicists to control the reactions of matter. I am not sure whether psychologists generally recognize this. My impression is that by and large they hold a laissez-faire attitude. Obviously Skinner and I do not hold this laissez-faire view, or we would not have written this article.

POINTS AT ISSUE

With these several points of basic and important agreement, are there then any issues that remain on which there are differences? I believe there are. They can be stated very briefly: Who will be controlled? Who will exercise control? What type of control will be exercised? Most important of all, toward what end or what purpose, or in the pursuit of what value, will control be exercised?

It is on questions of this sort that there exist ambiguities, misunderstandings, and probably deep differences. These differences exist among the general public in this country, and among various world cultures. Without any hope of achieving a final resolution of these questions, we can, I believe, put these issues in clearer form.

SOME MEANINGS

To avoid ambiguity and faulty communication, I would like to clarify the meanings of some of the terms we are using.

Behavioral science is a term that might be defined from several angles, but in the context of this discussion it refers primarily to knowledge that the existence of certain describable conditions in the human being and/or in his environment is followed by certain describable consequences in his actions.

Prediction means the prior identification of behaviors which then occur. Because it is important in some things I wish to say later, I would point out that one may predict a highly specific behavior, such as an eye blink, or one may predict a class of behaviors. One might correctly predict "avoidant behavior," for example, without being able to specify whether the individual will run away or simply close his eyes.

The word *control* is a very slippery one, which can be used with any one of several meanings. I would like to specify three that seem most important for our present purposes. *Control* may mean: (1) The setting of conditions by B for A, A having no voice in the matter, such that certain predictable behaviors then occur in A. I refer to this as external control. (2) The setting of conditions by B for A, A giving some degree of consent to these conditions, such that certain predictable behaviors then occur in A. I refer to this as the influence of B on A. (3) The setting of conditions by A such that certain predictable behaviors then occur in himself. I refer to this as internal control. It will be noted that Skinner lumps together the first two meanings, external control and influence, under the concept of control. I find this confusing.

USUAL CONCEPT OF CONTROL OF
HUMAN BEHAVIOR

With the underbrush thus cleared away (I hope), let us review very briefly the various elements that are involved in the usual concept of the control of human behavior as mediated by the behavioral sciences. I am drawing here on the previous writings of Skinner, on his present statements, on the writings of others who have considered in either friendly or antagonistic fashion the meanings that would be

involved in such control. I have not excluded the science fiction writers, as reported recently by Vandenbury, since they often show an awareness of the issues involved, even though the methods described are as yet fictional. These then are the elements that seem common to these different concepts of the application of science to human behavior.

1) There must first be some sort of decision about goals. Usually desirable goals are assumed, but sometimes, as in George Orwell's book *1984*, the goal that is selected is an aggrandizement of individual power with which most of us would disagree. In a recent paper Skinner suggests that one possible set of goals to be assigned to the behavioral technology is this: "Let men be happy, informed, skillful, well-behaved and productive." In the first draft of his part of this article, which he was kind enough to show me, he did not mention such definite goals as these, but desired "improved" educational practices, "wiser" use of knowledge in government, and the like. In the final version of his article he avoids even these value-laden terms, and his implicit goal is the very general one that scientific control of behavior is desirable, because it would perhaps bring "a far better world for everyone."

Thus the first step in thinking about the control of human behavior is the choice of goals, whether specific or general. It is necessary to come to terms in some way with the issue, "For what purpose?"

2) A second element is that, whether the end selected is highly specific or is a very general one such as wanting "a better world," we proceed by the methods of science to discover the means to these ends. We continue through further experimentation and investigation to discover more effective means. The method of science is self-correcting in thus arriving at increasingly effective ways of achieving the purpose we have in mind.

3) The third aspect of such control is that as the conditions or methods are discovered by which to reach the goal, some person or some group establishes these conditions and uses these methods, having in one way or another obtained the power to do so.

4) The fourth element is the exposure of individuals to the prescribed conditions, and this leads, with a high degree of probability, to behavior which is in line with the goals desired. Individuals are now happy, if that has been the goal, or well-behaved, or submissive, or what-

ever it has been decided to make them.

5) The fifth element is that if the process I have described is put in motion then there is a continuing social organization which will continue to produce the types of behavior that have been valued.

SOME FLAWS

Are there any flaws in this way of viewing the control of human behavior? I believe there are. In fact the only element in this description with which I find myself in agreement is the second. It seems to me quite incontrovertibly true that the scientific method is an excellent way to discover the means by which to achieve our goals. Beyond that, I feel many sharp differences, which I will try to spell out.

I believe that in Skinner's presentation here and in his previous writings, there is a serious underestimation of the problem of power. To hope that the power which is being made available by the behavioral sciences will be exercised by the scientists, or by a benevolent group, seems to me a hope little supported by either recent or distant history. It seems far more likely that behavioral scientists, holding their present attitudes, will be in the position of the German rocket scientists specializing in guided missiles. First they worked devotedly for Hitler to destroy the U.S.S.R. and the United States. Now, depending on who captured them, they work devotedly for the U.S.S.R. in the interest of destroying the United States, or devotedly for the United States in the interest of destroying the U.S.S.R. If behavioral scientists are concerned solely with advancing their science, it seems most probable that they will serve the purposes of whatever individual or group has the power.

But the major flaw I see in this review of what is involved in the scientific control of human behavior is the denial, misunderstanding, or gross underestimation of the place of ends, goals or values in their relationship to science. This error (as it seems to me) has so many implications that I would like to devote some space to it.

ENDS AND VALUES IN RELATION TO SCIENCE

In sharp contradiction to some views that have been advanced, I would like to propose a two-pronged thesis: (1) In any scientific endeavor—whether "pure" or applied science—there is a prior subjective choice of the purpose or value which that scientific work is perceived as serving. (2) This subjective value choice which brings the scientific endeavor into being must always lie outside of that endeavor and can never become a part of the science involved in that endeavor.

Let me illustrate the first point from Skinner himself. It is clear that in his earlier writing it is recognized that a prior value choice is necessary, and it is specified as the goal that men are to become happy, well-behaved, productive, and so on. I am pleased that Skinner has retreated from the goals he then chose, because to me they seem to be stultifying values. I can only feel that he was choosing these goals for others, not for himself. I would hate to see Skinner become "well-behaved," as that term would be defined for him by behavioral scientists. His recent article in the *American Psychologist* shows that he certainly does not want to be "productive" as that value is defined by most psychologists. And the most awful fate I can imagine for him would be to have him constantly "happy." It is the fact that he is very unhappy about many things which makes me prize him.

In the first draft of his part of this article, he also included such prior value choices, saying for example, "We must decide how we are to use the knowledge which a science of human behavior is now making available." Now he has dropped all mention of such choices, and if I understand him correctly, he believes that science can proceed without them. He has suggested this view in another recent paper, stating that "We must continue to experiment in cultural design . . . testing the consequences as we go. Eventually the practices which make for the greatest biological and psychological strength of the group will presumably survive."

I would point out, however, that to choose to experiment is a value choice. Even to move in the direction of perfectly random experimentation is a value choice. To test the consequences of an experiment is possible only if we have first made a subjective choice of a criterion value. And implicit in his statement is a valuing of biological and psychological strength. So even when trying to avoid such choice, it seems inescapable that a prior subjective value choice is necessary for any scientific endeavor, or for any application of scientific knowledge.

I wish to make it clear that I am not saying that values cannot be included as a subject of science. It is not true that science deals only with certain classes of "facts" and that these classes do not include values. It is a bit more complex than that, as a simple illustration or two may make clear.

If I value knowledge of the "three R's" as a goal of education, the methods of science can give me increasingly accurate information on how this goal may be achieved. If I value problem-solving ability as a goal of education, the scientific method can give me the same kind of help.

Now, if I wish to determine whether problem-solving ability is "better" than knowledge of the three R's, then scientific method can also study those two values but *only*—and this is very important—in terms of some other value which I have subjectively chosen. I may value college success. Then I can determine whether problem-solving ability or knowledge of the three R's is most closely associated with that value. I may value personal integration or vocational success or responsible citizenship. I can determine whether problem-solving ability or knowledge of the three R's is "better" for achieving any one of these values. But the value or purpose that gives meaning to a particular scientific endeavor must always lie outside of that endeavor.

Although our concern in this symposium is largely with applied science, what I have been saying seems equally true of so-called "pure" science. In pure science the usual prior subjective value choice is the discovery of truth. But this is a subjective choice, and science can never say whether it is the best choice, save in the light of some other value. Geneticists in the U.S.S.R., for example, had to make a subjective choice of whether it was better to pursue truth or to discover facts which upheld a governmental dogma. Which choice is "better"? We could make a scientific investigation of those alternatives but only in the light some other subjectively chosen value. If, for example, we value the survival of a culture, then we could begin to investigate with the methods of science the question of whether pursuit of truth or support of governmental dogma is most closely associated with cultural survival.

My point then is that any endeavor in science, pure or applied, is carried on in the pursuit of a purpose or value that is subjectively chosen by persons. It is important that this choice be made explicit, since the particular value which is being sought can never be tested or evaluated, confirmed or denied, by the scientific endeavor to which it gives birth. The initial

purpose or value always and necessarily lies outside the scope of the scientific effort which it sets in motion.

Among other things this means that if we choose some particular goal or series of goals for human beings and then set out on a large scale to control human behavior to the end of achieving those goals, we are locked in the rigidity of our initial choice, because such a scientific endeavor can never transcend itself to select new goals. Only subjective human persons can do that. Thus if we chose as our goal the state of happiness for human beings (a goal deservedly ridiculed by Aldous Huxley in *Brave New World*), and if we involved all of society in a successful scientific program by which people became happy, we would be locked in a colossal rigidity in which no one would be free to question this goal, because our scientific operations could not transcend themselves to question their guiding purposes. And without laboring this point, I would remark that colossal rigidity, whether in dinosaurs or dictatorships, has a very poor record of evolutionary survival.

If, however, a part of our scheme is to set free some "planners" who do not have to be happy, who are not controlled, and who are therefore free to choose other values, this has several meanings. It means that the purpose we have chosen as our goal is not a sufficient and a satisfying one for human beings but must be supplemented. It also means that if it is necessary to set up an elite group which is free, then this shows all too clearly that the great majority are only the slaves—no matter by what high-sounding name we call them—of those who select the goals.

Perhaps, however, the thought is that a continuing scientific endeavor will evolve its own goals; that the initial findings will alter the directions, and subsequent findings will alter them still further, and that science somehow develops its own purpose. Although he does not clearly say so, this appears to be the pattern Skinner has in mind. It is surely a reasonable description, but it overlooks one element in this continuing development, which is that subjective personal choice enters in at every point at which the direction changes. The findings of a science, the results of an experiment, do not and never can tell us what next scientific purpose to pursue. Even in the purest of science, the scientist must decide what the findings mean and must subjectively choose what next step will be most profitable in the pursuit of his purpose. And if we are speaking of the application of scientific knowledge, then it is distressingly clear that the increasing scientific knowledge of the structure of the atom carries with it no necessary choice as to the purpose to which this knowledge will be put. This is a subjective personal choice which must be made by many individuals.

Thus I return to the proposition with which I began this section of my remarks—and which I now repeat in different words. Science has its meaning as the objective pursuit of a purpose which has been subjectively chosen by a person or persons. This purpose or value can never be investigated by the particular scientific experiment or investigation to which it has given birth and meaning. Consequently, any discussion of the control of human beings by the behavioral sciences must first and most deeply concern itself with the subjectively chosen purposes which such an application of science is intended to implement.

IS THE SITUATION HOPELESS?

The thoughtful reader may recognize that, although my remarks up to this point have introduced some modifications in the conception of the processes by which human behavior will be controlled, these remarks may have made such control seem, if anything, even more inevitable. We might sum it up this way: Behavioral science is clearly moving forward; the increasing power for control which it gives will be held by someone or some group; such an individual or group will surely choose the values or goals to be achieved; and most of us will then be increasingly controlled by means so subtle that we will not even be aware of them as controls. Thus, whether a council of wise psychologists (if this is not a contradiction in terms), or a Stalin, or a Big Brother has the power, and whether the goal is happiness, or productivity, or resolution of the Oedipus complex, or submission, or love of Big Brother, we will inevitably find ourselves moving toward the chosen goal and probably thinking that we ourselves desire it. Thus, if this line of reasoning is correct, it appears that some form of *Walden Two* or of *1984* (and at a deep philosophic level they seem indistinguishable) is coming. The fact that it would surely arrive piecemeal, rather than all at once, does not greatly change the fundamental issues. In any event, as Skinner has indicated in his writings, we would then look back upon the concepts of human freedom, the capacity for choice, the re-

sponsibility for choice, and the worth of the human individual as historical curiosities which once existed by cultural accident as values in a prescientific civilization.

I believe that any person observant of trends must regard something like the foregoing sequence as a real possibility. It is not simply a fantasy. Something of that sort may even be the most likely future. But is it an inevitable future? I want to devote the remainder of my remarks to an alternative possibility.

ALTERNATIVE SET OF VALUES

Suppose we start with a set of ends, values, purposes, quite different from the type of goals we have been considering. Suppose we do this quite openly, setting them forth as a possible value choice to be accepted or rejected. Suppose we select a set of values that focuses on fluid elements of process rather than static attributes. We might then value: man as a process of becoming, as a process of achieving worth and dignity through the development of his potentialities; the individual human being as a self-actualizing process, moving on to more challenging and enriching experiences; the process by which the individual creatively adapts to an ever-new and changing world; the process by which knowledge transcends itself, as, for example, the theory of relativity transcended Newtonian physics, itself to be transcended in some future day by a new perception.

If we select values such as these we turn to our science and technology of behavior with a very different set of questions. We will want to know such things as these: Can science aid in the discovery of new modes of richly rewarding living? More meaningful and satisfying modes of interpersonal relationships? Can science inform us on how the human race can become a more intelligent participant in its own evolution—its physical, psychological and social evolution? Can science inform us on ways of releasing the creative capacity of individuals, which seem so necessary if we are to survive in this fantastically expanding atomic age? Oppenheimer has pointed out that knowledge, which used to double in millenia or centuries, now doubles in a generation or a decade. It appears that we must discover the utmost in release of creativity if we are to be able to adapt effectively. In short, can science discover the methods by which man can most readily become a continually developing and self-transcending process, in his behavior, his thinking, his knowledge? Can science predict and release an essentially "unpredictable" freedom?

It is one of the virtues of science as a method that it is as able to advance and implement goals and purposes of this sort as it is to serve static values, such as states of being well-informed, happy, obedient. Indeed we have some evidence of this.

SMALL EXAMPLE

I will perhaps be forgiven if I document some of the possibilities along this line by turning to psychotherapy, the field I know best.

Psychotherapy, as Meerloo and others have pointed out, can be one of the most subtle tools for the control of A by B. The therapist can subtly mold individuals in imitation of himself. He can cause an individual to become a submissive and conforming being. When certain therapeutic principles are used in extreme fashion, we call it brainwashing, an instance of the disintegration of the personality and a reformulation of the person along lines desired by the controlling individual. So the principles of therapy can be used as an effective means of external control of human personality and behavior. Can psychotherapy be anything else?

Here I find the developments going on in client-centered psychotherapy an exciting hint of what a behavioral science can do in achieving the kinds of values I have stated. Quite aside from being a somewhat new orientation in psychotherapy, this development has important implications regarding the relation of a behavioral science to the control of human behavior. Let me describe our experience as it relates to the issues of this discussion.

In client-centered therapy, we are deeply engaged in the prediction and influencing of behavior, or even the control of behavior. As therapists, we institute certain attitudinal conditions, and the client has relatively little voice in the establishment of these conditions. We predict that if these conditions are instituted, certain behavioral consequences will ensue in the client. Up to this point this is largely external control, no different from what Skinner has described, and no different from what I have discussed in the preceding sections of this article. But here any similarity ceases.

The conditions we have chosen to establish, predict such behavioral consequencies as these: that the client will become self-directing, less rigid, more open to the evidence of his senses, better organized and integrated, more similar to the ideal which he has chosen for himself. In other words, we have established by external control conditions which we predict will be followed by internal control by the individual, in pursuit of internally chosen goals. We have set the conditions which predict various classes of behaviors—self-directing behaviors, sensitivity to realities within and without, flexible adaptiveness—which are by their very nature unpredictable in their specifics. Our recent research indicates that our predictions are to a significant degree corroborated, and our commitment to the scientific method causes us to believe that more effective means of achieving these goals may be realized.

Research exists in other fields—industry, education, group dynamics—which seems to support our own findings. I believe it may be conservatively stated that scientific progress has been made in identifying those conditions in an interpersonal relationship which, if they exist in B, are followed in A by greater maturity in behavior, less dependence on others, an increase in expressiveness as a person, an increase in variability, flexibility and effectiveness of adaptation, an increase in self-responsibility and self-direction. And, quite in contrast to the concern expressed by some, we do not find that the creatively adaptive behavior which results from such self-directed variability of expression is a "happy accident" which occurs in "chaos." Rather, the individual who is open to his experience, and self-directing, is harmonious not chaotic, ingenious rather than random, as he orders his responses imaginatively toward the achievement of his own purposes. His creative actions are no more a "happy accident" than was Einstein's development of the theory of relativity.

Thus we find ourselves in fundamental agreement with John Dewey's statement: "Science has made its way by releasing, not by suppressing, the elements of variation, of invention and innovation, of novel creation in individuals" Progress in personal life and in group living is, we believe, made in the same way.

POSSIBLE CONCEPT OF THE CONTROL OF HUMAN BEHAVIOR

It is quite clear that the point of view I am expressing is in sharp contrast to the usual conception of the relationship of the behavioral sciences to the control of human behavior. In order to make this contrast even more blunt, I will state this possibility in paragraphs parallel to those used before.

1) It is possible for us to choose to value

man as a self-actualizing process of becoming, and to value creativity and the process by which knowledge becomes self-transcending.

2) We can proceed, by the methods of science, to discover the conditions which necessarily precede these processes and, through continuing experimentation, to discover better means of achieving these purposes.

3) It is possible for individuals or groups to set these conditions, with a minimum of power or control. According to present knowledge, the only authority necessary is the authority to establish certain qualities of interpersonal relationship.

4) Exposed to these conditions, present knowledge suggests that individuals become more self-responsible, make progress in self-actualization, become more flexible, and become more creatively adaptive.

5) Thus such an initial choice would inaugurate the beginnings of a social system or subsystem in which values, knowledge, adaptive skills, and even the concept of science would be continually changing and self-transcending. The emphasis would be upon man as a process of becoming.

I believe it is clear that such a view as I have been describing does not lead to any definable utopia. It would be impossible to predict its final outcome. It involves a step-by-step development, based on a continuing subjective choice of purposes, which are implemented by the behavioral sciences. It is in the direction of the "open society," as that term has been defined by Popper, Where individuals carry responsibility for personal decisions. It is at the opposite pole from his concept of the closed society, of which *Walden Two* would be an example.

I trust it is also evident that the whole emphasis is on process, not on end-states of being. I am suggesting that it is by choosing to value certain qualitative elements of the process of becoming that we can find a pathway toward the open society.

THE CHOICE

It is my hope that we have helped to clarify the range of choice which will lie before us and our children in regard to the behavioral sciences. We can choose to use our growing knowledge to enslave people in ways never dreamed of before, depersonalizing them, controlling them by means so carefully selected that they will perhaps never be aware of their loss of personhood. We can choose to utilize

our scientific knowledge to make men happy, well-behaved, and productive, as Skinner earlier suggested. Or we can insure that each person learns all the syllabus which we select and set before him, as Skinner now suggests. Or at the other end of the spectrum of choice we can choose to use the behavioral sciences in ways which will free, not control; which will bring about constructive variability, not conformity; which will develop creativity, not contentment; which will facilitate each person in his self-directed process of becoming; which will aid individuals, groups, and even the concept of science to become self-transcending in freshly adaptive ways of meeting life and its problems. The choice is up to us, and, the human race being what it is, we are likely to stumble about, making at times some nearly disastrous value choices and at other times highly constructive ones.

I am aware that to some, this setting forth of a choice is unrealistic, because a choice of values is regarded as not possible. Skinner has stated: "Man's vaunted creative powers . . . his capacity to choose and our right to hold him responsible for his choice—none of these is conspicuous in this new self-portrait (provided by science). Man, we once believed, was free to express himself in art, music, and literature, to inquire into nature, to seek salvation in his own way. He could initiate action and make spontaneous and capricious changes of course. . . . But science insists that action is initiated by forces impinging upon the individual, and that caprice is only another name for behavior for which we have not yet found a cause."

I can understand this point of view, but I believe that it avoids looking at the great paradox of behavioral science. Behavior, when it is examined scientifically, is surely best understood as determined by prior causation. This is one great fact of science. But responsible personal choice, which is the most essential element in being a person, which is the core experience in psychotherapy, which exists prior to any scientific endeavor, is an equally prominent fact in our lives. To deny the experience of responsible choice is, to me, as restricted a view as to deny the possibility of a behavioral science. That these two important elements of our experience appear to be in contradiction has perhaps the same significance as the contradiction between the wave theory and the corpuscular theory of light, both of which can be shown to be true, even though incompatible. We cannot profitably deny our subjective life, any more than we can deny the objective description of that life.

In conclusion then, it is my contention that science cannot come into being without a personal choice of the values we wish to achieve. And these values we choose to implement will forever lie outside of the science which implements them; the goals we select, the purposes we wish to follow, must always be outside of the science which achieves them. To me this has the encouraging meaning that the human person, with his capacity of subjective choice, can and will always exist, separate from and prior to any of his scientific undertakings. Unless as individuals and groups we choose to relinquish our capacity of subjective choice, we will always remain persons, not simply pawns of a self-created science.

III SKINNER

I cannot quite agree that the practice of science *requires* a prior decision about goals or a prior choice of values. The metallurgist can study the properties of steel and the engineer can design a bridge without raising the question of whether a bridge is to be built. But such questions are certainly frequently raised and tentatively answered. Rogers wants to call the answers "subjective choices of values." To me, such an expression suggests that we have had to abandon more rigorous scientific practices in order to talk about our own behavior. In the experimental analysis of other organisms I would use other terms, and I shall try to do so here. Any list of values is a list of reinforcers—conditioned or otherwise. We are so constituted that under certain circumstances food, water, sexual contact, and so on, will make any behavior which produces them more likely to occur again. Other things may acquire this power. We do not need to say that an organism chooses to eat rather than to starve. If you answer that it is a very different thing when a man chooses to starve, I am only too happy to agree. If it were not so, we should have cleared up the question of choice long ago. An organism can be reinforced by—can be made to "choose"—almost any given state of affairs.

Rogers is concerned with choices that involve multiple and usually conflicting consequences. I have dealt with some of these elsewhere in an analysis of self-control. Shall I eat these delicious strawberries today if I will then suffer an annoying rash tomorrow? The decision I am to make used to be assigned to the province

of ethics. But we are now studying similar combinations of positive and negative consequences, as well as collateral conditions which affect the result in the laboratory. Even a pigeon can be taught some measure of self-control! And this work helps us to understand the operation of certain formulas—among them value judgments—which folk-wisdom, religion, and psychotherapy have advanced in the interests of self-discipline. The observable effect of any statement of value is to alter the relative effectiveness of reinforcers. We may no longer enjoy the strawberries for thinking about the rash. If rashes are made sufficiently shameful, illegal, sinful, maladjusted, or unwise, we may glow with satisfaction as we push the strawberries aside in a grandiose avoidance response which would bring a smile to the lips of Murray Sidman.

People behave in ways which, as we say, conform to ethical, governmental, or religious patterns because they are reinforced for doing so. The resulting behavior may have far-reaching consequences for the survival of the pattern to which it conforms. And whether we like it or not, survival is the ultimate criterion. This is where, it seems to me, science can help—not in choosing a goal, but in enabling us to predict the survival value of cultural practices. Man has too long tried to get the kind of world he wants by glorifying some brand of immediate reinforcement. As science points up more and more of the remoter consequences, he may begin to work to strengthen behavior, not in a slavish devotion to a chosen value, but with respect to the ultimate survival of mankind. Do not ask me why I want mankind to survive. I can tell you why only in the sense in which the physiologist can tell you why I want to breathe. Once the relation between a given step and the survival of my group has been pointed out, I will take that step. And it is the business of science to point out just such relations.

The values I have occasionally recommended (and Rogers has not led me to recant) are transitional. Other things being equal, I am betting on the group whose practices make for healthy, happy, secure, productive, and creative people. And I insist that the values recommended by Rogers are transitional, too, for I can ask him the same kind of question. Man as a process of becoming—*what?* Self-actualization—for what? Inner control is no more a goal than external.

What Rogers seems to me to be proposing, both here and elsewhere is this: Let us use our increasing power of control to create individuals who will not need and perhaps will no longer respond to control. Let us solve the problem of our power by renouncing it. At first blush this seems as implausible as a benevolent despot. Yet power has occasionally been foresworn. A nation has burned its Reichstag, rich men have given away their wealth, beautiful women have become ugly hermits in the desert, and psychotherapists have become nondirective. When this happens, I look to other possible reinforcements for a plausible explanation. A people relinquish democratic power when a tyrant promises them the earth. Rich men give away wealth to escape the accusing finger of their fellowmen. A woman destroys her beauty in the hope of salvation. And a psychotherapist relinquishes control because he can thus help his client more effectively.

The solution that Rogers is suggesting is thus understandable. But is he correctly interpreting the results? What evidence is there that a client ever becomes truly *self*-directing? What evidence is there that he ever makes a truly *inner* choice of ideal or goal? Even though the therapist does not do the choosing even though he encourages "self-actualization"—he is not out of control as long as he holds himself ready to step in when occasion demands—when, for example, the client chooses the goal of becoming a more accomplished liar or murdering his boss. But supposing the therapist does withdraw completely or is no longer necessary—what about all the other forces acting upon the client? Is the self-chosen goal independent of his early ethical and religious training? of the folk-wisdom of his group? of the opinions and attitudes of others who are important to him? Surely not. The therapeutic situation is only a small part of the world of the client. From the therapist's point of view it may appear to be possible to relinquish control. But the control passes, not to a "self," but to forces in other parts of the client's world. The solution of the therapist's problem of power cannot be *our* solution, for we must consider *all* the forces acting upon the individual.

The child who must be prodded and nagged is something less than a fully developed human being. We want to see him hurrying to his appointment, not because each step is taken in response to verbal reminders from his mother, but because certain temporal contingencies, in which dawdling has been punished and hurrying reinforced, have worked a change in his

behavior. Call this a state of better organization, a greater sensitivity to reality, or what you will. The plain fact is that the child passes from a temporary verbal control exercised by his parents to control by certain inexorable features of the environment. I should suppose that something of the same sort happens in successful psychotherapy. Rogers seems to me to be saying this: Let us put an end, as quickly as possible, to any pattern of master-and-slave, to any direct obedience to command, to the submissive following of suggestions. Let the individual be free to adjust himself to more rewarding features of the world about him. In the end, let his teachers and counselors "wither away," like the Marxist state. I not only agree with this as a useful ideal, I have constructed a fanciful world to demonstrate its advantages. It saddens me to hear Rogers say that "at a deep philosophic level" *Walden Two* and George Orwell's *1984* "seem indistinguishable." They could scarcely be more unlike—at any level. The book *1984* is a picture of immediate aversive control for vicious selfish purposes. The founder of *Walden Two*, on the other hand, has built a community in which neither he nor any other person exerts any *current* control. His achievement lay in his original *plan*, and when he boasts of this ("It is enough to satisfy the thirstiest tyrant") we do not fear him but only pity him for his weakness.

Another critic of *Walden Two*, Andrew Hacker, has discussed his point in considering the bearing of mass conditioning upon the liberal notion of autonomous man. In drawing certain parallels between the Grand Inquisition passage in Dostoevsky's *Brothers Karamazov*, Huxley's *Brave New World*, and *Walden Two*, he attempts to set up a distinction to be drawn in any society between conditioners and conditioned. He assumes that "the conditioner can be said to be autonomous in the traditional liberal sense." But then he notes: "Of course the conditioner has been conditioned. But he has not been conditioned by the conscious manipulation of another *person*." But how does this affect the resulting behavior? Can we not soon forget the origins of the "artificial" diamond which is identical with the real thing? Whether it is an "accidental" cultural pattern, such as is said to have produced the founder of *Walden Two*, or the engineered environment which is about to produce his successors, we are dealing with sets of conditions generating human behavior which will ultimately be measured by their contribution to the strength of the group. We look to the future, not the past, for the test of "goodness" or acceptability.

If we are worthy of our democratic heritage we shall, of course, be ready to resist any tyrannical use of science for immediate or selfish purposes. But if we value the achievements and goals of democracy we must not refuse to apply science to the design and construction

of cultural patterns, even though we may then find ourselves in some sense in the position of controllers. Fear of control, generalized beyond any warrant, has led to a misinterpretation of valid practices and the blind rejection of intelligent planning for a better way of life. In terms which I trust Rogers will approve, in conquering this fear we shall become more mature and better organized and shall, thus, more fully actualize ourselves as human beings.

1956

GEORGE C. MARSHALL

1880-1959

BORN IN 1880 at Uniontown, Pennsylvania, George C. Marshall was graduated from the Virginia Military Institute in 1901 and from the United States Infantry-Cavalry School in 1907. By 1939 Marshall had become a major general, having served in the Philippines, in World War I, and as deputy and acting Chief of Staff of the United States Army. He was Chief of Staff during World War II and took an important part in diplomatic negotiations during the struggle and in the years immediately following the armistices. From January, 1947, to January, 1949, Marshall was Secretary of State. On June 5, 1947, he outlined in an address before the Harvard Alumni Association a program which became known as the Marshall Plan. It was implemented, and it accomplished many of its objectives.

General Marshall's Report, The Winning of the War in Europe and the Pacific, New York, 1945.
Selected Speeches and Statements of the General of the Army George C. Marshall, Washington, 1945.
William Frye, *Marshall, Citizen Soldier*, Indianapolis, New York, 1947.
Pierre S. R. Payne, *The Marshall Story*, New York, 1951.

» » *From:* EUROPEAN UNITY « «

I need not tell you gentlemen that the world situation is very serious. That must be apparent to all intelligent people. I think one difficulty is that the problem is one of such enormous complexity that the very mass of facts presented to the public by press and radio make it exceedingly difficult for the man in the street to reach a clear appraisement of the situation. Furthermore, the people of this country are distant from the troubled areas of the earth and it is hard for them to comprehend the plight and consequent reactions of the long-suffering peoples, and the effect of those reactions on their governments in connection with our efforts to promote peace in the world.

In considering the requirements for the re-

habilitation of Europe the physical loss of life, the visible destruction of cities, factories, mines and railroads was correctly estimated, but it has become obvious during recent months that this visible destruction was probably less serious than the dislocation of the entire fabric of European economy. For the past ten years conditions have been highly abnormal. The feverish preparation for war and the more feverish maintenance of the war effort engulfed all aspects of national economics. Machinery has fallen into disrepair or is entirely obsolete. Under the arbitrary and destructive Nazi rule, virtually every possible enterprise was geared into the German war machine. Long-standing commercial ties, private institutions, banks, insurance companies and shipping companies disappeared, through loss of capital, absorption through nationalization or by simple destruction. In many countries, confidence in the local currency has been severely shaken. The breakdown of the business structure of Europe during the war was complete. Recovery has been seriously retarded by the fact that two years after the close of hostilities a peace settlement with Germany and Austria has not been agreed upon. But even given a more prompt solution of these difficult problems, the rehabilitation of the economic structure of Europe quite evidently will require a much longer time and greater effort than had been foreseen.

There is a phase of this matter which is both interesting and serious. The farmer has always produced the foodstuffs to exchange with the city dweller for the other necessities of life. This division of labor is the basis of modern civilization. At the present time it is threatened with breakdown. The town and city industries are not producing adequate goods to exchange with the food-producing farmer. Raw materials and fuel are in short supply. Machinery is lacking or worn out. The farmer or the peasant cannot find the goods for sale which he desires to purchase. So the sale of his farm produce for money which he cannot use seems to him an unprofitable transaction. He, therefore, has withdrawn many fields from crop cultivation and is using them for grazing. He feeds more grain to stock and finds for himself and his family an ample supply of food, however short he may be on clothing and the other ordinary gadgets of civilization. Meanwhile people in the cities are short of food and fuel. So the governments are forced to use their foreign money and credits to procure these necessities abroad. This process exhausts funds which are urgently needed for reconstruction. Thus a very serious situation is rapidly developing which bodes no good for the world. The modern system of the division of labor upon which the exchange of products is based is in danger of breaking down.

The truth of the matter is that Europe's requirements for the next three or four years of foreign food and other essential products—principally from America—are so much greater than her present ability to pay that she must have substantial additional help, or face economic, social and political deterioration of a very grave character.

The remedy lies in breaking the vicious cir-cle and restoring the confidence of the European people in the economic future of their own countries and of Europe as a whole. The manufacturer and the farmer throughout wide areas must be able and willing to exchange their products for currencies the continuing value of which is not open to question.

Aside from the demoralizing effect on the world at large and the possibilities of disturbances arising as a result of the desperation of the people concerned, the consequences to the economy of the United States should be apparent to all. It is logical that the United States should do whatever it is able to do to assist in the return of normal economic health in the world, without which there can be no political stability and no assured peace. Our policy is directed not against any country or doctrine but against hunger, poverty, desperation and chaos. Its purpose should be the revival of a working economy in the world so as to permit the emergence of political and social conditions in which free institutions can exist. Such assistance, I am convinced, must not be on a piece-meal basis as various crises develop. Any assistance that this Government may render in the future should provide a cure rather than a mere palliative. Any government that is willing to assist in the task of recovery will find full cooperation, I am sure, on the part of the United States Government. Any government which maneuvers to block the recovery of other countries cannot expect help from us. Furthermore, governments, political parties or groups which seek to perpetuate human misery in order to profit therefrom politically or otherwise will encounter the opposition of the United States.

It is already evident that, before the United States Government can proceed much further in its efforts to alleviate the situation and help start the European world on its way to recovery, there must be some agreement among the countries of Europe as to the requirements of the situation and the part those countries themselves will take in order to give proper effect to whatever action might be undertaken by this Government. It would be neither fitting nor efficacious for this Government to undertake to draw up unilaterally a program designed to place Europe on its feet economically. This is the business of the Europeans. The initiative, I think, must come from Europe. The role of this country should consist of friendly aid in the drafting of a European

program and of later support of such a program so far as it may be practical for us to do
so. The program should be a joint one, agreed
to by a number, if not all European nations.

An essential part of any successful action
on the part of the United States is an understanding on the part of the people of America
of the character of the problem and the reme-

dies to be applied. Political passion and prejudice should have no part. With foresight, and
a willingness on the part of our people to face
up to the vast responsibility which history has
clearly placed upon our country, the difficulties I have outlined can and will be overcome.

1947

WALTER LIPPMANN

1889–

A GRADUATE OF Harvard in the class of 1910, Lippmann served as a captain in the
United States Military Intelligence during World War I, and, both before and after
the War, was an editor of *The New Republic*. He worked for the New York *World* and since
1931 has been a columnist for the New York *Herald Tribune*. A thoughtful analyst of foreign
affairs, Lippmann's opinions have carried considerable weight in many circles.

The following selection was given as an address to the Phi Beta Kappa Society at William
and Mary College on December 5, 1947.

Preface to Politics, 1913.
Phantom Public, 1925.
Preface to Morals, 1929.
United States in World Affairs, 1931.
United States Foreign Policy, 1943.
Marquis Childs and James Reston, eds., *Walter Lippmann and His Times*, New York, 1959.

» » From: PHILOSOPHY AND UNITED STATES FOREIGN POLICY « «

I must suppose that it has occurred to many
of you, as you looked at your program and
saw the title of my address, that anyone who
proposes to discuss philosophy and the foreign
policy of the United States has chosen a rather
wide and double-barreled subject. But I have
been studying a list of the subjects which were
debated here at William and Mary by the
founding members of our society, and I find
that tradition and historic precedents are with
me. Phi Beta Kappa never shrank from the
discussion of big subjects, or from questions
on which the speaker of the day must not have
been able to say the last word.

Thus, I find in Dr. Voorhees' History of Phi
Beta Kappa that on April 22, 1780 the subject
was: "Had William the Norman the right to
invade England?" On May 21 the subject was:

"Whether the execution of Charles the First
was justifiable?" On June 17 our reverend
founders had a debate on "Whether the rape
of the Sabine women was just." On August 27
they asked themselves "Whether all our affections and principles are not in some manner
deducible from self-love." And on September
12 "Whether polygamy is a dictate of nature
or not."

So I feel I am in good company, and I may
say that in coupling philosophy with the foreign policy of the United States, I did not
mean to tease you or to mystify you. For if,
as our society insists, philosophy is the guide
to life, then in philosophy we ought to find the
guide to the great difficulty which the American people have experienced—particularly in
the past 40 years—in forming a good and

workable foreign policy. I have come to think that the root of our difficulty is to be found in our philosophy. And that is what I should like to talk about this evening.

If we study the history of American foreign relations during the past 40 years, we must be struck by an extraordinary paradox. During this period the United States has emerged from its long isolation. It has become one of the leading powers of the world. Not once but twice during this period the American people have had to face the awful issues of war and peace. Can it be said that during this momentous period we have ever succeeded in forming and agreeing on a foreign policy which foresaw correctly and enabled us to deal successfully with the actual course of events? The record is, I think, clear. We have won both wars. But on the crucial issues our diplomacy has thus far always miscarried. It has been unable to prevent war. It has been unable to avoid war. It has not prepared us for war. It has not been able to settle the wars when they have been fought and won.

At no critical phase in this epoch has the actual outcome conformed with our declarations and our expectations. Never has the country been able to achieve any of the principal objectives to which again and again it has been so solemnly and fervently committed.

Thus from 1914 to 1917 the country believed and hoped that it could avoid participation in the First World War. Yet it was compelled to participate. And when it did participate, it was unprepared because it had believed that it would not have to participate. During that war the country hoped and believed that by a victory it would achieve a lasting and democratic peace. The victory was attained. But the peace which had been promised was not achieved. After the First World War the country again decided to believe that if there were another war, it would be able to remain out of it. Again it did not prepare for war. Once again it was unable to remain out of the war, when it came.

During the Second World War the country again decided to believe that with victory over the Germans there would begin an era in which all the victorious powers would agree and be harmonious and become unanimous on the terms and conditions of a just and durable peace. We have had the victory. But we have not been able to attain that peace.

Now, after two victorious world wars we find ourselves discussing the possibility of a third world war. And so we must ask ourselves whether we have become entangled in a degenerating cycle of wars that breed more wars, each more savage and more inconclusive than the last. It is a grim question. We must however face it, and I believe that we must answer it by saying that if our present estimates and calculations are no more correct than those on which we acted before, during and immediately after the first and second world wars, then we shall be surprised and disappointed again. Once more we shall not know how to prevent war, nor how to prepare for it correctly, or how, assuming we win it, to make peace after it. And if a second world war leads to the third, if we cannot make a settlement of the war we have just won, what ground is there to suppose that we could settle a third world war so that it did not lead to a fourth?

Is it not true that in the twentieth century we have witnessed on the one hand the rise of the United States to pre-eminence among the nations, to a position of great leadership and immense responsibility in shaping the destiny of mankind? And on the other hand, is it not also true that the course of events during the American rise to pre-eminence is strewn with debris and wreckage of high and hopeful declarations of policy—Wilson's neutrality, Wilson's Fourteen Points, the Covenant of the League of Nations; with the Washington treaties of disarmament and the Kellogg Pact to outlaw war, with the Dawes plan, and the Young plan, and the Hoover moratorium to reconstruct the world after the First World War, with the Stimson doctrine to prevent aggression, with the Neutrality Act before the Second World War, with the quarantine speech of Franklin Roosevelt, and the four freedoms, and Mr. Hull's 17 points, and the Atlantic Charter, and the Yalta declaration, and the so-called Truman doctrine?

Must we not say that it would not have been necessary to improvise in rapid succession so many new plans and new formulae if any of them had worked out as, at the time they were announced, we hoped and believed they would?

When we reflect on this experience of repeated declarations and repeated disappointments, we must be struck by the contrast between our capacity as a people to develop national power and our ability to use it and to manage it successfully.

It is plain that our failures lie in the field of policy—that is to say, in deciding correctly when, where, how, and to what ends we shall exert the enormous power and influence we are able to generate.

For it cannot be argued that the miscarriages of American diplomacy are due to the weakness of the American Nation. Among the powers of the world the United States is the least vulnerable to invasion, to blockade or, with existing weapons, to decisive assault. The United States has the material resources, and it has the productive capacity to develop enormous offensive power in time of war. And in time of peace it produces a great export surplus—a surplus above and beyond a high standard of life at home—which renders it economically invulnerable in the outer world. Two great wars have proved the valor of American troops, the fortitude of the American people, and the military competence of American military commanders. Our institutions and our traditions are respected. And on the whole our participation in world affairs is welcomed by the great masses of mankind as promising liberty, justice, peace, and plenty.

It is, therefore, a reasonable conclusion, I submit, that we must seek the cause of our diplomatic failures in our own minds. We must look for the cause of trouble not in material circumstances but in our own habits of thought when we are dealing with foreign affairs and with the formation of American policy. Now, I believe that an inquiry will show that in the period from Woodrow Wilson to President Truman our foreign policy has miscarried so regularly because there is interposed within our own minds, between the outer world and ourselves, a collection of stereotyped prejudices and sacred cows and wishful conceptions, which misrepresent the nature of things, which falsify our judgments of events, and which inhibit the formation of workable policies by which our available means can be devoted efficiently to realizable ends.

We have, I shall argue, brought along with us from our age of innocence, from the nineteenth century when we were isolated, and when we were sheltered from the rivalries of states and empires, an ideological picture of the world, a philosophical framework of preconceptions. We think this picture of the world is real and is noble. In fact it is imaginary and it is false. And because our philosophy of the nature of international life is imaginary and

false, all our efforts to play an effective part in world affairs are frustrated.

What then is it in our philosophy which, instead of guiding us, misguides us continually? I think that the question can be answered. The point, as I have already indicated, where our declarations of policy have regularly miscarried is in avoiding war, in preparing for war, and in settling wars. We must ask ourselves whether there is here some common factor of error which confuses all of us on the issues of war and peace. I think there is. I think the error is a refusal to recognize, to admit, to take as the premise of our thinking, the fact that rivalry and strife and conflict among states, communities, and factions is the normal condition of mankind. The popular American philosophy of international life refuses to recognize this fact. It denies that in the world as it is the struggle for existence is fundamental and in the nature of things. This, I am convinced, is the philosophical error which prevents us from forming an effective foreign policy.

In the American ideology the struggle for existence, and the rivalry of nations for advantages, is held to be wrong, abnormal and transitory. Our foreign policy throughout this period has been dominated by the belief that the struggle does not exist, or that it can be avoided, or that it can be abolished. Because of this belief our aim has not been to regulate and to moderate and to compose the conflicts and the issues, to check and to balance the contending forces. Our aim has been either to abstain from the struggle, or to abolish the struggle immediately, or to conduct crusades against those nations who most actively continue the struggle.

Yet in the world as it actually is, the struggle is not abnormal, and it is perceptually renewed. Twice during this period we have sought to abstain from the struggle by declaring our neutrality. We have not been able to stay out of it. Twice we have conducted victorious crusades against the chief troublemaker, believing what was soon disproved by events—that if he could be eliminated, we would then have eliminated all trouble makers. Twice we have sought, by forming universal societies like the League of Nations and the United Nations, to abolish the struggle. They have not abolished the struggle. But our efforts to use the universal society as if the struggle could be abolished has wrecked the

League of Nations and may yet wreck the United Nations.

Our refusal to recognize the struggle for existence as the normal state of mankind in international affairs has resulted in the repeated miscarriage of American policies. Our efforts to deal with events, as if they conformed or could be made to conform with our ideological picture of what they ought to be, has been rather like using a map of Utopia to find our way around New York City.

The American refusal to recognize the struggle for existence has in this century crystallized in a recognizable pattern of conduct—a neutrality which assumes that the struggle can be ignored and avoided, in crusades that assume that by defeating the chief trouble maker the struggle for existence will end, in the sponsorship of a universal society which assumes that the struggle can be abolished.

Since 1914 American relations with the outer world have oscillated among these three patterns of conduct. The great debates within this country have turned upon them. But the experience of these 40 years shows conclusively, I think, that if we insist on treating the conflict of States, communities, and factions as abnormal, as exceptional, as transitory, we are unable to form an efficient foreign policy. Our American ideology, which we have brought over from a time when we did not have to play a responsible part among the powers of the earth, distorts our judgment when we deal with the problems of power. It distorts our judgment when we determine our aims. It distorts our judgment when we have to calculate how a balance can be struck between our aims and our power to realize them.

Yet in practical judgments—and diplomacy, when the stakes are life and death, calls for very practical judgments—the criteria are always relative. For there is no such thing as absolute power. Whatever the wealth, the power and the prestige of a nation may be, its means are always limited. The problem of the maker of policy is to select objectives that are limited—not the best that could be desired but the best that can be realized without committing the whole power and the whole wealth and the very existence of the nation.

But if we examine the issues of foreign policy as they are presented to our people, we find an overwhelming disposition to regard the choices before us, not as relative but as absolute. We are disposed to think that the issue is either this or that, either all or nothing, either isolationism or globalism, either total peace or total war, either one world or no world, either disarmament or absolute weapons, either pious resolutions or atomic bombs, either nonintervention or a crusade, either democracy or tyranny, either the abolition of war or wars of annihilation, either disarmament or military supremacy, either appeasement or unconditional surrender, either nonresistance or a strategy of annihilation.

There is no place in this ideological pattern of the world for the adoption of limited ends or limited means, for the use of checks and balances among contending forces, for the demarcation of spheres of influence and of power and of interest, for accommodation and compromise and adjustment, for the stabilization of the status quo, for the restoration of an equilibrium. Yet this is the field of diplomacy. These are the substance and the matter of an efficient diplomacy.

Our ideologists, however, condemn it as power politics and as appeasement. They would exclude it, they would outlaw it, and they would excommunicate those who discuss it. They insist on treating the rivalry of nations as something that could not exist among right-thinking men. They will not regulate the rivalries because they hold that the rivalries ought not to exist. So they are left with our three patterns of policy—to ignore the rivalries by proclaiming our neutrality, or to deny the rivalry and to believe it will disappear if the nations are members of a universal society, or to conduct crusades of annihilation against the lions who do not wish to lie down with the lambs.

You will have been asking yourselves how what I have been saying bears upon the subject which preoccupies us all so anxiously and so profoundly—upon our relations with the Soviet Union, which is today our great rival in the world, with which we are now engaged in a world-wide diplomatic conflict. You are entitled to ask the question, and I must try briefly to answer it by indicating what a true philosophy of international life can do to guide us.

The beginning of wisdom on the Russian question is, I believe, to recognize the historic fact that the division between eastern and western Europe, the rivalry between Russia and the nations of the west, did not begin with Marx, Lenin, and Stalin nor would it end if the Soviet regime were overthrown or defeated. The cultural and ideological division of Europe is as old as the division of Christendom between Rome and Byzantium. The imperial rivalry of Russia and the nations of the west, in Europe, in the Danube Valley, in the Balkans, in the Middle East, and in the Far East did not begin with the Communists and will not end with communism. It has been one of the great fields of diplomacy under the czars as it is under the Communists. Rivalry with Russia is a new problem for the United States of America. But the British Foreign Office has been preoccupied with it for a hundred and fifty years. We had better make up our minds that we shall now be preoccupied with it for a very long time to come.

That being the case, we must give up the notion that the choice is between one world, in which the Russians are our partners, and two worlds in which we must annihilate the Russians or they must annihilate us. I do not believe that we must either marry the Russians or we must fight them, that we must have either a perfect peace or a total war. I believe that the best policy is to recognize that the rivalry will remain, and not to expect it to disappear, and not to think it could be abolished by the United Nations and not to think it could be abolished by a victorious war—and having recognized that the rivalry is a permanent fact to use our whole power and influence to regulate it, to keep it within bounds, to establish spheres of influence which limit the rivalry, and a balance of power in the world which checks it.

I do not believe that we can settle the Russian problem once and for all. I do believe we have enough power and influence, if we use them efficiently, to bring about a settlement in this generation with Russia. But it will have to be a settlement which aims not at

unanimity, not at ideological harmony, not at the abolition of all our differences and disagreements but at a truce in the cold war, a modus vivendi during which the nations can recover from the great war, at treaties which end in the withdrawal of the armies of occupation in Europe, and the restoration of Europe to the Europeans.

This will not be easy to achieve. It will require the pressure of power—which will offend those among us who do not like power politics. It will require political and economic compromises, which will offend those who regard all compromise as appeasement. But if a truce, and a modus vivendi, and a treaty are hard to achieve by power and by compromise, it is certain that without power on the one hand, and compromise on the other, nothing can be achieved.

If we will not or cannot use the classic procedure of diplomacy—which is always a combination of power and compromise—then the best we can look forward to is an era of disintegration in the civilized world, followed it may be by a war which once it began, would be savage, universal, and indecisive.

That must not happen. And it need not happen, if only our people will abjure their illusions about the nature of the world in which they have so recently become a leading power, and will permit and assist those who must form our policy, to go forward on the assumption that our aim is not to marry the Russians and then to live with them happily ever after, nor to fight them and let the whole world be devastated, but that our aim is to transact our necessary business with the Russians, at arms length, coolly, shrewdly, without fear and without extravagant hope, and with as much justice as may be possible where there is as yet no agreement on first principles and where the rivals do not live in the same moral order.

1947

REINHOLD NIEBUHR

1892–

AFTER BEING ordained in the ministry of the Evangelical Synod of North America, Niebuhr served as pastor of a Detroit church from 1915 to 1928. In that year he began his distinguished career as a member of the Union Theological Seminary faculty. The principal exponent of neo-orthodoxy, Niebuhr is one of America's most profound theologians. His writings are characterized by breadth and depth, by lucidity, irony, and intellectual sophistication, as well as by an exalted spiritual tone. The following piece is an address given on October 21, 1947, at the Sixteenth Annual Forum sponsored by the New York *Herald Tribune*.

The Nature and Destiny of Man, New York, 1941.
Moral Men and Immoral Society, New York, 1941.
The Irony of American History, New York, 1952.
Christian Realism and Political Problems, New York, 1953.
Hans Hoffman, *The Theology of Reinhold Niebuhr*, Louise P. Smith, trans., New York, 1956.
Holtan P. Odegard, *Sin and Science; Reinhold Niebuhr as Political Theologian*, Yellow Springs, Ohio, 1956.
Mary F. Thelen, *Man as Sinner in Contemporary American Realistic Theology*, New York, 1947.

From: AN ADEQUATE FAITH FOR THE
» » WORLD CRISIS « «

We might profitably distinguish between three dimensions of the world crisis and consider what resources are required to meet our situation in each of these dimensions. In the narrowest dimension, the crisis we confront consists of the peril in which a democratic civilization stands.

The second dimension of the crisis consists of the peril in which the whole of civilization stands, whether democratic or no. It is the dimension of the crisis which would exist, even if Russia were not a difficult partner in the world community. It would exist in any event because we have not yet developed the moral imagination or the political instruments for creating a world community.

The third level of the crisis is more explicitly religious and spiritual. It is created by the fact that the vicissitudes of our generation were not anticipated in our culture. We are experiencing tragic realities for which the optimism of modern culture had not prepared us, and we are consequently threatened by despair and a sense of the meaninglessness of life. Our perils are most obvious and most immediate in the first dimension and least so in the third: but the perils in the third dimension may be ultimately the most serious.

Perhaps it may seem foolish to speak of moral or religious resources for overcoming the peril in the first dimension. We face a truculent and ruthless foe, who is probably not as intent upon world dominion as some people imagine but who is certainly driven by peculiar dogmas and by a probable inferiority complex to defend himself against fancied or real enemies by rejecting every offer of co-operation and by stirring up as much confusion in the world community as possible.

It would seem that what is required to meet such a foe is not some great resource of imagination but simply common sense: the common sense which counsels us to be well armed and not to allow the foe to gain the strategic advantages in any part of the world which might prompt him to risk a martial adventure against us. But though the bitter experiences of the last decade have taught us that power is inevitably a factor in international relations, we would lack wisdom if we followed these precepts of common sense alone. *10*

The defense of civilization requires military strategy, but it also requires political and moral strategy. The best political strategy is prompted not so much by ordinary common sense as by humility—if you will, by religious humility. We call our civilization a democratic one and believe it worth defending. And so it is. But no civilization is as just, and no cause is as persuasive as it seems to its defenders and proponents. Our business is to make our cause *20* more deserving of defense, even though we must defend it strategically without reference to its virtues but because it is ours.

This is particularly true in facing a great center of power, a nation which has become a holy land of a secular religion. To millions of devotees, including many in our Western world, Russia has falsely become a fixed point of international virtue. This is a highly implausible faith. It is made the more implausible *30* by the fact that this holy land seems increasingly involved in every kind of political chicane and skulduggery which we once attributed only to Nazi tyrants. The fact that millions should still hold to this faith must be partly attributed to the generosity of the dream of a classless and just society which originally animated the Marxist cause.

Modern communism is a corruption of utopi- *40* anism and is thus different in principle from

the moral cynicism of nazism. We are therefore in a more difficult ideological battle than
when we engaged the Nazis. It is a battle
which we cannot win among the impoverished
and insecure people of Europe and of Asia if
we do not make it clearer than we have done
that we stand for freedom and justice, and not
for the preservation of privilege. To win the
ideological battle against communism it is not
enough to point to the crass corruptions of the
original dream of justice which we see in the
police states of Eastern Europe. It is more important to make our cause so just that it will
win the allegiance not of the comfortable but
of the insecure and the impoverished.

It is particularly important that America, as
the most powerful and wealthiest of the nations in the Western World, should acquire a
higher degree of humility. Without it we will
insist upon political creeds and political forms
which Europe regards not as the creed of democracy but as the characteristic prejudice of
a very wealthy nation. Europe is a vast ideological middle ground between communism
and American libertarianism. We are quite
wrong if we think that it does not cherish freedom as much as we do.

But it needs economic security more desperately than we. Its creeds are colored by that
fact even as our creeds are colored by the
fabulous character of our productivity and our
immediate, though not ultimate, lack of anxiety
about economic security. Without the humility
and the imagination to think beyond the
characteristic prejudices of American life we
cannot win the ideological battle against communism.

But even if the world's hopes had not been
frustrated by the irrelevancies and the trucu-
lence which the Communist creed has introduced into our situation, we still would have
been in a world crisis. For there is another
dimension of the crisis. A technical civilization
has produced a potential world community,
but not an actual one. There would be great
centers of power in the world not easily
brought under the dominion of a law higher
than their own will, even without this conflict
between a Communist and capitalist, a totalitarian and a democratic world. Even if we
survive the present tensions we will face for
decades the problem of achieving moral
strength and political imagination to bring
moral and political order in a world now related only by technics.

Our immediate perils tempt us to forget our
more ultimate danger caused not by Russian
policy but by the inability of all nations and
peoples to face new responsibilities. By clinging to ancient securities they make themselves
increasingly insecure in a new situation. It is
a tragic aspect of human history that men
learn so little from the lessons of history. They
are, as one of the prophets observed, wounded
by the Divine Judge but they do not grieve;
they are consumed but they will not receive
correction.

An adequate faith for such a day as this
must be a faith which induces repentance on
the part of all nations and all peoples; and a
consequent readiness to sacrifice any privilege
or prestige, incompatible with community on
the new and wider level of human community.
No dreams of world constitutions or contrivances of international law will avail if there is
not a wider and more resolute will to achieve
world community than is now apparent.

The first and the second level of the world
crisis—the peril in which a democratic civilization stands and in which civilization as such
stands—engage the minds of our generation.
These perils are obvious and immediate. I
should like to suggest, however, that there is
a third level or dimension of the crisis which
is not so obvious but which may be more important than the others. It is the crisis in our
culture caused by the fact that the faith of
modern man has not prepared him for the
tragedies which he experiences and does not
help him to interpret his urgent tasks as meaningful.

Our culture has been dominated by one
idea: the idea that history would solve all our
problems. We hoped that historical growth
and development would eliminate methods of
force and bring all politics under the dominion
of reason; that it would bring victory to democracy everywhere and eliminate tyranny;
that it would abolish poverty and injustice;
and that it would move inevitably toward a
parliament of mankind and a federation of the
world. These are false hopes.

Contemporary experience proves that history creates as many problems as it solves by
creating human power and freedom. A technical civilization created a vast interdependence of nations but not a world brotherhood
or even world community. It did not abolish
methods of force but ushered in total wars,
engaging the total resources of nations. It did

not insure man's increasing security. Rather it transmuted the perils of nature into perils of history and society. It made us safer against death by epidemic and less safe against death by atomic destruction. It did not gradually change our position from that of slavery to historical process to mastery over our own destiny. We remain now, as we have always been, both masters and tools of history. We are moved by forces vaster than our own power and are yet called upon to make fateful decisions.

It is because we had so completely miscalculated the character of human history that we are so frequently threatened by despair in this day of frustration and disappointed hopes. We fear atomic destruction partly because it is a great peril but also because it is the old peril of death in a new form. We thought we had banished the peril of death. We are driven to despair because the last war did not result in a stable peace, because we falsely thought that every task had to be justified by some completely new tomorrow. But no tomorrow is ever completely new. We must learn all over again not only that "sufficient unto the day are the evils thereof" but the duties thereof and the hopes thereof also. We must learn to exploit the qualitative meaning of our duties and tasks today without too much regard for what tomorrow may bring forth.

We are driven to despair because we cannot build out of hand the kind of stable world we desire, having discovered that recalcitrant forces in history stand against our will and our purposes. We must again acquire a faith which finds meaning in human life, even though no person or generation ever has the power to complete the ideal meaning of life. Our modern culture moved from a too simple optimism to a too deep despair: This cultural and religious confusion is dangerous for us, even on the lower level of the crisis, because the distraction of alternate moods of unjustified hopes and unjustified pessimism prevents us from doing our duties amidst the pressing and urgent tasks of today.

An adequate faith for a day of crisis will contain what modern men have completely dismissed, namely, a tragic sense of life and a recognition of the Cross as the final center of life's meaning. The Scripture describes the works of the night, as those of sleep and drunkenness: "They that sleep, sleep in the night and they that be drunken are drunken in the night." Let us who are of the day watch and be sober. We cannot afford either the sleep of complacency or the drunkenness of hysteria. We must watch and be sober. But this watchfulness and sobriety is the fruit of a profounder sense of the meaning of our existence, than any of the credos which have recently guided us. A much more modest estimate of human power and of human virtue might bring us nearer and quicker to the goal of a tolerable peace and a sufferable world order for all nations.

Finally, we had hoped that it was a fairly simple matter to achieve a universal culture or a universal religion as the basis of a universal community. Now we realize that the universal community remains full of partial and particular elements. It is characterized by differences in political, moral, and religious ideas. There is no possibility of achieving complete unity or identity of conviction. We must learn therefore that commnuty with our fellow men and other nations requires not so much a common culture as a recognition of the partial and particular character of our truth and our interest.

A religion adequate for community building on a world scale must cease to identify God with any particular culture or civilization, but sense, as the prophets of Israel did, that the judgment of God stands over all nations and that His mercy is available to all who are moved by that judgment. We can achieve accord with our fellow men in the proportion in which we recognize that both they and we hold facets of the truth and are loyal to aspects of justice imperfectly.

The wide variety of human aspirations is an old fact. We now face it in the new dimension of a world community. Every form of fanaticism has achieved new proportion of evil in this wider dimension. Religious forbearance of our fellow men has become even more urgent than when the words were spoken, "Let us judge not that we be not judged."   1947

DWIGHT D. EISENHOWER

1890–

THE EISENHOWER family moved from Denison, Texas, where Dwight was born, to Abilene, Kansas, where the boys received their schooling. Dwight worked at various jobs and received a nomination to enter the United States Military Academy, from which he was graduated in 1915. He was also graduated from the Army War College in 1928. During World War II he became Supreme Commander of American, British, and Canadian troops in Western Europe and after the War was appointed Chief of Staff of the United States Army. This office he resigned in 1948 to become President of Columbia University. In April, 1951 he became Supreme Commander of the Allied Powers in Europe. In 1952, he was elected to the Presidency of the United States. "An Atomic Stockpile for Peace, Dedicated to Serve the Needs Rather than the Fears of Mankind" was delivered before the General Assembly of the United Nations, December 8, 1953.

Dwight D. Eisenhower, *Crusade in Europe*, New York, 1948.
Robert J. Donovan, *Eisenhower; the Inside Story*, New York, 1956.
Merlo Pusey, *Eisenhower, the President*, New York, 1956.
Richard H. Rovere, *The Eisenhower Years; Affairs of State*, New York, 1956.

AN ATOMIC STOCKPILE FOR PEACE

Madame President, Members of the General Assembly:

When Secretary General Hammarskjold's invitation to address this General Assembly reached me in Bermuda, I was just beginning a series of conferences with the Prime Ministers and Foreign Ministers of Great Britain and France. Our subject was some of the problems that beset our world.

During the remainder of the Bermuda Conference, I had constantly in mind that ahead of me lay a great honor. That honor is mine today as I stand here, privileged to address the General Assembly of the United Nations.

At the same time that I appreciate the distinction of addressing you, I have a sense of exhilaration as I look upon this assembly.

Never before in history has so much hope for so many people been gathered together in a single organization. Your deliberations and decisions during these somber years have already realized part of those hopes.

But the great tests and the great accomplishments still lie ahead. And in the confident expectation of those accomplishments, I would use the office which, for the time being, I hold, to assure you that the Government of the United States will remain steadfast in its support of this body. This we shall do in the conviction that you will provide a great share of the wisdom, of the courage and the faith which can bring to this world lasting peace for all nations and happiness and well-being for all men.

Clearly, it would not be fitting for me to take this occasion to present to you a unilateral American report on Bermuda. Nevertheless, I assure you that in our deliberations on that lovely island we sought to invoke those same great concepts of universal peace and human dignity which are so clearly etched in your Charter.

Neither would it be a measure of this great opportunity merely to recite, however hopefully, pious platitudes.

I therefore decided that this occasion warranted my saying to you some of the things that have been on the minds and hearts of my legislative and executive associates and on mine for a great many months—thoughts I had originally planned to say primarily to the American people.

I know that the American people share my deep belief that if a danger exists in the world, it is a danger shared by all—and equally, that if hope exists in the mind of one nation, that hope should be shared by all.

Finally, if there is to be advanced any proposal designed to ease, even by the smallest measure, the tensions of today's world, what more appropriate audience could there be than the members of the General Assembly of the United Nations?

LANGUAGE OF ATOMIC WARFARE

I feel impelled to speak today in a language that, in a sense, is new—one, which I, who have spent so much of my life in the military profession, would have preferred never to use.

That new language is the language of atomic warfare.

The atomic age has moved forward at such a pace that every citizen of the world should have some comprehension, at least in comparative terms, of the extent of this development, of the utmost significance to every one of us. Clearly, if the peoples of the world are to conduct an intelligent search for peace, they must be armed with the significant facts of today's existence.

My recital of atomic danger and power is necessarily stated in United States terms, for these are the only incontrovertible facts that I know. I need hardly point out to this assembly, however, that this subject is global, not merely national in character.

On July 16, 1945, the United States set off the world's first atomic test explosion. Since that date in 1945, the United States has conducted forty-two test explosions.

Atomic bombs today are more than twenty-five times as powerful as the weapons with which the atomic age dawned, while hydrogen weapons are in the ranges of millions of tons of TNT equivalent. Today, the United States' stockpile of atomic weapons, which, of course, increases daily, exceeds by many times the explosive equivalent of the total of all bombs and all shells that came from every plane and every gun in every theatre of war through all the years of World War II.

A single air group, whether afloat or land based, can now deliver to any reachable target a destructive cargo exceeding in power all the bombs that fell on Britain in all of World War II.

In size and variety the development of atomic weapons has been no less remarkable. This development has been such that atomic weapons have virtually achieved conventional status within our armed services. In the United States services, the Army, the Navy, the Air Force and the Marine Corps are all capable of putting this weapon to military use.

But the dread secret and the fearful engines of atomic might are not ours alone.

In the first place, the secret is possessed by our friends and Allies, Great Britain and Canada, whose scientific genius made a tremendous contribution to our original discoveries and the designs of atomic bombs.

The secret is also known by the Soviet Union.

The Soviet Union has informed us that, over recent years, it has devoted extensive resources to atomic weapons. During this period the Soviet Union has exploded a series of atomic devices, including at least one involving thermonuclear reactions.

MONOPOLY ENDED

If at one time the United States possessed what might have been called a monopoly of atomic power, that monopoly ceased to exist several years ago. Therefore, although our earlier start has permitted us to accumulate what is today a great quantitative advantage, the atomic realities of today comprehend two facts of even greater significance.

First, the knowledge now possessed by several nations will eventually be shared by others, possibly all others.

Second, even a vast superiority in numbers of weapons, and a consequent capability of devastating retaliation is no preventive, of itself, against the fearful material damage and toll of human lives that would be inflicted by surprise aggression.

The free world, at least dimly aware of these facts, has naturally embarked on a large program of warning and defense systems. That program will be accelerated and expanded.

But let no one think that the expenditure of vast sums for weapons and systems of defense can guarantee absolute safety for the cities and the citizens of any nation. The awful arithmetic of the atomic bomb does not permit of such an easy solution. Even against the most powerful defense, an aggressor in possession of the effective minimum number of atomic bombs for a surprise attack could probably place a sufficient number of his bombs on the chosen targets to cause hideous damage.

Should such an atomic attack be launched against the United States, our reaction would be swift and resolute. But for me to say that the defense capabilities of the United States are such that they could inflict terrible losses upon an aggressor—for me to say that the retaliation capabilities of the United States are so great that such an aggressor's land would be laid waste—all this, while fact, is not the true expression of the purpose and the hope of the United States.

To pause there would be to confirm the hopeless finality of a belief that two atomic colossi are doomed malevolently to eye each other indefinitely across a trembling world. To stop there would be to accept helplessly the probability of civilization destroyed—the annihilation of the irreplaceable heritage of mankind handed down to us generation from generation—and the condemnation of mankind to begin all over again the age-old struggle upward from savagery toward decency and right and justice.

NO VICTORY IN DESOLATION

Surely no sane member of the human race could discover victory in such desolation. Could anyone wish his name to be coupled by history with such human degradation and destruction?

Occasional pages of history do record the faces of the "Great Destroyers" but the whole book of history reveals mankind's never-ending quest for peace and mankind's God-given capacity to build.

It is with the book of history, and not with isolated pages, that the United States will ever wish to be identified. My country wants to be constructive, not destructive. It wants agreements, not wars, among nations. It wants itself, to live in freedom and in the confidence that the people of every other nation enjoy equally the right of choosing their own way of life.

So my country's purpose is to help us move out of the dark chamber of horrors into the light, to find a way by which the minds of men, the hopes of men, the souls of men everywhere, can move forward toward peace and happiness and well-being.

In this quest, I know that we must not lack patience.

I know that in a world divided, such as ours today, salvation cannot be attained by one dramatic act.

I know that many steps will have to be taken over many months before the world can look at itself one day and truly realize that a new climate of mutually peaceful confidence is abroad in the world.

But I know, above all else, that we must start to take these steps—now.

The United States and its Allies, Great Britain and France, have, over the past months, tried to take some of these steps. Let no one say that we shun the conference table.

On the record has long stood the request of the United States, Great Britain and France, to negotiate with the Soviet Union the problems of a divided Germany.

On that record has long stood the request of the same three nations to negotiate an Austrian peace treaty.

On the same record still stands the request of the United Nations to negotiate the problems of Korea.

CONFERENCE WITH THE RUSSIANS

Most recently, we have received from the Soviet Union what is in effect an expression of willingness to hold a four-power meeting. Along with our Allies, Great Britain and France, we are pleased to see that this note did not contain the unacceptable preconditions previously put forward.

As you already know from our joint Bermuda communique, the United States, Great Britain and France have agreed promptly to meet with the Soviet Union.

The Government of the United States approaches this conference with hopeful sincerity. We will bend every effort of our minds to the single purpose of emerging from that conference with tangible results toward peace—the only true way of lessening international tension.

We never have, we never will, propose or suggest that the Soviet Union surrender what is rightfully theirs.

We will never say that the peoples of Russia are an enemy with whom we have no desire ever to deal or mingle in friendly and fruitful relationship.

On the contrary, we hope that this coming conference may initiate a relationship with the Soviet Union which will eventually bring about a free intermingling of the peoples of the

East and of the West—the one sure, human way of developing the understanding required for confident and peaceful relations.

Instead of the discontent which is now setting upon Eastern Germany, occupied Austria and the countries of eastern Europe, we seek a harmonious family of free European nations, with none a threat to the other, and least of all a threat to the peoples of Russia.

Beyond the turmoil and strife and misery of Asia, we seek peaceful opportunity for these peoples to develop their natural resources and to elevate their lot.

These are not idle words of shallow vision. Behind them lies a story of nations lately come to independence, not as a result of war but through free grant or peaceful negotiation. There is a record already written of assistance gladly given by nations of the West to needy peoples and to those suffering the temporary effects of famine, drought and natural disaster.

These are deeds of peace. They speak more loudly than promises or protestations of peaceful intent.

But I do not wish to rest either upon the reiteration of past proposals or the restatement of past deeds. The gravity of the time is such that every new avenue of peace, no matter how dimly discernible, should be explored.

There is at least one new avenue of peace which has not yet been well explored—an avenue now laid out by the General Assembly of the United Nations.

In its resolution of Nov. 18, 1953, this General Assembly suggested—and I quote—"that the Disarmament Commission study the desirability of establishing a subcommittee consisting of representatives of the powers principally involved, which should seek, in private, an acceptable solution—and report such a solution to the General Assembly and to the Security Council not later than 1 September, 1954."

The United States, heeding the suggestion of the General Assembly of the United Nations, is instantly prepared to meet privately with such other countries as may be "principally involved," to seek "an acceptable solution" to the atomic armaments race which overshadows not only the peace but the very life of the world.

We shall carry into these private or diplomatic talks a new conception.

The United States would seek more than the mere reduction or elimination of atomic materials for military purposes.

It is not enough to take this weapon out of the hands of the soldiers. It must be put into the hands of those who will know how to strip its military casing and adapt it to the arts of peace.

The United States knows that if the fearful trend of atomic military build-up can be reversed, this greatest of destructive forces can be developed into a great boon for the benefit of all mankind.

The United States knows that peaceful power from atomic energy is no dream of the future. That capability, already proved, is here now—today. Who can doubt if the entire body of the world's scientists and engineers had adequate amounts of fissionable material with which to test and develop their ideas, that this capability would rapidly be transformed into universal, efficient and economic usage?

To hasten the day when fear of the atom will begin to disappear from the minds of people and the governments of the East and West there are certain steps that can be taken now.

I therefore make the following proposals:

The governments principally involved to the extent permitted by elementary prudence, to begin now and continue to make joint contributions from their stockpiles of normal uranium and fissionable materials to an international atomic energy agency. We would expect that such an agency would be set up under the aegis of the United Nations.

The ratios of contributions, the procedures and other details would properly be within the scope of the "private conversations" I have referred to earlier.

The United States is prepared to undertake these explorations in good faith. Any partner of the United States acting in the same good faith will find the United States a not unreasonable or ungenerous associate.

Undoubtedly initial and early contributions to this plan would be small in quantity. However, the proposal has the great virtue that it can be undertaken without irritations and mutual suspicions incident to any attempt to set up a completely acceptable system of world-wide inspection and control.

The Atomic Energy Agency could be made responsible for the impounding, storage and protection of the contributed fissionable and other materials. The ingenuity of our scientists will provide special, safe conditions under which such a bank of fissionable material can be made essentially immune to surprise seizure.

The more important responsibility of this

atomic energy agency would be to devise methods whereby this fissionable material would be allocated to serve the peaceful pursuits of mankind. Experts would be mobilized to apply atomic energy to the needs of agriculture, medicine and other peaceful activities. A special purpose would be to provide abundant electrical energy in the power-starved areas of the world. Thus the contributing powers would be dedicating some of their strength to serve the needs rather than the fears of mankind.

EXPEDITE PEACEFUL USE

The United States would be more than willing—it would be proud—to take up with others "principally involved" the development of plans whereby such peaceful use of atomic energy would be expedited.

Of those "principally involved" the Soviet Union must, of course, be one.

I would be prepared to submit to the Congress of the United States, and with every expectation of approval, any such plan that would:

First, encourage world-wide investigation into the most effective peacetime uses of fissionable material; and with the certainty that they had all the material needed for the conduct of all experiments that were appropriate.

Second, begin to diminish the potential destructive power of the world's atomic stockpiles.

Third, allow all peoples of all nations to see that, in this enlightened age, the great powers of the earth, both of the East and of the West, are interested in human aspirations first rather than in building up armaments of war.

Fourth, open up a new channel for peaceful discussion and initiate at least a new approach to the many difficult problems that must be solved in both private and public conversations if the world is to shake off the inertia imposed by fear and is to make positive progress toward peace.

Against the dark background of the atomic bomb, the United States does not wish merely to present strength, but also the desire and the hope for peace.

The coming months will be fraught with fateful decisions in this Assembly, in the capitals and military headquarters of the world; in the hearts of men everywhere, be they governed or governors, may they be the decisions which will lead this world out of fear and into peace.

To the making of these fateful decisions, the United States pledges before you—and therefore before the world—its determination to help solve the fearful atomic dilemma—to devote its entire heart and mind to find the way by which the miraculous inventiveness of man shall not be dedicated to his death, but consecrated to his life. . . .

1953

EDWARD TELLER

1908–

and ALBERT L. LATTER

1920–

EDWARD TELLER was born in Budapest. After study at the University of Leipzig he pursued his researches in atomic physics at Copenhagen with the support of a Rockefeller Fellowship. During World War II Dr. Teller served as a staff member of the Los Alamos Scientific Laboratory and, subsequently, at various centers of atomic research and development. He has played an important part in advising the Atomic Energy Commission on policy and has popularized through his writings and television programs problems associated with the planning and prediction of the functions of atomic and hydrogen bombs. *Our Nuclear Future* (New York, 1958), written in collaboration with Albert L. Latter, is a strong plea for the continuation of atomic testing. Many competent reviewers took exception to its arguments and conclusions, but it is an able if controversial exposition of a position defended in influential government circles. Dr. Albert L. Latter, Dr. Teller's associate, is a theoretical physicist affiliated with the Rand Corporation.

Edward Teller and Francis Owen Rice, *The Structure of Matter*, New York, 1949.
Current Biography, December, 1954.

From: OUR NUCLEAR FUTURE

CHAPTER XV WHAT ABOUT FUTURE TESTS?

Many people feel that tests should be discontinued. This feeling is widespread and strong. The question of tests is obviously important. It may influence our security as individuals. It certainly will influence our security as a nation. If in a free, democratic country the majority believes that something should be done—it will be done. The sovereign power in a democracy is "the people." It is of the greatest importance that the people should be honestly and completely informed about all relevant facts. In no other way can a sound decision be reached. The basic and relevant facts are simple. The story can be presented without unnecessary frills or undue emotion. When this has been done, the right decision will be reached by common sense rather than by exceptional cleverness.

Unfortunately much of the discussion about continued experimentation with nuclear explosives has been carried out in a most emotional and confused manner. One argument concerning tests is so fantastic that it deserves to be mentioned for that very reason: It has been claimed that nuclear explosions may change the axis of the earth.

Of course, nuclear explosions do produce such changes. Only the changes are so small that they are impossible to observe and even difficult to estimate. Searching for effects connected with past tests that may displace the axis of the earth, or the position of the North Pole, we could find no effect that would have caused a change of position even as great as the size of an atom. One could design tests with the specific purpose to produce such a change, but these man-made effects could not be compared even remotely with the forces of nature. The motion of the Gulf Stream has a small effect on the North Pole; but this effect is incomparably greater than what any nuclear explosion could accomplish. It is good to know that the old top on which we live does have some stability.

The argument about world-wide radioactive fall-out is more serious. It is asserted that fall-out is dangerous and that we are ignorant of the extent of the danger.

In a narrow, literal sense both these statements are correct. But in the preceding chapters we have seen that the danger is limited. We do not know precisely how great it is. We do know, however, that the danger is considerably smaller than the danger from other radiations [10] to which we continue to expose ourselves without worry. The danger from the tests is quite small compared with the effects of x-rays used in medical practice. The fall-out produces only a fraction of the increase in cosmic ray effect to which a person subjects himself when he moves from the seashore to a place of higher altitude like Colorado. People may or may not be damaged by the fall-out. But it is quite certain that the damage is far below a level of [20] which we usually take notice.

Fall-out in the vicinity of the test sites did cause damage. In the past this damage was not great although in one Pacific test it was serious. Precautions have been increased and we may hope that future accidents will be avoided altogether. The safety record of the Atomic Energy Commission compares favorably with other enterprises of similar scale.

It seems probable that the root of the opposition to further tests is not connected with [30] fall-out. The root is deeper. The real reason against further tests is connected with our desire for disarmament and for peace.

There can be no doubt that the desire for peace is most deep, and this desire is felt by all thinking and honest people on our earth. All of us certainly hope that the catastrophe of war can be avoided. This great and universal wish for peace is the driving force behind the [40] desire for disarmament. In the minds of most people it would be an important step toward disarmament if the testing of nuclear weapons were stopped by all nations. This belief is widely held, but it is not necessarily well-founded. In fact, there are arguments on the other side which should be considered carefully.

It is generally believed that the First World War was caused by an arms race. For some strange reason most people forget that the Second World War was brought about by a situation which could be called a race in disarmament. The peace-loving and powerful nations divested themselves of their military power. When the Nazi regime in Germany adopted a program of rapid preparation for war, the rest of the world was caught unawares. At first they did not want to accept the fact of this menace. When the danger was unmistakable, it was too late to avert a most cruel war, and almost too late to stop Hitler short of world conquest. Unfortunately, disarmament is safe only when no one wants to impose his will by force of arms upon his neighbors.

In the uneasy world in which we live today no reasonable person will advocate unilateral disarmament. What people hope is that all sides will agree to reduce their military power and thereby contribute to a more peaceful atmosphere. The elimination of tests has appeared possible and proper for two reasons. One is that tests are conspicuous, and therefore it is believed that we can check whether or not testing has actually been stopped by everyone. The second reason is that nuclear explosives already represent such terrifying power that further tests appear useless and irrational These arguments are simple and almost universally accepted. They are based on misconceptions.

A nuclear explosion is a violent event, but in the great expanses of our globe such tests can be effectively hidden if appropriate care is taken to hide them. There can be no doubt that this is possible. The question is only how much it costs to hide a test and how big is the explosion that can be carried out in secret for a certain amount of expenditure.

If an agreement were made to discontinue the tests, the United States would surely keep such an agreement. The very social and political structure of our country excludes the possibility that many people would collaborate in breaking an international undertaking. Whether Russia would or would not keep such an agreement would depend on the ingenuity of the Russians, on their willingness to make economic sacrifices, and on their honesty. Of these three factors we can have a firm opinion about the first. The Russians are certainly ingenious

enough to devise secret methods of testing. As to the other questions, whether the Russians will want to invest the effort and whether they will be bound by their word, we feel that each man is entitled to his own opinion. According to past experience, an agreement to stop tests may well be followed by secret and successful tests behind the iron curtain.

In a more general way we may ask the question: Is it wise to make agreements which honesty will respect, but dishonesty can circumvent? Shall we put a free, democratic government at a disadvantage compared to the absolute power of a dictatorship? Shall we introduce prohibition in a new form, just to give rise to bootlegging on a much greater scale? It is almost certain that in the competition between prohibition and bootlegging, the bootlegger will win.

All of these arguments, however, would become irrelevant if it were true that further testing would not accomplish any further desirable result. It has been said and often repeated that we now possess adequate nuclear explosives to wipe out the cities of any enemy. What more do we need?

Our main purpose in further experimentation with nuclear bombs is not, of course, to make city-busters more horrible. We would prefer not to have to use our nuclear weapons at all. We keep them as a counterthreat against the danger that we ourselves should be subjected to a devastating attack. To understand what we are actually trying to do in the tests, we have to take a closer look at some military problems.

In the Second World War strategic bombing was used for the first time on a really massive scale. It may well be and, in fact, it is probable that such strategic bombing will not be repeated in the future.

There are two military reasons for the bombing of cities. One is that factories are located in cities, and these factories support the war effort. The other reason is that cities are centers of transportation through which the supplies of war materials pass. By destroying these centers the flow of the war supplies can be interrupted.

Nuclear warfare is likely to be quite different from past conflicts. The great concentration of firepower which a nuclear weapon represents makes it possible to attack an enemy anywhere, at very short notice. This is true no matter what the particular target is, whether one is trying to attack the planes, ships, tanks, or troop-concentrations of an enemy. The greater mobility of nuclear firepower makes it highly probable that the nuclear conflict will be short. What the factory produces during this conflict will not affect the outcome of the fighting. The only weapons on which anyone can rely are the weapons which are already stockpiled. Therefore, it will be militarily useless to bomb factories.

The same fact of mobility also implies that no great flow of war material will need to be maintained. Practically all movement can be executed by light and fast methods, by planes, submarines, and small battle groups. Under these conditions, the cities will lose their importance as centers of transportation.

The only purpose in bombing cities will be to spread terror among the enemy. This was rarely done in past wars. In fact, terror is self-defeating because it provokes retaliation from the other side.

We believe that the role of nuclear weapons in a future war is by no means the killing of millions of civilians. It is rather to stop the armed forces of an aggressor. This is not easy to do because it requires not only nuclear weapons, but very special kinds of nuclear weapons which are hard to develop and harder to perfect. But with proper experimentation and proper planning the defensive use of nuclear weapons is possible.

The idea of tactical nuclear weapons is not new. The possibility of using nuclear explosives in small wars has been frequently discussed. What kind of weapons do we need in order to fight these small wars and to defend the freedom of people wherever such defense becomes necessary? It has often been suggested that in small wars, small weapons will be used, while big weapons are appropriate for big wars. Such a statement is much too simple and has no relation to reality. In every case the right kind of weapon is the one which performs the job of stopping the enemy's armed forces without inflicting unnecessary loss on the innocent bystander. For this purpose we need a great number of weapons which are adaptable to specific purposes, which are easy to transport and easy to deliver, and give rise to the kind of effect which the situation requires.

For instance, a nuclear weapon may be carried by a fighter plane and used to shoot down an attacking bomber. Since the carrying capacity of the fighter plane is severely limited, the weapon for this purpose must be small and light. A major objective of the test program is to develop such purely defensive weapons.

The encounter between the fighter plane and the bomber may well take place in our own country over populated areas. This possibility would fill most people with alarm lest the population underneath the explosion should be hurt. Fortunately, in a recent nuclear test in Nevada, five well-informed and courageous Air Force officers demonstrated that there is complete safety to people on the ground. They did this 10 by standing directly beneath the explosion at ground zero.

This important test took place only a few months ago—on July 19, 1957. An F-89 jet fighter plane flying at 19,000 feet above sea level delivered an air-to-air atomic rocket to a preassigned point in the sky. The ground zero men were 15,000 feet immediately below. They wore no helmets, no sun-glasses, and no protective clothing. 20

At the instant of the explosion the men looked up, saw the fireball and felt the heat. There was no discomfort, only a gentle warmth. Then they waited for the shock wave to arrive —approximately ten seconds. When the shock came, it was actually just a loud noise. However, one of the men ducked his head instinctively.

The blast and the thermal pulse were over. But the Air Force men stood their ground. One 30 question still remained: Would there be any fall-out? They checked their radiation instruments and waited while the cloud drifted slowly away. There was no significant rise in the radiation level. The test had been a complete success. The effects of the explosion were utterly insignificant on the ground. But high in the air an enemy plane could have been demolished even if the nuclear explosion had missed it by a considerable distance. 40

In order that nuclear weapons should be effective against armed invaders, it is clear that great numbers of these weapons are needed. Such great numbers of weapons, some of which must be ground-burst, will produce a considerable amount of radioactive contamination, and this contamination will endanger friend and foe alike. In particular, the radio-activity is likely to kill people in the very country whose liberty we are trying to defend. For this reason 50 it is most important that we should be able to use nuclear weapons which cause the least possible contamination. In recent nuclear tests more and more attention has been paid to the development of such clean weapons, and most fortunately these efforts are well on the way toward success.

The radioactive fall-out from nuclear testing gives rise to a possible danger which is quite limited in size. The danger from the fall-out in a nuclear war, however, would be real and great. If we stop testing now, and if we should fail to develop to the fullest possible extent these clean weapons, we should unnecessarily kill a great number of noncombatants. Not to develop the explosives with the smallest radioactive fallout would indeed be completely inexcusable.

The only alternative is that nuclear weapons should not be used at all. Since these weapons have been presented as purely evil instruments, most people hope that they will never be used, and indeed one should hope that wars, and therefore the use of these weapons, can be avoided.

But in our conflict with the powerful communistic countries which strive for world domination, it may be too much to hope for uninterrupted peace. If we abandon our light and mobile weapons, we shall enable the Red bloc to take over one country after another, close to their borders, as opportunities arise. The free nations cannot maintain the massive armies throughout the world which would be required to resist such piecemeal aggression. On the other hand, the flexible power of clean nuclear explosives would put us in a position where we could resist aggression in any part of the world, practically at a moment's notice.

The announced policy of our country is to maintain peace and stability in the world. By being patient and prepared we are trying to arrive at a world order based on law and justice for all peoples. There is no doubt that this policy is supported by the overwhelming majority of Americans. Our armed forces need the greatest possible flexibility in order to give strength to this policy. Such flexibility we can possess only if we have in our possession the strongest, best developed weapons which are also the cleanest, so that they may be used for defense rather than for random destruction.

If we renounce nuclear weapons, we open the door to aggression. If we fail to develop clean explosives, we expose people to disaster from radioactive fallout in any serious military conflict. To our way of thinking these are weighty arguments in favor of continued experimentation and development of nuclear weapons. But still another, more general, point

of view should be considered.

The spectacular developments of the last centuries, in science, in technology, and in our everyday life, have been based on one important premise: to explore fearlessly any consequences to which greater knowledge and improved skills can lead us. When we talk about nuclear tests, we have in mind not only military preparedness but also the execution of experiments which will give us more insight and more ability to control the forces of nature. There are many specific political and military reasons why such experiments should not be abandoned. There also exists this very general reason—the tradition of exploring the unknown. We can follow this tradition, and we can at the same time be increasingly careful that radioactivity, carelessly dispersed, should not interfere with human life.

CHAPTER XIX

THE NUCLEAR AGE

The future depends on people. People are unpredictable. Therefore, the future is unpredictable. However, some general conditions of mankind depend on things like the development of technology, the control won by man over nature and the limitations of natural resources. These can be predicted with a little greater confidence. The future is unknown but in some respects its general outline can be guessed.

Such guesses are important. They influence our present outlook and our present actions.

The nuclear age has not yet started. Our sources of energy are not yet nuclear sources. Even in the military field, where development has been most rapid, the structure of the armed forces has not yet adjusted itself to the facts of the nuclear age in a realistic manner. In politics the atomic nucleus has entered as a promise and as a menace—not as a fact on which we can build and with which we can reckon.

Some technical predictions seem safe:

Nuclear energy will not render our older power plants obsolete in the near future. But nuclear energy will make it possible to maintain the pace—even the acceleration—of the industrial revolution. It will be possible to produce all the energy we need at a moderate cost. Furthermore—and this is the important point—this energy will be available at any place on the globe at a cost which is fairly uniform.

The greater the need for power, the sooner will it be feasible to satisfy the need with the help of nuclear reactors.

Nuclear energy can be made available at the most outlandish places. It can be used on the Antarctic continent. It can be made to work on the bottom of the ocean.

The expanding front of industrialization has been called the "revolution of rising expectations." That nuclear energy should be involved in the current and in the turbulence of this expanding front is inevitable.

One can say a little more about the effects of scientific and technological discoveries on the relations among the people of the globe. With added discoveries raw materials will no longer be needed with the old urgency. For most substances substitutes are being found. This may make for greater economic independence.

On the other hand, new possibilities will present themselves. We shall learn how to control the air and how to cultivate the oceans. This will call for co-operation and more interdependence.

The dangers from radioactive by-products will act in a similar direction. The radioactive cloud released from a reactor accident may be more dangerous than a nuclear explosion. Such a cloud will not stop at national boundaries. Some proper form of international responsibility will have to be developed.

What effect the existence of nuclear weapons will have upon the coexistence of nations is a question less understood and less explored than any other affecting our future. Most people turn away from it with a feeling of terror. It is not easy to look at the question with calm reason and with little emotion.

A few predictions seem disturbing but are highly probable:

Nuclear secrets will not keep. Knowledge of nuclear weapons will spread among nations—at least as long as independent nations exist.

Prohibition will not work. Laws or agreements which start with the word "don't" can be broken and will always be broken. If there is hope, it must lie in the direction of agreements which start with the word "do." The idea of "Atoms for Peace" succeeded because it resulted in concrete action.

An all-out nuclear war between the major powers could occur but we may have good hope that it will not occur if we remain prepared to strike back. No one will want to pro-voke the devastation of his own country.

Atomic bombs may be used against cities. But there will be no military advantage in destroying cities. In a short and highly mobile war neither centers of supply and communication nor massive means of production will count. If cities are bombed, this will be done primarily for reasons of psychological warfare. We must be and we are prepared for this kind of war but only as a measure of retaliation. There is good reason to believe that as long as we are prepared for all-out war, our civilian population will not suffer from a nuclear attack.

The certainty of a counterblow gives real protection against all-out war. No such protection exists against wars limited in territory and in aims. In the history of mankind such wars have been most frequent. There is no indication that these limited wars have ended. We must be prepared for these conflicts with effective and mobile units, and this requires the use of nuclear firepower.

Nuclear weapons will certainly have a profound effect upon such limited warfare. Not all of this effect need be and indeed it must not be in the direction of greater devastation.

In a nuclear war it will not make sense to use massed manpower. Any such concentration will provide too good a target for atomic weapons. To use big, costly and conspicuous machines of war will be unwise. Such machines will be defeated by nuclear explosions in the same way as the mailed knight went down before firearms.

Any fighting unit in a nuclear war will have to be small, mobile, inconspicuous, and capable of independent action. Such units whether on sea, land, or in the air cannot rely and will not rely on fixed lines of supply. There will be no possibility and no need to occupy territory and to fight at fixed and definite fronts. If a war should be fought for military reasons and for military advantage, it will consist of short and sharp local engagements involving skill and advanced techniques and not involving masses that slaughter and are being slaughtered.

If an invader adopts extreme dispersion, it will become impossible to defeat him with atomic weapons. But a very highly dispersed army can be defeated by a determined local population. Therefore the main role of nuclear weapons might well be to disperse any striking force so that the resistance of people defending their homes can become decisive. Nuclear weapons may well become the answer to massed armies and may put back the power into the hands where we believe it belongs: the hands of the people.

At this point we are brought back to the main topic of this book: radioactivity. In a limited nuclear war, the radioactive fall-out will probably kill many of the innocent bystanders. We have seen that the testing program gives rise to a danger which is much smaller than many risks which we take in our stride without any worry. In a nuclear war, even in a limited one, the situation will probably be quite different. That noncombatants suffer in wars is not new. In a nuclear war, this suffering may well be increased further due to the radioactive poisons which kill friend and foe, soldier and civilian alike.

Fortunately there exists a way out. Our early nuclear explosives have used fission. In the fission process a great array of radioactive products are formed, some of them intensely poisonous. More recently we have learned how to produce energy by fusion. Fusion produces fewer and very much less dangerous radioactivities. Actually the neutrons which are a by-product of the fusion reaction may be absorbed in almost any material and may again produce an assortment of radioactive nuclei. However, by placing only certain materials near the thermonuclear explosion, one may obtain a weapon in which the radioactivity is harmless. Thus the possibility of clean nuclear explosions lies before us.

Clean, flexible and easily delivered weapons of all sizes would make it possible to use these bombs as we want to use them: as tools of defense. When stopping an aggressor we would not let loose great quantities of radioactive atoms which would spread death where we wanted to defend freedom. Clean nuclear weapons would be the same as conveniently packaged high explosives. They would be nothing more.

The possibility of clean explosions opens up another development: the use of nuclear explosives for the purposes of peace. Conventional high explosives have been used in peace fully as much as in war. From mining to the building of dams there is a great variety of important jobs that dynamite has performed. Nuclear explosives have not been used in a similar way. The reason is the danger from radioactivity. Once we fully master the art of clean explosions peaceful applications will follow and another step will be made in controlling the forces of nature.

All this is of course only a small part of the process of the increasing power of man and the increasing responsibility of man. As the impossible of yesterday becomes the accomplished fact of today we have to be more and more aware of our neighbors on this shrinking planet. The arts of peace may lead to conflicting interest as easily as they may lead to fruitful co-operation. If we ever learn to control the climate of the world, a nation may find itself in the same relation to another nation as two farmers who have to use the waters of the same river.

Rivals are men who fight over the control of a river. When the same word "rivals" comes to mean co-operation for the best common use of the river or any other resource—that will be the time of law and of peace. Surely this sounds like Utopia and no one sees the way. But the general direction in which we should go is not to consider atomic explosives and radioactivity as the inventions of the devil. On the contrary, we must more fully explore all the consequences and possibilities that lie in nature, even when these possibilities seem frightening at first. In the end this is the way toward a better life. It may sound unusually optimistic in the atomic age, but we believe that the human race is tough and in the long run the human race is reasonable.   1958

NORMAN COUSINS

1912–

AFTER GRADUATING from Columbia University in 1933, Norman Cousins worked on the *New York Post* and *Current History*. In 1940 he began his affiliation with the *Saturday Review*, becoming editor two years later. His international and humane values found expression in the contributions he made to educational discussion and in his lectures in Japan, India, Pakistan and other countries as well as in his vigorous and courageous editorials. Norman Cousins is widely known as a forceful and eloquent champion of world federation and as a fearless opponent of atomic warfare and of everything that points in its direction. The following editorial appeared in the *Saturday Review* of February 1, 1958.

The Good Inheritance; the Democratic Chance, New York, 1942.
Modern Man Is Obsolete, New York, 1945.
Who Speaks for Man? New York, 1952.

WANTED: TWO BILLION ANGRY MEN

There is no point in talking about the possibility of a war breaking out. The war is already being fought. It is being waged by national sovereignties against human life.

It is true that national sovereignties are arrayed against each other under conflicting ideological banners. But the consequences of this conflict will not be victory by one over the other. The consequence can only be a mass cheapening of life or its elimination from this planet.

Everything being done by the national sovereignties to advance their supposed security succeeds only in intensifying the peril to life on earth. The weapons they are making are an advanced form of the competition between the sovereignties. Should these weapons be used, the nations behind the sovereignties will be pulverized and the humans along with them. The hope of the statesmen, of course, is to create a balance of terror so that neither side will dare to attack. But the same hideous momentum that produced the weapons can lead to their use. Neither side will be made secure by the fact that the other side possesses the means of instantaneous, devastating attack. Neither side will feel under obligation to wait until it is hit first. It is upon such a frail reed that the cause of life on earth is now made to rest.

It is wrong to say that nuclear explosives are being tested; they are being used. Every time one of the explosives is fired human beings are hurt. Just in the act of exploding a test nuclear bomb, life-destroying materials are put into the air. These explosions form no ordinary clouds; they are not dispersed by the winds; they retain their ability to poison and kill for more than two dozen years. With each bomb the canopy of poison above the earth grows heavier. Not long ago only one nation was involved in this kind of experimentation. Today, three nations are contributing to the general poisoning.[1]

Tomorrow, perhaps a half-dozen or more national sovereignties will insist on their right to add their own portions of poison to the sky.

There is no disagreement about one aspect of such general testing. All experts agree that at some point the burden of poison will become heavier than human life can sustain. The only disagreement has to do with when that point will be reached. Also, whether the amount of poison already in the air has caused widespread harm or only limited harm. In short, whether 10,000 persons will die this year of leukemia produced by the bomb poisons in the atmosphere or whether only one-fourth or one-fifth that number will die.

The men at the head of sovereign nations are helpless to deal with the onrushing peril. They are part of something unworkable as it concerns the making of world peace, for unfettered sovereignty today is an unworkable concept. It makes no difference how benign or well-intentioned are the men who represent the sovereignties. So long as their ultimate aim is to maintain the present station of a nation above law, the statesmen will work at opposite ends from what human life requires in order to be sustained on this planet.

In a very real sense, the statesmen are trying to deal with the problems of yesterday rather than the problems of today and tomorrow. It is true that the Second World War was brought on in large part because the free nations of the world were weak and disarmed. But if disarmament a generation ago was no answer, neither is an armaments race today the answer. If an arms race leads to war and if war leads to the liquidation of both freedom and life, then the arms race offers not military security but the prospect of mutual suicide.

[1] Early in 1960 France, in exploding atomic bombs in the Sahara, became the fourth nation to engage in production and testing (Ed.).

Here the advocates of unfettered national sovereignty argue that they would rather take their chances with an arms race ending in mutual suicide than with the danger of being disarmed in the face of almost certain Communist world conquest. If these were the only alternatives then something might be said for the arms race. But these are not the only alternatives. Neither disarmament nor armament can create a peace. Real peace depends on the amount of support that can be mobilized in the world for transforming the United Nations into a body with the effective powers of world law.

So long as peace is pursued under present methods; so long as each nation is allowed to retain the right and the capacity to destroy millions of human beings; so long as nations are allowed to engage in the kind of acts which are forbidden inside their countries to individual citizens; so long as lawlessness is the normal way of life among nations—so long as these conditions prevail there can be no peace.

It is not true that only the totalitarian states are opposed to a world under law. The free nations have yet to make the specific proposals that go as far beyond sovereignty as is necessary to make world law work.

Meanwhile, what the world needs today are two billion angry men who will make it clear to their national leaders that the earth does not exist for the purpose of being a stage for the total destruction of man. Two billion angry men can insist that the world's resources be utilized for human good. They can demand that the nations stop using the sky as an open sewer for radioactive poisons, and that an end be put to the uncontrolled devices that pursue future generations by way of damaged genes. They can compel the nations to end the long age of the cave and begin a real civilization. A war is now being waged against the world's peoples and they have the need and the duty to defend themselves.   1958

» » Appendix « «

» » « «

APPENDIX

» » THE DECLARATION OF INDEPENDENCE « «

When in the course of human events, it becomes necessary for one people to dissolve the political bands which have connected them with another, and to assume among the powers of the earth, the separate and equal station to which the Laws of Nature and of Nature's God entitle them, a decent respect to the opinions of mankind requires that they should declare the causes which impel them to the separation.

We hold these truths to be self-evident, that all men are created equal, that they are endowed by their Creator with certain unalienable Rights, that among these are Life, Liberty and the pursuit of Happiness. That to secure these rights, Governments are instituted among Men, deriving their just powers from the consent of the governed, That whenever any Form of Government becomes destructive of these ends, it is the Right of the People to alter or to abolish it, and to institute new Government, laying its foundation on such principles and organizing its powers in such form, as to them shall seem most likely to effect their Safety and Happiness. Prudence, indeed, will dictate that Governments long established should not be changed for light and transient causes; and accordingly all experience hath shewn, that mankind are more disposed to suffer, while evils are sufferable, than to right themselves by abolishing the forms to which they are accustomed. But when a long train of abuses and usurpations, pursuing invariably the same Object evinces a design to reduce them under absolute Despotism, it is their right, it is their duty, to throw off such Government, and to provide new Guards for their future security. Such has been the patient sufferance of these Colonies; and such is now the necessity which constrains them to alter their former Systems of Government. The history of the present King of Great Britain is a history of repeated injuries and usurpations, all having in direct object the establishment of an absolute Tyranny over these States. To prove this, let Facts be submitted to a candid world.

He has refused his Assent to Laws, the most wholesome and necessary for the public good.

He has forbidden his Governors to pass Laws of immediate and pressing importance, unless suspended in their operation till his Assent should be obtained; and when so suspended, he has utterly neglected to attend to them.

He has refused to pass other Laws for the accommodation of large districts of People, unless those People would relinquish the right of Representation in the legislature; a right inestimable to them and formidable to tyrants only.

He has called together legislative bodies at places unusual, uncomfortable, and distant from the depository of their Public Records, for the sole Purpose of fatiguing them into compliance with his measures.

He has dissolved Representative Houses repeatedly, for opposing, with manly firmness, his invasions on the rights of the People.

He has refused for a long time, after such dissolutions, to cause others to be elected; whereby the Legislative Powers, incapable of Annihilation, have returned to the People at large for their exercise; the State remaining in the mean time exposed to all the dangers of invasion from without, and convulsions within.

He has endeavoured to prevent the Population of these States; for that purpose obstructing the Laws for Naturalization of Foreigners; refusing to pass others to encourage their migrations hither, and raising the conditions of new Appropriations of Lands.

He has obstructed the Administration of Justice, by refusing his Assent to Laws for establishing Judiciary Powers.

He has made Judges dependent on his Will alone, for the tenure of their offices, and the amount and payment of their salaries.

He has erected a multitude of New Offices, and sent hither swarms of Officers to harass our People, and eat out their substance.

He has kept among us, in times of Peace, Standing Armies, without the Consent of our legislatures.

He has affected to render the Military independent of and superior to the Civil Power.

He has combined with others to subject us to a jurisdiction foreign to our constitution,

xxiii

and unacknowledged by our laws; giving his assent to their Acts of pretended Legislation:

For quartering large bodies of armed troops among us:

For protecting them, by a mock Trial, from Punishment for any Murders which they should commit on the Inhabitants of these States:

For cutting off our Trade with all parts of the world:

For imposing Taxes on us without our Consent:

For depriving us, in many cases, of the benefits of Trial by Jury:

For transporting us beyond Seas to be tried for pretended offences:

For abolishing the free System of English Laws in a neighbouring province, establishing therein an Arbitrary government, and enlarging its Boundaries, so as to render it at once an example and fit instrument for introducing the same absolute rule into these Colonies:

For taking away our Charters, abolishing our most valuable Laws, and altering fundamentally the Forms of our Governments:

For suspending our own Legislatures, and declaring themselves invested with Power to legislate for us in all cases whatsoever.

He has abdicated Government here by declaring us out of his protection, and waging War against us.

He has plundered our seas, ravaged our Coasts, burnt our towns, and destroyed the Lives of our People.

He is at this time transporting large Armies of foreign Mercenaries to compleat the works of death, desolation and tyranny, already begun with circumstances of Cruelty & perfidy scarcely paralleled in the most barbarous ages, and totally unworthy the Head of a civilized nation.

He has constrained our fellow Citizens taken Captive on the high Seas to bear Arms against their Country, to become the executioners of their friends and Brethren, or to fall themselves by their Hands.

He has excited domestic insurrections amongst us, and has endeavoured to bring on the inhabitants of our frontiers, the merciless Indian Savages, whose known rule of warfare, is an undistinguished destruction of all ages, sexes and conditions.

In every stage of these Oppressions We have Petitioned for Redress in the most humble terms: Our repeated Petitions have been answered only by repeated injury. A Prince, whose character is thus marked by every act which may define a Tyrant, is unfit to be the ruler of a free people.

Nor have We been wanting in attentions to our British brethren. We have warned them from time to time of attempts by their legislature to extend an unwarrantable jurisdiction over us. We have reminded them of the circumstances of our emigration and settlement here. We have appealed to their native justice and magnanimity, and we have conjured them by the ties of our common kindred to disavow these usurpations, which, would inevitably interrupt our connections and correspondence. They too have been deaf to the voice of justice and of consanguinity. We must, therefore, acquiesce in the necessity, which denounces our Separation, and hold them, as we hold the rest of mankind, Enemies in War, in Peace Friends.

We, therefore, the Representatives of the united States of America, in General Congress, Assembled, appealing to the Supreme Judge of the world for the rectitude of our intentions, do, in the Name, and by Authority of the good People of these Colonies, solemnly publish and declare, That these United Colonies are, and of Right ought to be Free and Independent States; that they are Absolved from all Allegiance to the British Crown, and that all political connection between them and the State of Great Britain, is and ought to be totally dissolved; and that as Free and Independent States, they have full Power to levy War, conclude Peace, contract Alliances, establish Commerce, and to do all other Acts and Things which Independent States may of right do. And for the support of this Declaration, with a firm reliance on the protection of divine Providence, we mutually pledge to each other our Lives, our Fortunes and our sacred Honor.

JOHN HANCOCK, *President*

[other signatures follow]

1776

» » THE CONSTITUTION OF THE UNITED STATES « «

PREAMBLE.

Preamble. We, the People of the United States, in Order to form a more perfect Union, establish Justice, insure domestic Tranquility, provide for the common defence, promote the general Welfare, and secure the Blessings of Liberty to ourselves and our Posterity, do ordain and establish this CONSTITUTION for the United States of America.

ARTICLE I.

LEGISLATIVE DEPARTMENT.

Section 1. All legislative Powers herein granted shall be vested in a Congress of the United States, which shall consist of a Senate and House of Representatives.

Section 2. [1] The House of Representatives shall be composed of Members chosen every second Year by the People of the several States, and the Electors in each State shall have the Qualifications requisite for Electors of the most numerous Branch of the State Legislature.

[2] No person shall be a Representative who shall not have attained to the Age of twenty-five Years, and been seven Years a Citizen of the United States, and who shall not, when elected, be an Inhabitant of that State in which he shall be chosen.

[3] [1] [Representatives and direct Taxes shall be apportioned among the several States which may be included within this Union, according to their respective Numbers, which shall be determined by adding to the whole Number of free Persons, including those bound to Service for a Term of Years, and excluding Indians not taxed, three-fifths of all other Persons.] The actual Enumeration shall be made within three Years after the first Meeting of the Congress of the United States, and within every subsequent Term of ten Years, in such Manner as they shall by Law direct. The Number of Representatives shall not exceed one for every thirty Thousand, but each State shall have at Least one Representative; and until such enumeration shall be made, the State of New Hampshire shall be entitled to chuse three, Massachusetts eight, Rhode-Island

and Providence Plantations one, Connecticut five, New-York six, New Jersey four, Pennsylvania eight, Delaware one, Maryland six, Virginia ten, North Carolina five, South Carolina five, and Georgia three.

[4] When vacancies happen in the Representation from any State, the Executive Authority thereof shall issue Writs of Election to fill such vacancies.

[5] The House of Representatives shall chuse their Speaker and other Officers; and shall have the sole power of Impeachment.

Section 3. [2] [1] The Senate of the United States shall be composed of two Senators from each State, chosen by the Legislature thereof, for six Years; and each Senator shall have one Vote.

[2] Immediately after they shall be assembled in Consequence of the first Election, they shall be divided as equally as may be into three Classes. The Seats of the Senators of the first Class shall be vacated at the Expiration of the second Year, of the second Class at the Expiration of the fourth Year, and of the third Class at the Expiration of the sixth Year, so that one-third may be chosen every second Year; and if Vacancies happen by Resignation, or otherwise, during the Recess of the Legislature of any State, the Executive thereof may make temporary Appointments [until the next Meeting of the Legislature, which shall then fill such Vacancies].

[3] No Person shall be a Senator who shall not have attained to the Age of thirty Years, and been nine years a Citizen of the United States, and who shall not, when elected, be an Inhabitant of that State for which he shall be chosen.

[4] The Vice President of the United States shall be President of the Senate, but shall have no Vote, unless they be equally divided.

[5] The Senate shall chuse their other Officers, and also a President pro tempore, in the absence of the Vice President, or when he shall exercise the Office of President of the United States.

[6] The Senate shall have the sole Power to try all Impeachments. When sitting for that Purpose, they shall be on Oath or Affirmation.

---

[1] The clause included in brackets is amended by the Fourteenth amendment, second section.

[2] The first paragraph of section three of article I, of the Constitution of the United States, and so much of paragraph two of the same section as relates to filling vacancies are amended by the seventeenth amendment to the Constitution.

When the President of the United States is tried, the Chief Justice shall preside: And no person shall be convicted without the Concurrence of two thirds of the Members present.

[7] Judgment in Cases of Impeachment shall not extend further than to removal from Office, and disqualification to hold and enjoy any Office of honor, Trust or Profit under the United States: but the Party convicted shall nevertheless be liable and subject to Indictment, Trial, Judgment and Punishment, according to Law.

Section 4. [1] The Times, Places and Manner of holding Elections for Senators and Representatives, shall be prescribed in each State by the Legislature thereof; but the Congress may at any time by Law make or alter such Regulations, except as to the Places of chusing Senators.

[2] The Congress shall assemble at least once in every Year, and such Meetings shall be on the first Monday in December, unless they shall by Law appoint a different day.

Section 5. [1] Each House shall be the Judge of the Elections, Returns and Qualifications of its own Members, and a Majority of each shall constitute a Quorum to do Business; but a smaller Number may adjourn from day to day, and may be authorized to compel the Attendance of absent Members, in such Manner, and under such Penalties as each House may provide.

[2] Each House may determine the Rules of its Proceedings, punish its Members for disorderly Behaviour, and, with the Concurrence of two thirds, expel a Member.

[3] Each House shall keep a Journal of its Proceedings, and from time to time publish the same, excepting such Parts as may in their Judgment require Secrecy; and the Yeas and Nays of the Members of either House on any question shall, at the Desire of one fifth of those Present, be entered on the Journal.

[4] Neither House, during the Session of Congress, shall, without the Consent of the other, adjourn for more than three days, nor to any other Place than that in which the two Houses shall be sitting.

Section 6. [1] The Senators and Representatives shall receive a Compensation for their Services, to be ascertained by Law, and paid out of the Treasury of the United States. They shall in all Cases, except Treason, Felony and Breach of the Peace, be privileged from Arrest during their Attendance at the Session of their respective Houses, and in going to and returning from the same; and for any Speech or Debate in either House, they shall not be questioned in any other Place.

[2] No Senator or Representative shall, during the Time for which he was elected, be appointed to any civil Office under the Authority of the United States, which shall have been created, or the emoluments whereof should have been increased during such time; and no Person holding any Office under the United States, shall be a Member of either House during his Continuance in Office.

Section 7. [1] All Bills for raising Revenue shall originate in the House of Representatives; but the Senate may propose or concur with Amendments as on other Bills.

[2] Every Bill which shall have passed the House of Representatives and the Senate, shall, before it becomes a Law, be presented to the President of the United States; if he approve he shall sign it, but if not he shall return it, with his Objections to that House in which it shall have originated, who shall enter the Objections at large on their Journal, and proceed to reconsider it. If after such Reconsideration two thirds of that House shall agree to pass the Bill, it shall be sent, together with the Objections, to the other House, by which it shall likewise be reconsidered, and if approved by two thirds of that House, it shall become a Law. But in all such Cases the Votes of both Houses shall be determined by Yeas and Nays, and the Names of the Persons voting for and against the Bill shall be entered on the Journal of each house respectively. If any Bill shall not be returned by the President within ten Days (Sundays excepted) after it shall have been presented to him, the Same shall be a Law, in like Manner as if he had signed it, unless the Congress by their Adjournment prevent its Return, in which Case it shall not be a Law.

[3] Every Order, Resolution, or Vote to which the Concurrence of the Senate and House of Representatives may be necessary (except on a question of Adjournment) shall be presented to the President of the United States; and before the Same shall take Effect, shall be approved by him, or being disapproved by him, shall be repassed by two thirds of the Senate and House of Representatives, according to the Rules and Limitations prescribed in the Case of a Bill.

Section 8. The Congress shall have Power [1] To lay and collect Taxes, Duties, Imposts and Excises, to pay the Debts and provide for the common defense and general Welfare of the United States; but all Duties, Imposts and Excises shall be uniform throughout the United States;

[2] To borrow money on the credit of the United States;

[3] To regulate Commerce with foreign Nations, and among the several States, and with the Indian Tribes;

[4] To establish an uniform Rule of Naturalization, and uniform Laws on the subject of Bankruptcies throughout the United States;

[5] To coin Money, regulate the Value thereof, and of foreign Coin, and fix the Standard of Weights and Measures;

[6] To provide for the Punishment of counterfeiting the Securities and current Coin of the United States;

[7] To establish Post Offices and post Roads;

[8] To promote the Progress of Science and useful Arts, by securing for limited Times to Authors and Inventors the exclusive Right to their respective Writings and Discoveries;

[9] To constitute Tribunals inferior to the supreme Court;

[10] To define and punish Piracies and Felonies committed on the high Seas, and Offenses against the Law of Nations;

[11] To declare War, grant Letters of Marque and Reprisal, and make Rules concerning Captures on Land and Water;

[12] To raise and support Armies; but no Appropriation of Money to that Use shall be for a longer Term than two years;

[13] To provide and maintain a Navy;

[14] To make Rules for the Government and Regulation of the land and naval Forces;

[15] To provide for calling forth the Militia to execute the Laws of the Union, suppress Insurrections and repel Invasions;

[16] To provide for organizing, arming, and disciplining the Militia, and for governing such Part of them as may be employed in the Service of the United States, reserving to the States respectively, the Appointment of the Officers, and the Authority of training the Militia according to the discipline prescribed by Congress;

[17] To exercise exclusive Legislation in all Cases whatsoever, over such District (not exceeding ten Miles square) as may, by Cession of particular States, and the acceptance of Congress, become the Seat of the Government of the United States, and to exercise like Au-

thority over all Places purchased by the Consent of the Legislature of the State in which the same shall be, for the Erection of Forts, Magazines, Arsenals, Dock-Yards, and other needful Buildings;—And

[18] To make all Laws which shall be necessary and proper for carrying into Execution the foregoing Powers, and all other Powers vested by this Constitution in the Government of the United States, or in any Department or   10 Officer thereof.

Section 9. [1] The Migration or Importation of such Persons as any of the States now existing shall think proper to admit, shall not be prohibited by the Congress prior to the Year one thousand eight hundred and eight, but a tax or duty may be imposed on such Importation, not exceeding ten dollars for each Person.

[2] The privilege of the Writ of Habeas Corpus shall not be suspended, unless when in   20 Cases of Rebellion or Invasion the public Safety may require it.

[3] No Bill of Attainder or ex post facto Law shall be passed.

[4] [1] No capitation, or other direct, Tax shall be laid, unless in Proportion to the Census or Enumeration herein before directed to be taken.

[5] No Tax or Duty shall be laid on Articles exported from any State.   30

[6] No preference shall be given by any Regulation of Commerce or Revenue to the Ports of one State over those of another: nor shall Vessels bound to, or from, one State, be obliged to enter, clear, or pay Duties in another.

[7] No Money shall be drawn from the Treasury, but in Consequence of Appropriations made by Law; and a regular Statement and Account of the Receipts and Expenditures   40 of all public Money shall be published from time to time.

[8] No Title of Nobility shall be granted by the United States: And no Person holding any Office of Profit or Trust under them, shall, without the Consent of the Congress, accept of any present, Emolument, Office, or Title, of any kind whatever, from any King, Prince, or foreign State.

Section 10. [1] No State shall enter into any   50 Treaty, Alliance, or Confederation; grant Letters of Marque and Reprisal; coin Money; emit Bills of Credit; make any Thing but gold and silver Coin a Tender in Payment of Debts;

[1] See XVI Amendment.

pass any Bill of Attainder, ex post facto Law, or Law impairing the Obligation of Contracts, or grant any Title of Nobility.

[2] No State shall, without the Consent of the Congress, lay any imposts or Duties on Imports or Exports, except what may be absolutely necessary for executing its inspection Laws: and the net Produce of all Duties and Imposts, laid by any State on Imports or Exports, shall be for the Use of the Treasury of the United States; and all such Laws shall be subject to the Revision and Controul of the Congress.

[3] No State shall, without the Consent of Congress, lay any duty of Tonnage, keep Troops, or Ships of War in time of Peace, enter into any Agreement or Compact with another State, or with a foreign Power, or engage in War, unless actually invaded, or in such imminent Danger as will not admit of delay.

ARTICLE II.

EXECUTIVE DEPARTMENT.

Section 1. [1] The executive Power shall be vested in a President of the United States of America. He shall hold his Office during the Term of four Years, and, together with the Vice President, chosen for the same Term, be elected, as follows:

[2] Each state shall appoint, in such Manner as the Legislature thereof may direct, a Number of Electors, equal to the whole number of Senators and Representatives to which the State may be entitled in the Congress: but no Senator or Representative, or Person holding an office of Trust or Profit under the United States, shall be appointed an Elector.

¹ [The Electors shall meet in their respective States, and vote by Ballot for two persons, of whom one at least shall not be an Inhabitant of the same State with themselves. And they shall make a List of all the Persons voted for, and of the Number of Votes for each; which List they shall sign and certify, and transmit sealed to the Seat of the Government of the United States, directed to the President of the Senate. The President of the Senate shall, in the Presence of the Senate and House of Representatives, open all the Certificates, and the Votes shall then be counted. The Person having the greatest Number of Votes shall be the

¹ This clause has been superseded by the twelfth amendment.

President, if such Number be a Majority of the whole Number of Electors appointed; and if there be more than one who have such Majority, and have an equal Number of Votes, then the House of Representatives shall immediately chuse, by Ballot one of them for President; and if no Person have a Majority, then from the five highest on the List, the said House shall in like Manner chuse the President. But in chusing the President, the Votes shall be taken by States, the Representation from each State having one Vote; a quorum for this Purpose shall consist of a Member or Members from two-thirds of the States, and a Majority of all the States shall be necessary to a choice. In every Case, after the Choice of the President, the Person having the greatest Number of Votes of the Electors shall be the Vice President. But if there should remain two or more who have equal Votes, the Senate shall chuse from them by Ballot the Vice President.]

[3] The Congress may determine the Time of chusing the Electors, and the Day on which they shall give their Votes; which Day shall be the same throughout the United States.

[4] No person except a natural born Citizen, or a Citizen of the United States, at the time of the adoption of this Constitution, shall be eligible to the Office of President; neither shall any Person be eligible to that office who shall not have attained to the Age of thirty-five Years and been fourteen Years a Resident within the United States.

[5] In Case of the Removal of the President from Office, or of his Death, Resignation, or inability to discharge the Powers and Duties of the said Office, the same shall devolve on the Vice President, and the Congress may by Law provide for the Case of Removal, Death, Resignation or Inability, both of the President and Vice President, declaring what Officer shall then act as President, and such Officer shall act accordingly, until the Disability be removed, or a President shall be elected.

[6] The President shall, at stated Times, receive for his Services, a Compensation, which shall neither be increased nor diminished during the Period for which he shall have been elected, and he shall not receive within that Period any other Emolument from the United States, or any of them.

[7] Before he enter on the Execution of his Office, he shall take the following Oath or Affirmation:—"I do solemnly swear (or affirm)

that I will faithfully execute the Office of President of the United States, and will to the best of my Ability, preserve, protect and defend the Constitution of the United States."

Section 2. [1] The President shall be Commander in Chief of the Army and Navy of the United States, and of the Militia of the several States, when called into the actual Service of the United States; he may require the Opinion, in writing, of the principal Officer in each of the executive Departments, upon any subject relating to the Duties of their respective Offices, and he shall have power to grant Reprieves and Pardons for Offenses against the United States, except in Cases of Impeachment.

[2] He shall have Power, by and with the Advice and Consent of the Senate, to make Treaties, provided two-thirds of the Senators present concur; and he shall nominate, and by and with the Advice and Consent of the Senate, shall appoint Ambassadors, other public Ministers and Consuls, Judges of the supreme Court, and all other Officers of the United States, whose Appointments are not herein otherwise provided for, and which shall be established by Law: but the Congress may by Law vest the Appointment of such inferior Offices, as they think proper, in the President alone, in the Courts of Law, or in the Heads of Departments.

[3] The President shall have Power to fill up all Vacancies that may happen during the Recess of the Senate, by granting Commissions which shall expire at the End of their next Session.

Section 3. He shall from time to time give to the Congress Information of the State of the union, and recommend to their Consideration such Measures as he shall judge necessary and expedient; he may, on extraordinary Occasions, convene both Houses, or either of them, and in Case of Disagreement between them, with Respect to the Time of Adjournment, he may adjourn them to such Time as he shall think proper; he shall receive Ambassadors and other public Ministers; he shall take Care that the Laws be faithfully executed, and shall Commission all the officers of the United States.

Section 4. The President, Vice President, and all civil Officers of the United States, shall be removed from Office on Impeachment for, and Conviction of, Treason, Bribery, or other high Crimes and Misdemeanors.

ARTICLE III.

JUDICIAL DEPARTMENT.

Section 1. The judicial Power of the United States, shall be vested in one supreme Court, and in such inferior Courts as the Congress may from time to time ordain and establish. The Judges, both of the supreme and Inferior Courts, shall hold their Offices during good Behaviour, and shall, at stated Times, receive for their Services a Compensation, which shall not be diminished during their Continuance in Office.

Section 2. [1] The judicial Power shall extend to all Cases, in Law and Equity, arising under this Constitution, the Laws of the United States, and Treaties made, or which shall be made, under their Authority;—to all Cases affecting Ambassadors, other public Ministers and Consuls;—to all Cases of admiralty and maritime Jurisdiction;—to Controversies to which the United States shall be a Party;—to Controversies between two or more states;—between a State and Citizens of another State;—between Citizens of different States;—between Citizens of the same State claiming Lands under Grants of different States, and between a State, or the Citizens thereof, and foreign States, Citizens or Subjects.

[2] In all Cases affecting Ambassadors, other public Ministers and Consuls, and those in which a State shall be Party, the supreme Court shall have original Jurisdiction. In all the other Cases before mentioned, the supreme Court shall have appellate Jurisdiction, both as to Law and Fact, with such Exceptions, and under such Regulations as the Congress shall make.

[3] The trial of all Crimes, except in Cases of Impeachment, shall be by Jury; and such Trial shall be held in the State where the said Crimes shall have been committed; but when not committed within any State, the Trial shall be at such Place or Places as the Congress may by Law have directed.

Section 3. [1] Treason against the United States, shall consist only in levying War against them, or in adhering to their Enemies, giving them Aid and Comfort. No Person shall be convicted of Treason unless on the Testimony of two Witnesses to the same overt Act, or on Confession in open Court.

[2] The Congress shall have power to declare the Punishment of Treason, but no At-

tainder of Treason shall work Corruption of Blood, or Forfeiture except during the Life of the Person attainted.

ARTICLE IV.

Section 1. Full Faith and Credit shall be given in each State to the public Acts, Records, and judicial Proceedings of every other State. And the Congress may by general Laws prescribe the Manner in which such Acts, Records and Proceedings shall be proved, and the Effect thereof.

Section 2. [1] The Citizens of each State shall be entitled to all Privileges and Immunities of Citizens in the several States.

[2] A Person charged in any State with Treason, Felony, or other Crime, who shall flee from Justice, and be found in another State, shall on demand of the executive Authority of the State from which he fled, be delivered up to be removed to the State having Jurisdiction of the Crime.

[3] No person held to Service or Labour in one State, under the Laws thereof, escaping into another, shall, in Consequence of any Law or Regulation therein, be discharged from such Service or Labour, but shall be delivered up on Claim of the Party to whom such Service or Labour may be due.

Section 3. [1] New States may be admitted by the Congress into this Union; but no new State shall be formed or erected within the Jurisdiction of any other State; nor any State be formed by the Junction of two or more States, or parts of States, without the Consent of the Legislatures of the States concerned as well as of the Congress.

[2] The Congress shall have Power to dispose of and make all needful Rules and Regulations respecting the Territory or other Property belonging to the United States; and nothing in this Constitution shall be so construed as to Prejudice any Claims of the United States, or any particular State.

Section 4. The United States shall guarantee to every State in this Union a Republican Form of Government, and shall protect each of them against Invasion; and on Application of the Legislature, or of the Executive (when the Legislature cannot be convened) against domestic Violence.

ARTICLE V.

The Congress, whenever two-thirds of both Houses shall deem it necessary, shall propose Amendments to this Constitution, or, on the Application of the Legislatures of two-thirds of the several States shall call a Convention for proposing Amendments, which, in either Case, shall be valid to all Intents and Purposes, as part of this Constitution, when ratified by the Legislatures of three-fourths of the several States, or by Conventions in three-fourths thereof, as the one or the other Mode of Ratification may be proposed by the Congress; Provided that no Amendment which may be made prior to the Year One thousand eight hundred and eight shall in any Manner affect the first and fourth Clauses in the Ninth Section of the first Article; and that no State, without its Consent, shall be deprived of its equal suffrage in the Senate.

ARTICLE VI.

[1] All Debts contracted and Engagements entered into, before the Adoption of this Constitution, shall be as valid against the United States under this Constitution, as under the Confederation.

[2] This Constitution, and the Laws of the United States which shall be made in Pursuance thereof; and all Treaties made, or which shall be made, under the Authority of the United States, shall be the supreme Law of the Land; and the Judges in every State shall be bound thereby, any Thing in the Constitution or Laws of any State to the Contrary notwithstanding.

[3] The Senators and Representatives before mentioned, and the Members of the several State Legislatures, and all executive and judicial officers, both of the United States and of the several States, shall be bound by Oath or Affirmation, to support this Constitution; but no religious Test shall ever be required as a Qualification to any Office or public Trust under the United States.

ARTICLE VII.

The Ratification of the Conventions of nine States, shall be sufficient for the Establishment of this Constitution between the States so ratifying the Same.

ARTICLES IN ADDITION TO, AND AMENDMENT OF, THE CONSTITUTION OF THE UNITED STATES OF AMERICA, PROPOSED BY CONGRESS, AND RATIFIED BY THE LEGISLA-

TURES OF THE SEVERAL STATES, PURSUANT TO THE FIFTH ARTICLE OF THE ORIGINAL CONSTITUTION.

ARTICLE I.

Congress shall make no law respecting an establishment of religion, or prohibiting the free exercise thereof; or abridging the freedom of speech, or of the press; or the right of the people peaceably to assemble, and to petition the Government for a redress of grievances.

ARTICLE II.

A well regulated Militia, being necessary to the security of a free State, the right of the people to keep and bear Arms, shall not be infringed.

ARTICLE III.

No Soldier shall, in time of peace be quartered in any house, without the consent of the Owner, nor in time of war, but in a manner to be prescribed by law.

ARTICLE IV.

The right of the people to be secure in their persons, houses, papers, and effects, against unreasonable searches and seizures, shall not be violated, and no Warrant shall issue, but upon probable cause, supported by Oath or affirmation, and particularly describing the place to be searched, and the persons or things to be seized.

ARTICLE V.

No person shall be held to answer for a capital, or otherwise infamous crime, unless on a presentment or indictment of a Grand Jury, except in cases arising in the land or naval forces, or in the Militia, when in actual service in time of War or public danger; nor shall any person be subject for the same offense to be twice put in jeopardy of life or limb; nor shall be compelled in any criminal case to be a witness against himself, nor be deprived of life, liberty, or property, without due process of law; nor shall private property be taken for public use, without just compensation.

ARTICLE VI.

In all criminal prosecutions, the accused shall enjoy the right to a speedy and public trial, by an impartial jury of the State and district wherein the crime shall have been committed, which district shall have been previously ascertained by law, and to be informed of the nature and cause of the accusation, to be confronted with the witnesses against him; to have compulsory process for obtaining witnesses in his favor, and to have the Assistance of Counsel for his defense.

ARTICLE VII.

In suits at common law, where the value in controversy shall exceed twenty dollars, the right of trial by jury shall be preserved, and no fact tried by a jury shall be otherwise re-examined in any Court of the United States, than according to the rules of the common law.

ARTICLE VIII.

Excessive bail shall not be required, nor excessive fines imposed, nor cruel and unusual punishments inflicted.

ARTICLE IX.

The enumeration in the Constitution, of certain rights, shall not be construed to deny or disparage others retained by the people.

ARTICLE X.

The powers not delegated to the United States by the Constitution, nor prohibited by it to the States, are reserved to the States respectively, or to the people.

ARTICLE XI.

The judicial power of the United States shall not be construed to extend to any suit in law or equity, commenced or prosecuted against one of the United States by citizens of another State, or by Citizens or Subjects of any foreign State.

ARTICLE XII.

The Electors shall meet in their respective states and vote by ballot for President and Vice President, one of whom, at least, shall not be an inhabitant of the same state with themselves; they shall name in their ballots the person voted for as President, and in distinct ballots the person voted for as Vice

President and they shall make distinct lists of all persons voted for as President, and of all persons voted for as Vice President, and of the number of votes for each, which lists they shall sign and certify, and transmit sealed to the seat of the government of the United States, directed to the President of the Senate; —The President of the Senate shall, in the presence of the Senate and House of Representatives, open all the certificates and the votes shall then be counted;—The person having the greatest number of votes for President, shall be the President, if such number be a majority of the whole number of Electors appointed; and if no person have such majority, then from the persons having the highest numbers not exceeding three on the list of those voted for as President, the House of Representatives shall choose immediately, by ballot, the President. But in choosing the President, the votes shall be taken by states, the representation from each state having one vote; a quorum for this purpose shall consist of a member or members from two-thirds of the states, and a majority of the states shall be necessary to a choice. And if the House of Representatives shall not choose a President whenever the right of choice shall devolve upon them, before the fourth day of March next following, then the Vice President shall act as President, as in the case of the death or other constitutional disability of the President. The person having the greatest number of votes as Vice President, shall be the Vice President, if such number be a majority of the whole number of Electors appointed, and if no person have a majority, then from the two highest numbers on the list, the Senate shall choose the Vice President; a quorum for the purpose shall consist of two-thirds of the whole number of Senators, and a majority of the whole number shall be necessary to a choice. But no person constitutionally ineligible to the Office of President shall be eligible to that of Vice President of the United States.

ARTICLE XIII.

Section 1. Neither slavery nor involuntary servitude, except as a punishment for crime whereof the party shall have been duly convicted, shall exist within the United States, or any place subject to their jurisdiction.

Section 2. Congress shall have power to enforce this article by appropriate legislation.

ARTICLE XIV.

Section 1. All persons born or naturalized in the United States, and subject to the jurisdiction thereof, are citizens of the United States and of the State wherein they reside. No State shall make or enforce any law which shall abridge the privileges or immunities of citizens of the United States; nor shall any State deprive any person of life, liberty, or property, without due process of law; nor deny to any person within its jurisdiction the equal protection of the laws.

Section 2. Representatives shall be apportioned among the several States according to their respective numbers, counting the whole number of persons in each State, excluding Indians not taxed. But when the right to vote at any election for the choice of electors for President and Vice President of the United States, Representatives in Congress, the Executive and Judicial Officers of a State, or the members of the Legislature thereof, is denied to any of the male inhabitants of such State, being twenty-one years of age, and citizens of the United States, or in any way abridged, except for participation in rebellion, or other crime, the basis of representation therein shall be reduced in the proportion which the number of such male citizens shall bear to the whole number of male citizens twenty-one years of age in such State.

Section 3. No person shall be a Senator or Representative in Congress, or elector of President and Vice President, or hold any office, civil or military, under the United States, or under any State, who, having previously taken an oath, as a member of Congress, or as an officer of the United States, or as a member of any State legislature, or as an executive or judicial officer of any State, to support the Constitution of the United States, shall have engaged in insurrection or rebellion against the same, or given aid or comfort to the enemies thereof. But Congress may by a vote of two-thirds of each House, remove such disability.

Section 4. The validity of the public debt of the United States, authorized by law, including debts incurred for payment of pensions and bounties for services in suppressing insurrection or rebellion, shall not be questioned. But neither the United States nor any State shall assume or pay any debt or obligation incurred in aid of insurrection or rebellion against the

United States, or any claim for the loss or emancipation of any slave; but all such debts, obligations and claims shall be held illegal and void.

Section 5. The Congress shall have power to enforce, by appropriate legislation, the provisions of this article.

ARTICLE XV.

Section 1. The right of citizens of the United States to vote shall not be denied or abridged by the United States or by any State on account of race, color, or previous condition of servitude.

Section 2. The Congress shall have power to enforce this article by appropriate legislation.

ARTICLE XVI.

The Congress shall have power to lay and collect taxes on incomes, from whatever source derived, without apportionment among the several States, and without regard to any census or enumeration.

ARTICLE XVII.

The Senate of the United States shall be composed of two Senators from each State, elected by the people thereof, for six years; and each Senator shall have one vote. The electors in each State shall have the qualifications requisite for electors of the most numerous branch of the State legislatures.

When vacancies happen in the representation of any State in the Senate, the executive authority of such State shall issue writs of election to fill such vacancies: *Provided,* That the legislature of any State may empower the executive thereof to make temporary appointment until the people fill the vacancies by election as the legislature may direct.

This amendment shall not be so construed as to affect the election or term of any Senator chosen before it becomes valid as part of the Constitution.

ARTICLE XVIII.

Section 1. After one year from the ratification of this article the manufacture, sale, or transportation of intoxicating liquors within, the importation thereof into, or the exportation thereof from the United States and all territory subject to the jurisdiction thereof for beverage purposes is hereby prohibited.

Section 2. The Congress and the several States shall have concurrent power to enforce this article by appropriate legislation.

Section 3. This article shall be inoperative unless it shall have been ratified as an amendment to the Constitution by the legislatures of the several States, as provided in the Constitution, within seven years from the date of the submission hereof to the States by the Congress.

ARTICLE XIX.

Section 1. The right of citizens of the United States to vote shall not be denied or abridged by the United States or by any State on account of sex.

Section 2. Congress shall have power, by appropriate legislation, to enforce the provisions of this article.

ARTICLE XX.

(Ratified Feb. 6, 1933)

Section 1. The terms of the President and Vice President shall end at noon on the 20th day of January, and the terms of Senators and Representatives at noon on the 3rd day of January, of the years in which such terms would have ended if this article had not been ratified; and the terms of their successors shall then begin.

Section 2. The Congress shall assemble at least once in every year, and such meeting shall begin at noon on the 3rd day of January, unless they shall by law appoint a different day.

Section 3. If, at the time fixed for the beginning of the term of the President, the President elect shall have died, the Vice President elect shall become President. If a President shall not have been chosen before the time fixed for the beginning of his term, or if the President elect shall have failed to qualify, then the Vice President elect shall act as President until a President shall have qualified; and the Congress may by law provide for the case wherein neither a President elect nor a Vice President elect shall have qualified, declaring who shall then act as President, or the manner in which one who is to act shall be selected, and such person shall act accordingly until a President or Vice President shall have qualified.

Section 4. The Congress may by law provide for the case of the death of any of the persons from whom the House of Representatives may choose a President whenever the right of choice shall have devolved upon them, and for the case of the death of any of the persons from whom the Senate may choose a Vice President whenever the right of choice shall have devolved upon them.

Section 5. Sections 1 and 2 shall take effect on the 15th day of October following the ratification of this article.

Section 6. This article shall be inoperative unless it shall have been ratified as an amendment to the Constitution by the legislatures of three-fourths of the several States within seven years from the date of its submission.

ARTICLE XXI.
(Ratified Dec. 5, 1933)

Section 1. The eighteenth article of amendment to the Constitution of the United States is hereby repealed.

Section 2. The transportation or importation into any State, Territory, or possession of the United States for delivery or use therein of intoxicating liquors, in violation of the laws thereof, is hereby prohibited.

Section 3. This article shall be inoperative unless it shall have been ratified as an amendment to the Constitution by conventions in the several States, as provided in the Constitution, within seven years from the date of the submission hereof to the States by the Congress.

ARTICLE XXII.
(Ratified Feb. 26, 1951)

Section 1. No person shall be elected to the office of the President more than twice, and no person who has held the office of President, or acted as President, for more than two years of a term to which some other person was elected President shall be elected to the office of the President more than once. But this article shall not apply to any person holding the office of President when this article was proposed by the Congress, and shall not prevent any person who may be holding the office of President, or acting as President, during the term within which this article becomes operative from holding the office of President or acting as President during the remainder of such term.

Section 2. This article shall be inoperative unless it shall have been ratified as an amendment to the Constitution by the legislatures of three-fourths of the several States within seven years from the date of its submission to the States by the Congress.

INDEX